# Koren Talmud Bavli
THE NOÉ EDITION

NIDDA

Steinsaltz
Center

KOREN

# תלמוד בבלי

# KOREN TALMUD BAVLI

THE NOÉ EDITION

## נידה

## NIDDA

COMMENTARY BY

Rabbi Adin Even-Israel Steinsaltz

EDITOR-IN-CHIEF

Rabbi Dr Tzvi Hersh Weinreb

EXECUTIVE EDITOR

Rabbi Joshua Schreier

STEINSALTZ CENTER

KOREN PUBLISHERS JERUSALEM

Supported by the Matanel Foundation

*Koren Talmud Bavli, The Noé Edition*
Volume 42: Tractate Nidda

Standard Size Color Edition, ISBN 978 965 301 603 3

First Hebrew/English Edition, 2019

Koren Publishers Jerusalem Ltd.
PO Box 4044, Jerusalem 9104001, ISRAEL
PO Box 8531, New Milford, CT 06776, USA
www.korenpub.com

Steinsaltz Center

*Steinsaltz Center is the parent organization of institutions established by Rabbi Adin Even-Israel Steinsaltz*

PO Box 45187, Jerusalem 91450 ISRAEL
Telephone: +972 2 646 0900, Fax +972 2 624 9454
www.steinsaltz-center.org



This book was published in cooperation with the Israel Institute for Talmudic Publications.


Printed in PRC

הִנֵּה יָמִים בָּאִים, נְאֻם אֲדֹנָי יֱהֹוִה, וְהִשְׁלַחְתִּי רָעָב בָּאָרֶץ,
לֹא־רָעָב לַלֶּחֶם וְלֹא־צָמָא לַמַּיִם, כִּי אִם־לִשְׁמֹעַ אֵת דִּבְרֵי יהוה.

Behold, days are coming – says the Lord God –
I will send a hunger to the land, not a hunger for bread
nor a thirst for water, but to hear the words of the Lord.

(Amos 8:11)

*The Noé edition of the Koren Talmud Bavli*
*with the commentary of Rabbi Adin Even-Israel Steinsaltz*
*is dedicated to all those who open its cover*
*to quench their thirst for Jewish knowledge,*
*in our generation of Torah renaissance.*

*This beautiful edition is for the young, the aged,*
*the novice and the savant alike,*
*as it unites the depth of Torah knowledge*
*with the best of academic scholarship.*

*Within its exquisite and vibrant pages,*
*words become worlds.*

*It will claim its place in the library of classics,*
*in the bookcases of the Beit Midrash,*
*the classrooms of our schools,*
*and in the offices of professionals and businesspeople*
*who carve out precious time to grapple with its timeless wisdom.*

*For the Student and the Scholar*

DEDICATED BY LEO AND SUE NOÉ

Steinsaltz Center

## Executive Director, Steinsaltz Center

Rabbi Meni Even-Israel

## Managing Editor

Rabbi Jason Rappoport

## Senior Content Editor

Rabbi Dr. Shalom Z. Berger

## Editors

Rabbi Dr. Joshua Amaru, *Coordinating Editor*
Rabbi Yehoshua Duker, *Final Editor*
Rabbi Yedidya Naveh, *Content Curator*
Rabbi Avishai Magence, *Content Curator*
Menucha Chwat
Rabbi Yonatan Shai Freedman
Rabbi Dov Foxbrunner
Rabbi Ayal Geffon
Yisrael Kalker
Elisha Loewenstern
Rabbi Simcha Mirvis
Rabbi Eli Ozarowski
Rabbi David Sedley
Avi Steinhart
Rabbi Yitzchak Twersky

## Copy Editors

Aliza Israel, *Coordinator*
Debbie Ismailoff, *Coordinator*
Ita Olesker
Sara Henna Dahan
Shira Finson
Ilana Sobel
Deena Nataf
Eliana Kurlantzick Yorav
Erica Hirsch Edvi
Oritt Sinclair

## Language Consultants

Dr. Stéphanie E. Binder, *Greek & Latin*
Rabbi Yaakov Hoffman, *Arabic*
Dr. Shai Secunda, *Persian*
Shira Shmidman, *Aramaic*

## Hebrew Edition Editors

Rabbi Avraham Gelbstein
Rabbi Gershon Kitsis

KOREN

## Design & Typesetting

Dena Landowne Bailey, *Typesetting*
Tomi Mager, *Typesetting*
Tani Bayer, *Jacket Design*
Raphaël Freeman, *Design & Typography*

## Images

Rabbi Eliahu Misgav, *Illustration & Image Acquisition*
Daniel Gdalevich, *Illustration & Image Acquisition*

*With love for those*

*Who gave, who give and who will give me life*

*Displaying their daily joy and sweetness*

*And who, with their deeds*

*Cared for other people and for their needs*

*To my grandparents*

***Jose Ephim Mindlin, Guita Kauffmann Mindlin,***
***Abrahão Jacob Lafer and Betty Lafer***

**יוסף אפרים בן אפרים מינדלין**
**גיטה בת יוסף**
**אברהם יעקב בן מאיר לאעפר**
**ביילע בת חיים נפתלי הערץ הכהן Beile**

*From Manuel Mindlin Lafer,*
*my wife Josie Berezin Lafer*
*and our son Lior Berezin Lafer*

**עמנואל בן זלמן לעפר**
**ג'וזי בת איתן הכהן**
**אברהם יעקב בן עמנואל לעפר**

# Contents



For the vocalized Vilna Shas layout, please open as a Hebrew book.

# Haskama

## Rabbi Moshe Feinstein

RABBI MOSES FEINSTEIN
455 F. D. R. DRIVE
New York N. Y. 10002
OREgon 7-1222

משה פיינשטיין
ר"ם תפארת ירושלים
בנוא יארק

בע"ה

בזה ראיתי הפירוש החשוב של הרב הגאון מוהר"ר עדין שטיינזלץ שליט"א מעיה"ק ירושלים, על מסכתות ביצה ור"ה. באמת כבר ידוע לי פירושו של הרה"ג הנ"ל על מסכתות מתלמוד בבלי, וכבר כתבתי מכתב הסכמה עליהם. ובאתי בזה רק להדגיש מחדש איך שהפירושים של הרה"ג הנ"ל, שכולל פירוש חדש על הגמרא עצמו וגם פירוש שיש בו סיכום להלכה מהנידונים שבגמרא, נוסף לעוד כמה חלקים, הם באמת עבודה גדולה, שיכולים להיות לתועלת לא רק לאלו שכבר מורגלים בלמוד הגמרא, ורוצים להעמק יותר, אלא גם לאלו שמתחילים ללמוד, להדריכם בדרכי התורה איך להבין ולהעמיק בים התלמוד.

והריני מברך להרה"ג הנ"ל שיצליחהו השי"ת בספריו אלו ושיזכה לחבר עוד ספרים, להגדיל תורה ולהאדירה, לתפארת השם ותורתו.

ועל זה באתי על החתום לכבוד התורה ביום ז' לחודש אייר תשמ"ג.

משה פיינשטיין

…These new commentaries – which include a new interpretation of the Talmud, a halakhic summary of the debated issues, and various other sections – are a truly outstanding work; they can be of great benefit not only to those familiar with talmudic study who seek to deepen their understanding, but also to those who are just beginning to learn, guiding them through the pathways of the Torah and teaching them how to delve into the sea of the Talmud.

I would like to offer my blessing to this learned scholar. May the Holy One grant him success with these volumes and may he merit to write many more, to enhance the greatness of Torah, and bring glory to God and His word…

Rabbi Moshe Feinstein
New York, 7 Adar 5743

**ר' משה פיינשטיין שליט"א**

הנה ראיתי את מסכת אחת מהש"ס שנקד אותה וגם צייר צורות הצמחים וכדומה מדברים שלא ידוע לכמה אנשים הרה"ג ר' עדין שטיינזלץ מירושלים שליט"א וגם הוסיף שם בגליון פירושים וחידושים וניכר שהוא ת"ח וראויין לעיין בהם ת"ח ובני הישיבה וטוב גם לקנותם בבתי כנסיות ובבתי מדרשות שיש שיהיו להם לתועלת. — ועל זה באתי עה"ח ג' אדר ב' תש"ל.

נאם משה פיינשטיין
ר"מ תפארת ירושלים, ניו־יורק, ארה"ב

I have seen one tractate from the Talmud to which the great scholar Rabbi Adin Steinsaltz שליט״א has added *nikkud* (vowels) and illustrations to explain that which is unknown to many people; he has also added interpretations and innovations, and is evidently a *talmid ḥakham*. *Talmidei ḥakhamim* and yeshiva students ought to study these volumes, and synagogues and *batei midrash* would do well to purchase them, as they may find them useful.

Rabbi Moshe Feinstein
New York, Adar 5730

# Haskama
## Rabbi Menachem Mendel Schneerson

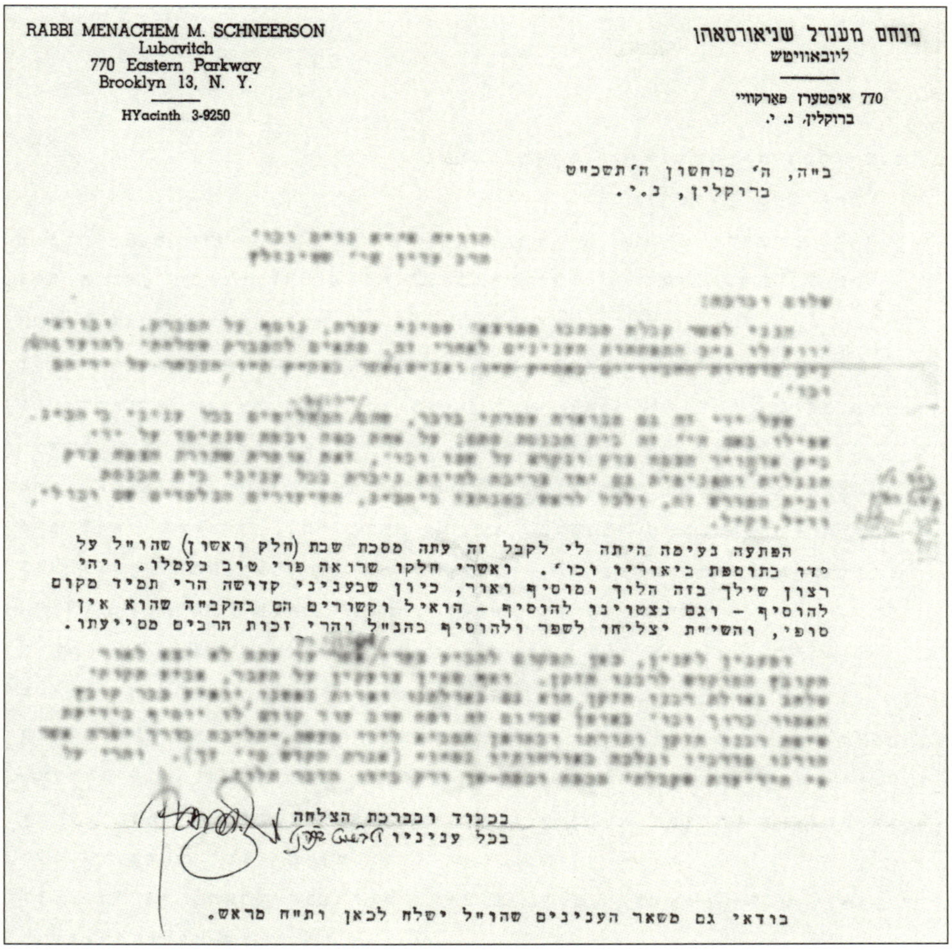

RABBI MENACHEM M. SCHNEERSON
Lubavitch
770 Eastern Parkway
Brooklyn 13, N. Y.
HYacinth 3-9250

מנחם מענדל שניאורסאהן
ליובאוויטש
770 איסטערן פארקוויי
ברוקלין, נ. י.

ב"ה, ה' מרחשון ה'תשכ"ט
ברוקלין, נ.י.

הפתעה נעימה היתה לי לקבל זה עתה מסכת שבת (חלק ראשון) שהו"ל על ידו בתוספת ביאוריו וכו'. ואשרי חלקו שרואה פרי טוב בעמלו. ויהי רצון שילך בזה הלוך ומוסיף ואור, כיון שבעניני קדושה הרי תמיד מקום להוסיף – וגם נצטוינו להוסיף – הואיל וקשורים הם בהקב"ה שהוא אין סופי, והשי"ת יצליחו לשפר ולהוסיף בהנ"ל והרי זכות הרבים מסייעתו.

בכבוד ובברכת הצלחה
בכל עניניו

בודאי גם משאר הענינים שהו"ל ישלח לכאן ותח"ח מראש.

…I have just had the pleasant surprise of receiving tractate *Shabbat* (part one), which has been published by [Rabbi Steinsaltz] along with his explanations, etc. Happy is the man who sees good fruits from his labors. May he continue in this path and increase light, for in the matters of holiness there is always room to add – and we have been commanded to add – for they are linked to the Holy One, Blessed be He, Who is infinite. And may the Holy One grant him success to improve and enhance this work, since the greater good strengthens his hand…

Rabbi Menachem Mendel Schneerson
The Lubavitcher Rebbe
Brooklyn, 5 Marḥeshvan 5729

# Haskama

## Rabbi Moshe Zvi Neria

הסכמה של הרב משה צבי נריה

ב"ה

"ושמעו ביום ההוא החרשים דברי ספר"
(ישעי' כט' יח')

תרגום ספרי קדמונים לשפת דורות אחרונים – היא משימתם של חכמי דור ודור. ובישראל שמצוות "ושננתם לבניך" מקיפה את כל חלקי האומה, ודאי שהיתה זאת המשימה בכל עידן ועידן.

בכל דור כך, ובדורנו אשר רבים בו הקרובים שנתרחקו וחוזרים ומתקרבים – לא כל שכן. כי רבים היום האומרים "מי ישקנו מים מבאר" התלמוד, ומועטים הם הדולים ומשקים.

ראוי אפוא להערכה מיוחדת נסיונו המבורך של הצעיר המופלא, הרב עדין שטיינזלץ, לפרש פרקי-תלמוד בהסברה מורחבת-תמציתית. אשר נוסף על הפרוש המלולי והעניני הוא מעלה גם את ההגיון של הדברים ומתרגמת אותם לשפת-המושגים של בן-דורנו.

דומה שכל הנגשים אל חומר למודי מתוך רצון להבינו – התלמיד החרוץ והמבוגר המשכיל – לא יתקלו בשום קושי בבואם ללמוד סוגיא תלמודית לפי פרוש זה. ולא עוד אלא שיש לקוות כי ההסברה הגיונית תעמידם מיד על טוב-הטעם של דף-הגמרא, והם ימשכו יותר ויותר אל הלמוד העיוני הזה אשר טובי המוחות בישראל לנו בעומקו, ואשר ממנו פינה, ממנו יתד לבנין חיינו.

נועם ד' על המפרש הנמרץ להמשיך במפעלו, וברוכים כל העוזרים להוצאתו לאור-עולם.

ביקר אורייתא

(חתימה)

The translation of the books of our past into the language of the present – this was the task of the sages of every generation. And in Israel, where the command to "teach them repeatedly to your children" applies to all parts of the nation, it was certainly the task of every era. This is true for every generation, and in our time – when many of those who have strayed far are once again drawing near – all the more so. For many today say, "Who will let us drink from the well" of Talmud, and few are those who offer up the waters to drink.

We must, therefore, particularly commend the blessed endeavor of Rabbi Adin Steinsaltz to explain the chapters of the Talmud in this extensive yet succinct commentary, which, in addition to its literal interpretation of the text, also explicates the latter's underlying logic and translates it into the language of our generation.

It appears that all those who seek to study Talmud – the diligent student and the learned adult – will have no difficulty understanding when using this commentary. Moreover, we may hope that the logical explanation will reveal to them the beauty of the talmudic page, and they will be drawn deeper and deeper into the intellectual pursuit which has engaged the best Jewish minds, and which serves as the cornerstone of our very lives…

Rabbi Moshe Zvi Neria

 THIS HASKAMA REFERS TO THE ORIGINAL HEBREW EDITION OF THE STEINSALTZ TALMUD, UPON WHICH THIS VOLUME IS BASED

# Haskama

**Rabbi Mordechai Eliyahu**

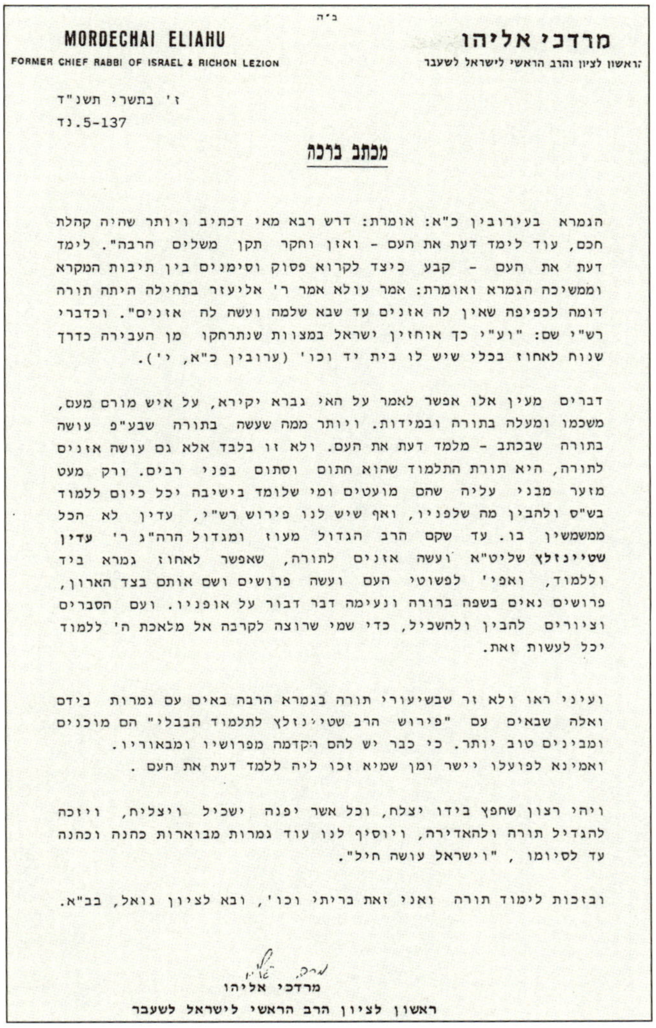

ב"ה

**MORDECHAI ELIAHU** — **מרדכי אליהו**

FORMER CHIEF RABBI OF ISRAEL & RICHON LEZION — ראשון לציון והרב הראשי לישראל לשעבר

ז' בתשרי תשנ"ד
נד.5-137

<u>מכתב ברכה</u>

הגמרא בעירובין כ"א: אומרת: דרש רבא מאי דכתיב ויותר שהיה קהלת חכם, עוד לימד דעת את העם - ואזן וחקר תקן משלים הרבה". לימד דעת את העם - קבע כיצד לקרוא פסוק וסימנים בין תיבות המקרא וממשיכה הגמרא ואומרת: אמר עולא אמר ר' אליעזר בתחילה היתה תורה דומה לכפיפה שאין לה אזנים עד שבא שלמה ועשה לה אזנים". וכדברי רש"י שם: "וע"י כך אוחזין ישראל במצוות שנתרחקו מן העבירה כדרך שנוח לאחוז בכלי שיש לו בית יד וכו' (ערובין כ"א, י').

דברים מעין אלו אפשר לאמר על האי גברא יקירא, על איש מורם מעם, משכמו ומעלה בתורה ובמידות. ויותר ממה שעשה בתורה שבע"פ עושה בתורה שבכתב - מלמד דעת את העם. ולא זו בלבד אלא גם עושה אזנים לתורה, היא תורת התלמוד שהוא חתום וסתום בפני רבים. ורק מעט מזער מבני עליה שהם מועטים ומי שלומד בישיבה יכל כיום ללמוד בש"ס ולהבין מה שלפניו, ואף שיש לנו פירוש רש"י, עדין לא הכל ממשמשין בו. עד שקם הרב הגדול מעוז ומגדול הרה"ג ר' **עדין שטיינזלץ** שליט"א ועשה אזנים לתורה, שאפשר לאחוז גמרא ביד וללמוד, ואפי' לפשוטי העם ועשה פרושים ושם אותם בצד הארון, פרושים נאים בשפה ברורה ונעימה דבר דבור על אופניו. ועם הסברים וציורים להבין ולהשכיל, כדי שמי שרוצה לקרבה אל מלאכת ה' ללמוד יכל לעשות זאת.

ועיני ראו ולא זר שבשיעורי תורה בגמרא הרבה באים עם גמרות בידם ואלה שבאים עם "פירוש הרב שטיינזלץ לתלמוד הבבלי" הם מוכנים ומבינים טוב יותר. כי כבר יש להם הקדמה מפרושיו ומבאוריו. ואמינא לפועלו יישר ומן שמיא זכו ליה ללמד דעת את העם .

ויהי רצון שחפץ בידו יצלח, וכל אשר יפנה ישכיל ויצליח, ויזכה להגדיל תורה ולהאדירה, ויוסיף לנו עוד גמרות מבוארות כהנה וכהנה עד לסיומו , "וישראל עושה חיל".

ובזכות לימוד תורה ואני זאת בריתי וכו', ובא לציון גואל, בב"א.

מרדכי אליהו
ראשון לציון הרב הראשי לישראל לשעבר

The Talmud in *Eruvin* 21b states: Rava continued to interpret verses homiletically. What is the meaning of the verse: "And besides being wise, Kohelet also taught the people knowledge; and he weighed, and sought out, and set in order many proverbs" (Ecclesiastes 12:9)? He explains: He taught the people knowledge; he taught it with the accentuation marks in the Torah, and explained each matter by means of another matter similar to it. And he weighed [*izen*], and sought out, and set in order many proverbs; Ulla said that Rabbi Eliezer said: At first the Torah was like a basket without handles [*oznayim*] until Solomon came and made handles for it. And as Rashi there explains: And thus were Israel able to grasp the mitzvot and distance themselves from transgressions – just as a vessel with handles is easily held, etc.

Such things may be said of this beloved and eminent man, a great sage of Torah and of virtue. And far more than he has done with the Oral Torah, he does with the Written Torah – teaching the people knowledge. And beyond that, he also affixes handles to the Torah, i.e., to the Talmud, which is obscure and difficult for many. Only the intellectual elite, which are a precious few, and those who study in yeshiva, can today learn the Talmud and understand what it says – and even though we have Rashi, still not everyone uses him. But now the great scholar Rabbi Adin Steinsaltz שליט"א has come and affixed handles to the Torah, allowing the Talmud to be held and studied, even by simple men. And he has composed a commentary alongside the text, a fine commentary in clear, comprehensible language, "a word fitly spoken" with explanations and illustrations, so that all those who seek to study the work of God can do so.

Rabbi Mordechai Eliyahu
Former Chief Rabbi of Israel, 7 Tishrei 5754

# Message from Rabbi Adin Even-Israel Steinsaltz

The Talmud is the cornerstone of Jewish culture. True, our culture originated in the Bible and has branched out in directions besides the Talmud, yet the latter's influence on Jewish culture is fundamental. Perhaps because it was composed not by a single individual, but rather by hundreds and thousands of Sages in *batei midrash* in an ongoing, millennium-long process, the Talmud expresses the deepest themes and values not only of the Jewish people, but also of the Jewish spirit. As the basic study text for young and old, laymen and learned, the Talmud may be said to embody the historical trajectory of the Jewish soul. It is, therefore, best studied interactively, its subject matter coming together with the student's questions, perplexities, and innovations to form a single intricate weave. In the entire scope of Jewish culture, there is not one area that does not draw from or converse with the Talmud. The study of Talmud is thus the gate through which a Jew enters his life's path.

The *Koren Talmud Bavli* seeks to render the Talmud accessible to the millions of Jews whose mother tongue is English, allowing them to study it, approach it, and perhaps even become one with it.

This project has been carried out and assisted by several people, all of whom have worked tirelessly to turn this vision into an actual set of books to be studied. It is a joyful duty to thank the many partners in this enterprise for their various contributions. Thanks to Koren Publishers Jerusalem, both for the publication of this set and for the design of its very complex graphic layout. Thanks of a different sort are owed to the Steinsaltz Center and its director, Rabbi Menachem Even-Israel, for their determination and persistence in setting this goal and reaching it. Many thanks to the translators, editors, and proofreaders for their hard and meticulous work. Thanks to the individuals and organizations that supported this project, chief among them the Matanel Foundation and the Noé family of London. And thanks in advance to all those who will invest their time, hearts, and minds in studying these volumes – to learn, to teach, and to practice.

Rabbi Adin Even-Israel Steinsaltz
Jerusalem 5773

# Acknowledgments

We are indeed privileged to dedicate this edition of the *Koren Talmud Bavli* in honor of the generous support of Leo and Sue Noé of London.

The name Noé is synonymous with philanthropy. The family's charitable endeavors span a vast range of educational projects, welfare institutions, and outreach organizations across the globe, with a particular emphasis on the "nurturing of each individual." Among so many other charitable activities, the Noés have been deeply involved with Kisharon, which provides the British Jewish community with vital support for hundreds of people with learning difficulties and their families; they provide steadfast support of SEED, which stands at the forefront of adult Jewish education in the UK, and Kemach, an organization in Israel that "helps Haredi students sustain themselves in dignity," providing both professional and vocational training for the Haredi community in Israel.

The Noés are not simply donors to institutions. They are partners. Donors think of a sum. Partners think of a cause, becoming rigorously and keenly involved, and giving of their time and energy. We are honored that they have chosen to partner with our two organizations, the Steinsaltz Center and Koren Publishers Jerusalem, enabling us to further and deepen learning among all Jews.

Leo and Sue are the proud parents and grandparents of five children and their families. The next generation has been taught by example that with life's gifts come the responsibilities to be active within and contribute to society – both Jewish and non-Jewish – as is consistent with the noblest of Jewish values.

Rabbi Adin Even-Israel Steinsaltz
Matthew Miller, Publisher
Jerusalem 5773

# Introduction by the Editor-in-Chief

The publication of tractate *Nidda* is another noteworthy achievement for the *Koren Talmud Bavli* project. With this, the first and only tractate of *Seder Teharot*, the Order of Ritual Purity, addressed by the Babylonian Talmud, we have reached a milestone: The completion of a new and unique translation of the Babylonian Talmud.

Presenting the English-speaking world with a translation that possesses all the merits of the original Hebrew work by Rabbi Steinsaltz, the *Koren Talmud Bavli* provides assistance for the beginner of any age who seeks to obtain the necessary skills to become an adept talmudist. Beginning with *Berakhot* and continuing through *Nidda*, the team has brought excellence to every aspect of the daunting task of translating Rabbi Adin Even-Israel Steinsaltz's masterful Hebrew translation of the Talmud into English. Rabbi Steinsaltz's work is much more than a mere translation. It includes a coherent interpretation of the Mishna and the Gemara, and an expansion of the text that provides an array of intriguing marginal notes. Rendering this masterpiece into English called for talents that include biblical and talmudic scholarship, literary skills, linguistic expertise, editorial acumen, graphic and visual creativity, and most of all, teamwork and diligence. Congratulations to every member of the team are in order, and celebration of our achievement is well deserved.

With the completion of this last volume, tractate *Nidda*, I thank the entire professional team for its dedication, diligence, and consummate skill. I express our gratitude to the Almighty for giving us the strength to persevere at this sacred task for the past several years. These years have been difficult ones for the Jewish people, and especially for those of us who dwell in Eretz Yisrael. But the difficulties have not diminished our ability to succeed in our goals. For that we thank the Master of the Universe. It has been a great privilege for all of us on the Talmud team to be involved in this enterprise. We hope these volumes will be a worthy tool for engagement with the Talmud, the most central text of our tradition.

Students of tractate *Nidda* will be both informed and inspired. They will be informed about the laws of marital intimacy, and will be inspired by our Sages' regard for the sanctity of the human birth process. As always, we consider our efforts successful if the reader comes away from the text a better person, and not just a better-informed person. For it is our contention that Talmud study fosters lifelong ethical development and a profound sensitivity to the needs and concerns of other human beings.

We have now had the opportunity to survey hundreds of responses submitted by our readers. Naturally, these include constructive criticism and reports of errors that are inevitable in such an undertaking. We have systematically preserved such responses so that we can correct them in future editions. Indeed, we have already begun to do so for the initial tractates in our series.

The most exciting result of our survey has been our discovery that "consumers" of the *Koren Talmud Bavli* are a remarkably diverse group. They range from beginners who have never before been exposed to a *blatt gemara*, to accomplished scholars who have completed the study of the entire Talmud more than once. Beginners find our work not only a helpful introduction to Talmud study, but an impetus to the further study of rabbinic texts. Experienced scholars report that our work provides them with unexpected insights and fresh perspectives that enhance their appreciation of texts with which they have long been acquainted.

Like all the preceding volumes, the forty-second and final volume, tractate *Nidda*, includes the entire original text, in the traditional configuration and pagination of the famed Vilna edition of the Talmud. This enables the student to follow the core text with the commentaries of Rashi, *Tosafot*, and the customary marginalia. It also provides a clear English translation in contemporary idiom, faithfully based upon the modern Hebrew edition.

At least equal to the linguistic virtues of this edition are the qualities of its graphic design. Rather than intimidate students by confronting them with a page-size block of text, we have divided the page into smaller thematic units. Thus, readers can focus their attention and absorb each discrete discussion before proceeding to the next unit. The design of each page allows for sufficient white space to ease the visual task of reading. The illustrations, one of the most innovative features of the Hebrew edition, have been substantially enhanced and reproduced in color.

The end result is a literary and artistic masterpiece. This has been achieved through the dedicated work of a large team of translators, headed by Rabbi Joshua Schreier; the unparalleled creative efforts of the gifted staff at Koren; and the inspired and impressive administrative skills of Rabbi Jason Rappoport, managing editor of the *Koren Talmud Bavli* project.

It is an honor for me to acknowledge the role of Matthew Miller of Koren Publishers Jerusalem in this historic achievement. Without him this work would never have begun. Its success is attributable to his vision and supervision. I owe a great personal debt to him for selecting me as editor-in-chief, and I am continually astounded by his commitment to Jewish learning, the Jewish people, and the Jewish homeland.

The group of individuals who surround Rabbi Steinsaltz and support his work deserve our thanks as well. I have come to appreciate their energy, initiative, and persistence. And I thank the indefatigable Rabbi Menachem Even-Israel, whom I cannot praise highly enough. The quality of his guidance and good counsel is surpassed only by his commitment to the dissemination and perpetuation of his father's precious teachings.

Finally, in humility, awe, and great respect, I acknowledge Rabbi Adin Even-Israel Steinsaltz. I thank him for the inspirational opportunity he has granted me to work with one of the outstanding sages of our time.

Rabbi Tzvi Hersh Weinreb
Jerusalem 5779

# Preface by the Executive Editor

The *Koren Talmud Bavli* concludes with its treatment of tractate *Nidda*, which delineates the laws of the menstruating woman, both in terms of ritual impurity and in terms of interaction with her husband. *Nidda* is the only tractate in the sixth and final order of the Talmud, *Seder Teharot*, the Order of Ritual Purity, addressed by the Babylonian Talmud. This order deals primarily with the sources of ritual impurity, the objects subject to ritual impurity, and the means of regaining ritual purity status.

The Talmud begins with tractate *Berakhot*, the only tractate in *Seder Zera'im* included in the Babylonian Talmud, and concludes with tractate *Nidda*, the only tractate in *Seder Teharot* included in the Babylonian Talmud. These bracket the four intervening orders, *Mo'ed*, *Nashim*, *Nezikin*, and *Kodashim*, which constitute the bulk of the Babylonian Talmud.

Well-known rabbinic sayings appear at the conclusion of both tractate *Berakhot* and tractate *Nidda*, sayings that are juxtaposed at the conclusion of the *Ein Keloheinu* prayer. At the conclusion of *Nidda*, the Gemara says: The school of Elijah taught: Anyone who studies *halakhot* every day is guaranteed that he is destined for the World-to-Come, as it is stated: "The ways of the world [*halikhot*] are his" (Habakkuk 3:6). Do not read the verse as *halikhot*; rather, read it as *halakhot*.

At the conclusion of *Berakhot*, the Gemara says: Rabbi Elazar said that Rabbi Ḥanina said: Torah scholars increase peace in the world, as it is said: "And all your children [*banayikh*] will be disciples of the Lord, and the peace of your children will be abundant" (Isaiah 54:13). Do not read: "Your children [*banayikh*]," but: Your builders [*bonayikh*] (*Berakhot* 63a).

The first tractate of the Babylonian Talmud and the final tractate of the Babylonian Talmud conclude with a common theme: Those who engage in Torah study, both those who study *halakhot* every day and those who are Torah scholars, have a constructive effect on the world. They positively affect their own lives, as they are guaranteed a place in the World-to-Come, and they positively affect their surroundings, as they increase peace in the world.

It is our hope and prayer that the *Koren Talmud Bavli* has contributed, and will continue to contribute, to bettering the lives of the individuals who regularly study *halakhot* from its pages, and that they, as Torah scholars, will in turn contribute to generating genuine peace in their immediate surroundings, among the entire Jewish people, and throughout the world.

My involvement in the production of the *Koren Talmud Bavli* has been both a privilege and a pleasure. The Steinsaltz Center, headed by Rabbi Menachem Even-Israel and devoted to the dissemination of the wide-ranging, monumental works of Rabbi Adin Even-Israel Steinsaltz, constitutes the Steinsaltz side of this partnership; while Koren Publishers Jerusalem constitutes the publishing side of this partnership. The combination of the inspiration, which is the hallmark of the Steinsaltz Center, with the creativity and professionalism for which Koren is renowned, is responsible for the exceptional quality of the *Koren Talmud Bavli* in terms of both content and form.

I would be remiss if I failed to mention the contribution of Raphaël Freeman, who guided this project from its inception and is largely responsible for transforming the content of the Steinsaltz Talmud into this aesthetic finished product, the *Koren Talmud Bavli*. He was succeeded by Dena Landowne Bailey, who facilitated a seamless transition and continued to ensure that the *Koren Talmud Bavli* lives up to the lofty standards that are the hallmark of Koren Publishers. Beginning with tractate *Menaḥot*, Tomi Mager assumed responsibility for the layout. She has proven herself a worthy successor to her predecessors in that role.

I would like to express my appreciation for Rabbi Dr. Tzvi Hersh Weinreb, the editor-in-chief, whose insight and guidance have been invaluable. Rabbi Jason Rappoport, the managing editor, has added a dose of professionalism to this project, systematizing the work of the large staff, and it is thanks to him that the project was completed with efficiency and excellence. Rabbi Dr. Joshua Amaru, the coordinating editor, oversees the work of the translators and editors, and is largely responsible for ensuring the consistently high quality of their work. The contribution of my friend and colleague, Rabbi Dr. Shalom Z. Berger, the senior content editor, cannot be overstated; his title does not begin to convey the excellent direction he has provided in all aspects of this project.

The staff of copy editors, headed by Aliza Israel, with Ita Olesker as production coordinator, pleasantly but firmly ensures that the finished product conforms to standards and is consistently excellent. The erudite and articulate men and women who serve as translators, editors, and copy editors generate the content that is ultimately the *raison d'être* of the *Koren Talmud Bavli*.

I would also like to express appreciation for the invaluable contribution of the technical staff. Without them, the jobs of the entire staff of translators and editors would be much more difficult. Thanks to Tani Bednarsh, Adena Frazer, Yaakov Shmidman, Shaltiel Shmidman, and Nava Wieder.

At the risk of being repetitious, I would like to thank Rabbi Dr. Berger for introducing me to the world of Steinsaltz. Finally, I would like to thank Rabbi Menachem Even-Israel, with whom it has been a pleasure working on this monumental project. I look forward to working together with him on additional projects dedicated to providing an ever-increasing audience greater access to the works of Rabbi Steinsaltz.

Rabbi Joshua Schreier
Jerusalem 5779

# Introduction by the Publisher

The Talmud has sustained and inspired Jews for thousands of years. Throughout Jewish history, an elite cadre of scholars has absorbed its learning and passed it on to succeeding generations. The Talmud has been the fundamental text of our people.

Beginning in the 1960s, Rabbi Adin Even-Israel Steinsaltz שליט״א created a revolution in the history of Talmud study. His translation of the Talmud, first into modern Hebrew and then into other languages, as well as the practical learning aids he added to the text, have enabled millions of people around the world to access and master the complexity and context of the world of Talmud.

It is thus a privilege to present the *Koren Talmud Bavli*, an English translation of the talmudic text with the brilliant elucidation of Rabbi Steinsaltz. The depth and breadth of his knowledge are unique in our time. His rootedness in the tradition and his reach into the world beyond it are inspirational.

Working with Rabbi Steinsaltz on this remarkable project has been not only an honor, but a great pleasure. Never shy to express an opinion, with wisdom and humor, Rabbi Steinsaltz sparkles in conversation, demonstrating his knowledge (both sacred and worldly), sharing his wide-ranging interests, and, above all, radiating his passion. I am grateful for the unique opportunity to work closely with him, and I wish him many more years of writing and teaching.

Our intentions in publishing this new edition of the Talmud are threefold. First, we seek to fully clarify the talmudic page to the reader – textually, intellectually, and graphically. Second, we seek to utilize today's most sophisticated technologies, both in print and electronic formats, to provide the reader with a comprehensive set of study tools. And third, we seek to help readers advance in their process of Talmud study.

To achieve these goals, the *Koren Talmud Bavli* is unique in a number of ways:

- The classic *tzurat hadaf* of Vilna, used by scholars since the 1800s, has been reset for greater clarity, and opens from the Hebrew "front" of the book. Full *nikkud* has been added to both the talmudic text and Rashi's commentary, allowing for a more fluent reading with the correct pronunciation; the commentaries of *Tosafot* have been punctuated. Upon the advice of many English-speaking teachers of Talmud, we have separated these core pages from the translation, thereby enabling the advanced student to approach the text without the distraction of the translation. This also reduces the number of volumes in the set. At the bottom of each *daf*, there is a reference to the corresponding English pages. In addition, the Vilna edition was read against other manuscripts and older print editions, so that texts which had been removed by non-Jewish censors have been restored to their rightful place.

- The English translation, which starts on the English "front" of the book, reproduces the *menukad* Talmud text alongside the English translation (in bold) and commentary and explanation (in a lighter font). The Hebrew and Aramaic text is presented in logical paragraphs. This allows for a fluent reading of the text for the non-Hebrew or non-Aramaic reader. It also allows for the Hebrew reader to refer easily to the text alongside. Where the original text features dialogue or poetry, the English text is laid out in a manner appropriate to the genre. Each page refers to the relevant *daf*.
- Critical contextual tools surround the text and translation: personality notes, providing short biographies of the Sages; language notes, explaining foreign terms borrowed from Greek, Latin, Persian, or Arabic; and background notes, giving information essential to the understanding of the text, including history, geography, botany, archaeology, zoology, astronomy, and aspects of daily life in the talmudic era.
- Halakhic summaries provide references to the authoritative legal decisions made over the centuries by the rabbis. They explain the reasons behind each halakhic decision as well as the ruling's close connection to the Talmud and its various interpreters.
- Photographs, drawings, and other illustrations have been added throughout the text – in full color in the Standard and Electronic editions, and in black and white in the Daf Yomi edition – to visually elucidate the text.

This is not an exhaustive list of features of this edition; it merely presents an overview for the English-speaking reader who may not be familiar with the "total approach" to Talmud pioneered by Rabbi Steinsaltz.

Several professionals have helped bring this vast collaborative project to fruition. My many colleagues are noted on the Acknowledgments page, and the leadership of this project has been exceptional.

RABBI MENACHEM EVEN-ISRAEL, DIRECTOR OF THE STEINSALTZ CENTER, was the driving force behind this enterprise. With enthusiasm and energy, he formed the happy alliance with Koren and established close relationships among all involved in the work.

RABBI DR. TZVI HERSH WEINREB שליט״א, EDITOR-IN-CHIEF, brought to this project his profound knowledge of Torah, intellectual literacy of Talmud, and erudition of Western literature. It is to him that the text owes its very high standard, both in form and content, and the logical manner in which the beauty of the Talmud is presented.

RABBI JOSHUA SCHREIER, EXECUTIVE EDITOR, assembled an outstanding group of scholars, translators, editors, and copy editors, whose standards and discipline enabled this project to proceed in a timely and highly professional manner.

RABBI MEIR HANEGBI, EDITOR OF THE HEBREW EDITION OF THE STEINSALTZ TALMUD, lent his invaluable assistance throughout the work process, supervising the reproduction of the Vilna pages.

RAPHAËL FREEMAN created this Talmud's unique typographic design which, true to the Koren approach, is both elegant and user-friendly.

It has been an enriching experience for all of us at Koren Publishers Jerusalem to work with the Steinsaltz Center to develop and produce the *Koren Talmud Bavli*. We pray that this publication will be a source of great learning and, ultimately, greater *avodat Hashem* for all Jews.

Matthew Miller, Publisher
Koren Publishers Jerusalem
Jerusalem 5773

# Introduction to **Nidda**

*Nidda* is the only tractate in *Seder Teharot*, the Order of Ritual Purity, for which there is a tractate of Gemara, in addition to its *mishnayot*, both in the Babylonian Talmud and a slim volume in the Jerusalem Talmud. The rest of the many and large tractates in this order have no Gemara written on them at all. The reason for this is that when the Temple was destroyed, the *halakhot* of ritual purity discussed in *Seder Teharot* became largely inapplicable. As the connection to the Temple and its concepts became increasingly distant, the necessity of studying *Teharot* correspondingly diminished. An exception to this trend is the study of the tractates in *Seder Kodashim*, which discusses the Temple and its offerings; the study of *Kodashim* can be understood as an expression of the eternal hope in the rebuilding of the Temple and of the redemption. The study of *Teharot*, which deals with the *halakhot* of ritual purity that are merely affiliated with the Temple, does not represent the same hope and indefatigable yearning.

The exception within *Seder Teharot* is tractate *Nidda*, as the status of a menstruating woman includes two aspects: One is that such a woman assumes ritual impurity status and transmits impurity. Her touch disqualifies consecrated items and renders ritually pure items impure. This aspect is similar to the other *halakhot* of impurity discussed throughout *Seder Teharot*. The second aspect is the status of a menstruating woman as one with whom intercourse is strictly forbidden, to the point that a man and woman who transgress this prohibition are liable to receive the grave punishment of *karet*. Although the first aspect of ritual impurity is just as impractical as the rest of *Teharot*, this second aspect of forbidden intercourse remains as applicable as ever. It is therefore necessary to delve into these *halakhot* and clarify them in every respect, in order to establish the *halakha* in practice.

This tractate deals not only with the *halakhot* of a menstruating woman, but also with a series of other related *halakhot* that have some connection to a menstruating woman. Many of these topics have no other corpus where they are elucidated in full. The *halakhot* concerning a menstruating woman are derived, in the main, from the verse: "And if a woman has an issue, and her issue in her flesh is blood, she shall be in her menstruation seven days, and whoever touches her shall be impure until the evening." (Leviticus 15:19). The subject closest to the case of a menstruating woman is a *zava* (see Leviticus 15:25–30). The discharge of *ziva* that applies to women has no medical similarity to that of a male *zav*. Whereas the *ziva* of a man is a specific, known condition with its own specifications, the *ziva* found in women is defined as the discharge of uterine blood not at the time of her menstruation. The status of a *zava* is generally even more stringent than that of a menstruating woman, as a greater *zava* requires a longer period of time to attain a status of purity: Seven days during which absolutely no blood is found. In addition, she must bring offerings upon the completion of her purification period.

A different type of ritual impurity is caused by the flow of blood of a woman after childbirth. The Torah states (see Leviticus 12:1–8) that there is a specific period of time after childbirth when any blood that the mother discharges has the same status as menstrual blood. Following that period of impurity there is a period of blood of purity, during which any blood that she emits does not transmit impurity. Different periods of impurity and purity are prescribed in accordance with the sex of the baby. A woman after childbirth is also required by Torah law to bring offerings after that period of purity, and only after their sacrifice is she permitted to partake of consecrated food and enter the Temple.

In addition to these categories of blood that transmit impurity by Torah law, there are other types of blood that exit via the vagina that do not transmit impurity by Torah law. They are blood from a torn hymen and blood from a wound along the vaginal canal. These types of blood are free of impurity, but one is not always able to distinguish between different types of blood to determine if blood that is found in that area is impure, pure, or a mixture of the two.

The Torah teaches what kinds of blood transmit impurity and which *halakhot* govern each particular type of blood. The discharges of these various types of blood are tangible, physical occurrences, and the ability to clarify and investigate physical phenomena is accessible to the experts of each generation.

Nevertheless, due to the grave nature of these prohibitions, the transgression of which can entail the punishment of *karet*, the Sages throughout the generations have cautioned and safeguarded not only against clear prohibitions, but also against any cases of uncertainty. One result of such concerns is that even the examinations recommended by the Talmud were not always relied upon in practice if they led to lenient rulings. Some of these examinations entail fine distinctions between shades of blood, and at times even differences in form or smell, and these distinctions cannot easily be expressed in words. Therefore, there is always a concern that our expertise in these areas might be lacking, and the tendency is to err on the side of caution when rendering practical rulings.

Tractate *Nidda* also analyzes the length of a woman's menstrual cycle. There are seven days of ritual impurity status caused by any discharge of menstrual blood, whether it flows throughout the seven days or only on some of them. This is followed by a period of purity that spans eleven days in between each period of menstruation. During that time, blood that a woman emits is not considered menstrual blood. If she does experience bleeding, it is defined as *ziva* blood, to which a different set of *halakhot* apply. Although there may be differences in practice, this cycle of seven days followed by eleven days is a set system with regard to the various *halakhot* of a menstruating woman and a *zava* that is accepted as a *halakha* transmitted to Moses from Sinai.

These fixed halakhic definitions and established principles often become confusing when applied to real-life scenarios. Menstrual cycles are complex and irregular. This is true not only of women in general, but even with regard to each woman's individual cycle. Whereas some woman have fixed, immutable menstrual cycles, both with regard to the dates on which menstruation occurs and its duration, others have more sporadic, variable cycles that are unpredictable both with regard to duration as well as the dates on which menstruation occurs or does not occur. Time is of utmost importance in this regard, as it is imperative to know in advance exactly when a woman may assume ritual impurity status and when she will have the presumptive status of ritual purity. As stated, there are no natural or fixed principles that can be followed in all cases, and the issue of how to deal with differences between one woman and the next, as well as the variations within each individual woman, occupies a significant portion of this tractate.

Another halakhic topic that has significant practical ramifications is with regard to blood stains. Many of the cases discussed in the tractate do not involve isolated blood, but rather blood that has been absorbed into clothing or found somewhere else. In most instances it is easy to verify the facts with regard to the source of a discovered blood stain and when it appeared. Yet, in many situations when blood is found absorbed in clothing or somewhere on the body, the time of its appearance and its origin are unclear. In such cases it might even be unknown whether the blood came from the body of a woman or from another source, such as an animal. Furthermore, even if it came from a woman, it may be uncertain whether it is uterine blood or blood from a wound found in the vaginal canal or from some other wound.

Tractate *Nidda* discusses the halakhic implications of all these aforementioned types of blood. It largely discusses an aspect that is still applicable nowadays, the prohibition of intercourse, and for that matter, all forms of physical intimacy with a menstruating woman. Apropos of this topic, it also discusses matters that are not relevant nowadays, specifically the study of ritual purity as it relates to the status of a menstruating woman.

There is one *halakha* that renders virtually obsolete a large proportion of the most basic halakhic concepts contained in this tractate. The Talmud refers to this *halakha* as the stringency that Jewish women accepted upon themselves, and it is considered by the authorities as the basic *halakha*.

This stringency is that every woman who sees even the most minuscule amount of possible menstrual blood automatically assumes the ritual impurity status of a *zava*. In many cases there is no perceivable basis for this concern, but nevertheless it determines all the relevant *halakhot*. Due to this accepted custom, there is no longer any practical significance to many of the details and discussions contained in this tractate.

The tractate also includes lengthy discussions of the *halakhot* of childbirth. The *halakhot* that apply to a normal childbirth are stated explicitly in the Torah. Yet, there are many questions with regard to irregular occurrences, such as caesarean births and various types of miscarriages, including instances where the fetus is deformed to the point where it does not have a human form. Another matter that requires clarification is the stage of pregnancy when a miscarriage is considered a full-fledged birth. The analysis of these issues is important both with regard to establishing whether any ensuing blood is considered menstrual blood, and for determining the purity status of the mother.

Another detailed discussion in this tractate is the various stages that a child passes through on his or her way to adulthood. What are the external physical signs that indicate the stages of a developed youth, and which subsequent signs are indicative of adulthood? These definitions are important with regard to both the *halakhot* of menstruation as well as the obligation to observe mitzvot and the liability for punishment that come with adulthood.

*Nidda* is considered one of the more difficult tractates of the Talmud. There are several reasons for this. One is that a significant portion of its discussions is either connected to, or entirely focused on, the *halakhot* of ritual impurity. As far back as talmudic times, the *halakhot* of ritual impurity have been considered one of the most complex systems of Torah law. The Rambam writes in his introduction to *Teharot* that even if one were to review them many times, he would still be lacking in his clear understanding of these matters. This is partly because their basic principles cannot be logically deduced, which results in many discrete *halakhot*, each of which is apparently dictated by its own logic or internal rationale.

Another difficulty in studying this tractate that obfuscates the basic reading of the text is that the Talmud often speaks in euphemistic terms, designed to mask material of a sexual or graphic nature. Metaphors, symbols, and analogies are often used for this purpose. Since the basic meaning of the words and the concepts in question is ambiguous, this can lead to difficulties in analyzing the text, both in terms of general ideas and with regard to the halakhic ramifications.

The vast majority of the tractate deals with the clarification of halakhic principles and how they may be applied. In addition, it also contains a certain amount of aggadic literature. In most cases the aggadic passages are closely related to the main topics of the tractate. Some are cited in order to help clarify ideas or situations, while others teach proper ethical behavior or delve into spiritual matters connected to the main discussion.

Tractate *Nidda* contains ten chapters. A single chapter might deal entirely with one topic, or a topic might span across more than one chapter. Likewise, there are chapters that focus on varied topics.

Chapter One discusses the point at which a menstruating woman transmits ritual impurity due to uncertainty. It also addresses the issue of which women are considered either temporarily or permanently pure due to their suspended menstruation.

Chapter Two deals with the ways in which a menstruating woman performs her self-examinations, as well as the various shades of blood that cause a woman to have the status of a menstruating woman.

The main topic of Chapter Three is miscarriages. The chapter defines what is considered to be a fully formed fetus and what is only an incomplete sac.

Chapter Four addresses two central topics: One is the *halakhot* of menstruation as they apply to Cuthean, Sadducee, and gentile women. The other is the menstruation or *ziva* status of a woman who is having difficulty giving birth and discharges blood for a substantial period of time.

Chapter Five continues with the previous topics, but its main focus is the stages at which girls and boys pass into adulthood.

Chapter Six further analyzes these topics, although it mostly contains a collection of varied *halakhot* and topics gathered together not due to their content, but due to their similar structure and style.

Chapter Seven deals with categories of ritual impurity for which wetness or dryness makes a difference. It also discusses the *halakhot* of impurity with regard to Cutheans.

Chapter Eight focuses on the *halakhot* of blood stains found on a woman's clothing or skin. It defines which stains cause impurity and which are treated leniently.

Chapter Nine discusses what to do when the origin of found blood is unknown. When is it assumed that the blood came from a certain woman and when can it be presumed that it came from other sources? In addition, the chapter explains how stains can be analyzed to determine if they are in fact blood or some other substance. This chapter also contains a discussion of the establishment of fixed menstrual cycles, whether they are based upon specific dates or upon particular physical phenomena.

Finally, Chapter Ten deals with a variety of topics, including bleeding from the torn hymen, examinations of various forms of ritual impurity where there is uncertainty as to the accuracy of the examination, blood of purity following childbirth, and the *halakha* of one who passes away in a state of ritual impurity. In addition, there is a discussion concerning a woman who engages in intercourse with her husband before she completes the full process required to attain ritual purity.

# Introduction to **Perek I**

*And if a woman has an issue, and her issue in her flesh is blood, she shall be in her menstruation seven days, and whoever touches her shall be impure until the evening.*

(Leviticus 15:19)

The Sages derived from the above verse that any woman who emits blood from her uterus becomes ritually impure, even if the blood never completely exits her body. Not only does she assume ritual impurity status from when she had the discharge of blood, but the Sages are concerned that she might have emitted blood earlier unawares. In this chapter, the Gemara discusses the length of time with regard to which she is retroactively considered impure due to this concern. Is it from the last time she performed a self-examination, or is it for a twenty-four-hour period?

This issue of retroactive impurity is analyzed and applied to several categories of women who have different types of menstrual cycles. Some have fixed menstrual cycles while others do not. There are older women whose menstrual cycles have ceased, and young girls who have not yet started menstruating. There are also pregnant and nursing women, whose cycles are suspended due to their current physical condition. The *halakha* of each of these classes of women requires clarification.

With regard to the determination of the time for which a woman assumes retroactive ritual impurity, various external factors must be addressed as well. One of these is the requirement to perform internal examinations before and after intercourse. Another is the significance of a contraceptive absorbent cloth a woman placed in her vaginal canal prior to her finding blood, or if she was awake and aware to the extent that she would have felt the discharge at its onset.

This chapter also includes a discussion of the ritually pure items that a menstruating woman had touched during the period of her retroactive impurity. Is there a difference between sacred items and non-sacred items in this regard? Furthermore, it considers whether the location of the pure items at the time she touched them makes any difference, as the issue of whether an item is in the public domain or private domain is generally of great importance in cases of uncertainty involving ritual purity.

מתני׳ שַׁמַּאי אוֹמֵר: כׇּל הַנָּשִׁים דַּיָּין שְׁעָתָן. הִלֵּל אוֹמֵר: מִפְּקִידָה לִפְקִידָה, וַאֲפִילּוּ לְיָמִים הַרְבֵּה.

**MISHNA** Shammai[P] **says: For all women** who do not have a fixed menstrual cycle, **their time is sufficient.** Women who discern that menstrual blood emerged do not need to be concerned that perhaps the flow of blood began before they noticed it. Rather, they assume their ritual impurity status begins at that moment, in terms of rendering impure *teruma* and ritually pure items with which they come in contact. **Hillel says: From examination [*mipekida*]**[B] **to examination,** i.e., she assumes ritual impurity status retroactive to the last time she examined herself and determined that she was ritually pure, **and** this is the *halakha* **even** if her examination took place **several days** earlier. Any ritually pure item with which she came in contact in the interim becomes ritually impure.

וַחֲכָמִים אוֹמְרִים: לֹא כְּדִבְרֵי זֶה וְלֹא כְּדִבְרֵי זֶה, אֶלָּא מֵעֵת לְעֵת – מְמַעֶטֶת עַל יַד מִפְּקִידָה לִפְקִידָה, וּמִפְּקִידָה לִפְקִידָה – מְמַעֶטֶת עַל יַד מֵעֵת לְעֵת.

**And the Rabbis say:** The *halakha* **is neither in accordance with the statement of this** *tanna* **nor in accordance with the statement of that** *tanna*; **rather,** the principle is: A twenty-four-hour **period**[N] **reduces** the time **from examination to examination.**[H] In other words, if her final self-examination took place more than twenty-four hours earlier, she need only concern herself with ritual impurity for the twenty-four-hour period prior to discerning the blood. **And from examination to examination reduces** the time **from** a twenty-four-hour **period.** In other words, if she examined herself in the course of the previous day and discovered no blood, she was certainly ritually pure prior to the examination.

כׇּל אִשָּׁה שֶׁיֵּשׁ לָהּ וֶסֶת – דַּיָּהּ שְׁעָתָהּ. וְהַמְשַׁמֶּשֶׁת בְּעֵדִים – הֲרֵי זוֹ כִּפְקִידָה, וּמְמַעֶטֶת עַל יַד מֵעֵת לְעֵת וְעַל יַד מִפְּקִידָה לִפְקִידָה.

For **any woman who has a fixed** menstrual **cycle [*veset*],**[HL] and she examined herself at that time and discovered blood, **her time is sufficient,** and it is only from that time that she transmits ritual impurity. **And** with regard to a woman **who engages in intercourse** while using **examination cloths [*be'edim*]**[NL] before and after intercourse, with which she ascertains whether her menstrual flow began, the halakhic status of such an action **is like that of an examination, and** therefore **it reduces** the time **from** a twenty-four-hour **period,** and reduces the time **from examination to examination.**

**HALAKHA**

**A twenty-four-hour period reduces the time from examination to examination** – מֵעֵת לְעֵת מְמַעֶטֶת עַל יַד מִפְּקִידָה לִפְקִידָה: A menstruating woman, a *zava*, a lesser *zava* who observes a clean day for a day she experiences a discharge, and a woman who recently gave birth, all assume ritual impurity status retroactive to the last time they examined themselves, or for the last twenty-four hours. For example, if a woman of ritually pure status who has no fixed menstrual cycle examines herself in the morning and finds herself clean of menstrual blood, and half a day later she examines herself again and finds menstrual blood, all the ritually pure items that she touched in between those two examinations are retroactively deemed ritually impure. Some note that this is only when she finds definite menstrual blood in her second examination and not in a case of uncertainty (*Mishne LaMelekh*). If the last time she examined herself was two or three days previously, then only the ritually pure items that she touched in the last twenty-four hours are retroactively deemed ritually impure. This is in accordance with the opinion of the Rabbis in the mishna (Rambam *Sefer Tahara, Hilkhot Metamei Mishkav UMoshav* 3:4).

**Any woman who has a fixed menstrual cycle** – כׇּל אִשָּׁה שֶׁיֵּשׁ לָהּ וֶסֶת: A woman who has a fixed menstrual cycle who experiences a flow of menstrual blood at her fixed time assumes ritual impurity status beginning at that moment. She does not assume impurity status retroactively (Rambam *Sefer Kedusha, Hilkhot Issurei Bia* 9:4).

**LANGUAGE**

**Fixed menstrual cycle [*veset*]** – וֶסֶת: The etymology of this word is unclear. Some maintain that it comes from the Greek ἔθος, *ethos*, which means routine or custom. Indeed, in the mishna and for many subsequent generations, the word was used in this sense. Over the course of time the word has become associated with a woman's regular menstrual cycle.

**Examination cloths [*edim*]** – עֵדִים: There are two different ways in which this word can be vowelized. According to the way this word is vowelized here, *edim*, it is connected to the word for witness, *ed*, or the word for an adornment, *adi* (see Isaiah 49:18). Others vowelize it as *idim*, in which case it refers to a worn piece of cloth (see Isaiah 64:5).

**PERSONALITIES**

**Shammai** – שַׁמַּאי: Shammai, occasionally referred to as Shammai the Elder, was the counterpart of Hillel the Elder; they constituted the last of the pairs of Sages of the early tannaitic period, approximately one hundred years prior to the destruction of the Temple, at the beginning of Herod's reign. Hillel was the *Nasi* and Shammai served as president of the court. Despite the fact that they founded two schools, Beit Hillel and Beit Shammai, whose disputes continued for many years after their passing, they themselves disagreed with regard to only three or four issues. The difference between Hillel and Shammai themselves was mainly a difference in character. Hillel related to himself and to others in an easygoing manner, avoiding conflict whenever possible. Shammai, by contrast, took a more exacting approach, closely scrutinizing people's motivation and conduct. Nevertheless, it was Shammai who was known for teaching: And greet every person with a pleasant countenance (*Avot* 1:15). Little is known about his personal life. He was apparently an architect or builder by trade, as he is described on several occasions standing with a builder's cubit, which was a common measuring stick, in his hand.

**BACKGROUND**

**Examination [*pekida*]** – פְּקִידָה: Some explain that in the context of the mishna, this word simply means: Examination. Others maintain that here *pekida* has the connotation of remembering (see Genesis 21:1), as women must constantly remember to perform their rabbinically obligated self-examinations twice daily. Another connotation of the word *pekida* is that of counting (see Numbers 1:3), as a woman relies on these self-examinations in the course of counting seven clean days.

**NOTES**

**A twenty-four-hour period** – מֵעֵת לְעֵת: This expression, which literally means: From time to time, is understood by some commentaries as referring to the same time of day yesterday, i.e., a full twenty-four-hour period (Rashi; Rambam). By contrast, some *ge'onim* maintain that it means a twelve-hour period, which is the amount of time a couple is required to separate from each other close to the woman's menstrual cycle (Responsa of the *Ge'onim*).

**A woman who engages in intercourse while using examination cloths** – וְהַמְשַׁמֶּשֶׁת בְּעֵדִים: The Gemara's final explanation (5a) is that the mishna is referring to the examination cloths used by both husband and wife. There is a variant reading of the text here: And she engages in intercourse while using examination cloths, i.e., every woman is required to examine herself with an examination cloth before and after intercourse.

## HALAKHA

A woman with a fixed cycle counts her menstrual days only from the moment that she saw blood – אֵינָהּ מוֹנָה אֶלָּא מִשָּׁעָה שֶׁרָאֲתָה: Although the Rabbis said that a woman who experiences a flow of menstrual blood not at the time of her fixed menstrual cycle transmits ritual impurity retroactively for a twenty-four-hour period; she counts her menstrual days only from the moment that she experiences a flow of blood or a stain (Rambam *Sefer Kedusha, Hilkhot Issurei Bia* 9:3).

כֵּיצַד דַּיָּהּ שָׁעָתָהּ? הָיְתָה יוֹשֶׁבֶת בַּמִּטָּה וַעֲסוּקָה בְּטָהֳרוֹת, וּפָרְשָׁה וְרָאֲתָה – הִיא טְמֵאָה וְהֵן טְהוֹרוֹת.

**Her time is sufficient, how so?** If the woman **was sitting in the bed**[B] **and engaged in** handling **ritually pure items, and she left** the bed **and saw** blood, **she is ritually impure and** those items **are ritually pure.**

אַף עַל פִּי שֶׁאָמְרוּ: מְטַמְּאָה מֵעֵת לְעֵת – אֵינָהּ מוֹנָה אֶלָּא מִשָּׁעָה שֶׁרָאֲתָה.

**Although** the Rabbis **said** that a woman without a fixed menstrual cycle **transmits ritual impurity** retroactively **for** a twenty-four-hour **period,** a woman with a fixed cycle **counts** her menstrual days **only from the moment that she saw** blood.[H]

גמ׳ מַאי טַעְמֵיהּ דְּשַׁמַּאי? קָסָבַר: הַעֲמֵד אִשָּׁה עַל חֶזְקָתָהּ, וְאִשָּׁה בְּחֶזְקַת טְהוֹרָה עוֹמֶדֶת. וְהִלֵּל, כִּי אָמַר הַעֲמֵד דָּבָר עַל חֶזְקָתוֹ הֵיכָא דְּלֵית לֵיהּ רֵיעוּתָא מִגּוּפֵיהּ, אֲבָל אִיתְּתָא

**GEMARA** The mishna teaches that when a woman discerns that her menstrual blood emerged, Shammai holds that her impurity status starts from that moment, while Hillel maintains that it begins from the time of her most recent self-examination. The Gemara asks: **What is the reason** for the opinion **of Shammai?** The Gemara answers: Shammai **holds** that as there is a principle that when the status of an item is uncertain it retains its presumptive status, here too: **Establish** the **woman in her presumptive status, and a woman remains with the presumptive status of** being **ritually pure. And** what is the reasoning of **Hillel?** He claims that **when** one **states** the principle: **Establish an item in its presumptive status,** that applies only **where there is no weakening** in the presumptive status that is a result **of** the item **itself. But** in the case of **a woman,**

## BACKGROUND

Bed – מִטָּה: In talmudic times, the bed was used for other purposes besides sleeping, consequently it was an important piece of furniture in the house. A typical bed was rectangular and stood on legs. Some had four additional bed-frame posts, and others had two bed poles, which were used to create a structure for a tent-like covering over the bed.

Terracotta bed, third century BCE

Perek **I**
Daf **2** Amud **b**

כֵּיוָן דְּמִגּוּפָהּ קָחָזְיָא – לָא אָמְרִינַן אוֹקְמַהּ אַחֶזְקָתָהּ.

**since** it is her nature **to see** blood flow **from her body**[N] at regular intervals, **we do not say: Establish her in her presumptive status** of ritual purity.[N] Her body is constantly changing, and therefore she has no such presumptive status.

## NOTES

Since it is her nature to see blood flow from her body – כֵּיוָן דְּמִגּוּפָהּ קָחָזְיָא: Various explanations are given for this statement. Some say that it means that a woman is prone to experience menstruation (Rashi) or that she regularly experiences menstruation (*Tosefot Rid*) and therefore she has no presumptive status of purity. Later authorities note that this reasoning applies even to a woman who has no fixed menstrual cycle (*Noda BiYehuda*). Others maintain that she has no presumptive status of ritual purity, as the menstrual blood is always lying dormant within her body (*Tosefot HaRosh*). Yet others explain the phrase more literally: Since her impurity comes from her body rather than from an external source, she has no presumptive status of purity (*Beit HaLevi*).

We do not say: Establish her in her presumptive status of ritual purity – לָא אָמְרִינַן אוֹקְמַהּ אַחֶזְקָתָהּ: Some question why this *halakha* is determined by the woman's status of impurity and not the presumed status of purity of the items that she touched? They answer that since the variable in question is the point in time that the woman's menstruation started, therefore the ritual status of the woman must first be determined, as the status of the items is dependent upon her (*Tosefot HaRosh*; *Tosefot Rid*; *Mayim Amukim*, *Yosef Da'at*).

וּמַאי שְׁנָא מִמִּקְוֶה? דִּתְנַן: מִקְוֶה שֶׁנִּמְדַּד וְנִמְצָא חָסֵר – כָּל טָהֳרוֹת שֶׁנַּעֲשׂוּ עַל גַּבָּיו לְמַפְרֵעַ, בֵּין בִּרְשׁוּת הָרַבִּים בֵּין בִּרְשׁוּת הַיָּחִיד, טְמֵאוֹת.

With regard to the opinions of both Shammai and Hillel, the Gemara asks: **And in what way is this case different from that of a ritual bath? As we learned** in a mishna (*Mikvaot* 2:2): In the case **of a ritual bath** that was known to have contained the requisite forty *se'a*, **which was** then **measured and found lacking**[HB] in its quantity of water, **all pure items that had been rendered** pure **in it,** i.e., any impure items that had been purified through immersion in this ritual bath, **retroactive** to when the ritual bath was last measured, **whether** this ritual bath is found **in the private domain or in the public domain, are impure.**

לְשַׁמַּאי – קַשְׁיָא לְמַפְרֵעַ.

The Gemara explains: **According to** the opinion of **Shammai,** the mishna poses **a difficulty from** its statement that the change in the ritual bath's status is assumed **retroactive** to the time when it was last measured, as he maintains that a menstruating woman's status changes only at the present moment, not retroactive to the last time she examined herself.

לְהִלֵּל קַשְׁיָא וַדַּאי, דְּאִילּוּ מֵעֵת לְעֵת שֶׁבְּנִדָּה תּוֹלִין, לֹא אוֹכְלִין וְלֹא שׂוֹרְפִין, וְאִילּוּ הָכָא – טוּמְאָה וַדַּאי!

**According to** the opinion of **Hillel,** the mishna also poses **a difficulty** with regard to its ruling that the items purified in the ritual bath are deemed impure with **certainty, whereas** a menstruating women does not assume retroactive impurity with certainty. In other words, although according to the Rabbis there is a twenty-four-hour **period** of retroactive ritual impurity in the case **of a menstruating woman,**[N] and according to Hillel the retroactive impurity extends back to her most recent examination, nevertheless any *teruma* that she touched during that period is not deemed definitely impure to the extent that it must be burned. Rather, the impure status of the items she touched is uncertain and the status of the *teruma* is **suspended,** i.e., one may **neither eat** it **nor burn** it. **Whereas here,** in the case of the ritual bath, any item purified in it is retroactively deemed **definitely impure.**

הָתָם מִשּׁוּם דְּאִיכָּא לְמֵימַר: הַעֲמֵד טָמֵא עַל חֶזְקָתוֹ, וְאֵימָא לֹא טָבַל. אַדְּרַבָּה, הַעֲמֵד מִקְוֶה עַל חֶזְקָתוֹ וְאֵימָא לֹא חָסַר! הֲרֵי חָסֵר לְפָנֶיךָ!

The Gemara answers: **There,** in the case of a ritual bath, it is different, **since it can be said: Establish** the **impure** item **in its presumptive status and say** that **it was not** properly **immersed.** In other words, the presumptive status of the item as ritually impure is in keeping with the current deficient state of the ritual bath. The Gemara raises a difficulty: **On the contrary,** one should **establish the ritual bath in its presumptive state** of validity[N] **and say that** the ritual bath **was not** previously **lacking** the requisite measure of water. The Gemara responds: There is no presumptive state of validity, as the ritual bath **is lacking before you,** i.e., at present, and this offsets the presumptive status that it was full.

**HALAKHA**

A ritual bath which was measured and found lacking – מִקְוֶה שֶׁנִּמְדַּד וְנִמְצָא חָסֵר: If a ritual bath was measured and found to be lacking in the requisite amount of water for a ritual bath, anything immersed in it, going back to the time when it was last inspected and found full, is considered to be impure. It makes no difference whether the ritual bath was in the public domain or the private domain. This *halakha* applies only to severe categories of impurity; but with regard to lenient forms of ritual impurity, such as one who ate impure food, the individual remains pure despite the uncertainty, since this type of impurity is rabbinic in origin. The Ra'avad maintains that even by rabbinic law an individual who immersed in it to purify himself of a primary category of impurity remains impure (Rambam *Sefer Tahara, Hilkhot Mikvaot* 10:6; *Shulḥan Arukh, Yoreh De'a* 201:71).

**BACKGROUND**

A ritual bath which was measured and found lacking – מִקְוֶה שֶׁנִּמְדַּד וְנִמְצָא חָסֵר: A valid ritual bath must have forty *se'a* of water in it. A *se'a* is one-thirtieth of a *kor*, or the equivalent of 144 egg-bulks. Forty *se'a* are the equivalent of eighty *hin* or 5,760 egg-bulks. The Talmud tells us that the dimensions of a ritual bath must be three cubits by one cubit by one cubit, and that its volume must be forty *se'a*. Consequently, according to the calculations of Rabbi Ḥayyim Na'e in *Shiuri Torah*, a ritual bath must contain at least slightly less than 332 liters of water, while according to the calculation of the *Ḥazon Ish*, it must contain at least 573 liters.

Ancient ritual bath in the western Negev

**NOTES**

There is a twenty-four-hour period of retroactive ritual impurity in the case of a menstruating woman – מֵעֵת לְעֵת שֶׁבְּנִדָּה: Some question why the Gemara refers to the opinion of the Rabbis that a menstruating woman assumes impurity for a retroactive twenty-four-hour period when it explains its challenge to the opinion of Hillel, who disagrees with them. Rashi explains that the Gemara means to broadly refer both to the Rabbis' twenty-four-hour period of retroactive impurity as well as Hillel's period of retroactive impurity that extends back to the time of her last self-examination.

Establish the ritual bath in its presumptive state of validity – הַעֲמֵד מִקְוֶה עַל חֶזְקָתוֹ: Based upon the Gemara's suggestion to affix the ritual bath's status based upon its presumptive status of validity, some authorities maintain that once a ritual bath has been properly filled with its requisite measure of water, going forward it always has a presumptive status of validity and it does not need to be checked on a regular basis (*Magen Avraham*; *Arukh LaNer*). Others disagree and maintain that no halakhic presumptive status may be affixed through human intervention. Therefore the human measurement that determines that a ritual bath contains its requisite measure may not be relied upon to create a presumptive status of validity and purity, and therefore the ritual bath must be regularly checked (*Baḥ*). Similarly they maintain that ritual fringes must constantly be checked to ensure their validity. Furthermore, there is an authority among those who are lenient with regard to the necessity to constantly check a ritual bath who agrees that in the case of ritual fringes, they must be constantly checked. Since this brief examination is easily performed one may not rely on a presumed status (*Magen Avraham*).

הָכָא נַמִי: הֲרֵי דָּם לְפָנֶיךָ! הָשְׁתָּא הוּא דַּחֲזַאי. הָכָא נַמִי: הָשְׁתָּא הוּא דַּחֲסַר!

The Gemara raises a difficulty: **Here too,** in the case of a menstruating woman, she is one who has experienced a discharge of **blood before you,** i.e., at present. Just as the ritual bath's presumptive status of validity is offset by its present lack of the requisite measure of water, so too the woman's previous presumptive status of ritual purity is offset by her present state of impurity due to menstruation. The Gemara answers: In the case of the menstruating woman, it is possible that **it is** only **now that she saw** the first emission of her menstrual blood. The Gemara retorts: One can say the same with regard to the ritual bath: **Here too, it is** only **now that** it **became lacking** in the requisite measure of water.

הָכִי הָשְׁתָּא? הָתָם – אִיכָּא לְמֵימַר חֲסַר וְאָתָא חֲסַר וַאֲתָא, הָכָא – מִי אִיכָּא לְמֵימַר חֲזַאי וְאָתָא חֲזַאי וַאֲתָא? וּמַאי קוּשְׁיָא? דִּלְמָא הַגַּס הַגַּס חֲזִיתֵיהּ?

The Gemara answers: **How can** these cases **be compared? There,** in the case of the ritual bath, **it can be said** that the water slowly trickled out and consequently the amount of water was **continuously diminishing.**[N] Therefore, it is possible that the ritual bath lost its valid status long ago without anyone realizing. By contrast, **here,** with regard to a menstruating woman, **can it be said** that she was **continuously seeing** menstrual blood? The Gemara responds: **And what is the difficulty?** The same possibility does in fact exist in the case of a menstruating woman, as **perhaps she saw** the blood depart **bit** [***hagas***][L] **by bit.**

הָתָם – אִיכָּא תַּרְתֵּי לְרֵיעוּתָא, הָכָא – אִיכָּא חֲדָא לְרֵיעוּתָא.

The Gemara states a different answer: **There,** in the case of the ritual bath, **there are two** factors **that weaken**[N] the suggestion that the items are ritually pure: First, the ritual bath is lacking at present; second, the item has a presumptive status of impurity. **Here,** by contrast, **there is** only **one** factor **that weakens** the possibility that the items touched by the currently menstruating woman were rendered ritually impure, i.e., that she is currently experiencing a menstrual flow. Therefore, according to Shammai she assumes impurity status only from that moment onward, and according to Hillel her retroactive impurity status applies only as an uncertainty.

וּמַאי שְׁנָא מֵחָבִית? דִּתְנַן: הָיָה בּוֹדֵק אֶת הֶחָבִית לִהְיוֹת מַפְרִישׁ עָלֶיהָ תְּרוּמָה וְהוֹלֵךְ, וְאַחַר כָּךְ נִמְצָא חוֹמֶץ, כָּל שְׁלֹשָׁה יָמִים (הָרִאשׁוֹנִים) – וַדַּאי,

§ The Gemara asks: **And** according to Shammai, who holds that her time is sufficient and there is no retroactive impurity, **what is different** in the case **of a barrel?**[B] **As it is taught** in a *baraita* (*Tosefta*, *Terumot* 2:8): If someone **would inspect** the contents of **a barrel**[HN] to see if it still contained enough wine **to continually** mentally **separate *teruma***[B] **from it,** i.e., to exempt other untithed wine of his until all the wine in this barrel will be *teruma*, **and afterward** the contents of the barrel **were found** to have turned to **vinegar,** which cannot be set aside as *teruma* for untithed wine, then for **all of the first three days** following his most recent inspection, it is **definitely** considered to have been wine. Therefore, any of the untithed wine for which *teruma* was separated during those days is tithed.

## HALAKHA

**If someone would inspect the contents of a barrel** – הָיָה בּוֹדֵק אֶת הֶחָבִית: If a person inspects the contents of a barrel and determines that it contains enough wine to separate *teruma* from it to exempt other untithed wine, and later he finds that the wine turned to vinegar, it is assumed that it was good wine for three days after it was initially inspected, and all the *teruma* separated during that period is valid. Any *teruma* separated afterward is in doubt and must be separated again (Rambam *Sefer Zera'im*, *Hilkhot Terumot* 5:24; see Radbaz and *Kesef Mishne* there).

## LANGUAGE

**A bit [*hagas*]** – הַגַּס: Some say *hagas* is related to the word *gis*, meaning a close relationship, i.e., the blood came out close to the present time, or it came out gently. Alternatively, it can sometimes mean large, which may be the case in this context as well, i.e., the blood accumulated (Rashi).

## BACKGROUND

**Barrel** – חָבִית: Generally barrels were made of clay and used for storing food items. Sometimes they were used to hold liquids like oil and honey, or solids such as grains, olives, and figs, but their main purpose was for wine storage. After they were filled, they were sealed with a plug. Often an inappropriate or ill-fitted plug would lead to the wine oxidizing and turning to vinegar.

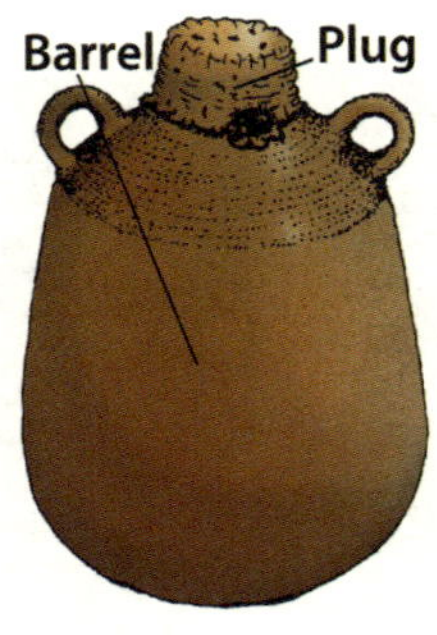


Earthenware barrel with a plug

***Teruma*** – תְּרוּמָה: Whenever the term *teruma* appears without qualification, it refers to *teruma gedola*. The Torah commands that "the first fruit of your grain, of your wine, and of your oil" be given to the priest (Deuteronomy 18:4; Numbers 18:12), but the Sages extended the scope of this mitzva, which applies only in Eretz Yisrael, to include all produce. After the first fruits have been separated, a certain portion of the produce must be separated for priests as *teruma*.

Although the Torah does not specify the amount of *teruma* that must be separated, and one may theoretically fulfill his obligation by giving even a single kernel of grain from an entire crop, the Sages established a measure: One-fortieth for a generous gift, one-fiftieth for an average gift, and one-sixtieth for a miserly gift. One first separates *teruma* and then separates the other tithes.

Teruma is considered sacred and may be eaten only by a priest and his household while they are in a state of ritual purity (see Leviticus 22:9–15). To emphasize the importance of this requirement, the Sages obligated the priests to wash their hands before partaking of *teruma*. This is the source for the practice of washing the hands before eating. A ritually impure priest or a non-priest who eats *teruma* is subject to death at the hand of Heaven. If *teruma* becomes ritually impure, it may no longer be eaten and must be burned. Nevertheless, it remains the property of the priest, and he may benefit from its burning.

Today, *teruma* is not given to priests because they have no definite proof of their priestly lineage and because everyone today is ritually impure. Nevertheless, the obligation to separate *teruma* remains, and a minuscule portion of the produce is separated.

## NOTES

**There it can be said that the water slowly trickled out and the amount was continuously diminishing** – הָתָם אִיכָּא לְמֵימַר חֲסַר וְאָתָא: The commentaries explain that it is normal for water to slowly seep out of a ritual bath and therefore one must assume ritual impurity retroactively. By contrast, in the case of a menstruating woman there is no reason to think that the blood emerged earlier (Ritva, citing Rashi).

**There are two factors that weaken, etc.** – אִיכָּא תַּרְתֵּי לְרֵיעוּתָא וכו׳: Some explain that the ritual bath's original presumptive status of validity is negated by the impure status of the item being immersed. The only status that remains is the ritual bath's current status of invalidity, which is then presumed to have been in effect since the bath was last measured (Responsa of Rabbi Akiva Eiger; *Penei Yehoshua* on *Kiddushin*; *Shev Shemateta*; *Yosef Da'at*). Others explain that it is not that the ritual bath's current status negates its original presumptive status of validity. Rather, the ritual bath's presumptive status is weakened by its current definite invalid state, and therefore we follow the presumptive impure status of the immersed item (*Hazon Ish*).

**If someone would inspect the contents of a barrel** – הָיָה בּוֹדֵק אֶת הֶחָבִית: Some commentaries explain that it is sufficient to smell the contents of the barrel to ascertain whether it is wine or vinegar. According to this opinion, it is prohibited to taste it, as the liquid is currently untithed (Ritva on *Kiddushin* 79b; Rashbam and *Tosafot* on *Bava Batra* 96b). By contrast, Rashi maintains that the inspection is performed by tasting the contents. Some state that according to Rashi the mere tasting of untithed foods is prohibited by rabbinic law only, and since he is planning to separate tithes from the rest of the barrel, the Sages were lenient in this case (Responsa of the Rivash; *Pithei Teshuva*).

מִכָּאן וְאֵילָךְ – סָפֵק. קַשְׁיָא לְשַׁמַּאי!

The *baraita* continues: **From that** point **forward,** i.e., more than three days after the most recent inspection, it is **uncertain** whether it had already turned to vinegar, and consequently any untithed wine for which *teruma* was separated during those days remains uncertainly tithed. This poses **a difficulty for Shammai,** who maintains that there is no such retroactive consideration in the case of a menstruating woman.

הָתָם, מִשּׁוּם דְּאִיכָּא לְמֵימַר: הַעֲמֵד טֶבֶל עַל חֶזְקָתוֹ, וְאֵימַר לֹא נִתְקַן. אַדְּרַבָּה, הַעֲמֵד יַיִן עַל חֶזְקָתוֹ וְאֵימַר לֹא הֶחְמִיץ!

The Gemara answers: **There,** in the case of the barrel, it is different, **since it can be said: Establish the untithed produce in its presumptive status,** as when it first grew it was definitely untithed, **and say** it was **not amended,** i.e., exempted, and its status continues to be untithed produce. The Gemara asks: **On the contrary,** one should **establish the wine in its presumptive status, and say** that it had **not turned to vinegar.**

הֲרֵי הֶחְמִיץ לְפָנֶיךָ! הָכָא נַמִי, הֲרֵי דָּם לְפָנֶיךָ! הַשְׁתָּא הוּא דַּחֲזַאי. הָתָם נַמִי, הַשְׁתָּא הוּא דְּהֶחְמִיץ!

The Gemara rejects this suggestion: This is impossible, as **it is turned to vinegar before you,** i.e., at present. The Gemara replies: **Here too,** in the case of a menstruating woman, one who has experienced a discharge of **blood** is **before you,** at present, so what is the difference? The Gemara explains: With regard to the woman, it is possible that **it is** only **now that she saw** the beginning of her menstrual blood. The Gemara responds: **There too,** it is possible that **it is** only **now that it turned to vinegar,** but not earlier.

הָכִי הַשְׁתָּא? הָתָם – אִיכָּא לְמֵימַר: הֶחְמִיץ וַאֲתָא הֶחְמִיץ וַאֲתָא, הָכָא – מִי אִיכָּא לְמֵימַר: חֲזַאי וַאֲתָא חֲזַאי וַאֲתָא? וּמַאי קוּשְׁיָא, דִּלְמָא הַגַּס הַגַּס חֲזִיתֵיהּ?

The Gemara again answers: **How can** these cases **be compared? There,** in the case of the wine, **it can be said** that it was **continuously turning to vinegar.** Therefore, it is possible that the wine turned to vinegar much earlier without anyone realizing. By contrast, in the case of the menstruating woman, **can it be said** that she was **continuously seeing** menstrual blood? Once again, the Gemara responds: **And what is the difficulty?** The same possibility does in fact exist in the case of a menstruating woman, as **perhaps she saw** the blood depart **bit by bit.**

הָתָם אִיכָּא תַּרְתֵּי לְרֵיעוּתָא, הָכָא אִיכָּא חֲדָא לְרֵיעוּתָא.

The Gemara provides a different answer: **There,** in the case of the barrel, there are **two** factors **that weaken** the suggestion that the wine is tithed: First, it is vinegar at present; second, the wine has a presumptive status that it is untithed. **Here,** by contrast, **there is** only **one** factor **that weakens** the possibility that the items touched by the menstruating woman were rendered ritually impure, i.e., that she is currently experiencing a menstrual flow.

וְרָמֵי חָבִית אַמִּקְוֶה: מַאי שְׁנָא הָכָא – וַדַּאי, וּמַאי שְׁנָא הָכָא – סָפֵק?

§ **And** the Gemara **raises a contradiction between** the *halakha* of the **barrel** and that **of the ritual bath: What is different here,** in the case of the ritual bath, where the items are **definitely** impure, **and what is different there,** with regard to the barrel, where it is only **uncertain** that the produce remains untithed? In both cases the current situation, that the ritual bath is deficient and the contents of the barrel have turned to vinegar, should lead to a definite status.

אָמַר רַבִּי חֲנִינָא מִסּוּרָא: מַאן תַּנָּא חָבִית – רַבִּי שִׁמְעוֹן הִיא, דִּלְגַבֵּי מִקְוֶה נַמִי סְפֵקָא מַשְׁוֵי לֵיהּ.

The Gemara answers: **Rabbi Ḥanina of Sura**[P] **says: Who** is the *tanna* who **taught** the *halakha* of the **barrel? It is Rabbi Shimon, who, with regard to a ritual bath also considers it** as a matter of **uncertainty,** rather than as definitely impure. Therefore, there is no contradiction between the two *halakhot.*

**PERSONALITIES**

Rabbi Ḥanina of Sura – רַבִּי חֲנִינָא מִסּוּרָא: Also known as Rabbi Ḥinnana, Rabbi Ḥanina was a sixth-generation Babylonian *amora*. A colleague of Mar Zutra and Rav Ashi, he was a well-known scholar in his own right and is mentioned many times throughout the Talmud.

דִּתְנַן: מִקְוֶה שֶׁנִּמְדַּד וְנִמְצָא חָסֵר. כׇּל הַטְּהָרוֹת שֶׁנַּעֲשׂוּ עַל גַּבָּיו לְמַפְרֵעַ, בֵּין בִּרְשׁוּת הָרַבִּים בֵּין בִּרְשׁוּת הַיָּחִיד – טְמֵאוֹת.

**As we learned** in a mishna (*Mikvaot* 2:2): In the case of **a ritual bath** that was known to have contained the requisite forty *se'a*, **which was** then **measured and found lacking** in its quantity of water, **all pure items that had been rendered** pure **in it,** i.e., any impure items that had been purified through immersion in this ritual bath, **retroactive** to when the ritual bath was last measured, **whether** this ritual bath is located **in the private domain or in the public domain, are impure.**

רַבִּי שִׁמְעוֹן אוֹמֵר: בִּרְשׁוּת הָרַבִּים – טְהוֹרוֹת, בִּרְשׁוּת הַיָּחִיד – תּוֹלִין.

The mishna continues: **Rabbi Shimon says:** If the impure items were immersed in a ritual bath that was **in the public domain,** they are deemed **pure.** But if they were immersed in a ritual bath that was **in a private domain,** the status of any *teruma* that touched them is **suspended,** i.e., it is neither consumed nor burned. Rabbi Shimon holds that even in the case of a ritual bath, the items are not retroactively deemed definitely impure. Rather the status is uncertain, just as in the case of the barrel.

Perek **I**
Daf **3** Amud **a**

**BACKGROUND**

*Sota* – סוֹטָה: The Torah describes the procedure governing a wife who secludes herself with a man about whom her husband had previously become suspicious and had warned her in the presence of witnesses to not be alone with him (see Numbers 5:11–31). Since she disobeyed this warning and is observed in seclusion with that man, she and her husband can no longer engage in marital relations until she has undergone a rite to determine whether she has committed adultery. The woman is taken to the Temple in Jerusalem and forced by the priests to stand in a public place while holding the unique meal offering that she is required to bring. There, she is again questioned about her behavior. If she continues to insist upon her fidelity and takes an oath to that effect, a scroll is brought and the curses of the *sota* in the Torah are written on it. If she does not then admit that she has committed adultery, the scroll is submerged in a clay vessel filled with water taken from the Temple basin and some earth from the Temple floor, and the scroll's writing is dissolved in the water. She is then forced to drink that water. If she did commit adultery, then, in the words of the Torah: "Her belly shall swell, and her thigh shall fall away" (Numbers 5:27), until ultimately she dies from the water's curse. If she is innocent, she is permitted to resume normal marital relations with her husband and the water will bring her blessing.

וּשְׁנֵיהֶם לֹא לְמָדוּהָ אֶלָּא מִסּוֹטָה.

The Gemara explains their reasoning: **And both** *tanna'im* **derived** their respective opinions **only from** the case of **a woman suspected by her husband of having been unfaithful** [*sota*],[B] who is forbidden to engage in intercourse with her husband just like a definite adulteress.

רַבָּנַן סָבְרִי: כִּי סוֹטָה, מַה סּוֹטָה – סָפֵק הִיא וַעֲשָׂאוּהָ כְּוַדַּאי, הָכָא נַמִּי – סָפֵק וַעֲשָׂאוּהָ כְּוַדַּאי.

**The Rabbis hold:** This case of a ritual bath is **like** the case of **a** ***sota.*** **Just as** in the case of **a** ***sota*** it is **uncertain** whether **she** was actually unfaithful, **and** nevertheless the Torah **rendered her like** one who **definitely** committed adultery in that she is forbidden to her husband until she drinks the water of a *sota*; **here too,** in the case of a ritual bath, it is **uncertain** whether it was lacking the requisite measure of water **and** yet the Torah **rendered it as** though it was **definitely** lacking water, to the extent that *teruma* that touched an item that had been immersed in it must be burned.

אִי מִסּוֹטָה, אֵימָא כִּי סוֹטָה, מַה סּוֹטָה – בִּרְשׁוּת הָרַבִּים טָהוֹר, הָכָא נַמִּי בִּרְשׁוּת הָרַבִּים טָהוֹר!

The Gemara raises a difficulty: **If** the *halakhot* of the ritual bath are derived **from** those of **a** ***sota,*** then one can **say** that it should be **like** the *halakha* of a ***sota*** in another respect: **Just as a** ***sota*** who is suspected of having been unfaithful **in a public domain** is considered **pure,** i.e., she does not undergo to rite of a *sota*, **here too,** any impure item that was immersed in a currently deficient ritual bath that is situated **in a public domain** should be considered **pure.**

הָכִי הָשְׁתָּא! הָתָם – מִשּׁוּם סְתִירָה הוּא, וּסְתִירָה בִּרְשׁוּת הָרַבִּים לֵיכָּא, הָכָא – מִשּׁוּם חָסֵר הוּא, מַה לִּי חָסֵר בִּרְשׁוּת הָרַבִּים, מַה לִּי חָסֵר בִּרְשׁוּת הַיָּחִיד?

The Gemara answers: **How can** these cases **be compared?** One cannot apply the *halakha* of a *sota* in a public domain to any other case. **There,** the reason why a *sota* is treated as having definitely been unfaithful is **due to** her **seclusion** with another man. **And** as a proper **seclusion in the public domain is not** possible, she does not assume the status of a *sota*. By contrast, **here,** in the case of the ritual bath, the uncertainty **is due to** the **lack** of the requisite measure of water in the ritual bath. If so, **what** difference is it **to me** if the ritual bath is **lacking in a public domain** or if it is **lacking in a private domain?**

וְכִי תֵּימָא: הָא כׇּל סְפֵק טוּמְאָה בִּרְשׁוּת הָרַבִּים טָהוֹר! כֵּיוָן דְּאִיכָּא תַּרְתֵּי לְרֵיעוּתָא – כְּוַדַּאי טוּמְאָה דָּמֵי.

The Gemara comments: **And if you would say** that the guiding principle in **any** case of **uncertainty** involving **impurity in a public domain** is that it is **ritually pure,** and therefore all items immersed in a ritual bath situated in the public domain should be pure even if there is uncertainty about its status of purity, that suggestion can be rejected, as follows: **Since there are two** factors **that weaken** the possibility that the items are ritually pure: First, the ritual bath is currently lacking, and second, the item has a presumptive status of impurity, it is therefore **considered as** an item of **definite impurity.**

וְרַבִּי שִׁמְעוֹן סָבַר: כִּי סוֹטָה, מַה סוֹטָה – בִּרְשׁוּת הָרַבִּים טָהוֹר, הָכָא נַמִּי – בִּרְשׁוּת הָרַבִּים טָהוֹר.

After analyzing the reasoning of the Rabbis, the Gemara turns to the opinion of Rabbi Shimon. **And Rabbi Shimon holds:** This case of a ritual bath is just **like** the case of **a** *sota*. **Just as a** *sota* who is suspected of having been unfaithful **in a public domain** is considered **pure, here too,** any impure item that was immersed in a currently deficient ritual bath that is situated **in a public domain** is considered **pure.**

אִי מִסּוֹטָה, אֵימָא כִּי סוֹטָה, מַה סוֹטָה – בִּרְשׁוּת הַיָּחִיד טְמֵאָה וַדַּאי, הָכָא נַמִּי – בִּרְשׁוּת הַיָּחִיד טְמֵאָה וַדַּאי!

The Gemara asks: **If** the *halakhot* of the ritual bath are derived **from** those of **a** *sota*, then one can **say** that it should be **like** the *halakha* of a *sota* in another respect: **Just as a** *sota* who secluded herself with the man **in a private domain** is deemed **definitely impure,** i.e., she is forbidden to her husband until she undergoes the rite of the *sota*, **here too,** any ritually impure item that was immersed in a currently deficient ritual bath situated **in a private domain** should be considered **definitely impure.** If so, any *teruma* that comes in contact with the immersed vessel should be burned. Why, then, does Rabbi Shimon rule that its status is suspended and it is neither consumed nor burned?

הָכִי הָשְׁתָּא! הָתָם – יֵשׁ רַגְלַיִם לַדָּבָר, שֶׁהֲרֵי קִינֵּא לָהּ וְנִסְתְּרָה. הָכָא – מַאי רַגְלַיִם לַדָּבָר אִיכָּא?

The Gemara answers: **How can** these cases **be compared? There,** in the case of a *sota*, **there is a basis for the matter.** She is considered definitely impure, **as** her husband **issued a warning to her** about this particular man **and she** then **secluded** herself with him. By contrast, **here,** in the case of a ritual bath, **what basis for the matter is there?** Why should one assume impurity with certainty?

וְאִי בָּעֵית אֵימָא, הַיְינוּ טַעְמָא דְּרַבִּי שִׁמְעוֹן: גָּמַר סוֹף טוּמְאָה מִתְּחִלַּת טוּמְאָה.

**And if you wish, say** instead that **this is** the **reason** for the opinion **of Rabbi Shimon:** He does not base his ruling on the case of a *sota*; rather, he **derives the end of impurity from the beginning of impurity,** i.e., he derives the *halakha* of the immersion of an impure item into a ritual bath from the *halakha* of the initial contraction of ritual impurity.

מַה תְּחִלַּת טוּמְאָה, סָפֵק נָגַע סָפֵק לֹא נָגַע – בִּרְשׁוּת הָרַבִּים טָהוֹר, אַף סוֹף טוּמְאָה, סָפֵק טָבַל סָפֵק לֹא טָבַל – בִּרְשׁוּת הָרַבִּים טָהוֹר.

The Gemara explains: **Just as** with regard to the **beginning of impurity,** if there is **uncertainty whether or not** a pure item **came into contact** with a source of impurity, if this occurred **in the public domain** it is considered ritually **pure; so too** in the case of the **end of impurity,** if there is **uncertainty whether or not** the impure item was **immersed** in a ritual bath with the requisite amount of water, the *halakha* is that if the ritual bath is located **in the public domain,** the item is considered **pure.**

וְרַבָּנַן – הָכִי הָשְׁתָּא! הָתָם – גַּבְרָא בְּחֶזְקַת טָהֳרָה קָאֵי, מִסְּפֵקָא לָא מַחְתִּינַן לֵיהּ לְטוּמְאָה. הָכָא – גַּבְרָא בְּחֶזְקַת טוּמְאָה קָאֵי, מִסְּפֵקָא לָא מַפְּקִינַן לֵיהּ מִטּוּמְאָתוֹ.

The Gemara asks: **And** how would **the Rabbis** respond to this claim? They would respond: **How can** these cases **be compared? There,** with regard to the beginning of impurity, **the man** who might have touched an impure item **remains with the presumptive status** of **ritual purity.** Consequently, **we do not lower his** status to one who has contracted **ritual impurity** merely **due to uncertainty. Here,** in the case of the ritual bath, **the man** who immerses in that ritual bath **has the presumptive status** of **ritual impurity.** Therefore, **we do not remove him** from **his** status **of ritual impurity due to uncertainty.**

וּמַאי שְׁנָא מִמָּבוֹי? דִּתְנַן: הַשֶּׁרֶץ שֶׁנִּמְצָא בְּמָבוֹי – מְטַמֵּא לְמַפְרֵעַ, עַד שֶׁיֹּאמַר ״בָּדַקְתִּי אֶת הַמָּבוֹי הַזֶּה, וְלֹא הָיָה בּוֹ שֶׁרֶץ״, אוֹ עַד שְׁעַת הַכִּיבּוּד!

§ The Gemara returns to its analysis of the mishna. Shammai said: For all women, their time is sufficient, i.e., women who discern that menstrual blood emerged do not need to be concerned that perhaps the flow of blood began before they noticed it. The Gemara asks: In **what way is** this case **different from** that of **an alleyway?**[B] **As we learned** in a mishna (66a): With regard to the carcass of **a creeping animal that is found in an alleyway,**[H] **it renders** any item in the alleyway **ritually impure retroactively to** the time **that** a person can **say: I examined this alleyway and there was no** carcass of **a creeping animal in it, or until the time of the** last **sweeping** of the alleyway.

BACKGROUND

Alleyway – מָבוֹי: The alleyway mentioned in the Talmud is one that is open to the public domain and its walls are composed of the walls of courtyards or of houses that open into the alleyway. An open alleyway is one that leads to a public domain at both ends. Although it is widely used as a passageway between main streets, it itself is too narrow to be a public thoroughfare and is therefore not considered a public domain. An enclosed alleyway is one that at one end leads to the public domain and on the other side is closed with a wall.

Open alleyway

Enclosed alleyway

HALAKHA

The carcass of a creeping animal that is found in an alleyway – הַשֶּׁרֶץ שֶׁנִּמְצָא בְּמָבוֹי: If one finds the carcass of a creeping animal in an alleyway, any item that was found there is considered ritually impure retroactively. This extends back to the last time that one can say he checked the alleyway and found it clean of creeping animals. Even if he had swept the alleyway in the interim, if he did not check it as well, the retroactive impurity still applies (Rambam *Sefer Tahara*, *Hilkhot She'ar Avot HaTumot* 18:4).

הָתָם נַמִי, כֵּיוָן דְּאִיכָּא שְׁרָצִים דְּגוּפֵיהּ, וּשְׁרָצִים דְּאָתוּ מֵעָלְמָא – כְּתַרְתֵּי לְרֵיעוּתָא דָּמֵי.

The Gemara answers: **There too,** one can explain: **Since there** are two types of carcasses of creeping animals that are likely to be found in the alleyway, **creeping animals from** the alleyway **itself and creeping animals that came from the world** at large, **it is compared to** a case where there **are two** factors **that weaken** the possibility that the items are ritually pure. Therefore, even Shammai agrees that in such a case the impurity extends retroactively back in time.

וְאִי בָּעֵית אֵימָא, הַיְינוּ טַעֲמָא דְּשַׁמַּאי: הוֹאִיל וְאִשָּׁה מַרְגֶּשֶׁת בְּעַצְמָהּ. וְהִלֵּל – כִּסְבוּרָה הַרְגָּשַׁת מֵי רַגְלַיִם הִיא.

**And if you wish, say** instead that **this is the reason** for the opinion **of Shammai: Since a women senses within herself** if she is experiencing a flow of blood, if she felt the flow only at present, it is certain that she did not experience a flow previously. **And Hillel** holds that she might have experienced a flow earlier while she was urinating and **she thought it** was all **the sensation of** her flow of **urine.**

וּלְשַׁמַּאי, הָאִיכָּא יְשֵׁנָה? יְשֵׁנָה נַמִי, אַגַּב צַעֲרָהּ מִיתְעֲרָא, מִידֵּי דַּהֲוָה אַהַרְגָּשַׁת מֵי רַגְלַיִם.

The Gemara asks: **And according to Shammai, isn't there** the case of **a sleeping** woman, who would not sense her flow of menstrual blood? The Gemara answers: **A sleeping** woman would **also** sense her flow, and **due to her discomfort** she **would awaken, just as it is with the sensation** of the need to **urinate.**

וְהָאִיכָּא שׁוֹטָה? מוֹדֶה שַׁמַּאי בְּשׁוֹטָה. הָא "כָּל הַנָּשִׁים" קָתָנֵי? כָּל הַנָּשִׁים פִּקְחוֹת.

The Gemara raises another difficulty with regard to the opinion of Shammai: **But there** is the case of **a mentally incompetent** woman, who does not properly understand what she is sensing. She might have previously experienced a flow of menstrual blood that she did not notice. The Gemara answers: **Shammai concedes** in the case **of a mentally incompetent** woman that she is impure retroactively. The Gemara asks: **But** the mishna explicitly **teaches** that Shammai mentioned **all women,** which apparently includes even the mentally incompetent. The Gemara answers: When the mishna teaches: **All women,** it is referring to all **mentally competent** women.

וְלִיתְנֵי "נָשִׁים"? לְאַפּוּקֵי מִדְּרַבִּי אֱלִיעֶזֶר, דְּאָמַר רַבִּי אֱלִיעֶזֶר: אַרְבַּע נָשִׁים, וְתוּ לָא. קָא מַשְׁמַע לָן כָּל הַנָּשִׁים.

The Gemara raises a difficulty: **But** if so, **let** the mishna **teach** that Shammai's opinion applies to: **Women,** rather than referring to all women. The Gemara answers: The inclusive statement: All women, serves **to exclude** the opinion **of Rabbi Eliezer. As Rabbi Eliezer said** in a mishna (7a): There are **four women** with regard to whom the *halakha* is that their time is sufficient. This indicates that there are only four, **and no more.** Therefore, the mishna **teaches us: All women,** to include all mentally competent women, not only the four mentioned by Rabbi Eliezer.

וְהָאִיכָּא כְּתָמִים, לֵימָא תְּנַן כְּתָמִים דְּלָא כְּשַׁמַּאי! אָמַר אַבַּיֵי: מוֹדֶה שַׁמַּאי בִּכְתָמִים, מַאי טַעֲמָא – בְּצִפּוֹר לֹא נִתְעַסְּקָה, בְּשׁוּק שֶׁל טַבָּחִים לֹא עָבְרָה, הַאי דָּם מֵהֵיכָא אָתֵי?

The Gemara raises yet another difficulty against the opinion of Shammai: **But there is** the case of blood **stains.** The mishna teaches (66a) that a woman who finds a blood stain is impure retroactive to the last time she examined her clothing and found them clean. **Shall we say** that **we learned** the mishna with regard to **stains not in accordance with** the opinion of **Shammai? Abaye said: Shammai concedes** in the case **of stains.** The Gemara asks: **What is the reason?** The reason is **that she neither engaged in** handling a slaughtered **bird nor** did **she pass through a marketplace of butchers.** If so, **from where** could **this blood** stain on her clothing have **come?** Since it must be from her last menstrual flow, Shammai agrees that she is impure retroactively.

אִי בָּעֵית אֵימָא, הַיְינוּ טַעְמֵיהּ דְּשַׁמַּאי: דְּאִם אִיתָא דַּהֲוָה דָּם – מֵעִיקָּרָא הֲוָה אָתֵי. וְהִלֵּל – כּוֹתְלֵי בֵית הָרֶחֶם הֶעֱמִידוּהוּ. וְשַׁמַּאי – כּוֹתְלֵי בֵית הָרֶחֶם לָא מוֹקְמֵי דָּם.

The Gemara suggests another analysis: **Or if you wish, say** that **this is the reason** for the opinion **of Shammai:** She is impure only from that point onward, **as, if it is so that there was** any menstrual **blood** previously, **it would have come** out **at the outset,** i.e., at the earlier time. The Gemara explains why Hillel maintains that there is ritual impurity retroactively, in light of this analysis: **And** as for **Hillel,** he holds that the **walls of the womb,** i.e., the walls of the vaginal canal, **held back** the menstrual blood from leaving the body entirely, and therefore there might have been a previous emission from the uterus into the vaginal canal that was not visible on the outside. The Gemara asks: **And** how does **Shammai** respond to this claim? The Gemara answers: Shammai maintains that the **walls of the womb do not hold back blood.**

מְשַׁמֶּשֶׁת בְּמוֹךְ מַאי אִיכָּא לְמֵימַר? אָמַר אַבַּיֵי: מוֹדֶה שַׁמַּאי בִּמְשַׁמֶּשֶׁת בְּמוֹךְ.

The Gemara asks: **With regard to** a woman who **engages in intercourse** while using a contraceptive absorbent **cloth** in the form of a wad that she inserts in her vagina at the opening of her womb so as not to become pregnant, **what is there to say?** In other words, how does Shammai explain why there is no retroactive impurity status in such a case, as it cannot be claimed that any previous menstrual blood would have flowed out earlier. **Abaye says: Shammai concedes with regard to** a woman who **engages in intercourse** while using a contraceptive **cloth** that she is impure retroactively.

רָבָא אָמַר: מוֹךְ נַמִי, אַגַּב זֵיעָה מִכְוְיץ כָּוְיץ. וּמוֹדֶה רָבָא בְּמוֹךְ דָּחוּק.

**Rava says:** Here **as well,** in a case where a woman engages in intercourse while using a contraceptive absorbent **cloth,** any previous menstrual blood would have flowed out, as the absorbent cloth does not hermetically seal the womb. The reason is that the cloth **wrinkles due to perspiration,** leaving space for blood to pass through. The Gemara adds: **And** nevertheless **Rava concedes** to Abaye that Shammai agrees that she is retroactively impure in a case **where** a woman engages in intercourse while using a tightly **packed** absorbent **cloth.**

וּמַאי אִיכָּא בֵּין הָנֵי לִישָּׁנֵי לְהָאֵיךְ לִישָּׁנָא?

§ The Gemara suggested that the reasoning for Shammai's opinion is that the woman would have felt any previous menstrual flow, or that any prior menstrual blood would have flowed out previously. Yet, earlier the Gemara suggested that his reason was that the woman retains her presumptive status of ritual purity. With regard to the explanations given for the opinion of Shammai, the Gemara asks: **What** difference **is there between these versions and that version** suggested earlier?

Perek **I**
Daf **3** Amud **b**

אִיכָּא בֵּינַיְיהוּ: לְמִרְמֵי חָבִית וּמִקְוֶה וּמָבוֹי. לְהָאֵיךְ לִישָּׁנָא – אִיכָּא לְמִרְמִינְהוּ, לְהָנֵי לִישָּׁנֵי – לֵיכָּא לְמִרְמֵי.

The Gemara answers: The difference **between** them is with regard to the possibility **of raising a contradiction**[N] between Shammai's ruling here and the cases of **a barrel, a ritual bath, and an alleyway. According to that version,** that Shammai's reasoning is based upon the principle that an item retains its presumptive status, **there is** room **to raise these contradictions,** as the Gemara explained. By contrast, **according to these** other **versions,** that the woman would have felt any previous menstrual flow or that any prior menstrual blood would have flowed out previously, **there is no** room **to raise** such **contradictions,** as those rulings do not contradict the *halakha* here, where a unique factor is relevant.

וּמַאי אִיכָּא בֵּין הַאי לִישָּׁנָא לְהָאֵיךְ לִישָּׁנָא? לְאַבַּיֵי – אִיכָּא מוֹךְ,

The Gemara further asks: **And what** difference **is there between this version,** that any prior menstrual blood would have flowed out, **and that version,** that she would have felt any previous menstrual flow? The Gemara answers: **According to Abaye,** who maintains that Shammai agrees that a woman who engages in intercourse while using a contraceptive cloth is impure retroactively, **there is** a difference in a case where the woman engages in intercourse while using a contraceptive **cloth.** If Shammai's reasoning is that a woman senses the emission of blood, in this case too it is assumed that she did not emit blood earlier. By contrast, if his reasoning is that any prior menstrual blood would have come out at the outset, it is possible that the cloth blocked the emission of blood, and she already emitted blood. Consequently, she is impure retroactively.

לְרָבָא – אִיכָּא מוֹךְ דָּחוּק.

**According to Rava,** who maintains that blood can emerge even if the woman engages in intercourse while using a contraceptive absorbent cloth, **there is** a difference between the two interpretations in a case where she engages in intercourse while using a tightly **packed** absorbent **cloth,** as such a cloth will prevent the blood from flowing out, but it does not affect her ability to sense an emission.

**NOTES**

**The difference between them is with regard to raising a contradiction – אִיכָּא בֵּינַיְיהוּ לְמִרְמֵי:** Some point out other differences could have been identified, such as the case of a mentally incompetent woman or a woman who engages in intercourse while using a contraceptive absorbent cloth. According to the first explanation that she should be kept in her presumptive status of purity, in both those cases Shammai would maintain that rendering her impure from the time of her menstruation is sufficient, whereas according to the other explanations Shammai would concede to render her impure retroactively.

תַּנְיָא כִּי הַאי לִישָּׁנָא דְּאִם אִיתָא דַּהֲוָה דָּם מֵעִיקָּרָא הֲוָה אָתֵי, אָמַר לוֹ הִלֵּל לְשַׁמַּאי: אִי אַתָּה מוֹדֶה בְּקוּפָּה שֶׁנִּשְׁתַּמְּשׁוּ בָּהּ טָהֳרוֹת בְּזָוִית זוֹ, וְנִמְצָא שֶׁרֶץ בְּזָוִית אַחֶרֶת – שֶׁטָּהֳרוֹת הָרִאשׁוֹנוֹת טְמֵאוֹת? אָמַר לוֹ: אֲבָל!

It is **taught** in a mishna (*Teharot* 4:4) **in accordance with this version**, i.e., that Shammai's reasoning is **that if it is so, that there was** menstrual **blood** previously, **it would have come out at the outset: Hillel said to Shammai: Don't you concede** to the following *halakha*: In the case **of a basket**[NH] that **was used** as a container for **ritually pure** items, and those items were placed **in one corner, and** subsequently the carcass of **a creeping animal was found in a different corner** of the basket, the *halakha* is **that the** items **initially** considered **ritually pure** are now retroactively considered **impure? Shammai said to him: Indeed,** that is correct.

וּמָה הֶפְרֵשׁ בֵּין זוֹ לָזוֹ? לָזוֹ – יֵשׁ לָהּ שׁוּלַיִם, לָזוֹ – אֵין לָהּ שׁוּלַיִם.

Hillel continues: **And** if so, **what difference** is there between **this** case of the pure items stored in the basket, which are now considered retroactively impure, **and that** case of the ritually pure woman who experiences a menstrual flow, who is impure only from that point onward? Shammai answers: **This** one, the basket, **has a base** on which it rests, and therefore the creeping animal might have been there earlier unseen. **That one,** the menstruating woman, **has no base,** i.e., there is nothing to impede her menstrual blood from flowing out. Shammai's response indicates that she is not retroactively impure because if she had experienced a previous menstruation it would have flowed at that stage.

רָבָא אָמַר: טַעְמָא דְּשַׁמַּאי – מִשּׁוּם בִּטּוּל פְּרִיָּה וּרְבִיָּה. תַּנְיָא נַמִי הָכִי, אָמַר לוֹ שַׁמַּאי לְהִלֵּל: אִם כֵּן, בִּטַּלְתָּ בְּנוֹת יִשְׂרָאֵל מִפְּרִיָּה וּרְבִיָּה.

§ **Rava says:** The **reason for** the opinion of **Shammai** that a woman who experiences menstruation is not deemed ritually impure retroactively is **due to the dereliction of** the mitzva to **be fruitful and multiply.** If woman is always deemed retroactively impure, she and her husband might abstain from engaging in sexual intercourse out of fear that she is already impure even if she has not yet experienced bleeding. The Gemara adds **that this** explanation **is also taught** in a *baraita*: **Shammai said to Hillel: If** it is **so,** that a woman is rendered retroactively impure as you claim, **you** will **have caused the Jewish women to be derelict in** the mitzva to **be fruitful and multiply.**[N]

וּמַאן דְּתָנֵי הַאי לִישָּׁנָא, הָא תַּנְיָא כִּי הָאֵיךְ לִישָּׁנָא דְּאִם אִיתָא דַּהֲוָה דָּם – מֵעִיקָּרָא הֲוָה אָתֵי! הָתָם, הִלֵּל הוּא דְּקָטָעֵי, הוּא סָבַר: טַעֲמָא דְּשַׁמַּאי דְּאִם אִיתָא דַּהֲוָה דָּם – מֵעִיקָּרָא הֲוָה אָתֵי, וְקָא מַקְשֵׁי לֵיהּ קוּפָּה.

The Gemara asks: **But** according to **the one who taught this version,** i.e., Rava, there is a difficulty: **Isn't it taught in** the aforementioned mishna **in accordance with that** other **version,** that Shammai's reasoning is **that if it is so, that there was** any menstrual **blood** previously, **it would have come out at the outset?** The Gemara answers: There, in that mishna, **it is Hillel who erred. He thought** the **reason** of **Shammai** is **that if it is so, that there was** any menstrual **blood** previously, **it would have come** out **at the outset. And** therefore, **he raises a difficulty** against Shammai's opinion from the case of the **basket.**

וַאֲמַר לֵיהּ שַׁמַּאי: טַעֲמָא דִּידִי – מִשּׁוּם בִּטּוּל פְּרִיָּה וּרְבִיָּה, וּלְמַאי דְּקָטָעִית נַמִי, דְּקָמַקְשִׁית קוּפָּה – לָזוֹ יֵשׁ לָהּ שׁוּלַיִם, וְלָזוֹ אֵין לָהּ שׁוּלַיִם.

**And Shammai said to** Hillel: You are mistaken. **My reasoning** is actually **due to the dereliction of** the mitzva to **be fruitful and multiply. But even according to your erroneous** reasoning **that** led **you to raise a difficulty** from the case of the **basket,** I have an answer for that as well: **This** basket **has a base,** and therefore the creeping animal could have been there earlier, unseen; **but that** menstruating woman **has no base.**

וּלְמַאן דְּתָנֵי הַאי לִישָּׁנָא, הָא תַּנְיָא כִּי הָאֵיךְ לִישָּׁנָא מִשּׁוּם בִּטּוּל פְּרִיָּה וּרְבִיָּה!

The Gemara asks the reverse question: **And according to the one** who **teaches this** other **version,** that Shammai's reasoning is that if there was previous menstrual blood it would have come out at the outset, **isn't it taught** in a *baraita* **in accordance with that** other **version,** that Shammai's reasoning is **due to the dereliction of** the mitzva to **be fruitful and multiply?**

הָכִי קָאָמַר לֵיהּ הִלֵּל לְשַׁמַּאי: אִין, טַעֲמָא קָאָמְרַתְּ דְּאִם אִיתָא דַּהֲוָה דָּם – מֵעִיקָּרָא הֲוָה אָתֵי, וּמִיהוּ – עֲשֵׂה סְיָיג לִדְבָרֶיךָ, דְּמַאי שְׁנָא מִכָּל הַתּוֹרָה כּוּלָּהּ דְּעָבְדִינַן סְיָיג?

The Gemara answers: That *baraita* was recorded at a later point in their discussion, as **this** is what **Hillel is saying to Shammai: Yes,** the **reason** that **you say** for your opinion has merit, **that if it is so, that there was** any menstrual **blood** previously, **it would have come** out **at the outset. Nevertheless,** you should **enact a safeguard for your statement** and render her retroactively impure, **as in what** way **is this** case **different from the rest of the entire Torah, where** the Sages **enact safeguards?**

NOTES

**Don't you concede in the case of a basket – אִי אַתָּה מוֹדֶה בְּקוּפָּה:** Seemingly, this case of a basket would present a question on Hillel's opinion as well, as although Hillel maintains that she assumes retroactive impurity status, that is only out of uncertainty and not a definite status, as the Gemara explains later. The Ramban answers utilizing the Gemara's forthcoming distinction: Since a basket has a base, the previously pure items are therefore deemed retroactively impure with certainty, while a woman has no base and therefore she is not deemed retroactively impure with certainty, as it is reasonable to assume that had there been a previous flow of menstrual blood she would have seen it. Nevertheless, Hillel's question to Shammai is that although the woman has no base, she does have an anatomical shape that forms something like the rim mentioned later in the Gemara, which could impede a flow of blood; therefore if one agrees to render the pure items in the basket retroactively impure, one should agree that there is a chance that the woman had previously menstruated and render her impure due to the uncertainty.

**You will have caused the Jewish women to be derelict in the mitzva to be fruitful and multiply – בִּטַּלְתָּ בְּנוֹת יִשְׂרָאֵל מִפְּרִיָּה וּרְבִיָּה:** The commentaries note that if the imposition of a rabbinic safeguard would certainly lead to the suspension of procreation, Hillel would agree that the Sages would not enact such a safeguard, but in this case, such an outcome is not certain. Nevertheless, Shammai is concerned for this possibility (Maharik; *Beit Yosef*).

HALAKHA

**The case of a basket – בְּקוּפָּה:** If a basket has a base or even just a curved rim with no base, and in one corner one stored ritually pure items and found the carcass of a creeping animal there after he moved the items to another corner, those items are deemed ritually impure. If the ritually pure item was *teruma* it is not burned. This is in accordance with the Rambam's interpretation of the opinion of Rabbi Yoḥanan later in the Gemara (Rambam *Sefer Tahara*, *Hilkhot She'ar Avot HaTumot* 17:2).

אָמַר לֵיהּ: אִם כֵּן בִּטַּלְתָּ בְּנוֹת יִשְׂרָאֵל מִפְּרִיָּה וּרְבִיָּה! וְהִלֵּל – מִפְּרִיָּה וּרְבִיָּה מִי קָאָמֵינָא? לְטָהֳרוֹת הוּא דְּקָאָמֵינָא!

Shammai **said to** Hillel: **If so,** i.e., if she is considered impure retroactively as a safeguard, **you** will **have caused the Jewish women to be derelict in** the mitzva to **be fruitful and multiply.** The Gemara asks: **And** how does **Hillel** respond to Shammai's reasoning with regard to the mitzva to be fruitful and multiply? The Gemara explains that Hillel would answer: Although I rule that she is retroactively impure, **did I say** that she is forbidden to her husband and must therefore abstain **from** the mitzva to **be fruitful and multiply? I said** only **that** she renders impure any **ritually pure** items that she touched.

וְשַׁמַּאי – לְטָהֳרוֹת נַמִי לָא, דְּאִם כֵּן – לִבּוֹ נוֹקְפוֹ וּפוֹרֵשׁ.

The Gemara asks: **And** how would **Shammai** reply to this? The Gemara answers: Shammai maintains that **even** a safeguard that renders **ritually pure** items impure should **not** be imposed. The reason is **that if** it were **so,** the **heart** of a scrupulous husband might **strike him** with pangs of conscience over sins that he could transgress **and he** would **separate** from his wife, out of fear that she is impure.

(שׁוּלַיִם, בְּדוּקִין, מְכוּסִּין, בְּזָוִית, סִימָן). אִיתְּמַר: קוּפָּה שֶׁנִּשְׁתַּמְּשׁוּ בָּהּ טָהֳרוֹת בְּזָוִית זוֹ, וְנִמְצָא שֶׁרֶץ בְּזָוִית אַחֶרֶת. חִזְקִיָּה אָמַר: טָהֳרוֹת הָרִאשׁוֹנוֹת טְהוֹרוֹת. רַבִּי יוֹחָנָן אָמַר: טָהֳרוֹת הָרִאשׁוֹנוֹת טְמֵאוֹת. וְהָא (בֵּית) שַׁמַּאי וְהִלֵּל מוֹדוּ בְּקוּפָּה דְּטָהֳרוֹת הָרִאשׁוֹנוֹת טְמֵאוֹת!

The Gemara provides **a mnemonic**[B] for the ensuing discussions: **A base; examined; covered; in a corner. It was stated:** If one has **a basket** that **was used** as a container for holding **ritually pure** produce, and those items were placed **in** one **corner** of the basket, **and** subsequently the carcass of **a creeping animal was found in a different corner** of the basket, **Ḥizkiyya says:** That produce **initially** considered **ritually pure** is still **pure. Rabbi Yoḥanan says:** The produce **initially** considered **ritually pure** is now retroactively deemed **impure.** The Gemara asks: **But** how can Ḥizkiyya rule that it is pure? After all, don't **Shammai and Hillel agree in** the case of the **basket that** the produce **initially** considered **pure** is now retroactively **impure?**

כִּי מוֹדוּ שַׁמַּאי וְהִלֵּל – בְּקוּפָּה שֶׁיֵּשׁ לָהּ שׁוּלַיִם, כִּי פְּלִיגִי חִזְקִיָּה וְרַבִּי יוֹחָנָן – בְּקוּפָּה שֶׁאֵין לָהּ שׁוּלַיִם.

The Gemara answers: **When** do **Shammai and Hillel agree** that all the produce is retroactively impure? **With regard to a basket that has a base.** In such a case, the carcass of the creeping animal might have previously been in the basket and it went unnoticed when one removed the pure produce items. **When Ḥizkiyya and Rabbi Yoḥanan disagree,** it is **with regard to a basket that has no base,** i.e., both ends were open and the basket was used while it was lying on its side. In that situation, the contents of the basket are emptied by raising one end, which causes all items inside to fall out. Consequently, any creeping animal that was found subsequently must have entered the basket only after that produce was removed, which is why Ḥizkiyya rules that the produce remains pure.

אֵין לָהּ שׁוּלַיִם – מַאי טַעְמָא דְּרַבִּי יוֹחָנָן? אֵין לָהּ שׁוּלַיִם וְיֵשׁ לָהּ אוֹגְנַיִם.

The Gemara asks: If this is referring to a case where the basket **has no base, what is the reasoning of Rabbi Yoḥanan** for ruling that the produce is ritually impure? The Gemara answers: The basket **has no base but it** does **have** an inward-curved **rim.** Therefore, it is possible that the carcass of a small creeping animal might have been held back by the rim and remained inside the basket even after it was turned over. Rabbi Yoḥanan rules that the produce is retroactively impure, due to the possibility that the creeping animal might have been in the basket previously together with the initially pure produce.

וְהָתַנְיָא, הַמַּדְלֶה עֲשָׂרָה דְּלָיִים מַיִם בְּזֶה אַחַר זֶה וְנִמְצָא שֶׁרֶץ בְּאֶחָד מֵהֶן – הוּא טָמֵא וְכוּלָּן טְהוֹרִין. וְאָמַר רֵישׁ לָקִישׁ מִשּׁוּם רַבִּי יַנַּאי: לֹא שָׁנוּ אֶלָּא שֶׁאֵין לָהּ אוֹגְנַיִם, אֲבָל יֵשׁ לָהּ אוֹגְנַיִם – כּוּלָּן טְמֵאִין.

The Gemara raises a difficulty: **But isn't it taught** in a *baraita*: With regard to **one who draws**[N] **ten pails of water**[H] **one after another,** i.e., he draws out water in one pail and from it he fills another ten pails with water, **and** the carcass of **a creeping animal is found in one of them, that** pail of water **is ritually impure but all** the rest **of them** are **pure. And Reish Lakish says in the name of Rabbi Yannai:** This *halakha* was **taught only** in a case **where** the pail **has no** inward-curved **rim.** Consequently, its contents are entirely emptied each time it is overturned, which means that the creeping animal must have entered only this pail. **But** if the pail **has a rim, all of** the water that had been drawn is **impure,** as the creeping animal might have entered the pail earlier and the rim held it back each time the pail was overturned.

**BACKGROUND**

Mnemonic – סִימָן: Because the Talmud was studied orally for many generations, mnemonic devices, or memory aids, were necessary to facilitate memorizing a series of *halakhot* and the order in which they were taught.

**NOTES**

**Isn't it taught in a *baraita* [*vehatanya*]: One who draws – וְהָתַנְיָא הַמַּדְלֶה:** Some point out that since this source is a mishna and not a *baraita*, the Gemara should read: Isn't it taught in a mishna [*vehatenan*], and not: Isn't it taught in a *baraita* [*vehatanya*] (*Baḥ*). From the early commentaries (Rosh; Rabbi Shimshon of Saens) who ask why the Gemara chose to raise its question from a *baraita* as opposed to a mishna, the later authorities deduce that the correct reading is, in fact: Isn't it taught in a *baraita* [*vehatanya*] (*Arukh LaNer*; *Kehillot Ya'akov*; *Yad Eliyahu*).

**HALAKHA**

**One who draws ten pails of water – הַמַּדְלֶה עֲשָׂרָה דְּלָיִים מַיִם וכו׳:** In a case where one draws out water in one pail and from it he fills another ten pails with water, if subsequently he finds the carcass of a creeping animal in one of them, that pail of water is deemed ritually impure while the rest remain ritually pure. This is the *halakha* only when the first pail does not have an inward-curved rim. If it did have a rim, all the pails of water are deemed ritually impure (Rambam *Sefer Tahara*, *Hilkhot She'ar Avot HaTumot* 17:1).

לֵימָא חִזְקִיָּה לֵית לֵיהּ דְּרַבִּי יַנַּאי! מַיָּא – שָׁרְקִי, פֵּירֵי – לָא שָׁרְקִי.

The Gemara explains the difficulty: **Shall we say** that **Ḥizkiyya,** who is not concerned that the rim of the basket might have held back the creeping animal, does **not agree** with the opinion **of Rabbi Yannai?** The Gemara answers that there is a difference between the two cases: **Water is slippery,** whereas **produce is not slippery.** In order to pour water out of the pail it is not necessary to turn it over completely. Therefore, the rim might hold back a creeping animal. By contrast, a basket must have one end fully raised in order to empty out all the produce it contains. In such a case Rabbi Yannai would agree that nothing could have been held back, and therefore the emptied produce remains pure.

אִי נַמִי: מַיָּא – לָא קָפֵיד עֲלַיְיהוּ, פֵּירֵי – קָפֵיד עֲלַיְיהוּ.

Alternatively, there is a different reason why one does not overturn a pail of water entirely: In the case of **water, one is not particular about it,** i.e., he does not mind if some is left over. Therefore he does not overturn the pail completely. By contrast, in the case of **produce one is particular about it,** so he raises one end of the basket entirely to ensure that every last piece of produce is emptied. Consequently, in the case of produce Rabbi Yannai would agree that even if the basket has a rim, all the produce remains pure.

וְאִי בָּעֵית אֵימָא: כִּי מוֹדוּ שַׁמַּאי וְהִלֵּל – בְּקוּפָּה שֶׁאֵינָהּ בְּדוּקָה,

As an alternative to its previous resolution that Ḥizkiyya is discussing the case of a rimmed receptacle, the Gemara suggests another resolution of the apparent contradiction between Ḥizkiyya's ruling and the opinions of Hillel and Shammai. **And if you wish, say: When** do **Shammai and Hillel agree? In** the case of **a basket that was not examined.** Since he did not examine the basket when he placed the pure produce there, a creeping animal might have already been inside. Consequently, they agree that the produce does not retain its presumptive state of purity but is considered retroactively impure.

Perek **I**
Daf **4** Amud **a**

כִּי פְּלִיגִי חִזְקִיָּה וְרַבִּי יוֹחָנָן – בְּקוּפָּה בְּדוּקָה. מָר סָבַר: הָא בְּדָקָהּ. וּמָר סָבַר: אֵימוּר, עִם סִילּוּק יָדוֹ נָפַל.

**When Ḥizkiyya and Rabbi Yoḥanan disagree,** it is **with regard to a basket** that was **examined.**[N] One **Sage,** Ḥizkiyya, **holds** that **since** it **was examined** before the produce was placed inside and was found to be clean of creeping animals, it is reasonable to assume that the creeping animal entered only after the ritually pure produce was removed. **And** one **Sage,** Rabbi Yoḥanan, **holds** that one can **say** that it is possible that **when he removed his hand** after feeling around to examine the basket, the creeping animal **fell** in.

וְהָא דּוּמְיָא דְּאִשָּׁה קָתָנֵי, וְאִשָּׁה בְּדוּקָה הִיא! כֵּיוָן דִּשְׁכִיחִי בָּהּ דָּמִים כְּשֶׁאֵינָהּ בְּדוּקָה דָּמְיָא.

The Gemara asks: **But isn't** the case of a basket **taught** as being **similar to** the case of a menstruating **woman?** Hillel had cited the case of the basket as a difficulty with regard to Shammai's opinion in the case of a menstruating woman. **And** since **a woman is** considered fully **examined,** since she examines herself with examination cloths twice a day, the other case must also be referring to a basket that had been examined. The Gemara answers: **Since blood is commonly found** flowing from **her,** as women regularly experience menstrual flows, it is **considered as** though she were **not examined.**

NOTES

**When Ḥizkiyya and Rabbi Yoḥanan disagree it is with regard to a basket that was examined – כִּי פְּלִיגִי חִזְקִיָּה וְרַבִּי יוֹחָנָן בְּקוּפָּה בְּדוּקָה:** *Tosafot* point out that Ḥizkiyya and Rabbi Yoḥanan disagreed only about a basket found in a private domain. By contrast, in the case of basket found in a public domain, all agree that the produce is pure, as the principle is that in a case of uncertainty with regard to impurity in a public domain, it is ruled to be ritually pure.

וְאִיבָּעֵית אֵימָא: כִּי מוֹדוּ שַׁמַּאי וְהִלֵּל – בְּקוּפָּה שֶׁאֵינָהּ מְכוּסָּה, כִּי פְּלִיגִי חִזְקִיָּה וְרַבִּי יוֹחָנָן – בְּקוּפָּה מְכוּסָּה. מְכוּסָּה, הֵיכִי נְפַל? כְּגוֹן שֶׁתַּשְׁמִישָׁהּ עַל יְדֵי כִּסּוּי.

The Gemara suggests another resolution of the apparent contradiction between the ruling of Ḥizkiyya and the opinions of Hillel and Shammai. **And if you wish, say: When Shammai and Hillel agree,** it is **with regard to a basket that is not covered. When** do **Ḥizkiyya and Rabbi Yoḥanan disagree? With regard to a basket** that is **covered.** The Gemara asks: If the basket **is covered, how did** the creeping animal **fall** inside? The Gemara answers: **For example, if** the basket **is used by** removing its **lid.** Ḥizkiyya holds that the creeping animal must have fallen in after the produce was removed, because as long as the produce was inside one would be careful not to allow anything else inside. Rabbi Yoḥanan is concerned that perhaps while the basket was uncovered a creeping animal could have fallen inside without one noticing.

וְהָא דּוּמְיָא דְּאִשָּׁה קָתָנֵי, וְאִשָּׁה מְכוּסָּה הִיא! כֵּיוָן דִּשְׁכִיחִי בָּהּ דָּמִים – כְּשֶׁאֵין מְכוּסָּה דָּמְיָא.

The Gemara raises a difficulty: But **isn't** the case of a basket **taught** as being **similar to** the case of a menstruating **woman? And** just as a woman **is considered covered,** since no outside blood can enter her, so too in the case of a basket, it must be one where it is constantly covered. The Gemara explains: **Since blood is commonly found** flowing from **her,** as women regularly experience menstrual flows, it is **considered as** though she is **not** always **covered.**

וְאִיבָּעֵית אֵימָא: כִּי מוֹדוּ שַׁמַּאי וְהִלֵּל – בְּזָוִית קוּפָּה, כִּי פְּלִיגִי חִזְקִיָּה וְרַבִּי יוֹחָנָן – בְּזָוִית בַּיִת. וְהָא קוּפָּה קָאָמַר!

The Gemara suggests another resolution. **And if you wish, say: When** do **Shammai and Hillel agree?** In a case where the produce was stored **in the corner of a basket.** By contrast, **when Ḥizkiyya and Rabbi Yoḥanan disagree,** it is in a case where the produce was stored **in the corner of a house.** The Gemara expresses puzzlement at this suggestion: **But** the Gemara on 3b explicitly **states** that they are referring to a case of **a basket.**

הָכִי קָאָמַר: קוּפָּה שֶׁנִּשְׁתַּמְּשׁוּ בָּהּ טָהֳרוֹת בְּזָוִית בַּיִת זוֹ, וְטִלְטְלוּהָ בְּזָוִית אַחֶרֶת, וְנִמְצָא שֶׁרֶץ בְּזָוִית אַחֶרֶת. חִזְקִיָּה סָבַר: לָא מַחְזְקִינַן טוּמְאָה מִמָּקוֹם לְמָקוֹם, וְרַבִּי יוֹחָנָן סָבַר: מַחְזְקִינַן.

The Gemara explains that **this** is what the Gemara on 3b **is saying:** If one has **a basket that was used** as a container for **ritually pure** produce **in this corner**[H] of the **house, and** after the produce was removed **it was** subsequently **carried to another corner, and** the carcass of **a creeping animal was found** in the basket while it was **in** that **other corner, Ḥizkiyya holds:** The produce remains ritually pure, as **we do not presume** that **ritual impurity** moved **from place to place.**[N] In other words, the impure creeping animal is not assumed to have moved from the first corner where the produce was kept. Instead, it fell inside while the basket was in the second corner, and therefore the produce that it previously contained remains pure. **And Rabbi Yoḥanan holds:** The produce is retroactively considered impure, as **we do presume** that ritual impurity, i.e., the carcass of the creeping animal in the basket, moved from place to place.

וּמִי מַחְזְקִינַן? וְהָתְנַן: נָגַע בְּאֶחָד בַּלַּיְלָה, וְאֵינוֹ יוֹדֵעַ אִם חַי אִם מֵת, וּלְמָחָר הִשְׁכִּים וּמְצָאוֹ מֵת – רַבִּי מֵאִיר מְטַהֵר,

The Gemara asks a question with regard to the opinion of Rabbi Yoḥanan: **And do we presume** that ritual impurity moved from place to place? **But didn't we learn** in a mishna (*Teharot* 5:7): If someone **touched one** other person **at night, and he does not know whether** the person he touched was **alive or dead, and on the following day he arose and found him dead,**[H] and he is uncertain whether or not he contracted ritual impurity from contact with a corpse, **Rabbi Meir deems him** ritually **pure.** It is assumed that the deceased was still alive until the point that it is known with certainty that he was dead.

**HALAKHA**

**A basket that was used for ritually pure produce in this corner, etc.** – **קוּפָּה שֶׁנִּשְׁתַּמְּשׁוּ בָּהּ טָהֳרוֹת בְּזָוִית...זוֹ וכו׳**: When a basket was emptied of its ritually pure produce and subsequently the carcass of a creeping animal was found in it, if it has a base or if it has a rim, all the produce that was stored therein is deemed ritually impure. This is the *halakha* even if the basket was thoroughly examined and covered with a lid, as the animal could have fallen in just as one was finishing his examination. Furthermore, even in a case where the basket was used to store produce in one corner and after it was emptied, it was placed in a different corner and there the carcass of a creeping animal was found inside, the produce is deemed impure, although *teruma* in that case would not be burned but rather held in suspension (Rambam *Sefer Tahara*, *Hilkhot She'ar Avot HaTumot* 17:2).

**If someone touched one other person at night… and on the following day he arose and found him dead** – **נָגַע בְּאֶחָד בַּלַּיְלָה...וּלְמָחָר הִשְׁכִּים וּמְצָאוֹ מֵת**: If one touched another person at night in a public domain, and he does not know whether the person he touched was alive or dead, and the following day he arose and found him dead, he is deemed ritually impure. This is in accordance with the principle that all ritually impure items are presumed to have been in the same state as they were at the time they were discovered (Rambam *Sefer Tahara*, *Hilkhot She'ar Avot HaTumot* 18:14).

**NOTES**

**Ḥizkiyya holds: We do not presume that ritual impurity moved from place to place** – **חִזְקִיָּה סָבַר לָא מַחְזְקִינַן טוּמְאָה מִמָּקוֹם לְמָקוֹם**: This dispute with regard to ritual impurity that moves from place to place does not apply in the case in the mishna of a menstruating woman. The commentaries explain that the place in which the impure menstrual blood of a woman is discovered is considered its original location, because anywhere she walks her impurity goes with her. Consequently, she herself is the designated place of the impurity, and the particular locale in which she is found is irrelevant (*Tosafot* on 2a).

וַחֲכָמִים מְטַמְּאִין, שֶׁכׇּל הַטְּמָאוֹת כְּשַׁעַת מְצִיאָתָן.

**And the Rabbis deem him** ritually **impure, as** it is presumed that **all** ritually **impure** items had already been in the same state as they were **at the time they were discovered.**[HN] Just as the deceased was found dead in the morning, so too, it is presumed that he was dead when he was touched in the middle of the night.

וְתָנֵי עֲלָהּ: כְּשַׁעַת מְצִיאָתָן, וּבִמְקוֹם מְצִיאָתָן!

The Gemara concludes its question: **And it is taught with regard to** this mishna: It is presumed that ritually impure items had been in the same state as they were **at the time they were discovered, but** only **in the place** in which **they were discovered.** In other words, if the corpse had been found in a different spot than he was at night, it is not presumed that he was already dead in the first spot, and the man who touched him remains ritually pure. If so, how can Rabbi Yoḥanan maintain that we presume impurity moved from place to place?

וְכִי תֵּימָא: הָנֵי מִילֵּי – לִשְׂרוֹף, אֲבָל לִתְלוֹת – תָּלֵינַן. וּמִי תָּלֵינַן?

**And if you would say** in response: **This statement,** that impurity is presumed only in the place in which it was discovered, applies specifically with regard to definite impure status, i.e., **to burn** *teruma*, **but** with regard to uncertain impurity, i.e., **to suspend** the status of *teruma*, **we** do in fact **suspend** its status and it may be neither burned nor eaten; is this distinction correct? **Do we** in fact **suspend** the status of ritually pure items in such a case, due to the concern that the dead man whom this individual touched might have already been dead in the first location?

וְהָתְנַן: מַחַט שֶׁנִּמְצֵאת מְלֵאָה חֲלוּדָה אוֹ שְׁבוּרָה – טְהוֹרָה, שֶׁכׇּל הַטְּמָאוֹת כְּשַׁעַת מְצִיאָתָן. וְאַמַּאי? לֵימָא: הַאי מֵעִיקָּרָא – מַחַט מְעַלַּיְיתָא הִיא, וְהָשְׁתָּא הוּא דְּהֶעֱלָה חֲלוּדָה!

**But didn't we learn** in a mishna (*Teharot* 3:5): With regard to a previously impure **needle that is found** on top of *teruma* and it is **full of rust or broken,** and therefore no longer contracts or transmit ritual impurity, the *teruma* remains **pure,**[N] **as** it is presumed that in **all** cases of **impurity,** the items in question had already been in the same state as they were **at the time they were discovered? But why** should that be the case? **Let us say** that **initially,** when it had fallen onto the *teruma*, **this needle was a proper,** non-rusty and unbroken, **needle,** capable of contracting and transmitting ritual impurity, **and it is** only **now that rust** had **formed** on it. The status of the *teruma* should at least be held in suspension. Rather, it is evident that the *teruma* is considered definitely pure and is not held in suspension due to the possibility that it might have become impure from the nail at a previous time or, presumably, in a previous place.

וְעוֹד, תְּנַן: מָצָא שֶׁרֶץ שָׂרוּף עַל גַּבֵּי הַזֵּיתִים, וְכֵן מַטְלִית הַמְהוּמְהָם – טָהוֹר, שֶׁכׇּל הַטְּמָאוֹת כְּשַׁעַת מְצִיאָתָן!

**And furthermore, we learned** in a mishna (*Teharot* 9:9): If one **found** the carcass of **a burned creeping animal on top of** a pile of **olives,** and that animal no longer transmits impurity as it is burned, **and similarly** if one finds **a tattered rag** of a *zav*, which likewise no longer transmits impurity, on top of a pile of olives, the olives are **pure.** The reason is **that** it is presumed in **all** cases of **impurity,** the items in question had already been in the same state as they were **at the time they were discovered.** Once again, this demonstrates that when this presumption is applied, the item is considered definitely pure, and is not held in suspension due to uncertainty.

**HALAKHA**

At the time they were discovered – כְּשַׁעַת מְצִיאָתָן: The guiding principle is that in all cases of impurity, the items in question are presumed to have been in the same state as they were at the time they were discovered. For example, if one finds the carcass of a burned creeping animal, or a needle that was known to be impure but is now rusted or broken, touching ritually pure items, one should not assume that it had touched the ritually pure items while it was impure. Rather, it is assumed that it had only touched them while in its current state of ritual purity (Rambam *Sefer Tahara, Hilkhot She'ar Avot HaTumot* 15:6, 10).

**NOTES**

All ritually impure items had already been in the same state as they were at the time they were discovered – כׇּל הַטְּמָאוֹת כְּשַׁעַת מְצִיאָתָן: Some ask: Why doesn't Shammai apply this principle to the case of a menstruating woman and say that the woman who discovers that she is ritually impure should presume that she was already in that state when she discovered her impurity? They answer that Shammai does not apply this principle here out of concern for the dereliction of the mitzva of procreation (*Tosefot HaRosh*; *Gilyon Tosafot* 2a). Apparently, they maintain that this principle is a presumption set by rabbinic law, as if it were by Torah law such an exception could not be made.

A needle that is found full of rust or broken, the *teruma* remains pure – מַחַט שֶׁנִּמְצֵאת מְלֵאָה חֲלוּדָה אוֹ שְׁבוּרָה טְהוֹרָה: Some explain that the case is where it is known that the needle had been ritually impure, but it is not known if it had fallen on the *teruma* while it was still unbroken and still impure or only after it was already broken, and therefore pure (Rashi). Others explain that it is unknown if the needle was at all ritually impure when it was in its proper, unbroken, state (Rambam's Commentary on the Mishna; Rabbi Ovadya Bartenura).

Ancient Roman needles

וְכִי תֵּימָא: כִּשְׁעַת מְצִיאָתָן – בֵּין לְקוּלָּא בֵּין לְחוּמְרָא וּבִמְקוֹם מְצִיאָתָן. אֲבָל שֶׁלֹּא בִּמְקוֹם מְצִיאָתָן – מִשְׂרָף לָא שָׂרְפִינַן, מִתְלָא תָּלֵינַן,

**And if you would say** that there is a difference between these last cases, where the items did not move, and the case of the basket that moved, this distinction is not correct. The suggestion is that in the last cases the items are treated entirely as if they had always been as they were **at the time they were discovered, whether** this leads **to a leniency,** as in the cases of the needle and the rag, **and whether** it leads **to a stringency,** in the case of one who touched someone at night, when he is considered to be definitely impure, **but** this is the *halakha* only with regard to the **place** where **they were discovered,** i.e., if they did not move. **But** with regard to a location that is **not the place** where **they were discovered,** we do suspect that ritual impurity moved from place to place, and therefore although **we do not burn** the *teruma* in question, **we hold it in suspension.**

וְהָתְנַן: כִּכָּר עַל גַּבֵּי הַדַּף, וּמַדָּף טָמֵא מוּנָּח תַּחְתָּיו, אַף עַל פִּי שֶׁאִם נָפְלָה אִי אֶפְשָׁר אֶלָּא אִם כֵּן נָגְעָה – טְהוֹרָה, שֶׁאֲנִי אוֹמֵר: אָדָם טָהוֹר נִכְנַס לְשָׁם וּנְטָלָהּ,

The Gemara refutes this suggestion: **But didn't we learn** in a *baraita* (*Tosefta, Teharot* 4:3): There was **a loaf** resting **on top of a shelf,**[H] **and** there was **an item of light impurity,** e.g., a garment of a *zav*, which transmits impurity to food but not to people or vessels, **lying underneath it,** and the loaf was later found on the ground. **Even though** the situation was such **that if** the loaf **fell** to the ground it would be **impossible** for it to have done anything **other than touch** the impure garment on its way down, nevertheless the loaf is **pure.** The reason is **that I say** that **a ritually pure man entered there and took it**[N] off the shelf and placed it onto the ground without it touching the impure garment.

עַד שֶׁיֹּאמַר: "בָּרִי לִי שֶׁלֹּא נִכְנַס אָדָם שָׁם", וְאָמַר רַבִּי אֶלְעָזָר: לֹא נִצְרְכָה אֶלָּא לִמְקוֹם מִדְרוֹן!

The *baraita* concludes: This ruling applies **unless someone says: It is clear to me that no person entered** there. **And Rabbi Elazar says:** This principle is **necessary only when** the top shelf is **an inclined surface.** In other words, even if it is very likely that the loaf rolled off the shelf and touched the garment on its way down to the ground, nevertheless it is assumed to be pure. This indicates that one does not presume that the loaf contracted impurity and then fell to the ground where it was found. Since such a possibility is not even entertained to the extent that the *teruma* is held in suspension, this demonstrates that in a case involving a movement from one place to another there is no presumption of ritual impurity at all.

הָתָם כִּדְקָתָנֵי טַעְמָא,

The Gemara explains that no proof can be cited from **there, as** that *baraita* explicitly **teaches** the **reason** for its ruling:

Perek **I**
Daf **4** Amud **b**

שֶׁאֲנִי אוֹמֵר: "אָדָם טָהוֹר נִכְנַס לְשָׁם, וּנְטָלָהּ".

The reason is not **that** one does not presume that ritual impurity moved from place to place, but because **I say** that **a ritually pure man entered there and took it** off the shelf and placed it onto the ground, avoiding the impure garment it would have hit had it fallen. When there is no such explanation, the principle that one presumes impurity moved from place to place does apply, e.g., in the case of the basket where the carcass of a creeping animal was found inside.

הָכָא נַמִי – נֵימָא: "עוֹרֵב אֲתָא, וּשְׁדָא"! אָדָם דְּבְכַוָּונָה – אָמְרִינַן, עוֹרֵב דְּשֶׁלֹּא בְּכַוָּונָה – לָא אָמְרִינַן.

The Gemara raises a difficulty: **Here, too, let us say** that **a raven,** which often touches creeping animals, **came and threw** the creeping animal into the basket when it was in the second corner, after the produce had been emptied from it. The Gemara rejects this claim: In the case of **a person, who** acts **with intent, we** can **say** that perhaps a person moved the loaf from the shelf onto the ground. By contrast, with regard to **a raven, which** does **not** act **with intent, we** do **not say** that perhaps it committed such a purposeful act.

**HALAKHA**

**There was a loaf resting on top of a shelf, etc.** – **כִּכָּר עַל גַּבֵּי הַדַּף וכו׳**: In the case of a loaf that was resting on top of a shelf and a garment that was impure with the impurity imparted by treading was lying underneath it, if the loaf is found lying on the ground, it is ritually pure, even if the situation was such that if the loaf had fallen it would certainly have touched the impure garment on its way down; nevertheless, since it is found in a pure spot, it is pure. The reason is that one can say that a ritually pure person entered there and took it off the shelf and placed it on that spot without it touching the impure garment (Rambam *Sefer Tahara, Hilkhot She'ar Avot HaTumot* 16:7).

**NOTES**

**That I say that a ritually pure man entered there and took it** – **שֶׁאֲנִי אוֹמֵר אָדָם טָהוֹר נִכְנַס לְשָׁם וּנְטָלָהּ**: Some commentaries cite other cases where, if vessels are found somewhere other than the places they were left, the *halakha* is that the vessels are deemed ritually impure, as it is assumed that a ritually impure person moved them. Why is it that in this case it is assumed that a ritually pure person moved the loaf? Some answer by differentiating between those cases involving vessels and this case about a food item. In the case of vessels, which are able to be purified by immersing them in a ritual bath, the Sages applied a stringent ruling to assume that they were touched by a ritually impure person. But in the case of food items, which have no possibility of being purified, they were lenient and assumed that a ritually pure person had moved them (*Sefer HaYashar*; *Tosafot*; Ritva). According to this explanation, in a case with an earthenware vessel, which also has no possibility of being purified in a ritual bath, it would share the same ruling and one would assume that it was moved only by a ritually pure person (Maharam).

מִכְּדֵי, הַאי כִּכָּר – סְפֵק טוּמְאָה בִּרְשׁוּת הַיָּחִיד הוּא, וְכָל סְפֵק טוּמְאָה בִּרְשׁוּת הַיָּחִיד – סְפֵקָה טָמֵא! מִשּׁוּם דְּהָוֵי דָּבָר שֶׁאֵין בּוֹ דַּעַת לִישָּׁאֵל, וְכָל דָּבָר שֶׁאֵין בּוֹ דַּעַת לִישָּׁאֵל, בֵּין בִּרְשׁוּת הָרַבִּים בֵּין בִּרְשׁוּת הַיָּחִיד – סְפֵקוֹ טָהוֹר.

The Gemara raises a difficulty with regard to the ruling of the *Tosefta*: **Now** the status of **this loaf** found on the ground **is** one of **uncertain impurity** found **in a private domain,**[H] **and** the guiding principle in **any** case of **uncertainty** involving **impurity in a private domain** is that the item with **uncertain** status is deemed **impure.** If so, shouldn't the loaf be deemed impure? The Gemara answers: No, **as** this **is an entity that lacks consciousness** in order for it **to be asked, and** the guiding principle is that with regard to **any entity that lacks consciousness** in order for it **to be asked,**[H] **whether** it is found **in a public domain or in a private domain,** the item with **uncertain** status is deemed **pure.**

וְאִי בָּעֵית אֵימָא: הָכָא בְּטוּמְאָה דְּרַבָּנַן. דַּיְקָא נַמִי, דְּקָתָנֵי "מַדָּף", כְּדִכְתִיב "עָלֶה נִדָּף".

**And if you wish, say** instead: That principle, that in any case of uncertainty involving impurity in a private domain the item with uncertain status is deemed impure, applies to a case of impurity by Torah law, whereas **here** we are dealing **with ritual impurity by rabbinic law.** The Gemara adds: The language of the *Tosefta* **is also precise, as it teaches:** There was a loaf resting on top of a shelf, and there was an item of light impurity [*madaf*] lying underneath it. The term ***madaf***[N] is similar to that **which is written: "A driven leaf [*niddaf*]"** (Leviticus 26:36), i.e., a light item. Likewise, the *Tosefta* is referring to a light, or rabbinic, impurity.

"וַחֲכָמִים אוֹמְרִים: לֹא כְּדִבְרֵי זֶה" כו׳. תָּנוּ רַבָּנַן, וַחֲכָמִים אוֹמְרִים: לֹא כְּדִבְרֵי זֶה וְלֹא כְּדִבְרֵי זֶה. לֹא כְּדִבְרֵי שַׁמַּאי – שֶׁלֹּא עָשָׂה סְיָיג לִדְבָרָיו, וְלֹא כְּדִבְרֵי הִלֵּל – שֶׁהִפְרִיז עַל מִדּוֹתָיו.

§ The mishna teaches: **And the Rabbis say:** The *halakha* is **neither in accordance with the statement of this** *tanna* nor in accordance with the statement of that *tanna*. **The Sages taught** in a *baraita*: **And the Rabbis say:** The *halakha* is **neither in accordance with the statement of this** *tanna* **nor in accordance with** the statement of **that** *tanna*. It is **not accordance with the statement of Shammai,** who rules that her time is sufficient and she does not need to be concerned that her menstrual flow started earlier, **as he did not enact** any **safeguard for his statement. And** is it **not in accordance with the statement of Hillel,** who rules that she assumes ritual impurity status retroactive to the time of her most recent examination, **as** he **went beyond** [*hifriz*][L] **his bounds** with his safeguard.

אֶלָּא: מֵעֵת לְעֵת מְמַעֶטֶת עַל יַד מִפְּקִידָה לִפְקִידָה, וּמִפְּקִידָה לִפְקִידָה – מְמַעֶטֶת עַל יַד מֵעֵת לְעֵת.

The Rabbis continue: **Rather,** a twenty-four-hour **period reduces** the time **from examination to examination,** i.e., if her most recent self-examination took place more than twenty-four hours earlier, she need concern herself with ritual impurity only for the twenty-four-hour period prior to discerning the blood. **And from examination to examination reduces** the time **from** a twenty-four-hour **period,** i.e., if she examined herself in the course of the previous day and discovered no blood, she was definitely pure prior to the examination.

מֵעֵת לְעֵת מְמַעֶטֶת עַל יַד מִפְּקִידָה לִפְקִידָה, כֵּיצַד? בָּדְקָה עַצְמָהּ בְּאֶחָד בְּשַׁבָּת וּמָצָאת טְהוֹרָה, וְיָשְׁבָה שֵׁנִי וּשְׁלִישִׁי וְלֹא בָּדְקָה, וְלָרְבִיעִי בָּדְקָה וּמְצָאָהּ טְמֵאָה – אֵין אוֹמְרִים: תִּטַּמֵּא מִפְּקִידָה לִפְקִידָה, אֶלָּא מֵעֵת לְעֵת.

The *baraita* elaborates: A twenty-four-hour **period reduces** the time[H] **from examination to examination, how so?** A woman **examined herself on Sunday and found** that she was **ritually pure, and** then **she sat** through **Monday and Tuesday and did not examine** herself. **And** then **on Wednesday she examined herself and found** that she was **impure.** In such a case **we do not say** that **she should be impure** retroactively **from** the time of this **examination** extending back **until** the time of her most recent **examination. Rather,** she is impure retroactively **for** a twenty-four-hour **period.**

HALAKHA

**Uncertain impurity found in a private domain** – **סְפֵק טוּמְאָה בִּרְשׁוּת הַיָּחִיד**: If one is uncertain as to whether or not he came into contact with an impure substance in the private domain, he is ritually impure (Rambam *Sefer Tahara, Hilkhot She'ar Avot HaTumot* 15:8).

**Any entity that lacks consciousness in order for it to be asked** – **דָּבָר שֶׁאֵין בּוֹ דַּעַת לִישָּׁאֵל**: An inanimate object, which lacks consciousness in order for it to be asked about a specific situation, or a person who lacks that knowledge, such as a deaf-mute, an imbecile, or a minor, is presumed ritually pure in cases of uncertain impurity (Rambam *Sefer Tahara, Hilkhot She'ar Avot HaTumot* 16:2).

**A twenty-four-hour period reduces the time, etc.** – **מֵעֵת לְעֵת מְמַעֶטֶת וכו׳**: A menstruating woman and a *zava* both assume ritual impurity status retroactively for twenty-four hours or extending back to their previous examination. For example, a ritually pure woman with no fixed menstrual cycle examines herself in the morning and finds that she is ritually pure. If she then examines herself later in the day and finds blood, all the ritually pure items that she handled from the time of her most recent examination that morning are rendered impure retroactively. If her second examination was not for another three days, all the ritually pure items that she had handled for the twenty-four-hour period preceding her second examination are rendered impure retroactively (Rambam *Sefer Tahara, Hilkhot Metamei Mishkav UMoshav* 3:4).

LANGUAGE

**Went beyond [*hifriz*]** – **הִפְרִיז**: The root of this word is similar to the root *peh, reish, tzadi*, meaning to break through. It is also similar to the word *perazot*, which refers to unwalled cities that are open and accessible. The expression: Went beyond his bounds, is used in contrast to the phrase: Enacted a safeguard for his words. This phraseology lends itself to the imagery that while one person constructs layers of protection, the other person is busy breaking them down.

NOTES

**The language of the *Tosefta* is also precise as it teaches *madaf*, etc.** – **דַּיְקָא נַמִי דְּקָתָנֵי מַדָּף וכו׳**: The Rambam writes that this section of the Gemara is not in the original Talmud. Rather, it was added by the *savora'im*, sixth-century Sages in Babylonia. It was originally added as a marginal note and was eventually incorporated into the text of the Gemara. With regard to the meaning of the word *madaf*, the Rambam writes that it is similar to the phrase: His odor spreads [*nodef*] (*Berakhot* 51a) (Rambam's Commentary on the Mishna). In this context of the ritually impure garment, this word is used to connote that the impure person's ritual impurity wafts through any layers above him and renders impure all garments that are on top of him (Maharatz Ḥayyut).

וּמִפְּקִידָה לִפְקִידָה מְמַעֶטֶת עַל יַד מֵעֵת לְעֵת, כֵּיצַד? בָּדְקָה עַצְמָהּ בְּשָׁעָה רִאשׁוֹנָה וּמָצְאָה טְהוֹרָה, וְיָשְׁבָה לָהּ שְׁנִיָּה וּשְׁלִישִׁית וְלֹא בָּדְקָה, וְלָרְבִיעִית בָּדְקָה וּמָצְאָה טְמֵאָה – אֵין אוֹמְרִים: תִּטַּמֵּא מֵעֵת לְעֵת, אֶלָּא מִפְּקִידָה לִפְקִידָה.

The *baraita* continues: And **from examination to examination reduces** the time **from** a twenty-four-hour **period, how so?** A woman **examined herself** in **the first hour** of a day **and found** that she was **ritually pure, and** then **she sat** through the **second and third** hours of the day **and did not examine** herself. **And** then **at the fourth** hour **she examined herself and found** that she was **impure.** In such a case **we do not say** that **she should be impure** retroactively **for** a twenty-four-hour **period. Rather,** she is impure retroactively **from** the time of this **examination** extending back **until** the time of her most recent **examination,** three hours earlier.

פְּשִׁיטָא, כֵּיוָן דְּבָדְקָה עַצְמָהּ בְּשָׁעָה רִאשׁוֹנָה וּמָצְאָה טְהוֹרָה – לָא מְטַמְּינַן לָהּ מֵעֵת לְעֵת! אַיְּידֵי דִּתְנָא "מֵעֵת לְעֵת מְמַעֶטֶת עַל יַד מִפְּקִידָה לִפְקִידָה", תְּנָא נַמִי "מִפְּקִידָה לִפְקִידָה מְמַעֶטֶת עַל יַד מֵעֵת לְעֵת".

The Gemara raises a difficulty: This *halakha* is **obvious. Since she examined herself at the first hour and found** that she was **pure,** there is **no** reason **to render her impure** retroactively **for** a twenty-four-hour **period.** Why does the *baraita* state such an obvious *halakha*? The Gemara answers: Since the *baraita* taught that according to the Rabbis a twenty-four-hour **period reduces** the time **from examination to examination,** it **also taught** the parallel case, that **from examination to examination reduces** the time **from** a twenty-four-hour **period,** despite the fact that this *halakha* is obvious.

אָמַר רַבָּה: מַאי טַעֲמַיְיהוּ דְּרַבָּנַן – אִשָּׁה מַרְגֶּשֶׁת בְּעַצְמָהּ. אֲמַר לֵיהּ אַבַּיֵי: אִם כֵּן, תְּהֵא דַּיָּהּ שַׁעְתָּהּ! וְרַבָּה – לְחַדּוּדֵי לְאַבַּיֵי הוּא דְּבָעֵי. אֶלָּא מַאי טַעֲמַיְיהוּ דְּרַבָּנַן?

**Rabba says: What** is the **reason** for the opinion **of the Rabbis? A woman** can **sense within herself** if she is experiencing a flow of blood. **Abaye**[P] **said to** Rabba: **If so, her time should be sufficient,** as there should be no concern that her flow began earlier. The Gemara explains: **And Rabba** did not in fact mean this explanation seriously; rather, he **wanted to hone**[N] the mind of **Abaye.** The Gemara asks: **But** if so, **what** is the real **reason** for the opinion **of the Rabbis?**

כִּי הָא דַּאֲמַר רַב יְהוּדָה, אָמַר שְׁמוּאֵל: חֲכָמִים תִּקְּנוּ לָהֶן לִבְנוֹת יִשְׂרָאֵל שֶׁיְּהוּ בּוֹדְקוֹת עַצְמָן שַׁחֲרִית וְעַרְבִית. שַׁחֲרִית – לְהַכְשִׁיר טָהֳרוֹת שֶׁל לַיְלָה, וְעַרְבִית – לְהַכְשִׁיר טָהֳרוֹת שֶׁל יוֹם.

The Gemara answers: It is **in accordance with that which Rav Yehuda said** that **Shmuel says: The Sages instituted that the Jewish women should examine themselves** twice each day, **morning and evening.**[H] The **morning** examination is in order **to render fit** the **ritually pure** items **of the night,**[N] i.e., any items that she touched the night before. **And** the **evening** examination is in order **to render fit** the **pure** items that she touched **during the day.**

וְזוֹ הוֹאִיל וְלֹא בָּדְקָה – הִפְסִידָה עוֹנָה. מַאי "עוֹנָה"? עוֹנָה יְתֵירָה.

The Gemara continues its explanation: **And this** woman, **since she did not examine** herself in accordance with the rabbinic enactment, **she loses** the status of the ritually pure items she touched over the **period** [*ona*][L] of a day or a night. The Gemara asks: **What** is meant by: **Period** of a day or a night? Doesn't her retroactive impurity status extend back for a twenty-four-hour period? The Gemara answers: It means **an additional period** of a day or a night, i.e., twenty-four hours in total.

אֲמַר לֵיהּ רַב פַּפָּא לְרָבָא: וְהָא זִימְנִין מַשְׁכַּחַתְּ לָהּ שָׁלֹשׁ עוֹנוֹת בְּמֵעֵת לְעֵת! הִשְׁווּ חֲכָמִים מִדּוֹתֵיהֶן, שֶׁלֹּא תַּחֲלוֹק בְּמֵעֵת לְעֵת.

**Rav Pappa says to Rava: But** occasionally **you find three periods** of day or night within a twenty-four-hour period. For example, if she examined herself on Monday afternoon and finds blood, then the twenty-four-hour period extending back to Sunday afternoon includes three periods of day or night: Monday day, Sunday night and Sunday day from the time of her most recent examination, as these twenty-four hours do not fit precisely into two such periods. The Gemara answers: **The Sages rendered their measures equal,** so that **one should not differentiate** between cases. In other words, they wanted to issue a uniform ruling that applies universally **and** therefore they established a set twenty-four-hour **period** of retroactive impurity, regardless of the circumstances.

**PERSONALITIES**

**Abaye – אַבַּיֵי:** One of the outstanding Sages of the Talmud, Abaye was a fourth-generation Babylonian *amora*. He lost both of his parents at an early age and was raised in the home of his uncle, Rabba bar Naḥmani. Some say that his real name was Naḥmani or Kilil, and Abaye was just a nickname. The woman who assisted Rabba in raising him left a profound impression upon him, and he cites many life lessons in her name in the Gemara. The Gemara relates several stories that illustrate his intelligence even as a child, including several where Rabba tests him with questions.

**NOTES**

**To hone – לְחַדּוּדֵי:** The practice of a Sage intentionally making an incorrect statement, acting improperly, or even praising an opinion that is directly contradicted by an established *halakha*, is an educational technique that is mentioned several times in the Gemara. The aim was not simply to test the students, but to require them to pay close attention and think independently (Rashi on *Eiruvin* 13a), or to remind them of matters that they had previously studied (Ritva on *Yoma* 43a).

**The morning examination is in order to render fit the ritually pure items of the night – שַׁחֲרִית לְהַכְשִׁיר טָהֳרוֹת שֶׁל לַיְלָה:** Some commentaries maintain that according to Shammai, who holds that a woman's time of examination is sufficient and she does not become impure retroactively, there is no such rabbinic institution of daily examinations (*Ḥazon Ish*; *Arukh LaNer*). By contrast, Rashi on 4a indicates that this institution is in effect even according to Shammai. Consequently, it has been suggested that according to Shammai the purpose of this examination was not to establish retroactive purity, but to provide current evidence of purity rather than relying on a presumptive status (*Ḥazon Ish*).

**HALAKHA**

**The Sages instituted…morning and evening – חֲכָמִים תִּקְּנוּ...שַׁחֲרִית וְעַרְבִית:** The Sages instituted that all Jewish women should examine themselves twice each day, morning and evening. The morning examination is in order to render fit the ritually pure items that she touched the night before. The evening examination is in order to render fit the ritually pure items that she touched during the day (Rambam *Sefer Tahara, Hilkhot Metamei Mishkav UMoshav* 4:7).

**LANGUAGE**

**Period [*ona*] – עוֹנָה:** The literal meaning of this word is a fluctuating period of time. It is used in reference to the rainy season, for example, which can be long or short, depending on the year. In this case, it is referring to a half-day period of either day or night. At an equinox, each period is exactly twelve hours. During the rest of the year each fluctuates based upon the sun's rising and setting.

**PERSONALITIES**

**Rabbi Dosa – רַבִּי דּוֹסָא:** When the name Rabbi Dosa is mentioned without any qualifiers in the Mishna, the reference is to Rabbi Dosa ben Harkinas. Rabbi Dosa ben Harkinas was one of the earliest *tanna'im*. He was already considered a Sage of great stature in the period of the Second Temple. He engaged in disputes with Akavya ben Mahalalel and Ḥananya the deputy High Priest, and he was apparently from the same generation as Rabban Yoḥanan ben Zakkai, whom he outlived. As a result of his longevity, he is described as participating in various deliberations during the time of Rabban Gamliel in Yavne, although he would not come to the study hall due to his old age. If this is the case, he lived well over a hundred years. See the Rambam's introduction to the Mishna, where his wondrously long life span is discussed.

Rabbi Dosa ben Harkinas was universally respected due to his old age and wisdom, and Rabbi Yehoshua asked his advice on several issues. He was apparently an expert in the history of the Jewish people, and he could recall even small details of events. He possibly preserved for himself relics from earlier eras, such as the mortar of the prophet Haggai. The story recounted here indicates that he was also extremely wealthy, but there are no records of his profession or family, besides the younger brother he himself mentions. His statements, which are also cited in the Mishna, deal with both *aggada* and *halakha*.

אִיבָּעֵית אֵימָא: שֶׁלֹּא יְהֵא חוֹטֵא נִשְׂכָּר.

**And if you wish, say** instead that they established the set twenty-four-hour period **so that the sinner should not profit** from his transgression. If the extent of retroactive impurity would be fixed at one additional period of day or night, a woman who remembers and examines herself in the early morning would be impure retroactively for a full twenty-four hours, back to early morning the previous day, whereas one who waits until noon would be impure only for the period of the morning and the previous night.

מַאי בֵּינַיְיהוּ? אִיכָּא בֵּינַיְיהוּ: דְּאִתְנִיסָה וְלָא בָּדְקָה.

The Gemara asks: **What is** the difference **between** these two answers? The Gemara answers: The difference **between** them is in a case **where she was prevented** by outside circumstances **and did not perform an examination.** According to the second answer she would not be considered a sinner and therefore she would be impure only for an additional period of a day or night. By contrast, according to the first answer her impure status would span twenty-four hours regardless of the circumstances.

״כָּל אִשָּׁה שֶׁיֵּשׁ לָהּ וֶסֶת״ [וכו׳]. לֵימָא מַתְנִיתִין רַבִּי דּוֹסָא הִיא וְלָא רַבָּנַן, דְּתַנְיָא, רַבִּי אֱלִיעֶזֶר אוֹמֵר: אַרְבַּע נָשִׁים דַּיָּין שָׁעָתָן, בְּתוּלָה, מְעוּבֶּרֶת, מֵנִיקָה, וּזְקֵנָה. רַבִּי דּוֹסָא אוֹמֵר: כָּל אִשָּׁה שֶׁיֵּשׁ לָהּ וֶסֶת – דַּיָּהּ שָׁעָתָהּ!

§ The mishna teaches: For **any woman who has a fixed** menstrual **cycle,** and she examined herself at that time and discovered blood, her time is sufficient, and she transmits impurity only from that time onward. The Gemara asks: **Shall we say** that the mishna **is** in accordance with the opinion of **Rabbi Dosa,**[P] **and not** in accordance with **the** opinion of **the Rabbis? As it is taught** in a *baraita* that **Rabbi Eliezer says: There are four** categories of **women** for whom the *halakha* is that **their time is sufficient: A virgin,** i.e., a girl who has never experienced menstruation, **a pregnant woman, a nursing** mother, **and an elderly woman. Rabbi Dosa says:** For **every woman who has a fixed** menstrual **cycle,** and she examined herself at that time and discovered blood, **her time is sufficient,** and it is only from that stage that she transmits ritual impurity.

אֲפִילּוּ תֵּימָא רַבָּנַן, עַד כָּאן לָא פְּלִיגִי רַבָּנַן עֲלֵיהּ דְּרַבִּי דּוֹסָא – אֶלָּא שֶׁלֹּא בִּשְׁעַת וְסְתָּהּ, אֲבָל בִּשְׁעַת וְסְתָּהּ – מוֹדוּ לֵיהּ, וּמַתְנִיתִין בִּשְׁעַת וְסְתָּהּ – וְדִבְרֵי הַכֹּל.

The Gemara answers: **You** may **even say** that the mishna is in accordance with the opinion of **the Rabbis. The Rabbis disagree with Rabbi Dosa only in** the case of a woman who discovers blood at an irregular time, **not at the fixed time of her** menstrual **cycle. But** if she discovers blood **at the fixed time of her** menstrual **cycle, they agree with him** that her time is sufficient and there is no retroactive impurity. **And the mishna** is referring to a woman who discovers blood **at the fixed time of her** menstrual **cycle, and** therefore **everyone agrees** that her time is sufficient.

מִכְּלָל דְּרַבִּי דּוֹסָא – אֲפִילּוּ שֶׁלֹּא בִּשְׁעַת וְסְתָּהּ אָמַר. מַאן תְּנָא לְהָא דְּתָנוּ רַבָּנַן: אִשָּׁה שֶׁיֵּשׁ לָהּ וֶסֶת כִּתְמָהּ טָמֵא לְמַפְרֵעַ, שֶׁאִם תִּרְאֶה שֶׁלֹּא בִּשְׁעַת וְסְתָּהּ – מְטַמְּאָה מֵעֵת לְעֵת,

The Gemara raises a difficulty: **By inference,** one can conclude **that Rabbi Dosa says** that her time is sufficient **even** if she discovers blood **not at the fixed time of her** menstrual **cycle.**[N] If so, **who** is the *tanna* who **taught** the following *baraita*? **As the Sages taught** in a *baraita*: With regard to **a woman who has a fixed** menstrual **cycle** who finds a blood stain, **her** blood **stain** is **impure retroactively**[N] from when the garment in question was laundered. The reason is **that if she sees** a flow of menstrual blood **not at the fixed time of her** menstrual **cycle,** it renders her impure retroactively **for** a twenty-four-hour **period.** Therefore, the blood stain likewise renders her retroactively impure.

**NOTES**

**Even if she discovers blood not at the fixed time of her menstrual cycle – אֲפִילּוּ שֶׁלֹּא בִּשְׁעַת וְסְתָּהּ:** The early commentaries explain that Rabbi Dosa's reasoning is that in between a woman's fixed menstruation times she is considered as temporarily having ceased to experience menstruation. Therefore she is not expected to find any blood until her fixed time of menstruation, and any blood that she does discover is an anomaly that causes her to assume impurity status only from then onward (*Bedek HaBayit*). In a case where she discovers blood after her fixed time of menstruation has passed, some maintain that she assumes impurity status only from then onward only if she performed a clean self-examination at her fixed time of menstruation. But if she neglected to perform a self-examination at that time, then she assumes retroactive impurity status extending back to her fixed time of menstruation, even according to Rabbi Dosa (*Ḥeshek Shlomo*).

**Her blood stain is impure retroactively – כִּתְמָהּ טָמֵא לְמַפְרֵעַ:** Rashi explains that she assumes impurity status retroactively extending back to the time that this stained garment was last laundered. The source for this explanation is the mishna (66a) that states that a blood stain causes her to assume ritual impurity status until the time that she can declare that she had examined the garment and found it free of stains, or extending back to the time that she last examined it, as the Gemara (66b) explains that it is presumed that every Jewish woman examines her garments upon laundering them.

נֵימָא רַבָּנַן הִיא וְלָא רַבִּי דּוֹסָא? אֲפִילּוּ תֵּימָא רַבִּי דּוֹסָא, עַד כָּאן לָא פָּלֵיג רַבִּי דּוֹסָא עֲלַיְיהוּ דְּרַבָּנַן – אֶלָּא בִּשְׁעַת וִסְתָּהּ, אֲבָל שֶׁלֹּא בִּשְׁעַת וִסְתָּהּ – מוֹדֵי לְהוּ. וּמַתְנִיתִין – בִּשְׁעַת וִסְתָּהּ, וְרַבִּי דּוֹסָא הִיא,

The Gemara concludes its question: **Shall we say** that this *baraita* **is** in accordance with the opinion of **the Rabbis and not** in accordance with the opinion of **Rabbi Dosa?** The Gemara answers: **You may even say** that it is in accordance with the opinion of **Rabbi Dosa,** as one can claim that **Rabbi Dosa disagrees with the Rabbis only** in a case where a woman sees menstrual blood **at the fixed time of her** menstrual **cycle. But** if she sees blood **not at the fixed time of her** menstrual **cycle, he agrees** with them that she is impure retroactively. **And** according to this answer **the mishna,** which deals with a woman who discovers blood **at the fixed time of her** menstrual **cycle,** is only in accordance with the opinion of **Rabbi Dosa,** in contrast to the earlier claim.

Perek **I**
Daf **5** Amud **a**

וּבָרַיְיתָא – דִּבְרֵי הַכֹּל.

**And** as for the ruling of **the** ***baraita,*** that a woman who discovers menstrual blood not at her fixed time for menstruation is impure retroactively, this is a *halakha* with which **everyone agrees.**

וְלוֹקְמָא אִיפְּכָא!

The Gemara raises a difficulty: **But let** us **interpret** the mishna in the **opposite** manner. Why interpret the mishna in accordance with the opinion of Rabbi Dosa and the *baraita* in accordance with everyone, when we can give precedence to the mishna, which is more authoritative, by interpreting it in accordance with all opinions, as was first explained, and the *baraita* only in accordance with the opinion of the Rabbis.

כֵּיוָן דְּאִיכָּא לְאוֹקוֹמֵי לְקוּלָּא וּלְחוּמְרָא – לְחוּמְרָא מוֹקְמִינַן.

The Gemara answers: **Since there is** a way **to interpret** it **as a leniency,**[N] i.e., that all agree that blood discovered at the fixed time of menstruation renders items impure only from that point onward, **and** it can also be interpreted in a manner that leads **to a stringency,** i.e., everyone agrees that blood discovered not at her fixed time for menstruation causes retroactive impurity, and furthermore the Rabbis hold that this is the *halakha* even when blood is discovered at her fixed time of menstruation, **we interpret** it the way that leads **to a stringency.**

קָתָנֵי: ״שֶׁאִם תִּרְאֶה שֶׁלֹּא בִּשְׁעַת וִסְתָּהּ – מְטַמְּאָה מֵעֵת לְעֵת״, טַעְמָא – דְּאִשָּׁה שֶׁיֵּשׁ לָהּ וֶסֶת הוּא, דִּפְלִיגִי רַבָּנַן בֵּין כִּתְמָהּ לִרְאִיָּיתָהּ,

§ It **is taught** in the *baraita*: If a woman who has a fixed menstrual cycle finds a blood stain, her blood stain is retroactively impure. The reason is **that if she sees** a flow of menstrual blood **not at the fixed time of her** menstrual **cycle,** it renders her ritually impure retroactively **for** a twenty-four-hour **period.** The Gemara analyzes this statement: The **reason** for this ruling is **that** she is **a woman who has a fixed** menstrual **cycle;** therefore, **the Rabbis distinguish between her** blood **stain,** which causes retroactive impurity like a sighting not at her fixed time, **and her sighting** of her menstrual flow at its fixed time, which does not cause retroactive impurity.

הָא שְׁאָר נָשִׁים שֶׁאָמְרוּ חֲכָמִים דַּיָּין שְׁעָתָן – כִּתְמָן כִּרְאִיָּיתָן.

It can be inferred from here that in the case of those **other women,** e.g., a pregnant or elderly woman, **with regard to** whom **the Sages stated: Their time is sufficient** and their menstrual flow never causes retroactive impurity, the same *halakha* applies to **their** blood **stains as** to **their sighting** of their menstrual flow, i.e., the stains do not cause retroactive impurity.

NOTES

**Since there is a way to interpret it as a leniency, etc.** – כֵּיוָן דְּאִיכָּא לְאוֹקוֹמֵי לְקוּלָּא וכו׳: The early commentaries ask: Since the idea of imposing retroactive impurity is a rabbinic safeguard to begin with, why it is preferable to interpret the mishna in a more stringent fashion? They answer that, nevertheless, a higher standard is warranted in the case of matters of ritual purity (Ritva).

מַנִּי? רַבִּי חֲנִינָא בֶּן אַנְטִיגְנוֹס הִיא. דְּאָמַר רַב יְהוּדָה, אָמַר שְׁמוּאֵל מִשּׁוּם רַבִּי חֲנִינָא בֶּן אַנְטִיגְנוֹס: כׇּל הַנָּשִׁים – כִּתְמָן טָמֵא לְמַפְרֵעַ. וְנָשִׁים שֶׁאָמְרוּ חֲכָמִים דַּיָּין שְׁעָתָן – כִּתְמָן כִּרְאִיָּיתָן, חוּץ מִתִּינוֹקֶת שֶׁלֹּא הִגִּיעַ זְמַנָּהּ לִרְאוֹת – שֶׁאֲפִילּוּ סְדִינִין שֶׁלָּהּ מְלוּכְלָכִין בְּדָם, אֵין חוֹשְׁשִׁין לָהּ.

The Gemara asks: In accordance with **whose** opinion is this *baraita* taught? The Gemara answers: **It is** in accordance with the opinion of **Rabbi Ḥanina ben Antigonus,**[P] **as Rav Yehuda said** that **Shmuel says in the name of Rabbi Ḥanina ben Antigonus:** The *halakha* **with regard to all women** is that **their** blood **stains are impure retroactively. But** any **women with regard to whom the Sages stated: Their time is sufficient, their** blood **stains** share the same ruling **as their sighting** of their menstrual flow, i.e., they do not cause retroactive impurity. This is the *halakha* **except** for the case **of a young girl whose time to see** the flow of menstrual blood **has not arrived.** With regard to her, **even if her sheets are soiled with blood one** need **not be concerned for it,**[N] i.e., her blood stains do not cause any impurity at all, even from that point onward.

וּמִי אִית לֵיהּ לְרַבִּי חֲנִינָא כֶּתֶם כְּלָל? וְהָתַנְיָא: כׇּל הַנָּשִׁים כִּתְמָן טָמֵא, וְנָשִׁים שֶׁאָמְרוּ חֲכָמִים דַּיָּין שְׁעָתָן – כִּתְמָן טָמֵא. רַבִּי חֲנִינָא בֶּן אַנְטִיגְנוֹס אוֹמֵר: נָשִׁים שֶׁאָמְרוּ חֲכָמִים דַּיָּין שְׁעָתָן – אֵין לָהֶן כֶּתֶם. מַאי לָאו: אֵין לָהֶן כֶּתֶם כְּלָל! לָא, אֵין לָהֶן כֶּתֶם לְמַפְרֵעַ, אֲבָל יֵשׁ לָהֶן כֶּתֶם מִכָּאן וּלְהַבָּא.

The Gemara asks: **And does Rabbi Ḥanina** ben Antigonus **hold** that a blood **stain** causes ritual impurity **at all? But isn't it taught** in a *baraita*: The *halakha* with regard to **all women** is that **their** blood **stains are impure. And** similarly, **women with regard to** whom **the Sages stated: Their time is sufficient, their** blood **stains are** also **impure. Rabbi Ḥanina ben Antigonus says:** The *halakha* of **women with regard to** whom **the Sages stated: Their time is sufficient,** is that **they do not have** the ritual impurity of a blood **stain. What, is it not** correct to say that this means **they have no** impurity caused by a blood **stain at all?** The Gemara answers: **No,** it means that **they do not have** impurity caused by a blood **stain retroactively, but they do have** the impurity caused by a blood **stain from here onward.**

מִכְּלָל דְּתַנָּא קַמָּא סָבַר: אֲפִילּוּ לְמַפְרֵעַ? אִין, רַבִּי מֵאִיר הִיא, דְּמַחְמִיר גַּבֵּי כְּתָמִים. דְּתַנְיָא: כׇּל הַנָּשִׁים – כִּתְמָן טָמֵא לְמַפְרֵעַ, וְנָשִׁים שֶׁאָמְרוּ חֲכָמִים דַּיָּין שְׁעָתָן – כִּתְמָן טָמֵא לְמַפְרֵעַ, דִּבְרֵי רַבִּי מֵאִיר.

The Gemara asks: **From the fact that** Rabbi Ḥanina ben Antigonus holds that a blood stain imparts ritual impurity from that point onward, does this not indicate that **the first *tanna* holds** that it causes ritual impurity **even retroactively?** The Gemara answers: **Yes,** the ruling of the first *tanna* **is** in accordance with the opinion of **Rabbi Meir, who is stringent with regard to blood stains. As it is taught** in a *baraita*: The *halakha* with regard to **all women** is that **their** blood **stains are impure retroactively.**[H] **And** similarly, **women with regard to** whom **the Sages stated: Their time is sufficient, their** blood **stains are** also **impure retroactively.** This is **the statement of Rabbi Meir.**

רַבִּי חֲנִינָא בֶּן אַנְטִיגְנוֹס אוֹמֵר: נָשִׁים שֶׁאָמְרוּ חֲכָמִים דַּיָּין שְׁעָתָן – כִּתְמָן כִּרְאִיָּיתָן. וְתִינוֹקֶת שֶׁהִגִּיעַ זְמַנָּהּ לִרְאוֹת – יֵשׁ לָהּ כֶּתֶם, וְשֶׁלֹּא הִגִּיעַ זְמַנָּהּ לִרְאוֹת – אֵין לָהּ כֶּתֶם. וְאֵימָתַי הִגִּיעַ זְמַנָּהּ לִרְאוֹת? מִשֶּׁהִגִּיעוּ יְמֵי הַנְּעוּרִים.

The *baraita* continues: **Rabbi Ḥanina ben Antigonus says:** The *halakha* of **women with regard to** whom **the Sages stated: Their time is sufficient,**[H] is that **their** blood **stains** share the same ruling **as their sighting** of their menstrual flow, i.e., they cause ritual impurity from that point onward. **And** in the case of **a young girl, if her time to see** the flow of menstrual blood **has arrived,**[N] then **she has** impurity status when she finds a blood **stain. But if her time to see** the flow of menstrual blood **has not** yet **arrived, she does not have** impurity status when she finds a blood **stain.** The Gemara asks: **And when does** a young girl **arrive** at **her time to see** the flow of menstrual blood? The Gemara answers: **When the days of** her **young womanhood have arrived.**[HN]

## PERSONALITIES

**Rabbi Ḥanina ben Antigonus – רַבִּי חֲנִינָא בֶּן אַנְטִיגְנוֹס:** The *tanna* Rabbi Ḥanina ben Antigonus, referred to in the Jerusalem Talmud as Rabbi Ḥananya ben Antigonus, lived through the period of the destruction of the Second Temple. Some of the early commentaries maintain that he was a priest. He was notably scrupulous in matters of ritual impurity and was very discerning with regard to whom he trusted to handle ritually pure items. He testifies that he personally saw the Levites performing their service in the Temple. Rabbi Ḥanina ben Antigonus discussed matters of Torah with the famous *tanna'im* Rabbi Yishmael and Rabbi Akiva.

## HALAKHA

**The *halakha* with regard to all women is that their blood stains are impure retroactively – כׇּל הַנָּשִׁים כִּתְמָן טָמֵא לְמַפְרֵעַ:** A woman who discovers a blood stain assumes impurity status retroactively for twenty-four hours, or extending back to the last time she examined her garment and found it clean within the last twenty-four hours. Even if she laundered the garment, one may not assume that the stain came after it was laundered. If she discovers a wet, seemingly fresh blood stain, nevertheless she assumes the same retroactive impurity status, as the blood stain may have been there for days with water recently falling upon it, thereby moistening it and giving it a fresh appearance (Rambam *Sefer Kedusha, Hilkhot Issurei Bia* 9:3 and *Sefer Tahara, Hilkhot Metamei Mishkav UMoshav* 3:7).

**The *halakha* of women with regard to whom the Sages stated: Their time is sufficient, etc. – נָשִׁים שֶׁאָמְרוּ חֲכָמִים דַּיָּין שְׁעָתָן וכו׳:** The Sages ruled that with regard to these four women, i.e., a woman who never experienced menstrual bleeding, a pregnant woman, a nursing mother, and an elderly woman, their time is sufficient. This means that neither their menstrual flow of blood nor a discovered blood stain causes them retroactive impurity, but only impurity going forward. This holds true until they experience three separate flows of menstrual blood (Rambam *Sefer Kedusha, Hilkhot Issurei Bia* 9:5 and *Sefer Tahara, Hilkhot Metamei Mishkav UMoshav* 3:8).

**When the days of her young womanhood have arrived – מִשֶּׁהִגִּיעוּ יְמֵי הַנְּעוּרִים:** The Sages instituted that only the blood stains found on the body or clothing of an adult woman cause ritual impurity. The blood stain of a young girl, who has not yet reached the normal time for menstruation, does not cause any ritual impurity. The normal time for menstruation is when she reaches the age of young womanhood, which is marked by her reaching the age of twelve plus the growth of two hairs in her pubic area. If she has only one of the two conditions, i.e., age or pubic hairs, her blood stain causes no impurity, even if she is a non-virgin and even if she discovered blood stains twice. If she discovers blood stains three times, her blood stains will then start to cause ritual impurity (Rambam *Sefer Kedusha, Hilkhot Issurei Bia* 9:5 and *Sefer Nashim, Hilkhot Ishut* 2:1; *Shulḥan Arukh, Yoreh De'a* 190:2).

## NOTES

**Even if her sheets are soiled with blood one need not be concerned for it – שֶׁאֲפִילּוּ סְדִינִין שֶׁלָּהּ מְלוּכְלָכִין בְּדָם אֵין חוֹשְׁשִׁין לָהּ:** One of the later authorities interprets this precisely, that it is only for blood stains on her sheets or garment that one need not be concerned; blood stains found on her body would cause ritual impurity (*Baḥ*). Others disagree and understand that with regard to young girls who are the under the age of menstruation, the Sages did not institute any ritual impurity (*Shakh*, citing *Tur* and *Shulḥan Arukh*).

**And in the case of a young girl if her time to see the flow of menstrual blood has arrived – וְתִינוֹקֶת שֶׁהִגִּיעַ זְמַנָּהּ לִרְאוֹת:** Some commentaries state that a young girl's time of menstruation has arrived only if she has experienced two or three flows of menstrual blood (Rashba; Meiri). Most commentaries maintain that if she is old enough she is designated as one whose time to begin menstruating has arrived even if she has not yet emitted blood (Rashi; Rashba; Ritva).

**When the days of her young womanhood have arrived – מִשֶּׁהִגִּיעוּ יְמֵי הַנְּעוּרִים:** The Gemara mentions two indicators that signify the transition from childhood to adulthood: The physical sign of at least two hairs in the pubic area, and the time factor of the age of twelve years. The early commentaries disagree whether one indicator is sufficient (Rashi) or if both indicators are necessary to signify her entrance into young womanhood.

״וְהַמְשַׁמֶּשֶׁת בְּעֵדִים״ כו׳. אָמַר רַב יְהוּדָה, אָמַר שְׁמוּאֵל: עֵד שֶׁלִּפְנֵי תַשְׁמִישׁ – אֵינוֹ מְמַעֵט כִּפְקִידָה.

§ The mishna teaches: **And** with regard to a woman **who engages in intercourse while** using **examination cloths,** with which she ascertains whether the menstrual flow began, since the halakhic status of that act is like that of an examination, it reduces the time from a twenty-four-hour period and reduces the time from examination to examination. **Rav Yehuda says** that **Shmuel says:** The **examination cloth** with **which** she examined herself **before intercourse**[H] **does not reduce** the time from a twenty-four-hour period **like** a regular **examination.**

מַאי טַעֲמָא? אָמַר רַב קְטִינָא: מִתּוֹךְ שֶׁמְּהוּמָה לְבֵיתָהּ. וְכִי מְהוּמָה לְבֵיתָהּ, מַאי הָוֵי? מִתּוֹךְ שֶׁמְּהוּמָה לְבֵיתָהּ – אֵינָהּ מַכְנֶסֶת לְחוֹרִין וְלִסְדָקִין.

The Gemara asks: **What is the reason** for the opinion of Shmuel? **Rav Ketina says: Since she is excited** [*shemehuma*][L] and hurried **for** intercourse with **her husband,** it is not considered a proper examination. The Gemara asks: **And** even **if she is excited for** intercourse with **her husband, what of it?** Why does that invalidate her examination? The Gemara answers: **Since she is excited** and hurried **for** intercourse with **her husband,**[N] **she does not insert** the examination cloth **into** her **recesses and folds.**

תְּנַן: הַמְשַׁמֶּשֶׁת בְּעֵדִים – הֲרֵי זוֹ כִּפְקִידָה, מַאי לָאו: חַד לִפְנֵי תַשְׁמִישׁ, וְחַד לְאַחַר תַּשְׁמִישׁ? לָא, אִידִי וְאִידִי – לְאַחַר תַּשְׁמִישׁ, וְאֶחָד לוֹ וְאֶחָד לָהּ. כִּדְתְנַן: דֶּרֶךְ בְּנוֹת יִשְׂרָאֵל מְשַׁמְּשׁוֹת בִּשְׁנֵי עֵדִים, אֶחָד לוֹ וְאֶחָד לָהּ.

The Gemara raises a difficulty: **We learned** in the mishna: And a woman **who engages in intercourse while** using **examination cloths,** the halakhic status of that act **is like that of an examination.** The mishna refers to examination cloths in the plural. **What, is it not** speaking of **one** cloth used **before intercourse and one** cloth used **after intercourse?** The Gemara answers: **No, this** cloth **and that** cloth are both used **after intercourse; and** the reason why the mishna uses the plural is that **one** cloth is **for his** use **and one** is **for her** use. **As we learned** in a mishna (14a): It is the **custom of Jewish women to engage in intercourse** with their husbands **with two examination cloths, one for his** use **and one for her** use.

הַאי מַאי? אִי אָמְרַתְּ בִּשְׁלָמָא חַד לִפְנֵי תַשְׁמִישׁ וְחַד לְאַחַר תַּשְׁמִישׁ – אִיצְטְרִיךְ, סָלְקָא דַעְתָּךְ אָמֵינָא: מִתּוֹךְ שֶׁמְּהוּמָה לְבֵיתָהּ – לָא בָּדְקָה שַׁפִּיר, קָא מַשְׁמַע לָן: הֲרֵי זוֹ כִּפְקִידָה. אֶלָּא אִי אָמְרַתְּ: אִידִי וְאִידִי לְאַחַר תַּשְׁמִישׁ – פְּשִׁיטָא!

The Gemara asks: **What is this? Granted, if you say** that the mishna is referring to **one** cloth used **before intercourse and one** used **after intercourse,** it **was necessary** for the mishna to mention both examinations, as it might **enter your mind to say** that **since she is excited** and hurried **for** intercourse with **her husband, she did not examine** herself **properly.** Therefore, the mishna **teaches us** that her examination with a cloth before intercourse **is** considered **as** a halakhically valid **examination. But if you say** that **this** cloth **and that** cloth are his and her cloths used **after intercourse,** isn't it **obvious** that they are treated as halakhic examinations? Why is this ruling necessary?

מַהוּ דְּתֵימָא: שֶׁמָּא תִּרְאֶה טִפַּת דָּם כְּחַרְדָּל, וּתְחַפֶּנָּה שִׁכְבַת זֶרַע – קָא מַשְׁמַע לָן.

The Gemara answers: The *halakha* that the examinations performed after intercourse count as valid examinations is necessary, **lest you say** that **perhaps** she might **see a drop of blood corresponding** to the size of **a mustard seed**[B] **and** a drop of **semen covered it.** In other words, it is possible that she discharged a tiny amount of menstrual blood that went undetected, as it was covered by a drop of semen. Therefore, the mishna **teaches us** that one does not need to be concerned for this possibility.

**HALAKHA**

**The examination cloth with which she examined herself before intercourse – עֵד שֶׁלִּפְנֵי תַשְׁמִישׁ:** A woman must examine herself with a cloth before and after intercourse. The examination following intercourse has the halakhic status of a regular examination. The examination prior to intercourse does not, as it is likely to be a substandard inspection performed in haste (Rambam *Sefer Tahara*, *Hilkhot Metamei Mishkav UMoshav* 3:4).

**LANGUAGE**

**Excited [*mehuma*] – מְהוּמָה:** The root of this word is *heh, mem, heh,* which means vocalizing a sound or making a noise. If there is a ruckus or if a person is performing an action in haste, there is often a resulting sound. Here the word is used to refer to an action that a person performs with haste spurred by passion or desire.

**BACKGROUND**

**Corresponding to the size of a mustard seed – כְּחַרְדָּל:** Edible mustard is derived from various plants, such as the white mustard plant, *Sinapis alba*, the black mustard plant, *Brassica nigra*, or some combination of them. These plants are members of the wild Brassicaceae family of plants. The black mustard plant is a very large strain that grows in Eretz Yisrael. Its height usually ranges between 0.5 and 2 m, although in some rare cases it can reach a height of 5 m. Mustard seeds are small, ranging between 1.5 and 2 mm in diameter, which is why they are chosen by the Gemara as a symbol of a minute entity.

Mustard flowers in a field

Black and white mustard seeds

**NOTES**

**Since she is excited and hurried for intercourse with her husband, etc. – מִתּוֹךְ שֶׁמְּהוּמָה לְבֵיתָהּ וכו׳:** Some authorities prove from here that the examination required before intercourse does not obligate the woman to insert the cloth into the recesses and folds of her vagina. They explain that the reason is that the requirement for this examination in the first place is a stringency enacted for the protection of ritually pure items, which, according to the Rambam, remained in force after the Temple period when standards of ritual purity were no longer practiced. Therefore what is required is not an inspection of recesses and folds, which was necessary when dealing with ritually pure items, but rather a general sweep of the vaginal area as far as the finger can reach (Ra'avad in *Ba'alei HaNefesh*; *Beit Yosef*; *Ḥavvot Da'at*).

וְאִיבָּעֵית אֵימָא: שְׁתֵּי בְדִיקוֹת אַצְרְכוּהָ רַבָּנַן, חַד – לִפְנֵי תַשְׁמִישׁ, וְחַד – לְאַחַר תַּשְׁמִישׁ, וְכִי קָתָנֵי ״הֲרֵי זוֹ כִּפְקִידָה״ – אַלְּאַחַר תַּשְׁמִישׁ. וְהָא ״הַמְשַׁמֶּשֶׁת״ קָתָנֵי! תְּנֵי: ״וּמְשַׁמֶּשֶׁת״.

**And if you wish, say** instead: The mishna is referring only to her examinations, but the reason the mishna mentions two examinations is not to give them the status of valid examinations, but to teach that they are both obligatory. As **the Sages required her** to perform **two examinations:**[H] **One before intercourse and one after intercourse. And when** the mishna **teaches:** The halakhic status of that act **is like that of an examination,** it is referring specifically **to** the examination performed **after intercourse.** The Gemara raises a difficulty: **But** the mishna **teaches:** A woman **who engages** in intercourse while using examination cloths. This formulation indicates that the examination is voluntary and is not mandated by the Sages. The Gemara explains that one should emend the text of the mishna so that it **teaches: And** a woman must **engage** in intercourse while using examination cloths.

״מְמַעֶטֶת עַל יַד מֵעֵת לְעֵת״. הָשְׁתָּא מֵעֵת לְעֵת מְמַעֶטֶת,

§ The mishna teaches: And with regard to a woman who engages in intercourse while using examination cloths, as the halakhic status of that act is like that of an examination, **it reduces** the time **from** a twenty-four-hour **period,** and reduces the time from examination to examination. The Gemara asks: **Now** that the mishna teaches that this examination **reduces** time **from** a twenty-four-hour **period,**

### HALAKHA

**The Sages required her to perform two examinations, etc.** – שְׁתֵּי בְדִיקוֹת אַצְרְכוּהָ רַבָּנַן וכו׳: According to some early authorities, a woman who has a fixed menstrual cycle should not perform self-examinations before or after intercourse. Not only is it not required, but she is advised not to examine herself, as this might cause her husband to become nervous that she may be menstruating and he may refrain from intercourse. The Rambam maintains that both the husband and wife should examine themselves after intercourse to determine if she discharged any menstrual blood during intercourse. The *halakha* follows the first opinion (*Roke'ah*; *Haggahot Maimoniyyot*).

In the case of a woman who does not have a fixed menstrual cycle, she and her husband are required to perform self-examinations before and after intercourse for the first three times that they engage in intercourse. If there is no blood found during those three sessions, she no longer requires any further examinations before or after intercourse. According to the Rambam and the Rosh, a woman with no fixed menstrual cycle always requires an examination before and after intercourse, and according to the Rambam the husband must examine himself after intercourse as well. Later authorities add that there is no need to perform an examination after each act of intercourse performed during the night; rather, one examination after everything is sufficient. The *Shakh* maintains that the examinations surrounding intercourse were instituted only to protect ritually pure items. Now that this is no longer relevant, there is no reason to perform those examinations. Moreover, even if a husband wants to impose a stringency upon himself to perform an examination, it may be done only after intercourse and not before (Rambam *Sefer Kedusha*, *Hilkhot Issurei Bia* 4:16; *Shulḥan Arukh*, *Yoreh De'a* 184:1 and 186:1–2 and in the comment of Rema).



מִפְּקִידָה לִפְקִידָה מִיבַּעְיָא!

is it **necessary** to teach that an examination reduces the time **from examination to examination,** which is less than twenty-four hours?

מַהוּ דְּתֵימָא: מֵעֵת לְעֵת – חָשׁוּ בָּהּ רַבָּנַן לִפְסֵידָא דְטָהֳרוֹת, אֲבָל מִפְּקִידָה לִפְקִידָה – לָא, קָא מַשְׁמַע לָן.

The Gemara answers: This ruling is necessary, **lest you say** that with regard to the significant passage of a twenty-four-hour **period** the **Sages are** concerned **for** the possible **loss of ritually pure items, but** with regard to the smaller period **from examination to examination,** the Sages are **not** concerned for the loss of pure items, and therefore the use of an examination cloth should not reduce the time of possible impurity between that and her next examination. Therefore, the mishna **teaches us** that it does reduce this time.

״כֵּיצַד דַּיָּהּ שְׁעָתָהּ״ וכו׳. לָמָּה לִי לְמִיתְנֵי ״הָיְתָה יוֹשֶׁבֶת בַּמִּטָּה, וַעֲסוּקָה בְטָהֳרוֹת״? לִיתְנֵי ״הָיְתָה עֲסוּקָה בְטָהֳרוֹת וּפֵרְשָׁה וְרָאֲתָה״!

§ The mishna teaches with regard to a woman who has a fixed menstrual cycle: **Her time is sufficient, how so?** If the woman was sitting in a bed and engaged in handling ritually pure items, and she left the bed and saw blood, she is impure and those items are pure. The Gemara asks: **Why do I** need the mishna **to teach:** If the woman **was sitting in a bed and engaged in** handling **pure items? Let** the mishna **teach** the same ruling without mentioning the bed: If she **was engaged in** handling **pure items and she left and saw** blood. The detail that she was sitting in a bed is apparently superfluous.

הָא קָא מַשְׁמַע לַן: טַעֲמָא – דְּדַיָּהּ שַׁעְתָּהּ, הָא מֵעֵת לְעֵת – מִטָּה נַמִּי מְטַמְּיָא. מְסַיַּיע לֵיהּ לִזְעֵירִי, דְּאָמַר זְעֵירִי: מֵעֵת לְעֵת שֶׁבְּנִדָּה – עוֹשָׂה מִשְׁכָּב וּמוֹשָׁב לְטַמֵּא אָדָם לְטַמֵּא בְּגָדִים.

The Gemara answers: **This** detail **teaches us** that the **reason** why the bed is not rendered impure is **that her time is sufficient** and there is no retroactive impurity. It can be inferred that in a case where she is impure retroactively for a twenty-four-hour **period, her bed is also rendered impure.** This **supports** the opinion **of Ze'eiri, as Ze'eiri said:** The level of impurity of the retroactive twenty-four-hour **period of a menstruating woman renders** impure **a bed**[H] upon which she lies **and a chair** upon which she sits,[N] **to** the extent that they **transmit impurity to a person** who comes in contact with them, **to** the extent that he **transmits impurity to the garments** he is wearing.

מִכְּדִי הַאי מִטָּה דָּבָר שֶׁאֵין בּוֹ דַּעַת לִישָּׁאֵל הוּא, וְכָל דָּבָר שֶׁאֵין בּוֹ דַּעַת לִישָּׁאֵל – סְפֵקוֹ טָהוֹר! תַּרְגְּמָהּ זְעֵירִי: כְּשֶׁחֲבֵרוֹתֶיהָ נוֹשְׂאוֹת אוֹתָהּ בְּמִטָּה, דְּהָוְיָא לֵיהּ יַד חֲבֵרוֹתֶיהָ.

This Gemara raises a difficulty: **Now, this bed** upon which she sat **is an entity that lacks consciousness** in order for it **to be asked,** and the principle with regard to **any entity that lacks consciousness** in order for it **to be asked** is that the item with **uncertain** status is deemed **pure.** The Gemara explains: **Ze'eiri interpreted** his ruling as applying specifically to a case **where her friends are carrying her in the bed, where** the bed **is** considered as the extended **hand of her friends.** In other words, it is part of an entity that has consciousness in order for it to be asked, and therefore the item with uncertain status is deemed impure.

וְהָשְׁתָּא דְּאָמַר רַבִּי יוֹחָנָן: סְפֵק טוּמְאָה הַבָּאָה בִּידֵי אָדָם – נִשְׁאָלִין עָלֶיהָ, אֲפִילּוּ בִּכְלִי מוּנָּח עַל גַּבֵּי קַרְקַע, כְּמִי שֶׁיֵּשׁ בּוֹ דַּעַת לִישָּׁאֵל – אַף עַל פִּי שֶׁאֵין חֲבֵרוֹתֶיהָ נוֹשְׂאוֹת אוֹתָהּ בְּמִטָּה.

The Gemara provides another answer: **And now that Rabbi Yoḥanan said:** In a case of **uncertain ritual impurity that comes** about **by the hand of a person,** i.e., through his involvement, the owner of the vessel must **consult** a Sage **about it,** i.e., it is considered an entity that has consciousness in order for it to be asked, as in such a case **even with regard to a vessel that is placed upon the ground,** which is certainly incapable of providing an answer if asked, its halakhic status is **like** that of **an item that has consciousness** in order for it **to be asked.** With this statement in mind, one can explain that according to Ze'eiri a menstruating woman transmits impurity to a bed **even though her friends are not carrying her in the bed.** Rather, as the bed's ritual impurity was caused by the hand of a person, it has the halakhic status of an item that has consciousness in order for it to be asked.

גּוּפָא, אָמַר רַבִּי יוֹחָנָן: סְפֵק טוּמְאָה הַבָּאָה בִּידֵי אָדָם – נִשְׁאָלִים עָלֶיהָ, אֲפִילּוּ בִּכְלִי הַמּוּנָּח עַל גַּבֵּי קַרְקַע – כְּמִי שֶׁיֵּשׁ בּוֹ דַּעַת לִישָּׁאֵל.

§ The Gemara discusses **the** matter of Rabbi Yoḥanan's statement **itself. Rabbi Yoḥanan says:** In a case of **uncertain ritual impurity** that **comes** about **by the hand of man,** its owner must **consult** a Sage **about it,** i.e., it is ritually impure, as in such a case **even with regard to a vessel that is placed upon the ground,** its halakhic status is **like** that of **an item that has consciousness** in order for it **to be asked.**

### HALAKHA

**The impurity of the retroactive period of a menstruating woman renders impure a bed, etc.** – מֵעֵת לְעֵת שֶׁבְּנִדָּה עוֹשָׂה מִשְׁכָּב וכו׳: Whether a woman assumes retroactive impurity status due to a menstrual flow or whether it was due to a blood stain, she renders a bed upon which she lay and a chair upon which she sat impure to the extent that they transmit impurity to a person who comes in contact with them, and he, in turn, transmits impurity to the garments he is wearing (Rambam *Sefer Tahara, Hilkhot Metamei Mishkav UMoshav* 3:8).

### NOTES

**Renders impure a bed upon which she lies and a chair upon which she sits, etc.** – עוֹשָׂה מִשְׁכָּב וּמוֹשָׁב וכו׳: Proof for this principle comes from the extraneous detail in the mishna that the menstruating woman was sitting in a bed. From this it is derived that she transmits impurity to the bed to the extent that it then transmits impurity to a person and he, in turn, transmits impurity to the garments that he is wearing. The mishna is written this way to include this principle, a principle unique to beds. Otherwise, the mishna could have simply depicted a case where ritual impurity was imparted to vessels through contact and not though lying in a bed (Ramban; *Yosef Da'at*; see *Tosafot*).

מֵיתִיבִי, הָיָה מִתְעַטֵּף בְּטַלִּיתוֹ וְטָהֳרוֹת וְטוּמְאוֹת בְּצִדּוֹ, וְטָהֳרוֹת וְטוּמְאוֹת לְמַעְלָה מֵרֹאשׁוֹ, סָפֵק נָגַע סָפֵק לֹא נָגַע – טָהוֹר. וְאִם אִי אֶפְשָׁר אֶלָּא אִם כֵּן נָגַע – טָמֵא.

The Gemara **raises an objection** from a *baraita* (*Tosefta*, *Teharot* 4:1): If a man who contracted ritual impurity **was wrapping** himself **in his cloak**[NH] **and** there were **pure** items **beside him; or** if he was pure and there were **impure** items **beside him** as he was wrapping his cloak; **or** if there were **pure** items and **impure** items **above his head** at the time and there is **uncertainty** whether he **touched** the impure items with his cloak and then touched the pure items with his cloak, and **uncertainty** whether it did **not touch** them, the *halakha* is that the pure items remain **pure. But if** it is **impossible** for him to have wrapped himself **unless** his cloak had **touched** the impure items in the process, then those previously pure items become **impure.**

רַבָּן שִׁמְעוֹן בֶּן גַּמְלִיאֵל אוֹמֵר: אוֹמְרִים לוֹ "שְׁנֵה", וְשׁוֹנֶה. אָמְרוּ לוֹ: אֵין שׁוֹנִים בְּטָהֳרוֹת,

The *baraita* continues: **Rabban Shimon ben Gamliel says** that **we say to him: Repeat** your action. **And he repeats** the action of wrapping himself with his cloak, and it can then be determined whether or not the cloak and the other items came in contact with each other. The Rabbis **said to him: We do** not rely on **repeated** actions **with regard to** the determination of ritually **pure** items. Since the second action may not exactly mimic the first, it cannot be relied upon to determine ritual purity status.

אַמַּאי? הָא סְפֵק טוּמְאָה הַבָּאָה בִּידֵי אָדָם הוּא!

The Gemara explains the objection: But according to the Rabbis, **why** is the *halakha* that the items in question remain pure? **Isn't** this a case of **uncertain ritual impurity that comes** about **by the hand of man,** which, according to Rabbi Yoḥanan, is considered as having consciousness in order for it to be asked? If so, these items should be ritually impure.

בַּר מִינֵּיהּ דְּהַהִיא, דְּתָנֵי רַב הוֹשַׁעְיָא: בִּרְשׁוּת הַיָּחִיד – סְפֵקוֹ טָמֵא, בִּרְשׁוּת הָרַבִּים – טָהוֹר.

The Gemara answers: **Except for that** one, i.e., do not raise a difficulty from that *baraita*, since it is referring to a specific case. **As Rav Hoshaya teaches** with regard to an item whose purity status is uncertain: When it is **in the private domain,** the item with **uncertain** status is deemed **impure;** when it is **in the public domain,** it is deemed **pure.** The *baraita* is referring to an item located in the public domain. Consequently, even if it is considered as having consciousness in order to be asked, nevertheless it is pure, as its uncertainty occurred in the public domain.

גּוּפָא, אָמַר זְעֵירִי: מֵעֵת לְעֵת שֶׁבְּנִדָּה – עוֹשָׂה מִשְׁכָּב וּמוֹשָׁב לְטַמֵּא אָדָם לְטַמֵּא בְּגָדִים.

§ The Gemara analyzes **the** matter of Ze'eiri's ruling **itself. Ze'eiri says:** The level of impurity assumed during the retroactive twenty-four-hour **period of a menstruating woman renders a bed** upon which she lies **and a chair** upon which she sits impure **to** the extent that they **transmit impurity to a person** who comes in contact with them **to** the extent that he **transmits impurity to the garments** he is wearing.

## NOTES

**A man who contracted ritual impurity was wrapping himself in his cloak, etc.** – **הָיָה מִתְעַטֵּף בְּטַלִּיתוֹ וכו׳**: The wording of the *Tosefta* is interpreted by the early commentaries as referring to three separate cases of uncertainty involving a man who was wrapping himself with his cloak: First, an impure cloak with pure items beside him; second, a pure cloak while there are impure items, such as carcasses of creeping animals, beside him; third, a pure cloak and pure and impure items above his head. In the first two cases the uncertainty is whether his cloak touched the other items. In the third case, the uncertainty is whether the cloak first touched the impure items and then touched the pure items, rendering them impure. The novelty of this third case is that it is not considered as a compound uncertainty, i.e., involving one uncertainty as to whether the cloak touched the impure items and another uncertainty as to whether it then touched the pure items. Rather, it is assumed that if it touched the impure items, it certainly touched the pure items as well (*Tosafot*).

## HALAKHA

**A man who contracted ritual impurity was wrapping himself in his cloak, etc.** – **הָיָה מִתְעַטֵּף בְּטַלִּיתוֹ וכו׳**: This is a case in which a person had ritually pure and impure items beside him when he wrapped himself in his cloak and there is doubt if he first touched the impure items with his cloak and then the pure items. If the case took place in the private domain, the pure items are deemed impure. This is due to the principle that when uncertain ritual impurity comes about by the hand of man, even an inanimate object is considered as if it has consciousness in order for it to be asked about its purity. It is therefore rendered impure, as is the ruling in all cases of uncertain impurity in a private domain. If the case took place in the public domain, the items remain ritually pure. If it is impossible for the person to enwrap himself in his cloak without having touched the pure items, they are rendered impure even in the public domain (Rambam *Sefer Tahara*, *Hilkhot She'ar Avot HaTumot* 16:6).

אִינִי, וְהָא כִּי אֲתָא אֲבִימִי מִבֵּי חוֹזָאֵי, אֲתָא וְאַיְיתֵי מַתְנִיתָא בִּידֵיהּ: מֵעֵת לְעֵת שֶׁבְּנִדָּה – מִשְׁכָּבָהּ וּמוֹשָׁבָהּ כְּמַגָּעָהּ. מַאי לָאו: מַה מַּגָּעָהּ לֹא מְטַמֵּא אָדָם – אַף מִשְׁכָּבָהּ לֹא מְטַמֵּא אָדָם!

The Gemara asks: **Is that so? But when Avimi**[LP] **came from Bei Ḥozai,**[B] **he came and brought** the following ***baraita*** **with him:** The level of impurity during the retroactive twenty-four-hour **period of a menstruating woman** renders **her bed** upon which she lies **and her chair** upon which she sits impure **like** the impurity level caused by **her touch.** The Gemara explains the difficulty: **What, is it not** correct to say that this means that **just as** an item rendered impure by **her touch** does **not render** another **person impure, so too, her bed** does **not render** another **person impure?**

אָמַר רָבָא: וְתִסְבְּרָא? קַל וָחוֹמֶר הוּא, וּמַה כְּלִי חֶרֶס הַמּוּקָּף צָמִיד פָּתִיל, הַנִּיצּוֹל בְּאוֹהֶל הַמֵּת – אֵינוֹ נִיצּוֹל בְּמֵעֵת לְעֵת שֶׁבְּנִדָּה. מִשְׁכָּבוֹת וּמוֹשָׁבוֹת, שֶׁאֵינָן נִיצּוֹלִין בְּאֹהֶל הַמֵּת – אֵינוֹ דִּין שֶׁאֵין נִיצּוֹלִין בְּמֵעֵת לְעֵת שֶׁבְּנִדָּה?

**Rava says: And** how can **you understand** it in that manner? There **is an** ***a fortiori*** inference here: **And if an earthenware vessel sealed** with **a tightly bound cover, which is spared** from impurity when it is **in a tent** that has **a corpse** in it,[H] is nevertheless **not spared** from impurity if the woman moved it **during** the twenty-four-hour **period** of retroactive impurity **of a menstruating woman** and is impure as though she moved it after she experienced bleeding; **so too,** with regard to **beds and chairs, which are not spared** from impurity **in a tent** that has **a corpse** in it, **is it not logical that they are** also **not spared** from impurity when used **during the** twenty-four-hour **period** of retroactive impurity **of a menstruating woman** and are impure as though she used them after she experienced bleeding?

וְהָא אֲבִימִי מִבֵּי חוֹזָאֵי מַתְנִיתָא קָאָמַר! אֵימָא: מִשְׁכָּבָהּ וּמוֹשָׁבָהּ

The Gemara asks: **But Avimi from Bei Ḥozai cited a** ***baraita*** that apparently does not accept Rava's *a fortiori* inference. The Gemara answers: One can **say** that the *baraita* does not mean that her bed and chair are rendered impure with the light level of impurity caused by her touch, but rather: **Her bed** upon which she lies **and her chair** upon which she sits

**LANGUAGE**

**Avimi – אֲבִימִי:** This name is shared by several Sages. It is a combined form of the words *avi imi*, my mother's father. It is meant to refer to the fact that he is named after his maternal grandfather.

**PERSONALITIES**

**Avimi – אֲבִימִי:** Some suggest that this is Avimi the son of Rabbi Abahu, a scholar of Eretz Yisrael during the fourth generation of *amora'im* there. He appears only occasionally in the Talmud, usually quoting early tannaitic sources. He was punctilious regarding the commandment of honoring his father and appears to have been a master of *aggada*.

Since Avimi is described as having business interactions in Bei Ḥozai, it appears that he was a wealthy merchant who brought back important traditions of Jewish law when he returned from his travels there.

**HALAKHA**

**Which is spared from impurity in a tent that has a corpse in it, etc. – הַנִּיצּוֹל בְּאוֹהֶל הַמֵּת וכו׳:** Even an earthenware vessel sealed with a tightly bound cover, which is spared from impurity when it is in a tent that has a corpse in it, is nevertheless rendered impure retroactively if it was moved by a woman who assumed impurity status retroactively from a newly discovered menstrual flow or even a blood stain (Rambam *Sefer Tahara*, *Hilkhot Metamei Mishkav UMoshav* 3:8).

**BACKGROUND**

**Bei Ḥozai – בֵּי חוֹזָאֵי:** This is the Aramaic name for the portion of the Persian kingdom near Shatt al Arab, the river formed by the confluence of the Euphrates and the Tigris. Bei Ḥozai is known today as Khuzestan, which is derived from the original name Ḥozai. This region was known for its agricultural development and fertile ground near reliable sources of water, and as a result many large Jewish communities took root there. The area was distant from the centers of Jewish life in Babylonia, however, due to the strong business relations between Bei Ḥozai and the other Jewish communities in Babylonia, there was constant contact between these places. Many Torah scholars traveled to Bei Ḥozai for business and returned home laden with Torah traditions, in addition to economic gains.

Location of Bei Ḥozai

Perek **I**
Daf **6** Amud **a**

כְּמַגַּע עַצְמָהּ, מַה מַּגַּע עַצְמָהּ – מְטַמֵּא אָדָם לְטַמֵּא בְּגָדִים, אַף מִשְׁכָּבָהּ וּמוֹשָׁבָהּ – מְטַמֵּא אָדָם לְטַמֵּא בְּגָדִים.

are **like** her **touch itself. Just as** her touch **transmits impurity to a person** who comes in contact with them **to** the extent that he **transmits impurity to the garments** he is wearing, **so too** her bed and her chair **transmit impurity to a person** who comes in contact with them **to** the extent that he **transmits impurity to the garments** he is wearing.

תַּנְיָא כְּוָותֵיהּ דְּרָבָא: הָרוֹאָה דָּם – מְטַמְּאָה מֵעֵת לְעֵת. וּמַה הִיא מְטַמְּאָה? מִשְׁכָּבוֹת וּמוֹשָׁבוֹת, אוֹכָלִין וּמַשְׁקִין, וּכְלִי חֶרֶס הַמּוּקָּף צָמִיד פָּתִיל, וְאֵינָהּ מְקוּלְקֶלֶת לְמִנְיָנָהּ, וְאֵינָהּ מְטַמְּאָה אֶת בּוֹעֲלָהּ לְמַפְרֵעַ. רַבִּי עֲקִיבָא אוֹמֵר: מְטַמָּא אֶת בּוֹעֲלָהּ. וְאֵינָהּ מוֹנָה אֶלָּא מִשָּׁעָה שֶׁרָאֲתָה.

§ It is taught in a *baraita* in accordance with the opinion of Rava: If a woman sees menstrual blood, it renders her impure retroactively for a twenty-four-hour period. And what does she render impure[H] during that period? Beds and chairs, food and drink, and an earthenware vessel sealed with a tightly bound cover [*tzamid patil*],[NL] if she moves it. But she does not disrupt her count of the periods of menstruation and *ziva*, i.e., she starts her cycle only from that day when she saw the blood, and she does not render impure retroactively a man who engaged in intercourse with her.[HN] Rabbi Akiva says: She does render impure a man who engaged in intercourse with her. And she counts her seven days of impurity only from the time that she saw her menstrual blood, not retroactively.

הָרוֹאָה כֶּתֶם מְטַמְּאָה לְמַפְרֵעַ, וּמַה הִיא מְטַמְּאָה? אוֹכָלִין וּמַשְׁקִין, מִשְׁכָּבוֹת וּמוֹשָׁבוֹת, וּכְלִי חֶרֶס הַמּוּקָּף צָמִיד פָּתִיל, וּמְקוּלְקֶלֶת לְמִנְיָנָהּ, וּמְטַמְּאָה אֶת בּוֹעֲלָהּ, וְאֵינָהּ מוֹנָה אֶלָּא מִשָּׁעָה שֶׁרָאֲתָה.

The *baraita* continues: With regard to a woman who sees a blood stain, it renders her impure retroactive to when the garment was last checked. And what does she render impure during that period?[H] Food and drink, beds and chairs, and an earthenware vessel sealed with a tightly bound cover, if she moves it. And it also disrupts her count[H] of eleven days during which emission of blood renders the woman a *zava*, as the time of the stain is unknown, and she renders ritually impure a man who engaged in intercourse with her.[H] And she counts her seven days of impurity only from the time that she saw her menstrual blood, not retroactively.

וְזֶה וְזֶה תּוֹלִין, לֹא אוֹכְלִין וְלֹא שׂוֹרְפִין.

The *baraita* further teaches: With regard to both this, one who sees menstrual blood, and that, one who sees a blood stain, if they had touched *teruma*, its status is suspended.[HN] It is not eaten, as impure *teruma* is prohibited in consumption, but it is not burned either, since it is prohibited to burn pure *teruma*.

וְרָבָא, אִי שְׁמִיעַ לֵיהּ מַתְנִיתָא – לֵימָא מַתְנִיתָא! וְאִי לָא שְׁמִיעַ לֵיהּ מַתְנִיתָא – קַל וָחוֹמֶר מְנָא לֵיהּ?

The Gemara raises a difficulty: And as for Rava, why is the *halakha* of an earthenware vessel more obvious to him than the *halakha* of a bed and a chair? If he had heard this *baraita*, which states the *halakha* of an earthenware vessel, then let him say that the *baraita* itself is proof for his opinion with regard to a bed and a chair as well, as the *baraita* states both *halakhot*. And if he had not heard this *baraita*, from where did he learn his *a fortiori* inference, which is based on the *halakha* that an earthenware vessel sealed with a tightly bound cover is not spared from impurity if a menstruating woman moved it during her twenty-four-hour period of retroactive impurity?

## HALAKHA

**If a woman sees menstrual blood…And what does she render impure, etc. – הָרוֹאָה דָּם...וּמַה הִיא מְטַמְּאָה וכו׳:** A woman who experiences a discharge of menstrual blood assumes impurity status retroactive to her most recent examination or twenty-four-hour period, which retroactively renders impure any bed that she sat on. That bed, in turn, transmits retroactive impurity to anyone who touched it to the extent that he then renders his garments impure. Her saliva and urine are also given the same level of retroactive impurity. She even renders impure an item inside an earthenware vessel sealed with a tightly bound cover (Rambam *Sefer Tahara, Hilkhot Metamei Mishkav UMoshav* 3:8).

**And she does not render impure retroactively a man who engaged in intercourse with her – וְאֵינָהּ מְטַמְּאָה אֶת בּוֹעֲלָהּ לְמַפְרֵעַ:** Although a woman who experiences a menstrual flow assumes impurity status retroactively, nevertheless one who engaged in intercourse with her does not have the more severe impurity status of one who engaged in intercourse with a menstruating woman. Rather he assumes the lighter impurity status of one touched by a menstruating woman (Rambam *Sefer Kedusha, Hilkhot Issurei Bia* 9:3).

**A woman who sees a blood stain…And what does she render impure – הָרוֹאָה כֶּתֶם...וּמַה הִיא מְטַמְּאָה וכו׳:** A woman who finds a blood stain on her body or clothing and therefore assumes impurity status retroactive to her most recent examination, renders impure any bed that she sat on. That bed, in turn, transmits retroactive impurity to anyone who touched it to the extent that he then renders his garments impure. Her saliva and urine are also given the same level of retroactive impurity. She even renders impure something inside an earthenware vessel sealed with a tightly bound cover (Rambam *Sefer Tahara, Hilkhot Metamei Mishkav UMoshav* 3:8).

**And it also disrupts her count – וּמְקוּלְקֶלֶת לְמִנְיָנָהּ:** A blood stain that causes a woman to assume impurity status retroactively also disrupts her count of the periods of menstruation and *ziva* (Rambam *Sefer Kedusha, Hilkhot Issurei Bia* 9:3).

**A woman who sees a blood stain…and she renders ritually impure a man who engaged in intercourse with her – הָרוֹאָה כֶּתֶם...וּמְטַמְּאָה אֶת בּוֹעֲלָהּ:** A woman who discovers a blood stain that causes her to assume impurity status retroactively does not retroactively render impure a man who engaged in intercourse with her (Rambam *Sefer Kedusha, Hilkhot Issurei Bia* 9:3).

**Both this and that, if they had touched *teruma* its status is suspended – וְזֶה וְזֶה תּוֹלִין:** Although a menstruating woman may assume impurity status retroactively for twenty-four hours or until her last self-examination, nevertheless since her impurity status is only out of doubt, if she had touched *teruma* or sacrificial foods during that retroactive period, they are held in suspension; they are neither eaten nor burned (Rambam *Sefer Kedusha, Hilkhot Issurei Bia* 9:3).

## LANGUAGE

**Tightly bound cover [*tzamid patil*] – צָמִיד פָּתִיל:** This expression is found in the Torah in the passage that deals with ritual impurity caused by a corpse, as it is written: "And every open vessel, which has no tightly bound cover upon it, is unclean" (Numbers 19:15). *Tzamid* refers to the cover that is connected [*tzamud*] to the vessel and *patil* refers to the seal that binds it.

## NOTES

**Sealed with a tightly bound cover – מוּקָּף צָמִיד פָּתִיל:** The Torah states that any person, vessel, or food under the same roof as a corpse becomes ritually impure. The Torah adds: "And every open vessel, which has no covering close-bound upon it, is impure" (Numbers 19:15). The Sages explain that the vessel referred to here is specifically an earthenware vessel, which does not contract ritual impurity when its exterior is exposed to impurity, but becomes impure only from its interior. Therefore, only such a vessel is spared from ritual impurity by being tightly sealed, whereas other vessels are rendered impure in any circumstance. The seal prevents the earthenware vessel and its contents from contracting impurity even if it is inserted within an impure earthenware vessel. But if the inner vessel contains an impure item, e.g., the carcass of a creeping animal, the outer vessel is rendered impure, as the seal prevents impurity from entering it, but it does not prevent it from spreading outward.

**And she does not render impure retroactively a man who engaged in intercourse with her – וְאֵינָהּ מְטַמְּאָה אֶת בּוֹעֲלָהּ לְמַפְרֵעַ:** Different explanations are given as why a menstruating woman does not transmit retroactive impurity to a man who engaged in intercourse with her. Some say that the Sages omitted this case when they instituted retroactive impurity, as it is an uncommon occurrence (*Tosefot HaRosh*). Others explain that they refrained from including a man who engaged in intercourse with her due to the concern that her husband might have misgivings when he engages in intercourse, for fear that he could later be rendered retroactively impure (*Tosafot* on 2a).

**Both this and that, if they had touched *teruma* its status is suspended – וְזֶה וְזֶה תּוֹלִין:** The reason why the purity status of the *teruma* is suspended and the *teruma* is not burned due to retroactive impurity is because the woman had a presumptive status of ritual purity at the time that she touched the *teruma* (*Tosafot* 2a).

לְעוֹלָם שְׁמִיעַ לֵיהּ מַתְנִיתָא, וְאִי מִמַּתְנִיתָא הֲוָה אָמֵינָא: אוֹ אָדָם אוֹ בְּגָדִים, אֲבָל אָדָם וּבְגָדִים – לָא, מִשּׁוּם הָכִי קָאָמַר קַל וָחוֹמֶר.

The Gemara answers: **Actually, he** did **hear** the ***baraita*. But if** his proof had been merely **from the *baraita*, I would say** that a different *halakha* applies to a bed and chair than to the earthenware vessels, as the *baraita* means that the bed and chair render impure **a person or garments** that they touch, **but** they do **not** render a **person** impure to the extent that he then transmits impurity to his **garments.** It is **due to that** reason that Rava **says** the ***a fortiori*** inference.

אָמַר רַב הוּנָא: מֵעֵת לְעֵת שֶׁבְּנִדָּה – לְקֹדֶשׁ, אֲבָל לֹא לִתְרוּמָה. אִי הָכִי, לִיתְנֵי גַּבֵּי מַעֲלוֹת! כִּי קָתָנֵי – הֵיכָא דְּאִית לֵיהּ דְּרָרָא דְּטוּמְאָה, אֲבָל הֵיכָא דְּלֵית לֵיהּ דְּרָרָא דְּטוּמְאָה – לָא קָתָנֵי.

§ **Rav Huna says:** The twenty-four-hour **period** of retroactive impurity **of a menstruating woman** applies only **to sacrificial** food **but not to *teruma*.** The Gemara asks: **If so, let** the mishna in *Ḥagiga* 20b **teach** this **among** the other higher **levels** of purity that apply to sacrificial foods but not to *teruma*. That mishna lists stringencies of ritual purity that are in effect with regard to sacrificial foods and not *teruma*. The Gemara answers: **When** that mishna **teaches** those higher levels of purity, it is referring only to types of impurity **that have a connection** [*derara*][L] **to impurity** as defined by Torah law.[N] **But** it **does not teach** a case **where there is no connection to impurity** as defined by Torah law, and the retroactive impurity of a menstruating woman is by rabbinic law.

מֵיתִיבִי: מַה הִיא מְטַמְּאָה – אוֹכָלִין וּמַשְׁקִין. מַאי לָאו: בֵּין דְּקֹדֶשׁ בֵּין דִּתְרוּמָה! לָא, דְּקֹדֶשׁ.

The Gemara **raises an objection** from the aforementioned *baraita* that deals with the retroactive impurity of a menstruating woman: What does **she render impure** during that period? **Food and drink.** The Gemara asks: **What, is it not** correct to say that this is referring **both to sacrificial** food **and to *teruma*? The** Gemara answers: **No,** it is referring only **to sacrificial** food, not to *teruma*.

תָּא שְׁמַע, רַבִּי יְהוּדָה אוֹמֵר: אַף בִּשְׁעַת עֲבָרָתָן מִלֶּאֱכוֹל בִּתְרוּמָה. וְהָוֵינַן בָּהּ: מַאי דַּהֲוָה הֲוָה!

The Gemara suggests: **Come** and **hear** a proof from a mishna (11a): With regard to women of priestly families who must examine themselves before partaking of *teruma*, **Rabbi Yehuda says: Even when they conclude partaking of *teruma*,** they still need to examine themselves. **And we discussed** this statement of Rabbi Yehuda and asked: Why do they need to examine themselves after they finish eating *teruma*? **What was, was;** i.e., if a woman was impure when she ate the *teruma*, what is achieved by an examination now?

אָמַר רַב חִסְדָּא: לֹא נִצְרְכָה אֶלָּא לְתַקֵּן שִׁירַיִם שֶׁבְּפָנֶיהָ!

And **Rav Ḥisda says** in explanation: **It was necessary only** in order **to amend the** situation of the **remaining** *teruma* that is left **before her,** i.e., to prevent it from being rendered ritually impure. In other words, if she later experiences a flow of menstrual blood, her retroactive impurity status will not render the remaining *teruma* impure. This ruling apparently contradicts the opinion of Rav Huna, who said that the retroactive impurity of a menstruating woman affects only sacrificial foods, not *teruma*.

רַב הוּנָא מַתְנֵי: לִישְׂרוֹף שִׁירַיִם שֶׁבְּיָדֶיהָ. שֶׁבָּדְקָה עַצְמָהּ כְּשִׁיעוּר וֶסֶת.

The Gemara answers: According to **Rav Huna,** Rabbi Yehuda **teaches** that since impure *teruma* must be burned, she must examine herself in order to determine whether it is correct **to burn** the **remaining** *teruma* that was **in her hands.** If she **examined herself** immediately after eating the *teruma*, in the **period of time** needed for the onset of **menstruation** (see 14b), and she found that she was impure, it is assumed as a certainty that she was impure when she ate the *teruma*. Consequently, the remaining *teruma* must be burned, in accordance with the *halakha* of *teruma* that was definitely rendered impure. But in fact, Rav Huna maintains that she does not render that remaining *teruma* impure retroactively, in a case where she did not examine herself.

## LANGUAGE

Connection [*derara*] – דְּרָרָא: Different explanations are given for this word. Some define it as referring to a connection or bond. Some say it means a loss or a lack. Others define it as referring to the root of something. Still others explain it as referring to a general topic or point of discussion.

## NOTES

**When it teaches those higher levels of purity that have a connection to impurity as defined by Torah law** – כִּי קָתָנֵי הֵיכָא דְּאִית לֵיהּ דְּרָרָא דְּטוּמְאָה: Rashi explains that the mishna lists only those cases that involve possible ritual impurity by Torah law. By contrast, impurities instituted by the Sages as mere stringencies, such as the retroactive impurity status of a menstruating woman who did not experience bleeding earlier, are not listed.

**LANGUAGE**

Worthy [*kedai*] – כְּדַי: The root of this word is *dai*, which means: Enough. *Kedai* in this context means it is enough, he is sufficient or worthy enough.

תָּא שְׁמַע, מַעֲשֶׂה וְעָשָׂה רַבִּי כְּרַבִּי אֱלִיעֶזֶר,

The Gemara further suggests: **Come** and **hear** another difficulty with regard to the opinion of Rav Huna from a *baraita*: There was **an incident** in which **Rabbi** Yehuda HaNasi **performed an action** by ruling that the *halakha* **is in accordance with** the opinion of **Rabbi Eliezer.** Rabbi Eliezer maintains that a woman who passed three expected menstrual cycles without experiencing bleeding is presumed not to be menstruating any longer, and therefore any menstrual blood that she emits later renders her ritually impure only from then onward, but not retroactively. By contrast, the Rabbis contend that this *halakha* applies only to an older woman, for whom it is natural to stop menstruating, but not to a young woman, even if three typical periods have passed without bleeding.

לְאַחַר שֶׁנִּזְכַּר אָמַר: כְּדַי הוּא רַבִּי אֱלִיעֶזֶר לִסְמוֹךְ עָלָיו

The *baraita* continues: **After** Rabbi Yehuda HaNasi **remembered** that Rabbi Eliezer's colleagues disagree with Rabbi Eliezer on this matter and that he had apparently ruled incorrectly, **he** nevertheless **said: Rabbi Eliezer is worthy** [***kedai***][L] **to rely upon**

Perek **I**
Daf **6** Amud **b**

**NOTES**

In exigent circumstances – בִּשְׁעַת הַדְּחָק: The early commentaries suggest different explanations of the exigent circumstances referred to here. Rashi explains that it was a time of famine and Rabbi Yehuda HaNasi did not want to issue a ruling that would cause the loss of sacrificial food or *teruma*.

*Tosafot* reject this explanation, as the Gemara on 9b states that the Rabbis concede to Rabbi Eliezer that one may be lenient in times of famine. Instead, they explain that the case involved a man who had touched a woman who later found a discharge of menstrual blood that rendered her impure retroactively. Since he had also handled some ritually pure items, he went to ask Rabbi Yehuda HaNasi about their status. Rabbi Yehuda HaNasi mistakenly decided leniently in accordance with Rabbi Eliezer, and it was only after the man went and handled many more ritually pure items that Rabbi Yehuda HaNasi realized his mistake. Nevertheless, he chose to remain with his initial ruling, due to the exigent circumstances of causing impurity to the large quantity of pure items. *Tosafot* similarly suggest that perhaps the questioner who had been given the mistaken ruling had already left the vicinity and it would take too much effort to track him down.

**LANGUAGE**

Exigent circumstances [*she'at hadeḥak*] – שְׁעַת הַדְּחָק: This expression refers to a time when various circumstances cause a pressing or distressful situation. Examples of this include famine, danger, and monetary loss.

בִּשְׁעַת הַדְּחָק. וְהָוֵינַן בָּהּ: מַאי ״לְאַחַר שֶׁנִּזְכַּר״? אִילֵימָא לְאַחַר שֶׁנִּזְכַּר דְּאֵין הֲלָכָה כְּרַבִּי אֱלִיעֶזֶר אֶלָּא כְּרַבָּנַן, בִּשְׁעַת הַדְּחָק הֵיכִי עָבֵיד כְּוָתֵיהּ?

**in exigent circumstances** [***bishe'at hadeḥak***].[NL] **And we discussed it** and asked: **What is** the meaning of: **After he remembered? If we say** that this means **after he remembered that the *halakha* is not in accordance with** the opinion of **Rabbi Eliezer but in accordance with** the opinion of **the Rabbis,** if so, **how could** Rabbi Yehuda HaNasi **act in accordance with** Rabbi Eliezer even **in exigent circumstances,** since the *halakha* has been decided against him?

אֶלָּא – (לָאו) דְּלָא אִיתְּמַר הִלְכְתָא לָא כְּמָר וְלָא כְּמָר, וְכֵיוָן שֶׁנִּזְכַּר – דְּלָאו יָחִיד פָּלֵיג עֲלֵיהּ אֶלָּא רַבִּים פְּלִיגִי עֲלֵיהּ, אָמַר ״כְּדַי הוּא רַבִּי אֱלִיעֶזֶר לִסְמוֹךְ עָלָיו בִּשְׁעַת הַדְּחָק״.

**Rather, is it not** correct that the ***halakha*** had **not been stated** on this matter, **neither in accordance with** the opinion of this **Sage,** Rabbi Eliezer, **nor in accordance with** the opinion of **that Sage,** i.e., the Rabbis. **And once** Rabbi Yehuda HaNasi **remembered that it was not a single** authority who **disagrees with** Rabbi Eliezer, **but** it was several Sages who **disagreed with him,** and there is a principle that the *halakha* follows the opinion of the many over that of an individual, **he** nevertheless **said: Rabbi Eliezer is worthy to rely upon in exigent circumstances.**

אִי אָמְרַתְּ בִּשְׁלָמָא לִתְרוּמָה – הַיְינוּ דַּהֲוַאי תְּרוּמָה בִּימֵי רַבִּי, אֶלָּא אִי אָמְרַתְּ לְקֹדֶשׁ – קֹדֶשׁ בִּימֵי רַבִּי מִי הֲוַאי?

The Gemara explains the proof from the *baraita*: **Granted, if you say** that it was a case **of** a menstruating woman who had touched ***teruma*** during the previous twenty-four hours, **this is** fine, **as *teruma*** still **existed in the days of Rabbi** Yehuda HaNasi. **But if** you say that it was a case **of** a woman who touched **sacrificial** food, **was there** still **sacrificial** food **in days of Rabbi** Yehuda HaNasi, after the destruction of the Temple? Clearly, the case involved *teruma*, and according to the Rabbis, whose opinion is accepted as *halakha*, this woman who had skipped three menstrual cycles nevertheless renders *teruma* impure retroactively. This ruling apparently contradicts the opinion of Rav Huna.

כִּדְעוּלָּא, דַּאֲמַר עוּלָּא: חַבְרַיָּא מַדְכָּן בְּגָלִילָא, הָכָא נַמִי בִּימֵי רַבִּי.

The Gemara answers: This can be answered **in accordance with** the testimony **of Ulla, as Ulla said: *Ḥaverim*[B] purify** their wine and oil **in the Galilee,**[N] i.e., they produce their wine and oil by the standards of purity used for sacrificial food, in the hope that the Temple will be rebuilt in their lifetime. **Here, too, in the days of Rabbi** Yehuda HaNasi there were those who kept the standards of purity observed for sacrificial food.

תָּא שְׁמַע: מַעֲשֶׂה בְּשִׁפְחָתוֹ שֶׁל רַבָּן גַּמְלִיאֵל שֶׁהָיְתָה אוֹפָה כִּכָּרוֹת שֶׁל תְּרוּמָה, וּבֵין כׇּל אַחַת וְאַחַת מְדִיחָה יָדָהּ בַּמַּיִם וּבוֹדֶקֶת. בָּאַחֲרוֹנָה בָּדְקָה וּמָצְאָה טְמֵאָה, וּבָאת וְשָׁאֲלָה אֶת רַבָּן גַּמְלִיאֵל, וְאָמַר לָהּ: כּוּלָּן טְמֵאוֹת. אָמְרָה לוֹ: רַבִּי, וַהֲלֹא בְּדִיקָה הָיְתָה לִי בֵּין כׇּל אַחַת וְאַחַת? אָמַר לָהּ: אִם כֵּן, הִיא טְמֵאָה וְכוּלָּן טְהוֹרוֹת.

The Gemara suggests: **Come and hear** a *baraita*: There was **an incident involving the maidservant of Rabban Gamliel, who was baking loaves of *teruma*** bread. **And in between each and every one she** would **wash her hand in water and examine** herself. **After** the **last** one she **examined** herself **and found** that she was **impure** due to menstrual blood, **and she came and asked Rabban Gamliel** about the status of the loaves. **And he said to her: They are all impure,** due to her retroactive impurity for the previous twenty-four hours. **She said to him: My teacher, didn't I perform an examination in between each and every one?** Rabban Gamliel **said to her: If so,** then **this** last one is **impure and** the rest are **all pure,** as your retroactive impurity is reduced until the time of the most recent examination.

קָתָנֵי מִיהַת ״כִּכָּרוֹת שֶׁל תְּרוּמָה״! מַאי ״תְּרוּמָה״? תְּרוּמַת לַחְמֵי תוֹדָה. תְּרוּמַת לַחְמֵי תוֹדָה בַּאֲפִיָּה מַאי בָּעְיָא?

The Gemara explains the difficulty: **In any event,** the *baraita* **teaches** that the case involved **loaves of *teruma*** bread. This apparently contradicts the opinion of Rav Huna, as Rabban Gamliel applied retroactive impurity in a case of *teruma*. The Gemara answers: What is meant by: *Teruma*? It means ***teruma* of the loaves of the thanks offering,** i.e., the four loaves of the thanks offering that were separated from the total of forty and eaten by the priests. These are sacrificial foods, not *teruma*. The Gemara raises a difficulty with regard to this interpretation: **What** was she **doing baking the *teruma* of the loaves of the thanks offering** alone? All forty loaves of the thanks offering are baked together, and only afterward are four set aside as *teruma* to be eaten by priests.

דְּאַפְרְשִׁינְהוּ בְּלִישַׁיְיהוּ. וְכִי הָא דַּאֲמַר רַב טוֹבִי בַּר רַב קְטִינָא: לַחְמֵי תוֹדָה שֶׁאֲפָאָן אַרְבַּע חַלּוֹת – יָצָא. וְהָוֵינַן בָּהּ: וְהָא בָּעֵינַן אַרְבָּעִים? לְמִצְוָה.

The Gemara answers: This is referring to a case **where** dough for the *teruma* loaves **was separated** and designated for the priests **during its kneading. And** this *halakha* is **in accordance with that which Rav Tovi bar Rav Ketina said: If one baked the loaves of the thanks offering as four loaves,**[H] rather than the requisite forty loaves, **he has fulfilled** his obligation. **And we discussed it** and asked: **Isn't one required** to bring **forty** loaves with the thanks offering, ten loaves of each of the four different types? The Gemara answers: One must bake forty loaves in order **to fulfill** the **mitzva** in the optimal fashion, but he has nevertheless fulfilled his obligation with four loaves, one of each type.

וְהָא בָּעֵינַן אַפְרוּשֵׁי תְּרוּמָה מִינַּיְיהוּ? וְכִי תֵּימָא דְּמַפְרִישׁ פְּרוּסָה מִכׇּל חַד וְחַד – ״אֶחָד״ אָמַר רַחֲמָנָא – שֶׁלֹּא יִטּוֹל פְּרוּסָה! וְאָמְרִינַן: דְּאַפְרְשִׁינְהוּ בְּלִישַׁיְיהוּ, הָכָא נַמִי – דְּאַפְרְשִׁינְהוּ בְּלִישַׁיְיהוּ.

The Gemara continues its answer by further elucidating the statement of Rav Tovi bar Rav Ketina. And we asked with regard to this opinion: **But he is required to separate *teruma* from it,** i.e., to designate one loaf from each type that is given to the priests. **And if you would say that he separates a slice from each one** of the four loaves and gives them to the priest, this cannot be the case, as **the Merciful One states** in the Torah: "And of it he shall present **one** out of each offering for a gift to the Lord; it shall be the priest's" (Leviticus 7:14). The word "one" indicates **that he may not take a slice,** but rather he takes a complete loaf. The Gemara answers: Rather, **we** must **say** that he **separated** dough for the *teruma* loaves **during its kneading. Here too, in** the incident involving Rabban Gamliel's maidservant, she **separated** the dough **during its kneading.**

**HALAKHA**

**If one baked the loaves of the thanks offering as four loaves, etc.** – לַחְמֵי תוֹדָה שֶׁאֲפָאָן אַרְבַּע חַלּוֹת וכו׳: If one baked four loaves rather than the forty loaves that should ideally be baked, he has fulfilled his obligation, because forty loaves are required only for the optimal performance of the mitzva. In this case one has to be sure that during the kneading process he separated dough for the *teruma* loaves given to the priests because after they are baked this is no longer possible, as one is required to give a complete loaf as *teruma* and not a slice of a baked loaf (Rambam *Sefer Avoda*, *Hilkhot Ma'aseh HaKorbanot* 9:22).

**BACKGROUND**

*Ḥaverim* – חַבְרַיָּא: Although this group lived many years after the destruction of the Temple, and in the Galilee, far from Jerusalem where the Temple was situated, they nevertheless scrupulously produced their wine and oil by the standards of ritual purity used for sacrificial food. They did so even though there was no way to transport these items to Jerusalem and keep them free from ritual impurity because they believed that when Elijah the prophet comes to herald the coming of the Messiah, he will also reveal a ritually secure method of transportation.

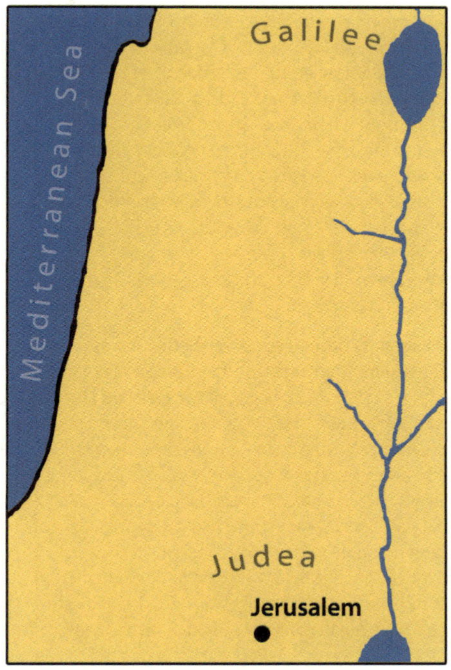


Location of the Galilee in relation to Jerusalem

**NOTES**

*Ḥaverim* purify their wine and oil in the Galilee – חַבְרַיָּא מַדְכָּן בְּגָלִילָא: Some suggest that these *ḥaverim* had the ashes of the red heifer, which they used for purifying themselves of ritual impurity (*Mishne LaMelekh*). Rabbeinu Ḥananel explains that the reason they would purify their food was because many Galileans would eat non-sacred food while following the *halakhot* of ritual purity for sacrificial food.

תָּא שְׁמַע: שׁוּב מַעֲשֶׂה בְּשִׁפְחָה שֶׁל רַבָּן גַּמְלִיאֵל שֶׁהָיְתָה גָּפָה חָבִיּוֹת שֶׁל יַיִן, וּבֵין כָּל אַחַת וְאַחַת מְדִיחָה יָדֶיהָ בַּמַּיִם וּבוֹדֶקֶת. וּבָאַחֲרוֹנָה בָּדְקָה וּמָצְאָה טְמֵאָה, וּבָאת וְשָׁאֲלָה לְרַבָּן גַּמְלִיאֵל, וְאָמַר לָהּ: כּוּלָּן טְמֵאוֹת. אָמְרָה לוֹ: וַהֲלֹא בְּדִיקָה הָיְתָה לִי בֵּין כָּל אַחַת וְאַחַת? אָמַר לָהּ: אִם כֵּן, הִיא טְמֵאָה וְכוּלָּן טְהוֹרוֹת.

The Gemara suggests: **Come** and **hear** a proof from a *baraita*: There was **another incident involving the maidservant of Rabban Gamliel who was sealing barrels**[B] **of wine. And in between each and every one** she would **wash her hands in water and examine** herself. **And after the last** one **she examined** herself **and found** that she was ritually **impure, and she came and asked Rabban Gamliel** about the wine. **And he said to her: They are all impure. She said to him:** My teacher, **didn't I perform an examination in between each and every one?** Rabban Gamliel **said to her: If so, this** last one is **impure and** the rest are **all pure.**

אִי אָמְרַתְּ בִּשְׁלָמָא חֲדָא דְּקֹדֶשׁ וַחֲדָא דִּתְרוּמָה הִיא, הַיְינוּ דַּהֲדָרָה וְשַׁיְּילָה, אֶלָּא אִי אָמְרַתְּ אִידִי וְאִידִי דְּקֹדֶשׁ, לָמָּה לָהּ לְמֶהְדַּר וְלְשַׁיְּילֵיהּ? מַעֲשֶׂה שֶׁהָיָה – בִּשְׁתֵּי שְׁפָחוֹת הָיָה.

The Gemara clarifies the difficulty with regard to Rav Huna's opinion: **Granted, if you say** that **one** incident involved a case **of sacrificial** food **and one** incident involved a case **of** ***teruma*****, this is** the reason **that she returned and** again **asked** Rabban Gamliel what to do. **But if you say** that both **this** incident **and that** incident **involved sacrificial** food, **why** did **she** need **to return and ask him** the same question a second time? The Gemara answers: Each **incident that occurred was** with sacrificial food and they happened **with two** different **maidservants.**

לִישָּׁנָא אַחֲרִינָא אָמְרִי לָהּ: אָמַר רַב הוּנָא מֵעֵת לְעֵת שֶׁבְּנִדָּה – מְטַמְּאָה בֵּין לְקֹדֶשׁ וּבֵין לִתְרוּמָה, מִמַּאי? מִדְּלָא קָתָנֵי לָהּ גַּבֵּי מַעֲלוֹת. אֲמַר לֵיהּ רַב נַחְמָן: וְהָא תָּנֵי תַּנָּא "לְקֹדֶשׁ אֲבָל לֹא לִתְרוּמָה"!

**Some say another version** of Rav Huna's statement. **Rav Huna says:** During the twenty-four-hour **period of** retroactive impurity of **a menstruating woman,** she **renders impure** both **sacrificial** food and ***teruma*****.** The Gemara asks: **From where** is this derived? The Gemara answers: It can be inferred **from** the fact **that** the mishna in *Ḥagiga* (20b) **does not teach** this matter **among** the other matters where higher **levels** of purity are required only for sacrificial foods but not for *teruma*. **Rav Naḥman said to** Rav Huna: **But doesn't** the ***tanna*** explicitly **teach** in a *baraita*: The retroactive impurity of a menstruating woman applies only **with regard to sacrificial** food but **not with regard to** ***teruma*****?**

קִבְּלָהּ מִינֵּיהּ רַב שְׁמוּאֵל בַּר רַב יִצְחָק: בְּחוּלִּין שֶׁנַּעֲשׂוּ עַל טׇהֳרַת קֹדֶשׁ, וְלֹא בְּחוּלִּין שֶׁנַּעֲשׂוּ עַל טׇהֳרַת תְּרוּמָה.

The Gemara answers: **Rav Shmuel bar Rav Yitzḥak**[P] **received** the following explanation **from** Rav Naḥman: The *baraita* means that this retroactive impurity applies **to non-sacred** food **that was prepared according to** the standards of **purity of sacrificial** food,[H] **but not to non-sacred** food **that was prepared** according to the standards of **purity of** ***teruma*****.** It does apply to *teruma* itself.

תְּנַן הָתָם: נוֹלַד לָהּ סְפֵק טוּמְאָה, עַד שֶׁלֹּא גִּלְגְּלָה – תֵּעָשֶׂה בְּטוּמְאָה, מִשֶּׁגִּלְגְּלָה – תֵּעָשֶׂה בְּטׇהֳרָה.

§ With regard to a non-sacred food prepared according to the standards of purity of *teruma*, **we learned** in a mishna **elsewhere** (*Ḥalla* 3:2): In a case of dough where **uncertainty developed** as to whether it was **ritually impure,**[H] if the uncertainty developed **before it was kneaded, it may be prepared** even **in** definite **impurity,** i.e., with impure vessels. If it developed **after it was kneaded, it** must **be prepared in purity.**

עַד שֶׁלֹּא גִּלְגְּלָה – תֵּעָשֶׂה בְּטוּמְאָה, חוּלִּין נִינְהוּ, וּמוּתָּר לִגְרוֹם טוּמְאָה לְחוּלִּין שֶׁבְּאֶרֶץ יִשְׂרָאֵל. מִשֶּׁגִּלְגְּלָה – תֵּעָשֶׂה בְּטׇהֳרָה, חוּלִּין הַטְּבוּלִין לְחַלָּה – כְּחַלָּה דָּמוּ, וְאָסוּר לִגְרוֹם טוּמְאָה לְחַלָּה.

The *baraita* elaborates: **Before it was kneaded it may be prepared** even **in** definite **impurity** because **it is non-sacred** food, **and the** *halakha* is that it is **permitted to cause impurity to non-sacred food in Eretz Yisrael.**[H] **After it was kneaded it** must **be prepared in purity,** since **non-sacred** food **that is untithed with regard to** the obligation to separate ***ḥalla*****,** i.e., its *ḥalla* has not yet been separated, **is considered like** ***ḥalla*****, and** it **is prohibited to cause impurity to** ***ḥalla*****.**

תָּנָא,

It is **taught** in a *baraita*:

**BACKGROUND**

**Sealing barrels – גָּפָה חָבִיּוֹת:** Barrels of wine were sealed with a seal made of soft clay. Gasses often formed in the barrel after it was closed, and therefore a small hole was left in the seal to allow them to escape.

**HALAKHA**

**Non-sacred food that was prepared according to the standards of purity of sacrificial food, etc. – חוּלִּין שֶׁנַּעֲשׂוּ עַל טׇהֳרַת קֹדֶשׁ וכו׳:** If, during the twenty-four-hour period of retroactive impurity of a menstruating woman, she touched non-sacred food that was prepared according to the standards of purity of sacrificial food, the food's ritual purity status is left uncertain. It is held in a suspended state; it is neither burned nor eaten. This is not the *halakha* with regard to non-sacred food that was prepared according to the standards of purity of *teruma*, where the food remains pure. This is in accordance with the statement of Rav Shmuel bar Rav Yitzḥak that he received from Rav Naḥman (Rambam *Sefer Tahara, Hilkhot Metamei Mishkav UMoshav* 3:9).

**Uncertainty developed as to whether it was ritually impure – נוֹלַד לָהּ סְפֵק טוּמְאָה:** In a case of dough with regard to which uncertainty developed as to whether it was ritually impure, if the uncertainty occurred before the dough was kneaded, the dough may be prepared in conditions of definite impurity, and its *ḥalla* should be burned. This is because it has the status of non-sacred food and it is permitted to cause impurity to non-sacred food in Eretz Yisrael. But if the uncertainty with regard to ritual impurity occurred after it had already been kneaded, it must be completed in conditions of purity, as the Sages issued a decree prohibiting rendering dough from which one is obligated to separate *ḥalla* ritually impure. This decree applies to any possible ritual impurity that would render non-sacred food impure. The *ḥalla* separated from this dough is then held in a suspended state; it is neither burned nor eaten by priests (Rambam *Sefer Zera'im, Hilkhot Bikkurim* 8:10).

**It is permitted to cause impurity to non-sacred food in Eretz Yisrael – מוּתָּר לִגְרוֹם טוּמְאָה לְחוּלִּין שֶׁבְּאֶרֶץ יִשְׂרָאֵל:** Just as it is permitted to eat and drink ritually impure non-sacred foods, so too it is permitted to cause impurity to non-sacred food in Eretz Yisrael (Rambam *Sefer Tahara, Hilkhot Tumat Okhalin* 16:9).

**PERSONALITIES**

**Rav Shmuel bar Rav Yitzḥak – רַב שְׁמוּאֵל בַּר רַב יִצְחָק:** Rav Shmuel bar Rav Yitzḥak was a second-generation *amora* who lived in Babylonia. His father, Rav Yitzḥak was a great Torah scholar, in addition to being a man of great piety. Rav Shmuel, too, was known for his righteousness. It is told that he fulfilled the mitzva of giving joy to a bride and groom with particular zest. He was a disciple of Rav and he transmitted many of his statements. He was a student in the Sura yeshiva under the leadership of Rav Huna, and he engaged in Torah discussions with Rav Naḥman. Despite being a noted scholar in Babylonia, toward the end of his life he emigrated to Eretz Yisrael where he joined the elite group of Rabbi Yoḥanan's disciples. It is told that upon his passing, God showed His respect in a spectacular manner, by causing a great pillar of fire to separate his body from the crowd of mourners.

וְחַלָּתָהּ תְּלוּיָה, לֹא אוֹכְלִין וְלֹא שׂוֹרְפִין. בְּאֵיזֶה סָפֵק אָמְרוּ? בִּסְפֵק חַלָּה. מַאי ״סְפֵק חַלָּה״?

**And as the *ḥalla* of** this kneaded, untithed dough is in a state of uncertain purity, its status is **suspended: It is neither eaten** like ritually pure *ḥalla*, **nor is it burned** like impure *ḥalla*. **With regard to which** uncertainty did **they state** this *halakha*? **With regard to *ḥalla*** of **uncertain** status. The Gemara asks: **What** is the meaning of the concept of ***ḥalla* of uncertain** status? This apparently indicates a scenario of possible ritual impurity that applies specifically to *ḥalla*, not to non-sacred food.

אַבַּיֵּי וְרָבָא דְּאָמְרִי תַּרְוַיְיהוּ: שֶׁלֹּא תֹּאמַר בְּהוֹכָחוֹת שָׁנִינוּ כְּמוֹ שְׁנֵי שְׁבִילִין, דְּהָתָם – חוּלִּין גְּרֵידָא נָמֵי מְטַמּוּ,

**Abaye and Rava both say: One should not say** that **we learned** this case of *ḥalla* of uncertain status among the cases of equal **proofs,** i.e., an unresolvable uncertainty, **such as** the case of **two paths,** where someone walked down one of two paths, one of which was ritually impure and the other ritually pure, and he does not remember which one he walked down. **As there,** even **regular non-sacred** food is **also rendered** ritually **impure** due to uncertainty.

אֶלָּא בְּנִשְׁעָן. דִּתְנַן: זָב וְטָהוֹר שֶׁהָיוּ פּוֹרְקִין מִן הַחֲמוֹר, אוֹ טוֹעֲנִין. בִּזְמַן שֶׁמַּשָּׂאָן כָּבֵד – טָמֵא, מַשָּׂאָן קַל – טָהוֹר, וְכוּלָּן טְהוֹרִין לִבְנֵי הַכְּנֶסֶת, וּטְמֵאִין לִתְרוּמָה.

**Rather,** the uncertainty referred to here is similar to the less likely case **of leaning, as we learned** in a mishna (*Zavim* 3:2): In a case of **a *zav* and a ritually pure** person **who were unloading** a package **from a donkey**[H] **or** who were **loading** a package onto a donkey, **when their package is heavy** the pure person is rendered **impure,** as perhaps the *zav* leaned on him while they handled the package together. If **their package is light,** he remains **pure. And** in **all those** cases,[N] he remains ritually **pure**[N] even if he is one of the **members of a synagogue** whose congregants handle non-sacred food according to the standards of sacrificial food, as this is not a true case of a *zav* moving a pure person. **But** he is **impure with regard to** matters involving ***teruma***, by rabbinic law.

וְחוּלִּין הַטְּבוּלִין לְחַלָּה כְּחַלָּה דָּמוּ? וְהָתַנְיָא: אִשָּׁה שֶׁהִיא טְבוּלַת יוֹם – לָשָׁה אֶת הָעִיסָּה, וְקוֹצָה הֵימֶנָּה חַלָּתָהּ, וּמַנִּיחַתָּהּ בִּכְפִישָׁה אוֹ בְּאַנְחוּתָא, וּמַקֶּפֶת וְקוֹרָא לָהּ שֵׁם,

The Gemara asks: **And is non-sacred** food **that is untithed with regard to** the obligation to separate ***ḥalla*** really **considered like *ḥalla*** to the extent that it is rendered impure even in a case of leaning? **But isn't it taught** in a *baraita*: With regard to **a woman who immersed that day** and is waiting for nightfall for the purification process to be completed, she may separate *ḥalla*: **She may knead the dough,**[H] **and separate its *ḥalla* from it, and place** the separated dough **into a wicker basket**[B] **or a wooden board** [***be'anḥuta***],[NL] **and** subsequently she may **bring** it **near** the rest of the dough,[N] **and** she may then **designate it** *ḥalla* **by name.**

מִפְּנֵי שֶׁהוּא שְׁלִישִׁי, וּשְׁלִישִׁי טָהוֹר בְּחוּלִּין. וְאִי אָמְרַתְּ חוּלִּין הַטְּבוּלִין לְחַלָּה כְּחַלָּה דָּמוּ – הָא טַמֵּיתִנְהוּ!

The *baraita* continues: The reason that this is allowed, despite her impurity, is **because** the dough **is** impure by **third**-degree ritual impurity, **and** an item that has **third**-degree impurity is considered **pure with regard to non-sacred** food.[H] The Gemara concludes its question: **And if you say** that **non-sacred** food **that is untithed with regard to** the obligation to separate ***ḥalla*** **is considered like *ḥalla***, then she should **render it impure** with her touch, just as she would render actual *ḥalla* impure.

**NOTES**

**And in all those cases** – **וְכוּלָּן**: It is not entirely clear what exactly is included by this phrase in the *baraita*. The early commentaries disagree here. Some say that it is referring to both types of packages mentioned earlier, the heavy and the light package. Others maintain that it is referring to those individuals listed earlier in that mishna (*Zavim* 3:2) who do not contract ritual impurity when moved by a *zav*.

**And in all those cases he remains ritually pure** – **וְכוּלָּן טְהוֹרִין**: A *zav* renders items impure by moving them. Since in this case, even if the ritually pure person was leaned on by the *zav*, he was not fully lifted or displaced by him, he remains ritually pure with regard to the stringency of handling non-sacred food according to the standards used for sacrificial foods (*Mishneh Aḥarona*).

**Into a wicker basket or a wooden board** – **בִּכְפִישָׁה אוֹ בְּאַנְחוּתָא**: These items are not susceptible to ritual impurity. The commentaries note that there is really no need for this added stringency, since even a regular receptacle does not contract third-degree ritual impurity and therefore it would not render the dough impure. The reason for this added step is simply to serve as a reminder (Rashi) that she is not entirely ritually pure and therefore she should take care not to touch the separated *ḥalla* after she officially designates it *ḥalla* by name (*Tosefot Ḥakhmei Angliyya*).

**And subsequently she may bring it near the rest of the dough** – **וּמַקֶּפֶת**: She draws the receptacle containing the separated dough near to the larger batch of dough because when one separates *teruma* and *ḥalla* from produce or dough, there is a *halakha* to bring the separated part near to the produce or dough that it comes to exempt, *ab initio* (Rashi).

**BACKGROUND**

**Wicker basket [*kefisha*]** – **כְּפִישָׁה**: A *kefisha* is a wicker basket. Some explain that it is a flask made from leather. It was used as a receptacle in the vineyard during the grape harvest, or inside the house for holding dough during kneading.

**LANGUAGE**

**Wooden board [*anḥuta*]** – **אַנְחוּתָא**: This Aramaic word developed from the Hebrew term *naḥat*, denoting an item on which things are placed. It is a simple receptacle that was made from wood according to some, and from hide according to others.

**HALAKHA**

**A *zav* and a ritually pure person who were unloading a package from a donkey** – **זָב וְטָהוֹר שֶׁהָיוּ פּוֹרְקִין מִן הַחֲמוֹר**: In the case of a *zav* and a pure person who were unloading a package from a donkey, or were loading a package onto a donkey, the following applies: If their package is a heavy one, the pure person is rendered ritually impure; if their package is light, he remains ritually pure (Rambam *Sefer Tahara, Hilkhot Metamei Mishkav UMoshav* 8:9).

**A woman who immersed that day, she may knead the dough, etc.** – **אִשָּׁה שֶׁהִיא טְבוּלַת יוֹם לָשָׁה אֶת הָעִיסָּה וכו׳**: A woman who immersed that day due to a type of ritual impurity from which she will become fully ritually pure upon nightfall, may separate *ḥalla*. She may knead the dough and separate a portion to be designated as *ḥalla*; she may place it into a receptacle and bring it near the rest of the dough, and then she may then designate it *ḥalla* by name. After she has designated it as *ḥalla* she may no longer touch it, lest it become disqualified by contracting ritual impurity (Rambam *Sefer Tahara, Hilkhot Tumat Okhalin* 8:17).

**Third-degree impurity is considered pure with regard to non-sacred food** – **וּשְׁלִישִׁי טָהוֹר בְּחוּלִּין**: Something that has second-degree impurity does not render non-sacred items impure with third-degree impurity (Rambam *Sefer Tahara, Hilkhot She'ar Avot HaTumot* 11:2).

אָמַר אַבָּיֵי: כָּל שֶׁוַּדַּאי מְטַמֵּא חוּלִּין – גָּזְרוּ עַל סְפֵקוֹ מִשּׁוּם חוּלִּין הַטְּבוּלִין לְחַלָּה. וְהַאי טְבוּל יוֹם, כֵּיוָן דְּלָא מְטַמֵּא וַדַּאי חוּלִּין – לֹא גָּזְרוּ עָלָיו מִשּׁוּם חוּלִּין הַטְּבוּלִין לְחַלָּה.

**Abaye says:** With regard to **any** item **that** when it is **definitely** impure **renders non-sacred** food **impure,** as in the case of the *zav*, the Sages **issued a decree**[H] that **its uncertain** impurity should also render non-sacred food items impure, **due to** its status as **non-sacred** food **that is untithed with regard to *ḥalla*. But** with regard to **this** case of **one who immersed that day, since** even when she is **definitely** impure she **does not render non-sacred food impure, they did not issue a decree** that she should render that dough impure **due to** its status as **non-sacred** food **that is untithed with regard to *ḥalla*.**

וְהָא מֵעֵת לְעֵת שֶׁבְּנִדָּה, דְּוַדַּאי מְטַמֵּא חוּלִּין – וְלֹא גָּזְרוּ עַל סְפֵקָהּ מִשּׁוּם חוּלִּין הַטְּבוּלִין לְחַלָּה!

The Gemara asks: **But** what about the twenty-four-hour **period** of retroactive impurity **of a menstruating woman? As a definitely** impure menstruating woman **renders non-sacred** food **impure and** nevertheless with regard to untithed dough the Sages **did not issue a decree** to treat **her uncertain** impurity as definite impurity **due to** the dough's status as **non-sacred** food **that is untithed with regard to *ḥalla*.**

דְּאָמַר מָר: קִבְּלָהּ מִינֵּיהּ רַב שְׁמוּאֵל בַּר רַב יִצְחָק בְּחוּלִּין שֶׁנַּעֲשׂוּ עַל טׇהֳרַת קֹדֶשׁ, וְלֹא בְּחוּלִּין שֶׁנַּעֲשׂוּ עַל טׇהֳרַת תְּרוּמָה!

The Gemara cites its source for this claim: **As the Master said: Rav Shmuel bar Rav Yitzḥak received** from Rav Naḥman: The retroactive impurity of a menstruating woman transmits impurity **to non-sacred** food items **that were prepared according to** the standards of **purity of sacrificial** food, **but not to non-sacred** food items **that were prepared** according to the standards of **purity of *teruma*.**[N] It is assumed that the level of purity required for non-sacred food items prepared according to the standards required of *teruma* is the same as that of dough from which *ḥalla* has not been separated, i.e., it is not treated as real *ḥalla*, which is rendered impure by her retroactive twenty-four-hour period of impurity.

הָתָם – לָא פְּתִיכָא בְּהוּ תְּרוּמָה, הָכָא – פְּתִיכָא בְּהוּ תְּרוּמָה.

The Gemara answers: The level of purity required for non-sacred food items that were prepared according to the standards of purity of *teruma* is actually lower than the level required for dough from which *ḥalla* has not been separated. The reason is that **there,** in the case of non-sacred food items, there is **no** actual ***teruma* mixed in it.** By contrast, **here,** in the case of untithed dough, there is ***teruma***, i.e., *ḥalla*, **mixed in it,** which will eventually be separated from this dough.

וְאִיבָּעֵית אֵימָא: הַנַּח מֵעֵת לְעֵת – דְּרַבָּנַן.

**If you wish, say** instead: **Leave** aside the twenty-four-hour **period** of retroactive impurity[H] of a menstruating woman, as it applies **by rabbinic law.**[N] One cannot raise a difficulty against the principle that untithed dough is treated with the same level of purity as *ḥalla* from the case of the retroactive impurity of a menstruating woman, since that retroactive impurity is a rabbinic decree, and therefore there is more room for leniency.

## HALAKHA

**With regard to any item that when definitely impure renders non-sacred food impure the Sages issued a decree – כָּל שֶׁוַּדַּאי מְטַמֵּא חוּלִּין גָּזְרוּ:** If untithed dough is in a situation of uncertain impurity where, had the particular impurity been certain, it would have certainly rendered something non-sacred impure, the Sages issued a decree to treat that untithed dough with the same ritual stringency as *ḥalla* itself. The dough must be prepared in ritual purity; *ḥalla* is then taken from it and the ritual status of the *ḥalla* remains suspended as it is neither eaten nor burned (Rambam *Sefer Tahara, Hilkhot She'ar Avot HaTumot* 11:16 and *Sefer Zera'im, Hilkhot Bikkurim* 8:10).

**The twenty-four-hour period of retroactive impurity – מֵעֵת לְעֵת:** The twenty-four-hour period of retroactive impurity of a menstruating woman is a rabbinic decree, and therefore her impurity status during that period is viewed as uncertain (Rambam *Sefer Tahara, Hilkhot Metamei Mishkav UMoshav* 3:9).

## NOTES

**But not to non-sacred food items that were prepared according to the standards of purity of *teruma* – וְלֹא בְּחוּלִּין שֶׁנַּעֲשׂוּ עַל טׇהֳרַת תְּרוּמָה:** The commentaries explain that at this point the Gemara assumes that dough that is untithed with regard to *ḥalla* is treated like *ḥalla* because it is prepared with same higher standards of ritual purity. This is similar to non-sacred food that is prepared according to the standards required for *teruma* and that is treated like *teruma* (Ritva).

**Leave aside the period of retroactive impurity as it applies by rabbinic law – הַנַּח מֵעֵת לְעֵת דְּרַבָּנַן:** The early commentaries ask: In the case of leaning, where the *zav* leans on a pure person in the course of handling a package together, he is also impure by rabbinic law. What is the difference between that case and the retroactive impurity of a menstruating woman? They answer that the retroactive impurity of a menstruating woman is more lenient, as it was instituted as a general safeguard and there is no specific concern that she was previously impure. By contrast, in the case of uncertainty of the leaning *zav* there is a specific concern of actual impurity (Ritva).

מתני׳ רַבִּי אֱלִיעֶזֶר אוֹמֵר, אַרְבַּע נָשִׁים דַּיָּין שְׁעָתָן: בְּתוּלָה, מְעוּבֶּרֶת, מֵינִיקָה, וּזְקֵינָה. אָמַר רַבִּי יְהוֹשֻׁעַ: אֲנִי לֹא שָׁמַעְתִּי אֶלָּא בְּתוּלָה,

**MISHNA** **Rabbi Eliezer**[P] **says:** Unlike the women with regard to whom it was taught that they transmit impurity retroactively, there are **four women** who discern menstrual blood and **their time is sufficient,**[HN] i.e., they transmit impurity only from the moment that they saw the blood: **A virgin, a pregnant woman, a nursing woman, and an elderly woman. Rabbi Yehoshua**[P] **says: I heard** this *halakha* from my teachers **only** with regard to **a virgin,**

### HALAKHA

**There are four women who discern menstrual blood and their time is sufficient – אַרְבַּע נָשִׁים דַּיָּין שְׁעָתָן:** There are four types of women who discern menstrual blood and their time is sufficient; that is, they transmit impurity only from the moment that they saw blood: A woman who has yet to experience menstrual bleeding, a pregnant woman, a nursing woman, and an elderly woman. This is in accordance with the opinion of Rabbi Eliezer and Rabbi Yehoshua in the mishna (Rambam *Sefer Tahara, Hilkhot Metamei Mishkav UMoshav* 4:1).

### NOTES

**There are four women who discern menstrual blood and their time is sufficient – אַרְבַּע נָשִׁים דַּיָּין שְׁעָתָן:** The commentaries explain that these four categories of women generally do not experience any flow of menstrual blood, and therefore there is no concern that they experienced a previous discharge and no reason to give them retroactive impurity status.

### PERSONALITIES

**Rabbi Eliezer – רַבִּי אֱלִיעֶזֶר:** This is the *tanna* Rabbi Eliezer ben Hyrcanus, also called Rabbi Eliezer the Great, who lived through the destruction of the Second Temple. Rabbi Eliezer was the son of a wealthy family that traced its lineage to Moses. He began to study Torah only at the age of twenty, when he went to Jerusalem to learn from Rabban Yoḥanan ben Zakkai. Rabban Yoḥanan ben Zakkai had great esteem for Rabbi Eliezer and considered him the greatest of his disciples, so much so that he claimed he was equal to all the Sages of Israel. Rabban Yoḥanan ben Zakkai described Rabbi Eliezer as: A plastered well that does not lose a drop, and Rabbi Eliezer's learning was based mostly on traditions that he received from Rabbi Yoḥanan ben Zakkai. Rabbi Eliezer's approach differed from that of his teacher in that Rabbi Eliezer accepted the rulings of Beit Shammai. Rabbi Eliezer began to teach Torah before the destruction of the Temple and was among Rabban Yoḥanan's students who joined him in founding the great yeshiva in Yavne.

Rabbi Eliezer married Imma Shalom, the sister of the *Nasi*, Rabban Gamliel of Yavne. Following a fundamental dispute between Rabbi Eliezer and the other Sages with regard to the process of halakhic decision-making, Rabban Gamliel had him excommunicated. Rabbi Eliezer's colleagues were the other disciples of Rabban Yoḥanan ben Zakkai, and in particular there are many recorded discussions between Rabbi Eliezer and Rabbi Yehoshua, who was Rabbi Eliezer's closest colleague. His principal student was Rabbi Akiva, but he taught other scholars in his generation as well. His son Hyrcanus was one of the talmudic Sages.

**Rabbi Yehoshua – רַבִּי יְהוֹשֻׁעַ:** This is Rabbi Yehoshua ben Ḥananya the Levite, one of the leading Sages in the generation following the destruction of the Second Temple. He served as one of the Levite singers in the Temple. After its destruction, he was among the students who followed their primary teacher, Rabban Yoḥanan ben Zakkai, to Yavne. Rabbi Yehoshua lived a life of poverty, working as a blacksmith, and was recognized by all as one of the leading Torah authorities. While he disagreed with Rabban Gamliel's rulings on several occasions, he ultimately accepted his authority as the *Nasi*. After Rabban Gamliel's death, he served as a leader of the Sages.

Perek **I**
Daf **7** Amud **b**

אֲבָל הֲלָכָה כְּרַבִּי אֱלִיעֶזֶר.

**but the *halakha* is in accordance with** the opinion of **Rabbi Eliezer.**

אֵיזוֹ הִיא בְּתוּלָה – כׇּל שֶׁלֹּא רָאֲתָה דָּם מִיָּמֶיהָ, אַף עַל פִּי שֶׁנְּשׂוּאָה. מְעוּבֶּרֶת – מִשֶּׁיִּוָּדַע עוּבָּרָהּ. מֵינִיקָה – עַד שֶׁתִּגְמוֹל אֶת בְּנָהּ. נָתְנָה בְּנָהּ לְמֵינִיקָה, גְּמָלַתּוּ, אוֹ מֵת, רַבִּי מֵאִיר אוֹמֵר: מְטַמְּאָה מֵעֵת לְעֵת, וַחֲכָמִים אוֹמְרִים: דַּיָּהּ שַׁעְתָּהּ.

**Who is** the woman characterized as **a virgin** in this context? It is **any** woman **who has not seen** the flow of menstrual **blood in all her days,**[H] **even if she was married** and has experienced bleeding as a result of intercourse consummating her marriage. The time of **a pregnant woman** is **from** the point in her pregnancy when the existence of **her fetus is known**[H] to all who see her. The time of a **nursing woman** is **until she weans her child**[NH] from nursing. If she stopped nursing, e.g., **she gave her child to a wet nurse, weaned him** from nursing, **or** her child **died,** and she saw menstrual blood, **Rabbi Meir says: She transmits impurity for** a twenty-four-hour **period** or from her most recent examination. **And the Rabbis say:** Even in those cases, **her time is sufficient.**

### NOTES

**Until she weans her child – עַד שֶׁתִּגְמוֹל אֶת בְּנָהּ:** The Rabbis, who disagree with Rabbi Meir, maintain that a woman retains the status of a nursing woman for a full twenty-four months after childbirth, regardless of whether or not she is actually nursing. Their reasoning is that it takes that long for her body to recover fully from childbirth (Rabbi Ovadya Bartenura; *Tosefot Yom Tov*).

### HALAKHA

**A virgin is any woman who has not seen the flow of menstrual blood in all her days – בְּתוּלָה כׇּל שֶׁלֹּא רָאֲתָה דָּם מִיָּמֶיהָ:** When the Rabbis stated that a virgin who sees a menstrual flow is rendered ritually impure only going forward and not retroactively, they were referring to a woman who never before saw a discharge of menstrual blood. Even if she saw hymenal bleeding after her first intercourse or blood from childbirth, she is nevertheless considered a virgin in this context (Rambam *Sefer Kedusha, Hilkhot Issurei Bia* 9:5 and *Sefer Tahara, Hilkhot Metamei Mishkav UMoshav* 4:1).

**The time of a pregnant woman is from when the existence of her fetus is known – מְעוּבֶּרֶת מִשֶּׁיִּוָּדַע עוּבָּרָהּ:** A pregnant woman who sees a menstrual flow is rendered impure only from then on and not retroactively. This applies after three months of pregnancy when she is noticeably pregnant (Rambam *Sefer Kedusha, Hilkhot Issurei Bia* 9:4 and *Sefer Tahara, Hilkhot Metamei Mishkav UMoshav* 4:1; *Shulḥan Arukh, Yoreh De'a* 189:33).

**The time of a nursing woman is until she weans her child – מֵינִיקָה עַד שֶׁתִּגְמוֹל אֶת בְּנָהּ:** When the Rabbis declared that a nursing woman who sees a flow of menstrual blood is impure only from that point on, and not retroactively, they included any woman within twenty-four months of childbirth in this category. Since this ruling is not given solely to women who are actually nursing, it applies even in a case where her child died, she weaned him from nursing, or she hired a wet nurse (Rambam *Sefer Kedusha, Hilkhot Issurei Bia* 9:4 and *Sefer Tahara, Hilkhot Metamei Mishkav UMoshav* 4:1; *Shulḥan Arukh, Yoreh De'a* 189:33).

איזוהי זְקֵנָה – כֹּל שֶׁעָבְרוּ עָלֶיהָ שָׁלֹשׁ עוֹנוֹת סָמוּךְ לְזִקְנָתָהּ. רַבִּי אֱלִיעֶזֶר אוֹמֵר: כׇּל אִשָּׁה שֶׁעָבְרוּ עָלֶיהָ שָׁלֹשׁ עוֹנוֹת – דַּיָּהּ שַׁעְתָּהּ. רַבִּי יוֹסֵי אוֹמֵר: מְעוּבֶּרֶת וּמֵנִיקָה שֶׁעָבְרוּ עֲלֵיהֶן שָׁלֹשׁ עוֹנוֹת – דַּיָּין שַׁעְתָּן.

Who is the woman characterized as **an elderly woman** in this context? It is **any** woman for **whom three** typical menstrual **cycles** of thirty days **passed**[H] during which she saw no menstrual blood, at a stage of her life **close to her old age. Rabbi Eliezer says:** In the case of **any woman** for **whom three** typical menstrual **cycles passed** during which she saw no menstrual blood, if she then experiences bleeding, **her time is sufficient. Rabbi Yosei says:** With regard to **a pregnant woman and a nursing woman** for **whom three** typical menstrual **cycles passed** during which they saw no menstrual blood, if they then saw blood, **their time is sufficient.**

וּבַמֶּה אָמַר דַּיָּהּ שַׁעְתָּהּ – בִּרְאִיָּיה רִאשׁוֹנָה, אֲבָל בַּשְּׁנִיָּה – מְטַמְּאָה מֵעֵת לְעֵת. וְאִם רָאֲתָה הָרִאשׁוֹנָה מֵאוֹנֶס – אַף הַשְּׁנִיָּה דַּיָּהּ שַׁעְתָּהּ.

**And** in the above cases, **with regard to what did** the *tanna* say **her time is sufficient?** It is **with regard to the first sighting** of blood,[H] **but with regard to the second sighting,** her status is like that of any other woman, and **she transmits impurity for** a twenty-four-hour **period** or from her most recent examination. **And if she saw the first** sighting as a result of **unnatural circumstances, even** with regard to **the second** sighting, the *halakha* is that **her time is sufficient.**

גמ׳ תַּנְיָא, אָמַר לוֹ רַבִּי אֱלִיעֶזֶר לְרַבִּי יְהוֹשֻׁעַ: אַתָּה לֹא שָׁמַעְתָּ, אֲנִי שָׁמַעְתִּי. אַתָּה לֹא שָׁמַעְתָּ אֶלָּא אַחַת, וַאֲנִי שָׁמַעְתִּי הַרְבֵּה.

**GEMARA** Rabbi Eliezer teaches in the mishna that there are four women who transmit impurity only from the moment that they saw menstrual blood, not retroactively. Rabbi Yehoshua said: I heard this *halakha* from my teachers only with regard to a virgin. The Gemara notes that **it is taught** in a *baraita* that **Rabbi Eliezer said to Rabbi Yehoshua: You did not hear,** but **I did hear** it. In other words, you may not have received a tradition from your teachers with regard to any other woman, but I did receive such a tradition. Furthermore, **you heard** a halakhic ruling with regard to **only one** woman, **and I heard** rulings with regard to **many** women.[N]

אֵין אוֹמְרִים לְמִי שֶׁלֹּא רָאָה אֶת הַחֹדֶשׁ: יָבֹא וְיָעִיד, אֶלָּא לְמִי שֶׁרְאָהוּ. כׇּל יָמָיו שֶׁל רַבִּי אֱלִיעֶזֶר הָיוּ עוֹשִׂין כְּרַבִּי יְהוֹשֻׁעַ, לְאַחַר פְּטִירָתוֹ שֶׁל רַבִּי אֱלִיעֶזֶר הֶחְזִיר רַבִּי יְהוֹשֻׁעַ אֶת הַדָּבָר לְיוֹשְׁנוֹ.

Rabbi Eliezer continued his rebuttal with a metaphor from the practice of sanctifying the new moon, which required the testimony of witnesses: **We do not say to one who had not seen the new moon** to **come and testify. Rather** we give such an instruction only **to he who saw it.** Similarly, my opinion is weightier with regard to this issue, as I heard many rulings about the matter, whereas you did not. The Gemara reports: **All the days of** the life of **Rabbi Eliezer, they would practice in accordance with** the opinion of **Rabbi Yehoshua,** i.e., only a virgin would be exempt from retroactive impurity. **After Rabbi Eliezer's passing, Rabbi Yehoshua returned the matter to its former** custom, which was to follow the opinion of Rabbi Eliezer.

כְּרַבִּי אֱלִיעֶזֶר בְּחַיָּיו מַאי טַעְמָא לָא? מִשּׁוּם דְּרַבִּי אֱלִיעֶזֶר שַׁמּוּתִי הוּא, וְסָבַר: אִי עָבְדִינַן כְּוָותֵיהּ בַּחֲדָא – עָבְדִינַן כְּוָותֵיהּ בְּאַחֲרָנְיָיתָא,

The Gemara asks: **What is the reason** that they **did not** act **in accordance with** the opinion of **Rabbi Eliezer during his lifetime?** The Gemara answers: **Because Rabbi Eliezer was a *Shammuti*,**[L] i.e., a follower of the rulings of Beit Shammai, and the *halakha* is generally in accordance with the opinion of Beit Hillel in their disputes with Beit Shammai. **And** the Sages **held** that **if we act in accordance with his** opinion **in one** matter, people will **act in accordance with his** opinion **in other** matters.

וּמִשּׁוּם כְּבוֹדוֹ דְּרַבִּי אֱלִיעֶזֶר לָא מָצֵינַן מְחֵינַן בְּהוּ. לְאַחַר פְּטִירָתוֹ שֶׁל רַבִּי אֱלִיעֶזֶר, דְּמָצֵינוּ מְחֵינַן בְּהוּ, הֶחְזִיר אֶת הַדָּבָר לְיוֹשְׁנוֹ.

**And** that would be a problem, as if so, then during his lifetime, **due to the honor of Rabbi Eliezer, we** will **not be able to protest** against **them.** But **after Rabbi Eliezer's passing, when we are able to protest** against **those** who act in accordance with Rabbi Eliezer's opinion in other matters, Rabbi Yehoshua **returned the matter to its former** custom of deciding the *halakha* in accordance with the opinion of Rabbi Eliezer in this matter.

אָמַר רַב יְהוּדָה, אָמַר שְׁמוּאֵל: הֲלָכָה כְּרַבִּי אֱלִיעֶזֶר בְּאַרְבַּע. חֲדָא – דַּאֲמַרַן.

§ The Gemara mentions other instances in which the *halakha* is in accordance with the opinion of Rabbi Eliezer. **Rav Yehuda says** that **Shmuel says:** The *halakha* is **in accordance with** the opinion **of Rabbi Eliezer in four** cases. **One** is the *halakha* **that we** just **mentioned,** of the four women who transmit ritual impurity only from the time of their sighting and onward.

**HALAKHA**

**An elderly woman is any woman for whom three typical menstrual cycles of thirty days passed – זְקֵנָה כֹּל שֶׁעָבְרוּ עָלֶיהָ שָׁלֹשׁ עוֹנוֹת:** An elderly woman who sees a menstrual flow is rendered impure only from that point on and not retroactively. This applies to an older woman who is not offended when she is openly called an elderly woman and for whom three typical menstrual cycles had passed during which she saw no menstrual blood (Rambam *Sefer Kedusha, Hilkhot Issurei Bia* 9:4 and *Sefer Tahara, Hilkhot Metamei Mishkav UMoshav* 4:1; *Shulḥan Arukh, Yoreh De'a* 189:28).

**Her time is sufficient with regard to the first sighting of blood – דַּיָּהּ שַׁעְתָּהּ בִּרְאִיָּיה רִאשׁוֹנָה:** A pregnant woman, a nursing woman, an elderly woman, and a virgin who saw one flow of menstrual blood are rendered impure only from that point on and not retroactively. If they see menstrual blood a second time, they assume the same impurity status as all women and are rendered impure retroactively. If that first sighting of menstrual blood was caused by unnatural circumstances, then such a woman does not assume retroactive impurity status upon her second sighting of menstrual blood (Rambam *Sefer Kedusha, Hilkhot Issurei Bia* 9:4 and *Sefer Tahara, Hilkhot Metamei Mishkav UMoshav* 4:1; see Ra'avad and *Kesef Mishne*).

**NOTES**

**You heard a halakhic ruling with regard to only one woman and I heard rulings with regard to many women – אַתָּה לֹא שָׁמַעְתָּ אֶלָּא אַחַת וַאֲנִי שָׁמַעְתִּי הַרְבֵּה:** This is in keeping with the known account of Rabbi Eliezer's diligent, punctilious, and faithful ways. It is said that none of his colleagues ever preceded him into the study hall, nor did he ever exit before anyone else. And he never taught anything that he did not first hear from his teacher (*Sukka* 28a).

**LANGUAGE**

***Shammuti* – שַׁמּוּתִי:** Some explain this term as referring to *shamta*, excommunication, as Rabbi Eliezer was excommunicated (Rashi). Others explain that it refers to the fact that he was a student of Beit Shammai (*Tosafot*).

וְאִידָךְ: הַמַּקְשָׁה כַּמָּה תִּשְׁפֶּה וּתְהֵא זָבָה – מֵעֵת לְעֵת, דִּבְרֵי רַבִּי אֱלִיעֶזֶר, וַהֲלָכָה כִּדְבָרָיו.

**And another** is taught in a *baraita* with regard to a woman **who** experiences **labor** pain as a result of which she sees a flow of blood. Her discharge is attributed to childbirth rather than *zava* blood. The *baraita* asks: For **how long** must she be **relieved** from pain in order **to be** considered **a** ***zava*** due to her flow of uterine blood? She must have relief **for a** twenty-four-hour **period.** This is **the statement of Rabbi Eliezer. And the** ***halakha*** **is in accordance with his statement.**

וְאִידָךְ: הַזָּב וְהַזָּבָה שֶׁבָּדְקוּ עַצְמָן יוֹם רִאשׁוֹן – וּמָצְאוּ טָהוֹר, יוֹם שְׁבִיעִי – וּמָצְאוּ טָהוֹר, וּשְׁאָר הַיָּמִים לֹא בָּדְקוּ, רַבִּי אֱלִיעֶזֶר אוֹמֵר: הֲרֵי אֵלּוּ בְּחֶזְקַת טָהֳרָה. רַבִּי יְהוֹשֻׁעַ אוֹמֵר: אֵין לָהֶן אֶלָּא יוֹם הָרִאשׁוֹן וְיוֹם הַשְּׁבִיעִי בִּלְבַד.

**And another** case in which the *halakha* follows Rabbi Eliezer is taught in a mishna (68b): A *zav* and a *zava* must observe seven days without a discharge in order to attain ritual purity. With regard to **a** ***zav***[B] **or a** ***zava***[B] **who examined themselves** on the **first day and found** themselves to be **pure,** and they examined themselves on the **seventh day and found** themselves to be **pure, but** on the **rest of the** intervening **days they did not examine** themselves, **Rabbi Eliezer says: The presumptive status of** the *zav* and the *zava* is one of **ritual purity. Rabbi Yehoshua says:** In that case, the *zav* and the *zava* **have** counted **only the first day and the seventh day,** two of the seven clean days, and they must count another five days to complete the tally.

רַבִּי עֲקִיבָא אוֹמֵר: אֵין לָהֶם אֶלָּא יוֹם שְׁבִיעִי בִּלְבַד. וְתַנְיָא, רַבִּי שִׁמְעוֹן וְרַבִּי יוֹסֵי אוֹמְרִים: נִרְאִין דִּבְרֵי רַבִּי אֱלִיעֶזֶר מִדִּבְרֵי רַבִּי יְהוֹשֻׁעַ, וְדִבְרֵי רַבִּי עֲקִיבָא מִדִּבְרֵי כּוּלָּן, אֲבָל הֲלָכָה כְּרַבִּי אֱלִיעֶזֶר.

The mishna continues: **Rabbi Akiva says:** Since any impure discharge that they might have experienced in between the first and seventh days would negate their count and require them to restart the seven-day period, the *zav* and the *zava* **have** counted **only the seventh day,** and must count another six days to complete the tally. And with regard to this dispute, it **is taught** in a *baraita* that **Rabbi Shimon and Rabbi Yosei say: The statement of Rabbi Eliezer appears** more correct **than the statement of Rabbi Yehoshua, and the statement of Rabbi Akiva** appears more correct **than the statement of all of them. But the** ***halakha*** **is in accordance with** the opinion of **Rabbi Eliezer.**

וְאִידָךְ, דִּתְנַן: אֲחוֹרֵי כֵלִים שֶׁנִּטְמְאוּ בְּמַשְׁקִין, רַבִּי אֱלִיעֶזֶר אוֹמֵר: מְטַמְּאִין אֶת הַמַּשְׁקִין וְאֵין פּוֹסְלִין אֶת הָאוֹכָלִין, מְטַמְּאִין אֶת הַמַּשְׁקִין – וַאֲפִילּוּ דְּחוּלִּין, וְאֵין פּוֹסְלִין אֶת הָאוֹכָלִין – וַאֲפִילּוּ דִּתְרוּמָה. רַבִּי יְהוֹשֻׁעַ אוֹמֵר: מְטַמְּאִין אֶת הַמַּשְׁקִין וּפוֹסְלִין אֶת הָאוֹכָלִין.

**And the other** case in which the *halakha* is in accordance with the opinion of Rabbi Eliezer is **as we learned** in a mishna (*Teharot* 8:7): With regard to **the exterior of vessels that contracted ritual impurity** through contact **with impure liquids,**[H] i.e., with liquids that had touched the carcass of a creeping animal, **Rabbi Eliezer says,** with regard to this impurity that applies by rabbinic law: These exteriors **transmit impurity to liquids** that come in contact with them, but **they do not disqualify foods**[H] with which they come into contact. The mishna elaborates: **They transmit impurity to** other **liquids, and even non-sacred** liquids. **And they do not disqualify foods, and even** ***teruma*****. Rabbi Yehoshua says:** These exteriors **transmit impurity to liquids and they disqualify** *teruma* **foods,** as well.

אָמַר רַבִּי יְהוֹשֻׁעַ: קַל וָחוֹמֶר, וּמָה טְבוּל יוֹם, שֶׁאֵין מְטַמֵּא מַשְׁקֶה חוּלִּין – פּוֹסֵל אוֹכְלֵי תְרוּמָה, אֲחוֹרֵי כֵלִים, שֶׁמְּטַמֵּא מַשְׁקֵה חוּלִּין – אֵינוֹ דִּין שֶׁפּוֹסֵל אוֹכְלֵי תְרוּמָה?

**Rabbi Yehoshua says:** I derived my ruling via **an** ***a fortiori*** inference from the *halakha* of one who was ritually impure, who immersed that day and is waiting for nightfall for the purification process to be completed. **And if one who immersed that day, who** has second-degree ritual impurity status and therefore he **does not transmit impurity to non-sacred liquids,** nevertheless **disqualifies** ***teruma*** **foods** with which he comes into contact, then with regard to the **exteriors of vessels, which do transmit impurity to non-sacred liquids, is it not logical that** they should **render** ***teruma*** **food disqualified?**

וְרַבִּי אֱלִיעֶזֶר – אֲחוֹרֵי כֵלִים דְּרַבָּנַן, וּטְבוּל יוֹם דְּאוֹרַיְיתָא, וְרַבָּנַן מִדְּאוֹרַיְיתָא לָא עָבְדִינַן קַל וָחוֹמֶר. דִּמְדְּאוֹרַיְיתָא אֵין אוֹכֶל מְטַמֵּא כְּלִי, וְאֵין מַשְׁקֶה מְטַמֵּא כְּלִי.

The Gemara asks: **And Rabbi Eliezer,** how does he refute this inference? The Gemara answers: He would counter that the *halakha* that the **exterior of vessels** are rendered impure through contact with impure foods or liquids is **by rabbinic law, and the** *halakhot* **of one who immersed that day** apply **by Torah law. And** there is a principle that one does not **apply** ***a fortiori*** inferences to derive conclusions **by rabbinic law from** cases that apply **by Torah law. As by Torah law** impure **foods do not transmit impurity to vessels, and** similarly, impure **liquids do not transmit impurity to vessels.**

---

**BACKGROUND**

*Zav* – זָב: The *halakhot* relating to the stringent ritual impurity caused by this condition appear in Leviticus, chapter 15, and in tractate *Zavim*. The *zav* becomes ritually impure as a result of secreting a white, pus-like discharge. A man who experiences this discharge on one occasion becomes ritually impure for one day, similar to a man who has discharged semen. If one experiences a second discharge on the same or the following day, or if the initial discharge is prolonged, he contracts the more severe ritual impurity of a *zav*, which lasts until he counts seven clean days. One who experiences a third discharge within the next day is obligated to bring an offering as part of his purification process. Not only does he become ritually impure, he also imparts ritual impurity through contact with vessels or people, by being moved by them, by moving them, and by lying or sitting on them. He also imparts impurity to items under a very heavy stone by sitting on the stone, although the stone itself does not thereby become impure. The fluids secreted by a *zav*, his saliva, urine, and semen, impart ritual impurity, and the articles on which he sits or lies become primary sources of ritual impurity and can themselves impart ritual impurity to other articles.

*Zava* – זָבָה: A *zava* is a woman who experiences a flow of menstrual-type blood on three consecutive days during a time of the month when she is not due to experience menstrual bleeding. The first secretion makes her ritually impure, but until the third secretion her status is that of a woman who observes a day for a day, i.e., she needs only one clean day in order to be purified. After experiencing bleeding on the third day, the woman is considered a *zava* and is obligated to count seven clean days and bring an offering as part of her purification process. A *zava* imparts ritual impurity in the same way as a *zav*. A *zav* does not require three days to attain his halakhic status, as even after three secretions on one day he is considered to be a *zav*. Today, all women who experience menstrual bleeding are considered to have the status of *zavot* and must wait seven clean days before immersing in a ritual bath.

**HALAKHA**

**The exterior of vessels that contracted ritual impurity through contact with impure liquids – אֲחוֹרֵי כֵלִים שֶׁנִּטְמְאוּ בְּמַשְׁקִין:** The exterior of a vessel that was rendered impure by contact with impure liquids then renders impure other liquids that come in contact with it, even if those liquids were non-sacred. They contract first-degree impurity and can therefore defile other vessels, which then become defiled with second-degree impurity (Rambam *Sefer Tahara, Hilkhot She'ar Avot HaTumot* 7:5).

**They transmit impurity to liquids but they do not disqualify foods – מְטַמְּאִין אֶת הַמַּשְׁקִין וְאֵין פּוֹסְלִין אֶת הָאוֹכָלִין:** By Torah law, impure food and drink that come in contact with the exterior of vessels do not render them impure. Nevertheless, as a safeguard against making a mistake with the secretions of a *zav* and *zava*, which do defile vessels according to Torah law, the Sages decreed that impure liquids render the exterior of vessels impure. Therefore, a vessel's exterior that was defiled by impure liquids will then render impure any other liquids that come in contact with it, even non-sacred liquids, but the impure exterior will not render impure foods that come into contact with it, even *teruma* (Rambam *Sefer Tahara, Hilkhot She'ar Avot HaTumot* 7:1–6).

**NOTES**

That a final *halakha* may not be learned directly from the Talmud – שֶׁאֵין לְמֵדִין הֲלָכָה מִפִּי תַלְמוּד: Some commentaries write that this principle applies only to a ruling of *halakha* that conflicts with an accepted principle of deciding *halakhot*. Otherwise, a *halakha* recorded in a mishna or *baraita* is accepted as the final *halakha* (Rashba).

וְרַבָּנַן הוּא דִּגְזוּר גְּזֵרָה מִשּׁוּם מַשְׁקִין דְּזָב וְזָבָה. מַשְׁקִין דַּעֲלוּלִין לְקַבֵּל טוּמְאָה – גָּזְרוּ בְּהוּ רַבָּנַן, אוֹכָלִין דְּאֵין עֲלוּלִין לְקַבֵּל טוּמְאָה – לָא גָּזְרוּ בְּהוּ רַבָּנַן.

The Gemara continues: **And** it was **the Sages who issued a decree** that the exterior of a vessel is rendered impure when it comes into contact with impure liquids, and they decreed that only liquids, not foods, are rendered impure when they come into contact with impure vessel exteriors. The reason for this is **due to the liquids** secreted **by a** ***zav*** **or** ***zava***, e.g., their saliva and urine, which have a primary degree of ritual impurity and therefore transmit impurity to vessels. Consequently, with regard to **liquids, which are apt to contract impurity, the Sages issued a decree that they** contract impurity when they come in contact with these impure vessel exteriors. But with regard to **foods, which are not** as **apt to contract impurity,** as they must first be rendered susceptible to impurity through contact with a liquid, **the Sages did not issue** such **a decree with regard to them.**

וּמַאי שְׁנָא אֲחוֹרֵי כֵלִים דְּנָקֵט – מִשּׁוּם דְּקִילִי, דִּתְנַן: כְּלִי שֶׁנִּטְמָא מֵאֲחוֹרָיו בְּמַשְׁקִין – אֲחוֹרָיו טָמֵא, תּוֹכוֹ, אָזְנוֹ, אוֹגְנוֹ, יָדָיו – טְהוֹרִין. נִטְמָא תּוֹכוֹ – כּוּלּוֹ טָמֵא.

The Gemara raises a difficulty: Rabbi Eliezer agrees that if the interior of a vessel is rendered impure by contact with impure liquids, it renders impure any *teruma* foods that come into contact with it. **But what is different** about the **exterior of vessels, that** Rabbi Eliezer **cited** them as having a more lenient status? The Gemara answers: This is **due to** the fact **that** their *halakhot* are more **lenient** than those of the other parts of the vessel. **As we learned** in a mishna (*Kelim* 25:6): With regard to **a vessel whose exterior was rendered impure by** contact with impure **liquids,**[H] its **exterior is impure,** while its others parts, such as **its interior, its ear,** i.e., its looped handle, **its rim,** the edge of the vessel that protrudes outward, and **its handles, are pure.** But if its **interior was rendered impure, it is all impure.**

מַאי קָא מַשְׁמַע לַן שְׁמוּאֵל? בְּכוּלְּהוּ תְּנַן הִלְכְתָא!

These are the four cases with regard to which Shmuel said that the *halakha* is in accordance with the opinion of Rabbi Eliezer. The Gemara asks: **What is Shmuel teaching us? In all** of these cases **we learned** explicitly that **the** ***halakha*** is in accordance with the opinion of Rabbi Eliezer.

וְכִי תֵּימָא: אֲחוֹרֵי כֵלִים קָא מַשְׁמַע לַן, דְּלָא תְּנַן; וְלֵימָא הֲלָכָה כְּרַבִּי אֱלִיעֶזֶר בַּאֲחוֹרֵי כֵלִים! אֶלָּא, הָא קָא מַשְׁמַע לַן: שֶׁאֵין לְמֵדִין הֲלָכָה מִפִּי תַלְמוּד.

**And if you would say** that he is **teaching us** the *halakha* with regard to the **exterior of vessels, whose** *halakha* **we did not learn** from the mishna, **let** Shmuel simply **state** that the ***halakha*** is **in accordance with** the opinion of **Rabbi Eliezer with regard to** the **exterior of vessels.** The Gemara explains: **Rather, this** is what Shmuel **teaches us: That** a final ***halakha*** **may not be learned** directly **from the Talmud,**[N] i.e., from a statement of a mishna or *baraita* that the *halakha* is in accordance with a specific opinion, unless the ruling is confirmed by *amora'im*.

וְתוּ לֵיכָּא? וְהָאִיכָּא דִּתְנַן, רַבִּי אֱלִיעֶזֶר אוֹמֵר:

The Gemara asks: **And is there nothing more** that can be added to the list of cases in which the *halakha* is in accordance with the opinion of Rabbi Eliezer? **But isn't there** another case **that we learned** in a mishna (*Yevamot* 109a): Two brothers married two sisters, one an adult and the other a minor. If the husband of the adult dies, the Torah obligation of levirate marriage applies to the other brother, which is not abrogated by the rabbinic prohibition of the *yevama* as the sister of his minor wife. In such a case, **Rabbi Eliezer says:**

**HALAKHA**

A vessel whose exterior was rendered impure by contact with impure liquids – כְּלִי שֶׁנִּטְמָא מֵאֲחוֹרָיו בְּמַשְׁקִין: Impure liquids that fall into the airspace of a vessel will render the entire vessel impure with second-degree impurity. If the impure liquids fall on the exterior of the vessel, only the outside is defiled, while the interior of the vessel remains pure. This applies to both earthenware vessels and metal vessels. All of these rulings hold true with regard to questions of impurity involving non-sacred items or *teruma*. With regard to items of sacrificial sanctity, once a vessel's exterior is defiled it renders the entire vessel impure with second-degree impurity (Rambam *Sefer Tahara, Hilkhot She'ar Avot HaTumot* 7:3, and see Ra'avad, *Kesef Mishne*, and *Leḥem Mishne* there).

מְלַמְּדִין אֶת הַקְּטַנָּה שֶׁתְּמָאֵן בּוֹ, וְאָמַר רַב יְהוּדָה אָמַר שְׁמוּאֵל: הֲלָכָה כְּרַבִּי אֱלִיעֶזֶר! כִּי אָמַר שְׁמוּאֵל, הֲלָכָה כְּרַבִּי אֱלִיעֶזֶר בְּאַרְבָּעָה – בְּסֵדֶר טְהָרוֹת, אֲבָל בִּשְׁאָר סְדָרִים – אִיכָּא טוּבָא.

**We instruct the minor,** i.e., the surviving brother's wife, **to refuse** to continue to stay married to **him**[N] so that her marriage is dissolved, and he may then enter into levirate marriage with her adult sister, the widow of his childless brother. **And Rav Yehuda says** that **Shmuel says:** The ***halakha*** **is in accordance with** the opinion of **Rabbi Eliezer.** The Gemara explains: **When Shmuel says** that the *halakha* **is in accordance with** the opinion of **Rabbi Eliezer in four** cases, what he meant was four cases **within** ***Seder Teharot*** in the Mishna, the order that deals with ritual purity. **But in the other orders, there are many** instances where the *halakha* is in accordance with the opinion of Rabbi Eliezer.

וְהָכִי נַמִּי מִסְתַּבְּרָא, דִּתְנַן, רַבִּי אֱלִיעֶזֶר אוֹמֵר: אַף הָרוֹדֶה וְנוֹתֵן לַסַּל – הַסַּל מְצָרְפָן לְחַלָּה. וְאָמַר רַב יְהוּדָה אָמַר שְׁמוּאֵל: הֲלָכָה כְּרַבִּי אֱלִיעֶזֶר, שְׁמַע מִינָּהּ.

The Gemara adds: **This too stands to reason, as we learned** in a mishna in the order of *Zera'im* (*Ḥalla* 2:4) that **Rabbi Eliezer says: Even** with regard to **one who removes** loaves of bread[B] from an oven **and places them in a basket,**[H] **the basket** serves to **combine them to** reach the quantity from which one is required to separate ***ḥalla,*** despite the fact that each of the loaves does not contain the necessary measure for *ḥalla* on its own. **And Rav Yehuda says** that **Shmuel says:** The ***halakha*** is **in accordance with** the opinion of **Rabbi Eliezer. Conclude from this** that Shmuel's general statement applies only to *Seder Teharot.*

וּמַאי אוּלְמֵיהּ דְּהַאי מֵהַאי? מִשּׁוּם דְּקָאֵי רַבִּי אֶלְעָזָר כְּוָתֵיהּ.

The Gemara raises a difficulty: The case of *ḥalla* was cited as proof that there is an exception to Shmuel's principle that there are only four cases where the *halakha* is in accordance with the opinion of Rabbi Eliezer, after a difficulty was raised from the case of levirate marriage with the sister of one's minor wife. **But in what** way is **this** case of *ḥalla* **greater** proof **than that** case of the levirate marriage? Neither case appears in *Seder Teharot.* The Gemara answers: The case of the levirate marriage is different, as there **Rabbi Elazar holds in accordance with** the opinion of Rabbi Eliezer.

דִּתְנַן, רַבִּי אֶלְעָזָר אוֹמֵר: מְלַמְּדִין אֶת הַקְּטַנָּה שֶׁתְּמָאֵן בּוֹ.

**As we learned** in the mishna (*Yevamot* 111b): A *yavam* may perform levirate marriage with only one of his deceased brother's wives. Once he does so, the other wives are forbidden to him, because they had been married to his brother. If a deceased brother had two wives, an adult and a minor, and the *yavam* engaged in sexual intercourse with the minor and then engaged in intercourse with the adult, the Rabbis maintain that he disqualifies the minor from staying married to him, as her levirate bond is uncertain, and the adult wife is also prohibited to him, because the levirate marriage with the minor is considered effective by rabbinic law. **Rabbi Elazar says:** The court **instructs the minor to refuse him,** thereby annulling her marriage retroactively, and he may then perform levirate marriage with the adult. Accordingly, the case of *ḥalla* is a stronger example, as there the *halakha* is in accordance with the opinion of Rabbi Eliezer exclusively, as his opinion is not supported by another *tanna.*

וּמִי קָאֵי? וְהָא אַצְרְכוּ מַצְרְכִינַן לְהוּ, וְלָא דָּמְיָין לַהֲדָדֵי! אֶלָּא מִשּׁוּם דְּקָאֵי רַבִּי יְהוּדָה בֶּן בָּבָא כְּוָתֵיהּ.

The Gemara asks: **And does** Rabbi Elazar in fact **hold** in accordance with the opinion of Rabbi Eliezer? **But doesn't** the Gemara (*Yevamot* 111b) explain that both the opinions of Rabbi Eliezer and Rabbi Elazar **are necessary,** as they apply to different cases, **and** therefore **they are not comparable to each other?** The Gemara suggests a new answer: **Rather,** the ruling with regard to levirate marriage is a weaker example of a case where the *halakha* is in accordance with the opinion of Rabbi Eliezer **because Rabbi Yehuda ben Bava holds in accordance with his opinion.**

### NOTES

We instruct the minor to refuse him – מְלַמְּדִין אֶת הַקְּטַנָּה שֶׁתְּמָאֵן בּוֹ: Rashi explains that this is referring to a case of two brothers who married two sisters, one adult and one a minor who was orphaned and married off by her mother or brother. The husband of the older sister passed away childless, thereby rendering her a *yevama* who must be married or perform *ḥalitza* with his brother, her sister's husband. This levirate marriage is barred by the prohibition against marrying one's wife's sister. To resolve this problem, the court instructs the wife, who is a minor, to dissolve her marriage by refusing to continue living with her husband. This enables the *yevama* to marry her late husband's brother.

### BACKGROUND

One who removes loaves of bread – הָרוֹדֶה: Ovens in talmudic times were made of earthenware. Dough would be inserted into the oven through special openings and stuck to its walls for baking. Removal of bread from the walls was done with a long, narrow paddle. Its length would allow for sticking the dough deep in the oven where its heat was most intense, and for turning the dough when necessary, as well as moving it to different locations within the oven.

Brick oven and paddle

### HALAKHA

One who removes loaves of bread from an oven and places them in a basket – הָרוֹדֶה וְנוֹתֵן לַסַּל: If one kneads together an amount of dough that is less than the requisite amount required to necessitate the separation of *ḥalla*, and he then bakes it and places it into a basket along with bread from another such dough that was baked separately, the basket serves to combine them to reach the requisite quantity and he must then separate *ḥalla* from them (Rambam *Sefer Zera'im, Hilkhot Bikkurim* 6:16; *Shulḥan Arukh, Yoreh De'a* 325:1).

דְּתַנְיָא, רַבִּי יְהוּדָה בֶּן בָּבָא הֵעִיד חֲמִשָּׁה דְּבָרִים: שֶׁמְּמָאֲנִים אֶת הַקְּטַנּוֹת,

As it is taught in a *baraita*: **Rabbi Yehuda ben Bava testified** about **five matters of** *halakha*: Normally, marriage refusals of girls married off by their mother or brothers are discouraged. Yet, in specific instances where it is clear that if the marriage were to remain in effect it would engender problems related to levirate marriage and *ḥalitza*, the court **persuades minor girls to refuse** to continue living with their husbands,[H] thereby resolving the complications involved in the case.

וְשֶׁמַּשִּׂיאִין אֶת הָאִשָּׁה עַל פִּי עֵד אֶחָד, וְשֶׁנִּסְקַל תַּרְנְגוֹל בִּירוּשָׁלַיִם עַל שֶׁהָרַג אֶת הַנֶּפֶשׁ, וְעַל יַיִן בֶּן אַרְבָּעִים יוֹם שֶׁנִּתְנַסֵּךְ עַל גַּבֵּי הַמִּזְבֵּחַ, וְעַל תָּמִיד שֶׁל שַׁחַר שֶׁקָּרַב בְּאַרְבַּע שָׁעוֹת.

**And** he also testified **that one may** allow **a woman** who seeks to remarry after hearing of her husband's death **to marry based on** the testimony of **one witness,**[H] as opposed to the two witnesses required for other matters of testimony. **And** he further testified **that a rooster**[B] **was stoned** to death **in Jerusalem for killing a person,**[HN] in order to teach that the Torah law requiring the stoning of an ox that killed a person (see Exodus 21:28) applies to other animals as well. **And** he testified **about forty-day-old wine that was** used for **libation on the altar.**[N] **And** finally, he testified **about** the **daily morning offering that was sacrificed at four hours**[HN] of the day.

מַאי "קְטַנּוֹת" – לָאו חֲדָא דְּרַבִּי אֶלְעָזָר וְחַד דְּרַבִּי אֱלִיעֶזֶר? לָא, מַאי "קְטַנּוֹת" – קְטַנּוֹת דְּעָלְמָא.

The Gemara concludes its proof: When the *baraita* teaches that Rabbi Yehuda ben Bava testified that the court persuades minor girls to refuse to continue living with their husbands, **what** is the significance of the reference to **minor girls** in the plural? Is this **not** referring to the **one** minor girl who is the subject of the ruling **of Rabbi Elazar and** the other **one** that is the subject of the ruling **of Rabbi Eliezer?** Apparently, Rabbi Yehuda ben Bava holds in accordance with the opinion of Rabbi Eliezer in the case of the minor's refusal. If so, this ruling is a weaker proof that the *halakha* is in accordance with the opinion of Rabbi Eliezer in cases outside of *Seder Teharot*. The Gemara answers: **No, what** is meant by the plural: **Minor girls?** It means **minor girls in general,** i.e., all minor girls in such cases where the ruling of Rabbi Elazar applies.

אִי הָכִי, גַּבֵּי אִשָּׁה נַמִי, נִתְנֵי "נָשִׁים", וְנֵימָא נָשִׁים דְּעָלְמָא! אֶלָּא, מִדְּהָכָא קָתָנֵי "אִשָּׁה", וְהָכָא קָתָנֵי "קְטַנּוֹת", שְׁמַע מִינָּהּ: דַּוְקָא קָתָנֵי, שְׁמַע מִינָּהּ.

The Gemara challenges: **If so, with regard to** the *halakha* listed in the *baraita* that one may allow **a woman** to marry based on the testimony of one witness, **let it also teach: Women,** in the plural, **and we will say** that it is referring to **women in general. Rather, from** the fact that **here** it **teaches: A woman, and** yet **here** it **teaches: Minor girls, conclude from** this discrepancy that Rabbi Yehuda ben Bava **is teaching** his ruling **specifically** about two minor girls: The one who is the subject of Rabbi Elazar's ruling and the one who is the subject of Rabbi Eliezer's ruling. The Gemara comments: Indeed, **conclude from it** that Rabbi Yehuda ben Bava holds in accordance with the opinion of Rabbi Eliezer.

**HALAKHA**

**The court persuades minor girls to refuse to continue living with their husbands – שֶׁמְּמָאֲנִים אֶת הַקְּטַנּוֹת:** There are certain cases where the court will persuade a minor orphan who was married off by her brother or mother to perform refusal and annul her marriage, for example, in a case where someone marries a deaf-mute woman and a minor. If he dies without children, since marriage to either will not exempt her rival wife, the court persuades the minor to perform refusal, thereby allowing him to enter into a levirate marriage with the deaf-mute woman. Another case is where two brothers marry two sisters, one an adult and the other a minor. If the husband of the adult sister dies without children, the court persuades the minor to perform refusal, thereby allowing him to enter into a levirate marriage with the adult sister. This *halakha* is in accordance with the opinion of Rabbi Eliezer and the testimony of Rabbi Yehuda ben Bava (Rambam *Sefer Nashim, Hilkhot Yibbum VaḤalitza* 5:30, 7:15; *Shulḥan Arukh, Even HaEzer* 171:1, 175:11).

**One may allow a woman to marry based on the testimony of one witness – מַשִּׂיאִין אֶת הָאִשָּׁה עַל פִּי עֵד אֶחָד:** If a woman's husband traveled overseas and she hears of his death and wishes to remarry, she may marry based upon the testimony of one witness (Rambam *Sefer Nashim, Hilkhot Geirushin* 12:15; *Shulḥan Arukh, Even HaEzer* 17:3).

**A rooster was stoned in Jerusalem for killing a person – נִסְקַל תַּרְנְגוֹל בִּירוּשָׁלַיִם עַל שֶׁהָרַג אֶת הַנֶּפֶשׁ:** A bird that kills a person is killed by stoning (Rambam *Sefer Nezikin, Hilkhot Nizkei Mamon* 10:2).

**The daily morning offering that was sacrificed at four hours – תָּמִיד שֶׁל שַׁחַר שֶׁקָּרַב בְּאַרְבַּע שָׁעוֹת:** Although the daily morning offering is sacrificed before sunrise, in exigent circumstances it may be sacrificed until the end of the fourth hour of the day (Rambam *Sefer Avoda, Hilkhot Temidin UMusafin* 1:2).

**BACKGROUND**

**Rooster – תַּרְנְגוֹל:** A rooster is considered to be an aggressive creature. A wild rooster tends to rage against other roosters that tread on its turf, and at times they attack other species as well. Some strains of roosters are especially aggressive and are trained to be violent, such as those raised to be fighting cocks. It is possible for a rooster to kill a person, particularly a baby, by pecking his head.

Roosters fighting, detail from Roman mosaic

**NOTES**

**And he testified that a rooster was stoned in Jerusalem for killing a person – וְשֶׁנִּסְקַל תַּרְנְגוֹל בִּירוּשָׁלַיִם עַל שֶׁהָרַג אֶת הַנֶּפֶשׁ:** Rashi (*Berakhot* 27a) explains that the rooster pecked at the soft spot of a baby's skull and punctured it. It was stoned in accordance with the *halakha* of an ox that gores and kills a person, as it is written: "But if the ox was wont to gore in time past, and warning has been given to its owner, and he has not kept it in, but it has killed a man or a woman, the ox shall be stoned" (Exodus 21:29).

**And he testified about forty-day-old wine that was used for libation on the altar – וְעַל יַיִן בֶּן אַרְבָּעִים יוֹם שֶׁנִּתְנַסֵּךְ עַל גַּבֵּי הַמִּזְבֵּחַ:** Wine from the presses that has not finished fermenting is unfit for a libation on the altar. All wine under forty-days old is in this category (Rashi).

**And about the daily morning offering that was sacrificed at four hours – וְעַל תָּמִיד שֶׁל שַׁחַר שֶׁקָּרַב בְּאַרְבַּע שָׁעוֹת:** There are different explanations as to when this event occurred. Some say that this is referring to the early days of the First Temple, when King Shlomo married Pharaoh's daughter. He stayed up the whole night and slept in the daytime until the fourth hour while the keys to the Temple lay under his head. It was then that the Sages declared that the morning daily offering may still be sacrificed, even in the fourth hour of the day (Rashi on *Mishlei* 31:1; *Tosafot* on *Menaḥot* 64b). Others say that this incident occurred in the Second Temple period, when the Hasmonean kings were waging war on each other and Jerusalem was under siege. Each day, those on the inside would lower down the walls two baskets of gold and those on the outside would send up two sheep for the daily offerings. One day those on the outside sent up two goats instead and the people inside thought they would be unable to sacrifice the daily offering, but they providentially found two inspected lambs left in the Chamber of the Lambs. It was at that time that Rabbi Yehuda ben Bava testified that the morning daily offering can be brought at the fourth hour (*Tosafot* on *Menaḥot* 64b; Rambam's Commentary on the Mishna, *Eduyyot* 6:1; Rav Ovadya Bartenura on *Eduyyot* 6:1, citing the Jerusalem Talmud, *Berakhot*, chapter 4).

וְכֵן אָמַר רַבִּי אֶלְעָזָר: הֲלָכָה כְּרַבִּי אֱלִיעֶזֶר בְּאַרְבָּעָה. וְתוּ לֵיכָּא? וְהָתְנַן רַבִּי אֱלִיעֶזֶר אוֹמֵר: מְלַמְּדִין אֶת הַקְּטַנָּה שֶׁתְּמָאֵן בּוֹ, וְאָמַר רַבִּי אֶלְעָזָר: הֲלָכָה כְּרַבִּי אֱלִיעֶזֶר! וְכִי תֵּימָא: כִּי אָמַר רַבִּי אֶלְעָזָר הֲלָכָה כְּרַבִּי אֱלִיעֶזֶר בְּאַרְבָּעָה – בְּסֵדֶר טָהֳרוֹת, אֲבָל בִּשְׁאָר סִדְרֵי – אִיכָּא, וּמִי אִיכָּא?

§ **And similarly, Rabbi Elazar says:** The ***halakha* is in accordance with** the opinion of **Rabbi Eliezer in four** cases. The Gemara asks: **And** are there **no more? But didn't we learn** in a mishna that **Rabbi Eliezer says:** The court **instructs the minor to refuse** to stay married **to him, and Rabbi Elazar said:** The ***halakha* is in accordance with** the opinion of **Rabbi Eliezer?** The Gemara adds: **And if you would say** that **when Rabbi Elazar said** that the ***halakha* is in accordance with** the opinion of **Rabbi Eliezer in four** cases, he meant four cases **within *Seder Teharot*, but in the other orders** of the Mishna **there are many** cases, **are there** really other such cases?

וְהָתְנַן: הַוֶּרֶד וְהַכּוֹפֶר וְהַלָּטוֹם וְהַקְּטָף – יֵשׁ לָהֶן שְׁבִיעִית, וְלִדְמֵיהֶן שְׁבִיעִית, יֵשׁ לָהֶן בִּיעוּר וְלִדְמֵיהֶן בִּיעוּר. וְאָמַר רַבִּי פְּדָת: מַאן תַּנָּא קְטָפָא פֵּירָא – רַבִּי אֱלִיעֶזֶר.

**But didn't we learn** in a mishna (*Shevi'it* 7:6) that the *halakha* of the following fragrant plants: **The rose,**[B] **the henna,**[B] **the rockrose,**[B] **and the balsam,**[B] is that **they have** the sanctity of the **Sabbatical** Year,[H] **and money** exchanged for **them has** the sanctity of the **Sabbatical** Year. Additionally, **they have** the *halakha* of **eradication and money** exchanged for **them has** the *halakha* of **eradication. And** with regard to this mishna, **Rabbi Pedat said: Who** is the *tanna* who **taught that balsam** has the status of **a fruit,** and is not merely sap, and therefore it has the sanctity of the Sabbatical Year? It is **Rabbi Eliezer.**

וַאֲמַר רַבִּי זֵירָא: חֲזֵי דְּמִינָּךְ וּמֵאֲבוּךְ קַשְׁרִיתוּ קְטָפָא לְעָלְמָא! אַתְּ אָמְרַתְּ מַאן תַּנָּא קְטָפָא פֵּירָא רַבִּי אֱלִיעֶזֶר, וַאֲבוּךְ אֲמַר הֲלָכָה כְּרַבִּי אֱלִיעֶזֶר בְּאַרְבָּעָה.

The Gemara continues: **And Rabbi Zeira said to** Rabbi Pedat: One can **see that from you and from your father,** i.e., between the two of you, **you have permitted balsam to the world,** since the ruling of Rabbi Eliezer is certainly not accepted. As **you said: Who** is the *tanna* who **taught that balsam** has the status of **a fruit?** It is **Rabbi Eliezer. And your father,** Rabbi Elazar, **said** that the ***halakha* is in accordance with** the opinion of **Rabbi Eliezer in** only **four** cases.

וְאִם אִיתָא, לֵימָא לֵיהּ: כִּי אָמַר אַבָּא הֲלָכָה כְּרַבִּי אֱלִיעֶזֶר בְּאַרְבָּעָה – בְּסֵדֶר טָהֳרוֹת, אֲבָל בִּשְׁאָר סִדְרֵי – אִיכָּא.

The Gemara explains the difficulty: **And if it is so,** that Rabbi Elazar was referring only to *Seder Teharot*, then **let** Rabbi Pedat **say to** Rabbi Zeira: **When** my **father said** that the ***halakha* is in accordance with** the opinion of **Rabbi Eliezer in four** cases, he meant only four cases **within *Seder Teharot*, but in the other orders there are** other such cases. From the fact that Rabbi Pedat did not reply in this manner, evidently there are no cases in the other orders of the Mishna where, according to Rabbi Elazar, the *halakha* is in accordance with the opinion of Rabbi Eliezer.

**HALAKHA**

**The rose, the henna, the rockrose, and the balsam, they have sanctity of the Sabbatical Year – הַוֶּרֶד וְהַכּוֹפֶר וְהַלָּטוֹם יֵשׁ לָהֶן שְׁבִיעִית וכו׳:** Even though the rose, henna, and rockrose are not classic fruit, nevertheless, they have sanctity in the Sabbatical Year, and money exchanged for them has sanctity as well. Sap that comes from the balsam tree is not considered its fruit unless it is a barren tree, in which case even its leaves and shoots are considered like its fruit and have sanctity in the Sabbatical Year (Rambam *Sefer Zera'im, Hilkhot Shemitta VeYovel* 7:19, and see *Kesef Mishne* there).

**BACKGROUND**

**Rose – וֶרֶד:** Referring to any of several species of the genus *Rosa*, this plant is used for decoration due to its beautiful, fragrant flower and for training onto fences due to its sharp thorns. Roses also grow wild on several continents. Other minor uses of the rose include medicinal use of oils produced from it and use of the fruit, called a rose hip, for food.

Rose hips

**Henna – כּוֹפֶר:** Henna, *Lawsonia inermis*, is also called kopro in Akkadian, or κύπρος, kupros, in Greek. It is native to North Africa and western Asia, and in Eretz Yisrael it is grown in the Jordan Valley. It has yellow or white blossoms that are arranged in clusters. Henna dye is produced from crushed henna leaves and is traditionally used in certain cultures to color hair or create decorative patterns on the skin.

Henna tree

Henna design on hand

**Rockrose – לָטוֹם:** This is the same as the *lot* plant mentioned in the Torah (Genesis 37:25), where the Ishmaelites who bought Joseph were carrying their "spices and balm and *lot*" down to Egypt. Some identify this plant as a member of the genus *Cistus*, known as the rockrose, shrubs with large white- or yellow-tinted flowers that grow in the mountains of Israel. Rockroses are sources of the resin known as labdanum, which was prized in antiquity for its scent and medicinal properties.

Sage-leaved rockrose

**Balsam – קְטָף:** The Arabian balsam tree, *Commiphora gileadensis*, is the source of balsam, known in biblical and rabbinic Hebrew as *tzori*, a resinous sap used in the incense mixture offered in the Temple (see *Karetot* 6a).

אֶלָּא קַשְׁיָא הַהִיא! מִשּׁוּם דְּקָאֵי רַבִּי אֶלְעָזָר כְּוָתֵיהּ, דִּתְנַן רַבִּי אֶלְעָזָר אוֹמֵר: מְלַמְּדִים אֶת הַקְּטַנָּה שֶׁתְּמָאֵן בּוֹ.

The Gemara asks: **But that** case, where the *amora* Rabbi Elazar said that the *halakha* is in accordance with the opinion of Rabbi Eliezer with regard to persuading a minor to refuse to stay married to her husband, is **difficult.** This apparently conflicts with the statement that there are only four cases in which Rabbi Elazar rules in accordance with the opinion of Rabbi Eliezer. The Gemara answers: There the *halakha* is in accordance with the opinion of Rabbi Eliezer only **because** the *tanna* **Rabbi Elazar holds in accordance with his** opinion. **As we learned** in a mishna that **Rabbi Elazar says:** The court **instructs the minor to refuse** to stay married to **him,** thereby annulling her marriage retroactively.

וּמִי קָאֵי? וְהָא אַצְרוּכֵי מַצְרְכִינַן לְהוּ, וְלָא דָּמְיָין לַהֲדָדֵי! אֶלָּא מִשּׁוּם דְּקָאֵי רַבִּי יְהוּדָה בֶּן בָּבָא כְּוָותֵיהּ.

The Gemara asks: **And does** Rabbi Elazar **hold** in accordance with the opinion of Rabbi Eliezer in that case of the minor? **But doesn't** the Gemara in *Yevamot* explain that both the opinions of Rabbi Eliezer and Rabbi Elazar **are necessary, and** therefore **they are not comparable to each other? Rather,** the *halakha* is in accordance with the opinion of Rabbi Eliezer in that case **because Rabbi Yehuda ben Bava holds in accordance with his opinion,** as explained earlier.

וְתוּ לֵיכָּא? וְהָתְנַן, רַבִּי עֲקִיבָא אוֹמֵר: אוֹמְרָהּ בְּרָכָה רְבִיעִית בִּפְנֵי עַצְמָהּ, רַבִּי אֱלִיעֶזֶר אוֹמֵר: אוֹמְרָהּ בְּהוֹדָאָה. וְאָמַר רַבִּי אֶלְעָזָר: הֲלָכָה כְּרַבִּי אֱלִיעֶזֶר!

The Gemara asks: **And** are there **no more** cases in which Rabbi Elazar maintains that the *halakha* is in accordance with Rabbi Eliezer? **But didn't we learn** in a mishna (*Berakhot* 33a): One recites the prayer of distinction between the holy and the profane [*havdala*], said in the evening prayer following Shabbat and festivals, in the fourth blessing of the *Amida* prayer: Who graciously grants knowledge. **Rabbi Akiva says: One recites** *havdala* as **a fourth blessing by itself. Rabbi Eliezer says** that **one recites it in** the blessing of **thanksgiving.** And with regard to this dispute, **Rabbi Elazar says:** The ***halakha*** is **in accordance with** the opinion of **Rabbi Eliezer.**

אָמַר רַבִּי אַבָּא: הַהוּא – דַּאֲמַר מִשּׁוּם רַבִּי חֲנִינָא בֶּן גַּמְלִיאֵל, דְּתַנְיָא, רַבִּי עֲקִיבָא אוֹמֵר: אוֹמְרָהּ בְּרָכָה רְבִיעִית בִּפְנֵי עַצְמָהּ, רַבִּי חֲנִינָא בֶּן גַּמְלִיאֵל אוֹמֵר: אוֹמְרָהּ בְּהוֹדָאָה.

**Rabbi Abba said,** in explanation: **That** case is different, **as** that is not the opinion of Rabbi Eliezer himself. Rather, he **stated** that ruling **in the name of Rabbi Ḥanina ben Gamliel, as it is taught** in a *baraita* that **Rabbi Akiva says: One recites** *havdala* as **a fourth blessing by itself; Rabbi Ḥanina ben Gamliel[P] says: One recites it in** the blessing of **thanksgiving.**

**PERSONALITIES**

Rabbi Ḥanina ben Gamliel – רַבִּי חֲנִינָא בֶּן גַּמְלִיאֵל: Rabbi Ḥanina ben Gamliel was the son of the *Nasi* Rabban Gamliel of Yavne, and his lifetime spanned the fourth and fifth generations of *tanna'im*. He probably learned Torah from both his father and Rabbi Tarfon, but he would also discuss matters of *halakha* with the students of Rabbi Akiva. His rulings on matters of *halakha* are reported by his brother Rabbi Yehuda ben Gamliel, by the *amora* Rabbi Abbahu, and by others. Being from a distinguished family, he was very strict with the members of his household (*Gittin* 7a). He apparently died young (*Bava Kamma* 83a) and therefore never became the *Nasi* himself, despite having been the elder child; instead, his brother Rabban Shimon ben Gamliel was the *Nasi*.

Perek **I**
Daf **8** Amud **b**

וְהָא קַשִּׁישׁ מִינֵּיהּ טוּבָא! אֶלָּא: מִשּׁוּם דְּקָאֵי רַבִּי חֲנִינָא בֶּן גַּמְלִיאֵל בְּשִׁיטָתֵיהּ.

The Gemara asks: **But** wasn't Rabbi Eliezer **much older than** Rabbi Ḥanina ben Gamliel?[N] How could Rabbi Eliezer have cited the opinion of Rabbi Ḥanina ben Gamliel? The Gemara answers: **Rather,** the reason Rabbi Elazar ruled that the *halakha* is in accordance with the opinion of Rabbi Eliezer in that case was **because Rabbi Ḥanina ben Gamliel held in accordance with his** opinion.

**NOTES**

**But wasn't Rabbi Eliezer much older than Rabbi Ḥanina ben Gamliel** – וְהָא קַשִּׁישׁ מִינֵּיהּ טוּבָא: Rabbi Ḥanina ben Gamliel was a fourth-generation *tanna* who lived in the post-Temple period. He was the son of Rabban Gamliel and the older brother of Rabban Shimon ben Gamliel, the two of whom served consecutively as the heads of the academy at Yavne. By contrast, Rabbi Eliezer was a second-generation *tanna* who studied under Rabban Yoḥanan ben Zakkai during the period before the destruction of the Temple. He was married to Imma Shalom, Rabban Gamliel's sister, and therefore was Rabbi Ḥanina ben Gamliel's uncle (Rashi).

וּמִי קָאֵי? וְהָתַנְיָא: אוֹר יוֹם הַכִּפּוּרִים – מִתְפַּלֵּל שֶׁבַע וּמִתְוַדֶּה, שַׁחֲרִית – מִתְפַּלֵּל שֶׁבַע וּמִתְוַדֶּה, מוּסָף – מִתְפַּלֵּל שֶׁבַע וּמִתְוַדֶּה, מִנְחָה – מִתְפַּלֵּל שֶׁבַע וּמִתְוַדֶּה, בִּנְעִילָה – מִתְפַּלֵּל שֶׁבַע וּמִתְוַדֶּה, בְּעַרְבִית – מִתְפַּלֵּל שֶׁבַע מֵעֵין שְׁמוֹנֶה עֶשְׂרֵה.

And does Rabbi Ḥanina ben Gamliel really **hold** in accordance with Rabbi Eliezer's opinion? **But isn't it taught** in a *baraita*: On **the night of Yom Kippur, one prays seven** blessings in the *Amida* prayer[H] **and confesses;** in the **morning prayer, one prays seven** blessings **and confesses;** in the **additional prayer, one prays seven** blessings **and confesses;** in the **afternoon prayer, one prays seven** blessings **and confesses;** and **in the** ***ne'ila*** **prayer, one** also **prays seven** blessings **and confesses. For the evening prayer** at the conclusion of Yom Kippur, **one prays seven** blessings in **an abridged** version of the **eighteen** blessings[N] of the weekday *Amida* prayer. One recites the first three blessings, the final three, and a middle blessing that includes an abbreviated form of the other weekday blessings.

רַבִּי חֲנִינָא בֶּן גַּמְלִיאֵל מִשּׁוּם אֲבוֹתָיו אוֹמֵר: מִתְפַּלֵּל שְׁמוֹנֶה עֶשְׂרֵה, מִפְּנֵי שֶׁצָּרִיךְ לוֹמַר הַבְדָּלָה בְּ״חוֹנֵן הַדַּעַת״. אָמַר רַב נַחְמָן בַּר יִצְחָק: אִיהוּ אָמַר מִשּׁוּם אֲבוֹתָיו, וְלֵיהּ לָא סְבִירָא לֵיהּ.

**Rabbi Ḥanina ben Gamliel says in the name of his forefathers: One recites** the complete **eighteen** blessings, **due to** the fact that he is **required to recite** ***havdala***[H] **in** the fourth blessing of the *Amida*: **Who graciously grants knowledge.** *Havdala* cannot be inserted into the abridged version. Evidently, Rabbi Ḥanina ben Gamliel does not agree with Rabbi Eliezer's ruling that one recites *havdala* in the blessing of thanksgiving, one of the final three blessings of the *Amida* prayer. **Rav Naḥman bar Yitzḥak says** in explanation: Rabbi Ḥanina ben Gamliel **said** this opinion **in the name of his forefathers, but** he **himself does not hold accordingly.**

אֲמַר לֵיהּ רַבִּי יִרְמְיָה לְרַבִּי זֵירָא: וְאַתְּ לָא תִּסְבְּרָא דְּמַאן תְּנָא קְטָפָא פֵּירָא – רַבִּי אֱלִיעֶזֶר הוּא? וְהָתְנַן, רַבִּי אֱלִיעֶזֶר אוֹמֵר: הַמַּעֲמִיד בִּשְׂרַף עָרְלָה – אָסוּר!

§ Earlier, Rabbi Zeira questioned the claim of Rabbi Pedat, son of Rabbi Eliezer, that the Sage who holds that balsam is considered to be fruit and therefore has the sanctity of the Sabbatical Year is Rabbi Eliezer. **Rabbi Yirmeya said to Rabbi Zeira: And you? Do you not hold** that the *tanna* **who taught** that **balsam** sap has the status of **fruit is Rabbi Eliezer? As, didn't we learn** in a mishna (*Orla* 1:7) that **Rabbi Eliezer says:** With regard to **one who curdles** cheese **in the sap of** ***orla***,[H] the cheese is **prohibited,** as the sap is considered to be fruit of the tree.

אֲפִילּוּ תֵּימָא רַבָּנַן, עַד כָּאן לָא פְּלִיגִי רַבָּנַן עֲלֵיהּ דְּרַבִּי אֱלִיעֶזֶר – אֶלָּא בִּקְטָפָא דְגַוְוזָא, אֲבָל בִּקְטָפָא דְפֵירָא – מוֹדוּ לֵיהּ. דִּתְנַן, אָמַר רַבִּי יְהוֹשֻׁעַ: שָׁמַעְתִּי בְּפֵירוּשׁ שֶׁהַמַּעֲמִיד בִּשְׂרַף הֶעָלִין, בִּשְׂרַף הָעִיקָּרִין – מוּתָּר, בִּשְׂרַף הַפַּגִּין – אָסוּר, מִפְּנֵי שֶׁהוּא פְּרִי.

The Gemara answers: **You** may **even say** that the mishna that deals with balsam is in accordance with the opinion of **the Rabbis.** As **the Rabbis disagree with Rabbi Eliezer only with regard to the sap of the tree,**[H] **but** in the case of the **sap of the fruit they agree with him. As we learned** in a mishna (*Orla* 1:7) that **Rabbi Yehoshua said: I heard explicitly that** in the case of **one who curdles** cheese **in the sap of the leaves** or **the sap of the roots** of an *orla* tree, the cheese is **permitted.** But if it is curdled **in the sap of unripe figs it is prohibited, because** that sap **is** considered to be **fruit.**

וְאִיבָּעֵית אֵימָא: כִּי פְּלִיגִי רַבָּנַן עֲלֵיהּ דְּרַבִּי אֱלִיעֶזֶר – בְּאִילָן הָעוֹשֶׂה פֵּירוֹת, אֲבָל בְּאִילָן שֶׁאֵינוֹ עוֹשֶׂה פֵּירוֹת – מוֹדוּ דִּקְטָפוֹ זֶהוּ פִּרְיוֹ. דִּתְנַן, רַבִּי שִׁמְעוֹן אוֹמֵר: אֵין לַקְּטָף שְׁבִיעִית, וַחֲכָמִים אוֹמְרִים: יֵשׁ לַקְּטָף שְׁבִיעִית, מִפְּנֵי שֶׁקְּטָפוֹ זֶהוּ פִּרְיוֹ.

**And if you wish,** say instead: **When the Rabbis disagree with Rabbi Eliezer,** it is **with regard to a tree that bears fruit. But in** the case of **a tree that does not bear fruit, they agree that its sap is** considered to be **its fruit. As we learned** in a mishna (*Shevi'it* 7:6) that **Rabbi Shimon says:** The sanctity of the **Sabbatical** Year **does not** apply **to sap. And the Rabbis say:** The sanctity of the **Sabbatical** Year **does** apply **to sap, because its sap is its fruit.**

מַאן חֲכָמִים? לָאו רַבָּנַן דִּפְלִיגִי עֲלֵיהּ דְּרַבִּי אֱלִיעֶזֶר? אָמַר לֵיהּ הַהוּא סָבָא, הָכִי אָמַר רַבִּי יוֹחָנָן: מַאן חֲכָמִים – רַבִּי אֱלִיעֶזֶר דְּאָמַר קְטָפוֹ זֶהוּ פִּרְיוֹ.

The Gemara explains the proof: **Who** are these **Rabbis?** Are they **not the Rabbis who disagree with Rabbi Eliezer?** If so, this demonstrates that they agree in the case of a tree that does not bear fruit. The Gemara rejects this proof: **A certain elder said to** Rabbi Zeira that **this is what Rabbi Yoḥanan says: Who** are **the Rabbis** in this mishna? It is **Rabbi Eliezer, who said** that **its sap is** considered to be **its fruit.**

**HALAKHA**

On the night of Yom Kippur one prays seven blessings in the *Amida* prayer – אוֹר יוֹם הַכִּפּוּרִים מִתְפַּלֵּל שֶׁבַע: On the night of Yom Kippur, one prays seven blessings in the *Amida* prayer: The three first blessings, the final three, and a middle blessing featuring the themes of the day (Rambam *Sefer Ahava*, *Hilkhot Tefilla UVirkat Kohanim* 2:7).

One recites the complete eighteen blessings due to the fact that he is required to recite *havdala* – מִתְפַּלֵּל שְׁמוֹנֶה עֶשְׂרֵה מִפְּנֵי שֶׁצָּרִיךְ לוֹמַר הַבְדָּלָה: On the evening after Yom Kippur, during the evening prayer, one prays the eighteen complete blessings of the *Amida* and includes *havdala* in the fourth blessing: Who graciously grants knowledge. This *halakha* is in accordance with the opinion of Rabbi Ḥanina ben Gamliel, in the name of his forefathers (*Shulḥan Arukh*, *Oraḥ Ḥayyim* 624:1; see Rambam *Sefer Ahava*, *Hilkhot Tefilla UVirkat Kohanim* 2:12).

One who curdles cheese in the sap of *orla* – הַמַּעֲמִיד בִּשְׂרַף עָרְלָה: If one curdles cheese in the sap of *orla*, the cheese is prohibited. Even though it is a type of food mixed with food not of its own kind, and even if it is a tiny amount, it is still prohibited and it is not nullified by the majority of permitted food. This is the *halakha* only when the sap is used as a curdling agent, because it is then that its effect is felt throughout the cheese (Rambam *Sefer Kedusha*, *Hilkhot Ma'akhalot Assurot* 16:26).

The Rabbis disagree with Rabbi Eliezer only with regard to the sap of the tree – עַד כָּאן לָא פְּלִיגִי רַבָּנַן עֲלֵיהּ דְּרַבִּי אֱלִיעֶזֶר אֶלָּא בִּקְטָפָא דְגַוְוזָא וכו׳: The *halakha* is in accordance with the opinion of Rabbi Yehoshua that sap that flows from trees or from tree trunks does not have sanctity in the Sabbatical Year. There are two cases where the Rabbis agree and the *halakha* there follows the unanimous opinion. One is with regard to sap that flows from unripe figs, where all agree that it does have sanctity of the Sabbatical Year, and money exchanged for the sap also has sanctity. And the other case is with regard to sap that flows from barren trees that bear no fruit. In that case, all agree that the sap is considered like its fruit and it has the sanctity of the Sabbatical Year (Rambam *Sefer Zera'im*, *Hilkhot Shemitta VeYovel* 7:19–20).

**NOTES**

For the evening prayer one prays seven blessings in an abridged version of the eighteen blessings – בְּעַרְבִית מִתְפַּלֵּל שֶׁבַע מֵעֵין שְׁמוֹנֶה עֶשְׂרֵה: Rashi explains that one recites the first three blessings, the final three, and a middle blessing that includes an abbreviated form of the other weekday blessings. This middle blessing begins with the words: Grant us understanding, and it was formulated as a special prayer for wayfarers who do not have time to pray a full *Amida*. Rashi explains that the Sages abbreviated the post-Yom Kippur evening services because the people were waiting to break their full-day fast.

BACKGROUND

Virgin sycamore – בְּתוּלַת שִׁקְמָה: The sycamore, *Ficus sycomorus*, is a tall and wide tree that is a species of fig. Even though a sycamore's fruits are edible, it is predominantly cultivated for its wood, because beams made from the sycamore are strong, relatively light, and generally free from imperfections found in other wood. Typically, a sycamore is left to grow until it reaches a significant height and then it is chopped down. The remaining part of the tree grows again and is chopped down again every few years.

Sycamore tree

Sycamore fruit

NOTES

As long as she has not engaged in intercourse, etc. – כָּל זְמַן שֶׁלֹּא נִבְעֲלָה וכו׳: The early commentaries note that these practical differences do not apply exclusively to a woman who has engaged in sexual intercourse, as even a woman whose hymen was torn accidentally is prohibited to marry a High Priest and her marriage contract is likewise less than two hundred dinars. Rather, the Gemara is referring to any woman who has not engaged in intercourse or any physical incident that resulted in the same effect (Ramban; Rashba; Ritva).

אִי רַבִּי אֱלִיעֶזֶר, מַאי אִירְיָא אִילָן שֶׁאֵינוֹ עוֹשֶׂה פְּרִי? אֲפִילּוּ אִילָן הָעוֹשֶׂה פְּרִי – קִטְפוֹ זֶהוּ פִּרְיוֹ! לְדִבְרֵיהֶם דְּרַבָּנַן קָאָמַר לְהוּ, לְדִידִי – אֲפִילּוּ אִילָן הָעוֹשֶׂה פֵּירוֹת נַמִי קִטְפוֹ זֶהוּ פִּרְיוֹ, לְדִידְכוּ – אוֹדוּ לִי מִיהַת בְּאִילָן שֶׁאֵינוֹ עוֹשֶׂה פֵּירוֹת דְּקִטְפוֹ זֶהוּ פִּרְיוֹ, וְרַבָּנַן אָמְרִי לֵיהּ: לָא שְׁנָא.

The Gemara asks: **If it is** the opinion of **Rabbi Eliezer, why** are they **specifically** discussing the case of **a tree that does not bear fruit? Even** in the case of **a tree that** does **bear fruit,** Rabbi Eliezer maintains that **its sap is** like **its fruit.** The Gemara answers: Rabbi Eliezer **stated** his opinion **to them in accordance with the statement of the Rabbis** themselves, as follows: **According to my** opinion, **even** with regard to **a tree that bears fruit, its sap** is **also** considered to be **its fruit.** But **according to your** opinion, you should **at least agree with me in** the case of **a tree that does not bear fruit,** that **its sap is** considered to be **its fruit. And the Rabbis said** in response **to** Rabbi Eliezer: **It is no different.** Sap is not considered fruit whether it comes from a fruit-bearing tree or a barren tree.

״אֵיזוֹ הִיא בְּתוּלָה – כָּל שֶׁלֹּא רָאֲתָה״ כו׳. תָּנוּ רַבָּנַן: נִשֵּׂאת וְרָאֲתָה דָּם מֵחֲמַת נִישּׂוּאִין, יָלְדָה וְרָאֲתָה דָּם מֵחֲמַת לֵידָה – עֲדַיִין אֲנִי קוֹרֵא לָהּ ״בְּתוּלָה״, שֶׁהֲרֵי בְּתוּלָה שֶׁאָמְרוּ – בְּתוּלַת דָּמִים, וְלֹא בְּתוּלַת בְּתוּלִים.

§ The mishna teaches: **Who is** the woman characterized as **a virgin** in this context? It is **any** woman **who did not see** the flow of menstrual blood in all her days, even if she was married and experienced bleeding resulting from intercourse consummating her marriage. **The Sages taught:** If she was **married and she saw** a flow of **blood due to her marriage,**[H] i.e., blood resulting from the tearing of her hymen; or if **she gave birth and saw blood due to the birth, I still call her a virgin** in this context. The reason is **that when they said: Virgin** here, they meant a menstrual **blood virgin,** i.e., one who did not yet see a menstrual flow, **and not a hymen**-blood **virgin,** i.e., one who did not experience bleeding from a torn hymen.

אִינִי, וְהָאָמַר רַב כָּהֲנָא, תָּנָא, שָׁלֹשׁ בְּתוּלוֹת הֵן: בְּתוּלַת אָדָם, בְּתוּלַת קַרְקַע, בְּתוּלַת שִׁקְמָה. בְּתוּלַת אָדָם – כָּל זְמַן שֶׁלֹּא נִבְעֲלָה, נָפְקָא מִינָּהּ – לְכֹהֵן גָּדוֹל, אִי נַמִי – לִכְתוּבָּתָהּ מָאתַיִם.

The Gemara asks: **Is that so? But didn't Rav Kahana say** that a Sage **taught: There are three** types of **virgins: A virgin human, virgin ground, and a virgin sycamore.**[B] **A virgin human** is a woman for **as long as she has not engaged in intercourse.**[N] **The relevance** of this designation is that only a virgin is permitted **to** marry **a High Priest** (see Leviticus 21:13–14). **Alternatively,** the relevance is **that her marriage contract is two hundred dinars,** instead of the one hundred dinars in the marriage contract of a non-virgin.

בְּתוּלַת קַרְקַע – כָּל זְמַן שֶׁלֹּא נֶעֶבְדָה, נָפְקָא מִינָּהּ – לְנַחַל אֵיתָן, אִי נַמִי – לְמִקָּח וּמִמְכָּר.

**Virgin ground** is ground for **as long as it has not been worked. The relevance** of this designation is **with regard to** the **rough** dried-up **stream** mentioned in the Torah. When the corpse of a murder victim is found between two towns and the murderer is unknown, the Torah states that a heifer's neck is broken in a place that was not worked. **Alternatively,** the relevance is **with regard to buying and selling.** If one stipulates that he is buying virgin land, it is defined as land that has never been worked.

בְּתוּלַת שִׁקְמָה – כָּל זְמַן שֶׁלֹּא נִקְצְצָה, נָפְקָא מִינָּהּ – לְמִקָּח וּמִמְכָּר, אִי נַמִי – לְמִקְצְצָהּ בַּשְּׁבִיעִית, כִּדְתְנַן: אֵין קוֹצְצִין בְּתוּלַת שִׁקְמָה בַּשְּׁבִיעִית, מִפְּנֵי שֶׁהִיא עֲבוֹדָה. וְאִם אִיתָא, לִיתְנֵי נַמִי הָא!

Finally, **a virgin sycamore** is a sycamore for **as long as it has not been felled,** i.e., cut to promote growth. **The relevance** of this designation is **with regard to buying and selling.** If one stipulates that he is buying virgin sycamore, it is defined as one that has never been felled. **Alternatively,** the relevance is **with regard to** the prohibition against **felling it in the Sabbatical** Year, **as we learned** in a mishna: (*Shevi'it* 4:5): **One may not fell a virgin sycamore in the Sabbatical** Year,[H] **because it is** considered **work,** as this promotes the growth of the tree. The Gemara explains its question: **And if it is so,** that there is a concept of a virgin from menstrual blood, **let** the *tanna* of this *baraita* **also teach this** type of virgin.

HALAKHA

If she was married and she saw a flow of blood due to her marriage – נִשֵּׂאת וְרָאֲתָה דָּם מֵחֲמַת נִישּׂוּאִין וכו׳: A virgin who experiences a menstrual flow is impure only from then on and does not assume retroactive impurity status. A virgin in this context is defined as a woman who had never before seen a menstrual flow, even if she had experienced bleeding due to a torn hymen after her first act of intercourse or in the course of childbirth (Rambam *Sefer Kedusha, Hilkhot Issurei Bia* 9:5 and *Sefer Tahara, Hilkhot Metamei Mishkav UMoshav* 4:1).

One may not fell a virgin sycamore in the Sabbatical Year – אֵין קוֹצְצִין בְּתוּלַת שִׁקְמָה בַּשְּׁבִיעִית: One may not fell, i.e., cut to promote growth, a virgin sycamore in the Sabbatical Year as he does during other years because it is considered working the tree, as cutting it down promotes the growth of the tree. If he needs its wood, he may trim off branches in an unusual manner that differs from the standard method of cutting for growth (Rambam *Sefer Zera'im, Hilkhot Shemitta VeYovel* 1:21).

אָמַר רַב נַחְמָן בַּר יִצְחָק: כִּי קָתָנֵי – מִידֵּי דְּלֵית לֵיהּ שֵׁם לְוַוי, אֲבָל מִידֵּי דְּאִית לֵיהּ שֵׁם לְוַוי – לָא קָתָנֵי. רַב שֵׁשֶׁת בְּרֵיהּ דְּרַב אִידִי אָמַר: כִּי קָתָנֵי – מִידֵּי דְּתָלֵי בְּמַעֲשֶׂה, מִידֵּי דְּלָא תָּלֵי בְּמַעֲשֶׂה – לָא קָתָנֵי.

The Gemara cites several answers. **Rav Naḥman bar Yitzḥak says: When** the Sage **teaches** the list of virgins, he includes only **an item that does not have a modifier, but he does not teach an item that has a modifier.** A virgin human, virgin land, and a virgin sycamore can be referred to without another modifier. Conversely, a virgin with regard to menstrual blood cannot be referred to simply by the unmodified term: Virgin. **Rav Sheshet, son of Rav Idi, says: When** the Sage **teaches** the list of virgins, he includes only **an item that is dependent upon** an outside **action,** e.g., intercourse in the case of a human virgin or felling in the case of a virgin sycamore. But **he does not teach an item that is not dependent upon** an outside **action,** such as a woman's menstrual flow.

רַבִּי חֲנִינָא בְּרֵיהּ דְּרַב אִיקָא אָמַר: כִּי קָתָנֵי – מִידֵּי דְּלָא הָדַר לִבְרִיָּיתוֹ, מִידֵּי דְּהָדַר לִבְרִיָּיתוֹ – לָא קָתָנֵי. רָבִינָא אָמַר: כִּי קָתָנֵי – מִידֵּי דְּקָפֵיד עֲלֵיהּ זְבִינָא, מִידֵּי דְּלָא קָפֵיד עֲלֵיהּ זְבִינָא – לָא קָתָנֵי.

**Rabbi Ḥanina, son of Rav Ika says: When** the Sage **teaches** the list of virgins, he includes only **an item that will not** later **revert to its** original **state.** But **he does not teach an item** that will later **revert to its** original **state,** such as a woman's menstrual flow that ceases when she reaches old age. **Ravina says: When** the Sage **teaches** the list of virgins, he includes only **an item about which a buyer is particular,** such as one who purchases a virgin sycamore tree. But **he does not teach an item about which a buyer is not particular,** e.g., a woman's menstrual blood.

וְלָא קָפְדִי? וְהָתַנְיָא, רַבִּי חִיָּיא אוֹמֵר: כְּשֵׁם שֶׁהַשְּׂאוֹר יָפֶה לָעִיסָּה – כָּךְ דָּמִים יָפִין לָאִשָּׁה, וְתַנְיָא מִשּׁוּם רַבִּי מֵאִיר: כָּל אִשָּׁה שֶׁדָּמֶיהָ מְרוּבִּין – בָּנֶיהָ מְרוּבִּין! אֶלָּא: כִּי קָתָנֵי – מִידֵּי דְּקָפֵיץ עֲלֵיהּ זְבִינָא, מִידֵּי דְּלָא קָפֵיץ עֲלֵיהּ זְבִינָא – לָא קָתָנֵי.

The Gemara asks: **And** is a buyer, i.e., a potential husband, **not particular** about her menstrual blood? **But isn't it taught** in a *baraita* that **Rabbi Ḥiyya says: Just as leaven is fortuitous for dough, so too, blood is fortuitous for a woman; and it is taught** in another *baraita* **in the name of Rabbi Meir: Any woman whose blood is plentiful, her children are plentiful?** A potential husband would certainly be particular about this factor. The Gemara provides an alternative answer: **Rather, when** the Sage **teaches** the list of virgins, he includes only **an item that buyers are eager** to purchase. But **he does not teach an item that buyers are not eager** to purchase, e.g., a woman without menstrual blood.

תָּנוּ רַבָּנַן: אֵיזוֹהִי בְּתוּלַת קַרְקַע – כָּל שֶׁמַּעֲלָה רְשׁוּשִׁין וְאֵין עֲפָרָהּ תִּיחוּחַ, נִמְצָא בָּהּ חֶרֶס – בְּיָדוּעַ שֶׁנֶּעֶבְדָה, צוּנְמָא – הֲרֵי זוֹ בְּתוּלַת קַרְקַע.

**The Sages taught** in a *baraita*: **What is virgin ground?** It is **any** ground **that raises up hard clumps** of **earth and whose dirt is not loose.** If one **finds** a shard of **earthenware in** the earth, **it is** thereby **known that it** was once **worked** and is not virgin ground. If one finds hard **rock, it is virgin ground.**

״מְעוּבֶּרֶת מִשֶּׁיִּוָּדַע עוּבָּרָהּ״. וְכַמָּה הַכָּרַת הָעוּבָּר? סוּמָכוֹס אוֹמֵר מִשּׁוּם רַבִּי מֵאִיר: שְׁלֹשָׁה חֳדָשִׁים. וְאַף עַל פִּי שֶׁאֵין רְאָיָה לַדָּבָר – זֵכֶר לַדָּבָר, שֶׁנֶּאֱמַר: ״וַיְהִי כְּמִשְׁלֹשׁ חֳדָשִׁים״ וְגוֹמֵר.

§ The mishna teaches: The time of **a pregnant woman** is sufficient **from** the point in her pregnancy when the existence of **her fetus is known** to all who see her. The Gemara asks: **And how much** time must pass for **the fetus to be known? Sumakhos says in the name of Rabbi Meir: Three months.**[NH] **And although** there is **no** explicit **proof for the matter,** that a fetus is discernable after three months of pregnancy, there is **an allusion to the matter, as it is stated: "And it came to pass about three months** after, that it was told to Judah, saying: Tamar your daughter-in-law has played the harlot" (Genesis 38:24).

״זֵכֶר לַדָּבָר״? קְרָא כְּתִיב, וּרְאָיָה גְּדוֹלָה הִיא! מִשּׁוּם דְּאִיכָּא דְּיָלְדָה לְתִשְׁעָה, וְאִיכָּא דְּיָלְדָה לְשִׁבְעָה.

The Gemara asks: Why does Rabbi Meir call this a mere **allusion to the matter?** An explicit **verse is written, and that is a significant proof.** The Gemara answers: It is only an allusion **because there are** some women **who give birth after nine** months **and there are** others **who give birth after seven** months. Although the verse indicates that a fetus is known to all after three months, it is possible that this applies only to a nine-month pregnancy. Since in the case of a nine-month pregnancy the fetus is recognizable after a third of the full term, with regard to a seven-month pregnancy, the fetus would likewise be noticeable after a third of the full pregnancy, i.e., at two and one-third months. Therefore, Rabbi Meir teaches that in all cases the fetus is known only after three months.

תָּנוּ רַבָּנַן: הֲרֵי שֶׁהָיְתָה בְּחֶזְקַת מְעוּבֶּרֶת וְרָאֲתָה דָּם, וְאַחַר כָּךְ הִפִּילָה רוּחַ אוֹ כָּל דָּבָר שֶׁאֵינוֹ שֶׁל קַיְּימָא – הֲרֵי הִיא בְּחֶזְקָתָהּ, וְדַיָּהּ שַׁעְתָּהּ.

**The Sages taught** in a *baraita*: With regard to a woman who **had a presumptive status that** she was **pregnant and she saw blood, and afterward** she **miscarried air,**[HB] **or anything that is not a viable** fetus, **she retains her presumptive status, and** therefore **her time is sufficient** from that flow of blood, i.e., it renders her impure only from then on, not retroactively, as even a non-viable fetus gives her full pregnancy status.

**NOTES**

**And how much time must pass for the fetus to be known…three months** – וְכַמָּה הַכָּרַת הָעוּבָּר...שְׁלֹשָׁה חֳדָשִׁים: The later authorities discuss the application of this *halakha* in contemporary times. Since modern pregnancy tests can determine pregnancy well before the three-month mark, perhaps this *halakha* should apply to a woman as soon as she has a positive test, especially in light of the fact that woman nowadays generally stop seeing all menstrual blood as soon as they become pregnant (see *Iggerot Moshe*; *Shevet HaLevi*; *Yosef Da'at*).

**HALAKHA**

**And how much time must pass for the fetus to be known…three months** – וְכַמָּה הַכָּרַת הָעוּבָּר...שְׁלֹשָׁה חֳדָשִׁים: The pregnant woman whose time is sufficient, for whom a flow of blood does not render her ritually impure retroactively, is one whose fetus is known to all. This occurs at the end of the third month of pregnancy, in accordance with the opinion of Rabbi Meir (Rambam *Sefer Kedusha*, *Hilkhot Issurei Bia* 9:4 and *Sefer Tahara*, *Hilkhot Metamei Mishkav UMoshav* 4:1; *Shulḥan Arukh*, *Yoreh De'a* 189:33).

**Afterward she miscarried air, etc.** – אַחַר כָּךְ הִפִּילָה רוּחַ וכו׳: If a woman had a presumptive status that she was pregnant and she saw a flow of blood, and afterward she miscarried air, or anything that is not a viable fetus, she retains her presumptive status and her time is sufficient (Rambam *Sefer Tahara*, *Hilkhot Metamei Mishkav UMoshav* 4:1).

**BACKGROUND**

**She miscarried air** – הִפִּילָה רוּחַ: Sometimes, due to psychological or physical factors, a woman may experience a false, or phantom, pregnancy. In such a case, the woman may feel her uterus expand, her period may stop, and sometimes she may experience labor pains, even though there is no fetus. This is what the Gemara is referring to when it says she miscarried air.

וְאַף עַל גַּב שֶׁאֵין רְאָיָה לַדָּבָר – זֵכֶר לַדָּבָר, שֶׁנֶּאֱמַר: ״הָרִינוּ חַלְנוּ כְּמוֹ יָלַדְנוּ רוּחַ״. מַאי ״זֵכֶר לַדָּבָר״? הֲרֵי רְאָיָה גְּדוֹלָה הִיא! כִּי כְּתִיב הַאי קְרָא – בִּזְכָרִים כְּתִיב.

**And even though there is no** explicit **proof for** this **matter,** that even a pregnancy that ends in a miscarriage is like a full-fledged pregnancy, there is **an allusion to the matter, as it is stated: "We have been with child, we have been in pain, we have as it were brought forth wind"** (Isaiah 26:18). This verse indicates that even one who miscarries wind is considered as having been with child. The Gemara asks: **What** is the reason that this is called a mere **allusion to the matter?** This explicit verse **is a significant proof.** The Gemara answers: **When that verse was written,** it was **written with regard to males** as bearing children. The allusion to child-bearing in the verse is symbolic, so halakhic inferences may not be drawn from it.

וּרְמִינְהִי: קָשְׁתָה שְׁנַיִם, וְלַשְּׁלִישִׁי הִפִּילָה רוּחַ אוֹ כָּל דָּבָר שֶׁאֵינוֹ שֶׁל קַיָּימָא – הֲרֵי זוֹ יוֹלֶדֶת בְּזוֹב. וְאִי אָמְרַתְּ לֵידָה מְעַלַּיְיתָא הִיא,

**And** the Gemara **raises a contradiction** from a *baraita*: If a woman experienced **labor** pain for **two** days, during which she saw a discharge of blood, **and on the third** day **she miscarried air or anything that is not a viable** fetus, **that** woman **gives birth as a *zava*,** and the blood is treated as blood of a *zava* in all regards. The Gemara explains the contradiction: **And if you say** that miscarrying a non-viable fetus **is** considered **a proper birth,** this is problematic,

Perek **I**
Daf **9** Amud **a**

HALAKHA

**She saw blood and only afterward her fetus became known** – רָאֲתָה וְאַחַר כָּךְ הוּכַּר עוּבָּרָהּ: If a pregnant woman saw menstrual blood and it was only afterward that her fetus became known, she assumes retroactive impurity status like any normal woman. This is in accordance with Rabbi Zeira's answer to Rabbi Yirmeya's question (Rambam *Sefer Tahara, Hilkhot Metamei Mishkav UMoshav* 4:1).

קוֹשִׁי סָמוּךְ לַלֵּידָה רַחֲמָנָא טַהֲרֵיהּ! אָמַר רַב פַּפֵּי: הַנַּח מֵעֵת לְעֵת – דְּרַבָּנַן.

as with regard to blood emitted while experiencing **labor** pain **close to** the time of a proper **birth, the Merciful One deems it pure,** and it should not be treated as the blood of a *zava*. **Rav Pappi says:** The miscarriage is not considered a proper birth and therefore her blood is considered the blood of a *zava*. And **leave** aside the first *baraita* and do not raise a contradiction from it, as the *halakha* that a woman who sees menstrual blood is retroactively impure **for** a twenty-four-hour **period,** which is the topic under discussion in that *baraita*, applies **by rabbinic law,** and they did not impose this stringency in the case of a woman who miscarries.

רַב פָּפָּא אָמַר: מִידֵּי הוּא טַעְמָא – אֶלָּא מִשּׁוּם דְּרֹאשָׁהּ כָּבֵד עָלֶיהָ וְאֵבָרֶיהָ כְּבֵדִין עָלֶיהָ, הָכָא נַמִי – רֹאשָׁהּ וְאֵבָרֶיהָ כְּבֵדִין עָלֶיהָ.

**Rav Pappa says: That reason** for the *halakha* that a pregnant woman is not retroactively impure when she experiences bleeding is **only because her head and limbs** feel **heavy to her.** Her physical state is compromised, which also causes her regular menstrual cycle to cease. **Here, too,** in the case of a pregnancy that precedes a miscarriage, even if it is not considered a proper birth, **her head and limbs** felt **heavy to her** during her pregnancy, and therefore it can be assumed that she did not experience a prior menstrual flow.

בְּעָא מִינֵּיהּ רַבִּי יִרְמְיָה מֵרַבִּי זֵירָא: רָאֲתָה וְאַחַר כָּךְ הוּכַּר עוּבָּרָהּ, מַהוּ? כֵּיוָן דִּבְעִידָּנָא דַּחֲזַאי לָא הוּכַּר עוּבָּרָהּ – מְטַמְּיָא, אוֹ דִלְמָא: כֵּיוָן דִּסְמוּךְ לַהּ חֲזַאי לָא מְטַמְּיָא?

With regard to the mishna's ruling that the time of a pregnant woman is sufficient, **Rabbi Yirmeya asked Rabbi Zeira:** If **she saw** blood **and** only **afterward her fetus became known**[H] to all who see her, **what is the** *halakha*? One can claim that **since at the time when she saw** the blood **her fetus was not** yet **known,** therefore she **becomes impure; or perhaps, since she saw** blood **in close** proximity **to** the time that her fetus became known, she does **not become impure.**

אָמַר לֵיהּ: מִידֵּי הוּא טַעְמָא – אֶלָּא מִשּׁוּם דְּרֹאשָׁהּ כָּבֵד עָלֶיהָ וְאֵבָרֶיהָ כְּבֵדִין עָלֶיהָ, בְּעִידָּנָא דַּחֲזַאי – אֵין רֹאשָׁהּ כָּבֵד עָלֶיהָ וְאֵין אֵבָרֶיהָ כְּבֵדִין עָלֶיהָ.

Rabbi Zeira **said to him: That reason** for the *halakha* that a pregnant woman's time is sufficient is **only because her head and limbs** feel **heavy to her.** In this case, where she was yet unaware of her pregnancy **at the time when she saw** her menstrual flow, **neither her head nor her limbs** felt **heavy to her.** Therefore she is impure retroactively, like any other woman.

בְּעָא מִינֵּיהּ הַהוּא סָבָא מֵרַבִּי יוֹחָנָן: הִגִּיעַ עֵת וִסְתָּהּ בִּימֵי עִבּוּרָהּ וְלֹא בָּדְקָה, מַהוּ? קָא מִיבַּעְיָא לִי אַלִּיבָּא דְּמַאן דַּאֲמַר וְסָתוֹת דְּאוֹרַיְיתָא. מַאי! כֵּיוָן דִּוְסָתוֹת דְּאוֹרַיְיתָא – בָּעֲיָא בְּדִיקָה, אוֹ דִּלְמָא: כֵּיוָן דְּדָמֶיהָ מְסוּלָּקִין, לָא בָּעֲיָא בְּדִיקָה?

§ **A certain elder asked Rabbi Yoḥanan:** If the **time** of a woman's fixed menstrual **cycle arrived during her pregnancy and she did not perform an examination, what is** the *halakha*? **I raise** this **dilemma** only **according to** the opinion **of the one who said** that the obligation for a woman to perform a self-examination during her fixed menstrual **cycle** applies **by Torah law. What** is the *halakha*? According to that opinion, one can claim that **since** the obligation of an examination during one's fixed menstrual **cycle** is **by Torah law,** she is **required** to perform **an examination** even during her pregnancy. **Or perhaps, since her blood has stopped,** as a pregnant woman generally does not experience a flow of menstrual blood, she is **not required** to perform **an examination.**

אֲמַר לֵיהּ, תְּנֵיתוּהָ: רַבִּי מֵאִיר אוֹמֵר, אִם הָיְתָה בְּמַחֲבֵא וְהִגִּיעַ שְׁעַת וִסְתָּהּ וְלֹא בָּדְקָה – טְהוֹרָה, שֶׁחֲרָדָה מְסַלֶּקֶת אֶת הַדָּמִים. טַעְמָא – דְּאִיכָּא חֲרָדָה, הָא לֵיכָּא חֲרָדָה וְהִגִּיעַ וִסְתָּהּ וְלֹא בָּדְקָה – טְמֵאָה,

Rabbi Yoḥanan **said to him: You learned** the answer to your dilemma from a mishna (39a): **Rabbi Meir says: If** a woman **was in hiding** from danger, **and the time of her** fixed menstrual **cycle came and she did not examine** herself,[H] nevertheless she is **ritually pure, as** it may be assumed that she did not experience bleeding because **fear dispels** the flow of menstrual **blood.** Rabbi Yoḥanan explains the proof: The **reason** she is pure is **that there is fear,** from which it may be inferred that in a case where **there is no fear and the time of her** fixed menstrual **cycle arrived and she did not examine** herself, she would be **impure.**

אַלְמָא: וְסָתוֹת דְּאוֹרַיְיתָא. וְכֵיוָן דְּאִיכָּא חֲרָדָה – דָּמֶיהָ מְסוּלָּקִין, וְלָא בָּעֲיָא בְּדִיקָה. הָכָא נַמִי – דָּמֶיהָ מְסוּלָּקִין, וְלָא בָּעֲיָא בְּדִיקָה.

Rabbi Yoḥanan concludes: **Evidently,** from the fact that Rabbi Meir rules that a woman is impure if the time of her period passed without a proper examination, he maintains that the obligation for a woman to perform an examination at the time of her fixed menstrual **cycle** applies **by Torah law. And,** nevertheless, **since there is fear, her blood has stopped and** she is **not required** to perform **an examination. Here, too,** in the case of a pregnant woman, **her blood has stopped and** therefore she is **not required** to perform **an examination.**

"מֵנִיקָה עַד שֶׁתִּגְמוֹל" וכו׳. תָּנוּ רַבָּנַן: מֵנִיקָה שֶׁמֵּת בְּנָהּ בְּתוֹךְ עֶשְׂרִים וְאַרְבַּע חֹדֶשׁ – הֲרֵי הִיא כְּכָל הַנָּשִׁים, וּמְטַמְּאָה מֵעֵת לְעֵת וּמִפְּקִידָה לִפְקִידָה. לְפִיכָךְ, אִם הָיְתָה מֵנִיקָתוֹ וְהוֹלֶכֶת אַרְבַּע אוֹ חָמֵשׁ שָׁנִים – דַּיָּהּ שָׁעָתָהּ, דִּבְרֵי רַבִּי מֵאִיר.

§ The mishna teaches: The time of **a nursing woman** is sufficient **until she weans** her child[H] from nursing. **The Sages taught** in a *baraita* (see *Tosefta* 2:1): With regard to **a nursing woman whose child dies within twenty-four months** of his birth, **she is like all** other **women** with regard to her impurity status after seeing menstrual blood, **and** therefore **she transmits ritual impurity** retroactively **for** a twenty-four-hour **period or from examination to examination. Therefore, if** a woman **continued to nurse** her child **for four or five years, her time is sufficient** and she does not retroactively transmit impurity for the entire four or five years. This is **the statement of Rabbi Meir.**

רַבִּי יְהוּדָה וְרַבִּי יוֹסֵי וְרַבִּי שִׁמְעוֹן אוֹמְרִים: דַּיָּין שָׁעָתָן כָּל עֶשְׂרִים וְאַרְבַּע חֹדֶשׁ, לְפִיכָךְ, אִם הָיְתָה מֵנִיקָתוֹ אַרְבַּע וְחָמֵשׁ שָׁנִים – מְטַמְּאָה מֵעֵת לְעֵת וּמִפְּקִידָה לִפְקִידָה.

**Rabbi Yehuda and Rabbi Yosei and Rabbi Shimon** all **say:** With regard to nursing women, **their time is sufficient** for **an entire twenty-four months. Therefore, if she nursed him for four or five years,**[H] then after the first twenty-four months have passed, **she transmits ritual impurity** retroactively **for** a twenty-four-hour **period or from examination to examination.**

**HALAKHA**

**If a woman was in hiding and the time of her fixed menstrual cycle came and she did not examine herself – הָיְתָה בְּמַחֲבֵא וְהִגִּיעַ שְׁעַת וִסְתָּהּ וְלֹא בָּדְקָה:** If a woman was in a hiding place to escape harm, she need not be concerned for her menstrual cycle if its time arrives while she is in hiding. The Rema cites an opinion that she is required to perform a self-examination *ab initio*. If she did not, she remains ritually pure as long as she did not feel an internal sensation that accompanies a menstrual flow (Rambam *Sefer Kedusha, Hilkhot Issurei Bia* 8:12; *Shulḥan Arukh, Yoreh De'a* 184:8).

**The time of a nursing woman is sufficient until she weans her child – מֵנִיקָה עַד שֶׁתִּגְמוֹל:** The *halakha* is in accordance with the opinion of Rabbi Eliezer that when a nursing woman sees menstrual blood, her time is sufficient and she does not transmit impurity retroactively until twenty-four months from the time of her child's birth. Even if the child dies or she weans him or gives him to a nursemaid within that time frame, nevertheless her time is sufficient (Rambam *Sefer Tahara, Hilkhot Metamei Mishkav UMoshav* 4:1).

**She nursed him for four or five years – הָיְתָה מֵנִיקָתוֹ אַרְבַּע וְחָמֵשׁ שָׁנִים:** The *halakha* is in accordance with the opinion of the opinion of Rabbi Yehuda, Rabbi Yosei, and Rabbi Shimon that if a woman was nursing her child for four or five years and she sees menstrual blood, she transmits impurity retroactively like any normal woman (Rambam *Sefer Tahara, Hilkhot Metamei Mishkav UMoshav* 4:1).

כְּשֶׁתִּמְצָא לוֹמַר, לְדִבְרֵי רַבִּי מֵאִיר – דָּם נֶעְכָּר וְנַעֲשֶׂה חָלָב, לְדִבְרֵי רַבִּי יוֹסֵי וְרַבִּי יְהוּדָה וְרַבִּי שִׁמְעוֹן – אֵבָרֶיהָ מִתְפָּרְקִין, וְאֵין נַפְשָׁהּ חוֹזֶרֶת עַד עֶשְׂרִים וְאַרְבַּע חֹדֶשׁ.

The Gemara discusses the reasoning of each opinion: **When** you analyze the matter **you will find** that one must **say that according to the statement of Rabbi Meir** the case is that menstrual **blood spoils and becomes milk.**[B] Therefore, it follows that this status continues for as long as she is nursing. By contrast, **according to the statement of Rabbi Yosei and Rabbi Yehuda and Rabbi Shimon, her limbs become dislocated**[B] **and her spirit,** i.e., her full strength and her regular menstrual cycle, **does not return** to her **until twenty-four months** have passed.

״לְפִיכָךְ״ דְּרַבִּי מֵאִיר לָמָּה לִי? מִשּׁוּם ״לְפִיכָךְ״ דְּרַבִּי יוֹסֵי.

The Gemara asks: **Why do I** need the statement **of Rabbi Meir: Therefore,** if a woman continued to nurse her child for four or five years, her time is sufficient? Since his reasoning is that the menstrual blood of a nursing woman spoils and becomes milk, it is obvious that this applies as long as she continues to nurse him. The Gemara answers: This statement is indeed extraneous. It merely serves to form a parallel between the statement of Rabbi Meir and that of the other Sages. In other words, it was appended **due to** the statement: **Therefore,** if she was nursing him for four or five years, then after the first twenty-four months have passed, she transmits ritual impurity retroactively for a twenty-four-hour period or from examination to examination, which is referring to the opinion **of Rabbi Yosei.**

וּ״לְפִיכָךְ״ דְּרַבִּי יוֹסֵי לָמָּה לִי? מַהוּ דְּתֵימָא: רַבִּי יוֹסֵי תַּרְתֵּי אִית לֵיהּ, קָא מַשְׁמַע לַן.

The Gemara further asks: **And why do I** need the statement: **Therefore,** if she was nursing him for four or five years, then after the first twenty-four months have passed, she transmits ritual impurity retroactively for a twenty-four-hour period or from examination to examination, which is referring to the opinion **of Rabbi Yosei?** The Gemara explains that this clause is necessary, **lest you say** that **Rabbi Yosei holds** that there are **two** reasons that a pregnant woman's time is sufficient, both because her blood spoils and because her limbs become dislocated. Therefore, the additional clause **teaches us** that Rabbi Yosei maintains that the reason is only that her limbs become dislocated, and consequently she transmits retroactive impurity after twenty-four months.

תַּנְיָא נַמִי הָכִי: דָּם נֶעְכָּר וְנַעֲשֶׂה חָלָב, דִּבְרֵי רַבִּי מֵאִיר. רַבִּי יוֹסֵי אוֹמֵר: אֵבָרֶיהָ מִתְפָּרְקִין, וְאֵין נַפְשָׁהּ חוֹזֶרֶת עָלֶיהָ עַד עֶשְׂרִים וְאַרְבַּע חֹדֶשׁ. אָמַר רַבִּי אֶלְעַאי: מַאי טַעְמָא דְּרַבִּי מֵאִיר – דִּכְתִיב: ״מִי יִתֵּן טָהוֹר מִטָּמֵא לֹא אֶחָד״.

**That** explanation **is also taught** in a *baraita*: Menstrual **blood spoils and becomes milk;** this is **the statement of Rabbi Meir. Rabbi Yosei says: Her limbs become dislocated and her spirit does not return to her until twenty-four months** have passed. The Gemara analyzes their respective reasons. **Rabbi Ilai says: What is the reason of Rabbi Meir?** It is based upon a verse, **as it is written: "Who can bring a pure thing out of an impure? Is it not the One?"** (Job 14:4). In other words, is it not true that the One, i.e., God, can bring a pure thing, such as milk, out of an impure thing, such as menstrual blood?

וְרַבָּנַן – אָמַר רַבִּי יוֹחָנָן: זוֹ שִׁכְבַת זֶרַע, שֶׁהוּא – טָמֵא, וְאָדָם הַנּוֹצָר מִמֶּנּוּ – טָהוֹר.

The Gemara asks: **And the** other **Sages,** i.e., Rabbi Yosei, Rabbi Yehuda, and Rabbi Shimon, how do they interpret this verse? **Rabbi Yoḥanan says** that according to those Sages **this** verse is referring to **semen, which is impure,** and yet **the person that is formed from it is pure.**

**BACKGROUND**

Blood spoils and becomes milk – דָּם נֶעְכָּר וְנַעֲשֶׂה חָלָב: In modern medical terms, this position could be understood to mean that nutrients and materials from the bloodstream are necessary to produce milk.

Her limbs become dislocated – אֵיבָרֶיהָ מִתְפָּרְקִין: According to this explanation, a nursing woman's lack of a menstrual cycle is caused by the pressure imposed on the body due to the birth and nursing. Alternatively, since this woman has a negative energy balance, i.e., she expends more energy than she brings in, the reproductive system does not function, the uterine lining is not developed, and she does not experience her menstrual cycle, which occurs when the uterine lining disintegrates if pregnancy has not been effected. It is interesting to note that various studies have shown that women or female animals with a healthy diet return to their normal menstrual cycle more quickly than those that do not have a healthy diet.

וְרַבִּי אֶלְעָזָר אוֹמֵר: אֵלּוּ מֵי הַנִּדָּה, שֶׁהַמַּזֶּה וּמַזִּין עָלָיו – טָהוֹר, וְנוֹגֵעַ – טָמֵא. וּמַזֶּה טָהוֹר? וְהָכְתִיב: ״וּמַזֵּה מֵי הַנִּדָּה יְכַבֵּס בְּגָדָיו״! מַאי ״מַזֶּה״ – נוֹגֵעַ.

**And Rabbi Elazar says:** Those Sages maintain that this verse is referring to **the water of sprinkling,** i.e., the purification water mixed with the ashes of the red heifer. **As** the individual who **sprinkles** the water and the one **upon whom** the water is **sprinkled** are both **pure,**[H] and yet one who **touches** the purification water is rendered **impure.** The Gemara asks: **Is** the **one who sprinkles** the water actually **pure? But isn't it written: "He who sprinkles the water of sprinkling will wash his clothes,** and he who touches the water of sprinkling will be impure until evening" (Numbers 19:21)? The Gemara responds: **What** is the meaning of the term: **"He who sprinkles"?** It means: **He who touches.**

וְהָכְתִיב ״מַזֶּה״, וְהָכְתִיב ״נוֹגֵעַ״? וְעוֹד, מַזֶּה – בָּעֵי כִּבּוּס, נוֹגֵעַ – לָא בָּעֵי כִּבּוּס! אֶלָּא: מַאי ״מַזֶּה״ – נוֹשֵׂא.

The Gemara asks: **But it is written: "He who sprinkles," and it is written** in the same verse: "And **he who touches."** How can these two terms be referring to the same individual? **And furthermore,** that verse states that **one who sprinkles requires** the **washing** of his **clothes,** indicating a severe level of impurity, whereas **one who touches does not require** the **washing** of his **clothes.** Evidently, the phrase "he who sprinkles" is not referring to one who touches. **Rather,** the Gemara explains: **What** is the meaning of: **"He who sprinkles"?** This is referring to **one who carries** the purification waters.

וְלִיכְתּוֹב ״נוֹשֵׂא״! קָא מַשְׁמַע לַן דְּעַד דְּהָוֵי כְּשִׁיעוּר הַזָּאָה. הָנִיחָא לְמַאן דְּאָמַר הַזָּאָה צְרִיכָה שִׁיעוּר, אֶלָּא לְמַאן דְּאָמַר אֵין צְרִיכָה שִׁיעוּר, מַאי אִיכָּא לְמֵימַר?

The Gemara asks: **But** if so, **let** the Torah **write** explicitly: **One who carries.** Why does it state "he who sprinkles" when it is referring to carrying? The Gemara answers: The use of the term sprinkling in reference to carrying **teaches us** that one becomes impure **only by carrying** the **measure** required for **sprinkling.** The Gemara asks: **This works out well according to the one who said** that **sprinkling requires** a minimum **measure** of water. **But according to the one who said** that **sprinkling does not require** a minimum **measure** of water, **what can be said?** According to this opinion, there is apparently no concept of a measure required for sprinkling.

אֲפִילּוּ לְמַאן דְּאָמַר אֵינָהּ צְרִיכָה שִׁיעוּר, הָנֵי מִילֵּי – אַגַּבָּא דְּגַבְרָא, אֲבָל בְּמָנָא – בָּעֵינָא שִׁיעוּר. כִּדְתְנַן: כַּמָּה יְהוּ בַּמַּיִם וִיהֵא בָּהֶן כְּדֵי הַזָּאָה? כְּדֵי שֶׁיִּטְבּוֹל רָאשֵׁי גִבְעוֹלִין וְיַזֶּה.

The Gemara answers: **Even according to the one who said** that **sprinkling does not require** a minimum **measure** of water, **that statement** applies only to the measure of purification water that must be sprinkled **onto the back,** i.e., onto the body, **of** the impure **man.** In this regard, any amount will suffice. **But with regard to the vessel** into which one dips the hyssop in order to sprinkle the water, it **requires** a certain **measure** of water. **As we learned** in a mishna (*Para* 12:5): **How much** water must **be in** the vessel so that it **will be enough for sprinkling?** It must be **enough to dip the tops of the stems** of the hyssop branch, used in the rite of purification, into the water **and sprinkle** it.[H]

וְהַיְינוּ דְּאָמַר שְׁלֹמֹה: ״אָמַרְתִּי אֶחְכָּמָה וְהִיא רְחוֹקָה מִמֶּנִּי״.

The Gemara concludes the discussion of the purification waters with the following observation: **And that is** the meaning of that **which** King **Solomon said: "I said I would become wise, but it eludes me"** (Ecclesiastes 7:23). According to tradition, even Solomon in his great wisdom could not understand the contradictory nature of the sprinkling of purification water, as it renders an impure person pure, and a pure person impure.

״אֵיזוֹ הִיא זְקֵנָה – כׇּל שֶׁעָבְרוּ עָלֶיהָ שָׁלֹשׁ עוֹנוֹת״ [סָמוּךְ לְזִקְנָתָהּ]. הֵיכִי דָּמֵי ״סָמוּךְ לְזִקְנָתָהּ״? אָמַר רַב יְהוּדָה: כׇּל שֶׁחַבְרוֹתֶיהָ אוֹמְרוֹת עָלֶיהָ ״זְקֵנָה הִיא״. וְרַבִּי שִׁמְעוֹן אוֹמֵר:

§ The mishna teaches: **Who is** the woman characterized as **an elderly woman** in this context? It is **any** woman for **whom three** typical menstrual **cycles** of thirty days **passed** at a stage of her life **close to her old age,** during which she saw no menstrual blood. The Gemara asks: **What is considered close to old age? Rav Yehuda says: Any** woman **about whom her friends say** that **she is an elderly woman. And Rabbi Shimon says:**[N]

## HALAKHA

**As the individual who sprinkles the water and the one upon whom the water is sprinkled are both pure, etc.** – שֶׁהַמַּזֶּה וּמַזִּין עָלָיו טָהוֹר וכו׳: A person or a vessel that comes into contact with a small amount of purification water before it is sprinkled is rendered impure, but it does not render his garments impure. If there was a minimum measure of water, then one who touches the water or carries it is rendered impure, and even his garments are rendered impure while he touches the water. The one who sprinkles the purification water on an impure person remains pure. Tradition teaches that the verse "He who sprinkles the purification waters will wash his clothes" is referring to a case where the water has the minimum measure. Only in that case are the garments of one who touches or carries the purification water rendered impure (Rambam *Sefer Tahara, Hilkhot Para Aduma* 15:1).

**It must be enough to dip the tops of the stems of the hyssop branch into the water and sprinkle it** – כְּדֵי שֶׁיִּטְבּוֹל רָאשֵׁי גִבְעוֹלִין וְיַזֶּה: The measure required for sprinkling the water of purification is equivalent to the measure required to dip the tops of the stems of the hyssop branch into the water and sprinkle it (Rambam *Sefer Tahara, Hilkhot Para Aduma* 15:1).

## NOTES

**Rav Yehuda says…and Rabbi Shimon says** – אָמַר רַב יְהוּדָה...וְרַבִּי שִׁמְעוֹן אוֹמֵר: Many commentaries note that this is not the *tanna* Rabbi Shimon but rather Rabbi Shimon ben Lakish, the *amora* (*Gilyon HaShas*, citing *Taz* and *Torat HaBayit*). This stands to reason, as an *amora* such as Rav Yehuda would not disagree with a *tanna*, and the Gemara certainly would not cite his opinion before that of a *tanna*. This claim is supported by variant texts as well as the Jerusalem Talmud, where the opinion of Reish Lakish is cited without a disputant.

**LANGUAGE**

Mother [*Imma*] – אִמָּא: *Imma* is the name one calls his own mother, but it was also the word used to describe a specific elderly woman: Mother so-and-so. It became a polite way to refer to elderly women.

**NOTES**

**It is any woman who is old enough that people call her: Mother, Mother – כָּל שֶׁקּוֹרִין לָהּ אִמָּא אִמָּא:** *Tosafot* cite a question posed by the Jerusalem Talmud: How can the test for determining if one is an elderly woman who does not experience regular menstruation be dependent upon her subjective perspective? They explain that the Gemara means: Any women who is old enough that it is fitting to call her: Mother, Mother.

**The average menstrual cycle is thirty days long – עוֹנָה בֵּינוֹנִית שְׁלֹשִׁים יוֹם:** There are three main opinions among the authorities with regard to the average menstrual cycle: Some claim that it means that the menstruation will begin on a particular day of the month, whether the month has twenty-nine days or thirty days. They explain that when the Gemara refers to an average thirty-day cycle, it is actually referring to a month, as the Sages referred to the period of a month as: Thirty days (*Shakh*). Others maintain that an average menstrual cycle recurs on the thirty-first day (*Ḥavvot Da'at*). The majority opinion is that it recurs on the thirtieth day (*Ḥakham Tzvi*; *Beit Yosef*; Rema; *Perisha*; *Baḥ*; *Levush*).

כָּל שֶׁקּוֹרִין לָהּ ״אִמָּא, אִמָּא״ וְאֵינָהּ בּוֹשָׁה. רַבִּי זֵירָא וְרַבִּי שְׁמוּאֵל בַּר רַב יִצְחָק, חַד אָמַר: כָּל שֶׁאֵינָהּ מַקְפֶּדֶת, וְחַד אָמַר: כָּל שֶׁאֵינָהּ בּוֹשָׁה. מַאי בֵּינַיְיהוּ? אִיכָּא בֵּינַיְיהוּ: בּוֹשָׁה וְאֵינָהּ מַקְפֶּדֶת.

It is any woman who is old enough **that** people **call her: Mother** [*Imma*],[L] **Mother,**[N] **and she is not embarrassed.**[H] **Rabbi Zeira and Rabbi Shmuel bar Rav Yitzḥak** disagree with regard to this matter. **One says** that the definition is **any** woman **who does not take offense** about being called: Mother, Mother. **And** the other **one says** that it is **any woman who is not embarrassed** by this. The Gemara asks: **What is the difference between** their definitions? The Gemara answers: The practical difference **between** them is in a case where a woman is **embarrassed but she does not take offense** when called: Mother.

וְכַמָּה עוֹנָה? אָמַר רֵישׁ לָקִישׁ מִשּׁוּם רַבִּי יְהוּדָה נְשִׂיאָה: עוֹנָה בֵּינוֹנִית, שְׁלֹשִׁים יוֹם. וְרָבָא אָמַר רַב חִסְדָּא: עֶשְׂרִים יוֹם. וְלָא פְּלִיגִי, מָר קָחָשֵׁיב יְמֵי טוּמְאָה וִימֵי טׇהֳרָה, וּמָר לָא חָשֵׁיב יְמֵי טוּמְאָה.

The Gemara asks: **And how long** is a typical menstrual **cycle?**[H] **Reish Lakish says in the name of Rabbi Yehuda Nesia:** The **average** menstrual **cycle** is **thirty days** long.[N] **And Rava says** that **Rav Ḥisda** says: It is **twenty days.** The Gemara notes: **And** they **do not disagree.** One **Sage,** Rav Yehuda Nesia, **counts** all the days of her cycle, including the **days of impurity and days of purity. And** the other **Sage,** Rav Ḥisda, **does not count** the **days of impurity,** i.e., the seven days of impurity of a menstruating woman and the three days of the sighting of *ziva*.

תָּנוּ רַבָּנַן: זְקֵנָה שֶׁעָבְרוּ עָלֶיהָ שָׁלֹשׁ עוֹנוֹת וְרָאֲתָה – דַּיָּהּ שַׁעְתָּהּ, וְעוֹד עָבְרוּ עָלֶיהָ שָׁלֹשׁ עוֹנוֹת וְרָאֲתָה – דַּיָּהּ שַׁעְתָּהּ, וְעוֹד עָבְרוּ עָלֶיהָ שָׁלֹשׁ עוֹנוֹת וְרָאֲתָה – הֲרֵי הִיא כְּכׇל הַנָּשִׁים, וּמְטַמְּאָה מֵעֵת לְעֵת וּמִפְּקִידָה לִפְקִידָה.

§ **The Sages taught** in a *baraita*: With regard to **an elderly woman** for **whom three** typical menstrual **cycles** of thirty days **passed**[H] **and** then **she saw** a discharge of menstrual blood, **her time is sufficient. And if a further three** typical menstrual **cycles** of thirty days **passed for her and she** subsequently **saw** a discharge of menstrual blood, **her time is sufficient. And** if yet **a further three** typical menstrual **cycles** of thirty days **passed for her and** then **she saw** a discharge of menstrual blood, after this third time **she is** now **like all** normal **women,** and she **transmits impurity** retroactively **for** a twenty-four-hour **period or from examination to examination.**

וְלָא (מִיבַּעְיָא) שֶׁכִּוְּונָה, אֶלָּא אֲפִילּוּ פִּיחֲתָה (וַאֲפִילּוּ) וְהוֹתִירָה.

The *baraita* continues: **And it is not necessary** to teach this *halakha* in a case **where she** experienced the three sightings in **even** intervals of ninety days, as in such a case it is obvious that she assumes the status of a normal woman who transmits impurity retroactively. **Rather, even if she** had intervals where she **decreased,** i.e., experienced bleeding at intervals smaller than that, **or even if she increased** and experienced bleeding at greater intervals, she still assumes the status of a woman who transmits impurity retroactively.

אֲפִילּוּ פִּיחֲתָה, וְלָא מִבָּעֲיָא כִּוְּונָה? אַדְּרַבָּה, כִּי כִּוְּונָה – קָבְעָה לָהּ וֶסֶת, וְדַיָּהּ שַׁעְתָּהּ!

The Gemara infers: The wording of the *baraita*: **Even if she** had intervals where she **decreased,** indicates that **it is not necessary** to teach the *halakha* in the case of a woman who experienced bleeding at **even** intervals. This is puzzling, as **on the contrary, if she** experienced bleeding at **even** intervals she thereby **fixes her** menstrual **cycle** as being every thirty days, **and** according to Rabbi Dosa (4b) the *halakha* is that **her time is sufficient.**

**HALAKHA**

**Any woman who is old enough that people call her: Mother, Mother, and she is not embarrassed – כָּל שֶׁקּוֹרִין לָהּ אִמָּא אִמָּא וְאֵינָהּ בּוֹשָׁה:** An elderly woman whose time is sufficient when she experiences a menstrual flow is defined as one who is old enough that when people call her an old woman she is not particular about it. This *halakha* is in accordance with the opinion of Rabbi Shimon, as Rabbi Zeira and Rabbi Shmuel bar Rav Yitzḥak seem to support it. It is also in accordance with Rabbi Shmuel bar Rav Yitzḥak, as he holds the more lenient opinion. This is a matter of rabbinic law, and the principle in the case of rabbinic law is that in cases of uncertainty the *halakha* is in accordance with the more lenient opinion (Rambam *Sefer Tahara*, *Hilkhot Metamei Mishkav UMoshav* 4:1).

**And how long is a typical menstrual cycle – וְכַמָּה עוֹנָה:** Any woman who does not have a fixed menstrual cycle must assume that she will experience menstruation on the thirtieth day from her last menstruation, as the average cycle lasts thirty days. Some say it is thirty-one days long (*Shulḥan Arukh*, *Yoreh De'a* 189:1, and see *Shakh* and *Ḥavvot Da'at* there).

**An elderly woman for whom three typical menstrual cycles of thirty days passed – זְקֵנָה שֶׁעָבְרוּ עָלֶיהָ שָׁלֹשׁ עוֹנוֹת:** If an elderly woman who had stopped menstruating experiences menstruation after a break of three typical menstrual cycles and then again after another three menstrual cycles, even if they are shorter or longer than the first set, she then returns to the status of normal women and transmits impurity retroactively (Rambam *Sefer Tahara*, *Hilkhot Metamei Mishkav UMoshav* 4:1, and see *Kesef Mishne* there).

וכי תימא: רבנן היא, דפליגי עליה דרבי דוסא, דאמרי אשה שיש לה וסת – מטמאה מעת לעת, איפכא מבעי ליה, ולימא: ולא שפיחתה והותירה, אלא אפילו כוונה!

**And if you would say** that this **is** in accordance with the opinion of **the Rabbis, who disagree with Rabbi Dosa, as they say** that **a woman who has** a fixed menstrual **cycle transmits impurity** retroactively **for** a twenty-four-hour **period,** then the *baraita* **should have** been written in the **opposite** fashion: **Let** it **say: And** the *halakha* that an elderly woman who sees menstrual blood at intervals returns to the status of normal women and transmits impurity retroactively applies **not** only to a case where she had intervals where **she decreased or increased,** i.e., she experienced bleeding less or more than ninety days apart, **but** this *halakha* applies **even** if she experienced bleeding at **even** intervals.

תני: לא שפיחתה והותירה אלא אפילו כוונה. ואיבעית אימא, הכי קאמר: ולא שכוונה אלא שפיחתה והותירה, אבל כוונה – קבעה לה וסת ודיה שעתה, ומני – רבי דוסא היא.

The Gemara answers: **Teach** in the *baraita* in accordance with this altered version: **And** the *halakha* applies **not** only to a case where she had intervals where **she decreased or increased, but** this is the *halakha* **even** if she experienced bleeding at **even** intervals. **And if you wish say** instead that **this** is what the *baraita* **is saying:** The *halakha* that an elderly woman is retroactively impure does **not** apply to a case when she saw menstrual blood at **even** intervals. **Rather,** it applies only if **she decreased or increased,** i.e., she experienced bleeding at intervals less or more than ninety days apart. **But** if she saw blood at **even** intervals, she thereby **fixes** a set menstrual **cycle** of ninety days and her time is sufficient. The Gemara adds: **And** if so, in accordance with **whose** opinion is this *baraita*? **It is** in accordance with the opinion of **Rabbi Dosa.**

"רבי אליעזר אומר: כל אשה שעברו עליה" וכו׳. תניא, אמר להם רבי אליעזר לחכמים: מעשה בריבה אחת בהיתלו שהפסיקה שלש עונות, ובא מעשה לפני חכמים ואמרו דיה שעתה.

§ The mishna teaches that **Rabbi Eliezer says:** With regard to **any woman** for **whom** three typical menstrual cycles **passed** during which she saw no menstrual blood, if she experiences bleeding, her time is sufficient. Rabbi Yosei says: In the case of a pregnant woman and a nursing woman for whom three menstrual cycles passed during which they saw no menstrual blood, if she then saw blood her time is sufficient. Rabbi Eliezer cites a proof for his opinion. It **is taught** in a *baraita*: There was **an incident involving a certain girl in** the village of **Hitlo who stopped** menstruating **for three** typical menstrual **cycles,** after which she experienced menstruation. **And the matter came before the Sages, and they said** that **her time is sufficient** and she does not transmit impurity retroactively.

אמרו לו: אין שעת הדחק ראיה. מאי "שעת הדחק"? איכא דאמרי: שני בצורת הוו, איכא דאמרי: טהרות אפיש לעבידא, וחשו רבנן להפסד דטהרות.

The other Sages **said to** Rabbi Eliezer: Decisions rendered **in exigent circumstances are no proof.** The Gemara asks: **What** were the **exigent circumstances? Some say** that **it was** during the **years of famine,** and **some say** that the girl had **handled many ritually pure** items **and the Sages were concerned for the loss** of those **pure** items if they were ruled retroactively impure.

תנו רבנן, מעשה ועשה רבי כרבי אליעזר, לאחר שנזכר אמר: כדי הוא רבי אליעזר לסמוך עליו בשעת הדחק. מאי "לאחר שנזכר"? אילימא – לאחר שנזכר דאין הלכה כרבי אליעזר אלא כרבנן, בשעת הדחק היכי עביד כוותיה?

**The Sages taught** in a *baraita*: There was **an incident** in which **Rabbi** Yehuda HaNasi **acted** by ruling that the *halakha* **is in accordance with** the opinion of **Rabbi Eliezer. After he remembered** that Rabbi Eliezer's colleagues disagree with him on this matter and that he had apparently ruled incorrectly, **he** nevertheless **said: Rabbi Eliezer is worthy to rely upon in exigent circumstances.** The Gemara asks: **What** is the meaning of: **After he remembered? If we say** that this means **after he remembered** that the ***halakha*** is **not in accordance with** the opinion of **Rabbi Eliezer, but in accordance with** the opinion of **the Rabbis,** if so, **how could he act in accordance with** Rabbi Eliezer even **in exigent circumstances,** since the *halakha* has been decided against him?

אלא – דלא איתמר הילכתא לא כמר ולא כמר, ומאי "לאחר שנזכר" – לאחר שנזכר דלאו יחיד פליג עליה, אלא רבים פליגי עליה, אמר: כדי הוא רבי אליעזר לסמוך עליו בשעת הדחק.

**Rather,** one must say **that** the ***halakha*** had **not been stated** on this matter, **neither in accordance with** the opinion of this **Sage,** Rabbi Eliezer, **nor in accordance with** the opinion of **that Sage,** the Rabbis. **And what** is the meaning of: **After he remembered? After** Rabbi Yehuda HaNasi **remembered that it was not a lone** authority who **disagrees with** Rabbi Eliezer, **but** it was several Sages who **disagreed with him,** and there is a principle that the *halakha* is in accordance with the opinion of the many over the opinion of an individual, he nevertheless **said: Rabbi Eliezer is worthy to rely upon in exigent circumstances.**

**HALAKHA**

A young girl whose time to see menstrual blood has not arrived and she saw menstrual blood – תִּינוֹקֶת שֶׁלֹּא הִגִּיעַ זְמַנָּהּ לִרְאוֹת וְרָאֲתָה: With regard to a young girl whose time to see menstrual blood has not arrived, as she is not yet twelve years and one day old (*Shakh*) even if she has two pubic hairs, or even if she is twelve years old but does not yet have two pubic hairs, and she saw menstrual blood once or twice, her time is sufficient. If she sees menstrual blood a third time, she transmits ritual impurity retroactively. If three months pass by and she does not see menstrual blood, when she again sees menstrual blood, her time is sufficient (*Kesef Mishne*). If three months again pass by and she does not see menstrual blood, when she again sees menstrual blood her time is sufficient. If three months pass by for a third time and she sees menstrual blood, she transmits ritual impurity retroactively, in accordance with the *baraita* (Rambam *Sefer Tahara, Hilkhot Metamei Mishkav UMoshav* 4:3; *Shulḥan Arukh, Yoreh De'a* 189:27).

A girl whose time to see menstrual blood has arrived – שֶׁהִגִּיעַ זְמַנָּהּ לִרְאוֹת: With regard to a girl whose time to see menstrual blood has arrived, and she sees menstrual blood for the first time, her time is sufficient. When she sees menstrual blood for the second time, she transmits ritual impurity retroactively. If three months pass without her seeing menstrual blood and then she sees menstrual blood, her time is sufficient. If three months again pass without her seeing menstrual blood and then she sees menstrual blood, she transmits ritual impurity retroactively (Rambam *Sefer Tahara, Hilkhot Metamei Mishkav UMoshav* 4:4).

תָּנוּ רַבָּנַן: תִּינוֹקֶת שֶׁלֹּא הִגִּיעַ זְמַנָּהּ לִרְאוֹת וְרָאֲתָה, פַּעַם רִאשׁוֹנָה – דַּיָּהּ שַׁעְתָּהּ, שְׁנִיָּה – דַּיָּהּ שַׁעְתָּהּ, שְׁלִישִׁית – הֲרֵי הִיא כְּכׇל הַנָּשִׁים, וּמְטַמְּאָה מֵעֵת לְעֵת וּמִפְּקִידָה לִפְקִידָה.

The Gemara continues the discussion of a woman who fails to experience menstruation for three typical menstrual cycles. **The Sages taught** in a *baraita*: With regard to **a young girl,** less than twelve years old, **whose time to see** the flow of menstrual blood **has not arrived and she saw** menstrual blood,[H] after the **first time her time is sufficient.** After the **second time,** again **her time is sufficient.** After the **third time, she is like all** normal adult **women, and** therefore **she transmits impurity** retroactively **for** a twenty-four-hour **period or from examination to examination.**

עָבְרוּ עָלֶיהָ שָׁלֹשׁ עוֹנוֹת וְרָאֲתָה – דַּיָּהּ שַׁעְתָּהּ, וְעוֹד עָבְרוּ עָלֶיהָ שָׁלֹשׁ עוֹנוֹת וְרָאֲתָה – דַּיָּהּ שַׁעְתָּהּ, וְעוֹד עָבְרוּ עָלֶיהָ שָׁלֹשׁ עוֹנוֹת וְרָאֲתָה – הֲרֵי הִיא כְּכׇל הַנָּשִׁים, וּמְטַמְּאָה מֵעֵת לְעֵת וּמִפְּקִידָה לִפְקִידָה.

The *baraita* continues: If she then **passed three** expected menstrual **cycles** without experiencing bleeding, **and** then **she saw** menstrual blood, she returns to the status of a young girl and **her time is sufficient. And** if it **further** happens that she again **passed three** expected menstrual **cycles** without experiencing bleeding, **and** then **she saw** menstrual **blood, her time is sufficient. And** if she **passed three further cycles** without experiencing bleeding, and **she** subsequently **saw** menstrual **blood, she is like all** normal adult **women.** She is considered a woman who experiences regular menstruation at long intervals with breaks of ninety days. **And** therefore **she transmits impurity** retroactively **for** a twenty-four-hour **period or from examination to examination.**

וּכְשֶׁהִגִּיעַ זְמַנָּהּ לִרְאוֹת, פַּעַם רִאשׁוֹנָה – דַּיָּהּ שַׁעְתָּהּ, שְׁנִיָּה – מְטַמְּאָה מֵעֵת לְעֵת וּמִפְּקִידָה לִפְקִידָה, עָבְרוּ עָלֶיהָ שָׁלֹשׁ עוֹנוֹת וְרָאֲתָה – דַּיָּהּ שַׁעְתָּהּ.

The *baraita* concludes: **And** with regard to a girl **whose time to see** the flow of menstrual blood **has arrived,**[H] i.e., she has reached the age of twelve, when she sees menstrual blood for the **first time, her time is sufficient.** After the **second** time, **she transmits impurity** retroactively **for** a twenty-four-hour **period or from examination to examination.** If **three** menstrual **cycles** then **passed** without her experiencing bleeding, **and** afterward **she saw** menstrual **blood, her time is sufficient.** This is in accordance with the opinion of Rabbi Eliezer, who holds that any woman who passed three expected menstrual cycles without experiencing bleeding is presumed not to be menstruating.

אָמַר מָר: עָבְרוּ עָלֶיהָ שָׁלֹשׁ עוֹנוֹת – דַּיָּהּ שַׁעְתָּהּ,

**The Master said** in the *baraita*: If the young girl who had started menstruating **passed three** expected menstrual **cycles** without experiencing bleeding and then saw menstrual blood, she returns to the status of a young girl and **her time is sufficient.**

Perek **I**
Daf **10** Amud **a**

**NOTES**

What is the *halakha* if she then sees menstrual blood at regular intervals of thirty-day cycles – הֲדַר קַחְזְיָא בְּעוֹנוֹת מַאי: Rashi explains that the Gemara's first question is referring to the first time she stops experiencing bleeding for three regular cycles. The question is if she reverts to her status of one whose does not emit blood, or if she has already attained the presumptive status of a woman who sees menstrual blood. If she is considered as one who does not emit blood, then she requires another three regular cycles for her to be considered like an adult woman who transmits impurity retroactively. The Gemara then repeats its question but this time with regard to the *halakha* after the second occasion that she stops experiencing bleeding for three regular menstrual cycles.

הֲדַר קַחְזְיָא בְּעוֹנוֹת מַאי? אָמַר רַב גִּידֵּל, אָמַר רַב: פַּעַם רִאשׁוֹנָה וּשְׁנִיָּה – דַּיָּהּ שַׁעְתָּהּ, שְׁלִישִׁית – מְטַמְּאָה מֵעֵת לְעֵת וּמִפְּקִידָה לִפְקִידָה.

The Gemara asks: **What is** the *halakha* if she **then sees** menstrual blood **at** regular intervals of thirty-day **cycles**? Is her time sufficient, or does she transmit impurity retroactively? **Rav Giddel says** that **Rav says:** With regard to the **first time and** the **second** time that she sees menstrual blood, **her time is sufficient.** After the **third** time, **she transmits impurity** retroactively **for** a twenty-four-hour **period or from examination to examination.**

וְעוֹד, עָבְרוּ עָלֶיהָ שָׁלֹשׁ עוֹנוֹת וְרָאֲתָה – דַּיָּהּ שַׁעְתָּהּ, הֲדַר קַחְזְיָא בְּעוֹנוֹת מַאי?

The *baraita* further teaches, with regard to a young girl who did not experience bleeding for three typical cycles and then saw blood, **and three further** expected menstrual **cycles passed** without her experiencing bleeding **and** then afterward **she saw** menstrual **blood,** that **her time is sufficient.** The Gemara asks: **What** is the *halakha* if she **then sees** menstrual blood **at** regular intervals of thirty-day **cycles?**[N]

אָמַר רַב כָּהֲנָא, אָמַר רַב גִּידֵּל אָמַר רַב: פַּעַם רִאשׁוֹנָה – דַּיָּהּ שַׁעְתָּהּ, שְׁנִיָּה – מְטַמְּאָה מֵעֵת לְעֵת וּמִפְּקִידָה לִפְקִידָה.

The Gemara answers: **Rav Kahana says** that **Rav Giddel says** that **Rav says:** The **first time** that she sees menstrual blood, **her time is sufficient.** After the **second** time, **she transmits impurity** retroactively **for** a twenty-four-hour **period or from examination to examination.**

מַנִּי? רַבִּי הִיא, דְּאָמַר: בִּתְרֵי זִימְנֵי הָוֵי חֲזָקָה.

The Gemara asks: **Who is the** *tanna* of the *baraita*? The Gemara answers: Since the *baraita* teaches that she attains the status of a regular adult woman upon the third sighting of menstrual blood, apparently it is **Rabbi** Yehuda HaNasi, **who said** that **presumption** is established **by two occasions.**[N]

אֵימָא סֵיפָא: עָבְרוּ עָלֶיהָ שָׁלֹשׁ עוֹנוֹת וְרָאֲתָה – דַּיָּהּ שְׁעָתָהּ, אֲתָאן לְרַבִּי אֱלִיעֶזֶר!

The Gemara raises a difficulty: **Say the latter clause:** If she then **passed three** expected menstrual **cycles** without experiencing bleeding, **and** then **she saw** menstrual blood, she returns to the status of a young girl and **her time is sufficient.** In this ruling **we come to the opinion of Rabbi Eliezer,**[N] who holds that any woman who passed three expected menstrual cycles without experiencing bleeding is presumed not to be menstruating and her time is sufficient. Is the *baraita* in accordance with the opinion of Rabbi Yehuda HaNasi or Rabbi Eliezer?

וְכִי תֵּימָא: רַבִּי הִיא, וּבְעוֹנוֹת סְבַר לַהּ כְּרַבִּי אֱלִיעֶזֶר, וּמִי סְבַר לַהּ? וְהָא "לְאַחַר שֶׁנִּזְכַּר" קָאָמַר! אֶלָּא: רַבִּי אֱלִיעֶזֶר הִיא, וּבְוֶסְתוֹת סְבַר לַהּ כְּרַבִּי.

**And if you would say** that the *tanna* of the *baraita* **is Rabbi** Yehuda HaNasi, **and in** the case of a woman who passes three menstrual **cycles** without experiencing bleeding, **he holds in accordance with** the opinion of **Rabbi Eliezer, but does he** really **hold** in accordance with **this** opinion? Doesn't the *baraita* **state** that **after** Rabbi Yehuda HaNasi **remembered** that several authorities disagreed with the ruling of Rabbi Eliezer, he said: Rabbi Eliezer is worthy to rely upon in exigent circumstances, i.e., only in exigent circumstances. The Gemara concludes: **Rather,** the *tanna* of the *baraita* **is Rabbi Eliezer, and with regard to** menstrual **cycles** he **holds in accordance with** the opinion of **Rabbi Yehuda HaNasi,** that a presumptive cycle is established after two occasions of seeing menstrual blood.

כֶּתֶם שֶׁבֵּין רִאשׁוֹנָה וּשְׁנִיָּה – טָהוֹר. שֶׁבֵּין שְׁנִיָּה וּשְׁלִישִׁית – חִזְקִיָּה אָמַר: טָמֵא, רַבִּי יוֹחָנָן אָמַר: טָהוֹר. חִזְקִיָּה אָמַר: טָמֵא, כֵּיוָן דְּאִילּוּ חָזְיָא – מְטַמְּאָה, כִּתְמָהּ נַמִּי – טָמֵא. וְרַבִּי יוֹחָנָן אָמַר: טָהוֹר, כֵּיוָן דְּלָא אִתַּחְזְקָה בְּדָם – כִּתְמָהּ נַמִּי לָא מְטַמְּינַן לַהּ.

§ With regard to a young girl who was just starting to menstruate, the Gemara states: If she finds a blood **stain between** the **first** and **second** time that she sees menstrual blood, she is **pure.**[HN] If it is **between** the **second and** the **third** time, **Ḥizkiyya says:** She is **impure; Rabbi Yoḥanan says:** She is **pure.** The Gemara explains the reasoning behind their respective opinions. **Ḥizkiyya says:** She is **impure, since if she had seen** menstrual blood it would **render her impure.** Consequently, her blood **stain is also impure. And Rabbi Yoḥanan says:** She is **pure, since she has not** yet attained the **presumptive status of** one who sees menstrual **blood.** Therefore, **we also do not render her impure** on account of **her** blood **stain.**

**HALAKHA**

If she finds a stain between the first and second time she sees menstrual blood she is pure – כֶּתֶם שֶׁבֵּין רִאשׁוֹנָה וּשְׁנִיָּה טָהוֹר: The blood stain of a minor who is a virgin and has never experienced menstruation is deemed pure until she experiences three separate cycles of menstruation (Rambam *Sefer Kedusha, Hilkhot Issurei Bia* 9:5; *Shulḥan Arukh, Yoreh De'a* 190:2–4).

**NOTES**

Presumption is established by two occasions – בִּתְרֵי זִימְנֵי הָוֵי חֲזָקָה: According to the opinion of Rabbi Yehuda HaNasi that presumption is established by two occasions, why doesn't she transmit impurity retroactively after the second time she sees menstrual blood? Following the opinion that a woman transmits impurity retroactively as a penalty for having missed a self-examination (4b), the early commentaries explain that since her presumptive status changed only upon experiencing bleeding the second time, there was no requirement for her to perform a self-examination beforehand. Consequently, no penalty is imposed and she transmits impurity only retroactively from the next time that she menstruates (Ramban; Ran).

Say the latter clause…we come to the opinion of Rabbi Eliezer – אֵימָא סֵיפָא...אֲתָאן לְרַבִּי אֱלִיעֶזֶר: In the case of a woman who stopped seeing menstrual blood for three typical menstrual cycles, only Rabbi Eliezer holds that any woman who passed three menstrual cycles without bleeding is presumed not to be menstruating. Therefore, the last clause of the *baraita*, which is about a girl whose time to see menstrual blood has arrived, can be explained only in accordance with his opinion. By contrast, in the first clause of the *baraita*, which is about a girl whose time to see menstrual blood has not yet arrived, there it is possible that even the Rabbis agree that after a cessation from menstruation for three menstrual cycles, her time is sufficient (Ramban; Rashba; Ritva; Ran).

If she finds a stain between the first and second time she sees menstrual blood she is pure – כֶּתֶם שֶׁבֵּין רִאשׁוֹנָה וּשְׁנִיָּה טָהוֹר: Rashi explains that the Gemara is referring to a young girl whose time to see menstrual blood has not yet arrived. This explanation is in keeping with Rashi's general understanding that once a woman's time to see menstrual blood has arrived, her blood stain will transmit impurity even if she has not yet experienced menstruation. This opinion is shared by the Rashba and the Ritva, although the Ritva (5a) cites a dissenting opinion.

**LANGUAGE**

Secretion [*sirfa*] – שִׁירְפָה: The meaning of this word is similar to that of the word *saraf*, sap, the liquid that comes out of plants, and it is being borrowed here to refer to a woman's blood. The precise definition of the word *sirfa* here is a dispute among the early commentaries.

Seafarers [*naḥotei yamma*] – נָחוֹתֵי יַמָּא: This phrase, which means seafarers or sailors, is similar to the Hebrew *yordei hayam*, which literally means those who go down to the sea.

**NOTES**

With regard to this menstrual virgin her secretion [*sirfah*] is common, etc. – זוֹ שִׁירְפָה מָצוּי וכו׳: Some commentaries explain that the term *sirfa* means a secretion. If so, Rabbi Zeira is answering that a newly married menstrual virgin commonly secretes blood from her torn hymen and it can therefore be assumed that this is the source of her stain, whereas a young girl who begins experiencing menstruation cannot ascribe her blood stain to any such source (Rashi; *Tosafot*; *Tosefot HaRosh*). Others maintain that *sirfa* means an illness, a medical condition. According to this explanation, Rabbi Zeira is saying that a young girl who has started experiencing menstruation has a regular condition in that she sees menstrual blood. Consequently, it is assumed that any blood stain she finds is from menstrual blood. Conversely, a menstrual virgin has no such condition and therefore her blood stain must have come from a different source, and it is deemed ritually pure (Rabbeinu Ḥananel; Ritva; Rashba).

**HALAKHA**

A young girl whose time to see the flow of menstrual blood has not arrived and she saw – תִּינוֹקֶת שֶׁלֹּא הִגִּיעַ זְמַנָּהּ לִרְאוֹת וְרָאֲתָה: The blood stain of a young girl who is still a minor and has never experienced menstruation is deemed ritually pure until she experiences menstruation three times. This *halakha* is in accordance with the opinion of Rabbi Yoḥanan, as well as Rabbi Shimon ben Yehotzadak, as reported by Ravin (Rambam *Sefer Kedusha*, *Hilkhot Issurei Bia* 9:5; *Shulḥan Arukh*, *Yoreh De'a* 190:2–4).

Continuously discharges menstrual blood – שׁוֹפַעַת: When a young girl whose time to see menstrual blood has not yet arrived, sees a continuous discharge of menstrual blood for a few days, or if she experiences a constant drip of menstrual blood, these are considered as one single sighting of menstrual blood. If they stop a bit and then start again three times, even in the course of a one day, they are considered as three separate sightings of menstrual blood; the young girl assumes the presumed status of a regular woman who has regular menstruation and therefore her blood stain is deemed ritually impure (Rashba; Rashi; *Tur*). Some say that her blood stain remains pure until she experiences three cycles of menstruation. The Rema rules that one should conduct himself in accordance with the more stringent former opinion (Rambam *Sefer Tahara*, *Hilkhot Metamei Mishkav UMoshav* 4:2; *Shulḥan Arukh*, *Yoreh De'a* 190:3).

מַתְקִיף לַהּ רַבִּי אִלְעַאי: וְכִי מָה בֵּין זוֹ לִבְתוּלָה שֶׁדָּמֶיהָ טְהוֹרִין? אֲמַר לֵיהּ רַבִּי זֵירָא: זוֹ – שִׁירְפָה מָצוּי, וְזוֹ – אֵין שִׁירְפָה מָצוּי.

**Rabbi Ilai objects to this** ruling of Ḥizkiyya: **And what** is the difference **between this** case of a girl who has not yet started menstruating **and** a recently married menstrual **virgin whose** stain is deemed pure for as long **as her blood is pure,** since the stain is presumed to be from her torn hymen? **Rabbi Zeira said** to him: With regard to **this** menstrual virgin, **her secretion** [*sirfah*][L] **is common,**[N] i.e., blood from her torn hymen is normally found during this period. Therefore, any blood stain that is found is also assumed to be from her hymen. **But** in the case of **this** young girl, **her secretion is not common.** Therefore, if a blood stain is found, it is assumed to be menstrual blood.

אָמַר עוּלָּא, אָמַר רַבִּי יוֹחָנָן מִשּׁוּם רַבִּי שִׁמְעוֹן בֶּן יְהוֹצָדָק: תִּינוֹקֶת שֶׁלֹּא הִגִּיעַ זְמַנָּהּ לִרְאוֹת וְרָאֲתָה, פַּעַם רִאשׁוֹנָה וּשְׁנִיָּה – רוּקָּהּ וּמִדְרָסָהּ בַּשּׁוּק טָהוֹר, כִּתְמָהּ נַמִי טָהוֹר, וְלָא יָדַעְנָא אִם דִּידֵיהּ אִם דְּרַבֵּיהּ.

§ **Ulla says** that **Rabbi Yoḥanan says in the name of Rabbi Shimon ben Yehotzadak:** With regard to **a young girl whose time to see** the flow of menstrual blood **has not arrived and she saw**[H] menstrual blood **one time and** then **a second** time, but not the third time that would render her a woman who regularly sees menstrual blood, **her saliva and her** garment that she **treads** upon that are found **in the marketplace** are **pure** if we do not know whether she has menstruated. Likewise, **her** blood **stain** is **also pure.** Ulla added: **And I do not know if** this ruling with regard to the stain is merely Rabbi Yoḥanan's own conclusion **or** if that is also part of the opinion **of his teacher.**

לְמַאי נָפְקָא מִינָּהּ? לְמֶיהֱוֵי דְּבָרָיו שֶׁל אֶחָד בִּמְקוֹם שְׁנַיִם.

The Gemara asks: **What difference is** there? That is, what does it matter who said it? The Gemara explains: It makes a difference **for it to be** considered the **statement of one** Sage **in the place of two** dissenting opinions. As stated above, Ḥizkiyya disagrees with this ruling and maintains that a young girl's blood stain is impure after she sees menstrual blood twice. If this statement is both Rabbi Shimon ben Yehotzadak's opinion and that of Rabbi Yoḥanan, then Ḥizkiyya's ruling is opposed by two Sages, which means that his is a minority opinion. If it is Rabbi Yoḥanan's opinion alone, then the two sides are equal, with one Sage maintaining each opinion.

כִּי אֲתָא רָבִין וְכׇל נָחוֹתֵי יַמָּא אַמְרוּהָ כְּרַבִּי שִׁמְעוֹן בֶּן יְהוֹצָדָק.

**When Ravin**[P] **came** from Eretz Yisrael to Babylonia along with **all the seafarers** [*naḥotei yamma*],[L] **they stated** this ruling **as** the statement of **Rabbi Shimon ben Yehotzadak.** If so, Rabbi Yoḥanan was relating his own opinion, which echoed that of his teacher, Rabbi Shimon ben Yehotzadak, and therefore the *halakha* is in accordance with this majority opinion.

אָמַר רַב חִלְקִיָּה בַּר טוֹבִי: תִּינוֹקֶת שֶׁלֹּא הִגִּיעַ זְמַנָּהּ לִרְאוֹת, אֲפִילּוּ שׁוֹפַעַת כׇּל שִׁבְעָה – אֵינָהּ אֶלָּא רְאִיָּה אַחַת. אֲפִילּוּ שׁוֹפַעַת – וְלָא מִבַּעְיָא פּוֹסֶקֶת? אַדְּרַבָּה, פּוֹסֶקֶת הָוְיָא לַהּ כִּשְׁתֵּי רְאִיּוֹת!

§ **Rav Ḥilkiya bar Tovi says:** With regard to **a young girl whose time to see** menstrual blood **has not arrived, even** if she **continuously discharges** menstrual blood[H] **for all seven** days of a typical menstrual period, it is considered as **only one sighting** of blood and she remains in the category of one who lacks blood until she sees menstrual blood twice more. The Gemara asks: Why did Rav Ḥilkiya bar Tovi stress: **Even** if she **continuously discharges** menstrual blood, which indicates that **it is not necessary** to teach that this is the *halakha* if she **stops** seeing a discharge and then starts again? **On the contrary,** if she **stops** and restarts **it is as** though she has had **two sightings** of menstrual blood.

**PERSONALITIES**

Ravin – רָבִין: Ravin's name is an abbreviation of Rabbi Avin. He is called Rabbi Bon in the Jerusalem Talmud. He was the most important of those who descended, i.e., who went from Eretz Yisrael to Babylonia, in the third and fourth generations of the Babylonian *amora'im*.

Rabbi Avin was born in Babylonia and immigrated to Eretz Yisrael at an early age. There he was fortunate to study Torah from Rabbi Yoḥanan, and later from his many students. Rabbi Avin was appointed an emissary to Babylonia to disseminate innovative Torah insights that were unknown in other lands, succeeding Rav Dimi. Ravin transmitted new and revised formulations of the *halakhot*; therefore, he is considered an authority and, in general, the *halakha* was decided in accordance with his opinions. Ravin returned to Eretz Yisrael several times, transmitting the Torah studied in Babylonia. His statements are often cited in the Jerusalem Talmud.

אֶלָּא: תִּינוֹקֶת שֶׁלֹּא הִגִּיעַ זְמַנָּהּ לִרְאוֹת, וְשׁוֹפַעַת כָּל שִׁבְעָה – אֵינָהּ אֶלָּא רְאִיָּה אַחַת.

The Gemara answers: **Rather,** this is what Rav Ḥilkiya bar Tovi meant: With regard to **a young girl whose time to see** menstrual blood **has not arrived, and** she then **continuously discharges** menstrual blood **for all seven** days of a typical menstrual period, it is considered as **only one sighting** of blood. In other words, he did not state the word: Even.

אָמַר רַב שִׁימִי בַּר חִיָּיא: מַדְלֶפֶת אֵינָהּ כְּרוֹאָה. וְהָא קָחָזְיָא! אֵימָא: אֵינָהּ כְּשׁוֹפַעַת אֶלָּא כְּפוֹסֶקֶת.

**Rav Shimi bar Ḥiyya says:** The case of woman who constantly **drips** menstrual blood is **not** considered **like** a full **sighting** of blood. The Gemara expresses surprise at this claim: **But** she **saw** blood. The Gemara answers: **Say** that what Rav Shimi bar Ḥiyya meant was that she is **not** considered **like** one who **continuously discharges** blood, but **rather like** one who **stops** and starts again, even if she drips constantly.

מִכְּלָל דְּשׁוֹפַעַת (נַמִי) – כִּי נַהֲרָא? אֶלָּא אֵימָא: אֵינָהּ אֶלָּא כְּשׁוֹפַעַת.

The Gemara raises a difficulty: **From the fact** that Rav Shimi bar Ḥiyya claims that a different *halakha* applies to a woman who constantly drips menstrual blood, it can be inferred **that** the blood of one who **continuously discharges** menstrual blood streams **like a river** for seven days. But this is physically impossible. The Gemara explains: **Rather, say** that Rav Shimi bar Ḥiyya meant that the status of a woman who constantly drips menstrual blood is **nothing other than** the status **of** a woman who **continuously discharges** blood. In both cases, it is all considered as one sighting.

תָּנוּ רַבָּנַן: חֲזָקָה, בְּנוֹת יִשְׂרָאֵל עַד שֶׁלֹּא הִגִּיעוּ לְפִרְקָן – הֲרֵי הֵן בְּחֶזְקַת טָהֳרָה, וְאֵין הַנָּשִׁים בּוֹדְקוֹת אוֹתָן. מִשֶּׁהִגִּיעוּ לְפִרְקָן – הֲרֵי הֵן בְּחֶזְקַת טוּמְאָה, וְנָשִׁים בּוֹדְקוֹת אוֹתָן.

§ **The Sages taught** in a *baraita*: The **presumption** with regard to the **daughters of Israel** is that **until they have reached their** physical **maturity they have** the **presumptive status of ritual purity,**[H] **and** adult **women do not** need to **examine them** to check if they are ritually pure before they handle consecrated items or *teruma*. **Once they have reached their** physical **maturity, they have** the **presumptive status of ritual impurity,** due to the possibility of an unnoticed menstrual discharge, **and** if they are still minors, adult **women** must **examine them** to check if they are ritually pure.

רַבִּי יְהוּדָה אוֹמֵר: אֵין בּוֹדְקִין אוֹתָן בַּיָּד – מִפְּנֵי שֶׁמְּעַוְּותוֹת אוֹתָן, אֶלָּא סָכוֹת אוֹתָן בְּשֶׁמֶן מִבִּפְנִים וּמְקַנְּחוֹת אוֹתָן מִבַּחוּץ, וְהֵן נִבְדָּקוֹת מֵאֵילֵיהֶן.

**Rabbi Yehuda says: They should not examine them by hand, because that** is likely to scratch them and **ruin their** status, as it will be assumed that they are ritually impure with menstrual blood. **Rather,** they **should smear them with oil inside and wipe them** off **on the outside. And** through this method **they are automatically examined,** i.e., if at that age they are ready to menstruate, the oil will cause the blood to flow.

״רַבִּי יוֹסֵי אוֹמֵר מְעוּבֶּרֶת״ וכו׳. תָּנֵי תַּנָּא קַמֵּיהּ דְּרַבִּי אֶלְעָזָר: רַבִּי יוֹסֵי אוֹמֵר מְעוּבֶּרֶת וּמֵינִיקָה שֶׁעָבְרוּ עָלֶיהָ שָׁלֹשׁ עוֹנוֹת – דַּיָּהּ שַׁעְתָּהּ, אֲמַר לֵיהּ: פָּתַחְתְּ בִּתְרֵי וְסָיְימַתְּ בַּחֲדָא!

§ The mishna teaches that **Rabbi Yosei says:** With regard to **a pregnant woman** and a nursing woman for whom three expected menstrual cycles passed during which they saw no menstrual blood, if she then saw blood, her time is sufficient. **A *tanna* taught** a *baraita* **before Rabbi Elazar: Rabbi Yosei says:** With regard to **a pregnant woman and a nursing woman for whom three** expected menstrual **cycles passed** during which they saw no menstrual blood, if she then experienced bleeding **her time is sufficient.** Rabbi Elazar **said to him:** The structure of your *baraita* is inconsistent. **You opened with two** categories of women: A pregnant woman and a nursing woman, **and you ended** your quote **with one,** as you concluded in the singular form: Her time is sufficient.

דִּלְמָא מְעוּבֶּרֶת וְהִיא מֵינִיקָה קָאָמְרַתְּ, וּמִילְּתָא אַגַּב אוֹרְחֵיהּ קָא מַשְׁמַע לָן – דִּימֵי עִיבּוּרָהּ עוֹלִין לָהּ לִימֵי מֵינִיקוּתָהּ וִימֵי מֵינִיקוּתָהּ עוֹלִין לָהּ לִימֵי עִיבּוּרָהּ. כִּדְתַנְיָא: יְמֵי עִיבּוּרָהּ עוֹלִין לָהּ לִימֵי מֵינִיקוּתָהּ, וִימֵי מֵינִיקוּתָהּ עוֹלִין לָהּ לִימֵי עִיבּוּרָהּ;

Rabbi Elazar continued: **Perhaps you are saying** that this is a case of **a pregnant woman who was also nursing. And** if so, the *baraita* **teaches us a matter in passing, that** with regard to tallying three menstrual cycles in which she saw no menstrual blood, **her days of pregnancy count** toward, i.e., combine with, **her days of nursing and her days of nursing count** toward **her days of pregnancy. As it is taught** in a *baraita*: **Her days of pregnancy count** toward **her days of nursing and her days of nursing count** toward **her days of pregnancy.**

HALAKHA

**Until they have reached their physical maturity they have the presumptive status of ritual purity – עַד שֶׁלֹּא הִגִּיעוּ לְפִרְקָן הֲרֵי הֵן בְּחֶזְקַת טָהֳרָה:** Before girls have reached physical maturity, the presumption is that they do not experience menstruation and are ritually pure. Therefore adult women do not need to examine them before they handle consecrated items or *teruma*. Once they have reached physical maturity, they need to be examined by adult women (Rambam *Sefer Tahara*, *Hilkhot Metamei Mishkav UMoshav* 4:8).

בֵּיצַד, הִפְסִיקָה שְׁתַּיִם בִּימֵי עִיבּוּרָהּ וְאַחַת בִּימֵי מֵנִיקוּתָהּ, שְׁתַּיִם בִּימֵי מֵנִיקוּתָהּ וְאַחַת בִּימֵי עִיבּוּרָהּ, אַחַת וּמֶחֱצָה בִּימֵי עִיבּוּרָהּ וְאַחַת וּמֶחֱצָה בִּימֵי מֵנִיקוּתָהּ – מִצְטָרְפוֹת לְשָׁלֹשׁ עוֹנוֹת.

The *baraita* continues: **How so?** If a woman **stopped** seeing menstrual blood for **two** expected menstrual cycles **during her days of pregnancy and** then for **one** more cycle **during her days of nursing**, or she passed **two** expected menstrual cycles **during her days of nursing and one** more **during her days of pregnancy**, or **one and a half** cycles **during her days of pregnancy and one and a half** cycles **during her days of nursing**, in all these cases the missed cycles spanning her pregnancy and nursing **combine to** a total of **three** missed **cycles**, and therefore her time is sufficient.

בִּשְׁלָמָא יְמֵי עִיבּוּרָהּ עוֹלִין לָהּ לִימֵי מֵנִיקוּתָהּ מַשְׁכַּחַתְּ לַהּ – דְּקָמֵנִיקָה וְאָזְלָא וּמִיעַבְּרָה, אֶלָּא יְמֵי מֵנִיקוּתָהּ עוֹלִין לָהּ לִימֵי עִיבּוּרָהּ הֵיכִי מַשְׁכַּחַתְּ לַהּ?

The Gemara asks: **Granted,** with regard to the claim that **her days of pregnancy count** toward **her days of nursing, you** can **find it** in a case where **she was nursing continuously and** then she **became pregnant. But** the scenario mentioned in the *baraita* where **her days of nursing count** toward **her days of pregnancy, how can you find these** circumstances? Since she certainly experienced bleeding when she gave birth, how can there be three consecutive menstrual cycles where she did not experience any discharge of blood?

אִיבָּעֵית אֵימָא: בְּלֵידָה יְבֵשְׁתָּא, וְאִיבָּעֵית אֵימָא: דַּם נִדָּה לְחוּד וְדַם לֵידָה לְחוּד, וְאִיבָּעֵית אֵימָא: תְּנֵי חֲדָא.

The Gemara provides several answers: **If you wish, say** that it is referring to a case **of a dry birth,** i.e., one without any discharge of blood. Or, **if you wish, say:** The **blood** of **a menstruating woman** is **discrete and** the **blood** seen during **birth** is **discrete.** Blood seen during birth does not disrupt the count of menstrual cycles during which a woman does not see menstrual blood. Therefore, the cycles before and after the birth combine to form the requisite three cycles according to Rabbi Eliezer. **Or, if you wish, say: Teach** only **one** of these scenarios. In other words, teach only the case where the days of pregnancy count toward the days of nursing, but not the case where the days of nursing count toward the days of pregnancy.

״בַּמֶּה אָמְרוּ דַּיָּהּ שְׁעָתָהּ״ וכו׳. אָמַר רַב: אַכּוּלְּהוּ,

§ The mishna teaches: **And with regard to what** did **they say** that **her time is sufficient?**[H] It is with regard to the first sighting of blood. But with regard to the second sighting, her status is like that of any other woman and she transmits impurity for a twenty-four-hour period or from her last examination. The Gemara inquires concerning which case this clause is referring to. **Rav says:** This qualification is stated **with regard to all of them,** i.e., all four cases of the mishna: The menstrual virgin, the elderly woman, the pregnant woman, and the nursing woman.

וּשְׁמוּאֵל אָמַר: לֹא שָׁנוּ אֶלָּא בְּתוּלָה וּזְקֵנָה, אֲבָל מְעוּבֶּרֶת וּמֵנִיקָה – דַּיָּין כׇּל יְמֵי עִיבּוּרָן, דַּיָּין כׇּל יְמֵי מְנִיקוּתָן.

**And Shmuel says: They taught** it **only** with regard to a menstrual **virgin and an elderly woman. But** in the case of **a pregnant woman and a nursing woman, their** time is **sufficient** for **all their days of pregnancy and their** time is **sufficient** for **all their days of nursing.**

וְכֵן אָמַר רַבִּי שִׁמְעוֹן בֶּן לָקִישׁ: אַכּוּלְּהוּ, וְרַבִּי יוֹחָנָן אָמַר: לֹא שָׁנוּ אֶלָּא בְּתוּלָה וּזְקֵנָה, אֲבָל מְעוּבֶּרֶת וּמֵנִיקָה – דַּיָּין כׇּל יְמֵי עִיבּוּרָן, דַּיָּין כׇּל יְמֵי מְנִיקוּתָן. כְּתַנָּאֵי, מְעוּבֶּרֶת וּמֵנִיקָה שֶׁהָיוּ

The Gemara notes that another pair of Sages had the same dispute. **And similarly, Rabbi Shimon ben Lakish says:** This qualification applies **to all of them; and Rabbi Yoḥanan says: They taught** it **only** with regard to a menstrual **virgin and an elderly woman. But** in the case of a **pregnant woman and a nursing woman, their** time is **sufficient** for **all their days of pregnancy and their** time is **sufficient** for **all their days of nursing.** The Gemara suggests: This is **like** a dispute between *tanna'im* in the following *baraita*: With regard to **a pregnant woman and a nursing woman who were**

**HALAKHA**

**And with regard to what did they say that her time is sufficient – בַּמֶּה אָמְרוּ דַּיָּהּ שְׁעָתָהּ:** There are four women whose time is sufficient and who assume impurity only from the time that they see menstrual blood: A pregnant woman, a nursing woman, a menstrual virgin, and an elderly woman. This is in accordance with the opinion of Rav and Rabbi Shimon ben Lakish (Rambam *Sefer Tahara, Hilkhot Metamei Mishkav UMoshav* 4:1, 5, and see Ra'avad and *Kesef Mishne* there).

שׁוֹפְעוֹת דָּם וּבָאוֹת – דַּיָּין כׇּל יְמֵי עִיבּוּרָן, וְדַיָּין כׇּל יְמֵי מְנִיקוּתָן, דִּבְרֵי רַבִּי מֵאִיר. רַבִּי יוֹסֵי וְרַבִּי יְהוּדָה וְרַבִּי שִׁמְעוֹן אוֹמְרִים: לֹא אָמְרוּ דַּיָּין שְׁעָתָן אֶלָּא בִּרְאִיָּיה רִאשׁוֹנָה, אֲבָל בַּשְּׁנִיָּה – מְטַמְּאָה מֵעֵת לְעֵת וּמִפְּקִידָה לִפְקִידָה.

**continuously discharging** menstrual **blood, their time is sufficient** for **all their days of pregnancy and their** time is **sufficient** for **all their days of nursing.** This is **the statement of Rabbi Meir. Rabbi Yosei and Rabbi Yehuda and Rabbi Shimon** all **say: They said** that **her time is sufficient only with regard to** the **first sighting** of blood, **but with regard to the second** sighting, her status is like that of any other woman, and she **transmits impurity for** a twenty-four-hour **period or from examination to examination.**

״וְאִם רָאֲתָה רִאשׁוֹנָה״ וכו׳. אָמַר רַב הוּנָא: קָפְצָה וְרָאֲתָה, קָפְצָה וְרָאֲתָה, קָפְצָה וְרָאֲתָה – קָבְעָה לָהּ וֶסֶת. לְמַאי? אִילֵּימָא לְיָמִים – הָא כׇּל יוֹמָא דְּלָא קָפֵיץ לָא חָזְיָא!

§ The mishna teaches: **And if she saw** the **first** sighting as a result of unnatural circumstances, then even with regard to the second sighting her time is sufficient. **Rav Huna says:** If she **jumped**[N] **and saw** menstrual blood, and again she **jumped and saw** menstrual blood, and a third time she **jumped and saw** menstrual blood, she has **established a fixed** menstrual **cycle.** The Gemara asks: **For what** occurrence has she established a fixed cycle? **If we say** that it is a cycle **of days** alone, **this** cannot be correct, **as every day that she did not jump,** she also **did not see** menstrual blood. Therefore, her cycle cannot be a mere pattern of days.

אֶלָּא לִקְפִיצוֹת, וְהָתַנְיָא: כׇּל שֶׁתִּקְבַּעְנָה מֵחֲמַת אוֹנֶס – אֲפִילּוּ כַּמָּה פְּעָמִים לֹא קָבְעָה וֶסֶת! מַאי לָאו – לֹא קָבְעָה וֶסֶת כְּלָל!

The Gemara explains: **Rather,** the established menstrual cycle is caused **by jumps,** i.e., by observing a pattern of jumping and seeing blood three times, she has established that jumping causes the onset of her menstrual period. The Gemara raises a difficulty: **But isn't it taught** in a *baraita*: **Any** woman who **establishes** a pattern of seeing menstrual blood **due to** a recurring **accident,**[H] **even if the** pattern repeats, still has **not established a fixed** menstrual **cycle?** An accidental menstrual pattern brought about by external causes does not create a menstrual cycle. The Gemara explains the difficulty: **What, is it not** correct to say that the *baraita* means that she has **not established a fixed** menstrual **cycle at all?**

לֹא, לֹא קָבְעָה וֶסֶת לְיָמִים לְחוּדַיְיהוּ וְלִקְפִיצוֹת לְחוּדַיְיהוּ, אֲבָל קָבְעָה לָהּ וֶסֶת לְיָמִים וְלִקְפִיצוֹת. לְיָמִים לְחוּדַיְיהוּ פְּשִׁיטָא! אָמַר רַב אַשִׁי: כְּגוֹן דְּקָפֵיץ בְּחַד בְּשַׁבָּת וַחֲזַאי, וְקָפֵיץ בְּחַד בְּשַׁבָּת וַחֲזַאי, וּבְשַׁבָּת קָפְצָה וְלָא חֲזַאי, וּלְחַד בְּשַׁבָּת חֲזַאי בְּלָא קְפִיצָה.

The Gemara answers: **No,** the *baraita* means that she has **not established a fixed** menstrual **cycle of days alone, nor of jumps alone, but** she has **established a fixed** menstrual **cycle for** a combination of **days and of jumps.** In other words, she has established a fixed menstrual cycle when she jumps on specific days. The Gemara asks: Isn't it **obvious** that she does not establish a cycle **for days alone?** Why is it necessary to state this? **Rav Ashi says:** It is necessary to teach this in a case **where** she **jumped on Sunday and saw** menstrual blood, **and** again she **jumped on Sunday and saw** menstrual blood, **and** then **on** the following **Shabbat she jumped and did not see** blood, **but on Sunday,** the next day, **she saw** menstrual blood **without jumping.**

מַהוּ דְּתֵימָא: אִיגַּלַּאי מִילְּתָא לְמַפְרֵעַ דְּיוֹמָא הוּא דְּקָגָרֵים וְלָא קְפִיצָה, קָא מַשְׁמַע לָן דִּקְפִיצָה נַמִי דְּאֶתְמוֹל גָּרְמָא, וְהַאי דְּלָא חֲזַאי – מִשּׁוּם דְּאַכַּתִּי לָא מְטָא זְמַן קְפִיצָה.

Rav Ashi explains: **Lest you say** that the **matter** is **revealed retroactively that it** was **the day that caused** her to experience menstruation **and** not the **jumping,** and therefore she has established a menstrual cycle of menstruating on Sundays, regardless of jumping, the *baraita* **teaches us that** it was **also** the jumping **of yesterday,** on Shabbat, that **caused** the menstruation today, on Sunday. **And** as for the fact **that she did not see** menstrual blood then, that was **because the time** when **jumping** causes menstruation had **not** yet **arrived.**

NOTES

Jumped – קָפְצָה: While Rav Huna discusses a case where jumping causes a woman to experience menstruation, this is only one example of an accidental outside circumstance that causes her to menstruate.

HALAKHA

Any woman who establishes a pattern of seeing menstrual blood due to a recurring accident – כׇּל שֶׁתִּקְבַּעְנָה מֵחֲמַת אוֹנֶס: If a woman's menstrual cycle seems fixed due to several instances where she experiences menstrual blood after jumping, she does not need to be concerned for that fixed cycle unless it also follows a pattern of set days. The Rema adds that, nevertheless, after three times that she sees menstrual blood through jumping, she treats it as an unfixed menstrual cycle and she must therefore be concerned that the next time she jumps, it may bring about menstrual blood. Later authorities add that if she sees menstrual blood once after jumping, she needs to be concerned only for a cycle following that span of days that passed since her last menstrual cycle (*Shakh*). For example, if she saw menstrual blood, and after twenty days she jumped and again saw menstrual blood, she needs to be concerned for a possible discharge of menstrual blood if she jumps twenty days later (Rambam *Sefer Kedusha, Hilkhot Issurei Bia* 8:5, and see Ra'avad there; *Shulhan Arukh, Yoreh De'a* 189:17).

## NOTES

Blood of purity – דַּם טוֹהַר: With regard to a woman who gives birth to a boy, the Torah states: "If a woman be delivered, and bear a male child, then she shall be impure seven days…And she shall continue in the blood of purity thirty-three days" (Leviticus 12:2–4). In the case of the birth of a girl, the verse states: "And if she bear a female child, then she shall be impure two weeks, as in her impurity; and she shall continue in the blood of purity sixty-six days" (Leviticus 12:5). During the period of the blood of purity, a woman remains ritually pure and permitted to her husband even if she experiences bleeding.

## BACKGROUND

They partake of *teruma* – אוֹכְלוֹת בִּתְרוּמָה: *Teruma* may be eaten only by a priest and the members of his household. These include his wife, his sons, his unmarried daughters, his Canaanite slaves, and his animals. When a priest dies or divorces his wife, if she is from an Israelite or Levite family she may no longer partake of *teruma* unless she has borne him a child, in which case she may continue to partake of *teruma* under certain circumstances (see Rambam *Sefer Zera'im*, *Hilkhot Terumot*, chapter 6).

לִישָּׁנָא אַחֲרִינָא, אָמַר רַב הוּנָא: קָפְצָה וְרָאֲתָה, קָפְצָה וְרָאֲתָה, קָפְצָה וְרָאֲתָה – קָבְעָה לָהּ וֶסֶת לְיָמִים וְלֹא לִקְפִיצוֹת. הֵיכִי דָּמֵי? אָמַר רַב אַשִׁי: דְּקָפֵיץ בְּחַד בְּשַׁבָּת וַחֲזַאי, וּקְפִיץ בְּחַד בְּשַׁבָּת וַחֲזַאי, וּבְשַׁבָּת קָפְצָה וְלָא חֲזַאי, וּלְחַד בְּשַׁבָּת (אַחֲרִינָא) חֲזַאי בְּלָא קְפִיצָה, דְּהָתָם אִיגַּלַּאי מִילְּתָא דְּיוֹמָא הוּא דְּקָא גָּרֵים.

The Gemara presents **another version** of Rav Huna's statement. **Rav Huna says:** If a woman **jumped and saw** menstrual blood, and again she **jumped and saw** menstrual blood, and a third time she **jumped and saw** menstrual blood,[H] she has **established a fixed** menstrual **cycle for** a pattern of **days and not for** a pattern of **jumps.** The Gemara asks: **What are the circumstances? Rav Ashi says:** This is referring to a case **where** she **jumped on Sunday and saw** menstrual blood, **and** then again she **jumped on Sunday and saw** menstrual blood, **and** then **on** the following **Shabbat she jumped and did not see** blood, **but on Sunday,** the next day, **she saw** menstrual blood **without jumping.** In that case **there,** the **matter** is **revealed retroactively** that it is **the day that causes** her to menstruate, not the jumping.

מתני׳ אַף עַל פִּי שֶׁאָמְרוּ דַּיָּהּ שְׁעָתָהּ – צְרִיכָה לִהְיוֹת בּוֹדֶקֶת, חוּץ מִן הַנִּדָּה וְהַיּוֹשֶׁבֶת עַל דַּם טוֹהַר.

**MISHNA** Although the Rabbis **said** that for a woman with a fixed menstrual cycle **her time is sufficient** and she does not transmit impurity retroactively, **she is required to examine herself**[H] each day to ensure that she is ritually pure and will not impurify pure items that she is handling. All women must examine themselves each day **except for a menstruating woman,** whose impure status is known, **and** a woman after childbirth **who is observing** the period of the **blood of purity,**[N] whose ritually pure status is known even if she experiences bleeding.

וּמְשַׁמֶּשֶׁת בְּעֵדִים – חוּץ מִיּוֹשֶׁבֶת עַל דַּם טוֹהַר, וּבְתוּלָה שֶׁדָּמֶיהָ טְהוֹרִים.

**And** even a woman with a fixed menstrual cycle **engages in intercourse while** using **examination cloths**[H] to ascertain whether her menstrual flow began, **except for** a woman after childbirth **who is observing** the period of the **blood of purity, and a virgin whose blood is ritually pure** for four days after engaging in intercourse for the first time.

וּפַעֲמַיִם צְרִיכָה לִהְיוֹת בּוֹדֶקֶת – שַׁחֲרִית וּבֵין הַשְּׁמָשׁוֹת, וּבְשָׁעָה שֶׁהִיא עוֹבֶרֶת לְשַׁמֵּשׁ אֶת בֵּיתָהּ. יְתֵירוֹת עֲלֵיהֶן כֹּהֲנוֹת בְּשָׁעָה שֶׁהֵן אוֹכְלוֹת בִּתְרוּמָה. רַבִּי יְהוּדָה אוֹמֵר: אַף בִּשְׁעַת עֲבָרָתָן מִלֶּאֱכוֹל בִּתְרוּמָה.

**And she is required to examine** herself **twice** each day:[H] In the **morning,** to ascertain if she menstruated during the night, **and** at **twilight,** to ascertain if she menstruated during the day. **And** she is also required to examine herself **at a time that she is about to engage in intercourse with her husband.** The obligation of **women of priestly** families is **greater than** that of other women,[H] as they are also required to examine themselves **when they** seek to **partake of** ***teruma***.[B] **Rabbi Yehuda says: Even when they conclude partaking of *teruma*** they are required to examine themselves, in order to ascertain whether they experienced bleeding while partaking of *teruma*.

## HALAKHA

**And a third time she jumped and saw menstrual blood, etc.** – קָפְצָה וְרָאֲתָה וכו׳: If a woman jumps and sees menstrual blood three times on the same day, she establishes a fixed menstrual cycle for jumping on that set day. For example, if she jumps and sees menstrual blood three times on the first day of the month, or on three consecutive Sundays, she has a fixed menstrual cycle when she jumps on the first of the month, or on Sundays. If, on the following first of the month, or the following Sunday, she does not jump, there is no need for concern that she may menstruate, as her fixed cycle is only for the combination of jumping on that specific day. Later authorities add that she uproots her fixed cycle when that specific day comes around three times and she jumps on that day without experiencing menstruation. This *halakha* is in accordance with the opinion of Rav Huna, as explained by Rav Ashi (Rambam *Sefer Kedusha*, *Hilkhot Issurei Bia* 8:5; *Shulḥan Arukh*, *Yoreh De'a* 189:18).

**Although the Rabbis said her time is sufficient she is required to examine herself** – אַף עַל פִּי שֶׁאָמְרוּ דַּיָּהּ שְׁעָתָהּ צְרִיכָה לִהְיוֹת בּוֹדֶקֶת: Every woman with a fixed menstrual cycle must examine herself each morning and evening before handling ritually pure items, and before engaging in intercourse, even though her time is sufficient. An exception to this rule is a menstruating woman who already transmits impurity, and a woman after childbirth whose blood is deemed pure, as in those cases examinations would not change her status (Rambam *Sefer Tahara*, *Hilkhot Metamei Mishkav UMoshav* 4:6).

**And even a woman with a fixed menstrual cycle engages in intercourse while using examination cloths** – וּמְשַׁמֶּשֶׁת בְּעֵדִים: A woman who has a fixed menstrual cycle and does not handle ritually pure items does not need to examine herself, not before engaging in intercourse or after. Not only is she not required to examine herself, but she is advised to refrain from doing so, as this would cause her husband to become nervous. By contrast, the Rambam maintains that both husband and wife should examine themselves after intercourse with their respective swatches to ascertain if she experienced bleeding as a result of the intercourse. Furthermore, he holds that especially virtuous women should examine themselves before intercourse as well. The Rema (citing *Roke'aḥ*; *Haggahot Maimoniyyot*) rules that the *halakha* and common practice is in accordance with the former opinion (Rambam *Sefer Tahara*, *Hilkhot Metamei Mishkav UMoshav* 4:7; see *Sefer Kedusha*, *Hilkhot Issurei Bia* 4:16 and Ra'avad and *Kesef Mishne* there; *Shulḥan Arukh*, *Yoreh De'a* 186:1).

**And she is required to examine herself twice each day** – וּפַעֲמַיִם צְרִיכָה לִהְיוֹת בּוֹדֶקֶת: Throughout her seven clean days, a woman is required to examine herself twice a day, once in the morning and once at twilight. Some maintain that even if she did not perform the required examinations throughout the seven days, they may still be counted, as long as she performed one examination during any of the seven days. This opinion should not be relied upon *ab initio*. The later authorities explain that this is aside from the initial examination that starts the seven days (*Shakh*). Others maintain that without at least one examination on each of the first and seventh days, she must restart the seven days (Rambam *Sefer Tahara*, *Hilkhot Metamei Mishkav UMoshav* 4:7; *Shulḥan Arukh*, *Yoreh De'a* 196:4).

**The obligation of women of priestly families is greater than that of other women** – יְתֵירוֹת עֲלֵיהֶן כֹּהֲנוֹת: Any woman of a priestly family that wishes to partake of *teruma* must examine herself prior to partaking (Rambam *Sefer Tahara*, *Hilkhot Metamei Mishkav UMoshav* 4:7).

גמ׳ ״חוץ מן הנדה״. דבתוך ימי נדתה לא בעי בדיקה.

**GEMARA** The mishna teaches: All women must examine themselves each day, **except for a menstruating woman.** The Gemara explains: Such a woman does not need to examine herself, **as during the days of her menstruation** she **does not need examination.**

הניחא לרבי שמעון בן לקיש דאמר אשה קובעת לה וסת בתוך ימי זיבתה, ואין אשה קובעת לה וסת בתוך ימי נדתה – שפיר; אלא לרבי יוחנן דאמר אשה קובעת לה וסת בתוך ימי נדתה – תבדוק, דילמא קבעה לה וסת!

The Gemara raises a difficulty: **This works out well according to** the opinion of **Rabbi Shimon ben Lakish, who said** that **a woman** can **establish a fixed** menstrual **cycle** even **during the days** that she **has *zava* status, but a woman does not establish a fixed** menstrual **cycle during the days of her** impurity due to **menstruation,** as any bleeding during these seven days is merely a continuation of her original menstruation. According to this opinion, it is **well,** and one can understand the mishna. **But according to** the opinion of **Rabbi Yoḥanan, who said** that **a woman** can **establish a fixed** menstrual **cycle during the days of her menstruation,**[H] **let her examine** herself, as **perhaps** she will **establish a fixed** menstrual **cycle.**

אמר לך רבי יוחנן: כי אמינא אנא – היכא דחזיתיה ממעין סתום, אבל חזיתיה ממעין פתוח – לא אמרי.

The Gemara explains that **Rabbi Yoḥanan** could **say to you: When I say** that a woman can establish a fixed menstrual cycle during the days of her menstruation, that applies only in a case **where** the first two instances of her fixed cycle were established when she first **saw** blood **from a stopped source,**[N] i.e., she saw blood on those particulars days at the outset of her period. **But** when she first **saw** blood **from an open source,** i.e., when the first two instances that she experienced bleeding on those particular days was in the middle of her menstrual period, **I did not say** that she establishes a fixed menstrual cycle, and therefore there is no need for her to examine herself.

״והיושבת על דם טוהר״. קא סלקא דעתך: מבקשת לישב על דם טוהר.

§ The mishna teaches: All women must examine themselves each day, except for a menstruating woman, whose impure status is known, **and** a woman after childbirth **who is observing** the period of the **blood of purity.** The Gemara explains: It may **enter your mind** that when the mishna mentions a woman who is observing the period of the blood of purity, it is referring to one who is finishing the period of impurity following a birth and is **anticipating observing** the period **of the blood of purity.** In other words, her days of impurity are ending and she is about to start her days of purity, and the mishna is stating that there is no need for an examination to conclude her days of impurity before starting her days of purity.

הניחא לרב דאמר מעין אחד הוא, התורה טמאתו והתורה טהרתו – שפיר,

The Gemara analyzes the mishna in accordance with this interpretation. **This works out well according to** the opinion of **Rav, who said** that blood after birth and blood of purity both come from **one source,**[H] and **the Torah deemed** blood after birth **impure, and the Torah deemed** blood of purity **pure.** According to this opinion, it is **well,** and one can understand the mishna, since even if she emits blood continuously through the end of her days of impurity into her days of purity, the blood during her days of purity is pure.

אלא ללוי דאמר שני מעינות הם – תבדוק, דילמא אכתי לא פסק ההוא מעין טמא! אמר לך לוי: הא מני?

But **according to** the opinion of **Levi, who said** that **there are two** distinct **sources,** one for blood after birth and one for blood of purity, **she should** be required to **examine** herself at the end of the period following birth, as **perhaps that impure source** of blood after birth had **not yet stopped** flowing. The Gemara explains that **Levi** could **say to you:** In accordance with **whose** opinion **is this** ruling?

**NOTES**

Where the instances of her fixed cycle were established when she first saw blood from a stopped source – היכא דחזיתיה ממעין סתום: The early commentaries explain that, according to Rabbi Yoḥanan, just as a woman cannot establish a fixed menstrual cycle during the days of her menstruation, so too there is no requirement for her to perform a self-examination on that day of expected menstruation in the future. In addition, they explain that from this *halakha* it is apparent that a menstrual cycle is established based only upon the onset of menstruation and not based upon the continuation of menstruation on subsequent days.

**HALAKHA**

A woman can establish a fixed menstrual cycle during the days of her menstruation – אשה קובעת לה וסת בתוך ימי נדתה: The Rambam maintains that a woman constantly cycles through seven *nidda* days and eleven *zava* days. During the seven days of *nidda*, a woman who saw menstrual blood can establish a fixed menstrual cycle. After experiencing bleeding once, though, any further blood she sees during the seven days of *nidda* cannot establish a fixed menstrual cycle (Rambam *Sefer Kedusha*, *Hilkhot Issurei Bia* 8:9).

Both come from one source – מעין אחד הוא: Menstrual blood seen during one's days of *nidda* or days of *zava*, blood from childbirth or blood emitted while experiencing labor pain, and the blood of purity after childbirth all come from the same source. Nonetheless, the blood can be deemed pure or impure based on when it is seen, in accordance with the opinion of Rav (Rambam *Sefer Kedusha*, *Hilkhot Issurei Bia* 6:1).

**NOTES**

**As perhaps she will find that she established a fixed menstrual cycle** – **דְּדִילְמָא קָבְעָה לָהּ וֶסֶת**: The period of purity after the birth of a daughter is sixty-six days. During that time it is entirely possible for a woman to establish a fixed menstrual cycle, either through examining herself and finding blood three times at twenty-day intervals, according to Rabban Shimon ben Gamliel, or at two thirty-day intervals, according to Rabbi Yehuda HaNasi, who holds that presumptions can be established after two instances. Therefore, the mishna needed to teach us that a possible cycle that may have been established during those days of purity does not transfer to her subsequent days of impurity (Rashi).

בֵּית שַׁמַּאי הִיא, דְּאָמְרִי מַעְיָן אֶחָד הוּא. וְסָתַם לָן תַּנָּא כְּבֵית שַׁמַּאי? סְתָם וְאַחַר כָּךְ מַחֲלוֹקֶת הוּא, וְכָל סְתָם וְאַחַר כָּךְ מַחֲלוֹקֶת – אֵין הֲלָכָה כִּסְתָם.

It is the opinion of **Beit Shammai, who say** that there **is** only **one source** for the two types of blood (see 35b). The Gemara asks: **But** can it be that **the** ***tanna*** **taught us an unattributed** mishna, which is generally accepted as the *halakha*, **in accordance with** the opinion of **Beit Shammai,** whose opinion is usually not accepted as *halakha*? The Gemara answers: **It is** a case where the mishna first records **an unattributed opinion and afterward** it records **a dispute** with regard to the same matter. **And** there is a principle that **any** time the mishna first records **an unattributed opinion and afterward** it records that the ruling is subject to **a dispute,** then the ***halakha*** is **not** necessarily **in accordance with the unattributed opinion.**

וְאִי בָּעֵית אֵימָא: מִי קָתָנֵי ״מְבַקֶּשֶׁת לֵישֵׁב״? ״יוֹשֶׁבֶת״ קָתָנֵי. אִי יוֹשֶׁבֶת, מַאי לְמֵימְרָא? מַהוּ דְּתֵימָא: תִּיבְדּוֹק, דְּדִילְמָא קָבְעָה לָהּ וֶסֶת – קָא מַשְׁמַע לָן דְּמַעְיָן טָהוֹר לְמַעְיָן טָמֵא לָא קָבְעָה.

**And if you wish, say** instead: **Does** the mishna **teach:** A woman is **anticipating observing** the period **of** the blood of purity? Rather, it teaches: **Who is observing** the period of the blood of purity. The Gemara asks: **If** the mishna is referring to a woman **who is** already **observing** the period of the blood of purity, **what** is the purpose **of stating** that she is exempt from performing examinations? Isn't this obvious? The Gemara answers: **Lest you say** that **she should examine** herself, **as perhaps** she will find that **she established a fixed** menstrual **cycle**[N] through blood found on her examination cloths, the mishna **teaches us that** a woman **does not establish** a cycle from sightings of blood that came from **a pure source** that transfers **to** the period when she sees blood from **an impure source.**

הָנִיחָא לְלֵוִי, דְּאָמַר שְׁנֵי מַעְיָנוֹת הֵם, אֶלָּא לְרַב דְּאָמַר מַעְיָן אֶחָד הוּא – תִּבְדּוֹק, דִּילְמָא קָבְעָה לָהּ וֶסֶת! אֲפִילּוּ הָכִי, מִימֵי טָהֳרָה לִימֵי טוּמְאָה – לָא קָבְעָה.

The Gemara raises a difficulty with regard to this answer: **This** answer **works out well according to Levi, who said** that **there are two** distinct **sources,** one for blood after birth and one for blood of purity; one can understand that she does not establish a cycle with regard to blood from one source, from a sighting of blood from a different source. **But according to Rav, who said** that blood after birth and blood of purity both come from **one source, she should** be required to **examine** herself during the period of the blood of purity, as **perhaps she established a fixed** menstrual **cycle.** The Gemara answers: **Even so,** i.e., that both types of blood come from the same source, nevertheless a woman **does not establish** a cycle **from** her **days of purity** that transfers **to** her **days of impurity.**

״וּמְשַׁמֶּשֶׁת בְּעֵדִים״ וכו׳. תְּנַן הָתָם: תִּינוֹקֶת שֶׁלֹּא הִגִּיעַ זְמַנָּהּ לִרְאוֹת וְנִשֵּׂאת, בֵּית שַׁמַּאי אוֹמְרִים: נוֹתְנִין לָהּ אַרְבַּע לֵילוֹת. וּבֵית הִלֵּל אוֹמְרִים: עַד שֶׁתִּחְיֶה הַמַּכָּה.

§ The mishna teaches: **And** even a woman with a fixed menstrual cycle **engages in intercourse while** using **examination cloths** to ascertain whether her menstrual flow began, except for a woman after childbirth who is observing the period of the blood of purity, and a virgin whose blood is ritually pure for four days after engaging in intercourse for the first time. In this connection, the Gemara notes that **we learned** in a mishna **there** (64b): With regard to **a young girl whose time to see** the flow of menstrual blood **has not arrived,** as she has not yet reached puberty, **and she married,**[H] **Beit Shammai say:** The Sages **give her four nights** after intercourse during which the blood is attributed to her torn hymen and she is ritually pure. Thereafter, any blood is menstrual blood and she is impure. **And Beit Hillel say:** The blood is attributed to the torn hymen **until the wound heals.**

**HALAKHA**

**A young girl whose time to see menstrual blood has not arrived and she married** – **תִּינוֹקֶת שֶׁלֹּא הִגִּיעַ זְמַנָּהּ לִרְאוֹת וְנִשֵּׂאת**: Blood attributed to a woman's torn hymen is deemed pure, as its source is not the womb, but her wound. The Rambam rules in accordance with Beit Hillel, that the blood seen by a new virgin bride who is a young girl, even if she previously experienced menstruation, is deemed pure until her wound has fully healed. This ruling does not reflect the practical *halakha*, as nowadays the leniency of ritually pure blood is not practiced. Rather, any blood, even if it is not menstrual blood, renders her impure (Rambam *Sefer Kedusha*, *Hilkhot Issurei Bia* 5:18, 25 and Ra'avad there, 11:8).

אָמַר רַב גִּידֵּל, אָמַר שְׁמוּאֵל: לֹא שָׁנוּ אֶלָּא שֶׁלֹּא פָּסְקָה מֵחֲמַת תַּשְׁמִישׁ, וְרָאֲתָה שֶׁלֹּא מֵחֲמַת תַּשְׁמִישׁ. אֲבָל פָּסְקָה מֵחֲמַת תַּשְׁמִישׁ וְרָאֲתָה – טְמֵאָה.

With regard to Beit Hillel's statement, **Rav Giddel says** that **Shmuel says:** They **taught** this **only** in a case **where** she **does not stop** seeing blood **due to intercourse.**[N] In other words, every time she engages in intercourse she experiences bleeding. In that case, even if **she saw** blood **not due to intercourse,** Beit Hillel still attribute the blood to the torn hymen. **But** if she **stops seeing** blood **due to intercourse, and** then she subsequently **saw** blood[H] on another occasion, that blood renders her **impure.**

עָבַר לַיְלָה אַחַת בְּלֹא תַּשְׁמִישׁ וְרָאֲתָה – טְמֵאָה. נִשְׁתַּנּוּ מַרְאֵה דָּמִים שֶׁלָּהּ – טְמֵאָה. מְתִיב רַבִּי יוֹנָה: וּבְתוּלָה שֶׁדָּמֶיהָ טְהוֹרִים, אַמַּאי? תְּשַׁמֵּשׁ בְּעֵדִים, דְּדִילְמָא נִשְׁתַּנּוּ מַרְאֵה דָּמִים שֶׁלָּהּ!

He continues: Similarly, if **one night passed without** them engaging in **intercourse and she** subsequently **saw** blood without connection to intercourse, this indicates that the blood is no longer from her torn hymen and therefore she is deemed **impure.** Likewise, if the **appearance** of **her blood** had changed since her initial blood from her torn hymen, she is **impure. Rabbi Yona raises an objection** to this last *halakha* from the mishna: **And a virgin whose blood is ritually pure** is not required to examine herself when she engages in intercourse. **Why** not? **She should engage in intercourse while** using **examination cloths, as perhaps** she will find that the **appearance of her blood** has **changed,** which would mean that her blood is no longer ritually pure blood from her torn hymen.

אָמַר רָבָא, אֵימָא רֵישָׁא: חוּץ מִן הַנִּדָּה וְהַיּוֹשֶׁבֶת עַל דַּם טוֹהַר – הוּא דְּלָא בָּעֲיָא בְּדִיקָה, אֲבָל בְּתוּלָה שֶׁדָּמֶיהָ טְהוֹרִין – בָּעֲיָא בְּדִיקָה. אֶלָּא קַשְׁיָין אַהֲדָדֵי!

**Rava says: Say the first clause:** All women must engage in intercourse while using examination cloths, **except for a menstruating woman** whose impure status is certain **and** a woman after childbirth **who is observing** the period of the **blood of purity.** It can be inferred from here that these two exceptions are not required for women to examine themselves, **but a virgin whose blood is pure** is **required** to perform **an examination.** This ruling apparently supports Shmuel's opinion that examination is required to determine if there is a change in the appearance of her blood. **But** if so, then the two clauses of the mishna are **difficult,** as they contradict **each other.**

כָּאן – שֶׁשִּׁמְּשָׁה, דְּאֵימָא שַׁמָּשׁ עֲכָרָן, כָּאן – שֶׁלֹּא שִׁמְּשָׁה.

The Gemara explains: **Here,** in the latter clause that indicates that a virgin requires no examination, it is referring to a case **where she had engaged in intercourse.** In such a situation an examination would be inconclusive, **as** even if the appearance of her blood had changed, one can **say** that it was because the man's **organ soiled it,** i.e., perhaps the intercourse caused the change of appearance in her blood. By contrast, **there,** in the first clause, it is referring to a case **where she** had **not engaged in intercourse,** and therefore she is required to perform an examination to determine if there was a change in appearance in her blood, as any difference in appearance would indicate a change from pure blood to impure blood.

תַּנְיָא נַמִי הָכִי: בַּמֶּה דְּבָרִים אֲמוּרִים – שֶׁלֹּא פָּסְקָה מֵחֲמַת תַּשְׁמִישׁ וְרָאֲתָה שֶׁלֹּא מֵחֲמַת תַּשְׁמִישׁ,

The Gemara notes **that** this *halakha* **is also taught** in a *baraita*. With regard to the opinion of Beit Hillel that blood is attributed to the torn hymen until the wound heals, the *baraita* asks: **In what** case **is this statement said?** In a case **where she does not stop** seeing blood **due to intercourse,** i.e., every time she engages in intercourse she experiences bleeding. If so, even when **she sees** blood **not due to intercourse,** it is deemed pure.

**NOTES**

**They taught this only where she does not stop seeing blood due to intercourse – לֹא שָׁנוּ אֶלָּא שֶׁלֹּא פָּסְקָה מֵחֲמַת תַּשְׁמִישׁ:** The time frame that the blood seen by a virgin after her first intercourse is deemed pure is dependent not upon the passage of time, but upon the conditions under which she experiences bleeding. As long as she continues to experience bleeding with each act of intercourse, any blood seen in between is presumed to be coming from her torn hymen, even if a couple of days have passed since her last act of intercourse. After one occurrence when she engaged in intercourse and did not experience bleeding, her hymen is presumed to be healed, and therefore any blood seen thereafter will render her impure. If she then continues to experience bleeding with intercourse, it must be suspected that it is menstrual blood that is being discharged due to intercourse (*Shulḥan Arukh Yoreh De'a* 187:13; see *Baḥ*).

Some say that even without that one occurrence where she engaged in intercourse without blood, engaging in intercourse one time without pain indicates that her wound has healed and any blood seen thereafter is suspected to be menstrual blood that is discharged due to intercourse. With regard to blood seen during her first act of intercourse, all agree that it is presumed to be from her torn hymen, even if she experiences no pain (Rema citing Maharam Padua).

Some later authorities question the first opinion above, noting that it can lead to the untenable situation where her menstrual blood is deemed as coming from the hymen long after it should have stopped bleeding. Rather, they explain that the ruling stated in the *Shulḥan Arukh* is limited to a few acts of intercourse, but not more (*Sidrei Tahara*; *Darkhei Teshuva*; *Tohorat HaBayit*; *Maasai Binyamin*). Some ask why a self-examination was not instituted to determine when bleeding from her hymen stops. They answer that the institution of self-examination was established only to determine if she is currently impure, and not to clarify her status in the future (*Tosefot HaRosh*).

**HALAKHA**

**She stops seeing blood due to intercourse and then she subsequently saw blood – פָּסְקָה מֵחֲמַת תַּשְׁמִישׁ וְרָאֲתָה:** After a virgin marries, blood that she sees in the course of intercourse is presumed to come from her torn hymen. This presumption continues until the first time she engages in intercourse without any bleeding.

By contrast, the Rema rules that as soon as she engages in intercourse without experiencing any pain, even if she continues to bleed during intercourse, it may no longer be presumed that the blood is from her wound. Some authorities are similarly reluctant to take a lenient stance after she has stopped experiencing pain from intercourse (*Beit Yosef*), while the *Baḥ* cites other authorities who have no qualms about ruling leniently until she engages in intercourse without bleeding (Rambam *Sefer Kedusha*, *Hilkhot Issurei Bia* 11:8; *Shulḥan Arukh*, *Yoreh De'a* 187:13).

אֲבָל פָּסְקָה מֵחֲמַת תַּשְׁמִישׁ וְרָאֲתָה – טְמֵאָה, עָבַר לַיְלָה אַחַת בְּלֹא תַּשְׁמִישׁ וְרָאֲתָה – טְמֵאָה, נִשְׁתַּנּוּ מַרְאֵה דָמִים שֶׁלָּהּ – טְמֵאָה.

**But** if she **stopped seeing** blood **due to intercourse, and** she subsequently **sees** blood at a different time, that sighting renders her **impure.** Similarly, if **one night passed without** her engaging in **intercourse and** then **she saw** blood without connection to intercourse, she is deemed **impure.** Furthermore, if she sees blood and the **appearance** of **her blood** had changed from her initial blood from her torn hymen, she is **impure.**

״פַּעֲמַיִם הִיא צְרִיכָה״ וכו׳. אָמַר רַב יְהוּדָה אָמַר שְׁמוּאֵל: לֹא שָׁנוּ אֶלָּא לְטָהֳרוֹת, אֲבָל לְבַעְלָהּ – מוּתֶּרֶת. פְּשִׁיטָא, ״שַׁחֲרִית״ תְּנַן!

§ The mishna teaches: **And she is required** to examine herself **twice** each day, in the morning and at twilight. **Rav Yehuda says** that **Shmuel says:** The mishna **taught** this *halakha* **only with regard to** touching ritually **pure** items. **But with regard to her husband, she is permitted** to him without any requirement to perform examinations. The Gemara asks: Isn't this **obvious,** as **we learn** in the mishna that she must examine herself twice a day, and the first time is in the **morning?** This indicates that the mishna is concerned about the status of ritually pure items that she will handle during the day, but not about intercourse with her husband, as a couple usually engages in relations at night rather than during the day.

אֶלָּא, אִי אִתְּמַר – אַסֵּיפָא אִתְּמַר: וּבְשָׁעָה שֶׁהִיא עוֹבֶרֶת לְשַׁמֵּשׁ אֶת בֵּיתָהּ. אָמַר רַב יְהוּדָה אָמַר שְׁמוּאֵל: לֹא שָׁנוּ אֶלָּא בְּאִשָּׁה עֲסוּקָה בְּטָהֳרוֹת, דְּמִגּוֹ דְּבָעֲיָא בְּדִיקָה לְטָהֳרוֹת – בָּעֲיָא נַמִי בְּדִיקָה לְבַעְלָהּ. אֲבָל אֵינָהּ עֲסוּקָה בְּטָהֳרוֹת – לָא בָּעֲיָא בְּדִיקָה.

The Gemara answers: **Rather, if** the statement of Rav Yehuda citing Shmuel **was stated,** it **was stated with regard to the latter clause** of the mishna: **And** she is also required to examine herself **at a time that she is about to engage in intercourse with her husband. Rav Yehuda says** that **Shmuel says:** The mishna **taught** this *halakha* **only with regard to a woman who is engaged in** handling **pure** items.[H] She alone is required to examine herself before intercourse. The reason is **that since** she is **required** to perform **an examination** in preparation **for** handling **pure** items,[N] she **also requires an examination** in preparation **for** intercourse with **her husband. But** with regard to a woman who **is not engaged in** handling **pure** items, she is **not required** to perform **an examination** in preparation for intercourse with her husband.

מַאי קָא מַשְׁמַע לָן? תְּנֵינָא: כׇּל הַנָּשִׁים בְּחֶזְקַת טָהֳרָה לְבַעֲלֵיהֶן! אִי מִמַּתְנִיתִין – הֲוָה אָמִינָא: הָנֵי מִילֵּי בְּאִשָּׁה שֶׁיֵּשׁ לָהּ וֶסֶת, אֲבָל אִשָּׁה שֶׁאֵין לָהּ וֶסֶת – בָּעֲיָא בְּדִיקָה.

The Gemara asks: **What is** Rav Yehuda **teaching us? We** already **learn** this from the mishna (15a): **All women have the presumptive status of purity to their husbands,** and therefore the husband does not need to ascertain whether she is ritually pure before engaging in intercourse. The Gemara answers: **If** this *halakha* is learned **from the mishna** alone, **I would say** that **this statement** applies only **to a woman who has** a fixed menstrual **cycle. But** in the case of **a woman who does not have** a fixed menstrual **cycle,** she is **required** to perform **an examination** before intercourse. Consequently, Rav Yehuda teaches us that even a woman who does not have a fixed menstrual cycle is not required to perform an examination before intercourse, unless she handles pure items.

וְהָא מַתְנִיתִין בְּאִשָּׁה שֶׁיֵּשׁ לָהּ וֶסֶת עָסְקִינַן! מַתְנִיתִין – בֵּין שֶׁיֵּשׁ לָהּ וֶסֶת בֵּין אֵין לָהּ וֶסֶת, וְהָא קָא מַשְׁמַע לָן: דְּאַף עַל גַּב דְּיֵשׁ לָהּ וֶסֶת, מִגּוֹ דְּבָעֲיָא בְּדִיקָה לְטָהֳרוֹת – בָּעֲיָא נַמִי בְּדִיקָה לְבַעְלָהּ.

The Gemara asks: **But aren't we are dealing** in **the mishna with** a case **of a woman who has** a fixed menstrual **cycle?** The Gemara answers: The mishna **is dealing both** with a case **where she has** a fixed menstrual **cycle** and with a case where **she does not have** a fixed menstrual **cycle. And this** is what the mishna **teaches us: That even though she has** a fixed menstrual **cycle,** and therefore one might think that she is exempt from examination, nevertheless if she handles pure items, **since** she is **required** to perform **an examination** in preparation **for** handling those **pure** items, she is **also required** to perform **an examination** in preparation **for** intercourse with **her husband.**

**HALAKHA**

**With regard to a woman who is engaged in handling pure items** – **בְּאִשָּׁה עֲסוּקָה בְּטָהֳרוֹת:** The Rambam rules that a woman who is required to examine herself because she handles ritually pure items is also required to examine herself before engaging in intercourse with her husband, even if she has a fixed menstrual cycle. If she does not handle ritually pure items, then, if she has a fixed menstrual cycle, she is not required to examine herself before engaging in intercourse with her husband. The Ra'avad disagrees and maintains that even if she does not have a fixed menstrual cycle, she is not required to examine herself before intercourse if she does not handle ritually pure items. The Rema, citing *Roke'ah*, rules that the *halakha* and common practice is in accordance with the latter opinion (Rambam *Sefer Tahara*, *Hilkhot Metamei Mishkav UMoshav* 4:7, and see *Kesef Mishne* there; *Shulḥan Arukh*, *Yoreh De'a* 186:1).

**NOTES**

**Since she is required to perform an examination in preparation for handling pure items, etc.** – **דְּמִגּוֹ דְּבָעֲיָא בְּדִיקָה לְטָהֳרוֹת וכו׳:** Why is there is a greater requirement for examination for the purpose of handling pure items than for intercourse with her husband? Isn't the sin of intercourse while she is menstruating, which is punishable by *karet*, more serious than rendering ritually pure items impure? The later commentaries suggest that the Sages were particularly concerned with regard to ritual impurity, just as the Torah shows great concern in this regard, as demonstrated by the many offerings prescribed by the Torah for one who consumes sacred items or enters into the Temple in a state of ritual impurity.

וְהָא אֲמָרָהּ שְׁמוּאֵל חֲדָא זִימְנָא! דַּאֲמַר רַבִּי זֵירָא, אָמַר רַבִּי אַבָּא בַּר יִרְמְיָה, אָמַר שְׁמוּאֵל: אִשָּׁה שֶׁאֵין לָהּ וֶסֶת – אֲסוּרָה לְשַׁמֵּשׁ עַד שֶׁתִּבְדּוֹק. וְאוֹקִימְנָא: בַּעֲסוּקָה בְּטָהֳרוֹת! חֲדָא מִכְּלַל חֲבֶרְתָּהּ אִתְּמַר.

The Gemara asks: **But didn't Shmuel** already **state** this *halakha* on **another occasion? As Rabbi Zeira said** that **Rabbi Abba bar Yirmeya says** that **Shmuel says:** With regard to **a woman who does not have** a fixed menstrual **cycle**, it is **forbidden** for her to engage in intercourse with her husband **until she examines** herself and determines that she is pure. **And we interpreted** this *halakha* as referring to a case **where she is engaged in** handling **pure** items. The Gemara answers: Shmuel did not in fact issue two statements; rather, **one was stated by inference from the other.** In other words, Shmuel said one of these statements explicitly; the other was reported by his students in his name based on an inference from what he had said.

תַּנְיָא נָמֵי הָכִי: בַּמֶּה דְּבָרִים אֲמוּרִים – לְטָהֳרוֹת, אֲבָל לְבַעְלָהּ – מוּתֶּרֶת. בַּמֶּה דְּבָרִים אֲמוּרִים – שֶׁהִנִּיחָהּ בְּחֶזְקַת טְהוֹרָה, אֲבָל הִנִּיחָהּ בְּחֶזְקַת טְמֵאָה – לְעוֹלָם הִיא בְּטוּמְאָתָהּ, עַד שֶׁתֹּאמַר לוֹ "טְהוֹרָה אָנִי".

The Gemara adds: **This is also taught** in a *baraita*: **In what** case **is this statement**, that a woman requires an examination, **said?** It is said with regard to a woman who is preparing **for** handling **pure** items. **But** with regard to engaging in intercourse **with her husband, she is permitted**[N] to do so without performing an examination. The *baraita* qualifies this ruling: And **in what** case **is this statement,** that she is not required to perform an examination, **said?** It is said **when** her husband traveled and **left her with the presumptive status of ritual purity.**[H] If so, upon his return she does not need to perform an examination before they engage in intercourse. **But if he left her with the presumptive status of ritual impurity,** she remains **forever in her status of impurity, until she says to him: I am ritually pure.**

**NOTES**

**But with regard to engaging in intercourse with her husband she is permitted – אֲבָל לְבַעְלָהּ מוּתֶּרֶת:** The early commentaries disagree concerning this *halakha*. Some say that a woman is not required to perform an examination prior to intercourse or after intercourse (Rashi). Others rule, based on their interpretation of the Gemara on 12b, that such a woman is required to perform two examinations, one before intercourse and one after intercourse (Rabbeinu Ḥananel and Rosh).

**HALAKHA**

**When her husband traveled and left her with the presumptive status of ritual purity – שֶׁהִנִּיחָהּ בְּחֶזְקַת טְהוֹרָה:** Every woman with a fixed menstrual cycle has the presumptive status of purity to her husband until she declares that she is impure or her neighbors know her to be a *nidda*. If, when a husband traveled, he left his wife in a presumptive status of purity, upon his return he does not need to ask her if she is still ritually pure. He may engage in intercourse with her, even if she is groggy and is unable to clarify her status to him. If when he left she was impure, he may not engage in intercourse with her until she declares her purity to him (Rambam *Sefer Tahara, Hilkhot Metamei Mishkav UMoshav* 4:7 and *Sefer Kedusha, Hilkhot Issurei Bia* 4:9).

Perek **I**
Daf **12** Amud **a**

בְּעָא מִינֵּיהּ רַבִּי זֵירָא מֵרַב יְהוּדָה: אִשָּׁה מַהוּ שֶׁתִּבְדּוֹק עַצְמָהּ לְבַעְלָהּ? אֲמַר לֵיהּ: לֹא תִּבְדּוֹק. וְתִבְדּוֹק, וּמָה בְּכָךְ? אִם כֵּן – לִבּוֹ נוֹקְפוֹ וּפוֹרֵשׁ.

§ **Rabbi Zeira raised a dilemma before Rav Yehuda: What is** the *halakha* as to whether **a woman should examine herself** before engaging in intercourse **with her husband?**[HN] Rav Yehuda **said to him: She should not examine** herself. Rabbi Zeira asked: **And let her examine** herself; **what** would be the problem **with that?** Rav Yehuda answered: **If so,** the **heart** of a scrupulous husband might **strike him** with pangs of conscience over sins that he could transgress, **and he** will **separate** from his wife out of fear that she is impure.

בְּעָא מִינֵּיהּ רַבִּי אַבָּא מֵרַב הוּנָא: אִשָּׁה מַהוּ שֶׁתִּבְדּוֹק עַצְמָהּ כְּשִׁיעוּר וֶסֶת, כְּדֵי לְחַיֵּיב בַּעְלָהּ חַטָּאת?

**Rabbi Abba raised** a similar **dilemma before Rav Huna: What is** the *halakha* as to whether **a woman should examine herself** immediately after engaging in intercourse, within the minimum **period of time** needed for the onset of **menstruation, in order to render her husband liable to** bring **a sin offering** for engaging in intercourse with a menstruating woman?

אֲמַר לֵיהּ: מִי מַשְׁכַּחַתְּ לָהּ לִבְדִיקָה כְּשִׁיעוּר וֶסֶת? וְהָתַנְיָא: אֵיזֶהוּ שִׁיעוּר וֶסֶת – מָשָׁל לְשַׁמָּשׁ וְעֵד שֶׁעוֹמְדִים בְּצַד הַמַּשְׁקוֹף, בִּיצִיאוֹת הַשַּׁמָּשׁ – נִכְנָס עֵד,

Rav Huna **said to him:** Can **you find** a case **where** it is physically possible to perform a full examination after intercourse within the **period of time** needed for the onset of **menstruation? But isn't it taught** in a *baraita*: **What is** the **period of time** needed for the onset of **menstruation?** This is **comparable to** a male **organ and an examination cloth that are standing alongside the doorpost,** i.e., at the entrance to the vagina; **upon the exit of** the **organ** the **examination cloth** immediately **enters.**

**HALAKHA**

**What is the** *halakha* **as to whether a woman should examine herself before engaging in intercourse with her husband – אִשָּׁה מַהוּ שֶׁתִּבְדּוֹק עַצְמָהּ לְבַעְלָהּ:** Not only is a woman who has a fixed menstrual cycle not required to perform self-examinations when she engages in intercourse, but she should not perform them even if she wishes to, as it will make her husband nervous and he may worry that perhaps he will engage in intercourse with a menstruating woman. By contrast, the Rambam rules that both wife and husband should examine themselves after intercourse with their respective swatches to determine if there was any blood discharged during intercourse. He also notes that scrupulous women should even examine themselves before intercourse. Nevertheless, the Rema, citing *Roke'aḥ*, rules in accordance with the first opinion that no examination should be performed, and he adds that this is the prevalent custom (Rambam *Sefer Tahara, Hilkhot Metamei Mishkav UMoshav* 4:7; see *Sefer Kedusha, Hilkhot Issurei Bia* 4:16, and Ra'avad and *Kesef Mishne* there; *Shulḥan Arukh, Yoreh De'a* 186:1).

**NOTES**

**What is the** *halakha* **as to whether a woman should examine herself before engaging in intercourse with her husband – אִשָּׁה מַהוּ שֶׁתִּבְדּוֹק עַצְמָהּ לְבַעְלָהּ:** It is unclear to which examination Rabbi Zeira is referring. The early commentaries differ in their explanations. Some claim that he is inquiring about an examination after intercourse, as although the examination after intercourse is not obligatory, it is customary for scrupulous women to perform that examination. The Rambam adds that he is referring only to an examination immediately after intercourse, but both the woman and the man are obligated to examine themselves sometime after intercourse to determine that there was no blood (see Rambam *Sefer Kedusha, Hilkhot Issurei Bia* 4:16, and *Haggahot Maimoniyyot* there). Others say that Rabbi Zeira is referring to both examinations, before intercourse and after intercourse. Rav Yehuda replied that she should not perform any examination (Rashi; *Tosafot*), and that is the *halakha* in practice (Ramban).

**HALAKHA**

And this is the examination cloth of virtuous women – וְזֶהוּ עֵדָן שֶׁל צְנוּעוֹת: In the case of a woman without a fixed menstrual cycle, she and her husband must examine themselves with their respective swatches before and after each intercourse. If, after three occasions, no blood is found, she then attains the presumptive status that intercourse does not bring upon her a menstrual flow, and from then on they no longer need to perform any examinations before or after intercourse. The Rambam and Rosh maintain that a woman without a fixed menstrual cycle must always examine herself before and after intercourse, and the Rambam adds that her husband must also examine himself. There are those who maintain that all these examinations are necessary only for a woman who is also handling ritually pure items (*Shulḥan Arukh*, *Yoreh De'a* 186:2, and see *Shakh* there).

הֲוֵי: וֶסֶת שֶׁאָמְרוּ – לְקִנּוּחַ וְלֹא לִבְדִיקָה. אֶלָּא: מַהוּ שֶׁתְּקַנֵּחַ?

The Gemara explains: **It is** apparent that **the period of time that they stated** is the time required **for** an external **wipe, and not** for a full internal **examination.** Therefore, if she did an internal examination and found blood, one cannot be certain that she was already menstruating during intercourse and thereby render the husband liable to bring a sin offering. **Rather,** this is Rabbi Abba's dilemma: **What is** the *halakha* as to whether a woman **should wipe** herself immediately after engaging in intercourse? Since this action can be performed quickly, if she were to find blood her husband would be liable to bring a sin offering.

אִיכָּא דְּאָמְרִי, הָכִי בְּעָא מִינֵּיהּ: אִשָּׁה מַהוּ שֶׁתִּבְדּוֹק עַצְמָהּ, כְּדֵי לְחַיֵּיב בַּעְלָהּ אָשָׁם תָּלוּי? אָמַר לוֹ: לֹא תִּבְדּוֹק. וְתִבְדּוֹק, וּמַה בְּכָךְ? אִם כֵּן – לִבּוֹ נוֹקְפוֹ וּפוֹרֵשׁ.

**Some say** that **this** is the dilemma that Rabbi Abba **raised before** Rav Huna: **What is** the *halakha* as to whether **a woman should examine herself** immediately after engaging in intercourse, **in order to render her husband liable to** bring **a provisional guilt offering** brought by one who is uncertain as to whether he committed a sin that requires a sin offering? Rav Huna **said to him: She should not examine** herself. Rabbi Abba asked: **And** let **her examine** herself; **what** would be the problem **with that?** Rav Huna answered: **If so,** the **heart** of a scrupulous husband might **strike him** with pangs of conscience over sins that he could transgress, **and he** will **separate** from his wife out of fear that she is impure.

״וּבְשָׁעָה שֶׁהִיא עוֹבֶרֶת״ וכו׳. אָמַר רַבִּי אַמִי אָמַר רַבִּי יַנַּאי: וְזֶהוּ עֵדָן שֶׁל צְנוּעוֹת. אָמַר לֵיהּ רַבִּי אַבָּא בַּר מֶמֶל לְרַבִּי אַמִי: תַּנָּא תָּנֵי ״צְרִיכוֹת״ וְאַתְּ תָּנֵי ״צְנוּעוֹת״! אָמַר לֵיהּ: שֶׁאֲנִי אוֹמֵר כָּל הַמְקַיֵּים דִּבְרֵי חֲכָמִים נִקְרָא ״צָנוּעַ״.

§ The mishna teaches: **And** she is also required to examine herself **at a time that she is about to** engage in intercourse with her husband. **Rabbi Ami says** that **Rabbi Yannai says: And this** examination performed before intercourse is known as: The **examination cloth of virtuous women,**[H] as this examination is not strictly required. **Rabbi Abba bar Memel said to Rabbi Ami:** The *tanna* teaches that women **are required** to perform this examination, **and** yet **you teach** that only **virtuous women** perform it. Rabbi Ami **said to him:** Yes, **as I say** that **anyone who fulfills the statements of the Sages is called virtuous.** Rabbi Ami did not mean that this examination is beyond the letter of the law. He was simply praising those who abide by the established *halakha*.

אָמַר רָבָא: וְשֶׁאֵינוֹ מְקַיֵּים דִּבְרֵי חֲכָמִים, ״צָנוּעַ״ הוּא דְּלָא מִקְּרֵי, הָא ״רָשָׁע״ לָא מִקְּרֵי? אֶלָּא אָמַר רָבָא: צְנוּעוֹת, עֵד שֶׁבָּדְקוּ בּוֹ עַצְמָן לִפְנֵי תַּשְׁמִישׁ זֶה – אֵין בּוֹדְקוֹת בּוֹ לִפְנֵי תַּשְׁמִישׁ אַחֵר; וְשֶׁאֵינָן צְנוּעוֹת – בּוֹדְקוֹת וְלֹא אִיכְפַּת לְהֶן.

With regard to Rabbi Ami's claim, **Rava says: And** according to your opinion, with regard to one **who does not fulfill the statements of the Sages, he is not called virtuous. But** this indicates that **he is not called wicked** either. This cannot be correct, as one who does not heed the instructions of the Sages is certainly wicked. **Rather, Rava said: Virtuous women** are those who do not reuse **the examination cloth that they used to examine themselves before this intercourse.** Even if no blood was found on it, **they do not examine themselves with it prior to another** act of **intercourse,** as once it was used once, it is not as clean as before. **And those who are not virtuous women** reuse the same examination cloths and **examine** themselves with them **and they are not particular** about this matter.

גּוּפָא, אָמַר רַבִּי זֵירָא, אָמַר רַבִּי אַבָּא בַּר יִרְמְיָה, אָמַר שְׁמוּאֵל: אִשָּׁה שֶׁאֵין לָהּ וֶסֶת – אֲסוּרָה לְשַׁמֵּשׁ עַד שֶׁתִּבְדּוֹק. אֲמַר לֵיהּ רַבִּי זֵירָא לְרַבִּי אַבָּא בַּר יִרְמְיָה: אֵין לָהּ וֶסֶת – בָּעֲיָא בְּדִיקָה, יֵשׁ לָהּ וֶסֶת – לָא בָּעֲיָא בְּדִיקָה?

§ The Gemara returns to **the** matter **itself: Rabbi Zeira says** that **Rabbi Abba bar Yirmeya says** that **Shmuel says:** With regard to **a woman who does not have** a fixed menstrual **cycle,** it is **forbidden** for her **to engage in intercourse until she examines** herself. **Rabbi Zeira said to Rabbi Abba bar Yirmeya:** Does Shmuel mean that if **she does not have** a fixed menstrual **cycle** she is **required** to perform **an examination,** but if **she has** a fixed menstrual **cycle** she is **not required** to perform **an examination?** This is difficult, as the mishna teaches that even a woman with a fixed menstrual cycle is required to perform an examination before she engages in intercourse.

אֲמַר לֵיהּ: יֵשׁ לָהּ וֶסֶת, עֵרָה – בָּעֲיָא בְּדִיקָה, יְשֵׁנָה – לָא בָּעֲיָא בְּדִיקָה. אֵין לָהּ וֶסֶת; בֵּין עֵרָה בֵּין יְשֵׁנָה – בָּעֲיָא בְּדִיקָה.

Rabbi Abba bar Yirmeya **said to him:** The mishna means that if **she has** a fixed menstrual **cycle** and she is **awake,** she is **required** to perform **an examination;** if she is **sleeping** she is **not required** to perform **an examination** before intercourse, as this would involve much effort. If **she does not have** a fixed menstrual **cycle,** then **whether** she is **awake or sleeping,** she is **required** to perform **an examination.**

אָמַר רָבָא, וְלֵימָא לֵיהּ: יֵשׁ לָהּ וֶסֶת, לְטָהֳרוֹת – בָּעֲיָא בְּדִיקָה, לְבַעְלָהּ – לָא בָּעֲיָא בְּדִיקָה, אֵין לָהּ וֶסֶת – אֲפִילּוּ לְבַעְלָהּ נַמִי בָּעֲיָא בְּדִיקָה; וּמִדְּלָא אֲמַר לֵיהּ הָכִי, שְׁמַע מִינָּהּ קָסָבַר שְׁמוּאֵל: כׇּל לְבַעְלָהּ – לָא בָּעֲיָא בְּדִיקָה.

Rava says: And let Rabbi Abba bar Yirmeya say a different answer to Rabbi Zeira: Shmuel means that if **she has** a fixed menstrual **cycle,** then **in** the case of a woman who handles **pure** items, she is **required** to perform **an examination** for the sake of intercourse as well. If she does not handle pure items, then **for** the sake of intercourse with **her husband** alone she is **not required** to perform **an examination.** By contrast, if she **does not have** a fixed menstrual **cycle,** then she is **required** to perform **an examination even for** the sake of intercourse with **her husband.** Rava concludes: **And from** the fact **that** Rabbi Abba bar Yirmeya **did not say this** answer, one can **learn from** it that **Shmuel holds** that in **any** case where an examination is only **for** the purpose of intercourse with **her husband,** she is **not required** to perform **an examination.**

תָּנוּ רַבָּנַן: חַמָּרִין וּפוֹעֲלִין וְהַבָּאִין מִבֵּית הָאֵבֶל וּמִבֵּית הַמִּשְׁתֶּה – נְשֵׁיהֶם לָהֶם בְּחֶזְקַת טָהֳרָה, וּבָאִין וְשׁוֹהִין עִמָּהֶם, בֵּין יְשֵׁנוֹת בֵּין עֵרוֹת. בַּמֶּה דְּבָרִים אֲמוּרִים – שֶׁהִנִּיחָן בְּחֶזְקַת טָהֳרָה, אֲבָל הִנִּיחָן בְּחֶזְקַת טוּמְאָה – לְעוֹלָם הִיא טְמֵאָה, עַד שֶׁתֹּאמַר לוֹ ״טְהוֹרָה אֲנִי״.

§ **The Sages taught** in a *baraita*: With regard to **donkey drivers and laborers** who return home, **and those who come** home **from the house of mourning or from the house of feasting** for a wedding, **their wives** remain **in a presumptive status of purity.**[H] **And** therefore **they may come and remain with them,** i.e., engage in intercourse with them, **whether they are sleeping**[N] **or awake.** The *baraita* clarifies: **In what** case **is this statement said? When** the husbands **left** their wives **in a presumptive state of purity. But** if the husbands **left them in a presumptive state of impurity, she** remains **forever** in a status of **impurity, until she says to him: I am ritually pure.**

וְהָא, שְׁמוּאֵל בְּמַאי מוֹקֵי לַהּ? אִי בְּשֶׁיֵּשׁ לָהּ וֶסֶת – קַשְׁיָא עֵרָה! וְאִי בְּשֶׁאֵין לָהּ וֶסֶת – קַשְׁיָא בֵּין עֵרָה בֵּין יְשֵׁנָה!

The Gemara asks: **But** according to Rabbi Abba bar Yirmeya, **with regard to what** case does **Shmuel interpret this** *baraita*? If the *baraita* is dealing **with** a woman **who has** a fixed menstrual **cycle,** it is **difficult,** as Shmuel holds that such a woman who is **awake** is required to perform an examination, whereas the *baraita* indicates that no examination is necessary. **And if** the *baraita* is referring **to** a woman **who does not have** a fixed menstrual **cycle,** it is also **difficult,** as Shmuel holds that she always is required to perform an examination, **whether** she is **awake or sleeping.**

לְעוֹלָם בְּשֶׁיֵּשׁ לָהּ וֶסֶת, וְכֵיוָן שֶׁתְּבָעָהּ – אֵין לְךָ בְּדִיקָה גְּדוֹלָה מִזּוֹ. אֲמַר לֵיהּ רַב פַּפָּא לְרָבָא: מַהוּ לְמֶעְבַּד כִּי הָא מַתְנִיתָא?

The Gemara answers: **Actually,** the *baraita* is referring to a case **where she has** a fixed menstrual **cycle, and since** her husband came home from his travels and **requested of her** that they engage in intercourse, **there is no greater examination than this.**[N] Since she had time to consider the matter while he was asking her, she would have remembered had she sensed the onset of her menstrual cycle, whereas under regular circumstances she might not have time to recall. Based upon this explanation, **Rav Pappa**[P] **said to Rava: What is** the *halakha* with regard **to acting in accordance with this** *baraita*? Perhaps it is necessary to wake her and ask her whether she is ritually pure.

HALAKHA

**Donkey drivers and laborers…their wives remain in a presumptive status of purity – חַמָּרִין וּפוֹעֲלִין...נְשֵׁיהֶם לָהֶם בְּחֶזְקַת טָהֳרָה:** Every woman with a fixed menstrual cycle has the presumptive status of purity to her husband until she declares that she is impure or her neighbors know her to be a *nidda*. If, when a husband traveled, he left his wife in a presumptive status of purity, upon his return he does not need to ask her if she is still ritually pure. He may engage in intercourse with her, even if she is unable to clarify her status to him. If when he left she was impure, he may not engage in intercourse with her until she declares her purity to him (Rambam *Sefer Tahara, Hilkhot Metamei Mishkav UMoshav* 4:7 and *Sefer Kedusha, Hilkhot Issurei Bia* 4:9).

NOTES

**Whether they are sleeping – בֵּין יְשֵׁנוֹת:** Although it is prohibited to engage in intercourse with one's wife while she is sleeping (see *Nedarim* 20b), the *baraita* is dealing only with her status as a menstruating woman, irrespective of other considerations (*Tosafot*). Alternatively, *Tosafot* suggest that the *baraita* is referring to a woman who is not fully asleep; she is merely not alert enough to declare whether or not she is ritually pure.

**There is no greater examination than this – אֵין לְךָ בְּדִיקָה גְּדוֹלָה מִזּוֹ:** *Tosafot* explain that those people discussed in the *baraita* have a tendency to take more time enticing their wives before requesting of them to engage in intercourse. Therefore, she would have remembered during that time if she was expecting the onset of her menstrual period. This would not apply to a standard case of a husband who requests of his wife to engage in intercourse.

PERSONALITIES

**Rav Pappa – רַב פַּפָּא:** Rav Pappa belonged to the fifth generation of the *amora'im* of Babylon. He was a student of both Abaye and Rava in Pumbedita. Rav Pappa established an academy in Neresh, where he was joined by his close friend Rav Huna, son of Rav Yehoshua, who was appointed chief lecturer. After Rava's death, many of his students came to study under Rav Pappa, who had more than two hundred students attending his lectures. Rav Pappa's father was a wealthy merchant and supported him in order to allow him to study. Rav Pappa also became a wealthy businessman; he was a successful brewer of date beer and he prospered in other business ventures as well. The Talmud records that he engaged in trade with both Jews and gentiles and had a reputation for fairness and generosity in his business dealings.

Perek **I**
Daf **12** Amud **b**

אֲמַר לֵיהּ: סוּדָנִי, לָא, דְּמִגַּנְיָא בְּאַפֵּיהּ. אָמַר רַב כָּהֲנָא: שְׁאַלְתִּינְהוּ לְאֵינָשֵׁי בֵּיתֵיהּ דְּרַב פַּפָּא וּדְרַב הוּנָא בְּרֵיהּ דְּרַב יְהוֹשֻׁעַ, כִּי אָתוּ רַבָּנַן מִבֵּי רַב מַצְרְכִי לְכוּ בְּדִיקָה? וַאֲמַרוּ לִי: לָא. וְלִישַׁיְּילִינְהוּ לְדִידְהוּ! דִּילְמָא אִינְהוּ קָא מַחְמִירִי אַנַּפְשַׁיְיהוּ.

Rava **said to** Rav Pappa: **Wise one** [*sudani*]![L] **No, won't she be demeaned before him?** It is embarrassing for her if she is awoken and has to think about whether or not she is pure. **Rav Kahana says: I asked the members of the households,** i.e., the wives, **of Rav Pappa and of Rav Huna, son of Rav Yehoshua: When the Sages,** your husbands, **came** home **from** the **study hall,** did they **require you** to perform **an examination prior** to intercourse? **And they said to me: No.** The Gemara asks: **But** why ask their wives? Why not **ask** those Sages **themselves?** The Gemara answers: **Perhaps** they might rule leniently for others, while **acting stringently with themselves.** Therefore, their wives were asked, to determine how the Sages conducted themselves in their personal lives.

LANGUAGE

**Wise one [*sudani*] – סוּדָנִי:** Several explanations are given for this nickname. Some say that it comes from the Hebrew word *sod*, which means secret, as in the verse: "The secret [*sod*] of the Lord is with them that fear Him" (Psalms 25:14). Rashi explains that Rav Pappa was called by this name due to his stature as a Torah scholar. Others explain that it was because of his piety (*Arukh*). Alternatively, this moniker refers to one who manufactures or sells wine (Rashi on *Berakhot* 44b).

תָּנוּ רַבָּנַן: אִשָּׁה שֶׁאֵין לָהּ וֶסֶת – אֲסוּרָה לְשַׁמֵּשׁ, וְאֵין לָהּ לֹא כְּתוּבָּה וְלֹא פֵּירוֹת וְלֹא מְזוֹנוֹת וְלֹא בְּלָאוֹת, וְיוֹצִיא וְלֹא מַחֲזִיר עוֹלָמִית, דִּבְרֵי רַבִּי מֵאִיר.

§ **The Sages taught** in a *baraita*: With regard to **a woman who does not have** a fixed menstrual **cycle,** she is **forbidden to engage in intercourse, and she does not have** the right to receive payment of her **marriage contract** if divorced or widowed, **nor** is she entitled to payment from her husband for the **produce** of her property[N] that he consumed, **nor** is she entitled to provisions for her **sustenance** from his estate, **nor** does she get back her **worn clothes**[N] or other items she brought with her to her marriage as part of her dowry. And furthermore, her husband **must divorce** her **and he may never remarry** her. This is **the statement of Rabbi Meir.**

רַבִּי חֲנִינָא בֶּן אַנְטִיגְנוֹס אוֹמֵר: מְשַׁמֶּשֶׁת בִּשְׁנֵי עֵדִים, הֵן עִוּוּתָהּ הֵן תַּקָּנָתָהּ. מִשּׁוּם אַבָּא חָנָן אָמְרוּ: אוֹי לוֹ לְבַעְלָהּ.

**Rabbi Ḥanina ben Antigonus says:** She is permitted to **engage in intercourse** with her husband, but she must examine herself **with two examination cloths,** one prior to intercourse and one afterward. **They** may be to **her detriment** if she finds blood on the cloths, or **they** may lead to **her betterment,** since if she finds no blood she is permitted to her husband. **They said in the name of Abba Ḥanan: Woe to her husband!**

אֲסוּרָה לְשַׁמֵּשׁ – דִּילְמָא מְקַלְקֶלֶת לֵיהּ. וְאֵין לָהּ כְּתוּבָּה – כֵּיוָן דְּלָא חַזְיָא לְבִיאָה לֵית לַהּ כְּתוּבָּה,

The Gemara explains each clause of the *baraita*: She is **forbidden to engage in intercourse,** as **perhaps she will ruin** her husband if she emits blood during intercourse. **And** with regard to the *halakha* that **she does not have** the right to receive payment of her **marriage contract,** the reason is that **since** she is **not fit for intercourse, she is not** entitled to payment of her **marriage contract.**

וְלֹא פֵּירוֹת, וְלֹא מְזוֹנוֹת, וְלֹא בְּלָאוֹת – תְּנָאֵי כְּתוּבָּה כִּכְתוּבָּה דָּמוּ.

The Gemara continues its explanation: **And** she is **not** entitled to payment for the **produce** of her property, **nor** is she entitled to provisions for her **sustenance** from his estate, **nor** does she get back her **worn clothes.** The reason for all these is because **stipulations in the marriage contract are considered like the marriage contract** itself. Since she is not entitled to a marriage contract, she is likewise not entitled to these additional provisions that are stipulated in the marriage contract.

״וְיוֹצִיא וְלֹא יַחֲזִיר עוֹלָמִית״ פְּשִׁיטָא! לָא צְרִיכָא – דְּהַדְרָה וְאִתַּקְנָה, מַהוּ דְּתֵימָא לִיהַדְרַהּ, קָא מַשְׁמַע לַן דְּזִימְנִין דְּאָזְלָא וּמִנַּסְבָא וּמִתַּקְנָא,

The Gemara analyzes the next clause in the *baraita*: Her husband **must divorce** her **and he may never remarry** her. The Gemara asks: Isn't that **obvious?** The Gemara answers: **No,** it is **necessary** to teach this in a case **where** her situation **was subsequently amended,** i.e., she established a fixed menstrual cycle. **Lest you say** that he **may remarry her,** the *baraita* **teaches us** that this is not permitted, **as sometimes** such a woman might **go and marry** someone else **and** her status is **subsequently amended.**

וְאָמַר: ״אִילּוּ הָיִיתִי יוֹדֵעַ שֶׁכָּךְ הָיָה – אֲפִילּוּ הֱיִיתֶם נוֹתְנִין לִי מֵאָה מָנֶה לֹא הָיִיתִי מְגָרְשָׁהּ״, וְנִמְצָא גֵּט בָּטֵל וּבָנֶיהָ מַמְזֵרִין.

**And** the problem in this scenario is that her first husband might **say: If I would have known that it is like this,** that she would be cured, **even if you would have given me one hundred** times **one hundred dinars**[B] to divorce her **I would not have divorced her.**[N] **And** if so, the **bill of divorce** will be **found** to be **void, and her children** from her second husband will be considered ***mamzerim.*** Therefore it must be made clear to him from the outset that this divorce is final.

״מִשּׁוּם אַבָּא חָנָן אָמְרוּ: אוֹי לוֹ לְבַעְלָהּ״. אִיכָּא דְּאָמְרִי: לְרַבִּי מֵאִיר אָמַר לֵיהּ – דְּבָעֵי לְאַגְבּוּיַהּ כְּתוּבְּתָהּ. אִיכָּא דְּאָמְרִי: לְרַבִּי חֲנִינָא בֶּן אַנְטִיגְנוֹס קָאָמַר לֵיהּ – דִּמְקַלְקֶלֶת לֵיהּ.

The Gemara analyzes the final clause of the *baraita*: **They said in the name of Abba Ḥanan: Woe to her husband! Some say** that **he said this to Rabbi Meir, as** Abba Ḥanan maintains that the husband is **required to settle** her payment of **her marriage contract** upon their divorce. And **some say** that **he said this to Rabbi Ḥanina ben Antigonus,** since Abba Ḥanan disagrees with his opinion and holds that it is forbidden to engage in intercourse with her, **as** perhaps **she will ruin him** if they engage in intercourse when she is menstruating.

אָמַר רַב יְהוּדָה, אָמַר שְׁמוּאֵל: הֲלָכָה כְּרַבִּי חֲנִינָא בֶּן אַנְטִיגְנוֹס. וּבְמַאי? אִי בַּעֲסוּקָה בְּטָהֳרוֹת – הָא אֲמָרָהּ שְׁמוּאֵל חֲדָא זִימְנָא!

**Rav Yehuda says** that **Shmuel says:** The ***halakha*** **is in accordance with** the opinion of **Rabbi Ḥanina ben Antigonus.** The Gemara asks: **And with regard to what** case did Shmuel issue this ruling of *halakha*? The Gemara elaborates: **If** it is referring to a woman who **is engaged in** handling ritually **pure** items, **didn't Shmuel** already **say** on **another occasion** that a woman without a fixed menstrual cycle must examine herself prior to intercourse?

NOTES

**Nor produce of her property** – וְלֹא פֵּירוֹת: This is referring to the benefits that the husband received from the usufruct property that his wife brought into the marriage. One might have thought that as she has no right to receive payment of her marriage contract, it is evident that she was never really his wife, and therefore he must reimburse her for the benefit that he received from her property. Therefore, the *baraita* teaches that she is not entitled to any such reimbursement (Rashi).

**Nor does she get back her worn clothes** – וְלֹא בְּלָאוֹת: There are certain items that a woman brings into a marriage, such as clothing, whose value is guaranteed to be returned to her upon divorce or her husband's death. These are known as guaranteed property. Her husband is permitted to use them, even if they become worn through his use. Rashi maintains that in a case such as this, when there is an obligation to divorce her, she is not entitled to those worn clothes and items, even if they remain intact. Other early commentaries maintain that any guaranteed property that is intact must be returned to her, and the worn clothes mentioned here are clothes and items that are entirely worn out, to the point that they are unusable. According to this opinion, the *baraita* means that the husband is not responsible for reimbursement with regard to those items. Furthermore, according to this opinion, the woman is also entitled to the additional sum that her husband voluntarily added to her marriage contract.

**I would not have divorced her** – לֹא הָיִיתִי מְגָרְשָׁהּ: The early commentaries are puzzled as to how this man could possibly claim that he would not have divorced his wife. Isn't he obligated to divorce her due to her lack of a fixed menstrual cycle? They answer that since the court does not actually force him to divorce her, he is able to make such an assertion. Therefore, he is able to claim that he would have stayed married to her until she attained a fixed menstrual cycle, as she did while she was married to her second husband (Ran).

BACKGROUND

**One hundred times one hundred dinars** [*maneh*] – מֵאָה מָנֶה: The *maneh* is a coin worth one hundred dinars. To evaluate the purchasing power of one hundred *maneh*, it should be kept in mind that a worker's daily wages amounted to roughly four dinars. One hundred *maneh* were worth approximately seven years of the average worker's wages.

וְאִי בְּשֶׁאֵינָהּ עֲסוּקָה בְּטָהֳרוֹת – הָא אָמַר כׇּל לְבַעְלָהּ – לָא בָּעְיָא בְּדִיקָה, דְּאָמַר רַבִּי זֵירָא, אָמַר רַבִּי אַבָּא בַּר יִרְמְיָה, אָמַר שְׁמוּאֵל: אִשָּׁה שֶׁאֵין לָהּ וֶסֶת – אֲסוּרָה לְשַׁמֵּשׁ עַד שֶׁתִּבְדּוֹק, וְאוֹקִימְנָא לַהּ – בַּעֲסוּקָה בְּטָהֳרוֹת! מַאן דְּמַתְנֵי הָא, לָא מַתְנֵי הָא.

הדרן עלך שמאי אומר

**And if** it is referring to a woman **who is not engaged in** handling ritually **pure** items, **doesn't** Shmuel **say** that in **any** case where an examination is only **for** the purpose of intercourse with **her husband,** not for handling pure items, she is **not required** to perform **an examination? As Rabbi Zeira said** that **Rabbi Abba bar Yirmeya says** that **Shmuel says: A woman who does not have** a fixed menstrual **cycle is forbidden to engage in intercourse until she examines** herself, **and we interpreted this** statement as referring to cases **where she is engaged in** handling ritually **pure** items.[H] The Gemara answers: **He who teaches this does not teach that,**[N] i.e., Shmuel's ruling is in fact referring to a woman engaged in handling pure items, and the two rulings were cited in his name by different Sages.

### HALAKHA

**A woman who does not have a fixed menstrual cycle… where she is engaged in handling ritually pure items – אִשָּׁה שֶׁאֵין לָהּ וֶסֶת...בַּעֲסוּקָה בְּטָהֳרוֹת:** The Rambam writes that a woman who does not have a fixed menstrual cycle must examine herself before and after intercourse with two separate swatches. It appears that this ruling applies even to a woman who does not handle ritually pure items. The Ra'avad disagrees and rules that it should apply only to a woman who handles ritually pure items, while a woman who does not handle pure items is not required to examine herself just for intercourse with her husband. Most authorities follow the Ra'avad's opinion, which is supported by the Gemara's conclusion with regard to Shmuel's opinion (see *Shakh*; *Haggahot Maimoniyyot*; *Kesef Mishne*). With regard to the *halakha* as it is practiced, some say that in a place where the prevalent custom is to be lenient, one should not act stringently, while anywhere else one should act stringently as set down in the *Shulḥan Arukh* (*Pitḥei Teshuva*, citing *Torat Shelamim*). Others maintain that even the lenient opinion is only lenient in that a full internal examination is not required, but a surface wiping is necessary, and the swatch must be left on her for the amount of time needed for the onset of menstruation (Rambam *Sefer Kedusha*, *Hilkhot Issurei Bia* 4:16 and *Sefer Tahara*, *Hilkhot Metamei Mishkav UMoshav* 4:7; *Shulḥan Arukh*, *Yoreh De'a* 186:2).

### NOTES

**He who teaches this does not teach that – מַאן דְּמַתְנֵי הָא לָא מַתְנֵי הָא:** Some explain that two *amora'im* reported the same statement in the name of Shmuel. According to this explanation, Shmuel holds that a woman who handles ritually pure items must perform an examination before and after intercourse, even if she has a fixed menstrual cycle. Whereas a woman who does not handle ritually pure items needs no examination, even if she does not have a fixed menstrual cycle (Rashi; Rid). Others understand that the case is that the *amora'im* reported opposing opinions in the name of Shmuel. According to Rabbi Abba bar Yirmeya, Shmuel holds that even when she does not handle pure items, she is required to perform an examination if she does not have a fixed menstrual cycle, while according to Rabbi Yehuda, Shmuel holds that if she does not handle ritually pure items she need not examine herself (Rambam; Rabbeinu Ḥananel; Rabbeinu Tam in *Sefer HaYashar*).

# Summary of **Perek I**

This chapter clarified the *halakhot* and details with regard to a woman who assumes ritual impurity upon experiencing a discharge of menstrual blood. It discussed the possibility of blood leaving her uterus before it was physically discovered, and the status of ritually pure items that she handled prior to that discovery.

In the case of a woman who has a fixed menstrual cycle, her time is sufficient, i.e., she assumes ritual impurity status only from the time of her discovery of menstrual blood, not retroactively. But with regard to a woman who does not have a fixed menstrual cycle, the Sages disagree. Some maintain that she too need not worry about retroactive impurity. Several reasons are given for this opinion. One is that this woman had a presumptive status of ritual purity until that moment, and therefore any uncertainty in the interim is resolved by reliance on that presumptive status. Another reason is that had menstrual blood been in the womb previously, it would have come out at that stage. Since it was discovered only later, at that moment, it can be assumed that it was there only at that point in time.

Yet another reason for not imposing retroactive impurity is that every woman who has a menstrual flow clearly senses that flow. Consequently, if a woman felt her flow only at that particular time, it stands to reason that she had no previous discharge. According to this last reason, woman who are unable to perceive such physical sensations, such as mentally incompetent women, would transmit impurity retroactively. One more rationale for this ruling is that if women were deemed impure retroactively, their husbands might be too apprehensive to engage in intercourse with them, which would cause them to be derelict in the mitzva to procreate.

With regard to the scope of a woman's retroactive impurity, some say that it extends back to her last examination, even if that occurred several days earlier. Others hold that it extends back to the shorter of the following two periods: Either a twenty-four-hour period, or since the last time she performed an examination. The *halakha* is in accordance with this opinion. The dispute among the Sages applies only to a case where a woman discovers a flow of menstrual blood. If she discovered a blood stain, all agree that it transmits impurity retroactively.

The Sages disagree with regard to a woman's retroactive impurity for sacred items that she might have touched during that period, but with regard to non-sacred items that one treats in the manner of sacred items for the purposes of ritual purity, all agree that a menstruating woman renders them impure only from that point onward, not retroactively, as the elevated status of these items is merely a stringency to protect the sanctity of consecrated items.

There are certain categories of women with regard to whom all agree that they transmit impurity only from the time that they find menstrual blood, even if the blood is emitted outside of their regular menstrual cycle. Four such categories of women are enumerated in this chapter: The first is a menstrual virgin, who has yet to see menstrual blood, even if she was married and experienced bleeding after her first intercourse. The second is a pregnant woman, starting from the third month of her pregnancy, which is the point at which her fetus is recognizable to others. The third is a nursing woman, a status that continues for a period of twenty-four months following birth. Finally, the fourth is an elderly woman who has passed through three regular menstrual cycles of thirty days without experiencing bleeding.

# Introduction to **Perek II**

*And he shall sacrifice it before the Lord, and make atonement for her; and she shall be purified from the source of her blood. This is the law for she who bears, whether a male or a female.*

(Leviticus 12:7)

*And if a woman has an issue, and her issue in her flesh is blood, she shall be in her menstruation seven days, and whoever touches her shall be impure until the evening.*

(Leviticus 15:19)

*If there arise a matter too hard for you in judgment, between blood and blood, between plea and plea, and between leprous mark and leprous mark, even matters of controversy within your gates, then you shall arise, and get up unto the place that the Lord your God shall choose.*

(Deuteronomy 17:8)

The verse "and if a woman has an issue, and her issue in her flesh is blood" teaches that a menstruating woman is rendered ritually impure. Therefore, a woman must examine herself to see whether she has contracted this impurity, so that she does not transmit impurity to other items or partake of *teruma*, the portion of the produce designated for the priest, in a state of ritual impurity. This basic *halakha* leads to the secondary question of how women who are not halakhically competent can be examined so that they may partake of *teruma*. With regard to the examination itself, it must be determined how the woman should perform it, and at what intervals it should be conducted. A similar inquiry applies to a man who wishes to examine himself for the impurity of a seminal emission or a gonorrhea-like discharge [*ziva*].

It is derived from the phrase "her issue in her flesh is blood" that not all fluids that are discharged from the uterus are ritually impure; only blood is. But the Torah does not specify the precise appearance of impure blood. Since there are many shades of red, as well as other reddish colors, it is necessary to establish the exact color of this blood. Furthermore, sometimes blood can change in color, and therefore the status of every reddish tinge must be established.

In addition, the phrase "between blood and blood" indicates that certain types of blood are ritually pure, as only blood from the uterus whose color is the proper shade of red renders the woman impure. This is derived from the phrase "from the source of her blood," which refers to the uterus.

If a woman examined herself and discovered blood, but is unsure whether or not the blood is impure, she requires the ruling of a halakhic authority. Many questions arise with regard to this examination by a halakhic authority, e.g., in what manner it should be performed, and whether one halakhic authority can deem blood pure after another halakhic authority has already deemed it impure.

These and other related matters are discussed in this chapter.

מתני׳ כָּל הַיָּד הַמַּרְבָּה לִבְדּוֹק, בַּנָּשִׁים – מְשׁוּבַּחַת, וּבָאֲנָשִׁים – תִּקָּצֵץ.

**MISHNA** With regard to **any hand that is diligent to examine** bodily emissions to ascertain ritual impurity, **among women**[H] such a hand **is praiseworthy. But among men**[H] such a hand **should be severed,** as this action is apt to lead to a seminal emission for naught.

גמ׳ מַאי שְׁנָא נָשִׁים וּמַאי שְׁנָא אֲנָשִׁים? נָשִׁים לָאו בְּנוֹת הַרְגָּשָׁה נִינְהוּ – מְשׁוּבָּחוֹת, אֲנָשִׁים דִּבְנֵי הַרְגָּשָׁה נִינְהוּ – תִּקָּצֵץ.

**GEMARA** The Gemara asks: **What is different** about **women and what is different** about **men,** that women are praised for examining for bodily emissions while men are castigated for the same? The Gemara answers: **Women are not susceptible to** sexual **arousal** by this action, and therefore when a woman is diligent to examine herself she is considered **praiseworthy;** whereas **men, who are susceptible to** sexual **arousal**[N] and may experience a seminal emission as a result of this contact, may not do so, and the hand of a man who conducts frequent examinations for emissions **should be severed.**

אִי הָכִי, מַאי אִירְיָא מַרְבָּה? כִּי לֹא מַרְבָּה נַמִי! כִּי קָתָנֵי ״מַרְבָּה״ – אַנָּשִׁים.

The Gemara asks: **If so, why** does the mishna state **specifically** among men that only the hand that is **diligent** to examine, i.e., that does so often, should be severed? Even **when** a man **is not diligent** to examine, but does so occasionally, this action is **also** apt to cause a seminal emission. The Gemara answers: **When** the mishna **teaches:** Any hand that is **diligent** to examine, it states this only **with regard to women,** as men should not examine even occasionally.

תָּנָא: בַּמֶּה דְּבָרִים אֲמוּרִים – לְעִנְיַן שִׁכְבַת זֶרַע, אֲבָל לְעִנְיַן זוֹב – אַף הוּא מְשׁוּבָּח כַּנָּשִׁים.

The Gemara continues to discuss the examination of men for seminal emissions. It is **taught** in a *baraita*: **In what** case **is this statement,** that men should not examine themselves, **said?** It is said **with regard to** an examination for **semen. But with regard to** a man who examines himself for gonorrhea-like **discharge** [*zov*], **he too is praiseworthy** for examining diligently, **as women** are. The reason is that a man who experiences two such discharges is ritually impure but is not obligated to bring an offering, whereas one who experiences three such emissions must bring an offering as a *zav*. Therefore, it is important for a man who experiences a gonorrhea-like discharge to examine and count his emissions carefully.

וַאֲפִילּוּ לְעִנְיַן שִׁכְבַת זֶרַע, אִם בָּא לִבְדּוֹק בִּצְרוֹר אוֹ בְּחֶרֶס – בּוֹדֵק.

The *baraita* adds: **And even with regard to semen, if one wants to examine** himself **with a rock or with** a piece of **earthenware,** which are hard and will not warm the body, **he may examine** himself in this manner.

וּבְמַטְלִית לֹא? וְהָתַנְיָא: בּוֹדֵק עַצְמוֹ בְּמַטְלִית וּבְכָל דָּבָר שֶׁרוֹצֶה! כִּדְאָמַר אַבָּיֵי: בְּמַטְלִית עָבָה, הָכָא נַמִי – בְּמַטְלִית עָבָה.

The Gemara asks: **And** may a man **not** examine himself **with** a linen **cloth? But isn't it taught** in a *baraita*: A man **may examine himself with a cloth,** to see if he has emitted semen, **or with any** similar **item that he wants?** The Gemara answers: Just **as Abaye said,** with regard to a different issue, that it is referring **to a coarse cloth,** which will not warm one's body, **here too,** the *baraita* is referring **to a coarse cloth,** which will not lead to a seminal emission.

וְהֵיכָא אִיתְּמַר דְּאַבָּיֵי? אַהָא, דִּתְנַן: הָיָה אוֹכֵל בִּתְרוּמָה וְהִרְגִּישׁ שֶׁנִּזְדַּעְזְעוּ אֵיבָרָיו – אוֹחֵז בְּאַמָּתוֹ וּבוֹלֵעַ אֶת הַתְּרוּמָה.

The Gemara asks: **And where was** this statement **of Abaye stated?** It was stated **with regard to that which we learned** in a mishna (40a): If a priest **was eating *teruma* and he sensed that his limbs quaked,**[H] indicating that a seminal emission was imminent, he should firmly **hold his penis** to prevent the emission from leaving his body, **and swallow the *teruma*** while ritually pure.

**HALAKHA**

**Any hand that is diligent to examine among women – כָּל הַיָּד הַמַּרְבָּה לִבְדּוֹק בַּנָּשִׁים:** A woman who is diligent to examine herself, whether when she is counting the days for her purity or when she has not yet experienced bleeding, is considered praiseworthy. This is the case even if she has a fixed menstrual period. But she should not do so at the time of intercourse (Rambam *Sefer Kedusha*, *Hilkhot Issurei Bia* 8:11; *Shulḥan Arukh*, *Yoreh De'a* 184:1).

**Among men – בָּאֲנָשִׁים:** It is prohibited for an unmarried man to handle his penis, so that he does not arouse himself. He should not even place his hand below his navel, for the same reason. When he urinates, he should do so without taking hold of his penis. It is permitted for a married man to take hold of his penis when urinating, even if his wife is not present (*Beit Shmuel*). But even a married man should touch his penis only when he needs to urinate (Rambam *Sefer Kedusha*, *Hilkhot Issurei Bia* 21:23; *Shulḥan Arukh*, *Even HaEzer* 23:4).

**If a priest was eating *teruma* and he sensed that his limbs quaked – הָיָה אוֹכֵל בִּתְרוּמָה וְהִרְגִּישׁ שֶׁנִּזְדַּעְזְעוּ אֵיבָרָיו:** If a priest was eating *teruma* and realized that his limbs were quaking, he should take hold of his penis, preferably above the corona (Radbaz), and swallow the *teruma* (Rambam *Sefer Zera'im*, *Hilkhot Terumot* 7:4).

**NOTES**

**Men, who are susceptible to arousal – אֲנָשִׁים דִּבְנֵי הַרְגָּשָׁה נִינְהוּ:** Various explanations have been suggested by the early commentaries for this difference between men and women. Some say that the constant handling of the penis can lead to a seminal emission, whereas women do not experience seminal emissions (*Tosafot* on *Yevamot* 12b; Rashi; Ramban; Rashba; Ritva; Ran; Meiri). Others claim that women who touch their private parts could also destroy any semen that might be there, but as they are not obligated in the mitzva to be fruitful and multiply the prohibition against wasting seed does not apply to them (*Tosafot* on *Yevamot* 12b, citing Rabbeinu Tam; see *Gilyon* of *Tosafot*).

## HALAKHA

**Anyone who holds his penis and urinates – כָּל הָאוֹחֵז בְּאַמָּתוֹ וּמַשְׁתִּין:** One should be careful not to hold his penis and urinate, as this might cause him to emit semen for naught. It is permitted for a married man to urinate in this manner, although some commentaries maintain that this leniency applies only if his wife is with him and she is not menstruating (*Magen Avraham*). Others rule that this is the *halakha* even if his wife is not present (*Beit Shmuel*). It is an attribute of piety to be careful in this regard even when one is married, in accordance with the opinion of Rabbi Eliezer, as explained by Rav Naḥman later. In any case it is permitted to handle one's testicles for this purpose, as stated by Abba, son of Rabbi Binyamin bar Ḥiyya. If one holds his penis from the corona and below, i.e., toward the tip of the penis, it is permitted in all cases, even if he had an erection (*Mishna Berura*), in accordance with the opinion of Rabbi Abbahu citing Rabbi Yoḥanan (Rambam *Sefer Kedusha, Hilkhot Issurei Bia* 21:23; *Shulḥan Arukh, Even HaEzer* 23:4 and *Oraḥ Ḥayyim* 3:14–15).

**Let a person stand on an elevated place and urinate downward or urinate into an area where there is loose soil – יַעֲמוֹד אָדָם בְּמָקוֹם גָּבוֹהַּ וְיַשְׁתִּין, אוֹ יַשְׁתִּין בְּעָפָר תִּיחוּחַ:** A man should not urinate when standing, because of the drops that might spray onto his legs, unless he is situated at the high end of an inclined plane or if he urinates into soft dirt, e.g., plowed earth (Rambam *Sefer Ahava, Hilkhot Tefillin UMezuza VeSefer Torah* 4:18; *Shulḥan Arukh, Oraḥ Ḥayyim* 3:13).

אוֹחֵז? וְהָתַנְיָא, רַבִּי אֱלִיעֶזֶר אוֹמֵר: כָּל הָאוֹחֵז בְּאַמָּתוֹ וּמַשְׁתִּין – כְּאִילּוּ מֵבִיא מַבּוּל לָעוֹלָם! אָמַר אַבָּיֵי: בִּמַטְלִית עָבָה.

A difficulty was raised with regard to this mishna: May he actually **hold** his penis? **But isn't it taught** in a *baraita* that **Rabbi Eliezer says:** With regard to **anyone who holds his penis**[N] **and urinates,**[H] it is considered **as though he is bringing a flood to the world,** as masturbation was one of the sins that led to the flood (*Sanhedrin* 108b)? **Abaye says** in resolution of this difficulty that the mishna is referring to one who holds his penis **with a coarse cloth.**

רָבָא אָמַר: אֲפִילּוּ תֵּימָא בְּמַטְלִית רַכָּה, כֵּיוָן דְּעָקַר – עֲקַר. וְאַבָּיֵי – חָיֵישׁ דִּלְמָא אָתֵי לְאוֹסוֹפֵי, וְרָבָא – לָא חָיֵישׁ דִּלְמָא אָתֵי לְאוֹסוֹפֵי.

**Rava says** with regard to that mishna: **You may even say** that it is referring to a priest who holds his penis **with a soft cloth,** and the reason it is permitted is that **once** the semen **has** already been **uprooted** from his body, it is **uprooted,** and his subsequent holding of the penis, even with a soft cloth, does not increase the emission of semen. **And Abaye** prohibits the use of a soft cloth even here, as he is **concerned** that **perhaps** due to the contact of this cloth one might **come to increase** the emission of semen. **But Rava is not concerned** that **perhaps** one might **come to increase** the emission.

וְלָא? וְהָתַנְיָא: הָא לְמָה זֶה דּוֹמֶה – לְנוֹתֵן אֶצְבַּע בָּעַיִן, שֶׁכָּל זְמַן שֶׁאֶצְבַּע בָּעַיִן – עַיִן מְדַמַּעַת וְחוֹזֶרֶת וּמְדַמַּעַת!

The Gemara asks: **And** is Rava **not** concerned for this possibility? **But isn't it taught** in a *baraita*: **To what is this** repeated examination of a man **comparable? To** one who **places a finger in** his **eye, for as long as** the **finger** is **in the eye,** the **eye will tear and continue to tear.** Here too, the priest's action will lead to an increased emission of semen.

וְרָבָא – כָּל אִחֲמוּמֵי וַהֲדַר אִחֲמוּמֵי, בְּשַׁעְתֵּיהּ – לָא שְׁכִיחַ.

The Gemara answers: **And Rava** would claim that if the priest's limbs were not quaking and the semen was coming out in drops, there is indeed a concern that an examination might increase the emission. But when he feels his limbs quaking, this concern does not apply. The reason is that with regard to **any warming** of the body that leads to a seminal emission **and** that is **then** followed by another **warming at the time** when the semen is being uprooted, it is **uncommon** for the latter warming to increase the emission. Consequently, in this case the priest may hold his penis even with a soft cloth.

גּוּפָא, רַבִּי אֱלִיעֶזֶר אוֹמֵר: כָּל הָאוֹחֵז בָּאַמָּה וּמַשְׁתִּין – כְּאִילּוּ מֵבִיא מַבּוּל לָעוֹלָם. אָמְרוּ לוֹ לְרַבִּי אֱלִיעֶזֶר: וַהֲלֹא נִצוֹצוֹת נִתָּזִין עַל רַגְלָיו, וְנִרְאֶה כִּכְרוּת שָׁפְכָה, וְנִמְצָא מוֹצִיא לַעַז עַל בָּנָיו שֶׁהֵן מַמְזֵרִים!

The Gemara discusses **the** matter **itself. Rabbi Eliezer says:** With regard to **anyone who holds** his **penis and urinates,** it is considered **as though he is bringing a flood to the world.** The Rabbis **said to Rabbi Eliezer: But** if one does not hold his penis, **small drops are sprayed on his legs, and he appears as one whose penis has been severed.** A man with that affliction is incapable of fathering children. People who see urine on his legs might suspect that he is suffering from that condition **and as a result** they will **cast aspersions about his children** and say **that they are children born from a forbidden relationship** [*mamzerim*].

אָמַר לָהֶן: מוּטָב שֶׁיּוֹצִיא לַעַז עַל בָּנָיו שֶׁהֵן מַמְזֵרִים, וְאַל יַעֲשֶׂה עַצְמוֹ רָשָׁע שָׁעָה אַחַת לִפְנֵי הַמָּקוֹם.

Rabbi Eliezer **said to them: It is preferable that** people **cast aspersions about his children that they are** *mamzerim*, **and he should not render himself wicked** even **one moment before the Omnipresent.**

תַּנְיָא אִידָךְ, אָמַר לָהֶן רַבִּי אֱלִיעֶזֶר לַחֲכָמִים: אֶפְשָׁר, יַעֲמוֹד אָדָם בְּמָקוֹם גָּבוֹהַּ וְיַשְׁתִּין, אוֹ יַשְׁתִּין בְּעָפָר תִּיחוּחַ, וְאַל יַעֲשֶׂה עַצְמוֹ רָשָׁע שָׁעָה אַחַת לִפְנֵי הַמָּקוֹם.

With regard to the same issue, it **is taught** in **another** *baraita* that **Rabbi Eliezer said to** the other **Rabbis** in response: It is **possible** for one to avoid spraying urine on his legs. How so? **Let a person stand on an elevated place and urinate** downward, **or urinate into** an area where there is **loose soil,**[H] which absorbs the urine, so that it does not ricochet upward, **and he should not render himself wicked** even **one moment before the Omnipresent.**

## NOTES

**Anyone who holds his penis – כָּל הָאוֹחֵז בְּאַמָּתוֹ:** According to the conclusion of the Gemara, there are six conditions under which it is permitted for a man to hold his penis while urinating. The early commentaries state that although these cases are introduced as alternatives, with the phrase: And if you wish say, nevertheless they are all accepted as *halakha*, as they complement one another (*Arukh*; Ritva). Some maintain that these answers are in conflict with each other, which is why the Rambam cited only the leniency that a married man may hold his penis (Gra).

הֵי אֲמַר לְהוּ בְּרֵישָׁא? אִילֵימָא קַמַּיְיתָא אֲמַר לְהוּ בְּרֵישָׁא, בָּתַר דַּאֲמַר לְהוּ אִיסּוּרָא הֲדַר אֲמַר לְהוּ תַּקַּנְתָּא?!

The Gemara asks: **Which** of these replies **did** Rabbi Eliezer **say to** the Rabbis **first? If we say** that it was the **first** statement, i.e., that one should not hold his penis even if people might cast aspersions about his children, that he **said to** the Rabbis **first,** and subsequently he told them that there was a way to avoid urine being sprayed on his legs, this is difficult; **after saying to them** that it is **a prohibition, would he then say to them** a practical **remedy?** By saying that one can avoid urine being sprayed on his legs, Rabbi Eliezer indicated that if one cannot do so he may hold his penis, which contradicts his other statement.

אֶלָּא, הָא אֲמַר לְהוּ בְּרֵישָׁא. וְאָמְרוּ לֵיהּ: אֵין לוֹ מָקוֹם גָּבוֹהַּ וְעָפָר תִּיחוּחַ מַאי? אֲמַר לָהֶן: מוּטָב שֶׁיּוֹצִיא לַעַז עַל בָּנָיו, וְאַל יַעֲשֶׂה עַצְמוֹ רָשָׁע שָׁעָה אַחַת לִפְנֵי הַמָּקוֹם,

**Rather,** clearly **he said this** practical solution **to the Rabbis first, and they** then **said to him: If one does not have an elevated place or loose earth** upon which he can urinate, **what** should he do? In response to this question, **he said to them: It is preferable** that people **cast aspersions about his children that they are *mamzerim*, and he should not render himself wicked** even **one moment before the Omnipresent.**

וְכׇל כָּךְ לָמָּה? מִפְּנֵי שֶׁמּוֹצִיא שִׁכְבַת זֶרַע לְבַטָּלָה. דְּאָמַר רַבִּי יוֹחָנָן: כׇּל הַמּוֹצִיא שִׁכְבַת זֶרַע לְבַטָּלָה – חַיָּיב מִיתָה, שֶׁנֶּאֱמַר: ״וַיֵּרַע בְּעֵינֵי ה׳ (אֶת) אֲשֶׁר עָשָׂה וַיָּמֶת גַּם אֹתוֹ״.

The Gemara asks: **And** why must one refrain **to that extent** from holding his penis? **Because** as the result of holding his penis **he** might **emit semen for naught. As Rabbi Yoḥanan says: Anyone who emits semen for naught**[H] **is liable** to receive the punishment of **death** at the hand of Heaven, **as it is stated** with regard to Onan, son of Judah: "And it came to pass, when he engaged in intercourse with his brother's wife, that he spilled it on the ground, lest he should give seed to his brother. **And the thing that he did was evil in the eyes of the Lord, and He slew him also**" (Genesis 38:9–10).

רַבִּי יִצְחָק וְרַבִּי אַמִי אָמְרִי: כְּאִילּוּ שׁוֹפֵךְ דָּמִים, שֶׁנֶּאֱמַר: ״הַנֵּחָמִים בָּאֵלִים תַּחַת כׇּל עֵץ רַעֲנָן שֹׁחֲטֵי הַיְלָדִים בַּנְּחָלִים תַּחַת סְעִפֵי הַסְּלָעִים״, אַל תִּקְרֵי ״שׁוֹחֲטֵי״ אֶלָּא ״סוֹחֲטֵי״.

**Rabbi Yitzḥak and Rabbi Ami say:** One who emits semen for naught is considered **as though he sheds blood, as it is stated:** "But draw near here, you sons of the sorceress, the seed of the adulterer and the harlot… Are you not children of transgression, a seed of falsehood, **you that inflame yourselves among the terebinths, under every leafy tree, that slay [*shoḥatei*] the children in the valleys, under the clefts of the rocks?**" (Isaiah 57:3–5). **Do not read** this word as ***shoḥatei*; rather,** read it as ***soḥatei*,** i.e., one who squeezes out [*soḥet*] semen is considered to have shed the blood of the children who could have been born from that seed.

רַב אַסִי אָמַר: כְּאִילּוּ עוֹבֵד עֲבוֹדָה זָרָה, כְּתִיב הָכָא ״תַּחַת כׇּל עֵץ רַעֲנָן״ וּכְתִיב הָתָם ״עַל הֶהָרִים הָרָמִים וְתַחַת כׇּל עֵץ רַעֲנָן״.

**Rav Asi says:** It is considered **as though he worships idols,** as **it is written here: "Under every leafy tree," and it is written there,** with regard to the mitzva of eradicating idols from Eretz Yisrael: "You shall destroy all the places, where the nations that you are to dispossess worshipped their gods, **upon the high mountains,** and upon the hills, **and under every leafy tree**" (Deuteronomy 12:2).

רַב יְהוּדָה וּשְׁמוּאֵל הָווּ קָיְימִי אַאִיגָּרָא דְּבֵי כְּנִישְׁתָּא דְּשָׁף וְיָתֵיב בִּנְהַרְדְּעָא. אֲמַר לֵיהּ רַב יְהוּדָה לִשְׁמוּאֵל: צָרִיךְ אֲנִי לְהַשְׁתִּין. אֲמַר לֵיהּ: שִׁינָּנָא, אֱחוֹז בְּאַמָּתְךָ וְהַשְׁתֵּן לַחוּץ.

§ With regard to the issue of holding one's penis for the purpose of urinating, the Gemara relates that **Rav Yehuda**[P] **and Shmuel**[P] **were standing on the roof of the synagogue that was destroyed and rebuilt**[B] **in Neharde'a. Rav Yehuda said to Shmuel:** What can I do? **I need to urinate.** Shmuel **said to him: *Shinnana*,**[L] **hold your penis,** so that the water does not fall onto the synagogue roof, **and urinate outward,** away from the synagogue.

### HALAKHA

Anyone who emits semen for naught – כׇּל הַמּוֹצִיא שִׁכְבַת זֶרַע לְבַטָּלָה: It is prohibited to emit semen for naught, and this is more severe than any of the transgressions of the Torah. Therefore, one may not perform coitus interruptus. With regard to those who commit adultery with their hand and waste their seed, not only is this a great sin, but they are ostracized by Heaven, and some say that the earthly court should ostracize them (*Tosafot*; Ramban; see *Beit Shmuel*).

Some commentaries state that if one is scared that if he does not emit semen he might sin with a married or a menstruating woman, it is preferable for him to emit semen. But to atone for this act he should fast forty days in the summer, or sit out in the cold in the winter (Rambam *Sefer Kedusha*, *Hilkhot Issurei Bia* 21:18; *Shulḥan Arukh*, *Even HaEzer* 23:1 and *Ḥelkat Meḥokek* there).

### PERSONALITIES

Rav Yehuda – רַב יְהוּדָה: Rav Yehuda bar Yeḥezkel, who is referred to throughout the Talmud simply as Rav Yehuda, was a second-generation *amora*. He studied under Rav, and following Rav's death he studied under Shmuel in Neharde'a. Shmuel recognized his intellectual prowess as well as his extreme piety, as indicated here. Rav Yehuda had a tremendous memory and was careful to quote halakhic statements in the name of those he heard them from; he is mentioned as quoting a *halakha* in the name of Rav or Shmuel over four hundred times in the Talmud. Rav Yehuda was known as a lover of Eretz Yisrael, but he believed it was prohibited to move there, in accordance with the verse: "They shall be carried to Babylon, and there shall they be, until the day that I remember them" (Jeremiah 27:22). After Shmuel's death, Rav Yehuda established the celebrated yeshiva in Pumbedita, which he headed for forty years. The yeshiva focused on the study of the *halakhot* of damages, as Rav Yehuda believed that the main expression of one's piety is demonstrated through proper conduct toward other people (see *Bava Kamma* 30a). In his later years, Rav Yehuda became blind.

Shmuel – שְׁמוּאֵל: Shmuel was a first-generation *amora* who was born and ultimately died in Neharde'a. A child prodigy, he was famous not only for his Torah learning, but for his secular knowledge as well. The Gemara is replete with stories of his expertise in such areas as language, medicine, astronomy, and the natural sciences.

Shmuel traveled to Eretz Yisrael to study with the students of Rabbi Yehuda HaNasi, and Rabbi Yehuda HaNasi regretted that he was unable to find an opportunity to ordain him. The Gemara records that Shmuel treated Rabbi Yehuda HaNasi's eye ailment. After his return to Babylonia, Shmuel was appointed as one of the judges of the Diaspora community.

Together with his colleague, Rav, Shmuel raised the standard of Torah study in Babylonia to such a level that thousands of students chose to remain there rather than to travel to Eretz Yisrael. Shmuel considered Babylonia second in sanctity to Eretz Yisrael and ruled that it was prohibited to leave Babylonia to travel to other locations in the Diaspora.

Shmuel had a close friendship with King Shapur I of Persia, a benevolent monarch who tolerated religious diversity in his kingdom.

Shmuel lived to an old age, leaving behind two daughters renowned for their wisdom and modesty.

### BACKGROUND

The synagogue that was destroyed and rebuilt – בֵּי כְּנִישְׁתָּא דְּשָׁף וְיָתֵיב: This was an extremely ancient synagogue. The *ge'onim* record a tradition that this synagogue was called the one that was destroyed and rebuilt because when the Jews were exiled they took stones and materials from the Temple and used them to build the synagogue in Neharde'a (see Rashi). It was known as a sacred place, and it was said that the Divine Presence rested there. The greatest Sages of Babylonia used this synagogue.

### LANGUAGE

*Shinnana* – שִׁינָּנָא: This moniker given by Shmuel to his disciple Rav Yehuda appears many times in the Talmud (see, e.g., 17a and 25b). According to Rashi, *shinnana* means sharp or witty, and the term reflects a degree of respect bestowed by Shmuel on his foremost student. The *ge'onim* explain that according to oral tradition *shinnana* means big toothed, and that this was a nickname for Rav Yehuda based on his appearance.

הֵיכִי עָבֵיד הָכִי? וְהָתַנְיָא, רַבִּי אֱלִיעֶזֶר אוֹמֵר: כׇּל הָאוֹחֵז בְּאַמָּתוֹ וּמַשְׁתִּין – כְּאִילּוּ מֵבִיא מַבּוּל לָעוֹלָם!

The Gemara asks: **How could** Rav Yehuda **do so? But isn't it taught** in a *baraita* that **Rabbi Eliezer says:** With regard to **anyone who holds his penis and urinates,** it is considered **as though he is bringing a flood to the world?**

אָמַר אַבָּיֵי: עֲשָׂאוֹ כְּבוֹלֶשֶׁת. דִּתְנַן: בּוֹלֶשֶׁת שֶׁנִּכְנַס לָעִיר. בִּשְׁעַת שָׁלוֹם, חָבִיּוֹת פְּתוּחוֹת – אֲסוּרוֹת, סְתוּמוֹת – מוּתָּרוֹת. בִּשְׁעַת מִלְחָמָה – אֵלּוּ וָאֵלּוּ מוּתָּרוֹת, לְפִי שֶׁאֵין לָהֶן פְּנַאי לְנַסֵּךְ. אַלְמָא: דְּכֵיוָן דְּבָעִיתִי – לָא אָתֵי לְנַסּוֹכֵי, הָכָא נַמִי – כֵּיוָן דְּבָעִיתִי לָא אָתֵי לְהַרְהוּרֵי.

**Abaye says:** The Sages **rendered** the halakhic status of this situation **like** that of **a troop of marauders, as we learned** in a mishna (*Avoda Zara* 70b): With regard to **a troop of marauders that entered a town,**[H] if they did so **in a time of peace, open casks** of wine **are forbidden,** in case the marauders used the wine for libations in idol worship, whereas **sealed** casks **are permitted. In a time of war,** both **these and those are permitted, because** the marauders **do not have leisure to pour libations. Evidently, since** these marauders **are afraid, they will not come to pour libations. Here too,** in this incident involving Rav Yehuda, **since he is afraid he will not come to have** sexual **thoughts.**

וְהָכָא מַאי בְּעִיתוּתָא אִיכָּא? אִיבָּעֵית אֵימָא: בִּיעֲתוּתָא דְּלֵילְיָא וּדְאִיגָּרָא. וְאִיבָּעֵית אֵימָא: בִּיעֲתוּתָא דְּרַבֵּיהּ. וְאִיבָּעֵית אֵימָא: בִּיעֲתוּתָא דִּשְׁכִינָה. וְאִיבָּעֵית אֵימָא: אֵימָתָא דְּמָרֵיהּ עֲלֵיהּ, דְּקָרֵי שְׁמוּאֵל עֲלֵיהּ: אֵין זֶה יְלוּד אִשָּׁה.

The Gemara asks: **And what fear is there here,** in the case of Rav Yehuda? The Gemara explains: **If you wish, say** that there is **the fear of the night and of the roof,** i.e., that he might fall. **And if you wish, say** that **the awe of his teacher,** Shmuel, is upon him. **And if you wish, say** that **the awe of the Divine Presence** that dwells in the synagogue is upon Rav Yehuda. **And if you wish, say** that **the awe of his Master,** God, is upon him. Rav Yehuda was renowned for his fear of Heaven, **as Shmuel declared about** him: **This one is not born of a woman,** but is like an angel.

וְאִיבָּעֵית אֵימָא: נָשׂוּי הֲוָה, דַּאֲמַר רַב נַחְמָן: אִם הָיָה נָשׂוּי – מוּתָּר.

**And if you wish, say** a different answer, that Rav Yehuda was allowed to hold his penis while urinating because he **was married; as Rav Naḥman said: If one is married,** it is **permitted** for him to hold his penis while urinating, as his improper sexual urges are not as strong.

וְאִיבָּעֵית אֵימָא: כִּי הָא אוֹרֵי לֵיהּ, דְּתָנֵי אַבָּא בְּרֵיהּ דְּרַבִּי בִּנְיָמִין בַּר חִיָּיא: אֲבָל מְסַיֵּיעַ בַּבֵּיצִים מִלְּמַטָּה. וְאִיבָּעֵית אֵימָא: כִּי הָא אוֹרֵי לֵיהּ, דַּאֲמַר רַבִּי אַבָּהוּ, אָמַר רַבִּי יוֹחָנָן: גְּבוּל יֵשׁ לוֹ, מֵעֲטָרָה וּלְמַטָּה – מוּתָּר,

**And if you wish, say** that Shmuel **ruled for** Rav Yehuda **in accordance with this** *baraita,* **which Abba, son of Rabbi Binyamin bar Ḥiyya, teaches:** One may not hold the penis itself while urinating, **but** a man who wishes to urinate **may assist** the process **by** holding the **testicles from below.** Shmuel instructed Rav Yehuda to act in this manner. **And if you wish, say** that **Shmuel ruled** for Rav Yehuda **in accordance with that which Rabbi Abbahu said** that **Rabbi Yoḥanan says: There is** a clear **demarcation** in the prohibition against holding one's penis while urinating: **From the corona and below,** toward the tip of the penis, it is **permitted** to hold, as this will not lead to arousal.

#### HALAKHA

**A troop of marauders that entered a town, etc. –** **בּוֹלֶשֶׁת שֶׁנִּכְנַס לָעִיר וכו׳:** With regard to a troop of marauders that came into a town and entered Jewish homes, if this occurred in a time of peace, then open casks, even if they were corked, are prohibited, but casks that are sealed with a clay stopper are permitted. In a time of war, all the casks are permitted. This applies only to casks that had been open beforehand (Ran), but one should not partake of wine from casks that were sealed and later found opened (Rambam *Sefer Kedusha, Hilkhot Ma'akhalot Assurot* 12:24; *Shulḥan Arukh, Yoreh De'a* 129:12).

Perek **II**
Daf **13** Amud **b**

מֵעֲטָרָה וּלְמַעְלָה – אָסוּר.

**From the corona and above,** toward the body, it is **prohibited.**

אָמַר רַב: הַמַּקְשֶׁה עַצְמוֹ לְדַעַת – יְהֵא בְּנִדּוּי. וְלֵימָא "אָסוּר"! דְּקָמְגָרֵי יֵצֶר הָרָע אַנַּפְשֵׁיהּ. וְרַבִּי אַמִי אָמַר: נִקְרָא "עֲבַרְיָין", שֶׁכָּךְ אוּמָּנְתּוֹ שֶׁל יֵצֶר הָרָע, הַיּוֹם אוֹמֵר לוֹ: "עֲשֵׂה כָּךְ", וּלְמָחָר אוֹמֵר לוֹ: "עֲשֵׂה כָּךְ", וּלְמָחָר אוֹמֵר לוֹ: "לֵךְ עֲבוֹד עֲבוֹדָה זָרָה", וְהוֹלֵךְ וְעוֹבֵד.

§ **Rav says: One who intentionally causes himself an erection**[H] **shall be ostracized.**[N] The Gemara suggests: **And let** Rav **say** simply that it is **prohibited.** The Gemara explains that it is proper to ostracize such a man, **as he arouses the evil inclination upon himself. And Rabbi Ami says: He is called** a habitual **transgressor, as this is the craft of the evil inclination. Today he says to** a person: **Do this** sin, **and** when the individual obeys his inclination, **on the following day** the evil inclination **says to him: Do that** sin, **and on the following day he says to him:** Go and **worship idols, and he goes and worships** idols.

#### NOTES

**One who intentionally causes himself an erection shall be ostracized – הַמַּקְשֶׁה עַצְמוֹ לְדַעַת יְהֵא בְּנִדּוּי:** The commentaries discuss the meaning of the clause: Shall be ostracized. Some say that the Sages are obligated to ostracize him for his behavior, but he is not automatically ostracized (*Tosafot*; Ramban; Rashba). Others claim that he is considered ostracized even without a formal declaration to this effect, as the Sages ostracized at the outset anyone who intentionally gives himself an erection. The *Maggid Mishne* maintains that this is the opinion of the Rambam, who writes: He shall sit in a state of ostracism (*Sefer Kedusha, Hilkhot Issurei Bia* 21:18).

#### HALAKHA

**One who intentionally causes himself an erection – הַמַּקְשֶׁה עַצְמוֹ לְדַעַת:** It is prohibited to give oneself an erection on purpose or to entertain lascivious thoughts. If such thoughts come to mind, one should turn his attention from worthless matters to Torah (Rambam *Sefer Kedusha, Hilkhot Issurei Bia* 21:19; *Shulḥan Arukh, Even HaEzer* 23:3).

אִיכָּא דְּאָמְרִי, אָמַר רַבִּי אַמִי: כָּל הַמֵּבִיא עַצְמוֹ לִידֵי הִרְהוּר – אֵין מַכְנִיסִין אוֹתוֹ בִּמְחִיצָתוֹ שֶׁל הַקָּדוֹשׁ בָּרוּךְ הוּא. כְּתִיב הָכָא: ״וַיֵּרַע בְּעֵינֵי ה׳״, וּכְתִיב הָתָם: ״כִּי לֹא אֵל חָפֵץ רֶשַׁע אָתָּה לֹא יְגֻרְךָ רָע״.

**Some say** that **Rabbi Ami says:** With regard to **anyone who brings himself into** a state of **arousal,** they **do not bring him within the boundary of the Holy One, Blessed be He.** The proof is that **it is written here,** with regard to Onan, son of Judah: **"And the thing that he did was evil in the eyes of the Lord,** and He slew him also" (Genesis 38:10), **and it is written there: "For You are not a God who has pleasure in wickedness; evil shall not sojourn with You.** The boasters shall not stand in Your sight…But as for me, in the abundance of Your kindness will I come into Your house; I will bow down toward Your holy Temple in fear of You" (Psalms 5:5–8). This demonstrates that whoever does evil, like Onan, shall not sojourn with God.

וְאָמַר רַבִּי אֶלְעָזָר: מַאי דִּכְתִיב ״יְדֵיכֶם דָּמִים מָלֵאוּ״ – אֵלּוּ הַמְנָאֲפִים בַּיָּד. תָּנָא דְּבֵי רַבִּי יִשְׁמָעֵאל: ״לֹא תִנְאָף״ – לֹא תְּהֵא בְּךָ נִיאוּף, בֵּין בַּיָּד בֵּין בָּרֶגֶל.

**And Rabbi Elazar says,** with regard to the severity of this transgression: **What** is the meaning of that **which is written:** "And when you spread forth your hands, I will hide My eyes from you; even when you make many prayers, I will not hear; **your hands are full of blood"** (Isaiah 1:15)? **These are** those men **who commit adultery with the hand,** by masturbating. Likewise, **the school of Rabbi Yishmael taught:** When it is stated in the Ten Commandments: **"You shall not commit adultery"** (Exodus 20:13), this means that **there shall not be adultery among you, whether** you masturbate **by hand** or **whether with** one's **foot.**

תָּנוּ רַבָּנַן: הַגֵּרִים וְהַמְשַׂחֲקִין בְּתִינוֹקוֹת – מְעַכְּבִין אֶת הַמָּשִׁיחַ. בִּשְׁלָמָא גֵּרִים – כִּדְרַבִּי חֶלְבּוֹ, דְּאָמַר רַבִּי חֶלְבּוֹ: קָשִׁין גֵּרִים לְיִשְׂרָאֵל כְּסַפַּחַת. אֶלָּא מְשַׂחֲקִין בְּתִנוֹקוֹת מַאי הִיא?

§ **The Sages taught** in a *baraita*: **Converts and those who play with children delay** the coming of **the Messiah.** The Gemara asks: **Granted** with regard to **converts,** this is **in accordance with** the opinion **of Rabbi Ḥelbo,**[P] **as Rabbi Ḥelbo says: Converts are as harmful to the Jewish people as a leprous scab**[NH] on the skin, as they are not proficient in the performance of the mitzvot and born Jews learn from them. **But** with regard to the category of **those who play with children,** to **what is it** referring?

אִילֵימָא מִשְׁכַּב זָכוּר – בְּנֵי סְקִילָה נִינְהוּ! אֶלָּא דֶּרֶךְ אֵבָרִים – בְּנֵי מַבּוּל נִינְהוּ!

**If we say** that this is referring to **homosexuality,** such men **are liable to** be executed by **stoning,** and their behavior is criticized not simply because they delay the Messiah. **Rather,** one might suggest that this is referring to those who emit semen **by way of** other **limbs,** i.e., without engaging in intercourse; if so, **they are** considered as though they are bringing a flood, and are therefore **liable to** be punished themselves with **a flood.**

אֶלָּא דְּנָסְיבִי קְטַנּוֹת, דְּלָאו בְּנוֹת אוֹלוּדֵי נִינְהוּ. דְּאָמַר רַבִּי יוֹסֵי: אֵין בֶּן דָּוִד בָּא עַד שֶׁיִּכְלוּ כָּל הַנְּשָׁמוֹת שֶׁבַּגּוּף, שֶׁנֶּאֱמַר: ״כִּי רוּחַ מִלְּפָנַי יַעֲטוֹף וּנְשָׁמוֹת אֲנִי עָשִׂיתִי״.

**Rather,** the *baraita* means **that they marry minor girls**[H] **who are not** yet **capable of bearing children,** consequently emitting semen for naught. **As Rabbi Yosei said: The** Messiah, **son of David, will not come until all the souls of the body**[N] **have been finished,** i.e., until all souls that are destined to inhabit physical bodies do so. **As it is stated: "For the spirit that enwraps itself is from Me, and the souls that I have made"** (Isaiah 57:16). The verse is interpreted as follows: The spirit, i.e., the souls about which it has been decreed by Me that they are to be born, if they are not born, they enwrap the Messiah and prevent him from coming.

### PERSONALITIES

**Rabbi Ḥelbo – רַבִּי חֶלְבּוֹ:** Rabbi Ḥelbo was a Babylonian *amora* of the third generation, who moved to Eretz Yisrael. He was a student of Rav Huna and apparently received most of his Torah education from him; indeed, he often quotes Rav Huna. It appears that he went to Eretz Yisrael near the time of Rav Huna's death and was there when his coffin was brought for burial. In Eretz Yisrael he was a student and colleague of the greatest disciples of Rabbi Yoḥanan. He became one of the leaders of his generation and a halakhic codifier, and in the field of *aggada* he was a student of Rabbi Shmuel bar Naḥmani, in whose name he quotes aggadic traditions. Rabbi Ḥelbo settled in Tiberias and was close to Rabbi Yehuda Nesia. The Talmud relates that he had no children and lived in extremely humble quarters. It is also related that when he became sick there was no one to visit him.

### HALAKHA

**Converts are as harmful to the Jewish people as a leprous scab – קָשִׁין גֵּרִים לְיִשְׂרָאֵל כְּסַפַּחַת:** Since converts are often accepted without having been properly examined, and they do not convert for the sake of Heaven, many of them return to their former ways and cause Jews to err. It was for this reason that the Sages said that converts are as difficult for the Jewish people as a scab (Rambam *Sefer Kedusha, Hilkhot Issurei Bia* 13:18).

**That they marry minor girls – דְּנָסְיבִי קְטַנּוֹת:** It is prohibited to marry a minor girl who is too young to bear children. This is included in the prohibition against emitting semen for naught, as stated in the *baraita* (Rambam *Sefer Kedusha, Hilkhot Issurei Bia* 21:18; *Shulḥan Arukh, Even HaEzer* 23:1).

### NOTES

**Converts are as harmful to the Jewish people as a leprous scab – קָשִׁין גֵּרִים לְיִשְׂרָאֵל כְּסַפַּחַת:** Many different interpretations of this statement have been suggested. Rashi states that as converts are not experts in the performance of mitzvot, their sins bring punishment upon the Jewish people. One explanation, suggested by the Rambam, is that it is common for converts to revert to their old ways and beliefs, at which point they exert a corrupting influence on other Jews. This is similar to the mixed multitude who accompanied the Jewish people in the exodus from Egypt and caused the sin of the Golden Calf (see Rashi on *Kiddushin* 70b). *Tosafot* on *Kiddushin* 70b cite the statement of the Gemara that the continuing exile and dispersion of the Jewish people occurs in order to provide an opportunity for converts to join them. Consequently, converts are an indirect cause of the exile. *Tosafot* also cite the opinion of Rabbi Avraham the convert. He claims that converts are generally punctilious and strict with regard to the mitzvot, and therefore their behavior discredits the practice of those born Jews who are not as vigilant.

**All the souls of the body [*guf*] – כָּל הַנְּשָׁמוֹת שֶׁבַּגּוּף:** Rashi explains that this *guf* means a chamber, i.e., *guf* is the name of a special place where the souls that will be born are kept. Others state that it is comparable to a curtain upon which these souls are embroidered (*Arukh*).

NOTES

Below his navel – לְמַטָּה מִטַּבּוּרוֹ: The commentaries dispute the precise meaning of navel in this context. Some say it is a euphemism for the penis, and that the same applies to the mention of the belly (*Magen Avraham*). Alternatively, it means the actual navel, i.e., one should not place his hand on the area of the body below the navel.

And they may partake of *teruma* – וְהֵן אוֹכְלוֹת בִּתְרוּמָה: The later commentaries infer from this statement concerning preparation for the purpose of partaking of *teruma*, that these women do not require an examination before and after intercourse.

״בְּאֲנָשִׁים תִּקְצֵץ״. אִיבַּעְיָא לְהוּ: דִּינָא תְּנַן, אוֹ לְטוּתָא תְּנַן? דִּינָא תְּנַן – כִּי הָא דְּרַב הוּנָא קָץ יְדָא, אוֹ לְטוּתָא תְּנַן?

§ The mishna teaches that with regard to any hand that is diligent to examine bodily emissions, **among men,** such a hand **should be severed. A dilemma was raised before** the Sages: **Do we learn** this statement as a practical ***halakha***, i.e., that the court should actually sever his hand, **or do we learn** it as a mere **curse,** but not as an actual instruction to punish him in that manner? The Gemara elaborates: **Do we learn** it as a practical ***halakha*** **like that** prohibition against striking another, in which the same expression is used: With regard to anyone who raises his hand upon another, his hand should be severed, and **Rav Huna** indeed acted accordingly and **severed the hand** of an offender? **Or** perhaps **do we learn** it as a mere **curse?**

תָּא שְׁמַע, דְּתַנְיָא, רַבִּי טַרְפוֹן אוֹמֵר: יָד לְאַמָּה – תִּקָּצֵץ יָדוֹ עַל טַבּוּרוֹ. אָמְרוּ לוֹ: יָשַׁב לוֹ קוֹץ בִּכְרֵיסוֹ לֹא יִטְּלֶנּוּ? אָמַר לָהֶן: לָא. וַהֲלֹא כְּרֵיסוֹ נִבְקַעַת! אָמַר לָהֶן: מוּטָב תִּבָּקַע כְּרֵיסוֹ, וְאַל יֵרֵד לִבְאֵר שַׁחַת.

The Gemara suggests: **Come** and **hear, as it is taught** in a *baraita* that **Rabbi Tarfon says:** If one's **hand** goes **to** his **penis, his hand should be severed upon his navel.** The Rabbis **said to him:** If so, in a case where **a thorn was stuck in** one's **belly, should he not remove it?** Rabbi Tarfon **said to them:** Indeed, he should **not** remove it, and if he does so his hand should be severed. The Rabbis replied: **But** if his hand is severed while it is upon his navel, **won't his belly be split open?** Rabbi Tarfon **said to them: It is preferable that the belly of** one who acts in this manner **should be split open, and he should not descend into the pit of destruction.**

אִי אָמְרַתְּ בִּשְׁלָמָא דִּינָא תְּנַן – הַיְינוּ דְּאָמְרִי ״וַהֲלֹא כְּרֵיסוֹ נִבְקַעַת״, אֶלָּא אִי אָמְרַתְּ לְטוּתָא תְּנַן – מַאי ״כְּרֵיסוֹ נִבְקַעַת״? אֶלָּא מַאי – דִּינָא תְּנַן? לָא סַגִּי דְּלָאו עַל טַבּוּרוֹ?

The Gemara analyzes this discussion: **Granted, if you say** that **we learn** the statement in the mishna as a practical ***halakha***, **this is** the meaning of that **which** the Rabbis **said: But** if his hand is severed upon his navel, **won't his belly be split open? But if you say** that **we learn** the statement in the mishna as a mere **curse, what** is the meaning of the phrase: Won't **his belly be split open?** The Gemara responds: **Rather, what** explanation is the alternative? That **we learn** the mishna as stating a practical ***halakha***? That would not explain the exchange between the Rabbis to Rabbi Tarfon, because is it **not sufficient that** the hand be severed **not upon his navel?** In other words, even if the hand must actually be severed, it is not clear why it should be severed while it is upon his navel.

אֶלָּא, הָכִי קָאָמַר רַבִּי טַרְפוֹן: כׇּל הַמַּכְנִיס יָדוֹ לְמַטָּה מִטַּבּוּרוֹ – תִּקָּצֵץ, אָמְרוּ לוֹ לְרַבִּי טַרְפוֹן: יָשַׁב לוֹ קוֹץ בִּכְרֵיסוֹ, לֹא יִטְּלֶנּוּ? אָמַר לָהֶן: לָא. וַהֲלֹא כְּרֵיסוֹ נִבְקַעַת! אָמַר לָהֶן: מוּטָב תִּבָּקַע כְּרֵיסוֹ, וְאַל יֵרֵד לִבְאֵר שַׁחַת.

**Rather, this** is what **Rabbi Tarfon is saying:** With regard to **anyone who inserts his hand below his navel,**[NH] his hand **should be severed.** The Rabbis **said to Rabbi Tarfon: If a thorn was stuck in** one's **belly, should he not remove it?** Rabbi Tarfon **said to them:** He should **not.** They responded: **But won't his belly be split open** due to the thorn? Rabbi Tarfon **said to them: It is preferable that his belly be split open, and he should not descend into the pit of destruction.**

מתני׳ הַחֵרֶשֶׁת וְהַשּׁוֹטָה וְהַסּוּמָא וְשֶׁנִּטְרְפָה דַּעְתָּהּ, אִם יֵשׁ לָהֶם פִּקְחוֹת – מְתַקְּנוֹת אוֹתָן, וְהֵן אוֹכְלוֹת בִּתְרוּמָה.

**MISHNA** In the case of a woman **who is deaf** [*haḥereshet*], **or an imbecile, or blind, or who went insane,** and is therefore unable to examine herself reliably, **if** such women **have competent** friends, those friends **prepare them** by examining them and immersing them in a ritual bath. **And** on that basis the incompetent women **may partake**[H] **of *teruma***[N] after the sun sets.

גמ׳ ״חֵרֶשֶׁת״. אִיהִי תִּבְדּוֹק לְנַפְשַׁהּ! דְּתַנְיָא, אָמַר רַבִּי: חֵרֶשֶׁת הָיְתָה בִּשְׁכוּנָתֵינוּ, לֹא דַּיָּהּ שֶׁבּוֹדֶקֶת לְעַצְמָהּ – אֶלָּא שֶׁחַבְרוֹתֶיהָ רוֹאוֹת וּמַרְאוֹת לָהּ!

**GEMARA** The mishna states that competent women must assist **a deaf woman.** The Gemara asks: **Let her examine herself; as it is taught** in a *baraita* that **Rabbi** Yehuda HaNasi **said: There was a deaf woman in our neighborhood** who was so proficient in these matters that **not only did she examine herself, but** when **her friends would see** stains similar to blood **and** were unsure whether or not the stains were ritually impure, they would **show her** the stains.

HALAKHA

Anyone who inserts his hand below his navel – כׇּל הַמַּכְנִיס יָדוֹ לְמַטָּה מִטַּבּוּרוֹ: It is prohibited to place one's hand below the navel, in case this leads to lascivious thoughts (Rambam *Sefer Kedusha, Hilkhot Issurei Bia* 21:23; *Shulḥan Arukh, Even HaEzer* 23:4).

A woman who is deaf…may partake – הַחֵרֶשֶׁת...אוֹכְלוֹת: A deaf-mute woman, an imbecile, and one who went insane due to illness may partake of *teruma* if their friends prepare them for purification from ritual impurity by examining them and immersing them in a ritual bath (Rambam *Sefer Tahara, Hilkhot Metamei Mishkav UMoshav* 4:9; *Shulḥan Arukh, Yoreh De'a* 196:8).

הָתָם – בִּמְדַבֶּרֶת וְאֵינָהּ שׁוֹמַעַת, הָכָא – בְּשֶׁאֵינָהּ מְדַבֶּרֶת וְאֵינָהּ שׁוֹמַעַת. כִּדְתְנַן: חֵרֵשׁ שֶׁדִּבְּרוּ חֲכָמִים בְּכָל מָקוֹם – אֵינוֹ שׁוֹמֵעַ וְאֵינוֹ מְדַבֵּר.

The Gemara answers: **There,** Rabbi Yehuda HaNasi is referring **to** a woman who **can speak but cannot hear.** It is possible for such a woman to be an expert in examining blood. But **here,** the mishna is dealing **with** a woman **who can neither speak nor hear,** and she is therefore considered incompetent and incapable of examining herself. **As we learned** in a mishna (*Terumot* 1:2): The **deaf person of whom the Sages spoke everywhere** is one **who can neither hear nor speak,**[NH] i.e., a deaf-mute.

"הַסּוּמָא". אִיהִי תִּבְדּוֹק לְנַפְשָׁהּ וְתֶיחֱזֵי לַחֲבֶירְתָּהּ! אָמַר רַבִּי יוֹסֵי בְּרַבִּי חֲנִינָא: סוּמָא אֵינָהּ מִשְׁנָה.

§ The mishna further teaches that competent women must assist **a blind** woman. The Gemara similarly asks: **Let her examine herself and show** the cloth **to her friend.**[H] **Rabbi Yosei, son of Rabbi Ḥanina, says:** The correct version of the **mishna** does **not** mention **a blind** woman.

"וְשֶׁנִּטְרְפָה דַּעְתָּהּ". הַיְינוּ שׁוֹטָה! שֶׁנִּטְרְפָה דַּעְתָּהּ מֵחֲמַת חוֹלִי.

§ The mishna also states that competent women must assist **a woman who went insane.** The Gemara asks: With regard to her ability to examine herself, **isn't this** the same as **an imbecile,** who is already mentioned in the mishna? The Gemara answers: Here, the mishna is referring to a woman **who went insane due to illness,** which is a different category than that of an imbecile.

תָּנוּ רַבָּנַן: כֹּהֵן שׁוֹטֶה – מַטְבִּילִין אוֹתוֹ וּמַאֲכִילִין אוֹתוֹ תְּרוּמָה לָעֶרֶב, וּמְשַׁמְּרִין אוֹתוֹ שֶׁלֹּא יִישַׁן, יָשַׁן – טָמֵא, לֹא יָשַׁן – טָהוֹר.

The Gemara further discusses *halakhot* pertaining to an imbecile. **The Sages taught** in a *baraita*: With regard to **an imbecile priest** who was ritually impure, competent men deal with his purification: **They immerse him,**[H] **and** then **enable him to partake of *teruma* in the evening,** like any other priest who was impure. **And** those taking care of him must **watch over him** to ensure **that he does not sleep** before he partakes of *teruma*, in case he experiences a seminal emission, which would render him impure. **If he slept,** he is once again **impure,** and may not partake of *teruma*; if he **did not sleep** he is **pure.**

רַבִּי אֱלִיעֶזֶר בְּרַבִּי צָדוֹק אוֹמֵר: עוֹשִׂין לוֹ כִּיס שֶׁל עוֹר. אָמְרוּ לוֹ: כׇּל שֶׁכֵּן שֶׁמֵּבִיא לִידֵי חִימּוּם! אָמַר לָהֶן: לְדִבְרֵיכֶם שׁוֹטֶה אֵין לוֹ תַּקָּנָה!

**Rabbi Eliezer, son of Rabbi Tzadok, says** that there is another method of allowing an imbecile priest to partake of *teruma*: **One prepares for him a leather pouch,** which is wrapped around his penis, and before giving him *teruma* to partake of one checks this pouch to see if he has emitted semen. The other Sages **said to him:** It is improper to do this, as **all the more so** he will be prevented from partaking of *teruma*; this pouch **warms him** and increases the likelihood of a seminal emission. Rabbi Eliezer, son of Rabbi Tzadok, **said to them: According to your statement, an imbecile** priest **has no remedy** that will enable him to partake of *teruma*.

אָמְרוּ לוֹ: לְדִבְרֵינוּ, יָשַׁן – טָמֵא, לֹא יָשַׁן – טָהוֹר, לְדִבְרֶיךָ – שֶׁמָּא יִרְאֶה טִפָּה כְּחַרְדָּל וְתִבָּלַע בַּכִּיס!

**They said to him: According to our statement** there is a way he can partake of *teruma*, as stated above: If **he slept,** he is **impure;** if he **did not sleep** he is **pure.** But **according to your statement,** that one wraps a pouch around his penis, this is not a reliable method, as **perhaps he will see,** i.e., experience the emission of, **a drop** of semen as small **as a mustard** seed, **and it will be absorbed in the pouch** and will not be noticed, which would mean that he is eating *teruma* in a state of ritual impurity.

תָּנָא, מִשּׁוּם רַבִּי אֶלְעָזָר אָמְרוּ: עוֹשִׂין לוֹ כִּיס שֶׁל מַתֶּכֶת.

The Gemara continues to discuss the methods by which an imbecile priest can partake of *teruma*. It was **taught** in a *baraita* that the Sages **said in the name of Rabbi Elazar: One prepares for him a metal pouch,** which is placed on his penis and does not warm it.

אָמַר אַבָּיֵי: וְשֶׁל נְחֹשֶׁת. כִּדְתַנְיָא, רַבִּי יְהוּדָה אוֹמֵר: רוֹאִין אוֹתָן גִּבְעוֹלִין שֶׁל אֵזוֹב כְּאִילּוּ הֵן שֶׁל נְחֹשֶׁת.

In explanation of this statement, **Abaye says: And** when this *tanna* speaks of metal, he means that the pouch should be made **of copper,** which does not absorb liquid, and therefore any drop of semen would be visible. This is **as it is taught** in a mishna (*Para* 12:5), with regard to the amount of water of purification that must be sprinkled on an individual who is impure due to impurity imparted by a corpse, that **Rabbi Yehuda says: One considers those hyssop stems,** with which the waters of purification are sprinkled, **as though they are** made **of copper,** which does not absorb any of the water.

**NOTES**

**The deaf person of whom the Sages spoke everywhere is one who can neither hear nor speak – חֵרֵשׁ שֶׁדִּבְּרוּ חֲכָמִים בְּכָל מָקוֹם אֵינוֹ שׁוֹמֵעַ וְאֵינוֹ מְדַבֵּר:** Rashi on *Ḥagiga* 2b explains that the Sages had a tradition that one who neither hears nor speaks is not halakhically competent, even if he does not display the signs of an imbecile (Responsa *Ḥatam Sofer*). The *Ḥatam Sofer* adds that this is possibly a *halakha* transmitted to Moses from Sinai.

**HALAKHA**

**The deaf person [*ḥeresh*] of whom the Sages spoke everywhere is one who can neither hear nor speak – חֵרֵשׁ שֶׁדִּבְּרוּ חֲכָמִים בְּכָל מָקוֹם אֵינוֹ שׁוֹמֵעַ וְאֵינוֹ מְדַבֵּר:** Whenever the Sages speak of a *ḥeresh* they are referring to one who neither hears nor speaks. One who can speak but not hear, or hear but not speak, is considered halakhically competent (Rambam *Sefer Nashim, Hilkhot Ishut* 2:26).

**The examination of a blind woman – בְּדִיקַת הַסּוּמָא:** A blind woman performs an examination on herself and shows the examination cloth to her friends (Rambam *Sefer Kedusha, Hilkhot Issurei Bia* 8:15; *Shulḥan Arukh, Yoreh De'a* 196:7).

**With regard to an imbecile priest they immerse him, etc. – כֹּהֵן שׁוֹטֶה מַטְבִּילִין אוֹתוֹ וכו׳:** A ritually impure priest who is a deaf-mute or an imbecile is immersed and then fed *teruma* after sunset. Such individuals are watched so that they do not sleep after their immersion. If they do sleep they are impure, unless a copper pouch was prepared for them, which would clearly indicate whether they had experienced a seminal emission (Radbaz). The *halakha* is in accordance with the opinion of Rabbi Elazar, because Abaye analyzed and interpreted his ruling (Rambam *Sefer Zera'im, Hilkhot Terumot* 7:5).

LANGUAGE

Riding trousers [*pamalanya*] – פָּמָלַנְיָא: From the Latin feminalia, referring to bandages for the upper part of the thighs.

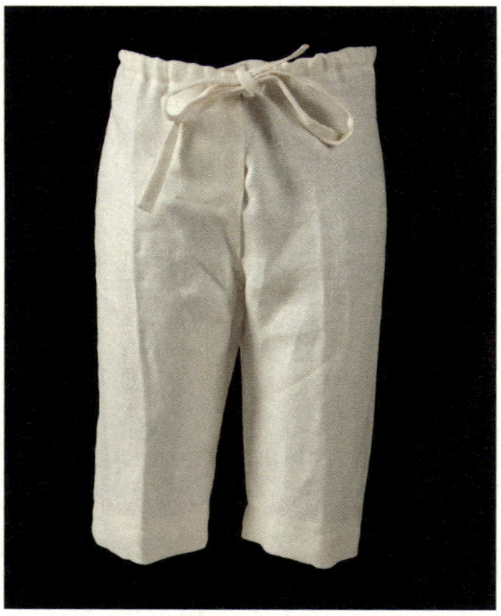

Reproduction of the priests' trousers worn during the Temple service

אָמַר רַב פַּפָּא: שְׁמַע מִינַּהּ – מִכְנָסַיִם אֲסוּרִים. וְהָכְתִיב ״וַעֲשֵׂה לָהֶם מִכְנְסֵי בָד לְכַסּוֹת בְּשַׂר עֶרְוָה״!

**Rav Pappa says:** One can **learn from** the statement of the Rabbis that a pouch wrapped around one's penis can warm it enough to cause a seminal emission, that **trousers are prohibited**[H] to be worn, as they too warm the penis, by being placed so they are tight against it. The Gemara asks: **But isn't it written** with regard to the priestly garments: **"And you shall make them linen trousers to cover the flesh of their nakedness,** from the loins even to the thighs they shall reach" (Exodus 28:42)?

הַהוּא – כִּדְתַנְיָא: מִכְנְסֵי כֹהֲנִים לְמָה הֵן דּוֹמִין? כְּמִין פָּמָלַנְיָא שֶׁל פָּרָשִׁים. לְמַעְלָה – עַד מָתְנַיִם, לְמַטָּה – עַד יְרֵכַיִם, וְיֵשׁ לָהֶם שְׁנָצִים, וְאֵין לָהֶם לֹא בֵּית הַנֶּקֶב וְלֹא בֵּית הָעֶרְוָה.

The Gemara explains: **That** garment, the trousers worn by priests, was different, **as it is taught** in a *baraita*: **The trousers of priests, to what are they comparable?**[H] They are **similar to riding trousers** [*pamalanya*][L] **of horsemen,** and this is what they look like: **Above,** they reach **up to the loins; below,** they go **down to the thighs, and they have straps, and they have no opening,** neither **at the back nor at the front.**

אָמַר אַבַּיֵּי:

**Abaye says:**

HALAKHA

Trousers are prohibited – מִכְנָסַיִם אֲסוּרִים: The Rema writes: The Gemara indicates that it is prohibited to wear trousers unless they have proper leggings, as wearing them can lead to a seminal emission. It can be claimed that the Gemara is referring to the impurity of the body only with regard to the consumption of *teruma*, but as the Rosh cites this statement in his rulings, wearing them is apparently prohibited even nowadays (*Shulḥan Arukh*, *Even HaEzer* 23:6, and see *Pitḥei Teshuva* there).

The trousers of priests, to what are they comparable – מִכְנְסֵי כֹהֲנִים לְמָה הֵן דּוֹמִין: The trousers of both the High Priest and of ordinary priests stretch from the loins to the thighs, i.e., from above the navel, near the heart, until the end of the thigh, the knee. They have straps, and they have no openings at the back or at the front, but are surrounded by a kind of pouch, as explained in the *baraita* (Rambam *Sefer Avoda*, *Hilkhot Kelei HaMikdash* 8:18).

Perek **II**
Daf **14** Amud **a**

NOTES

It is prohibited for camel riders to partake of *teruma* – רוֹכְבֵי גְמַלִּים אֲסוּרִין לֶאֱכוֹל בִּתְרוּמָה: Rashi explains that while the priests ride on the camels their penises might warm up due to friction with the body of the animal. This can lead to a seminal emission, which disqualifies them from partaking of *teruma*. Others explain that riding on the camel leads them to lascivious thoughts, which might cause a seminal emission (*Tosafot*).

HALAKHA

It is prohibited for camel riders to partake of *teruma* – רוֹכְבֵי גְמַלִּים אֲסוּרִין לֶאֱכוֹל בִּתְרוּמָה: Camel riders may not partake of *teruma* until they have immersed and waited for sunset. The reason is that they have the presumptive status of ritual impurity due to the warming caused by riding on the camel, as stated by Abaye. If the driver sits on a saddle or saddlecloth placed on the camel, it is permitted for him to partake of *teruma* (Rambam *Sefer Zera'im*, *Hilkhot Terumot* 7:6 and Radbaz there; see *Shulḥan Arukh*, *Even HaEzer* 23:6).

רוֹכְבֵי גְמַלִּים אֲסוּרִין לֶאֱכוֹל בִּתְרוּמָה. תַּנְיָא נַמִי הָכִי: רוֹכְבֵי גְמַלִּים – כּוּלָּם רְשָׁעִים, הַסַּפָּנִים – כּוּלָּם צַדִּיקִים,

**It is prohibited for camel riders to partake of *teruma*,**[NH] due to the concern for a seminal emission that might result from the friction. The Gemara notes: **This** opinion of Abaye **is also taught** in a *baraita*: **Camel riders are all wicked,** as they are suspected of emitting semen for naught. **Sailors are all righteous,** because they are in a constant state of danger at sea, and therefore their hearts are always turned to God in prayer.

הַחַמָּרִים – מֵהֶן רְשָׁעִים מֵהֶן צַדִּיקִים. אִיכָּא דְּאָמְרִי: הָא – דְּמֵכַף, הָא – דְּלָא מֵכַף, וְאִיכָּא דְּאָמְרִי: הָא – דְּמִטַּרְטֵין, הָא – דְּלָא מִטַּרְטֵין.

The *baraita* continues: As for **donkey drivers,** some **of them are wicked** while some **of them are righteous.** With regard to the difference between wicked and righteous donkey drivers, **there are** those **who say** that **this** donkey driver is righteous, **as** his donkey **is saddled,** and therefore his penis does not rub against it, whereas **that** donkey driver is wicked, **as** his donkey **is not saddled,** which can cause a seminal emission. **And there are** those **who say: This** donkey driver is wicked, **as he spreads** [*demittartein*][L] his thighs on either side of the donkey, whereas **that** donkey driver is righteous **as he does not spread** his thighs in this manner, but rides with both legs on one side of the donkey, so that his penis does not rub against the donkey.

LANGUAGE

Spreads [*mittartein*] – מִטַּרְטֵין: From *turtani*, meaning scales. *Turtani* is derived from the Greek τρυτάνη, *trutanē*, which also means scales. The word *turtani* came to mean any item similar in shape to a balance scale. Therefore, it is used as a description of the manner of riding a donkey, due to the position of the rider's legs on either side of the animal.

רַבִּי יְהוֹשֻׁעַ בֶּן לֵוִי לָיֵיט אַמַּאן דְּגָנֵי אַפַּרְקִיד. אִינִי, וְהָאָמַר רַב יוֹסֵף: פְּרַקְדָּן לֹא יִקְרָא קְרִיַּת שְׁמַע, קְרִיַּת שְׁמַע הוּא דְּלָא יִקְרָא, הָא מַגְנָא – שַׁפִּיר דָּמֵי!

The Gemara further discusses actions that are apt to lead to a seminal emission. **Rabbi Yehoshua ben Levi would curse one who sleeps lying on his back** [*aparkeid*],[NH] as this might lead to a seminal emission. The Gemara asks: **Is that so? But doesn't Rav Yosef say:** One who is **lying on his back may not recite** ***Shema***?[H] From this it may be inferred that **it is only** ***Shema*** **that one may not recite** in this position, **but** to sleep **lying** in that position is **permitted.**

לְעִנְיַן מַגְנָא – כִּי מַצְלֵי שַׁפִּיר דָּמֵי, לְעִנְיַן קְרִיאַת שְׁמַע – כִּי מַצְלֵי אָסוּר. וְהָא רַבִּי יוֹחָנָן מַצְלֵי וְקָרֵי קְרִיאַת שְׁמַע! שָׁאנֵי רַבִּי יוֹחָנָן דְּבַעַל בָּשָׂר הֲוָה.

The Gemara answers: **With regard to** the prohibition against **sleeping** while lying on one's back, **when one leans slightly** to the side it is **permitted.** But **with regard to reciting** ***Shema*** while lying face upward, even **when one leans slightly** to the side it is **prohibited.** The Gemara asks: **But wouldn't Rabbi Yoḥanan**[P] lie on his back **leaning slightly** to the side **and recite** ***Shema*** in this manner? The Gemara answers: The *halakha* in the case of **Rabbi Yoḥanan is different, as he was corpulent,** and consequently he could lean only slightly.

מתני׳ דֶּרֶךְ בְּנוֹת יִשְׂרָאֵל מְשַׁמְּשׁוֹת בִּשְׁנֵי עֵדִים, אֶחָד לוֹ וְאֶחָד לָהּ. וְהַצְּנוּעוֹת מְתַקְּנוֹת שְׁלִישִׁי, לְתַקֵּן אֶת הַבַּיִת.

**MISHNA** It is **the custom of Jewish women** that **they engage in intercourse** with their husbands **while** using **two examination cloths,**[NH] **one for** the husband, to see if there is any of the wife's blood on him after intercourse, **and one for her,** to ascertain after intercourse whether her menstrual flow has begun. **And the modest** women **prepare a third** examination cloth,[H] **to** examine themselves and **prepare** the pubic **area** for intercourse.

## HALAKHA

**Would curse one who sleeps lying on his back – לָיֵיט אַמַּאן דְּגָנֵי אַפַּרְקִיד:** It is prohibited to sleep on one's back, with his face upward. Instead, one should tilt his body slightly, to prevent an erection. This *halakha* is in accordance with the opinion of Rabbi Yehoshua ben Levi (Rambam *Sefer Kedusha*, *Hilkhot Issurei Bia* 21:19; *Shulḥan Arukh*, *Even HaEzer* 23:3).

**One who is lying on his back may not recite** ***Shema*** **– פְּרַקְדָּן לֹא יִקְרָא קְרִיַּת שְׁמַע:** One may not recite *Shema* while lying facing the ground, or on his back with his face upward, as he appears like one who is accepting the yoke of Heaven in a manner of haughtiness. If he recited *Shema* in this fashion, he has fulfilled the mitzva after the fact (*Peri Megadim*). He may recite *Shema* if he tilts his body slightly to the side. The Rema writes that this leniency applies only if he is already lying down and it would take a great effort for him to stand and to dress himself once again (*Magen Avraham*). If he is fully turned to the side, he may recite *Shema* in this manner *ab initio* (*Beit Yosef*; *Taz*; *Magen Avraham*). Others claim that one may not recite *Shema* in this manner *ab initio* (Rabbeinu Yona; see Rabbi Akiva Eiger). If he is extremely fat and cannot turn over to the side, or if he is sick, he may tilt his body slightly and recite *Shema* (Rambam *Sefer Ahava*, *Hilkhot Keriat Shema* 2:2; *Shulḥan Arukh*, *Oraḥ Ḥayyim* 63:1).

**It is the custom of Jewish women that they engage in intercourse with their husbands while using two examination cloths – דֶּרֶךְ בְּנוֹת יִשְׂרָאֵל מְשַׁמְּשׁוֹת בִּשְׁנֵי עֵדִים:** With regard to a woman who does not have a fixed time for her menstrual period, on the first three occasions of intercourse in their marriage she and her husband must examine themselves before and after intercourse, each with their own cloth. If it is established on these occasions that she does not experience a flow of blood due to intercourse, she no longer requires these examinations. Some commentaries maintain that as long as she has no fixed time for her menstrual period she always requires these examinations before and after intercourse, and according to the Rambam the husband must do the same every time. The *halakha* is in accordance with the opinion of Rabbi Ami, citing Rabbi Yannai (Rambam *Sefer Kedusha*, *Hilkhot Issurei Bia* 4:16, 8:3; *Shulḥan Arukh*, *Yoreh De'a* 186:2, and see *Shakh* there).

**And the modest women prepare a third examination cloth, etc. – וְהַצְּנוּעוֹת מְתַקְּנוֹת שְׁלִישִׁי וכו׳:** A woman who has a fixed time for her menstrual period does not require examination either before or after intercourse. On the contrary, she should not examine herself before intercourse in the presence of her husband, so that he will not be worried that she is impure and refrain from engaging in intercourse with her. The *halakha* is in accordance with the opinion of Rav Yehuda. The Rambam requires the husband and wife to examine themselves with their respective cloths after intercourse in case she experienced bleeding during intercourse. According to his opinion, the modest women mentioned here examine themselves even before intercourse. The Rema writes, citing *Roke'aḥ*, *Haggahot Maimoniyyot*, and most of his teachers, that the *halakha* and general custom follow the first opinion (Rambam *Sefer Tahara*, *Hilkhot Metamei Mishkav UMoshav* 4:7; see *Sefer Kedusha*, *Hilkhot Issurei Bia* 4:16 and Ra'avad and *Kesef Mishne* there; *Shulḥan Arukh*, *Yoreh De'a* 186:1).

## NOTES

**One who sleeps lying on his back [*aparkeid*] – אַמַּאן דְּגָנֵי אַפַּרְקִיד:** The early commentaries disagree as to the meaning of the term *aparkeid*. Some say that it refers to one who sleeps on his back, with his face upward (Rashi; *Tosafot*). Others claim the opposite, that it means one who lies face downward (*Arukh*). There are commentaries who rule stringently in accordance with both interpretations (Rambam *Sefer Ahava*, *Hilkhot Keriat Shema* 2:2).

As for the reason for the prohibition against sleeping on one's back, the early commentaries cite various explanations: Some say that this might cause one to have an erection while sleeping, and it would be demeaning for him for his penis to be revealed to others in this fashion (Rashi, first interpretation). Furthermore, this manner of lying might lead him to place his hand on his penis while sleeping, which can warm it up and cause a seminal emission (Rashi, second interpretation).

**It is the custom of Jewish women that they engage in intercourse with their husbands while using two examination cloths – דֶּרֶךְ בְּנוֹת יִשְׂרָאֵל מְשַׁמְּשׁוֹת בִּשְׁנֵי עֵדִים:** The reason they examine themselves after engaging in intercourse is due to the concern that the act of intercourse might have caused a flow of blood (Rashi on 16b; Ramban on 11b).

## PERSONALITIES

**Rabbi Yoḥanan – רַבִּי יוֹחָנָן:** This is Rabbi Yoḥanan bar Nappaḥa, one of the greatest *amora'im*, whose statements are fundamental components of both the Babylonian Talmud and the Jerusalem Talmud. He resided in Tiberias and lived to an advanced age.

Rabbi Yoḥanan was orphaned when he was young, and although his family apparently owned considerable property, he devoted virtually all of his resources to the study of Torah, until he eventually became impoverished. In his youth, he had the privilege of studying under Rabbi Yehuda HaNasi, the redactor of the Mishna, but most of his Torah study was done under Rabbi Yehuda HaNasi's students: Ḥizkiyya ben Ḥiyya, Rabbi Oshaya, Rabbi Ḥanina, and Rabbi Yannai. In time, he became the head of the yeshiva in Tiberias, at which point his fame and influence increased greatly. For a long time Rabbi Yoḥanan was the leading rabbinic scholar of the entire Jewish world, not only in Eretz Yisrael but in Babylonia as well, where he was respected by the Babylonian Sages, many of whom immigrated to Eretz Yisrael to become his students.

Rabbi Yoḥanan was renowned as a handsome man (*Bava Metzia* 84a), and much was said in praise of his good looks. It is known that his life was full of suffering, as ten of his sons died in his lifetime.

HALAKHA

**If blood was found on his cloth, etc.** – **נִמְצָא עַל שֶׁלּוֹ וכו׳**: If a man engages in intercourse with his wife near the time of the onset of her period, expecting that he will be able to complete the act of intercourse before she experiences bleeding, and blood was later found on his cloth, they are both ritually impure and are each liable to bring a sin offering. In a case where blood was found on her cloth, if she wiped herself immediately after intercourse, they are ritually impure and are each liable to bring a sin offering. If she waited enough time for her to place her hand under the cushion or blanket to pick up the cloth for the examination, they are impure as a matter of uncertainty and are both exempt from bringing a sin offering. If she waited sufficiently long for her to descend from the bed and rinse her pubic area, then even if blood was found on her cloth her husband is ritually pure. The *halakha* is in accordance with the opinion of the first *tanna* (Rambam *Sefer Korbanot*, *Hilkhot Shegagot* 5:6).

**In the case of a woman who sees a blood stain, that she transmits seven-day impurity to the man with whom she engaged in intercourse** – **בְּרוֹאָה כֶּתֶם שֶׁמְּטַמְּאָה אֶת בּוֹעֲלָהּ**: Even with regard to a woman concerning whom the Sages stated that her time is sufficient (see 2a), a man who engages in intercourse with her after she finds a blood stain, before she was properly purified, is impure as one who engaged in intercourse with a menstruating woman. This ruling is unanimous, as the Rabbis concede to Rabbi Akiva in this case (Rambam *Sefer Tahara*, *Hilkhot Metamei Mishkav UMoshav* 3:8).

LANGUAGE

**Immediately [*otyom*]** – **אוֹתְיוֹם**: From the Greek εὐθέος, *eutheos*, meaning directly or immediately.

נִמְצָא עַל שֶׁלּוֹ – טְמֵאִין, וְחַיָּיבִין קׇרְבָּן. נִמְצָא עַל שֶׁלָּהּ אוֹתְיוֹם – טְמֵאִין, וְחַיָּיבִין בְּקׇרְבָּן. נִמְצָא עַל שֶׁלָּהּ לְאַחַר זְמַן – טְמֵאִין מִסָּפֵק, וּפְטוּרִין מִן הַקׇּרְבָּן.

If blood **was found on his** cloth,[H] the woman and her husband are both **ritually impure** for seven days, in accordance with the *halakha* of a menstruating woman and of one who engages in intercourse with a menstruating woman, **and are** each **liable to** bring a sin **offering** for unwittingly performing an action punishable with excision from the World-to-Come [*karet*]. If blood **was found on her** cloth **immediately** [***otyom***][L] after intercourse, the woman and her husband are likewise **ritually impure** for seven days **and are** each **liable to** bring a sin **offering.** If blood **was found on her** cloth **after time** passed, they are both **ritually impure due to uncertainty,** as it is possible that the blood appeared only after intercourse, **and they are exempt from** bringing **the** sin **offering.**

אֵיזֶהוּ ״אַחַר זְמַן״? כְּדֵי שֶׁתֵּרֵד מִן הַמִּטָּה וְתָדִיחַ פָּנֶיהָ, וְאַחַר כָּךְ מְטַמְּאָה מֵעֵת לְעֵת, וְאֵינָהּ מְטַמְּאָה אֶת בּוֹעֲלָהּ. רַבִּי עֲקִיבָא אוֹמֵר: אַף מְטַמְּאָה אֶת בּוֹעֲלָהּ.

**What is** considered as being: **After time** passed? It is a period of time **equivalent to** the time needed **for her to descend from the bed and rinse her face,** a euphemism for her pubic area. **And afterward, she** retroactively **transmits impurity** to all ritually pure items with which she came into contact **for** the preceding twenty-four-hour **period,** by rabbinic law, **but she does not transmit** seven-day **impurity to the man with whom she engaged in intercourse.** He is impure with this impurity by rabbinic law only until the evening, like one who came in contact with a menstruating woman. **Rabbi Akiva says:** In the case where blood was found on her cloth after time passed, **she even transmits** seven-day **impurity** by rabbinic law **to the man with whom she engaged in intercourse.**

מוֹדִים חֲכָמִים לְרַבִּי עֲקִיבָא בְּרוֹאָה כֶּתֶם שֶׁמְּטַמְּאָה אֶת בּוֹעֲלָהּ.

The mishna concludes: **The Rabbis concede to Rabbi Akiva in** the case of a woman who **sees** a blood **stain** and then engages in intercourse, **that she transmits** seven-day **impurity to the man with whom she engaged in intercourse,**[H] although this impurity also applies by rabbinic law.

גמ׳ וְנֵיחוּשׁ דִּלְמָא דַּם מַאֲכוֹלֶת הוּא! אָמַר רַבִּי זֵירָא: אוֹתוֹ מָקוֹם בָּדוּק הוּא אֵצֶל מַאֲכוֹלֶת, וְאִיכָּא דְּאָמְרִי: דָּחוּק הוּא אֵצֶל מַאֲכוֹלֶת.

**GEMARA** The mishna states that if blood is found on the husband's cloth after intercourse the husband and wife are both definitely impure. The Gemara asks: **But let us be concerned** that **perhaps it is the blood of a louse,** as it is possible that there was a louse in the woman's pubic area that was squashed during intercourse, and its blood was found on the husband's penis. Accordingly, it should be uncertain if they are impure. **Rabbi Zeira says:** There is no concern for this possibility, as **that place,** a woman's genitals, **is** considered **examined** [***baduk***] **with regard to** the appearance of **a louse,** i.e., it is clear that no louse was there. **And some say** a different version of Rabbi Zeira's statement: **That place is** too **narrow** [***daḥuk***] **for a louse** to enter, and therefore this is not a concern.

מַאי בֵּינַיְיהוּ? אִיכָּא בֵּינַיְיהוּ – דְּאִשְׁתַּכַּח מַאֲכוֹלֶת רְצוּפָה, לְהָךְ לִישָּׁנָא דַּאֲמַר בָּדוּק הוּא – הָא מֵעָלְמָא אֲתַאי, לְהָךְ לִישָּׁנָא דַּאֲמַר דָּחוּק הוּא – אֵימָא שַׁמָּשׁ רְצָפָהּ.

The Gemara asks: **What is** the practical difference **between** these two versions of Rabbi Zeira's statement? The Gemara answers: There is a practical difference **between them** in a case **where a squashed louse was found**[H] on the husband's cloth, near the blood: **According to this version, which states** that a woman's genitals are considered **examined with regard to a louse, this** louse certainly **came from elsewhere,** as a louse is never found in her pubic area, so the blood on the cloth is clearly from the woman, and therefore the couple is ritually impure. By contrast, **according to that version, which states** that the place **is** too **narrow for a louse** to enter, one can **say** that although it is generally too narrow, in this case one did enter and the man's **organ squashed it** during intercourse, and therefore their impurity is uncertain.

HALAKHA

**Where a squashed louse was found** – **דְּאִשְׁתַּכַּח מַאֲכוֹלֶת רְצוּפָה**: If a woman examined herself with a cloth that was examined by her before its use, and she found a blood stain on it, then even if it was as small as a mustard seed she is ritually impure, whether it was round or elongated. Furthermore, even if a squashed louse was found on the blood stain she is impure, as it is proper to be stringent in this case (Rambam *Sefer Kedusha*, *Hilkhot Issurei Bia* 4:18 and *Maggid Mishne* there; *Shulḥan Arukh*, *Yoreh De'a* 190:33).

אִתְּמַר, בָּדְקָה בְּעֵד הַבָּדוּק לָהּ, וְטָחֲתוֹ בִּירֵכָהּ, וּלְמָחָר מָצְאָה עָלֶיהָ דָּם, אָמַר רַב: טְמֵאָה נִדָּה. אֲמַר לֵיהּ רַב שִׁימִי בַּר חִיָּיא: וְהָא חוֹשֶׁשֶׁת אָמְרַתְּ לָן!

It **was stated:** If the woman **examined** herself **with a cloth that was examined by her** before she used it and found free of blood, **and** after the examination **she pressed it against her thigh,**[H] and did not look at the cloth, **and on the following day she found blood on** her thigh, **Rav says:** In such a case she is definitely **impure** as **a menstruating woman.** Since it is known that the cloth was clear of blood before the examination, the blood on her thigh must be from her examination, and it must have passed onto her thigh after the cloth was pressed there. **Rav Shimi bar Ḥiyya said to** Rav: **But didn't you say to us** with regard to this case that **she** needs to be **concerned** for ritual impurity, which indicates that her impurity is uncertain?

אִיתְּמַר נַמִי, אָמַר שְׁמוּאֵל: טְמֵאָה נִדָּה. וְכֵן מוֹרִין בֵּי מִדְרְשָׁא: טְמֵאָה נִדָּה.

In this regard it **was also stated** that **Shmuel says: She** is definitely **impure** as **a menstruating woman. And they likewise rule** as a practical *halakha* in **the study hall** that this woman is definitely **impure** as **a menstruating woman.**

אִתְּמַר, בָּדְקָה בְּעֵד שֶׁאֵינוֹ בָּדוּק לָהּ וְהִנִּיחָתוֹ בְּקוּפְסָא, וּלְמָחָר מָצְאָה עָלָיו דָּם, אָמַר רַב יוֹסֵף: כָּל יָמָיו שֶׁל רַבִּי חִיָּיא טִימֵּא, וּלְעֵת זִקְנָתוֹ טִיהֵר.

With regard to a similar case, it **was stated:** If a woman **examined** herself **with a cloth that was not examined by her** before its use,[H] **and** she then **placed it in a box** without looking at it, **and on the following day she found blood on** this cloth, the question is whether the blood was on the cloth before the examination and the woman is consequently not impure, or whether the blood is from the examination, and she is impure. **Rav Yosef says: All the days of Rabbi Ḥiyya he would deem** such a woman **impure, but in his old age he would deem** her **pure.**

אִיבַּעְיָא לְהוּ: הֵיכִי קָאָמַר? כָּל יָמָיו טִימֵּא מִשּׁוּם נִדָּה, וּלְעֵת זִקְנָתוֹ – טִיהֵר מִשּׁוּם נִדָּה וְטִימֵּא מִשּׁוּם כֶּתֶם.

**A dilemma was raised before** the Sages with regard to this statement of Rav Yosef: With regard to **what** type of impurity status **is he speaking?** Does he mean that **all his days** Rabbi Ḥiyya **would deem** the woman definitely **impure as a menstruating woman,** and therefore any *teruma* with which she came into contact required burning; **and in his old age he would deem** her **pure** from the definite impurity status of **a menstruating woman, but would deem** her **impure as** a woman who discovered **a stain,** which is an uncertain source of impurity? If so, according to his ruling from his old age any *teruma* she touches is not burned but may not be eaten.

אוֹ דִּלְמָא: כָּל יָמָיו טִימֵּא מִשּׁוּם כֶּתֶם, וּלְעֵת זִקְנָתוֹ טִיהֵר מִוּלָּא כְלוּם?

**Or perhaps** does Rav Yosef mean that **all his days** Rabbi Ḥiyya **would deem** the woman **impure** as a matter of uncertainty **due to the stain, and in his old age he would deem** her **pure from any** type of impurity status?

תָּא שְׁמַע, דְּתַנְיָא: בָּדְקָה בְּעֵד שֶׁאֵינוֹ בָּדוּק לָהּ וְהִנִּיחָתוֹ בְּקוּפְסָא, וּלְמָחָר מָצְאָה עָלָיו דָּם, רַבִּי אוֹמֵר: טְמֵאָה מִשּׁוּם נִדָּה, וְרַבִּי חִיָּיא אָמַר: טְמֵאָה מִשּׁוּם כֶּתֶם.

The Gemara suggests: **Come and hear** a resolution for this dilemma, **as it is taught** in a *baraita*: If a woman **examined** herself **with a cloth that was not examined by her** before its use, **and she placed it in a box, and on the following day she found blood on** this cloth, **Rabbi** Yehuda HaNasi **says: She is** definitely **impure as a menstruating woman, and Rabbi Ḥiyya says: She is impure** as a matter of uncertainty **due to the stain.**

### HALAKHA

**If the woman examined herself with a cloth that was examined by her and she pressed it against her thigh, etc.** – **בָּדְקָה בְּעֵד הַבָּדוּק לָהּ וְטָחָתוֹ בִּירֵכָהּ וכו׳:** With regard to a woman who examined herself with a cloth that she knew was clean, and she pressed it against her thigh and on the next day found a blood stain on that thigh, if the stain is elongated she is impure, no matter how small the stain. This *halakha* is in accordance with the opinion of Rabbi Yehuda HaNasi. If the stain is round and less than the size of a split bean, she is pure. The Ramban and others maintain that even if it is round and of minimal size she is impure (Rambam *Sefer Kedusha, Hilkhot Issurei Bia* 4:19; *Shulḥan Arukh, Yoreh De'a* 190:35).

**If a woman examined herself with a cloth that was not examined by her before its use** – **בָּדְקָה בְּעֵד שֶׁאֵינוֹ בָּדוּק לָהּ:** If a woman examined herself with a cloth that had not been previously examined by her, if she found blood on it that was slightly larger in size than a split bean, she is impure. This *halakha* is in accordance with the opinion of Rabbi Yehuda HaNasi (Rambam *Sefer Kedusha, Hilkhot Issurei Bia* 4:19; *Shulḥan Arukh, Yoreh De'a* 190:36).

Perek **II**
Daf **14** Amud **b**

אָמַר לוֹ רַבִּי חִיָּיא: אִי אַתָּה מוֹדֶה שֶׁצְּרִיכָה כִּגְרִיס וְעוֹד? אָמַר לוֹ: אֲבָל. אָמַר לוֹ: אִם כֵּן, (אַתָּה) אַף אַתָּה עֲשִׂיתוֹ כֶּתֶם.

**Rabbi Ḥiyya said to** Rabbi Yehuda HaNasi: **Do you not concede that** for her to become ritually impure **she requires** that the size of the blood stain on the cloth be **more than** the size of **a split bean?** If the stain is smaller, it is assumed to have been caused by a squashed louse. Rabbi Yehuda HaNasi **said to him: Indeed** [*aval*],[L] that is correct. Rabbi Ḥiyya **said to him: If so, you too render** this blood found on the cloth in the box **a stain,** which renders one impure as a matter of uncertainty. If you had considered it definitely impure, there would have been no distinction between a small stain and a large one.

### LANGUAGE

**Indeed** [*aval*] – **אֲבָל:** This word usually means however or but. In addition, it was used by the *tanna'im* as a response to the question that begins: Do you not concede that. When the responder states: *Aval*, he means: Indeed, that is correct (Rashi on *Eiruvin* 41a). This term also appears in the Bible, for example: "Indeed [*aval*] Sarah your wife" (Genesis 17:19), and: "Indeed [*aval*], we are guilty" (Genesis 42:21; see Rashi there).

וְרַבִּי סָבַר: בָּעֵינַן כִּגְרִיס וְעוֹד – לְאַפּוּקֵי מִדַּם מַאֲכוֹלֶת, וְכֵיוָן דִּנְפַק לָהּ מִדַּם מַאֲכוֹלֶת – וַדַּאי מִגּוּפָהּ אֲתָא.

The Gemara comments: **And Rabbi** Yehuda HaNasi, who deems the woman definitely impure in this case, **maintains** that although **we require** that the size of the blood stain be **more than** the size of **a split bean,** this is necessary only **to exclude** the possibility that this is **the blood of a louse; and since** the possibility that it is **the blood of a louse has been excluded,** as its size is more than that of a split bean, **it certainly came from her body,** and therefore she is definitely impure.

מַאי לָאו בְּזִקְנוּתוֹ קָאֵי? הָא בְּיַלְדוּתוֹ – טִימֵּא מִשּׁוּם נִדָּה! שְׁמַע מִינָּהּ.

The Gemara analyzes this statement of Rabbi Ḥiyya with reference to the dilemma under discussion: **What, is it not** correct to assume that Rabbi Ḥiyya **was in his old age** when he disagreed with his teacher, Rabbi Yehuda HaNasi? He would not have done so when he was young. And if he deemed the woman impure as a matter of uncertainty in his old age, it can be inferred that **in his youth he would deem** her definitely **impure as a menstruating woman.** The Gemara concludes: Indeed, **conclude from** here that this is the case.

מִשְׁתַּבַּח לֵיהּ רַבִּי לְרַבִּי יִשְׁמָעֵאל בְּרַבִּי יוֹסֵי בְּרַבִּי חָמָא בַּר בִּיסָא דְּאָדָם גָּדוֹל הוּא. אָמַר לוֹ: לִכְשֶׁיָּבֹא לְיָדְךָ, הֲבִיאֵהוּ לְיָדִי.

§ The Gemara relates: **Rabbi** Yehuda HaNasi would **praise Rabbi Ḥama bar Bisa**[P] **to Rabbi Yishmael, son of Rabbi Yosei,** by saying **that he is a great man.** Rabbi Yishmael **said to** Rabbi Yehuda HaNasi: **When he comes to you, bring him to me.**

כִּי אֲתָא, אֲמַר לֵיהּ: בְּעֵי מִינַּאי מִילְּתָא. בְּעָא מִינֵּיהּ: בָּדְקָה בְּעֵד שֶׁאֵינוֹ בָּדוּק לָהּ, וְהִנִּיחָתוֹ בְּקוּפְסָא, וּלְמָחָר מָצְאָה עָלָיו דָּם, מַהוּ?

**When** Rabbi Ḥama **came** before him, Rabbi Yishmael **said to him: Ask me** about a halakhic **matter.** Rabbi Ḥama **asked him:** If a woman **examined** herself **with a cloth that was not examined by her** before its use, **and she placed it in a box, and on the following day she found blood on** this cloth, **what is** the *halakha*?

אָמַר לוֹ: כְּדִבְרֵי אַבָּא אֵימָא לָךְ, אוֹ כְּדִבְרֵי רַבִּי אֵימָא לָךְ? אֲמַר לֵיהּ: כְּדִבְרֵי רַבִּי אֵימָא לִי.

Rabbi Yishmael **said to him: Shall I say to you** an answer **in accordance with the statement of father,** Rabbi Yosei, **or shall I say to you** an answer **in accordance with the statement of Rabbi** Yehuda HaNasi? Which would you prefer? Rabbi Ḥama **said to him: Say to me** an answer **in accordance with the statement of Rabbi** Yehuda HaNasi.

אָמַר רַבִּי יִשְׁמָעֵאל: זֶהוּ שֶׁאוֹמְרִין עָלָיו דְּאָדָם גָּדוֹל הוּא?! הֵיאַךְ מַנִּיחִין דִּבְרֵי הָרַב וְשׁוֹמְעִין דִּבְרֵי הַתַּלְמִיד?!

**Rabbi Yishmael said:** Is **this** the one **that** Rabbi Yehuda HaNasi **says about him that he is a great man? How can he neglect the statement of the teacher,** Rabbi Yosei, **and listen to the statement of the student,** Rabbi Yehuda HaNasi?

וְרַבִּי חָמָא בַּר בִּיסָא סָבַר: רַבִּי – רֵישׁ מְתִיבְתָּא הוּא, וּשְׁכִיחִי רַבָּנַן קַמֵּיהּ, וּמְחַדְּדִי שְׁמַעְתָּתֵיהּ.

The Gemara explains: **And Rabbi Ḥama bar Bisa** did so because he **maintains** that the opinion of **Rabbi** Yehuda HaNasi is preferable, as **he is the head of the yeshiva, and the Sages are frequently in his presence,**[N] **and** due to the constant disputes **his statements are sharper** than those of Rabbi Yosei, despite the fact that Rabbi Yosei was his teacher.

מַאי רַבִּי וּמַאי רַבִּי יוֹסֵי? אָמַר רַב אַדָּא בַּר מַתָּנָא, תָּנָא: רַבִּי – מְטַמֵּא, וְרַבִּי יוֹסֵי – מְטַהֵר.

The Gemara asks: **What** is this statement of **Rabbi** Yehuda HaNasi, **and what** is the statement of **Rabbi Yosei,** referred to by Rabbi Yishmael? **Rav Adda bar Mattana says** that the reference is to that which was **taught** in a *baraita* with regard to this case: **Rabbi** Yehuda HaNasi **deems** the woman **impure and Rabbi Yosei deems** her **pure.**

וְאָמַר רַבִּי זֵירָא: כְּשֶׁטִּימֵּא רַבִּי – כְּרַבִּי מֵאִיר, וּכְשֶׁטִּיהֵר רַבִּי יוֹסֵי – לְעַצְמוֹ טִיהֵר.

**And Rabbi Zeira says,** in explanation of this dispute: **When Rabbi** Yehuda HaNasi **deemed** the woman **impure,** he ruled **in accordance with** the line of reasoning of **Rabbi Meir, and when Rabbi Yosei deemed** her **pure, he deemed** her **pure in accordance with his own** line of reasoning.

**NOTES**

**Rabbi Yehuda HaNasi is preferable as he is the head of the yeshiva and the Sages are frequently in his presence, etc.** – **רַבִּי רֵישׁ מְתִיבְתָּא הוּא וּשְׁכִיחִי רַבָּנַן קַמֵּיהּ וכו׳**: The commentaries note that although Rabbi Ḥama maintains that Rabbi Yehuda HaNasi had qualities that his teacher Rabbi Yosei did not possess, in that his status as head of the yeshiva enabled him to make halakhic rulings after extensive deliberation, nevertheless there is a principle that the *halakha* is in accordance with the opinion of Rabbi Yosei in his disputes with Rabbi Yehuda HaNasi (Introduction to the Talmud of Rabbi Shimon HaNaggid; *Seder Tanna'im VaAmora'im*). By contrast, some commentaries infer from this passage that the *halakha* follows the opinion of Rabbi Yehuda HaNasi even when in dispute with Rabbi Yosei (New Responsa of Maharil). The particular issue at hand is a matter of dispute among the major ruling authorities. Some state that the woman is impure as a matter of uncertainty, in accordance with the opinion of Rabbi Yosei (Rosh), whereas others rule in accordance with the opinion of Rabbi Yehuda HaNasi (Rambam *Sefer Kedusha, Hilkhot Issurei Bia* 4:19; see *Likkutei Halakhot*).

**PERSONALITIES**

**Rabbi Ḥama bar Bisa** – **רַבִּי חָמָא בַּר בִּיסָא**: Rabbi Ḥama was from the last generation of *tanna'im*, and was apparently a member of Rabbi Yehuda HaNasi's rabbinical court. He probably lived in the southern part of Judea, perhaps in Lod, and served as a city judge. On most occasions when his statements are quoted in the Babylonian Talmud or the Jerusalem Talmud, he is referred to by the name of his son: Rabbi Ḥama, father of Rabbi Oshaya. This is because Rabbi Oshaya was one of the leaders of the generation, who compiled a collection of important *baraitot*. Very little is known about Rabbi Bisa, and only one *halakha* is quoted in his name, in a case where he ruled in accordance with the opinion of his grandson Rabbi Oshaya, and against his son Rabbi Ḥama.

דְּתַנְיָא, הָאִשָּׁה שֶׁהָיְתָה עוֹשָׂה צְרָכֶיהָ וְרָאֲתָה דָּם, רַבִּי מֵאִיר אוֹמֵר: אִם עוֹמֶדֶת – טְמֵאָה, אִם יוֹשֶׁבֶת – טְהוֹרָה.

**As it is taught** in a mishna (59b): In the case of **a woman who was urinating and saw blood** mixed in the urine, **Rabbi Meir says: If** she urinated while **standing,** she is **impure,** as the blood could have originated in the uterus. **If** she was **sitting,** she is **pure,** as the blood is clearly from the urethra.

רַבִּי יוֹסֵי אוֹמֵר: בֵּין כָּךְ וּבֵין כָּךְ טְהוֹרָה.

**Rabbi Yosei says: Whether** she urinates in **this** manner, standing, **or whether** she urinates in **that** manner, sitting, she is **pure.** Like Rabbi Meir, who disregards the possibility that the blood originated in the urethra in a case where the woman was standing, Rabbi Yehuda HaNasi deems a woman impure in the case where blood is found on the cloth in the box, despite the possibility that it could have been on the cloth before she used it to examine herself. Rabbi Yosei, by contrast, maintains that wherever there is a reasonable uncertainty, the woman is not impure.

אֲמַר לֵיהּ רַב אַחָא בְּרֵיהּ דְּרָבָא לְרַב אַשִׁי: וְהָא אָמַר רַבִּי יוֹסֵי בְּרַבִּי חֲנִינָא: כְּשֶׁטִּימֵּא רַבִּי מֵאִיר – לֹא טִימֵּא אֶלָּא מִשּׁוּם כֶּתֶם, וְאִילּוּ רַבִּי מִשּׁוּם נִדָּה קָאָמַר! אֲמַר לֵיהּ, אֲנַן הָכִי קָאָמְרִינַן: כִּי אִיתְּמַר הַהִיא – מִשּׁוּם נִדָּה אִיתְּמַר.

**Rav Aḥa, son of Rava, said to Rav Ashi: But doesn't Rabbi Yosei, son of Rabbi Ḥanina, say** that **when Rabbi Meir deemed** the woman **impure** in the case involving urination, **he merely deemed her impure** as a matter of uncertainty, **due to** contact with a blood **stain, whereas Rabbi** Yehuda HaNasi **said** that in the case involving a stained cloth the woman is definitely impure **as a menstruating woman?** Rav Ashi **said to** Rav Aḥa, son of Rava: **This is what we are saying: When that** comment of Rabbi Yosei, son of Rabbi Ḥanina, concerning the ruling of Rabbi Meir **was stated, it was stated** that he deemed the woman impure **as a menstruating woman.**

״נִמְצָא עַל שֶׁלָּהּ אוֹתִיּוֹם טְמֵאִין״ וכו׳. תָּנוּ רַבָּנַן: אֵיזֶהוּ שִׁיעוּר וֶסֶת? מָשָׁל לְשַׁמָּשׁ וְעֵד שֶׁעוֹמְדִין בְּצַד הַמַּשְׁקוֹף, בִּיצִיאַת שַׁמָּשׁ נִכְנָס עֵד,

§ The mishna states: If blood **was found on her** cloth **immediately** after intercourse, the woman and her husband are both **ritually impure** and are each liable to bring a sin offering. **The Sages taught** in a *baraita*: **What is** the **period of time** needed for the onset of **menstruation,** i.e., what is considered to be immediately after intercourse? This is **comparable to** a male **organ and a cloth that are standing alongside the doorpost,** i.e., at the entrance to the vagina; **at the exit of** the **organ** the **cloth** immediately **enters.**

הָוֵי: וֶסֶת שֶׁאָמְרוּ – לְקִינּוּחַ, אֲבָל לֹא לִבְדִיקָה.

The Gemara comments: **This is the period of time** concerning **which** the Sages **said:** During this period any blood on the cloth renders both the woman and the man ritually impure and liable to bring a sin offering. Yet this period is referring only **to** an external **wipe** of the pubic area with the cloth after intercourse, to see if there was a flow of blood during intercourse. **But** this time frame was **not** stated **with regard to** a full internal **examination.** If the woman conducts a full examination of herself, too much time would have passed since the intercourse for the man to be considered definitely impure.

״נִמְצָא עַל שֶׁלָּהּ לְאַחַר זְמַן״ וכו׳. תָּנָא: וְחַיָּיבִין אָשָׁם תָּלוּי. וְתַנָּא דִּידַן מַאי טַעְמָא?

§ The mishna further states: If blood **was found on her** cloth **after time** passed, they are both ritually impure due to uncertainty, as it is possible that the blood appeared only after intercourse, and therefore they are exempt from bringing the sin offering. The Gemara notes that it is **taught** in a *baraita*: **But they are** each **liable to** bring a **provisional guilt offering**[B] brought by one who is uncertain as to whether he committed a sin that requires a sin offering. The Gemara asks: **And the *tanna* of our** mishna, **what is the reason** that he does not render each of them liable to bring a provisional guilt offering?

בָּעֵינַן חֲתִיכָה מִשְּׁתֵּי חֲתִיכוֹת.

The Gemara answers: The *tanna* of our mishna holds that one is not liable to bring a provisional guilt offering in every case involving the uncertain violation of a prohibition that, were it certain, would render one liable to bring a sin offering. Rather, **we require** it to be a case akin to that of one **piece from two pieces,**[H] e.g., one had two pieces of meat before him, one of which was definitely forbidden while the other was permitted, and he does not know for certain which he ate. But when the uncertainty involves a single item, which may or may not have been forbidden, one does not bring a provisional guilt offering. In the case discussed in the mishna there is only one woman, as it is uncertain whether or not engaging in intercourse with her was permitted, which depends on whether menstruation began before or after intercourse.

**BACKGROUND**

**Provisional guilt offering** – **אָשָׁם תָּלוּי**: The provisional guilt offering is mentioned in the Torah (see Leviticus 5:17–19), and its various *halakhot* are delineated in tractate *Karetot*. The standard case of a provisional guilt offering involves a situation where there is uncertainty whether or not a transgression warranting a sin offering has been committed. For example, if a piece of forbidden fat and a piece of permitted fat were placed alongside one another and one thought that they were both permitted and ate one of them, and he does not know which of them he ate, he must bring a provisional guilt offering. This offering protects him from punishment until he determines whether or not he actually sinned. If he did, he must bring a sin offering.

**HALAKHA**

**We require it to be a case of one piece from two pieces** – **בָּעֵינַן חֲתִיכָה מִשְּׁתֵּי חֲתִיכוֹת**: One is liable to bring a provisional guilt offering only in a case that involves uncertainty concerning an established prohibited item. For example, in a case where there were two pieces of meat before a person, one of which is definitely forbidden fat, and the other of which is definitely permitted fat, and he does not know which of them he ate, he is liable to bring a provisional guilt offering. But if there was only one piece of meat before him, concerning which it is uncertain if it is forbidden or permitted fat, he is exempt from bringing a provisional guilt offering. The *halakha* is in accordance with the opinion of the *tanna* of the mishna (Rambam *Sefer Korbanot*, *Hilkhot Shegagot* 8:2).

"אֵיזֶהוּ אַחַר זְמַן" וכו'. וּרְמִינְהִי, אֵיזֶהוּ "אַחַר זְמַן"? פֵּירֵשׁ רַבִּי אֱלִיעֶזֶר בְּרַבִּי צָדוֹק: כְּדֵי שֶׁתּוֹשִׁיט יָדָהּ תַּחַת הַכַּר אוֹ תַּחַת הַכֶּסֶת וְתִטּוֹל עֵד וְתִבְדּוֹק בּוֹ!

§ The mishna states: **What is** considered **after time** passed? It is a period of time equivalent to the time needed for the woman to descend from the bed and rinse her pubic area. The Gemara **raises a contradiction** from a *baraita*: **What is** considered **after time** passed? **Rabbi Eliezer, son of Rabbi Tzadok, explained:** It is a period **equivalent** to the time in **which she may extend her hand under the cushion or under the blanket and take a cloth and examine** herself **with it.** This is a shorter period than that required for her to get out of bed and rinse her pubic area.

אָמַר רַב חִסְדָּא: מַאי "אַחַר" – אַחַר אַחַר.

**Rav Ḥisda says: What** is the meaning of: **After,** in the mishna? **After, after.** In other words, this is referring to the period after the period of time mentioned by Rabbi Eliezer, son of Rabbi Tzadok, who said it is after the amount of time it takes for the woman to extend her hand under the cushion and take a cloth and examine herself. The mishna is referring to the period of time that follows the time frame referred to by Rabbi Eliezer, son of Rabbi Tzadok, as: After time passed. If blood is found after this amount of time has elapsed the man is not ritually impure for a seven-day period, but only until evening, according to the Rabbis.

וְהָא קָתָנֵי עֲלָהּ "נִמְצָא עַל שֶׁלָּהּ לְאַחַר זְמַן – טְמֵאִין מִסָּפֵק וּפְטוּרִין מִן הַקָּרְבָּן. אֵיזֶהוּ 'אַחַר זְמַן' – כְּדֵי שֶׁתֵּרֵד מִן הַמִּטָּה וְתָדִיחַ פָּנֶיהָ"!

The Gemara raises a difficulty: **But isn't it taught** in the mishna **with regard to** this time period: If blood **was found on her** cloth **after time** passed, they are both **ritually impure due to uncertainty, and they are exempt from** bringing **the** sin **offering.** And the mishna continues: **What is** considered **after time** passed? It is a period of time **equivalent to** the time needed **for her to descend from the bed and rinse her face,** i.e., her pubic area. This indicates that the period of time that follows the ability to perform an immediate examination is that which is mentioned in the mishna, and the mishna is not discussing the third time frame concerning which the husband is impure only until the evening.

הָכִי קָאָמַר: אֵיזֶהוּ "אַחַר זְמַן"? כְּדֵי שֶׁתּוֹשִׁיט יָדָהּ לְתַחַת הַכַּר אוֹ לְתַחַת הַכֶּסֶת וְתִטּוֹל עֵד וְתִבְדּוֹק בּוֹ, וּכְדֵי שֶׁתֵּרֵד מִן הַמִּטָּה וְתָדִיחַ אֶת פָּנֶיהָ – מַחֲלוֹקֶת רַבִּי עֲקִיבָא וַחֲכָמִים.

The Gemara explains that **this** is what the mishna **is saying: What is** considered **after time** passed? It is a period **equivalent** to the time in **which she may extend her hand under the cushion or under the blanket and take a cloth and examine** herself **with it,** as stated by Rabbi Eliezer, son of Rabbi Tzadok. **And** with regard to the other time frame, i.e., **equivalent to** the time needed **for her to descend from the bed and rinse her face,** i.e., her pubic area, there is **a dispute between Rabbi Akiva and the Rabbis** as to whether the man is impure for seven days or only until the evening.

וְהָא "אַחַר כָּךְ" קָתָנֵי! הָכִי קָאָמַר: וְזֶהוּ "אַחַר כָּךְ" שֶׁנֶּחְלְקוּ רַבִּי עֲקִיבָא וַחֲכָמִים.

The Gemara raises a difficulty: **But** with regard to the dispute between Rabbi Akiva and the Rabbis, **doesn't** the mishna **teach: Afterward,** which indicates that they disagree concerning blood found in the time period that comes after the period in which she can descend from the bed and rinse her pubic area? The Gemara answers that **this** is what the mishna **is saying: And this** time frame, i.e., which is equivalent to the time needed for her to descend from the bed and rinse her pubic area, **is** that period of time labeled: **Afterward,** with regard to **which Rabbi Akiva and the Rabbis disagree.**

רַב אַשִׁי אָמַר: אִידִי וְאִידִי חַד שִׁיעוּרָא הוּא, עֵד בְּיָדָהּ – כְּדֵי שֶׁתֵּרֵד מִן הַמִּטָּה וְתָדִיחַ אֶת פָּנֶיהָ, אֵין עֵד בְּיָדָהּ – כְּדֵי שֶׁתּוֹשִׁיט יָדָהּ לְתַחַת הַכַּר אוֹ לְתַחַת הַכֶּסֶת וְתִטּוֹל עֵד וְתִבְדּוֹק בּוֹ.

**Rav Ashi says** a different resolution of the apparent contradiction between the mishna and the *baraita*: Both **this and that are one period,** as it all depends on the situation. If the **cloth** is already **in her hand,** she does not need to extend her hand, and therefore the time frame is as stated in the mishna: **Equivalent to** the time needed **for her to descend from the bed and rinse her face.** If the **cloth is not in her hand,** the period is **equivalent** to the time in **which she may extend her hand under the cushion or under the blanket and take a cloth and examine** herself **with it,** while she is still in bed.

מֵיתִיבִי: אֵיזֶהוּ "אַחַר זְמַן"? דָּבָר זֶה שָׁאַל רַבִּי אֶלְעָזָר בְּרַבִּי צָדוֹק לִפְנֵי חֲכָמִים בְּאוּשָׁא, וְאָמַר לָהֶם:

The Gemara **raises an objection** to Rav Ashi's interpretation from a *baraita*: **What is** considered **after time** passed, at which point the blood found on the woman's cloth renders them both impure as a matter of uncertainty for seven days? About **this matter Rabbi Elazar, son of Rabbi Tzadok, asked the Sages in Usha,**[B] **and he said to them:**

**BACKGROUND**

**Usha – אוּשָׁא:** Usha was a town in the Galilee and was the seat of the Sanhedrin for a generation, around 140 CE. After the bar Kokheva revolt, which took place during the years 132–135 CE, the Jewish community in Eretz Yisrael was almost completely destroyed. Those scholars who survived the upheavals assembled in Usha, where the *Nasi* of the Sanhedrin, Rabban Shimon ben Gamliel II, lived. The surviving students of Rabbi Akiva accepted his spiritual leadership. Although they were scattered throughout the Galilee, they recognized Usha as the center of Torah study and the seat of the Sanhedrin. In Usha, the Sages of that generation instituted many important ordinances, known as the rabbinical ordinances instituted in Usha. From there the Sanhedrin moved to Shefaram, apparently for a brief period.

Usha is located in the western part of the Lower Galilee, in a place nowadays called Hurvat Usha. It lies east of Kiryat Ata.

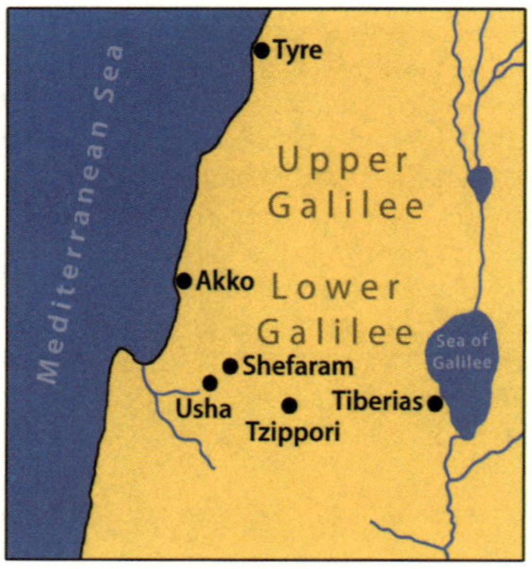


Location of Usha

שֶׁמָּא כְּרַבִּי עֲקִיבָא אַתֶּם אוֹמְרִים, שֶׁמְּטַמְּאָה אֶת בּוֹעֲלָהּ? אָמְרוּ לוֹ: לֹא שָׁמַעְנוּ.

**Perhaps you say in accordance with** the opinion of **Rabbi Akiva,** that the woman **transmits impurity to the man with whom she engaged in intercourse,** just as she retroactively transmits impurity to any pure items she touched in the preceding twenty-four-hour period? The Sages of Usha **said to** Rabbi Eliezer, son of Rabbi Tzadok: **We have not heard** this opinion of Rabbi Akiva, i.e., we do not accept it as *halakha*, and therefore we would like to know what this period of: After time passed, is.

אָמַר לָהֶם, כָּךְ פֵּירְשׁוּ חֲכָמִים בְּיַבְנֶה: לֹא שֶׁהָתָה כְּדֵי שֶׁתֵּרֵד מִן הַמִּטָּה וְתָדִיחַ אֶת פָּנֶיהָ – תּוֹךְ זְמַן הוּא זֶה, וּטְמֵאִין מִסָּפֵק, וּפְטוּרִין מִקׇּרְבָּן, וְחַיָּיבִין בְּאָשָׁם תָּלוּי.

Rabbi Eliezer, son of Rabbi Tzadok, **said to them: This** is how **the Sages of Yavne**[B] **explained** it: As long as the woman **did not wait** before examining herself after intercourse for a period of time **equivalent to** the time in **which she may descend from the bed and rinse her face, this is** considered **within** the period of **time** referred to in the mishna as: After time passed. **And** if blood is found on the cloth she used to examine herself during this period, they are both **impure** for seven days **due to uncertainty, and they are exempt from** bringing a sin **offering,** as this offering is brought only for an unwitting sin that was definitely committed. **But they are** each **obligated to** bring **a provisional guilt offering.**

שֶׁהָתָה כְּדֵי שֶׁתֵּרֵד מִן הַמִּטָּה וְתָדִיחַ אֶת פָּנֶיהָ – אַחַר הַזְּמַן הוּא זֶה.

If **she waited** before examining herself after intercourse for a period of time **equivalent to** the time in **which she may descend from the bed and rinse her face, this is** considered: **After time,** i.e., after the time frame referred to in the mishna as: After time passed.

וְכֵן כְּשֶׁשָּׁהֲתָה מֵעֵת לְעֵת וּמִפְּקִידָה לִפְקִידָה – בּוֹעֲלָהּ מְטַמֵּא מִשּׁוּם מַגָּע, וְאֵינוֹ מְטַמֵּא מִשּׁוּם בּוֹעֵל. רַבִּי עֲקִיבָא אוֹמֵר: אַף מְטַמֵּא מִשּׁוּם בּוֹעֵל. רַבִּי יְהוּדָה בְּנוֹ שֶׁל רַבָּן יוֹחָנָן בֶּן זַכַּאי אוֹמֵר: בַּעְלָהּ נִכְנָס לַהֵיכָל וּמַקְטִיר קְטוֹרֶת.

In this case, **and likewise** in a case **when she waited for** a twenty-four-hour **period or from examination to examination,**[H] i.e., she examined herself before intercourse and was pure, and then examined herself within twenty-four hours after intercourse and was impure, **the man with whom she engaged in intercourse becomes impure** until evening **due to contact** with a menstruating woman, **but he does not become impure** for seven days **as one who engaged in intercourse** with a menstruating woman. **Rabbi Akiva says: He even becomes impure** for seven days **as one who engaged in intercourse** with a menstruating woman. **Rabbi Yehuda, son of Rabban Yoḥanan ben Zakkai, says:** In such a case, not only is **her husband** not impure for seven days, but he is not even deemed impure until evening by rabbinic law. Therefore, if he is a priest **he may enter the Sanctuary and burn incense.**

בִּשְׁלָמָא לְרַב חִסְדָּא – הַיְינוּ דִּמְטַהֲרִי רַבָּנַן.

The Gemara explains the difficulty with Rav Ashi's interpretation of the mishna according to this *baraita*: **Granted, according to** the opinion of **Rav Ḥisda,** who maintains that the period of: After time passed, during which if the woman found blood on her cloth the man with whom she engaged in intercourse is rendered impure for seven days, is equivalent to the time it takes for her to extend her hand and examine herself, **this is** the reason **that the Rabbis deem** him **pure** if she discovered blood after this period has passed.

אֶלָּא לְרַב אַשִׁי – אַמַּאי מְטַהֲרִי רַבָּנַן?

**But according to** the opinion of **Rav Ashi,** who holds that if she has a cloth in her hand then she renders the man with whom she engaged in intercourse impure if she discovers blood within the amount of time it takes for her to descend from the bed and rinse or clean her pubic area with the cloth she is holding in her hand, **why do the Rabbis deem** him **pure** if the amount of time that has passed is the time it takes for her to descend and clean her pubic area? She should still render him impure during that time span.

**HALAKHA**

**When she waited for a twenty-four-hour period or from examination to examination** – כְּשֶׁשָּׁהֲתָה מֵעֵת לְעֵת וּמִפְּקִידָה לִפְקִידָה: With regard to all women who render items impure retroactively when they experience bleeding, even though they transmit impurity to items on which they sit or ride and likewise their saliva and urine transmit impurity retroactively, nevertheless they do not retroactively render impure the man with whom they engaged in intercourse as one who engaged in intercourse with a menstruating woman, but only as one who came into contact with a menstruating woman (Rambam *Sefer Tahara, Hilkhot Metamei Mishkav UMoshav* 3:8).

**BACKGROUND**

**Yavne** – יַבְנֶה: An ancient city, Yavne is identified as the biblical city of Yavne'el in the region of the tribal lands of Judah. It is just over 1 km from the coast and almost due west of Jerusalem. After the destruction of the Second Temple, Yavne became an important Torah center and the seat of the Sanhedrin. Apparently, Yavne had been a center of Torah study even before the Temple was destroyed, but it attained prominence only after the destruction, when Rabban Yoḥanan ben Zakkai reestablished the Sanhedrin there. Until the bar Kokheva revolt, Yavne was the spiritual center of the entire Jewish population in Eretz Yisrael. The Yavne yeshiva, initially headed by Rabban Yoḥanan ben Zakkai and later by Rabban Gamliel II of Yavne, attracted many of the greatest Torah scholars of that era, and numerous ordinances were instituted there to maintain Jewish religious and spiritual life after the destruction of the Temple.

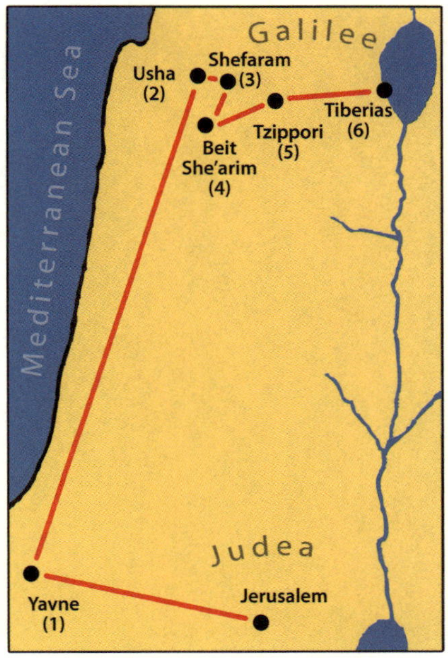


Route of the Sanhedrin in exile

וְכִי תֵּימָא: דְּאֵין עֵד בְּיָדָהּ, הַאי "עֵד בְּיָדָהּ" וְ"אֵין עֵד בְּיָדָהּ" מִיבָּעֵי לֵיהּ! קַשְׁיָא.

**And if you would say** that the *baraita* is dealing with a case **where** the **cloth is not in her hand,** and for this reason the time period that it is referring to is after the amount of time it would take for the woman to extend her hand and examine herself, this cannot be the case, as if so, the *tanna* of the *baraita* **should have** taught two cases: **A cloth is in her hand, and: A cloth is not in her hand,** to differentiate between the situations. The Gemara concludes: Indeed, this *baraita* poses **a difficulty** to the opinion of Rav Ashi.

"רַבִּי יְהוּדָה בְּנוֹ שֶׁל רַבָּן יוֹחָנָן בֶּן זַכַּאי אוֹמֵר: בַּעְלָהּ נִכְנָס לַהֵיכָל וּמַקְטִיר קְטוֹרֶת". וְתֵיפּוֹק לֵיהּ דַּהֲוָה נוֹגֵעַ בִּמֵעֵת לְעֵת שֶׁבְּנִדָּה!

§ The *baraita* teaches that **Rabbi Yehuda, son of Rabban Yoḥanan ben Zakkai, says:** If the examination took place following this period called: After time passed, **her husband** is not ritually impure at all, and therefore if he is a priest he **may enter the Sanctuary and burn incense.** The Gemara asks: **And let him derive that** the husband is impure because **he is one who touched a menstruating woman during** the twenty-four-hour **period** before she discovered blood, as the Sages decreed that pure items touched by a menstruating woman in the twenty-four hours before she noticed the bleeding are impure retroactively.

הוּא דַּאֲמַר כְּשַׁמַּאי, דַּאֲמַר: כָּל הַנָּשִׁים דַּיָּין שְׁעָתָן.

The Gemara answers that Rabbi Yehuda, son of Rabban Yoḥanan ben Zakkai, **who said** the ruling, holds **like Shammai, who said** in a mishna (2a): For **all women, their time is sufficient,** i.e., women who discern the emergence of menstrual blood do not need to be concerned that the flow of blood began before they noticed it, and they assume ritual impurity status only from that moment.

וְתֵיפּוֹק לֵיהּ דַּהֲוָה בַּעַל קֶרִי! בְּשֶׁלֹּא גָּמַר בִּיאָתוֹ.

The Gemara raises another difficulty with the opinion of Rabbi Yehuda, son of Rabban Yoḥanan ben Zakkai: **And let him derive** that the husband is impure **because he is one who experienced a seminal emission.** The Gemara answers that he is referring **to** a case where the husband **did not complete his** act of **intercourse.**

"וּמוֹדִים חֲכָמִים לְרַבִּי עֲקִיבָא בְּרוֹאָה כֶּתֶם". אָמַר רַב: לְמַפְרֵעַ, וְרַבִּי מֵאִיר הִיא.

§ The mishna states: **And the Rabbis concede to Rabbi Akiva in** the case of a woman who **sees** a blood **stain,** that she transmits seven-day impurity to the man with whom she engaged in intercourse. The Gemara cites a dispute of *amora'im* in this regard. **Rav says** that she renders the man with whom she engaged in intercourse impure **retroactively, and** this **is** in accordance with the opinion of **Rabbi Meir,** who maintains that a woman who sees a blood stain renders pure items impure retroactively (see 5a).

וּשְׁמוּאֵל אָמַר: מִכָּאן וּלְהַבָּא, וְרַבָּנַן הִיא. מִכָּאן וּלְהַבָּא, פְּשִׁיטָא!

**And Shmuel says** that she does not render him impure retroactively, but only if he engages in intercourse with her **from now and onward,**[H] i.e., after she sees the blood stain, **and** this **is** in accordance with the opinion of **the Rabbis,** who hold that a woman who sees a blood stain renders pure items impure only from that moment onward. The Gemara raises a difficulty with the opinion of Shmuel: Why does the mishna find it necessary to state that she renders him impure **from now and onward?** Isn't it **obvious?**

מַהוּ דְּתֵימָא: הוֹאִיל וּמֵעֵת לְעֵת דְּרַבָּנַן, וּכְתָמִים דְּרַבָּנַן, מַה מֵּעֵת לְעֵת – לֹא מְטַמְּאָה אֶת בּוֹעֲלָהּ, אַף כְּתָמִים – לֹא מְטַמְּאָה אֶת בּוֹעֲלָהּ, קָא מַשְׁמַע לָן.

The Gemara explains that it was necessary for the mishna to state this ruling, **lest you say: Since** the woman's retroactive impurity for a twenty-four-hour **period** is a decree that applies **by rabbinic law, and** the impurity of blood **stains** also applies **by rabbinic law,** one might claim as follows: **Just as** her retroactive impurity of a twenty-four-hour **period does not render impure the man with whom she engaged in intercourse, so too,** her blood **stains** should **not render impure the man with whom she engaged in intercourse.** Therefore, the mishna **teaches us** that she does render him impure from that point onward.

---

**HALAKHA**

From now and onward – מִכָּאן וּלְהַבָּא: If she saw a blood stain then a man who engages in intercourse with her from that moment forward is impure as one who engaged in intercourse with a menstruating woman (Rambam *Sefer Tahara, Hilkhot Metamei Mishkav UMoshav* 3:8, and see *Kesef Mishne* there).

וְאֵימָא הָכִי נַמִי! הָתָם – אֵין שׁוֹר שָׁחוּט לְפָנֶיךָ, הָכָא – יֵשׁ שׁוֹר שָׁחוּט לְפָנֶיךָ.

The Gemara asks: **But** perhaps one can **say** that **indeed,** she does not transmit impurity to him? The Gemara explains that there is a difference between the two types of rabbinic impurity: **There,** with regard to retroactive impurity, it is **not** a case of: The **slaughtered ox is before you,**[N] i.e., the evidence of impurity did not exist at the time, as she had yet to experience menstruation. Therefore, the Sages did not apply the stringency of retroactive impurity to the husband. By contrast, **here,** with regard to the impurity of blood stains, it **is** a case of: The **slaughtered ox is before you,** as blood has appeared on the cloth.

וְכֵן אָמַר רֵישׁ לָקִישׁ: לְמַפְרֵעַ, וְרַבִּי מֵאִיר הִיא. רַבִּי יוֹחָנָן אָמַר: מִכָּאן וּלְהַבָּא, וְרַבָּנַן הִיא.

The Gemara notes: **And Reish Lakish similarly says,** like Rav, that the woman transmits impurity to the man with whom she engaged in intercourse **retroactively, and** this **is** in accordance with the opinion of **Rabbi Meir.** But **Rabbi Yoḥanan says,** like Shmuel: She renders him impure **from now and onward,** i.e., after she sees the blood stain, **and** this **is** in accordance with the opinion of **the Rabbis.**

מתני׳ כָּל הַנָּשִׁים בְּחֶזְקַת טָהֳרָה לְבַעֲלֵיהֶן. הַבָּאִין מִן הַדֶּרֶךְ – נְשֵׁיהֶן לָהֶן בְּחֶזְקַת טָהֳרָה.

**MISHNA All women have the presumptive status of purity for their husbands,**[H] and therefore one is not required to ascertain whether his wife is ritually pure before engaging in intercourse with her. Even with regard to husbands **returning from a journey,** if their wives were ritually pure when they left, **their wives have the presumptive status of purity for them.**

גמ׳ לָמָּה לֵיהּ לְמִתְנֵי ״הַבָּאִין מִן הַדֶּרֶךְ״? סָלְקָא דַּעְתָּךְ אָמֵינָא: הָנֵי מִילֵּי – הֵיכָא דְּאִיתֵיהּ בְּמָתָא, דְּרַמְיָא אַנַּפְשָׁהּ וּבָדְקָה, אֲבָל הֵיכָא דְּלֵיתָא בְּמָתָא – דְּלָא רַמְיָא אַנַּפְשָׁהּ – לָא, קָא מַשְׁמַע לַן.

**GEMARA** Why does the *tanna* of the mishna need **to teach** the *halakha* of husbands **returning from a journey?** In what manner are they different from other husbands? The Gemara explains that it might **enter your mind to say: This statement,** that women have the presumptive status of purity, applies only in a case **where** the husband **is in the city** of his residence, **as** the woman **takes upon herself** the responsibility of being ready for her husband at all times, **and** therefore **she examines** herself. **But** in a case **where** the husband **is not in the city, since she does not take upon herself** the responsibility of being constantly ready for him, perhaps she should **not** have the presumptive status of purity. Therefore, the *tanna* of the mishna **teaches us** that even in this case she has a presumptive status of purity.

אָמַר רֵישׁ לָקִישׁ מִשּׁוּם רַבִּי יְהוּדָה נְשִׂיאָה: וְהוּא שֶׁבָּא וּמְצָאָהּ בְּתוֹךְ יְמֵי עוֹנָתָהּ.

The Gemara notes that in this regard, **Reish Lakish says in the name of Rabbi Yehuda Nesia: And** this *halakha* that the wife of a husband returning from a journey has a presumptive status of purity **is** applicable only in a case **where** the husband **came and found** that his wife was **within the days of her** projected **period,**[N] i.e., within thirty days of her previous menstruation. In this case he may assume that she has not yet experienced a new period, and therefore he may rely on her presumptive status of purity. But if he arrived after thirty days had elapsed from her previous menstruation, it is assumed that she experienced menstruation at the usual time and therefore it is not permitted for him to engage in intercourse with her unless she examined herself and found herself pure.

אָמַר רַב הוּנָא: לֹא שָׁנוּ אֶלָּא שֶׁאֵין לָהּ וֶסֶת. אֲבָל יֵשׁ לָהּ וֶסֶת – אָסוּר לְשַׁמֵּשׁ.

§ With regard to the presumptive status of purity of wives, **Rav Huna says:** The Sages **taught** this *halakha* **only** in the case of a woman **who does not have** a fixed menstrual **cycle. But** with regard to a woman **who does have** a fixed menstrual **cycle, it is prohibited** for her husband **to engage in intercourse** with her.

### NOTES

**There with regard to retroactive impurity it is not a case of the slaughtered ox is before you, etc. – הָתָם אֵין שׁוֹר שָׁחוּט לְפָנֶיךָ וכו׳:** Some commentaries say that the case of a blood stain is called: The slaughtered ox is before you, because there is no other source to attribute the blood on the garment to, as she had not touched the blood of a bird nor passed by a slaughterhouse. By contrast, retroactive impurity is not like: The slaughtered ox is before you, as she did not experience bleeding the day before, and the impurity is merely a preventive measure (Rashi; *Tosefot Rid*; *Arukh*).

**And this is applicable only in a case where the husband came and found that his wife was within the days of her projected period – וְהוּא שֶׁבָּא וּמְצָאָהּ בְּתוֹךְ יְמֵי עוֹנָתָהּ:** Reish Lakish does not specify what kind of woman he is referring to. Some explain that it is referring either to a woman who does not have a fixed time in which she expects her period to begin, or that she does have a fixed time, but that fixed time is less than thirty days from the onset of her previous period. In these two cases, if more than thirty days have passed since the onset of her previous period, there is cause to suspect that she might have experienced bleeding (see Ramban and Rashba). Others explain that this is referring to a woman who has a fixed time in which she expects her period to begin, and the husband arrives home at that time (see Rif and Rambam).

### HALAKHA

**All women have the presumptive status of purity for their husbands, etc. – כָּל הַנָּשִׁים בְּחֶזְקַת טָהֳרָה לְבַעֲלֵיהֶן וכו׳:** Every woman who has a fixed period has a presumptive status of purity for her husband unless she tells him that she is impure, or until she has the presumptive status of a menstruating woman among her neighbors. If her husband left for a different country when she was pure, when he returns he does not have to ask her if she is pure. Therefore, even if she is asleep when he arrives he may engage in intercourse with her. Some say that this lenient ruling applies only if he arrived when she was within thirty days of her previous sighting of blood, which is the average cycle for most women (*Haggahot Maimoniyyot* and *Kesef Mishne*, citing Ramban and Rashi). If she was menstruating when he left, she remains prohibited until she informs him that she is pure. The *halakha* is in accordance with the opinion of Reish Lakish, citing Rabbi Yehuda Nesia (Rambam *Sefer Tahara*, *Hilkhot Metamei Mishkav UMoshav* 4:7 and *Sefer Kedusha*, *Hilkhot Issurei Bia* 4:9).

**BACKGROUND**

Isn't it the opposite [*kelapei layya*] – כְּלַפֵּי לַיָּיא: This phrase expresses a sense of astonishment: Your statement is puzzling, as the opposite makes sense. Some commentaries explain that this expression should be read as: Toward the tail [*kelapei alya*], i.e., the statement is focusing on the tail instead of the head (Rabbeinu Ḥananel; *Arukh*).

**NOTES**

The concern for impurity of women at the projected time of their periods applies by Torah law – וְסָתוֹת דְּאוֹרַיְיתָא: The early commentaries explain that it is a *halakha* transmitted to Moses from Sinai that a woman who does not examine herself at the projected time of her period has a status of uncertain impurity (Rashi; see Rashi on 9a and Rosh at the beginning of the tractate). Consequently, if she wants to be presumed pure she must examine herself at that time. Others state that according to the opinion that the concern for impurity of women at the projected time of their periods applies by Torah law, if she does not examine herself it is considered as though she definitely experienced bleeding (*Tosafot*).

**HALAKHA**

The concern for impurity of women at the projected time of their periods applies by rabbinic law – וְסָתוֹת דְּרַבָּנַן: The impurity of a woman at the projected time of her period applies by rabbinic law, and it is due to uncertainty. Therefore, one does not burn *teruma* or sacred food with which this woman came into contact, although one may not eat them either (Rambam *Sefer Tahara, Hilkhot Metamei Mishkav UMoshav* 3:9 and *Kesef Mishne* there).

כְּלַפֵּי לַיָּיא? אַדְּרַבָּה, אִיפְּכָא מִסְתַּבְּרָא! אֵין לָהּ וֶסֶת – אֵימָא חֲזַאי, יֵשׁ לָהּ וֶסֶת – וֶסֶת קְבִיעַ לָהּ!

The Gemara asks: **Isn't it the opposite?**[B] **On the contrary;** the **reverse** claim **stands to reason:** If the wife **does not have** a fixed **cycle,** one can **say** that perhaps **she saw** blood, and therefore she should be forbidden to him; whereas if **she has** a fixed **cycle,** since **her cycle is fixed for her** she knows when she will become impure and is presumed to be pure beforehand.

אֶלָּא, אִי אִיתְּמַר – הָכִי אִיתְּמַר, אָמַר רַב הוּנָא: לֹא שָׁנוּ אֶלָּא שֶׁלֹּא הִגִּיעַ שְׁעַת וִסְתָּהּ, אֲבָל הִגִּיעַ שְׁעַת וִסְתָּהּ – אֲסוּרָה. קָסָבַר: וְסָתוֹת דְּאוֹרַיְיתָא.

**Rather,** if Rav Huna's differentiation **was stated,** it **was stated like this: Rav Huna says:** The Sages **taught** this *halakha* **only** in a case **when the** projected **time of** the woman's **period had not arrived** before her husband returned from his journey. **But if the** projected **time of her period had arrived, she is forbidden** to him. Rav Huna **maintains** that the concern for impurity of women at the projected time of their **periods** applies **by Torah law,**[N] as this is a *halakha* transmitted to Moses from Sinai. If a woman did not examine herself at this time she is presumed to have experienced bleeding, even if she did not sense the emission of blood, though there is no formal obligation to examine herself at this time. Accordingly, a husband returning home from a journey cannot rely on the assumption that his wife has examined herself at the projected time of her period, unless he positively establishes that she has done so.

רַבָּה בַּר בַּר חָנָה אָמַר: אֲפִילּוּ הִגִּיעַ שְׁעַת וִסְתָּהּ – נַמִי מוּתֶּרֶת, קָסָבַר: וְסָתוֹת דְּרַבָּנַן.

By contrast, **Rabba bar bar Ḥana says: Even** if **the** projected **time of her period had arrived, she is permitted** to her husband. Rabba bar bar Ḥana **maintains** that the concern for impurity of women at the projected time of their **periods** applies **by rabbinic law,**[H] and therefore she is not considered to have experienced bleeding, though by rabbinic law she must still examine herself to ascertain that she is pure.

רַב אָשֵׁי מַתְנֵי הָכִי, אָמַר רַב הוּנָא:

**Rav Ashi teaches** the opinions of Rav Huna and Rabba bar bar Ḥana **like this: Rav Huna says:**

Perek **II**
Daf **15** Amud **b**

**HALAKHA**

The Sages taught this only where she does not have a menstrual cycle of days – לֹא שָׁנוּ אֶלָּא שֶׁאֵין לָהּ וֶסֶת לְיָמִים: With regard to a woman who has a period that comes by days alone, and the date of her period arrived, her husband may not engage in intercourse with her unless he first asks her whether she is pure. Some say that even if she is awake and lying beside him, this is not enough, as he must ask her and she must explicitly state that she is pure (*Ḥavvat Da'at*). If she does not have a fixed period, the thirtieth day after her previous sighting is considered the projected time of her period. If the husband waited after her period enough time for her to have counted her days of purity and immerse herself, he may engage in intercourse with her without asking her if she is pure (*Shulḥan Arukh, Yoreh De'a* 184:11–12).

לֹא שָׁנוּ אֶלָּא שֶׁאֵין לָהּ וֶסֶת לְיָמִים אֶלָּא יֵשׁ לָהּ וֶסֶת לְיָמִים וְלִקְפִיצוֹת, כֵּיוָן דִּבְמַעֲשֶׂה תַּלְיָא מִילְּתָא – אֵימָא לֹא קָפֵיץ וְלֹא חֲזַאי. אֲבָל יֵשׁ לָהּ וֶסֶת לְיָמִים – אֲסוּרָה לְשַׁמֵּשׁ.

The Sages **taught** this *halakha*, that a woman has a presumptive status of purity to her husband, **only** in a case **where she does not have** a menstrual **cycle of days**[H] alone, **but has** a menstrual **cycle** that is determined both **by** fixed **days and by** physical actions she might perform, such as **jumps.** The reason is that **since the matter is** also **dependent on** a particular **action,** one can **say** that **she did not jump and** therefore **she did not see** blood, and consequently she is presumed to be pure. **But** with regard to a woman who **has** a menstrual **cycle of days** alone, and the projected day of her period arrived, **it is prohibited for her to engage in intercourse** with her husband.

קָסָבַר – וְסָתוֹת דְּאוֹרַיְיתָא.

The Gemara explains that Rav Huna **maintains** that the concern for impurity of women at the projected time of their **periods** applies **by Torah law.** Since she has an uncertain status of impurity by Torah law when the projected day of her period arrives, it is permitted for her to engage in intercourse with her husband only after an examination.

רַבָּה בַּר בַּר חָנָה אָמַר: אֲפִילּוּ יֵשׁ לָהּ וֶסֶת לְיָמִים – מוּתֶּרֶת, קָסָבַר – וְסָתוֹת דְּרַבָּנַן.

**Rabba bar bar Ḥana says: Even** if **she has** a menstrual **cycle of days** alone, **she is permitted** to her husband. Rabba bar bar Ḥana **maintains** that the concern for impurity of women at the projected time of their **periods** applies **by rabbinic law.** Consequently, she is not considered to have experienced bleeding, though by rabbinic law she should have examined herself to ascertain if she was pure.

אָמַר רַב שְׁמוּאֵל מִשְּׁמֵיהּ דְּרַבִּי יוֹחָנָן: אִשָּׁה שֶׁיֵּשׁ לָהּ וֶסֶת – בַּעְלָהּ מְחַשֵּׁב יְמֵי וִסְתָּהּ וּבָא עָלֶיהָ.

**Rav Shmuel says in the name of Rabbi Yoḥanan:** With regard to **a woman who has** a fixed menstrual **cycle,** and her husband was away for seven days after the expected onset of her period, at which point he returned home, **her husband calculates the days of her cycle; and** if in the elapsed time it was possible for her to immerse and purify herself, he can presume that she did so, and **he may engage in intercourse with her** even without asking her whether she is pure.

אֲמַר לֵיהּ רַב שְׁמוּאֵל בַּר יֵיבָא לְרַבִּי אַבָּא: אָמַר רַבִּי יוֹחָנָן אֲפִילּוּ יַלְדָּה, דְּבִיזְיָא לְמִטְבַּל?

**Rav Shmuel bar Yeiva said to Rabbi Abba:** Did **Rabbi Yoḥanan state** this ruling **even** with regard to **a young girl, who is embarrassed to** go and **immerse** herself,[N] in which case one can claim that if her husband was away she would not have gone to the ritual bath?

אֲמַר לֵיהּ: אַטּוּ וַדַּאי רָאֲתָה מִי אָמַר רַבִּי יוֹחָנָן? אֵימַר דְּאָמַר רַבִּי יוֹחָנָן – סָפֵק רָאֲתָה סָפֵק לֹא רָאֲתָה, וְאִם תִּמְצָא לוֹמַר רָאֲתָה – אֵימָא טָבְלָה,

Rabbi Abba **said to** Rav Shmuel bar Yeiva: **Is that to say** that Rabbi Yoḥanan applied this *halakha* to all cases? **Did Rabbi Yoḥanan say** that a woman who **definitely saw** blood is also permitted to her husband? You can **say that Rabbi Yoḥanan said** his ruling with regard to a case where **it is uncertain** whether the woman **saw** blood and **it is uncertain** whether **she did not see** blood, **and** therefore her husband may engage in intercourse with her, as one can reason as follows: **If you say** that **she saw** blood, one can still **say** that perhaps **she immersed.**[N]

אֲבָל וַדַּאי רָאֲתָה – מִי יֵימַר דְּטָבְלָה? הָוֵה לֵיהּ סָפֵק וְוַדַּאי, וְאֵין סָפֵק מוֹצִיא מִידֵי וַדַּאי.

**But** if **she definitely saw** blood, it is not permitted for the husband to engage in intercourse with her. The reason is: **Who is to say that she immersed? It is** a conflict between **an uncertainty** as to whether or not she immersed, **and a certainty** that she saw blood, **and** there is a principle that **an uncertainty does not override a certainty.** In the case of a young girl, since it is uncertain whether she saw blood, and it is uncertain whether she immersed, she is permitted to her husband.

וְלָא? וְהָתַנְיָא: חָבֵר שֶׁמֵּת וְהִנִּיחַ מְגוּרָה מְלֵאָה פֵּירוֹת, אֲפִילּוּ הֵן בְּנֵי יוֹמָן – הֲרֵי הֵן בְּחֶזְקַת מְתוּקָּנִין. וְהָא הָכָא, וַדַּאי טֶבֶל, סָפֵק מְעוּשָּׂר סָפֵק אֵינוֹ מְעוּשָּׂר, וְקָאָתֵי סָפֵק וּמוֹצִיא מִידֵי וַדַּאי!

The Gemara raises a difficulty with this principle: **And** does an uncertainty **not** override a certainty? **But isn't it taught** in a *baraita*: In the case of a ***ḥaver***[B] **who died and left a storehouse filled with produce,**[H] **even** if the produce was there only **that day,** it has the **presumptive status** of produce that was ritually **prepared,** i.e., properly tithed. This is due to the presumption that the *ḥaver* tithed the produce himself or instructed others to do so. The Gemara infers: **And here,** the produce was **definitely untithed** at the outset, and there is **uncertainty** whether the *ḥaver* **tithed it,** and there is **uncertainty** whether **he did not tithe it. And** despite this conflict, **the uncertainty** whether it was tithed **comes and overrides the certainty** that it was untithed produce.

**BACKGROUND**

*Ḥaver* – חָבֵר: The term *ḥaver* refers to one who belonged to the group or movement of *ḥaverim* in the mishnaic period and later. *Ḥaverim* accepted upon themselves, through a special ritual, to keep the matter of *ḥaverim*, i.e., the meticulous observance of mitzvot, especially the *halakhot* of ritual purity, *teruma*, and tithes. In practice, every Torah scholar would certainly become a *ḥaver*, but there were also many *ḥaverim* who were not Torah scholars.

**NOTES**

**A young girl [*yalda*], who is embarrassed [*beziza*] to go and immerse herself** – יַלְדָּה דְּבִיזְיָא לְמִטְבַּל: The early commentaries dispute the meaning of this statement. Some say that *yalda* is used as a noun, meaning young girl, while *beziza* refers to embarrassment. In other words, a minor requires persuasion from her husband before she will agree to immerse herself. Consequently, it is questionable whether Rabbi Yoḥanan's leniency applies in a case when the husband is not in town. Others claim that *yalda* is used as a verb, meaning: Gave birth, and Rav Shmuel bar Yeiva is referring to a woman who has given birth. According to this interpretation, *beziza* means fear, as this woman who has recently given birth is worried that in her weak state she will become ill when she goes to immerse herself.

**If you say that she saw blood one can still say that perhaps she immersed** – וְאִם תִּמְצָא לוֹמַר רָאֲתָה אֵימָא טָבְלָה: Rabbi Abba does not specify whether Rabbi Yoḥanan's ruling applies by Torah law or by rabbinic law. The early commentaries disagree concerning this point. Some say that according to Rabbi Yoḥanan the concern that women are impure at the projected time of their periods applies by Torah law, and yet he maintains that as seven days have passed since this woman's period she has the presumptive status of purity (Rashi). Others contend that in Rabbi Yoḥanan's opinion the concern that the woman had an emission at the projected time of her period applies by rabbinic law (*Tosafot*).

**HALAKHA**

**A *ḥaver* who died and left a storehouse filled with produce** – חָבֵר שֶׁמֵּת וְהִנִּיחַ מְגוּרָה מְלֵאָה פֵּירוֹת: If a *ḥaver* who is known to have been scrupulous about separating *terumot* and tithes died and left a storehouse full of produce, it has the presumptive status of having been tithed, even if it came into his possession on the day he died. The reason is that a *ḥaver* would not allow produce that had not been properly tithed to become available to others. The *halakha* is in accordance with the *baraita* and the explanation of Rav Ḥanina Ḥoza'a (Rambam *Sefer Zera'im*, *Hilkhot Ma'aser* 10:2, 10).

## LANGUAGE

Olive gatherer [*massik*] – מַסִּיק: A *massik* is one who harvests olives. In parallel discussions the word is *matzik* (see *Avoda Zara* 42a), which means a violent man or one who would collaborate with the Roman authorities after the subjugation of the Jewish revolt.

הָתָם וַדַּאי וְוַדַּאי הוּא, כְּדְרַב חֲנִינָא חוֹזָאָה. דְּאָמַר רַב חֲנִינָא חוֹזָאָה: חֲזָקָה עַל חָבֵר שֶׁאֵינוֹ מוֹצִיא מִתַּחַת יָדוֹ דָּבָר שֶׁאֵינוֹ מְתוּקָּן.

The Gemara rejects this claim: **There,** the conflict that leads to the question with regard to the produce's status **is between certainty and certainty,** as the *ḥaver* certainly tithed the produce. This presumption is **in accordance with** the statement **of Rav Ḥanina Ḥoza'a; as Rav Ḥanina Ḥoza'a said:** There is **a presumption with regard to a *ḥaver* that he does not release an item from his possession that is not** ritually **prepared.**

וְאִיבָּעֵית אֵימָא: סָפֵק וְסָפֵק הוּא, וְכִדְרַבִּי אוֹשַׁעְיָא. דְּאָמַר רַבִּי אוֹשַׁעְיָא: מַעֲרִים אָדָם עַל תְּבוּאָתוֹ וּמַכְנִיסָהּ בְּמוֹץ שֶׁלָּהּ, כְּדֵי שֶׁתְּהֵא בְּהֶמְתּוֹ אוֹכֶלֶת וּפְטוּרָה מִן הַמַּעֲשֵׂר.

**And if you wish, say** instead that in that case the conflict **is** between **uncertainty and uncertainty,** as it is possible that there was never an obligation to tithe this produce, **in accordance with** the opinion **of Rabbi Oshaya. As Rabbi Oshaya said: A person can employ artifice** to circumvent obligations incumbent upon him in dealing **with his grain, and bring it into** his courtyard **in its chaff,**[HN] **so that his animal may eat** from it, **and** this grain **is exempt from tithe.** Although the obligation to tithe produce applies even to animal fodder, it is permitted to feed one's animal untithed produce that was brought into one's home before being fully processed. Consequently, the case involving produce is a conflict between two uncertain factors, as it is uncertain whether or not the owner was obligated to tithe the produce in the first place, and even if he was required to do so, it is uncertain whether or not he tithed it.

וְאַכַּתִּי, אֵין סָפֵק מוֹצִיא מִידֵי וַדַּאי? וְהָתַנְיָא: מַעֲשֶׂה בְּשִׁפְחָתוֹ שֶׁל מַסִּיק אֶחָד בְּרִימּוֹן, שֶׁהִטִּילָה נֵפֶל לַבּוֹר, וּבָא כֹּהֵן וְהֵצִיץ בּוֹ לֵידַע אִם זָכָר אִם נְקֵבָה,

The Gemara challenges: **And still,** is it correct that **an uncertainty does not override a certainty? But isn't it taught** in a *baraita*: There was **an incident involving the maidservant of a certain olive gatherer** [*massik*][L] **in** the city of **Rimon, who cast a non-viable newborn into a pit,**[HN] **and a priest came and looked** into the pit **to ascertain whether** the baby was **male**[N] or **whether** it was **female,** as the length of time of a woman's ritual impurity after childbirth, even if she gave birth to a non-viable newborn, depends on whether the child was male or female (see Leviticus, chapter 12).

## HALAKHA

**A person can employ artifice with his grain, and bring it into his courtyard in its chaff** – מַעֲרִים אָדָם עַל תְּבוּאָתוֹ וּמַכְנִיסָהּ בְּמוֹץ שֶׁלָּהּ: It is permitted to employ artifice by bringing grain into one's courtyard while it is still mixed with chaff, and to feed it to his animals. He is exempt from tithing it, even if he winnows it a little bit at a time after bringing it into his house, as stated by Rabbi Oshaya (Rambam *Sefer Zera'im, Hilkhot Ma'aser* 3:6; *Shulḥan Arukh, Yoreh De'a* 331:84).

**Who cast a non-viable newborn into a pit** – שֶׁהִטִּילָה נֵפֶל לַבּוֹר: If one leans over a pit in which there might be a non-viable newborn or there might be a mass that is not considered a non-viable newborn, and there are martens or similar animals in the area, the assumption is that an animal took the non-viable newborn and ate it, and the person leaning over the pit is ritually pure. If a non-viable newborn was definitely thrown there, one who leans over it is ritually impure by Torah law (Rambam *Sefer Tahara, Hilkhot Tumat Met* 9:11).

## NOTES

**A person can employ artifice with his grain and bring it into his courtyard in its chaff** – מַעֲרִים אָדָם עַל תְּבוּאָתוֹ וּמַכְנִיסָהּ בְּמוֹץ שֶׁלָּהּ: *Halakha* dictates that one is obligated to tithe the grain that has been threshed and piled, regardless of the ultimate purpose for which the grain was intended. This is because this is classified as grain, and the verse states: "The first fruits of your grain, of your wine, and of your oil, and the first of the fleece of your sheep, you shall give him" (Deuteronomy 18:4). Nevertheless, any produce that is used only as animal feed and is never eaten by people is exempt from tithes. By Torah law, one is exempt from tithing grain that was not threshed and is still in its chaff. Furthermore, even after it has been threshed, the produce is not included in the mitzva of tithing until it enters through the front of the house, through which people enter and exit, in accordance with the verse: "I have removed the consecrated from the house" (Deuteronomy 26:13). By rabbinic law, it is prohibited to eat grain that has not entered the house in the framework of a meal, although feeding it to animals is permitted without first tithing it.

The early commentaries on *Pesaḥim* 9a ask why the Gemara suggests that a *ḥaver*, who is scrupulous in the performance of mitzvot, might employ artifice to exempt his produce from tithes. Some explain that the *ḥaver* does so only as a temporary measure until he finishes processing the grain, as he plans to tithe all the produce afterward (Maharam Ḥalawa). Others maintain that he intends to tithe the produce himself, but he employs this artifice to prevent a situation where members of his household forget to tithe the produce and unwittingly eat it untithed (*Tosefot Rid*).

**Who cast a non-viable newborn into a pit** – שֶׁהִטִּילָה נֵפֶל לַבּוֹר: Some learn from here that there is no obligation to bury non-viable newborns (*Ḥavvot Ya'ir*). Others dispute this proof, as this act can be seen as a form of burial. Alternatively, this case involves an entity whose status as a non-viable newborn is uncertain (*Magen Avraham*).

**To ascertain whether the baby was male** – לֵידַע אִם זָכָר: The early commentaries learn from here that the *halakhot* of the impurity of birth apply equally to a Canaanite maidservant as to a Jewish woman (*Tosafot* on *Avoda Zara* 42a).

וּבָא מַעֲשֶׂה לִפְנֵי חֲכָמִים וְטִהֲרוּהוּ, מִפְּנֵי שֶׁחוּלְדָּה וּבַרְדְּלָס מְצוּיִים שָׁם.

**And** the **incident came before the Sages** to rule whether or not the priest contracted ritual impurity while standing over the corpse, **and they deemed him ritually pure.** The basis for this ruling was: **Due to** the fact **that martens**[B] **and hyenas**[B] **are common there,** it is likely that the body was dragged away before the priest arrived at the pit.

וְהָא הָכָא - דְּוַדַּאי הִטִּילָה נֵפֶל, סָפֵק גְּרָרוּהוּ סָפֵק לֹא גְּרָרוּהוּ, וְקָאָתֵי סָפֵק וּמוֹצִיא מִידֵי וַדַּאי!

The Gemara explains the challenge from this *baraita*: **And here, where it is certain** that the maidservant **cast** the **non-viable newborn** into the pit, and it is **uncertain** whether an animal **dragged it** away and it is **uncertain** whether **no** animal **dragged it** away, the Sages nevertheless ruled that **an uncertainty comes and overrides a certainty.**

לָא תֵּימָא "הִטִּילָה נֵפֶל לַבּוֹר", אֶלָּא אֵימָא

The Gemara rejects this challenge: **Do not say** in the *baraita* **that** the woman certainly **cast a non-viable newborn into a pit; rather, say**

**BACKGROUND**

Marten [*ḥulda*] – חוּלְדָּה: The *ḥulda* of the Talmud, which is probably the same as the *ḥoled* of Leviticus 11:29, is described here as a predator; in tractate *Ta'anit* 8a it is also referenced as killing a human baby. Yisrael Aharoni, an influential early twentieth-century Israeli zoologist, proposed that it is the brown rat, which is indeed predatory. As a result, *ḥulda* became the name for the rat in modern Hebrew. It is now known that brown rats reached the Middle East from Norway only very recently; in the talmudic era, the only rat in the region was the black rat, a much smaller rodent, which is not predatory. A more likely explanation is that of the medieval European rabbinic tradition, which identifies the *ḥulda* as a member of the weasel family. The weasel itself does not live in the Middle East, although it did live there in the early biblical era and possibly survived through to talmudic times. Yet, it is exclusively carnivorous, and would not drag leavened bread, a case mentioned in the first chapter of tractate *Pesaḥim*. The marten, which belongs to the same family, is found in Israel and it may be the *ḥulda*.

Black rat

Marten

Hyena [*bardelas*] – בַּרְדְּלָס: The *bardelas* is also mentioned in the mishna in *Bava Kamma* 15b. The mishna there is using a variation of the Greek term πάρδαλις, *pardalis*, which denotes spots and refers to the leopard. While it seems that this was the Hebrew name given to the cheetah during the mishnaic era, the Gemara on that mishna posits that it is referring to the striped hyena. The *bardelas* described here, listed alongside the *ḥulda*, is clearly not referring to the cheetah, which does not feed on carrion and avoids humans. It therefore seems most likely that it refers to the hyena here as well.

Hyena

Perek **II**
Daf **16** Amud **a**

כְּמִין נֵפֶל.

that she cast an item **similar to a non-viable newborn** into a pit. Perhaps it was not a non-viable newborn; it might simply have been congealed blood, which does not transmit impurity. Therefore, this is a conflict between uncertainty and uncertainty. It is unclear whether there was anything in the pit that could have rendered the priest ritually impure, and even if there was, it might already have been dragged away.

וְהָא "לֵידַע אִם זָכָר אִם נְקֵבָה" קָתָנֵי!

The Gemara challenges: **But isn't it taught** in the *baraita*: And a priest came and looked into the pit **to ascertain whether** it was **male** or **whether** it was **female?** This indicates that the only uncertainty was with regard to its sex; it was certainly a non-viable newborn.

הָכִי קָאָמַר: וּבָא כֹּהֵן וְהֵצִיץ בּוֹ לֵידַע אִם נֵפֶל הִפִּילָה אִם רוּחַ הִפִּילָה, וְאִם תִּמְצֵי לוֹמַר נֵפֶל הִפִּילָה – לֵידַע אִם זָכָר אִם נְקֵבָה.

The Gemara answers that **this** is what the *baraita* **is saying: And a priest came and glanced at** the baby **to ascertain whether** the woman **discharged a non-viable newborn,** or **whether she discharged an amorphous mass.**[N] **And if you say** that **she discharged a non-viable newborn,** he sought **to ascertain whether** it was **male** or **whether** it was **female.**

וְאִיבָּעֵית אֵימָא: כֵּיוָן דְּחוּלְדָּה וּבַרְדְּלָס מְצוּיִים שָׁם – וַדַּאי גְּרָרוּהוּ.

**And if you wish, say** instead that this was not a conflict between certainty and uncertainty; rather, it was between two certainties. **Since martens and hyenas are common there, they certainly dragged it** away immediately. Consequently, the ruling in this case does not contradict the principle that an uncertainty does not override a certainty.

בָּעוּ מִינֵּיהּ מֵרַב נַחְמָן: וְסָתוֹת דְּאוֹרָיְיתָא אוֹ דְּרַבָּנַן?

§ The Gemara returns to the issue of a woman's examination at the projected time of her period. The Sages **asked Rav Naḥman:** Does the concern for impurity of women at the projected time of their **periods,** and in turn the obligation for her to perform an examination at that time, apply **by Torah law?** If so, if a woman did not examine herself she is ritually impure, even if she later examined herself and did not find any blood, as it is assumed that she emitted blood without her seeing it. **Or** perhaps the concern for impurity of women at the projected time of their periods, and in turn the obligation for her to perform an examination at that time, applies **by rabbinic law?** If so, a woman who did not examine herself at the time and did not sense the emission of blood can still examine herself after that time and would be ritually pure.

אֲמַר לְהוּ: מִדַּאֲמַר הוּנָא חַבְרִין מִשְּׁמֵיהּ דְּרַב, אִשָּׁה שֶׁיֵּשׁ לָהּ וֶסֶת, וְהִגִּיעַ שְׁעַת וִסְתָּהּ וְלֹא בָּדְקָה, וּלְבַסּוֹף רָאֲתָה – חוֹשֶׁשֶׁת לְוִסְתָּהּ וְחוֹשֶׁשֶׁת לִרְאִיָּיתָהּ, אַלְמָא – וְסָתוֹת דְּאוֹרָיְיתָא.

Rav Naḥman **said to them:** A resolution can be found for your dilemma **from that which Huna our colleague said**[N] **in the name of Rav:** With regard to **a woman who has** a fixed menstrual **cycle, and the** projected **time of her period arrived and she did not examine herself, and ultimately,** when she did examine herself, **she saw** blood, the *halakha* is that **she must be concerned for** ritual impurity from the projected time of **her period** and that therefore any pure items she touched since then are impure. **And** additionally, **she must be concerned** for ritual impurity with regard to the twenty-four hours prior **to her seeing** the blood, and any items she touched during those twenty-four hours are impure, even if she saw the blood a short while after the projected time of her period. **Evidently,** the concern for impurity of women at the projected time of their **periods** applies **by Torah law,** which is why the *halakha* is stringent.

אִיכָּא דְּאָמְרִי, הָכִי קָאָמַר לְהוּ: טַעְמָא – דְּרָאֲתָה, הָא לֹא רָאֲתָה – אֵין חוֹשְׁשִׁין, אַלְמָא – וְסָתוֹת דְּרַבָּנַן.

**There are** those **who say** that **this is what** Rav Naḥman **said to** the other Sages: The **reason** for Rav's ruling that pure items she touched are retroactively considered impure is **that** she ultimately **saw** blood, from which it may be inferred that if **she did not see** blood, one is **not concerned** about the status of pure items that she touched from the projected time of her period, despite the fact that she neglected to examine herself at the time. **Evidently,** the concern for impurity of women at the projected time of their **periods** applies **by rabbinic law.**[N]

אִיתְּמַר: אִשָּׁה שֶׁיֵּשׁ לָהּ וֶסֶת, וְהִגִּיעַ שְׁעַת וִסְתָּהּ וְלֹא בָּדְקָה, וּלְבַסּוֹף בָּדְקָה. אָמַר רַב: בָּדְקָה וּמָצְאָה טְמֵאָה – טְמֵאָה, טְהוֹרָה – טְהוֹרָה. וּשְׁמוּאֵל אָמַר: אֲפִילּוּ בָּדְקָה וּמָצְאָה טְהוֹרָה – נַמִי טְמֵאָה, מִפְּנֵי שֶׁאוֹרַח בִּזְמַנּוֹ בָּא.

§ Since the Gemara mentioned Rav's ruling it cites the dispute between Rav and Shmuel with regard to this *halakha*. **It was stated** that these *amora'im* disagree about **a woman who has** a fixed menstrual **cycle, and the** projected **time of her period arrived and she did not examine herself, and ultimately she examined** herself. **Rav says:** If **she examined** herself at this later time **and found** that she was **ritually impure,**[H] **she is impure;** and if she found that she was **pure, she is pure.**[H] **And Shmuel says: Even if she** later **examined** herself **and found** that she was **pure, she is impure.** This is **because** the **manner** of women, i.e., a women's menstrual period, **comes at its** usual **time.**

## NOTES

**Glanced at the baby to ascertain whether the woman discharged a non-viable newborn or…an amorphous mass – הֵצִיץ לֵידַע אִם נֵפֶל הִפִּילָה אִם רוּחַ הִפִּילָה:** The commentaries disagree as to why the priest looked in the pit, exposing himself to the possibility that he would be rendered ritually impure in the process. Some commentaries have counted eleven different explanations of this matter (*Yosef Da'at*). Many suggest that this priest was an *am ha'aretz*, who was unaware that it is prohibited for a priest to become ritually impure, or that he was a child sent by the woman to examine the pit (*Tosafot*). Others claim that he sought to provide a halakhic answer to a question he was asked with regard to the days of her ritual purity and impurity. It is also possible that the woman lived in his house, and he sought to ascertain whether she was ritually pure or impure so as to keep the food of the house in a state of ritual purity. Alternatively, he sought to ascertain whether the time of her obligation to bring an offering would coincide with his priestly watch in the Temple (Rashi).

**From that which Huna our colleague said, etc. – מִדַּאֲמַר הוּנָא חַבְרִין:** The early commentaries are puzzled by this claim, as it was stated previously that Rav Huna himself maintains that this obligation applies by Torah law. They explain that the earlier statement represents the opinion of Rav Huna himself, whereas this *halakha* that Rav Naḥman learned from him reflects the opinion of Rav, which Rav Huna cited but does not accept (*Tosafot*).

**There are those who say…evidently the concern for impurity of women at the projected time of their periods applies by rabbinic law – אִיכָּא דְּאָמְרִי...אַלְמָא וְסָתוֹת דְּרַבָּנַן:** The commentaries explain that the two versions of the discussion differ with regard to the significance of the clause: Ultimately she saw. According to the first version, this phrase is merely serving to emphasize that she should be concerned that she will see blood, but it makes no practical difference whether she saw blood at this stage or not, as either way she is impure. This indicates that her examination is a requirement by Torah law. According to the second version, the phrase: Ultimately she saw, indicates that if she did not see blood at that stage then she is pure, which proves that her examination is a rabbinic requirement (Rashi).

## HALAKHA

**She examined herself and found that she was ritually impure – בָּדְקָה וּמָצְאָה טְמֵאָה:** Every woman who has a fixed period must examine herself at the projected time of her period. If the expected time for her period passed and she did not examine herself and did not sense the emission of blood, she is pure. Some say that if she has a fixed period, or if she does not have a fixed period but thirty days have passed from her previous sighting of blood, she is pure only if she examined herself and found that she was pure. The Rema notes that this is the accepted custom (Rambam *Sefer Tahara, Hilkhot Metamei Mishkav UMoshav* 3:5 and *Sefer Kedusha, Hilkhot Issurei Bia* 8:13; *Shulḥan Arukh, Yoreh De'a* 184:9).

**If she found that she was pure she is pure – טְהוֹרָה טְהוֹרָה:** With regard to a woman who has a fixed period and who did not examine herself at the projected time of her period, but a few days later she examined herself and found blood, she is retroactively impure. She has the presumptive status of a menstruating woman from the projected time of her period. If this later examination indicated that she was pure, she is pure retroactively, as stated by Rav (Rambam *Sefer Tahara, Hilkhot Metamei Mishkav UMoshav* 3:5 and *Sefer Kedusha, Hilkhot Issurei Bia* 8:13).

לֵימָא בְּוֶסֶתוֹת קָמִיפַּלְגִי, דְּמָר סָבַר – דְּאוֹרָיְיתָא, וּמָר סָבַר – דְּרַבָּנַן!

The Gemara suggests: **Shall we say** that Rav and Shmuel **disagree with regard to** the concern for impurity of women at the projected time of their **periods? As one Sage,** Shmuel, who rules that the woman is impure in both cases, **holds** that this concern for impurity applies **by Torah law, and** one **Sage,** Rav, who says that if her subsequent examination came out clean then she remains pure, **holds** that this concern for impurity applies **by rabbinic law.**

אָמַר רַבִּי זֵירָא – דְּכוּלֵּי עָלְמָא – וֶסֶתוֹת דְּאוֹרָיְיתָא, כָּאן – שֶׁבָּדְקָה עַצְמָהּ כְּשִׁיעוּר וֶסֶת, כָּאן – שֶׁלֹּא בָּדְקָה עַצְמָהּ כְּשִׁיעוּר וֶסֶת.

**Rabbi Zeira says:** It is possible **that everyone,** even Rav, agrees that the concern for impurity of women at the projected time of their **periods** applies **by Torah law,** and the reason Rav deems the woman pure in this case is that **here** it is a situation **where she examined herself within the period of time** needed for the onset of **menstruation,** i.e., very close to the projected time of her period, and therefore it is assumed that if there was blood at the projected time of her period she would have seen it upon this examination. By contrast, **there,** in other cases of subsequent examinations, **she did not examine herself within the period of time** needed for the onset of **menstruation.**

רַב נַחְמָן בַּר יִצְחָק אָמַר: בְּוֶסֶתוֹת גּוּפַיְיהוּ קָמִיפַּלְגִי, דְּמָר סָבַר – וֶסֶתוֹת דְּאוֹרָיְיתָא, וּמָר סָבַר – וֶסֶתוֹת דְּרַבָּנַן.

**Rav Naḥman bar Yitzḥak says:** Actually, Rav and Shmuel **disagree with regard to** the matter of the projected time of their **periods itself, as one Sage,** Shmuel, **holds** that the concern for impurity of women at the projected time of their **periods** applies **by Torah law, and one Sage,** Rav, **holds** that the concern for impurity of women at the projected time of their **periods** applies **by rabbinic law.**

אָמַר רַב שֵׁשֶׁת: כְּתַנָּאֵי, רַבִּי אֱלִיעֶזֶר אוֹמֵר טְמֵאָה נִדָּה,

The Gemara continues to discuss this dispute between Rav and Shmuel. **Rav Sheshet says:** This disagreement between Rav and Shmuel is **parallel to** a dispute between ***tanna'im*: Rabbi Eliezer says** that a woman who has a fixed menstrual cycle but who did not examine herself at the projected time of her period **is ritually impure as a menstruating woman,** which indicates that in his opinion the examination at the projected time of a woman's period applies by Torah law.

וְרַבִּי יְהוֹשֻׁעַ אוֹמֵר תִּבָּדֵק. וְהָנֵי תַּנָּאֵי כִּי הָנֵי תַּנָּאֵי, דְּתַנְיָא, רַבִּי מֵאִיר אוֹמֵר: טְמֵאָה נִדָּה, וַחֲכָמִים אוֹמְרִים: תִּבָּדֵק.

**And Rabbi Yehoshua says** that **she should be examined** now, despite the elapsed time, and if the examination came out clean she is pure retroactively as well. Apparently, Rabbi Yehoshua maintains that this examination applies by rabbinic law. The Gemara adds: **And** the dispute of **these *tanna'im* is parallel to** the dispute of **those *tanna'im*, as it is taught** in a *baraita* that **Rabbi Meir says: She is ritually impure as a menstruating woman, and the Rabbis say: She should be examined** now.

אָמַר אַבָּיֵי: אַף אֲנַן נַמִּי תְּנֵינָא, דִּתְנַן, רַבִּי מֵאִיר אוֹמֵר: אִם הָיְתָה בְּמַחֲבוֹא, וְהִגִּיעַ שְׁעַת וִסְתָּהּ וְלֹא בָּדְקָה – טְהוֹרָה, שֶׁחֲרָדָה מְסַלֶּקֶת אֶת הַדָּמִים. טַעְמָא – דְּאִיכָּא חֲרָדָה, הָא לֵיכָּא חֲרָדָה – טְמֵאָה, אַלְמָא – וֶסֶתוֹת דְּאוֹרָיְיתָא.

**Abaye said: We, too, learn** likewise in a mishna, **as we learned** in a mishna (39a): **Rabbi Meir says: If** a woman **was in hiding**[HB] from danger, **and the** projected **time of her period arrived and she did not examine** herself, nevertheless she is **ritually pure, as** it may be assumed that she did not experience bleeding because **fear dispels** the flow of menstrual **blood,** and therefore there is no concern that she might have emitted blood without sensing it. By inference, **the reason** she is pure is **that there is fear** of danger; **but if there is no fear** upon this woman, **she is impure. Evidently,** Rabbi Meir maintains that the concern for impurity of women at the projected time of their **periods** applies **by Torah law.**

לֵימָא הָנֵי תַּנָּאֵי בְּהָא נַמִּי פְּלִיגִי, דְּתַנְיָא: הָרוֹאָה דָּם מֵחֲמַת מַכָּה – אֲפִילּוּ בְּתוֹךְ יְמֵי נִדָּתָהּ, טְהוֹרָה, דִּבְרֵי רַבָּן שִׁמְעוֹן בֶּן גַּמְלִיאֵל.

The Gemara further suggests: **Shall we say** that **these** following ***tanna'im* also disagree with regard to this** matter of whether the examination at the projected time of a woman's period is required by Torah law? **As it is taught** in a *baraita*: With regard to a woman **who sees blood due to a wound**[H] in her pubic area, **even** if she saw the blood **during the days of her menstruation,** including the projected time of her period, **she is pure,** as it is assumed that the blood came from the wound; this is **the statement of Rabban Shimon ben Gamliel.**

**HALAKHA**

**If a woman was in hiding – אִם הָיְתָה בְּמַחֲבוֹא:** If the expected time for a woman's period arrived when she was hiding out of fear, she does not need to be concerned with regard to impurity. Some commentaries say that this *halakha* applies only if the expected time for her period had passed and she did not examine herself or sense the emission of blood. But she is obligated to examine herself at the projected time of her period *ab initio* (see *Beit Yosef*). This *halakha* is in accordance with the opinion of Rabbi Meir (*Shulḥan Arukh, Yoreh De'a* 184:8).

**A woman who sees blood due to a wound – הָרוֹאָה דָּם מֵחֲמַת מַכָּה:** If a woman has a wound in her pubic area and she sees blood, it is presumed to come from the wound, and she and the blood are pure. If the blood from the wound is different from the blood she sees, she is impure. The Rema writes that this applies only to a woman who has a fixed period, and who sees this blood when it was not the projected time of her period. In such a case it is assumed that the blood was from the wound, despite the uncertainty. Similarly, if she does not have a fixed period and it is uncertain whether the blood came from her uterus or from the inner walls of the vagina, she is pure because this is a compound uncertainty, as even if the blood came from her uterus it might be the blood of the wound. But if she does not have a fixed period and the blood certainly came from the uterus, it is not assumed that it is from the wound unless she knows for certain that her wound is bleeding. In any case, at the projected time of her period, or, in the case of a woman who does not have a fixed period, thirty days after her previous sighting, the blood cannot be assumed to come from the wound, as otherwise she would never be impure as a menstruating woman. With regard to blood stains, she can assume that they are from the wound in all cases (Rambam *Sefer Kedusha, Hilkhot Issurei Bia* 8:14; *Shulḥan Arukh, Yoreh De'a* 187:5, and see 187:6).

**BACKGROUND**

**If a woman was in hiding – אִם הָיְתָה בְּמַחֲבוֹא:** Archaeological evidence suggests that this is not merely theoretical; in the Judean Desert, caves have been found that were clearly used as dwelling places at the time of the bar Kokheva rebellion. Under stressful conditions like this, regular ovulation could be affected.

Bell caves in Beit Guvrin, one area of bar Kokheva's activity

רַבִּי אוֹמֵר: אִם יֵשׁ לָהּ וֶסֶת – חוֹשֶׁשֶׁת לְוִסְתָּהּ.

**Rabbi** Yehuda HaNasi **says** that if the woman does not have a fixed menstrual cycle then the blood can be attributed to the wound. But **if she has** a fixed menstrual **cycle,** and she saw blood on the projected day of her period, even if the blood was from the wound **she must be concerned that** blood from **her period** might be mixed with this blood from the wound, and must therefore observe impurity status.

מַאי לָאו, בְּהָא קָמִיפַּלְגִי, דְּמָר סָבַר – וְסָתוֹת דְּאוֹרַיְיתָא, וּמָר סָבַר – וְסָתוֹת דְּרַבָּנַן!

The Gemara clarifies its suggestion: **What, is it not** the case that these Sages **disagree with regard to this** matter, i.e., **that** one **Sage,** Rabbi Yehuda HaNasi, **holds** that the concern for impurity of women at the projected time of their **periods** applies **by Torah law,** and though she can examine herself and ascertain that she is pure, if she did not she is presumed impure, and therefore he is stringent in the case of a woman who has a fixed menstrual cycle; **and** one **Sage,** Rabban Shimon ben Gamliel, **holds** that the concern for impurity of women at the projected time of their **periods** applies **by rabbinic law,** and consequently he rules leniently even with regard to a woman who has a fixed cycle?

אָמַר רָבִינָא: לָא, דְּכוּלֵּי עָלְמָא – וְסָתוֹת דְּרַבָּנַן, וְהָכָא – בִּמְקוֹר מְקוֹמוֹ טָמֵא קָמִיפַּלְגִי.

**Ravina says:**[H] **No;** they do not necessarily disagree with regard to this point, as it is possible **that everyone,** even Rabbi Yehuda HaNasi, agrees that the concern for impurity of women at the projected time of their **periods** applies **by rabbinic law, and here they disagree** as **to** whether **the location of** a woman's **source,** i.e., her uterus, **is impure,** and therefore any blood that passes through there is impure, even if it is blood from a wound.

רַבָּן שִׁמְעוֹן בֶּן גַּמְלִיאֵל סָבַר: אִשָּׁה – טְהוֹרָה, וְדָם טָמֵא – דְּקָאָתֵי דֶּרֶךְ מָקוֹר.

**Rabban Shimon ben Gamliel holds** that the **woman** herself **is pure** from the seven-day impurity status of a menstruating woman, as the requirement of an examination upon the projected time of her period applies by rabbinic law, **but** the **blood is impure,** even if it is from a wound, **as it came through** her **source,** and was thereby rendered impure. Consequently, the blood renders the woman impure until the evening.

וַאֲמַר לֵיהּ רַבִּי: אִי חָיְישַׁתְּ לְוֶסֶת – אִשָּׁה נַמִי טְמֵאָה, וְאִי לָא חָיְישַׁתְּ לְוֶסֶת – מָקוֹר מְקוֹמוֹ טָהוֹר הוּא.

**And Rabbi** Yehuda HaNasi **said to** Rabban Shimon ben Gamliel: **If you are concerned** due **to** the possibility that this is blood of her menstrual **period,** then the **woman** should **also** be **impure** as a menstruating woman. **And if you are not concerned** due **to** the possibility that this is blood of her menstrual **period,** then her **source** does not transmit impurity to the blood that passes through **its location,** as that blood **is pure.**

**מתני׳** בֵּית שַׁמַּאי אוֹמְרִים: צְרִיכָה שְׁנֵי עֵדִים עַל כָּל תַּשְׁמִישׁ וְתַשְׁמִישׁ, אוֹ תְּשַׁמֵּשׁ לְאוֹר הַנֵּר. בֵּית הִלֵּל אוֹמְרִים: דַּיָּהּ בִּשְׁנֵי עֵדִים כָּל הַלַּיְלָה.

**MISHNA** **Beit Shammai say:** A woman is **required** to examine herself with **two cloths,** once before and once after **each and every** act of **intercourse** in which she engages throughout the night, and she must inspect them for blood the following morning, **or** she must **engage in intercourse by the light of a lamp** and inspect the cloths before and after each act of intercourse. **Beit Hillel**[N] **say:** She is not required to examine herself between each act of intercourse. Rather, it is **sufficient** for her to examine herself **with two cloths throughout the night,**[H] once before the first act of intercourse and once after the final act of intercourse.

**NOTES**

**Beit Shammai…Beit Hillel – בֵּית שַׁמַּאי...בֵּית הִלֵּל:** Some commentaries explain that according to the opinion of Beit Shammai she requires two fresh cloths for an examination, once before and once after each act of intercourse. On the following day she must check each of these cloths for blood. Alternatively, she can engage in intercourse by the light of a lamp and inspect the cloths before and after each act of intercourse. Beit Hillel maintain that it is enough for her to use two cloths for the entire night (Rashi).

**HALAKHA**

**Ravina says, etc. – אָמַר רָבִינָא וכו׳:** In a case where a woman experienced bleeding due to a wound in her pubic area, even if she saw the blood at the projected time of her period she and the blood are pure. Therefore, she may partake of *teruma* and consecrated foods. The *halakha* is in accordance with Ravina's explanation of the dispute between Rabbi Yehuda HaNasi and Rabban Shimon ben Gamliel (Rambam *Sefer Kedusha, Hilkhot Issurei Bia* 8:14; see *Sefer Tahara, Hilkhot Metamei Mishkav UMoshav* 3:9 and *Kesef Mishne* there).

**It is sufficient for her to examine herself with two cloths throughout the night – דַּיָּהּ בִּשְׁנֵי עֵדִים כָּל הַלַּיְלָה:** If a husband engages in intercourse with his wife many times over the course of a single night, the pair do not have to examine their cloths after each and every act of intercourse. Rather, they wipe themselves with their respective cloths after each act of intercourse, and on the following day they look at the cloths. If they find blood on his cloth or on her cloth, she is impure (Rambam *Sefer Kedusha, Hilkhot Issurei Bia* 4:17; *Shulḥan Arukh, Yoreh De'a* 186:2 in the comment of Rema).

גמ׳ תָּנוּ רַבָּנַן, אַף עַל פִּי שֶׁאָמְרוּ ״הַמְשַׁמֵּשׁ מִטָּתוֹ לְאוֹר הַנֵּר – הֲרֵי זֶה מְגוּנֶּה״, בֵּית שַׁמַּאי אוֹמְרִים: צְרִיכָה שְׁנֵי עֵדִים עַל כׇּל תַּשְׁמִישׁ, אוֹ תְּשַׁמֵּשׁ לְאוֹר הַנֵּר. וּבֵית הִלֵּל אוֹמְרִים: דַּיָּהּ בִּשְׁנֵי עֵדִים כׇּל הַלַּיְלָה.

**GEMARA** The mishna teaches that according to Beit Shammai it is permitted to engage in intercourse by the light of a lamp. In this regard, **the Sages taught** in a *baraita*: **Even though** the Sages **said** with regard to **one who engages in intercourse by the light of a lamp,**[N] that **this is disgraceful,**[N] **Beit Shammai say: A woman is required** to examine herself with **two cloths,** once before and once after **each** act of **intercourse, or** she must **engage in intercourse by the light of a lamp. And Beit Hillel say:** It is **sufficient** for her to examine herself **with two cloths throughout the night,** once before the first act of intercourse and once after the final act of intercourse.

תַּנְיָא, אָמְרוּ לָהֶם בֵּית שַׁמַּאי לְבֵית הִלֵּל: לְדִבְרֵיכֶם, לֵיחוּשׁ שֶׁמָּא תִּרְאֶה טִיפַּת דָּם כְּחַרְדָּל בְּבִיאָה רִאשׁוֹנָה, וְתַחְפֶּנָּה שִׁכְבַת זֶרַע בְּבִיאָה שְׁנִיָּה!

It **is taught** in a *baraita* that **Beit Shammai said to Beit Hillel: According to your statement** that a woman may engage in intercourse several times in one night without an examination between each act of intercourse, **let us be concerned lest she will see,** i.e., emit, **a drop of blood the size of a mustard** seed **during the first** act of **intercourse,** and will thereby become impure, **and semen from the second** act of **intercourse will cover it.** Since the examination after the last act of intercourse will not reveal the drop of blood, the woman will erroneously think she is pure.

אָמְרוּ לָהֶם בֵּית הִלֵּל: אַף לְדִבְרֵיכֶם – לֵיחוּשׁ עַד שֶׁהָרוֹק בְּתוֹךְ הַפֶּה שֶׁמָּא נִימּוֹק וְהוֹלֵךְ לוֹ!

**Beit Hillel said to them** in response: **Even according to your statement, let us be concerned** that **while the saliva** was still **in the mouth,** i.e., while the blood was in her vagina, **perhaps it was squashed and disappeared.** Even if she examines herself after each act of intercourse, as mandated by Beit Shammai, it is possible that the semen of that act covered the blood, and it will not be revealed by the examination.

אָמְרוּ לָהֶם: לְפִי שֶׁאֵינוֹ דּוֹמֶה נִימּוֹק פַּעַם אַחַת לְנִימּוֹק שְׁתֵּי פְּעָמִים.

Beit Shammai **said to** Beit Hillel: One cannot compare the two situations, **as a squashed** drop of blood after the woman has engaged in intercourse **once is not similar to a squashed** drop of blood after the woman has engaged in intercourse **twice,** and therefore our concern is more reasonable.

תַּנְיָא, אָמַר רַבִּי יְהוֹשֻׁעַ: רוֹאֶה אֲנִי אֶת דִּבְרֵי בֵית שַׁמַּאי. אָמְרוּ לוֹ תַּלְמִידָיו: רַבִּי, כַּמָּה הֶאֱרַכְתָּ עָלֵינוּ! אָמַר לָהֶם: מוּטָב שֶׁאַאֲרִיךְ עֲלֵיכֶם בָּעוֹלָם הַזֶּה, כְּדֵי שֶׁיַּאֲרִיכוּ יְמֵיכֶם לָעוֹלָם הַבָּא.

It **is taught** in a *baraita* that **Rabbi Yehoshua said: I see** as correct **the statement of Beit Shammai** in this case. **His students said to him:** Our **teacher, how you have weighed** [*he'erakhta*] **us down**[N] with this stringent ruling. Rabbi Yehoshua **said to them: It is preferable that I weigh you down in this world, so that** you do not sin by engaging in prohibited intercourse, i.e., so that **your days in the World-to-Come will be lengthened** [*sheya'arikhu*].

אָמַר רַבִּי זֵירָא: מִדִּבְרֵי כּוּלָּם נִלְמַד – בַּעַל נֶפֶשׁ לֹא יִבְעוֹל וְיִשְׁנֶה.

§ **Rabbi Zeira says: From the statements of all of them,** i.e., both Beit Shammai, who permit engaging in intercourse a second time only after an examination, and Beit Hillel, who rule that the second examination must be performed only after the final act of intercourse of the night, **we can learn** that their dispute relates only to that which is permitted after the fact. But **a pious person** [*ba'al nefesh*][L] **should not engage in intercourse and repeat** his act without an examination between each act.

רָבָא אָמַר: בּוֹעֵל וְשׁוֹנֶה, כִּי תַּנְיָא הַהִיא – לְטָהֳרוֹת.

**Rava says:** Even a pious person **may engage in intercourse and repeat** the act without an examination in between, as **when that** *baraita* **is taught,** it is referring **to** a woman who handles **pure items.** But with regard to intercourse with her husband, there is no cause for concern.

NOTES

One who engages in intercourse by the light of a lamp – הַמְשַׁמֵּשׁ מִטָּתוֹ לְאוֹר הַנֵּר: The early commentaries discuss whether or not this is a ruling of *halakha*, similar to Rabbi Yoḥanan's statement that one may not engage in intercourse by day. Some claim that this is in fact a prohibition, but just as there are ways, explained later, in which it is permitted to engage in intercourse by day, with regard to intercourse by the light of a lamp the same exceptions apply (Rabbeinu Efrayim on the Torah).

This is disgraceful – הֲרֵי זֶה מְגוּנֶּה: The commentaries state that there is room for leniency in the case of the first act of intercourse after marriage, as the bridegroom might otherwise be concerned that he will be unable to tell if she is in fact a virgin (*Orḥot Ḥayyim*; *Torah Leshma*). Some reject this leniency with regard to the first act of intercourse of a virgin (*Tzitz Eliezer*; *Yosef Da'at*).

You have weighed [*he'erakhta*] us down – הֶאֱרַכְתָּ עָלֵינוּ: Rashi explains that this *he'erakhta* is an expression of severity: The acceptance of the opinion of Beit Shammai would entail an examination between each act of intercourse. The later commentaries note that according to this interpretation, the same phrase is used by Rabbi Yehoshua in his response with an entirely different meaning. They therefore explain that *he'erakhta* also refers to length of time, as the examinations required by Beit Shammai would increase the time needed to engage in intercourse, and Rabbi Yehoshua's students did not wish to be overly burdened in that way (see *Nedarim* 20b). According to this interpretation, Rabbi Yehoshua's response with regard to the length of days in the World-to-Come is commensurate with the students' comment to him: Better that you lengthen the time needed to engage in intercourse in this world so that your days in the World-to-Come will be increased (*Amtaḥat Binyamin*). In addition, the students wanted to engage in intercourse more than once in one night so that they would have male children, in accordance with the statement of Rava: One who wants all his children to be males should engage in intercourse with his wife and repeat the act (*Eiruvin* 100b).

LANGUAGE

Pious person [*ba'al nefesh*] – בַּעַל נֶפֶשׁ: This expression, which comes from Proverbs 23:2, means someone who is careful about his behavior and acts in a pious manner. The Ra'avad called his book on the *halakhot* of menstruating women *Ba'alei HaNefesh*.

**NOTES**

**Rabbi Yoḥanan says it is prohibited for a person to engage in intercourse by day** – **אָמַר רַבִּי יוֹחָנָן אָסוּר לְאָדָם שֶׁיְּשַׁמֵּשׁ מִטָּתוֹ בַּיּוֹם**: The later commentaries discuss whether Rava's statement later in the discussion, i.e., that there are ways in which it is permitted to engage in intercourse during the day, contradicts this ruling of Rabbi Yoḥanan. Some claim that Rava basically agrees with Rabbi Yoḥanan, but he maintains that if it is absolutely necessary it is possible to engage in intercourse by day in a permitted manner.

תַּנְיָא נַמִי הָכִי: בַּמֶּה דְּבָרִים אֲמוּרִים – לְטָהֳרוֹת, אֲבָל לְבַעְלָהּ – מוּתֶּרֶת. וּבַמֶּה דְּבָרִים אֲמוּרִים – שֶׁהִנִּיחָהּ בְּחֶזְקַת טָהֳרָה, אֲבָל הִנִּיחָהּ בְּחֶזְקַת טְמֵאָה – לְעוֹלָם הִיא בְּחֶזְקָתָהּ עַד שֶׁתֹּאמַר לוֹ ״טְהוֹרָה אֲנִי״.

This opinion **is also taught** in a *baraita*: **In what** case **is this statement said,** i.e., that a woman must examine herself before and after every act of intercourse according to Beit Shammai, or before the first act and after the last act, according to Beit Hillel? It was said **with regard to** a woman who handles **pure items; but** a woman **is permitted to her husband** even without any examination, and he is not required to ask her if she is pure. **But in what** case **is this** lenient **statement said? When** her husband traveled and **left her with the presumptive status of ritual purity. But** if he **left her with the presumptive status of ritual impurity,** she remains **forever in her presumptive status** of impurity **until she says to him: I am pure.**

אָמַר רַבִּי אַבָּא, אָמַר רַבִּי חִיָּיא בַּר אָשֵׁי, אָמַר רַב: בָּדְקָה בְּעֵד, וְאָבַד – אֲסוּרָה לְשַׁמֵּשׁ עַד שֶׁתִּבְדּוֹק. מַתְקִיף לַהּ רַבִּי אִילָא: אִילּוּ אִיתָא – מִי לָא מְשַׁמְּשָׁה וְאַף עַל גַּב דְּלָא יָדְעָה? הַשְׁתָּא נַמִי – תְּשַׁמֵּשׁ!

§ **Rabbi Abba says** that **Rabbi Ḥiyya bar Ashi says** that **Rav says:** If a woman **examined** herself at night **with a cloth, and** the cloth **was** then immediately **lost,**[H] **it is prohibited for her to engage in intercourse** again **until she examines** herself with another cloth, as perhaps there was blood on the cloth that was lost. **Rabbi Ila objects to this: If** this cloth **were intact,** i.e., if it were not lost, **couldn't** this woman **engage in intercourse** with her husband that night, on the basis that she will examine the cloth only the following day, **and** isn't this the *halakha* **even though she does not know** at the time of intercourse whether there is blood on the cloth? **Now too,** although the cloth is lost, **let her engage in intercourse** with her husband.

אֲמַר לֵיהּ רָבָא: זוֹ – מוֹכִיחָהּ קַיָּים, וְזוֹ – אֵין מוֹכִיחָהּ קַיָּים.

**Rava said to him:** There is a difference between the two cases, as when the cloth is intact, **this** woman's **proof exists,** and if she discovers on the following day that she was impure they will be obligated to bring sin offerings for engaging in intercourse in a state of ritual impurity. **But** with regard to **that** woman who lost her cloth, **her proof does not exist,** and therefore they will never know if they require atonement.

אָמַר רַבִּי יוֹחָנָן: אָסוּר לְאָדָם שֶׁיְּשַׁמֵּשׁ מִטָּתוֹ בַּיּוֹם. אָמַר רַב הַמְנוּנָא מַאי קְרָא? שֶׁנֶּאֱמַר: ״יֹאבַד יוֹם אִוָּלֶד בּוֹ וְהַלַּיְלָה אָמַר הֹרָה גָבֶר״ – לַיְלָה נִיתַּן לְהֵרָיוֹן, וְיוֹם לֹא נִיתַּן לְהֵרָיוֹן. רֵישׁ לָקִישׁ אָמַר מֵהָכָא: ״בּוֹזֵה דְרָכָיו יָמוּת״.

§ **Rabbi Yoḥanan says: It is prohibited for a person to engage in intercourse by day.**[NH] **Rav Hamnuna says: What is the verse** from which this is derived? **As it is stated: "Let the day perish on which I was born, and the night on which it was said: Conceived is a man-child"** (Job 3:3). It is derived from here that **nighttime is meant for conception, but daytime is not meant for conception. Reish Lakish says** that the proof is **from here: "But he who despises his ways shall die"** (Proverbs 19:16). One might see something unpleasing in his wife in the daylight and come to despise her.

וְרֵישׁ לָקִישׁ, הַאי קְרָא דְּרַבִּי יוֹחָנָן מַאי דָּרֵישׁ בֵּיהּ? מִבָּעֵי לֵיהּ לִכְדְדָרֵישׁ רַבִּי חֲנִינָא בַּר פַּפָּא. דְּדָרֵישׁ רַבִּי חֲנִינָא בַּר פַּפָּא: אוֹתוֹ מַלְאָךְ הַמְּמוּנֶּה עַל הַהֵרָיוֹן, ״לַיְלָה״ שְׁמוֹ, וְנוֹטֵל טִפָּה וּמַעֲמִידָהּ לִפְנֵי הַקָּדוֹשׁ בָּרוּךְ הוּא, וְאוֹמֵר לְפָנָיו: רִבּוֹנוֹ שֶׁל עוֹלָם, טִפָּה זוֹ מָה תְּהֵא עָלֶיהָ? גִּבּוֹר אוֹ חַלָּשׁ, חָכָם אוֹ טִיפֵּשׁ, עָשִׁיר אוֹ עָנִי?

The Gemara asks: **And how does Reish Lakish interpret this verse** cited **by Rabbi Yoḥanan?** The Gemara answers that **he requires** that verse **for that which Rabbi Ḥanina bar Pappa taught. As Rabbi Ḥanina bar Pappa interpreted** that verse in the following manner: **That angel that is appointed over conception is called: Night. And** that angel **takes the drop** of semen from which a person will be formed **and presents it before the Holy One, Blessed be He, and says before Him: Master of the Universe, what will be of this drop?** Will the person fashioned from it be **mighty or weak?** Will he be **clever or stupid?** Will he be **wealthy or poor?**

**HALAKHA**

**If a woman examined herself at night with a cloth and the cloth was lost** – **בָּדְקָה בְּעֵד וְאָבַד**: With regard to a woman who engaged in intercourse and then wiped herself with a cloth, if the cloth was subsequently lost, she must examine herself with another cloth before she engages in intercourse again, in case there was blood on the lost cloth. The *halakha* is in accordance with the opinion of Rabbi Yoḥanan (Rambam *Sefer Kedusha, Hilkhot Issurei Bia* 4:17; *Shulḥan Arukh, Yoreh De'a* 186:2).

**It is prohibited for a person to engage in intercourse by day** – **אָסוּר לְאָדָם שֶׁיְּשַׁמֵּשׁ מִטָּתוֹ בַּיּוֹם**: One may not engage in intercourse by day, but it is permitted to do so in a dark house. According to some commentaries a Torah scholar may cause darkness with his garment and engage in intercourse even during the day. The reason is that a Torah scholar is modest (*Tur*) and will not look (Rashi). The *Tur* and the *Baḥ* write that this is permitted only in a case of great need, e.g., when he is overcome by his desire (*Magen Avraham*). The *halakha* is in accordance with the opinion of Rabbi Yoḥanan (Rambam *Sefer Kedusha, Hilkhot Issurei Bia* 21:10; *Shulḥan Arukh, Oraḥ Ḥayyim* 240:11 and *Even HaEzer* 25:5).

וְאִילּוּ "רָשָׁע אוֹ צַדִּיק" – לָא קָאָמַר, כִּדְרַבִּי חֲנִינָא. דְּאָמַר רַבִּי חֲנִינָא: הַכֹּל בִּידֵי שָׁמַיִם – חוּץ מִיִּרְאַת שָׁמַיִם, שֶׁנֶּאֱמַר: "וְעַתָּה יִשְׂרָאֵל מָה ה' אֱלֹהֶיךָ שֹׁאֵל מֵעִמָּךְ כִּי אִם לְיִרְאָה" וגו'.

The Gemara notes: **But** this angel **does not say:** Will he be **wicked or righteous?** This is **in accordance with** a statement **of Rabbi Ḥanina, as Rabbi Ḥanina said: Everything is in the hand of Heaven, except for fear of Heaven.**[N] People have free will to serve God or not, **as it is stated: "And now, Israel, what does the Lord your God ask of you other than to fear** the Lord your God" (Deuteronomy 10:12). The fact that God asks of the Jewish people to fear Him indicates that it is a person's choice to do so.

וְרַבִּי יוֹחָנָן – אִם כֵּן נִכְתּוֹב קְרָא "גֶּבֶר הוֹרָה", מַאי "הוֹרָה גָבֶר"? לַיְלָה נִיתָּן לְהֵרָיוֹן, וְיוֹם לֹא נִיתַּן לְהֵרָיוֹן.

The Gemara explains: **And Rabbi Yoḥanan** derives two *halakhot* from the verse "and the night on which it was said: Conceived is a man-child," as he holds as follows: **If so,** i.e., if it is referring only to the statement of the angel, **let the verse write:** And the night that said: **A man-child is conceived. What** is the meaning of: **"Conceived is a man-child"?** It is derived from the juxtaposition of the word "night" and the word "conceived" that **nighttime is meant for conception but daytime is not meant for conception.**

וְרַבִּי יוֹחָנָן, הַאי קְרָא דְּרֵישׁ לָקִישׁ מַאי דָּרֵישׁ בֵּיהּ? מִבְּעֵי לֵיהּ לְכִדְכְתִיב בְּסֵפֶר בֶּן סִירָא: "שְׁלֹשָׁה שָׂנֵאתִי, וְאַרְבָּעָה לֹא אֲהַבְתִּי: שַׂר הַנִּרְגָּל בְּבֵית הַמִּשְׁתָּאוֹת, וְאָמְרִי לַהּ: שַׂר הַנִּרְגָּן וְאָמְרִי לַהּ: שַׂר הַנִּרְגָּז,

The Gemara asks: **And Rabbi Yoḥanan, how does he interpret that verse** cited **by Reish Lakish?** The Gemara answers that Rabbi Yoḥanan **requires** that verse: "But he who despises his ways shall die," **to** teach **that which is written in the book of ben Sira:**[B] **Three** people **I have hated, and a fourth I have not loved: A minister who frequents [*hanirgal*] drinking houses,** as he disgraces himself and leads himself to ruin and death; **and some say** a different version of the text: **A minister who chats [*hanirgan*]** in drinking houses; **and some say** a third version: **A minister who is short-tempered [*hanirgaz*]** when in drinking houses.

וְהַמּוֹשִׁיב שֶׁבֶת בִּמְרוֹמֵי קֶרֶת, וְהָאוֹחֵז בָּאַמָּה וּמַשְׁתִּין מַיִם, וְהַנִּכְנָס לְבֵית חֲבֵירוֹ פִּתְאוֹם". אָמַר רַבִּי יוֹחָנָן: וַאֲפִילּוּ לְבֵיתוֹ.

That is the first that he hated. **And** the others are **one who dwells at the highest point of the city,** where everyone sees him; **and one who holds** his **penis and urinates. And** the fourth, whom he has not loved, is **one who enters the house of another suddenly,** without warning. **Rabbi Yoḥanan says: And** this includes **even** one who comes **into his** own **house** without prior warning, as the members of his household might be engaged in private activities.

אָמַר רַבִּי שִׁמְעוֹן בֶּן יוֹחַאי: אַרְבָּעָה דְּבָרִים הַקָּדוֹשׁ בָּרוּךְ הוּא שׂוֹנְאָן וַאֲנִי אֵינִי אוֹהֲבָן: הַנִּכְנָס לְבֵיתוֹ פִּתְאוֹם, וְאֵין צָרִיךְ לוֹמַר – לְבֵית חֲבֵירוֹ. וְהָאוֹחֵז בָּאַמָּה וּמַשְׁתִּין מַיִם,

The Gemara cites a similar saying. **Rabbi Shimon ben Yoḥai says: Four matters the Holy One, Blessed be He, hates, and I do not love them,**[N] and they are: **One who enters his house suddenly, and needless to say** one who suddenly enters **the house of another;** and **one who holds** his **penis and urinates;**

## NOTES

**Everything is in the hand of Heaven except for fear of Heaven** – **הַכֹּל בִּידֵי שָׁמַיִם חוּץ מִיִּרְאַת שָׁמַיִם**: *Tosafot* ask: This statement indicates that all other matters, apart from fear of Heaven, are in the hand of Heaven, whereas elsewhere the Gemara states that everything is in the hand of Heaven apart from cold and hot (*Ketubot* 30a). They explain that the Gemara here is referring to one's inherited qualities and the natural course of his life, whereas there the Gemara is speaking of incidents and occurrences that might befall a person, such as illnesses and other misfortunes.

**Four matters the Holy One Blessed be He hates and I do not love them** – **אַרְבָּעָה דְּבָרִים הַקָּדוֹשׁ בָּרוּךְ הוּא שׂוֹנְאָן וַאֲנִי אֵינִי אוֹהֲבָן**: There are many interpretations of this statement; see *Yosef Da'at* for a summary. Some explain that God hates those who act in such a fashion on a regular basis, and Rabbi Shimon ben Yoḥai added that he does not love those who perform these acts even irregularly (Ya'avetz). Others note that it is stated about the righteous that the Divine Presence speaks through their mouths, and therefore Rabbi Shimon ben Yoḥai's comment: And I do not love them, can be attributed to God, i.e., God hates these people and does not love them (*Marit HaAyin*). Alternatively, the phrase: And I do not love them, means that Rabbi Shimon ben Yoḥai does not like to pray on their behalf that they be spared punishment (*Marit HaAyin*). Others explain that Rabbi Shimon ben Yoḥai is saying that by nature he merely does not love the wicked, but since God hates them, he too hates them (*Ben Yehoyada*).

## BACKGROUND

**Book of ben Sira** – **סֵפֶר בֶּן סִירָא**: The book of ben Sira was widely accepted by the Jews in the time of the Second Temple. It was possibly written by Yehoshua ben Sira, a contemporary of the High Priest Shimon HaTzaddik. The Sages did not canonize it among the books of the Bible, in contrast to some translators of the Bible, such as those in Egypt, who included the book of ben Sira among the books of the Bible. It can still be found nowadays in many foreign language editions of the Bible based on this translation.

The book was originally composed in Hebrew, but only excerpts of the original Hebrew text have survived, including some excavated at Masada and in the Judean Desert, as well as in the Cairo Geniza. Expanded versions of the wisdom of ben Sira have survived in other languages. These versions contain various matters, including superstitions and fantastical stories. It is possible that external material was incorporated into early Aramaic folk editions of the work, and for this reason the book was not respected by the Sages. This could be a central reason that it was not included in the books of the Bible.

It is noteworthy that the Talmud quotes passages from the book of ben Sira just as it quotes the Bible, introduced by the phrase that appears here: Which is written in the book of ben Sira. There are even places where it treats these passages as if they are a part of the Bible. It may be deduced from this that the Sages had no basic objection to the original book of ben Sira, but did not wish to ascribe sanctity to the later admixture of superstition and nonsense.

וּמַשְׁתִּין מַיִם עָרוֹם לִפְנֵי מִטָּתוֹ, וְהַמְשַׁמֵּשׁ מִטָּתוֹ בִּפְנֵי כׇּל חַי. אֲמַר לֵיהּ רַב יְהוּדָה לִשְׁמוּאֵל: וַאֲפִילּוּ לִפְנֵי עַכְבָּרִים? אֲמַר לֵיהּ: שִׁינְנָא, לָא, אֶלָּא כְּגוֹן שֶׁל בֵּית פְּלוֹנִי – שֶׁמְּשַׁמְּשִׁין מִטּוֹתֵיהֶן בִּפְנֵי עַבְדֵיהֶם וְשִׁפְחוֹתֵיהֶם.

and a man who **urinates naked next to his bed;**[N] **and one who engages in intercourse in the presence of any living being.**[N] **Rav Yehuda said to Shmuel:** Does the phrase: In the presence of any living being, mean **even in the presence of mice?** Shmuel **said to him:** ***Shinnana***, that is **not** the case. **Rather,** it is referring to a situation **such as in so-and-so's house, where they engage in intercourse in the presence of their** Canaanite **slaves and maidservants.**[H]

וְאִינְהוּ מַאי דְּרוּשׁ? ״שְׁבוּ לָכֶם פֹּה עִם הַחֲמוֹר״ – עַם הַדּוֹמֶה לַחֲמוֹר.

The Gemara asks: **And those** members of that household, who act in that manner, **what** verse **do they interpret** in a manner that allows them to do so? The Gemara answers: They reference the verse in which Abraham said to his two servants: **"Remain here with [*im*] the donkey"** (Genesis 22:5). This verse is interpreted as meaning that they are **a nation [*am*] comparable to a donkey.** The members of the aforementioned household thought that it is permitted to engage in intercourse in the presence of animals, and therefore one can do so in the presence of his Canaanite slaves and maidservants.

רַבָּה בַּר רַב הוּנָא מְקַרְקֵשׁ זָגֵי דְּכִילְּתָא, אַבַּיֵּי בָּאלֵי דִּידְבֵי, רָבָא בָּאלֵי פְּרוּחֵי.

The Gemara cites practices of modesty observed by the Sages. **Rabba bar Rav Huna** would **sound the bells [*zagei*]**[L] **of the canopy**[B] above his bed when engaging in intercourse, so that people would know to keep away. **Abaye** would even **drive away flies [*didevei*]**[L] from around his bed, so that he would not engage in intercourse in their presence, and **Rava** would **drive away gnats [*peruḥei*].**[L]

אָמַר רַבִּי שִׁמְעוֹן בֶּן יוֹחַי: חֲמִשָּׁה דְּבָרִים הֵן שֶׁהָעוֹשֶׂה אוֹתָן מִתְחַיֵּיב בְּנַפְשׁוֹ וְדָמוֹ בְּרֹאשׁוֹ: הָאוֹכֵל שׁוּם קָלוּף, וּבָצָל קָלוּף, וּבֵיצָה קְלוּפָה, וְהַשּׁוֹתֶה מַשְׁקִין מְזוּגִין שֶׁעָבַר עֲלֵיהֶן הַלַּיְלָה, וְהַלָּן בְּבֵית הַקְּבָרוֹת, וְהַנּוֹטֵל צִפׇּרְנָיו וְזוֹרְקָן לִרְשׁוּת הָרַבִּים, וְהַמַּקִּיז דָּם וּמְשַׁמֵּשׁ מִטָּתוֹ.

**Rabbi Shimon ben Yoḥai** further **says:** There are **five** actions with regard to **which one who performs them** is held **liable for his own life, and his blood is upon his** own **head,** i.e., he bears responsibility for his own demise. They are as follows: **One who eats peeled garlic or a peeled onion or a peeled egg, and one who drinks diluted drinks;** all these are referring to items only **when they were left overnight. And one who sleeps** at night **in a cemetery, and one who removes his nails and throws them into a public area, and one who lets blood**[HB] **and** immediately afterward **engages in intercourse.**

## HALAKHA

**Where they engage in intercourse in the presence of their Canaanite slaves and maidservants – שֶׁמְּשַׁמְּשִׁין מִטּוֹתֵיהֶן בִּפְנֵי עַבְדֵיהֶם וְשִׁפְחוֹתֵיהֶם:** It is prohibited to engage in intercourse in the presence of any person who is awake, even when separated by a screen that is ten handbreadths tall, unless those on the other side of the screen are unable to discern what is going on (*Mishna Berura*). It is permitted to engaging in intercourse in the presence of a child who is unable to talk (*Shulḥan Arukh, Oraḥ Ḥayyim* 240:6).

**And one who lets blood – וְהַמַּקִּיז דָּם:** One should not engage in intercourse on the day he lets blood, as stated by Rabbi Shimon ben Yoḥai (Rambam *Sefer HaMadda, Hilkhot Deot* 4:19).

## BACKGROUND

**Canopy [*kilta*] – כִּילְּתָא:** Like *kila*, *kilta* refers to a canopy spread above a bed, either for protection from flies and mosquitoes, or for reasons of modesty. By extension, the bed over which such a canopy is spread is also called a *kilta*.

Bed with mosquito netting

**Bloodletting – הַקָּזַת דָּם:** Bloodletting involves spilling small quantities of blood. It was used both as a cure and as a general preventive therapy that was believed to keep a person healthy. Bloodletting was based on an ancient system of medicine in which blood and other bodily fluids were considered to be humors, the proper balance of which was believed to maintain health. It was the most common medical practice performed by doctors on both humans and animals from antiquity through the late nineteenth century. Today it is well established that bloodletting is not effective for the treatment of most diseases. The only remaining condition for which it is used is polycythemia vera, a disease in which the body produces too many red blood cells. Among the symptoms of this illness are bleeding gums, excessive bleeding from ordinary cuts and bruises, and a reddish color of the skin.

## NOTES

**And a man who urinates naked next to his bed – וּמַשְׁתִּין מַיִם עָרוֹם לִפְנֵי מִטָּתוֹ:** The commentaries explain that although Rabbi Shimon ben Yoḥai specified that one may not urinate next to his bed when he is naked, he means that one may not do so even when dressed. He mentioned nakedness merely because this is the usual case, as one who is naked does not want to go to the trouble of dressing in order to go out to urinate (Rashi on *Shabbat* 62b; *Magen Avraham* on *Shulḥan Arukh, Oraḥ Ḥayyim* 241:1). The reason for this prohibition is that God wants people to act in a clean and holy manner, and this is a repulsive, dirty practice (*Levush*; *Mishna Berura*).

**In the presence of any living being – בִּפְנֵי כׇּל חַי:** Despite the mention of any living being, the Gemara concludes that this prohibition applies only to engaging in intercourse in the presence of people, and those *amora'im* who would chase away all living creatures when engaging in intercourse did so as a stringency. With regard to engaging in intercourse in the presence of people, the commentaries state that one may do so in the case of a child who is not yet able to talk. Furthermore, the prohibition applies only if the other people are awake, but one may engage in intercourse in the presence of sleeping individuals. Nevertheless, the prohibition includes people behind a screen, as they can sense that the couple is engaging in intercourse (*Tur, Oraḥ Ḥayyim* 240; *Ba'alei HaNefesh*; *Shulḥan Arukh, Oraḥ Ḥayyim* 240:6). If the people behind the screen are paying no attention to them whatsoever, it is permitted (*Ḥokhmat Adam*; *Kaf HaḤayyim*). The authorities further add that although it is permitted to engage in intercourse if the other people are asleep, it is appropriate to block them with a screen *ab initio* (*Beur Halakha*). Some comment that the most proper course of action is to follow the example of those *amora'im* who would not engage in intercourse in the presence of any living creature (*Olat Tamid*; *Eliya Rabba*; *Kaf HaḤayyim*).

## LANGUAGE

**Bells [*zagei*] – זָגֵי:** The Aramaic word *zagei*, like its Hebrew counterpart *zog*, refers to the outer part of the bell, upon which the tongue or clapper of the bell strikes to produce the noise. Like *zag*, the term *zagei* also refers to the outer peel of a grape.

**Flies [*didevei*] – דִּידְבֵי:** *Didevei*, or *dudvei*, refers to flies. These are corruptions of the original word, *divava*. See the *Targum* on the verse: "Dead flies [*zevuvei*] make the ointment of the perfumer fetid and putrid" (Ecclesiastes 10:1), as well as: "For the bee [*zevuv*] that is in the land of Assyria" (Isaiah 7:18), which is translated by *Targum Yonatan* as *devuvya*.

**Gnats [*peruḥei*] – פְּרוּחֵי:** The name of these insects is derived from *periḥa*, meaning blossoming or flowering. It is possible that the reason for this name is that they hover and surround one's bed like a small hat or ribbon used to gather hairs that protrude [*peruḥei*] from a headdress (see *Shabbat* 57b).

״הָאוֹכֵל שׁוּם קָלוּף״ כו׳. וְאַף עַל גַּב דְּמַנְחִי בְּסִילְתָּא, וּמְצַיְירִי וַחֲתִימִי – רוּחַ רָעָה שׁוֹרָה עֲלֵיהֶן. וְלָא אֲמַרַן אֶלָּא דְּלָא שַׁיַּיר בָּהֶן עִיקָּרָן אוֹ קְלִיפָּתָן, אֲבָל שַׁיַּיר בָּהֶן עִיקָּרָן אוֹ קְלִיפָּתָן – לֵית לָן בָּהּ.

The Gemara analyzes this statement of Rabbi Shimon ben Yoḥai, beginning with the case of **one who eats peeled garlic,** a peeled onion, or a peeled egg, when they were left overnight. The Gemara notes: **And** these peeled foods are dangerous **even if they are placed in a basket**[B] **and they are tied and sealed** in that basket throughout the night, as **an evil spirit rests upon them. And we said** that eating them is dangerous **only if one did not leave on them their roots or their shells. But if one left on them their roots or their shells, we have no** problem **with it.**

״וְהַשּׁוֹתֶה מַשְׁקִין מְזוּגִין שֶׁעָבַר עֲלֵיהֶן הַלַּיְלָה״. אָמַר רַב יְהוּדָה אָמַר שְׁמוּאֵל: וְהוּא שֶׁלָּנוּ בִּכְלֵי מַתָּכוֹת. אָמַר רַב פָּפָּא: וּכְלֵי נֶתֶר כִּכְלֵי מַתָּכוֹת דָּמוּ. וְכֵן אָמַר רַבִּי יוֹחָנָן: וְהוּא שֶׁלָּנוּ בִּכְלֵי מַתָּכוֹת, וּכְלֵי נֶתֶר כִּכְלֵי מַתָּכוֹת דָּמוּ.

Rabbi Shimon ben Yoḥai further mentions **one who drinks diluted drinks that were left overnight. Rav Yehuda says** that **Shmuel says: And** that **is** dangerous only **when they were left overnight in metal vessels. Rav Pappa says: And natron vessels**[B] are considered **like metal vessels** in this regard. **And Rabbi Yoḥanan likewise says: And** that **is** dangerous only **when they were left overnight in metal vessels, and natron vessels are considered like metal vessels** in this regard.

״וְהַלָּן בְּבֵית הַקְּבָרוֹת״, כְּדֵי שֶׁתִּשְׁרֶה עָלָיו רוּחַ טוּמְאָה – זִימְנִין דִּמְסַכְּנִין לֵיהּ.

Rabbi Shimon ben Yoḥai also says: **And one who sleeps in a cemetery** places himself in danger. The Gemara notes that this is the case if he does so **in order that a spirit of impurity will rest upon him,** as **sometimes** the evil spirits in the cemetery **endanger** the one who sleeps there.

״וְהַנּוֹטֵל צִפָּרְנָיו וְזוֹרְקָן לִרְשׁוּת הָרַבִּים״ – מִפְּנֵי שֶׁאִשָּׁה מְעוּבֶּרֶת עוֹבֶרֶת עֲלֵיהֶן וּמַפֶּלֶת. וְלָא אֲמַרַן אֶלָּא דְּשָׁקֵיל בִּגְנוֹסְטְרֵי. וְלָא אֲמַרַן אֶלָּא דְּשָׁקֵיל דִּידֵיהּ וְדִכְרָעֵיהּ. וְלָא אֲמַרַן אֶלָּא דְּלָא גָּז מִידֵּי בָּתְרַיְיהוּ, אֲבָל גָּז מִידֵּי בָּתְרַיְיהוּ – לֵית לָן בָּהּ. וְלָא הִיא, לְכוּלָּה מִילְּתָא חָיְישִׁינַן.

The next case is **one who removes his nails and throws them into a public area.** The Gemara explains that this is dangerous **because a pregnant woman** might **pass over them, and** this can cause her to **miscarry. And we said** this *halakha* **only when one removes** his nails **with scissors** [*bigenosteri*].[L] **And** furthermore, **we said** this *halakha* **only when one removes** the nails **of his hand and his foot** together. **And we said** this *halakha* **only when he did not cut anything** else **after** his nails, **but if he cut something** else **after them, we have no** problem **with it.** The Gemara comments: **And** that **is not so;** rather, **we are concerned with regard to the entire matter,** i.e., in all cases.

תָּנוּ רַבָּנַן: שְׁלֹשָׁה דְּבָרִים נֶאֶמְרוּ בְּצִפָּרְנַיִם: שׂוֹרְפָן – חָסִיד, קוֹבְרָן – צַדִּיק, זוֹרְקָן – רָשָׁע.

With regard to removing one's nails, **the Sages taught: Three matters were stated with regard to** removing **nails:** One who **burns them** is **pious,** as he eradicates them entirely; one who **buries them** is on the slightly lower level of **a righteous** individual, as they might be dug up; and one who simply **throws them** where a person might step upon them is **wicked.**

״וְהַמַּקִּיז דָּם וּמְשַׁמֵּשׁ מִטָּתוֹ״. דְּאָמַר מָר: מַקִּיז דָּם וּמְשַׁמֵּשׁ מִטָּתוֹ – הָוְיָין לוֹ בָּנִים וִיתָּקִין. הִקִּיזוּ שְׁנֵיהֶם וְשִׁמְּשׁוּ – הָוְיָין לוֹ בָּנִים בַּעֲלֵי רָאתָן. אָמַר רַב: וְלָא אֲמַרַן אֶלָּא דְּלָא טָעֵים מִידֵּי, אֲבָל טָעֵים מִידֵּי – לֵית לָן בָּהּ.

The Gemara discusses the final clause of Rabbi Shimon ben Yoḥai's statement: **And one who lets blood and** immediately afterward **engages in intercourse.** This is **as the Master said:** With regard to one who **lets blood and** afterward **engages in intercourse, he will have weak** [*vittakin*][L] **children** conceived from this act of intercourse. If **both of them,** husband and wife, **let blood and engaged in intercourse, he will have children afflicted with** a disease known as *ra'atan*.[B] **Rav says: And we said** this **only** in a case **when he did not taste anything** after letting blood, **but if he tasted something** then **we have no** problem **with it.**

אָמַר רַב חִסְדָּא: אָסוּר לוֹ לְאָדָם שֶׁיְּשַׁמֵּשׁ מִטָּתוֹ בַּיּוֹם, שֶׁנֶּאֱמַר: ״וְאָהַבְתָּ לְרֵעֲךָ כָּמוֹךָ״. מַאי מַשְׁמַע? אָמַר אַבָּיֵי: שֶׁמָּא יִרְאֶה בָּהּ דָּבָר מְגוּנֶּה, וְתִתְגַּנֶּה עָלָיו. אָמַר רַב הוּנָא: יִשְׂרָאֵל קְדוֹשִׁים הֵם, וְאֵין מְשַׁמְּשִׁין מִטּוֹתֵיהֶן בַּיּוֹם.

§ **Rav Ḥisda says:** It is **prohibited for a person to engage in intercourse by day, as it is stated: "And you shall love your fellow as yourself"** (Leviticus 19:18). The Gemara asks: **From where** is this **inferred? Abaye says:** If one engages in intercourse by day, **perhaps** the husband **will see some repulsive matter in** his wife **and she will become repugnant to him,** which will cause him to hate her, and he will thereby violate this mitzva. **Rav Huna says: Jews are holy, and they do not engage in intercourse by day.**

## BACKGROUND

**Basket** [*silta*] – **סִילְתָּא**: A *silta* is a woven basket, typically made from soft palm or willow branches. It was used mainly for transporting food, but also served to store it. It was most commonly used for bread, although people would also place other edibles, such as fruit, in a *silta*.

Mosaic from late antiquity depicting a basket used in the grape harvest

**Natron vessels** – **כְּלֵי נֶתֶר**: Natron is a type of sodium carbonate, $NaC_2O_3$. It occurs naturally in colorless deposits in desert plains, and in ancient times it was often produced from seaweed as well. The Gemara elsewhere (*Avoda Zara* 33b) indicates that people would craft vessels from excavated mixtures of earth and natron. These vessels could not normally be used to hold liquids, but in a dry climate, it is conceivable that they could have done so for a limited time.

***Ra'atan*** – **רָאתָן**: This disease, mentioned in the Talmud and various *midrashim*, has not been definitively identified, and there are several theories as to its nature. The most likely explanation is that it refers to Hansen's disease, colloquially known as leprosy, which is distinct from *tzara'at*, the biblical disease discussed at length in the Talmud, which has commonly been translated as leprosy.

Hansen's disease appears in different forms, one of which is in line with the descriptions of the disease in the Talmud. In addition to a severe toughening of the skin that causes a loss of feeling in that area or to the entire limb, the ailment also causes a great deal of mucus to flow from the nose. For various reasons, in later stages this illness causes serious wounds and gangrene, which rots away the external limbs. The disease is infectious but it requires close, prolonged contact for contagion to occur. Nevertheless, due to the severity of this illness and the inability of those in talmudic times to treat it, they were extremely careful about any kind of contact, which included not only direct contact with the infected patient but even with flies that touched their secretions, or anything the patient may have touched.

## LANGUAGE

**Scissors** [*genosteri*] – **גְּנוֹסְטְרֵי**: The origin of this word is Greek. Some say it is from κνηστήρ, *knēstēr*, meaning scraping knife, slayer, or destroyer. Others suggest that it is from ὄνυξ, *onux*, meaning nail, and ῥίνη, *rhinē*, a file or rasp.

**Weak** [*vittakin*] – **וִיתָּקִין**: The source of this word and its meaning remain unclear. According to Rabbi Binyamin Musafya it is derived from the Greek φθισικός, *fthisikos*, meaning consumptive. Some assert that it is from the Greek ἑκτικός, *ektikos*, meaning hectic or consumptive.

BACKGROUND

**King Munbaz** – מוּנְבַּז הַמֶּלֶךְ: Munbaz was the king of Adiabene at the end of the Second Temple period. This tiny principality, located in northern Aram Naharaim, in the area of modern-day Kirkuk and Mosul, was a functionally independent vassal of the Parthian empire. Members of the royal family of Adiabene, and some of the military, joined the rebels against Rome during the Great Rebellion before the destruction of the Temple. Queen Helene and her two sons, Munbaz and Izitus, called Zutus in the talmudic sources, converted to Judaism and scrupulously kept the mitzvot (see *Bereshit Rabba* 46). Initially, Munbaz abdicated the throne in favor of his brother, but he accepted the kingship upon his brother's death.

Sarcophagus of Queen Helene, mother of Munbaz

NOTES

**And they would practice ritual impurity and purity with regard to snow** – וְנוֹהֲגִין טוּמְאָה וְטָהֳרָה בִּשְׁלָגִים: The later commentaries suggest an explanation of the praiseworthy practice: Although the *halakha* is that snow is susceptible to ritual impurity only if one intended to drink it, nevertheless the members of the household of King Munbaz would apply the *halakhot* of impurity and purity to all snow, as there is no way to discern whether someone had intended to use the snow for drinking.

**As at night there is a risk of being overcome by sleep and consequently she might be repulsive to him** – דְּאַגַּב דְּאִיכָּא אוֹנֶס שֵׁינָה מִגַּנְיָא בְּאַפֵּיהּ: The commentaries explain that even according to this suggestion, this conduct is considered praiseworthy only in the case of the household of King Munbaz, who were occupied with royal matters all day and were therefore too tired at night to engage in intercourse. The same applies to Torah scholars, who learn Torah day and night, but not to ordinary people (Ya'avetz).

**One may examine a bed only with a cloth of linen or…clean and soft wool** – אֵין בּוֹדְקִין אֶת הַמִּטָּה אֶלָּא בְּפָקוֹלִין או...צֶמֶר נָקִי וָרַךְ: The commentaries explain that one is not required to examine with these particular cloths. Rather, all types of cloths are fit for this purpose provided that they have been checked to see that they absorb blood. This excludes cloths made of synthetic materials that do not absorb blood, such as nylon (*Shiurei Shevet HaLevi*).

אָמַר רָבָא: וְאִם הָיָה בֵּית אָפֵל – מוּתָּר. וְתַלְמִיד חָכָם – מַאֲפִיל בִּכְסוּתוֹ וּמְשַׁמֵּשׁ.

**Rava says: And if** the **house is dark,** it is **permitted** to engage in intercourse by day there. **And** in the case of **a Torah scholar, he may cause darkness with his garment and engage in intercourse** even during the daytime, as he will certainly do so with modesty.

תְּנַן: אוֹ תְּשַׁמֵּשׁ לְאוֹר הַנֵּר! אֵימָא: תִּבְדּוֹק לְאוֹר הַנֵּר.

The Gemara challenges: **We learned** in the mishna: **Or** she must **engage in intercourse by the light of a lamp.** This indicates that one may engage in intercourse in the light. The Gemara answers: **Say** that the mishna reads: **She must examine** the cloth **by the light of a lamp,** but not engage in intercourse in this manner.

תָּא שְׁמַע: אַף עַל פִּי שֶׁאָמְרוּ הַמְשַׁמֵּשׁ מִטָּתוֹ לְאוֹר הַנֵּר הֲרֵי זֶה מְגוּנֶּה! אֵימָא: ״הַבּוֹדֵק מִטָּתוֹ לְאוֹר הַנֵּר הֲרֵי זֶה מְגוּנֶּה״.

The Gemara cites a relevant source. **Come** and **hear** a *baraita*: **Even though** the Sages **said** that **one who engages in intercourse by the light of a lamp is repulsive,** nevertheless Beit Shammai say: Or she must engage in intercourse by the light of a lamp and inspect the cloths before and after each act of intercourse. The Gemara similarly explains: **Say** that the *baraita* reads: **One who examines** herself before or after **intercourse by the light of a lamp is repulsive,** as this examination would not be conducted properly, since the light of the lamp may not be sufficient. Nevertheless Beit Shammai say that a woman who engages in many acts of intercourse in one night must examine the cloth by the light of a lamp.

תָּא שְׁמַע: וְשֶׁל בֵּית מוּנְבַּז הַמֶּלֶךְ הָיוּ עוֹשִׂין שְׁלֹשָׁה דְּבָרִים וּמַזְכִּירִין אוֹתָן לְשֶׁבַח. הָיוּ מְשַׁמְּשִׁין מִטּוֹתֵיהֶם בַּיּוֹם, וּבוֹדְקִין מִטּוֹתֵיהֶם בְּמֵילָא פַּרְהָבָא, וְנוֹהֲגִין טוּמְאָה וְטָהֳרָה בִּשְׁלָגִים. קָתָנֵי מִיהָא ״מְשַׁמְּשִׁין מִטּוֹתֵיהֶן בַּיּוֹם״!

The Gemara further suggests: **Come** and **hear** a *baraita*: **And the household of King Munbaz**[B] **would perform three matters, and** the Sages **would mention them favorably** for their behavior in this regard. **They would engage in intercourse by day; and they** would **examine** before and after **intercourse with wool** [*bemeila*][L] **of Parhava,** which is very white and would show any stain; **and they** would **practice ritual impurity and purity with regard to snow.**[N] Regardless of the meaning of the last two matters, **in any event** this *baraita* **teaches** that they would **engage in intercourse by day,** which indicates that this practice is not prohibited.

אֵימָא: ״בּוֹדְקִין מִטּוֹתֵיהֶם בַּיּוֹם״. הָכִי נַמִי מִסְתַּבְּרָא, דְּאִי סָלְקָא דַּעְתָּךְ מְשַׁמְּשִׁין – מַזְכִּירִין אוֹתָן לְשֶׁבַח? אִין הָכִי נַמִי – דְּאַגַּב דְּאִיכָּא אוֹנֶס שֵׁינָה מִגַּנְיָא בְּאַפֵּיהּ.

The Gemara answers: **Say** that they would **examine their beds,** i.e., check the examination cloths, **by day.** The Gemara adds: **So too, it is reasonable** that this is the correct explanation, **as if** it should **enter your mind** that it means that they would **engage in intercourse** by day, even if it is permitted, would the Sages have **mentioned them favorably** for this practice? The Gemara refutes this proof: **Yes,** it **is indeed so.** There is a praiseworthy aspect to engaging in intercourse by day, **as at night there is** a risk of being **overcome by sleep,** because the husband might be too tired after the exertions of the day, and **consequently** his wife who desires sexual intercourse might **be repulsive to him.**[N]

״וּבוֹדְקִין מִטּוֹתֵיהֶן בְּמֵילָא פַּרְהָבָא״. מְסַיֵּיעַ לֵיהּ לִשְׁמוּאֵל, דַּאֲמַר שְׁמוּאֵל: אֵין בּוֹדְקִין אֶת הַמִּטָּה אֶלָּא בְּפָקוֹלִין, אוֹ בְּצֶמֶר נָקִי וָרַךְ. אָמַר רַב: הַיְינוּ דְּכִי הֲוַאי הָתָם בְּעַרְבֵי שַׁבָּתוֹת הָווּ אָמְרִי ״מַאן בָּעֵי פָּקוֹלֵי בְּנַהֲמָא״, וְלָא יָדַעְנָא מַאי קָאָמְרִי.

The Gemara further analyzes the *baraita,* which teaches: **And the** household of King Munbaz would **examine** before and after **intercourse, with wool of Parhava.** The Gemara notes: This statement **supports** the opinion **of Shmuel, as Shmuel said: One may examine a bed,** i.e., use an examination cloth for intercourse, **only with** a cloth made of **linen** [*befakolin*],[L] **or with** one made of **clean and soft wool.**[N] **Rav says: This is** the explanation of **that** which I heard **when I was there,** in Eretz Yisrael, **on Shabbat evenings,** which is the time when Torah scholars engage in intercourse with their wives; people **would** offer and **say: Who needs linen** cloths for eating **bread** [***benahama***],[L] a euphemism for intercourse. **And I did not know what they were saying** until now.

LANGUAGE

**Wool** [*meila*] – מֵילָא: *Meila*, or *meilat* as it is more commonly known, means soft wool. Apparently, it is from the Greek μηλωτή, *mēlotē*, meaning sheepskin or any rough woolly skin. There are those who say that this word is related to the name of the city of Miletus, which was a center for wool trading.

**Linen** [*pakolin*] – פָּקוֹלִין: The word *pakolin* refers to bundles of flax, or linen towels. It may be derived from the Greek φάκελος, *fakelos*, meaning bundle, and λίνον, *linon*, meaning linen. One who deals with *pakolin* is called a *pakuli*. For example, the *tanna* who arranged the eighteen blessings before Rabban Gamliel, the *Nasi* of the Sanhedrin, was called Shimon HaPakuli, a reference to his profession.

**Bread** [*nahama*] – נַהֲמָא: Bread is used as a euphemism for intercourse in many places in the Bible, e.g.: "Save the bread that he did eat" (Genesis 39:6), which refers to Potiphar's wife (see Rashi there).

אָמַר רָבָא: הָנֵי שְׁחָקֵי דְּכִיתָּנָא מַעֲלֵי לִבְדִיקָה. אִינִי, וְהָא תָּנָא דְּבֵי מְנַשֶּׁה: אֵין בּוֹדְקִין אֶת הַמִּטָּה לֹא בְּעֵד אָדוֹם, וְלֹא בְּעֵד שָׁחוֹר, וְלֹא בְּפִשְׁתָּן, אֶלָּא בְּפַקּוֹלִין אוֹ בְּצֶמֶר נָקִי וְרַךְ!

**Rava says: Those worn-out flax** clothes are **good for examination.** The Gemara asks: **Is that so? But didn't the school of Menashe teach: One may not examine a bed with a red cloth,**[H] **nor with a black cloth, nor with flax,**[B] **but with** a cloth made of **linen, or with** one made of **clean and soft wool?**

לָא קַשְׁיָא, הָא – בְּכִיתָּנָא, הָא – בְּמָאנֵי דְּכִיתָּנָא. וְאִיבָּעֵית אֵימָא: הָא וְהָא בְּמָאנֵי דְּכִיתָּנָא, הָא – בַּחֲדַתֵּי, הָא – בִּשְׁחָקֵי.

The Gemara answers that this is **not difficult,** as **this** statement that one may not examine with flax is referring **to flax** itself, whereas **that** statement of Rava, that flax is good for an examination, is referring **to flax garments. And if you wish, say** instead that both **this** statement **and that** statement are referring **to flax garments,** and the difference is that **this** ruling that one may not use flax is referring **to new** garments, whereas **that** ruling of Rava is referring specifically **to worn-out** garments,[N] which are brighter.

"נוֹהֲגִין טוּמְאָה וְטׇהֳרָה בִּשְׁלָגִין". תְּנַן הָתָם: שֶׁלֶג אֵינוֹ לֹא אוֹכֶל וְלֹא מַשְׁקֶה. חִישֵּׁב עָלָיו לַאֲכִילָה – אֵינוֹ מְטַמֵּא טוּמְאַת אוֹכָלִין, לְמַשְׁקֶה – מְטַמֵּא טוּמְאַת מַשְׁקִין.

It was further stated that the household of King Munbaz was praised by the Sages because its members would **practice ritual impurity and purity with regard to snow.** The Gemara comments: **We learned** in a *baraita* **there** (see *Tosefta, Teharot* 2:5): **Snow is neither food nor drink**[H] with regard to ritual impurity. **If one designated it for consumption,** his intention is disregarded, and **it does not impart the ritual impurity of food.** But if one planned to use it as **a drink, it imparts the ritual impurity of liquid.**

נִטְמָא מִקְצָתוֹ – לֹא נִטְמָא כּוּלּוֹ, נִטְהַר מִקְצָתוֹ – נִטְהַר כּוּלּוֹ.

If **part of** the snow **became impure, it does not all become impure,** but only the area that came into contact with the item of ritual impurity, as a pile of snow is not considered a single unit. If impure snow in a vessel is lowered into a ritual bath, even if the waters of the ritual bath touched only the snow on the mouth of the vessel, since **part of** the snow **is purified, all of it is purified.**

הָא גּוּפָא קַשְׁיָא, אָמְרַתְּ נִטְמָא מִקְצָתוֹ – לֹא נִטְמָא כּוּלּוֹ, וַהֲדַר תָּנֵי נִטְהַר מִקְצָתוֹ – נִטְהַר כּוּלּוֹ, לְמֵימְרָא דְּנִטְמָא כּוּלּוֹ!

The Gemara analyzes the *baraita*: **This** *baraita* **itself** is **difficult. You** initially **said** that if **part of** the snow **became impure, it does not all become impure, and then** the *baraita* **teaches** that if **part of** the snow **is purified, all of it is purified,** which is **to say that all of it became impure.** In other words, the last clause of the *baraita* is dealing with a lump of snow all of which is ritually impure, whereas according to the previous clause this is impossible: How could the source of the impurity have touched all of the snow?

אָמַר אַבָּיֵי: כְּגוֹן שֶׁהֶעֱבִירוֹ עַל אֲוִיר תַּנּוּר, דְּהַתּוֹרָה הֵעִידָה עַל כְּלִי חֶרֶס,

**Abaye says:** It is possible for all the snow to become impure, in a case **where one passed** the snow **within the airspace of** an earthenware vessel, such as **an oven,** in which the source of impurity was located. This renders the entire lump of snow impure, **as the Torah testifies with regard to an earthenware vessel** that contains a source of impurity that all items inside its airspace are rendered impure, as the verse states: "Whatever is in it shall be impure" (Leviticus 11:33).

Perek **II**
Daf **17** Amud **b**

אֲפִילּוּ מָלֵא חַרְדָּל.

Therefore, **even** if the earthenware vessel was **full** of items as small as **mustard** seeds, only a few of which touched the sides of the vessel or the impure item inside it, all the items inside the vessel are rendered ritually impure. Likewise, with regard to snow that passes through the vessel's airspace, all of it becomes impure.

**HALAKHA**

One may not examine a bed with a red cloth, etc. – אֵין בּוֹדְקִין אֶת הַמִּטָּה לֹא בְּעֵד אָדוֹם וכו׳: For all her examinations, a woman should use a piece of old white flax clothing, cotton wool, or white, clean, soft wool. The *halakha* is in accordance with the opinion of the school of Menashe (Rambam *Sefer Kedusha, Hilkhot Issurei Bia* 4:15; *Shulḥan Arukh, Yoreh De'a* 196:6).

Snow is neither food nor drink, etc. – שֶׁלֶג אֵינוֹ לֹא אוֹכֶל וְלֹא מַשְׁקֶה וכו׳: Snow is considered neither food nor drink with regard to ritual impurity. If one intended to use it for food his intention is disregarded. If one planned to use it as a drink, it is susceptible to ritual impurity as a liquid. If part of the snow became impure, it does not all become impure. But if one passed the snow within the airspace of an earthenware vessel containing a source of impurity it is all rendered impure. The *halakha* is as stated in the *Tosefta* in *Oholot*, in accordance with the explanation of Abaye (Rambam *Sefer Tahara, Hilkhot Tumat Okhalin* 1:22).

**BACKGROUND**

Flax – פִּשְׁתָּן: Cultivated flax, *Linum usitatissimum* L., is an annual plant that grows to a height of 40–120 cm. Its flowers are blue or white. Its stiff stalks contain flax fibers, and oil is extracted from its seeds. After the plant is cut, the stalks are soaked in water for several days. Various bacteria cause the materials that attach the fibers to the stalks to decompose. Afterward, the shell is beaten and opened and the fibers are extracted, to be used in weaving linen.

**NOTES**

**This ruling is referring to new garments whereas that ruling is referring specifically to worn-out garments – הָא בַּחֲדַתֵּי הָא בִּשְׁחָקֵי:** The Gemara does not provide the reason for this difference. Various explanations are suggested by the early commentaries. Some say that worn-out clothes are very white, which aids the examination (Rashi; see *Tosafot*). Others state that it is not easy to fold new clothes, and therefore they are not as convenient for such examinations as softer, worn-out clothes are (*Tosafot*; Maharam of Rothenburg). Furthermore, new clothes, being hard, might scratch the skin and cause an emission that is not menstrual blood, which would mislead the woman (Rashba).

**מתני׳** מָשָׁל מָשְׁלוּ חֲכָמִים בָּאִשָּׁה: הַחֶדֶר וְהַפְּרוֹזְדוֹר וְהָעֲלִיָּיה.

**MISHNA** A woman's reproductive organs are composed of different parts, and the halakhic status of blood that emerges from one part differs from the halakhic status of blood that emerges from another part. **The Sages stated a parable with regard to** the structure of the sexual organs of **a woman,**[H] based on the structure of a house: **The** inner **room**[N] represents the uterus, **and the corridor** [*perozdor*][LN] leading to the inner room represents the vaginal canal, **and the upper story**[BN] represents the bladder.

דַּם הַחֶדֶר – טָמֵא, דַּם הָעֲלִיָּיה – טָהוֹר, נִמְצָא בַּפְּרוֹזְדוֹר – סְפֵקוֹ טָמֵא, לְפִי שֶׁחֶזְקָתוֹ מִן הַמָּקוֹר.

Blood from **the** inner **room**[H] **is ritually impure. Blood** from **the upper story is ritually pure.** If blood **was found in the corridor,** there is uncertainty whether it came from the uterus and is impure, or from the bladder and is pure. Despite **its** state of **uncertainty,** it is deemed definitely **impure, due to** the fact **that its presumptive status** is of blood that came **from the source,** i.e., the uterus, and not from the bladder.

**גמ׳** רָמִי בַּר שְׁמוּאֵל וְרַב יִצְחָק בְּרֵיהּ דְּרַב יְהוּדָה תָּנוּ נִדָּה בֵּי רַב הוּנָא. אַשְׁכַּחִינְהוּ רַבָּה בַּר רַב הוּנָא דְּיָתְבִי וְקָאָמְרִי: הַחֶדֶר מִבִּפְנִים, וְהַפְּרוֹזְדוֹר מִבַּחוּץ, וַעֲלִיָּיה בְּנוּיָה עַל שְׁתֵּיהֶן, וְלוּל פָּתוּחַ בֵּין עֲלִיָּיה לַפְּרוֹזְדוֹר.

**GEMARA** **Rami bar Shmuel and Rav Yitzḥak, son of Rav Yehuda, were learning** tractate *Nidda* in **the study hall of Rav Huna. Rabba bar Rav Huna found them sitting and saying** an interpretation of this mishna: **The room,** i.e., the uterus, is the **inner** part of the reproductive organs, **and the corridor** is the **outer** part. **And the upper story,** the bladder, **is built,** i.e., found, **above them both. And** there is **an open vestibule**[B] **between** the **upper story and the corridor.**

נִמְצָא מִן הַלּוּל וְלִפְנִים – סְפֵקוֹ טָמֵא, מִן הַלּוּל וְלַחוּץ – סְפֵקוֹ טָהוֹר.

They continued: If blood is **found from** the opening of this **vestibule and inward** toward the uterus, i.e., inside the vagina, there is uncertainty whether it came from the uterus and is impure, or from the bladder and is pure, but **its** state of **uncertainty** renders it definitely **impure.**[N] If it is found in the area **from the** opening of this **vestibule and outward,** on the outer surface of the vulva, the blood is more likely to have come from the bladder, through the urethra, and therefore **its** state of **uncertainty** renders it **pure.**

## LANGUAGE

**Corridor** [*perozdor*] – **פְּרוֹזְדוֹר:** From the Greek, although there is no consensus as to its exact source. Some maintain that it is from προστάδος, *prostados*, which is the genitive case of προστάς, *prostas*, meaning entrance or corridor. Alternatively, it may be from πρόθυρον, *prothuron*, which has a similar meaning. *Perozdor* is a euphemism for the vaginal canal.

## BACKGROUND

**Upper story** – **עֲלִיָּיה:** In the talmudic period buildings were often two stories tall. They consisted of an entrance hall, or corridor, interior rooms, and an upper story. Sometimes the size of the upper story was equal to that of the house underneath, while in other cases it occupied only part of the area of the house.

Facade of a two-story villa in Pompeii

**Vestibule** [*lul*] – **לוּל:** A *lul* is an opening that connects the upper and lower stories, usually by means of a ladder. A *lul* can also be a space in the earth for transporting items above or below ground, as in the verse: "And they went up by vestibules [*lullim*] into the middle row, and out of the middle into the third" (I Kings 6:8).

## HALAKHA

**The Sages stated a parable with regard to the structure of the sexual organs of the woman, etc.** – **מָשָׁל מָשְׁלוּ חֲכָמִים בָּאִשָּׁה וכו׳:** The Sages compared the structure of the reproductive organs of the woman to a building: The inner room represents the uterus, which is the source from which the blood of a menstruating woman and a *zava* flow. The corridor leading to the inner room represents the entire vaginal canal, which leads to the uterus. Above the room and the corridor, situated between them, is the upper story, with the woman's two ovaries. Lastly, there is a kind of hole between the upper story and the roof of the corridor, which is called the vestibule (Rambam *Sefer Kedusha, Hilkhot Issurei Bia* 5:3–4).

**Blood from the inner room, etc.** – **דַּם הַחֶדֶר וכו׳:** If a woman experienced a flow of blood from her source she is impure and must observe seven clean days. This *halakha* applies if she sensed the emission of the blood, or even if she sensed its movement, despite the fact that it did not emerge. With regard to blood found in the corridor, if it was found from the vestibule and inward, it is ritually impure, as it is presumed to come from the room. Therefore, one burns any *teruma* that came into contact with it or with the woman, and she must bring an offering if she enters the Temple in that impure state. If the blood was found in the corridor outward of the vestibule it is impure as a matter of uncertainty, as it might have come from the room, in which case it is impure, or it might have flowed from the upper story by way of the vestibule, and therefore is pure. Due to the uncertainty, she does not bring an offering if she enters the Temple, and one does not burn *teruma* due to it (Rambam *Sefer Kedusha, Hilkhot Issurei Bia* 5:5; *Shulḥan Arukh, Yoreh De'a* 183).

## NOTES

**The inner room** – **הַחֶדֶר:** The blood of a menstruating woman is impure only if it comes from the source, i.e., the uterus, as it is stated: "And she shall be purified from the source of her blood" (Leviticus 12:7; *Torat Kohanim*).

**And the corridor** – **וְהַפְּרוֹזְדוֹר:** The precise identification of this corridor is a matter of much dispute among the early commentaries. The *Ḥatam Sofer* writes that he conducted extensive investigation of written and oral sources and found that the explanations of Rashi and *Tosafot* do not accord with the physical reality. He concludes: We must rely on the interpretation of the Rambam in his ruling of *halakha* (*Sefer Kedusha, Hilkhot Issurei Bia* 5:3–4) as well as in Rambam's Commentary on the Mishna. The Rambam's opinion is that the corridor represents the entire vaginal canal, possibly including the vulva, and it is called a corridor because it leads to the uterus. Alternatively, it refers to the cervix (*Ḥatam Sofer*). Some commentaries claim that Rashi and *Tosafot* do not disagree with the Rambam in this regard (*Ḥazon Ish*).

**And the upper story** – **וְהָעֲלִיָּיה:** The are various opinions among the early commentaries with regard to the precise identification of the upper story. The Rambam claims that it refers to a woman's ovaries (*Sefer Kedusha, Hilkhot Issurei Bia* 5:4). Others contend that it is the bladder (*Arukh*).

**From this vestibule and inward its uncertainty renders it definitely impure** – **מִן הַלּוּל וְלִפְנִים סְפֵקוֹ טָמֵא:** Rashi explains that if this blood came from the upper story it should be found from the vestibule and outward. The reason is that when the blood flows from the upper story through the vestibule to the corridor it is found on the outside and does not return inside. Rashi notes that according to this reasoning it is unclear why the blood is only impure as a matter of uncertainty and not definitely impure.

אֲתָא וַאֲמַר לֵיהּ לַאֲבוּהּ: סְפֵקוֹ טָמֵא אָמְרַתְּ לָן מָר? וְהָא אֲנַן ״שֶׁחֶזְקָתוֹ מִן הַמָּקוֹר״ תְּנַן!

Rabba **came and said to his father,** Rav Huna: With regard to the *halakha* of blood that is found from the vestibule and inward, **did the Master say to us** that its state of **uncertainty** renders it **impure,** as I heard in the study hall, from which it may be inferred that this is a case of uncertain impurity? **But didn't we learn** in the mishna: The blood is impure **due to** the fact **that its presumptive status** is of blood that came **from the source,**[N] i.e., the uterus? This indicates that it is a case of definite impurity. If so, the mishna cannot be referring either to blood found from the vestibule and inward or from the vestibule and outward.

אֲמַר לֵיהּ, אֲנָא הָכִי קָאָמִינָא: מִן הַלּוּל וְלִפְנִים – וַדַּאי טָמֵא, מִן הַלּוּל וְלַחוּץ – סְפֵקוֹ טָמֵא.

Rav Huna **said to** his son Rabba: **This is what I said:**[N] If the blood was found **from the vestibule inward** it is **definitely impure,** as it is presumed to come from the uterus. This is the case mentioned in the mishna. If the blood was found **from the vestibule outward its** state of **uncertainty** renders it **impure.** Although it can be claimed that if this was blood from the uterus it would not have been found in this area, it is possible that when the woman bent over, the blood went from the uterus into this area. Consequently, she is impure due to the uncertainty.

אָמַר אַבַּיֵי: מַאי שְׁנָא מִן הַלּוּל וְלַחוּץ דִּסְפֵקוֹ טָמֵא – דִּדִלְמָא שָׁחֲתָה, וּמֵחֶדֶר אֲתָא; מִן הַלּוּל וְלִפְנִים נָמֵי, אֵימָא אִיזְדַּקְרָה – וּמֵעֲלִיָּיה אֲתָא!

**Abaye says: What is different** about a situation where the blood was found **from the vestibule outward, where its** state of **uncertainty** renders it **impure?** The reason for that *halakha* is **that perhaps** the woman **bent over** and leaned forward, **and** the blood **came from the room,** i.e., the uterus. If so, in the case where the blood was found **from the vestibule inward,** concerning which you ruled that she is definitely impure, you can **also say** that it is possible that the woman **staggered** backward **and** as a result the blood **came from** the **upper story** to the back of the canal. Accordingly, she should be impure merely out of uncertainty.

אֶלָּא אָמַר אַבַּיֵי: אִי בָּתַר חֲשָׁשָׁא אָזְלַתְּ – אִידֵי וְאִידֵי סָפֵק הוּא, וְאִי בָּתַר חֲזָקָה אָזְלַתְּ – מִן הַלּוּל וְלִפְנִים – וַדַּאי טָמֵא, מִן הַלּוּל וְלַחוּץ – וַדַּאי טָהוֹר.

**Rather, Abaye says: If you follow the concern,** i.e., if your ruling of *halakha* is based on a concern that the blood might have moved due to the woman leaning forward or backward, then in both **this** case **and that,** whether the blood is found in the inner or outer section of the canal, the source of the blood **is uncertain. And if you follow** the **presumption** based on where the blood found in a particular place is usually from, then blood found **from the vestibule inward is definitely impure,** whereas blood found **from the vestibule outward is definitely pure.**

תָּנֵי רַבִּי חִיָּיא: דָּם הַנִּמְצָא בִּפְרוֹזְדוֹר – חַיָּיבִין עָלָיו עַל בִּיאַת מִקְדָּשׁ, וְשׂוֹרְפִין עָלָיו אֶת הַתְּרוּמָה. וְרַב קְטִינָא אָמַר: אֵין חַיָּיבִין עָלָיו עַל בִּיאַת מִקְדָּשׁ, וְאֵין שׂוֹרְפִין עָלָיו אֶת הַתְּרוּמָה.

**Rabbi Ḥiyya teaches: Blood that is found in the corridor** is considered definite menstrual blood, and therefore if she engages in intercourse, both she and her partner would be **liable as a result of** this blood to receive *karet* **for entering the Temple** intentionally when ritually impure, or to bring an offering for entering unwittingly. **And one burns** *teruma* **due to it,** if the woman touches such produce. **And Rav Ketina says:** It is impure merely as a matter of uncertainty; therefore, the woman **is not obligated, due to** that blood, to bring an offering **for entering the Temple** when ritually impure, **and one does not burn** *teruma* **on its account.**

לְהַךְ לִישָּׁנָא דַּאֲמַר אַבַּיֵי אִי בָּתַר חֲשָׁשָׁא אָזְלַתְּ – מְסַיַּיע לֵיהּ לְרַב קְטִינָא וּפְלִיגָא דְּרַבִּי חִיָּיא,

The Gemara discusses the relationship between this dispute and the previous statements of *amora'im*. **According to this formulation,** i.e., option, **that Abaye stated: If you follow the concern** that the blood might have moved due to the woman leaning forward or backward, there is uncertainty whether the blood was found in the inner or outer section of the canal, this **supports** the opinion **of Rav Ketina,** who likewise deems blood found in the canal impure due to uncertainty. **And** this option suggested by Abaye **contradicts** the opinion **of Rabbi Ḥiyya,** who deems the blood definitely impure.

לְהַךְ לִישָּׁנָא דְּאָמְרַתְּ אִי בָּתַר חֲזָקָה אָזְלַתְּ – מְסַיַּיע לֵיהּ לְרַבִּי חִיָּיא,

**According to that formulation that Abaye stated: If you follow** the **presumption** that blood found in the inner section is definitely impure, while blood found in the outer section is definitely pure, this **supports** the opinion of **Rabbi Ḥiyya,** whose ruling that the blood is definitely impure is understood as referring to blood found in the inner section.

NOTES

**Didn't we learn in the mishna: It is impure due to the fact that its presumptive status is of blood that came from the source** – **וְהָא אֲנַן שֶׁחֶזְקָתוֹ מִן הַמָּקוֹר תְּנַן**: The early commentaries are puzzled by this question of Rabba, son of Rav Huna, as the mishna also states that its impurity is uncertain, similar to the comment of Rami bar Shmuel and Rav Yitzḥak, son of Rav Yehuda. What, then, is the difficulty from the mishna? Perhaps his statement also meant that the blood is definitely impure, as explained in the mishna. One explanation is that the mishna indicates that it is definitely impure when it is found from the vestibule and inward, as the term: Its presumptive status, is indicative of definite impurity (Rashi).

**This is what I said** – **אֲנָא הָכִי קָאָמִינָא**: According to Rav Huna, the mishna is not in accordance with the opinion of Rami bar Shmuel and Rav Yitzḥak, son of Rav Yehuda. Some commentaries explain the mishna according to Rami bar Shmuel and Rav Yitzḥak, son of Rav Yehuda, as follows: The mishna is referring only to a case where the blood is found on the floor of the corridor, i.e., the lower part of the vaginal canal, whereas they are speaking of a case where it is found on the roof of the corridor (Rashi).

וּפְלִיגָא דְּרַב קְטִינָא.

**And** this option **contradicts** the opinion **of Rav Ketina,** who deems the blood impure due to uncertainty.

לְרַב הוּנָא – לָא פְּלִיגִי, כָּאן – מִן הַלּוּל וְלִפְנִים, כָּאן – מִן הַלּוּל וְלַחוּץ.

**And according to** the opinion of **Rav Huna,** who said that if the blood was found in the inner section it is definitely impure, as it is presumed to come from the uterus, and if the blood was found in the outer section it is impure due to uncertainty, one can say that Rabbi Ḥiyya and Rav Ketina **do not disagree,** as they were referring to different cases. **Here,** where Rabbi Ḥiyya deems the blood definitely impure, he is speaking of blood found **from the vestibule and inward,** whereas **there,** Rav Ketina deems it impure due to uncertainty when it is found **from the vestibule and outward.**

אֶלָּא לְרָמִי בַּר שְׁמוּאֵל וּלְרַב יִצְחָק בְּרֵיהּ דְּרַב יְהוּדָה, דְּאָמְרִי מִן הַלּוּל וְלַחוּץ – סְפֵקוֹ טָהוֹר, מִן הַלּוּל וְלִפְנִים – סְפֵקוֹ טָמֵא הָנֵי בְּמַאי מִתּוֹקְמָא – מִן הַלּוּל וְלִפְנִים,

**But according to** the opinion of **Rami bar Shmuel**[N] **and Rav Yitzḥak, son of Rav Yehuda, who say** that if the blood is found **from the vestibule and outward, its** state of **uncertainty** renders it **pure,** whereas if it is found in the area **from the vestibule and inward, its** state of **uncertainty** renders it **impure, with regard to what** case can the dispute between **these** Sages, Rabbi Ḥiyya and Rav Ketina, be **interpreted?** It must be referring to a situation where the blood was found **from the vestibule and inward,** as according to Rami bar Shmuel and Rav Yitzḥak, son of Rav Yehuda, if the blood is found from the vestibule and outward it is pure.

לֵימָא פְּלִיגָא דְּרַבִּי חִיָּיא!

If so, **shall we say** that Rami bar Shmuel and Rav Yitzḥak, son of Rav Yehuda, **disagree** with the opinion **of Rabbi Ḥiyya,** who deems the blood definitely impure, whereas they maintain that it is impure merely due to uncertainty?

לָא קַשְׁיָא, כָּאן – כְּשֶׁנִּמְצָא בְּקַרְקַע פְּרוֹזְדוֹר, וְכָאן – שֶׁנִּמְצָא בְּגַג פְּרוֹזְדוֹר.

The Gemara answers: This is **not difficult.** It is possible that Rami bar Shmuel and Rav Yitzḥak, son of Rav Yehuda, agree with the opinion of Rabbi Ḥiyya, as they maintain that there is no dispute between Rav Ketina and Rabbi Ḥiyya. Once again the reason is that Rav Ketina and Rabbi Ḥiyya might be referring to two different cases: **Here,** Rabbi Ḥiyya deems the blood definitely impure because he is speaking of a case **where it is found on the floor of** the **corridor,** in which case the blood is presumed to come from the uterus rather than the bladder. **And there,** Rav Ketina, who deems the blood impure due to uncertainty, is referring to blood **that is found on the roof of** the **corridor,**[N] and therefore it is uncertain whether the blood came from the bladder or the uterus.

## NOTES

**But according to the opinion of Rami bar Shmuel** – אֶלָּא לְרָמִי בַּר שְׁמוּאֵל: This passage presents four different opinions of Sages with regard to the status of blood found in the corridor and the resulting impurity of the woman, with differentiations based on whether the blood was found from the vestibule and inward or from the vestibule and outward. The Gemara further offers various suggestions concerning the relationship between these opinions and the dispute between Rabbi Ḥiyya and Rav Ketina, which accounts for the complexity of this discussion; see the chart below.

**Here a case where it is found on the floor…and there is referring to blood that is found on the roof of the corridor** – כָּאן כְּשֶׁנִּמְצָא בְּקַרְקַע פְּרוֹזְדוֹר וְכָאן שֶׁנִּמְצָא בְּגַג פְּרוֹזְדוֹר: The early commentaries are puzzled as to why this distinction is not mentioned earlier, where the Gemara discusses the relationship between Abaye's first proposal and the dispute of Rabbi Ḥiyya and Rav Ketina. Instead of determining that this suggestion of Abaye is in conflict with the opinion of Rabbi Ḥiyya, the Gemara could have said that Abaye is referring to the roof of the corridor, which is why the blood is impure due to uncertainty, whereas Rabbi Ḥiyya is referring to blood found on the floor of the corridor, and therefore it is definitely impure. The commentaries explain that this distinction cannot be applied to the opinion of Abaye, as he said that there is a concern that the blood might have reached its current location due to the woman's movement. This possibility applies to blood found on the floor of the corridor as well, and therefore Abaye would maintain that this blood is also impure only due to uncertainty (Rashi).

| | From the vestibule and inward | From the vestibule and outward | Rabbi Ḥiyya: Definitely impure | Rav Ketina: Impure as a matter of uncertainty |
|---|---|---|---|---|
| Rami bar Shmuel and Rav Yitzḥak, son of Rav Yehuda | The item's uncertain impurity renders it impure | The item's uncertainty leaves it pure | Refers to the floor of the corridor | Refers to the roof of the corridor |
| Rav Huna | Definitely impure | The item's uncertain impurity renders it impure | Refers to the area from the vestibule and inward | Refers to the area from the vestibule and outward |
| Abaye's first formulation: Concern of bending over or straightening | The item's uncertain impurity renders it impure | The item's uncertainty leaves it impure | Disagrees with his opinion | Agrees with his opinion |
| Abaye's second formulation | Definitely impure | Definitely pure | Refers to the area from the vestibule and inward | Disagrees with his opinion |

אָמַר רַבִּי יוֹחָנָן: בִּשְׁלֹשָׁה מְקוֹמוֹת הָלְכוּ בּוֹ חֲכָמִים אַחַר הָרוֹב וַעֲשָׂאוּם כְּוַדַּאי: מָקוֹר, שִׁלְיָא, חֲתִיכָה. מָקוֹר – הָא דַּאֲמַרַן,

§ **Rabbi Yoḥanan says: In three places** where there is uncertainty **the Sages followed the majority, and** based on that majority **they established** the *halakha* in these cases **as** though they involved **a certainty.** The three cases are as follows: The **source,** the **afterbirth** [*shilya*],[BL] and **a shaped** limb. The Gemara elaborates: The **source** is **that which we** just **said,** i.e., that blood found in the corridor from the vestibule and inward it is ritually impure, because the majority of blood found there is from the uterus.

שִׁלְיָא – דִּתְנַן: שִׁלְיָא בַּבַּיִת – הַבַּיִת טָמֵא, וְלֹא שֶׁהַשִּׁלְיָא וָלָד, אֶלָּא שֶׁאֵין שִׁלְיָא בְּלֹא וָלָד. רַבִּי שִׁמְעוֹן אוֹמֵר: נִמּוֹק הַוָּלָד עַד שֶׁלֹּא יָצָא.

The **afterbirth** is **as we learned** in a mishna (26a): If a woman miscarried and **the afterbirth** is **in the house,**[H] **the house is ritually impure,** in the sense that everything under the roof becomes impure due to impurity imparted by a corpse. **And** the reason is **not that the afterbirth** itself has the status of **an offspring; rather,** it is **that there is no afterbirth without an offspring.** It is clear that the afterbirth contained an offspring, which disintegrated after the miscarriage. That offspring renders the contents of the house impure. **Rabbi Shimon says:** The **offspring was squashed before it emerged** with the afterbirth. Consequently, the house is not rendered impure, because the squashed fetus is nullified by the majority of blood that accompanied the miscarriage.

חֲתִיכָה – דִּתְנַן: הַמַּפֶּלֶת יָד חֲתוּכָה וְרֶגֶל חֲתוּכָה – אִמּוֹ טְמֵאָה לֵידָה, וְאֵין חוֹשְׁשִׁין שֶׁמָּא מִגּוּף אָטוּם בָּאת.

The third case of an uncertainty where the Sages followed the majority is that of **a shaped** limb, **as we learned** in a *baraita*: In the case of a woman **who miscarries a shaped hand,** i.e., its fingers are discernible, **or a shaped foot,**[H] **its mother is impure** with the impurity of a woman after **childbirth,** as it certainly came from a full-fledged fetus, **and we are not concerned** that **perhaps it came from** a fetus with **a sealed,** i.e., deficient **body,** in which case the miscarriage does not have the status of childbirth with regard to ritual impurity. The reason is that most pregnant women give birth to a fully formed fetus, and therefore it is presumed that the hand or foot came from a whole fetus that was squashed during childbirth. Once again the Sages established the impurity as a certainty, based on a majority.

וְתוּ לֵיכָּא? וְהָאִיכָּא תֵּשַׁע חֲנוּיוֹת!

The Gemara asks: **And are there no more** cases of uncertainty in which the Sages determined the *halakha* according to the status of the majority, treating the case as though it involved a certainty? **But isn't there** the case of **nine stores?**[H]

דְּתַנְיָא: תֵּשַׁע חֲנוּיוֹת כּוּלָּן מוֹכְרוֹת בְּשַׂר שְׁחוּטָה, וְאַחַת מוֹכֶרֶת בְּשַׂר נְבֵלָה, וְלָקַח מֵאַחַת מֵהֶן וְאֵינוֹ יוֹדֵעַ מֵאֵיזֶה מֵהֶן לָקַח – סְפֵקוֹ אָסוּר,

**As it is taught** in a *baraita*: With regard to **nine stores** in a city, **all of which sell** kosher **meat** from **slaughtered** animals, **and one** other store that **sells meat** from unslaughtered **animal carcasses, and** a person **bought** meat **from one of** the stores **and he does not know from which** store **he bought** the meat, in this case of **uncertainty,** the meat **is prohibited.** With regard to an item of uncertain status, if it separated from its fixed location it is presumed to have separated from the majority[B] of items like it in that location, and has their halakhic status. But in the case of an item that remained in its fixed location, i.e., didn't separate, it is viewed as an uncertainty that is equally balanced, and one does not follow the majority. This ruling is based on the principle: The halakhic status of uncertainty with regard to any item fixed in its place is that of an uncertainty that is equally balanced, and one does not follow the majority. In this case, when it comes to determining whether or not this meat comes from a kosher store, since the uncertainty stems from the act of buying the meat in the store, and the stores are fixed in their places, the two types of stores are regarded as though they were equal in number.

וּבְנִמְצָא – הַלֵּךְ אַחַר הָרוֹב.

The *baraita* continues: **And in the** case of meat **found** in the street, outside the stores, **follow the majority** of stores. If most stores in the city sell kosher meat one can assume that the meat he found is kosher, based on the principle: Any item separated, i.e., not fixed in its place, is presumed to have been separated from the majority. Similar to the previous cases, this meat is treated as certainly kosher on the basis of a majority.

### LANGUAGE

**Afterbirth** [*shilya*] – **שִׁלְיָא:** In modern Hebrew, the word *shilya* refers specifically to the placenta, but in the Gemara the term refers to the placenta, the fetal membranes, and the umbilical cord that are expelled from a woman's body following delivery (see 26a and *Tosefta* 4:9). For this reason, the translation used here is afterbirth. See also the verse: "And against her afterbirth [*uveshilyatah*] that comes out from between her feet" (Deuteronomy 28:57). The term is derived from the Akkadian word *elitu*.

### BACKGROUND

**Afterbirth** – **שִׁלְיָא:** The placenta is a mass filled with blood vessels affixed to the wall of the uterus, through which the fetus is nourished, by way of the umbilical cord. Shortly after birth, usually within the first hour, the placenta separates from the uterus and is expelled from the body, but there are cases where the placenta is retained in the body for periods of up to several days, which is potentially life-threatening to the mother. The existence of a placenta is clear evidence that a woman or a female animal was pregnant. Such a sign is important when there is uncertainty whether there was a birth, which is relevant for the *halakhot* of impurity and for defining whether the subsequent offspring will have the status of a firstborn. If a placenta is expelled, even if there is no fetus present it is assumed that it was either delivered and then taken away, or that it did not develop properly and therefore is not discernible.

**If it separated from its fixed location it is presumed to have separated from the majority** – **כָּל דְּפָרֵישׁ מֵרוּבָּא פָּרֵישׁ:** This principle applies to many dilemmas with regard to the *halakhot* of forbidden and permitted mixtures. If an item or person whose status is unclear is found separated from a group, it can be assumed that it shares common status with the majority of items in that group. One may rely on this principle only in cases where the item spontaneously emerged from a mixture whose proportions are known. That is not the case when the item remains in the mixture. In that case, the sample is flawed and there is room for concern that the item in question is not really from the majority component. Then the principle is: Anything that is fixed, i.e., anything that remains in the mixture, is considered part of an evenly balanced uncertainty, and the item is not attributed to the majority.

### HALAKHA

**The afterbirth is in the house, etc.** – **שִׁלְיָא בַּבַּיִת וכו׳:** If a woman miscarried an afterbirth inside a house, that house is definitely impure, as there is a presumption that there is no afterbirth without a fetus (Rambam *Sefer Tahara, Hilkhot Tumat Met* 25:10, and see *Sefer Kedusha, Hilkhot Issurei Bia* 10:14).

**A woman who miscarries a shaped hand or a shaped foot, etc.** – **הַמַּפֶּלֶת יָד חֲתוּכָה וְרֶגֶל חֲתוּכָה:** If a woman miscarried a hand with distinctly formed fingers or a foot with distinctly formed toes, the presumption is that it came from a whole fetus, and therefore she is impure as a childbearing woman (Rambam *Sefer Kedusha, Hilkhot Issurei Bia* 10:11).

**Nine stores, etc.** – **תֵּשַׁע חֲנוּיוֹת וכו׳:** If the majority of stores in a city sell kosher meat and a minority sell non-kosher meat, and someone entered one of the stores and purchased meat and does not know which store he entered, as there is a fixed majority the meat's halakhic status is that of having a balanced uncertainty, and the meat is prohibited. If the meat was found in the marketplace or in the hands of a gentile, it is permitted, as most of the stores sell kosher meat, and there is a principle that any item separated, i.e., not fixed in its place, is presumed to have been separated from the majority. This is the *halakha* by Torah law, but the Sages prohibited this meat even if all the slaughterers and all the sellers are Jews. The Rema explains that one follows the principle: Any item separated is presumed to have been separated from the majority, only when the item was not separated in one's presence, but if it was separated in his presence or if he saw the gentile take it, it is considered as if he himself separated it from there, and it is prohibited (Rambam *Sefer Kedusha, Hilkhot Ma'akhalot Assurot* 8:11 and *Sefer Tahara, Hilkhot She'ar Avot HaTumot* 17:8; *Shulḥan Arukh, Yoreh De'a* 110:3).

**HALAKHA**

**Nine frogs, etc.** – **תֵּשַׁע צְפַרְדְּעִין וכו׳**: If there were nine frogs and one ritually impure creeping animal in the private domain, and a person touched one of them but he does not know which, he is ritually impure, as uncertain ritual impurity in the private domain is deemed ritually impure (Rambam *Sefer Tahara, Hilkhot She'ar Avot HaTumot* 18:2).

**NOTES**

**In the private domain the item's uncertain impurity renders it impure, etc.** – **בִּרְשׁוּת הַיָּחִיד סְפֵקוֹ טָמֵא וכו׳**: The *halakhot* of the uncertain transmission of ritual impurity are derived from the case of the woman suspected by her husband of having been unfaithful [*sota*], which is the paradigm of a situation in which there is uncertainty as to whether or not a person has become defiled. Since a *sota* is rendered prohibited to her husband due to suspicion only if she secludes herself with another man in a private domain, in other cases too, people are rendered impure based on a suspicion only if the potential impurity was contracted in a private domain. Although the case of a *sota* involves her being prohibited to her husband, i.e., it does not involve ritual impurity, cases of ritual impurity are nevertheless derived from it since the Torah uses the term "impurity" with regard to a *sota* (see, e.g., Numbers 5:14).

טוּמְאָה – קָאָמְרִינַן, אִיסּוּר – לָא קָאָמְרִינַן.

The Gemara answers: **We say** that this list of cases mentioned by Rabbi Yoḥanan is referring to matters of **ritual impurity,** whereas **we do not say** that the list includes cases that involve **prohibitions,** such as that of non-kosher meat.

וְהָאִיכָּא, תֵּשַׁע צְפַרְדְּעִין וְשֶׁרֶץ אֶחָד בֵּינֵיהֶם, וְנָגַע בְּאֶחָד מֵהֶן וְאֵינוֹ יוֹדֵעַ בְּאֵיזֶה מֵהֶן נָגַע, בִּרְשׁוּת הַיָּחִיד – סְפֵקוֹ טָמֵא, בִּרְשׁוּת הָרַבִּים – סְפֵקוֹ טָהוֹר,

The Gemara further asks: **But isn't there** the case where there were **nine** dead **frogs,**[H] which do not impart ritual impurity, **and one** carcass of a **creeping animal among them,** which does impart impurity, **and** someone **touched one of** these ten dead creatures, **and he does not know which of them he touched?** The *halakha* is as follows: If this occurred **in the private domain** the item's **uncertain** impurity renders it **impure,**[N] as it is derived from the Torah that in cases of uncertainty with regard to ritual impurity in the private domain, the item is deemed impure. If the contact occurred **in the public domain,** the item's **uncertainty** leaves it **pure.**

וּבְנִמְצָא – הַלֵּךְ אַחַר הָרוֹב!

The Gemara continues: **And in** a case where one of these creatures was separated from the rest and **was found** elsewhere, and the person touched it there, **follow the majority.** Since most of the animals do not impart ritual impurity, this individual remains pure. This is another case involving uncertain impurity where the Sages established the *halakha* as certain based on the majority.

טוּמְאָה דְּאִשָּׁה – קָאָמְרִינַן, טוּמְאָה בְּעָלְמָא – לָא קָאָמְרִינַן.

The Gemara explains: **We say** that Rabbi Yoḥanan's list is referring to matters of **ritual impurity of a woman,** whereas **we do not say** that the list includes cases that involve **ritual impurity in general.**

וְהָאִיכָּא הָא דְּאָמַר רַבִּי יְהוֹשֻׁעַ בֶּן לֵוִי: עָבְרָה בַּנָּהָר

The Gemara further asks: **But isn't there that which Rabbi Yehoshua ben Levi said:** With regard to a pregnant woman who **passed across a river**

Perek **II**
Daf **18** Amud **b**

וְהִפִּילָה – מְבִיאָה קָרְבָּן וְנֶאֱכָל,

**and she miscarried**[H] her fetus into the river, but she does not know whether or not the fetus was fully formed, **she brings** the **offering** of a woman after childbirth, i.e., a burnt offering and a sin offering. **And** the sin offering, which is a bird, **is eaten** after the nape of its neck has been severed, in the manner of a regular bird sin offering. This is the *halakha* despite the uncertainty, i.e., this fetus might not have been fully formed, in which case the woman is not obligated to bring this offering, and a bird that is not an offering may not be eaten if its nape was severed.

הַלֵּךְ אַחַר רוֹב נָשִׁים, וְרוֹב נָשִׁים וָלָד מְעַלְּיָא יָלְדָן.

Rabbi Yehoshua ben Levi explains the reasoning behind this ruling: One must **follow the majority of** pregnant **women, and most** pregnant **women give birth to full-fledged offspring.** If so, this is another case involving an uncertainty where the Sages established the *halakha* as a certainty based on the majority. Furthermore, this case involves the ritual impurity of a woman. Why then did Rabbi Yoḥanan list only three cases of this kind?

מַתְנִיתִין קָאָמְרִינַן, שְׁמַעְתְּתָא – לָא קָאָמְרִינַן.

The Gemara answers: **We say** that only cases taught in **the Mishna** or a *baraita* are included in this list, whereas **we do not say** that those derived from an amoraic **halakhic statement,** e.g., the statement of Rabbi Yehoshua ben Levi, are included.

**HALAKHA**

**Passed across a river and she miscarried** – **עָבְרָה בַּנָּהָר וְהִפִּילָה**: If a woman was known to be pregnant, and she gave birth but did not know the form of what she birthed, e.g., if she miscarried into a river, she is presumed to have given birth to a fully formed child, and she is ritually impure as a woman after childbirth. Since she does not know whether the child was male or female, she must accept the stringencies of both the birth of a male child and a female child, i.e., a longer period of impurity and a shorter period of purity. Since she is considered a definite childbearing woman, she must bring the offerings of a woman who has given birth, and her sin offering is eaten. The *halakha* is in accordance with the opinion of Rabbi Yehoshua ben Levi (Rambam *Sefer Kedusha, Hilkhot Issurei Bia* 10:19 and *Sefer Korbanot, Hilkhot Meḥusrei Kappara* 1:6).

וְהָא כִּי אֲתָא רָבִין אֲמַר: מְתִיב רַבִּי יוֹסֵי בַּר רַבִּי חֲנִינָא טוֹעָה, וְלָא יָדַעְנָא מַאי תְּיוּבְתֵּיה,

The Gemara raises a difficulty with regard to this explanation: **But when Ravin came** from Eretz Yisrael to Babylonia **he said** that **Rabbi Yosei bar Rabbi Ḥanina raises an objection** against the opinion of Rabbi Yehoshua ben Levi from a *baraita* that deals with **an unsure woman,**[N] i.e., one who does not know when she gave birth. Ravin added: **And I do not know what his objection** was[N] from that *baraita.*

מַאי לָאו: לָא תְּיוּבְתָּא אֶלָּא סַייעְתָּא?

The Gemara discusses Ravin's statement: **What, is it not** correct to say that Ravin meant that this *baraita* is **not a refutation** of the opinion of Rabbi Yehoshua ben Levi **but** actually provides **support**[N] for that opinion? If so, that would mean that Rabbi Yehoshua ben Levi's opinion is effectively taught in a *baraita* as well, and therefore according to the above consideration Rabbi Yoḥanan should have included it in his list.

לָא, דִּלְמָא: לָא תְּיוּבְתָּא וְלָא סַייעְתָּא.

The Gemara answers: This is **not** necessarily the correct inference, as **perhaps** Ravin meant simply that the ruling of this *baraita* is **neither a refutation nor a support** for the opinion of Rabbi Yehoshua ben Levi.

לְמַעוּטֵי מַאי?

§ When Rabbi Yoḥanan says that in three places where there is uncertainty the Sages followed the majority and established the *halakha* as though it involved a certainty, he is clearly indicating that some cases are excluded from this category. The Gemara asks: Rabbi Yoḥanan says this **to exclude what?**

אִילֵימָא לְמַעוּטֵי רוּבָּא דְּאִיכָּא חֲזָקָה בַּהֲדֵיהּ, דְּלָא שָׂרְפִינַן עֲלֵיהּ אֶת הַתְּרוּמָה – וְהָא אֲמַרָהּ רַבִּי יוֹחָנָן חֲדָא זִימְנָא!

**If we say** that he says this **to exclude** an uncertain case where on the one hand there is **a majority that** indicates the woman should be deemed ritually impure and on the other hand **there is a presumptive status along with it** that opposes that majority, **which** is why the uncertainty is not treated as a certainty, and therefore **one does not burn *teruma* due to** contact with that impurity, this cannot be the case. The reason is that Rabbi Yoḥanan already **said it** on **another occasion,** with regard to other cases of ritual impurity, that if the consideration of a majority indicates that an item should be impure while its presumptive status indicates that it should be pure, it is not considered definitely impure.

דִּתְנַן: תִּינוֹק הַנִּמְצָא בְּצַד הָעִיסָּה וּבָצֵק בְּיָדוֹ – רַבִּי מֵאִיר מְטַהֵר, וַחֲכָמִים מְטַמְּאִין, שֶׁדַּרְכּוֹ שֶׁל תִּינוֹק לְטַפֵּחַ.

The Gemara cites the source for Rabbi Yoḥanan's opinion in this regard. **As we learned** in a mishna (*Teharot* 3:8): If a ritually impure **child is found alongside** ritually pure **started dough** that has not yet risen, **and** he has **risen dough in his hand**[H] that may have been removed from the larger portion of started dough, **Rabbi Meir deems** the started dough **pure,** since there is no proof the child touched it, as he might have been given the piece by someone else. **And the Rabbis deem it impure,** as they assume that he touched the started dough. The child is presumed to be impure, **because it is the norm of a child to handle** items.

וְאָמְרִינַן: מַאי טַעְמָא דְּרַבִּי מֵאִיר – קָסָבַר: רוֹב תִּינוֹקוֹת מְטַפְּחִין, וּמִיעוּט אֵין מְטַפְּחִין, וְעִיסָּה זוֹ בְּחֶזְקַת טְהוֹרָה עוֹמֶדֶת, סְמוֹךְ מִיעוּטָא לַחֲזָקָה – וְאִיתְרַע לֵיהּ רוּבָּא.

**And we say** with regard to this dispute: **What is the reason** for the opinion **of Rabbi Meir? He holds** that **a majority of children handle** items that are within reach, in this case the dough, **and a minority do not handle** items within reach, **and this dough retains a presumptive status of purity,** since its impurity has not been definitively determined. Therefore, one should **append** the fact that the **minority** of children do not handle items within reach **to the presumptive status** of purity of the dough, **and** the force of the **majority** of children who handle items within reach **is weakened.** Therefore, the dough is considered pure.

## NOTES

**Unsure woman – טוֹעָה:** The Gemara here alludes to a discussion that is cited in full on 29b. There, the Gemara cites a *baraita* that deals with a woman who left her house when she was pregnant and returned a long while afterward, no longer pregnant. The problem is that she knows nothing about when she gave birth or the nature of the child. Furthermore, since her return, three weeks of purity passed, i.e., three weeks without her experiencing a blood flow, after which there was another ten-week period that consisted alternately of a week where she experienced bleeding every day, followed by a week in which she did not experience bleeding at all. The *halakha* is that this woman may engage in intercourse with her husband only on the thirty-fifth day from her arrival, which is the end of the fifth week.

**What his objection was – מַאי תְּיוּבְתֵּיהּ:** Rabbi Yosei bar Rabbi Ḥanina's objection is explained in the Gemara on 29b. He asked: Why does the *baraita* teach that the woman may engage in intercourse with her husband only at the end of the fifth week from her arrival? It is clear that she is not permitted to him in the first week, as she might have given birth to a male child just before she arrived, in which case this week is included in the seven days of impurity a woman must observe upon the birth of a male child. Likewise, she may not engage in intercourse with her husband in the second week, in case she gave birth to a female just before her return, and she must therefore observe two weeks of impurity. Furthermore, they are forbidden to each other in the third week of her return as well, as she might have given birth to a female while in a state of a *zava*, i.e., she might have experienced a blood flow for three days before the birth that was not due to childbirth. In such a case she must count the seven pure days of a *zava* after the two weeks of impurity for the birth of a female. But why is she prohibited to her husband in the fourth week following her return? Even if she experiences bleeding that week, it should be considered ritually pure. The reason it should be considered ritually pure is that the majority of women give birth to fully formed children, and therefore this woman should also be treated as one who gave birth to a fully formed child, which means that she has a period of purity during which her blood is ritually pure. The fact that the *baraita* does not accept this opinion is a proof against the claim of Rabbi Yehoshua ben Levi that one follows the majority of women, who give birth to fully formed children.

**But provides support – אֶלָּא סַייעְתָּא:** This interpretation of Ravin's statement is not discussed by the Gemara on 29b, which deals with this *baraita* in detail. The early commentaries explain why the *baraita* could be understood as providing support of Rabbi Yehoshua ben Levi's ruling: If the *baraita* did not accept Rabbi Yehoshua ben Levi's opinion that one follows the majority of women, who give birth to fully formed children, then this woman who returned no longer pregnant should not be considered impure at all. The reason is that there is a compound uncertainty here: Perhaps she did not give birth to a fully formed child, and even if she did, perhaps she gave birth long before her arrival, in which case all the days of her impurity have ended. Once Rabbi Yehoshua ben Levi's opinion has been accepted, there is only one uncertainty left, which is that she might have given birth just before her arrival, and therefore she is considered impure, in accordance with the principle that the *halakha* is stringent when only one uncertainty is involved.

## HALAKHA

**If a ritually impure child is found alongside ritually pure started dough and he has risen dough in his hand – תִּינוֹק הַנִּמְצָא בְּצַד הָעִיסָּה וּבָצֵק בְּיָדוֹ:** If an impure child is found alongside a started dough while holding a piece of risen dough, the entire dough is impure, as the presumption is that a child will handle items within reach. Nevertheless, if the dough was *teruma* it is not burned based on this presumption, in accordance with the opinion of the Rabbis, as explained by Rabbi Yoḥanan (Rambam *Sefer Tahara, Hilkhot She'ar Avot HaTumot* 16:3).

וְרַבָּנַן – מִיעוּטָא – כְּמַאן דְּלֵיתֵיהּ דָּמֵי, וְרוּבָּא וַחֲזָקָה – רוּבָּא עָדִיף.

**And the Rabbis** contend that in a case where the majority is followed, **the minority is considered like it does not exist. And** consequently, there is a conflict between the determining factors of **the majority** of impure children who handle items within reach **and the presumptive status** of purity of the dough. Therefore, **the majority takes precedence.**[N]

וְאָמַר רֵישׁ לָקִישׁ מִשּׁוּם רַבִּי אוֹשַׁעְיָא: זוֹ הִיא חֲזָקָה שֶׁשּׂוֹרְפִין עָלֶיהָ אֶת הַתְּרוּמָה, וְרַבִּי יוֹחָנָן אָמַר: אֵין זוֹ חֲזָקָה שֶׁשּׂוֹרְפִין עָלֶיהָ אֶת הַתְּרוּמָה!

**And Reish Lakish says in the name of Rabbi Oshaya: This** *halakha* of a child **is** an example of **a presumption,** that children handle items within reach, **over which** ***teruma*** **is burned,** as the Rabbis hold that it is sufficiently certain that the dough has become impure to allow it to be burned. **And Rabbi Yoḥanan says: This is not a presumption over which** ***teruma*** **is burned.** Rather, the dough is left aside, and can be neither eaten nor burned, due to the uncertainty whether it is impure. In this context, Rabbi Yoḥanan has already stated that when a majority is contradicted by a presumption, the status of uncertainty applies. Therefore, there was no need for him to specify the three cases he mentioned in order to exclude situations of this kind.

אֶלָּא לְמַעוּטֵי רוּבָּא דְּרַבִּי יְהוּדָה. דִּתְנַן, הַמַּפֶּלֶת חֲתִיכָה, אִם יֵשׁ עִמָּהּ דָּם – טְמֵאָה, וְאִם לָאו – טְהוֹרָה. רַבִּי יְהוּדָה אוֹמֵר: בֵּין כָּךְ וּבֵין כָּךְ טְמֵאָה.

**Rather,** Rabbi Yoḥanan's statement that there are only three cases in which uncertainty is treated as certainty is meant **to exclude** a specific situation involving **a majority,** as discussed by **Rabbi Yehuda. As we learned** in a mishna (21a): In the case of a woman **who miscarries** an amorphous **piece**[H] of flesh, **if there is blood** that emerges **with it,** the woman **is ritually impure** with the impurity of a menstruating woman. **And if not, she is pure,** as she is neither a menstruating woman nor a woman after childbirth. **Rabbi Yehuda says:** In **both this** case, where blood emerged, **and that** case, where no blood emerged, the woman **is impure** with the impurity of a menstruating woman, as there was certainly undetected blood that emerged with the flesh.

וְאָמַר רַב יְהוּדָה, אָמַר שְׁמוּאֵל: לֹא טִימֵּא רַבִּי יְהוּדָה אֶלָּא בַּחֲתִיכָה שֶׁל אַרְבַּע מִינֵי דָּמִים, אֲבָל שְׁאָר מִינֵי דָּמִים – טְהוֹרָה. וְרַבִּי יוֹחָנָן אָמַר: שֶׁל אַרְבַּע מִינֵי דָּמִים – דִּבְרֵי הַכֹּל טְמֵאָה, וְשֶׁל שְׁאָר דָּמִים – דִּבְרֵי הַכֹּל טְהוֹרָה. לֹא נֶחְלְקוּ אֶלָּא כְּשֶׁהִפִּילָה

**And Rav Yehuda says** that **Shmuel says: Rabbi Yehuda deemed** the woman **impure,** despite the fact that no blood emerged, **only in** the case of **a piece** of flesh that has the color **of** one of the **four types of** ritually impure **blood,** as stated in the mishna below (19a). **But** if it has the color **of other types of blood,** the woman is **pure. And Rabbi Yoḥanan says:** If a woman miscarries a piece of flesh that has the color **of** one of the **four types of** ritually impure **blood, all,** i.e., Rabbi Yehuda and the Rabbis, **agree** that she **is impure. And** likewise, if the piece has the color **of other types of blood, all agree** that **she is pure.** The Rabbis and Rabbi Yehuda **disagree only** with regard to a case **where** the woman **miscarried** an amorphous piece of flesh,

וְאֵינָהּ יוֹדַעַת מָה הִפִּילָה. רַבִּי יְהוּדָה סָבַר: זִיל בָּתַר רוֹב חֲתִיכוֹת, וְרוֹב חֲתִיכוֹת שֶׁל אַרְבַּע מִינֵי דָּמִים הָוְיָין. וְרַבָּנַן סָבְרִי: ״זִיל בָּתַר רוֹב חֲתִיכוֹת״ לָא אָמְרִינַן.

**and she** herself **does not know** exactly **what** the appearance of the piece of flesh that **she miscarried** was, e.g., if it was lost. In this case **Rabbi Yehuda holds: Follow the majority of** miscarriages of amorphous **pieces** of flesh, **and the majority of pieces** of flesh have the appearance **of** one of the **four types of** impure **blood. And the Rabbis hold: We do not say: Follow the majority of** miscarriages of amorphous **pieces** of flesh. Therefore, Rabbi Yoḥanan's mention of three cases is meant to exclude this statement of Rabbi Yehuda, who rules that the woman is definitely impure based on a majority.

**NOTES**

**The majority takes precedence** – רוּבָּא עָדִיף: The dispute between Rabbi Meir and the Rabbis concerns the basic question of which factor takes precedence in a conflict between a majority and a presumption. What weight is granted to the minority, which supports the presumption? According to the Rabbis the minority is entirely discounted, and therefore there is simply a majority versus a presumption, in which case the majority takes precedence. Rabbi Meir contends that the minority is not completely negated; it combines with the presumption to override the majority, as two factors are more powerful than one (Rashi). If so, this preference of a presumption and a minority over a majority applies by Torah law, not rabbinic law.

**HALAKHA**

**One who miscarries a piece, etc.** – הַמַּפֶּלֶת חֲתִיכָה וכו׳: With regard to a woman who miscarries a piece of flesh, even if it is red she is ritually impure only if there is blood with it. Furthermore, even if the piece of flesh was torn open and discovered to be full of blood, she is pure, as this is not the blood of her menstruation but the blood of the piece of flesh (Rambam). Others hold that as the Rabbis maintain that there is always an emergence of blood when the uterus opens, and the *halakha* is in accordance with their opinion, she must certainly have experienced bleeding when she miscarried (Ra'avad). Consequently, she is ritually impure (Rambam *Sefer Kedusha, Hilkhot Issurei Bia* 5:13, and see *Maggid Mishne* there).

Perek **II**
Daf **19** Amud **a**

מתני׳ חֲמִשָּׁה דָמִים טְמֵאִים בָּאִשָּׁה: הָאָדוֹם, וְהַשָּׁחוֹר, וּכְקֶרֶן כַּרְכּוֹם, וּכְמֵימֵי אֲדָמָה, וּכְמָזוּג. בֵּית שַׁמַּאי אוֹמְרִים: אַף כְּמֵימֵי תִלְתָּן, וּכְמֵימֵי בְשַׂר צָלִי, וּבֵית הִלֵּל מְטַהֲרִים. הַיָּרוֹק, עֲקַבְיָא בֶּן מַהֲלַלְאֵל מְטַמֵּא, וַחֲכָמִים מְטַהֲרִין.

**MISHNA** There are **five** distinct colors of **ritually impure blood in a woman:**[H] **Red, and black, and like the bright** color of the **crocus** [*karkom*][L] flower,[BN] **and like water** that inundates red **earth, and like diluted** wine. **Beit Shammai say: Even** blood **like the water** in which **a fenugreek**[B] plant is soaked, **and like the liquid** that drips from **roast meat,** are ritually impure, **and Beit Hillel deem** blood of those colors **ritually pure.** With regard to blood that is **green,**[BHN] **Akavya ben Mahalalel deems** it **impure and the Rabbis deem** it **pure.**

אָמַר רַבִּי מֵאִיר: אִם אֵינוֹ מְטַמֵּא מִשּׁוּם כֶּתֶם – מְטַמֵּא מִשּׁוּם מַשְׁקֶה. רַבִּי יוֹסֵי אוֹמֵר: לֹא כָךְ וְלֹא כָךְ.

**Rabbi Meir said:** Even **if** the green blood **does not transmit impurity due to** the *halakhot* of a blood **stain** or the blood of a menstruating woman, it is blood in that **it renders** food susceptible to **ritual impurity due to** its status as one of the seven **liquids** that render food susceptible to impurity. **Rabbi Yosei says: Neither** in **this** sense, as the blood of a menstruating woman according to Akavya ben Mahalalel, **nor** in **that** sense, as a liquid that renders food susceptible to impurity according to Rabbi Meir, is green blood considered blood.

אֵיזֶהוּ אָדוֹם? כְּדַם הַמַּכָּה. שָׁחוֹר? כְּחֶרֶת. עָמוֹק מִכֵּן – טָמֵא, דֵּיהֶה מִכֵּן – טָהוֹר. וּכְקֶרֶן כַּרְכּוֹם? כַּבָּרוּר שֶׁבּוֹ.

The mishna asks: **What is** the **red** color that is impure?[H] It is as red **as the blood** that flows from **a wound.** What is the **black** color that is impure? It is blood as black **as *ḥeret*.**[N] If the black is **deeper than that,** the blood is **ritually impure;** if the black is **lighter than that,** the blood is **ritually pure.**[HN] **And** what is the color that is **like the bright** color of the **crocus** flower that is impure? It is **like the brightest** part **in** the flower, which is harvested to produce the orange-colored spice saffron.

HALAKHA

**There are five distinct colors of ritually impure blood in a woman** – **חֲמִשָּׁה דָמִים טְמֵאִים בָּאִשָּׁה:** All types of red blood that flow from a woman, whether they are very dark or deep, are ritually impure. The same applies to all forms of black blood (Rambam *Sefer Kedusha, Hilkhot Issurei Bia* 5:7; *Shulḥan Arukh, Yoreh De'a* 188:1).

**Green** – **הַיָּרוֹק:** If white or green fluid flowed from a woman, even if it is similar to wax or to gold in color, it is pure, and all the more so if it is green like a leek or like grass. Some claim that blue blood is considered like green blood (Rema). The *halakha* is in accordance with the opinion of the Rabbis (Rambam *Sefer Kedusha, Hilkhot Issurei Bia* 5:6 and *Sefer Tahara, Hilkhot Metamei Mishkav UMoshav* 1:8; *Shulḥan Arukh, Yoreh De'a* 188:1).

**What is the red color that is impure** – **אֵיזֶהוּ אָדוֹם:** The red color of blood that the Sages said is impure in a woman is like the first flow of blood from someone's wound, as explained by Rav Naḥman in the Gemara later (Rambam *Sefer Kedusha, Hilkhot Issurei Bia* 5:8).

**If the black is deeper than that it is ritually impure, if the black is lighter than that it is ritually pure** – **עָמוֹק מִכֵּן טָמֵא, דֵּיהֶה מִכֵּן טָהוֹר:** With regard to a woman who saw one of the types of blood listed in the mishna, if it was the same as described in the mishna or deeper, it is impure; if it was lighter, it is pure. How so? If black blood was darker than dried ink, she is impure. If it was lighter than that, e.g., if it was like a black olive, or tar, or the black of a raven, it is pure (Rambam *Sefer Kedusha, Hilkhot Issurei Bia* 5:9).

NOTES

**And like the bright color of the crocus flower [*keren karkom*]** – **וּכְקֶרֶן כַּרְכּוֹם:** All the commentaries agree that *karkom* refers to the crocus flower. With regard to *keren*, Rashi suggests two possible explanations: First, that it means a corner, as in the common talmudic expression *keren zavit*, the angle of a corner. In this context, it is the color of a crocus flower in the corner of a garden, not one in the center of the garden. Second, that it means shining and brightness, as in the verse: "The skin of his face sent forth beams [*karan*]" (Exodus 34:29); in other words, the phrase means: The bright color of the crocus flower.

**Blood that is green [*yarok*]** – **הַיָּרוֹק:** There are various opinions with regard to the precise nature of this green that is the subject of the dispute between the Rabbis and Akavya ben Mahalalel. Some say that their dispute applies only to the green color of an *etrog* fruit, which has a reddish tinge, but that if it is leek green, even Akavya ben Mahalalel concedes that it is pure (*Tosafot*). The commentaries infer from here that all shades of *yarok* are pure, even one that is waxy green, greenish gold, or similar in appearance to the yolk of an egg (*Tur, Yoreh De'a* 188; *Shulḥan Arukh, Yoreh De'a* 188:1).

***Ḥeret*** – **חֶרֶת:** This refers to an extremely dark black, like the color used by tanners and shoemakers to dye hides.

**If the black is deeper than that it is ritually impure, if the black is lighter [*deiha*] than that it is ritually pure** – **עָמוֹק מִכֵּן טָמֵא דֵּיהֶה מִכֵּן טָהוֹר:** The early commentaries disagree as to the meaning of this statement. Some say that the clause: If the black is deeper than that the blood is ritually impure, means that it is deeper than ink, whereas *deiha* means that it is a lighter black (Rashi; Ramban; Rashba). Others maintain the reverse, that the term: Deeper, means that it is less black, whereas *deiha* means that it is very black (Ramban, citing Rabbeinu Shmuel). The Ramban rejects this opinion, claiming that the stronger shade of any color is always described as deeper.

LANGUAGE

**Crocus [*karkom*]** – **כַּרְכּוֹם:** The earliest source for this word is apparently the Sanskrit *kunkuma*, which found its way into many other languages with a shift from the letter *n* to *r*, in forms such as *karkom* and the Latin word crocus.

BACKGROUND

**Crocus flower** – **כַּרְכּוֹם:** Saffron crocus, *Crocus sativus* L., is a plant of the Iridaceae family. The plant is notable for the fact that it flowers early in the winter, and for its flowers, from which the orange-colored spice saffron is extracted. Due to its pleasant odor it is mentioned in the Bible and in rabbinic sources as being a source of perfume.

Crocus flower with saffron-producing stigmata and styles

**Fenugreek** – **תִּלְתָּן:** *Trigonella foenum-graecum* L., known in modern Hebrew as *ḥilbe*, belongs to the legume family. It is a short plant, growing to less than 1 m high. The plant has hollow, hairy stems, light green leaves arranged in threes, and white flowers. The fruit is found in small pods that are up to 15 cm long and contain flat seeds about 5 mm long. While the plant is generally grown for its seeds, which are used as a spice for food, the shoots are also edible when cooked. In some countries, fenugreek is used as animal fodder and as fertilizer.

Fenugreek

**Green [*yarok*]** – **יָרוֹק:** Green is not a primary color; it is located between blue and yellow on the spectrum of visible light. The term *yarok*, as it is used by the Sages, includes a wide variety of shades, from dark green to yellow. For this reason there are numerous opinions with regard to the precise definition of *yarok* in different areas of *halakha*.

**BACKGROUND**

**Beit Kerem Valley – בִּקְעַת בֵּית הַכֶּרֶם:** The Beit Kerem Valley is in the Lower Galilee. Some say it is the Shagor stream, between Majd al-Krum and Carmiel. This identification is based on the *baraita* cited later, which states: In order to examine blood that is like water that inundates red earth, one brings fertile earth from the Beit Kerem Valley and inundates the earth with enough water until it pools on the surface; this is the statement of Rabbi Meir. Rabbi Akiva says: One brings earth from the Yodfat Valley. Rabbi Yosei says: From the Sikhnei Valley. Rabbi Shimon says: One can even bring earth from the Genosar Valley or from similar places. These valleys mentioned in the *baraita* are all in the Lower Galilee.

This Beit Kerem Valley, like the surrounding valleys, was known for its fertile soil. It is not the same as the Beit Kerem mentioned in *Middot* 3:4, which is near Jerusalem and which was renowned for the quality of its stones.

וּכְמֵימֵי אֲדָמָה? מִבִּקְעַת בֵּית כֶּרֶם, וּמֵיצֵף מַיִם. וּכְמָזוּג? שְׁנֵי חֲלָקִים מַיִם וְאֶחָד יַיִן, מִן הַיַּיִן הַשָּׁרוֹנִי.

**And** what is the color that is **like water** that inundates red **earth** that is impure? It is specifically earth **from the Beit Kerem Valley**[B] **and** specifically when **one inundates** the earth with enough **water** until it pools on the surface. **And** what is the color that is **like diluted** wine that is impure? It is specifically when the dilution consists of **two parts water and one** part **wine,** and specifically when it is **from the wine of the Sharon** region in Eretz Yisrael.

גמ׳ מְנָלַן דְּאִיכָּא דָּם טָהוֹר בָּאִשָּׁה? דִּלְמָא כׇּל דָּם דְּאָתֵי מִינַּהּ טָמֵא!

**GEMARA** The fact that the mishna discusses the colors of ritually impure blood in a woman indicates that there is blood that is not impure. The Gemara asks: **From where do we** derive **that there is pure blood in a woman?**[N] **Perhaps any** type of **blood that emerges from** a woman **is impure?**

אָמַר רַבִּי חָמָא בַּר יוֹסֵף אָמַר רַבִּי אוֹשַׁעְיָא, אָמַר קְרָא: ״כִּי יִפָּלֵא מִמְּךָ דָבָר לַמִּשְׁפָּט בֵּין דָּם לְדָם״ – בֵּין דָּם טָהוֹר לְדָם טָמֵא.

**Rabbi Ḥama bar Yosef says** that **Rabbi Oshaya says:** The **verse states** with regard to those who come before the court: **"If there arise a matter too hard for you in judgment, between blood and blood,** between plea and plea, and between leprous mark and leprous mark, even matters of controversy within your gates, then you shall arise, and get up unto the place that the Lord your God shall choose" (Deuteronomy 17:8). When the verse states: "Between blood and blood," it means **between pure blood and impure blood,**[N] which demonstrates that there must be types of pure blood that are emitted by a woman.

אֶלָּא מֵעַתָּה ״בֵּין נֶגַע לָנֶגַע״, הָכִי נַמִּי בֵּין נֶגַע טָמֵא לְנֶגַע טָהוֹר? וְכִי תֵּימָא: הָכִי נַמִּי – נֶגַע טָהוֹר מִי אִיכָּא? וְכִי תֵּימָא: ״כֻּלּוֹ הָפַךְ לָבָן טָהוֹר הוּא״ – הַהוּא ״בּוֹהַק״ מִקְּרֵי!

The Gemara raises a difficulty: **If that is so,** then does the other expression in the verse: **"Between leprous mark and leprous mark," also** mean: **Between a pure leprous mark and an impure leprous mark? And if you would say** that **indeed,** this is what it means, **is there** a type of **pure leprous mark? And if you would say** that there is in fact a pure leprous mark, according to the verse: "Then the priest shall look; and behold, if the leprosy has covered all his flesh, he shall pronounce pure the one that has the leprous mark; **it is all turned white: He is pure"** (Leviticus 13:13), **that** mark is not classified as a leprous mark; rather, it **is called a paleness,** as a leprous mark is by definition impure.

אֶלָּא: בֵּין נִגְעֵי אָדָם לְנִגְעֵי בָתִּים וּלְנִגְעֵי בְגָדִים – וְכוּלָּן טְמֵאִין, הָכָא נַמִּי – בֵּין דַּם נִדָּה לְדַם זִיבָה – וְכוּלָּן טְמֵאִין!

**Rather,** the phrase "between leprous mark and leprous mark" must mean the following: **Between the leprous marks** that afflict **man** (see Leviticus 13:1–46) **and the leprous marks of houses** (see Leviticus 14:33–53) **and the leprous marks of garments** (see Leviticus 13:47–59), as different *halakhot* pertain to these categories of leprous marks, **and** yet **they are all ritually impure.** Therefore, **here too,** when the verse states: "Between blood and blood," it means: **Between the blood of a menstruating woman and the blood of a discharge** [*ziva*], **and they are all ritually impure.** If so, this verse cannot be cited as proof that there is a type of blood emitted by a woman that is pure.

**NOTES**

That there is pure blood in a woman – דְּאִיכָּא דָּם טָהוֹר בָּאִשָּׁה: The early commentaries disagree as to the reason all other types of blood, i.e., those not listed in the mishna, are pure. Some say that even those types of blood come from the uterus, but the Torah declared them pure (see Rambam *Sefer Kedusha, Hilkhot Issurei Bia* 5:6–7). The *Tur* likewise writes: Not all blood from the source is impure, but only these five types (see *Terumat HaDeshen*). Others state that the difference between the types of blood listed in the mishna and all other types is that those other types do not come from the uterus (*Smag*; *Sefer HaḤinnukh*; *Tosefot Rid*), but are caused by wounds (Abravanel's Commentary on the Torah).

Between pure blood and impure blood – בֵּין דָּם טָהוֹר לְדָם טָמֵא: The commentaries state that only the greatest of Sages are qualified to rule with regard to the differences between these types of blood. Similarly, the Jerusalem Talmud (2:7) cites Rav's statement that one may issue rulings with regard to the types of blood only if he is an expert in their appearances and in their names. Even in talmudic times there were Sages who would refrain from examining blood. Nowadays, when people have less understanding (*Smak*), the requisite expertise is lacking (Meiri; *Tur*), and people are unable to discern properly the differences between the types of blood (*Sefer HaEshkol*), one may not rely on his own judgment to distinguish between the impure and pure shades of red; all shades of red blood must be treated as impure.

הַאי מַאי? בִּשְׁלָמָא הָתָם – אִיכָּא לְאִפְּלוּגֵי בְּנִגְעֵי אָדָם, וּבִפְלוּגְתָּא דְּרַבִּי יְהוֹשֻׁעַ וְרַבָּנַן,

The Gemara questions this interpretation: This verse serves as the source for the areas of *halakha* for which a rebellious elder is liable to receive the death penalty for publicly ruling in contradiction to a decision of the Sanhedrin, as it states: "And the man who does presumptuously, in not listening to the priest that stands to minister there before the Lord your God, or to the judge, that man shall die; and you shall exterminate the evil from Israel" (Deuteronomy 17:12). With this in mind, the Gemara asks: **What is this** explanation? **Granted, there,** with regard to leprous marks, even if all the leprous marks are impure, **one can disagree** with the Sanhedrin **with regard to the leprous marks** that afflict **man, and** therefore the rebellious elder could potentially disagree with the court **with regard to** the issue that is the subject of **the dispute of Rabbi Yehoshua and the Rabbis.**

דִּתְנַן, אִם בַּהֶרֶת קוֹדֶם לִשְׂעָר לָבָן – טָמֵא, וְאִם שֵׂעָר לָבָן קוֹדֵם לְבַהֶרֶת – טָהוֹר, סָפֵק – טָמֵא, וְרַבִּי יְהוֹשֻׁעַ אוֹמֵר: כֵּהָה. וְאָמַר רַבָּה: כֵּהָה וְטָהוֹר.

**As we learned** in a mishna (*Nega'im* 4:11): **If the snow-white leprous mark** [*baheret*], which is one sign of leprosy, **preceded** the **white hair,** which is another sign, he is **ritually impure,** as stated in the Torah (see Leviticus 13:3). **And if** the **white hair preceded** the *baheret* he is **pure,** as this is not considered a sign of impurity. If there is **uncertainty** as to which came first, he is **impure. And Rabbi Yehoshua says:** It is **dull** [*keha*].[L] **And Rabba says,** explaining the statement of Rabbi Yehoshua: In the case of uncertainty, the leprous mark is deemed as though it is of **a dull** shade, and therefore the person is **ritually pure.**

בְּנִגְעֵי בָתִּים – כִּי הָא פְּלוּגְתָּא דְּרַבִּי אֶלְעָזָר בְּרַבִּי שִׁמְעוֹן וְרַבָּנַן, דִּתְנַן, רַבִּי אֶלְעָזָר בְּרַבִּי שִׁמְעוֹן אוֹמֵר: לְעוֹלָם אֵין הַבַּיִת טָמֵא עַד שֶׁיֵּרָאֶה כִּשְׁנֵי גְרִיסִין עַל שְׁנֵי אֲבָנִים, בִּשְׁנֵי כוֹתָלִים, בְּקֶרֶן זָוִית, אׇרְכּוֹ כִּשְׁנֵי גְרִיסִין וְרׇחְבּוֹ כִּגְרִיס.

Likewise, **with regard to the leprous marks of houses** one can find a case where the rebellious elder might dispute the ruling of the Sanhedrin, such **as that dispute between Rabbi Elazar, son of Rabbi Shimon, and the Rabbis. As we learned** in a mishna (*Nega'im* 12:3): **Rabbi Elazar, son of Rabbi Shimon, says: A house is never** deemed **impure**[H] with leprosy **unless** the leprous mark **will be seen** to be the size **of two split beans,**[B] and it is found **on two stones on two walls in a corner** between two walls. **The length of** the mark **is** that of **two split beans, and its width is** that of one **split bean.**

מַאי טַעְמָא דְּרַבִּי אֶלְעָזָר בְּרַבִּי שִׁמְעוֹן? כְּתִיב: "קִיר" וּכְתִיב: "קִירוֹת", אֵיזֶהוּ קִיר שֶׁהוּא כִּשְׁנֵי קִירוֹת – הֱוֵי אוֹמֵר: זֶה קֶרֶן זָוִית.

The Gemara explains: **What is the reason** for the opinion **of Rabbi Elazar, son of Rabbi Shimon?** The word **"wall" is written** in the verse, **and** the word **"walls" is written** in the same verse: "And he shall see the leprous mark…in the walls of the house with hollow streaks, greenish or reddish, and their appearance is lower than the wall" (Leviticus 14:37). **Which is** one **wall that is like two walls? You must say: This is a corner** between two walls.

בְּנִגְעֵי בְגָדִים – בִּפְלוּגְתָּא דְּרַבִּי יוֹנָתָן בֶּן אַבְטוּלְמוֹס וְרַבָּנַן. דְּתַנְיָא, רַבִּי יוֹנָתָן בֶּן אַבְטוּלְמוֹס אוֹמֵר: מִנַּיִן לִפְרִיחַת בְּגָדִים שֶׁהִיא טְהוֹרָה?

Similarly, **with regard to the leprous marks on garments,** it is possible that the rebellious elder disputed the ruling of the Sanhedrin **with regard to** the issue that is the subject of **the dispute between Rabbi Yonatan ben Avtolemos**[L] **and the Rabbis. As it is taught** in a *baraita* that **Rabbi Yonatan ben Avtolemos says: From where** is it derived **with regard to** a case where there is **a spread** of leprosy **in garments** that culminates with the garment's being completely covered with leprous marks, **that** the garment **is pure,** just as the *halakha* is with regard to a leprous mark that fully covers a person?

נֶאֱמַר "קָרַחַת" וְ"גַבַּחַת" בִּבְגָדִים, וְנֶאֱמַר "קָרַחַת" וְ"גַבַּחַת" בְּאָדָם,

It is derived via a verbal analogy: **A bareness within** [*karaḥat*] **and a bareness without** [*gabbaḥat*] **are stated with regard to** leprosy of **garments:** "And the priest shall look, after that the mark is washed; and, behold, if the mark has not changed its color, and the mark has not spread, it is impure; you shall burn it in the fire; it is a fret, whether the bareness be within or without" (Leviticus 13:55); **and a bald head** [*karaḥat*] **and a bald forehead** [*gabbaḥat*] **are stated with regard to** leprosy of **a person:** "But if there is in the bald head, or the bald forehead, a reddish-white mark, it is leprosy breaking out in his bald head, or his bald forehead" (Leviticus 13:42).

### LANGUAGE

**Dull** [*keha*] – **כֵּהָה:** Rashi cites a version that reads *keha* with the letter *kuf* instead of *kaf*. This term may indicate that Rabbi Yehoshua doubted the matter or was uncomfortable with it. Since the meaning of this term was unclear, it was necessary for Rabba to explain that Rabbi Yehoshua's ruling was that the leprous mark is pure.

**Avtolemos – אַבְטוּלְמוֹס:** Some say that this name is from the Greek εὔτολμος, *eutolmos*, meaning brave or a mighty warrior.

### BACKGROUND

**Split bean** [*geris*] – **גְּרִיס:** A *geris* is a broken grain or bean. When a bean or a grain is broken in half, its inner surface is flat and convenient for use in measuring. The Sages defined the bean mentioned here with regard to the leprous mark as the split bean (*Kelim* 17:12), now known as the broad bean or fava bean. The area of this bean, which is considered particularly great, is equal to a square made up of nine lentils, i.e., three lentils by three lentils, which is the same as six barley grains by six barley grains (*Nega'im* 6:1). In the Jerusalem Talmud (*Ma'asrot* 5:3), Rabban Shimon ben Gamliel is cited as saying that this bean was square shaped.

### HALAKHA

**A house is never deemed impure, etc. – לְעוֹלָם אֵין הַבַּיִת טָמֵא וכו׳:** For a house to have the potential to become impure with leprosy it must contain at least eight stones, two for each wall. The reason is that a house is rendered impure only if the leprous mark is the size of two split beans, on two stones, as indicated by the plural form in the verse: "The stones in which the leprous mark is" (Leviticus 14:40). If the leprous mark is smaller the house is not impure (Rambam *Sefer Tahara*, *Hilkhot Tumat Tzara'at* 14:7).

**BACKGROUND**

Blackens only when it is removed from the body – כְּשֶׁנֶּעֱקַר הוּא מַשְׁחִיר: When blood is inside the body it does not receive enough oxygen to oxidize its hemoglobin. Once the blood flows from the body, the oxygen in the air oxidizes the iron in the hemoglobin, causing the blood to blacken.

מַה לְּהַלָּן – פָּרַח בְּכוּלּוֹ טָהוֹר, אַף כָּאן נַמִי – פָּרַח בְּכוּלּוֹ טָהוֹר.

**Just as there,** with regard to a person, if the leprosy **spread to his entire** body he is **pure,** as the verse states: "Then the priest shall look; and behold, if the leprosy has covered all his flesh, he shall pronounce pure the one who has the leprous mark; it is all turned white: He is pure" (Leviticus 13:13), **so too here,** with regard to garments, if the leprosy **spread to the entire** garment[H] it is **pure.**

אֶלָּא הָכָא, אִי דָּם טָהוֹר לֵיכָּא, בְּמַאי פְּלִיגִי?

The Gemara concludes: **But here,** concerning the phrase "between blood and blood," **if there is no** type of **pure blood** at all, **with regard to what** issue could the rebellious elder **disagree** with the Sanhedrin? It must be that this verse is alluding to the fact that there is a type of blood of a woman that is pure.

וּמִמַּאי דְּהָנֵי טְהוֹרִין וְהָנֵי טְמֵאִין? אָמַר רַבִּי אַבָּהוּ, דְּאָמַר קְרָא: ״וַיִּרְאוּ מוֹאָב אֶת הַמַּיִם אֲדֻמִּים כַּדָּם״. לְמֵימְרָא דְּדָם אָדוֹם הוּא, אֵימָא אָדוֹם וְתוּ לָא!

§ Once it has been established that there are types of blood that are pure and other types that are impure, the Gemara asks: **And from where** is it derived **that those** types of blood that are not listed in the mishna are **pure, and these** ones that are mentioned in the mishna are **impure? Rabbi Abbahu said that the verse states:** "And the sun shone upon the water, **and the Moabites saw the water** some way off **as red as blood"** (II Kings 3:22), which indicates that blood is red. The Gemara asks: **Is this to say that blood is red?** If so, one can **say** that only blood that is **red** like the blood of a wound is ritually impure, **and no more** colors of blood are impure.

אָמַר רַבִּי אַבָּהוּ: אָמַר קְרָא ״דָּמֶיהָ״ ״דָּמֶיהָ״ – הֲרֵי כָּאן אַרְבָּעָה.

**Rabbi Abbahu said** in response: **The verse states,** with regard to a menstruating woman: "And she shall be purified from the source of **her blood** [*dameha*]" (Leviticus 12:7). The plural form of the word blood, *dameha,* indicates at least two types of blood. And another verse states: "And if a man shall lie with a woman having her sickness, and shall uncover her nakedness, he has made naked her source, and she has uncovered the source of **her blood** [*dameha*]; both of them shall be cut off from among their people" (Leviticus 20:18). The use of the plural form of blood once again indicates another two types, which means that **there are four** types of blood stated **here.**

וְהָא אֲנַן ״חֲמִשָּׁה״ תְּנַן! אָמַר רַבִּי חֲנִינָא: שָׁחוֹר – אָדוֹם הוּא, אֶלָּא שֶׁלָּקָה.

The Gemara asks: **But didn't we learn** in the mishna that there are **five** types of impure blood in a woman, whereas the verses indicate that there are only four? **Rabbi Ḥanina says:** The **black** blood mentioned in the mishna **is** actually **red, but** its color **has faded,** which is why it looks black. Therefore, although the mishna lists five kinds of blood, there are only four basic types.

תַּנְיָא נַמִי הָכִי: שָׁחוֹר – כְּחֶרֶת, עָמוֹק מִכֵּן – טָמֵא, דֵּיהָה אֲפִילּוּ כְּכָחוֹל – טָהוֹר. וְשָׁחוֹר זֶה, לֹא מִתְּחִלָּתוֹ הוּא מַשְׁחִיר, אֶלָּא כְּשֶׁנֶּעֱקַר הוּא מַשְׁחִיר, מָשָׁל לְדַם מַכָּה – לִכְשֶׁנֶּעֱקַר הוּא מַשְׁחִיר.

**This** opinion, that black blood is actually red blood, **is also taught** in a *baraita*: The **black** color of blood that is impure is blood as black **as** ***ḥeret.*** If the black is **deeper than that,** the blood is **ritually impure;** if the black is **lighter** than that, **even** if it is still as dark **as blue,** the blood is **ritually pure. And this black** blood **does not blacken from its outset,** when it is inside the body; **rather, it blackens** only **when it is removed** from the body.[B] This is **comparable to the blood of a wound,** which is initially red, but **when it is removed** from the body **it blackens.**

״בֵּית שַׁמַּאי אוֹמְרִים: אַף כְּמֵימֵי תִלְתָּן״. וְלֵית לְהוּ לְבֵית שַׁמַּאי ״דָּמֶיהָ״ ״דָּמֶיהָ״ הֲרֵי כָּאן אַרְבָּעָה?

§ The mishna states that **Beit Shammai say: Even** blood **like the water** in which **a fenugreek** plant is soaked, and like the liquid that drips from roast meat, are ritually impure. The Gemara asks: **But do Beit Shammai not accept** the exposition of Rabbi Abbahu that the two mentions of the plural form of blood: **"*Dameha*"** (Leviticus 12:7), and **"*Dameha*"** (Leviticus 20:18), indicate that **there are four** types of blood **here?**

**HALAKHA**

If the leprosy spread to the entire garment – פָּרַח בְּכוּלּוֹ: If a garment was quarantined by a priest due to a possible leprous mark, and the mark spread throughout the entire garment, which turned greenish or reddish, the garment is pure. If it spread throughout the entire garment after he washed the garment, the garment must be burned. The *halakha* is in accordance with the opinion of Rabbi Yonatan ben Avtolemos (Rambam *Sefer Tahara, Hilkhot Tumat Tzara'at* 12:8).

איבָּעֵית אֵימָא: לֵית לְהוּ. וְאִיבָּעֵית אֵימָא: אִית לְהוּ, מִי לָא אָמַר רַבִּי חֲנִינָא שָׁחוֹר – אָדוֹם הוּא, אֶלָּא שֶׁלָּקָה, הָכִי נַמִי – מִלְקָא הוּא דְּלָקֵי.

The Gemara answers: **If you wish, say** that Beit Shammai **do not accept** this opinion of Rabbi Abbahu, and they maintain that there are more than four types of blood in a woman. **And if you wish, say** instead that Beit Shammai **do accept** Rabbi Abbahu's exposition, and the apparent contradiction can be resolved as follows: **Didn't Rabbi Ḥanina say** with regard to the **black** blood mentioned in the mishna that it is not an additional type, as it **is** actually **red but** its color **has faded? So too,** with regard to the colors of blood mentioned by Beit Shammai, that of water in which a fenugreek plant is soaked, and that of the liquid that drips from roast meat, one can say that these are not additional types of blood. Rather, they too were initially red but their color **faded.**

"וּבֵית הִלֵּל מְטַהֲרִין". הַיְינוּ תַּנָּא קַמָּא!

§ The mishna states: **And Beit Hillel deem** blood of those colors, i.e., the color of water in which a fenugreek plant is soaked or of the liquid that drips from roast meat, **ritually pure.** The Gemara asks: **Isn't this** opinion of Beit Hillel identical to the opinion of **the first *tanna*?**

אִיכָּא בֵּינַיְיהוּ

The Gemara explains: **There is** a practical difference **between them**

Perek **II**
Daf **19** Amud **b**

לְתְלוֹת.

with regard to whether **to leave in abeyance,** i.e., to treat as uncertain, blood the color of water in which a fenugreek plant is soaked, or the color of the liquid that drips from roast meat. According to the first *tanna* of the mishna there are five types of blood that are definitely impure, whereas other types, such as those mentioned by Beit Shammai, are deemed impure due to uncertainty. By contrast, Beit Hillel maintain that blood of these colors is entirely pure.

הַיָּרוֹק עֲקַבְיָא בֶּן מַהֲלַלְאֵל מְטַמֵּא. וְלֵית לֵיהּ לַעֲקַבְיָא "דָּמֶיהָ" "דָּמֶיהָ" הֲרֵי כָּאן אַרְבָּעָה?

§ The mishna states: Blood that is **green, Akavya ben Mahalalel deems** it **impure.**[N] The Gemara asks: **But does Akavya** ben Mahalalel **not accept** the exposition of Rabbi Abbahu that the two verses: ***"Dameha"*** (Leviticus 12:7), and: ***"Dameha"*** (Leviticus 20:18), indicate that **there are four** types of blood **here?**

אִיבָּעֵית אֵימָא: לֵית לֵיהּ, וְאִיבָּעֵית אֵימָא: אִית לֵיהּ, מִי לָא אָמַר רַבִּי חֲנִינָא שָׁחוֹר – אָדוֹם הוּא אֶלָּא שֶׁלָּקָה, הָכָא נַמִי – מִלְקָא הוּא דְּלָקֵי.

The Gemara answers: **If you wish, say** that Akavya ben Mahalalel **does not accept** this opinion of Rabbi Abbahu, as he maintains that there are more than four types of blood in a woman. **And if you wish, say** instead that Akavya ben Mahalalel **accepts** Rabbi Abbahu's exposition, and the apparent contradiction can be resolved as follows: **Didn't Rabbi Ḥanina say,** with regard to the **black** blood mentioned in the mishna, that it **is** actually **red but** its color **has faded? Here too,** with regard to the green mentioned by Akavya ben Mahalalel, one can say that it was initially red but its color **faded**[N] and turned green.

"וַחֲכָמִים מְטַהֲרִין". הַיְינוּ תַּנָּא קַמָּא! אִיכָּא בֵּינַיְיהוּ לְתְלוֹת.

§ The mishna states with regard to blood that is green: **And the Rabbis deem** it **pure.** The Gemara asks: **Isn't this** opinion of the Rabbis identical to the opinion of **the first *tanna*?** The Gemara answers: **There is** a practical difference **between them** with regard to whether **to leave in abeyance** blood that is green. According to the first *tanna* of the mishna there are five types of blood that are definitely impure, whereas other types, such as green, are impure due to uncertainty. By contrast, the Rabbis maintain that green blood is entirely pure.

"אָמַר רַבִּי מֵאִיר: אִם אֵינוֹ מְטַמֵּא מִשּׁוּם כֶּתֶם" כו'.

§ The mishna states that **Rabbi Meir said:** Even **if** the green blood **does not transmit impurity due to** the *halakhot* of a blood **stain** or the blood of a menstruating woman, it is blood in that it renders food susceptible to ritual impurity due to its status as one of the seven liquids that render food susceptible.

**NOTES**

**Blood that is green Akavya ben Mahalalel deems it impure – הַיָּרוֹק עֲקַבְיָא בֶּן מַהֲלַלְאֵל מְטַמֵּא:** Some early commentaries cite the opinion of Akavya ben Mahalalel as proof that the green discussed here is similar in color to the *etrog* fruit, i.e., yellow with a reddish tinge, rather than the color of a leek. Their reasoning is that it is unlikely that Akavya ben Mahalalel would deem impure even blood of a shade of green that has no reddish tinge at all (*Tosafot*).

**Here too it faded – הָכָא נַמִי מִלְקָא הוּא דְּלָקֵי:** According to this answer, Rabbi Ḥanina's statement that the color of deteriorated blood can change applies also to a change from red to green. Some commentaries differentiate between various shades of red in this regard, claiming that when there is a deterioration of blood that was like the bright color of the crocus flower, it will turn green (Rambam's Commentary on the Mishna).

אָמַר רַבִּי יוֹחָנָן: יָרַד רַבִּי מֵאִיר לְשִׁיטַת עֲקַבְיָא בֶּן מַהֲלַלְאֵל, וְטִימֵּא. וְהָכִי קָאָמַר לְהוּ לְרַבָּנַן: נְהִי דְּהֵיכָא דְּקָא מַשְׁכַּחַת כֶּתֶם יָרוֹק אַמָּנָא לָא מְטַמְּאִיתוּ, הֵיכָא דְּקָחָזְיָא דָּם יָרוֹק מִגּוּפָהּ – תִּטַּמֵּא.

**Rabbi Yoḥanan says: Rabbi Meir accepted the opinion of Akavya ben Mahalalel and deemed** green blood **impure** as blood of a menstruating woman. **And** as for his statement in the mishna, **this** is what Rabbi Meir **was saying to the Rabbis: Granted that** in a case **where** a woman **finds a green stain on** an article of **clothing you do not deem** her **ritually impure,** as its greenness is an indication that it did not come from her body. But in a case **where she** actually **sees green blood** come **from her body, she shall be impure.**

אִי הָכִי, "אִם אֵינוֹ מְטַמֵּא מִשּׁוּם כֶּתֶם, מְטַמֵּא מִשּׁוּם מַשְׁקֶה", "מִשּׁוּם רוֹאָה" מִבָּעְיָא לֵיהּ!

The Gemara raises a difficulty with this interpretation: **If so,** why did Rabbi Meir say: Even **if it does not transmit impurity due to** the *halakhot* of a blood **stain, it renders** food susceptible to **ritual impurity due to** its status as **a liquid?** According to the above explanation, he **should have** said: If the woman **saw** the emission of this blood, she is impure **as** a menstruating woman.

אֶלָּא הָכִי קָאָמַר לְהוּ: נְהִי הֵיכָא דְּקָא חַזְיָא דָּם יָרוֹק מֵעִיקָּרָא לָא מְטַמְּאִיתוּ, הֵיכָא דְּחָזְיָא דָּם אָדוֹם וַהֲדַר חַזְיָא דָּם יָרוֹק – תִּטַּמֵּא, מִידֵּי דַּהֲוָה אַמַּשְׁקֵה זָב וְזָבָה.

**Rather, this** is what Rabbi Meir **was saying to** the Rabbis: **Granted** that in a case **where** the woman **sees green blood from the outset you do not deem** her **ritually impure,** but in a case **where she sees red blood and then sees green blood, she shall be impure.** This is **just as it is with regard to** the *halakha* of **the fluids of a man who experiences a gonorrhea-like discharge** [*zav*] **and a woman who experiences a discharge of uterine blood after her menstrual period** [*zava*]. All fluids emitted by a *zav* or *zava*, such as saliva and urine, are impure. Likewise, green blood that is emitted by this woman who has already emitted red blood should be impure.

וְרַבָּנַן – דּוּמְיָא דְּרוֹק, מָה רוֹק שֶׁמִּתְעַגֵּל וְיוֹצֵא, אַף כָּל שֶׁמִּתְעַגֵּל וְיוֹצֵא, לְאַפּוּקֵי הַאי – דְּאֵין מִתְעַגֵּל וְיוֹצֵא. אִי הָכִי – שַׁפִּיר קָאָמְרִי לֵיהּ רַבָּנַן לְרַבִּי מֵאִיר!

The Gemara asks: **And** how would **the Rabbis** respond to this? The Gemara answers: They maintain that the impure fluids of a menstruating woman are only those that are **similar to saliva: Just as** when **saliva** leaves one's mouth it **is** first **gathered** together **and** then **expelled**[H] from the body, **so too, all** impure fluids are those that are **gathered** together **and** then **expelled.** This definition serves **to exclude this** green blood, **which is not gathered** together **and expelled.** The Gemara asks: **If so, the Rabbis spoke well to Rabbi Meir,** i.e., their answer is convincing. Why does Rabbi Meir deem green blood impure?

אֶלָּא הָכִי קָאָמַר לְהוּ: לֶהֱוֵי כְּמַשְׁקֶה לְהַכְשִׁיר אֶת הַזְּרָעִים. וְרַבָּנַן – בָּעֵי "דַּם חֲלָלִים" וְלֵיכָּא. אִי הָכִי, שַׁפִּיר קָאָמְרִי לֵיהּ רַבָּנַן לְרַבִּי מֵאִיר!

**Rather, this** is what Rabbi Meir **was saying to** the Rabbis: **Let** green blood **be** at least **like** one of the seven **liquids that render seeds** upon which they fall **susceptible** to ritual impurity. Why is green blood deemed pure even with regard to this matter? **And the Rabbis** disagree because they **require** that every type of blood that renders food susceptible to ritual impurity be like that mentioned in the verse: "And drink **the blood of the slain**" (Numbers 23:24), i.e., the blood that flows at the time of death; **and** green blood is **not** the type that flows at the time of death. Therefore, it does not render food susceptible to ritual impurity. The Gemara again asks: **If so, the Rabbis spoke well to Rabbi Meir.** Why does he disagree with them?

אֶלָּא הָכִי קָאָמַר לְהוּ – אַלְפוּהָ בִּגְזֵירָה שָׁוָה, כְּתִיב הָכָא: "שְׁלָחַיִךְ פַּרְדֵּס רִמּוֹנִים" וּכְתִיב הָתָם: "וְשֹׁלֵחַ מַיִם עַל פְּנֵי חוּצוֹת".

**Rather, this** is what Rabbi Meir **was saying to** the Rabbis: **Learn** this *halakha* that green blood renders food susceptible to ritual impurity **from** the following **verbal analogy: It is written here,** in a description of the beloved woman that alludes to her menstrual blood: "**Your shoots** [*shelaḥayikh*] **are an orchard of pomegranates**" (Song of Songs 4:13), **and it is written there:** "Who gives rain upon the earth, **and sends** [*veshole'aḥ*] **waters upon the fields**" (Job 5:10). This verbal analogy indicates that menstrual blood is similar to water in that both render food susceptible to ritual impurity.

**HALAKHA**

**Just as saliva is first gathered together and then expelled, etc.** – מָה רוֹק שֶׁמִּתְעַגֵּל וְיוֹצֵא וכו׳: If a woman saw green blood, it is pure. It is not considered like her saliva or her other impure fluids, as saliva is gathered together before it is expelled, whereas this green blood flows from her body (Rambam *Sefer Tahara*, *Hilkhot Metamei Mishkav UMoshav* 1:8).

וְרַבָּנַן – אָדָם דָּן קַל וָחוֹמֶר מֵעַצְמוֹ, וְאֵין אָדָם דָּן גְּזֵרָה שָׁוָה מֵעַצְמוֹ.

**And the Rabbis** disagree with Rabbi Meir, as they do not have a tradition that this is an accepted verbal analogy, and there is a principle that although **a person may derive an *a fortiori*** inference **on his own,** i.e., even though he was not taught that particular logical argument by his teachers, **a person may not derive a verbal analogy on his own,**[N] but only if he received it by tradition.

״רַבִּי יוֹסֵי אוֹמֵר לֹא כָּךְ״ וכו׳. הַיְינוּ תַּנָּא קַמָּא! הָא קָא מַשְׁמַע לָן: מַאן תַּנָּא קַמָּא – רַבִּי יוֹסֵי, וְכָל הָאוֹמֵר דָּבָר בְּשֵׁם אוֹמְרוֹ מֵבִיא גְאוּלָּה לָעוֹלָם.

§ The mishna states that **Rabbi Yosei says: Neither** in **this** sense, as the blood of a menstruating woman according to Akavya ben Mahalalel, nor in that sense, as a liquid that renders food susceptible according to Rabbi Meir, is green blood considered blood. The Gemara raises a difficulty: **Isn't this** the same as the opinion of **the first *tanna*?** The Gemara answers that **this** is what the mishna **is teaching us: Who is the first *tanna*?** **Rabbi Yosei. And** the reason Rabbi Yosei's name is mentioned is due to the principle that **anyone who reports a statement in the name of the one who said it brings redemption to the world.**

״אֵיזֶהוּ אָדוֹם כְּדַם הַמַּכָּה״. מַאי ״כְּדַם הַמַּכָּה״? אָמַר רַב יְהוּדָה, אָמַר שְׁמוּאֵל: כְּדַם שׁוֹר שָׁחוּט.

§ The mishna states: **What is** the **red** color of blood that is impure? It is as red **as the blood** that flows from **a wound.**[N] The Gemara asks: **What** is the meaning of the phrase: **As the blood** that flows from **a wound? Rav Yehuda says** that **Shmuel says: Like the blood of a slaughtered ox.**

וְלֵימָא: כְּדַם שְׁחִיטָה! אִי אָמַר כְּדַם שְׁחִיטָה – הֲוָה אָמֵינָא כְּכוּלָּהּ שְׁחִיטָה, קָא מַשְׁמַע לָן כְּדַם הַמַּכָּה – כִּתְחִילַּת הַכָּאָה שֶׁל סַכִּין.

The Gemara inquires: **But** if so, **let** the *tanna* of the mishna **say** explicitly that it is as red **as the blood of slaughter.** The Gemara explains: **If** the *tanna* had **said** that it is as red **as the blood of slaughter, I would say** that it means as red **as** the blood that flows throughout **the entire slaughter,** and it would apply to the shades of all blood emitted during the process. Therefore, the *tanna* **teaches us** that it is as red **as the blood** that flows from **a wound,** i.e., **as** the blood that flows at **the beginning of the slitting with** the slaughtering **knife.**

עוּלָּא אָמַר: כְּדַם צִפּוֹר חַיָּה. אִיבַּעְיָא לְהוּ: חַיָּה – לְאַפּוֹקֵי שָׁחוּט, אוֹ דִלְמָא לְאַפּוֹקֵי כָּחוּשׁ? תֵּיקוּ.

The Gemara cites other definitions of the color described in the mishna as: Red as the blood that flows from a wound. **Ulla says:** It is red **like the blood** that flows from **a living bird** that was wounded. **A dilemma was raised before** the Sages: When Ulla specified that the bird is **living,** did he mean that it was not dead, **to exclude** the blood of **a slaughtered** bird? **Or perhaps** he meant that the bird was healthy, **to exclude** the blood of **a weak** bird. No answer was found, and therefore the Gemara concludes that the dilemma **shall stand** unresolved.

זְעֵירִי, אָמַר רַבִּי חֲנִינָא: כְּדַם מַאֲכוֹלֶת שֶׁל רֹאשׁ. מֵיתִיבִי: הָרְגָה מַאֲכוֹלֶת – הֲרֵי זֶה תּוֹלָה בָּהּ, מַאי לָאו – דְּכוּלֵּיהּ גּוּפָהּ! לָא, דְּרֹאשָׁהּ.

The Gemara cites another definition: **Ze'eiri** says that **Rabbi Ḥanina says:** It is red **like the blood** that comes from a squashed **head louse.** The Gemara **raises an objection** from a mishna that discusses a stain found on a woman's garment (58b): If a woman **killed a louse**[H] and subsequently found a blood stain on her garment or body, **this** woman **may attribute** the stain **to** that louse, and she remains pure. The Gemara explains the objection: **What, is it not** correct to say that this is referring to a louse **from all** parts of **her body,** not just the head, as claimed by Rabbi Ḥanina? If so, the color of impure blood is like the color of the blood of a louse from anywhere on the body. The Gemara answers: **No;** this *halakha* is referring specifically to a louse that was **on her head.**

**HALAKHA**

**If a woman killed a louse – הָרְגָה מַאֲכוֹלֶת:** If a woman killed an insect and subsequently found a blood stain on her clothing or body, she may attribute a stain up to the size of a lupine to that creature. The *halakha* is in accordance with the ruling of the *baraita* (Rambam *Sefer Kedusha, Hilkhot Issurei Bia* 9:23; *Shulḥan Arukh, Yoreh De'a* 190:7, and see 190:26).

**NOTES**

**A person may not derive a verbal analogy on his own – אֵין אָדָם דָּן גְּזֵרָה שָׁוָה מֵעַצְמוֹ:** The verbal analogy is one of the hermeneutical principles of the Torah and is included in all the lists of these principles, e.g., the seven principles of Hillel the Elder, the thirteen principles of Rabbi Yishmael, and the thirty-two principles of Rabbi Elazar, son of Rabbi Yosei HaGelili. A verbal analogy may be drawn only if a Sage received it as a tradition from his teachers that was passed down from one generation to another as a *halakha* transmitted to Moses from Sinai (Rashi; see Rashi on *Sukka* 11b).

**As the blood that flows from a wound – כְּדַם הַמַּכָּה:** The early commentaries explain that these *amora'im* who offer various descriptions of this blood are not in dispute. Rather, each was familiar with a particular appearance of blood, all of which are included in the category of blood that is red as the blood that flows from a wound (Ramban; Rashba; Ritva). The Rambam cites one definition alone, that of Rav Naḥman (*Sefer Kedusha, Hilkhot Issurei Bia* 5:8, 11).

PERSONALITIES

Ami of Vardina – אַמִי וַרְדִּינָאָה: Ami of Vardina, from the third generation of *amora'im* in Eretz Yisrael, is mentioned in several places in the Talmud. He taught in the household of the *Nasi*. According to Rashi, he is also known as Ami the Handsome [*Shefir Na'eh*], which is possibly a translation of Vardina or an analogous name. Others say that the name alludes to the idea that he was as beautiful as a rose [*vered*].

HALAKHA

She may attribute a blood stain she finds on her garment to her son or to her husband – תּוֹלָה בִּבְנָהּ וּבְבַעְלָהּ: If a woman's son or husband had been in contact with blood stains or had suffered an injury, she may attribute a blood stain on her clothing to them. But if there were no stains on their persons, she may not attribute her stain to them, unless their activity was such that the blood would have sprayed, e.g., the act of slaughter (Rambam *Sefer Kedusha, Hilkhot Issurei Bia* 9:24; *Shulḥan Arukh, Yoreh De'a* 190:19).

אַמִי וַרְדִּינָאָה, אָמַר רַבִּי אַבָּהוּ: כְּדַם אֶצְבַּע קְטַנָּה שֶׁל יָד, שֶׁנִּגְּפָה וְחָיְיתָה וְחָזְרָה וְנִגְּפָה, וְלֹא שֶׁל כׇּל אָדָם אֶלָּא שֶׁל בָּחוּר שֶׁלֹּא נָשָׂא אִשָּׁה. וְעַד כַּמָּה? עַד בֶּן עֶשְׂרִים.

The Gemara cites yet another definition of the color described in the mishna as: Red as the blood that flows from a wound. The Sage **Ami of Vardina**[P] says that **Rabbi Abbahu says:** It is red **as the blood** that flows from the **smallest finger of** the **hand, which was wounded and** later **healed and was** subsequently **wounded again. And** this is **not** referring to the finger **of any person, but** specifically to the finger **of a young man who has not** yet **married a woman. And** furthermore, this does not mean any young man; rather, **until what** age must he be? **Until twenty** years **old.**

מֵיתִיבִי: תּוֹלָה בִּבְנָהּ וּבְבַעְלָהּ, בִּשְׁלָמָא בִּבְנָהּ – מַשְׁכַּחַתְּ לַהּ, אֶלָּא בַּעְלָהּ – הֵיכִי מַשְׁכַּחַתְּ לַהּ?

The Gemara **raises an objection** from the aforementioned mishna (58b): If the woman's husband or son suffered an injury, **she may attribute** a blood stain she finds on her garment **to her son or to her husband,**[H] and she remains pure. The Gemara analyzes this *halakha*: **Granted, with regard to** the ruling that she may attribute it to **her son, you can find** a case where this meets all the requirements specified by Rabbi Abbahu, i.e., he could be younger than twenty and unmarried. **But** with regard to the ruling that she may attribute it to **her husband, how can you find** a case where her husband is unmarried?

אָמַר רַב נַחְמָן בַּר יִצְחָק: כְּגוֹן שֶׁנִּכְנְסָה לַחוּפָּה וְלֹא נִבְעֲלָה.

**Rav Naḥman bar Yitzḥak says:** It is possible in a case **where** this woman **entered the** marriage **canopy but has not** yet **engaged in intercourse** with her husband. In such a situation, although he is her husband he is physically akin to an unmarried young man. Therefore, she can attribute the blood stain to his wound.

רַב נַחְמָן אָמַר: כְּדַם הַקָּזָה. מֵיתִיבִי: מַעֲשֶׂה וְתָלָה רַבִּי מֵאִיר

**Rav Naḥman says:** This red is **like the blood** spilled in the process **of bloodletting.** The Gemara **raises an objection** from a *baraita*: **An incident** occurred involving a blood stain found on a woman's garment, **and Rabbi Meir attributed**

Perek **II**
Daf **20** Amud **a**

LANGUAGE

Eye salve [*kilor*] – קִילוֹר: From the Greek κολλύριον, *kollurion*, meaning a salve for the eyes.

בְּקִילוֹר, וְרַבִּי תָּלָה בְּשְׂרַף שִׁקְמָה. מַאי לָאו – אָדוֹם?

it **to an eye salve** [*bekilor*],[L] which the woman had previously handled. **And** likewise, **Rabbi** Yehuda HaNasi **attributed** a stain **to the sap of a sycamore**[B] tree the woman had touched. The Gemara explains the objection: **What, is it not** the case that Rabbi Meir and Rabbi Yehuda HaNasi attributed red bloodstains **to** these causes because they are **red,** albeit not as red as blood? Evidently, the color of impure blood can be similar to such shades of red as well, which means that all these distinctions mentioned by the *amora'im* above are irrelevant.

לָא, אַשְּׁאָר דָּמִים.

The Gemara answers: **No;** Rabbi Meir and Rabbi Yehuda HaNasi attributed stains **to** an eye salve and the sap of a sycamore tree because those stains were like the **other** types of **blood** mentioned in the mishna.

BACKGROUND

Sycamore – שִׁקְמָה: The sycamore, *Ficus sycomorus* L., is a tall, wide tree similar to a fig tree. Although it is possible to eat the fruits of a sycamore tree, it is usually grown for its wood, as the trunk is wide, large, and relatively light. Typically, a sycamore is left to grow until it reaches a significant size, at which point it is chopped down. The remaining part of the tree grows again, and it is chopped down every few years. Sycamore trees thrive in heat and grow primarily in plains, not in mountainous regions.

אַמֵימָר וּמָר זוּטְרָא וְרַב אַשִׁי הָווּ יָתְבִי קַמֵּיהּ אוּמָּנָא, שָׁקְלִי לֵיהּ קַרְנָא קַמַּיְיתָא לְאַמֵימָר, חַזְיֵיהּ, אֲמַר לְהוּ: אָדוֹם דִּתְנַן – כִּי הַאי. שָׁקְלִי לֵיהּ אַחֲרִיתֵי, אֲמַר לְהוּ: אִשְׁתַּנִּי. אֲמַר רַב אַשִׁי: כְּגוֹן אֲנָא, דְּלָא יָדַעְנָא בֵּין הַאי לְהַאי – לָא מִבָּעֵי לִי לְמֶחֱזֵי דָּמָא.

The Gemara relates that **Ameimar and Mar Zutra and Rav Ashi were sitting before a bloodletter,**[B] to receive treatment. The bloodletter **removed** blood in a bloodletter's **horn**[B] **from Ameimar** for his **first** treatment. Ameimar **saw** the blood and **said to** his colleagues: The **red** color **that we learned** about in the mishna is **like this** blood in the horn. The bloodletter again **removed** blood from Ameimar, this time using **another** horn. Upon seeing the blood in this horn, Ameimar **said to them:** The color of this blood **has changed** compared to the blood in the first horn. **Rav Ashi,** who saw both types of blood, **said:** Any Sage **such as myself, as I do not know** how to distinguish **between this** blood **and that** blood, **should not see,** i.e., examine, different types of **blood** to issue a ruling as to whether they are pure or impure.

"שָׁחוֹר כְּחֶרֶת". אָמַר רַבָּה בַּר רַב הוּנָא: חֶרֶת שֶׁאָמְרוּ – דְּיוֹ. תַּנְיָא נַמִי הָכִי: שָׁחוֹר – כְּחֶרֶת, וְשָׁחוֹר שֶׁאָמְרוּ – דְּיוֹ. וְלֵימָא דְּיוֹ! אִי אָמַר דְּיוֹ – הֲוָה אָמִינָא: כִּי פַּכְחוּתָא דִּדְיוֹתָא, קָא מַשְׁמַע לָן – כִּי חָרוּתָא דִּדְיוֹתָא.

§ The mishna teaches: What is the **black** color that is impure? It is blood as black **as** ***ḥeret.*** **Rabba bar Rav Huna says:** This ***ḥeret*** **of which** the Sages **spoke is ink.**[BH] The Gemara notes that **this** opinion **is also taught** in a *baraita*: This **black** color is **like** ***ḥeret,*** **and the black of which** the Sages **spoke is ink.** The Gemara asks: **But** if so, why does the *tanna* of this *baraita* mention both terms? **Let him say** simply: **Ink.** The Gemara explains: **If** the *tanna* had **said** only: **Ink, I would say** that he means that it is **like the clear part of the ink,** i.e., the upper portion of ink in an inkwell, which is very bright. Therefore, the *tanna* of the *baraita* **teaches us** that it is **like the blackness** [*ḥaruta*] **of the ink,** the lower part of the inkwell, which is darker.

אִיבַּעְיָא לְהוּ: בְּלַחָה אוֹ בִּיבֵשְׁתָּא? תָּא שְׁמַע: דְּרַבִּי אַמִי פָּלֵי קוֹרְטָא דִּדְיוֹתָא וּבָדֵיק בָּהּ.

**A dilemma was raised before** the Sages: To which type of *ḥeret* were the Sages referring? Were they referring **to moist or dry** *ḥeret*? **Come** and **hear** a resolution from a practical ruling, **as** when black blood was brought before **Rabbi Ami** he would **break up pieces of** dried **ink and examine** blood **with it.**

אָמַר רַב יְהוּדָה, אָמַר שְׁמוּאֵל: כְּקִיר, כִּדְיוֹ, וּכְעֵנָב – טְמֵאָה, וְזוֹהִי שֶׁשָּׁנִינוּ "עָמוֹק מִכֵּן – טְמֵאָה". אָמַר רַבִּי אֶלְעָזָר: כְּזַיִת, כְּזֶפֶת, וּכְעוֹרֵב – טָהוֹר, וְזוֹהִי שֶׁשָּׁנִינוּ "דֵּיהָה מִכֵּן – טָהוֹר".

§ The mishna states that if the blackness of the blood is deeper than ink, it is impure, whereas if it is lighter it is pure. In this regard, **Rav Yehuda says** that **Shmuel says:** If a woman saw blood whose color was **like** black **wax** [***kekir***][L] or **like** black **ink**[N] **or like** a black **grape, she is ritually impure. And this is** the meaning of **that which we learned** in the mishna: If the black is **deeper than that,** it is **ritually impure. Rabbi Elazar says:** If a woman saw blood whose color was **like** a black **olive,** or **like** black **tar,**[BH] **or like** a black **raven,**[B] this blood is **pure. And this is** the meaning of that **which we learned** in the mishna: If the black is **lighter than that,** it is **ritually pure.**

## NOTES

**Like black ink** – **כִּדְיוֹ:** The commentaries are puzzled by this statement of Rav Yehuda citing Shmuel, as a *baraita* quoted earlier says the black mentioned in the mishna is like ink, whereas here Rav Yehuda says that ink is blacker than that. They explain that there is a difference between fresh ink, which is what the black referred to in the mishna is like, and old ink, which is very black (Rashba).

## HALAKHA

**This** ***ḥeret*** **of which the Sages spoke is ink** – **חֶרֶת שֶׁאָמְרוּ דְּיוֹ:** The black color of blood that the Sages said is impure in the case of a woman is like dried ink, as stated by Rabba bar Rav Huna (Rambam *Sefer Kedusha*, *Hilkhot Issurei Bia* 5:8).

**Like a black olive or like black tar, etc.** – **כְּזַיִת כְּזֶפֶת וכו׳:** If the blood was blacker than dried ink it is impure. If it was less black than that, e.g., it was like a black olive, or tar, or a raven, it is pure. An analogous *halakha* applies to the other colors of impure blood (Rambam *Sefer Kedusha*, *Hilkhot Issurei Bia* 5:9).

## BACKGROUND

**Bloodletter** – **אוּמָּנָא:** This was a quasi-medical profession. Typically a bloodletter performed only the letting of blood, which was considered for many generations a healing treatment for various ailments and a method of ensuring general health. On occasion, a bloodletter would also perform simple surgeries such as circumcision (see, e.g., *Shabbat* 133b).

Bloodletting scene depicted on a Greek earthenware vessel

**Horn** – **קַרְנָא:** According to Rashi, blood was drawn from incisions in the flesh, into a ram's or cow's horn, by creating a vacuum through heating, or by sucking. It is also possible that these horns were used for storing the blood.

**Ink** – **דְּיוֹ:** In the talmudic period, ink was primarily a combination of soot and oil, and various substances were added to it before it was mixed with water. Although it came in different colors, ink was generally black. On most parchment, this ink was erasable and could be blotted out with water. Certain substances, e.g., copper sulfate, were occasionally used to render the ink more permanent.

**Tar** – **זֶפֶת:** In ancient times tar was prepared by slowly burning wood, which would transform into charcoal while releasing various fluids, from which tar and pitch would be made. Tar is the thicker of the two, and its foul odor is due to additional materials found in the fluid. Tar was sometimes made from naturally occurring asphalt.

**Raven [*orev*]** – **עוֹרֵב:** The word *orev* is an umbrella term for a group of birds characterized by their large bodies and powerful cries. This group includes the black *orev*, or raven, all of whose feathers are black. Due to its color, the raven is used in the imagery of items that are thick black, as in the verse: "His locks are curled, and black as a raven" (Song of Songs 5:11).

Black raven

## LANGUAGE

**Wax [*kir*]** – **קִיר:** From the Greek κηρός, *kēros*, or the Latin cera, meaning wax.

עוּלָּא אָמַר: כִּלְבוּשָׁא סִיוָאָה. עוּלָּא אִיקְּלַע לְפוּמְבְּדִיתָא, חַזְיֵיהּ לְהַהוּא טַיָּיעָא דִּלְבוּשׁ לְבוּשָׁא אוּכָּמָא. אֲמַר לְהוּ: ״שָׁחוֹר״ דִּתְנַן – כִּי הַאי. מָרְטוּ מִינֵּיהּ פּוּרְתָּא פּוּרְתָּא, יְהַבוּ בֵּיהּ אַרְבַּע מְאָה זוּזֵי.

**Ulla says:** When the mishna states that black blood is impure, it means **like** the garments of the inhabitants of **Siva'a,** which were extremely black. The Gemara relates that when **Ulla happened** to go **to Pumbedita, he saw a certain Arab** [*tayya'a*][L] **who was dressed in a black garment.** Ulla **said to** the Sages of Pumbedita: The **black** color **that we learned** about in the mishna is **like this** color. Since people wanted a sample of the shade of blood mentioned in the mishna, **they tore** the Arab's garment **from him bit by bit,** and in recompense **they gave him four hundred dinars.**

רַבִּי יוֹחָנָן אָמַר: אֵלּוּ כֵּלִים הָאוֹלְיָירִין הַבָּאִים מִמְּדִינַת הַיָּם. לְמֵימְרָא דְּאוּכָּמֵי נִינְהוּ? וְהָאָמַר לְהוּ רַבִּי יַנַּאי לְבָנָיו: בָּנַי, אַל תִּקְבְּרוּנִי לֹא בְּכֵלִים שְׁחוֹרִים וְלֹא בְּכֵלִים לְבָנִים. שְׁחוֹרִים – שֶׁמָּא אֶזְכֶּה, וְאֶהְיֶה כְּאָבֵל בֵּין הַחֲתָנִים, לְבָנִים – שֶׁמָּא לֹא אֶזְכֶּה, וְאֶהְיֶה כְּחָתָן בֵּין הָאֲבֵלִים, אֶלָּא בְּכֵלִים הָאוֹלְיָירִין הַבָּאִים מִמְּדִינַת הַיָּם.

**Rabbi Yoḥanan says:** The black blood that the mishna says is impure is like **these cloths of the bath attendants** [*haolyarin*][L] **who come from overseas.** The Gemara asks: **Is that to say that these are black** cloths? **But didn't Rabbi Yannai say to his sons: My sons, do not bury me in black cloths nor in white cloths.**[N] Not in **black, lest I be acquitted** in judgment **and I will be** among the righteous **like a mourner among the grooms.** And not in **white, lest I not be acquitted**[N] in judgment **and I will be** among the wicked **like a groom among the mourners. Rather,** bury me **in the cloths of the bath attendants who come from overseas,** which are neither black nor white. **Apparently,** these cloths of the bath attendants **are not black.**

אַלְמָא – לָאו אוּכָּמֵי נִינְהוּ! לָא קַשְׁיָא, הָא – בִּגְלִימָא, הָא – בִּפְתוֹרָא.

The Gemara answers: This is **not difficult,** as a distinction can be made. When Rabbi Yannai indicates that they are not black, **that** is referring **to** a regular **garment,** whereas with regard to the statement of Rabbi Yoḥanan that indicates that they are black, **that** is referring **to** a cloth placed on an item such as **a table** or a bed.

אָמַר רַב יְהוּדָה, אָמַר שְׁמוּאֵל: וְכוּלָּם אֵין בּוֹדְקִין אֶלָּא עַל גַּבֵּי מַטְלִית לְבָנָה. אָמַר רַב יִצְחָק בַּר אֲבוּדִימִי: וְשָׁחוֹר – עַל גַּבֵּי אָדוֹם.

§ With regard to the examination of the five types of blood mentioned in the mishna, **Rav Yehuda says** that **Shmuel says: And** with regard to **all of them,** in their various shades, **one examines them only** when they are placed **on a white** linen **cloth,**[H] as only in this fashion can one properly discern the precise color of the blood. **Rav Yitzḥak bar Avudimi says: And** in the case of **black** blood, one must place it **on a red** linen cloth.

אָמַר רַב יִרְמְיָה מִדִּפְתִּי: וְלָא פְּלִיגִי, הָא – בְּשָׁחוֹר, הָא – בִּשְׁאָר דָּמִים. מַתְקִיף לָהּ רַב אַשִׁי: אִי הָכִי, לֵימָא שְׁמוּאֵל ״חוּץ מִשָּׁחוֹר״! אֶלָּא אָמַר רַב אַשִׁי: בְּשָׁחוֹר גּוּפֵיהּ קָמִיפַּלְגִי.

**Rav Yirmeya of Difti says: And** Shmuel and Rav Yitzḥak bar Avudimi **do not disagree,** as **this** statement of Rav Yitzḥak bar Avudimi is referring specifically **to black** blood, whereas **that** ruling of Shmuel that one must use a white cloth is referring **to the other** four types of **blood** listed in the mishna. **Rav Ashi objects to this** interpretation: **If so, let Shmuel say:** With regard to all of them **except for black,** one examines them only when they are placed on a white linen cloth. **Rather, Rav Ashi says:** Shmuel and Rav Yitzḥak bar Avudimi **disagree with regard to black** blood **itself,** whether it should be examined against the background of a white or a red cloth.

אָמַר עוּלָּא: כּוּלָּן – עָמוֹק מִכָּאן – טָמֵא, דֵּיהָה מִכָּאן – טָהוֹר, כְּשָׁחוֹר.

**Ulla says:** With regard to **all of** these five types of blood enumerated in the mishna, if the color is **deeper than** that which is described in the mishna the blood is **ritually impure;** if it is **lighter than it,** the blood is **ritually pure,**[NH] **as** explicitly stated in the mishna with regard to **black.**

## LANGUAGE

**Arab** [*tayya'a*] – **טַיָּיעָא:** This word is similar to the name of the Arab nomadic tribe طاي, *ṭā'ī*. Apparently, the members of this tribe were so common in the area close to Babylonia at that time that any unidentified Arab was referred to as *tayya'a*.

**Bath attendants** [*olyarin*] – **אוֹלְיָירִין:** The origin of this word and its meaning are unclear. Its root might be from the Latin olearius, which relates to oil. Since the garments of bath attendants were imported from overseas and were not familiar to all, there were disputes with regard to their color. Some commentaries state that the term is from the Greek ὀλερόν, *oleron*, meaning unclean or faded.

## NOTES

**Not…in black cloths nor in white cloths – לֹא בְּכֵלִים שְׁחוֹרִים וְלֹא בְּכֵלִים לְבָנִים:** Although certain Sages, such as Rabbi Yannai here, commanded their descendants not to bury them in white, other Sages, e.g., Rabbi Yoshiya, expressed a desire to be buried specifically in white. This is the practice nowadays as well, and it is the proper custom (Rambam *Sefer Shofetim, Hilkhot Evel* 4:1; *Shulḥan Arukh, Yoreh De'a* 352:2).

**Lest I be acquitted…lest I not be acquitted – שֶׁמָּא אֶזְכֶּה...שֶׁמָּא לֹא אֶזְכֶּה:** Rashi explains that this refers to the judgment with regard to receiving a portion in the World-to-Come. The grooms are the righteous, while the mourners are the wicked in Gehenna.

**With regard to all of these, if it is deeper than that in the mishna it is ritually impure; if it is lighter…it is ritually pure – כּוּלָּן עָמוֹק מִכָּאן טָמֵא דֵּיהָה...טָהוֹר:** The early commentaries explain that although the color that is lighter than red is deeper than the bright color of the crocus flower, and the color that is lighter than the bright color of the crocus flower is deeper than the color of water that inundates red earth, all these intermediate shades are ritually pure. The reason is that it is derived from the verses that there are four types of blood, and the Sages have a tradition that women see only these four types during menstruation, and not in-between shades (*Tosefot HaRosh*).

## HALAKHA

**One examines them only when they are placed on a white linen cloth – אֵין בּוֹדְקִין אֶלָּא עַל גַּבֵּי מַטְלִית לְבָנָה:** One must place the blood on a white linen cloth in order to examine it, as stated by Rav Yehuda, citing Shmuel (Rambam *Sefer Kedusha, Hilkhot Issurei Bia* 5:12).

**If the color is deeper than that which is described in the mishna it is ritually impure; if it is lighter than it, it is ritually pure – עָמוֹק מִכָּאן טָמֵא דֵּיהָה מִכָּאן טָהוֹר:** With regard to the colors of impure blood, if a woman saw blood that was the same or deeper than the shade mentioned in the mishna, the blood is impure. If it was lighter than that, it is pure. How so? If the blood was blacker than dried ink, it is impure. If it was less black than that, e.g., like a black olive, or tar, or a raven, it is pure. An analogous *halakha* applies to the other colors of impure blood, in accordance with the opinion of bar Kappara (Rambam *Sefer Kedusha, Hilkhot Issurei Bia* 5:9).

וְאֶלָּא מַאי שְׁנָא שָׁחוֹר דְּנָקֵט? סָלְקָא דַּעְתָּךְ אָמֵינָא: הוֹאִיל וְאָמַר רַבִּי חֲנִינָא שָׁחוֹר – אָדוֹם הוּא, אֶלָּא שֶׁלָּקָה, הִילְכָּךְ – אֲפִילּוּ דֵּיהֶה מִכֵּן נַמִי לִיטַמֵּא, קָמַשְׁמַע לַן.

The Gemara asks: **But** if so, **what is different** about **black, that** the mishna **mentions** this *halakha* only with regard to that color? The Gemara answers: The reason is that it might **enter your mind to say** that **since Rabbi Ḥanina says:** The **black** blood mentioned in the mishna **is** actually **red but** its color **has faded, therefore, even** if it is **lighter than** that which is described in the mishna, **it should also be impure.** Consequently, the mishna **teaches us** that even with regard to black blood, if the color is lighter than the shade mentioned in the mishna, it is pure.

רַבִּי אַמִי בַּר אַבָּא אָמַר: וְכוּלָּן, עָמוֹק מִכֵּן – טָמֵא, דֵּיהֶה מִכֵּן – נַמִי טָמֵא, חוּץ מִשָּׁחוֹר. אֶלָּא מַאי אַהֲנֵי שִׁיעוּרֵיהּ דְּרַבָּנַן? לְאַפּוֹקֵי דֵּיהֶה דְּדֵיהֶה.

**Rabbi Ami bar Abba says: And** with regard to **all of** these five types of blood, if the color is **deeper than** that which is described in the mishna, the blood is **ritually impure;** if it is **lighter than** that which is described in the mishna, it is also **ritually impure, except for black,** which is pure if it is lighter. The Gemara asks: **But** if these types of blood, except for black, are impure whether they are deeper or lighter than the specific shade described in the mishna, **what purpose do the measures** specified **by the Sages** in the mishna **serve?** The Gemara answers that these descriptions are **to the exclusion of** a color that is **lighter than lighter,** i.e., the color is so faint that it does not qualify as impure blood.

וְאִיכָּא דְּאָמְרִי, רָמִי בַּר אַבָּא אָמַר: וְכוּלָּן, עָמוֹק מִכֵּן – טָהוֹר, דֵּיהֶה מִכֵּן – טָהוֹר, חוּץ מִשָּׁחוֹר. וּלְהָכִי מְהַנֵּי שִׁיעוּרֵיהּ דְּרַבָּנַן.

**And there are** those **who say** a different version of the above statement. **Rami bar Abba says: And** with regard to **all of** these five types of blood, if the color is **deeper than that** which is described in the mishna, it is **ritually pure;** if it is **lighter than that,** it is also **ritually pure, except for black,** which is impure if it is deeper. **And for this** reason **the measures,** i.e., descriptions, **of the Sages are effective,** as any discrepancy from these descriptions means that the blood is pure.

בַּר קַפָּרָא אָמַר: וְכוּלָּן, עָמוֹק מִכֵּן – טָמֵא, דֵּיהֶה מִכֵּן – טָהוֹר. חוּץ מִמָּזוּג, שֶׁעָמוֹק מִכֵּן – טָהוֹר, דֵּיהֶה מִכֵּן – טָהוֹר. בַּר קַפָּרָא אַדְיוּהוּ לֵיהּ – וְדַכֵּי, אַעֲמִיקוּ לֵיהּ – וְדַכֵּי. אָמַר רַבִּי חֲנִינָא: כַּמָּה נְפִישׁ גַּבְרָא דְּלִבֵּיהּ כְּמִשְׁמַעְתֵּיהּ!

**Bar Kappara says: And** with regard to **all of them,** if the color is **deeper than that,** the blood is **impure;** if it is **lighter than that,** it is **pure, except** for blood the color of **diluted** wine,[H] with regard to **which** if the color is **deeper than that,** the blood is **pure,** and if it is **lighter than that,** it is also **pure.** The Gemara relates that in an effort to test **bar Kappara,** the Sages brought before him blood that had the appearance of diluted wine and **they lightened it, and** bar Kappara **deemed it pure.** On another occasion **they deepened** the color of blood that looked like diluted wine, **and** again bar Kappara **deemed it pure. Rabbi Ḥanina says** in astonishment: **How great** is this **man whose heart,** which is so sensitive it can distinguish between such similar shades of blood, **is in accordance with his** ruling of ***halakha.***

״וּכְקֶרֶן כַּרְכּוֹם״. תָּנָא: לַח וְלֹא יָבֵשׁ.

§ The mishna teaches, with regard to the colors of impure blood: **And** what is the color that is **like the bright** color of the **crocus** flower that is impure? It is like the brightest part of the flower, which is used to produce the orange-colored spice saffron. The Sages **taught:** This is referring to the appearance of **moist** saffron that is still fresh **and not** to its **dry** counterpart.

תָּנֵי חֲדָא: כַּתַּחְתּוֹן לֹא כָּעֶלְיוֹן, וְתַנְיָא אִידָךְ: כָּעֶלְיוֹן וְלֹא כַּתַּחְתּוֹן, וְתַנְיָא אִידָךְ: כָּעֶלְיוֹן, וְכׇל שֶׁכֵּן כַּתַּחְתּוֹן, וְתַנְיָא אִידָךְ: כַּתַּחְתּוֹן, וְכׇל שֶׁכֵּן כָּעֶלְיוֹן.

With regard to this color, it **is taught** in **one** *baraita* that it is **like** the **lower** part of the crocus flower, **not like** its **upper** part; **and** it **is taught** in **another** *baraita* that it is **like** the **upper** part of the flower **and not like** its **lower** part; **and** it **is taught** in **another** *baraita* that it is **like** its **upper** part, **and all the more so** blood whose color is **like** its **lower** part is impure; **and** it **is taught** in yet **another** *baraita* that it is **like** its **lower** part, **and all the more so** blood whose color is **like** its **upper** part is impure.

**HALAKHA**

**Except for diluted wine – חוּץ מִמָּזוּג:** How does one examine blood that is similar in appearance to diluted wine? One mixes one part fresh undiluted wine from the Sharon region in Eretz Yisrael with two parts water. If the blood was deeper or lighter than this mixture, it is pure, as stated by bar Kappara (Rambam *Sefer Kedusha*, *Hilkhot Issurei Bia* 5:10).

## BACKGROUND

**Yodfat Valley** – בִּקְעַת יוֹדְפַת: Like the other valleys mentioned here, the Valley of Yodfat, or Yotvat, is located in the Lower Galilee. As for its precise location, some say that it is in the upper wadis of the Yodfat River. Others maintain that the reference is to the delta of the Yodfat River, which is near Khirbet Qana. Yet others identify the Valley of Yodfat with Beit Netofa Valley.

Yodfat Valley

Beit Netofa Valley

**Sikhnei Valley** – בִּקְעַת סִכְנֵי: The Sikhnei Valley is somewhere near Sakhnin, with the Shagor mountain range to the north and the Yodfat range to the south.

**Genosar Valley** – בִּקְעַת גְּנוֹסָר: This valley has been identified as the delta of the Tzalmon River, in the Lower Galilee. Like the other valleys listed here, it is named after a nearby settlement, in this case Genosar, which is probably the site occupied later by the Arab village Ghuwayr Abu Shusha.

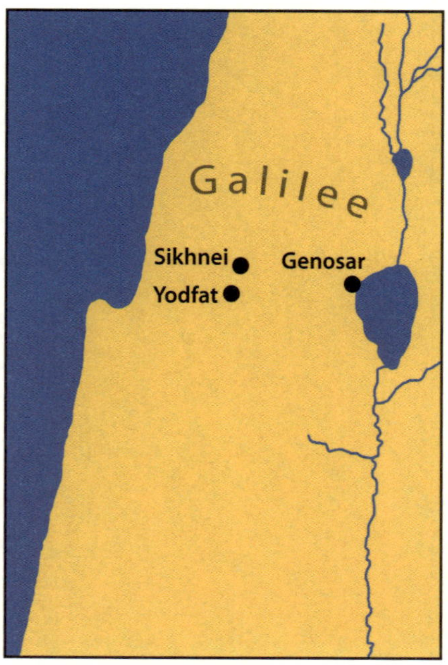

Locations of Yodfat, Sikhnei, and Genosar

אָמַר אַבַּיֵי: תְּלָתָא דָּרֵי וּתְלָתָא טַרְפָּן הָווּיָין,

**Abaye says** that these *baraitot* do not contradict one another, as the crocus has **three layers** of the brightly colored parts of the crocus flower harvested for saffron, one above the other, **and** in each layer **there are three leaves,**[H] i.e., styles or stigmata.

נְקוֹט דָּרָא מְצִיעָאָה וְטַרְפָּא מְצִיעֲתָא בִּידָךְ.

In order to examine blood whose color is similar to saffron, you should **grasp** the **middle leaf** of the **middle layer in your hand** and compare it to the blood. If they are similar, the blood is impure. Consequently, the four *baraitot* do not contradict one another: The first two *baraitot* are referring to the layer of leaves that must be examined. The first *baraita* says that it is the lower one, as the middle layer is lower than the upper one, while the second *baraita* states the reverse because the middle layer is higher than the lower one. Meanwhile, the last two *baraitot* are dealing with the leaves within the middle layer. The *baraita* that states: Like its lower part, and all the more so like its upper part, means: Like the lowest of the three leaves and all the more so like the middle leaf, which is above that leaf, while the other *baraita* states a similar idea with regard to the upper and middle leaves. In any event, all four *baraitot* are referring to the part of the crocus flower that is called by the mishna its brightest part.

כִּי אָתוּ לְקַמֵּיהּ דְּרַבִּי אַבָּהוּ, אָמַר לְהוּ: בְּגוּשַׁיְיהוּ שָׁנִינוּ.

The Gemara relates: **When** people **would come before Rabbi Abbahu** for him to examine blood whose color was similar to saffron, **he** would **say to them: We learned** that the mishna is referring specifically to crocus flowers that are still **in their clumps** of earth in which they grew, as once they are detached from that earth their color changes.

"וּכְמֵימֵי אֲדָמָה". תָּנוּ רַבָּנַן: כְּמֵימֵי אֲדָמָה – מֵבִיא אֲדָמָה שְׁמֵנָה מִבִּקְעַת בֵּית כֶּרֶם, וּמֵצִיף עָלֶיהָ מַיִם, דִּבְרֵי רַבִּי מֵאִיר. רַבִּי עֲקִיבָא אוֹמֵר: מִבִּקְעַת יוֹדְפַת. רַבִּי יוֹסֵי אוֹמֵר: מִבִּקְעַת סִכְנֵי. רַבִּי שִׁמְעוֹן אוֹמֵר: אַף מִבִּקְעַת גְּנוֹסָר וְכַיּוֹצֵא בָּהֶן.

§ The mishna states: **And** what is the color that is **like water** that inundates red **earth** that is impure? In this regard **the Sages taught** in a *baraita*: In order to examine blood that is **like water** that inundates red **earth, one brings fertile earth from the Beit Kerem Valley and one inundates** the earth with enough **water** until it pools on the surface; this is **the statement of Rabbi Meir. Rabbi Akiva says:** One brings earth **from the Yodfat Valley.**[B] **Rabbi Yosei says: From the Sikhnei Valley.**[BH] **Rabbi Shimon says:** One can **even** bring earth **from the Genosar Valley**[B] **or** from **similar** places.

תַּנְיָא אִידָךְ: וּכְמֵימֵי אֲדָמָה – מֵבִיא אֲדָמָה שְׁמֵנָה מִבִּקְעַת בֵּית כֶּרֶם, וּמֵצִיף עָלֶיהָ מַיִם כִּקְלִיפַּת הַשּׁוּם, וְאֵין שִׁיעוּר לַמַּיִם – מִשּׁוּם דְּאֵין שִׁיעוּר לֶעָפָר. וְאֵין בּוֹדְקִין אוֹתָן צְלוּלִין אֶלָּא עֲכוּרִין. צָלְלוּ – חוֹזֵר וְעוֹכְרָן. וּכְשֶׁהוּא עוֹכְרָן – אֵין עוֹכְרָן בַּיָּד אֶלָּא בַּכְּלִי.

**It is taught** in **another** *baraita*: **And** to test whether blood is **like water** that inundates red **earth, one brings fertile earth from the Beit Kerem Valley and one inundates** the earth with an amount of **water** that rises above the earth by the thickness **of the husk of garlic. And there is no** required **measure for the water, because there is no** required **measure for** the **earth** with which the examination must be performed; it is sufficient to use a small amount of earth with a small amount of water. **And one does not examine it** when the water is **clear,** as it does not have the color of the earth, but **rather** when it is **muddy** from the earth. And if the water **became clear** because the earth settled, **one must muddy it again. And when one muddies it he does not muddy it by hand** but **rather with a vessel.**

## HALAKHA

**Three layers and…three leaves, etc.** – תְּלָתָא דָּרֵי וּתְלָתָא טַרְפָּן וכו׳: How does one examine blood that is similar in appearance to the bright color of the crocus flower? One brings a moist crocus flower still attached to its clump of earth, and takes the brightest part of the plant. This is the middle leaf of the middle layer, as there are three layers, each of which contains three leaves. One places the blood next to that leaf and compares their appearances. The *halakha* is in accordance with the opinion of bar Kappara (Rambam *Sefer Kedusha*, *Hilkhot Issurei Bia* 5:8).

**From the Sikhnei Valley** – מִבִּקְעַת סִכְנֵי: How does one examine blood that is similar in appearance to water that inundates red earth? One brings earth from the Sikhnei Valley, or from a location where the earth is similarly red, and one places water in a vessel until it covers the earth by the thickness of a garlic husk. There is no requisite amount for the water or the earth. Then, one muddies the water in the vessel for the examination. This examination is effective only in the location the earth was taken, and right after it was taken. If the water cleared, one must muddy it again. The *halakha* is in accordance with the opinion of Rabbi Yosei (Rambam *Sefer Kedusha*, *Hilkhot Issurei Bia* 5:8).

איבעיא להו: אין עוכרין אותן ביד אלא בכלי – דלא לרמיה בידיה ולעכרינהו, אבל במנא, כי עכר ליה בידיה – שפיר דמי, או דלמא: דלא לעכרינהו בידיה, אלא במנא?

A dilemma was raised before the Sages: Does the statement that one does not muddy it by hand but rather with a vessel mean that one should not put the dirt into his hand and muddy the water with dirt in his hand, but in a case where the earth is in a vessel, when one muddies it by mixing the earth and water with his hand one may well do so? Or perhaps the *baraita* means that even when the earth is in a vessel one should not muddy the water by mixing it with earth with his hand, but rather with a vessel?

תא שמע: כשהוא בודקן – אין בודקן אלא בכוס. ועדיין תבעי לך: בדיקה – בכוס, עכירה במאי? תיקו.

The Gemara suggests: Come and hear a *baraita*: When one examines this water, he examines it only with a cup. Evidently, it is necessary to use a vessel. The Gemara rejects this proof: But you still have a dilemma. This *baraita* merely states that the examination must be performed while the water is in a cup, but with what is the muddying performed? Must this be done by means of a vessel alone, or may one use his hand as well? The Gemara concludes: The dilemma shall stand unresolved.

כי אתו לקמיה דרבה בר אבוה, אמר להו: במקומה שנינו. רבי חנינא פלי קורטא דגרגשתא ובדיק ביה, לייט עליה רבי ישמעאל ברבי יוסי באסכרה.

§ The Gemara relates: When people would come before Rabba bar Avuh to examine blood that is similar to water that inundates red earth, he would say to them: We learned that the examination must be conducted in its place, i.e., the location the earth was taken from. But if the earth was transported elsewhere, the examination is no longer effective. The Gemara further relates that Rabbi Ḥanina would break up a clump of earth and examine with it, without mixing it in water. Rabbi Yishmael, son of Rabbi Yosei, would curse anyone who used this method that they should be punished with diphtheria.[B]

**BACKGROUND**

Diphtheria [*askara*] – אַסְכָּרָה: *Askara* is diphtheria, an infectious disease of the throat that causes the mucous membrane in the throat to swell, bringing on a choking sensation. Diphtheria was once very common among children, and until the discovery of a vaccine against it, the disease was extremely common and very deadly; those who contracted the illness would die of asphyxiation. During the Second Temple period, members of the non-priestly watch would fast once a week so that *askara* would not befall young children.

Perek **II**
Daf **20** Amud **b**

רבי חנינא הוא דחכים, כולי עלמא – לאו חכימי הכי.

Rabbi Yishmael, son of Rabbi Yosei, explained: It is only Rabbi Ḥanina who is permitted to examine the blood in this fashion, as he is wise, but everyone else is not so wise that they can successfully perform the examination without water.

אמר רבי יוחנן: חכמתא דרבי חנינא גרמא לי דלא אחזי דמא, מטמינא – מטהר, מטהרנא – מטמא. אמר רבי אלעזר: ענוותנותא דרבי חנינא גרמא לי דחזאי דמא, ומה רבי חנינא דענותן הוא – מחית נפשיה לספק וחזי, אנא לא אחזי?

Rabbi Yoḥanan says: Rabbi Ḥanina's wisdom causes me not to see blood for a halakhic examination. When I would examine blood and deem it impure, he would deem it pure, and when I would deem it pure, he would deem it impure. Conversely, Rabbi Elazar says: Rabbi Ḥanina's humility causes me to see blood, as I reason to myself: If Rabbi Ḥanina, who is humble, places himself into a situation of uncertainty and sees various types of blood to determine their status, should I, who am not nearly as humble, not see blood for an examination?

אמר רבי זירא: טבעא דבבל גרמא לי דלא חזאי דמא, דאמינא: בטבעא לא ידענא, בדמא ידענא?

Rabbi Zeira says: The complex nature of the residents of Babylonia causes me not to see blood for a halakhic examination, as I say to myself: Even matters involving the complex nature of people I do not know; can I then claim that I know about matters of blood?

למימרא דבטבעא תליא מלתא, והא רבה הוא דידע בטבעא ולא ידע בדמא! כל שכן קאמר, ומה רבה דידע בטבעא – לא חזא דמא, ואנא אחזי?

The Gemara asks: Is this to say that the matter of the appearance of blood is dependent on the nature of people, i.e., that it changes in accordance with their nature? But Rabba is an example of someone who knew about the complex nature of the people of Babylonia, and yet he did not know how to distinguish between different types of blood. The Gemara answers: Rabbi Zeira took this factor into account and said to himself: All the more so; if Rabba, who knew about the complex nature of these people, nevertheless would not see blood, should I, who am unknowledgeable about the nature of these people, see blood for examination?

## PERSONALITIES

**Rabbi Elazar – רַבִּי אֶלְעָזָר:** This is Rabbi Elazar ben Pedat, an *amora* from the third generation of *amora'im* of Eretz Yisrael. Rabbi Elazar ben Pedat, who was probably a priest, was born in Babylonia, where he studied Torah from Rav and Shmuel. Later, he ascended to Eretz Yisrael and learned from the Sages there. His primary teacher was Rabbi Yoḥanan. When Rabbi Elazar stated the *halakhot* of Rabbi Yoḥanan he did not deem it necessary to attribute them directly to Rabbi Yoḥanan, as it was obvious that he was citing his teacher. Accordingly, there are disputes with regard to certain statements as to whether they were formulated originally by Rabbi Yoḥanan or were stated by Rabbi Elazar himself. Rabbi Elazar ben Pedat was considered Rabbi Yoḥanan's greatest student. After Rabbi Yoḥanan passed away, Rabbi Elazar took over his post as head of the academy at Tiberias, and was called the master of Eretz Yisrael, as stated here. According to the epistle of Rav Sherira Gaon, Rabbi Elazar died in the same year as Rabbi Yoḥanan. Little is known of Rabbi Elazar's private life other than the fact that he was very poor, to the extent that he often went hungry, yet he still refused to accept charity from others. It is also known that he had at least one son, called Rabbi Pedat, after Rabbi Elazar's father.

**Ifera Hurmiz – אִפְרָא הוּרְמִיז:** Queen Ifera Hurmiz was the mother of Shapur II, king of Persia, who ruled between 309 and 379 CE. Since Shapur became king as a child, his mother maintained considerable influence over him for many years. Ifera Hurmiz is mentioned on several occasions in the Gemara as an admirer of Judaism and its Sages, and she even gave money to several Sages to distribute as charity and for the performance of mitzvot.

**King Shapur – שָׁבוֹר מַלְכָּא:** King Shapur, or Shavor Malka, was the name of several Persian kings. The Gemara is apparently referring to the second King Shapur, who lived 303–380 CE, during the period of the third and fourth generations of *amora'im* in Babylonia. He was a zealous supporter of Zoroastrianism, a religion he tried to impose on the minorities under his rule, especially Christians. During his reign, the Jewish community suffered from taxes, levies, and various decrees. When the Persian army was stationed in the city of Meḥoza, the local population, most of which was comprised of Jews, was obliged to maintain it.

## BACKGROUND

**Comb for killing lice – סְרִיקוּתָא דְּמַקְטְלָא כַּלְמֵי:**

Ancient lice comb

עוּלָּא אִקְּלַע לְפוּמְבְּדִיתָא, אַיְיתוּ לְקַמֵּיהּ דְּמָא וְלָא חֲזָא. אֲמַר: וּמָה רַבִּי אֶלְעָזָר דְּמָרָא דְּאַרְעָא דְּיִשְׂרָאֵל הֲוָה, כִּי מִקְּלַע לְאַתְרָא דְּרַבִּי יְהוּדָה – לָא חָזֵי דְּמָא, אֲנָא אֶחֱזֵי?

The Gemara relates that **Ulla happened** to come **to Pumbedita,** where **they brought blood before him** for an examination, **but he would not see** it, as **he said: If Rabbi Elazar,**[P] **who was the master of Eretz Yisrael** in wisdom, **when he would happen** to come **to the locale of Rabbi Yehuda, he would not see blood, shall I see blood** here?

וְאַמַּאי קָרוּ לֵיהּ ״מָרָא דְּאַרְעָא דְּיִשְׂרָאֵל״? דְּהַהִיא אִתְּתָא דְּאַיְיתָא דְּמָא לְקַמֵּיהּ דְּרַבִּי אֶלְעָזָר, הֲוָה יָתֵיב רַבִּי אַמִּי קַמֵּיהּ. אַרְחֵיהּ, אֲמַר לָהּ: הַאי דַּם חִימּוּד הוּא. בָּתַר דִּנְפַקָה אִטַּפַּל לָהּ רַבִּי אַמִּי. אָמְרָה לֵיהּ: בַּעְלִי הָיָה בַּדֶּרֶךְ וְחִמַּדְתִּיו. קָרֵי עֲלֵיהּ: ״סוֹד ה׳ לִירֵאָיו״.

The Gemara asks: **And why would they call** Rabbi Elazar **the master of Eretz Yisrael** in wisdom? The Gemara explains that there was an incident **involving a certain woman who brought blood before Rabbi Elazar** for examination, and **Rabbi Ami was sitting before him.** Rabbi Ami observed that Rabbi Elazar **smelled** the blood and **said to** the woman: **This is blood of desire,**[N] i.e., your desire for your husband caused you to emit this blood, and it is not the blood of menstruation. **After** the woman **left** Rabbi Elazar's presence, **Rabbi Ami caught up with her** and inquired into the circumstances of her case. **She said to him: My husband was** absent **on a journey, and I desired him.** Rabbi Ami **read** the following verse **about** Rabbi Elazar: **"The counsel of the Lord is with those who fear Him;** and His covenant, to make them know it" (Psalms 25:14), i.e., God reveals secret matters to those who fear Him.

אִפְרָא הוּרְמִיז אִמֵּיהּ דְּשָׁבוֹר מַלְכָּא שַׁדְרָה דְּמָא לְקַמֵּיהּ דְּרָבָא, הֲוָה יָתֵיב רַב עוֹבַדְיָה קַמֵּיהּ, אַרְחֵיהּ, אֲמַר לָהּ: הַאי דַּם חִימּוּד הוּא. אָמְרָה לֵיהּ לִבְרֵיהּ: תָּא חָזֵי כַּמָּה חַכִּימֵי יְהוּדָאֵי! אֲמַר לָהּ: דִּלְמָא כְּסוּמָא בַּאֲרוּבָּה?

The Gemara further relates that **Ifera Hurmiz,**[P] **the mother of King Shapur,**[P] **sent blood before Rava** for examination, as she sought to convert and was practicing the *halakhot* of menstruation. At that time **Rav Ovadya was sitting before** Rava. Rav Ovadya observed that Rava **smelled**[N] the blood and later **said to the woman: This is blood of desire. She said to her son: Come** and **see how wise the Jews** are, as Rava is correct. Her son **said to her: Perhaps** Rava was **like a blind man** who escapes **from a chimney,** i.e., it was a lucky guess.

הֲדַר שַׁדְרָה לֵיהּ שִׁתִּין מִינֵי דְּמָא, וְכוּלְּהוּ אָמְרִינְהוּ. הַהוּא בַּתְרָא דַּם כִּנִּים הֲוָה, וְלָא יָדַע, אִסְתַּיַּיע מִילְּתָא וְשַׁדַּר לָהּ סְרִיקוּתָא דְּמַקְטְלָא כַּלְמֵי. אָמְרָה: יְהוּדָאֵי, בְּתַוְונֵי דְּלִבָּא יָתְבִיתוּ!

Ifera Hurmiz **then sent** Rava **sixty** different types of **blood,** some impure and others pure, **and** with regard to **all of them** Rava accurately **told her** their origin. The Gemara adds: **That last** sample of blood sent by Ifera Hurmiz **was blood of lice, and** Rava **did not know** what it was. He received **support** in this **matter** in the form of heavenly guidance, as he unwittingly **sent her** as a gift **a comb for killing lice.**[B] **She said** in exclamation: **Jews, you** must **dwell in the chamber of** people's **hearts.**

אָמַר רַב יְהוּדָה: מֵרֵישָׁא הֲוָה חָזֵינָא דְּמָא, כֵּיוָן דְּאָמְרָה לִי אִמֵּיהּ דְּיִצְחָק בְּרִי: הַאי טִיפְּתָא קַמַּיְיתָא לָא מַיְיתִינַן לָהּ קַמַּיְיהוּ דְּרַבָּנַן, מִשּׁוּם דְּזִהֲימָא – לָא חָזֵינָא,

§ The Gemara cites more statements of the Sages with regard to the examination of blood. **Rav Yehuda says: At first I would see blood,** i.e., perform examinations of blood, but I changed my conduct **when the mother of my son Yitzḥak,** i.e., my wife, **said to me** that she acts as follows: With regard to **this first drop** of blood that I see, **I do not bring it before the Sages, because it is not pristine** blood, i.e., other substances are mixed with it. After hearing this, I decided I would **no** longer **see** blood, as it is possible that the first drop, which I do not get to see, was impure.

## NOTES

**This is blood of desire – הַאי דַּם חִימּוּד הוּא:** Rabbi Elazar merely stated that this blood resulted from the woman's desire for her husband; he did not say if it was pure or impure. The early commentaries engage in a dispute concerning this matter. Some claim that the Sages had a tradition that such blood of desire is pure, as it does not come from the uterus (*Ḥeshek Shlomo*; see *Ḥazon Ish*). One difficulty with this opinion is that the Gemara (66a) states that if a woman is asked for her hand in marriage and she accepts, she must observe seven clean days after she accepts, as she might have experienced bleeding due to her desire for the man. This indicates that a woman's desire can cause an emission of menstrual blood. The commentaries explain that the blood of desire itself is pure, but it is possible that a woman's desire might lead to the emission of menstrual blood as well, which was not observed in the case examined by Rabbi Elazar (Ran; see *Ḥatam Sofer* and *Ma'aneh Eliyahu*). Others claim that the blood of desire is in fact impure, and they cite proof for this opinion from that passage on 66a (Rashba; *Tosefot HaRosh*).

**Rav Ovadya was sitting before Rava, he smelled – הֲוָה יָתֵיב רַב עוֹבַדְיָה קַמֵּיהּ אַרְחֵיהּ:** It is unclear from the Gemara which of the Sages smelled the blood, whether it was Rava or his student Rav Ovadya. Some say that it was Rava who smelled the blood, whether because he knew how to identify types of blood by this method (*Tosafot*), or because a miracle was performed for him in this case (Rashi), or because the incident involved a particular kind of blood whose odor Rava was able to identify (*Arukh LaNer*).

בֵּין טְמֵאָה לִטְהוֹרָה וַדַּאי חָזֵינָא.

Rav Yehuda continues: But with regard to the examination of blood that a woman who gave birth emitted after the completion of her days of purity, i.e., at least forty days after giving birth to a male, or eighty after giving birth to a female (see Leviticus, chapter 12), in order to determine **whether she is ritually impure or pure, I certainly see** this blood and determine her status based on its color. This blood is clean, as the woman has been bleeding for a long period of time.

יַלְתָּא אַיְיתָא דָּמָא לְקַמֵּיהּ דְּרַבָּה בַּר בַּר חָנָה – וְטַמְּי לַהּ, הֲדַר אַיְיתָא לְקַמֵּיהּ דְּרַב יִצְחָק בְּרֵיהּ דְּרַב יְהוּדָה – וְדַכְּי לַהּ.

§ The Gemara relates that **Yalta,**[P] Rav Naḥman's wife, **brought blood before Rabba bar bar Ḥana, and he deemed her ritually impure. She then brought** it **before Rav Yitzḥak, son of Rav Yehuda, and he deemed her pure.**

וְהֵיכִי עָבֵיד הָכִי? וְהָתַנְיָא: חָכָם שֶׁטִּימֵּא – אֵין חֲבֵירוֹ רַשַּׁאי לְטַהֵר, אָסַר – אֵין חֲבֵירוֹ רַשַּׁאי לְהַתִּיר!

The Gemara asks: **But how could** Rav Yitzḥak, son of Rav Yehuda, **act in this manner? But isn't it taught** in a *baraita*: In the case of **a halakhic authority who deemed** an item **impure,**[H] **another** halakhic authority **is not allowed to deem** it **pure;** if one halakhic authority **deemed** a matter **prohibited, another** halakhic authority **is not allowed to deem** it **permitted?**

מֵעִיקָּרָא טַמּוּיֵי הֲוָה מְטַמֵּי לַהּ, כֵּיוָן דְּאָמְרָה לֵיהּ: דְּכׇל יוֹמָא הֲוָה מְדַכֵּי לִי כִּי הַאי גַּוְונָא, וְהָאִידָּנָא הוּא דְּחָשׁ בְּעֵינֵיהּ – דַּכְּי לַהּ.

The Gemara explains that **initially** Rav Yitzḥak, son of Rav Yehuda, **deemed her impure,** but he changed his mind **when** Yalta **said to him: Every day** that I bring blood **of this kind** of color to Rabba bar bar Ḥana **he deems me pure, and specifically now** he issued a different ruling, **as he feels** pain **in his eye.** Upon hearing this, Rav Yitzḥak, son of Rav Yehuda, **deemed her pure.**

וּמִי מְהֵימְנִי? אִין. וְהָתַנְיָא: נֶאֱמֶנֶת אִשָּׁה לוֹמַר ״כָּזֶה רָאִיתִי וְאִבַּדְתִּיו״.

The Gemara asks: **But** are people **deemed credible** to present claims such as the one presented by Yalta? The Gemara answers: **Yes; and** likewise **it is taught** in a *baraita*: **A woman is deemed credible** if she **says: I saw** blood **like this** color, **but I lost it**[H] before it could be examined.

אִיבַּעְיָא לְהוּ: ״כָּזֶה טִיהֵר אִישׁ פְּלוֹנִי חָכָם״ מַהוּ?

**A dilemma was raised before** the Sages: If a woman states to her friend who showed her blood: My blood, which has an appearance **like this, so-and-so, the halakhic authority, deemed** it **pure,**[H] **what is** the *halakha*?[N] Is she deemed credible concerning its status?

תָּא שְׁמַע: נֶאֱמֶנֶת אִשָּׁה לוֹמַר ״כָּזֶה רָאִיתִי וְאִבַּדְתִּיו״. שָׁאנֵי הָתָם – דְּלֵיתֵיהּ לְקַמָּהּ.

The Gemara suggests: **Come** and **hear** a resolution to this dilemma from the *baraita* cited above: **A woman is deemed credible** if she **says: I saw** blood **like this** color, **but I lost it.** This demonstrates that a woman may issue claims of this kind. The Gemara rejects this proof: **There** it **is different,** as in that case the blood **is not before her,** and therefore the Sages were lenient. But here, the woman's friend can take her blood to a halakhic authority for examination.

תָּא שְׁמַע: דְּיַלְתָּא אַיְיתָא דָּמָא לְקַמֵּיהּ דְּרַבָּה בַּר בַּר חָנָה – וְטַמְּי לַהּ. לְקַמֵּיהּ דְּרַב יִצְחָק בְּרֵיהּ דְּרַב יְהוּדָה – וְדַכְּי לַהּ. וְהֵיכִי עָבֵיד הָכִי? וְהָתַנְיָא: חָכָם שֶׁטִּימֵּא אֵין חֲבֵירוֹ רַשַּׁאי לְטַהֵר וכו׳,

The Gemara further suggests: **Come** and **hear** the incident cited above, **as Yalta brought blood before Rabba bar bar Ḥana, and he deemed her ritually impure;** she then brought it **before Rav Yitzḥak, son of Rav Yehuda, and he deemed her pure. And** the Gemara asked: **How could** Rav Yitzḥak, son of Rav Yehuda, **act in this manner? But isn't it taught** in a *baraita*: In the case of **a halakhic authority who deemed** an item **impure, another** halakhic authority **is not allowed to deem** it **pure?**

## PERSONALITIES

**Yalta – יַלְתָּא:** Yalta, Rav Naḥman's wife, was from the family of the Exilarch, possibly the daughter of the Exilarch himself. Some say that her father was the Sage Rabba bar Avuh, who was from the family of the Exilarch. As indicated from several passages in the Talmud, in addition to hailing from a wealthy family of distinguished lineage, Yalta was a woman of firm opinions. Rav Naḥman treated her with great honor, and she herself demanded respect from various Sages. It is related that she would listen and contribute to Rav Naḥman's discussions with other Sages, from which it may be inferred that she was well versed in Torah.

## HALAKHA

**A halakhic authority who deemed an item impure, etc. – חָכָם שֶׁטִּימֵּא וכו׳:** If one halakhic authority deemed an item prohibited, another halakhic authority may not deem it permitted based merely on his own reasoning. Some commentaries maintain that this applies even if the second halakhic authority is greater than the first (*Shakh*), while others claim that this is the *halakha* only if the two halakhic authorities are equal, whereas if the second is greater he may permit the item. The commentaries further state that this *halakha* applies only if the ruling of the first authority has already gone into effect, but if they are still in the study hall the second authority may issue a different ruling. If the second halakhic authority claims, based on a tradition, that the first halakhic authority erred, or if the first halakhic authority made a mistake in a matter that appears in the Mishna, i.e., an obvious error, the second halakhic authority may deem the item permitted. Some commentaries rule that he may not permit it based on a tradition (*Shakh*; see *Pitḥei Teshuva*). If the first halakhic authority erred in his reasoning, the second halakhic authority should discuss the matter with him until he retracts his errant ruling. Therefore, if someone asked one halakhic authority and he deemed the item prohibited, the person may turn to another halakhic authority provided that he informs the second halakhic authority of the ruling of the first. This *halakha* applies only if both halakhic authorities are dealing with the same case, but if another incident occurred it is permitted for the second halakhic authority to rule as he sees fit. The *halakha* is in accordance with the ruling of the *baraita* (*Shulḥan Arukh*, *Yoreh De'a* 242:31 in the comment of Rema).

**A woman is deemed credible if she says: I saw blood like this color but I lost it – נֶאֱמֶנֶת אִשָּׁה לוֹמַר כָּזֶה רָאִיתִי וְאִבַּדְתִּיו:** If a woman says: I saw blood of this color but I lost it, she is deemed credible. Therefore, if it was white or green, she is pure. This *halakha* is in accordance with the ruling of the *baraita* (Rambam *Sefer Kedusha*, *Hilkhot Issurei Bia* 5:10; *Shulḥan Arukh*, *Yoreh De'a* 188:2).

**Like this, so-and-so the halakhic authority deemed it pure – כָּזֶה טִיהֵר אִישׁ פְּלוֹנִי חָכָם:** In a case where a woman brought blood before a halakhic authority, if he established its presumptive status as impure or even if he was uncertain, and the woman says: So-and-so deemed blood of mine that had a similar appearance pure, her claim is not accepted (*Shulḥan Arukh*, *Yoreh De'a* 188:2).

## NOTES

**Like this, so-and-so the halakhic authority deemed it pure, what is the *halakha* – כָּזֶה טִיהֵר אִישׁ פְּלוֹנִי חָכָם מַהוּ:** The commentaries explain that the blood in question was brought before a Sage who was either uncertain as to its status or thought that it was impure. The issue is whether the other woman's statement concerning her own blood can be relied upon to resolve the Sage's uncertainty, or whether her claim is entirely disregarded in favor of the Sage's inclination to rule that the blood is impure. If blood is not brought before a Sage at all, one may rely upon the other woman's contention that she showed blood of a similar appearance to a certain Sage who deemed it pure, and there is no need to show the blood to another Sage (Rashba; Ritva; *Tur*; *Beit Yosef*; *Baḥ*).

וְאָמְרִינַן: טַמּוּיֵי הֲוָה מְטַמֵּי לַהּ, כֵּיוָן דַּאֲמַרָה לֵיהּ דְּכָל יוֹמָא מְדַכֵּי לַהּ כִּי הַאי גַּוְנָא, וְהָאִידָּנָא הוּא דְּחָשׁ בְּעֵינֵיהּ. הֲדַר דַּכְיַי לַהּ, אַלְמָא: מְהֵימְנָא לַהּ!

**And we say** in response that initially Rav Yitzḥak, son of Rav Yehuda, **deemed her impure**, but he changed his mind **when she said to him that every day** that she brings blood **of this kind** of color to Rabba bar bar Ḥana **he deems her pure, and specifically now** he issued a different ruling, **as he feels** pain **in his eye.** The Gemara summarizes: The conclusion of the story was that upon hearing this, Rav Yitzḥak, son of Rav Yehuda, **then deemed her pure. Evidently,** when a woman issues claims with regard to blood that is presented, **we deem her** claims **credible.**

רַב יִצְחָק בַּר יְהוּדָה – אַגְמָרֵיהּ סָמַךְ.

The Gemara answers: That incident does not provide proof, as **Rav Yitzḥak, son of Rav Yehuda, relied on his studies** in his lenient ruling. At first, he was reluctant to issue his ruling, in deference to Rabba bar bar Ḥana, who had said the blood was impure. But when he heard Yalta's explanation he deemed the blood pure, as he had originally thought. Therefore, there is no proof from there that a woman's statements of this kind are accepted.

רַבִּי רָאָה דָּם בַּלַּיְלָה – וְטִימֵּא, רָאָה בַּיּוֹם – וְטִיהֵר, הִמְתִּין שָׁעָה אַחַת – חָזַר וְטִימֵּא, אָמַר: אוֹי לִי שֶׁמָּא טָעִיתִי!

§ The Gemara further relates: **Rabbi** Yehuda HaNasi once **saw** a woman's **blood at night and deemed** it **impure. He** again **saw** that blood **in the day,** after it had dried, **and deemed** it **pure. He waited one hour** and then **deemed** it **impure again.** It is assumed that Rabbi Yehuda HaNasi did not conduct another examination at this point; rather, he reasoned that the previous night's examination had been correct, and the blood's color should be deemed impure because of how it had looked when it was moist. Rabbi Yehuda HaNasi then **said: Woe is me! Perhaps I erred** by declaring the blood impure, as based on its color it should be pure.

״שֶׁמָּא טָעִיתִי״?! וַדַּאי טָעָה! דְּתַנְיָא: לֹא יֹאמַר חָכָם ״אִילּוּ הָיָה לַח הָיָה וַדַּאי טָמֵא״,

The Gemara questions this statement: **Perhaps I erred? He certainly erred, as it is taught** in a *baraita* that **a halakhic authority may not say: If** the blood **were moist it would certainly have been impure,** and yet here, Rabbi Yehuda HaNasi deemed the blood impure based on that type of reasoning.

אֶלָּא אָמַר אֵין לוֹ לַדַּיָּין אֶלָּא מַה שֶּׁעֵינָיו רוֹאוֹת. מֵעִיקָּרָא אַחְזְקֵיהּ בְּטָמֵא, כֵּיוָן דַּחֲזָא לְצַפְרָא דְּאִשְׁתַּנִּי אֲמַר (לֵיהּ): וַדַּאי טָהוֹר הֲוָה, וּבַלַּיְלָה הוּא דְּלָא אִתַּחְזִי שַׁפִּיר. כֵּיוָן דַּחֲזָא דַּהֲדַר אִשְׁתַּנִּי, אֲמַר: הַאי – טָמֵא הוּא, וּמִפְכַּח הוּא דְּקָא מִפְכַּח וְאָזִיל.

The Gemara explains that the incident did not unfold as initially assumed. **Rather,** Rabbi Yehuda HaNasi examined the blood three times, as he **said: A judge has only what his eyes see** as the basis for his ruling. **Initially,** Rabbi Yehuda HaNasi **established the presumptive status** of the blood **as ritually impure,** but **when he saw in the morning that** its color had **changed, he said: It was definitely pure** last night as well, **and only** because it was **at night** I thought that it was impure, **because it could not be seen well.** Subsequently, **when he saw** after a short while **that** its color **again changed,** Rabbi Yehuda HaNasi **said: This** blood **is impure, and it is gradually becoming lighter** as its color fades.

רַבִּי בָּדֵיק לְאוֹר הַנֵּר, רַבִּי יִשְׁמָעֵאל בְּרַבִּי יוֹסֵף בָּדֵיק בְּיוֹם הַמְעוּנָּן בֵּינֵי עַמּוּדֵי. אָמַר רַב אַמֵּי בַּר שְׁמוּאֵל: וְכוּלָּן אֵין בּוֹדְקִין אוֹתָן אֶלָּא בֵּין חַמָּה לְצֵל. רַב נַחְמָן אָמַר רַבָּה בַּר אֲבוּהּ: בַּחַמָּה, וּבְצֵל יָדוֹ.

With regard to the manner in which the Sages would examine blood, the Gemara relates that **Rabbi** Yehuda HaNasi **would examine** blood **by candlelight. Rabbi Yishmael, son of Rabbi Yosef, would examine** blood **between the pillars** of the study hall even **on a cloudy day,** despite the fact that it was not very light there. **Rav Ami bar Shmuel says: And** in **all these** cases, **one examines** blood **only between sunlight and shade.**[H] **Rav Naḥman** says that **Rabba bar Avuh says:** One stands **in** a place lit by the **sun, and** he conducts the examination **under the shadow of his hand,** i.e., he places his hand over the blood. In this manner the color of the blood can be best discerned.

״וּכְמָזוּג שְׁנֵי חֲלָקִים״ כו׳. תָּנָא,

§ The mishna states: **And** what is the color that is **like diluted** wine that is impure? It is specifically when the dilution consists of **two parts** water and one part wine, and specifically when it is from the wine of the Sharon region in Eretz Yisrael. The Sages **taught** in a *baraita*:

**HALAKHA**

**And in all these cases one examines blood only between sunlight and shade** – וְכוּלָּן אֵין בּוֹדְקִין אוֹתָן אֶלָּא בֵּין חַמָּה לְצֵל: One must examine blood in sunlight, while forming a shadow over the blood with his hand. The examiner himself stands in the sun, as in this manner he can best see the color of the blood. The *halakha* is in accordance with the opinion of Rav Ami bar Shmuel (Rambam *Sefer Kedusha, Hilkhot Issurei Bia* 5:12).

הַשָּׁרוֹנִי נִידּוֹן כְּכַּרְמְלִי, חַי – וְלֹא מָזוּג, חָדָשׁ – וְלֹא יָשָׁן.

For the purposes of the examination of blood, **the** wine **of the Sharon** region[B] in Eretz Yisrael **has the same status as undiluted Carmelite**[B] wine[N] **and not diluted** Carmelite wine, **new** Carmelite wine **and not old** Carmelite wine.

אָמַר רַב יִצְחָק בַּר אֲבוּדִימִי: וְכוּלָּן אֵין בּוֹדְקִין אוֹתָן אֶלָּא בְּכוֹס טִבֶרְיָא פָּשׁוּט. מַאי טַעֲמָא? אָמַר אַבַּיֵי: שֶׁל כָּל הָעוֹלָם כּוּלּוֹ, מַחֲזִיק לוֹג – עוֹשִׂין אוֹתוֹ מִמָּנֶה, שְׁנֵי לוּגִּין – עוֹשִׂין אוֹתוֹ מִמָּאתַיִם. כּוֹס טִבֶרְיָא פָּשׁוּט, אֲפִילּוּ מַחֲזִיק שְׁנֵי לוּגִּין – עוֹשִׂין אוֹתוֹ מִמָּנֶה, וְאַיְּידֵי דְּקָלִישׁ – יְדִיעַ בֵּיהּ טְפֵי.

**Rav Yitzḥak bar Avudimi**[P] **says: And** in **all** cases of blood that has the color of diluted wine, **one examines** blood **only with a simple Tiberian cup.** The Gemara asks: **What is the reason? Abaye says:** Containers are designed according to **a universal** standard, such that a cup that can **contain a** ***log***[B] of wine, **one fashions it from** material weighing **one hundred dinars,**[B] whereas a cup that can contain **two** ***log*****, one fashions it from** material weighing **two hundred dinars.** By contrast, in the case of **a simple Tiberian cup, even** one that can **contain two** ***log*****, one fashions it from** material weighing **one hundred dinars. And since** the material from which the cup is made **is weak,** it is more transparent and therefore the redness of the wine inside is **more noticeable.**[N] Consequently, one must compare the blood to wine in a cup of this kind.

הדרן עלך כל היד

## BACKGROUND

**Sharon region** – **שָׁרוֹנִי**: Until the last few centuries, the Sharon region was densely forested. The Sharon is located in the coastal plains and is notable for the many rivers that pass through it, as well as its numerous springs and wells. The Sharon is also known for its fertile soil, especially in its center. The major products of the Sharon include wine, which was named after the region, Sharon wine.

**Carmelite** – **כַּרְמְלִי**: The Carmel region is basically a range of mountains with many steep inclines, as well as rocky terrain in the wadis. The climate of the Carmel region is rainy. Consequently, this region is well suited to various agricultural plantations, to the extent that the name Carmel became synonymous with a place of quality fruits, as in the verse: "And I brought you to a land of fruitful fields [*HaCarmel*]" (Jeremiah 2:7). The wine produced from the vineyards of this region was known as Carmelite wine.

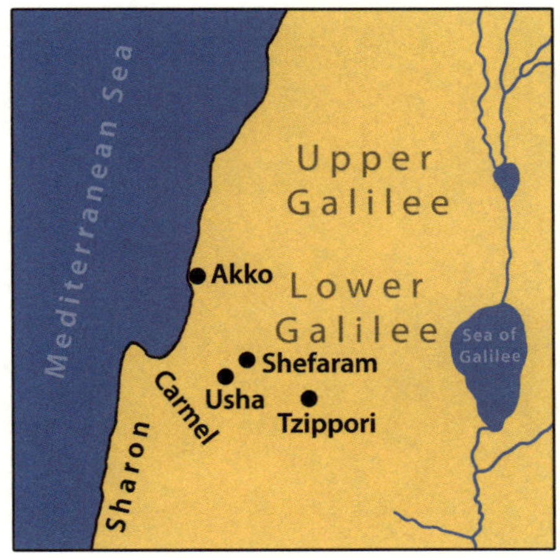


Location of the Sharon and Carmel regions

***Log*** – **לוֹג**: This is the basic liquid measure used by the Sages. It is equivalent to the volume of six eggs, one-quarter of a *kav*, or one twenty-fourth of a *se'a*. A range of modern opinions estimates this volume at 300–600 ml.

**One hundred dinars [*maneh*]** – **מָנֶה**: This refers to a specific weight in silver, equal in value to one hundred dinars. There is a difference between the weight of the Greek and the Roman *maneh*; here the reference is most likely to the Roman *maneh*, which weighed about 327 g.

## NOTES

**The wine of the Sharon has the same status as undiluted Carmelite wine, etc.** – **הַשָּׁרוֹנִי נִידּוֹן כְּכַרְמְלִי חַי וכו׳**: Rashi cites two versions of this statement. According to the version that appears here, the *baraita* is comparing Sharon wine to Carmelite wine. In other words, one may examine blood in comparison to Sharon wine when it is one part wine and two parts water, whether it is old or new. By contrast, an examination with Carmelite wine depends on two factors: The wine must be undiluted and new.

**Since the material is weak it is more noticeable** – **אַיְּידֵי דְּקָלִישׁ יְדִיעַ בֵּיהּ טְפֵי**: The commentaries explain the advantage to performing an examination with a Tiberian cup. Since its glass is thin, to the extent that its weight is half that of other cups that contain a similar volume, the appearance of the wine inside will be clearer (*Ḥeshek Shlomo*, explaining Rambam *Sefer Kedusha*, *Hilkhot Issurei Bia* 5:11).

## PERSONALITIES

**Rav Yitzḥak bar Avudimi** – **רַב יִצְחָק בַּר אֲבוּדִימִי**: The Talmud mentions two Sages of this name. The other Sage lived in the transitional generation between the *tanna'im* and the *amora'im*, whereas the Rav Yitzḥak bar Avudimi mentioned here was a third- and fourth-generation Babylonian *amora*. He was probably a disciple-colleague of Rav Ḥisda, and was famous for his breadth of knowledge of the Bible, as well as for his unique method of study, by which he would seek out and find evidence and allusion to all statements of the Sages in the Bible itself. Rava said of him that any verse that Rav Yitzḥak bar Avudimi did not explain cannot be elucidated (*Zevaḥim* 43b). Numerous *halakhot* are stated in Rav Yitzhak bar Avudimi's name, and his interpretations of verses appear in many places in the Talmud. Occasionally he disagrees with Rav Ḥisda with regard to the interpretation of a verse. Apparently, both Abaye and Rava were his disciples concerning matters of biblical explication, as they attribute various traditions to him.

# Summary of **Perek II**

Although by Torah law a woman is rendered ritually impure as a menstruating woman only if she experiences bleeding, and no regular examinations are required, the Sages deemed it proper and praiseworthy for a woman to examine herself frequently at times when she might have become impure, to ensure that she does not partake of *teruma* in a state of ritual impurity. This applies only to a woman; a man is prohibited from examining himself for a possible seminal emission in case this examination leads to one. But if the man has experienced a gonorrhea-like discharge and wishes to examine himself in case he experiences three such discharges and is consequently obligated to bring an offering, this too is considered praiseworthy.

A woman who is not halakhically competent can be examined and immersed by a competent woman, and it is thereby permitted for her to partake of *teruma*.

With regard to the proper method of examination, a woman should examine herself only with a white linen cloth, which must be soft enough that it can be inserted into all the crevices without injuring her. If a man and woman examined themselves after engaging in intercourse and blood is found on the man's cloth, they are impure and are each obligated to bring a sin offering. If the blood is found on her cloth after she had examined herself immediately after intercourse, they are likewise impure and must each bring a sin offering. If she waited a little while after intercourse before the examination, they are impure due to uncertainty, and if she conducted the examination a long time after engaging in intercourse, she is retroactively impure by rabbinic law, while the man who engaged in intercourse with her is impure only until the evening.

It is derived from the verse: "Her issue in her flesh is blood" (Leviticus 15:19), that not all fluids that come from the uterus are impure; only blood is. This applies even if a fluid is as thick as blood; any fluid that differs in color from blood is not impure. The Sages derive that there are five types of impure blood in a woman, while all others are pure. They specify which of the various colors and shades are included in the types of impure blood and which are excluded from these categories.

The proper manner for a Sage to examine blood brought to him for examination is to compare the blood to the most similar color listed by the Sages. This examination should be conducted against the background of a white cloth. Various practices of Sages are cited in this chapter concerning the time of day when they would perform the examination, and in which places and under what conditions of light they would look at the blood. It is further stated that under certain conditions a Sage may deem blood pure even after another Sage has deemed it impure.

This chapter also addresses the issue of appropriate modest conduct during sexual intercourse, which leads to a discussion of practices that must be avoided.

# Introduction to **Perek III**

*If a woman conceives and gives birth to a male, she shall be impure seven days, as in the days of her menstrual flow she shall be impure. And on the eighth day the flesh of his foreskin shall be circumcised. And she shall continue in the blood of her purification thirty-three days; she shall touch no consecrated item, nor come into the Sanctuary, until the days of her purification are fulfilled. But if she gives birth to a female, then she shall be impure two weeks, as in her menstruation; and she shall continue in the blood of purification sixty-six days.*

(Leviticus 12:2–5)

The Torah states that a woman who gave birth is ritually impure whether she bore a male or a female, and whether she gave birth to a viable newborn or to a non-viable newborn, and even if she discharged the fetus at an early stage of her pregnancy. In all of these cases, she has the ritual impurity status of a woman after childbirth.

But if a woman discharged an item that cannot be considered an offspring at all, she does not have the status of a woman after childbirth. This raises questions with regard to the definition of an offspring: Can an item that has the appearance of an animal, or another creature, be considered a human offspring? What if the offspring has some human features but not others? Other problematic cases include a woman who discharged an amorphous piece of tissue or items that have the appearance of hairs or shells; and a woman who discharged a gestational sac or an afterbirth, or a fetus that looks like it was deformed, in the form of a sandal fish. A similar question is, for how long must a woman be pregnant for a miscarriage to render her a woman after childbirth. All of these issues are discussed in this chapter.

Another case addressed in this chapter is an offspring of uncertain sex. This can happen when the fetus is too tiny for its sex to be recognized, when the newborn infant is a hermaphrodite, or when the infant is a *tumtum*, i.e., its sexual organs are indeterminate. In such a situation, it is unclear for how long the woman must observe the *halakhot* of a woman after childbirth, as this depends on the sex of the newborn.

With regard to a case where a woman discharged an item that is not considered a full-fledged fetus and therefore she does not have the status of a woman after childbirth, the chapter examines whether she automatically assumes the impurity status of a menstruating woman, due to the assumption that miscarriage is always accompanied by bleeding, or whether the woman remains pure unless she experienced bleeding.

One tangential issue examined in this chapter is whether a woman who inserted a tube into her vagina and found blood in the tube assumes the impurity status of a menstruating woman. The underlying question here is whether a woman is rendered impure by the emission of menstruation itself, or whether she is rendered impure through the contact between her menstrual blood and her skin. A similar question applies to the bodily emissions of a male that render him impure, i.e., semen and a gonorrhea-like discharge [*ziva*].

מתני׳ הַמַּפֶּלֶת חֲתִיכָה, אִם יֵשׁ עִמָּהּ דָּם – טְמֵאָה, וְאִם לָאו – טְהוֹרָה. רַבִּי יְהוּדָה אוֹמֵר: בֵּין כָּךְ וּבֵין כָּךְ – טְמֵאָה.

**MISHNA** In the case of a woman **who discharges** an amorphous **piece** of tissue,[H] **if there is blood** that emerges **with it,** the woman is **ritually impure**[N] with the impurity of a menstruating woman. **And if not, she is pure,** as she is neither a menstruating woman nor a woman after childbirth. **Rabbi Yehuda says:** In **both this** case, where blood emerged, **and that** case, where no blood emerged, the woman **is impure** with the impurity of a menstruating woman, as there was certainly undetected blood that emerged with the flesh.

הַמַּפֶּלֶת כְּמִין קְלִיפָּה, כְּמִין שְׂעָרָה, כְּמִין עָפָר, כְּמִין יַבְחוּשִׁין אֲדוּמִּים – תַּטִּיל לְמַיִם, אִם נִמּוֹחוּ – טְמֵאָה, וְאִם לָאו – טְהוֹרָה.

In the case of a woman **who discharges** an item **similar to a shell,** or **similar to a hair,**[N] or **similar to soil,** or **similar to mosquitoes,** if such items are **red,**[N] **she should cast** them **into water** to ascertain their nature: **If they dissolved,** it is blood, and the woman **is impure** with the impurity of a menstruating woman; **and if not, she is pure.**

הַמַּפֶּלֶת כְּמִין דָּגִים, חֲגָבִים, שְׁקָצִים וּרְמָשִׂים, אִם יֵשׁ עִמָּהֶם דָּם – טְמֵאָה, וְאִם לָאו – טְהוֹרָה.

In the case of a woman **who discharges** an item **similar to fish** or to **grasshoppers, repugnant creatures, or creeping animals, if there is blood** that emerges **with them,** the woman **is impure** with the impurity of a menstruating woman. **And if not, she is pure.**

הַמַּפֶּלֶת מִין בְּהֵמָה חַיָּה וָעוֹף, בֵּין טְמֵאִין בֵּין טְהוֹרִין, אִם זָכָר – תֵּשֵׁב לְזָכָר, וְאִם נְקֵבָה – תֵּשֵׁב לִנְקֵבָה,

With regard to a woman **who discharges** tissue in the form of **a type of domesticated animal, undomesticated animal, or bird, whether** it had the form of **a non-kosher** species or **a kosher** species, **if** it was **a male** fetus, then **she observes** the periods of impurity, seven days, and purity, thirty-three days, established in the Torah (see Leviticus 12:2–5) **for** a woman who gives birth to **a male. And if** the fetus was **a female,** the woman **observes** the periods of impurity, fourteen days, and purity, sixty-six days, established in the Torah **for** a woman who gives birth to **a female.**

וְאִם אֵין יָדוּעַ – תֵּשֵׁב לְזָכָר וְלִנְקֵבָה, דִּבְרֵי רַבִּי מֵאִיר. וַחֲכָמִים אוֹמְרִים: כֹּל שֶׁאֵין בּוֹ מִצּוּרַת אָדָם – אֵינוֹ וָלָד.

**And if** the sex of the fetus **is unknown, she observes** the strictures that apply to a woman who gave birth both **to a male and to a female.** Accordingly, she is prohibited from engaging in intercourse for fourteen days, but after that, she will be permitted to engage in intercourse despite a discharge of uterine blood until thirty-three days pass after the seven days she would have been prohibited if the fetus were male. The prohibition to enter the Temple will continue until eighty days have passed from the discharge of the fetus. This is **the statement of Rabbi Meir. And the Rabbis say: Any** fetus **that is not of human form is not** regarded as **an offspring** with regard to observance of these periods, and she is permitted to engage in intercourse provided that she does not experience a discharge of uterine blood.

גמ׳ אָמַר רַב יְהוּדָה, אָמַר שְׁמוּאֵל: לֹא טִימֵּא רַבִּי יְהוּדָה אֶלָּא בַּחֲתִיכָה שֶׁל אַרְבַּעַת מִינֵי דָמִים, אֲבָל שֶׁל שְׁאָר מִינֵי דָמִים – טְהוֹרָה.

**GEMARA** The mishna teaches that if a woman discharges an amorphous piece of tissue and no blood emerges with it, the Rabbis say that she is pure, whereas Rabbi Yehuda says that she is impure. **Rav Yehuda says** that **Shmuel says: Rabbi Yehuda deemed** the woman **impure,** despite the fact that no blood emerged, **only in** the case of **a piece** of tissue that has the appearance **of** one of **the four types of** ritually impure **blood,** as in such a case the piece has the status of blood. **But** if it has the appearance **of other types of blood,** the woman **is pure.**

**NOTES**

**A woman who discharges an amorphous piece of tissue, if there is blood with it she is ritually impure – הַמַּפֶּלֶת חֲתִיכָה אִם יֵשׁ עִמָּהּ דָּם טְמֵאָה:** She has the ritual impurity of a menstruating woman. In the Rambam's Commentary on the Mishna, it says that if there is a bone in the piece of tissue, she is impure with the impurity of a woman after childbirth.

**A woman who discharges an item similar to a shell or similar to a hair – הַמַּפֶּלֶת כְּמִין קְלִיפָּה כְּמִין שְׂעָרָה:** In this case, Rabbi Yehuda concedes that if the item is not dissolved in water, the woman is ritually pure. This is because the reason Rabbi Yehuda deems the woman impure in a case where she discharged an amorphous piece of tissue, according to the conclusion of the Gemara, is that he holds that blood automatically emerges when the womb opens. That reasoning is not relevant in these cases, as the items are so small that the womb does not open (early commentaries on 22b, including *Tosafot*, Ramban, Ran, Rashba, and Ra'avad).

**Similar to mosquitoes if they are red – כְּמִין יַבְחוּשִׁין אֲדוּמִּים:** The commentaries explain that the condition that the item must be red applies not only to when it is similar to a mosquito, but to the previous cases as well, i.e., if it is similar to a shell, hair, or soil. In other words, in all these cases, if the item is not red, there is no need to examine it by casting it into water, as the woman is definitely pure. This is also the ruling of the Rambam (*Sefer Kedusha, Hilkhot Issurei Bia* 5:14).

**HALAKHA**

**A woman who discharges an amorphous piece of tissue, etc. – הַמַּפֶּלֶת חֲתִיכָה וכו׳:** The Rambam holds that in a case where a woman discharges an amorphous piece of tissue, if blood emerges with it she is impure, but if blood does not emerge with it, even if it is red, she is ritually pure. This is the *halakha* even if the piece of tissue is torn open and is discovered to be full of blood, as the blood is not menstrual blood, but rather the blood of the piece of tissue. The Ra'avad writes that since the Rabbis in the *baraita* hold that when the womb opens, blood automatically emerges, the woman is impure in any case, as blood certainly emerged during the miscarriage. The *Maggid Mishne* rules in accordance with the opinion of the Rambam (Rambam *Sefer Kedusha, Hilkhot Issurei Bia* 5:13).

וְרַבִּי יוֹחָנָן אָמַר: שֶׁל אַרְבַּעַת מִינֵי דָמִים – דִּבְרֵי הַכֹּל טְמֵאָה, שֶׁל שְׁאָר מִינֵי דָמִים – דִּבְרֵי הַכֹּל טְהוֹרָה.

**And Rabbi Yoḥanan says** there is a different explanation of the dispute: If a woman discharges a piece of tissue that has the appearance **of** one of **the four types of** ritually impure **blood, everyone,** i.e., Rabbi Yehuda and the Rabbis, **agrees** that she **is impure.** Likewise, if it has the appearance **of other types of blood, everyone agrees** that **she is pure.**

לֹא נֶחְלְקוּ אֶלָּא שֶׁהִפִּילָה וְאֵינָהּ יוֹדַעַת מַה הִפִּילָה. רַבִּי יְהוּדָה סָבַר: זִיל בָּתַר רוֹב חֲתִיכוֹת, וְרוֹב חֲתִיכוֹת שֶׁל (מִינֵי) אַרְבַּעַת מִינֵי דָמִים הָוְיָין. וְרַבָּנַן סָבְרִי: לָא אָמְרִינַן רוֹב חֲתִיכוֹת שֶׁל אַרְבַּעַת מִינֵי דָמִים.

**They disagree only** with regard to a case **where** the woman **discharged** an amorphous piece of tissue, **and** she herself **does not know** exactly **what** was the appearance of the piece of tissue that **she discharged,** e.g., if it was lost. **Rabbi Yehuda holds: Follow the majority of** discharges of amorphous **pieces** of tissue, **and the majority of pieces** of tissue **are** of the appearance **of** one of the **four types of** impure **blood. And the Rabbis hold: We do not say** that **the majority of pieces** of flesh have the appearance **of** one of the **four types of** impure **blood.**

אִינִי, וְהָא כִּי אֲתָא רַב הוֹשַׁעְיָא מִנְּהַרְדְּעָא, אֲתָא וְאַיְיתֵי מַתְנִיתָא בִּידֵיהּ: הַמַּפֶּלֶת חֲתִיכָה אֲדוּמָּה, שְׁחוֹרָה, יְרוּקָּה, וּלְבָנָה, אִם יֵשׁ עִמָּהּ דָּם – טְמֵאָה, וְאִם לָאו – טְהוֹרָה. רַבִּי יְהוּדָה אוֹמֵר: בֵּין כָּךְ וּבֵין כָּךְ טְמֵאָה. קַשְׁיָא לִשְׁמוּאֵל בַּחֲדָא, וּלְרַבִּי יוֹחָנָן בְּתַרְתֵּי.

The Gemara asks: **Is that so? But when Rav Hoshaya came from Neharde'a,**[B] **he came and brought a** ***baraita*** **with him** that states: In the case of a woman **who discharges a piece** of tissue that is **red, black, green, or white, if there is blood** that emerges **with it,** the woman **is impure, and if not, she is pure. Rabbi Yehuda says: Both** in **this** case, where blood emerged, **and** in **that** case, where no blood emerged, the woman **is impure.** This *baraita* poses **a difficulty to** the statement of **Shmuel with regard to one** aspect of his opinion, **and** it poses a difficulty **to** the statement of **Rabbi Yoḥanan with regard to two** aspects of his opinion.

לִשְׁמוּאֵל בַּחֲדָא – דַּאֲמַר שְׁמוּאֵל: לֹא טִימֵּא רַבִּי יְהוּדָה אֶלָּא בַּחֲתִיכָה שֶׁל אַרְבַּעַת מִינֵי דָמִים, וְהָא קָתָנֵי יְרוּקָּה וּלְבָנָה, וּפָלֵיג רַבִּי יְהוּדָה!

The Gemara elaborates: It poses a difficulty **to** the statement of **Shmuel with regard to one** aspect of his opinion, **as Shmuel said** that **Rabbi Yehuda deemed** the woman **impure only in** the case of **a piece** of tissue that has the appearance **of** one of **the four types of** impure **blood, and** yet the *baraita* **teaches** that according to the Rabbis the woman is pure if the piece of tissue is **green or white,** which are not among the four colors of ritually impure blood, **and** that Rabbi Yehuda **disagrees** with their opinion.

וְכִי תֵּימָא: כִּי פָּלֵיג רַבִּי יְהוּדָה – אַאֲדוּמָּה וּשְׁחוֹרָה, וְאַיְּרוּקָּה וּלְבָנָה – לָא, אֶלָּא יְרוּקָּה וּלְבָנָה לְמַאן קָתָנֵי לָהּ?

**And if you would say** that **when Rabbi Yehuda disagrees** with the Rabbis, it is **with regard to** the case of **a red or black** piece of tissue, as these are among the four colors of ritually impure blood, **but with regard to** the case of **a green or white** piece he does **not** disagree with them, i.e., he concedes that the woman is pure, this cannot be correct. The Gemara explains why that explanation of the *baraita* is not possible: **But** if so, **for** the sake of clarifying **whose** opinion **does** the *baraita* **teach** the case of **a green or white** piece of tissue?

אִילֵימָא רַבָּנַן – הָשְׁתָּא אֲדוּמָּה וּשְׁחוֹרָה מְטַהֲרִי רַבָּנַן, יְרוּקָּה וּלְבָנָה מִיבַּעְיָא? אֶלָּא לָאו – לְרַבִּי יְהוּדָה, וּפָלֵיג!

**If we say** that it comes to clarify the opinion of **the Rabbis,** that is unnecessary: **Now** that in a case of **a red or black** piece of tissue, which are among the four colors of ritually impure blood, **the Rabbis deem** the woman **pure, is** it **necessary** to state that they deem her pure in a case of **a green or white** piece? **Rather,** is it **not** coming **to** clarify the opinion of **Rabbi Yehuda,** teaching that the Rabbis deem the woman pure in this case, **but** Rabbi Yehuda **disagrees** with them and deems her impure? This contradicts the explanation of Shmuel.

---

**BACKGROUND**

**Neharde'a – נְהַרְדְּעָא:** A city on the Euphrates, near the Malka River, Neharde'a was one of the oldest Jewish communities in Babylonia. According to tradition, Jews lived in Neharde'a as early as the First Temple period, in the sixth century BCE, beginning with the exile of King Jehoiachin of Judah. Furthermore, Neharde'a was one of the most important Jewish communities in Babylonia. It was a center of Torah learning from an early period, and its yeshiva was the oldest in Babylonia. Many of the greatest *tanna'im* visited Neharde'a, among them Rabbi Akiva, who intercalated the calendar there (*Yevamot* 122b). During Rav's time, the first half of the third century CE, the yeshiva in Neharde'a was headed by Rav Sheila, and after him by Shmuel. Since the city lay near the border between the Roman and the Persian Empires, it frequently suffered from the wars between the two, and Pappa ben Nazer Odonathus, king of Tadmor, destroyed it completely in 259 CE. Later, Jews resettled there, and many Torah scholars remained in Neharde'a even after its yeshiva split and was reestablished in Meḥoza and Pumbedita.

וְתוּ, לְרַבִּי יוֹחָנָן דְּאָמַר: שֶׁל אַרְבַּעַת מִינֵי דָמִים – דִּבְרֵי הַכֹּל טְמֵאָה, הָא קָתָנֵי אֲדוּמָּה וּשְׁחוֹרָה, וּפְלִיגִי רַבָּנַן!

**And furthermore,** the *baraita* poses an additional difficulty **to** the opinion of **Rabbi Yoḥanan,** in addition to the first difficulty explained above, **as he said** that if the piece of tissue has the appearance **of** one of **the four types of** ritually impure **blood** then **everyone agrees** that the woman **is impure,** and yet the *baraita* **teaches** the case of **a red or black** piece **and** states that **the Rabbis disagree** with Rabbi Yehuda and deem the woman pure.

וְכִי תֵּימָא: כִּי פְּלִיגִי רַבָּנַן – אַיְּרוּקָּה וּלְבָנָה, אֲבָל אַאֲדוּמָּה וּשְׁחוֹרָה – לָא, אֶלָּא אֲדוּמָּה וּשְׁחוֹרָה לְמַאן קָתָנֵי לָהּ?

**And if you would say** that **when the Rabbis disagree** with Rabbi Yehuda, it is **with regard to** the case of **a green or white** piece of tissue, **but in** the case of **a red or black** piece they do **not** disagree with him, as they concede that the woman is impure; **but** if that is so, then **for** the sake of clarifying **whose** opinion **does** the *baraita* **teach** the case of **a red or black** piece?

אִילֵימָא רַבִּי יְהוּדָה – הַשְׁתָּא יְרוּקָּה וּלְבָנָה טְמֵאָה, אֲדוּמָּה וּשְׁחוֹרָה מִיבַּעְיָא? אֶלָּא לָאו – רַבָּנַן, וּפְלִיגִי!

**If** we **say** that it comes to clarify the opinion of **Rabbi Yehuda,** this is unnecessary: **Now** that Rabbi Yehuda holds that in a case of **a green or white** piece the woman **is impure,** despite the fact that they are not among the four colors of ritually impure blood, **is it necessary** to state that she is impure in a case of **a red or black** piece? **Rather,** is it **not** coming to clarify the opinion of **the Rabbis,** teaching that Rabbi Yehuda deems the woman impure in this case, **but the Rabbis disagree** with him and maintain that she is pure?

אֶלָּא אָמַר רַב נַחְמָן בַּר יִצְחָק: בְּאֶפְשָׁר לִפְתִיחַת הַקֶּבֶר בְּלֹא דָּם קָמִיפַּלְגִי, וּבִפְלוּגְתָּא דְּהָנֵי תַּנָּאֵי, דְּתַנְיָא: קָשְׁתָה שְׁנַיִם וְלַשְּׁלִישִׁי הִפִּילָה, וְאֵינָהּ יוֹדַעַת מַה הִפִּילָה,

**Rather, Rav Naḥman bar Yitzḥak says** there is a different explanation of the dispute between the Rabbis and Rabbi Yehuda: **They disagree with regard to** whether or not **opening of the womb is possible without** a discharge of **blood. And** they disagree **with regard to** the issue that is the subject of **the dispute between these** *tanna'im*,[N] **as it is taught** in a *baraita*: If a woman experienced **difficulty in labor** during which blood emerged on **two** consecutive days, **and on the third** day **she discharged,**[H] **but she does not know what she discharged,** i.e., whether it was a stillborn human fetus, and whether blood emerged during the miscarriage,

**NOTES**

**And they disagree with regard to the dispute between these** ***tanna'im*** **– וּבִפְלוּגְתָּא דְּהָנֵי תַּנָּאֵי:** The early commentaries question this comparison between the dispute in the mishna and the dispute in the *baraita*, as in the *baraita* the dispute is whether it is certain or uncertain that the woman is impure, whereas the Rabbis in the mishna hold that she is definitely pure. They answer that the mishna is referring to a case where the woman examined herself and did not find blood. Therefore the Rabbis hold that she is pure for certain (Ramban).

**HALAKHA**

**If she experienced difficulty in labor during which blood emerged on two days and on the third day she discharged, etc. – קָשְׁתָה שְׁנַיִם וְלַשְּׁלִישִׁי הִפִּילָה וכו׳:** If a woman experienced bleeding on two consecutive days, and on the third day she discharged but does not know whether she discharged a full-fledged fetus, she assumes the status of a woman about whom it is uncertain whether she gave birth, and of an uncertain *zava*, as it is possible for a womb to open up without a discharge of blood. Therefore, she brings an offering, but it is not eaten by the priests. This is in accordance with the opinion of the first *tanna* (Rambam *Sefer Kedusha, Hilkhot Issurei Bia* 7:4).

Perek **III**
Daf **21** Amud **b**

הֲרֵי זוֹ סְפֵק לֵידָה סְפֵק זִיבָה, מְבִיאָה קָרְבָּן וְאֵינוֹ נֶאֱכָל.

**it is uncertain** whether **that** woman has the status of one who gave **birth,** and it is **uncertain** whether she has the status of a woman who experiences **an irregular discharge of blood from the uterus** [*ziva*].[N] Therefore, **she brings an offering,** like any woman after childbirth or after *ziva*, **but** the offering **is not eaten** by the priests. The reason is that perhaps she neither gave birth nor experienced *ziva*, and is therefore exempt from bringing an offering. Consequently, her bird sin offering is disqualified, and is forbidden in consumption, as a bird offering is killed by pinching its neck, which is not the valid manner of slaughtering a non-sacred bird.

רַבִּי יְהוֹשֻׁעַ אוֹמֵר: מְבִיאָה קָרְבָּן וְנֶאֱכָל, שֶׁאִי אֶפְשָׁר לִפְתִיחַת הַקֶּבֶר בְּלֹא דָּם.

**Rabbi Yehoshua says:** The woman **brings an offering, and it is eaten.** The reason is that she is certainly either a woman after childbirth or a *zava*, **as opening of the womb is not possible without** a discharge of **blood.** The *tanna'im* in the *baraita* disagree about whether opening of the womb is possible without a discharge of blood. Rav Naḥman bar Yitzḥak maintains that this is also the issue in dispute between Rabbi Yehuda and the Rabbis in the mishna.

לִישָּׁנָא אַחֲרִינָא אָמְרִי לָהּ, אָמַר רַב יְהוּדָה, אָמַר שְׁמוּאֵל: לֹא טִימֵּא רַבִּי יְהוּדָה אֶלָּא בַּחֲתִיכָה שֶׁל אַרְבָּעָה מִינֵי דָמִים, אֲבָל שֶׁל שְׁאָר מִינֵי דָמִים – טְהוֹרָה.

§ **Some say another version**[N] of the above discussion. **Rav Yehuda says** that **Shmuel says: Rabbi Yehuda deemed** the woman **impure,** despite the fact that no blood emerged, **only in** the case of **a piece** of tissue that has the appearance **of** one of the **four types of** ritually impure **blood, but** if it has the appearance **of other types of blood,** the woman **is pure.**

**NOTES**

**It is uncertain whether that woman has the status of one who gave birth and uncertain whether she experiences** ***ziva*** **– הֲרֵי זוֹ סְפֵק לֵידָה סְפֵק זִיבָה:** Rashi explains that there are two uncertainties, which lead to three possible outcomes. The uncertainties are whether the woman discharged a full-fledged fetus, and whether or not blood emerged during her miscarriage. If she discharged a full-fledged fetus, she assumes the status of a woman who gave birth, and is impure. She is not considered a *zava* even if blood emerged during the miscarriage and that was the third consecutive day on which she saw blood during her days of *ziva*, as blood that emerges during childbirth does not render a woman a *zava*. If it was not a full-fledged fetus, and blood emerged during the miscarriage, she is a *zava*, as this miscarriage does not have the halakhic status of childbirth. Finally, if it was not a full-fledged fetus and blood did not emerge during the miscarriage, the woman is pure. Consequently, the woman must bring an offering, due to the first two possibilities, but it is not eaten, due to the possibility that she is pure, in which case the offering is disqualified.

**Another version – לִישָּׁנָא אַחֲרִינָא:** The only difference between this version and the previous version is that in this version the explanation of Rabbi Yoḥanan is omitted.

אִינִי, וְהָא כִּי אֲתָא רַב הוֹשַׁעְיָא מִנְּהַרְדְּעָא, אֲתָא וְאַיְיתֵי מַתְנִיתָא בִּידֵיהּ: הַמַּפֶּלֶת חֲתִיכָה אֲדוּמָּה וּשְׁחוֹרָה יְרוּקָּה וּלְבָנָה, אִם יֵשׁ עִמָּהּ דָּם – טְמֵאָה, וְאִם לָאו – טְהוֹרָה. וְרַבִּי יְהוּדָה אוֹמֵר: בֵּין כָּךְ וּבֵין כָּךְ – טְמֵאָה.

The Gemara asks: **Is that so? But when Rav Hoshaya came from Neharde'a, he came and brought a *baraita* with him** that states: In the case of a woman **who discharges a piece** of tissue that is **red, or black, green, or white, if there is blood** that emerges **with it,** the woman **is impure, and if not, she is pure. And Rabbi Yehuda says:** In **both this** case, where blood emerged, **and that** case, where no blood emerged, the woman **is impure.**

קָתָנֵי ״אֲדוּמָּה וּשְׁחוֹרָה יְרוּקָּה וּלְבָנָה״ – וּפָלֵיג רַבִּי יְהוּדָה!

The Gemara concludes its challenge: The *baraita* **teaches** both a case where the piece of tissue is **red or black,** and a case where it is not one of the four types of impure blood but it is **green or white,** i.e., in all of these cases the Rabbis hold that the woman is pure, **and** yet **Rabbi Yehuda disagrees** with their opinion.

וְכִי תֵּימָא: כִּי פָּלֵיג רַבִּי יְהוּדָה – אַאֲדוּמָּה וּשְׁחוֹרָה, אֲבָל יְרוּקָּה וּלְבָנָה – לָא, אֶלָּא יְרוּקָּה וּלְבָנָה מַאן קָתָנֵי לַהּ?

**And if you would say** that **when Rabbi Yehuda disagrees** with the Rabbis, it is **with regard to** the case of **a red or black** piece of tissue, **but** with regard to the case of a **green or white** piece he does **not** disagree with them, as he concedes that the woman is pure; **but** if that is so, **for** the sake of clarifying **whose** opinion does the *baraita* **teach** the case of **a green or white** piece of tissue?

אִילֵימָא לְרַבָּנַן – הַשְׁתָּא אֲדוּמָּה וּשְׁחוֹרָה קָא מְטַהֲרִי רַבָּנַן, יְרוּקָּה וּלְבָנָה מִיבַּעְיָא? אֶלָּא לָאו – לְרַבִּי יְהוּדָה, וּפָלֵיג!

**If we say** that it comes **to** clarify the opinion of **the Rabbis,** that is unnecessary: **Now** that in the case of **a red or black** piece of tissue **the Rabbis deem** the woman **pure, is it necessary** to state that they deem her pure in a case of **a green or white** piece? **Rather, is it not** coming **to** clarify the opinion of **Rabbi Yehuda,** teaching that the Rabbis deem the woman pure in this case, **but** Rabbi Yehuda **disagrees** with them and deems her impure? This contradicts the explanation of Shmuel.

אֶלָּא אָמַר רַב יְהוּדָה: בְּאֶפְשָׁר לִפְתִיחַת הַקֶּבֶר בְּלֹא דָּם קָמִיפַּלְגִי, וּבִפְלוּגְתָּא דְּהָנֵי תַּנָּאֵי, דְּתַנְיָא: קָשְׁתָה שְׁנַיִם וְלַשְּׁלִישִׁי הִפִּילָה, וְאֵינָהּ יוֹדַעַת מַה הִפִּילָה – הֲרֵי זוֹ סְפֵק לֵידָה סְפֵק זִיבָה, מְבִיאָה קָרְבָּן וְאֵינוֹ נֶאֱכָל.

**Rather, Rav Yehuda says** there is a different explanation of the dispute between the Rabbis and Rabbi Yehuda: **They disagree with regard to** whether or not **opening of the womb is possible without** a discharge of **blood. And** they disagree **with regard to** the issue that is the subject of **the dispute between these *tanna'im*, as it is taught** in a *baraita*: If a woman experienced **difficulty in labor** during which blood emerged on **two** consecutive days, **and on the third** day **she discharged, but she does not know what she discharged, it is uncertain** whether she has the status of a woman who gave **birth,** and it is **uncertain** whether she has the status of a woman who experienced ***ziva***. Therefore **she brings an offering, but it is not eaten** by the priests.

רַבִּי יְהוֹשֻׁעַ אוֹמֵר: מְבִיאָה קָרְבָּן וְנֶאֱכָל, לְפִי שֶׁאִי אֶפְשָׁר לִפְתִיחַת הַקֶּבֶר בְּלֹא דָּם.

**Rabbi Yehoshua says:** The woman **brings an offering, and it is eaten.** The reason is that she is certainly either a woman after childbirth or a *zava*, **as opening of the womb is not possible without** a discharge of **blood.** This is also the matter in dispute between the Rabbis and Rabbi Yehuda.

תָּנוּ רַבָּנַן: הַמַּפֶּלֶת חֲתִיכָה, סוּמָכוֹס אוֹמֵר מִשּׁוּם רַבִּי מֵאִיר, וְכֵן הָיָה רַבִּי שִׁמְעוֹן בֶּן מְנַסְיָא אוֹמֵר כִּדְבָרָיו: קוֹרְעָהּ, אִם יֵשׁ דָּם בְּתוֹכָהּ – טְמֵאָה, וְאִם לָאו – טְהוֹרָה.

§ **The Sages taught** in a *baraita*: In the case of a woman **who discharges** an amorphous **piece** of tissue, **Sumakhos says in the name of Rabbi Meir, and likewise Rabbi Shimon ben Menasya would say in accordance with his statement:** A Sage who is presented with this piece of tissue should **tear it** to examine it. **If there is blood inside it,** the woman is **ritually impure, and if not, she is pure.**

כְּרַבָּנַן, וַעֲדִיפָא מִדְּרַבָּנַן, כְּרַבָּנַן – דְּאָמְרִי אֶפְשָׁר לִפְתִיחַת הַקֶּבֶר בְּלֹא דָּם, וַעֲדִיפָא מִדְּרַבָּנַן – דְּאִינְהוּ סָבְרִי עִמָּהּ – אִין, בְּתוֹכָהּ – לָא, וְסוּמָכוֹס סָבַר: אֲפִילּוּ בְּתוֹכָהּ.

The Gemara compares this *baraita* to the ruling of the mishna: This statement is basically **in accordance with** the opinion of **the Rabbis** in the mishna, **but it is** more **far-reaching,** i.e., more stringent, **than that** ruling **of the Rabbis. It is in accordance with** the opinion **of the Rabbis, as they say** that **opening of the womb is possible without** a discharge of **blood,** whereas Rabbi Yehuda maintains that opening of the womb is impossible without a discharge of blood. **But** the ruling of the *baraita* is more **far-reaching than that** ruling **of the Rabbis, as they hold** that if blood emerges **with** the piece of tissue, then **yes,** the woman is impure, but if blood is found **inside** the piece of tissue, she is **not** impure; **and Sumakhos holds** that **even** if blood is found **inside** the piece, the woman is impure.

וְתַנְיָא אִידָךְ, הַמַּפֶּלֶת חֲתִיכָה, רַבִּי אַחָא אוֹמֵר: קוֹרְעָהּ, אִם תּוֹכָהּ מַאֲדִים – טְמֵאָה, וְאִם לָאו – טְהוֹרָה.

**And it is taught** in **another** *baraita* with regard to a woman **who discharges** an amorphous **piece** of tissue, that **Rabbi Aḥa says:** One **tears it** open, and **if its interior looks red,** even if it contains no blood, the woman **is impure;**[N] **and if** it does **not** have a red appearance, **she is pure.**

כְּסוּמָכוֹס, וַעֲדִיפָא מִסּוּמָכוֹס.

The Gemara compares this *baraita* to the aforementioned opinion of Sumakhos: This ruling of Rabbi Aḥa is basically **in accordance with** the opinion of **Sumakhos,** as Rabbi Aḥa also requires that the interior of the piece of tissue must be examined to see if there is blood on the inside, **but** it is more **far-reaching than** the opinion of **Sumakhos,** as Rabbi Aḥa deems the woman impure even if the piece of tissue merely looks red on the inside but does not contain blood.

וְתַנְיָא אִידָךְ, הַמַּפֶּלֶת חֲתִיכָה, רַבִּי בִּנְיָמִין אוֹמֵר: קוֹרְעָהּ, אִם יֵשׁ בָּהּ עֶצֶם – אִמּוֹ טְמֵאָה לֵידָה. אָמַר רַב חִסְדָּא: וּבַחֲתִיכָה לְבָנָה. וְכֵן כִּי אֲתָא זוּגָא דְּמִן חַדְיַיב, אֲתָא וְאַיְיתֵי מַתְנִיתָא בִּידֵיהּ: הַמַּפֶּלֶת חֲתִיכָה לְבָנָה – קוֹרְעָהּ, אִם יֵשׁ בָּהּ עֶצֶם – אִמּוֹ טְמֵאָה לֵידָה.

**And it is taught** in **another** *baraita* with regard to a woman **who discharges** an amorphous **piece** of tissue, that **Rabbi Binyamin says** one **tears it** open to examine it. **If it contains a bone,** it is considered a fetus, and **its mother is impure** with the impurity of a woman who gave **birth. Rav Ḥisda says: And** this applies **in** the case of **a white piece**[H] of flesh; only in such a situation does the existence of a bone render it a fetus. **And likewise, when a pair** of Torah scholars **came from Ḥadyab,**[B] **they came and brought a** ***baraita*** **with them:** In the case of a woman **who discharges a white piece** of tissue, one **tears it** open to examine it, and **if it contains a bone, its mother is impure** with the impurity of a woman who gave **birth.**

אָמַר רַבִּי יוֹחָנָן מִשּׁוּם רַבִּי שִׁמְעוֹן בֶּן יוֹחַי: הַמַּפֶּלֶת חֲתִיכָה – קוֹרְעָהּ, אִם יֵשׁ בָּהּ דָּם אָגוּר – טְמֵאָה, וְאִם לָאו – טְהוֹרָה. כְּסוּמָכוֹס וְקִילָּא מִכּוּלְּהוּ.

**Rabbi Yoḥanan says in the name of Rabbi Shimon ben Yoḥai:** With regard to a woman **who discharges** an amorphous **piece** of tissue, one **tears it** open to examine it. **If it contains** a quantity of **accumulated blood,**[N] the woman **is impure; and if not, she is pure.** The Gemara comments: This is basically **in accordance with** the opinion of **Sumakhos,** that blood found inside the piece of tissue renders the woman impure, **but it is more lenient than all** the previous opinions, i.e., Sumakhos and Rabbi Aḥa, as according to Rabbi Shimon ben Yoḥai the woman is rendered impure only if there is a quantity of accumulated blood.

בְּעָא מִינֵּיהּ רַבִּי יִרְמְיָה מֵרַבִּי זֵירָא: הָרוֹאָה דָּם בִּשְׁפוֹפֶרֶת מַהוּ? ״בִּבְשָׂרָהּ״ אָמַר רַחֲמָנָא – וְלֹא בִּשְׁפוֹפֶרֶת, אוֹ דִּלְמָא הַאי ״בִּבְשָׂרָהּ״ מִיבְּעֵי לֵיהּ – שֶׁמִּטַּמְּאָה מִבִּפְנִים כְּבַחוּץ?

§ **Rabbi Yirmeya asked Rabbi Zeira:** In the case of a woman **who** inserted a tube into her vagina and **sees blood,** i.e., she found blood **in the tube,**[H] **what is** the *halakha*? Rabbi Yirmeya clarified his question: Since it is stated: "And if a woman has an issue, and her issue **in her flesh** is blood, she shall be in her impurity seven days" (Leviticus 15:19), perhaps **the Merciful One states** in this verse that the woman is impure only if the blood is discharged through "her flesh" **and not through a tube. Or perhaps this** term: **"In her flesh,"** is **necessary** to teach the *halakha* **that** a woman **becomes impure** by finding blood **inside** her vagina **just as** she becomes impure by experiencing bleeding **outside** her vagina, i.e., once the blood enters the vaginal canal from the uterus the woman is ritually impure.

## NOTES

**If its interior looks red the woman is impure – אִם תּוֹכָהּ מַאֲדִים טְמֵאָה:** The Gemara states that this is at variance with the Rabbis in the mishna. According to this opinion, if the interior of the piece of tissue is red, the woman is impure even if the exterior does not look red. If the exterior looks red, even if the interior is not red, the woman is impure.

**Rabbi Yoḥanan says in the name of Rabbi Shimon ben Yoḥai…if it contains accumulated blood – אָמַר רַבִּי יוֹחָנָן מִשּׁוּם רַבִּי שִׁמְעוֹן בֶּן יוֹחַי...אִם יֵשׁ בָּהּ דָּם אָגוּר:** This ruling apparently contradicts Rabbi Yoḥanan's earlier statement (21a), that if the piece of tissue has the appearance of one of the four types of impure blood, the woman is impure, but otherwise the woman is pure. He does not require that the piece of tissue must be torn for examination. Some commentaries explain that Rabbi Yoḥanan's statement here is not his own opinion, but that of Rabbi Shimon ben Yoḥai. Rabbi Yoḥanan's own opinion is cited earlier.

## BACKGROUND

**Ḥadyab – חַדְיַיב:** Ḥadyab is a region in northern Syria adjacent to the Tigris River. During the period before the destruction of the Second Temple, there existed in the region a small autonomous kingdom under the supreme rule of the Parthian Empire. Its monarchs, Queen Heleni and her sons Munbaz and Izates, converted to Judaism.

Location of Ḥadyab

## HALAKHA

**In the case of a white piece – בַּחֲתִיכָה לְבָנָה:** In a case where a woman discharges a white piece of tissue, and it is torn open for examination and a bone is found inside, the woman is impure with the status of a woman who gave birth. Since it is uncertain whether the fetus is male or female, she observes the period of impurity established in the Torah for a woman who gives birth to a female (*Shakh*). This is in accordance with the opinion of Rabbi Binyamin, as explained by Rav Ḥisda (Rambam *Sefer Kedusha*, *Hilkhot Issurei Bia* 10:4, and see *Maggid Mishne* and *Kesef Mishne* there).

**A woman who sees blood in the tube – הָרוֹאָה דָּם בִּשְׁפוֹפֶרֶת:** If a woman inserted a tube into her vagina, and blood came out, she is ritually pure. This is because it is derived from the verse: "Her discharge in her flesh is blood," that a woman is impure only if she finds blood in her body, which is the normal way that women find blood, as it is not the norm for a woman to find blood in a tube. This is in accordance with the opinion of Rabbi Zeira (Rambam *Sefer Kedusha*, *Hilkhot Issurei Bia* 5:16; *Shulḥan Arukh*, *Yoreh De'a* 188:3).

**HALAKHA**

**Where the piece of tissue is cracked – דִּפְלֵי פְּלוֹיֵי:** If a woman discharges an amorphous piece of tissue that has blood in it, even if the piece of tissue is cracked and the blood in the cracks comes in contact with the woman's body, she is pure, as menstrual blood does not normally emerge this way. This is in accordance with the Gemara's interpretation of the opinion of the Rabbis (*Shulḥan Arukh, Yoreh De'a* 188:3).

אֲמַר לֵיהּ: ״בִּבְשָׂרָהּ״ אָמַר רַחֲמָנָא – וְלֹא בִּשְׁפוֹפֶרֶת. דְּאִי ״בִּבְשָׂרָהּ״ מִבָּעֵי לֵיהּ שֶׁמְּטַמְּאָה מִבִּפְנִים כְּבַחוּץ – אִם כֵּן נֵימָא קְרָא ״בְּבָשָׂר״, מַאי ״בִּבְשָׂרָהּ״ – שְׁמַע מִינַּהּ תַּרְתֵּי.

Rabbi Zeira **said to** Rabbi Yirmeya: **The Merciful One states: "In her flesh,"** meaning that the woman is impure only if the blood is discharged through "her flesh" **and not through a tube. As, if the** term **"in her flesh" is necessary** to teach **that** a woman **becomes impure** by finding blood **inside** her vagina **just as** by seeing blood **outside** her vagina, **if so, let the verse say: In the flesh. What** is the significance of the fact that the verse states: **"In her flesh"? Conclude two** conclusions **from** the term, both that a woman becomes impure by the presence of blood inside her vagina, and that a woman who experiences bleeding that emerged through a tube is ritually pure.

וְהָא אָמַר רַבִּי יוֹחָנָן מִשּׁוּם רַבִּי שִׁמְעוֹן בֶּן יוֹחַי: הַמַּפֶּלֶת חֲתִיכָה – קוֹרְעָהּ, אִם יֵשׁ בָּהּ דָּם אָגוּר – טְמֵאָה, וְאִם לָאו – טְהוֹרָה!

The Gemara asks: **But doesn't Rabbi Yoḥanan say in the name of Rabbi Shimon ben Yoḥai:** With regard to a woman **who discharges** an amorphous **piece** of tissue, one **tears it** open to examine it; **if it contains** a quantity of **accumulated blood,** the woman **is impure, and if not, she is pure?** If a woman who sees blood that emerged inside a piece of tissue becomes impure, the same should apply to a woman who sees blood that emerged through a tube.

הָכִי הָשְׁתָּא? הָתָם – דַּרְכָּהּ שֶׁל אִשָּׁה לִרְאוֹת דָּם בַּחֲתִיכָה, הָכָא – אֵין דַּרְכָּהּ שֶׁל אִשָּׁה לִרְאוֹת דָּם בִּשְׁפוֹפֶרֶת.

The Gemara responds: **How can** these cases **be compared? There,** with regard to a piece of tissue, the woman is impure, as **it is the manner of a woman to see blood inside** such **a piece** of tissue. Therefore, this blood fulfills the condition stated in the verse: "In her flesh." By contrast, **here,** in the case of a tube, the woman should not be impure, as **it is not the manner of a woman to see blood** that emerged **through a tube.**

לֵימָא שְׁפוֹפֶרֶת תַּנָּאֵי הִיא. דְּתַנְיָא: הַמַּפֶּלֶת חֲתִיכָה, אַף עַל פִּי שֶׁמְּלֵאָה דָּם, אִם יֵשׁ עִמָּהּ דָּם – טְמֵאָה, וְאִם לָאו – טְהוֹרָה. רַבִּי אֱלִיעֶזֶר אוֹמֵר: ״בִּבְשָׂרָהּ״ – וְלֹא בְּשָׁפִיר, וְלֹא בַּחֲתִיכָה.

The Gemara suggests: **Shall we say** that the *halakha* in the case of **a tube is** subject to a dispute between ***tanna'im*? As it is taught** in a *baraita*: With regard to a woman **who discharges** an amorphous **piece** of tissue, **even though** the piece **is full of blood, if there is blood** on the outside that emerges **with it,** the woman **is impure; and if not, she is pure. Rabbi Eliezer says:** The term **"in her flesh"** teaches that a woman is rendered impure only by blood that emerges through direct contact with her flesh, **and not** by blood that emerges **in a gestational sac, nor** by blood that emerges **in** an amorphous **piece** of tissue.

רַבִּי אֱלִיעֶזֶר הַיְינוּ תַּנָּא קַמָּא! אֵימָא: שֶׁרַבִּי אֱלִיעֶזֶר אוֹמֵר ״בִּבְשָׂרָהּ״ – וְלֹא בְּשָׁפִיר וְלֹא בַּחֲתִיכָה,

The Gemara interrupts its citation of the *baraita* and asks: **Isn't the** opinion of **Rabbi Eliezer** identical to that of **the first *tanna*?** The first *tanna* also says that a woman does not become impure due to blood found in a piece of tissue. Rather, the entire *baraita* is the opinion of Rabbi Eliezer, and one must **say** that the *baraita* should read as follows: Even if the piece of tissue is full of blood the woman is pure, **as Rabbi Eliezer says** that the term **"in her flesh"** teaches that a woman is rendered impure only by blood that emerges through direct contact with her flesh, **and not** by blood that emerges **in a gestational sac, nor** by blood that emerges **in a piece** of tissue.

וַחֲכָמִים אוֹמְרִים: אֵין זֶה דַּם נִדָּה אֶלָּא דַּם חֲתִיכָה. תַּנָּא קַמָּא נָמֵי טַהוֹרֵי מְטַהֵר! אֶלָּא דִּפְלֵי פְּלוֹיֵי אִיכָּא בֵּינַיְיהוּ,

The *baraita* continues: **And the Rabbis say:** If there is blood in the piece of tissue, **this is not menstrual blood, but rather the blood of the piece** of tissue. The Gemara asks: Doesn't **the first *tanna* also deem** the woman **pure?** What is the difference between the opinion of the Rabbis and that of the first *tanna*? The Gemara answers: **Rather,** the difference **between** the opinion of the first *tanna* and that of the Rabbis **is** with regard to a case **where** the piece of tissue is **cracked,**[H] and its blood comes in direct contact with the woman's body.

תַּנָּא קַמָּא סָבַר: ״בִּבְשָׂרָהּ״ – וְלֹא בְּשָׁפִיר וְלֹא בַּחֲתִיכָה, וְהוּא הַדִּין לִשְׁפוֹפֶרֶת. וְהָנֵי מִילֵּי – הֵיכָא דְּשִׁיעָא, אֲבָל פְּלֵי פְּלוֹיֵי – טְמֵאָה, מַאי טַעְמֵיהּ – ״בִּבְשָׂרָהּ״ קָרֵינָא בֵּיהּ.

**The first *tanna* holds** that the term **"in her flesh"** teaches that a woman is rendered impure only by blood that emerges through direct contact with her flesh, **and not** by blood that emerges **in a gestational sac, nor** by blood that emerges **in a piece** of tissue. **And the same is true with regard to** blood that emerges through **a tube. But this statement** applies only in a case **where** the piece of tissue is **smooth, but** if it is **cracked,** the woman is **impure. What is the reason for** this exception? Since the blood comes in direct contact with the woman's flesh, **we read** the term **"in her flesh" with regard to it,** i.e., it fulfills that condition.

וְאָתוּ רַבָּנַן לְמֵימַר: אַף עַל גַּב דְּפָלֵי פַּלּוּיֵי – אֵין זֶה דַּם נִדָּה אֶלָּא דַּם חֲתִיכָה. הָא דַּם נִדָּה – וַדַּאי טָמֵא, וַאֲפִילּוּ בִּשְׁפוֹפֶרֶת נָמֵי!

**And the Rabbis come to say: Even though** the piece of tissue **is cracked,** the woman is pure, as **this is not menstrual blood but rather the blood of** the **piece** of tissue. It can be inferred from here **that** if the blood is **menstrual blood,** the woman **is certainly impure, and** this is true **even** if the blood emerges **through a tube.** Accordingly, the *halakha* in the case of a tube is subject to a dispute between *tanna'im*.

אָמַר אַבָּיֵי: בִּשְׁפוֹפֶרֶת כּוּלֵּי עָלְמָא לָא פְּלִיגִי דִּטְהוֹרָה,

**Abaye says** that this suggestion should be rejected: **In** the case of **a tube, everyone agrees that** the woman **is pure,** as derived from the term "in her flesh."



כִּי פְּלִיגִי – בַּחֲתִיכָה. מָר סָבַר דַּרְכָּהּ שֶׁל אִשָּׁה לִרְאוֹת דָּם בַּחֲתִיכָה, וּמָר סָבַר אֵין דַּרְכָּהּ שֶׁל אִשָּׁה לִרְאוֹת דָּם בַּחֲתִיכָה.

**When they disagree,** it is **with regard to** the case of blood that is found in **a piece** of tissue. One Sage, the first *tanna*, who follows the opinion of Rabbi Eliezer, **holds** that **it is the manner of a woman to see** menstrual **blood in a piece** of tissue that she discharges. Therefore, the term "in her flesh" applies to the blood in the cracks. **And one Sage,** i.e., the Rabbis, **holds** that **it is not the manner of a woman to see** menstrual **blood in a piece** of tissue that she discharges. Therefore, the blood found in the piece of tissue is not considered menstrual blood, and it does not render the woman impure.

רָבָא אָמַר: דְּכוּלֵּי עָלְמָא אֵין דַּרְכָּהּ שֶׁל אִשָּׁה לִרְאוֹת דָּם בַּחֲתִיכָה,

**Rava says** there is another explanation of this dispute: **Everyone,** both the first *tanna* and the Rabbis, agrees that **it is not the manner of a woman to see** menstrual **blood in a piece** of tissue that she discharges. Consequently, the blood that emerges from the cracks in the piece of tissue is not considered menstrual blood, and it does not render the woman impure.

וְהָכָא בְּאִשָּׁה טְהוֹרָה וּמָקוֹר מְקוֹמוֹ טָמֵא קָמִיפַּלְגִי. דְּרַבִּי אֱלִיעֶזֶר סָבַר: אִשָּׁה טְהוֹרָה, וְדָם טָמֵא – דְּהָא אָתֵי דֶּרֶךְ מָקוֹר. וְרַבָּנַן סָבְרִי: אִשָּׁה טְהוֹרָה, וּמָקוֹר מְקוֹמוֹ טָהוֹר.

**And here, they disagree** as **to** whether it is possible that the **woman** herself is **pure but the location of the source,** i.e., the uterus, **is impure. As Rabbi Eliezer holds** that the **woman is pure,** i.e., she was not rendered a menstruating woman with the discharge of the blood, **but the blood is impure,** despite the fact that it emerged in a piece of tissue, **as it emerged through the source,** which is impure. Therefore, when the blood comes into contact with the woman's body she contracts first-degree impurity, and the woman subsequently transmits impurity to foods that she touches. **And the Rabbis hold** that the **woman** is entirely **pure, and the location of the source** is also **pure.** Therefore, pure food that she touches is not rendered impure.

בְּעָא מִינֵּיהּ רַבָּה מֵרַב הוּנָא: הָרוֹאֶה קֶרִי בְּקֵיסָם מַהוּ? "מִמֶּנּוּ" אָמַר רַחֲמָנָא – עַד דְּנָפֵיק מִבְּשָׂרוֹ – וְלֹא בְּקֵיסָם. אוֹ דִּלְמָא הַאי "מִמֶּנּוּ" – עַד שֶׁתֵּצֵא טוּמְאָתוֹ לַחוּץ, וַאֲפִילּוּ בְּקֵיסָם נָמֵי?

§ **Rabba asked Rav Huna** a similar question to the case of the tube: With regard to a man **who sees semen**[B] by extracting it from his penis **with a sliver of wood,**[H] **what is the** *halakha*? Does he assume the impurity status of one who experiences a seminal emission? The Gemara explains the question. The verse states: "A man from whom the flow of semen emerges" (Leviticus 22:4). Since **the Merciful One states: "From whom,"** is it derived that the man is not impure **unless** the semen **emerges from his flesh** by itself, **and not** when it is extracted **with a sliver of wood? Or perhaps** from **this** term: **"From whom,"** it is derived merely that the man is not impure **unless his impurity,** i.e., his semen, **emerges outside** his body, **but** he is impure **even** if this is achieved **with a sliver of wood.**

**BACKGROUND**

A man who sees semen – בַּעַל קֶרִי: When a man experiences a seminal emission, whether involuntarily, intentionally, or during sexual intercourse, he becomes ritually impure. To purify himself, he must immerse in a ritual bath, and after nightfall on the day of his immersion he again becomes ritually pure (see Leviticus 15:16–17). While he is ritually impure, it is prohibited for him to enter the Temple Mount and to come in contact with various sacred items such as *teruma*. Ezra instituted that one who experienced a seminal emission was prohibited from engaging in Torah study, praying, or reciting *Shema* until he immersed himself. In subsequent generations that ordinance was repealed, and one who experienced a seminal emission was permitted to engage in all those activities without immersion. This remains the prevalent custom.

**HALAKHA**

A man who sees semen with a sliver of wood – הָרוֹאֶה קֶרִי בְּקֵיסָם: A man who experiences a seminal emission is impure only if the semen leaves his body and comes in contact with the tip of the penis, as it is stated in the verse: "A man from whom the flow of semen emerges." Accordingly, one is impure even if he extracted the semen with a needle, provided the semen comes in contact with the tip of the penis. This *halakha* is in accordance with the opinion of Rav Huna (Rambam *Sefer Tahara*, *Hilkhot She'ar Avot HaTumot* 5:1, and see Ra'avad there).

## BACKGROUND

Gonorrhea-like discharge [*ziva*] – זִיבָה: Gonorrhea is a sexually transmitted disease caused by the bacteria *Neisseria gonorrhoeae*. The bacteria causes severe infection of the sexual organs, and one of its primary symptoms is a thin or thick mucous discharge from these organs. Traces of these discharges can also be found in the urine of infected persons. According to some researchers, this is the disease associated with the status known in *halakha* as *zav*. It is also possible that the *zav* is afflicted with a different, similar condition.

## HALAKHA

So too a seminal emission negates – אַף שִׁכְבַת זֶרַע נַמִּי סוֹתֵר: If a *zav* experiences a seminal emission during his count of seven clean days, that day alone is negated, after which he completes his count and brings his offering. For example, if he experiences a seminal emission on the fifth day of his count, he counts three days after that day, immerses in a ritual bath on the third day, and brings his offering on the fourth day (Rambam *Sefer Korbanot*, *Hilkhot Meḥusrei Kappara* 3:2).

## LANGUAGE

Bits of [*tzaḥtzoḥei*] – צַחְצוֹחֵי: Some interpret this word based on the Arabic ضحضاح, *ḍaḥḍāḥ*, which means a tiny amount of liquid.

אֲמַר לֵיהּ: תֵּיפוֹק לֵיהּ דְּהוּא עַצְמוֹ אֵינוֹ מְטַמֵּא אֶלָּא בַּחֲתִימַת פִּי הָאַמָּה.

Rav Huna **said to** Rabba: **Derive** that the man is pure from the fact **that** semen **itself becomes impure only in** a case where the discharge is substantial enough to cause **a blockage of the tip of the penis.**[N] Since this amount cannot be extracted with a sliver of wood, it is not impure.

לְמֵימְרָא דְּנוֹגֵעַ הָוֵי? אֶלָּא מֵעַתָּה – אַל יִסְתּוֹר בְּזִיבָה!

Rabba replied to Rav Huna: Since a minimum measure is required for this impurity, **is this to say that** the reason a man who experiences a seminal emission is impure **is** that his penis **touches** the semen after it is emitted? If he was rendered impure merely by the emission of the semen then no minimum measure would apply, as is the *halakha* with regard to a menstruating woman. But **if that is so,** then a seminal emission **should not negate** the count of seven clean days **for** a man who experienced a gonorrhea-like **discharge** [*ziva*].[B] A *zav* does not stop his counting when he touches a source of impurity, e.g., the carcass of a creeping animal.

אַלְמָה תַּנְיָא: ״זֹאת תּוֹרַת הַזָּב וַאֲשֶׁר תֵּצֵא מִמֶּנּוּ שִׁכְבַת זֶרַע״ מָה זִיבָה סוֹתֶרֶת – אַף שִׁכְבַת זֶרַע נַמִּי סוֹתֵר?

If so, **why is it taught** in a *baraita*: It is derived from the verse's juxtaposition between a *zav* and one who experienced a seminal emission: **"This is the law of the *zav*, and of one from whom the flow of semen emerges"** (Leviticus 15:32), that **just as *ziva*** during the seven clean days **negates** the count, **so too, a seminal emission negates**[H] the count. If it is not the emission itself that renders the man impure but only his contact with the semen, why does the emission negate the count of seven clean days?

אֲמַר לֵיהּ: סְתִירָה, הַיְינוּ טַעְמָא דְּסוֹתֵר – לְפִי שֶׁאִי אֶפְשָׁר לָהּ בְּלֹא צַחְצוֹחֵי זִיבָה.

Rav Huna **said to** Rabba in response: The *halakha* of **negation** is not difficult, as **this is the reason that** a seminal emission **negates** the count of seven clean days: **Because it is impossible for** a *zav* to experience a seminal emission **without** it containing **bits of** [*tzaḥtzoḥei*][L] ***ziva.***

אֶלָּא מֵעַתָּה תִּסְתּוֹר כׇּל שִׁבְעָה! אַלְמָה תַּנְיָא: ״זֹאת תּוֹרַת הַזָּב״ וגו׳ מָה זִיבָה סוֹתֶרֶת – אַף שִׁכְבַת זֶרַע סוֹתֵר,

Rabba further objected: **If that is so,** then a seminal emission **should negate the entire** count of **seven** clean days, just like an emission of *ziva*, not merely the day on which the seminal emission occurred. But then **why is it taught** in the *baraita*: It is derived from the verse: **"This is the law of the *zav*,** and of one from whom the flow of semen emerges, so that he is impure by it" (Leviticus 15:32), that **just as *ziva*** during the seven clean days **negates** the count, **so too, a seminal emission negates** the count.

אִי מָה זִיבָה סוֹתֶרֶת כׇּל שִׁבְעָה, אַף שִׁכְבַת זֶרַע נַמִּי סוֹתֵר כׇּל שִׁבְעָה? תַּלְמוּד לוֹמַר ״לְטׇמְאָה בָהּ״ – אֵין לְךָ בָּהּ אֶלָּא מַה שֶּׁאָמוּר בָּהּ – סוֹתֶרֶת יוֹם אֶחָד?

The *baraita* continues: **If** a seminal emission is compared to *ziva*, then it might be suggested that **just as *ziva* negates the entire** count **of seven** days, **so too, a seminal emission** should **also negate the entire** count of **seven** days. Therefore, **the verse states: "So that he is impure by it,"** to teach that **in** the case of a seminal emission **you have** a negation of the count that is equivalent **only** to the impurity **that is stated by it,** i.e., impurity for one day. Accordingly, a seminal emission **negates** only **one day** of the count, not the entire count. This apparently contradicts Rav Huna's statement that the reason a seminal emission negates the count at all is that the seminal emission of a *zav* always contains *ziva*.

## NOTES

That semen itself becomes impure only in a blockage of the tip of the penis – דְּהוּא עַצְמוֹ אֵינוֹ מְטַמֵּא אֶלָּא בַּחֲתִימַת פִּי הָאַמָּה: The early commentaries disagree with regard to the meaning of this *halakha* and its ramification in a case where semen is extracted with a needle. Some explain that the minimum amount of semen that is impure is an amount substantial enough to block the tip of the penis. Therefore, since the needle itself takes up part of the area of the tip, the extracted amount is not enough. Accordingly, it makes no difference whether or not there is a hole in the needle (Rashi; *Ḥiddushei Tzemaḥ Tzedek*). By contrast, other commentaries explain that for the semen to render the man impure it must touch the tip of the penis. Therefore, if it came out through a hollow needle and did not touch the tip of the penis, the man remains pure. In their opinion, the needle in question is one that has a hole in it through which the semen is discharged. Since the needle interposes between the semen and the tip, the man is not impure (Rashba; Meiri; *Tosefot HaRosh*; *Tosefot Ḥakhmei Angliyya*).

אמר ליה: גזירת הכתוב היא, זיבה גמורה דלא ערבה בה שכבת זרע – סותרת כל שבעה, צחצוחי זיבה דערבה בה שכבת זרע – לא סותרת אלא יום אחד.

Rav Huna **said to** Rabba: **It is a Torah edict** that an emission that is **purely *ziva*, when semen is not mixed in it, negates the entire** count of **seven** days, whereas **bits of *ziva* in which** some **semen is mixed negate only one day** of the count.

בעא מיניה רבי יוסי ברבי חנינא מרבי אלעזר: דם יבש מהו? "כי יזוב זוב דמה" אמר רחמנא – עד דמידב דייב ליה, לח – אין, יבש – לא, או דלמא: האי "כי יזוב זוב דמה" – אורחא דמילתא היא, ולעולם אפילו יבש נמי?

§ **Rabbi Yosei, son of Rabbi Ḥanina, asked Rabbi Elazar:** If a woman discharges **dry blood,**[H] **what is** the *halakha*? Does she have the status of a menstruating woman? The Gemara explains the dilemma: Since **the Merciful One states:** "And **if** a woman **has a flow of her blood** many days" (Leviticus 15:25), does this indicate **that** the woman is not impure **unless** the blood **flows,** i.e., if it is **wet, yes,** she is impure, whereas if it is **dry** she is **not** impure? **Or perhaps this** phrase: **"If** a woman **has a flow of her blood," is** merely referring to **the normal manner** that menstrual blood emerges, **but actually even dry** blood renders the woman impure.

אמר ליה: תניתוה, דם הנדה ובשר המת – מטמאין לחים ויבשים. אמר ליה: לח ונעשה יבש לא קא מיבעיא לי, כי מיבעיא לי – יבש מעיקרא.

Rabbi Elazar **said to him: You learned** the solution to your dilemma in a mishna (54b): **The blood of a menstruating woman and the flesh of a corpse**[H] **impart impurity** whether they are **wet or dry.** Rabbi Yosei, son of Rabbi Ḥanina, **said to him** in response: **I do not raise the dilemma** about blood that was **wet** when it came out **and** subsequently **dried,** as such blood is certainly impure. **When I raise the dilemma,** it is with regard to blood that was **dry at the outset,** when it emerged.

הא נמי תניתוה: המפלת כמין קליפה, כמין שערה, כמין עפר, כמין יבחושין אדומין – תטיל למים,

Rabbi Elazar responded: **You learned** the solution to **this** dilemma **as well,** in the mishna here: In the case of a woman **who discharges** an item **similar to a shell,**[H] or **similar to a hair,** or **similar to soil,** or **similar to mosquitoes,** if these are **red, she should cast** them **into water** to ascertain their nature.

HALAKHA

**Dry blood** – דם יבש: If a woman experiences a discharge of blood from her uterus, she is impure, whether the blood is wet or dry (Rambam *Sefer Tahara, Hilkhot Metamei Mishkav UMoshav* 2:1 and *Sefer Kedusha, Hilkhot Issurei Bia* 5:14; *Shulḥan Arukh, Yoreh De'a* 188:4).

**And the flesh of a corpse** – ובשר המת: An olive-bulk of flesh from a corpse imparts impurity just like a complete corpse, whether it is moist or it is as dry as earthenware (Rambam *Sefer Tahara, Hilkhot Tumat Met* 2:1).

**A woman who discharges an item similar to a shell, etc.** – המפלת כמין קליפה וכו׳: A woman who discharges blood, whether it is wet or dry, is ritually impure. Even if a woman discharges a red item similar to a shell, hair, or mosquito, she is impure, but only if this item can be dissolved within twenty-four hours in lukewarm water that stays lukewarm for that entire period. The required temperature of the water is that of water that was drawn from a river or a well in the summer and was kept indoors. This is the required temperature in the winter as well. It is no higher than the temperature of saliva (*Beit Yosef*, citing Ritva). If the discharged item is not dissolved within twenty-four hours, even if one can mash it against his nails, the woman is pure. If one cannot mash it against his nails, the woman is certainly pure, and it is unnecessary to examine the item by soaking it in water (Rambam *Sefer Kedusha, Hilkhot Issurei Bia* 5:14, and see *Maggid Mishne* there; *Shulḥan Arukh, Yoreh De'a* 188:4).

Perek **III**
Daf **22** Amud **b**

אם נמוחו – טמאה. אי הכי – בלא נמוחו נמי! אמר רבה: כי לא נמוחו – בריה בפני עצמה היא.

**If they dissolved,** it is blood, and the woman **is impure;** and if not, she is ritually pure. Evidently, dry blood is impure, as these items are all dry until they are soaked in water. The Gemara asks: **If so,** that dry blood is impure, these items are impure **also in** a case where **they do not dissolve** in water. Why is this examination necessary at all? **Rabba says:** In a case **where they do not dissolve,** this indicates that the item is not blood at all; rather, **it is a distinct entity.**

וּמִי אִיכָּא כִּי הַאי גַּוְונָא? אִין, וְהָתַנְיָא, אָמַר רַבִּי אֶלְעָזָר בְּרַבִּי צָדוֹק, שְׁנֵי מַעֲשִׂים הֶעֱלָה אַבָּא מִטִּבְעִין לְיַבְנֶה.

The Gemara asks with regard to these instances discussed in the mishna: **But are there** actually **cases like this?** The Gemara answers: **Yes** there are, **and it is taught** likewise in a *baraita* that **Rabbi Elazar, son of Rabbi Tzadok,**[P] **says: My father raised two incidents from Tivin**[B] **to** the Sages in **Yavne**[B] for discussion.

מַעֲשֶׂה בְּאִשָּׁה שֶׁהָיְתָה מַפֶּלֶת כְּמִין קְלִיפּוֹת אֲדוּמּוֹת, וּבָאוּ וְשָׁאֲלוּ אֶת אַבָּא, וְאַבָּא שָׁאַל לַחֲכָמִים, וַחֲכָמִים שָׁאֲלוּ לָרוֹפְאִים, וְאָמְרוּ לָהֶם: אִשָּׁה זוֹ מַכָּה יֵשׁ לָהּ בְּתוֹךְ מֵעֶיהָ שֶׁמִּמֶּנָּה מַפֶּלֶת כְּמִין קְלִיפּוֹת, תַּטִּיל לַמַּיִם, אִם נִמּוֹחוּ – טְמֵאָה.

The first was **an incident involving a woman who would** repeatedly **discharge** items **similar to red shells, and** the local residents **came and asked my father** whether this rendered the woman impure. **And my father asked the** other **Sages, and the Sages asked the doctors**[N] what causes this to happen. **And** the doctors **said to them: This woman has a wound in her womb from which she discharges** red items **similar to shells.** The Sages therefore ruled that the woman **should cast** them **into water** to ascertain their nature. **If they dissolved,** it is blood and the woman **is impure.**

וְשׁוּב מַעֲשֶׂה בְּאִשָּׁה שֶׁהָיְתָה מַפֶּלֶת כְּמִין שְׂעָרוֹת אֲדוּמּוֹת, וּבָאָה וְשָׁאֲלָה אֶת אַבָּא, וְאַבָּא שָׁאַל לַחֲכָמִים, וַחֲכָמִים לָרוֹפְאִים, וְאָמְרוּ לָהֶם: שׁוּמָא יֵשׁ לָהּ בְּתוֹךְ מֵעֶיהָ, שֶׁמִּמֶּנָּה מַפֶּלֶת כְּמִין שְׂעָרוֹת אֲדוּמּוֹת, תַּטִּיל לַמַּיִם, אִם נִמּוֹחוּ – טְמֵאָה.

**And again** there was a similar **incident involving a woman who would discharge** items **similar to red hairs, and she came and asked my father** whether she was impure. **And my father asked the** other **Sages, and the Sages asked the doctors, and** the doctors **said to them:** The woman **has a mole in her womb from which she discharges** items **similar to red hairs.** The Sages therefore ruled that the woman **should cast** them **into water,** and **if they dissolved, she is impure.**

אָמַר רֵישׁ לָקִישׁ: וּבְפוֹשְׁרִין. תַּנְיָא נַמִי הָכִי: תַּטִּיל לַמַּיִם, וּבְפוֹשְׁרִין. רַבָּן שִׁמְעוֹן בֶּן גַּמְלִיאֵל אוֹמֵר: מְמַעֲכָתוֹ בְּרוֹק עַל גַּבֵּי הַצִּפּוֹרֶן. מַאי בֵּינַיְיהוּ? אָמַר רָבִינָא: מָעוּךְ עַל יְדֵי הַדְּחָק אִיכָּא בֵּינַיְיהוּ.

§ **Reish Lakish says: And** this examination is conducted only **with lukewarm** [*uvefoshrin*][L] water. **This is also taught** in a *baraita*: The woman **should cast** the item **into water, and** this examination is conducted only **with lukewarm** water. **Rabban Shimon ben Gamliel says:** The woman **mashes** the item **with saliva,** using the fingers of one hand **on a fingernail** of her other hand. The Gemara asks: **What** is the difference **between** the two opinions? **Ravina says:** The difference **between them is** whether an item is considered blood if it can be **mashed by pressing** on it, or only if the item dissolves by itself.

הָתָם תְּנַן: כַּמָּה הִיא שְׁרִיָּיתָן בְּפוֹשְׁרִין – מֵעֵת לְעֵת, הָכָא מַאי? מִי בָּעֵינָא מֵעֵת לְעֵת, אוֹ לֹא?

**We learned** in the mishna **there** (54b) with regard to an animal carcass or the carcass of a creeping animal that dried up, which is examined by soaking it in water to determine whether or not it still imparts impurity: For **how long is its soaking in lukewarm** water necessary? It is **for** a twenty-four-hour **period.** The Gemara asks: **Here,** with regard to the examination of an item discharged by a woman, **what** is the *halakha*? **Do I need** it to be soaked in lukewarm water **for** a twenty-four-hour **period, or not?**

שֶׁרֶץ וּנְבֵלָה דְּאַקּוּשִׁי – בָּעֵינַן מֵעֵת לְעֵת, אֲבָל דָּם דְּרַכִּיךְ – לָא, אוֹ דִּלְמָא לָא שְׁנָא? תֵּיקוּ.

The Gemara explains the question: Perhaps with regard to a carcass of **a creeping animal and an unslaughtered animal carcass, which are hard** when they dry up, **we require** soaking **for** a twenty-four-hour **period, but blood, which is** relatively **soft** after it dries up, does **not** need to be soaked for that long. In other words, if the item did not dissolve after even a shorter period of time, it is not blood. **Or perhaps** the examination of a discharged item **is no different,** and it also must be soaked for twenty-four hours. The Gemara concludes: The dilemma **shall stand** unresolved.

BACKGROUND

Tivin – טִבְעִין: Tivin is identified as modern-day Tivon, in the northern Jezreel Valley, southwest of Tiberias.

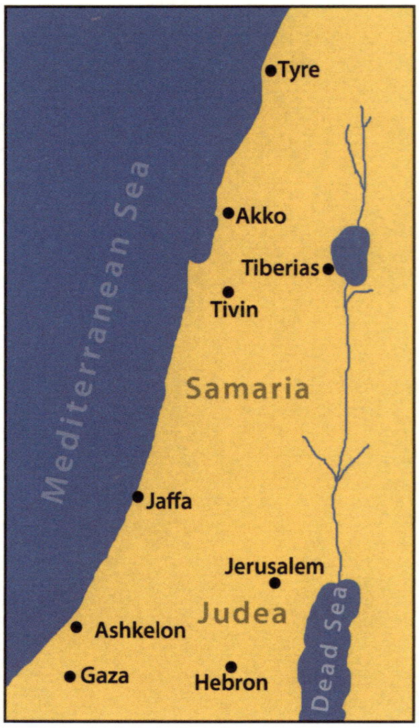


Location of Tivin

Yavne – יַבְנֶה: Yavne is located slightly more than 1 km from the Mediterranean coast, due west of Jerusalem. It is identified with Yavne'el, mentioned in the Bible as a city in the tribal lands of Judah. It was a Philistine city for many years, and it is listed as one of the cities whose walls were breached by King Uzziah of Judah.

Later Yavne was conquered by Vespasian during the campaign to quash the Great Revolt that culminated in the destruction of the Second Temple. It seems that several Sages who did not support the revolt settled there. When Rabban Yoḥanan ben Zakkai joined them, Yavne became the spiritual center of Eretz Yisrael and the seat of the Sanhedrin for many years, apparently until the bar Kokheva rebellion. The main yeshiva there was called Kerem BeYavne, meaning the vineyard in Yavne.

NOTES

And the Sages asked the doctors – וַחֲכָמִים שָׁאֲלוּ לָרוֹפְאִים: Some commentaries prove from here that one can rely on the opinion of an expert with regard to matters of ritual law. This applies even in cases of prohibitions by Torah law (*Mekom Shmuel*), and even with regard to prohibitions punishable by *karet* (Maharik). There are authorities who infer from the plural term doctors that one should rely only on several doctors, not on one alone. Some of these authorities also require that the doctors be Jewish (Responsa of the *Baḥ*). Others maintain that two doctors, one Jewish and the other gentile, suffice (*Shevut Ya'akov*).

LANGUAGE

Lukewarm [*poshrin*] – פּוֹשְׁרִין: The original meaning of the root *peh*, *shin*, *reish* is apparently to melt, and it came to refer to any liquid that is neither hot nor cold. Some say that the Hebrew word for soak, *heshra*, is also connected to this root.

PERSONALITIES

Rabbi Tzadok – רַבִּי צָדוֹק: The reference is apparently to Rabbi Tzadok the priest, who in his later years was one of the greatest Sages of Israel at the time of the destruction of the Second Temple. It is said that he fasted frequently over the period of forty years prior to the destruction of the Temple as a plea that the Temple not be destroyed. The leader of that generation, Rabban Yoḥanan ben Zakkai, held him in such high regard that he requested of the emperor Vespasian to procure a special doctor to care for him, since he had become so emaciated by his fasts. Rabban Yoḥanan ben Zakkai also said of Rabbi Tzadok that if there had been another person as righteous as him, Jerusalem would not have been destroyed.

After the destruction of the Temple, Rabbi Tzadok resided in the town of Tivin. He maintained contact with the Sages of Yavne and would ask them questions and testify before them about various halakhic traditions. It is related that when he would visit Yavne, Rabban Gamliel HaNasi would honor him greatly, as did Rabbi Yehoshua and Rabbi Eliezer, the greatest Sages of Yavne in that generation.

"הַמַּפֶּלֶת כְּמִין דָּגִים". וְלִיפְלוֹג נַמִּי רַבִּי יְהוּדָה בְּהָא!

§ The mishna teaches: In the case of a woman **who discharges** an item **similar to fish**[H] or to grasshoppers, repugnant creatures, or creeping animals, if blood emerges with it, the woman is impure, and if not, she is pure. The Gemara asks: **But let Rabbi Yehuda disagree** with the Rabbis **with regard to this** *halakha* **as well,** just as he disagrees with them in the first clause of the mishna, in the case where a woman discharges an amorphous piece of tissue, as he maintains that she is impure whether or not blood emerges with it.

אָמַר רֵישׁ לָקִישׁ: בְּמַחֲלוֹקֶת שְׁנוּיָה, וְרַבָּנַן הִיא. וְרַבִּי יוֹחָנָן אָמַר: אֲפִילּוּ תֵּימָא רַבִּי יְהוּדָה. עַד כָּאן לָא קָאָמַר רַבִּי יְהוּדָה הָתָם אֶלָּא גַּבֵּי חֲתִיכָה – דְּעָבֵיד דָּם דְּקָרֵישׁ וְהָוֵי חֲתִיכָה, אֲבָל בְּרִיָּה – לָא הָוֵי.

**Reish Lakish says:** This case is also **subject to the dispute** between Rabbi Yehuda and the Rabbis, **and** the opinion cited in the mishna **is** that of **the Rabbis. And Rabbi Yoḥanan says: You** may **even say** that the ruling of the mishna is in accordance with the opinion of **Rabbi Yehuda,** as when **Rabbi Yehuda says** that the woman is impure even if blood does not emerge, it is **only there, in** the case of an amorphous **piece** of tissue, **as** the **blood is likely to dry and turn into** the form of **a piece** of tissue. **But** blood is **not** likely to **become** the form of **a creature,** such as a fish or a grasshopper.

וּלְהַךְ לִישָּׁנָא דְּאָמַר רַבִּי יוֹחָנָן: בְּאִי אֶפְשָׁר לִפְתִיחַת הַקֶּבֶר בְּלֹא דָּם קָמִיפַּלְגִי, לִפְלוֹג נַמִּי רַבִּי יְהוּדָה בְּהָא!

The Gemara challenges: **But** this is difficult **according to that version** in **which Rabbi Yoḥanan says** that Rabbi Yehuda and the Rabbis **disagree with regard to** whether **opening of the womb is impossible without** a discharge of **blood**[N] (see 21b). Since **Rabbi Yehuda** holds that blood automatically emerges whenever the womb opens, and therefore the woman is impure even if she did not notice any blood, he **should disagree** with the Rabbis **in this** case **too,** i.e., if a woman discharges an item similar to a fish or one of the other creatures.

מַאן דְּמַתְנֵי הַךְ לִישָּׁנָא מַתְנֵי הָכִי: רַבִּי יוֹחָנָן וְרֵישׁ לָקִישׁ דְּאָמְרִי תַּרְוַיְיהוּ בְּמַחֲלוֹקֶת שְׁנוּיָה, וְרַבָּנַן הִיא.

The Gemara answers: **The one who teaches that version** of the above discussion **teaches** an alternative version of Rabbi Yoḥanan's opinion here as well, **like this:** With regard to a woman who discharges an item similar to fish, or to grasshoppers, repugnant creatures, or creeping animals, **Rabbi Yoḥanan and Reish Lakish both say** that this case is **subject to a dispute** between Rabbi Yehuda and the Rabbis, **and** the opinion stated in the mishna **is** that of **the Rabbis.**

"הַמַּפֶּלֶת כְּמִין בְּהֵמָה" [וכו'].

§ The mishna teaches: In the case of a woman **who discharges** tissue in the form of **a type of domesticated animal,** undomesticated animal, or bird, whether of a kosher or non-kosher species, if it is male, the woman observes the periods of impurity and purity for a woman who gives birth to a male. If it is female, the woman observes the periods of impurity and purity for a woman who gives birth to a female. And if its sex is unknown, the woman observes the strictures of a woman who gave birth to both a male and a female. This is the statement of Rabbi Meir.

אָמַר רַב יְהוּדָה, אָמַר שְׁמוּאֵל: מַאי טַעְמָא דְּרַבִּי מֵאִיר – הוֹאִיל וְנֶאֶמְרָה בּוֹ יְצִירָה כְּאָדָם.

**Rav Yehuda says** that **Shmuel says: What is the reason** for the opinion **of Rabbi Meir,** that a woman who discharges a fetus in the form of an animal has the same status as one who discharges a fetus with human form or gives birth to a human? It is **since** the Torah uses a similar formulation in the two cases, as a term of **formation is stated with regard to** the creation of these types of animals, in the verse: "And out of the ground the Lord God formed every animal of the field, and every fowl of the air" (Genesis 2:19), **just as** it is stated with regard to the creation of **man:** "And the Lord God formed man" (Genesis 2:7).

HALAKHA

**A woman who discharges an item similar to fish, etc.** – הַמַּפֶּלֶת כְּמִין דָּגִים וכו׳: If a woman discharged an item similar to a grasshopper, fish, repugnant creature, or creeping animal, the woman is impure only if blood emerged with it; otherwise, she is pure. Nowadays, the woman is considered impure regardless of the shape of the discharged item, as the halakhic authorities today are not proficient in the differences between the different forms of discharged items (Rambam *Sefer Kedusha, Hilkhot Issurei Bia* 5:15; *Shulḥan Arukh, Yoreh De'a* 194:3).

NOTES

**Rabbi Yoḥanan says they disagree…whether opening of the womb is impossible without blood** – אָמַר רַבִּי יוֹחָנָן...אִי אֶפְשָׁר לִפְתִיחַת הַקֶּבֶר בְּלֹא דָּם קָמִיפַּלְגִי: According to the standard version of the Gemara on 21b, it is Rav Yehuda, not Rabbi Yoḥanan, who says this. Nevertheless, apparently the correct version is that this statement was issued by Rabbi Yoḥanan, as indicated by the Gemara here.

אֶלָּא מֵעַתָּה, הַמַּפֶּלֶת דְּמוּת תַּנִּין תְּהֵא אִמּוֹ טְמֵאָה לֵידָה הוֹאִיל וְנֶאֱמַר בּוֹ יְצִירָה כְּאָדָם, שֶׁנֶּאֱמַר "וַיִּבְרָא אֱלֹהִים אֶת הַתַּנִּינִם הַגְּדוֹלִים"!

The Gemara asks: **If that is so,** then with regard to a woman **who discharges** an item with **the form of a sea monster, its mother should be impure** with the impurity of a woman after **childbirth, since** the concept of **formation is stated with regard to** its creation, **just as** it is stated with regard to the creation of **man. As it is stated: "And God created the great sea monsters"** (Genesis 1:21).

אָמְרִי: דָּנִין יְצִירָה מִיצִירָה, וְאֵין דָּנִין בְּרִיאָה מִיצִירָה.

The Sages **say** in response: **One derives** *halakhot* of a matter with regard to which **formation** is stated by means of a verbal analogy **from** another matter with regard to which **formation** is stated, **but one does not derive** *halakhot* of a matter with regard to which **creation** is stated **from** a matter with regard to which **formation** is stated.

מַאי נָפְקָא מִינַּהּ? הָא תָּנָא דְּבֵי רַבִּי יִשְׁמָעֵאל: "וְשָׁב הַכֹּהֵן" "וּבָא הַכֹּהֵן" – זוֹ הִיא שִׁיבָה זוֹ הִיא בִּיאָה!

The Gemara asks: **What difference is** there between formation and creation? A verbal analogy can be drawn between different words with similar meanings. For example, **the school of Rabbi Yishmael taught** a verbal analogy with regard to leprosy of houses.[B] The verse states: **"And the priest shall return** [*veshav*] on the seventh day" (Leviticus 14:39), and another verse with regard to the priest's visit seven days later states: **"And the priest shall come**[N] [*uva*] and look" (Leviticus 14:44). **This returning** and **this coming** have the same meaning, and one can therefore derive by verbal analogy that the *halakha* that applies if the leprosy had spread at the conclusion of the first week applies if it had spread again by the end of the following week.

וְעוֹד: נִגְמַר בְּרִיאָה מִבְּרִיאָה, דִּכְתִיב "וַיִּבְרָא אֱלֹהִים אֶת הָאָדָם בְּצַלְמוֹ"!

**And furthermore,** the *halakha* of a woman who discharges an item similar to a sea monster, with regard to which **creation** is stated, can be **derived** by a different verbal analogy **from** the *halakha* of human offspring, since here it also states **creation, as it is written: "And God created man in His own image"** (Genesis 1:27).

אָמְרִי: "וַיִּבְרָא" – לְגוּפֵיהּ, "וַיִּיצֶר" לְאַפְנוּיֵי, וְדָנִין יְצִירָה מִיצִירָה.

The Sages **say** in response: The verse **"And** God **created** man" is necessary **to** teach the matter **itself,** i.e., the creation of man. By contrast, the term **"And** the Lord God **formed** man," serves **to render it free,** i.e., the mention of the formation of man is superfluous in its context and was stated for the purpose of establishing a verbal analogy. **And** therefore **one derives** the *halakhot* of animals, with regard to which **formation** is stated, **from** the *halakhot* of man, with regard to which **formation** is stated.

אַדְּרַבָּה: "וַיִּיצֶר" – לְגוּפֵיהּ, "וַיִּבְרָא" – לְאַפְנוּיֵי, וְדָנִין בְּרִיאָה מִבְּרִיאָה!

The Gemara raises a difficulty: **On the contrary,** one can say that the verse **"And** the Lord God **formed** man" was stated **to** teach the matter **itself,** whereas the term **"And** God **created** man" serves **to render it free; and** therefore **one derives** the *halakhot* of sea monsters, with regard to which **creation** is stated, **from** the *halakhot* of man, with regard to which **creation** is stated.

אֶלָּא: "וַיִּיצֶר" – מוּפְנֶה מִשְּׁנֵי צְדָדִין, מוּפְנֶה גַּבֵּי אָדָם וּמוּפְנֶה גַּבֵּי בְּהֵמָה. "וַיִּבְרָא" – גַּבֵּי אָדָם מוּפְנֶה, גַּבֵּי תַּנִּינִים אֵינוֹ מוּפְנֶה.

The Gemara answers: **Rather,** the reason it is animals and not sea monsters that are compared to man is that the term **"and…formed"** is **free on both sides,** i.e., **it is free with regard to man and it is free with regard to animals.** By contrast, the term **"and…created" is free with regard to man,** but **it is not free with regard to sea monsters.**

מַאי מוּפְנֶה גַּבֵּי בְּהֵמָה? אִילֵימָא מִדִּכְתִיב "וַיַּעַשׂ אֱלֹהִים אֶת חַיַּת הָאָרֶץ" וּכְתִיב "וַיִּיצֶר [ה'] אֱלֹהִים מִן הָאֲדָמָה כָּל חַיַּת הַשָּׂדֶה" – גַּבֵּי תַּנִּין נַמִי אַפְנוּיֵי מוּפְנֶה, דִּכְתִיב "וְאֵת כָּל רֶמֶשׂ הָאֲדָמָה", וּכְתִיב "וַיִּבְרָא אֱלֹהִים אֶת הַתַּנִּינִים הַגְּדוֹלִים"!

The Gemara asks: **What** is the reason that the term "and…formed" that appears **with regard to animals** is considered **free? If we say** it is due to the fact **that it is written: "And God made the animals of the earth** after its kind, and the cattle after their kind, and everything that creeps on the ground after its kind" (Genesis 1:25), **and it is** similarly **written: "And out of the ground the Lord God formed every animal of the field"** (Genesis 2:19), and therefore this verse is superfluous, but **with regard to** the **sea monster as well,** the expression "and…created" is **free, as it is written:** "And God made… **and everything that creeps on the ground** after its kind" (Genesis 1:25), **and it is** also **written: "And God created the great sea monsters."** Consequently, the term "and…created" is also free on both sides of the verbal analogy.

**BACKGROUND**

**Leprosy of houses** – **נִגְעֵי בָתִּים**: By Torah law (see Leviticus 14:33–57), if leprous marks appear in a house, all the items in the house must be removed in order to prevent them from becoming ritually impure in the event that the house is declared impure. A priest is then brought to examine the house. If he confirms that the marks are leprous, the house is left uninhabited for a week, after which it is reexamined. If the leprous marks darken or disappear, the house is declared ritually pure. If the marks are unchanged, the house is quarantined for a second week, after which it is reexamined. If by that point the marks have darkened, the house is ritually impure and must undergo a purification process involving birds, cedarwood, and scarlet thread, similar to the purification process through which a leprous person is purified. But if the marks have remained unchanged, the affected parts of the house are removed and replaced with new construction materials, after which the house is quarantined a third time. If the marks reappear, the entire house must be destroyed, and its stones are disposed of in a ritually impure place. If they do not reappear, the house undergoes a purification process.

**NOTES**

**And the priest shall return, and the priest shall come** – **וְשָׁב הַכֹּהֵן וּבָא הַכֹּהֵן**: The verses could lead to the conclusion that if the priest comes in the second week after the initial discovery of the leprosy and finds that the leprosy spread through the walls of the house, he orders the demolition of the house. But based on the verbal analogy, it is derived that the priest conducts himself in the second week as he did in the first week: He orders the affected area cut and that area of the wall plastered. The house is then quarantined for another week.

״רֶמֶשׂ״ דִּכְתִיב הָתָם – דְּיַבָּשָׁה הוּא. וּמַאי נָפְקָא מִינָּהּ בֵּין מוּפְנֶה מִצַּד אֶחָד לְמוּפְנֶה מִשְּׁנֵי צְדָדִין?

The Gemara answers: The **creeping animal that is written there is** referring to creeping animals **of the land,** not of the sea. Therefore, the term: "And…created," stated with regard to sea monsters is not superfluous. The Gemara asks: **But what difference is** there **between** a verbal analogy that is **free on one side and** a verbal analogy that is **free on both sides?**

נָפְקָא מִינָּהּ דַּאֲמַר רַב יְהוּדָה אָמַר שְׁמוּאֵל מִשּׁוּם רַבִּי יִשְׁמָעֵאל: כׇּל גְּזֵירָה שָׁוָה שֶׁאֵינָהּ מוּפְנָה כׇּל עִיקָּר – אֵין לְמֵדִין הֵימֶנָּה. מוּפְנָה מִצַּד אֶחָד, לְרַבִּי יִשְׁמָעֵאל – לְמֵדִין וְאֵין מוֹשִׁיבִין, לְרַבָּנַן – לְמֵדִין וּמְשִׁיבִין. מוּפְנָה מִשְּׁנֵי צְדָדִין, דִּבְרֵי הַכֹּל – לְמֵדִין וְאֵין מְשִׁיבִין.

The Gemara answers: The **difference** is with regard to that **which Rav Yehuda said** that **Shmuel says in the name of Rabbi Yishmael,** with regard to the exegetical principle of verbal analogy: With regard to **any verbal analogy that is not free at all, one cannot derive** *halakhot* **from it.** If the verbal analogy is **free on one side, according to Rabbi Yishmael one can derive** *halakhot* from it, **and one cannot refute** it through logic, even if there are valid counterarguments. **According to the Rabbis, one can derive** *halakhot* **from it, but one can** also **refute** it logically if there are grounds to distinguish between the two cases. If a verbal analogy is **free on both sides,**[NB] **everyone agrees** that **one can derive** *halakhot* from it **and one cannot refute** it logically.

וְרַבִּי יִשְׁמָעֵאל, מַאי אִיכָּא בֵּין מוּפְנָה מִצַּד אֶחָד לְמוּפְנֶה מִשְּׁנֵי צְדָדִין? נָפְקָא מִינָּהּ דְּהֵיכָא דְּאִיכָּא מוּפְנָה מִצַּד אֶחָד וּמוּפְנָה מִשְּׁנֵי צְדָדִין, שָׁבְקִינַן מוּפְנָה מִצַּד אֶחָד

The Gemara asks: **And** according to **Rabbi Yishmael, what** difference **is there between** a verbal analogy that is **free on one side and** a verbal analogy that is **free on both sides?** In both cases, he holds that one can derive *halakhot* from it and one cannot refute it. The Gemara answers: He holds that the **difference** is **that** in a case **where there** are two mutually exclusive verbal analogies, one that is **free on one side and** one that is **free on both sides, we disregard** the analogy that is **free on one side,**

**NOTES**

Free on both sides – מוּפְנָה מִשְּׁנֵי צְדָדִין: The reason that *halakhot* derived from a verbal analogy that is free on both sides cannot be refuted is that it is considered as though the *halakha* were written explicitly in the Torah (Rashi on *Shabbat* 64a).

**BACKGROUND**

Verbal analogy…free on both sides – גְּזֵירָה שָׁוָה...מוּפְנָה מִשְּׁנֵי צְדָדִין: A verbal analogy is a fundamental rabbinic principle of biblical interpretation, appearing in all standard lists of exegetical principles. If the same word or phrase appears in two places in the Torah, and a certain *halakha* is explicitly stated in one of these places, the Sages may infer on the basis of verbal analogy that the same *halakha* must apply in the other case as well. In its simplest form, the verbal analogy is a type of linguistic interpretation by means of which the meaning of an obscure word or phrase is inferred on the basis of another occurrence of the same word or phrase in a clearer context. It is often used not only to determine the meaning of obscure words and phrases but to transfer entire *halakhot* from one context to another. Verbal analogies are unique among the exegetical principles in that they are based on verbal rather than conceptual similarity. For this reason there are several limitations placed on its use. For example, many hold that the analogy is binding only if the key words are free, or superfluous, in the sense that they are not needed as a source for some other *halakha*. If the key words are not superfluous, the verbal analogy may be refuted logically.

Perek **III**
Daf **23** Amud **a**

וְיָלְפִינַן מוּפְנָה מִשְּׁנֵי צְדָדִין. וּלְהָכִי אַפְנְיַהּ רַחֲמָנָא לִבְהֵמָה מִשְּׁנֵי צְדָדִין, כִּי הֵיכִי דְּלָא נִגְמַר מִן מוּפְנָה מִצַּד אֶחָד.

**and derive** the *halakha* from the analogy that is **free on both sides. And** it is **for this** reason that **the Merciful One rendered** the verbal analogy between **animal** and man **free on both sides, so that one would not derive** the *halakha* **from** the verbal analogy between sea monster and man, which is **free on** only **one side.**

רַב אַחָא בְּרֵיהּ דְּרָבָא מַתְנֵי לַהּ מִשְּׁמֵיהּ דְּרַבִּי אֶלְעָזָר לְקוּלָּא: כׇּל גְּזֵירָה שָׁוָה שֶׁאֵינָהּ מוּפְנָה כׇּל עִיקָּר – לְמֵדִין וּמְשִׁיבִין. מוּפְנָה מִצַּד אֶחָד, לְרַבִּי יִשְׁמָעֵאל – לְמֵדִין וְאֵין מְשִׁיבִין, לְרַבָּנַן – לְמֵדִין וּמְשִׁיבִין. מוּפְנָה מִשְּׁנֵי צְדָדִין, דִּבְרֵי הַכֹּל – לְמֵדִין וְאֵין מְשִׁיבִין.

**Rav Aḥa, son of Rava, teaches in the name of Rabbi Elazar** a more **lenient** version of the aforementioned principle of exegesis of verbal analogy: With regard to **any verbal analogy that is not free at all, one can derive** *halakhot* from it, **but one can** also **refute** it logically. If the verbal analogy is **free on one side, according to Rabbi Yishmael one can derive** *halakhot* from it, **and one cannot refute** it. **According to the Rabbis, one can derive** *halakhot* from it, **but one can** also **refute** it. If the verbal analogy is **free on both sides, everyone agrees** that **one can derive** *halakhot* from it **and one cannot refute** it.

וּלְרַבָּנַן, מַאי אִיכָּא בֵּין מוּפְנָה מִצַּד אֶחָד לְשֶׁאֵינָהּ מוּפְנָה כׇּל עִיקָּר?

The Gemara asks: **But** if so, **according to the Rabbis, what** difference **is there between** a verbal analogy that is **free on one side and** one **that is not free at all?** In both cases, the Rabbis hold that one can derive *halakhot* from such a verbal analogy but one can also refute it.

נָפְקָא מִינָּהּ הֵיכָא דְּמִשְׁכַּחַתְּ לַהּ מוּפְנָה מִצַּד אֶחָד וְשֶׁאֵינָהּ מוּפְנָה כׇּל עִיקָּר, וְלָאו לְהַאי אִית לֵיהּ פִּירְכָא, וְלָאו לְהַאי אִית לֵיהּ פִּירְכָא – שָׁבְקִינַן שֶׁאֵינָהּ מוּפְנָה כׇּל עִיקָּר, וְגָמְרִינַן מִמּוּפְנָה מִצַּד אֶחָד.

The Gemara answers: The **difference** is in a case **where you find** two mutually exclusive verbal analogies, one that is **free on one side and** one **that is not free at all, and neither** does **this one have** a logical **refutation nor** does **that one have** a logical **refutation.** In such a case, **we disregard** the analogy **that is not free at all, and we derive** the *halakha* **from** the one that is **free on one side.**

NOTES

As it is stated, for He Who forms the mountains and creates the wind – שֶׁנֶּאֱמַר כִּי הִנֵּה יוֹצֵר הָרִים וּבוֹרֵא רוּחַ: This verbal analogy cannot be refuted, as it is free on both sides, i.e., the word "forms" is superfluous in its context, since the verse could have stated instead: For He Who creates the mountains and the wind (*Tosafot*; *Tosefot HaRosh*).

It is a stone that she discharges – אֶבֶן הִיא דְּקָא מַפֶּלֶת: An alternative explanation for the *halakha* that a woman who discharges an item that looks like a mountain is not impure is offered in the Jerusalem Talmud: Although in other biblical contexts the concept of formation is written with regard to mountains, it is not so written in the context of the creation in Genesis.

One does not derive matters stated in the Torah from the words of the tradition – אֵין דָּנִין דִּבְרֵי תוֹרָה מִדִּבְרֵי קַבָּלָה: Rashi (*Hullin* 137a) explains that the Torah was given to all generations, whereas each prophecy was issued for a specific generation.

וְהָכָא מַאי פִּירְכָא אִיכָּא? מִשּׁוּם דְּאִיכָּא לְמִיפְרַךְ: מָה לְאָדָם – שֶׁכֵּן מִטַּמֵּא מֵחַיִּים.

The Gemara asks: **And here,** with regard to the verbal analogy between man and sea monster, which was rejected because it is free on only one side, **what** logical **refutation is there** on account of which this verbal analogy is rejected? The Gemara answers: The verbal analogy between man and sea monster is rejected **because it can be refuted** as follows: **What** is unique **about man?** Man is unique **in that** a person can **become impure while he is alive,** unlike an animal, which can become impure only after it dies, or a sea monster, which cannot become impure at all.

וְכֵן אָמַר רַבִּי חִיָּיא בַּר אַבָּא, אָמַר רַבִּי יוֹחָנָן: הַיְינוּ טַעְמָא דְּרַבִּי מֵאִיר – הוֹאִיל וְנֶאֶמְרָה בּוֹ "יְצִירָה" כְּאָדָם.

**And likewise, Rabbi Ḥiyya bar Abba said** that **Rabbi Yoḥanan said: This is the reason** for the opinion **of Rabbi Meir,** that a woman who discharges an item similar to a domesticated animal, an undomesticated animal, or a bird is impure: It is **because formation is stated with regard to** the creation of these animals, **just as** it is stated with regard to the creation of **man.**

אֲמַר לֵיהּ רַבִּי אַמִּי: אֶלָּא מֵעַתָּה, הַמַּפֶּלֶת דְּמוּת הַר, אִמּוֹ טְמֵאָה לֵידָה – שֶׁנֶּאֱמַר: "כִּי הִנֵּה יוֹצֵר הָרִים וּבוֹרֵא רוּחַ"! אֲמַר לֵיהּ: הַר מִי קָא מַפֶּלֶת? אֶבֶן הִיא דְּקָא מַפֶּלֶת, הַהוּא – "גּוּשׁ" אִיקְרֵי.

**Rabbi Ami said to him: If that is so,** then in the case of a woman **who discharges** an item that has **the shape of a mountain, its mother** should be **impure** with the impurity of a woman after **childbirth, as it is stated** with regard to the creation of mountains: **"For He Who forms the mountains and creates the wind"** (Amos 4:13).[N] Rabbi Ḥiyya bar Abba **said to him: Does she discharge a mountain?** The discharged item cannot possibly be that large. **It is** an item with the form of **a stone that she discharges,**[N] and **that is called a clod,** not a mountain.

אֶלָּא מֵעַתָּה, הַמַּפֶּלֶת רוּחַ, תְּהֵא אִמּוֹ טְמֵאָה לֵידָה – הוֹאִיל וְנֶאֶמְרָה בּוֹ "בְּרִיאָה" כְּאָדָם, דִּכְתִיב: "וּבוֹרֵא רוּחַ"! וְכִי תֵּימָא: לָא מוּפְנֶה – מִדַּהֲוָה לֵיהּ לְמִכְתַּב "יוֹצֵר הָרִים וְרוּחַ", וּכְתִיב "וּבוֹרֵא רוּחַ" – שְׁמַע מִינָּהּ לְאַפְנוּיֵי!

Rabbi Ami further inquired: **If that is so,** in the case of a woman **who discharges** an item having **an amorphous form** [*ruaḥ*], **its mother should be impure** with the impurity of a woman after **childbirth, since creation is stated with regard to it, just as** it is stated with regard to **man, as it is written: "And creates the wind** [*ruaḥ*]." **And if you would say** that no verbal analogy can be drawn here, because the verse **is not free,** i.e., it is not superfluous, as it is necessary to recount the creation of the wind, that is not so. Rabbi Ami explains: **From** the fact **that** the verse **could have written: Who forms the mountains and the wind, and** instead **it is written:** "Who forms the mountains **and creates the wind," conclude from it** that the superfluous word "creates" serves **to render it free** for drawing a verbal analogy between *ruaḥ* and man.

אֲמַר לֵיהּ: דָּנִין דִּבְרֵי תוֹרָה מִדִּבְרֵי תוֹרָה, וְאֵין דָּנִין דִּבְרֵי תוֹרָה מִדִּבְרֵי קַבָּלָה.

Rabbi Ḥiyya bar Abba **said to** Rabbi Ami: **One derives matters** that are stated in the **Torah from matters** that are stated in the **Torah,** i.e., from verses in the Torah, **but one does not derive matters** that are stated in the **Torah from the words of the tradition,**[N] i.e., verses in the Prophets or the Writings, such as the verse in Amos.

(אָמַר) רַבָּה בַּר בַּר חָנָה, אָמַר רַבִּי יוֹחָנָן: הַיְינוּ טַעְמָא דְּרַבִּי מֵאִיר – הוֹאִיל וְעֵינֵיהֶם דּוֹמוֹת כְּשֶׁל אָדָם.

§ **Rabba bar bar Ḥana** said that **Rabbi Yoḥanan said: This is the reason** for the opinion **of Rabbi Meir: Since the eyes of** these animals **are similar to those of a human,** a woman who discharges an item of that type is impure.

אֶלָּא מֵעַתָּה הַמַּפֶּלֶת דְּמוּת נָחָשׁ, תְּהֵא אִמּוֹ טְמֵאָה לֵידָה – הוֹאִיל וְגַלְגַּל עֵינוֹ עֲגוּלָּה כְּשֶׁל אָדָם! וְכִי תֵּימָא: הָכִי נָמֵי – לִיתְנֵי נָחָשׁ!

The Gemara objects: **If that is so,** then in the case of a woman **who discharges** an item that has **the form of a snake,**[H] **its mother should** likewise **be impure** with the impurity of a woman after **childbirth, since the pupil of** a snake **is round, like** that **of a human. And if you would say** that **indeed,** this is the *halakha*, then **let** the mishna **teach** this case of a woman who discharges an item that has the form of a **snake** among the other cases where the woman discharges an item of an unusual form.

HALAKHA

A woman who discharges the form of a snake – הַמַּפֶּלֶת דְּמוּת נָחָשׁ: The Rambam maintains that a woman who discharges an item that has the form of a snake is impure with the impurity of a woman after childbirth, since the pupil of a snake is round, like that of a human. The Ra'avad holds that the woman is not impure, in accordance with the opinion of the Rabbis. The *Maggid Mishne* points out the apparent contradiction between the Rambam's ruling in this case and his ruling in the case of a woman who discharges an item having the form of a domesticated animal, an undomesticated animal, or a bird, which follows the opinion of the Rabbis (Rambam *Sefer Kedusha*, *Hilkhot Issurei Bia* 10:10, and see *Kesef Mishne* there).

אִי תְּנָא נָחָשׁ, הֲוָה אָמִינָא: בְּנָחָשׁ הוּא דִּפְלִיגִי רַבָּנַן עֲלֵיהּ דְּרַבִּי מֵאִיר – דְּלָא כְּתִיב בֵּיהּ ״יְצִירָה״, אֲבָל בְּהֵמָה וְחַיָּה – לָא פְּלִיגִי, דִּכְתִיבָא בְּהוּ ״יְצִירָה״.

The Gemara explains: If the mishna had **taught** the case of **a snake, I would say** that it **is** only **in** the case of a woman who discharges an item having the form of **a snake that the Rabbis disagree with Rabbi Meir** and rule that the woman is not impure, **as** a term of **formation is not written with regard to** the creation of the snake. **But** with regard to a woman who discharges an item having the form of **a domesticated animal or an undomesticated animal, they do not disagree** with Rabbi Meir, **as** the concept of **formation is written with regard to them.**

וְהָא גַּבֵּי מוּמִין קָתָנֵי לָהּ אֶת שֶׁגַּלְגַּל עֵינוֹ עָגוֹל כְּשֶׁל אָדָם! לָא קַשְׁיָא, הָא – בְּאוּכָּמָא, הָא – בְּצִירָיָא.

The Gemara raises a difficulty: **But with regard to** the *halakhot* of **blemishes** that render the slaughter of a firstborn animal permitted, **it is taught** in a mishna (*Bekhorot* 40a) that an animal **whose pupil is round like** that **of a human**[BH] is considered blemished. Evidently, the eyes of animals are dissimilar to those of humans. The Gemara answers that it is **not difficult; this** statement, that the eyes of animals are similar to those of humans, is referring **to** the **pupil,** and **that** statement, that the eyes of animals are not similar to those of humans, is referring **to** the entire eyeball in the **socket.**

רַבִּי יַנַּאי אָמַר: הַיְינוּ טַעְמָא דְּרַבִּי מֵאִיר – הוֹאִיל וְעֵינֵיהֶם הוֹלְכוֹת לִפְנֵיהֶם כְּשֶׁל אָדָם. וַהֲרֵי עוֹף, דְּאֵין עֵינָיו הוֹלְכוֹת לְפָנָיו, וְקָאָמַר רַבִּי מֵאִיר דְּטָמֵא! אָמַר אַבַּיֵי: בְּקָרְיָא וְקִיפוֹפָא, וּבִשְׁאָר עוֹפוֹת – לָא.

§ **Rabbi Yannai said: This is the reason** for the opinion **of Rabbi Meir:** It is **because the eyes of** these animals **are fixed in the front of** their heads **like** those **of a human,** unlike the eyes of birds and snakes, a woman who discharges an item of that kind is impure. The Gemara raises a difficulty: **But** there is the case of a woman who discharges an item similar to **a bird, whose eyes are not fixed in the front of** its head, **and** nevertheless **Rabbi Meir says that** the woman **is impure.** This apparently contradicts Rabbi Yannai's explanation. **Abaye said:** Rabbi Meir is referring **to the little owl** [***bekarya***] **and** the **great owl** [***vekifofa***],[B] whose eyes are fixed in the front of their heads, **but in** the case of a woman who discharges any of the **other** species of **birds,** Rabbi Meir does **not** deem her impure.

מֵיתִיבֵי: רַבִּי חֲנִינָא בֶּן אַנְטִיגְנוֹס אוֹמֵר: נִרְאִין דִּבְרֵי רַבִּי מֵאִיר בִּבְהֵמָה וְחַיָּה, וְדִבְרֵי חֲכָמִים בְּעוֹפוֹת,

The Gemara **raises an objection** to this answer from a *baraita*: **Rabbi Ḥanina ben Antigonus says: The statement of Rabbi Meir seems** correct **in** the case of a woman who discharges the form of **a domesticated animal or an undomesticated animal, and the statement of the Rabbis** seems correct **in** the case of **birds.**

מַאי עוֹפוֹת? אִילֵימָא בְּקָרְיָא וְקִיפוֹפָא, מַאי שְׁנָא בְּהֵמָה וְחַיָּה – דְּעֵינֵיהֶן הוֹלְכוֹת לִפְנֵיהֶן כְּשֶׁל אָדָם, קָרְיָא וְקִיפוֹפָא – נַמִי!

The Gemara asks: To **what birds** is Rabbi Ḥanina ben Antigonus referring? **If we say** he is referring **to the little owl and** the **great owl, what is the difference** between this case and the cases of **a domesticated animal or an undomesticated animal,** with regard to which Rabbi Ḥanina ben Antigonus accepts the opinion of Rabbi Meir? If the key factor is **that their eyes are fixed in the front of** their heads **like** those **of a human,** Rabbi Ḥanina ben Antigonus should accept the opinion of Rabbi Meir in the case of **a little owl or a great owl as well,** as their eyes are also fixed in the front of their heads.

**BACKGROUND**

**Whose pupil is round like that of a human** – **גַּלְגַּל עֵינוֹ עָגוֹל כְּשֶׁל אָדָם:**

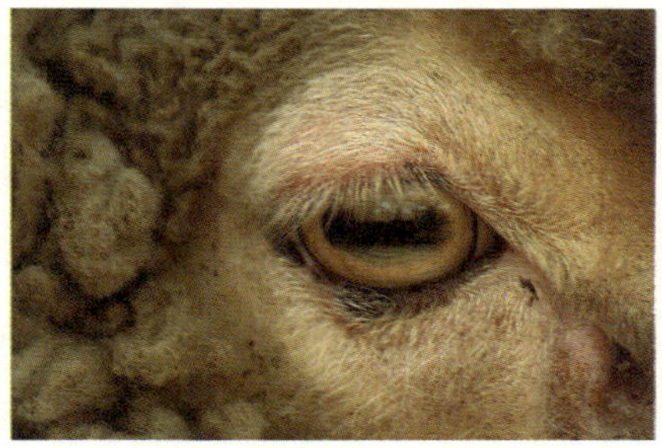

Eye of a sheep, with rectangular pupil

**Little owl [*karya*] and great owl [*kifofa*]** – **קָרְיָא וְקִיפוֹפָא:** Several identifications have been suggested for the *karya* and *kifofa*, which are referred to in the Torah as the *kos* and the *yanshuf*, respectively (see *Targum Onkelos* on Leviticus 11:17). It is generally assumed that both are types of owls. Since the faces of these nocturnal birds have a peculiar appearance different from other birds of prey, seeing them in a dream is considered a bad sign.

Eurasian eagle-owl, posited to be the *karya*

Little owl, also posited to be the *karya*

Barn owl, posited to be the *kifofa*

**HALAKHA**

**Whose pupil [*galgal eino*] is round like that of a human** – **שֶׁגַּלְגַּל עֵינוֹ עָגוֹל כְּשֶׁל אָדָם:** The normal pupil of an animal is not round like that of a human. If its pupil is round like that of a human, this is a blemish that disqualifies the animal from being brought as an offering. In the *Kesef Mishne* it is stated that *galgal eino* refers to the iris; if the entire eyeball is round like that of a human, that is not considered a blemish. The *Kesef Mishne* does note that the Rambam does not mention this distinction (Rambam *Sefer Avoda*, *Hilkhot Issurei Mizbe'aḥ* 2:2).

**PERSONALITIES**

Rabbi Yirmeya – רַבִּי יִרְמְיָה: Born in Babylonia, Rabbi Yirmeya was one of the leading *amora'im* of the third and fourth generations. He studied in Babylonia in his youth, but soon thereafter immigrated to Eretz Yisrael, where he became a disciple of some of the most prominent Sages of the generation, Rabbi Zeira and Rabbi Abbahu, who were the preeminent students of Rabbi Yoḥanan. Rabbi Yirmeya had a special dialectical method of great acuity, and he would pose provocative questions to his teachers and colleagues. Since these questions gave the impression that Rabbi Yirmeya was seeking to undermine the accepted conventions of halakhic dialectic, he was criticized, and was even removed from the study hall for a brief period (see *Bava Batra* 23b). Rabbi Yirmeya's statements are quoted extensively in both the Babylonian Talmud and the Jerusalem Talmud, so much so that when the Babylonian Talmud simply says: They say in the West, i.e., in Eretz Yisrael, it generally refers to the opinion of Rabbi Yirmeya.

Rabbi Zeira – רַבִּי זֵירָא: One of the greatest of the third-generation Babylonian *amora'im*, Rabbi Zeira was educated in the Babylonian tradition and studied mainly with the disciples of Rav and Shmuel. He immigrated to Eretz Yisrael, where he studied under Rabbi Yoḥanan and was a colleague of Rabbi Yoḥanan's foremost disciples. When Rabbi Zeira reached Eretz Yisrael he was extremely impressed by the method of learning he found there, which he adopted in full. Accordingly, he undertook one hundred fasts to help him forget the Babylonian method of learning. He also fasted to prevent the fires of Gehenna from ruling over him. When he performed tests to see if fire would affect him, the calves of his legs were burned. For this reason he became known as the short man with the scorched calves (*Bava Metzia* 85a). Rabbi Zeira was famous for his great piety, his modesty, and his affable and accommodating nature. He was greatly loved and honored by his peers. Rabbi Zeira had many disciples throughout Eretz Yisrael, and his statements are widely quoted in both the Babylonian Talmud and the Jerusalem Talmud. He had a son who was also a Sage, Rabbi Ahava.

אֶלָּא פְּשִׁיטָא – בִּשְׁאָר עוֹפוֹת, מִכְּלָל דְּרַבִּי מֵאִיר פָּלֵיג בִּשְׁאָר עוֹפוֹת!

**Rather,** it is **obvious** that when Rabbi Ḥanina ben Antigonus says that he does not accept the opinion of Rabbi Meir, he is referring **to the other** species of **birds. From the fact** that it is necessary for Rabbi Ḥanina ben Antigonus to reject Rabbi Meir's opinion in those cases, it may be concluded that **Rabbi Meir** himself **disagrees** with the Rabbis **with regard to** the **other** species of **birds** as well, despite the fact that their eyes are not fixed in the front of their heads.

חַסּוּרֵי מִיחַסְּרָא וְהָכִי קָתָנֵי, רַבִּי חֲנִינָא בֶּן אַנְטִיגְנוֹס אוֹמֵר: נִרְאִין דִּבְרֵי רַבִּי מֵאִיר בִּבְהֵמָה וְחַיָּה, וְהוּא הַדִּין לְקָרְיָא וְקִיפּוֹפָא, וְדִבְרֵי חֲכָמִים בִּשְׁאָר עוֹפוֹת, שֶׁאַף רַבִּי מֵאִיר לֹא נֶחְלַק עִמָּהֶם אֶלָּא בְּקָרְיָא וְקִיפּוֹפָא, אֲבָל בִּשְׁאָר עוֹפוֹת מוֹדֵי לְהוּ.

The Gemara explains that the *baraita* **is incomplete, and this** is what **it is teaching: Rabbi Ḥanina ben Antigonus says: The statement of Rabbi Meir seems** correct **in** the case of **a domesticated animal or an undomesticated animal, and the same is true with** regard **to a little owl or a great owl. And the statement of the Rabbis** appears correct even to Rabbi Meir **with regard to** the **other** species of **birds.** The reason is **that even Rabbi Meir** agrees that if a woman discharges an item that has the form of one of the other species of birds, she is not impure, i.e., he **disagrees with them only with regard to a little owl or a great owl, but he concedes to** their opinion **with regard to** the **other** species of **birds.**

וְהָתַנְיָא, אָמַר רַבִּי אֶלְעָזָר בְּרַבִּי צָדוֹק: הַמַּפֶּלֶת מִין בְּהֵמָה וְחַיָּה, לְדִבְרֵי רַבִּי מֵאִיר – וָלָד, וּלְדִבְרֵי חֲכָמִים – אֵינוֹ וָלָד, בְּעוֹפוֹת – תִּיבָּדֵק.

The Gemara cites proof for Abaye's claim that Rabbi Meir differentiates between an owl and other species of birds, **as it is taught** in a *baraita* that **Rabbi Elazar, son of Rabbi Tzadok, says:** In the case of a woman **who discharges** an item that has the form of **a type of domesticated animal or undomesticated animal, according to the statement of Rabbi Meir** it has the halakhic status of a full-fledged **offspring, and according to the statement of the Rabbis,** it does **not** have the status of a full-fledged **offspring. In** the case of a woman who discharges an item that has the form of **birds, it must be examined.**

לְמַאן, תִּיבָּדֵק? לָאו לְדִבְרֵי רַבִּי מֵאִיר דְּאָמַר קָרְיָא וְקִיפּוֹפָא – אִין, שְׁאָר עוֹפוֹת – לָא?

The Gemara asks: **According to whom must it be examined?** Is this **not** referring **to the statement of Rabbi Meir, who said** that if a woman discharges an item that has the form of **a little owl or a great owl, yes,** she is impure, but if she discharges an item that has the form of **other birds,** she is **not** impure? Consequently, the item must be examined to determine what type of bird it resembles.

אָמַר רַב אַחָא בְּרֵיהּ דְּרַב אִיקָא: לָא, תִּיבָּדֵק לְרַבָּנַן, דְּאָמְרִי קָרְיָא וְקִיפּוֹפָא – אִין, שְׁאָר עוֹפוֹת – לָא.

**Rav Aḥa, son of Rav Ika, said: No,** this *baraita* does not prove that Rabbi Meir differentiates between owls and other species of birds, as perhaps the statement that the discharged item **must be examined** applies **according to the Rabbis, as they say** that if a woman discharges an item that has the form of **a little owl or a great owl, yes,** she is impure, but if a woman discharges an item that has the form of **other birds,** she is **not** impure.

וּמַאי שְׁנָא קָרְיָא וְקִיפּוֹפָא מִבְּהֵמָה וְחַיָּה? הוֹאִיל וְיֵשׁ לָהֶן לְסָתוֹת כְּאָדָם.

The Gemara asks: **But** if the Rabbis hold that a woman who discharges an item similar to a land animal is not impure, why would they hold that if she discharges an item that has the form of owls she is impure? **What is the difference** between **a little owl and a great owl** on the one hand, and **a domesticated animal and an undomesticated animal** on the other? The Gemara answers: **Since** owls **have cheeks like** those of **a human,** therefore a woman who discharges an item similar to an owl is impure, whereas if she discharges an item that has the form of a land animal she is pure, despite the fact that their eyes are fixed in the front of their heads.

בְּעָא מִינֵּיהּ רַבִּי יִרְמְיָה מֵרַבִּי זֵירָא: לְרַבִּי מֵאִיר דְּאָמַר בְּהֵמָה בִּמְעֵי אִשָּׁה וָלָד מְעַלְּיָא הוּא, קִבֵּל בָּהּ אָבִיהָ קִידּוּשִׁין מַהוּ? לְמַאי נָפְקָא מִינַּהּ – לְאִיתְסוּרֵי בַּאֲחוֹתָהּ.

§ **Rabbi Yirmeya**[P] **asked Rabbi Zeira:**[P] **According to Rabbi Meir, who said** that **an animal in the womb of a woman is** considered **a full-fledged offspring, what is** the *halakha* in a case where it is a female, and **her father accepted betrothal for her,** i.e., he married her off by accepting betrothal money from a man, or a document of betrothal? Is such a betrothal valid? Rabbi Yirmeya elaborated: **What** practical **difference is** there whether it is valid? The difference is **with regard to** whether it is **prohibited** for the man **to** marry **her sister.** If the betrothal is valid, it is prohibited for the husband to marry her sister, as one may not marry his wife's sister.

לְמֵימְרָא דְּחָיֵי? וְהָאָמַר רַב יְהוּדָה, אָמַר רַב: לֹא אָמְרָה רַבִּי מֵאִיר אֶלָּא הוֹאִיל וּבְמִינוֹ מִתְקַיֵּים! אָמַר רַב אַחָא בַּר יַעֲקֹב: עַד כָּאן הֱבִיאוֹ רַבִּי יִרְמְיָה לְרַבִּי זֵירָא לִידֵי גִּיחוּךְ וְלָא גָּחֵיךְ.

The Gemara asks: **Is this to say that** such an offspring **can live?** This factor is important, as a man is prohibited from marrying his wife's sister only during his wife's lifetime. **But doesn't Rav Yehuda say** that **Rav says: Rabbi Meir said** that a woman who discharges an item that has the form of an animal is impure **only since** there are other animals **of its type** that can **live,** i.e., there are animals similar to the discharged item that do survive, but not that creature itself. **Rav Aḥa bar Ya'akov says: Rabbi Yirmeya tried this hard to cause Rabbi Zeira to laugh, but he did not laugh.** In other words, Rabbi Yirmeya was not asking his question seriously.

גּוּפָא, אָמַר רַב יְהוּדָה, אָמַר רַב: לֹא אָמְרָה רַבִּי מֵאִיר אֶלָּא הוֹאִיל וּבְמִינוֹ מִתְקַיֵּים. אָמַר רַב יִרְמְיָה מִדִּפְתִּי:

The Gemara discusses **the** matter **itself. Rav Yehuda says** that **Rav says: Rabbi Meir said** that a woman who discharges an item that has the form of an animal is impure **only since** there are animals **of its type** that can **live. Rav Yirmeya of Difti says:**

Perek **III**
Daf **23** Amud **b**

אַף אֲנַן נַמִּי תְּנֵינָא: הַמַּפֶּלֶת כְּמִין בְּהֵמָה חַיָּה וְעוֹף – (וָלָד מְעַלְּיָא הוּא), דִּבְרֵי רַבִּי מֵאִיר. וַחֲכָמִים אוֹמְרִים: עַד שֶׁיְּהֵא בּוֹ מִצּוּרַת אָדָם.

**We, too, learn** in a mishna (*Bekhorot* 46a) that the fetus of a woman that has the form of an animal cannot survive: In the case of a woman **who** had previously **discharged a fetus** with the appearance **similar to** that **of a domesticated animal, an undomesticated animal, or bird** before giving birth to any children, and subsequently she gives birth to a son, the son is considered a firstborn with regard to the *halakhot* of inheritance, but he does not require redemption, as the fetus is considered a full-fledged offspring in that regard. This is **the statement of Rabbi Meir. And the Rabbis say:** The son is not exempted from the requirement of redemption from a priest **unless** it follows the birth of a fetus **that takes the form of a person;** otherwise, it is not considered the offspring that "opens the womb" (Exodus 13:2), and the son requires redemption as a firstborn.

וְהַמַּפֶּלֶת סַנְדָּל, אוֹ שִׁלְיָא, אוֹ שַׁפִיר מְרוּקָּם, וְהַיּוֹצֵא מְחוּתָּךְ – הַבָּא אַחֲרָיו בְּכוֹר לְנַחֲלָה וְאֵינוֹ בְּכוֹר לְכֹהֵן. וְאִי סָלְקָא דַּעְתָּךְ דְּחָיֵי, הַבָּא אַחֲרָיו בְּכוֹר לְנַחֲלָה מִי הָוֵי?

**And** in the case of a woman **who discharges** a fetus in the form of **a sandal fish,**[B] **or** from whom **an afterbirth or a gestational sac** in which **tissue developed** emerged, **or** who delivered a fetus **that emerged in pieces,** the son **that follows them is** considered **a firstborn with regard to inheritance but is not a firstborn with regard to** redemption from **a priest.**[N] The Gemara explains the proof: **And if it enters your mind that** a fetus that has the form of an animal **can survive, is the** son **that follows it a firstborn with regard to inheritance?**

אָמַר רָבָא: לְעוֹלָם – דְּחָיֵי, וְשָׁאנֵי הָתָם דְּאָמַר קְרָא "רֵאשִׁית אֹנוֹ" – מִי שֶׁלִּבּוֹ דָּוֶה עָלָיו, יָצָא זֶה שֶׁאֵין לִבּוֹ דָּוֶה עָלָיו.

**Rava said,** in rejection of this proof: **Actually,** it is possible **that** a fetus shaped like an animal **can survive; but it is different there,** with regard to inheritance. The son that follows such a fetus has the status of a firstborn, **as the verse states** with regard to the inheritance of a firstborn: "By giving him a double portion of all that he has; for he is **the first fruits of his strength** [*ono*]; the right of the firstborn is his" (Deuteronomy 21:17). It is derived from the verse that the status of a firstborn applies only to a son **over whose** death a father would **mourn.** The word *ono* is interpreted homiletically based on its similarity to the word *onen*, acute mourner. **This** offspring that has the form of an animal is therefore **excluded, as** its father **would not mourn over its** death.

**BACKGROUND**

Sandal fish – סַנְדָּל: This fish is referred to today as the sole, a group of flatfish. The name is derived from the Latin solea, referring to both the fish and the sole of a shoe. The common sole, *Solea solea*, possesses an interesting feature: Both of its eyes are on the right side of its body.

**NOTES**

Is a firstborn with regard to inheritance but is not a firstborn with regard to a priest – בְּכוֹר לְנַחֲלָה וְאֵינוֹ בְּכוֹר לְכֹהֵן: The Torah states two *halakhot* with regard to a firstborn: He must be redeemed through payment of five *sela* to a priest, and he receives a portion double that of his brothers in his father's inheritance. The definition of a firstborn differs with regard to these two matters. A firstborn must be redeemed if he opened the womb of his mother, i.e., he is her firstborn. Such a firstborn requires redemption even if he is not the firstborn of his father, i.e., a man who has multiple wives must redeem the firstborn of each. Conversely, with regard to the *halakhot* of inheritance, it is the father's firstborn son who receives a double share, even if he is not his mother's firstborn, as it is stated in the verse: "For he is the first fruits of his strength, the right of the firstborn is his" (Deuteronomy 21:17).

בְּעָא מִינֵּיהּ רַב אַדָּא בַּר אַהֲבָה מֵאַבַּיֵי: לְרַבִּי מֵאִיר דְּאָמַר בְּהֵמָה בִּמְעֵי אִשָּׁה – וָלָד מְעַלְּיָא הוּא, אָדָם בִּמְעֵי בְהֵמָה מַאי? לְמַאי נָפְקָא מִינֵּיהּ – לְאִשְׁתַּרוּיֵי בַּאֲכִילָה.

§ **Rav Adda bar Ahava asked Abaye: According to Rabbi Meir, who said** that an item that is similar to **an animal in the womb of a woman is** considered **a full-fledged offspring, what** is the *halakha* with regard to **a human** fetus **in the womb of an animal?** The Gemara explains: **What is the** practical **difference** of this inquiry? The difference is **with regard to permitting** the fetus **in consumption.** A full-fledged fetus found inside its slaughtered mother is permitted to be eaten, despite the fact that it was not slaughtered itself.

וְתִפְשׁוֹט לֵיהּ מֵהָא דְּרַבִּי יוֹחָנָן, דְּאָמַר רַבִּי יוֹחָנָן: הַשּׁוֹחֵט אֶת הַבְּהֵמָה וּמָצָא בָּהּ דְּמוּת יוֹנָה – אֲסוּרָה בַּאֲכִילָה!

The Gemara suggests: **But** one can **resolve** the dilemma **from that** statement **of Rabbi Yoḥanan, as Rabbi Yoḥanan said:** In the case of **one who slaughters an animal and finds in it** an item that has **the form of a pigeon,**[H] the pigeon **is prohibited for consumption.** Evidently, the ritual slaughter of a pregnant animal renders its fetus permitted to be eaten only if the fetus is of the same species as the mother. Accordingly, if the fetus has the form of a human, it is prohibited for consumption.

הָכִי הַשְׁתָּא? הָתָם – לָא פְּרָסוֹת אִיכָּא וְלָא פַּרְסָה אִיכָּא, הָכָא – נְהִי דִּפְרָסוֹת לֵיכָּא, פַּרְסָה מִיהָא אִיכָּא.

The Gemara rejects this suggestion: **How can** these cases **be compared? There,** with regard to a pigeon fetus, **there are no** split **hooves, and there is not** even **a hoof** at all. Since a pigeon is completely different from the slaughtered animal, the fetus is forbidden. By contrast, **here,** in the case of a human fetus, **although there are no** split **hooves, there is at least a hoof,** i.e., solid feet. Therefore, it is possible that the human fetus is permitted for consumption, and the dilemma remains unresolved.

״וַחֲכָמִים אוֹמְרִים כָּל שֶׁאֵין בּוֹ״ כו׳. אָמַר רַב יִרְמְיָה בַּר אַבָּא, אָמַר רַב: הַכֹּל מוֹדִים, גּוּפוֹ תַּיִישׁ וּפָנָיו אָדָם – אָדָם, גּוּפוֹ אָדָם וּפָנָיו תַּיִישׁ – וְלֹא כְלוּם,

§ The mishna teaches: **And the Rabbis say: Any** discharged entity **that is not** of human form does not render the woman impure. **Rav Yirmeya bar Abba says** that **Rav says: All concede** that if a woman discharged an entity **whose body is** that of **a goat**[B] **and whose face is** that of **a human,** it is considered **a human** offspring, i.e., even the Rabbis rule that the woman is impure in this case. Likewise, if **its body is** that of **a human and its face is** that of **a goat,** Rabbi Meir concedes that **it is nothing,** and the woman is pure.

לֹא נֶחְלְקוּ אֶלָּא שֶׁפָּנָיו אָדָם וְנִבְרָא בְּעַיִן אַחַת כִּבְהֵמָה. שֶׁרַבִּי מֵאִיר אוֹמֵר: מִצּוּרַת אָדָם. וַחֲכָמִים אוֹמְרִים: כָּל צוּרַת אָדָם.

**They disagree only** in a case **where its face is** that of **a human, but it was created with** one human eye and **one eye like** that of **an animal. As Rabbi Meir says** that if the offspring has part **of the form of a human** face, even if one eye is not like that of a human, it is considered a human offspring, and the woman is impure. **And the Rabbis say** that it must have **the entire form of a human** face to be considered a human offspring, and otherwise the woman is not impure.

אֲמַר לוֹ לְרַב יִרְמְיָה בַּר אַבָּא: וְהָא אִיפְּכָא תַּנְיָא, רַבִּי מֵאִיר אוֹמֵר: ״כָּל צוּרַת״, וַחֲכָמִים אוֹמְרִים: ״מִצּוּרַת״! אֲמַר לְהוּ: אִי תַּנְיָא – תַּנְיָא.

One of the Sages **said to Rav Yirmeya bar Abba: But isn't the opposite taught** in a *baraita*: **Rabbi Meir says** that a woman who discharged is impure if the fetus has **any** part of the **form** of a human face, **and the Rabbis say** that the woman is impure only if the fetus has a recognizable part **of the form of** a human face, e.g., half of a human face? According to this *baraita*, Rabbi Meir does not even require that a significant part of it must look human. In his opinion, even if it has only one human eye or one human cheek and the rest of the face is like that of an animal, the woman is impure. Rav Yirmeya bar Abba **said to** the Sages: **If this** *baraita* **is taught, it is taught,** and I cannot take issue with it. I have my tradition from Rav, and you should rule in accordance with the *baraita* that you received.

אָמַר רַבִּי יִרְמְיָה בַּר אַבָּא, אָמַר רַבִּי יוֹחָנָן: מֵצַח, וְהַגְּבִינִים, וְהָעֵינַיִם, וְהַלְּסָתוֹת, וְגַבּוֹת הַזָּקָן – עַד שֶׁיְּהוּ כּוּלָּם כְּאֶחָד. רָבָא אָמַר חָסָא: מֵצַח, וְהַגָּבִן, וְהָעַיִן, וְהַלֶּסֶת, וְגַבַּת הַזָּקָן – עַד שֶׁיְּהוּ כּוּלָּם כְּאַחַת.

**Rabbi Yirmeya bar Abba says** that **Rabbi Yoḥanan says:** A woman who discharges an entity is impure only if the entire face of the fetus has a human form. This includes its **forehead, and the eyebrows, and the eyes,**[H] **and the cheeks, and** its **chin.** The woman is not impure **unless** these facial features **all as one** have the human form. **Rava says** that **Ḥasa says:** It is sufficient for the fetus to have the appearance of a human on one side of its face; its **forehead, and** one **eyebrow, and** one **eye, and** one **cheek, and** its **chin** are enough. The woman is not impure **unless** these facial features **all as one** have the human form.

**HALAKHA**

**One who slaughters an animal and finds in it the form of a pigeon – הַשּׁוֹחֵט אֶת הַבְּהֵמָה וּמָצָא בָּהּ דְּמוּת יוֹנָה:** If one slaughters a pregnant animal and finds in its womb an item that has the form of a bird, even a kosher bird, the fetus is forbidden for consumption. A fetus found in the womb of a slaughtered animal is permitted for consumption only if it has hooves. The *Shakh* adds that according to the Rambam and the *Shulḥan Arukh*, even if the fetus has the appearance of an animal that has hooves, if it does not actually have hooves, it is forbidden. The Rema writes that it is not necessary for its hooves to be split, i.e., if it looks like an animal with hooves, even one that does not have split hooves, it is permitted for consumption (Rambam *Sefer Kedusha, Hilkhot Ma'akhalot Assurot* 1:7; *Shulḥan Arukh, Yoreh De'a* 13:5).

**Its forehead and the eyebrows and the eyes, etc. – מֵצַח וְהַגְּבִינִים וְהָעֵינַיִם וכו׳:** If a woman discharged a type of domesticated animal, undomesticated animal, or bird, if it has a human face, it is considered human. Therefore, if it is male, the woman observes the periods of impurity and purity established in the Torah for a woman who gives birth to a male, and if it is female, she observes the periods established in the Torah for a woman who gives birth to a female. If the sex of the offspring is indiscernible, the woman observes the strictures of a woman who gave birth to a male and to a female. If the fetus does not have a human face, then even if the rest of its body looks human, including its hands and legs, and its sex is clear as well, nevertheless, it is not considered a human fetus, and the woman does not have the impurity status of a woman after childbirth. For a fetus to be defined as having a human face it must have a human forehead and chin, and human eyebrows, eyes, and cheeks. If it has these human features, it is considered a human offspring, even if its mouth, ears, and nose resemble those of animals. Nowadays, the woman is considered impure regardless of the shape of the discharged item, as the halakhic authorities today are not proficient in the differences between the various forms of discharged items (Rambam *Sefer Kedusha, Hilkhot Issurei Bia* 10:8–9, and see *Maggid Mishne* there; *Shulḥan Arukh, Yoreh De'a* 194:3).

**BACKGROUND**

**Goat [*tayish*] – תַּיִישׁ:** A *tayish* is a buck, or male goat, and can be recognized by its beard. There are over three hundred breeds of goats, which differ substantially in their coloring, build, and genetics. The goats generally discussed in the Mishna and Talmud are of a species similar to *Capra mambrica*, which is native to Eretz Yisrael.

וְלָא פְּלִיגִי, הָא – כְּמַאן דְּאָמַר ״כׇּל צוּרַת״, הָא – כְּמַאן דְּאָמַר ״מִצּוּרַת״.

**And** Rabbi Yoḥanan and Ḥasa **do not disagree** about whether the *halakha* is in accordance with the opinion of Rabbi Meir or that of the Rabbis, as they both accept the opinion of the Rabbis. The difference between them is that **this** *amora*, Rabbi Yoḥanan, holds **like the one who says** that the Rabbis require **the entire form of** the face to be human, and **that** *amora*, Ḥasa, holds **like the one who says** that the Rabbis require only a recognizable part **of the form of** a human face.

מֵיתִיבִי: צוּרַת פָּנִים שֶׁאָמְרוּ – אֲפִילּוּ פַּרְצוּף אֶחָד מִן הַפַּרְצוּפִין, חוּץ מִן הָאוֹזֶן. לְמֵימְרָא דְּמֵחַד נַמִי סַגִּי!

Ḥasa evidently interprets the version of the Rabbis' statement that only part of a human face is required as referring to half of a human face. The Gemara **raises an objection** to this interpretation from a *baraita*: The miscarriage of a fetus with **the form of** a human **face, which** the Rabbis **said** renders the woman impure, includes **even one of the facial features, apart from the ear.** Apparently, **that is to say that** even **if** the fetus has only **one** facial feature of a human, this **is also sufficient** to render the woman impure.

אָמַר אַבָּיֵי: כִּי תַּנְיָא הַהִיא – לְעַכֵּב תַּנְיָא, וּכְמַאן דְּאָמַר ״כׇּל צוּרַת״. וְאִיבָּעֵית אֵימָא: לְעוֹלָם כְּמַאן דְּאָמַר ״מִצּוּרַת״, וּמַאי ״אֶחָד״ – אֶחָד אֶחָד.

**Abaye says: When that** *baraita* **is taught, it is taught with regard to** the *halakha* of **rendering** all of the facial features **indispensable** for the fetus to be defined as human, except for the ear. **And** this ruling **is in accordance with the one who says** that the Rabbis require that **the entire form of** the face must be human. **And if you wish, say** that **actually** this ruling **is in accordance with the one who says** that the Rabbis require only a recognizable part **of the form of** a human face. **And what** is the meaning of the claim that it is sufficient for the fetus to have **one** facial feature of a human? It means **one of each** facial feature of which a human has two, i.e., one eye, one eyebrow, and so on.

אָמַר רָבָא: נִבְרָא בְּעַיִן אַחַת וּבְיָרֵךְ אֶחָד, מִן הַצַּד – אִמּוֹ טְמֵאָה, בָּאֶמְצַע – אִמּוֹ טְהוֹרָה.

**Rava says:** In a case where a fetus **was created with one eye or with one thigh,**[H] if the eye is located **to the side** on the middle of the face, or the thigh is located at the side of the hip, where a human eye or thigh is normally located, the fetus is considered human, and **its mother is impure.** If it appears **in the middle** of the face or hip, the fetus is not considered human, and **its mother is pure.**

אָמַר רָבָא: וֶשֶׁט נָקוּב – אִמּוֹ טְמֵאָה, וֶשֶׁט אָטוּם – אִמּוֹ טְהוֹרָה.

**Rava says:** If **its esophagus is punctured,** although the fetus is considered a *tereifa*, i.e., one that has a wound that will cause it to die within twelve months, **its mother is impure.**[N] But if **its esophagus is sealed,**[H] i.e., it is closed at one end, it does not have the status of a human fetus, and therefore **its mother is pure.**

תָּנוּ רַבָּנַן: הַמַּפֶּלֶת גּוּף אָטוּם – אֵין אִמּוֹ טְמֵאָה לֵידָה. וְאֵיזֶהוּ גּוּף אָטוּם? רַבִּי אוֹמֵר: כְּדֵי שֶׁיִּנָּטֵל מִן הַחַי וְיָמוּת.

§ **The Sages taught** in a *baraita*: In the case of a woman **who discharges** a fetus that has **a sealed body,**[H] **its mother is not impure** with the impurity of a woman after **childbirth. And what is a sealed body? Rabbi** Yehuda HaNasi **says:** It is a body which is lacking a limb that **when removed from a living** person would cause him to **die.**

וְכַמָּה יִנָּטֵל מִן הַחַי וְיָמוּת? רַבִּי זַכַּאי אוֹמֵר:

**And how much** of the lower part of a person's body **when removed from a living** person would cause him to **die,** because one cannot survive such a wound? **Rabbi Zakkai says:**

**NOTES**

**Rava says: If its esophagus is punctured its mother is impure – אָמַר רָבָא וֶשֶׁט נָקוּב אִמּוֹ טְמֵאָה:** Some explain that Rava conforms to his opinion elsewhere that it is possible for a *tereifa* to live beyond twelve months. By contrast, according to the opinion that a *tereifa* is not capable of surviving beyond twelve months, the mother is not impure (Rashi; *Tosafot*). Nevertheless, *Tosafot* demonstrate that there are places where Rava rules in accordance with the opinion that a *tereifa* cannot live for more than twelve months. Others explain that even according to the opinion that a *tereifa* is not capable of surviving beyond twelve months, still the mother is impure, due to the capability of the newborn to survive for a significant period of time, even if less than twelve months. Furthermore, it is possible that the esophagus was punctured after the baby was born, in which case the blemish is irrelevant to the status of the woman (Ramban; Rashba).

**HALAKHA**

Where a fetus was created with one eye or with one thigh – נִבְרָא בְּעַיִן אַחַת וְיָרֵךְ אֶחָד: If a woman discharges a fetus that has only one eye or one thigh, if it is located in the part of the body where it is supposed to be located, i.e., the eye is to the side on the middle of the face and the thigh is at the side of the hip, the fetus is considered half-human, and the woman is impure with the impurity of a woman after childbirth. If the eye or thigh is located in the middle of the face or hip, the fetus is considered a separate entity, and the woman is pure (Rambam *Sefer Kedusha*, *Hilkhot Issurei Bia* 10:10).

Its esophagus is sealed – וֶשֶׁט אָטוּם: If the esophagus of a fetus is sealed from its formation, it is not considered an offspring, and its mother is not impure with the impurity of a woman after childbirth (Rambam *Sefer Kedusha*, *Hilkhot Issurei Bia* 10:11).

A woman who discharges a fetus that has a sealed body – הַמַּפֶּלֶת גּוּף אָטוּם: If a woman discharges a fetus lacking the part of the body below the navel, it is not considered an offspring, and its mother is not impure with the impurity of a woman after childbirth. This is in accordance with the interpretation of the *baraita* by Rabbi Yoḥanan, citing Rabbi Yosei ben Yehoshua (Rambam *Sefer Kedusha*, *Hilkhot Issurei Bia* 10:11).

עַד הָאַרְכּוּבָה. רַבִּי יַנַּאי אוֹמֵר: עַד לִנְקָבָיו. רַבִּי יוֹחָנָן אוֹמֵר מִשּׁוּם רַבִּי יוֹסֵי בֶּן יְהוֹשֻׁעַ: עַד מְקוֹם טַבּוּרוֹ.

Until above **the knee. Rabbi Yannai says: Until his orifices. Rabbi Yoḥanan says in the name of Rabbi Yosei ben Yehoshua: Until the location of his navel.**[N]

בֵּין רַבִּי זַכַּאי לְרַבִּי יַנַּאי אִיכָּא בֵּינַיְיהוּ טְרֵפָה חָיָה, מָר סָבַר: טְרֵפָה חָיָה, וּמָר סָבַר: טְרֵפָה אֵינָהּ חָיָה.

The Gemara explains the dispute between the *amora'im*: The difference **between** the opinion of **Rabbi Zakkai and** that of **Rabbi Yannai** is whether **a *tereifa* can survive** beyond twelve months. One **Sage,** Rabbi Yannai, **holds** that **a *tereifa* can survive** beyond twelve months. Therefore, although one whose legs were removed until above the knee has the status of a *tereifa,* if a woman discharges a fetus of this form she is impure. Only if the fetus lacks legs until his orifices is the woman pure, as such a person cannot survive. **And** one **Sage,** Rabbi Zakkai, **holds** that **a *tereifa* cannot survive** beyond twelve months. Therefore, even if the fetus lacks legs only from above the knee and not from his orifices, the woman is not impure.

בֵּין רַבִּי יַנַּאי לְרַבִּי יוֹחָנָן אִיכָּא בֵּינַיְיהוּ דְּרַבִּי אֶלְעָזָר, דְּאָמַר רַבִּי אֶלְעָזָר: נִיטַּל יָרֵךְ וַחֲלָלָהּ שֶׁלָּהּ – נְבֵלָה.

The difference **between** the opinion of **Rabbi Yannai and** the opinion of **Rabbi Yoḥanan,** who both agree that a *tereifa* can survive, is with regard to a statement **of Rabbi Elazar, as Rabbi Elazar said:** If the **thigh,** i.e., the hind leg of the animal, **and its recess were removed** from an animal before slaughter, the animal is considered **an unslaughtered carcass;** consequently, it is forbidden in consumption and imparts ritual impurity even while still alive. Rabbi Yannai agrees with the statement of Rabbi Elazar, and accordingly holds that if the lower part of a person's body until his orifices is missing or removed, the person immediately assumes the halakhic status of a corpse. Rabbi Yoḥanan disagrees with Rabbi Elazar and holds that one whose lower part of his body was missing or removed has the status of a corpse only if it is removed until his navel.

אָמַר רַב פַּפָּא: מַחֲלוֹקֶת מִלְּמַטָּה לְמַעְלָה, אֲבָל מִלְמַעְלָה לְמַטָּה – אֲפִילּוּ כָּל דְּהוּ טְהוֹרָה. וְכֵן אָמַר רַב גִּידֵּל, אָמַר רַבִּי יוֹחָנָן: הַמַּפֶּלֶת אֶת שֶׁגּוּלְגָּלְתּוֹ אֲטוּמָה – אִמּוֹ טְהוֹרָה.

**Rav Pappa says:** The **dispute** between the *amora'im* is with regard to a fetus that is lacking part of its body **from below** to **above,** i.e., the lower part of his body; **but** if it is lacking part of its body **from above** to **below, even any amount** of its skull, the woman **is pure. And likewise, Rav Giddel says** that **Rabbi Yoḥanan says:** In the case of a woman **who discharges** a fetus **whose skull is sealed,** i.e., deficient,[H] **its mother is pure.**

וְאָמַר רַב גִּידֵּל, אָמַר רַבִּי יוֹחָנָן: הַמַּפֶּלֶת כְּמִין אַפַּקְתָא דְּדִיקְלָא – אִמּוֹ טְהוֹרָה.

The Gemara cites another *halakha*: **And Rav Giddel says** that **Rabbi Yoḥanan says:** In the case of a woman **who discharges** a fetus that looks **like** the part **of a palm tree** that **branches out,**[B] i.e., the lower part of its body is formless while the upper part has arms and legs coming out of its shoulders like branches, **its mother is pure.**

אִיתְּמַר, הַמַּפֶּלֶת מִי שֶׁפָּנָיו מוּסְמָסִים, רַבִּי יוֹחָנָן אָמַר: אִמּוֹ טְמֵאָה, רֵישׁ לָקִישׁ אָמַר: אִמּוֹ טְהוֹרָה.

§ It **was stated** with regard to a woman **who discharges** a fetus **whose face is mashed** but not completely flattened, that **Rabbi Yoḥanan says its mother is impure,** and **Reish Lakish says its mother is pure.**

אֵיתִיבֵיהּ רַבִּי יוֹחָנָן לְרֵישׁ לָקִישׁ: הַמַּפֶּלֶת יָד חֲתוּכָה וְרֶגֶל חֲתוּכָה – אִמּוֹ טְמֵאָה לֵידָה, וְאֵין חוֹשְׁשִׁין שֶׁמָּא מִגּוּף אָטוּם בָּאתָה. וְאִם אִיתָא – לִיתְנֵי שֶׁמָּא מִגּוּף אָטוּם אוֹ מִמִּי שֶׁפָּנָיו מוּסְמָסִין!

**Rabbi Yoḥanan raised an objection to Reish Lakish** from a *baraita*: In the case of a woman **who discharges a shaped hand,** i.e., a hand whose fingers are discernible, **or a shaped foot, its mother is impure** with the impurity of a woman after **childbirth,** as it certainly came from a full-fledged fetus, **and we are not concerned** that **perhaps it came from** a fetus with **a sealed,** i.e., deficient, **body. And if it is so,** that a fetus with a mashed face does not render its mother impure, **let** the *baraita* **teach:** We are not concerned that **perhaps** it came **from** a fetus with **a sealed body or from one whose face is mashed.**

### NOTES

**Until the location of his navel** – עַד מְקוֹם טַבּוּרוֹ: The early authorities disagree with regard to the halakhic ruling in this dispute. Some rule in accordance with the opinion of Rabbi Zakkai, that if the offspring lacks legs from above the knee the woman is not impure, based on the halakhic ruling that a *tereifa* cannot survive beyond twelve months, and one who lacks legs from above the knee is considered a *tereifa.* Likewise, these authorities rule that if the thigh and its recess were removed from an animal before slaughter the animal is considered an unslaughtered carcass and is forbidden for consumption (Ra'avad). Other authorities rule in accordance with the opinion of Rabbi Yoḥanan, as he cites Rabbi Yosei ben Yehoshua, who was a *tanna* (Rambam).

### BACKGROUND

**The part of a palm tree that branches out** – אַפַּקְתָא דְּדִיקְלָא:

Palm tree

### HALAKHA

**A woman who discharges a fetus whose skull is sealed** – הַמַּפֶּלֶת אֶת שֶׁגּוּלְגָּלְתּוֹ אֲטוּמָה: If a woman discharges a fetus whose skull is deficient, it is not considered an offspring, and its mother is not impure with the impurity of a woman after childbirth (Rambam *Sefer Kedusha, Hilkhot Issurei Bia* 10:11).

אָמַר רַב פַּפִּי: בְּפָנָיו מוּסְמָסִין – כּוּלֵּי עָלְמָא לָא פְּלִיגִי דִּטְמֵאָה, כִּי פְּלִיגִי – בְּפָנָיו טוּחוֹת, וְאִיפְּכָא אִיתְּמַר, רַבִּי יוֹחָנָן אָמַר: אִמּוֹ טְהוֹרָה, וְרֵישׁ לָקִישׁ אָמַר: אִמּוֹ טְמֵאָה.

**Rav Pappi says: In** a case where **its face is mashed, everyone agrees that** the woman **is impure. When they disagree,** it is **in** a case where **its face is** completely **flat,**[H] i.e., none of its features are discernible; **and the opposite was stated: Rabbi Yoḥanan says** that **its mother is pure, and Reish Lakish says** that **its mother is impure.**

וְלוֹתְבֵיהּ רֵישׁ לָקִישׁ לְרַבִּי יוֹחָנָן מֵהָא! מִשּׁוּם דְּשָׁנֵי לֵיהּ: הַיְינוּ גּוּף אָטוּם, הַיְינוּ מִי שֶׁפָּנָיו טוּחוֹת.

The Gemara raises a difficulty: **But** according to this version of the dispute, **let Reish Lakish raise an objection to** the opinion of **Rabbi Yoḥanan from this** *baraita*, from which Rabbi Yoḥanan raised an objection to the opinion of Reish Lakish according to the previous version of the dispute: If a woman who discharges a fetus whose face is flat is pure, the *baraita* should have stated that there is no concern that the hand or foot might have come from a fetus with a sealed body or one whose face is flat. The Gemara answers: Reish Lakish did not raise the objection, **because Rabbi Yoḥanan** would have **responded to him** that the status of **a sealed body is** the same as that of **one whose face is flat.** There is no reason to mention both types of deformities.

בְּנֵי רַבִּי חִיָּיא נְפַק לְקִרְיָיתָא, אָתוּ לְקַמֵּיהּ דַּאֲבוּהוֹן, אָמַר לְהֶם: כְּלוּם בָּא מַעֲשֶׂה לְיֶדְכֶם? אָמְרוּ לוֹ: פָּנִים טוּחוֹת בָּא לְיָדֵינוּ, וְטִימֵּאנוּהָ.

The Gemara relates: **The sons of Rabbi Ḥiyya went out to the villages** to inspect their father's fields. When **they came** back **to their father, he said to them:** Wasn't **any incident brought to you** for a halakhic ruling? **They said to him:** A case of a woman who discharged a fetus with **a flat face was brought to us, and we deemed her impure** with the impurity of a woman after childbirth.

אָמַר לָהֶם: צְאוּ וְטַהֲרוּ מַה שֶּׁטִּמֵּאתֶם. מַאי דַּעְתַּיְיכוּ – לְחוּמְרָא, חוּמְרָא דְּאָתְיָא לִידֵי קוּלָּא הִיא, דְּקָיְהֲבִיתוּ לָהּ יְמֵי טוֹהַר.

Rabbi Ḥiyya **said to them: Go out and deem pure that which you have deemed impure. What was your thinking** when you ruled that she is impure? Did you reason that as the matter is subject to a dispute, one should rule **stringently?** But your ruling **is a stringency that leads to a leniency, as you have given** the woman thirty-three **days of purity** after the birth of a male, following her period of impurity, which are the minimum days of purity established in the Torah for a woman who gave birth.

אִיתְּמַר, הַמַּפֶּלֶת בְּרִיָּה שֶׁיֵּשׁ לָהּ שְׁנֵי גַּבִּים וּשְׁנֵי שִׁדְרָאוֹת. אָמַר רַב: בְּאִשָּׁה – אֵינוֹ וָלָד, בִּבְהֵמָה – אָסוּר בַּאֲכִילָה. וּשְׁמוּאֵל אָמַר: בְּאִשָּׁה – וָלָד, בִּבְהֵמָה – מוּתָּר בַּאֲכִילָה.

§ **It was stated:** With regard to a woman or female animal **who discharges an entity that has two backs and two spines,**[H] **Rav says** that **in** the case of the **woman,** her discharged fetus **is not** considered **an offspring,** as it cannot survive, and therefore the woman does not have the ritual impurity caused by childbirth, and **in** the case of the **animal,**[H] its fetus **is prohibited for consumption. And Shmuel says: In** the case of **a woman,** the discharged fetus is considered **an offspring,** and the woman is impure, and **in** the case of **an animal,** the fetus is **permitted for consumption.**

**HALAKHA**

In a case where its face is flat – בְּפָנָיו טוּחוֹת: If the face of a discharged fetus is flat, i.e., its facial features are not discernible, it is not considered an offspring, and the woman is not impure with the impurity of a woman after childbirth, in accordance with the opinion of Rabbi Yoḥanan in the version of the dispute presented by Rav Pappi (Rambam *Sefer Kedusha*, *Hilkhot Issurei Bia* 10:11).

A woman who discharges an entity that has two backs and two spines – הַמַּפֶּלֶת בְּרִיָּה שֶׁיֵּשׁ לָהּ שְׁנֵי גַּבִּים וּשְׁנֵי שִׁדְרָאוֹת: If a woman discharges an entity that has two backs and two spines, it is not considered an offspring, and the woman is not impure with the impurity of a woman after childbirth, in accordance with the opinion of Rav (Rambam *Sefer Kedusha*, *Hilkhot Issurei Bia* 10:11).

An animal who discharges an entity that has two backs and two spines – הַמַּפֶּלֶת בְּרִיָּה שֶׁיֵּשׁ לָהּ שְׁנֵי גַּבִּים וּשְׁנֵי שִׁדְרָאוֹת: If a kosher animal gives birth, and the newborn has two backs and two spines, or if the mother is slaughtered and such a fetus is found in its womb, it is forbidden for consumption. The *halakha* is in accordance with the opinion of Rav, as his opinion in ritual matters is accepted in his disputes with Shmuel. This is what the word *hashesua* is referring to in the verse: "Nevertheless these you shall not eat of them that only chew the cud, or of them that only have the hoof cloven [*hashesua*]," as an animal that has two backs and two spines looks like an entirely cloven animal (Rambam *Sefer Kedusha*, *Hilkhot Ma'akhalot Assurot* 1:6; *Shulḥan Arukh*, *Yoreh De'a* 13:6).

בְּמַאי קָמִיפַּלְגִי? בִּדְרַב חָנִין בַּר אַבָּא, דְּאָמַר רַב חָנִין בַּר אַבָּא: ״הַשְּׁסוּעָה״ – בְּרִיָּה שֶׁיֵּשׁ לָהּ שְׁנֵי גַּבִּין וּשְׁנֵי שִׁדְרָאוֹת.

The Gemara asks: **With regard to what do** Rav and Shmuel **disagree?** The Gemara answers: They disagree **concerning** the statement **of Rav Ḥanin bar Abba, as Rav Ḥanin bar Abba said:** The verse states: "Nevertheless these you shall not eat of them that only chew the cud, or of them that only have the hoof cloven [*umimafrisei haparsa hashesua*]: The camel, and the hare, and the rock badger" (Deuteronomy 14:7). The apparently superfluous term ***hashesua*** is not a redundant description of the cloven hoof; it is referring to a separate **entity that has two backs and two spines** and therefore looks like an entirely cloven animal.

רַב אָמַר: בְּרִיָּה בְּעָלְמָא – לֵיתָא, וְכִי אַגְמְרֵיהּ רַחֲמָנָא לְמֹשֶׁה – בִּמְעֵי אִמָּהּ אַגְמְרֵיהּ. וּשְׁמוּאֵל אָמַר: בְּרִיָּה בְּעָלְמָא – אִיתָא, וְכִי אַגְמְרֵיהּ רַחֲמָנָא לְמֹשֶׁה – בְּעָלְמָא אַגְמְרֵיהּ, אֲבָל בִּמְעֵי אִמָּהּ – שַׁרְיָא.

It is with regard to this prohibition that Rav and Shmuel disagree. **Rav says** that **there is no** such living **entity in the world, and when the Merciful One taught** this prohibition **to Moses, he taught** it **to** him with regard to a fetus that has two backs and two spines that is found **in the womb of its mother** after slaughter. **And Shmuel says** that **there is** such **an entity in the world,**[N] **and when the Merciful One taught** this prohibition **to Moses, he taught** it **to him** with regard to a living animal **in the world, but** a fetus that has two backs and two spines **in the womb of its mother is permitted** for consumption.

אֵיתִיבֵיהּ רַב שִׁימִי בַּר חִיָּיא לְרַב: רַבִּי חֲנִינָא בֶּן אַנְטִיגְנוֹס אוֹמֵר, כֹּל שֶׁיֵּשׁ לוֹ שְׁנֵי גַּבִּין וּשְׁנֵי שִׁדְרָאוֹת – פָּסוּל לַעֲבוֹדָה, אַלְמָא דְּחַיֵּי! וְקַשְׁיָא לְרַב. אֲמַר לֵיהּ: שִׁימִי אַתְּ! שֶׁשִּׁדְרָתוֹ עֲקוּמָּה.

**Rav Shimi bar Ḥiyya**[P] **raised an objection to Rav** from a *baraita*: **Rabbi Ḥanina ben Antigonus says: Any** priest **who has two backs and two spines is disqualified from** the Temple **service,** as he is blemished. **Evidently,** an entity **that** has two backs and two spines **can survive, and** this is **difficult for** the opinion of **Rav. Rav said to him: You are** clearly **Shimi,**[N] i.e., you asked well. Yet the statement of Rabbi Ḥanina ben Antigonus is not referring to one who literally has two backs and two spines, but rather **to** one **whose spine is crooked**[HB] and therefore appears as though he has two spines. One who actually has two backs and two spines cannot survive.

מֵיתִיבֵי: יֵשׁ בְּעוּבָּרִין שֶׁהֵן אֲסוּרִין. בֶּן אַרְבָּעָה – לְדַקָּה, בֶּן שְׁמֹנָה – לְגַסָּה, הֵימֶנּוּ וּלְמַטָּה – אָסוּר. יָצָא מִי שֶׁיֵּשׁ לוֹ שְׁנֵי גַּבִּין וּשְׁנֵי שִׁדְרָאוֹת.

The Gemara **raises an objection** from a *baraita*: Among discharged animal **fetuses, there are those that are forbidden** in consumption, as they have the halakhic status of carcasses of unslaughtered animals. Specifically, if an animal fetus is **born** in the **fourth** month of pregnancy in the case **of small** domesticated animals, where the pregnancy is normally five months long, or it is **born** in the **eighth** month of pregnancy in the case **of large** livestock,[H] where the pregnancy is normally nine months long, or if the miscarriage occurred **from this** stage of the pregnancy **and earlier,** i.e., if the pregnancy ended before this stage, the animal is **forbidden.** This **excludes one that has two backs and two spines.**

מַאי ״יָצָא״? לָאו, יָצָא מִכְּלַל עוּבָּרִין שֶׁאֲפִילּוּ בִּמְעֵי אִמָּן אֲסוּרִין?

The Gemara asks: **What** does the *baraita* mean when it states that an animal with two backs and two spines is **excluded? Does** it **not** mean that it is **excluded from the category of** those **fetuses,** which are permitted for consumption if found inside their mother's womb, **as** such animals are **forbidden even** while they are **in the wombs of their mothers?** This contradicts the opinion of Shmuel, who holds that an animal fetus of that type is permitted for consumption.

**NOTES**

And Shmuel says that there is such an entity in the world – וּשְׁמוּאֵל אָמַר בְּרִיָּה בְּעָלְמָא אִיתָא: The early commentaries disagree concerning the meaning of this statement. Rashi maintains that there is a unique species that has two backs and two spines. The majority of the early commentaries hold that there is no such species and that the reference is to a mutation of an existing species that has two backs and two spines; according to this opinion, Shmuel contends that such an animal can survive (Rabbeinu Tam; Ramban; Rashba; Rabbeinu Ḥananel; Rambam). According to Rashi, Shmuel would concede that an animal with such a mutation cannot survive, and it is therefore prohibited for consumption like any stillborn animal.

Rav said to him, you are clearly Shimi – אֲמַר לֵיהּ שִׁימִי אַתְּ: In several places Rav addresses Rav Shimi bar Ḥiyya in this manner. Rashi suggests three interpretations of the statement. One interpretation, which Rashi accepts, is that Rav would address Rav Shimi fondly since he was his grandson, as if to say: You, Shimi, definitely know how to raise objections to my statements. Another interpretation is that as Rav would always be looking downward, as a practice of modesty, he had to ask if it was in fact Rav Shimi. Rashi rejects this interpretation, as there is no record of Rav addressing anyone else in this manner. The third explanation is that Rav Shimi's objections were especially sharp, i.e., it was an exclamation of praise.

**PERSONALITIES**

Rav Shimi bar Ḥiyya – רַב שִׁימִי בַּר חִיָּיא: Rav Shimi bar Ḥiyya was a second-generation *amora* in Babylonia. He was a grandson of Rav and apparently his preeminent disciple and much beloved by him. Even during his grandfather's lifetime, Rav Shimi was recognized as a significant Torah scholar. The Talmud records numerous halakhic statements of his, both those he transmitted citing his grandfather and those of his own. In certain cases he even disagreed with the rulings of his grandfather.

**HALAKHA**

Whose spine is crooked – שֶׁשִּׁדְרָתוֹ עֲקוּמָּה: A crooked spine is considered a blemish, and a priest with this blemish is disqualified from the Temple service, in accordance with the opinion of Rav (Rambam *Sefer Avoda, Hilkhot Biat HaMikdash* 8:10).

Born in the fourth month in the case of small animals or born in the eighth month in the case of large livestock – בֶּן אַרְבָּעָה לְדַקָּה בֶּן שְׁמֹנָה לְגַסָּה: If an animal gave birth after a full period of gestation, i.e., nine months for cattle and five months for sheep and goats, the newborn may be slaughtered and eaten immediately, and one need not be concerned that its limbs were crushed during the birth. If it is unclear whether the period of gestation was full, the newborn is forbidden for consumption until the beginning of the night before the eighth day after its birth (Rambam *Sefer Kedusha, Hilkhot Ma'akhalot Assurot* 4:4; *Shulḥan Arukh, Yoreh De'a* 15:2).

**BACKGROUND**

Whose spine is crooked – שִׁדְרָתוֹ עֲקוּמָּה:

Illustration of crooked spine

רַב מְתָרֵץ לְטַעְמֵיהּ, וּשְׁמוּאֵל מְתָרֵץ לְטַעְמֵיהּ. רַב מְתָרֵץ לְטַעְמֵיהּ: בֶּן אַרְבָּעָה – לְדַקָּה, בֶּן שְׁמוֹנָה – לְגַסָּה, הֵימֶנּוּ וּלְמַטָּה – אָסוּר.

The Gemara answers: **Rav explains** the *baraita* **according to his** line of **reasoning, and Shmuel explains** the *baraita* **according to his** line of **reasoning. Rav explains** the *baraita* **according to his** line of **reasoning**, as was assumed above: If an animal fetus is **born** in the **fourth** month of pregnancy in the case **of small** domesticated animals, or it is **born** in the **eighth** month of pregnancy in the case **of large** livestock, or if it was born **from this** stage of the pregnancy **and earlier**, the animal is **forbidden.**

בַּמֶּה דְּבָרִים אֲמוּרִים – כְּשֶׁיָּצָא לַאֲוִיר הָעוֹלָם, אֲבָל בִּמְעֵי אִמּוֹ – שָׁרֵי, יָצָא מִי שֶׁיֵּשׁ לוֹ שְׁנֵי גַבִּין וּשְׁנֵי שִׁדְרָאוֹת, דַּאֲפִילּוּ בִּמְעֵי אִמּוֹ נָמֵי אָסוּר.

**In what** case **is this statement said?** In a case **where** the animal **emerged into the airspace of the world; but** if it was found **in its mother's womb**[H] after its mother was slaughtered, **it is permitted for** consumption. This **excludes** the case of a fetus **that has two backs and two spines, as even** if it is found **in the womb of its mother it is prohibited.**

**HALAKHA**

In its mother's womb – בִּמְעֵי אִמּוֹ: If one ritually slaughtered a female animal and found a fetus in its womb after eight months of gestation, whether dead or alive, the fetus is permitted for consumption and does not require ritual slaughter (Rambam *Sefer Kedusha, Hilkhot Ma'akhalot Assurot* 5:13–14; *Shulḥan Arukh, Yoreh De'a* 13:2).



וּשְׁמוּאֵל מְתָרֵץ לְטַעְמֵיהּ: בֶּן אַרְבָּעָה לְדַקָּה, בֶּן שְׁמוֹנָה לְגַסָּה, הֵימֶנּוּ וּלְמַטָּה – אָסוּר. בַּמֶּה דְּבָרִים אֲמוּרִים – בְּשֶׁלֹּא כָּלוּ לוֹ חֳדָשָׁיו, אֲבָל כָּלוּ לוֹ חֳדָשָׁיו – מוּתָּר. יָצָא מִי שֶׁיֵּשׁ לוֹ שְׁנֵי גַבִּין וּשְׁנֵי שִׁדְרָאוֹת, דְּאַף עַל גַּב דְּכָלוּ לוֹ חֳדָשָׁיו, אִם יָצָא לַאֲוִיר הָעוֹלָם – אָסוּר, בִּמְעֵי אִמּוֹ – שָׁרֵי.

**And Shmuel explains** the *baraita* **according to his** line of **reasoning**, in the following manner: If an animal fetus is **born** in the **fourth** month of pregnancy in the case **of small** domesticated animals, or it is **born** in the **eighth** month of pregnancy in the case **of large** livestock, or if it was born **from this** stage of the pregnancy **and earlier,** the animal is **forbidden. In what** case **is this statement said?** In a case **when** the fetus's **months** of gestation **were not completed; but** in a case when **its months** of gestation **were completed, it is permitted** for consumption even outside the womb. This **excludes** a fetus **that has two backs and two spines, as even in** a case where **its months** of gestation **were completed, if it emerged into the airspace of the world, it is forbidden,** whereas if it is found **in the womb of its mother, it is permitted.**

תָּנֵי תַּנָּא קַמֵּיהּ דְּרַב: הַמַּפֶּלֶת בְּרִיַּית גּוּף שֶׁאֵינוֹ חָתוּךְ, וּבְרִיַּית רֹאשׁ שֶׁאֵינוֹ חָתוּךְ, יָכוֹל תְּהֵא אִמּוֹ טְמֵאָה לֵידָה – תַּלְמוּד לוֹמַר ״אִשָּׁה כִּי תַזְרִיעַ וְיָלְדָה זָכָר וגו׳ וּבַיּוֹם הַשְּׁמִינִי יִמּוֹל״ וגו׳

**A** *tanna* **taught** a *baraita* **before Rav:** In the case of a woman **who discharges an entity** that has **a shapeless body,** i.e., it does not have the outline of limbs, **or an entity** that has **a shapeless head,** one **might** have thought that **its mother should be impure** with the impurity of a woman after **childbirth.** Therefore, **the verse states: "If a woman bears seed and gives birth to a male,** she shall be impure seven days; as in the days of the menstruation of her sickness she shall be impure. **And on the eighth day** the flesh of his foreskin **shall be circumcised"** (Leviticus 12:2–3).

מִי שֶׁרָאוּי לִבְרִית שְׁמֹנָה יָצְאוּ אֵלּוּ שֶׁאֵינָן רְאוּיִין לִבְרִית שְׁמֹנָה. אֲמַר לֵיהּ רַב: וְסַיֵּים בָּהּ הָכִי וְשֶׁיֵּשׁ לוֹ שְׁנֵי גַבִּין וּשְׁנֵי שִׁדְרָאוֹת.

Those verses teach that the impurity of a woman after childbirth applies only to one who gave birth to a child **that is fit for circumcision** on the **eighth** day, **excluding these** cases, **where** the child **is not fit for circumcision** on the **eighth** day, as it cannot survive that long. Consequently, this woman does not have the impurity of a woman after childbirth. **Rav said to** the *tanna*: **And conclude** the *baraita* **like this:** Excluding these cases, where the child is not fit for circumcision on the eighth day, **and** excluding the case of a woman who discharges a child **that has two backs and two spines.**

רַבִּי יִרְמְיָה בַּר אַבָּא סָבַר לְמֶעְבַּד עוֹבָדָא כְּוָותֵיהּ דִּשְׁמוּאֵל, אֲמַר לֵיהּ רַב הוּנָא: מַאי דַּעְתָּיךְ – לְחוּמְרָא? חוּמְרָא דְּאָתֵי לִידֵי קוּלָּא הוּא, דְּקָיְהַבְתְּ לַהּ דְּמֵי טוֹהַר. עֲבֵיד מִיהָא כְּוָותֵיהּ דְּרַב, דְּקַיְימָא לַן: הִלְכְתָא כְּרַב בְּאִיסּוּרֵי, בֵּין לְקוּלָּא בֵּין לְחוּמְרָא.

**Rabbi Yirmeya bar Abba thought to perform an action,** i.e., to issue a ruling, **in accordance with** the opinion **of Shmuel,** that a woman who gives birth to a child with two backs and two spines is impure. **Rav Huna said to him: What is your thinking?** That as this matter is subject to a dispute, one should rule **stringently?** Your ruling **is a stringency that leads to a leniency, as you have given** the woman a period of thirty-three days following her period of impurity when any blood that emerges is **blood of purity. In any event,** you should **perform,** i.e., issue your ruling, **in accordance with** the opinion **of Rav, as we maintain** that **the** *halakha* **is in accordance with** the opinion of **Rav with regard to ritual matters, whether** his opinion leads **to a leniency or to a stringency.**

אָמַר רָבָא: הֲרֵי אָמְרוּ אִשָּׁה יוֹלֶדֶת לְתִשְׁעָה וְיוֹלֶדֶת לְשִׁבְעָה, בְּהֵמָה גַּסָּה יוֹלֶדֶת לְתִשְׁעָה יוֹלֶדֶת לְשִׁבְעָה אוֹ לֹא יָלְדָה?

§ **Rava says:** The Sages **said** that **a woman can give birth** to a viable offspring **after nine** months of pregnancy **or after seven** months of pregnancy; but if a woman gives birth after eight months of pregnancy, the child cannot survive and is stillborn. Similarly, **a large domesticated animal gives birth** to a viable offspring **after nine** months of pregnancy, and if it discharges a fetus after only eight months, the newborn animal cannot survive. With this in mind, Rava asked: Can a large domesticated animal **give birth** to a viable offspring **after seven** months of pregnancy, like a human, **or** can such an animal **not give birth** to a viable offspring after only seven months?

אֲמַר רַב נַחְמָן בַּר יִצְחָק: תָּא שְׁמַע, הֵימֶנּוּ וּלְמַטָּה – אָסוּר, מַאי לָאו אַגַּסָּה? לָא, אַדַּקָּה.

**Rav Naḥman bar Yitzḥak said: Come** and **hear** a resolution to this dilemma from the aforementioned *baraita*: If an animal discharges **from this** stage of the pregnancy **and earlier,** the fetus is **forbidden** in consumption as an unslaughtered animal carcass. **What, is it not** referring **to large** livestock, which indicates that large livestock do not give birth to a viable offspring after only seven months of pregnancy? The Gemara answers: **No,** the reference is specifically **to small** domesticated animals, which do not give birth to a viable offspring until after five months of pregnancy.

הַאי מַאי? אִי אָמְרַתְּ בִּשְׁלָמָא אַגַּסָּה – אִיצְטְרִיךְ, סָלְקָא דַּעְתָּךְ אָמִינָא: הוֹאִיל וּבְאִשָּׁה חַיֵּי – בִּבְהֵמָה נַמִי חַיֵּי, קָא מַשְׁמַע לָן דְּלָא חַיֵּי.

The Gemara raises a difficulty with regard to this answer: **What is this? Granted, if you say** that the reference is **to large** livestock, it is **necessary** for the *baraita* to state that an animal does not give birth to a viable offspring after less than a complete period of pregnancy, as otherwise it might **enter your mind to say** that **since in** the case of **a woman** who gives birth after seven months the baby **survives,** it is logical that **in** the case of a large domesticated **animal** that gives birth after seven months the newborn **also survives,** and it is therefore permitted for consumption. Consequently, the *baraita* **teaches us that** such an animal **does not survive.**

אֶלָּא אִי אָמְרַתְּ אַדַּקָּה אִיתְּמַר, פְּשִׁיטָא! בַּת תְּלָתָא יַרְחֵי מִי קָא חַיֵּי?!

**But if you say** that the ruling in the *baraita*, that if an animal discharged a fetus before the period of gestation was completed then the fetus is prohibited, **was stated with regard to small** domesticated animals, isn't it **obvious** that if a sheep or goat fetus was discharged at this stage it cannot survive? **Can it survive after** only **three months** of gestation?

אִיצְטְרִיךְ, סָלְקָא דַּעְתָּךְ אָמִינָא: כׇּל בְּצִיר תְּרֵי יַרְחֵי חַיֵּי – קָא מַשְׁמַע לָן.

The Gemara answers that in fact **it is necessary** for the *baraita* to state this *halakha* with regard to small domesticated animals, as otherwise it might **enter your mind to say** that **any** mammal that is born **two months less** than its complete gestation **survives,** just as a human born at seven months of gestation survives. Therefore, the *baraita* **teaches us** that a sheep or goat that is born at three months of gestation cannot survive and is forbidden for consumption.

אָמַר רַב יְהוּדָה, אָמַר שְׁמוּאֵל: הַמַּפֶּלֶת דְּמוּת לִילִית – אִמּוֹ טְמֵאָה לֵידָה. וָלָד הוּא, אֶלָּא שֶׁיֵּשׁ לוֹ כְּנָפַיִם. תַּנְיָא נַמִי הָכִי, אָמַר רַבִּי יוֹסֵי: מַעֲשֶׂה בְּסִימוֹנִי בְּאַחַת שֶׁהִפִּילָה דְּמוּת לִילִית, וּבָא מַעֲשֶׂה לִפְנֵי חֲכָמִים, וְאָמְרוּ וָלָד הוּא אֶלָּא שֶׁיֵּשׁ לוֹ כְּנָפַיִם.

§ **Rav Yehuda says** that **Shmuel says:** In the case of a woman **who discharges** a fetus that has **the form of a lilith,**[N] a female demon with wings and a human face, **its mother is impure** with the impurity of a woman after **childbirth,** as **it is** a viable **offspring, only it has wings. This is also taught** in a *baraita*: **Rabbi Yosei said: An incident** occurred **in Simoni**[B] **involving a certain** woman **who discharged** a fetus that had **the form of a lilith, and the incident was brought before the Sages; and they said** that **it is** a viable **offspring, only it has wings.**[H]

**BACKGROUND**

**Simoni – סִימוֹנִי:** Simoni, or Simonia, is identified as the biblical city of Shimron, which dates back to the Canaanite period; its king was one of the thirty-one kings Joshua overcame in his conquest of Eretz Yisrael. During the Second Temple period it was called Shimonia, and during the mishnaic and talmudic periods, Simonia. One of the major battles of the Jewish revolt against the Romans prior to the destruction of the Second Temple took place in Simonia. It had a prominent Jewish community with well-known leaders throughout the ages.

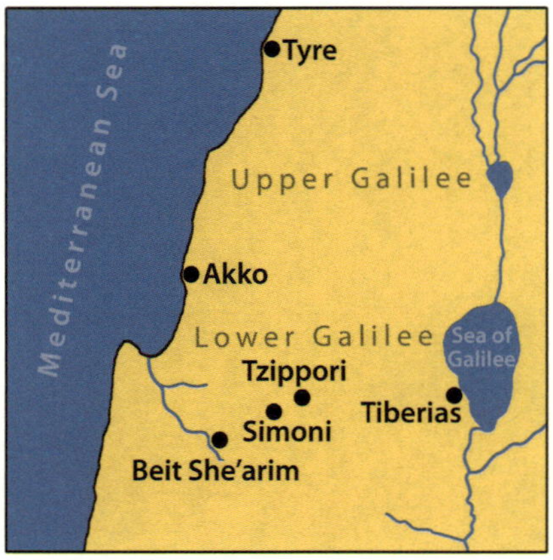


Location of Simoni

**HALAKHA**

**A woman who discharged the form of a lilith…only it has wings – הַמַּפֶּלֶת דְּמוּת לִילִית...שֶׁיֵּשׁ לוֹ כְּנָפַיִם:** If a woman discharged a fetus that looks like a human but has wings of flesh, the woman is impure with the impurity of a woman after childbirth (Rambam *Sefer Kedusha, Hilkhot Issurei Bia* 10:10).

**NOTES**

**A woman who discharges a fetus that has the form of a lilith – הַמַּפֶּלֶת דְּמוּת לִילִית:** The early commentaries disagree with regard to the definition and appearance of a lilith. Rashi explains that it is a female demon, as demons were known to have wings and human faces. The Rambam does not mention the word lilith explicitly. Instead, he writes: A woman who discharges an item that looks like a human with wings of flesh (*Sefer Kedusha, Hilkhot Issurei Bia* 10:10). In this manner, the Rambam cites this *halakha* while conforming to his general opinion that demons and ghosts are mere figments of the imagination (see *Ein Mishpat*; *Maggid Mishne*; *Beit Yosef*).

הַמַּפֶּלֶת דְּמוּת נָחָשׁ, הוֹרָה חֲנִינָא בֶּן אָחִיו שֶׁל רַבִּי יְהוֹשֻׁעַ: אִמּוֹ טְמֵאָה לֵידָה. הָלַךְ רַבִּי יוֹסֵף וְסִפֵּר דְּבָרִים לִפְנֵי רַבָּן גַּמְלִיאֵל, שָׁלַח לוֹ: רַבִּי יְהוֹשֻׁעַ, הַנְהֵג בֶּן אָחִיךָ וּבֹא.

There was a case of a woman **who discharged** an item that had **the form of a snake. Ḥanina,** the **son of Rabbi Yehoshua's brother, ruled** that **its mother is impure** with the impurity of a woman after **childbirth. Rabbi Yosef went and told** this **matter to Rabban Gamliel.** Rabban Gamliel **sent to Rabbi Yehoshua:**[P] **Take** hold of **your nephew and come** to me, so that I may admonish him for his ruling.

בַּהֲלִיכָתָן יָצְתָה כַּלַּת (רַבִּי) חֲנִינָא לִקְרָאתוֹ, אָמְרָה לוֹ: רַבִּי, הַמַּפֶּלֶת כְּמִין נָחָשׁ מַהוּ? אָמַר לָהּ: אִמּוֹ טְהוֹרָה. אָמְרָה לוֹ: וַהֲלֹא מִשְּׁמְךָ אָמְרָה לִי חֲמוֹתִי אִמּוֹ טְמֵאָה? וְאָמַר לָהּ מֵאֵיזֶה טַעַם – הוֹאִיל וְגַלְגַּל עֵינוֹ עָגוֹל כְּשֶׁל אָדָם! מִתּוֹךְ דְּבָרֶיהָ נִזְכַּר רַבִּי יְהוֹשֻׁעַ, שָׁלַח לוֹ לְרַבָּן גַּמְלִיאֵל: מִפִּי הוֹרָה חֲנִינָא.

**While they were going** to Rabban Gamliel, **Ḥanina's daughter-in-law went out to greet** Rabbi Yehoshua, and **said to him: My teacher, what is** the *halakha* with regard to a woman **who discharges** an item that looks **like a snake?** Rabbi Yehoshua **said to her: Its mother is pure. She said to him: But my mother-in-law said to me in your name** that **its mother is impure** in such a case, and that you **said to her: For what reason** is she impure? It is **because the pupil of** a snake **is round like that of a human. Due to her statement, Rabbi Yehoshua remembered** that he had issued such a ruling. He subsequently **sent** a message **to Rabban Gamliel: Ḥanina issued the ruling based on my** own statement.

אָמַר אַבַּיֵי, שְׁמַע מִינָּהּ: צוּרְבָא מֵרַבָּנַן דְּאָמַר מִילְּתָא, לֵימָא בָּהּ טַעֲמָא, דְּכִי מַדְכְּרוּ לֵיהּ – מִדְּכַר.

**Abaye said: Conclude from** this incident that **a Torah scholar** [*tzurva merabbanan*][L] **who says** a halakhic **matter should say the reason** for his statement, **so that when** his colleagues **remind him** of his reasoning, **he will remember** that ruling, as happened to Rabbi Yehoshua.

**מתני׳** הַמַּפֶּלֶת שָׁפִיר מָלֵא מַיִם, מָלֵא דָּם, מָלֵא גְּנוּנִים – אֵינָהּ חוֹשֶׁשֶׁת לְוָלָד, וְאִם הָיָה מְרוּקָּם – תֵּשֵׁב לְזָכָר וְלִנְקֵבָה. הַמַּפֶּלֶת סַנְדָּל אוֹ שִׁלְיָא – תֵּשֵׁב לְזָכָר וְלִנְקֵבָה.

**MISHNA** A woman **who discharges a gestational sac full of fluid,**[H] **full of blood,** or **full of** different **colors**[N] need **not be concerned that** it was **an offspring. But if** the sac **was** one in which **tissue developed,**[H] her halakhic status is that of a woman after childbirth. Since the sex of the embryo is unknown, the woman **observes** the strictures of a woman who gave birth both **to a male and to a female;** she is impure for fourteen days like a woman who gave birth to a female, but blood that she sees thereafter is pure only until forty days after birth, like a woman who gave birth to a male. A woman **who discharges a sandal** fetus,[H] i.e., one that has the form of a sandal fish, **and** one who discharges **an afterbirth**[H] **observes** the strictures of a woman who gave birth both **to a male and to a female.**

**גמ׳** בִּשְׁלָמָא דָּם וּמַיִם – לָאו כְּלוּם הִיא, אֶלָּא גְּנוּנִים – נֵיחוּשׁ שֶׁמָּא וָלָד הֲוָה וְנִימּוֹחַ? אָמַר אַבַּיֵי: כַּמָּה יַיִן חַי שָׁתַת אִמּוֹ שֶׁל זֶה שֶׁנִּמּוֹחַ עוּבָּרָהּ בְּתוֹךְ מֵעֶיהָ?

**GEMARA** The Gemara raises a difficulty: **Granted,** one can understand why a woman who discharges a gestational sac full of **blood or water** is pure, as such an item **is nothing,** i.e., it is not an offspring. **But** if the gestational sac was full of different **colors, let us be concerned** that **perhaps it was an offspring and** it **liquefied. Abaye says** in response: **How much undiluted wine,** which can be harmful to an embryo, **did the mother of this** purported embryo **drink, that her embryo was liquefied in her womb?** In other words, there is no such concern.

רָבָא אָמַר: ״מָלֵא״ תְּנַן, וְאִם אִיתָא דְּאִתְמוּחֵי אִתְמַח – מִחְסַר חָסַר. רַב אַדָּא בַּר אַהֲבָה אָמַר: ״גְּוָונִים״ תְּנַן, וְאִם אִיתָא דְּאִתְמוּחֵי אִתְמַח – כּוּלָּהּ בְּחַד גַּוְונָא הָוֵי קָאֵי.

**Rava says** that there is a different explanation: **We learned** in the mishna that the gestational sac was **full** of different colors, **and if it is so,** that there was an embryo in the sac **that liquefied,** the sac would have been **lacking** some of the mass of the liquified portion. **Rav Adda bar Ahava says** that there is yet another explanation: **We learned** in the mishna that the gestational sac is full of different **colors, and if it is so,** that there was an embryo there **that liquefied, it would all be of one color.**

**LANGUAGE**

Torah scholar [*tzurva merabbanan*] – צוּרְבָא מֵרַבָּנַן: While this appellation for a Torah scholar is commonly used throughout the Talmud, its source and precise meaning are unclear. Some say that it derives from the word *tzarav*, sear, as scholars are seared by the fire of Torah. Others say that the word *tzarav* is related to the Arabic root *ḍrb*, meaning hard and strong, in which case the phrase itself would refer to a Sage who is forceful and incisive (Rav Hai Gaon).

**HALAKHA**

A woman who discharges a gestational sac full of fluid, etc. – הַמַּפֶּלֶת שָׁפִיר מָלֵא מַיִם וכו׳: In a case where a woman discharged a gestational sac full of water, full of blood, full of different colors, or full of flesh, since the embryo has not taken shape, the woman does not need to be concerned that it was an offspring, and she is pure (Rambam *Sefer Kedusha, Hilkhot Issurei Bia* 10:4).

In which tissue developed – מְרוּקָּם: If a woman discharged a gestational sac in which tissue developed and which contains even a tiny, barely recognizable form of a human embryo, the woman observes the strictures of a woman who gave birth both to a male and to a female (Rambam *Sefer Kedusha*, *Hilkhot Issurei Bia* 10:2).

A woman who discharges a sandal fetus – הַמַּפֶּלֶת סַנְדָּל: If a woman discharged a fetus in the form of a sandal fish, she observes the strictures of a woman who gave birth both to a male and to a female (Rambam *Sefer Kedusha, Hilkhot Issurei Bia* 10:12).

A woman who discharges…afterbirth – הַמַּפֶּלֶת...שִׁלְיָא: If a woman discharged an afterbirth, she observes the strictures of a woman who gave birth both to a male and to a female. The reason is not that an afterbirth has the halakhic status of an offspring, but that there is no afterbirth without an offspring (Rambam *Sefer Kedusha*, *Hilkhot Issurei Bia* 10:14; *Shulḥan Arukh*, *Yoreh De'a* 194:3).

**NOTES**

Full of different colors [*genonim*] – מָלֵא גְּנוּנִים: The early commentaries disagree with regard to the meaning of *genonim*. Some write that the reference is to colors (Rashi), in accordance with the interpretation of Rav Adda bar Ahava in the Gemara. Others write that it is a kind of worm. Accordingly, the mishna means that a woman who discharges pieces of flesh shaped like worms need not be concerned that it might be a mashed embryo (Rambam's Commentary on the Mishna).

**PERSONALITIES**

Rabbi Yehoshua – רַבִּי יְהוֹשֻׁעַ: Rabbi Yehoshua ben Ḥananya was one of the leading Sages in the generation following the destruction of the Second Temple. As a Levite he served as a singer in the Temple, and after its destruction, he was among the students who followed their primary teacher, Rabban Yoḥanan ben Zakkai, to Yavne. Rabbi Yehoshua lived a life of poverty, working as a blacksmith, and was recognized by all as a leading Torah authority. While he disagreed with Rabban Gamliel's rulings on several occasions, Rabbi Yehoshua ultimately accepted his authority as *Nasi*. Rabbi Yehoshua was exceptionally long lived, and he had many famous religious debates with the imperial family in Rome.

**LANGUAGE**

Attendant [*dayyala*] – **דַּיָּילָא**: Some linguists assert that this word is derived from the Greek δοῦλος, *doulos*, meaning slave or servant. Others maintain that it has a Semitic root. The word is used for a police officer or court attendant.

תַּנְיָא, אַבָּא שָׁאוּל אוֹמֵר: קוֹבֵר מֵתִים הָיִיתִי וְהָיִיתִי מִסְתַּכֵּל בְּעַצְמוֹת שֶׁל מֵתִים. הַשּׁוֹתֶה יַיִן חַי – עַצְמוֹתָיו שְׂרוּפִין, מָזוּג – עַצְמוֹתָיו סְכוּיִין, כָּרָאוּי – עַצְמוֹתָיו מְשׁוּחִין. וְכָל מִי שֶׁשְּׁתִיָּיתוֹ מְרוּבָּה מֵאֲכִילָתוֹ – עַצְמוֹתָיו שְׂרוּפִין, אֲכִילָתוֹ מְרוּבָּה מִשְּׁתִיָּיתוֹ – עַצְמוֹתָיו סְכוּיִין, כָּרָאוּי – עַצְמוֹתָיו מְשׁוּחִין.

With regard to the effect of drinking wine on a person's body, **it is taught** in a *baraita* that **Abba Shaul**[P] **says: I used to be a gravedigger, and I would observe the bones of corpses.** I discovered that **the bones of one who drinks** too much **undiluted wine** during his lifetime look **burnt, the bones of** one who drinks too much **diluted** wine **are black,** and **the bones of** one who drinks the **appropriate** amount of wine **are fat,** i.e., full of marrow. **And** furthermore, I discovered that **the bones of anyone who drinks** much **more than he eats** look **burnt, the bones of** one who **eats** much **more than he drinks are black,** and **the bones of one who** eats and drinks **appropriate** amounts **are fat.**

תַּנְיָא, אַבָּא שָׁאוּל אוֹמֵר, וְאִיתֵּימָא רַבִּי יוֹחָנָן: קוֹבֵר מֵתִים הָיִיתִי, פַּעַם אַחַת רַצְתִּי אַחַר צְבִי, וְנִכְנַסְתִּי בְּקוּלִית שֶׁל מֵת, וְרַצְתִּי אַחֲרָיו שָׁלֹשׁ פַּרְסָאוֹת, וּצְבִי לֹא הִגַּעְתִּי וְקוּלִית לֹא כָּלְתָה. כְּשֶׁחָזַרְתִּי לַאֲחוֹרַי אָמְרוּ לִי: שֶׁל עוֹג מֶלֶךְ הַבָּשָׁן הָיְתָה.

**It is taught** in a *baraita* that **Abba Shaul says** the following, **and some say** that **Rabbi Yoḥanan** said it: **I used to be a gravedigger. Once I ran after a deer, and I entered the thighbone of a corpse;**[N] **and** it was so large that **I ran after** the deer for **three parasangs** inside the thighbone, **and** although **I did not reach** the **deer,** the **thighbone did not end. When I came back** and related this to the Sages, **they said to me: It was** evidently the thighbone **of Og, king of Bashan,** a known giant.

תַּנְיָא, אַבָּא שָׁאוּל אוֹמֵר: קוֹבֵר מֵתִים הָיִיתִי, פַּעַם אַחַת נִפְתְּחָה מְעָרָה תַּחְתַּי, וְעָמַדְתִּי בְּגַלְגַּל עֵינוֹ שֶׁל מֵת עַד חוֹטְמִי. כְּשֶׁחָזַרְתִּי לַאֲחוֹרַי אָמְרוּ: עַיִן שֶׁל אַבְשָׁלוֹם הָיְתָה.

It is likewise **taught** in a *baraita* that **Abba Shaul says: I used to be a gravedigger. Once** a burial **cave opened up underneath** where I was standing, **and I** found myself **standing in the eye socket of a corpse until my nose. When I came back** and told this to the Sages, **they said to me: It was** evidently **the eye of Absalom.**

וְשֶׁמָּא תֹּאמַר: אַבָּא שָׁאוּל נַנָּס הֲוָה – אַבָּא שָׁאוּל אָרוֹךְ בְּדוֹרוֹ הֲוָה וְרַבִּי טַרְפוֹן מַגִּיעַ לְכִתְפוֹ, וְרַבִּי טַרְפוֹן אָרוֹךְ בְּדוֹרוֹ הֲוָה וְרַבִּי מֵאִיר מַגִּיעַ לְכִתְפוֹ, רַבִּי מֵאִיר אָרוֹךְ בְּדוֹרוֹ הֲוָה וְרַבִּי מַגִּיעַ לְכִתְפוֹ, רַבִּי אָרוֹךְ בְּדוֹרוֹ הֲוָה

**And lest you say** that **Abba Shaul was a midget,** and therefore he was capable of standing in an eye socket until his nose, **Abba Shaul was the tallest** person **in his generation. And Rabbi Tarfon reached** only **his shoulder, and Rabbi Tarfon was the tallest** person **in his generation. And Rabbi Meir reached** only **the shoulder of** Rabbi Tarfon, and **Rabbi Meir was the tallest** person **in his generation. And Rabbi** Yehuda HaNasi **reached** only **the shoulder of** Rabbi Meir, and **Rabbi** Yehuda HaNasi **was the tallest** person **in his generation.**

וְרַבִּי חִיָּיא מַגִּיעַ לְכִתְפוֹ, וְרַבִּי חִיָּיא אָרוֹךְ בְּדוֹרוֹ הֲוָה וְרַב מַגִּיעַ לְכִתְפוֹ, רַב אָרוֹךְ בְּדוֹרוֹ הֲוָה וְרַב יְהוּדָה מַגִּיעַ לְכִתְפוֹ, וְרַב יְהוּדָה אָרוֹךְ בְּדוֹרוֹ הֲוָה וְאַדָּא דַּיָּילָא מַגִּיעַ לְכִתְפוֹ,

The Gemara continues: **And Rabbi Ḥiyya reached** only **the shoulder of** Rabbi Yehuda HaNasi, **and Rabbi Ḥiyya was the tallest** person **in his generation. And Rav reached** only **the shoulder of** Rabbi Ḥiyya, and **Rav was the tallest** person **in his generation. And Rav Yehuda reached** only **the shoulder of** Rav, **and Rav Yehuda was the tallest** person **in his generation. And Adda the attendant** [*dayyala*][L] **reached** only **the shoulder of** Rav Yehuda,

**PERSONALITIES**

**Abba Shaul – אַבָּא שָׁאוּל:** Abba was an appellation of deference used when addressing prominent Sages in early generations, before the title Rabbi was in use. Based on his statements that relate to the Temple service and specific activities that took place there, Abba Shaul appears to have been one of the *tanna'im* who lived when the Second Temple still stood. He may have been a younger contemporary of Rabbi Akiva and a student of Rabban Yoḥanan ben Zakkai. As is clear from the Gemara, he served as a gravedigger, suggesting that he placed great emphasis on the mitzva of burial of the dead.

Tomb of Abba Shaul, near Safed

**NOTES**

**Once I ran after a deer and I entered the thighbone of a corpse – פַּעַם אַחַת רַצְתִּי אַחַר צְבִי וְנִכְנַסְתִּי בְּקוּלִית שֶׁל מֵת:** Since Abba Shaul worked with the dead it is not surprising that he chose to express his thoughts using that imagery. In this case he is using the deer and the thighbone as metaphors for enticing, base desires, which are difficult to overcome. This is evident from the statement that the thighbone belonged to Og, king of Bashan, whose desire to battle the Jewish people even after seeing the defeat of the Amorite King Sihon brought about his downfall (see Numbers 21:21–35). In a similar vein, the description of Abba Shaul's standing in an eye socket symbolizes how an individual can be tempted by his eyes. The message of these stories is that even a prominent Sage and pious individual like Abba Shaul, who was great in stature in comparison to his peers, could be drawn by his desires, emphasizing how careful every individual must be when faced with objects of desire (*Midrash Shlomo*).

פַּרַשְׁתְּבִינָא דְּפוּמְבְּדִיתָא קָאֵי לֵיהּ לְאַדָּא דַּיָּילָא עַד פַּלְגֵיהּ, וְכוּלֵּי עָלְמָא קָאֵי לְפָרַשְׁתְּבִינָא דְּפוּמְבְּדִיתָא עַד חַרְצֵיהּ.

and when **the governor** [*parashtevina*][N] **of Pumbedita would stand** next **to Adda the attendant,** he would reach only **half of his** height. **And** when **everyone** else **in the world would stand** next **to the governor of Pumbedita,** they would reach only **his loins** [***ḥartzeih***].[L]

שָׁאֲלוּ לִפְנֵי רַבִּי: הַמַּפֶּלֶת שָׁפִיר מָלֵא בָּשָׂר, מַהוּ? אָמַר לָהֶם: לֹא שָׁמַעְתִּי.

§ The students **asked Rabbi** Yehuda HaNasi: In the case of a woman **who discharges a gestational sac full of flesh, what is** the *halakha*? Does she have the impurity of a woman after childbirth? Rabbi Yehuda HaNasi **said to them: I have not heard** from my teachers the *halakha* in this case.

אָמַר לְפָנָיו רַבִּי יִשְׁמָעֵאל בְּרַבִּי יוֹסֵי, כָּךְ אָמַר אַבָּא: מָלֵא דָּם – טְמֵאָה נִדָּה, מָלֵא בָּשָׂר – טְמֵאָה לֵידָה.

**Rabbi Yishmael, son of Rabbi Yosei, said to him: This** is what **my father,** i.e., Rabbi Yosei ben Ḥalafta, one of Rabbi Yehuda HaNasi's teachers, **said:** If a woman discharged a gestational sac **full of blood, she is impure** with the impurity of **a menstruating woman.** If it is **full of flesh, she is impure** with the impurity of a woman after **childbirth.**

אֲמַר לֵיהּ: אִילְמָלֵי דָּבָר חָדָשׁ אָמַרְתָּ לָנוּ מִשּׁוּם אָבִיךָ – שְׁמַעֲנוּךָ, עַכְשָׁיו,

Rabbi Yehuda HaNasi **said to him: If you had told us** an entirely **new statement in the name of your father,** no part of which was also stated by another Sage, **we would have listened to you,** i.e., we would have accepted the statement as *halakha*. But **now** that you stated two *halakhot*, one with regard to a woman who discharged a gestational sac full of blood, and the other with regard to a woman who discharged a gestational sac full of flesh, the entire statement cannot be accepted as *halakha*.

מִדְּהָא קַמַּיְיתָא כִּיחִידָאָה קָאָמַר – כְּסוּמָכוֹס שֶׁאָמַר מִשּׁוּם רַבִּי מֵאִיר, הָא נַמִּי – שֶׁמָּא כְּרַבִּי יְהוֹשֻׁעַ אֲמָרָהּ, וְאֵין הֲלָכָה כְּרַבִּי יְהוֹשֻׁעַ.

Rabbi Yehuda HaNasi explains: **From** the fact that Rabbi Yosei **said this first clause** of his statement, with regard to a gestational sac full of blood, **in accordance with an individual** opinion, i.e., **in accordance with** the opinion of **Sumakhos, who said in the name of Rabbi Meir** that the woman is impure, contrary to the opinion of the other Sages, it follows that with regard to **this** latter statement **as well,** with regard to a gestational sac full of flesh, one can say that **perhaps** Rabbi Yosei **said it in accordance with** the opinion of another individual Sage, **Rabbi Yehoshua. And** the ***halakha*** is **not in accordance with** the opinion of **Rabbi Yehoshua.**

דְּתַנְיָא, הַמַּפֶּלֶת שָׁפִיר שֶׁאֵינוֹ מְרוּקָּם – רַבִּי יְהוֹשֻׁעַ אוֹמֵר: וָלָד, וַחֲכָמִים אוֹמְרִים: אֵינוֹ וָלָד.

**As it is taught** in a *baraita*: In the case of a woman **who discharges a gestational sac in which tissue did not develop, Rabbi Yehoshua says:** It has the status of **an offspring,** and the woman has the impurity of a woman after childbirth; **and the Rabbis say: It is not an offspring,** and the woman is pure. The opinion of Rabbi Yosei that a woman who discharged a gestational sac full of flesh is impure might be in accordance with the ruling of Rabbi Yehoshua, which is not accepted as *halakha*, since the majority of the other Sages disagree with him. Therefore, the *halakha* cannot be decided in accordance with either part of the statement of Rabbi Yosei.

אָמַר רַבִּי שִׁמְעוֹן בֶּן לָקִישׁ מִשּׁוּם רַבִּי אוֹשַׁעְיָא: מַחֲלוֹקֶת – בְּעָכוּר, אֲבָל בְּצָלוּל – דִּבְרֵי הַכֹּל אֵינוֹ וָלָד. וְרַבִּי יְהוֹשֻׁעַ בֶּן לֵוִי אָמַר: בְּצָלוּל מַחֲלוֹקֶת.

**Rabbi Shimon ben Lakish says in the name of Rabbi Oshaya:** The **dispute** between Rabbi Yehoshua and the Rabbis applies **in** a case where the amniotic fluid is **turbid,** as Rabbi Yehoshua holds that the turbidity indicates that there was likely an embryo in the sac that liquefied. **But in** a case where the amniotic fluid is **clear, everyone agrees** that the discharged sac **is not** considered **an offspring.**[N] **And Rabbi Yehoshua ben Levi says:** The **dispute** applies **in** a case where the amniotic fluid is **clear.**

**NOTES**

**Governor** [*parashtevina*] – **פָּרַשְׁתְּבִינָא:** The early commentaries disagree about the meaning of this word. Some say that it is the name of a particular person who lived in Pumbedita and was known for his height (Rashi; *Arukh*). Others challenge this interpretation, as in that case the Gemara would have written: Parashtevina from Pumbedita, and not: Parashtevina of Pumbedita. Therefore they explain that the reference is to a certain rank of authority in the city government (*Tosafot*; Rashbam).

**Applies in a case where it is turbid but in a case where it is clear everyone agrees it is not an offspring – בְּעָכוּר אֲבָל בְּצָלוּל דִּבְרֵי הַכֹּל אֵינוֹ וָלָד:** Rashi explains that the terms turbid and clear are referring to the amniotic fluid: If it is turbid, the woman is impure, as the sac might have contained an embryo that liquefied, whereas if the fluid is clear, the woman is pure. Accordingly, Rabbi Yehoshua disagrees with the ruling of the mishna that if a woman discharges a gestational sac full of water, she is pure, as the mishna does not differentiate between turbid fluid and clear fluid.

*Tosafot* reject this interpretation, claiming that there is no reason for the *halakha* of a sac full of amniotic fluid to be more stringent than that of a sac full of blood, with regard to which the woman does not have the impurity of one after childbirth, but only that of a menstruating woman, even according to Rabbi Yehoshua. Therefore, *Tosafot* explain that the reference is to a gestational sac full of flesh. According to *Tosafot*, *akhur* means dissolved, while *tzalul* means not dissolved.

**LANGUAGE**

**Loins** [*ḥartza*] – **חַרְצָא:** The meaning of this Aramaic word is loins, as in the translation by Onkelos of the verse: "And put sackcloth upon his loins" (Genesis 37:34). It is similar to the Hebrew word for loins, *ḥalatzim*, as the letters *lamed* and *reish* are commonly switched in Hebrew and Aramaic words that are similar to each other.

איבַּעְיָא לְהוּ: בְּצָלוּל מַחֲלוֹקֶת – אֲבָל בְּעָכוּר דִּבְרֵי הַכֹּל וָלָד, אוֹ דִּלְמָא – בֵּין בָּזֶה וּבֵין בָּזֶה מַחֲלוֹקֶת? תֵּיקוּ.

**A dilemma was raised before** the Sages: What does Rabbi Yehoshua ben Levi mean? Does he mean that the **dispute** applies only **in** a case where the amniotic fluid is **clear, but in** a case where it is **turbid, everyone agrees** that it has the halakhic status of **an offspring? Or perhaps** Rabbi Yehoshua ben Levi means that the **dispute** applies **in this** case **and in that** case, i.e., the Rabbis hold that the sac does not have the status of an offspring even if the amniotic fluid is turbid. The Gemara concludes that the dilemma **shall stand** unresolved.

מֵיתִיבֵי, אֶת זוֹ דָּרַשׁ רַבִּי יְהוֹשֻׁעַ בֶּן חֲנַנְיָא: ״וַיַּעַשׂ ה׳ אֱלֹהִים לְאָדָם וּלְאִשְׁתּוֹ כָּתְנוֹת עוֹר וַיַּלְבִּשֵׁם״ – מְלַמֵּד שֶׁאֵין הַקָּדוֹשׁ בָּרוּךְ הוּא עוֹשֶׂה עוֹר לָאָדָם אֶלָּא אִם כֵּן נוֹצָר.

The Gemara **raises an objection** to the opinion that the dispute between Rabbi Yehoshua and the Rabbis applies only in a case where the amniotic fluid is turbid. It is taught in a *baraita* that **Rabbi Yehoshua ben Ḥananya,** who is the same Rabbi Yehoshua who disagrees with the Rabbis with regard to the case of a woman who discharges a gestational sac in which tissue did not develop, **taught this** following proof for his opinion that the woman is impure: It is stated: **"And the Lord God made for Adam and for his wife garments of skins, and clothed them"** (Genesis 3:21). This **teaches that the Holy One, Blessed be He, does not make skin for a person unless he is** already **created,** as God first created Adam and Eve, and then gave them skin. Consequently, the existence of a gestational sac proves that there is an offspring.

אַלְמָא: בְּעוֹר תַּלְיָא מִילְּתָא, לָא שְׁנָא עָכוּר וְלָא שְׁנָא צָלוּל.

**Evidently,** according to Rabbi Yehoshua **the matter** of whether or not an embryo is considered offspring **is dependent on** whether or not there is **skin,** and there **is no difference** whether the amniotic fluid is **turbid, and** there **is no difference** whether it is **clear.**

אִי אָמְרַתְּ בִּשְׁלָמָא בְּצָלוּל מַחֲלוֹקֶת – הַיְינוּ דְּאִיצְטְרִיךְ קְרָא, אֶלָּא אִי אָמְרַתְּ בְּעָכוּר מַחֲלוֹקֶת – לָמָּה לִי קְרָא? סְבָרָא בְּעָלְמָא הוּא! אֶלָּא שְׁמַע מִינָּהּ: בְּצָלוּל מַחֲלוֹקֶת, שְׁמַע מִינָּהּ.

**Granted, if you say** that the **dispute** applies **in** a case where it is **clear, that is** why it **was necessary** for Rabbi Yehoshua to derive from **a verse** that an embryo that has skin is considered an offspring. **But if you say** that the **dispute** applies **in** a case where the amniotic fluid is **turbid,** but Rabbi Yehoshua concedes that the woman is pure if it is clear, **why do I need a verse** to teach that if the amniotic fluid is turbid the woman is impure? **It is logical** that where the amniotic fluid is turbid there was probably an embryo that liquefied. **Rather, conclude from it** that the **dispute** applies **in** a case where the amniotic fluid is **clear.** The Gemara concludes: **Conclude from it** that this is correct.

וְכֵן אָמַר רַב נַחְמָן אָמַר רַבָּה בַּר אֲבוּהּ: מַחֲלוֹקֶת בְּעָכוּר, אֲבָל בְּצָלוּל – דִּבְרֵי הַכֹּל אֵינוֹ וָלָד.

**And likewise,** just as Rabbi Oshaya interprets the dispute between Rabbi Yehoshua and the Rabbis as referring to a case where the amniotic fluid is turbid, **Rav Naḥman says** that **Rabba bar Avuh says:** The **dispute** between Rabbi Yehoshua and the Rabbis applies **in** a case where the amniotic fluid is **turbid; but in** a case where the amniotic fluid is **clear, everyone agrees** that the discharged sac **is not** considered **an offspring.**

אֵיתִיבֵיהּ רָבָא לְרַב נַחְמָן: אֶלָּא אָמְרוּ, סִימַן וָלָד בִּבְהֵמָה דַּקָּה – טִינּוּף, בְּגַסָּה – שִׁלְיָא, בְּאִשָּׁה – שָׁפִיר וְשִׁלְיָא.

**Rava raised an objection to** the opinion of **Rav Naḥman** from a mishna that specifies the obligations that apply to firstborn animals [B] (*Bekhorot* 19b): **But** the Sages **said** that not only does a viable offspring exempt any subsequent offspring from being counted a firstborn, but the same applies to **an indication of the offspring** that is discharged from the womb. The indication **in a small animal**[H] is a **murky discharge** from the womb, **in a large** animal it is the emergence of **an afterbirth,**[H] and **in a woman** the indication is **a gestational sac or an afterbirth.**

**BACKGROUND**

Firstborn animal – בְּכוֹר: The male firstborn of cattle, sheep, or goats belonging to a Jew is sacred from birth and must be given to a priest to be sacrificed on the altar in the Temple, with its meat eaten by the priests and their families (see Numbers 18:17–18). If a firstborn animal develops a physical blemish that disqualifies it from being sacrificed as an offering, it still has to be given to a priest, but it can be slaughtered and eaten like any other non-sacred kosher animal.

The obligations of primogeniture with regard to humans are limited to the obligation that one redeem his firstborn son from a priest for five pieces of silver.

**HALAKHA**

An indication of the offspring in a small animal – סִימַן וָלָד בִּבְהֵמָה דַּקָּה: The discharge of turbid fluid from the womb of a small female animal indicates the existence of an embryo that was crushed and exempts subsequent births from the obligations of firstborn status. One must show the discharge to an expert shepherd to determine whether it is actually a crushed embryo (Rambam *Sefer Korbanot, Hilkhot Bekhorot* 4:10; *Shulḥan Arukh, Yoreh De'a* 315:7).

An indication of the offspring…in a large animal is the afterbirth – סִימַן...בְּגַסָּה שִׁלְיָא: If a large animal discharges an afterbirth from its womb, its subsequent births are exempt from the obligations of firstborn status, as there is no afterbirth without the existence of an embryo (*Shulḥan Arukh, Yoreh De'a* 315:7, and *Shakh* there).

וְאִילּוּ שָׁפִיר בִּבְהֵמָה – לָא פָּטַר. אִי אָמְרַתְּ בִּשְׁלָמָא בְּצָלוּל מַחֲלוֹקֶת – מִשּׁוּם הָכִי.

Rava infers: **And yet** the miscarriage of **a gestational sac in** the case of a large **animal does not exempt** the animal's subsequent offspring from being counted a firstborn. **Granted, if you say** that the **dispute** between Rabbi Yehoshua and the Rabbis applies **in** a case where the amniotic fluid is **clear**, it is **due to that** reason that the mishna differentiates between a large animal and a woman with regard to a gestational sac.

אִשָּׁה דְּרַבִּי בָּהּ קְרָא – פָּטַר בָּהּ שָׁפִיר, בִּבְהֵמָה דְּלָא רַבִּי קְרָא – לָא פָּטַר בָּהּ שָׁפִיר.

Rava explains: **With regard to a woman, as the** aforementioned **verse:** "And the Lord God made for Adam and for his wife garments of skins," **includes** in the definition of offspring a gestational sac, i.e., skin, one can say that such **a gestational sac exempts** subsequent births from the obligations of primogeniture. By contrast, **in** the case of **an animal, as the verse does not include** a gestational sac in the definition of offspring, discharging **a gestational sac does not exempt** the animal's subsequent offspring from being considered a firstborn.

אֶלָּא אִי אָמְרַתְּ בְּעָכוּר מַחֲלוֹקֶת, מִכְּדִי סְבָרָא הוּא, מַאי שְׁנָא אִשָּׁה וּמַאי שְׁנָא בְּהֵמָה?

**But if you say** that the **dispute** applies **in** a case where the amniotic fluid is **turbid**, and Rabbi Yehoshua deems the woman impure due to the likelihood that there was an embryo that liquefied, **since** this *halakha* **is** based on **logic, what is different** in the case of **a woman, and what is different** in the case of **an animal?** Rabbi Yehoshua's reasoning applies equally to both. Evidently, the dispute applies in a case where the amniotic fluid is clear.

מִי סָבְרַתְּ, רַבִּי יְהוֹשֻׁעַ מִפְשַׁט פְּשִׁיט לֵיהּ? רַבִּי יְהוֹשֻׁעַ סְפוּקֵי מְסַפְּקָא לֵיהּ, וְאָזֵיל הָכָא לְחוּמְרָא, וְהָכָא לְחוּמְרָא.

The Gemara answers: **Do you hold** that **it is obvious to Rabbi Yehoshua** that a gestational sac in which the amniotic fluid is turbid has the halakhic status of an offspring? That is not so; rather, **Rabbi Yehoshua is uncertain** of its halakhic status, **and** therefore **here,** in this case, he rules **stringently, and there** he also rules **stringently.**

גַּבֵּי אִשָּׁה דְּמָמוֹנָא הוּא – סְפֵק מָמוֹנָא לְקוּלָּא.

The Gemara elaborates: First of all, **with regard to** a situation where **a woman** discharged a gestational sac in which the amniotic fluid was turbid, in **which** case the obligation of primogeniture **is a monetary matter,** i.e., the obligation to redeem the newborn child by paying money to a priest, the subsequent births are exempt, in accordance with the principle that **uncertainty** with regard to **monetary matters** is treated **leniently.**

גַּבֵּי בְּהֵמָה דְּאִיסּוּרָא הוּא, דְּאִיכָּא לְגַבֵּי גִּיזָּה וַעֲבוֹדָה – סְפֵק אִיסּוּרָא לְחוּמְרָא. הָכִי נַמִי גַּבֵּי אִשָּׁה – סְפֵק טוּמְאָה לְחוּמְרָא.

By contrast, **with regard to an animal,** in **which** case firstborn status **is a ritual matter, as there are** prohibitions **involving,** i.e., against, **shearing** the animal's wool **and** using the animal for **labor** before it incurs a blemish, the discharged gestational sac is not considered an offspring and does not exempt subsequent births from the obligations of firstborn status, as **uncertainty** with regard to **ritual matters** is treated **stringently. So too, with regard to** the impurity of **a woman** who discharged a gestational sac, she is deemed impure, as **uncertainty** with regard to **impurity** is treated **stringently,** which means that for the purposes of this *halakha* a gestational sac is considered an offspring.

וּמִי מְסַפְּקָא לֵיהּ? וְהָא קְרָא קָאָמַר! מִדְּרַבָּנַן, וּקְרָא – אַסְמַכְתָּא בְּעָלְמָא הוּא.

The Gemara asks: **And is** Rabbi Yehoshua **uncertain** about the *halakha* of a woman who discharges a gestational sac? **But doesn't he cite a verse** as proof that the woman has the impurity of one who gave birth? The Gemara answers: Rabbi Yehoshua maintains that the woman is impure **by rabbinic** law, **and the verse** he cites **is a mere support** for this *halakha*; it is not the actual source.

אֲמַר לֵיהּ רַב חֲנִינָא בַּר שְׁלַמְיָא לְרַב: הָא רַבִּי, הָא רַבִּי יִשְׁמָעֵאל בְּרַבִּי יוֹסֵי, וְהָא רַבִּי אוֹשַׁעְיָא, וְהָא רַבִּי יְהוֹשֻׁעַ בֶּן לֵוִי, מָר כְּמַאן סְבִירָא לֵיהּ?

**Rav Ḥanina bar Shelamya said to Rav: This** is the opinion of **Rabbi** Yehuda HaNasi, who told his students that he did not hear from his teachers the *halakha* in the case of a woman who discharged a gestational sac full of flesh; and **this** is the opinion of **Rabbi Yishmael, son of Rabbi Yosei,** who cited his father's opinion that in such a case the woman is impure. **And this** is the opinion of **Rabbi Oshaya,** that the dispute between Rabbi Yehoshua and the Rabbis applies only in a case where the amniotic fluid is turbid; **and** finally **this** is the opinion of **Rabbi Yehoshua ben Levi,** who holds that the dispute applies if the amniotic fluid is clear. **In accordance with whose** opinion **does the Master hold?**

אֲמַר לֵיהּ: אֲנִי אוֹמֵר, אֶחָד זֶה וְאֶחָד זֶה – אֵינָהּ חוֹשֶׁשֶׁת.

Rav **said to** Rav Ḥanina bar Shelamya: **I say** that **both** in **this** case, where the amniotic fluid is turbid, **and in that** case, where the fluid is clear, the woman does **not** need to be **concerned** that she has the status of a woman who gave birth to an offspring.

וּשְׁמוּאֵל אָמַר: אֶחָד זֶה וְאֶחָד זֶה – חוֹשֶׁשֶׁת. וְאַזְדָא שְׁמוּאֵל לְטַעְמֵיהּ, דְּכִי אֲתָא רַב דִּימִי אָמַר: מֵעוֹלָם לָא דַּכּוּ שָׁפִיר בִּנְהַרְדְּעָא, לְבַר מֵהַהוּא שְׁפִירָא דַּאֲתָא לְקַמֵּיהּ דִּשְׁמוּאֵל, דְּמַנַּח עֲלֵיהּ חוּט הַשַּׂעֲרָה מֵהַאי גִּיסָא וְחָזְיָא מֵהַאי גִּיסָא, אֲמַר: אִם אִיתָא דְּוָלָד הֲוַאי – לָא הֲוָה זִיג כּוּלֵּי הַאי.

**And Shmuel says:** In **both this** case **and that** case, the woman must be **concerned** that the discharged gestational sac has the status of an offspring, and therefore she is considered impure like a woman who gave birth. **And Shmuel follows his** standard line of **reasoning** here, **as when Rav Dimi came** and transmitted many halakhic traditions, the latter **said: In Nehardе'a** the Sages **never deemed** a woman who discharged **a gestational sac pure, except for** the case of **a certain gestational sac that came before Shmuel, who placed a hair on this side** of that sac, **and it was visible from that side.** Shmuel **said,** based on this test: **If it were so, that** there **was an offspring** in the sac, **it would not have been so transparent.** He therefore deemed the woman pure, but his ruling applied only in that extreme case.

״וְאִם הָיָה מְרוּקָּם״ וכו׳. תָּנוּ רַבָּנַן, אֵיזֶהוּ שָׁפִיר מְרוּקָּם? אַבָּא שָׁאוּל אוֹמֵר: תְּחִלַּת בְּרִיָּיתוֹ מֵרֹאשׁוֹ, וּשְׁתֵּי עֵינָיו כִּשְׁתֵּי טִיפִּין שֶׁל זְבוּב. תָּנֵי רַבִּי חִיָּיא: מְרוּחָקִין זֶה מִזֶּה. שְׁנֵי חוֹטָמִין – כִּשְׁתֵּי טִיפִּים שֶׁל זְבוּב.

§ The mishna teaches: **But if** the sac **was** one in which **tissue developed,** the halakhic status of the woman is that of a woman after childbirth. Since the sex of the embryo is unknown, she observes the strictures of a woman who gave birth both to a male and to a female; she is impure for fourteen days like a woman who gave birth to a female, but blood that she sees thereafter is pure only until forty days after birth, like a woman who gave birth to a male. **The Sages taught** in a *baraita*: **What is** the definition of **a gestational sac** in which **tissue developed?**[H] **Abba Shaul says: The beginning of the formation of** the embryo **is from its head, and its two eyes** look **like two drops,** similar to the eyes **of a fly. Rabbi Ḥiyya teaches:** These eyes must be **distant from each other.** Furthermore, **its two nostrils** look **like two drops,** similar to the nostrils **of a fly.**

תָּנֵי רַבִּי חִיָּיא: וּמְקוֹרָבִין זֶה לָזֶה. וּפִיו מָתוּחַ כְּחוּט הַשַּׂעֲרָה, וּגְוִיָּיתוֹ כַּעֲדָשָׁה, וְאִם הָיְתָה נְקֵבָה – נִדּוֹנָה כִּשְׂעוֹרָה לְאׇרְכָּהּ.

**Rabbi Ḥiyya teaches: And** these eyes must be **close to each other. And its mouth stretches** along the width of its face **like a strand of hair. And its body**[N] **is like** the size of **a lentil.**[B] **And if it was female,** its vagina can be **discerned** by the appearance **of** a line like a cracked grain of **barley** oriented **along the length of** its body.

וְחִתּוּךְ יָדַיִם וְרַגְלַיִם אֵין לוֹ, וְעָלָיו מְפוֹרָשׁ בַּקַּבָּלָה ״הֲלֹא כֶחָלָב תַּתִּיכֵנִי וְכַגְּבִינָה תַּקְפִּיאֵנִי. עוֹר וּבָשָׂר תַּלְבִּישֵׁנִי וַעֲצָמוֹת וְגִידִים תְּסוֹכְכֵנִי. חַיִּים וָחֶסֶד עָשִׂיתָ עִמָּדִי וּפְקֻדָּתְךָ שָׁמְרָה רוּחִי״.

**And it does not have the shape of arms and legs** at this stage. **And it is said with regard to** an embryo at this stage, **in the texts of tradition,** the Prophets: **"Have You not poured me out as milk, and curdled me like cheese? You have clothed me with skin and flesh, and knit me together with bones and sinews. You have granted me life and favor, and Your providence has preserved my spirit"** (Job 10:10–12).

וְאֵין בּוֹדְקִין אוֹתוֹ בְּמַיִם – שֶׁהַמַּיִם עַזִּין

**And one does not examine it with water**[H] to discover its sex, **as water is too strong,**

**HALAKHA**

What is a gestational sac in which tissue developed – אֵיזֶהוּ שָׁפִיר מְרוּקָּם: What is the definition of a gestational sac in which tissue developed, which renders a woman who discharges it impure with the impurity of a woman after childbirth? It is a sac that contains an embryo whose body looks like a lentil; whose eyes look like two drops, like the eyes of a fly, and are distant from each other; whose nostrils look the same, but are close to each other; whose mouth is open just to the length of a hair. It does not need to have the shape of arms and legs (Rambam *Sefer Kedusha, Hilkhot Issurei Bia* 10:3).

And one does not examine it with water, etc. – וְאֵין בּוֹדְקִין אוֹתוֹ בְּמַיִם וכו׳: If the form of a discharged embryo is more developed than it was at the outset of its formation, but its sex is still indiscernible, it should be examined after cleaning it with oil, not water (Rambam *Sefer Kedusha, Hilkhot Issurei Bia* 10:3).

**NOTES**

Its body [*geviyyato*] – גְּוִיָּיתוֹ: Some commentaries interpret this word as referring to the penis (Rashi; *Tosafot*). Others explain that the reference is to the entire body (Rambam).

**BACKGROUND**

Like a lentil – כַּעֲדָשָׁה: When a lentil is mentioned in the Mishna and Talmud, the reference is generally to the red lentil, whose diameter is 4 mm.

Perek **III**
Daf **25** Amud **b**

וְטוֹרְדִין אוֹתוֹ, אֶלָּא בּוֹדְקִין אוֹתוֹ בְּשֶׁמֶן – שֶׁהַשֶּׁמֶן רַךְ וּמְצַחְצְחוֹ. וְאֵין רוֹאִין אֶלָּא בַּחַמָּה.

**and dissolves it. Rather, one examines it with oil, as oil is soft and cleans** the embryo so that its sex can be discerned. **And one views** it **only** in the light of **the sun.**

כֵּיצַד בּוֹדְקִין אוֹתוֹ? כֵּיצַד בּוֹדְקִין אוֹתוֹ? כִּדְאָמְרִינַן! אֶלָּא: בַּמֶּה בּוֹדְקִין אוֹתוֹ לֵידַע אִם זָכָר הוּא אִם נְקֵבָה הִיא?

The *baraita* continues: **How does one examine** the embryo? The Gemara expresses surprise at this question: **How does one examine it** to determine whether it has the halakhic status of an offspring? Clearly, one examines it **as we** just **said. Rather,** the question is as follows: **In what** manner **does one examine it to ascertain whether it is male**[H] **or** whether **it is female?**

**HALAKHA**

In what manner does one examine it to ascertain whether it is male, etc. – בַּמֶּה בּוֹדְקִין אוֹתוֹ לֵידַע אִם זָכָר הוּא וכו׳: The examination of a discharged fetus whose sex is indiscernible is performed by running a sliver of wood whose top is smooth along the fetus's sex organ from top to bottom. If the sliver's movement is not smooth, the fetus is evidently male. If the sex organ looks like a cracked grain of barley, the fetus is clearly female, and further examination is unnecessary (Rambam *Sefer Kedusha, Hilkhot Issurei Bia* 10:3).

אַבָּא שָׁאוּל בַּר נַשׁ, וְאָמְרִי לַהּ אַבָּא שָׁאוּל בַּר רְמַשׁ אוֹמֵר: מֵבִיא קֵיסָם שֶׁרֹאשׁוֹ חָלָק וּמְנַעְנֵעַ בְּאוֹתוֹ מָקוֹם. אִם מְסַכְסֵךְ – בְּיָדוּעַ שֶׁזָּכָר הוּא, וְאִם לָאו – בְּיָדוּעַ שֶׁנְּקֵבָה הִיא.

**Abba Shaul bar Nash, and some say Abba Shaul bar Remash, says: One brings a sliver of wood whose top is smooth, and he moves** it along the embryo **in that place,** i.e., the sex organ. **If the sliver is caught,** i.e., its movement is not smooth, **it is known that** the embryo **is male,** as its member interfered with the movement of the sliver. **And if** the sliver is **not** caught, **it is known that it is female.**

אָמַר רַב נַחְמָן אָמַר רַבָּה בַּר אֲבוּהּ: לֹא שָׁנוּ אֶלָּא מִלְּמַטָּה לְמַעְלָה, אֲבָל מִן הַצְּדָדִין – אֵימָא: כּוֹתְלֵי בֵּית הָרֶחֶם נִינְהוּ.

**Rav Naḥman says that Rabba bar Avuh says: They taught** this *halakha,* that if the movement of the sliver is not smooth then the embryo is male, **only** if the sliver was moved along the sex organ of the embryo **from below to above;**[N] **but** if it was moved **from the sides,** from one side to the other, the fact that it was not smooth does not prove that the embryo is male, as one can **say** that **the sides of the womb** interfered.

אָמַר רַב אַדָּא בַּר אַהֲבָה: תָּנָא, אִם הָיְתָה נְקֵבָה – נִדּוֹנָה כִּשְׂעוֹרָה סְדוּקָה. מַתְקִיף לַהּ רַב נַחְמָן: וְדִילְמָא חוּט שֶׁל בֵּיצִים נִינְהוּ? אֲמַר אַבָּיֵי: הָשְׁתָּא בֵּיצִים גּוּפַיְיהוּ – לָא יְדִיעִי, חוּט שֶׁל בֵּיצִים – יְדִיעַ?!

**Rav Adda bar Ahava says:** The complete version of the *baraita* is **taught** as follows: **If it was female,** its vagina can be **discerned** by the appearance **of** a line like **a cracked** grain of **barley** oriented along the length of its body. **Rav Naḥman objects to this: But perhaps it** is not the vagina but **the recess between the testes,** and the embryo is male. **Abaye said** to him: **Now,** at this stage of development, **the testes** of the embryo **themselves are not discernible.** Is it possible that **the recess between the testes is discernible?**

אָמַר רַבִּי עַמְרָם, תָּנָא: שְׁתֵּי יְרֵכוֹתָיו – כִּשְׁנֵי חוּטִין שֶׁל זְהוֹרִית. וְאָמַר רַבִּי עַמְרָם עֲלָהּ: כְּשֶׁל עֵרֶב. וּשְׁנֵי זְרוֹעוֹתָיו כִּשְׁנֵי חוּטִין שֶׁל זְהוֹרִית, וְאָמַר רַבִּי עַמְרָם עֲלָהּ: כְּשֶׁל שְׁתִי.

The *baraita* teaches that at this stage an embryo does not have the shape of arms and legs. **Rabbi Amram says** that **it is taught** in a *baraita* that when an embryo's arms and legs start to take shape, **its two thighs** look **like two strings of crimson** thread [*zehorit*].[B] **And Rabbi Amram says with regard to** this matter that the thighs look **like** two strings **of the woof,** which are thicker than those of the warp. The *baraita* adds: **And its two arms** look **like two strings of crimson** thread. **And Rabbi Amram says with regard to** this matter that the arms look **like** two strings **of the warp.**[B]

אֲמַר לֵיהּ שְׁמוּאֵל לְרַב יְהוּדָה: שִׁינָּנָא, לָא תַּעֲבֵיד עוּבְדָא עַד שֶׁיִּשְׂעִיר. וּמִי אָמַר שְׁמוּאֵל הָכִי? וְהָאָמַר שְׁמוּאֵל: אַחַת זוֹ וְאַחַת זוֹ – חוֹשֶׁשֶׁת!

**Shmuel said to Rav Yehuda:** *Shinnana,*[L] **do not perform an action,** i.e., do not issue a practical ruling deeming a woman who discharges an embryo at this stage of development impure, **unless** the embryo **has grown hair.**[H] The Gemara asks: **And did Shmuel** actually **say that? But doesn't Shmuel say** with regard to a woman who discharged a gestational sac that **both in this** case, where the amniotic fluid is turbid, **and in that** case, where the fluid is clear, the woman must be **concerned** that the discharged gestational sac might have the status of an offspring, which would mean that she is impure even without the growth of hair on the embryo?

**BACKGROUND**

Crimson thread [*zehorit*] – זְהוֹרִית: *Zehorit* is a woven material made of wool or silk and dyed crimson. Crimson pigment is produced from the eggs of the scale insect of the genus *Kermes*, which is found among trees. Crimson-dyed material was used in various items in the Temple and for decorative purposes outside of the Temple.

Left to right: Dried female *Kermes echinatus* with eggs, dyed string, dyed wool

Warp – שְׁתִי: In the craft of weaving, threads of the warp are normally fixed on the loom, forming the foundation of the fabric. The threads of the woof are crossed between the threads of the warp in different ways. Since the threads of the warp hold the weave together, they need to be much stronger than the threads of the woof. Nevertheless, they are often thinner than the threads of the woof. Therefore, the spinning of the threads for the warp required greater care than the spinning of the threads for the woof.

Reconstructed ancient loom

**NOTES**

**They taught only from below to above** – לֹא שָׁנוּ אֶלָּא מִלְּמַטָּה לְמַעְלָה: The later commentaries infer from the statement of Rabba bar Avuh that the sliver should be run along the sex organ of the fetus specifically from bottom to top, and not from top to bottom. The reason for this is that if one runs the sliver along the sex organ from top to bottom, he may inadvertently skip over the penis, whereas if one runs it from bottom to top, the penis will invariably interfere. By contrast, the Rambam writes that one runs the sliver along the sex organ from top to bottom (*Arukh LaNer*).

**HALAKHA**

**Do not perform an action unless the embryo has grown hair** – לָא תַּעֲבֵיד עוּבְדָא עַד שֶׁיִּשְׂעִיר: A woman who discharged an underdeveloped fetus does not observe the period of purity that a woman after childbirth observes unless the fetus has grown hair. This is in accordance with Shmuel's instruction to Rav Yehuda and Rav Ami's interpretation of his statement (Rambam *Sefer Kedusha, Hilkhot Issurei Bia* 10:3).

**LANGUAGE**

*Shinnana* – שִׁינָּנָא: This is a nickname for Rav Yehuda, appearing in several places in the Talmud. According to Rashi, the name means sharp or brilliant. By contrast, the *ge'onim* assert that they are certain that this is an expression describing one with large teeth [*shinayim*], noting that the expression was still employed in their time.

## BACKGROUND

Fish of the sea – דָּג שֶׁל יָם: The sandal fish mentioned in the Gemara is generally identified with flatfish in the genus *Bothus*, which lie flat on the ocean floor.

Fish of the genus *Bothus*

## NOTES

This mishna is taught from the testimony of Rabbi Neḥunya – מֵעֵדוּתוֹ שֶׁל רַבִּי נְחוּנְיָא נִשְׁנֵית מִשְׁנָה זוֹ: Rashi explains that the ruling in this *baraita* is an individual opinion, and therefore one cannot use it as the basis of an objection. The early commentaries derive from here that the *halakha* is that a sandal fetus is considered an offspring even if it does not have the shape of a face. Although Rabbi Yoḥanan, who states that this *baraita* is an individual opinion, is quoted earlier (24a) as stating that if a woman discharges a fetus whose face is flat, she is pure, the case of a sandal fetus is different, as it was originally a normal offspring, and was mashed by its twin (Rashba; Ritva).

אָמַר רַב אַמִי בַּר שְׁמוּאֵל, לְדִידִי מְפָרְשָׁא לִי מִינֵּיהּ דְּמָר שְׁמוּאֵל: לָחוּשׁ – חוֹשֶׁשֶׁת, יְמֵי טׇהֳרָה – לָא יָהֲבִינַן לָהּ עַד שֶׁיִּשְׂעִיר.

**Rav Ami bar Shmuel says:** This matter was **explained to me by Mar Shmuel:** As for **being concerned** that perhaps she is impure, the woman must be **concerned,** due to the uncertainty whether she discharged an offspring. But **we do not give her** the **days of purity** that follow the period of impurity for a woman who gave birth, **unless** the embryo **has grown hair.**

לְמֵימְרָא דִּמְסַפְּקָא לֵיהּ לִשְׁמוּאֵל? וְהָא הַהוּא שְׁפִירָא דַּאֲתַאי לְקַמֵּיהּ דְּמָר שְׁמוּאֵל, אֲמַר: הָא בַּר אַרְבְּעִין וְחַד יוֹמָא, וְחָשֵׁיב מִיּוֹמָא דַּאֲזַלָא לִטְבִילָה עַד הַהוּא יוֹמָא, וְלָא הָוֵה אֶלָּא אַרְבְּעִין יוֹמִין,

The Gemara asks: **Is that to say that Shmuel is uncertain** whether a gestational sac has the halakhic status of an offspring? **But** there was an incident involving **a certain gestational sac that was brought before Mar Shmuel,** and Shmuel **said: This** embryo **is forty-one days old. And** Shmuel subsequently **calculated** the amount of time that had passed **from the day that** the woman **went to** perform **immersion** in a ritual bath **until that day, and it was only forty days.**

וַאֲמַר לְהוּ: הַאי בְּנִדָּה בָּעַל. כַּפְתֵיהּ – וְאוֹדִי! שָׁאנֵי שְׁמוּאֵל דְּרַב גּוּבְרֵיהּ.

**And he said to** the local court: **This** husband **engaged in intercourse with** his wife when she was **a menstruating woman. They bound** the husband **and he confessed.** Since Shmuel was so proficient in embryology, why was he unsure about the halakhic status of a gestational sac? The Gemara answers: **Shmuel** himself **is different, as his strength,** i.e., his proficiency, was **great.** His general ruling that the halakhic status of a gestational sac is uncertain applies to people who are not as proficient as he is.

״הַמַּפֶּלֶת סַנְדָּל״ וכו׳. תָּנוּ רַבָּנַן, סַנְדָּל דּוֹמֶה לְדָג שֶׁל יָם, מִתְּחִלָּתוֹ וָלָד הוּא אֶלָּא שֶׁנִּרְצַף. רַבָּן שִׁמְעוֹן בֶּן גַּמְלִיאֵל אוֹמֵר: סַנְדָּל דּוֹמֶה לְלָשׁוֹן שֶׁל שׁוֹר הַגָּדוֹל. מִשּׁוּם רַבּוֹתֵינוּ הֵעִידוּ: סַנְדָּל צָרִיךְ צוּרַת פָּנִים.

§ The mishna teaches that a woman **who discharges a sandal** fetus or one who discharges an afterbirth observes the strictures of a woman who gave birth both to a male and to a female. **The Sages taught** in a *baraita*: **A sandal** fetus has **a similar** appearance **to** a certain **fish of the sea**[B] known as a sandal fish; it looks as though **it is** a full-fledged **offspring from the outset, but it was mashed. Rabban Shimon ben Gamliel says: A sandal** fetus has an appearance that is **similar to the tongue of the large bull.**[H] Students **testified in the name of our teachers** that for a **sandal** fetus to have the halakhic status of an offspring, it **requires the shape of a face.**

אָמַר רַב יְהוּדָה, אָמַר שְׁמוּאֵל: הֲלָכָה – סַנְדָּל צָרִיךְ צוּרַת פָּנִים. אָמַר רַב אַדָּא, אָמַר רַב יוֹסֵף, אָמַר רַבִּי יִצְחָק: סַנְדָּל צָרִיךְ צוּרַת פָּנִים, וַאֲפִילּוּ מֵאֲחוֹרָיו. מָשָׁל לְאָדָם שֶׁסָּטַר אֶת חֲבֵירוֹ, וְהֶחֱזִיר פָּנָיו לַאֲחוֹרָיו.

**Rav Yehuda says** that **Shmuel says:** The ***halakha*** is that **a sandal** fetus **requires the shape of a face** for it to have the status of an offspring. **Rav Adda says** that **Rav Yosef says** that **Rabbi Yitzḥak says: A sandal** fetus **requires the shape of a face, but** the face does not need to be in its proper location; **even** if the face is **on the back of its** head, the fetus has the status of an offspring. **A parable to** which this situation can be compared is that of **a person who slapped another** in the face **and pushed his face back.** Here too, the face of the sandal fetus was pushed back due to external pressure.

בִּימֵי רַבִּי יַנַּאי בִּקְּשׁוּ לְטַהֵר אֶת הַסַּנְדָּל שֶׁאֵין לוֹ צוּרַת פָּנִים, אָמַר לָהֶם רַבִּי יַנַּאי: טִיהַרְתֶּם אֶת הַוְּולָדוֹת!

The Gemara relates: **In the days of Rabbi Yannai,** the other Sages **wished to deem pure** a woman who discharges **a sandal** fetus **that does not have the shape of a face. Rabbi Yannai said to them: You have deemed pure** women who discharge **offspring.** Rabbi Yannai holds that even a sandal fetus that does not have the shape of a face is considered an offspring.

וְהָתַנְיָא, מִשּׁוּם רַבּוֹתֵינוּ הֵעִידוּ: סַנְדָּל צָרִיךְ צוּרַת פָּנִים! אָמַר רַב בֵּיבַי בַּר אַבָּיֵי אָמַר רַבִּי יוֹחָנָן: מֵעֵדוּתוֹ שֶׁל רַבִּי נְחוּנְיָא נִשְׁנֵית מִשְׁנָה זוֹ. אָמַר רַבִּי זֵירָא: זָכָה בָּהּ רַב בֵּיבַי בִּשְׁמַעְתֵּיהּ, דַּאֲנָא וְהוּא הֲוֵינָא יָתְבִינַן קַמֵּיהּ דְּרַבִּי יוֹחָנָן כִּי אֲמָרָהּ לְהָא שְׁמַעְתָּא, וְקָדֵים אִיהוּ וַאֲמַר וְזָכָה בָּהּ.

The Gemara asks: **But isn't it taught** in a *baraita* that students **testified in the name of our teachers** that for **a sandal** fetus to have the halakhic status of an offspring it **requires the shape of a face? Rav Beivai bar Abaye says** that **Rabbi Yoḥanan says** in response: **This mishna,** i.e., the ruling to which the students testified, **is taught from the testimony of Rabbi Neḥunya.**[N] In other words, this ruling is the opinion of an individual *tanna*, which is not accepted. **Rabbi Zeira says: Rav Beivai merited that his** ruling of ***halakha,*** which he transmitted in the name of Rabbi Yoḥanan, was accepted. **As he and I were** both **sitting before Rabbi Yoḥanan when** Rabbi Yoḥanan **said this *halakha*, but** Rav Beivai **said it first** to the other Sages, **and** thereby **merited** that **it** was ascribed to him.

## HALAKHA

A sandal fetus has an appearance similar to the tongue of the large bull – סַנְדָּל דּוֹמֶה לְלָשׁוֹן שֶׁל שׁוֹר הַגָּדוֹל: Sometimes part of the blood from which a human fetus is formed solidifies and forms the shape of a bull's tongue, and it is wrapped around part of the fetus's body. This item is referred to as a sandal fetus. This is in accordance with the opinion of Rabban Shimon ben Gamliel (Rambam *Sefer Kedusha*, *Hilkhot Issurei Bia* 10:12).

לָמָּה הִזְכִּירוּ סַנְדָּל, וַהֲלֹא אֵין סַנְדָּל שֶׁאֵין עִמּוֹ וָלָד?

§ The Gemara asks: **Why** does the mishna **mention** that if a woman discharged **a sandal** fetus she observes the strictures of a woman who gave birth both to a male and to a female? Since **there is no** such thing as **a sandal** fetus **that** does **not** have another **offspring with it,** which mashed it and gave it the form of a sandal fish, in any case the woman has the impurity of a woman after childbirth.

אִי דְּאִתְיְלִידָא נְקֵבָה בַּהֲדֵיהּ – הָכִי נַמִי, הָכָא בְּמַאי עָסְקִינַן – דְּאִתְיְלִיד זָכָר בַּהֲדֵיהּ.

The Gemara answers: **If** it is **a female** offspring that **is born with** the sandal fetus, it is **indeed** unnecessary to mention the *halakha* of the sandal fetus, as the woman is in any case impure for two weeks. But **here we are dealing with** a case **where a male is born with it,**[H] on account of which the woman would be impure for only seven days were it not for the sandal fetus.

מַהוּ דְּתֵימָא, הוֹאִיל וְאָמַר רַב יִצְחָק בַּר אַמִי: אִשָּׁה מַזְרַעַת תְּחִילָּה – יוֹלֶדֶת זָכָר, אִישׁ מַזְרִיעַ תְּחִלָּה – יוֹלֶדֶת נְקֵבָה, מִדְּהָא זָכָר – הָא נַמִי זָכָר,

In this case, it is necessary for the mishna to state that the woman observes the strictures of one who gave birth both to a male and to a female, **lest you say** that **since Rav Yitzḥak bar Ami says** that the sex of a fetus is determined at the moment of conception, as, if the **woman emits seed first she gives birth to a male** and if the **man emits seed first she gives birth to a female,** therefore, it can be concluded **from** the fact **that this** offspring that was born with the sandal fetus **is male,** that **this** sandal fetus **is also male.**

קָא מַשְׁמַע לָן: אֵימָא שְׁנֵיהֶם הִזְרִיעוּ בְּבַת אַחַת, הַאי זָכָר וְהַאי נְקֵבָה.

Lest this reasoning be accepted, the mishna **teaches us** that the woman must observe the strictures of a woman who gave birth to a female as well. This is because one can **say** that perhaps **both** the man and the woman **emitted seed at the same time,** and consequently **this** offspring **is male and that** sandal fetus **is female.**

דָּבָר אַחֵר: שֶׁאִם תֵּלֵד נְקֵבָה לִפְנֵי שְׁקִיעַת הַחַמָּה, וְסַנְדָּל לְאַחַר שְׁקִיעַת הַחַמָּה,

**Alternatively,** it can be suggested that it is necessary for the mishna to state this *halakha* even with regard to a case where the twin of the sandal fetus is female, **as, if** the woman **gives birth to** the **female before sunset and** gives birth to the **sandal** fetus **after sunset,** which is considered the next day, the sex of the sandal fetus affects the count of the woman's periods of impurity and purity.

מוֹנָה תְּחִלַּת נִדָּה לָרִאשׁוֹן וּתְחִלַּת נִדָּה לָאַחֲרוֹן.

If the sandal fetus is male, the woman's status as a woman after childbirth ends after the eightieth day from the birth of the female offspring, and **she counts the beginning of** the period when seeing blood renders her impure as **a menstruating woman from** the birth of **the first** offspring, i.e., the female. **But** if the sandal fetus is female, the woman has the status of a woman after childbirth until after the eightieth day from its birth, which is the eighty-first day from the birth of the first offspring. If so, she counts **the beginning of** the period when seeing blood renders her impure as **a menstruating woman from** the birth of **the last** offspring, i.e., the sandal fetus.

סַנְדָּל דִּתְנַן

The Gemara discusses why the case of a woman who discharged a sandal fetus is mentioned in other *mishnayot*, given that a sandal fetus always has a twin. First the Gemara discusses the *halakha* of a woman who discharged **a sandal** fetus **that we learned** in a mishna

**HALAKHA**

**Where a male is born with it** – דְּאִתְיְלִיד זָכָר בַּהֲדֵיהּ: Occasionally, when the abdomen of a pregnant woman is struck, the fetus is disfigured and assumes the shape of a sandal fetus. Sometimes the face remains, and other times the fetus dries up and is so disfigured and covered by solidified blood that no facial features remain. Therefore, if a woman discharges a male fetus and a sandal fetus, she must observe the strictures of a woman who gives birth to both a male and a female, as the sandal fetus might be female. The Sages instituted this stringency treating a sandal fetus as an offspring even if it does not have the shape of a face, because the woman is anyway impure with the impurity of a woman after childbirth due to the full-fledged offspring that is born with it (Rambam *Sefer Kedusha*, *Hilkhot Issurei Bia* 10:12).

Perek **III**
Daf **26** Amud **a**

גַּבֵּי בְּכוֹרוֹת לְמַאי הִלְכְתָא?

**with regard to firstborns** (*Bekhorot* 46a), which states that the son who is born after a sandal fetus has the status of a firstborn with regard to inheritance but not with regard to the obligation of redemption from a priest. The Gemara asks: **For what** matter is that ***halakha*** relevant? Since the sandal fetus has a twin that is born with it, the subsequent son is in any case exempt from redemption.

לַבָּא אַחֲרָיו – בְּכוֹר לְנַחֲלָה וְאֵין בְּכוֹר לְכֹהֵן.

The Gemara answers: That *halakha* is relevant **for** a case where the sandal fetus's twin **comes** out of the womb **after it.** The mishna teaches that as the sandal fetus was born first, its twin is considered **a firstborn with regard to inheritance,**[H] **but** it is **not a firstborn with regard to** redemption from **a priest.**[H]

סַנְדָּל דִּתְנַן גַּבֵּי כְּרֵיתוֹת לְמַאי הִלְכְתָא?

The Gemara discusses the *halakha* with regard to a woman who discharged **a sandal** fetus **that we learned** in a mishna **in** tractate *Karetot* (7b), which states that such a woman brings the offering of a woman who gave birth. The Gemara asks: **For what** matter is that *halakha* relevant? In any case that woman is obligated to bring the offering of a woman who gave birth, due to the twin.

שֶׁאִם תֵּלֵד וָלָד דֶּרֶךְ דּוֹפֶן, וְסַנְדָּל דֶּרֶךְ רֶחֶם – דְּמַיְיתָא קׇרְבָּן אַסַּנְדָּל.

The Gemara answers: It is necessary for the mishna to state **that if** a woman **gives birth to** a full-fledged **offspring by means of caesarean section, and** to **a sandal** fetus in a regular manner **through** the **womb,** in such a case **she brings an offering for** giving birth to the **sandal**[H] fetus, despite the fact that she does not bring an offering for the full-fledged offspring, as one does not bring an offering for a birth by caesarean section.

וּלְרַבִּי שִׁמְעוֹן דַּאֲמַר יוֹצֵא דֶּרֶךְ דּוֹפֶן – וָלָד מְעַלְּיָא הוּא מַאי אִיכָּא לְמֵימַר?

The Gemara asks: **But according to Rabbi Shimon, who said** that an offspring which is **delivered by means of caesarean section**[B] **is** considered **a full-fledged offspring,** and its mother does bring an offering, **what is there to say?** Why is it necessary for the mishna to state this *halakha* if the woman must bring an offering regardless of the sandal fetus?

אָמַר רַבִּי יִרְמְיָה: שֶׁאִם תֵּלֵד וָלָד בִּהְיוֹתָהּ גּוֹיָה, וְסַנְדָּל לְאַחַר שֶׁנִּתְגַּיְּירָה – דְּמַיְיתָא קׇרְבָּן אַסַּנְדָּל.

**Rabbi Yirmeya says:** It is necessary for the mishna to state **that if** a woman **gives birth to** the full-fledged **offspring while she is a gentile,** when the *halakhot* of a woman after childbirth do not apply to her, and she immediately converts to Judaism **and** gives birth to the **sandal** fetus **after she converted** and became obligated to observe the *halakhot* of a woman after childbirth, **that she brings an offering for the sandal** fetus.

אֲמַרוּהָ רַבָּנַן קַמֵּיהּ דְּרַב פַּפָּא: וּמִי אִיתְנְהוּ לְהָנֵי שִׁינּוּיֵי? וְהָא תַּנְיָא: כְּשֶׁהֵן יוֹצְאִין – אֵין יוֹצְאִין אֶלָּא כְּרוּכִין!

**The Sages said** the answers to these questions **before Rav Pappa, and** they asked him: **And are these answers** correct? Can it be suggested that the sandal fetus was born before or after the twin fetus? **But isn't it taught** in a *baraita* that **when** a sandal fetus and the full-fledged offspring **exit** the womb, **they exit only wrapped** around one another?

אָמַר רַב פַּפָּא: שְׁמַע מִינָּהּ מִכְרַךְ כָּרֵיךְ לֵיהּ וָלָד לְסַנְדָּל אַפַּלְגֵיהּ, וּמְשַׁלְחִיף לֵיהּ כְּלַפֵּי רֵישֵׁיהּ. גַּבֵּי בְּכוֹרוֹת – כְּגוֹן שֶׁיָּצְאוּ דֶּרֶךְ רָאשֵׁיהֶם, דְּסַנְדָּל קָדֵים וְנָפֵיק. גַּבֵּי כְּרֵיתוֹת – שֶׁיָּצְאוּ דֶּרֶךְ מַרְגְּלוֹתֵיהֶם, דְּוָלָד קָדֵים וְנָפֵיק.

**Rav Pappa said** in response: **Conclude from it** that the sandal fetus and its twin do not lie side by side, but rather the full-fledged **offspring encounters the sandal** fetus **at half its** height, i.e., the head of the full-fledged offspring presses into the abdomen of the sandal fetus. **And** when they are born, the full-fledged offspring **pushes** the sandal fetus **toward** the direction **its head** is pointing, to the entrance of the womb, causing the sandal fetus to be born first. Therefore, the mishna **with regard to firstborns** can be explained as referring to a case **where** the fetuses **exited** the womb **with their heads** first, **as** in such a case the **sandal** fetus **emerges first.** By contrast, the mishna **in** tractate ***Karetot*** is referring to a case **where they emerged with their feet** first, **as** in such a case the full-fledged **offspring emerges first.**

רַב הוּנָא בַּר תַּחְלִיפָא מִשְּׁמֵיהּ דְּרָבָא אָמַר: אֲפִילּוּ תֵּימָא מְצוּמְצָמִין, וְאֵיפוֹךְ שְׁמַעְתְּתָא, גַּבֵּי בְּכוֹרוֹת – שֶׁיָּצְאוּ דֶּרֶךְ מַרְגְּלוֹתֵיהֶם, וָלָד דְּאִית בֵּיהּ חִיּוּתָא – סָרֵיךְ וְלָא נָפֵיק, סַנְדָּל דְּלֵית בֵּיהּ חִיּוּתָא – שָׁרֵיק וְנָפֵיק. גַּבֵּי כְּרֵיתוֹת – שֶׁיָּצְאוּ דֶּרֶךְ רָאשֵׁיהֶן, וָלָד דְּאִית בֵּיהּ חִיּוּתָא – מִדְּנָפֵיק רֵישֵׁיהּ הָוְיָא לֵידָה, סַנְדָּל – עַד דְּנָפֵיק רוּבֵּיהּ.

**Rav Huna bar Taḥlifa says in the name of Rava: You** may **even say** that the two fetuses lie **precisely** side by side, **and** you should **reverse** Rav Pappa's *halakha* so that it reads as follows: **With regard to firstborns,** the reference is to a case **where** the fetuses **emerged with their feet** first. In such a case, the full-fledged **offspring, which has life, hangs on and does not emerge** so quickly, whereas the **sandal** fetus, **which does not have life, slides out and emerges** first. **In** tractate ***Karetot,*** it is referring to a case **where** the fetuses **came out with their heads** first. In such an instance, with regard to the full-fledged **offspring, which has life, once its head emerges it is** considered **a birth,** whereas the **sandal** fetus is considered to have been born **only when the majority of its** body **emerges.**[N]

**HALAKHA**

The *halakha* of a sandal fetus with regard to inheritance – סַנְדָּל לְעִנְיַן נַחֲלָה: A son who is born after stillborn babies is considered the firstborn with regard to inheritance (*Sefer Mishpatim, Hilkhot Naḥalot* 2:10; *Shulḥan Arukh, Ḥoshen Mishpat* 277:6).

The *halakha* of a sandal fetus with regard to redemption from a priest – סַנְדָּל לְעִנְיַן כֹּהֵן: In a case where a woman discharged an afterbirth, a gestational sac in which tissue developed, or an embryo in the form of a sandal fish, or in a case where she gave birth to a fetus that emerged in pieces, if she subsequently gives birth to a son, it is not considered as though he "opens the womb" (Exodus 13:2), and he does not require redemption (Rambam *Sefer Zera'im, Hilkhot Bikkurim* 11:14,15; *Shulḥan Arukh, Yoreh De'a* 305:22).

She brings an offering for giving birth to the sandal – דְּמַיְיתָא קׇרְבָּן אַסַּנְדָּל: If a woman discharges a full-fledged male fetus and a sandal fetus, she observes the strictures of a woman who gave birth to both a male and a female, due to the uncertain sex of the sandal fetus. This is not the fundamental *halakha* but rather a stringency of the Sages (Rambam *Sefer Kedusha, Hilkhot Issurei Bia* 10:12, and see *Or Same'aḥ* there; *Sefer Korbanot, Hilkhot Meḥusrei Kappara* 1:6).

**BACKGROUND**

Delivered by caesarean section – יוֹצֵא דֶּרֶךְ דּוֹפֶן: This refers to an offspring that was born by caesarean section. There is no record of such an operation being performed in the ancient world on a woman who was still alive, but only on a woman who died during childbirth, in order to save the offspring. Only in the modern era is this operation performed on women who are still alive. Nevertheless, various *mishnayot* and discussions in the Talmud indicate that among Jews these operations were performed on living women even in antiquity, and some who were operated upon not only survived but even managed to become pregnant and have children again.

**NOTES**

The sandal fetus is considered to have been born only when the majority of its body emerges – סַנְדָּל עַד דְּנָפֵיק רוּבֵּיהּ: The early commentaries explain that although in general an offspring is considered to have been born once its head comes out, a sandal fetus is stillborn, and a stillborn fetus is considered to have been born only when the majority of its body emerges (Rashi).

**מתני׳** שִׁלְיָא בַּבַּיִת – הַבַּיִת טָמֵא. לֹא שֶׁהַשִּׁלְיָא וָלָד, אֶלָּא שֶׁאֵין שִׁלְיָא בְּלֹא וָלָד.

**MISHNA** If there is **an afterbirth in the house,**[H] **the house is ritually impure,** in the sense that everything under the roof contracts impurity imparted by a corpse. The reason is **not that** the status of **an afterbirth** is that of **an offspring;**[H] **rather,** it is **that there is no afterbirth without an offspring.** It is clear that the afterbirth contained an offspring that disintegrated after the miscarriage. That offspring rendered the contents of the house impure.

רַבִּי שִׁמְעוֹן אוֹמֵר: נִימּוֹק הַוָּלָד עַד שֶׁלֹּא יָצָא.

**Rabbi Shimon says:** The house does not become a tent over a corpse, as although there had been an offspring in the afterbirth, **the offspring disintegrated,** turning to blood, **before it emerged** from the womb, and it was negated by the majority of blood that accompanied the miscarriage.

**גמ׳** תָּנוּ רַבָּנַן: שִׁלְיָא תְּחִלָּתָהּ דּוֹמָה לְחוּט שֶׁל עֵרֶב, וְסוֹפָהּ דּוֹמָה כְּתוּרְמוּס, וַחֲלוּלָה כַּחֲצוֹצֶרֶת, וְאֵין שִׁלְיָא פְּחוּתָה מִטֶּפַח. רַבִּי שִׁמְעוֹן בֶּן גַּמְלִיאֵל אוֹמֵר: שִׁלְיָא דּוֹמָה לְקוּרְקְבָן שֶׁל תַּרְנְגוֹלִין, שֶׁהַדַּקִּין יוֹצְאִין מִמֶּנָּה.

**GEMARA** **The Sages taught** in a *baraita* with regard to the appearance of the afterbirth: At **the outset of** the pregnancy, the **afterbirth** is so thin that it is **similar to a string of the woof,**[H] **and** at the **end of** the pregnancy it is much wider, **similar** in width **to a lupine.**[B] **And** the afterbirth is **hollow like a trumpet,**[B] **and there is no afterbirth** whose length is **less than a handbreadth.**[B] **Rabbi Shimon ben Gamliel says: An afterbirth is similar to the craw of roosters, from which the small** intestine **emerges.**

**HALAKHA**

**Afterbirth in the house – שִׁלְיָא בַּבַּיִת:** If a woman discharged an afterbirth, the house where she discharged it is definitely impure, due to the presumption that there is no afterbirth without an offspring (Rambam *Sefer Tahara, Hilkhot Tumat Met* 25:10).

**Not that an afterbirth is an offspring – לֹא שֶׁהַשִּׁלְיָא וָלָד:** If a woman discharged an afterbirth, she observes the strictures of a woman who gave birth to both a male and a female, not because the status of an afterbirth is that of an offspring, but rather because there is no such thing as an afterbirth without an offspring (Rambam *Sefer Kedusha, Hilkhot Issurei Bia* 10:14).

**Afterbirth is so thin that it is similar to a string of the woof – שִׁלְיָא תְּחִלָּתָהּ דּוֹמָה לְחוּט שֶׁל עֵרֶב:** The thick membrane that is like a gourd in which the fetus is formed and that surrounds the fetus and the sandal, if there is a sandal with it, is called the afterbirth. When it is time for the offspring to be born, it tears the afterbirth and emerges. When it is first formed, the afterbirth is similar to a string of the woof, hollow like a trumpet, and thick like the craw of a rooster. An afterbirth is at least one handbreadth long (Rambam *Sefer Kedusha, Hilkhot Issurei Bia* 10:13).

**BACKGROUND**

**Lupine – תּוּרְמוּס:** Lupine is the name for several plants from the legume family. The cultivated lupine, *Lupinus termis*; the yellow lupine, *L. luteus*; and the Israeli lupine, *L. palaestinus*, are particularly common. Lupine seeds, which are round with a diameter of up to 15 mm in the cultivated lupine, grow inside pods. The seeds are extremely bitter, due to their alkaloid content, and must be boiled in water to be edible. The water is then poured out and the seeds are boiled again or soaked.

White lupines

Yellow lupine

Israeli lupines

**Trumpet – חֲצוֹצֶרֶת:**

Ancient Persian trumpet from Persepolis

**Handbreadth – טֶפַח:** A handbreadth [*tefaḥ*], which is the width of a clenched fist, is one of the standard measures of length used in the Talmud. One handbreadth is equal to four fingerbreadths. This is equivalent to five times the width of the middle finger or six times the width of the little finger. According to the opinion of Rabbi Ḥayyim Na'e, a handbreadth is 8 cm long. According to the opinion of the *Ḥazon Ish*, a handbreadth is 9.6 cm long. In the Bible a handbreadth is sometimes called a *tofaḥ*, and the Talmud occasionally uses the word *pushḥa*.

תַּנְיָא, רַבִּי אוֹשַׁעְיָא זְעֵירָא דְּמִן חַבְרַיָּא: חֲמִשָּׁה שִׁיעוּרָן טֶפַח, וְאֵלּוּ הֵן: שִׁלְיָא, שׁוֹפָר, שִׁדְרָה, דּוֹפֶן סוּכָּה, וְהָאֵזוֹב.

Since the *baraita* states that the minimum length of an afterbirth is a handbreadth, the Gemara cites another *baraita* that lists different items whose halakhic status is dependent on a minimum measure of a handbreadth. **It is taught** by **Rabbi Oshaya, the youngest** [*ze'eira*] **of the company** [*demin ḥavrayya*][P] of Sages: There are **five** items **whose** minimum **measure** is one **handbreadth, and these are they: An afterbirth,** the **shofar** for blowing on Rosh HaShana, the **spine** of a *lulav* that must be taken on *Sukkot*, the width of **the wall of a *sukka*, and the hyssop** [*veha'ezov*].[B] Hyssop is used for the purification of a leper and for the preparation of the ashes of a red heifer in order to sprinkle them with water on someone who is ritually impure due to impurity imparted by a corpse.

שִׁלְיָא – הָא דַּאֲמַרַן. שׁוֹפָר – דְּתַנְיָא, כַּמָּה יְהֵא שִׁיעוּר שׁוֹפָר? פֵּירֵשׁ רַבִּי שִׁמְעוֹן בֶּן גַּמְלִיאֵל: כְּדֵי שֶׁיֹּאחֲזֶנּוּ בְּיָדוֹ וְיֵרָאֶה לְכָאן וּלְכָאן טֶפַח.

The Gemara elaborates: The *halakha* with regard to **an afterbirth is that which we stated** above. The *halakha* of **a shofar** is **as it is taught** in a *baraita*: **How much is the measure** of the length **of a shofar**[H] for blowing on Rosh HaShana? **Rabbi Shimon ben Gamliel explained:** It must be long **enough that when one holds it in his hand** with four fingers, **it can be seen** protruding **on one side** of his hand **and on the other side,** i.e., at least one **handbreadth.**

שִׁדְרָה מַה הִיא? דַּאֲמַר רַבִּי פַּרְנָךְ, אָמַר רַבִּי יוֹחָנָן: שִׁדְרוֹ שֶׁל לוּלָב צָרִיךְ שֶׁיְּהֵא יוֹצֵא מִן הַהֲדַס טֶפַח. דּוֹפֶן סוּכָּה – דְּתַנְיָא: שְׁתַּיִם כְּהִלְכָתָן, שְׁלִישִׁית – אֲפִילּוּ טֶפַח. אֵזוֹב – דְּתָנֵי רַבִּי חִיָּיא: אֵזוֹב – טֶפַח.

**What is** the *halakha* with regard to **a spine** of a *lulav*? It is **as Rabbi Parnakh said** that **Rabbi Yoḥanan says: The spine of a *lulav***[H] **must protrude** at least one **handbreadth beyond the myrtle branch** that is tied together with it. The *halakha* of **the wall of a *sukka***[H] **is as it is taught** in a *baraita*: A *sukka* is valid only if it has **two** full-fledged partitions **in the standard sense,** completely closing each of those two sides and measuring at least seven handbreadths, **and a third** wall that measures **even** one **handbreadth.** If the third wall is less than a handbreadth long, the *sukka* is unfit. Finally, the *halakha* with regard to the **hyssop** is stated in a *baraita* **that Rabbi Ḥiyya teaches:** The **hyssop**[H] used for the purification of a leper and for the preparation of the ashes of a red heifer must measure at least one **handbreadth.**

אָמַר רַבִּי חֲנִינָא בַּר פַּפָּא, דָּרֵישׁ שֵׁילָא אִישׁ כְּפַר תְּמַרְתָּא: תְּלָת מַתְנִיתָא וְתַרְתֵּי שְׁמַעְתָּתָא – שִׁיעוּרָא טֶפַח. תַּרְתֵּי? חֲדָא הִיא! אָמַר אַבַּיֵי: אֵימָא אָמַר רַבִּי חִיָּיא אֵזוֹב טֶפַח.

**Rabbi Ḥanina bar Pappa says** that **Sheila of Kefar Temarta**[B] **taught** as a mnemonic: There are **three *baraitot*,** with regard to an afterbirth, a shofar, and the wall of a *sukka*, **and** there are **two** independent ***halakhot*** of *amora'im*, of the spine of a *lulav* and the hyssop, where the minimum **measure** of one **handbreadth** is required. The Gemara asks: Are there **two** *halakhot* of *amora'im* in this list? There **is** only **one**[N] statement, with regard to the spine of a *lulav*. The *halakha* of the hyssop is taught in a *baraita* by Rabbi Ḥiyya. **Abaye says:** Revise the wording of that statement, so that it should not read that Rabbi Ḥiyya taught a *baraita*; rather, **say** that **Rabbi Ḥiyya says** himself that the **hyssop** must measure at least one **handbreadth,** i.e., that *halakha* is not taught in a *baraita*.

**PERSONALITIES**

Rabbi Oshaya the youngest [*ze'eira*] of the company [*demin ḥavrayya*] – רַבִּי אוֹשַׁעְיָא זְעֵירָא דְּמִן חַבְרַיָּא: This Sage, who is mentioned on a few occasions, may be Rav Oshaya from Babylonia. The meaning of his title is unclear, as he might be called Oshaya the Young, who came from a place called Ḥavrayya, perhaps to differentiate from another Oshaya. Alternatively, as translated here, he might be known as Oshaya, the youngest of the group of Sages.

**BACKGROUND**

Hyssop [*ezov*] – אֵזוֹב: While the Sages were unsure of the precise identification of the *ezov* plant mentioned in the Torah, from the various descriptions it seems that it is bible hyssop, *Majorana syriaca*. Bible hyssop, a fragrant plant that reaches a height of 50–100 cm, grows in rocky terrain in Eretz Yisrael and in surrounding countries. The plant spreads out from its base into rigid wooden branches, which annually produce straight stems that dry out and die in winter. The white flowers of the hyssop plant are tightly bunched at the tips of its branches. Dried leaves of bible hyssop are used in the spice za'atar.

Bible hyssop

Kefar Temarta – כְּפַר תְּמַרְתָּא: Kefar Temarta was a town in the Galilee east of the modern-day town Ir Dor. Its name is preserved in the nearby Arab town called Tamra.

**NOTES**

Are there two *halakhot* of *amora'im* in this list, there is only one – תַּרְתֵּי חֲדָא הִיא: Why doesn't the Gemara similarly question Sheila's statement that there are three *baraitot* that require the minimum measure of a handbreadth, as there are actually four *baraitot*? One possibility is that Sheila disagrees with the *halakha* taught by Rabbi Ḥiyya, and therefore he does not consider his statement equivalent to the other *baraitot*. Alternatively, the Gemara could in fact have asked this question, but this is in effect the same difficulty that the Gemara raises, merely from a different perspective (Ramban).

**HALAKHA**

The measure of a shofar – שִׁיעוּר שׁוֹפָר: The minimum length of a shofar sufficient for blowing on Rosh HaShana is enough that when one holds it in his hand with four fingers, it can be seen protruding from both sides of his fingers, i.e., one handbreadth (Rambam *Sefer Zemanim*, *Hilkhot Shofar VeSukka VeLulav* 1:5 and *Haggahot Maimoniyyot* there; *Shulḥan Arukh*, *Oraḥ Ḥayyim* 586:9).

The measure of…the spine of a *lulav* – שִׁיעוּר...שִׁדְרוֹ שֶׁל לוּלָב: The spine of a *lulav* must be at least four handbreadths long, not including the top of its leaves. Since the myrtle branch and the willow branch that are taken with the *lulav* must be at least three handbreadths long, when one ties the *lulav* with the myrtle branch and the willow branch, the *lulav* should protrude beyond the myrtle branch and the willow branch at least one handbreadth, in accordance with the opinion of Rabbi Yoḥanan (Rambam *Sefer Zemanim*, *Hilkhot Shofar VeSukka VeLulav* 7:8).

The measure of…the wall of a *sukka* – שִׁיעוּר...דּוֹפֶן סוּכָּה: A *sukka* that does not have three walls is unfit. If it has two full-fledged partitions standing perpendicular to each other, forming an L shape, one can render the *sukka* fit by adding a wall that is one handbreadth wide at a distance of less than three handbreadths from one of the preexisting partitions. The third wall consists of the one-handbreadth-wide wall and the established form of a doorway (Rambam *Sefer Zemanim*, *Hilkhot Shofar VeSukka VeLulav* 4:2).

The measure of…the hyssop – שִׁיעוּר...הָאֵזוֹב: The hyssop used for the purification of a leper and for the purification of a person who has contracted impurity imparted by a corpse must be at least one handbreadth long (Rambam *Sefer Tahara*, *Hilkhot Tumat Tzara'at* 11:1; Rambam *Sefer Tahara*, *Hilkhot Para Aduma* 3:2).

וְתוּ לֵיכָּא? וְהָאִיכָּא: טֶפַח עַל טֶפַח עַל רוּם טֶפַח מְרוּבָּע – מֵבִיא אֶת הַטּוּמְאָה וְחוֹצֵץ בִּפְנֵי הַטּוּמְאָה!

The Gemara asks: **And are there no more** cases where the minimum measure is one handbreadth, other than those five listed by Rabbi Oshaya? **But isn't there** the following mishna (*Oholot* 3:7) that deals with the minimum size of a tent that transmits ritual impurity: **A cubic** space measuring one **handbreadth by** one **handbreadth with a height of** one **handbreadth transmits ritual impurity.** If a corpse is in that space, the impurity is transmitted to all people, vessels, and food in that space. **And** a space of that size **serves as a barrier before,** i.e., stops the spread of, **ritual impurity**[H] beyond that space.

טֶפַח – קָאָמְרִינַן, טֶפַח עַל טֶפַח לָא קָאָמְרִינַן.

The Gemara answers: **We said** that there are five items whose minimum measure is one **handbreadth; we did not say** anything about a space whose measure is one **handbreadth by** one **handbreadth.**

וְהָא אִיכָּא: אֶבֶן הַיּוֹצֵא מִן הַתַּנּוּר טֶפַח וּמִן הַכִּירָה שָׁלֹשׁ אֶצְבָּעוֹת – חִבּוּר!

The Gemara further asks: **But isn't there** the following mishna (*Kelim* 5:2): **A stone that protrudes from the oven**[H] by one **handbreadth,** which is used as a handle for lifting and carrying the oven, **and** similarly a stone that protrudes **from the stove**[B] **three fingerbreadths** is considered as having **a connection** to the oven or stove with regard to ritual impurity. Consequently, if the oven or stove becomes impure, then the stone handle, which is classified as part of the oven, is likewise rendered impure. If the handle is longer than that, the additional length will be removed, so it is not considered to be part of the oven.

כִּי קָאָמְרִינַן – הֵיכָא דִּבְצִיר מִטֶּפַח לָא חָזֵי, אֲבָל הָכָא – כׇּל שֶׁכֵּן דִּבְצִיר מִטֶּפַח יַד תַּנּוּר הוּא.

The Gemara answers: **When we said** that there are five items whose minimum measure is one handbreadth, we were referring to cases **where** if it **less than** one **handbreadth** it **is unfit** for the purpose of the item. **But here,** where a protruding stone one handbreadth long is considered a handle of the oven, it is **all the more so** the case **that** a protruding stone **less than** one **handbreadth** long **is** considered **a handle of** the **oven.**

וְהָאִיכָּא

The Gemara asks: **But aren't there**

**HALAKHA**

**The measure of a tent with regard to transmitting ritual impurity and serving as a barrier before ritual impurity** – **שִׁיעוּר אֹהֶל לַהֲבָאַת הַטּוּמְאָה וְלַחֲצִיצָה מִפְּנֵי הַטּוּמְאָה**: Any space with a base one handbreadth by one handbreadth and a height of one handbreadth is considered a tent. If a corpse is in that space, the impurity is transmitted to all people, vessels, and food in that space, but it does not spread beyond that space (Rambam *Sefer Tahara*, *Hilkhot Tumat Met* 13:1).

**A stone that protrudes from the oven** – **אֶבֶן הַיּוֹצֵא מִן הַתַּנּוּר**: With regard to the handle of a vessel, if it is necessary for the use of the vessel, it is considered part of the vessel with regard to ritual impurity. Therefore, if the vessel becomes impure, the handle becomes impure as well. If the handle is not necessary for the use of the vessel, it is not considered part of the vessel, and if the vessel becomes impure, the handle remains pure. Accordingly, a stone that protrudes one handbreadth from an oven or three fingerbreadths from a stove is considered part of the oven or stove, and if the oven or stove becomes impure, the stone becomes impure too, and it transmits impurity to any food or liquids that come in contact with it. If the stone protrudes more than one handbreadth from the oven, or more than three fingerbreadths from the stove, food or liquids that come in contact with the part of the stone that is more than one handbreadth or three fingerbreadths away from the oven or stove, respectively, remain pure (Rambam *Sefer Tahara*, *Hilkhot Kelim* 17:1).

**BACKGROUND**

**Oven and stove** – **תַּנּוּר וְכִירָה**: Ovens and stoves that were used in homes in antiquity were generally large clay vessels similar in form to a very large jug. They were heated by kindling a large fire inside. The difference between them in shape was that ovens were narrow on top and wide on the bottom, so that the heat could be contained in the oven for a significant amount of time. Stoves, on the other hand, had the same width both on top and on the bottom, and had two holes on top for pots to be placed on them. The heat in a stove was not contained as well as in an oven.

Perek **III**
Daf **26** Amud **b**

תַּנּוּרֵי בְּנוֹת טֶפַח, דִּתְנַן: תַּנּוּר – תְּחִלָּתוֹ אַרְבָּעָה וּשְׁיָרָיו אַרְבָּעָה, דִּבְרֵי רַבִּי מֵאִיר.

toy **ovens with** which **girls** play, whose minimum measure with regard to ritual impurity is also one **handbreadth? As it is taught** in a mishna (*Kelim* 5:1): A clay **oven** in **its original,** unbroken, **state** is susceptible to ritual impurity if it is **four** handbreadths tall. **And** with regard to an oven that became impure and was subsequently broken, if **its remains** include a piece **four** handbreadths tall, that piece remains impure. This is **the statement of Rabbi Meir.**

**HALAKHA**

**The measure of the remains of an oven with regard to ritual impurity – שִׁיעוּר שְׁיָרֵי תַּנּוּר לְעִנְיַן טוּמְאָה:** If a large oven breaks and a piece four handbreadths high remains intact, or if a small oven breaks and most of it remains intact, that piece is still susceptible to impurity. If less than this measure remains intact, it is no longer susceptible to impurity. Likewise, if a large oven is impure, and is shattered until less than four handbreadths remain intact, or, in the case of a small oven, if most of the oven does not remain intact, it is pure. Otherwise, that large piece is still impure (Rambam *Sefer Tahara*, *Hilkhot Kelim* 16:1).

**The measure of an oven with regard to ritual impurity – שִׁיעוּר תַּנּוּר לְעִנְיַן טוּמְאָה:** If one began to make a large oven, it is susceptible to ritual impurity once it is four handbreadths high and heated with fire, in accordance with the opinion of the Rabbis in the mishna in tractate *Kelim* (Rambam *Sefer Tahara*, *Hilkhot Kelim* 15:2).

**NOTES**

**Rabbi Oshaya is not dealing with consecrated items – בְּקָדָשִׁים לָא קָמַיְירֵי:** The early commentaries note that the Gemara could have cited this answer in response to the question of why the frame of the Table in the Temple is not listed. This is not difficult, as it is normal for the Gemara to state several different explanations even when one would have been sufficient (Ritva).

**Was silent – אִישְׁתִּיק:** It is unclear from the Gemara why Rav Yitzḥak bar Shmuel was initially silent and did not respond to the contradiction that Rav Kahana raised, and only when Rav Kahana suggested a resolution to the contradiction, Rav Yitzḥak responded that Rav had already said this explanation himself.

וַחֲכָמִים אוֹמְרִים: בַּמֶּה דְּבָרִים אֲמוּרִים – בְּגָדוֹל, אֲבָל בְּקָטָן – תְּחִלָּתוֹ כָּל שֶׁהוּא, מִשֶּׁתִּגָּמֵר מְלַאכְתּוֹ, וּשְׁיָרָיו – בְּרוּבּוֹ.

**And the Rabbis say: In what** case **is this statement said?** It is said **in** the case of **a large** oven, made for regular use; **but with regard to a small** oven made for girls to play with, in **its original state, any size** is sufficient for it to be susceptible to contract impurity. **Once its construction is completed,** if the oven then becomes impure and is subsequently broken, if **its remains include** a piece that contains **the majority of** the oven, that piece remains impure.[H]

וְכַמָּה ״כָּל שֶׁהוּא״? אָמַר רַבִּי יַנַּאי: טֶפַח, שֶׁכֵּן עוֹשִׂין תַּנּוּרֵי בָנוֹת טֶפַח! בִּפְלוּגְתָּא לָא קָמַיְירִי.

The Gemara explains: **And how** small is the size defined by the mishna as **any size? Rabbi Yannai says:** One **handbreadth,**[H] **as** people **fashion** toy **ovens for girls** one **handbreadth** high. This is another example of an item that has a minimum measure of one handbreadth, in addition to the five items listed by Rabbi Oshaya. The Gemara answers: Rabbi Oshaya **is not speaking of** matters that are subject to **dispute,** such as the minimum measure of an oven.

הַשְׁתָּא דְּאָתֵית לְהָכִי – הָא נַמִי פְּלוּגְתָּא הִיא. דְּקָתָנֵי סֵיפָא: אָמַר רַבִּי יְהוּדָה, לֹא אָמְרוּ טֶפַח – אֶלָּא מִן הַתַּנּוּר וְלַכּוֹתֶל.

The Gemara adds: **Now that you have arrived at this** answer, the fact that Rabbi Oshaya does not mention a stone protruding from an oven can be explained in the same manner, since **this** *halakha* **is also** subject to **a dispute. As the latter clause** of that mishna (*Kelim* 5:2) **teaches** that **Rabbi Yehuda said:** When the Sages **said** that a stone protruding from an oven is considered a handle if it protrudes one **handbreadth,** they said so **only** with regard to a stone that protrudes **from the oven and toward the wall.** If the stone protrudes more than that, it is not considered a handle, as it is likely to be removed so that the oven can be moved closer to the wall. But if the stone protrudes toward the airspace of the house, it is considered an oven handle even if it protrudes more than one handbreadth.

וְהָאִיכָּא מִסְגֶּרֶת טֶפַח! בְּדִכְתִיבָן לָא קָא מַיְירֵי. וְהָאִיכָּא כַּפּוֹרֶת טֶפַח! בְּקָדָשִׁים לָא קָמַיְירֵי.

The Gemara raises a difficulty: **But isn't there** the **frame** of the Table in the Temple, which is one **handbreadth** wide, as stated in the Torah (Exodus 25:25)? The Gemara answers: Rabbi Oshaya **is not dealing with** matters **that are written** in the Torah. The Gemara further asks: **But isn't there the Ark Cover,** which is one **handbreadth** thick, and its measure is not written explicitly in the Torah? The Gemara answers: Rabbi Oshaya **is not dealing with consecrated** items.[N]

וְהָאִיכָּא: דַּיָּהּ לְקוֹרָה שֶׁהִיא רְחָבָה טֶפַח! בִּדְרַבָּנַן לָא קָמַיְירִי, אֶלָּא בִּדְכְתִיבָן וְלָא מְפָרְשִׁי שִׁיעוּרַיְיהוּ.

The Gemara asks: **But isn't there** the *halakha* of a cross beam, which is placed over the entrance to an alleyway in order to permit carrying items in the alleyway on Shabbat, and the *halakha* is that **it is enough for** a cross **beam to be** one **handbreadth wide?** The Gemara answers: Rabbi Oshaya **is not dealing with matters of rabbinic law. Rather,** he is speaking only **of** matters **that are written** in the Torah **but whose measure is not explicit** in the Torah.

יָתֵיב רַב יִצְחָק בַּר שְׁמוּאֵל בַּר מָרְתָא קַמֵּיהּ דְּרַב כָּהֲנָא וְיָתֵיב וְקָאָמַר, אָמַר רַב יְהוּדָה, אָמַר רַב: כָּל שְׁלֹשָׁה יָמִים הָרִאשׁוֹנִים – תּוֹלִין אֶת הַשִּׁלְיָא בְּוָלָד, מִכָּאן וְאֵילָךְ – חוֹשְׁשִׁין לְוָלָד אַחֵר.

§ **Rav Yitzḥak bar Shmuel bar Marta sat before Rav Kahana, and he sat and said** that **Rav Yehuda says** that **Rav says:** For **all of the first three days** after a woman gives birth, if she discharges afterbirth, **we attribute the afterbirth to the offspring.** There is no concern that this afterbirth indicates the miscarriage of another offspring. **From this** point **forward,** once three days have passed since the birth, if the woman discharges an afterbirth, **we are concerned that** there might have been **another offspring** in the afterbirth, and the *halakhot* of a woman who discharged an offspring apply to her.

אָמַר לֵיהּ: וּמִי אָמַר רַב הָכִי? וְהָאָמַר רַב: אֵין הַוָּלָד מִתְעַכֵּב אַחַר חֲבֵירוֹ כְּלוּם! אִישְׁתִּיק. אָמַר לֵיהּ: דִּלְמָא כָּאן – בְּנֵפֶל, כָּאן – בְּבֶן קַיָּימָא?

Rav Kahana **said to** Rav Yitzḥak bar Shmuel: **And did Rav say this? But didn't Rav say** that **an offspring does not remain** in the womb **at all after another** offspring was born? Rav Yitzḥak bar Shmuel **was silent.**[N] Rav Kahana **said to him: Perhaps** there is no contradiction between Rav's two statements, as **here,** where he indicates that a second offspring can emerge even three days after the first, the reference is **to** a case where the first offspring is **a non-viable newborn,** whereas **there,** in the statement that a second offspring does not remain in the womb after the first offspring was born, he is referring **to** a case where the first offspring is **a viable** offspring.

אֲמַר לֵיהּ: אַתְּ אָמְרַתְּ לִשְׁמַעְתֵּיהּ דְּרַב? בְּפֵירוּשׁ אֲמַר רַב הָכִי: הִפִּילָה נֵפֶל, וְאַחַר כָּךְ הִפִּילָה שִׁלְיָא – כָּל שְׁלֹשָׁה יָמִים תּוֹלִין אֶת הַשִּׁלְיָא בְּוָלָד, מִכָּאן וְאֵילָךְ – חוֹשְׁשִׁין לְוָלָד אַחֵר. יָלְדָה וְאַחַר כָּךְ הִפִּילָה שִׁלְיָא – אֲפִילּוּ מִכָּאן וְעַד עֲשָׂרָה יָמִים אֵין חוֹשְׁשִׁין לְוָלָד אַחֵר.

Rav Yitzḥak bar Shmuel **said to him:** Are **you** the one who **says** this explanation **of Rav's *halakha*** of your own accord? Indeed, **Rav said this explicitly:** If a woman **discharged a non-viable newborn and subsequently discharged an afterbirth,** for **all of the first three days we attribute the afterbirth to the offspring. From this** point **forward,** if she discharged an afterbirth **we are concerned that** it contained **another offspring.** If she **gave birth** to a viable offspring **and subsequently discharged an afterbirth, even from now until ten days** after the birth **we are not concerned that** the afterbirth contained **another offspring.**

שְׁמוּאֵל וְתַלְמִידֵי דְּרַב וְרַב יְהוּדָה הָווּ יָתְבִי. חָלֵיף וְאָזֵיל רַב יוֹסֵף בְּרֵיהּ דְּרַב מְנַשְּׁיָא מִדְּוִיל לְאַפַּיְיהוּ, בָּאלֵי וְאָתֵי, אֲמַר: אָתֵי לָן גַּבְרָא דְּרָמֵינַן לֵיהּ בְּגִילָא דְּחִטְּתָא, וּמִרְמֵי וּמִדְּחִי.

The Gemara relates: **Shmuel, Rav's students, and Rav Yehuda were sitting** together. **Rav Yosef, son of Rav Menashya of D'vil,**[P] **was passing** by **and walking toward them,** i.e., he was walking in their direction, and **he was hurrying and coming** along. Shmuel **said** to his company: **A man is coming toward us whom one can knock** down **with a straw of wheat, and he falls and stays down.** In other words, he cannot refute even a minor challenge to his opinions.

אַדְּהָכִי אֲתָא. אֲמַר לֵיהּ שְׁמוּאֵל: מַאי אֲמַר רַב בְּשִׁלְיָא? אֲמַר לֵיהּ, הָכִי אֲמַר רַב: אֵין תּוֹלִין אֶת הַשִּׁלְיָא אֶלָּא בְּדָבָר שֶׁל קַיָּימָא. שַׁיְילִינְהוּ שְׁמוּאֵל לְכָל תַּלְמִידֵי דְּרַב וְאָמְרִי לֵיהּ הָכִי, הֲדַר חַזְיֵיהּ לְרַב יְהוּדָה בִּישׁוּת.

**In the meantime,** Rav Yosef, son of Rav Menashya, **arrived. Shmuel said to him: What did Rav say with regard to an afterbirth?** Rav Yosef **said to him** that **this is what Rav said: One attributes an afterbirth only to a viable item,**[NH] i.e., a viable offspring. **Shmuel** subsequently **asked all of Rav's students** who were present whether Rav actually said this, **and they said to him** that Rav indeed said **so.** Shmuel **then looked at Rav Yehuda harshly,** as Rav Yehuda was also a student of Rav, but he had not transmitted this *halakha* to Shmuel after Rav's death.

בְּעָא מִינֵּיהּ רַבִּי יוֹסֵי בֶּן שָׁאוּל מֵרַבִּי: הַמַּפֶּלֶת דְּמוּת עוֹרֵב וְשִׁלְיָא מַהוּ? אֲמַר לֵיהּ: אֵין תּוֹלִין אֶלָּא בְּדָבָר שֶׁיֵּשׁ בְּמִינוֹ שִׁלְיָא.

§ **Rabbi Yosei ben Shaul asked Rabbi** Yehuda HaNasi: In the case of a woman **who discharges** an item in **the form of a crow and** there is also **an afterbirth, what is** the *halakha*? Is the afterbirth attributed to the discharged item, or is there concern that the afterbirth might have contained another offspring? Rabbi Yehuda HaNasi **said to him: One attributes** an afterbirth **only to an item whose species has an afterbirth.** Since crows do not have an afterbirth, the afterbirth cannot be associated with that discharged item.

קְשׁוּרָה בּוֹ מַהוּ? אֲמַר לֵיהּ: דָּבָר שֶׁאֵינוֹ שָׁאַלְתָּ. אֵיתִיבֵיהּ: הַמַּפֶּלֶת מִין בְּהֵמָה חַיָּה וְעוֹף וְשִׁלְיָא עִמָּהֶן, בִּזְמַן שֶׁהַשִּׁלְיָא קְשׁוּרָה עִמָּהֶן – אֵין חוֹשְׁשִׁין לְוָלָד אַחֵר, אֵין שִׁלְיָא קְשׁוּרָה עִמָּהֶן – חוֹשְׁשִׁין לְוָלָד אַחֵר, הֲרֵינִי מַטִּיל עֲלֵיהֶן

Rabbi Yosei ben Shaul then asked Rabbi Yehuda HaNasi: If the afterbirth is **tied to** the item that has the form of a crow, **what is** the *halakha*? Rabbi Yehuda HaNasi **said to him: You asked** about a **matter that does not exist.** Rabbi Yosei ben Shaul **raised an objection to** this response from a *baraita*: With regard to a woman **who discharges a type of domesticated animal, undomesticated animal, or bird, and** she discharges **an afterbirth with them,**[H] in an instance **when the afterbirth is tied to them we are not concerned about** the possibility of **another offspring.** If the **afterbirth is not tied to them, we are concerned that** the afterbirth contained **another offspring. And I impose upon them**

**PERSONALITIES**

**Rav Yosef son of Rav Menashya of D'vil – רַב יוֹסֵף בְּרֵיהּ דְּרַב מְנַשְּׁיָא מִדְּוִיל:** Although this second-generation *amora* was a disciple of Rav, after Rav's death he addressed his questions to Shmuel. Although the disciples of Rav did not hold his scholarship in high regard, he did transmit several important traditions from Rav. He apparently lived a long life, as it is recorded that his widow went to court before Rav Yosef, a third-generation *amora*.

**NOTES**

**Only to a viable item – אֶלָּא בְּדָבָר שֶׁל קַיָּימָא:** It is unclear what exactly is referred to as a viable item. Some commentaries maintain that the reference is specifically to a viable offspring, i.e., to one that survives. Other commentaries explain that a stillborn baby is also considered a viable item in this regard, as long as a fetus of its shape and degree of development is capable of surviving. But if a woman discharges a fetus that is incapable of surviving, e.g., one whose thigh is in the middle of its body, or whose body is deficient, or that looks like a type of animal, the afterbirth is not associated with it, even if the woman discharged the afterbirth within three days of her miscarriage. Rather, the presumption is that the afterbirth contained another offspring (Rashi; *Tosafot*).

**HALAKHA**

**One attributes an afterbirth only to a viable item – אֵין תּוֹלִין אֶת הַשִּׁלְיָא אֶלָּא בְּדָבָר שֶׁל קַיָּימָא:** If a woman discharged a stillborn baby and then discharged an afterbirth, the afterbirth is ascribed to another offspring, as an afterbirth can be associated only with a viable offspring, in accordance with the opinion of Rav (Rambam *Sefer Kedusha, Hilkhot Issurei Bia* 10:14; see *Shulḥan Arukh, Yoreh De'a* 194:4).

**A woman who discharges a type of domesticated animal, undomesticated animal, or bird, and an afterbirth with them – הַמַּפֶּלֶת מִין בְּהֵמָה חַיָּה וְעוֹף וְשִׁלְיָא עִמָּהֶן:** In a case where a woman discharged a type of domesticated animal, undomesticated animal, or bird, and discharged afterbirth, if the afterbirth was tied to the discharged item, there is no concern that it contained another offspring. If the afterbirth was not tied to the discharged item, there is concern that the afterbirth contained another offspring. Consequently, even if the discharged item appears to be male, the woman must observe the period of impurity of a woman who gave birth to a female, due to the uncertainty (*Shakh*) that perhaps the afterbirth contained a female offspring. The *Shakh* adds that nowadays a woman who discharges an item that has the shape of an animal observes the period of impurity of a woman who gave birth to a female regardless of the *halakha* of the afterbirth, as the halakhic authorities nowadays are not proficient in the differences between different discharged items (Rambam *Sefer Kedusha, Hilkhot Issurei Bia* 10:16; see *Shulḥan Arukh, Yoreh De'a* 194:7).

חומר שני ולדות, שאני אומר: שמא נמוח שפיר של שליא, ונמוח שליא של שפיר! תיובתא.

the **stringency of two offspring, as I say: Perhaps** the **gestational sac of** this **afterbirth,** which contained the offspring, **disintegrated, and** the **afterbirth of** the **gestational sac** containing the fetus shaped like an animal also **disintegrated.** If so, there are two offspring, and as it is possible that one is male and the other female, the mother must observe the strictures of one who gave birth to both a male and a female. In any event, this *baraita* is **a conclusive refutation** of Rabbi Yehuda HaNasi's claim that it is impossible for an afterbirth to be tied to a fetus that has the form of a bird.

אמר רבה בר שילא, אמר רב מתנה, אמר שמואל: מעשה ותלו את השליא בולד עד עשרה ימים, ולא אמרו תולין – אלא בשליא הבאה אחר הולד.

§ **Rabba bar Sheila says** that **Rav Mattana says** that **Shmuel says: An incident** occurred where the Sages **attributed the afterbirth** that a woman discharged **to an offspring** that was born **up to ten days** beforehand. **And** Shmuel added that the Sages **said** that one **attributes** an afterbirth to an offspring that was born **only** in the case **of an afterbirth that emerges after the offspring**[H] is born. By contrast, an afterbirth that emerges before the offspring is born is not attributed to that offspring.

אמר רבה בר בר חנה, אמר רבי יוחנן: מעשה ותלו את השליא בולד עד עשרים ושלשה ימים. אמר ליה רב יוסף – עד עשרים וארבעה אמרת לן.

**Rabba bar bar Ḥana says** that **Rabbi Yoḥanan says:** There was **an incident** where the Sages **attributed the afterbirth to an offspring** that was born **up to twenty-three days** beforehand. **Rav Yosef said to him** a correction of his statement: **You said to us** on another occasion that the offspring was born **up to twenty-four** days beforehand.

אמר רב אחא בריה דרב עוירא, אמר רבי יצחק: מעשה ונשתהה הולד אחר חבירו שלשים ושלשה יום. אמר ליה רב יוסף: שלשים וארבעה אמרת לן.

**Rav Aḥa, son of Rav Avira, says** that **Rabbi Yitzḥak says:** There was **an incident** where a woman was pregnant with twins, **and** one **offspring remained** in the womb for **thirty-three days after the other** offspring was born. **Rav Yosef said to him: You said to us** on another occasion that the second offspring was born **thirty-four**[N] days after the first.

הניחא למאן דאמר יולדת לתשעה יולדת למקוטעין – משכחת לה: אחד נגמרה צורתו לסוף שבעה, ואחד נגמרה צורתו לתחלת תשעה. אלא למאן דאמר יולדת לתשעה אינה יולדת למקוטעין, מאי איכא למימר?

The Gemara asks: **This works out well according to the one who says** that if a woman **gives birth** to a baby **in** her **ninth** month, **she can give birth prematurely** (see *Rosh HaShana* 11a). **You find** a situation where there could be such a difference between the births of the two twins if **the form of one** of the twin fetuses **was completed at the end of the seventh** month, and it is born at that stage, **and the form of** the other **one was completed at the beginning of the ninth** month, and it is born then. In such a case, there can be a difference of thirty-four days between the births. **But according to the one who says** that a woman who **gives birth** to a baby **in** her **ninth** month **cannot give birth prematurely,** but rather she gives birth at the end of the ninth month, **what is there to say?**

איפוך שמעתתא: שלשים ושלשה – לשליא, עשרים ושלשה – לולד.

The Gemara answers that one should **reverse the statements:** The difference of **thirty-three** days was stated **with regard to** a case of **an afterbirth** that was discharged an extended period after the birth of the offspring, whereas the gap of **twenty-three** days was stated **with regard to** a case of an **offspring** that was born after its twin.

**HALAKHA**

**And the Sages said that one attributes only in the case of an afterbirth that emerges after the offspring – ולא אמרו תולין אלא בשליא הבאה אחר הולד:** If a woman gave birth to a viable offspring and subsequently discharged an afterbirth within twenty-three days from the day she gave birth, not including the day she gave birth (*Shakh*), she need not be concerned that the afterbirth contained another offspring; she may ascribe the afterbirth to the offspring to whom she knows she gave birth. If a woman discharged a stillborn fetus and subsequently discharged an afterbirth, she must take into account that perhaps the afterbirth contained an additional offspring (Rambam *Sefer Kedusha*, *Hilkhot Issurei Bia* 10:14; see *Shulḥan Arukh*, *Yoreh De'a* 194:4).

**NOTES**

**You said to us up to twenty-four…you said to us thirty-four – עד עשרים וארבעה אמרת לן...שלשים וארבעה אמרת לן:** The *Arukh LaNer* explains that the tradition that there were twenty-three and thirty-three days refers to twenty-four-hour periods, whereas the tradition that there were twenty-four and thirty-four days refers to the days and not to the nights. Therefore there is no contradiction between the two versions.

אָמַר רַבִּי אָבִין בַּר רַב אַדָּא, אָמַר רַב מְנַחֵם אִישׁ כְּפַר שְׁעָרִים, וְאָמְרִי לַהּ בֵּית שְׁעָרִים: מַעֲשֶׂה וְנִשְׁתַּהָה וָלָד אֶחָד אַחַר חֲבֵירוֹ שְׁלֹשָׁה חֳדָשִׁים, וַהֲרֵי הֵם יוֹשְׁבִים לְפָנֵינוּ בְּבֵית הַמִּדְרָשׁ. וּמַאן נִינְהוּ? יְהוּדָה וְחִזְקִיָּה בְּנֵי רַבִּי חִיָּיא.

**Rabbi Avin bar Rav Adda says** that **Rav Menaḥem of the village of She'arim, and some say** that he was from **Beit She'arim,**[B] **says: An incident** occurred where **one offspring remained** in the womb **after the other** was born for **three months, and** both twins **are sitting before us in the study hall. And who are they?** They are **Yehuda and Ḥizkiyya, the sons of Rabbi Ḥiyya.**[PN]

וְהָא אָמַר מָר: אֵין אִשָּׁה מִתְעַבֶּרֶת, וְחוֹזֶרֶת וּמִתְעַבֶּרֶת! אָמַר אַבָּיֵי: טִיפָּה אַחַת הָיְתָה וְנִתְחַלְּקָה לִשְׁתַּיִם, אֶחָד נִגְמְרָה צוּרָתוֹ בִּתְחִלַּת שִׁבְעָה, וְאֶחָד בְּסוֹף תִּשְׁעָה.

The Gemara asks: **But didn't the Master say** that **a woman cannot become pregnant and again become pregnant**[N] with another offspring while she is pregnant with the first? **Abaye says:** Both twins were conceived at the same time; **it was one drop** of semen **and it split into two. The form of one was completed at the beginning of the seventh** month, **and** the form of the other **one** was completed **at the end of the ninth** month.

״שִׁלְיָא בַּבַּיִת הַבַּיִת טָמֵא״. תָּנוּ רַבָּנַן: שִׁלְיָא בַּבַּיִת – הַבַּיִת טָמֵא. לֹא שֶׁהַשִּׁלְיָא וָלָד, אֶלָּא שֶׁאֵין שִׁלְיָא שֶׁאֵין וָלָד עִמָּהּ, דִּבְרֵי רַבִּי מֵאִיר. רַבִּי יוֹסֵי וְרַבִּי יְהוּדָה וְרַבִּי שִׁמְעוֹן מְטַהֲרִין.

§ The mishna teaches that if there is **an afterbirth in the house, the house is impure** in the sense that everything under the roof contracts impurity imparted by a corpse. **The Sages taught** in a *baraita*: If there is **an afterbirth in the house, the house is impure.** The reason is **not that the** status of **an afterbirth** is that of **an offspring; rather,** it is **that there is no afterbirth without an offspring,** and the offspring rendered the contents of the house impure. This is **the statement of Rabbi Meir. Rabbi Yosei and Rabbi Yehuda and Rabbi Shimon deem** the contents of the house **pure.**

אָמְרוּ לוֹ לְרַבִּי מֵאִיר: אִי אַתָּה מוֹדֶה שֶׁאִם הוֹצִיאוּהוּ בְּסֵפֶל לְבַיִת הַחִיצוֹן שֶׁהוּא טָהוֹר? אָמַר לָהֶן: אֲבָל! וְלָמָּה – לְפִי שֶׁאֵינוֹ.

These Sages **said to Rabbi Meir: Do you not concede that if** people **removed** the afterbirth **to the outer room** of the house **in a basin, that** the room **is pure?** Rabbi Meir **said to them** in response: **Indeed,** that room is pure; **but why** so? **Because** the offspring **does not exist** anymore, i.e., it presumably disintegrated while it was moved from place to place.

אָמְרוּ לוֹ: כְּשֵׁם שֶׁאֵינוֹ בְּבַיִת הַחִיצוֹן – כָּךְ אֵינוֹ בְּבַיִת הַפְּנִימִי! אָמַר לָהֶן: אֵינוֹ דּוֹמֶה נִמּוֹק פַּעַם אַחַת לְנִמּוֹק שְׁתֵּי פְעָמִים.

These Sages **said to him: Just as** the offspring **does not exist** when the afterbirth is moved **to the outer room, so too, it does not exist** when the afterbirth is **in the inner room** either. In other words, the offspring presumably disintegrated while it was moved from the woman's womb to the place in the house where it is located. Rabbi Meir **said to them:** A situation in which the offspring **disintegrated once,** when the afterbirth was moved to its first location in the house, **is not comparable to** a case where the offspring **disintegrated twice,** i.e., when the afterbirth was first moved to the interior room of the house and then moved to the outer room.

**PERSONALITIES**

**Yehuda and Ḥizkiyya the sons of Rabbi Ḥiyya – יְהוּדָה וְחִזְקִיָּה בְּנֵי רַבִּי חִיָּיא:** Yehuda and Ḥizkiyya, twin sons of Rabbi Ḥiyya and his wife, Yehudit, were among the most prominent first-generation *amora'im* of Eretz Yisrael. They studied Torah in poverty throughout their lives, and were eventually recognized as outstanding Torah scholars.

Yehuda and Ḥizkiyya moved from Babylonia to Eretz Yisrael with their parents. Like his father, Ḥizkiyya compiled collections of *baraitot*, cited occasionally in the Gemara with the introduction: A Sage from the school of Ḥizkiyya taught. He had many students, some of whom became prominent Torah scholars, including Rabbi Yoḥanan. Ḥizkiyya lived in Tiberias.

Yehuda, who was apparently the firstborn, married the daughter of Rabbi Yannai and died during his father-in-law's lifetime. Rabbi Yannai held his son-in-law Yehuda in high esteem; he nicknamed him Sinai and would stand before him.

**NOTES**

**They are Yehuda and Ḥizkiyya the sons of Rabbi Ḥiyya – יְהוּדָה וְחִזְקִיָּה בְּנֵי רַבִּי חִיָּיא:** The early commentaries note that the three-month difference between the births of Yehuda and Ḥizkiyya contradicts the statement of Rav (26b) that when a woman is pregnant with two fetuses, one of the fetuses does not remain in the womb after the other is born. Furthermore, as Yehuda and Ḥizkiyya were cousins of Rav, Rav must have been aware of the circumstances of their birth.

Some of the early commentaries claim that Rav was in fact not aware that Yehuda and Ḥizkiyya were born in this manner, but the Ramban writes that this is highly implausible. Others explain that Rav's statement is referring to a case where both fetuses have developed sufficiently to be born; if one of the fetuses has not yet developed sufficiently, it might remain in the womb after its twin is born, even for an extended period of time. This was the case with Yehuda and Ḥizkiyya (Ran). Yet others maintain that although Rav was aware of the possibility of the birth of one offspring a significant period of time after the other, he considered it a rare case that need not be taken into account (*Tosafot*).

**A woman cannot become pregnant and again become pregnant – אֵין אִשָּׁה מִתְעַבֶּרֶת וְחוֹזֶרֶת וּמִתְעַבֶּרֶת:** The early commentaries disagree with regard to the exact meaning of this statement. Some maintain that a pregnant woman cannot become pregnant with another offspring at all (Rabbeinu Tam). Others hold that a pregnant woman can become pregnant with another offspring, but that offspring becomes a sandal fetus (Rashi on 45a). Another opinion is that the first offspring becomes a sandal fetus (*Tosefot Rid*). *Tosafot* on tractate *Sota* (42b) cite the Jerusalem Talmud, where it is suggested that a woman can be pregnant from several men simultaneously.

**BACKGROUND**

**Beit She'arim – בֵּית שְׁעָרִים:** Beit She'arim was a small village in the Jezreel Valley, in an area that is today called Sheikh Abreik. The Sanhedrin was located there during the lifetime of Rabbi Yehuda HaNasi, and he was buried there, despite the fact that before he died he moved to Tzippori for health reasons. The cemetery of Beit She'arim consequently became prestigious, and for several centuries prominent families from Eretz Yisrael as well as from the Diaspora buried their deceased there. This large cemetery was revealed in recent years.

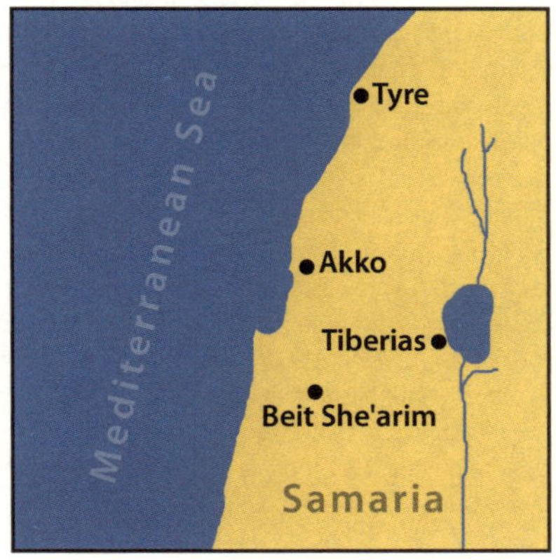


Location of Beit She'arim

Rabbi Yehuda HaNasi's burial site in Beit She'arim

Remains of ancient synagogue in Beit She'arim

## LANGUAGE

Ladle [*tarvad*] – תַּרְוָד: This term, which means ladle, also exists in other Semitic languages. Because ladles do not have a uniform size, the Gemara (50b) defines the size of the halakhic measurement referred to as a ladleful.

## NOTES

A ladleful of dust into which any amount of dirt fell – מְלֹא תַּרְוָד רָקָב שֶׁנָּפַל לְתוֹכוֹ עָפָר כׇּל שֶׁהוּ: The early commentaries explain that according to the Sages of Rav's study hall, who maintain that the house is pure according to Rabbi Shimon because the measure of the dust of a corpse in the mixture is insufficient to render the house impure, this is referring to precisely a ladleful of dust. If there is a larger amount of dust of a corpse, a tiny amount of dirt does not nullify its impurity. But according to Rabba, who explains that Rabbi Shimon rules that the dust of a corpse has the impurity status of a corpse only if it is not mingled, the reference is to any amount of dust. If so, the reason the *baraita* mentions specifically a ladleful of dust is in order to emphasize that according to the Rabbis even this minimal amount renders the house impure, despite the fact that there is some dirt mixed with it (Ritva).

## HALAKHA

A ladleful of dust into which any amount of dirt fell – מְלֹא תַּרְוָד רָקָב שֶׁנָּפַל לְתוֹכוֹ עָפָר כׇּל שֶׁהוּ: In a case where the dust of a corpse is impure, as it was buried naked in a marble or glass coffin, if a minimal amount of dirt is mixed in the dust, it remains impure, in accordance with the opinion of the Rabbis (Rambam *Sefer Tahara*, *Hilkhot Tumat Met* 3:4).

יְתֵיב רַב פָּפָּא אֲחוֹרֵי דְּרַב בֵּיבָי קַמֵּיהּ דְּרַב הַמְנוּנָא, וִיתֵיב וְקָאָמַר: מַאי טַעְמָא דְּרַבִּי שִׁמְעוֹן – קָסָבַר כׇּל טוּמְאָה שֶׁנִּתְעָרֵב בָּהּ מִמִּין אַחֵר – בָּטְלָה.

§ **Rav Pappa sat behind Rav Beivai** in the study hall **before** their teacher **Rav Hamnuna, and he sat and said: What is the reason** for the opinion **of Rabbi Shimon,** that a house in which there is an afterbirth is pure? **He holds** that with regard to **any** item that has **ritual impurity with which** there **was mixed** an item **of another type,** it **is nullified** by the other item and is pure. Consequently, in the case of an offspring that disintegrated, the disintegrated offspring is nullified by the blood of the childbirth.

אֲמַר לְהוּ רַב פָּפָּא: הַיְינוּ נָמֵי טַעְמַיְיהוּ דְּרַבִּי יְהוּדָה וְרַבִּי יוֹסֵי. אַחִיכוּ עֲלֵיהּ: מַאי שְׁנָא? פְּשִׁיטָא!

**Rav Pappa said to** Rav Beivai, who was a greater scholar than he, and to Rav Hamnuna his teacher: **This is also the reason** for the opinion **of Rabbi Yehuda and Rabbi Yosei,** who agree with Rabbi Shimon in the above *baraita*. Rav Beivai and Rav Hamnuna **laughed at him: What is different** about the opinion of Rabbi Yehuda and Rabbi Yosei? Since the statement of Rabbi Shimon is attributed to them as well, it is **obvious** that their reasoning is the same.

אָמַר רַב פָּפָּא: אֲפִילּוּ כִּי הָא מִילְּתָא לֵימָא אִינִישׁ וְלָא נִשְׁתּוֹק קַמֵּיהּ רַבֵּיהּ, מִשּׁוּם שֶׁנֶּאֱמַר "אִם נָבַלְתָּ בְהִתְנַשֵּׂא וְאִם זַמּוֹתָ יָד לְפֶה".

**Rav Pappa said** with regard to this incident: **A person should say a matter even** as obvious **as this** one, **and one should not be silent in the presence of his teacher,** despite the possibility that other people might laugh at him, **because it is stated: "If you have done foolishly in lifting up yourself, or if you have planned devices [*zammota*], lay your hand over your mouth"** (Proverbs 30:32). One who acts "foolishly" over matters of Torah by not hesitating to issue statements that might be ridiculed will ultimately be exalted and lifted up. Conversely, one who muzzles [*zamam*] himself due to embarrassment will end up with his hand over his mouth, unable to answer questions that are posed to him.

וְאָזְדָא רַבִּי שִׁמְעוֹן לְטַעְמֵיהּ, דְּתַנְיָא: מְלֹא תַּרְוָד רָקָב שֶׁנָּפַל לְתוֹכוֹ עָפָר כׇּל שֶׁהוּ – טָמֵא, וְרַבִּי שִׁמְעוֹן מְטַהֵר.

With regard to Rabbi Shimon's opinion that the woman is pure because the offspring is nullified by the blood of childbirth, the Gemara notes: **And Rabbi Shimon follows his** standard line of **reasoning, as it is taught** in a *baraita*: In the case of **a ladleful** [***melo tarvad***][L] **of dust** from a corpse, which is the minimum amount that renders everything in a house impure, **into which any amount of dirt fell,**[NH] the house is **impure; and Rabbi Shimon deems** it **pure.**

מַאי טַעְמָא דְּרַבִּי שִׁמְעוֹן? אָמַר רַבָּה, אַשְׁכַּחְתִּינְהוּ לְרַבָּנַן דְּבֵי רַב דְּיָתְבִי וְקָאָמְרִי: אִי אֶפְשָׁר שֶׁלֹּא יִרְבּוּ שְׁתֵּי פְרִידוֹת עָפָר עַל פְּרִידָה אַחַת שֶׁל רָקָב, וְחָסֵיר לֵיהּ.

The Gemara asks: **What is the reason** for the opinion **of Rabbi Shimon?** Why is the house pure when it contains a ladleful of dust from a corpse? **Rabba said: I found the Sages of the study hall of Rav sitting and saying:** The reason Rabbi Shimon deems the house pure is that **it is impossible for** there **not to be two grains of dirt** that are **more than one grain of dust** from the corpse, in a certain place in the mixture. **And** as that grain of dust from the corpse is nullified by the dirt, the amount of dust that remains **is insufficient** for rendering the house impure.

וְאָמֵינָא לְהוּ: אַדְּרַבָּה, אִי אֶפְשָׁר שֶׁלֹּא יִרְבּוּ שְׁתֵּי פְרִידוֹת רָקָב עַל פְּרִידָה אַחַת עָפָר וְנָפֵיל לֵיהּ שִׁיעוּרָא!

**And I said to them: On the contrary,** according to this reasoning the house should certainly be impure, as **it is impossible for** there **not to be two grains of dust** from the corpse that are **more than one grain of dirt** in a certain place in the mixture. That grain of dirt is thereby nullified by the dust of the corpse, **and** consequently **the measure** of the dust **increases.**[N]

Perek **III**
Daf **27** Amud **b**

## NOTES

And the measure of the dust increases – וְנָפֵיל לֵיהּ שִׁיעוּרָא: The standard text of the Gemara reads: And the measure of the dust falls [*venafeil*]. In *Masoret HaShas* the text is emended to read: Increases [*venafeish*].

אֶלָּא אֲמַר רַבָּה: הַיְינוּ טַעֲמָא דְּרַבִּי שִׁמְעוֹן, סוֹפוֹ כִּתְחִלָּתוֹ, מַה תְּחִלָּתוֹ – נַעֲשָׂה לוֹ דָּבָר אַחֵר גַּנְגִּילוֹן, אַף סוֹפוֹ – נַעֲשָׂה לוֹ דָּבָר אַחֵר גַּנְגִּילוֹן.

**Rather, Rabba said** that **this is the reason** for the opinion **of Rabbi Shimon:** The *halakha* with regard to a corpse in **its ultimate state** of dust **is like** the *halakha* in **its initial state** of decomposition: **Just** as with regard to **its initial state,** if **another matter** is mixed with the decomposing corpse it **serves as a nullification** [*gangilon*][L] **of** the corpse's impurity, as the dust of a decomposed corpse can impart impurity only if it is not mingled with the dust of any other substance, **so too,** in the corpse's **ultimate state** of dust, if **another matter** is mixed with it, that **serves as a nullification of** the impurity of the dust.[N]

מַאי הִיא? דְּתַנְיָא: אֵיזֶהוּ מֵת שֶׁיֵּשׁ לוֹ רָקָב וְאֵיזֶהוּ מֵת שֶׁאֵין לוֹ רָקָב: נִקְבַּר עָרוֹם בְּאָרוֹן שֶׁל שַׁיִשׁ, אוֹ עַל גַּבֵּי רִצְפָּה שֶׁל אֲבָנִים – זֶהוּ מֵת שֶׁיֵּשׁ לוֹ רָקָב,

The Gemara asks: **What is** the source for the *halakha* that the dust of a corpse imparts impurity only if it is not mingled with the dust of any other substance? The Gemara answers: **As it is taught** in a *baraita*: **Which is a corpse that has** the *halakha* **of dust,**[H] i.e., whose dust imparts impurity; **and which is a corpse that does not have** the *halakha* of **dust?** If a corpse **was buried naked in a marble coffin or on a stone floor,**[N] **that is a corpse that has** the *halakha* **of dust** that imparts impurity. Since any dust found there must have come from the corpse, it imparts impurity.

וְאֵיזֶהוּ מֵת שֶׁאֵין לוֹ רָקָב – נִקְבַּר בִּכְסוּתוֹ, אוֹ בְּאָרוֹן שֶׁל עֵץ, אוֹ עַל גַּבֵּי רִצְפָּה שֶׁל לְבֵנִים – זֶהוּ מֵת שֶׁאֵין לוֹ רָקָב. וְלֹא אָמְרוּ רָקָב – אֶלָּא לַמֵּת בִּלְבַד, לְמַעוּטֵי הָרוּג – דְּלָא.

**And what is a corpse that does not have** the *halakha* **of dust?** If a corpse **was buried in its cloak, or in a wooden coffin, or on a brick floor, that is a corpse that does not have** the *halakha* **of dust** that imparts impurity, as it is assumed that some of the dust is from particles of the clothes, wood, or bricks, and the dust from a decomposed corpse imparts impurity only if it is not mingled with the dust of any other substance. The *baraita* adds another *halakha* with regard to the impurity of the dust of a corpse: **And** the Sages **said** that the **dust** of a corpse is impure **only with regard to** the corpse of a person who **died** naturally,[H] **excluding one who was killed, whose** dust **is not** impure.

גּוּפָא: מְלֹא תַּרְוָד רָקָב שֶׁנָּפַל לְתוֹכוֹ עָפָר כָּל שֶׁהוּא – טָמֵא, וְרַבִּי שִׁמְעוֹן מְטַהֵר. מְלֹא תַּרְוָד רָקָב שֶׁנִּתְפַּזֵּר בַּבַּיִת – הַבַּיִת טָמֵא, וְרַבִּי שִׁמְעוֹן מְטַהֵר.

§ The Gemara returns to discuss **the** matter **itself,** i.e., the *baraita* cited above that clarifies the opinion of Rabbi Shimon: In the case of **a ladleful of dust** from a corpse **into which any amount of dirt fell,** the house **is impure; and Rabbi Shimon deems** it **pure.** The *baraita* continues: In the case of **a ladleful of dust** from a corpse **that was scattered in the house,**[H] **the house is impure.** Provided that there is a sufficient amount of dust in the house, the house is impure, even if the dust is scattered. **And Rabbi Shimon deems** it **pure.**

וּצְרִיכָא. דְּאִי אַשְׁמְעִינַן קַמַּיְיתָא – בְּהַהִיא קָאָמְרִי רַבָּנַן – מִשּׁוּם דִּמְכַנִּיף, אֲבָל נִתְפַּזֵּר – אֵימָא מוֹדוּ לוֹ לְרַבִּי שִׁמְעוֹן דְּאֵין מַאֲהִיל וְחוֹזֵר וּמַאֲהִיל.

The Gemara comments: **And it is necessary** for the *baraita* to state both of these *halakhot*. **As, if** the *baraita* had **taught us** only **the first** *halakha*, with regard to dust from a corpse in which dirt was mixed, one might have thought that it is specifically **in that** case that **the Rabbis say** the house is impure, **because** the dust is **concentrated** in one place; **but** if the dust **was scattered,** one might **say** that the Rabbis **concede to Rabbi Shimon that** the house is pure. The reasoning is **that** if an item **overlies** a collection of dust of a corpse that is insufficient to render it impure **and also overlies** another collection of similar size, where together these collections constitute a sufficient amount to render the item and everything under it impure, it **is not** impure.

**LANGUAGE**

Nullification [*gangilon*] – גַּנְגִּילוֹן: Some explain this term as referring to a matter that contradicts another matter, nullifying and ruining it (Rashi). Others explain that it refers to a matter that is rolled up with another matter (*Tosafot*; *Arukh*). Another interpretation is that this term derives from the Latin word cingula, meaning belt, i.e., an item that surrounds other items (see Rabbi Shimshon of Saens).

**HALAKHA**

**Which is a corpse that has the *halakha* of dust, etc. – אֵיזֶהוּ מֵת שֶׁיֵּשׁ לוֹ רָקָב וכו׳:** The dust of a corpse imparts impurity only if the corpse was buried naked in a marble or glass coffin and is whole. If a limb is missing, or if the corpse was buried in its garment, or if it was buried in a wooden or metal coffin, the dust does not impart impurity, as the dust of the garment or wood, or the rust of the metal, mixes with the dust of the corpse (Rambam *Sefer Tahara, Hilkhot Tumat Met* 3:4).

**The Sages said the dust is impure only with regard to the corpse of a person who died naturally – וְלֹא אָמְרוּ רָקָב אֶלָּא לַמֵּת בִּלְבַד:** The *halakha* that the dust of a corpse imparts impurity applies only in the case of a person who died naturally, i.e., one who was not killed (Rambam *Sefer Tahara, Hilkhot Tumat Met* 3:4).

**A ladleful of dust from a corpse that was scattered in the house – מְלֹא תַּרְוָד רָקָב שֶׁנִּתְפַּזֵּר בַּבַּיִת:** Two handfuls of dust of a corpse that is scattered in a house renders the house impure, in accordance with the opinion of the first *tanna* of the *baraita* (Rambam *Sefer Tahara, Hilkhot Tumat Met* 4:10).

**NOTES**

**So too, in its ultimate state, another matter serves as a nullification of it – אַף סוֹפוֹ נַעֲשָׂה לוֹ דָּבָר אַחֵר גַּנְגִּילוֹן:** According to this interpretation of Rabbi Shimon's opinion, the case of an afterbirth cannot be compared to that of dust from a corpse (Rashi).

**In a marble coffin or on a stone floor – בְּאָרוֹן שֶׁל שַׁיִשׁ אוֹ עַל גַּבֵּי רִצְפָּה שֶׁל אֲבָנִים:** This wording indicates that one or the other suffices; if the corpse is buried either in a marble coffin or on a stone floor, its dust is impure. By contrast, in the *Tosefta* this *halakha* reads: In a marble coffin and on a stone sheet. The early commentaries conclude from the version of the Gemara that for the dust to be impure, the corpse must be buried naked in a marble or stone coffin that has a marble covering, so that nothing mixes with its dust (Rambam's Commentary on the Mishna). It is added that a glass coffin also suffices, as long as the corpse is whole. By contrast, the dust of a corpse that is buried in a metal coffin is not impure (Rambam *Sefer Tahara, Hilkhot Tumat Met* 3:4).

HALAKHA

A ladleful of dirt from a cemetery and slightly more – מְלֹא תַּרְוָד וְעוֹד עֲפַר בֵּית הַקְּבָרוֹת: If more than two handfuls of dirt is found under a corpse or in a grave, and it is unclear whether it is dust from a corpse and therefore imparts impurity to items that are under the same roof, or whether it is merely dirt that absorbed the decomposed flesh and blood of the corpse, the dirt imparts impurity to items that are under the same roof and to one who carries the dirt, in accordance with the opinion of the first *tanna* of the mishna in tractate *Oholot*. This is because even if dirt mixed with the dust, there are presumably two handfuls of dust in the mixture. The Rambam adds that this *halakha* is apparently rabbinic law (Rambam *Sefer Tahara, Hilkhot Tumat Met* 3:8).

A large animal that expelled a mass of congealed blood – בְּהֵמָה גַּסָּה שֶׁשָּׁפְעָה חֲרָרַת דָּם: If a large animal discharged a mass of congealed blood, its future offspring is exempt from being counted a firstborn. Although the mass has no sanctity, it is buried in order to publicize that the animal's subsequent offspring does not have the status of a firstborn. Despite this exemption, the mass does not transmit impurity to one who touches it or to one who carries it, unless it has the form of a stillborn fetus. The reason for this is that the offspring is nullified, as there is a majority of other substances that are discharged with it (Rambam *Sefer Korbanot, Hilkhot Bekhorot* 4:11 and *Sefer Tahara, Hilkhot She'ar Avot HaTumot* 1:16; *Shulḥan Arukh, Yoreh De'a* 315:7).

NOTES

In order to publicize that the animal is exempt from having its future offspring being counted a firstborn – כְּדֵי לְפַרְסְמָהּ שֶׁהִיא פְּטוּרָה מִן הַבְּכוֹרָה: Rashi on tractate *Bekhorot* (22a) explains that burial of the mass of blood publicizes that the mass is considered an offspring and has firstborn status; otherwise, people might assume that it is not considered offspring.

וְאִי אַשְׁמְעִינַן בְּהָא – בְּהָא קָאָמַר רַבִּי שִׁמְעוֹן דְּאֵין מַאֲהִיל וְחוֹזֵר וּמַאֲהִיל, אֲבָל בְּהָא – אֵימָא מוֹדֶה לְהוּ לְרַבָּנַן, צְרִיכָא.

**And if** the *baraita* had **taught us** the *halakha* only **with regard to this** second case, where the dust of the corpse was scattered, one might have thought that it is specifically **in this** case that **Rabbi Shimon says** that the house is pure, as an item that **overlies** an insufficient collection of the dust of a corpse **and also overlies** another collection, where together these collections constitute a sufficient amount to render the item impure, **is not** impure. **But in that** first case, where dirt was mixed with the dust of the corpse, one might **say** that Rabbi Shimon **concedes to the Rabbis** that the house is impure. Therefore, it is **necessary** for the *baraita* to teach both cases.

תַּנְיָא אִידָךְ: מְלֹא תַּרְוָד וְעוֹד עֲפַר בֵּית הַקְּבָרוֹת – טָמֵא. וְרַבִּי שִׁמְעוֹן מְטַהֵר. מַאי טַעְמַיְיהוּ דְּרַבָּנַן? לְפִי שֶׁאִי אֶפְשָׁר לִמְלֹא תַּרְוָד וְעוֹד עֲפַר בֵּית הַקְּבָרוֹת שֶׁאֵין בּוֹ מְלֹא תַּרְוָד רָקָב.

There is a different dispute between Rabbi Shimon and the Rabbis that **is taught** in **another** mishna (*Oholot* 2:2): If a house contains **a ladleful of dirt from a cemetery and** slightly **more,**[H] the house **is impure; and Rabbi Shimon deems** it **pure.** The Gemara asks: **What is the reason** for the opinion **of the Rabbis?** The Gemara answers: They deem the house impure **as it is impossible for** slightly **more than a ladleful of dirt from a cemetery not to contain a ladleful of dust** from a corpse.

הַשְׁתָּא דַּאֲמַרְתְּ טַעְמָא דְּרַבִּי שִׁמְעוֹן מִשּׁוּם סוֹפוֹ כִּתְחִלָּתוֹ, גַּבֵּי שִׁלְיָא מַאי טַעְמָא? אָמַר רַבִּי יוֹחָנָן: מִשּׁוּם בִּטּוּל בְּרוֹב נָגְעוּ בָּהּ.

§ The Gemara asks: **Now that you say** that **the reason that Rabbi Shimon** deems the house pure, in a case where it contains dust from a corpse in which dirt was mixed, is **that** in his opinion the *halakha* of a corpse in **its ultimate state** of dust **is like** the *halakha* in **its initial state** of decomposition, then **with regard to** a case where there is **an afterbirth** in the house, **what is the reason** that Rabbi Shimon deems the house pure? **Rabbi Yoḥanan says:** The Sages **touched upon it,** i.e., deemed the house pure, **due to** the **nullification** of the disintegrated offspring **by** the **majority** of the blood that emerged during the miscarriage, in which the afterbirth was mixed.

וְאָזְדָא רַבִּי יוֹחָנָן לְטַעְמֵיהּ, דְּאָמַר רַבִּי יוֹחָנָן: רַבִּי שִׁמְעוֹן וְרַבִּי אֱלִיעֶזֶר בֶּן יַעֲקֹב אָמְרוּ דָּבָר אֶחָד. רַבִּי שִׁמְעוֹן – הָא דַּאֲמַרַן. רַבִּי אֱלִיעֶזֶר – דִּתְנַן, רַבִּי אֱלִיעֶזֶר בֶּן יַעֲקֹב אוֹמֵר: בְּהֵמָה גַּסָּה שֶׁשָּׁפְעָה חֲרָרַת דָּם – הֲרֵי זוֹ תִּקָּבֵר, וּפְטוּרָה מִן הַבְּכוֹרָה.

**And Rabbi Yoḥanan follows his** line of **reasoning** in this regard, **as Rabbi Yoḥanan says: Rabbi Shimon and Rabbi Eliezer ben Ya'akov** both **said the same thing,** i.e., they both issued rulings based on the same principle. The relevant statement of **Rabbi Shimon** is **that which we said,** i.e., that if a woman discharged an afterbirth the house is pure, as the offspring is nullified by the blood that emerged during the miscarriage. **Rabbi Eliezer** ben Ya'akov said that **which is taught** in a mishna (*Bekhorot* 21a): **Rabbi Eliezer ben Ya'akov says:** In the case of **a large animal that expelled a mass of** congealed **blood,**[H] **that** mass **must be buried,** as perhaps there was a male fetus there, which was consecrated as a firstborn when it emerged, **and** the animal **is exempt from** having any future offspring being counted **a firstborn.**

וְתָנֵי רַבִּי חִיָּיא עֲלַהּ: אֵינָהּ מְטַמְּאָה לֹא בְּמַגָּע וְלֹא בְּמַשָּׂא. וּמֵאַחַר שֶׁאֵינָהּ מְטַמְּאָה לֹא בְּמַגָּע וְלֹא בְּמַשָּׂא, אַמַּאי תִּקָּבֵר? כְּדֵי לְפַרְסְמָהּ שֶׁהִיא פְּטוּרָה מִן הַבְּכוֹרָה.

**And Rabbi Ḥiyya teaches** a *baraita* **with regard to that** *halakha*: The mass of congealed blood **does not impart ritual impurity, neither through** physical **contact nor through carrying** it. It does not have the status of an unslaughtered animal carcass, which does impart impurity in such manners. The Gemara asks: **But since** the mass **does not impart impurity, neither through contact nor through carrying,** which indicates that it is not considered a fetus, **why** must it be **buried?** The Gemara answers: It must be buried **in order to publicize that** the animal **is exempt from** having its future offspring being counted **a firstborn.**[N]

אַלְמָא וָלָד מְעַלְּיָא הוּא, וְאַמַּאי תָּנֵי רַבִּי חִיָּיא אֵינָהּ מְטַמְּאָה לֹא בְּמַגָּע וְלֹא בְּמַשָּׂא? אָמַר רַבִּי יוֹחָנָן: מִשּׁוּם בִּטּוּל בְּרוֹב נָגְעוּ בָּהּ.

The Gemara asks: If the animal's subsequent offspring is not counted a firstborn, **evidently** the mass **is** treated like **a full-fledged offspring. But** if so, **why does Rabbi Ḥiyya teach** that **it does not impart impurity, neither through** physical **contact nor through carrying? Rabbi Yoḥanan says:** It is **due to** the halakhic **nullification** of a foreign substance **in a majority** of permitted substances that the Sages **touched upon it,** to exclude it from impurity through contact or carrying. In other words, the fetus is considered a full-fledged offspring, but it does not impart impurity, because it is nullified by the rest of the congealed mass.

אָמַר רַבִּי אַמִי, אָמַר רַבִּי יוֹחָנָן: וּמוֹדֶה רַבִּי שִׁמְעוֹן שֶׁאִמּוֹ טְמֵאָה לֵידָה.

§ The Gemara resumes its discussion of the opinion of Rabbi Shimon that if a woman discharges an afterbirth in a house, the house is pure. **Rabbi Ami says** that **Rabbi Yoḥanan says: And Rabbi Shimon concedes that its mother is impure** with the impurity of a woman after **childbirth.**

אֲמַר הַהוּא סָבָא לְרַבִּי אַמִי: אַסְבְּרָא לָךְ טַעְמָא דְּרַבִּי יוֹחָנָן, דַּאֲמַר קְרָא ״אִשָּׁה כִּי תַזְרִיעַ וְיָלְדָה זָכָר״ וגו׳ – אֲפִילּוּ לֹא יָלְדָה אֶלָּא כְּעֵין שֶׁהִזְרִיעָה – טְמֵאָה לֵידָה.

**A certain elder said to Rabbi Ami: I will explain to you the reason** for the statement **of Rabbi Yoḥanan. As the verse states: "If a woman bears seed and gives birth to a male,** she shall be impure seven days, as in the days of the menstruation of her sickness she shall be impure" (Leviticus 12:2). This indicates that **even** if a woman **gives birth to** an offspring that is **similar only to the seed that she bore,** i.e., if the offspring liquefied and became similar to semen, the woman is **impure** with the impurity of a woman after **childbirth.**

רֵישׁ לָקִישׁ אָמַר: שָׁפִיר שֶׁטְּרָפוּהוּ בְּמֵימָיו – נַעֲשָׂה כְּמֵת שֶׁנִּתְבַּלְבְּלָה צוּרָתוֹ.

§ **Reish Lakish says:** In the case of a fetus in **a gestational sac, that was mashed in its** amniotic **fluid**[H] by being shaken violently, **it is rendered like a corpse that was deformed,** and therefore it does not impart impurity to other items that are under the same roof.

אֲמַר לֵיהּ רַבִּי יוֹחָנָן לְרֵישׁ לָקִישׁ: מֵת שֶׁנִּתְבַּלְבְּלָה צוּרָתוֹ מְנָלַן דְּטָהוֹר? אִילֵימָא מֵהָא דְּאָמַר רַבִּי שַׁבְּתַאי אָמַר רַבִּי יִצְחָק מִגְדְּלָאָה, וְאָמְרִי לַהּ אָמַר רַבִּי יִצְחָק מִגְדְּלָאָה אָמַר רַבִּי שַׁבְּתַאי: מֵת שֶׁנִּשְׂרַף וְשִׁלְדּוֹ קַיֶּימֶת – טָמֵא, מַעֲשֶׂה הָיָה וְטִמְּאוּ לוֹ פְּתָחִים גְּדוֹלִים,

**Rabbi Yoḥanan said to Reish Lakish: From where do we** derive **that a corpse that was deformed**[H] **is pure? If we say** it is derived **from that which Rabbi Shabbtai**[P] **says** that **Rabbi Yitzḥak from Migdal** [*Migdala'a*][P] **says, and some say** from that which **Rabbi Yitzḥak from Migdal says** that **Rabbi Shabbtai says,** that cannot be correct. The Gemara cites the relevant statement: With regard to **a corpse that was burned but its form** [*veshildo*] still **exists,**[NH] i.e., it still has the form of a human corpse, it **is impure. There was an incident** involving such a corpse, **and** the Sages **deemed impure** all items that were under the **large openings** of the house where the corpse was located, as these openings were fit for the removal of the corpse from the house through them.

**NOTES**

A corpse that was burned but its form [*shildo*] exists – מֵת שֶׁנִּשְׂרַף וְשִׁלְדּוֹ קַיֶּימֶת: The early commentaries disagree with regard to the meaning of the word *shildo*. Some say that it means its body or form, i.e., although the corpse was burned, the ashes did not scatter, either because it was only charred, or because it was burned in a box or coffin (Rashi; Meiri). Others interpret the word as referring to the spine and ribs, which are the main part of a skeleton, a *sheled* (*Arukh*; Rambam *Sefer Tahara*, *Hilkhot Tumat Met* 3:9).

**HALAKHA**

A gestational sac that was mashed in its fluid – שָׁפִיר שֶׁטְּרָפוּהוּ בְּמֵימָיו: A gestational sac in which tissue developed that was mashed in its amniotic fluid is pure, because the fetus was deformed. This is in accordance with the opinion of Reish Lakish (Rambam *Sefer Tahara*, *Hilkhot Tumat Met* 3:9).

A corpse that was deformed – מֵת שֶׁנִּתְבַּלְבְּלָה צוּרָתוֹ: A corpse that was deformed as a result of being burned is pure, in accordance with the opinion of Reish Lakish (Rambam *Sefer Tahara*, *Hilkhot Tumat Met* 3:9).

A corpse that was burned but its form exists – מֵת שֶׁנִּשְׂרַף וְשִׁלְדּוֹ קַיֶּימֶת: If a corpse was burned but its spine and ribs remain intact, it imparts impurity like a whole corpse. Needless to say, if a corpse was merely charred, it still has the status of a whole corpse (Rambam *Sefer Tahara*, *Hilkhot Tumat Met* 3:9).

**PERSONALITIES**

Rabbi Shabbtai – רַבִּי שַׁבְּתַאי: This second-generation *amora* in Eretz Yisrael transmitted *halakhot* in the name of Ḥizkiyya, and great Sages of Eretz Yisrael such as Rabbi Yoḥanan, Reish Lakish, and Rabbi Asi cite *halakhot* in his name and discuss them. His two sons Rabbi Kruspedai and Rabbi Ḥiyya were also well-known Torah scholars.

Rabbi Yitzḥak from Migdal [*Migdala'a*] – רַבִּי יִצְחָק מִגְדְּלָאָה: A first- and second-generation *amora* in Eretz Yisrael, Rabbi Yitzḥak from Migdal is cited as stating a *halakha* in the name of Rabbi Yehuda HaNasi. Some assert that the appellation *Migdala'a* is appended to Rabbi Yitzḥak's name because he lived in Migdal, a town that was located on the coast of the Sea of Galilee, north of Tiberias. Others suggest that the appellation alludes to a *halakha* that he stated with regard to one who finds coins configured in well-ordered towers [*migdalim*] (*Bava Metzia* 25a).

Perek **III**
Daf **28** Amud **a**

וְטִהֲרוּ לוֹ פְּתָחִים קְטַנִּים. וְקָא דָיְיקַתְּ מִינַּהּ: טַעְמָא – דְּשִׁלְדּוֹ קַיֶּימֶת, הָא לָאו הָכִי – טָהוֹר.

**But they deemed pure** all items that were under the **small openings** to the house, i.e., those whose width was less than four handbreadths. **And you infer from** this statement that **the reason** the large openings are impure in such a case is **that the form of** the corpse still **exists; but otherwise,** i.e., if the corpse was deformed, then even the large openings are **pure.**[N]

אַדְּרַבָּה, דּוּק מִינַּהּ לְהַאי גִּיסָא: שִׁלְדּוֹ קַיֶּימֶת – הוּא דְּטִהֲרוּ לוֹ פְּתָחִים קְטַנִּים, הָא לָאו הָכִי – פְּתָחִים קְטַנִּים נָמֵי טְמֵאִין, דְּכׇל חַד וְחַד חֲזֵי לְאַפּוּקֵי חַד חַד אֵבֶר!

The Gemara explains why one cannot infer from here that a deformed corpse does not impart impurity to other items that are under the same roof: **On the contrary,** one can **infer from** this statement **in the opposite manner: It is** only because **the form** of the corpse still **exists that** the Sages **deemed pure** the **small openings** of the house; **but otherwise,** the **small openings are also impure, as each and every one** of them **is fit for taking out** the corpse through them, **each limb one** by **one.** Consequently, no proof can be derived from this statement in support of the opinion of Reish Lakish.

**NOTES**

But otherwise pure – הָא לָאו הָכִי טָהוֹר: An alternative explanation in the early commentaries holds that Rabbi Yoḥanan agrees with Reish Lakish that a burned corpse is pure; their dispute is with regard to the reason for this *halakha*. Whereas Reish Lakish holds that a burned corpse is pure because it is deformed, and therefore disintegrated afterbirth is also pure, Rabbi Yoḥanan maintains that the reason a burned corpse is pure is that it is considered to have been completely eradicated. Therefore, Rabbi Yoḥanan holds that the *halakha* of afterbirth that disintegrated cannot be compared to the *halakha* of a burned corpse (*Tosafot*; Ramban).

אָמַר לֵיהּ רָבִינָא לְרַב אָשֵׁי: רַבִּי יוֹחָנָן דְּאָמַר כְּמַאן – כְּרַבִּי אֱלִיעֶזֶר. דִּתְנַן, אֵפֶר שְׂרוּפִין, רַבִּי אֱלִיעֶזֶר אוֹמֵר: שִׁיעוּרֵיהּ בְּרוֹבַע.

**Ravina said to Rav Ashi: In accordance with whose** opinion **did Rabbi Yoḥanan say** that a deformed corpse imparts impurity to items that are under the same roof? It is **in accordance with** the opinion of **Rabbi Eliezer,**[N] **as we learned** in a mishna (*Oholot* 2:2): With regard to **the ashes of burned** corpses that are not mixed with other types of ashes or dirt, **Rabbi Eliezer says** that **its measure for** imparting impurity to items that are under the same roof is a **quarter** of a *kav*. Clearly, Rabbi Eliezer maintains that a deformed corpse imparts impurity to items that are under the same roof.

הֵיכִי דָּמֵי מֵת שֶׁנִּשְׂרַף וְשִׁלְדּוֹ קַיֶּימֶת? אָמַר אַבָּיֵי: כְּגוֹן שֶׁשְּׂרָפוֹ עַל גַּבֵּי קַטַבְלָא. רָבָא אָמַר: כְּגוֹן שֶׁשְּׂרָפוֹ עַל גַּבֵּי אַפּוֹדְרִים. רָבִינָא אָמַר: כְּגוֹן דְּאִיחַרְכֵי אַחְרוּכֵי.

The Gemara asks: **What are the circumstances** of this case of **a corpse that was burned but its form** still **exists?** How is this possible? **Abaye says:** It is possible in a case **where** one **burned** the corpse **on top of** a hard **leather spread** [***katavla***],[L] which does not burn, and therefore the corpse retains its shape even after it is burned. **Rava says:** It is possible in a case **where** one **burned** the corpse **on top of a marble slate** [***apoderim***].[NL] **Ravina says:** It is possible in a case **where** the corpse **was charred**[NH] without being reduced to ashes.

תָּנוּ רַבָּנַן: הַמַּפֶּלֶת יָד חֲתוּכָה וְרֶגֶל חֲתוּכָה – אִמּוֹ טְמֵאָה לֵידָה, וְאֵין חוֹשְׁשִׁין שֶׁמָּא מִגּוּף אָטוּם בָּאוּ.

§ **The Sages taught** in a *baraita*: In the case of a woman **who discharges a shaped hand,** i.e., its fingers are discernible, **or a shaped foot,**[H] **its mother is impure** with the impurity of a woman after **childbirth,** as the hand or foot certainly came from a full-fledged fetus. **And we are not concerned** that **perhaps they came from** a fetus with **a sealed,** i.e., deficient, **body,** in which case the miscarriage does not have the status of childbirth with regard to ritual impurity. The reason is that most pregnant women give birth to a fully formed fetus, and therefore it is presumed that the hand or foot came from a whole fetus that was squashed during childbirth.

רַב חִסְדָּא וְרַבָּה בַּר רַב הוּנָא דְּאָמְרִי תַּרְוַיְיהוּ: אֵין נוֹתְנִין לָהּ יְמֵי טוֹהַר, מַאי טַעְמָא – אֵימָא הִרְחִיקָה לֵידָתָהּ.

**Rav Ḥisda and Rabba bar Rav Huna both say:** Although the woman observes the period of impurity of a woman after childbirth, **we do not give her** the **days of purity** following the period of impurity. **What is the reason?** Although it is presumed that the discharged limbs came from a full-fledged fetus, it is unknown whether or when the woman discharged the rest of the fetus, and the principle is that a woman who discharges observes her periods of impurity and purity when the majority of the limbs of the fetus emerge. Therefore, one can **say** that perhaps **her childbirth was distant,** i.e., the woman discharged the majority of the limbs of the fetus long before she discharged this hand or foot, and consequently her period of purity has already ended.

מֵתִיב רַב יוֹסֵף: הַמַּפֶּלֶת וְאֵין יָדוּעַ מַה הִפִּילָה – תֵּשֵׁב לְזָכָר וְלִנְקֵבָה. וְאִי סָלְקָא דַּעְתָּךְ, כָּל כְּהַאי גַּוְונָא אֵימָא הִרְחִיקָה לֵידָתָהּ – לִתְנֵי וּלְנִדָּה!

**Rav Yosef raises an objection** from a mishna (29a): In the case of a woman **who discharges and it is not known what** sex fetus **she discharged, she shall observe** the strictures of a woman who gave birth both **to a male and to a female. And if it enters your mind** that in **any case like this** one should **say** that perhaps the woman's **childbirth was distant, let** the mishna **teach** that the woman shall observe the strictures of a woman who gave birth to both a male and a female, **and** also observes the strictures **of a menstruating woman.** Since it is possible that the item she discharged was a limb from a fetus the majority of which she discharged a long time beforehand, then she must forgo the period of purity observed by a woman who gave birth, and treat any blood that emerges during this period like the blood of a menstruating woman.

**NOTES**

In accordance with whose opinion did Rabbi Yoḥanan say…Rabbi Eliezer – רַבִּי יוֹחָנָן דְּאָמַר כְּמַאן כְּרַבִּי אֱלִיעֶזֶר: By inference, if Rabbi Yoḥanan's opinion is in accordance with the opinion of Rabbi Eliezer, then the opinion of Reish Lakish is in accordance with the opinion of the Rabbis, who deem ashes of a burned corpse pure. The commentaries write that it is for this reason that the Rambam rules in accordance with the opinion of Reish Lakish; the *halakha* follows the majority opinion (*Kesef Mishne*).

Where one burned the corpse on top of a marble slate – כְּגוֹן שֶׁשְּׂרָפוֹ עַל גַּבֵּי אַפּוֹדְרִים: Rashi explains that a hard leather spread and a marble slate [*apoderim*] are similar in that both are hard surfaces that are not burned with the corpse. Furthermore, both have sides that prevent the ashes from scattering.

Where the corpse was charred – כְּגוֹן דְּאִיחַרְכֵי אַחְרוּכֵי: Rashi states that the corpse was burned but was not reduced to ashes. The later commentaries explain that Rashi clearly does not mean that the interior of the corpse remained intact, as if so, it would have the status of a whole corpse. Rather, Rashi means that the corpse was burned both on the inside and on the outside, and it turned to hard charcoal, thereby retaining its shape. The commentaries similarly explain that according to the Rambam this is referring to a case where the spine and ribs were burned, but they remained connected to the rest of the body, which retained its shape (*Ḥazon Ish*).

**LANGUAGE**

Leather spread [*katavla*] – קַטַבְלָא: This word, which appears in several different forms, derives from the Greek καταβολή, *katabolē*, meaning spread. The term refers to a leather sheet used for covering items or for placing items on it.

Marble slate [*apoderim*] – אַפּוֹדְרִים: This term refers to a specific type of marble slate that comes in a fixed shape and is used mainly for a table. Some suggest that the word derives from the Aramaic word for table, *petora*. Others suggest that it derives from *peresh*, a Hebrew word for animal manure, which hardens over time.

**HALAKHA**

The corpse was charred – אִיחַרְכֵי אַחְרוּכֵי: If a corpse was charred but its spine and ribs remain, it imparts impurity like a whole corpse (Rambam *Sefer Tahara*, *Hilkhot Tumat Met* 3:9).

Who discharges a shaped hand or a shaped foot – הַמַּפֶּלֶת יָד חֲתוּכָה וְרֶגֶל חֲתוּכָה: If a woman discharges a shaped hand or a shaped foot, it presumably came from a full-fledged offspring. If it can be assumed that the woman already discharged most of the limbs of the fetus, e.g., she no longer appears to be pregnant (see *Mirkevet HaMishne*), she assumes the impurity status of a woman after childbirth (Rambam *Sefer Kedusha*, *Hilkhot Issurei Bia* 10:11).

אָמַר אַבַּיֵי: אִי תְּנָא לְנִדָּה, הֲוָה אָמֵינָא – מְבִיאָה קָרְבָּן וְאֵינוֹ נֶאֱכָל, קָא מַשְׁמַע לָן – דְּנֶאֱכָל.

**Abaye says** in response: **If** the mishna had **taught** that the woman observes the strictures **of a menstruating woman, I would say** that as her status as a woman after childbirth is uncertain, since she observes the strictures of a menstruating woman with regard to any blood that emerges, **she brings an offering**[H] like any woman after childbirth, **but it is not eaten** by the priests. It might be thought that perhaps the woman did not give birth at all and is not obligated to bring the offering, and therefore her bird sin offering cannot be eaten. By omitting the *halakha* that the woman observes the strictures of a menstruating woman, the mishna **teaches us that** her offering **is eaten.** This indicates that she certainly discharged an offspring; the uncertainty is only about when she discharged it.

אָמַר רַב הוּנָא: הוֹצִיא עוּבָּר אֶת יָדוֹ וְהֶחֱזִירָהּ – אִמּוֹ טְמֵאָה לֵידָה. שֶׁנֶּאֱמַר: ״וַיְהִי בְלִדְתָּהּ וַיִּתֶּן יָד״.

§ **Rav Huna says:** If **a fetus extended its hand out** of the womb **and then returned it,**[H] **its mother is impure** with the impurity of a woman after childbirth. This is considered childbirth, **as it is stated** with regard to Tamar, Judah's daughter-in-law: **"And it happened when she gave birth that one put out a hand**…and it happened that as he drew back his hand, his brother came out" (Genesis 38:28–29). Evidently, the fetus extending out its hand was considered childbirth, despite the fact that it subsequently drew back the hand.

מְתִיב רַב יְהוּדָה: הוֹצִיא עוּבָּר אֶת יָדוֹ – אֵין אִמּוֹ חוֹשֶׁשֶׁת לְכׇל דָּבָר! אָמַר רַב נַחְמָן: לְדִידִי מִיפָּרְשָׁא לִי מִינֵּיהּ דְּרַב הוּנָא, לָחוּשׁ – חוֹשֶׁשֶׁת, יְמֵי טוֹהַר – לָא יָהֲבִינַן לַהּ עַד דְּנָפֵיק רוּבֵּיהּ.

**Rav Yehuda raises an objection** from a *baraita*: If **a fetus extended its hand out** of the womb, **its mother** need **not be concerned** that she is considered a woman after childbirth **with regard to any matter. Rav Naḥman says** in response: The meaning of this statement **was explained to me** personally **by Rav Huna** himself: **With regard to being concerned** that she has the status of a woman after childbirth, the woman must be **concerned,** i.e., she must observe the strictures of a woman after childbirth. But **we do not give her** a period of **days of purity** like any woman after childbirth, **until most of** the fetus **emerges.**

וְהָא ״אֵין אִמּוֹ חוֹשֶׁשֶׁת לְכׇל דָּבָר״ קָאָמַר! אָמַר אַבַּיֵי: אֵינָהּ חוֹשֶׁשֶׁת לְכׇל דָּבָר – מִדְּאוֹרָיְיתָא, אֲבָל מִדְּרַבָּנַן – חוֹשֶׁשֶׁת. וְהָא קְרָא קָאָמַר! מִדְּרַבָּנַן, וּקְרָא – אַסְמַכְתָּא בְּעָלְמָא.

The Gemara asks: **But doesn't** the *baraita* **say** that **its mother** need **not be concerned** that she is considered a woman after childbirth **with regard to any matter? Abaye says:** The *baraita* means that the woman need **not be concerned with regard to any matter by Torah law; but by rabbinic law** she must be **concerned,** i.e., she is required to observe the strictures of a woman after childbirth. The Gemara asks: **But doesn't** Rav Huna **cite a verse** as proof for his statement that if a fetus extended its hand out it is considered childbirth? The Gemara answers: This *halakha* applies **by rabbinic law, and the verse is** cited as **mere support** for it, i.e., it is not an actual source.

מתני׳ הַמַּפֶּלֶת טוּמְטוּם וְאַנְדְּרוֹגִינוֹס – תֵּשֵׁב לְזָכָר וְלִנְקֵבָה.

**MISHNA** A woman **who discharges** or gives birth to **a *tumtum*,**[L] whose sexual organs are obscured, **or to a hermaphrodite** [*ve'androginos*],[LBH] who has both male and female sexual organs, **shall observe** the strictures of a woman who gave birth both **to a male and to a female.** She is impure for fourteen days like a woman who gave birth to a female, but blood that she sees thereafter is pure only until forty days after birth, like for a woman who gave birth to a male.

## LANGUAGE

*Tumtum* – טוּמְטוּם: From the root *tet*, *mem*, *mem*, meaning sealed, i.e., an individual whose sexual organs are covered and concealed.

Hermaphrodite [*androginos*] – אַנְדְּרוֹגִינוֹס: From the Greek ἀνδρόγυνος, *androgunos*, which translates literally as man-woman, meaning one who has both male and female sexual characteristics.

## BACKGROUND

*Tumtum* or hermaphrodite – טוּמְטוּם וְאַנְדְּרוֹגִינוֹס: These are people whose sexual development is abnormal, usually during gestation. A *tumtum* has no external signs of sex at all. Sometimes the person is a male whose sexual development was delayed for some reason. Occasionally, the person has testicles but not a penis. Whether the individual is male or female might become apparent later in life, as developmental changes take place.

A hermaphrodite has both male and female sexual organs. Some *tanna'im* hold that a hermaphrodite has a distinct sex, neither male nor female. Others consider a hermaphrodite's sex to be uncertain, like the status of a *tumtum*.

The *halakhot* of a *tumtum* and a hermaphrodite are discussed at length in the Talmud, not due to their practical frequency, but because they present a point of departure for clarifying many points of practical *halakha*.

## HALAKHA

She brings an offering, etc. – מְבִיאָה קָרְבָּן וכו׳: If a woman who was not known to be pregnant discharged, and she does not know whether the fetus that she discharged was developed enough that she is obligated to bring an offering as a woman after childbirth, the miscarriage is deemed uncertain childbirth. The woman brings an offering, but it is not eaten (Rambam *Sefer Korbanot*, *Hilkhot Meḥusrei Kappara* 1:7).

A fetus extended its hand out and returned it – הוֹצִיא עוּבָּר אֶת יָדוֹ וְהֶחֱזִירָהּ: If a fetus extended its hand out of the womb and then returned it, the woman assumes the impurity status of a woman after childbirth by rabbinic law. She observes the period of purity only after the entire offspring, or the majority of its limbs, emerge (Rambam *Sefer Kedusha*, *Hilkhot Issurei Bia* 10:7; *Shulḥan Arukh*, *Yoreh De'a* 194:11).

Who discharges a *tumtum* or a hermaphrodite – הַמַּפֶּלֶת טוּמְטוּם וְאַנְדְּרוֹגִינוֹס: If a woman gives birth to a *tumtum* or a hermaphrodite, she observes the period of impurity that a woman observes after giving birth to a female, namely, fourteen days, and she then observes the period of purity that a woman observes after giving birth to a male, i.e., until forty days after she gave birth (Rambam *Sefer Kedusha*, *Hilkhot Issurei Bia* 10:18; *Shulḥan Arukh*, *Yoreh De'a* 194:8).

## NOTES

**They are not liable for entering the Temple – אֵין חַיָּיבִין עַל בִּיאַת מִקְדָּשׁ:** One who enters the Temple in a state of impurity is liable to receive lashes if he does so intentionally after being forewarned. If he acted unwittingly, e.g., he forgot that he was ritually impure, he is obligated to bring an offering.

טוּמְטוּם וְזָכָר, אַנְדְּרוֹגִינוֹס וְזָכָר – תֵּשֵׁב לְזָכָר וְלִנְקֵבָה. טוּמְטוּם וּנְקֵבָה, אַנְדְּרוֹגִינוֹס וּנְקֵבָה – תֵּשֵׁב לִנְקֵבָה בִּלְבַד.

In a case where she gave birth to twins, if they are **a** ***tumtum*** **and a male,** or **a hermaphrodite and a male,**[H] **she observes** the strictures of a woman who gave birth both **to a male and to a female.** But if the twins are **a** ***tumtum*** **and a female,** or **a hermaphrodite and a female,**[H] **she shall observe** the periods of purity and impurity established by the Torah **for** a woman who gives birth to **a female alone.** Regardless of the status of the *tumtum* and the hermaphrodite, the woman's seven days of impurity and her succeeding thirty-three days of purity are subsumed in the fourteen days of impurity and sixty-six days of purity for a female.

יָצָא מְחוּתָּךְ אוֹ מְסוֹרָס, מִשֶּׁיָּצָא רוּבּוֹ – הֲרֵי הוּא כְּיָלוּד. יָצָא כְּדַרְכּוֹ – עַד שֶׁיֵּצֵא רוֹב רֹאשׁוֹ. וְאֵיזֶהוּ רוֹב רֹאשׁוֹ – מִשֶּׁיֵּצֵא פַּדַּחְתּוֹ.

If the fetus **emerged in pieces, or** if it emerged **reversed,**[H] i.e., feetfirst rather than headfirst, **when most of its** limbs **emerge,** its status **is like** that of a child **born,** with regard to the impurity of a woman after childbirth. If the fetus **emerged in** the **usual manner,** headfirst, it is not considered born **until most of its head emerges. And what is** considered **most of its head?** It is **from when its forehead emerges.**

גמ׳ הַשְׁתָּא טוּמְטוּם לְחוּדֵיהּ וְאַנְדְּרוֹגִינוֹס לְחוּדֵיהּ אָמַר תֵּשֵׁב לְזָכָר וְלִנְקֵבָה, טוּמְטוּם וְזָכָר אַנְדְּרוֹגִינוֹס וְזָכָר מִיבָּעֲיָא?!

**GEMARA** The Gemara asks: **Now** that with regard to a woman who gives birth to **a** ***tumtum*** **alone, or a hermaphrodite alone,** the mishna **states** that **she shall observe** the strictures of a woman who gave birth both **to a male and to a female,** as the sex of the offspring is uncertain, **is it necessary** for the mishna to rule that if a woman gives birth to twins, a ***tumtum*** **and a male,** or **a hermaphrodite and a male,** she shall observe the strictures of a woman who gave birth to both a male and a female?

אִיצְטְרִיךְ, מַהוּ דְּתֵימָא, הוֹאִיל וְאָמַר רַבִּי יִצְחָק: אִשָּׁה מַזְרַעַת תְּחִלָּה – יוֹלֶדֶת זָכָר, אִישׁ מַזְרִיעַ תְּחִלָּה – יוֹלֶדֶת נְקֵבָה, אֵימָא: מִדְּהַאי זָכָר – הַאי נַמִּי זָכָר, קָא מַשְׁמַע לָן – אֵימָא שְׁנֵיהֶם הִזְרִיעוּ בְּבַת אַחַת, זוֹ זָכָר וְזֶה נְקֵבָה.

The Gemara answers: **It was necessary** for the mishna to state this *halakha*, **lest you say** that **since Rabbi Yitzḥak says** that the sex of a fetus is determined at the moment of conception, in that if the **woman emits seed first she gives birth to a male,** and if the **man emits seed first she gives birth to a female,** therefore one might **say** that **since this** offspring that was born with the *tumtum* or hermaphrodite **is male, that** *tumtum* or hermaphrodite **is also male.** Consequently, the mishna **teaches us** that the woman shall observe the strictures of a woman who gave birth to a female as well, as one can **say** that perhaps **both** the man and the woman **emitted seed at the same time,** which would mean that **this** offspring **is male and that** *tumtum* or hermaphrodite **is female.**

אָמַר רַב נַחְמָן אָמַר רַב: טוּמְטוּם וְאַנְדְּרוֹגִינוֹס שֶׁרָאוּ לוֹבֶן אוֹ אוֹדֶם – אֵין חַיָּיבִין עַל בִּיאַת מִקְדָּשׁ, וְאֵין שׂוֹרְפִין עֲלֵיהֶם אֶת הַתְּרוּמָה.

§ **Rav Naḥman says** that **Rav says:** In the case of **a** ***tumtum*** **and a hermaphrodite who saw a white** gonorrhea-like discharge [*ziva*], for which a man is impure, **or** who emitted **a red** discharge[H] that had the appearance of menstrual blood, for which a woman is impure, if they entered the Temple **they are not liable for entering the Temple**[N] in a state of impurity, as perhaps they are pure, in accordance with their true sex. **And** if they touched *teruma* after such a discharge, **one does not burn the** ***teruma*** **due to their** contact, as although impure *teruma* must be burned, the impurity in this case is uncertain.

## HALAKHA

**A *tumtum* and a male, a hermaphrodite and a male – טוּמְטוּם וְזָכָר אַנְדְּרוֹגִינוֹס וְזָכָר:** If a woman gave birth to twins, one male and one *tumtum* or hermaphrodite, she observes the period of impurity for giving birth to a female and the period of purity for giving birth to a male (Rambam *Sefer Kedusha*, *Hilkhot Issurei Bia* 10:18).

**A *tumtum* and a female, a hermaphrodite and a female – טוּמְטוּם וּנְקֵבָה אַנְדְּרוֹגִינוֹס וּנְקֵבָה:** If a woman gave birth to twins, one female and one *tumtum* or hermaphrodite, she observes the periods of impurity and purity for giving birth to a female (Rambam *Sefer Kedusha*, *Hilkhot Issurei Bia* 10:18).

**Emerged in pieces or reversed – יָצָא מְחוּתָּךְ אוֹ מְסוֹרָס:** If a fetus fell apart in the womb and emerged limb by limb, the woman assumes the impurity status of a woman after childbirth when the majority of the limbs have emerged, whether they emerged in order or out of order (Rambam *Sefer Kedusha*, *Hilkhot Issurei Bia* 10:6; *Shulḥan Arukh*, *Yoreh De'a* 194:10).

**A *tumtum* and a hermaphrodite who saw a white or red discharge – טוּמְטוּם וְאַנְדְּרוֹגִינוֹס שֶׁרָאוּ לוֹבֶן אוֹ אוֹדֶם:** A *tumtum* or hermaphrodite must observe the halakhic strictures of both a man and a woman. Therefore, if a *tumtum* or hermaphrodite emitted a red or white discharge, he is impure due to his uncertain status. Because his impurity is uncertain, if he touches *teruma* or sacred items, they are not burned, and he is not liable for entering the Temple or rendering sacred items impure (Rambam *Sefer Tahara*, *Hilkhot Metamei Mishkav UMoshav* 1:7).

רָאוּ לוֹבֶן וְאוֹדֶם כְּאֶחָד – אֵין חַיָּיבִין עַל בִּיאַת מִקְדָּשׁ, אֲבָל שׂוֹרְפִין עֲלֵיהֶם אֶת הַתְּרוּמָה, שֶׁנֶּאֱמַר: ״מִזָּכָר וְעַד נְקֵבָה

If a *tumtum* and a hermaphrodite **saw white *ziva* and red** blood **as one,**[H] i.e., they emitted both *ziva* and blood and are therefore impure regardless of their sex, **they are** still **not liable for entering the Temple, but one does burn *teruma* due to their** contact. The reason they are not liable for entering the Temple, despite the fact that they are definitely impure, is **that it is stated: "Both male and female**

**HALAKHA**

Saw white and red as one – רָאוּ לוֹבֶן וְאוֹדֶם כְּאֶחָד: If a *tumtum* or hermaphrodite emitted both *ziva* and blood and subsequently came in contact with *teruma* or sacrificial foods, these items are burned; but he is not liable for entering the Temple or eating sacrificial foods (Rambam *Sefer Tahara, Hilkhot Metamei Mishkav UMoshav* 1:7).

Perek **III**
Daf **28** Amud **b**

תְּשַׁלֵּחוּ״ – זָכָר וַדַּאי, נְקֵבָה וַדָּאִית, וְלֹא טוּמְטוּם וְאַנְדְּרוֹגִינוֹס.

**you shall send out,** out of the camp you shall send them, so that they not impurify their camp, in the midst of which I dwell" (Numbers 5:3). It is derived from the verse that only **a definite male** or **a definite female** is liable for entering the Temple in a state of impurity, **but not a *tumtum* or a hermaphrodite.**[N]

לֵימָא מְסַיַּיע לֵיהּ: טוּמְטוּם וְאַנְדְּרוֹגִינוֹס שֶׁרָאוּ לוֹבֶן אוֹ אוֹדֶם – אֵין חַיָּיבִין עַל בִּיאַת מִקְדָּשׁ, וְאֵין שׂוֹרְפִין עֲלֵיהֶם אֶת הַתְּרוּמָה. רָאוּ לוֹבֶן וְאוֹדֶם כְּאַחַת – אֵין חַיָּיבִין עַל בִּיאַת מִקְדָּשׁ, אֲבָל שׂוֹרְפִין עֲלֵיהֶם אֶת הַתְּרוּמָה.

The Gemara suggests: **Let us say** that the following *baraita* **supports** the opinion of Rav: In the case of **a *tumtum* and a hermaphrodite who saw white *ziva* or red** blood, **they are not liable for entering the Temple** in a state of impurity, **and** if they touch *teruma*, **one does not burn the *teruma* due to their** contact. If they **saw white *ziva* and red** blood **as one,** i.e., they emitted both *ziva* and blood, **they are** still **not liable for entering the Temple, but one burns *teruma* due to their** contact.

מַאי טַעְמָא? לָאו מִשּׁוּם שֶׁנֶּאֱמַר ״מִזָּכָר וְעַד נְקֵבָה תְּשַׁלֵּחוּ״ – זָכָר וַדַּאי, נְקֵבָה וַדָּאִית, וְלֹא טוּמְטוּם וְאַנְדְּרוֹגִינוֹס? אָמַר עוּלָּא: לָא, הָא מַנִּי – רַבִּי אֱלִיעֶזֶר הִיא.

The Gemara reasons: **What is the reason** that they are not liable for entering the Temple despite the fact that they are definitely impure? Is it **not because it is stated** in the verse: **"Both male and female you shall send out,"** from which it is derived that only **a definite male** or **a definite female** could be liable for entering the Temple in a state of impurity, **but not a *tumtum* or a hermaphrodite? Ulla says: No,** Rav's opinion cannot be proved from this *baraita*, as in accordance with **whose** opinion **is this** *baraita*? **It is** in accordance with the opinion of **Rabbi Eliezer.**

דִּתְנַן, רַבִּי אֱלִיעֶזֶר אוֹמֵר: ״הַשֶּׁרֶץ וְנֶעְלַם מִמֶּנּוּ״ – עַל הֶעְלֵם שֶׁרֶץ הוּא חַיָּיב, וְאֵינוֹ חַיָּיב עַל הֶעְלֵם מִקְדָּשׁ.

**As we learned** in a mishna (*Shevuot* 14b) that **Rabbi Eliezer says:** With regard to the sliding-scale offering the verse states: "Or if a person touches any impure thing…or the carcass of a non-kosher **creeping animal, and it is hidden from him**" (Leviticus 5:2). A precise reading of this verse indicates that **if** one has **a lapse of awareness** that he contracted ritual impurity by touching a carcass of **a creeping animal,** he is **liable** to bring a sliding-scale offering for defiling the Temple or the sacrificial food, **but he is not liable** to bring such an offering **for a lapse of awareness** that he is entering the **Temple** or partaking of sacrificial food.

רַבִּי עֲקִיבָא אוֹמֵר: ״וְנֶעְלַם מִמֶּנּוּ וְהוּא טָמֵא״ – עַל הֶעְלֵם טוּמְאָה הוּא חַיָּיב, וְאֵינוֹ חַיָּיב עַל הֶעְלֵם מִקְדָּשׁ.

**Rabbi Akiva says** that it is derived from the phrase: **"And it is hidden from him, so that he is impure"** (Leviticus 5:2), that **for a lapse of awareness** that one had contracted **ritual impurity,** he is **liable** to bring a sliding-scale offering, **but** he **is not liable** to bring an offering **for a lapse of awareness** that he is entering the **Temple** or partaking of sacrificial food.

**NOTES**

Hermaphrodite – אַנְדְּרוֹגִינוֹס: The early commentaries disagree with regard to the halakhic status of a hermaphrodite. There are those who hold that a hermaphrodite is a separate entity, neither male nor female (Ramban). Others reject this opinion (Rosh; *Tosafot*), and some rule that with regard to the prohibition of homosexual intercourse, a hermaphrodite has the status of a definite male (Ri, cited in *Tur*, *Yoreh De'a* 265). The opinion of the most prominent halakhic authorities, i.e., the Rif, the Rambam, the *Tur*, and the *Shulḥan Arukh*, is that the sex of a hermaphrodite is uncertain, and they are treated as one whose status as male or female is uncertain. An additional opinion is that they are a half-male, half-female (Ra'avad).

**NOTES**

**Whether he contracted impurity from a carcass of a creeping animal or…an unslaughtered animal carcass – אִי בְּשֶׁרֶץ אִיטַּמֵּי אִי…נְבֵילָה אִיטַּמֵּי:** These are examples of two distinct categories of sources of impurity, which have different measures; if the one who entered the Temple in a state of impurity did not know initially by what category he was rendered impure, Rabbi Eliezer holds that he does not bring an offering, as that is not considered knowledge of his sin. If the person knows by what category he was rendered impure, but not by what specific item, e.g., he does not know whether he came in contact with the carcass of an unslaughtered domesticated animal or undomesticated large animal, or whether he touched the carcass of one type of creeping animal or another type, he must bring an offering (Ritva on *Shevuot* 18b).

וְאָמְרִינַן: מַאי בֵּינַיְיהוּ? וְאָמַר חִזְקִיָּה: שֶׁרֶץ וּנְבֵלָה אִיכָּא בֵּינַיְיהוּ, דְּרַבִּי אֱלִיעֶזֶר סָבַר בָּעֵינַן עַד דְּיָדַע אִי בְּשֶׁרֶץ אִיטַּמֵּי אִי בִּנְבֵילָה אִיטַּמֵּי, וְרַבִּי עֲקִיבָא סָבַר לָא בָּעֵינַן.

**And we say** with regard to this mishna: **What** is the difference **between** the opinions of Rabbi Eliezer and Rabbi Akiva? They are apparently stating the same *halakha*. **And Ḥizkiyya says: There is** a practical difference **between them** in a case where one initially knew that he had contracted ritual impurity, but he did not know whether the impurity was contracted from a carcass of **a creeping animal or** from **the carcass of an unslaughtered animal. As Rabbi Eliezer holds** that for one to be liable to bring an offering, **we require that he** initially **know whether he contracted impurity from** a carcass of **a creeping animal** or **whether he contracted impurity from an unslaughtered animal carcass,**[N] and if he never knew this, he does not bring an offering. **And Rabbi Akiva holds** that for him to be liable to bring an offering, **we do not require**[H] that he know this detail, since he knows in general terms that he contracted impurity.

לָאו אָמַר רַבִּי אֱלִיעֶזֶר הָתָם בָּעֵינַן דְּיָדַע אִי בְּשֶׁרֶץ אִיטַּמֵּי אִי בִּנְבֵלָה אִיטַּמֵּי, הָכָא נַמִּי – בָּעֵינַן דְּיָדַע אִי בְּלוֹבֶן אִיטַּמֵּי, אִי בְּאוֹדֶם אִיטַּמֵּי.

The Gemara infers: **Doesn't Rabbi Eliezer say there,** in that mishna, that **we require** one to bring an offering for entering the Temple in a state of impurity only **if he knew** initially **whether he contracted impurity from** a carcass of **a creeping animal** or **whether he contracted impurity from an unslaughtered animal carcass? Here, too,** with regard to a hermaphrodite or a *tumtum* who emitted both *ziva* and blood, they are not obligated to bring an offering according to Rabbi Eliezer, as **we require** one to bring an offering only **if he knew whether he became impure due to** the **white** *ziva* he emitted or **whether he became impure due to** the **red** blood he emitted.

אֲבָל לְרַבִּי עֲקִיבָא, דַּאֲמַר מִשּׁוּם טוּמְאָה מִיחַיַּיב, הָכָא נַמִּי – מִשּׁוּם טוּמְאָה מִיחַיַּיב.

**But according to Rabbi Akiva, who said** that one **is obligated** to bring an offering **due to** his initial knowledge of his **impurity** even if he did not know the exact cause of his impurity, **here too,** in the case of a hermaphrodite or a *tumtum* who emitted both *ziva* and blood, **he is obligated** to bring an offering **due to** his initial knowledge of his **impurity,** despite the fact that he does not know whether he is impure due to the blood or the *ziva*.

וְרַב, מַאי שְׁנָא בִּיאַת מִקְדָּשׁ דְּלָא – דִּכְתִיב ״מִזָּכָר וְעַד נְקֵבָה תְּשַׁלֵּחוּ״ – זָכָר וַדַּאי, נְקֵבָה וַדָּאִית, וְלֹא טוּמְטוּם וְאַנְדְּרוֹגִינוֹס.

The Gemara asks: **And** according to **Rav,** who holds that an impure *tumtum* or hermaphrodite is not liable for entering the Temple but that any *teruma* that he touches is burned, **what is different** with regard to **entering the Temple,** for **which** he is **not** liable? The reason it is different is **that it is written: "Both male and female you shall send out,"** from which it is derived that **a definite male** or **a definite female** is liable for entering the Temple in a state of impurity, **but not a** ***tumtum*** **or a hermaphrodite.**

אִי הָכִי – תְּרוּמָה נַמִּי לָא נִשְׂרוֹף, דִּכְתִיב ״וְהַזָּב אֶת זוֹבוֹ לַזָּכָר וְלַנְּקֵבָה״ – זָכָר וַדַּאי, נְקֵבָה וַדָּאִית, וְלֹא טוּמְטוּם וְאַנְדְּרוֹגִינוֹס!

**If so, we should not burn** ***teruma*** that he touches either, **as it is written** in a verse dealing with these types of impurity: "This is the law of the *zav*, and of one from whom the flow of semen emerges, so that he is thereby impure; and of her that is sick with her menstrual status, **and they who have an issue, whether a male or a female**" (Leviticus 15:32–33). It can similarly be derived from this verse that these types of impurity apply only to **a definite male** or **a definite female, but not** to **a** ***tumtum*** **or a hermaphrodite.**

הַהוּא מִבָּעֵי לֵיהּ לְכִדְרַבִּי יִצְחָק, דַּאֲמַר רַבִּי יִצְחָק: ״לַזָּכָר״ – לְרַבּוֹת אֶת הַמְּצוֹרָע לְמַעְיְנוֹתָיו, ״וְלַנְּקֵבָה״ – לְרַבּוֹת אֶת הַמְּצוֹרַעַת לְמַעְיְנוֹתֶיהָ.

The Gemara answers: **That** verse **is necessary for the** *halakha* **of Rabbi Yitzḥak, as Rabbi Yitzḥak said:** The term **"whether a male"** serves **to include a male leper** as a primary source of impurity **with regard to the sources of his** bodily emissions. In other words, the various emissions of a leper, e.g., his saliva and urine, have the status of a primary source of impurity, and therefore they transmit impurity to a person or utensil that touches them. And the term **"or a female"** serves **to include a female** as a primary source of impurity **with regard to the sources of her** bodily emissions.

**HALAKHA**

**A carcass of a creeping animal or the carcass of an unslaughtered animal…we do not require – שֶׁרֶץ וּנְבֵלָה…לָא בָּעֵינַן:** If a person became impure, and was aware that he became impure but did not know with what primary source of impurity he made contact, and he was also aware that he was about to enter the Temple or eat a consecrated item, but then he forgot that he was impure and entered the Temple or ate the consecrated item, and he subsequently found out with what primary source of impurity he made contact, in this case, the person is obligated to bring an offering, in accordance with the opinion of Rabbi Akiva. This is because although he did not know initially with what primary source of impurity he made contact, he knew that he was impure (Rambam *Sefer Korbanot*, *Hilkhot Shegagot* 11:2).

הַאי נַמִּי מִבָּעֵי לֵיהּ – בְּמִי שֶׁיֵּשׁ לוֹ טׇהֳרָה בְּמִקְוֶה, פְּרָט לִכְלִי חֶרֶס – דִּבְרֵי רַבִּי יוֹסֵי!

The Gemara raises a difficulty: **This** verse: "Both male and female you shall send out" (Numbers 5:3), from which Rav derives that the prohibition against an impure person entering the Temple does not apply to one whose sex is uncertain, **is also necessary** for another *halakha*. That *halakha* is that the obligation to remove from the Temple any impure person or item applies only **to one that has** the option of attaining ritual **purity** by immersing **in a ritual bath; this excludes** an impure **earthenware vessel,** which cannot be purified by immersing it in a ritual bath. This is **the statement of Rabbi Yosei.** Consequently, Rav's *halakha* cannot be derived from that verse.

אִם כֵּן – נִכְתּוֹב רַחֲמָנָא "אָדָם",

The Gemara answers: **If so,** that the verse serves to teach Rabbi Yosei's *halakha* alone, **let the Merciful One write:** Any **person** you shall send out, as this would also exclude earthenware vessels. Rav's *halakha* is derived from the fact that the wording of the verse is: "Both male and female."

וְכִי תֵּימָא אִי כְּתַב רַחֲמָנָא "אָדָם" הֲוָה אָמִינָא – כְּלֵי מַתָּכוֹת לָא, מִ"כֹּל טָמֵא לָנָפֶשׁ" נָפְקָא! "זָכָר וּנְקֵבָה" לָמָּה לִי – לְכִדְרַב.

**And if you would say** in response that **if the Merciful One had written:** Any **person** you shall send out, **I would say** that impure **metal vessels** need **not** be removed from the Temple either, as they are not included in the term: Any person, this is not correct. The Gemara elaborates: The *halakha* that impure metal vessels must be removed from the Temple **is derived from** the previous verse: "That they put out of the camp every leper, and every one that has an issue, and **whatever is impure by the dead**" (Numbers 5:2).[N] Therefore, **why do I** need the verse to write: **"Both male and female** you shall send out," instead of simply stating: Any person you shall send out? Clearly, the phrase: "Both male and female," is necessary **for** the *halakha* **of Rav.**

וְאֵימָא: כּוּלֵּיהּ לְכִדְרַב הוּא דַּאֲתָא! אִם כֵּן, נִכְתּוֹב "זָכָר וּנְקֵבָה", מַאי "מִזָּכָר וְעַד נְקֵבָה" – עַד כׇּל דָּבָר שֶׁיֵּשׁ לוֹ טׇהֳרָה בְּמִקְוֶה.

The Gemara asks: **But** if so, one can **say** that **the entire** phrase **comes for Rav's** *halakha*, and not the *halakha* of Rabbi Yosei. The Gemara answers: **If so, let** the verse **write: Male and female. What** is the meaning of the phrase: **"Both male and female"?** The verse is referring **to any** ritually impure **item that has** the same *halakha* that applies to both males and females, i.e., it can attain **purity by** being immersed in **a ritual bath;** this excludes earthenware vessels.

אִי הָכִי, כִּי אִיטַּמֵּי בִּשְׁאָר טוּמְאוֹת – לָא לִישַׁלְּחוּ! אָמַר קְרָא: "מִזָּכָר" – מְטוּמְאָה הַפּוֹרֶשֶׁת מִן הַזָּכָר.

With regard to Rav's *halakha* that the prohibition of entering the Temple in a state of ritual impurity does not apply to one who is a *tumtum* or a hermaphrodite, the Gemara asks: **If so,** then even **when they become impure with other types of impurity,** in addition to the impurity of a *zav* or a menstruating woman, a *tumtum* and a hermaphrodite **should** likewise **not be sent out** of the Temple, as the passage from which a *tumtum* and a hermaphrodite are excluded is also referring to other types of impurity: "That they put out of the camp every leper, and every one that has an issue, and whatever is impure by the dead" (Numbers 5:2). The Gemara answers: **The** next **verse states: "Both male,"** which is referring **to impurity** caused by a substance **that is emitted from the male** organ, i.e., *ziva*.

וְכׇל הֵיכָא דִּכְתִיב "מִזָּכָר עַד נְקֵבָה" לְמַעוּטֵי טוּמְטוּם וְאַנְדְּרוֹגִינוֹס הוּא דַּאֲתָא? וְהָא גַּבֵּי עֲרָכִין, דִּכְתִיב "הַזָּכָר",

The Gemara raises a difficulty with regard to Rav's derivation: **And** is it correct that **anywhere that** the phrase **"both male and female" is written** in the Torah, this **comes to exclude a *tumtum* and a hermaphrodite? But isn't** a similar expression stated **with regard to valuations,**[B] **as it is written:** "For **the male…** fifty shekels of silver, after the shekel of the Sanctuary. And if she is a female, then your valuation shall be thirty shekels" (Leviticus 27:3–4).

וְתַנְיָא: "הַזָּכָר" – וְלֹא טוּמְטוּם וְאַנְדְּרוֹגִינוֹס, יָכוֹל לֹא יְהֵא בְּעֶרֶךְ אִישׁ אֲבָל יְהֵא בְּעֶרֶךְ אִשָּׁה – תַּלְמוּד לוֹמַר "הַזָּכָר וְאִם נְקֵבָה" – זָכָר וַדַּאי, נְקֵבָה וַדָּאִית, וְלֹא טוּמְטוּם וְאַנְדְּרוֹגִינוֹס.

**And it is taught** in a *baraita* that it is derived from the term **"the male": But not a *tumtum* or a hermaphrodite.** One **might** have thought that a *tumtum* or a hermaphrodite **shall not be** valuated **according to the valuation of a man,** which is fifty shekels, **but shall be** valuated **according to the valuation of a woman,** which is thirty shekels. Therefore, **the verse states: "The male,"** and the following verse states: **"And if she is a female,"** indicating that these *halakhot* apply only to **a definite male** or **a definite female, but not** to **a *tumtum*** or **a hermaphrodite.**[H]

NOTES

**Is derived from whatever is impure by the dead** – מִכֹּל טָמֵא לָנֶפֶשׁ נָפְקָא: The early commentaries ask how the obligation to remove impure metal vessels from the Temple would have been derived from this verse if it had stated explicitly: "Any person you shall send out." They answer that it would have been derived by means of the method of biblical exegesis known as: A generalization, and a detail, and a generalization; the word "any" is a generalization, the word "person" is a detail, and the term "you shall send out" is a generalization. It can therefore be derived that the verse pertains to any item that is similar to a person in this context, namely, any item that can be purified via immersion in a ritual bath (Ritva).

BACKGROUND

**Valuations** – עֲרָכִין: The *halakhot* of valuations appear in Leviticus 27:1–8, and are clarified in tractate *Arakhin*. A valuation is a vow to donate the value of a particular individual to the Temple treasury. The sum to be paid is not determined by the individual's social stature or by his value as a slave; rather, the Torah provides fixed sums based upon age and sex. If one vows to donate the valuation of a particular limb, his vow is of no consequence, as only a whole person has a valuation. By contrast, one can vow to donate the actual monetary value of a limb to the Temple treasury. Notwithstanding this distinction, if someone vows to donate the valuation of a critical organ or limb, e.g., if he says: I am obligated in the valuation of my head, it is as though he vowed to donate his full valuation, because one cannot live without a head.

HALAKHA

**The valuation of a *tumtum* or a hermaphrodite** – טוּמְטוּם וְאַנְדְּרוֹגִינוֹס בַּעֲרָכִין: A *tumtum* and a hermaphrodite do not have a valuation, as the Torah defines valuations only for definite males or females. Therefore, if a *tumtum* or a hermaphrodite obligates himself in his own valuation, or if another person vows to pay his valuation, he is not liable to pay anything (Rambam *Sefer Hafla'a*, *Hilkhot Arakhin VaHaramim* 1:5).

טַעְמָא – דִּכְתִיב "הַזָּכָר וְאִם נְקֵבָה", הָא "מִזָּכָר וּנְקֵבָה" – לָא מְמַעֵט! הַהוּא מִבָּעֵי לֵיהּ

The Gemara explains the difficulty: **The reason** a *tumtum* and a hermaphrodite are excluded is **that it is written: "The male…and if she is a female,"** which indicates **that** if the verse had written: **Male and female,** without the superfluous words "the" and "if," it would **not** have been derived that the verse **excludes** a *tumtum* and a hermaphrodite. This apparently contradicts the opinion of Rav, who excludes a *tumtum* and a hermaphrodite from the prohibition of entering the Temple in a state of impurity merely due to the phrase: "Male and female" (Numbers 5:3). The Gemara answers: In **that** verse with regard to valuations, the words "male" and "female" are themselves **necessary**

Perek **III**
Daf **29** Amud **a**

לְחַלֵּק בֵּין עֵרֶךְ אִישׁ לְעֵרֶךְ אִשָּׁה.

in order **to differentiate between the valuation of a man and the valuation of a woman.** Therefore, it could not have been derived from that verse that a *tumtum* and a hermaphrodite are excluded from the *halakha* of valuations, were it not for the superfluous words "the" and "if."

"יָצָא מְחוּתָּךְ אוֹ מְסוֹרָס" וכו׳. אָמַר רַבִּי אֶלְעָזָר: אֲפִילּוּ הָרֹאשׁ עִמָּהֶן.

§ The mishna teaches that if the fetus **emerged in pieces, or** if it emerged **reversed,** i.e., feetfirst rather than headfirst; when most of its limbs emerge, its status is like that of a child born, with regard to the impurity of a woman after childbirth. **Rabbi Elazar says: Even** if **the head is among** the limbs that emerged, provided that the majority of the limbs did not yet emerge, the fetus is not considered born.

וְרַבִּי יוֹחָנָן אָמַר: לֹא שָׁנוּ אֶלָּא שֶׁאֵין הָרֹאשׁ עִמָּהֶן, אֲבָל הָרֹאשׁ עִמָּהֶן – הָרֹאשׁ פּוֹטֵר.

**And Rabbi Yoḥanan says: They taught** in the mishna that the woman is not impure unless most of the fetus's limbs emerged **only** in a case **where the head is not among** the limbs that emerged; **but** if **the head is among them, the head exempts** the woman's future offspring from the obligation of primogeniture, as the fetus is considered born.

לֵימָא בִּדְשְׁמוּאֵל קָמִיפַּלְגִי, דְּאָמַר שְׁמוּאֵל: אֵין הָרֹאשׁ פּוֹטֵר בִּנְפָלִים.

The Gemara asks: **Shall we say** that these Sages **disagree with regard to** the opinion **of Shmuel? As Shmuel said** that if a woman is pregnant with twins, and **the head** of one of the fetuses emerges and then disappears back into the womb, this **does not exempt** the other fetus from the obligation of primogeniture should it be born first. Shmuel says this specifically **in** a case of **non-viable newborns,** i.e., where the fetus whose head emerged was a non-viable newborn and the one that was eventually born first is a viable offspring. But if both are viable offspring, the emergence of the head is considered birth. The suggestion is that Rabbi Elazar agrees with the opinion of Shmuel, whereas Rabbi Yoḥanan disagrees with the opinion of Shmuel and maintains that the emergence of the head is considered birth even in the case of a non-viable newborn.

בְּשָׁלֵם – דְּכוּלֵּי עָלְמָא לָא פְּלִיגִי, כִּי פְּלִיגִי – בִּמְחוּתָּךְ. דְּמָר סָבַר: בְּשָׁלֵם הוּא דְּקָחָשֵׁיב, בִּמְחוּתָּךְ – לָא קָחָשֵׁיב. וּמָר סָבַר: בִּמְחוּתָּךְ נַמִי חָשֵׁיב.

The Gemara rejects this suggestion, as it is possible that **in** the case of **a whole** non-viable newborn, **everyone,** i.e., Rabbi Elazar and Rabbi Yoḥanan, **agrees** that the emergence of the head is considered a birth, contrary to the opinion of Shmuel. **When they disagree,** it is **in** the case of a fetus that emerged **in pieces. As** one **Sage,** Rabbi Elazar, **holds** that **it is** specifically **in** the case of **a whole** non-viable newborn **that** the emergence of the head **is considered** birth, whereas **with regard to** a fetus that emerged **in pieces** it **is not considered** birth; **and** one **Sage,** Rabbi Yoḥanan, **holds** that **in** the case of a fetus that emerged **in pieces as well,** the emergence of the head **is considered** birth.

לִישָּׁנָא אַחֲרִינָא: טַעְמָא – דְּיָצָא מְחוּתָּךְ אוֹ מְסוֹרָס, הָא כְּתִקְנוֹ – הָרֹאשׁ פּוֹטֵר, תַּרְוַיְיהוּ לֵית לְהוּ דִּשְׁמוּאֵל, דְּאָמַר שְׁמוּאֵל: אֵין הָרֹאשׁ פּוֹטֵר בִּנְפָלִים.

The Gemara cites **another version** of this discussion. **The reason** it is necessary for most of the limbs of the fetus to emerge for it to be considered born is **that it emerged in pieces, or** that it emerged **reversed,** i.e., feet first. It may be inferred from here that if it emerged **in its proper manner,** headfirst and whole, it is considered born, even according to Rabbi Elazar. Therefore, if the woman is pregnant with twins, the emergence of **the head exempts** the other twin from the obligations of primogeniture. Evidently, **both** Rabbi Yoḥanan and Rabbi Elazar **do not hold** in accordance with the opinion **of Shmuel, as Shmuel said** that the emergence of **the head** of one of the twins **does not exempt** the other **in** a case of **non-viable newborns.**

אִיכָּא דְּמַתְנֵי לַהּ לְהָא שְׁמַעְתְּתָא בְּאַפֵּי נַפְשַׁהּ, אָמַר רַבִּי אֶלְעָזָר: אֵין הָרֹאשׁ כְּרוֹב אֵבָרִים, וְרַבִּי יוֹחָנָן אָמַר: הָרֹאשׁ כְּרוֹב אֵבָרִים. וְקָמִיפַּלְגִי בִּדְשְׁמוּאֵל.

**There are those who teach this *halakha* by itself,**[N] i.e., not in reference to the mishna: **Rabbi Elazar says:** The emergence of **the head** of a non-viable newborn **is not** considered **like** the emergence of **most of the limbs;**[N] **and Rabbi Yoḥanan says:** The emergence of **the head** of a non-viable newborn **is** considered **like** the emergence of **most of the limbs. And they disagree with regard to** the opinion **of Shmuel;** Rabbi Elazar holds in accordance with Shmuel's opinion, whereas Rabbi Yoḥanan does not accept the opinion of Shmuel.

תְּנַן: יָצָא מְחוּתָּךְ אוֹ מְסוֹרָס, מִשֶּׁיָּצָא רוּבּוֹ – הֲרֵי הוּא כְּיָלוּד. מִדְּקָאָמַר מְסוֹרָס, מִכְּלָל דִּמְחוּתָּךְ – כְּתִקְנוֹ, וְקָאָמַר מִשֶּׁיֵּצֵא רוּבּוֹ – הֲרֵי זֶה כְּיָלוּד. קַשְׁיָא לְרַבִּי יוֹחָנָן!

The Gemara raises a difficulty: **We learned** in the mishna that if the fetus **emerged in pieces or** if it emerged **reversed, when most of its** limbs **emerge,** its status **is like** that of a child **born.** The Gemara infers: **From the fact that** the mishna **states: Or reversed, by inference** in the case of a fetus **that** emerged **in pieces** it emerged **in its proper manner,** i.e., the head first and then the body, **and** nevertheless the mishna **states** that it is only **when most of its** limbs **emerge** that its status **is like** that of a child **born.** This is **difficult for** the opinion of **Rabbi Yoḥanan,**[N] as he maintains that once the head emerges, the fetus is considered born.

אָמַר לָךְ רַבִּי יוֹחָנָן: אֵימָא ״יָצָא מְחוּתָּךְ וּמְסוֹרָס״.

The Gemara explains that **Rabbi Yoḥanan** could have **said to you: Say** that the mishna is referring to a case where the fetus **emerged in pieces and reversed,** whereas if it emerged with its head first, it is considered born even if most of its limbs did not emerge yet.

וְהָא ״אוֹ״ קָתָנֵי! הָכִי קָאָמַר: יָצָא מְחוּתָּךְ אוֹ שָׁלֵם, וְזֶה וָזֶה מְסוֹרָס – מִשֶּׁיֵּצֵא רוּבּוֹ הֲרֵי זֶה כְּיָלוּד.

The Gemara asks: **But doesn't** the mishna **teach** that the fetus emerged in pieces **or** reversed? If so, it cannot be explained as referring to a case where the fetus emerged both in pieces and reversed. The Gemara answers that **this** is what the mishna **is saying:** If the fetus **emerged in pieces or whole, and** in both **this** case **and that** case it emerged **reversed,** then **when most of its** limbs **emerge,** its status **is like** that of a child **born.**

**NOTES**

**There are those who teach this *halakha* by itself** – אִיכָּא דְּמַתְנֵי לַהּ לְהָא שְׁמַעְתְּתָא בְּאַפֵּי נַפְשַׁהּ: Rashi writes that the issue of whether or not the dispute between Rabbi Elazar and Rabbi Yoḥanan was originally stated in reference to the mishna affects the understanding of their opinions. If the dispute was in reference to the mishna, it was presumably with regard to the case of a fetus that emerged in pieces alone; but in the case of a fetus that emerged whole, Rabbi Elazar agrees with Rabbi Yoḥanan that when the head emerges, the fetus is considered born. But if the dispute was stated without reference to the mishna, it presumably relates to the case of a fetus that emerged whole as well.

**The emergence of the head is not considered like the emergence of most of the limbs** – אֵין הָרֹאשׁ כְּרוֹב אֵבָרִים: Rashi notes that this is referring to a non-viable newborn alone, as with regard to a viable offspring, the mishna states that if it emerges in the proper manner it has the status of a born child when most of its head emerges.

**Difficult for the opinion of Rabbi Yoḥanan** – קַשְׁיָא לְרַבִּי יוֹחָנָן: The later commentaries write that this challenge to Rabbi Yoḥanan's opinion is according to both versions of it; although in the second version Rabbi Yoḥanan's statement was not specifically in reference to the mishna, nevertheless, since he did not specify the case to which he was referring, he was presumably referring both to a case where the fetus emerged whole and to a case where it emerged in pieces. In both cases, Rabbi Yoḥanan holds that when the head emerges, the fetus is considered born, even if most of its limbs did not yet emerge (Maharsha).

אָמַר רַב פַּפָּא: כְּתַנָּאֵי. יָצָא מְחוּתָּךְ אוֹ מְסוֹרָס – מִשֶּׁיָּצָא רוּבּוֹ הֲרֵי הוּא כְּיָלוּד, רַבִּי יוֹסֵי אוֹמֵר: מִשֶּׁיֵּצֵא כְּתִקְנוֹ. מַאי קָאָמַר?

**Rav Pappa says:** This dispute between Rabbi Elazar and Rabbi Yoḥanan is **parallel to** a dispute between *tanna'im*, as it is stated in a *baraita*: If the fetus **emerged in pieces or reversed, when most of its** limbs **emerge** its status **is like** that of a child **born. Rabbi Yosei says:** Its status is like that of a child born **when it emerges in its proper manner.** The Gemara asks: **What is** Rabbi Yosei **saying?** His statement apparently indicates that if a fetus emerges with its feet first, then even after most of its limbs emerge it is not considered born.

אָמַר רַב פַּפָּא, הָכִי קָאָמַר: יָצָא מְחוּתָּךְ וּמְסוֹרָס – מִשֶּׁיָּצָא רוּבּוֹ הֲרֵי הוּא כְּיָלוּד, הָא כְּתִקְנוֹ – הָרֹאשׁ פּוֹטֵר. רַבִּי יוֹסֵי אוֹמֵר – מִשֶּׁיֵּצֵא רוּבּוֹ כְּתִקְנוֹ.

**Rav Pappa says** that **this** is what the *baraita* **is saying:** If the fetus **emerged in pieces or reversed, when most of its** limbs **emerge** its status **is like** that of a child **born; but** by inference, if the fetus emerged **in its proper manner,** then the emergence of **the head exempts** its twin, should it eventually be born first, from the obligations of primogeniture. And **Rabbi Yosei says:** The status of a fetus that emerged in pieces is like that of a child born **when most of its** limbs **emerge,** provided that it emerged **in its proper manner,** i.e., both requirements are necessary. The suggestion is that the opinion of Rabbi Yoḥanan is in accordance with the ruling of the first *tanna*, that even if a fetus emerges in pieces, once its head emerges it is considered born; whereas the opinion of Rabbi Elazar follows the ruling of Rabbi Yosei that even if such a fetus emerges headfirst, it is not considered born.

מַתְקִיף לַהּ רַב זְבִיד: מִכְּלָל דְּבִמְסוֹרָס – רוּבּוֹ נָמֵי לָא פּוֹטֵר, הָא קַיְימָא לַן דְּרוּבּוֹ כְּכוּלּוֹ!

**Rav Zevid objects to** Rav Pappa's interpretation of the *baraita*: Since Rabbi Yosei issued his statement that both requirements are necessary, i.e., a majority of limbs and emergence in the proper manner, with regard to the two cases mentioned by the first *tanna*, **by inference in** the other case, **where** the fetus emerged **reversed, even** when **most of its** limbs emerge **it does not exempt** its twin from the obligations of primogeniture. But this is difficult, as **we maintain that the majority of** an item is considered **like all** of it. Accordingly, when most of the fetus's limbs emerge it should be considered born even if it came out feetfirst.

אֶלָּא אָמַר רַב זְבִיד, הָכִי קָאָמַר: יָצָא מְחוּתָּךְ וּמְסוֹרָס – מִשֶּׁיָּצָא רוּבּוֹ הֲרֵי זֶה כְּיָלוּד, הָא כְּתִקְנוֹ – הָרֹאשׁ פּוֹטֵר. רַבִּי יוֹסֵי אוֹמֵר: מִשֶּׁיֵּצֵא כְּתִקְנוֹ לְחַיִּים.

**Rather, Rav Zevid says** that **this** is what the *baraita* **is saying:** If the fetus **emerged in pieces and reversed, when most of its** limbs **emerge** its status **is like** that of a child **born; but** by inference, if the fetus emerged **in its proper manner** then the emergence of **the head exempts** its twin from the obligations of primogeniture, even if it was born in pieces. **Rabbi Yosei says:** The fetus is considered born once its head emerges only in a case **when it emerges in its proper manner alive;** if it emerges in pieces, the fetus is considered born only when most of its limbs emerge.

תַּנְיָא נָמֵי הָכִי: יָצָא מְחוּתָּךְ (אוֹ) מְסוֹרָס – מִשֶּׁיָּצָא רוּבּוֹ הֲרֵי זֶה כְּיָלוּד, הָא כְּתִקְנוֹ – הָרֹאשׁ פּוֹטֵר. רַבִּי יוֹסֵי אוֹמֵר: מִשֶּׁיֵּצֵא כְּתִקְנוֹ לְחַיִּים.

**This** explanation **is also taught** explicitly in another *baraita*: If the fetus **emerged in pieces** and **reversed,** then **when most of its** limbs **emerge** its status **is like** that of a child **born; but** if the fetus emerged **in its proper manner,** the emergence of **the head exempts** its twin. **Rabbi Yosei says:** The fetus is considered born once its head emerges only in a case **where it emerges in its proper manner alive.**

וְאֵיזֶהוּ כְּתִקְנוֹ לְחַיִּים – מִשֶּׁיֵּצֵא רוֹב רֹאשׁוֹ. וְאֵיזֶהוּ רוֹב רֹאשׁוֹ? רַבִּי יוֹסֵי אוֹמֵר: מִשֶּׁיֵּצְאוּ צְדָעָיו, אַבָּא חָנָן מִשּׁוּם רַבִּי יְהוֹשֻׁעַ אוֹמֵר: מִשֶּׁיֵּצֵא פַּדַּחְתּוֹ, וְיֵשׁ אוֹמְרִים: מִשֶּׁיֵּרָאוּ קַרְנֵי רֹאשׁוֹ.

**And what is** the exact stage when a fetus that emerged **in its proper manner alive** is considered born? **When most of its head emerges. And what is** the stage when **most of its head** emerges? **Rabbi Yosei says: When its temples emerge.**[H] **Abba Ḥanan says in the name of Rabbi Yehoshua: When its forehead emerges. And some say: When the corners of its head,** i.e., the projection of the head above the neck, **are visible.**

**HALAKHA**

The head is tantamount to most of the limbs…when its temples emerge – הָרֹאשׁ כְּרוֹב אֵבָרִים מִשֶּׁיֵּצְאוּ פַּדַּחְתּוֹ: If the fetus's head emerges together whole, the woman assumes the impurity status of a woman after childbirth, just as in a case where most of the limbs of the fetus emerge, in accordance with the opinion of Rabbi Yoḥanan. If the fetus is not in pieces and emerges headfirst, it is considered born once its temples emerge, even if it subsequently falls apart. Emergence refers to leaving the vaginal canal (Rambam *Sefer Kedusha, Hilkhot Issurei Bia* 10:6; *Shulḥan Arukh, Yoreh De'a* 194:10).

מתני׳ הַמַּפֶּלֶת וְאֵין יָדוּעַ מַהוּ – תֵּשֵׁב לְזָכָר וְלִנְקֵבָה, אֵין יָדוּעַ אִם וָלָד הָיָה אִם לָאו – תֵּשֵׁב לְזָכָר וְלִנְקֵבָה וּלְנִדָּה.

**MISHNA** In the case of a woman **who discharges and it is not known what is** the fetus's sex,[H] she **shall observe** the strictures of a woman who gave birth both **to a male and to a female.** She is impure for fourteen days, like a woman who gave birth to a female, and any blood the woman sees only until forty days after birth, not eighty days thereafter, is pure, like a woman who gave birth to a male. If **it is unknown whether it was** a male or female **offspring** or **whether** it was **not** an offspring at all, **she shall observe** the period of impurity **for** a woman who gave birth to **a male and for** a woman who gave birth to **a female; and for** any blood that she sees, she observes the *halakhot* of **a menstruating woman.** Since it is possible that what she discharged was not an offspring at all, any blood she sees might be due to menstruation, not childbirth.

גמ׳ אָמַר רַבִּי יְהוֹשֻׁעַ בֶּן לֵוִי: עָבְרָה נָהָר וְהִפִּילָה – מְבִיאָה קׇרְבָּן וְנֶאֱכָל, הַלֵּךְ אַחַר רוֹב נָשִׁים, וְרוֹב נָשִׁים וָלָד מְעַלְּיָא יָלְדָן.

**GEMARA Rabbi Yehoshua ben Levi says:** With regard to a pregnant woman who **passed across a river and she discharged** her fetus into the river, and she does not know whether the fetus was fully formed, **she brings** the **offering** of a woman after childbirth, which is a burnt offering and a sin offering. **And** the sin offering, which is a bird, **is eaten** after the nape of its neck has been pinched, in the manner of a regular bird sin offering. This is the *halakha* despite the uncertainty that this fetus might not have been fully formed, in which case the woman would not be obligated to bring this offering, and a bird that is not an offering may not be eaten if its nape was pinched. Rabbi Yehoshua ben Levi explains the reasoning behind this ruling: One must **follow the majority of** pregnant **women, and most** pregnant **women give birth to full-fledged offspring.**[N]

תְּנַן: אֵין יָדוּעַ אִם וָלָד הָיָה – תֵּשֵׁב לְזָכָר וְלִנְקֵבָה וּלְנִדָּה. אַמַּאי תֵּשֵׁב לְנִדָּה? לֵימָא: הַלֵּךְ אַחַר רוֹב נָשִׁים, וְרוֹב נָשִׁים וָלָד מְעַלְּיָא יָלְדָן!

The Gemara analyzes this claim. **We learned** in the mishna: If **it is unknown whether** what the woman discharged **was** a male or female **offspring** or whether it was not an offspring at all, **she shall observe** the period of impurity **for** a woman who gave birth to **a male and for** a woman who gave birth to **a female; and for** any blood that she sees, she observes the *halakhot* of **a menstruating woman.** The Gemara asks: According to the statement of Rabbi Yehoshua ben Levi, **why must** the woman **observe** the *halakhot* of **a menstruating woman? Let us say** that one must **follow the majority of women, and the majority of women give birth to full-fledged offspring.** If so, she should observe a period of purity, during which any blood she sees is pure, after her period of impurity, like all women after childbirth.

מַתְנִיתִין – בְּשֶׁלֹּא הוּחְזְקָה עוּבָּרָה, וְכִי קָאָמַר רַבִּי יְהוֹשֻׁעַ בֶּן לֵוִי – כְּשֶׁהוּחְזְקָה עוּבָּרָה.

The Gemara answers: The *halakha* in **the mishna** is referring **to** a case **where** the woman **had not been presumed** to be **pregnant**[N] prior to her miscarriage; **and when Rabbi Yehoshua ben Levi says** that a woman who discharges is presumed to have discharged an offspring, he was speaking of a case **where** the woman **had been presumed** to be **pregnant**[H] prior to her miscarriage.

תָּא שְׁמַע: בְּהֵמָה שֶׁיָּצְאָה מְלֵאָה וּבָאָה רֵיקָנִית – הַבָּא אַחֲרָיו בְּכוֹר מִסָּפֵק.

The Gemara suggests: **Come** and **hear** a difficulty with regard to the opinion of Rabbi Yehoshua ben Levi from a *baraita*: There is the case of a kosher **animal** that had not yet given birth, **which went** to the pasture **full,** i.e., pregnant, **and came** back the same day **empty,**[H] i.e., with no live offspring. It clearly discharged, but it is unknown whether or not it discharged an offspring, which would exempt the animal's subsequent offspring from the status of a firstborn. In this case, the offspring **that comes after it** is **a firstborn** of **uncertain** status.

**NOTES**

**And most pregnant women give birth to full-fledged offspring** – וְרוֹב נָשִׁים וָלָד מְעַלְּיָא יָלְדָן: The early commentaries point out an apparent contradiction between the *halakha* of Rabbi Yehoshua ben Levi, that the woman's offering is eaten, and a *baraita* stating that if a woman discharges and does not know what she discharged, she brings an offering, but it is not eaten due to the possibility that what she discharged was not an offspring. The commentaries resolve this contradiction in a similar manner to the Gemara's resolution to the contradiction to the statement of Rabbi Yehoshua ben Levi from the mishna: The *baraita* is referring to a case where the woman had not been presumed to be pregnant at all, whereas Rabbi Yehoshua ben Levi is referring to a case where the woman had been presumed to be pregnant (Ramban).

**Where the woman had not been presumed to be pregnant** – הוּחְזְקָה עוּבָּרָה: The later commentaries disagree over the definition of a woman who had been presumed to be pregnant. Some maintain that she is presumed to be pregnant after three months of pregnancy, as at this stage her situation is recognizable to other people (*Noda BiYehuda*). Others claim that the interruption of her menstrual cycle is also required, as well as other signs noticeable by a woman's neighbors (*Ḥatam Sofer*).

**HALAKHA**

**A woman who discharges and it is not known what is the fetus's sex** – הַמַּפֶּלֶת וְאֵין יָדוּעַ מַהוּ: If a woman experiences a miscarriage but does not know what she discharged, she observes the ritual impurity status of a woman who gave birth to a female, even if she had not been presumed to be pregnant (Rambam *Sefer Kedusha, Hilkhot Issurei Bia* 10:19; *Shulḥan Arukh, Yoreh De'a* 194:9).

**Passed across a river and discharged…presumed to be pregnant** – עָבְרָה בְּנָהָר וְהִפִּילָה...כְּשֶׁהוּחְזְקָה עוּבָּרָה: If a woman who had been presumed to be pregnant discharged, and it is unknown what she discharged, e.g., she discharged while passing across a river, or into a hole in the ground, or an animal carried the discharged item away, it is presumed that the woman discharged a full-fledged offspring, and she observes the strictures of a woman who gave birth to both a male and a female, in accordance with the opinion of Rabbi Yehoshua ben Levi. If a woman who had not been presumed to be pregnant discharged, and it is unknown what she discharged, she assumes the status of a woman about whom it is uncertain if she gave birth, and she observes the strictures of a woman who gave birth to both a male and a female as well as those of a menstruating woman. She brings an offering, but her sin-offering is not eaten, due to the uncertainty (Rambam *Sefer Korbanot, Hilkhot Meḥusrei Kappara* 1:6–7).

**An animal that went full and came empty** – בְּהֵמָה שֶׁיָּצְאָה מְלֵאָה וּבָאָה רֵיקָנִית: If an animal pregnant with its first offspring came back from the pasture empty, it clearly discharged; consequently, the animal's subsequent offspring is a firstborn of uncertain status, as perhaps the animal did not discharge a full-fledged offspring. Therefore, its subsequent offspring is not exempt from firstborn status (Rambam *Sefer Korbanot, Hilkhot Bekhorot* 4:13; *Shulḥan Arukh, Yoreh De'a* 315:4).

**BACKGROUND**

When Ravin came – כִּי אֲתָא רָבִין: Ravin was one of the Sages who descended, i.e., would often travel from Eretz Yisrael to Babylonia, primarily to transmit the Torah of Eretz Yisrael to the Torah centers of the Diaspora, although occasionally he traveled on business as well. Consequently, many questions, particularly those concerning the Torah of Eretz Yisrael, would remain unresolved until the messenger from Eretz Yisrael would arrive and elucidate the *halakha*, the novel expression, or the unique circumstances pertaining to a particular statement that required clarification.

וְאַמַּאי? הַלֵּךְ אַחַר רוֹב בְּהֵמוֹת, וְרוֹב בְּהֵמוֹת וָלָד מְעַלְּיָא יָלְדָן, וְהַאי – פָּשׁוּט הוּא!

The Gemara asks: **But why** is this the *halakha*? According to Rabbi Yehoshua ben Levi, one should **follow** the reality among **the majority of animals, and the majority of animals give birth to full-fledged offspring. And** if so, **this** subsequent offspring of the animal **is a regular** offspring, i.e., it is definitely not a firstborn.

אָמַר רָבִינָא: מִשּׁוּם דְּאִיכָּא לְמֵימַר, רוֹב בְּהֵמוֹת יוֹלְדוֹת דָּבָר הַפּוֹטֵר מִבְּכוֹרָה, וּמִיעוּטָן יוֹלְדוֹת דָּבָר שֶׁאֵינוֹ פּוֹטֵר מִבְּכוֹרָה, וְכָל הַיּוֹלְדוֹת – מְטַנְּפוֹת, וְזוֹ הוֹאִיל וְלֹא טִנְּפָה – אִתְרַע לָהּ רוּבָּא.

**Ravina says** in response: In this case, the *halakha* does not follow the majority of animals, **because it can be said** that **the majority of animals give birth to an item that exempts** the animal's subsequent offspring **from firstborn** status, **but a minority of** animals **give birth to an item that does not exempt** the animal's subsequent offspring **from firstborn** status, i.e., an item that is not a full-fledged offspring. **And** an additional factor is that **all** animals **that give birth** to full-fledged offspring **discharge turbid liquids** one day before giving birth, **and since this** animal **did not discharge turbid liquids** before going to the pasture, **the** effect of the **majority is undermined.** Consequently, the status of the animal's birth is uncertain, and for this reason its subsequent offspring is considered a firstborn of uncertain status.

אִי כָּל הַיּוֹלְדוֹת מְטַנְּפוֹת, הָא – מִדְּלָא מְטַנְּפָה – בְּכוֹר מְעַלְּיָא הוּא! אֶלָּא אֵימָא: רוֹב יוֹלְדוֹת מְטַנְּפוֹת, וְזוֹ הוֹאִיל וְלֹא טִנְּפָה – אִתְרַע לָהּ רוּבָּא.

The Gemara raises a difficulty: **If all** animals **that give birth** to full-fledged offspring **discharge turbid liquids** before giving birth, then it should be concluded **from** the fact **that this** animal **did not discharge turbid liquids** that it did not discharge a full-fledged offspring, and therefore the animal's subsequent offspring **is a proper firstborn,** not a firstborn of uncertain status. **Rather,** one should **say** that Ravina meant the following: **The majority of** animals that **give birth discharge turbid liquids** beforehand, **and** therefore, **since this** animal **did not discharge turbid liquids, the** effect of the **majority is undermined.**

כִּי אֲתָא רָבִין אֲמַר: מְתִיב רַבִּי יוֹסֵי בְּרַבִּי חֲנִינָא טוֹעָה, וְלָא יָדַעְנָא מַאי תְּיוּבְתָּא. מַאי הִיא? דְּתַנְיָא,

§ **When Ravin came**[B] from Eretz Yisrael to Babylonia, **he said: Rabbi Yosei, son of Rabbi Ḥanina, raises an objection** to the opinion of Rabbi Yehoshua ben Levi from the *halakha* **of a forgetful woman; but I do not know what the objection is.** The Gemara asks: This *halakha* of a forgetful woman, which forms the basis of the objection, **what is it?** The Gemara explains: **As it is taught** in a *baraita*:

Perek **III**
Daf **29** Amud **b**

**NOTES**

A woman left full and came back empty – אִשָּׁה שֶׁיָּצְתָה מְלֵאָה וּבָאָה רֵיקָנִית: The *baraita* does not describe the woman's version of the events. Some early commentaries maintain that the woman provides no information whatsoever. Others derive from the fact that the woman is considered a *zava* of uncertain status, as explained in the Gemara later, that the woman attests to having experienced a discharge of uterine blood besides her miscarriage, but she does not remember when this began or how long it lasted. But if the woman does not mention this, there is no concern that the woman is a *zava*, from either before or after her miscarriage. As proof for this opinion, it is posited that if a woman who does not know whether or not she experienced a discharge of blood is considered a *zava* of uncertain status, then a woman who is a deaf-mute, an imbecile, or a minor girl who had already experienced a discharge of blood once, should be prohibited from ever engaging in intercourse, as perhaps she experienced a discharge of blood without noticing (Ramban).

אִשָּׁה שֶׁיָּצְתָה מְלֵאָה וּבָאָה רֵיקָנִית, וְהֵבִיאָה לְפָנֵינוּ שְׁלֹשָׁה שָׁבוּעִין טְהוֹרִין, וַעֲשָׂרָה שָׁבוּעוֹת אֶחָד טָמֵא וְאֶחָד טָהוֹר.

**A woman left** home for an extended period of time while she was **full,** i.e., pregnant, **and came** back when she was **empty,**[N] as she discharged the fetus, but it is unknown exactly when and what she discharged; **and she spent three weeks in our presence** during which she was **pure,** i.e., she did not experience any bleeding, **and** for the following **ten weeks** she alternated between **one impure** week, in which she experienced bleeding every day, **and one pure** week, in which she did not experience bleeding at all.

מְשַׁמֶּשֶׁת לָאוֹר שְׁלֹשִׁים וְחָמֵשׁ, וּמַטְבִּילִין אוֹתָהּ תִּשְׁעִים וְחָמֵשׁ טְבִילוֹת, דִּבְרֵי בֵּית שַׁמַּאי. וּבֵית הִלֵּל אוֹמְרִים: שְׁלֹשִׁים וְחָמֵשׁ. רַבִּי יוֹסֵי בְּרַבִּי יְהוּדָה אוֹמֵר: דַּיָּהּ לִטְבִילָה שֶׁתְּהֵא בָּאַחֲרוֹנָה.

In such a case, the woman **may engage in intercourse** with her husband at the end of the fifth week following her return, **on the eve of the thirty-fifth** day, after which she is again prohibited from engaging in intercourse with her husband. **And we require her to immerse** in a ritual bath a total of **ninety-five immersions.** This is **the statement of Beit Shammai. And Beit Hillel say** that she is required to immerse **thirty-five** times. **Rabbi Yosei, son of Rabbi Yehuda, says:** She is required to immerse only once, as **it is sufficient for the immersion to be at the end** of the period when she is required to immerse every day. The entire *baraita* will be explained below.

בִּשְׁלָמָא שָׁבוּעַ רִאשׁוֹן לֹא מְשַׁמֶּשֶׁת – אֵימַר: יוֹלֶדֶת זָכָר הִיא, שָׁבוּעַ שֵׁנִי – אֵימַר: יוֹלֶדֶת נְקֵבָה הִיא,

The Gemara explains the objection from the *baraita* to the opinion of Rabbi Yehoshua ben Levi: **Granted** in the **first week** following her arrival the woman **may not engage in intercourse** with her husband, despite the fact that she did not experience bleeding during that week, as one can **say** that perhaps **she is a woman who gave birth to a male** just before her arrival, which would mean that the first week is her seven-day period of impurity. Likewise, it is clear that the woman may not engage in intercourse with her husband during the **second week** after her arrival, as one can **say** that **she is a woman who gave birth to a female,** and consequently her period of impurity is two weeks long.

שָׁבוּעַ שְׁלִישִׁי – אֵימַר: יוֹלֶדֶת נְקֵבָה בְּזוֹב הִיא,

It is also clear why she may not engage in intercourse during the **third week,** as one can **say** that perhaps **she is a woman who gave birth to a female as a *zava*,** i.e., a woman who experienced a discharge of uterine blood after her menstrual period for three days without the pain of labor, and therefore assumed the status of a *zava* before giving birth. If so, she must count seven clean days after her two-week period of impurity, and subsequently immerse.

אֶלָּא שָׁבוּעַ רְבִיעִי – אַף עַל גַּב דְּקָא חַזְיָא דָּם – תְּשַׁמֵּשׁ, דְּהָא דָּם טָהוֹר הוּא! לָאו מִשּׁוּם דְּלָא אָזְלִינַן בָּתַר רוּבָּא?

**But** in the **fourth week, even though** the woman **sees blood** during that period, **let her engage in intercourse** with her husband, **as it is pure blood.** At this stage the woman's period of purity is certainly underway. Why does the *baraita* state that she may not engage in intercourse with her husband in this week? Is it **not due to** the concern **that** she might have discharged an item that was not a full-fledged offspring? Evidently, although most pregnant women give birth to full-fledged offspring, **we do not follow the majority,** which contradicts the opinion of Rabbi Yehoshua ben Levi.

אֶלָּא מַאי "לָא יָדַעְנָא מַאי תְּיוּבְתָּא"? אֵימַר: הִרְחִיקָה לֵידָתָהּ.

The Gemara asks: **Rather,** as this is apparently a valid objection, **what** is the reason that Ravin said: **I do not know what the objection** to the opinion of Rabbi Yehoshua ben Levi **is?** The Gemara explains: Perhaps it is in fact assumed that the woman gave birth to a full-fledged offspring, in accordance with the opinion of Rabbi Yehoshua ben Levi, and the reason she is not considered pure in the fourth week after her arrival is that one can **say** that **her birth was distant,** i.e., she gave birth a long time before her arrival, and therefore her period of purity had already ended before the fourth week.

הַךְ שָׁבוּעַ חֲמִישִׁי דְּטָהוֹר הוּא, תְּשַׁמֵּשׁ!

§ The Gemara further analyzes the above *baraita*: During **this fifth week, when** the woman **is pure,** as she did not experience any bleeding, **let her engage in intercourse** with her husband. Why is she permitted to do so only on the eve of the thirty-fifth day, at the end of the fifth week?

הַךְ שָׁבוּעַ רְבִיעִי, כָּל יוֹמָא וְיוֹמָא מְסַפְּקִין בְּסוֹף לֵידָה וּבִתְחִלַּת נִדָּה. וְעֶשְׂרִין וּתְמַנְיָא גּוּפֵיהּ, אֵימַר: תְּחִלַּת נִדָּה הִיא, וּבָעְיָא לְמֵיתַב שִׁבְעָה לְנִדָּתָהּ.

The Gemara answers: During **this fourth week,** when she experiences bleeding every day, **we are uncertain** with regard to **each and every day as** to whether it is **the end of** the woman's period of purity as a woman after **childbirth, and that** it is therefore **the beginning of** the seven-day period that she must observe as **a menstruating woman. And** with regard to the **twenty-eighth** day **itself,** the last day of the fourth week, one can also **say** that **it is** after the last day of her period of purity and **the beginning of** her period as **a menstruating woman, and** therefore **she is required to observe seven** days **for her menstruation,** which end on the thirty-fourth day after her arrival. Consequently, the woman may engage in intercourse with her husband only on the eve of the thirty-fifth day.

בְּעֶשְׂרִים וְחַד תְּשַׁמֵּשׁ!

The Gemara further inquires: As explained above, the reason it is prohibited for the woman to engage in intercourse during the third week is that she might have given birth just before arriving and had been a *zava* at the time, and therefore after observing the two weeks of impurity of a woman after childbirth, she must observe an additional seven days of impurity as a *zava*. A *zava* may undergo her purification process on the seventh day of her impurity, following which she is permitted to engage in intercourse. Accordingly, **let** the woman **engage in intercourse on** the **twenty-first** day after her arrival.

רַבִּי שִׁמְעוֹן הִיא, דַּאֲמַר: אָסוּר לַעֲשׂוֹת כֵּן, שֶׁמָּא תָּבֹא לִידֵי סָפֵק. לְאוּרְתָּא תְּשַׁמֵּשׁ! כְּשֶׁרָאֲתָה בָּעֶרֶב.

The Gemara answers: The *halakha* in this *baraita* **is** in accordance with the opinion of **Rabbi Shimon, who said** that **it is prohibited** for a woman **to do so,** i.e., to engage in intercourse on the seventh day of her *ziva* after immersing in a ritual bath, **lest she come to** a case of **uncertainty.** If she engages in intercourse on that seventh day after immersion, and subsequently experiences bleeding on that same day, it retroactively nullifies her entire seven clean days, and it turns out that she engaged in intercourse while she was impure. The Gemara continues to ask: Even so, **let her engage in intercourse that night,** after having completed seven clean days. The Gemara answers: The *baraita* is referring to a case **when** the woman **saw** blood **in the evening,** i.e., her fourth week of experiencing bleeding started in the nighttime.

״וּמַטְבִּילִין אוֹתָהּ תִּשְׁעִים וְחָמֵשׁ טְבִילוֹת״. שָׁבוּעַ קַמָּא מַטְבִּילִין אוֹתָהּ בְּלֵילְוָתָא – אֵימַר: יוֹלֶדֶת זָכָר הִיא.

§ The Gemara analyzes the statement of Beit Shammai: **And we require** the woman **to immerse** in a ritual bath for a total of **ninety-five immersions.** The Gemara explains: During **the first week she** is required **to immerse at night,** every night of the week. The reason is that as the date of her childbirth and the sex of the offspring are unknown, one can **say** that **she is a woman who gave birth to a male.** If so, the seven days of impurity might have ended on any night of the first week, and therefore she must immerse in a ritual bath on each night.

שָׁבוּעַ שֵׁנִי מַטְבִּילִין אוֹתָהּ בְּלֵילְוָתָא – אֵימַר: יוֹלֶדֶת נְקֵבָה הִיא, בִּימָמָא – אֵימַר: יוֹלֶדֶת זָכָר בְּזוֹב הִיא.

During the **second week, she** is required **to immerse at night,** every night, as one can **say** that **she is a woman who gave birth to a female,** and therefore it is possible that her fourteen-day period of impurity ended on any of the nights of the second week. She must also immerse every day of the second week **in the daytime,** as one can **say** that **she is a woman who gave birth to a male as a *zava*.**[N] If so, it is possible that her seven-day period of impurity as a woman after childbirth ended on any given day during the first week, after which she must start to count seven clean days as a *zava*. These seven days necessarily culminate during the second week, and the *halakha* is that a woman must immerse in a ritual bath on the morning when her seven clean days of *ziva* conclude.

שָׁבוּעַ שְׁלִישִׁי מַטְבִּילִין לָהּ בִּימָמָא – אֵימַר: יוֹלֶדֶת נְקֵבָה בְּזוֹב הִיא,

During the **third week, she** is required **to immerse** every day **in the daytime,** as one can **say** that **she is a woman who gave birth to a female as a *zava*,** and consequently her fourteen-day period of impurity as a woman after childbirth ended during the second week. Therefore, the woman's seven clean days as a *zava* might end on any day of the third week, and she is obligated to immerse on that morning.

בְּלֵילְוָתָא – בֵּית שַׁמַּאי לְטַעֲמַיְיהוּ, דְּאָמְרִי: טְבוּלַת יוֹם אָרוֹךְ בָּעֵי טְבִילָה.

She is also required to immerse **on** every **night** of the third week, according to Beit Shammai. **Beit Shammai** conform **to their** line of **reasoning, as they say** in a mishna (71b) that a woman who finished her period of purity after childbirth, referred to as **a woman who immersed that long day**[N] and is waiting for her purification process to be completed, **requires immersion** at the end of this period. The woman must therefore immerse on every night of the third week, in case that night is the end of her period of purity, for a total of thirty-five immersions by the end of the week. She must continue to immerse every night until her period of purity is certainly over, no matter when she gave birth, i.e., until the eightieth day since her arrival.

NOTES

**In the daytime say she is a woman who gave birth to a male as a *zava* – בִּימָמָא אֵימַר יוֹלֶדֶת זָכָר בְּזוֹב הִיא:** The early commentaries explain that the woman's nightly immersions do not purify her from her status as a *zava*, as it is stated: "But if she is purified of her issue, then she shall count to herself seven days, and after that she shall be pure" (Leviticus 15:28). This verse teaches that a *zava* must count at least part of the daytime. Although in general the halakhic status of part of the day is like that of an entire day, in this case that principle does not apply to part of the night (*Tosefot Rid*).

**A woman who immersed that long day – טְבוּלַת יוֹם אָרוֹךְ:** In a mishna (71b), there is a dispute between Beit Shammai and Beit Hillel as to whether a woman after childbirth must immerse at the end of her period of purity, i.e., forty days after giving birth to a male and eighty days after giving birth to a female. Beit Shammai hold that in order to be permitted to enter the Temple, and, in the case of the daughter or wife of a priest, to be permitted to partake of *teruma*, she is required to immerse. Beit Hillel maintain that this immersion is not necessary.

מִכְּדִי, יְמֵי טָהֳרָה כַּמָּה הָווּ – שִׁתִּין וְשִׁיתָּא, דַּל שָׁבוּעַ שְׁלִישִׁי דְּאַטְבְּלִינַן לָהּ – פָּשׁוּ לְהוּ שִׁתִּין נְכִי חֲדָא, שִׁתִּין נְכִי חֲדָא וּתְלָתִין וְחָמֵשׁ – תִּשְׁעִין וְאַרְבַּע הָוְיָין, תִּשְׁעִין וְחָמֵשׁ מַאי עֲבִידְתַּיְיהוּ?

The Gemara asks: **Now** consider, **how many days of purity are there,** in the case of a woman who gave birth to a female? There are **sixty-six** days. Therefore, in order to account for all of the nights that might occur immediately after the woman's period of purity, she must immerse on sixty-six nights, according to Beit Shammai. **Remove** from this sum the immersions of the **third week, when we require** the woman **to immerse** seven times, and **sixty less one are left.** These **sixty-less-one** times she immerses after the third week **and** the **thirty-five** times she immerses during the first three weeks **are** together **ninety-four** immersions. If so, those **ninety-five** immersions, required by Beit Shammai, **what is their purpose?** Why do they require an extra immersion?

אָמַר רַב יִרְמְיָה מִדִּפְתִּי: כְּגוֹן שֶׁבָּאת לְפָנֵינוּ בֵּין הַשְּׁמָשׁוֹת, דְּיָהֲבִינַן לָהּ טְבִילָה יְתֵירְתָּא.

**Rav Yirmeya of Difti says:** The *baraita* is referring to a case **where** the woman **came before us,** i.e., she returned from her journey, **during twilight,** when it is halakhically uncertain whether it is day or night. The ruling is **that** in this case **we give her another immersion,** i.e., she is obligated to immerse on an additional day, in case she completed her days of impurity on the day she arrived, and that night is the night she must immerse.

וּלְבֵית הִלֵּל דְּאָמְרִי טְבוּלַת יוֹם אָרוֹךְ – לָא בָּעֵי טְבִילָה, תְּלָתִין וְחָמֵשׁ מַאי עֲבִידְתַּיְיהוּ?

The Gemara asks: **And according to Beit Hillel, who say** that **a woman who immersed that long day,** i.e., a woman observing her period of purity after childbirth, **does not require immersion** once her period of purity is over, those **thirty-five** immersions that they require, **what is their purpose?**

עֶשְׂרִים וּתְמַנְיָא – כִּדְאֲמָרַן, הַךְ שָׁבוּעַ חֲמִישִׁי מַטְבְּלִינַן כָּל לֵילְיָא וְלֵילְיָא, אֵימַר סוֹף נִדָּה הִיא.

The Gemara answers: **Twenty-eight** immersions are required **as we said** above, i.e., due to the end of the period of impurity in case the woman gave birth to a male or to a female, and due to the completion of the woman's seven clean days in case she gave birth as a *zava*. In addition, during **this fifth week we require** the woman **to immerse each and every night,** as one can **say** that **it is the end of** her seven-day period as **a menstruating woman.**

עֲשָׂרָה שָׁבוּעִין לָמָּה לִי? בִּתְמַנְיָא וּפַלְגָּא סָגֵי!

The Gemara raises a further difficulty: **Why do I** need the *baraita* to state that after the woman did not experience any bleeding for the first three weeks after arriving, she alternated for **ten weeks** between experiencing bleeding every day for a week and not experiencing any bleeding for a week. How does this detail contribute to Beit Shammai's ruling that the woman must immerse ninety-five times? After all, **eight and a half** weeks **are sufficient.** Combined with the first three weeks after the woman's arrival, this period amounts to eighty days, which is the number of days on which the woman must immerse according to Beit Shammai, as each day might be the last of her period of purity.

אַיְּידֵי דְּתָנָא פַּלְגָּא דְּשָׁבוּעַ – מַסֵּיק לֵיהּ, וְאַיְּידֵי דְּתָנָא שָׁבוּעַ טָמֵא – תָּנָא נַמִי שָׁבוּעַ טָהוֹר.

The Gemara answers: Although eight and a half weeks are sufficient, **since** the *baraita* must **teach half a week, it completes** that week, for a total of nine weeks. **And since** the *baraita* **teaches** with regard to the ninth **week** that the woman is **impure, it also taught** with regard to the tenth **week** that the woman is **pure,** in accordance with the pattern of a week of purity following every week of impurity.

וְהָאִיכָּא טְבִילַת זָבָה!

With regard to the opinion of Beit Hillel that the woman immerses only thirty-five times, the Gemara asks: **But isn't there the immersion** that the woman is obligated to perform **due to** the possibility that she is **a *zava*?** It is possible that by the fourth week, the woman's period of purity after childbirth has already ended, and the bleeding she experiences that week is menstrual blood, in which case the next week that she sees blood renders her a *zava*. If so, she must immerse at the end of that week, after counting seven clean days. The same applies to all the other weeks on which she experiences bleeding, apart from the fourth. Consequently, there are additional immersions not counted by Beit Hillel.

דִּלְפְנֵי תַּשְׁמִישׁ – קָחָשֵׁיב, דִּלְאַחַר תַּשְׁמִישׁ – לָא קָחָשֵׁיב.

The Gemara answers: Beit Hillel **count** only the times **that** the woman is obligated to immerse **before** she is permitted to engage in **intercourse** with her husband, which amount to thirty-five. They **do not count** the times **that** she must immerse **after** she is permitted to engage in **intercourse** with her husband.

וּלְבֵית שַׁמַּאי, דְּחָשֵׁיב דִּלְאַחַר תַּשְׁמִישׁ – נִיחְשׁוֹב נַמִי טְבִילַת זָבָה! בְּלֵידָה – קָמַיְירִי, בְּזִיבָה – לָא קָמַיְירִי.

The Gemara asks: **But according to Beit Shammai, who count** the times **that** the woman is obligated to immerse **after** she is permitted to engage in **intercourse** in their total of ninety-five immersions, **let them also count** those **immersions** in which the woman is obligated **due to** the possibility that she is **a *zava*.** The Gemara answers: Beit Shammai **deal with** immersions that are due to the woman's **childbirth;** they do **not deal with** immersions that are due to the possibility of ***ziva*.**

וְהָאִיכָּא יוֹלֶדֶת בְּזוֹב! יוֹלֶדֶת בְּזוֹב – קָחָשֵׁיב, זִיבָה גְּרֵידְתָּא – לָא קָחָשֵׁיב.

The Gemara questions this response: **But there are** immersions counted by Beit Shammai that are due to the possibility that she is **a woman who gave birth as a *zava*.** These immersions serve to purify the woman from her status as a *zava*, not as a woman after childbirth. The Gemara answers: Beit Shammai **count** immersions that are due to the possibility that she is **a woman who gave birth as a *zava*.** In such a scenario, immersion is delayed due to the childbirth, and is performed when the woman's impurity period of *ziva* following childbirth is over. Therefore, these immersions are considered as connected to the childbirth. But Beit Shammai **do not count** immersions that are due to ***ziva* alone.**

שָׁבוּעֲתָא קַמָּא דְּאָתְיָא לְקַמַּן לִיטְבְּלָה בְּיוֹמָא, דִּילְמָא כׇּל יוֹמָא וְיוֹמָא שְׁלִימוּ לַהּ סְפוּרִים דִּידַהּ!

§ With regard to the statement of the *baraita* that the woman immerses on every night of the first week in case her period of impurity after childbirth just ended, the Gemara asks: Besides immersing on every night of **the first week after she came before us, let** the woman **immerse during the daytime** of every day of that week as well, **as perhaps** she is a *zava*, and on **each and every day** it is possible that **her counting** of clean days **are completed,** and she must therefore immerse that morning. Accordingly, seven more immersions should be added to the count.

הָא מַנִּי – רַבִּי עֲקִיבָא הִיא, דְּאָמַר: בָּעֵינַן סְפוּרִים בְּפָנֵינוּ.

The Gemara answers: In accordance with **whose** opinion **is this** statement? **It is** in accordance with the opinion of **Rabbi Akiva, who said** that **we require** that the seven clean days of a *zava* must be **counted in our presence,** i.e., they must actually be counted. Since she did not know she should count before she arrived, she did not begin counting prior to her arrival. Therefore, her seven clean days begin only once she arrives, and she cannot immerse from her status as a *zava* of uncertain status before the end of the first week.

סוֹף שָׁבוּעַ קַמָּא לִיטְבְּלָה! חַד בְּשָׁבוּעַ לָא קָמַיְירִי.

The Gemara raises a further difficulty: Even so, **let her immerse** at **the end of the first week,** on the morning of the seventh day, after counting seven clean days following her return. This adds one more immersion to the count. The Gemara answers: The *baraita* **is not dealing with** immersions that the woman is obligated to perform **once a week.**

יוֹמָא קַמָּא דְּאָתְיָא לְקַמַּן לִיטְבְּלָה, דִּילְמָא שׁוֹמֶרֶת יוֹם כְּנֶגֶד יוֹם הִיא! בְּזָבָה גְּדוֹלָה – קָמַיְירִי, בְּזָבָה קְטַנָּה – לָא קָמַיְירִי.

The Gemara further inquires: **Let** the woman **immerse** on **the first day that she came before us, as perhaps she is** a lesser *zava*, i.e., **a woman who** experienced a discharge of uterine blood after her menstrual period for one or two consecutive days, and who therefore **observes** a clean **day for a day** she experiences a discharge. The Gemara answers: The *baraita* **is dealing with a greater *zava*** alone, i.e., one who experienced a discharge for three consecutive days and must therefore count seven clean days before immersing; **it is not dealing with a lesser *zava*.**

שְׁמַע מִינַּהּ תְּלָת: שְׁמַע מִינַּהּ – רַבִּי עֲקִיבָא הִיא, דְּאָמַר: בָּעֵינַן סְפוּרִים בְּפָנֵינוּ.

§ The Gemara summarizes its analysis of the *baraita*: **Conclude from it three** conclusions. **Conclude from it** that the *baraita* **is** in accordance with the opinion of **Rabbi Akiva, who said** that **we require** that the seven clean days of a *zava* must be **counted in our presence.**

וּשְׁמַע מִינָּהּ – רַבִּי שִׁמְעוֹן הִיא, דְּאָמַר: אֲבָל אָמְרוּ חֲכָמִים אָסוּר לַעֲשׂוֹת כֵּן, שֶׁמָּא תָּבֹא לִידֵי סָפֵק.

**And conclude from it** that the *baraita* **is** in accordance with the opinion of **Rabbi Shimon, who says** that it is permitted in principle for a *zava* to engage in intercourse with her husband on her seventh clean day after immersing in a ritual bath, **but** that **the Sages said** that **it is prohibited** for her **to do so, lest she come to** a case of **uncertainty,** i.e., in case she experiences a discharge of blood after engaging in intercourse, which retroactively nullifies her entire seven clean days and renders her impure.

וּשְׁמַע מִינָּהּ – טְבִילָה בִּזְמַנָּהּ מִצְוָה. וְרַבִּי יוֹסֵי בְּרַבִּי יְהוּדָה אוֹמֵר: דַּיָּהּ לִטְבִילָה בָּאַחֲרוֹנָה, וְלָא אָמְרִינַן טְבִילָה בִּזְמַנָּהּ מִצְוָה.

And finally, **conclude from it** that **immersion at its proper time is a mitzva,**[N] which is why the woman immerses every day despite the fact it remains prohibited for her to engage in intercourse. **But Rabbi Yosei, son of Rabbi Yehuda, says: It is sufficient for the immersion to be at the end, and we do not say** that **immersion at its proper time is a mitzva** in its own right. Consequently, the woman is obligated to perform only one immersion.

מתני׳ הַמַּפֶּלֶת לְיוֹם אַרְבָּעִים – אֵינָהּ חוֹשֶׁשֶׁת לְוָלָד, לְיוֹם אַרְבָּעִים וְאֶחָד – תֵּשֵׁב לְזָכָר וְלִנְקֵבָה וּלְנִדָּה.

**MISHNA** A woman **who discharges on the fortieth day**[H] since she immersed herself and engaged in intercourse with her husband need **not be concerned that** it might have been **an offspring**[N] and she became impure with its miscarriage, as the formation of the offspring in the womb occurs only forty days after conception. But in the case of a woman who discharges **on the forty-first day** after immersion, there is concern that perhaps it was an offspring. Since its sex is unknown, **she shall observe** the period of impurity **for** a woman who gave birth to **a male and for** a woman who gave birth to **a female; and for** any blood that she sees, she observes the *halakhot* of **a menstruating woman.**

רַבִּי יִשְׁמָעֵאל אוֹמֵר: יוֹם אַרְבָּעִים וְאֶחָד – תֵּשֵׁב לְזָכָר וּלְנִדָּה, יוֹם שְׁמוֹנִים וְאֶחָד – תֵּשֵׁב לְזָכָר וְלִנְקֵבָה וּלְנִדָּה, שֶׁהַזָּכָר נִגְמָר לְאַרְבָּעִים וְאֶחָד וְהַנְּקֵבָה לִשְׁמוֹנִים וְאֶחָד. וַחֲכָמִים אוֹמְרִים: אֶחָד בְּרִיַּית הַזָּכָר וְאֶחָד בְּרִיַּית הַנְּקֵבָה – זֶה וָזֶה אַרְבָּעִים וְאֶחָד.

**Rabbi Yishmael says:** A woman who discharges on the **forty-first day** after immersion **observes** the seven days of impurity **for** a woman who gave birth to **a male; and for** any blood that she sees after seven days, she observes the *halakhot* of **a menstruating woman.** But a woman who discharges on the **eighty-first day** after immersion **observes** the strictures of a woman who gave birth both **to a male and to a female, and** also the strictures **of a menstruating woman, as** the formation of **the male** offspring **concludes on** the **forty-first** day **and** the formation of **the female** offspring concludes **on** the **eighty-first** day. **And the Rabbis say:** With regard to **both the formation of the male and the formation of the female, this and that** conclude on the **forty-first**[H] day.

גמ׳ לָמָּה הוּזְכַּר זָכָר?

**GEMARA** The Gemara discusses the statement of the mishna that a woman who discharges on the forty-first day after immersion observes the strictures of a woman who gave birth to both a male and a female, and the strictures of a menstruating woman. **Why** are the strictures of a woman who gave birth to **a male mentioned** in this statement? What additional strictures must the woman observe due to the possibility that she gave birth to a male, over and above those she observes for the birth of a female?

### NOTES

**Immersion at its proper time is a mitzva – טְבִילָה בִּזְמַנָּהּ מִצְוָה:** It is a positive mitzva for a ritually impure person to purify himself by immersing in a ritual bath. This mitzva is counted among the six hundred and thirteen mitzvot of Torah law (Rav Se'adya Gaon, *Sefer HaMitzvot*, positive mitzva 170; Rambam, *Sefer HaMitzvot*, positive mitzva 109; *Smag*, positive mitzva 148; *Sefer HaḤinnukh*, mitzva 175).

Nevertheless, there is a dispute among the *tanna'im* as to whether the mitzva is to immerse as soon as one is halakhically capable of purifying himself, or whether one may delay his immersion to a later date. Beit Shammai and Beit Hillel, as well as Rabbi Yosei (*Shabbat* 121a) and Rabbi Meir (*Yoma* 8a), hold that it is a mitzva to immerse at the first halakhic opportunity. Therefore, if one is capable of immersing at night, he may not wait until the morning to immerse. This is derived from the verse: "But it shall be, when evening comes in, he shall bathe himself in water" (Deuteronomy 23:12), and from the verse: "And the pure person shall sprinkle upon the impure on the third day, and on the seventh day; and on the seventh day he shall purify him; and he shall wash his clothes, and bathe himself in water, and shall be pure at evening" (Numbers 19:19). By contrast, Rabbi Yosei, son of Rabbi Yehuda, holds that there is no mitzva to immerse at the first opportunity. The indication of these verses that one should immerse when he is first able is, according to Rabbi Yosei, son of Rabbi Yehuda, a mere suggestion.

**A woman who discharges on the fortieth day need not be concerned that it might have been an offspring – הַמַּפֶּלֶת לְיוֹם אַרְבָּעִים אֵינָהּ חוֹשֶׁשֶׁת לְוָלָד:** In the Rambam's Commentary on the Mishna it says that the reference here is to the fortieth day after the woman engaged in intercourse with her husband. Rashi maintains that it is the fortieth day after she immersed in a ritual bath.

### HALAKHA

**A woman who discharges on the fortieth day – הַמַּפֶּלֶת לְיוֹם אַרְבָּעִים:** A woman who discharges on the fortieth day after immersing (*Be'er Heitev*) need not be concerned that perhaps she discharged an offspring, and does not assume the impurity status of a woman after childbirth. She assumes the impurity status of a menstruating woman even if she did not experience any bleeding during the miscarriage; the Rema explains that whenever the womb opens, blood automatically emerges. After counting seven clean days and immersing, the woman is permitted to engage in intercourse with her husband (Rambam *Sefer Kedusha*, *Hilkhot Issurei Bia* 10:2; *Shulḥan Arukh*, *Yoreh De'a* 194:2).

**Both the formation of the male and the formation of the female, this and that conclude on the forty-first – אֶחָד בְּרִיַּית הַזָּכָר וְאֶחָד בְּרִיַּית הַנְּקֵבָה זֶה וָזֶה אַרְבָּעִים וְאֶחָד:** The formation of an offspring is complete no earlier than the fortieth day of gestation, whether it is male or female, in accordance with the opinion of the Rabbis (Rambam *Sefer Kedusha*, *Hilkhot Issurei Bia* 10:1).

אִי לִימֵי טוּמְאָה, הָא קָתָנֵי נְקֵבָה, וְאִי לִימֵי טָהֳרָה,

**If** these strictures are mentioned due **to the days of impurity** that a woman who gave birth to a male must observe, **doesn't** the mishna in any case **teach** that the woman observes the strictures of a woman who gave birth to **a female?** The seven days of impurity that are observed by a woman who gave birth to a male are included in the fourteen days of impurity that she observes for a female. **And if** these strictures are mentioned due **to the days of purity** that are observed by a woman who gave birth to a male, which are fewer than the days of purity that are observed for the birth of a female,

Perek **III**
Daf **30** Amud **b**

הָא קָתָנֵי נִדָּה!

**doesn't** the mishna **teach** that the woman observes the strictures of **a menstruating woman,** i.e., she is considered ritually impure every time she experiences bleeding, and does not observe any period of purity at all?

שֶׁאִם תִּרְאֶה יוֹם שְׁלוֹשִׁים וְאַרְבָּעָה, וְתַחֲזוֹר וְתִרְאֶה יוֹם אַרְבָּעִים וְאֶחָד – תְּהֵא מְקוּלְקֶלֶת עַד אַרְבָּעִים וּשְׁמוֹנָה.

The Gemara answers: The mishna mentions that the woman observes the strictures of a woman who gave birth to a male to teach **that if she sees** blood on the **thirty-fourth day** after her miscarriage **and again sees** blood on the **forty-first day,** her purity status **shall be ruined,** i.e., she shall be prohibited from engaging in intercourse, **until** the **forty-eighth** day. If she were not observing the strictures of a woman who gave birth to a male, but only those of a menstruating woman and one who gave birth to a female, she would not have to wait seven days after seeing blood on the forty-first day. Instead, she would wait only one day, as her possible seven-day period of menstruation began on the thirty-fourth day and ended on the fortieth. Yet, as she might have given birth to a male, the forty-first day might be the first day after her period of purity, and therefore the first of her seven days of menstruation. Consequently, she must consider herself impure until the forty-eighth day.

וְכֵן לְעִנְיַן נְקֵבָה, שֶׁאִם תִּרְאֶה יוֹם שִׁבְעִים וְאַרְבָּעָה, וְתַחֲזוֹר וְתִרְאֶה יוֹם שְׁמוֹנִים וְאֶחָד – תְּהֵא מְקוּלְקֶלֶת עַד שְׁמוֹנִים וּשְׁמוֹנָה.

**And similarly, with regard to** the *halakha* that she observes the strictures of a woman who gave birth to **a female,** one ramification is **that if she sees** blood on the **seventy-fourth day**[H] **and again sees** blood on the **eighty-first day,** her purity status **shall be ruined until** the **eighty-eighth** day. Although she observes ritual impurity after discovering bleeding on the seventy-fourth day, as perhaps she has the status of a menstruating woman, when she discovers bleeding on the eighty-first day she must begin the count of seven days of menstruation again, in case the seventy-fourth day was during her period of purity after having given birth to a female.

״רַבִּי יִשְׁמָעֵאל אוֹמֵר יוֹם אַרְבָּעִים וְאֶחָד תֵּשֵׁב לְזָכָר וּלְנִדָּה״ כו׳. תַּנְיָא, רַבִּי יִשְׁמָעֵאל אוֹמֵר: טִימֵּא וְטִיהֵר בְּזָכָר, וְטִימֵּא וְטִיהֵר בִּנְקֵבָה,

§ The mishna teaches that **Rabbi Yishmael says:** A woman who discharges on the **forty-first day** after immersion **observes** both the strictures of a woman who gave birth **to a male, and** those **of a menstruating woman,** but not the strictures of a woman who gave birth to a female, as the formation of a male offspring takes forty-one days, whereas the formation of a female offspring takes eighty-one days. **It is taught** in a *baraita* that **Rabbi Yishmael says,** in explanation of his opinion: **In** the case of a woman who gave birth to **a male,** the verse **deems** her **impure** for seven days **and deems** her **pure** for an additional thirty-three days, for a total of forty days; **and with regard to** a woman who gave birth to **a female,** the verse **deems** her **impure** for fourteen days **and deems** her **pure** for another sixty-six days, for a total of eighty days.

**HALAKHA**

**That if she sees on the thirty-fourth day…that if she sees on the seventy-fourth day – שֶׁאִם תִּרְאֶה יוֹם שְׁלוֹשִׁים וְאַרְבָּעָה...שֶׁאִם תִּרְאֶה יוֹם שִׁבְעִים וְאַרְבָּעָה:** Whenever a woman must observe the strictures of a woman who gave birth to both a male and a female, and also the strictures of a menstruating woman, the *halakha* is as follows: The woman is prohibited to engage in intercourse with her husband for fourteen days, just like a woman who gave birth to a female. If she discovers bleeding on the eighty-first day, she assumes the status of a menstruating woman of uncertain status. Similarly, if she experiences bleeding on the seventy-fourth day and the eighty-first day, she assumes the status of a menstruating woman of uncertain status. Likewise, if she experiences bleeding on the forty-first day, she is a menstruating woman of uncertain status even if she already experienced bleeding on the thirty-fourth day. She is prohibited from engaging in intercourse with her husband until the eve of the forty-eighth day, as is the *halakha* in the case of a woman who gave birth to a male. She receives no period of purity, like a menstruating woman.

The following *halakhot* apply with regard to any bleeding that she discovers from the day on which she discharged until the eightieth day. If she experiences bleeding during her menstrual period, she is a menstruating woman of uncertain status. If she experiences bleeding during her period of *ziva*, she is a *zava* of uncertain status, as throughout the period after childbirth, the previous patterns concerning the expected times of menstruation do not apply.

Similarly, if she experiences bleeding on the eighty-first day, even if she does not experience bleeding for more than one day consecutively, she is still considered a menstruating woman of uncertain status, due to the lack of an established pattern. Once she establishes a pattern of menstruation after eighty days, her status of uncertainty ceases, and she is either definitely a menstruating woman or definitely a *zava*. Furthermore, if the woman discharged during her menstrual period, she has the status of a definite menstruating woman (Rambam *Sefer Kedusha, Hilkhot Issurei Bia* 10:21).

מַה כְּשֶׁטִּימֵּא וְטִיהֵר בְּזָכָר – יְצִירָתוֹ כַּיּוֹצֵא בּוֹ, אַף כְּשֶׁטִּימֵּא וְטִיהֵר בִּנְקֵבָה – יְצִירָתָהּ כַּיּוֹצֵא בָּהּ. אָמְרוּ לוֹ: אֵין לְמֵדִין יְצִירָה מִטּוּמְאָה.

It can therefore be inferred that **just as when** the verse **deems** a woman **impure and** then **deems** her **pure** for a total of forty days **in** the case of a **male, its** amount of time **is parallel to** the time of **the formation of** a male embryo; **so too, when** the verse **deems** a woman **impure and deems** her **pure** for a total of eighty days **in** the case of **a female, its** amount of time **is parallel to** the time of **the formation of** a female embryo.[N] Accordingly, the formation of a female ends on the eighty-first day after conception. The Rabbis **said to** Rabbi Yishmael in response: **One cannot derive** the amount of time of the **formation** of an embryo **from** the extent of a woman's period of **impurity** after giving birth.

אָמְרוּ לוֹ לְרַבִּי יִשְׁמָעֵאל: מַעֲשֶׂה בְּקְלֵיאוֹפַּטְרָא מַלְכַּת אֲלֶכְּסַנְדְּרוּס שֶׁנִּתְחַיְּיבוּ שִׁפְחוֹתֶיהָ הֲרֵיגָה לַמַּלְכוּת, וּבְדָקָן וּמְצָאָן זֶה וְזֶה לְאַרְבָּעִים וְאֶחָד! אָמַר לָהֶן: אֲנִי מֵבִיא לָכֶם רְאָיָה מִן הַתּוֹרָה, וְאַתֶּם מְבִיאִין לִי רְאָיָה מִן הַשּׁוֹטִים?!

Furthermore, the Rabbis **said to Rabbi Yishmael** that there is a proof against his opinion from **an incident involving Cleopatra,**[P] **Queen of Alexandria.**[B] **Since her maidservants were sentenced to death by the government, she** took advantage of the opportunity and **experimented on them** in order to examine the amount of time it takes for an embryo to develop. She had her maidservants engage in intercourse and operated on them following their execution in order to determine the stage at which an embryo is fully formed, **and found** that both in **this** case, when the embryo is male, **and that** case, when it is female, the formation is complete **on the forty-first** day after conception. Rabbi Yishmael **said to them** in response: **I bring you proof from the Torah, and you bring me proof from the fools?**

מַאי רְאָיָה מִן הַתּוֹרָה? אִילֵימָא "טִימֵּא וְטִיהֵר בְּזָכָר וְטִימֵּא וְטִיהֵר בִּנְקֵבָה" כו׳ – הָא קָאָמְרִי לֵיהּ: אֵין דָּנִין יְצִירָה מִטּוּמְאָה!

The Gemara asks: **What proof from the Torah** does Rabbi Yishmael bring for his opinion? **If we say** that his proof is the aforementioned derivation that **in** the case of a woman who gave birth to **a male,** the verse **deems** her **impure** for seven days **and deems** her **pure** for an additional thirty-three days, for a total of forty days; **and in** the case of **a female,** the verse **deems** her **impure** for fourteen days **and deems** her **pure** for an additional sixty-six days, for a total of eighty days, **didn't** the Rabbis **say to him** in response that **one cannot derive** the amount of time that the **formation** of an embryo takes **from** the extent of a woman's period of **impurity** after giving birth?

אָמַר קְרָא "תֵּלֵד" – הוֹסִיף לָהּ הַכָּתוּב לֵידָה אַחֶרֶת בִּנְקֵבָה.

The Gemara answers: Rabbi Yishmael's derivation is that **the verse states:** "If a woman bears seed and gives birth to a male ... and if **she gives birth** to a female" (Leviticus 12:2–5). **The verse adds another** explicit mention of **childbirth with regard to a female,** besides the mention of childbirth in the case of a male, when it could have simply stated: And if it is a female. Rabbi Yishmael derives from here that not only are the periods of ritual impurity and purity of one who gives birth to a female double those of a woman who gives birth to a male, but the formation of a female embryo also takes twice the time.

וּמַאי "רְאָיָה מִן הַשּׁוֹטִים"? אֵימַר: נְקֵבָה קָדֵים וְאִיעַבּוּר אַרְבְּעִין יוֹמִין קַמֵּי זָכָר.

The Gemara asks: **And** for **what** reason does Rabbi Yishmael refer to the proof that the Rabbis cited from Cleopatra's experiment as **a proof from the fools?** The Gemara answers: One can **say** that the maidservant who was pregnant with **a female** embryo **became pregnant first, forty days before** the maidservant who was pregnant with **a male** embryo. Consequently, it took the female embryo eighty days to be develop, not forty.

**PERSONALITIES**

Cleopatra – קְלֵיאוֹפַּטְרָא: Cleopatra is the Greek name Κλεοπάτρα, Kleopatra, which was given to many Egyptian queens. From the incident related in the Gemara it is difficult to determine which Cleopatra it is referring to.

**BACKGROUND**

Alexandria – אֲלֶכְּסַנְדְּרוּס: Alexandria, a major Egyptian city on the coast of the Mediterranean Sea, was named after Alexander the Great, to whom the city's establishment in the fourth century BCE is attributed. The city was referred to among the Jews as Noe Amon, based on *Targum Yonatan* on the verse: "The multitude of Noe" (Ezekiel 30:15). At its prime, Alexandria was the most important cultural center in the world, and it also had great astronomers and mathematicians. Expert physicians settled in Alexandria and they performed many complicated medical procedures on both animals and humans.

Location of Alexandria

**NOTES**

Its amount of time is parallel to the time of the formation of a female embryo – יְצִירָתָהּ כַּיּוֹצֵא בָּהּ: The later commentaries ask: According to Rabbi Yishmael, who holds that the formation of a female embryo takes forty days longer than that of a male, why does its gestation not last forty days longer? They explain that once a female embryo is formed, it develops more quickly than a male, just as a girl reaches puberty before a boy (*Hatam Sofer*).

**LANGUAGE**

Steward [*apotropos*] – אַפּוֹטְרוֹפּוֹס: From the Greek ἐπίτροπος, *epitropos*, meaning trustee, administrator, or appointee. Usually this word refers to an individual appointed to tend to the estate of minors or others incapable of doing so themselves. It may also refer to one appointed by an individual to tend to his estate.

וְרַבָּנַן – סַמָּא דְּנַפְצָא אַשְׁקִינְהוּ. וְרַבִּי יִשְׁמָעֵאל – אִיכָּא גּוּפָא דְּלָא מְקַבֵּל סַמָּא.

The Gemara asks: **And** how would **the Rabbis** respond to this claim? The Gemara answers: Cleopatra **gave** the maidservants **a purgative medicine**[N] **to drink** before they engaged in intercourse, which would have terminated any previous pregnancy. **And Rabbi Yishmael** would respond that **there are bodies that are not affected by** this **medicine,** i.e., certain pregnancies are not terminated by the medicine. Consequently, the maidservant who was pregnant with a female embryo might have been pregnant prior to the experiment.

אָמַר לָהֶם רַבִּי יִשְׁמָעֵאל: מַעֲשֶׂה בְּקִלַּפְּטְרָא מַלְכַּת יְוָונִית שֶׁנִּתְחַיְּיבוּ שִׁפְחוֹתֶיהָ הֲרִיגָה לַמַּלְכוּת, וּבְדָקָן וּמְצָאָן זָכָר לְאַרְבָּעִים וְאֶחָד, וּנְקֵבָה לִשְׁמוֹנִים וְאֶחָד! אָמְרוּ לוֹ: אֵין מְבִיאִין רְאָיָה מִן הַשּׁוֹטִים.

The Gemara cites another *baraita* that presents a different version of this exchange between Rabbi Yishmael and the Rabbis: **Rabbi Yishmael said to** the Rabbis that there is a proof for his opinion from **an incident involving Cleopatra, the Greek queen, as her maidservants were sentenced to death by the government, and she experimented on them and found** that **a male** embryo is fully formed **on the forty-first** day after conception, **and a female** embryo is formed **on the eighty-first** day. The Rabbis **said to him: One does not bring proof from the fools.**

מַאי טַעֲמָא? הַךְ דִּנְקֵבָה אַיְיתְרָה אַרְבְּעִין יוֹמִין, וַהֲדַר אִיעַבַּר.

The Gemara explains: **What is the reason** the Rabbis consider this a proof from the fools? They claim that it is possible that **this** woman **who** was pregnant with **a female** embryo did not conceive when Cleopatra had her engage in intercourse; rather, she **waited forty days, and then became pregnant** when she again engaged in intercourse. Therefore, the embryo was formed in forty days.

וְרַבִּי יִשְׁמָעֵאל – לְשׁוֹמֵר מְסָרִינְהוּ, וְרַבָּנַן – אֵין אַפּוֹטְרוֹפּוֹס לַעֲרָיוֹת, אֵימָא שׁוֹמֵר גּוּפֵיהּ בָּא עָלֶיהָ.

**And** how would **Rabbi Yishmael** respond to this claim? He would claim that the maidservants could not have conceived on a later date, as Cleopatra **transferred them to** the custody of **a steward,** who made sure that they did not engage in intercourse during the experiment. **And the Rabbis** would say that **there is no steward** [***apotropos***][L] **for** restraining **sexual intercourse,**[N] and therefore one can **say** that the **warden himself engaged in intercourse with** the maidservant.

וְדִילְמָא אִי קָרְעוּהוּ לְהַךְ דִּנְקֵבָה בְּאַרְבְּעִין וְחַד הֲוָה מִשְׁתַּכְחָא כְּזָכָר? אָמַר אַבַּיֵּי: בְּסִימָנֵיהוֹן שָׁוִין.

The Gemara raises a difficulty with regard to Rabbi Yishmael's proof: **But** how can one be sure that the female embryo was formed after eighty-one days? **Perhaps if** the womb **of** the woman carrying **this female** embryo **would have been torn** open **on the forty-first** day after conception, the female embryo **would have** already **been found** in it, **just as** in the case of **a male** embryo. **Abaye says** in response: It was a case **where the indications of** the ages of the two embryos, e.g., their hairs and fingernails, **were identical.** Evidently, the female embryo developed in eighty days to the same degree that the male embryo developed in forty days.

״וַחֲכָמִים אוֹמְרִים אֶחָד בְּרִיַּית זָכָר וְאֶחָד בְּרִיַּית נְקֵבָה״ וכו׳. חֲכָמִים הַיְינוּ תַּנָּא קַמָּא!

§ The mishna teaches: **And the Rabbis say: Both the formation of the male and the formation of the female** conclude on the forty-first day. The Gemara asks: The statement of **the Rabbis is** identical to the statement of **the first *tanna*.** Why does the mishna repeat this opinion in the name of the Rabbis?

**NOTES**

A purgative [*naftza*] medicine – סַמָּא דְּנַפְצָא: Rashi explains that this medicine causes a miscarriage and also scatters [*menapetz*] any semen that may already be in the woman's body after sexual intercourse, preventing pregnancy.

There is no steward for restraining sexual intercourse – אֵין אַפּוֹטְרוֹפּוֹס לַעֲרָיוֹת: It is for this reason that it is stated in the Jerusalem Talmud that even an exceptionally pious person may not be appointed as a warden for women with whom he is prohibited from engaging in sexual intercourse. The halakhic authorities cite this *halakha* (Rambam *Sefer Kedusha, Hilkhot Issurei Bia* 22:15; *Shulḥan Arukh, Even HaEzer* 22:15), and the later authorities add that this prohibition exists even if the warden's wife is generally present while he is on the job, lest he sin while she is absent (*Arugat HaBosem*).

וְכִי תֵּימָא: לְמִסְתְּמָא רֵישָׁא כְּרַבָּנַן, וְיָחִיד וְרַבִּים הֲלָכָה כְּרַבִּים, פְּשִׁיטָא!

And if you would say that the purpose is to teach that the unattributed opinion mentioned in **the first clause** of the mishna is **in accordance with** the opinion of **the Rabbis, and** therefore it is the *halakha*, as when there is a disagreement between **an individual** Sage **and many** Sages, the ***halakha*** **is in accordance with** the opinion of the **many,** this cannot be the reason. The Gemara explains: It is **obvious** that the *halakha* is in accordance with the unattributed opinion mentioned in the first clause of the mishna, as this is a general halakhic principle.

מַהוּ דְּתֵימָא: מִסְתַּבְּרָא טַעְמָא דְּרַבִּי יִשְׁמָעֵאל, דִּקְמְסַיַּיע לֵיהּ קְרָאֵי, קָא מַשְׁמַע לַן.

The Gemara answers: **Lest you say** that **from** the fact that **the explanation of** the opinion of **Rabbi Yishmael stands to reason, as the verses** apparently **support it,** the *halakha* should be in accordance with his opinion, therefore the mishna **teaches us** that the majority of Sages agree with the unattributed opinion mentioned in the first clause of the mishna.

דָּרַשׁ רַבִּי שַׂמְלַאי: לְמָה הַוָּלָד דּוֹמֶה בִּמְעֵי אִמּוֹ – לְפִנְקָס שֶׁמְּקוּפָּל, וּמוּנָּח יָדָיו עַל שְׁתֵּי צְדָעָיו, שְׁתֵּי אֲצִילָיו עַל שְׁתֵּי אַרְכּוּבוֹתָיו, וּשְׁנֵי עֲקֵבָיו עַל שְׁתֵּי עַגְבוֹתָיו, וְרֹאשׁוֹ מוּנָּח לוֹ בֵּין בִּרְכָּיו, וּפִיו סָתוּם וְטַבּוּרוֹ פָּתוּחַ, וְאוֹכֵל מִמַּה שֶּׁאִמּוֹ אוֹכֶלֶת, וְשׁוֹתֶה מִמַּה שֶּׁאִמּוֹ שׁוֹתָה, וְאֵינוֹ מוֹצִיא רְעִי שֶׁמָּא יַהֲרוֹג אֶת אִמּוֹ. וְכֵיוָן שֶׁיָּצָא לַאֲוִיר הָעוֹלָם – נִפְתַּח הַסָּתוּם וְנִסְתַּם הַפָּתוּחַ, שֶׁאִלְמָלֵא כֵּן אֵינוֹ יָכוֹל לִחְיוֹת אֲפִילּוּ שָׁעָה אַחַת.

§ **Rabbi Samlai taught: To what is a fetus in its mother's womb comparable? To a folded notebook** [***lefinkas***].[L] **And it rests with its hands on its two sides** of its head, at the temples, **its two arms** [***atzilav***][N] **on its two knees, and its two heels on its two buttocks, and its head rests between its knees,**[N] **and its mouth is closed, and its umbilicus is open. And it eats from what its mother eats, and it drinks from what its mother drinks, and it does not emit excrement**[N] **lest it kill its mother. But once it emerges into the airspace of the world, the closed** limb, i.e., its mouth, **opens, and the open** limb, its umbilicus, **closes, as otherwise it cannot live** for **even one hour.**[N]

וְנֵר דָּלוּק לוֹ עַל רֹאשׁוֹ וְצוֹפֶה וּמַבִּיט מִסּוֹף הָעוֹלָם וְעַד סוֹפוֹ, שֶׁנֶּאֱמַר: "בְּהִלּוֹ נֵרוֹ עֲלֵי רֹאשִׁי לְאוֹרוֹ אֵלֶךְ חֹשֶׁךְ". וְאַל תִּתְמַהּ, שֶׁהֲרֵי אָדָם יָשֵׁן כָּאן וְרוֹאֶה חֲלוֹם בְּאַסְפַּמְיָא.

**And a candle is lit for it above its head, and it gazes from one end of the world to the other, as it is stated: "When His lamp shined above my head, and by His light I walked through darkness"** (Job 29:3). **And do not wonder** how one can see from one end of the world to the other, **as a person can sleep here,** in this location, **and see a dream** that takes place **in** a place as distant as **Spain** [***beAspamya***].[B]

וְאֵין לְךָ יָמִים שֶׁאָדָם שָׁרוּי בְּטוֹבָה יוֹתֵר מֵאוֹתָן הַיָּמִים, שֶׁנֶּאֱמַר: "מִי יִתְּנֵנִי כְיַרְחֵי קֶדֶם כִּימֵי אֱלוֹהַּ יִשְׁמְרֵנִי", וְאֵיזֶהוּ יָמִים שֶׁיֵּשׁ בָּהֶם יְרָחִים וְאֵין בָּהֶם שָׁנִים – הֱוֵי אוֹמֵר: אֵלּוּ יַרְחֵי לֵידָה.

**And there are no days when a person is in a more blissful state than those days** when he is a fetus in his mother's womb, **as it is stated** in the previous verse: **"If only I were as in the months of old, as in the days when God watched over me"** (Job 29:2). **And the** proof that this verse is referring to gestation is as follows: **Which** are the **days that have months but do not have years? You must say** that **these are the months of gestation.**

**LANGUAGE**

Notebook [*pinkas*] – פִּנְקָס: From the Greek πίναξ, *pinax*, meaning tablet or board on which one writes. Over time, the *pinkas* became several tablets connected to each other in the form of a small book. The notebooks in the time of the Talmud varied in shape and were made from various materials. Apparently the most common of them was a notebook made of tablets of wood on which they smeared a layer of wax, in which they would carve words and erase them to write again.

Fresco of woman with wax tablet and man with scroll, Pompeii, second century BCE

**BACKGROUND**

Spain [*Aspamya*] – אַסְפַּמְיָא: Aspamia or Aspania is generally identified as Spain, which is called Aspamia in Greek and Latin. In biblical Hebrew, Sepharad, mentioned in the verse: "And the captivity of Jerusalem that is in Sepharad shall possess the cities of the South" (Obadiah 1:20), is identified by the commentaries as Spain (*Targum Yonatan*; Abravanel on II Kings). Since Spain was on the other end of the Mediterranean Sea from Eretz Yisrael and Babylonia, and journeys by sea would be conducted in proximity to the coast, with several stops along the way, a trip to Spain would take a very long time, and Spain was considered a prototypical very distant country.

**NOTES**

Its two arms [*atzilav*] – שְׁתֵּי אֲצִילָיו: Rashi explains that the reference is to the armpits. Others interpret this word as referring to the elbows, in accordance with *Targum Yonatan* on the verse (Ezekiel 13:18): "Upon all elbows [*atzilei yadai*]" (*Tosafot*; *Arukh*).

And its head rests between its knees – וְרֹאשׁוֹ מוּנָּח לוֹ בֵּין בִּרְכָּיו: The *ge'onim* write that the *halakha* that one must bow his head to the height of his knees while reciting the blessing of *modim* during the *Amida* prayer is because a fetus lies with its head between its thighs (*Shibbolei HaLeket*; *Tanya Rabbati*; *Emek Berakha*).

And it does not emit excrement – וְאֵינוֹ מוֹצִיא רְעִי: The Maharsha writes that the life of a fetus is comparable to that of the Jewish people in the wilderness, when they would eat manna and drink from Miriam's well, and would therefore not emit excrement, as manna was divine food that would not turn into excrement.

As otherwise it cannot live for even one hour – שֶׁאִלְמָלֵא כֵּן אֵינוֹ יָכוֹל לִחְיוֹת אֲפִילּוּ שָׁעָה אַחַת: Some of the early commentaries delete the phrase: For even one hour, as one can close his mouth for several hours without endangering his life (Maharam of Rothenburg, cited by *Tashbetz* and Abudirham). Others maintain this phrase, as the reference is to the moment that an infant is born; if its mouth is closed and its umbilicus is open, even for a short while, it cannot survive (*Tur*). As result of this dispute, the halakhic authorities disagree as to whether the phrase: Even one hour, is included in the blessing of *Asher Yatzar*, said after using the bathroom. The *Magen Avraham* (*Oraḥ Ḥayyim* 6:2) rules that this phrase should not be included, but the *Taz* (*Oraḥ Ḥayyim* 6:2) rules that the phrase should be included.

NOTES

And a fetus is taught the entire Torah – וּמְלַמְּדִין אוֹתוֹ כׇּל הַתּוֹרָה כּוּלָּהּ: This is interpreted as a metaphor for free will in the development and birth of every child. While still in the womb, the developing embryo receives raw abilities and intelligence that will allow the person to engage in and understand God's Torah. But upon its exit from the womb the newborn is overwhelmed and enticed with the sensations of a physical world that draw one away from Torah, and as he grows he must choose the path of righteousness (*Midrash Shlomo*).

וּמְלַמְּדִין אוֹתוֹ כׇּל הַתּוֹרָה כּוּלָּהּ, שֶׁנֶּאֱמַר: ״וַיֹּרֵנִי וַיֹּאמֶר לִי יִתְמׇךְ דְּבָרַי לִבֶּךָ שְׁמֹר מִצְוֹתַי וֶחְיֵה״, וְאוֹמֵר: ״בְּסוֹד אֱלוֹהַּ עֲלֵי אׇהֳלִי״.

**And a fetus is taught the entire Torah**[N] while in the womb, **as it is stated: "And He taught me and said to me: Let your heart hold fast My words; keep My commandments, and live"** (Proverbs 4:4). **And it** also **states:** "As I was in the days of my youth, **when the converse of God was upon my tent"** (Job 29:4).

מַאי ״וְאוֹמֵר״? וְכִי תֵּימָא נָבִיא הוּא דְּקָאָמַר – תָּא שְׁמַע: ״בְּסוֹד אֱלוֹהַּ עֲלֵי אׇהֳלִי״.

The Gemara asks: **What is** the purpose of the statement: **And it** also **states:** "When the converse of God was upon my tent"? Why is it necessary to cite this verse in addition to the previously quoted verse from Proverbs? The Gemara explains: **And if you would say** that the verse in Proverbs is insufficient, as **it is a prophet who is saying** that he was taught the entire Torah in his mother's womb, but this does not apply to ordinary people, **come** and **hear** the verse in Job: **"When the converse of God was upon my tent."**

וְכֵיוָן שֶׁבָּא לַאֲוִיר הָעוֹלָם – בָּא מַלְאָךְ וְסְטָרוֹ עַל פִּיו, וּמְשַׁכְּחוֹ כׇּל הַתּוֹרָה כּוּלָּהּ, שֶׁנֶּאֱמַר: ״לַפֶּתַח חַטָּאת רֹבֵץ״.

**And once** the fetus **emerges into the airspace of the world, an angel comes and slaps it on its mouth, causing it to forget the entire Torah, as it is stated: "Sin crouches at the entrance"** (Genesis 4:7), i.e., when a person enters the world he is immediately liable to sin due to his loss of Torah knowledge.

וְאֵינוֹ יוֹצֵא מִשָּׁם עַד שֶׁמַּשְׁבִּיעִין אוֹתוֹ, שֶׁנֶּאֱמַר: ״כִּי לִי תִּכְרַע כׇּל בֶּרֶךְ תִּשָּׁבַע כׇּל לָשׁוֹן״, ״כִּי לִי תִּכְרַע כׇּל בֶּרֶךְ״ – זֶה יוֹם הַמִּיתָה, שֶׁנֶּאֱמַר: ״לְפָנָיו יִכְרְעוּ כׇּל יוֹרְדֵי עָפָר״, ״תִּשָּׁבַע כׇּל לָשׁוֹן״ – זֶה יוֹם הַלֵּידָה, שֶׁנֶּאֱמַר: ״נְקִי כַפַּיִם וּבַר לֵבָב אֲשֶׁר לֹא נָשָׂא לַשָּׁוְא נַפְשׁוֹ וְלֹא נִשְׁבַּע לְמִרְמָה״.

**And** a fetus **does not leave** the womb **until** the angels **administer an oath to it, as it is stated: "That to Me every knee shall bow, every tongue shall swear"** (Isaiah 45:23). The verse is interpreted as follows: **"That to Me every knee shall bow"; this is** referring to **the day of** one's **death, as it is stated: "All those who go down to the dust shall kneel before Him"** (Psalms 22:30). **"Every tongue shall swear"; this is** referring to **the day of** one's **birth, as it is stated** in description of a righteous person: **"He who has clean hands, and a pure heart, who has not taken My name in vain, and has not sworn deceitfully"** (Psalms 24:4), i.e., he has kept the oath that he took before he was born.

וּמָה הִיא הַשְּׁבוּעָה שֶׁמַּשְׁבִּיעִין אוֹתוֹ – תְּהִי צַדִּיק וְאַל תְּהִי רָשָׁע, וַאֲפִילּוּ כׇּל הָעוֹלָם כּוּלּוֹ אוֹמְרִים לָךְ: צַדִּיק אַתָּה – הֱיֵה בְּעֵינֶיךָ כְּרָשָׁע. וֶהֱוֵי יוֹדֵעַ שֶׁהַקָּדוֹשׁ בָּרוּךְ הוּא טָהוֹר וּמְשָׁרְתָיו טְהוֹרִים, וּנְשָׁמָה שֶׁנָּתַן בְּךָ טְהוֹרָה הִיא, אִם אַתָּה מְשַׁמְּרָהּ בְּטׇהֳרָה – מוּטָב, וְאִם לָאו – הֲרֵינִי נוֹטְלָהּ מִמְּךָ.

**And what is the oath that** the angels **administer to** the fetus? **Be righteous and do not be wicked. And even if the entire world says to you: You are righteous, consider yourself wicked. And know that the Holy One, Blessed be He, is pure, and His ministers are pure, and the soul that He gave you is pure. If you preserve it in** a state of **purity,** all is **well, but if** you do **not** keep it pure, **I,** the angel, **shall take it from you.**

תָּנָא דְּבֵי רַבִּי יִשְׁמָעֵאל: מָשָׁל לְכֹהֵן שֶׁמָּסַר תְּרוּמָה לְעַם הָאָרֶץ, וְאָמַר לוֹ: אִם אַתָּה מְשַׁמְּרָהּ בְּטׇהֳרָה – מוּטָב, וְאִם לָאו – הֲרֵינִי שׂוֹרְפָהּ לְפָנֶיךָ.

**The school of Rabbi Yishmael taught a parable:** This matter is comparable **to a priest who gave** ***teruma***, the portion of the produce designated for the priest, **to one who is unreliable with regard to ritual impurity [*am ha'aretz*]**, and therefore it is suspected that he might not maintain the purity of the *teruma*. **And** the priest **said to him: If you keep it in** a state of **ritual purity,** all is **well, but if** you do **not** keep it pure, **I shall burn it before you.**

אָמַר רַבִּי אֶלְעָזָר:

**Rabbi Elazar said:**

Perek **III**
Daf **31** Amud **a**

מַאי קְרָא ״מִמְּעֵי אִמִּי אַתָּה גוֹזִי״. מַאי מַשְׁמַע דְּהַאי ״גּוֹזִי״ לִישָּׁנָא דְּאִשְׁתַּבּוּעֵי הוּא? דִּכְתִיב: ״גׇּזִּי נִזְרֵךְ וְהַשְׁלִיכִי״.

**What is the verse** from which it is derived that a fetus is administered an oath on the day of its birth? "Upon You I have relied from birth; **You are He Who took me out [*gozi*] of my mother's womb"** (Psalms 71:6). **From where may it be inferred that this** word: **"*Gozi*," is a term of administering an oath? As it is written: "Cut off [*gozi*] your hair and cast it away"** (Jeremiah 7:29), which is interpreted as a reference to the vow of a nazirite, who must cut off his hair at the end of his term of naziriteship.

וְאָמַר רַבִּי אֶלְעָזָר: לְמָה וָלָד דּוֹמֶה בִּמְעֵי אִמּוֹ? לֶאֱגוֹז מוּנָּח בְּסֵפֶל שֶׁל מַיִם, אָדָם נוֹתֵן אֶצְבָּעוֹ עָלָיו – שׁוֹקֵעַ לְכָאן וּלְכָאן.

**And Rabbi Elazar says: To what is a fetus in its mother's womb comparable?** It is comparable **to a nut placed in a basin** full **of water,** floating on top of the water. If **a person puts his finger on top of** the nut, **it sinks** either **in this direction or in that direction.**

תָּנוּ רַבָּנַן: שְׁלֹשָׁה חֳדָשִׁים הָרִאשׁוֹנִים – וָלָד דָּר בַּמָּדוֹר הַתַּחְתּוֹן, אֶמְצָעִיִּים – וָלָד דָּר בַּמָּדוֹר הָאֶמְצָעִי, אַחֲרוֹנִים – וָלָד דָּר בַּמָּדוֹר הָעֶלְיוֹן. וְכֵיוָן שֶׁהִגִּיעַ זְמַנּוֹ לָצֵאת – מִתְהַפֵּךְ וְיוֹצֵא, וְזֶהוּ חֶבְלֵי אִשָּׁה.

§ **The Sages taught** in a *baraita*: During **the first three months** of pregnancy, the **fetus resides in the lower compartment** of the womb; in the **middle** three months, the **fetus resides in the middle compartment;** and during the **last** three months of pregnancy the **fetus resides in the upper compartment. And once its time to emerge arrives, it turns upside down and emerges; and this is** what causes **labor pains.**

וְהַיְינוּ דִּתְנַן: חֶבְלֵי שֶׁל נְקֵבָה מְרוּבִּין מִשֶּׁל זָכָר.

With regard to the assertion that labor pains are caused by the fetus turning upside down, the Gemara notes: **And this is** the explanation for **that which we learned** in a *baraita*: **The labor pains experienced by** a woman who gives birth to **a female are greater than** those **experienced by** a woman who gives birth to **a male.** The Gemara will explain this below.

וְאָמַר רַבִּי אֶלְעָזָר: מַאי קְרָא? "אֲשֶׁר עֻשֵּׂיתִי בַסֵּתֶר רֻקַּמְתִּי בְּתַחְתִּיּוֹת אָרֶץ". "דַּרְתִּי" לֹא נֶאֱמַר, אֶלָּא "רֻקַּמְתִּי",

**And Rabbi Elazar says: What is the verse** from which it is derived that a fetus initially resides in the lower part of the womb? **"When I was made in secret, and I was woven together in the lowest parts of the earth"** (Psalms 139:15). Since it **is not stated: I resided** in the lowest parts of the earth, **but rather: "I was woven together** in the lowest parts of the earth," this teaches that during the initial stage of a fetus's development, when it is woven together, its location is in the lower compartment of the womb.

מַאי שְׁנָא חֶבְלֵי נְקֵבָה מְרוּבִּין מִשֶּׁל זָכָר. זֶה בָּא כְּדֶרֶךְ תַּשְׁמִישׁוֹ וְזֶה בָּא כְּדֶרֶךְ תַּשְׁמִישׁוֹ, זוֹ הוֹפֶכֶת פָּנֶיהָ וְזֶה אֵין הוֹפֵךְ פָּנָיו.

The Gemara asks: **What is different** about **the labor pains experienced by** a woman who gives birth to **a female,** that they **are greater than those experienced by** a woman who gives birth to **a male?** The Gemara answers: **This** one, a male fetus, **emerges in the manner in which it engages in intercourse.** Just as a male engages in intercourse facing downward, so too, it is born while facing down. **And that** one, a female fetus, **emerges in the manner in which it engages in intercourse,**[N] i.e., facing upward. Consequently, **that** one, a female fetus, **turns its face around** before it is born, **but this** one, a male fetus, **does not turn its face around** before it is born.

תָּנוּ רַבָּנַן: שְׁלֹשָׁה חֳדָשִׁים הָרִאשׁוֹנִים – תַּשְׁמִישׁ קָשֶׁה לָאִשָּׁה וְגַם קָשֶׁה לַוָּלָד, אֶמְצָעִיִּים – קָשֶׁה לָאִשָּׁה וְיָפֶה לַוָּלָד, אַחֲרוֹנִים – יָפֶה לָאִשָּׁה וְיָפֶה לַוָּלָד, שֶׁמִּתּוֹךְ כָּךְ נִמְצָא הַוָּלָד מְלוּבָּן וּמְזוֹרָז.

§ **The Sages taught** in a *baraita*: During **the first three months** of pregnancy, **sexual intercourse is difficult** and harmful **for the woman and is also difficult for the offspring.**[N] During the **middle** three months, intercourse is **difficult for the woman but is beneficial for the offspring.** During the **last** three months, sexual intercourse is **beneficial for the woman and beneficial for the offspring; as a result of it the offspring is found to be strong and fair skinned.**

**NOTES**

**That emerges in the manner in which it engages in intercourse** – זֶה בָּא כְּדֶרֶךְ תַּשְׁמִישׁוֹ: Some later commentaries explain that although in previous generations a male infant would be born facedown and a female would be born faceup, this is no longer the case. Nowadays there is no difference between the position of male and female infants during childbirth. This is one of several differences between ancient times and the modern era with regard to childbirth (*Sefer HaBerit*).

**During the first three months sexual intercourse is difficult for the woman and is also difficult for the offspring** – שְׁלֹשָׁה חֳדָשִׁים הָרִאשׁוֹנִים תַּשְׁמִישׁ קָשֶׁה לָאִשָּׁה וְגַם קָשֶׁה לַוָּלָד: Rashi explains that it is difficult for the offspring because it is in the lower compartment of the womb. Others state that although intercourse renders the offspring uncomfortable, it does not harm it (Responsa of the Rivash). Some add that the Sages could have prohibited intercourse during this period due to the effect on the offspring, but they did not do so, as most people would be unable to adhere to a three-month ban on intercourse, which might cause the couple to have sinful thoughts (*Sefer Ḥasidim*).

**LANGUAGE**

**Countenance** [*kelaster*] **– קְלַסְתֵּר:** Possibly from the Latin caelatura, meaning a graven image. Others claim that it derives from the Greek εἰκών, *eikon*, meaning likeness or image, and ἀστήρ, *aster*, meaning star, flame, or light, yielding the meaning: The image or radiance of the countenance.

**BACKGROUND**

**Flask that is tied – חֵמֶת צְרוּרָה:** This refers to a leather sack that was used for liquids, e.g., drinking water. The opening of the flask would be tied closed, and it would be opened only in order to fill the flask or to pour water out. Flasks were sometimes used to store solid items as well, but this was not considered a recommended way to keep an item safe, as a flask could easily be untied by anyone.

Relief of servant carrying wineskin, Persepolis, 480 BCE

תָּנָא: הַמְשַׁמֵּשׁ מִטָּתוֹ לְיוֹם תִּשְׁעִים – כְּאִילּוּ שׁוֹפֵךְ דָּמִים. מְנָא יָדַע? אֶלָּא אָמַר אַבַּיֵּי: מְשַׁמֵּשׁ וְהוֹלֵךְ, וְ״שֹׁמֵר פְּתָאִים ה׳״.

The Sages **taught** in a *baraita*: With regard to **one who engages in intercourse** with his wife **on the ninetieth day** of her pregnancy, **it is as though he spills** her **blood.** The Gemara asks: **How does one know** that it is the ninetieth day of her pregnancy? **Rather, Abaye says: One should go ahead and engage in intercourse** with his wife even if it might be the ninetieth day, **and** rely on God to prevent any ensuing harm, as the verse states: **"The Lord preserves the simple"** (Psalms 116:6).

תָּנוּ רַבָּנַן: שְׁלֹשָׁה שׁוּתָּפִין יֵשׁ בָּאָדָם, הַקָּדוֹשׁ בָּרוּךְ הוּא וְאָבִיו וְאִמּוֹ. אָבִיו – מַזְרִיעַ הַלּוֹבֶן, שֶׁמִּמֶּנּוּ עֲצָמוֹת וְגִידִים וְצִפׇּרְנַיִם וּמוֹחַ שֶׁבְּרֹאשׁוֹ וְלוֹבֶן שֶׁבָּעַיִן. אִמּוֹ – מַזְרַעַת אוֹדֶם, שֶׁמִּמֶּנּוּ עוֹר וּבָשָׂר וּשְׂעָרוֹת וְשָׁחוֹר שֶׁבָּעַיִן. וְהַקָּדוֹשׁ בָּרוּךְ הוּא – נוֹתֵן בּוֹ רוּחַ וּנְשָׁמָה וּקְלַסְתֵּר פָּנִים וּרְאִיַּית הָעַיִן וּשְׁמִיעַת הָאוֹזֶן וְדִבּוּר פֶּה וְהִילּוּךְ רַגְלַיִם וּבִינָה וְהַשְׂכֵּל.

§ **The Sages taught: There are three partners in** the creation of **a person: The Holy One, Blessed be He, and his father, and his mother. His father emits the white seed,**[N] **from which** the following body parts are formed: The **bones,** the **sinews,** the **nails,** the **brain that is in its head, and** the **white of the eye. His mother emits red seed, from which** are formed the **skin,** the **flesh,** the **hair, and** the **black of the eye. And the Holy One, Blessed be He, inserts into him a spirit, a soul,** his **countenance** [*ukelaster*],[L] **eyesight, hearing of the ear,** the capability of **speech** of **the mouth,** the capability of **walking** with **the legs, understanding, and wisdom.**

וְכֵיוָן שֶׁהִגִּיעַ זְמַנּוֹ לְהִפָּטֵר מִן הָעוֹלָם, הַקָּדוֹשׁ בָּרוּךְ הוּא נוֹטֵל חֶלְקוֹ, וְחֵלֶק אָבִיו וְאִמּוֹ מַנִּיחַ לִפְנֵיהֶם. אָמַר רַב פָּפָּא: הַיְינוּ דְּאָמְרִי אֱינָשֵׁי ״פּוּץ מִלְחָא, וּשְׁדֵי בִּשְׂרָא לְכַלְבָּא״.

**And when** a person's **time to depart from the world arrives, the Holy One, Blessed be He, retrieves His part, and He leaves the part of** the person's **father and mother before them. Rav Pappa said: This** is in accordance with the adage **that people say: Remove the salt** from a piece of meat, **and** you may then **toss the meat to a dog,** as it has become worthless.

דָּרַשׁ רַב חִינָּנָא בַּר פַּפָּא: מַאי דִּכְתִיב ״עֹשֶׂה גְדֹלוֹת עַד אֵין חֵקֶר וְנִפְלָאוֹת עַד אֵין מִסְפָּר״ – בֹּא וּרְאֵה שֶׁלֹּא כְּמִדַּת הַקָּדוֹשׁ בָּרוּךְ הוּא, מִדַּת בָּשָׂר וָדָם. מִדַּת בָּשָׂר וָדָם – נוֹתֵן חֵפֶץ בְּחֵמֶת צְרוּרָה וּפִיהָ לְמַעְלָה. סָפֵק מִשְׁתַּמֵּר, סָפֵק אֵין מִשְׁתַּמֵּר. וְאִילּוּ הַקָּדוֹשׁ בָּרוּךְ הוּא – צָר הָעוּבָּר בִּמְעֵי אִשָּׁה פְּתוּחָה, וּפִיהָ לְמַטָּה, וּמִשְׁתַּמֵּר.

§ **Rav Ḥinnana bar Pappa taught: What** is the meaning of that **which is written: "Who does great deeds beyond comprehension, wondrous deeds without number"** (Job 9:10)? **Come and see that the attribute of flesh and blood is unlike the attribute of the Holy One, Blessed be He. The attribute of flesh and blood** is that if one **puts an article in a flask,** even if the flask is **tied**[B] **and its opening** faces **upward, it is uncertain whether** the item **is preserved** from getting lost, **and it is uncertain whether it is not preserved** from being lost. **But the Holy One, Blessed be He, forms the fetus in a woman's open womb, and its opening** faces **downward, and** yet the fetus **is preserved.**

דָּבָר אַחֵר: אָדָם נוֹתֵן חֲפָצָיו לְכַף מֹאזְנַיִם – כׇּל זְמַן שֶׁמַּכְבִּיד, יוֹרֵד לְמַטָּה. וְאִילּוּ הַקָּדוֹשׁ בָּרוּךְ הוּא – כׇּל זְמַן שֶׁמַּכְבִּיד הַוָּלָד, עוֹלֶה לְמַעְלָה.

**Another matter** that demonstrates the difference between the attributes of God and the attributes of people is that when **a person places his articles on a scale** to be measured, **the heavier** the item **is,** the more **it descends. But** when **the Holy One, Blessed be He,** forms a fetus, **the heavier the offspring gets,** the more **it ascends upward** in the womb.

דָּרַשׁ רַבִּי יוֹסֵי הַגְּלִילִי: מַאי דִּכְתִיב ״אוֹדְךָ (ה׳) עַל כִּי נוֹרָאוֹת נִפְלֵיתִי נִפְלָאִים מַעֲשֶׂיךָ וְנַפְשִׁי יֹדַעַת מְאֹד״? בֹּא וּרְאֵה, שֶׁלֹּא כְּמִדַּת הַקָּדוֹשׁ בָּרוּךְ הוּא מִדַּת בָּשָׂר וָדָם. מִדַּת בָּשָׂר וָדָם – אָדָם נוֹתֵן זֵרְעוֹנִים בַּעֲרוּגָה, כׇּל אַחַת וְאַחַת עוֹלֶה בְּמִינוֹ. וְאִילּוּ הַקָּדוֹשׁ בָּרוּךְ הוּא – צָר הָעוּבָּר בִּמְעֵי אִשָּׁה, וְכוּלָּם עוֹלִין לְמִין אֶחָד.

**Rabbi Yosei HaGelili taught: What** is the meaning of that **which is written: "I will give thanks to You, for I am fearfully and wonderfully made; wonderful are Your works, and that my soul knows very well"** (Psalms 139:14)? **Come and see that the attribute of flesh and blood is unlike the attribute of the Holy One, Blessed be He. The attribute of flesh and blood** is that when **a person plants seeds** of different species **in** one **garden bed, each and every one** of the seeds **emerges** as a grown plant **according to its species. But the Holy One, Blessed be He, forms the fetus in a woman's womb, and all of** the seeds, i.e., those of both the father and the mother, **emerge** when the offspring is formed **as one** sex.

**NOTES**

**His father emits the white seed, etc. – אָבִיו מַזְרִיעַ הַלּוֹבֶן וכו׳:** In *Mishḥat Aharon* it is pointed out that five elements are attributed to the father, namely, the bones, the sinews, the nails, the brain, and the white of the eye; four are attributed to the mother, namely, the skin, the flesh, the hair, and the black of the eye; and nine elements are attributed to God, an amount that is equal to that of both parents put together, namely, the spirit, the soul, the countenance, eyesight, hearing, speech, walking, understanding, and wisdom. A total of eighteen elements are counted, which is the numerical value of the Hebrew word *ḥai*, alive. Therefore, when God removes the elements that He contributed, the person is no longer alive.

דָּבָר אַחֵר: צַבָּע נוֹתֵן סַמָּנִין לְיוֹרָה – כּוּלָּן עוֹלִין לְצֶבַע אֶחָד. וְאִילּוּ הַקָּדוֹשׁ בָּרוּךְ הוּא, צָר הָעוּבָּר בִּמְעֵי אִשָּׁה – כָּל אַחַת וְאַחַת עוֹלָה לְמִינוֹ.

**Alternatively,** when **a dyer puts herbs in a cauldron** [*leyora*],[L] **they all emerge as one color** of dye, **whereas the Holy One, Blessed be He, forms the fetus in a woman's womb,** and **each and every one** of the seeds **emerges as its own type.** In other words, the seed of the father form distinct elements, such as the white of the eye, and the seed of the mother forms other elements, such as the black of the eye, as explained above.

דָּרַשׁ רַב יוֹסֵף: מַאי דִּכְתִיב ״אוֹדְךָ ה׳ כִּי אָנַפְתָּ בִּי יָשֹׁב אַפְּךָ וּתְנַחֲמֵנִי״, בַּמֶּה הַכָּתוּב מְדַבֵּר?

**Rav Yosef taught: What** is the meaning of that **which is written:** "And on that day you shall say: **I will give thanks to You, Lord, for You were angry with me; Your anger is turned away, and You comfort me"** (Isaiah 12:1)? **With regard to what** matter **is the verse speaking?**

בִּשְׁנֵי בְּנֵי אָדָם שֶׁיָּצְאוּ לִסְחוֹרָה. יָשַׁב לוֹ קוֹץ לְאֶחָד מֵהֶן, הִתְחִיל מְחָרֵף וּמְגַדֵּף. לְיָמִים שָׁמַע שֶׁטָּבְעָה סְפִינָתוֹ שֶׁל חֲבֵירוֹ בַּיָּם, הִתְחִיל מוֹדֶה וּמְשַׁבֵּחַ. לְכָךְ נֶאֱמַר ״יָשֹׁב אַפְּךָ וּתְנַחֲמֵנִי״.

It is referring, for example, **to two people who left** their homes to go **on a business** trip. **A thorn penetrated** the body **of one of them,** and he was consequently unable to go with his colleague. **He started blaspheming and cursing** in frustration. **After a period of time, he heard that the ship of the other** person **had sunk in the sea,** and realized that the thorn had saved him from death. He then **started thanking** God **and praising** Him for his delivery due to the slight pain caused to him by the thorn. This is the meaning of the statement: I will give thanks to You, Lord, for You were angry with me. **Therefore, it is stated** at the end of the verse: **"Your anger is turned away, and You comfort me."**

וְהַיְינוּ דַּאֲמַר רַבִּי אֶלְעָזָר: מַאי דִּכְתִיב ״עֹשֵׂה נִפְלָאוֹת (גְּדוֹלוֹת) לְבַדּוֹ. וּבָרוּךְ שֵׁם כְּבוֹדוֹ לְעוֹלָם״? אֲפִילּוּ בַּעַל הַנֵּס אֵינוֹ מַכִּיר בְּנִסּוֹ.

**And this** statement **is** identical to **that which Rabbi Elazar said: What** is the meaning of that **which is written:** "Blessed be the Lord God, the God of Israel, **Who does wondrous things alone; and blessed be His glorious name forever"** (Psalms 72:18–19)? What does it mean that God "does wondrous things alone"? It means that **even the one for whom the miracle was performed does not recognize the miracle** that was performed for **him.**

דָּרֵישׁ רַבִּי חֲנִינָא בַּר פַּפָּא: מַאי דִּכְתִיב ״אָרְחִי וְרִבְעִי זֵרִיתָ וְכָל דְּרָכַי הִסְכַּנְתָּה״? מְלַמֵּד שֶׁלֹּא נוֹצָר אָדָם מִן כָּל הַטִּפָּה, אֶלָּא מִן הַבָּרוּר שֶׁבָּהּ. תָּנָא דְּבֵי רַבִּי יִשְׁמָעֵאל: מָשָׁל לְאָדָם שֶׁזּוֹרֶה בְּבֵית הַגְּרָנוֹת, נוֹטֵל אֶת הָאוֹכֶל וּמַנִּיחַ אֶת הַפְּסוֹלֶת.

**Rabbi Ḥanina bar Pappa taught: What** is the meaning of that **which is written: "You measure** [*zerita*] **my going about** [*orḥi*] **and my lying down** [*riv'i*], **and are acquainted with all my ways"** (Psalms 139:3)? This verse **teaches that a person is not created from the entire drop** of semen, **but from its clear** part. *Zerita* can mean to winnow, while *orḥi* and *riv'i* can both be explained as references to sexual intercourse. Therefore the verse is interpreted homiletically as saying that God separates the procreative part of the semen from the rest. **The school of Rabbi Yishmael taught a parable:** This matter is comparable **to a person who winnows** grain **in the granary; he takes the food and leaves the waste.**

כְּדְרַבִּי אַבָּהוּ, דְּרַבִּי אַבָּהוּ רָמֵי: כְּתִיב ״וַתַּזְרֵנִי חַיִל״, וּכְתִיב ״הָאֵל הַמְאַזְּרֵנִי חָיִל״ – אָמַר דָּוִד לִפְנֵי הַקָּדוֹשׁ בָּרוּךְ הוּא: רִבּוֹנוֹ שֶׁל עוֹלָם, זֵירִיתַנִי וְזֵרַזְתַּנִי.

This is **in accordance with** a statement **of Rabbi Abbahu, as Rabbi Abbahu raises a contradiction: It is written** in one of King David's psalms: **"For You have girded me** [*vatazreni*] **with strength for battle"** (II Samuel 22:40), without the letter *alef* in *vatazreni*; **and it is written** in another psalm: **"Who girds me** [*hame'azreni*] **with strength"** (Psalms 18:33), with an *alef* in *hame'azreini*. What is the difference between these two expressions? **David said before the Holy One, Blessed be He: Master of the Universe, You selected me** [*zeiritani*], i.e., You separated between the procreative part and the rest of the semen in order to create me, **and You have girded me** [*zeraztani*] **with strength.**

דְּרַשׁ רַבִּי אַבָּהוּ: מַאי דִּכְתִיב ״מִי מָנָה עֲפַר יַעֲקֹב וּמִסְפָּר אֶת רֹבַע יִשְׂרָאֵל״? מְלַמֵּד שֶׁהַקָּדוֹשׁ בָּרוּךְ הוּא יוֹשֵׁב וְסוֹפֵר אֶת רְבִיעִיּוֹתֵיהֶם שֶׁל יִשְׂרָאֵל, מָתַי תָּבֹא טִיפָּה שֶׁהַצַּדִּיק נוֹצָר הֵימֶנָּה.

**Rabbi Abbahu taught: What** is the meaning of that **which is written** in Balaam's blessing: **"Who has counted the dust of Jacob, or numbered the stock** [*rova*] **of Israel"** (Numbers 23:10)? The verse **teaches that the Holy One, Blessed be He, sits and counts the times that the Jewish people engage in intercourse** [*revi'iyyoteihem*], anticipating the time **when the drop from which the righteous person will be created will arrive.**

**LANGUAGE**

Cauldron [*yora*] – יוֹרָה: Some explain that this term derives from the word *ur*, fire, as a cauldron is placed on a fire for cooking.

**NOTES**

**With his daughter Dinah – וְאֵת דִּינָה בִתּוֹ:** The Sages (*Berakhot* 60a; *Midrash Tanḥuma*) state that Dinah was, in fact, conceived as a male, but miraculously turned into a female after Leah prayed that she would not give birth to another one of the twelve predestined sons of Jacob, leaving Rachel with only one son, less than the maidservants Bilhah and Zilpah. The Gemara in tractate *Berakhot* infers from this statement that Leah must have emitted seed first, contrary to the statement of the Gemara here, but concludes that they apparently emitted seed simultaneously.

וְעַל דָּבָר זֶה נִסְמֵית עֵינוֹ שֶׁל בִּלְעָם הָרָשָׁע. אָמַר: מִי שֶׁהוּא טָהוֹר וְקָדוֹשׁ, וּמְשָׁרְתָיו טְהוֹרִים וּקְדוֹשִׁים, יָצִיץ בְּדָבָר זֶה?! מִיָּד נִסְמֵית עֵינוֹ, דִּכְתִיב: ״נְאֻם הַגֶּבֶר שְׁתֻם הָעָיִן״.

And it was **due to this matter** that **the eye of wicked Balaam went blind. He said: Should** God, **who is pure and holy, and whose ministers are pure and holy, peek at this matter? Immediately his eye was blinded** as a divine punishment, **as it is written: "The saying of the man whose eye is shut"** (Numbers 24:3).

וְהַיְינוּ דַּאֲמַר רַבִּי יוֹחָנָן מַאי דִּכְתִיב ״וַיִּשְׁכַּב עִמָּהּ בַּלַּיְלָה הוּא״? מְלַמֵּד שֶׁהַקָּדוֹשׁ בָּרוּךְ הוּא סִיֵּיעַ בְּאוֹתוֹ מַעֲשֶׂה, שֶׁנֶּאֱמַר: ״יִשָּׂשכָר חֲמוֹר גָּרֶם״ – חֲמוֹר גָּרַם לוֹ לְיִשָּׂשכָר.

**And this** statement **is** the same as that **which Rabbi Yoḥanan said: What** is the meaning of that **which is written,** with regard to Leah's conceiving Issachar: **"And he lay with her that night"** (Genesis 30:16)? The verse **teaches that the Holy One, Blessed be He, contributed to that act.** The manner in which God contributed to this act is derived from another verse, **as it is stated: "Issachar is a large-boned [*garem*] donkey"** (Genesis 49:14). This teaches that God directed Jacob's **donkey** toward Leah's tent so that he would engage in intercourse with her, thereby **causing [*garam*]** Leah's conceiving **Issachar.**

אָמַר רַבִּי יִצְחָק, אָמַר רַבִּי אַמִי: אִשָּׁה מַזְרַעַת תְּחִילָּה – יוֹלֶדֶת זָכָר, אִישׁ מַזְרִיעַ תְּחִילָּה – יוֹלֶדֶת נְקֵבָה. שֶׁנֶּאֱמַר: ״אִשָּׁה כִּי תַזְרִיעַ וְיָלְדָה זָכָר״.

§ **Rabbi Yitzḥak says** that **Rabbi Ami says:** The sex of a fetus is determined at the moment of conception. If the **woman emits seed first, she gives birth to a male,** and if the **man emits seed first, she gives birth to a female, as it is stated: "If a woman bears seed and gives birth to a male"** (Leviticus 12:2).

תָּנוּ רַבָּנַן: בָּרִאשׁוֹנָה הָיוּ אוֹמְרִים, אִשָּׁה מַזְרַעַת תְּחִילָּה – יוֹלֶדֶת זָכָר, אִישׁ מַזְרִיעַ תְּחִלָּה – יוֹלֶדֶת נְקֵבָה, וְלֹא פֵּירְשׁוּ חֲכָמִים אֶת הַדָּבָר. עַד שֶׁבָּא רַבִּי צָדוֹק וּפֵירְשׁוֹ: ״אֵלֶּה בְּנֵי לֵאָה אֲשֶׁר יָלְדָה לְיַעֲקֹב בְּפַדַּן אֲרָם וְאֵת דִּינָה בִתּוֹ״ – תָּלָה הַזְּכָרִים בַּנְּקֵבוֹת וּנְקֵבוֹת בַּזְּכָרִים.

**The Sages taught: At first,** people **would say** that if the **woman emits seed first she gives birth to a male,** and if the **man emits seed first, she gives birth to a female. But the Sages did not explain** from which verse this **matter** is derived, **until Rabbi Tzadok came and explained** that **it** is derived from the following verse: **"These are the sons of Leah, whom she bore to Jacob in Paddan Aram, with his daughter Dinah"**[N] (Genesis 46:15). From the fact that the verse **attributes the males to the females,** as the males are called: The sons of Leah, **and** it attributes **the females to the males,** in that Dinah is called: His daughter, it is derived that if the woman emits seed first she gives birth to a male, whereas if the man emits seed first, she bears a female.

״וַיִּהְיוּ בְנֵי אוּלָם אֲנָשִׁים גִּבּוֹרֵי חַיִל דֹּרְכֵי קֶשֶׁת וּמַרְבִּים בָּנִים וּבְנֵי בָנִים״ – וְכִי בְּיָדוֹ שֶׁל אָדָם לְהַרְבּוֹת בָּנִים וּבְנֵי בָנִים? אֶלָּא מִתּוֹךְ

This statement is also derived from the following verse: **"And the sons of Ulam were mighty men of valor, archers, and had many sons and sons' sons"** (1 Chronicles 8:40). **Is it in a person's power to have many sons and sons' sons? Rather, because**

Perek **III**
Daf **31** Amud **b**

**NOTES**

**Engage in intercourse and repeat – יִבְעוֹל וְיִשְׁנֶה:** Rashi explains that after the wife is aroused by the first act, during the second act she emits seed before the husband, which causes her to become pregnant with a male.

**A woman becomes pregnant only close to the onset of her menstrual cycle – אֵין אִשָּׁה מִתְעַבֶּרֶת אֶלָּא סָמוּךְ לְוִסְתָּהּ:** In tractate *Sota* (27a) Rashi explains that this is referring to the day before the onset of the woman's menstruation. The early commentaries write that despite the Gemara's apparently unequivocal statement, in fact all opinions agree that a woman is capable of becoming pregnant at different stages of her menstrual cycle.

שֶׁמְּשָׁהִין עַצְמָן בַּבֶּטֶן, כְּדֵי שֶׁיַּזְרִיעוּ נְשׁוֹתֵיהֶן תְּחִלָּה, שֶׁיְּהוּ בְּנֵיהֶם זְכָרִים – מַעֲלֶה עֲלֵיהֶן הַכָּתוּב כְּאִילּוּ הֵם מַרְבִּים בָּנִים וּבְנֵי בָנִים. וְהַיְינוּ דַּאֲמַר רַב קְטִינָא: יָכוֹלְנִי לַעֲשׂוֹת כָּל בָּנַי זְכָרִים. אָמַר רָבָא: הָרוֹצֶה לַעֲשׂוֹת כָּל בָּנָיו זְכָרִים – יִבְעוֹל וְיִשְׁנֶה.

**they delay** while **in** their wives' **abdomen,** initially refraining from emitting semen **so that their wives will emit seed first,** in order **that their children will be male, the verse ascribes them** credit **as though they have many sons and sons' sons. And this** statement **is** the same as that **which Rav Ketina said: I could have made all of my children males,** by refraining from emitting seed until my wife emitted seed first. **Rava says** another method through which one can cause his children to be males: **One who wishes to make all of his children males should engage in intercourse** with his wife **and repeat**[N] the act.

וְאָמַר רַבִּי יִצְחָק, אָמַר רַבִּי אַמִי: אֵין אִשָּׁה מִתְעַבֶּרֶת אֶלָּא סָמוּךְ לְוִסְתָּהּ, שֶׁנֶּאֱמַר: ״הֵן בְּעָווֹן חוֹלָלְתִּי״.

§ **And Rabbi Yitzḥak says** that **Rabbi Ami says: A woman becomes pregnant only** by engaging in intercourse **close to the onset of her** menstrual **cycle,**[N] **as it is stated: "Behold, I was brought forth in iniquity"** (Psalms 51:7). This iniquity is referring to intercourse close to the woman's menstrual cycle, when intercourse is prohibited. Accordingly, David is saying that his mother presumably conceived him at this time.

ורבי יוחנן אמר: סמוך לטבילה, שנאמר: "ובחטא יחמתני אמי".

**And Rabbi Yoḥanan says:** A woman becomes pregnant only by engaging in intercourse **near** the time of her **immersion**[N] in a ritual bath, through which she is purified from her status as a menstruating woman, **as it is stated** in the continuation of the same verse: "**And in sin** [*uvḥet*] **did my mother conceive me**" (Psalms 51:7).

מאי משמע דהאי "חטא" לישנא דדכויי הוא? דכתיב: "וחטא את הבית", ומתרגמינן: וידכי ית ביתא. ואי בעית אימא מהכא "תחטאני באזוב ואטהר".

The Gemara explains this derivation: **From where may it be inferred that this term "*ḥet*" is a reference to purity?** The Gemara answers: **As it is written** with regard to leprosy of houses: "*Veḥittei* **the house**" (Leviticus 14:52), **and we translate** the verse into Aramaic as: **And he shall purify the house. And if you wish, say** that the interpretation is derived **from here: "Purge me** [*teḥatte'eni*] **with hyssop, and I shall be pure**" (Psalms 51:9). Evidently, the root *ḥet, tet, alef* refers to purification.

ואמר רבי יצחק אמר רבי אמי: כיון שבא זכר בעולם – בא שלום בעולם, שנאמר "שלחו כר מושל ארץ", "זכר" – זה כר.

§ **And Rabbi Yitzḥak** says that **Rabbi Ami says: When a male comes into the world,** i.e., when a male baby is born, **peace comes to the world, as it is stated: "Send the lambs** [*khar*] **for the ruler of the land"** (Isaiah 16:1). This *khar*, or *kar*, a gift one sends the ruler, contributes to the stability of the government and peace, and the word **male** [*zakhar*] can be interpreted homiletically as an abbreviation of: **This is a *kar*** [***zeh kar***].

ואמר רבי יצחק דבי רבי אמי: בא זכר בעולם – בא ככרו בידו. "זכר" – זה כר, דכתיב: "ויכרה להם כרה גדולה".

**And Rabbi Yitzḥak from the school of Rabbi Ami says: When a male comes into the world, his loaf** of bread, i.e., his sustenance, **comes into his possession.** In other words, a male can provide for himself. This is based on the aforementioned interpretation of the word **male** [*zakhar*] as an abbreviation of: **This is a *kar*** [***zeh kar***], and the term *kar* refers to sustenance, **as it is written: "And he prepared great provision** [*kera*] **for them"** (II Kings 6:23).

נקבה – אין עמה כלום, "נקבה" – נקייה באה. עד דאמרה "מזוני" – לא יהבי לה, דכתיב: "נקבה שכרך עלי ואתנה".

By contrast, **when a female comes into the world, nothing,** i.e., no sustenance, comes **with her.** This is derived from the homiletic interpretation of the word **female** [*nekeva*] as an abbreviation of the phrase: **She comes clean** [*nekiya ba'a*], i.e., empty. Furthermore, **until she says:** Give me **sustenance,** people **do not give her, as it is written** in Laban's request of Jacob: "**Appoint me** [*nokva*] **your wages, and I will give it**" (Genesis 30:28). Laban used the word *nokva*, similar to *nekeva*, when he said that he would pay Jacob only if he explicitly demanded his wages.

שאלו תלמידיו את רבי שמעון בן יוחי: מפני מה אמרה תורה יולדת מביאה קרבן? אמר להן: בשעה שכורעת לילד – קופצת ונשבעת שלא תזקק לבעלה. לפיכך אמרה תורה: תביא קרבן.

**The students of Rabbi Shimon ben Yoḥai asked him: For what** reason **does the Torah say** that **a woman after childbirth brings an offering? He said to them: At the time that** a woman **crouches to give birth,** her pain is so great that **she impulsively takes an oath**[N] **that she will not engage in intercourse with her husband** ever again, so that she will never again experience this pain. **Therefore, the Torah says** that **she must bring an offering** for violating her oath and continuing to engage in intercourse with her husband.

NOTES

And Rabbi Yoḥanan says: Near her immersion – וְרַבִּי יוֹחָנָן אָמַר סָמוּךְ לִטְבִילָה: Some later commentaries write that because nowadays women wait longer after menstruation before immersing, it is no longer true that a woman becomes pregnant by engaging in intercourse soon after her immersion (Responsa *Malbushei Yom Tov*). Others have claimed that the later a woman engages in intercourse after her immersion the more likely that she will become pregnant, citing physicians of the time (Responsa *Dovev Meisharim*).

She impulsively takes an oath – קוֹפֶצֶת וְנִשְׁבַּעַת: The later commentaries explain that this means a mental, rather than a spoken oath, which she undertakes while experiencing labor pains (*Ein Ya'akov*; *Arukh LaNer*). Some commentaries further add that the reason her husband cannot exercise his right to nullify her oaths is that she did not take this oath contingent upon his consent (*Anaf Yosef*).

מַתְקִיף לַהּ רַב יוֹסֵף: וְהָא מְזִידָה הִיא, וּבַחֲרָטָה תַּלְיָא מִילְּתָא! וְעוֹד, קׇרְבַּן שְׁבוּעָה בָּעֵי אֵיתוּיֵי.

**Rav Yosef objects to this** answer: **But isn't** the woman **an intentional violator** of her oath? **And** if she wishes that her oath be dissolved, so that she may engage in intercourse with her husband, **the matter depends on** her **regret** of her oath. One is obligated to bring an offering for violating an oath of an utterance only if his transgression is unwitting. **And furthermore,** if the purpose of the offering that a woman brings after childbirth is to atone for violating an oath, then **she** should be **required to bring** a female lamb or goat as **an offering,** which is the requirement of one who violated **an oath,** rather than the bird offering brought by a woman after childbirth.

וּמִפְּנֵי מָה אָמְרָה תּוֹרָה זָכָר לְשִׁבְעָה וּנְקֵבָה לְאַרְבָּעָה עָשָׂר? זָכָר, שֶׁהַכֹּל שְׂמֵחִים בּוֹ – מִתְחָרֶטֶת לְשִׁבְעָה. נְקֵבָה, שֶׁהַכֹּל עֲצֵבִים בָּהּ – מִתְחָרֶטֶת לְאַרְבָּעָה עָשָׂר.

**And** the students of Rabbi Shimon ben Yoḥai further inquired of him: **For what** reason **does the Torah say** that a woman who gives birth to **a male** is ritually impure **for seven** days, **but** a woman who gives birth to **a female** is impure **for fourteen** days? Rabbi Shimon ben Yoḥai answered them: When a woman gives birth to **a male, over which everyone is happy, she regrets** her oath, that she will never again engage in intercourse with her husband, already **seven** days after giving birth. By contrast, after giving birth to **a female, over which everyone is unhappy,**[N] **she regrets** her oath only **fourteen** days after giving birth.

וּמִפְּנֵי מָה אָמְרָה תּוֹרָה מִילָה לִשְׁמוֹנָה? שֶׁלֹּא יְהוּ כּוּלָּם שְׂמֵחִים וְאָבִיו וְאִמּוֹ עֲצֵבִים.

**And** the students further asked him: **For what** reason **does the Torah say** that **circumcision** is performed only **on the eighth** day of the baby's life, and not beforehand? He answered them: It is **so that** there **will not be** a situation where **everyone** is **happy** at the circumcision ceremony **but the father and mother of** the infant **are unhappy,**[N] as they are still prohibited from engaging in intercourse.

תַּנְיָא, הָיָה רַבִּי מֵאִיר אוֹמֵר: מִפְּנֵי מָה אָמְרָה תּוֹרָה נִדָּה לְשִׁבְעָה? מִפְּנֵי שֶׁרָגִיל בָּהּ וְקָץ בָּהּ. אָמְרָה תּוֹרָה: תְּהֵא טְמֵאָה שִׁבְעָה יָמִים, כְּדֵי שֶׁתְּהֵא חֲבִיבָה עַל בַּעְלָהּ כִּשְׁעַת כְּנִיסָתָהּ לַחוּפָּה.

**It is taught** in a *baraita* that **Rabbi Meir would say: For what** reason **does the Torah say** that **a menstruating woman** is prohibited from engaging in intercourse with her husband **for seven** days? It **is because** if a woman were permitted to engage in intercourse with her husband all the time, her husband would be too **accustomed to her, and** would eventually be **repulsed by her.** Therefore, **the Torah says** that a menstruating woman **shall be ritually impure** for **seven days,** during which she is prohibited from engaging in intercourse with her husband, **so that** when she becomes pure again **she will be dear to her husband as at the time when she entered the wedding canopy** with him.

שָׁאֲלוּ תַּלְמִידָיו אֶת רַבִּי דּוֹסְתַּאי בְּרַבִּי יַנַּאי: מִפְּנֵי מָה אִישׁ מְחַזֵּר עַל אִשָּׁה, וְאֵין אִשָּׁה מְחַזֶּרֶת עַל אִישׁ? מָשָׁל לְאָדָם שֶׁאָבַד לוֹ אֲבֵידָה, מִי מְחַזֵּר עַל מִי? בַּעַל אֲבֵידָה מְחַזֵּיר עַל אֲבֵידָתוֹ.

§ **The students of Rabbi Dostai, son of Rabbi Yannai, asked him: For what** reason is it the norm that **a man pursues a woman** for marriage, **but a woman does not pursue a man?** Rabbi Dostai answered them by citing **a parable of a person who lost an item. Who searches for what?** Certainly **the owner of the lost item searches for his item;** the item does not search for its owner. Since the first woman was created from the body of the first man, the man seeks that which he has lost.

וּמִפְּנֵי מָה אִישׁ פָּנָיו לְמַטָּה, וְאִשָּׁה פָּנֶיהָ לְמַעְלָה כְּלַפֵּי הָאִישׁ? זֶה מִמָּקוֹם שֶׁנִּבְרָא וְזוֹ מִמָּקוֹם שֶׁנִּבְרֵאת.

**And** the students of Rabbi Dostai further asked him: **For what** reason does **a man** engage in intercourse **facing down, and a woman** engage in intercourse **facing up toward the man?** Rabbi Dostai answered them: **This** man faces **the place from which he was created,** i.e., the earth, **and that** woman faces **the place from which she was created,** namely man.

NOTES

A male over which everyone is happy…a female over which everyone is unhappy – זָכָר שֶׁהַכֹּל שְׂמֵחִים בּוֹ נְקֵבָה שֶׁהַכֹּל עֲצֵבִים בָּהּ: Some commentaries explain that the reason people are happy when a male is born is that he will never have to suffer the pains of labor (Maharsha). Others explain that the difference is due to the fact that the labor pains that a woman experiences while giving birth to a male are less severe than those she experiences when giving birth to a female (*Mei Nidda*).

But the father and mother are unhappy – וְאָבִיו וְאִמּוֹ עֲצֵבִים: The later commentaries note that according to the *halakha* nowadays, the prohibition against the parents engaging in intercourse lasts much longer than seven days. Other reasons why circumcision is performed on the eighth day are not mentioned in the Gemara, and those reasons are relevant nowadays as well (*Marit HaAyin*). Furthermore, the interpretations mentioned in the Gemara here for various *halakhot* of the Torah are mere homiletics and have no halakhic ramifications (*Anaf Yosef*).

וּמִפְּנֵי מָה הָאִישׁ מְקַבֵּל פִּיּוּס, וְאֵין אִשָּׁה מְקַבֶּלֶת פִּיּוּס? זֶה מִמָּקוֹם שֶׁנִּבְרָא וְזוֹ מִמָּקוֹם שֶׁנִּבְרֵאת.

**And** the students also inquired: **For what** reason is **a man** who is angry likely to **accept appeasement, but a woman** is **not** as likely to **accept appeasement?** Rabbi Dostai answered them: It is **because this** man behaves like **the place from which he was created,** i.e., the earth, which yields to pressure, **and that** woman behaves like **the place from which she was created,** i.e., from bone, which cannot be molded easily.

מִפְּנֵי מָה אִשָּׁה קוֹלָהּ עָרֵב, וְאֵין אִישׁ קוֹלוֹ עָרֵב? זֶה מִמָּקוֹם שֶׁנִּבְרָא וְזוֹ מִמָּקוֹם שֶׁנִּבְרֵאת. שֶׁנֶּאֱמַר ״כִּי קוֹלֵךְ עָרֵב וּמַרְאֵךְ נָאוֶה״.

The students continued to ask Rabbi Dostai: **For what** reason **is a woman's voice pleasant, but a man's voice is not pleasant?** He answered: **This** man is similar to **the place from which he was created,** the earth, which does not issue a sound when it is struck, **and that** woman is similar to **the place from which she was created,** a bone, which makes a sound when it is struck. The proof that a woman's voice is pleasant is **that it is stated** in Song of Songs that the man says to his beloved: **"For sweet is your voice, and your countenance is beautiful"** (Song of Songs 2:14).

הדרן עלך המפלת חתיכה

# Summary of **Perek III**

A woman who miscarried assumes the ritual impurity status of a woman after childbirth. Nevertheless, the Sages determined that if she discharged an embryo that is less than forty days old, or if the fetus does not have the shape of a human being, she is not impure. If the fetus has a human face, the woman is impure.

In certain cases, the discharged item is not considered a full-fledged human offspring, e.g., if she discharged an amorphous piece of tissue, or a piece that looks like a shell or a hair. In these cases as well, the *halakha* is that the woman does not have the impurity status of a woman after childbirth.

With regard to those instances where the woman is not impure, the Sages disagree as to whether she assumes the impurity status of a menstruating woman if she examined herself and did not discover bleeding during the miscarriage. Some hold that in such a case the woman is pure, whereas others maintain that miscarriage is always accompanied by bleeding, and consequently she is impure. Everyone agrees that if the woman did not examine herself she is impure, although if the opening of the womb was minor, e.g., in a case where she discharged small pieces of flesh, she is pure.

If a woman discharged a gestational sac in which tissue developed, she must observe the impurity of a woman after childbirth. Since the sex of the offspring is unknown, she must observe the strictures of a woman who gave birth to both a male and a female. This is also the *halakha* if she discharged a deformed fetus that looks like a sandal fish, or if the sex of a full-fledged offspring is uncertain, e.g., a hermaphrodite or a *tumtum,* i.e., a fetus whose sexual organs are indeterminate. If a woman discharges an afterbirth, it is presumed that she was pregnant and that the fetus dissolved in the womb. Consequently, she observes the strictures of a woman who gave birth to both a male and a female, as the sex of the dissolved fetus is unknown.

In a case where the offspring's sex is unknown, the woman observes the strictures of one who gave birth to both a male and a female. In a case where it is uncertain whether a woman was pregnant with a full-fledged offspring at all, she also observes the strictures of a menstruating woman. The reason is that if she did not discharge a full-fledged offspring, the bleeding from her uterus renders her a menstruating woman.

The Sages determined the stage of birth at which the infant is considered born and the woman becomes impure: If an infant is born headfirst, the woman is impure when most of the infant's forehead emerges. If it is born feetfirst, or if it is a non-viable newborn and emerges limb by limb, it is considered born when most of its body emerges.

If a woman inserted a tube into her vagina and discovered blood in the tube, she does not become ritually impure, even by rabbinic law. There is a disagreement among the early commentaries as to whether contact is required for her to contract ritual impurity or if she is not ritually impure because this is not the normal way that a woman discovers bleeding.

# Introduction to **Perek IV**

*And if a woman has an issue, and her issue in her flesh is blood, she shall be in her menstruation seven days, and whoever touches her shall be impure until the evening.*

(Leviticus 15:19)

*And if a woman has an issue of her blood many days, not in the time of her menstruation, or if she has an issue beyond the time of her menstruation, all the days of the issue [zov] of her impurity she shall be as in the days of her menstruation: She is impure.*

(Leviticus 15:25)

The verse states that a woman who experiences menstrual bleeding is rendered a menstruating woman and is impure for seven days. But the Torah does not describe the conditions of such bleeding: Is the verse referring to a woman who experiences a continuous discharge of blood, or even to a woman who experiences a single discharge?

Additionally, the phrase "And her issue in her flesh is blood" requires clarification. Is this referring to any issue of blood that emanates from her flesh, or to a specific type of emission that is known as "her issue in her flesh"?

The Torah also treats the case of a woman who "has an issue of her blood many days, not in the time of her menstruation," and states that such a woman is rendered a *zava*. But the Torah does not explain what is considered the time of her menstruation, and what is not considered the time of her menstruation, or how they are determined. Several other issues likewise require clarification: What are the circumstances in which a woman is rendered a *zava*? What is considered "many days," and what is the *halakha* with regard to a woman who had an issue for only one day "not in the time of her menstruation"?

Once the two time periods, of menstruation and *ziva*, are clearly defined, one must clarify how a woman should act during the days of her *ziva*, when she is ritually pure provided she does not emit blood. Is she required to examine herself, just as she must do during her days of menstruation?

Additionally, when the verse states: "And if a woman has an issue of her blood," is this referring only to blood that comes of its own accord, or even to blood that is emitted because of some additional factor, e.g., blood emitted due to labor pains?

Furthermore, when the verse speaks of "a woman," is it referring specifically to an adult woman, which would mean that a minor girl is not included in these *halakhot*, or is it referring to all females who have a menstrual cycle, including minors? It is also necessary to determine the status of women who do not observe *halakhot* of family purity in the proper manner, such as Sadducee and Samaritan women.

These are the main subjects discussed in this chapter.

מתני׳ בְּנוֹת כּוּתִים נִדּוֹת מֵעֲרִיסָתָן. וְהַכּוּתִים מְטַמְּאִים מִשְׁכָּב תַּחְתּוֹן כָּעֶלְיוֹן, מִפְּנֵי שֶׁהֵן בּוֹעֲלֵי נִדּוֹת,

**MISHNA** Samaritan[B] **girls**[N] are considered **menstruating women from** the time they lie in **their cradle. And the Samaritan** men **impart ritual impurity** to the **lower bedding like the upper** bedding, i.e., all layers of bedding beneath them are impure, and their status is like the bedding above a man who experiences a gonorrhea-like discharge [*zav*]: The status of both levels of bedding is that of first-degree ritual impurity, which can impart impurity to food and drink. This is **due to** the fact **that** Samaritan men are considered men who **engage in intercourse with menstruating women.**

וְהֵן יוֹשְׁבוֹת עַל כָּל דָּם וָדָם.

**And** they are considered men who engage in intercourse with menstruating women because Samaritan women **observe** the seven-day menstrual period of ritual impurity **for each and every** emission of **blood,** even for blood that does not render them impure. Accordingly, if a Samaritan woman has an emission of impure blood during the seven-day period, she will nevertheless continue counting seven days from the first emission. It is therefore possible that the Samaritan men will engage in intercourse with their wives while they are still halakhically considered menstruating women, as the seven-day period of impurity should have been counted from the emission of the impure blood.

וְאֵין חַיָּיבִין עֲלֵיהֶן עַל בִּיאַת מִקְדָּשׁ, וְאֵין שׂוֹרְפִין עֲלֵיהֶם אֶת הַתְּרוּמָה, מִפְּנֵי שֶׁטּוּמְאָתָן סָפֵק.

**But** one who enters the Temple while wearing **those** garments upon which a Samaritan had lain **is not liable** to bring an offering **for entering the Temple**[NH] in a status of impurity, **nor does one burn** ***teruma*** that came into contact with **those** garments, **because their impurity** is **uncertain.**

גמ׳ הֵיכִי דָּמֵי, אִי דְּקָא חַזְיָין – אֲפִילּוּ דִּידָן נַמִי, וְאִי דְּלָא קָחַזְיָין – דִּידְהוּ נַמִי לָא!

**GEMARA** The mishna teaches that Samaritan girls are considered menstruating women from the time they lie in their cradle. The Gemara asks: **What are the circumstances** of this statement? **If** the mishna is referring to girls **who** already **see** menstrual blood, then **even our own,** i.e., Jewish girls, are **also** considered menstruating women under such circumstances. **And if** it is referring to girls **who do not** yet **see** menstrual blood, then **their** girls, i.e., those of the Samaritans, should **also not** have the status of menstruating women.

**BACKGROUND**

Samaritans [*Kutim*] – כּוּתִים: The term *Kutim*, Samaritans, actually is referring to members of a community that included several nations and which was only partly populated by Kutim, Cutheans (II Kings 17:24). In the period of the First Temple, Cutheans were brought to Eretz Yisrael by the Assyrians to replace the Jews who had recently been exiled to Babylonia. They settled in Samaria, and for this reason they are also called Samaritans. The Bible (II Kings, chapter 17) relates how these nations partially accepted the Jewish faith out of fear of wild lions which were prevalent in Samaria. This led to the expression: Converts of lions. Although their conversion was suspect, it did inspire the Samaritans to abandon idol worship by and large.

In the beginning of the Second Temple period, hostility escalated between Jews and Samaritans and their allies. The Samaritans resorted to informing, incitement, and even military action to prevent the construction of the walls of Jerusalem and the Temple. Nevertheless, in later times some Jewish families in Judea, including the priestly class, intermarried and assimilated with the Samaritans. This clearly aggravated the already deep animosity between the two peoples, to the extent that Yoḥanan Hyrcanus, leader of Judea and the High Priest, even traveled to Samaria and destroyed their temple on Mount Gerizim. But there were also occasions in which Jews and Samaritans allied themselves together somewhat, e.g., during the bar Kokheva revolt.

There are various opinions among the Sages not just with regard to marriages between Jews and Samaritans but concerning their overall status in *halakha*. After much deliberation, the Sages decided that due to the prevalence of idolatry in their community, fostered by Greek and Roman influence, Samaritans should be considered gentiles in all regards. In the past few hundred years there has been a reawakening of similar dilemmas and conflicts of opinion.

Samaritans at Mount Gerizim

**NOTES**

Samaritan girls – בְּנוֹת כּוּתִים: According to some commentaries, this mishna is only in accordance with the opinion that Samaritans are true converts. Moreover, is stated that when the Samaritans observed the Torah they were more particular about the mitzvot they upheld than were the Jews (see *Kiddushin* 79a). Nevertheless, in certain aspects the Sages treated Samaritans differently from regular Jews, as they did not accept the traditions of the Oral Law (Meiri). According to the opinion that Samaritans converted under duress and their conversion was therefore ineffective, and certainly after the Sages found that they worshipped the image of a dove (see *Ḥullin* 6a), they are considered like full-fledged gentiles in all regards and in all areas of Torah law, including in the *halakhot* of ritual purity and impurity (Rambam's Commentary on the Mishna; *Tosafot*).

But one who enters the Temple while wearing those is not liable to bring an offering for entering the Temple – וְאֵין חַיָּיבִין עֲלֵיהֶן עַל בִּיאַת מִקְדָּשׁ: Some commentaries maintain that the term: Those, is not referring to the garments, which is how Rashi understands the term. Rather, it is referring to the Samaritans themselves. In other words, the mishna is teaching that one who touches a Samaritan and enters the Temple is not thereby rendered liable to bring an offering (Rashash; *Arukh LaNer*).

**HALAKHA**

But one…is not liable to bring an offering for entering the Temple – וְאֵין חַיָּיבִין...עַל בִּיאַת מִקְדָּשׁ: By Torah law gentiles are not susceptible to the ritual impurity of a *zav*, a menstruating woman, or a woman after childbirth, but the Sages decreed that all gentiles impart impurity like a *zav*; this *halakha* applies to males from the age of nine years and one day and to females from the age of three years and one day.

This decree was not applied to the semen of a male gentile, which remains ritually pure, as is the *halakha* by Torah law. The reason for this exception was to make known that the ritual impurity of semen applies by rabbinic law, as everyone is aware that the semen of an actual *zav* is a primary source of ritual impurity. Since people will realize that the impurity of gentiles applies by rabbinic law only, they will refrain from burning *teruma* and consecrated food on account of this impurity.

Consequently, the gonorrhea-like discharge of gentiles, the blood of a menstruating woman, the blood of a *ziva*, the blood of childbirth, and a gentile man and woman themselves, including their saliva, urine, and the bedding on which they lie and the saddles upon which they ride, all have the status of a primary source of ritual impurity by rabbinic law only. Therefore, one who comes into contact with one of these and subsequently enters the Temple is not liable to bring an offering, nor does one burn *teruma* that touches one of them. They all impart impurity to people and vessels, and they impart ritual impurity by carrying, as does a *zav*, in all respects, except that the impurity applies by rabbinic law (Rambam *Sefer Tahara, Hilkhot Metamei Mishkav UMoshav* 2:10).

אָמַר רָבָא בְּרֵיהּ דְּרַב אַחָא בַּר רַב הוּנָא אָמַר רַב שֵׁשֶׁת: הָכָא בְּמַאי עָסְקִינַן בִּסְתָמָא, דְּכֵיוָן דְּאִיכָּא מִיעוּטָא דְּחָזְיָין – חָיְישִׁינַן. וּמַאן תַּנָּא דְּחָיֵישׁ לְמִיעוּטָא,

**Rava, son of Rav Aḥa bar Rav Huna, says** that **Rav Sheshet says: Here we are dealing with an unspecified** case, i.e., it is unknown whether these girls have experienced their first menstrual period. **Since there is a minority** of girls **who see** menstrual blood, **we are concerned** with regard to each Samaritan girl that she might be from this minority. The Gemara asks: **And who is the** *tanna* who **taught that one must be concerned for the minority?**

Perek **IV**
Daf **32** Amud **a**

רַבִּי מֵאִיר הִיא. דְּתַנְיָא, קָטָן וּקְטַנָּה – לֹא חוֹלְצִין וְלֹא מְיַבְּמִין, דִּבְרֵי רַבִּי מֵאִיר.

The Gemara responds: **It is Rabbi Meir, as it is taught** in a *baraita*: **A minor boy**[H] **and a minor girl**[H] **may not perform the ritual through which a** *yavam* **frees a** *yevama* **of her levirate bonds [*ḥalitza*], nor may they enter into levirate marriage.**[B] In other words, a minor boy whose brother died childless may not perform *ḥalitza* with his brother's widow, nor may he enter into levirate marriage with her, even if she is an adult. Likewise, a minor girl whose husband died childless may not perform *ḥalitza* with her husband's brother, nor may she enter into levirate marriage with him, even if he is an adult. This is **the statement of Rabbi Meir.**

אָמְרוּ לוֹ לְרַבִּי מֵאִיר: יָפֶה אָמַרְתָּ שֶׁאֵין חוֹלְצִין – ״אִישׁ״ כָּתוּב בַּפָּרָשָׁה, וּמַקְּשִׁינַן אִשָּׁה לְאִישׁ, וּמַה טַּעַם אֵין מְיַבְּמִין?

The Rabbis **said to Rabbi Meir: You have aptly stated that they may not perform *ḥalitza*,** since **"man" is written in the passage** of the Torah discussing *ḥalitza* (Deuteronomy 25:7), **and we compare a woman to a man,** as the aforementioned verse states: "And if the man does not want to take his brother's wife." Consequently, neither a minor boy nor a minor girl may perform *ḥalitza*. **But what is the reason** that **they may not enter into levirate marriage?**

אָמַר לָהֶן: קָטָן – שֶׁמָּא יִמָּצֵא סָרִיס, קְטַנָּה – שֶׁמָּא תִּמָּצֵא אַיְלוֹנִית, וְנִמְצְאוּ פּוֹגְעִין בְּעֶרְוָה שֶׁלֹּא בִּמְקוֹם מִצְוָה.

Rabbi Meir **said to them: A minor boy** may not enter into levirate marriage **lest,** once he is older, **he be found** to be **a sexually underdeveloped man,**[B] who is incapable of fathering children. Likewise, **a minor girl** may not enter into levirate marriage **lest,** once she is older, **she be found** to be **a sexually underdeveloped woman.**[B] **And** if a sexually underdeveloped boy or girl enters into levirate marriage **they will be found** to be **infringing upon** prohibitions against **forbidden sexual intercourse where no mitzva applies,** as the entire purpose of levirate marriage is to bear children in the name of the deceased.

וְרַבָּנַן: זִיל בָּתַר רוּבָּא דִּקְטַנִּים – וְרוֹב קְטַנִּים לָאו סָרִיסִים נִינְהוּ, זִיל בָּתַר רוּבָּא דִּקְטַנּוֹת – וְרוֹב קְטַנּוֹת לָאו אַיְלוֹנִית נִינְהוּ.

The Gemara notes: **And the Rabbis** maintain that one **follows the majority of minor boys, and most minor boys are not** going to be **sexually underdeveloped men;** likewise, one **follows the majority of** minor girls, **and most** minor girls **are not** going to be **sexually underdeveloped women.** In any event, the *baraita* indicates that Rabbi Meir is concerned for the minority.

אֵימַר דְּשָׁמְעַתְּ לֵיהּ לְרַבִּי מֵאִיר מִיעוּטָא דִּשְׁכִיחַ, אֲבָל מִיעוּטָא דְּלָא שְׁכִיחַ מִי שָׁמְעַתְּ לֵיהּ?

The Gemara objects: You can **say that you heard that Rabbi Meir** is concerned for **a common minority,** e.g., the minority of sexually underdeveloped men and sexually underdeveloped women. **But did you hear him** say that one is concerned for **an uncommon minority,** such as the minority of young girls who menstruate?

**BACKGROUND**

Levirate marriage and *ḥalitza* – יִבּוּם וַחֲלִיצָה: The *halakhot* of levirate marriage and *ḥalitza* appear in the Torah (see Deuteronomy 25:5–10) and are articulated at length in tractate *Yevamot*, which is devoted primarily to this topic. The basic concept is that if a man dies with no living descendants, his wife is obligated by a levirate bond to her husband's brother. The brother must either take her as a wife through levirate marriage or sever the bond by means of the ceremony of *ḥalitza*. As long as the levirate bond is intact, it is prohibited for her to marry a different man. Any continued involvement on her part with another man prior to *ḥalitza* is considered an ongoing transgression.

Sexually underdeveloped man [*saris*] – סָרִיס: The Sages use the term *saris*, which generally means a eunuch, to refer not only to one who has had a significant portion of his genitals removed but to any male with a major physical or genetic defect on account of which he is unable to father children. Consequently, even when no blemish is discernable, it is possible that any minor boy might eventually have such a defect.

Sexually underdeveloped woman [*ailonit*] – אַיְלוֹנִית: An *ailonit* is a woman who is sexually underdeveloped to the extent that she is incapable of bearing children. This is a general term for women who have basic flaws in their reproductive systems. Sometimes the secondary reproductive signs of these women are not present at all or are barely developed. A comprehensive inquiry into the definition of an *ailonit*, from both a biological and a halakhic perspective, can be found in tractate *Yevamot* 80b.

**HALAKHA**

A minor boy with regard to *ḥalitza* – קָטָן בְּדִין חֲלִיצָה: A minor boy is not halakhically capable of performing *ḥalitza*. He can do so only when he reaches the age of thirteen years and one day and has been examined and found to have two pubic hairs (Rambam *Sefer Nashim*, *Hilkhot Yibbum VaḤalitza* 1:16; *Shulḥan Arukh*, *Even HaEzer* 167:3).

A minor girl with regard to *ḥalitza* – קְטַנָּה בְּדִין חֲלִיצָה: A minor girl is not halakhically capable of performing *ḥalitza* until she reaches the age of twelve years and one day, and has been examined and found to have two pubic hairs (Rambam *Sefer Nashim*, *Hilkhot Yibbum VaḤalitza* 1:17; *Shulḥan Arukh*, *Even HaEzer* 167:4).

הָא נַמִּי מִיעוּטָא דִּשְׁכִיחַ הוּא. דְּתַנְיָא, אָמַר רַבִּי יוֹסֵי: מַעֲשֶׂה בְּעֵין בּוּל – וְהִטְבִּילוּהָ קוֹדֶם לְאִמָּהּ. וְאָמַר רַבִּי: מַעֲשֶׂה בְּבֵית שְׁעָרִים – וְהִטְבִּילוּהָ קוֹדֶם לְאִמָּהּ. וְאָמַר רַב יוֹסֵף: מַעֲשֶׂה בְּפוּמְבְּדִיתָא – וְהִטְבִּילוּהָ קוֹדֶם לְאִמָּהּ.

The Gemara explains: **This** minority of young girls who menstruate **is also a common minority. As it is taught** in a *baraita* that **Rabbi Yosei said:** There was **an incident in** the town of **Ein Bul**[B] where **they immersed** a baby girl in a ritual bath **before her mother.**[N] In other words, the baby girl experienced bleeding so soon after birth that her immersion in a ritual bath occurred before her mother immersed fourteen days after giving birth. **And Rabbi** Yehuda HaNasi likewise **said:** There was **an incident in Beit She'arim**[B] where **they immersed** a baby girl **before her mother. And Rav Yosef said:** There was **an incident in Pumbedita**[B] where **they immersed** a baby girl[N] **before her mother.**

בִּשְׁלָמָא דְּרַבִּי יוֹסֵי וּדְרַבִּי – מִשּׁוּם תְּרוּמַת אֶרֶץ יִשְׂרָאֵל, אֶלָּא דְּרַב יוֹסֵף לָמָּה לִי? וְהָא אָמַר שְׁמוּאֵל: אֵין תְּרוּמַת חוּץ לָאָרֶץ אֲסוּרָה – אֶלָּא בְּמִי שֶׁטּוּמְאָה יוֹצְאָה מִגּוּפוֹ, וְהָנֵי מִילֵּי – בַּאֲכִילָה, אֲבָל בִּנְגִיעָה – לָא!

The Gemara asks: **Granted,** the immersions reported **by Rabbi Yosei and by Rabbi** Yehuda HaNasi are understandable, **due to the** *teruma*[B] **of Eretz Yisrael,** i.e., these incidents occurred in Eretz Yisrael, where the touch of a menstruating girl disqualifies *teruma*. **But** in the incident reported **by Rav Yosef,** which occurred in Babylonia, **why do I** need to immerse the baby girl? **But doesn't Shmuel say:** The ***teruma*** **of outside of Eretz Yisrael**[H] **is prohibited only to one whose impurity** is due to **an emission from his body,** e.g., a menstruating woman, or one who experiences a gonorrhea-like discharge [*zav*]. **And this statement** applies only **with regard to eating** *teruma*, **but with regard to touching** *teruma*, there is **no** prohibition. Since the touch of a menstruating woman does not disqualify *teruma* outside Eretz Yisrael, why was it necessary to immerse the baby girl in the incident reported by Rav Yosef?

**HALAKHA**

**The prohibition of ritual impurity with regard to the *teruma* outside of Eretz Yisrael – אִיסּוּר טוּמְאָה בִּתְרוּמַת חוּץ לָאָרֶץ:** Since *teruma* outside of Eretz Yisrael applies by rabbinic law, it is prohibited in consumption only to a priest whose impurity is due to an emission from his body, i.e., one who experienced a seminal emission; a *zav*; a *zava*; a menstruating woman; and a woman who gave birth. According to some commentaries, once these individuals have immersed they may eat this *teruma* even before sunset, which is not the *halakha* with regard to *teruma* in Eretz Yisrael (Rambam). Others disagree and rule that if a minor priest is available then such *teruma* is not given to such an adult priest before sunset (Ra'avad; see Radbaz and *Kesef Mishne*). The *halakha* is in accordance with the opinion of Shmuel (Rambam *Sefer Zera'im, Hilkhot Terumot* 7:8).

**NOTES**

**They immersed a baby girl before her mother – הִטְבִּילוּהָ קוֹדֶם לְאִמָּהּ:** The early commentaries disagree as to the reason for this immersion. Some state it was to prevent any *teruma* the girl might touch from becoming ritually impure (Rashi). Others claim that it is unlikely that such a young child would come into contact with *teruma*. Furthermore, as the baby would once again be rendered ritually impure when she touches her mother, who herself is impure from childbirth, the immersion does not resolve this problem. They therefore explain that the immersion is due to a concern that people who touch the baby girl, who imparts impurity to them as a primary source of ritual impurity, might subsequently come into contact with *teruma* (*Tosefot HaRosh*; Rashba).

**They immersed a baby girl – הִטְבִּילוּהָ:** The later commentaries explain that although immersion in a ritual bath requires intent, and a baby girl has no halakhic intent, the main requirement for intent applies to the one who immerses her in the water. This is comparable to the immersion of impure vessels, where the necessary intent is fulfilled by the one performing the action (*Ḥatam Sofer*).

**BACKGROUND**

**Ein Bul – עֵין בּוּל:** The town of Ein Bul, also called Inbul, is identified with the village Ein Avel, in southern Lebanon.

**Beit She'arim – בֵּית שְׁעָרִים:** Beit She'arim was a small village in the Jezreel Valley, in a place now known as Sheikh Abreik. It was the seat of the Sanhedrin in the days of Rabbi Yehuda HaNasi. Although Rabbi Yehuda HaNasi moved to Tzippori toward the end of his life for health reasons, he was nevertheless buried in Beit She'arim. This is likely the reason the burial grounds at Beit She'arim gained importance, as for hundreds of years distinguished families in Eretz Yisrael and the Diaspora would bring their dead to be buried there. In recent times this large cemetery has been unearthed, with many of the ossuaries and epitaphs on the tombstones remaining intact.

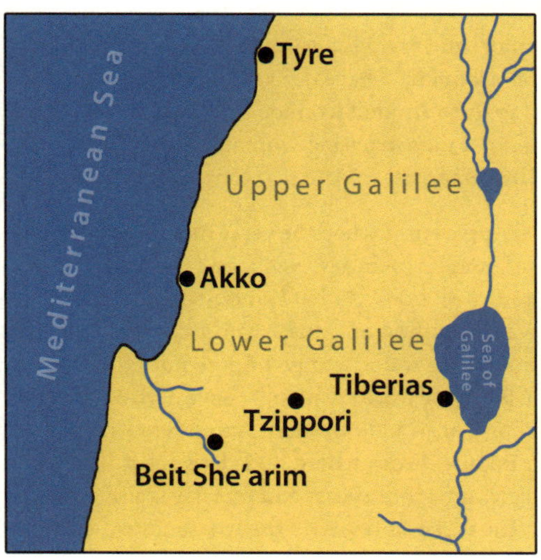


Location of Beit She'arim

**Pumbedita – פּוּמְבְּדִיתָא:** A city on the Euphrates River, northwest of Neharde'a, Pumbedita was an important center of the Babylonian Jewish community for many generations. As early as the Second Temple period Pumbedita was called simply: The Diaspora, as it was considered the center of Babylonian Jewry. After the destruction of Neharde'a, some scholars from its yeshiva relocated to Pumbedita, and from then on Torah study continued there without interruption until the end of the geonic period.

The scholars of Pumbedita were particularly famous for their acumen. The most famous heads of the Pumbedita Yeshiva were its founder Rav Yehuda, as well as Rabba, Rav Yosef, Abaye, Rav Naḥman bar Yitzhak, Rav Zevid, and Rafram bar Pappa. The Pumbedita Yeshiva was prominent in the geonic period as well, often overshadowing the yeshiva in Sura. The last heads of the Pumbedita Yeshiva were the renowned *ge'onim* Rav Sherira Gaon and his son, Rav Hai Gaon.

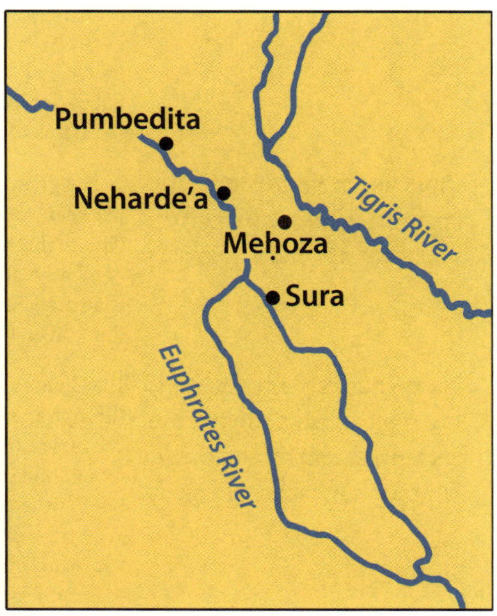


Location of Pumbedita

***Teruma* – תְּרוּמָה:** Whenever the term *teruma* appears without qualification it is referring to *teruma gedola*. The Torah commands that "the first fruit of your grain, of your wine, and of your oil" be given to the priest (Deuteronomy 18:4; see Numbers 18:12). The Sages extended the scope of this mitzva to include all produce grown in Eretz Yisrael. *Teruma* is sacred and may be eaten only by a priest and his household while they are in a state of ritual purity (see Leviticus 22:9–15). Today *teruma* may not be eaten, as there is no way to ensure that the priest who eats it is ritually pure, and priests today do not have definitive proof of their status. Therefore, the *halakha* reverts to Torah law, and in practice only a minimal portion of the produce is separated.

**NOTES**

**To include one who smears like one who drinks** – לְרַבּוֹת אֶת הַסָּךְ כַּשּׁוֹתֶה: Some commentaries claim that the verse is merely cited in support, as by Torah law one is liable only for eating and drinking *teruma*, not for anointing one's body. According to this opinion, the statement that anointing is like drinking applies by rabbinic law (*Tosafot*; Ramban). Others maintain this is a full-fledged derivation from the verse and therefore applies by Torah law, but only with regard to *teruma*. By contrast, with regard to other *halakhot*, e.g., forbidden fat, anointing is not considered like drinking by Torah law (Ritva; see Ramban). Yet others contend that in the case of *teruma* the verse is cited as mere support of a rabbinic law, whereas with regard to other prohibitions anointing is not considered like drinking even by rabbinic law (*Tosafot*, citing Rabbeinu Tam; Rashba; Meiri).

**HALAKHA**

**To include one who smears like one who drinks** – לְרַבּוֹת אֶת הַסָּךְ כַּשּׁוֹתֶה: In a case where a non-priest unwittingly anointed himself with an olive-bulk of *teruma* (see Radbaz), if that produce is normally used for anointing then he must pay the principal and an additional one-fifth, whether the *teruma* was ritually pure or impure (Rambam *Sefer Zera'im*, *Hilkhot Terumot* 10:2).

**A one-day-old girl with regard to menstruation** – תִּינוֹקֶת בַּת יוֹם אֶחָד לְנִדָּה: If a one-day-old baby girl emits blood, she imparts ritual impurity as a menstruating woman. This is in accordance with a tradition that there is no difference between an adult woman and a minor with regard to the impurity of menstruation and a gonorrhea-like discharge (Rambam *Sefer Kedusha*, *Hilkhot Issurei Bia* 4:1 and *Sefer Tahara*, *Hilkhot Metamei Mishkav UMoshav* 1:3).

**A girl aged three years and one day with regard to sexual intercourse** – תִּינוֹקֶת בַּת שָׁלֹשׁ שָׁנִים וְיוֹם אֶחָד לְבִיאָה: Like all those with whom engaging in intercourse is forbidden, one who engages in even the initial stage of intercourse with a menstruating woman, including a girl aged three years and one day, is liable to excision from the World-to-Come [*karet*]. The reason is that a girl can become ritually impure as a menstruating woman from the day of her birth, while a ten-day-old girl can contract the ritual impurity of *ziva*, and intercourse with a girl aged three years and one day is halakhically considered an act of intercourse (Rambam *Sefer Kedusha*, *Hilkhot Issurei Bia* 4:1; see *Sefer Tahara*, *Hilkhot Metamei Mishkav UMoshav* 1:3).

אָמַר מָר זוּטְרָא: לֹא נִצְרְכָה אֶלָּא לְסוֹכָה שֶׁמֶן שֶׁל תְּרוּמָה. דְּתַנְיָא: ״וְלֹא יְחַלְּלוּ אֶת קׇדְשֵׁי בְּנֵי יִשְׂרָאֵל אֲשֶׁר יָרִימוּ לַה׳״ – לְרַבּוֹת אֶת הַסָּךְ וְאֶת הַשּׁוֹתֶה.

**Mar Zutra**[P] **says:** That immersion **was necessary only for smearing oil of *teruma*** of outside of Eretz Yisrael. Since smearing is equivalent to eating, it would have been prohibited to smear such oil on the baby girl, were it not for her immersion in a ritual bath. And from where is it derived that smearing is like eating with regard to *teruma*? **As it is taught** in a *baraita*: The verse discussing the prohibition against consuming *teruma* in a state of ritual impurity states: **"And they shall not desecrate the sacred items of the children of Israel, which they set apart for the Lord"** (Leviticus 22:15). The verse serves **to include** in this prohibition **one who smears and one who drinks.**

שׁוֹתֶה לָמָּה לִי קְרָא? שְׁתִיָּה בִּכְלַל אֲכִילָה! אֶלָּא, לְרַבּוֹת אֶת הַסָּךְ כַּשּׁוֹתֶה. וְאִיבָּעֵית אֵימָא מֵהָכָא: ״וַתָּבֹא כַמַּיִם בְּקִרְבּוֹ וְכַשֶּׁמֶן בְּעַצְמוֹתָיו״.

Mar Zutra continues: **Why do I** need **a verse** to teach that one who **drinks** *teruma* in a state of impurity is liable? Isn't **drinking included** in the category **of eating? Rather,** the *baraita* means that the verse serves **to include one who smears,** teaching that he is **like one who drinks.**[NH] **And if you wish, say** that one may derive that smearing is like drinking **from here: "And it came into his innards like water, and like oil into his bones"** (Psalms 109:18).

אִי הָכִי – דִּידַן נָמֵי!

As it stands, the *halakha* that Samaritan girls are considered menstruating women from the time they lie in their cradle is in accordance with the opinion of Rabbi Meir, who is concerned for the minority of young girls who menstruate. The Gemara objects: **If so,** let us be concerned for the same minority with regard to **our** girls **as well.**

אֲנַן דְּדָרְשִׁינַן ״אִשָּׁה״ ״וְאִשָּׁה״, וְכִי חָזְיָין מַפְרְשִׁי לְהוּ – לָא גְּזַרוּ בְּהוּ רַבָּנַן. אִינְהוּ דְּלָא דָּרְשִׁי ״אִשָּׁה״ ״וְאִשָּׁה״, וְכִי חָזְיָין לָא מַפְרְשִׁי לְהוּ – גְּזַרוּ בְּהוּ רַבָּנַן.

The Gemara explains: There is no need to be concerned with regard to **our** young girls, **as we interpret** the verse: "And if a woman has an issue" (Leviticus 15:19), and derive from the fact that the verse does not merely state: **"A woman,"** but: **"And if a woman,"** that even minor girls are included in the *halakhot* of a menstruating woman. **And** consequently, **when** our girls **see** menstrual blood, **we separate them** in the manner of all menstruating women. Therefore, **the Sages did not decree with regard to them** that all young Jewish girls assume the status of menstruating women. By contrast, with regard to **them,** Samaritans, **who do not interpret** the difference between **"a woman"** and **"and if a woman," when** their girls **see** menstrual blood **they do not separate them,** and therefore **the Sages decreed with regard to them** that all Samaritan girls assume the status of menstruating women.

מַאי ״אִשָּׁה״ ״וְאִשָּׁה״? דְּתַנְיָא: ״אִשָּׁה״ – אֵין לִי אֶלָּא אִשָּׁה, תִּינוֹקֶת בַּת יוֹם אֶחָד לְנִדָּה מִנַּיִן? תַּלְמוּד לוֹמַר: ״וְאִשָּׁה״.

§ The Gemara asks: **What** is this interpretation of the difference between **"a woman"** and **"and if a woman"? As it is taught** in a *baraita* that from **"a woman" I have** derived **only** that the *halakhot* of menstruation apply to an adult **woman. From where** do I derive **that** the *halakhot* of **a menstruating woman** also apply to **a one-day-old girl?**[H] **The verse states: "And if a woman."**

אַלְמָא, כִּי מְרַבֵּי קְרָא – בַּת יוֹם אֶחָד מְרַבֵּי, וּרְמִינְהוּ: ״אִשָּׁה״ – אֵין לִי אֶלָּא אִשָּׁה, תִּינוֹקֶת בַּת שָׁלֹשׁ שָׁנִים וְיוֹם אֶחָד לְבִיאָה מִנַּיִן? תַּלְמוּד לוֹמַר: ״וְאִשָּׁה״!

The Gemara asks: **Apparently, when the verse includes** young girls through the word "and" it **includes** even **a one-day-old. But** you can **raise a contradiction** from another *baraita*, which discusses the verse: "And the woman with whom a man shall lie carnally, they shall both bathe themselves in water, and be impure until the evening" (Leviticus 15:18). From the word **"woman" I have** derived **only** that the sexual intercourse of an adult **woman** is considered intercourse that renders her impure. **From where** do I derive that the **sexual intercourse of a girl aged three years and one day** is also classified as intercourse?[H] **The verse states: And the woman.** Evidently, the word "and" includes only a girl aged three years and one day.

**PERSONALITIES**

**Mar Zutra** – מָר זוּטְרָא: A colleague of Rav Ashi, Mar Zutra was one of the leading Sages of his generation. He was a disciple-colleague of Rav Pappa and Rav Naḥman bar Yitzḥak. Beyond his greatness in *halakha* and *aggada*, Mar Zutra was a noted preacher, and his homiletic interpretations are cited throughout the Talmud. He apparently held an official position as the scholar and preacher in the house of the Exilarch. Late in life he was appointed head of the academy in Pumbedita. The Talmud frequently mentions meetings between Mar Zutra, Ameimar, and Rav Ashi, some of which may have been formal conferences of the leaders of Babylonian Jewry of that generation.

אֲמַר רָבָא: הִלְכְתָא נִינְהוּ, וְאַסְמְכִינְהוּ רַבָּנַן אַקְרָאֵי. הֵי קְרָא וְהֵי הִלְכְתָא? אִילֵימָא בַּת יוֹם אֶחָד – הִלְכְתָא, בַּת שָׁלֹשׁ שָׁנִים וְיוֹם אֶחָד – קְרָא, קְרָא סְתָמָא כְּתִיב!

**Rava said: These are** ***halakhot*** transmitted to Moses from Sinai,[N] **and the Sages** merely **supported them with verses.** There is therefore no contradiction. The Gemara asks: **Which** *halakha* is derived from **a verse and which** is **a** ***halakha*** transmitted to Moses from Sinai? **If we say** that the *halakha* that the status of a menstruating woman may apply to **a one-day-old** girl is **a** ***halakha*** transmitted to Moses from Sinai, and the *halakha* that the intercourse of a girl **aged three years and one day** is considered intercourse is derived from **a verse,** then one may object: But **the verse is written** in **an unspecified** manner; consequently, a one-day-old girl should be included by the verse in the same manner as a three-year-old girl.

אֶלָּא, בַּת שָׁלֹשׁ שָׁנִים וְיוֹם אֶחָד – הִלְכְתָא, בַּת יוֹם אֶחָד – קְרָא. וּמֵאַחַר דְּהִלְכְתָא, קְרָא לָמָּה לִי?

**Rather,** the *halakha* with regard to the intercourse of a girl **aged three years and one day** is **a** ***halakha*** transmitted to Moses from Sinai, whereas the *halakha* with regard to the menstruation of a **one-day-old** girl is derived from **a verse.** The Gemara asks: **And now that** it has been established that the *halakha* with regard to the intercourse of a three-year-old girl is **a** ***halakha*** transmitted to Moses from Sinai, **why do I** need **a verse?**

**NOTES**

**These are** ***halakhot*** **transmitted to Moses from Sinai** – **הִלְכְתָא נִינְהוּ**: In other words, one of these *halakhot* is transmitted to Moses from Sinai, whereas the other may be derived from the verse itself (Rashi).

Perek **IV**
Daf **32** Amud **b**

לְמַעוּטֵי אִישׁ מֵאוֹדֶם.

The Gemara responds: The verse serves **to exclude a man from** contracting ritual impurity due to **red** semen.[H]

וְהָא דְּתַנְיָא: "אִשָּׁה" – אֵין לִי אֶלָּא אִשָּׁה, בַּת עֲשָׂרָה יָמִים לְזִיבָה מִנַּיִן – תַּלְמוּד לוֹמַר "וְאִשָּׁה". לָמָּה לִי? לִיגְמַר מִנִּדָּה!

The Gemara objects: **But** what about **that which is taught** in a *baraita* with regard to a woman who experiences a discharge of uterine blood after her menstrual period [*zava*]: The verse states: "And if a woman has an issue of her blood many days" (Leviticus 15:25). From the word **"woman" I have** derived **only** that *ziva* applies to an adult **woman. From where** do I derive **that a ten-day-old** girl is included in the *halakhot* of ***ziva*****?**[BH] **The verse states: "And** if **a woman." Why do I** need the verse? **Let one derive** that a ten-day-old girl is included in the *halakhot* of *ziva* **from** the fact that a one-day-old girl is included in the *halakhot* of **a menstruating woman,** as a woman may become a *zava* only after seven days of menstruation and three subsequent days of experiencing uterine discharge.

צְרִיכָא, דְּאִי כְּתַב רַחֲמָנָא בְּנִדָּה – הֲוָה אָמֵינָא: נִדָּה – מִשּׁוּם דְּכִי חָזְיָא חַד יוֹמָא, בָּעֲיָא לְמֵיתַב שִׁבְעָה. אֲבָל זָבָה, דְּאִי חָזְיָא חַד יוֹמָא – בְּשׁוֹמֶרֶת יוֹם כְּנֶגֶד יוֹם סַגִּי לַהּ, אֵימָא: לָא, צְרִיכָא.

The Gemara responds: It was **necessary** for the verse to teach that the *halakhot* of *ziva* apply to a ten-day-old girl. **As, if the Merciful One had written** only that a one-day-old girl is included **in the** *halakhot* of **a menstruating woman, I would say:** The *halakhot* of **a menstruating woman** apply to a one-day-old girl **because** of their stringency, **as when** a woman **sees blood** on only **one day she is required to sit** for the **seven** days of menstruation. **But** with regard to **a** ***zava*****,**[B] since the *halakha* is **that if** a woman **sees** blood on only **one day** she has the status of a lesser *zava*, and it is **enough for her** to **observe** a clean **day for a day** she experiences a discharge, one might **say** that the *halakhot* of *ziva* do **not** apply to a ten-day-old girl. It was therefore **necessary** for the verse to indicate otherwise.

**BACKGROUND**

Gonorrhea-like discharge [*ziva*] – **זִיבָה**: Gonorrhea is a sexually transmitted disease caused by the bacteria *Neisseria gonorrhoeae*. The bacteria causes severe infection of the sexual organs, and one of its primary symptoms is a thin or thick mucous discharge from these organs. Traces of these discharges can also be found in the urine of infected persons. According to some researchers, this is the disease associated with the status known in *halakha* as *zav*. It is also possible that the *zav* is afflicted with a different, albeit similar condition.

The female counterpart of the *zav* is the *zava*. Although from a halakhic standpoint the *halakhot* governing the ritual impurity of the two are virtually identical, a *zava* is not one who suffers from a gonorrhea-like discharge but rather from uterine bleeding extending beyond the duration of her normal menstrual period. This can be caused by hormonal disruptions of the menstrual cycle, or by other conditions.

*Zava* – **זָבָה**: This is a woman who experiences a flow of menstrual-type blood on three consecutive days during a time of the month when she is not due to experience menstrual bleeding. The first discharge renders her ritually impure, but until the third discharge her status is that of a woman who observes a clean day for a day she experiences a discharge, and she is not subject to all the halakhic rulings of a *zava*. After experiencing bleeding on the third day, the woman is considered a *zava* and is obligated to bring an offering as part of her purification process. A *zava* imparts ritual impurity in the same manner as a *zav*. In addition, a man who engages in sexual intercourse with her becomes a primary source of ritual impurity and imparts ritual impurity to others.

**HALAKHA**

To exclude a man due to red semen – **לְמַעוּטֵי אִישׁ מֵאוֹדֶם**: Red semen is ritually pure. Only white, viscous semen is impure (Rambam *Sefer Tahara, Hilkhot Metamei Mishkav UMoshav* 1:6 and *Hilkhot She'ar Avot HaTumot* 5:3).

A ten-day-old girl is included in the *halakhot* of *ziva* – **בַּת עֲשָׂרָה יָמִים לְזִיבָה**: A ten-day-old minor girl can contract the impurity of *ziva*, as stated in the *baraita* (Rambam *Sefer Tahara, Hilkhot Metamei Mishkav UMoshav* 1:3 and *Sefer Kedusha, Hilkhot Issurei Bia* 4:1).

וְלִיכְתּוֹב רַחֲמָנָא בְּזָבָה, וְלָא בָּעֵי בְּנִדָּה, וַאֲנָא יָדַעְנָא דְּאֵין זָבָה בְּלֹא נִדָּה! אִין הָכִי נַמִי. וְאֶלָּא קְרָא לָמָּה לִי? לְמַעוּטֵי אִישׁ מֵאוֹדֶם.

The Gemara objects: **And let the Merciful One write** that a ten-day-old girl is included **in** the *halakhot* of **a *zava*, and** it would **not** be **required** to write that a one-day-old girl is included **in** the *halakhot* of **a menstruating woman, and I would know that** as a girl **cannot** become **a *zava* without** first assuming the status of **a menstruating woman,** she must also be included in the *halakhot* of a menstruating woman. The Gemara responds: **Yes, it is indeed so;** the fact that a one-day-old girl is included in the *halakhot* of a menstruating woman can be derived from the fact that a ten-day-old girl is included in the *halakhot* of a *zava*. **Rather, why do I** need the **verse:** "And if a woman," that is stated with regard to a menstruating woman? The verse serves **to exclude a man from** contracting ritual impurity due to **red** semen.

הָא מִיעַטְתֵּיהּ חֲדָא זִימְנָא? חַד – לְמַעוּטֵי מִשְׁכְּבַת זֶרַע, וְחַד – לְמַעוּטֵי מִדָּם.

The Gemara objects: **But** the Torah already **excluded this** case on **another occasion,** as stated earlier. The Gemara explains: **One** verse serves **to exclude** a man **from** contracting ritual impurity due to red **semen, and one** verse **serves to exclude** a man **from** being rendered a *zav* due to **blood** that emanates from his penis.

וְכֵן לְעִנְיַן זְכָרִים. דְּתַנְיָא: "אִישׁ אִישׁ", מַה תַּלְמוּד לוֹמַר "אִישׁ אִישׁ"? לְרַבּוֹת תִּינוֹק בֶּן יוֹם אֶחָד, שֶׁהוּא מְטַמֵּא בְּזִיבָה, דִּבְרֵי רַבִּי יְהוּדָה.

§ The Gemara discusses the *halakha* of *ziva* with regard to a male: **And so with regard to males,** the *halakhot* of a *zav* apply even to minor boys. **As it is taught** in a *baraita*: The verse states concerning a *zav*: "When **any man** has an issue out of his flesh, his issue is impure" (Leviticus 15:2). **What** is the meaning when **the verse states "any man"?** The verse serves **to include a one-day-old baby,** teaching **that** even **he is susceptible to impurity of *ziva*.**[NH] This is **the statement of Rabbi Yehuda.**

רַבִּי יִשְׁמָעֵאל בְּנוֹ שֶׁל רַבִּי יוֹחָנָן בֶּן בְּרוֹקָה אוֹמֵר: אֵין צָרִיךְ, הֲרֵי הוּא אוֹמֵר: "לַזָּכָר וְלַנְּקֵבָה", "לַזָּכָר" – כָּל שֶׁהוּא זָכָר, בֵּין שֶׁהוּא גָּדוֹל בֵּין שֶׁהוּא קָטָן. "וְלַנְּקֵבָה" – כָּל שֶׁהִיא נְקֵבָה, בֵּין גְּדוֹלָה בֵּין קְטַנָּה. אִם כֵּן מַה תַּלְמוּד לוֹמַר "אִישׁ אִישׁ"? דִּבְּרָה תּוֹרָה כִּלְשׁוֹן בְּנֵי אָדָם.

**Rabbi Yishmael, son of Rabbi Yoḥanan ben Beroka, says:** This derivation **is not necessary, as the verse states:** "And of them that have an issue, **whether it be a male or a female**" (Leviticus 15:33). **"Whether it be a male"** includes **anyone who is a male, whether he is an adult** or **whether he is a minor; "or a female"** includes **anyone who is a female, whether** she is **an adult** or **whether** she is **a minor. If so, what** is the meaning when **the verse states "any man"? The Torah spoke in the language of people,**[N] and one is not meant to derive anything from this verse.

אַלְמָא, כִּי מְרַבֵּי קְרָא – בֶּן יוֹם אֶחָד מְרַבֵּי. וּרְמִינְהוּ: "אִישׁ" – אֵין לִי אֶלָּא אִישׁ, בֶּן תֵּשַׁע שָׁנִים וְיוֹם אֶחָד מִנַּיִן? תַּלְמוּד לוֹמַר: "וְאִישׁ"!

The Gemara asks: **Apparently, when the verse includes** a minor boy it **includes** even **a one-day-old. But raise a contradiction** from another *baraita*, which addresses the verse: "And if the flow of seed go out from a man, then he shall bathe all his flesh in water and be impure until the evening" (Leviticus 15:16). From the word **"man" I have** derived **only** that **a man** is rendered ritually impure through a seminal emission. **From where** do I derive that the seminal emission of a boy **aged nine years and one day** renders him impure as well? **The verse states: "And a man."** Evidently, the verse does not include a one-day-old boy.

אֲמַר רָבָא: הִלְכְתָא נִינְהוּ, וְאַסְמְכִינְהוּ רַבָּנַן אַקְּרָאֵי. הֵי הִלְכְתָא וְהֵי קְרָא? אִילֵימָא בֶּן יוֹם אֶחָד – הִלְכְתָא, וּבֶן תֵּשַׁע שָׁנִים וְיוֹם אֶחָד – קְרָא, קְרָא סְתָמָא כְּתִיב!

**Rava said: These are *halakhot*** transmitted to Moses from Sinai, **and the Sages** merely **supported them with verses.** Therefore, there is no contradiction. The Gemara asks: **Which is a *halakha*** transmitted to Moses from Sinai, **and which** *halakha* **is** derived from **a verse? If we say** that the *halakha* that **a one-day-old** boy is included in the *halakhot* of a *zav* is **a *halakha*** transmitted to Moses from Sinai, **and** the *halakha* that the seminal emission of a boy **aged nine years and one day** renders him impure is derived from **a verse,** then one may object: But **the verse is written** in **an unspecified** manner; consequently, even a one-day-old boy should be included in the verse.

אֶלָּא בֶּן תֵּשַׁע שָׁנִים וְיוֹם אֶחָד – הִלְכְתָא, וּבֶן יוֹם אֶחָד – קְרָא. וְכִי מֵאַחַר דְּהִלְכְתָא הִיא, קְרָא לָמָּה לִי? לְמַעוּטֵי אִשָּׁה מִלּוֹבֶן.

**Rather,** the *halakha* with regard to the seminal emission of a boy **aged nine years and one day** is **a *halakha*** transmitted to Moses from Sinai, **and** the *halakha* that **a one-day-old** boy is included in the *halakhot* of a *zav* is derived from **a verse.** The Gemara asks: **And now that** the *halakha* with regard to the seminal emission of a boy aged nine years and one day renders **is a *halakha*** transmitted to Moses from Sinai, **why do I** need **a verse?** The Gemara answers: The verse serves **to exclude a woman from** contracting the impurity of a *zava* due to **a white** discharge.[NH]

## NOTES

A one-day-old baby that he is susceptible to impurity of *ziva* – תִּינוֹק בֶּן יוֹם אֶחָד שֶׁהוּא מְטַמֵּא בְּזִיבָה: It can be inferred from here that a one-day-old baby boy does not become impure by a seminal emission. This ritual impurity applies only to a male who is at least nine years and one day old (see Rambam *Sefer Tahara, Hilkhot She'ar Avot HaTumot* 5:2).

The Torah spoke in the language of people – דִּבְּרָה תּוֹרָה כִּלְשׁוֹן בְּנֵי אָדָם: The verse states *ish ish*, literally "man man." The later commentaries explain that just as people sometimes repeat a term in their speech without intending to indicate a novelty, the Torah does the same.

To exclude a woman from the impurity of a *zava* due to a white discharge – לְמַעוּטֵי אִשָּׁה מִלּוֹבֶן: Although it was already explained on 19a that a woman contracts ritual impurity by five types of blood alone, and white blood is not included in that list, it is still necessary for a verse to teach this *halakha*, lest one seek to derive by an *a fortiori* inference from the case of a man that a woman becomes impure by a white discharge (*Tosafot*).

## HALAKHA

A one-day-old baby with regard to *ziva* – תִּינוֹק בֶּן יוֹם אֶחָד לְזִיבָה: A one-day-old minor boy can contract the impurity of *ziva*, as stated in the *baraita* (Rambam *Sefer Tahara, Hilkhot Metamei Mishkav UMoshav* 1:4 and *Sefer Korbanot, Hilkhot Meḥusrei Kappara* 3:6).

To exclude a woman from contracting impurity due to a white discharge – לְמַעוּטֵי אִשָּׁה מִלּוֹבֶן: A woman does not become ritually impure as a result of a white discharge (Rambam *Sefer Tahara, Hilkhot Metamei Mishkav UMoshav* 1:6).

לָמָּה לִי לְמִכְתַּב בִּזְכָרִים, וְלָמָּה לִי לְמִכְתַּב בִּנְקֵבוֹת?

The Gemara asks: **Why do I** need for the Merciful One **to write** that a one-day-old is included in the *halakhot* of *ziva* **with regard to males, and why do I** need for the Merciful One **to write** that a one-day-old is included in the *halakhot* of a menstruating woman and a ten-day-old is included in the *halakhot* of *ziva* **with regard to females?**

צְרִיכִי, דְּאִי כְּתַב רַחֲמָנָא בִּזְכָרִים – מִשּׁוּם דְּמִטַּמְּאוּ בִּרְאִיּוֹת כְּבְיָמִים, אֲבָל נְקֵבוֹת דְּלָא מִטַּמְּאוּ בִּרְאִיּוֹת כְּבְיָמִים – אֵימָא לָא.

The Gemara answers that both verses **are necessary. As, if the Merciful One had written** only **concerning males,** one might say: A one-day-old boy is included in the *halakhot* of *ziva* **because** the *halakha* is more stringent with regard to males, **as they are rendered impure through** three **sightings** of *ziva* on one day just **like through** sightings on three consecutive **days.**[H] **But** with regard to **females, who are not rendered impure through** three **sightings** on one day **as** they are **through** sightings on three consecutive **days,** one might **say** that the *halakhot* of *ziva* do **not** apply to ten-day-old girls.

וְאִי כְּתַב רַחֲמָנָא בִּנְקֵבוֹת – מִשּׁוּם דְּקָמִטַּמְּאוּ בְּאוֹנֶס, אֲבָל זְכָרִים דְּלָא מִטַּמְּאוּ בְּאוֹנֶס – אֵימָא: לָא, צְרִיכָא.

**And** by contrast, **if the Merciful One had written** only **with regard to females,** one might say: The *halakhot* of *ziva* apply to ten-day-old girls, **because** of the fact that **they are rendered impure** even on account of sightings that occur **due to circumstances beyond** their **control.**[H] **But** with regard to **males, who are not rendered impure** on account of sightings that occur **due to circumstances beyond** their **control,** one might **say** that one-day-old boys are **not** included in the *halakhot* of *ziva*. Therefore, both verses are **necessary.**

״הַכּוּתִים מְטַמְּאִין מִשְׁכָּב תַּחְתּוֹן כָּעֶלְיוֹן״. מַאי ״מִשְׁכָּב תַּחְתּוֹן כָּעֶלְיוֹן״? אִילֵימָא דְּאִי אִיכָּא עֲשָׂרָה מַצָּעוֹת וְיָתֵיב עֲלַיְיהוּ – מְטַמּוּ לְהוּ, פְּשִׁיטָא, דְּהָא דָּרֵס לְהוּ!

§ The mishna teaches: **And the Samaritan** men **impart ritual impurity** to the **lower bedding like** the **upper** bedding. The Gemara asks: **What** is the meaning of the clause: The **lower bedding like** the **upper** bedding? **If we say** it means **that if there are ten mattresses** stacked one upon the other **and** a Samaritan man **sat upon them,** the lowest mattress, like the upper mattresses, is **rendered impure,** this *halakha* is **obvious, since he presses** on all of **them** when he sits on them. In other words, since Samaritan men impart impurity to the bedding beneath them because they are considered men who engage in intercourse with menstruating women, there is no reason to distinguish between the lowest mattress and the other mattresses above it.

אֶלָּא שֶׁיְּהֵא תַּחְתּוֹנוֹ שֶׁל בּוֹעֵל נִדָּה כְּעֶלְיוֹנוֹ שֶׁל זָב, מָה עֶלְיוֹנוֹ שֶׁל זָב – אֵינוֹ מְטַמֵּא אֶלָּא אוֹכָלִין וּמַשְׁקִין, אַף תַּחְתּוֹנוֹ שֶׁל בּוֹעֵל נִדָּה – אֵינוֹ מְטַמֵּא אֶלָּא אוֹכָלִין וּמַשְׁקִין.

**Rather,** the mishna means **that** the status of the lowest mattress **beneath** a man who **engages in intercourse with a menstruating woman**[HN] **is like** that of the bedding **above a *zav*,** i.e., the bedding beneath a Samaritan man assumes first-degree ritual impurity and does not become a primary source of impurity like the bedding beneath a *zav*. That is, **just as the upper** bedding **of a *zav*** is not a primary source of impurity and **imparts impurity only** to **food and drink** but not people or vessels, **so too,** the bedding **beneath** a man who **engages in intercourse with a menstruating woman imparts ritual impurity only** to **food and drink.**

עֶלְיוֹנוֹ שֶׁל זָב מְנָלַן? דִּכְתִיב ״וְכָל הַנֹּגֵעַ בְּכֹל אֲשֶׁר יִהְיֶה תַחְתָּיו יִטְמָא״, מַאי ״תַּחְתָּיו״?

The Gemara asks: **From where do we** derive that the bedding **above a *zav*** imparts ritual impurity only to food and drink? **As it is written** with regard to a *zav*: **"And whoever touches any thing that was under him shall be impure"** (Leviticus 15:10). **What** is the meaning of the expression **"under him"?**

**HALAKHA**

**Through three sightings of *ziva* on one day just like through sightings on three consecutive days – בִּרְאִיּוֹת כְּבְיָמִים:** A man who emits one discharge of *ziva* has the status of one who experienced a seminal emission. If he had two sightings he is a *zav*, and therefore must count seven clean days and then immerse, but he is not obligated to bring an offering. If he experienced three sightings he is a full-fledged *zav* who is liable to bring an offering. These *halakhot* are all traditions transmitted to Moses from Sinai (Rambam *Sefer Korbanot, Hilkhot Meḥusrei Kappara* 2:6).

**With regard to females because they are rendered impure due to circumstances beyond their control – בִּנְקֵבוֹת מִשּׁוּם דְּקָמִטַּמְּאוּ בְּאוֹנֶס:** Unlike a man, a woman becomes impure due to an accident, both with regard to the impurity of menstruation and the impurity of *ziva*. How so? If, for example, she leaped from one place to another, or saw animals, beasts, or fowl engaging in intercourse and had lustful thoughts, and she subsequently experienced a blood flow, she is rendered impure by any amount of blood (Rambam *Sefer Kedusha, Hilkhot Issurei Bia* 5:1).

**That the status of the lowest mattress beneath a man who engages in intercourse with a menstruating woman, etc. – שֶׁיְּהֵא תַּחְתּוֹנוֹ שֶׁל בּוֹעֵל נִדָּה וכו׳:** The bedding of a man who engaged in intercourse with a menstruating woman and the saddle upon which he rides have first-degree ritual impurity status, like vessels he touches. Consequently, they impart impurity to food and drink, but not to people or vessels (Rambam *Sefer Tahara, Hilkhot Metamei Mishkav UMoshav* 3:2).

**NOTES**

**That the status of the lowest mattress beneath a man who engages in intercourse with a menstruating woman, etc. – שֶׁיְּהֵא תַּחְתּוֹנוֹ שֶׁל בּוֹעֵל נִדָּה וכו׳:** The early commentaries disagree with regard to the *halakha* of the upper bedding of a *zav*. Some maintain that its impurity applies by rabbinic law (Rambam *Sefer Tahara, Hilkhot Metamei Mishkav UMoshav* 6:3), and the verse is cited merely in support (*Kesef Mishne*). Accordingly, this bedding does not impart impurity to vessels at all. Others claim that the status of the upper bedding of a *zav* is derived from the verses as a Torah law (Ra'avad; Rashi on 4b), and it has first-degree ritual impurity status and renders vessels impure by touch. The consensus among the later commentaries is that the upper bedding of a *zav* imparts impurity by Torah law, as that is the opinion of the majority of the early commentaries (*Likkutei Halakhot*).

## BACKGROUND

*Zav* – זָב: The *halakhot* relating to the stringent ritual impurity caused by this condition appear in Leviticus, chapter 15, and in tractate *Zavim*. The *zav* becomes ritually impure as a result of secreting a white, pus-like discharge. A man who experiences this discharge on one occasion becomes ritually impure for one day, similar to a man who discharged semen. If he experiences a second discharge on the same or the following day, or if the initial discharge is prolonged, he contracts the more severe ritual impurity of a *zav*, which lasts until after he experiences seven clean days. One who experiences a third discharge within the day following the second discharge is obligated to bring an offering as part of his purification process.

Not only does a *zav* become impure, he also imparts impurity through contact with vessels or people, by being moved by them, by moving them, and by lying or sitting on them. Likewise, he imparts impurity to items under a very heavy stone by sitting on the stone, although the stone itself does not thereby become impure. The fluids secreted by a *zav*, his saliva, urine, and semen, all impart impurity, and the articles on which he sits or lies become primary sources of ritual impurity and themselves impart impurity to other items.

## HALAKHA

Just as she imparts impurity to people and earthenware vessels – מַה הִיא מְטַמְּאָה אָדָם וּכְלֵי חֶרֶס: A *zava*, a menstruating woman, and a woman after childbirth are all primary sources of ritual impurity. Consequently, they impart impurity to vessels by touch, and to people by touch and by carrying them, as stated in the *baraita* (Rambam *Sefer Tahara*, *Hilkhot Metamei Mishkav UMoshav* 1:1).

אִילֵימָא תַּחְתָּיו דְּזָב – מִ״וְאִישׁ אֲשֶׁר יִגַּע בְּמִשְׁכָּבוֹ״ נָפְקָא, אֶלָּא הַנּוֹגֵעַ בְּכָל אֲשֶׁר יִהְיֶה הַזָּב תַּחְתָּיו, וּמַאי נִיהוּ – עֶלְיוֹן שֶׁל זָב,

If we say the verse is teaching that a mattress **beneath a *zav***[B] is impure, this is already **derived from** the verse: **"And whoever touches his bed"** (Leviticus 15:5). **Rather,** the verse is referring to that **which touches any** item **under which the *zav* will be. And what is this** item? It is the bedding **above a *zav*.** The verse teaches that the bedding above a *zav* imparts ritual impurity.

וְהַנּוֹשֵׂא נַמִי יִטְמָא, וּמַאי נִיהוּ – נִישָּׂא, מַאי טַעְמָא? ״וְהַנִּשָּׂא״ כְּתִיב.

The verse further states: "And he who bears [*vehanoseh*] these things shall wash his clothes and bathe himself in water, and be impure until the evening" (Leviticus 15:10), indicating that **he who bears also becomes impure. And what is this?** This is an item **borne** [*nisa*] by a *zav*. **What is the reason,** i.e., how is this indicated by the verse? The term ***vehanisa* is written**[N] in the verse.

נִתְּקוֹ הַכָּתוּב מִטּוּמְאָה חֲמוּרָה וֶהֱבִיאוֹ לִידֵי טוּמְאָה קַלָּה, לוֹמַר לְךָ שֶׁאֵינוֹ מְטַמֵּא אֶלָּא אוֹכָלִין וּמַשְׁקִין.

The Gemara continues: **The verse removed** the *halakha* of the bedding above a *zav* **from** the status of **severe impurity and brought it to** the status of **lesser impurity, to tell you that it imparts impurity only** to **food and drink,** but not to people or garments.

אֵימַר: נִתְּקוֹ הַכָּתוּב מִטּוּמְאָה חֲמוּרָה – דְּלָא מְטַמֵּא אָדָם לְטַמֵּא בְּגָדִים, אֲבָל אָדָם אוֹ בְּגָדִים לִיטַמֵּא! אָמַר קְרָא ״יִטְמָא״ – טוּמְאָה קַלָּה מַשְׁמַע.

The Gemara objects: **Say** that **the verse removed** the bedding above a *zav* **from severe impurity,** in the sense **that it does not impart impurity** to **a person to** the extent that he may in turn **impart impurity** to the **garments** he is wearing. **But let** the bedding above a *zav* **impart impurity** to **people or garments.** The Gemara explains that **the verse states:** "And whoever touches anything that was under him **shall be impure"** (Leviticus 15:10), which **indicates lesser impurity.**

וְתַחְתּוֹנוֹ שֶׁל בּוֹעֵל נִדָּה, מְנָלַן? דְּתַנְיָא ״וּתְהִי נִדָּתָהּ עָלָיו״,

§ The mishna teaches that Samaritan men are considered men who engage in intercourse with menstruating women, and consequently they impart impurity to the bedding beneath them. The Gemara asks: **And from where do we** derive that the bedding **beneath** one who **engages in intercourse with a menstruating woman** is impure? **As it is taught** in a *baraita*: The verse states with regard to a menstruating woman: "And if any man lie with her, **and her impurity be upon him,** he shall be impure seven days, and every bed upon which he lies shall be impure" (Leviticus 15:24).

יָכוֹל יַעֲלֶה לְרַגְלָהּ – תַּלְמוּד לוֹמַר ״יִטְמָא שִׁבְעַת יָמִים״.

The *baraita* explains: One **might** have thought that the phrase: "And her impurity be upon him," indicates that the man assumes the impure status of the menstruating woman with whom he engaged in intercourse, such that if they were together on the sixth day of her menstruation **he may elevate** himself **at her time,** i.e., he may immerse in a ritual bath the next day, just like the menstruating woman. Therefore, **the verse states: "He shall be impure seven days."**

וּמַה תַּלְמוּד לוֹמַר ״וּתְהִי נִדָּתָהּ עָלָיו״? שֶׁיָּכוֹל לֹא יְטַמֵּא אָדָם וּכְלֵי חֶרֶס, תַּלְמוּד לוֹמַר ״וּתְהִי נִדָּתָהּ עָלָיו״, מַה הִיא מְטַמְּאָה אָדָם וּכְלֵי חֶרֶס – אַף הוּא מְטַמֵּא אָדָם וּכְלֵי חֶרֶס.

But if so, **what is** the meaning when **the verse states: "And her impurity be upon him"?** As, one **might** have thought that a man who engages in intercourse with a menstruating woman **will not impart impurity** to **people and earthenware vessels.** Therefore, **the verse states: "And her impurity be upon him,"** to teach that he imparts impurity like a menstruating woman. In other words, **just as she imparts impurity** to **people and earthenware vessels,**[H] **so too, he imparts impurity** to **people**[N] **and earthenware vessels.**

## NOTES

*Vehanisa* is written – וְהַנִּשָּׂא כְּתִיב: The Gemara indicates that the word *vehanoseh* is written in the defective form, without a *vav*, which allows it to be read as *vehanisa*. This is difficult, as in the standard text of the Bible the word is spelled plene, i.e., with a *vav*. The commentaries explain that sometimes the version of a verse discussed in the Gemara is not in accordance with the standard text in use today (see *Shabbat* 55b). For example, the later commentaries note many slight differences between verses as we have them and their citation in the Talmud and *midrashim* (see *Gilyonei HaShas* on *Shabbat* 55b). With regard to the *halakha*, the early commentaries write that whenever there is a conflict between the standard text of our Torah scrolls and the version of the verse found in the Talmud or *midrashim*, one follows the standard text (*Sefer HaEshkol*).

So too he imparts impurity to people, etc. – אַף הוּא מְטַמֵּא אָדָם וכו׳: In other words, the touch of a man who has intercourse with a menstruating woman is like the touch of a menstruating woman herself, and their *halakhot* are also the same with regard to carrying, as they both impart impurity to a person and to the garments he is wearing (Rashi; Ritva; see *Mishne LaMelekh* on Rambam *Sefer Tahara*, *Hilkhot Metamei Mishkav UMoshav* 3:1 and *Hilkhot She'ar Avot HaTumot* 6:12).

אִי מַה הִיא עוֹשָׂה מִשְׁכָּב וּמוֹשָׁב לְטַמֵּא אָדָם לְטַמֵּא בְּגָדִים, אַף הוּא עוֹשֶׂה מִשְׁכָּב וּמוֹשָׁב לְטַמֵּא אָדָם לְטַמֵּא בְּגָדִים? תַּלְמוּד לוֹמַר: ״וְכׇל הַמִּשְׁכָּב אֲשֶׁר יִשְׁכַּב עָלָיו יִטְמָא״.

If so, i.e., that one who engages in intercourse with a menstruating woman is compared to the woman herself, then say: **Just as she renders the bedding** beneath her **and** the **seat** upon which she sits[H] impure **to** the extent that they **impart impurity** to **a person to** in turn **impart impurity** to **the garments** he is wearing, **so too, he renders** the **bedding** beneath him **and** the **seat** upon which he sits impure **to** the extent that they **impart impurity** to **a person to** in turn **impart impurity** to **the garments** he is wearing. Therefore, **the verse states: "And every bed upon which he lies shall be impure"** (Leviticus 15:24).

שֶׁאֵין תַּלְמוּד לוֹמַר ״וְכׇל הַמִּשְׁכָּב אֲשֶׁר יִשְׁכַּב עָלָיו יִטְמָא״, וּמַה תַּלְמוּד לוֹמַר ״וְכׇל הַמִּשְׁכָּב אֲשֶׁר״ וגו׳ – נִתְּקוֹ הַכָּתוּב מִטּוּמְאָה חֲמוּרָה וֶהֱבִיאוֹ לִידֵי טוּמְאָה קַלָּה, לוֹמַר לְךָ שֶׁאֵינוֹ מְטַמֵּא אֶלָּא אוֹכָלִין וּמַשְׁקִין.

The *baraita* elaborates: **As,** there is **no** need for **the verse to state: "And every bed upon which he lies shall be impure,"** since it is already written: "And her impurity be upon him," which indicates that just as a menstruating woman imparts impurity to her bedding, so too does one who has intercourse with her. **And** if so, **what** is the meaning when **the verse states: "And every bed upon** which he lies shall be impure"? **The verse separated** the *halakha* of one who has intercourse with a menstruating woman **from** the **severe impurity** of the menstruating woman herself, **and brought him to lesser impurity, to tell you that he imparts impurity only** to **food and drink,** but not to people or garments.

פָּרֵיךְ רַב אַחַאי: אֵימָא נִתְּקוֹ הַכָּתוּב מִטּוּמְאָה חֲמוּרָה וֶהֱבִיאוֹ לְטוּמְאָה קַלָּה – דְּלָא לִיטַמֵּא אָדָם לְטַמּוֹיֵי בְּגָדִים, אֲבָל אָדָם וּבְגָדִים לִיטַמֵּא! אָמַר רַב אַסִי: ״יִטְמָא״ – טוּמְאָה קַלָּה מַשְׁמַע.

**Rav Aḥai**[P] **refutes**[B] this derivation: **Say that the verse removed** the *halakha* of one who has intercourse with a menstruating woman **from severe impurity and brought it to lesser impurity,** in the sense **that** his bedding **does not impart impurity** to **a person to** in turn **impart impurity** to the **garments** upon him. **But let** his bedding **impart impurity** to **people or garments. Rav Asi says:** The verse states: "And every bed upon which he lies **shall be impure,"** which **indicates a lesser impurity.**

אֵימָא: ״וּתְהִי נִדָּתָהּ עָלָיו״ – כְּלָל, ״וְכׇל הַמִּשְׁכָּב״ – פְּרָט, כְּלָל וּפְרָט – אֵין בִּכְלָל אֶלָּא מַה שֶּׁבִּפְרָט: מִשְׁכָּב וּמוֹשָׁב – אִין, מִידֵּי אַחֲרִינָא – לָא!

The Gemara objects: But **say** that the phrase: **"And her impurity be upon him,"** is **a generalization,** and the phrase: **"And every bed** upon which he lies shall be impure," is **a detail.** If so, the verse constitutes **a generalization and a detail,** and it is a hermeneutical principle that in such a case **the generalization** is referring **only** to **that which** is specified **in the detail.** Accordingly, with regard to the **bedding and seat** upon which the man rests, **yes,** they are rendered impure, but **other items** are **not.**

אָמַר אַבָּיֵי: ״יִטְמָא שִׁבְעַת יָמִים״ מַפְסִיק הָעִנְיָן, הָוֵי כְּלָל וּפְרָט הַמְרוּחָקִין זֶה מִזֶּה, וְכׇל כְּלָל וּפְרָט הַמְרוּחָקִין זֶה מִזֶּה – אֵין דָּנִין אוֹתוֹ בִּכְלָל וּפְרָט.

**Abaye says** that when the verse states: **"He shall be impure seven days,"** between the generalization and the detail, this **interrupts the matter.** Accordingly, **this is** a case of **a generalization and a detail that are distant from one another, and** with regard to **any generalization and detail that are distant from one another, one does not derive** a *halakha* from them in accordance with the principle **of a generalization and a detail.**

רָבָא אָמַר: לְעוֹלָם דָּנִין, ״וְכׇל״ – רִיבּוּיָא הוּא.

**Rava says: Actually, one may derive** a *halakha* from a generalization and a detail that are distant from one another. But this verse does not constitute a case of a generalization and a detail, as the verse states: "And every bed upon which he lies." The term **"and every" is an amplification.**

מַתְקִיף לַהּ רַבִּי יַעֲקֹב: אֵימָא כְּהִיא, מַה הִיא – לֹא חִלַּקְתָּ בָּהּ בֵּין מַגָּעָהּ לְמִשְׁכָּבָהּ לְטַמֵּא אָדָם וּלְטַמֵּא בְּגָדִים לְחוּמְרָא, אַף הוּא – לֹא תַּחֲלוֹק בּוֹ בֵּין מַגָּעוֹ לְמִשְׁכָּבוֹ לְטַמֵּא אָדָם וּלְטַמֵּא בְּגָדִים לְקוּלָּא!

**Rabbi Ya'akov objects to this: Say** that as the verse compares a man who engages in intercourse with a menstruating woman to the woman herself, the man should be **like her,** i.e., **just as** with regard to **her you did not differentiate between her touch and her bedding in terms of imparting impurity** to **a person and imparting impurity to garments,** as the *halakha* is **stringent** concerning both in that her touch and her bedding impart impurity to people to in turn impart impurity to their garments; **so too,** with regard to **him, you shall not differentiate between his touch and his bedding in terms of imparting impurity** to **a person and imparting impurity to garments,** and the *halakha* should be **lenient** in both cases: Neither his bedding nor his touch should impart impurity to people to in turn impart impurity to their garments.

**HALAKHA**

**She renders the bedding beneath her and the seat upon which she sits, etc.** – **הִיא עוֹשָׂה מִשְׁכָּב וּמוֹשָׁב וכו׳:** A *zava*, a menstruating woman, and a woman after childbirth are all primary sources of ritual impurity. Therefore, they impart impurity to the bedding, seat, and saddle underneath them and render those items a primary source of ritual impurity (Rambam *Sefer Tahara, Hilkhot Metamei Mishkav UMoshav* 1:1).

**PERSONALITIES**

**Rav Aḥai** – **רַב אַחַאי:** The early commentaries disagree as to the identity of this Rav Aḥai. Some maintain he is an *amora* (Rabbeinu Tam). Others claim that the reference here is to Rav Aḥai Gaon, the author of *She'iltot deRav Aḥai Gaon* and the foremost Sage of his generation, whose statements were accepted as though they were written in the Talmud (Responsa of the Rivash). Since he lived after the period of the *amora'im*, his statements are introduced by the unusual expression Rav Aḥai refutes, or Rav Aḥai resolved (*Tosafot* on *Ketubot* 2b, citing Rashbam).

Alternatively, the Rav Aḥai mentioned here refers to one of the *Savora'im*, a member of the post-amoraic generation responsible for the redaction of the Talmud, following Ravina and Rav Ashi (*Tosafot* on *Zevaḥim* 102b). If so, he is Rav Aḥai, son of Rav Huna. There is also an opinion that this is the Rav Aḥai who lived in the generation of Rav Shmuel, son of Rav Abbahu, with regard to whom it is stated that the Sages from Eretz Yisrael sent the following statement to Babylonia: Respect the opinion of our teacher Aḥai, as he enlightens the eyes of the exile (*Ḥullin* 59b).

**BACKGROUND**

**Rav Aḥai refutes** – **פָּרֵיךְ רַב אַחַאי:** The early commentaries note that the Talmud deploys standard expressions with regard to particular Sages, e.g., Rabbi Abbahu ridiculed it; Rabbi Yoḥanan wondered about this; and Abaye cursed it. The phrase that appears here, Rav Aḥai refutes, is another example of such a conventional phrase. One can also find the expressions Rav Aḥai resolved, and Rav Aḥai discussed it.

אָמַר רָבָא: ״עָלָיו״ – לְהַטְעִינוֹ מַשְׁמַע.

**Rava says** in response that when the verse states: "And her impurity be **upon him,**" this **indicates** that the Torah intends for the impurity **to weigh upon him,** i.e., in a stringent manner.

״מִפְּנֵי שֶׁהֵן בּוֹעֲלֵי נִדּוֹת״ וכו׳. אַטּוּ כּוּלְּהוּ בּוֹעֲלֵי נִדּוֹת נִינְהוּ? אָמַר רַבִּי יִצְחָק מִגְּדָלָאָה: בִּנְשׂוּאוֹת שָׁנוּ.

§ The mishna teaches that the impurity of Samaritan men is **due to** the fact **that** Samaritan men are considered men who **engage in intercourse with menstruating women,** and this is because they observe the seven-day menstrual period of impurity for each and every emission of blood. The Gemara asks: **Is this to say** that **all** Samaritan men **are** considered men who **engage in intercourse with menstruating women?** Aren't there some unmarried men who do not engage in intercourse with menstruating women? **Rabbi Yitzḥak of Migdal says: They taught** this *halakha* only **with regard to** men to whom women are **married.**

״וְהֵן יוֹשְׁבוֹת עַל דָּם״ וכו׳. תַּנְיָא, אָמַר רַבִּי מֵאִיר: אִם הֵן יוֹשְׁבוֹת עַל כָּל דָּם וְדָם – תַּקָּנָה גְּדוֹלָה הִיא לָהֶן,

The mishna further teaches: **And** Samaritan men are considered men who engage in intercourse with menstruating women because **they observe** the seven-day menstrual period of impurity **for** each and every emission of **blood.** In this regard **it is taught** in a *baraita* that **Rabbi Meir said: If** Samaritan women would begin **observing** a seven-day period of impurity **for each and every** emission of **blood, it** would be **a great remedy for them,** i.e., this practice would not lead to sin, as they would observe a seven-day period from each emission. But this is not their practice.

אֶלָּא – שֶׁרוֹאוֹת דָּם אָדוֹם וּמַשְׁלִימוֹת אוֹתוֹ לְדַם יָרוֹק.

**Rather,** when Samaritan women see green blood, which does not render them impure, they begin counting seven days of impurity from that emission. **As,** if **they see red blood,** which is impure, during that period, they do not begin observing another seven days. Instead, they consider it an additional emission of blood **and they complete** the remaining days from the seven days they began observing **for** the **green blood.**[N] Consequently, the women will have immersed in a ritual bath while still impure.

דָּבָר אַחֵר: יוֹם שֶׁפּוֹסֶקֶת בּוֹ, סוֹפַרְתּוֹ לְמִנְיַן שִׁבְעָה.

**Alternatively,** a Samaritan woman is considered ritually impure because she **counts** the **day** on **which she ceases** to experience three consecutive days of emissions of *ziva* **toward** the **total** of **seven** clean days that a *zava* must experience before being able to immerse in a ritual bath. Accordingly, she does not wait seven full days, as is required by *halakha*.

מַתְקִיף לַהּ רָמִי בַּר חָמָא: וְתִסְפְּרֶנּוּ, וַאֲנַן נַמִי נִיסְפְּרֵיהּ, דְּקַיְימָא לָן מִקְצָת הַיּוֹם כְּכוּלּוֹ!

**Rami bar Ḥama objects to this: And let her count that** day on which she ceases to experience emissions of *ziva*, **and we,** i.e., Jewish women, **shall also count it,**[N] **as we maintain** that the halakhic status of **part of the day is like** that **of an entire** day.[N]

אָמַר רָבָא: אִם כֵּן שִׁכְבַת זֶרַע דְּסָתַר בְּזִיבָה הֵיכִי מַשְׁכַּחַת לַהּ? וְהָא מִקְצָת הַיּוֹם כְּכוּלּוֹ!

**Rava says** in response: **If so,** that even with regard to *ziva* the halakhic status of part of the day is like that of an entire day, one can object: It is taught in a *baraita* that if a *zav* experiences an emission of **semen** while counting seven clean days toward his purity, the seminal emission **negates** the day on which he experiences it. **How can you find the** circumstances of this *halakha* **with regard to** *ziva***? Isn't** the halakhic status of **part of the day is like** that **of an entire** day? If so, let the remainder of the day on which he experiences the emission count as a day.

**NOTES**

**As they see red blood and they complete the remaining days for the green blood** – שֶׁרוֹאוֹת דָּם אָדוֹם וּמַשְׁלִימוֹת אוֹתוֹ לְדַם יָרוֹק: The early commentaries are puzzled by this statement of Rabbi Meir, as he himself holds in accordance with the opinion of Akavya ben Mahalalel that green blood renders a woman impure (see 19b). They explain that Rabbi Meir deems her impure only if the blood is dark green, not if it is light green, whereas Samaritan women observe the seven-day menstrual period of impurity even for light green blood (*Tosafot*).

**And we shall also count it** – וַאֲנַן נַמִי נִיסְפְּרֵיהּ: The early commentaries explain that Rami bar Ḥama is challenging the previous explanation. Although he subsequently refuted Rava's question against his own opinion, even he does not maintain that women should count such part days in practice (*Tosafot*; Ramban; Meiri; Rashba). The consensus among all the ruling authorities is that the day on which the emission of *ziva* ceases is not included in the seven days of her counting (*Beit Yosef* on *Tur*, beginning of *Yoreh De'a* 196).

**The halakhic status of part of the day is like that of an entire day** – מִקְצָת הַיּוֹם כְּכוּלּוֹ: The commentaries disagree as to the precise definition of part of a day. Some say it includes only part of the daytime, not a part of the night (*Tosafot* on *Moed Katan* 21b; Responsa *Halakhot Ketannot*; Rabbeinu Yona). Others rule more leniently, allowing a part of the night to also be considered like part of the day (Ramban). The *halakha* is that part of the day is like the entire day only if some of the daytime passed, not part of the night (*Shulḥan Arukh*, *Yoreh De'a* 395:1).

אִי דַּחֲזַאי בְּפַלְגָּא דְּיוֹמָא – הָכִי נַמִי, הָכָא בְּמַאי עָסְקִינַן – דַּחֲזַאי סָמוּךְ לִשְׁקִיעַת הַחַמָּה.

The Gemara rejects this suggestion: Perhaps even with regard to *ziva* the halakhic status of part of the day is like that of an entire day, and **if** the *zav* **sees** the seminal emission **in the middle of the day,** the remainder of the day is **indeed** counted as a whole day. But **here we are dealing with** a *zav* **who sees** a seminal emission **adjacent to sunset,** when there is no remaining time in the day that can be counted as an entire day.

וְלֵיקוּם וְלֵימָא לֵיהּ לִקְרָא: כִּי כְּתִיבָא סָמוּךְ לִשְׁקִיעַת הַחַמָּה כְּתִיבָא? אִין, עַל כָּרְחָךְ שַׁבְקֵיהּ לִקְרָא, דְּאִיהוּ דָּחֵיק וּמוֹקֵי אַנַּפְשֵׁיהּ.

The Gemara objects: **But** the *halakha* that a seminal emission negates a day from the count of a *zav* is derived from the verse: "This is the law of the *zav*, and of him from whom the flow of seed goes out, so that he is impure thereby" (Leviticus 15:32). Is it right that one **will stand and say about the verse** that **when it is written, it is written** specifically with regard to a seminal emission that occurs **adjacent to sunset?** The Gemara explains: **Yes, perforce you must leave** aside the plain meaning **of this verse, as it compels itself to be established** as referring to such limited circumstances because it must conform to the principle that the halakhic status of part of the day is like that of an entire day.

בָּעֵי רָמֵי בַּר חָמָא: פּוֹלֶטֶת שִׁכְבַת זֶרַע, מַהוּ שֶׁתִּסְתּוֹר בְּזִיבָה? רוֹאָה הָיְתָה – וְסוֹתֶרֶת,

§ The Gemara mentioned earlier that if a *zav* experiences a seminal emission while counting seven clean days toward his purity, the seminal emission negates the day on which he experiences it. On a similar note, **Rami bar Ḥama raises a dilemma:** In the case of a woman who **discharges semen**[N] after engaging in intercourse with her husband, **what is** the *halakha*[H] as to whether **she negates** her counting **with regard to *ziva*?** Rami bar Ḥama elaborates: In general, a woman who discharges semen is impure, but the reason for this *halakha* is uncertain. Is it because **she was** considered one who **saw** semen, i.e., the emission of semen itself renders her impure just like a man who experiences a seminal emission? **And** if so, this woman **negates** her count.

### NOTES

**A woman who discharges semen – פּוֹלֶטֶת שִׁכְבַת זֶרַע:** The mishna in tractate *Shabbat* (86a) states: From where is it derived that a woman who discharges semen even on the third day after engaging in intercourse is ritually impure, just like one who touches semen? As the verse states: "And he said to the people: Prepare yourselves for three days; do not approach a woman" (Exodus 19:15). In other words, do not engage in intercourse with your wives from three days prior to the Revelation at Sinai, so that even if a woman discharges semen on the fourth day she will be pure. Although the Torah had not yet been given at that time, it can be assumed that this command is in keeping with the requirements of the Torah as would later be revealed at Sinai (*Tosafot* on *Shabbat* 86a). The commentaries further note that a woman who discharges semen is rendered ritually impure only if the semen leaves her body. But if it remains in a concealed part of the body she is pure, as the touch of a concealed part of the body does not impart impurity (Rashi on 42a).

### HALAKHA

**In the case of a woman who discharges semen what is the *halakha*, etc. – פּוֹלֶטֶת שִׁכְבַת זֶרַע מַהוּ וכו׳:** A woman who discharges semen during the period of impurity for her *ziva* negates one day of her counting, like a *zav* who experiences a seminal emission (Rambam *Sefer Kedusha*, *Hilkhot Issurei Bia* 6:16).

Perek **IV**
Daf **33** Amud **b**

אוֹ דִּילְמָא, נוֹגַעַת הָיְתָה – וְלָא סָתְרָה?

**Or perhaps** it is because **she was touching** the semen, **and** if so **she has not** thereby **negated**[N] her count, just as a *zav* does not negate his count if he touches semen.

אָמַר רָבָא: לְפוּם חוּרְפָּא שִׁבַּשְׁתָּא, נְהִי נַמִי דְּסָתְרָה, כַּמָּה תִּסְתּוֹר? תִּסְתּוֹר שִׁבְעָה – דַּיָּהּ כְּבוֹעֲלָהּ.

**Rava says: Commensurate with the sharpness** of Rami bar Ḥama is the extent of his **error,** as this is not a dilemma at all, since **even** if one could suggest **that** a *zava* who discharges semen has **indeed negated** her count, one must ask: **How much should she negate?** If one suggests **she should negate** all **seven** days of her counting, this is untenable, as **it is enough for her** that she should negate her count **like** the man who **engages in intercourse with her,** i.e., like a *zav* who discharges semen, who negates only one day.

תִּסְתּוֹר יוֹם אֶחָד – "וְאַחַר תִּטְהָר" אָמַר רַחֲמָנָא "אַחַר" – אַחַר לְכוּלָּן, שֶׁלֹּא תְּהֵא טוּמְאָה מַפְסֶקֶת בֵּינֵיהֶם.

And if one suggests that **she should negate one day** alone, this too is untenable, as **the Merciful One states:** "But if she is purified from her *ziva* then she shall count to herself seven days, **and after that she shall be pure"** (Leviticus 15:28). The word **"after"** indicates that she shall be pure only **after all of them,** i.e., after seven consecutive clean days, such **that there should be no impurity separating between them.** If so, there cannot be a situation where a *zava* negates a single day, and consequently it cannot be that a *zava* who discharges semen negates any part of her count.

### NOTES

**Or perhaps she was touching the semen and if so she has not thereby negated – אוֹ דִּילְמָא נוֹגַעַת הָיְתָה וְלָא סָתְרָה:** The exact circumstances of this dilemma are somewhat difficult to understand, as a discharge of semen renders a woman impure only if it occurred within three days of engaging in intercourse. If it is determined that the woman is a *zava*, she was prohibited to her husband for at least three days. How, then, can the semen render her impure? According to Rashi, Rami bar Ḥama is referring to a case where the husband and wife engaged in forbidden sexual intercourse. The later commentaries add that Rashi indicates that the couple was engaging in intercourse while she was actually experiencing a blood flow.

**BACKGROUND**

Tavakh – תואך: Apparently this is the name of a town near Neresh, or Nares, located on the caravan routes to Bei Ḥozai. Towns with the similar name Tauk are found in several places in Babylonia.

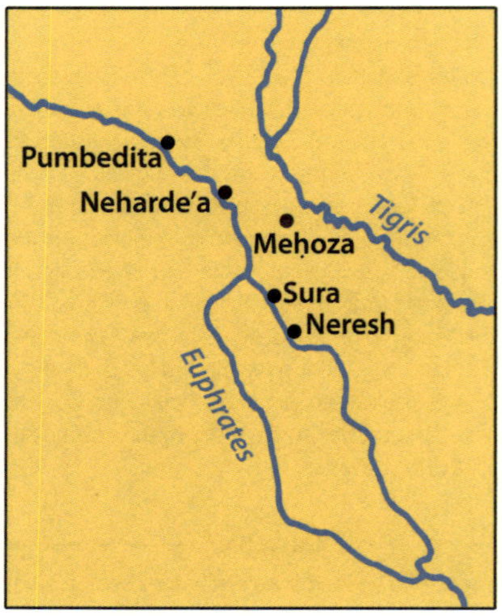


Location of Neresh

**NOTES**

I may conclude from it that he is a God-fearing individual, etc. – שמע מינה ירא שמים הוא וכו׳: The later commentaries explain that Rav Pappa initially intended to visit any Torah scholar in the study hall. This was an accepted act of respect even if the visiting rabbi was greater than the Torah scholar. When he heard that Rav Shmuel was not only considered a Torah scholar but was also renowned as a God-fearing individual, he decided that it was appropriate to pay him a visit in his own home (*Ben Yehoyada*).

**HALAKHA**

The uncertain case of the garments of an *am ha'aretz* – ספק בגדי עם הארץ: One burns *teruma* for uncertainty involving the purity of the garments of an *am ha'aretz*. This is one of six cases of uncertain impurity in which one burns the *teruma* that came into contact with a suspect item. In other words, if *teruma* came into contact with the garments of an *am ha'aretz* it must be burned, despite the fact that this impurity applies only due to uncertainty. The reason is that if this impurity were certain then the *am ha'aretz* would be a *zav*, whose impurity applies by Torah law (Rambam *Sefer Tahara*, *Hilkhot She'ar Avot HaTumot* 13:13).

וליטעמיך, זב גופיה היכי סתר? ״לטהרתו״ אמר רחמנא – שלא תהא טומאה מפסקת ביניהן!

The Gemara rejects Rava's response: **And according to your reasoning, how does a *zav* himself negate** only one day from his count due to a seminal emission? After all, **the Merciful One states:** "And when the *zav* is purified of his *ziva*, then he shall count for himself seven days for his purification, and wash his clothes, and bathe his flesh in running water, and he shall be pure" (Leviticus 15:13). The phrase: "Seven days **for his purification,**" indicates **that there should be no impurity separating between them.**

אלא מאי אית לך למימר – שלא תהא טומאת זיבה מפסקת ביניהן, הכא נמי – שלא תהא טומאת זיבה מפסקת ביניהן.

**Rather, what have you to say?** The verse means only **that there should not be an impurity of *ziva* separating between them. Here too,** with regard to a *zava*, the verse means only **that there should not be an impurity of *ziva* separating between them;** a discharge of semen is not included in this restriction. It is therefore possible that a discharge of semen from a *zava* negates only one day from her count. Accordingly, the dilemma raised by Rami bar Ḥama remains in place.

״ואין חייבין עליהן על ביאת מקדש״ וכו׳. רב פפא איקלע לתואך. אמר: אי איכא צורבא מרבנן הכא, איזיל אקביל אפיה. אמרה ליה ההיא סבתא: איכא הכא צורבא מרבנן, ורב שמואל שמיה, ותני מתניתא, יהא רעוא דתהוי כוותיה!

§ The mishna teaches: **But** one who enters the Temple while wearing **those** garments upon which a Samaritan had lain **is not liable** to bring an offering **for entering the Temple,** nor does one burn *teruma* that came into contact with those garments, because their impurity is uncertain. In connection to these *halakhot*, the Gemara relates that **Rav Pappa**[P] **happened** to come **to** the city of **Tavakh.**[B] **He said: If there is a Torah scholar here I will go and greet him. A certain elderly woman said to him: There is a Torah scholar here and Rav Shmuel is his name, and he teaches *mishnayot*; may it be** God's **will that you should be like him.**

אמר: מדקמברכי לי בגוויה – שמע מינה ירא שמים הוא. אזל לגביה. רמא ליה תורא, רמא ליה מתניתין אהדדי. תנן: אין חייבין עליהן על ביאת מקדש, ואין שורפין עליהן את התרומה, מפני שטומאתה ספק. אלמא – מספיקא לא שרפינן תרומה,

Rav Pappa **said** to himself: **From** the fact **that they bless me through** this Rav Shmuel that I should be like him, I may **conclude from it** that **he is a God-fearing** individual.[N] Rav Pappa **went to** visit **him,** and Rav Shmuel **raised a bull for him,** i.e., he slaughtered a bull in honor of Rav Pappa, and he also **raised** a difficulty between two ***mishnayot*** that apparently contradict **one another: We learn** in the mishna: One who enters the Temple while wearing **those** garments upon which a Samaritan had lain is **not liable** to bring an offering **for entering the Temple, nor does one burn *teruma*** that came into contact with **those** garments, **because their impurity is uncertain. Evidently, we do not burn *teruma* due to uncertain** impurity.

ורמינהי: על ששה ספקות שורפין את התרומה, על ספק בגדי עם הארץ!

**And** one can **raise a contradiction** from another mishna (*Teharot* 4:5): **For six** cases of **uncertain** impurity **one burns the *teruma*** if it came into contact with them, or if a person came into contact with them and subsequently touched the *teruma*. One of these is **for the uncertain** case **of the garments of one who is unreliable with regard to ritual impurity** [***am ha'aretz***].[H] Such garments impart impurity through contact and through carrying, due to a concern that the wife of the *am ha'aretz* might have sat on them while she was menstruating. Evidently, one burns *teruma* due to uncertain impurity.

**PERSONALITIES**

Rav Pappa – רב פפא: Rav Pappa belonged to the fifth generation of the *amora'im* of Babylonia. He was a student of both Abaye and Rava in Pumbedita. Rav Pappa established an academy in Neresh, where he was joined by his close friend Rav Huna, son of Rav Yehoshua, who was appointed chief lecturer. After Rava's death, many of his disciples came to study under Rav Pappa, who had more than two hundred students attending his lectures.

Rav Pappa's father was a wealthy merchant who supported him through many years of Talmud study. Rav Pappa became a wealthy businessman in his own right; he was a successful brewer of date beer, and he also prospered in other business ventures. The Talmud records that he engaged in trade with both Jews and gentiles and had a reputation for fairness and generosity in his business dealings (see *Ketubot* 97a). Rav Huna, who was his partner in many such undertakings, grew wealthy as well.

Rav Pappa had great respect for other Sages, and upon entering a city would immediately call upon the rabbinic head of the community. On one occasion Rav Pappa felt that he had spoken inappropriately about one of the Sages, and he took upon himself a personal fast as penance for his act (*Sanhedrin* 100a). He was reluctant to offer final rulings in areas of *halakha*, and he often chose to be stringent in accordance with both opinions in the Talmud rather than rule in accordance with a single opinion.

Rav Pappa was blessed with ten sons, all of whom were Torah scholars. Traditionally, the names of the ten sons of Rav Pappa are recited as part of the ceremony at the completion of the study of a tractate. Although the source of this tradition is unclear and the identities of the sons are uncertain as well, the Rema suggests that it commemorates the celebrations Rav Pappa performed with his sons upon completing a course of study.

אָמַר רַב פָּפָּא: יְהֵא רַעֲוָא דְּלִתְאֲכֵיל הַאי תּוֹרָא לִשְׁלָמָא, הָכָא בְּמַאי עָסְקִינַן בְּכוּתִי חָבֵר.

**Rav Pappa** began his response with a supplication and **said: May it be** God's **will that this bull shall be eaten peacefully,** i.e., that I will provide a satisfactory resolution of this contradiction. Since the bull was slaughtered in my honor, failing to resolve the contradiction might spoil the meal. Rav Pappa continued: **Here we are dealing with a Samaritan** who is **devoted to the meticulous observance of mitzvot, especially *halakhot* of ritual purity, *teruma*, and tithes** [***ḥaver***].[B] There is therefore less concern with regard to his ritual purity than that of an *am ha'aretz*. Consequently, the mishna here states that *teruma* is not burned on account of him.

כּוּתִי חָבֵר בּוֹעֵל נִדָּה מְשַׁוֵּית לֵיהּ?

Rav Shmuel rejected this response: Since the mishna is referring to men who engage in intercourse with menstruating women, **are you equating a Samaritan *ḥaver*** with a man who **engages in intercourse with a menstruating woman?**

שַׁבְקֵיהּ, וַאֲתָא לְקַמֵּיהּ דְּרַב שִׁימִי בַּר אַשִׁי. אֲמַר לֵיהּ: מַאי טַעְמָא לָא מְשַׁנֵּית לֵיהּ; בְּכוּתִי שֶׁטָּבַל וְעָלָה, וְדָרַס עַל בִּגְדֵי חָבֵר, וְאָזְלוּ בִּגְדֵי חָבֵר וְנָגְעוּ בִּתְרוּמָה.

Rav Pappa **left** Rav Shmuel in embarrassment **and came before Rav Shimi bar Ashi,** to whom he related this incident. Rav Shimi bar Ashi **said to him: What is the reason** that **you did not respond to him** that the ruling of the mishna is stated **with regard to a Samaritan who immersed** in a ritual bath **and arose** from his impure status, **and** subsequently **trod on the garments of a *ḥaver*,** which means they are now considered the bedding of the Samaritan, **and** then those **garments of** the ***ḥaver*** **went and touched *teruma*?** In such a case one does not burn the *teruma*.

דְּאִי מִשּׁוּם טוּמְאַת עַם הָאָרֶץ – הָא טְבֵיל לֵיהּ, וְאִי מִשּׁוּם בּוֹעֵל נִדָּה – סָפֵק בָּעַל בְּקָרוֹב סָפֵק לֹא בָּעַל בְּקָרוֹב.

**As, if** one would say to burn it **due to the impurity of an *am ha'aretz*, he** has **immersed** in a ritual bath. **And if** one were to suggest that it should be burned **because** the Samaritan is one who **engages in intercourse with a menstruating woman,** this too is an unsatisfactory reason. This is because it is **uncertain** whether **he recently engaged in intercourse** with his wife, in which case his immersion does not remove his impurity; and it is **uncertain** whether **he did not recently engage in intercourse** with his wife, in which case he is in fact pure.

וְאִם תִּמְצֵי לוֹמַר בָּעַל בְּקָרוֹב – סָפֵק הִשְׁלִימָתוֹ יָרוֹק סָפֵק לֹא הִשְׁלִימָתוֹ, וְהָוֵי סְפֵק סְפֵיקָא, וְאַסְּפֵק סְפֵיקָא לָא שָׂרְפִינַן תְּרוּמָה.

**And** even **if you say** that **he recently engaged in intercourse** with his wife, another uncertainty remains: It is **uncertain** whether his wife began counting seven days from an emission of green blood and ignored any subsequent emission of red blood and **completed** her count for the **green** blood, which would mean that she was in fact a menstruating woman when she engaged in sexual intercourse with her husband; and it is **uncertain** whether **she did not complete** a count of seven days from the emission of the green blood, rather from the emission of red blood, in which case she was not a menstruating woman when her husband engaged in intercourse with her. **And** therefore **this is a compound uncertainty, and** there is a principle that **one does not burn *teruma*** **on** account of **a compound uncertainty.**[H]

**BACKGROUND**

*Ḥaver* – חָבֵר: The *ḥaverim* were members of a group or class of people who were meticulous in their observance of several mitzvot that most common people [*amei ha'aretz*] were not strict in observing. One who sought to enter a society of this kind had to accept its practices formally in the presence of three other members, who served as a kind of court for this purpose. The main emphasis of these groups was the strict observance of the *halakhot* of *teruma* and tithes and careful adherence to the *halakhot* of ritual purity, to the extent that they would eat even non-sacred food in a state of purity. As a rule, a Torah scholar was typically a *ḥaver*, but a *ḥaver* was not necessarily a Torah scholar. Acceptance as a member of this group removed an individual from the category of a common, uneducated person, and his statements with regard to tithes and ritual purity were deemed reliable. In later generations, the term took on a more restricted meaning and was used in reference only to prominent scholars.

**HALAKHA**

**And one does not burn *teruma* on account of a compound uncertainty** – וְאַסְּפֵק סְפֵיקָא לָא שָׂרְפִינַן תְּרוּמָה: If it is uncertain whether or not *teruma* touched the garments of an *am ha'aretz* one does not burn the *teruma*, but it remains in abeyance. The reason is that this impurity itself applies only due to uncertainty, and even if the *am ha'aretz* is impure it is uncertain whether the *teruma* touched him. Accordingly, this is a compound uncertainty and the *halakha* is that in a case of a compound uncertainty one leaves the *teruma* in abeyance (Rambam *Sefer Tahara*, *Hilkhot She'ar Avot HaTumot* 13:13).

וְתֵיפּוֹק לֵיהּ מִשּׁוּם בִּגְדֵי עַם הָאָרֶץ, דְּאָמַר מָר: בִּגְדֵי עַם הָאָרֶץ מִדְרָס לִפְרוּשִׁין! אֲמַר לֵיהּ: בְּכוּתִי עָרוֹם.

Rav Pappa raised an objection to Rav Shimi bar Ashi: **And let** one **derive** that the garments of the *ḥaver* are impure **because** they came into contact with the **garments of an *am ha'aretz*. As the Master said:** The **garments of an *am ha'aretz***[H] are considered impure with the ritual impurity imparted by the **treading** of a *zav*, which means they impart impurity to people and to garments, **for individuals who are scrupulous with regard to impurity [*perushin*].**[B] Rav Shimi bar Ashi **said to** Rav Pappa: The mishna is referring **to a naked Samaritan.** Consequently, none of his garments came into contact with the garments of the *ḥaver*.

**מתני׳** בְּנוֹת צְדוֹקִין, בִּזְמַן שֶׁנָּהֲגוּ לָלֶכֶת בְּדַרְכֵי אֲבוֹתֵיהֶן – הֲרֵי הֵן כְּכוּתִיּוֹת, פֵּרְשׁוּ לָלֶכֶת בְּדַרְכֵי יִשְׂרָאֵל – הֲרֵי הֵן כְּיִשְׂרְאֵלִית. רַבִּי יוֹסֵי אוֹמֵר: לְעוֹלָם הֵן כְּיִשְׂרְאֵלִית, עַד שֶׁיִּפְרְשׁוּ לָלֶכֶת בְּדַרְכֵי אֲבוֹתֵיהֶן.

**MISHNA** With regard to **Sadducee**[B] **girls,**[N] **when they were accustomed to follow in the ways of their** Sadducee **ancestors their** status **is like** that of **Samaritan women,** whose *halakha* was discussed in the previous mishna. If the Sadducee women **abandoned** the customs of their ancestors in order **to follow in the ways of the Jewish people** their status **is like** that of **a Jewish woman. Rabbi Yosei says: Their** status **is always like** that of **a Jewish woman, until they will abandon** the ways of the Jewish people in order **to follow in the ways of their** Sadducee **ancestors.**

**גמ׳** אִיבַּעְיָא לְהוּ: סְתָמָא מַאי? תָּא שְׁמַע: בְּנוֹת צְדוֹקִין, בִּזְמַן שֶׁנּוֹהֲגוֹת לָלֶכֶת בְּדַרְכֵי אֲבוֹתֵיהֶן – הֲרֵי הֵן כְּכוּתִיּוֹת, הָא סְתָמָא – כְּיִשְׂרְאֵלִית. אֵימָא סֵיפָא: פֵּרְשׁוּ לָלֶכֶת בְּדַרְכֵי יִשְׂרָאֵל – הֲרֵי הֵן כְּיִשְׂרְאֵלִית, הָא סְתָמָא – כְּכוּתִיּוֹת! אֶלָּא מֵהָא לֵיכָּא לְמִשְׁמַע מִינַּהּ.

**GEMARA** **A dilemma was raised before** the Sages: **What** is the *halakha* in **an unspecified** case, i.e., when the custom of a Sadducee woman is unknown? The Gemara suggests: **Come** and **hear** evidence from the mishna: With regard to **Sadducee girls, when they are accustomed to follow in the ways of their** Sadducee **ancestors their** status **is like** that of **Samaritan women.** It can be inferred from the mishna **that** in **an unspecified** case their status **is like** that of **a Jewish woman.** The Gemara rejects this suggestion: **Say the latter clause:** If the Sadducee women **abandoned** the customs of their ancestors in order **to follow in the ways of the Jewish people their** status **is like** that of **a Jewish woman.** One may infer from this **that** in **an unspecified** case their status **is like** that of **Samaritan women. Rather, no** inference is **to be learned from this** mishna.

תָּא שְׁמַע, דִּתְנַן רַבִּי יוֹסֵי אוֹמֵר: לְעוֹלָם הֵן כְּיִשְׂרְאֵלִית עַד שֶׁיִּפְרְשׁוּ לָלֶכֶת בְּדַרְכֵי אֲבוֹתֵיהֶן. מִכְּלָל דְּתַנָּא קַמָּא סָבַר: סְתָמָא כְּכוּתִיּוֹת, שְׁמַע מִינַּהּ.

The Gemara suggests: **Come** and **hear** the last clause of the mishna, **as we learned** in the mishna that **Rabbi Yosei says: Their** status **is always like** that of **a Jewish woman, until they will abandon** the ways of the Jewish people in order **to follow in the ways of their** Sadducee **ancestors. By inference,** one may conclude **that the first *tanna* holds** that in **an unspecified** case their status **is like** that of **Samaritan women.** The Gemara affirms: **Conclude from it** that this is the case.

### HALAKHA

**The garments of an *am ha'aretz*, etc.** – **בִּגְדֵי עַם הָאָרֶץ וכו׳**: An *am ha'aretz*, although he is a full-fledged Jew, and even if he is versed in Torah and mitzvot, has the presumptive status of ritual impurity, and his garments have the ritual impurity imparted by the treading of a *zav* for those who are scrupulous with regard to impurity. Consequently, his garments impart impurity to food or drink they touch, and likewise they render impure an earthenware vessel through its airspace. Furthermore, although this impurity is due to uncertainty, one burns *teruma* that came into contact with these garments (Rambam *Sefer Tahara, Hilkhot Metamei Mishkav UMoshav* 10:1).

### NOTES

**Sadducee girls** – **בְּנוֹת צְדוֹקִין**: The early commentaries write that Sadducees are considered Jews in all regards, but as they deny basic articles of faith in the Torah, in practice the halakhic status of their women depends on their behavior (Meiri). Some commentaries maintain that after the Sadducees went astray and ceased acting in accordance with the strictures of *halakha* they became considered like full-fledged gentiles (*Shita Mekubbetzet*).

### BACKGROUND

***Perushin*** – **פְּרוּשִׁין**: The name *perushin*, or Pharisees, is usually understood as referring to the rabbinic Sages, particularly during the late Second Temple period. Depending on context, the name can be an antonym of *amei ha'aretz* or Sadducees. The Sages rarely referred to themselves with this term, which was used more often by their opponents. The root *peh, reish, shin* can denote both interpretation and separation. Therefore, while some suggest the term *perushin* means those who interpret or expound, i.e., those who expound the Written Torah, many explain that it means separatists. The reference to the Sages as separatists who reject community norms could be either a positive or a negative appellation, depending on one's perspective on general society at the time. It can also refer to separation from forbidden sexual intercourse. The greatest of the *perushin* were the *tanna'im* of the Mishna.

**Sadducees** – **צְדוֹקִין**: At the end of the Second Temple period and in subsequent years, groups of Jews strayed from the path of the Sages to various degrees. The first Christians were among these sects, which by and large consisted of different types of Gnostics. Although these groups differed from one another, they all deviated from the accepted *halakha*. They also leveled accusations against the Sages, often claiming that the Sages themselves did not observe the *halakha* in an absolute manner and instead interpreted the *halakha* as they saw fit.

The source of the name Sadducees is a man called Tzadok, who was a student of Antigonus of Sokho, a Sage from the start of the period of the *zugot*, or Pairs, the early period of the *tanna'im*. Tzadok did not believe in the reality of the World-to-Come. A similar group was called the Boethusians, named after Baitos, another heretical disciple of Antigonus of Sokho.

The conflicts between the Sages and the Sadducees were manifested in various areas, both ideological and political. In addition to denying the reality of the World-to-Come, the Sadducees rejected the halakhic traditions espoused by the Sages, choosing to interpret the Torah according to their own rationale and understanding. Although the Sadducees themselves eventually enacted various ordinances of their own, these were not rooted in any tradition. While the Sadducees comprised only a minority of the population they enjoyed a great deal of political influence, as they maintained close ties to the later Hasmonean kings. They used this influence to exacerbate the conflict between the king and the Sages, and to rebuff the Sages wherever possible. As a result, the Sages responded in kind and rejected all Sadducee practices, even if they were perfectly acceptable from a halakhic perspective. They also enacted certain decrees specifically against Sadducee customs, in the formula of the Gemara: To remove a misconception from the heart of the Sadducees.

תָּנוּ רַבָּנַן: מַעֲשֶׂה בִּצְדוֹקִי אֶחָד שֶׁסִּפֵּר עִם כֹּהֵן גָּדוֹל בַּשּׁוּק, וְנִתְּזָה צִנּוֹרָא מִפִּיו וְנָפְלָה לְכֹהֵן גָּדוֹל עַל בְּגָדָיו, וְהוֹרִיקוּ פָּנָיו שֶׁל כֹּהֵן גָּדוֹל, וְקָדַם אֵצֶל אִשְׁתּוֹ.

§ **The Sages taught:** There was **an incident involving a certain Sadducee who was conversing with the High Priest in the marketplace, and** as he was speaking, **saliva** [*tzinora*][L] **sprayed from his mouth and fell onto the garments of the High Priest. And the face of the High Priest turned green,**[N] as he feared that his garments had been rendered ritually impure. **And he rushed to** the Sadducee's **wife**[N] to inquire whether she properly observed the *halakhot* of menstruation, in which case his garments were not rendered impure by the saliva of her husband, as he is not considered one who engages in intercourse with a menstruating woman.

אָמְרָה לוֹ: אַף עַל פִּי שֶׁנְּשֵׁי צְדוֹקִים הֵן – מִתְיָרְאוֹת מִן הַפְּרוּשִׁים, וּמַרְאוֹת דָּם לַחֲכָמִים.

**She said to him: Even though** women such as myself **are the wives of Sadducees,** who do not follow in the ways of the *perushim*, **they are scared of the *perushim* and they show** their **blood to the Sages** when an uncertainty arises. The garments of the High Priest are therefore pure, as the Sadducee wives properly observe the *halakhot* of menstruation.

אָמַר רַבִּי יוֹסֵי: בְּקִיאִין אָנוּ בָּהֶן יוֹתֵר מִן הַכֹּל, וְהֵן מַרְאוֹת דָּם לַחֲכָמִים, חוּץ מֵאִשָּׁה אַחַת שֶׁהָיְתָה בִּשְׁכוּנָתֵינוּ, שֶׁלֹּא הֶרְאָת דָּם לַחֲכָמִים וּמֵתָה.

**Rabbi Yosei says: We are familiar with the** wives of Sadducees **more so than everyone** else, as they are our neighbors, **and** I can testify that **they** all **show** their **blood to the Sages, except for a certain woman who was** living **in our neighborhood who did not show** her **blood to the Sages, and she died,** as a punishment for her behavior.

וְתֵיפּוֹק לֵיהּ מִשּׁוּם צִנּוֹרָא דְּעַם הָאָרֶץ! אָמַר אַבַּיֵי: בִּצְדוֹקִי חָבֵר. אָמַר רָבָא: צְדוֹקִי חָבֵר, בּוֹעֵל נִדָּה מְשַׁוֵּית לֵיהּ? אֶלָּא אָמַר רָבָא:

The Gemara objects: **And let** the High Priest **derive** that his garments are impure **due to the saliva of an *am ha'aretz*,** which imparts impurity. **Abaye said:** That case involved **a Sadducee *ḥaver*,** who was particular with regard to the *halakhot* of ritual purity. **Rava said: Are you equating a Sadducee *ḥaver*** with a man who **engages in intercourse with a menstruating woman?** After all, the High Priest was initially concerned that the Sadducee might engage in intercourse with his wife while she is still menstruating. **Rather, Rava said:**

**LANGUAGE**

Saliva [*tzinora*] – צִנּוֹרָא: The origin of this word in unclear, but it is apparently related to *tzinor*, a hollow pipe or spout through which water flows. *Tzinora* can also refer to a trickle of liquid, or in this case a spray of saliva.

**NOTES**

And the face of the High Priest turned green – וְהוֹרִיקוּ פָּנָיו שֶׁל כֹּהֵן גָּדוֹל: The later commentaries note that this story parallels the incident recounted in *Yoma* (47a) involving Rabbi Yishmael ben Kimḥit, who was in fact a High Priest. The Gemara there relates that he was talking with a certain officer in the marketplace when the officer's saliva sprayed onto his clothes, and the commentaries explain that this occurred on Yom Kippur (Rashi) or on the eve of Yom Kippur (Maharsha, citing the Jerusalem Talmud). According to the *Tosefta*, Rabbi Yishmael ben Kimḥit went to converse with the king. Similarly, one can say that the incident here also occurred on Yom Kippur, and it was necessary for the High Priest to speak with the Sadducee for matters of public importance. It was for this reason that the High Priest was so upset, since if he contracted ritual impurity he would be unable to perform the Yom Kippur service.

And he rushed to the Sadducee's wife – וְקָדַם אֵצֶל אִשְׁתּוֹ: The early commentaries ask why the High Priest relied on the statement of the Sadducee's wife, in light of the principle that one who is suspected with regard to a certain matter is not deemed credible to testify about it (see *Bekhorot* 35a). They further ask why he did not inquire about her status from the Sadducee himself. They explain that even one who is suspected concerning a matter is deemed credible if he speaks offhandedly. As the Sadducee himself had seen the High Priest's reaction he would have known how important his response would be, and therefore any answer he would give could not have been accepted. By contrast, his wife could be classified as one who speaks offhandedly, provided that her husband had not yet informed her of the incident. Therefore, the High Priest rushed to ask her before she spoke to her husband (Ran; Ritva). Others explain that one who is suspected with regard to a certain matter is not deemed credible to testify about it if he stands to gain in some form from his testimony, whereas here the Sadducee woman would not benefit from lying (Meiri).



רֶגֶל הֲוָה, וְטוּמְאַת עַם הָאָרֶץ בָּרֶגֶל – כְּטָהֳרָה שַׁוְּינְהוּ רַבָּנַן, דִּכְתִיב: "וַיֵּאָסֵף כָּל אִישׁ יִשְׂרָאֵל אֶל הָעִיר כְּאִישׁ אֶחָד חֲבֵרִים" – הַכָּתוּב עֲשָׂאָן כּוּלָּן חֲבֵרִים.

This incident occurred during **a pilgrimage Festival,** either Passover, *Sukkot*, or *Shavuot*, **and the Sages rendered the ritual impurity of an *am ha'aretz* during a pilgrimage Festival as purity.**[H] **As it is written: "And all the men of Israel gathered to the city, like one man, united [*ḥaverim*]"** (Judges 20:11).[N] Whenever all the Jewish people gather in a single place, such as on a pilgrimage Festival, **the verse renders all of them *ḥaverim*,** even one who is an *am ha'aretz*. There was therefore no concern for impurity due to the saliva of an *am ha'aretz*. Yet, the High Priest was concerned that this Sadducee was one who engages in intercourse with a menstruating woman.

**HALAKHA**

The impurity of an *am ha'aretz* during a pilgrimage Festival – טוּמְאַת עַם הָאָרֶץ בָּרֶגֶל: During pilgrimage Festivals, all members of the Jewish people are considered *ḥaverim* and are ritually pure, including their vessels, drinks, and food. They are likewise deemed credible with regard to all purity, whether that of sacrificial food or *teruma*. Once the Festival has ended, they return to their impure state. The *halakha* is in accordance with the opinion of Rava (Rambam *Sefer Tahara*, *Hilkhot Metamei Mishkav UMoshav* 11:9).

**NOTES**

As it is written…like one man united [*ḥaverim*] – דִּכְתִיב...כְּאִישׁ אֶחָד חֲבֵרִים: In the Jerusalem Talmud, in *Hagiga*, chapter 3, a different source verse is cited: "Jerusalem, that is built as a city that is compact [*ḥubbera*] together" (Psalms 122:3), which is interpreted to mean that Jerusalem renders all who are inside it into *ḥaverim*. And when is this the case? As the verse states: "When the tribes went up there, the tribes of the Lord" (Psalms 122:4). By contrast, see Jerusalem Talmud *Bava Kamma*, chapter 7, where a different interpretation of this verse is stated: Jerusalem is a city which joins [*meḥaberet*] all Jews together.

The later commentaries explain that the two interpretations complement each other, as on the pilgrimage Festivals the hearts of Jews are drawn close together (Maharatz Ḥayyut).

The Rambam provides a logical rationale for this principle: It can be assumed that all people purify themselves properly in order to bring the Festival offerings, and therefore one may rely upon them all. He adds this reason because the verses adduced by the Talmud are intended merely as allusions, and consequently it is necessary to provide a more substantial justification for this *halakha* (*Tosefot Yom Tov*).

מתני׳ דַּם גּוֹיָה וְדַם טׇהֳרָה שֶׁל מְצוֹרַעַת, בֵּית שַׁמַּאי מְטַהֲרִים, וּבֵית הִלֵּל אוֹמְרִים: כְּרוּקָּהּ וּכְמֵימֵי רַגְלֶיהָ.

**MISHNA** With regard to the **blood of** a menstruating **gentile woman**[H] or a gentile *zava*, **and the blood** discharged **by** a female Jewish **leper** during the days **of purity**[H] of a woman who gives birth, **Beit Shammai deem** them **ritually pure, and Beit Hillel say:** The halakhic status of the blood of the gentile woman is **like** that of **her saliva and her urine,**[N] which impart impurity only while moist. Likewise, the blood discharged by a Jewish leper during the days of purity imparts impurity only when moist.

דַּם הַיּוֹלֶדֶת שֶׁלֹּא טָבְלָה, בֵּית שַׁמַּאי אוֹמְרִים: כְּרוּקָּהּ וּכְמֵימֵי רַגְלֶיהָ, וּבֵית הִלֵּל אוֹמְרִים: מְטַמֵּא לַח וְיָבֵשׁ.

With regard to **the blood of a woman who gave birth** and reached the conclusion of her days of impurity, i.e., seven days after giving birth to a male or fourteen days after giving birth to a female, but **who did not** yet **immerse** in a ritual bath, **Beit Shammai say:** Although she has yet to immerse in a ritual bath, the blood does not retain the halakhic status of menstrual blood. Rather, the status of the blood is **like** that of **her saliva and her urine,** and it imparts impurity only while moist. **And Beit Hillel say:** Since she did not immerse in a ritual bath, her blood is considered like that of a menstruating woman, and it **imparts impurity** whether it is **moist or dry.**[N]

וּמוֹדִים בְּיוֹלֶדֶת בְּזוֹב – שֶׁהִיא מְטַמְּאָה לַח וְיָבֵשׁ.

**And** Beit Shammai **concede** to Beit Hillel **in** the case of **a woman who gives birth as a *zava*,** where the woman must count seven clean days from the conclusion of her days of impurity, **that** any blood **she** sees during those seven days **imparts impurity** whether it is **moist or dry.**

גמ׳ וְלֵית לְהוּ לְבֵית שַׁמַּאי ״דַּבֵּר אֶל בְּנֵי יִשְׂרָאֵל וְאָמַרְתָּ אֲלֵיהֶם אִישׁ אִישׁ כִּי יִהְיֶה זָב״ – בְּנֵי יִשְׂרָאֵל מְטַמְּאִין בְּזִיבָה, וְאֵין הַגּוֹיִם מְטַמְּאִין בְּזִיבָה, אֲבָל גָּזְרוּ עֲלֵיהֶן שֶׁיְּהוּ כְּזָבִין לְכָל דִּבְרֵיהֶם?

**GEMARA** The mishna teaches that according to Beit Shammai the blood of a gentile woman does not impart impurity. The Gemara objects: **And do Beit Shammai not accept** that which is taught with regard to the verse: **"Speak to the children of Israel and say to them, when any man has an issue** [*zav*] out of his flesh, his issue is impure" (Leviticus 15:2), from which it is inferred: By Torah law, **the children of Israel become impure through *ziva* and gentiles do not become impure through *ziva*, but** the Sages **decreed concerning them that they shall be like *zavin* in all their matters**[NH] of ritual purity.

אָמְרִי לָךְ בֵּית שַׁמַּאי: (הַהוּא בִּזְכָרִים אִיתְּמַר, דְּאִי בִּנְקֵבוֹת) הֵיכִי לַעֲבֵיד? לִיטַמֵּא לַח וְיָבֵשׁ – עֲשִׂיתוֹ כְּשֶׁל תּוֹרָה, לִיטַמֵּי לַח וְלָא לִיטַמֵּי יָבֵשׁ – חָלַקְתָּ בְּשֶׁל תּוֹרָה.

The Gemara responds: **Beit Shammai** could **say to you** that **this was stated** only **with regard to males,** not females. **As, if** it was stated even **with regard to females, how should one act** with regard to this impurity? **Should** their blood **impart impurity** whether it is **moist or dry?** If so, **you have rendered it like** blood that imparts impurity **by Torah** law, and people will mistakenly come to burn *teruma* that comes into contact with it. Perhaps one will suggest that it **should impart impurity** only while it is **moist and it should not impart impurity** when it is **dry.** But if so, **you** will have **differentiated** between moist and dry blood even **with regard to** blood **that** is impure by **Torah** law, i.e., one might mistakenly conclude that the blood of Jewish women imparts impurity only when it is moist, when in fact it imparts impurity whether it is moist or dry.

**NOTES**

**And Beit Hillel say the blood of a gentile is like that of her saliva and her urine** – **וּבֵית הִלֵּל אוֹמְרִים כְּרוּקָּהּ וּכְמֵימֵי רַגְלֶיהָ**: This dispute between Beit Shammai and Beit Hillel is cited by Rabbi Yehuda at the beginning of the fifth chapter of *Eduyyot*, as a rare dispute in which Beit Shammai maintain a more lenient opinion than that of Beit Hillel. But the Rabbis do not agree with Rabbi Yehuda in this regard. Some commentaries maintain that according to the Rabbis the opinions should be reversed, so that Beit Shammai rule more stringently than Beit Hillel, while others contend that according to the Rabbis Beit Shammai and Beit Hillel did not disagree with regard to this *halakha* at all (see *Tosefot Yom Tov*).

**And Beit Hillel say her blood imparts impurity whether moist or dry** – **וּבֵית הִלֵּל אוֹמְרִים מְטַמֵּא לַח וְיָבֵשׁ**: Beit Hillel maintain that the blood of a woman after childbirth remains impure by Torah law until she immerses in a ritual bath. The early commentaries dispute whether she is rendered a menstruating woman due to this blood. Some claim that any blood she sees during her days of purity after childbirth does not render her a menstruating woman, even if she has not immersed, despite the fact that the blood itself is impure (Rashba; Ritva; *Tosafot* on 36a; Rambam *Sefer Kedusha, Hilkhot Issurei Bia* 7:8). Others contend that this blood does render her a menstruating woman. This latter opinion is cited by the Meiri on 35b, although the Meiri himself rejects it.

**The Sages decreed concerning them that they shall be like *zavin* in all their matters** – **גָּזְרוּ עֲלֵיהֶן שֶׁיְּהוּ כְּזָבִין לְכָל דִּבְרֵיהֶם**: The Gemara in *Shabbat* 17b indicates that this is one of the so-called eighteen matters, the decrees issued by the students of Beit Shammai and Beit Hillel which were in accordance with the opinion of Beit Shammai. By contrast, it can be inferred from *Avoda Zara* 36b that this decree dates back to the period of the Hasmonean kings. Some commentaries explain that the initial decree referred only to an adult gentile who saw an emission of *ziva*, and the students of Beit Shammai and Beit Hillel later extended it to include even gentile minors, even when they did not experience an emission (Maharsha on *Shabbat* 21b).

**HALAKHA**

**The blood of a menstruating gentile woman** – **דַּם גּוֹיָה**: With regard to the blood of a gentile menstruating woman or a gentile *zava*, and the blood of a gentile woman after childbirth, although they do not impart impurity by Torah law, they do impart impurity by rabbinic law while they are moist. They are considered as a primary source of ritual impurity, and therefore they impart impurity to vessels through contact, and to people through contact and by carrying. This impurity applies by rabbinic law. One is not liable to bring an offering for entering the Temple in the state of ritual impurity imparted by them, and one does not burn *teruma* and consecrated items that come into contact with them. The *halakha* is in accordance with the opinion of Beit Hillel (Rambam *Sefer Tahara, Hilkhot Metamei Mishkav UMoshav* 2:10).

**Blood discharged by a female Jewish leper during the days of purity** – **דַּם טׇהֳרָה שֶׁל מְצוֹרַעַת**: In the case of a female leper who gave birth and who immersed seven days after the birth of a male or fourteen days after the birth of a female, her blood of purity is ritually impure like the saliva and urine of a regular leper. The *halakha* is in accordance with the opinion of Beit Hillel (Rambam *Sefer Tahara, Hilkhot Metamei Mishkav UMoshav* 5:5).

**The Sages decreed concerning them that they shall be like *zavin* in all their matters** – **גָּזְרוּ עֲלֵיהֶן שֶׁיְּהוּ כְּזָבִין לְכָל דִּבְרֵיהֶם**: Although by Torah law the impurities of menstruation, *ziva*, and a woman after childbirth do not apply to gentiles, the Sages decreed that all gentiles, male and female, should always be considered like *zavim* with regard to ritual impurity (Rambam *Sefer Tahara, Hilkhot Metamei Mishkav UMoshav* 2:10 and *Sefer Kedusha, Hilkhot Issurei Bia* 4:4).

אִי הָכִי, רוּקָּהּ וּמֵימֵי רַגְלֶיהָ נַמִי! כֵּיוָן דְּעָבְדִינַן הֶיכֵּרָא בְּדָמָהּ – מֵידַע יְדִיעַ דְּרוּקָּהּ וּמֵימֵי רַגְלֶיהָ דְּרַבָּנַן.

The Gemara objects: **If so,** then with regard to **the saliva and urine of** a gentile *zava*, which impart impurity by rabbinic law only when moist, Beit Shammai should **also** rule that they do not impart impurity at all, in order to distinguish their saliva and urine from that of a Jewish *zava*, which by Torah law impart impurity only when moist (see 54b). The Gemara responds: **Since we implement a conspicuous marker with regard to the blood of** a gentile woman, i.e., it is clear that her status is different from that of a Jewish woman in that her blood does not impart impurity whatsoever, everyone **will know that** the impurity of **her saliva and her urine** is only **by rabbinic** law, and there is no concern that people might come to mistakenly burn *teruma* that comes into contact with the saliva and urine of a gentile *zava*.

וְלַעֲבֵיד הֶיכֵּרָא בְּרוּקָּהּ וּמֵימֵי רַגְלֶיהָ, וּלְטַמּוּיֵי לְדָמָהּ! רוּקָּהּ וּמֵימֵי רַגְלֶיהָ דִּשְׁכִיחִי – גָּזְרוּ בְּהוּ רַבָּנַן, דָּמָהּ דְּלָא שְׁכִיחָא – לָא גָּזְרוּ בֵּיהּ רַבָּנַן.

The Gemara persists: **And let them implement a conspicuous marker with regard to the saliva and urine of** a gentile woman, that they should not impart impurity whatsoever, **and let them deem her blood impure** even when dry. In this manner, everyone will know that the impurity of a gentile woman applies only by rabbinic law, and they will not come to treat that which is impure by Torah law in the same manner. The Gemara responds: With regard to **her saliva and her urine, which are** relatively **common, the Sages decreed** that **they** are impure, but with regard to **her blood, which is not** as **common, the Sages did not decree** that **it** is impure.

אָמַר רָבָא: זוֹבוֹ טָמֵא – אֲפִילּוּ לְבֵית שַׁמַּאי, קֶרְיוֹ טָהוֹר – אֲפִילּוּ לְבֵית הִלֵּל.

§ With regard to a gentile man, **Rava says: The** *ziva* **of** a gentile man is **ritually impure,**[H] **even according to** the opinion of **Beit Shammai,** who maintain that the *ziva* of a gentile woman does not impart impurity whatsoever. By contrast, **the semen of** a gentile is **pure,**[H] **even according to** the opinion of **Beit Hillel,** who hold that the blood of menstruating gentiles and the blood of their *ziva* imparts impurity when it is moist.

זוֹבוֹ טָמֵא אֲפִילּוּ לְבֵית שַׁמַּאי – דְּהָא אִיכָּא לְמֶעְבַּד הֶיכֵּרָא בְּקֶרְיוֹ,

Rava elaborates: **The** *ziva* **of** a gentile man is **impure, even according to** the opinion of **Beit Shammai, as it is** possible **to implement a conspicuous marker with his semen,** i.e., since his semen does not impart impurity whatsoever, everyone will know that the impurity imparted by the *ziva* of a gentile applies by rabbinic law, and they will not come to burn *teruma* that comes in contact with the *ziva* of a gentile.

קֶרְיוֹ טָהוֹר אֲפִילּוּ לְבֵית הִלֵּל – עֲבוּד בֵּיהּ רַבָּנַן הֶיכֵּרָא, כִּי הֵיכִי דְּלָא לִשְׂרוֹף עֲלֵיהּ תְּרוּמָה וְקָדָשִׁים.

And **the semen of** a gentile is **ritually pure, even according to** the opinion of **Beit Hillel.** This is because **the Sages** had to **implement a conspicuous marker with regard to it**[HN] to indicate that the *ziva* of a gentile imparts impurity only by rabbinic law **in order that they will not** come **to burn** ***teruma*** **and consecrated** items **that** come into contact with their *ziva*, as must be performed with *teruma* and consecrated items that contract impurity by Torah law.

וְלַעֲבֵיד הֶיכֵּרָא בְּזוֹבוֹ וּלְטַמּוּיֵי לְקֶרְיוֹ! זוֹבוֹ דְּלָא תָּלֵי בְּמַעֲשֶׂה – גָּזְרוּ בֵּיהּ רַבָּנַן, קֶרְיוֹ דְּתָלֵי בְּמַעֲשֶׂה – לָא גָּזְרוּ בֵּיהּ רַבָּנַן.

The Gemara objects: **And let** the Sages **implement a conspicuous marker with regard to the** ***ziva*** **of** a gentile man, that it should not impart impurity whatsoever, **and let them deem his semen impure.** The Gemara explains: With regard to **his** ***ziva,*** **which is not dependent on an action** he performs but is emitted on its own, **the Sages decreed** that **it** is impure; with regard to **his semen, which is dependent on an action** he performs, **the Sages did not decree** that **it** is impure.

לֵימָא מְסַיַּיע לֵיהּ: גּוֹיָה שֶׁפָּלְטָה שִׁכְבַת זֶרַע מִיִּשְׂרָאֵל – טְמֵאָה, וּבַת יִשְׂרָאֵל שֶׁפָּלְטָה שִׁכְבַת זֶרַע מִן הַגּוֹי – טְהוֹרָה. מַאי לָאו טְהוֹרָה גְּמוּרָה? לָא, טְהוֹרָה – מִדְּאוֹרַיְיתָא, טְמֵאָה – מִדְּרַבָּנַן.

The Gemara suggests: **Let us say** that the following mishna (*Mikvaot* 8:4) **supports** Rava's opinion: In the case of **a gentile woman who discharged semen** that came **from a Jew**[H] who engaged in intercourse with her, the semen is **impure,** as it came from a Jew. **And** in the case of **a Jewish woman who discharged semen** that came **from a gentile,**[H] the semen is **pure. What, is it not** correct to say that the mishna means the semen of the gentile is **entirely pure,** in accordance with the opinion of Rava? The Gemara refutes this suggestion: **No,** perhaps the mishna means that the semen of a gentile is **pure by Torah law** but **impure by rabbinic law,** whereas according to Rava, the semen of a gentile is pure even by rabbinic law.

## HALAKHA

**The *ziva* of a gentile man is ritually impure – זוֹבוֹ טָמֵא:** Although gentiles do not contract the impurity of *ziva* by Torah law, the Sages decreed they should contract the impurity of *ziva*, in the case of a male from the age of nine years and one day, and a female from three years and one day. They did not apply this decree to children younger than that age (Rambam *Sefer Tahara*, *Hilkhot Metamei Mishkav UMoshav* 2:10).

**The semen of a gentile is pure – קֶרְיוֹ טָהוֹר:** Although the Sages decreed impurity on the *ziva* emission of gentiles, they did not decree likewise with regard to their semen, and it is ritually pure even by rabbinic law. The *halakha* is in accordance with the opinion of Rava (Rambam *Sefer Tahara*, *Hilkhot Metamei Mishkav UMoshav* 2:10 and *Hilkhot She'ar Avot HaTumot* 5:17).

**The Sages implement a conspicuous marker with regard to it – עֲבוּד בֵּיהּ רַבָּנַן הֶיכֵּרָא:** Why didn't the Sages decree impurity on the semen of gentiles? In order to make known that their impurity of *ziva* applies by rabbinic law, as people would realize that if a gentile was a *zav* by Torah law then his semen would be a primary source of ritual impurity like the semen of a *zav*. Since they will know that the impurity is by rabbinic law, they will not burn *teruma* and consecrated items which came into contact with them (Rambam *Sefer Tahara*, *Hilkhot Metamei Mishkav UMoshav* 2:10).

**A gentile woman who discharged semen that came from a Jew – גּוֹיָה שֶׁפָּלְטָה שִׁכְבַת זֶרַע מִיִּשְׂרָאֵל:** In the case of a gentile woman who discharged semen that came from a Jew, if this happened within three twelve-hour periods after engaging in intercourse, the semen is ritually impure. If it occurred later than that, it is uncertain whether or not it is still classified as semen (Rambam *Sefer Tahara*, *Hilkhot She'ar Avot HaTumot* 5:16).

**A Jewish woman who discharged semen that came from a gentile – בַּת יִשְׂרָאֵל שֶׁפָּלְטָה שִׁכְבַת זֶרַע מִן הַגּוֹי:** In the case of a Jewish woman who discharged semen that came from a gentile, since the semen of a gentile is not ritually impure, she is pure even if three twelve-hour periods had not passed since she engaged in intercourse with him (Rambam *Sefer Tahara*, *Hilkhot She'ar Avot HaTumot* 5:17 and *Kesef Mishne* there).

## NOTES

**The Sages implement a conspicuous marker with regard to it – עֲבוּד בֵּיהּ רַבָּנַן הֶיכֵּרָא:** Since the *ziva* of a Jewish male imparts impurity only when moist, the only available conspicuous marker is to deem some emission of a gentile male ritually pure (Rashi).

The Gemara here indicates that the semen of a gentile is ritually pure, but in the Jerusalem Talmud (*Shabbat* 1:4) it is stated that the eighteen matters include the decree that the semen of gentiles is impure. The Gemara there states that this is puzzling, as Rabbi Yoḥanan rules that the semen of a gentile is pure. The answer given is that the decree was due to the fact that in practice it is impossible for semen to be emitted without some trace of urine (see *Korban HaEda*).

תָּא שְׁמַע, נִמְצֵאתָ אוֹמֵר: שִׁכְבַת זֶרַע שֶׁל יִשְׂרָאֵל – טְמֵאָה בְּכָל מָקוֹם,

The Gemara cites another source that possibly supports Rava's opinion: **Come and hear** a *baraita*: **You are found** to **say the semen of a Jew is impure wherever** it is found,

Perek **IV**
Daf **34** Amud **b**

וַאֲפִילּוּ בִּמְעֵי גוֹיָה. וְשֶׁל גּוֹי – טְהוֹרָה בְּכָל מָקוֹם וַאֲפִילּוּ בִּמְעֵי יִשְׂרְאֵלִית, חוּץ מִמֵּי רַגְלַיִם שֶׁבָּהּ.

**even** if it is **in the womb of a gentile woman.** If she discharges this semen, it imparts ritual impurity. **And** by contrast, the semen **of a gentile is ritually pure wherever** it is found, **even** if it is **in the womb of a Jewish woman, except for** any **urine that** intermingled **with it.**[N] In other words, if the semen of a gentile intermingled with his urine, the mixture is impure due to the urine it contains, as the Sages decreed that a gentile is considered like a *zav* in all matters. Consequently, his urine imparts impurity.

וְכִי תֵּימָא הָכִי נַמִּי טְהוֹרָה מִדְּאוֹרַיְיתָא, אֲבָל טְמֵאָה מִדְּרַבָּנַן, אַטּוּ מֵי רַגְלֶיהָ מִדְּאוֹרַיְיתָא מִי מְטַמְּאוּ? אֶלָּא שְׁמַע מִינַּהּ: טְהוֹרָה אֲפִילּוּ מִדְּרַבָּנַן, שְׁמַע מִינַּהּ.

The Gemara continues: **And if you would say** in rejection of this proof: Here **as well,** the *baraita* means that the semen of a gentile is **ritually pure by Torah law but impure by rabbinic** law, one may respond: Since the *baraita* states that the urine of a gentile is impure, **is that to say** that **her urine,** i.e., the urine of the gentile that intermingled with his semen and is now inside the womb of the Jewish woman, is **ritually impure by Torah law?** Isn't it impure only by rabbinic law? **Rather, conclude from** the *baraita* that the semen of a gentile is **pure even by rabbinic law.** The Gemara concludes: Indeed, **conclude from it** that this is so.

אָמַר מָר: שִׁכְבַת זֶרַע שֶׁל יִשְׂרָאֵל – טְמֵאָה בְּכָל מָקוֹם, אֲפִילּוּ בִּמְעֵי גוֹיָה. תִּפְשׁוֹט דִּבְעֵי רַב פָּפָּא. דִּבְעֵי רַב פָּפָּא: שִׁכְבַת זֶרַע שֶׁל יִשְׂרָאֵל בִּמְעֵי גוֹיָה מַהוּ?

**The Master said** above in a *baraita*: **The semen of a Jew is impure wherever** it is found, **even** if it is **in the womb of a gentile woman.** The Gemara suggests: **Let one resolve** from this *baraita* a dilemma **that Rav Pappa raises. As Rav Pappa raises a dilemma: What is** the *halakha* with regard to the **semen of a Jew in the womb of a gentile woman?** Let one conclude from the *baraita* that the semen is impure.

בְּתוֹךְ שְׁלֹשָׁה – לָא קָמִיבַּעְיָא לֵיהּ לְרַב פָּפָּא, כִּי קָמִיבַּעְיָא לֵיהּ – לְאַחַר שְׁלֹשָׁה מַאי?

The Gemara rejects this suggestion: Rav Pappa **does not raise his dilemma** with regard to the semen of a Jew that is in the womb of a gentile woman **within three** days of their intercourse, as such semen is impure. Rather, **when** Rav Pappa **raises his dilemma** it is with regard to semen in the womb of the gentile more than **three** days **after** their intercourse. **What is** the *halakha* in such a case?

יִשְׂרָאֵל דְּדָיְיגִי בְּמִצְוֹת – חֲבִיל גּוּפַיְיהוּ וּמַסְרִיחַ, גּוֹיִם דְּלָא דָּיְיגִי בְּמִצְוֹת – לָא חֲבִיל גּוּפַיְיהוּ וְלָא מַסְרִיחַ. אוֹ דִּילְמָא: כֵּיוָן דְּאָכְלִי שְׁקָצִים וּרְמָשִׂים – חֲבִיל גּוּפַיְיהוּ, וּמַסְרִיחַ? תֵּיקוּ.

The Gemara explains the sides of the dilemma: Do we say that as **Jewish** women **are concerned about** the proper fulfillment of **mitzvot, their bodies are hot and** semen in their wombs **becomes foul** within three days, whereas **gentile** women **are not concerned about** the proper fulfillment of **mitzvot** and therefore **their bodies are not hot and** semen in their wombs **does not become foul** within three days? **Or perhaps, since** gentiles **eat repugnant creatures and creeping animals, their bodies are** also **hot and** semen in their wombs **becomes foul** within three days? Since no resolution is found, the Gemara concludes: The dilemma **shall stand** unresolved.[N]

## NOTES

Except for any urine intermingled with it – חוּץ מִמֵּי רַגְלַיִם שֶׁבָּהּ: The commentaries disagree as to the meaning of this clause, of which there are slightly different versions. Some say it serves to exclude the urine of the gentile, i.e., the decree of the Sages with regard to the impurity of the urine of a gentile applies even when it is mixed with his semen (Rashi). The later commentaries explain that according to Rashi's interpretation, the correct version of the text should be: Apart from his urine inside it. Others accept the standard version of the text, and maintain that it is referring to the woman's urine. This urine is impure because it touched the woman, who herself is ritually impure due to her contact with the *zav* in a place that is not a concealed part of the body (Rashash).

The dilemma shall stand unresolved – תֵּיקוּ: The ruling authorities disagree as to the *halakha* in this case. Some write that as the dilemma is left unresolved by the Gemara one should be stringent due to uncertainty (*Tashbetz*). Others maintain that one should add a day and deem semen impure even on the fourth day after intercourse (Meiri). The Rambam in *Sefer Tahara, Hilkhot She'ar Avot HaTumot* 5:16, leaves this issue as an uncertainty and does not rule that one should treat it stringently, and the later commentaries analyze his opinion (*Arukh LaNer*).

״דַּם טָהֳרָה שֶׁל מְצוֹרַעַת בֵּית שַׁמַּאי״ כו׳. מַאי טַעְמָא דְּבֵית הִלֵּל? אָמַר רַבִּי יִצְחָק: ״לַזָּכָר״ – לְרַבּוֹת מְצוֹרָע לְמַעְיְנוֹתָיו, ״וְלַנְּקֵבָה״ – לְרַבּוֹת מְצוֹרַעַת לְמַעְיְנוֹתֶיהָ.

§ The mishna teaches: With regard to **blood** discharged **by** a female Jewish **leper** during the days **of purity** of a woman who gives birth, **Beit Shammai** deem it ritually pure and Beit Hillel say it imparts impurity only while moist. The Gemara asks: **What is the reasoning of Beit Hillel,** i.e., from where is their opinion derived? **Rabbi Yitzḥak says:** The verse states at the conclusion of the passage discussing impure individuals: "Whether it be a male or a female" (Leviticus 15:33). **"Whether it be a male"** serves **to include the sources** of bodily emissions **of a male leper,** teaching that they also impart impurity. Likewise, the phrase **"or a female"** serves **to include the sources** of bodily emissions **of a female leper,** teaching that they too impart impurity.

מַאי ״מַעְיְנוֹתֶיהָ״? אִילֵימָא שְׁאָר מַעְיְנוֹתֶיהָ – מִזָּכָר נָפְקָא, אֶלָּא לְדָמָהּ – לְטַמֵּא דַּם טָהֳרָה שֶׁלָּהּ.

**What** is meant by the **sources** of bodily emissions of a female leper? **If we say** that this is referring to **the rest of her sources,** e.g., her saliva and urine, this can be **derived from** the *halakha* of **a male** leper. **Rather,** it is referring **to her blood,** and the verse serves **to render impure** the **blood** of a leper discharged during the days of **her purity.**

וּבֵית שַׁמַּאי? נְקֵבָה מִזָּכָר לָא אָתְיָא, דְּאִיכָּא לְמִיפְרַךְ: מַה לְּזָכָר – שֶׁכֵּן טָעוּן פְּרִיעָה וּפְרִימָה, וְאָסוּר בְּתַשְׁמִישׁ הַמִּטָּה, תֹּאמַר בִּנְקֵבָה – דְּלָא.

The Gemara asks: **And** how do **Beit Shammai,** who maintain the blood is ritually pure, interpret the verse? They contend that the *halakha* with regard to the emissions of **a female** leper **cannot be derived from** that of **a male** leper, **as** such a comparison **can be refuted** as follows: **What** is unique **about a male** leper? He is unique **in that he is required to let his hair grow and rend his garments, and he is prohibited to** engage in **sexual intercourse.** Can **you say,** then, that the same *halakhot* should apply to the emissions **of a female** leper, **to** whom all the aforementioned requirements do **not** apply? Consequently, the verse is necessary to teach that the saliva and urine of a female leper are impure.

וּבֵית הִלֵּל? לִכְתּוֹב רַחֲמָנָא בִּנְקֵבָה, וְלָא בָּעֵי זָכָר. וַאֲנָא אָמֵינָא: וּמַה נְּקֵבָה שֶׁאֵינָהּ טְעוּנָה פְּרִיעָה וּפְרִימָה, וְאֵינָהּ אֲסוּרָה בְּתַשְׁמִישׁ הַמִּטָּה – רַבֵּי רַחֲמָנָא מַעְיְנוֹתֶיהָ. זָכָר – לֹא כׇּל שֶׁכֵּן!

The Gemara asks: **And** how do **Beit Hillel** respond? They respond as follows: If the verse serves to include only the saliva and urine of a female leper, then **let the Merciful One write** this *halakha* only **with regard to a female** leper. **And** there will be **no need** to write it with regard to **a male** leper, as **I will say** that the saliva and urine of a male leper are impure by an *a fortiori* inference: **And what,** if with regard to **a female** leper, **who is not required to let her hair grow and rend her garments,**[N] **and** it **is not prohibited** for her **to** engage in **sexual intercourse, the Merciful One** nevertheless **includes her sources** of bodily emissions as impure, then in the case of **a male** leper, to whom all the aforementioned requirements apply, is it **not all the more so** that his emissions are impure?

אִם אֵינוֹ עִנְיָן לְזָכָר – תְּנֵהוּ עִנְיָן לִנְקֵבָה, וְאִם אֵינוֹ עִנְיָן לְמַעְיְנוֹתֶיהָ – תְּנֵהוּ עִנְיָן לְדָמָהּ, לְטַמֵּא דַּם טָהֳרָה שֶׁלָּהּ.

Therefore, **if** the phrase "whether it be a male" **is not** needed for the **matter of a male** leper, as this *halakha* may be derived by an *a fortiori* inference, **apply it** to the **matter of a female** leper. **And if it is not** needed for the **matter of her** other **sources** of bodily emissions, as they are derived from the phrase "or a female," **apply it** to the **matter of her blood,** i.e., **to render impure** the **blood of her** days of **purity.**

וּבֵית שַׁמַּאי? זָכָר מִנְּקֵבָה לָא אָתְיָא, דְּאִיכָּא לְמִיפְרַךְ: מַה לִּנְקֵבָה – שֶׁכֵּן מְטַמְּאָה מֵאוֹנֶס, תֹּאמַר בְּזָכָר דְּלָא.

The Gemara asks: **And** how do **Beit Shammai** respond? They would answer that the *halakha* with regard to the emissions of **a male** leper **cannot be derived** by an *a fortiori* inference **from** the *halakha* of **a female** leper, **as** it **can be refuted** as follows: **What** is unique **about a female?** She is unique **in that she is rendered impure** as a *zava* even by sightings that occur **due to circumstances beyond** her **control.** Can **you say** that the same *halakhot* should apply to the emissions **of a male,** for **whom** this is **not** the case?

וּבֵית הִלֵּל? קָיְימִי בִּמְצוֹרָע וּפָרְכִי מִילֵּי דְּזָב? וּבֵית שַׁמַּאי? שׁוּם טוּמְאָה פָּרְכִי.

The Gemara asks: **And** how do **Beit Hillel** respond? They respond as follows: Can it be that we are **standing** and dealing **with** the *halakhot* of **a leper, and** Beit Shammai are attempting to **refute** the *a fortiori* inference by citing **matters** pertaining **to a *zav*?** The Gemara asks: **And** as for **Beit Shammai?** According to Beit Shammai, this is a legitimate refutation of the *a fortiori* inference, as **they refute** it through the common **name of impurity** that applies to both a leper and a *zav*.

**NOTES**

**A female leper, who is not required to let her hair grow and rend her garments – נְקֵבָה שֶׁאֵינָהּ טְעוּנָה פְּרִיעָה וּפְרִימָה:** The Torah states with regard to a confirmed leper: "And the leper in whom the plague is, his clothes shall be rent, and the hair of his head shall go loose" (Leviticus 13:45). The Sages derived from the phrase: "He is a leprous man" (Leviticus 13:44), that these obligations apply only a to male leper (*Karetot* 8b).

וְאִיבָּעֵית אֵימָא, אָמְרִי לָךְ בֵּית שַׁמַּאי: הַאי "לַזָּכָר" מִיבָּעֵי לֵיהּ, "לַזָּכָר" – כָּל שֶׁהוּא זָכָר, (הַאי) בֵּין גָּדוֹל בֵּין קָטָן. וּבֵית הִלֵּל? נָפְקָא לְהוּ מִ"זֹּאת תּוֹרַת הַזָּב" – בֵּין גָּדוֹל בֵּין קָטָן.

**And if you wish, say** that **Beit Shammai** could **say to you: That** phrase **"whether it be a male" is necessary to** teach another *halakha*, that the phrase **"whether it be a male"** serves to include **anyone who is a male, whether an adult or a minor,** in the *halakhot* of a *zav*. **And** how do **Beit Hillel** respond? **They derive** this *halakha* **from** the following verse: **"This is the law of the *zav*,** and of him from whom the flow of seed goes out, so that he is unclean through it" (Leviticus 15:32). The verse indicates that the *halakhot* of a *zav* apply to any male, **whether** he is **an adult or whether** he is **a minor.**[H]

אָמַר רַב יוֹסֵף, כִּי פָּשֵׁיט רַבִּי שִׁמְעוֹן בֶּן לָקִישׁ בְּזָב, בָּעֵי הָכִי: רְאִיָּיה רִאשׁוֹנָה שֶׁל זָב קָטָן, מַהוּ שֶׁתְּטַמֵּא בְּמַגָּע? "זֹאת תּוֹרַת הַזָּב וַאֲשֶׁר תֵּצֵא מִמֶּנּוּ שִׁכְבַת זֶרַע" אָמַר רַחֲמָנָא,

§ The Gemara mentioned earlier that a minor is included in the *halakhot* of a *zav*. In this regard **Rav Yosef says: When Rabbi Shimon ben Lakish taught** the *halakhot* **of a *zav*, he raised this dilemma:** With regard to the **first sighting** of *ziva* **of a *zav*** who is a **minor, what is** the *halakha* as to whether **it imparts impurity through contact?** Does one say that as **the Merciful One states: "This is the law of the *zav*, and of him from whom the flow of seed goes out"** (Leviticus 15:32), one's *ziva* is thereby compared to his semen?

כָּל שֶׁשִּׁכְבַת זֶרַע שֶׁלּוֹ מְטַמָּא – רְאִיָּיה רִאשׁוֹנָה שֶׁלּוֹ מְטַמְּאָה, וְהַאי – כֵּיוָן דְּשִׁכְבַת זֶרַע שֶׁלּוֹ לָא מְטַמְּאָה – רְאִיָּיה רִאשׁוֹנָה נַמִי לָא תְּטַמֵּא. אוֹ דִּילְמָא: כֵּיוָן דְּאִילּוּ אִיהוּ חָזֵי תַּרְתֵּי – מִצְטָרְפָא, מְטַמְּיָא?

Accordingly, with regard to **any** male **whose semen imparts impurity, his first sighting** of *ziva* **imparts impurity. And** with regard to **this** minor, **since his semen does not impart impurity,**[N] **his first sighting does not impart impurity either. Or perhaps, since if** this minor **sees two** emissions of *ziva* the first sighting **combines** with the second sighting to render him impure as a *zav* for seven days, this indicates that the first sighting of a minor is significant, and consequently it should **render him impure** until the evening, just like an adult male.

אָמַר רָבָא: תָּא שְׁמַע, "זֹאת תּוֹרַת הַזָּב" – בֵּין גָּדוֹל בֵּין קָטָן, מַה גָּדוֹל – רְאִיָּיה רִאשׁוֹנָה שֶׁלּוֹ מְטַמָּא, אַף קָטָן – רְאִיָּיה רִאשׁוֹנָה נַמִי מְטַמָּא.

**Rava says: Come** and **hear** a proof from a *baraita*: **"This is the law of the *zav*," whether** he is **an adult** or **whether** he is **a minor.** Since the verse equates an adult and a minor, **just as** with regard to **an adult his first sighting imparts impurity, so too,** with regard to **a minor,** his **first sighting imparts impurity as well.**

בָּעֵי רַב יוֹסֵף: רְאִיָּיה רִאשׁוֹנָה שֶׁל מְצוֹרָע מַהוּ שֶׁתְּטַמֵּא בְּמַשָּׂא? מְקוֹם זִיבָה מַעְיָן הוּא – וּמְטַמֵּא, אוֹ דִּילְמָא לָאו מַעְיָן הוּא?

The Gemara earlier stated that the phrase "whether it be a male" serves to include the sources of bodily emissions of a male leper, teaching that they impart impurity. In this regard **Rav Yosef raises a dilemma:** Granted, the first sighting of *ziva* of an otherwise ritually pure individual imparts impurity only through contact, as stated above, and only the second sighting imparts impurity through carrying. But with regard to the **first sighting** of *ziva* **of a leper, what is** the *halakha* **as to** whether **it imparts impurity** even **through carrying?** Does one say that the **place of *ziva*** in one's body **is** considered **a source, and** therefore his *ziva* **imparts impurity** through carrying, like all the sources of bodily emissions of a leper? **Or perhaps** the place of *ziva* **is not** considered **a source,** in which case the first sighting of *ziva* does not impart impurity through carrying.

אָמַר רָבָא: תָּא שְׁמַע, "זוֹבוֹ טָמֵא הוּא" – לִימֵּד עַל הַזּוֹב שֶׁהוּא טָמֵא. בְּמַאי? אִילֵימָא בְּזָב גְּרֵידָא,

**Rava says: Come** and **hear** proof from a *baraita*: The verse states: "When any man has an issue out of his flesh, **his issue** [*zovo*] **is unclean"** (Leviticus 15:2). The verse **teaches with regard to the *zov* that it is impure,**[N] and that it imparts impurity through carrying. **To what** case is the verse referring? **If we say** it is referring **to** one who is **just a *zav*** and not a leper as well, and the verse is teaching that any drop of *ziva* emitted by him imparts impurity through carrying,

NOTES

**His semen does not impart impurity – שִׁכְבַת זֶרַע שֶׁלּוֹ לָא מְטַמְּאָה:** The minor referred to here is a boy less than nine years old. It was stated in 32b that it is a *halakha* transmitted to Moses from Sinai that the semen of such a minor does not impart impurity. Nevertheless, there are different opinions among the later commentaries with regard to the *halakha* of a minor. Some write that the statement that a minor does not transmit the impurity of a seminal discharge does not mean that his semen does not impart impurity. Rather, it means that it is assumed that as a minor he has not experienced a seminal discharge. But if it is known for certain that he did have a seminal discharge, he is ritually impure even if he is one day old (*Magen Avraham*). Others question this opinion, as the wording of the Gemara here: His semen does not impart impurity, is apparently referring to the semen itself, not the presumptive status of the minor (*Dagul MeRevava*; *Ḥok Ya'akov*; *Ḥatam Sofer*). Some say that this opinion, that the semen of a minor younger than nine years old does not impart impurity, is the ruling of the Rambam in *Sefer Tahara*, *Hilkhot She'ar Avot HaTumot* 5:2. Yet others maintain that although the semen of a minor does not impart impurity to others, it does render the minor himself ritually impure, like any other male who had a seminal emission (*Noda BiYehuda*).

**The verse teaches with regard to the *zov* that it is impure – לִימֵּד עַל הַזּוֹב שֶׁהוּא טָמֵא:** The Gemara later on (55a) explains that it is unnecessary for the verse to state that *ziva* imparts impurity through contact, as its status should be no less stringent than semen, which itself imparts impurity through contact. Accordingly, the verse must be coming to add to the impurity of *ziva*, i.e., that it imparts impurity through carrying as well.

HALAKHA

**This is the law of the *zav* whether he is an adult or whether he is a minor – זֹאת תּוֹרַת הַזָּב בֵּין גָּדוֹל בֵּין קָטָן:** The *ziva* discharge of a *zav* is a primary source of ritual impurity, like the *zav* himself. Consequently, even the smallest discharge imparts impurity by touch from the first sighting, and by carrying from the second sighting, whether the *zav* is an adult male or a minor (Rambam *Sefer Tahara*, *Hilkhot Metamei Mishkav UMoshav* 1:12).

לַאֲחֵרִים גּוֹרֵם טוּמְאָה, לְעַצְמוֹ לֹא כׇּל שֶׁכֵּן? אֶלָּא פְּשִׁיטָא – בְּזָב מְצוֹרָע,

there is no need for the verse to teach this. After all, if this drop of *ziva* **causes impurity for others,** i.e., if the person emitting the drop imparts impurity through carrying, is it **not all the more so** that the drop **itself** imparts impurity through carrying? **Rather,** it is **obvious** that the verse is referring **to** a drop of *ziva* from **a** ***zav*** who is also a **leper.**[B] And it was necessary for the verse to teach this *halakha*, as it could not be derived by means of the *a fortiori* inference. This is because this drop of *ziva* is not what causes the leper to impart impurity through carrying; rather, it is his leprosy that causes him to impart impurity through carrying.

וּמִדְּאִיצְטְרִיךְ קְרָא לְרַבּוֹיֵי בְּרְאִיָּיה שְׁנִיָּה – שְׁמַע מִינַּהּ: מְקוֹם זִיבָה לָאו מַעְיָן הוּא.

Rava concludes: **And** as the verse mentions the word "issue" twice, it is evident that it is referring to a second sighting of *ziva*. **From** the fact that **a verse was necessary to include a second sighting** of *ziva* of a leper, teaching that his *ziva* imparts impurity through carrying, **conclude from it** that the **place of** ***ziva*** **is not** considered **a source.** If it were a source, then even the first sighting of *ziva* would impart impurity through carrying.

אֲמַר לֵיהּ רַב יְהוּדָה מִדִּסְקַרְתָּא לְרָבָא: מִמַּאי? דִּילְמָא לְעוֹלָם אֵימָא לָךְ – בְּזָב גְּרִידָא, וּדְקָאָמְרַתְּ לַאֲחֵרִים גּוֹרֵם טוּמְאָה, לְעַצְמוֹ לֹא כׇּל שֶׁכֵּן – שָׂעִיר הַמִּשְׁתַּלֵּחַ יוֹכִיחַ, שֶׁגּוֹרֵם טוּמְאָה לַאֲחֵרִים – וְהוּא עַצְמוֹ טָהוֹר!

**Rav Yehuda of Diskarta**[B] **said to Rava: From where** do you know that the verse is referring to a *zav* who is also a leper? **Actually, perhaps I will say to you** that the verse is referring **to** the *ziva* of one who is **just a** ***zav***. **And** as for **that** *a fortiori* inference **that you said:** If this drop of *ziva* **causes impurity for others,** is it **not all the more so** that the drop **itself** imparts impurity through carrying, one can counter that inference. The case of the **scapegoat**[B] brought on Yom Kippur **will prove** that this *a fortiori* inference is not valid, **as it causes impurity to others,** since the dispatcher of the scapegoat is rendered ritually impure, **and** yet the goat **itself is pure,** as a living animal cannot be rendered impure.

אָמַר אַבָּיֵי: מַאי תִּבְעֵי לֵיהּ? וְהָא הוּא דְּאָמַר "זֹאת תּוֹרַת הַזָּב" – בֵּין גָּדוֹל בֵּין קָטָן, וְכֵיוָן דְּנָפְקָא לֵיהּ מֵהָתָם – אִייַּתַּר לֵיהּ "לַזָּכָר" לְרַבּוֹת מְצוֹרָע לְמַעְיְנוֹתָיו, "נְקֵבָה" – לְרַבּוֹת מְצוֹרַעַת לְמַעְיְנוֹתֶיהָ,

With regard to the dilemma raised by Rav Yosef about the first sighting of *ziva* of a leper, **Abaye said: What** is the reason **he raises** such **a dilemma? But it was he who said** that when the verse states: **"This is the law of the** ***zav***" (Leviticus 15:32), it thereby teaches that the *halakhot* of a *zav* apply **whether** he is **an adult** or **whether** he is **a minor. And since he derives** this *halakha* **from there,** the verse: "And of them that have an issue [*vehazav*] of *ziva*, whether it be a male or a female" (Leviticus 15:33), **remains** available **for him** to derive as follows: **"Whether it be a male"** serves **to include a male leper** with regard **to his sources** of bodily emissions,[N] and **"or a female"** serves **to include a female leper** with regard **to her sources** of bodily emissions.

וְאַקְשְׁיֵהּ רַחֲמָנָא מְצוֹרָע לְזָב גָּמוּר, מָה זָב גָּמוּר – מְטַמֵּא בְּמַשָּׂא, אַף רְאִיָּיה רִאשׁוֹנָה שֶׁל מְצוֹרָע – מְטַמֵּא בְּמַשָּׂא.

**And** as this verse discusses a full-fledged *zav*, and the word "issue" is mentioned twice, **the Merciful One compares a leper to a full-fledged** ***zav***: **Just as a full-fledged** ***zav*** **imparts impurity through carrying, so too,** the **first sighting** of *ziva* **of a leper**[H] **imparts impurity through carrying.**

## BACKGROUND

**Leprosy** – צָרַעַת: Traditionally rendered as leprosy, the term used in the Torah is not necessarily the medical equivalent of that disease. The Torah term is referring to symptoms that cause severe ritual impurity. The *halakhot* governing these symptoms are articulated at length in Leviticus, chapters 13–15, and in tractate *Nega'im* of the Mishna. There can be leprosy of the skin, the hair, articles of clothing, and houses. When a symptom appears, it is examined by a priest, as only a priest is authorized to determine whether to quarantine the affected person for a certain period or to declare immediately that the symptom is or is not leprosy.

Leprosy is one of the primary sources of ritual impurity, and it is particularly severe in that it imparts ritual impurity to items found in the same enclosure with it, like the impurity caused by a corpse. A person afflicted with leprosy is sent out of the Israelite camp and must live alone until his affliction is cured. A cured leper undergoes certain rites outside the city and a purification ceremony in the Temple itself. As part of his purification, he is obligated to bring specific offerings.

**Diskarta** – דִּסְקַרְתָּא: Diskarta is the name of a place, derived from the Middle Persian dastagird, meaning an inherited plot of land.

**Scapegoat** – שָׂעִיר הַמִּשְׁתַּלֵּחַ: On Yom Kippur, the Torah requires lots to be drawn between two goats, one to be sacrificed as a sin-offering in the Temple and one to be sent to Azazel (see Leviticus, chapter 16). This goat was thrown from a high desert cliff, 12–15 km from Jerusalem. Before sending the goat to its death, the High Priest would symbolically burden it with all the sins of the Jewish people, both their intentional and their unwitting violations. Afterward, he would send the goat to the desert with a man specifically designated for this task. The service associated with this goat, an essential part of the Yom Kippur ritual, atoned for sins for which no other offering atoned.

## HALAKHA

**The first sighting of a leper** – רְאִיָּיה רִאשׁוֹנָה שֶׁל מְצוֹרָע: The first *ziva* sighting of a leper imparts impurity through carrying by Torah law. The *halakha* is in accordance with the opinion of Abaye (Rambam *Sefer Tahara, Hilkhot Metamei Mishkav UMoshav* 1:13).

## NOTES

**To include a male leper with regard to his sources of bodily emissions** – לְרַבּוֹת מְצוֹרָע לְמַעְיְנוֹתָיו: The early commentaries dispute Abaye's exposition of the phrase "for a male" in reference to a male leper, in light of the statement on 34b that according to Beit Hillel this phrase is not necessary for the case of a male leper but is referring to the blood of purity of a female leper (see *Tosafot*; Rashba; Ran). Some explain that there is no contradiction between the two statements, as "for a male" is referring to both matters (see Rashba).

## HALAKHA

**Sighting of a *zav*…due to circumstances beyond his control – רְאִיָּה...שֶׁל זָב...מֵחֲמַת אוֹנְסוֹ:** If a *zav* who experienced an emission was examined and it was found that his first emission was caused by an accident while the second was not caused by an accident, he is a *zav*, but the first sighting does not count with two others to render him liable to bring an offering (Rambam *Sefer Korbanot, Hilkhot Meḥusrei Kappara* 2:5, and see also 2:2).

אָמַר רַב הוּנָא: רְאִיָּה רִאשׁוֹנָה שֶׁל זָב מְטַמְּאָה בְּאוֹנֶס, שֶׁנֶּאֱמַר: ״זֹאת תּוֹרַת הַזָּב וַאֲשֶׁר תֵּצֵא מִמֶּנּוּ שִׁכְבַת זָרַע״, מַה שִּׁכְבַת זֶרַע – מְטַמָּא בְּאוֹנֶס, אַף רְאִיָּה רִאשׁוֹנָה שֶׁל זָב – מְטַמְּאָה בְּאוֹנֶס.

§ **Rav Huna says:** The **first sighting** of *ziva* **of a** ***zav*** **imparts ritual impurity** to one who comes into contact with it, even if the emission occurred **due to circumstances beyond** his **control, as it is stated: "This is the law of the** ***zav*****, and of him from whom the flow of seed goes out"** (Leviticus 15:32). The verse compares the first sighting of *ziva* to a seminal emission: **Just as semen imparts impurity** even if it occurs **due to circumstances beyond** his **control, so too,** the **first sighting of a** ***zav***[N] **imparts impurity** even if it occurs **due to circumstances beyond** his **control.**

תָּא שְׁמַע: רָאָה רְאִיָּה רִאשׁוֹנָה – בּוֹדְקִין אוֹתוֹ. מַאי לָאו – לְטוּמְאָה? לָא, לְקׇרְבָּן.

The Gemara analyzes the statement of Rav Huna: **Come** and **hear** a mishna (*Zavim* 2:2): With regard to a man who **saw a first sighting** of *ziva*, **one examines him**[N] to determine whether the discharge was caused by circumstances beyond his control. **What, is it not** that the purpose of this examination is **to** clarify that he does not have **ritual impurity,** i.e., if the discharge was due to circumstances beyond his control he remains pure, which contradicts the statement of Rav Huna? The Gemara responds: **No,** the purpose of this examination is **to** determine whether he will be obligated to bring **an offering** if he experiences another two discharges of *ziva*. If the first sighting was caused by circumstances beyond his control, it is not counted toward the three sightings that render one liable to bring an offering.

תָּא שְׁמַע: בַּשְּׁנִיָּה בּוֹדְקִין אוֹתוֹ. לְמַאי? אִילֵימָא לְקׇרְבָּן, אֲבָל לְטוּמְאָה לָא, אִקְרִי כָּאן ״מִבְּשָׂרוֹ״ – וְלֹא מֵחֲמַת אוֹנְסוֹ, אֶלָּא לָאו – לְטוּמְאָה, וּמִדְּסֵיפָא לְטוּמְאָה – רֵישָׁא נַמִי לְטוּמְאָה!

The Gemara suggests: **Come** and **hear** the latter clause of the same mishna: **When** he experiences **the second** sighting of *ziva*, **one examines him** to determine whether the discharge was caused by circumstances beyond his control. **For what** purpose does one examine him? **If we say** that it is **to** exempt him from bringing **an offering** in the event that he experiences a third discharge **but not to** clarify that he does not have **ritual impurity,** this is untenable, as one may **read here** the verse: "An issue **out of his flesh**" (Leviticus 15:2), from which it is derived that one is **not** rendered a *zav* if the discharge occurred **due to circumstances beyond his control.**[H] **Rather, is it not** that the examination serves **to** clarify that he does not have **ritual impurity? And from** the fact **that** the examination in **the latter clause** is **for** purposes of **impurity,** one may conclude that the examination of **the first clause** is **also for** purposes of **impurity.**

מִידֵּי אִירְיָא? הָא – כִּדְאִיתָא, וְהָא – כִּדְאִיתָא.

The Gemara rejects this: **Are the cases comparable? This** case is **as it is, and that** case is **as it is.** In other words, it is possible that each examination is intended for a different purpose. In particular, the first examination is meant to exempt him from bringing an offering, and the second examination pertains to both the offering and ritual impurity.

תָּא שְׁמַע, רַבִּי אֱלִיעֶזֶר אוֹמֵר: אַף בַּשְּׁלִישִׁי בּוֹדְקִין אוֹתוֹ מִפְּנֵי הַקׇּרְבָּן. מִכְּלָל דְּתַנָּא קַמָּא – מִפְּנֵי הַטּוּמְאָה קָאָמַר!

The Gemara suggests: **Come** and **hear** the same mishna, which states that **Rabbi Eliezer says: Even** after **the third** discharge **one examines him, because of the offering.** In other words, if the third discharge occurred due to circumstances beyond his control, he is not liable to bring an offering. From the fact that according to Rabbi Eliezer the examination is due to the offering, one may conclude **by inference that the first** ***tanna*** **is saying** the examinations are **for ritual impurity.** If so, then according to the mishna one who has an initial discharge of *ziva* due to circumstances beyond his control remains pure.

## NOTES

**Just as semen imparts impurity due to circumstances beyond his control so too the first sighting of a** ***zav*** **– מַה שִּׁכְבַת זֶרַע מְטַמָּא בְּאוֹנֶס אַף רְאִיָּה רִאשׁוֹנָה שֶׁל זָב:** The statement that semen imparts impurity if it occurs due to accident is based on the fact that a seminal emission is caused by the accidental heating of the body (Rashi).

**One examines him – בּוֹדְקִין אוֹתוֹ:** The mishna in tractate *Zavim* (2:2) lists seven possible causes of an emission that occurs due to circumstances beyond one's control: Food, i.e., excessive consumption of food, or consumption of food items that are known to cause *ziva*; excessive drinking; lifting a burden; jumping; sickness; an arousing sight of a woman, even if he was not led to think about her; and the thought of a woman, even if he did not see her. If any of these circumstances were present before a *zav* experienced a second discharge, it is assumed to be the cause of this emission, and the drops of *ziva* do not impart impurity through carrying.

לָא, דְּכוּלֵּי עָלְמָא לְקׇרְבָּן, וְהָכָא בְּ"אֶתִים" קָא מִיפַּלְגִי, רַבָּנַן לָא דָּרְשִׁי "אֶתִים", וְרַבִּי אֱלִיעֶזֶר דָּרֵישׁ "אֶתִים".

The Gemara rejects this suggestion: **No,** this is not the proper explanation of the mishna. Rather, **everyone agrees** that the examination serves **to** exempt him from bringing **an offering. And here they disagree with regard to** whether one interprets instances of the word **"*et*"** in a verse. With regard to a *zav*, the verse states: "And of them that have an issue of *ziva* [*vehazav et zovo*], whether it be a male or a female" (Leviticus 15:33). **The Rabbis do not interpret** instances of the word **"*et*," and Rabbi Eliezer interprets** instances of the word **"*et*."**

רַבָּנַן לָא דָּרְשִׁי "אֶתִים": "הַזָּב" – חֲדָא, "זוֹבוֹ" – תַּרְתֵּי, "לַזָּכָר" – בַּשְּׁלִישִׁי אַקְשֵׁיהּ רַחֲמָנָא לִנְקֵבָה.

The Gemara elaborates: **The Rabbis do not interpret** instances of the word **"*et*."** Therefore, they explain the verse as follows: **"*Hazav*"** is referring to **one** sighting; **"*zovo*"** makes **two** sightings, and when the verse states: **"Whether it be a male,"** this indicates that **for the third** sighting **the Merciful One compares** the *halakha* of a male **to** that of **a female,** i.e., just as a woman is rendered impure even through an emission of *ziva* due to circumstances beyond her control, so too, the third sighting of *ziva* by a man renders him impure even if it occurs due to circumstances beyond his control. Accordingly, the Rabbis maintain that there is no need for an examination after the third sighting.

וְרַבִּי אֱלִיעֶזֶר דָּרֵישׁ "אֶתִים": "הַזָּב" – חֲדָא, "אֶת" – תַּרְתֵּי, "זוֹבוֹ" – תְּלָת, בָּרְבִיעִי אַקְשֵׁיהּ רַחֲמָנָא לִנְקֵבָה.

**And Rabbi Eliezer interprets** instances of the word **"*et*."** Therefore, he explains the verse as follows: **"*Hazav*"** is referring to **one** sighting; **"*et*"** makes **two** sightings; **"*zovo*"** totals **three** sightings. Accordingly, even for the third sighting of *ziva* one must examine whether it was caused due to circumstances beyond his control. If it was, he is not liable to bring an offering. When the verse states: "Whether it be a male," this indicates that **for the fourth** sighting **the Merciful One compares** the *halakha* of a male **to** that of **a female,**[N] in that it is counted as a sighting even if it occurred due to circumstances beyond his control.

תָּא שְׁמַע, רַבִּי יִצְחָק אוֹמֵר: וַהֲלֹא זָב בִּכְלַל בַּעַל קֶרִי הָיָה, וְלָמָּה יָצָא – לְהָקֵל עָלָיו וּלְהַחְמִיר עָלָיו. לְהָקֵל עָלָיו, שֶׁאֵין מְטַמֵּא בְּאוֹנֶס, וּלְהַחְמִיר עָלָיו,

The Gemara attempts to refute the statement of Rav Huna: **Come** and **hear** that which **Rabbi Yitzḥak says: But wasn't a *zav* included in** the category of **one who experienced a seminal emission? Why,** then, **was he taken out** and discussed in a separate passage? In order **to be lenient with him and to be stringent with him** relative to the *halakhot* of one who experienced a seminal emission. Rabbi Yitzḥak elaborates: The separate passage serves **to be lenient with him, as he is not rendered impure through** an emission that occurs **due to circumstances beyond** his **control,** unlike one who experienced a seminal emission. **And** the separate passage serves **to be stringent with him,**

Perek **IV**
Daf **35** Amud **b**

שֶׁהוּא עוֹשֶׂה מִשְׁכָּב וּמוֹשָׁב.

**as he renders** impure the **bedding** upon which he lies **and** the **seat** upon which he sits, like a primary source of ritual impurity, which is not the case for one who experienced a seminal emission.

אֵימַת? אִילֵימָא בִּרְאִיָּיה שְׁנִיָּיה – הֵיכָא הֲוָה בִּכְלַל בַּעַל קֶרִי? אֶלָּא פְּשִׁיטָא – בִּרְאִיָּיה רִאשׁוֹנָה, וְקָתָנֵי "לְהָקֵל עָלָיו שֶׁאֵינוֹ מְטַמֵּא בְּאוֹנֶס"!

The Gemara analyzes Rabbi Yitzḥak's statement: **When** does this statement apply, i.e., to which sighting of *ziva* is Rabbi Yitzḥak referring? **If we say** he is referring **to** the **second sighting** this is untenable, for **where** in the verse **was** such a person **included in** the category of **one who experienced a seminal emission?** After the second sighting one is considered a full-fledged *zav*. **Rather,** it is **obvious** that he is referring **to** the **first sighting. And** yet Rabbi Yitzḥak **teaches:** The separate passage discussing a *zav* serves **to be lenient with him,** as a *zav* **is not rendered impure through** an emission that occurs **due to circumstances beyond** his **control.** This contradicts the statement of Rav Huna.

**NOTES**

**For the fourth sighting the Merciful One compares the *halakha* of a male to that of a female – בָּרְבִיעִי אַקְשֵׁיהּ רַחֲמָנָא לִנְקֵבָה:** In other words, the Rabbis maintain that if one experiences a fourth emission of *ziva*, it negates any clean days counted thus far, even if the *ziva* was emitted due to circumstances beyond his control.

וְתִסְבְּרָא ״לְהַחְמִיר עָלָיו שֶׁהוּא עוֹשֶׂה מִשְׁכָּב וּמוֹשָׁב״, בִּרְאִיָּה רִאשׁוֹנָה בַּר מִשְׁכָּב וּמוֹשָׁב הוּא?

The Gemara rejects this: **And how can you understand** that Rabbi Yitzḥak is referring **to** the first sighting of *ziva*? But Rabbi Yitzḥak also says: The separate passage serves **to be stringent with him, as he renders** impure the **bedding** upon which he lies **and the seat** upon which he sits. **With the first sighting** of *ziva* **is** one **fit** to render impure his **bedding or** his **seat?**

אֶלָּא הָכִי קָאָמַר, רַבִּי יִצְחָק אוֹמֵר: וַהֲלֹא זָב בִּכְלַל בַּעַל קֶרִי הָיָה בִּרְאִיָּה רִאשׁוֹנָה, וְלָמָּה יָצָא בִּרְאִיָּה שְׁנִיָּיה – לְהָקֵל עָלָיו וּלְהַחְמִיר עָלָיו, לְהָקֵל עָלָיו – שֶׁאֵינוֹ מְטַמֵּא בְּאוֹנֶס, וּלְהַחְמִיר עָלָיו – שֶׁהוּא עוֹשֶׂה מִשְׁכָּב וּמוֹשָׁב.

**Rather, this** is what **he is saying: Rabbi Yitzḥak says: But wasn't a** *zav* **with** his **first sighting included** in the category of **one who experienced a seminal emission? Why,** then, **was he taken out** and discussed in a separate passage **with regard to** his **second sighting?** In order **to be lenient with him and to be stringent with him.** In other words, the passage serves **to be lenient with him, as he is not rendered impure** through an emission that occurs **due to circumstances beyond** his **control. And** it serves **to be stringent with him, as he renders** impure the **bedding** upon which he lies **and the seat** upon which he sits.

אָמַר רַב הוּנָא: זוֹב דּוֹמֶה לְמֵי בָּצֵק שֶׁל שְׂעוֹרִים, זוֹב בָּא מִבְּשַׂר הַמֵּת, שִׁכְבַת זֶרַע בָּא מִבְּשַׂר הַחַי. זוֹב – דֵּיהֶה, וְדוֹמֶה לְלוֹבֶן בֵּיצָה הַמּוּזֶרֶת, שִׁכְבַת זֶרַע – קְשׁוּרָה, וְדוֹמָה לְלוֹבֶן בֵּיצָה שֶׁאֵינָהּ מוּזֶרֶת.

With regard to *ziva*, **Rav Huna says:** The discharge of ***ziva* is similar to water of barley dough.**[H] Whereas the discharge of *ziva* **comes from dead flesh,** i.e., when one's penis is flaccid, **semen comes from living flesh,** when one's penis is erect. Moreover, the discharge of *ziva* **is runny, and is similar** in appearance **to the white of a unfertilized egg.** By contrast, **semen is viscous, and** it **is similar** in appearance **to the white of an egg that is not unfertilized,** i.e., a fertilized egg.

״דַּם הַיּוֹלֶדֶת שֶׁלֹּא טָבְלָה״ וכו׳.

§ The mishna teaches that Beit Shammai and Beit Hillel disagree with regard to **the blood of a woman who gave birth** and reached the conclusion of her days of impurity, but **did not** yet **immerse** in a ritual bath. Beit Shammai say: The blood does not retain the halakhic status of menstrual blood; rather, it imparts impurity only while moist. And Beit Hillel say: Since she did not immerse in a ritual bath, her blood is considered like that of a menstruating woman, and it imparts impurity whether it is moist or dry.

תַּנְיָא, אָמְרוּ לָהֶן בֵּית הִלֵּל לְבֵית שַׁמַּאי: אִי אַתֶּם מוֹדִים בְּנִדָּה שֶׁלֹּא טָבְלָה וְרָאֲתָה דָּם, שֶׁהִיא טְמֵאָה? אָמְרוּ לָהֶם בֵּית שַׁמַּאי: לֹא אִם אֲמַרְתֶּם בְּנִדָּה – שֶׁאֲפִילּוּ טָבְלָה וְרָאֲתָה, טְמֵאָה. תֹּאמְרוּ בְּיוֹלֶדֶת – שֶׁאִם טָבְלָה וְרָאֲתָה, שֶׁהִיא טְהוֹרָה.

With regard to this dispute, it **is taught** in a *baraita* that **Beit Hillel said to Beit Shammai: Do you not concede with regard to a menstruating woman who did not immerse** after seven days **and** thereafter **saw blood, that she is impure** as a menstruating woman in every sense? If so, a woman who failed to immerse after childbirth should likewise be impure as a menstruating woman. **Beit Shammai said to them: No,** this is not a legitimate comparison. Even **if you say** this is true **with regard to a menstruating woman,** there the *halakha* **is that even** in a case where **she immersed and** immediately **saw** blood thereafter, she is **impure. Will you say** that this *halakha* applies **with regard to a woman who gave birth,** where the *halakha* **is that if she immersed and** then **saw** blood **she is pure?** Therefore, even if a woman who gave birth neglected to immerse and experienced bleeding, she is not considered a full-fledged menstruating woman, and the blood does not impart impurity whether it is moist or dry.

אָמְרוּ לָהֶם: יוֹלֶדֶת בְּזוֹב תּוֹכִיחַ, שֶׁאִם טָבְלָה וְרָאֲתָה לְאַחַר יְמֵי סְפִירָה – טְהוֹרָה, לֹא טָבְלָה וְרָאֲתָה – טְמֵאָה!

Beit Hillel **said to** Beit Shammai: The *halakha* of **a woman who gives birth as a** ***zava*** **will prove** this is in fact a legitimate comparison. A woman who gives birth as a *zava* may immerse only after experiencing seven clean days. The *halakha* is **that if she immersed** in her days of purity **and** then **saw** blood **after** the seven **days of counting** for *ziva*, she is **pure,** as she is in her days of purity. But if **she did not immerse and she saw** blood, she is **impure.**[N] If so, the same should apply to a woman who gave birth and did not immerse at the conclusion of her days of impurity: She should be considered a full-fledged menstruating woman as long as she has not immersed.

אָמְרוּ לָהֶם: הוּא הַדִּין, וְהִיא הַתְּשׁוּבָה.

Beit Shammai **said to them: The same is true and** this **is the refutation,** i.e., we maintain that even in the case of a woman who gave birth as a *zava* and failed to immerse after seven clean days, her blood imparts impurity only while moist. Accordingly, one cannot compare this case to that of a typical menstruating woman.

**HALAKHA**

**The discharge of *ziva* is similar to water of barley dough, etc.** – **זוֹב דּוֹמֶה לְמֵי בָּצֵק שֶׁל שְׂעוֹרִים וכו׳**: The *ziva* mentioned in the Torah is a discharge that results from a disease of the places in the body in which semen is collected. It is not discharged from an erect penis like semen, and is not due to lust, nor does its release provide pleasure. Rather, it emerges watery like dough water of dark barley flour, and is similar in appearance to the white of an unfertilized egg. By contrast, semen is viscous and similar in appearance to the white of an egg that is fertilized. The *halakha* is in accordance with the opinion of Rav Huna (Rambam *Sefer Korbanot, Hilkhot Meḥusrei Kappara* 2:1).

**NOTES**

**If she did not immerse and she saw blood she is impure** – **לֹא טָבְלָה וְרָאֲתָה טְמֵאָה**: The later commentaries explain that the wording of the Gemara here apparently indicates that Beit Hillel maintain that even in a case where she counted seven clean days, if she did not immerse and she subsequently experienced bleeding, she forfeits all seven days and is prohibited to her husband until she counts another seven clean days. Nevertheless, the Rambam rules that at this stage she immerses and is permitted to her husband immediately, without having to count seven clean days anew (Rambam *Sefer Kedusha, Hilkhot Issurei Bia* 7:8).

לְמֵימְרָא דִּפְלִיגִי? וְהָתְנַן: וּמוֹדִים בְּיוֹלֶדֶת בְּזוֹב שֶׁהִיא מְטַמְּאָה לַח וְיָבֵשׁ!

The Gemara asks: **Is this to say that** Beit Shammai and Beit Hillel **disagree** with regard to a woman who gave birth as a *zava* and counted seven clean days but did not immerse? **But didn't we learn** in the mishna: **And** Beit Shammai **concede** to Beit Hillel **in** the case of **a woman who gives birth as a *zava*, that** any blood **she** sees **imparts impurity** whether it is **moist or dry?**

לָא קַשְׁיָא, כָּאן – שֶׁסָּפְרָה, כָּאן – שֶׁלֹּא סָפְרָה.

The Gemara responds: This is **not difficult. Here,** in the *baraita*, Beit Hillel and Beit Shammai disagree with regard to a woman **who counted** seven clean days for her *ziva*.[H] In such a case Beit Shammai maintain that any blood she sees imparts impurity only when moist. **There,** in the mishna, they agree with regard to a woman **who did not** yet **count** seven clean days for her *ziva*. In such an instance, even Beit Shammai concede that her blood imparts impurity whether it is moist or dry.

וְהָתַנְיָא: יוֹלֶדֶת בְּזוֹב שֶׁסָּפְרָה וְלֹא טָבְלָה וְרָאֲתָה, הָלְכוּ בֵּית שַׁמַּאי לְשִׁיטָתָן וּבֵית הִלֵּל לְשִׁיטָתָן.

The Gemara notes: **And it is taught** likewise in a *baraita*: With regard to **a woman who gives birth as a *zava*, who counted** seven clean days after the conclusion of her days of impurity **but did not** yet **immerse, and** she subsequently **saw** blood, **Beit Shammai follow their opinion** with regard to any woman who gave birth and concluded her days of impurity but did not yet immerse, **and Beit Hillel** likewise **follow their opinion.** In other words, according to Beit Shammai her blood imparts impurity only while moist, whereas according to Beit Hillel it imparts impurity whether moist or dry.

אִיתְּמַר, רַב אָמַר: מַעְיָן אֶחָד הוּא, הַתּוֹרָה טִמְּאַתּוּ וְהַתּוֹרָה טִהֲרָתוֹ.

§ With regard to blood emitted by a woman during her days of purity after childbirth, **it was stated** that there is a dispute between the Sages. **Rav says: It is from one source**[H] in a woman's body that pure and impure blood are emitted, but **the Torah rendered impure** the blood emitted during her days of impurity **and the Torah rendered pure** the blood emitted during her days of purity.

וְלֵוִי אָמַר: שְׁנֵי מַעְיָנוֹת הֵם, נִסְתַּם הַטָּמֵא – נִפְתַּח הַטָּהוֹר, נִסְתַּם הַטָּהוֹר – נִפְתַּח הַטָּמֵא.

**And Levi says: There are two sources**[N] in a woman's body. Blood emitted during her days of impurity emerges from one source, while blood emitted during her days of purity emerges from the other, and these two sources are not active simultaneously. Rather, when **the** source of the **impure** blood **is closed,** i.e., following her days of impurity, **the** source of the **pure** blood **opens,** and when **the** source of the **pure** blood **is closed,** at the conclusion of her days of purity, either thirty-three days for a male child or sixty-six days for a female child, **the** source of the **impure** blood **is opened.**

מַאי בֵּינַיְיהוּ? אִיכָּא בֵּינַיְיהוּ: שׁוֹפַעַת מִתּוֹךְ שִׁבְעָה לְאַחַר שִׁבְעָה, וּמִתּוֹךְ אַרְבָּעָה עָשָׂר לְאַחַר אַרְבָּעָה עָשָׂר, וּמִתּוֹךְ אַרְבָּעִים לְאַחַר אַרְבָּעִים, וּמִתּוֹךְ שְׁמוֹנִים לְאַחַר שְׁמוֹנִים,

The Gemara asks: **What is** the practical difference **between** the opinions of Rav and Levi? The Gemara responds: **There is** a practical difference **between them** with regard to the following cases: A woman who **continuously discharges** menstrual blood **from within seven** days of giving birth to a male until sometime **after** those **seven** days, during her days of purity; **and** likewise, a woman who continuously discharges menstrual blood **from within fourteen** days of giving birth to a female until sometime **after** those **fourteen** days, during her days of purity; **and** a woman who continuously discharges menstrual blood **from within forty** days of giving birth to a male until sometime **after** those **forty** days, i.e., after the conclusion of her days of purity; **and** a woman who continuously discharges menstrual blood **from within eighty** days of giving birth to a female until sometime **after** those **eighty** days, i.e., after the conclusion of her days of purity.

### HALAKHA

**Here with regard to a woman who counted seven clean days for her *ziva*, etc. – כָּאן שֶׁסָּפְרָה וכו׳:** A woman who gives birth in the state of *ziva*, whose flow of blood did not stop, does not have days of purity. Rather, every emission of blood she sees is considered like the blood of *ziva*. If she counted seven clean days, and her fourteen days of impurity for the birth of a female ended and she immersed, and she subsequently experienced bleeding during the eighty days after the birth of the female, or forty days after the birth of a male, this is blood of her days of purity (Rambam *Sefer Kedusha, Hilkhot Issurei Bia* 7:7).

**It is from one source, etc. – מַעְיָן אֶחָד הוּא וכו׳:** The blood of menstruation, the blood of *ziva*, the blood that accompanies labor, the blood of a woman who gives birth, and the blood of purity of a woman after childbirth are all one type of blood which comes from one source. The status of the woman is established in accordance with the time and the circumstances of the emission, which determines whether it renders her a menstruating woman or a *zava*, or whether it is the blood of purity (Rambam *Sefer Kedusha, Hilkhot Issurei Bia* 6:1).

### NOTES

**There are two sources – שְׁנֵי מַעְיָנוֹת הֵם:** Some commentaries maintain that according to Levi the blood of menstruation and the blood of *ziva* also come from two sources, which is why the sightings of the days of menstruation do not combine with the sightings of the days of *ziva* to establish a fixed period (*Levush*). Others dispute this claim, citing the Rambam's explicit statement that they come from the same source. They further maintain that this matter does not depend on the dispute between Rav and Levi.

לְרַב – רֵישָׁא לְקוּלָּא וְסֵיפָא לְחוּמְרָא,

The Gemara elaborates: **According to Rav,** who maintains that both pure and impure blood emerge from the same source, in the cases described in **the first clause,** i.e., if she continuously discharged menstrual blood from within her days of impurity until sometime during her days of purity, one is **to be lenient,** In other words, any blood emitted during her days of purity is pure, since the Torah rendered it pure. **And** in the cases described in **the latter clause,** when the discharge begins during her days of purity and continues until after the conclusion of her days of purity, one is **to be stringent,** as the Torah deemed impure any blood emitted after her days of purity.

לְלֵוִי – רֵישָׁא לְחוּמְרָא וְסֵיפָא לְקוּלָּא.

**According to Levi,** who says that there are two different sources in the body, in the cases described in **the first clause** one is **to be stringent,** as the continuous flow of blood indicates this blood is emanating from the source of the impure blood, and the Torah deemed pure only the blood that emerges from the source of the pure blood. **And** in the cases described in **the latter clause** one is **to be lenient,** as the continuous flow of blood indicates this blood is from the source of the pure blood.

מֵיתִיבִי, דַּם הַיּוֹלֶדֶת שֶׁלֹּא טָבְלָה, בֵּית שַׁמַּאי אוֹמְרִים: כְּרוּקָּהּ וּכְמֵימֵי רַגְלֶיהָ, וּבֵית הִלֵּל אוֹמְרִים: מְטַמֵּא לַח וְיָבֵשׁ.

The Gemara **raises an objection** from the mishna: With regard to **the blood of a woman who gave birth** and reached the conclusion of her days of impurity but **did not** yet **immerse, Beit Shammai say:** The blood is **like her saliva and urine,** and it imparts impurity only while moist. **And Beit Hillel say:** Her blood is considered like that of a menstruating woman, and it **imparts impurity** whether **moist or dry.**

קָא סָלְקָא דַּעְתָּךְ דְּפָסְקָה, בִּשְׁלָמָא לְרַב דַּאֲמַר מַעְיָן אֶחָד הוּא – מִשּׁוּם הָכִי מְטַמֵּא לַח וְיָבֵשׁ, אֶלָּא לְלֵוִי, דַּאֲמַר שְׁנֵי מַעְיָנוֹת הֵן, אַמַּאי מְטַמֵּא לַח וְיָבֵשׁ?

It **enters your mind** to explain **that** the mishna is referring to a case where a woman's discharge of menstrual blood **ceased** during her days of impurity, and she subsequently experienced bleeding after the conclusion of her days of impurity. If so, **granted** the mishna is clear **according to** the opinion of **Rav, who said** pure and impure blood emanate from **one source,** as it is **due to that** reason that Beit Hillel maintain that the blood **imparts impurity** whether it is **moist or dry,** since she did not yet immerse. **But according to** the opinion of **Levi, who said there are two** separate **sources, why** do Beit Hillel maintain that the blood **imparts impurity** whether it is **moist or dry?** After all, blood emitted during her days of purity comes from the source of pure blood.

אָמַר לָךְ לֵוִי: הָכָא בְּמַאי עָסְקִינַן – בְּשׁוֹפַעַת. אִי בְּשׁוֹפַעַת – מַאי טַעְמָא דְּבֵית שַׁמַּאי? קָסָבְרִי בֵּית שַׁמַּאי: מַעְיָן אֶחָד הוּא.

The Gemara explains that **Levi** could **say to you: Here we are dealing with** a woman who **continuously discharges** menstrual blood from within her days of impurity until sometime during her days of purity. Since the continuous flow of blood indicates that this blood emanates from the source of the impure blood, Beit Hillel rule that it imparts impurity whether it is moist or dry. The Gemara asks: **If** the mishna is dealing **with** a woman who **continuously discharges** menstrual blood, **what is the reason that Beit Shammai** maintain this blood imparts impurity only while moist? Isn't it evident that it is impure menstrual blood? The Gemara responds: **Beit Shammai hold** that **it is** from **one source** that pure and impure blood emanate, and the Torah deemed pure any blood emitted during her days of purity.

בִּשְׁלָמָא לְלֵוִי – הַיְינוּ דְּאִיכָּא בֵּין בֵּית שַׁמַּאי וּבֵית הִלֵּל, אֶלָּא לְרַב מַאי בֵּינַיְיהוּ?

The Gemara questions the opinion of Rav: **Granted,** the mishna is clear **according to Levi,** who maintains there are two separate sources, as **that is** how there is a practical difference **between** the opinions of **Beit Shammai and Beit Hillel.** Beit Hillel hold there are two sources, and the continuous flow of blood from her days of impurity into her days of purity indicates that the blood emanates from the source of the impure blood, whereas Beit Shammai contend that pure and impure blood emanate from one source, and the Torah deemed pure the blood of her days of purity. **But according to Rav, what is** the reason for the difference **between them?**

אִיכָּא בֵּינַיְיהוּ יוֹמֵי וּטְבִילָה, דְּבֵית שַׁמַּאי סָבְרִי בְּיוֹמֵי תָּלָה רַחֲמָנָא, וּבֵית הִלֵּל סָבְרִי בְּיוֹמֵי וּטְבִילָה.

The Gemara responds: The difference **between them** is due to their opinions with regard to the significance of the **days and** the **immersion** at the conclusion of her days of impurity. **As, Beit Shammai hold** that **the Merciful One rendered** the purity of her blood **dependent on days,** which means that once she begins her days of purity her blood is pure regardless of whether or not she immersed. **And Beit Hillel hold** that it is dependent **on** both **days and immersion.**[H] Accordingly, if she fails to immerse after her days of impurity, any blood she sees is impure.

תָּא שְׁמַע: וּמוֹדִים בְּיוֹלֶדֶת בְּזוֹב שֶׁהִיא מְטַמְּאָה לַח וְיָבֵשׁ. סָלְקָא דַּעְתָּךְ הָכָא נַמִי דְּפָסְקָה,

The Gemara suggests: **Come** and **hear** proof from the continuation of the mishna: **And** Beit Shammai **concede** to Beit Hillel **in** the case of **a woman who gives birth as a** *zava*, **that** any blood **she** sees **imparts impurity** whether it is **moist or dry.** It **enters your mind** to explain that **here too,** the mishna is referring to a case **where** a woman's discharge of menstrual blood **ceased** during her days of impurity, and she then experienced bleeding during her days of purity. Since she is still a *zava* at the beginning of her days of purity, the blood imparts impurity whether it is moist or dry.

בִּשְׁלָמָא לְרַב דְּאָמַר מַעְיָן אֶחָד הוּא – מִשּׁוּם הָכִי מְטַמְּאָה לַח וְיָבֵשׁ, אֶלָּא לְלֵוִי דְּאָמַר שְׁנֵי מַעְיָינוֹת הֵן, אַמַּאי מְטַמְּאָה לַח וְיָבֵשׁ?

The Gemara continues: If so, **granted,** the mishna is clear **according to Rav, who said** that pure and impure blood emanate from **one source,** as it is **due to that** reason that the blood **imparts impurity** whether it is **moist or dry,** since she is still a *zava* and the Torah has not yet deemed her pure. **But according to Levi, who said there are two sources, why** does the blood **impart impurity** whether it is **moist or dry?** Let it be considered like the saliva or urine of a *zava*, which imparts impurity only when moist.

אָמַר לָךְ: הָכָא נַמִי בְּשׁוֹפַעַת. אִי בְּשׁוֹפַעַת – לְמַאי אִיצְטְרִיךְ?

The Gemara explains that **Levi** could **say to you: Here too,** we are dealing **with** a woman who **continuously discharges** menstrual blood from within her days of impurity until her days of purity. The continuous flow of blood indicates that the blood emanates from the source of the impure blood. The Gemara asks: **If** the mishna is dealing **with** a woman who **continuously discharges** menstrual blood, **for what** purpose **was** it **necessary** for the mishna to teach this *halakha*? It is obvious that this blood is impure.

לְבֵית שַׁמַּאי אִיצְטְרִיךְ, אַף עַל גַּב דְּקָאָמְרִי בֵּית שַׁמַּאי מַעְיָן אֶחָד הוּא וּבְיוֹמֵי תָּלָה רַחֲמָנָא, הָנֵי מִילֵּי – בְּיוֹלֶדֶת גְּרֵידְתָּא, דִּשְׁלִימוּ לְהוּ יוֹמֵי, אֲבָל יוֹלֶדֶת בְּזוֹב דְּבָעֵי סְפִירָה – לָא.

The Gemara answers that it **was necessary for** the opinion of **Beit Shammai.** The mishna is teaching that **even though Beit Shammai say** there **is one source, and the Merciful One rendered** the purity of her blood **dependent on days** alone, **that statement** applies only **in** the case of **a woman who only gave birth,** as her **days** of impurity **have been completed** at this point. **But** with regard to **a woman who gives birth as a** *zava*, **who requires** the **counting** of seven clean days from the end of her days of impurity, that statement does **not** apply, and blood emitted before she counted seven clean days imparts impurity whether moist or dry, like the blood of a menstruating woman.

תָּא שְׁמַע: ״דְּוֹתָהּ תִּטְמָא״ – לְרַבּוֹת אֶת בּוֹעֲלָהּ,

The Gemara suggests: **Come** and **hear** a *baraita*, which addresses the verse: "If a woman be delivered, and bear a male, then she shall be impure seven days; as in the days of her menstrual sickness she shall be impure" (Leviticus 12:2). The superfluous phrase **"her** menstrual **sickness she shall be impure"** serves **to include** a man **who engages in intercourse with her,**[HN] teaching that he is rendered impure like a menstruating woman and imparts impurity like her.

**HALAKHA**

**On both days and immersion – בְּיוֹמֵי וּטְבִילָה:** If a woman who gave birth did not immerse after seven days following the birth of a male or fourteen days following the birth of a female, any blood she sees imparts impurity whether it is moist or dry, like the blood of a menstruating woman, even if she is in her days of purity. This is because the Torah did not render the status of her blood dependent merely on her days, but rather on two factors: her days and her immersion. The *halakha* is in accordance with the opinion of Beit Hillel (Rambam *Sefer Tahara, Hilkhot Metamei Mishkav UMoshav* 5:2).

**To include a man who engages in intercourse with her – לְרַבּוֹת אֶת בּוֹעֲלָהּ:** A man who engaged in intercourse with a menstruating woman has the status of a primary source of ritual impurity by Torah law, like her. He imparts impurity to vessels by touch and to people by touch and carrying. Furthermore, he imparts impurity through movement, and he renders impure the bedding upon which he lies and the seat upon which he sits, like a menstruating woman (Rambam *Sefer Tahara, Hilkhot Metamei Mishkav UMoshav* 3:1).

**NOTES**

**To include a man who engages in intercourse with her – לְרַבּוֹת אֶת בּוֹעֲלָהּ:** In other words, she renders the man who engages in intercourse with her ritually impure like a menstruating woman (Rashi). By contrast, the Gemara in *Pesaḥim* 68a explicitly states that one who engages in intercourse with a menstruating woman has the status of one who became impure through impurity imparted by a corpse. Some commentaries explain that with regard to matters in which the Torah explicitly compares one who engages in intercourse with a menstruating woman to a menstruating woman herself, the same *halakhot* apply. But with regard to matters in which the Torah did not expressly compare him to a menstruating woman, he is compared to one who became impure from a corpse, as they both become impure through contact with a source of impurity, and are not themselves sources of impurity.

"דּוֹתָהּ תִּטְמָא" – לְרַבּוֹת הַלֵּילוֹת, "דּוֹתָהּ תִּטְמָא" – לְרַבּוֹת הַיּוֹלֶדֶת בְּזוֹב שֶׁצְּרִיכָה שֶׁתֵּשֵׁב שִׁבְעָה יָמִים נְקִיִּים. בִּשְׁלָמָא לְרַב דַּאֲמַר מַעְיָן אֶחָד הוּא – מִשּׁוּם הָכִי בָּעֲיָא שִׁבְעָה יָמִים נְקִיִּים,

Furthermore, the phrase "Her menstrual **sickness she shall be impure**" serves **to include the nights;** although the verse states: "As in the days," she is impure during the night as well. Finally, "**her** menstrual **sickness she shall be impure**" serves **to include a woman who gives birth as a** ***zava*****,** teaching **that she must observe seven clean days.**[H] The Gemara analyzes this *baraita*: **Granted,** the *baraita* is clear **according to Rav, who said** there **is one source,** as it is **due to that** reason that a woman who gives birth as a *zava* **requires seven clean days.**

HALAKHA

**A woman who gives birth as a** ***zava*****…must observe seven clean days** – הַיּוֹלֶדֶת בְּזוֹב שֶׁצְּרִיכָה שֶׁתֵּשֵׁב שִׁבְעָה יָמִים נְקִיִּים: A woman who gives birth as a *zava* must observe seven clean days and immerse, only after which is she permitted to her husband. At this stage she begins her days of purity and subsequently brings the offerings for her *ziva* and for her childbirth. The *halakha* is in accordance with the ruling of the *baraita* (Rambam *Sefer Kedusha, Hilkhot Issurei Bia* 7:5).

Perek **IV**
Daf **36** Amud **a**

אֶלָּא לְלֵוִי דַּאֲמַר שְׁנֵי מַעְיָנוֹת הֵן, לָמָּה לִי שִׁבְעָה? בְּמַשֶּׁהוּ סַגְיָא!

**But according to Levi, who said there are two sources, why do I** need this woman to wait **seven** clean days? It should be **enough** for her to wait seven days after experiencing **any amount** of cleanliness from the conclusion of her days of impurity. After all, according to Levi, once the blood ceases to flow from her days of impurity, any blood emitted thereafter is from the source of pure blood. Consequently, even if she experiences a flow of blood during the seven clean days this should not negate her count.

הָכִי קָאָמַר: צְרִיכָה שֶׁתִּפְסוֹק מַשֶּׁהוּ, שֶׁיַּעֲלוּ לָהּ לְשִׁבְעָה נְקִיִּים.

The Gemara explains that **this** is what the *baraita* **is saying: She requires that** the blood flow **should stop** for **any amount** of time after her days of impurity, so **that** she will have entered her days of purity, and consequently, the next seven days **will be considered for her as** the **seven clean** days required by a *zava*.

תָּא שְׁמַע: יְמֵי עִיבּוּרָהּ עוֹלִים לָהּ לִימֵי מֵנִיקוּתָהּ, וִימֵי מֵנִיקוּתָהּ עוֹלִים לָהּ לִימֵי עִיבּוּרָהּ.

The Gemara suggests: **Come** and **hear** a *baraita*: There are certain women with regard to whom the *halakha* is that if they notice an emission of menstrual blood they are deemed impure only from when they saw the blood, and one is not concerned they might have experienced the emission from an earlier time. Two such women are one who is pregnant and one who is nursing. This applies only to a pregnant woman who has been noticeably pregnant for three periods, each thirty days in length, and has not experienced bleeding during the three periods; and to a nursing woman who has been nursing for three periods, each also thirty days in length, and did not experience bleeding during that time. With regard to this the *baraita* teaches: **The days of her pregnancy** in which she saw no blood **count for her toward the days of her nursing** in which she saw no blood, to complete three periods, **and** likewise, **the days of her nursing count for her toward the days of her pregnancy.**

כֵּיצַד? הִפְסִיקָה שְׁתַּיִם בִּימֵי עִיבּוּרָהּ וְאַחַת בִּימֵי מֵנִיקוּתָהּ, שְׁתַּיִם בִּימֵי מֵנִיקוּתָהּ וְאַחַת בִּימֵי עִיבּוּרָהּ, אַחַת וּמֶחֱצָה בִּימֵי עִיבּוּרָהּ וְאַחַת וּמֶחֱצָה בִּימֵי מֵנִיקוּתָהּ – עוֹלִין לָהּ לְשָׁלֹשׁ עוֹנוֹת.

The *baraita* elaborates: **How** so? If a woman **stopped** experiencing bleeding for **two** periods **during her days of pregnancy and one** period **during her days of nursing;** or if she did not experience bleeding for **two** periods **during her days of nursing and one** period **during her days of pregnancy;** or if she did not experience bleeding for **one and a half** periods **during her days of pregnancy and one and a half** periods **during her days of nursing,** the days **count for her as three periods** in which she did not experience bleeding, and if she experiences bleeding she is deemed impure only from the hour that she saw the blood.

בִּשְׁלָמָא לְרַב דְּאָמַר מַעְיָן אֶחָד הוּא – מִשּׁוּם הָכִי בָּעֵי הֶפְסֵק שָׁלֹשׁ עוֹנוֹת, אֶלָּא לְלֵוִי דְּאָמַר שְׁנֵי מַעְיָנוֹת הֵן – לָמָּה לִי הֶפְסֵק שָׁלֹשׁ עוֹנוֹת? בְּמַשֶּׁהוּ סַגִּי!

The Gemara analyzes this *baraita*: **Granted,** the *baraita* is clear **according to Rav, who said there is one source,** as it is **due to that** reason that the woman **requires a cessation** of menstrual emissions for **three periods** in order that she may be considered a woman whose menstrual emissions have ceased. **But according to Levi, who said there are two sources, why do I** need **a cessation** of menstrual emissions for **three periods?** Provided the woman's menstrual emissions cease for **any amount** of time at the completion of her days of impurity, it should be **enough,** as any blood she may emit thereafter is pure and should not negate her count of three periods.

הָכִי קָאָמַר: צְרִיכָה שֶׁתִּפְסוֹק מַשֶּׁהוּ, כְּדֵי שֶׁיַּעֲלוּ לָהּ לְשָׁלֹשׁ עוֹנוֹת.

The Gemara explains that **this** is what the *baraita* **is saying: She requires that** the blood flow **should stop** for **any amount** of time at the conclusion of her days of impurity, **in order that** her days of purity **will be counted for her as** part of the **three periods,** even if she experiences bleeding during her days of purity.

תָּא שְׁמַע: וְשָׁוִין בְּרוֹאָה אַחַר דַּם טוֹהַר שֶׁדַּיָּהּ שְׁעָתָהּ.

The Gemara suggests: **Come** and **hear** a *baraita*: **And** although Shammai and Hillel disagree with regard to all women who experience bleeding (see 2a), as Shammai maintains they are impure only from when they saw the blood while Hillel holds that they assume ritual impurity status retroactively from the last time they examined themselves and were found to be pure, **they agree**[N] **with regard to** a woman who **sees** blood **after** seeing **blood** during her days **of purity, that it is sufficient for her** to be considered impure from the **hour** of **her** seeing the blood.

בִּשְׁלָמָא לְלֵוִי דְּאָמַר שְׁנֵי מַעְיָנוֹת הֵן – מִשּׁוּם הָכִי דַּיָּהּ שְׁעָתָהּ, אֶלָּא לְרַב דְּאָמַר מַעְיָן אֶחָד הוּא אַמַּאי דַּיָּהּ שְׁעָתָהּ? תִּטְמָא מֵעֵת לְעֵת!

The Gemara analyzes the *baraita*: **Granted,** the *baraita* is clear **according to Levi, who said there are two sources,**[N] as it is **due to that** reason that **it is sufficient for her** to be considered impure from the **hour** of **her** seeing the blood. In other words, although she experienced bleeding during her days of purity, until this emission she was still considered a woman whose menstrual emissions have ceased. **But according to Rav, who said there is one source,** if this woman experienced bleeding during her days of purity, she cannot be considered a woman whose menstrual emissions have ceased. If so, **why is it sufficient for her** to be considered impure from the **hour** of **her** seeing the blood? **She should be** considered **impure** retroactively **for** a twenty-four-hour **period,** like all other women.

דְּלֵיכָּא שָׁהוּת.

The Gemara responds: The *baraita* is referring to a case **where there is no time**[H] between the conclusion of her days of purity and the subsequent emission of blood. In such a situation, she cannot be considered impure retroactively for a twenty-four-hour period, as the previous twenty-four hours are part of her days of purity.

**HALAKHA**

**Where there is no time** – **דְּלֵיכָּא שָׁהוּת**: With regard to a woman who experiences bleeding within twenty-four hours of the conclusion of the days of her blood of purity, it is sufficient for her to be ritually impure from the time she first saw blood, as stated in the *baraita* (Rambam *Sefer Tahara*, *Hilkhot Metamei Mishkav UMoshav* 4:6).

**NOTES**

**And they agree, etc.** – **וְשָׁוִין וכו׳**: Rashi explains that when the *baraita* states: They agree, it is referring to the opinions of Shammai and Hillel at the start of the tractate (2a). They disagree with regard to regular women who experience bleeding, whether it is sufficient for them to be ritually impure from the time they first saw blood, according to Shammai, or if they impart impurity retroactively from examination to examination, as maintained by Hillel. The later commentaries question this interpretation, as the following Gemara suggests that according to Rav she should impart impurity retroactively for a twenty-four-hour period, and neither Shammai nor Hillel maintain that she imparts impurity in this manner (Rabbi Akiva Eiger; *Arukh LaNer*; *Ḥiddud Halakhot*). One answer is that the Gemara's question applies according to the opinion of the Rabbis in that mishna, who maintain that she imparts impurity retroactively for a twenty-four-hour period, and that Hillel agrees with this ruling (*Arukh LaNer*). Alternatively, the phrase: They agree, is referring to Rabbi Meir and the Rabbis, who disagree on 11a with regard to a nursing woman, whether it is sufficient for her to be ritually impure from the time she first saw blood all the days of her nursing (Ramban).

**It is clear according to Levi who said there are two sources, etc.** – **לְלֵוִי דְּאָמַר שְׁנֵי מַעְיָנוֹת הֵן וכו׳**: Rashi explains that her time is sufficient because her blood has stopped, as several days have passed without her experiencing bleeding from this source. Consequently, this is considered like a woman's first sighting, and a nursing woman is one of those with regard to whom the *halakha* is that her time is sufficient. Other early commentaries question this interpretation, since if the *baraita* is referring to a nursing woman, why does it present a difficulty to the opinion of Rav? After all, Rav agrees that in this case her time is sufficient regardless of the fact that the blood comes from one source. This is because the blood cycle of a nursing woman stops, since the blood is spoiled and becomes milk (see 9a). They therefore maintain that the *baraita* is referring to a woman who is not nursing, e.g., she had a miscarriage or her baby died. Consequently, the reason her time is sufficient is because she experienced bleeding after her blood of purity. This presents a difficulty to the opinion of Rav, since if the blood comes from one source why should her time be sufficient? (*Tosefot Rid*).

NOTES

**Since there is no possibility of her being impure retroactively for a twenty-four-hour period, etc.** – כֵּיוָן דְּמֵעֵת לְעֵת לֵיכָּא וכו׳: This answer is based on the standard manner in which the Sages enacted their decrees: In order to ensure that a decree would be established and observed, they would not differentiate and apply it only in certain cases, i.e., they would not issue a decree by half-measures (Ramban in *Milḥamot HaShem* on *Beitza*).

וְתִטַמֵּא מִפְּקִידָה לִפְקִידָה! כֵּיוָן דְּמֵעֵת לְעֵת לֵיכָּא, מִפְּקִידָה לִפְקִידָה נַמִּי לָא גְּזוּר בָּהּ רַבָּנַן.

The Gemara raises a difficulty: **But** still, why is she impure only from when she sees the blood? **She should be** considered **impure from examination to examination,** i.e., from the last time she examined herself and found that she was pure. The Gemara responds: **Since there is no** possibility of her being impure retroactively **for** a twenty-four-hour **period,**[N] with regard to impurity **from examination to examination as well, the Sages did not decree** impurity **with regard to her.**

תָּא שְׁמַע: יוֹלֶדֶת בְּזוֹב שֶׁסָּפְרָה וְלֹא טָבְלָה וְרָאֲתָה, הָלְכוּ בֵּית שַׁמַּאי לְשִׁיטָתָן וּבֵית הִלֵּל לְשִׁיטָתָן.

The Gemara further suggests: **Come and hear** a *baraita*: With regard to **a woman who gives birth as a** *zava*, **who counted** seven clean days after the conclusion of her days of impurity **but did not** yet **immerse, and** subsequently **saw** blood, **Beit Shammai follow their opinion** with regard to any woman who gave birth and concluded her days of impurity but did not yet immerse, **and Beit Hillel** likewise **follow their opinion.** In other words, according to Beit Shammai her blood imparts impurity only while moist, whereas according to Beit Hillel it imparts impurity whether it is moist or dry.

בִּשְׁלָמָא לְרַב דְּאָמַר מַעְיָן אֶחָד הוּא – מִשּׁוּם הָכִי מְטַמֵּא לַח וְיָבֵשׁ, אֶלָּא לְלֵוִי דְּאָמַר שְׁנֵי מַעְיָנוֹת הֵן אַמַּאי מְטַמֵּא לַח וְיָבֵשׁ?

The Gemara analyzes the *baraita*: **Granted,** the *baraita* is clear **according to Rav, who said there is one source,** as it is **due to that** reason Beit Hillel maintain that the blood **imparts impurity** whether it is **moist** or **dry.** In other words, as she has not yet immersed, the Torah does not deem pure her menstrual emissions. **But according to Levi, who said there are two sources,** any blood she may emit after counting seven clean days must have come from the source of pure blood. If so, **why does** it **impart impurity** whether it is **moist or dry?**

אָמַר לָךְ לֵוִי: אֲנָא דַּאֲמַרִי – כְּתַנָּא דְּשָׁוִין.

The Gemara explains that **Levi** could **say to you: I say** my opinion **in accordance with** the opinion of **the** ***tanna*** of the *baraita* cited above, **that** Shammai and Hillel **agree** that with regard to a woman who experiences bleeding after experiencing bleeding during her days of purity, it is sufficient for her to be considered impure from the hour that she saw the blood. That *baraita* apparently indicates that there are in fact two sources.

וְאִיבָּעֵית אֵימָא: בְּשׁוֹפַעַת. וְהָא ״סָפְרָה״ קָתָנֵי!

**And if you wish, say** instead that this *baraita* is referring **to a** woman who **continuously discharges** menstrual blood from within her days of impurity into her days of purity. Accordingly, the blood she sees during her days of purity is still from the source of impure blood. The Gemara objects: **But** the *baraita* **teaches** that the woman **counted** seven clean days.

הָכָא בְּיוֹלֶדֶת נְקֵבָה בְּזוֹב עָסְקִינַן, דְּשָׁבוּעַ קַמָּא פָּסְקָה, שָׁבוּעַ בַּתְרָא לָא פָּסְקָה, וְקָסָבַר: יְמֵי לֵידָתָהּ שֶׁאֵין רוֹאָה בָּהֶן – עוֹלִין לָהּ לִסְפִירַת זִיבָתָהּ.

The Gemara explains: **Here we are dealing with a woman who gave birth to a female as a** ***zava***, and therefore her days of impurity are two weeks in length. And this is a case **where** in the **first week** her menstrual emissions **ceased,** and in the **latter week** her menstrual emissions **did not cease,** and they continued until her days of purity. **And** the *tanna* of this *baraita* **holds: The days of her birth,** i.e., the days of impurity, **in which she does not see** blood,[H] **count for her toward the counting of her** ***ziva***. Accordingly, although she is considered to have counted seven clean days, the blood emitted during her days of purity is from the source of impure blood.

HALAKHA

**The days of her birth in which she does not see blood** – יְמֵי לֵידָתָהּ שֶׁאֵין רוֹאָה בָּהֶן: If a woman does not experience bleeding during the days of the impurity of her birth or the days of her menstrual impurity, they are counted toward the seven clean days. This *halakha* is in accordance with the Gemara here and the opinion of Rava on 37a. Some authorities rule that they do not count toward the seven clean days, as maintained by Abaye (Rambam *Sefer Kedusha*, *Hilkhot Issurei Bia* 7:11, and see *Haggahot Maimoniyyot* there; *Shulḥan Arukh*, *Yoreh De'a* 194:1).

אֲמַר לֵיהּ רָבִינָא לְרַב אָשֵׁי, אֲמַר לָן רַב שֶׁמֶן מִסִּכְרָא, אִקְלַע מָר זוּטְרָא לְאַתְרִין וְדָרַשׁ: הִילְכְתָא כְּוָותֵיהּ דְּרַב לְחוּמְרָא, וְהִלְכְתָא כְּוָותֵיהּ דְּלֵוִי לְחוּמְרָא.

§ With regard to the dispute between Rav and Levi, **Ravina said to Rav Ashi: Rav Shemen from Sikhra**[B] **said to us: Mar Zutra happened to** come to **our locale, and he taught** that **the *halakha* is in accordance with** the opinion **of Rav as a stringency,**[N] **and the *halakha* is in accordance with** the opinion **of Levi as a stringency.** In other words, if a woman continuously discharges menstrual blood from within her days of purity until sometime after the conclusion of her days of purity, the blood emitted after her days of purity is impure, in accordance with the opinion of Rav. By contrast, if she continuously discharges menstrual blood from within her days of impurity into her days of purity, the blood emitted during her days of purity is impure, in accordance with the opinion of Levi.

רַב אָשֵׁי אָמַר: הִלְכְתָא כְּוָותֵיהּ דְּרַב, בֵּין לְקוּלָּא בֵּין לְחוּמְרָא. דָּרֵישׁ מָרֵימָר: הִלְכְתָא כְּוָותֵיהּ דְּרַב, בֵּין לְקוּלָּא בֵּין לְחוּמְרָא. וְהִלְכְתָא כְּוָותֵיהּ דְּרַב בֵּין לְקוּלָּא בֵּין לְחוּמְרָא.

**Rav Ashi said: The *halakha*** is **in accordance with** the opinion **of Rav, whether as a leniency or as a stringency.** Likewise, **Mareimar taught: The *halakha*** is **in accordance with** the opinion **of Rav, whether as a leniency or as a stringency.** The Gemara concludes: **And the *halakha*** is **in accordance with** the opinion **of Rav, whether as a leniency or as a stringency.**

### NOTES

**The *halakha* is in accordance with the opinion of Rav as a stringency, etc.** – הִילְכְתָא כְּוָותֵיהּ דְּרַב לְחוּמְרָא וכו׳: The Gemara explicitly states that the *halakha* is in accordance with the opinion of Rav in cases where this ruling leads to a stringency (*Ḥasdei David*; *Yad Malakhi*). In this instance, one does not follow the principle that whenever there is a dispute between Rav and Levi the *halakha* is always in accordance with the opinion of Levi (*Maggid Mishne* on Rambam *Sefer Kedusha*, *Hilkhot Ma'akhalot Assurot* 9:1).

The early commentaries are puzzled by the statement that the *halakha* is in accordance with the opinion of both Rav and Levi, as their opinions contradict one another, and the Gemara (*Eiruvin* 6b; *Ḥullin* 44a) applies the verse: "The fool walks in darkness" (Ecclesiastes 2:14) to one who adopts the stringencies of two contradictory opinions. They explain that the Gemara there is referring to a case where one of the opinions is accepted as *halakha*, e.g., in a dispute between Beit Shammai and Beit Hillel, as the *halakha* is in accordance with the opinion of Beit Hillel. By contrast, here, as it is uncertain whose opinion is accepted as *halakha*, it is permitted to act in accordance with the stringencies of two opinions despite the fact that they contradict one another (*Tosafot*; *Tosefot HaRosh*; Rashba).

### BACKGROUND

**Sikhra** – סִכְרָא: The city of Sikhra, which was one of the most important in Babylonia, was probably named for the water dam [*sekher*] of the Tigris, as it was located to the west of that dam. Sikhra was a major commercial center, and various types of merchandise were brought there from the south by means of carrier boats that traversed a network of canals. The city was also known for its great Sages, including the Rav Shemen mentioned here. Due to its significance, Sages such as Mar Zutra would visit Sikhra and teach *halakhot* there. Their statements were preserved by the local scholars.

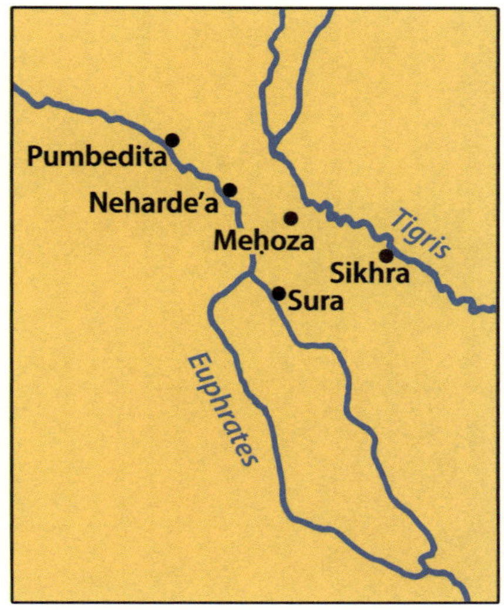


Location of Sikhra

Perek **IV**
Daf **36** Amud **b**

מתני׳ הַמַּקְשָׁה – נִדָּה. קָשְׁתָה שְׁלֹשָׁה יָמִים בְּתוֹךְ אַחַד עָשָׂר יוֹם, וְשָׁפְתָה מֵעֵת לְעֵת, וְיָלְדָה – הֲרֵי זוֹ יוֹלֶדֶת בְּזוֹב, דִּבְרֵי רַבִּי אֱלִיעֶזֶר.

**MISHNA** With regard to a pregnant woman **who experiences** labor **pains,** and they are accompanied by an emission of blood, her status is that of **a menstruating woman. If she experienced** these **pains** accompanied by emissions of blood for **three** consecutive **days within the eleven days** between periods of menstruation, during which time emissions of blood render a woman a *zava*, **and she rested** from labor **for** a twenty-four-hour **period,** i.e., the pangs subsided, **and** she then **gave birth,** it indicates that the emissions were not due to her imminent labor, and **this** woman **is** considered **one who gives birth as a *zava*.**[N] This is **the statement of Rabbi Eliezer.**

רַבִּי יְהוֹשֻׁעַ אוֹמֵר: לַיְלָה וָיוֹם, כְּלֵילֵי שַׁבָּת וְיוֹמוֹ. שֶׁשָּׁפְתָה מִן הַצַּעַר, וְלֹא מִן הַדָּם.

**Rabbi Yehoshua says:** She is considered a *zava* only if the pangs subsided for a twenty-four-hour period of **a night and** the following **day, like Shabbat evening and its** accompanying **day.**[N] Additionally, she is considered a *zava* in a case **where she rested from the pain** of labor **but not** necessarily **from the** flow of **blood.** In other words, the presence of labor pangs determines whether this blood is due to labor or the impure blood of *ziva*. Accordingly, if the pangs cease for twenty-four hours, she is considered a *zava* even if blood was discharging continuously from when she experienced her labor pains.

### NOTES

**Gives birth as a *zava*** – יוֹלֶדֶת בְּזוֹב: By Torah law, a woman who begins to emit blood from her uterus is rendered a menstruating woman. Provided her emissions cease within seven days of her initial emission, she remains a menstruating woman. Such a woman is impure for seven days, which are counted from her initial emission; on the eve of the eighth day she may immerse and is deemed pure. The eleven days following these days of menstruation are called the days of *ziva*, and any woman who emits blood during these days has the status of a *zava*.

**Rabbi Yehoshua says a night and the following day, like Shabbat evening and its accompanying day** – רַבִּי יְהוֹשֻׁעַ אוֹמֵר לַיְלָה וָיוֹם כְּלֵילֵי שַׁבָּת וְיוֹמוֹ: Some commentaries explain that according to Rabbi Yehoshua a short amount of time must be added before and after the day, as is the case on Shabbat, when one adds from the non-sacred time to the sacred (Rashba; Ritva, citing *Tosafot*). They further note that Rabbi Yehoshua said: Like Shabbat evening and the day that follows it, in order to indicate that the day follows the night in this context (Ritva).

כַּמָּה הִיא קִישׁוּיָהּ? רַבִּי מֵאִיר אוֹמֵר: אֲפִילּוּ אַרְבָּעִים וַחֲמִשִּׁים יוֹם. רַבִּי יְהוּדָה אוֹמֵר: דַּיָּהּ חָדְשָׁהּ. רַבִּי יוֹסֵי וְרַבִּי שִׁמְעוֹן אוֹמְרִים: אֵין קִישּׁוּי יוֹתֵר מִשְּׁתֵּי שַׁבָּתוֹת.

**How long** before birth **is** pain attributable to **her** labor **pains,** which means that the blood is not considered blood of *ziva*? **Rabbi Meir says: Even forty or fifty days** before the birth, any blood she sees during the eleven days of *ziva* is not considered blood of *ziva*. **Rabbi Yehuda says:** It is **sufficient** that this *halakha* applies only from within one **month of her** due date. **Rabbi Yosei and Rabbi Shimon say:** Labor **pains** do **not** occur **more than two weeks** before birth. Accordingly, if she experiences bleeding for three consecutive days during eleven days of *ziva* that occur before this time, she is a *zava*.

גמ׳ אֵטוּ כׇּל הַמַּקְשָׁה נִדָּה הִיא?

**GEMARA** The mishna teaches that a pregnant woman who experiences an emission of menstrual blood due to labor pains is considered a menstruating woman. This statement apparently applies to all blood due to labor. The Gemara therefore asks: **Is this to say that any** woman **who experiences** an emission due to labor **pains is a menstruating woman?** But if a woman experiences an emission due to labor pains in the eleven days of *ziva*, she is not rendered a *zava*, nor can this render her a menstruating woman.

אֲמַר רַב: נִדָּה לְיוֹמָא. וּשְׁמוּאֵל אֲמַר: חָיְישִׁינַן שֶׁמָּא תִּשָּׁפֶה.

**Rav said:** It is correct that a woman who experiences an emission of blood due to labor during the eleven days of *ziva* is not rendered a *zava*, or even a lesser *zava*, who must observe one clean day for the day she experienced an emission. But she is **a menstruating woman for** one **day,** i.e., she is prohibited to her husband on the day of the emission, and in the evening she may immerse and become permitted to him. **And Shmuel said:** It is a rabbinic decree that she must observe a clean day, as **we are concerned**[N] **lest she rest** from labor[N] and thereby be rendered a lesser *zava*, as the cessation of pangs would indicate that her emission was not due to her imminent labor.

וְרַבִּי יִצְחָק אֲמַר: הַמַּקְשָׁה אֵינָהּ כְּלוּם. וְהָקָתָנֵי ״הַמַּקְשָׁה – נִדָּה״!

**And Rabbi Yitzḥak said:** A woman **who experiences** labor **pains** during the eleven days of *ziva* **is nothing,** i.e., she is completely pure and is permitted to her husband. The Gemara asks: **But isn't it taught** in the mishna that a woman **who experiences** labor **pains** is **a menstruating woman?** This apparently includes all women who experience an emission due to labor, even if it occurs during the eleven days of *ziva*.

אֲמַר רָבָא: בִּימֵי נִדָּה – נִדָּה, בִּימֵי זִיבָה – טְהוֹרָה. וְהָתַנְיָא, הַמַּקְשָׁה בִּימֵי נִדָּה – נִדָּה, בִּימֵי זִיבָה – טְהוֹרָה.

**Rava said:** The mishna means that if she experienced an emission due to labor **during the days of menstruation,** she is considered **a menstruating woman;**[N] if she experienced the emission **during the days of *ziva*,** she is **pure. And it is taught** likewise in a *baraita*: A woman **who experiences** labor **pains during the days of menstruation** is a menstruating woman; if she experiences them **during the days of *ziva*,** she is **pure.**

**NOTES**

**We are concerned, etc.** – חָיְישִׁינַן וכו׳: The early commentaries disagree with regard to the precise dispute between Rav, Shmuel, and Rabbi Yitzḥak, and the case to which they are referring. Some maintain that both Rav and Shmuel are dealing with the *halakha* of a woman who experiences labor pains in her days of *ziva*. Rav holds that although such a woman cannot become a *zava*, the Sages decreed that she has the status of a menstruating woman for one day. By contrast, Shmuel rules that she must observe a clean day for each day that she experiences a discharge, lest it turn out in retrospect that it was not blood due to labor. Rabbi Yitzḥak disagrees with both of them, as he contends that the Sages did not decree at all with regard to one who experiences labor pains in the days of *ziva*, but only if this occurs during her days of menstruation (Rashi; Ritva).

**And Shmuel said, as we are concerned lest she rest from labor** – וּשְׁמוּאֵל אֲמַר חָיְישִׁינַן שֶׁמָּא תִּשָּׁפֶה: As for why Rav does not entertain this concern, the early commentaries explain that he maintains this is a rare occurrence, as most women who experience labor pains do not rest from such pains for a night and day prior to giving birth (*Tosafot*; *Tosefot HaRosh*).

**An emission due to labor during the days of menstruation, she is considered a menstruating woman** – בִּימֵי נִדָּה נִדָּה: According to the majority of the early commentaries, the days of menstruation are the days that follow the eleven days of *ziva*. The Rambam has a different calculation with regard to the days of menstruation and the days of *ziva* (see Rashba; Meiri).

בֵּיצַד, קָשְׁתָה יוֹם אֶחָד וְשָׁפְתָה שְׁנַיִם, אוֹ שֶׁקָּשְׁתָה שְׁנַיִם וְשָׁפְתָה יוֹם אֶחָד, אוֹ שֶׁשָּׁפְתָה וְקָשְׁתָה וְחָזְרָה וְשָׁפְתָה – הֲרֵי זוֹ יוֹלֶדֶת בְּזוֹב.

The *baraita* continues: **How** so, i.e., when does an emission during the eleven days of *ziva* render a woman one who gives birth as a *zava*? If **she experienced** labor **pains** for **one day and** then **rested** from labor for **two** days, and she experienced an emission on all three days; **or** if **she experienced** labor **pains** for **two** days **and rested** from labor for **one day,** and she experienced bleeding on all three days; **or** if **she rested** from labor for one day **and she** then **experienced** labor **pains** for one day, **and again rested** from labor for one day, and she experienced bleeding on all three days; in each of these cases **this** woman **is** considered **one who gives birth as a** *zava,* as the cessation of labor pains indicates that the emission of blood is not due to her imminent labor.

אֲבָל שָׁפְתָה יוֹם אֶחָד וְקָשְׁתָה שְׁנַיִם, אוֹ שֶׁשָּׁפְתָה שְׁנַיִם וְקָשְׁתָה יוֹם אֶחָד, אוֹ שֶׁקָּשְׁתָה וְשָׁפְתָה וְחָזְרָה וְקָשְׁתָה – אֵין זוֹ יוֹלֶדֶת בְּזוֹב. כְּלָלוֹ שֶׁל דָּבָר: קוֹשִׁי סָמוּךְ לַלֵּידָה – אֵין זוֹ יוֹלֶדֶת בְּזוֹב, שׁוֹפִי סָמוּךְ לַלֵּידָה – הֲרֵי זוֹ יוֹלֶדֶת בְּזוֹב.

**But** if she **rested** from labor for **one day and** then **experienced** labor **pains** for **two** days; **or** if **she rested** from labor for **two** days **and experienced** labor **pains** for **one day; or** if **she experienced** labor **pains** for one day **and** then **rested** from labor for one day, **and again experienced** labor **pains** for one day; **this** woman **is not** considered **one who gives birth as a** *zava,* since the labor pains indicate that the blood is due to her imminent labor. This is **the principle of the matter:** If she experienced labor **pains adjacent to** giving **birth, this** woman **is not** considered **one who gives birth as a** *zava*; if she was **resting** from labor **adjacent to** giving **birth,**[H] **this** woman **is** considered **one who gives birth as a** *zava.*

חֲנַנְיָא בֶּן אֲחִי רַבִּי יְהוֹשֻׁעַ אוֹמֵר: כׇּל שֶׁחָל קִישׁוּיָהּ בִּשְׁלִישִׁי שֶׁלָּהּ, אֲפִילּוּ כׇּל הַיּוֹם כּוּלּוֹ בְּשׁוֹפִי – אֵין זוֹ יוֹלֶדֶת בְּזוֹב.

**Ḥananya, son of Rabbi Yehoshua's brother, says:** In **any** situation **where** she experiences an emission due to **her** labor **pains** that **occur on her third day,**[H] she is not a *zava.* **Even** if she was in a state **of resting** from labor for **the entire** third **day,** with the exception of one hour of labor pains, **this** woman **is not** considered **one who gives birth as a** *zava,* since a woman is considered to be resting from labor on the third day only if she was resting for the entire day.

״כְּלָלוֹ שֶׁל דָּבָר״ לְאֵתוֹיֵי מַאי? לְאֵתוֹיֵי דַּחֲנַנְיָא.

The Gemara asks: The statement that this is **the principle of the matter** serves **to add what?** The Gemara answers: It serves **to add** the ruling **of Ḥananya,** son of Rabbi Yehoshua's brother, that for a woman to be considered one who gives birth as a *zava,* she must have rested from labor for the entire third day.

מְנָא הָנֵי מִילֵּי? דְּתָנוּ רַבָּנַן: ״דָּמָהּ״ – דָּמָהּ מֵחֲמַת עַצְמָהּ וְלֹא מֵחֲמַת וָלָד.

§ The mishna teaches that if a woman experiences bleeding due to labor pains during the eleven days of *ziva* she is not considered a *zava.* The Gemara asks: **From where are these matters** derived? **As the Sages taught** in a *baraita*: The verse states with regard to a *zava*: "And if a woman has an issue of her blood many days" (Leviticus 15:25). The term **"her blood"** indicates that only **her blood** that comes **due to herself** is impure as blood of *ziva,* **but not** blood that comes **due to** her **child.**

---

**HALAKHA**

**If she was resting from labor adjacent to giving birth** – שׁוֹפִי סָמוּךְ לַלֵּידָה: If a woman experienced bleeding on one day without labor pains, and then saw a discharge of blood for two days with labor pains and subsequently gave birth; or for two days without labor pains and experienced labor pains for one day and gave birth; or if she experienced labor pains one day and rested from labor one day, and again experienced labor pains one day and gave birth, that woman is not considered one who gives birth as a *zava.* But if she experienced bleeding one day with labor pains and two without such pain and then gave birth; or if she experienced labor pains two days and rested from labor for one day and gave birth; or if she rested from labor one day, and experienced labor pains one day, and again rested from labor one day, before giving birth, that woman gives birth as a *zava.* The principle is that if she experienced labor pains near the time of birth, she does not give birth as a *zava*; if she was resting from labor near the time of birth, she gives birth as a *zava,* as stated in the *baraita* (Rambam *Sefer Kedusha, Hilkhot Issurei Bia* 7:3).

**An emission due to labor pains that occur on her third day** – שֶׁחָל קִישׁוּיָהּ בִּשְׁלִישִׁי שֶׁלָּהּ: If on the third day of her sighting blood a woman gave birth, she is not considered one who gave birth as a *zava,* even if she rested from labor pains all day. The *halakha* is in accordance with the opinion of Ḥananya, son of Rabbi Yehoshua's brother, as explained by the Rambam (Rambam *Sefer Kedusha, Hilkhot Issurei Bia* 7:4, and *Maggid Mishne* there).

אַתָּה אוֹמֵר מֵחֲמַת וָלָד, אוֹ אֵינוֹ אֶלָּא מֵחֲמַת אוֹנֶס? כְּשֶׁהוּא אוֹמֵר ״וְאִשָּׁה כִּי יָזוּב זוֹב דָּמָהּ״ – הֲרֵי אוֹנֶס אָמוּר, הָא מָה אֲנִי מְקַיֵּים ״דָּמָהּ״? דָּמָהּ מֵחֲמַת עַצְמָהּ וְלֹא מֵחֲמַת וָלָד.

The Gemara analyzes the *baraita*: **Do you say** the verse excludes blood that comes **due to** her **child? Or is it only** excluding blood that comes **due to circumstances beyond** her **control? When** the verse **states: "And if a woman has an issue of her blood,"** the inclusion of *ziva* due to **circumstances beyond** her **control is** already **stated** in the inclusive phrase: Has an issue. If so, **how do I realize** the meaning of the term **"her blood"?** The verse is teaching that only **her blood** that comes **due to herself** is impure as blood of *ziva,* **but not** blood that comes **due to** her **child.**

וּמָה רָאִיתָ לְטַהֵר אֶת הַוָּלָד וּלְטַמֵּא בְּאוֹנֶס? מְטַהֵר אֲנִי בְּוָלָד – שֶׁיֵּשׁ טָהֳרָה אַחֲרָיו, וּמְטַמֵּא אֲנִי בְּאוֹנֶס – שֶׁאֵין טָהֳרָה אַחֲרָיו.

The Gemara asks: **But** given that the verse contains both an inclusion and an exclusion, **what did you see to deem pure** the blood emitted due to **the child, and to deem impure** the blood she sees **due to circumstances beyond** her **control?** Perhaps the opposite is the case, that blood emitted due to circumstances beyond her control is pure, whereas blood caused by labor is impure. The Gemara answers: **I deem pure** the blood emitted **due to the child, as there is** a period of **purity after it,** i.e., her days of purity following her days of impurity; **and I deem impure** the blood she sees **due to circumstances beyond** her **control, as there is no** period of **purity after it.**

אַדְּרַבָּה, מְטַהֵר אֲנִי בְּאוֹנֶס – שֶׁכֵּן אוֹנֶס בְּזָב טָהוֹר! הָשְׁתָּא מִיהָא בְּאִשָּׁה קָיְימִינַן, וְאוֹנֶס בְּאִשָּׁה לָא אַשְׁכַּחַן.

The Gemara objects: **On the contrary,** I should **deem** the blood **pure in** a case where it was emitted due to **circumstances beyond** her **control, as** an emission of *ziva* due **to circumstances beyond** one's **control** in the case **of** a male ***zav*** **is pure.** The Gemara explains: **Now, in any event, we are dealing with** the *halakha* of **a woman, and in** the case of **a woman we do not find** that an emission caused by **circumstances beyond** her **control** is pure.[H] It is therefore preferable to deem impure an emission caused by circumstances beyond her control, and to deem pure an emission due to childbirth.

וְאִיבָּעֵית אֵימָא: מַאי דַּעְתֵּיךְ – לְטַהוּרֵי בְּאוֹנֶס וּלְטַמּוּיֵי בְּוָלָד? אֵין לְךָ אוֹנֶס גָּדוֹל מִזֶּה!

The Gemara adds: **And if you wish, say** instead: **What is your opinion, that** one should **deem** the blood **pure in** a case where it was emitted due to **circumstances beyond** her **control, and deem** the blood **impure** in a case where it was emitted **due to the child?** But **you have no greater** instance of **circumstances beyond** her **control than this,** the experience of labor pains.

אִי הָכִי, נִדָּה נַמִי נֵימָא ״זֹבָהּ״ – זוֹבָהּ מֵחֲמַת עַצְמָהּ וְלֹא מֵחֲמַת וָלָד.

The Gemara objects: **If** it is **so** that the above verse is interpreted in such a manner, then in the case **a menstruating woman as well,** with regard to whom the verse states: "And a woman, if she has an issue, and her issue in her flesh is blood, she shall be in her menstruation seven days" (Leviticus 15:19), **let us say** that when the verse states **"her issue"** this indicates that only **her issue** that comes **due to herself** renders her a menstruating woman, **but not** an issue that comes **due to** her **child.**

אַתָּה אוֹמֵר וָלָד, אוֹ אֵינוֹ אֶלָּא אוֹנֶס? כְּשֶׁהוּא אוֹמֵר ״וְאִשָּׁה כִּי תִהְיֶה זָבָה״ – הֲרֵי אוֹנֶס אָמוּר, הָא מָה אֲנִי מְקַיֵּים ״זֹבָהּ״ – זוֹבָהּ מֵחֲמַת עַצְמָהּ, וְלֹא מֵחֲמַת וָלָד!

The Gemara elaborates: **Do you say** that the verse excludes an issue that comes due to her **child? Or** is it excluding **only** an issue that comes due to **circumstances beyond** her **control? When** the verse **states: "And a woman if she has an issue,"** the inclusion of an issue due to **circumstances beyond** her **control is** already **stated.** If so, **how do I realize** the meaning of the term **"her issue"?** The verse is teaching that only **her issue** that comes **due to herself** renders her a menstruating woman, **but not** an issue that comes **due to** her **child.** If the verse can be interpreted in this manner, why does the *baraita* teach that a woman who experiences labor pains during the days of menstruation is considered a menstruating woman?

**HALAKHA**

**In the case of a woman we do not find that an emission… beyond her control is pure – אוֹנֶס בְּאִשָּׁה לָא אַשְׁכַּחַן:** If a woman sensed an emission of blood from her source she is ritually impure, regardless of the cause of the emission. The *halakha* is in accordance with the *baraita* (Rambam *Sefer Kedusha, Hilkhot Issurei Bia* 5:1; *Shulḥan Arukh, Yoreh De'a* 183:1).

אֲמַר רֵישׁ לָקִישׁ: אָמַר קְרָא ״תֵּשֵׁב״ – יֵשׁ לָךְ יְשִׁיבָה אַחֶרֶת שֶׁהִיא כָּזוֹ, וְאֵיזוֹ זוֹ – זוֹ קוֹשִׁי בִּימֵי זִיבָה. וְאֵימָא: זוֹ קוֹשִׁי בִּימֵי נִדָּה!

**Reish Lakish said:** The **verse states** with regard to the days of purity after childbirth: **"She shall observe** the blood of purity" (Leviticus 12:5). This indicates that **you have another** instance of an **observance that is like this one**, i.e., where the woman is not rendered impure by an emission of blood. **And which is this** other case? **This** is the case of blood that is emitted due to labor **pains during** the eleven **days of** *ziva*. An emission during the days of menstruation, by contrast, renders the woman a menstruating woman. The Gemara asks: **But** one can **say** that **this** other case is where a woman has an emission of blood due to labor **pains during the days of menstruation,** not where she experiences an emission during the days of *ziva*.

אֶלָּא אָמַר אֲבוּהּ דִּשְׁמוּאֵל: אָמַר קְרָא ״וְטָמְאָה שְׁבֻעַיִם כְּנִדָּתָהּ״ – וְלֹא כְּזִיבָתָהּ, מִכְּלָל דְּזִיבָתָהּ טָהוֹר, וְאֵיזוֹ זוֹ – זוֹ קוֹשִׁי בִּימֵי זִיבָה.

**Rather, Shmuel's father said** the **verse states: "And she shall be impure two weeks, as in her menstruation"** (Leviticus 12:5), **and not: As in her** *ziva*. **By inference,** one may conclude **that** there is an instance in which an emission of blood that occurs during **her** days of *ziva* **is pure. And which** case **is this? This** is the case of blood that is emitted due to labor **pains during** the eleven **days of** *ziva*.

וְהַשְׁתָּא דִּכְתִיב ״וְטָמְאָה שְׁבֻעַיִם כְּנִדָּתָהּ״, ״דָּמֶהָ״ לָמָּה לִי? אִי לָאו ״דָּמֶהָ״ הֲוָה אָמִינָא כְּנִדָּתָהּ וְלֹא כְּזִיבָתָהּ, וַאֲפִילּוּ בְּשׁוֹפִי – קָא מַשְׁמַע לָן.

The Gemara asks: **And now that it is written: "And she shall be impure two weeks as in her menstruation," why do I** need the term **"her blood"** (Leviticus 15:25) from which it is likewise derived that blood emitted due to labor pains during the eleven days of *ziva* is pure? The Gemara answers: **If not** for the term **"her blood," I would say** the verse is teaching that a woman who gives birth is impure **as in her menstruation, and not as in her** *ziva*, **and** therefore, **even** if she experienced bleeding during her days of *ziva* **in** a state of **resting** from labor pains, she remains pure. Consequently, the term "her blood" **teaches us** that this *halakha* applies only if she experiences bleeding due to labor pains.

שֵׁילָא בַּר אָבִינָא עֲבַד עוּבְדָא כְּוָותֵיהּ דְּרַב. כִּי קָא נָח נַפְשֵׁיהּ דְּרַב, אֲמַר לֵיהּ לְרַב אַסִּי: זִיל צַנְעֵיהּ, וְאִי לָא צָיֵית – גָּרְיֵיהּ. הוּא סָבַר ״גַּדְּיֵיהּ״ אֲמַר לֵיהּ.

§ According to Rav, a woman who emits blood during the eleven days of *ziva* due to labor pains is considered like a menstruating woman for that day, i.e., she is prohibited to her husband until she immerses in the evening. The Gemara relates that **Sheila bar Avina**[P] **ruled** in an actual **case in accordance with** the opinion **of Rav.** The Gemara further relates that **when Rav was dying, he said to Rav Asi:**[P] Go and **hide** this *halakha*, i.e., inform Sheila bar Avina that my ruling is incorrect. **And if he does not listen** to you, **drag him** [*garyei*] to your side with convincing claims. Rav Asi misheard and **thought** that Rav **said to him** *gadyei*, excommunicate him.

בָּתַר דְּנָח נַפְשֵׁיהּ דְּרַב, אֲמַר לֵיהּ: הֲדַר בָּךְ! דַּהֲדַר בֵּיהּ רַב. אֲמַר לֵיהּ: אִם אִיתָא דַּהֲדַר בֵּיהּ – לְדִידִי הֲוָה אֲמַר לִי. לָא צָיֵית. גַּדְּיֵיהּ. אֲמַר לֵיהּ: וְלָא מִסְתְּפֵי מָר מִדְּלֵיקְתָא?

**After Rav died,** Rav Asi went to Sheila bar Avina and **said to him: Retract your** ruling, **as Rav** himself **retracted his** opinion.[N] Sheila bar Avina **said to** Rav Asi: **If it is so, that he retracted his** opinion, **he would have told me,** as I was his student; he would not have sent a messenger to inform me of such a retraction. Consequently, Sheila bar Avina **did not listen** to Rav Asi. Rav Asi **excommunicated him,** as he thought that this was Rav's instruction. Sheila bar Avina **said to** Rav Asi: **But is the Master not afraid of the fire,** i.e., of a punishment for offending me?

אֲמַר לֵיהּ: אֲנָא אִיסִי בֶּן יְהוּדָה, דְּהוּא אִיסִי בֶּן גּוּר אַרְיֵה, דְּהוּא אִיסִי בֶּן גַּמְלִיאֵל, דְּהוּא אִיסִי בֶּן מַהֲלַלְאֵל – אָסִיתָא דִּנְחָשָׁא, דְּלָא שַׁלִּיט בֵּיהּ רָקְבָא. אֲמַר לֵיהּ: וַאֲנָא שֵׁילָא בַּר אָבִינָא – בּוּכְנָא דְּפַרְזְלָא, דְּמִתְבַּר אָסִיתָא דִּנְחָשָׁא.

Rav Asi **said to him,** linking in a fanciful manner his own name to the various names of an important *tanna*: **I am Isi ben Yehuda,**[P] **who is Isi ben Gur Arye, who is Isi ben Gamliel, who is Isi ben Mahalalel,** and this name alludes to **a copper mortar** [*asita*], **over which rot has no power,** i.e., no harm will befall me. Sheila bar Avina **said to** Rav Asi: **And I am Sheila bar Avina,** and my father's name alludes to **an iron pestle** [*bukhna*], **which smashes a copper mortar,** i.e., harm may befall you through the merit of my ancestors.

## PERSONALITIES

**Sheila bar Avina – שֵׁילָא בַּר אָבִינָא:** Little is known of this Sage, other than the fact that he transmitted statements citing Rav. Apparently, Sheila bar Avina was a man of forceful opinions, who accepted the rulings of his teacher as the *halakha* in practice.

**Rav Asi – רַב אַסִּי:** This Rav Asi was the preeminent disciple of Rav, to the extent that he, as well as Rav Kahana, was virtually considered Rav's peer.

Another Sage of the same name, Rav Asi the priest, lived one generation later and was a student of Rav Huna. Consequently, there is much confusion with regard to the events of their respective lives. According to the Gemara here, this Rav Asi remained in Babylonia until his passing, unlike Rav Asi the priest, who ascended to Eretz Yisrael.

**Isi ben Yehuda – אִיסִי בֶּן יְהוּדָה:** Isi ben Yehuda was a *tanna* who lived in the generation before Rabbi Yehuda HaNasi. He is known as Yosef HaBavli because he was a native of Babylonia, from Hutzal, a significant center of Jewish life and scholarship. Isi is one of the Aramaic nicknames for Yosef, and as his father's name was Yehuda he was dubbed *Gur Arye*, the lion's whelp (see Genesis 49:9). There is a tradition that a harsh decree was enacted where Yosef HaBavli lived forced him to flee and change his name to Isi ben Gamliel.

When he came to Eretz Yisrael, Isi studied with several of the students of Rabbi Akiva. According to the Jerusalem Talmud he was also called Rabbi Yosef Katnuta, who is mentioned in the Mishna as one of the last of the famous pious Sages (see *Sota* 49a). His halakhic and aggadic statements are cited in *baraitot* and in the Talmud.

## NOTES

**As Rav himself retracted his opinion – דַּהֲדַר בֵּיהּ רַב:** Some commentaries explain that Rav retracted in favor of the ruling of Rabbi Yitzhak that she is entirely pure (Rashi). Other early commentaries raise a difficulty against this interpretation: If so, why did Rav Ashi excommunicate Sheila bar Avina? After all, a Sage is permitted to accept a more stringent ruling if he so chooses (Ramban; Ran). The later commentaries suggest various answers (see *Arukh LaNer*; *Ḥokhmat Betzalel*). Some contend that Rav ruled more stringently than he did initially (Rashba; Ritva).

חֲלַשׁ רַב אַסִי. עַיְילוּהּ בַּחֲמִימֵי אַפְּקוּהּ מִקְּרִירֵי, עַיְילוּהּ בִּקְרִירֵי אַפְּקוּהּ מֵחֲמִימֵי, נָח נַפְשֵׁיהּ דְּרַב אַסִי.

The Gemara relates that **Rav Asi fell ill** and contracted one sickness after another, so that when **he entered the heat** of a fever, **he exited** a sickness where he felt **cold,** and when **he entered into** a sickness where he felt **cold, he exited the heat** of a fever. Eventually, **Rav Asi died.**

Perek **IV**
Daf **37** Amud **a**

**LANGUAGE**

Provisions [*zevadata*] – זְוָודְתָא: The modern Hebrew word *mizvada*, suitcase, is derived from this root. *Targum Onkelos* uses this word in his translation of Genesis 42:25: "And to give them provision for the way."

**BACKGROUND**

Myrtle [*asa*] – אָסָא: The *asa* is the branch of the myrtle tree, *Myrtus*, which typically grows in the northern coastal regions of Eretz Yisrael. This ornamental plant, which is used for various purposes, is one of the four species that must be taken on the festival of *Sukkot*, in accordance with the verse: "Boughs of thick trees" (Leviticus 23:40).

There was a custom to place a myrtle branch on the bier of the dead, which was considered a mark of honor. Due to the importance of a custom performed in honor of the dead, the Sages permitted the cutting of myrtle branches for this purpose even on the second day of a Festival in the Diaspora. In a very different setting, myrtle branches were used in honor of a groom on his wedding day.

Blossoming myrtle branch

אֲזַל שֵׁילָא אֲמַר לִדְבֵיתְהוּ: צְבֵית לִי זְוָודְתָא, דְּלָא לֵיזִיל וְלֵימָא לֵיהּ לְרַב מִילֵּי עִילָּוַאי. צְבִיתָה לֵיהּ זְוָודְתָא, נָח נַפְשֵׁיהּ דְּשֵׁילָא. חֲזוֹ דְּפָרְחָא אָסָא מֵהַאי פּוּרְיָא לְהַאי פּוּרְיָא, אָמְרִי: שְׁמַע מִינַּהּ, עֲבַדוּ רַבָּנַן פַּיְיסָא.

Immediately upon Rav Asi's death, **Sheila** bar Avina **went** and **said to his wife: Prepare for me provisions** [*zevadata*],[LN] i.e., shrouds for my burial, as I will soon die. This is in order **that** Rav Asi **will not go and tell Rav matters** of criticism **about me,** that I did not listen to Rav Asi and that I caused his death because I took offense when he excommunicated me. His wife **prepared for him** the **provisions,** and **Sheila passed away.** The biers of Rav Asi and Sheila bar Avina were brought together for burial. Those accompanying the dead **saw that** the **myrtle**[B] that was customarily placed on a bier was **flying from this bier to that bier.**[N] **They said: Conclude from it** that **the Sages,** i.e., Rav Asi and Sheila bar Avina, **have made peace** with one another.

בָּעֵי רָבָא: קוֹשִׁי מַהוּ שֶׁתִּסְתּוֹר בְּזִיבָה?

§ The mishna teaches that a woman who experiences an emission of blood due to labor pains is not rendered a *zava* if she sees the blood in days when she can become a *zava*, but rather a menstruating woman if she sees the blood on days during which she can be a menstruating woman. In this regard **Rava raises a dilemma:** In general, if a *zava* experiences an emission of blood while counting seven clean days, her count is negated and she must begin a new count of seven clean days. But **what is** the *halakha* with regard to a *zava* who experienced an emission of blood due to labor **pains?** Does this emission **negate** her count **with regard to *ziva*?**

דָּבָר הַמְטַמֵּא סוֹתֵר – וְהַאי נָמֵי מְטַמֵּא כִּימֵי נִדָּה הוּא, אוֹ דִּילְמָא: דָּבָר הַגּוֹרֵם סוֹתֵר, וְהַאי – לָאו גּוֹרֵם הוּא?

Rava elaborates: Does every **substance that imparts impurity negate** the count of seven clean days? If so, as **this** emission **imparts impurity like** blood of **the days of menstruation,** it negates her count as well. **Or perhaps** only **a substance that causes** a woman to become a *zava* **negates** her count,[N] **and** as **this** blood **is not** a substance that **causes** her to become a *zava* it does not negate her count.

אָמַר לֵיהּ אַבָּיֵי: אוֹנֶס בְּזִיבָה יוֹכִיחַ, שֶׁאֵינוֹ גּוֹרֵם – וְסוֹתֵר!

**Abaye said to** Rava: The case of an emission **of *ziva*** due to **circumstances beyond** one's **control will prove** the *halakha* with regard to this dilemma, **as** such an emission **does not cause** one to be rendered a *zav*, **and** yet **it negates** one's count of seven clean days.

**NOTES**

Prepare for me provisions – צְבֵית לִי זְוָודְתָא: The later commentaries explain that Sheila bar Avina instructed his wife to act in this manner because he sensed that he was about to die (Maharsha). Some claim that Sheila willingly brought about his own death, as the righteous can pass on to the upper world when they choose to do so, even if their time has not yet come (see *Or HaḤayyim* on Leviticus 26:11).

The myrtle…from this bier to that bier – אָסָא מֵהַאי פּוּרְיָא לְהַאי פּוּרְיָא: The later commentaries discuss this Gemara in the context of the issue whether or not it is permitted to place flowers other than myrtles on the bier of the dead. Some say the reason why a myrtle was placed on these biers was because the righteous are called myrtles, as in the verse: "And he stood among the myrtle trees" (Zechariah 1:8; Maharsha). If so, this custom applies only to the myrtle and only to the biers of the righteous (*Naḥalat Meir*). Others permit the placement of other flowers on the biers of all individuals (*Kiryat Ḥana David*; *Yabia Omer*).

Only a substance that causes a woman to become a *zava* negates her count, etc. – דָּבָר הַגּוֹרֵם סוֹתֵר וכו׳: Some of the early commentaries maintain that Rava's dilemma refers only to blood that accompanies labor pains, whereas if a woman who gives birth as a *zava* experiences bleeding of purity, she negates her counting of seven days. The difference is that according to Rav the blood of both impurity and purity come from the same source, and had she not given birth the blood would have caused impurity of menstruation or *ziva*. It is not comparable to the blood emitted when a woman is experiencing labor pains, as that blood does not cause the impurity of *ziva* at all (*Tosafot*).

אֲמַר לֵיהּ: לָאֵי, הַאי נַמִּי גּוֹרֵם הוּא. דִּתְנַן, רָאָה רְאִיָּה רִאשׁוֹנָה – בּוֹדְקִין אוֹתוֹ, שְׁנִיָּה – בּוֹדְקִין אוֹתוֹ, שְׁלִישִׁית – אֵין בּוֹדְקִין אוֹתוֹ.

Rava said to him: This is not so [*la'ei*],[L] as this emission of *ziva* due to circumstances beyond one's control is also a substance that causes one to be rendered a *zav*, as we learned in a mishna (*Zavim* 2:2): With regard to a man who saw a first sighting of *ziva*,[H] one examines him to determine whether the discharge was caused by circumstances beyond his control. After the second sighting of *ziva* as well, one examines him. But after the third sighting one does not examine him, as even if the third sighting occurred due to circumstances beyond his control he is nevertheless rendered a *zav* on its account.

וּלְרַבִּי אֱלִיעֶזֶר, דְּאָמַר אַף בִּשְׁלִישִׁי בּוֹדְקִין אוֹתוֹ, הָכִי נַמִּי כֵּיוָן דְּלָא גָּרֵים לָא סָתַר? אֲמַר לֵיהּ: לְרַבִּי אֱלִיעֶזֶר, הָכִי נַמִּי.

Abaye asked Rava: **And according to Rabbi Eliezer, who said: Even** after **the third** discharge **one examines him,** will you **indeed** say that **since** an emission of *ziva* due to circumstances beyond one's control **does not cause** one to be rendered a *zav*, **it does not negate** his count? Rava **said to** Abaye: **According to Rabbi Eliezer,** this is **indeed** the case.

תָּא שְׁמַע, רַבִּי אֱלִיעֶזֶר אוֹמֵר: אַף בִּשְׁלִישִׁית בּוֹדְקִין אוֹתוֹ, בָּרְבִיעִית – אֵין בּוֹדְקִין אוֹתוֹ. מַאי לָאו – לִסְתִירָה?

The Gemara attempts to reject Rava's explanation of the opinion of Rabbi Eliezer: **Come** and **hear** a *baraita*: **Rabbi Eliezer says: Even** after **the third** discharge **one examines him** to establish whether he must bring an offering, but after **the fourth** discharge **one does not examine him. What, is it not** correct to say that as he was already rendered a *zav* after three discharges, an examination after the fourth discharge is **for** the matter of **negating** any clean days counted thus far? If so, Rabbi Eliezer maintains that an emission of *ziva* due to circumstances beyond one's control negates one's count.

לָא, לְטַמּוּיֵיהּ לְהַהִיא טִיפָּה בְּמַשָּׂא.

The Gemara rejects this suggestion: **No,** it is possible that the purpose of the examination after the fourth discharge is to determine whether **to render impure that drop** of *ziva* such that it imparts impurity **through carrying.** According to Rabbi Eliezer, the discharge of a *zav* imparts impurity through carrying, even if the discharge occurred due to circumstances beyond his control.

תָּא שְׁמַע, בִּשְׁלִישִׁית, רַבִּי אֱלִיעֶזֶר אוֹמֵר: בּוֹדְקִין אוֹתוֹ, בָּרְבִיעִית – אֵין בּוֹדְקִין אוֹתוֹ, לְקָרְבָּן אָמַרְתִּי וְלֹא לִסְתִירָה.

The Gemara suggests: **Come** and **hear** another *baraita*: **With regard to the third** discharge, **Rabbi Eliezer says** that **one examines him,** but after **the fourth** discharge **one does not examine him.** The reason is as **I said,** that the purpose of these examinations is **to** determine liability to bring **an offering, and** they do **not** pertain **to** the matter of **negating** any clean days counted thus far. Since the fourth sighting does not affect liability to bring an offering there is no need for an examination. Evidently, Rabbi Eliezer maintains that a discharge that occurs due to circumstances beyond one's control does negate his count.

אֶלָּא לְרַבִּי אֱלִיעֶזֶר, תִּפְשׁוֹט דְּדָבָר שֶׁאֵינוֹ גּוֹרֵם – סוֹתֵר, לְרַבָּנַן מַאי?

The Gemara concedes: **Rather, according to Rabbi Eliezer,** one can **resolve** the dilemma and conclude **that** even **a substance that does not cause** one to be rendered a *zav* **negates** one's count. But **what** is the *halakha* **according to** the opinion of **the Rabbis?**

תָּא שְׁמַע, דְּתָנֵי אֲבוּהּ דְּרַבִּי אָבִין: מָה גָּרַם לוֹ זוֹבוֹ – שִׁבְעָה, לְפִיכָךְ – סוֹתֵר שִׁבְעָה, מָה גָּרַם לוֹ קִרְיוֹ – יוֹם אֶחָד, לְפִיכָךְ – סוֹתֵר יוֹם אֶחָד.

The Gemara suggests: **Come** and **hear that** which **the father of Rabbi Avin teaches** with regard to the question of why a discharge of *ziva* causes a *zav* to negate his entire count of clean days, whereas a seminal emission negates only the day of the emission itself: **What did his *ziva* cause for him?** An impurity of **seven** days. **Therefore,** a discharge of *ziva* causes him to **negate** his count of **seven** clean days. By contrast, **what did his seminal emission cause for him?** An impurity of **one day** alone. **Therefore,** a seminal emission causes him to **negate** only **one day** of his count.

**HALAKHA**

With regard to a man who saw a first sighting of *ziva*, etc. – רָאָה רְאִיָּה רִאשׁוֹנָה וכו׳: In order to determine whether a *zav* has to bring an offering, he is examined with regard to seven ways in which his discharge might have been caused by accident. This applies only to the first and second sightings. He is not examined for the third discharge, as even if it was due to an accident he is liable to bring an offering (Rambam *Sefer Korbanot*, *Hilkhot Meḥusrei Kappara* 2:5).

**LANGUAGE**

Not so [*la'ei*] – לָאֵי: The root of the word and its meaning are not entirely clear. According to Rashi, it means in truth or indeed. Some maintain that it is a shortened form of the Hebrew expression *lo hi* or the Aramaic phrase *la hai*, both of which mean not so. Alternatively, it is a shortened form of the Aramaic expression *kelapei laya*, just the opposite, which often appears in the Talmud in a discussion between Sages. The *Arukh* claims that it is a compound of two words, the Aramaic *la* and the Greek υἱός, *huios*, meaning son. If so, the word *la'ei* would mean: No, my son.

In any event, the expression introduces an inescapable conclusion; it indicates that the statement that follows must be accepted as true.

מַאי ״שִׁבְעָה״? אִילֵימָא דִּמְטַמֵּא שִׁבְעָה – הַאי ״מַה זּוֹבוֹ טָמֵא שִׁבְעָה״ מִבְּעֵי לֵיהּ, אֶלָּא לָאו: דָּבָר הַגּוֹרֵם – סוֹתֵר, דָּבָר שֶׁאֵינוֹ גּוֹרֵם – אֵינוֹ סוֹתֵר, שְׁמַע מִינָּהּ.

The Gemara analyzes this statement: **What** is the meaning of the claim that *ziva* causes an impurity of **seven** days? **If we say** it means merely **that** *ziva* **renders him impure** for **seven** days, then the father of Rabbi Avin **should have** stated: **Just as his *ziva*** causes him to be impure for **seven** days, so too, it negates his count of seven clean days. **Rather, is it not** that the mention of causation indicates that this is what he is saying: **A substance that causes** one to be rendered a *zav* **negates** one's count of seven clean days, whereas **a substance that does not cause** one to be rendered a *zav*, e.g., an emission of blood due to labor pains, **does not negate** one's count. The Gemara concludes: Indeed, **conclude from it** that this is the opinion of the Rabbis.

אֲמַר אַבַּיֵי: נָקְטִינַן, אֵין קוֹשִׁי סוֹתֵר בְּזִיבָה. וְאִי מַשְׁכַּחַתְּ תַּנָּא דַּאֲמַר סוֹתֵר – הַהוּא רַבִּי אֱלִיעֶזֶר הִיא.

With regard to the *halakha*, **Abaye said: We have a tradition** that blood emitted by a woman due to labor **pains does not negate** the seven clean days **of *ziva*,**[NH] in accordance with the opinion of the Rabbis. **And if you a find *tanna* who said** that it does **negate** them, the statement of **that** *tanna* **is** in accordance with the opinion of **Rabbi Eliezer.**

תַּנְיָא, רַבִּי מָרִינוּס אוֹמֵר: אֵין לֵידָה סוֹתֶרֶת בְּזִיבָה. אִיבַּעְיָא לְהוּ: מַהוּ שֶׁתַּעֲלֶה? אַבַּיֵי אָמַר: אֵינָהּ סוֹתֶרֶת וְאֵינָהּ עוֹלָה. רָבָא אָמַר: אֵינָהּ סוֹתֶרֶת וְעוֹלָה.

§ It **is taught** in a *baraita* that **Rabbi Marinus**[P] **says:** In the case of a *zava* who gave birth in the middle of counting seven clean days, the **birth does not negate** her count of seven clean days **of *ziva*.**[NH] With regard to this statement, **a dilemma was raised before** the Sages: **What is** the *halakha* as to whether her days of impurity **may be counted** toward the seven clean days of *ziva*? **Abaye says:** The birth **does not negate** her count, **but it does not count**[N] toward the seven clean days. **Rava says:** The birth **does not negate** her count **and** it also **counts** toward the seven days.

אֲמַר רָבָא: מְנָא אָמִינָא לָהּ – דְּתַנְיָא, ״וְאַחַר תִּטְהָר״ – אַחַר אַחַר לְכוּלָּן, שֶׁלֹּא תְּהֵא טוּמְאָה מַפְסֶקֶת בֵּינֵיהֶם.

**Rava said: From where do I say** that the birth is counted toward the seven days? **As it is taught** in a *baraita*: The verse states: "But if she is purified from her *ziva* then she shall count for herself seven days, **and after that she shall be pure**" (Leviticus 15:28). The word "**after**" indicates that she shall be pure only **after** counting **all of them,** i.e., **that there should not be an impurity separating between** any of the seven clean days.

אִי אָמְרַתְּ בִּשְׁלָמָא עוֹלָה – הַיְינוּ דְּלָא מַפְסֶקֶת טוּמְאָה, אֶלָּא אִי אָמְרַתְּ אֵינָהּ עוֹלָה – אַפְסֵיק לֵיהּ לֵידָה! וְאַבַּיֵי אֲמַר לָךְ: שֶׁלֹּא תְּהֵא טוּמְאַת זִיבָה מַפְסֶקֶת בֵּינֵיהֶם.

Rava explains: **Granted, if you say** the birth **counts** toward the seven clean days, **this is** in accordance with the requirement **that there should not be an impurity separating** between any of the seven clean days, as they remain consecutive. **But if you say** the birth **does not count** toward the seven clean days, then the **birth separates between** the seven clean days. The Gemara notes: **And Abaye** could have **said to you** that the *baraita* means **that there should not be an impurity of *ziva* separating between them.** There is no problem with a separation due to birth.

### NOTES

**Blood emitted due to labor pains does not negate the seven days of *ziva* – אֵין קוֹשִׁי סוֹתֵר בְּזִיבָה:** This conclusion applies only to the negation of the seven clean days of *ziva*. In this regard Abaye determined that the *halakha* is in accordance with the opinion of the Rabbis, not Rabbi Eliezer. The early commentaries disagree as to whether this blood that accompanies labor pains is included in the seven days. Some maintain that not only does it not negate the clean days, but that day itself is even included in the seven days (Ramban *Sefer Kedusha, Hilkhot Issurei Bia* 7:10; Ritva, citing Rabbeinu Ḥananel and Ramban). By contrast, in the extant commentary of the Ramban it is stated that this day is not included, and the *Likkutei Halakhot* writes that this is in fact the opinion of most of the halakhic authorities (see Ra'avad; *Tosefot Rid*).

**The birth does not negate her count of seven days of *ziva* – אֵין לֵידָה סוֹתֶרֶת בְּזִיבָה:** According to Rashi, the Gemara is referring to a case where a woman gave birth without emitting any blood. In such a situation, Abaye and Rava disagree whether her days of birth are counted toward her seven clean days. Although Rava himself maintains it is impossible for a woman to give birth without emitting some blood, which means that the birth will necessarily negate her count, he is speaking in accordance with the opinion of Rabbi Marinus, who holds that it is in fact possible for a woman to give birth without emitting blood (*Tosafot*).

**Abaye says the birth does not negate her count but it does not count, etc. – אַבַּיֵי אָמַר אֵינָהּ סוֹתֶרֶת וְאֵינָהּ עוֹלָה וכו׳:** There is a principle that the *halakha* is in accordance with Rava in his disputes with Abaye, with six exceptions (see, e.g., *Kiddushin* 52a). According to some opinions, this case is one of the six in which the *halakha* is in accordance with the opinion of Abaye. If so, a woman who gives birth as a *zava* must count seven clean days after the days of impurity, which are seven for the birth of a male and fourteen for the birth of a female (*Tosafot*, citing Rabbeinu Tam; Responsa of the *Ge'onim*). Others maintain this is not one of the six exceptions, and rule that the *halakha* is in accordance with the opinion of Rava, who holds that the days of her birth in which she does not experience bleeding are included in the seven clean days of *ziva* (Rif; Rabbeinu Ḥananel; Ramban; Meiri). The Ritva and the *Maggid Mishne* claim this is the consensus opinion among the commentaries and the *ge'onim*.

### HALAKHA

**Blood emitted by a woman due to labor pains does not negate the seven days of *ziva* – אֵין קוֹשִׁי סוֹתֵר בְּזִיבָה:** If a *zava* began counting seven clean days after the cessation of her blood flow and she emitted blood due to labor pains during those seven days, she does not negate the days she has already counted. According to the Rambam, the days in which she experienced labor pains are included in the seven clean days, although the Ra'avad disagrees (Rambam *Sefer Kedusha, Hilkhot Issurei Bia* 7:10).

**The birth does not negate her count of seven days of *ziva* – אֵין לֵידָה סוֹתֶרֶת בְּזִיבָה:** If a woman gave birth during the seven clean days of her *ziva* she does not negate the days she has counted, in accordance with the opinion of Rabbi Marinus. The days of impurity for her birth are included in the seven clean days despite the fact that she is ritually impure, in accordance with the opinion of Rava (Rambam *Sefer Kedusha, Hilkhot Issurei Bia* 7:10).

### PERSONALITIES

**Rabbi Marinus – רַבִּי מָרִינוּס:** Only a few statements of Rabbi Marinus, who was from the fifth generation of *tanna'im*, have been preserved in the *Tosefta* and *baraitot*. It is known that he discussed *halakhot* before Rabbi Ḥama, Rabbi Oshaya's father, and before bar Kappara, and that he had a son, Shabbtai. Marinus is a Latin name. Originally a Roman family name, it is either from the name Marius, which in itself may derive from the Roman name Mars, the Roman god of war, or from the Latin word marinus, meaning of the sea.

אֲמַר רָבָא: מְנָא אָמִינָא לַהּ – דְּתַנְיָא, "מִזּוֹבָהּ" – מִזּוֹבָהּ וְלֹא מִנִּגְעָהּ, מִזּוֹבָהּ – וְלֹא מִלֵּידָתָהּ. וְאַבָּיֵי אָמַר לָךְ: תְּנֵי חֲדָא "מִזּוֹבָהּ וְלֹא מִנִּגְעָהּ", וְלָא תִּתְנֵי "וְלֹא מִלֵּידָתָהּ".

Rava further **said: From where do I say** that the birth is counted toward the seven clean days? **As it is taught** in a *baraita*: The verse states: "But if she is purified **from her *ziva*** then she shall count for herself seven days" (Leviticus 15:28). This indicates that she counts seven clean days **from her *ziva* and not from her leprosy,**[H] i.e., she begins counting seven days from the cessation of her *ziva*, even if she is a leper. Likewise, she counts seven clean days **from her *ziva* and not from her** giving **birth,** as she counts seven clean days even if they continue through her days of impurity. The Gemara notes: **And Abaye** could have **said to you:** From this verse **teach one** derivation, i.e., **from her *ziva* and not from her leprosy, but do not teach:** From her *ziva* **and not from her** giving **birth.**

וְרָבָא – הַאי מַאי? אִי אָמְרַתְּ בִּשְׁלָמָא "מִזּוֹבָהּ וְלֹא מִלֵּידָתָהּ", אַיְּידֵי דְּאִצְטְרִיךְ לֵיהּ לֵידָה – תָּנָא נִגְעָהּ אַטּוּ לֵידָה, אֶלָּא אִי אָמְרַתְּ "מִזּוֹבָהּ וְלֹא מִנִּגְעָהּ" – הַאי מִ"וְּכִי יִטְהַר הַזָּב מִזּוֹבוֹ" נָפְקָא – מִזּוֹבוֹ וְלֹא מִנִּגְעוֹ!

**And Rava** would respond: **What is this** suggestion? **Granted, if you say** that the *tanna* of the *baraita* taught: **From her *ziva* and not from her** giving **birth,** one can understand why the *tanna* also teaches: From her *ziva* and not from her leprosy: **Since it was necessary for** the *tanna* to teach this *halakha* with regard to **birth,** he **taught** it with regard to **her leprosy, due to** the fact that he taught it with regard to **birth. But if you say** that the *tanna* taught only: **From her *ziva* and not from her leprosy,** then the verse is unnecessary, as **this** *halakha* **is** already **derived from** another verse: **"And when the *zav* is purified of his *ziva*"** (Leviticus 15:13), i.e., **from his *ziva*** and **not from his leprosy.**

וְאַבָּיֵי – חַד בְּזָב וְחַד בְּזָבָה. וּצְרִיכִי, דְּאִי כְּתַב רַחֲמָנָא

**And Abaye** could respond: **One** verse discusses the case **of a *zav*** and the other **one** discusses the case **of a *zava*, and** both verses **are necessary. As, if the Merciful One had written**

**HALAKHA**

**From her *ziva* and not from her leprosy – מִזּוֹבָהּ וְלֹא מִנִּגְעָהּ:** With regard to a *zava* who began counting seven clean days after the cessation of her blood flow, even if she contracts another form of ritual impurity, such as leprosy, she includes those days in her counting, as those other types of impurity do not negate her counting. The *halakha* is in accordance with the ruling of the *baraita* (Rambam *Sefer Kedusha, Hilkhot Issurei Bia* 7:10).

Perek **IV**
Daf **37** Amud **b**

בְּזָב – מִשּׁוּם דְּלָא מְטַמֵּא בְּאוֹנֶס, אֲבָל זָבָה דְּמִטַּמְּאָה בְּאוֹנֶס – אֵימָא לָא, צְרִיכָא.

this *halakha* only **with regard to a *zav*,** one might have thought that the Torah was lenient solely in the case of a *zav*, **because** a *zav* **is not rendered impure** on account of an emission that occurs **due to circumstances beyond** his **control. But** in the case of **a *zava*, who is rendered impure** on account of an emission that occurs **due to circumstances beyond** her **control,** one might **say** this *halakha* does **not** apply. It was therefore **necessary** for the verse to teach that a *zava* may count her seven clean days even if she is a leper.

וְאִי כְּתַב רַחֲמָנָא בְּזָבָה, מִשּׁוּם דְּלָא מִטַּמְּאָה בִּרְאִיּוֹת כְּבְיָמִים, אֲבָל זָב דְּמִטַּמֵּא בִּרְאִיּוֹת כְּבְיָמִים – אֵימָא לָא, צְרִיכָא.

**And if the Merciful One had written** this *halakha* only **with regard to a *zava*,** one might have thought that the Torah was lenient with regard to a *zava*, **because she is not rendered impure through** three **sightings** on one day, **as** she is **through** sightings on three consecutive **days. But** with regard to **a *zav*, who is rendered impure through** three **sightings** on one day, **as** he is **through** sightings on three consecutive **days,** one might **say** that this *halakha* does **not** apply. It was therefore **necessary** for the verse to teach that a *zav* may count his seven clean days even if he is a leper.

אָמַר אַבָּיֵי: מְנָא אָמִינָא לַהּ – דְּתַנְיָא: "דְּוֹתָהּ תִּטְמָא" – לְרַבּוֹת אֶת בּוֹעֲלָהּ,

**Abaye says: From where do I say** that although the birth does not negate the count of a *zava*, it does not count toward the seven clean days? **As it is taught** in a *baraita* which addresses the verse: "If a woman be delivered, and bear a male, then she shall be impure seven days; as in the days of her menstrual sickness she shall be impure" (Leviticus 12:2). The superfluous phrase: **"Her** menstrual **sickness she shall be impure,"** serves **to include** a man **who engages in intercourse with her,**[N] teaching that he is rendered impure as a menstruating woman and imparts impurity like her.

**NOTES**

**Her menstrual sickness she shall be impure, serves to include a man who engages in intercourse with her – דְּוֹתָהּ תִּטְמָא לְרַבּוֹת אֶת בּוֹעֲלָהּ:** The later commentaries question the need for this exposition, as the Sages already derived from the verse: "And if any man lie with her, and her impurity be upon him, he shall be impure seven days, and every bed upon which he lies shall be impure" (Leviticus 15:24), that one who engages in sexual intercourse with a menstruating woman acquires her status of impurity. They suggest that the exposition here is teaching that if the woman gave birth to a female and is therefore impure for fourteen days, the man who engages in intercourse with her is likewise impure for fourteen days (*Nezer HaKodesh*).

## LANGUAGE

Aḥadevoi – אַחְדְּבוֹי: This Aramaic name is a contraction of *aḥa d'avuha*, which literally means father's brother, or uncle. Certain people used this as a first name, similar to the name Abba, father.

## PERSONALITIES

Rav Aḥadevoi bar Ami – רַב אַחְדְּבוֹי בַּר אַמֵּי: From the third to fourth generation of Babylonian *amora'im*, Rav Aḥadevoi bar Ami was a student of Rav Sheshet. He appears in discussions with Rav Ḥisda. The *amora'im* of the following generation learned from Rav Aḥadevoi bar Ami and they analyze his statements.

"דְּוֹתָהּ תִּטְמָא" – לְרַבּוֹת אֶת הַלֵּילוֹת, "דְּוֹתָהּ תִּטְמָא" – לְרַבּוֹת אֶת הַיּוֹלֶדֶת בְּזוֹב שֶׁצְּרִיכָה שֶׁתֵּשֵׁב שִׁבְעָה נְקִיִּים.

Furthermore, the phrase: **"Her** menstrual **sickness she shall be impure,"** serves **to include the nights,** i.e., although the verse states: "As in the days," she is impure during the night as well. Finally, the phrase: **"Her** menstrual **sickness she shall be impure,"** serves **to include a woman who gives birth as a** ***zava***, teaching **that she must observe seven clean days.**

מַאי לָאו נְקִיִּים מִלֵּידָה? לָא, מִדָּם.

Abaye continues: **What, is it not** correct that the *baraita* means she must observe seven days that are **clean from** the impurity of **birth?** Evidently, her days of impurity do not count toward her count of seven clean days. The Gemara rejects this suggestion: **No,** the *baraita* means that these days must be clean **of blood.** If she does not experience bleeding during her days of impurity, they may be counted toward her seven clean days.

וְאָמַר אַבַּיֵי: מְנָא אָמֵינָא לַהּ – דְּתַנְיָא: כִּימֵי נִדָּתָהּ כָּךְ יְמֵי לֵידָתָהּ, מָה יְמֵי נִדָּתָהּ – אֵין רְאוּיִן לְזִיבָה וְאֵין סְפִירַת שִׁבְעָה עוֹלָה מֵהֶן, אַף יְמֵי לֵידָתָהּ שֶׁאֵין רְאוּיִן לְזִיבָה – אֵין סְפִירַת שִׁבְעָה עוֹלָה מֵהֶן.

**And Abaye said: From where do I say** that the birth does not count toward the seven clean days? **As it is taught** in a *baraita* with regard to the aforementioned verse: The verse compares the *halakha* of the impurity of birth to the impurity of menstruation, indicating that **the days of her menstruation are like the days of her** giving **birth: Just as the days of her menstruation are unfit for** ***ziva***, as a woman may be rendered a *zava* only through emissions during the eleven days following the seven days of menstruation, **and the counting of seven** clean days of *ziva* **is not reckoned from them** because as long as she remains a *zava* she cannot be deemed a menstruating woman; **so too,** with regard to **the days of her** giving **birth, which are unfit for** ***ziva*** because a woman cannot be rendered a *zava* on account of blood emitted due to childbirth, the **counting of seven** clean days of *ziva* **is not reckoned from them.**

וְרָבָא – הָא מַנִּי רַבִּי אֱלִיעֶזֶר הִיא, דְּאָמַר מִסְתַּר נָמֵי סָתְרָה.

The Gemara notes: **And Rava,** who maintains that the days of impurity may be counted toward the seven clean days, could say to you: In accordance with **whose** opinion **is this** *baraita*? **It is** in accordance with the opinion of **Rabbi Eliezer, who said** that not only is the birth not counted toward the seven clean days, it **also negates** any days counted thus far.

וְכִי דָּנִין אֶפְשָׁר מִשֶּׁאִי אֶפְשָׁר?

The Gemara analyzes the aforementioned *baraita*, which compares the *halakha* of the impurity of birth to the impurity of menstruation, with regard to *ziva*: **But does one derive** the **possible from** the **impossible?** In other words, how can the *halakha* with regard to impurity after giving birth be derived from that of the days of menstruation? While it is possible for a woman to give birth as a *zava*, it is impossible for a *zava* to simultaneously attain the status of a menstruating woman.

אָמַר רַב אַחְדְּבוֹי בַּר אַמֵּי: רַבִּי אֱלִיעֶזֶר הִיא, דְּאָמַר דָּנִין אֶפְשָׁר מִשֶּׁאִי אֶפְשָׁר. וְרַב שֵׁשֶׁת אָמַר: עַל כָּרְחָךְ הִקִּישָׁן הַכָּתוּב. אִיכָּא דְּאָמְרִי, אָמַר רַב אַחְדְּבוֹי בַּר אַמֵּי אָמַר רַב שֵׁשֶׁת: רַבִּי אֱלִיעֶזֶר הִיא, דְּאָמַר דָּנִין אֶפְשָׁר מִשֶּׁאִי אֶפְשָׁר, וְרַב פַּפָּא אָמַר: עַל כָּרְחָךְ הִקִּישָׁן הַכָּתוּב.

Rav Aḥadevoi[L] bar Ami[P] **says:** This *baraita* **is** in accordance with the opinion of **Rabbi Eliezer, who said** that **one derives** the **possible from** the **impossible. And Rav Sheshet says** a different explanation: Although generally one does not derive the possible from the impossible, **perforce the verse juxtaposed** the days of impurity after birth and those of menstruation,[N] and a juxtaposition in the verse is expounded even if one case is possible while the other is not. **Some say** a different attribution of these answers, that **Rav Aḥadevoi bar Ami says** that **Rav Sheshet says:** This *baraita* **is** in accordance with the opinion of **Rabbi Eliezer, who said** that **one derives** the **possible from** the **impossible. And Rav Pappa says: Perforce the verse juxtaposed** the days of impurity after birth and those of menstruation.

## NOTES

Perforce the verse juxtaposed the days of impurity after birth and of menstruation – עַל כָּרְחָךְ הִקִּישָׁן הַכָּתוּב: There is a principle that one cannot refute a derivation based on juxtaposition by drawing distinctions between the two juxtaposed cases (Rashi; *Tosafot*). According to the commentaries, this is because one cannot state juxtapositions by himself; they must be learned as a tradition from one's rabbi, who in turn learned it from his rabbi, as a *halakha* transmitted to Moses from Sinai. Since a juxtaposition is not based on reason, it cannot be refuted by logical argument alone (Rashi on *Menaḥot* 82b).

"קָשְׁתָה שְׁלֹשָׁה יָמִים" וכו'.

§ The mishna teaches that if a woman **experienced** labor **pains** accompanied by emissions of blood for **three** consecutive **days** within the eleven days between periods of menstruation, and the pangs subsided for a twenty-four-hour period, and she then gave birth, this indicates that the emissions were not due to her imminent labor, and this woman is considered one who gives birth as a *zava*. Additionally, the mishna states that she is considered a *zava* in a case where she rested from the pain of labor, but not necessarily from the flow of blood. Accordingly, if the pangs cease for twenty-four hours, she is considered a *zava* even if blood was discharging continuously.

אִיבַּעְיָא לְהוּ: שָׁפְתָה מִזֶּה וּמִזֶּה מַהוּ? רַב חִסְדָּא אָמַר: טְמֵאָה, רַבִּי חֲנִינָא אָמַר: טְהוֹרָה.

In this regard, **a dilemma was raised before** the Sages: If **she rested from** both **this and that,** from labor pains and emissions of blood, **what is** the *halakha*? **Rav Ḥisda says** that as she rested from labor pains it is evident that the emissions of blood were not due to her imminent labor, and she is **ritually impure. Rabbi Ḥanina says** that as the emissions of blood also ceased it is apparent that they were due to her imminent labor, and she is **ritually pure.**

אָמַר רַבִּי חֲנִינָא: מָשָׁל לְמֶלֶךְ שֶׁיָּצָא וְחַיָּילוֹתָיו לְפָנָיו, בְּיָדוּעַ שֶׁחַיָּילוֹתָיו שֶׁל מֶלֶךְ הֵן.

**Rabbi Ḥanina says,** in explanation of his opinion: Hear **a parable;** to what is this case comparable? It is comparable **to a king who left** his palace, **and his soldiers** left **before him.** Although the king travels behind them, **it is known that they are the soldiers of the king.** Likewise, although both the labor pains and the blood subsided, it is clear that the blood she emitted was due to the approaching birth, and therefore she is not a *zava*.

וְרַב חִסְדָּא אָמַר: כׇּל שֶׁכֵּן דְּבָעֵי נְפֵישׁ חַיָּילוֹת טְפֵי.

**And Rav Ḥisda says:** By the same parable, i.e., assuming that the soldiers arrive before the king, **all the more so that** there **must** be **many more soldiers** accompanying the king upon his arrival. The lack of soldiers before the arrival of the king indicates that they are not in fact soldiers of the king. Likewise, the cessation of labor pains before the birth indicates that the previous emissions of blood were not due to her imminent labor. She is therefore rendered a *zava*.

תְּנַן, רַבִּי יְהוֹשֻׁעַ אוֹמֵר: לַיְלָה וְיוֹם כְּלֵילֵי שַׁבָּת וְיוֹמוֹ, שֶׁשָּׁפְתָה מִן הַצַּעַר וְלֹא מִן הַדָּם. טַעְמָא – דְּמִן הַצַּעַר וְלֹא מִן הַדָּם, הָא מִזֶּה וּמִזֶּה – טְהוֹרָה. תְּיוּבְתָּא דְּרַב חִסְדָּא?

The Gemara raises an objection against the opinion of Rav Ḥisda: **We learned** in the mishna that **Rabbi Yehoshua says:** She is considered a *zava* only if the pangs subsided for a twenty-four-hour period of **a night and** the following **day, like Shabbat evening and its** accompanying **day.** Additionally, she is considered a *zava* in a case **where she rested from the pain** of labor **but not from the** flow of **blood.** The Gemara infers: **The reason** she is rendered a *zava* is **that** she rested **from the pain** of labor **and not from the** flow of **blood. But** if she rested **from** both **this and that,** from labor pains and emissions of blood, she is **ritually pure.** The mishna is apparently **a conclusive refutation of** the opinion of **Rav Ḥisda.**

אָמַר לָךְ רַב חִסְדָּא: לָא מִבַּעְיָא מִזֶּה וּמִזֶּה – דִּטְמֵאָה, דְּפָסְקִי לְהוּ חַיָּילוֹת לְגַמְרֵי, אֲבָל מִן הַצַּעַר וְלֹא מִן הַדָּם, אֵימָר: כִּי הֵיכִי דְּמִדָּם לָא פָּסְקָה – מִקּוֹשִׁי נָמֵי לָא פָּסְקָה, וְהָא – תּוּנְבָּא בְּעָלְמָא הוּא דְּנָקֵט לַהּ, קָא מַשְׁמַע לַן.

The Gemara explains that **Rav Ḥisda** could **say to you: It is not necessary** to teach **that** if she rested **from** both **this and that** she is **impure, as,** in terms of the above parable, the king's **soldiers have ceased entirely,** i.e., both the labor pains and the blood have completely subsided. **But** with regard to a case where she rested **from the pain but not from the blood,** one might **say** that **just as she did not cease** emitting **blood, so too, she did not cease** experiencing labor **pains, and** the fact **that** she does not sense any pain **is** because **she was seized by a general disorientation,** i.e., she was so weakened by the labor that she was unable to discern pain. Consequently, she should remain pure. Therefore, the mishna **teaches us** that if she does not feel labor pains, this is indicative that the previous emissions of blood were not due to her imminent labor, and she is a *zava*.

תְּנַן: קָשְׁתָה שְׁלֹשָׁה יָמִים בְּתוֹךְ אַחַד עָשָׂר יוֹם, וְשָׁפְתָה מֵעֵת לְעֵת וְיָלְדָה – הֲרֵי זוֹ יוֹלֶדֶת בְּזוֹב.

The Gemara poses a difficulty with regard to the opinion of Rabbi Ḥanina: **We learned** in the mishna: If a woman **experienced** labor **pains** for **three** consecutive **days within the eleven days** between periods of menstruation, **and she rested** from labor **for a** twenty-four-hour **period, and** she then **gave birth, this** woman **is** considered **one who gives birth as a** ***zava***.

הֵיכִי דָּמֵי? אִילֵימָא כִּדְקָתָנֵי – לָמָּה לִי שָׁלֹשׁ? בִּתְרֵי בְּקוֹשִׁי וְחַד בְּשׁוֹפִי סַגִּי!

The Gemara analyzes the mishna: **What are the circumstances** of the scenario described in the mishna? **If we say that** it is **as is taught,** i.e., she rested from labor pains but continued to emit blood, then **why do I** need for her to experience **three** days of labor pains accompanied by emissions of blood in order for her to be rendered a *zava*? If she experienced bleeding **during two** days **of** labor **pains** and **one** day **of resting,** it would be **sufficient** to render her a *zava,* as she experienced bleeding even on the day she rested from labor pains.

אֶלָּא לָאו הָכִי קָאָמַר: קָשְׁתָה שְׁלֹשָׁה וְשָׁפְתָה מִזֶּה וּמִזֶּה, אוֹ שֶׁקָּשְׁתָה שְׁנַיִם וְשָׁפְתָה מֵעֵת לְעֵת – הֲרֵי זוֹ יוֹלֶדֶת בְּזוֹב, וּתְיוּבְתָּא דְּרַבִּי חֲנִינָא!

**Rather, is it not** correct that **this** is what the mishna **is saying:** If **she experienced** labor **pains** accompanied by emissions of blood for **three days and she** then **rested from** both **this and that, or if** she experienced labor **pains** for **two** days **and she** then **rested** from labor pains **for** a twenty-four-hour **period, this** woman **is** considered **one who gives birth as a** ***zava*****? And** if so, the mishna is **a conclusive refutation of** the opinion of **Rabbi Ḥanina.**

אָמַר לָךְ רַבִּי חֲנִינָא: לָא, לְעוֹלָם כִּדְקָתָנֵי, וְהָא קָא מַשְׁמַע לַן: דְּאַף עַל גַּב דְּמַתְחִיל קִישּׁוּי בַּשְּׁלִישִׁי, וְשָׁפְתָה מֵעֵת לְעֵת – טְמֵאָה, לְאַפּוֹקֵי מֵרַבִּי חֲנִינָא.

The Gemara explains that **Rabbi Ḥanina** could **say to you: No, actually** the mishna is to be understood **as** it **is taught,** that she experienced labors pains for three days and then rested from the pain but continued to emit blood. **And this** is what the mishna **is teaching us: That even though** she **began** experiencing labor **pains** at beginning **of the third** day, **and she** then **rested** from labor pains **for** a twenty-four-hour **period** during which she continued to emit blood, **she is impure.** And this serves **to exclude** the opinion **of Rabbi Ḥanina,** i.e., Ḥananya, son of Rabbi Yehoshua's brother, who maintains that if a woman experiences labor pains during even part of her third day of experiencing emissions of blood she is not a *zava,* even if the pain then subsided for a twenty-four-hour period (see 36b).

״כַּמָּה הִיא קְשׁוּיָה רַבִּי מֵאִיר אוֹמֵר״ וכו׳. הַשְׁתָּא חֲמִשִּׁים מִקַּשְׁיָא, אַרְבָּעִים מִיבַּעְיָא? אָמַר רַב חִסְדָּא: לָא קַשְׁיָא, כָּאן – לַחוֹלָה, כָּאן – לַבְּרִיאָה.

The mishna teaches: **How long** before birth **is** pain attributable to **her** labor **pains,** such that the blood is not considered blood of *ziva*? **Rabbi Meir says:** Even forty or fifty days before the birth. The Gemara asks: **Now** that you have said that even **fifty** days before the due date a woman can experience labor **pains, is** it **necessary** to teach that she can experience them **forty** days before? **Rav Ḥisda says:** This is **not difficult. Here,** where the mishna states that she can experience labor pains fifty days before birth, it is referring **to a sick woman; there,** where the mishna states that she can experience labor pains forty days before birth, it is referring **to a healthy woman.**

אָמַר רַבִּי לֵוִי: אֵין הַוָּלָד מְטַהֵר אֶלָּא יָמִים הָרְאוּיִין לִהְיוֹת בָּהֶן זָבָה, וְרַב אָמַר: אֲפִילּוּ בְּיָמִים הָרְאוּיִין לִסְפִירַת זָבָה. אָמַר רַב אַדָּא בַּר אַהֲבָה: וּלְטַעְמֵיהּ דְּרַב,

§ With regard to the *halakha* that a woman who experiences labor pains does not contract the impurity of *ziva,* **Rabbi Levi says: The** birth of **a child renders** the mother **ritually pure** from *ziva* **only** if she experienced bleeding during the eleven **days that are fit** for her **to become a** ***zava*****.** But if she experienced bleeding due to labor pains during the days of menstruation that precede or follow those eleven days, she is a menstruating woman. **And Rav says: Even** if she continued to experience bleeding **during** the **days that are fit for the counting of a** ***zava*****,** i.e., in the seven days following the eleven days of *ziva,* which are also part of her days of menstruation, she remains pure. **Rav Adda bar Ahava says: And according to the reasoning of Rav,**

Perek **IV**
Daf **38** Amud **a**

אֲפִילּוּ יָמִים הָרְאוּיִין לִסְפִירַת סְתִירַת זָבָה.

**even** if she continues to experience bleeding **during** the **days that are fit for the** new **counting** following **the negation** of the days counted by **a** ***zava*****,** she remains pure. If a woman experiences bleeding during her seven clean days, she negates any days counted thus far, and must begin a new count of seven clean days. Accordingly, all the days that follow her days of *ziva* are effectively considered days that are fit for the counting of a *zava*. Therefore, blood emitted due to labor pains during these days is also ritually pure. Consequently, the blood that accompanies labor pains is ritually impure only if she begins to emit it during her days of menstruation.

תְּנַן, כַּמָּה הוּא קִשּׁוּיָהּ? רַבִּי מֵאִיר אוֹמֵר: אַרְבָּעִים וַחֲמִשִּׁים יוֹם.

The Gemara poses a difficulty with regard to the opinion of Levi: **We learned** in the mishna: **How long** before birth **is** pain attributable to **her** labor **pains? Rabbi Meir says:** Even **forty or fifty days** before the birth. Rabbi Meir apparently maintains that a woman who experiences continuous labor pains accompanied by emissions of blood for forty or fifty days remains pure.

בִּשְׁלָמָא לְרַב – מַשְׁכַּחַתְּ לָהּ, כְּרַב אַדָּא בַּר אַהֲבָה, אֶלָּא לְלֵוִי קַשְׁיָא!

The Gemara explains the difficulty: **Granted,** the mishna is clear **according to Rav,** as **you find** that it is possible that she will remain pure for such a long period, i.e., **in accordance with** the explanation of **Rav Adda bar Ahava** that Rav deems the blood pure even during the days that are fit for the new counting following the negation of the days counted by a *zava*. Accordingly, as long as the woman begins to experience labor pains during her days of *ziva*, she remains pure until birth, provided the labor pains continue without a twenty-four-hour period of resting. **But according to Levi,** who maintains that blood accompanying labor pains is pure only during the days of *ziva*, the mishna is **difficult,** as it is impossible for her blood to remain pure due to labor pains for fifty days.

אָמַר לָךְ לֵוִי: מִי קָתָנֵי "טְהוֹרָה בְּכוּלָּן"? בִּימֵי נִדָּה – נִדָּה, בִּימֵי זִיבָה – טְהוֹרָה.

The Gemara explains that **Levi** could **say to you: Does** the mishna **teach** that she is **pure during all** these days, i.e., that she remains pure throughout the days of menstruation and *ziva*? Not so. Rather, if she emitted blood due to labor pains **during the days of menstruation** she has the status of **a menstruating woman,** whereas if she emitted the blood **during the days of *ziva*** she is **pure.** The mishna is teaching only that she will not be deemed a *zava* on account of this blood.

לִישָּׁנָא אַחֲרִינָא אָמְרִי, אָמַר רַבִּי לֵוִי: אֵין הַוָּלָד מְטַהֵר אֶלָּא יָמִים הָרְאוּיִין לִהְיוֹת בָּהֶן זָבָה גְּדוֹלָה, מַאי טַעְמָא "דָּמָהּ יָמִים רַבִּים" כְּתִיב.

Some Sages **state another version** of the above disagreement: **Rabbi Levi says: The** birth of **a child renders** the mother **ritually pure only** if she experienced bleeding during the eleven **days that are fit** for her **to become a greater *zava*,** i.e., if she experienced bleeding on three consecutive days during that time. But if she experienced bleeding on only one or two days she is rendered a lesser *zava*, and she must observe a clean day for each day she experiences a discharge. **What is the reason?** It **is written:** "And if a woman has an issue of **her blood many days**… all the days of the issue of her impurity she shall be as in the days of her menstruation: She is impure" (Leviticus 15:25). The verse is referring specifically to a greater *zava*, indicating that the *halakha* that a woman is not rendered a *zava* on account of an emission of blood caused by labor pains applies only to a greater *zava*.

אַבָּא שָׁאוּל מִשְּׁמֵיהּ דְּרַב אָמַר: אֲפִילּוּ יָמִים הָרְאוּיִין לִהְיוֹת בָּהֶן זָבָה קְטַנָּה, מַאי טַעְמָא – "יְמֵי" וְ"כׇל יְמֵי" הָתָם כְּתִיבִי.

**Abba Shaul says in the name of Rav:** The birth of a child renders the mother ritually pure **even** if she experienced bleeding on the **days that are fit** for her **to become a lesser *zava*. What is the reason? "Days" and "many days" are written there,** from which the impurity of a lesser *zava* is derived. Accordingly, the verse includes a lesser *zava* in this *halakha* as well.

תְּנַן, כַּמָּה הוּא קִשּׁוּיָהּ? רַבִּי מֵאִיר אוֹמֵר: אֲפִילּוּ אַרְבָּעִים וַחֲמִשִּׁים יוֹם, קַשְׁיָא לְתַרְוַיְיהוּ! מִי קָתָנֵי "טְהוֹרָה בְּכוּלָּן"? קָשְׁתָה בִּימֵי נִדָּתָהּ – נִדָּה, בִּימֵי זִיבָתָהּ – טְהוֹרָה.

The Gemara raises a difficulty: **We learned** in the mishna: **How long** before birth **is** pain attributable to **her** labor **pains? Rabbi Meir says: Even forty or fifty days** before the birth. Rabbi Meir apparently maintains that a woman who experiences continuous labor pains accompanied by emissions of blood for forty or fifty days remains pure. If so, the mishna is **difficult according to both** opinions, as all agree that only emissions of blood due to labor pains that occur during her days of *ziva* are pure. The Gemara responds: **Does** the mishna **teach** that **she is pure during all** fifty days? Not so. Rather, if **she experienced** labor **pains** accompanied by emissions of blood **during the days of menstruation** she has the status of **a menstruating woman,** whereas if she experienced them **during the days of *ziva* she is pure.**

תַּנְיָא, הָיָה רַבִּי מֵאִיר אוֹמֵר: יֵשׁ מַקְשָׁה מֵאָה וַחֲמִשִּׁים יוֹם וְאֵין זִיבָה עוֹלָה בָּהֶן. כֵּיצַד, שְׁנַיִם בְּלֹא עֵת,

With regard to the above statement of Rabbi Meir, it **is taught** in a *baraita* that **Rabbi Meir would say: There is** a scenario in which a woman **experiences** labor **pains** accompanied by emissions of blood for **one hundred and fifty days, and** the impurity of ***ziva* is not included in those** days, i.e., she will not be rendered a greater *zava*. **How so?** First, a woman emits blood for **two days not at the time** of her menstruation, e.g., she experiences bleeding on the tenth and eleventh days of *ziva*. She is not rendered a menstruating woman by these emissions, as they occurred during the days of *ziva*, nor does she become a greater *zava*, since she experienced bleeding on only two days.

NOTES

**Womb [*kever*] – קֶבֶר:** Although the Talmud does not shy away from discussing any issue, as all aspects of life require talmudic study, the Sages consistently employ euphemisms. In this case, the word *kever*, literally grave, is a euphemism for the womb. This particular euphemism was influenced by the verse in which these two items are listed together among things that are never satisfied: "The grave and the barren womb" (Proverbs 30:16).

**That it is possible for there to be an opening of the womb without blood – דְּאֶפְשָׁר לִפְתִיחַת הַקֶּבֶר בְּלֹא דָם:** Since it is possible for a woman to give birth without experiencing an emission of blood, then in a case where she has not actually seen an emission of blood, it is assumed she did not experience one, and she is therefore pure from *ziva*. According to the opinion that it is impossible for there to be an opening of the womb without an emission of blood, it is certain that in this scenario she experienced a third emission of blood with the birth. Rashi explains that the *baraita* is referring to a case where she did not experience any labor pains; accordingly, this emission renders her a greater *zava* (Rashi).

וְשִׁבְעָה נִדָּה, וּשְׁנַיִם שֶׁל אַחַר הַנִּדָּה, וַחֲמִשִּׁים שֶׁהַוָּלָד מְטַהֵר,

Rabbi Meir continues: **And** then she continues to experience bleeding throughout the **seven** days of **menstruation.** She is not considered to have experienced bleeding of *ziva* for three consecutive days, as the third emission occurred during her days of menstruation. **And** she then experiences bleeding for the first **two** days **after the** days of **menstruation,** i.e., on the first and second days of the eleven days of *ziva*. **And** on the third day of *ziva* she begins the period of **fifty** days before giving birth, during **which the child renders** her **pure.** This constitutes a period of sixty-one days during which she is not rendered a greater *zava*.

וּשְׁמוֹנִים שֶׁל נְקֵבָה, וְשִׁבְעָה נִדָּה, וּשְׁנַיִם שֶׁל אַחַר הַנִּדָּה.

Rabbi Meir continues: **And** this period is followed by **eighty** days **of** purity from *ziva* after giving birth to **a female,** for a total of 141 days during which she does not become a greater *zava* on account of blood emitted. **And** there are then **seven** days of **menstruation** following her days of purity, **and** another **two** days **after the** days of **menstruation,** i.e., the first and second days of *ziva*, during which she experiences bleeding, for a total of 150 days during which she does not become a greater *zava* on account of blood emitted.

אָמְרוּ לוֹ: אִם כֵּן, יֵשׁ מַקְשָׁה כׇּל יָמֶיהָ וְאֵין זִיבָה עוֹלָה בָּהֶן!

The Rabbis **said to** Rabbi Meir: **If so, there is** also a scenario in which a woman **experiences** emissions of blood due to labor **pains** for **all the days of her** life, **and** the impurity of ***ziva* is not included in them.** For example, she gives birth to a female, and at the conclusion of her days of impurity engages in intercourse with her husband and becomes pregnant. She continues to experience bleeding throughout her days of purity, after which she experiences bleeding during the seven days of menstruation and the first two days of the next cycle of *ziva*. She then experiences labor pains accompanied by blood for fifty days, after which she miscarries a female. She subsequently becomes pregnant again within eighty days of the miscarriage, and the above process repeats itself. In this manner, she will never become a greater *zava*.

אָמַר לָהֶן: מַאי דַּעְתַּיְיכוּ – מִשּׁוּם נְפָלִים, אֵין קוֹשִׁי לִנְפָלִים.

Rabbi Meir **said to them: What is your opinion,** that a woman is not rendered a *zava* **due to** the birth of **non-viable newborns?** The *halakha* that blood emitted due to labor **pains** does not render a woman a *zava* does **not** apply **to non-viable newborns.**[H]

תָּנוּ רַבָּנַן: יֵשׁ רוֹאָה מֵאָה יוֹם וְאֵין זִיבָה עוֹלָה בָּהֶן. כֵּיצַד, שְׁנַיִם בְּלֹא עֵת, וְשִׁבְעָה נִדָּה, וּשְׁנַיִם שֶׁל אַחַר הַנִּדָּה, וּשְׁמוֹנִים שֶׁל נְקֵבָה, וְשִׁבְעָה נִדָּה, וּשְׁנַיִם שֶׁל אַחַר הַנִּדָּה.

**The Sages taught** in a *baraita*: **There is** a scenario in which a woman **sees** blood for **one hundred days, and** the impurity of greater ***ziva* is not included in them. How** so? She emits blood for **two** days **not at the time** of her menstruation, **and** then throughout the **seven** days of **menstruation, and** then for the first **two** days **after the** days of **menstruation. And** this period is followed by **eighty** days **of** purity from *ziva* after giving birth to **a female, and seven** days of **menstruation** following her days of purity, **and** another **two** days **after the** days of **menstruation.** This amounts to one hundred days.

מַאי קָא מַשְׁמַע לַן? לְאַפּוֹקֵי מִמַּאן דְּאָמַר אִי אֶפְשָׁר לִפְתִיחַת הַקֶּבֶר בְּלֹא דָם – קָא מַשְׁמַע לַן: דְּאֶפְשָׁר לִפְתִיחַת הַקֶּבֶר בְּלֹא דָם.

The Gemara asks: **What is** this *baraita* **teaching us?** The Gemara responds: The *baraita* serves **to exclude** the opinion of **the one who said** that **it is impossible for** there to be **an opening of the womb** [***hakever***][N] **without** an emission of **blood.** According to this opinion, if a woman gives birth after experiencing bleeding on the first two days after the days of menstruation, it is certain she experienced bleeding on the third day as well, as every birth is accompanied by an emission of blood. Consequently, she has experienced bleeding on three consecutive days during the days of *ziva* and is rendered a greater *zava*. The *baraita* **teaches us that it is possible for** there to be **an opening of the womb without** an emission of **blood.**[N] Therefore, if she gave birth on the third day of *ziva* and she did not experience bleeding, she is not rendered a greater *zava*.

HALAKHA

**The *halakha* that blood emitted due to labor pains does not apply to non-viable newborns – אֵין קוֹשִׁי לִנְפָלִים:** With regard to a pregnant woman who began to feel labor pains and started emitting blood before birth, this is considered the blood that accompanies labor pains, which is ritually pure in the days of *ziva*. This *halakha* applies only to the birth of a viable child, not if she had a miscarriage. The *halakha* is in accordance with the opinion of Rabbi Meir, since Rava on the following *amud* rules in accordance with his opinion, and the *halakha* follows Rava because he is a late *amora* (Rambam *Sefer Kedusha*, *Hilkhot Issurei Bia* 7:1).

״רַבִּי יְהוּדָה אוֹמֵר דַּיָּהּ״ וכו׳. תַּנְיָא, רַבִּי יְהוּדָה אוֹמֵר מִשּׁוּם רַבִּי טַרְפוֹן: דַּיָּהּ חָדְשָׁהּ, וְיֵשׁ בַּדָּבָר לְהָקֵל וּלְהַחְמִיר.

§ The mishna teaches that **Rabbi Yehuda says:** It is **sufficient** that a woman is not rendered a *zava* on account of blood that is emitted due to labor pains only from within one month of her due date. In this regard, it **is taught** in a *baraita* that **Rabbi Yehuda says in the name of Rabbi Tarfon:** It is **sufficient for her** not to be rendered a *zava* from within one **month of her** due date. **And there is** an aspect of **leniency and** an aspect of **stringency in the matter.**

כֵּיצַד, קָשְׁתָה שְׁנַיִם בְּסוֹף שְׁמִינִי וְאֶחָד בִּתְחִלַּת תְּשִׁיעִי, וַאֲפִילּוּ בִּתְחִלַּת תְּשִׁיעִי יָלְדָה – הֲרֵי זוֹ יוֹלֶדֶת בְּזוֹב.

The *baraita* explains: **How** so? If **she experienced** labor **pains** accompanied by an emission of blood for **two** days **at the end of** her **eighth** month of pregnancy, which are days in which she can be rendered a *zava*, **and** for **one** day **at the beginning of** her **ninth** month, then **even** if she **gave birth** at **the beginning of** the **ninth** month, the one day from the ninth month joins together with the two days from the eighth month, and **this** woman is considered **one who gives birth as a *zava*.** This is an aspect of stringency.

אֲבָל קָשְׁתָה יוֹם אֶחָד בְּסוֹף שְׁמִינִי וּשְׁתַּיִם בִּתְחִלַּת תְּשִׁיעִי, וַאֲפִילּוּ בְּסוֹף תְּשִׁיעִי יָלְדָה – אֵין זוֹ יוֹלֶדֶת בְּזוֹב.

**But** if **she experienced** labor **pains** accompanied by an emission of blood for **one day at the end of** her **eighth** month, **and** for only **two** days **at the beginning of** her **ninth** month, then **even** if she **gave birth at the end of** the **ninth** month, **this** woman **is not** considered **one who gives birth as a *zava*,** and she is pure. This is an aspect of leniency.

אָמַר רַב אַדָּא בַּר אַהֲבָה: שְׁמַע מִינַּהּ, קָסָבַר רַבִּי יְהוּדָה שִׁיפּוּרָא גָּרֵים. אִינִי, וְהָא אָמַר שְׁמוּאֵל: אֵין אִשָּׁה מִתְעַבֶּרֶת וְיוֹלֶדֶת אֶלָּא לְמָאתַיִם וְשִׁבְעִים וְאֶחָד יוֹם, אוֹ לְמָאתַיִם וְשִׁבְעִים וּשְׁנַיִם יוֹם, אוֹ לְמָאתַיִם וְשִׁבְעִים וּשְׁלֹשָׁה!

**Rav Adda bar Ahava says: Conclude from** the *baraita* that **Rabbi Yehuda holds** that the blast of **the shofar** at the beginning of the ninth month **causes**[N] the blood emitted during that month to be pure. That is to say, once the ninth months begins, any blood emitted does not render her a *zava*. The Gemara asks: **Is that so,** that the entire ninth month of pregnancy is suitable for giving birth, and therefore any blood seen during the ninth month is attributed to the imminent labor? **But doesn't Shmuel say** that **a woman becomes pregnant and gives birth only after 271 days,** which is a full nine months, **or after 272 days, or after 273** days? She will not, however, give birth during the ninth month itself.

הוּא דְּאָמַר כַּחֲסִידִים הָרִאשׁוֹנִים, דְּתַנְיָא: חֲסִידִים הָרִאשׁוֹנִים לֹא הָיוּ מְשַׁמְּשִׁין מִטּוֹתֵיהֶן אֶלָּא בִּרְבִיעִי בְּשַׁבָּת, שֶׁלֹּא יָבוֹאוּ נְשׁוֹתֵיהֶן

The Gemara responds: Shmuel **said** his statement **in accordance with** the opinion of **the early** generations of **pious men. As it is taught** in a *baraita*: **The early** generations of **pious** men **would engage in sexual intercourse only on a Wednesday, so that their wives should not come**

**NOTES**

**The shofar at the beginning of the month causes – שִׁיפּוּרָא גָּרֵים:** Rashi explains that this is referring to the shofar blast by the court at the time of the sanctification of the new month. Some write that this does not mean, as might be inferred from a literal reading, that the sanctification of the month by the court is a factor with regard to the time of birth, since a woman does not give birth in coordination with the lunar months. Rather, the Gemara is speaking of the months of pregnancy in terms of the months of the year. Furthermore, labor pains can be compared to a shofar blast, in keeping with the parable of a king and his soldiers (see 37b), since when a king leaves a city his soldiers blast the shofar to herald his approach (Ritva).

Perek **IV**
Daf **38** Amud **b**

לִידֵי חִלּוּל שַׁבָּת. בִּרְבִיעִי וְתוּ לָא? אֵימָא: מֵרְבִיעִי וְאֵילָךְ.

**to a desecration of Shabbat.** If they were to engage in sexual intercourse on a Sunday, Monday, or Tuesday, their wives might give birth on Shabbat, either 271, 272, or 273 days after conception either. The Gemara asks: If this was indeed the concern of the early generations of pious men, why would they engage in intercourse only **on a Wednesday, and nothing more?** After all, if they engaged in intercourse on a Thursday, Friday, or Shabbat, they would likewise avoid any desecration of Shabbat. The Gemara answers: **Say** that the *baraita* means that the early generations of pious men would engage in intercourse each week only **from Wednesday onward.**[N]

אָמַר מָר זוּטְרָא: מַאי טַעְמַיְיהוּ דַּחֲסִידִים הָרִאשׁוֹנִים – דִּכְתִיב ״וַיִּתֵּן [ה׳] לָהּ הֵרָיוֹן״ ״הֵרָיוֹן״ בְּגִימַטְרִיָּא מָאתַן וְשִׁבְעִים וְחַד הָווּ.

**Mar Zutra said: What is the reasoning of the early** generations of **pious** men, who state that a woman does not give birth before 271 days have passed from the time of insemination? **As it is written** with regard to Boaz and Ruth: "And he went in unto her, **and the Lord gave her conception** [***herayon***]" (Ruth 4:13). The letters that constitute the word ***herayon*** **are 271 in numerical value.**

**NOTES**

**From Wednesday onward – מֵרְבִיעִי וְאֵילָךְ:** Some commentaries explain that the early generation of pious men would engage in intercourse with their wives only on Wednesdays due to a concern that the conception might not begin until three days later, in which case she might give birth on Shabbat (Ritva). Others maintain that they were concerned that even if their wives did not give birth on Shabbat they might have the child within three days of Shabbat, and the *halakha* is that one desecrates Shabbat for a childbearing woman in the first three days after the birth (Ran).

אָמַר מָר זוּטְרָא: אֲפִילּוּ לְמַאן דְּאָמַר יוֹלֶדֶת לְתִשְׁעָה – אֵינָהּ יוֹלֶדֶת לְמִקּוּטָּעִים, יוֹלֶדֶת לְשִׁבְעָה – יוֹלֶדֶת לְמִקּוּטָּעִים, שֶׁנֶּאֱמַר "וַיְהִי לִתְקֻפוֹת הַיָּמִים וַתַּהַר חַנָּה וַתֵּלֶד בֵּן", מִיעוּט "תְּקוּפוֹת" – שְׁנַיִם, מִיעוּט "יָמִים" – שְׁנַיִם.

**Mar Zutra says: Even according to the one who said,** e.g., Shmuel and the early generations of pious men, that a woman **who gives birth at nine** months **does not give birth after an incomplete** number of months,[N] i.e., she carries for a full nine months, nevertheless, a woman **who gives birth at seven months can give birth after an incomplete** number of months. **As it is stated** with regard to the birth of Samuel: **"And it came to pass, when the seasons of the days had come, that Hannah conceived, and bore a son"** (I Samuel 1:20). **The minimal** number of **"seasons" is two,** and as each season of the year is three months, this amounts to six months. And **the minimal** number of **"days" is two.**[N] If so, Samuel was born in the seventh month of Hannah's pregnancy.

"רַבִּי יוֹסֵי וְרַבִּי שִׁמְעוֹן אוֹמְרִים אֵין קוֹשִׁי יוֹתֵר מִשְּׁתֵּי שַׁבָּתוֹת". אָמַר שְׁמוּאֵל: מַאי טַעְמַיְיהוּ דְּרַבָּנַן – דִּכְתִיב "וְטָמְאָה שְׁבֻעַיִם כְּנִדָּתָהּ" – כְּנִדָּתָהּ וְלֹא כְּזִיבָתָהּ, מִכְּלָל – דְּזִיבָתָהּ טְהוֹרָה, וְכַמָּה – שְׁבוּעַיִם.

§ The mishna teaches that **Rabbi Yosei and Rabbi Shimon say:** Labor **pains** do **not** occur **more than two weeks** before birth. **Shmuel said: What is the reasoning of the Rabbis,** i.e., Rabbi Yosei and Rabbi Shimon? **As it is written** with regard to a woman who gives birth to a female: **"And she shall be impure two weeks, as in her menstruation"** (Leviticus 12:5). The verse indicates that she is impure **as in her menstruation but not as in her** ***ziva*****. By inference,** one may conclude **that her** ***ziva*** **is pure,** i.e., if she emits blood accompanied by labor pains she is not rendered a *zava*. **And** for **how** long is this the case? For **two weeks.**

תָּנוּ רַבָּנַן: יֵשׁ מַקְשָׁה עֶשְׂרִים וַחֲמִשָּׁה יוֹם וְאֵין זִיבָה עוֹלָה בָּהֶן. כֵּיצַד, שְׁנַיִם בְּלֹא עֵת, וְשִׁבְעָה נִדָּה, וּשְׁנַיִם שֶׁלְּאַחַר נִדָּה, וְאַרְבָּעָה עָשָׂר שֶׁהַוָּלָד מְטַהֵר.

With regard to the *halakha* that blood emitted due to labor pains does not impart impurity of *ziva*, **the Sages taught: There is** a scenario in which a woman **experiences** labor **pains** accompanied by emissions of blood for **twenty-five days** before birth, **and** the impurity of greater ***ziva*** **is not included in them. How** so? She emits blood for **two** days **not at the time** of her menstruation, i.e., on the tenth and eleventh days of *ziva*, **and** then for the **seven** days of **menstruation, and** then for the first **two** days of *ziva* **that** come **after** the days of **menstruation. And** this period is followed by **fourteen** days during **which the** impending birth of **a child renders pure** the blood she sees.

וְאִי אֶפְשָׁר שֶׁתִּתְקַשֶּׁה עֶשְׂרִים וְשִׁשָּׁה יוֹם בְּלֹא וָלָד, וְלֹא תְּהֵא יוֹלֶדֶת בְּזוֹב.

The *baraita* continues: **And it is impossible for** a woman **to experience** labor **pains** accompanied by emissions of blood for **twenty-six days without a child,** such that **she will not be** a woman **who gives birth as a** ***zava*****.** Since a span of twenty-six days includes at least five days of *ziva*, there will inevitably be three consecutive days of *ziva* during which she experienced bleeding, therefore rendering her a greater *zava*.

"בְּלֹא וָלָד"? בִּתְלָתָא נַמִּי סַגִּי! אָמַר רַב שֵׁשֶׁת, אֵימָא: בְּמָקוֹם שֶׁיֵּשׁ וָלָד. אֲמַר לֵיהּ רָבָא: וְהָא "בְּלֹא וָלָד" קָתָנֵי!

The Gemara analyzes the *baraita*: Is the *baraita* really dealing with a case **without a child,** i.e., where she is not even pregnant? If there is no child, then experiencing bleeding **on three** consecutive days after the days of menstruation **is also sufficient** to render her a greater *zava*. **Rav Sheshet said** one should **say** the *baraita* as follows: Twenty-six days **in a case where there is a child,** i.e., where she is pregnant. **Rava said to** Rav Sheshet: **But** the *baraita* explicitly **teaches: Without a child.**

**NOTES**

**A woman who gives birth at nine months does not give birth after an incomplete number of months – יוֹלֶדֶת לְתִשְׁעָה אֵינָהּ יוֹלֶדֶת לְמִקּוּטָּעִים:** The early commentaries disagree as to the *halakha* in the case of a woman who gives birth midway through her ninth month. Some say the child is considered viable in all regards, if it is known that its term of gestation was completed (Ramban). According to some authorities, the nine months must be full and complete for the child to be considered viable (Rambam *Sefer Nashim, Hilkhot Yibbum VaḤalitza* 1:5 and *Sefer Shofetim, Hilkhot Evel* 1:7).

Nowadays, even women with normal pregnancies often give birth in the middle of the ninth month (see *Tosafot* on *Avoda Zara* 24b). The Rema likewise rules that a child born anytime in the ninth month is considered viable (*Shulḥan Arukh, Even HaEzer* 156:4, in the comment of Rema).

**The minimal number of days is two – מִיעוּט יָמִים שְׁנַיִם:** There is a principle that whenever a verse uses a plural form without further specification it is assumed to be referring to the smallest possible number (see *Yoma* 80a). With regard to the matter at hand, this means two days (see Gemara and Rashi on *Sukka* 5b).

אֶלָּא אֲמַר רָבָא, הָכִי קָאָמַר: אִי אֶפְשָׁר שֶׁתִּתְקַשֶּׁה עֶשְׂרִים וְשִׁשָּׁה יוֹם בְּמָקוֹם שֶׁיֵּשׁ וָלָד וְלֹא תְּהֵא יוֹלֶדֶת בְּזוֹב, וּבְמָקוֹם שֶׁאֵין וָלָד אֶלָּא נֵפֶל – בִּתְלָתָא נַמִי הָוְיָא זָבָה, מַאי טַעְמָא – אֵין קוֹשִׁי לִנְפָלִים.

Rather, Rava said that **this** is what the *baraita* **is saying: It is impossible for** a woman **to experience** labor **pains** accompanied by emissions of blood for **twenty-six days in a case where there is a child,** such that **she will not be** a woman **who gives birth as a** *zava***. And in a case where there is no child** born **but** there is a **non-viable newborn, with three** consecutive days of emissions **she also becomes a** *zava***. What is the reason?** The *halakha* that blood emitted due to labor **pains** does not render a woman a *zava* does **not** apply **to non-viable newborns.**

מתני׳ הַמַּקְשָׁה בְּתוֹךְ שְׁמוֹנִים שֶׁל נְקֵבָה – כׇּל דָּמִים שֶׁהִיא רוֹאָה טְהוֹרִין, עַד שֶׁיֵּצֵא הַוָּלָד, וְרַבִּי אֱלִיעֶזֶר מְטַמֵּא.

**MISHNA** A woman **who experiences** labor **pains within eighty** days **of** giving birth to **a female,**[NH] e.g., she conceived during the sixty-six days of purity, or she initially conceived twins and she gave birth to a female and the birth of the second fetus was delayed, **all blood that she sees is ritually pure,** as she is currently within her days of purity. And this remains the *halakha* **until the child emerges** from the womb, at which point she is rendered impure as a woman who gives birth. **And Rabbi Eliezer deems ritually impure** the blood that occurs due to these labor pains.

אָמְרוּ לוֹ לְרַבִּי אֱלִיעֶזֶר: וּמָה בְּמָקוֹם שֶׁהֶחְמִיר בְּדַם הַשּׁוֹפִי – הֵיקֵל בְּדַם הַקּוֹשִׁי, מָקוֹם שֶׁהֵיקֵל בְּדַם הַשּׁוֹפִי – אֵינוֹ דִּין שֶׁנָּקֵל בְּדַם הַקּוֹשִׁי?

The Rabbis **said to Rabbi Eliezer: And what,** if **in an instance where** the verse **was stringent with regard to blood** emitted while **resting,** namely if a pregnant woman emits blood after her days of purity without any labor pains she is rendered impure, the verse **was lenient with regard to blood** that accompanies **the** labor **pains;** then in **an instance where** the verse **was lenient with regard to blood** emitted while **resting,** i.e., during a woman's days of purity, **is it not right that we will be lenient with regard to blood** that accompanies **the** labor **pains?**

אָמַר לָהֶן: דַּיּוֹ לַבָּא מִן הַדִּין לִהְיוֹת כַּנִּדּוֹן, מִמָּה הֵיקֵל עָלֶיהָ – מִטּוּמְאַת זִיבָה, אֲבָל טְמֵאָה טוּמְאַת נִדָּה.

Rabbi Eliezer **said to them:** When deriving a *halakha* by means of an *a fortiori* inference, there is a principle that **it is sufficient for the** conclusion that **emerges from** an *a fortiori* **inference to be like** its **source.**[B] In other words, the status of blood emitted due to labor pains during her days of purity should not be more lenient than that of blood emitted due to labor pains after her days of purity. Rabbi Eliezer elaborates: **Concerning what** type of impurity **was** the verse **lenient with regard to** a woman who experiences an emission of blood due to labor pains? **Concerning the impurity of** *ziva***. But she** may still be rendered **ritually impure** with **the impurity of a menstruating woman.** So too, if a woman experiences emissions of blood due to labor pains during her days of purity, she is rendered a menstruating woman.

גמ׳ תָּנוּ רַבָּנַן: ״תֵּשֵׁב״ – לְרַבּוֹת הַמַּקְשָׁה בְּתוֹךְ שְׁמוֹנִים שֶׁל נְקֵבָה, שֶׁכׇּל דָּמִים שֶׁהִיא רוֹאָה טְהוֹרִין, עַד שֶׁיֵּצֵא הַוָּלָד. וְרַבִּי אֱלִיעֶזֶר מְטַמֵּא.

**GEMARA** With regard to the dispute between Rabbi Eliezer and the Rabbis concerning a woman who emits blood due to labor pains during her days of purity, **the Sages taught** a *baraita* that addresses a verse discussing a woman who gives birth to a female: "And sixty-six days she shall observe the blood of purity" (Leviticus 12:5). The term **"She shall observe"** serves **to include** a woman **who experiences** labor **pains within eighty** days **of** giving birth to **a female,** teaching **that all blood that she sees is ritually pure.** And this remains the case **until the child emerges** from the womb. **And Rabbi Eliezer deems ritually impure** the blood that occurs due to these labor pains.

**BACKGROUND**

It is sufficient [*dayyo*] for the conclusion that emerges from an *a fortiori* inference to be like its source – דַּיּוֹ לַבָּא מִן הַדִּין לִהְיוֹת כַּנִּדּוֹן: This halakhic principle, referred to in shorthand as *dayyo*, restricts the conclusions that may be derived from an *a fortiori* inference. It prevents the implementation of limitless leniencies or stringencies from an *a fortiori* inference by creating limits for its implementation. The principle of *dayyo* establishes that an *a fortiori* inference teaches in the following manner: Just as X is more stringent than Y with regard to point A, X is no less stringent than Y with regard to point B. It does not teach: Just as X is more stringent than Y with regard to point A, X is similarly more stringent than Y with regard to point B. If that were the case, there would be no limit to the conclusions derived from such an inference.

**NOTES**

A woman who experiences labor pains within eighty days of giving birth to a female – הַמַּקְשָׁה בְּתוֹךְ שְׁמוֹנִים שֶׁל נְקֵבָה: The mishna does not refer to the forty days following the birth of a male because this case involves a woman who became pregnant again during her days of purity. Such a scenario is not possible after the birth of a male, as the days of purity end forty days after his birth, and a fetus within forty days of conception is not classified as a fetus with regard to the *halakhot* of experiencing labor pains and birth.

**HALAKHA**

A woman who experiences labor pains within eighty days of giving birth to a female – הַמַּקְשָׁה בְּתוֹךְ שְׁמוֹנִים שֶׁל נְקֵבָה: If a woman gives birth to a female and after her fourteen days of impurity becomes pregnant again and emits blood while experiencing labor pains within eighty days of the birth of the female, this is considered blood of purity, despite the fact that the *halakha* of blood accompanying labor pains does not apply to miscarriages. The reason is that any blood she sees during her days of purity is pure until she has a miscarriage, at which point she has the impurity of a woman after childbirth, for the amount of days for a male or female depending on the sex of the miscarried fetus. The *halakha* is in accordance with the opinion of the first *tanna* (Rambam *Sefer Kedusha*, *Hilkhot Issurei Bia* 7:9).

אָמְרוּ לוֹ לְרַבִּי אֱלִיעֶזֶר: וּמָה בְּמָקוֹם שֶׁהֶחְמִיר בְּשׁוֹפִי שֶׁלִּפְנֵי הַוָּלָד – הֵיקֵל בְּשׁוֹפִי שֶׁלְּאַחַר הַוָּלָד. מָקוֹם שֶׁהֵיקֵל בְּקוֹשִׁי שֶׁלִּפְנֵי הַוָּלָד – אֵינוֹ דִּין שֶׁנָּקֵל בְּקוֹשִׁי שֶׁלְּאַחַר הַוָּלָד?

The Rabbis **said to Rabbi Eliezer: And what, if in an instance where** the verse **was stringent with regard to** blood that is emitted while **resting before** the birth of **the child,** as such blood renders her a *zava*, the verse **was lenient with regard to** blood that is emitted while **resting after** the birth of **the child,** i.e., during her days of purity; then in **an instance where** the verse **was lenient with regard to** blood emitted due to labor **pains before** the birth of **the child, is it not right that we will be lenient with regard to** blood that is emitted due to labor **pains after** the birth of **the child?**

אָמַר לָהֶם: דַּיּוֹ לַבָּא מִן הַדִּין לִהְיוֹת כַּנִּדּוֹן, מִמָּה הֵיקֵל עָלֶיהָ – מִטּוּמְאַת זִיבָה, אֲבָל מְטַמְּאָה טוּמְאַת נִדָּה.

Rabbi Eliezer **said to them: It is sufficient for the** conclusion that **emerges from** an *a fortiori* **inference to be like** its **source.** Rabbi Eliezer elaborates: **Concerning what** type of impurity **was** the verse **lenient with regard to** a woman who experiences an emission of blood due to labor pains? **Concerning the impurity of *ziva*. But** an emission of blood **renders her impure** with **the impurity of a menstruating woman.** So too, if a woman experiences emissions of blood due to labor pains during her days of purity, she is rendered a menstruating woman.

אָמְרוּ לוֹ: הֲרֵי אָנוּ מְשִׁיבִין לָךְ לָשׁוֹן אַחֵר, וּמָה בְּמָקוֹם שֶׁהֶחְמִיר בְּשׁוֹפִי שֶׁלִּפְנֵי הַוָּלָד – הֵיקֵל בְּקוֹשִׁי שֶׁעִמּוֹ. מָקוֹם שֶׁהֵיקֵל בְּשׁוֹפִי שֶׁלְּאַחַר הַוָּלָד – אֵינוֹ דִּין שֶׁנָּקֵל בְּקוֹשִׁי שֶׁעִמּוֹ?

The Rabbis **said to him: But we** will **respond to you** with **another version** of the *a fortiori* inference: **And what, if in an instance where** the verse **was stringent with regard to** blood that is emitted while **resting before** the birth of **the child** the verse **was lenient with regard to** blood that is emitted due to labor **pains that** come **with it,** i.e., which precede the birth of the child; then in **an instance where** the verse **was lenient with regard to** blood emitted while **resting,** namely during a woman's days of purity, **is it not right that we will be lenient with regard to** blood that accompanies **the** labor **pains that** come **with it?**

אָמַר לָהֶם: אֲפִילּוּ אַתֶּם מְשִׁיבִין כׇּל הַיּוֹם כּוּלּוֹ – דַּיּוֹ לַבָּא מִן הַדִּין לִהְיוֹת כַּנִּדּוֹן, מִמָּה הֵיקֵל עָלֶיהָ – מִטּוּמְאַת זִיבָה, אֲבָל מְטַמְּאָה טוּמְאַת נִדָּה.

Rabbi Eliezer **said to them: Even** if **you respond** by citing *a fortiori* inferences of that type throughout **the entire day,** the principle remains that **it is sufficient for the** conclusion that **emerges from** an *a fortiori* **inference to be like** its **source. Concerning what** type of impurity **was** the verse **lenient with regard to** a woman who experiences an emission of blood due to labor pains? **Concerning the impurity of *ziva*. But** an emission of blood **renders her impure** with **the impurity of a menstruating woman.**

אָמַר רָבָא: בְּהָא זְכִינְהוּ רַבִּי אֱלִיעֶזֶר לְרַבָּנַן, לָאו אָמְרִיתוּ ״דָּמָהּ״ – דָּמָהּ מֵחֲמַת עַצְמָהּ וְלֹא מֵחֲמַת וָלָד, הָכִי נָמֵי – ״וְטָהֲרָה מִמְּקוֹר דָּמֶיהָ״ – דָּמֶיהָ מֵחֲמַת עַצְמָהּ וְלֹא מֵחֲמַת וָלָד.

**Rava said: With this** response **Rabbi Eliezer triumphed over the Rabbis: Didn't you say** that the reason why a woman is not rendered a *zava* on account of blood that is emitted due to labor pains before birth is because the verse states: "And if a woman has an issue of her blood many days" (Leviticus 15:25)? The term **"her blood"** indicates that only **her blood** that comes **due to herself** is impure due to *ziva*, **but not** blood that comes **due to** her **child. So too,** one can say that as the verse states with regard to a woman who gives birth: **"And she shall be purified from the fountain of her blood"** (Leviticus 12:7), this indicates that only **her blood** that comes **due to herself** is pure from *ziva*, **but not** blood that comes **due to** her **child.**

אֵימָא: בִּימֵי נִדָּה – נִדָּה, בִּימֵי זִיבָה – טְהוֹרָה! אָמַר קְרָא: ״תֵּשֵׁב״ – יְשִׁיבָה אַחַת לְכוּלָּן.

This Gemara raises a difficulty against the opinion of Rabbi Eliezer: If so, one can **say** that if she emits blood due to labor pains **during the days of menstruation** she is **a menstruating woman,** but if she emits blood **in the days of *ziva*,** i.e., after the days of menstruation, she is **pure.** The Gemara explains that **the verse states: "She shall observe** the blood of purity" (Leviticus 12:5), which indicates that there is **one observance for all** the days of her purity, i.e., all the blood she emits due to labor pains during her days of purity is either pure or impure.

**מתני׳** כׇּל אַחַד עָשָׂר יוֹם בְּחֶזְקַת טָהֳרָה.

**MISHNA** For **all** the **eleven days** of *ziva* that follow the seven days of menstruation, a woman **has the presumptive status of ritual purity,**[H] as it is unusual for her to experience bleeding on these days.

HALAKHA

**All eleven days a woman has the presumptive status of ritual purity – כׇּל אַחַד עָשָׂר יוֹם בְּחֶזְקַת טָהֳרָה:** A woman has the status of purity for all the eleven days after the seven days of menstruation. Consequently, she does not need to examine herself on these days (Rambam *Sefer Kedusha, Hilkhot Issurei Bia* 8:11).

יָשְׁבָה לָהּ וְלֹא בָּדְקָה, שׁוֹגֵג, אָנוּס, מֵזִיד וְלֹא בָּדְקָה – טְהוֹרָה.

If a woman **sat and did not examine** herself[H] every morning and evening to determine whether she emitted blood and is impure, it makes no difference whether she failed to examine herself **unwittingly** or due to **circumstances beyond her control,** or even if she acted **intentionally and did not examine** herself; she remains **ritually pure.** She is rendered impure only if she examined herself and was found to have emitted blood.

הִגִּיעַ שְׁעַת וֶסְתָּהּ וְלֹא בָּדְקָה – הֲרֵי זוֹ טְמֵאָה. רַבִּי מֵאִיר אוֹמֵר: אִם הָיְתָה בְּמַחֲבוֹא, וְהִגִּיעַ שְׁעַת וֶסְתָּהּ וְלֹא בָּדְקָה – הֲרֵי זוֹ טְהוֹרָה, מִפְּנֵי שֶׁחֲרָדָה מְסַלֶּקֶת אֶת הַדָּמִים.

By contrast, if **the time of her** menstrual **cycle arrived,** when she is required to examine herself, **and she did not examine** herself, **that** woman **is ritually impure,** as it is typical for a woman to discharge blood at that time. **Rabbi Meir says:** If a woman **was in hiding**[B] from danger, **and the time of her** menstrual **cycle arrived and she did not examine** herself[H] on that day, **that** woman **is pure,**[N] **because fear drives away blood.**[N] There is therefore no concern that she might have emitted blood.

אֲבָל יְמֵי הַזָּב וְהַזָּבָה, וְשׁוֹמֶרֶת יוֹם כְּנֶגֶד יוֹם – הֲרֵי אֵלּוּ בְּחֶזְקַת טוּמְאָה.

But with regard to the seven clean **days of the** ***zav*** **and the** ***zava*****, and** with regard to a woman who **observes** a clean **day for a day** she experiences a discharge during her days of *ziva*, if she fails to examine herself on those days, **these** women **have a presumptive status of ritual impurity,** as they already experienced a discharge.

**גמ׳** לְמַאי הִלְכְתָא? אָמַר רַב יְהוּדָה: לוֹמַר שֶׁאֵינָהּ צְרִיכָה בְּדִיקָה. וְהָא מִדְּקָתָנֵי סֵיפָא ״יָשְׁבָה וְלֹא בָּדְקָה״ – מִכְּלָל דִּלְכַתְּחִלָּה בָּעְיָא בְּדִיקָה!

**GEMARA** The mishna teaches that throughout the eleven days of *ziva* that follow the seven days of menstruation, a woman has the presumptive status of ritual purity. The Gemara asks: **With regard to what** ***halakha*** is this stated? **Rav Yehuda says:** This serves **to say that she does not require an examination** during these days. The Gemara objects: **But from** the fact **that the latter clause teaches:** If **she sat and did not examine** herself she remains ritually pure, **it can be inferred that she requires examination** ***ab initio*****.**

סֵיפָא אֲתָאן לִימֵי נִדָּה, וְהָכִי קָאָמַר: כָּל אַחַד עָשָׂר בְּחֶזְקַת טָהֳרָה – וְלָא בָּעְיָא בְּדִיקָה, אֲבָל בִּימֵי נִדָּתָהּ – בָּעְיָא בְּדִיקָה. יָשְׁבָה וְלֹא בָּדְקָה, שׁוֹגֵג, אָנוּס, מֵזִיד וְלֹא בָּדְקָה – טְהוֹרָה.

The Gemara explains: In **the latter clause we arrive at** the case of a woman who is in the **days of menstruation,** not in the days of *ziva*. **And this** is what the mishna **is saying:** For **all** the **eleven days** of *ziva* that follow the days of menstruation, a woman **has the presumptive status of ritual purity and she does not require examination. But during the days of her menstruation she requires examination.** Nevertheless, if **she sat and did not examine** herself, whether **unwittingly** or due to **circumstances beyond her control,** or even if she acted **intentionally and did not examine** herself, she remains **ritually pure.**

רַב חִסְדָּא אָמַר: לָא צְרִיכָא אֶלָּא לְרַבִּי מֵאִיר, דְּאָמַר: אִשָּׁה שֶׁאֵין לָהּ וֶסֶת אֲסוּרָה לְשַׁמֵּשׁ, הָנֵי מִילֵּי – בִּימֵי נִדָּתָהּ, אֲבָל בִּימֵי זִיבָתָהּ – בְּחֶזְקַת טָהֳרָה קַיְימָא.

**Rav Ḥisda said** a different answer: The first clause of the mishna **is necessary only for** the opinion of **Rabbi Meir, who said:** With regard to a **woman who does not have** a fixed menstrual **cycle,** she is **forbidden to engage in intercourse,** lest she emit blood during intercourse. The mishna is teaching that **this statement** applies only **during the days of her menstruation, but during the days of her** ***ziva*** even Rabbi Meir concedes that she **stands in** her **presumptive status of purity** and may engage in intercourse with her husband.

**BACKGROUND**

If a woman was in hiding – אִם הָיְתָה בְּמַחֲבוֹא: Archaeological evidence suggests that this is not merely a theoretical construct, as situations like these were not uncommon during the bar Kokheva rebellion. Caves have been found in the Judean Desert that were clearly used as dwelling places, and under such stressful situations regular ovulation would likely have been affected.

**NOTES**

That woman is pure – הֲרֵי זוֹ טְהוֹרָה: According to some of the early commentaries, this means she is completely pure and she is not even required examine herself *ab initio* (Ba'al HaMaor; Rashba). Others explain that she is pure only after the fact, i.e., she is required to examine herself *ab initio*, but if she failed to do so she remains pure (Rashi; Ra'avad).

Fear drives away blood – חֲרָדָה מְסַלֶּקֶת אֶת הַדָּמִים: The Gemara later explains that certain mental states, such as fear, anxiety, and terror, can affect a woman's blood flow (71a). As the Gemara states elsewhere in this regard: Trepidation generated by extended worry contracts the muscles and prevents blood from flowing, and sudden fear relaxes the muscles and causes the blood to flow (*Sota* 20b).

The later commentaries ask why this is not cited by the ruling authorities as a *halakha* that whenever a woman experiences a sudden panic there is a concern for the emission of blood and she is required to examine herself (*Arukh HaShulḥan*). Some of the later commentaries do in fact maintain that she must perform an examination under such circumstances (*Darkhei Teshuva*; *Gufei Halakha*; *Tziyunei Tahara*; *Taharat Yisrael*). Others disagree with this conclusion, claiming that the Gemara is merely saying that in such a situation a woman will certainly feel an emission of blood; it does not mean that even if she does not have such a sensation she is assumed to have had a discharge. Consequently, she is not obligated to examine herself (*Ḥatam Sofer*; Responsa *Meshiv Davar*).

**HALAKHA**

If a woman sat and did not examine herself, etc. – יָשְׁבָה לָהּ וְלֹא בָּדְקָה וכו׳: If a woman did not examine herself after the eleven days of her *ziva*, whether due to circumstances beyond her control or willingly, she has the presumptive status of ritual purity until she examines herself and finds that she is impure (Rambam *Sefer Kedusha*, *Hilkhot Issurei Bia* 8:12; see also *Sefer Tahara*, *Hilkhot Metamei Mishkav UMoshav* 3:5; *Shulḥan Arukh*, *Yoreh De'a* 184:9).

If woman was in hiding and the time of her menstrual cycle arrived and she did not examine herself – הָיְתָה בְּמַחֲבוֹא וְהִגִּיעַ שְׁעַת וֶסְתָּהּ וְלֹא בָּדְקָה: If the time for a woman's period arrived when she was hiding out of fear, she need not be concerned for impurity. Some commentaries say this *halakha* applies only if the time for her period had passed and she did not examine herself or sense any emission of blood, but she is obligated to examine herself at the time of her period *ab initio* (see *Shulḥan Arukh*, *Yoreh De'a* 184:8, and in the comment of Rema).

אִי הָכִי, אַמַּאי אֲמַר רַבִּי מֵאִיר יוֹצִיא וְלֹא יַחֲזִיר עוֹלָמִית? דִּלְמָא אָתְיָא לְקִלְקוּלָא בִּימֵי נִדָּה.

The Gemara asks: **If so,** that even according to Rabbi Meir there are days in which a woman who does not have a fixed menstrual cycle is permitted to engage in sexual intercourse with her husband, **why did Rabbi Meir say** that her husband **must divorce** her **and he may never take** her **back,** even if she eventually develops a fixed menstrual cycle? Let them engage in intercourse during the eleven days of *ziva*. The Gemara answers: He must divorce her **lest** the matter **lead to failure during the days of menstruation,** i.e., in case they come to engage in intercourse during the days of menstruation, when she might experience regular menstrual bleeding.

הָא מִדְּקָתָנֵי סֵיפָא ״הִגִּיעַ שְׁעַת וִסְתָּהּ וְלֹא בָּדְקָה״ – מִכְּלָל דְּבְאִשָּׁה שֶׁיֵּשׁ לָהּ וֶסֶת עָסְקִינַן! חַסּוּרֵי מִחַסְּרָא וְהָכִי קָתָנֵי: כָּל אַחַד עָשָׂר בְּחֶזְקַת טָהֳרָה וְשָׁרְיָא לְבַעְלָהּ, וּבִימֵי נִדָּה אֲסוּרָה.

The Gemara objects: But **from** the fact **that the latter clause teaches:** If **the time of her** menstrual **cycle arrived and she did not examine** herself, that woman is ritually impure, **it can be inferred that we are dealing with a woman who has** a fixed menstrual **cycle.** The Gemara explains: The mishna **is incomplete and this** is what **it is teaching:** For **all** the **eleven** days of *ziva* that follow the days of menstruation, a woman **has the presumptive status of ritual purity and she is permitted to her husband, but during the days of menstruation she is prohibited** to her husband.

בַּמֶּה דְּבָרִים אֲמוּרִים – בְּאִשָּׁה שֶׁאֵין לָהּ וֶסֶת, אֲבָל יֵשׁ לָהּ וֶסֶת – מוּתֶּרֶת, וּצְרִיכָה בְּדִיקָה. יָשְׁבָה וְלֹא בָּדְקָה, שָׁגְגָה, נֶאֶנְסָה, הֵזִידָה וְלֹא בָּדְקָה – טְהוֹרָה, הִגִּיעַ שְׁעַת וִסְתָּהּ וְלֹא בָּדְקָה – טְמֵאָה.

**In what** case **is this statement said? In** the case of **a woman who does not have** a fixed menstrual **cycle,** where there is a concern she might experience bleeding during any of the days of menstruation. **But** in the case of a woman who **has** a fixed menstrual **cycle, she is permitted** to engage in sexual intercourse with her husband, **and she requires examination.** Nevertheless, if **she sat and did not examine** herself, whether **unwittingly** or due to **circumstances beyond her control,** or even if she acted **intentionally and did not examine** herself, she remains **ritually pure.** If **the time of her** menstrual **cycle arrived and she did not examine** herself, she is **impure.**

הָא מִדְּסֵיפָא רַבִּי מֵאִיר – רֵישָׁא לָאו רַבִּי מֵאִיר! כּוּלָּהּ רַבִּי מֵאִיר הִיא, וְהָכִי קָאָמַר: אִם לֹא הָיְתָה בְּמַחֲבֵא, וְהִגִּיעַ שְׁעַת וִסְתָּהּ וְלֹא בָּדְקָה – טְמֵאָה, שֶׁרַבִּי מֵאִיר אוֹמֵר, אִם הָיְתָה בְּמַחֲבֵא וְהִגִּיעַ שְׁעַת וִסְתָּהּ וְלֹא בָּדְקָה – טְהוֹרָה, שֶׁחֲרָדָה מְסַלֶּקֶת אֶת הַדָּמִים.

The Gemara objects: But **from** the fact that **the last clause** is in accordance with the opinion of **Rabbi Meir,** it can be inferred that **the first clause** is **not** in accordance with the opinion of **Rabbi Meir.** The Gemara explains that **the entire** mishna **is** in accordance with the opinion of **Rabbi Meir, and this** is what it **is saying: If she was not in hiding and the time of her** menstrual **cycle arrived and she did not examine** herself, she is **impure, as Rabbi Meir says:** If a woman **was in hiding and the time of her** menstrual **cycle arrived and she did not examine** herself, she is **pure, as fear drives away blood.**

רָבָא אָמַר: לוֹמַר שֶׁאֵינָהּ מְטַמְּאָה מֵעֵת לְעֵת.

**Rava says** a different explanation of the first clause of the mishna: The mishna is coming **to say that** if a woman experiences bleeding during the eleven days of *ziva*, as she previously had the presumptive status of purity **she does not impart impurity** retroactively **for** a twenty-four-hour **period** to any ritually pure items she touched. It is assumed that she did not emit any blood before this emission.

מֵיתִיבֵי: הַנִּדָּה, וְהַזָּבָה, וְהַשּׁוֹמֶרֶת יוֹם כְּנֶגֶד יוֹם, וְהַיּוֹלֶדֶת – כּוּלָּן מְטַמְּאוֹת מֵעֵת לְעֵת. תְּיוּבְתָּא.

The Gemara **raises an objection** from a *baraita*: With regard to **a menstruating woman, and a *zava*, and a woman who observes a day for a day,**[H] **and a woman who gave birth, they all impart impurity** retroactively **for** a twenty-four-hour **period.** A woman who observes a day for a day is one who experiences bleeding for one or two days during her days of *ziva*, and the *baraita* teaches that even such a woman imparts impurity retroactively for a twenty-four-hour period. If so, this is **a conclusive refutation** of Rava's explanation.

רַב הוּנָא בַּר חִיָּיא אָמַר שְׁמוּאֵל: לוֹמַר שֶׁאֵינָהּ קוֹבַעַת לָהּ וֶסֶת בְּתוֹךְ יְמֵי זִיבָתָהּ. אֲמַר רַב יוֹסֵף: לָא שְׁמִיעַ לִי הָא שְׁמַעְתְּתָא.

**Rav Huna bar Ḥiyya says** another explanation of the first clause of the mishna in the name of **Shmuel:** The mishna is coming **to say that** a woman **does not fix** a menstrual **cycle for herself during the days of her *ziva*.**[HN] In other words, a sighting during these days does not combine with sightings during the previous two periods of *ziva* to establish a fixed menstrual cycle. The Gemara relates that this statement was recited before **Rav Yosef,** who **said: I did not hear this *halakha*** from Shmuel.

**HALAKHA**

**A menstruating woman, a *zava*, and a woman who observes a day for a day, etc.** – הַנִּדָּה וְהַזָּבָה וְהַשּׁוֹמֶרֶת יוֹם כְּנֶגֶד יוֹם וכו׳: A menstruating woman, a *zava*, a woman who observes a day for a day, and a woman after childbirth all impart impurity retroactively for twenty-four hours, or from their last examination before they experienced bleeding. This *halakha* applies by rabbinic law, and this is the twenty-four-hour period mentioned with regard to a menstruating woman. How so? If a woman who was ritually pure and has no fixed period examined herself in the morning and found that she was pure, and then at midday she performed another examination and discovered that she certainly (*Mishne LaMelekh*) had an emission, all pure items she touched in between the two examinations are retroactively impure. Likewise, if she examined herself on one day and she was pure, and two or three days later examined herself again and found blood, all pure items she handled in the previous twenty-four hours are retroactively impure. The *halakha* is in accordance with the opinion of the Rabbis (Rambam *Sefer Kedusha, Hilkhot Issurei Bia* 9:3 and *Sefer Tahara, Hilkhot Metamei Mishkav UMoshav* 3:4).

**A woman does not fix a menstrual cycle for herself during the days of her *ziva*** – אֵינָהּ קוֹבַעַת לָהּ וֶסֶת בְּתוֹךְ יְמֵי זִיבָתָהּ: A woman does not fix a period during the eleven days of her *ziva*. If she regularly experiences bleeding on the same day during her days of *ziva*, she must be concerned for impurity at that time. The *halakha* is in accordance with the opinion of Rav Pappa (Rambam *Sefer Kedusha, Hilkhot Issurei Bia* 8:9).

**NOTES**

**A woman does not fix a menstrual cycle for herself during the days of her *ziva*** – אֵינָהּ קוֹבַעַת לָהּ וֶסֶת בְּתוֹךְ יְמֵי זִיבָתָהּ: Some early commentaries write that these sightings during the days of *ziva* are considered accidental and are disregarded altogether. Consequently, if a woman experiences bleeding every fifteen days, the occurrences on the days of *ziva* are ignored as though they did not happen at all, and therefore her fixed period is on the twenty-ninth day (Ra'avad in *Ba'alei HaNefesh*). Other early commentaries are puzzled by this conclusion, as it is unreasonable to allow an actual interval of fifteen days to be ignored in favor of a supposed regular interval that is not regular at all (Ramban; Rashba; Ba'al HaMaor; Meiri).

אֲמַר לֵיהּ אַבַּיֵי: אַתְּ אֲמַרְתְּ נִיהֲלָן, וְאַהָא אֲמַרְתְּ לָן, הָיְתָה לְמוּדָה לִהְיוֹת רוֹאָה יוֹם חֲמִשָּׁה עָשָׂר (יוֹם), וְשִׁינְּתָה לְיוֹם עֶשְׂרִים – זֶה וָזֶה אֲסוּרִין לְשַׁמֵּשׁ. שִׁינְּתָה פַּעֲמַיִם לְיוֹם עֶשְׂרִים – זֶה וָזֶה אֲסוּרִין.

**Abaye said to him:** But **you** yourself **told us** this *halakha*,[B] **and** it was **with regard to that** mishna **you told** it to **us,** as we learned in a mishna (63b): If the woman **was accustomed to see** an emission of blood on the **fifteenth day,** so that this was her fixed menstrual cycle, **and she deviated**[H] from her cycle **to** see an emission on the **twentieth day,** then on both **this** day, the fifteenth, **and that** day, the twentieth, it is **prohibited** for her to engage in sexual intercourse due to the concern that she might have an emission on either day. If **she deviated** from her cycle **twice, to** see an emission on the **twentieth day,** then on both **this** day **and that** day it is **prohibited** for her to engage in intercourse. If she deviates a third time to see on the twentieth she has established for herself a new fixed menstrual cycle.

וַאֲמַרְתְּ לָן עֲלָהּ אֲמַר רַב יְהוּדָה אֲמַר שְׁמוּאֵל: לָא שְׁנָא אֶלָּא חֲמִשָּׁה עָשָׂר לִטְבִילָתָהּ שֶׁהֵן עֶשְׂרִים וּשְׁנַיִם לִרְאִיָּיתָהּ, דְּהָתָם בִּימֵי נִדָּתָהּ קָאֵי לָהּ, אֲבָל חֲמִשָּׁה עָשָׂר לִרְאִיָּיתָהּ, דְּבִימֵי זִיבָתָהּ קָאֵי – לָא קָבְעָה.

Abaye continues: **And you said to us with regard to this** mishna that **Rav Yehuda said** that **Shmuel said: They taught** this *halakha* **only** with regard to a woman who normally experiences bleeding **fifteen** days **from her immersion, which are twenty-two** days **from her sighting** of menstrual blood. This means **that there, she stands in her days of menstruation. But** if she normally experiences bleeding **fifteen** days **from her sighting** of menstrual blood, so **that she stands in her days of *ziva*,** she **has not fixed** a menstrual cycle, and the previous cycle is uprooted even if she deviates from it only once.

אֲמַר רַב פַּפָּא, אֲמַרִיתָא לִשְׁמַעְתָּא קַמֵּיהּ רַב יְהוּדָה מִדִּסְקַרְתָּא: מִקְבַּע לָא קָבְעָה, מֵיחַשׁ מַהוּ דְּנֵיחוּשׁ לָהּ?

§ With regard to the ruling that a woman's menstrual cycle cannot be fixed during her days of *ziva*, **Rav Pappa said: I said** this ***halakha* before Rav Yehuda of Diskarta,** and I asked him for a clarification of the following matter: Granted, **she does not fix** a menstrual cycle during the days of *ziva*, and there is no need for three deviations to uproot her cycle; rather, it is uprooted by even one deviation. But **what is** the *halakha* with regard to whether **we should be concerned** that **she** might experience bleeding? In other words, if she normally experiences bleeding on a particular day during her days of *ziva*, must she avoid engaging in sexual intercourse with her husband on that day out of concern that she might emit blood?

אִישְׁתִּיק וְלָא אֲמַר לֵיהּ וְלָא מִידֵּי. אֲמַר רַב פַּפָּא: נֶחֱזֵי אֲנַן, הָיְתָה לְמוּדָה לִהְיוֹת רוֹאָה לְיוֹם חֲמִשָּׁה עָשָׂר, וְשִׁינְּתָה לְיוֹם עֶשְׂרִים – זֶה וָזֶה אֲסוּרִין.

Rav Yehuda of Diskarta **was silent and did not say anything to** Rav Pappa. Therefore, **Rav Pappa said: Let us see** and try to resolve this **ourselves.** The mishna cited above states: If the woman **was accustomed to see** an emission of blood **on the fifteenth day, and she deviated** from her cycle **to** see an emission on the **twentieth day,** then on both **this** day **and that** day it is **prohibited** for her to engage in sexual intercourse.

Perek **IV**
Daf **39** Amud **b**

וַאֲמַר רַב יְהוּדָה אֲמַר שְׁמוּאֵל, לָא שְׁנָא אֶלָּא חֲמִשָּׁה עָשָׂר לִטְבִילָתָהּ שֶׁהֵן עֶשְׂרִים וּשְׁנַיִם לִרְאִיָּיתָהּ,

**And** with regard to this mishna, **Rav Yehuda said** that **Shmuel said: They taught** this *halakha* **only** with regard to a woman who normally experiences bleeding **fifteen** days **from her immersion, which are twenty-two** days **from her sighting** of menstrual blood, which means that there, she stands in her days of menstruation.

וְשִׁינְּתָה לְיוֹם עֶשְׂרִים וְשִׁבְעָה, דְּכִי הָדְרִי וְאָתוּ עֶשְׂרִין וְתַרְתֵּי – קָיְימָא לָהּ בְּתוֹךְ יְמֵי זִיבָתָהּ, וְקָתָנֵי "זֶה וָזֶה אֲסוּרִין" – אַלְמָא דְּחָיְישִׁינַן לָהּ.

**And** when the mishna states that **she deviated** from her cycle and experienced bleeding on the twentieth day, it means she experienced bleeding twenty days from her immersion, i.e., **twenty-seven days from** her previous sighting, not twenty-two. This means **that when twenty-two days again elapse** from when she usually experiences bleeding, **she stands within** what is now the eleven **days of her *ziva*. And** the mishna **teaches** that both **this,** the twenty-second day, **and that,** the twenty-seventh day, **are prohibited,** despite the fact that the twenty-second day now stands during her days of *ziva*. **Evidently, we are concerned** for an emission of blood during the days of *ziva* if she is accustomed to experiencing bleeding on that day.

**BACKGROUND**

**You yourself told us this *halakha* – אַתְּ אֲמַרְתְּ נִיהֲלָן:** Rav Yosef, who is Rav Yosef bar Ḥiyya, from the third generation of *amora'im*, was one of the greatest *amora'im* of Babylonia. Among his fine qualities he was praised by being called Sinai, i.e., extremely erudite and possessing an extensive knowledge of Mishna and *baraitot* (see *Berakhot* 64a). Unfortunately, a severe illness caused him to forget much of his Torah knowledge and also left him blind. On many occasions the Gemara relates that Rav Yosef was unable to recall *halakhot* that he himself had stated, and had to be reminded of them by his great student Abaye.

**HALAKHA**

**And she deviated, etc. – וְשִׁינְּתָה וכו׳:** If a woman was accustomed to seeing a flow of blood on the twentieth day, and she deviated to see blood on the thirtieth, she is prohibited to engage in intercourse with her husband on both the twentieth and the thirtieth days of the following cycle. Upon the twentieth day after her sighting on the thirtieth, she is prohibited due to her initial fixed time, and if she does not experience bleeding on that day she must be concerned for a discharge on the thirtieth day. If she again sees a flow of blood on the thirtieth day, both days remain prohibited. If she sees blood for a third time on the thirtieth day but not on the twentieth day, the thirtieth becomes her new accustomed time to see, and the twentieth day of the following cycle is permitted. If after experiencing bleeding once or twice on the thirtieth day she emits blood on the twentieth day, her fixed period returns to the twentieth and she is permitted on the thirtieth. The *halakha* is in accordance with the opinion of Rav Yosef, as explained by Abaye (Rambam *Sefer Kedusha, Hilkhot Issurei Bia* 8:8; *Shulḥan Arukh, Yoreh De'a* 189:14).

וְקָסָבַר רַב פַּפָּא: עֶשְׂרִין וְתַרְתֵּין – מֵעֶשְׂרִין וְתַרְתֵּין מָנֵינַן, נִדָּה וּפִתְחָהּ – מֵעֶשְׂרִין וְשִׁבְעָה מָנֵינַן.

The Gemara elaborates: **And Rav Pappa holds** that **we count twenty-two** days of her menstrual cycle **from twenty-two** days, i.e., from when she usually begins to menstruate, whereas **we count the beginning** of the days of **menstruation**[N] **from** day **twenty-seven,** when she actually experiences bleeding. Consequently, the twenty-second day of her normal menstrual cycle falls during the days of *ziva*, according to the actual day of menstruation.

אֲמַר לֵיהּ רַב הוּנָא בְּרֵיהּ דְּרַב יְהוֹשֻׁעַ לְרַב פַּפָּא: מִמַּאי? דִּלְמָא עֶשְׂרִין וְתַרְתֵּין נַמִי מֵעֶשְׂרִין וְשִׁבְעָה מָנֵינַן, דְּכִי הָדְרִי וְאָתוּ עֶשְׂרִין וְתַרְתֵּין – קָיְימָא לַהּ בְּתוֹךְ יְמֵי נִדּוּתָהּ.

**Rav Huna, son of Rav Yehoshua, said to Rav Pappa: From where**[N] do you know this is the correct reckoning of her days? **Perhaps one also counts** those **twenty-two** days **from** day **twenty-seven,** such **that when twenty-two days again arrive** from day twenty-seven, **she stands within her days of menstruation.** Accordingly, there is no proof from the mishna with regard to a sighting during the days of *ziva*.

וְהָכִי נַמִי מִסְתַּבְּרָא. דְּאִי לָא תֵּימָא הָכִי, הַאי תַּרְנְגוֹלְתָּא דְּרָמְיָא יוֹמָא וְכָבְשָׁה יוֹמָא, וְרָמְיָא יוֹמָא וְכָבְשָׁה יוֹמָא, וְכָבְשָׁה תְּרֵי יוֹמֵי וְרָמְיָא חַד יוֹמָא,

Rav Huna, son of Rav Yehoshua, adds: **And so too, it is reasonable** that the twenty-two days are counted from when she actually experiences bleeding. **As if you do not say so,** then consider the case of **this chicken that** normally **lays** an egg on one **day and withholds** an egg the next **day, and lays** an egg on the third **day and withholds** an egg on the fourth **day. And** the chicken deviated from its routine, so that after laying eggs on the first day and third day, it **withheld** an egg for **two days and** then **laid** an egg on **one day,** i.e., on the sixth day.

כִּי הָדְרָה נָקְטָה – כִּדְלְקַמֵּיהּ נָקְטָה אוֹ כִּדְמֵעִיקָּרָא נָקְטָה? עַל כָּרְחָךְ כִּדְלְקַמֵּיהּ נָקְטָה!

When this chicken **again takes hold** of its previous routine and starts laying an egg on one day and withholding an egg on the next, does **it take hold of** the order of the routine **ahead of it,** i.e., will it withhold an egg on the next day, **or** does **it take hold** of its routine **as it** was **from the outset,** so that it will lay an egg on the seventh day, as if there had been no deviation? **Perforce it takes hold of** the order of the routine **ahead of it.** Likewise, a woman who deviated from her normal menstrual cycle counts the days of her cycle according to the order of the cycle ahead of her, i.e., from the time that she experiences bleeding.

אֲמַר לֵיהּ רַב פַּפָּא, אֶלָּא הָא דַּאֲמַר רֵישׁ לָקִישׁ: אִשָּׁה קוֹבַעַת לָהּ וֶסֶת בְּתוֹךְ יְמֵי זִיבָתָהּ, וְאֵין אִשָּׁה קוֹבַעַת לָהּ וֶסֶת בְּתוֹךְ יְמֵי נִדּוּתָהּ. וְרַבִּי יוֹחָנָן אָמַר: אִשָּׁה קוֹבַעַת לָהּ וֶסֶת בְּתוֹךְ יְמֵי נִדּוּתָהּ, הֵיכִי דָּמֵי?

**Rav Pappa said to** Rav Huna, son of Rav Yehoshua: **But** if so, a question arises with regard to **that which Reish Lakish said: A woman fixes** a menstrual **cycle for herself during the days of her *ziva*, but a woman does not fix** a menstrual **cycle for herself during the days of her menstruation,** i.e., when she is already a menstruating woman. **And Rabbi Yoḥanan says: A woman fixes** a menstrual **cycle for herself during the days of her menstruation.** One could ask: **What are the circumstances** of this dispute? Rabbi Yoḥanan cannot be referring to a case where all her sightings occurred while she was a menstruating woman, as everyone agrees that a woman's menstrual cycle is not fixed in such a situation (see 11a).

לָאו כְּגוֹן דַּחֲזַאי רֵישׁ יַרְחָא, וְחַמְשָׁא בְּיַרְחָא, וְרֵישׁ יַרְחָא, וְחַמְשָׁא בְּיַרְחָא, וְהַשְׁתָּא חֲזַאי בְּחַמְשָׁא בְּיַרְחָא, וּבְרֵישׁ יַרְחָא לָא חֲזַאי,

Rather, **is it not** referring to a case **where she saw** blood on the **first of the month; and** then again on **the fifth of** that same **month,** when she was a menstruating woman; **and** subsequently she saw blood on the **first of the** next **month and** then again on **the fifth of** that **month; and now** in the third month she **saw** blood **on the fifth of the month but on the first of the month she did not see** blood? In such a situation, the woman experienced an emission of blood on the fifth of the month for three consecutive months.

וְקָאָמַר: אִשָּׁה קוֹבַעַת לָהּ וֶסֶת בְּתוֹךְ יְמֵי נִדּוּתָהּ – אַלְמָא, מֵרֵישׁ יַרְחָא מָנֵינָא!

Rav Pappa concludes: **And** it is with regard to this case that Rabbi Yoḥanan **says: A woman fixes** a menstrual **cycle for herself during the days of her menstruation.** Although she was not actually a menstruating woman before she experienced bleeding on the fifth day of the third month, this is nevertheless considered a sighting during her days of menstruation. **Evidently, one counts** her menstrual cycle **from the first of the month,**[N] despite the fact that she did not actually experience bleeding. Likewise, with regard to the case involving twenty-two days, one counts from when she generally experiences bleeding, not from the day she emitted blood in practice.

NOTES

**The beginning of the days of menstruation – נִדָּה וּפִתְחָהּ:** According to Rashi, this phrase is referring to her entire menstrual cycle, i.e., the days of menstruation and *ziva* combined, as counted from the first day of her cycle. Alternatively, it means the day on which she is certain that she experienced bleeding, from when she begins to count her days of menstruation. Others explain that this phrase, which literally means: A menstruating woman and her opening, is referring euphemistically to the three places in a woman's body where the blood she emits can be found: The room; the corridor; and the upper story (Rabbeinu Yona).

**From where – מִמַּאי:** The early commentaries disagree with regard to the opinion of Rav Huna, son of Rav Yehoshua. Some maintain he is merely rejecting Rav Pappa's proof but not Rav Pappa's opinion, as indicated by the word: Perhaps (Ritva; Meiri). Others explain that if Rav Huna goes to the trouble of rejecting Rav Pappa's proof from the mishna he certainly disagrees with his conclusion. Determining if Rav Huna disagrees with Rav Pappa is significant for the following reason: Since the *halakhot* that determine a woman's fixed period apply by rabbinic law, one would follow Rav Huna's lenient ruling and not be concerned for establishing a menstrual cycle during the days of *ziva*, as neither opinion can be inferred from the mishna (Ramban on 39a; see Ra'avad in *Ba'alei HaNefesh*; *Beit Yosef* on *Yoreh De'a* 189).

**One counts her menstrual cycle from the first of the month – מֵרֵישׁ יַרְחָא מָנֵינָא:** The reason a woman would count this way is that according to Rav Pappa the day of the New Moon causes her to experience bleeding (*Tosafot*; see *Tosafot* on *Bava Kamma* 37b). This is similar to the Gemara's statement on 38a that the blast of the shofar announcing the new moon is the decisive cause of her beginning to experience bleeding. According to some commentaries, the principle in this regard is that if the earthly court sanctifies the month, the heavenly court follows suit (see *Rosh HaShana* 8b), and this applies even to the effect of the heavenly court on the workings of the human body (Jerusalem Talmud, *Ketubot* 5:2).

אֲמַר לֵיהּ: לָא, הָכִי אֲמַר רַבִּי יוֹחָנָן: כְּגוֹן דַּחֲזַאי רֵישׁ יַרְחָא, וְרֵישׁ יַרְחָא, וְעֶשְׂרִין וַחֲמִשָּׁה בְּיַרְחָא, וְרֵישׁ יַרְחָא, דְּאָמְרִינַן דְּמֵי יְתֵירֵי הוּא דְּאִתּוֹסְפוּ בָּהּ.

Rav Huna, son of Rav Yehoshua, **said to** Rav Pappa: These are **not** the circumstances of the dispute. Rather, **this** is what **Rabbi Yoḥanan said:** The dispute is referring to a case **where she saw** blood on the **first of the month; and** then again on the **first of the** next **month, and** then again on **the twenty-fifth** day **of** that **month; and** again on the **first of the** next **month,** which occurs during her days of menstruation. Rabbi Yoḥanan maintains that although she is in her days of menstruation, this sighting on the first of the third month serves to fix her menstrual cycle, **as we say** with regard to the sighting on the twenty-fifth day of the previous month that **it is extra blood that gathered inside her.**[N] Therefore, it does not negate her regular cycle.

וְכֵן כִּי אֲתָא רָבִין וְכָל נָחוֹתֵי יַמָּא, אַמְרוּהָ כְּרַב הוּנָא בְּרֵיהּ דְּרַב יְהוֹשֻׁעַ.

The Gemara notes: **And likewise, when Ravin and all** the **seafarers**[B] **came**[N] from Eretz Yisrael to Babylonia and transmitted statements of Rabbi Yoḥanan, **they said** this statement of Rabbi Yoḥanan **in accordance with** the explanation of **Rav Huna, son of Rav Yehoshua.**

הדרן עלך בנות כותים

**NOTES**

**It is extra blood that gathered inside her – דְּמֵי יְתֵירֵי הוּא דְּאִתּוֹסְפוּ בָּהּ:** The early commentaries explain that as a result of the collection of a large amount of blood in her body, some of it was emitted on the twenty-fifth day of the month. But when she once again sees a flow of blood on the first of the following month, this is clearly the beginning of her actual menstrual cycle (Rashba; *Torat HaBayit*).

**When Ravin and all seafarers came, etc. – כִּי אֲתָא רָבִין וְכָל נָחוֹתֵי יַמָּא וכו׳:** The early commentaries write that the *halakha* should indeed follow the opinion of Rav Huna, son of Rav Yehoshua, with regard to whether a woman counts from the day she actually experienced bleeding, or from the menstrual cycle, despite the fact that she did not experience bleeding. The *halakha* is not in accordance with the opinion of Rav Pappa, following the statement of Ravin and the other scholars who came from Eretz Yisrael (Ran; see Rambam *Sefer Kedusha, Hilkhot Issurei Bia* 8:8; *Shulḥan Arukh, Yoreh De'a* 189:14).

**BACKGROUND**

**Seafarers – נָחוֹתֵי יַמָּא:** In this context the term is referring to Sages who came from Eretz Yisrael to Babylonia for commercial purposes. When they arrived in Babylonia they would recite statements of *halakha* they had heard in Eretz Yisrael.

# Summary of **Perek IV**

With regard to the definition of a woman's "time of her menstruation" (Leviticus 15:25), it was determined in this chapter that a woman is rendered a menstruating woman immediately upon experiencing a menstrual discharge. Whether she continued to emit blood or the emission ceased immediately after the initial discharge, she is impure as a menstruating woman for seven days. Assuming her emissions ceased before the end of these seven days, she immerses in a ritual bath on the eve of the eighth day and is then deemed pure. These seven days of menstruation are referred to in the verse as the "time of her menstruation."

The period called: "Not in the time of her menstruation" (Leviticus 15:25), is the period of eleven days following the days of menstruation. If a woman experiences bleeding during this time, the blood is not considered the blood of menstruation but the blood of *ziva*, and she is rendered a *zava*. The Sages call this period the days of *ziva*, as although a woman remains ritually pure during this time provided she does not experience a discharge, these eleven days constitute the only period in which she may be rendered a *zava*.

At the conclusion of her days of *ziva*, the woman once again enters a period in which any blood she sees renders her a menstruating woman. The Sages call this period the days of menstruation, as any blood she sees during this time renders her a menstruating woman for seven days. When she again experiences bleeding she becomes impure for seven days. When seven days are over she again enters the days of *ziva*. Accordingly, the days of *ziva* are also referred to as the course of eleven days between menstrual periods.

The Sages distinguish between a woman who experienced bleeding on one or two days during the days of *ziva* and one who experienced blood on three consecutive days during this period. A woman who emitted blood on only one or two days is called a lesser *zava*, and she must observe the *halakhot* of a woman who observes a clean day for each day she experiences a discharge, i.e., she waits one day to see if her emissions have ceased; if they have indeed ceased she immerses in the evening and is deemed pure. A woman who experienced a discharge of blood on three consecutive days is rendered a greater *zava*, who remains ritually impure until she has successfully counted seven clean days. After counting seven clean days she immerses in a ritual bath, and on the following day she brings an offering and is deemed ritually pure.

Since a woman may be rendered a *zava* only during her days of *ziva*, if she experienced a discharge on the tenth and eleventh days of *ziva*, and again on the following day, she is not rendered a greater *zava*. Rather, this third emission is considered the beginning of her days of menstruation.

It was also taught in this chapter that a woman is not required to examine herself during her days of *ziva* as she must during the days of menstruation, since it is uncommon for a woman to experience an emission of blood during her days of *ziva*. It is typical for a woman to experience bleeding during her days of menstruation.

With regard to a woman who experiences an emission of blood accompanied by labor pains, it was concluded that if the emission occurred during her days of menstruation she is rendered a menstruating woman; if it occurred during the days of *ziva* she remains pure, as the emission is attributed to an external factor, e.g., childbirth, and such an emission does not render a woman a *zava*.

Other matters relating to the *halakhot* of ritual purity were addressed in this chapter, in particular the status of Samaritan women, who are considered ritually impure from birth, as well as the status of Sadducee women.

# Introduction to **Perek V**

*If a woman conceives and gives birth to a male, then she shall be impure seven days; as in the days of her menstrual flow she shall be impure. And on the eighth day the flesh of his foreskin shall be circumcised. And she shall continue in the blood of purification thirty-three days; she shall touch no consecrated item, nor come into the Sanctuary, until the days of her purification are fulfilled. But if she gives birth to a female, then she shall be impure two weeks, as in her menstruation; and she shall continue in the blood of purification sixty-six days. And when the days of her purification are fulfilled, for a son, or for a daughter, she shall bring a lamb of its first year for a burnt offering, and a young pigeon, or a dove, for a sin offering, to the door of the Tent of Meeting, to the priest.*

(Leviticus 12:2–6)

*And if a woman has an issue, and her issue in her flesh is blood, she shall be in her menstruation seven days, and whoever touches her shall be impure until the evening.*

(Leviticus 15:19)

One of the *halakhot* of ritual impurity that applies uniquely to a woman, apart from the impurity of menstruation and of a *zava*, is the impurity of a woman after childbirth. The Torah states that a woman who gives birth has the status of a primary source of ritual impurity, and she is prohibited from engaging in intercourse with her husband just as when she menstruates. This is the *halakha* whether she gives birth to a boy or to a girl, and it applies even if the baby is stillborn.

This status of impurity differs from that of menstruation in that it is not a result of the emission of blood. Even if the woman did not emit blood at all during the birth, this impurity status still applies. Another distinctive feature of this impurity is that there is a difference between the birth of a boy and of a girl: If the woman gives birth to a boy she is impure for seven days, whereas if she bears a girl her impurity lasts for fourteen days. These are called the days of impurity.

Once the days of impurity have concluded, the woman enters a period termed the days of purity. It is called this because even if she emits blood during this time, she is not rendered impure by Torah law, neither as a menstruating woman nor as a *zava*, and she remains permitted to engage in intercourse with her husband. Like the days of impurity, the length of this period depends on whether a woman gave birth to a boy or a girl: It lasts thirty-three days in the case of a boy and sixty-six days in the case of a girl. When the days of purity end, she is still not entirely pure with regard to partaking of *teruma* and consecrated food or entering the Temple until she brings the requisite offerings.

The Torah does not state the *halakha* of a birth via caesarean section. In such a case, it is necessary for the Sages to determine the status of the mother with regard to her days of impurity and days of purity, as well as her offerings.

Another issue that requires clarification is the minimum age from which the ritual impurity of a menstruating woman and *ziva* apply.

These are the main issues discussed in this chapter.

מתני׳ יוצא דופן – אין יושבין עליו יְמֵי טוּמְאָה וִימֵי טָהֳרָה, וְאֵין חַיָּיבִין עָלָיו קָרְבָּן. רַבִּי שִׁמְעוֹן אוֹמֵר: הֲרֵי זֶה כְּיָלוּד.

**MISHNA** After the birth of an offspring by caesarean **section,**[HB] the mother **does not observe** seven or fourteen **days of impurity**[N] **and** thirty-three or sixty-six **days of purity for** male and female offspring, respectively, **and she is not obligated to** bring **for it** the **offering** brought by a woman after childbirth. **Rabbi Shimon says:** The halakhic status of **that** offspring is **like** that of an offspring **born** in a standard birth.

כָּל הַנָּשִׁים מְטַמְּאוֹת בְּבַיִת הַחִיצוֹן, שֶׁנֶּאֱמַר ״דָּם יִהְיֶה זוֹבָהּ בִּבְשָׂרָהּ״. אֲבָל הַזָּב וּבַעַל קֶרִי – אֵינָן מְטַמְּאִין, עַד שֶׁתֵּצֵא טוּמְאָתָן לַחוּץ.

**All women become ritually impure** with the flow of blood from the uterus **into the outer chamber,**[H] i.e., the vagina, although it did not leave the woman's body, **as it is stated: "And her issue in her flesh shall be blood,** she shall be in her menstruation seven days" (Leviticus 15:19), indicating that even if her menstrual blood remains in her flesh, she becomes impure. **But one who experiences a gonorrhea-like discharge** [*zav*] **and one who experiences a seminal emission**[H] **do not become ritually impure until their** emission of **impurity emerges outside** the body.

הָיָה אוֹכֵל בִּתְרוּמָה, וְהִרְגִּישׁ שֶׁנִּזְדַּעְזְעוּ אֵבָרָיו – אוֹחֵז בָּאַמָּה, וּבוֹלֵעַ אֶת הַתְּרוּמָה. וּמְטַמְּאִין בְּכׇל שֶׁהוּא, אֲפִילּוּ כְּעֵין הַחַרְדָּל וּבְפָחוֹת מִכֵּן.

If a priest **was partaking of *teruma*,** the portion of the produce designated for the priest, **and sensed a quaking of his limbs**[H] indicating that a seminal emission was imminent, he should firmly **hold** his **penis** to prevent the emission from leaving his body, **and swallow the *teruma*** while ritually pure. **And** the emission of a *zav* and a seminal emission **impart impurity in any amount,**[HN] **even like** the size of **a mustard seed or even smaller than that.**[N]

גמ׳ אָמַר רַבִּי מָנִי בַּר פָּטִישׁ: מַאי טַעְמַיְיהוּ דְּרַבָּנַן, אָמַר קְרָא ״אִשָּׁה כִּי תַזְרִיעַ וְיָלְדָה זָכָר״ – עַד שֶׁתֵּלֵד בְּמָקוֹם שֶׁהִיא מַזְרַעַת.

**GEMARA** The mishna cites a dispute as to whether or not a birth by caesarean section is considered a birth with regard to the *halakhot* pertaining to childbirth. **Rabbi Mani bar Patish**[P] **said: What is the reason** for the opinion **of the Rabbis,** who say that it is not considered a birth? It is because **the verse states: "If a woman emitted seed and gave birth to a male,** then she shall be impure seven days… And when the days of her purification are fulfilled, for a son, or for a daughter, she shall bring a lamb of the first year for a burnt offering, and a pigeon or a dove for a sin offering" (Leviticus 12:2–6). It is derived from here that the *halakhot* mentioned in that passage do not apply **unless she gives birth through the place where she emits seed.**

וְרַבִּי שִׁמְעוֹן – הַהִיא, דַּאֲפִילּוּ לֹא יָלְדָה אֶלָּא כְּעֵין שֶׁהִזְרִיעָה, אִמּוֹ טְמֵאָה לֵידָה.

The Gemara asks: **And** how does **Rabbi Shimon** interpret the term "emitted seed"? The Gemara answers: **That** word serves to teach **that even** if **she gave birth only** to a fluid that **resembles the seed that she emitted,** i.e., the fetus died and entirely decomposed and dissolved before emerging, **its mother is ritually impure** due to **childbirth.**

**NOTES**

**The mother does not observe seven or fourteen days of impurity** – **אֵין יוֹשְׁבִין עָלָיו יְמֵי טוּמְאָה**: A mother is ritually pure after a caesarean birth, even if blood emerged together with the child. The reason is that vaginal blood alone renders a woman impure, as Rabbi Yoḥanan states later in this chapter (41b). The blood itself is ritually impure, in accordance with the opinion that all blood originating in the uterus is impure; see 16a (*Divrei Ḥamudot*; *Shulḥan Arukh*, *Yoreh De'a* 194:14).

**Impart impurity in any amount** – **מְטַמְּאִין בְּכׇל שֶׁהוּא**: This is referring to the aforementioned emission of a *zav* and a seminal emission: Even the slightest amount of emission of these fluids renders the one who emits them impure (Rambam's Commentary on the Mishna; Rabbi Ovadya Bartenura). According to some of the later commentaries this also refers to menstrual blood, which was mentioned earlier in the mishna as well (Rashash; see *Baḥ*, explaining Rashi).

**Even like the size of a mustard seed or even smaller than that** – **אֲפִילּוּ כְּעֵין הַחַרְדָּל וּבְפָחוֹת מִכֵּן**: Rabbi Zeira taught: The daughters of Israel have accepted upon themselves the stringency that even if they emit a drop of blood as small as a mustard seed, they observe seven clean days before undergoing purification (66a). The commentaries explain that this stringency applies to blood even smaller than the size of a mustard seed (*Shakh*, citing *Agur* and *Sha'arei Dura*).

**HALAKHA**

**Caesarean section** – **יוֹצֵא דוֹפֶן**: In the case of birth by caesarean section, if no blood emerged through the vagina, the mother is ritually pure from the impurities of childbirth, menstruation, and *ziva*, in accordance with the opinion of the first *tanna* (Rambam *Sefer Kedusha*, *Hilkhot Issurei Bia* 10:5; *Shulḥan Arukh*, *Yoreh De'a* 194:14).

**All women become ritually impure with the flow of blood from the uterus into the outer chamber** – **כׇּל הַנָּשִׁים מְטַמְּאוֹת בְּבַיִת הַחִיצוֹן**: A woman becomes ritually impure as soon as blood emerges from the uterus, even if it has not yet emerged from the body. This is the *halakha* only if the woman feels the emergence of the blood from the uterus; if she does not feel it, she is not impure by Torah law. Some hold that she is impure by rabbinic law (Rambam *Sefer Kedusha*, *Hilkhot Issurei Bia* 5:2; *Shulḥan Arukh*, *Yoreh De'a* 183:1 and *Shakh* there).

**A *zav* and one who experiences a seminal emission, etc.** – **הַזָּב וּבַעַל קֶרִי וכו׳**: One who experiences a seminal emission is ritually impure only when the semen emerges from his body (Rambam *Sefer Tahara*, *Hilkhot She'ar Avot HaTumot* 5:1).

**If a priest was partaking of *teruma* and sensed a quaking of his limbs** – **הָיָה אוֹכֵל בִּתְרוּמָה וְהִרְגִּישׁ שֶׁנִּזְדַּעְזְעוּ אֵבָרָיו**: If one was partaking of *teruma* and he sensed that his limbs were quaking in the manner that precedes a seminal emission, he should firmly hold his penis to prevent the emission from leaving his body, and swallow the *teruma* (Rambam *Sefer Zera'im*, *Hilkhot Terumot* 7:4).

**Impart impurity in any amount** – **מְטַמְּאִין בְּכׇל שֶׁהוּא**: Blood of menstruation, blood of *ziva*, and blood of childbirth all impart impurity to those who touch or move it, even if it is the most minute amount of blood (Rambam *Sefer Kedusha*, *Hilkhot Issurei Bia* 5:1 and *Sefer Tahara*, *Hilkhot Metamei Mishkav UMoshav* 1:8; *Shulḥan Arukh*, *Yoreh De'a* 183:1).

**BACKGROUND**

**Birth by caesarean section [*yotze dofen*]** – **יוֹצֵא דוֹפֶן**: The term *yotze dofen*, which literally means that which emerges from the side of the body, refers to an offspring born not in the natural way, but by medical intervention through an incision of the abdomen or side. Such procedures were known in ancient times, but it is not mentioned in outside sources as an option for a living woman; rather, it was carried out only in cases where the mother had died carrying a live fetus. It is only in modern times that it became possible to perform such an operation on a living woman, who would survive the procedure. Nevertheless, the Talmud's discussions of this procedure indicate that the practice was carried out among the Jews even on living women.

**PERSONALITIES**

**Rabbi Mani bar Patish** – **רַבִּי מָנִי בַּר פָּטִישׁ**: A second-generation *amora* who lived in Eretz Yisrael, Rabbi Mani bar Patish is apparently identical to the Sage Rabbi Mana, who is mentioned frequently in the Jerusalem Talmud. In the Babylonian Talmud he is referred to by the slightly altered form Mani, along with the name of his father, Patish. He was a friend of Reish Lakish, and the two of them would discuss talmudic topics in the presence of Rabbi Yoḥanan. Rabbi Mani was one of the preservers and transmitters of the Torah knowledge of Rabbi Yannai.

וְרַבִּי שִׁמְעוֹן מַאי טַעְמֵיהּ? אֲמַר רֵישׁ לָקִישׁ: אֲמַר קְרָא ״תֵּלֵד״ – לְרַבּוֹת יוֹצֵא דוֹפֶן.

The Gemara further asks: **And Rabbi Shimon, what is the reason** for **his** opinion that the *halakhot* of childbirth apply in the case of a caesarean section? **Reish Lakish said** that it is because the **verse states:** "But if **she gives birth** to a female" (Leviticus 12:5). The term "she gives birth" is superfluous in the context of the passage, as it was mentioned previously, and it therefore serves **to include** the birth of an offspring by **caesarean section.**

וְרַבָּנַן – הַאי מִבָּעֵי לֵיהּ לְרַבּוֹת טוּמְטוּם וְאַנְדְּרוֹגִינוֹס. דְּסָלְקָא דַּעְתָּךְ אָמִינָא: ״זָכָר״ וּ״נְקֵבָה״ כְּתִיב – זָכָר וַדַּאי, נְקֵבָה וַדָּאִית, וְלֹא טוּמְטוּם וְאַנְדְּרוֹגִינוֹס, קָא מַשְׁמַע לָן.

The Gemara asks: **And** what do **the Rabbis** derive from this superfluous expression? The Gemara answers: In their opinion, **that** expression **is necessary to include** the birth of a child **whose sexual organs are indeterminate** [*tumtum*] **or a hermaphrodite. As** it might **enter your mind to say** that as the words **"male"** (Leviticus 12:2) **and "female"** (Leviticus 12:5) are **written** in the passage, these *halakhot* apply only to **a definite male** and **a definite female, but not** to **a *tumtum* or a hermaphrodite.** Therefore, the term "she gives birth" **teaches us** that it is the birth itself, not the sex of the offspring, that matters.

וְרַבִּי שִׁמְעוֹן – נָפְקָא לֵיהּ מִדְּתָנֵי בַּר לִיוַאי. דְּתָנֵי בַּר לִיוַאי: ״לְבֵן״ – לְבֵן מִכָּל מָקוֹם, ״לְבַת״ – לְבַת מִכָּל מָקוֹם.

The Gemara asks: **And** from where does **Rabbi Shimon** derive that these *halakhot* apply to a *tumtum* and a hermaphrodite? The Gemara answers: **He derives it from** that **which bar Livai teaches, as bar Livai teaches** a *baraita* that discusses the verse: "And when the days of her purity are fulfilled, for a son, or for a daughter" (Leviticus 12:6). Since the verse uses the terms "son" and "daughter," rather than male and female, it is derived from the term **"for a son"** that these *halakhot* apply **to a son in any case,** even if his masculinity is not definite. Similarly, the term **"for a daughter"** teaches that these *halakhot* apply **to a daughter in any case,** even if her femininity is not definite.

וְרַבָּנַן – הַאי מִבָּעֵי לֵיהּ לְחַיֵּיב עַל כָּל בֵּן וּבֵן, וּלְחַיֵּיב עַל כָּל בַּת וּבַת.

The Gemara asks: **And** what do **the Rabbis** derive from the terms "for a son" and "for a daughter"? The Gemara answers: In their opinion, **that** term **is necessary to obligate** the mother to bring an offering **for each and every son** to whom she gives birth, rather than one offering after having given birth to several sons; **and likewise to obligate** her to bring an offering **for each and every daughter** to whom she gives birth.

וְרַבִּי שִׁמְעוֹן – נָפְקָא לֵיהּ מִדְּתָנֵי תַּנָּא קַמֵּיהּ דְּרַב שֵׁשֶׁת: ״זֹאת תּוֹרַת הַיֹּלֶדֶת״ – מְלַמֵּד שֶׁמְּבִיאָה קָרְבָּן אֶחָד עַל וְלָדוֹת הַרְבֵּה. יָכוֹל תָּבִיא עַל לֵידָה וְעַל זִיבָה כְּאַחַת?

The Gemara asks: **And** from where does **Rabbi Shimon** derive this *halakha*? The Gemara answers that **he derives it from** a *baraita* **that a *tanna* taught before Rav Sheshet:** The verse states: **"This is the law for one who gives birth,** whether to a male or a female" (Leviticus 12:7). This **teaches that** a woman **brings a single offering for many offspring**[H] born within a short time, e.g., after a multiple birth. One **might** have thought that **she may bring** an offering **for** her **childbirth and** an offering **for** an irregular **discharge** of blood from the uterus [*ziva*], in a case where she is required to bring one, **as one,** i.e., that she may fulfill her two obligations with a single offering.

אֶלָּא יוֹלֶדֶת דְּאָכְלָה דָּם, וְיוֹלֶדֶת דְּאָכְלָה חֵלֶב – בְּחַד קָרְבָּן תִּסְגֵּי לָהּ?!

The Gemara interrupts the *baraita* to raise a difficulty: **But** how could it possibly enter your mind that a woman may bring one offering for two obligations? In the case of **a woman after childbirth who consumed blood, or a woman after childbirth who ate** forbidden **fat, is one offering sufficient for her?** One who eats blood or forbidden fat is obligated to bring a sin offering for atonement (see Leviticus 7:25–27). There is no reason to think that a woman after childbirth, who is required to bring a sin offering for a reason other than her childbirth, may bring one offering for both obligations. Similarly, there are no grounds for suggesting that a single offering might suffice for both childbirth and *ziva*.

## HALAKHA

**This teaches that she brings a single offering for many offspring – מְלַמֵּד שֶׁמְּבִיאָה קָרְבָּן אֶחָד עַל וְלָדוֹת הַרְבֵּה:** One who gives birth, whether to live or dead offspring, to one child or several children, may bring a single childbirth offering for all these births. This is the *halakha* only if all the births occurred within the period of postpartum purification of the first child, i.e., forty days for a male child and eighty days for a female. Any birth that occurs after this period of time requires its own offering, in accordance with the *baraita* that the *tanna* taught before Rav Sheshet (Rambam *Sefer Korbanot*, *Hilkhot Meḥusrei Kappara* 1:8).

אֶלָּא: יָכוֹל תָּבִיא עַל לֵידָה שֶׁלִּפְנֵי מְלֹאת וְעַל לֵידָה שֶׁלְּאַחַר מְלֹאת כְּאַחַת – תַּלְמוּד לוֹמַר ״זֹאת״. וְרַבָּנַן – אַף עַל גַּב דִּכְתִיב ״זֹאת״, אִיצְטְרִיךְ ״לְבֵן אוֹ לְבַת״,

**Rather,** the statement of the *baraita* should be revised, as follows: One **might** have thought that a woman **may bring** an offering **for a childbirth that** occurred **before the completion** of her term of postpartum purity, **and for** a second **childbirth that** happened **after the completion** of that period, **as one,** i.e., she may fulfill her two obligations with a single offering. Therefore, **the verse states:** "**This** is the law for one who gives birth" (Leviticus 12:7), indicating that each birth, unless it occurred within the period of purity following another birth, requires its own offering. The Gemara asks: **And** how do **the Rabbis** respond to this derivation? The Gemara answers that in their opinion, **even though it is written: "This** is the law," **it was** still **necessary** for the verse to state: **"For a son, or for a daughter."**

סָלְקָא דַּעְתָּךְ אָמִינָא: בִּתְרֵי עִיבּוּרֵי (דְּחַד הָוֵי נֵפֶל), אֲבָל בְּחַד עִבּוּרָא, כְּגוֹן יְהוּדָה וְחִזְקִיָּה בְּנֵי רַבִּי חִיָּיא, אֵימַר בְּחַד קָרְבָּן סַגִּי לָהּ – קָא מַשְׁמַע לָן.

The Gemara explains: Had the Torah stated only the verse: "This is the law," it might **enter your mind to say** that one offering does not suffice for two births that occurred as a result **of two pregnancies,** as the second one was a miscarriage whose conception occurred during the woman's period of purity following the first birth. **But** if both births occurred as a result **of one pregnancy, such as** in the case of **Yehuda and Ḥizkiyya,** the twin **sons of Rabbi Ḥiyya,** who were born three months apart (see 27a), **I would say that one offering** for both births is **sufficient for her.** Therefore, the verse "for a son, or for a daughter" **teaches us** otherwise.

אָמַר רַבִּי יוֹחָנָן: וּמוֹדֶה רַבִּי שִׁמְעוֹן בְּקָדָשִׁים – שֶׁאֵינוֹ קָדוֹשׁ. מַאי טַעֲמָא, גָּמַר לֵידָה לֵידָה מִבְּכוֹר, מַה הָתָם – פֶּטֶר רֶחֶם, אַף כָּאן – פֶּטֶר רֶחֶם.

§ **Rabbi Yoḥanan says: And Rabbi Shimon,** who maintains that childbirth by caesarean section has the halakhic status of regular childbirth, **concedes in** the case of **consecrated** animals[H] **that** if one attempts to consecrate an animal born by caesarean section, it **is not consecrated. What is the reason** for this opinion? **He derives** it by means of a verbal analogy **from** the word **birth** that is written with regard to consecrated animals (see Leviticus 22:27), and the word **birth** that is written in connection with a **firstborn** animal (see Deuteronomy 15:19). **Just as there,** in the case of the firstborn, the *halakhot* apply specifically to one who **"opens the womb"** (Exodus 13:15), **so too here,** in the case of consecrated animals, the *halakhot* apply only to one who **opens the womb.**

וְלִגְמַר לֵידָה לֵידָה מֵאָדָם, מַה הָתָם – יוֹצֵא דוֹפֶן, אַף כָּאן – יוֹצֵא דוֹפֶן?

The Gemara objects: **And let** Rabbi Shimon **derive** a different conclusion by a similar verbal analogy, as the word **birth** is written with regard to consecrated animals, and the word **birth** is also written **with regard to a person,** i.e., a woman who gives birth (see Leviticus 12:2): **Just as there,** in the case of humans, childbirth by **caesarean section** has the status of childbirth according to Rabbi Shimon, **so too here,** in the case of consecrated animals, an animal born by **caesarean section** is considered the same as an animal born via a natural birth.

מִסְתַּבְּרָא, מִבְּכוֹר הֲוָה לֵיהּ לְמֵילַף, שֶׁכֵּן ״אִמּוֹ״ מֵ״אִמּוֹ״. אַדְּרַבָּה, מֵאָדָם הֲוָה לֵיהּ לְמֵילַף, שֶׁכֵּן פָּשׁוּט מִפָּשׁוּט!

The Gemara answers: It **is** more **reasonable for** Rabbi Shimon **to derive** the *halakha* of a consecrated animal **from a firstborn** animal, rather than from the *halakha* of childbirth, **as** it is written with regard to a consecrated animal: **"Its mother"** (Leviticus 22:27), and it is likewise written **with regard to** a firstborn animal: **"Its mother"** (Exodus 22:29). The Gemara objects: **On the contrary, he should derive** it **from human** births, **as** that would be a derivation of the *halakha* concerning consecrated animals that are **ordinary,** i.e., not firstborns, **from** the *halakha* concerning human births of children that are **ordinary,** and not firstborns.

אֶלָּא, מִבְּכוֹר הֲוָה לֵיהּ לְמֵילַף, שֶׁכֵּן: אֵם, בֶּהֱמַת קֳדָשִׁים, פִּגּוּל, נוֹתָר, וְטָמֵא.

The Gemara adopts a different line of reasoning: **Rather,** Rabbi Shimon **should derive** it **from a firstborn** animal, **as** they both share the following five characteristics: In both cases it is written: "its **mother"**; both are cases of **a sacrificial animal;** both are subject to ***piggul,*** the disqualification of an offering through improper intent during its sacrificial rites; both are subject to ***notar,*** the disqualification of sacrificial meat after a prescribed time; **and** finally, both are subject to disqualification by becoming **ritually impure.** By contrast, humans do not share any of these characteristics.

HALAKHA

**And Rabbi Shimon concedes in the case of consecrated animals – וּמוֹדֶה רַבִּי שִׁמְעוֹן בְּקָדָשִׁים:** An animal born by caesarean section may not be used as an offering, even if it is unblemished. This ruling is unanimous, as even Rabbi Shimon, who maintains that caesarean births are like regular births, agrees that this does not apply to sacrificial animals, as stated by Rabbi Yoḥanan (Ramban *Sefer Avoda, Hilkhot Issurei Mizbe'aḥ* 3:4, 11).

אַדְּרַבָּה, מֵאָדָם הֲוָה לֵיהּ לְמֵילַף, שֶׁכֵּן: פָּשׁוּט, זָכָר, קָדוֹשׁ, בְּמַתָּנָה! הָנָךְ נְפִישָׁן.

The Gemara objects: **On the contrary, he should derive** it **from human** births, **as** both cases share the following four characteristics: They are both instances of **ordinary,** non-firstborn offspring; they both apply to the offspring of either sex, and are not exclusively **males;** they are both dealing with offspring that are not automatically **sacred** at birth; and they both apply **to** offspring that are not **a gift** to a priest, but belong to an individual non-priest. By contrast, firstborn animals do not share any of these characteristics. The Gemara answers that the comparison to firstborn animals is preferable to the comparison to human childbirth because **these** shared characteristics **are more** numerous. The comparison to consecrated animals includes five shared characteristics, whereas the comparison to human births involves only four.

אָמַר רַב חִיָּיא בְּרֵיהּ דְּרַב הוּנָא מִשְּׁמֵיהּ דְּרָבָא: תַּנְיָא דְּמְסַיֵּיעַ לֵיהּ לְרַבִּי יוֹחָנָן, רַבִּי יְהוּדָה אוֹמֵר: ״זֹאת תּוֹרַת הָעֹלָה הִיא הָעֹלָה״ – הֲרֵי אֵלּוּ שְׁלֹשָׁה מִיעוּטִין,

**Rav Ḥiyya, son of Rav Huna, said in the name of Rava:** A *baraita* **is taught which supports** the statement **of Rabbi Yoḥanan: Rabbi Yehuda says: "This is the law of the burnt offering; that is the burnt offering** that goes up on the pyre upon the altar" (Leviticus 6:2). It is derived from this verse that the *halakha* is that if a part of a disqualified offering is taken up to the altar it should be burned there, rather than taken down, despite its unfit status. **There are three** expressions which indicate **exclusion** in this verse: The term "this is," which indicates this one and not another one; the term "that is," indicating that one and not another one; and the term "the burnt offering" instead of "a burnt offering."



פְּרָט לְנִשְׁחֲטָה בַּלַּיְלָה, וְשֶׁנִּשְׁפַּךְ דָּמָהּ, וְשֶׁיָּצָא דָּמָהּ חוּץ לַקְּלָעִים – שֶׁאִם עָלְתָה תֵּרֵד.

These three expressions allude **to the exclusion of** the following three cases from the above principle: An offering that was disqualified because it was **slaughtered at night,**[H] **and** an offering **whose blood spilled** before it could be sprinkled on the altar, **and** an offering **whose blood** was disqualified because it **was taken outside the curtains** [*lakela'im*][L] surrounding the courtyard of the Tabernacle in the wilderness, i.e., it left the Temple courtyard. These three cases are excluded, **as** in these instances, **if** parts of the disqualified offering **ascended,** i.e., were brought upon the altar, **they must descend,** i.e., be taken down.

רַבִּי שִׁמְעוֹן אוֹמֵר: ״עֹלָה״ – אֵין לִי אֶלָּא עוֹלָה כְּשֵׁרָה, מִנַּיִן לְרַבּוֹת שֶׁנִּשְׁחֲטָה בַּלַּיְלָה, וְשֶׁנִּשְׁפַּךְ דָּמָהּ, וְשֶׁיָּצָא דָּמָהּ חוּץ לַקְּלָעִים, וְהַלָּן, וְהַיּוֹצֵא, וְהַטָּמֵא, וְהַנּוֹתָר, וְשֶׁנִּשְׁחַט חוּץ לִזְמַנּוֹ וְחוּץ לִמְקוֹמוֹ,

**Rabbi Shimon says:** From the verse's reference to **a burnt offering, I have** derived **only** that **a valid burnt offering** should not be taken down from the altar. **From where** is it derived that the verse also serves **to include** the following disqualified offerings: An offering **that** is invalid because it **was slaughtered at night; and** one **whose blood spilled** before sprinkling; **and** one **whose blood was taken outside the curtains,** i.e., the Temple courtyard; **and** one whose blood **was left overnight; and** one **that was** itself **taken out** of the Temple courtyard;[H] **and** one **that** became **ritually impure; and** one **that was left overnight; and** one **that was slaughtered** with the intent to eat its flesh **beyond its** designated **time or outside its** designated **area.**

## HALAKHA

To the exclusion of an offering that was slaughtered at night – פְּרָט לְנִשְׁחֲטָה בַּלַּיְלָה: A sacrificial animal that was slaughtered at night is disqualified. Even if it was placed upon the altar it must be taken down, in accordance with the opinion of Rabbi Yehuda (Rambam *Sefer Korbanot, Hilkhot Pesulei HaMukdashin* 3:6).

And one whose blood was left overnight and one that was itself taken out of the Temple courtyard, etc. – וְהַלָּן וְהַיּוֹצֵא וכו׳: If the blood or flesh of sacrificial animals, whether the parts that should be consumed or the parts that should be burned on the altar, remained beyond its permitted time frame, it should not be placed on the altar. If it was placed on the altar it should not be taken down. The same applies to sacrificial flesh that left the precincts of the Temple courtyard, and sacrificial flesh that became ritually impure, and an offering that was disqualified because one of its rites was performed with the wrong intent, and one which was disqualified because its blood was collected or sprinkled by ritually impure priests, and one that was disqualified because its blood was sprinkled in the wrong place on the altar, and an offering of the most sacred order that was slaughtered, or whose blood was collected, at the south side of the altar. All these offerings are disqualified and should not be placed on the altar, but if they were placed there they should not be taken down (Rambam *Sefer Korbanot, Hilkhot Pesulei HaMukdashin* 3:7).

## LANGUAGE

Curtains [*kela'im*] – קְלָעִים: The term curtains, or hangings, refers to the partition that delineated the limits of the courtyard of the Tabernacle built by the Israelites in the wilderness. In the Temple, the corresponding limits were demarcated by solid walls. Although the *baraita* is dealing with the *halakhot* of offerings in the Temple, the term curtains is retained as an allusion to the original manner in which the demarcation was delineated. In fact, curtains were used initially in the Second Temple as well (see *Zevaḥim* 107b).

וְשֶׁקִּבְּלוּ פְּסוּלִין וְזָרְקוּ אֶת דָּמָן, וְהַנִּתָּנִין לְמַעְלָה שֶׁנְּתָנָן לְמַטָּה, וְהַנִּתָּנִין לְמַטָּה שֶׁנְּתָנָן לְמַעְלָה, וְהַנִּתָּנִין בַּחוּץ שֶׁנְּתָנָן בִּפְנִים, וְהַנִּתָּנִין בִּפְנִים שֶׁנְּתָנָן בַּחוּץ, וְהַפֶּסַח וְהַחַטָּאת שֶׁשְּׁחָטָן שֶׁלֹּא לִשְׁמָן, מִנַּיִן?

**And** likewise, from where is it derived that the verse serves to include offerings **that** those who are **unfit** for performing the Temple service **collected or sprinkled their blood; and** offerings **whose** blood is supposed to be **placed above** the red line of the altar[B] but **which one placed below** that line; **and** offerings **whose** blood is supposed to be **placed below** the red line of the altar but **which one placed above** it; **and** offerings **whose** blood should be **placed** on the altar situated **outside** the Sanctuary but **which one** instead **placed** on the altar **inside** the Sanctuary; **and** offerings **whose** blood should be **placed** on the altar **inside** the Sanctuary but **which one placed** on the altar **outside; and a Paschal offering and a sin offering that one slaughtered not for their** own **sake,**[N] i.e., while slaughtering he actually intended to sacrifice a different offering? **From where** is it derived that although these offerings are disqualified, if they were brought up to the altar they are not taken down?

תַּלְמוּד לוֹמַר – ״זֹאת תּוֹרַת הָעֹלָה״. רִיבָּה תּוֹרָה אַחַת לְכָל הָעוֹלִין – שֶׁאִם עָלוּ לֹא יֵרְדוּ.

**The verse states: "This is the law of the burnt offering."** The verse thereby **included** in **one law all** items **that ascend** upon the altar, even disqualified offerings, teaching **that if they ascended** the altar, **they shall not descend.**

יָכוֹל שֶׁאֲנִי מְרַבֶּה אֶת הָרוֹבֵעַ, וְהַנִּרְבָּע, וְהַמּוּקְצֶה, וְהַנֶּעֱבָד, וְאֶתְנָן, וְהַמְּחִיר, וְהַכִּלְאַיִם, וְהַטְּרֵפָה, וְיוֹצֵא דוֹפֶן. תַּלְמוּד לוֹמַר ״זֹאת״.

Rabbi Shimon continues: One **might** have thought **that I** should also **include an animal that copulated with a person;**[H] **and an animal that was the object of bestiality; and** an animal **that** was **set aside** for idol worship; **and** an animal **that was worshipped** as a deity; **and** an animal that was given as **payment** to a prostitute **or** as **the price** of a dog; **and** an animal that is an offspring of **diverse kinds,** i.e., crossbreeding; **and an animal with a wound that will cause it to die within twelve months** [*tereifa*]; **and** an animal born by **caesarean section.** Therefore, **the verse states: "This,"** to exclude these disqualifications.

וּמָה רָאִיתָ לְרַבּוֹת אֶת אֵלּוּ וּלְהוֹצִיא אֶת אֵלּוּ?

Rabbi Shimon elaborates: **And what did you see,** i.e., what is the reason **to include these** particular cases **and to exclude those** particular cases?

**BACKGROUND**

**Offerings whose blood is supposed to be placed above the red line of the altar, etc.** – הַנִּתָּנִין לְמַעְלָה וכו׳: The terms above and below, in regard to the altar, refer to the two sections of the external altar of the Temple. The border between them is designated by a red line surrounding the altar at the midpoint of its height. The blood of certain offerings, notably the sin offering, must be placed on the top of the altar, whereas the blood of others, such as the burnt offering, the guilt offering, and the peace offering, must be placed on the bottom half.

View of the altar from the south, with the red line at its midpoint

**NOTES**

**And a Paschal offering and a sin offering that one slaughtered not for their own sake** – וְהַפֶּסַח וְהַחַטָּאת שֶׁשְּׁחָטָן שֶׁלֹּא לִשְׁמָן: With regard to the Paschal offering, the later commentaries note that this is referring specifically to an offering that was slaughtered on the afternoon of the fourteenth of Nisan, which is the proper time for the slaughter of Paschal offerings. A Paschal offering slaughtered any other time of the year is not disqualified at all if it is slaughtered not for its own sake, as it has the status of a peace offering.

**HALAKHA**

**One might have thought that I should also include an animal that copulated with a person, etc.** – יָכוֹל שֶׁאֲנִי מְרַבֶּה אֶת הָרוֹבֵעַ וכו׳: All animals that are disqualified from being sacrificed upon the altar, e.g., a male animal that copulated with a woman, a female animal that copulated with a man, an animal that had been set aside for idolatry, an animal that was worshipped as a deity, an animal that was given as payment to a prostitute, an animal that was exchanged for a dog, a *tereifa*, and an animal born by caesarean section, may not be placed upon the altar, and should be taken down if they were placed there. The reason is that they were unfit for sacrifice from the outset (Rambam *Sefer Avoda, Hilkhot Pesulei HaMukdashin* 3:5).

Perek **V**
Daf **41** Amud **a**

אַחַר שֶׁרִיבָּה הַכָּתוּב וּמִיעֵט, אָמַרְתָּ: מְרַבֶּה אֲנִי אֶת אֵלּוּ – שֶׁהָיָה פְּסוּלָן בַּקֹּדֶשׁ, וּמוֹצִיא אֲנִי אֶת אֵלּוּ – שֶׁלֹּא הָיָה פְּסוּלָן בַּקֹּדֶשׁ.

Rabbi Shimon explains: **After the verse** both **included** some disqualified offerings in this principle **and excluded** others, **you should say: I include** in the items that should not be taken down if they had been placed on the altar **those whose disqualification** occurred **in the sacred** area,[N] i.e., the Temple courtyard, in the course of the sacrificial service, e.g., an offering that was slaughtered at night, or whose blood spilled before sprinkling. **And I exclude those whose disqualification was not in the sacred** area, such as an animal that copulated with a person, as these animals were disqualified before their sacrificial process began. This concludes the *baraita*.

**NOTES**

**Those whose disqualification occurred in the sacred area** – שֶׁהָיָה פְּסוּלָן בַּקֹּדֶשׁ: This translation follows the commentary of Rashi, who says that this category is referring specifically to disqualifications that occurred while the animal was inside the sacred grounds of the Temple, not those which occurred beforehand. Other commentaries indicate that the phrase means disqualification in sanctity, and is referring to disqualifications that are due to the performance of the sacrificial rites, not those that occurred to the animal itself (see *Tosafot*; *Tosefot HaRosh*).

קָתָנֵי מִיהַת יוֹצֵא דוֹפֶן דְּלָא, מַאי לָאו – יוֹצֵא דוֹפֶן דְּקָדָשִׁים? אֲמַר רַב הוּנָא בְּרֵיהּ דְּרַב נָתָן: לָא, יוֹצֵא דוֹפֶן דִּבְכוֹר.

The Gemara explains how this *baraita* supports the opinion of Rabbi Yoḥanan. The *baraita* **teaches, in any event, that** an animal **born by caesarean section** is **not** fit for sacrifice. **What, is it not** referring to one who consecrates an animal born by **caesarean section** and renders it **a sacrificial** animal? Evidently, although Rabbi Shimon maintains that a human birth by caesarean section has the halakhic status of a regular birth, he concedes that animals born in this manner are unfit for sacrifice. **Rav Huna, son of Rav Natan, said: No,** the *baraita* is dealing **with a firstborn** animal born by **caesarean section,** and it is this animal that is disqualified as an offering. A firstborn animal is sacred only if it emerged from the womb.

בְּכוֹר – מִ״פֶּטֶר רֶחֶם״ נָפְקָא!

The Gemara objects to this interpretation of the *baraita*: How can it be referring to **a firstborn** animal? The *halakha* that firstborn status does not apply to an animal born by caesarean section is **derived from** the phrase **"opens the womb,"** which teaches that only animals born in the natural manner are endowed with the sanctity of firstborn animals and may be sacrificed on the altar. Since an animal born by caesarean section is not sacred at all, and it is clear that a non-sacred animal cannot be sacrificed upon the altar, it is obvious that the animal must be taken down if it was placed there in error.

אֶלָּא מַאי, דְּקָדָשִׁים? מֵ״אִמּוֹ״ ״אִמּוֹ״ נָפְקָא!

The Gemara responds to this objection: **Rather, what** would you say? Would you say that the *baraita* is referring to an ordinary animal, not a firstborn, **that** had been consecrated as **a sacrificial** animal? But this animal is not sacred either, as **derived from** the verbal analogy of the term **"its mother"** stated with regard to the firstborn and the term **"its mother"** stated in connection with consecrated animals, as Rabbi Yoḥanan taught earlier. If one seeks to consecrate as an offering an animal that was born by caesarean section, it is not rendered sacred at all. Accordingly, the same reasoning applies as before: It is evident that a non-sacred animal may not be placed on the altar, and it must be removed if placed there in error.

הַאי מַאי, אִי אָמְרַתְּ בִּשְׁלָמָא דְּקָדָשִׁים – הַיְינוּ דְּאִצְטְרִיכִי תְּרֵי קְרָאֵי, חַד – לִבְהֵמַת חוּלִּין דְּאוֹלִיד דֶּרֶךְ דּוֹפֶן וְאַקְדְּשָׁהּ,

The Gemara rejects this response: **What is this** comparison between firstborn animals and consecrated animals? **Granted, if you say** that the *baraita* is referring to animals **that are consecrated** to be offerings, **that is why two verses are necessary: One** verse, the verbal analogy between consecrated animals and firstborn animals, teaches **that a non-sacred animal** whose mother **gave birth** to it **by caesarean section and** whose owner subsequently **consecrated it** as an offering is not sacred at all, and must therefore be removed from the altar if it was placed there in error.

וְחַד – לִבְהֵמַת קָדָשִׁים דְּאוֹלִיד דֶּרֶךְ דּוֹפֶן, וְקָסָבַר וַלְדוֹת קָדָשִׁים בַּהֲוָיָיתָן הֵן קְדוֹשִׁים. אֶלָּא אִי אָמְרַתְּ דִּבְכוֹר – מִ״פֶּטֶר רֶחֶם״ נָפְקָא!

**And one** verse: "This is the law of the burnt offering; that is the burnt offering that goes up on the pyre upon the altar" (Leviticus 6:2), teaches **with regard to a sacrificial animal that gave birth by caesarean section,** that although the offspring is sacred by virtue of its mother's sanctity, it may not be sacrificed and must be removed from the altar if placed there in error. **And the** *tanna* of this *baraita* **maintains** that the **offspring of sacrificial animals are** automatically **sacred upon their emergence**[N] from the womb. **But if you say** that the *baraita* is referring **to a firstborn** animal that was born by caesarean section, the *halakha* that this animal is not sacred **is derived from** the phrase **"opens the womb."**

NOTES

**Offspring of sacrificial animals are automatically sacred upon their emergence – וַלְדוֹת קָדָשִׁים בַּהֲוָיָיתָן הֵן קְדוֹשִׁים:** There is a dispute with regard to the sacred status of animals born to consecrated mothers: Some maintain that the sacred status applies at birth, whereas others claim that the sanctity is attained already in the fetal stage. Since the relevance of this dispute to the Gemara's discussion here is not apparent, Rashi recommends deleting this line altogether (see *Tosafot* for a possible explanation).

הָכִי נַמִּי מִסְתַּבְּרָא, מִדְּקָתָנֵי ״הָרוֹבֵעַ וְהַנִּרְבָּע וְהַמּוּקְצֶה וְהַנֶּעֱבָד וְהַכִּלְאַיִם״.

The Gemara adds: **So too, it is reasonable** to interpret the *baraita* in this manner, that it is referring to an offspring born to a sacrificial animal by caesarean section, **from the fact that** the *baraita* **teaches** that **an animal that copulated with a person, and an animal that was the object of bestiality, and** an animal **that** was **set aside** for idol worship, **and** an animal **that was worshipped** as a deity, **and** an animal that is an offspring of **diverse kinds,** must all be removed from the altar if placed there in error.

הָנֵי מֵהָכָא נָפְקָא? מֵהָתָם נָפְקָא! ״מִן הַבְּהֵמָה״ – לְהוֹצִיא הָרוֹבֵעַ וְהַנִּרְבָּע. ״מִן הַבָּקָר״ – לְהוֹצִיא אֶת הַנֶּעֱבָד. ״מִן הַצֹּאן״ – לְהוֹצִיא אֶת הַמּוּקְצֶה. ״וּמִן הַצֹּאן״ – לְהוֹצִיא אֶת הַנּוֹגֵחַ.

The Gemara explains: Now **are these** disqualifications **derived from here,** from the verse adduced by the *baraita*? No, they are **derived from elsewhere,** as taught in a *baraita*: The verse states: "You shall bring your offering from the cattle, even from the herd or from the flock" (Leviticus 1:2). The expression **"from the cattle"** serves **to exclude** from eligibility as an offering **an animal that copulated with a person**[H] **and an animal that was the object of bestiality.** The expression **"from the herd"** serves **to exclude** an animal **that was worshipped**[H] as a deity. **"From the flock"** serves **to exclude** an animal **set aside** for idol worship. The word "or" in the expression **"or from the flock"** serves **to exclude** an animal **that gored**[H] a person, killing him. In all these cases the animal cannot be consecrated at all, and therefore it is not necessary for the Torah to teach that they must be removed from the altar if placed there in error.

וְתוּ, כִּלְאַיִם, מֵהָכָא נָפְקָא? מֵהָתָם נָפְקָא: ״שׁוֹר אוֹ כֶשֶׂב אוֹ עֵז״. ״שׁוֹר״ – פְּרָט לְכִלְאַיִם, ״אוֹ עֵז״ – פְּרָט לְנִדְמֶה!

**And furthermore,** is the disqualification of an animal born of a mixture of **diverse kinds derived from here?** No, it is **derived from elsewhere,** as taught in a *baraita*: The verse states: "When **a bull or a sheep or a goat** is born, it shall be seven days under its mother; but from the eighth day and onward it may be accepted for an offering" (Leviticus 22:27). The term **"a bull"** serves **to exclude** an offspring of **diverse kinds**[H] from being used as an offering, The phrase **"or a goat"** serves **to exclude** an animal that **resembles** another,[H] i.e., a sheep that is the offspring of sheep but that looks like a goat, or vice versa. Once again, as these animals cannot be consecrated at all, it is not necessary for the Torah to teach that they must be removed from the altar if placed there in error.

אֶלָּא: אִיצְטְרִיכוּ תְּרֵי קְרָאֵי, חַד – לְבֶהֱמַת חוּלִּין, וְחַד – לְבֶהֱמַת קָדָשִׁים, הָכָא נַמִּי – אִיצְטְרִיךְ תְּרֵי קְרָאֵי.

**Rather,** it must be that **two verses are necessary** for each of these cases: **One to** teach that **a non-sacred animal** that is subject to any of these disqualifications cannot be consecrated, **and** the other **one to** teach that with regard to **a sacrificial animal** that was born with this status by virtue of its mother's sanctity, if it is subject to one of these disqualifications it may not be sacrificed and must be removed from the altar if placed there in error. Accordingly, it stands to reason that **here too,** in the case of an animal born by caesarean section, **two verses** are **necessary** for the same reason: One for a non-sacred animal, to teach that it cannot be consecrated, and another for the offspring of a sacrificial animal.

תָּנוּ רַבָּנַן: הַמַּקְשָׁה שְׁלֹשָׁה יָמִים, וְיָצָא וָלָד דֶּרֶךְ דּוֹפֶן – הֲרֵי זוֹ יוֹלֶדֶת בְּזוֹב. וְרַבִּי שִׁמְעוֹן אוֹמֵר: אֵין זוֹ יוֹלֶדֶת בְּזוֹב. וְדָם הַיּוֹצֵא מִשָּׁם – טָמֵא, וְרַבִּי שִׁמְעוֹן מְטַהֵר.

§ **The Sages taught** in a *baraita*: Although a woman who experiences a discharge of uterine blood after her menstrual period is rendered a *zava* and must count seven clean days before immersing and purifying herself, if a pregnant woman **experiences** birth **pangs** accompanied by bleeding for **three days**[N] after her menstrual period, at the end of which she gives birth, she is not rendered a *zava*, as the bleeding is attributed to the childbirth. **And** if the **offspring emerged by caesarean section,**[H] **she is** considered **one who has given birth during** a period of *ziva*. **But Rabbi Shimon says: She is not** considered **one who has given birth during** a period of *ziva*. **And** the **blood that emerges from there is ritually impure, but Rabbi Shimon deems it pure.**

NOTES

**If a pregnant woman experiences birth pangs accompanied by bleeding for three days, etc.** – הַמַּקְשָׁה שְׁלֹשָׁה יָמִים וכו׳: As the Gemara stated earlier (36b), once a woman begins experiencing labor pains, any bleeding that occurs at that time, even over a period of several days, does not render her impure as a *zava*, provided that it is immediately followed by a live birth. If there is a daylong pause between the bleeding and the birth, or if there is no birth at all, the blood renders her impure as a *zava*. Since Rabbi Shimon and the Rabbis disagree whether or not a birth by caesarean section is halakhically considered a birth, it follows that they also disagree whether bleeding followed by a caesarean birth renders the woman ritually impure.

HALAKHA

**To exclude an animal that copulated with a person, etc.** – לְהוֹצִיא הָרוֹבֵעַ וכו׳: An animal that copulated with either a woman or a man may not be sacrificed upon the altar, although it is permitted to eat its meat (Rambam *Sefer Avoda, Hilkhot Issurei Mizbe'aḥ* 3:6).

**To exclude an animal that was worshipped** – לְהוֹצִיא אֶת הַנֶּעֱבָד: An animal that was worshipped as a deity, and likewise one set aside to be used as an idolatrous sacrifice, may not be sacrificed upon the altar, although it is permitted to eat their meat. This *halakha* is in accordance with the mishna on *Temura* 28a (Rambam *Sefer Avoda, Hilkhot Issurei Mizbe'aḥ* 3:6).

**To exclude an animal that gored** – לְהוֹצִיא אֶת הַנּוֹגֵחַ: An animal or bird that killed a person may not be sacrificed upon the altar (Rambam *Sefer Avoda, Hilkhot Issurei Mizbe'aḥ* 3:6).

**To exclude an offspring of diverse kinds** – פְּרָט לְכִלְאַיִם: An offspring of diverse kinds may not be sacrificed upon the altar, even if it is unblemished (Rambam *Sefer Avoda, Hilkhot Issurei Mizbe'aḥ* 3:4).

**To exclude an animal that resembles another** – פְּרָט לְנִדְמֶה: An animal that resembles a different species, even if it is not a hybrid, may not be sacrificed upon the altar. How so? If a ewe gives birth to an offspring that resembles a goat, or if a goat gives birth to an animal that resembles a sheep, the offspring may not be sacrificed, even if it has certain characteristics that cause it to resemble its mother. It is similar to a blemished animal, as there is no greater blemish that an abnormal appearance (Rambam *Sefer Avoda, Hilkhot Issurei Mizbe'aḥ* 3:5).

**And if the offspring emerged by caesarean section** – וְיָצָא וָלָד דֶּרֶךְ דּוֹפֶן: If a pregnant woman experienced labor pains accompanied by bleeding, and subsequently gave birth by caesarean section, the blood that emerged from the vagina is ritually impure, either as menstrual blood or blood of *ziva*, depending on the time in the woman's *ziva* cycle when it emerged. Whatever blood emerged from the abdominal incision is impure. If no blood emerged from the vagina, the woman is ritually pure; she is not rendered impure for seven days by the blood that emerged from the abdominal incision (Rambam *Sefer Kedusha, Hilkhot Issurei Bia* 10:5 and *Sefer Tahara, Hilkhot Metamei Mishkav UMoshav* 1:9).

בִּשְׁלָמָא רֵישָׁא – רַבִּי שִׁמְעוֹן לְטַעְמֵיהּ, וְרַבָּנַן לְטַעֲמַיְיהוּ, אֶלָּא סֵיפָא – בְּמַאי פְּלִיגִי? אָמַר רָבִינָא: כְּגוֹן שֶׁיָּצָא וָלָד דֶּרֶךְ דּוֹפֶן,

The Gemara analyzes the *baraita*: **Granted, the first clause** of the *baraita* is clear: **Rabbi Shimon** conforms **to his** line of **reasoning,** cited in the mishna, that birth via caesarean section has the halakhic status of childbirth; **and the Rabbis,** i.e., the first *tanna*, conform **to their** line of **reasoning,** that birth via caesarean section does not have the halakhic status of childbirth. **But** in **the latter clause, with regard to what** matter **do they disagree? Ravina said:** The latter clause is referring to a case **where the offspring emerged by caesarean section,**

Perek **V**
Daf **41** Amud **b**

**NOTES**

**The location of a woman's source is ritually impure – מָקוֹר מְקוֹמוֹ טָמֵא:** Rashi explains that the blood that comes from the uterus becomes impure through its contact with the uterus, and it imparts ritual impurity to the woman when it leaves her body and comes into contact with the outside of her body. Since it does not render her impure as a menstruating woman, she is permitted to her husband.

וְדַם דֶּרֶךְ רֶחֶם, וְאָזְדָא רַבִּי שִׁמְעוֹן לְטַעְמֵיהּ וְרַבָּנַן לְטַעֲמַיְיהוּ.

**and blood** emerged **through the womb,** i.e., vaginally, during the three days preceding the birth. **And Rabbi Shimon** conforms **to his** line of **reasoning,** that a caesarean birth is a full-fledged birth, and therefore the blood that emerged prior to the birth is ritually pure, **and the Rabbis** conform **to their** line of **reasoning,** that a caesarean birth is not halakhically considered a birth, which means that the blood which emerged beforehand is considered the blood of *ziva*, and is ritually impure.

מַתְקִיף לַהּ רַב יוֹסֵף: חֲדָא – דְּהַיְינוּ רֵישָׁא, וְעוֹד, "מִשָּׁם" – מָקוֹם וָלָד מַשְׁמַע!

**Rav Yosef objects to this** explanation: **One** difficulty is that according to this interpretation, the latter clause of the *baraita* is superfluous, as the dispute recorded there **is** identical to that of **the first clause. And furthermore,** the words: **From there,** in the phrase: The blood that emerges from there, **indicate** that this is referring to a place already mentioned in the *baraita*, i.e., the **place** from which the **offspring** emerged, which is the abdominal incision of the caesarean section, not the vagina.

אֶלָּא אָמַר רַב יוֹסֵף: כְּגוֹן שֶׁיָּצָא וָלָד וְדָם דֶּרֶךְ דּוֹפֶן,

**Rather, Rav Yosef said** that this is the explanation of the latter clause of the *baraita*: It is referring to a situation **where** both the **offspring and blood emerged through** the incision in the **abdomen.**[H] It is in such a case that the first *tanna* deems the blood which emerged impure and Rabbi Shimon deems it pure.

וּבְמָקוֹר מְקוֹמוֹ טָמֵא קָמִיפַּלְגִי, מָר סָבַר – מָקוֹר מְקוֹמוֹ טָמֵא, וּמָר סָבַר – מָקוֹר מְקוֹמוֹ טָהוֹר.

**And** the matter **with regard to** which they **disagree** is whether or not **the location** of a woman's **source,** i.e., her uterus, is ritually **impure.** One **Sage,** the first *tanna*, **holds** that **the location** of a woman's **source** is ritually **impure,**[NH] and therefore any blood that emerges from it, regardless of how it came out of her body, is impure as well. **And** one **Sage,** Rabbi Shimon, **holds** that **the location** of a woman's **source** is **pure,** and blood that emerges from there is also pure. Only uterine blood which emerges vaginally is impure.

**HALAKHA**

**Where both the offspring and blood emerged through the incision in the abdomen – שֶׁיָּצָא וָלָד וְדָם דֶּרֶךְ דּוֹפֶן:** If a woman experienced pain associated with childbirth and gave birth to a child by caesarean section, both the blood that emerged vaginally and that which emerged through the abdominal incision are ritually impure. If no blood emerged vaginally, the woman is pure, despite the fact that the blood emerging from the abdomen is impure. This ruling is in accordance with the opinion of the first *tanna* of the *baraita* (Rambam *Sefer Kedusha, Hilkhot Issurei Bia* 10:5 and *Sefer Tahara, Hilkhot Metamei Mishkav UMoshav* 1:9).

**The location of a woman's source is ritually impure – מָקוֹר מְקוֹמוֹ טָמֵא:** If a woman gave birth by caesarean section and blood emerged from the abdomen along with the child, that blood is a primary source of ritual impurity, just like the vaginal blood of menstruation, childbirth, and *ziva*. The reason is that the place of a woman's source, i.e., the uterus, is ritually impure. The woman herself is not rendered impure except when emitting blood vaginally (Rambam *Sefer Tahara, Hilkhot Metamei Mishkav UMoshav* 1:9, and see *Sefer Kedusha, Hilkhot Issurei Bia* 10:5).

אָמַר רֵישׁ לָקִישׁ: לְדִבְרֵי הַמְטַמֵּא בְּדָם – מְטַמֵּא בְּאִשָּׁה, לְדִבְרֵי הַמְטַהֵר בְּדָם – מְטַהֵר בְּאִשָּׁה. וְרַבִּי יוֹחָנָן אָמַר: אַף לְדִבְרֵי הַמְטַמֵּא בְּדָם – מְטַהֵר בְּאִשָּׁה.

§ **Reish Lakish says: According to the statement of the one who deems the blood impure,** the first *tanna*, **he deems the woman impure**[N] as well, as though it were blood of menstruation. Likewise, **according to the statement of the one who deems the blood pure,** Rabbi Shimon, **he deems the woman pure** as well. **But Rabbi Yoḥanan says: Even according to the statement of the one who deems the blood impure,** the first *tanna*, **he deems the woman pure.**

וְאָזְדָא רַבִּי יוֹחָנָן לְטַעְמֵיהּ, דְּאָמַר רַבִּי יוֹחָנָן מִשּׁוּם רַבִּי שִׁמְעוֹן בֶּן יוֹחַי: מִנַּיִן שֶׁאֵין אִשָּׁה טְמֵאָה עַד שֶׁיֵּצֵא מַדְוֶה דֶּרֶךְ עֶרְוָתָהּ, שֶׁנֶּאֱמַר: "וְאִישׁ אֲשֶׁר יִשְׁכַּב אֶת אִשָּׁה דָּוָה וְגִלָּה אֶת עֶרְוָתָהּ אֶת מְקוֹרָהּ הֶעֱרָה" – מְלַמֵּד שֶׁאֵין אִשָּׁה טְמֵאָה עַד שֶׁיֵּצֵא מַדְוֶה דֶּרֶךְ עֶרְוָתָהּ.

**And Rabbi Yoḥanan follows his** standard line of **reasoning** here, **as Rabbi Yoḥanan said in the name of Rabbi Shimon ben Yoḥai: From where** is it derived **that a woman does not become impure** due to menstruation **unless the flow** of blood **emerges from her nakedness,** i.e., genitalia? **As it is stated: "And a man who lies with a woman having her flow, and shall uncover her nakedness, he has made naked her source"** (Leviticus 20:18) This **teaches that a woman is not impure** due to menstruation **unless the flow emerges from her nakedness.**

אָמַר רֵישׁ לָקִישׁ מִשּׁוּם רַבִּי יְהוּדָה נְשִׂיאָה: מָקוֹר שֶׁנֶּעֱקַר וְנָפַל לָאָרֶץ – טְמֵאָה, שֶׁנֶּאֱמַר "יַעַן הִשָּׁפֵךְ נְחָשְׁתֵּךְ וַתִּגָּלֶה עֶרְוָתֵךְ".

**Reish Lakish says in the name of Rabbi Yehuda Nesia:**[P] If a woman's **source,** i.e., her uterus, **became dislodged and fell** out of her body **onto the ground, she is ritually impure, as it is stated: "Because your foundation was poured out, and your nakedness was uncovered"** (Ezekiel 16:36). The word "foundation" alludes to the uterus, and the verse is referring to it after it has been "poured out," i.e., detached, as an uncovering of nakedness, which indicates that it is still a source of impurity even after it has been detached from its place.

לְמַאי? אִילֵּימָא לְטוּמְאַת שִׁבְעָה – "דָּם" אָמַר רַחֲמָנָא, וְלֹא חֲתִיכָה! אֶלָּא לְטוּמְאַת עֶרֶב.

The Gemara asks: **To what** kind of impurity is this woman subject in this situation? **If we say** that she is subject **to the impurity of seven** days of menstruating women, that is impossible, as **the Merciful One states** in the Torah that such impurity is caused by **"blood"** (Leviticus 15:19), **and not a piece** of flesh. **Rather,** she is subject **to impurity** that lasts until the **evening,** as a result of the surface of her body having come into contact with the uterus, which is a source of impurity.

אָמַר רַבִּי יוֹחָנָן: מָקוֹר שֶׁהִזִּיעַ כִּשְׁתֵּי טִיפֵּי מַרְגָּלִיּוֹת – טְמֵאָה. לְמַאי? אִילֵּימָא לְטוּמְאַת שִׁבְעָה – חֲמִשָּׁה דָּמִים טְמֵאִין בְּאִשָּׁה, וְתוּ לָא! אֶלָּא לְטוּמְאַת עֶרֶב. וְדַוְקָא תַּרְתֵּי, אֲבָל חֲדָא – אֵימָא מֵעָלְמָא אָתְיָא.

**Rabbi Yoḥanan says:** In the case of a woman's **source that discharged two** whitish, clear, **pearl-like** [*margaliyyot*][L] **drops,**[H] **she is impure.** The Gemara asks: **To what** kind of impurity is this woman subject in this situation? **If we say** that she is subject **to the impurity of seven** days of menstruating women, that is impossible, as the mishna (*Nidda* 19a) states that there are **five** distinct colors of **ritually impure blood in a woman, but no more,** and pearly white is not one of those colors. **Rather,** she is subject **to impurity** that lasts until the **evening,** as a result of her body having come into contact with a discharge from the uterus, which is a source of impurity. **And** this is the *halakha* **specifically** if there were **two** drops, **but** if there was only **one** such drop she is not impure, as **I can say** that the drop **came from elsewhere,**[H] not from the uterus.

### PERSONALITIES

**Rabbi Yehuda Nesia – רַבִּי יְהוּדָה נְשִׂיאָה:** Three different Sages were known by this name, each the grandson of his namesake. The first, who lived during the first and second generations of *amora'im* in Eretz Yisrael, was the son of Rabban Gamliel, who was himself the son of Rabbi Yehuda HaNasi, the redactor of the Mishna. In order to distinguish him from his grandfather, also named Yehuda, the grandson was called Rabbi Yehuda Nesia, the Aramaic form of Yehuda the *Nasi*, or patriarch. Like his grandfather, he is sometimes referred to simply as Rabbi. The grandson of this Rabbi Yehuda, a disciple of Rabbi Yoḥanan and Reish Lakish, was also known as Rabbi Yehuda Nesia. The grandson of this later Rabbi Yehuda Nesia, a fourth-generation *amora* in Eretz Yisrael and a contemporary of Rabbi Yirmeya, was likewise called by the same name.

### LANGUAGE

**Pearls [*margaliyyot*] – מַרְגָּלִיּוֹת:** The source of this word is the Greek μαργαρίτης, *margaritēs*, with a shift from the letter *r* to the letter *l*. The meaning of the word in Greek, as in Hebrew, is pearl. There is a similar Greek word which denotes a precious stone. In talmudic Hebrew the word can likewise have both meanings.

### HALAKHA

**A woman's source that discharged two whitish clear pearl-like drops – מָקוֹר שֶׁהִזִּיעַ כִּשְׁתֵּי טִיפֵּי מַרְגָּלִיּוֹת:** If a woman's source, i.e., her uterus, discharged two pearl-like, i.e., clear white, drops, she is impure until the evening. She is not a menstruating woman, which would entail seven days of ritual impurity, unless she emits one of the five types of blood listed in the mishna on 19a. This is in accordance with the opinion of Rabbi Yoḥanan (Rambam *Sefer Tahara, Hilkhot Metamei Mishkav UMoshav* 1:10).

**If there was only one drop she is not impure as I can say it came from elsewhere – חֲדָא אֵימָא מֵעָלְמָא אָתְיָא:** If a woman discharges a single pearl-like drop she is not rendered impure, as it is assumed that it did not originate in the uterus. This is in accordance with the opinion of Rabbi Yoḥanan (Rambam *Sefer Tahara, Hilkhot Metamei Mishkav UMoshav* 1:11).

### NOTES

**According to the statement of the one who deems the blood impure he deems the woman impure – לְדִבְרֵי הַמְטַמֵּא בְּדָם מְטַמֵּא בְּאִשָּׁה:** Reish Lakish, like Rav Yosef, maintains that the latter clause of the *baraita* is referring to blood that emerges from the abdominal incision. Yet his explanation differs from the previous explanations of this clause in that he holds that according to the first *tanna*, the blood is considered menstrual blood despite its emergence from a place other than the vagina.

With regard to Reish Lakish's explanation of the opinion of Rabbi Shimon in this latter clause of the *baraita*, there are two opinions among the early commentaries. According to one opinion, Rabbi Shimon agrees that in theory, uterine blood which emerges due to an abdominal incision can render a woman a menstruating woman or a *zava*. But in this particular case, since the bleeding was followed by a birth, it is considered pure, as is the case with any painful bleeding followed by a birth. The first *tanna*, by contrast, does not consider a caesarean birth a full-fledged birth, and therefore he rules that the woman's bleeding does render her impure. Consequently, the dispute between Rabbi Shimon and the first *tanna* in the latter clause of the *baraita* is directly related to their dispute in the first clause (*Tosafot*; *Tosefot HaRosh*).

According to the other opinion, Reish Lakish maintains that Rabbi Shimon disagrees altogether with the basic assertion of the first *tanna* that uterine blood emerging from anywhere other than the vagina can be considered blood of menstruation or *ziva*. Therefore, the woman experiencing such bleeding remains pure (Ramban; Ran).

**NOTES**

**Is the area between the teeth-like projections itself considered as internal or as external – בֵּין הַשִּׁינַּיִם כְּלִפְנִים או כְּלַחוּץ:** This question is due to the ambiguity of the word: Until. The Talmud often discusses whether this term includes or excludes the specified endpoint.

**The place of threshing – מְקוֹם דִּישָׁה:** According to the Rambam (*Sefer Kedusha, Hilkhot Issurei Bia* 5:2), this place of threshing is a description of the area previously called: Between the teeth-like projections (Rashbatz).

״כׇּל הַנָּשִׁים מְטַמְּאִין בַּבַּיִת הַחִיצוֹן״. הֵי נִיהוּ ״בַּיִת הַחִיצוֹן״? אָמַר רֵישׁ לָקִישׁ: כׇּל שֶׁתִּינוֹקֶת יוֹשֶׁבֶת וְנִרְאֵית.

§ The mishna teaches: **All women become ritually impure** with the flow of blood from the uterus **into the outer chamber,** i.e., the vagina, as it is stated: "And her issue in her flesh shall be blood" (Leviticus 15:19). The Gemara asks: **What** exactly **is the outer chamber? Reish Lakish says: Any** place **which can be seen when a little girl sits** with her legs spread. When the blood reaches that area in the vagina, the woman becomes ritually impure.

אֲמַר לֵיהּ רַבִּי יוֹחָנָן: אוֹתוֹ מָקוֹם – גָּלוּי הוּא אֵצֶל שֶׁרֶץ! אֶלָּא אָמַר רַבִּי יוֹחָנָן: עַד בֵּין הַשִּׁינַּיִם.

**Rabbi Yoḥanan said to** Reish Lakish in objection: **That place is** considered **exposed** even **with regard to** contact with the carcass of a **creeping animal.** If one comes into contact with the carcass of a creeping animal he becomes impure. This is the *halakha* only if the animal touches a part of the body that is exposed, not an internal cavity such as the inside of the mouth. Since the area of the vagina described by Reish Lakish is considered an exposed part of the body for the purposes of the impurity imparted by the carcass of a creeping animal, it should not be necessary for the mishna to derive the *halakha* of her impurity from the expression "in her flesh." **Rather, Rabbi Yoḥanan says:** The term outer chamber extends **until** the area **between the teeth**-like projections[H] inside the vagina.

אִיבַּעֲיָא לְהוּ: בֵּין הַשִּׁינַּיִם. כְּלִפְנִים אוֹ כְּלַחוּץ? תָּא שְׁמַע, דְּתָנֵי רַבִּי זַכַּאי: עַד בֵּין הַשִּׁינַּיִם, בֵּין הַשִּׁינַּיִם עַצְמָן – כְּלִפְנִים.

**A dilemma was raised before** the Sages: Is the area **between the teeth**-like projections itself considered **as internal,** which would mean that blood there would not render the woman impure, **or as external?**[N] **Come** and **hear** a resolution, **as Rabbi Zakkai teaches** a *baraita*: The term outer chamber extends **to** the area **between the teeth**-like projections, but the area **between the teeth**-like projections **themselves** is considered **as internal.**

בְּמַתְנִיתָא תָּנָא: מְקוֹם דִּישָׁה. מַאי ״מְקוֹם דִּישָׁה״? אָמַר רַב יְהוּדָה: מָקוֹם שֶׁהַשַּׁמָּשׁ דָּשׁ.

**It was taught in a** *baraita* that a woman becomes impure when the blood reaches the **place of threshing,**[N] which is a euphemism. The Gemara asks: **What** is the meaning of this euphemism, the **place of threshing? Rav Yehuda says:** It is referring to the **place** in the vagina **where the penis threshes,** i.e., reaches, during intercourse.

תָּנוּ רַבָּנַן: ״בִּבְשָׂרָהּ״ – מְלַמֵּד שֶׁמְּטַמְּאָה בִּפְנִים כְּבַחוּץ. וְאֵין לִי אֶלָּא נִדָּה, זָבָה מִנַּיִן – תַּלְמוּד לוֹמַר ״זוֹבָהּ בִּבְשָׂרָהּ״.

§ **The Sages taught** in a *baraita*: It is written concerning a menstruating woman: "And if a woman has an issue, and her flow in her flesh shall be blood, she shall be in her menstruation seven days" (Leviticus 15:19). The term **"in her flesh" teaches that she becomes impure** while the blood is still **inside** her flesh just **as** when the blood emerges **outside** her body. **I have** derived **only** that this applies in the case of **a menstruating woman. From where** is it derived that it applies to a ***zava*** as well? **The** same **verse states: "Her flow** [*zovah*] **in her flesh."**

פּוֹלֶטֶת שִׁכְבַת זֶרַע מִנַּיִן – תַּלְמוּד לוֹמַר ״יִהְיֶה״. וְרַבִּי שִׁמְעוֹן אוֹמֵר: דַּיָּהּ כְּבוֹעֲלָהּ, מַה בּוֹעֲלָהּ – אֵינוֹ מְטַמֵּא עַד שֶׁתֵּצֵא טוּמְאָה לַחוּץ, אַף הִיא – אֵינָהּ מְטַמְּאָה עַד שֶׁתֵּצֵא טוּמְאָתָהּ לַחוּץ.

**From where** is it derived that this also applies to a woman who **discharges semen** after intercourse?[H] **The** same **verse states** the apparently superfluous term **"shall be." And Rabbi Shimon says:** In the case of discharging semen, **it is sufficient for her** to be **like the man who engaged in intercourse with her: Just as the man who engaged in intercourse with her does not become impure until** the source of **impurity,** the semen, **emerges outside** his body, **so too, she does not become impure until her** source of **impurity,** the semen, **emerges outside** her body. It does not render her impure while it is still inside her body.

**HALAKHA**

**Until the area between the teeth-like projections – עַד בֵּין הַשִּׁינַּיִם:** Blood that emerges from the uterus, even if it has not yet left the body, renders the woman impure by Torah law once it has gone beyond the area between the teeth-like projections, as all women become ritually impure with the flow of blood from the uterus into the outer chamber. This is the *halakha* only if the woman feels the blood discharged from the uterus. If she does not feel it she is not rendered impure by Torah law, but only by rabbinic law (*Shakh*). The area of the teeth-like projections is equivalent to the place where the penis reaches during intercourse. If the blood reaches the area of the teeth-like projections itself, without going beyond it, it is considered as though the blood has not yet been emitted, in accordance with the opinion of Rabbi Yannai (Rambam *Sefer Kedusha, Hilkhot Issurei Bia* 5:2).

**A woman who discharges semen after intercourse – פּוֹלֶטֶת שִׁכְבַת זֶרַע:** A woman who discharged semen is rendered impure like a man who emits semen, provided that it is emitted within three time periods after intercourse, with each time period consisting of an entire day or night. Even if the semen did not leave the woman's body, she becomes impure as soon as it reaches the area between the teeth-like projections, in accordance with the opinion of the first *tanna* in the *baraita* (Rambam *Sefer Tahara, Hilkhot She'ar Avot HaTumot* 5:11).

וְסָבַר רַבִּי שִׁמְעוֹן דַּיָּהּ כְּבוֹעֲלָהּ? וְהָתַנְיָא, "וְרָחֲצוּ בַמַּיִם וְטָמְאוּ עַד הָעָרֶב". אָמַר רַבִּי שִׁמְעוֹן: וְכִי מָה בָּא זֶה לְלַמְּדֵנוּ? אִם לְעִנְיַן נוֹגֵעַ בְּשִׁכְבַת זֶרַע – הֲרֵי כְּבָר נֶאֱמַר לְמַטָּה "אוֹ אִישׁ",

The Gemara asks: **And does Rabbi Shimon** in fact **hold** that **it is sufficient for her** to be **like the man who engaged in intercourse with her? But isn't it taught** to the contrary in a *baraita*: The verse states: "The woman also with whom a man shall lie carnally, **they shall both bathe themselves in water, and be impure until the evening**" (Leviticus 15:18). **Rabbi Shimon said: And what does this** verse **come to teach us? If** it teaches **with regard to** one who **comes into contact with semen** that they are impure, **it is already stated below** (Leviticus 22:4): **"Or a man** from whom the flow of seed goes out," from which it is derived that coming into contact with semen renders one impure.

אֶלָּא מִפְּנֵי שֶׁטּוּמְאַת בֵּית הַסְּתָרִים הִיא, וְטוּמְאַת בֵּית הַסְּתָרִים אֵינָהּ מְטַמְּאָה, אֶלָּא שֶׁגְּזֵירַת הַכָּתוּב הוּא!

**Rather,** this verse is necessary **because** in the case of intercourse the contact with the source of **impurity** occurs in **a concealed part** of the body, **and** contact with **impurity** by **a concealed part** of the body generally **does not render** one **impure.**[H] **But** here **it is a Torah edict** that the woman does become impure in this manner. This *baraita* proves that according to Rabbi Shimon a woman is rendered impure by semen even when it is inside her body.

לָא קַשְׁיָא, כָּאן – בִּמְשַׁמֶּשֶׁת, כָּאן – בְּפוֹלֶטֶת.

The Gemara answers that this is **not difficult. Here,** this second *baraita* is dealing **with** a woman who **engages in intercourse,** whereas **there,** the first *baraita* is dealing **with** a woman who **discharges** semen after intercourse. It is only during the act of intercourse that a woman becomes impure due to the semen. If she later discharges semen, she does not become impure, according to Rabbi Shimon, until the semen leaves her body and touches her on the outside.

פּוֹלֶטֶת – תֵּיפוֹק לֵיהּ דְּהָא שִׁמְּשָׁה! בְּשֶׁטָּבְלָה לְשִׁמּוּשָׁהּ.

The Gemara objects: But in the case of a woman who **discharges** semen, one can **derive** that she is impure **due to** the fact **that she engaged in intercourse** prior to the discharge.[N] The Gemara answers: Rabbi Shimon is referring to a case **where she immersed herself,** thereby purifying herself **from** the impurity **from her intercourse,** and she subsequently discharged semen.

לְמֵימְרָא דִּמְשַׁמֶּשֶׁת בְּטוּמְאַת עֶרֶב סַגִּי לַהּ? וְהָא אָמַר רָבָא: מְשַׁמֶּשֶׁת – כׇּל שְׁלֹשָׁה יָמִים אֲסוּרָה לֶאֱכוֹל בִּתְרוּמָה, שֶׁאִי אֶפְשָׁר לָהּ שֶׁלֹּא תִּפְלוֹט!

The Gemara asks: **Is this to say that** in the case of a woman who **engages in intercourse it is sufficient for her** to simply immerse herself, and then she is **in** a state of **impurity** only until **evening? But didn't Rava say:** A woman who **engages in intercourse is prohibited from partaking of *teruma*,** even if she is married to a priest, for **the entire three days**[H] following the intercourse, **as it is impossible for her not to discharge** semen throughout this period, and *teruma* may not be consumed by one who is impure?

הָכָא בְּמַאי עָסְקִינַן – שֶׁהִטְבִּילוּהָ בְּמִטָּה. מִכְּלָל דְּכִי קָאָמַר רָבָא – דְּאָזְלָה אִיהִי בְּכַרְעַהּ וְטָבְלָה, דִּילְמָא בַּהֲדֵי דְּקָאָזְלָה שַׁדְיָתַהּ?

The Gemara answers: **Here we are dealing with** a case **where** others **immersed** the woman while she was still **in bed,** and she remained there. If she remains lying down, it is possible for her not to discharge semen following intercourse, and the immersion after intercourse purifies her. The Gemara asks: **By inference,** one can conclude **that when Rava said** that a woman is in a constant state of impurity for three days after intercourse, he was referring to a case **where she walked** to the ritual bath **by foot and immersed** herself. But if so, **perhaps while she was walking she released** all the semen in her body even before the three days were over, and therefore will not subsequently become impure.

**HALAKHA**

**Contact with impurity by a concealed part of the body does not render one impure – וְטוּמְאַת בֵּית הַסְּתָרִים אֵינָהּ מְטַמְּאָה:** Ritual impurity is imparted to a woman who engages in intercourse not due to the contact with semen, as this contact takes place internally, and contact with an impure substance in a concealed part of the body is not considered contact. Rather, the woman's impurity is imposed by Torah law because of the act of intercourse itself, as explained by Rabbi Shimon (Rambam *Sefer Tahara, Hilkhot She'ar Avot HaTumot* 5:9; see also *Hilkhot Tumat Met* 1:3).

**A woman who engages in intercourse is prohibited from partaking of *teruma* for the entire three days – מְשַׁמֶּשֶׁת כׇּל שְׁלֹשָׁה יָמִים אֲסוּרָה לֶאֱכוֹל בִּתְרוּמָה:** With regard to a woman after intercourse, if she did not turn over during intercourse, she may immerse immediately and partake of *teruma* in the evening. This immersion would have to be performed while she is still lying in bed (Ra'avad; see Radbaz and *Kesef Mishne*). If she did turn over during intercourse, she is prohibited from partaking of *teruma* for three days, as it is impossible that she did not emit some semen over this period, thereby rendering herself impure, in accordance with the statement of Rava (Rambam *Sefer Zera'im, Hilkhot Terumot* 7:7).

**NOTES**

**One can derive that she is impure due to the fact that she engaged in intercourse prior to the discharge – פּוֹלֶטֶת תֵּיפוֹק לֵיהּ דְּהָא שִׁמְּשָׁה:** The Gemara first explained that according to Rabbi Shimon, a woman is subject to ritual impurity by insemination in two distinct ways, through intercourse and through discharge of semen. The Gemara proceeds to ask: What is the point of these two separate categories, as a discharge of semen is necessarily preceded by intercourse in any event? The question could not be posed to the first *tanna*, as according to him it is possible that there are not two categories, but rather, the Torah declares a woman impure after intercourse only because of the discharge of semen that necessarily follows it (Ramban; Ran). See *Tosafot* for a different explanation.

**NOTES**

**Here he is referring to a woman who turns around, there he is speaking of a woman who does not turn around – כָּאן בְּמִתְהַפֶּכֶת כָּאן בְּשֶׁאֵינָהּ מִתְהַפֶּכֶת:** Rashi offers two different interpretations of this sentence. The first is that the turning around mentioned by the Gemara is referring to the woman's movement after she has immersed. If she turned from side to side after the immersion, Rava maintains that she certainly discharges semen throughout the three-day period and is therefore impure. When Rabbi Shimon indicates that it is possible for her to remain pure after immersion, he is referring to a case where she does not turn from side to side. The majority of the early commentaries adopt this interpretation (Ramban; Rashba; Ritva; Rashbatz).

Rashi's second explanation is that the turning around mentioned by the Gemara is referring to her position at the time of intercourse. If she remained still at that time, the semen is better absorbed inside her body and is not necessarily discharged thereafter. If she turned from side to side during that time, she will constantly be discharging semen over the next three days, as stated by Rava. The Rambam explains the Gemara in accordance with this second interpretation.

וְכִי תֵּימָא: דִּילְמָא אִשְׁתַּיֵּיר, אִי הָכִי – ״חָיְישִׁינַן שֶׁמָּא נִשְׁתַּיֵּיר״ מִבָּעֵי לֵיהּ!

**And if you would say** that it is certainly possible that she released all the semen, but Rava's concern was that **perhaps** some of it might have **remained, if so, he should have** said: **We are concerned** that **perhaps** some semen **remained** and will be discharged, rather than: It is impossible for her not to discharge semen throughout this period.

אֶלָּא לְרָבָא נַמִי – שֶׁהִטְבִּילוּהָ בְּמִטָּה, וְלָא קַשְׁיָא, כָּאן – בְּמִתְהַפֶּכֶת, כָּאן – בְּשֶׁאֵינָהּ מִתְהַפֶּכֶת.

**Rather, according to Rava too,** this is referring even to a case **where** others **immersed her** while she was still **in bed** and she remained there for three days. **And** the contradiction is **not difficult: Here,** in the statement of Rava, he is referring to a woman **who turns around** in bed from side to side. It is therefore certain that she will discharge semen over the course of three days. **There,** in the statement of Rabbi Shimon, he is speaking of a woman lying in bed **who does not turn around**[N] from side to side. Such a woman will not discharge semen at all.

וְרָבָא אַקְּרָא קָאֵי, וְהָכִי קָאָמַר: כִּי כָּתַב רַחֲמָנָא ״וְרָחֲצוּ בַמַּיִם וְטָמְאוּ עַד הָעָרֶב״ – בְּשֶׁאֵינָהּ מִתְהַפֶּכֶת, אֲבָל בְּמִתְהַפֶּכֶת – כָּל שְׁלֹשָׁה יָמִים אֲסוּרָה לֶאֱכוֹל בִּתְרוּמָה, שֶׁאִי אֶפְשָׁר לָהּ שֶׁלֹּא תִּפְלוֹט.

**And** the statement of **Rava is referring to a verse** in the Torah, **and this** is what **he is saying: When the Merciful One writes** in the Torah, with regard to a man and woman who engaged in intercourse: **"They shall both bathe themselves in water, and be impure until the evening"** (Leviticus 15:18), which indicates that when evening comes the woman's purification is complete, it is dealing with a case **where she** is in bed and **does not turn around** from side to side. **But** in a case **where she does turn around, she is prohibited from partaking of *teruma*** for **the entire three days** following the intercourse, **as it is impossible for her not to discharge** semen throughout this period.

בְּעָא מִינֵּיהּ רַב שְׁמוּאֵל בַּר בִּיסְנָא מֵאַבַּיֵי: פּוֹלֶטֶת שִׁכְבַת זֶרַע, רוֹאָה הָוְיָא אוֹ נוֹגַעַת הָוְיָא?

**Rav Shmuel bar Bisna asked Abaye:** With regard to a woman who **discharges semen, is her** status that of **one who experienced** an emission of an impure substance, **or is her** status that of **one who came into contact** with an impure substance?

נָפְקָא מִינָּהּ: לִסְתּוֹר, וּלְטַמֵּא בְּמַשֶּׁהוּ, וּלְטַמֵּא בִּפְנִים כְּבַחוּץ.

The practical **difference** between these two possibilities is threefold: Whether or not the discharge **negates** her counting of seven clean days at the end of the *ziva* period, whether or not it **renders** her **impure by any amount, and** whether or not it **renders** her **impure** while still **inside** her body **as** it would after emerging **out** of her body. If it is considered an emission of an impure substance, it negates her count of seven clean days, and it renders her impure even in the slightest amount, and it renders her impure even before it emerges from her body. If it renders her impure because she came into contact with it, it does not negate her count, it renders her impure only if a certain minimum amount emerges, and it renders her impure only after touching the outside of her body.

מַה נַּפְשָׁךְ, אִי שְׁמִיעַ לֵיהּ מַתְנִיתִין, לְרַבָּנַן – רוֹאָה הָוְיָא, וּלְרַבִּי שִׁמְעוֹן – נוֹגַעַת הָוְיָא.

Before addressing the dilemma, the Gemara raises a difficulty with Rav Shmuel bar Bisna's question itself: **Whichever** way **you** look at it, the question is problematic. **If he had heard the *baraita*** cited above, the answer is obvious: **According to the Rabbis, her status is** that of one who **experienced** an emission of an impure substance, as the *baraita* clearly states that in the Rabbis' opinion the woman is rendered impure even before the semen emerges from her body. **And according to Rabbi Shimon, her status is** that of one who **came into contact with** the impure substance, as Rabbi Shimon states that the woman is impure only when the semen emerges from her body.

וְאִי לָא שְׁמִיעַ לֵיהּ מַתְנִיתִין, מִסְתַּבְּרָא – נוֹגַעַת הָוְיָא!

**And if** Rav Shmuel bar Bisna **did not hear the *baraita*** and was unaware of it, it **is** certainly more **reasonable** to assume that **her** status should be that of one who **came into contact** with the semen. Why would he think otherwise, as after all, the emitted substance did not originate in her body?

לְעוֹלָם שְׁמִיעַ לֵיהּ מַתְנִיתִין, וְאַלִּיבָּא דְּרַבָּנַן – לָא קָמִיבַּעְיָא לֵיהּ, כִּי קָא מִיבַּעְיָא לֵיהּ – אַלִּיבָּא דְּרַבִּי שִׁמְעוֹן.

The Gemara answers: **Actually,** Rav Shmuel bar Bisna **had heard the *baraita*, and he did not raise the dilemma according to** the opinion **of the Rabbis.** According to their opinion it is clear that the woman has the status of one who experienced an emission of an impure bodily substance. Rather, **when he raises the dilemma,** it is **according to** the opinion **of Rabbi Shimon.**

וּלְטַמֵּא בִּפְנִים כְּבַחוּץ – לָא קָמִיבַּעְיָא לֵיהּ, כִּי קָמִיבַּעְיָא לֵיהּ – לִסְתּוֹר וּלְטַמֵּא בְּכׇל שֶׁהוּא, מַאי?

**And he does not raise the dilemma with regard to** the question of whether or not the semen **renders** her **impure** when it is **inside** the body **as** it would after emerging **outside** the body, as Rabbi Shimon states explicitly that the woman is impure only when the semen leaves her body. Rather, **when he raises the dilemma,** it is only with regard to the other two issues mentioned above: Whether or not the discharge **negates** her counting of seven clean days at the end of the *ziva* period, **and** whether or not it **renders** her **impure in any amount.** He therefore asked: **What** is the status of her discharge of semen with respect to these two matters?

כִּי קָאָמַר רַבִּי שִׁמְעוֹן דַּיָּהּ כְּבוֹעֲלָהּ – הָנֵי מִילֵּי לְטַמּוּיֵי בִּפְנִים כְּבַחוּץ, אֲבָל לִסְתּוֹר וּלְטַמֵּא בְּכׇל שֶׁהוּא – רוֹאָה הָוְיָא, אוֹ דִּילְמָא – לָא שְׁנָא?

The Gemara explains the sides of the dilemma: It is possible that **when Rabbi Shimon says: It is sufficient for her** to be **like the man who engaged in intercourse with her, this statement** applies only with regard to the question of whether or not the semen **renders** her **impure** when it is **inside** the body **as** it would after emerging **outside** the body. It does not render her impure unless it touches her body on the outside. **But** with regard to the question of whether or not the discharge **negates** her counting of seven clean days at the end of the *ziva* period **and** whether or not it **renders** her **impure in any amount,** perhaps **she is** considered impure as one who **experienced** an emission of an impure substance. **Or perhaps** there **is no difference.** Rather, with regard to all three issues she has the status of one who came into contact with an impure substance.

אִיכָּא דְּאָמְרִי: לְעוֹלָם לָא שְׁמִיעַ לֵיהּ מַתְנִיתָא, וְהָכִי קָמִיבַּעְיָא לֵיהּ, מִדְּאַחְמִיר רַחֲמָנָא אַבַּעֲלֵי קְרָיִין בְּסִינַי – רוֹאָה הָוְיָא.

**There are** those **who say** a different explanation of Rav Shmuel bar Bisna's dilemma: **Actually, he did not hear the *baraita*** and was unaware of it. **And** as for the question of why he would think that the woman should have the status of one who experienced an emission of an impure bodily substance, **this was his dilemma: Since the Merciful One was stringent** before the giving of the Torah **on** Mount **Sinai with regard to** men **who had experienced a seminal emission,** in that they were prohibited from attending that event, as it is stated: "Be ready on the third day; do not come near a woman" (Exodus 19:15), whereas those who had come into contact with other impure items were not prohibited from attending, perhaps the stringency of this particular source of impurity should likewise be applied to a woman who discharges semen. If so, **her** status should be like one who **experienced** a seminal emission, rather than one who merely came into contact with semen.

אוֹ דִּילְמָא: לָא גָּמְרִינַן מִסִּינַי, דְּחִדּוּשׁ הוּא, דְּהָא זָבִין וּמְצוֹרָעִים דַּחֲמִירֵי – וְלָא אַחְמִיר בְּהוּ רַחֲמָנָא?

The Gemara explains the other side of the dilemma: **Or perhaps we should not derive** any *halakhot* **from** the instructions given before the revelation at **Sinai, as that** was **a novelty.** The Gemara cites a proof for this claim: **As** that was the case with regard to ***zavin* and lepers, whose** impurity is even more **stringent** than that of one who experiences a seminal emission, **but** nevertheless **the Merciful One was not stringent with regard to them,** as He permitted them to attend the ceremony of the giving of the Torah.

אֲמַר לֵיהּ: רוֹאָה הָוְיָא. אֲתָא שַׁיְילֵיהּ לְרָבָא, אֲמַר לֵיהּ: רוֹאָה הָוְיָא. אֲתָא לְקַמֵּיהּ דְּרַב יוֹסֵף, אֲמַר לֵיהּ: רוֹאָה הָוְיָא. הֲדַר אֲתָא לְקַמֵּיהּ דְּאַבָּיֵי, אֲמַר לֵיהּ: כּוּלְּכוּ בְּרוּקָא חֲדָא תְּפִיתוּ.

After clarifying Rav Shmuel bar Bisna's dilemma, the Gemara cites Abaye's answer to him. Abaye **said to him:** The woman's status **is** that of one who **experienced** an emission of semen. Rav Shmuel bar Bisna **came** and **asked Rava** the same question, and **he** too **said to him:** The woman's status **is** that of one who **experienced** an emission. **He came before Rav Yosef,** and **he** too **said to him: Her** status **is** that of one who **experienced** an emission. Rav Shmuel bar Bisna **came back to Abaye** and **said to him: You are all spewing the same saliva.** None of you are teaching anything new, as you all repeat the same unsatisfactory answer.

אֲמַר לֵיהּ: שַׁפִּיר אָמְרִי לָךְ, עַד כָּאן לָא קָאֲמַר רַבִּי שִׁמְעוֹן דַּיָּהּ כְּבוֹעֲלָהּ – אֶלָּא לְטַמֵּא בִּפְנִים כְּבַחוּץ, אֲבָל לִסְתּוֹר וּלְטַמֵּא בְּכָל שֶׁהוּא – רוֹאָה הָוְיָא.

Abaye **said to him: I said well to you,** i.e., my response was correct. **Rabbi Shimon says** that **it is sufficient for** the woman to be **like the man who engaged in intercourse with her only with regard to** the question of whether or not the semen **renders** her **impure** while still **inside** her body **as** it would after emerging **out** of her body. Rabbi Shimon rules that it does not render her impure until it touches her on the outside. **But with regard to** the other two issues, i.e., **negating** the woman's count of seven clean days at the end of a *ziva* period **and rendering** her **impure in any amount,** Rabbi Shimon maintains that the woman's status **is** that of one who **experienced** an emission. Therefore, the discharge negates her count and renders her impure by any amount.

תָּנוּ רַבָּנַן: הַנִּדָּה, וְהַזָּבָה, וְהַשּׁוֹמֶרֶת יוֹם כְּנֶגֶד יוֹם, וְהַיּוֹלֶדֶת – כּוּלָּן מְטַמְּאוֹת בִּפְנִים כְּבַחוּץ.

§ The Gemara continues to discuss types of ritual impurity that apply whether the impure substance is still inside the body or has been discharged from it. **The Sages taught** in a *baraita*: With regard to **a menstruating woman, a** *zava*, a woman **who observes** a clean **day for a day** she experiences a discharge, **and a woman after childbirth, they all become impure** while the blood is still **inside** their bodies just **as** they would be when the blood emerges **outside** their bodies.[H]

בִּשְׁלָמָא כּוּלְּהוּ – לְחַיֵּי, אֶלָּא יוֹלֶדֶת, אִי בִּימֵי נִדָּה – נִדָּה, אִי בִּימֵי זִיבָה – זִיבָה!

The Gemara asks: **Granted,** with regard to **all those** other cases, **it is well,** i.e., one can understand this ruling with regard to blood that has not left the body. **But** the *halakha* of **a woman after childbirth** is puzzling, since **if** this is referring to blood that she discharges **in** her **days of menstruation,** then she is **a menstruating woman,** and she is included in the earlier category. Likewise, **if** the *baraita* is referring to blood that she discharges **in** her **days of** *ziva*, she has the status of ***ziva***, and once again is included in a previously mentioned category.

לָא צְרִיכָא – שֶׁיָּרְדָה לִטְבּוֹל מִטּוּמְאָה לְטָהֳרָה.

The Gemara answers: **No,** the mention of a woman after childbirth is **necessary** only in a case **where** the days of ritual impurity after childbirth, which are seven for a male and fourteen for a female, have passed, and the woman **descended to immerse** in a ritual bath in order to emerge **from** her status of **impurity to purity.**

וְכִי הָא דְּאָמַר רַבִּי זֵירָא אָמַר רַבִּי חִיָּיא בַּר אַשִׁי, אָמַר רַב: יוֹלֶדֶת שֶׁיָּרְדָה לִטְבּוֹל מִטּוּמְאָה לְטָהֳרָה, וְנֶעֱקַר מִמֶּנָּה דָּם, בִּירִידָה – טְמֵאָה, בַּעֲלִיָּיה – טְהוֹרָה.

**And** the *halakha* here is **like that which Rabbi Zeira said** that **Rabbi Ḥiyya bar Ashi said** that **Rav said:** In the case of **a woman after childbirth who descended to immerse** in a ritual bath in order to emerge **from** her status of **impurity to purity,**[H] **and blood was uprooted from her** uterus but it did not leave her body, her status is as follows: If this occurred **on** her **descent** to the ritual bath, she remains **impure,** as the immersion is ineffective. If it happened **on** her **ascent** from the bath, she is **pure,** as her period of purity, which is thirty-three days for a male and sixty-six for a female, has commenced.

אֲמַר לֵיהּ רַבִּי יִרְמְיָה לְרַבִּי זֵירָא: בִּירִידָה אַמַּאי טְמֵאָה? טוּמְאָה בְּלוּעָה הִיא! אֲמַר לֵיהּ: זִיל שַׁיְילֵיהּ לְרַבִּי אָבִין, דְּאַסְבְּרִית נִיהֲלֵיהּ, וְכַרְכִּישׁ לִי בְּרֵישֵׁיהּ בֵּי מִדְרָשָׁא.

**Rabbi Yirmeya said to Rabbi Zeira,** with regard to this *halakha*: If the blood emerged **on** her **descent** to immerse, **why** is she **impure?** After all, the blood **is** a substance of **impurity** that is **encapsulated** inside a body,[N] and there is a *halakha* that an encapsulated source of impurity does not impart impurity to other items (see *Ḥullin* 71a). Rabbi Zeira **said to** Rabbi Yirmeya: **Go** and **ask Rabbi Avin, as I explained to him** the reason for this *halakha*, **and he nodded** [***vekharkish***][L] **his head to me** in **the study hall,** in affirmation of my explanation.

**HALAKHA**

**They all become impure while the blood is inside their bodies just as when it emerges outside their bodies** – **כּוּלָּן מְטַמְּאוֹת בִּפְנִים כְּבַחוּץ**: If blood emerged from a woman's uterus, she is ritually impure by Torah law even if it did not leave her body (*Shakh*), as all women are rendered impure by blood in the outer chamber, i.e., the vagina. This is the *halakha* only if the woman senses the emergence of the blood from the uterus; if she does not feel it, she is not impure by Torah law, although the *Shakh* maintains that she is impure by rabbinic law (Rambam *Sefer Kedusha, Hilkhot Issurei Bia* 5:2; *Shulḥan Arukh, Yoreh De'a* 183:1).

**A woman after childbirth who descended to immerse to emerge from her status of impurity to purity, etc.** – **יוֹלֶדֶת שֶׁיָּרְדָה לִטְבּוֹל מִטּוּמְאָה לְטָהֳרָה וכו׳**: If a woman after childbirth descended to immerse in order to transition from her days of impurity to her days of purity, and blood emerged from her uterus and left the area between the teeth-like projections inside the vagina, she is impure. The immersion was ineffective with regard to this blood, despite the fact that it is still in her flesh. If the blood emerged from her uterus upon her ascent from the ritual bath, she is pure, as the immersion was effective for any blood encapsulated in her limbs to render it the blood of her days of purity. The *halakha* is in accordance with the statement that Rabbi Zeira said that Rabbi Ḥiyya bar Ashi said that Rav said (Rambam *Sefer Tahara, Hilkhot Metamei Mishkav UMoshav* 5:3).

**LANGUAGE**

**He nodded [*karkish*]** – **כַּרְכִּישׁ**: This phrase means that he tipped his head toward another, which is a gesture of acquiescence to the other's comment.

**NOTES**

**It is a substance of impurity that is encapsulated inside a body** – **טוּמְאָה בְּלוּעָה הִיא**: There is a *halakha* with regard to ritual impurity that an impure item which is encapsulated inside another item does not transfer impurity. Likewise, if a ritually pure item is inside another item, it is not susceptible to impurity. For example, a vessel inside someone's intestines is not considered part of his body, neither with regard to purity, i.e., if the vessel was impure it remains so even if he immersed in a ritual bath, nor with regard to impurity, i.e., if the vessel was pure it is not rendered impure when the individual who swallowed it contracts impurity.

This principle is derived from a verse discussing an animal carcass: "And he who eats of its carcass shall wash his clothes, and be impure until the evening" (Leviticus 11:40). Since this verse applies even to one who ate from the carcass near sunset, this means that it was still undigested at sunset, and yet he still becomes pure in the evening. Evidently, an impure item inside a person does not render the individual impure (see *Ḥullin* 71a).

אֲזַל שַׁיְילֵיהּ, אֲמַר לֵיהּ: עֲשָׂאוּהָ כְּנִבְלַת עוֹף טָהוֹר, שֶׁמְּטַמְּאָה בְּגָדִים בְּבֵית הַבְּלִיעָה. מִי דָּמֵי?

The Gemara relates that Rabbi Yirmeya indeed **went** and **asked** Rabbi Avin the reason, and Rabbi Avin **said to** Rabbi Yirmeya: The Sages **rendered** this blood **like the unslaughtered carcass of a kosher bird,**[H] **which imparts impurity** even **to** the **garments** of the one who eats it, when there is an olive-bulk of it **in** his **throat,** despite the fact that this source of impurity is encapsulated in his body. Rabbi Yirmeya asked Rabbi Avin: **Are** these cases **comparable?** How can one compare the impurity of a woman after childbirth to the impurity of one who eats the unslaughtered carcass of a kosher bird?

**HALAKHA**

**The unslaughtered carcass of a kosher bird, etc. – נִבְלַת עוֹף טָהוֹר וכו׳:** An unslaughtered carcass of a kosher bird imparts impurity by Torah law. It does not transfer impurity by touch or carrying, or when it is in one's mouth, but only while an olive-bulk is in the throat. One who contracts impurity in this manner renders his garments impure until he separates from his impurity. How so? If one swallowed an olive-bulk of an unslaughtered carcass of a kosher bird and touched vessels at the time, the vessels have first-degree ritual impurity. Once he has swallowed the carcass, he does not impart impurity to other vessels, as he is comparable to an object that has first-degree ritual impurity and has separated from the source of its impurity. Such an object does not impart impurity to vessels, despite the fact that it requires immersion and the passing of sunset before it becomes ritually pure. This *halakha* is in accordance with the *baraita* in *Torat Kohanim* (Rambam *Sefer Tahara, Hilkhot She'ar Avot HaTumot* 3:1).

Perek **V**
Daf **42** Amud **b**

הָתָם – אֵין לָהּ טוּמְאָה בַּחוּץ, הָכָא – כִּי נָפֵיק לְבָרַאי לִיטַמֵּי! הָכָא נַמִי – כְּשֶׁיָּצָא לַחוּץ.

Rabbi Yirmeya elaborates: **There,** with regard to the impurity contracted by swallowing an unslaughtered bird carcass, this unusual type of impurity **does not have** an equivalent form of **impurity outside,** since if one merely touches an unslaughtered bird carcass, he and his garments remain pure. By contrast, **here,** with regard to the blood of a woman after childbirth, **let it become impure** only **when it emerges outside** her body, like all other items that impart impurity by contact once they are no longer encapsulated. Rather, due to this difficulty one must explain that **here too,** Rabbi Zeira is referring to a case **where** the blood **emerged outside** her body after her immersion; otherwise she remains pure.

אִי יָצָא לַחוּץ – מַאי לְמֵימְרָא? מַהוּ דְּתֵימָא: מִגּוֹ דִּמְהַנְּיָא טְבִילָה לְדָם דְּאִיכָּא גַּוָּאֵי – תְּהַנֵּי נַמִי לְהַאי, קָא מַשְׁמַע לָן.

The Gemara asks: **If** the reason that the woman is pure is that the blood **emerged outside** her body, **what** is the purpose **of stating** this *halakha*? Certainly, this blood renders the woman impure upon contact. The Gemara answers that this ruling is necessary, **lest you say: Since** the woman's **immersion is effective for** any **blood that is inside** her, i.e., it prevents that blood from rendering her impure, **let it also be effective for this** blood, which did not leave her body until after the immersion. Therefore, Rabbi Zeira **teaches us** that this is not the *halakha*.

שְׁמַעְתִּין – אִיפְּרִיק, אֶלָּא יוֹלֶדֶת, אִי בִּימֵי נִדָּה – נִדָּה, אִי בִּימֵי זִיבָה – זִיבָה!

The Gemara objects: **We have resolved our** ***halakha,*** the statement of Rabbi Zeira, **but** the difficulty remains with regard to the case of **a woman after childbirth.** In light of the explanation of Rabbi Zeira's opinion, the *baraita* cited at the beginning of the discussion, which states that a woman after childbirth becomes impure by blood that is still inside her body, cannot be interpreted in accordance with his opinion, as Rabbi Zeira maintains that the blood does not render her impure unless it emerges outside her body. Accordingly, the original difficulty remains: **If** the *baraita* is referring to blood that she discharges **in** her **days of menstruation,** then she is **a menstruating woman,** and **if** the *baraita* is referring to her **days of** ***ziva,*** it has the status of ***ziva,*** both are which are already listed in the *baraita*.

הָכָא בְּמַאי עָסְקִינַן – בְּלֵידָה יְבֵשְׁתָּא. לֵידָה יְבֵשְׁתָּא מַאי ״מְטַמֵּא בִּפְנִים כְּבַחוּץ״ אִיכָּא?

The Gemara explains: **Here we are dealing with a dry birth,** without the emission of blood, and the *baraita* is teaching that the woman is rendered impure despite the fact that no blood emerged. The Gemara asks: If the *baraita* is referring to **a dry birth, what** blood **is there** that **becomes impure** while still **inside** the woman's body just **as** it would when emerging **outside** her body? There is no blood at all in the case of a dry birth.

## BACKGROUND

**Circumcision on Shabbat – מִילָה בְּשַׁבָּת:** By Torah law, all male Jews must be circumcised (see Genesis 17:10–14). This obligation is assigned to the father of a son eight days after birth. The Sages derived that the obligation to circumcise on the eighth day overrides the prohibitions of Shabbat (see Leviticus 12:3). Nevertheless, if the circumcision had been postponed due to the infant's illness or if there exists some uncertainty as to whether Shabbat is truly the eighth day after birth, the circumcision may be performed only on a weekday.

## HALAKHA

**A child making a noise at nightfall on Shabbat eve but it was not born until Shabbat – וָלָד דִּצְוִיץ אַפַּנְיָא דְּמַעֲלֵי שַׁבְּתָא וְלָא אִתְיְלִיד עַד שַׁבְּתָא:** If a child reached its head out from the corridor on Shabbat eve, or if he was heard crying, even if he fully emerged only on Shabbat he is not circumcised on Shabbat. Rather, his circumcision is performed on the following Shabbat eve, which is the eighth day after the emergence of his head. The *halakha* is in accordance with the opinion of Rava (Rambam *Sefer Ahava, Hilkhot Mila* 1:15; *Shulḥan Arukh, Yoreh De'a* 262:4).

**Where another woman inserted an olive-bulk of an animal carcass into that place – תָּחֲבָה לָהּ חֲבֵירְתָּהּ כְּזַיִת נְבֵלָה בְּאוֹתוֹ מָקוֹם:** If one inserted a ritually impure object with a stick into the body cavity of a woman below, without the impure object touching her flesh, she is not rendered impure by this contact, as internal contact is not considered touching with regard to this *halakha*. This ruling is in accordance with the opinion of Rava (Rambam *Sefer Tahara, Hilkhot Tumat Met* 1:3; see 1:8).

כְּגוֹן שֶׁהוֹצִיא וָלָד רֹאשׁוֹ חוּץ לַפְּרוֹזְדוֹר, וְכִדְרַב אוֹשַׁעְיָא. דְּאָמַר רַב אוֹשַׁעְיָא: גְּזֵרָה שֶׁמָּא יוֹצִיא הַוָּלָד רֹאשׁוֹ חוּץ לַפְּרוֹזְדוֹר.

The Gemara answers that this clause is not referring to blood; rather, this is a situation **where the offspring put his head out of the corridor,** in which case it is considered born and renders its mother impure, despite the fact that the rest of its body has not emerged. **And** this is **in accordance with** the statement **of Rav Oshaya, as Rav Oshaya said:** If a midwife inserted her hand into the womb of a woman whose fetus is dead, she is rendered impure due to contact with a corpse. This is a rabbinic **decree lest** the midwife touch it after **the offspring puts his head out of the corridor** and it dies afterward, in which case the fetus is considered born and therefore she would be ritually impure by Torah law.

וְכִי הַהוּא דַּאֲתָא לְקַמֵּיהּ דְּרָבָא, אֲמַר לֵיהּ: מַהוּ לְמִמְהַל בְּשַׁבְּתָא? אֲמַר לֵיהּ: שַׁפִּיר דָּמֵי. בָּתַר דִּנְפַק, אֲמַר רָבָא: סָלְקָא דַּעְתָּךְ דְּהַהוּא גַּבְרָא לָא יָדַע דְּשָׁרֵי לְמִמְהַל בְּשַׁבְּתָא?! אֲזַל בַּתְרֵיהּ, אֲמַר לֵיהּ: אֵימָא לִי אִיזִי, גּוּפָא דְּעוּבְדָא הֵיכִי הֲוָה?

The Gemara adds: **And** this is **similar to** an incident involving **a certain man who came before Rava** and **said to him: What is** the *halakha* **with regard to** whether one **may circumcise on Shabbat?**[B] Rava **said to him:** One may **well** do so. **After** that man **left, Rava said** to himself, perplexed: Can it **enter your mind that that man did not know that** it is **permitted to circumcise on Shabbat,** and he approached me to inquire about such a basic matter? There must be an unstated aspect to his question. Rava therefore **went after him** and **said to him: Say to me, my friend** [*izi*],[L] **how did the incident itself happen?**

אֲמַר לֵיהּ: שְׁמָעִית וָלָד דִּצְוִיץ אַפַּנְיָא דְּמַעֲלֵי שַׁבְּתָא, וְלָא אִתְיְלִיד עַד שַׁבְּתָא. אֲמַר לֵיהּ: הַאי – הוֹצִיא רֹאשׁוֹ חוּץ לַפְּרוֹזְדוֹר הוּא, וַהֲוֵי מִילָה שֶׁלֹּא בִּזְמַנָּהּ, וְכׇל מִילָה שֶׁלֹּא בִּזְמַנָּהּ – אֵין מְחַלְּלִין עָלֶיהָ אֶת הַשַּׁבָּת.

The man **said to** Rava: **I heard** the **child making a noise at nightfall on Shabbat eve,** before Shabbat began, **but it was not born until Shabbat.**[H] Rava **said to him: This is** a baby who **put his head out of the corridor,** as otherwise his voice would not have been heard. Consequently, it is considered born already on Friday, which means that it should be circumcised on the following Friday, the eighth day after its birth. **And** if it is circumcised afterward, this **is a circumcision** performed **not at its** appointed **time, and** there is a *halakha* that although circumcision on the eighth day overrides Shabbat, nevertheless, with regard to **any circumcision** performed **not at its** appointed **time, one does not desecrate Shabbat for its** performance.

אִיבַּעְיָא לְהוּ: אוֹתוֹ מָקוֹם שֶׁל אִשָּׁה, בָּלוּעַ הָוֵי אוֹ בֵּית הַסְּתָרִים הָוֵי?

§ **A dilemma was raised before** the Sages: With regard to **that place in a woman,** i.e., her vagina, how is it defined? **Is** an impure substance located there considered **encapsulated, or is it** considered to be located in **a concealed part** of the body?

לְמַאי נָפְקָא מִינָּהּ? כְּגוֹן שֶׁתָּחֲבָה לָהּ חֲבֵירְתָּהּ כְּזַיִת נְבֵלָה בְּאוֹתוֹ מָקוֹם. אִי אָמְרַתְּ בָּלוּעַ הָוֵי – טוּמְאָה בְּלוּעָה לָא מְטַמְּאָה, וְאִי אָמְרַתְּ בֵּית הַסְּתָרִים הָוֵי – נְהִי דִּבְמַגָּע לָא מִטַּמְיָא, בְּמַשָּׂא מִיהָא מִטַּמְיָא!

The Gemara explains: **What is the** practical **difference** as to whether it is considered encapsulated or concealed? The difference is in a case **where another** woman **inserted an olive-bulk of an animal carcass,** which is the size that imparts impurity, **into that place.**[H] **If you say** that **it is** considered **encapsulated, an encapsulated** source of **impurity does not impart impurity. But if you say** that **it is** considered located in **a concealed part** of the body, **although** the woman **does not become impure by contact, she at least becomes impure by carrying** the olive-bulk of the carcass.

אַבַּיֵי אֲמַר: בָּלוּעַ הָוֵי. רָבָא אֲמַר: בֵּית הַסְּתָרִים הָוֵי. אֲמַר רָבָא: מְנָא אָמִינָא לַהּ – דְּתַנְיָא, אֶלָּא מִפְּנֵי שֶׁטּוּמְאַת בֵּית הַסְּתָרִים הִיא,

**Abaye said: It is** considered **encapsulated. Rava said: It is** considered located in **a concealed part** of the body. **Rava** further **said: From where do I say** this? **As it is taught** in a *baraita*: The verse states: "The woman also with whom a man shall lie carnally, they shall both bathe themselves in water, and be impure until the evening" (Leviticus 15:18). Rabbi Shimon said: Now what does this verse teach? If it teaches that one who touches semen is rendered impure, this is derived from the verse: "Or a man from whom the flow of seed goes out" (Leviticus 22:4). **Rather,** it must be teaching that a woman who engages in intercourse is rendered impure by the man's semen, despite the fact that the semen did not touch her on the outside of her body.

## LANGUAGE

**My friend** [*izi*] **– אִיזִי:** Some commentaries maintain that this word means my friend, and is a term of affection and closeness, as translated here. However, the source and the definition of the word *izi* and its alternative form *izo* are unclear. Some claim that it is a form of an Aramaic phrase meaning: Therefore, or: If so. Alternatively, it is related to the Persian zi, meaning: Now, rendering the phrase in the Gemara as: Say to me now.

וְטוּמְאַת בֵּית הַסְּתָרִים לֹא מְטַמְּאָה, אֶלָּא שֶׁגְּזֵירַת הַכָּתוּב הִיא.

The *baraita* continues: This is a novelty **because** the semen **is** a source of **impurity** located in **a concealed part** of the body, **and** ordinarily contact with a source of **impurity** by **a concealed part** of the body **does not render** one **impure. But** here **it is a Torah edict** that the woman does become impure in this manner. Evidently, an impure substance in the vagina is considered located in a concealed part of the body.

וְאַבַּיֵּי – חֲדָא וְעוֹד קָאָמַר, חֲדָא – דְּטוּמְאָה בְּלוּעָה הִיא, וְעוֹד – אֲפִילּוּ אִם תִּמְצֵי לוֹמַר טוּמְאַת בֵּית הַסְּתָרִים הִיא – אֵינָהּ מְטַמְּאָה, אֶלָּא שֶׁגְּזֵירַת הַכָּתוּב הִיא.

The Gemara asks: **And Abaye,** how does he respond to Rava's proof? The Gemara answers that Abaye would explain that the *tanna* of this *baraita*, Rabbi Shimon, **states one** reason **and** adds **another: One** reason **that** this *halakha* is a novelty is that semen in the vagina **is an encapsulated** substance of **impurity, and another** reason is that **even if you were to say** that the semen **is** considered located in **a concealed part** of the body, which ordinarily **does not render** one **impure, but** here, **it is a Torah edict** that the woman does become impure in this manner.

אִיבַּעְיָא לְהוּ: מְקוֹם נִבְלַת עוֹף טָהוֹר, בָּלוּעַ הָוֵי אוֹ בֵּית הַסְּתָרִים הָוֵי?

§ A similar **dilemma was raised before** the Sages: With regard to the **place** in a person's throat where **an unslaughtered carcass of a kosher bird** renders him ritually impure, how is it defined? **Is** the meat of the carcass considered **encapsulated, or is it** considered located in **a concealed part** of the body?

לְמַאי נָפְקָא מִינָּהּ כְּגוֹן שֶׁתָּחַב לוֹ חֲבֵירוֹ כְּזַיִת נְבֵלָה לְתוֹךְ פִּיו. אִי אָמְרַתְּ בָּלוּעַ הָוֵי – טוּמְאָה בְּלוּעָה לָא מְטַמְּיָא. (אֶלָּא אִי) אָמְרַתְּ בֵּית הַסְּתָרִים הָוֵי – נְהִי נַמִי דִּבְמַגָּע לָא מְטַמֵּא, בְּמַשָּׂא מִיהָא מְטַמֵּא.

The Gemara explains: **What is the** practical **difference?** The difference is in a case **where another** individual **inserted an olive-bulk of an animal carcass into his mouth.**[NH] **If you say** that an impure item located in one's throat **is** considered **encapsulated, an encapsulated** source of **impurity does not impart impurity.** But **if you say** that **it is** considered located in **a concealed part** of the body, **although** the one swallowing the meat of the carcass **indeed does not become impure by contact, he at least becomes impure by carrying**[H] the meat.

אַבַּיֵּי אָמַר: בָּלוּעַ הָוֵי, וְרָבָא אָמַר: בֵּית הַסְּתָרִים הָוֵי. אָמַר אַבַּיֵּי: מְנָא אָמִינָא לַהּ – דְּתַנְיָא, יָכוֹל תְּהֵא נִבְלַת בְּהֵמָה מְטַמְּאָה בְּגָדִים אַבֵּית הַבְּלִיעָה – תַּלְמוּד לוֹמַר ״נְבֵלָה וּטְרֵפָה לֹא יֹאכַל לְטָמְאָה בָהּ״,

Abaye and Rava disagree with regard to this issue as well. **Abaye said: It is** considered **encapsulated, and Rava said: It is** considered located in **a concealed part** of the body. **Abaye** further **said: From where do I say** that it is considered encapsulated? **As it is taught** in a *baraita*: One **might** have thought that **an animal carcass should impart impurity to garments** when it is **in** one's **throat,** like an unslaughtered carcass of a kosher bird. Therefore, **the verse states: "That which dies of itself, or is torn of animals, he shall not eat to render himself impure through it"** (Leviticus 22:8).

מִי שֶׁאֵין לָהּ טוּמְאָה אֶלָּא אֲכִילָתָהּ, יָצְתָה זוֹ שֶׁטְּמֵאָה קוֹדֶם שֶׁיֹּאכְלֶנָּה.

The *baraita* continues: This verse, which is dealing with impurity through eating, applies to **that which has impurity only** by means of **its consumption,** i.e., an unslaughtered carcass of a kosher bird, which imparts impurity solely when it is in one's throat. Therefore, the verse **excludes this** animal carcass from impurity by consumption, **as it is impure,** i.e., it imparts impurity, even **before one eats it,** by touch and carrying. This ruling, that other sources of impurity do not impart impurity in the throat, supports Abaye's opinion that an item located in the throat is considered encapsulated, which is why it does not impart impurity.

**NOTES**

**Where another individual inserted an olive-bulk of an animal carcass into his mouth – שֶׁתָּחַב לוֹ חֲבֵירוֹ כְּזַיִת נְבֵלָה לְתוֹךְ פִּיו:** The Gemara does not say that one inserted the olive-bulk into his own mouth, as in such a case he would already be rendered impure because he touched the animal carcass (Rashi).

**HALAKHA**

**Another individual inserted an olive-bulk of an animal carcass into his mouth – תָּחַב לוֹ חֲבֵירוֹ כְּזַיִת נְבֵלָה לְתוֹךְ פִּיו:** If someone inserted with a stick a ritually impure food into the throat of a pure individual, without the impure object touching his tongue, the one who swallows it is not rendered impure. The reason is that internal contact is not considered touching. This ruling is in accordance with the opinion of Rava (Rambam *Sefer Tahara, Hilkhot Tumat Met* 1:3; see 1:8).

**He at least becomes impure by carrying – בְּמַשָּׂא מִיהָא מְטַמֵּא:** If one carries in a concealed part of his body an impure item which imparts impurity by carrying, he is rendered impure. The reason is that although he is not considered to be touching the item, he is nevertheless carrying it. If he swallowed the impure item he does not become impure through carrying it, as the contact of an impure item in one's stomach is of no consequence, neither with regard to touching nor with regard to carrying. This *halakha* is in accordance with the opinion of Rava (Rambam *Sefer Tahara, Hilkhot Tumat Met* 1:8; see 1:1).

LANGUAGE

Fold [*kummat*] – קוּמָט: From the root *kuf, mem, tet*, this word is used to describe limbs in the body which shrink as a result of various movements. See the verse "And you have shriveled me up [*vatikmeteni*], which is a witness against me" (Job 16:8).

וְתֵיתֵי בְּקַל וָחוֹמֶר מִנִּבְלַת עוֹף טָהוֹר: וּמָה נִבְלַת עוֹף טָהוֹר, שֶׁאֵין לָהּ טוּמְאָה בַּחוּץ – יֵשׁ לָהּ טוּמְאָה בִּפְנִים, זוֹ שֶׁיֵּשׁ לָהּ טוּמְאָה בַּחוּץ – אֵינוֹ דִּין שֶׁיֵּשׁ לָהּ טוּמְאָה בִּפְנִים?

The Gemara raises a difficulty with regard to the *baraita*: **And let it be derived** that an animal carcass imparts impurity to garments when it is in one's throat **by an *a fortiori* inference from** the *halakha* **of an unslaughtered carcass of a kosher bird,** in the following manner: **If an unslaughtered carcass of a kosher bird,** whose status is relatively lenient, **as it does not have impurity outside** the body, since if one touched it or carried it he is not rendered impure, and yet **it has impurity inside** the throat, then with regard to **this** animal carcass, whose status is more stringent, **as it does have impurity outside** the body, **is it not right that it** should **have impurity inside** the throat?

אָמַר קְרָא "בָּהּ" – בָּהּ וְלֹא בְּאַחֶרֶת.

The Gemara answers that **the verse states:** "That which dies of itself, or is torn of animals, he shall not eat to become impure **through it,**" which indicates that one becomes impure when the item is in the throat only **through it,** i.e., an unslaughtered carcass of a kosher bird, **and not through another,** i.e., an animal carcass.

אִם כֵּן מַה תַּלְמוּד לוֹמַר "וְהָאֹכֵל"?

The Gemara asks: **If so, what** is the meaning when **the verse states** with regard to an animal carcass: **"And he who eats** of its carcass shall wash his clothes and be impure until the evening" (Leviticus 11:40), which indicates that an animal carcass does impart impurity by means of consumption?

לִיתֵּן שִׁיעוּר לַנּוֹגֵעַ וְלַנּוֹשֵׂא כְּאוֹכֵל, מָה אוֹכֵל – בִּכְזַיִת, אַף נוֹגֵעַ וְנוֹשֵׂא – בִּכְזַיִת.

The Gemara explains that this verse is written **to provide a measure** for the impurity of an animal carcass, but this measure applies only **to one who touches and to one who carries** it, not to one who eats the carcass. This measure is **like** the amount that one **eats. Just as** the minimum amount that one **eats** is **an olive-bulk,** i.e., this is the minimum measure that has the halakhic status of consumption, **so too,** the minimum measure of an animal carcass that imparts impurity to one who **touches or carries** it is **an olive-bulk.**

אָמַר רָבָא: שֶׁרֶץ בְּקוּמְטוֹ – טָהוֹר, נְבֵלָה בְּקוּמְטוֹ – טָמֵא.

§ The Gemara further discusses the impurity of a concealed part of the body. **Rava says:** If the carcass of a **creeping animal** is found **in the folds** [*bekometo*][L] **of** one's body, e.g., the armpit, he is **ritually pure.** If the flesh of **an animal carcass** is found **in the folds of** one's body, he is **impure.**

שֶׁרֶץ בְּקוּמְטוֹ טָהוֹר – שֶׁרֶץ בִּנְגִיעָה הוּא דִּמְטַמֵּא, וּבֵית הַסְּתָרִים לָאו בַּר מַגָּע הוּא. נְבֵלָה בְּקוּמְטוֹ – טָמֵא, נְהִי דִּבְמַגָּע לָא מְטַמֵּא – בְּמַשָּׂא מִיהָא מְטַמֵּא.

Rava elaborates: If the carcass of a **creeping animal** is found **in the folds of** one's body he is **ritually pure,** as **it is through contact that a creeping animal imparts impurity, and a concealed part** of the body **is not susceptible to** impurity through **contact.** By contrast, if the flesh of **an animal carcass** is found **in the folds of** one's body he is **impure,** as **although it does not impart impurity through contact,** since it is in a concealed part of the body, **it at least imparts impurity by carrying,** and he is considered to be carrying the animal carcass.

שֶׁרֶץ בְּקוּמְטוֹ, וְהִכְנִיסוֹ לַאֲוִיר הַתַּנּוּר – טָמֵא. פְּשִׁיטָא! מַהוּ דְּתֵימָא: "תּוֹכוֹ" אָמַר רַחֲמָנָא,

Rava further said: If there was the carcass of **a creeping animal in the folds of** one's body, **and he brought** the creeping animal that was in the fold **into the airspace of** a large earthenware vessel, such as **an oven,** the oven is thereby rendered **impure,**[H] as is the *halakha* when a creeping animal is placed in its airspace. The Gemara asks: Isn't this **obvious?** The Gemara answers: **Lest you say** that as **the Merciful One states** with regard to the impurity of creeping animals: "And any earthenware vessel into **whose interior** any of them fall, whatever is in it shall be impure, and it you shall break" (Leviticus 11:33), this teaches that impurity applies only if the creeping animal fell inside the vessel itself,

HALAKHA

If there was the carcass of a creeping animal in the folds of one's body and he brought it into the airspace of an oven it is impure – שֶׁרֶץ בְּקוּמְטוֹ וְהִכְנִיסוֹ לַאֲוִיר הַתַּנּוּר טָמֵא: If one had a lentil-bulk of the carcass of a creeping animal in one of the folds of his body, and he brought it into the airspace of an oven, the oven is rendered ritually impure, despite the fact that the impure item is inside a fold. This *halakha* is in accordance with the opinion of Rava (Rambam *Sefer Tahara, Hilkhot Kelim* 14:5).

וְלֹא תּוֹךְ תּוֹכוֹ, קָא מַשְׁמַע לַן.

**and not** if it was in **the interior of its interior,** i.e., contained within something else, such as a fold, which is inside the vessel, therefore Rava **teaches us** that a fold in one's body is not considered like the interior of the interior of a vessel. Rather, this definition applies only when the carcass of the creeping animal was actually inside another vessel whose opening was outside the oven.

אָמַר רֵישׁ לָקִישׁ: קָנֶה בְּקוֹמְטוֹ שֶׁל זָב, וְהֵסִיט בּוֹ אֶת הַטָּהוֹר – טָהוֹר. קָנֶה בְּקוֹמְטוֹ שֶׁל טָהוֹר, וְהֵסִיט בּוֹ אֶת הַזָּב – טָמֵא.

§ The Gemara continues to discuss the folds in the body with regard to ritual impurity. **Reish Lakish says:** If there was **a pole** or a stick placed **in the folds of** an individual impure with the impurity of **a *zav*,**[H] **and he moved a ritually pure** person **with it,** that individual is **pure,** despite the fact that a *zav* imparts impurity by moving an item. If the **pole** was placed **in the folds of one who is pure, and he moved the *zav* with it,**[NH] the pure individual is thereby rendered **impure,** as is the *halakha* of one who carries a *zav*.

מַאי טַעְמָא – דְּאָמַר קְרָא "וְכֹל אֲשֶׁר יִגַּע בּוֹ הַזָּב וְיָדָיו לֹא שָׁטַף בַּמָּיִם" – זֶהוּ הֶסֵּיטוֹ שֶׁל זָב, שֶׁלֹּא מָצִינוּ לוֹ טוּמְאָה בְּכָל הַתּוֹרָה כּוּלָּהּ.

The Gemara explains: **What is the reason** that if a *zav* moved another with a pole in his own folds he does not render the other person impure? **As the verse states: "And whoever a *zav* touches, without having rinsed his hands in water,**[N] he shall wash his clothes, and bathe himself in water" (Leviticus 15:11). **This is** referring to the impurity imparted by **the movement of a *zav*, as we have not found an impurity** similar **to it in the entire Torah.** Only a *zav* imparts impurity to items by moving them.

וְאַפְקֵיהּ רַחֲמָנָא בִּלְשׁוֹן נְגִיעָה, לְמֵימְרָא דְּהֶיסֵּט וּנְגִיעָה כְּיָדָיו, מָה הָתָם – מֵאַבְּרַאי, אַף הָכָא – מֵאַבְּרַאי.

**And the Merciful One expresses** this impurity imparted **by** movement using **the language of touch,** in order **to say that** the **moving and touch** of a *zav* **are like his hands: Just as there,** with regard to the impurity imparted by contact with the hands, it occurs **external** to the body, **so too here,** impurity by means of movement applies only to moving an item with the **external** portions of the body of the *zav*.

"אֲבָל הַזָּב וּבַעַל קֶרִי אֵינָן מְטַמְּאִין" וכו׳. זָב – דִּכְתִיב "כִּי יִהְיֶה זָב מִבְּשָׂרוֹ", עַד שֶׁיֵּצֵא זוֹבוֹ מִבְּשָׂרוֹ. בַּעַל קֶרִי – דִּכְתִיב: "וְאִישׁ כִּי תֵצֵא מִמֶּנּוּ שִׁכְבַת זָרַע".

§ The mishna teaches that a woman becomes ritually impure with the flow of blood from the uterus into the vagina, even if it did not leave the woman's body. **But the *zav* and one who experiences a seminal emission do not become ritually impure** until their emission of impurity emerges outside the body. The Gemara explains: This is the *halakha* with regard to **a *zav*, as it is written: "When** any man **has an issue out of his flesh"** (Leviticus 15:2). The verse teaches that a *zav* is not impure **until his issue emerges out of his flesh.** With regard to **one who experiences a seminal emission,** the reason is **that it is written: "And if the flow of seed goes out from a man"** (Leviticus 15:16),[N] which indicates that the flow must exit his body.

"הָיָה אוֹכֵל בִּתְרוּמָה וְהִרְגִּישׁ" וכו׳. אוֹחֵז? וְהָתַנְיָא, רַבִּי אֱלִיעֶזֶר אוֹמֵר: כָּל הָאוֹחֵז בְּאַמָּה וּמַשְׁתִּין, כְּאִילּוּ מֵבִיא מַבּוּל לָעוֹלָם!

§ The mishna further states that if a priest **was partaking of *teruma* and sensed** a quaking in his limbs, indicating that a seminal emission was imminent, he should firmly hold his penis to prevent the emission from leaving his body, and swallow the *teruma* while ritually pure. The Gemara asks: May one **hold** his penis? **But isn't it taught** in a *baraita* that **Rabbi Eliezer says: Anyone who holds** his **penis and urinates** is considered **as though he is bringing a deluge to the world,** as masturbation was one of the sins that led to the flood?

**NOTES**

**If the pole was in the folds of one who is pure and he moved the *zav* with it, etc. – קָנֶה בְּקוֹמְטוֹ שֶׁל טָהוֹר וְהֵסִיט בּוֹ אֶת הַזָּב וכו׳:** Rashi explains that the individual is impure because he carried a *zav*. A *zav* imparts impurity by being carried, as it is stated: "And whoever touches anything that was under him shall be impure until the evening; and he that bears those things shall wash his clothes, and bathe himself in water, and be impure until the evening" (Leviticus 15:10). If one becomes impure by carrying that which was under a *zav*, this applies *a fortiori* with regard to carrying the *zav* himself.

**And whoever a *zav* touches without having rinsed his hands in water, etc. – וְכֹל אֲשֶׁר יִגַּע בּוֹ הַזָּב וְיָדָיו לֹא שָׁטַף בַּמַּיִם וכו׳:** The *halakha* that a *zav* imparts impurity by moving an item is derived from the first part of this verse: "And whoever he that has the issue touch." This section of the verse is superfluous, as it is already stated earlier in the chapter: "And he who touches the flesh of him who has the issue shall wash his clothes, and bathe himself in water, and be impure until the evening" (Leviticus 15:7). Therefore, the verse is expounded as referring not to touch but to the impurity of movement.

**And if the flow of seed goes out from a man – וְאִישׁ כִּי תֵצֵא מִמֶּנּוּ שִׁכְבַת זָרַע:** The Gemara does not explain how this *halakha*, that one who experiences a seminal emission becomes impure only after his emission emerges outside his body, is derived from the verse. On 22a it is stated that the *halakha* is learned from the word "from." Some claim that the derivation is based on the term "goes out," which indicates that the flow has entirely left its previous place (Malbim).

**HALAKHA**

**A pole in the folds of a *zav*, etc. – קָנֶה בְּקוֹמְטוֹ שֶׁל זָב וכו׳:** If a *zav* had a pole placed in the folds of his body and he moved a ritually pure individual or vessel with it, they remain ritually pure. The *halakha* is in accordance with the opinion of Reish Lakish (Rambam *Sefer Tahara*, *Hilkhot Metamei Mishkav UMoshav* 8:5).

**The pole was in the folds of one who is pure and he moved the *zav* with it – קָנֶה בְּקוֹמְטוֹ שֶׁל טָהוֹר וְהֵסִיט בּוֹ אֶת הַזָּב:** If a ritually pure individual had a pole placed in the folds of his body and he moved a *zav* with it, he is rendered impure. The reason is that the impurity caused by moving an impure individual or item is similar to carrying it, and just as carrying impurity in a concealed part of the body imparts impurity, the same applies to movement by a concealed part of the body. The *halakha* is in accordance with the opinion of Reish Lakish (Rambam *Sefer Tahara*, *Hilkhot Metamei Mishkav UMoshav* 8:5).

אֲמַר אַבַּיֵי: בְּמַטְלִית עָבָה. וְרָבָא אֲמַר: אֲפִילּוּ תֵּימָא בְּמַטְלִית רַכָּה, כֵּיוָן דְּעָקַר – עָקַר. וְאַבַּיֵי – חָיֵישׁ דִּילְמָא אָתֵי לְאוֹסוּפֵי, וְרָבָא – לְאוֹסוּפֵי לָא חָיֵישׁ.

**Abaye said,** in resolution of this difficulty, that the mishna is referring to one who holds his penis **with a coarse cloth. Rava said: You** may **even say** that the mishna is referring to a priest who holds his penis **with a soft cloth,** and the reason it is permitted is that **once** the semen **has** already **been uprooted** from his body, it is **uprooted,** and his subsequent holding of the penis, even with a soft cloth, does not increase the flow of semen. **And Abaye** prohibits the use of a soft cloth, as he is **concerned** that **perhaps** one might **come to increase** the emission of semen, due to the contact of this cloth. **But Rava is not concerned** that one might **come to increase** the emission.

וְהָתַנְיָא: לְמָה זֶה דּוֹמֶה – לְנוֹתֵן אֶצְבַּע בָּעַיִן, שֶׁכָּל זְמַן שֶׁאֶצְבַּע בָּעַיִן – מְדַמַּעַת וְחוֹזֶרֶת וּמְדַמַּעַת!

The Gemara raises a difficulty with regard to the opinion of Rava. **Isn't it taught** in a *baraita*: **To what is this** holding of a penis **comparable?** It is comparable **to** one who **places a finger in** his **eye,** in **that as long as** the **finger** is **in the eye,** the eye **will tear and continue to tear.** Here too, the priest's action will lead to an increased emission of semen.

וְרָבָא – כָּל אִחֲמוּמֵי וַהֲדַר אִחֲמוּמֵי בְּשַׁעְתָּא – לָא שְׁכִיחַ.

The Gemara answers that **Rava** would maintain that if the priest's limbs were not quaking and the semen was coming out in drops, there is indeed a concern that holding the penis might increase the emission. But when he feels his limbs quaking, this concern does not apply. The reason is that **any** such event, i.e., **a heating** of the body that leads to a seminal emission **and** which is **then** followed by another **heating** of that kind **at the time** when the semen has been uprooted, is **uncommon.** Consequently, in this case the priest may hold his penis even with a soft cloth.

אָמַר שְׁמוּאֵל: כָּל שִׁכְבַת זֶרַע שֶׁאֵין כָּל גּוּפוֹ מַרְגִּישׁ בָּהּ – אֵינָהּ מְטַמְּאָה. מַאי טַעֲמָא? "שִׁכְבַת זָרַע" אָמַר רַחֲמָנָא – בְּרְאוּיָה לְהַזְרִיעַ.

**Shmuel says: Any** emission of **semen that is not felt by one's entire body**[H] **does not render** him **impure. What is the reason? The Merciful One states: "The flow of seed"** (Leviticus 15:16), which indicates that it is referring to an emission **that is fit to fertilize,** i.e., it is referring only to the kind of emission which is felt as it exits the body.

מֵיתִיבֵי: הָיָה מְהַרְהֵר בַּלַּיְלָה, וְעָמַד וּמָצָא בְּשָׂרוֹ חַם – טָמֵא! תִּרְגְּמָא רַב הוּנָא: בִּמְשַׁמֵּשׁ מִטָּתוֹ בַּחֲלוֹמוֹ, דְּאִי אֶפְשָׁר לְשַׁמֵּשׁ בְּלֹא הַרְגָּשָׁה.

The Gemara **raises an objection** from a mishna (*Mikvaot* 8:3): If one **was having** sexual **thoughts at night and he arose and found** that **his flesh** was **warm, he is ritually impure,** despite the fact that he did not sense the emission of semen. This shows that the impurity of a seminal emission applies even if one did not feel it in his entire body. The Gemara answers: **Rav Huna interpreted** this mishna as referring **to** one who **engaged in intercourse in his dream.**[H] **Since it is impossible to engage in intercourse without** the accompanying **sensation,** he certainly must have felt it, despite the fact that he was unaware of this when he awoke.

לִישָּׁנָא אַחֲרִינָא, אָמַר שְׁמוּאֵל: כָּל שִׁכְבַת זֶרַע שֶׁאֵינוֹ יוֹרֶה כְּחֵץ – אֵינָהּ מְטַמְּאָה. מַאי אִיכָּא בֵּין הַאי לִישָּׁנָא לְהַאי לִישָּׁנָא? אִיכָּא בֵּינַיְיהוּ: נֶעֶקְרָה בְּהַרְגָּשָׁה, וְיָצְאָה שֶׁלֹּא בְּהַרְגָּשָׁה.

The Gemara cites **another version** of the above statement. **Shmuel says: Any semen that is not shot like an arrow does not render** one **impure.** The Gemara asks: **What** practical difference **is there between this version** of Shmuel's ruling **and that version** of Shmuel's ruling? The Gemara answers that the difference **between them** is a case where the semen **was uprooted** accompanied **by a sensation, but it emerged without a sensation.**[H] According to the first version the man is rendered impure, as he sensed the uprooting of the semen, whereas according to the second version he is not impure, as this is not considered semen shot like an arrow.

## HALAKHA

**Any emission of semen that is not felt by one's entire body** – **כָּל שִׁכְבַת זֶרַע שֶׁאֵין כָּל גּוּפוֹ מַרְגִּישׁ בָּהּ:** Any emission of semen that is not felt by one's entire body does not cause ritual impurity. Therefore, if one emitted semen without an erection and without any lustful thoughts, he does not have the impurity of one who experienced a seminal emission. This *halakha* is in accordance with the opinion of Shmuel, following the first and second versions of his statement (Rambam). The Ra'avad maintains that the *halakha* follows the last version of Shmuel's ruling, and he is impure (Rambam *Sefer Tahara, Hilkhot She'ar Avot HaTumot* 5:4 and *Kesef Mishne* there).

**One who engaged in intercourse in his dream** – **בִּמְשַׁמֵּשׁ מִטָּתוֹ בַּחֲלוֹמוֹ:** If one was thinking impure thoughts at night and he saw himself engaging in intercourse in a dream, and upon awakening he found that his penis was warm, even if he did not find any semen he is impure. The reason is that as he dreamed of engaging in intercourse he must certainly have experienced an emission accompanied by a sensation, which is why his penis was warm. As for why he did not find any semen, that is because he emitted only a small amount which was rubbed away on his skin or clothing. This *halakha* is in accordance with the *baraita* as explained by Rav Huna (Rambam *Sefer Tahara, Hilkhot She'ar Avot HaTumot* 5:5).

**Was uprooted accompanied by a sensation but it emerged without a sensation** – **נֶעֶקְרָה בְּהַרְגָּשָׁה וְיָצְאָה שֶׁלֹּא בְּהַרְגָּשָׁה:** If semen was uprooted from a man accompanied by a sensation, he is impure, even if there was no sensation when it emerged. This *halakha* is in accordance with the second version of the opinion of Shmuel (Rambam *Sefer Tahara, Hilkhot She'ar Avot HaTumot* 5:4).

מִילְּתָא דִּפְשִׁיטָא לֵיהּ לִשְׁמוּאֵל מִיבַּעְיָא לֵיהּ לְרָבָא. דְּבָעֵי רָבָא: נֶעֶקְרָה בְּהַרְגָּשָׁה, וְיָצְתָה שֶׁלֹּא בְּהַרְגָּשָׁה, מַהוּ?

The Gemara notes that this **matter, which is obvious to Shmuel, is raised as a dilemma by Rava. As Rava raises a dilemma:** If semen **was uprooted** accompanied **by a sensation but it emerged without a sensation, what is** the *halakha*? Is the man ritually impure or not?

תָּא שְׁמַע: בַּעַל קֶרִי שֶׁטָּבַל וְלֹא הֵטִיל מַיִם, לִכְשֶׁיָּטִיל מַיִם טָמֵא. שָׁאנֵי הָתָם דְּרוּבָּה בְּהַרְגָּשָׁה נְפַק.

The Gemara suggests: **Come** and **hear** a proof from a mishna (*Mikvaot* 8:3): With regard to **one who experienced a seminal emission,** and who subsequently **immersed but did not urinate** before doing so,[H] **when he** later **urinates** he is rendered **impure,** as some semen will also be emitted. The reason that he is rendered impure by this emission, which he does not sense, must be because the uprooting of the semen was accompanied by a sensation. The Gemara refutes this proof: **There it is different, as the majority** of the semen **emerged** accompanied **by a sensation,** and therefore he is rendered impure by this small amount even without a sensation.

לִישָּׁנָא אַחֲרִינָא, אָמְרִי לַהּ אָמַר שְׁמוּאֵל: כׇּל שִׁכְבַת זֶרַע שֶׁאֵינוֹ יוֹרֶה כַּחֵץ – אֵינָהּ מַזְרַעַת, אַזְרוֹעֵי הוּא דְּלָא מַזְרְעָא, הָא טַמּוּיֵי – מְטַמְּיָא, שֶׁנֶּאֱמַר: ״כִּי יִהְיֶה בְךָ אִישׁ אֲשֶׁר לֹא יִהְיֶה טָהוֹר מִקְּרֵה״ – אֲפִילּוּ קֶרִי בָּעוֹלָם.

Some say **another version** of the previous discussion. **Shmuel says: Any semen that is not shot like an arrow cannot fertilize,** i.e., impregnate a woman. The Gemara infers: **It cannot fertilize, but it does render** the man who emits it **ritually impure, as it is stated: "If there be among you any man who is not ritually pure by reason of that which happened to him** by night" (Deuteronomy 23:11). This teaches that **even mere semen** which cannot fertilize renders one impure.

בָּעֵי רָבָא: גּוֹי שֶׁהִרְהֵר, וְיָרַד וְטָבַל, מַהוּ?

**Rava raises** a similar **dilemma:** With regard to **a gentile who had** sexual **thoughts,** on account of which semen was uprooted but not emitted from his body, **and he** subsequently **descended and immersed**[H] for the purpose of conversion, which means that he is now Jewish, and he then emitted semen, **what is** the *halakha* with regard to his status of ritual purity?

אִם תִּמְצֵי לוֹמַר בָּתַר עֲקִירָה אָזְלִינַן, הָנֵי מִילֵּי – לְחוּמְרָא, אֲבָל הָכָא דִּלְקוּלָּא – לָא אָמְרִינַן, אוֹ דִּילְמָא לָא שְׁנָא? תֵּיקוּ.

The Gemara explains the dilemma: Even **if you say** that **we follow** the moment of **uprooting,** at which point he was still a gentile, one can maintain that **this statement** applies only when it entails **a stringency,** as is the case with regard to a born Jew. **But here, where** this would lead **to a leniency,** as the gentile would be ritually pure, perhaps **we do not say** that one follows the moment of uprooting. **Or perhaps** there **is no difference** in the application of this principle between a born Jew and a convert, but rather, one always follows the moment of uprooting. The Gemara concludes that the dilemma **shall stand** unresolved.

בָּעֵי רָבָא: זָבָה שֶׁנֶּעֶקְרוּ מֵימֵי רַגְלֶיהָ וְיָרְדָה וְטָבְלָה, מַהוּ?

**Rava raises** a further **dilemma:** With regard to **a woman who experienced a discharge of uterine blood after her menstrual period [*zava*], whose urine,** which imparts impurity like all liquids that she discharges vaginally, **was uprooted** but not emitted from her body, **and she descended** to the ritual bath **and immersed** to purify herself from her *ziva*, and urinated afterward, **what is** the *halakha*?

אִם תִּמְצָא לוֹמַר בָּתַר עֲקִירָה אָזְלִינַן, הָנֵי מִילֵּי שִׁכְבַת זֶרַע, דְּלָא מָצֵי נָקֵיט לַהּ, אֲבָל מֵימֵי רַגְלֶיהָ דְּמָצְיָא נָקְטָא לְהוּ – לָא, אוֹ דִּילְמָא לָא שְׁנָא? תֵּיקוּ.

The Gemara explains the sides of the dilemma: Even **if you say** that generally **we follow** the moment of **uprooting,** and therefore she should be impure, since the urine was uprooted when she was a *zava*, nevertheless one can claim that **this statement** applies only with regard to **semen, as** the man **cannot hold it** back from emission. **But** with regard to the **urine of** a *zava*, **which she can hold in,** one does **not** follow the moment of uprooting. **Or perhaps** there **is no difference** in the application of this principle between urine and semen, but rather, in both cases one follows the moment of uprooting. Here too, the Gemara concludes that the dilemma **shall stand** unresolved.

בָּעֵי רָבָא: גּוֹיָה זָבָה שֶׁנֶּעֶקְרוּ מֵימֵי רַגְלֶיהָ,

**Rava raises** yet another **dilemma:** With regard to **a gentile *zava*,** who is not impure by Torah law, although by rabbinic law she is considered a *zava* in all regards, **whose urine was uprooted** when she was a gentile,

HALAKHA

**One who experienced a seminal emission who immersed but did not urinate before doing so – בַּעַל קֶרִי שֶׁטָּבַל וְלֹא הֵטִיל מַיִם:** If one who experienced a seminal emission immersed for his ritual purification but did not urinate beforehand, when he later urinates he is rendered impure by the drops of semen which invariably accompany this urination. This applies only to a sick or elderly individual, but with regard to a young, healthy man, even if he urinates only after immersion he remains pure, as his semen is shot like an arrow and all of it is emitted from his body (Rambam *Sefer Tahara, Hilkhot She'ar Avot HaTumot* 5:7).

**A gentile who had sexual thoughts and he subsequently descended and immersed – גּוֹי שֶׁהִרְהֵר וְיָרַד וְטָבַל:** If a gentile sensed that semen had been uprooted from his body and he then converted and immersed, after which he felt the emission of semen, he is uncertainly impure, as this dilemma is left unresolved by the Gemara (Rambam *Sefer Tahara, Hilkhot She'ar Avot HaTumot* 5:18).

**HALAKHA**

And she descended and immersed – וְיָרְדָה וְטָבְלָה: In the case of gentile *zava* whose urine was uprooted, and who subsequently converted, immersed, and then urinated, it is uncertain whether we follow the moment of uprooting, and therefore she is impure, or if we follow the moment of emission, which would mean that her urine is like that of a ritually pure Jew (Rambam *Sefer Tahara, Hilkhot Metamei Mishkav UMoshav* 2:9).

A *zav* must experience a discharge substantial enough to cause a blockage of the tip of the penis – זָב צָרִיךְ כַּחֲתִימַת פִּי הָאַמָּה: There is no minimum measure of discharge necessary to cause impurity as a *zav*, but rather, one who sees even a minute amount becomes ritually impure. This *halakha* is in accordance with the opinion of the *tanna* of the mishna, not Rabbi Yishmael (Rambam *Sefer Korbanot, Hilkhot Meḥusrei Kappara* 2:9).

A discharge which is moist imparts impurity but a dry discharge does not impart impurity – לַח מְטַמֵּא וְאֵינוֹ מְטַמֵּא יָבֵשׁ: The issue, saliva, and semen of a *zav* impart impurity only when they are moist, not when they are overly dry. This ruling is unanimous, as the Rabbis and Rabbi Yishmael disagree only with regard to the source of the *halakha* (Rambam *Sefer Tahara, Hilkhot Metamei Mishkav UMoshav* 2:1).

The verse teaches with regard to a *zav* who experienced three emissions that he is obligated to bring an offering – לִימֵּד עַל זָב בַּעַל שָׁלֹשׁ רְאִיּוֹת שֶׁחַיָּיב בְּקׇרְבָּן: A *zav* who experienced three emissions must bring an offering. This *halakha* is learned by a tradition transmitted to Moses at Sinai (Rambam *Sefer Korbanot, Hilkhot Meḥusrei Kappara* 2:6).

וְיָרְדָה וְטָבְלָה, מַהוּ?

**and she descended** to the ritual bath **and immersed**[H] for the sake of conversion, **what is the** *halakha*?

אִם תִּמְצֵי לוֹמַר בָּתַר עֲקִירָה אָזְלִינַן אַף עַל גַּב דְּמָצֵי נָקֵיט לְהוּ, הָנֵי מִילֵּי – יִשְׂרְאֵלִית דִּטְמֵאָה דְּאוֹרַיְיתָא, אֲבָל גּוֹיָה זָבָה, דִּטְמֵאָה דְּרַבָּנַן – לָא, אוֹ דִּילְמָא – לָא שְׁנָא? תֵּיקוּ.

Once again, the Gemara explains the dilemma: **If you say** that **we follow** the moment of **uprooting even though she can hold in** the urine, nevertheless one can claim that **this statement** applies specifically to **a Jewish woman, who is impure by Torah law. But** with regard to **a gentile** ***zava*****, who is impure by rabbinic law,** it is possible that one does **not** follow the moment of uprooting. **Or perhaps** there **is no difference** in the application of this principle between the case of a Jewish woman and a gentile woman, as in both cases one follows the moment of uprooting. The Gemara again concludes that the dilemma **shall stand** unresolved.

״וּמְטַמְּאִין בְּכׇל שֶׁהֵן״. אָמַר שְׁמוּאֵל: זָב צָרִיךְ כַּחֲתִימַת פִּי הָאַמָּה, שֶׁנֶּאֱמַר: ״אוֹ הֶחְתִּים בְּשָׂרוֹ מִזּוֹבוֹ״.

§ The mishna teaches that the emission of a *zav* and a seminal emission **impart impurity in any amount. Shmuel says:** In order for **a** ***zav*** to become ritually impure, he **must** experience a discharge substantial enough **to cause a blockage of the tip of the penis,**[H] **as it is stated:** "And this shall be his impurity in his issue: Whether his flesh run with his issue, **or his flesh be stopped from his issue,** it is his impurity" (Leviticus 15:3).

וְהָאֲנַן תְּנַן: מְטַמְּאִין בְּכׇל שֶׁהֵן! הוּא דְּאָמַר כְּרַבִּי נָתָן. דְּתַנְיָא, רַבִּי נָתָן אוֹמֵר מִשּׁוּם רַבִּי יִשְׁמָעֵאל: זָב צָרִיךְ כַּחֲתִימַת פִּי הָאַמָּה, וְלֹא הוֹדוּ לוֹ.

The Gemara asks: **But didn't we learn** in the mishna that the emission of a *zav* and a seminal emission **impart impurity in any amount?** The Gemara answers that Shmuel **said** his ruling **in accordance with** the statement of **Rabbi Natan, as it is taught** in a *baraita* that **Rabbi Natan says in the name of Rabbi Yishmael:** In order for **a** ***zav*** to become ritually impure, he **must** experience a discharge substantial enough **to cause a blockage of the tip of the penis, but** the Rabbis **did not concede to his** opinion, as they maintain that any amount is sufficient. The *tanna* of the mishna agrees with the opinion of the Rabbis, whereas Shmuel agrees with the statement of Rabbi Natan in the name of Rabbi Yishmael.

מַאי טַעְמָא דְּרַבִּי יִשְׁמָעֵאל? דְּאָמַר קְרָא ״אוֹ הֶחְתִּים בְּשָׂרוֹ מִזּוֹבוֹ״.

The Gemara asks: **What is the reason** for the opinion **of Rabbi Yishmael,** i.e., what is the source in the Torah for his ruling? The Gemara answers: His source is, as mentioned above, **that the verse states:** "And this shall be his impurity in his issue: Whether his flesh run with his issue, **or his flesh be stopped from his issue,** it is his impurity" (Leviticus 15:3). This verse indicates that the emission must be enough to cause a blockage of his penis.

וְרַבָּנַן? הַהוּא מִבְּעֵי לֵיהּ לַח מְטַמֵּא, וְאֵינוֹ מְטַמֵּא יָבֵשׁ.

The Gemara asks: **And the Rabbis,** who disagree with Rabbi Yishmael, what do they derive from this verse? The Gemara explains that according to the Rabbis, **that** verse **is necessary** to teach a different *halakha* with regard to a *zav*, that it is only a discharge which is **moist,** and which therefore could cause a blockage of the organ, that **imparts impurity, but a dry** discharge does **not impart impurity.**[H]

וְרַבִּי יִשְׁמָעֵאל? הַהוּא מֵ״רָר״ נָפְקָא.

The Gemara asks: **And** from where does **Rabbi Yishmael** derive that only a moist discharge imparts impurity? The Gemara answers: **That** *halakha* **is derived from** the word **"run"** in the verse "And this shall be his impurity in his issue: Whether his flesh run with his issue."

וְרַבָּנַן? הַהוּא לְמִנְיָנָא הוּא דַּאֲתָא: ״זוֹבוֹ״ – חֲדָא, ״רָר בְּשָׂרוֹ״ – תְּרֵי, ״אֶת זוֹבוֹ״ – תְּלָת, לִימֵּד עַל זָב בַּעַל שָׁלֹשׁ רְאִיּוֹת שֶׁחַיָּיב בְּקׇרְבָּן.

The Gemara asks: **And** what do **the Rabbis** derive from this word? The Gemara explains that according to the Rabbis, **that** verse **comes to** teach the **number** of emissions by which a *zav* is rendered impure, as follows: The term **"his issue"** is **one** emission, the term **"his flesh run"** is another emission so that there are **two** emissions, and the term **"with his issue"** makes a total of **three** emissions. The verse thereby **teaches with regard to a** ***zav*** **who experienced three emissions that** he **is obligated to** bring **an offering**[H] as part of his purification process.

"אוֹ הֶחְתִּים בְּשָׂרוֹ מִזּוֹבוֹ טֻמְאָה" – מִקְצָת זוֹבוֹ טָמֵא, לִימֵּד עַל זָב בַּעַל שְׁתֵּי רְאִיּוֹת שֶׁמְּטַמֵּא מִשְׁכָּב וּמוֹשָׁב. וְרַבִּי יִשְׁמָעֵאל מִנְיָנָא מְנָא לֵיהּ? נָפְקָא לֵיהּ מִדְּרַבִּי סִימַאי,

The Gemara continues: From the last section of the verse: **"Or his flesh be stopped from his issue,** it is his **impurity,"** it is derived that one is **impure** even by means of **part of his issue,** i.e., even if he did not experience three emissions. Here the verse **teaches with regard to a** *zav* **who experienced two emissions that** although he is not obligated to bring an offering, he **renders** a surface designated for **lying and** a surface designated for **sitting ritually impure** by lying or sitting on them, even without touching them directly. The Gemara asks: **And Rabbi Yishmael, from where does he** derive this *halakha* of the requisite **number** of emissions? The Gemara answers that **he derives it from that** which **Rabbi Simai** said.

דְּתַנְיָא, רַבִּי סִימַאי אוֹמֵר: מָנָה הַכָּתוּב שְׁתַּיִם – וּקְרָאוֹ "טָמֵא", שָׁלֹשׁ – וּקְרָאוֹ "טָמֵא". הָא כֵּיצַד? שְׁתַּיִם – לְטוּמְאָה, וְשָׁלֹשׁ – לְקׇרְבָּן.

**As it is taught** in a *baraita* that **Rabbi Simai says: The verse enumerated two** emissions **and called** the *zav* **impure:** "When any man has an emission out of his flesh, due to his issue he is impure" (Leviticus 15:2). And yet, another verse enumerates **three** emissions **and** it too **called him impure:** "And this shall be his impurity in his emission: Whether his flesh runs with his emission, or his flesh be stopped from his emission, it is his impurity" (Leviticus 15:3). **How** can **these** verses be reconciled? If one is impure after two emissions, for what purpose does the Torah mention three? It is to teach that **two** emissions are necessary **to** establish **impurity,**[H] **and three** are necessary **to** render a *zav* liable to bring **an offering.**

וּלְמַאן דְּנָפְקָא לֵיהּ תַּרְוַויְיהוּ מִ"זֹּאת תִּהְיֶה טוּמְאָתוֹ בְּזוֹבוֹ", "אִישׁ אִישׁ כִּי יִהְיֶה זָב מִבְּשָׂרוֹ" מַאי עָבֵיד לֵיהּ? מִבָּעֵי לֵיהּ – עַד שֶׁיֵּצֵא מִבְּשָׂרוֹ.

The Gemara asks: **And according to the one who derives both** the *halakha* of impurity and the obligation to bring an offering **from** the single verse: "And **this shall be his impurity in his issue,"** what **do they,** i.e., the Rabbis, **do with** the other verse: **"When any man has an emission out of his flesh"?** The Gemara answers that this verse is **necessary** to teach the *halakha* that a *zav* is not impure **unless** the discharge **emerges from his flesh.**

"זוֹבוֹ טָמֵא" לָמָּה לִי? לִימֵּד עַל הַזּוֹב שֶׁהוּא טָמֵא.

The Gemara further asks: **Why do I** need the last part of the previous verse, which can be read as: **His issue is impure** (Leviticus 15:2)?[H] The Gemara explains that this **teaches with regard to the issue** itself **that it is impure,** i.e., not only does it render the man who emitted it impure, but the substance itself is impure and imparts impurity to others by contact.

אָמַר רַב חֲנִילַאי מִשּׁוּם רַבִּי אֶלְעָזָר בְּרַבִּי שִׁמְעוֹן: שִׁכְבַת זֶרַע, לָרוֹאֶה – בְּמַשֶּׁהוּ, לַנּוֹגֵעַ – בְּכַעֲדָשָׁה. וְהָאֲנַן "מְטַמְּאִין בְּכׇל שֶׁהֵן" תְּנַן! מַאי לָאו – לַנּוֹגֵעַ? לָא, לָרוֹאֶה.

§ With regard to the statement of the mishna that the issue of the *zav* and a seminal emission render them impure in any amount, **Rav Ḥanilai says in the name of Rabbi Elazar, son of Rabbi Shimon: Semen** imparts impurity **to** the man who **emits** it **in any amount,**[H] whereas **with regard to one who touches** semen, it imparts impurity only **in** the amount of **a lentil-bulk.** The Gemara asks: **But didn't we learn** in the mishna that the emission of a *zav* and a seminal emission **impart impurity in any amount? What, is it not** referring to **one who touches** semen? The Gemara answers: **No,** the mishna is referring **to** the man who **emits** it.

## HALAKHA

**Two emissions to establish impurity – שְׁתַּיִם לְטוּמְאָה:** One who experiences two emissions of *ziva* is a *zav* and must count seven days clean of emissions and immerse in spring water to become ritually pure. Nevertheless, he is not obligated to bring an offering. This *halakha* is also learned by tradition, as transmitted to Moses at Sinai (Rambam *Sefer Korbanot, Hilkhot Meḥusrei Kappara* 2:6).

**His issue is impure – זוֹבוֹ טָמֵא:** The issue of a *zav*, like the *zav* himself, is a primary source of ritual impurity and imparts impurity by touch and carrying in any amount. This *halakha* does not apply equally to all emissions of a *zav*. His first emission imparts impurity by touch alone, whereas his second emission imparts impurity by touch and carrying (Rambam *Sefer Tahara, Hilkhot Metamei Mishkav UMoshav* 1:12).

**Semen imparts impurity to the man who emits it in any amount, etc. – שִׁכְבַת זֶרַע לָרוֹאֶה בְּמַשֶּׁהוּ וכו׳:** Semen is a primary source of ritual impurity, and it imparts impurity to people and vessels by touch and to earthenware vessels when it is in their airspace. It does not impart impurity by carrying, nor does one who contracted impurity from semen render his garments impure while he is in contact with it. There is no difference in this regard between one who touches semen and one who experiences an emission of semen, as both have first-degree ritual impurity by Torah law. Nevertheless, there is a difference between them with regard to the amount by which they are rendered impure, as one who touches semen becomes impure only if it is at least a lentil-bulk, whereas one who experiences a seminal emission is rendered impure by any amount. This *halakha* is in accordance with the opinion of Rav Ḥanilai, citing Rabbi Elazar, son of Rabbi Shimon (Rambam *Sefer Tahara, Hilkhot She'ar Avot HaTumot* 5:1).

NOTES

So too the impurity discussed in the *baraita* with regard to semen is imparted by contact – אַף שִׁכְבַת זֶרַע בִּנְגִיעָה: It is for this reason that the early authorities write that one should be careful that there should be no semen on his body or his clothes (*Sefer Ḥasidim*, 509). Some later commentaries add that semen on one's skin is considered like excrement with regard to the prohibition of reciting *Shema* in its presence (*Shulḥan Arukh, Oraḥ Ḥayyim* 76:4, in the comment of Rema). If the semen is only on his garments and it is covered, it is permitted to recite *Shema* (*Shulḥan Arukh, Oraḥ Ḥayyim* 76:4 and *Magen Avraham* there).

תָּא שְׁמַע: חוֹמֶר בְּשִׁכְבַת זֶרַע מִבְּשֶׁרֶץ, וְחוֹמֶר בְּשֶׁרֶץ מִבְּשִׁכְבַת זֶרַע. חוֹמֶר בְּשֶׁרֶץ – שֶׁהַשֶּׁרֶץ אֵין חֲלוּקָה טוּמְאָתוֹ, מַה שֶּׁאֵין כֵּן בְּשִׁכְבַת זֶרַע. חוֹמֶר בְּשִׁכְבַת זֶרַע – שֶׁהַשִּׁכְבַת זֶרַע מְטַמֵּא בְּכׇל שֶׁהוּא, מַה שֶּׁאֵין כֵּן בְּשֶׁרֶץ.

The Gemara suggests: **Come** and **hear** a proof from a *baraita*: There is an element of **stringency** which applies **to** the impurity of **semen that** does not apply **to** the impurity of the carcass of **a creeping animal, and** likewise there is an element of **stringency** which applies **to** the impurity of the carcass of **a creeping animal that** does not apply **to** the impurity of **semen.** The *baraita* elaborates: The **stringency** which applies **to** the carcass of **a creeping animal** but not to semen is **that** with regard to the carcass of **a creeping animal there is no differentiation in its impurity, which is not the case with regard to semen,** as certain types of semen impart impurity while others do not. The **stringency** which applies **to semen** but not to the carcass of a creeping animal is **that semen imparts impurity in any amount, which is not the case with regard to** the carcass of **a creeping animal,** which must be at least a lentil-bulk.

מַאי לָאו – לְנוֹגֵעַ? לָא, לְרוֹאֶה.

The Gemara analyzes this *baraita*: **What, is it not** referring **to one who touches** semen, and the *baraita* rules that he is rendered impure by any amount? The Gemara again answers: **No,** the *baraita* is speaking **of** the man who **emits** semen, whereas one who touches it becomes impure only if it is at least as large as a lentil-bulk.

וְהָא דּוּמְיָא דְּשֶׁרֶץ קָתָנֵי, מָה שֶׁרֶץ – בִּנְגִיעָה, אַף שִׁכְבַת זֶרַע – בִּנְגִיעָה! אָמַר רַב אַדָּא בַּר אַהֲבָה: שׁוּם שֶׁרֶץ קָתָנֵי, וְשׁוּם שִׁכְבַת זֶרַע קָתָנֵי.

The Gemara raises a difficulty with regard to this answer: **But** the *baraita* **teaches** the case of semen as **similar to** that of the carcass of **a creeping animal,** which indicates that **just as** the impurity of the carcass of **a creeping animal** is imparted **by contact, so too,** the impurity discussed in the *baraita* with regard to **semen** is imparted **by contact.**[N] **Rav Adda bar Ahava said** in response: The *baraita* **teaches the category of** the carcass of **a creeping animal, and** it likewise **teaches the category of semen,** i.e., it is referring to these types of impurity in general, but this does not mean that these types of impurity are contracted in the same manner.

וְשֶׁרֶץ לָא מְטַמֵּא בְּמַשֶּׁהוּ? וְהָא אֲנַן תְּנַן: הָאֵבָרִים אֵין לָהֶם שִׁיעוּר. פָּחוֹת מִכַּזַּיִת בְּשַׂר הַמֵּת, וּפָחוֹת מִכַּזַּיִת בְּשַׂר נְבֵלָה, וּפָחוֹת מִכַּעֲדָשָׁה מִן הַשֶּׁרֶץ!

The Gemara asks: **And does** the carcass of **a creeping animal not impart impurity in any amount? But didn't we learn** in a mishna (*Oholot* 1:7): **The limbs** of impure bodies that are whole **have no** minimum **measure** with regard to imparting ritual impurity. Even if a limb is **less than an olive-bulk of** a human **corpse,**[H] **or less than an olive-bulk of an animal carcass,**[H] **or less than a lentil-bulk of** the carcass of **a creeping animal,**[H] it imparts ritual impurity. If so, how can the *baraita* state that there is a minimum measure of a lentil-bulk with regard to the impurity of a creeping animal?

שָׁאנֵי אֵבֶר – דְּכוּלֵּיהּ בִּמְקוֹם עֲדָשָׁה קָאֵי, דְּהָא אִילּוּ חָסֵר פּוּרְתָּא – אֵבֶר מִי קָמְטַמְּיָא?

The Gemara answers that the *halakha* of **a limb is different, as** when **all of it** is intact **it stands in place of a lentil**-bulk, i.e., a whole limb is considered like a lentil-bulk of the carcass of a creeping animal, regardless of its actual size. The proof is **that if** it were **lacking** any slight **bit,** thereby causing this **limb** of a creeping animal to be less than a lentil-bulk, **would it impart impurity?** Certainly not. Clearly, then, the impurity of a limb is due to its wholeness, not its size.

HALAKHA

**Less than an olive-bulk of a corpse – פָּחוֹת מִכַּזַּיִת בְּשַׂר הַמֵּת:** A limb cut from a living person is considered like a whole corpse, and it imparts impurity by touch, carrying, and through the impurity of a tent. This applies even to a small limb of a one-day-old baby, as there is no minimum measure with regard to the impurity of limbs. This is the *halakha* only if the limb is whole, including the flesh, sinews, and bones. If any amount was lacking from the bone of the limb, the entire limb is pure. In a case where some of the flesh is lacking, if there is enough flesh left on the limb to heal it were it attached to a living person, it imparts impurity by touch, carrying, and through the impurity of a tent. If there is not enough flesh for healing, it imparts impurity by touch and carrying, but not through the impurity of a tent. The *halakha* is in accordance with the ruling of the mishna in *Oholot* (Rambam *Sefer Tahara, Hilkhot Tumat Met* 2:3).

**Less than an olive-bulk of an animal carcass – פָּחוֹת מִכַּזַּיִת בְּשַׂר נְבֵלָה:** With regard to ritual impurity, the limbs of an animal, whether kosher or non-kosher, have no minimum measure. Even if the limb is only the size of a barley seed, or even less than that, it renders one ritually impure, whether it came from a living animal or from a fetus inside it. This is the *halakha* only when the limb is whole, with its bones and sinews and enough flesh for the limb to heal. If there is not enough flesh for healing, the person who came in contact with it remains pure. This *halakha* is in accordance with the mishna in *Oholot* (Rambam *Sefer Tahara, Hilkhot She'ar Avot HaTumot* 2:3).

**Less than a lentil-bulk of a creeping animal – פָּחוֹת מִכַּעֲדָשָׁה מִן הַשֶּׁרֶץ:** Although the flesh of a creeping animal imparts impurity only in the amount of a lentil-bulk, there is no minimum measure for its limbs when they are whole. This *halakha* is in accordance with the mishna in *Oholot* (Rambam *Sefer Tahara, Hilkhot She'ar Avot HaTumot* 4:2–3).

שִׁכְבַת זֶרַע דַּחֲלוּקָה טוּמְאָתוֹ מַאי הִיא? אִילֵימָא בֵּין יִשְׂרָאֵל לְגוֹיִם – הָכִי נָמֵי אִיכָּא עַכְבָּר דְּיָם וְעַכְבָּר דְּיַבָּשָׁה!

The *baraita* teaches: The stringency that applies to the carcass of a creeping animal but not to semen is that with regard to a creeping animal there is no differentiation concerning its impurity, which is not the case with regard to semen. The Gemara asks: **What is the differentiation** with regard to **the impurity of semen? If we say** that this is referring to the difference **between** the semen of **Jews,** to which this impurity applies, **and** the semen **of gentiles,**[H] to which it does not apply, **there is also** a differentiation with regard to the impurity of the carcass of a creeping animal between **a sea mouse,**[HN] which is not impure, and **a land mouse,**[B] which is impure.

אֶלָּא – בֵּין קָטָן לְגָדוֹל.

**Rather,** the *baraita* is referring to the differentiation **between** the emission of **a minor,** which is not classified as semen and which does not render him impure, **and** that of **an adult,**[H] which does render him impure. By contrast, there is no such differentiation with regard to the impurity of the carcass of a creeping animal, as it imparts impurity regardless of its age and size.

אָמַר רַב פַּפָּא: כְּתַנָּאֵי, מִנַּיִן לְרַבּוֹת נוֹגֵעַ בְּשִׁכְבַת זֶרַע – תַּלְמוּד לוֹמַר ״אוֹ אִישׁ״.

§ **Rav Pappa said:** The amount of semen which imparts impurity to one who touches it is **subject to** a dispute between ***tanna'im***, as it is stated in a *baraita*: **From where** is it derived **that** the Torah **includes one who touches semen,** in addition to one who emits semen, as impure? **The verse states** with regard to the impurity of the carcass of a creeping animal: **"Or whoever** touches any creeping animal, whereby he may become impure" (Leviticus 22:5). It is inferred from the inclusive phrase "or whoever" that one who touches semen is also impure.

וּפְלִיגִי תַּנָּאֵי בְּעָלְמָא, דְּאִיכָּא דְּאָמְרִי דּוּן מִינָּהּ וּמִינָּהּ, וְאִיכָּא דְּאָמְרִי דּוּן מִינָּהּ וְאוֹקֵי בְּאַתְרָא.

**And in general, *tanna'im* disagree** with regard to the possibility of deriving a *halakha* in this manner. **As some say** with regard to a *halakha* that is inferred from another *halakha*: **Infer from it, and** derive the details of the *halakha* **from it** as well. **And some say** with regard to such a *halakha*: **Infer from it, but interpret** the *halakha* according **to its** own **place,** i.e., not all aspects of the source case are applied to this *halakha*.

לְמַאן דְּאָמַר דּוּן מִינָּהּ וּמִינָּהּ: מָה שֶּׁרֶץ – בִּנְגִיעָה, אַף שִׁכְבַת זֶרַע – בִּנְגִיעָה. וּמִינָּהּ, מָה שֶּׁרֶץ – בְּכַעֲדָשָׁה, אַף שִׁכְבַת זֶרַע – בְּכַעֲדָשָׁה.

The Gemara explains how this general dispute applies to the case at hand. **According to the one who says** that one **infers from it and** again **from it,** the derivation is as follows: **Just as** the carcass of **a creeping animal** imparts impurity **by contact, so too, semen** imparts impurity **by contact. And** one again infers **from** the impurity of the carcass of a creeping animal that **just as** the carcass of **a creeping animal** imparts impurity **in** the amount of **a lentil-bulk, so too, semen** imparts impurity **in** the amount of **a lentil-bulk.**

וּלְמַאן דְּאָמַר דּוּן מִינָּהּ וְאוֹקֵי בְּאַתְרָא: מָה שֶּׁרֶץ – בִּנְגִיעָה, אַף שִׁכְבַת זֶרַע – בִּנְגִיעָה. וְאוֹקֵי בְּאַתְרָא: מָה שִׁכְבַת זֶרַע לָרוֹאֶה – בְּמַשֶּׁהוּ, אַף לַנּוֹגֵעַ – בְּמַשֶּׁהוּ.

**And according to the one who says: Infer from it, but interpret** the *halakha* according **to its own place,** one derives as follows: **Just as** the carcass of **a creeping animal** imparts impurity **by contact, so too, semen** imparts impurity **by contact. But** one must **interpret** the *halakha* according **to its own place: Just as semen** imparts impurity **to the one who emits** it **in any amount, so too,** it imparts impurity **to the one who touches** it **in any amount.**

**HALAKHA**

Between Jews and that of gentiles – בֵּין יִשְׂרָאֵל לְגוֹיִם: The semen of a gentile is ritually pure (Rambam *Sefer Tahara, Hilkhot She'ar Avot HaTumot* 5:17 and *Hilkhot Metamei Mishkav UMoshav* 2:10).

Sea mouse – עַכְבָּר דְּיָם: Vessels fashioned from the bones or skin of sea creatures are ritually pure (Rambam *Sefer Tahara, Hilkhot Kelim* 1:3).

Between the emission of a minor and that of an adult – בֵּין קָטָן לְגָדוֹל: The semen of a minor does not impart impurity until he is nine years and one day old (Rambam *Sefer Tahara, Hilkhot She'ar Avot HaTumot* 5:2).

**BACKGROUND**

Sea mouse and land mouse – עַכְבָּר יָם וְעַכְבָּר יַבָּשָׁה: Some maintain that a sea mouse is a type of snail which lives near water (see *Sanhedrin* 91a), whereas others claim that it is a sea creature which bears a resemblance to a land mouse. This latter suggestion may refer to what is now known as the sea mouse, *Aphrodita aculeate*, which is a type of marine worm covered in hair-like structures that can be found in the Mediterranean.

As for the term land mouse, this refers to the house mouse, *Mus musculus*, a small rodent that grows up to 8 cm. It is gray in color and has a white underbelly. This mouse feeds on various remnants it finds around the house, particularly bread crumbs.

Freshwater snails

Sea mouse

**NOTES**

Sea mouse – עַכְבָּר דְּיָם: This creature does not impart impurity, as a *baraita* teaches that the verse: "And these are they which are impure to you among the creeping animals that creep on the earth" (Leviticus 11:29), indicates that this impurity applies only to the carcasses of creeping animals that traverse the earth, not those of the sea (Rashi; see *Ḥullin* 126b). This follows Rashi's opinion that a mouse of the sea is a fish which looks like a mouse. All creatures of the sea are ritually pure (see *Kelim* 17:13).

אֲמַר לֵיהּ רַב הוּנָא בְּרֵיהּ דְּרַב נָתָן לְרַב פַּפָּא: מִמַּאי דְּמֵ״אוֹ אִישׁ״ דְּשֶׁרֶץ קָמְרַבֵּי לֵיהּ, דִּילְמָא מֵ״אוֹ אִישׁ אֲשֶׁר תֵּצֵא מִמֶּנּוּ שִׁכְבַת זָרַע״ קָמְרַבֵּי לֵיהּ. וּדְכוּלֵּי עָלְמָא דּוֹן מִינָּהּ וּמִינָּהּ?

**Rav Huna, son of Rav Natan, said to Rav Pappa: From where** do you infer **that** the *tanna* of the *baraita* **derives** the impurity of one who touches semen **from** the phrase **"or whoever"** that is stated with regard to the impurity **of** the carcass of **a creeping animal? Perhaps he derives it from** the previous verse: **"Or from whoever the flow of seed goes out"** (Leviticus 22:4), **and everyone** agrees that when a *halakha* is derived from a verse dealing with the same matter, one should **infer from it and** derive the details of the *halakha* **from it** as well. If so, the amount of semen that imparts impurity by contact should be derived from the amount that renders the one who emitted it impure, which is any amount.

שַׁיְילִינְהוּ לְתַנָּאֵי, אִיכָּא דְּתָנֵי כְּרַב פַּפָּא, וְאִיכָּא דְּתָנֵי כְּרַב הוּנָא בְּרֵיהּ דְּרַב נָתָן.

The Gemara relates that the Sages **asked the** ***tanna'im***, i.e., those who recite *mishnayot* and *baraitot*, whether the derivation of the *baraita* is from the verse dealing with the carcass of a creeping animal or from the one dealing with semen. They discovered that **there are those who teach** this *halakha* **in accordance with** the assumption of **Rav Pappa,** that it is derived from a creeping animal, **and there are those who teach** this *halakha* **in accordance with** the opinion of **Rav Huna, son of Rav Natan,** that the source is the verse referring to semen.

מתני׳ תִּנוֹקֶת בַּת יוֹם אֶחָד – מִטַּמְּאָה בְּנִדָּה, בַּת עֲשָׂרָה יָמִים – מִטַּמְּאָה בְּזִיבָה.

**MISHNA A baby girl,** even one who is **one day old,** who experiences an emission of blood, **becomes impure with** the impurity of **a menstruating woman.**[H] A baby girl who is **ten days old** who experiences an emission of blood for three consecutive days after the conclusion of the seven days fit for menstruation **becomes impure with** the impurity of ***ziva,*** and is therefore obligated to observe seven clean days before immersion.

תִּנוֹק בֶּן יוֹם אֶחָד – מִטַּמֵּא בְּזִיבָה, וּמִטַּמֵּא בִּנְגָעִים, וּמִטַּמֵּא בִּטְמֵא מֵת, וְזוֹקֵק לְיִבּוּם, וּפוֹטֵר מִן הַיִּבּוּם, וּמַאֲכִיל בִּתְרוּמָה, וּפוֹסֵל (אֶת) [מִן] הַתְּרוּמָה,

**A baby boy,** even one who is **one day old, becomes impure with** the impurity of ***ziva;***[H] **and becomes impure with** the impurity of **leprous marks;**[H] **and becomes impure with impurity** imparted by **a corpse;**[H] **and he creates** a levirate bond requiring the widow of his childless brother **to** enter into **levirate marriage** with him;[H] **and he exempts** his widowed mother **from the** obligation of **levirate marriage,**[H] freeing her to marry anyone she chooses; **and he enables** his mother, an Israelite woman who is no longer married to his father, a priest, to continue **to partake of** ***teruma;***[B] **and he disqualifies** his mother, the daughter of a priest who is no longer married to his father, an Israelite man, **from** continuing to partake of ***teruma,*** because the child is unfit to partake of *teruma;*

BACKGROUND

*Teruma* – תְּרוּמָה: Whenever the term *teruma* appears without qualification, it refers to *teruma gedola*, the great *teruma*. The Torah commands that *teruma* must be separated from grain, wine, and oil and must be given to the priest (see Deuteronomy 18:4 and Numbers 18:12). The Sages extended the scope of this mitzva to include all produce. This mitzva applies only in Eretz Yisrael. *Teruma* is sacred and may be consumed only by a priest and his household while they are in a state of ritual purity (see Leviticus 22:9–15).

HALAKHA

**A baby girl even one day old becomes impure with the impurity of a menstruating woman** – **תִּנוֹקֶת בַּת יוֹם אֶחָד מִטַּמְּאָה בְּנִדָּה:** A female can become impure and impart the impurity of menstruation even on the day of her birth. This is a *halakha* learned by tradition, that there is no difference between a minor and an adult woman with regard to the impurities of menstruation and *ziva* (Rambam *Sefer Tahara, Hilkhot Metamei Mishkav UMoshav* 1:3 and *Sefer Kedusha, Hilkhot Issurei Bia* 4:1).

**A baby boy one day old becomes impure with the impurity of** ***ziva*** – **תִּנוֹק בֶּן יוֹם אֶחָד מִטַּמֵּא בְּזִיבָה:** A one-day-old baby boy can become impure with the impurity of *ziva* (Rambam *Sefer Tahara, Hilkhot Metamei Mishkav UMoshav* 1:4).

**And becomes impure with the impurity of leprous marks** – **וּמִטַּמֵּא בִּנְגָעִים:** A one-day- old baby boy can become impure with the impurity of leprous marks (Rambam *Sefer Tahara, Hilkhot Tumat Tzara'at* 9:1).

**And becomes impure with impurity imparted by a corpse** – **וּמִטַּמֵּא בִּטְמֵא מֵת:** A minor Jew, even one who is one day old, can become ritually impure with all forms of impurity, including the impurity imparted by a corpse, like an adult. Therefore, if he touched, carried, or formed a tent over the dead, he has the impurity of one who came into contact with the dead. This is the *halakha* only if the baby was born after nine months of pregnancy, but if he was born after eight months he is considered like a stone and is not susceptible to ritual impurity (Rambam *Sefer Tahara, Hilkhot Tumat Met* 1:14).

**And he creates a levirate bond requiring the widow of his childless brother to enter into levirate marriage with him** – **וְזוֹקֵק לְיִבּוּם:** If a deceased, childless husband had a paternal brother, even a one-day-old baby, he creates a levirate bond requiring the widow to enter into levirate marriage with him, provided that his head and most of his body emerged into the world before the husband's death (Rambam *Sefer Nashim, Hilkhot Yibbum VaḤalitza* 1:6; *Shulḥan Arukh, Even HaEzer* 157:1).

**And he exempts his widowed mother from the obligation of levirate marriage** – **וּפוֹטֵר מִן הַיִּבּוּם:** In a case where a husband died childless and was survived by a pregnant wife, if she gave birth to a living child, she is exempt from the obligation of *ḥalitza* and levirate marriage, even if the child subsequently died. By rabbinic law this child renders the mother exempt only if it is established for certain that it was born after a full nine months of pregnancy. The Rema writes that according to some opinions, in the present time, even if the mother entered into the first day of her ninth month, not including the day on which she became pregnant, the child is considered viable and she is exempt, as the nature of pregnancies has changed from the time of the Gemara (Rambam *Sefer Nashim, Hilkhot Yibbum VaḤalitza* 1:5; *Shulḥan Arukh, Even HaEzer* 156:4).

וְנוֹחֵל וּמַנְחִיל, וְהַהוֹרְגוֹ חַיָּיב, וַהֲרֵי הוּא לְאָבִיו וּלְאִמּוֹ וּלְכׇל קְרוֹבָיו כְּחָתָן שָׁלֵם.

**and he inherits**[B] the estate of his mother if she died on the day of his birth; **and** if he dies, **he bequeaths**[H] that inheritance to his paternal brothers; **and one who kills him is liable** for his murder,[HN] as it is written: "And he that smites any man mortally shall be put to death" (Leviticus 24:17), i.e., any man, including a child who is one day old; **and** if he dies, **his** status in relation **to his father and to his mother and to all his relatives,** in terms of the *halakhot* of mourning, is **like** that of **a full-fledged groom** [***keḥatan shalem***],[L] whose death is deeply mourned.

גמ׳ מְנָהָנֵי מִילֵּי? דְּתָנוּ רַבָּנַן: "אִשָּׁה" – אֵין לִי אֶלָּא אִשָּׁה, בַּת יוֹם אֶחָד לְנִדָּה מִנַּיִן? תַּלְמוּד לוֹמַר "וְאִשָּׁה".

**GEMARA** The Gemara asks: **From where is this matter,** that the *halakhot* of menstruation apply even to a one-day-old baby girl, derived? **As the Sages taught** in a *baraita*: The verse states: "And if a woman has an issue, and her issue in her flesh is blood, she shall be in her impurity seven days" (Leviticus 15:19). When the verse states **"a woman," I have** derived **only** that the *halakhot* of menstruation apply to an adult **woman. From where** do I derive that the impurity **of a menstruating woman** also applies to **a one-day-old** baby? **The verse states: "And a woman,"**[N] to include even a baby girl.

"בַּת עֲשָׂרָה יָמִים לְזִיבָה". מְנָא הָנֵי מִילֵּי? דְּתָנוּ רַבָּנַן: "אִשָּׁה" – אֵין לִי אֶלָּא אִשָּׁה, בַּת עֲשָׂרָה יָמִים לְזִיבָה מִנַּיִן? תַּלְמוּד לוֹמַר "וְאִשָּׁה".

The mishna further teaches that a baby girl who is **ten days old** who experiences an emission of blood for three consecutive days after the conclusion of the seven days fit for menstruation, becomes impure with the impurity **of *ziva*.** Again, the Gemara asks: **From where are these matters** derived? **As the Sages taught** in a *baraita*: The verse states: "And if a woman has an issue of her blood many days not in the time of her menstruation ... she shall be as in the days of her menstruation: She is impure" (Leviticus 15:25). When the verse states **"a woman," I have** derived **only** that the *halakhot* of a *zava* apply to an adult **woman. From where** do I derive that the impurity **of *ziva*** also applies to **a ten-day-old** baby? **The verse states: "And a woman,"** to include even a baby girl.

"תִּינוֹק בֶּן יוֹם אֶחָד" כו׳. מְנָא הָנֵי מִילֵּי? דְּתָנוּ רַבָּנַן: "אִישׁ אִישׁ". מַה תַּלְמוּד לוֹמַר "אִישׁ אִישׁ"? לְרַבּוֹת בֶּן יוֹם אֶחָד שֶׁמִּטַּמֵּא בְּזִיבָה, דִּבְרֵי רַבִּי יְהוּדָה.

The mishna further teaches that **a baby boy,** even one who is **one day old,** can become impure with the impurity of *ziva*. Once again, the Gemara asks: **From where are these matters** derived? **As the Sages taught** in a *baraita*: The verse states with regard to a *zav*: "When **any man** has an issue out of his flesh, his issue is impure" (Leviticus 15:2). It would have been enough for the verse to state "a man." **Why** must **the verse state "any man"?** It is in order **to include** even **a one-day-old** baby boy who has such a discharge, to teach **that he becomes impure with** the impurity of ***ziva*.** This is **the statement of Rabbi Yehuda.**

רַבִּי יִשְׁמָעֵאל בְּנוֹ שֶׁל רַבִּי יוֹחָנָן בֶּן בְּרוֹקָא אוֹמֵר: אֵינוֹ צָרִיךְ, הֲרֵי הוּא אוֹמֵר "וְהַזָּב אֶת זוֹבוֹ לַזָּכָר וְלַנְּקֵבָה". "לַזָּכָר" – כׇּל שֶׁהוּא, בֵּין גָּדוֹל בֵּין קָטָן. "לַנְּקֵבָה" – כׇּל שֶׁהִיא, בֵּין גְּדוֹלָה בֵּין קְטַנָּה. אִם כֵּן מַה תַּלְמוּד לוֹמַר "אִישׁ אִישׁ"? דִּבְּרָה תוֹרָה כִּלְשׁוֹן בְּנֵי אָדָם.

**Rabbi Yishmael, son of Rabbi Yoḥanan ben Beroka, says** that this derivation **is not necessary,** as the verse **states: "And of those who have an issue, whether it be a male or a female"** (Leviticus 15:33). The phrase **"whether it be a male"** includes **anyone** who is a male, **whether** he is **an adult** or **whether** he is **a minor; "or a female"** includes **anyone** who is a female, **whether** she is **an adult** or **whether** she is **a minor. If so, why** must **the** earlier **verse state "any man"? The Torah spoke in the language of people,** i.e., this emphasis is not unusual and therefore one should not derive a *halakha* from the superfluous word.

### HALAKHA

**And he inherits and he bequeaths – וְנוֹחֵל וּמַנְחִיל:** If a mother predeceased her son, even if he was a one-day-old baby he inherits from her, and his heirs from his father's family inherit from him. The Rema writes that if she died while pregnant the fetus does not inherit from her to bequeath to his heirs from his father's family, because the assumption is that the fetus died before the mother, in accordance with the opinion of Rav Sheshet (Rambam *Sefer Mishpatim, Hilkhot Naḥalot* 1:13; *Shulḥan Arukh, Ḥoshen Mishpat* 276:5).

**And one who kills him is liable for his murder – וְהַהוֹרְגוֹ חַיָּיב:** One who kills a one-day-old baby, whether male or female, is like one who killed an adult, and he is liable to be put to death if he did so intentionally, or to exile if he acted unwittingly. This applies only to a baby whose months of pregnancy were fully completed, but one born before nine months is considered like a stillborn until thirty days have passed. Consequently, if someone kills him within thirty days, he is not liable to be put to death (Rambam *Sefer Nezikin, Hilkhot Rotze'aḥ UShmirat HaNefesh* 2:6).

### NOTES

**And one who kills him is liable for his murder – וְהַהוֹרְגוֹ חַיָּיב:** The early commentaries note that this applies only to a one-day-old baby, whereas one who kills a fetus is not liable to be put to death, as a fetus is not classified as "any man" (*Tosafot*; Ramban; Rashba; Ritva; Ran). Even so, it is prohibited to kill a fetus, although the early commentaries disagree with regard to the nature of this prohibition. Some say that it applies by rabbinic law (see *Tosafot* on *Nidda* 44a; *Tzitz Eliezer* 9:51:3), whereas others maintain that it is by Torah law (Rabbeinu Ḥayyim HaLevi Soloveitchik on Rambam *Sefer Nezikin, Hilkhot Rotze'aḥ UShmirat HaNefesh* 1:39).

**The verse states: And a woman – תַּלְמוּד לוֹמַר וְאִשָּׁה:** The commentaries note that although this one-day-old baby girl remains ritually impure until she has immersed, one who engages in intercourse with her is not liable, as any act of intercourse with a girl less than three years and one day old is not considered intercourse (Rambam *Sefer Kedusha, Hilkhot Issurei Bia* 4:1 and *Maggid Mishne* there).

### LANGUAGE

**Full-fledged groom [*ḥatan shalem*] – חָתָן שָׁלֵם:** The term *ḥatan* generally refers to a man who is about to marry a woman. His prospective father-in-law is called a *ḥoten*, his future mother-in-law a *ḥotenet*, and the ceremony itself a *ḥatuna*, wedding. The term is also used in reference to those experiencing a joyful event of a great mitzva, e.g., a circumcision, a bar mitzva, and those celebrating achievements in Torah study.

### BACKGROUND

**Inheritance – נַחֲלָה:** This is referring to the right of a relative to inherit the property of his deceased kin. The basic *halakhot* of inheritance are stated in the Torah (see Numbers 27:8–11). The main provisions are that a father's property is inherited by his sons, with the firstborn son receiving a double share. If the deceased had no sons, or if his sons died and left no heirs, his daughters receive the inheritance. If he has no offspring at all, the inheritance passes to his father, and then to his father's heirs. The process continues generation by generation, moving back through the paternal family. With regard to this matter the Sages established the principle that in matters of inheritance a father takes precedence over all his offspring.

HALAKHA

**Which excludes a pregnant woman – פְּרָט לִמְעוּבֶּרֶת:** A fetus renders one disqualified from partaking of *teruma* and does not enable one to partake of *teruma*. How so? An Israelite woman who was pregnant from a priest may not partake of *teruma* on account of the fetus. By contrast, if the daughter of a priest was pregnant from an Israelite, she is prohibited from partaking of *teruma* due to the fetus (Rambam *Sefer Zera'im, Hilkhot Terumot* 8:2).

״וּמִטַּמֵּא בִּנְגָעִים״. דִּכְתִיב: ״אָדָם כִּי יִהְיֶה בְעוֹר בְּשָׂרוֹ״ – אָדָם כׇּל שֶׁהוּ.

The mishna teaches: **And** a one-day-old baby **becomes impure with** the impurity of **leprous marks.** The Gemara explains that this is derived from that **which is written** with regard to leprous marks: **"When a person shall have in the skin of his flesh"** (Leviticus 13:2). This serves to include **anyone who is a person,** irrespective of age.

״וּמִטַּמֵּא בְּטָמֵא מֵת״. דִּכְתִיב: ״וְעַל הַנְּפָשׁוֹת אֲשֶׁר הָיוּ שָׁם״ – נֶפֶשׁ כׇּל דְּהוּ.

The mishna further teaches: **And** a one-day-old baby **becomes impure with impurity** imparted by **a corpse.** The Gemara explains that this is derived from that **which is written** in the context of purification from impurity imparted by a corpse: "And a pure person shall take hyssop, and dip it in the water, and sprinkle it upon the tent, and upon all the vessels, **and upon the people that were there"** (Numbers 19:18). This apparently superfluous mention of "people" serves to include **anyone who is a person,** irrespective of age.

״וְזוֹקֵק לְיִבּוּם״. דִּכְתִיב ״כִּי יֵשְׁבוּ אַחִים יַחְדָּו״ – אַחִים שֶׁהָיָה לָהֶם יְשִׁיבָה אַחַת בָּעוֹלָם.

The mishna also teaches: **And** a one-day-old baby **creates** a levirate bond requiring the widow of his childless brother **to** enter into **levirate marriage** with him. The Gemara explains that this is derived from that **which is written: "If brothers dwell together** and one of them dies, and he has no child, the wife of the dead man shall not be married outside of the family to one not of his kin. Her brother-in-law will have intercourse with her and take her to him to be his wife, and consummate the levirate marriage" (Deuteronomy 25:5). This verse is referring to **brothers who had one dwelling in the world,** i.e., who were alive at the same time, which includes a baby who was born the day his brother died.

״וּפוֹטֵר מִן הַיִּבּוּם״. ״וּבֵן אֵין לוֹ״ אָמַר רַחֲמָנָא – וְהָא אִית לֵיהּ.

The mishna teaches: **And** a one-day-old baby **exempts** his widowed mother **from the** obligation of **levirate marriage.** The Gemara explains the derivation: **The Merciful One states:** "And one of them dies, **and he has no child"** (Deuteronomy 25:5), **and this** late husband **has** a child, albeit one who is one day old.

״וּמַאֲכִיל בִּתְרוּמָה״. דִּכְתִיב: ״וִילִיד בֵּיתוֹ הֵם יֹאכְלוּ בְלַחְמוֹ״, קְרֵי בֵּיהּ: ״יַאֲכִילוּ בְּלַחְמוֹ״.

The mishna teaches: **And** a one-day-old baby **enables** his mother, an Israelite woman who is no longer married to his father, a priest, to continue **to partake of *teruma*.** The Gemara explains that this is **as it is written,** with regard to those who are entitled to partake of *teruma* on account of a priest: **"And those who are born in his house, they may eat [*yokhelu*] of his bread"** (Leviticus 22:11). **Read into** the verse: Those who are born in his house **enable others to eat [*ya'akhilu*] of his bread,** i.e., on account of her son the priest, the Israelite mother may continue to partake of *teruma* even after the death of his father.

״וּפוֹסֵל מִן הַתְּרוּמָה״. ״וְזֶרַע אֵין לָהּ״ אָמַר רַחֲמָנָא – וְהָא אִית לַהּ.

§ The mishna also teaches: **And** a one-day-old baby **disqualifies** his mother, the daughter of a priest who is no longer married to his father, an Israelite man, **from** continuing to partake of ***teruma*.** The Gemara explains that the reason is that **the Merciful One states:** "But if a priest's daughter becomes a widow, or divorced, **and has no child,** and is returned to her father's house, as in her youth, she may eat of her father's bread" (Leviticus 22:13), **and this** daughter of a priest **has** a child.

מַאי אִירְיָא זֶרַע? אֲפִילּוּ עוּבָּר נָמֵי, דִּכְתִיב: ״כִּנְעוּרֶיהָ״ – פְּרָט לִמְעוּבֶּרֶת!

The Gemara asks: **Why** state **specifically** that she has **a child? Even** if she has **a fetus** in her womb from an Israelite man, the same *halakha* applies, **as it is written: "As in her youth,"** which **excludes a pregnant woman,**[H] since her pregnancy has changed her physical state from that of her youth.

וּצְרִיכִי, דְּאִי כְּתַב רַחֲמָנָא ״וְזֶרַע אֵין לָהּ״ – מִשּׁוּם דְּמֵעִיקָּרָא חַד גּוּפָא וְהָשְׁתָּא תְּרֵי גּוּפֵי, אֲבָל הָכָא – דְּמֵעִיקָּרָא חַד גּוּפָא וְהָשְׁתָּא חַד גּוּפָא – אֵימָא תֵּיכוֹל, כְּתַב רַחֲמָנָא ״כִּנְעוּרֶיהָ״.

The Gemara answers that both derivations **are necessary.** As, **if the Merciful One had written** only: **"And has no child,"** I would say that the reason the daughter of a priest who has a child from an Israelite man may no longer partake of *teruma* is **due to** the fact **that at the outset,** before she married, she was **one body, and now** she has developed into **two bodies,** herself and her child. **But here,** in a case when she is merely pregnant, **when at the outset** she was **one body and now** she remains **one body,** one might **say** that **she should** be permitted to **partake** of *teruma*. Therefore, **the Merciful One writes: "As in her youth."**

וְאִי כְּתַב רַחֲמָנָא "כִּנְעוּרֶיהָ" – מִשּׁוּם דְּמֵעִיקָּרָא גּוּפָהּ סְרִיקָא וְהָשְׁתָּא גּוּפָהּ מַלְיָא, אֲבָל הָכָא – דְּמֵעִיקָּרָא גּוּפָהּ סְרִיקָא וְהָשְׁתָּא גּוּפָהּ סְרִיקָא – אֵימָא תֵּיכוּל, צְרִיכָא.

**And** by contrast, **if the Merciful One had written** only: **"As in her youth,"** I would say that the reason that the daughter of a priest who is pregnant from an Israelite man may no longer partake of *teruma* is **due to** the fact **that at the outset** she had **an empty body and now** she has **a full body,** and consequently she is not returning to her father's household in her initial state. **But here,** after she has given birth, **where at the outset** she had **an empty body and now** she still has **an empty body,** one might **say** that **she should** be permitted to **partake** of *teruma*. Therefore, the Merciful One writes: "And has no child." Therefore, both derivations are **necessary.**

קְרָאֵי – אִתְרוּץ, אֶלָּא מַתְנִיתִין, מַאי אִרְיָא בֶּן יוֹם אֶחָד – אֲפִילּוּ עוּבָּר נָמֵי! אָמַר רַב שֵׁשֶׁת: הָכָא בְּמַאי עָסְקִינַן – בְּכֹהֵן שֶׁיֵּשׁ לוֹ שְׁתֵּי נָשִׁים אַחַת גְּרוּשָׁה וְאַחַת שֶׁאֵינָהּ גְּרוּשָׁה, וְיֵשׁ לוֹ בָּנִים מִשֶּׁאֵינָהּ גְּרוּשָׁה, וְיֵשׁ לוֹ בֵּן יוֹם אֶחָד מִן הַגְּרוּשָׁה,

The Gemara asks: The need for both **verses** has been **resolved, but the mishna** remains difficult: **What** is the reason the mishna is referring **specifically** to a baby who is **one day old,** when, as stated above, the same *halakha* applies **even** to **a fetus? Rav Sheshet said: Here we are dealing with a priest who has two wives: One** who is **a divorcée,** as she was previously divorced from another man, and who was therefore married to this priest in violation of *halakha*, **and one who is not a divorcée. And he has sons from** the wife **who is not a divorcée, and he has** a baby boy who is **one day old from the** wife who is **a divorcée.** This son is disqualified from the priesthood and may not partake of *teruma*.

דְּפוֹסֵל בְּעַבְדֵי אָבִיו מִלֶּאֱכוֹל בִּתְרוּמָה. וּלְאַפּוֹקֵי מִדְּרַבִּי יוֹסֵי דְּאָמַר עוּבָּר נָמֵי פּוֹסֵל, קָא מַשְׁמַע לַן: בֶּן יוֹם אֶחָד – אִין, עוּבָּר – לָא.

Rav Sheshet continues: The mishna is teaching **that** this baby **disqualifies his father's** Canaanite **slaves from partaking of** ***teruma*** again. Since this child is entitled to a portion of his father's inheritance, which includes his slaves, they may no longer partake of *teruma* due to his presence in the world. **And** the mishna teaches this **to exclude** the opinion **of Rabbi Yosei, who said** that **a fetus also disqualifies** his father's slaves from partaking of *teruma*. For this reason, the *tanna* of the mishna **teaches us** that with regard to **a one-day-old** baby boy, **yes,** he disqualifies his father's slaves from partaking of *teruma*, but **a fetus** does **not.**[H]

"נוֹחֵל וּמַנְחִיל". נוֹחֵל מִמַּאן? מֵאָבִיו, וּמַנְחִיל לְמַאן? לְאֶחָיו מֵאָבִיו, אִי בָּעֵי – מֵאֲבוּהּ לִירְתֵי וְאִי בָּעֵי – מִינֵּיהּ לִירְתֵי!

§ The mishna teaches that this baby **inherits and he bequeaths.** The Gemara asks: **From whom does he inherit?** It must be **from his father. And to whom does he bequeath?** Presumably, he bequeaths **to his paternal brother,** in a case where the baby inherited his father's property and then died on the same day, as maternal half-brothers do not inherit from each other. The Gemara raises a difficulty with regard to this interpretation: What is the novelty of the *halakha* that the brother of this one-day-old baby inherits from him? After all, **if** the surviving brother **wants, let him inherit from his father, and if he wants, let him inherit from** the one-day-old baby. Either way, he receives his late father's property.

אָמַר רַב שֵׁשֶׁת: נוֹחֵל בְּנִכְסֵי הָאֵם, לְהַנְחִיל לְאֶחָיו מִן הָאָב. וְדַוְקָא בֶּן יוֹם אֶחָד, אֲבָל עוּבָּר – לָא. מַאי טַעְמָא – דְּהוּא מָיֵית בְּרֵישָׁא, וְאֵין הַבֵּן יוֹרֵשׁ אֶת אִמּוֹ

**Rav Sheshet said:** The mishna is teaching that a one-day-old baby **inherits his mother's property** if she died on the day he was born, so that he is able **to bequeath** it, even if he dies after a day, **to** his heirs who are not the mother's heirs, e.g., **a paternal half-brother. And** in such a case it is **specifically** when he is at least **one day old** that he inherits from his mother and bequeaths the property to his paternal half-brothers, **but a fetus,** whose mother died before he emerged, does **not** inherit from his mother. **What is the reason** for this? The reason is **that** presumably the fetus **died first,**[N] before its mother died, **and** there is a *halakha* that **a son does not inherit from his mother**

### HALAKHA

**A one-day-old baby boy yes but a fetus does not – בֶּן יוֹם אֶחָד אִין עוּבָּר לָא:** If an Israelite woman was pregnant from her husband, a priest, and he died, her slaves may not partake of *teruma* on account of the fetus. The reason is that only a child enables one to partake of *teruma*, not a fetus. Consequently, if the fetus was disqualified from the priesthood, e.g., his mother is a divorcée, he does not disqualify the slaves from partaking of *teruma*; rather, they may partake of *teruma* on account of his brothers who are of unflawed lineage until the fetus is born and disqualifies them (Rambam). The Ra'avad disagrees and maintains that these slaves may not partake of *teruma*, due to the portion of the disqualified son in his father's inheritance even when he is a fetus (Rambam *Sefer Zera'im*, *Hilkhot Terumot* 8:4).

### NOTES

**The reason is that presumably the fetus died first – דְּהוּא מָיֵית בְּרֵישָׁא:** The commentaries explain that this applies only if the mother died by the hand of Heaven, but not if she was killed, as in that case the fetus might have survived (*Tosafot*; see *Arakhin* 7a). Furthermore, if she died during labor it is also possible that the fetus might survive, as once it has been uprooted from its place to emerge from the womb, it would no longer die. This is similar to the statement of Shmuel on *Arakhin* 7a with regard to a woman who was in the throes of labor and died on Shabbat, that one should bring a knife and tear open her abdomen and remove the fetus, as it may still be alive and it might be possible to save its life.

בַּקֶּבֶר לְהַנְחִיל לְאָחִיו מִן הָאָב.

while **in the grave,** i.e., after death, **in order to bequeath to his paternal half-brother.**

אִינִי, וְהָא הֲוָה עוּבְדָא וּפִרְכֵּס עַד תְּלָת פִּרְכּוּסֵי! אֲמַר מָר בְּרֵיהּ דְּרַב אַשִׁי: מִידֵּי דַּהֲוָה אַזְּנַב הַלְּטָאָה דִּמְפַרְכֶּסֶת.

The Gemara asks: **Is that so,** that it is presumed that the fetus died before its mother? **But wasn't there an incident** in which the mother died **and** the fetus **made up to three spasmodic motions** afterward? **Mar, son of Rav Ashi, said:** That is **just as it is with the tail of the lizard,**[B] **which twitches**[B] after being severed from the lizard, but it is merely a spasmodic motion which does not indicate that it is still alive.

מָר בְּרֵיהּ דְּרַב יוֹסֵף מִשְּׁמֵיהּ דְּרָבָא אֲמַר: לוֹמַר שֶׁמְּמַעֵט בְּחֵלֶק בְּכוֹרָה. וַאֲמַר מָר בְּרֵיהּ דְּרַב יוֹסֵף מִשְּׁמֵיהּ דְּרָבָא: בֵּן שֶׁנּוֹלַד אַחַר מִיתַת הָאָב – אֵינוֹ מְמַעֵט בְּחֵלֶק בְּכוֹרָה, מַאי טַעֲמָא – ״וְיָלְדוּ לוֹ״ בָּעֵינַן.

**Mar, son of Rav Yosef, said** a different explanation of the mishna's ruling **in the name of Rava:** The mishna teaches that a one-day-old baby inherits in order **to say that** such a child **reduces the portion of the firstborn.**[HN] A firstborn is entitled to a double portion of the inheritance, which is calculated by taking into account the portion due to his dead brother. **And Mar, son of Rav Yosef,** further **said in the name of Rava: A son who was born after his father's death does not reduce the portion of the firstborn.**[H] Therefore, the *halakha* in the mishna does not apply to a fetus. **What is the reason** for this? **We require** fulfillment of the verse: "If a man has two wives, the one beloved, and the other hated, **and they bore him children**" (Deuteronomy 21:15), and this does not apply to a fetus not yet born at the time of the father's death.

בְּסוּרָא מַתְנוּ הָכִי. בְּפוּמְבְּדִיתָא מַתְנוּ הָכִי: אֲמַר מָר בְּרֵיהּ דְּרַב יוֹסֵף מִשְּׁמֵיהּ דְּרָבָא, בְּכוֹר שֶׁנּוֹלַד לְאַחַר מִיתַת אָבִיו – אֵינוֹ נוֹטֵל פִּי שְׁנַיִם, מַאי טַעֲמָא – ״יַכִּיר״ בָּעֵינַן, וְהָא לֵיכָּא.

The Gemara notes: **In Sura they taught** Mar's statement **that** way, whereas **in Pumbedita**[B] **they taught** it **this way: Mar, son of Rav Yosef, said in the name of Rava: A firstborn who was born after his father's death**[H] **does not receive a double** portion.[N] **What is the reason** for this? **We require** fulfillment of the verse: "But **he shall acknowledge** the firstborn... by giving him a double portion" (Deuteronomy 21:17), **and** in this case the father **is not there**[N] to acknowledge him.

וְהִלְכְתָא כְּכׇל הָנֵי לִישָּׁנֵי דְּמָר בְּרֵיהּ דְּרַב יוֹסֵף מִשְּׁמֵיהּ דְּרָבָא.

The Gemara concludes: **And the *halakha* is in accordance with all these versions of** the statement of **Mar, son of Rav Yosef, in the name of Rava,** i.e., a one-day-old baby reduces the portion of the firstborn, a son born after his father's death does not reduce the portion of the firstborn, and a firstborn born after his father's death does not receive a double portion.

## BACKGROUND

Lizard [*leta'a*] – לְטָאָה: The *leta'a* is almost certainly one of the many species of lizards from the Lacertidae family. These lizards range in length from 15 to 25 cm, and they have developed limbs that allow them to run quickly. Their skin is generally so soft that it wrinkles, although in some species the skin is tight on the body.

Small-spotted lizard, native to Eretz Yisrael

The tail of the lizard which twitches – זְנַב הַלְּטָאָה דִּמְפַרְכֶּסֶת: After a limb, e.g., the tail of a lizard, is severed, the nerves continue functioning in an involuntary manner for a brief period. This is caused by the release of neurotransmitters, which cause a twitching of the muscles. Nevertheless, such neurological activity is not a sign of life. Likewise, the twitching of a fetus might be a neurological reaction which does not prove that it is alive.

In Sura...in Pumbedita – בְּסוּרָא...בְּפוּמְבְּדִיתָא: In the first generations of *amora'im*, two main academies were established in Babylonia, those of Sura and Pumbedita. On occasion these academies, for various reasons, were disbanded or split up, but overall they continued for many years. From the outset the methodology of the academy of Sura was probably more similar than that of Pumbedita to that of Eretz Yisrael, with an emphasis on broad knowledge, from the Bible to statements of *tanna'im*.

## HALAKHA

A one-day-old child reduces the portion of the firstborn – מְמַעֵט בְּחֵלֶק בְּכוֹרָה: A one-day-old child reduces the portion of the firstborn, in accordance with the ruling of Mar, son of Rav Yosef, citing Rava, as the Gemara on *Bava Batra* 142a accepts this opinion as *halakha* (Rambam *Sefer Mishpatim*, *Hilkhot Naḥalot* 2:5; *Shulḥan Arukh*, *Ḥoshen Mishpat* 277:5).

A son who was born after his father's death does not reduce the portion of the firstborn – בֵּן שֶׁנּוֹלַד אַחַר מִיתַת הָאָב אֵינוֹ מְמַעֵט בְּחֵלֶק בְּכוֹרָה: A son who was born after his father's death does not reduce the firstborn's share, in accordance with the opinion of Mar, son of Rav Yosef, citing Rava, as the Gemara on *Bava Batra* 142a accepts this opinion as *halakha* (Rambam *Sefer Mishpatim*, *Hilkhot Naḥalot* 2:5; *Shulḥan Arukh*, *Ḥoshen Mishpat* 277:5).

A firstborn who was born after his father's death – בְּכוֹר שֶׁנּוֹלַד לְאַחַר מִיתַת אָבִיו: A firstborn son who was born after his father's death does not receive a double portion in his father's inheritance, in accordance with the opinion of Rava as cited by Mar, son of Rav Yosef (Rambam *Sefer Mishpatim*, *Hilkhot Naḥalot* 2:2; *Shulḥan Arukh*, *Ḥoshen Mishpat* 277:3).

## NOTES

To say that such a child reduces the portion of the firstborn – לוֹמַר שֶׁמְּמַעֵט בְּחֵלֶק בְּכוֹרָה: A fetus inherits his father just like a one-day-old child. The difference between them is how they affect the portion of the firstborn. If the son was not yet born at the time of the father's death, and in addition to him there was a firstborn and an ordinary son, the firstborn receives one-third of the inheritance as his firstborn portion, as though the fetus does not exist, and the remainder is divided into three portions, i.e., for the firstborn, the fetus, and the other brother. If that fetus dies after it is born (Ri Migash on *Bava Batra* 142a), the firstborn and the ordinary son divide his portion of the inheritance evenly between them. By contrast, if he was a one-day-old child, he reduces the portion of the firstborn: The firstborn receives one-fourth as his firstborn portion, and the remainder is divided in the manner described above.

A firstborn who was born after his father's death does not receive a double portion – בְּכוֹר שֶׁנּוֹלַד לְאַחַר מִיתַת אָבִיו אֵינוֹ נוֹטֵל פִּי שְׁנַיִם: The commentaries explain that there are two ways in which a firstborn born after his father's death might have a brother. Either he is a twin, or his father had several wives who all gave birth after his death.

We require fulfillment of the verse: But he shall acknowledge, and in this case the father is not there – יַכִּיר בָּעֵינַן וְהָא לֵיכָּא: The early commentaries disagree with regard to this condition. Some say that it does not mean that the father must acknowledge his firstborn in practice; rather, he must have the potential to acknowledge him. Accordingly, even if the father was overseas when his firstborn son was born, that firstborn is entitled to a double portion of his inheritance (Rashbam on *Bava Batra* 142a, citing Rabbeinu Ḥananel). Likewise, if the birth of the firstborn occurred while the father was on his deathbed, provided that he is still alive he is considered able to acknowledge him, despite the fact that he cannot actually do so (Meiri). Others disagree, maintaining that the father must be physically capable of acknowledging his firstborn in practice, which excludes a case where he is dying (Rashbatz and *Nimmukei Yosef* on *Bava Batra* 142a).

״וְהַהוֹרְגוֹ חַיָּיב״. דִּכְתִיב: ״וְאִישׁ כִּי יַכֶּה כָּל נֶפֶשׁ״ – מִכׇּל מָקוֹם.

§ The mishna teaches: **And one who kills** a one-day-old baby is **liable** for his murder. The Gemara explains that the reason for this **is as it is written: "And he who smites any man mortally** shall be put to death" (Leviticus 24:17), where the phrase "any man" indicates that this verse applies **in any case,**[N] even in the case of a one-day-old baby.

״וַהֲרֵי הוּא לְאָבִיו וּלְאִמּוֹ וּלְכׇל קְרוֹבָיו כְּחָתָן שָׁלֵם״. לְמַאי הִלְכְתָא? אֲמַר רַב פַּפָּא: לְעִנְיַן אֲבֵילוּת.

The mishna further teaches: **And** if a one-day-old baby dies, **his** status in relation **to his father and to his mother and to all his relatives is like** that of **a full-fledged groom.** The Gemara asks: **With regard to what *halakha*** is this stated? **Rav Pappa said: With regard to mourning.**[H]

כְּמַאן? דְּלָא כְּרַבָּן שִׁמְעוֹן בֶּן גַּמְלִיאֵל, דַּאֲמַר: כׇּל שֶׁשָּׁהָה שְׁלֹשִׁים יוֹם בָּאָדָם – אֵינוֹ נֵפֶל, הָא לֹא שָׁהָה – סָפֵק הָוֵי! הָכָא בְּמַאי עָסְקִינַן – דְּקִים לֵיהּ שֶׁכָּלוּ לוֹ חֳדָשָׁיו.

The Gemara comments: **In accordance with whose** opinion is this stated? It is **not in accordance with** the opinion of **Rabban Shimon ben Gamliel,**[N] **who said: With regard to humans, any** child **that remained** alive **thirty days** after birth **is not** considered **a non-viable newborn.** It can be inferred from this statement that if **he did not remain** alive for thirty days after birth, **he is** of **uncertain** status. The Gemara refutes this proof: **Here we are dealing with** a case **where one is certain that its months** of gestation **were completed,** and therefore it is certainly a viable newborn.

מתני׳ בַּת שָׁלֹשׁ שָׁנִים וְיוֹם אֶחָד מִתְקַדֶּשֶׁת בְּבִיאָה. וְאִם בָּא עָלֶיהָ יָבָם – קְנָאָהּ, וְחַיָּיבִין עָלֶיהָ מִשּׁוּם אֵשֶׁת אִישׁ,

**MISHNA** A girl who is **three years and one day old,** whose father arranged her betrothal, **is betrothed through intercourse,**[H] as the halakhic status of intercourse with her is that of intercourse in all halakhic senses. **And** in a case where the childless husband of a girl three years and one day old dies, **if** his brother the ***yavam* engages in intercourse with her,**[H] **he acquires her** as his wife; **and** if she is married, a man other than her husband **is liable for** engaging in intercourse with **her due to** violation of the prohibition against intercourse with **a married woman.**[H]

וּמְטַמְּאָה אֶת בּוֹעֲלָהּ לְטַמֵּא מִשְׁכָּב תַּחְתּוֹן כְּעֶלְיוֹן.

**And** if she is impure due to menstruation, **she imparts impurity to one who engages in intercourse with her**[H] who then **renders impure** all the layers of **bedding beneath** him, rendering them impure **like the upper** bedding covering a *zav*, in the sense that it assumes first-degree ritual impurity and does not become a primary source of ritual impurity, and it renders impure food and drink, but it does not render impure people and vessels.

**NOTES**

As it is written: And he who smites any man mortally shall be put to death, where this applies in any case – דִּכְתִיב וְאִישׁ כִּי יַכֶּה כׇּל נֶפֶשׁ מִכׇּל מָקוֹם: In other words, the verse is referring to any human being (*Tosefot HaRosh*). Some commentaries read a clearer version of the text: And he that smites any man mortally, any sort of man (*Tosafot*).

It is not in accordance with the opinion of Rabban Shimon ben Gamliel – דְּלָא כְּרַבָּן שִׁמְעוֹן בֶּן גַּמְלִיאֵל: The early commentaries disagree as to the meaning of this statement. Some say that it is referring to the entire mishna (Rashi). Although this claim is mentioned only in connection with the end of the mishna, the Gemara first explained all the *halakhot* of the mishna before stating that it is not in accordance with the opinion of Rabban Shimon ben Gamliel. Others maintain that the statement is referring only to the last clause of the mishna, with regard to mourning (Rambam).

**HALAKHA**

With regard to mourning – לְעִנְיַן אֲבֵילוּת: If a baby died within thirty days of birth, including the thirtieth day, one does not mourn for him, even if his hair and nails were fully developed. If he died later than that point one does mourn for him, unless it is known that he was born after eight months of pregnancy. If it is known for certain that he completed a full term of gestation, then one mourns for him even if he died on the day of birth. The *halakha* is in accordance with the opinion of Rav Pappa, not Rabban Shimon ben Gamliel (Rambam *Sefer Shofetim, Hilkhot Evel* 1:6–7; *Shulḥan Arukh, Yoreh De'a* 374:8).

A girl who is three years and one day old is betrothed through intercourse – בַּת שָׁלֹשׁ שָׁנִים וְיוֹם אֶחָד מִתְקַדֶּשֶׁת בְּבִיאָה: A girl who is three years and one day old can be betrothed by means of sexual intercourse, with her father's consent. If she is younger than that she cannot be betrothed in this manner (Rambam *Sefer Nashim, Hilkhot Ishut* 3:11; *Shulḥan Arukh, Even HaEzer* 37:1).

If his brother the *yavam* engages in intercourse with her – אִם בָּא עָלֶיהָ יָבָם: Intercourse with a *yevama* aged less than three years and one day does not effect levirate marriage. If she was older than that and the *yavam* engaged in intercourse with her, he acquires her as his wife. Nevertheless, she cannot perform *ḥalitza* until she is twelve years and one day old, and she has been examined and found to have two pubic hairs (*Shulḥan Arukh, Even HaEzer* 167:4).

A man other than her husband is liable…due to the prohibition against intercourse with a married woman – חַיָּיבִין...מִשּׁוּם אֵשֶׁת אִישׁ: If a father accepts betrothal for his minor daughter, and another man engages in intercourse with her, the second man is executed by strangulation, while she is exempt from punishment. If she was married off by her mother or brothers, i.e., in a situation where her father was not alive, such a marriage does not take effect by Torah law and she does not require a bill of divorce to leave her husband. Therefore, if she refused her husband, the second man is exempt from the death penalty, but the court administers lashes for rebelliousness (Rambam *Sefer Kedusha, Hilkhot Issurei Bia* 3:2).

She imparts impurity to one who engages in intercourse with her, etc. – מְטַמְּאָה אֶת בּוֹעֲלָהּ וכו׳: One who engages in intercourse with a minor girl who is menstruating is rendered impure, as is the case with any menstruating woman. This applies only if he is at least nine years and one day old, and she is at least three years and one day old (Rambam *Sefer Tahara, Hilkhot Metamei Mishkav UMoshav* 3:3).

NOTES

If she marries a priest she may partake of *teruma* – נִשֵּׂאת לְכֹהֵן תֹּאכַל בִּתְרוּמָה: Although the betrothal of a girl younger than three years old is valid when performed by her father, a marriage canopy does not take effect in her case, as the purpose of a marriage canopy is to permit intercourse between a couple, and she is too young for intercourse (Rashi). Therefore, she has the status of a betrothed woman, not a married one, and the Sages say that a woman betrothed to a priest should not partake of *teruma* before she enters the marriage canopy (Rashi on *Sanhedrin* 55b).

נִשֵּׂאת לְכֹהֵן – תֹּאכַל בִּתְרוּמָה. בָּא עָלֶיהָ אֶחָד מִן הַפְּסוּלִין – פְּסָלָהּ מִן הַכְּהוּנָּה. בָּא עָלֶיהָ אֶחָד מִכׇּל הָעֲרָיוֹת הָאֲמוּרוֹת בַּתּוֹרָה – מוּמָתִין עָלֶיהָ, וְהִיא פְּטוּרָה.

If **she marries a priest, she may partake of** ***teruma*****,**[NH] like any other wife of a priest; if she is unmarried and **one of the** men **who are unfit** for the priesthood, e.g., a *mamzer* or *ḥalal*, **engaged in intercourse with her,**[H] **he disqualifies her from** marrying into **the priesthood,** and if she is the daughter of a priest, she is disqualified from partaking of *teruma*. Finally, if **one of all those with whom relations are forbidden,** as **stated in the Torah,** e.g., her father or her husband's father, **engaged in intercourse with her,**[H] **they are executed** by the court **for** engaging in intercourse with **her, and she is exempt,** because she is a minor.

פָּחוֹת מִכָּאן – כְּנוֹתֵן אֶצְבַּע בָּעַיִן.

If the girl is **less than that** age, younger than three years and one day, the status of intercourse with her is not that of intercourse in all halakhic senses; rather, it is **like placing a finger into the eye.** Just as in that case, the eye constricts, sheds tears, and then returns to its original state, so too, in a girl younger than three years and one day old, the hymen returns to its original state.

גמ׳ תָּנוּ רַבָּנַן: בַּת שָׁלֹשׁ שָׁנִים מִתְקַדֶּשֶׁת בְּבִיאָה, דִּבְרֵי רַבִּי מֵאִיר. וַחֲכָמִים אוֹמְרִים: בַּת שָׁלֹשׁ שָׁנִים וְיוֹם אֶחָד. מַאי בֵּינַיְיהוּ? אָמְרִי דְּבֵי רַבִּי יַנַּאי: עֶרֶב רֹאשׁ הַשָּׁנָה אִיכָּא בֵּינַיְיהוּ.

**GEMARA** **The Sages taught** in a *baraita*: **A girl** who is **three years** old **is betrothed through intercourse;** this is **the statement of Rabbi Meir. And the Rabbis say:** She must be **three years and one day old.** The Gemara asks: **What** is the difference **between** their opinions, as both agree that she cannot be betrothed before the age of three? The Sages **of the school of Rabbi Yannai said:** There is a difference **between** their opinions in the case of a girl on **the eve of the first day of** the fourth **year** of her life. According to Rabbi Meir, she can be betrothed through intercourse, as on this day three years are complete, whereas the Rabbis maintain that she cannot be betrothed in this manner, as she has not yet entered the first day of her fourth year.

וְרַבִּי יוֹחָנָן אָמַר: שְׁלֹשִׁים יוֹם בַּשָּׁנָה חֲשׁוּבִין שָׁנָה אִיכָּא בֵּינַיְיהוּ.

**And Rabbi Yoḥanan said:** There is a difference **between** their opinions with regard to the issue of whether **thirty days in a year are considered** equivalent to **a year.** Rabbi Meir maintains that thirty days in a year are considered equivalent to a year, and therefore a girl aged two years and thirty days is already considered like a three-year-old and may be betrothed through intercourse. By contrast, the Rabbis contend that thirty days in a year are not considered equivalent to a year, and she may be betrothed through intercourse only upon reaching the age of three years and one day.

מֵיתִיבִי, בַּת שָׁלֹשׁ שָׁנִים, וַאֲפִילּוּ בַּת שְׁתֵּי שָׁנִים וְיוֹם אֶחָד מִתְקַדֶּשֶׁת בְּבִיאָה – דִּבְרֵי רַבִּי מֵאִיר. וַחֲכָמִים אוֹמְרִים: בַּת שְׁלֹשָׁה שָׁנִים וְיוֹם אֶחָד.

The Gemara **raises an objection** against the explanation of Rabbi Yannai from a *baraita*: A girl who is **three years old, and even** one who is **two years and one day old, is betrothed through intercourse;** this is **the statement of Rabbi Meir. And the Rabbis say:** She must be **three years and one day old.**

HALAKHA

If she marries a priest she may partake of *teruma* – נִשֵּׂאת לְכֹהֵן תֹּאכַל בִּתְרוּמָה: The daughter of a non-priest who marries a priest may partake of *teruma* and eat the breast and thigh, which are portions designated to priests from peace offerings, even if she is only three years and one day old (Rambam *Sefer Zera'im*, *Hilkhot Terumot* 6:3).

If she is unmarried and one of the men who are unfit for the priesthood engaged in intercourse with her – בָּא עָלֶיהָ אֶחָד מִן הַפְּסוּלִין: With regard to any woman who engages in intercourse with a man to whom she is forbidden by a prohibition that would give her the status of a *zona*, whether she was raped or acted willingly or unwittingly, and whether it was regular or anal intercourse, once the man has performed the initial stage of intercourse she is considered a *zona* and thereby disqualified from marrying into the priesthood, and she may not partake of *teruma*. This is the *halakha* provided that she is three years and one day old, and he is at least nine years and one day old (Rambam *Sefer Kedusha*, *Hilkhot Issurei Bia* 18:6; *Shulḥan Arukh*, *Even HaEzer* 6:9; see 7:10).

If one of all those with whom relations are forbidden as stated in the Torah engaged in intercourse with her – בָּא עָלֶיהָ אֶחָד מִכׇּל הָעֲרָיוֹת הָאֲמוּרוֹת בַּתּוֹרָה: If a man engages in intercourse with a girl to whom he is forbidden and who is three years and one day old, he is liable to receive the death penalty, *karet*, or lashes, depending on the circumstances, e.g., whether he did so intentionally or unwittingly, and the nature of the forbidden relationship, whereas she is exempt from any punishment. If she was younger than this, this act is not considered intercourse and they are both exempt (Rambam *Sefer Kedusha*, *Hilkhot Issurei Bia* 1:13).

בִּשְׁלָמָא לְרַבִּי יוֹחָנָן, כִּי הֵיכִי דְּאִיכָּא תַּנָּא דְּקָאָמַר: יוֹם אֶחָד בַּשָּׁנָה חָשׁוּב שָׁנָה, הָכִי נַמִי אִיכָּא תַּנָּא דְּאָמַר: שְׁלֹשִׁים יוֹם בַּשָּׁנָה חֲשׁוּבִין שָׁנָה.

The Gemara asks: **Granted, according to** the opinion of **Rabbi Yoḥanan, just as there is a *tanna* who says** that **one day in a year is considered** equivalent to a year, **so too, there is a *tanna* who** says that **thirty days in a year are considered** equivalent to **a year.**[N] The *baraita* states that according to Rabbi Meir, a girl two years and one day old is considered like a three-year-old, following the opinion that one day in a year is equivalent to a full year. Similarly, Rabbi Yoḥanan maintains that there is a second *tanna* who says that thirty days in a year are considered equivalent to a full year, and therefore a girl can be betrothed by intercourse from the age of two years and thirty days.

אֶלָּא לְרַבִּי יַנַּאי קַשְׁיָא! קַשְׁיָא.

**But according to** the opinion of **Rabbi Yannai,**[N] that Rabbi Meir requires a full three years, this *baraita* is **difficult,** as it explicitly states that in Rabbi Meir's opinion even a girl aged two years and one day can be betrothed by intercourse. The Gemara concludes: Indeed, this *baraita* is **difficult**[N] according to the opinion of Rabbi Yannai.

״פָּחוֹת מִכָּאן כְּנוֹתֵן אֶצְבַּע בָּעַיִן״. אִיבַּעְיָא לְהוּ: הָנֵי בְּתוּלִין מֵיזַל אָזְלִי וְאָתוּ, אוֹ דִּלְמָא אִתְצוּדֵי הוּא דְּלָא מִתְצַדְיָי עַד לְאַחַר שָׁלֹשׁ?

§ The last clause of the mishna teaches that if the girl is **less than that** age, i.e., younger than three years and one day, the status of intercourse with her is **like placing a finger into the eye.**[N] **A dilemma was raised before** the Sages: What happens to **this hymen,** i.e., to the hymen of a girl under three with whom a man engaged in intercourse? Does it **disappear and come** back again[H] later, **or perhaps it is not removed at all until after** she reaches the age of **three?**

לְמַאי נַפְקָא מִינַּהּ? כְּגוֹן שֶׁבָּעַל בְּתוֹךְ שָׁלֹשׁ וּמָצָא דָּם, וּבָעַל לְאַחַר שָׁלֹשׁ וְלֹא מָצָא דָּם. אִי אָמְרַתְּ מֵיזַל אָזְלִי וְאָתוּ – שָׁהוּת הוּא דְּלָא הָוְיָא לְהוּ.

The Gemara asks: **What difference is** there in *halakha* between these two suggestions? The Gemara answers that there is a practical ramification in a case **where** a priest **engaged in intercourse** with a girl to whom he is married **within** her first **three** years, **and found blood** on her due to that intercourse, **and** again **engaged in intercourse** with her many times, including **after** she turned **three, but** on that occasion **he did not find blood. If you say** that after engaging in intercourse when the girl is younger than three, the hymen **disappears and comes** back again, here one can maintain that it disappeared due to the first time they engaged in intercourse and did not grow back because **there was not enough time** without intercourse **for it** to grow back.

אֶלָּא אִי אָמְרַתְּ אִתְצוּדֵי הוּא דְּלָא מִתְצַדְיָי עַד לְאַחַר שָׁלֹשׁ, הָא – אַחֵר בָּא עָלֶיהָ, מַאי?

**But if you say** that the hymen **is not removed** at all **until after** she reaches the age of **three,** the fact that **this** girl did not emit blood after three years must be because **another** man **engaged in intercourse with her**[N] after she turned three, in which case she is classified as a *zona*, a woman who has engaged in sexual intercourse with a man forbidden to her by the Torah, and is forbidden to her husband the priest. The Gemara reiterates: **What,** then, is the resolution of the dilemma?

**NOTES**

**So too there is a *tanna* who says that thirty days in a year are considered a year** – הָכִי נַמִי אִיכָּא תַּנָּא דְּאָמַר שְׁלֹשִׁים יוֹם בַּשָּׁנָה חֲשׁוּבִין שָׁנָה: According to Rabbi Yoḥanan, one can explain that the two *tanna'im* who taught these two *baraitot* agree that Rabbi Meir maintains that part of a year is considered like a complete year. They disagree with regard to Rabbi Meir's exact opinion on how much of a year this must be. According to the *tanna* of one *baraita*, a single day of a year is enough to count as a full year, whereas according to the *tanna* of the other *baraita*, a complete month is required. By contrast, according to Rabbi Yannai, who holds that Rabbi Meir is of the opinion that a full three years are required, there is no way of reconciling his ruling with the opinion cited in the second *baraita*.

**But according to Rabbi Yannai** – אֶלָּא לְרַבִּי יַנַּאי: The early commentaries explain that everyone agrees that in many areas of *halakha*, thirty days are considered a year. The Rabbis disagree with Rabbi Meir only with regard to this specific case of the intercourse of a minor girl, as they had a tradition that her physical signs of virginity are removed due to intercourse only if she is at least three years and one day old. Consequently, an act of intercourse with a girl younger than that is not considered intercourse and she cannot be betrothed through them (Ritva).

**This *baraita* is difficult [*kashya*]** – קַשְׁיָא: The term *kashya*, meaning: This is difficult, indicates that there is a problem here which must be addressed, but the opinion itself is not necessarily rejected. By contrast, the corresponding term *teyuvta*: Conclusive refutation, which also appears often in the Gemara, is an indication of a severe difficulty for which there is no answer and on account of which the opinion is rejected.

**Less than that is like placing a finger into the eye** – פָּחוֹת מִכָּאן כְּנוֹתֵן אֶצְבַּע בָּעַיִן: Everyone agrees that an act of intercourse with a girl younger than three is not considered intercourse. Therefore, when she grows older and marries her marriage contract is two hundred dinar, like that of a virgin (Rashi on *Ketubot* 11b). The commentaries further note that as an act of intercourse with such a young girl is not classified as intercourse, it does not render her a *zona* and she is not forbidden to a priest (Responsa of the Rashba).

**The fact that this girl did not emit blood after three years must be because another man engaged in intercourse with her** – הָא אַחֵר בָּא עָלֶיהָ: This suggestion has halakhic ramifications. Although there is a principle that the seduction of a minor girl is considered rape (see *Yevamot* 33b), if the minor who was raped was married to a priest, she is rendered prohibited to him. This is because the wife of a priest is forbidden to him due to any act of intercourse with another man, even if she was raped. By contrast, if the girl who was raped was married to an Israelite man, she is not rendered forbidden to him (*Tosafot*; see Rashi, Ritva, and Meiri).

**HALAKHA**

**This hymen of a girl under three, does it disappear and come back again, etc.** – הָנֵי בְּתוּלִין מֵיזַל אָזְלִי וְאָתוּ וכו׳: If a man engaged in intercourse with a girl or a woman who is a virgin and she did not bleed, and he again engaged in intercourse with her and this time she did bleed, even if she was a minor and not of an age at which a girl usually menstruates, but older than three years of age, this is considered to be blood of menstruation. The reason for this is that if it was the blood from the tearing of the hymen, one could assume she would have bled the first time they engaged in intercourse. If a man engages in intercourse with a girl younger than three years of age and she bleeds, this is assumed to be blood from the tearing of the hymen, in accordance with Rav Ḥisda's resolution of the Gemara's dilemma (Rambam *Sefer Kedusha*, *Hilkhot Issurei Bia* 5:25).

מַתְקִיף לָהּ רַב חִיָּיא בְּרֵיהּ דְּרַב אִיקָא: וּמַאן לֵימָא לַן דְּמַכָּה שֶׁבְּתוֹךְ שָׁלֹשׁ אֵינָהּ חוֹזֶרֶת לְאַלְתַּר? שֶׁמָּא חוֹזֶרֶת לְאַלְתַּר, וְהָא – אַחֵר בָּא עָלֶיהָ!

**Rav Ḥiyya, son of Rav Ika, objects to this** explanation of the practical ramifications of the dilemma: **But** even if one maintains that the hymen of a girl younger than three disappears and grows back, one can still contend that this girl engaged in intercourse with another man, as **who will say to us that a wound that** was inflicted **within three years** of a girl's birth **is not restored** and healed **immediately? Perhaps it is restored immediately, and this** girl did not emit blood because **another** man **engaged in intercourse with her** previously, and she is therefore a *zona* who is forbidden to a priest.

אֶלָּא נַפְקָא מִינָּהּ: כְּגוֹן שֶׁבָּעַל בְּתוֹךְ שָׁלֹשׁ וּמָצָא דָּם, וּבָעַל לְאַחַר שָׁלֹשׁ וּמָצָא דָּם. אִי אָמְרַתְּ מֵיזַל אָזְלֵי וְאָתוּ – הַאי דַּם בְּתוּלִין הוּא, אֶלָּא אִי אָמְרַתְּ אִתְצוּדֵי הוּא דְּלָא מִתְצְדֵי אֶלָּא עַד לְאַחַר שָׁלֹשׁ – הַאי דַּם נִדָּה הוּא, מַאי?

**Rather,** the practical **difference** between the two suggestions relates to a case **where** the husband **engaged in intercourse** with this girl **within** her first **three** years, **and found blood, and engaged in intercourse** with her again **after** she turned **three, and** again **found blood. If you say** that the hymen **disappears and comes** back again, **this** blood emitted when she is less than three years old **is blood** from the tearing of **the hymen,** which does not render her impure. **But if you say** that the hymen **is not removed** at all **until after** she reaches the age of **three,** then **this** blood she emitted when she was younger than three **is menstrual blood,** which renders her impure. **What,** then, is the resolution of the dilemma?

אָמַר רַב חִסְדָּא: תָּא שְׁמַע, פָּחוֹת מִכָּאן – כְּנוֹתֵן אֶצְבַּע בָּעַיִן, לָמָּה לִי לְמִתְנֵי ״כְּנוֹתֵן אֶצְבַּע בָּעַיִן״? לִתְנֵי ״פָּחוֹת מִכָּאן – וְלֹא כְלוּם״, מַאי לָאו – הָא קָא מַשְׁמַע לַן: מָה עַיִן – מְדַמַּעַת וְחוֹזֶרֶת וּמְדַמַּעַת, אַף בְּתוּלִין – מֵיזַל אָזְלֵי וְאָתֵי.

**Rav Ḥisda said: Come** and **hear** the mishna: If the girl is **less than that** age of three years and one day, intercourse with her is **like placing a finger into the eye. Why do** I need the mishna **to teach: Like placing a finger into the eye? Let** it **teach** simply: If she is **less than that** age, intercourse with her is **nothing. What, is it not** correct that **this** is what the mishna **teaches us,** by its comparison to an eye: **Just as** placing a finger in **an eye** causes it to **tear and tear again,** when another finger is placed in it, **so too** after the intercourse of a girl under three the **hymen disappears and comes** back again?

תָּנוּ רַבָּנַן, מַעֲשֶׂה בְּיוּסְטְנִי בִּתּוֹ שֶׁל אַסְוֵירוּס בֶּן אַנְטוֹנִינוּס שֶׁבָּאת לִפְנֵי רַבִּי. אָמְרָה לוֹ: רַבִּי, אִשָּׁה בְּכַמָּה נִיסֵּת? אָמַר לָהּ: בַּת שָׁלֹשׁ שָׁנִים וְיוֹם אֶחָד.

§ **The Sages taught** in a *baraita*: There was **an incident involving** a gentile woman called **Yusteni,**[L] **the daughter of Asveirus, son of Antoninus,**[B] a Roman emperor, **who came before Rabbi** Yehuda HaNasi. **She said to him: My teacher, at what** age is **a woman** fit to **marry,** i.e., at what age is it appropriate for a woman to engage in intercourse, which would therefore be the appropriate time to marry? Rabbi Yehuda HaNasi **said to her:** She must be at least **three years and one day old.**

וּבְכַמָּה מִתְעַבֶּרֶת? אָמַר לָהּ: בַּת שְׁתֵּים עֶשְׂרֵה שָׁנָה וְיוֹם אֶחָד. אָמְרָה לוֹ: אֲנִי נִשֵּׂאתִי בְּשֵׁשׁ וְיָלַדְתִּי בְּשֶׁבַע, אוֹי לְשָׁלֹשׁ שָׁנִים שֶׁאִבַּדְתִּי בְּבֵית אַבָּא!

Yusteni further inquired: **And at what** age is **she** fit to **become pregnant?** Rabbi Yehuda HaNasi **said to her:** When she is at least **twelve years and one day old. She said to him: I married when** I was **six, and gave birth** a year later, **when** I was **seven. Woe for** those **three years,** between the age of three, when I was fit for intercourse, and the age of six, when I married, **as I wasted** those years **in my father's house** by not engaging in intercourse.

וּמִי מִעַבְּרָה? וְהָתָנֵי רַב בֵּיבַי קַמֵּיהּ דְּרַב נַחְמָן: שָׁלֹשׁ נָשִׁים מְשַׁמְּשׁוֹת בְּמוֹךְ, קְטַנָּה מְעוּבֶּרֶת וּמֵנִיקָה.

The Gemara asks: **And can** a minor of that age **become pregnant? But didn't Rav Beivai teach** a *baraita* **before Rav Naḥman: Three women** may **engage in intercourse** while **using** a contraceptive absorbent **cloth,** a soft fabric placed at the entrance to the womb to prevent conception, despite the fact that this practice generally is prohibited. They are **a minor; a pregnant woman; and a nursing woman.**

קְטַנָּה – שֶׁמָּא תִּתְעַבֵּר וְתָמוּת, מְעוּבֶּרֶת – שֶׁמָּא תַּעֲשֶׂה עוּבָּרָהּ סַנְדָּל, מֵנִיקָה – שֶׁמָּא תִּגְמוֹל אֶת בְּנָהּ וְיָמוּת.

The *baraita* specifies the reason for allowing these women to use contraceptive absorbent cloths: **A minor, lest she become pregnant and** perhaps **die** from this pregnancy; **a pregnant woman, lest** she be impregnated a second time and **her** older **fetus become** deformed into the shape of **a sandal** fish, by being squashed by the pressure of the second fetus; and **a nursing woman, lest** she become pregnant and her milk dry up, in which case **she weans her son** too early, thereby endangering him, **and he dies.**

**LANGUAGE**

**Yusteni – יוּסְטְנִי:** The name Yusteni, or Justina for a woman, and the name Justin and similar variations for a man, were common names in the Roman period. They are all derived from the Latin justus, meaning righteous.

**BACKGROUND**

**Asveirus son of Antoninus – אַסְוֵירוּס בֶּן אַנְטְנִינוּס:** Some claim that this Antoninus is Marcus Aurelius Antoninus, the emperor nicknamed Caracalla, who ruled from 211 to 217 CE. He was known for his close relations with the Jews, with stories of such an affinity dating back to his childhood. Others assert that the reference here is to a different emperor: the Emperor Septimius Severus, Caracalla's father, who ruled from 193 to 211 CE. He, too, maintained friendly relations with the Jews. Yet others contend that this is Marcus Aurelius Antoninus, who ruled from 161 to 180 CE.

Bust of Caracalla

וְאֵיזוֹהִי קְטַנָּה – מִבַּת אַחַת עֶשְׂרֵה שָׁנָה וְיוֹם אֶחָד וְעַד שְׁתֵּים עֶשְׂרֵה שָׁנָה וְיוֹם אֶחָד. פָּחוֹת מִכָּאן, אוֹ יָתֵר עַל כֵּן – מְשַׁמֶּשֶׁת וְהוֹלֶכֶת – דִּבְרֵי רַבִּי מֵאִיר.

The *baraita* continues: **And who is considered a minor?** It is a girl **from the age of eleven years and one day until** the age of **twelve years and one day.** If she was **younger than that or older than that, she may go ahead and engage in intercourse** in her usual manner, i.e., without contraception. This is **the statement of Rabbi Meir.** Since it is assumed that a minor who is less than eleven years old cannot become pregnant, she is considered to be in no danger.

וַחֲכָמִים אוֹמְרִים: אַחַת זוֹ וְאַחַת זוֹ – מְשַׁמֶּשֶׁת כְּדַרְכָּהּ וְהוֹלֶכֶת, וּמִן הַשָּׁמַיִם יְרַחֲמוּ, שֶׁנֶּאֱמַר ״שׁוֹמֵר פְּתָאִים ה׳״!

**And the Rabbis say: Both** in **this** case of a minor girl who can become pregnant **and** in **that** case of a minor girl who cannot become pregnant, she **may go ahead and engage in intercourse in her usual manner, and Heaven will have mercy** upon her and prevent any mishap, **as it is stated: "The Lord preserves the simple"** (Psalms 116:6). In light of the statement of Rabbi Meir, how could Yusteni have become pregnant at age seven?

אִיבָּעֵית אֵימָא: ״אֲשֶׁר בְּשַׂר חֲמוֹרִים בְּשָׂרָם״. וְאִיבָּעֵית אֵימָא: ״אֲשֶׁר פִּיהֶם דִּבֶּר שָׁוְא וִימִינָם יְמִין שָׁקֶר״.

The Gemara answers: **If you wish, say** that Yusteni was able to become pregnant at such a young age because she was a gentile, and the verse states with regard to gentiles: **"Their flesh is the flesh of donkeys"** (Ezekiel 23:20). **And if you wish, say** instead that Yusteni was lying when she said she became pregnant at age seven, as it is stated with regard to gentiles: **"Whose mouth speaks falsehood, and their right hand is a right hand of lying"** (Psalms 144:8).

תָּנוּ רַבָּנַן, מַעֲשֶׂה בְּאִשָּׁה אַחַת שֶׁבָּאת לִפְנֵי רַבִּי עֲקִיבָא, אָמְרָה לוֹ: רַבִּי, נִבְעַלְתִּי בְּתוֹךְ שָׁלֹשׁ שָׁנִים, מָה אֲנִי לִכְהוּנָּה? אָמַר לָהּ: כְּשֵׁרָה אַתְּ לִכְהוּנָּה.

**The Sages taught** in a *baraita*: There was **an incident involving a certain woman who came before Rabbi Akiva and said to him: My teacher, I engaged in intercourse within three years** of my birth; **what is my** status with regard to marrying **into the priesthood?** Rabbi Akiva **said to her: You are fit** to marry **into the priesthood.**

אָמְרָה לוֹ: רַבִּי, אֶמְשׁוֹל לְךָ מָשָׁל, לְמָה הַדָּבָר דּוֹמֶה – לְתִינוֹק שֶׁטָּמְנוּ לוֹ אֶצְבָּעוֹ בִּדְבַשׁ. פַּעַם רִאשׁוֹנָה וּשְׁנִיָּה – גּוֹעֵר בָּהּ, שְׁלִישִׁית – מְצָצָהּ. אָמַר לָהּ: אִם כֵּן – פְּסוּלָה אַתְּ לִכְהוּנָּה.

**She said to him: My teacher, I will tell you a parable; to what is this matter comparable?** It is comparable **to a baby whose finger** one forcibly **dipped in honey.** On the **first time and** the **second** time, **he moans at** his mother for doing so, but on the **third** occasion, once he is used to the taste of honey, he willingly **sucks** the finger dipped in honey. She was insinuating to Rabbi Akiva that she engaged in intercourse several times, and although the first couple of times were against her will, the third incident was with her consent. Rabbi Akiva **said to her: If so, you are disqualified** from marrying **into the priesthood.**

רָאָה הַתַּלְמִידִים מִסְתַּכְּלִים זֶה בָּזֶה. אָמַר לָהֶם: לָמָּה הַדָּבָר קָשֶׁה בְּעֵינֵיכֶם? [אָמְרוּ לֵיהּ]: כְּשֵׁם שֶׁכָּל הַתּוֹרָה הֲלָכָה לְמֹשֶׁה מִסִּינַי, כָּךְ פְּחוּתָה מִבַּת שָׁלֹשׁ שָׁנִים – כְּשֵׁרָה לִכְהוּנָּה הֲלָכָה לְמֹשֶׁה מִסִּינַי. וְאַף רַבִּי עֲקִיבָא לֹא אֲמָרָהּ אֶלָּא לְחַדֵּד בָּהּ אֶת הַתַּלְמִידִים.

Rabbi Akiva **saw** his **students looking at each other,** puzzling over this ruling. **He said to them: Why is this matter difficult in your eyes? They said to him: Just as the entire Torah is a *halakha*** transmitted **to Moses from Sinai, so too** this *halakha* of a girl who engaged in intercourse when she was **less than three years old,** i.e., that she is **fit** to marry **into the priesthood,** is a ***halakha*** transmitted **to Moses from Sinai,** and it applies whether she engaged intercourse against her will or with her consent. The Gemara notes: **And even Rabbi Akiva did not say** to the woman that she was unfit to marry into the priesthood because that is the *halakha*; rather, he did so **only to sharpen** the minds[H] of his **students with** his statement, to see how they would respond.

מתני׳ בֶּן תֵּשַׁע שָׁנִים וְיוֹם אֶחָד שֶׁבָּא עַל יְבִמְתּוֹ – קְנָאָהּ, וְאֵין נוֹתֵן גֵּט עַד שֶׁיַּגְדִּיל.

**MISHNA** In the case of a boy, **nine years and one day old,** whose brother had died childless, **who engaged in intercourse with his *yevama*,**[H] his brother's widow, the status of the intercourse is that of halakhic intercourse and **he acquires her** as his wife; **but he cannot give** her **a bill of divorce,** if he chooses to end the marriage, **until he reaches majority.**

וּמְטַמֵּא בְּנִדָּה לְטַמֵּא מִשְׁכָּב תַּחְתּוֹן כָּעֶלְיוֹן.

**And he becomes ritually impure** after engaging in intercourse **with a menstruating woman**[H] **to** the degree that he **renders impure** all the layers of **bedding beneath** him, such that they become impure **like the upper** bedding covering a *zav*. Accordingly, the bedding assumes first-degree ritual impurity status and does not become a primary source of ritual impurity, and it renders impure food and drink and does not render impure people and vessels.

**HALAKHA**

**To sharpen the minds, etc. – לְחַדֵּד בָּהּ וכו׳:** It is proper for a teacher to mislead his students occasionally through speech or action in order to test them and see if they recall their studies (Rambam *Sefer HaMadda, Hilkhot Talmud Torah* 4:6; *Shulḥan Arukh, Yoreh De'a* 246:12).

**A boy nine years and one day old whose brother had died childless, who engaged in intercourse with his *yevama* – בֶּן תֵּשַׁע שָׁנִים וְיוֹם אֶחָד שֶׁבָּא עַל יְבִמְתּוֹ:** With regard to a boy who is nine years and one day old who engages in intercourse with his *yevama*, his act effects acquisition like the levirate betrothal of an adult. Although he acquires the *yevama* as his wife, he cannot divorce her with a bill of divorce until he reaches majority and then engages in intercourse with her. If he does not engage in intercourse with her after reaching majority and he wishes to divorce her, she requires a bill of divorce and *ḥalitza* (Rambam *Sefer Nashim, Hilkhot Yibbum VaḤalitza* 1:16; *Shulḥan Arukh, Even HaEzer* 167:2).

**And he becomes ritually impure after engaging in intercourse with a menstruating woman – וּמְטַמֵּא בְּנִדָּה:** A boy who is a minor and engages in intercourse with a menstruating woman becomes ritually impure to the same degree as an adult man who does so. This is the *halakha* provided that she is at least three years and one day old, and he is at least nine years and one day old (Rambam *Sefer Tahara, Hilkhot Metamei Mishkav UMoshav* 3:3).

וּפוֹסֵל וְאֵינוֹ מַאֲכִיל בִּתְרוּמָה, וּפוֹסֵל אֶת הַבְּהֵמָה מֵעַל גַּבֵּי הַמִּזְבֵּחַ, וְנִסְקֶלֶת עַל יָדוֹ. וְאִם בָּא עַל אַחַת מִכׇּל הָעֲרָיוֹת הָאֲמוּרוֹת בַּתּוֹרָה – מוּמָתִין עַל יָדוֹ, וְהוּא פָּטוּר.

**And** if he is disqualified from the priesthood and the woman with whom he engages in intercourse is the daughter of a priest, **he disqualifies** her from partaking of *teruma*; **but** if he is a priest who marries an Israelite woman, **he does not enable** her **to partake of** ***teruma*****.**[H] **And** if he engages in bestiality, **he disqualifies the animal from** being sacrificed **upon the altar,**[H] **and** the animal **is stoned due to his** act. **And if he engaged in intercourse with one of all those with whom relations are forbidden,** as **stated in the Torah,**[H] e.g., his aunt or his mother, **they are executed** by the court **due to** having engaged in intercourse with **him,** because they are adults; **but he is exempt,** as he is a minor.

גמ׳ וְלִכְשֶׁיַּגְדִּיל, בְּגֵט סַגִּי לָהּ? וְהָתַנְיָא: עָשׂוּ בִּיאַת בֶּן תֵּשַׁע כְּמַאֲמָר בְּגָדוֹל,

**GEMARA** The mishna teaches that a boy aged nine years and one day cannot give his *yevama* a bill of divorce until he reaches majority. The Gemara asks: **And** even **when he reaches majority, is a bill of divorce enough to** enable **her** to marry any man? **But isn't it taught** in a *baraita* that the Sages **rendered the** halakhic status of the act of **intercourse of** a boy **nine** years and one day **old like** that of **levirate betrothal** by means of money or a document performed **by an adult man,**[H] which is an acquisition by rabbinic law? Accordingly, she is not his full-fledged wife.

מַה מַּאֲמָר בְּגָדוֹל צָרִיךְ גֵּט לְמַאֲמָרוֹ וַחֲלִיצָה לְזִיקָתוֹ, אַף בִּיאַת בֶּן תֵּשַׁע – צָרִיךְ גֵּט לְמַאֲמָרוֹ וַחֲלִיצָה לְזִיקָתוֹ!

Therefore, one can assert as follows: **Just as** after **a levirate betrothal** performed **by an adult man,** the *yavam* **must** give the *yevama* **a bill of divorce to** release her from **his levirate betrothal and** perform ***ḥalitza*** **to** release her from **his** levirate **bond, so too** with regard to **the intercourse of** a boy **nine** years and one day **old,** the *halakha* should be that he **must** give her **a bill of divorce for his levirate betrothal and** perform ***ḥalitza*** **to** release her from **his** levirate **bond.**

אֲמַר רַב, הָכִי קָאָמַר,

**Rav said** in response that **this** is what the *tanna* of the mishna **is saying:**

HALAKHA

**And he disqualifies her but he does not enable her to partake of *teruma*** – **וּפוֹסֵל וְאֵינוֹ מַאֲכִיל בִּתְרוּמָה**: If a woman engages in intercourse with a minor boy forbidden to her who has reached the age of nine and one day, she is disqualified from marrying into the priesthood. If she is the daughter of a priest, she is disqualified from partaking of *teruma*. But if an Israelite woman marries a nine-year-old priest, the *halakha* is different: Although her engaging in intercourse with him has the halakhic status of intercourse, his marriage to her does not enable her to partake of *teruma* until he reaches majority (Rambam *Sefer Zera'im, Hilkhot Terumot* 8:11).

**And if he engages in bestiality he disqualifies the animal from being sacrificed upon the altar** – **וּפוֹסֵל אֶת הַבְּהֵמָה מֵעַל גַּבֵּי הַמִּזְבֵּחַ**: A nine-year-old boy who copulates with an animal disqualifies it from being sacrificed as an offering. If he is under the age of nine, he does not disqualify it (Rambam). The Ra'avad disagrees, maintaining that this applies only when the animal is passive in the act of copulation; but if the animal is the active party, the age of the boy makes no difference, as the animal is disqualified in any case (Rambam *Sefer Avoda, Hilkhot Issurei Mizbe'aḥ* 4:3, and see *Kesef Mishne* and *Leḥem Mishne* there).

**And if he engaged in intercourse with one of all those with whom relations are forbidden as stated in the Torah** – **בָּא עַל אַחַת מִכׇּל הָעֲרָיוֹת הָאֲמוּרוֹת בַּתּוֹרָה**: If a minor boy who is at least nine years old engages in intercourse with an adult female relative who is forbidden to him, she is liable to receive the death penalty, excision, or lashes, depending on the circumstances, e.g., what type of forbidden relation she is, whereas he is exempt. If he is under the age of nine, they are both exempt (Rambam *Sefer Kedusha, Hilkhot Issurei Bia* 1:13).

**The Sages rendered the intercourse of a boy nine years and one day old like that of levirate betrothal by an adult man** – **עָשׂוּ בִּיאַת בֶּן תֵּשַׁע כְּמַאֲמָר בְּגָדוֹל**: If a minor *yavam* aged nine years and one day engaged in intercourse with his *yevama*, the intercourse does not fully consummate the levirate marriage. Rather, it is equivalent to an adult's betrothal to his *yevama*, which applies by rabbinic law. The *halakha* is in accordance with the ruling of the *baraita* (Rambam *Sefer Nashim, Hilkhot Yibbum VaḤalitza* 5:18; *Shulḥan Arukh, Even HaEzer* 167:1).

Perek **V**
Daf **45** Amud **b**

לִכְשֶׁיַּגְדִּיל יִבְעוֹל וְיִתֵּן גֵּט.

**When he reaches majority he may engage in intercourse with her,** and thereby acquire her as his full-fledged wife, **and** if he wished to divorce her **he** can then **give her a bill of divorce**[NH] without having to perform *ḥalitza*.

NOTES

**When he reaches majority he may engage in intercourse with her and he can give her a bill of divorce** – **לִכְשֶׁיַּגְדִּיל יִבְעוֹל וְיִתֵּן גֵּט**: When the *yavam* engages in intercourse with his *yevama* as an adult man, their levirate marriage is consummated and she becomes his wife in all halakhic senses. Consequently, if he wishes to divorce her, she does not require *ḥalitza* but only a bill of divorce. This *halakha* is derived from the verse: "Her husband's brother shall go in unto her, and take her to him to wife, and perform the duty of a husband's brother unto her" (Deuteronomy 25:5), i.e., once he has performed that duty she is considered his wife in all regards (Rashi).

HALAKHA

**When he reaches majority he may engage in intercourse with her and he can give her a bill of divorce** – **לִכְשֶׁיַּגְדִּיל יִבְעוֹל וְיִתֵּן גֵּט**: If a boy aged nine years and one day engaged in intercourse with his *yevama*, he cannot divorce her with a bill of divorce until he reaches majority and then engages in intercourse with her. If he does not engage in intercourse with her after reaching majority and he wishes to divorce her, she requires a bill of divorce and *ḥalitza*. The bill of divorce is required by virtue of the fact that he engaged in intercourse with her, creating a situation that is parallel to levirate betrothal; and she also requires *ḥalitza* because his initial act of intercourse did not serve to acquire her as his wife in all regards (Rambam *Sefer Nashim, Hilkhot Yibbum VaḤalitza* 5:21; *Shulḥan Arukh, Even HaEzer* 167:2).

מתני׳ בַּת אַחַת עֶשְׂרֵה שָׁנָה וְיוֹם אֶחָד – נְדָרֶיהָ נִבְדָּקִין, בַּת שְׁתֵּים עֶשְׂרֵה שָׁנָה וְיוֹם אֶחָד – נְדָרֶיהָ קַיָּימִין, וּבוֹדְקִין כָּל שְׁתֵּים עֶשְׂרֵה.

**MISHNA** With regard to a girl who is **eleven years and one day old, her vows**[B] **are examined** to ascertain whether she is aware of the meaning of her vow and in Whose name she vowed. Once she is **twelve years and one day old** and has grown two pubic hairs, which is a sign of adulthood, even without examination **her vows are in effect. And one examines** her vows throughout **the entire twelfth** year until her twelfth birthday.

בֶּן שְׁתֵּים עֶשְׂרֵה שָׁנָה וְיוֹם אֶחָד – נְדָרָיו נִבְדָּקִין, בֶּן שְׁלֹשׁ עֶשְׂרֵה שָׁנָה וְיוֹם אֶחָד – נְדָרָיו קַיָּימִין, וּבוֹדְקִין כָּל שְׁלֹשׁ עֶשְׂרֵה.

With regard to a boy who is **twelve years and one day old,**[H] **his vows are examined**[N] to ascertain whether he is aware of the meaning of his vow and in Whose name he vowed. Once he is **thirteen years and one day old** and has grown two pubic hairs, even without examination **his vows are in effect.**[N] **And one examines** his vows throughout **the entire thirteenth** year until his thirteenth birthday.

קוֹדֶם לַזְּמַן הַזֶּה, אַף עַל פִּי שֶׁאָמְרוּ ״יוֹדְעִין אָנוּ לְשֵׁם מִי נָדַרְנוּ, לְשֵׁם מִי הִקְדַּשְׁנוּ״ – אֵין נִדְרֵיהֶם נֶדֶר, וְאֵין הֶקְדֵּשָׁן הֶקְדֵּשׁ. לְאַחַר הַזְּמַן הַזֶּה, אַף עַל פִּי שֶׁאָמְרוּ ״אֵין אָנוּ יוֹדְעִין לְשֵׁם מִי נָדַרְנוּ, לְשֵׁם מִי הִקְדַּשְׁנוּ״ – נִדְרָן נֶדֶר וְהֶקְדֵּשָׁן הֶקְדֵּשׁ.

**Prior to that time,** eleven years and one day for a girl and twelve years and one day for a boy, **even if they said: We know in Whose name we vowed** and **in Whose name we consecrated, their vow is not** a valid **vow and their consecration is not** a valid **consecration. After that time,** twelve years and one day for a girl and thirteen years and one day for a boy, **even if they said: We do not know in Whose name we vowed** and **in Whose name we consecrated, their vow is** a valid **vow and their consecration is** a valid **consecration.**

גמ׳ וְכֵיוָן דְּתָנָא ״בַּת אַחַת עֶשְׂרֵה שָׁנָה וְיוֹם אֶחָד – נְדָרֶיהָ נִבְדָּקִין״, ״בַּת שְׁתֵּים עֶשְׂרֵה שָׁנָה וְיוֹם אֶחָד – נְדָרֶיהָ קַיָּימִין״ לָמָּה לִי? סָלְקָא דַּעְתָּךְ אָמִינָא: בּוֹדְקִין לְעוֹלָם, קָא מַשְׁמַע לָן.

**GEMARA** The Gemara asks: **But since** the mishna **teaches:** With regard to a girl who is **eleven years and one day old her vows are examined, why do I** need the mishna to further state: Once she is **twelve years and one day old her vows are in effect?** After all, by this stage she is already an adult. The Gemara answers that this ruling is necessary, as it might **enter your mind to say** that **one examines** her vows **forever,** even when she is an adult. Therefore, the mishna **teaches us** that the vows of an adult are valid even without examination.

וְכֵיוָן דְּתָנֵי ״בַּת שְׁתֵּים עֶשְׂרֵה שָׁנָה וְיוֹם אֶחָד – נְדָרֶיהָ קַיָּימִין״, ״בּוֹדְקִין כָּל שְׁתֵּים עֶשְׂרֵה״ לָמָּה לִי? סָלְקָא דַּעְתָּךְ אָמִינָא: הוֹאִיל וְאָמַר מָר שְׁלֹשִׁים יוֹם בַּשָּׁנָה חֲשׁוּבִים שָׁנָה, הֵיכָא דְּבָדַקְנָא שְׁלֹשִׁים וְלֹא יָדְעָה לְהַפְלוֹת – אֵימָא: תּוּ לָא לִיבְדּוֹק, קָא מַשְׁמַע לָן.

The Gemara further asks: **And since** the mishna **teaches:** Once she is **twelve years and one day old her vows are in effect, why do I** need it to further state: **One examines** her vows throughout **the entire twelfth** year? The Gemara answers that this ruling is necessary, as it might **enter your mind to say: Since the Master says** that **thirty days in a year are considered** equivalent to **a year,** in a case **where we examine her** for **thirty** days after she turned eleven **and she did not know** how **to utter** a vow **properly,** i.e., she did not have a clear understanding of the meaning of the vow, one might **say** that **one should examine** her **no further** until she reaches the age of twelve. Therefore, the mishna **teaches us** that she is examined throughout her twelfth year.

וְלִתְנֵי הָנֵי תַּרְתֵּי בָּבֵי: ״בַּת שְׁתֵּים עֶשְׂרֵה שָׁנָה וְיוֹם אֶחָד – נְדָרֶיהָ קַיָּימִין, וּבוֹדְקִין כָּל שְׁתֵּים עֶשְׂרֵה״, ״בַּת אַחַת עֶשְׂרֵה וְיוֹם אֶחָד – נְדָרֶיהָ נִבְדָּקִין״ לָמָּה לִי?

The Gemara asks: **And let** the mishna **teach** only **these two clauses:** Once she is **twelve years and one day old her vows are in effect, and one examines** her vows throughout **the entire twelfth** year. Once both of these have been taught, **why do I** need the ruling: With regard to a girl who is **eleven years and one day old, her vows are examined?**

**HALAKHA**

**A girl eleven years and one day old…a boy twelve years and one day old, etc.** – **בַּת אַחַת עֶשְׂרֵה שָׁנָה וְיוֹם אֶחָד...בֶּן שְׁתֵּים עֶשְׂרֵה שָׁנָה וְיוֹם אֶחָד וכו׳:** The vows of a boy or girl in the year before reaching majority, and who understands the nature of vows, are valid, as are those of one who has reached the age of adulthood who lacks this understanding, even if he or she has not reached maturity through the appearance of two pubic hairs. If a male who is twelve years old or a female who is eleven years old utters a vow, the court examines it. Before the male reaches the age of twelve and the female the age of eleven, their vows are invalid even if they know in Whose name they vowed (Rambam *Sefer Hafla'a, Hilkhot Nedarim* 11:1–3; *Shulḥan Arukh, Yoreh De'a* 233:1).

**BACKGROUND**

**Vows** – **נְדָרִים:** This is referring to a personal vow, i.e., a voluntary obligation to refrain from deriving benefit from a specific item or from deriving benefit from a specific person. This is, in effect, a type of reverse consecration. The person pledges to regard an item or person as consecrated to the Temple. Such a vow can take effect with regard to any item, and one who fails to fulfill his vow violates the mitzva: "He shall not profane his word" (Numbers 30:3). It is also possible to prohibit one's own property to another by means of a vow; the other person must then treat that property as consecrated. Nevertheless, one cannot prohibit another's property to anyone other than himself.

The Sages were very strongly opposed to the taking of vows and encouraged people who had vowed to have them dissolved. If one issues a statement worded in the form of a vow, and it is evident that the intention was not to utter a vow but rather to make a point by means of exaggeration or hyperbole, such a vow is not binding.

**NOTES**

**With regard to a boy who is twelve years and one day old his vows are examined** – **בֶּן שְׁתֵּים עֶשְׂרֵה שָׁנָה וְיוֹם אֶחָד נְדָרָיו נִבְדָּקִין:** The Sages call this period in which vows are examined the age of vows, and the child is called a discriminating minor on the brink of adulthood [*mufla samukh le'ish*], following the verse: "When a man or a woman shall clearly utter [*yafli*] a vow" (Numbers 6:2). The Sages distinguish between two stages of maturity with respect to vows. The first is within a year of reaching majority, e.g., a boy between twelve and thirteen. During that stage, if he is able to utter clearly [*lehafli*] and articulate that his vow is in the name of God, his vows are valid. The second stage is when has reached the age of majority, e.g., a boy from age thirteen but who has yet to produce physical signs of puberty, according to one opinion. At this point, his vows are valid even if he is unable to articulate that his vow is in the name of God. Accordingly, the phrase means one who took a vow [*hifli*] when he was on the brink of adulthood.

The *amora'im* on 46b disagree whether the vows of a discriminating minor on the brink of adulthood take effect by Torah law or by rabbinic law. There are also divergent opinions among early commentaries with regard to the period of a discriminating minor on the brink of adulthood. Some maintain that it applies one year before adulthood, i.e., a year before the age of twelve and the development of pubic hairs for a girl, and a year before the age of thirteen and the development of pubic hairs for a boy (*Tosafot* on 46b; Rashba; Ritva). Other commentaries refer to two different periods: A girl from the age of eleven to the age of twelve; and then from the age of twelve until she develops pubic hairs, and for a boy from the age of twelve to the age of thirteen, and then from the age of thirteen until he develops pubic hairs (Rambam).

**His vows are in effect** – **נְדָרָיו קַיָּימִין:** The only condition mentioned in the mishna for the vows of a boy to be in effect is that he is thirteen years and one day old. But the commentaries explain that it means that he has reached this age and has also developed two pubic hairs, a sign of maturation. The majority of the early commentaries maintain that this is the requirement for all Torah obligations, that he must reach that age and have the physical signs, and vows are no exception (e.g., Rabbi Betzalel Ronsburg). Others contend that once a boy is thirteen years and one day old his vows are valid, even if he does not have two pubic hairs (Rambam *Sefer Hafla'a, Hilkhot Nedarim* 11:3). If so, the *halakha* of vows is unique in that the determination of the age of vows is based solely on one's age, not the physical signs of maturation. Some explain that this is due to a concern that he might have grown two pubic hairs and they have fallen out (Rabbi Akiva Eiger).

אִיצְטְרִיךְ, סָלְקָא דַעְתָּךְ אָמִינָא: סְתָמָא – בִּשְׁתֵּים עֶשְׂרֵה בָּעֲיָא בְּדִיקָה, בְּאַחַת עֶשְׂרֵה – לָא בָּעֲיָא בְּדִיקָה. וְהֵיכָא דַּחֲזֵינַן לַהּ דַּחֲרִיפָא טְפֵי – מִיבְדְּקָה בְּאַחַת עֶשְׂרֵה, קָא מַשְׁמַע לַן.

The Gemara answers that this clause **was necessary,** as it might **enter your mind to say:** In **an ordinary** case, a girl **requires examination** in her **twelfth** year, whereas **in** her **eleventh** year she **does not require examination. But** in a case **where we discern about her that she** has **a very sharp** mind, perhaps **she should be examined** already **in** her **eleventh** year. Therefore, the *tanna* **teaches us** that she is not examined in her eleventh year irrespective of how intelligent she is, as she is too young.

״קוֹדֶם הַזְּמַן הַזֶּה״ וְ״אַחַר הַזְּמַן הַזֶּה״ לָמָּה לִי? סָלְקָא דַעְתָּךְ אָמִינָא: הָנֵי מִילֵּי – הֵיכָא דְּלָא קָאָמְרִי אִינְהוּ, אֲבָל הֵיכָא דְּקָאָמְרִי אִינְהוּ – נִסְמוֹךְ עֲלַיְיהוּ, קָא מַשְׁמַע לַן.

The Gemara asks: **Why do I** need the mishna to teach that **prior to that time** their vows and consecration are always not valid **and after that time** they are always valid? These *halakhot* can be inferred from the previous statements of the mishna. The Gemara answers that these rulings are necessary, as it might **enter your mind to say: These matters** apply only in a case **where they do not say:** We know in Whose name we vowed, when they are younger than the periods mentioned in the mishna, or: We do not know in Whose name we vowed, when they are older. **But** in a case **where they do say** such statements, perhaps **we rely on their** claim. Therefore, the *tanna* **teaches us** that when they are younger than the periods stated in the mishna their vows are never valid, and when they are older, their vows are always valid.

תָּנוּ רַבָּנַן, אֵלּוּ דִּבְרֵי רַבִּי. רַבִּי שִׁמְעוֹן בֶּן אֶלְעָזָר אוֹמֵר: דְּבָרִים הָאֲמוּרִים בְּתִינוֹקֶת – בְּתִינוֹק אֲמוּרִים, דְּבָרִים הָאֲמוּרִים בְּתִינוֹק – בְּתִינוֹקֶת אֲמוּרִים.

§ The mishna indicates that the intellectual development of a girl is faster than that of a boy. In this regard, **the Sages taught** in a *baraita*: **This** opinion, with regard to the periods of vows for girls and boys, is in accordance with **the statement of Rabbi** Yehuda HaNasi. But **Rabbi Shimon ben Elazar says** the opposite, that the **matter stated** here **with regard to a girl is** actually **stated with regard to a boy,** whereas the **matter stated with regard to a boy is** in fact **stated with regard to a girl,** as the intellectual development of males is faster than that of females.

אָמַר רַב חִסְדָּא: מַאי טַעְמָא דְּרַבִּי – דִּכְתִיב ״וַיִּבֶן ה׳ [אֱלֹהִים] אֶת הַצֵּלָע״ – מְלַמֵּד שֶׁנָּתַן הַקָּדוֹשׁ בָּרוּךְ הוּא בִּינָה יְתֵירָה בָּאִשָּׁה יוֹתֵר מִבָּאִישׁ.

**Rav Ḥisda said: What is the reason of Rabbi** Yehuda HaNasi? **As it is written,** with regard to the creation of woman: **"And the rib,** which **the Lord God** had taken from the man, **He made** [*vayyiven*] a woman, and brought her to the man" (Genesis 2:22). This **teaches that the Holy One, Blessed be He, granted a woman a greater understanding** [*bina*] **than** that **of a men.**

וְאִידָּךְ – הַהוּא מִבָּעֵי לֵיהּ לְכִדְרֵישׁ לָקִישׁ, דְּאָמַר רֵישׁ לָקִישׁ מִשּׁוּם רַבִּי שִׁמְעוֹן בֶּן מְנַסְיָא: ״וַיִּבֶן ה׳ [אֱלֹהִים] אֶת הַצֵּלָע אֲשֶׁר לָקַח מִן הָאָדָם לְאִשָּׁה וַיְבִאֶהָ אֶל הָאָדָם״ – מְלַמֵּד שֶׁקִּלְּעָהּ הַקָּדוֹשׁ בָּרוּךְ הוּא לְחַוָּה וֶהֱבִיאָהּ אֵצֶל אָדָם הָרִאשׁוֹן, שֶׁכֵּן בִּכְרַכֵּי הַיָּם קוֹרִין לְקִלְעִיתָא – בְּנָיְיתָא.

The Gemara asks: **And** what does **the other** *tanna*, Rabbi Shimon ben Elazar, derive from this verse? The Gemara answers: **He requires that** verse **for that which Reish Lakish** taught, **as Reish Lakish said in the name of Rabbi Shimon ben Menasya** with regard to the verse: **"And the rib, which the Lord God had taken from the man, He made a woman, and brought her to the man."** This **teaches that the Holy One, Blessed be He, braided** the hair of **Eve, and** then **brought her to Adam the first** man. **As in the cities overseas** [*bikhrakei hayyam*][L] **they call braiding** hair, **building** [*benayita*].

וְרַבִּי שִׁמְעוֹן בֶּן אֶלְעָזָר מַאי טַעְמָא? אָמַר רַב שְׁמוּאֵל בַּר רַב יִצְחָק: מִתּוֹךְ שֶׁהַתִּינוֹק מָצוּי בְּבֵית רַבּוֹ, נִכְנֶסֶת בּוֹ עַרְמוּמִית תְּחִלָּה.

The Gemara asks: **And Rabbi Shimon ben Elazar, what is the reason** that he maintains that the intellectual development of males is faster than that of females? **Rav Shmuel bar Rav Yitzḥak says: Since a boy frequents his teacher's house, cleverness enters his** mind **first.**

**LANGUAGE**

**The cities overseas** [*kerakei hayyam*] – **כְּרַכֵּי הַיָּם**: The term *kerakh* generally refers to a large city, typically one surrounded by a wall. Some claim that it is from the Greek **χάραξ**, *kharax*, which can mean a place fortified by beams. Others maintain that it has a Semitic origin, related to the root *kaf, reish, kaf,* meaning revolution or circumference, which matches the appearance of a walled city.

The term *hayyam* is a shortened version of *medinot hayyam*, meaning overseas countries. It refers to places outside of Eretz Yisrael on the shore of the Mediterranean Sea, and is used in the Gemara as a broad term for any country outside of Eretz Yisrael.

אִיבַּעְיָא לְהוּ: תּוֹךְ זְמַן, כִּלְפְנֵי זְמַן אוֹ כִּלְאַחַר זְמַן?

§ The mishna teaches that there are three periods in the development of girls and boys: When their vows are examined, i.e., the twelfth year for a girl and the thirteenth year for a boy, which will be termed below: During the time; the period beforehand, when their vows are entirely invalid, called: Before the time; and after that period, when their vows are always valid, known as: After the time. But the mishna does not address the issue of their physical development during these periods, with regard to the appearance of two pubic hairs. In this regard, **a dilemma was raised before** the Sages: If a boy or girl developed pubic hairs **during** the **time,** is this year considered **like** the development of signs indicating puberty **before** the **time** that the child reaches majority, and therefore they are not treated as signs indicating puberty, **or** is it considered **as after** the **time?**

לְמַאי הִלְכְתָא? אִי לִנְדָרִים – לָאו כִּלְפְנֵי זְמַן דָּמְיָא, וְלָאו כִּלְאַחַר זְמַן דָּמְיָא.

The Gemara asks: **With regard to what *halakha*** is this dilemma raised? **If** it is **with regard to vows,** the development of pubic hairs **is not considered as before** the **time, but** it **is not considered as after** the **time** either. Instead, the status of the vow is determined in accordance with the examination of the child's understanding, as stated in the mishna.

אֶלָּא, לְעוֹנָשִׁין מַאי? רַב וְרַבִּי חֲנִינָא דְּאָמְרִי תַּרְוַיְיהוּ: תּוֹךְ זְמַן – כִּלְפְנֵי זְמַן, רַבִּי יוֹחָנָן וְרַבִּי יְהוֹשֻׁעַ בֶּן לֵוִי דְּאָמְרִי תַּרְוַיְיהוּ: תּוֹךְ זְמַן – כִּלְאַחַר זְמַן.

**Rather,** the dilemma is raised **with regard to punishments,** i.e., whether such a boy or girl is punished like an adult for violating the prohibitions of the Torah. **What,** then, is the *halakha*? The Sages disagree. **Rav and Rabbi Ḥanina both say:** The development of pubic hairs **during** that **time** is considered **as before** the **time,** and therefore the boy or girl is not liable to receive punishment for his or her actions. **Rabbi Yoḥanan and Rabbi Yehoshua ben Levi both say:** The development of pubic hairs **during** that **time** is considered **as after** the **time,** and they are punished.

אָמַר רַב נַחְמָן בַּר יִצְחָק, וְסִימָנֵיךְ: ״וְזֹאת לְפָנִים בְּיִשְׂרָאֵל״.

**Rav Naḥman bar Yitzḥak says: And your mnemonic,** to remember which Sages said which ruling, is the verse: **"Now this** [***vezot***] **was the custom in former times in Israel"** (Ruth 4:7). The Sage whose name has a feminine form like the word *vezot,* namely, Rav Ḥanina, maintains that the development of pubic hairs during the time is considered as before the time, like the former times mentioned in the verse.

מְתִיב רַב הַמְנוּנָא: אַחַר זְמַן הַזֶּה, אַף עַל פִּי שֶׁאָמְרוּ ״אֵין אָנוּ יוֹדְעִים לְשֵׁם מִי נָדַרְנוּ, לְשֵׁם מִי הִקְדַּשְׁנוּ״ – נִדְרֵיהֶם נֶדֶר וְהֶקְדֵּשָׁן הֶקְדֵּשׁ, הָא תּוֹךְ זְמַן – כִּלְפְנֵי זְמַן!

**Rav Hamnuna raises an objection** to the opinion of Rabbi Yoḥanan and Rabbi Yehoshua ben Levi from the mishna: **After that time,** twelve years and one day for a girl and thirteen years and one day for a boy, **even if they say: We do not know in Whose name we vowed** and **in Whose name we consecrated, their vow is** a valid **vow and their consecration is** a valid **consecration.** Rav Hamnuna infers from this ruling that if they issued this statement **during** the **time,** it is considered **as before** the **time,** even if they had developed two hairs.

אֲמַר לֵיהּ רָבָא: אֵימָא רֵישָׁא, קוֹדֶם הַזְּמַן הַזֶּה, אַף עַל פִּי שֶׁאָמְרוּ ״יוֹדְעִים אָנוּ לְשֵׁם מִי נָדַרְנוּ, לְשֵׁם מִי הִקְדַּשְׁנוּ״ – אֵין נִדְרֵיהֶם נֶדֶר, וְאֵין הֶקְדֵּשָׁן הֶקְדֵּשׁ, הָא תּוֹךְ זְמַן – כִּלְאַחַר זְמַן!

**Rava said to** Rav Hamnuna, in rejection of this proof: **Say the former clause** in the mishna: **Prior to that time,** eleven years and one day for a girl and twelve years and one day for a boy, **even if they said: We know in Whose name we vowed** and **in Whose name we consecrated, their vow is not** a valid **vow and their consecration is not** a valid **consecration.** One can infer the opposite from here, that if they issued this statement **during** the **time,** it is considered **as after** the **time.**

וְלָא הִיא, רָבָא קָטָעֵי. הוּא סָבַר: רַב הַמְנוּנָא מִמִּשְׁנָה יְתֵירָה קָדָייק, וְאַדְּדָייק מִסֵּיפָא – לֵידוּק מֵרֵישָׁא.

The Gemara responds: **And that is not so,** as **Rava erred. He thought** that **Rav Hamnuna inferred from the superfluous** statement of the **mishna,** i.e., that the clause Rav Hamnuna cites is unnecessary for the *halakha* it states, which is why Rav Hamnuna inferred his conclusion from it. **And** therefore Rava responded that **rather than inferring from the latter clause** of the mishna that if the boy or girl claims not to know in Whose name he or she vowed during the time, it is considered as before the time, **let him infer from the former clause** that it is considered as after the time, as Rava demonstrated.

וְלָא הִיא, רַב הַמְנוּנָא מִגּוּפָא דְּמַתְנִיתִין קָא דָּיֵיק, הָא לְאַחַר זְמַן הֵיכִי דָּמֵי? אִי דְּלָא אַיְיתִי שְׁתֵּי שְׂעָרוֹת – קָטָן הוּא, אֶלָּא לָאו – דְּאַיְיתִי שְׁתֵּי שְׂעָרוֹת,

The Gemara continues: **But it is not so;** rather, **Rav Hamnuna inferred** that it is considered as before the time **from the** statement of **the mishna itself,** without assuming that it is superfluous, as follows: In **that** mention in the mishna of: **After** that **time, what are the circumstances? If** it is referring to a case **where** the boy **has not** yet **developed two** pubic **hairs, he is a minor. Rather, is it not** referring to a case **where** the boy **has developed two** pubic **hairs,**

Perek **V**
Daf **46** Amud **a**

**HALAKHA**

A nine-year-old boy who developed two hairs, etc. – בֶּן תֵּשַׁע שָׁנִים שֶׁהֵבִיא שְׁתֵּי שְׂעָרוֹת וכו׳: If a boy grows two hairs before the age of thirteen, these are considered merely the hairs of a mole. If he developed two pubic hairs when he is at least thirteen years and one day old, he is classified as an adult (Rambam *Sefer Nashim*, *Hilkhot Ishut* 2:10).

**BACKGROUND**

Sign indicating puberty – סִימָן: The physical sign marking the transition from childhood to adulthood, according to *halakha*, is the appearance of at least two hairs in the pubic area. There is no precise time for the appearance of this sign, and several variables affect its earlier or later appearance, such as genetics, nutrition, and climate. Nevertheless, there are average ages for the growth of this hair in boys and girls. The appearance of such hair extremely early is not usually a sign of adulthood, except in rare cases of disease, and it should instead be treated as being only a mole.

וְטַעְמָא דִּלְאַחַר זְמַן הוּא דְּגָמְרָא לֵהּ לְמִילְּתֵיהּ, הָא תּוֹךְ זְמַן – כְּלִפְנֵי זְמַן.

**and the reason** that the development of two hairs renders him an adult is **that** the onset of **his matter,** i.e., his reaching puberty, **was completed for him after the time?** Rav Hamnuna infers from here that if the child developed two hairs **during** the **time,** it is considered **as before** the **time,** and he or she is not classified as an adult.

וְעוֹד, מְתִיב רַבִּי זֵירָא: ״אִישׁ כִּי יַפְלִא לִנְדֹּר נֶדֶר״ מַה תַּלְמוּד לוֹמַר ״אִישׁ״ – לְרַבּוֹת בֶּן שְׁלֹשׁ עֶשְׂרֵה שָׁנָה וְיוֹם אֶחָד, שֶׁאַף עַל פִּי שֶׁאֵינוֹ יוֹדֵעַ לְהַפְלִיא – נְדָרָיו קַיָּימִין.

**And furthermore, Rabbi Zeira raises an objection** to the opinion that the development of signs indicating puberty during the time is equivalent to their development after the time. It is taught in a *baraita* which deals with the verse: "Speak to the children of Israel and say to them: **When** either **man** or a woman **shall clearly utter a vow"** (Numbers 6:2). **What** is the meaning when **the verse states "man,"** after it has already stated "the children of Israel"? This serves **to include** anyone who is **thirteen years and one day old, that even if he does not know** how **to utter clearly** and articulate the meaning of his statements, **his vows are in effect.**

הֵיכִי דָּמֵי? אִי דְּלָא אַיְיתִי שְׁתֵּי שְׂעָרוֹת – קָטָן הוּא. אֶלָּא לָאו דְּאַיְיתִי שְׁתֵּי שְׂעָרוֹת, וְטַעְמָא – דְּבֶן שְׁלֹשׁ עֶשְׂרֵה וְיוֹם אֶחָד הוּא דַּהֲוָה לֵיהּ ״אִישׁ״, הָא תּוֹךְ זְמַן – כְּלִפְנֵי זְמַן! תְּיוּבְתָּא.

Rabbi Zeira analyzes this *baraita*. **What are the circumstances? If** it is referring to a case **where** the boy **has not** yet **developed two** pubic **hairs,** then **he is a minor,** and the *halakha* with regard to him cannot be derived from the word "man." **Rather, is it not** referring to a case **where** the boy **has developed two** pubic **hairs? And** by inference, **the reason that he is** considered **a man** due to his development of pubic hairs **is that he is thirteen years and one day old, but** if the boy developed two hairs **during** the **time,** it is considered **as before** the **time.** The Gemara concludes: This is indeed **a conclusive refutation** of the opinion of Rabbi Yoḥanan and Rabbi Yehoshua ben Levi that developing pubic hairs during the time is equivalent to developing hairs after the time.

אָמַר רַב נַחְמָן: כְּתַנָּאֵי, בֶּן תֵּשַׁע שָׁנִים שֶׁהֵבִיא שְׁתֵּי שְׂעָרוֹת – שׁוּמָא, מִבֶּן תֵּשַׁע וְעַד שְׁתֵּים עֶשְׂרֵה שָׁנָה וְיוֹם אֶחָד – שׁוּמָא. רַבִּי יוֹסֵי בְּרַבִּי יְהוּדָה אוֹמֵר: סִימָן. בֶּן שְׁלֹשׁ עֶשְׂרֵה שָׁנָה וְיוֹם אֶחָד – דִּבְרֵי הַכֹּל סִימָן.

**Rav Naḥman said** that the *baraita* is not a refutation of the opinion of Rabbi Yoḥanan and Rabbi Yehoshua ben Levi, as this matter is **subject to** a dispute between ***tanna'im***, since there is another *baraita* which teaches the following: Everyone agrees with regard to **a nine-year-old** boy **who developed two hairs**[H] that this is not considered a sign of puberty, as they are treated as hairs that grow on **a mole. From nine** years of age **until** the age of **twelve years and one day,** even if the hairs have not fallen out, this is still considered **a mole. Rabbi Yosei, son of Rabbi Yehuda, says:** At this stage it is **a sign** indicating puberty.[B] If he is **thirteen years and one day old** and has grown two hairs, **all agree** that it is **a sign** indicating puberty.

הָא גּוּפָא קַשְׁיָא, אָמְרַתְּ מִבֶּן תֵּשַׁע וְעַד שְׁתֵּים עֶשְׂרֵה שָׁנָה וְיוֹם אֶחָד – שׁוּמָא, הָא שְׁלֹשׁ עֶשְׂרֵה שָׁנָה גּוּפָא – סִימָן. וַהֲדַר תָּנֵי בֶּן שְׁלֹשׁ עֶשְׂרֵה שָׁנָה וְיוֹם אֶחָד – סִימָן, הָא שְׁלֹשׁ עֶשְׂרֵה שָׁנָה גּוּפָא – שׁוּמָא!

Rav Naḥman analyzes the *baraita*. **This** *baraita* **itself** is **difficult,** as **you** initially **said** that **from nine** years **of age until** the age of **twelve years and one day** it is **a mole,** from which it can be inferred that if he developed two pubic hairs in **the thirteenth year itself,** it is **a sign** indicating puberty. **And then** the *baraita* **teaches** that if he is **thirteen years and one day old** and has grown two hairs, this is **a sign** indicating puberty, which indicates that if he developed the hairs in **the thirteenth year itself,** it is **a mole.**

מַאי לָאו – תַּנָּאֵי הִיא, דְּמָר סָבַר: תּוֹךְ זְמַן – כִּלְאַחַר זְמַן, וּמָר סָבַר: תּוֹךְ זְמַן – כִּלְפְנֵי זְמַן!

Rav Naḥman concludes: **What, is it not** correct to say that there **is a** dispute between ***tanna'im*, as one Sage,** the *tanna* who states the first line of the *baraita*, **holds** that **during** that **time** is considered **as after** the **time, and one Sage,** the *tanna* of the last line of the *baraita*, **holds** that **during** that **time** is considered **as before** the **time?** If so, the opinion of Rabbi Yoḥanan and Rabbi Yehoshua ben Levi is one side of a dispute between *tanna'im*.

לָא, דְּכוּלֵּי עָלְמָא תּוֹךְ זְמַן כִּלְפְנֵי זְמַן, וְאִידִי וְאִידִי בְּתִינוֹקֶת. וְרֵישָׁא – רַבִּי, וְסֵיפָא – רַבִּי שִׁמְעוֹן בֶּן אֶלְעָזָר.

The Gemara rejects this suggestion: **No, everyone,** i.e., the *tanna'im* of both clauses of the *baraita*, agrees that **during** that **time** is considered **as before** the **time, and this** clause **and that** clause of the *baraita* are both referring **to a young girl. And** the difference between them is that **the first clause** of the *baraita* is in accordance with the opinion of **Rabbi** Yehuda HaNasi, who maintains that the thirteenth year for a female is considered after the time, and therefore the development of two pubic hairs at this stage is a sign of maturation; **and the last clause** is in accordance with the opinion of **Rabbi Shimon ben Elazar,** who holds that the thirteenth year for a female is considered before the time.

וְאִיבָּעֵית אֵימָא: הָא וְהָא בְּתִינוֹק, וְרֵישָׁא – רַבִּי שִׁמְעוֹן בֶּן אֶלְעָזָר, וְסֵיפָא – רַבִּי.

**And if you wish, say** that **this** clause **and that** clause are both dealing **with a young boy, and the first clause** is in accordance with **Rabbi Shimon ben Elazar and the last clause** is in accordance with the opinion of **Rabbi** Yehuda HaNasi, who maintains that the thirteenth year for a boy is considered before the time.

וְאִיבָּעֵית אֵימָא: הָא וְהָא רַבִּי, הָא – בְּתִינוֹק, הָא – בְּתִינוֹקֶת. וְאִיבָּעֵית אֵימָא: הָא וְהָא רַבִּי שִׁמְעוֹן בֶּן אֶלְעָזָר, הָא – בְּתִינוֹק, הָא – בְּתִינוֹקֶת.

**And if you wish, say** that both **this** clause **and that** clause are in accordance with the opinion of **Rabbi** Yehuda HaNasi, and the difference between them is that **this** last clause of the *baraita* is referring **to a young boy,** whereas **that** first clause is referring **to a young girl. And if you wish, say** that both **this** clause **and that** clause are in accordance with the opinion of **Rabbi Shimon ben Elazar,** and **that** first clause of the *baraita* is referring **to a young boy,** whereas **this** last clause is referring **to a young girl.**

רַבִּי יוֹסֵי בְּרַבִּי יְהוּדָה אוֹמֵר: סִימָן. אָמַר רַבִּי כְּרוּסְפְּדַאי בְּרֵיהּ דְּרַבִּי שַׁבְּתַאי: וְהוּא שֶׁעוֹדָן בּוֹ.

The *baraita* further teaches that **Rabbi Yosei, son of Rabbi Yehuda, says** with regard to hairs from nine years of age until the age of twelve years and one day, that it is **a sign** indicating puberty. In explanation of this opinion, **Rabbi Keruspedai, son of Rabbi Shabbtai, says: And this is** the *halakha* only **when** the hairs **are still upon him,** i.e., they had not fallen out when he reached the age of puberty, as otherwise they are considered a mole.

תַּנְיָא נַמִי הָכִי, בֶּן תֵּשַׁע שָׁנִים וְיוֹם אֶחָד שֶׁהֵבִיא שְׁתֵּי שְׂעָרוֹת – שׁוּמָא, מִבֶּן תֵּשַׁע וְעַד שְׁתֵּים עֶשְׂרֵה שָׁנָה וְיוֹם אֶחָד וְעוֹדָן בּוֹ – שׁוּמָא. רַבִּי יוֹסֵי בְּרַבִּי יְהוּדָה אוֹמֵר: סִימָן.

The Gemara notes that **this** opinion **is also taught** in a *baraita*: With regard to a boy **nine years and one day old who developed two hairs,** this is considered **a mole.** If the boy is **from nine** years **of age until** the age of **twelve years and one day, and** the hairs **are still upon him,**[H] it is still considered **a mole. Rabbi Yosei, son of Rabbi Yehuda, says:** It is **a sign** indicating puberty.

אָמַר רָבָא: הִילְכְתָא תּוֹךְ זְמַן – כִּלְפְנֵי זְמַן. רַב שְׁמוּאֵל בַּר זוּטְרָא מַתְנֵי לַהּ לִשְׁמַעְתָּא דְּרָבָא בְּהַאי לִישָּׁנָא, אָמַר רָבָא: קְטַנָּה, כׇּל שְׁתֵּים עֶשְׂרֵה שָׁנָה – מְמָאֶנֶת וְהוֹלֶכֶת, מִכָּאן וְאֵילָךְ – אֵינָהּ מְמָאֶנֶת וְאֵינָהּ חוֹלֶצֶת.

§ In summary of the rulings cited above, **Rava said: The *halakha*** is that the development of two hairs **during** the **time** is considered **as before** the **time,** and it does not render one an adult. **Rav Shmuel bar Zutra teaches this *halakha* of Rava in this formulation: Rava says:** With regard to **a minor girl** whose father has passed away and whose mother or brothers accepted betrothal on her behalf, a form of betrothal instituted by the Sages, throughout her **entire twelfth year she** has the **continuous** right to **perform refusal**[H] **with regard to** this marriage and thereby annul it. **From that** point **forward,** when she is already an adult, **she may no** longer **perform refusal, and she may not perform *ḥalitza*** with the brother of her husband, if he died without children.

**HALAKHA**

**From nine years of age until twelve years and one day and the hairs are still upon him** – מִבֶּן תֵּשַׁע וְעַד שְׁתֵּים עֶשְׂרֵה שָׁנָה וְיוֹם אֶחָד וְעוֹדָן בּוֹ: If a boy grows two hairs at the age of twelve, they are considered merely the hairs of a mole even if they remain after the individual has reached the age of maturity, as stated in the *baraita* (Rambam *Sefer Nashim*, *Hilkhot Ishut* 2:18).

**Throughout her entire twelfth year she has the continuous right to perform refusal** – כׇּל שְׁתֵּים עֶשְׂרֵה שָׁנָה מְמָאֶנֶת וְהוֹלֶכֶת: A minor has the right to perform refusal until she develops two pubic hairs after she reaches the age of twelve, or until she gives birth. The *halakha* is in accordance with the opinion of Rava (see Rambam *Sefer Nashim*, *Hilkhot Geirushin* 11:4; *Shulḥan Arukh*, *Even HaEzer* 155:12).

הָא גּוּפָא קַשְׁיָא, אָמְרַתְּ אֵינָהּ מְמָאֶנֶת – אַלְמָא גְּדוֹלָה הִיא, אִי גְּדוֹלָה הִיא – תַּחֲלוֹץ!

The Gemara asks: **This** statement of Rava **itself is difficult: You** first **said** that once she is twelve **she may not perform refusal. Evidently, she is an adult woman.** But **if she is an adult woman, let her perform *ḥalitza*,** like any other adult woman.

וְכִי תֵּימָא – מִסַּפְּקָא לֵיהּ, וּמִי מִסַּפְּקָא לֵיהּ? וְהָאָמַר רָבָא: קְטַנָּה שֶׁהִגִּיעָה לִכְלַל שְׁנוֹתֶיהָ – אֵינָהּ צְרִיכָה בְּדִיקָה, חֲזָקָה הֵבִיאָה סִימָנִין!

**And if you would say** that Rava **is uncertain** whether a twelve-year-old girl is presumed to have developed two hairs and is therefore an adult, or whether it is presumed that she has not yet grown two hairs and remains a minor, and consequently he is stringent on both counts, that she may not perform refusal, like an adult, but she may also not perform *ḥalitza*, like a minor, this suggestion is problematic, as **is** Rava actually **uncertain** in this regard? **But doesn't Rava say: A minor girl who reached her full age** of maturity,[H] i.e., twelve years and one day, **does not require examination** to determine whether she has grown two hairs, as there is **a presumption** that **she has developed signs** indicating puberty.

הָנֵי מִילֵּי בִּסְתָמָא, אֲבָל הָכָא דְּבָדְקוּ וְלָא אַשְׁכְּחוּ – לָא.

The Gemara answers that **this statement,** that it is presumed that a twelve-year-old girl has developed two hairs, applies only **in an ordinary** situation. **But here** Rava is referring to a case **where they examined** her **and did not find** hairs.[H] In such an instance, Rava did **not** say that the presumption is in effect.

אִי הָכִי, תְּמָאֵן! חוֹשְׁשִׁין שֶׁמָּא נָשְׁרוּ.

The Gemara asks: **If so,** that she was actually examined, she should be considered a minor in all regards and **she should** be able to **perform refusal.** The Gemara answers: **We are concerned** that **perhaps** the girl had already developed pubic hairs but **they fell out.** Consequently, although the girl is not treated with the presumption that she is an adult, she does not have the certain status of a minor either, and cannot perform refusal.

הָנִיחָא לְמַאן דְּאָמַר חוֹשְׁשִׁין, אֶלָּא לְמַאן דְּאָמַר אֵין חוֹשְׁשִׁין, מַאי אִיכָּא לְמֵימַר? דְּאִיתְּמַר, רַב פַּפָּא אָמַר: אֵין חוֹשְׁשִׁין שֶׁמָּא נָשְׁרוּ, רַב פַּפִּי אָמַר: חוֹשְׁשִׁין. הָנֵי מִילֵּי – לְעִנְיַן חֲלִיצָה, אֲבָל לְעִנְיַן מֵיאוּן – חוֹשְׁשִׁין.

The Gemara objects: **This works out well according to the one who says** that **we are concerned** that the pubic hairs fell out. **But according to the one who says** that **we are not concerned** that they have fallen out, **what is there to say? As it was stated** that *amora'im* disagreed with regard to this matter. **Rav Pappa says: We are not concerned** that **perhaps** the pubic hairs **fell out; Rav Pappi says: We are concerned** that they might have fallen out. The Gemara answers that **this statement** of Rav Pappa, that there is no concern that perhaps the pubic hairs fell out, applies only **with regard to *ḥalitza*, but with regard to refusal** everyone agrees that **we are concerned** that they might have fallen out.

מִכְּלָל דְּמַאן דְּאָמַר חוֹשְׁשִׁין – חוֹלֶצֶת? וְהָא "חוֹשְׁשִׁין" בְּעָלְמָא קָאָמַר?

The Gemara asks: **By inference, does the one who says** that **we are concerned** that perhaps the hairs fell out maintain that this twelve-year-old **performs *ḥalitza*? But** this cannot be correct, as **he says** that **we are merely concerned** that the hairs might have fallen out, not that this is certainly the case. How, then, can she perform *ḥalitza* like an adult?

אֶלָּא, לְעוֹלָם – דְּלָא בְּדָקָהּ, וּלְעִנְיַן חֲלִיצָה – חָיְישִׁינַן, וְכִי קָאָמַר רָבָא חֲזָקָה – לְמֵיאוּן, אֲבָל לַחֲלִיצָה – בָּעֲיָא בְּדִיקָה.

**Rather,** Rava is **actually** referring to a case **where one did not examine** the girl, **and with regard to *ḥalitza* we are concerned** that she might not have developed hairs and is still a minor. **And when Rava said** that there is **a presumption** that a twelve-year-old has developed signs indicating puberty, he was referring **to refusal, but with regard to *ḥalitza* she requires examination.**

**HALAKHA**

A minor girl who reached her full age of maturity, etc. – קְטַנָּה שֶׁהִגִּיעָה לִכְלַל שְׁנוֹתֶיהָ וכו׳: A girl aged twelve years and one day who has not been examined to see if she has grown two pubic hairs may not perform refusal, as there is a presumption that she has developed two hairs and is an adult. Nevertheless, she may not perform *ḥalitza* until she has been examined and found to have two hairs (Rambam *Sefer Nashim*, *Hilkhot Geirushin* 11:4 and *Hilkhot Yibbum VaḤalitza* 1:17; *Shulḥan Arukh*, *Even HaEzer* 155:19).

Where they examined her and did not find hairs – דְּבָדְקוּ וְלָא אַשְׁכְּחוּ: If a twelve-year-old girl was examined and hairs were not found, she is considered a minor and she may therefore perform refusal. If she remains this way, she continues to be a minor until the age of twenty, when she is retroactively established to be an *ailonit*, a sexually underdeveloped woman (Rambam *Sefer Nashim*, *Hilkhot Ishut* 2:3–4; *Shulḥan Arukh*, *Even HaEzer* 155:12).

אָמַר רַב דִּימִי מִנְּהַרְדְּעָא: הִלְכְתָא, חוֹשְׁשִׁין שֶׁמָּא נָשְׁרוּ.

With regard to the issue of whether there is concern that hairs might have fallen out, **Rav Dimi of Neharde'a said: The *halakha*** is that if a girl reached the age of twelve and she was examined and the signs of puberty were not found, **we are concerned** that **perhaps** the pubic hairs **fell out.**[H] Consequently, if her mother or brothers had accepted betrothal for her when she was a minor, she cannot perform refusal at that stage.

וְהָנֵי מִילֵּי – הֵיכָא דְּקִדְּשָׁהּ בְּתוֹךְ זְמַן וּבָעַל לְאַחַר זְמַן, דְּאִיכָּא סְפֵיקָא דְּאוֹרָיְיתָא, אֲבָל מֵעִיקָּרָא – לָא.

The Gemara adds: **And this statement** applies only in a case **where** her husband **betrothed her during** the **time,** before she reached the age of twelve years and one day, **and engaged in intercourse** with her **after** the **time,** when she was already twelve years and one day old. This is a situation **where there is an uncertainty** with regard to **Torah law,** since if she had developed two hairs and is an adult, the marriage applies by Torah law, due to the intercourse. **But** if he engaged in intercourse with her only **at the outset,** before she turned twelve, there is **no** concern that perhaps she developed pubic hairs and they fell out, as this marriage applies by rabbinic law.

אָמַר רַב הוּנָא: הִקְדִּישׁ וְאָכַל – לוֹקֶה,

§ With regard to a minor who vowed, **Rav Huna says:** If the minor is aware of the meaning of his vow and in Whose name he or she vowed, and the minor's age is during the time, i.e., the twelfth year for a girl or the thirteenth year for a boy, and he **consecrated** an item of food **and** subsequently **ate** it, **he is flogged,**[N] which is the punishment for one who eats consecrated food.

שֶׁנֶּאֱמַר "אִישׁ כִּי יַפְלִא לִנְדֹּר" וְ"לֹא יַחֵל דְּבָרוֹ", כׇּל שֶׁיֶּשְׁנוֹ בְּהַפְלָאָה – יֶשְׁנוֹ בְּבַל יַחֵל, וְכׇל שֶׁאֵינוֹ בְּהַפְלָאָה – אֵינוֹ בְּבַל יַחֵל.

Rav Huna explains: **As it is stated: "When** either **a man** or a woman **shall clearly utter a vow"** (Numbers 6:2), from which it is derived that if one on the brink of adulthood is able to articulate that his vow is in the name of God, his vows are valid. **And** another verse states: **"He shall not profane his word"** (Numbers 30:3). This indicates that **any** person **who is** included **in explicitness** of intent **is** also included **in** the prohibition: **"He shall not profane** his word," **and anyone who is not** included **in explicitness** of intent **is not** included **in** the prohibition: **"He shall not profane** his word."

מְתִיב רַב הוּנָא בַּר יְהוּדָה (לְרָבָא) לְסַיּוּעֵי לְרַב הוּנָא:

**Rav Huna bar Yehuda raises an objection** to Rava, **in support** of the opinion **of Rav Huna:**

Perek **V**
Daf **46** Amud **b**

לְפִי שֶׁמָּצִינוּ שֶׁהִשְׁוָה הַכָּתוּב הַקָּטָן כְּגָדוֹל לְזָדוֹן שְׁבוּעָה, וְלָאִיסָּר, וּלְבַל יַחֵל, יָכוֹל יְהֵא חַיָּיב עַל הֶקְדֵּשׁוֹ קׇרְבָּן?

**Since we find that the verse equates a minor,** i.e., one on the brink of adulthood, **to an adult with regard to an intentional** violation of **an oath and with regard to** a vow of **prohibition,** where one renders an item prohibited to himself through a vow, **and with regard to** the prohibition of **he shall not profane** his word, one **might** have thought that this minor, like an adult, **should** also **be liable** to bring **an offering for** misuse of **his consecrated** property, e.g., if he ate an item that he consecrated.

תַּלְמוּד לוֹמַר "זֶה הַדָּבָר".

Therefore, **the verse states** with regard to vows: **"This is the matter** which the Lord has commanded. When a man vows a vow to the Lord, or takes an oath" (Numbers 30:2–3). The emphasis of "this" indicates that it is only with regard to this matter, i.e., prohibitions resulting from vows, that a discriminating minor on the brink of adulthood is considered an adult, but he is not rendered liable to bring an offering for his misuse.

HALAKHA

**We are concerned that perhaps the pubic hairs fell out – חוֹשְׁשִׁין שֶׁמָּא נָשְׁרוּ:** If a young girl was betrothed by her mother or brothers following the death of her father, and her husband engaged in intercourse with her after she reached the age of twelve years and one day, she may no longer perform refusal. This is the *halakha* even if no pubic hairs are found on her, as there a concern that they might have fallen off. The reason for this stringent ruling is that this is an uncertainty involving a matter of Torah law, since if he knew that she had two hairs before engaging in intercourse with her, he would have done so with the intent of effecting betrothal by Torah law. This would mean that theirs is a full-fledged betrothal, and if another man had betrothed her afterward she would not even require a bill of divorce from him. Since it is an uncertainty involving a matter of Torah law, one must be concerned that she might have had two hairs before the intercourse, and therefore she requires a bill of divorce for her to be permitted to another. If she performed refusal after they engaged in intercourse, and she was examined and was not found to have hairs, and subsequently accepted betrothal from another, she requires a bill of divorce from the first man due to uncertainty and is prohibited to return to him. If she married another man, she must leave both men, and any child born from either man is one whose status as a *mamzer* is uncertain (Rambam *Sefer Nashim*, *Hilkhot Geirushin* 11:5; *Shulḥan Arukh*, *Even HaEzer* 155:20).

NOTES

**If he consecrated an item of food and subsequently ate it he is flogged – הִקְדִּישׁ וְאָכַל לוֹקֶה:** Although boys younger than thirteen and girls younger than twelve are not liable to punishment in all other areas of Torah law, because they are still minors, nevertheless in the unique case of vows they are considered as adults and are flogged for their violation (Rashi).

HALAKHA

**If a minor consecrated a food item and others ate it they are flogged – הִקְדִּישׁ הוּא וְאָכְלוּ אֲחֵרִים לוֹקִין:** If a minor boy aged thirteen, who does not have pubic hairs, consecrated an item and an adult derived benefit from that item, e.g., he ate it, he is liable to receive lashes, as the vows of the boy are valid by Torah law. The *halakha* is in accordance with the opinion of Rabbi Yoḥanan and Reish Lakish (Rambam *Sefer Hafla'a*, *Hilkhot Nedarim* 11:5).

**A discriminating minor on the brink of adulthood is an adult by Torah law – מוּפְלָא סָמוּךְ לְאִישׁ דְּאוֹרָיְיתָא:** The consecrations and vows of a discriminating minor on the brink of adulthood are valid by Torah law. But he is not liable to receive lashes for violating his vow until he reaches majority and develops two hairs. This *halakha* is in accordance with the opinion of Rabbi Yoḥanan and Reish Lakish (Rambam *Sefer Hafla'a*, *Hilkhot Nedarim* 11:4).

קָתָנֵי מִיהַת לְאִיסָּר וּלְבַל יַחֵל – חַיָּיב. אֵימָא: לְאִיסּוּר בַּל יַחֵל.

The Gemara analyzes the *baraita*. **In any event,** the *baraita* **teaches** that a discriminating minor on the brink of adulthood is considered an adult **with regard to** a vow of **prohibition and with regard to** the prohibition of **he shall not profane** his word, which indicates that he is **liable** for violating this prohibition. This supports the opinion of Rav Huna that a minor is flogged for eating food he consecrated. The Gemara refutes this proof: There is room to **say** that the word: And, in the phrase: With regard to a vow of prohibition and with regard to the prohibition of he shall not profane his word, should be omitted, and the *baraita* is comparing a minor to an adult **with regard to the prohibition** of **he shall not profane** his word, but it does not indicate that he is liable to receive lashes for violating this prohibition.

אִיסּוּר בַּל יַחֵל, מַה נַּפְשָׁךְ, אִי מוּפְלָא סָמוּךְ לְאִישׁ דְּאוֹרָיְיתָא – מִילְקָא נָמֵי לִילְקֵי, וְאִי מוּפְלָא סָמוּךְ לְאִישׁ לָאו דְּאוֹרָיְיתָא – אִיסּוּר נָמֵי לֵיכָּא! לְאוֹתָן הַמּוּזְהָרִים עָלָיו.

The Gemara asks: Can the *baraita* actually mean that a minor is compared to an adult with regard to **the prohibition** of **he shall not profane** his word, but he is not flogged? **Whichever way you** look at it, this is problematic: **If a discriminating** minor **on the brink of adulthood** is considered an adult **by Torah law, he should be flogged too,** for his violation. **And if a discriminating** minor **on the brink of adulthood** is **not** considered an adult **by Torah law, there is no prohibition** violated here **either.** The Gemara answers that according to the *baraita* the prohibition does not apply to the minor himself, but **to those who are warned to** keep **him** away from the prohibited item.

שְׁמַע מִינַּהּ: קָטָן אוֹכֵל נְבֵלוֹת – בֵּית דִּין מְצוּוִּין עָלָיו לְהַפְרִישׁוֹ! הָכָא בְּמַאי עָסְקִינַן – כְּגוֹן שֶׁהִקְדִּישׁ הוּא וְאָכְלוּ אֲחֵרִים.

The Gemara raises a difficulty: If so, one can **conclude from** the *baraita* that if **a minor eats** meat from unslaughtered **animal carcasses**[N] or violates other prohibitions, **the court is commanded to prevent him** from doing so. This is problematic, as elsewhere it is stated that this matter is subject to dispute (see *Yevamot* 114a). The Gemara explains: **Here we are dealing with** a case **where** the minor **consecrated** the food item **and others ate** it. They are liable to receive lashes for their consumption, but if he ate it he is not liable.

הָנִיחָא לְמַאן דַּאֲמַר הִקְדִּישׁ הוּא וְאָכְלוּ אֲחֵרִים – לוֹקִין, אֶלָּא לְמַאן דַּאֲמַר אֵין לוֹקִין, מַאי אִיכָּא לְמֵימַר? דְּאִיתְּמַר, הִקְדִּישׁ הוּא וְאָכְלוּ אֲחֵרִים, רַב כָּהֲנָא אָמַר: אֵין לוֹקִין, רַבִּי יוֹחָנָן וְרֵישׁ לָקִישׁ דְּאָמְרִי תַּרְוַיְיהוּ: לוֹקִין!

The Gemara raises another difficulty: **This works out well according to the one who said** that if a minor **consecrated** a food item **and others ate** it, **they are flogged.**[H] **But according to the one who said** that in such a case **they are not flogged, what can be said? As it was stated** that *amora'im* disagreed with regard to this issue: If a minor **consecrated** a food item **and others ate** it, **Rav Kahana says** that **they are not flogged; Rabbi Yoḥanan and Reish Lakish both say** that **they are flogged.**

מִדְּרַבָּנַן, וּקְרָא אַסְמַכְתָּא בְּעָלְמָא.

The Gemara therefore reverts to the interpretation that the *baraita* is referring to the prohibition of he shall not profane his word, not the punishment for violation of the vow. And the reason lashes are not administered is that the prohibition is **by rabbinic law. And** as for the **verse** mentioned in the *baraita*, when it states that the verse equates a minor to an adult, which indicates that it is dealing with Torah law, this verse is **a mere support** for a rabbinic law.

גּוּפָא, הִקְדִּישׁ וְאָכְלוּ אֲחֵרִים. רַב כָּהֲנָא אָמַר: אֵין לוֹקִין, רַבִּי יוֹחָנָן וְרֵישׁ לָקִישׁ דְּאָמְרִי תַּרְוַיְיהוּ: לוֹקִין. בְּמַאי קָמִיפַּלְגִי? מָר סָבַר: מוּפְלָא סָמוּךְ לְאִישׁ – דְּאוֹרָיְיתָא, וּמָר סָבַר: מוּפְלָא סָמוּךְ לְאִישׁ – מִדְּרַבָּנַן.

§ The Gemara discusses **the** matter **itself,** i.e., the dispute cited above. If a minor **consecrated** a food item **and others ate** it, **Rav Kahana says** that **they are not flogged; Rabbi Yoḥanan and Reish Lakish both say** that **they are flogged. With regard to what** principle **do** these Sages **disagree?** One **Sage,** i.e., Rabbi Yoḥanan and Reish Lakish, **holds** that **a discriminating** minor **on the brink of adulthood** is considered an adult **by Torah law,**[H] which is why others are liable for eating an item he consecrated; **and** one **Sage,** Rav Kahana, **holds** that **a discriminating** minor **on the brink of adulthood** is considered an adult **by rabbinic law.**

NOTES

**If a minor eats meat from unslaughtered animal carcasses, etc. – קָטָן אוֹכֵל נְבֵלוֹת וכו׳:** Rashi notes that this matter is subject to a dispute on *Yevamot* 114a. Other early commentaries are puzzled by this observation, as everyone agrees that the court is not commanded to prevent a minor from sinning with regard to matters which apply by rabbinic law, and as the status of a discriminating minor on the brink of adulthood applies by rabbinic law, his consumption of the food he consecrated would be a violation by rabbinic law. They explain that Rashi simply means that this general issue of preventing a minor from eating meat of unslaughtered animals is discussed in tractate *Yevamot*, not that this is the *halakha* with regard to a discriminating minor on the brink of adulthood (Rashba).

מְתִיב רַב יִרְמְיָה: יְתוֹמָה שֶׁנָּדְרָה – בַּעְלָהּ מֵפֵר לָהּ. אִי אָמְרַתְּ בִּשְׁלָמָא מוּפְלָא סָמוּךְ לְאִישׁ דְּרַבָּנַן, אָתוּ נִשּׂוּאִין דְּרַבָּנַן – וּמְבַטְּלִי נִדְרָא דְּרַבָּנַן. אֶלָּא אִי אָמְרַתְּ דְּאוֹרַיְיתָא – אָתוּ נִשּׂוּאִין דְּרַבָּנַן וּמְבַטְּלִי נִדְרָא דְּאוֹרַיְיתָא?!

**Rav Yirmeya raises an objection** from a *baraita*: In the case of a minor girl who is **an orphan** from her father and her mother or brothers accepted betrothal on her behalf, **who vowed, her husband may nullify her** vow,[B] like any other husband, despite the fact that this marriage is valid merely by rabbinic law. Rav Yirmeya analyzes this *baraita*: **Granted, if you say** that **a discriminating** minor **on the brink of adulthood** is considered an adult **by rabbinic law,** one can explain that a husband whose **marriage** is **by rabbinic law comes and negates a vow** that also applies **by rabbinic law. But if you say** that a discriminating minor on the brink of adulthood is considered an adult **by Torah law,** can a husband whose **marriage** is **by rabbinic law come and negate a vow** that applies **by Torah law?**

אָמַר רַב יְהוּדָה, אָמַר שְׁמוּאֵל: בַּעְלָהּ מֵפֵר לָהּ מִמָּה נַפְשָׁךְ, אִי דְּרַבָּנַן – דְּרַבָּנַן הוּא, אִי דְּאוֹרַיְיתָא – קָטָן אוֹכֵל נְבֵלוֹת הוּא, וְאֵין בֵּית דִּין מְצֻוִּין עָלָיו לְהַפְרִישׁוֹ.

**Rav Yehuda says** that **Shmuel says: Her husband may nullify her** vows, **whichever** way **you** look at it: **If** the validity of the vows of such a minor applies **by rabbinic law,** the husband may nullify her vows, as the validity of their marriage **is** likewise **by rabbinic law.** And **if** the validity of a vow by a discriminating minor on the brink of adulthood is **by Torah law,** which means she would be violating a Torah prohibition, this **is** the same as the case of **a minor** who **may eat** meat from unslaughtered **animal carcasses** or violate other prohibitions, **and the court** or any other adult, including her husband in this case, **is not commanded to prevent him**[HN] from doing so, and it does not matter if his nullification was not effective.

וְהָא כִּי גָּדְלָה, אָכְלָה בַּהֲפָרָה קַמַּיְיתָא!

The Gemara raises a difficulty: **But** there is still concern for a violation, as **when she grows** and becomes an adult **she will eat** the food that she rendered forbidden to herself, relying **on the initial nullification** of her vow by her husband, which was not valid. At that stage she is an adult, whom the court is certainly commanded to prevent from violating prohibitions.

אָמַר רַבָּה בַּר לִיוַאי: בַּעְלָהּ מֵפֵר לָהּ כׇּל שָׁעָה וְשָׁעָה, וְהוּא שֶׁבָּעַל.

**Rabba bar Livai said** that this is not a concern, as **her husband nullifies her** vows **each and every moment,** and therefore when she reaches majority he will nullify her vow in a manner that is valid by Torah law. **And this is** the *halakha*, that the nullification takes effect by Torah law, only in a case **where** her husband **engaged in intercourse** with her after she became an adult, thereby rendering their marriage valid by Torah law.

וְהָא אֵין בַּעַל מֵפֵר בְּקוֹדְמִין! כִּדְרַב פִּינְחָס מִשְּׁמֵיהּ דְּרָבָא, דְּאָמַר רַב פִּנְחָס מִשְּׁמֵיהּ דְּרָבָא: כׇּל הַנּוֹדֶרֶת – עַל דַּעַת בַּעְלָהּ הִיא נוֹדֶרֶת.

The Gemara raises another difficulty: **But** there is a principle that **a husband cannot nullify** vows of his wife that **preceded** their marriage;[H] and as she is considered his wife by Torah law only when she becomes an adult, her vow when she was a minor preceded their marriage. The Gemara answers that he can still nullify her vow, **in accordance with** the statement **of Rav Pinehas in the name of Rava, as Rav Pinehas said in the name of Rava: Any** woman **who takes a vow,** it is from the outset contingent **on her husband's consent** that **she takes the vow.**[N] Since the minor was married by rabbinic law, she vowed on the condition that her husband should agree to her vow, and therefore the nullification is valid by Torah law.

**BACKGROUND**

**Nullification of vows – הֲפָרַת נְדָרִים:** The Torah authorizes a father to nullify the vows of his daughter before she either attains the age of majority or marries (see Numbers 30:4–6). Similarly, a husband is entitled to nullify vows uttered by his wife. If a girl is betrothed before she attains the age of majority, her vows may be nullified by her husband and father acting together. The vow must be nullified on the same day on which the father or husband hear of it. A husband is empowered to nullify only those vows that directly or indirectly affect the personal relationship between him and his wife. According to many opinions, this restriction applies to the father as well.

**HALAKHA**

**A minor may eat from unslaughtered animal carcasses and the court is not commanded to prevent him – קָטָן אוֹכֵל נְבֵלוֹת הוּא וְאֵין בֵּית דִּין מְצֻוִּין עָלָיו לְהַפְרִישׁוֹ:** If a minor is eating meat from unslaughtered animals, or violating any other prohibition, of his own accord (*Mishna Berura*), the court is not commanded to separate him from the act. But his father is commanded to reprimand him and stop him. This requirement does not apply to his mother (*Magen Avraham*), although some authorities disagree (*Mishna Berura*). If the prohibition applies by Torah law and the father does not stop him, the court rebukes the father, but not if the prohibition was by rabbinic law (*Magen Avraham* and *Taz*; see *Mishna Berura*). Some claim that if the child has reached the suitable age for education, the court is obligated to prevent him from transgression (Rema, based on *Tosafot*), whereas the *Beit Yosef* maintains that the mitzva of education applies to the father alone (Rambam *Sefer Kedusha, Hilkhot Ma'akhalot Assurot* 17:27–28; *Shulḥan Arukh, Yoreh De'a* 343).

**A husband cannot nullify vows of his wife that preceded their marriage – אֵין בַּעַל מֵפֵר בְּקוֹדְמִין:** If a betrothed woman vowed and her father nullified her vow by himself, and her betrothed did not hear about it until they were married, he cannot nullify it after the marriage, as a husband cannot nullify vows of his wife which preceded their marriage (Rambam *Sefer Hafla'a, Hilkhot Nedarim* 11:20; *Shulḥan Arukh, Yoreh De'a* 234:35).

**NOTES**

**And the court is not commanded to prevent him – וְאֵין בֵּית דִּין מְצֻוִּין עָלָיו לְהַפְרִישׁוֹ:** The early commentaries are puzzled by this statement, as even if the court is not commanded to prevent a minor from transgressing, they are certainly prohibited from actively feeding a minor forbidden food. In this case, by nullifying her vow, her husband is effectively telling her that she may eat the food, which is tantamount to feeding her actively. The commentaries answer that the Gemara could have raised this difficulty, but in any event reaches a conclusion according to which this is not difficult (Rashba). Others suggest that nullifying a vow is not equivalent to feeding someone, as the husband does not compel her to eat; he merely indicates to her that she may do so if she chooses (Ritva; Meiri).

**On her husband's consent that she takes the vow – עַל דַּעַת בַּעְלָהּ הִיא נוֹדֶרֶת:** Rashi claims that this opinion is cited in explanation of how this husband can nullify his wife's vow when the vow preceded their marriage (see *Tosefot HaRosh*). The later commentaries maintain that it is apparent from Rashi's commentary that he understands that the Gemara here is retracting from its previous interpretation that the husband nullifies her vows each and every moment. Instead, the Gemara is referring to the earlier difficulty of how a husband whose marriage is only by rabbinic law can come and negate a vow which applies by Torah law. The Gemara's answer is that this is because even when she was a minor, she took her vow contingent on her husband's consent. If so, Rashi's explanation is in line with that of the majority of the early commentaries (see *Tosafot*, *Tosefot HaRosh*, and *Eizehu Mekoman*).

אֲמַר אַבַּיֵי: תָּא שְׁמַע, קָטָן שֶׁלֹּא הֵבִיא שְׁתֵּי שְׂעָרוֹת, רַבִּי יְהוּדָה אוֹמֵר: אֵין תְּרוּמָתוֹ תְּרוּמָה, רַבִּי יוֹסֵי אוֹמֵר: עַד שֶׁלֹּא בָּא לְעוֹנַת נְדָרִים – אֵין תְּרוּמָתוֹ תְּרוּמָה, מִשֶּׁבָּא לְעוֹנַת נְדָרִים – תְּרוּמָתוֹ תְּרוּמָה.

§ The Gemara continues to discuss the validity of the vows of a discriminating minor on the brink of adulthood. **Abaye said: Come** and **hear** a mishna (*Terumot* 1:3): With regard to **a minor who has not grown two hairs, Rabbi Yehuda says: His *teruma* is not** valid ***teruma*. Rabbi Yosei says: Until he has reached the age of vows,** i.e., when he does not yet have the status of a discriminating minor on the brink of adulthood, **his *teruma* is not** valid ***teruma*,**[H] but **once he has reached the age of vows, his *teruma* is *teruma*.**

סַבְרוּהָ: קָסָבַר רַבִּי יוֹסֵי תְּרוּמָה בַּזְּמַן הַזֶּה – דְּאוֹרַיְיתָא. אִי אָמְרַתְּ בִּשְׁלָמָא מוּפְלָא סָמוּךְ לְאִישׁ, דְּאוֹרַיְיתָא – אָתֵי גַּבְרָא דְּאוֹרַיְיתָא וּמְתַקֵּן טִבְלָא דְּאוֹרַיְיתָא. אֶלָּא אִי אָמְרַתְּ דְּרַבָּנַן – אָתֵי גַּבְרָא דְּרַבָּנַן וּמְתַקֵּן טִבְלָא דְּאוֹרַיְיתָא?! לָא, קָסָבַר רַבִּי יוֹסֵי תְּרוּמָה בַּזְּמַן הַזֶּה דְּרַבָּנַן.

The Sages **assumed** that **Rabbi Yosei holds** that ***teruma* in the present**[H] applies **by Torah law.** They therefore objected: **Granted, if you say** that a **discriminating** minor **on the brink of adulthood** is an adult **by Torah law,** one can understand that one who is **a man by Torah law** with regard to vows **can come and prepare untithed produce** [***tivla***][L] for consumption by tithing it, which also applies **by Torah law. But if you say** that a discriminating minor on the brink of adulthood is an adult **by rabbinic law,** can one who is **a man by rabbinic law come and prepare untithed produce,** which is prohibited **by Torah law?** The Gemara refutes this proof: **No,** perhaps **Rabbi Yosei holds** that ***teruma* in the present** applies **by rabbinic law,**[N] and this is why he rules that a minor on the brink of adulthood can set aside *teruma*.

וְסָבַר רַבִּי יוֹסֵי תְּרוּמָה בַּזְּמַן הַזֶּה דְּרַבָּנַן? וְהָתַנְיָא בְּסֵדֶר עוֹלָם: ״אֲשֶׁר יָרְשׁוּ אֲבוֹתֶיךָ וִירִשְׁתָּהּ״,

The Gemara asks: **And does Rabbi Yosei hold** that ***teruma* in the present** applies **by rabbinic law? But isn't it taught** in a ***baraita* in** the anthology called ***Seder Olam*:**[B] The verse that states with regard to the Jewish people's return to Eretz Yisrael following their exile: "And the Lord your God will bring you into the land **that your fathers possessed, and you shall possess it"** (Deuteronomy 30:5).

יְרוּשָּׁה רִאשׁוֹנָה וּשְׁנִיָּה – יֵשׁ לָהֶן, שְׁלִישִׁית – אֵין לָהֶן.

These two expressions of possession indicate that the Jewish people had **a first possession** of Eretz Yisrael in the days of Joshua, when Eretz Yisrael was first sanctified with regard to the obligation of its mitzvot, **and they had a second** possession at the time of Ezra and the return of the Babylonian exile. In other words, the sanctity of the land lapsed when the First Temple was destroyed and the Jews were exiled to Babylonia, and therefore a second sanctification was necessary when they returned to their land. But **they** will **not have a third** possession. That is, it will never be necessary to sanctify the land a third time, as the second sanctification was permanent.

וַאֲמַר רַבִּי יוֹחָנָן: מַאן תְּנָא סֵדֶר עוֹלָם – רַבִּי יוֹסֵי!

**And Rabbi Yoḥanan said: Who** is the *tanna* that **taught *Seder Olam*? Rabbi Yosei.** Since Rabbi Yosei maintains that the second sanctification of Eretz Yisrael did not lapse even after the destruction of the Second Temple, he must also maintain that *teruma* in the present applies by Torah law.

רַבִּי יוֹסֵי תְּנֵי לָהּ, וְלָא סָבַר לָהּ. הָכִי נַמִי מִסְתַּבְּרָא, דְּתַנְיָא: עִיסָּה שֶׁנִּדְמְעָה אוֹ שֶׁנִּתְחַמְּצָה בִּשְׂאוֹר שֶׁל תְּרוּמָה

The Gemara answers that **Rabbi Yosei taught** *Seder Olam* **but he does not maintain** in accordance with **its** ruling here. The Gemara adds: **So too, it is reasonable** that this is so, **as it is taught** in a *baraita*: With regard to non-sacred **dough that became mixed** with *teruma* dough, **or which was leavened with leaven of *teruma*,**

**LANGUAGE**

Untithed produce [*tivla*] – טִבְלָא: This refers to produce from which the priestly dues of *teruma* have not been separated, or dough from which *ḥalla* has not been separated. It is more commonly known as *tevel*.

Some suggest that *tevel*, which is spelled with the letter *tet*, is from the Hebrew word *tevel* with a *tav*, which means mixed, as *tevel* is produce which contains a mixture of tithes and non-sacred food.

**NOTES**

*Teruma* in the present applies by rabbinic law – תְּרוּמָה בַּזְּמַן הַזֶּה דְּרַבָּנַן: The majority of the early commentaries maintain that *teruma* in the present time applies by rabbinic law (Rambam *Sefer Zera'im*, *Hilkhot Terumot* 1:26, 13:14; *Smag*; *Sefer HaTeruma*; Rashba). Others add that although there is a dissenting opinion that even in the present the obligation of *teruma* in Eretz Yisrael is by Torah law, the practice is not in accordance with this opinion (*Shulḥan Arukh*, *Yoreh De'a* 331:2, and in the comment of Rema).

**BACKGROUND**

*Seder Olam* – סֵדֶר עוֹלָם: *Seder Olam* is a book from the period of the Mishna that deals with the chronology of biblical times and continues until the destruction of the Second Temple. Woven into its thirty chapters are various *halakhot* and non-halakhic statements. The work is based on verses and ancient traditions. The Gemara here and elsewhere states that the *tanna* who taught *Seder Olam* is Rabbi Yosei.

The book is also called *Seder Olam Rabba*, in order to distinguish it from a similar book composed in a later period, called *Seder Olam Zuta*. *Seder Olam* has been published over the generations in many editions, some of which include additional commentaries.

**HALAKHA**

**Until he has reached the age of vows his *teruma* is not *teruma*** – עַד שֶׁלֹּא בָּא לְעוֹנַת נְדָרִים אֵין תְּרוּמָתוֹ תְּרוּמָה: If a minor has reached the age of vows, i.e., when he is a discriminating minor on the brink of adulthood, his *teruma* is *teruma*, even if he has not yet grown two pubic hairs. This is the *halakha* even with regard to *teruma* by Torah law, as his vows and consecrations are valid by Torah law. The *halakha* is in accordance with the opinion of Rabbi Yosei, following the ruling of Rabbi Yoḥanan and Reish Lakish that the status of a discriminating minor on the brink of adulthood applies by Torah law (Rambam *Sefer Zera'im*, *Hilkhot Terumot* 4:5).

***Teruma* in the present** – תְּרוּמָה בַּזְּמַן הַזֶּה: The *halakhot* of *teruma* apply in the present by rabbinic decree only, even in those places settled by the Jews who returned from Babylonia in the time of Ezra. By Torah law, these *halakhot* are in effect only in Eretz Yisrael and only when the entire Jewish people dwells there. The Rambam adds: It would appear to me that the same applies to tithes, that their obligation in the present applies by rabbinic law, like *teruma*. The Ra'avad disagrees and claims that *teruma* in the present is by Torah law (Rambam *Sefer Zera'im*, *Hilkhot Terumot* 1:26).

חַיֶּיבֶת בְּחַלָּה, וְאֵינָהּ נִפְסֶלֶת בִּטְבוּל יוֹם, דִּבְרֵי רַבִּי מֵאִיר וְרַבִּי יְהוּדָה. רַבִּי יוֹסֵי וְרַבִּי שִׁמְעוֹן פּוֹטְרִין מִן הַחַלָּה.

it is **subject to the obligation** of separating ***ḥalla*****,**[NB] the portion of the dough designated for the priest. **And** although *teruma* fell into it, that produce does not have the status of *teruma*, as the *teruma* was nullified by a majority of non-sacred produce. Consequently, **it is not rendered unfit** for consumption, i.e., rendered ritually impure, **by one** who was ritually impure **who immersed that day**[H] and is waiting for nightfall for his purification process to be completed. This is **the statement of Rabbi Meir and Rabbi Yehuda. Rabbi Yosei and Rabbi Shimon deem** the dough **exempt from the** obligation of separating ***ḥalla*****,**[NH] as this obligation does not apply to *teruma*, and the entire dough is exempt due to the mixture of *teruma* it contains.

סַבְרוּהָ: מַאן דַּאֲמַר תְּרוּמָה דְּאוֹרַיְיתָא – חַלָּה דְּאוֹרַיְיתָא, מַאן דַּאֲמַר תְּרוּמָה דְּרַבָּנַן – חַלָּה דְּרַבָּנַן. אִי אָמְרַתְּ בִּשְׁלָמָא, קָסָבַר רַבִּי יוֹסֵי חַלָּה בִּזְמַן הַזֶּה דְּרַבָּנַן – אָתֵי דִּמּוּעַ דְּרַבָּנַן וּמַפְקַע חַלָּה דְּרַבָּנַן.

The Sages **assumed** that **the one who said** that ***teruma*** in the present applies **by Torah law** maintains that ***ḥalla*** likewise applies in the present **by Torah law,** whereas **the one who said** that ***teruma*** in the present applies **by rabbinic law** holds that ***ḥalla*** also applies **by rabbinic law.**[H] If so, **granted, if you say** that **Rabbi Yosei holds** that ***ḥalla* in the present** applies **by rabbinic law,** one can understand that **a mixture** which has the status of *teruma* **by rabbinic law comes and abrogates** the obligation of separating ***ḥalla*****,** which also applies **by rabbinic law.**

אֶלָּא אִי אָמְרַתְּ חַלָּה דְּאוֹרַיְיתָא – אָתֵי דִּמּוּעַ דְּרַבָּנַן וּמַפְקַע חַלָּה דְּאוֹרַיְיתָא?!

**But if you say** that ***ḥalla*** in the present applies **by Torah law,** can a **mixture** that has the status of *teruma* **by rabbinic law come and abrogate** the mitzva of ***ḥalla*** which is **by Torah law?** Evidently, according to Rabbi Yosei the obligation of separating *ḥalla* in the present is by rabbinic law, and therefore *teruma* likewise applies by rabbinic law. If so, Rabbi Yosei does not agree with the opinion he cites in *Seder Olam*, according to which *teruma* applies in the present by Torah law.

וְדִלְמָא קָסָבַר רַבִּי יוֹסֵי תְּרוּמָה בִּזְמַן הַזֶּה – דְּאוֹרַיְיתָא, וְחַלָּה – דְּרַבָּנַן?

The Gemara rejects this proof: **But perhaps Rabbi Yosei maintains** that ***teruma* in the present** applies **by Torah law and** yet ***ḥalla*** applies **by rabbinic law,** and therefore the mixture discussed in the above *baraita*, which has the status of *teruma* by Torah law, abrogates the obligation of *ḥalla*, which is by rabbinic law.

וְכִדְאַהֲדַר רַב הוּנָא בְּרֵיהּ דְּרַב יְהוֹשֻׁעַ. דַּאֲמַר רַב הוּנָא בְּרֵיהּ דְּרַב יְהוֹשֻׁעַ, אַשְׁכַּחְתִּינְהוּ לְרַבָּנַן דְּבֵי רַב דְּיָתְבִי וְקָאָמְרִי: אֲפִילּוּ לְמַאן דַּאֲמַר תְּרוּמָה בִּזְמַן הַזֶּה דְּרַבָּנַן – חַלָּה דְּאוֹרַיְיתָא,

The Gemara adds: **And** this answer is **as Rav Huna, son of Rav Yehoshua, responded** to the statement of the other Sages. **As Rav Huna, son of Rav Yehoshua, said:** I once **found the Sages of the study hall of Rav sitting and saying: Even according to the one who said** that ***teruma* in the present** applies **by rabbinic law,** the obligation to separate ***ḥalla*** is **by Torah law.**

שֶׁהֲרֵי שֶׁבַע שֶׁכִּבְּשׁוּ וְשֶׁבַע שֶׁחִלְּקוּ – נִתְחַיְּיבוּ בְּחַלָּה וְלֹא נִתְחַיְּיבוּ בְּמַעֲשֵׂר.

The reason is **that** during the **seven** years **that** the Jewish people **conquered** Eretz Yisrael led by Joshua **and** during the **seven** years **that they divided** the land, **they were obligated to** separate ***ḥalla*** **but they were not obligated to** separate *teruma* and **tithe.** In the present as well, although there is no obligation to set aside *teruma* in Eretz Yisrael by Torah law, the obligation to separate *ḥalla* applies by Torah law.

## NOTES

**Subject to the obligation of *ḥalla* – חַיֶּיבֶת בְּחַלָּה:** The *teruma* in the dough does not exempt the entire mixture from the obligation of *ḥalla*, i.e., although *teruma* itself is not obligated in *ḥalla*, this obligation does apply to a mixture of *teruma* and non-sacred produce. The reason is that by Torah law when a unit of prohibited substance becomes intermingled with two units of a permitted substance, the prohibited substance is nullified by the majority. It was the Sages who required a ratio of one in one hundred parts in order for a non-sacred substance to nullify *teruma*. Consequently, a substance which is prohibited by rabbinic law, such as this mixture, does not negate an obligation by Torah law, as according to the opinion of Rabbi Meir and Rabbi Yehuda the obligation to set aside *ḥalla* nowadays applies by Torah law (Rashi).

**Rabbi Yosei and Rabbi Shimon deem it exempt from the obligation of *ḥalla* – וְרַבִּי יוֹסֵי וְרַבִּי שִׁמְעוֹן פּוֹטְרִין מִן הַחַלָּה:** The wording of the *baraita* indicates that Rabbi Yosei and Rabbi Shimon disagree with Rabbi Meir and Rabbi Yehuda only with regard to the *halakha* of the *ḥalla* in this dough, but they concur that it is not disqualified by one who was ritually impure who immersed that day. Yet, a mishna in *Tevul Yom* (3:4) explicitly states that if dough became mixed with *teruma* dough or was leavened with leaven of *teruma*, Rabbi Yosei and Rabbi Shimon maintain that it is disqualified by the touch of one who was ritually impure who immersed that day. The reason that this opinion is not mentioned in the *baraita* is that the *tanna* assumes familiarity with the mishna in *Tevul Yom*.

The later commentaries explain that this dispute is based on a fundamental disagreement concerning the principle that a permitted food flavored by a forbidden food assumes the halakhic status of the forbidden food. This principle is stated in connection to prohibitions, and the dispute is whether it also applies to the *halakhot* of ritual purity. According to Rabbi Meir and Rabbi Yehuda this principle does not apply to impurity, and therefore the dough which has absorbed the taste of *teruma* is not disqualified by the touch of an impure person. By contrast, Rabbi Yosei and Rabbi Shimon maintain that the status of the flavored food changes even with regard to ritual impurity, and therefore this dough is rendered impure by one who was ritually impure who immersed that day (*Beit Yitzḥak*).

## BACKGROUND

***Ḥalla* – חַלָּה:** The Torah mandates the giving of a portion of dough to the priests (Numbers 15:20–21). This portion is called *ḥalla* and is governed by all the *halakhot* pertaining to *teruma*, the priests' portion of the crop. The Torah does not specify a measure for *ḥalla*, but the Sages required a private person to give one twenty-fourth of his dough and a commercial baker to give one forty-eighth. *Ḥalla* must be taken from all dough made from any one of the five types of grain, provided that the quantity of flour is at least one-tenth of an ephah in volume. If *ḥalla* is not separated, the dough is considered untithed and may not be eaten. Today, when all Jews are considered ritually impure, *ḥalla* is governed by the same *halakhot* as ritually impure *teruma* and must be burned. Accordingly, the aforementioned measures no longer apply; instead, a small portion is separated from the dough and burned, after which the rest of the dough may be used.

## HALAKHA

**And it is not rendered unfit by one who was ritually impure who immersed that day – וְאֵינָהּ נִפְסֶלֶת בִּטְבוּל יוֹם:** Non-sacred dough that became mixed with *teruma* dough or which was leavened with leaven of *teruma* is not disqualified by one who was ritually impure who immersed that day. The *halakha* is in accordance with the opinion of the first *tanna* in the mishna in *Tevul Yom* (Rambam *Sefer Tahara, Hilkhot Tumat Okhalin* 8:15).

**Deem it exempt from the obligation of *ḥalla* – פּוֹטְרִין מִן הַחַלָּה:** If non-sacred dough became mixed with *teruma* it is exempt from the obligation of *ḥalla*, in accordance with the opinion of Rabbi Yosei and Rabbi Shimon (Rambam *Sefer Zera'im, Hilkhot Bikkurim* 6:4).

***Ḥalla* applies by rabbinic law – חַלָּה דְּרַבָּנַן:** The Torah obligation of *ḥalla* is in effect only in Eretz Israel and only when the entire Jewish people is within its borders. Therefore, even after the return to Eretz Yisrael and the construction of the Second Temple, *ḥalla* was in effect only by rabbinic law, in accordance with the opinion of Rav Huna, son of Rav Yehoshua (Rambam *Sefer Zera'im, Hilkhot Bikkurim* 5:5; *Shulḥan Arukh, Yoreh De'a* 322:2).

וְאָמִינָא לְהוּ אֲנָא: אֲפִילּוּ לְמַאן דַּאֲמַר תְּרוּמָה בַּזְּמַן הַזֶּה דְּאוֹרַיְיתָא – חַלָּה דְּרַבָּנַן, דְּתַנְיָא: אִי ״בְּבֹאֲכֶם״, יָכוֹל מִשֶּׁנִּכְנְסוּ לָהּ שְׁנַיִם וּשְׁלֹשָׁה מְרַגְּלִים? תַּלְמוּד לוֹמַר ״בְּבֹאֲכֶם״ – בְּבִיאַת כּוּלְּכֶם אָמַרְתִּי, וְלֹא בְּבִיאַת מִקְצָתְכֶם,

Rav Huna, son of Rav Yehoshua, continued: **And I said to them:** On the contrary, **even according to the one who said** that *teruma* **in the present** applies **by Torah law,** the obligation to separate *ḥalla* applies **by rabbinic law, as it is taught** in a *baraita*: The verse states with regard to *ḥalla*: "When you come into the land where I bring you… from the first of your dough you shall set apart a cake for a gift" (Numbers 15:18–20). **If** the obligation applies **"when you come"** into the land, one **might** have thought that it took effect **from** the moment **that two or three spies entered** the land. Therefore **the verse states: "When you come,"** from which it is derived that the Torah is saying: **I said** that the obligation applies **when all of you come, and not when some of you come.**

וְכִי אַסְּקִינְהוּ עֶזְרָא – לָא כּוּלְּהוּ סְלוּק.

According to this *baraita*, the separation of *ḥalla* is an obligation by Torah law only when the entire Jewish people come to Eretz Yisrael. **And when Ezra brought** the Jewish people to Eretz Yisrael at the beginning of the Second Temple period, **not all of them ascended.** Since the majority of the Jewish people stayed behind, separating *ḥalla* was not restored to the status of an obligation by Torah law.

**מתני׳** מָשָׁל מָשְׁלוּ חֲכָמִים בָּאִשָּׁה: פַּגָּה, בּוֹחַל, וְצֶמֶל. פַּגָּה – עוֹדָהּ תִּינוֹקֶת, בּוֹחַל – אֵלּוּ יְמֵי נְעוּרֶיהָ.

**MISHNA** **The Sages stated a parable** based on the development of the fruit of a fig tree with regard to the three stages of development **in a woman:** Minority, young womanhood, and grown womanhood. **An unripe fig, a ripening fig, and a ripe fig.**[B] **An unripe fig** represents the stage when **she is still a child** and has not yet developed the signs of puberty; **a ripening fig** represents **the days of her young womanhood,** when she reaches twelve years and one day and has developed two pubic hairs.

בָּזוֹ וּבָזוֹ אָמְרוּ: אָבִיהָ זַכַּאי בִּמְצִיאָתָהּ, וּבְמַעֲשֵׂה יָדֶיהָ, וּבַהֲפָרַת נְדָרֶיהָ. צֶמֶל – כֵּיוָן שֶׁבָּגְרָה, שׁוּב אֵין לְאָבִיהָ רְשׁוּת בָּהּ.

With regard to the periods both **during this** stage, minority, **and during that** stage, young womanhood, the Sages **said** that **her father is entitled to** any lost object that **she finds**[H] that cannot be returned to its owner, **and to her earnings, and to nullification of her vows.**[H] **A ripe fig** represents the stage of grown womanhood: **Once she has reached her majority, her father no longer has authority over her.** He can no longer nullify her vows, and he does not have a claim to lost objects found by her and her earnings belong to her.

אֵיזֶהוּ סִימָנִין? רַבִּי יוֹסֵי הַגְּלִילִי אוֹמֵר: מִשֶּׁיַּעֲלֶה הַקֶּמֶט תַּחַת הַדַּד. רַבִּי עֲקִיבָא אוֹמֵר: מִשֶּׁיַּטּוּ הַדַּדִּים. בֶּן עַזַּאי אוֹמֵר: מִשֶּׁיַּשְׁחִיר הַפִּיטוֹמֶת. רַבִּי יוֹסֵי אוֹמֵר: כְּדֵי שֶׁיְּהֵא נוֹתֵן יָדוֹ עַל הָעוֹקֶץ, וְהוּא שׁוֹקֵעַ וְשׁוֹהֶא לַחֲזוֹר.

**What are the signs**[NH] that indicate grown womanhood? **Rabbi Yosei HaGelili says:** Grown womanhood begins **from when** her breast **grows** sufficiently so that **a fold appears below the breast. Rabbi Akiva says:** It begins **from when the breasts sag** onto the chest. **Ben Azzai says:** It begins **from when the areola** at the tip of the breast **darkens. Rabbi Yosei says:** It begins when the breasts have developed to **a size where** a person **places his hand on the nipple and it depresses and slows to return.**

## BACKGROUND

**Unripe fig [*paga*], ripening fig [*boḥal*], ripe fig [*tzemel*] – פַּגָּה בּוֹחַל צֶמֶל:** These terms refer to three stages in the growth of a fig. The first development of an unripe fig, called a *pag*, corresponds to a girl who has yet to reach young womanhood. During the second stage, until a fig is fit for consumption, it is called *boḥal*, meaning that it is ripening. In the third stage, the fig becomes fully ripe and is called *tzemel*.

Unripe fig

Ripening fig

Ripe fig

## NOTES

**What are the signs – אֵיזֶהוּ סִימָנִין:** The mishna does not specify whether it is referring here to the stage of an unripe fig, a ripening fig, or a ripe fig. The early commentaries explain that these are the signs of grown womanhood (Rashi; Rabbeinu Ḥananel). The commentaries note that these signs are indicative of maturity only if the woman has reached the appropriate age, as they are not more significant than two pubic hairs, which have halakhic significance only if the girl is of age (*Maggid Mishne* on Rambam *Sefer Nashim*, *Hilkhot Ishut* 2:7).

## HALAKHA

**Her father is entitled to any lost object that she finds – אָבִיהָ זַכַּאי בִּמְצִיאָתָהּ:** A father is entitled to lost items that his daughter has found and to her earnings, until she becomes a grown woman. This is the *halakha* even if she is not financially dependent upon him (Rambam *Sefer Nezikin*, *Hilkhot Gezeila VaAveda* 17:13 and *Sefer Nashim*, *Hilkhot Ishut* 3:11; *Shulḥan Arukh*, *Ḥoshen Mishpat* 270:2 and *Even HaEzer* 37:1).

**And to nullification of her vows – וּבַהֲפָרַת נְדָרֶיהָ:** A father may nullify his daughter's vows when she is a minor or a young woman, i.e., she is aged twelve years and one day and has grown two hairs (*Shakh*). This applies only to vows that involve affliction of the girl or that are between him and her, i.e., vows which negatively impact their relationship (*Shakh*), even if her vow was taken based on the consent of the public (Rambam *Sefer Hafla'a*, *Hilkhot Nedarim* 11:6; *Shulḥan Arukh*, *Yoreh De'a* 234:1).

**What are the signs – אֵיזֶהוּ סִימָנִין:** There are signs of maturity in the upper part of a girl's body which are called the upper signs: From when the breast has grown enough so that if she were to stretch out her arms, it would appear as there is a fold below the breast, as stated by Rabbi Yosei HaGelili; from when the areola at the tip of the breast darkens, as maintained by ben Azzai; from when the breasts have developed to a size where if a hand were placed on the nipple, the nipple is depressed and takes time to return to its original shape, as stated by Rabbi Yosei; and from when the end of the protrusion splits, which is the opinion of Rav Ashi in the *baraita*. In this regard, the Rambam adds: My teachers explain that this means from when the protrusion itself splits.

Other signs are from when the breasts sag onto the chest, which is stated by Rabbi Akiva in the mishna; from when the breasts knock against each other due to their size, in accordance with the opinion of Rabbi Elazar, son of Rabbi Tzadok, in the *baraita*; from when the protuberance above the womb, the mons pubis, is surrounded by a circle, which the Rambam maintains is the opinion of Rabbi Yosei in the *baraita*; and from when the mons pubis softens and is not hard, as stated by Rabbi Shimon in the *baraita*.

These total eight signs. The Rambam rules that any of these signs is sufficient, in accordance with one version of Rabbi Yehuda HaNasi's statement on the following *amud* (Rambam *Sefer Nashim*, *Hilkhot Ishut* 2:7–8).

**גמ׳** פַּגָּה – עוֹדָהּ תִּינוֹקֶת, כְּדִכְתִיב ״הַתְּאֵנָה חָנְטָה פַגֶּיהָ״. בּוֹחַל – אֵלּוּ יְמֵי הַנְּעוּרִים, כִּדְתְנַן: הַתְּאֵנִים – מִשֶּׁיִּבָּחֲלוּ, וְאָמַר רַבָּה בַּר בַּר חָנָה, אָמַר רַב: מִשֶּׁיַּלְבִּין רָאשֵׁיהֶן.

**GEMARA** The mishna teaches that **an unripe fig** [*paga*] represents the stage when a woman **is still a child.** The Gemara explains that the meaning of the word *paga* is **as it is written: "The fig tree puts forth her green fruits** [*fageha*]" (Song of Songs 2:13). The mishna further teaches that **a ripening fig** [*boḥal*] represents **the days of her young womanhood.** The Gemara explains that the meaning of this word is **as we learned** in a mishna (*Ma'asrot* 1:2): The obligation of tithes applies to **the figs from when they begin to ripen** [*misheyyibaḥalu*];[H] **and Rabba bar bar Ḥana says** that **Rav says** that this means **from when the heads** of the figs **whiten.**

וְאִיבָּעֵית אֵימָא מֵהָכָא: ״וַתִּקְצַר נַפְשִׁי בָּהֶם וְגַם נַפְשָׁם בָּחֲלָה בִי״. צֶמֶל – כְּמַאן דַּאֲמַר: יָצְתָה מְלֵאָה.

The Gemara adds: **And if you wish, say** instead that the source is **from here: "For My soul became impatient of them, and their soul also grew in disgust** [*baḥala*] **toward Me"** (Zechariah 11:8). The verse indicates that this word denotes growth. As for the third term in the mishna, **a ripe fig** [*tzemel*], it is **as one would say:** A fruit **has come forth complete** [*yatzeta mele'a*].

וְאֵיזֶהוּ סִימָנִים? רַבִּי יוֹסֵי הַגְּלִילִי אוֹמֵר: מִשֶּׁיַּעֲלֶה הַקֶּמֶט. אָמַר שְׁמוּאֵל: לֹא מִשֶּׁיַּעֲלֶה הַקֶּמֶט מַמָּשׁ, אֶלָּא כְּדֵי שֶׁתַּחֲזִיר יָדֶיהָ לַאֲחוֹרֶיהָ, וְנִרְאֵית כְּמִי שֶׁיַּעֲלֶה הַקֶּמֶט תַּחַת הַדַּד.

§ The mishna teaches: **And what are the signs** that indicate grown womanhood? **Rabbi Yosei HaGelili says:** Grown womanhood begins **from when** her breast **grows** sufficiently so that **a fold** appears below the breast. **Shmuel says:** This does **not literally** mean **from when** her breast **grows** sufficiently so that a permanent **fold** appears below the breast. **Rather,** it means that the breast has grown enough **so that** if she were to **stretch her hand behind her** back, **it would appear as though** her breast has **grown** sufficiently that there is **a fold below the breast.**

שְׁמוּאֵל בָּדַק בְּאַמְתֵּיהּ, וִיהַב לָהּ אַרְבָּעָה זוּזֵי דְּמֵי בּוֹשְׁתָּהּ. שְׁמוּאֵל לְטַעְמֵיהּ, דַּאֲמַר שְׁמוּאֵל: ״לְעֹלָם בָּהֶם תַּעֲבֹדוּ״ – לַעֲבוֹדָה נְתַתִּים וְלֹא לְבוּשָׁה.

The Gemara relates that **Shmuel examined** these stages **in his** Canaanite **maidservant, and** subsequently **gave her four dinars** as **payment for her humiliation.** The Gemara notes that in this regard **Shmuel** conforms **to his** line of **reasoning, as Shmuel said** that the verse: **"You may enslave them forever"** (Leviticus 25:46) teaches: **I gave them** to you **for** the **service** of slaves, **but not for humiliation.**[H] Consequently, if a master humiliated his Canaanite slave, he must pay him damages.

שְׁמוּאֵל מְיַיחֵד לָהֶן, רַב נַחְמָן מַחֲלִיף לָהֶן, רַב שֵׁשֶׁת מָסַר לָהֶן לַעֲרָבִי, וַאֲמַר לָהֶן: אִזְדַּהֲרוּ מִיִּשְׂרָאֵל.

The Gemara further relates, with regard to the attitude toward maidservants, that **Shmuel** would **designate**[N] a particular slave **for** each of his maidservants for intercourse, and he would not allow his slaves to engage in intercourse with whichever maidservant they chose. By contrast, **Rav Naḥman** would **exchange** his maidservants between his slaves, while **Rav Sheshet handed** his maidservants **to an Arab, and said to them:** You may engage in intercourse with whomever you choose, but **take care** not to engage in intercourse **with a Jew.**

״רַבִּי יוֹסֵי אוֹמֵר״ כּו׳. מַאי ״עוֹקֶץ״? אֲמַר שְׁמוּאֵל: עוּקְצוֹ שֶׁל דַּד.

§ The mishna teaches that **Rabbi Yosei says:** Grown womanhood begins when the breasts have developed to a size where if a person places his hand on the nipple [*oketz*] it depresses and slows to return. The Gemara asks: **What** is the meaning of ***oketz*? Shmuel said:** It means **the protrusion** [*oketz*] **of the breast,** i.e., the nipple.

תָּנוּ רַבָּנַן: אֵלּוּ הֵן סִימָנֵי בַגְרוּת? רַבִּי אֶלְעָזָר בְּרַבִּי צָדוֹק אוֹמֵר: מִשֶּׁיִּתְקַשְׁקְשׁוּ הַדַּדִּין. רַבִּי יוֹחָנָן בֶּן בְּרוֹקָה אוֹמֵר: מִשֶּׁיַּכְסִיף רֹאשׁ הַחוֹטֶם. מִשֶּׁיַּכְסִיף? אַזְקוּנָה לָהּ! אֶלָּא אֲמַר רַב אַשִׁי: מִשֶּׁיַּפְצִיל רֹאשׁ הַחוֹטֶם. רַבִּי יוֹסֵי אוֹמֵר: מִשֶּׁתַּקִּיף הָעֲטָרָה, רַבִּי שִׁמְעוֹן אוֹמֵר: מִשֶּׁנִּתְמַעֵךְ

**The Sages taught** in a *baraita*: **What are the signs of maturity? Rabbi Elazar, son of Rabbi Tzadok, says: From when the breasts knock against each other,** due to their size. **Rabbi Yoḥanan ben Beroka says: From when the head** of the protrusion in the center **of the nipple darkens.** The Gemara asks with regard to this suggestion: **From when it darkens? One** thereby **renders her old,** i.e., if one accepts this sign, the beginning of maturity is delayed significantly. **Rather, Rav Ashi said: From when the head of the protrusion splits. Rabbi Yosei says: From when the nipple** grows to such an extent that it **is surrounded by a circle. Rabbi Shimon says: From when** there is **a softening**

**HALAKHA**

**The obligation of tithes applies to the figs from when they begin to ripen – הַתְּאֵנִים מִשֶּׁיִּבָּחֲלוּ:** Figs are obligated in tithes from when they become soft to the extent that twenty-four hours after they are gathered, they are fit for consumption (Rambam *Sefer Zera'im*, *Hilkhot Ma'aser* 2:5).

**I gave them to you for the service of slaves but not for humiliation – לַעֲבוֹדָה נְתַתִּים וְלֹא לְבוּשָׁה:** One may not debase his Canaanite slave, neither physically nor verbally, as the slave is given to him for service, not for humiliation. This *halakha* is in accordance with the practice of Shmuel (Rambam *Sefer Kinyan*, *Hilkhot Avadim* 9:8).

**NOTES**

**Shmuel would designate, etc. – שְׁמוּאֵל מְיַיחֵד וכו׳:** Shmuel wanted to treat his maidservants in a more honorable manner and therefore he would not allow his slaves the freedom to engage in intercourse with them as they saw fit (Rashi). By contrast, Rav Naḥman, who was not particular with regard to the humiliation of his maidservants, would swap the arrangements between his slaves and maidservants, whereas Rav Sheshet would allow them to engage in intercourse even with gentile outsiders (Rashi). Others suggest that Rav Naḥman would pass each maidservant before a slave, so that she should find favor in his eyes and he would willingly marry her (Rif).

**HALAKHA**

What is a Tyrian courtyard which renders food brought inside it to be required to be tithed – אֵיזוֹהִי חָצֵר צוֹרִית שֶׁחַיֶּיבֶת בְּמַעֲשֵׂר: Which type of courtyard renders produce brought there obligated in tithes? It is any courtyard in which vessels are guarded, as stated by Rabbi Shimon; or where people are not ashamed to eat, in accordance with the opinion of Neḥemya; or where one cannot enter without being asked about his purpose there, which is the opinion of Rabbi Yosei; and likewise a courtyard which has two residents or which belongs to two partners, where one of them opens it and enters, and the other walks through and locks it, as stated by Rabbi Akiva (see Jerusalem Talmud). The Rambam accepts all these opinions as stringencies, in accordance with the statement of Rabbi Yehuda HaNasi, following the explanation that Rabbi Yehuda HaNasi was referring to a Tyrian courtyard (Rambam *Sefer Zera'im*, *Hilkhot Ma'aser* 4:8).

**BACKGROUND**

Tyre – צוֹר: The city of Tyre in Lebanon is one of the most ancient cities in the Near East. It is located on the shore of the Mediterranean Sea, roughly 23 km north of Akko. Tyre was known for its great wealth, as it served as a port city for international trade between places near the Mediterranean. Merchants from Tyre established settlements in various areas, including North Africa, southern Europe, and Mediterranean islands. These seafaring, mercantile peoples are also known as Phoenicians, and they enabled Tyre to control the surrounding regions.

The impressive wealth of Tyre is described on many occasions in the Bible (see, e.g., Ezekiel 26; Zechariah 9:2–3). It remained an important commercial and political center until the end of the thirteenth century.

Due to the significance and wealth of the city, various items of good quality are called Tyrian, including the widely respected Tyrian coinage.

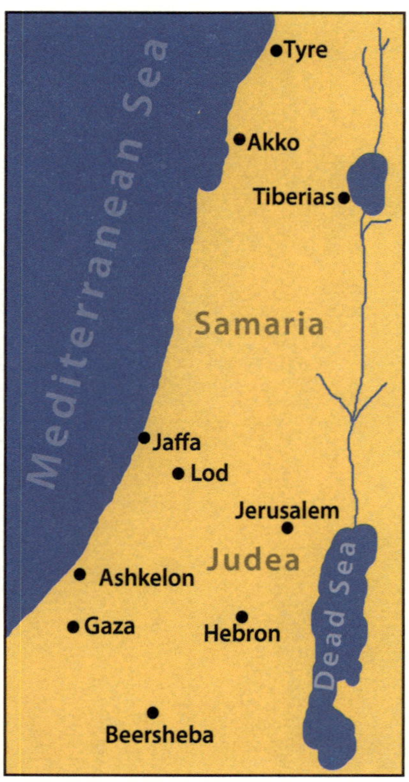


Location of Lod

הַכַּף.

of **the protuberance above the womb,** the mons pubis.

וְכֵן הָיָה רַבִּי שִׁמְעוֹן (בֶּן יוֹחַי) אוֹמֵר: שְׁלֹשָׁה סִימָנִין נָתְנוּ חֲכָמִים בָּאִשָּׁה מִלְּמַטָּה, וּכְנֶגְדָּן מִלְּמַעְלָה. פַּגָּה מִלְּמַעְלָה – בְּיָדוּעַ שֶׁלֹּא הֵבִיאָה שְׁתֵּי שְׂעָרוֹת. בּוֹחַל מִלְּמַעְלָה – בְּיָדוּעַ שֶׁהֵבִיאָה שְׁתֵּי שְׂעָרוֹת. צֶמֶל מִלְּמַעְלָה – בְּיָדוּעַ שֶׁנִּתְמַעֵךְ הַכַּף.

**And Rabbi Shimon** ben Yoḥai **would likewise say: The Sages provided three signs** indicating puberty **in a woman below,** i.e., near her vagina, **and** they stated three **corresponding** signs **above.** If a woman has the signs of **an unripe fig above, it is known that she has not grown two** pubic **hairs;** if she has the signs of **a ripening fig above, it is known that she has grown two hairs;** and if she has the signs of **a ripe fig above, it is known that the protuberance has softened.**

מַאי "כַּף"? אָמַר רַב הוּנָא: מָקוֹם תָּפוּחַ יֵשׁ לְמַעְלָה מֵאוֹתוֹ מָקוֹם, כֵּיוָן שֶׁמַּגְדֶּלֶת – מִתְמַעֵךְ וְהוֹלֵךְ. שָׁאֲלוּ אֶת רַבִּי: הֲלָכָה כְּדִבְרֵי מִי? שָׁלַח לְהוּ: כְּדִבְרֵי כּוּלָּן לְהַחְמִיר.

The Gemara asks: **What is** this **protuberance? Rav Huna says: There is a swollen place** in a woman's body, **above that place,** a euphemism for the vagina. It is initially hard, but **when** a girl **grows it increasingly softens.** The Sages **asked Rabbi** Yehuda HaNasi: With regard to the signs of maturity in woman, **in accordance with whose statement is the** ***halakha*****? He sent them** in response: The ***halakha*** **is stringent in accordance with all of their statements,** i.e., if any one of these signs mentioned by the Sages cited above appears in a girl, she must be treated as an adult with regard to all stringent aspects of this classification.

רַב פַּפָּא וְרַב חִינְּנָא בְּרֵיהּ דְּרַב אִיקָא, חַד מַתְנֵי – אַהָא, וְחַד מַתְנֵי – אַחָצֵר צוֹרִית. דִּתְנַן, אֵיזוֹהִי חָצֵר צוֹרִית שֶׁחַיֶּיבֶת בְּמַעֲשֵׂר? רַבִּי שִׁמְעוֹן אוֹמֵר: חָצֵר הַצּוֹרִית, שֶׁהַכֵּלִים נִשְׁמָרִים בְּתוֹכָהּ.

**Rav Pappa and Rav Ḥinnana, son of Rav Ika,** disagree about the context of this statement of Rabbi Yehuda HaNasi that the *halakha* is stringent in accordance with all of the Sages' statements. **One** of them **teaches** it **with regard to this** matter, of a woman's signs of puberty, **and the other one teaches** it **with regard to** the case of **a Tyrian courtyard, as we learned** in a mishna (*Ma'asrot* 3:5): **What is a Tyrian courtyard, which** renders food brought inside it to be **required to be tithed?**[H] **Rabbi Shimon says: A Tyrian courtyard** is one **inside of which vessels are safe.**

מַאי "חָצֵר הַצּוֹרִית"? אָמַר רַבָּה בַּר בַּר חָנָה, אָמַר רַבִּי יוֹחָנָן: שֶׁכֵּן בְּצוֹר מוֹשִׁיבִין שׁוֹמֵר עַל פֶּתַח הֶחָצֵר. רַבִּי עֲקִיבָא אוֹמֵר: כָּל שֶׁאֶחָד פּוֹתֵחַ וְאֶחָד נוֹעֵל – פְּטוּרָה.

The Sages discuss this mishna: **What** is the meaning of **a Tyrian courtyard? Rabba bar bar Ḥana says** that **Rabbi Yoḥanan says:** The courtyard is called by this name **as** the custom **in** the city **of Tyre**[B] is to **place a watchman at the entrance of the courtyard** to guard the articles inside. Consequently, any courtyard in which vessels are safe is called a Tyrian courtyard. **Rabbi Akiva says:** In **any** courtyard **where** there is no permanent watchman who locks and unlocks it, but rather **one** of its residents **opens** the courtyard **and** another **one locks** it, e.g., a courtyard shared by several partners, each of whom can do as he chooses without asking the other, the produce inside it is **exempt** from the obligation of separating tithe, as such a courtyard is not considered one in which vessels are safe.

רַבִּי נְחֶמְיָה אוֹמֵר: כָּל שֶׁאֵין אָדָם בּוֹשׁ לֶאֱכוֹל בְּתוֹכָהּ – חַיֶּיבֶת. רַבִּי יוֹסֵי אוֹמֵר: כָּל שֶׁנִּכְנָסִים לָהּ, וְאֵין אוֹמְרִים לוֹ "מָה אַתָּה מְבַקֵּשׁ" – פְּטוּרָה.

**Rabbi Neḥemya says: Any** courtyard **which** is hidden from the gaze of outsiders, and therefore **a person is not ashamed to eat inside it,** that courtyard renders produce inside it **obligated** to have tithe separated from it. **Rabbi Yosei says: Any** courtyard **that** one who does not live there **can enter it, and** the residents **do not say to him: What do you want** here, produce inside such a courtyard is **exempt** from tithe.

רַבִּי יְהוּדָה אוֹמֵר: שְׁתֵּי חֲצֵרוֹת זוֹ לִפְנִים מִזּוֹ, הַפְּנִימִית – חַיֶּיבֶת, וְהַחִיצוֹנָה – פְּטוּרָה.

**Rabbi Yehuda says:** If there are **two courtyards, one within the other,** positioned in such a manner that the residents of the inner courtyard cannot enter their houses without passing through the outer courtyard, whereas the residents of the outer courtyard do not traverse the inner one, **the inner** courtyard renders any produce located inside it **obligated** to have tithe separated from it, **but** produce located in **the outer** courtyard is **exempt** from tithe. It is not safe, as residents of a different courtyard pass freely through it.

שָׁאֲלוּ אֶת רַבִּי: הֲלָכָה כְּדִבְרֵי מִי? אֲמַר לְהוּ: הֲלָכָה כְּדִבְרֵי כּוּלָּן לְהַחְמִיר.

According to the opinion of one of the *amora'im* mentioned above, i.e., either Rav Pappa or Rav Ḥinnana, son of Rav Ika, it was with regard to this issue that the Sages **asked Rabbi** Yehuda HaNasi: **In accordance with whose statement is the *halakha*? He said to them: The *halakha* is stringent in accordance with all of** the Sages' **statements.** In other words, with regard to any courtyard in which produce must be tithed according to any of these opinions, the *halakha* is that tithe must be separated from this produce.

**מתני׳** בַּת עֶשְׂרִים שָׁנָה שֶׁלֹּא הֵבִיאָה שְׁתֵּי שְׂעָרוֹת, תָּבִיא רְאָיָה שֶׁהִיא בַּת עֶשְׂרִים שָׁנָה – וְהִיא אַיְילוֹנִית, לֹא חוֹלֶצֶת וְלֹא מִתְיַבֶּמֶת.

**MISHNA** A girl twelve years and one day old who grew two pubic hairs is classified as a young woman. Six months later, she becomes a grown woman. But a woman who is **twenty years old who did not grow two** pubic **hairs**[H] and was never classified as a young woman **shall bring proof that she is twenty years old, and** from that point forward **she** assumes the status of **a sexually underdeveloped woman** [*ailonit*], who is incapable of bearing children. If she married and her husband died childless, **she neither performs *ḥalitza* nor does she enter into levirate marriage,** as the mitzva of levirate marriage applies only to a woman capable of conceiving a child. An *ailonit* is excluded from that mitzva.

בֶּן עֶשְׂרִים שָׁנָה שֶׁלֹּא הֵבִיא שְׁתֵּי שְׂעָרוֹת, יָבִיאוּ רְאָיָה שֶׁהוּא בֶּן עֶשְׂרִים שָׁנָה – וְהוּא סָרִיס, לֹא חוֹלֵץ וְלֹא מְיַבֵּם, אֵלּוּ דִּבְרֵי בֵּית הִלֵּל. בֵּית שַׁמַּאי אוֹמְרִים: זֶה וָזֶה – בֶּן שְׁמוֹנֶה עֶשְׂרֵה.

In the case of a man who is **twenty years old who did not grow two** pubic **hairs, they shall bring proof that he is twenty years old and he** assumes the status of **a sexually underdeveloped man** [*saris*], who is excluded from the mitzva of levirate marriage. Therefore, if his married brother dies childless, **he neither performs *ḥalitza* nor enters into levirate marriage** with his *yevama*. **This is the statement of Beit Hillel. Beit Shammai say:** For both **this** case of a woman **and that** case of a man, they shall bring proof that they are **eighteen years old,** and they assume the status of a sexually underdeveloped woman and man respectively.

רַבִּי אֱלִיעֶזֶר אוֹמֵר: הַזָּכָר – כְּדִבְרֵי בֵּית הִלֵּל, וְהַנְּקֵבָה – כְּדִבְרֵי בֵּית שַׁמַּאי, שֶׁהָאִשָּׁה מְמַהֶרֶת לָבֹא לִפְנֵי הָאִישׁ.

**Rabbi Eliezer says:** The status of **the male** is determined **in accordance with the statement of Beit Hillel,** i.e., he assumes the status of a sexually underdeveloped man at the age of twenty; **and** the status of **the female** is determined **in accordance with the statement of Beit Shammai,** i.e., she assumes the status of a sexually underdeveloped woman at the age of eighteen. The reason is **that the woman is quick to reach** physical maturity, and reaches that stage **before the man** reaches physical maturity.

**גמ׳** וּרְמִינְהִי: אֶחָד לִי בֶּן תֵּשַׁע שָׁנִים וְיוֹם אֶחָד, וְאֶחָד לִי בֶּן עֶשְׂרִים שֶׁלֹּא הֵבִיא שְׁתֵּי שְׂעָרוֹת!

**GEMARA** The mishna teaches that a sexually underdeveloped man does not enter into levirate marriage with the widow of his childless brother. **And** the Gemara **raises a contradiction** from another mishna (*Yevamot* 96b): A boy who is **nine years and one day old,** who has not developed two hairs, **and a** man who is **twenty years old who has not grown two hairs, are one and the same to me**[H] with regard to levirate marriage, in that if they engaged in intercourse with the widow of their childless brother, this levirate marriage is partially effective, to the extent that this woman requires both a bill of divorce and *ḥalitza*.

אָמַר רַב שְׁמוּאֵל בַּר רַב יִצְחָק, אָמַר רַב: וְהוּא שֶׁנּוֹלְדוּ בּוֹ סִימָנֵי סָרִיס. אֲמַר רָבָא: דַּיְקָא נַמִי, דְּקָתָנֵי "וְהוּא סָרִיס", שְׁמַע מִינָּהּ.

**Rav Shmuel bar Yitzḥak says** that **Rav says** in explanation of the ruling of the mishna here: **And this** *halakha* applies only in a case **where he developed** physical **signs of a sexually underdeveloped man** (see *Yevamot* 80b) by the age of twenty. By contrast, the mishna in *Yevamot* is referring to one who did not develop signs of a sexually underdeveloped man. **Rava said:** The language of the mishna **is also precise, as it teaches: And he is a sexually underdeveloped man,** which indicates that he had already developed physical signs of such a condition. The Gemara concludes: **Conclude from it** that this is the correct interpretation of the mishna.

וְכִי לֹא נוֹלְדוּ לוֹ סִימָנֵי סָרִיס, עַד כַּמָּה? תָּנֵי רַבִּי חִיָּיא: עַד רוֹב שְׁנוֹתָיו.

The Gemara asks a question with regard to the *halakha* itself: **And** in a case **where he does not develop the signs of a sexually underdeveloped man, until what** age is he considered a minor? **Rabbi Ḥiyya teaches: Until most of his years** have passed,[N] i.e., until he reaches the age of thirty-five, halfway to seventy, which is the standard length of a person's life.

**HALAKHA**

**A woman who is twenty years old who did not grow two pubic hairs – בַּת עֶשְׂרִים שָׁנָה שֶׁלֹּא הֵבִיאָה שְׁתֵּי שְׂעָרוֹת:** If a woman reaches the age of twenty without growing two pubic hairs and exhibits the signs of an *ailonit*, she is considered an *ailonit*. Once she reaches the age of thirty-five without growing two pubic hairs, she is considered an *ailonit* even if she did not exhibit the signs of an *ailonit*. The *halakha* is in accordance with the opinion of the first *tanna* (Rambam *Sefer Nashim, Hilkhot Ishut* 2:4–5; *Shulḥan Arukh, Even HaEzer* 155:13).

**A boy nine years and one day old and a man twenty years old...are one and the same to me, etc. – אֶחָד לִי בֶּן תֵּשַׁע שָׁנִים וְיוֹם אֶחָד וְאֶחָד לִי בֶּן עֶשְׂרִים וכו׳:** With regard to a man who reached the age of thirteen years and one day and failed to develop two pubic hairs, even if he showed the signs of sexual underdevelopment, he is nevertheless considered a minor until his twentieth year. If he reached the age of twenty, i.e., thirty days into his twentieth year (Ra'avad), and showed the signs of a sexually underdeveloped man, he has the status of adults.

If he does not show the signs of a sexually underdeveloped man he remains a minor until he develops two pubic hairs or reaches the age of thirty-five and one day. The *halakha* is in accordance with the opinion of Rav Shmuel bar Yitzḥak citing Rav, and in accordance with the opinion of Rabbi Ḥiyya (Rambam *Sefer Nashim, Hilkhot Ishut* 2:11).

**NOTES**

**Until most of his years have passed – עַד רוֹב שְׁנוֹתָיו:** The early commentaries disagree as to the precise age when most of one's years are considered to have passed. Some say that it means exactly thirty-six years of age. According to the verse, this is the majority of one's life, as the verse states: "The days of our years are seventy" (Psalms 90:10), from which it can be inferred that half of one's years are thirty-five, and anything beyond that is most of his years (Ran; Rashbam, Rabbeinu Gershom Meor HaGola, and *Nimmukei Yosef* on *Bava Batra* 155b; *Tur, Even HaEzer* 155). Others maintain that since thirty days are considered as a year, the majority of one's life is thirty-five years and thirty days (Rema), or thirty-five years and one day (Rambam; see *Divrei Ḥamudot*).

כִּי אָתוּ לְקַמֵּיהּ דְּרַבִּי חִיָּיא, אִי כָּחִישׁ, אֲמַר לְהוּ: אַבְרִיוּהּ. אִי בָּרִיא, אֲמַר לְהוּ: אַכְחֲשׁוּהּ, דְּהָנֵי סִימָנִים – זִימְנִין דְּאָתוּ מֵחֲמַת כְּחִישׁוּתָא, זִימְנִין דְּאָתוּ מֵחֲמַת בְּרִיאוּתָא.

The Gemara relates: **When** people **would come before Rabbi Ḥiyya** to inquire about someone who had reached the age of puberty but had not yet developed the physical signs of maturity, **if** the person in question was **thin, he** would **say to them: Go** and **fatten him** up before we decide on his status. **If** he was **fat,** Rabbi Ḥiyya would **say to them: Go** and **make him thin. As these signs** indicating puberty **sometimes come due to thinness** and **sometimes they come due to fatness.** It is therefore possible that after his bodily shape is properly adjusted this individual will develop the signs indicating puberty and will not have the status of a sexually underdeveloped man.

אֲמַר רַב: הִלְכְתָא בְּכוּלֵּי פִּרְקָא – מֵעֵת לְעֵת. וְעוּלָּא אֲמַר: דִּתְנַן – תְּנַן, וּדְלָא תְּנַן – לָא תְּנַן.

§ **Rav said: The** ***halakha*** **in** this **entire chapter** with regard to all of the places where an age is mentioned in years is that even when the phrase: And one day, is not explicitly noted, they are all calculated **from** the **time** of year of birth **until** that same **time** of year in the age specified. **And Ulla said:** With regard to cases **where we learned** in the mishna a quantity of years including the phrase: And one day, **we learned** that the reference is to full years; **and** with regard to cases **where we did not learn** this phrase, i.e., where a quantity of years is mentioned in the mishna without the phrase: And one day, **we did not learn** it, and part of the final year is equivalent to a whole year.

בִּשְׁלָמָא לְעוּלָּא, הַיְינוּ דְּקָתָנֵי הָכָא "יוֹם אֶחָד" וְהָכָא לָא קָתָנֵי. אֶלָּא לְרַב, לִיתְנֵי!

The Gemara discusses these two opinions. **Granted, according to Ulla, this** is the reason **that** the *tanna* **teaches there,** in previous *mishnayot* (44b, 45a, 45b): And **one day; and here,** in this mishna, the *tanna* **does not teach** this phrase. **But according to Rav, let** the *tanna* be consistent and **teach** this phrase in all cases, including the mishna here.

וְעוֹד, תָּנֵי, רַבִּי יוֹסֵי בֶּן כֵּיפַר אוֹמֵר מִשּׁוּם רַבִּי אֱלִיעֶזֶר: שְׁנַת עֶשְׂרִים שֶׁיָּצְאוּ מִמֶּנָּה שְׁלֹשִׁים יוֹם – הֲרֵי הִיא כִּשְׁנַת עֶשְׂרִים לְכָל דְּבָרֶיהָ. וְכֵן הוֹרָה רַבִּי בְּלוֹד: שְׁנַת שְׁמֹנֶה עֶשְׂרֵה שֶׁיָּצְאוּ מִמֶּנָּה שְׁלֹשִׁים יוֹם – הֲרֵי הִיא כִּשְׁנַת שְׁמֹנֶה עֶשְׂרֵה לְכָל דְּבָרֶיהָ.

**And furthermore, it is taught** in a *baraita* that **Rabbi Yosei ben Keifar**[P] **says in the name of Rabbi Eliezer** with regard to the *halakhot* of a sexually underdeveloped man and a sexually underdeveloped woman: **The twentieth year, of which thirty days have passed,** i.e., from the age of nineteen and thirty days, **is** considered **like the twentieth year in all regards;**[H] **and Rabbi** Yehuda HaNasi **similarly issued** a practical **ruling** of *halakha* **in** the city of **Lod,**[B] that **the eighteenth year of which thirty days have passed is** considered **like the eighteenth year in all regards.**

בִּשְׁלָמָא דְּרַבִּי וּדְרַבִּי יוֹסֵי בֶּן כֵּיפַר לָא קַשְׁיָא, הָא – כְּבֵית שַׁמַּאי, הָא – כְּבֵית הִילֵּל, אֶלָּא לְרַב קַשְׁיָא!

**Granted,** according to the opinion of Ulla, it is **not difficult that Rabbi** Yehuda HaNasi is referring to the eighteenth year whereas **Rabbi Yosei ben Keifar** discusses the twentieth year, as **this** statement of Rabbi Yehuda HaNasi is **in accordance with** the opinion of **Beit Shammai** with regard to the age of a sexually underdeveloped woman, and **that** statement of Rabbi Yosei ben Keifar is **in accordance with** the opinion of **Beit Hillel. But according to** the opinion of **Rav,** who maintains that full years are required for a sexually underdeveloped man or woman, this *baraita* poses **a difficulty.**

### PERSONALITIES

**Rabbi Yosei ben Keifar – רַבִּי יוֹסֵי בֶּן כֵּיפַר:** This Sage from the last generation of *tanna'im* is mentioned in the *Tosefta* and in *baraitot*, although not in the Mishna. He was a primary disciple of Rabbi Elazar ben Shammua, and most of the statements he cites are in this teacher's name. It is related that he was one of the emissaries sent to Babylonia to raise funds for the scholars of Eretz Yisrael. He is grouped together historically with Rabbi Dostai, son of Rabbi Yehuda, and Rabbi Dostai, son of Rabbi Yannai, who were also among the last of the *tanna'im*.

A Sage by the name of Rabbi Yosei ben Keifar is mentioned in relation to an important mission of the Sages of Eretz Yisrael, who wanted to quash the attempts of Ḥananya to determine the calendar outside Eretz Yisrael. Based on the timeline of these events, this was apparently a different Sage of the same name.

### HALAKHA

**The twentieth year of which thirty days have passed is considered like the twentieth year in all regards – שְׁנַת עֶשְׂרִים שֶׁיָּצְאוּ מִמֶּנָּה שְׁלֹשִׁים יוֹם הֲרֵי הִיא כִּשְׁנַת עֶשְׂרִים לְכָל דְּבָרֶיהָ:** If a twenty-year-old woman developed the signs of an *ailonit*, she is considered an adult with regard to performing refusal and similar matters, retroactively from when she was twelve, even if she later grew two hairs (Rema). A woman aged nineteen years and thirty days has the status of a twenty-year-old, as thirty days in a year are considered a year. Some say that she is considered twenty years old only when she is within thirty days of her twentieth birthday (see Rambam *Sefer Nashim*, *Hilkhot Ishut* 2:11; *Shulḥan Arukh*, *Even HaEzer* 155:12).

### BACKGROUND

**Lod – לוֹד:** Lod was one of the oldest towns in Judea. The Sages maintain that Lod dates back to the time of Joshua, son of Nun. Due to its location at the center of the coastal region, it was an important city for many generations.

As it was situated at the heart of a fertile agricultural area, Lod was a commercial center, while due to its position at the crossroads of Eretz Yisrael, it also served as an administrative center. In the talmudic period there was a large Jewish community in Lod, headed by well-known Sages, including the *tanna'im* Rabbi Eliezer ben Hyrcanus the Great and Rabbi Tarfon. Several significant ordinances were instituted in the upper chamber of the house of Nitza, in Lod. After the bar Kokheva revolt, the town remained an important place of Torah, the center for scholars in the south of Eretz Yisrael. Among the great *amora'im* who lived there were Rabbi Yehoshua ben Levi, Rabbi Simlai, Rabbi Yitzḥak bar Naḥmani, Rabbi Aḥa, and Rabbi Shimon ben Pazi and his son, Rabbi Yehuda.

תַּנָּאֵי הִיא, דְּתַנְיָא: שָׁנָה הָאֲמוּרָה בְּקָדָשִׁים, שָׁנָה הָאֲמוּרָה בְּבָתֵּי עָרֵי חוֹמָה, שְׁתֵּי שָׁנִים שֶׁבִּשְׂדֵה אֲחוּזָּה,

The Gemara answers that this matter **is** a dispute between ***tanna'im***, and Rav maintains in accordance with the opinion that full years are required. **As it is taught** in a *baraita*: Full years are required with regard to the period of one **year stated with regard to sacrificial** animals, e.g., "a lamb in its first year" (Leviticus 12:6); the one **year stated with regard to houses of walled cities,**[N] during which one can redeem a house he has sold in a walled city (see Leviticus 25:29); and the **two years** stated **with regard to an ancestral field,**[N] during which one cannot yet redeem an ancestral field he has sold (see Leviticus 25:15).

שֵׁשׁ שָׁנִים שֶׁבְּעֶבֶד עִבְרִי, וְכֵן שֶׁבְּבֵן וְשֶׁבְּבַת – כּוּלָּן מֵעֵת לְעֵת.

The **six years** stated **with regard to a Hebrew slave** (see Exodus 21:2) **and similarly** the years **of a son and of a daughter,** as will be explained, **all of** these are years **from the time** of the first year **until** that same **time** of year in the year specified,[H] i.e., these periods are units of whole years instead of expiring on predetermined dates, as at the end of the calendar year. This supports the opinion of Rav that the years mentioned with regard to a sexually underdeveloped man or woman are full years.

שָׁנָה הָאֲמוּרָה בְּקָדָשִׁים מְנָא לַן? אָמַר רַב אַחָא בַּר יַעֲקֹב: אָמַר קְרָא "כֶּבֶשׂ בֶּן שְׁנָתוֹ" – שְׁנָתוֹ שֶׁלּוֹ, וְלֹא שָׁנָה שֶׁל מִנְיַן עוֹלָם.

The Gemara asks: **From where do we** derive that the one **year stated with regard to sacrificial** animals is calculated by whole years and not by calendar years? **Rav Aḥa bar Ya'akov said** that **the verse states: "A lamb in its first year"** (Leviticus 12:6). Since the verse does not state: A one-year-old lamb, it means **a year** based on calculation of **its** life, **and not a year of the universal count,** i.e., the calendar year.

שָׁנָה הָאֲמוּרָה בְּבָתֵּי עָרֵי חוֹמָה מְנָלַן? אָמַר קְרָא: "עַד תֹּם שְׁנַת מִמְכָּרוֹ" – מִמְכָּרוֹ שֶׁלּוֹ, וְלֹא שְׁנַת שֶׁל מִנְיַן עוֹלָם. שְׁתֵּי שָׁנִים שֶׁבִּשְׂדֵה אֲחוּזָּה מְנָלַן? אָמַר קְרָא: "בְּמִסְפַּר

The Gemara further asks: **From where do we** derive the *halakha* that the one **year stated with regard to houses of walled cities** is calculated by a whole year and not by calendar year? **The verse states:** "Then he may redeem it **within a whole year after it is sold,** for a full year he shall have the right of redemption" (Leviticus 25:29). The verse is referring to a year counted from the day **of its own sale, and not the year of the universal count. From where do we** derive that the **two years** stated **with regard to an ancestral field** are whole years? **The verse states:** "According the number of years after the Jubilee you shall buy from your neighbor, and **according to the number**

**HALAKHA**

**All of these are years from the time of the first year until that same time of year specified** – **כּוּלָּן מֵעֵת לְעֵת**: All the years mentioned with regard to a son and a daughter, valuations, and other *halakhot*, are not counted by lunar years or solar years, but by the calendar, which can be regular or intercalated, in accordance with the decision of the court (Rambam *Sefer Nashim*, *Hilkhot Ishut* 2:21, and *Mishne LaMelekh* there).

**NOTES**

**The one year stated with regard to houses of walled cities** – **שָׁנָה הָאֲמוּרָה בְּבָתֵּי עָרֵי חוֹמָה**: The various *halakhot* of houses of walled cities are discussed in the ninth chapter of tractate *Arakhin*. The source in the Torah for this topic is Leviticus 25:29–30. The basic *halakha* is that if one sells a house located in a walled city, he has the right to redeem that house for up to a year of the sale. If he fails to do so, the house becomes the permanent possession of the purchaser.

**The two years stated with regard to an ancestral field** – **שְׁתֵּי שָׁנִים שֶׁבִּשְׂדֵה אֲחוּזָּה**: The details of the *halakhot* of the sale of ancestral fields are clarified in tractate *Arakhin*. Whoever sells an ancestral field is permitted, and even commanded, to redeem his field from the buyer. But he may not do so within two years of the sale. If he did not redeem the field by the Jubilee Year, the field reverts to the possession of the seller, as the sale of land in Eretz Yisrael is merely temporary, until the Jubilee. When the owner redeems the field from the buyer, the redemption price of the field varies, reflecting the number of years that the field would have remained in the buyer's possession.

It should be noted that only years when the field yields produce are counted; the Sabbatical Year, and likewise years of blight and mildew, are disregarded. By contrast, as one sells the field based on the number of years, not the number of yields, if he sold it at the end of the year when it was full of produce, the purchaser may return it to him two years later when it is empty of produce.

Perek **V**
Daf **48** Amud **a**

שְׁנֵי תְבוּאוֹת יִמְכָּר לָךְ" – פְּעָמִים שֶׁאַתָּה מוֹכֵר שְׁלֹשָׁה תְּבוּאוֹת בִּשְׁתֵּי שָׁנִים.

**of years of the crops he shall sell to you"** (Leviticus 25:15). The plural form of both "years" and "crops" indicates that the number of years does not necessarily correspond to the quantity of crops. Consequently, **sometimes you** might **sell three** yields of **crops in two years.**[N] If one purchases a field in the summer, when the produce has not yet been harvested, and he harvests that yield and subsequently grows and harvests two more crops before the completion of the whole two years, he will have gained three yields in less than two years.

**NOTES**

**Sometimes you might sell three yields of crops in two years** – **פְּעָמִים שֶׁאַתָּה מוֹכֵר שְׁלֹשָׁה תְּבוּאוֹת בִּשְׁתֵּי שָׁנִים**: Rashi explains that the plural term "years" indicates a minimum of two. When the verse states "crops," this means all the crops of two years, i.e., even a third yield that grew in those two years (see Rashi and *Tosafot* on *Arakhin* 18b).

שֵׁשׁ שָׁנָה שֶׁבְּעֶבֶד עִבְרִי מְנָלַן? אֲמַר קְרָא: ״שֵׁשׁ שָׁנִים יַעֲבֹד וּבַשְּׁבִיעִת״ – וּבַשְּׁבִיעִית נַמִי יַעֲבוֹד.

The Gemara asks: **From where do we** derive the *halakha* that the **six years** stated **with regard to a Hebrew slave** is calculated by whole years? The Gemara answers that **the verse states: "Six years he shall work, and in the seventh** he shall go out free for nothing" (Exodus 21:2). The word "and" in the phrase **"and in the seventh"** indicates that **he shall also work**[N] in the seventh calendar year, if six full years have not passed since he was sold. For example, if he was sold in the month of Nisan, it means that five years and six months have passed when Tishrei, the first month of the seventh year, arrives; he has not yet completed six years of service, and he must work in this seventh calendar year as well, until the date on which he was sold.

שֶׁבַּבֵּן וְשֶׁבַּבַּת לְמַאי הִלְכְתָא? אָמַר רַב גִּידֵּל, אָמַר רַב: לְעִנְיַן עֲרָכִין. וְרַב יוֹסֵף אָמַר: לְפִרְקִין דְּ״יוֹצֵא דוֹפֶן״.

The *baraita* mentions the years **of a son and of a daughter** among those calculated as full years. The Gemara asks: **With regard to what *halakha*** is this stated? **Rav Giddel says** that **Rav says: With regard to valuations,** i.e., the age of a valuated male or female is calculated in whole years from the date of his birth, not by calendar years. **And Rav Yosef says:** The *halakha* is stated **with regard to** the matters taught in **our** fifth **chapter** in tractate *Nidda,* which is named after its opening words: ***Yotze Dofen,*** meaning an offspring born by caesarean section. In other words, when a mishna in this chapter mentions years, it means full years, even when it does not state this explicitly.

אֲמַר לֵיהּ אַבַּיֵי: מִי פְּלִיגַתְּ? אֲמַר לֵיהּ: לָא, הוּא אֲמַר חֲדָא, וַאֲנָא אָמִינָא חֲדָא, וְלָא פְּלִיגִינַן.

**Abaye said to** Rav Yosef: **Do you** and Rav **disagree** with regard to this matter? In other words, as you interpreted the mention of a son and a daughter differently, does each of you reject the halakhic application of the other? Rav Yosef **said to** Abaye: **No, he said one** matter, **and I said one** different matter, **but we do not disagree.**

וְהָכִי נַמִי מִסְתַּבְּרָא, דְּאִי סָלְקָא דַּעְתָּךְ פְּלִיגִי, מַאן דַּאֲמַר לַעֲרָכִין לָא אָמַר לְ״יוֹצֵא דוֹפֶן״? וְהָאָמַר רַב: הִלְכְתָא בְּכוּלָּהּ פִּרְקִין מֵעֵת לְעֵת!

The Gemara notes: **And this, too, stands to reason, as if it enters your mind** that they **disagree** with regard to this matter, then **the one who said** full years are required **for** determining **valuations** does **not say** that full years are necessary **for** the *halakhot* of this chapter, ***Yotze Dofen.* But doesn't Rav say,** like Rav Yosef, that **the *halakha* in** this **entire chapter** with regard to all of the places where an age is mentioned in years is that even when the phrase: And one day, is not explicitly noted, they are all calculated **from the time** of year of birth **until** that same **time** of year in the age specified, not by calendar years?

אֶלָּא לְמַאן דַּאֲמַר לַעֲרָכִין, מַאי טַעְמָא לָא אָמַר לְ״יוֹצֵא דוֹפֶן״? דּוּמְיָא דְּהָנָךְ, מַה הָנָךְ דִּכְתִיבָן, אַף הָנֵי נַמִי – דִּכְתִיבָן.

The Gemara asks: **But** if that is correct, then **according to** Rav, who is **the one who said** that full years are required **for** determining **valuations, what is the reason** that **he does not say** in his interpretation of the *baraita* that full years are required **for** the *halakhot* of ***Yotze Dofen*?** The Gemara answers: Rav maintains that the years of a son and of a daughter mentioned in the *baraita* are **similar to those** other cases mentioned in the *baraita*: **Just as those** numbers of years **are written** in the Torah, **so too these** years of a son and of a daughter are referring to matters **where** the years **are written** in the Torah, i.e., the years of valuations, unlike the topics discussed in *Yotze Dofen,* where the years are not mentioned explicitly in the Torah.

**NOTES**

**And in the seventh, and in the seventh indicates that he shall also work – וּבַשְּׁבִיעִת וּבַשְּׁבִיעִית נַמִי יַעֲבוֹד:** The commentaries disagree concerning this derivation from the verse: "Six years he shall work and in the seventh he shall go out free for nothing." The basic issue is whether the phrase "and in the seventh" should be read as part of the previous phrase, without a comma, i.e., six years he shall work and in the seventh, or whether it is part of the second clause of the verse.

According to Rashi, the phrase "and in the seventh" is referring back to the previous part of the verse, i.e., he shall work six full years and even in the seventh calendar year, as his six years end on the same date they begun (see Maharam and Maharsha). Others maintain that the phrase "and in the seventh" should be read together with the end of the verse. According to this opinion, the Gemara is saying that one should not think that thirty days of the sixth year is enough, despite the fact that thirty days of a year generally is considered a year, as "in the seventh he shall go out free for nothing," i.e., he must work until the very beginning of the seventh year (*Tosafot*, as explained by Maharsha and Maharam).

וְאִידָּךְ – הַאי "שֶׁבַּבֵּן וְשֶׁבַּבַּת", "שֶׁבַּזָּכָר וְשֶׁבַּנְּקֵבָה" מִבָּעֵי לֵיהּ!

The Gemara asks: **And** how would **the other** *amora*, Rav Yosef, respond to this contention? The Gemara answers: He would maintain that if the *baraita* were referring to the years of valuations, which are written in the Torah, then **this** expression in the *baraita*: **Of a son and of a daughter,** is unsuitable. Rather, the *baraita* **should have** stated: **Of the male and of the female,** which are the terms the Torah uses with regard to valuations, whereas the terms: Son and daughter, are used in *Yotze Dofen*.

אָמַר רַב יִצְחָק בַּר נַחְמָנִי, אָמַר רַבִּי אֶלְעָזָר: הֲלָכָה כְּרַבִּי יוֹסֵי בֶּן כֵּיפַר שֶׁאָמַר מִשּׁוּם רַבִּי אֱלִיעֶזֶר. אֲמַר רַבִּי זֵירָא: אֶזְכֶּה וְאֵיסַק וְאֶגְמַר לִשְׁמַעְתָּא מִפּוּמֵיהּ דְּמָרָא!

§ **Rav Yitzḥak bar Naḥmani says** that **Rabbi Elazar**[P] **says:** The ***halakha*** is **in accordance with** the opinion of **Rabbi Yosei ben Keifar, who said** his ruling **in the name of Rabbi Eliezer,** that a man nineteen years and thirty days of age who has not developed signs of puberty is deemed a sexually underdeveloped man. In this regard, the Gemara relates that **Rabbi Zeira**[P] **said:** May it be God's will that **I merit to ascend** to Eretz Yisrael, **and** that **I learn** this ***halakha*** **from the mouth of its Master,** Rabbi Elazar.

כִּי סְלֵיק אַשְׁכְּחֵיהּ לְרַבִּי אֶלְעָזָר, אֲמַר לֵיהּ: אָמְרַתְּ הֲלָכָה כְּרַבִּי יוֹסֵי בֶּן כֵּיפַר? אֲמַר לֵיהּ: מִסְתַּבְּרָא אָמְרִי, מִדְּכוּלֵּיהּ פִּירְקִין תָּנֵי "יוֹם אֶחָד", וְהָכָא לָא קָתָנֵי – שְׁמַע מִינַּהּ מִסְתַּבְּרָא כְּוָתֵיהּ.

The Gemara recounts that **when** Rabbi Zeira eventually **ascended** to Eretz Yisrael **he** indeed **found Rabbi Elazar** and **said to him: Did you say** that the ***halakha*** is **in accordance with** the opinion of **Rabbi Yosei ben Keifar?** Rabbi Elazar **said to him: I said** that it **stands to reason** that the *halakha* is in accordance with his opinion. He elaborated: **From** the fact **that** throughout **the entire chapter** the Mishna **teaches:** And **one day, but here,** in the last mishna, **it does not teach** this phrase, one can **conclude from it** that it **stands to reason** that there is a reason for this discrepancy, **in accordance with the opinion of** Rabbi Yosei ben Keifar.

הדרן עלך יוצא דופן

PERSONALITIES

Rabbi Elazar – רַבִּי אֶלְעָזָר: In the Gemara, citations of Rabbi Elazar, with no patronymic, refer to Rabbi Elazar ben Pedat, a second-generation *amora* in Eretz Yisrael. He was born in Babylonia, and was a student of both Rav and Shmuel. In his youth, he immigrated to Eretz Yisrael, married there, and became the primary student of Rabbi Yoḥanan. The connection between them was so close that when the Gemara raises a contradiction between their statements, it also indicates surprise that they would hold different opinions.

Rabbi Zeira – רַבִּי זֵירָא: One of the greatest of the third generation of Babylonian *amora'im*, Rabbi Zeira was educated in the Babylonian tradition and studied mainly with the disciples of Rav and Shmuel. He immigrated to Eretz Yisrael, where he studied under Rabbi Yoḥanan and was a colleague of Rabbi Yoḥanan's foremost disciples. When Rabbi Zeira reached Eretz Yisrael he was extremely impressed by the method of learning he found there, which he adopted in full. Accordingly, he undertook one hundred fasts to help him forget the Babylonian method of learning. He also fasted so that the fires of Gehenna should not rule over him. When he performed tests to see if fire would affect him, the calves of his legs were burned. For this reason he became known as the short man with the scorched calves (*Bava Metzia* 85a). Rabbi Zeira was famous for his great piety, his modesty, and his affable, accommodating nature. He was greatly loved and honored by his peers. Rabbi Zeira had many disciples throughout Eretz Yisrael, and his statements are widely quoted in both the Babylonian Talmud and the Jerusalem Talmud. He had a son who was also a Sage, Rabbi Ahava.

# Summary of **Perek V**

This chapter discussed the dispute between *tanna'im* as to whether a woman who gave birth via caesarean section has the status of a woman after natural childbirth. The dispute focuses on the ramifications both with regard to impurity and purity, and the offerings she is obligated to bring.

Some maintain that the *halakha* regarding the status of a woman after a caesarean section is derived from the verse: "If a woman conceives and gives birth" (Leviticus 12:2), which teaches that for the *halakhot* of a woman after childbirth to apply, she must give birth from the same place where she conceived. This interpretation excludes a birth by caesarean section.

Others contend that the phrase: "But if she gives birth to a female" (Leviticus 12:5), teaches that a birth by caesarean section has the status of childbirth in all respects. This derivation is based on the explanation that once the Torah has stated: "If a woman conceives and gives birth to a male," there was no need for it to add: "And if she gives birth to a female," as it could simply have written: "And if it is a female." The seemingly superfluous mention of the phrase "gives birth" indicates that other types of birth are also included, i.e., a caesarean section.

With regard to the definition of a menstruating woman, who is rendered impure through the emission of blood, the Sages derive from the verse: "And if a woman has an issue, and her issue in her flesh is blood" (Leviticus 15:19), that it is the blood which emerges from the uterus that renders a woman impure. Furthermore, it is derived from the phrase "her issue in her flesh is blood" that once the blood reaches the vagina, even if it did not leave the woman's body, she has the status of a menstruating woman. In this regard the impurity of a menstruating woman differs from that of both a *zav* and a man who experienced a seminal emission, about whom it is stated: "When any man has an issue out of his flesh" (Leviticus 15:2), and: "And if the flow of seed go out from a man" (Leviticus 15:16), which indicate that the flow must go out of their bodies for them to become ritually impure.

It was further clarified in this chapter that the reference to a woman in the verse "And if a woman has an issue" refers to a girl or woman of any age, and it even includes the case of a one-day-old baby girl who emitted blood; she too becomes impure.

In addition, the chapter also addressed the developmental stages of a woman and how they are relevant to various areas of *halakha*: Until what age is a girl considered a minor? When does she reach the age of young womanhood? When does she achieve grown womanhood? In this context, the chapter listed the various physical signs indicating puberty and explored their halakhic significance.

# Introduction to **Perek VI**

*And if a woman has an issue, and her issue in her flesh is blood, she shall be in her menstruation seven days, and whoever touches her shall be impure until the evening.*

(Leviticus 15:19)

A woman is rendered impure as a menstruating woman by Torah law only when she actually sees a discharge of blood that emanated from her uterus, not merely blood on her body or a stain on her garment. This is derived from the verse: "And if a woman has an issue, and her issue in her flesh is blood" (Leviticus 15:19). The phrase "her issue in her flesh" indicates that she becomes impure due to menstruation only if she senses that she emitted blood from her uterus, as opposed to merely discovering a stain.

This is the *halakha* only with regard to Torah law. Due to various concerns, the Sages decreed that a woman who discovers a stain is likewise impure. The extent and details of this *halakha* are the subject of a later chapter, Chapter Eight. One of the important issues involves the question of timing. By rabbinic decree, a woman who discovers a stain has to assume an emission of blood, but she does not know when this emission occurred. As a result, she does not know from when she should begin counting her seven menstrual days and the subsequent eleven days of *ziva*.

This issue in turn leads to various problematic cases, e.g., that of a woman who discovered a stain on a garment that she wore for three days during the days on which she can assume the status of a *zava*. If the size of the stain is equivalent to the area of at least three split beans, perhaps one should be concerned that this stain is due to three emissions on three days, each of which was the requisite measure of at least one split bean. If so, the woman would be a greater *zava*.

Before these issues are addressed, the chapter first completes the discussion of signs of maturation that began in the previous chapter. In this regard, the chapter deals with the appearance of the lower sign of puberty, two pubic hairs, as well as the upper sign, the development of the breasts. The assumption, according to one opinion among the *tanna'im*, is that the lower signs invariably appear first. The question is raised with regard to the status of a female whose upper sign has appeared, but no pubic hairs are discovered upon examination.

The chapter also deals tangentially with other matters where there are two asymmetrical *halakhot*. They are mentioned together here for structural reasons, due to the similar form of the various rulings, and they involve varied areas of *halakha*, such as ritual purity and impurity, judges and witnesses, tithes and gifts for the poor.

מתני׳ בָּא סִימָן הַתַּחְתּוֹן עַד שֶׁלֹּא בָּא הָעֶלְיוֹן – אוֹ חוֹלֶצֶת אוֹ מִתְיַבֶּמֶת.

**MISHNA** **If the lower sign**[N] of puberty, two pubic hairs, **appeared** in a young woman **before the upper** sign,[H] development of the breasts, **appeared,** then she is an adult, as the pubic hairs are an unequivocal sign. Therefore, if her childless husband died and she came before her husband's brother [*yavam*] for levirate marriage, **she either performs the ritual through which a *yavam* frees a *yevama* of her levirate bonds [*ḥalitza*] or enters into levirate marriage** with her husband's brother.

בָּא הָעֶלְיוֹן עַד שֶׁלֹּא בָּא הַתַּחְתּוֹן, אַף עַל פִּי שֶׁאִי אֶפְשָׁר, רַבִּי מֵאִיר אוֹמֵר: לֹא חוֹלֶצֶת וְלֹא מִתְיַבֶּמֶת,

If **the upper** sign indicating puberty **appeared before the lower** sign **appeared,** i.e., the two pubic hairs are not visible, **although that** order of development is apparently **impossible, Rabbi Meir says:** In fact, it is possible for the breasts to develop before the growth of two pubic hairs, and the concern is that the two hairs did not grow and fall out but rather they never grew in the first place, which would mean that she remains a minor. Therefore, if her childless husband dies, **she neither performs *ḥalitza* nor does she enter into levirate marriage** with her husband's brother.

וַחֲכָמִים אוֹמְרִים: אוֹ חוֹלֶצֶת אוֹ מִתְיַבֶּמֶת. מִפְּנֵי שֶׁאָמְרוּ, אֶפְשָׁר לַתַּחְתּוֹן לָבֹא עַד שֶׁלֹּא בָּא הָעֶלְיוֹן, אֲבָל אִי אֶפְשָׁר לָעֶלְיוֹן לָבֹא עַד שֶׁלֹּא בָּא הַתַּחְתּוֹן.

**And the Rabbis say:** She has reached majority, and therefore if her childless husband dies **she either performs *ḥalitza* or enters into levirate marriage** with her husband's brother. That is **due to** the fact **that** the Sages **said:** It is **possible for the lower** sign of puberty **to appear before the upper** sign **appears; but** it is **impossible for the upper** sign **to appear before the lower** sign **appears.**

גמ׳ "אַף עַל פִּי שֶׁאִי אֶפְשָׁר", וַהֲלֹא בָּא! "בָּא" – לְרַבִּי מֵאִיר, "אַף עַל פִּי שֶׁאִי אֶפְשָׁר" – לְרַבָּנַן.

**GEMARA** The mishna teaches that Rabbi Meir and the Rabbis disagree with regard to the *halakha* when the upper sign of puberty appears before the lower sign. The mishna stated about that case: **Although that** order of development is **impossible.** The Gemara raises a difficulty: **But** the mishna explicitly states that it is referring to a situation where the upper sign **did appear** before the lower one. The Gemara explains: When the mishna states that it **did appear,** that is **according to** the opinion of **Rabbi Meir,** who maintains that such an occurrence is possible, whereas when the mishna teaches: **Although that** order of development is **impossible,** it is referring **to** the opinion of **the Rabbis,** who contend that it is not possible.

וְלִתְנֵי "בָּא הָעֶלְיוֹן, רַבִּי מֵאִיר אוֹמֵר: לֹא חוֹלֶצֶת וְלֹא מִתְיַבֶּמֶת. וַחֲכָמִים אוֹמְרִים: אוֹ חוֹלֶצֶת אוֹ מִתְיַבֶּמֶת", וַאֲנָא יָדַעְנָא מִשּׁוּם דְּאִי אֶפְשָׁר הוּא!

The Gemara objects: **But** why is it necessary at all to mention the phrase: Although that order of development is impossible. Instead, let the mishna simply **teach:** If **the upper** sign of puberty **appeared, Rabbi Meir says: She neither performs *ḥalitza* nor does she enter into levirate marriage** with her husband's brother; **and the Rabbis say: She either performs *ḥalitza* or enters into levirate marriage** with her husband's brother. **And I would know** that the ruling of the Rabbis is **due to** the fact **that it is impossible** for the upper sign of puberty to appear before the lower sign.

אִי לָא תְּנָא "אַף עַל פִּי שֶׁאִי אֶפְשָׁר", הֲוָה אָמֵינָא: רוֹב נָשִׁים – תַּחְתּוֹן אָתֵי בְּרֵישָׁא, וּמִיעוּט – עֶלְיוֹן אָתֵי בְּרֵישָׁא. וְרַבִּי מֵאִיר לְטַעְמֵיהּ – דְּחָיֵישׁ לְמִיעוּטָא, וְרַבָּנַן לְטַעְמַיְיהוּ – דְּלָא חָיְישִׁי – לְמִיעוּטָא.

The Gemara explains: **If** the mishna **had not taught: Although that** order of development is **impossible, I would say** that with regard to **most women the lower** sign **appears first,** before the upper sign; **but** in **a minority of women, the upper** sign **appears first. And Rabbi Meir,** who rules that she is a minor who may not perform either *ḥalitza* or enter into levirate marriage, conforms **to his** standard line of **reasoning, that one must be concerned for the minority.** In other words, Rabbi Meir takes into account the minority of women in whom the upper sign appears first, and therefore he considers her to be a minor. **And the Rabbis** likewise conform to their standard line of **reasoning that one need not be concerned for the minority,** and therefore they consider the young woman to have reached majority.

**NOTES**

**The lower sign** – **סִימָן הַתַּחְתּוֹן**: This sign is the growth of two pubic hairs. It is called the lower sign because it is located in the lower portion of the body, whereas the upper sign is located in the upper portion of the body. The specifics of this sign are not stated here, although they are discussed in somewhat further detail later in the chapter. The Rambam writes (*Sefer Nashim, Hilkhot Ishut* 2:17) that the pubic hairs constitute a sign of having reached majority only if certain conditions are met. First, they must be located in the pubic area, broadly defined. In addition, the two hairs must be in close proximity to each other. The hairs must also have follicles, although they can share one follicle. If there are two follicles alongside one another, they constitute a sign even if they do not contain hair, based on the assumption that there are no follicles without hair, and therefore there must have been hairs that fell out.

**HALAKHA**

**If the lower sign appeared before the upper sign** – **בָּא סִימָן הַתַּחְתּוֹן עַד שֶׁלֹּא בָּא הָעֶלְיוֹן**: A girl aged at least twelve years and one day who developed two hairs on her lower body in the places where hair typically grows has the status of a young woman (Rambam *Sefer Nashim, Hilkhot Ishut* 2:1).

וְהָנֵי מִילֵּי – בִּסְתָמָא, אֲבָל הֵיכָא דִּבְדַקְןָ וְלָא אַשְׁכַּחַן – אֵימַר מוֹדוּ לֵיהּ רַבָּנַן לְרַבִּי מֵאִיר דְּעֶלְיוֹן קָדֵים,

**And this statement,** that one can rely on the assumption that if a woman has the upper sign then she certainly has the lower sign, while the minority of cases are not taken into account, applies only **in an ordinary** case, where the woman was not examined to determine if she had the lower sign. **But** in a case **where we examined** her **and did not find** the lower sign, one might **say** that **the Rabbis concede to Rabbi Meir that** the **upper** sign appeared **before** the lower sign, and therefore she neither performs *ḥalitza* nor enters into levirate marriage with her husband's brother.

קָא מַשְׁמַע לָן דְּאִי אֶפְשָׁר. וַדַּאי אָתֵי, וּמִנְתַּר הוּא דְּנְתַר.

Therefore, the mishna **teaches us that** according to the Rabbis it is **impossible** for the upper sign to precede the lower sign, which means that even if she was examined and no lower sign was found, the assumption is that the two hairs of the lower sign had **certainly appeared, but** later they **fell out.**

בִּשְׁלָמָא לְרַבִּי מֵאִיר – הַיְינוּ דִּכְתִיב ״שָׁדַיִם נָכֹנוּ וּשְׂעָרֵךְ צִמֵּחַ״, אֶלָּא לְרַבָּנַן – אִיפְּכָא מִבָּעֵי לֵיהּ! הָכִי קָאָמַר: כֵּיוָן שֶׁ״שָּׁדַיִם נָכֹנוּ״ – בְּיָדוּעַ שֶׁ״שְּׂעָרֵךְ צִמֵּחַ״.

The Gemara raises a difficulty: **Granted, according to** the opinion of **Rabbi Meir,** who holds that it is possible for the upper sign to precede the lower, **that** accounts for that verse **which is written** with regard to a maturing young woman: "And you increased and grew up, and you came to excellent beauty; **your breasts were fashioned, and your hair was grown"** (Ezekiel 16:7). This verse mentions the upper sign before the lower sign. **But according to** the opinion of **the Rabbis,** the verse **should have** said the **reverse,** first stating "your hair has grown," and then stating "your breasts were fashioned." The Gemara answers that **this** is what the verse **is saying: Since your breasts were fashioned, it is known that your hair was** already **grown.**

בִּשְׁלָמָא לְרַבִּי מֵאִיר – הַיְינוּ דִּכְתִיב ״בַּעְשׂוֹת מִמִּצְרַיִם דַּדַּיִךְ לְמַעַן שְׁדֵי נְעוּרָיִךְ״, אֶלָּא לְרַבָּנַן – אִיפְּכָא מִבָּעֵי לֵיהּ!

The Gemara raises a further difficulty: **Granted, according to** the opinion of **Rabbi Meir,** this accounts for **that which is written: "When they from Egypt bruised your breasts for the sprouting forth of your young womanhood"** (Ezekiel 23:21). This verse, which compares the Jewish people to a promiscuous girl, describes how, in her childhood, Egyptian men would play with her by pressing her breasts in order to engage in licentious sexual intercourse with her when she became a young woman, i.e., once the pubic hairs that indicate puberty developed. This indicates that it is possible for the upper sign to appear before the lower sign. **But according to** the opinion of **the Rabbis,** the verse **should have** said the **reverse.**

הָכִי קָאָמַר: כֵּיוָן שֶׁבָּאוּ דַּדַּיִךְ – בְּיָדוּעַ שֶׁבָּאוּ נְעוּרַיִךְ. וְאִיבָּעֵית אֵימָא: מַאי ״שְׁדֵי״ – כּוּלָּהּ בְּדַדֵּי כְּתִיב, וְהָכִי קָאָמַר הַקָּדוֹשׁ בָּרוּךְ הוּא לְיִשְׂרָאֵל:

The Gemara similarly answers that **this** is what the verse **is saying: Since your breasts appeared, it is known that** the pubic hairs, which are the sign of **your young womanhood, have** already **appeared.** Or **if you wish, say** instead: **What** is the meaning of the phrase: **The sprouting forth of** [*shedei*] your young womanhood? It is not speaking of the lower sign, but rather of the upper sign, i.e., the **entire** verse **is written** in reference **to the breasts,** *shadayim* in Hebrew. **And this** is what **the Holy One, Blessed be He, is saying to the Jewish people:**

Perek **VI**
Daf **48** Amud **b**

אִיכְּרְפוּ דַּדַּיִךְ – לָא הַדְרַתְּ בָּךְ, אִישְׁתְּדוּ דַּדַּיִךְ – נַמִי לָא הַדְרַתְּ בָּךְ.

Although **your breasts began to develop, you** still **did not reform** your ways, and you continued to act licentiously. And furthermore, even when **your breasts grew fully, you also did not reform** your ways.

דְּכוּלֵּי עָלְמָא מִיהָא – אַתַּחְתּוֹן סָמְכִינַן, מְנָלַן? אָמַר רַב יְהוּדָה, אָמַר רַב, וְכֵן תָּנָא דְּבֵי רַבִּי יִשְׁמָעֵאל: אָמַר קְרָא "אִישׁ אוֹ אִשָּׁה כִּי יַעֲשׂוּ מִכָּל חַטֹּאת הָאָדָם" – הִשְׁוָה הַכָּתוּב אִשָּׁה לְאִישׁ לְכָל עוֹנָשִׁין שֶׁבַּתּוֹרָה, מָה אִישׁ – בְּסִימָן אֶחָד, אַף אִשָּׁה – בְּסִימָן אֶחָד.

§ The Gemara asks: **In any event, everyone,** both Rabbi Meir and the Rabbis, agrees that **we rely on the lower** sign. **From where do we** derive that we rely exclusively on the lower sign and do not require the appearance of the upper sign as well? **Rav Yehuda said** that **Rav said, and likewise** a Sage of **the school of Rabbi Yishmael taught: The verse states: "A man or woman, when they commit any of the sins of men"** (Numbers 5:6). **The Torah** thereby **rendered a woman equal to a man with regard to all punishments of the Torah. Just as a man** is considered to have reached majority based **on one sign,** i.e., the lower sign of two pubic hairs, **so too, a woman** reaches majority based **on one sign,** the lower sign.

וְאֵימָא: אוֹ הַאי אוֹ הַאי! כְּאִישׁ, מָה אִישׁ – תַּחְתּוֹן וְלֹא עֶלְיוֹן, אַף אִשָּׁה – תַּחְתּוֹן וְלֹא עֶלְיוֹן.

The Gemara raises a difficulty: **But** one can **say** that although a woman's status, like that of a man, depends on one sign, in the case of a woman she reaches majority **either** through **this,** the lower sign, **or that,** the upper sign. From where is it derived that it must be specifically the lower sign? The Gemara answers: This is based on the same comparison of men and women. Her *halakha* is **like** that **of a man: Just as a man** reaches majority based on the **lower** sign **and not** the **upper** sign, as this is not applicable to him, **so too, a woman** reaches majority based on the **lower** sign **and not** the **upper** sign.

תַּנְיָא נָמֵי הָכִי, אָמַר רַבִּי אֱלִיעֶזֶר בְּרַבִּי צָדוֹק, כָּךְ הָיוּ מְפָרְשִׁין בְּיַבְנֶה, וְאָמְרוּ: כֵּיוָן שֶׁבָּא תַּחְתּוֹן – שׁוּב אֵין מַשְׁגִּיחִין עַל עֶלְיוֹן.

The Gemara notes that **this** *halakha*, that the lower sign is sufficient by itself for a woman, **is also taught** in a *baraita*. **Rabbi Eliezer, son of Rabbi Tzadok, said:** This is **how** the Sages **would explain it** in the study hall of **Yavne. They said:** Once the **lower** sign has **appeared, we no longer concern ourselves with** the appearance of the **upper** sign[H] in order to establish a woman's status, as she is considered to have reached her majority by virtue of the lower sign.

תַּנְיָא, רַבָּן שִׁמְעוֹן בֶּן גַּמְלִיאֵל אוֹמֵר: בְּנוֹת כְּרַכִּים – תַּחְתּוֹן מְמַהֵר לָבֹא, מִפְּנֵי שֶׁרְגִילוֹת בְּמֶרְחֲצָאוֹת. בְּנוֹת כְּפָרִים – עֶלְיוֹן מְמַהֵר לָבֹא, מִפְּנֵי שֶׁטּוֹחֲנוֹת בָּרֵחַיִם.

§ It **is taught** in a *baraita*, with regard to the appearance of signs indicating puberty in young women, that **Rabban Shimon ben Gamliel says:**[N] In the case of young **women** who reside in **cities,** the **lower** sign **appears** more **quickly** than the upper sign, **because they frequent the bathhouses,** which stimulates the growth of the hair. By contrast, in the case of young **women** who reside in **villages,** the **upper** sign **appears** more **quickly** than the lower sign, **because they grind with mills,**[N] which develops their breasts.

רַבִּי שִׁמְעוֹן בֶּן אֶלְעָזָר אוֹמֵר: בְּנוֹת עֲשִׁירִים – צַד יָמִין מְמַהֵר לָבֹא, שֶׁנִּישּׁוֹף בְּאַפִּקְרִיסוּתָן. בְּנוֹת עֲנִיִּים – צַד שְׂמֹאל מְמַהֵר לָבֹא, מִפְּנֵי שֶׁשּׁוֹאֲבוֹת כַּדֵּי מַיִם עֲלֵיהֶן, וְאִיבָּעֵית אֵימָא: מִפְּנֵי שֶׁנּוֹשְׂאִין אֲחֵיהֶן עַל גַּסֵּיהֶן.

**Rabbi Shimon ben Elazar says:**[N] There are differences in the rate of development of the breasts. In the case of **the daughters of the wealthy,** the growth of the breast on the **right side arrives** more **quickly** than that of the left side, **as it rubs against their upper body cloaks,** which are worn by the wealthy. By contrast, in the case of **the daughters of the poor,** the growth of the breast on the **left side arrives** more **quickly** than that of the right side, **because they draw jugs of water on** that side. **And if you wish, say** instead that the left breast develops more quickly **because they carry their** younger **brothers on their** left **sides.**

תָּנוּ רַבָּנַן, צַד שְׂמֹאל קוֹדֵם לְצַד יָמִין, רַבִּי חֲנִינָא בֶּן אֲחִי רַבִּי יְהוֹשֻׁעַ אוֹמֵר: מֵעוֹלָם לֹא קָדַם צַד שְׂמֹאל לְצַד יָמִין, חוּץ מֵאַחַת שֶׁהָיְתָה בִּשְׁכוּנָתִי, שֶׁקָּדַם צַד שְׂמֹאל לְצַד יָמִין, וְחָזַר לְאֵיתָנוֹ.

**The Sages taught** in a *baraita*: The growth of the breast on the **left side** arrives **before** that of the **right side. Rabbi Ḥanina, son of the brother of Rabbi Yehoshua, says:** It **never** occurred that the growth of the breast on the **left side** arrived **before** that of the **right side, except for** the case of **one** young woman **who was in my neighborhood, as** the growth of the breast on her **left side** arrived **before** that of the **right side, and** later the right breast **returned to its normal condition** and developed normally.

**NOTES**

**Rabban Shimon ben Gamliel says – רַבָּן שִׁמְעוֹן בֶּן גַּמְלִיאֵל אוֹמֵר:** There are various explanations among the commentaries with regard to the opinion of Rabban Shimon ben Gamliel, as well as the subsequent opinion of Rabbi Shimon ben Elazar, and the relationship between their statements and the rulings of Rabbi Meir and the Rabbis in the mishna.

Some contend that Rabban Shimon ben Gamliel disagrees both with the opinion of the Rabbis, who hold that the lower sign indicating puberty always appears first, and with the opinion of Rabbi Meir, as neither of them accept his distinction between young women who reside in villages and those who live in cities (*Tosafot*; *Tosefot HaRosh*).

Others maintain that Rabban Shimon ben Gamliel and Rabbi Shimon ben Elazar fundamentally agree with the Rabbis, that the appearance of the upper sign indicates the appearance of the lower one as well. Rabban Shimon ben Gamliel merely qualifies their opinion, claiming that one relies on the upper sign alone only in the case of young women who reside in cities. Rabbi Shimon ben Elazar adds another stipulation, that one relies on the upper sign only with regard to the right breast in the case of the daughters of the wealthy, and the left breast in the case of the daughters of the poor (Rashba; Meiri).

**The upper sign appears more quickly than the lower because they grind with mills – עֶלְיוֹן מְמַהֵר לָבֹא מִפְּנֵי שֶׁטּוֹחֲנוֹת בָּרֵחַיִם:** Since grinding requires extensive movement of the arms, young women residing in villages, who regularly engage in this activity, will have their breasts develop more quickly. Therefore, in these cases the upper sign indicating puberty appears before the lower sign (Rashi). By contrast, girls who live in cities frequent the bathhouses, which stimulates the growth of pubic hair. Consequently, in their case the lower sign appears first.

Traditional hand mill

**Rabbi Shimon ben Elazar says – רַבִּי שִׁמְעוֹן בֶּן אֶלְעָזָר אוֹמֵר:** The practical ramification of this observation is that if the left breast atypically developed first in the case of the daughters of the wealthy, this is not considered a sign indicating puberty but a chance occurrence (Rashba; Meiri).

**HALAKHA**

**Once the lower sign appeared we no longer concern ourselves with the upper sign – כֵּיוָן שֶׁבָּא תַּחְתּוֹן שׁוּב אֵין מַשְׁגִּיחִין עַל עֶלְיוֹן:** A girl who is twelve years old or younger is considered a minor, regardless of what signs indicating puberty she has developed. Once she is twelve and one day old she is considered to have reached majority as soon as the lower sign appears, and there is no concern about the appearance of any other signs. This is in accordance with the tradition that Rabbi Eliezer, son of Rabbi Tzadok, cited in the name of the Sages of Yavne (Rambam *Sefer Nashim*, *Hilkhot Ishut* 2:8).

תָּנוּ רַבָּנַן, כׇּל הַנִּבְדָּקוֹת – נִבְדָּקוֹת עַל פִּי נָשִׁים, וְכֵן הָיָה רַבִּי אֱלִיעֶזֶר מוֹסֵר לְאִשְׁתּוֹ, וְרַבִּי יִשְׁמָעֵאל מוֹסֵר לְאִמּוֹ.

§ **The Sages taught** in a *baraita*: **All** girls who **are examined** to determine whether or not their signs indicating puberty have appeared **are examined based on** the testimony of **women.**[NH] **And likewise, Rabbi Eliezer** would follow this *halakha* in practice and **give** the girls **to his wife** to examine, **and Rabbi Yishmael** would similarly **give** the girls **to his mother** to examine.

רַבִּי יְהוּדָה אוֹמֵר: לִפְנֵי הַפֶּרֶק וּלְאַחַר הַפֶּרֶק – נָשִׁים בּוֹדְקוֹת אוֹתָן, תּוֹךְ הַפֶּרֶק – אֵין נָשִׁים בּוֹדְקוֹת אוֹתָן, שֶׁאֵין מַשִּׂיאִין סְפֵקוֹת עַל פִּי נָשִׁים. רַבִּי שִׁמְעוֹן אוֹמֵר: אַף תּוֹךְ הַפֶּרֶק – נָשִׁים בּוֹדְקוֹת אוֹתָן. וְנֶאֱמֶנֶת אִשָּׁה לְהַחְמִיר אֲבָל לֹא לְהָקֵל.

The *baraita* continues: **Rabbi Yehuda says: Before the** minimum **age** at which pubic hair is considered a sign, i.e., eleven years and one day, when any hair that is found is considered to be merely a mole and not a sign, **and** similarly **after the age** of majority, twelve years and one day, when a female is presumed to have grown pubic hair like most girls her age, **women may examine them** and their testimony is accepted. But **during the time** between eleven years and one day and twelve years and one day, **women may not examine them.** The reason is **that one does not resolve** cases of **uncertainty based on** the testimony of **women. Rabbi Shimon says: Even during the time** between eleven years and one day and twelve years and one day, **women may examine them. And a woman is deemed credible,** and her testimony is accepted, **to be stringent but not to be lenient.**

כֵּיצַד, ״גְּדוֹלָה הִיא״ – שֶׁלֹּא תְּמָאֵן, ״קְטַנָּה הִיא״ – שֶׁלֹּא תַּחֲלוֹץ.

The *baraita* continues: **How so,** i.e., how is a woman's testimony accepted with regard to the girl she has examined as a stringency but not a leniency? If the woman said that the girl is **a female who reached majority,** her claim is accepted to the extent **that she does not perform refusal.** The refusal of a husband, which applies in the case of a girl whose father had died and who was married off by her mother or brother, can be performed by the girl only until she reaches majority. If the woman said that this girl is **a minor,** her testimony is accepted to the extent **that she does not perform *ḥalitza*.**

אֲבָל אֵין נֶאֱמֶנֶת לוֹמַר ״קְטַנָּה הִיא״ – שֶׁתְּמָאֵן, – וּ״גְדוֹלָה הִיא״ – שֶׁתַּחֲלוֹץ.

The *baraita* concludes: **But** the woman who examined the girl is **not deemed credible to say** that she **is a minor girl** to the extent **that she performs refusal. And** likewise, the woman is not deemed credible to say that she **is a female who reached majority to** the extent **that she performs *ḥalitza*.**

אָמַר מָר, רַבִּי יְהוּדָה אוֹמֵר: לִפְנֵי הַפֶּרֶק וּלְאַחַר הַפֶּרֶק – נָשִׁים בּוֹדְקוֹת אוֹתָן. בִּשְׁלָמָא לִפְנֵי הַפֶּרֶק – בָּעֵי בְּדִיקָה, דְּאִי מִשְׁתַּכְּחִי לְאַחַר הַפֶּרֶק – שׁוּמָא נִינְהוּ.

The Gemara analyzes the *baraita*. **The Master said** that **Rabbi Yehuda says: Before the** minimum **age** at which pubic hair is considered a sign, **and** similarly **after the age** of majority, **women may examine them.** The Gemara raises a difficulty: **Granted,** one can understand that **before the** minimum **age** there is **a requirement** for **examination,** so **that if** they **find** hair **after the** minimum **age** which they already saw before the minimum age, these hairs **are** evidently a mere **mole,** not a sign of maturity.

אֶלָּא לְאַחַר הַפֶּרֶק לָמָּה לִי בְּדִיקָה? וְהָאֲמַר רָבָא: קְטַנָּה שֶׁהִגִּיעָה לִכְלַל שְׁנוֹתֶיהָ – אֵינָהּ צְרִיכָה בְּדִיקָה, חֲזָקָה הֵבִיאָה סִימָנִין! כִּי אֲמַר רָבָא חֲזָקָה – לְמֵיאוּן, אֲבָל לַחֲלִיצָה – בָּעֲיָא בְּדִיקָה.

**But why do I** need a girl to undergo **an examination after the age** of majority? **Didn't Rava say: A minor girl who reached her full years,** i.e., her age of majority, twelve years and one day, **does not require an examination,** as there is **a presumption** that **she has developed signs** indicating puberty? The Gemara explains: **When Rava said** that one relies on this **presumption,** he was referring specifically **to** her inability from now on to perform **refusal. But with regard to *ḥalitza*,** she **requires an examination** to determine that she has reached maturity.

תּוֹךְ הַפֶּרֶק – אֵין נָשִׁים בּוֹדְקוֹת אוֹתָן, – קָסָבַר: תּוֹךְ הַפֶּרֶק כִּלְאַחַר הַפֶּרֶק (דָּמֵי),

The *baraita* stated that according to Rabbi Yehuda, women are deemed credible to examine girls who are either younger than eleven years and one day or older than twelve years and one day. But **during the time** between eleven years and one day and twelve years and one day, **women may not examine them.** The Gemara explains that Rabbi Yehuda **holds** that the period **during** this **time** is considered like **after the age** of majority. In other words, the signs indicating puberty that a girl develops during this time are considered to be full-fledged signs, which means that she has reached majority even before the age of twelve and one day. Accordingly, the testimony of women is not accepted for this period, as her change of status enables her to perform *ḥalitza* with her husband's brother.

**NOTES**

**Are examined based on the testimony of women – נִבְדָּקוֹת עַל פִּי נָשִׁים:** The early commentaries ask: How can the testimony of women be accepted for the determination of a young woman's status, in light of the principle that testimony involving forbidden sexual intercourse requires no fewer than two male witnesses? Some explain that it is because this is a matter that is likely to be revealed, with regard to which it is presumed that people do not lie. Furthermore, the woman is not testifying directly about a matter of forbidden sexual intercourse but is referring only to the existence of the hairs. Therefore, this is considered like testimony about a regular prohibition of the Torah, with regard to which women are deemed credible. An additional reason that their testimony is accepted is that it is preferable for the girl to be examined by women, as it is prohibited for a man to look at her nakedness (Rivash).

**HALAKHA**

**All girls who are examined are examined based on the testimony of women – כׇּל הַנִּבְדָּקוֹת נִבְדָּקוֹת עַל פִּי נָשִׁים:** The examination of young women to determine whether or not signs indicating puberty have appeared is performed by trustworthy women. One woman is sufficient to carry out this examination, and her testimony with regard to the young woman's status is accepted, even if she is a relative of that young woman. This *halakha* applies throughout her twelfth year, as well as before and afterward. This ruling is in accordance with the *baraita* as well as the precedent of Rabbi Elazar, who had his wife inspect the young women, and Rabbi Yishmael, who had his mother examine them (Rambam *Sefer Nashim, Hilkhot Ishut* 2:20; *Shulḥan Arukh, Even HaEzer* 155:15).

וּלְאַחַר הַפֶּרֶק דְּאִיכָּא חֲזָקָה דְּרָבָא – סָמְכִינַן אַנָּשִׁים וּבָדְקִי, תּוֹךְ הַפֶּרֶק דְּלֵיכָּא חֲזָקָה דְּרָבָא – לָא סָמְכִינַן אַנָּשִׁים, וְלָא בָּדְקִי נָשִׁים.

**But after the** minimum **age** of twelve years and one day, **when there is the presumption of Rava** that a girl has already developed signs indicating puberty, one **may rely on women and** have them **examine** the girl. **During** this **age**, between eleven and twelve, **when there is no presumption of Rava** that she has already developed signs indicating puberty, one **may not rely on women, and** therefore **women may not examine** the girl.

רַבִּי שִׁמְעוֹן אוֹמֵר: אַף תּוֹךְ הַפֶּרֶק נָשִׁים בּוֹדְקוֹת אוֹתָן, קָסָבַר: תּוֹךְ הַפֶּרֶק – כְּלִפְנֵי הַפֶּרֶק, וּבָעֲיָא בְּדִיקָה, דְּאִי מִשְׁתַּכְּחִי לְאַחַר הַפֶּרֶק – שׁוּמָא נִינְהוּ.

By contrast, **Rabbi Shimon says** that **even during** this **age,** between eleven years and one day and twelve years and one day, **women may examine** girls to determine if they have grown pubic hair. This is because Rabbi Shimon **holds** that the period **during** this **age** is considered **like before the** minimum **age,** which means that the girl is a minor based on her age, regardless of the results of the examination. **And** the only reason she **requires an examination** is **that if** they **find** hair **after the** minimum **age,** which they had already seen before the minimum age, these hairs **are** deemed a mere **mole,** not a sign of maturity.

וְנֶאֱמֶנֶת אִשָּׁה לְהַחְמִיר אֲבָל לֹא לְהָקֵל. הַאי מַאן קָתָנֵי לַהּ? אִיבָּעֵית אֵימָא: רַבִּי יְהוּדָה – וְאַתּוֹךְ הַפֶּרֶק,

The *baraita* further teaches: **And a woman is deemed credible** to testify **to be stringent** with regard to the girl who she examined **but not to be lenient.** The Gemara asks: **Who taught this** *halakha*? The Gemara answers: **If you wish, say** that it is in accordance with the opinion of **Rabbi Yehuda, and** it is referring to **during** the **age** between eleven years and one day and twelve and one day.

Perek **VI**
Daf **49** Amud **a**

וְאִיבָּעֵית אֵימָא: רַבִּי שִׁמְעוֹן, וּלְאַחַר הַפֶּרֶק, וְלֵית לֵיהּ חֲזָקָה דְּרָבָא.

**And if you wish, say** instead that the *tanna* who taught this ruling was **Rabbi Shimon,** and the *baraita* is referring to an examination conducted **after the age** of majority. **And** Rabbi Shimon **does not** accept **the presumption of Rava** that a girl of this age has already developed signs indicating puberty.

״מִפְּנֵי שֶׁאָמְרוּ אֶפְשָׁר״ כו׳. הָא תּוּ לָמָּה לִי? הָא תָּנָא לֵיהּ רֵישָׁא!

§ The mishna teaches that according to the Rabbis a young woman who apparently developed the upper sign before the lower sign has reached majority, and therefore if her childless husband died she either performs *ḥalitza* or enters into levirate marriage with her husband's brother. This ruling is **due to** the fact **that** the Sages **said:** It is **possible** for the lower sign of puberty to appear before the upper sign, but it is impossible for the upper sign to appear before the lower sign. The Gemara asks: **Why do I need this additional** repetition of this point? **It was** already **taught in the first clause** that it is impossible for the upper sign to appear without the lower sign having already appeared.

וְכִי תֵּימָא: מִשּׁוּם דְּקָא בָּעֵי לְמִסְתְּמָה כְּרַבָּנַן – פְּשִׁיטָא, יָחִיד וְרַבִּים הֲלָכָה כְּרַבִּים!

**And if you would say** that it is repeated **because** the *tanna* **wants** to teach **an unattributed** mishna **in accordance with** the opinion of **the Rabbis,** in order to establish that the *halakha* follows their opinion in their dispute with Rabbi Meir, that cannot be the case. The Gemara explains why this suggestion is incorrect: This is **obvious,** as there is a principle that in a dispute between **an individual** Sage **and a majority** of other Sages, the ***halakha*** is always decided **in accordance with** the opinion of **the majority.**

מהו דתימא: מסתברא טעמא דרבי מאיר, דקא מסייע ליה קראי – קא משמע לן. ואיבעית אימא: משום דקא בעי למתני "כיוצא בו".

The Gemara answers: It is necessary for the *tanna* to state that the *halakha* is in accordance with the opinion of the Rabbis despite the fact that they are the majority, **lest you say that the rationale for** the opinion of **Rabbi Meir is** more **reasonable.** One might have thought this, **as the verses** cited above **support it:** "Your breasts were fashioned, and your hair was grown," and: "When they from Egypt bruised your breasts for the sprouting forth of your young womanhood." Therefore, the mishna **teaches us** that the *halakha* is in accordance with the opinion of the Rabbis. **And if you wish, say** instead that the *tanna* repeated the claim that the upper sign cannot precede the lower one **because** he **wants to teach** a case in the next mishna which is **similar to** this one, i.e., this summary provides a transition to the *halakha* brought in the following mishna.

מתני׳ כיוצא בו: כל כלי חרס שהוא מכנים – מוציא, ויש שמוציא ואינו מכנים.

**MISHNA** **Similar to** the order of the appearance of the signs of puberty in a girl, where it is impossible for the upper sign to appear before the lower sign, there is an analogous principle with regard to the mutual dependency of two items: **Any earthenware vessel** with a hole **that enables entry** of liquid into the vessel certainly **enables exit** of liquid through that hole, and it thereby ceases to be a vessel fit for sanctification of the waters mixed with the ashes of the red heifer. **And there are** holes **that enable exit** of liquids from the earthenware vessels **but do not enable entry** of liquids from outside the vessel, and therefore it remains a vessel.

כל אבר שיש בו צפורן – יש בו עצם, ויש שיש בו עצם ואין בו – צפורן.

Likewise, **in any limb** of the body **where there is a nail, there is** certainly **a bone**[N] **in it** as well. If it is the limb of a corpse, it transmits ritual impurity through contact, movement, and in a tent, even if its size is less than that of an olive-bulk. **And there are** limbs **in which there is a bone but** yet **there is not a nail in it.** That limb does not transmit impurity in a tent if its size is less than that of an olive-bulk.

כל המטמא מדרס – מטמא טמא מת, ויש שמטמא טמא מת ואינו מטמא מדרס.

Similarly, **any** item **that becomes ritually impure** with impurity of a *zav* imparted by **treading,** e.g., a vessel designated for sitting, **becomes ritually impure** with **impurity imparted by a corpse.**[N] **And there are** vessels **that become ritually impure** with **impurity imparted by a corpse but do not become ritually impure** with impurity of a *zav* imparted by **treading.**

גמ׳ מכנים – פסול למי חטאת, ופסול משום גסטרא, מוציא – כשר למי חטאת, ופסול משום גסטרא.

**GEMARA** The mishna teaches that any earthenware vessel with a hole that enables entry of liquid into the vessel certainly enables exit of liquid through that hole, whereas there are holes that enable exit of liquids but do not enable entry. The Gemara explains the halakhic significance of this distinction. A vessel that contains a hole that is large enough to enable liquid to **enter** is no longer considered a vessel and is therefore **unfit to** contain the **water of purification.**[H] **And** it is also **disqualified as a shard** [*gastera*][L] of a vessel. A shard still has some utility and is therefore susceptible to ritual impurity. By contrast, an earthenware vessel that contains a small hole **that enables** only the **exit** of liquids is **fit for** the **water of purification,**[HB] **but** is **disqualified as a shard** of a vessel.

### HALAKHA

**A hole large enough to enable liquid to enter is unfit to contain the water of purification – מכנים פסול למי חטאת:** An earthenware vessel which contains a hole that is large enough to enable liquid to enter it may not be used for drawing or consecrating the water of purification (Rambam *Sefer Tahara, Hilkhot Para Aduma* 6:6).

**A hole that enables only the exit of liquids is fit for water of purification – מוציא כשר למי חטאת:** An earthenware vessel containing a small hole that enables only the exit of liquids is fit for the consecration of the water of purification (Rambam *Sefer Tahara, Hilkhot Kelim* 19:1–2).

### LANGUAGE

Shard [*gastera*] – גסטרא: Apparently from the Greek γάστρα, *gastra*, meaning the bottom portion, or belly, of an earthenware vessel. The Sages use this term to refer to a partially damaged earthenware vessel. Apparently, it also attained the derivative meaning of anything that was damaged or broken. According to some opinions, it can refer to splitting an object in two, particularly in the middle.

### BACKGROUND

Water of purification – מי חטאת: This is water mixed with the ashes of the red heifer, which was used to purify people and items that had contracted ritual impurity imparted by a corpse. Running spring water was placed in a container, to which a small amount of ashes from the red heifer was added. The resulting mixture, called the water of purification, or water of separation, was sprinkled on the people or items to be purified. The process of mixing the ashes with water is called the sanctification of the water of purification. The act of purification is performed by taking a bundle of three hyssop branches, dipping them in the water of purification, and, using the branches, sprinkling the purification waters on the impure individual on the third and the seventh day after he became ritually impure.

### NOTES

In any limb where there is a nail there is a bone – כל אבר שיש בו צפורן יש בו עצם: Rashi explains that this is referring to an extra limb that grew, over and above the standard limbs of the body. For example, if a sixth finger grew on one's hand and it contained a nail, it is known that it contains a bone, and it is considered a significant limb. If it is not an extra limb, then even if it does not have a nail it is considered a limb and transmits ritual impurity in the normal manner of limbs.

Becomes ritually impure with impurity imparted by a corpse – מטמא טמא מת: There is no vessel that is capable of being rendered impure as a seat upon which a *zav* sat which is not also capable of being rendered impure by all other forms of impurity. The reason the mishna specifically mentions impurity imparted by a corpse, despite the fact that it could refer to all forms of impurity, is that impurity imparted by a corpse is comparable to the impurity of a *zav* imparted by treading, in that both are primary sources of impurity (Rashi).

אָמַר רַב אַסִי, שׁוֹנִין: כְּלִי חֶרֶס – שִׁיעוּרוֹ בְּכוֹנֵס מַשְׁקֶה, וְלֹא אָמְרוּ "מוֹצִיא מַשְׁקֶה" – אֶלָּא לְעִנְיַן גִּסְטְרָא בִּלְבַד. מַאי טַעְמָא? אָמַר מָר זוּטְרָא בְּרֵיהּ דְּרַב נַחְמָן: לְפִי שֶׁאֵין אוֹמְרִים "הָבֵא גִּסְטְרָא לְגִסְטְרָא".

**Rav Asi says** that **they teach** the following *halakha*: In the case of **an earthenware vessel, its measure** of a hole that renders it no longer ritually impure is one that is large enough **to enable liquid to enter** it. **And they said** that the measure of a small hole is that **which enables** the **exit of liquids only with regard to a shard.** The Gemara inquires: **What is the reason** for this? **Mar Zutra, son of Rav Naḥman, said:** It is **because** people **do not say: Bring** another **shard to** seal the leak of **a shard**; rather, they throw it out immediately. A shard is used as a plate beneath a perforated earthenware vessel. If the shard itself is also perforated and leaks, it is no longer of any use.

תָּנוּ רַבָּנַן: כֵּיצַד בּוֹדְקִין כְּלִי חֶרֶס לֵידַע אִם נִיקַּב בְּכוֹנֵס מַשְׁקֶה אִם לָאו? יָבִיא עֲרֵיבָה מְלֵאָה מַיִם וְנוֹתֵן קְדֵרָה לְתוֹכָהּ, אִם כָּנְסָה – בְּיָדוּעַ שֶׁכּוֹנֵס מַשְׁקֶה, וְאִם לָאו – בְּיָדוּעַ שֶׁמּוֹצִיא מַשְׁקֶה.

§ On the topic of holes in earthenware vessels, **the Sages taught** in a *baraita*: **How does one test** a broken **earthenware vessel**[H] **to know if it was pierced** with a hole **that enables liquid to enter** it **or not? One brings a tub filled with water and places** the broken **pot into it. If** the water from the tub **enters** the pot, **it is known that** the pot contains a hole **that enables liquid to enter. And if** the water does **not** enter the pot, **it is known that** the vessel contains only a small hole **that** merely **enables** the **exit** of **liquids.**

**HALAKHA**

**How does one test a broken earthenware vessel, etc.** – **כֵּיצַד בּוֹדְקִין כְּלִי חֶרֶס וכו׳**: An earthenware vessel that is used to hold liquids and that was pierced after it became impure is rendered ritually pure if the measure of the hole enables liquid to enter. If the hole is any smaller than that, the vessel remains impure. How does one test it? The vessel is placed on the liquid. If the liquid enters the vessel by means of the hole, then the vessel is no longer considered functional, and it is pure. This ruling is in accordance with the *baraita* (Rambam *Sefer Tahara*, *Hilkhot Kelim* 19:1).

Perek **VI**
Daf **49** Amud **b**

רַבִּי יְהוּדָה אוֹמֵר: כּוֹפֵף אׇזְנֵי קְדֵרָה לְתוֹכָהּ, וּמֵצִיף עָלֶיהָ מַיִם, וְאִם כּוֹנֵס – בְּיָדוּעַ שֶׁכּוֹנֵס מַשְׁקֶה, וְאִם לָאו – בְּיָדוּעַ שֶׁמּוֹצִיא מַשְׁקֶה.

**Rabbi Yehuda says** that the method for determining whether an earthenware vessel contains a hole that allows liquid to enter is as follows: One takes the **handles of the pot and turns it over,** placing it upside down **in** an empty tub,[N] **and** he then **covers** the pot with **water. If** water **enters** the pot, **it is known that** it contains a hole **that enables liquid to enter, and if** the water does **not** enter the pot, **it is known that** the vessel contains a small hole **that enables** only the **exit** of **liquids.**

אוֹ שׁוֹפְתָהּ עַל גַּבֵּי הָאוּר, אִם הָאוּר מַעֲמִידָהּ – בְּיָדוּעַ שֶׁמּוֹצִיא מַשְׁקֶה, וְאִם לָאו – בְּיָדוּעַ שֶׁמַּכְנִיס מַשְׁקֶה.

**Or** one can determine the size of the hole by the following method: One **places** the pot, with liquid in it, **on the fire. If the fire holds** the liquid back and does not allow it to exit the vessel, then **it is known** that the vessel contains a small hole **that enables** only the **exit** of **liquids. And if** the fire does **not** hold the liquid back and does not prevent it from exiting the vessel, then **it is known** that it contains a hole **that enables liquid to enter.**

רַבִּי יוֹסֵי אוֹמֵר: אַף לֹא שׁוֹפְתָהּ עַל גַּבֵּי הָאוּר – מִפְּנֵי שֶׁהָאוּר מַעֲמִידָהּ, אֶלָּא שׁוֹפְתָהּ עַל גַּבֵּי הָרֶמֶץ. אִם רֶמֶץ מַעֲמִידָהּ – בְּיָדוּעַ שֶׁמּוֹצִיא מַשְׁקֶה, וְאִם לָאו – בְּיָדוּעַ שֶׁכּוֹנֵס מַשְׁקֶה. הָיָה טוֹרֵד טִיפָּה אַחַר טִיפָּה – בְּיָדוּעַ שֶׁכּוֹנֵס מַשְׁקֶה.

**Rabbi Yosei says: One should not place** the pot with liquid in it **on the fire.** This is not a reliable test for determining the size of the hole, as it is possible that the hole is actually large enough to enable liquid to enter, but nevertheless **the fire prevents** the liquid from exiting. **Rather, one places** the pot with liquid in it **on hot ash. If the hot ash holds** the liquid back and does not allow it to exit the vessel, then **it is known** that the vessel contains a small hole **that enables** only the **exit** of **liquids. But if** the hot ash does **not** hold the liquid back and does not prevent it from exiting the vessel, **it is known** that it contains a hole **that enables liquid to enter.** Another manner of testing is to fill the vessel with liquid. If it **drips** one **drop after** another **drop, it is known** that it contains a hole **that enables liquid to enter.**

**NOTES**

**One takes the handles of the pot and turns it over in an empty tub** – **כּוֹפֵף אׇזְנֵי קְדֵרָה לְתוֹכָהּ**: Rabbi Yehuda does not state the deficiency in the method of the first *tanna*, nor why his own method is more effective. Rashi explains that according to Rabbi Yehuda, pushing the vessel into the tub of water involves a certain amount of force. This can cause water to enter a small hole which would normally not allow water to enter. By contrast, when the vessel is placed in an empty tub and water is added afterward, the entry of water accurately indicates that there is a significant hole which allows the entry of liquid.

BACKGROUND

Our great rabbi – רַבֵּינוּ הַגָּדוֹל: This honorific appellation, used specifically in reference to Rav, i.e., Rabbi Abba bar Ivo, expresses the lofty status of Rav for those in his generation, such as his great disciple Rav Ḥisda, as well as Sages of later generations.

Rav is considered the father of Torah in Babylonia. He was the first and greatest of the Babylonian *amora'im*. The yeshiva he founded at Sura existed for centuries, until the end of the period of the *ge'onim*.

His plain title, our great rabbi, or simply Rav, is similar to that of Rabbi Yehuda HaNasi, who was referred to as our holy rabbi, or Rabbi. He was called this because he was the rabbi, or teacher, of all the Jews of the exile (Rashi on *Beitza* 9b).

Rav was also called Abba the Tall, as he was the tallest in his generation (see 24b).

An extra finger – אֶצְבַּע יְתֵרָה:

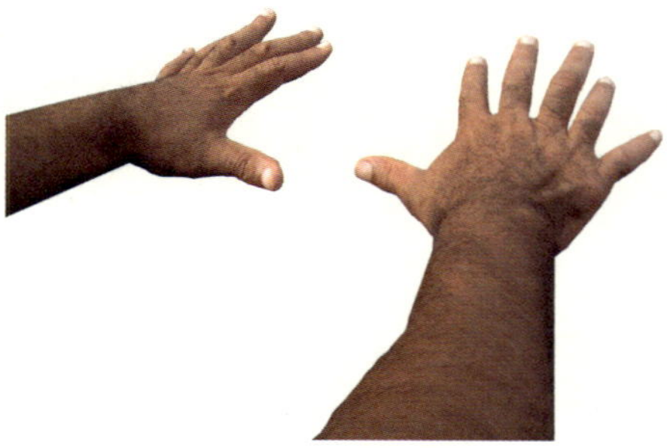

Man with six fingers on each hand

LANGUAGE

Half-*se'a* [*tarkav*] – תַּרְקַב: A *tarkav* is a vessel used to measure a half-*se'a*. The early commentaries explain that it is derived from the words two [*trei*] and *kav*, i.e., two *kav* plus another *kav*, three *kav* in all, as a *se'a* consists of six *kav*. It is likely, however, that it is actually derived from the Greek τρίκαβος, *trikabos*, meaning three *kav*.

מַאי אִיכָּא בֵּין תַּנָּא קַמָּא לְרַבִּי יְהוּדָה? אֲמַר עוּלָּא: כִּינּוּס עַל יְדֵי הַדְּחָק אִיכָּא בֵּינַיְיהוּ.

The Gemara asks: **What** difference **is there between** the method of testing stated by **the first *tanna*,** placing the vessel in a tub of water, and that **of Rabbi Yehuda,** placing the vessel upside down into the tub and then covering it with water? **Ulla said:** The difference **between** their opinions is whether liquid that **enters** through a hole **with difficulty,** i.e., as the result of force, is considered entering. According to Rabbi Yehuda, placing the vessel directly into a tub of water constitutes the use of force to a certain degree, and he maintains that if water enters the vessel in such a case, this does not count as liquid entering the vessel. Therefore, he rejects the testing method of the first *tanna*.

״כׇּל אֵבֶר שֶׁיֵּשׁ בּוֹ צִפּוֹרֶן״ וכו׳. יֵשׁ בּוֹ צִפּוֹרֶן – מְטַמֵּא בְּמַגָּע וּבְמַשָּׂא וּבְאֹהֶל, יֵשׁ בּוֹ עֶצֶם וְאֵין בּוֹ צִפּוֹרֶן – מְטַמֵּא בְּמַגָּע וּבְמַשָּׂא, וְאֵינוֹ מְטַמֵּא בְּאֹהֶל.

§ The mishna teaches: **In any limb** of the body **where there is a nail,** there is certainly a bone in it as well. But it is possible for there to be limbs that contain a bone without a nail. The Gemara explains the halakhic significance of this distinction. A limb **in which there is a nail** and which therefore certainly contains a bone has the status of a full-fledged limb. Therefore, it **transmits impurity** through **contact, movement, and in a tent,** even if its size is less than that of an olive-bulk. By contrast, if **there is a bone in** the limb **but there is no nail,** it **transmits impurity** through **contact and movement** even if its size is less than that of an olive-bulk, **but** it does **not transmit impurity in a tent** unless its size is that of an olive-bulk.

אָמַר רַב חִסְדָּא, דָּבָר זֶה רַבֵּינוּ הַגָּדוֹל אָמְרוֹ, הַמָּקוֹם יִהְיֶה בְּעֶזְרוֹ. אֶצְבַּע יְתֵרָה שֶׁיֵּשׁ בּוֹ עֶצֶם וְאֵין בּוֹ צִפּוֹרֶן – מְטַמֵּא בְּמַגָּע וּבְמַשָּׂא, וְאֵינוֹ מְטַמֵּא בְּאֹהֶל.

**Rav Ḥisda says: The** following **matter was stated by our great rabbi,**[B] Rav, **may the Omnipresent** come **to his assistance. An extra finger**[BH] on one's hand **in which there is a bone but there is no nail transmits impurity** through **contact and movement** even if its size is less than that of an olive-bulk, **but** it does **not transmit impurity in a tent.**

אָמַר רַבָּה בַּר בַּר חָנָה אָמַר רַבִּי יוֹחָנָן: וּכְשֶׁאֵינָהּ נִסְפֶּרֶת עַל גַּב הַיָּד.

**Rabba bar bar Ḥana says that Rabbi Yoḥanan said: And** this is the *halakha*, that it must contain both bone and a nail for it to be considered a limb, only in a case **where** this finger **cannot be counted along the back of the hand,** i.e., the extra finger is not aligned with the others. But if it is aligned with the other fingers then it is considered like any other limb and imparts impurity in a tent, whether or not it contains a nail.

״כׇּל הַמְטַמֵּא מִדְרָס״ וכו׳. כׇּל דַּחֲזִי לְמִדְרָס – מְטַמֵּא טְמֵא מֵת.

§ The mishna further teaches: Similarly, **any** item that **becomes ritually impure** with impurity of a *zav* imparted by **treading** becomes ritually impure with impurity imparted by a corpse. The Gemara explains that this means that **any item that is fit to** become impure with the impurity of a *zav* imparted by **treading**[H] is fit to **become ritually impure** with **impurity imparted by a corpse.**

״וְיֵשׁ שֶׁמְּטַמֵּא טְמֵא מֵת – וְאֵין מְטַמֵּא מִדְרָס״, לְאֵתוּיֵי מַאי? לְאֵתוּיֵי סְאָה וְתַרְקַב,

The mishna continues: **And there are** vessels **that become ritually impure** with **impurity imparted by a corpse but do not become ritually impure** with impurity of a *zav* imparted by **treading.** The Gemara asks: **What is added** by this statement? The Gemara answers: This serves **to add** a measuring vessel, e.g., the measure of **a *se'a* or a half-*se'a* [*vetarkav*].**[L]

HALAKHA

An extra finger – אֶצְבַּע יְתֵרָה: According to the Sages, the male body consists of 248 limbs, each containing flesh, sinews, and bone. This number does not include the teeth. A woman's body contains 251 limbs. Any limb that is separated in its entirety from a body, whether from a living person or a corpse, imparts impurity through contact, by being carried, and in a tent, with the exception of the three additional limbs found in a woman's body, which do not impart impurity in a tent.

An extra finger that contains a bone but not a nail, and which is positioned in line with the other fingers, is considered like any other limb and imparts impurity in a tent. If it is not aligned with the other fingers, it imparts impurity through contact and by being carried but not in a tent, and its impurity applies by rabbinic law. If it contains a nail it has the same status as a regular limb. This ruling is in accordance with the opinion of Rav Ḥisda and Rabba bar bar Ḥana, citing Rabbi Yoḥanan (Rambam *Sefer Tahara*, *Hilkhot Tumat Met* 2:7).

**Any item that is fit to become impure with the impurity of a *zav* imparted by treading, etc.** – כׇּל דַּחֲזֵי לְמִדְרָס וכו׳: Any item that can become impure with the impurity of a *zav* imparted by treading can become ritually impure with impurity imparted by a corpse. There are items that can become impure with impurity imparted by a corpse but cannot become impure with the impurity of a *zav* imparted by treading (Rambam *Sefer Tahara*, *Hilkhot Kelim* 27:16).

דְּתַנְיָא: ״וְהַיּוֹשֵׁב עַל הַכְּלִי״, יָכוֹל כְּפָה סְאָה וְיָשַׁב עָלֶיהָ, אוֹ תַּרְקַב וְיָשַׁב עָלָיו יְהֵא טָמֵא

As it is taught in a *baraita*: The verse states with regard to the impurity of the treading of a *zav*: **"And he who sits on** any **object** whereon the *zav* sits shall wash his clothes and bathe himself in water, and is impure until the evening" (Leviticus 15:6). One **might** have thought that if a *zav* **turned over** a vessel used to measure **a** ***se'a*** **and sat on it, or** if he turned over a vessel used to measure **a half-*****se'a*** **and sat on it,** that vessel **should be** rendered **impure** as a seat upon which a *zav* sat.

תַּלְמוּד לוֹמַר ״אֲשֶׁר יֵשֵׁב עָלָיו הַזָּב״ – מִי שֶׁמְּיוּחָד לִישִׁיבָה, יָצָא זֶה שֶׁאוֹמְרִים לוֹ ״עֲמוֹד וְנַעֲשֶׂה מְלַאכְתֵּנוּ״.

Therefore, **the verse states:** "And he who sits on any object **whereon the** ***zav*** **sits"** (Leviticus 15:6). The wording of the verse indicates that it is speaking of an object **that is designated for sitting,**[N] i.e., upon which people generally sit, **excluding such** a vessel, with regard to **which we say to** someone sitting on it: **Stand up and** allow us to use it to **do our work,** i.e., to measure. This is not defined as a vessel used for sitting, as it serves another function.

**מתני׳** כָּל הָרָאוּי לָדוּן דִּינֵי נְפָשׁוֹת – רָאוּי לָדוּן דִּינֵי מָמוֹנוֹת, וְיֵשׁ שֶׁרָאוּי לָדוּן דִּינֵי מָמוֹנוֹת וְאֵינוֹ רָאוּי לָדוּן דִּינֵי נְפָשׁוֹת.

**MISHNA** Any person **who is fit to adjudicate** cases **of capital law is fit to adjudicate** cases of **monetary law, and there are those who are fit to adjudicate** cases of **monetary law but are unfit to adjudicate** cases of **capital law.**[H]

**גמ׳** אָמַר רַב יְהוּדָה: לַאֲתוּיֵי מַמְזֵר.

**GEMARA** **Rav Yehuda said:** The statement of the mishna that some are fit to adjudicate cases of monetary law but are unfit to adjudicate cases of capital law serves **to add** the case of a ***mamzer***.[NH] Although he may not adjudicate cases of capital law, nevertheless he may adjudicate cases of monetary law.

תְּנֵינָא חֲדָא זִימְנָא: הַכֹּל כְּשֵׁרִין לָדוּן דִּינֵי מָמוֹנוֹת, וְאֵין הַכֹּל כְּשֵׁרִין לָדוּן דִּינֵי נְפָשׁוֹת. וְהָוֵינַן בָּהּ: לַאֲתוּיֵי מַאי? וַאֲמַר רַב יְהוּדָה: לַאֲתוּיֵי מַמְזֵר! חֲדָא – לַאֲתוּיֵי גֵּר, וַחֲדָא – לַאֲתוּיֵי מַמְזֵר.

The Gemara asks: Why is it necessary to teach this here? **We** already **learned** this on **another occasion,** in a mishna (*Sanhedrin* 32a): **All are fit to judge** cases of **monetary law, but not all are fit to judge** cases of **capital law. And we discussed it,** and asked **what is added** by the phrase: All are fit to judge. **And Rav Yehuda said** in response that this serves **to add** the case of **a** ***mamzer***. The Gemara answers: **One** mishna serves **to add** the case of **a convert,**[H] **and one** other mishna serves **to add** the case of **a** ***mamzer***.

וּצְרִיכִי, דְּאִי אַשְׁמְעִינַן גֵּר – מִשּׁוּם דְּרָאוּי לָבֹא בַּקָּהָל, אֲבָל מַמְזֵר דְּאֵין רָאוּי לָבֹא בַּקָּהָל – אֵימָא לָא.

The Gemara explains: **And** both additions **are necessary. As, if** the *mishnayot* had **taught us** only that **a convert** is fit to judge cases of monetary law, one might have said that the *halakha* is lenient in the case of a convert **because** he is **fit to enter into the congregation,** i.e., marry a Jewish woman. **But** with regard to **a** ***mamzer*****, who is unfit to enter into the congregation,** one might **say** that **he** is **not** fit to judge cases of monetary law.

וְאִי אַשְׁמְעִינַן מַמְזֵר – מִשּׁוּם דְּקָאָתֵי מִטִּפָּה כְּשֵׁרָה, אֲבָל גֵּר דְּקָאָתֵי מִטִּפָּה פְּסוּלָה – אֵימָא לָא, צְרִיכָא.

**And if** the *mishnayot* had **taught us** only that **a** ***mamzer*** is fit to judge cases of monetary law, one might have said that the *halakha* is lenient in the case of a *mamzer* **because he comes from a fit drop** of semen, i.e., his father is Jewish. **But** with regard to **a convert, who comes from an unfit drop,** as he was born a gentile, one might **say** that he is **not** fit to judge cases of monetary law. Therefore, it is **necessary** to teach the *halakhot* of both a convert and a *mamzer*.

## NOTES

**That is designated for sitting – מִי שֶׁמְּיוּחָד לִישִׁיבָה:** Rashi in tractate *Shabbat* (59a) explains that this is derived from the fact that the Torah states with regard to the impurity of a bed on which a *zav* lay: "Every bed whereon he that has the issue lies shall be impure" (Leviticus 15:4). The same verse states with regard to the impurity of a seat on which he sat: "And everything whereon he sits shall be impure." The fact that the verse does not speak of that which he lay or sat on, but rather "lies" or "sits" on, suggests that it is referring to an object that is commonly used for these purposes.

**To add the case of a *mamzer* – לַאֲתוּיֵי מַמְזֵר:** A *mamzer* is fit to adjudicate cases of monetary law but not capital law. The Sages (*Sanhedrin* 36b) derive this from the verse: "You are all fair, my love; and there is no blemish in you" (Song of Songs 4:7). This teaches that as well as being flawless with regard to justice, judges must also be without imperfection in general. This excludes a *mamzer*, who is considered blemished (Rashi). The commentaries further explain that a *mamzer* may not be included in the courts of twenty-three judges, which adjudicate cases of capital law, as every Sanhedrin, including these small ones, must consist of members described as follows in the verse: "And they shall bear the burden of the people with you" (Numbers 11:17), i.e., the judges must be similar to Moses. Just as he was of distinguished lineage, so too, the members of the Sanhedrin must be of distinguished lineage (Rashi on *Sanhedrin* 36b).

## HALAKHA

**And there are those who are fit to adjudicate cases of monetary law but are unfit to adjudicate cases of capital law – וְיֵשׁ שֶׁרָאוּי לָדוּן דִּינֵי מָמוֹנוֹת וְאֵינוֹ רָאוּי לָדוּן דִּינֵי נְפָשׁוֹת:** All are fit to adjudicate cases of monetary law, including a convert, provided that his mother was Jewish. Even if his mother was not Jewish, he may judge a fellow convert. Similarly, a *mamzer* or one who is blind in one eye may adjudicate cases of monetary law. By contrast, cases of capital law may be adjudicated only by priests, Levites, and Israelites who are of sufficiently fit lineage that their daughters may marry a member of the priesthood, and who have sight in both eyes. This *halakha* is in accordance with the opinion of Rav Yehuda in the Gemara (Rambam *Sefer Shofetim, Hilkhot Sanhedrin* 11:11).

**To add the case of a *mamzer* – לַאֲתוּיֵי מַמְזֵר:** A court of three is fit to adjudicate cases even if any or all of them are *mamzerim*. This ruling is in accordance with the opinion of Rav Yehuda (Rambam *Sefer Shofetim, Hilkhot Sanhedrin* 2:9; *Shulḥan Arukh, Ḥoshen Mishpat* 7:2).

**To add the case of a convert – לַאֲתוּיֵי גֵּר:** A court of three, one of whom is a convert, is unfit to judge a Jew (Rambam *Sefer Shofetim, Hilkhot Sanhedrin* 2:9; *Shulḥan Arukh, Ḥoshen Mishpat* 7:1).

**מתני׳** כָּל הַכָּשֵׁר לָדוּן – כָּשֵׁר לְהָעִיד, וְיֵשׁ שֶׁכָּשֵׁר לְהָעִיד וְאֵינוֹ כָּשֵׁר לָדוּן.

**MISHNA** Any person **who is fit to adjudicate** a case and serve as a judge **is fit to testify**[N] as a witness, **and there are** those **who are fit to testify but are not fit to adjudicate.**

**גמ׳** לַאֲתוּיֵי מַאי? אֲמַר רַבִּי יוֹחָנָן: לַאֲתוּיֵי סוּמָא בְּאַחַת מֵעֵינָיו. וּמַנִּי?

**GEMARA** The Gemara asks: **What is added** by this statement, that some people are fit to testify but not to adjudicate? **Rabbi Yoḥanan said:** This serves **to add one who is blind in one of his eyes. And** in accordance with **whose** opinion is this ruling?

**NOTES**

**Any person who is fit to adjudicate a case and serve as a judge is fit to testify – כָּל הַכָּשֵׁר לָדוּן כָּשֵׁר לְהָעִיד:** The early commentaries analyze this generalization in depth, particularly with regard to the status of women. On the one hand, there are indications that women can be judges, as the verse states with regard to Deborah: "She judged Israel at that time" (Judges 4:4). On the other hand, a woman is unfit to testify in court. The commentaries address this difficulty in various ways.

Some suggest that the mishna is referring only to men (*Tosafot*, first interpretation). Alternatively, women are in fact unfit to be judges, and Deborah was an exception who acted based on divine instruction (*Tosafot*, second interpretation; see *Tosafot* on *Yevamot* 45b).



רַבִּי מֵאִיר הִיא. דְּתַנְיָא, הָיָה רַבִּי מֵאִיר אוֹמֵר: מַה תַּלְמוּד לוֹמַר "עַל פִּיהֶם יִהְיֶה כָּל רִיב וְכָל נָגַע" – וְכִי מָה עִנְיַן רִיבִים אֵצֶל נְגָעִים? מַקִּישׁ רִיבִים לִנְגָעִים: מַה נְּגָעִים בַּיּוֹם, דִּכְתִיב "וּבְיוֹם הֵרָאוֹת בּוֹ" – אַף רִיבִים בַּיּוֹם.

It is the opinion of **Rabbi Meir, as it is taught** in a *baraita* that **Rabbi Meir would say: What** is the meaning when **the verse states: "According to their word shall every dispute and every leprous mark be"** (Deuteronomy 21:5)? **What do disputes have to do with leprous marks?** The verse **juxtaposes disputes to leprous marks,** to teach that **just as leprous marks** are viewed by a priest only **in the daytime,**[H] **as it is written** with regard to leprous marks: **"And on the day when** raw flesh **appears in him** he shall be impure" (Leviticus 13:14), **so too, disputes** are adjudicated only **in the daytime.**[H]

וּמַה נְּגָעִים שֶׁלֹּא בְּסוּמָא, דִּכְתִיב "לְכָל מַרְאֵה עֵינֵי הַכֹּהֵן" – אַף רִיבִים שֶׁלֹּא בְּסוּמָא. וּמַקִּישׁ נְגָעִים לְרִיבִים, מָה רִיבִים – שֶׁלֹּא בִּקְרוֹבִים, אַף נְגָעִים – שֶׁלֹּא בִּקְרוֹבִים.

**And just as leprous marks** are seen by priests who can see, but **not by blind** priests, **as it is written: "As far as appears to the priest"** (Leviticus 13:12), which teaches that they must be viewed by priests who can see with both eyes, **so too, disputes are not** adjudicated **by blind judges,** even if they are blind in only one eye. **And the** verse **juxtaposes leprous marks to disputes** to teach that **just as disputes may not** be judged **by relatives** of the litigants, **so too, leprous marks may not** be viewed **by** a priest who is **a relative** of the afflicted party.

אִי מָה רִיבִים – בִּשְׁלֹשָׁה, אַף נְגָעִים – בִּשְׁלֹשָׁה? וְדִין הוּא, מָמוֹנוֹ – בִּשְׁלֹשָׁה, גּוּפוֹ – לֹא כָּל שֶׁכֵּן! תַּלְמוּד לוֹמַר "וְהוּבָא אֶל אַהֲרֹן הַכֹּהֵן אוֹ אֶל אַחַד מִבָּנָיו הַכֹּהֲנִים" – הָא לָמַדְתָּ, שֶׁאֲפִילּוּ כֹּהֵן אֶחָד רוֹאֶה אֶת הַנְּגָעִים.

The *baraita* continues: **If** these two *halakhot* are compared, one can also say that **just as disputes** are judged specifically **by three** judges, **so too, leprous marks** must be viewed **by three** priests. **And this** suggestion is supported by **a logical inference:** If a case that only involves **one's money** is adjudicated **by three** judges, **all the more** so is it **not** clear that leprous marks, which afflict the person **himself,** should be viewed by three priests? To counter this notion, **the verse states: "And he shall be brought to Aaron the priest or to one of his sons, the priests"** (Leviticus 13:2). **You** have **learned** from this **that even one priest may view leprous marks.**

הַהוּא סַמְיָא דַּהֲוָה בִּשְׁבָבוּתֵיהּ דְּרַבִּי יוֹחָנָן, דַּהֲוָה קָדַיֵּין דִּינָא, וְלָא קָאָמַר לֵיהּ וְלָא מִידֵּי. הֵיכִי עָבֵיד הָכִי? וְהָאֲמַר רַבִּי יוֹחָנָן: הֲלָכָה כִּסְתַם מִשְׁנָה,

The Gemara relates: There was **a certain blind person**[HN] **who was** living **in the neighborhood of Rabbi Yoḥanan who would render judgments, and** Rabbi Yoḥanan **did not say anything to him.** The Gemara asks: **How could** Rabbi Yoḥanan **do this? But didn't Rabbi Yoḥanan** himself **say** that the ***halakha*** is **in accordance with** the ruling of **an unattributed mishna?**

וּתְנַן: כָּל הַכָּשֵׁר לָדוּן – כָּשֵׁר לְהָעִיד, וְיֵשׁ כָּשֵׁר לְהָעִיד וְאֵין כָּשֵׁר לָדוּן. וְאָמְרִינַן: לַאֲתוּיֵי מַאי? וַאֲמַר רַבִּי יוֹחָנָן: לַאֲתוּיֵי סוּמָא בְּאַחַת מֵעֵינָיו!

**And we learned** in the mishna: **Any** person **who is fit to adjudicate** a case and serve as a judge **is fit to testify** as a witness, **and there are** those who are **fit to testify but** are **not fit to adjudicate. And we said: What is added** by this *halakha*, **and Rabbi Yoḥanan said:** It serves **to add one who is blind in one of his eyes,** as he is fit to testify but unfit to judge. Since Rabbi Yoḥanan evidently maintains that one who is blind even in one of his eyes is not fit to judge, why did he not admonish this judge?

**HALAKHA**

**Leprous marks are viewed by a priest only in the daytime – נְגָעִים בַּיּוֹם:** Leprous marks may be examined only during the day, whether the ruling is that the leper should be quarantined, declared a confirmed leper, or declared pure. With regard to all cases the verse uses the term: "On the day," or something similar. This *halakha* is in accordance with the opinion of Rabbi Meir (Rambam *Sefer Tahara, Hilkhot Tumat Tzara'at* 9:6).

**Disputes are adjudicated only in the daytime – רִיבִים בַּיּוֹם:** A court may not start adjudicating a case at night unless both litigants agree to do so (*Sma* and *Shakh*, citing Maharam of Rothenburg). If the court began to adjudicate a case of monetary law during the day, they may complete the case at night. Some maintain that if the court judged a case during the night, its ruling is valid after the fact (Rashbam; *Baḥ*), but the majority of the early commentaries hold that it is not valid; see Ramban, Ran, Rosh, *Tur*, *Kesef Mishne*, and *Shakh* (Rambam *Sefer Shofetim*, *Hilkhot Sanhedrin* 3:3; *Shulḥan Arukh*, *Ḥoshen Mishpat* 5:2).

**Blind person – סַמְיָא:** A court of three judges where each is blind in one eye is fit, but in the case of a Sanhedrin, the court is unfit. One who is blind in both eyes is unfit to judge all cases. Some maintain that if one who is blind in both eyes serves as a judge it is valid after the fact; see *Baḥ* (Rambam *Sefer Shofetim*, *Hilkhot Sanhedrin* 2:9; *Shulḥan Arukh*, *Ḥoshen Mishpat* 7:2).

**NOTES**

**A certain blind person – הַהוּא סַמְיָא:** The Gemara does not specify the extent of this man's blindness. Some early commentaries write that he was blind in one eye (Ran on *Sanhedrin* 36b; Rav Sherira Gaon; Rif). Since he was blind in only one eye he could serve as a judge. One who is totally blind is disqualified to serve in this capacity, as a fully blind individual is unfit to testify, and therefore he is certainly unfit to judge (Rambam *Sefer Shofetim*, *Hilkhot Sanhedrin* 2:9; *Shulḥan Arukh*, *Ḥoshen Mishpat* 7:2). Others maintain that even one who is entirely blind is fit to judge (*Tosafot*) in cases of monetary law (Mordekhai on *Sanhedrin*).

רַבִּי יוֹחָנָן סְתָמָא אַחֲרִינָא אַשְׁכַּח, דִּתְנַן: דִּינֵי מָמוֹנוֹת דָּנִין בַּיּוֹם וְגוֹמְרִין בַּלַּיְלָה.

The Gemara answers: **Rabbi Yoḥanan found another unattributed mishna** which indicates a different conclusion. **As we learned** in the mishna in tractate *Sanhedrin* (32a): In cases of **monetary law,** the court **judges during the daytime, and concludes** the deliberations and issues their ruling even **at night.** This is not the *halakha* with regard to leprous marks, which may not be viewed at night at all. Accordingly, one does not compare judging cases of monetary law to viewing leprous marks. Since this comparison was the source for disqualifying a blind judge, one cannot derive from it that a blind judge is disqualified.

וּמַאי אוּלְמֵיהּ דְּהַאי סְתָמָא מֵהַאי סְתָמָא? אִיבָּעֵית אֵימָא: סְתָמָא דְּרַבִּים עָדִיף, וְאִיבָּעֵית אֵימָא: מִשּׁוּם דְּקָתָנֵי לָהּ גַּבֵּי הִלְכְתָא דְּדַיָּינֵי.

The Gemara asks: **And** in **what** manner is **the strength of that unattributed** mishna in tractate *Sanhedrin* greater **than** the strength of **this unattributed** mishna here? Why did Rabbi Yoḥanan accept the ruling of that mishna? The Gemara explains: **If you wish, say** that **an unattributed** mishna that records the opinion **of many** Sages, as in *Sanhedrin,* is **preferable,** whereas the mishna here was established as in accordance with the individual opinion of Rabbi Meir. **And if you wish, say** instead that it is **because** the mishna in *Sanhedrin* **teaches this** *halakha* **in the context of the** ***halakhot*** **of judges.** Since that chapter is the primary source for all of the *halakhot* of court matters, its rulings are of greater weight.

מתני׳ כׇּל שֶׁחַיָּיב בְּמַעַשְׂרוֹת – מְטַמֵּא טוּמְאַת אוֹכָלִין, וְיֵשׁ שֶׁמְּטַמֵּא טוּמְאַת אוֹכָלִין וְאֵינוֹ חַיָּיב בְּמַעַשְׂרוֹת.

**MISHNA** Any food from **which** one is **obligated to** separate **tithes becomes impure with the ritual impurity of food; and there is** food **that becomes impure with the ritual impurity of food but** from **which one is not obligated to** separate **tithes.**

גמ׳ לְאֵתוֹיֵי מַאי? לְאֵתוֹיֵי בָּשָׂר וְדָגִים וּבֵיצִים.

**GEMARA** The Gemara asks: **What is added** by the last clause of this mishna? The Gemara answers: This serves **to add meat, fish, and eggs.**[H] Although they are subject to the ritual impurity of food, one is not obligated to separate tithes from them.

מתני׳ כׇּל שֶׁחַיָּיב בְּפֵאָה – חַיָּיב בְּמַעַשְׂרוֹת, וְיֵשׁ שֶׁחַיָּיב בְּמַעַשְׂרוֹת וְאֵינוֹ חַיָּיב בְּפֵאָה.

**MISHNA** With regard to **any** produce from **which** one is **obligated to** designate **produce in the corner of the field given to the poor** [***pe'a***], as commanded in the Torah (see Leviticus 19:9, 23:22), one is **obligated to** separate **tithes** from it; **and there is** produce from **which** one is **obligated to** separate **tithes but** from **which one is not obligated to** designate ***pe'a.***

גמ׳ לְאֵתוֹיֵי מַאי? לְאֵתוֹיֵי תְּאֵנָה, וְיָרָק שֶׁאֵינוֹ חַיָּיב בְּפֵאָה. דִּתְנַן, כְּלָל אָמְרוּ בְּפֵאָה: כׇּל שֶׁהוּא אוֹכֶל, וְנִשְׁמָר, וְגִידּוּלוֹ מִן הָאָרֶץ, וּלְקִיטָתוֹ כְּאֶחָד, וּמַכְנִיסוֹ לְקִיּוּם – חַיָּיב בְּפֵאָה.

**GEMARA** The Gemara asks: **What is added** by the last clause of the mishna? The Gemara answers: It serves **to add figs and vegetables,** for **which** one is **not obligated** to designate ***pe'a,*** although the obligation of tithes does apply to them. **As we learned** in a mishna (*Pe'a* 1:4): The Sages **stated a principle with regard to** the *halakhot* of ***pe'a:*** With regard to **anything that is food, and is protected, and** that **grows from the earth, and is gathered as one,** i.e., there is one fixed time for gathering it, **and** that one **brings in** to store **for preservation,** its owner **is obligated to** designate ***pe'a.***[H]

HALAKHA

**Meat, fish, and eggs – בָּשָׂר וְדָגִים וּבֵיצִים:** Any food that is normally intended for human consumption, e.g., meat and fish, is susceptible to becoming ritually impure. Food that is not generally used for human consumption is not susceptible to ritual impurity unless it was specifically designated for human consumption. In all cases, food is not susceptible to impurity until it comes into contact with one of the seven liquids, which are water, dew, oil, wine, milk, blood, and honey (Rambam *Sefer Tahara, Hilkhot Tumat Okhalin* 1:1, 3:3).

**Obligated to designate *pe'a* – חַיָּיב בְּפֵאָה:** The obligation of *pe'a* applies to any food that grows from the earth, is protected, is all gathered as one, and that one brings in to store for preservation (Rambam *Sefer Zera'im, Hilkhot Mattenot Aniyyim* 2:1).

אוֹכֶל – לְמַעוּטֵי סְפִיחֵי סֵטִים וְקוֹצָה, וְנִשְׁמָר – לְמַעוּטֵי הֶפְקֵר, וְגִידּוּלוֹ מִן הָאָרֶץ – לְמַעוּטֵי כְּמֵהִים וּפִטְרִיּוֹת, וּלְקִיטָתוֹ כְּאֶחָד – לְמַעוּטֵי תְּאֵנָה, וּמַכְנִיסוֹ לְקִיּוּם – לְמַעוּטֵי יָרָק.

The Gemara analyzes each criterion of the mishna. The clause: **Anything that is food,** serves **to exclude** the ***sefiḥin***, produce that grew without being intentionally planted, **of woad** [***setim***][B] **and safflower** [***vekotza***].[B] These plants are used as dyes rather than for food. The clause: **And is protected,** serves **to exclude ownerless** crops, which no one protects. The clause: **And grows from the earth,** serves **to exclude truffles**[B] **and mushrooms,** which do not draw sustenance from the ground. The clause: **And is gathered as one,** serves **to exclude** the **fig** tree, whose fruit is gathered over an extended period, as the figs do not all ripen at the same time. Finally, the clause: **And** that **one brings in** to storage **for preservation,** serves **to exclude vegetables,** which cannot be stored for lengthy periods.

וְאִילּוּ גַּבֵּי מַעֲשֵׂר תְּנַן: כָּל שֶׁהוּא אוֹכֶל, וְנִשְׁמָר, וְגִידּוּלוֹ מִן הָאָרֶץ – חַיָּיב בְּמַעַשְׂרוֹת, וְאִילּוּ "לְקִיטָתוֹ כְּאֶחָד, וּמַכְנִיסוֹ לְקִיּוּם" לָא קָתָנֵי.

**And yet** in the case **of tithe, we learned** in a mishna (*Ma'asrot* 1:1) with regard to the *halakhot* of tithes: **Anything that is food, and is protected, and grows from the earth is obligated in tithes.**[H] **And whereas** some of the conditions overlap, the following criteria **are not taught** with regard to tithes: **Gathered as one, and that one brings in** to storage **for preservation.** Evidently, the obligation of tithes applies to fig trees and vegetables, despite the fact that the obligation of *pe'a* does not apply.

אִם הָיוּ בָּהֶם שׁוּמִים וּבְצָלִין – חַיָּיבִין, דִּתְנַן, מַלְבְּנוֹת בְּצָלִים שֶׁבֵּין הַיָּרָק, רַבִּי יוֹסֵי אוֹמֵר: פֵּאָה מִכָּל אַחַת וְאַחַת, וַחֲכָמִים אוֹמְרִים: מֵאַחַת עַל הַכֹּל.

The Gemara notes that **if** these vegetables that are exempt from *pe'a* **contained garlic and onions,** which are stored for an extended period of time, then they are **obligated** in *pe'a* as well. **As we learned** in a mishna (*Pe'a* 3:4): If one has **garden beds of onions that are between the vegetables,**[H] **Rabbi Yosei says** that one leaves a separate ***pe'a* from each and every one** of the beds. **And the Rabbis say** one leaves *pe'a* **from one** garden bed **for all** of them.

אָמַר רַבָּה בַּר בַּר חָנָה אָמַר רַבִּי יוֹחָנָן: עוֹלְשִׁין שֶׁזְּרָעָן מִתְּחִילָּה לִבְהֵמָה, וְנִמְלַךְ עֲלֵיהֶן לְאָדָם,

§ **Rabba bar bar Ḥana says** that **Rabbi Yoḥanan says:** In the case of **endives**[B] **that were initially planted** to be fed **to animals, and** later the owner **reconsidered their** designation and decided to use them **for human** consumption[H]

## HALAKHA

**Obligated in tithes – חַיָּיב בְּמַעַשְׂרוֹת:** The obligation of *teruma* applies to any food normally intended for human consumption that grows from the earth and is protected. This obligation is a mitzva by Torah law (Rambam *Sefer Zera'im*, *Hilkhot Terumot* 2:1).

**Garden beds of onions that are between the vegetables – מַלְבְּנוֹת בְּצָלִים שֶׁבֵּין הַיָּרָק:** In a case of garden beds of onions that are between the vegetables, one leaves *pe'a* from one garden bed for all of the onions, despite the fact that the vegetables separate the beds of onions. This *halakha* is in accordance with the opinion of the Rabbis in the mishna in tractate *Pe'a* (Rambam *Sefer Zera'im*, *Hilkhot Mattenot Aniyyim* 3:10).

**And the owner reconsidered their designation and decided to use them for human consumption – וְנִמְלַךְ עֲלֵיהֶן לְאָדָם:** With regard to endives that were initially planted for feeding to an animal, where later the owner reconsidered and decided to use them for human consumption, they are not susceptible to ritual impurity unless they were designated for human consumption after they were detached from the earth. This is due to the fact that intent to designate the produce is ineffective while it is attached to the earth. The *halakha* is in accordance with the opinion of Rabba bar bar Ḥana, citing Rabbi Yoḥanan (Rambam *Sefer Tahara*, *Hilkhot Tumat Okhalin* 3:3).

## BACKGROUND

**Woad [*setim*] – סֵטִים:** Woad, *Isatis tinctoria*, is a biennial or multiannual plant from the Brassicaceae family, reaching up to 1 m in height, with simple leaves and yellow flowers. By means of various compressing and fermenting processes, a highly durable indigo-blue dye can be extracted from its leaves. Nowadays, the use of woad for dye production has all but ceased, as dye producers manufacture a less expensive synthetic indigo dye. Although it is no longer cultivated, woad can be found growing naturally in many places in Eretz Yisrael.

Woad

**Safflower [*kotza*] – קוֹצָה:** Safflower, *Cartamus tinctorus*, is mentioned in the Talmud by the names of *ḥariya*, *morika*, and *kotza*. It is a thorny plant from the Asteraceae family whose flowers were used to make yellow dye. Nowadays its leaves are used as a high-quality fodder for animals and its seeds for producing oil.

**Truffles – כְּמֵהִים:** Truffles belong to the *Tuber* genus, a special genus of fungi that grows entirely underground, including its fruit. The body of the fruit looks like a slightly rounded mass that is black, brown, and whitish. Truffles generally grow up to 3–5 cm in height and up to 10 cm in diameter, and a large truffle can weigh as much as 1 kg. Truffles are harvested by removing the earth from above them, a task sometimes performed by specially trained animals. Most truffles are edible at early stages of their growth and are regarded as a delicacy.

Truffles

Safflower

**Endives – עוֹלְשִׁין:** This refers to *Cichorium endivia*, a winter vegetable similar to lettuce. It has a flower that is usually blue, but sometimes it is pink and white. Its leaves, which grow clustered tightly together around the base of the plant, have a pleasant taste when they are young but grow bitter as the plant matures. There are several varieties of endives, including curly endive and broad-leaved endive. One type of endive, *Chicorium intybus*, or common chicory, is mainly harvested today for its root, which can be used as a substitute for coffee.

Endive

צְרִיכוֹת מַחֲשָׁבָה לִכְשֶׁיִּתָּלְשׁוּ. קָסָבַר: מַחֲשֶׁבֶת חִבּוּר לֹא שְׁמָהּ מַחֲשָׁבָה.

**they require intent**[N] to be used for human consumption **once they are detached** from the ground, in order for them to be susceptible to ritual impurity. Rabbi Yoḥanan rules in this manner because he **holds** that **intent** to designate produce while it is **attached** to the ground **is not considered intent.**[N]

אֲמַר רָבָא: אַף אֲנַן נַמִּי תְּנֵינָא, שְׁלֹשָׁה עָשָׂר דְּבָרִים נֶאֶמְרוּ בְּנִבְלַת עוֹף טָהוֹר, וְזֶה אֶחָד מֵהֶן – צְרִיכָה מַחֲשָׁבָה וְאֵינָהּ צְרִיכָה הֶכְשֵׁר. אַלְמָא: מַחֲשֶׁבֶת חַיִּים – לֹא שְׁמָהּ מַחֲשָׁבָה, הָכָא נַמִּי – מַחֲשֶׁבֶת חִבּוּר לֹא שְׁמָהּ מַחֲשָׁבָה.

**Rava said: We learn** in a mishna (*Teharot* 1:1) **as well: Thirteen matters were stated with regard to the carcass of a kosher bird,**[H] **and this is one of them:** In order for such a carcass to be susceptible to impurity and to be capable of imparting impurity to food through contact, it **requires** a person's **intention** to eat it, **but it does not require** exposure to liquid to be **rendered susceptible** to impurity. Even if one had intent to eat the bird while it was still alive, intent is still required after it became a carcass for it to transmit impurity. Rava concludes: **Evidently, intent** that the bird be eaten while the bird is **alive is not considered intent. Here too, intent** to designate produce while it is **attached** to the ground **is not considered intent.**

רַבִּי זֵירָא אָמַר: הָכָא בְּגוֹזָל שֶׁנָּפַל מִן הָרוּם עָסְקִינַן, דְּלָא הֲוָה קַמָּן דְּלִיחְשׁוֹב עֲלֵיהּ.

**Rabbi Zeira said:** Rava's proof is inconclusive, as **here we are dealing with a young bird that fell from a height, where** the bird **was not before us** prior to it becoming a carcass, **so that** one could have had **intent that it** is food. Consequently, it requires intent afterward for it to impart impurity, but had there been intent while it was still alive, that would have sufficed.

אֲמַר לֵיהּ אַבַּיֵי: תַּרְנְגוֹלֶת שֶׁבְּיַבְנֶה, מַאי אִיכָּא לְמֵימַר? אֲמַר לֵיהּ: תַּרְנְגוֹל בָּרָא הֲוָה.

**Abaye said to** Rabbi Zeira: **What is there to say** about the case of the **chicken in Yavne?** In that instance the Sages deemed the chicken impure due to intent only after it became a carcass, despite the fact that it was present before them while it was alive. This apparently indicates that intent which occurred while the bird was alive is not considered intent. Rabbi Zeira **said to** Abaye: That **was** actually **a wild chicken,**[B] which was not before them while it was alive, and therefore there was no intent that it should be food while it was alive.

אַחִיכוּ עֲלֵיהּ: תַּרְנְגוֹל בָּרָא – עוֹף טָמֵא הוּא, וְעוֹף טָמֵא מִי קָמְטַמֵּא? אֲמַר לְהוּ אַבַּיֵי: גַּבְרָא רַבָּה אֲמַר מִילְּתָא לָא תְּחִיכוּ עֲלֵיהּ, בְּתַרְנְגוֹלֶת שֶׁמָּרְדָה, וּמַאי בָּרָא – דְּאִיבְּרַאי מִמָּרָה.

Those who heard this comment **laughed at** Rabbi Zeira's interpretation: **A wild chicken is a non-kosher bird, and does a non-kosher bird impart impurity? Abaye said to them: A great man has stated a matter; do not laugh at him.** Rabbi Zeira means that this is referring **to a chicken that rebelled** against its owner, ran away to the wild, and raised its kosher chicks there. One of those chicks subsequently returned from the wild. Consequently, it had not been present before the Sages while it was alive. **And what** did Rabbi Zeira mean when he mentioned **a wild** [*bara*] chicken? He meant one **that was created** [*de'ivrai*] **from** a chicken **that rebelled.**

## NOTES

**They require intent** – צְרִיכוֹת מַחֲשָׁבָה: Since endives are customarily grown for consumption by animals, they require intent to use them for human consumption after they are detached in order for them to be susceptible to ritual impurity. Such intent is effective despite the fact that when they were attached to the ground the owner planned to use them to feed his animals, as he has retracted the original designation (Rashi).

With regard to the nature of this designation, some maintain that one must retract the prior designation verbally, in accordance with the general opinion of Rashi and *Tosafot* (*Bava Metzia* 43b) that when the Gemara refers to intention it means a verbal statement (*Tosefot Yom Tov* on *Kelim* 25:9). Others contend that mere thought suffices in order for these to be rendered impure with the impurity of food (Rabbi Ovadya Bartenura). Some claim that this matter is an unresolved dispute between the early commentaries (*Tiferet Yisrael* on *Kelim* 25:9).

**Intent to designate produce while it is attached to the ground is not considered intent** – מַחֲשֶׁבֶת חִבּוּר לֹא שְׁמָהּ מַחֲשָׁבָה: Food items that are attached to the ground are not susceptible to ritual impurity. Even food that was already impure loses its impurity when it is planted. The commentaries explain that anything attached to the ground is not defined as food, and therefore cannot attain, or even retain, the status of impure food (Rashi on *Pesaḥim* 34a).

## HALAKHA

**The carcass of a kosher bird** – נִבְלַת עוֹף טָהוֹר: The unslaughtered carcass of a kosher bird does not require intent for it to be classified as human food, nor does it require contact with liquid to become susceptible to the ritual impurity of food. The reason is that it is customarily grown for human consumption, and any item that is generally grown for human consumption does not require intent to become susceptible to impurity of food, as it will ultimately transmit impurity to people and vessels by an olive-bulk. It also does not require contact with a liquid, in accordance with the principle that an item that will contract a severe form of ritual impurity does not require contact with liquid to be rendered susceptible to impurity, as stated in the mishna in tractate *Okatzin* (Rambam *Sefer Tahara*, *Hilkhot Tumat Okhalin* 3:3).

## BACKGROUND

**Wild chicken** – תַּרְנְגוֹל בָּרָא: Red junglefowl, *Gallus gallus*, are the untamed ancestors of the domesticated chicken. However, they are indigenous to the forests of Asia, and there is no basis for the assumption that these were found in Babylonia. It is possible that the term wild chicken also refers to other wild fowl that are similar in appearance to chickens, e.g., the partridge or the pheasant.

Red junglefowl

Rock partridges

רַב פַּפָּא אֲמַר: תַּרְנְגוֹלְתָּא דְּאַגְמָא הֲוַאי. רַב פַּפָּא לְטַעְמֵיהּ, דְּאָמַר רַב פַּפָּא: תַּרְנְגוֹל דְּאַגְמָא – אָסוּר, תַּרְנְגוֹלְתָּא דְּאַגְמָא – שָׁרְיָא,

**Rav Pappa stated** an alternative interpretation: **It was a marsh** [*de'agma*][B] **hen.**[B] Since no one lives in a marsh, there was no opportunity for intent while it was alive, and therefore intent was necessary afterward. The Gemara adds: **Rav Pappa** conforms **to his** standard line of **reasoning** in this regard, **as Rav Pappa said:** The animal called **the marsh rooster is prohibited,** as it is a non-kosher bird, whereas **the marsh hen is** kosher and **permitted.**

וְסִימָנֵיךְ – עַמּוֹנִי וְלֹא עַמּוֹנִית. דָּרַשׁ מָרֵימָר: תַּרְנְגוֹלְתָּא דְּאַגְמָא – אֲסִירָא. חַזְיוּהָ רַבָּנַן דְּדָרְסָה וְאָכְלָה, וְהַיְינוּ גֵּירוּתָא.

**And your mnemonic** to remember which animal is permitted and which is prohibited is the well-known statement of the Sages with regard to the verse: "An Ammonite or a Moabite shall not enter into the assembly of the Lord" (Deuteronomy 23:4). **An Ammonite** man is unfit to enter the assembly **but not an Ammonite woman.** Here too, the animal with a female name is permitted, whereas the one with a male name is prohibited. **Mareimar taught: The marsh hen is prohibited,** contrary to the opinion of Rav Pappa, as **the Sages saw that it mauled and ate** its prey. **And this is the *geiruta*,** a non-kosher bird.

תָּנוּ רַבָּנַן, גּוֹזָל שֶׁנָּפַל לַגַּת, וְחִישֵּׁב עָלָיו לְהַעֲלוֹתוֹ לְכוּתִי – טָמֵא, לְכֶלֶב – טָהוֹר. רַבִּי יוֹחָנָן בֶּן נוּרִי אוֹמֵר: אַף לְכֶלֶב – טָמֵא.

§ Apropos the case of a young kosher bird that fell and died, **the Sages taught** in a *baraita*: **A young** kosher **bird that fell into a winepress**[BH] and died there, **where** the owner **intended to draw it up** from the press **for a Samaritan** to eat, is **ritually impure,** like any carcass of a kosher bird. If he intended to draw it up from the press **for a dog** to eat, it is **ritually pure. Rabbi Yoḥanan ben Nuri says: Even** if he intended to draw it up from the press **for a dog** to eat, it is **impure,** as the bird does not require intent for it to be impure.

אָמַר רַבִּי יוֹחָנָן בֶּן נוּרִי: קַל וָחוֹמֶר, אִם מְטַמֵּא טוּמְאָה חֲמוּרָה שֶׁלֹּא בְּמַחֲשָׁבָה, לֹא יְטַמֵּא טוּמְאָה קַלָּה שֶׁלֹּא בְּמַחֲשָׁבָה?

**Rabbi Yoḥanan ben Nuri says** in explanation of his opinion: This *halakha* can be derived by the following ***a fortiori*** inference: **If** the carcass of a kosher bird **transmits severe** ritual **impurity,** i.e., it renders one's garments impure when an olive-bulk of it is in the throat, **without thought,** i.e., even if no one had intent that a person should eat it, should it **not transmit a lenient impurity** of food, by touch alone, likewise **without thought?**

אָמְרוּ לוֹ: לֹא, אִם אָמַרְתָּ בְּטוּמְאָה חֲמוּרָה – שֶׁכֵּן אֵינָהּ יוֹרֶדֶת לְכָךְ, תֹּאמַר בְּטוּמְאָה קַלָּה – שֶׁכֵּן יוֹרֶדֶת לְכָךְ!

The Rabbis **said to** Rabbi Yoḥanan ben Nuri: **No,** this is not a valid *a fortiori* inference. **If you said** that there is no requirement of intent **with regard to severe** ritual **impurity, that** is because severe ritual impurity **does not assume** its status **with that** requirement of thought, i.e., intent is not relevant to that type of impurity. **Shall you** also **say** that there is no requirement of thought **with regard to lenient impurity, which does assume** its status **with that** requirement of thought? The Gemara will soon explain the precise meaning of this concept of assuming its status with the requirement of thought.

אָמַר לָהֶן: תַּרְנְגוֹלֶת שֶׁבְּיַבְנֶה תּוֹכִיחַ, שֶׁיּוֹרֶדֶת לְכָךְ – וְטִמְּאוּהָ שֶׁלֹּא בְּמַחֲשָׁבָה. אָמְרוּ לוֹ: מִשָּׁם רְאָיָה? כּוּתִים הָיוּ שָׁם, וְחָשְׁבוּ עָלֶיהָ לַאֲכִילָה.

Rabbi Yoḥanan ben Nuri **said to** the Rabbis: The case of the **chicken in Yavne can prove** that the question of whether or not intent is required does not depend on that factor. The case in Yavne involved an item **that does assume** its status **with that** requirement of thought, **and** yet the Sages **declared it impure without intent.** The Rabbis **said to** Rabbi Yoḥanan ben Nuri: Will you cite **proof from there?** In that case **there were Samaritans there, and** the people in Yavne **intended that it be eaten** by the Samaritans.

**BACKGROUND**

Marsh [*agma*] – אַגְמָא: The term *agma*, like its Hebrew counterpart *agam*, refers to a place next to a river or a pond abundant in vegetation such as reeds, low trees, and grass. Since the region of Babylonia is flat with a large amount of river erosion, it has many swamps, which form marshes. These marshes, which were swampy, boggy areas that occasionally flood when the rivers overflow, were ownerless but were often used as grazing pasture for animals.

Marsh hen – תַּרְנְגוֹלְתָּא דְּאַגְמָא: In contrast to kosher animals and fish, the Torah does not mention the characteristic signs that distinguish birds as kosher. Rather, the verses (Leviticus 11:13–19; Deuteronomy 14:12–19) simply list the non-kosher birds. Nevertheless, the Sages provide three identification signs of a kosher bird: One of its toes is significantly longer than the others; it has a discernible crop; and its craw, the thick, muscular stomach, is easily peeled away. Moreover, it is not a bird of prey. The discovery that a given bird attacked its prey is a clear indication that it is not kosher. Despite these signs, the Sages declared that in practice a species of bird should be considered kosher only if there is an accepted tradition to that effect.

A young bird that fell into a winepress – גּוֹזָל שֶׁנָּפַל לַגַּת: The winepresses in the time of the Mishna and Gemara were typically carved into a rock where grapes were placed and pressed. Between the upper press, where the grapes were pressed, and the lower press, where the wine was collected, there was a small pipe carved into the rock through which the liquid flowed.

Both the upper and lower presses were uncovered, which is why it was common for young birds to fall in and drown in the juice that accumulated there.

Winepress, first century CE

**HALAKHA**

A young kosher bird that fell into a winepress – גּוֹזָל שֶׁנָּפַל לַגַּת: If a young kosher bird fell into a winepress and died, it requires intent to become susceptible to the impurity of food. This is the case even in a city. If one intended it to be eaten by a gentile when he drew it out of the press, it is susceptible to impurity, as it was designated for human consumption. But if he intended it to be fed to a dog, it is not susceptible to impurity (Rambam *Sefer Tahara*, *Hilkhot Tumat Okhalin* 3:10).

בְּמַאי עָסְקִינַן? אִילֵּימָא בִּכְרַכִּים – לָמָּה לָהּ מַחֲשָׁבָה? וְהָתְנַן: נִבְלַת בְּהֵמָה טְהוֹרָה בְּכָל מָקוֹם, וְנִבְלַת עוֹף טָהוֹר וְהַחֵלֶב בִּכְרַכִּים – אֵין צְרִיכִין לֹא מַחֲשָׁבָה וְלֹא הֶכְשֵׁר!

The Gemara analyzes the case of a young kosher bird that fell into a winepress: **What** type of situation **are we dealing with? If we say** that we are dealing **with cities,** where there are many people available to consume all sorts of food, including the carcass of a kosher bird, **why does it** require **intent? But didn't we learn** in a mishna (*Okatzin* 3:3): **An unslaughtered carcass of a kosher animal in any location,**[H] whether the population is large or small, **and the carcass of a kosher bird or the fat** of a kosher animal found **in cities** [***bakerakim***],[L] **require neither intent** for human consumption **nor** contact with liquid for them to be rendered **susceptible** to impurity?

אֶלָּא בִּכְפָרִים, וּמִי אִיכָּא לְמַאן דַּאֲמַר דְּלָא בָּעֲיָא מַחֲשָׁבָה? וְהָתְנַן: נִבְלַת בְּהֵמָה טְמֵאָה בְּכָל מָקוֹם, וְנִבְלַת עוֹף טָהוֹר בִּכְפָרִים – צְרִיכָה מַחֲשָׁבָה, וְאֵינָהּ צְרִיכָה הֶכְשֵׁר!

**Rather,** it must be referring **to villages,** where the population is small and there are not many people who would eat the carcass. **But** this too is difficult: **Is there anyone who said that intent is not required** in the case of a carcass of a non-kosher bird for the impurity of food? **Didn't we learn** in the beginning of that same mishna: **A carcass of a non-kosher animal** found **in any location,**[N] **and an unslaughtered carcass of a kosher bird in the villages**[H] both **require intent** to consume them, **but they do not require** contact with a liquid to become **susceptible** to ritual impurity?

אָמַר רַבִּי זְעֵירָא בַּר חֲנִינָא: לְעוֹלָם – בִּכְרַךְ, וְגִתּוֹ – מְאַסְתּוֹ וַעֲשָׂאַתּוּ כִּכְפָר.

**Rabbi Zeira bar Ḥanina says: Actually,** the *baraita* is referring to a case that occurred **in a city,** and even so intent is required. The reason is that the young bird fell into a winepress, **and the winepress rendered it disgusting and** thereby **rendered it like** the carcass of a kosher bird in **a village,** where there are few people who would eat it.

אָמַר רַבִּי יוֹחָנָן בֶּן נוּרִי: קַל וָחוֹמֶר, אִם מְטַמְּאָה טוּמְאָה חֲמוּרָה שֶׁלֹּא בְּמַחֲשָׁבָה – לֹא תְּטַמֵּא טוּמְאָה קַלָּה שֶׁלֹּא בְּמַחֲשָׁבָה?

The Gemara analyzes the exchange cited above. **Rabbi Yoḥanan ben Nuri says** that this *halakha* can be derived by **an *a fortiori*** inference: **If** the carcass of a kosher bird **transmits severe** ritual **impurity without thought,** should it **not transmit lenient impurity without thought?**

אָמְרוּ לוֹ: לֹא, אִם אָמַרְתָּ בְּטוּמְאָה חֲמוּרָה – שֶׁכֵּן אֵינָהּ יוֹרֶדֶת לְכָךְ.

The Rabbis **said to** Rabbi Yoḥanan ben Nuri: **No,** this is not a valid *a fortiori* inference. **If you said** so **with regard to severe ritual impurity, that** is because it **does not assume** its status **with that** requirement of thought.

מַאי "אֵינָהּ יוֹרֶדֶת לְכָךְ"? אָמַר רָבָא, הָכִי קָאָמְרִי לֵיהּ: לֹא, אִם אָמַרְתָּ

The Gemara asks: **What** is the meaning of the clause: It **does not assume** its status **with that** requirement of thought? In what manner is thought required for the lenient impurity of food it imparts in the case of a bird carcass but not required for the severe impurity it imparts when it is in the throat? **Rava said** that **this is what** the Rabbis **said to** Rabbi Yoḥanan ben Nuri: **No, if you said** that there is no requirement of thought

**LANGUAGE**

Cities [*kerakim*] – כְּרַכִּים: This refers to large cities that were typically surrounded by a wall. Some maintain that the term is from the Greek χάραξ, *kharax*, a place fortified by beams. Others contend that it has a Semitic, or perhaps Assyrian source, related to the root *kaf*, *reish*, *kaf*, meaning encirclement, which is a fitting description for a walled city.

**NOTES**

A carcass of a non-kosher animal found in any location – נִבְלַת בְּהֵמָה טְמֵאָה בְּכָל מָקוֹם: Rashi explains that as the carcass of a non-kosher animal is generally not considered food, it requires intent for consumption in order for it to be susceptible to impurity as food. It can be claimed that the question of whether or not it is subject to impurity as food is irrelevant, since in any case it will transmit the impurity of a carcass to people and vessels, and certainly to food and liquids, when it is of the volume of an olive-bulk. Nevertheless, the issue of its impurity as food is important in a case where there is other impure food that is less than the minimum measure for impurity as food, i.e., an egg-bulk, and there is less than an olive-bulk of the carcass of a non-kosher animal. Since this piece is less than an olive-bulk it does not transmit impurity as a carcass. But if it is subject to impurity as food it can combine with the other impure food to complete the measure for impurity of an egg-bulk.

**HALAKHA**

An unslaughtered carcass of a kosher animal in any location, etc. – נִבְלַת בְּהֵמָה טְהוֹרָה בְּכָל מָקוֹם וכו׳: The unslaughtered carcass of a kosher animal in any location, the carcass of a kosher bird in any location, and the fat of a kosher animal found in cities require neither intent for human consumption nor contact with liquid for them to be rendered susceptible to impurity. The reason is that they are designated for human consumption, and anything that is designated for human consumption does not require intent to become susceptible to the impurity of food. No contact with liquid is required, as they will ultimately transmit impurity to people and vessels in the amount of an olive-bulk. This ruling is in accordance with the mishna in tractate *Okatzin* (Rambam *Sefer Tahara*, *Hilkhot Tumat Okhalin* 3:3).

A carcass of a non-kosher animal in any location and an unslaughtered carcass of a kosher bird in the villages – נִבְלַת בְּהֵמָה טְמֵאָה בְּכָל מָקוֹם וְנִבְלַת עוֹף טָהוֹר בִּכְפָרִים: The carcass of a kosher bird in the villages and the unslaughtered carcass of a non-kosher animal in any location require intent for human consumption, but not contact with liquid, to be rendered susceptible to impurity. This *halakha* applies only when they are less than an olive-bulk in volume. But if there is an olive-bulk of the carcass it is a primary source of ritual impurity even in the absence of intention. This ruling is in accordance with the mishna in tractate *Okatzin* (Rambam *Sefer Tahara*, *Hilkhot Tumat Okhalin* 3:3).

בְּטוּמְאָה חֲמוּרָה – שֶׁכֵּן אֵינָהּ עוֹשָׂה כַּיּוֹצֵא בָּהּ, תֹּאמַר בְּטוּמְאָה קַלָּה – שֶׁעוֹשָׂה כַּיּוֹצֵא בָּהּ.

in a case of **severe** ritual **impurity,** i.e., when the carcass of a kosher bird renders one's garments impure while it is in his throat, **which does not render** impure another item **similar to it,** i.e., a person who is rendered impure by the carcass does not render another man impure; **shall you** also **say** that there is no requirement of thought **in** the case of **lenient impurity,** i.e., when the carcass transmits impurity as food, **which does render** impure another item **similar to it?** Food that became impure transmits impurity to other food, albeit by rabbinic law.

אֲמַר לֵיהּ אַבָּיֵי: כׇּל דְּכֵן הוּא, וּמָה טוּמְאָה חֲמוּרָה דְּקִילָּא – דְּאֵינָהּ עוֹשָׂה כַּיּוֹצֵא בָּהּ – מְטַמְּאָה שֶׁלֹּא בְּמַחְשָׁבָה. טוּמְאָה קַלָּה דַּחֲמִירָא, דְּעוֹשָׂה כַּיּוֹצֵא בָּהּ – אֵינוֹ דִּין שֶׁמְּטַמְּאָה שֶׁלֹּא בְּמַחְשָׁבָה?

**Abaye said to** Rava: But in that case, **all the more so** impurity as food should apply without thought. **If severe impurity,** i.e., the unique impurity of the carcass of a kosher bird, **which is lenient** in the sense **that it does not render** impure another item **similar to it,** nevertheless **imparts impurity without thought,** i.e., without one knowing what is in his throat, then with regard to **lenient impurity,** i.e., the carcass's impurity as food, **which is** more **severe** in the sense **that it renders** impure another item **similar to it, isn't it logical that it** should **impart impurity without thought?**

אֶלָּא אָמַר רַב שֵׁשֶׁת, הָכִי קָאָמַר: לֹא אִם אָמַרְתָּ בְּטוּמְאָה חֲמוּרָה – שֶׁכֵּן אֵינָהּ צְרִיכָה הֶכְשֵׁר, תֹּאמַר בְּטוּמְאָה קַלָּה – שֶׁצְּרִיכָה הֶכְשֵׁר.

**Rather, Rav Sheshet said** that **this** is what the Rabbis, who replied to Rabbi Yoḥanan ben Nuri, **are saying: No, if you said** that thought is not required **with regard to severe impurity,** i.e., the carcass of a kosher bird in the throat, **as it does not require** contact with a liquid for it to be rendered **susceptible** to ritual impurity, **shall you** also **say** that thought is not required **with regard to lenient impurity,** i.e., its impurity as food, **where** it **does require** contact with a liquid for it to be rendered **susceptible** to ritual impurity?

וּמִי צְרִיכָה הֶכְשֵׁר? וְהָתְנַן, שְׁלֹשָׁה דְּבָרִים נֶאֶמְרוּ בְּנִבְלַת עוֹף טָהוֹר: צְרִיכָה מַחְשָׁבָה, וְאֵינָהּ מְטַמְּאָה אֶלָּא בְּבֵית הַבְּלִיעָה, וְאֵינָהּ צְרִיכָה הֶכְשֵׁר!

The Gemara asks: **And does** the carcass of a kosher bird **require** contact with a liquid for it to be rendered **susceptible** to impurity as food? **But didn't we learn** in a *baraita*: **Three matters were stated with regard to the carcass of a kosher bird:** In order for it to be susceptible to impurity as food, it **requires** a person's **intent** to eat it; **and it transmits impurity** to garments by rendering one who swallows it ritually impure **only** when an olive-bulk of it is **in the throat;**[H] **and it does not require** contact with a liquid for it to be rendered **susceptible** to ritual impurity?[H]

נְהִי דְּהֶכְשֵׁר שֶׁרֶץ לָא בָּעֲיָא, הֶכְשֵׁר מַיִם בָּעֲיָא.

The Gemara answers: **Although it does not require** contact **with a creeping animal** for it to be rendered **susceptible** to impurity, i.e., it is inherently impure, nevertheless **it does require** contact with **water**[N] or another liquid for it to be rendered **susceptible** to ritual impurity.

מַאי שְׁנָא הֶכְשֵׁר שֶׁרֶץ דְּלָא בָּעֲיָא, כִּדְתָנָא דְּבֵי רַבִּי יִשְׁמָעֵאל, הֶכְשֵׁר מַיִם נָמֵי לָא תִּבְעֵי, כִּדְתָנָא דְּבֵי רַבִּי יִשְׁמָעֵאל!

The Gemara asks: **What is different** about being rendered **susceptible** to ritual impurity by contact with **a creeping animal that it does not require** this contact? This ruling is **in accordance with that which the school of Rabbi Yishmael taught.** If so, it should **also not require** contact with **water** or another liquid for it to be rendered **susceptible** to ritual impurity, likewise **in accordance with that which the school of Rabbi Yishmael taught.**

**NOTES**

**It does require contact with water** – הֶכְשֵׁר מַיִם בָּעֲיָא: In order for an item to be considered food with regard to susceptibility to ritual impurity, one of the seven liquids: Water, dew, oil, wine, milk, blood, or honey, must fall on it with the owner's knowledge and in accordance with his wishes (see *Makhshirin* 6:7).

**HALAKHA**

**It transmits impurity to garments only when an olive-bulk is in the throat** – אֵינָהּ מְטַמְּאָה אֶלָּא בְּבֵית הַבְּלִיעָה: Carcasses of kosher birds impart ritual impurity by Torah law, but not to one who touches or carries them, nor when it is still in his mouth. Rather, one who eats an olive-bulk of the meat of such a carcass contracts impurity when the meat is in his throat. One who is thereby rendered impure imparts impurity to any clothing or vessels that are in contact with him at the moment of swallowing, except for earthenware vessels (Rambam *Sefer Tahara, Hilkhot She'ar Avot HaTumot* 3:1).

**It does not require contact to be rendered susceptible to impurity** – אֵינָהּ צְרִיכָה הֶכְשֵׁר: The unslaughtered carcass of a kosher bird does not require intent to be classified as human food, nor does it require contact with liquid to become susceptible to the impurity of food. The reason is that it is customarily grown for human consumption, and anything that is customarily grown for human consumption does not require intent in order to become susceptible to the impurity of food. It also does not require contact with liquid, in accordance with the principle that an item that will contract a severe form of ritual impurity does not require contact with liquid to be rendered susceptible to impurity. This *halakha* is in accordance with the mishna in tractate *Okatzin* (Rambam *Sefer Tahara, Hilkhot Tumat Okhalin* 3:3).

דְּתָנָא דְּבֵי רַבִּי יִשְׁמָעֵאל: ״עַל כָּל זֶרַע זֵרוּעַ אֲשֶׁר יִזָּרֵעַ״,

As the school of Rabbi Yishmael taught in a *baraita*: The verse states that seeds contract impurity from the carcass of a creeping animal only if they first come into contact with water: "And if any part of their carcass fall **upon any sowing seed that is to be sown,** it is pure. But if water be put upon the seed, and any part of their carcass fall thereon, it is impure unto you" (Leviticus 11:37–38). This passage teaches that as long as water did not fall on the seeds, they are not susceptible to ritual impurity. This *halakha* applies to all items similar to seeds.

מָה זְרָעִים שֶׁאֵין סוֹפָן לְטַמֵּא טוּמְאָה חֲמוּרָה – צְרִיכִין הֶכְשֵׁר, אַף כָּל שֶׁאֵין סוֹפָן לְטַמֵּא טוּמְאָה חֲמוּרָה – צְרִיכִין הֶכְשֵׁר, יָצְתָה נִבְלַת עוֹף טָהוֹר שֶׁסּוֹפָהּ לְטַמֵּא טוּמְאָה חֲמוּרָה – שֶׁאֵין צָרִיךְ הֶכְשֵׁר.

Accordingly, **just as seeds, which will never transmit impurity severe** enough to transmit to humans,[N] like any food, **require** contact with liquid to be rendered **susceptible** to impurity, **so too, all** items **that will never transmit severe impurity require** contact with liquid to be rendered **susceptible** to impurity. This **excludes the carcass of a kosher bird, which will ultimately transmit impurity severe** enough to be transmitted to a human, i.e., when it is in his throat, and therefore **it does not require** contact with liquid for it to be rendered **susceptible** to ritual impurity.

אֶלָּא אָמַר רָבָא וְאִיתֵּימָא רַב פַּפָּא: שׁוּם טוּמְאָה חֲמוּרָה בְּעוֹלָם, שׁוּם טוּמְאָה קַלָּה בְּעוֹלָם.

**Rather, Rava said, and some say** that it was **Rav Pappa** who said: The Rabbis' rejection of Rabbi Yoḥanan ben Nuri's *a fortiori* inference is not based on the specific *halakha* of impurity of food imparted by the carcass of a bird. Rather, they are referring to the fact that **in general** there is no item under the common **name of severe impurity** that requires contact with a liquid for it to be rendered susceptible to ritual impurity. By contrast, with regard to the common **name of lenient impurity** as food, **in general** the items in this category require contact with a liquid for them to be rendered susceptible to impurity, despite the fact that the particular case of the carcass of a kosher bird is an exception. Therefore, intent is required for lenient impurity even in the case of a carcass of a kosher bird.

אָמַר רָבָא: וּמוֹדֶה רַבִּי יוֹחָנָן לְעִנְיַן מַעֲשֵׂר, דְּמַחְשֶׁבֶת חִיבּוּר – שְׁמָהּ מַחֲשָׁבָה. אָמַר רָבָא: מְנָא אָמֵינָא לַהּ – דִּתְנַן, הַסֵּיאָה וְהָאֵזוֹב וְהַקּוֹרָנִית שֶׁבְּחָצֵר, אִם הָיוּ נִשְׁמָרִין – חַיָּיבִין.

§ **Rava says: And Rabbi Yoḥanan concedes with regard to** the obligation to **tithe, that intent** while the produce is **attached** to the ground **is considered intent. Rava said: From where do I say** that **this** is the *halakha*? It is **as we learned** in a mishna (*Ma'asrot* 3:9) that deals with the obligation to tithe: **Savory, hyssop** [*veha'ezov*],[B] **and thyme** [*vehakoranit*],[B] i.e., various types of hyssop plants, that were growing **in a courtyard,**[H] are eaten by some people although they are not specifically intended for human consumption. Therefore, **if they were protected** by the owners, those owners are **obligated** to separate tithes from them.

הֵיכִי דָּמֵי? אִילֵימָא דְּזַרְעִינְהוּ מֵתְּחִלָּה לְאָדָם – צְרִיכָא לְמֵימַר? אֶלָּא לָאו דְּזַרְעִינְהוּ מִתְּחִלָּה לִבְהֵמָה, וְקָתָנֵי: ״אִם הָיוּ נִשְׁמָרִין חַיָּיבִין״.

The Gemara clarifies the mishna: **What are the circumstances** of this ruling? **If we say** that it is referring to a case **where one initially planted them for human** consumption, does it **need to be said** that there is an obligation to tithe if they are protected by the owners? It is clear that in such a situation the criteria for the obligation to tithe, i.e., that it is human food which is protected, have been met. **Rather,** is it **not** referring to a case **where one initially planted them** to be fed **to an animal,** and nevertheless the mishna **teaches: If** the owner reconsidered their designation and decided to use them for human consumption and **they were protected** by the owners, the owners are **obligated** to tithe them. This apparently indicates that intent while the produce is attached to the ground is considered intent.

**NOTES**

Seeds which will never transmit impurity severe enough to transmit to humans – זְרָעִים שֶׁאֵין סוֹפָן לְטַמֵּא טוּמְאָה חֲמוּרָה: Seeds cannot contract severe ritual impurity, as food does not contract impurity severe enough to be transmitted to people. Furthermore, food cannot become a primary source of impurity (Rashi on *Ḥullin* 121a). Even if food touches a corpse, which is the ultimate primary source of impurity and renders that which it touches a primary source of impurity, the food does not become a primary source of impurity that renders a person and vessels impure.

**BACKGROUND**

Hyssop [*ezov*] – אֵזוֹב: The Sages were unsure of the precise identification of the *ezov* plant mentioned in the Torah. From the various descriptions in the rabbinic sources it is apparently the common hyssop plant, *Majorna syriaca*.

The hyssop is a fragrant plant that grows to a height of 50–100 cm. The plant spreads out from its base into rigid wooden branches, which annually produce straight stems that dry out and die in winter. The white flowers of the hyssop plant grow in crowded bunches on the ends of its branches. This plant grows in rocky terrain and in the undergrowth in Eretz Yisrael and in surrounding countries. Dried hyssop leaves are used in the spice za'atar.

Bible hyssop

Thyme [*koranit*] – קוֹרָנִית: *Koranit*, according to various identifications in the Talmud, is probably the plant called conehead thyme, *Thymus capitatus*, of the Lamiaceae family. It is a branched shrub 10–50 cm in height, with small, short branches up to 5 mm long, whose flowers are pink and emit a fragrance. Conehead thyme grows wild in most areas of Eretz Yisrael. Thyme has also been posited as the identity of *sei'a*, translated here as savory.

Conehead thyme

**HALAKHA**

Savory, hyssop, and thyme that were growing in a courtyard – הַסֵּיאָה וְהָאֵזוֹב וְהַקּוֹרָנִית שֶׁבֶּחָצֵר: If savory, hyssop, and thyme were planted from the outset for human consumption, their owners are obligated to tithe them. If they were planted to be used as food for animals, and later the owners changed their minds before they were harvested and decided to use them for human consumption, they are exempt from tithes. The reason is that intent while produce is attached to the ground is ineffective. If they grew by themselves in a courtyard that is secure, the obligation of tithes applies, as they are generally intended for human consumption unless they were specifically designated as food for animals. If the courtyard is not secure, their owner is exempt. This ruling is in accordance with the mishna in tractate *Ma'asrot*, as interpreted by Rav Ashi (Rambam *Sefer Zera'im*, *Hilkhot Terumot* 2:2).

אֲמַר רַב אַשִׁי: הָכָא בְּחָצֵר שֶׁעָלוּ מֵאֵילֵיהֶן עָסְקִינַן, וּסְתָמָא – לְאָדָם קָיְימִי. וְהָכִי קָאָמַר: אִם הֶחָצֵר מְשַׁמֶּרֶת פֵּירוֹתֶיהָ – חַיָּיבִין, וְאִם לָאו – פְּטוּרִין.

**Rav Ashi said** that Rava's proof is inconclusive, for the following reason: **Here we are dealing with a courtyard where** these various types of hyssop plants **grew by themselves, and** where they are **unspecified,** they are **intended for human** consumption. Therefore, they meet the first criteria for the obligation to tithe, as they are considered food. **And** the mishna addresses the second requirement, that the food must be protected, and **this** is what it **is saying: If the courtyard protects its produce,** the owners **are obligated** in tithes, **and if not, they are exempt.**

מְתִיב רַב אַשִׁי: כָּל שֶׁחַיָּיבִין בְּמַעַשְׂרוֹת – מְטַמְּאִין טוּמְאַת אוֹכָלִין. וְאִם אִיתָא, הָא אִיכָּא הָנֵי – דְּקָחַיָּיבִין – בְּמַעֲשֵׂר וְאֵין מְטַמְּאִין טוּמְאַת אוֹכָלִין!

**Rav Ashi raises** a further **objection** to Rava's explanation from a mishna (50a): **Any** food from **which** one is **obligated to** separate **tithes becomes impure with the ritual impurity of food. But if it is so,** as Rava claimed, that intent while the produce is attached to the ground is considered intent with respect to the obligation to tithe, despite the fact that it is not considered intent with regard to impurity, then the mishna's blanket statement is inaccurate. Rav Ashi elaborates: After all, **there are these** endives that were initially planted in order to feed to an animal and later the owner reconsidered their designation and decided to use them for human consumption, from **which** one is **obligated to** separate **tithe, but which do not become impure with the ritual impurity of food.**

אֲמַר רָבָא, הָכִי קָאֲמַר: כָּל מִין שֶׁחַיָּיב בְּמַעֲשֵׂר – מִטַּמֵּא טוּמְאַת אוֹכָלִין.

**Rava said** in response that **this** is what the mishna **is saying: Any type** of food from **which** one is **obligated to** separate **tithe becomes impure with the ritual impurity of food.** In other words, this is referring to types of food, not to all situations. It is possible for a particular circumstance to be an exception to this principle.

הָכִי נַמִי מִסְתַּבְּרָא, מִדְּקָתָנֵי סֵיפָא: כָּל שֶׁחַיָּיב בְּרֵאשִׁית הַגֵּז – חַיָּיב בְּמַתָּנוֹת, וְיֵשׁ שֶׁחַיָּיב בְּמַתָּנוֹת וְאֵין חַיָּיב בְּרֵאשִׁית הַגֵּז.

The Gemara adds that **this too stands to reason,** that the mishna is referring only to types of food, not situations, **from** the fact **that the latter clause teaches** (51b): With regard to **any** animal from **which** the owner is **obligated to** give **the first shearing** of its wool, he is **obligated to** have **gifts** of the priesthood taken from it, i.e., the foreleg, the jaw, and the maw, if it was slaughtered. **And there are** animals from **which** one is **obligated to** have **gifts** of the priesthood taken from it, **but** from which he is **not obligated to** give **the first shearing.**

וְאִם אִיתָא, הָאִיכָּא טְרֵפָה – דְּחַיֶּיבֶת בְּרֵאשִׁית הַגֵּז, וְאֵינָהּ חַיֶּיבֶת בְּמַתָּנוֹת!

**And if it is so,** that the principles of the mishna are all-inclusive, one can raise the following difficulty: **But there is** the specific case of **an animal with a wound that will cause it to die within twelve months** [*tereifa*], from **which** one is **obligated to** give **the first shearing,**[H] **but one is not obligated to** have **gifts** of the priesthood taken from it,[H] as it may not be eaten. This proves that Rava is correct, that the mishna is not referring to all circumstances, but only to general categories.

אֲמַר רָבִינָא: הָא מַנִּי – רַבִּי שִׁמְעוֹן הִיא, דִּתְנַן: רַבִּי שִׁמְעוֹן פּוֹטֵר אֶת הַטְּרֵפָה מֵרֵאשִׁית הַגֵּז.

**Ravina said,** rejecting this proof: It is possible that the mishna is referring to all circumstances, and as for the difficulty with regard to a *tereifa,* one can say that in accordance with **whose** opinion **is this** mishna? **It is** in accordance with the opinion of **Rabbi Shimon, as we learned** in a *baraita*: **Rabbi Shimon exempts the** owner of **a *tereifa*** from the mitzva of **the first shearing.**

אֲמַר רַב שִׁימִי בַּר אַשִׁי, תָּא שְׁמַע: הַמַּפְקִיר אֶת כַּרְמוֹ, וְהִשְׁכִּים בַּבֹּקֶר וּבְצָרוֹ – חַיָּיב בְּפֶרֶט, וּבְעוֹלְלוֹת, וּבְשִׁכְחָה, וּבְפֵאָה, וּפָטוּר מִן הַמַּעֲשֵׂר.

**Rav Shimi bar Ashi said: Come** and **hear** a proof from a *baraita* that the mishna is not referring to all circumstances, but only to general categories: With regard to **one who declares his vineyard ownerless, and who arose the** next **morning and picked grapes**[H] from the vineyard before anyone else took possession of them, he is **obligated in** the mitzva of leaving for the poor **individual fallen** grapes [*peret*], **and in** the mitzva of leaving for them **incompletely formed clusters** of grapes [*uve'olelot*], **and in** the mitzva of **forgotten** clusters, **and in *pe'a*.** The Torah includes such cases in the phrase: "Leave them for the poor and for the stranger" (Leviticus 19:10, 23:22), which is written with regard to all these mitzvot. **And he is exempt from** the obligation to separate **the tithe** from the grapes. Since the vineyard is ownerless, there is no obligation to tithe the produce.

**HALAKHA**

*Tereifa* from which one is obligated to give the first shearing – טְרֵפָה דְּחַיֶּיבֶת בְּרֵאשִׁית הַגֵּז: The obligation of the first shearing applies to a *tereifa* (Rambam *Sefer Zera'im, Hilkhot Bikkurim* 10:7).

But one is not obligated to have gifts of the priesthood taken from it – וְאֵינָהּ חַיֶּיבֶת בְּמַתָּנוֹת: If one slaughtered an animal and discovered that it was a *tereifa*, or even if there was uncertainty whether it is a *tereifa* (*Shakh*), there is no obligation to give the gifts of the priesthood (*Shulḥan Arukh, Yoreh De'a* 61:6).

One who declares his vineyard ownerless and who arose the next morning and picked grapes – הַמַּפְקִיר אֶת כַּרְמוֹ וְהִשְׁכִּים בַּבֹּקֶר וּבְצָרוֹ: One who declared his vineyard ownerless and in the morning reacquired the field for himself and harvested it is obligated to leave for the poor *peret*, *olelot*, forgotten grape clusters, and *pe'a*. Nevertheless, he is exempt from tithes, in accordance with the *baraita* (Rambam *Sefer Zera'im, Hilkhot Mattenot Aniyyim* 5:27).

וְהָא אֲנַן תְּנַן: כָּל שֶׁחַיָּיב בְּפֵאָה – חַיָּיב בְּמַעַשְׂרוֹת! אֶלָּא לָאו שְׁמַע מִינָּהּ: מִין קָתָנֵי, שְׁמַע מִינָּהּ.

The Gemara explains the proof: **But didn't we learn** in the mishna (50a): With regard to **any** produce from **which** one is **obligated to** designate ***pe'a***, one is likewise **obligated to** separate **tithes? Rather,** must one **not conclude from** the mishna that Rava is correct in asserting that the mishna **is teaching** only principles with regard to each **type** of produce, but there are exceptions in certain circumstances? The Gemara answers that one should in fact **conclude from** the mishna that Rava is correct.

תְּנַן הָתָם: מוֹדִים חֲכָמִים לְרַבִּי עֲקִיבָא בְּזוֹרֵעַ שֶׁבֶת אוֹ חַרְדָּל בִּשְׁנַיִם וּשְׁלֹשָׁה מְקוֹמוֹת, שֶׁנּוֹתֵן פֵּאָה מִכָּל אֶחָד וְאֶחָד.

§ With regard to the obligations of *pe'a* and tithes, the Gemara notes that **we learned** in a mishna **elsewhere** (*Pe'a* 3:2): The Rabbis and Rabbi Akiva disagree with regard to a case where one harvested several separate patches in a field. Rabbi Akiva rules that each patch requires its own *pe'a*, whereas the Rabbis maintain that one *pe'a* is required for all of the patches. Nevertheless, **the Rabbis concede to Rabbi Akiva in** the case of **one who sows dill**[B] **or mustard in two or three** separate **locations**[H] in a single field, **that he leaves *pe'a* for each and every one** of these plots on its own, rather than one corner for all of them.

**BACKGROUND**

**Dill – שֶׁבֶת:** Dill, *Anethum graveolens*, is an annual or biennial herb that belongs to the Apiaceaa family. The dill plant reaches a height of 50–80 cm and produces small, yellow flowers that are grouped in umbels. Its thread-like leaves, which have a unique scent, are used as a spice. Its seeds and the oil extracted from them were once used for medicinal purposes. In the time of the Mishna dill was commonly grown in herb gardens. Today it is cultivated in gardens on a limited basis and grows wild in various places.

Dill

**HALAKHA**

**Sows dill or mustard in two or three separate locations – זוֹרֵעַ שֶׁבֶת אוֹ חַרְדָּל בִּשְׁנַיִם וּשְׁלֹשָׁה מְקוֹמוֹת:** When one plants a type of vegetable that is planted in garden beds, such as dill or mustard, he leaves *pe'a* for each and every bed individually. This *halakha* is in accordance with the opinions of all the *tanna'im* in the mishna in *Pe'a*, as the Rabbis concede to Rabbi Akiva in this case (Rambam *Sefer Zera'im*, *Hilkhot Mattenot Aniyyim* 3:11).

Perek **VI**
Daf **51** Amud **b**

וְהָא שֶׁבֶת דְּמִיחַיַּיב בְּפֵאָה, וּמִיחַיַּיב בְּמַעֲשֵׂר, דִּתְנַן: כָּל שֶׁחַיָּיב בְּפֵאָה – חַיָּיב בְּמַעֲשֵׂר.

The Gemara asks: **But** with regard to **dill,** from **which** one is **obligated to** designate ***pe'a,*** as stated in the mishna, one must also **be obligated to** separate **tithe,** since if the obligation of *pe'a* applies then the obligation of tithes likewise applies. **As we learned** in the mishna (50a): With regard to **any** produce from **which** one is **obligated to** designate ***pe'a,*** one is likewise **obligated to** separate **tithe.**

וּמִדְּחַיָּיב בְּמַעֲשֵׂר – מְטַמֵּא טוּמְאַת אוֹכָלִין, אַלְמָא: כָּל מִילֵּי דַּעֲבִיד לְטַעֲמָא – מְטַמֵּא טוּמְאַת אוֹכָלִין, דְּהַאי שֶׁבֶת לְטַעֲמָא עֲבִידָא.

**And from** the fact that with regard to dill one is **obligated to** separate **tithe,** it follows that it **becomes impure with the ritual impurity of food.** As the mishna on 50a states: Any food that is obligated in tithes becomes impure with the ritual impurity of food. **Apparently, any item that is prepared** in order **to** add **taste** to food, such as dill, **becomes impure with the ritual impurity of food, as this dill is prepared** in order **to** add **taste** to food.

## HALAKHA

They do not become impure with the ritual impurity of food – אֵין מְטַמְּאִין טוּמְאַת אוֹכָלִין: Although people do partake of spices such as costus, amomum, chief spices, root of crowfoot, asafoetida, peppers, and a cake of safflower, they are not considered food to the extent that they become impure with the ritual impurity of food, as they are used only for flavoring or to enhance the aroma or appearance of the food. This ruling is in accordance with the mishna in *Okatzin* and the opinion of Rabbi Yoḥanan ben Nuri (Rambam *Sefer Tahara, Hilkhot Tumat Okhalin* 1:6).

They should also not be bought with second-tithe money – אַף הֵם לֹא יִלָּקְחוּ בְּכֶסֶף מַעֲשֵׂר: Although people do eat spices such as costus, amomum, chief spices, root of crowfoot, asafoetida, peppers, and a cake of safflower, they may not be bought with second-tithe money, as they are used only for flavoring or to enhance the aroma or appearance of the food. This *halakha* is in accordance with the opinion of Rabbi Yoḥanan ben Nuri (Rambam *Sefer Zera'im, Hilkhot Ma'aser Sheni* 7:9).

וּרְמִינְהִי: הַקּוֹשְׁטְ, וְהַחִימּוּם, וְרָאשֵׁי בְשָׂמִים, וְהַתֵּיאָה, וְהַחִלְתִּית, וְהַפִּלְפְּלִין, וְחַלַּת חָרִיעַ – נִקָּחִין בְּכֶסֶף מַעֲשֵׂר, וְאֵין מְטַמְּאִין טוּמְאַת אוֹכָלִין – דִּבְרֵי רַבִּי עֲקִיבָא.

And the Gemara **raises a contradiction** to this conclusion from a mishna (*Okatzin* 3:5), which deals with the ritual impurity of food: With regard to spices such as **costus,**[B] **amomum,**[B] **chief spices, root of crowfoot,**[B] **asafoetida,**[B] **peppers, and a cake of safflower,** although their function is merely to add taste to food, they are considered food for the purposes of the following *halakha*: They **may be bought with** second-**tithe money,** which must be taken to Jerusalem and used to purchase food. **But** they are not considered food insofar as **they do not become impure with the ritual impurity of food.**[H] This is **the statement of Rabbi Akiva.**

אָמַר לוֹ רַבִּי יוֹחָנָן בֶּן נוּרִי: אִם נִקָּחִין בְּכֶסֶף מַעֲשֵׂר – מִפְּנֵי מָה אֵין מְטַמְּאִין טוּמְאַת אוֹכָלִין? וְאִם אֵינָן מְטַמְּאִין – אַף הֵם לֹא יִלָּקְחוּ בְּכֶסֶף מַעֲשֵׂר!

**Rabbi Yoḥanan ben Nuri said to** Rabbi Akiva: **If** they are considered food to the extent that **they may be bought with** second-**tithe money, for what** reason are **they not** considered food in terms of **becoming impure with the ritual impurity of food? And if they do not become impure** with the ritual impurity of food because they are not considered food, then **they should also not be bought with** second-**tithe money.**[H]

## BACKGROUND

Costus – קוֹשְׁטְ: This is a substance derived from the root of the aromatic plant of the same name, *Costus speciosus*, or crêpe ginger, from the family of ginger plants. It was used as an ingredient in the incense in the Temple, and the stem of its root was utilized for medicinal purposes.

Crêpe ginger

Amomum – חִימּוּם: The amomum plant, which is identified as a member of the ginger family, is characterized by its pungent odor.

Amomum

Crowfoot [*tei'a*] – תֵּיאָה: This possibly refers to one or many species in the buttercup family, genus *Ranunculus*, which includes several species known as crowfoot.

Asafoetida – חִלְתִּית: *Ferula assa-foetida*, also known as devil's dung or giant fennel, is a perennial plant of the celery family. It has a thick root and a stem with leafed branches. The asafoetida grows to a height of 2–3 m. It is native mainly to Afghanistan and the neighboring regions, though related species, such as the *Ferula communis*, the giant fennel, can be found elsewhere in the Middle East, including Eretz Yisrael. The plant grows for several years until it blossoms and produces fruit, after which it dies.

Medicinal asafoetida is manufactured from the resin found in the root of the plant. It was used, and is still used today, as a medicine in the form of powder, creams, pills, and in other forms, both for intestinal diseases and for strengthening the nervous system. In certain places, asafoetida is even used as a spice. Consumption of asafoetida in amounts of more than 1 g is toxic both to ruminants and to humans.

Asafoetida

Common water crowfoot, indigenous to Eretz Yisrael

וְאָמַר רַבִּי יוֹחָנָן בֶּן נוּרִי: נִמְנוּ וְגָמְרוּ שֶׁאֵין נִקָּחִין בְּכֶסֶף מַעֲשֵׂר, וְאֵין מִטַּמְּאִין טוּמְאַת אוֹכָלִין.

**And Rabbi Yoḥanan ben Nuri said** with regard to this *halakha*: **They counted** the opinions of the Sages, **and they concluded that** these spices **may not be bought with** second-**tithe money, and** they do **not become impure** with the ritual **impurity of food.** This apparently contradicts the previous claim that dill, which is a spice, becomes impure with the ritual impurity of food.

אָמַר רַב חִסְדָּא: כִּי תַּנְיָא הַהִיא – בְּשֶׁבֶת הָעֲשׂוּיָה לִכְמָךְ.

**Rav Ḥisda says** the following resolution of the difficulty: **When that** *baraita*, which indicates that dill is considered food and can contract the impurity of food, **is taught,** it is referring **to dill that is prepared for a spice dish** [*likhmakh*],[N] i.e., to be ground and placed in a Babylonian spice, *kutaḥ*, which is used as a dip.

אָמַר רַב אַשִׁי אָמְרִיתָהּ לִשְׁמָעֲתֵיהּ קַמֵּיהּ דְּרַב כָּהֲנָא: (אָמַר) לָא תֵּימָא בְּשֶׁבֶת הָעֲשׂוּיָה לִכְמָךְ – הָא סְתָמָא לִקְדֵרָה, אֶלָּא – סְתַם שֶׁבֶת לִכְמָךְ עֲשׂוּיָה, דִּתְנַן: הַשֶּׁבֶת מִשֶּׁנָּתְנָה טַעַם בַּקְּדֵרָה – אֵין בָּהּ מִשּׁוּם תְּרוּמָה, וְאֵינָהּ מְטַמְּאָה טוּמְאַת אוֹכָלִין.

**Rav Ashi said: I said this** *halakha* of Rav Ḥisda's **before Rav Kahana,** and he commented: **Do not say** that the *baraita* is referring specifically to a case **where** the **dill** was prepared **for a spice dish** from the outset, which would indicate that if dill is **undesignated** then it is intended to be an ingredient **in a pot** of food. **Rather, undesignated dill** is also **prepared for a spice dish. As we learned** in a mishna (*Okatzin* 3:4): With regard to *teruma* **dill, once it imparted flavor in a pot**[H] of food and was removed from the pot, it **is no** longer **subject to** the prohibition of a non-priest partaking of *teruma*, **and it can no** longer **become impure with the ritual impurity of food.**

הָא עַד שֶׁלֹּא נָתְנָה טַעַם בַּקְּדֵרָה – יֵשׁ בָּהּ מִשּׁוּם תְּרוּמָה, וּמְטַמְּאָה טוּמְאַת אוֹכָלִין. וְאִי סָלְקָא דַּעְתָּךְ סְתָמָא לִקְדֵרָה – כִּי לָא נָתְנָה נַמִי, סְתָמָא לִקְדֵרָה! אֶלָּא לָאו שְׁמַע מִינָּהּ – סְתָמָא לִכְמָךְ עֲשׂוּיָה. שְׁמַע מִינָּהּ.

Rav Kahana explains the proof: It can be inferred from this mishna that **until** the dill has **imparted flavor in a pot** of food it **is subject to** the prohibition of a non-priest partaking of *teruma*, **and it can become impure with the ritual impurity of food. And if** it **enters your mind** that **undesignated** dill is intended as an ingredient **in a pot** of food, then **even when** one did **not place** the dill in a pot, the same *halakha* with respect to *teruma* and impurity should apply, as when it is **undesignated** the dill is intended as an ingredient **in a pot** of food. **Rather,** must one **not conclude from** the mishna that **undesignated** dill is **prepared for a spice dish?**[N] The Gemara concludes: **Learn from** the mishna that this is the case.

מתני׳ כָּל שֶׁחַיָּיב בְּרֵאשִׁית הַגֵּז – חַיָּיב בְּמַתָּנוֹת, וְיֵשׁ שֶׁחַיָּיב בְּמַתָּנוֹת וְאֵינוֹ חַיָּיב בְּרֵאשִׁית הַגֵּז.

**MISHNA** With regard to **any** animal, i.e., sheep and rams, from **which one is obligated** by Torah law (see Deuteronomy 18:4) **to** give **the first shearing** of its wool to a priest, he **is obligated to** have **gifts** of the priesthood, i.e., the foreleg, the jaw, and the maw, which must be removed from slaughtered animals, taken from it (see Deuteronomy 18:3). **And there are** animals from **which one is obligated to** have **gifts** of the priesthood taken from them, e.g., cattle and goats, **but** from which **he is not obligated to** give **the first shearing.**

כָּל שֶׁיֵּשׁ לוֹ בִּיעוּר – יֵשׁ לוֹ שְׁבִיעִית, וְיֵשׁ שֶׁיֵּשׁ לוֹ שְׁבִיעִית וְאֵין לוֹ בִּיעוּר.

The mishna teaches a similar principle: For **all** Sabbatical-Year produce **to which there** applies the obligation of **eradication**[B] from the house when it ceases to be available to the animals in the field, **there is** the sanctity of **Sabbatical**-Year produce upon **it,**[H] i.e., it may not be used for commerce and is ownerless while it is attached to the ground. **And there** is produce **for which there is** the sanctity of **Sabbatical**-Year produce, **but** for which **there is no** obligation of **eradication** from the house, e.g., produce that is preserved in the ground and does not cease to be available in the field.

**NOTES**

**Referring to dill that is prepared for a spice dish [*likhmakh*] – בְּשֶׁבֶת הָעֲשׂוּיָה לִכְמָךְ:** Some commentaries maintain that the dill is ground up to be used as an ingredient in the Babylonian spice *kutaḥ*. Accordingly, it is meant to be eaten as food, not merely as flavoring (Rashi; *Arukh*). Others explain that the dill is eaten unprocessed, as a kind of vegetable dessert (Rambam's Commentary on the Mishna on tractate *Okatzin*; *Sefer Tahara, Hilkhot Tumat Okhalin* 1:7). If so, *likhmakh* means to eat as a dessert, rather than to include in a *kutaḥ* (*Arukh LaNer*). The commentary here follows the first interpretation.

**Undesignated dill is prepared for a spice dish – סְתָמָא לִכְמָךְ עֲשׂוּיָה:** Some early commentaries maintain that undesignated dill is intended to be used as a food, like any other vegetable. If one intended to use it for flavoring it is no longer considered a food, and it cannot become impure with the ritual impurity of food (Rambam *Sefer Tahara, Hilkhot Tumat Okhalin* 1:7, and see Ra'avad there).

**HALAKHA**

***Teruma* dill once it imparted flavor in a pot – הַשֶּׁבֶת מִשֶּׁנָּתְנָה טַעַם בַּקְּדֵרָה:** Dill that was not designated for a specific purpose is intended to be eaten, like other vegetables. If one designated it for use as flavoring, it can no longer become impure with the ritual impurity of food. Furthermore, once dill has imparted flavor in a pot, it is considered refuse and can no longer become impure with the impurity of food (Rambam). Others maintain that thought alone does not exempt it from contracting the ritual impurity of food (Ra'avad). Rather, it remains subject to becoming impure until it has imparted flavor in a pot (Rambam *Sefer Tahara, Hilkhot Tumat Okhalin* 1:7 and *Kesef Mishne* there).

**There is the sanctity of Sabbatical-Year produce upon it – יֵשׁ לוֹ שְׁבִיעִית:** The leaves of the wild arum and the ceterach, and likewise their value, are subject to the sanctity of Sabbatical-Year produce and eradication, since they are not preserved in the ground, and they are used for human consumption. The *halakha* is in accordance with the mishna in tractate *Shevi'it* (Rambam *Sefer Zera'im, Hilkhot Shemitta VeYovel* 7:13).

**BACKGROUND**

**Eradication – בִּיעוּר:** There are two primary opinions with regard to the requirement to remove produce that grows during the Sabbatical Year. Between those who hold each opinion, there is a disagreement with regard to the details of the *halakha*. One opinion is that eradication must be performed after a certain species is no longer found in the field. It is carried out by destroying the produce that remains in the house, either by burning it, throwing it into the sea, or a similar action (Rashi; Rambam; Ra'avad). According to others, the process entails removing the produce from one's house and then declaring it ownerless. When a given type of produce is no longer in the field, one removes it from his home and declares it ownerless, thereby rendering it available to both the poor and the wealthy to eat in the field (*Tosafot*; *Smag*; Ramban). According to some *tanna'im*, it may be eaten only by the poor.

גמ׳ כְּגוֹן עָלֵה הַלּוּף שׁוֹטֶה, וְהַדַּנְדַּנָּה. יֵשׁ שֶׁיֵּשׁ לוֹ שְׁבִיעִית וְאֵין לוֹ בִּיעוּר – עִיקַּר הַלּוּף שׁוֹטֶה, וְעִיקַּר הַדַּנְדַּנָּה.

**GEMARA** The mishna teaches that the sanctity of Sabbatical-Year produce applies to any produce upon which there is an obligation of eradication, but the converse is not necessarily the case. The Gemara cites an example of plants whose various parts illustrate these *halakhot*: Plants **such as the wild arum**[B] **leaf and the ceterach,**[B] which cease to be available in the field during the rainy season, are subject to eradication and to the sanctity of the Sabbatical Year. Examples of the second *halakha* of the mishna, that **there is** produce **for which there is** the sanctity of **Sabbatical**-Year produce **but** for which **there is no** obligation of **eradication** from the house, include the **root of the wild arum**[H] **and the root of the ceterach.**

דִּכְתִיב ״וְלִבְהֶמְתְּךָ וְלַחַיָּה אֲשֶׁר בְּאַרְצֶךָ תִּהְיֶה כָל תְּבוּאָתָהּ לֶאֱכֹל״, כׇּל זְמַן שֶׁחַיָּה אוֹכֶלֶת מִן הַשָּׂדֶה – אַתָּה מַאֲכִיל לִבְהֶמְתְּךָ בַּבַּיִת, כָּלָה לַחַיָּה מִן הַשָּׂדֶה – כַּלֵּה לִבְהֶמְתְּךָ שֶׁבַּבַּיִת, וְהָנֵי לָא כָּלוּ לְהוּ.

The Gemara explains **that it is written** in connection to the Sabbatical Year: **"And for the cattle and the beasts that are in your land, all its produce may be eaten"** (Leviticus 25:7), from which it is derived: **As long as the undomesticated animals eat** a type of produce **from the field, you may feed** that type of produce **to your domesticated animal in the house,** as it still remains in the field. But if that type of produce **has ceased for the undomesticated animals in the field, you must cease** feeding it **to your domesticated animal in the house.** This is the obligation of eradication. **And these,** the root of the wild arum and the ceterach, **have not ceased for undomesticated animals** in the field, and therefore there is no obligation of eradication.

מתני׳ כׇּל שֶׁיֵּשׁ לוֹ קַשְׂקֶשֶׂת – יֵשׁ לוֹ סְנַפִּיר, וְיֵשׁ שֶׁיֵּשׁ לוֹ סְנַפִּיר וְאֵין לוֹ קַשְׂקֶשֶׂת. כׇּל שֶׁיֵּשׁ לוֹ קַרְנַיִם – יֵשׁ לוֹ טְלָפַיִם, וְיֵשׁ שֶׁיֵּשׁ לוֹ טְלָפַיִם וְאֵין לוֹ קַרְנַיִם.

**MISHNA** It is written: "Whatever has fins and scales in the waters, in the seas, and in the rivers, you may eat them" (Leviticus 11:9). There is a principle with regard to the signs indicating that fish are kosher: **Any** fish **that has scales has fins;**[N] **and there are** fish **that have fins but do not have scales.**[H] Similarly, with regard to kosher animals it is written: "Whatever parts the hoof, and is wholly cloven-footed, and chews the cud, among the beasts, that you may eat" (Leviticus 11:3). **Any** animal **that has horns has hooves; and there are** animals **that have hooves but do not have horns.**

גמ׳ כׇּל שֶׁיֵּשׁ לוֹ קַשְׂקֶשֶׂת – דָּג טָהוֹר, יֵשׁ שֶׁיֵּשׁ לוֹ סְנַפִּיר וְאֵין לוֹ קַשְׂקֶשֶׂת – דָּג טָמֵא. מִכְּדִי, אַקַּשְׂקֶשֶׂת סָמְכִינַן, ״סְנַפִּיר״ דִּכְתַב רַחֲמָנָא לָמָּה לִי?

**GEMARA** The mishna teaches that **any** fish **that has scales** also has fins and therefore is **a kosher fish.** The mishna also stated that **there are** fish **that have fins but do not have scales.** Such a fish is **a non-kosher fish.** The Gemara asks: **Since we rely** exclusively **upon** the sign of the **scales,** as a fish that has scales necessarily has fins as well, **why do I** need the sign of **fins that the Merciful One writes** in the Torah as one of the criteria of kosher fish?

אִי לָא כְּתַב רַחֲמָנָא סְנַפִּיר, הֲוָה אָמֵינָא: מַאי ״קַשְׂקֶשֶׂת״ דִּכְתִיב – סְנַפִּיר, וַאֲפִילּוּ דָּג טָמֵא – כְּתַב רַחֲמָנָא ״סְנַפִּיר וְקַשְׂקֶשֶׂת״.

The Gemara answers: **If the Merciful One** had **not** also **written** the sign of **fins** in the Torah, **I would say: What** does the word ***kaskeset***, scales, **that is written** in the Torah mean? It does not mean scales, but **fins. And** I would therefore say that **even a non-kosher fish,** which has fins but no scales, is permitted. Therefore, **the Merciful One writes** both signs, **fins and scales.**

וְהָשְׁתָּא דִּכְתַב רַחֲמָנָא סְנַפִּיר וְקַשְׂקֶשֶׂת, מְנָלַן דְּקַשְׂקֶשֶׂת לְבוּשָׁא הוּא? דִּכְתִיב ״וְשִׁרְיוֹן קַשְׂקַשִּׂים הוּא לָבוּשׁ״.

The Gemara further asks: **But now that the Merciful One wrote** in the Torah **fins and *kaskeset*, from where do we** derive that ***kaskeset*** denotes **clothing,** i.e., scales, rather than fins? The Gemara answers: We derive it from a verse, **as it is written** about Goliath the Philistine: **"And he was clad with a coat of mail [*kaskasim*]"** (I Samuel 17:5).

**NOTES**

Any fish that has scales has fins – כׇּל שֶׁיֵּשׁ לוֹ קַשְׂקֶשֶׂת יֵשׁ לוֹ סְנַפִּיר: Some commentaries maintain that there is in fact a fish that has scales and not fins, but it is so rare that it is not taken into account (*Kereti UFleti*, citing Ritva). Others hold that as the Torah asserts that any fish having scales also has fins, it is assumed that no fish exists that has scales and does not have fins (*Taz; Peri Megadim; Maḥazik Berakha*).

**BACKGROUND**

Wild arum – לוּף שׁוֹטֶה: This plant is generally identified as the arum of Eretz Yisrael, *Arum palaestinum*, of the Araceae family. The plant has a bulb in the ground from which large leaves sprout. The arum's inflorescence has a unique structure and is covered with a special type of leaf called a spathe. All parts of the plant contain calcium oxalate, $CaC_2O_4$, which is poisonous and causes extreme itching to any skin that it comes in contact with. Consequently, arum is not eaten by people in its raw state, and few animals draw sustenance from it. The bulb and leaves are cooked or roasted to make them edible for human consumption. The plant grows in the wild in all regions of Eretz Yisrael.

Ceterach – דַּנְדַּנָּה: *Ceterach officinarum*, commonly known as rustyback, is a short fern plant. In Eretz Yisrael it grows mainly in mountainous regions. It can serve as food for humans in exigent circumstances.

Rustyback

**HALAKHA**

Root of the wild arum – עִיקַּר הַלּוּף שׁוֹטֶה: With regard to the root of the wild arum and the root of the ceterach, which are not used for human consumption, fodder, or dye, since they are not utilized as firewood, they and their value are subject to the sanctity of Sabbatical-Year produce. Nevertheless, the obligation of eradication does not apply to them, despite the fact that they are not preserved in the ground. Rather, one may use them, and their value may be used until Rosh HaShana. This ruling is in accordance with the mishna in tractate *Shevi'it* (Rambam *Sefer Zera'im, Hilkhot Shemitta VeYovel* 7:14).

Any fish that has scales has fins and there are fish that have fins but do not have scales – כׇּל שֶׁיֵּשׁ לוֹ קַשְׂקֶשֶׂת יֵשׁ לוֹ סְנַפִּיר וְיֵשׁ שֶׁיֵּשׁ לוֹ סְנַפִּיר וְאֵין לוֹ קַשְׂקֶשֶׂת: Any fish that has scales has fins as well, but there are fish that have fins but do not have scales. Therefore, if one found a piece of a fish containing scales, one may eat it without investigating whether or not it has fins. If he found one containing fins, he may not eat it until he ascertains that it also has scales (Rambam *Sefer Kedusha, Hilkhot Ma'akhalot Assurot* 1:24; *Shulḥan Arukh, Yoreh De'a* 83:3).

וְלִכְתּוֹב רַחֲמָנָא ״קַשְׂקֶשֶׂת״ וְלָא בָּעֵי ״סְנַפִּיר״! אָמַר רַבִּי אַבָּהוּ, וְכֵן תָּנָא דְּבֵי רַבִּי יִשְׁמָעֵאל: ״יַגְדִּיל תּוֹרָה וְיַאְדִּיר״.

The Gemara asks: **But** if there is proof that *kaskeset* means scales, the question returns: **Let the Merciful One write** only **"scales" and** then there would be **no need** to write **"fins." Rabbi Abbahu says, and likewise** a Sage of **the school of Rabbi Yishmael taught,** that this is in accordance with the verse: "The Lord was pleased, for His righteousness' sake, **to make Torah great and glorious"**[N] (Isaiah 42:21). In this context, this means that it is fitting for the Torah to state all the characteristics of a kosher animal rather than merely state that which is absolutely necessary.

מתני׳ כָּל הַטָּעוּן בְּרָכָה לְאַחֲרָיו – טָעוּן בְּרָכָה לְפָנָיו, וְיֵשׁ שֶׁטָּעוּן בְּרָכָה לְפָנָיו וְאֵין טָעוּן בְּרָכָה לְאַחֲרָיו.

**MISHNA** This mishna teaches a generalization that is similar to the previous ones: **Anything that requires a blessing after** one partakes of **it requires a blessing beforehand.**[H] **And there exist** items **that require a blessing before but** do **not require a blessing thereafter.**

גמ׳ לְאַתּוֹיֵי מַאי? לְאַתּוֹיֵי יָרָק. וּלְרַבִּי יִצְחָק דִּמְבָרֵךְ אַיָּרָק, לְאַתּוֹיֵי מַאי? לְאַתּוֹיֵי מַיָּא.

**GEMARA** The mishna teaches that there are items that require a blessing before but not after. The Gemara inquires: **What** case does this *halakha* in the mishna **add?** The Gemara answers: It serves **to add** the case of **vegetables,** as one recites a blessing before eating them but not afterward. The Gemara asks: **And according to** the opinion of **Rabbi Yitzḥak, who** maintains that one **recites a blessing on vegetables** after eating them, **what** case does this *halakha* in the mishna **add?** The Gemara answers: It serves **to add** the case of **water,** as one recites a blessing before drinking it but not afterward.

וּלְרַב פַּפָּא דִּמְבָרֵךְ אַמַּיָּא, לְאַתּוֹיֵי מַאי? לְאַתּוֹיֵי מִצְוֹת. וְלִבְנֵי מַעֲרָבָא דִּמְבָרְכִי בָּתַר דְּסָלְקִי תְּפִילַּיְיהוּ ״אֲשֶׁר קִדְּשָׁנוּ בְּמִצְוֹתָיו וְצִוָּנוּ לִשְׁמוֹר חוּקָּיו״, לְאַתּוֹיֵי מַאי? לְאַתּוֹיֵי

The Gemara further asks: **And according to** the opinion of **Rav Pappa, who** rules that **one recites a blessing on water** after drinking it, **what** case does this *halakha* in the mishna serve **to add?** The Gemara answers that the mishna, which does not explicitly mention food, serves **to add mitzvot.** In other words, one recites a blessing before performing a mitzva, e.g., wearing ritual fringes or taking the *lulav* and the like, but one does not recite a blessing after its fulfillment. The Gemara asks: **And according to** the **residents of the West,** Eretz Yisrael, **who recite** the following **blessing after they remove their phylacteries: Who sanctified us with His mitzvot and commanded us to keep His laws, what** does this *halakha* in the mishna **come to add?** The Gemara answers: It serves **to add** the case of

Perek **VI**
Daf **52** Amud **a**

רֵיחָנֵי.

fragrant **spices.**[HN]

מתני׳ תִּינוֹקֶת שֶׁהֵבִיאָה שְׁתֵּי שְׂעָרוֹת – אוֹ חוֹלֶצֶת אוֹ מִתְיַבֶּמֶת, וְחַיֶּיבֶת בְּכׇל מִצְוֹת הָאֲמוּרוֹת בַּתּוֹרָה.

**MISHNA** **A young girl who** reached the age of puberty and **grew two** pubic **hairs** is an adult. If her childless husband dies, **she either performs *ḥalitza***[H] and is thereby permitted to marry anyone, **or enters into levirate marriage** with her husband's brother. **And** furthermore, such a girl is **obligated to** fulfill **all the mitzvot stated in the Torah** in which women are obligated.

**NOTES**

To make Torah great and glorious – יַגְדִּיל תּוֹרָה וְיַאְדִּיר: The Torah is enhanced when it clarifies itself, rather than requiring elucidation from elsewhere, e.g., the narrative of Goliath, as in this case, or from other verses in the Prophets and Writings (*Tosafot*).

Fragrant spices – רֵיחָנֵי: Since one derives only minor pleasure from smelling spices, he recites the blessing: Who creates spice trees, only before smelling them, but not afterward (Rashi). Others explain that the reason for not reciting a blessing afterward is that unlike eating food, where one derives pleasure even after the food is eaten, until digestion has been completed, there is no residual benefit to the body after one finishes smelling the fragrance (*Magen Avraham*, citing *Kolbo*). It is therefore comparable to the case of food that has already been digested, for which one no longer recites a blessing (*Taz*).

**HALAKHA**

Anything that requires a blessing after one partakes of it requires a blessing beforehand – כָּל הַטָּעוּן בְּרָכָה לְאַחֲרָיו טָעוּן בְּרָכָה לְפָנָיו: Any food item that requires a blessing after consuming it requires a blessing beforehand as well (Rambam *Sefer Ahava*, *Hilkhot Berakhot* 8:8).

Fragrant spices – רֵיחָנֵי: It is prohibited to derive pleasure from a pleasant fragrance without first reciting a blessing. No blessing is recited after smelling a fragrance (*Shulḥan Arukh*, *Oraḥ Ḥayyim* 216:1).

Performs *ḥalitza* – חוֹלֶצֶת: A young girl does not perform *ḥalitza* until she is twelve years and one day old and has grown two pubic hairs (Rambam *Sefer Nashim*, *Hilkhot Yibbum VaḤalitza* 1:17; *Shulḥan Arukh*, *Even HaEzer* 167:4).

וְכֵן תִּינוֹק שֶׁהֵבִיא שְׁתֵּי שְׂעָרוֹת – חַיָּיב בְּכָל מִצְוֹת הָאֲמוּרוֹת בַּתּוֹרָה, וְרָאוּי לִהְיוֹת בֵּן סוֹרֵר וּמוֹרֶה, מִשֶּׁיָּבִיא שְׁתֵּי שְׂעָרוֹת עַד שֶׁיַּקִּיף זָקָן.

**And likewise, a young boy who** reached the age of puberty and **grew two** pubic **hairs** is an adult and is **obligated to** fulfill **all the mitzvot stated in the Torah. And he is fit to be** declared **a stubborn and rebellious son**[H] if he performs the actions that warrant that designation, **from when he grows two** pubic **hairs until** his **beard will form a circle.** During that period, although he is an adult and punishable for his actions, he is incapable of fathering a child. Consequently, as he is a son and not a father, he can be designated a stubborn and rebellious son.

הַתַּחְתּוֹן וְלֹא הָעֶלְיוֹן, אֶלָּא שֶׁדִּבְּרוּ חֲכָמִים בְּלָשׁוֹן נְקִיָּה.

The mishna explains that the reference is to **the lower,** pubic, hair, **and not to the upper,** facial, hair. **But** the term beard is used, despite its being subject to misinterpretation, due to the fact **that the Sages spoke euphemistically.**

תִּינוֹקֶת שֶׁהֵבִיאָה שְׁתֵּי שְׂעָרוֹת אֵינָהּ יְכוֹלָה לְמָאֵן. רַבִּי יְהוּדָה אוֹמֵר: עַד שֶׁיִּרְבֶּה הַשָּׁחוֹר.

**A young girl who** reached the age of puberty and **grew two** pubic **hairs can no** longer **perform refusal**[HB] to end a marriage with a husband to whom she was married as a minor by her mother and brothers after her father's death. **Rabbi Yehuda says:** She retains the right to perform refusal **until** the pubic hair will grow to the extent **that the black** hair **will be preponderant** in the pubic area.

**גמ׳** וְכֵיוָן דִּתְנַן "חַיֶּיבֶת בְּכָל מִצְוֹת הָאֲמוּרוֹת בַּתּוֹרָה", "אוֹ חוֹלֶצֶת אוֹ מִתְיַבֶּמֶת" לָמָּה לִי?

**GEMARA** The Gemara raises an objection: **But since we learned** in the mishna that a young girl who reached the age of puberty and grew two pubic hairs is considered an adult and is **obligated to** fulfill **all the mitzvot stated in the Torah, why do I** need the mishna to also teach: **She either performs *ḥalitza* or enters into levirate marriage.** These specific examples are included in the broader statement.

לְאַפּוּקֵי מִדְּרַבִּי יוֹסֵי, דַּאֲמַר: "אִישׁ" כָּתוּב בַּפָּרָשָׁה, אֲבָל אִשָּׁה – בֵּין גְּדוֹלָה וּבֵין קְטַנָּה, קָא מַשְׁמַע לָן: דְּאִי אַיְיתֵי שְׁתֵּי שְׂעָרוֹת – אִין, אִי לָא – לָא. מַאי טַעְמָא? אִשָּׁה כְּאִישׁ.

The Gemara explains: This emphasis serves **to exclude** the opinion **of Rabbi Yosei, who said: Man,** i.e., an adult man, **is written in the passage** of *ḥalitza*: "And if the man does not wish to take his brother's wife" (Deuteronomy 25:7). **But** with regard to the **woman, whether** she is **an adult or whether** she is **a minor,** she can be released by *ḥalitza*, as the Torah does not specify her age. The mishna **teaches us that** the *halakha* is not in accordance with the opinion of Rabbi Yosei. Rather, **if** she **grew two** pubic **hairs,** then **yes,** she can perform *ḥalitza*, whereas **if** she did **not** grow two hairs, she may **not** perform *ḥalitza* or enter into levirate marriage. **What is the reason** for this ruling? It is that the *halakha* of the **woman** is **like** that of the **man,** as a woman is juxtaposed to man in this passage.

וְכֵיוָן דִּתְנָא "וְכֵן הַתִּינוֹק שֶׁהֵבִיא שְׁתֵּי שְׂעָרוֹת", "חַיָּיב בְּכָל הַמִּצְוֹת הָאֲמוּרוֹת בַּתּוֹרָה" לָמָּה לִי?

The Gemara asks further: **And since we learned** in the continuation of the mishna: **And likewise, a young boy who** reached the age of puberty and **grew two** pubic **hairs** is an adult, **why do I** need the mishna to add explicitly: Is **obligated to** fulfill **all the mitzvot stated in the Torah?**

וְכִי תֵּימָא: מִשּׁוּם דְּקָבָעֵי לְמִתְנֵי "וְרָאוּי לִהְיוֹת בֵּן סוֹרֵר וּמוֹרֶה" – תְּנֵינָא חֲדָא זִימְנָא: אֵימָתַי הוּא בֵּן סוֹרֵר וּמוֹרֶה – מִשֶּׁיָּבִיא שְׁתֵּי שְׂעָרוֹת וְעַד שֶׁיַּקִּיף זָקָן, הַתַּחְתּוֹן וְלֹא הָעֶלְיוֹן, אֶלָּא שֶׁדִּבְּרוּ חֲכָמִים בְּלָשׁוֹן נְקִיָּה!

**And if you would say** that the mishna specified this **because** it **wanted to teach** the particular *halakha*: **And he is fit to be** declared **a stubborn and rebellious son,** that cannot be the reason, as **we** already **learned** that ***halakha*** on **another occasion** in a mishna (*Sanhedrin* 68b): **When** is such a boy liable to receive the death penalty imposed upon **a stubborn and rebellious son? From when he grows two** pubic **hairs until** his **beard will form a circle.** The reference is to **the lower,** pubic, hair **and not to the upper,** facial hair, **but** the term beard is used, due to the fact **that the Sages spoke euphemistically.**

### HALAKHA

**And he is fit to be declared a stubborn and rebellious son – וְרָאוּי לִהְיוֹת בֵּן סוֹרֵר וּמוֹרֶה:** According to the tradition of the Sages, one can be declared a stubborn and rebellious son only from the age of thirteen and one day, and from when he has grown two pubic hairs until the hair completely surrounds his organ. At that point he is independent and is no longer liable to be executed by stoning in this manner (Rambam *Sefer Shofetim*, *Hilkhot Mamrim* 7:5).

**A young girl who reached puberty and grew two hairs can no longer perform refusal – תִּינוֹקֶת שֶׁהֵבִיאָה שְׁתֵּי שְׂעָרוֹת אֵינָהּ יְכוֹלָה לְמָאֵן:** Until when can a young girl perform refusal to end a marriage with her husband to whom she was married as a minor by her mother or brothers after her father's death? Until she grows two pubic hairs after she reaches the age of twelve and one day, or gives birth. As long as she has not yet grown two hairs or given birth, she is considered a minor, even if she developed signs of being a sexually underdeveloped woman. But if she is twenty years old and she developed signs of a sexually underdeveloped woman, she is considered an adult retroactively from the age of twelve and one day. This is the *halakha* even if she later grew two hairs. Consequently, she may no longer perform refusal (Rambam *Sefer Nashim*, *Hilkhot Geirushin* 11:4; *Shulḥan Arukh*, *Even HaEzer* 155:12).

### BACKGROUND

**Refusal – מֵיאוּן:** A girl under the age of twelve can be married off by her father. But if her father is no longer alive then by Torah law she cannot marry while still a minor. Nevertheless, the Sages instituted that her mother or brothers may marry her off with her consent. Since her consent is not halakhically valid until she reaches the age of maturity, the girl may terminate this marriage once she reaches twelve years of age by performing refusal, i.e., by declaring that she does not desire this marriage. In such cases, no bill of divorce is necessary. When a girl performs refusal, the marriage is nullified retroactively, and it is considered as though she had never been married at all.

אִין הָכִי נַמִי, אֶלָּא – אַיְּידֵי דְּפָרֵישׁ מִילֵּי דְּתִינוֹקֶת – קָמְפָרֵשׁ נַמִי מִילֵּי דְּתִינוֹק.

The Gemara answers: **Yes, it is indeed so,** i.e., it is not necessary for the mishna to specify with regard to a boy that he is obligated to fulfill all the mitzvot stated in the Torah. **But since** the mishna **specified** this **matter** in the case **of a young girl,** it **also specified** this **matter** in the case **of a young boy.**

״תִּינוֹקֶת שֶׁהֵבִיאָה״ כו׳. אָמַר רַבִּי אַבָּהוּ, אָמַר רַבִּי אֶלְעָזָר: הֲלָכָה כְּרַבִּי יְהוּדָה.

§ The mishna teaches: **A young girl who** reached the age of puberty and **grew** two pubic hairs can no longer perform refusal to end a marriage with a husband to whom she was married as a minor by her mother and brothers after her father's death. Rabbi Yehuda maintains that she retains the right of refusal until the pubic hair grows to the extent that the black hair is preponderant in the pubic area. **Rabbi Abbahu says** that **Rabbi Elazar says:** The *halakha* **is in accordance with** the opinion of **Rabbi Yehuda.**

וּמוֹדֶה רַבִּי יְהוּדָה שֶׁאִם נִבְעֲלָה לְאַחַר שֶׁהֵבִיאָה שְׁתֵּי שְׂעָרוֹת – שׁוּב אֵינָהּ יְכוֹלָה לְמָאֵן.

**And Rabbi Yehuda concedes** to the Rabbis **that if she engaged in intercourse** with her husband **after she grew two** pubic **hairs,** she **can no longer perform refusal.** This is because the act of intercourse renders her betrothed to him by Torah law, and refusal is a rabbinic enactment that is effective only with regard to a betrothal that applies by rabbinic law.

חַבְרוֹהִי דְּרַב כָּהֲנָא סְבוּר לְמֶעְבַּד עוּבְדָא כְּרַבִּי יְהוּדָה, וְאַף עַל גַּב דְּנִבְעֲלָה.

**Rav Kahana's colleagues thought to perform an action in accordance with** the opinion of **Rabbi Yehuda** in the mishna, **and** to permit a young girl who had grown two pubic hairs to perform refusal, **even though she** had **engaged in intercourse** with her husband after growing two hairs. They held that until the pubic hair grows to the extent that the black hair is preponderant in the pubic area, her betrothal does not apply by Torah law.

אֲמַר לְהוּ רַב כָּהֲנָא: לֹא כָּךְ הָיָה מַעֲשֶׂה בְּבִתּוֹ שֶׁל רַבִּי יִשְׁמָעֵאל, שֶׁבָּאת לְבֵית הַמִּדְרָשׁ לְמָאֵן, וּבְנָהּ מוּרְכָּב לָהּ עַל כְּתֵפָהּ. וְאוֹתוֹ הַיּוֹם הוּזְכְּרוּ דְּבָרָיו שֶׁל רַבִּי יִשְׁמָעֵאל בְּבֵית הַמִּדְרָשׁ, וּבָכְתָה בְּכִיָּיה גְּדוֹלָה בְּבֵית הַמִּדְרָשׁ.

**Rav Kahana said to** his colleagues: **Didn't the incident involving Rabbi Yishmael's daughter,** who was married as a minor by her mother and brothers after her father's death, transpire **in that manner? As she came to the study hall to refuse** her marriage, **and her son was riding on her shoulders. And on that** very **day, Rabbi Yishmael's statement,** that a young girl may perform refusal even if she engaged in intercourse with her husband after growing two hairs, **was mentioned in the study hall. And she cried** with **a great weeping in the study hall,** as a result of the incident.

אָמְרוּ: דָּבָר שֶׁאָמַר אוֹתוֹ צַדִּיק – יִכָּשֵׁל בּוֹ זַרְעוֹ?

The Sages who were in the study hall **said:** Could it be that with regard to **a matter that that righteous** Rabbi Yishmael **said,** i.e., that she can perform refusal, **his offspring would stumble upon it?** The consequence of her refusal is that she is considered to have borne the child retroactively out of wedlock.

דַּאֲמַר רַב יְהוּדָה, אָמַר שְׁמוּאֵל מִשּׁוּם רַבִּי יִשְׁמָעֵאל: ״וְהִיא לֹא נִתְפָּשָׂה״ – אֲסוּרָה, הָא נִתְפְּשָׂה – מוּתֶּרֶת. וְיֵשׁ לָךְ אַחֶרֶת, שֶׁאַף עַל פִּי שֶׁלֹּא נִתְפְּשָׂה – מוּתֶּרֶת, וְאֵיזוֹ זוֹ – שֶׁקִּדּוּשֶׁיהָ קִדּוּשֵׁי טָעוּת, שֶׁאַף עַל פִּי שֶׁבְּנָהּ מוּרְכָּב עַל כְּתֵפָהּ – מְמָאֶנֶת וְהוֹלֶכֶת לָהּ.

**As Rav Yehuda said** that **Shmuel says in the name of Rabbi Yishmael:** The verse states with regard to a *sota*: **"And neither was she taken"** (Numbers 5:13), i.e., raped. In this case **she is prohibited** to her husband. It may be inferred that if she **was taken** forcefully **she is permitted**[H] to her husband. **And there is** a case of **another** woman **where, even though she was not taken** forcefully, but was willing, she nevertheless remains **permitted. And which** case **is this?** This is referring to one **whose betrothal** was **a mistaken betrothal, as, even if her son** from this marriage **is riding on her shoulders she may perform refusal and go** off as pleases **her.** Although she engaged in intercourse with her husband after growing two pubic hairs, she was relying on the original betrothal, which was a mistaken betrothal, and did not intend to become betrothed to him by means of this intercourse, which would have rendered her betrothed by Torah law. She may therefore nullify the betrothal by means of refusal.

וְנִמְנוּ וְגָמְרוּ: עַד מָתַי הַבַּת מְמָאֶנֶת – עַד שֶׁתָּבִיא שְׁתֵּי שְׂעָרוֹת! פְּרוּשׁ וְלָא עֲבוּד עוּבְדָא.

**And** the Gemara relates that as a result of the event involving Rabbi Yishmael's daughter, the Sages assembled, **counted** the votes, **and concluded: Until when may** a young **girl perform refusal? Until** she **grows two** pubic **hairs.** Once Rav Kahana's colleagues heard this, they **retracted** and **did not perform an action** in accordance with the opinion of Rabbi Yehuda in the mishna, to permit the girl to perform refusal as they had originally planned.

**HALAKHA**

**If she was taken forcefully she is permitted – נִתְפְּשָׂה מוּתֶּרֶת:** The wife of an Israelite who was raped is permitted to her husband (Rambam *Sefer Kedusha, Hilkhot Issurei Bia* 18:7; *Shulḥan Arukh, Even HaEzer* 6, 14).

## LANGUAGE

Constable [*ballasha*] – בַּלָּשָׁא: From the Aramaic *balash*, meaning search. The Gemara refers to *ballashim*, who were policemen or soldiers sent to conduct searches and seize property. Apparently Rabbi Yehuda Nesia had such forces at his disposal, possibly assigned to him by the government.

Forelock [*belorit*] – בְּלוֹרִית: Many derivations have been suggested for this word, mostly based on Latin and Greek words, none of which fit perfectly. This hairstyle involved letting one's hair grow long, particularly on the back of the head, and then shaving it off in a ritual of idolatrous worship.

## HALAKHA

Must have follicles at their roots – צָרִיךְ שֶׁיְּהֵא בְּעִיקָּרָן גּוּמוֹת: The two hairs which serve as a sign of adulthood must be in the area of the sexual organs, and they must have follicles at their roots. The hairs serve as a sign even if they both occupy a single follicle (Rambam *Sefer Nashim*, *Hilkhot Ishut* 2:17; *Shulḥan Arukh*, *Even HaEzer* 155:16).

Even if there are no hairs – אַף עַל פִּי שֶׁאֵין שְׂעָרוֹת: If there are two follicles next to each other, they constitute a sign of adulthood even if they contain no hairs. The assumption is that follicles do not exist without hair, and therefore they must have contained hair that fell out. This is in accordance with the ruling of Rav Malkiyyu, citing Rav Adda bar Ahava (Rambam *Sefer Nashim*, *Hilkhot Ishut* 2:17; *Shulḥan Arukh*, *Even HaEzer* 155:16).

רַבִּי יִצְחָק וְתַלְמִידֵי דְּרַבִּי חֲנִינָא עֲבוּד עוֹבְדָא כְּרַבִּי יְהוּדָה, וְאַף עַל גַּב דְּנִבְעֲלָה. אֲזַל רַב שֶׁמֶן בַּר אַבָּא אֲמַרָהּ קַמֵּיהּ דְּרַבִּי יוֹחָנָן, אֲזַל רַבִּי יוֹחָנָן אֲמַרָהּ קַמֵּיהּ דְּרַבִּי יְהוּדָה נְשִׂיאָה. שְׁדַר בַּלָּשָׁא, וְאַפְּקוּהָ.

The Gemara further relates that **Rabbi Yitzḥak and the disciples of Rabbi Ḥanina performed an action in accordance with** the opinion of **Rabbi Yehuda** in the mishna, **and** permitted a young girl who had grown two pubic hairs to perform refusal, **even though she** had **engaged in intercourse** with her husband after growing two hairs. **Rav Shemen bar Abba** subsequently **went** and **stated** this story **before Rabbi Yoḥanan,** and **Rabbi Yoḥanan went** and **stated it before Rabbi Yehuda Nesia.** Rabbi Yehuda Nesia **sent a constable** [***ballasha***][L] **and removed** that girl from her second husband.

אָמַר רַב חִסְדָּא, אָמַר מָר עוּקְבָא: לֹא שֶׁיִּרְבֶּה הַשָּׁחוֹר מַמָּשׁ, אֶלָּא כְּדֵי שֶׁיִּהְיוּ שְׁתֵּי שְׂעָרוֹת שׁוֹכְבוֹת, וְנִרְאוֹת כְּמִי שֶׁיִּרְבֶּה הַשָּׁחוֹר עַל הַלָּבָן. רָבָא אָמַר: שְׁתֵּי שְׂעָרוֹת הַמַּקִּיפוֹת מִשָּׂפָה לְשָׂפָה.

With regard to Rabbi Yehuda's opinion, that the black hair must be preponderant in the pubic area, **Rav Ḥisda says** that **Mar Ukva says:** This does **not** mean **that** the **black** hair must **literally be preponderant** in the pubic area. **Rather, there must be two hairs lying down, so that it appears as though the black** hairs in the pubic area cover an area **greater than the white** area uncovered by hair. **Rava says:** Rabbi Yehuda means that there are **two hairs that surround** the pubic area **from end to end.**

אָמַר רַבִּי חֶלְבּוֹ, אָמַר רַב הוּנָא: שְׁתֵּי שְׂעָרוֹת שֶׁאָמְרוּ – צָרִיךְ שֶׁיְּהֵא בְּעִיקָּרָן גּוּמוֹת. רַב מַלְכִּיוּ אָמַר רַב אַדָּא בַּר אַהֲבָה: גּוּמוֹת אַף עַל פִּי שֶׁאֵין שְׂעָרוֹת.

§ The mishna teaches that the growth of two hairs is a sign of becoming an adult. The Gemara clarifies the details of this *halakha*. **Rabbi Ḥelbo says** that **Rav Huna says:** These **two hairs that** the Sages **said** are a sign of adulthood **must have follicles at their roots.**[H] **Rav Malkiyyu says** that **Rav Adda bar Ahava** says: If there are two **follicles** next to each other, they constitute a sign of adulthood **even if there are no hairs**[H] in them. The assumption is that follicles do not exist without hair, and therefore there must have been hairs there that fell out.

אָמַר רַב חֲנִינָא בְּרֵיהּ דְּרַב אִיקָא: שַׁפּוּד, שְׁפָחוֹת, וְגוּמוֹת – רַב מַלְכִּיוּ; בְּלוֹרִית, אֵפֶר מִקְלֶה, וּגְבִינָה – רַב מַלְכִּיָּא.

This *halakha* was stated by a Sage by the name of Rav Malkiyyu. To prevent confusion between his rulings and those of the similarly named Rav Malkiyya, **Rabbi Ḥanina, son of Rav Ika, says:** The *halakha* involving **a skewer,** the *halakha* with regard to **maidservants, and** the *halakha* involving hair **follicles**[N] were all stated by **Rav Malkiyyu.** By contrast, the *halakha* with regard to the **forelock** [***belorit***],[L] the *halakha* involving **burnt ashes, and** the *halakha* with regard to **cheese** were all stated by a different Sage named **Rav Malkiyya.**

רַב פַּפָּא אָמַר: מַתְנִיתִין וּמַתְנִיתָא – רַב מַלְכִּיָּא, שְׁמַעְתָּתָא – רַב מַלְכִּיוּ, וְסִימָנָא: מַתְנִיתָא מַלְכְּתָא.

**Rav Pappa says:** The aforementioned *halakhot* that relate to **a mishna or a *baraita*** were stated by **Rav Malkiyya,** whereas ***halakhot*** that do not refer to a mishna or *baraita* but are independent statements of *amora'im* were taught by **Rav Malkiyyu. And a mnemonic** to remember this is: **The mishna is a queen** [***malketa***], i.e., the comments that are referring to a mishna were issued by Rav Malkiyya, whose name is similar to the Aramaic term for queen.

מַאי בֵּינַיְיהוּ? אִיכָּא בֵּינַיְיהוּ שְׁפָחוֹת.

The Gemara asks: **What is** the difference **between** the opinion of Rabbi Ḥanina, son of Rav Ika, and Rav Pappa? The Gemara answers: The difference **between them** is with regard to which Sage taught the *halakha* involving **maidservants.** Rav Pappa maintains that it was taught by Rav Malkiyya, as it is referring to a dispute in a mishna. By contrast, according to Rabbi Ḥanina, this *halakha* was stated by Rav Malkiyyu.

## NOTES

A skewer, maidservants, and hair follicles – שַׁפּוּד שְׁפָחוֹת וְגוּמוֹת: The term skewer is referring to a *halakha* of the Festivals, that one may not move a skewer on which meat was roasted but that he must rather allow it to fall in its place (see *Beitza* 28b). The term maidservants is a reference to one of the *halakhot* of a marriage contract. This ruling is in accordance with the opinion in the mishna (see *Ketubot* 59b) that even if a wife brought into the marriage a large dowry including one hundred maidservants, she may not remain idle but is required to perform at least some minimal household tasks.

The term forelock, mentioned in the *halakhot* of Rav Malkiyya, refers to the *halakhot* of idol worship. Idolaters would grow forelocks in deference to their idol. It is taught in a *baraita* that a Jew who cuts the hair of a gentile must distance his hand from the forelock. The Gemara rules that the barber must avoid cutting hair within three fingerbreadths of the forelock (see *Avoda Zara* 29a). The term burnt ashes is referring to the prohibition against tattoos. One may not place burnt ashes on a wound for medicinal purposes, as this creates the appearance of a tattoo (see *Makkot* 21a). Finally, the term cheese is a reference to a *halakha* proscribing the consumption of cheese produced by gentiles (see *Avoda Zara* 29b), because they smooth it with forbidden fat (see *Avoda Zara* 35b).

אָמַר רַב אַשִׁי, אָמַר לִי מָר זוּטְרָא, קָשֶׁה בָּהּ רַבִּי חֲנִינָא מִסּוּרָא: לָא לִישְׁתַּמִּיט תַּנָּא וְאַשְׁמוֹעִינַן גּוּמוֹת! אִי אַשְׁמוֹעִינַן גּוּמוֹת – הֲוָה אָמִינָא: עַד שֶׁיְּהוּ שְׁתֵּי שְׂעָרוֹת בִּשְׁתֵּי גּוּמוֹת, קָא מַשְׁמַע לָן – דַּאֲפִילּוּ שְׁתֵּי שְׂעָרוֹת בְּגוּמָּא אַחַת.

With regard to the *halakha* of Rav Malkiyyu itself, concerning follicles, **Rav Ashi says: Mar Zutra told me** that **Rabbi Ḥanina of Sura** posed the following **difficulty:** If it is correct that follicles suffice as a sign of adulthood, **let the *tanna*** of the mishna **not evade** the issue, **but** rather let him **teach us** explicitly that **follicles** are a sign of adulthood even if they do not contain hair. The Gemara answers: **If** the mishna had **taught us** the case of **follicles, I would say** that they are not considered a sign of adulthood **until there are two hairs in two follicles.** By omitting any mention of follicles in the mishna, the *tanna* **teaches us that even two hairs in one follicle**[H] are a sign of adulthood.

וּמִי אִיכָּא כְּהַאי גַּוְונָא? וְהָכְתִיב ״אֲשֶׁר בִּשְׂעָרָה יְשׁוּפֵנִי וְהִרְבָּה פְצָעַי חִנָּם״, וְאָמַר רָבָא: אִיּוֹב בִּסְעָרָה חֵירֵף, בִּסְעָרָה הֱשִׁיבוּהוּ. בִּסְעָרָה חֵירֵף – אָמַר לְפָנָיו: רִבּוֹנוֹ שֶׁל עוֹלָם, שֶׁמָּא רוּחַ סְעָרָה עָבְרָה לְפָנֶיךָ וְנִתְחַלְּפָה לְךָ בֵּין אִיּוֹב לְאוֹיֵב? בִּסְעָרָה הֱשִׁיבוּהוּ – ״וַיַּעַן ה׳ אֶת

The Gemara asks: **And is there** actually **a case like this,** of two hairs in one follicle? **But isn't it written: "He crushes me with a tempest, and multiplies my wounds without cause"** (Job 9:17); **and Rava said** with regard to this verse: **Job blasphemed with a tempest,** and **with a tempest he was answered. He blasphemed with a tempest,** as Job **said before** God: **Master of the Universe, perhaps a tempest passed before You and You confused Iyyov,** Job, **with *oyev*,** enemy. **With a tempest he was answered,** as the verse states: **"Then the Lord answered**

Two hairs in one follicle – שְׁתֵּי שְׂעָרוֹת בְּגוּמָּא אַחַת: Two pubic hairs in one follicle are a sign of adulthood. This *halakha* is in accordance with the opinion of Rav Ashi (Rambam *Sefer Nashim, Hilkhot Ishut* 2:17; *Shulḥan Arukh, Even HaEzer* 155:16).

Perek **VI**
Daf **52** Amud **b**

אִיּוֹב מִן הַסְּעָרָה, וַיֹּאמַר״ אֵלָיו: שׁוֹטֶה שֶׁבָּעוֹלָם, הַרְבֵּה נִימִין בָּרָאתִי בְּרֹאשׁוֹ שֶׁל אָדָם, וּלְכָל נִימָא וְנִימָא בָּרָאתִי לוֹ גּוּמָּא בִּפְנֵי עַצְמָהּ שֶׁלֹּא יִהְיוּ שְׁתַּיִם יוֹנְקוֹת מִגּוּמָּא אַחַת, שֶׁאִלְמָלֵא שְׁתַּיִם יוֹנְקוֹת מִגּוּמָּא אַחַת – מַכְחִישׁ מְאוֹר עֵינָיו שֶׁל אָדָם. גּוּמָּא בְּגוּמָּא לֹא נִתְחַלֵּף לִי, אִיּוֹב בְּאוֹיֵב נִתְחַלֵּף לִי?

**Job out of the tempest, and said"** (Job 38:1–3) **to him:** Greatest **imbecile in the world! I have created many hairs on a person's head, and for each and every hair I created** its own **distinct follicle, so that two hairs should not draw** sustenance **from one follicle. As, were two** hairs **to draw** sustenance **from one follicle,** it would **weaken a man's vision.** Now **if I did not confuse one follicle with another, would I confuse** a man named **Iyyov with *oyev*?** This indicates that two hairs do not grow from one follicle.

לָא קַשְׁיָא, הָא – בְּגוּפָא, הָא – בְּרֵישָׁא.

The Gemara answers: It is **not difficult; that** statement above, that two hairs in one follicle is a valid sign of adulthood, is referring to the hairs **in** the rest of a person's **body,** whereas **this** statement, that there cannot be two hairs in one follicle, is referring to the hairs **on** a person's **head.**

אָמַר רַב יְהוּדָה, אָמַר שְׁמוּאֵל: שְׁתֵּי שְׂעָרוֹת שֶׁאָמְרוּ – אֲפִילּוּ אַחַת עַל הַכַּף וְאַחַת עַל הַבֵּיצִים.

**Rav Yehuda says** that **Shmuel says:** The **two hairs that** the Sages **said** are signs of adulthood are valid signs **even if** they are not adjacent; but rather **one** hair is **on the spoon**-shaped area[H] above his organ **and one** is **on the** young boy's **testicles.**

HALAKHA

**The two hairs that the Sages said are signs of adulthood are valid even if one hair is on the spoon-shaped area** – שְׁתֵּי שְׂעָרוֹת שֶׁאָמְרוּ אֲפִילּוּ אַחַת עַל הַכַּף: The two pubic hairs that are a sign of adulthood must be located in the genital area. Hairs that are located anywhere on the entire pubic area are valid signs, whether they are higher or lower or on the reproductive organs themselves. But the two hairs must be adjacent to each other, in accordance with the opinion of the Rabbis (see *Kesef Mishne* and *Beit Shmuel*). Others maintain that even if one hair is on her back and another on her lower abdomen, or one on her finger joints and one on her toe joints (see *Leḥem Mishne* and *Maggid Mishne*), she is considered an adult with regard to refusing her marriage, but not with regard to performing *ḥalitza* (Rambam *Sefer Nashim, Hilkhot Ishut* 2:17; *Shulḥan Arukh, Even HaEzer* 155:17).

## BACKGROUND

**Village of Akko** – כְּפַר עַכּוֹ: The village of Akko, as indicated by its name, was one of the settlements that enveloped the city of Akko, or Acre. This city served as a center for the residents of the entire area, providing them with essential services. The village of Akko, like other villages near the city of Acre, supplied the city with agricultural products. It was an especially important village among those situated near Acre, as it was located on the main route leading to Lebanon and Syria.

Some identify the village of Akko with the settlement of Kafr Yasif, east of the city of Acre. In the past there was a large Jewish presence there. Indeed, Josephus calls the place the village of Akko and lists it among the areas he fortified in anticipation of the battle with the Romans. The village was inhabited by Jews throughout the entire period of the Mishna and the Gemara, and even afterward, until recent times. The remains of many graves have been discovered at this site, as well as other important archaeological findings.

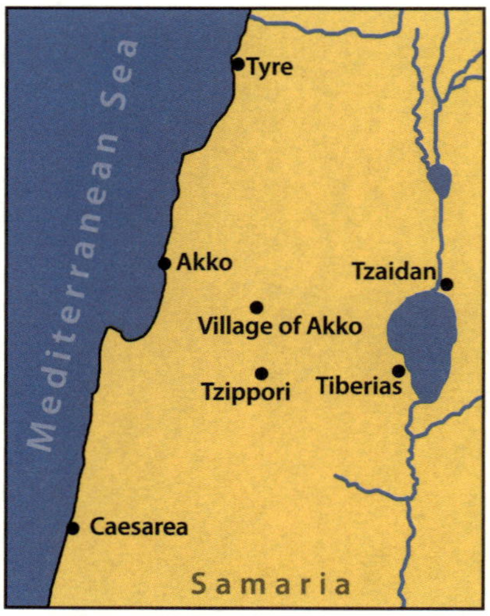


Location of the village of Akko

**Tzaidan** – צַיְדָן: Tzaidan, which was also called Beit Tzayda or Bethsaida, and was referred to by Josephus as Julias, its Roman name, was a village on the northern side of the Sea of Galilee, adjacent to the estuary of the Jordan River. It was home to various Sages during the mishnaic period, as well as afterward.

## PERSONALITIES

**Ḥanina ben Ḥakhinai** – חֲנִינָא בֶּן חֲכִינַאי: Ḥanina, or Ḥananya, ben Ḥakhinai is identified by the Gemara as one of those referred to by the appellation: They deliberated before the Sages in Yavne, who knew seventy languages. He was a preeminent disciple of Rabbi Akiva. Traditions and *halakhot* cited in his name can be found throughout the Mishna, the *Tosefta*, various halakhic *midrashim*, and the Talmud. In one midrash, Ḥanina ben Ḥakhinai is listed among the ten martyrs.

## LANGUAGE

**Filling with hair [*kilkul*]** – כִּלְכּוּל: This word has a similar meaning in Syriac, i.e., a head full of hair. In the Mishna its precise meaning is the hair located on the temples, although it is also used in reference to a mass of hair elsewhere on the body, as in this case.

**Pair [*zug*]** – זוּג: From the Greek ζυγόν, *zugon*, meaning a pair of a certain item. It is therefore used to refer to utensils that come in pairs, particularly scissors.

תַּנְיָא נַמִּי הָכִי: שְׁתֵּי שְׂעָרוֹת שֶׁאָמְרוּ – אֲפִילּוּ אַחַת בְּגַבָּהּ וְאַחַת בִּכְרֵיסָהּ, אַחַת עַל גַּבֵּי קִשְׁרֵי אֶצְבְּעוֹתֶיהָ שֶׁל יָד וְאַחַת עַל גַּבֵּי קִשְׁרֵי אֶצְבְּעוֹתֶיהָ שֶׁל רֶגֶל, דִּבְרֵי רַבִּי שִׁמְעוֹן בֶּן יְהוּדָה אִישׁ כְּפַר עַכּוֹ שֶׁאָמַר מִשּׁוּם רַבִּי שִׁמְעוֹן. וְרַבָּנַן אָמַר רַב חִסְדָּא: עַד שֶׁיְּהוּ שְׁתֵּי שְׂעָרוֹת בְּמָקוֹם אֶחָד.

The Gemara notes **that** this **is also taught** in a *baraita*: The **two hairs that** the Sages **said** are signs of adulthood are valid signs **even** if **one** hair is **on** the young girl's **back,** below her pubic area, **and one on her lower abdomen.**[N] The same applies if **one** hair is **on the finger joints of her hand and one** hair is **on the toe joints of her foot.** This is **the statement of Rabbi Shimon ben Yehuda, of the village of Akko,**[B] **who said** it **in the name of Rabbi Shimon. And** what do **the Rabbis** say about this matter? **Rav Ḥisda says:** According to the Rabbis, they are not a valid sign of adulthood **unless** the **two hairs are in one place.**[N]

תָּנוּ רַבָּנַן: עַד מָתַי הַבַּת מְמָאֶנֶת? עַד שֶׁתָּבִיא שְׁתֵּי שְׂעָרוֹת, דִּבְרֵי רַבִּי מֵאִיר. רַבִּי יְהוּדָה אוֹמֵר: עַד שֶׁיִּרְבֶּה הַשָּׁחוֹר. רַבִּי יוֹסֵי אוֹמֵר: עַד שֶׁתַּקִּיף הָעֲטָרָה. בֶּן שְׁלָקוֹת אוֹמֵר: עַד שֶׁתְּכַלְכֵּל.

§ The mishna teaches that Rabbi Yehuda and the Rabbis disagree with regard to when a young girl can perform refusal. According to the Rabbis, it is until she grows two pubic hairs after she reaches the age of twelve years and one day. According to Rabbi Yehuda she still retains the right to perform refusal at that point, until the majority of the pubic area is filled with hair. In this regard, **the Sages taught** in a *baraita*: **Until when can a young girl perform refusal? Until she grows two** pubic **hairs;** this is **the statement of Rabbi Meir. Rabbi Yehuda says:** She can perform refusal **until** the area covered by the **black** pubic hairs **is greater** than the white skin of the genital area. **Rabbi Yosei says: Until the nipple is surrounded** by hair. **Ben Shelakot says: Until** the pubic area is **filled with hair.**

וְאָמַר רַבִּי שִׁמְעוֹן, מְצָאַנִי חֲנִינָא בֶּן חֲכִינַאי בְּצַיְדָן, וְאָמַר: כְּשֶׁאַתָּה מַגִּיעַ אֵצֶל רַבִּי עֲקִיבָא אֱמוֹר לוֹ "עַד מָתַי הַבַּת מְמָאֶנֶת"? אִם יֹאמַר לְךָ "עַד שֶׁתָּבִיא שְׁתֵּי שְׂעָרוֹת", אֱמוֹר לוֹ "וַהֲלֹא בֶּן שְׁלָקוֹת הֵעִיד בְּמַעֲמַד כּוּלְּכֶם בְּיַבְנֶה עַד שֶׁתְּכַלְכֵּל, וְלֹא אֲמַרְתֶּם לוֹ דָּבָר"!

**And Rabbi Shimon said: Ḥanina ben Ḥakhinai**[P] **found me in** the city of **Tzaidan**[B] **and said** to me: **When you reach Rabbi Akiva, say to him: Until when can a young girl perform refusal? If he says to you** that she may perform refusal **until she grows two** pubic **hairs, say to him: But didn't ben Shelakot testify in the presence of all of you in Yavne** that she may perform refusal **until** the pubic area **is filled with hair** [*shetekhalkel*], **and you did not say anything to him,** thereby indicating that you conceded to him?

כְּשֶׁבָּאתִי אֵצֶל רַבִּי עֲקִיבָא, אָמַר לִי: כִּלְכּוּל זֶה – אֵינִי יוֹדֵעַ מַהוּ, בֶּן שְׁלָקוֹת – אֵינִי מַכִּיר, עַד מָתַי הַבַּת מְמָאֶנֶת – עַד שֶׁתָּבִיא שְׁתֵּי שְׂעָרוֹת.

Rabbi Shimon continued: **When I reached Rabbi Akiva,** and I said what I had been told to say to him, **he said to me: I do not know what this filling with hair** [*kilkul*][L] **is, I don't know** any **ben Shelakot,** and my opinion with regard to your question, **until when can a young girl perform refusal,** is that she can perform refusal **until she grows two** pubic **hairs.**

מתני׳ שְׁתֵּי שְׂעָרוֹת הָאֲמוּרוֹת בְּפָרָה, וּבִנְגָעִים, וְהָאֲמוּרוֹת בְּכָל מָקוֹם – כְּדֵי לָכוֹף רֹאשָׁן לְעִיקָּרָן – דִּבְרֵי רַבִּי יִשְׁמָעֵאל, רַבִּי אֱלִיעֶזֶר אוֹמֵר: כְּדֵי לִקְרוֹץ בְּצִיפּוֹרֶן, רַבִּי עֲקִיבָא אוֹמֵר: כְּדֵי שֶׁיְּהוּ נִיטָּלוֹת בְּזוּג.

**MISHNA** The **two** white or black **hairs that are mentioned with regard to** disqualification of a red **heifer; and** the two white hairs mentioned **with regard to leprous marks,** i.e., that if they grow within a white leprous mark, it is impure; **and** the two hairs **that are mentioned in every place,** i.e., with regard to a young boy and girl, are significant only if they are long **enough to bend the top** of the hairs **to reach their roots.** This is **the statement of Rabbi Yishmael. Rabbi Eliezer says:** They must be long **enough to** grasp them and **cut** them **with a fingernail. Rabbi Akiva says:** They must be long **enough to be cut with a pair** [*bezug*][L] of scissors.

## NOTES

**Even if one hair is on her back and one on her lower abdomen** – אֲפִילּוּ אַחַת בְּגַבָּהּ וְאַחַת בִּכְרֵיסָהּ: The commentaries disagree whether the reference to her back and lower abdomen is meant literally or euphemistically. Some maintain that they allude to areas of her genitalia (Rashi; Rashba), as the Sages spoke euphemistically concerning these matters (Meiri).

**Unless two hairs are in one place** – עַד שֶׁיְּהוּ שְׁתֵּי שְׂעָרוֹת בְּמָקוֹם אֶחָד: The early commentaries disagree with regard to the opinion of the Rabbis. Some maintain that although the Rabbis rule that the two hairs must be in one location, they agree with Rabbi Shimon that they are not required to be in the pubic area. Even if they grow on the finger joints, they are a sign of adulthood. According to this interpretation, the Rabbis disagree with Rabbi Shimon only insofar as they require that the two hairs must be adjacent (Ramban; Rashba; Ritva; Ran).

Some early commentaries further conclude that the same applies to a young boy. They contend that two hairs in any part of the body where hair does not usually grow until adulthood are considered a sign of adulthood (Ran). It has been noted that this is a lone opinion (*Eizehu Mekoman*), and the authorities rule that only pubic hairs are a sign of adulthood. This is stated explicitly by *Tosafot* on *Yevamot* 80b.

גמ׳ אָמַר רַב חִסְדָּא, אָמַר מָר עוּקְבָא: הֲלָכָה כְּדִבְרֵי כּוּלָּן לְהַחְמִיר.

**GEMARA** **Rav Ḥisda says** that **Mar Ukva says** with regard to the various opinions in the mishna on the measure of hairs: The ***halakha*** **is in accordance with the statements of all of them to be stringent.**[H] One should consider it hair only if all of the criteria are met, or consider it to be hair if any one condition is met, depending on which standard yields the more stringent result.

מתני׳ הָרוֹאָה כֶּתֶם – הֲרֵי זוֹ מְקוּלְקֶלֶת

**MISHNA** With regard to a woman **who sees** a red **stain**[H] on her garment, **that** woman's reckoning **is distorted.** Since she does not know when the blood that caused the stain appeared, she does not know when the seven days of menstrual flow end and when the eleven days of the flow of the *zava* begin.

וְחוֹשֶׁשֶׁת מִשּׁוּם זוֹב – דִּבְרֵי רַבִּי מֵאִיר, וַחֲכָמִים אוֹמְרִים: אֵין בִּכְתָמִים מִשּׁוּם זוֹב.

**And** therefore she must be **concerned due to** the possibility that it might have been caused by the **flow of a** ***zava.*** If she wore the same garment for three days on which she can assume the status of a *zava*, and subsequently discovered a stain with an area that is the size of at least three split beans, the concern is that on each of those three days a stain with the area of at least one split bean, the minimum area that transmits impurity, was formed. The result is that she is a greater *zava* and is required to count seven clean days before immersion. This is **the statement of Rabbi Meir. And the Rabbis say: No** configuration **of stains** leads to concern **due to the flow of a** ***zava.***

גמ׳ מַאן חֲכָמִים? רַבִּי חֲנִינָא בֶּן אַנְטִיגְנוֹס הִיא, דְּתַנְיָא, רַבִּי חֲנִינָא בֶּן אַנְטִיגְנוֹס אוֹמֵר: כְּתָמִים אֵין בָּהֶן מִשּׁוּם זוֹב. וּפְעָמִים שֶׁהַכְּתָמִים מְבִיאִין לִידֵי זִיבָה.

**GEMARA** The Gemara asks: **Who are the Rabbis** in this mishna? **It is Rabbi Ḥanina ben Antigonus, as it is taught** in a *baraita* that **Rabbi Ḥanina ben Antigonus says: Stains do not** lead to concern **due to the flow of a** ***zava,*** **but stains can sometimes lead to** ***ziva.***

כֵּיצַד – לָבְשָׁה שְׁלֹשָׁה חֲלוּקוֹת הַבְּדוּקוֹת לָהּ וּמָצְאָה עֲלֵיהֶם כֶּתֶם, אוֹ שֶׁרָאֲתָה שְׁנֵי יָמִים וְחָלוּק אֶחָד – הֵן הֵן הַכְּתָמִים הַמְבִיאִין לִידֵי זִיבָה.

**How so,** i.e., how can stains lead to *ziva* according to Rabbi Ḥanina ben Antigonus? If a woman **wore three** different **robes that** had been **examined by her** for blood stains, **and** she then **found a stain on** each of **them;**[H] **or** if she **saw** blood flowing from her body on **two** consecutive **days and** on the third day she saw a stain on **one** of the **robes**[H] that she wore that day, **those are the stains that lead to** ***ziva.***

הַשְׁתָּא שְׁלֹשָׁה חֲלוּקוֹת דְּלָאו מִגּוּפָהּ קָחָזְיָא – חָיְישִׁינַן, שְׁנֵי יָמִים וְחָלוּק אֶחָד מִיבַּעְיָא?

The Gemara raises a difficulty with regard to the above statement: According to the opinion of Rabbi Ḥanina ben Antigonus, **now** that in a case where she sees stains on **three robes we are concerned** for *ziva*, despite the fact **that** she **does not see** the blood flowing **from her body, is it necessary** to state that we are concerned if she experiences bleeding from her body on **two days and** sees a stain on **one** of the **robes?**

מַהוּ דְּתֵימָא – כָּל כִּי הַאי גַּוְונָא מְבִיאָה קָרְבָּן וְנֶאֱכָל, קָא מַשְׁמַע לָן.

The Gemara answers: It is necessary to state that, **lest you say** that in **any case like this,** where she experiences bleeding from her body on two days and on the third day she sees a stain on one of the robes, **she brings an offering and it is consumed,** like one who is definitely a *zava*. Therefore, Rabbi Ḥanina ben Antigonus **teaches us** that her status as a *zava* is uncertain, and consequently she brings a bird for a sin offering that is due to uncertainty, which is not eaten.

אָמַר רָבָא, בְּהָא זָכִינְהוּ רַבִּי חֲנִינָא בֶּן אַנְטִיגְנוֹס לְרַבָּנַן: מַאי שְׁנָא פָּחוּת מִשְּׁלֹשָׁה גְּרִיסִין בְּמָקוֹם אֶחָד דְּלָא חָיְישִׁינַן – דְּאָמְרִינַן: בִּתְרֵי יוֹמֵי חֲזֵיתֵיהּ, שְׁלֹשָׁה גְּרִיסִין בְּמָקוֹם אֶחָד נַמִי – נֵימָא: תַּרְתֵּי וּפַלְגָא מִגּוּפָהּ חֲזֵיתֵיהּ, וְאִידַּךְ אַגַּב זוּהֲמָא דַּם מַאֲכוֹלֶת הוּא.

**Rava said: With this** claim **Rabbi Ḥanina ben Antigonus bested the** other **Rabbis,** who agree with the opinion of Rabbi Meir in the mishna: **What is different** about a stain that is **less than three split beans in one place, that we are not concerned** she might be a *zava*? The reason is **that we say** she **saw** blood **on** only **two days.** But in a case where she discovered a stain on her robe with the area of at least **three split beans in one place,** one can **also say:** The area of **two and a half** split beans should be attributed to blood **seen from her body, but the other is** the **blood of a louse that** was there **due to the dirt** associated with her bleeding.

**HALAKHA**

**The** ***halakha*** **is in accordance with the statements of all of them to be stringent** – **הֲלָכָה כְּדִבְרֵי כּוּלָּן לְהַחְמִיר**: The two white or black hairs that are mentioned with regard to disqualification of a red heifer; and the two white hairs mentioned with regard to leprosy, that if they grow within a white leprous mark, it is impure; and likewise the two hairs mentioned with regard to the signs of adulthood for a young boy or girl are all significant only if they are long enough to bend the top of the hairs to reach their roots, or to grasp them and cut them with a fingernail, or to be cut with scissors, whichever standard is the most stringent. This ruling is in accordance with the opinions of Rabbi Yishmael, Rabbi Eliezer, and Rabbi Akiva, following the statement of Rav Ḥisda citing Mar Ukva, that the *halakha* is in accordance with all of them to be stringent (Rambam *Sefer Tahara, Hilkhot Para Aduma* 1:4 and *Hilkhot Tumat Tzara'at* 2:1, and *Sefer Nashim, Hilkhot Ishut* 2:16; *Shulḥan Arukh, Even HaEzer* 155:18).

**A woman who sees a red stain** – **הָרוֹאָה כֶּתֶם**: With regard to a woman who sees a red stain when it is not her fixed time of menstruation, her reckoning is distorted, as it might be menstrual blood. This ruling is in accordance with the *baraita* (Rambam *Sefer Kedusha, Hilkhot Issurei Bia* 9:3).

**Wore three different robes that had been examined by her and she found a stain on them** – **לָבְשָׁה שְׁלֹשָׁה חֲלוּקוֹת הַבְּדוּקוֹת לָהּ וּמָצְאָה עֲלֵיהֶם כֶּתֶם**: If a woman wore three different robes that she had examined for blood stains after the seven days of menstrual flow ended, and she wore them for three days during the eleven days of *ziva*, and she then found a stain on each of them, even if she discovered three stains in the same location on the three robes, she is only a *zava* of uncertain status. This is in accordance with the opinion of the Rabbis, i.e., Rabbi Ḥanina ben Antigonus (Rambam *Sefer Kedusha, Hilkhot Issurei Bia* 9:12).

**Saw blood flowing on two consecutive days and on the third saw a stain on one of the robes** – **רָאֲתָה שְׁנֵי יָמִים וְחָלוּק אֶחָד**: If a woman sees blood flowing from her body on two consecutive days when it is not her fixed time of menstruation and on the third day she sees a stain, she is a *zava* of uncertain status. This *halakha* is in accordance with the opinion of the Rabbis, i.e., Rabbi Ḥanina ben Antigonus (Rambam *Sefer Kedusha, Hilkhot Issurei Bia* 9:14).

**HALAKHA**

**If the area is large enough to be divided into three split beans – אִם יֵשׁ בּוֹ כְּדֵי לְחַלֵּק שְׁלֹשָׁה גְּרִיסִין:** With regard to a woman who wears a robe for three or more days when it is not her fixed time of menstruation, and then discovers three stains on it, or one large stain the size of three stains, she is a *zava* of uncertain status. This is due to a concern that blood might have emerged from her each of the three days, as stated in the *baraita* (Rambam *Sefer Kedusha*, *Hilkhot Issurei Bia* 9:12).

**NOTES**

**She must be concerned – חוֹשֶׁשֶׁת:** This is due to the fact that seeing during twilight is considered like seeing twice, as part of it is considered as seeing during the day while part of the sighting is considered to have occurred at night.

וְרַבָּנַן, כֵּיוָן דְּאִיכָּא לְפַלּוּגֵי בִּגְרִיס וְעוֹד לְכָל יוֹמָא – לָא תָּלֵינַן.

The Gemara asks: **And** how do **the Rabbis** respond to this claim? The Gemara answers: They maintain that **since it is possible to divide** the stain into **at least one split bean for each** of the three **days, we do not attribute** the stain to the blood of a louse.

וְרַבִּי חֲנִינָא בֶּן אַנְטִיגְנוֹס שְׁלֹשָׁה גְּרִיסִין בְּמָקוֹם אֶחָד הוּא דְּלָא חָיְישִׁינַן, הָא בִּשְׁלֹשָׁה מְקוֹמוֹת – חָיְישִׁינַן? הָא אָמְרַתְּ בִּשְׁלֹשָׁה חֲלוּקוֹת – אִין, בִּשְׁלֹשָׁה מְקוֹמוֹת – לָא!

The Gemara raises a difficulty with regard to the statement of Rava: **And** according to the opinion of **Rabbi Ḥanina ben Antigonus,** one can infer that **it is** specifically in the case of a stain with the area of at least **three split beans in one place that we are not concerned** she might be a *zava*. It can be inferred from here that if it is **in three places, we are concerned.** But **didn't you say** that if she discovered stains **in three robes, yes,** we are concerned, which indicates that if it is **in three places** on a single robe we are **not** concerned.

לְדִבְרֵיהֶם דְּרַבָּנַן קָאָמַר לְהוּ, לְדִידִי – בִּשְׁלֹשָׁה חֲלוּקוֹת – אִין, בִּשְׁלֹשָׁה מְקוֹמוֹת – לָא; אֶלָּא לְדִידְכוּ, אוֹדוּ לִי מִיהַת דְּהֵיכָא דַּחֲזַאי שְׁלֹשָׁה גְּרִיסִין בְּמָקוֹם אֶחָד, דְּאָמְרִינַן – תְּרֵי וּפַלְגָא מִגּוּפָהּ חֲזֵיתֵיהּ, וְאִידָּךְ – אַגַּב זוּהֲמָא דַּם מַאֲכוֹלֶת הוּא!

The Gemara answers that it was **in accordance with the statement of the Rabbis** that Rabbi Ḥanina ben Antigonus **stated** his opinion **to them,** as follows: **According to my** opinion, if she discovered stains **in three robes, yes** we are concerned, whereas if it is **in three places** we are **not** concerned. **But according to your** opinion, **at least concede to me that where** she **saw** a stain on her robe with the area of at least **three split beans in one place, that we say** that the area of **two and a half** split beans can be attributed to blood **seen from her body, and the other is** the **blood of a louse** that was there **due to the dirt** associated with her bleeding.

וְרַבָּנַן – כֵּיוָן דְּאִיכָּא לְפַלּוּגֵי בִּגְרִיס וְעוֹד לְכָל יוֹמָא – לָא תָּלֵינַן.

The Gemara asks: **And** how do **the Rabbis** respond to this claim? The Gemara answers: They maintain that **since it is possible to divide** the stain into **at least one split bean for each** of the three **days, we do not attribute** the stain to the blood of a louse.

תָּנוּ רַבָּנַן: הָרוֹאָה כֶּתֶם, אִם יֵשׁ בּוֹ כְּדֵי לְחַלֵּק שְׁלֹשָׁה גְּרִיסִין, שֶׁהֵן כִּגְרִיס וְעוֹד – חוֹשֶׁשֶׁת, וְאִם לָאו – אֵינָהּ חוֹשֶׁשֶׁת.

§ With regard to a woman who finds a stain on her robe, **the Sages taught** in a *baraita*: In the case of a woman **who sees** a red **stain** on her garment that she wore for a number of days and she does not know when and where it is from, what is her status? **If** the area is large **enough to be divided** into three parts, where the total area is the size of **three split beans,**[H] each of **which is** the minimum measure to render her a *zava*, i.e., an area the size of **at least a split bean,** she must be **concerned** that she is a *zava*, as this stain might be the result of seeing a sufficient measure of blood on each of three occasions. **But if** the stain is **not** that size, she does **not** need to **be concerned.**

רַבִּי יְהוּדָה בֶּן אַגְרָא אוֹמֵר מִשּׁוּם רַבִּי יוֹסֵי: אַחַת זוֹ וְאַחַת זוֹ – חוֹשֶׁשֶׁת.

**Rabbi Yehuda ben Agra says in the name of Rabbi Yosei: Both** in **this** case, where she saw a stain large enough to be divided into three parts, where the total area is the size of three split beans, **and that** case, where the stain was not that large, she must be **concerned**[N] that she might be a *zava*. This is due to the fact that she possibly saw stains of sufficient size on only two occasions, but one was during twilight, which counts as two days, amounting to a total of three days.

Perek **VI**
Daf **53** Amud **a**

אָמַר רַבִּי: נִרְאִין דִּבְרֵי רַבִּי יְהוּדָה בֶּן אַגְרָא – בְּשֶׁלֹּא בָּדְקָה, וְדִבְרֵי חֲכָמִים – בְּשֶׁבָּדְקָה.

**Rabbi** Yehuda HaNasi **says** that the dispute between Rabbi Yehuda ben Agra and the Rabbis should be decided as follows: **The statement of Rabbi Yehuda ben Agra,** who maintains that there is a concern for the possibility that the woman might have seen blood at twilight, **appears** to be correct **in** a case **where she did not examine. And the statement of the Rabbis,** who are not concerned about that possibility, appears to be correct **in** a case **where she did examine.**

מַאי בָּדְקָה וּמַאי לֹא בָּדְקָה? אָמַר רָבָא, אַשְׁכַּחְתִּינְהוּ לְרַבָּנַן דְּבֵי רַב דְּיָתְבִי וְקָאָמְרִי: הָכָא בְּמַאי עָסְקִינַן – כְּגוֹן שֶׁבָּדְקָה עַצְמָהּ וְלֹא בָּדְקָה חֲלוּקָהּ, וְאַף עַצְמָהּ לֹא בָּדְקָה אֶלָּא בֵּין הַשְּׁמָשׁוֹת דְּרַבִּי יְהוּדָה, וּבְבֵין הַשְּׁמָשׁוֹת דְּרַבִּי יוֹסֵי לֹא בָּדְקָה.

The Gemara asks: **What** did Rabbi Yehuda HaNasi mean by: Where she **did examine, and what** did he mean by: Where she **did not examine? Rava says: I found the Sages in the study hall of Rav sitting and saying** the following explanation of the *baraita*: **Here we are dealing with** a case **where** the woman **examined herself but did not examine her robe. And even** with regard to **herself, she examined** herself **only** during **twilight** [*bein hashemashot*][NL] as defined **by Rabbi Yehuda,**[N] i.e., the time it takes to walk a half *mil* before the emergence of the stars. **But during twilight** as defined **by Rabbi Yosei**, i.e., the blink of an eye before the emergence of the stars, **she did not examine** herself.

דְּרַבָּנַן סָבְרִי בְּבֵין הַשְּׁמָשׁוֹת דְּרַבִּי יוֹסֵי – לֵילְיָא הוּא, וְהָא בָּדְקָה בְּבֵין הַשְּׁמָשׁוֹת דְּרַבִּי יְהוּדָה. וְרַבִּי יוֹסֵי לְטַעְמֵיהּ, דְּאָמַר בֵּין הַשְּׁמָשׁוֹת סְפֵיקָא הָוֵי.

**As the Rabbis hold** that **during** the period of **twilight** as defined **by Rabbi Yosei it is** already **night,** and therefore it does not matter that she did not examine herself then. **And** as **she did examine** herself **during** the period of **twilight** as defined **by Rabbi Yehuda,** and she found no blood, there is no concern that she saw during twilight, which would count as two sightings. **And Rabbi Yosei** conforms **to his** line of **reasoning, as** Rabbi Yosei, in whose name Rabbi Yehuda ben Agra said his ruling, **stated** that the time that he defines as **twilight is** considered **uncertain,** i.e., it is not definitely night or day, and therefore there is a concern that she might have seen blood at that time, which would count as seeing twice.

וְאָמִינָא לְהוּ אֲנָא: אִילְמָלֵי יָדֶיהָ בְּעֵינֶיהָ כׇּל בֵּין הַשְּׁמָשׁוֹת – יָפֶה אַתֶּם אוֹמְרִים, עַכְשָׁיו – שֶׁמָּא עִם סִלּוּק יָדֶיהָ רָאֲתָה? וְאָמְרוּ לִי: כִּי קָאָמְרִינַן – כְּשֶׁנָּתְנָה יָדֶיהָ בְּעֵינֶיהָ כׇּל בֵּין הַשְּׁמָשׁוֹת.

Rava continues: **And I said to** those Sages: **Had** the woman's **hands** been **in her eyes**, a euphemism for her private parts, for **the entire twilight** period, what **you say** would be **fine.** But **now** that this is not the case, **perhaps when she removed her hands** from examining herself **she saw** blood. **And** those Sages **said to me:** The case about which **we said** that opinion **was where she placed her hands in her eyes** for **the entire twilight**[H] period.

אָמַר רַבִּי: נִרְאִין דִּבְרֵי רַבִּי יְהוּדָה בֶּן אַגְרָא כְּשֶׁלֹּא בָּדְקָה. מַאי ״לֹא בָּדְקָה״?

The Gemara further clarifies the *baraita*. **Rabbi** Yehuda HaNasi **says: The statement of Rabbi Yehuda ben Agra** in the name of Rabbi Yosei, who maintains that one needs to be concerned for the possibility that the woman saw blood at twilight, which would count as though she saw blood twice, **appears** to be correct **in** a case **where she did not examine.** The Gemara asks: **What** is meant by: Where she did **not examine?**

אִילֵימָא דְּבָדְקָה בִּדְרַבִּי יְהוּדָה וְלֹא בָּדְקָה בִּדְרַבִּי יוֹסֵי, מִכְּלָל דְּרַבִּי יְהוּדָה סָבַר אַף עַל גַּב דְּבָדְקָה בְּתַרְוַיְיהוּ – חָיְישָׁא? הָא בָּדְקָה!

**If we say that she examined** herself **during** the period **that is** defined by **Rabbi Yehuda** as twilight, **but** she **did not examine** herself **during** the time period **that is** defined by **Rabbi Yosei** as twilight, this is difficult: If Rabbi Yehuda HaNasi accepted the opinion of Rabbi Yehuda ben Agra only in such a case, this indicates, **by inference, that Rabbi Yehuda** ben Agra himself, whose ruling is more strict than that of the Rabbis, **holds** that **even though** she **examined** herself **during** the twilight period as defined by **both** Rabbi Yehuda and Rabbi Yosei, **she must be concerned.** This conclusion is untenable, as **she examined** herself throughout twilight and there was no blood.

## NOTES

**Twilight – בֵּין הַשְּׁמָשׁוֹת:** Everyone accepts the basic definition of twilight as an uncertain period in terms of day and night. There are three possibilities with regard to the status of this period of time: The entire period of twilight is night, the entire period is day, or part of it is day and part of it is night. Every moment during this period is subject to these three possibilities (Rabbeinu Tam, cited in *Tosafot* on *Shabbat* 34b).

**Twilight as defined by Rabbi Yehuda – בֵּין הַשְּׁמָשׁוֹת דְּרַבִּי יְהוּדָה:** There are different explanations of Rabbi Yehuda's opinion; see *Shabbat* 34b. According to Rabba, Rav Yehuda maintains that the period of twilight begins when the sun sets and continues for as long as the eastern face of the sky is reddened. If the lower segment of the sky closest to the horizon has lost its color, and the upper segment has not yet lost its color, that is the twilight period. Rashi interprets this losing of color as darkening, while others claim that it is whitening (*Arukh*). Some commentaries maintain that Rashi and the *Arukh* do not actually disagree, as they are both referring to the diminishing of sunlight (*Arukh HaShulḥan*). According to Rav Yosef, Rav Yehuda maintains that twilight starts a little later. This discussion is with regard to the opinion of Rav Yehuda. Rabbi Neḥemya disagrees with Rav Yehuda and holds that the twilight period is equivalent to the time it takes for one to walk a half of a *mil*, starting from sunset. According to Rabbi Yosei, the duration of the twilight period is like the blink of an eye; night enters and day departs, and it is impossible to calculate the period due to its brevity. The Gemara on *Shabbat* 35a explains that the phrase: The eastern face of the sky is reddened, is referring to the face that reddens the east, i.e., when the sun sets, its rays redden the sky (Rashi).

## LANGUAGE

Twilight [*bein hashemashot*] – בֵּין הַשְּׁמָשׁוֹת: This term is used to describe the time of transition from day to night, which is considered an uncertain period in terms of whether it is day or night. There are various suggestions with regard to the actual meaning of the term. One possibility is that it means between the days, as days are referred to as *shemesh*, sun. If so, *bein hashemashot* means between the day that passed and the following day. Another possible meaning is the period between the different stages of the gradual disappearance of the sun's light, i.e., between sunset and total darkness.

## HALAKHA

**Where she placed her hands in her eyes for the entire twilight – כְּשֶׁנָּתְנָה יָדֶיהָ בְּעֵינֶיהָ כׇּל בֵּין הַשְּׁמָשׁוֹת:** With regard to a woman who discovered on her robe, on the third day of wearing that robe, a stain of an area less than the size of three split beans, after examining herself on the twilight of the first day and not finding blood but without examining the robe at that stage, she does not need to be concerned that she is a *zava*. In a case where she did not examine herself throughout the twilight period, as she did not examine the robe and she wore it for three days during the time that she could become a *zava*, she must be concerned that she is a *zava*, even if the area of the stain is not equivalent to the measure of three stains (Rambam *Sefer Kedusha*, *Hilkhot Issurei Bia* 9:13).

אֶלָּא פְּשִׁיטָא – דְּלֹא בָּדְקָה לֹא בִּדְרַבִּי יְהוּדָה וְלֹא בִּדְרַבִּי יוֹסֵי, אֲבָל בָּדְקָה בִּדְרַבִּי יְהוּדָה וְלֹא בָּדְקָה בִּדְרַבִּי יוֹסֵי – לֹא חָיְישָׁא.

**Rather,** it is **obvious** that when Rabbi Yehuda HaNasi referred to a case where she did not examine herself, he meant **that she examined** herself **neither during** the period **that Rabbi Yehuda** defines as twilight, **nor during** the period **that Rabbi Yosei** defines as twilight. **But** if she **examined** herself **during** the period **that Rabbi Yehuda** defines as twilight, **but** she **did not examine** herself **during** the period **that Rabbi Yosei** defines as twilight, then she does **not** need to be **concerned.**

אַלְמָא: בֵּין הַשְּׁמָשׁוֹת דְּרַבִּי יוֹסֵי – לְרַבִּי לֵילְיָא הוּא. אֵימָא סֵיפָא ״וְדִבְרֵי חֲכָמִים כְּשֶׁבָּדְקָה״. מַאי ״בָּדְקָה״?

**Evidently,** the time period **that Rabbi Yosei** defines as **twilight is** considered **nighttime** according **to Rabbi** Yehuda HaNasi. But if so, **say the latter clause: And the statement of the Rabbis** appears to be correct **in** a case **where she did examine. What** is meant by: Where she did **examine?**

אִילֵּימָא דְּבָדְקָה בִּדְרַבִּי יְהוּדָה וְלֹא בָּדְקָה בִּדְרַבִּי יוֹסֵי, מִכְּלָל דְּרַבָּנַן סָבְרִי אַף עַל גַּב דְּלֹא בָּדְקָה בִּתַרְוַיְיהוּ – לָא חָיְישִׁינַן, הָא לֹא בָּדְקָה!

**If we say that she examined** herself **during** the period **that is** defined **by Rabbi Yehuda** as twilight, **but** she **did not examine** herself **during** the period **that is** defined **by Rabbi Yosei** as twilight, this is difficult: If Rabbi Yehuda HaNasi accepted the opinion of the Rabbis only in such a case, this indicates **by inference that the Rabbis** themselves **hold** that **even though** she **did not examine** herself **during** the twilight period as defined by **both** Rabbi Yehuda and Rabbi Yosei, nevertheless, **we are not concerned. But** in such a case, **she did not examine** herself at twilight at all.

אֶלָּא פְּשִׁיטָא – דְּבָדְקָה בֵּין בִּדְרַבִּי יְהוּדָה וּבֵין בִּדְרַבִּי יוֹסֵי, אֲבָל בָּדְקָה בִּדְרַבִּי יְהוּדָה וְלֹא בָּדְקָה בִּדְרַבִּי יוֹסֵי – חָיְישִׁינַן.

**Rather,** it is **obvious that** she **examined** herself **both during** the period **that Rabbi Yehuda** defines as twilight, **and during** the period **that Rabbi Yosei** defines as twilight. **But** if she **examined** herself **during** the period **that Rabbi Yehuda** defines as twilight, **and** she **did not examine** herself **during** the period **that Rabbi Yosei** defines as twilight, then **we** are **concerned.**

אַלְמָא: בֵּין הַשְּׁמָשׁוֹת דְּרַבִּי יוֹסֵי – לְרַבִּי סְפֵקָא הָוֵי. קַשְׁיָא דְּרַבִּי אַדְּרַבִּי!

**Evidently,** the time period **that Rabbi Yosei** defines as **twilight is** considered to be of **uncertain** status regarding whether it is day or night **according to Rabbi** Yehuda HaNasi. The Gemara asks: If so, one statement **of Rabbi** Yehuda HaNasi poses **a difficulty for** another statement **of Rabbi** Yehuda HaNasi, as the inferences from the two parts of Rabbi Yehuda HaNasi's observation contradict one another.

הָכִי קָאָמַר: נִרְאִין דִּבְרֵי רַבִּי יְהוּדָה בֶּן אַגְרָא לְרַבָּנַן דְּלֹא בָּדְקָה כְּלָל, לֹא בִּדְרַבִּי יְהוּדָה וְלֹא בִּדְרַבִּי יוֹסֵי, שֶׁאַף חֲכָמִים לֹא נֶחְלְקוּ עָלָיו אֶלָּא דְּבָדְקָה בִּדְרַבִּי יְהוּדָה, וְלֹא בָּדְקָה בִּדְרַבִּי יוֹסֵי. אֲבָל הֵיכָא דְּלֹא בָּדְקָה כְּלָל – מוֹדוּ לֵיהּ.

The Gemara explains that **this** is what Rabbi Yehuda HaNasi **is saying: The statement of Rabbi Yehuda ben Agra appears** correct **to the Rabbis** in a case **where she did not examine** herself **at all, neither during** the period **that Rabbi Yehuda** defines as twilight, **nor during** the period **that Rabbi Yosei** defines as twilight. **As, even the Rabbis disagree with** Rabbi Yehuda ben Agra **only** in a case **where** she **examined** herself **during** the period **that Rabbi Yehuda** defines as twilight **but** she **did not examine** herself **during** the time period **that Rabbi Yosei** defines as twilight. **But** in a case **where** she **did not examine** herself **at all, they concede to him** that we are concerned that she might have emitted blood at twilight.

וּרְמִינְהוּ: הָרוֹאָה כֶּתֶם, לִרְאִיָּה מְרוּבָּה – חוֹשֶׁשֶׁת, לִרְאִיָּה מוּעֶטֶת – אֵינָהּ חוֹשֶׁשֶׁת, זוֹ דִּבְרֵי רַבִּי יְהוּדָה בֶּן אַגְרָא שֶׁאָמַר מִשּׁוּם רַבִּי יוֹסֵי.

**And** the Gemara **raises a contradiction** from a *baraita*: In the case of a woman **who sees** a red **stain,** if she **saw a large** stain, covering an area the size of at least three split beans, she must be **concerned** that she might be a *zava*. But if she **saw a small** stain, covering an area of less than the size of three split beans, she does **not** need to **be concerned** that she is a *zava*. **This** is **the statement of Rabbi Yehuda ben Agra, who said** it **in the name of Rabbi Yosei.**

אָמַר רַבִּי: אֲנִי שָׁמַעְתִּי מִמֶּנּוּ שֶׁאַחַת זוֹ וְאַחַת זוֹ – חוֹשֶׁשֶׁת, וּמִן הַטַּעַם הַזֶּה אָמַר לִי: וּמָה אִילּוּ נִדָּה שֶׁלֹּא הִפְרִישָׁה בְּטָהֳרָה מִן הַמִּנְחָה וּלְמַעְלָה – לֹא תְּהֵא בְּחֶזְקַת טְמֵאָה? וְנִרְאִין דְּבָרָיו כְּשֶׁבָּדְקָה.

**Rabbi** Yehuda HaNasi **said: I heard from** Rabbi Yosei **that** with regard to both **this one and that one,** i.e., whether it is a large or small stain, she **must be concerned** that she is a *zava*. **And** Rabbi Yosei **said** this *halakha* **to me based on this reasoning: And what** would be the case **if a menstruating woman did not** perform the examination marking the first step in her **transition** from ritual impurity **to ritual purity** on the seventh day **from *minḥa*** time **onward?** Would she **not** have a **presumptive status of ritual impurity?** Rabbi Yehuda HaNasi added: **And** Rabbi Yosei's **statement appears** to be correct **with regard to** the case **where she examined.**

מַאי בָּדְקָה? אִילֵימָא דְּבָדְקָה בִּדְרַבִּי יְהוּדָה וְלֹא בָּדְקָה בִּדְרַבִּי יוֹסֵי, מִכְּלָל דְּרַבִּי יְהוּדָה בֶּן אַגְרָא סָבַר, אַף עַל גַּב דְּלֹא בָּדְקָה לֹא בִּדְרַבִּי יְהוּדָה וְלֹא בִּדְרַבִּי יוֹסֵי – לֹא חָיְישָׁא? וְהָא לֹא בָּדְקָה!

Once again, the Gemara asks: **What** is meant by the term: Where she **examined? If we say that she examined** herself **during** the period **that is** defined **by Rabbi Yehuda** as twilight, **but** she **did not examine** herself **during** the period **that is** defined **by Rabbi Yosei** as twilight, this indicates **by inference that Rabbi Yehuda ben Agra,** who disagrees in the second *baraita* with this version of Rabbi Yosei's opinion and rules more leniently, **holds** that **even though** she **did not examine** herself **during** the twilight period as defined by **both Rabbi Yehuda and Rabbi Yosei,** nevertheless, **she** does **not** need to **be concerned** that she is a *zava*. **But** this conclusion is untenable, as **she did not examine** herself at twilight at all.

אֶלָּא פְּשִׁיטָא – דְּבָדְקָה בֵּין בִּדְרַבִּי יְהוּדָה וּבֵין בִּדְרַבִּי יוֹסֵי, מִכְּלָל דְּרַבִּי יְהוּדָה בֶּן אַגְרָא סָבַר: בָּדְקָה בִּדְרַבִּי יְהוּדָה וְלֹא בָּדְקָה בִּדְרַבִּי יוֹסֵי – לֹא חָיְישָׁא,

**Rather,** it is **obvious that** Rabbi Yehuda HaNasi is referring to a case **where** she examined herself **both during** the period **that Rabbi Yehuda** defines as twilight **and during** the period **that Rabbi Yosei** defines as twilight. This indicates, **by inference, that Rabbi Yehuda ben Agra holds** that if she **examined** herself **during** the period **that Rabbi Yehuda** defines as twilight, **but** she **did not examine** herself **during** the time period **that Rabbi Yosei** defines as twilight, then she does **not** need to be **concerned,** as a sighting at that time would not count as two.

אַלְמָא: בֵּין הַשְּׁמָשׁוֹת דְּרַבִּי יוֹסֵי לְרַבִּי יְהוּדָה בֶּן אַגְרָא – לֵילְיָא הוּא. קַשְׁיָא דְּרַבִּי יְהוּדָה בֶּן אַגְרָא אַדְּרַבִּי יְהוּדָה בֶּן אַגְרָא!

**Evidently,** the period **that Rabbi Yosei** defines as **twilight is** considered to be **nighttime according to Rabbi Yehuda ben Agra.** If so, one statement **of Rabbi Yehuda ben Agra** poses **a difficulty with regard to** another statement **of Rabbi Yehuda ben Agra,** as earlier it was stated that according to Rabbi Yehuda ben Agra twilight is not definitely night.

בִּשְׁלָמָא בְּלָא רַבִּי – לָא קַשְׁיָא, הָתָם – דְּבָדְקָה בִּדְרַבִּי יְהוּדָה וְלֹא בָּדְקָה בִּדְרַבִּי יוֹסֵי, הָכָא – דְּבָדְקָה נַמִּי בִּדְרַבִּי יְהוּדָה וּבִדְרַבִּי יוֹסֵי. אֶלָּא בִּדְרַבִּי קַשְׁיָא!

**Granted, without** the statement of **Rabbi** Yehuda HaNasi, the apparent contradiction between these statements of Rabbi Yehuda ben Agra in the two *baraitot* is **not difficult,** as one could explain as follows: **There,** with regard to the first *baraita*, it is referring to a case **where she examined** herself **during** the period **that is** defined **by Rabbi Yehuda** as twilight, **but** she **did not examine** herself **during** the period **that is** defined **by Rabbi Yosei** as twilight. By contrast, **here** it is referring to a case **where she examined** herself **both during** the period **that is** defined **by Rabbi Yehuda** as twilight **and during** the period **that is** defined **by Rabbi Yosei** as twilight. **But in** light of the statement **of Rabbi** Yehuda HaNasi, one cannot explain in this manner, and therefore the contradiction poses **a difficulty.**

תְּרֵי תַּנָּאֵי וְאַלִּיבָּא דְּרַבִּי יְהוּדָה בֶּן אַגְרָא; הַאי תַּנָּא סָבַר: שָׁלֵים בֵּין הַשְּׁמָשׁוֹת דְּרַבִּי יְהוּדָה,

The Gemara answers: This is not a contradiction, as there are **two *tanna'im* and** they disagree **with regard to** the opinion **of Rabbi Yehuda ben Agra. This *tanna* holds** that **Rabbi Yehuda's twilight ends,**

Perek **VI**
Daf **53** Amud **b**

וַהֲדַר חָיֵיל בֵּין הַשְּׁמָשׁוֹת דְּרַבִּי יוֹסֵי. וְהַאי תַּנָּא סָבַר: בֵּין הַשְּׁמָשׁוֹת דְּרַבִּי יוֹסֵי מֵישַׁךְ שַׁיָּיךְ בִּדְרַבִּי יְהוּדָה.

**and** only **thereafter** the twilight **of Rabbi Yosei begins,** when there is uncertainty, and there is a concern that perhaps she saw blood at that time. **And that *tanna*** of the second *baraita* **holds** that the **twilight of Rabbi Yosei is subsumed within** and occurs at the end of the twilight **of Rabbi Yehuda.** According to the opinion of this *tanna*, since she examined herself throughout the twilight of Rabbi Yehuda, she also necessarily examined herself throughout the twilight of Rabbi Yosei and therefore there is no need to be concerned about her status.

תָּנוּ רַבָּנַן: הָרוֹאָה כֶּתֶם – מְטַמְּאָה עַצְמָהּ וְקָדָשִׁים לְמַפְרֵעַ – דִּבְרֵי רַבִּי.

§ On the topic of a woman seeing a stain, **the Sages taught** in a *baraita*: A woman **who sees** a red **stain** on her garment **renders herself and consecrated items** that she touched **impure retroactively,**[H] from the time when that garment was last laundered. This is **the statement of Rabbi** Yehuda HaNasi.

רַבִּי שִׁמְעוֹן בֶּן אֶלְעָזָר אוֹמֵר: קֳדָשִׁים – מְטַמְּאָה, עַצְמָהּ – אֵינָהּ מְטַמְּאָה, שֶׁלֹּא יְהֵא כִּתְמָהּ חָמוּר מֵרְאִיָּיתָהּ.

**Rabbi Shimon ben Elazar says:** She does **render consecrated items** that she touched **impure** retroactively, but she **does not render herself impure** with regard to rendering impure objects that she touched since the time the garment was last laundered. The reason is **that her stain should not be more stringent than her** actual **seeing** of blood. If she experiences bleeding, she renders impure only objects that she touched during the previous twenty-four-hour period.

וְהָא מָצִינוּ כִּתְמָהּ חָמוּר מֵרְאִיָּיתָהּ לְעִנְיַן קֳדָשִׁים!

The Gemara asks: **But don't we find** that Rabbi Shimon ben Elazar himself holds that **her stain** is **more stringent than her** actual **seeing** of blood **with regard to consecrated** items? Her stain renders such items impure retroactively from the time that the garment was laundered, whereas her actually seeing blood renders impure only those items that she touched during the past twenty-four-hour period.

אֶלָּא תְּנֵי הָכִי: רַבִּי שִׁמְעוֹן בֶּן אֶלְעָזָר אוֹמֵר אַף קֳדָשִׁים אֵינָהּ מְטַמְּאָה, שֶׁלֹּא יְהֵא כִּתְמָהּ חָמוּר מֵרְאִיָּיתָהּ לְכָל דָּבָר.

The Gemara answers: **Rather, teach** the *baraita* **like this: Rabbi Shimon ben Elazar says** that she does **not even render consecrated** items that she touched **impure** retroactively from the time that the garment was laundered, but only those items that she touched during the past twenty-four-hour period. The reason is **that her stain should not be more stringent than her** actual **seeing** of blood **with regard to any matter.**

תָּנוּ רַבָּנַן: רָאֲתָה כֶּתֶם וְאַחַר כָּךְ רָאֲתָה דָּם – תּוֹלָה כִּתְמָהּ בִּרְאִיָּיתָהּ מֵעֵת לְעֵת, דִּבְרֵי רַבִּי.

§ **The Sages taught** in a *baraita*: In the case of a woman **who saw** a red **stain** on her garment, **and afterward saw blood,**[H] what is the *halakha*? She **attributes her stain to her seeing** blood, i.e., the stain is treated as part of the seeing of blood, which means that she is impure only from when she found the stain, as it assumed that it appeared no earlier. This is the *halakha* provided that she saw the blood within a twenty-four-hour **period** of her discovery of the stain. But if more than twenty-four hours passed, she cannot attribute the stain to her sighting. This is **the statement of Rabbi** Yehuda HaNasi.

רַבִּי שִׁמְעוֹן בֶּן אֶלְעָזָר אוֹמֵר: יוֹמוֹ. אָמַר רַבִּי: נִרְאִין דְּבָרָיו מִדְּבָרַי, שֶׁהוּא – מְתַקְּנָהּ, וַאֲנִי – מְעַוְּותָהּ.

**Rabbi Shimon ben Elazar says:** She may attribute the stain to the sighting only if she experienced bleeding on the **day of** discovering the stain. If she experienced bleeding after that day, even if it was within twenty-four hours, she may not attribute the stain to the sighting, which means that she is impure retroactively from when she found the stain, in case it appeared earlier. **Rabbi** Yehuda HaNasi **said: The statement of** Rabbi Shimon ben Elazar **appears** to be more correct **than mine,**[N] **as he fixes her** situation, i.e., he is lenient, **and I ruin her** situation, as my ruling is stringent. Since the impurity of a stain applies by rabbinic law, one should follow the more lenient opinion.

**NOTES**

**The statement of Rabbi Shimon ben Elazar appears more correct than mine** – **נִרְאִין דְּבָרָיו מִדְּבָרַי**: Rabbi Yehuda HaNasi is saying that he thinks Rabbi Shimon ben Elazar's opinion is the more reasonable. Based purely on logical reasoning, Rabbi Yehuda HaNasi would have reached the same conclusion as did Rabbi Shimon ben Elazar. But he did not adopt that opinion because he had a tradition to the contrary (Ritva).

**HALAKHA**

**A woman who sees a red stain on her garment renders herself and consecrated items she touched impure retroactively** – **הָרוֹאָה כֶּתֶם מְטַמְּאָה עַצְמָהּ וְקָדָשִׁים לְמַפְרֵעַ**: A woman who sees a red stain when it is not her fixed time of menstruation is considered impure retroactively for the past twenty-four-hour period, by rabbinic law. This *halakha* is in accordance with the opinion of Rabbi Yehuda HaNasi (Rambam *Sefer Kedusha*, *Hilkhot Issurei Bia* 9:3).

**A woman who saw a red stain on her garment and afterward saw blood** – **רָאֲתָה כֶּתֶם וְאַחַר כָּךְ רָאֲתָה דָּם**: A woman who saw a red stain and then experiences bleeding may attribute her stain to the blood, provided that she experienced the bleeding within a twenty-four-hour period of discovering the stain. This is the *halakha* whether or not she examined herself at the time she discovered the stain and determined that she was ritually pure. This ruling is in accordance with the opinion of Rabbi Yehuda HaNasi, whose opinion is accepted as *halakha* when he and a single colleague disagree, and with the opinion of Rabbi Yoḥanan, whose opinion is likewise accepted against that of one colleague. This follows the Rambam's interpretation of the Gemara (Rambam *Sefer Kedusha*, *Hilkhot Issurei Bia* 9:15, and see *Maggid Mishne* there).

מְתַקְנָהּ? עַוּותֵי מְעַוֵּית לַהּ! אָמַר רָבִינָא: אֵיפוּךְ.

The Gemara asks: But does Rabbi Shimon ben Elazar actually **fix her** situation? Does he not **ruin her** situation? If she experiences bleeding the day after she found the stain, but within twenty-four hours of finding the stain, according to Rabbi Shimon ben Elazar she renders items impure retroactively. By contrast, according to Rabbi Yehuda HaNasi she renders objects impure only from when she discovered the stain. **Ravina says: Reverse**[N] Rabbi Yehuda HaNasi's statement, so that it states: My statement appears to be more correct than that of Rabbi Shimon ben Elazar, as I fix her situation and he ruins her situation.

רַב נַחְמָן אָמַר: לְעוֹלָם לָא תֵּיפוּךְ, שֶׁהוּא מְתַקֵּן הִלְכוֹתֶיהָ לִידֵי זִיבָה,

**Rav Naḥman says: Actually, do not reverse** Rabbi Yehuda HaNasi's statement, as Rabbi Yehuda HaNasi meant the following: Rabbi Shimon ben Elazar's opinion appears to be more correct, **as he fixes her *halakhot* with regard to *ziva*.** If she experiences bleeding on the day after discovering the stain, the count of her seven days of menstrual flow begins on that day of her actual sighting, not from when she saw the stain. This is due to the fact that the stain is not attributable to the seeing of the blood. Therefore, if she experiences bleeding on the seventh day after first experiencing bleeding, which is the eighth day after discovering the stain, she is not considered a lesser *zava*, and she can be purified from her status as a menstruating woman.

וַאֲנִי מְעַוֵּות הִלְכוֹתֶיהָ לִידֵי זִיבָה.

**But I,** Rabbi Yehuda HaNasi, **ruin her *halakhot* with regard to *ziva*.** Since the stain is attributable to the seeing of the blood within twenty-four hours, her counting starts from when she found the stain, and therefore the blood that she sees on the eighth day after discovering the stain is considered *ziva*. Consequently, she is considered a lesser *zava* and must observe a clean day for each day she experiences a discharge.

בְּעִי מִינֵּיהּ רַבִּי זֵירָא מֵרַבִּי אַסִּי: כְּתָמִים צְרִיכִין הֶפְסֵק טׇהֳרָה אוֹ לָא? אִשְׁתִּיק וְלָא אָמַר לֵיהּ וְלָא מִידֵּי.

§ **Rabbi Zeira asked Rabbi Asi:** Are **stains** like the actual sight of blood, in that they **require** an examination in which she is clean of blood, marking the first step in her **transition** from impurity to **purity** before immersion on the night following the seventh day, **or not?** Rabbi Asi **was silent and said nothing to** Rabbi Zeira.

זִימְנִין אַשְׁכְּחֵיהּ דְּיָתֵיב וְקָאָמַר: תּוֹלָה כִּתְמָהּ בִּרְאִיָּיתָהּ מֵעֵת לְעֵת – דִּבְרֵי רַבִּי.

The Gemara relates that on another **occasion** Rabbi Zeira **found** Rabbi Asi **sitting and saying** that a woman who sees a stain and afterward experiences bleeding **attributes her stain to her seeing** blood, if she saw the blood within a twenty-four-hour **period** of when she discovered the stain. This is **the statement of Rabbi** Yehuda HaNasi.

אָמַר רֵישׁ לָקִישׁ: וְהוּא שֶׁבָּדְקָה, וְרַבִּי יוֹחָנָן אָמַר: אַף עַל פִּי שֶׁלֹּא בָּדְקָה.

Rabbi Asi added that there is a dispute with regard to the details of this *halakha*. **Reish Lakish says:** This applies only in a case **where she examined** herself at the end of the seventh day from the discovery of the stain. This examination indicates that the stain is related to her experiencing bleeding, and therefore the standard *halakha* of a woman who becomes pure at the end of her seven menstrual days applies to her. By contrast, if she examined herself only at the end of the eighth day, the stain is not attributable to her bleeding. **And Rabbi Yoḥanan says:** The stain is attributable to her bleeding under all circumstances, **even if she did not examine** herself until the eighth day.

**NOTES**

**Ravina says: Reverse – אָמַר רָבִינָא אֵיפוּךְ:** It is unclear exactly what Ravina and Rav Naḥman are referring to in their dispute about reversing the statement. The early commentaries disagree about this matter. Some understand it to mean that Rabbi Yehuda HaNasi's statement should be revised to state: My statement appears to be more correct than his, i.e., that of Rabbi Shimon ben Elazar (Rashi). Others explain that Rabbi Yehuda HaNasi's statement should be revised to state: Because I fix her situation, and he ruins her situation (*Tosafot*).

אֲמַר לֵיהּ: מִכְּלָל – דִּכְתָמִים צְרִיכִין הַפְסָקַת טׇהֳרָה? אֲמַר לֵיהּ: אִין. וְהָא זִימְנִין סַגִּיאִין בְּעָא מִינָּךְ וְלָא אָמַרְתְּ וְלָא מִידִי, דִּלְמָא אַגַּב שִׁיטְפָּךְ אֲתָיָא לָךְ? אֲמַר לֵיהּ: אִין, אַגַּב שִׁיטְפַאי אֲתָיָא לִי.

Upon hearing this, Rabbi Zeira **said to** Rabbi Asi: Does that mean, **by inference, that stains require** an examination marking the first step in her **transition** from impurity to **purity?**[H] Rabbi Asi **said to** Rabbi Zeira: **Yes,** that is the *halakha*. Rabbi Zeira further said to Rabbi Asi: **But** on **many occasions I asked you** about this matter **and you did not say anything to me. Perhaps in the course** of your studies this *halakha* **came** back **to you?** Rabbi Asi **said to him: Yes, in the course** of my studies this *halakha* **came** back **to me.**

**מתני׳** הָרוֹאָה יוֹם אַחַד עָשָׂר בֵּין הַשְּׁמָשׁוֹת – תְּחִלַּת נִדָּה וְסוֹף נִדָּה, תְּחִלַּת זִיבָה וְסוֹף זִיבָה,

**MISHNA** In the case of a woman **who sees** an emission of blood during **twilight** on the **eleventh day** of the days in which she can assume the status of a *zava*, as there is uncertainty whether the emission was during the day and it is the flow of a *zava* or whether it was at night and it is menstrual flow, she observes seven days of impurity like **the beginning of** the seven days of **menstruation and the end of menstruation.** If she experienced an emission on the two previous days as well, she observes seven clean days before immersion like **the beginning of the flow of *ziva* and the end of the flow of *ziva*.**

יוֹם אַרְבָּעִים לְזָכָר, וְיוֹם שְׁמוֹנִים לִנְקֵבָה, בֵּין הַשְּׁמָשׁוֹת לְכוּלָּן – הֲרֵי אֵלּוּ טוֹעוֹת.

Similarly, in the case of a woman who experiences an emission of blood during twilight on **the fortieth day** after the birth **of a male or the eightieth day** after the birth **of a female,** there is uncertainty whether it is considered daytime and therefore part of the final day of the blood of purity, or night that is part of the following day when the blood is impure. With regard to experiencing bleeding during **twilight in all** those cases, **these** women **are mistaken** in their calculation of the days of menstrual flow and the flow of a *zava*. Consequently, if they experience bleeding for three consecutive days at the beginning or at the end of the eleven days of *ziva*, they bring the offering of a *zava* but it is not eaten, as it was brought based on uncertainty.

אָמַר רַבִּי יְהוֹשֻׁעַ: עַד שֶׁאַתֶּם מְתַקְּנִים אֶת הַשּׁוֹטוֹת, בּוֹאוּ וְתַקְּנוּ אֶת הַפִּקְחוֹת.

**Rabbi Yehoshua said: Instead of** making provisions to **remedy** the uncertainties **of the misguided, come and remedy** the uncertainties of **the competent** women who know what day they saw the blood but require guidance, due to the multitude of emissions that they experienced.

**גמ׳** תְּחִלַּת נִדָּה וְסוֹף נִדָּה? תְּחִלַּת נִדָּה וְסוֹף זִיבָה הִיא!

**GEMARA** The mishna teaches that if a woman experiences bleeding during twilight on the eleventh day of the days on which she can assume the status of a *zava*, the flow is considered to be **the beginning of** the seven days of **menstruation and the end of menstruation.** The Gemara raises a difficulty: But the concern **is** only that this flow might be either **the beginning of** the seven days of **menstruation,** if twilight is treated as night, **or the end of *ziva*,** if twilight is treated as day.

אָמַר רַב חִסְדָּא, הָכִי קָאָמַר: הָרוֹאָה יוֹם אַחַד עָשָׂר בֵּין הַשְּׁמָשׁוֹת – תְּחִלַּת נִדָּה וְסוֹף זִיבָה,

**Rav Ḥisda says** that **this** is what the mishna **is saying:** A woman **who sees** an emission of blood during **twilight** on the **eleventh day**[H] of the days on which she can assume the status of a *zava* must be concerned both for the possibility that it is **the beginning of** the seven days of **menstruation and** for the possibility that it is **the end of the flow of *ziva*.** If she had also seen an emission on the two previous days, she observes seven clean days before immersion, due to uncertainty.

**HALAKHA**

**Stains require an examination in her transition from impurity to purity** – כְּתָמִים צְרִיכִין הַפְסָקַת טׇהֳרָה: By Torah law, a woman is ritually impure and prohibited to her husband only if she experiences a sensation of flow of blood. But the Sages decreed that even if she did not have a sensation, and even if she examined herself and found no blood, she is impure and prohibited to her husband if she discovered a stain on herself or on her garment. She then requires an examination to determine that she is no longer bleeding, marking the first step in her transition from impurity to purity, before she can begin counting seven clean days, just as she would if she has actually experienced bleeding. This ruling is in accordance with the opinion of Rabbi Yoḥanan, whose opinion is accepted when he and a single colleague disagree (see Rambam *Sefer Kedusha, Hilkhot Issurei Bia* 9:17–18; *Shulḥan Arukh, Yoreh De'a* 190:1).

**Who sees an emission of blood during twilight on the eleventh day** – הָרוֹאָה יוֹם אַחַד עָשָׂר בֵּין הַשְּׁמָשׁוֹת: If a woman experiences bleeding on the ninth and tenth days of the days on which she can assume the status of a *zava* and during twilight at the end of the eleventh day, she is a *zava* of uncertain status. This is based on the possibility that the last occurrence was in the daytime of the eleventh day. That would mean that she has experienced bleeding three days in a row during the days on which she can assume the status of a *zava*. This ruling is in accordance with the interpretation of Rav Ḥisda (Rambam *Sefer Kedusha, Hilkhot Issurei Bia* 6:19).

וּבַשְּׁבִיעִי לְנִדָּתָהּ – סוֹף נִדָּה וּתְחִלַּת זִיבָה.

With regard to the continuation of the mishna, which states: The beginning of the flow of *ziva* and the end of the flow of *ziva*, this should be understood as follows: **And** in the case of a woman who experiences an emission of blood during twilight **on the seventh** day of the seven days of the flow **of her menstruation,** she must be concerned both for the possibility that it is **the end of** the seven days of **menstruation and** for the possibility that it is **the beginning of the flow of** ***ziva*****.**[H]

"אָמַר רַבִּי יְהוֹשֻׁעַ עַד שֶׁאַתֶּם מְתַקְּנִין אֶת הַשּׁוֹטוֹת" כו׳. הָנֵי

§ The mishna teaches that **Rabbi Yehoshua said** to the Rabbis: **Instead of** making provisions to **remedy** the uncertainties **of the misguided,** come and remedy the uncertainties of the competent women. The Gemara asks: **Are these** women who experience bleeding during twilight

**HALAKHA**

**The beginning of the flow of** ***ziva*** **– תְּחִלַּת זִיבָה:** If a woman experienced bleeding on the twilight of the end of the seventh day of the seven days of the flow of menstruation and then again on the ninth and tenth days, she is a *zava* of uncertain status. This ruling is based on the possibility that the first time was in the nighttime of the eighth day, which would mean that she has seen three days in a row during the days on which she can assume the status of a *zava*. This *halakha* is in accordance with the opinion of Rav Ḥisda (Rambam *Sefer Kedusha, Hilkhot Issurei Bia* 6:19).

Perek **VI**
Daf **54** Amud **a**

שׁוֹטוֹת נִינְהוּ? טוֹעוֹת נִינְהוּ! אֶלָּא תְּנֵי: טוֹעוֹת

actually **misguided?** Since they are in doubt as to their status, would it not be more accurate to say that **they are mistaken?** The Gemara answers: **Rather,** this is how one should **teach** the statement of Rabbi Yehoshua in the mishna: Instead of making provisions to remedy the uncertainties of the **mistaken,** come and remedy the uncertainties of the competent women.

דְּתַנְיָא: יוֹם אֶחָד טָמֵא וְיוֹם אֶחָד טָהוֹר – מְשַׁמֶּשֶׁת שְׁמִינִי וְלֵילוֹ עִמּוֹ,

**As it is taught** in a *baraita* with regard to these competent women: What is the *halakha* in the case of a woman who consistently has the following pattern for each pair of days: **One day** she is **impure,** i.e., she experiences bleeding, **and one day** she is **pure,**[H] she does not experience bleeding? In what manner is it permitted for her to engage in intercourse with her husband? She **may engage in intercourse** with her husband on the **eighth day** from the first time that she experienced bleeding **and its accompanying night.**[N] At that time she is pure from her menstruation, as she immersed and purified herself on the night of the seventh day. It is permitted for her to engage in intercourse during the eighth day and the following night, as she will not experience bleeding until the ninth day.

וְאַרְבָּעָה לֵילוֹת מִתּוֹךְ שְׁמוֹנָה עָשָׂר יוֹם. וְאִם הָיְתָה רוֹאָה מִבָּעֶרֶב – אֵינָהּ מְשַׁמֶּשֶׁת אֶלָּא שְׁמִינִי בִּלְבַד.

In addition, she may engage in intercourse **four nights out of** the cycle of **eighteen days,** which consist of the seven menstrual days and the eleven days of the flow of the *zava*. This woman will never become a greater *zava*, as she does not emit blood on consecutive days. Since she must observe a day of purity during the eleven days of *ziva* each time she experiences bleeding, she may engage in intercourse with her husband on the night following the tenth, twelfth, fourteen, and sixteenth days. The night after the eighteenth day is considered part of the next cycle of menstruation and *ziva*. **But if** she **sees** blood **in the evening,** she **may engage in intercourse** with her husband **only** on the **eighth** night and its day. During the eleven days of *ziva* she either experiences bleeding at night or is observing a day of purity for the blood she had emitted earlier.

שְׁנֵי יָמִים טְמֵאִין וּשְׁנֵי יָמִים טְהוֹרִין – מְשַׁמֶּשֶׁת שְׁמִינִי, וּשְׁנֵים עָשָׂר, וְשִׁשָּׁה עָשָׂר, וְעֶשְׂרִים.

If in every set of four days, **two days** she is **impure,** i.e., experiences bleeding, **and two days** she is **pure,**[H] she **may engage in intercourse** with her husband on the **eighth** day, in the day or at night, **and** also on the **twelfth** day, after observing the eleventh as a day of purity for the sightings of the ninth and tenth days, **and** by a similar calculation on the **sixteenth** day **and** on the **twentieth** day, as she has not yet seen the blood of menstruation in this new cycle.

**HALAKHA**

**One day she is impure and one day she is pure – יוֹם אֶחָד טָמֵא וְיוֹם אֶחָד טָהוֹר:** A woman whose established pattern is that she experiences bleeding one day and does not on the next day may initially engage in intercourse with her husband on the entire eighth day, which consists of the night and the following day, which is the day after her menstrual days. In addition, she may engage in intercourse with him on four more nights out of each set of eighteen days. This *halakha* is in accordance with the ruling of the *baraita* (Rambam *Sefer Kedusha, Hilkhot Issurei Bia* 7:14).

**Two days she is impure and two days she is pure – שְׁנֵי יָמִים טְמֵאִין וּשְׁנֵי יָמִים טְהוֹרִין:** With regard to a woman whose established pattern is that she experiences bleeding for two days and does not on the next two days, she may engage in intercourse with her husband on the eighth day, the twelfth day, the sixteenth day, and the twentieth day, in accordance with the ruling of the *baraita* (Rambam *Sefer Kedusha, Hilkhot Issurei Bia* 7:15).

**NOTES**

**She may engage in intercourse on the eighth day and its accompanying night – מְשַׁמֶּשֶׁת שְׁמִינִי וְלֵילוֹ עִמּוֹ:** Some commentaries explain that the term: On the eighth day, includes the full twenty-four hours, while the term: Its accompanying night, refers to the following night, which is the beginning of the ninth day (Rashi; Rabbi Betzalel Ronsburg). Others maintain that it refers to the night of the eighth day (Rambam *Sefer Kedusha, Hilkhot Issurei Bia* 7:14). The Rambam does not mention the night of the ninth at all. The later commentaries note that the difference between the opinions is due to variant texts of the Gemara used by those early commentaries. Contrary to the standard text of his commentary, Rashi probably had the version: And a night with it. By contrast, the Rambam had the version: And its accompanying night, as in the standard text of the Gemara. The translation and commentary here follow the interpretation of Rashi.

וְתְשַׁמֵּשׁ נַמִי בִּתְשַׁסַר! אָמַר רַב שֵׁשֶׁת: זֹאת אוֹמֶרֶת, גַּרְגְּרָן דִּתְנַן – אָסוּר.

The Gemara objects: **And let her also engage in intercourse** with her husband on the **nineteenth** day, as the eleven days of the flow of the *zava* have already passed at the end of the eighteenth day, and she is no longer required to observe a clean day for each day she experiences a discharge. **Rav Sheshet says: That is to say that when we learned** in a mishna (72a) that a husband who could not wait for the conclusion of the day after the last day of *ziva* before engaging in intercourse is **a glutton,** it means that it is actually **prohibited**[H] for them to engage in intercourse.

רַב אַשִׁי אָמַר: נְהִי דְּחַד עָשָׂר לָא בָּעֵי שִׁימּוּר, עֲשִׂירִי מִיהָא בָּעֵי שִׁימּוּר.

**Rav Ashi says:** In fact, it is not prohibited for a woman to engage in intercourse with her husband on the day after the end of the days of the flow of the *zava* even by rabbinic decree, as it is already the beginning of her menstrual days, and she is no longer required to observe a clean day for each day she experiences a discharge. But **although** there is **no requirement** to **observe** a clean day **for** the **eleventh day** of *ziva*, which is the eighteenth day of the full cycle, **in any event** there is **a requirement** to **observe** a clean day for the **tenth day,** i.e., the seventeenth of the entire cycle. Since she did not observe a clean day on the eighteenth day, as she saw blood on that day as well, she must observe the nineteenth day in purity.

שְׁלֹשָׁה יָמִים טְמֵאִין וּשְׁלֹשָׁה יָמִים טְהוֹרִין מְשַׁמֶּשֶׁת שְׁנֵי יָמִים, וְשׁוּב אֵינָהּ מְשַׁמֶּשֶׁת לְעוֹלָם.

If out of every set of six days, **three days** she is **impure, and three days** she is **pure,**[H] she **may engage in intercourse** with her husband during **two** of the **days, and thereafter** she may **never again engage in intercourse** with him. The eighth and ninth days, which are the first days of the flow of *ziva*, are the second and third of the three days on which she experiences bleeding. Therefore, she can immerse and purify herself on the night of the eleventh, and engage in intercourse with her husband on the eleventh and twelfth days. These are the only two days on which she is permitted to engage in intercourse with her husband, as afterward she will experience bleeding for three days during the days of the flow of the *zava*, and is thereby rendered a greater *zava*. Accordingly, she requires seven clean days to become pure again, which she will never attain, as she never has more than three clean days.

אַרְבָּעָה יָמִים טְמֵאִים וְאַרְבָּעָה יָמִים טְהוֹרִין – מְשַׁמֶּשֶׁת יוֹם אֶחָד, וְשׁוּב אֵינָהּ מְשַׁמֶּשֶׁת לְעוֹלָם.

If out of every set of eight days, **four days** she is **impure, and four days** she is **pure,**[H] she **may engage in intercourse** with her husband during **one** of the **days,** the eighth, after her purification for menstruation, as it is the last of her first set of four days without blood, **and thereafter** she may **never again engage in intercourse** with him, as she will be rendered a greater *zava* by experiencing bleeding on the next three days.

## HALAKHA

**When we learned that a husband is a glutton it means that it is prohibited – גַּרְגְּרָן דִּתְנַן אָסוּר:** If a woman experienced bleeding on the eleventh day of the days on which she can assume the status of a *zava* and then immersed herself on the following night, i.e., the twelfth, and subsequently engaged in intercourse with her husband, they are impure and impart ritual impurity to that upon which they lie or sit. Nevertheless, they are not liable to receive *karet*, because the twelfth day does not combine with the eleventh to render her a *zava*, and her immersion exempts her from the obligation to bring an offering. Some commentaries maintain that the husband is labeled a glutton (see Ra'avad and *Maggid Mishne*). This *halakha* is in accordance with the opinion of Rav Sheshet (Rambam *Sefer Kedusha*, *Issurei Bia* 6:17).

**Three days she is impure and three days she is pure – שְׁלֹשָׁה יָמִים טְמֵאִין וּשְׁלֹשָׁה יָמִים טְהוֹרִין:** With regard to a woman whose established pattern is that she experiences bleeding for three days and does not on the next three days, she may engage in intercourse with her husband on two of her three clean days that follow her menstrual days. It is prohibited for her to engage in intercourse with her husband on the first of these days, as she must observe a clean day for each day she experiences a discharge. After those two days, it is never again permitted for her to engage in intercourse with her husband. This is due to the fact that when she experiences bleeding for three days during the days of the flow of a *zava*, she is rendered a greater *zava*. She subsequently requires seven clean days to become pure again, which she will never attain, as she never has more than three clean days. This *halakha* is in accordance with the ruling of the *baraita* (Rambam *Sefer Kedusha*, *Issurei Bia* 7:16).

**Four days she is impure and four days she is pure – אַרְבָּעָה יָמִים טְמֵאִים וְאַרְבָּעָה יָמִים טְהוֹרִין:** If a woman experiences bleeding for four days and four days she is pure, she may engage in intercourse with her husband on the one day after her menstrual days are completed, and thereafter she may never again engage in intercourse with him. This ruling is in accordance with the ruling of the *baraita* (Rambam *Sefer Kedusha*, *Hilkhot Issurei Bia* 7:17).

חֲמִשָּׁה יָמִים טְמֵאִים וַחֲמִשָּׁה יָמִים טְהוֹרִין – מְשַׁמֶּשֶׁת שְׁלֹשָׁה יָמִים, וְשׁוּב אֵינָהּ מְשַׁמֶּשֶׁת לְעוֹלָם. שִׁשָּׁה יָמִים טְמֵאִין וְשִׁשָּׁה יָמִים טְהוֹרִין – מְשַׁמֶּשֶׁת חֲמִשָּׁה יָמִים, וְשׁוּב אֵינָהּ מְשַׁמֶּשֶׁת לְעוֹלָם.

If out of every set of ten days, **five days** she is **impure, and five days** she is **pure,**[H] she **may engage in intercourse** with her husband during **three** of the **days,** i.e., the eighth, ninth, and tenth, as she has completed her menstruation period and has not yet emitted the blood of *ziva,* **and thereafter** she may **never again engage in intercourse** with him. Similarly, if out of every set of twelve days, **six days** she is **impure, and six days** she is **pure,**[H] she **may engage in intercourse** with her husband during **five** of the **days,** i.e., the eighth to the twelfth, **and thereafter** she may **never again engage in intercourse** with him.

שִׁבְעָה יָמִים טְמֵאִין וְשִׁבְעָה יָמִים טְהוֹרִין – מְשַׁמֶּשֶׁת רְבִיעַ יָמֶיהָ, מִתּוֹךְ עֶשְׂרִים וּשְׁמוֹנָה יָמִים.

If out of every set of fourteen days, **seven days** she is **impure, and seven days** she is **pure,**[H] she **may engage in intercourse** with her husband during **a quarter** of the **days of her** life, i.e., seven **out of** every **twenty-eight days.** In the first seven days she is a menstruating woman, but during the next seven days she is pure. In the third set of seven days, when she again experiences bleeding, she becomes a *zava,* which means that in her last seven days, which are without blood, she counts the clean days for her *ziva,* after which this cycle of twenty-eight days begins afresh.

שְׁמוֹנָה יָמִים טְמֵאִין וּשְׁמוֹנָה יָמִים טְהוֹרִין – מְשַׁמֶּשֶׁת חֲמִשָּׁה עָשָׂר יוֹם מִתּוֹךְ אַרְבָּעִים וּשְׁמוֹנָה.

If out of every set of sixteen days, **eight days** she is **impure, and eight days** she is **pure,**[H] she **may engage in intercourse** with her husband **fifteen days out of** every **forty-eight** days. The first eight days during which she experiences bleeding are the seven days of menstruation and one day of *ziva,* which renders her a lesser *zava.* Therefore, she must observe one clean day, after which she is pure for seven days. The first two days of the third set of eight are her last days of *ziva,* and the bleeding she experiences renders her again a lesser *zava,* while the next six are during her days of menstruation. Then she starts her fourth set of eight days, which are without blood. The first of these completes her days of menstruation, after which she may engage in intercourse for the subsequent seven days. During the fifth set of eight days she experiences bleeding, rendering her a greater *zava.* She counts her clean days in the sixth set, leaving her one day of purity, after which the cycle of forty-eight days starts again.

## HALAKHA

**Five days she is impure and five days she is pure – חֲמִשָּׁה יָמִים טְמֵאִים וַחֲמִשָּׁה יָמִים טְהוֹרִין:** If a woman experiences bleeding for five days, and for five days she is pure, she may engage in intercourse with her husband during the three days following her menstrual days, and thereafter she may never again engage in intercourse with him, as stated in the *baraita* (Rambam *Sefer Kedusha, Hilkhot Issurei Bia* 7:18).

**Six days she is impure and six days she is pure – שִׁשָּׁה יָמִים טְמֵאִין וְשִׁשָּׁה יָמִים טְהוֹרִין:** If a woman experiences bleeding for six days, and for six days she is pure, she may engage in intercourse with her husband during the five days following her menstrual days, and she may never again engage in intercourse with him. This *halakha* is in accordance with the ruling of the *baraita* (Rambam *Sefer Kedusha, Hilkhot Issurei Bia* 7:19).

**Seven days she is impure and seven days she is pure – שִׁבְעָה יָמִים טְמֵאִין וְשִׁבְעָה יָמִים טְהוֹרִין:** If a woman experiences bleeding for seven days, and seven days she is pure, she may engage in intercourse with her husband during the week after her menstrual days are completed. When she experiences bleeding the following week she becomes a greater *zava.* She then requires seven clean days to become pure again, and therefore it is prohibited for her to engage in intercourse with her husband during that week. Consequently, it is permitted for her to engage in intercourse with her husband only during one week out of every four weeks.

Throughout her lifetime, she may engage in intercourse with her husband eighteen days out of every eighteen weeks. How so? During the fifth week, she is a *zava.* In the sixth week, during which she does not experience bleeding, she counts seven clean days. In the seventh week, she is again a *zava.* The eighth week, during which she does not experience bleeding, she counts seven clean days. During the ninth week she experiences bleeding. The first five days are menstrual days, and the last two are the first two days of the flow of a *zava.* During the tenth week, she observes one clean day on the first day of that week, and on the other six days it is permitted for her to engage in intercourse with her husband. During the eleventh week she experiences bleeding. The first two days of the week are the final days on which she can assume the status of a *zava,* while the remaining five days are the beginning of her menstrual days. She may engage in intercourse with her husband for five of the days of the twelfth week, during which she does not experience bleeding. During the thirteenth week, she is a *zava.* In the fourteenth week, during which she does not experience bleeding, she counts seven clean days. During the fifteenth week, once again she is a *zava.* The sixteenth week, in which she does not experience bleeding, she counts seven clean days. In the seventeenth week she is a *zava.* In the eighteenth week, in which she does not experience bleeding, she counts seven clean days.

This pattern is repeated for the rest of her life. Consequently, throughout her lifetime she may engage in intercourse with her husband eighteen days out of every eighteen weeks. Were she not afflicted in this manner but experienced bleeding for the seven menstrual days and was then clean for the following eleven days, it would be permitted for her to engage in intercourse with her husband for eleven weeks, i.e., seventy-seven days, out of the eighteen weeks. This *halakha* is in accordance with the *baraita,* as understood by the Rambam (Rambam *Sefer Kedusha, Issurei Bia* 7:20 and *Maggid Mishne* there).

**Eight days she is impure and eight days she is pure – שְׁמוֹנָה יָמִים טְמֵאִין וּשְׁמוֹנָה יָמִים טְהוֹרִין:** If a woman experiences bleeding for eight days, and for eight days she is pure, she may engage in intercourse with her husband during fifteen out of forty-eight days. How so? The first seven days of the first set of eight impure days are menstrual days, while the eighth is the flow of a *zava.* On the first of the eight pure days she observes the first of the eight pure days as a clean day. It is then permitted for her to engage in intercourse with her husband during the remaining seven days. Next she experiences bleeding for eight days. The first two days are the final days on which she can assume the status of a *zava,* while the remaining six are the beginning of her menstrual days. She subsequently has eight clean days, the first of which is the final day of her menstrual days. During the other seven it is once again permitted for her to engage in intercourse with her husband. These days are followed by eight impure days. Of these, the first four are the final days on which she can assume the status of a *zava,* and the remaining four are the start of her menstrual days. But as she was already rendered a greater *zava,* she is required to count seven clean days in order to become pure again. Consequently, during the next set of eight clean days she counts seven clean days and then may engage in intercourse with her husband on the final day. In this manner, it is permitted for her to engage in intercourse with her husband fifteen days out of every forty-eight days. This ruling is in accordance with the *baraita* (Rambam *Sefer Kedusha, Issurei Bia* 7:22).

הֲרֵי אַרְבֵּיסַר הָווּ!

The Gemara objects: **But** the days during which she is permitted **are** actually only **fourteen,** not fifteen. This objection is based on the assumption that a woman cannot count her clean days for *ziva* during days that are fit for menstruation. Consequently, the last four days of the fifth cycle are actually part of her days of menstruation, as her eleven days of *ziva* ended after the fourth day of that cycle. If so, the sixth set of eight days consists of three menstrual days followed by five days of *ziva*. Although she is not a menstruating woman in those three days, as she did not previously count seven clean days, they still do not count for her seven clean days of *ziva*, since they are fit to be menstrual days. She can start counting her seven clean days only on day forty-four, but on day forty-nine, before the seven clean days are finished, she will again experience bleeding. Therefore, it should not be permitted for her to engage in intercourse with her husband on the forty-eighth night.

אָמַר רַב אַדָּא בַּר יִצְחָק: זֹאת אוֹמֶרֶת: יְמֵי נִדָּתָהּ שֶׁאֵין רוֹאָה בָּהֶן – עוֹלִין לִסְפִירַת זִיבָתָהּ. דְּאִיבַּעְיָא לְהוּ:

**Rav Adda bar Yitzḥak says** that this premise should be rejected: **That is to say** that **her menstrual days on which she does not** actually **see** blood **do count toward her counting of her** seven clean days of ***ziva*.** In other words, she begins counting the seven clean days during these menstrual days. **As a dilemma was raised before** the Sages with regard to this issue:

Perek **VI**
Daf **54** Amud **b**

יְמֵי לֵידָה שֶׁאֵינָהּ רוֹאָה בָּהֶן, מַהוּ שֶׁיַּעֲלוּ לִסְפִירַת זִיבָתָהּ?

**What is** the *halakha* in the case of a woman who gave birth when she was a *zava*? There are seven **days of** impurity following the **birth** of a son and fourteen days of impurity following the birth of a daughter, during which the mother is impure even if she did not experience bleeding. With regard to those days during this period **on which she does not see** blood, are they **reckoned in the counting of her** seven clean days required to become purified from the status of ***ziva*?**

אָמַר רַב כָּהֲנָא: תָּא שְׁמַע, רָאֲתָה שְׁנַיִם, וְלַשְּׁלִישִׁי הִפִּילָה, וְאֵינָהּ יוֹדַעַת מַה הִפִּילָה

**Rav Kahana says: Come** and **hear** a *baraita*: A woman **saw** blood on **two** consecutive days during the period of *ziva*, **and on the third** day **she miscarried, but she does not know what she miscarried,** i.e., whether it was a stillborn human fetus for which a woman contracts the impurity of childbirth, or whether she discharged an amorphous piece of tissue. In addition, she does not know whether she emitted blood during the miscarriage.

הֲרֵי זוֹ סְפֵק זִיבָה סְפֵק לֵידָה.

In such a case, **it is uncertain** whether **she** has the status of one who experienced ***ziva* or** whether she has the status of a woman who gave **birth.** If she gave birth to a fetus and did not emit blood, she is a woman after childbirth but not a *zava*. If the discharge was an amorphous piece of tissue and she saw blood, she is a *zava*. If it was a human fetus and she saw blood, she is one who gives birth as a *zava*. Finally, if she did not emit blood and it was a discharge of an amorphous piece of tissue, she is not obligated to bring an offering at all.

מְבִיאָה קׇרְבָּן וְאֵינוֹ נֶאֱכָל, וִימֵי לֵידָתָהּ שֶׁאֵין רוֹאָה בָּהֶן – עוֹלִין לָהּ לִסְפִירַת זִיבָתָהּ.

Consequently, **she brings an offering but it is not eaten** by the priests, as it is uncertain whether it is an offering of *ziva* or an offering for her childbirth, or whether it is non-sacred. **And the days of** impurity following this uncertain **birth, on which she does not see** blood, **are reckoned in the counting of her** seven clean days required to become purified from the status of ***ziva*.** This resolves the dilemma raised by the Sages.

אָמַר רַב פַּפָּא: שָׁאנֵי הָתָם, כֵּיוָן דְּאִיכָּא לְמֵימַר יוֹלֶדֶת זָכָר הִיא, וְכׇל הָנֵי שִׁבְעָה יְתֵירֵי דְּקָיָהֲבִינַן לַהּ – סָלְקִי לַהּ לִסְפִירַת זִיבָתָהּ.

**Rav Pappa says** that this does not resolve the dilemma, as it **is different there, since it can be said** that **she is a woman who gave birth to a male, and** it is only for that reason that **all of these additional seven** days **that we give her** due to the concern that she might have given birth to a female, which would render her impure for fourteen days, **are reckoned in the counting of her** seven clean days of ***ziva***. But if it was certain that she gave birth to a female, those days after the birth would not count toward her period of *ziva*.

אֲמַר לֵיהּ רַב הוּנָא בְּרֵיהּ דְּרַב יְהוֹשֻׁעַ לְרַב פַּפָּא: בְּיוֹלֶדֶת זָכָר – אִיכָּא לְסַפּוּקֵי, בְּיוֹלֶדֶת נְקֵבָה – לֵיכָּא לְסַפּוּקֵי? אֶלָּא לָאו שְׁמַע מִינַּהּ: עוֹלִין, שְׁמַע מִינַּהּ.

**Rav Huna, son of Rav Yehoshua, said to Rav Pappa:** Is there **uncertainty that** perhaps she is **a woman who gave birth to a male,** but **there** is **no uncertainty that** she might be **a woman who gave birth to a female?** In fact, both possibilities must be taken into account. And yet, despite the fact that she might have given birth to a female, these seven days are included in the counting of her seven clean days. **Rather, isn't it** correct to **conclude from** it that such days **are reckoned** in the counting? The Gemara comments: Indeed, **conclude from** the *baraita* that these days do count.

תִּשְׁעָה יָמִים טְמֵאִין וְתִשְׁעָה יָמִים טְהוֹרִין – מְשַׁמֶּשֶׁת שְׁמוֹנָה יָמִים מִתּוֹךְ שְׁמוֹנָה עָשָׂר.

The Gemara concludes its citation of the *baraita*: In the case of a woman whose set pattern is that **nine days** she is **impure,** i.e., experiences bleeding, **and nine days** she is **pure,** she **may engage in intercourse** with her husband during **eight days out of eighteen.** The last two days of the nine with blood are part of her *ziva* period, after which she must observe one clean day, leaving her with eight days when she may engage in intercourse before the cycle begins again.

עֲשָׂרָה יָמִים טְמֵאִין וַעֲשָׂרָה יָמִים טְהוֹרִים – יְמֵי שִׁמּוּשָׁהּ כִּימֵי זִיבָתָהּ. וְכֵן לְמֵאָה וְכֵן לְאֶלֶף.

In the case of a woman whose set pattern is that **ten days** she is **impure and ten days** she is **pure,** the number of **days of her** being permitted to **engage in intercourse** with her husband **is equivalent to** the number of **days of her** experiencing the flow of ***ziva***. In the first seven days she is a menstruating woman, followed by three days of blood that render her a *zava*. She must count seven of the ten days without blood to be purified from her *ziva*, which leaves her three days in which she may engage in intercourse, exactly the same as the three days of *ziva* on which she saw blood. **And so too,** the same applies in the case **of one hundred** days, as she experiences bleeding of *ziva* for ninety-three days, and is subsequently permitted to her husband for ninety-three days, **and so too** in the case **of one thousand** days.

הדרן עלך בא סימן

# Summary of **Perek VI**

A woman is not rendered impure as a menstruating woman by Torah law when she discovers blood on her body or a stain on her garment. This is derived from the verse: "And if a woman has an issue, and her issue in her flesh is blood" (Leviticus 15:19). Two important *halakhot* are derived from the verse with regard to this matter. First, she becomes impure when she sees an actual discharge of blood, not merely blood on her body or a stain on her garment. Second, she becomes impure only when she has an accompanying physical sensation that she emitted blood from her uterus.

This is the *halakha* only by Torah law, as the Sages decreed impurity on a woman who discovers a stain on her body or on her garment. They instituted that stains render her impure so that people would not treat the impurity of her blood lightly. This is related to the fact that there are two basic ramifications to an emission of blood from the uterus. First, it renders her impure as a menstruating woman. Second, the blood itself is ritually impure and renders one who touches it impure until the evening. Although by discovering a stain a woman is not rendered impure as a menstruating woman by Torah law, nevertheless, the Sages decreed that she is impure so that people would not be lenient with regard to the impurity of the blood itself.

In addition, the Sages were concerned about the possibility that a woman might have actually sensed the emission of the blood that produced this stain, but didn't realize it, which would mean that she is in fact impure by Torah law.

The Sages disagreed with regard to the case of a woman who discovered a stain the size of at least three split beans on a garment that she wore for three days during the period on which she can assume the status of a *zava*. Some rule that she is considered a *zava* in all respects, due to the concern that this stain might consist of three stains from three days, each of which is the requisite measure of at least one split bean. Others maintain that there is no concern about this possibility. All agree that a woman who discovered on three different garments three different stains, each the requisite size of at least one split bean, on three different days of the days of *ziva*, is rendered a greater *zava*.

The chapter first continued the previous chapter's recounting of the stages in the maturation of a young woman. This consists of an analysis of the appearance of the lower sign, two pubic hairs, as well as the upper sign, the development of the breasts. The assumption according to one opinion among the *tanna'im* is that the lower sign invariably appears first. The status of a young woman whose upper sign appeared but did not yet develop the lower sign is the subject of a dispute among the *tanna'im*.

Much of the rest of the chapter does not deal with the *halakhot* of a menstruating woman at all, but with tangential issues. Those matters are cited here due to the structural similarity between their formulation and a ruling stated with regard to the upper and lower signs, where there are two asymmetrical *halakhot*.

# Introduction to **Perek VII**

*And if a woman has an issue, and her issue in her flesh is blood, she shall be in her menstruation seven days, and whoever touches her shall be impure until the evening.*

(Leviticus 15:19)

*This is the law of him that has an issue, and of him from whom the semen is emitted, so that he is impure thereby. And of her who experiences the flow of her menstrual impurity, and of one who emits his issue, in the case of a male or a female, and of him who lies with her who is impure.*

(Leviticus 15:32–33)

The verse "And if a woman has an issue, and her issue in her flesh is blood" deals with the impurity of menstruation. It teaches that a woman is rendered impure by a discharge of blood from the uterus. From that point onward she has the status of a primary source of ritual impurity; she renders vessels impure by contact with them, and renders people impure if they come into contact with her or carry her. In addition to the woman herself, her blood transmits impurity to anyone who touches or carries it. This is derived from the phrase "and of her who experiences the flow of her menstrual impurity," which compares the status of the menstrual flow to the status of the menstruating woman.

Exactly how menstrual blood transmits impurity requires clarification. Is it a source of impurity only when it is in a liquid state, similar to substances emitted by a *zav*, such as his saliva and semen, which transmit impurity only when moist? Or does dry menstrual blood also transmit impurity? If it is established that dry menstrual blood also transmits impurity, it is necessary to clarify whether this applies only to blood that was initially moist or even to a menstrual discharge that was dry from the outset.

Similar to the dry blood of a menstruating woman, the dried-out flesh of a corpse also imparts ritual impurity. It is necessary to define what constitutes dried-out flesh, as at some point it is no longer called by this name and ceases to transmit impurity. Apropos the discussion with regard to the blood of a menstruating woman and the flesh of a corpse, the chapter discusses whether other sources of impurity transmit impurity even when they are dry, e.g., the various impure emissions of a *zav*, an animal carcass, and semen.

The previous and following chapters discuss the *halakhot* of blood stains found on a woman's garments. These stains do not render her impure by Torah law, but they render her impure by rabbinic law. A woman who finds a blood stain on her garments is rendered impure just as in the case of a woman who experienced a discharge of uterine blood. Since the blood stain might have been caused some time ago the woman is rendered impure retroactively, and any pure items she touched previously are rendered impure. This leads to the question of how far back in time the woman is rendered impure retroactively.

This decree of the Sages with regard to blood stains applies only to stains of Jewish women. Although the Sages decreed that gentiles have the status of *zavim* in all regards, they did not apply the status of impurity to the blood stains of gentile women. Consequently, concerning the status of blood stains that come from places inhabited by both Jews and gentiles, it is necessary to establish whether these stains are ritually pure or impure.

**מתני׳** דַּם הַנִּדָּה וּבְשַׂר הַמֵּת – מְטַמְּאִין לַחִין וּמְטַמְּאִין יְבֵשִׁין. אֲבָל הַזּוֹב, וְהַנִּיעַ, וְהָרוֹק, וְהַשֶּׁרֶץ, וְהַנְּבֵלָה, וְהַשִּׁכְבַת זֶרַע – מְטַמְּאִין לַחִין וְאֵין מְטַמְּאִין יְבֵשִׁין. וְאִם יְכוֹלִין לְהִשְׁרוֹת וְלַחֲזוֹר לִכְמוֹת שֶׁהֵן – מְטַמְּאִין לַחִין וּמְטַמְּאִין יְבֵשִׁין.

**MISHNA** **The blood of a menstruating woman**[H] **and the flesh of a corpse**[H] **transmit impurity** by contact and by carrying when they are **moist, and** likewise **transmit impurity** when they are **dry. But** with regard to **the** gonorrhea-like **discharge of a** ***zav*** **[*ziva*], and the mucus and the saliva** of a *zav*,[H] **and** the carcass of a **creeping animal,**[H] **and an animal carcass,**[H] **and semen,**[H] all **transmit impurity** when they are **moist but do not transmit impurity** when they are **dry. And if one could soak** those dry substances in water **and** thereby **restore** them **to their** previous **state, they transmit impurity** when **moist and transmit impurity** when **dry.**

וְכַמָּה הִיא שְׁרִיָּיתָן? בְּפוֹשְׁרִין מֵעֵת לְעֵת. רַבִּי יוֹסֵי אוֹמֵר: בְּשַׂר הַמֵּת יָבֵשׁ, וְאֵינוֹ יָכוֹל לְהִשָּׁרוֹת וְלַחֲזוֹר לִכְמוֹת שֶׁהָיָה – טָהוֹר.

The mishna asks: **And how long is the** process of **soaking these** substances that determines whether they can be restored to their previous state? This is referring to soaking them **in lukewarm** water **for** a twenty-four-hour **period.**[N] **Rabbi Yosei says:** With regard to **the flesh of a corpse** that is **dry and cannot be soaked to restore** it **to** its **previous state,** it is **ritually pure,** in the sense that an olive-bulk of the flesh does not transmit impurity imparted by a corpse. But a ladleful of the flesh transmits the impurity of the decayed flesh of a corpse.

**גמ׳** מְנָא הָנֵי מִילֵּי? אָמַר חִזְקִיָּה, דְּאָמַר קְרָא ״וְהַדָּוָה בְּנִדָּתָהּ״, מַדְוֶה כְּמוֹתָהּ, מַה הִיא מְטַמְּאָה, אַף מַדְוֶה מְטַמְּאָה.

**GEMARA** The mishna teaches that the blood of a menstruating woman transmits impurity by contact and by carrying both when moist and when dry. The Gemara asks: **From where are these matters** derived?[N] **Ḥizkiyya says:** They are derived from a verse, **as the verse states** with regard to a menstruating woman: "This is the law of him that has an issue… **And of her who experiences the flow of her menstrual impurity**" (Leviticus 15:32–33). The verse compares the status of the menstrual flow to that of the menstruating woman. This teaches that the status of **the menstrual flow is like** the status of the woman **herself: Just as she transmits impurity** by contact and by carrying, **so too, the menstrual flow transmits impurity** by contact and by carrying.

אַשְׁכְּחַן לַח, יָבֵשׁ מְנָלַן? אָמַר רַבִּי יִצְחָק: אָמַר קְרָא ״יִהְיֶה״ – בַּהֲוָיָיתוֹ יְהֵא.

The Gemara asks: **We found** a source for the impurity of the menstrual blood when it is **moist,** since it is called the menstrual flow; **from where do we** derive that **dry** menstrual blood also transmits impurity? **Rabbi Yitzḥak says** that **the verse states** with regard to menstrual impurity: "And if a woman should have an issue, and her issue in her flesh **shall be** blood, she shall be in her impurity seven days, and whoever touches her shall be impure until the evening" (Leviticus 15:19). The term "shall be" indicates that the blood **shall** remain **in its** impure **status** even once it is dry.

**NOTES**

For a twenty-four-hour period – מֵעֵת לְעֵת: Some commentaries maintain that this examination in lukewarm water for a twenty-four-hour period applies to all the substances listed earlier in the mishna: The discharge of a *zav*, his mucus and saliva, and the rest (Rambam *Sefer Tahara, Hilkhot Metamei Mishkav UMoshav* 2:1). Others claim that the examination as detailed in the mishna refers only to the carcass of a creeping animal and an animal carcass (Ra'avad). With regard to the other substances, which were initially moist, it is enough to soak them in lukewarm water for a short period of time (*Kesef Mishne*). It should be noted that the wording of the mishna supports the opinion of the Rambam.

From where are these matters derived – מְנָא הָנֵי מִילֵּי: This question is referring to the *halakha* stated at the beginning of the mishna that the blood of a menstruating woman transmits impurity both when moist and when dry. Rashi adds that the question refers to the *halakha* that this blood transmits impurity by contact and by carrying.

**HALAKHA**

The blood of a menstruating woman – דַּם הַנִּדָּה: The blood of a menstruating woman, whether moist or dry, transmits impurity (Rambam *Sefer Tahara, Hilkhot Metamei Mishkav UMoshav* 2:1).

And the flesh of a corpse – וּבְשַׂר הַמֵּת: An olive-bulk of the flesh of a corpse, whether it is moist or dry as a shard, transmits ritual impurity like a whole corpse (Rambam *Sefer Tahara, Hilkhot Tumat Met* 2:1).

The discharge of a *zav* and the mucus and the saliva of a *zav* – הַזּוֹב וְהַנִּיעַ וְהָרוֹק: The emission and saliva of a *zav* transmit ritual impurity only when moist, but not if they are overly dry. How much is considered dry? If one could soak those dry substances in lukewarm water for a twenty-four-hour period and they would be restored to their previous state, they transmit impurity, even if the water is lukewarm only at the beginning at not at the end. The method of conducting this examination is learned by tradition (Rambam *Sefer Tahara, Hilkhot Metamei Mishkav UMoshav* 2:1).

And the carcass of a creeping animal – וְהַשֶּׁרֶץ: With regard to the flesh of a creeping animal that became dry as a shard, if it would return to its former state if soaked in lukewarm water for a twenty-four-hour period, it transmits ritual impurity. If not, it is ritually pure and does not transmit impurity even in the manner of impure foods (Rambam *Sefer Tahara, Hilkhot She'ar Avot HaTumot* 4:12).

And an animal carcass – וְהַנְּבֵלָה: With regard to the flesh of an animal carcass that dried, if after soaking in lukewarm water for a twenty-four-hour period it would once again become moist and fit to be eaten by a dog, then it transmits ritual impurity. If not, it is ritually pure and does not transmit impurity even in the manner of impure foods (Rambam *Sefer Tahara, Hilkhot She'ar Avot HaTumot* 1:13).

And semen – וְהַשִּׁכְבַת זֶרַע: Semen transmits ritual impurity only when moist. If it is dry as a shard it is ritually pure. If when soaked in lukewarm water for a twenty-four-hour period it would once again become moist, it is impure (Rambam *Sefer Tahara, Hilkhot She'ar Avot HaTumot* 5:14 and *Hilkhot Metamei Mishkav UMoshav* 2:1).

וְאֵימָא: הָנֵי מִילֵּי בְּלַח וְנַעֲשָׂה יָבֵשׁ, יָבֵשׁ מֵעִיקָּרוֹ מְנָלַן? וְתוּ, הָא דִּתְנַן: הַמַּפֶּלֶת כְּמִין קְלִיפָּה, כְּמִין עָפָר, כְּמִין שְׂעָרָה, כְּמִין יַבְחוּשִׁין אֲדוּמִּים – תַּטִּיל לַמַּיִם, אִם נִמּוֹחוּ טְמֵאָה מְנָלַן? ״יִהְיֶה״ רִבּוּיָא הוּא.

**The Gemara objects: But** one may **say** that **this statement** applies only **to** blood that was initially **moist and** subsequently **became dry,** as it retains its initial status. With regard to blood that was **dry at the outset, from where do we** derive that it too transmits impurity? **And furthermore,** this inference does not provide a source for **that which we learned** in a mishna (21a): In the case of a woman **who discharges** an item whose shape is **similar to a type of shell, similar to a type of soil, similar to a type of hair,** or **similar to a type of mosquito,**[B] if such items are **red, she should cast** them **into water** to ascertain their nature. **If they dissolved,** it is blood, and the woman is **impure. From where do we** derive that even this type of blood is impure? The Gemara explains: The term **"shall be" is an amplification,** indicating that menstrual blood in all these forms is impure.

אִי מַה הִיא עוֹשָׂה מִשְׁכָּב וּמוֹשָׁב לְטַמֵּא אָדָם וּלְטַמֵּא בְּגָדִים, אַף דָּמָהּ נַמִּי עוֹשֶׂה מִשְׁכָּב וּמוֹשָׁב לְטַמֵּא אָדָם וּלְטַמֵּא בְּגָדִים? אַטּוּ דָּמָהּ בַּר מִשְׁכָּב וּמוֹשָׁב הוּא?

The Gemara objects: **If** so, one can likewise infer the following: **Just as she,** a menstruating woman, **renders** an item designated for **lying or sitting** impure[B] **to** the extent that it **transmits impurity to a person and** to the extent that that person **transmits impurity to** his **garments,** despite the fact that the garments did not come into contact with the couch, **so too, her blood also renders** items designated for **lying or sitting** impure **to** the extent that they **transmit impurity to a person and** to the extent that he **transmits impurity to** his **garments,** in the manner of a primary source of ritual impurity. The Gemara replies: **Is that to say** that the concepts of **lying and sitting apply** to **her** menstrual **blood?** These categories of impurity are limited to people.

וּלְטַעֲמִיךְ, אֶבֶן מְנוּגַּעַת בַּת מִשְׁכָּב וּמוֹשָׁב הִיא, דְּאִיצְטְרִיךְ קְרָא לְמַעוּטֵי? דְּתַנְיָא: יָכוֹל תְּהֵא אֶבֶן מְנוּגַּעַת עוֹשָׂה מִשְׁכָּב וּמוֹשָׁב לְטַמֵּא אָדָם לְטַמֵּא בְּגָדִים.

The Gemara asks: **But according to your reasoning** that this category of impurity is limited to people, **do** the concepts of **lying and sitting apply** to **a stone afflicted** with leprosy,[H] so **that a verse was necessary to exclude** it? **As it is taught** in a *baraita*: One **might** have thought that **a stone afflicted** with leprosy **should render** an item designated for **lying or sitting** impure **to** the extent that it **transmits impurity to a person and** to the extent that he **transmits impurity to** his **garments.**

וְדִין הוּא, וּמַה זָּב שֶׁאֵינוֹ מְטַמֵּא בְּבִיאָה עוֹשֶׂה מִשְׁכָּב וּמוֹשָׁב לְטַמֵּא אָדָם לְטַמֵּא בְּגָדִים, אֶבֶן מְנוּגַּעַת שֶׁמְּטַמְּאָה בְּבִיאָה אֵינוֹ דִּין שֶׁמְּטַמְּאָה מִשְׁכָּב וּמוֹשָׁב לְטַמֵּא אָדָם לְטַמֵּא בְּגָדִים.

The *baraita* explains: **And** this ruling might be derived by **logical inference:** If one enters a house where there is a stone afflicted with leprosy he becomes impure, but one who enters a house together with a man who experienced a gonorrhea-like discharge [*zav*] does not become impure. One may therefore infer as follows: **If a *zav*, who does not transmit impurity by entering** a house, nevertheless **renders** an item designated for **lying or sitting** impure **to** the extent that it **transmits impurity to a person** and to the extent that that person **transmits impurity to** his **garments,** then with regard to **a stone afflicted** with leprosy, **which does transmit impurity by entering** a house, **is it not logical that** it **renders** an item designated for **lying or sitting impure to** the extent that it **transmits impurity to a person** and to the extent that he **transmits impurity to** the **garments** he is wearing?

תַּלְמוּד לוֹמַר ״הַזָּב״, הַזָּב – וְלֹא אֶבֶן מְנוּגַּעַת. טַעֲמָא דְּמַעֲטֵיהּ קְרָא, הָא לָאו הָכִי מְטַמְּאָה!

The *baraita* concludes: Therefore, **the verse states:** "Every bed upon which the *zav* lies shall be impure, and every item upon which he sits shall be impure" (Leviticus 15:4). The term **"the *zav*"** indicates that only **the *zav*, and not a stone afflicted** with leprosy, renders items designated for lying or sitting impure. The Gemara infers from the *baraita*: **The reason** a stone afflicted with leprosy does not transmit impurity to items designated for lying or sitting is **that the verse excluded it, but** were it **not so,** the stone **would transmit impurity** to items designated for lying or sitting, despite the fact that the concepts of lying and sitting do not apply to a stone.

**BACKGROUND**

**Mosquitoes – יַבְחוּשִׁין:** This refers to many kinds of biting midges in the *Culicoides* genus, which includes mosquitoes. Mosquitoes are common the world over, but certain species are unique to particular geographical areas. In Eretz Yisrael, mosquitoes are active throughout the year, although their numbers dwindle in the winter and increase from the spring, reaching their height in September and October. Their eggs and larvae develop in moist spots, e.g., puddles and streams, and they can transmit diseases.

Magnified image of a biting midge

**Renders an item designated for lying or sitting impure – עוֹשָׂה מִשְׁכָּב וּמוֹשָׁב:** This form of ritual impurity is also known as impurity imparted by treading. It is imparted by a *zav*, a *zava*, a woman after childbirth, and a menstruating woman. These individuals render items upon which they stand, sit, lie, or lean ritually impure even if they did not actually touch it with their bodies. Such an item becomes a primary source of ritual impurity, like the individual who imparted the impurity, and in turn, it imparts ritual impurity to people or items that touch or carry it. Only items that are specifically intended for sitting or lying upon are susceptible to this impurity imparted by treading; other items upon which the impure individual stands or sits do become ritually impure, but are considered only secondary sources of ritual impurity.

According to the some commentaries, susceptible items become impure only if the impure individual actually touched them (Rambam). Others maintain they are rendered impure as secondary sources even if the impure individual stands, sits, or lies on them without touching them directly (Rabbeinu Tam).

**HALAKHA**

**The ritual impurity of a stone afflicted with leprosy – טוּמְאַת אֶבֶן מְנוּגַּעַת:** A stone removed from a house with leprosy is a primary source of ritual impurity. An olive-bulk of such a stone transmits impurity to people and vessels by contact, carrying, and entering. How does it transmit impurity by entering? If this olive-bulk was brought into a ritually pure house, all items and people in the house are rendered ritually impure (Rambam *Sefer Tahara, Hilkhot Tzara'at* 16:1).

וּמִינָּהּ, לָאו מִי אָמְרַתְּ הַזָּב – וְלֹא אֶבֶן מְנוּגַּעַת, הָכִי נַמִּי אָמַר קְרָא: "אֲשֶׁר הִיא יוֹשֶׁבֶת עָלָיו" – הִיא וְלֹא דָּמָהּ.

The Gemara replies that **from this** same derivation one can infer that menstrual blood does not render items designated for lying or sitting impure: **Didn't you say** that the term "the *zav*" teaches that only **the *zav*, and not a stone afflicted** with leprosy, renders items designated for lying or sitting impure? **So too,** a verse excludes menstrual blood from this category of impurity, as **the verse states:** "And he if is on the bed, or on any item **upon which she sits,** when he touches it, he shall be impure until the evening" (Leviticus 15:23). The term "she" indicates that **she,** the menstruating woman, **but not her blood,** transmits impurity to items designated for lying or sitting.

Perek **VII**
Daf **55** Amud **a**

אִי מָה הִיא מְטַמְּאָה בְּאֶבֶן מְסָמָא, אַף מִדְוָה נַמִּי מְטַמְּאָה בְּאֶבֶן מְסָמָא?

The Gemara raises an objection: There is a unique *halakha* with regard to the impurity of a *zav* and a menstruating woman: In a case where one of them sits on an item, including one that cannot become ritually impure, e.g., a stone, and beneath that item is a vessel, that vessel becomes impure, even if their weight has no effect on the vessel, as in the case of a very heavy stone. **If** the verse compares the status of the menstrual blood to the status of the menstruating woman, as derived above, one can infer as follows: **Just as** a menstruating woman **transmits impurity to** items that lie beneath **a very heavy stone,**[N] **so too, her menstrual flow also transmits impurity to** items that lie beneath **a very heavy stone.**

אָמַר רַב אַשִׁי: אָמַר קְרָא "וְהַנּוֹשֵׂא אוֹתָם", "אוֹתָם" – מִיעוּטָא הוּא.

**Rav Ashi said** in response: Items designated for lying or sitting also transmit impurity to items that lie beneath a very heavy stone. **The verse states** with regard to an item of this kind, which was rendered impure by a *zav*: "And whoever touches anything that was under him shall be impure until the evening, **and he that carries them** shall wash his clothes, and bathe himself in water, and he shall be impure until the evening" (Leviticus 15:10). The term **"them" is an exclusion,** indicating that items designated for lying or sitting transmit impurity to items that lie beneath a very heavy stone, but menstrual blood does not.

"וּבְשַׂר הַמֵּת". מְנָלַן? אָמַר רֵישׁ לָקִישׁ: אָמַר קְרָא "לְכֹל טֻמְאָתוֹ" – לְכָל טוּמְאוֹת הַפּוֹרְשׁוֹת מִמֶּנּוּ.

§ The mishna teaches: **And the flesh of a corpse** transmits impurity both when moist and when dry. The Gemara asks: **From where do we** derive this *halakha*? **Reish Lakish said** that this is as **the verse states:** "Or whoever touches any creeping thing by which he may be made impure, or a man from whom he may be made impure, **from any impurity that he has**" (Leviticus 22:5). The term "from any" is an amplification, indicating that one may become impure **from any impurities that come from** a dead person, whether they are moist or dry.

רַבִּי יוֹחָנָן אָמַר: "אוֹ בְעֶצֶם אָדָם אוֹ בְקָבֶר", אָדָם דּוּמְיָא דְּעֶצֶם, מָה עֶצֶם – יָבֵשׁ, אַף כָּאן – יָבֵשׁ.

**Rabbi Yoḥanan said** that this *halakha* is derived from the verse: "And whoever touches in the open field one who is slain with a sword, or one who died, **or the bone of a man, or a grave,** shall be impure seven days" (Numbers 19:16). The verse indicates that the impurity of a dead **man** is **similar to** the impurity of **a bone: Just as a bone** is **dry, so too here,** with regard to the impurity of a corpse, it transmits impurity even when it is **dry.**

מַאי בֵּינַיְיהוּ? אִיכָּא בֵּינַיְיהוּ – דְּאַפְרִיךְ אַפְרוּכֵי.

The Gemara asks: **What is** the practical difference **between** the inferences of Reish Lakish and Rabbi Yoḥanan? The Gemara answers that the practical difference **between them** is the case of a corpse which is so dry **that it crumbles.** Reish Lakish maintains it is impure, as the term "from any" indicates that a corpse transmits impurity in any form, whereas Rabbi Yoḥanan maintains it is ritually pure, as it is unlike a bone, which does not crumble.

**NOTES**

A very heavy stone – אֶבֶן מְסָמָא: According to the commentaries, the source of this term is from the verse: "And a stone [*even*] was brought, and laid [*vesumat*] on the mouth of the den" (Daniel 6:18). The verse indicates that the stone was heavier than the weight a single person could move and it was meant to remain in one place. It is therefore called *even mesama*, which is related to the word for placed, *hasama*.

There are different opinions as to the exact nature of this method of transmitting impurity. According to Rashi, the stone itself does not weigh on the vessels beneath it. Some claim that the stone weighs on the vessels beneath it, while the additional weight of the one sitting on the stone is entirely insignificant (*Tosafot*). The Meiri states that some understand from Rashi that impurity is transferred even if the stone does not touch the vessels at all, although the Meiri himself prefers to explain that according to Rashi the stone touches the vessels, and in fact he maintains that Rashi explains the matter in a similar manner to *Tosafot*.

According to all opinions, the impurity is transmitted only when the impure individual is sitting on the stone. The status of the stone is unlike that of a couch upon which a *zav* lies or a seat upon which he sits, as it cannot become ritually impure. Nevertheless, impurity is transmitted from the one sitting atop the stone to the vessels beneath it.

מֵיתִיבֵי: בְּשַׂר הַמֵּת שֶׁהוּפְרַךְ – טָהוֹר! הָתָם – דְּאִקְמַח וַהֲוֵי עַפְרָא.

The Gemara **raises an objection** to the opinion of Reish Lakish from a *baraita*: **The flesh of a corpse that crumbled**[H] **is ritually pure.** The Gemara answers that this is not difficult, as the *baraita* **there** is referring to where the flesh is so dry **that it has become** like **flour and is** therefore classified as **dust.**

מֵיתִיבֵי: כָּל שֶׁבַּמֵּת – מְטַמֵּא, חוּץ מִן הַשִּׁינַּיִם, וְהַשֵּׂעָר, וְהַצִּפּוֹרֶן. וּבִשְׁעַת חִבּוּרָן – הַכֹּל טָמֵא!

The Gemara **raises an objection** to the opinions of both Reish Lakish and Rabbi Yoḥanan from a mishna (*Oholot* 3:3): **Everything that is in a corpse transmits impurity,**[H] **except for the teeth, and the hair, and the nails.** This is the *halakha* only when these items are separated from the body, **but when they are attached** to the corpse they are **all impure.** According to Rabbi Yoḥanan teeth should transmit impurity because they are similar to bones, while according to Reish Lakish they should be included in the term "from any."

אֲמַר רַב אַדָּא בַּר אַהֲבָה: דּוּמְיָא דְּעֶצֶם, מָה עֶצֶם – שֶׁנִּבְרָא עִמּוֹ, אַף כָּל – שֶׁנִּבְרָא עִמּוֹ. וְהָאִיכָּא שֵׂעָר וְצִפּוֹרֶן, שֶׁנִּבְרְאוּ עִמּוֹ – וּטְהוֹרִין!

**Rav Adda bar Ahava said:** Only items that are **similar to a bone** transmit impurity: **Just as a bone** is an item **that was created with him** at the time of birth, **so too, all** items that transmit impurity are those **that were created with him,** whereas teeth are not present at the time of birth. The Gemara asks: **But are there not** the cases of **hair and nails, which were created with him, and** yet the mishna states that **they are ritually pure?**

אֶלָּא אֲמַר רַב אַדָּא בַּר אַהֲבָה: דּוּמְיָא דְּעֶצֶם, מָה עֶצֶם – שֶׁנִּבְרָא עִמּוֹ וְאֵין גִּזְעוֹ מַחֲלִיף, אַף כָּל שֶׁנִּבְרָא עִמּוֹ וְאֵין גִּזְעוֹ מַחֲלִיף. יָצְאוּ הַשִּׁינַּיִם – שֶׁלֹּא נִבְרְאוּ עִמּוֹ. יָצְאוּ שֵׂעָר וְצִפּוֹרֶן, שֶׁאַף עַל פִּי שֶׁנִּבְרְאוּ עִמּוֹ – גִּזְעוֹ מַחֲלִיף.

**Rather, Rav Adda bar Ahava said** a different explanation: Only those items that are **similar to a bone** transmit impurity: **Just as a bone** is an item **that was created with him and its root does not renew**[N] itself, i.e., if a bone is removed a new bone does not grow in its place, **so too, any item that was created with him and whose root does not renew** itself transmits impurity. **The teeth were excluded** from this category, **as they were not created with him.** The **hair and nails were excluded, as even though they were created with him** their **roots renew** themselves, since they grow again after they are cut off.

וַהֲרֵי עוֹר, דְּגִזְעוֹ מַחֲלִיף, וּתְנַן: הַגְּלוּדָה, רַבִּי מֵאִיר מַכְשִׁיר. וַחֲכָמִים – פּוֹסְלִין. וַאֲפִילּוּ רַבָּנַן לָא קָפָסְלִי אֶלָּא דְּאַדְּהָכִי וְהָכִי שָׁלֵיט בָּהּ אֲוִירָא וּמֵתָה, וּלְעוֹלָם גִּזְעוֹ מַחֲלִיף. וְתָנֵינַן: אֵלּוּ שֶׁעוֹרוֹתֵיהֶם כִּבְשָׂרָן – עוֹר הָאָדָם!

The Gemara objects: **But isn't there** the case of **skin, whose root renews** itself, **and** this is as **we learned** in a mishna (*Ḥullin* 54a): In the case of an animal **whose hide was removed** [*hageluda*],[NLH] **Rabbi Meir deems** it **kosher,** as the skin renews itself, **and the Rabbis deem** it an animal with a wound that will cause it to die within twelve months [*tereifa*] and **unfit** for consumption. The Gemara explains: **And even the Rabbis deem** it **unfit only** due to the fact **that in the meantime,** between the removal of the old hide and the growth of the new one, **the air affects it and** as a result **it** will **die, but** they concede that **actually** the skin's **root renews** itself. **And** nevertheless **we learned** in a mishna (*Ḥullin* 122a): **These** are the entities **whose skin** has the same halakhic status **as their flesh: The skin of a dead person,**[H] and the skin of a domesticated pig…and the skin of the hump of a young camel, etc.

NOTES

And its root does not renew – וְאֵין גִּזְעוֹ מַחֲלִיף: Literally this term means: Whose trunk does not replenish itself. The expression originates from the *halakhot* of the prohibition against eating the fruit of a tree during the first three years after its planting [*orla*], where part of the definition of a tree for which one has to observe the *halakhot* of *orla* is that it has a trunk that does not sprout anew each year from the ground.

An animal whose hide was removed – הַגְּלוּדָה: The early commentaries provide different explanations for why this animal's hide was removed. Some say it was due to overwork; others say that the animal suffered from some kind of skin disease (Rashi; see Rashi on *Ḥullin* 54a).

LANGUAGE

Whose hide was removed [*geluda*] – גְּלוּדָה: From the root *gimmel*, *lamed*, *dalet*, meaning skin; see Job 16:15: "I have sewn sackcloth on my skin [*gildi*] and have laid my horn in the dust." *Geluda* accordingly refers to one whose skin has been removed. It is possible that the word is derived from *galud*, ice (see *Halakhot Gedolot*).

HALAKHA

The flesh of a corpse that crumbled – בְּשַׂר הַמֵּת שֶׁהוּפְרַךְ: If flesh of a corpse crumbled and became flour-like, it is ritually pure. The *halakha* is in accordance with the opinion of Reish Lakish (Rambam *Sefer Tahara*, *Hilkhot Tumat Met* 3:10 and *Kesef Mishne* there).

Everything that is in a corpse transmits impurity, etc. – כָּל שֶׁבַּמֵּת מְטַמֵּא וכו׳: Everything that is in a corpse is impure except for the teeth, hair, and nails. When they are attached to the corpse they are all impure. How so? If a corpse is outside a house but the hair attached to it is inside, all items inside the house are rendered ritually impure. Likewise, anyone who touches a corpse's hair, teeth, or nails while these body parts are attached to the corpse becomes impure. The *halakha* is in accordance with the mishna in *Oholot* (Rambam *Sefer Tahara*, *Hilkhot Tumat Met* 3:13).

An animal whose hide was removed – הַגְּלוּדָה: If an animal's hide was removed entirely, either by human intervention or due to disease, it is a *tereifa*. If pieces of skin, each the size of a *sela*, remained in three specific areas of the body the animal is kosher (Rambam *Sefer Kedusha*, *Hilkhot Sheḥita* 9:7; *Shulḥan Arukh*, *Yoreh De'a* 59:1).

The skin of a person – עוֹר הָאָדָם: The skin of a dead person is impure like his flesh. If one tanned it or trod on it for the period of time required for tanning, it is ritually pure by Torah law. By rabbinic law it transmits impurity if it is the volume of an olive-bulk like the flesh of the dead, lest one tan human skin and fashion mats from it. The *halakha* is in accordance with the opinion of Ulla (Rambam *Sefer Tahara*, *Hilkhot Tumat Met* 3:11).

הָא אִיתְּמַר עֲלַהּ, אֲמַר עוּלָּא: דְּבַר תּוֹרָה – עוֹר אָדָם, טָהוֹר. וּמַאי טַעֲמָא אָמְרוּ טָמֵא – גְּזֵרָה שֶׁמָּא יַעֲשֶׂה אָדָם עוֹרוֹת אָבִיו וְאִמּוֹ שְׁטִיחִין לַחֲמוֹר.

The Gemara explains that **it was stated with regard to that** mishna that **Ulla said: By Torah law, the skin of** a dead **person is ritually pure. And what is the reason** the Sages **said** that it is **impure?** It is a rabbinic **decree lest a person should fashion rugs for a donkey** out of **the skins of his** deceased **father and mother.**[N]

וְאִיכָּא דְּאָמְרִי: הֲרֵי עוֹר, דְּאֵין גִּזְעוֹ מַחֲלִיף, וּתְנַן ״וַחֲכָמִים פּוֹסְלִין״. וַאֲפִילּוּ רַבִּי מֵאִיר לָא קָא מַכְשַׁר אֶלָּא דְּקָרִיר בִּשְׂרָא וְחַיְיא, וּלְעוֹלָם אֵין גִּזְעוֹ מַחֲלִיף, וַאֲמַר עוּלָּא: דְּבַר תּוֹרָה – עוֹר אָדָם טָהוֹר!

**And some say** a different version of the above discussion: **Isn't there** the case of **skin, whose root does not renew** itself,[N] **and** this is as **we learned** in a mishna (*Ḥullin* 54a): In the case of an animal whose hide was removed, Rabbi Meir deems it kosher, **and the Rabbis deem** it a *tereifa* and **unfit** for consumption, as its skin does not regrow? The Gemara explains: **And even Rabbi Meir deems** it **fit only because the flesh cools and** the animal **heals, but** he concedes that **actually** the skin's **root does not renew** itself. Accordingly, the skin of a corpse should be impure. **But Ulla said: By Torah law, the skin of** a dead **person is ritually pure.**

כִּי אִיתְּמַר דְּעוּלָּא – אַסֵּיפָא אִיתְּמַר: וְכוּלָּן שֶׁעִבְּדָן אוֹ שֶׁהִילֵּךְ בָּהֶן כְּדֵי עֲבוֹדָה – טְהוֹרִין, חוּץ מֵעוֹר אָדָם. וַאֲמַר עוּלָּא: דְּבַר תּוֹרָה – עוֹר אָדָם כִּי עִבְּדוֹ, טָהוֹר. וּמַה טַּעַם אָמְרוּ טָמֵא – גְּזֵרָה שֶׁמָּא יַעֲשֶׂה אָדָם עוֹר אָבִיו וְאִמּוֹ שְׁטִיחִין.

The Gemara answers that **when** the opinion **of Ulla was stated, it was stated with regard to the latter clause** of that mishna: **And** for **all of** these skins, in a case **where one tanned them**[H] **or where one** spread them on the ground and **trod on them** for the same amount of time it takes **for tanning,** they are no longer classified as flesh and **are ritually pure, except for the skin of** a dead **person,** which maintains the status of flesh. **And** with regard to this **Ulla said** that **by Torah law the skin of** a dead **person, when one tanned it, is ritually pure. And what is the reason** the Sages **said** it is **impure?** It is a rabbinic **decree lest a person should fashion rugs** out of **the skin of his** deceased **father and mother.**

וַהֲרֵי בָּשָׂר, דְּגִזְעוֹ מַחֲלִיף וְטָמֵא! אָמַר מָר בַּר רַב אַשִׁי: בָּשָׂר נַעֲשָׂה מְקוֹמוֹ צַלֶּקֶת.

The Gemara asks: **But isn't there** the case of **flesh, whose root renews** itself, as when one's flesh is cut it regrows and heals, **and** yet it is **impure? Mar bar Rav Ashi says: Flesh** does not renew itself, as although when someone is cut his flesh regrows and heals, **a scar is formed** in **its place.**

״אֲבָל הַזּוֹב״. זוֹב מְנָלַן? דְּתַנְיָא: ״זוֹבוֹ טָמֵא״ – לִימֵּד עַל הַזּוֹב שֶׁהוּא טָמֵא.

§ The mishna teaches: **But** *ziva* transmits impurity when moist, although not when dry. The Gemara asks: **From where do we** derive that *ziva* transmits impurity? **As it is taught** in a *baraita* that discusses the verse: "When any man has an issue out of his flesh, **his issue,** it is **impure**" (Leviticus 15:2). This **taught with regard to** *ziva* **that it is impure.**

וַהֲלֹא דִּין הוּא, לַאֲחֵרִים – גּוֹרֵם טוּמְאָה, לְעַצְמוֹ – לֹא כׇּל שֶׁכֵּן? שָׂעִיר הַמִּשְׁתַּלֵּחַ יוֹכִיחַ, שֶׁגּוֹרֵם טוּמְאָה לַאֲחֵרִים – וְהוּא עַצְמוֹ, טָהוֹר. אַף אַתָּה אַל תִּתְמַהּ עַל זֶה, שֶׁאַף עַל פִּי שֶׁגּוֹרֵם טוּמְאָה לַאֲחֵרִים – הוּא עַצְמוֹ טָהוֹר. תַּלְמוּד לוֹמַר: ״זוֹבוֹ טָמֵא״ – לִימֵּד עַל הַזּוֹב שֶׁהוּא טָמֵא.

The *baraita* asks: Why is this derivation necessary? **Could this not** be derived through an *a fortiori* **inference?** Since *ziva* **causes impurity to others,** i.e., to the one who emitted the discharge, is it **not all the more so** that *ziva* **itself** is impure? The *baraita* replies that the case of the **scapegoat** brought on Yom Kippur **may prove** that this inference is not valid, **as it causes impurity to others,** i.e., the dispatcher of the scapegoat is rendered impure, **and** yet the goat **itself is pure. So too, you should not be surprised about this,** the discharge of *ziva,* **that even though it causes impurity to others,** *ziva* **itself is pure.** Therefore, **the verse states: "His issue,** it **is impure."** This **taught with regard to** *ziva* **that it is impure.**

**NOTES**

**Lest a person should fashion rugs for a donkey out of the skins of his deceased father and mother – שֶׁמָּא יַעֲשֶׂה אָדָם עוֹרוֹת אָבִיו וְאִמּוֹ שְׁטִיחִין לַחֲמוֹר:** The mention of a donkey indicates that these skins would be used in a degrading manner. Some versions of the text omit the term: For a donkey (*Tosafot*). Rashi on *Ḥullin* 122a explains that these rugs were used as upholstery for beds and expensive chairs. Other early commentaries maintain that the aim of this practice was to honor one's parents by keeping their memories alive and present. Nevertheless, there are two prohibitions involved in such an act: Failing to bury a dead body and degrading the deceased (Ritva; Ramban).

Some claim this practice was a form of sorcery, and that the use of skins of a close relative provided a more powerful sorcery (Responsa of the Radbaz). The commentaries ask: Since it is in any case prohibited to derive benefit from a corpse, why is a rabbinic decree of ritual impurity necessary to prohibit this practice? *Tosafot* give two answers: One is that people treat matters of impurity more stringently than they treat other prohibitions, and the other is that the skin is not included with the flesh in the prohibition against deriving benefit from a corpse. Others suggest that using mats fashioned from skins is not considered deriving benefit (*Mei Nidda*).

**And some say, isn't there the case of skin whose root does not renew itself – וְאִיכָּא דְּאָמְרִי הֲרֵי עוֹר דְּאֵין גִּזְעוֹ מַחֲלִיף:** In other words, according to this opinion, if skin is removed it will not grow again (Rashi). The later commentaries are puzzled by this claim, as it is unusual to find a dispute in the Gemara with regard to reality, in a situation where one can simply see whether new skin grows in place of skin that has been removed. They therefore explain that everyone agrees new skin will grow to replace removed skin, but there are distinguishing marks that indicate it is not the same skin. According to the second version of the discussion, due to these marks skin is considered an item whose root does not replenish itself, whereas according to the first version, since new skin does grow it is in the category of an entity that replenishes itself.

**HALAKHA**

**And all of these skins where one tanned them, etc. – וְכוּלָּן שֶׁעִבְּדָן וכו׳:** With regard to the hide of a domesticated pig, the skin of the hump of a young camel that is still soft, the skin of the womb, the skin of an animal fetus in the womb of a slaughtered animal, and the skin beneath the tail of a ewe, if one tanned them or spread them on the ground and trod on them for the period of time required for tanning, they are ritually pure, as stated in the mishna in *Ḥullin* (Rambam *Sefer Tahara*, *Hilkhot She'ar Avot HaTumot* 1:9).

וְאֵימָא: הָנֵי מִילֵּי – בְּמַגָּע, אֲבָל בְּמַשָּׂא – לָא, מִידֵּי דַּהֲוָה אַשֶּׁרֶץ! אֲמַר רַב בֵּיבָי בַּר אַבַּיֵי: בְּמַגָּע לָא אִיצְטְרִיךְ קְרָא – דְּלָא גָּרַע מִשִּׁכְבַת זֶרַע,

The Gemara objects: **But** one **may say** that **this statement,** that the discharge of *ziva* transmits impurity, applies only to transmitting impurity **by contact. But** with regard to transmitting impurity **by carrying** it does **not** transmit impurity, **just as it is with regard to** the carcass of **a creeping animal,** which transmits impurity by contact but not by carrying. **Rav Beivai bar Abaye said: A verse was not necessary** to teach that *ziva* transmits ritual impurity **by contact,** as the *halakha* with regard to *ziva* is **no less** stringent **than** with regard to **semen,** which transmits impurity by contact.

Perek **VII**
Daf **55** Amud **b**

כִּי אִיצְטְרִיךְ קְרָא – לְמַשָּׂא. וְאֵימָא: בְּמַשָּׂא – מְטַמֵּא אָדָם וּבְגָדִים. וּבְמַגָּע, אָדָם – מְטַמֵּא, בְּגָדִים – לֹא לְטַמֵּא, מִידֵּי דַּהֲוָה אַמַּגַּע נְבֵלָה!

**When the verse was necessary,** it was **to** teach that *ziva* transmits impurity by **carrying.** The Gemara asks: **And** yet one may **say** that *ziva* **transmits impurity** to **a person and** to his **garments** only **by carrying, but** as for impurity **by contact,** although *ziva* **transmits impurity** to the **person** who touches it, **it does not transmit impurity** to his **garments, just as is** the *halakha* **with regard to contact** with an unslaughtered **animal carcass.**[N] If one touches a carcass he is rendered impure but his garments remain pure, despite the fact that if one carries a carcass his garments are also rendered impure.

לָא סָלְקָא דַּעְתָּךְ, דְּתַנְיָא, אֲחֵרִים אוֹמְרִים: ״הַזָּב אֶת זוֹבוֹ לַזָּכָר וְלַנְּקֵבָה״ – מַקִּישׁ זוֹבוֹ לוֹ. מַה הוּא – לֹא חִלַּקְתָּ בֵּין מַגָּעוֹ לְמַשָּׂאוֹ לְטַמֵּא אָדָם וּלְטַמֵּא בְּגָדִים, אַף זוֹבוֹ – כֵּן.

The Gemara answers: This could **not enter your mind, as it is taught** in a *baraita* that *Aḥerim* **say,** with regard to the verse: "This is the law of him that has an issue… And of her who experiences the flow of her menstrual impurity, and **of one who emits his issue** [*zovo*], **in the case of a male or a female**" (Leviticus 15:32–33). The verse **juxtaposes** the impurity of **the issue of the** *zav* **to** the impurity of the *zav* **himself: Just as** with regard to **him you did not distinguish between** impurity transmitted by **contact with him and** impurity transmitted by **carrying him, as** in both cases the *zav* **transmits impurity to a person and transmits impurity to** his **garments, so too,** with regard to **the issue of the** *zav* the *halakha* is **the same.**[H]

וְהַשְׁתָּא דְּנָפְקָא לָן מֵ״הַזָּב אֶת זוֹבוֹ״, ״זוֹבוֹ טָמֵא״ לָמָּה לִי?

The Gemara asks: **And now that we have derived** the impurity of the discharge of a *zav* **from** the verse: "And **of one who emits his issue**" (Leviticus 15:33), **why do I** need the verse: "When any man has an issue out of his flesh, **his issue,** it is **impure**" (Leviticus 15:2)?

אֲמַר רַב יְהוּדָה מִדִּסְקַרְתָּא: אִיצְטְרִיךְ, סָלְקָא דַּעְתָּךְ אָמִינָא: שָׂעִיר הַמִּשְׁתַּלֵּחַ יוֹכִיחַ – שֶׁגּוֹרֵם טוּמְאָה לַאֲחֵרִים וְהוּא עַצְמוֹ טָהוֹר, וְאִי מִשּׁוּם ״הַזָּב אֶת זוֹבוֹ״ – לְמִנְיָינָא הוּא דַּאֲתָא.

**Rav Yehuda of Diskarta said:** This verse **was necessary,** as it might **enter your mind to say** that the case of the **scapegoat may prove** that the discharge of a *zav* is not impure, **as** the scapegoat **causes impurity to others and** yet the goat **itself is pure.** Likewise, one might conclude that although the discharge of a *zav* causes impurity to others, *ziva* itself is pure. **And if** one were to dismiss this possibility, **due to** the verse: "And **of one who emits his issue** [*zovo*], in the case of a male or a female" (Leviticus 15:33), one could reply **that** it does not indicate the impurity of *ziva*. Rather, **it comes to** teach the **number** of emissions by which one becomes impure with the impurity of a *zav*.[N]

״זוֹב״ – חַד, ״זוֹבוֹ״ – תַּרְתֵּי, וּבַשְּׁלִישִׁי אַקְּשֵׁיהּ רַחֲמָנָא לִנְקֵבָה!

Rav Yehuda of Diskarta clarifies this interpretation of the verse. The term: **An issue** [*zov*], would indicate **one** emission of *ziva*. Since the verse uses the term "**his issue** [*zovo*]," the superfluous addition indicates **two** emissions of *ziva*. With regard to these two emissions, the verse states: "In the case of a male," indicating that the status of a male *zav* differs from the status of a female *zava* in that he is not rendered impure if the emission occurred due to an accident, which would render a female impure. **But in** the case of **the third** emission of *ziva* **the Merciful One juxtaposed** the status of a male *zav* **to** that of **a female,**[N] as the verse states: "Or a female," indicating that even if the third emission was due to an accident he is nevertheless obligated to bring an offering.

**NOTES**

**Just as is the *halakha* with regard to contact with an animal carcass** – מִידֵּי דַּהֲוָה אַמַּגַּע נְבֵלָה: An animal carcass transmits impurity by touch only to the one who touched it, not to the garments he is wearing, whereas if one carries a carcass both he and the clothing or non-earthenware vessels with which he is in contact while touching the carcass become impure (Rashi). This is because the verse states with regard to the impurity of an animal carcass: "And if any animal of which you may eat dies, he who touches its carcass shall be impure until the evening…he who also bears its carcass shall wash his clothes, and be impure until the evening" (Leviticus 11:39–40).

**The number of emissions by which one becomes impure with the impurity of a *zav*** – לְמִנְיָינָא: If a person experiences one gonorrhea-like discharge [*ziva*], he becomes impure for one day, and his impurity is equivalent to the impurity of one who experiences a seminal discharge. Only when one experiences two emissions of *ziva*, on the same day or on two consecutive days, does he become impure with the more severe impurity of a *zav*, which lasts seven days, and for which he requires seven clean days to become pure. If the person experiences a third emission of *ziva* on the same day or on the next day, he must bring an offering as part of his purification process.

**In the case of the third emission the Merciful One juxtaposed the status of a male *zav* to that of a female** – בַּשְּׁלִישִׁי אַקְּשֵׁיהּ רַחֲמָנָא לִנְקֵבָה: The Gemara is teaching that there is a distinction between the first two emissions of a *zav* and the third emission. The first two emissions do not render him impure if they occurred due to an accident, e.g., due to excessive consumption of food, rather than a disease (see *Zavim* 2:2). In this regard, the *halakha* of a male *zav* differs from that of a female *zava*, i.e., a woman who experiences a discharge of uterine blood after her menstrual period, as a *zava* is rendered impure by any discharge of blood from the uterus, irrespective of the cause. The Gemara is stating that with regard to the third emission of a *zav*, his *halakha* does not differ from that of a *zava*, and therefore it renders him obligated to bring an offering even if it occurred due to an accident (see 35a).

**HALAKHA**

**The emission of a *zav* with regard to impurity by carrying** – זוֹב לְעִנְיַן טוּמְאַת מַשָּׂא: The *ziva* of a *zav*, like the *zav* himself, is a primary source of ritual impurity, and it transmits impurity by touch and carrying in any amount (Rambam *Sefer Tahara*, *Hilkhot Metamei Mishkav UMoshav* 1:12).

כְּתַב רַחֲמָנָא ״זוֹבוֹ טָמֵא״. וְהָשְׁתָּא דַּאֲמַר רַחֲמָנָא ״זוֹבוֹ טָמֵא הוּא״ – דְּרוֹשׁ בֵּיהּ נַמִי הַאי.

Since one would not have derived the impurity of *ziva* from this verse, **the Merciful One wrote: "His issue, it is impure"** (Leviticus 15:2). **And now that the Merciful One states: "His issue, it is impure,"** one **may derive from** the verse "and of one who emits his issue" not only the number of emissions, but **also this** interpretation, that there is no difference between the impurity imparted by *ziva* by contact and by carrying.

״וְהָרוֹק״. רוֹק מְנָלַן? דְּתַנְיָא: ״וְכִי יָרֹק״, יָכוֹל אַף עַל פִּי שֶׁלֹּא נָגַע – תַּלְמוּד לוֹמַר ״בַּטָּהוֹר״ – עַד שֶׁיִּגַּע בַּטָּהוֹר.

§ The mishna teaches: And the mucus **and the saliva** of a *zav* transmit impurity when moist but not when dry. The Gemara asks: **From where do we** derive the ritual impurity of the **saliva** of a *zav*? The Gemara answers that this is derived **as it is taught** in a *baraita*: The verse states: **"And if** one who has an issue **spits** on the pure person, then he shall wash his clothes, and bathe himself in water, and he is impure until the evening" (Leviticus 15:8). One **might** have thought that the saliva transmits impurity even if the *zav* merely spat in the direction of a pure person, **despite** the fact **that it did not** come into **contact** with him. Therefore, **the verse states:** "And if one who has an issue spits **on the pure person,"** which teaches that **unless** the saliva comes into **contact with the pure person** he is not rendered impure.

אֵין לִי אֶלָּא רוּקוֹ, כִּיחוֹ וְנִיעוֹ וּמֵי הָאַף שֶׁלּוֹ מִנַּיִן? תַּלְמוּד לוֹמַר ״וְכִי יָרֹק״.

The *baraita* continues: **I have** derived **only** that **his saliva** is impure. **From where** is it derived that **his phlegm, his mucus, and his nasal fluids** are also impure?[H] **The verse states: "And if** one who has an issue **spits."** The superfluous "and" is an amplification, indicating that these substances also transmit impurity.

אֲמַר מָר: יָכוֹל אַף עַל פִּי שֶׁלֹּא נָגַע, מֵהֵיכָא תֵּיתֵי?

**The Master said** above: One **might** have thought that the saliva transmits impurity even if the *zav* merely spat in the direction of a pure person, **despite** the fact **that it did not** come into **contact** with him. The Gemara asks: **From where would this be derived?** Why would one think that a person becomes impure from saliva that did not come into contact with him, making it necessary for a verse to exclude this possibility?

סָלְקָא דַּעְתָּךְ אָמִינָא: נֵילַף ״רוֹק״ ״רוֹק״ מִיבָמָה, מַה הָתָם – אַף עַל פִּי דְּלָא נָגַע, אַף הָכָא נַמִי – דְּלָא נָגַע, קָא מַשְׁמַע לָן.

The Gemara explains: It might **enter your mind to say** that **we should derive** a verbal analogy **from** the term **saliva** in the verse "and if one who has an issue spits," and the term **saliva** stated in connection with **a *yevama*,**[B] a widow whose husband died childless and who participates in *ḥalitza*, as the verse states: "His *yevama* shall approach him, before the Elders, and remove his shoe from on his foot and spit before him" (Deuteronomy 25:9). **Just as there,** with regard to *ḥalitza*, the ritual is valid **even though** the saliva **did not touch** her brother-in-law, **so too here,** with regard to the saliva of a *zav*, it transmits impurity despite the fact **that it did not** come into **contact** with the pure person. Therefore, the verse **teaches us** that the saliva of a *zav* transmits impurity only if it comes into contact with the pure person.

וְאֵימַר: הָנֵי מִילֵּי – בְּמַגָּע, אֲבָל בְּמַשָּׂא – לָא, מִידֵּי דַּהֲוָה אַשֶּׁרֶץ! אֲמַר רֵישׁ לָקִישׁ, תָּנָא דְּבֵי רַבִּי יִשְׁמָעֵאל. אֲמַר קְרָא ״בַּטָּהוֹר״ – מַה שֶּׁבְּיַד טָהוֹר טִמֵּאתִי לָךְ.

The Gemara objects: **And** yet one **may say** that **this statement,** that the saliva of a *zav* transmits impurity, applies only to transmitting impurity **by contact. But** with regard to transmitting impurity **by carrying** it does **not** transmit impurity, **just as is** the *halakha* **with regard to** the carcass of a **creeping animal,** which transmits impurity by contact but not by carrying. **Reish Lakish said** that **the school of Rabbi Yishmael taught** in a *baraita*: **The verse states:** "And if one who has an issue spits **on the pure person."** The term "on the pure person" is interpreted to mean that in any case where **something** of the saliva **is in the hand of** the **pure person I deemed** him **impure for you,** even if he did not come into direct contact with the saliva but merely carried it.

וְאֵימָא: בְּמַשָּׂא – מְטַמֵּא אָדָם וּבְגָדִים, בְּמַגָּע – אָדָם לְטַמֵּא, בְּגָדִים – לָא לְטַמֵּא, מִידֵּי דַּהֲוָה אַמַּגַּע נְבֵלָה!

The Gemara objects: **But** one may **say** that although the saliva of a *zav* transmits impurity both by carrying and by contact, nevertheless there is the following difference between them: **By carrying** the saliva of a *zav*, **it transmits impurity** to **a person and** to his **garments,** but **by contact,** although it **transmits impurity** to the **person** who touches it, **it does not transmit impurity** to his **garments, just as is** the *halakha* **with regard to contact** with an unslaughtered **animal carcass.**

HALAKHA

**His phlegm, his mucus, and his nasal fluids are also impure – כִּיחוֹ וְנִיעוֹ וּמֵי הָאַף שֶׁלּוֹ:** The phlegm, mucus, saliva, and nasal fluids of a *zav* are considered like his saliva in all regards, and each of these transmits impurity by touch and carrying to people and vessels in any amount (Rambam *Sefer Tahara, Hilkhot Metamei Mishkav UMoshav* 1:16).

BACKGROUND

*Yevama* – **יְבָמָה:** When a man dies without children, the Torah requires his brother to perform levirate marriage with the wife of the deceased. If the brother does not wish to marry the widow he may perform the *ḥalitza* ceremony, thereby releasing her from her bond, and she is then allowed to remarry out of the family (see Deuteronomy 25:7–10). The term *ḥalitza* is derived from the central element of this ceremony, which involves the widow removing [*holetzet*] a special sandal from the foot of the brother. *Ḥalitza* must be performed before a rabbinical court.

אֲמַר רֵישׁ לָקִישׁ, וְכֵן תָּנָא דְּבֵי רַבִּי יִשְׁמָעֵאל: אֲמַר קְרָא ״בַּטָּהוֹר״ – טָהֳרָה שֶׁטִּהַרְתִּי לְךָ בְּמָקוֹם אַחֵר טִמֵּאתִי לְךָ כָּאן, וְאֵיזֶה זֶה – זֶה מַגַּע נְבֵלָה.

**Reish Lakish said, and so too the school of Rabbi Yishmael taught,** that **the verse states:** "And if one who has an issue spits **on the pure person."** The term "on the pure person" teaches that a case of **purity,** i.e., that **which I deemed pure for you in a different case, I have deemed impure for you here. And which** case **is this? This** is referring to **contact** with **an animal carcass,** which renders only the one touching it impure, but not his garments, whereas the saliva of a *zav* renders them both impure.

וְאֵימָא כְּמַשָּׂא דְּשֶׁרֶץ! אִם כֵּן נִכְתּוֹב קְרָא ״בָּאָדָם״, מַאי ״בַּטָּהוֹר״ – שְׁמַע מִינָּהּ תַּרְתֵּי.

The Gemara objects: **But** one can **say** that the case deemed pure elsewhere but deemed impure here is that **of carrying** the carcass of **a creeping animal.** Perhaps the verse is teaching that whereas a creeping animal does not transmit impurity by carrying, the saliva of a *zav* does transmit impurity by carrying. By contrast, contact with the saliva of a *zav* renders only the one touching it impure, but not his garments, as is the *halakha* with regard to an animal carcass. The Gemara responds: **If that is so, let the verse write:** If one who has an issue spits **on the person. What** is the reason the verse states specifically: **"On the pure person"? Conclude two** conclusions **from it,**[N] both that the saliva of a *zav* transmits impurity by carrying and that contact with the saliva renders impure both the person and his garments.

״וּמֵי הָאַף״. מַאי ״מֵי הָאַף״? אָמַר רַב: בְּנִגְרָרִין דֶּרֶךְ הַפֶּה, לְפִי שֶׁאִי אֶפְשָׁר לְמֵי הָאַף בְּלֹא צִחְצוּחֵי הָרוֹק. וְרַבִּי יוֹחָנָן אָמַר: אֲפִילּוּ בְּנִגְרָרִין דֶּרֶךְ הַחוֹטֶם, אַלְמָא קָסָבַר: מַעְיָין הוּא, וְרַחֲמָנָא רַבְּיֵיהּ.

§ The aforementioned *baraita* teaches: **And the nasal fluids** of a *zav* also transmit impurity. The Gemara asks: **What are these nasal fluids? Rav says:** This is referring to fluids **that are emitted via the mouth** of a person. They are impure **because** it is **impossible for the nasal fluids** to flow through the mouth **without** containing **traces of saliva,** which are impure. **And Rabbi Yoḥanan says:** The *baraita* is referring **even** to fluids **that are emitted via the nose. Evidently,** Rabbi Yoḥanan **maintains** that nasal fluids **are** categorized as **a flow** of bodily fluids, **and the Merciful One included it** among the impure bodily fluids of a *zav*, by the amplification: "And if one who has an issue spits."

וְרַב, נַחְשׁוֹב נַמִי דִּמְעַת עֵינוֹ! דַּאֲמַר רַב: הַאי מַאן דְּבָעֵי דְּלִסְתַּמְיֵהּ לְעֵינֵיהּ – לִיכְחוֹל מִגּוֹי. וְלֵוִי אֲמַר: הַאי מַאן דְּבָעֵי דְּלֵימוּת – לִיכְחוֹל מִגּוֹי.

The Gemara asks: **But** according to **Rav,** who maintains that nasal fluids are impure because they contain traces of saliva, this is difficult: **Let** the mishna **also count** among the impure bodily fluids of the *zav* **the tears of his eye, as Rav said: He who desires to blind his eye should have a gentile paint** [*likhḥol*][L] his eye, as the gentile is apt to add a substance that causes blindness. **And Levi said: He who desires to die should have a gentile paint** his eye, as the gentile is apt to add poison to the paint.

וַאֲמַר רַב חִיָּיא בַּר גּוּרְיָא: מַאי טַעֲמָא דְּרַב דְּלָא אֲמַר הָא מַאן דְּבָעֵי דְּלֵימוּת – הוֹאִיל וְיָכוֹל לְגוֹרְרָן וּלְהוֹצִיאָן דֶּרֶךְ הַפֶּה! וְרַב, נְהִי דְּזִיהֲרָא – נָפֵיק, דִּמְעָתָא גּוּפָא – לָא נָפֵיק.

The Gemara continues: **And Rav Ḥiyya bar Gurya said: What is the reasoning of Rav, that he did not say** like Levi: **He who desires to die** should have a gentile paint his eye? Rav did not say this because he maintains one can prevent the poisonous substances from killing him, **since he can suck** the poisonous substances into his mouth by inhaling **and emit them via the mouth.** This indicates that the fluids of the eye can also be emitted through the mouth, and if so, the tears of a *zav* should likewise transmit impurity. The Gemara answers: **And Rav** would say that **although the poison** [*dezihara*][L] placed in one's eye can **exit** the body via the mouth, **the tears themselves do not exit** the body through the mouth.

תָּא שְׁמַע, תִּשְׁעָה מַשְׁקִין הַזָּב הֵן: הַזֵּיעָה, וְהַלֵּיחָה סְרוּחָה, וְהָרֵיעִי – טְהוֹרִין מִכְּלוּם. דִּמְעַת עֵינוֹ, וְדַם מַגֵּפָתוֹ, וַחֲלֵב הָאִשָּׁה – מְטַמְּאִין טוּמְאַת מַשְׁקִין בִּרְבִיעִית. אֲבָל זוֹבוֹ, רוּקוֹ, וּמֵימֵי רַגְלָיו – מְטַמְּאִין טוּמְאָה חֲמוּרָה. וְאִילּוּ ״מֵי הָאַף״ לָא קָתָנֵי.

The Gemara states: With regard to the above dispute between Rav and Rabbi Yoḥanan, **come** and **hear** a *baraita*: **There are nine** types of **fluids of the *zav*.**[H] **The sweat, the foul secretion** from an infected wound, **and the excrement are pure from any** form of impurity. The **tears** that emerge **from his eye,** the **blood from his wound, and the milk of a woman** who is a *zava* all **transmit the ritual impurity of liquids,** i.e., they render food and liquids impure, as other impure liquids do, in a situation **where** there is at least **a quarter-*log*** of the fluid. **But his *ziva*, his saliva, and his urine** all **transmit a severe** form of **ritual impurity.** The Gemara comments: The *baraita* lists many substances, **and yet it does not teach** that **nasal fluids** are impure.

**NOTES**

**What is the reason the verse states specifically on the pure person, conclude two conclusions from it – מַאי בַּטָּהוֹר שְׁמַע מִינָּהּ תַּרְתֵּי:** It is derived from the term "pure person [*tahor*]" that the touch of the saliva of a *zav* transmits impurity both to a person and the garments he is wearing. The impurity of carrying is derived from the term "on," as the word in full reads *batahor*, on the pure person.

**LANGUAGE**

**Paint [*keḥol*] – כְּחוֹל:** The material known in the Talmud as *keḥol* was a blue substance that contained antimony oxide. It was ordinarily used as a cosmetic, but was sometimes applied in order to heal various ailments of the eyes and as a disinfectant, due to the antimony. Furthermore, there was a special brush known as a *mikhḥol*, which was used to apply the cosmetic to the eyes, and this brush also served to apply various other remedies, such as ointments and the like. Consequently, every treatment of the eye by means of ointments is called *keḥila*.

**Poison [*zihara*] – זִיהֲרָא:** From the Middle Persian zahr, meaning venom and anger.

**HALAKHA**

**Nine types of fluids of the *zav*, etc. – תִּשְׁעָה מַשְׁקִין הַזָּב וכו׳:** There are nine types of fluids emitted by the *zav*. Three of them are a primary source of ritual impurity: His saliva, semen, and urine. Each of these transmits impurity to people and vessels in any amount. Three others have the status of a secondary source of ritual impurity: His tears, blood from his wound, and the milk of a woman who is a *zava*. These are like impure liquids that do not transmit impurity to people, but they do render vessels impure by rabbinic law. Finally, three fluids of the *zav* are ritually pure: His sweat, his foul secretion, and his excrement (Rambam *Sefer Tahara, Hilkhot Metamei Mishkav UMoshav* 1:16).

בִּשְׁלָמָא לְרַב לָא קָתָנֵי – דְּלָא פְּסִיקָא לֵיהּ לְמִתְנֵי, זִימְנִין דְּאָתֵי דֶּרֶךְ הַפֶּה וְזִימְנִין דְּאָתֵי דֶּרֶךְ הַחוֹטֶם. אֶלָּא לְרַבִּי יוֹחָנָן – לִיתְנֵי!

Granted, according to the opinion of **Rav**, the *tanna* of the *baraita* **does not teach** that nasal fluids are impure, **as he could not teach it categorically,** since **sometimes** the nasal fluid **comes via the mouth,** and is impure, **and sometimes it comes via the nose,** and is not impure. **But according to** the opinion of **Rabbi Yoḥanan, let** the *tanna* **teach** that nasal fluids are impure.

וּלְטַעֲמִיךְ – ״כִּיחוֹ וְנִיעוֹ״ מִי קָתָנֵי? אֶלָּא: תָּנָא רוֹק וְכָל דַּאֲתָא מֵרִבּוּיָא, הָכָא נַמִי – תָּנָא רוּקוֹ, וְכָל דַּאֲתָא מֵרִבּוּיָא.

The Gemara responds: **And according to your reasoning, does** this *tanna* **teach** that **his phlegm and his mucus** are impure? **Rather, he taught** that **saliva** is impure, **and** this includes the impurity of **all** substances **that are derived from** its **amplification,** e.g., his phlegm and his mucus. **Here too,** with regard to nasal fluids, the *tanna* **taught** the *halakha* of **his saliva, and** this includes **all** substances **that are derived from** its **amplification,** including nasal fluids.

דִּמְעַת עֵינוֹ – דִּכְתִיב ״וַתַּשְׁקֵמוֹ בִּדְמָעוֹת שָׁלִישׁ״. וְדַם מַגֵּפָתוֹ – דִּכְתִיב ״וְדַם חֲלָלִים יִשְׁתֶּה״, מַה לִּי קַטְלֵיהּ כּוּלֵּיהּ, מַה לִּי קַטְלֵיהּ פַּלְגֵיהּ. חֲלֵב הָאִשָּׁה – דִּכְתִיב ״וַתִּפְתַּח אֶת נֹאוד הֶחָלָב וַתַּשְׁקֵהוּ״.

The *baraita* teaches that in the case of a *zav* or *zava*, the tears of their eyes and the blood from their wounds, as well as the milk of a *zava*, all transmit the ritual impurity of liquids. The Gemara cites the source for these cases of impurity: **The tears of his eye** are classified as a liquid, **as it is written:** "You have fed them with the bread of tears, **and given them tears to drink in great measure**" (Psalms 80:6). **And** the **blood from his wound** is classified as a liquid, **as it is written: "And he shall drink the blood of the slain"** (Numbers 23:24). Although the verse is referring to the blood of a dead person, and not to the blood of a wound, **what** difference does it make **to me** if one **killed all of him,** and **what** difference does it make **to me** if one **killed part of him,** i.e., wounded him? With regard to the **milk of a woman,** it too is classified as a liquid, **as it is written: "And she opened the bottle of milk, and gave him to drink"** (Judges 4:19).

מֵימֵי רַגְלָיו מְנָלַן? דְּתַנְיָא: ״זוֹבוֹ טָמֵא... וְזֹאת״ – לְרַבּוֹת מֵימֵי רַגְלָיו לְטוּמְאָה. וַהֲלֹא דִּין הוּא, וּמָה רוֹק הַבָּא מִמְּקוֹם טָהֳרָה – טָמֵא, מֵימֵי רַגְלָיו הַבָּאִין

The *baraita* teaches that the urine of a *zav* transmits a severe form of ritual impurity, as do his *ziva* and his saliva. The Gemara asks: **From where do we** derive that the **urine** of a *zav* is impure? **As it is taught** in a *baraita*: The verse states: "When any man has an issue out of his flesh, **his issue,** it is **impure. And this** shall be his impurity" (Leviticus 15:2–3). The term "and this" comes **to include his urine with regard to** a severe form of **ritual impurity.** The *baraita* asks: **And could this not be** derived through an *a fortiori* **inference? If saliva, which comes from a place of purity,** i.e., one's mouth, whose secretions are not usually impure, is nevertheless **impure,** then with regard to **his urine, which comes**

Perek **VII**
Daf **56** Amud **a**

מִמָּקוֹם טָמֵא – אֵינוֹ דִּין שֶׁיְּהוּ טְמֵאִין? דָּם הַיּוֹצֵא מִפִּי הָאַמָּה יוֹכִיחַ, שֶׁבָּא מִמָּקוֹם טָמֵא – וְטָהוֹר, אַף אַתָּה אַל תִּתְמַהּ עַל זֶה, שֶׁאַף עַל פִּי שֶׁבָּא מִמְּקוֹם טוּמְאָה – יִהְיֶה טָהוֹר, תַּלְמוּד לוֹמַר ״זוֹבוֹ טָמֵא... וְזֹאת״ – לְרַבּוֹת מֵימֵי רַגְלָיו לְטוּמְאָה.

**from a place of impurity,** the same place that emits *ziva*, **is it not logical that it should be impure?** The *baraita* answers: The case of **blood that issues from the opening of the penis may prove** that this inference is invalid, as the blood **comes from a place of impurity and yet it is pure. Likewise, you should not be surprised about this,** the urine of a *zav*, **that even though it comes from a place of impurity it should be pure.** Therefore, **the verse states:** "When any man has an issue out of his flesh, **his issue,** it is **impure. And this** shall be his impurity" (Leviticus 15:2–3). The term "and this" comes **to include his urine with regard to** the severe form of **ritual impurity.**

דָּם הַיּוֹצֵא מִפִּי הָאַמָּה מְנָלַן דְּטָהוֹר? דְּתַנְיָא: יָכוֹל יְהֵא דָּם הַיּוֹצֵא מִפִּיו וּמִפִּי הָאַמָּה טְמֵאִין – תַּלְמוּד לוֹמַר ״זוֹבוֹ טָמֵא הוּא״ – הוּא טָמֵא, וְאֵין דָּם הַיּוֹצֵא מִפִּיו וּמִפִּי הָאַמָּה טָמֵא, אֶלָּא טָהוֹר.

The Gemara asks: **From where do we** derive **that blood that issues from the opening of the penis is pure? As it is taught** in a *baraita* concerning a *zav*: One **might** have thought that **blood that issues from his mouth or from the opening of the penis**[H] **is impure,** like his saliva and urine. Therefore, **the verse states: "His issue, it is impure"** (Leviticus 15:2). The term "it" is an exclusion, indicating that **it,** *ziva*, **is impure, but blood that issues from his mouth or from the opening of the penis is not impure; rather, it is pure.**

וְאֵיפּוֹךְ אֲנָא! אָמַר רַבִּי יוֹחָנָן מִשּׁוּם רַבִּי שִׁמְעוֹן בֶּן יוֹחַי: דּוּמְיָא דְּרוֹק, מָה רוֹק – שֶׁמִּתְעַגֵּל וְיוֹצֵא, אַף כָּל – שֶׁמִּתְעַגֵּל וְיוֹצֵא, יָצָא דָּם – שֶׁאֵין מִתְעַגֵּל וְיוֹצֵא.

The Gemara suggests: **But** perhaps **I should reverse** the *halakhot*. One could derive from the amplification "and this" that blood issuing from the penis of the *zav* is impure, and from the exclusion "it" that his urine is pure. **Rabbi Yoḥanan said in the name of Rabbi Shimon ben Yoḥai:** Urine, rather than blood, should be included among the impure fluids of the *zav*, as it is **similar to saliva: Just as saliva** is a fluid **that** first **gathers together and** then **comes out** of the mouth, **so too, all** impure fluids are those **that gather together and** then **come out** of the body. **Blood** is therefore **excluded, as** it **does not** first **gather together and** then **come out** of the body.

וַהֲרֵי חָלָב שֶׁבָּאִשָּׁה, שֶׁמִּתְעַגֵּל וְיוֹצֵא, וַאֲמַר מָר: חָלָב שֶׁבָּאִשָּׁה – מְטַמֵּא טוּמְאַת מַשְׁקִין. טוּמְאַת מַשְׁקִין – אִין, אֲבָל לֹא טוּמְאָה חֲמוּרָה!

The Gemara objects: **But there is** the case of the **milk that** is emitted **from a woman, which** first **gathers together and** then **comes out** of the body, and it should therefore transmit a severe form of ritual impurity, like saliva and *ziva*. **And** yet **the Master said** in the aforementioned *baraita*: The **milk of a woman transmits the ritual impurity of liquids.** One may infer that with regard to **the ritual impurity of liquids, yes,** it transmits impurity, **but** it does **not** transmit **a severe** form of **ritual impurity.**

אֶלָּא אָמַר רַבִּי יוֹחָנָן מִשּׁוּם רַבִּי שִׁמְעוֹן בֶּן יוֹחַי: דּוּמְיָא דְּרוֹק, מָה רוֹק – מִתְעַגֵּל וְיוֹצֵא וְחוֹזֵר וְנִבְלָע, אַף כָּל – מִתְעַגֵּל וְיוֹצֵא וְחוֹזֵר וְנִבְלָע, יָצָא דָּם – שֶׁאֵינוֹ מִתְעַגֵּל וְיוֹצֵא, יָצָא חָלָב שֶׁבָּאִשָּׁה – שֶׁאַף עַל פִּי שֶׁמִּתְעַגֵּל וְיוֹצֵא, אֵינוֹ חוֹזֵר וְנִבְלָע.

**Rather, Rabbi Yoḥanan said in the name of Rabbi Shimon ben Yoḥai:** In order to transmit a severe form of impurity the fluid must be **similar to saliva: Just as saliva** first **gathers together and** then **comes out** of the mouth, **and** if it is not expectorated **it is reabsorbed, so too, all** impure fluids first **gather together and** then **come out** of the body, **and are reabsorbed** by the body if they are not emitted. **Blood** is therefore **excluded, as** it **does not** first **gather together and** then **come out** of the body. The **milk that** is emitted **from a woman** is also **excluded, as even though it gathers together and** then **comes out** of the body **it cannot be reabsorbed.**

וְנֵילַף מִזּוֹבוֹ: מָה זוֹבוֹ שֶׁאֵין מִתְעַגֵּל וְיוֹצֵא – מְטַמֵּא, אַף כָּל! אָמַר רָבָא: מִזּוֹבוֹ לֵיכָּא לְמֵילַף – שֶׁכֵּן גּוֹרֵם טוּמְאָה לַאֲחֵרִים.

The Gemara further objects: **But let us derive from** the case of *ziva* that both blood and breast milk transmit impurity: **Just as his** *ziva* **does not** first **gather together and** then **come out** of the body, and yet it **transmits impurity, so too, all** the fluids of a *zav* should transmit impurity, even if they do not gather together before they are emitted from the body. **Rava said** in explanation: **One cannot derive** the *halakha* with regard to the blood and breast milk of a *zav* or *zava* **from** the *halakha* with regard to **his** *ziva*, **as** the case of *ziva* is unique **in that** it **causes impurity to others,** i.e., to the one who emitted *ziva*.

״וְהַשֶּׁרֶץ״. אָמַר רֵישׁ לָקִישׁ: שֶׁרֶץ שֶׁיָּבַשׁ וְשִׁלְדּוֹ קַיֶּימֶת – טָמֵא. וְהָאֲנַן תְּנַן: מְטַמְּאִין לַחִין וְאֵין מְטַמְּאִין יְבֵשִׁין! אָמַר רַבִּי זֵירָא: לָא קַשְׁיָא, הָא – בְּכוּלָּן, הָא – בְּמִקְצָתָן.

§ The mishna teaches: **And the** carcass of **a creeping animal**[B] transmits impurity when moist but not when dry. **Reish Lakish says:** With regard to the carcass of **a creeping animal that dried up but its skeleton is intact,**[HN] i.e., its bone structure remains in place, it **is ritually impure.** The Gemara asks: **But didn't we learn** in the mishna that the items it lists, including the creeping animal, all **transmit impurity** when they are **moist, but they do not transmit impurity** when they are **dry? Rabbi Zeira said:** It is **not difficult. This** statement of Reish Lakish, that creeping animals transmit impurity even when dry, is referring **to** a case where **all of** the bones are intact. By contrast, **that** ruling of the mishna, that they do not transmit impurity when dry, is referring **to** a situation where only **part of** the bones are intact.

**HALAKHA**

**Blood that issues from his mouth or from the opening of the penis – דָּם הַיּוֹצֵא מִפִּיו וּמִפִּי הָאַמָּה:** Blood that flows from the penis of a *zav* or that issues from his mouth is considered like blood from the wound of a *zav*, and it causes ritual impurity only at the level of second-degree ritual impurity. When the Gemara states that the blood in these two cases is ritually pure, it means that it does not transmit impurity as a *zav*, but it does transmit impurity in the manner of impure liquids. This is explicitly stated in the *Tosefta* in *Zavim* 5:3 (Rambam *Sefer Tahara, Hilkhot Metamei Mishkav UMoshav* 1:16 and *Kesef Mishne* there).

**A creeping animal that dried up but its skeleton is intact – שֶׁרֶץ שֶׁיָּבַשׁ וְשִׁלְדּוֹ קַיֶּימֶת:** With regard to the carcass of a creeping animal that dried but its skeleton is intact, since its entire structure is there it transmits ritual impurity. The *halakha* is in accordance with the opinion of Reish Lakish. The Rambam adds: It would seem to me that this impurity applies by rabbinic law (Rambam *Sefer Tahara, Hilkhot She'ar Avot HaTumot* 4:12 and *Kesef Mishne* there).

**BACKGROUND**

**Carcass of a creeping animal – שֶׁרֶץ:** There are eight creeping animals, which are small mammals and lizards, whose carcasses impart ritual impurity upon contact (Leviticus 11:29–30). There is no clear oral tradition with regard to the identities of the animals listed in the Torah. Consequently, the determination of their identity involves educated conjecture. Among the suggestions offered are that *ḥoled* is a rat, *akhbar* a mouse, *tzav* a dab lizard, *anaka* a gecko, *koaḥ* a monitor, *leta'a* a lizard, *ḥomet* a skink, and *tinshemet* a chameleon.

**NOTES**

**The carcass of a creeping animal that dried up but its skeleton is intact – שֶׁרֶץ שֶׁיָּבַשׁ וְשִׁלְדּוֹ קַיֶּימֶת:** The early commentaries suggest various descriptions of this dried creeping animal whose skeleton remains intact. Some say its overall structure is still there, i.e., its bones have not broken and it retains its form (Rashi). Others explain that its spine appears whole and its ribs are still attached (Rambam *Sefer Tahara, Hilkhot Tumat Met* 3:9; Rambam's Commentary on the Mishna).

דְּתַנְיָא, אָמַר רַבִּי יִצְחָק בְּרַבִּי בִּיסְנָא, אָמַר רַבִּי שִׁמְעוֹן בֶּן יוֹחַי: ״בָּהֶם״, יָכוֹל בְּכוּלָּן? תַּלְמוּד לוֹמַר ״מֵהֶם״.

This is **as it is taught** in a *baraita* that **Rabbi Yitzḥak, son of Rabbi Bisna, says** that **Rabbi Shimon ben Yoḥai says:** The verse states with regard to creeping animals: "Whoever touches **them** when they are dead shall be impure until the evening" (Leviticus 11:31). One **might** have thought that the carcasses of creeping animals transmit impurity only if one comes into contact **with all of them,** i.e., with creeping animals that are completely intact. Therefore, **the verse states:** "And upon whatever any **of them** falls when they are dead shall be impure" (Leviticus 11:32). The term "any of them" indicates that this *halakha* applies even if one comes into contact with only part of a creeping animal.

אִי ״מֵהֶם״ – יָכוֹל בְּמִקְצָתָן? תַּלְמוּד לוֹמַר – ״בָּהֶם״. הָא כֵּיצַד? כָּאן – בְּלַח, כָּאן – בְּיָבֵשׁ.

**If** the *halakha* is derived from the term **"of them,"** one **might** have thought that even if one comes into contact **with a part of them** he is rendered impure. Therefore, **the verse states:** "Whoever touches **them,**" which indicates completely intact creeping animals. The *baraita* concludes: **How** can **these** texts be reconciled? **Here,** where the verse indicates that even part of them transmits impurity, it is referring **to a moist** creeping animal. **There,** where the verse teaches that only a complete creeping animal transmits impurity, it is speaking **of a dry** creature.

אֲמַר רָבָא: הָנֵי זְבוּגֵי דִּמְחוֹזָא, כִּי שִׁלְדָּן קַיֶּימֶת – טְמֵאִין. וְאָמַר רֵישׁ לָקִישׁ: שֶׁרֶץ שֶׁנִּשְׂרַף וְשִׁלְדּוֹ קַיֶּימֶת – טָמֵא.

**Rava said:** With regard to **these lizards of** the city of **Meḥoza,**[B] **when their skeleton is intact** they **are impure.** The dab lizard is one of the creeping animals listed in the Torah. **And Reish Lakish says:** With regard to the carcass of **a creeping animal that was burned but its skeleton is intact,**[H] it **is ritually impure.**

מֵיתִיבֵי: נִמְצָא שֶׁרֶץ שָׂרוּף עַל גַּבֵּי הַזֵּיתִים, וְכֵן מַטְלִית הַמְהוּהָא – טְהוֹרִין, שֶׁכׇּל הַטְּמָאוֹת כִּשְׁעַת מְצִיאָתָן! אֲמַר רַבִּי זֵירָא: לָא קַשְׁיָא, הָא – בְּכוּלָּן, הָא – בְּמִקְצָתָן.

The Gemara **raises an objection** from a mishna that indicates a burnt carcass of a creeping animal is pure (*Teharot* 9:9): In a case where **a burnt creeping animal was found on top of** a pile of **olives, and likewise,** if the **tattered rag** of a *zav*[H] was found on a pile of olives, the olives and the rag **are pure.** One is not concerned that the carcass of the creeping animal touched the olives or rag before it was burned, because **with regard to all** matters of **impurity,** it is assumed that when the item in question came into contact with the potential sources of impurity, the potential sources of impurity were in the same state **as** they were at **the time they were found,** and a burnt carcass does not transmit impurity. **Rabbi Zeira said:** It is **not difficult; this** statement of Reish Lakish refers **to** a case where **all of** the bones are intact, whereas **that** ruling of the mishna is referring **to** a situation where only **part of** the bones are intact.

דְּתַנְיָא, אָמַר רַבִּי יִצְחָק בְּרַבִּי בִּיסְנָא מִשּׁוּם רַבִּי שִׁמְעוֹן בֶּן יוֹחַי: ״בָּהֶם״, יָכוֹל בְּכוּלָּן? תַּלְמוּד לוֹמַר ״מֵהֶם״.

**As it is taught** in a *baraita* that **Rabbi Yitzḥak, son of Rabbi Bisna, says in the name of Rabbi Shimon ben Yoḥai:** When the verse states: "Whoever touches **them** when they are dead shall be impure" (Leviticus 11:31), one **might** have thought that creeping animals transmit impurity only if one comes into contact **with all of them,** i.e., with creeping animals that are completely intact. Therefore, **the verse states:** "And upon whatever any **of them** falls when they are dead shall be impure" (Leviticus 11:32), indicating that even a part of them transmits impurity.

אִי ״מֵהֶם״ – יָכוֹל בְּמִקְצָתָן? תַּלְמוּד לוֹמַר – ״בָּהֶם״. הָא כֵּיצַד? כָּאן – בְּשָׂרוּף, כָּאן – בְּשֶׁאֵינוֹ שָׂרוּף.

**If** the *halakha* is derived from the term **"of them,"** one **might** have thought that even contact **with a part of them** transmits impurity. Therefore, **the verse states:** "Whoever touches **them.**" **How** can **these** texts be reconciled? **Here,** where the verse teaches that only the complete carcass of a creeping animal transmits impurity, it is referring **to a burnt** creeping animal.[N] **There,** where the verse indicates that even a part of them transmits impurity, it is referring **to** the carcass of a creeping animal **that is not burnt.**

### NOTES

**Here it is referring to a burnt creeping animal, etc. – כָּאן בְּשָׂרוּף וכו׳:** Although Rabbi Yitzḥak, son of Rabbi Bisna, earlier interpreted these verses in a different manner, as referring to moist and dry creatures, this is not a contradiction. The reason is that these two expositions are one and the same, as a burnt creeping animal is equivalent to a dry one, and the *halakha* in both cases is derived from the word "them." Likewise, an animal that is not burnt and one that is moist are the same, and both of these are derived from the term "of them" (Rashba).

### BACKGROUND

**Meḥoza – מְחוֹזָא:** Meḥoza was a large city on the banks of the Tigris River. It served as a major center of commerce, but the Jewish inhabitants' great wealth corrupted them. Rava, who was the head of the yeshiva in Meḥoza, sharply criticized the traits of the inhabitants of the city when he taught them and was often able to point out the corruption in the city, due to his close familiarity with the goings-on there.

Location of Meḥoza

### HALAKHA

**A creeping animal that was burned but its skeleton is intact – שֶׁרֶץ שֶׁנִּשְׂרַף וְשִׁלְדּוֹ קַיֶּימֶת:** With regard to the carcass of a creeping animal that was burned but its skeleton is intact, as its entire structure remains intact it transmits ritual impurity. The *halakha* is in accordance with the opinion of Reish Lakish. The Rambam notes: It would seem to me that this impurity applies by rabbinic law (Rambam *Sefer Tahara*, *Hilkhot She'ar Avot HaTumot* 4:12 and *Kesef Mishne* there).

**A burnt creeping animal was found on top of a pile of olives and likewise the tattered rag of a *zav* – שֶׁרֶץ שָׂרוּף עַל גַּבֵּי הַזֵּיתִים וְכֵן מַטְלִית הַמְהוּהָא:** With regard to a burnt creeping animal that was found on top of food, and likewise an impure, worn-out rag of a *zav* that was found among vessels, the food is ritually pure whether it is in the public or in the private domain. One does not need to be concerned that the creeping animal was burned after it touched the food, or that the rag came into contact with the other vessels before it wore out and became pure, as it is presumed that all ritually impure items had already been in the same state they were in at the time they were found (Rambam *Sefer Tahara*, *Hilkhot She'ar Avot HaTumot* 15:10).

״מְטַמְּאִין לַחִין״. זָב – דִּכְתִיב ״רָר בְּשָׂרוֹ״. כִּיחוֹ וְנִיעוֹ וְרוּקוֹ – דִּכְתִיב ״כִּי יָרֹק הַזָּב״, כְּעֵין רוֹק.

§ The mishna teaches that the *ziva* of a *zav*, the mucus and saliva of a *zav*, the carcass of a creeping animal, an animal carcass, and semen all **transmit impurity** when they are **moist,** but they do not transmit impurity when they are dry. The Gemara cites the sources for these *halakhot*: The *ziva* of **a zav** transmits impurity only when moist, **as it is written: "His flesh runs** with his issue" (Leviticus 15:3), which is referring to a moist discharge. **His phlegm and his mucus and his saliva** likewise transmit impurity only when moist, **as it is written:** "And **if one who has an issue spits"** (Leviticus 15:8), which is referring to a substance **that is like saliva,** which is moist.

שֶׁרֶץ – ״בְּמוֹתָם״ אֲמַר רַחֲמָנָא, כְּעֵין מִיתָה. שִׁכְבַת זֶרַע – הָרְאוּיָה לְהַזְרִיעַ. נְבֵלָה – דִּכְתִיב ״כִּי יָמוּת״ – כְּעֵין מִיתָה.

The carcass of **a creeping animal** transmits impurity only when moist, as **the Merciful One states:** "Whoever touches them **when they are dead** shall be impure" (Leviticus 11:31). This indicates that they transmit impurity when they are in a state **similar to** their state at the time of **death,** when creatures are still moist. **Semen** transmits impurity only when moist, as it must be **fit to inseminate. An animal carcass** transmits impurity only when moist, **as it is written:** "And **if** any animal of which you may eat **dies,** he who touches its carcass shall be impure until the evening" (Leviticus 11:39), which teaches that the carcass transmits impurity when it is in a state **similar to** its state at the time of **death.**

״אִם יְכוֹלִין לְהַשְׁרוֹת״. בָּעֵי רַבִּי יִרְמְיָה: תְּחִילָּתוֹ וְסוֹפוֹ בְּפוֹשְׁרִין, אוֹ דִּלְמָא תְּחִילָּתוֹ אַף עַל פִּי שֶׁאֵין סוֹפוֹ?

§ The mishna teaches that **if one could soak** those dry substances in water and restore them to their previous state they would transmit impurity both when moist and when dry. The mishna further teaches that this is referring to soaking them in lukewarm water for a twenty-four-hour period. **Rabbi Yirmeya raises a dilemma:** Does the mishna mean that the soaking must be performed **in lukewarm** water from **the beginning of** the soaking until **its end, or perhaps** it is sufficient if the water is lukewarm at **the beginning of** the soaking, **even if** at **the end of** the soaking the water **is not** lukewarm?

תָּא שְׁמַע, דְּתַנְיָא: כַּמָּה הִיא שְׁרִיָּיתָן בְּפוֹשְׁרִין? יְהוּדָה בֶּן נְקוֹסָא אוֹמֵר: מֵעֵת לְעֵת, תְּחִילָּתוֹ אַף עַל פִּי שֶׁאֵין סוֹפוֹ. רַבָּן שִׁמְעוֹן בֶּן גַּמְלִיאֵל אוֹמֵר: צְרִיכִין שֶׁיְּהוּ פּוֹשְׁרִין מֵעֵת לְעֵת.

The Gemara explains: **Come** and **hear, as it is taught** in a *baraita*: **How much** time **is their soaking in lukewarm** water?[H] **Yehuda ben Nekosa**[P] **says:** This is referring to a twenty-four-hour **period,** and it is sufficient if the water is lukewarm at **its beginning, even if it is not** lukewarm **at its end. Rabban Shimon ben Gamliel says:** The water **must be lukewarm for** the entire twenty-four-hour **period.**

״רַבִּי יוֹסֵי אוֹמֵר בְּשַׂר הַמֵּת״ כו׳. אָמַר שְׁמוּאֵל: טָהוֹר מִלְּטַמֵּא בְּכַזַּיִת, אֲבָל מְטַמֵּא טוּמְאַת רָקָב. תַּנְיָא נַמִּי הָכִי, רַבִּי יוֹסֵי אוֹמֵר: בְּשַׂר הַמֵּת שֶׁיָּבַשׁ וְאֵין יָכוֹל לִשְׁרוֹת וְלַחֲזוֹר כְּמוֹת שֶׁהָיָה – טָהוֹר מִלְּטַמֵּא בְּכַזַּיִת, אֲבָל טָמֵא טוּמְאַת רָקָב.

§ The mishna teaches that **Rabbi Yosei says:** With regard to **the flesh of a corpse** that is dry and cannot be soaked to restore it to its previous state, it is ritually pure. **Shmuel says:** It **is pure from transmitting impurity by** the amount of **an olive-bulk, but** if there is a ladleful of the flesh it **transmits the impurity of** the **decayed** flesh of a corpse. **This is also taught** in a *baraita*: **Rabbi Yosei says:** With regard to **the flesh of a corpse that dried up and cannot be soaked and restored** to its **previous state, it is ritually pure from transmitting impurity by** the amount of **an olive-bulk, but it is impure** with the **impurity** of the **decayed** flesh of a corpse.

מתני׳ הַשֶּׁרֶץ שֶׁנִּמְצָא בְּמָבוֹי – מְטַמֵּא לְמַפְרֵעַ, עַד שֶׁיֹּאמַר ״בָּדַקְתִּי אֶת הַמָּבוֹי הַזֶּה, וְלֹא הָיָה בּוֹ שֶׁרֶץ״, אוֹ עַד שְׁעַת כִּבּוּד.

**MISHNA** The carcass of **a creeping animal that was found in an alleyway**[HB] **renders** pure items **impure retroactively.** All items that passed through that alleyway **from** the time about which **one may state: I examined this alleyway and there was no** carcass of **a creeping animal in it, or from the time** of the **sweeping** of the alleyway, are impure.

**HALAKHA**

**How much time is their soaking in lukewarm water** – **כַּמָּה הִיא שְׁרִיָּיתָן בְּפוֹשְׁרִין**: The *ziva* and saliva of a *zav* transmit impurity only when they are moist, but not when they are dry. To what extent is this the case? If one could soak them for a twenty-four-hour period to restore them to their previous state, they transmit impurity provided the water is lukewarm at the beginning of the soaking, even if it is not lukewarm at the end. This *halakha* is in accordance with the opinion of Yehuda ben Nekosa and is learned by tradition (Rambam *Sefer Tahara, Hilkhot Metamei Mishkav UMoshav* 2:1).

**The carcass of a creeping animal that was found in an alleyway** – **הַשֶּׁרֶץ שֶׁנִּמְצָא בְּמָבוֹי**: The carcass of a creeping animal that was found in an alleyway transmits ritual impurity retroactively, from the time about which one would state before the court: I examined this alleyway on such-and-such a day and there was no creeping animal in it. Even in a case where one swept the alleyway, if he neglected to examine it, the creeping animal transmits ritual impurity retroactively, from before the time of sweeping. This is the *halakha* only if the creeping animal was found dry; if it was found moist it transmits impurity retroactively only from when it could have died and still been moist when it was found. The *halakha* is in accordance with the opinion of Rabbi Shimon, as explained by Rabbi Elazar in the Gemara (Rambam *Sefer Tahara, Hilkhot She'ar Avot HaTumot* 18:4).

**BACKGROUND**

**Alleyway** – **מָבוֹי**: The alleyway mentioned in the Talmud refers to one that is open to the public domain, and whose walls are those of courtyards or houses that open up to the alleyway. An open alleyway is one that leads to a public domain at both ends. Although it is widely used as a passageway between main streets, it itself is too narrow to serve as a public thoroughfare and is therefore not considered a public domain. An enclosed alleyway refers to one that is closed with a wall on one end and whose open end leads to the public domain.

**PERSONALITIES**

**Yehuda ben Nekosa** – **יְהוּדָה בֶּן נְקוֹסָא**: Rabbi Yehuda ben Nekosa, who is sometimes referred to without his title, lived in the generation of his apparently older peer, Rabbi Yehuda HaNasi. Like many Sages of his generation, he studied under Rabbi Yehuda HaNasi's tutelage. Nevertheless, Yehuda ben Nekosa transmitted Torah in the name of other Sages who lived in the previous generation, who were apparently his primary teachers. The statements of Rabbi Yehuda ben Nekosa are cited in both the Jerusalem Talmud and the Babylonian Talmud. The Midrash relates that he argued with the heretics of his day and was victorious in his debates with them.

וְכֵן כֶּתֶם שֶׁנִּמְצָא בְּחָלוּק – מְטַמֵּא לְמַפְרֵעַ, עַד שֶׁיֹּאמַר ״בָּדַקְתִּי אֶת הֶחָלוּק הַזֶּה, וְלֹא הָיָה בּוֹ כֶּתֶם״, אוֹ עַד שְׁעַת הַכִּבּוּס.

**And likewise,** a blood **stain that was discovered on** the robe[B] of a woman **renders** her **impure retroactively.** Any pure items that she handled **from** the time about which **one may state: I examined this robe and there was no** blood **stain on it, or from the time of the laundering** of the robe, are impure.

וּמְטַמֵּא בֵּין לַח בֵּין יָבֵשׁ. רַבִּי שִׁמְעוֹן אוֹמֵר: הַיָּבֵשׁ – מְטַמֵּא לְמַפְרֵעַ, וְהַלַּח – אֵינוֹ מְטַמֵּא אֶלָּא עַד שְׁעַת שֶׁיְּהֵא יָכוֹל לַחֲזוֹר וְלִהְיוֹת לַח.

**And** the carcass of a creeping animal or a blood stain **renders** items **impure** retroactively **whether** they are still **moist** or are already **dried out. Rabbi Shimon says: The dry** one **renders** items **impure retroactively, but the moist** one **does not render** items **impure** from the aforementioned times, **but** only **from** such **a time that it could still be moist** from then up to the moment it was discovered.

**גמ׳** אִיבַּעְיָא לְהוּ: עַד שְׁעַת כִּבּוּד חֶזְקָתוֹ בָּדוּק, אוֹ דִּלְמָא חֶזְקָתוֹ מִתְכַּבֵּד?

**GEMARA** With regard to the case of the carcass of a creeping animal that was found in an alleyway, **a dilemma was raised before** the Sages: The mishna teaches that any pure items that passed through that alleyway **from the time of** the **sweeping** of the alleyway are impure. Does this mean that once the alleyway is swept **its presumptive status** is that it has been **examined,** as it is examined during the sweeping and any impure item would have been discovered, and therefore any pure items that passed through the alleyway beforehand remain pure? **Or perhaps** the mishna means that once the alleyway is swept **its presumptive status** is that it has been entirely **swept,** and therefore any creeping animal would have been removed by the sweeping.

וּמַאי נָפְקָא מִינָּהּ – דְּאָמַר ״כַּבִּיד וְלָא בְּדֵיק״. אִי אָמְרַתְּ חֶזְקָתוֹ בָּדוּק – הָא לָא בְּדַק, אִי אָמְרַתְּ חֶזְקָתוֹ מִתְכַּבֵּד – הָא מִתְכַּבֵּד.

The Gemara asks: **And what is the** practical **difference** that arises from this dilemma? The Gemara answers: There is a difference in a case **where** the one who swept the alleyway **said he swept** it **but did not examine** it. **If you say** that items that were present in the alleyway before it was swept remain pure because **the presumptive status of** a swept alleyway is that it has been **examined,** in **this** case the man explicitly said that **he did not examine** it, so it does not have this presumptive status. By contrast, **if you say** that the items remain pure because **the presumptive status of** the alleyway is that it has been completely **swept,** in **this** case too it has been **swept,** and therefore the items that were present earlier remain pure.

Perek **VII**
Daf **56** Amud **b**

אִי נַמִּי – דְּאִשְׁתַּכַּח בְּגוּמָּא. אִי אָמְרַתְּ חֶזְקָתוֹ בָּדוּק, מַאן דְּבָדַק – בְּגוּמָּא נַמִּי בָּדֵיק, אִי אָמְרַתְּ חֶזְקָתוֹ מִתְכַּבֵּד – גּוּמָּא לָא מִתְכַּבְּדָא.

**Alternatively,** there is a difference between these explanations in a case **where** the creeping animal **was found in a hole** in the ground. **If you say the presumptive status of** a swept alleyway is that it has been **examined,** it is clear that **one who examines** the alleyway **also examines** any **holes,** and any items that were in the alleyway beforehand should remain pure. By contrast, **if you say its presumptive status** is that it has been completely **swept,** this applies only to items that are on the ground, whereas **a hole is not** considered to have been **swept.** Consequently, even items that passed through the alleyway before it was swept should be deemed impure.

״וְכֵן הַכֶּתֶם״ וכו׳. אִיבַּעְיָא לְהוּ: עַד שְׁעַת כִּבּוּס חֶזְקָתוֹ בָּדוּק, אוֹ דִּלְמָא חֶזְקָתוֹ מִתְכַּבֵּס?

The mishna teaches: **And likewise,** a blood **stain** that was discovered on the robe of a woman renders her impure retroactively. With regard to this *halakha* as well **a dilemma was raised before** the Sages: The mishna states that any pure items the woman handled **from** the **time of laundering** are impure. Does this mean that once the robe has been laundered **its presumptive status** is that it has been **examined,** as when it is laundered it is examined thoroughly, and any blood stain would have been discovered? **Or perhaps** the mishna means that **its presumptive status** is that **it is** thoroughly **laundered,** and any blood stain would have been removed by the laundering.

BACKGROUND

Robe [*ḥaluk*] – חָלוּק: A *ḥaluk* is a garment whose upper half is divided [*meḥulak*] into two. The upper part of the garment, which is tied together with lacing, is called the key of the robe.

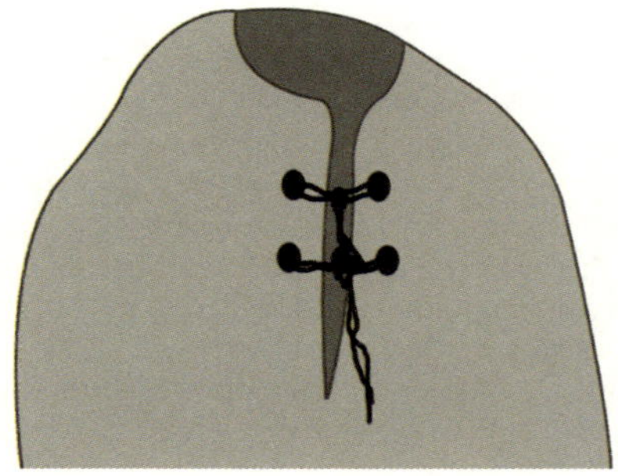

Robe

לְמַאי נָפְקָא מִינָּהּ – דַּאֲמַר כִּיבֵּס וְלָא בְּדַק. אִי אָמְרַתְּ חֶזְקָתוֹ בָּדוּק – הָא לָא בְּדַק, אִי אָמְרַתְּ חֶזְקָתוֹ מִתְכַּבֵּס – הָא מִתְכַּבֵּס.

The Gemara asks: **What is the** practical **difference** that arises from this dilemma? The Gemara replies: There is a difference in a case **where** the person who laundered the robe **said he laundered** it **but did not examine** it. **If you say its presumptive status** is that it has been **examined,** in **this** case the man explicitly said that **he did not examine** the robe, so it does not have this presumptive status. By contrast, **if you say its presumptive status** is that **it is** thoroughly **laundered,** in **this** case too it has been **laundered.**

אִי נַמִי, דְּאִשְׁתַּכְּחָה בְּסִטְרָא. אִי אָמְרַתְּ חֶזְקָתוֹ בָּדוּק – מַאן דִּבְדַק, בְּסִטְרָא נַמִי בָּדֵיק. אִי אָמְרַתְּ חֶזְקָתוֹ מִתְכַּבֵּס – בְּסִטְרָא לָא מִתְכַּבֵּס.

**Alternatively,** there is a difference between these explanations in a case **where** the blood stain **was found on the side** of the robe, in an area where there are folds and stitches. **If you say its presumptive status** is that it has been **examined,** it is clear that **one who examines** the robe **also examines the side** of the robe, and therefore any items that the woman handled before the robe was laundered should remain pure. By contrast, **if you say its presumptive status** is that **it is** thoroughly **laundered,** this applies only to the main part of the robe, but **on** its **side** it **is not laundered** thoroughly enough to remove a blood stain.

מַאי? תָּא שְׁמַע, דְּתַנְיָא, אָמַר רַבִּי מֵאִיר: מִפְּנֵי מָה אָמְרוּ הַשֶּׁרֶץ שֶׁנִּמְצָא בְּמָבוֹי – מְטַמֵּא לְמַפְרֵעַ, עַד שֶׁיֹּאמַר ״בָּדַקְתִּי אֶת הַמָּבוֹי הַזֶּה, וְלֹא הָיָה בּוֹ שֶׁרֶץ״, אוֹ עַד שְׁעַת כִּיבּוּד? מִפְּנֵי שֶׁחֶזְקַת בְּנֵי יִשְׂרָאֵל בּוֹדְקִין מְבוֹאוֹתֵיהֶן בִּשְׁעַת כִּבּוּדֵיהֶם, וְאִם לֹא בָּדְקוּ – הִפְסִידוּהוּ לְמַפְרֵעַ.

**What** is the *halakha* with regard to these two dilemmas? **Come** and **hear, as it is taught** in a *baraita* that **Rabbi Meir says: For what** reason **did** the Sages **say** that the carcass of **a creeping animal that was found in an alleyway renders** pure items **impure retroactively from** the time about which **one may state: I examined this alleyway and there was no creeping animal in it, or from** the **time of** the **sweeping** of the alleyway? It is **due to** the fact **that** there is **a presumption with regard to Jewish people** that **they examine their alleyways at the time of their sweeping. And** therefore, **if they did not examine** the alleyway **they retroactively lose** the purity of any items that were there from the last time it was examined.

וּמִפְּנֵי מָה אָמְרוּ כֶּתֶם שֶׁנִּמְצָא בְּחָלוּק מְטַמֵּא לְמַפְרֵעַ, עַד שֶׁיֹּאמַר ״בָּדַקְתִּי אֶת הֶחָלוּק וְלֹא הָיָה בּוֹ כֶּתֶם״, אוֹ עַד שְׁעַת הַכִּבּוּס? מִפְּנֵי שֶׁחֶזְקַת בְּנוֹת יִשְׂרָאֵל בּוֹדְקוֹת חֲלוּקֵיהֶן בִּשְׁעַת כִּבּוּסֵיהֶן, וְאִם לֹא בָּדְקוּ – הִפְסִידוּ לְמַפְרֵעַ.

**And** similarly, **for what** reason **did** the Sages **say** that a blood **stain that was found on** the **robe** of a woman **renders** her **impure retroactively from** the time about which **one may state: I examined the robe and there was no** blood **stain on it, or from the time of the laundering** of the robe? It is **due to** the fact **that** there is **a presumption with regard to the Jewish women** that **they examine their robes at the time of their laundering. And** therefore, **if they did not examine** the robe **they retroactively lose** the purity of any items they handled since it was last examined.

רַבִּי אַחָא אָמַר: תַּחֲזוֹר וּתְכַבְּסֶנּוּ, אִם נִדְחֶה מַרְאִיתוֹ – בְּיָדוּעַ שֶׁלְּאַחַר כִּבּוּס, וְאִם לָאו – בְּיָדוּעַ שֶׁלִּפְנֵי הַכִּבּוּס.

**Rabbi Aḥa says:** Even in a case where the robe was not examined when it was laundered and a blood stain was subsequently found on it, and it is unknown whether the stain was present before the laundering, there is a remedy to the dilemma: **Let her launder it again. If the appearance of** the blood stain **changes** as a result of this laundering **it is known that** the robe became stained **after** the previous **laundering,** which is why the present laundering affected its appearance. Consequently, those pure items that the woman handled before the earlier laundering remain pure. **And if** the blood stain's appearance does **not** change due to the second laundering **it is known that** the robe became stained **before the** previous **laundering,** and therefore the items that she handled before the laundering are impure.

רַבִּי אוֹמֵר: אֵינוֹ דּוֹמֶה כֶּתֶם שֶׁלְּאַחַר הַכִּבּוּס לְכֶתֶם שֶׁלִּפְנֵי הַכִּבּוּס, שֶׁזֶּה מַקְדִּיר וְזֶה מַגְלִיד. שְׁמַע מִינָּהּ: חֶזְקָתוֹ בָּדוּק, שְׁמַע מִינָּהּ.

**Rabbi** Yehuda HaNasi **says:** One can differentiate between a blood stain that was on the robe before it was laundered and one that stained the robe afterward by inspecting the stain itself. This is because the appearance of a blood **stain after the laundering is not similar to** the appearance of a blood **stain before the laundering,**[H] **as this** stain, from after the laundering, **penetrates** [*makdir*][L] the garment, **and that** stain, from before the laundering, **forms a crust** [*maglid*][LN] that can be scraped off the robe. With regard to the Gemara's dilemma, one may **conclude from** Rabbi Meir's statement that **the presumptive status of** a swept alleyway or a laundered robe is that it has been **examined.** The Gemara concludes: Indeed, **conclude from it** that this is so.

**HALAKHA**

**The appearance of a stain after the laundering is not similar to the appearance…before the laundering – אֵינוֹ דּוֹמֶה כֶּתֶם שֶׁלְּאַחַר הַכִּבּוּס...שֶׁלִּפְנֵי הַכִּבּוּס:** In a case of a woman who wore a robe while she was menstruating and it was laundered, and she subsequently wore it again when she was ritually pure without examining it, if it was laundered by a Jewish woman who is not present and one can ask her, she is presumed to have examined it when laundering and therefore it cannot be assumed that the blood stain was from when the owner of the robe was menstruating. If the woman who laundered it is present and says that she did not examine the robe, its owner may presume that the blood stain was there beforehand and was not removed by the laundering. The same applies if it was laundered by a Canaanite maidservant or a gentile woman, even if they are not present, as they are not presumed to have examined it when laundering. In a case where the owner knows how to discern between different types of blood stains, if the stain passes through the robe it was evidently present before laundering, and if it remains hard on the outside, it came after laundering. If she is not expert in this examination she must be stringent. It should be noted that the *Shulḥan Arukh* follows a different interpretation of the terms *makdir* and *maglid* than Rashi. The *halakha* is in accordance with the opinion of Rabbi Yehuda HaNasi (*Shulḥan Arukh, Yoreh De'a* 190:46, and see 47).

**LANGUAGE**

**Penetrates [*makdir*] – מַקְדִּיר:** The basic meaning of this root is unclear. Some explain that *kadar* refers to a hole that has been bored [*nekev*], or to a deep insertion. Others claim it belongs to the category of roots that can have opposite meanings, and therefore *kadar* can mean shine as well as darkness. Alternatively, it means to heat or boil, which leads to the common term *kedeira*, a pot used for cooking.

**Forms a crust [*maglid*] – מַגְלִיד:** The root *gimmel, lamed, dalet* has several meanings, first and foremost of which is a description of the skin covering human flesh, as in the verse: "I have sewed sackcloth on my skin [*gildi*] and have laid my horn in the dust" (Job 16:15). From this, its meaning has extended to refer to any substance that hardens as a membrane. Accordingly, part of the healing process of a wound on the human body is called *hagladato*, which refers to the scab that covers it.

**NOTES**

**This stain penetrates [*makdir*] the garment and that stain forms a crust [*maglid*] – זֶה מַקְדִּיר וְזֶה מַגְלִיד:** Rabbi Yehuda HaNasi does not clarify which of the types of blood stain is which. Furthermore, the terms *makdir* and *maglid* are left unexplained. Rashi states that *makdir* refers to a blood stain that was caused after laundering, and it means the stain penetrated the garment, whereas *maglid* refers to a blood stain that was on the garment before laundering, which hardens over the outside of the garment. Others maintain that *makdir* means the blood stain darkens, which occurs after laundering. Yet others explain that *makdir* means only a thin blood stain is visible in the material of the garment, and this indicates that the stain was already laundered, whereas *maglid* means a thicker blood stain is visible above the fabric, which indicates that the staining occurred after the laundering (Ramban; Rashba).

״וּמְטַמֵּא בֵּין לַח״ וכו׳. אָמַר רַבִּי אֶלְעָזָר: לֹא שָׁנוּ – אֶלָּא שֶׁרֶץ, אֲבָל כֶּתֶם לַח – נַמִּי מְטַמֵּא לְמַפְרֵעַ, אֵימַר יָבֵשׁ הָיָה וּמַיָּא נָפֵיל עֲלֵיהּ.

§ The mishna teaches: **And** the carcass of a creeping animal or a blood stain **renders** items **impure** retroactively **whether** they are still **moist** or are already dried out. Rabbi Shimon says: The dry one renders items impure retroactively, whereas the moist one does not render items impure since the aforementioned times, but only from such a time that it could still be moist from then up to the moment it was discovered. With regard to the opinion of Rabbi Shimon, **Rabbi Elazar says:** The mishna **taught** this *halakha* **only** with regard to the carcass of **a creeping animal, but** Rabbi Shimon concedes that **a moist** blood **stain also renders** the woman **impure retroactively**[H] from the time that the robe was examined. This is because one can **say** the blood stain **was dry** beforehand **and water fell upon it,** causing it to become moist.

שֶׁרֶץ נַמִּי, אֵימַר: יָבֵשׁ הָיָה וּמַיָּא נָפֵיל עֲלֵיהּ! אִם אִיתָא דְּהָכִי הוּא – אִמַּרְטוּטֵי אִימַּרְטֵט.

The Gemara asks: With regard to the moist carcass of **a creeping animal as well,** one can **say it was dried out** beforehand **and water fell on it.** It should therefore render items impure retroactively from the time that the alleyway was swept. The Gemara answers: **If it is so, that this is** what occurred, the dead creeping animal **would be sundered apart** and would not have its current appearance.

מתני׳ כָּל הַכְּתָמִין הַבָּאִין מֵרֶקֶם – טְהוֹרִין. רַבִּי יְהוּדָה מְטַמֵּא, מִפְּנֵי שֶׁהֵם גֵּרִים וְטוֹעִין. הַבָּאִין מִבֵּין הַגּוֹיִם – טְהוֹרִין. מִבֵּין יִשְׂרָאֵל וּמִבֵּין הַכּוּתִים – רַבִּי מֵאִיר מְטַמֵּא, וַחֲכָמִים מְטַהֲרִים, מִפְּנֵי שֶׁלֹּא נֶחְשְׁדוּ עַל כִּתְמֵיהֶן.

**MISHNA** Any blood **stains** on garments **that come from** the town of **Rekem**[B] **are ritually pure,** as most of the residents there are gentiles, and the blood stains of gentile women are not ritually impure. **Rabbi Yehuda deems** those stains **impure because** in his opinion the residents of Rekem are not gentiles; rather, **they are converts** whose halakhic status is that of Jews, **but they are misguided** and do not put away their blood-stained garments. The blood stains on garments **that come from among the gentiles**[H] **are ritually pure.** With regard to blood stains on garments that come **from among the Jews and from among the Samaritans,**[B] **Rabbi Meir deems** them **impure,** as they may have come from the Jews. **And the Rabbis deem** them **ritually pure due to** the fact **that** Jews **are not suspected of** failing to put away **their** garments on which there are blood **stains.**

## HALAKHA

**A moist stain also renders her impure retroactively – כֶּתֶם לַח נַמִּי מְטַמֵּא לְמַפְרֵעַ:** If a woman sees a blood stain on her body she is impure retroactively from her last examination. Similarly, if a blood stain is found on the garment of a woman it is impure retroactively from the time about which she can say: I examined this robe and there was no blood stain on it. Even in a case where she laundered the robe, if she did not examine it then the robe is impure retroactively from the most recent examination. Furthermore, even if the blood stain was moist when found, it transmits ritual impurity retroactively from the moment of the examination of the robe, as it is assumed the stain was present from that moment onward and is moist now because water fell on it, as stated by Rabbi Elazar (Rambam *Sefer Tahara, Hilkhot Metamei Mishkav UMoshav* 3:7).

**The stains on garments that come from among the gentiles – הַבָּאִין מִבֵּין הַגּוֹיִם:** Blood stains on garments that come from among the gentiles have the presumptive status of ritual purity (Rambam *Sefer Tahara, Hilkhot Metamei Mishkav UMoshav* 4:10).

## BACKGROUND

**Rekem – רֶקֶם:** The location of Rekem is not entirely clear from the sources, as it is mentioned infrequently. Nevertheless, most Aramaic translations of the Torah render Kadesh Barnea (see, e.g., Deuteronomy 1:2) as Rekem. If so, it is a city in the southeastern part of Eretz Yisrael, near the ancient Nabatean site of Petra. Apparently, after this area was conquered by the Hasmoneans and its inhabitants converted to Judaism it became a place of Jewish settlement. It can therefore be used as a marker of the southern border of Eretz Yisrael.

**Samaritans [*Kutim*] – כּוּתִים:** The name *Kutim* refers to the members of the nations, only some of whom were actually from Kuta, who were brought to Eretz Yisrael by the Assyrian kings to replace the Jews exiled from there. These gentiles settled in Samaria and are therefore also known as Samaritans. It is related in II Kings, chapter 17, that they accepted upon themselves some of the strictures of Judaism only out of fear of lions that were attacking them. For this reason some of the Sages maintained their conversion was invalid and therefore their halakhic status is that of gentiles. Apparently, they also did not entirely abandon idolatry.

At the beginning of the Second Temple era, when the Jews returned from Babylonia, relations with the Samaritans and their allies deteriorated. The Samaritans attempted to prevent and undermine the construction of the Temple and the wall of Jerusalem by a host of means, including informing on the Jews to the Persian government and even taking military action. During this period there was also assimilation and intermarriage between Jews and Samaritans. Later, the Samaritans established a center of worship on Mount Gerizim, as they claimed that the sanctity of that mountain was established in the Torah. Over time, attitudes toward the Samaritans fluctuated: There were periods when deep feelings of hatred separated Samaritans and Jews. Yoḥanan Hyrcanus even waged war against Samaria and destroyed their temple on Mount Gerizim. In other eras there was some measure of cooperation between the two communities, such as during the bar Kokheva revolt.

The Sages initially disagreed over the halakhic status of the Samaritans and the validity of their conversion. Ultimately, the opinion prevailed that halakhically the Samaritans are gentiles, especially after it was discovered that they persisted in various idolatrous practices, which was partly due to Greek and Roman influences.

Mount Gerizim

**BACKGROUND**

**Tarmod** – **תַּרְמוֹד**: The city of Tarmod, or Tadmor, known in English as Palmyra, is located in an oasis in the Syrian desert. Tadmor is an ancient city whose name dates back thousands of years. In the Bible the city is also called Tamar, meaning palm. For many generations Tadmor was an important center of commerce and served as a crossroads for different trading routes across Syria, Arabia, and Babylonia.

The Bible relates that King Solomon built and fortified Tadmor (see I Kings 9:18–19; II Chronicles 8:4). This is the source for the claim that Solomon's bond servants lived there, as well as the reason for the Jewish influence on the city's religion and culture.

The kingdom of Tadmor grew powerful in the middle of the third century CE, as its ruler, Odaenathus, called Papa bar Nasser in the Gemara, established Tadmor as a great power under Roman patronage, along with his wife, Zenobia. Papa bar Nasser destroyed the city of Neharde'a, and his wife even reigned over Eretz Yisrael. Apparently, the Jews opposed these rulers and treated them with hostility and contempt. In the year 273 CE the Roman emperor Aurelian conquered Tadmor, and from that point onward its influence waned considerably. Nevertheless, although it has been conquered and partially destroyed several times, certain parts of the city remain standing to this day.

Ruins of ancient temple in Palmyra

גמ׳ קָפְסֵיק וְתָנֵי, אֲפִילּוּ מִתַּרְמוֹד! אָמַר רַבִּי יוֹחָנָן, זֹאת אוֹמֶרֶת: מְקַבְּלִין גֵּרִים מִתַּרְמוֹד.

**GEMARA** The mishna **categorically teaches** that any blood stains on garments that come from among the gentiles are ritually pure, thereby indicating that this applies **even** to garments that come **from** among the gentile population of **Tarmod.**[B] **Rabbi Yoḥanan says: That is to say, one may accept converts from Tarmod,** i.e., there is no concern with regard to whether they are actually Jews of flawed lineage, who may not marry Jews of fit lineage.

אִינִי, וְהָא רַבִּי יוֹחָנָן וְסָבַיָּא דְּאָמְרִי תַּרְוַיְיהוּ: אֵין מְקַבְּלִין גֵּרִים מִתַּרְמוֹד!

The Gemara asks: **Is that so? But** aren't there **Rabbi Yoḥanan and the Elders who both say** that **one may not accept converts from Tarmod?** This is due to a concern that the daughters of the ten tribes exiled during the First Temple period might have intermingled with them, and according to Rabbi Yoḥanan the offspring of a Jewish woman and a gentile is a *mamzer*, who may not marry a Jew of fit lineage.

וְכִי תֵּימָא: ״זֹאת״, וְלָא סְבִירָא לֵיהּ, וְהָאָמַר רַבִּי יוֹחָנָן: הֲלָכָה כִּסְתָם מִשְׁנָה!

**And if you would say** that Rabbi Yoḥanan merely infers that this is the opinion of the mishna, as indicated by the term: **That** is to say, **but he** himself **does not hold accordingly,** that is not so. **Didn't Rabbi Yoḥanan say** a principle that the ***halakha* is in accordance with** the ruling of **an unattributed mishna,** as is the case here?

אֲמוֹרָאֵי נִינְהוּ, וְאַלִּיבָּא דְּרַבִּי יוֹחָנָן.

The Gemara answers: **They are *amora'im*, and** they disagree **with regard to** the opinion **of Rabbi Yoḥanan.** According to one *amora*, Rabbi Yoḥanan maintains that converts from Tarmod are not accepted, and he did not state that it is a principle that the *halakha* is in accordance with the ruling of an unattributed mishna. According to another *amora*, Rabbi Yoḥanan holds that the *halakha* is in accordance with the unattributed mishna, and therefore one may accept converts from Tarmod.

״מִבֵּין יִשְׂרָאֵל״ וכו׳. וְרַבָּנַן, אִי דְּיִשְׂרָאֵל מְטַהֲרִי, דְּמַאן מְטַמּוּ?

§ The mishna teaches with regard to blood stains on garments that come **from among the Jews** and from among the Samaritans that Rabbi Meir deems them impure, and the Rabbis deem them ritually pure. The Gemara asks: **But** with regard to the opinion of **the Rabbis, if they deem** stains that come **from a Jewish** woman **pure, whose** stains **do they deem impure?**

חַסּוּרֵי מִחַסְּרָא, וְהָכִי קָתָנֵי: מִבֵּין יִשְׂרָאֵל – טָמֵא. מִבֵּין הַכּוּתִים – רַבִּי מֵאִיר מְטַמֵּא, דְּכוּתִים גֵּרֵי אֱמֶת הֵן. וַחֲכָמִים מְטַהֲרִין, דְּכוּתִים גֵּרֵי אֲרָיוֹת הֵן.

The Gemara answers: The mishna **is incomplete and this** is what **it is teaching:** Everyone agrees that blood stains on garments that come **from among the Jews are impure.** With regard to blood stains that come **from among the Samaritans, Rabbi Meir deems** them **impure, as** he maintains the **Samaritans are true converts** and have the halakhic status of Jews, whose blood stains are impure. **And the Rabbis deem** them **ritually pure, as** they maintain the **Samaritans are converts** who converted under duress **due to** the threat posed by **lions,** and therefore their conversion is void, and their halakhic status is that of gentiles.

אִי הָכִי, ״שֶׁלֹּא נֶחְשְׁדוּ עַל כִּתְמֵיהֶן״ – ״גֵּרֵי אֲרָיוֹת״ מִבָּעֵי לֵיהּ!

The Gemara asks: **If so,** why does the mishna state that according to the Rabbis the blood stains of the Samaritans are ritually pure due to the fact **that they are not suspected of** failing to put away **their** garments on which there are blood **stains?** The mishna **should** state that their blood stains are pure, as they are **converts** who converted **due to** the threat of **lions.**

אֶלָּא הָכִי קָאָמַר: מִבֵּין יִשְׂרָאֵל וּמִבֵּין הַכּוּתִים – טְמֵאִין, דְּכוּתִים גֵּרֵי אֱמֶת הֵן. הַנִּמְצָאִין בְּעָרֵי יִשְׂרָאֵל – טְהוֹרִין, שֶׁלֹּא נֶחְשְׁדוּ עַל כִּתְמֵיהֶם, וְאִצְנוֹעֵי מִצְנְעֵי לְהוּ.

**Rather, this** is what the mishna **is saying:** Blood stains on garments that come **from among the Jews and from among the Samaritans are ritually impure, as** everyone agrees the **Samaritans are true converts.** With regard to blood stains **that are found in** the **towns of Jews,**[H] **they are pure, as they are not suspected of** failing to put away **their** garments on which there are blood **stains, and they** certainly **put them away.** Therefore, the stains necessarily come from gentiles.

**HALAKHA**

**Stains that are found in towns of Jews** – **הַנִּמְצָאִין בְּעָרֵי יִשְׂרָאֵל**: Blood stains found in cities of Jews have the presumptive status of ritual purity, as they are not suspected of failing to put away their garments on which there are blood stains (Rambam *Sefer Tahara, Hilkhot Metamei Mishkav UMoshav* 4:10).

הַנִּמְצָאִין בְּעָרֵי כוּתִים – רַבִּי מֵאִיר מְטַמֵּא, דְּנֶחְשְׁדוּ עַל כִּתְמֵיהֶם. וַחֲכָמִים מְטַהֲרִין, שֶׁלֹּא נֶחְשְׁדוּ עַל כִּתְמֵיהֶן.

The Gemara continues paraphrasing the mishna: With regard to blood stains **that are found in** the **towns of Samaritans, Rabbi Meir deems** them **impure, as** the inhabitants **are suspected of** failing to put away **their** garments on which there are blood **stains. And the Rabbis deem** them **pure, as** they maintain that even Samaritans **are not suspected of** failing to put away **their** garments on which there are blood **stains,** and the stains are necessarily from gentiles.

מתני׳ כָּל הַכְּתָמִים הַנִּמְצָאִים בְּכָל מָקוֹם – טְהוֹרִין, חוּץ מִן הַנִּמְצָאִים בַּחֲדָרִים וּבִסְבִיבוֹת בֵּית הַטְּמְאוֹת.

**MISHNA** All blood **stains** on garments **that are found anywhere**[H] where Jews and gentiles reside **are ritually pure,** since they must not belong to Jews, who put away their stained garments. This is the *halakha* **except for** the stained garments **that are found in the** inner **rooms** of the house, as these might be garments that the Jews put away there; **and** except for the stained garments found **in proximity to the house of impurity,** i.e., the room that women used when they were impure due to menstruation.

בֵּית הַטְּמְאוֹת שֶׁל כּוּתִים מְטַמְּאִין בְּאֹהֶל, מִפְּנֵי שֶׁהֵם קוֹבְרִין שָׁם אֶת הַנְּפָלִים. רַבִּי יְהוּדָה אוֹמֵר: לֹא הָיוּ קוֹבְרִין, אֶלָּא מַשְׁלִיכִין, וְחַיָּה גּוֹרַרְתּוֹ.

**The house of impurity of Samaritans imparts** the **impurity** that is imparted by a corpse **by means of a tent,**[B] **due to** the fact **that they bury the stillborn** children **there. Rabbi Yehuda says:** The house of impurity of Samaritans does not impart that impurity, as **they would not bury** a stillborn child there. **Rather, they would cast** it outside **and an animal would drag it** away.

נֶאֱמָנִים לוֹמַר "קָבַרְנוּ שָׁם אֶת הַנְּפָלִים", אוֹ "לֹא קָבַרְנוּ". נֶאֱמָנִים לוֹמַר עַל הַבְּהֵמָה אִם בִּכְּרָה אִם לֹא בִּכְּרָה. נֶאֱמָנִים עַל צִיּוּן קְבָרוֹת.

Samaritans **are deemed credible to state: We buried the stillborn** children **there,** in a certain place, and it transmits ritual impurity; **or** to state: **We did not bury** the stillborn children there, and it does not transmit ritual impurity. **They are** likewise **deemed credible to state about an animal whether it** previously **gave birth** or **whether it did not** previously **give birth;** and their testimony is accepted with regard to determining whether the animal's offspring has the status of a firstborn animal,[B] which is sacred. They **are** also **deemed credible** to testify **about the marking of graves,** i.e., that where they marked is deemed a grave and where they did not mark is deemed a place where there is no grave.

וְאֵין נֶאֱמָנִין לֹא עַל הַסְּכָכוֹת, וְלֹא עַל הַפְּרָעוֹת, וְלֹא עַל בֵּית הַפְּרָס.

**But** with regard to the following cases, in which the exact location of a grave is unknown, the Samaritans **are not deemed credible** to testify: They are **not** deemed credible to testify **about the overhanging boughs, nor about the protrusions**[N] that jut out of stone fences and cover the ground. If it is unknown which bough or protrusion hangs over a grave, forming a tent that transmits the impurity of a corpse, and if a Samaritan testifies that the grave is not beneath a particular bough or protrusion his testimony is not accepted. **And** likewise they are **not** deemed credible to testify **about a *beit haperas*.**[BL] The Sages issued a decree that in such a case, the area that was plowed is impure as far as one hundred cubits from the original grave, due to the concern that the bones were dispersed by the plow.

זֶה הַכְּלָל: דָּבָר שֶׁחֲשׁוּדִים בּוֹ – אֵין נֶאֱמָנִין עָלָיו.

**This is the principle** governing the credibility of Samaritans: In the case of any **matter** of *halakha* **that they are suspected** of not fulfilling, **they are not deemed credible** to testify **about it.**

**HALAKHA**

**All stains on garments that are found anywhere – כָּל הַכְּתָמִים הַנִּמְצָאִים בְּכָל מָקוֹם:** Blood stains on garments that are found anywhere are ritually pure, except for the stained garments found in inner rooms in the house and those found proximate to the house of impurity. These are considered ritually impure due to uncertainty (Rambam *Sefer Tahara, Hilkhot Metamei Mishkav UMoshav* 4:10).

**BACKGROUND**

**Imparts the impurity that is imparted by a corpse by means of a tent – מְטַמְּאִין בְּאֹהֶל:** The *halakhot* of the impurity imparted by a corpse, including that imparted by a tent covering a corpse, are cited in great detail in tractate *Oholot*. The essential *halakhot* of a tent over a corpse appear in the Torah (Numbers, chapter 19). The Sages derived from the verses that any structure that has a cavity of at least one cubic handbreadth in volume and contains a corpse or part of a corpse, e.g., its flesh, bones, or limbs, becomes a tent over a corpse. Any person or item subject to ritual impurity that enters the structure becomes ritually impure and becomes a primary source of ritual impurity, i.e., imparts ritual impurity to other people and items.

**Firstborn animal – בְּכוֹר:** A male firstborn calf, lamb, or kid belonging to a Jew is sanctified from birth and must be given to a priest to be sacrificed on the altar in the Temple (see Numbers 18:17–18). If a firstborn animal develops a physical blemish that disqualifies it from being sacrificed as an offering, it is slaughtered and eaten like any other non-sacred kosher animal. It is prohibited to intentionally inflict a disqualifying blemish on a firstborn animal. A firstborn animal may not be used for any mundane purpose, e.g., for work or for its fleece, even if it is blemished. The *halakhot* of a firstborn animal are detailed in tractate *Bekhorot*.

***Beit haperas* – בֵּית הַפְּרָס:** A *beit haperas* is a place that the Sages decreed ritually impure, as though it were a cemetery. There are three cases that are defined as a *beit haperas*: The first type is a field known to contain a grave but the location of the grave within the field in unknown. Therefore, the concern is that the grave might be located in any part of the field (*Tosafot*). The second type is a field in which a grave was plowed over, and there is a concern that the bones might have been scattered throughout an area the size of a one-hundred-cubit furrow, as will be explained (*Oholot* 17:1; Rambam *Sefer Tahara, Hilkhot Tumat Met* 10:1). The third kind is a field in which people would eulogize the dead. It is considered a *beit haperas* because part of a corpse might have fallen there (*Oholot* 18:2–4).

**NOTES**

**Overhanging boughs…protrusions – סְכָכוֹת...פְּרָעוֹת:** The commentaries dispute the meaning of these concepts. Rashi maintains it is referring to trees or walls adjacent to a cemetery where there is a concern that a corpse or part of a corpse might be buried beneath them. Others explain that there is certainly a corpse buried underneath the branch or protrusion from the wall, but there is doubt as to the precise location of the corpse.

**LANGUAGE**

***Beit haperas* – בֵּית הַפְּרָס:** Opinions are divided as to the origin of this term. Rashi and *Tosafot* explain that the word *peras* means broken, as the field became impure when it was plowed and the bones were broken and scattered about. The Rambam apparently understands the term in the sense of spreading, *perisa*, as the impurity spreads over the entire area. Some contend it is derived from the Greek πάρος, *paros*, meaning before, in the sense of both time and place. Finally, there are those who claim that it is from the Greek ἄπορος, aporos, which means without passage.

**NOTES**

What did they interpret – מַאי דְּרוּשׁ: It is unclear to which of the rulings of the mishna this is referring. According to Rashi, the reference is to Rabbi Yehuda's statement that Samaritans would not bury their stillborn children. Others explain that the Gemara is referring to the opinion of the Rabbis that Samaritans bury their stillborn children outside the cemetery (Rambam; Meiri).

You shall not remove your fellow's boundary marker which was bounded by the first ones in your inheritance – לֹא תַסִּיג גְּבוּל רֵעֲךָ אֲשֶׁר גָּבְלוּ רִאשֹׁנִים בְּנַחֲלָתְךָ: This main part of this exposition appears in the *Sifrei*, which interprets this verse as referring to one who sells his ancestors' graves (Rashi). An ancestral burial ground is a designated bounded area inherited from "the first ones." The Samaritans extended this concept and inferred that the mitzva of burial applies only to those who are candidates to inherit, which excludes stillborn children. The commentaries dispute whether this exposition is valid, notwithstanding the fact that it is the Samaritans' interpretation. Some authorities reject it and rule that it is an obligation to bury stillborn children (*Magen Avraham*; Responsa of the Radbaz). Others claim that the exposition is correct, and there is no obligation by Torah law to bury stillborn children, although by rabbinic law one must do so (*Ha'amek Davar*; *Shulḥan Arukh*, *Oraḥ Ḥayyim* 526:10; *Haggahot Maimoniyyot*). The *Ḥazon Ish* is of this opinion, and adds that the Samaritans did not invent this exposition but received it as a tradition.

Where a priest is standing there – בְּכֹהֵן עוֹמֵד שָׁם: The Gemara must be referring to a Samaritan who is a priest, as otherwise there would be no reason to rely on the statement of the Samaritan that the place is pure (Rashi). This is problematic: How can a Samaritan be a priest, as priests must be descendants of Aaron, whereas Samaritans were converts? Some explain that the Gemara is speaking of those individuals appointed by the Samaritans to serve as their priests, who observe the *halakhot* of actual priests (Responsa of the Rashba).

**גמ׳** מַאי דְּרוּשׁ? ״לֹא תַסִּיג גְּבוּל רֵעֲךָ אֲשֶׁר גָּבְלוּ רִאשֹׁנִים בְּנַחֲלָתְךָ״,

**GEMARA** The mishna teaches that the Samaritans do not observe burial customs for stillborn children. The Gemara asks: **What** verse **did they interpret**[N] as a source for this practice? The Gemara replies that they interpreted the verse: **"You shall not remove your fellow's boundary marker, which was bounded by the first ones, in your inheritance**[N] that you shall inherit, in the land that the Lord your God gives you to possess it" (Deuteronomy 19:14).

כָּל שֶׁיֵּשׁ לוֹ נַחֲלָה – יֵשׁ לוֹ גְּבוּל, כָּל שֶׁאֵין לוֹ נַחֲלָה – אֵין לוֹ גְּבוּל.

The Gemara explains: The Sages derived from this verse that it is prohibited to sell one's ancestral burial ground. In accordance with this interpretation of the verse, the Samaritans derived that **any** individual **who has an inheritance,** i.e., who stands to inherit land, **has a boundary,** i.e., a burial place, whereas **any** individual **who does not have an inheritance** in the land, e.g., a stillborn child, **does not have a boundary,** i.e., a burial place. The Samaritans therefore concluded that the mitzva of burial does not apply to stillborn children.

״נֶאֱמָנִים לוֹמַר קָבַרְנוּ״. וְהָא לֵית לְהוּ ״וְלִפְנֵי עִוֵּר לֹא תִתֵּן מִכְשֹׁל״! אָמַר רַבִּי אַבָּהוּ: בְּכֹהֵן עוֹמֵד שָׁם.

The mishna teaches that Samaritans **are deemed credible to state: We buried** the stillborn children in a certain place, or to state that they did not bury the stillborn children there, and that place does not transmit ritual impurity. The Gemara objects: **But** the Samaritans **do not accept** the Sages' interpretation of the verse: **"And you shall not put a stumbling block before the blind"** (Leviticus 19:14), that one may not cause another to sin. Since they are not concerned about misleading others, why is their testimony accepted? **Rabbi Abbahu says:** The mishna is referring to a case **where** a Samaritan **priest is standing there,**[N] on that spot, which indicates that he genuinely maintains it is not impure with the impurity of a corpse.

וְדִילְמָא כֹּהֵן טָמֵא הוּא? דְּנָקִיט תְּרוּמָה בִּידֵיהּ. וְדִילְמָא תְּרוּמָה טְמֵאָה הִיא? דְּקָאָכֵיל מִינַּהּ.

The Gemara objects: **But perhaps he is an impure priest** and therefore he does not refrain from standing in an impure place. The Gemara explains: The mishna is referring to a situation **where** the priest **is holding** ***teruma*** **in his hand,** which indicates he is ritually pure. The Gemara further objects: **But perhaps it is impure** ***teruma.*** The Gemara explains: The mishna is referring to a case **where** the priest **is partaking of** the *teruma*, which indicates that it is not impure, as it is prohibited to consume impure *teruma*.

אִי הָכִי, מַאי לְמֵימְרָא? מַהוּ דְּתֵימָא: לָא בְּקִיאִי בִּיצִירָה, קָא מַשְׁמַע לָן.

The Gemara asks: **If so,** i.e., if this is the circumstance, it is obvious that the Samaritan priest's testimony can be accepted. Then **what** is the purpose **of stating** this *halakha*? The Gemara answers: The ruling of the mishna is necessary, **lest you say** that the Samaritans **are not knowledgeable with regard to** the stages of the **formation** of an embryo, and they might bury a fetus believing that it is an unformed fetus that does not transmit impurity, when it is actually a forty-day-old fetus, which is impure. Therefore, the mishna **teaches us** that they are sufficiently knowledgeable, and their testimony is accepted.

״נֶאֱמָנִין עַל הַבְּהֵמָה״ וכו׳. וְהָא לֵית לְהוּ ״וְלִפְנֵי עִוֵּר לֹא תִתֵּן מִכְשֹׁל״! אָמַר רַבִּי חִיָּיא בַּר אַבָּא, אָמַר רַבִּי יוֹחָנָן: בְּגוֹזֵז וְעוֹבֵד.

The mishna teaches that the Samaritans are **deemed credible** to state **with regard to an animal** that it previously gave birth, and its subsequent offspring does not have the sacred status of a firstborn animal. The Gemara objects: **But** the Samaritans **do not accept** the Sages' interpretation of the verse: **"And you shall not put a stumbling block before the blind,"** that one may not cause another to sin. Why, then, is their testimony accepted? **Rabbi Ḥiyya bar Abba says** that **Rabbi Yoḥanan says:** The mishna is referring to a case **where** the Samaritan **is shearing and working** the offspring of the animal. Since the Samaritans are meticulous with regard to Torah law, it is evident that it is not a firstborn.

אִי הָכִי, מַאי לְמֵימְרָא? מַהוּ דְּתֵימָא: לָא בְּקִיאִי בְּטִינּוּף, קָא מַשְׁמַע לַן.

The Gemara asks: **If so,** i.e., if this is the circumstance, **what** is the purpose **of stating** this *halakha*? The Gemara answers: The ruling of the mishna is necessary, **lest you say** that the Samaritans **are not knowledgeable with regard to a murky** discharge emitted from the uterus, which is indicative of a fetus and exempts subsequent births from the mitzva of the firstborn (see *Bekhorot* 21a). It is possible that the Samaritan mistakenly believes the animal previously emitted a murky discharge and therefore its offspring is not a firstborn. Therefore, the mishna **teaches us** that they are sufficiently knowledgeable, and their testimony is accepted.

״נֶאֱמָנִין עַל צִיּוּן״ וכו׳. וְאַף עַל גַּב דִּמְדְּרַבָּנָן הוּא, כֵּיוָן דִּכְתִיבָא – מִזְהַר זְהִירִי בֵּיהּ, דִּכְתִיב: ״וְרָאָה עֶצֶם אָדָם וּבָנָה אֶצְלוֹ צִיּוּן״.

The mishna further teaches that the Samaritans **are deemed credible** to testify **with regard to** the **marking** of graves, as the Samaritans mark their graves, and we rely on their marking as an indication that a corpse is buried there. Therefore, any place where there is no marking is considered ritually pure. The Gemara explains: **Even though** the marking of graves **is** required only **by rabbinic law,** and Samaritans generally do not observe rabbinic law, **since it is written** in the Bible, the Samaritans **are meticulous with regard to it, as it is written:** "And those that pass through shall pass through the land, **and when one sees a human bone he shall set up a marking by it,** until the buriers have buried it in the valley of Hamon-gog" (Ezekiel 39:15).

״אֲבָל אֵין נֶאֱמָנִין לֹא עַל הַסְּכָכוֹת״ וכו׳. סְכָכוֹת – דִּתְנַן: אֵלּוּ הֵן סְכָכוֹת – אִילָן הַמֵּיסֵךְ עַל הָאָרֶץ. פְּרָעוֹת – דִּתְנַן: אֲבָנִים פְּרָעוֹת הַיּוֹצְאוֹת מִן הַגָּדֵר.

The mishna teaches: **But** with regard to the following cases in which the exact location of a grave is unknown, the Samaritans **are not deemed credible** to testify: They are **not** deemed credible to testify **about overhanging boughs,** nor about the protrusions that jut out of stone fences. The Gemara explains these terms: The term **overhanging boughs** should be understood **as we learned** in a mishna (*Oholot* 8:2): **These are overhanging boughs: A tree that hangs over the ground.** The term **protrusions** should be understood **as we learned** in the *Tosefta* (*Oholot* 9:4): **Protruding stones that jut out of a fence.**

״בֵּית הַפְּרָס״ – אָמַר רַב יְהוּדָה, אָמַר רַב שְׁמוּאֵל: מְנַפֵּחַ אָדָם בֵּית הַפְּרָס וְהוֹלֵךְ.

§ The mishna teaches that the Samaritans are not deemed credible to testify about **a *beit haperas*.** With regard to a *beit haperas*, **Rav Yehuda says** that **Rav Shmuel says:** The reason the Sages deemed a *beit haperas* impure is due to the concern that the bones, but not the flesh of the corpse, were dispersed by the plow throughout the field. The *halakha* is that a bone transmits impurity by carrying or by contact, if it is at least the size of a barley grain, but it does not transmit impurity by means of a tent. Therefore, if **a person** is carrying ritually pure items, or if he wishes to remain ritually pure so that he may consume consecrated items, and yet he must pass through a *beit haperas*, he **may blow** on the earth of the ***beit haperas*** before each step, so that if there is a bone beneath the dust he will expose it and avoid it. **And** in this manner he may **walk** across the area[H] while remaining ritually pure, even though he might step over a bone.

רַב יְהוּדָה בַּר אַמֵּי מִשְּׁמֵיהּ דְּרַב יְהוּדָה אָמַר: בֵּית הַפְּרָס שֶׁנִּידַּשׁ – טָהוֹר. וְתָנָא: הַחוֹרֵשׁ בֵּית הַקְּבָרוֹת – הֲרֵי זֶה עוֹשֶׂה בֵּית הַפְּרָס. וְעַד כַּמָּה הוּא עוֹשֶׂה? מְלֹא מַעֲנָה מֵאָה אַמָּה, בֵּית אַרְבַּעַת סְאִין. רַבִּי יוֹסֵי אוֹמֵר: חָמֵשׁ.

**Rav Yehuda bar Ami says in the name of Rav Yehuda: A *beit haperas* that has been trodden** underfoot by many people **is pure,** as it may be assumed that any bone fragments at least as large as a barley grain that were on the surface were either broken or removed. **And it was taught** in a *baraita*: In the case of **one who plows a graveyard, this** individual thereby **renders** it a ***beit haperas*. And to what** extent[H] **does he render** it a *beit haperas*, i.e., how far does the concern apply that bones might have been dispersed? The field is rendered a *beit haperas* to the extent of **a full furrow** [***ma'ana***],[L] **one hundred cubits** by one hundred cubits, which is the **area** required for sowing **four *se'a*** of seed.[B] **Rabbi Yosei says:** The area rendered a *beit haperas* is the area required for sowing **five** *se'a* of seed.

## HALAKHA

A person may blow on the earth of the *beit haperas* and in this manner walk across the area – מְנַפֵּחַ אָדָם בֵּית הַפְּרָס וְהוֹלֵךְ: One who must pass through a *beit haperas* may blow on the ground before each step. If he does not find a bone the size of a grain of barley, he retains his ritual purity and slaughters and partakes of the Paschal offering. In addition, if the ground of a *beit haperas* is well trodden, those who pass through it must partake of the Paschal offering. The reason is that in the case of an obligation involving excision from the World-to-Come [*karet*], such as the bringing of the Paschal offering, the Sages were not strict with regard to the ritually impure status of a *beit haperas*, as it applies by rabbinic law. The *halakha* is in accordance with the opinion of Rav Yehuda, citing Shmuel (Rambam *Sefer Korbanot, Hilkhot Korban Pesaḥ* 6:8).

And to what extent, etc. – וְעַד כַּמָּה וכו׳: A *beit haperas* is an area where a grave was plowed over, causing its bones to be scattered over a wide area. How far does a *beit haperas* extend? One hundred cubits by one hundred cubits from the spot of the grave (Rambam *Sefer Tahara, Hilkhot Tumat Met* 10:1).

## LANGUAGE

Furrow [*ma'ana*] – מַעֲנָה: The term *ma'ana* is connected to the act of plowing in a field, although its precise meaning is a matter of dispute among the early commentaries. Some maintain it means furrow, and therefore the term: A full furrow, is the area of a furrow plowed in one act of plowing (Rashi on *Temura* 13a). Others claim it refers to the sign the one plowing marks in the ground, as an indication of the exact spot where he wants to plow in his field.

## BACKGROUND

Area for sowing four *se'a* of seed – בֵּית אַרְבַּעַת סְאִין: The *se'a* is a dry volume measure. It is one of the basic measures of volume in the Bible and the Talmud.

Areas in the Talmud are based on an estimation of how large a field must be for the sowing of a certain amount of wheat. The standard measure is a *beit se'a*, i.e., the amount of land required for a *se'a*, which is 2,500 square cubits, or fifty by fifty cubits. Accordingly, an area for sowing four *se'a* is ten thousand square cubits.

BACKGROUND

Shabbat boundary – תְּחוּם שַׁבָּת: By rabbinic decree, and some say by Torah law, one is not permitted to travel more than a certain distance from the place where he established his residence at the onset of Shabbat. That distance is known as the Shabbat boundary or limit. Even animals and inanimate objects have a limit, determined by that of the one to whose care they are entrusted, and beyond which they may not be taken. Generally, the Shabbat boundary is defined as two thousand cubits outside of one's city, in all directions.

Wine used for a libation – יֵין נֶסֶךְ: In its strict sense this term refers to wine used in the rites of idolatry. It is prohibited to drink or benefit from such wine (see Deuteronomy 32:38). The Sages extended the scope of this prohibition to include any wine touched by gentiles even if it was not used, or intended, for idolatry.

וְלָא מְהֵימְנִי? וְהָתַנְיָא: שָׂדֶה שֶׁאָבַד בָּהּ קֶבֶר – נֶאֱמָן כּוּתִי לוֹמַר "אֵין שָׁם קֶבֶר".

With regard to the ruling of the mishna that the Samaritans are not deemed credible to testify about a *beit haperas*, the Gemara asks: **And aren't they deemed credible? But isn't it taught** in a *baraita*: With regard to **a field in which a grave was lost,** which has the status of a *beit haperas,* **a Samaritan is deemed credible to say: There is no grave there?**

לְפִי שֶׁאֵינוֹ מֵעִיד אֶלָּא עַל גּוּפוֹ שֶׁל קֶבֶר. אִילָן שֶׁהוּא מֵיסֵךְ עַל הָאָרֶץ – נֶאֱמָן לוֹמַר "אֵין תַּחְתָּיו קֶבֶר", לְפִי שֶׁאֵינוֹ מֵעִיד אֶלָּא עַל גּוּפוֹ שֶׁל קֶבֶר!

The *baraita* explains: This is **due to** the fact **that he is not** considered to be **testifying** about a case of uncertain impurity; **rather,** he is testifying **about** the location of the **grave itself,** which is a matter of Torah law, and the Samaritans are deemed credible with regard to a matter of Torah law. Likewise, in the case of **a tree that is hanging over the ground,** a Samaritan **is deemed credible to say: There is no grave beneath it, as he is testifying only about** the location of the **grave itself.** This indicates that the Samaritans are deemed credible with regard to overhanging boughs and protrusions.

אָמַר רַבִּי יוֹחָנָן: בִּמְהַלֵּךְ וּבָא עַל פְּנֵי כּוּלָּהּ.

**Rabbi Yoḥanan says** in explanation: The *baraita* is referring to a case **where** the Samaritan **is walking** to **and fro over the entire** area, and therefore if there was a grave there he would certainly have become impure. Consequently, one may rely on his statement with regard to the purity of the place. By contrast, the mishna is speaking of a case where the Samaritan did not traverse the entire area, and therefore his testimony is not accepted, as they are not meticulous with regard to cases of uncertainty.

אִי הָכִי, מַאי לְמֵימְרָא? מַהוּ דְּתֵימָא: רְצוּעָה נָפְקָא, קָא מַשְׁמַע לַן.

The Gemara asks: **If so,** it is obvious that his testimony is credible, and **what** is the purpose **of stating** this *halakha*? The Gemara answers: The ruling of the *baraita* is necessary, **lest you say** that perhaps a narrow **strip** of land, which is called by the same name as this field, **extends** into a nearby field, and the Samaritan presumes the grave is located in that strip of land. If so, even if the Samaritan traversed the entire field his testimony cannot be accepted, as he traversed the field because he considered it merely a case of uncertain impurity. The *baraita* therefore **teaches us** that if the Samaritan traverses the entire field his testimony is accepted, as this concern is not an issue.

"זֶה הַכְּלָל" כו׳. "זֶה הַכְּלָל" לְאֵתוֹיֵי מַאי? לְאֵתוֹיֵי תְּחוּמִין וְיֵין נֶסֶךְ.

The mishna teaches: **This is the principle** governing the credibility of Samaritans: In the case of any matter of *halakha* that they are suspected of not fulfilling, they are not deemed credible to testify about it. The Gemara asks: **What is added** by the term: **This is the principle?** The Gemara answers: It serves **to add** that Samaritans are not deemed credible with regard to Shabbat **boundaries,**[B] i.e., to say that a Shabbat boundary extends until a certain point, as the *halakha* of Shabbat boundaries applies by rabbinic law. **And** likewise, the Samaritans are not deemed credible with regard to the status of **wine** used for **a libation**[B] in idol worship, as the Samaritans do not refrain from drinking wine touched by a gentile.

הדרן עלך דם הנדה

# Summary of **Perek VII**

Just as a woman becomes ritually impure by a discharge of blood from the uterus and consequently has the status of a primary source of ritual impurity, which means that her touch transmits impurity to people and vessels, her blood is likewise impure and transmits impurity through contact and by being carried. Not only does moist blood transmit impurity, as derived from the verse: "And of her who experiences the flow of her menstrual impurity" (Leviticus 15:33), but so does dry blood. In this regard the blood of a menstruating woman differs from the secretions of a *zav*, such as his saliva, mucus, and semen, which transmit impurity only in a moist state.

It was further established in this chapter that not only does blood transmit impurity if it was initially moist and subsequently dried, but it does so even if it was dry from the outset. This is derived from the verse: "And her issue in her flesh shall be blood" (Leviticus 15:19), which indicates that the blood is in its impure state even it was dry from the outset. Furthermore, just as a menstruating woman transmits impurity to one who carries her, rendering him impure with first-degree ritual impurity, so too, one who carries menstrual blood is rendered impure with first-degree ritual impurity.

Like the blood of a menstruating woman, the flesh of a corpse also transmits impurity. The definition of the flesh of a corpse is disputed by the Sages. Some say that any flesh dry enough to crumble is no longer categorized as dried flesh that transmits impurity. Others say that it transmits impurity even if it crumbles, provided it is not so dry that it has become like flour and is therefore classified as dust.

Apropos the discussion of the impurity of the blood of a menstruating woman and the flesh of a corpse, the chapter examined whether other sources of ritual impurity, such as the impurity of a *zav*, an animal carcass, and semen, also transmit impurity when dry. It was determined that these transmit impurity only when moist. If after being soaked in lukewarm water for a twenty-four-hour period they would return to their former state, they transmit ritual impurity even when they are dry.

It was taught in the previous chapter that by Torah law a woman is not rendered impure by blood stains found on her body or her clothing. Nevertheless, the Sages issued a decree deeming a woman who finds a blood stain on her garment ritually impure just as in the case of a woman who experienced a discharge of uterine blood. The woman is rendered impure retroactively, and any pure items she touched previously are rendered impure. As for the question of how far back in time she is rendered impure retroactively, it was established that any items she touched since she last laundered the garment are rendered impure. By contrast, those pure items that she touched before the garment was last laundered are not rendered impure, as it was evident to the Sages that a woman examines her robes thoroughly when laundering them, and therefore any blood stain present at that time would have been discovered.

The decree of the Sages with regard to blood stains applies only to the stains of Jewish women. Although the Sages decreed that gentiles have the status of *zavim* in all regards, they did not apply the status of impurity to the stains of gentile women. Therefore, bloodstained garments that come from places inhabited exclusively by gentiles are ritually pure. Even if both gentiles and Jews live in that city the stains are deemed pure, as there is a presumption with regard to Jewish women that they do not fail to put away their bloodstained garments, and therefore the stains are necessarily from gentile women.

# Introduction to **Perek VIII**

*And if a woman has an issue, and her issue in her flesh is blood, she shall be in her menstruation seven days, and whoever touches her shall be impure until the evening.*

(Leviticus 15:19)

As explained in the introduction to Chapter Six, it is derived from the verse "And if a woman has an issue, and her issue in her flesh is blood" that a woman is rendered ritually impure only by an actual sighting of blood from her source, i.e., from the uterus, and not by a stain on her body or clothing. The phrase "and her issue in her flesh" teaches that in order to render a woman impure, the emission must be accompanied by a sensation in her body, which does not occur when she simply finds a stain and did not feel anything.

Due to various concerns, however, the Sages decreed impurity with regard to stains as well, and therefore the status of different kinds of stains must be determined. To what extent did the Sages impose this decree? In what circumstances may a stain be attributed to a source other than the woman's body? For example, if she had passed through a place where blood is frequently sprayed, e.g., a butchers' marketplace, it can be claimed that the stain should be attributed to that source. Likewise, if she had a wound, may she presume that the blood is from that part of her body and therefore it does not render her impure?

An additional factor that must be taken into account is the location of the stain on the woman's body. Is every blood stain assumed to come from her uterus, or are there cases where she can conclude that blood from her uterus could not possibly have left a stain on that part of her body or in that location on her garment? Furthermore, does this decree apply to stains of all sizes, even those smaller than a bean, or does it apply only to larger stains?

Likewise, is there any difference in the *halakha* with regard to the item on which the stain was found, or did the Sages decree that all stains that might have come from a woman's body render her impure regardless of the surface upon which they are discovered? In general, were the Sages stringent with regard to this decree of the ritual impurity of stains, or were they typically lenient in the many cases of uncertainty that arise?

These are the main topics dealt with in this chapter.

מתני׳ הָרוֹאָה כֶּתֶם עַל בְּשָׂרָהּ, כְּנֶגֶד בֵּית הַתּוּרְפָּה – מְטַמְּאָה, וְשֶׁלֹּא כְּנֶגֶד בֵּית הַתּוּרְפָּה – טְהוֹרָה. עַל עֲקֵבָהּ וְעַל רֹאשׁ גּוּדָלָהּ – טְמֵאָה.

**MISHNA** A woman **who sees** a blood **stain on her flesh**[H] **adjacent to** her **vagina** [***beit haturpa***],[L] i.e., a place where blood that originated in her vagina could be found, **becomes ritually impure,**[N] as there is a concern that it originated in the uterus and is menstrual blood. **And** if it was discovered on her flesh in an area **not adjacent to** her **vagina** she remains **ritually pure,** as it certainly did not originate in the uterus. If the stain was discovered **on her heel or on the tip of her large toe,** although it is not adjacent to her vagina she is **ritually impure,** as blood from the uterus could have reached there.

עַל שׁוֹקָהּ וְעַל פַּרְסוֹתֶיהָ, מִבִּפְנִים – טְמֵאָה, מִבַּחוּץ – טְהוֹרָה, וְעַל הַצְּדָדִין מִכָּאן וּמִכָּאן – טְהוֹרָה.

In a case where the stain was discovered **on her leg or on her feet,** if it was **on the inner** side she is **ritually impure,** as blood from the uterus could have reached there. If it was **on the outer** side she is **ritually pure, and** if it was **on the sides,** either **from here,** i.e., on the front of her leg or foot, **or from there,** i.e., on the back of her leg or foot, she is also **ritually pure,** as blood from the uterus could not have reached there.

רָאֲתָה עַל חֲלוּקָהּ, מִן הַחֲגוֹר וּלְמַטָּה – טְמֵאָה, מִן הַחֲגוֹר וּלְמַעְלָה – טְהוֹרָה. רָאֲתָה עַל בֵּית יָד שֶׁל חָלוּק, אִם מַגִּיעַ כְּנֶגֶד בֵּית הַתּוּרְפָּה – טְמֵאָה, וְאִם לָאו – טְהוֹרָה.

In a case where the woman **saw** a blood stain **on her robe,**[H] if it was **from the belt and below** she is **ritually impure,** as blood from the uterus could have reached there; if it was **from the belt and above** she is **ritually pure.** In a case where **she saw** the stain **on the** end of the **sleeve of the robe,**[H] **if** the sleeve can **reach adjacent to** her **vagina** she is **ritually impure; and if not,** i.e., if the stain is in a place on the sleeve that does not reach adjacent to the vagina, she is **ritually pure.**

הָיְתָה פּוֹשַׁטְתּוֹ וּמִתְכַּסָּה בּוֹ בַּלַּיְלָה, כָּל מָקוֹם שֶׁנִּמְצָא בּוֹ כֶּתֶם – טְמֵאָה, מִפְּנֵי שֶׁהוּא חוֹזֵר. וְכֵן בַּפּוֹלְיוֹס.

If it was a robe which **she would remove and with which she would cover** herself **at night, wherever** on the robe **that the stain is found,** the stain renders her **ritually impure, due to** the fact **that** the robe **moves** while the woman is asleep and therefore the blood could have originated in the uterus. **And likewise with regard to a kerchief** [***bapoleyos***],[L] no matter where the blood is found on the kerchief, the woman is impure.

### HALAKHA

**A woman who sees a blood stain on her flesh – הָרוֹאָה כֶּתֶם עַל בְּשָׂרָהּ:** A woman is not rendered ritually impure by a blood stain found anywhere on her body, but only if it is found in those areas where it might have come from her uterus. How so? If it was discovered on her heel she is impure, and the same applies if it was found anywhere on the inner parts of her leg or foot, which are the parts that press together when she stands with her feet together. Likewise, she is impure if it was discovered on the tip of her large toe, and the Rema adds that she is certainly impure if it was on the top of her foot itself. But if it was found on the outside of her leg or foot she is pure (Rambam *Sefer Kedusha, Hilkhot Issurei Bia* 9:8; *Shulḥan Arukh, Yoreh De'a* 190:11).

**The woman saw a blood stain on her robe – רָאֲתָה עַל חֲלוּקָהּ:** If a stain was found on a woman's robe from the belt and below, or on the belt itself, she is ritually impure, even if it was on the outer side of the garment. The Rema adds that there is no difference whether it was discovered on the part of the robe worn on the front, back, or side, as these garments will typically sway from one side of the body to the other with her movements (Rambam *Sefer Kedusha, Hilkhot Issurei Bia* 9:10; *Shulḥan Arukh, Yoreh De'a* 190:12).

**She saw the stain on the end of the sleeve of the robe – רָאֲתָה עַל בֵּית יָד שֶׁל חָלוּק:** With regard to a stain that was found on the sleeve of a robe, if that portion of the sleeve can reach adjacent to her vagina she is ritually impure, even if it reaches there only if she extends herself. If it cannot reach adjacent to her vagina she is ritually pure (Rambam *Sefer Kedusha, Hilkhot Issurei Bia* 9:10; *Shulḥan Arukh, Yoreh De'a* 190:13).

### LANGUAGE

**Vagina [*beit haturpa*] – בֵּית הַתּוּרְפָּה:** The term in this context is clearly a euphemism for the vagina. There are various suggestions as to why the word *turpa* bears this meaning. Some maintain that it means degradation, as this, more than anywhere else on her body, is the area of which a woman is ashamed in the presence of others. Some associate it with the word *toref*, which means the essence of a matter, e.g., *toref* is the name given to the essential part of a document. Likewise, this place can be considered the essence of womanhood. Alternatively, the word *turpa* stems from the word weakness [*rifayon*], and therefore the term used for vagina, *beit haturpa*, would refer to the most sensitive and vulnerable part of a woman's body.

**Kerchief [*poleyos*] – פּוֹלְיוֹס:** *Poleyos*, or *poleyon* or *poleyom*, is from the Greek φελώνης, *palinis*, which may come from the Latin pallium, meaning a cloak or upper garment. It is a kind of kerchief used for covering the head, somewhat similar to a hood. This garment was considered one of the basic items of a woman's clothing. In certain situations this cloth had a different function, as in a barber's shop, where it was placed over the customer's knees. In this case it was called the barber's wrap (see *Shabbat* 9b).

### NOTES

**A woman who sees a blood stain on her flesh adjacent to her vagina becomes ritually impure – הָרוֹאָה כֶּתֶם עַל בְּשָׂרָהּ כְּנֶגֶד בֵּית הַתּוּרְפָּה מְטַמְּאָה:** The early commentaries discuss the reason for the decree of the Sages that stains are ritually impure. Some suggest it is a decree due to uncertainty, in case the blood of the stain came from the uterus (Rambam *Sefer Kedusha, Hilkhot Issurei Bia* 9:2). This interpretation is problematic, as there is actually a compound uncertainty here: Perhaps the blood did not come from the woman's body at all, and even if it did come from her body, it is possible that it is from the vaginal canal and she would be pure. If so, she should not be rendered ritually impure, as the *halakha* is generally lenient in cases involving compound uncertainties.

Some explain that the Sages instituted a decree in this case despite the existence of a compound uncertainty due to the severity of the impurity of a menstruating woman. Others maintain that as the blood of a woman generally comes from the uterus, the possibility that it might come from the vaginal canal is disregarded (*Taz*; *Tosafot* on 62a).

## NOTES

**If a woman examined the ground and sat upon it and found blood on it she is ritually pure – בָּדְקָה קַרְקַע עוֹלָם וְיָשְׁבָה עָלֶיהָ וּמָצְאָה דָּם עָלֶיהָ טְהוֹרָה:** The commentaries note that Shmuel's statement indicates she is entirely pure, not only by Torah law but by rabbinic law as well. This conclusion can likewise be inferred from the initial stages of the Gemara's discussion of his opinion. If so, the reason Shmuel cites a verse in support of his opinion, which might be taken as an indication that his ruling applies by Torah law alone, is to illustrate that since she is pure by Torah law, the Sages did not see fit to deem her impure. But according to the conclusion of Rav Yirmeya later on, Shmuel does concede that she is impure by rabbinic law (Rashba).

גמ׳ אָמַר שְׁמוּאֵל: בָּדְקָה קַרְקַע עוֹלָם וְיָשְׁבָה עָלֶיהָ, וּמָצְאָה דָּם עָלֶיהָ – טְהוֹרָה, שֶׁנֶּאֱמַר ״בִּבְשָׂרָהּ״ – עַד שֶׁתַּרְגִּישׁ בִּבְשָׂרָהּ.

**GEMARA** With regard to the cases discussed in the mishna concerning a blood stain found on a woman, **Shmuel says:** If a woman **examined the ground** beneath her to see if it was clean from blood and other substances, and she found nothing, **and** subsequently she **sat upon it and** then **found blood on it,** although it might be assumed that this blood came from her, **she is ritually pure.**[NH] The reason is **as it is stated:** "And her issue **in her flesh** shall be blood, she shall be in her menstrual state seven days" (Leviticus 15:19). This verse teaches that a woman does not become impure **unless she senses,** i.e., experiences some type of sensation, **in her flesh** that she emitted blood from her uterus. Since this woman did not sense an emission of blood, she is pure.

הַאי ״בִּבְשָׂרָהּ״ – מִיבָּעֵי לֵיהּ שֶׁמְּטַמְּאָה בִּפְנִים כְּבַחוּץ! אִם כֵּן, לֵימָא קְרָא ״בְּבָשָׂר״, מַאי ״בִּבְשָׂרָהּ״ – שְׁמַע מִינָּהּ: עַד שֶׁתַּרְגִּישׁ בִּבְשָׂרָהּ.

The Gemara asks: How can Shmuel interpret the verse in this manner? After all, **he requires this** term: **"In her flesh,"** to teach a different *halakha,* **that** a woman **becomes impure** by finding blood **inside** her body **just as** by seeing blood **outside** her body, i.e., provided that the blood is uterine blood, even if it is currently situated inside her vaginal canal, she is impure. The Gemara answers: **If so,** if it serves to teach only that blood inside is like blood outside, **let the verse say: In the flesh. What** is the reason that the verse states: **"In her flesh"? Conclude from** this term that a woman does not become impure **unless she senses in her flesh.**

וְאַכַּתִּי מִיבָּעֵי לֵיהּ: ״בִּבְשָׂרָהּ״ – וְלֹא בְּשָׁפִיר, וְלֹא בַּחֲתִיכָה! תַּרְתֵּי שְׁמַע מִינָּהּ.

The Gemara asks: **And still,** Shmuel **requires** the term **"in her flesh"** to teach that she is impure only if the blood touches her flesh, **and not** through blood found **in a gestational sac, nor** through blood found **in** an amorphous **piece** of tissue that she emitted. The Gemara answers: **Conclude two** conclusions **from** this verse, as the plain meaning of the term teaches all these *halakhot.*

תָּא שְׁמַע, הָאִשָּׁה שֶׁהִיא עוֹשָׂה צְרָכֶיהָ וְרָאֲתָה דָּם, רַבִּי מֵאִיר אוֹמֵר: אִם עוֹמֶדֶת – טְמֵאָה, וְאִם יוֹשֶׁבֶת – טְהוֹרָה.

With regard to the opinion of Shmuel, the Gemara suggests: **Come** and **hear** a mishna at the beginning of the next chapter (59b): In the case of **a woman who is urinating and sees blood**[H] intermingled with the urine, **Rabbi Meir says: If** she urinates while **she is standing** she is **ritually impure,** as the blood could have originated in the uterus. **And if she is sitting** she is **ritually pure,** as it is clear that the blood is from a wound.

הֵיכִי דָּמֵי? אִי דְּאַרְגְּשָׁה – יוֹשֶׁבֶת אַמַּאי טְהוֹרָה? אֶלָּא לָאו – דְּלָא אַרְגְּשָׁה, וְקָתָנֵי: עוֹמֶדֶת – טְמֵאָה!

The Gemara analyzes this mishna: **What are the circumstances? If she sensed** while urinating, then in the case where **she is sitting, why is she ritually pure,** according to Shmuel? **Rather, is it not** referring to a case **where she did not sense** while urinating? **And** yet the mishna **teaches** that if she urinates while **she is standing** she is **ritually impure.** This indicates that her status does not depend on her sensing, which contradicts the statement of Shmuel.

לְעוֹלָם – דְּאַרְגְּשָׁה, וְאֵימוּר: הַרְגָּשַׁת מֵי רַגְלַיִם הֲוַאי. עוֹמֶדֶת – הֲדוּר מֵי רַגְלַיִם לַמָּקוֹר, וְאַיְיתֵי דָּם, וְיוֹשֶׁבֶת טְהוֹרָה.

The Gemara answers: This affords no proof, as the mishna is **actually** referring to a case **where she sensed** while urinating, **and** yet since this feeling accompanied urination, one might **say** it **was the sensation of urine.** Consequently, if she urinated while **standing,** the **urine would return to** her **uterus and bring blood** with it. **But** if she urinated while **sitting** the urine cannot return to the uterus and therefore she is **pure,** as the sensation is attributed to her urine.

## HALAKHA

**If a woman examined the ground and sat upon it and found blood on it she is ritually pure – בָּדְקָה קַרְקַע עוֹלָם וְיָשְׁבָה עָלֶיהָ וּמָצְאָה דָּם עָלֶיהָ טְהוֹרָה:** The Sages did not decree impurity on a stain found on an item that is not susceptible to ritual impurity. Therefore, if a woman examined the ground beneath her, or a toilet that is not susceptible to ritual impurity (Rema), or any similar item, and she sat on it and subsequently found a stain, she is pure. This *halakha* is in accordance with the opinion of Shmuel (Rambam *Sefer Kedusha, Hilkhot Issurei Bia* 9:7; *Shulḥan Arukh, Yoreh De'a* 190:10).

**A woman who is urinating and sees blood – הָאִשָּׁה שֶׁהִיא עוֹשָׂה צְרָכֶיהָ וְרָאֲתָה דָּם:** If a woman sees blood in her urine, whether she urinated while standing or while sitting, she remains ritually pure. Even if she feels her body trembling she does not need to be concerned, as this is simply the sensation of the urine leaving the bladder, whereas the blood must be from a wound of some sort. The Rema writes that some say she is ritually pure only if she was sitting while urinating (*Tur,* citing Rosh). Likewise, if she was standing and urinating in a steady stream, and she found blood in the basin into which she urinated, she remains pure. But if the urine was found on the edge of a basin she is impure.

Others claim that even when she is sitting, she is pure only if she urinates in a steady stream into a basin; while if she finds blood on the edge of the basin she is impure. Furthermore, if she was standing while urinating and found blood, she is impure in any event (Mordekhai; *Haggahot Maimoniyyot*). The Rema writes that the custom in practice is to follow this opinion (Rambam *Sefer Kedusha, Hilkhot Issurei Bia* 5:17; *Shulḥan Arukh, Yoreh De'a* 191:1).

תָּא שְׁמַע: עַד שֶׁהָיָה נָתוּן תַּחַת הַכַּר וְנִמְצָא עָלָיו דָּם, אִם עָגוֹל – טָהוֹר, וְאִם מָשׁוּךְ – טָמֵא.

The Gemara further suggests: **Come** and **hear** the mishna below (58b): With regard to **an examination cloth that was placed beneath the pillow and blood was** later **found on** the cloth,[H] and it is unclear whether it is the blood of an examination or the blood of a louse that was crushed beneath it, **if** the stain is **round** it is **ritually pure.** There is no concern that this blood might have come from her examination, as a woman examines through an act of wiping and a stain produced in this manner would not be round. **And if** the stain is **elongated** it is **ritually impure,** as this shape can be formed by an examination.

הֵיכִי דָּמֵי? אִי דְּאַרְגִּישָׁה – עָגוֹל אַמַּאי טָהוֹר? אֶלָּא לָאו – דְּלָא אַרְגִּישָׁה, וְקָתָנֵי: מָשׁוּךְ – טָמֵא!

The Gemara analyzes the mishna: **What are the circumstances? If she sensed,** then in the case where the stain is **round why** is it **pure? Rather, is it not** referring to a case **where she did not sense? And** yet the mishna **teaches** that **an elongated** stain is **impure.** This contradicts the opinion of Shmuel that a woman is rendered impure only if she sensed.

לָא, לְעוֹלָם – דְּאַרְגִּישָׁה, וְאֵימוּר: הַרְגָּשַׁת עֵד הֲוַאי, מָשׁוּךְ – וַדַּאי מִגּוּפָהּ אֲתָא, עָגוֹל – טָהוֹר.

The Gemara answers: **No,** the mishna is **actually** referring to a case **where she sensed, but** since she also performed an examination one might **say** this **was the sensation of the examination cloth.** Consequently, if the stain was **elongated,** as appropriate for a stain produced by an examination, the blood **certainly came from her body,** whereas if the stain was **round** it is **pure,** as this is not the usual appearance of a stain from an examination.

תָּא שְׁמַע: נִמְצָא עַל שֶׁלּוֹ – טְמֵאִין וְחַיָּיבִין בְּקׇרְבָּן, נִמְצָא עַל שֶׁלָּהּ אוֹתְיוֹם – טְמֵאִין, וְחַיָּיבִין בְּקׇרְבָּן. נִמְצָא עַל שֶׁלָּהּ לְאַחַר זְמַן – טְמֵאִים מִסָּפֵק, וּפְטוּרִין מִן הַקׇּרְבָּן.

The Gemara suggests: **Come** and **hear** another mishna (14a): If blood **was found on his,** i.e., the husband's, examination cloth following intercourse, the woman and her husband are both **ritually impure** for seven days, in accordance with the *halakha* of a menstruating woman and one who engages in intercourse with her, **and they are** each **liable to** bring a sin **offering** for unwittingly performing an action punishable with excision from the World-to-Come [*karet*]. If blood **was found on her** cloth **immediately** after intercourse, the woman and her husband are likewise **ritually impure** for seven days **and are** each **liable to** bring a sin **offering.** If blood **was found on her** swatch **after time** passed, they are both **ritually impure due to uncertainty,** as it is possible that the blood appeared only after intercourse, **and they are exempt from** bringing **the** sin **offering.**

הֵיכִי דָּמֵי? אִי דְּאַרְגִּישָׁה – לְאַחַר זְמַן אַמַּאי פְּטוּרִין מִן הַקׇּרְבָּן? אֶלָּא לָאו – דְּלָא אַרְגִּישָׁה, וְקָתָנֵי: נִמְצָא עַל שֶׁלָּהּ אוֹתְיוֹם – טְמֵאִין, וְחַיָּיבִין בְּקׇרְבָּן! לָא, לְעוֹלָם – דְּאַרְגִּישָׁה, וְאֵימָא: הַרְגָּשַׁת שַׁמָּשׁ הֲוָה.

The Gemara analyzes this mishna: **What are the circumstances? If** it is referring to a situation **where she sensed,** then in the case where blood was found on her cloth **after time** passed, **why are they exempt from** bringing **the** sin **offering? Rather, is it not** referring to a case **where she did not sense? And** yet the mishna **teaches** that if blood **was found on her** cloth **immediately** after intercourse, they are **ritually impure** for seven days **and are** each **liable to** bring a sin **offering.** Once again, this contradicts the opinion of Shmuel. The Gemara answers: **No,** the mishna is **actually** referring to a case **where she sensed, but** since she was engaging in intercourse at the time, one might **say** this **was the sensation** of the male **organ.**

**HALAKHA**

**An examination cloth that was placed beneath the pillow and blood was later found on it – עַד שֶׁהָיָה נָתוּן תַּחַת הַכַּר וְנִמְצָא עָלָיו דָּם:** In a case where a woman examined herself with her cloth and placed it under a pillow, and on the following day blood was found on it, if the stain is elongated it is impure, as it is presumed to have come from her examination. If it is round and no larger than the size of a bean she is pure, as it is assumed to be the blood of a louse that was killed beneath the pillow. This ruling is in accordance with the mishna. Some authorities rule that the same applies even if blood was found on the cloth immediately (*Pitḥei Teshuva*, citing *Meir Netivim*).

In addition, the Beit Yosef and Rema maintain that in a case where the stain is round but is larger than a bean, if she can attribute it to an external source she is pure (Rambam *Sefer Kedusha*, *Hilkhot Issurei Bia* 4:18; *Shulḥan Arukh*, *Yoreh De'a* 190:34).

תָּא שְׁמַע: נִמְצֵאתָ אַתָּה אוֹמֵר, שְׁלֹשָׁה סְפֵקוֹת בָּאִשָּׁה: עַל בְּשָׂרָהּ, סָפֵק טָמֵא סָפֵק טָהוֹר – טָמֵא; עַל חֲלוּקָהּ, סָפֵק טָמֵא סָפֵק טָהוֹר – טָהוֹר; וּבְמַגָּעוֹת וּבְהֶיסֵּטוֹת – הַלֵּךְ אַחַר הָרוֹב.

The Gemara suggests: **Come and hear** from a *baraita*: **You are found to say** that there are **three uncertainties** involving cases where blood is found **on a woman** or her garments. If a stain is discovered **on her flesh** and there is **uncertainty whether it is impure or pure,** the *halakha* is that it is **impure.** If it is found **on her robe** and there is **uncertainty whether it is impure or pure,** the *halakha* is that it is **pure. And** in the case of a woman whose status as a menstruating woman is uncertain, **with regard to** her **touching** items **and with regard to** her **moving** items, one should **follow the majority.**

מַאי ״הַלֵּךְ אַחַר הָרוֹב״? לָאו אִם רוֹב יָמֶיהָ טְמֵאִין – טְמֵאָה, וְאַף עַל גַּב דְּלָא אַרְגְּשָׁה!

The Gemara analyzes the *baraita*: **What** is the meaning of the phrase: **Follow the majority,** with regard to this woman of uncertain status? Does this **not** mean that **if** for **the majority of her days** she is in a state of **ritual impurity,** as she emits impure blood on many days, then **she is** considered **impure** even when her status is uncertain? **And** since this *baraita* does not differentiate between cases where she did and did not sense, the ruling that one follows the majority, and that she is impure, evidently applies **even though she did not sense,** which contradicts the opinion of Shmuel.

לָא, אִם רוֹב יָמֶיהָ בְּהַרְגָּשָׁה חָזְיָא – טְמֵאָה, דְּאֵימוּר: אַרְגְּשָׁה וְלָאו אַדַּעְתָּהּ.

The Gemara answers: **No** proof may be brought from here, as this is what the *baraita* means: **If** on **the majority of her days** this woman **sees** blood accompanied **by a sensation, she is impure,** despite the fact that she is uncertain whether she had a sensation, **as** one can **say she sensed** on this occasion as well, **but** it was **not on her mind,** i.e., she did not pay attention to it at the time.

אָמַר מָר: עַל בְּשָׂרָהּ, סָפֵק טָמֵא סָפֵק טָהוֹר – טָמֵא; עַל חֲלוּקָהּ, סָפֵק טָמֵא סָפֵק טָהוֹר – טָהוֹר.

Before returning to the opinion of Shmuel, the Gemara analyzes the other clauses of this *baraita*. **The Master said** above: If a stain is discovered **on her flesh** and there is **uncertainty whether it is impure or pure,** it is **impure;** if it is found **on her robe**[H] and there is **uncertainty whether it is impure or pure,** it is **pure.** The juxtaposition of these two cases indicates that the blood is found in the same area in both instances.

הֵיכִי דָּמֵי? אִי מֵחֲגוֹר וּלְמַטָּה – עַל חֲלוּקָהּ אַמַּאי טָהוֹר? וְהָא תְּנַן: מִן הַחֲגוֹר וּלְמַטָּה – טָמֵא! וְאִי מֵחֲגוֹר וּלְמַעְלָה – עַל בְּשָׂרָהּ אַמַּאי טָמֵא? וְהָתְנַן: רָאֲתָה דָּם עַל בְּשָׂרָהּ שֶׁלֹּא כְּנֶגֶד בֵּית הַתּוּרְפָּה – טְהוֹרָה!

The Gemara asks: **What are the circumstances? If** the blood was discovered **from the belt and below,** then when it was found **on her robe why is she pure? But didn't we learn** in the mishna: In a case where the woman saw a blood stain on her robe, if it was **from the belt and below** she is **ritually impure? And if** the blood was **from the belt and above,** then if it was discovered **on her flesh why is she impure? But didn't we learn** in the mishna that if **she saw blood on her flesh** in an area **not adjacent to** her **vagina** she remains **ritually pure?**

אִיבָּעֵית אֵימָא: מֵחֲגוֹר וּלְמַטָּה, וְאִיבָּעֵית אֵימָא: מֵחֲגוֹר וּלְמַעְלָה. אִי בָּעֵית אֵימָא: מֵחֲגוֹר וּלְמַטָּה – כְּגוֹן שֶׁעָבְרָה בְּשׁוּק שֶׁל טַבָּחִים, עַל בְּשָׂרָהּ – מִגּוּפָהּ אֲתַאי, דְּאִי מֵעָלְמָא אֲתַאי – עַל חֲלוּקָהּ מִיבָּעֵי לֵיהּ אִשְׁתַּכּוּחֵי. עַל חֲלוּקָהּ – מֵעָלְמָא אֲתָא, דְּאִי מִגּוּפָהּ אֲתָא – עַל בְּשָׂרָהּ מִיבָּעֵי לֵיהּ אִשְׁתַּכּוּחֵי.

The Gemara answers: **If you wish, say** that the blood was discovered **from the belt and below, and if you wish, say** instead that it was found **from the belt and above.** The Gemara elaborates: **If you wish, say** that the blood was found **from the belt and below,** as the *baraita* is referring to a situation where the blood can be attributed to an external factor, **e.g.,** a case **where she passed through a marketplace of butchers** [*tabbaḥim*].[HL] Consequently, if the blood is found **on her flesh** it is assumed that **it came from her body, as, if it came from the** outside **world, it should have been found on her robe** as well. If it is discovered **on her robe** it is assumed that **it came from the** outside **world,** as, **if it came from her body, it should have been found on her flesh** as well.

**HALAKHA**

On her flesh…on her robe – עַל בְּשָׂרָהּ...עַל חֲלוּקָהּ: With regard to all stains about which the Sages stated that they render a woman ritually impure, in a case where a woman can attribute the stain to some external factor the following distinction applies: If the stain is discovered on a garment she is pure, as the Sages were lenient with regard to stains on a garment. If the stain was found on her body she is impure and she may not attribute it to an outside source, as in such a case the blood would have been present on her garments as well. But if there is a reasonable explanation as to why there should be blood on her body even when it is not found on her clothes, e.g., she had a wound that could reopen and bleed, she may attribute the blood to that source and she is pure (Rambam *Sefer Kedusha, Hilkhot Issurei Bia* 9:19, 22; see *Beit Yosef* on *Tur* 190:11).

Where she passed through a marketplace of butchers – שֶׁעָבְרָה בְּשׁוּק שֶׁל טַבָּחִים: If a woman passed through a marketplace of butchers or was handling items that cause stains and a blood stain was found on her robe, she may attribute it to that external source, regardless of where on the robe it was found. In a case where the stain was found on her flesh alone, then if it is from her belt and below she is impure. If she had jumped, then even if the stain is from her belt and above she is impure. The reason is that if this blood was from the external source it should have been present on her clothes as well (Rambam *Sefer Kedusha, Hilkhot Issurei Bia* 9:19–21, and see *Kesef Mishne* there; *Shulḥan Arukh, Yoreh De'a* 190:11–12).

**LANGUAGE**

Butchers [*tabbaḥim*] – טַבָּחִים: In the Bible and talmudic literature the term *tabbaḥ* refers to a slaughterer and butcher, i.e., one who slaughters the animal and then cuts it into pieces. Likewise, the word in modern Hebrew for kitchen, *mitbaḥ*, indicates that it is the place where meat is found. Naturally, in a marketplace of butchers there is a lot of blood, and it would not be unusual for blood to be sprayed on a passerby.

וְאִיבָּעֵית אֵימָא: מֵחֲגוֹר וּלְמַעְלָה – כְּגוֹן דְּאִיזְדַּקְרָה. עַל בְּשָׂרָהּ – וַדַּאי מִגּוּפָהּ אֲתַאי, דְּאִי מֵעָלְמָא אֲתַאי – עַל חֲלוּקָהּ אִיבָּעֵי לֵיהּ אִשְׁתַּכּוּחֵי, עַל חֲלוּקָהּ – מֵעָלְמָא אֲתַאי, דְּאִי מִגּוּפָהּ אֲתַאי – עַל בְּשָׂרָהּ אִיבָּעֵי לֵיהּ אִשְׁתַּכּוּחֵי.

**And if you wish, say** instead that the blood was found **from the belt and above,** and the *baraita* is referring to a situation where it is possible the blood came from her body, **e.g.,** a case **where she jumped** backward. Therefore, if the blood is found **on her flesh it certainly came from her body, as, if it came from the** outside **world, it should have been found on her robe** as well. And if it is discovered **on her robe** the assumption is that **it came from** the outside **world, as, if it came from her body, it should have been found on her flesh** as well.

קָתָנֵי מִיהַת "עַל בְּשָׂרָהּ סָפֵק טָמֵא סָפֵק טָהוֹר – טָמֵא", וְאַף עַל גַּב דְּלָא הִרְגִּישָׁה! וְעוֹד, תְּנַן: הָרוֹאָה כֶּתֶם עַל בְּשָׂרָהּ כְּנֶגֶד בֵּית הַתּוּרְפָּה – טְמֵאָה, וְאַף עַל גַּב דְּלָא הִרְגִּישָׁה! אָמַר רַב יִרְמְיָה מִדִּפְתִּי: מוֹדֶה שְׁמוּאֵל שֶׁהִיא טְמֵאָה

The Gemara raises an objection from the *baraita* to the opinion of Shmuel: **In any event,** the *baraita* **teaches** that if a stain is discovered **on her flesh** and there is **uncertainty whether it is impure or pure,** it is **impure, and** this is the *halakha* **even though she did not sense,** which contradicts the opinion of Shmuel. **And furthermore, we learned** in the mishna that a woman **who sees** a blood **stain on her flesh adjacent to** her **vagina becomes ritually impure, and** this is apparently the *halakha* **even though she did not sense. Rav Yirmeya of Difti says:** The ruling of Shmuel that a woman must sense in order to be rendered impure applies only by Torah law. But **Shmuel concedes that** in all the cases cited above, where it is indicated that a woman is impure despite the fact that she did not sense, **she is impure**

Perek **VIII**
Daf **58** Amud **a**

מִדְּרַבָּנַן.

**by rabbinic law.** Accordingly, Shmuel agrees that if she examined the ground, found it clean, sat upon it, and later found blood, even if she did not sense that she emitted blood she is impure by rabbinic law.

רַב אַשִׁי אָמַר: שְׁמוּאֵל הוּא דְּאָמַר כְּרַבִּי נְחֶמְיָה. דִּתְנַן, רַבִּי נְחֶמְיָה אוֹמֵר: כָּל דָּבָר שֶׁאֵינוֹ מְקַבֵּל טוּמְאָה – אֵינוֹ מְקַבֵּל כְּתָמִים.

**Rav Ashi said: Shmuel said** this woman is pure even by rabbinic law, **in accordance with** the opinion of **Rabbi Neḥemya,**[N] **as we learned** in a mishna (59b) that **Rabbi Neḥemya says: Any item that is not susceptible to ritual impurity,** e.g., the ground, **is not susceptible to** ritual impurity due to blood **stains.** This is because the decree of impurity of blood stains was limited to items susceptible to ritual impurity. According to Rav Ashi, all the sources cited above that indicate she is impure even if she did not sense an emission are referring to cases where the stain was found on an item that is susceptible to ritual impurity.

בִּשְׁלָמָא לְרַב אַשִׁי – הַיְינוּ דְּקָאָמַר קַרְקַע, אֶלָּא לְרַב יִרְמְיָה – מַאי אִירְיָא קַרְקַע? אֲפִילּוּ גְּלִימָא נָמֵי! לָא מִיבַּעְיָא קָאָמַר,

The Gemara asks: **Granted, according to** the opinion of **Rav Ashi** with regard to Shmuel's opinion, **that is** why Shmuel **says** the woman examined **the ground** beneath her, as the ground is not susceptible to ritual impurity. **But according to** the opinion of **Rav Yirmeya, why** does Shmuel refer **specifically** to **the ground?** The same *halakha* should apply **even** if she sat on **a cloak** and did not sense an emission of blood. The Gemara answers that Shmuel **is speaking** utilizing the style of: **It is not necessary.**

לָא מִיבַּעְיָא גְּלִימָא – דְּלָא מִבְדַּק שַׁפִּיר, וְאִיכָּא לְמֵימַר מֵעָלְמָא אֲתָא, אֶלָּא אֲפִילּוּ קַרְקַע דְּמִבְדַּק שַׁפִּיר, דְּאִיכָּא לְמֵימַר מִגּוּפָהּ אֲתְיָא – טָהוֹר.

The Gemara elaborates: **It is not necessary** to state that if a woman examined **a cloak,** found it pure, sat upon it, and then saw a blood stain on it, she is pure. The reason is **that** it is **not** easy to **examine** a cloak **well,** due to its creases, **and** therefore **there is** room **to say** the stain on the cloak **came from the** outside **world,** i.e., from some external factor. **Rather, even** in the case of the **ground, which** one can **examine well** and therefore **there is** room **to say** the stain on the ground must have **come from her body** when she sat upon it, Shmuel teaches that the blood is nevertheless **ritually pure.**

NOTES

**Rav Ashi said, Shmuel said in accordance with the opinion of Rabbi Neḥemya** – **רַב אַשִׁי אָמַר שְׁמוּאֵל הוּא דְּאָמַר כְּרַבִּי נְחֶמְיָה:** The commentaries explain that according to Rav Ashi, Shmuel maintains that a woman who experiences bleeding without an accompanying sensation is entirely pure, both by Torah law and by rabbinic law. Furthermore, since Shmuel said his statement in accordance with the opinion of Rabbi Neḥemya, the *halakha* should follow his ruling (Rashba). The Ran writes that this is the ruling of the Ra'avad, although, as noted by the *Arukh LaNer*, he is probably referring to the Rambam (*Sefer Kedusha*, *Hilkhot Issurei Bia* 9:7), as the Ra'avad holds that the *halakha* is not in accordance with the opinion of Rabbi Neḥemya. The *Shulḥan Arukh* rules in accordance with Rav Ashi's explanation that the Sages did not apply their decree to items that are not susceptible to ritual impurity (*Yoreh De'a* 190:10).

LANGUAGE

Place of the joint [*mekom ḥavak*] – מְקוֹם חֲבָק: In general this expression refers to a location where tendons cause two limbs of the body to embrace [*leḥabek*], or join, one another. In this particular instance, the Gemara is referring to the ligaments next to the knee that join the thigh and the shin.

״עַל עֲקֵבָהּ וְעַל רֹאשׁ גּוּדָלָהּ טְמֵאָה״ וכו׳. בִּשְׁלָמָא עֲקֵבָהּ – עָבֵיד דְּנָגַע בְּאוֹתוֹ מָקוֹם, אֶלָּא רֹאשׁ גּוּדָלָהּ, מַאי טַעְמָא? וְכִי תֵּימָא: זִימְנִין דְּנָגַע בַּעֲקֵבָהּ, וּמִי מַחְזְקִינַן טוּמְאָה מִמָּקוֹם לְמָקוֹם?

§ The mishna teaches: If a stain was discovered on her heel or on the tip of her large **toe,** although it is not adjacent to her vagina **she is ritually impure,** as blood from the uterus could have reached there. The Gemara comments: **Granted,** when blood is found on **her heel** she is impure, as **it is wont to touch that place,** her vagina, when she kneels. **But** if the blood is discovered **on the tip of her large toe, what is the reason** she is thereby rendered impure? **And if you would say** the reason is that **sometimes** the tip of one large toe might **touch her heel,** i.e., the heel of the other foot, **do we presume** that **ritual impurity** travels **from place to place?** Since that is not presumed, the stain on the large toe of one foot cannot be presumed to come from the heel of the other foot.

וְהָתַנְיָא: הָיְתָה לָהּ מַכָּה בְּצַוָּארָהּ שֶׁתּוּכַל לִתְלוֹת – תּוֹלָה, עַל כְּתֵפָהּ שֶׁאֵינָהּ יְכוֹלָה לִתְלוֹת – אֵינָהּ תּוֹלָה,

The Gemara cites the source of this principle. **But isn't it taught** in a *baraita*: If a woman **had a wound on her neck**[H] in an area **where she can attribute** the blood she found adjacent to her vagina to that wound, **she may attribute** the blood to the wound and she is pure. But if the wound was **on her shoulder,** which is a place **where she cannot attribute** the blood she found adjacent to her vagina to that wound, **she may not attribute** it to the wound, and she is ritually impure.

וְאֵין אוֹמְרִים שֶׁמָּא בְּיָדָהּ נְטָלַתּוּ וֶהֱבִיאַתּוּ לְשָׁם! אֶלָּא: שָׁאנֵי רֹאשׁ גּוּדָלָהּ, דִּבְהַדֵּי דְּפָסְעָה, עָבֵיד דְּמִתְרַמֵּי.

The Gemara explains the proof from the *baraita*: **And** it is clear from this *baraita* that **we do not say** that **perhaps she took** blood from her wounded shoulder **in her hand and brought it there,** near her vagina. **Rather,** this is the reason for the ruling of the mishna: **The tip of her large toe is different,**[H] **as when she walks it might happen** that the tip of this toe is positioned under her vagina and blood drips onto it from there. For this reason she is rendered impure by a stain on that toe.

וְלָא מַחְזְקִינַן טוּמְאָה מִמָּקוֹם לְמָקוֹם? וְהָתַנְיָא: נִמְצֵאת עַל קִשְׁרֵי אֶצְבְּעוֹתֶיהָ – טְמֵאָה, מִפְּנֵי שֶׁיָּדַיִם עַסְקָנִיּוֹת הֵן.

The Gemara asks: **And do we not presume** that **ritual impurity** travels **from place to place? But isn't it taught** in a *baraita*: If blood **was found on the joints of her fingers** on the back of her hand **she is impure,** despite the fact that blood from her source is not usually found on that part of her hand **because hands are active?**

מַאי טַעְמָא – לָאו מִשּׁוּם דְּאָמְרִינַן: בָּדְקָה בְּחַד יְדָא וְנָגְעָה בְּאִידָּךְ יְדָא? לָא, שָׁאנֵי יָדָהּ – דְּכוּלָּה עֲבִידָא דְּנָגְעָה.

The Gemara analyzes the *baraita*: **What is the reason** for this *halakha*? Is it **not due to** the fact **that we say she examined with one hand and** then **touched** the back **of the other hand?** If so, this indicates that ritual impurity is presumed to travel from place to place. The Gemara answers: **No,** the reason she is impure when blood is found on the back of her hand is that **her hand is different,**[H] **as** with regard to the **entire** hand, including the back, it might **happen that it touched** the vagina, as one's hands are active.

״עַל שׁוֹקָהּ וְעַל פַּרְסוֹתֶיהָ מִבִּפְנִים״ וכו׳. מִבִּפְנִים עַד הֵיכָא? אָמְרִי דְּבֵי רַבִּי יַנַּאי: עַד מְקוֹם חֲבָק.

§ The mishna teaches: In a case where the stain was discovered **on her leg or on her feet,** if it was **on the inner** side she is ritually impure, as blood from the uterus could have reached there. If it was on the outer side of the leg or foot she is ritually pure. The Gemara asks: With regard to the term: **On the inner** side, **until where** does it extend? The students of **the school of Rabbi Yannai said: Until the place of the joint** [*mekom ḥavak*][L] of the thigh and shin, the ligaments on the inside of the kneecap.

HALAKHA

If a woman had a wound on her neck – הָיְתָה לָהּ מַכָּה בְּצַוָּארָהּ: One does not presume that ritual impurity traveled from one place to another. How so? If a woman had a wound on her shoulder and she found a stain on her thigh, it is not assumed that perhaps she touched the wound with her hand and then touched her thigh with the same hand and stained it. Likewise, one may not attribute a stain in this manner to any other part of her body or clothing, as stated in the *baraita* (Rambam *Sefer Kedusha, Hilkhot Issurei Bia* 9:25; *Shulḥan Arukh, Yoreh De'a* 190:11, 18).

The tip of her large toe is different – שָׁאנֵי רֹאשׁ גּוּדָלָהּ: If a blood stain was found on the tip of a woman's large toe she is impure, as blood from her vagina might have dripped on it as she was walking. This is in accordance with the ruling of the Gemara (Rambam *Sefer Kedusha, Hilkhot Issurei Bia* 9:8; *Shulḥan Arukh, Yoreh De'a* 190:11).

Her hand is different – שָׁאנֵי יָדָהּ: If blood was discovered on a woman's hand, including on the joints of her fingers on the back of her hand, she is impure. This is because her hand might have touched her vagina, as hands are active. This ruling is in accordance with the Gemara (Rambam *Sefer Kedusha, Hilkhot Issurei Bia* 9:8; *Shulḥan Arukh, Yoreh De'a* 190:11).

אִיבַּעְיָא לְהוּ: מְקוֹם חֲבָק כִּלְפְנִים אוֹ כִּלְחוּץ? תָּא שְׁמַע, דְּתָנֵי רַב קְטִינָא: עַד מְקוֹם חֲבָק, וַחֲבָק עַצְמוֹ – כִּלְפְנִים. רַב חִיָּיא בְּרֵיהּ דְּרַב אַוְיָא מַתְנֵי לָהּ בְּהֶדְיָא, אָמְרִי דְּבֵי רַבִּי יַנַּאי: עַד מְקוֹם חֲבָק, וַחֲבָק עַצְמוֹ – כִּלְפְנִים.

In this regard, **a dilemma was raised before** the Sages: Is **the place of the joint** itself considered **as** part of **the inner** side **or** as part of **the outer** side? **Come and hear, as Rav Ketina** explicitly **teaches:** The inner side extends **until the place of the joint, and the joint itself** is considered **as** part of **the inner** side. The Gemara adds that **Rav Ḥiyya, son of Rav Avya, teaches it explicitly** that the students of **the school of Rabbi Yannai** themselves **said:** The inner side extends **until the place of the joint, and the joint itself** is considered **as** part of **the inner** side.

בָּעֵי רַבִּי יִרְמְיָה: כְּשִׁיר מַהוּ, כְּשׁוּרָה מַהוּ, טִיפִּין טִיפִּין מַהוּ, לְרוֹחַב יְרֵכָהּ מַהוּ?

**Rabbi Yirmeya raises a dilemma:** If the stain on a woman's body was in the shape **of a bracelet,**[B] **what is** the *halakha*? Likewise, if it was in the shape **of a straight line, what is** the *halakha*? If it was not in a single defined shape but was **a series of drops, what is** the *halakha*? Furthermore, if the stain extended **along the width of her thigh,**[H] **what is** the *halakha*? Is there a concern in these cases that the blood might have come from her uterus?

תָּא שְׁמַע: עַל בְּשָׂרָהּ סָפֵק טָמֵא סָפֵק טָהוֹר – טָמֵא. עַל בְּשָׂרָהּ – מַאי לָאו כִּי הַאי גַּוְונָא? לָא, דִּלְמָא דַּעֲבִיד כִּרְצוּעָה.

The Gemara suggests: **Come** and **hear** a *baraita*: If a stain is discovered **on her flesh** and there is **uncertainty whether it is impure or pure,** it is **impure. What, is it not** that the case of blood found **on her flesh** is referring to **a case like this,** i.e., those cases mentioned by Rabbi Yirmeya, and therefore she is impure? The Gemara answers: There is **no** proof from here, as **perhaps** the *baraita* is referring to a stain **shaped like a strip** along the length of her thigh, as this is the usual form of a stain from the vagina.

הַהִיא אִיתְּתָא דְּאִשְׁתַּכַּח לַהּ דָּמָא בְּמַשְׁתִּיתָא, אֲתַאי לְקַמֵּיהּ דְּרַבִּי יַנַּאי, אֲמַר לַהּ: תֵּיזִיל וְתֵיתֵי.

The Gemara relates that there was **a certain woman who discovered blood in the warp**[BH] on the loom where she was weaving. She was concerned that while she was weaving, the threads of the warp might have come between her legs and been stained. **She came before Rabbi Yannai** to inquire about the status of this blood. Rabbi Yannai **said to her: Let her go and come,** i.e., she should go and weave in her usual manner. Since this involves a repetitive action, it will soon become clear whether the threads stretch between her legs.

וְהָתַנְיָא: אֵין שׁוֹנִין בְּטָהֳרוֹת! כִּי אָמְרִינַן ״אֵין שׁוֹנִין״ – לְקוּלָּא, אֲבָל לְחוּמְרָא – שׁוֹנִין.

The Gemara asks: **But isn't it taught** in a *baraita* that **one does not** rely on **repeated** actions **with regard to ritually pure** items? Since the second action might not precisely mimic the first it cannot be relied upon to determine ritual-purity status. The Gemara answers that **when we say one does not** rely on **repeated** actions it is only in cases where it would lead **to a leniency. But** if it leads **to a stringency,** as in this case where the woman is currently pure, since the blood was not found on her body or her garments **one does** rely on **repeated** actions. If the repeated action indicates that the threads of the warp come between her legs while weaving, she is impure.

״הָיְתָה פּוֹשַׁטְתּוֹ״ וכו׳. תַּנְיָא, אָמַר רַבִּי אֱלִיעֶזֶר בְּרַבִּי יוֹסֵי: דָּבָר זֶה הוֹרֵיתִי בְּעִיר רוֹמִי לְאִיסּוּר. וּכְשֶׁבָּאתִי אֵצֶל חֲכָמִים שֶׁבַּדָּרוֹם אָמְרוּ לִי יָפֶה הוֹרֵיתָה.

§ The mishna teaches: If it was a robe that **she would remove** and cover herself with at night, no matter where on the robe the stain is found, she is ritually impure because the robe moves while the woman is asleep, and therefore the blood could have originated in the uterus. The Gemara comments: It **is taught** in a *baraita* that **Rabbi Eliezer, son of Rabbi Yosei, said:** With regard to **this matter** of blood found on a robe worn at night, **I issued a prohibitive ruling in the city of Rome.**[B] **And when I came to the Sages in the south** of Eretz Yisrael **they said to me: You issued a proper ruling.**

**BACKGROUND**

**Bracelet – שִׁיר:** This is a round decorative object encircling a body part. They were used by women as ornaments, and were often tied to the necks or legs of animals as ornaments as well.

Anklet found in Iran, 650 BCE

**Warp [*mashtita*] – מַשְׁתִּיתָא:** This word is the Aramaic equivalent of the Hebrew word for the loom used for weaving [*masekhet*]. The act of weaving is performed using the threads of the warp, which are mainly fixed in the loom. In certain cases these threads can be lifted up, but generally they are firmly attached. The threads of the warp form the basis of the woven material, while the threads of the weft are passed through those of the warp by various means.

Warp and weft

**I issued a prohibitive ruling in the city of Rome – הוֹרֵיתִי בְּעִיר רוֹמִי לְאִיסּוּר:** As related elsewhere in the Talmud (see *Me'ila* 17a–b), Rabbi Eliezer, son of Rabbi Yosei, traveled to Rome together with Rabbi Shimon bar Yoḥai in order to persuade the authorities to rescind Roman decrees of persecution against the Jews. Rabbi Eliezer, son of Rabbi Yosei, recounts his experiences over the course of that visit, which included seeing important items in the Caesar's treasuries, such as the Sanctuary Curtain.

**HALAKHA**

**If the stain was in the shape of a bracelet…of a straight line…a series of drops…along the width of her thigh – כְּשִׁיר...כְּשׁוּרָה...טִיפִּין טִיפִּין...לְרוֹחַב יְרֵכָהּ:** If a blood stain was found on a woman's body, whether it was long like a strip or round, or in the form of a series of drops, or the length of it extended along the width of her thigh, or it looked as though it came from below to above, she is impure when it is adjacent to her vagina. This *halakha* is in accordance with the ruling of the *baraita* (Rambam *Sefer Kedusha, Hilkhot Issurei Bia* 9:9, and see *Maggid Mishne* there; *Shulḥan Arukh, Yoreh De'a* 190:9).

**A certain woman who discovered blood in the warp – הַהִיא אִיתְּתָא דְּאִשְׁתַּכַּח לַהּ דָּמָא בְּמַשְׁתִּיתָא:** If a woman was occupied with her work and discovered blood on a particular item that she had been occupied with, if the item had been previously examined and found to be pure, and if it was susceptible to ritual impurity (Rema), she should repeat the activity in which she was occupied. If when she repeats the activity the item is adjacent to the area between her legs (*Derisha*; *Shakh*), she is impure. If not, she is pure (*Shulḥan Arukh, Yoreh De'a* 190:32).

תָּנוּ רַבָּנַן: אֲרוּכָּה שֶׁלָּבְשָׁה חֲלוּקָהּ שֶׁל קְצָרָה, וּקְצָרָה שֶׁלָּבְשָׁה חֲלוּקָהּ שֶׁל אֲרוּכָּה, אִם מַגִּיעַ כְּנֶגֶד בֵּית הַתּוּרְפָּה שֶׁל אֲרוּכָּה – שְׁתֵּיהֶן טְמֵאוֹת. וְאִם לָאו, אֲרוּכָּה – טְהוֹרָה, וּקְצָרָה – טְמֵאָה.

With regard to blood discovered on a robe, **the Sages taught** in a *baraita*: In the case of **a tall** woman **who wore the robe of a short** woman[H] without first examining it to see if it was clean of stains, **and** likewise **a short** woman **who wore the robe of a tall** woman, if a stain was subsequently found on the robe and it is unknown from which woman it came, the *halakha* is as follows: **If** the location of the stain **reaches adjacent to the vagina of the tall** woman **they are both ritually impure.** The reason is that in this case it certainly reached that area of the short woman. **And if** it does **not** reach adjacent to the vagina of the tall woman, **the tall** woman **is pure,** as the stain is definitely not from her, **and the short** woman **is impure.**

תַּנְיָא אִידַךְ: בָּדְקָה חֲלוּקָהּ וְהִשְׁאִילַתּוּ לַחֲבֵירְתָּהּ, הִיא – טְהוֹרָה, וַחֲבֵירְתָּהּ – תּוֹלָה בָּהּ. אָמַר רַב שֵׁשֶׁת: וּלְעִנְיַן דִּינָא תְּנַן, אֲבָל לְעִנְיַן טוּמְאָה – הִיא טְהוֹרָה, וַחֲבֵירְתָּהּ טְמֵאָה.

It **is taught** in **another** *baraita*: If a woman **examined her robe** and did not find a stain, **and** then **lent it to another** woman,[H] after which a stain was discovered on the robe, what is the *halakha*? **She,** the woman who lent the robe, **is pure, and the other** woman, the one who borrowed the robe, **may attribute** the stain **to** the woman who lent the robe to her, i.e., she may say that she does not rely on the lender's examination. **Rav Sheshet said** in explanation of this *baraita*: **And we learn** this ruling that the borrower can say she does not rely on the lender only **with regard to the matter of** a monetary **judgment** as to which of the women must pay for the laundering of the robe. **But with regard to the matter of ritual impurity, she,** the lender, **is pure, and the other** woman, the borrower, **is impure.**

**HALAKHA**

A tall woman who wore the robe of a short woman – אֲרוּכָּה שֶׁלָּבְשָׁה חֲלוּקָהּ שֶׁל קְצָרָה: In a case where a tall woman wore the robe of a short woman, and a stain was subsequently found on that robe, if the location of the stain reaches the area adjacent to the vagina of the tall woman she is impure. If it does not reach then she is pure, as the stain is from the short woman, as stated in the *baraita* (Rambam *Sefer Kedusha*, *Hilkhot Issurei Bia* 9:31; *Shulḥan Arukh*, *Yoreh De'a* 190:48).

If a woman examined her robe and did not find a stain and then lent it to another woman – בָּדְקָה חֲלוּקָהּ וְהִשְׁאִילַתּוּ לַחֲבֵירְתָּהּ: If a woman examined her robe after wearing it and found that it was pure, and then lent it to another, who wore it, and a blood stain was subsequently discovered on it, the first woman is pure and the second woman is impure, as stated in the *baraita* and as explained by Rav Sheshet (Rambam *Sefer Kedusha*, *Hilkhot Issurei Bia* 9:30; *Shulḥan Arukh*, *Yoreh De'a* 190:40).

Perek **VIII**
Daf **58** Amud **b**

מַאי שְׁנָא מֵהָא דְּתַנְיָא: שְׁתֵּי נָשִׁים שֶׁנִּתְעַסְּקוּ בְּצִפּוֹר אֶחָד, וְאֵין בּוֹ אֶלָּא כְּסֶלַע דָּם, וְנִמְצָא כְּסֶלַע עַל זוֹ וּכְסֶלַע עַל זוֹ – שְׁתֵּיהֶן טְמֵאוֹת? שָׁאנֵי הָתָם – דְּאִיכָּא סֶלַע יְתֵירָה.

The Gemara asks: In **what** way **is this** case **different from that which is taught**[N] in a *baraita*: With regard to **two women who were occupied with one** slaughtered **bird,**[H] **and** the bird **contained only** an amount of **blood** capable of producing a stain as big **as a *sela***[B] coin, **and** blood the size **of a *sela* was found on this** woman **and** blood the size **of a *sela*** was found **on that** woman, **they are both impure,** despite the fact that the blood of one of them can be attributed to the bird. Likewise, in the case of Rav Sheshet the lender should be impure as well, as she might not have examined the robe properly. The Gemara answers: **There it is different, as there is an additional *sela*.**

**BACKGROUND**

*Sela* – סֶלַע: The *sela* is a coin worth four silver shekels. It was minted by the Roman emperor Nero in 85–96 CE. *Sela* is used as a general name for various coins mentioned by the Sages, as from the period of Nero the Romans began minting coins in the region of Eretz Yisrael. The diameter of the *sela* ranges from 5.2 to 6.2 cm, and this was also the size of coins minted in later times, until the end of the period of the *tanna'im*.

**HALAKHA**

Two women who were occupied with one slaughtered bird – שְׁתֵּי נָשִׁים שֶׁנִּתְעַסְּקוּ בְּצִפּוֹר אֶחָד: If two women were involved with one slaughtered bird that contained an amount of blood the size of a *sela*, and a stain the size of a *sela* was found on each one of them, they are both impure, as stated in the *baraita* (Rambam *Sefer Kedusha*, *Hilkhot Issurei Bia* 9:26; *Shulḥan Arukh*, *Yoreh De'a* 190:25).

**NOTES**

In what way is this case different from that which is taught, etc. – מַאי שְׁנָא מֵהָא דְּתַנְיָא וכו׳: The commentaries are puzzled by the suggested comparison between a stain found on a robe used by two women and a stain the size of a *sela* discovered by two women who were occupied with one slaughtered bird. In the case of the bird, the possibility that the blood is from the bird applies equally to both women, just as the other blood stain might have come from either of their bodies. By contrast, in the case of the robe there is a logical reason to declare the first woman pure, as she examined the robe before she lent it out, whereas the woman who borrowed it neglected to examine it before wearing it.

*Tosafot* cite Rabbeinu Tam's answer that this *baraita* is likewise dealing with a case where one of the women was occupied with the bird before the other came along. Had the second woman not arrived, the first one could have attributed the blood on her to the bird, but since there are two of them and the amount of blood found was of a larger quantity than that of the bird, they are both deemed impure. The Gemara is claiming that the same logic should apply in the case of the borrowed robe: Since the second woman can attribute the blood to the first woman, one can claim that both of them should be considered impure.

תָּנוּ רַבָּנַן: לָבְשָׁה שְׁלֹשָׁה חֲלוּקוֹת הַבְּדוּקִין לָהּ, אִם יְכוֹלָה לִתְלוֹת – תּוֹלָה, וַאֲפִילּוּ בַּתַּחְתּוֹן. אֵין יְכוֹלָה לִתְלוֹת – אֵינָהּ תּוֹלָה, וַאֲפִילּוּ בָּעֶלְיוֹן.

**The Sages taught** in a *baraita*: In the case of a woman who **wore three robes,** one on top of the other, **that had been examined by her**[NH] for blood stains, and she subsequently found a stain on one of the robes, **if she can attribute** the blood on the robe to an external source, **she may attribute** it to that source, and she is pure. **And** this is the *halakha* **even** if the stain was **on the lower** robe, closest to her skin. But if she **cannot** reasonably **attribute** the blood to an external factor **she may not attribute** it to an external factor, and she is impure, **and** this is the *halakha* **even** if the stain was **on the upper** robe.

כֵּיצַד, עָבְרָה בְּשׁוּק שֶׁל טַבָּחִים – תּוֹלָה, אֲפִילּוּ בַּתַּחְתּוֹן. לֹא עָבְרָה בְּשׁוּק שֶׁל טַבָּחִים – אַף בָּעֶלְיוֹן אֵינָהּ תּוֹלָה.

The *baraita* elaborates: **How so?** If **she passed through a marketplace of butchers,** where blood could have sprayed on her clothes, **she may attribute** a stain on her garment to the butchers and she is pure, **even** if the stain was **on the lower** robe. If **she did not pass through a marketplace of butchers** or anywhere else with a lot of blood, then **even** if the stain was **on the upper** robe she **may not attribute** the blood to an external source and she is impure.

מתני׳ וְתוֹלָה בְּכָל דָּבָר שֶׁהִיא יְכוֹלָה לִתְלוֹת: שָׁחֲטָה בְּהֵמָה חַיָּה וְעוֹף, נִתְעַסְּקָה בִּכְתָמִים, אוֹ שֶׁיָּשְׁבָה בְּצַד הָעֲסוּקִין בָּהֶן, הָרְגָה מַאֲכוֹלֶת – הֲרֵי זוֹ תּוֹלָה בָּהּ.

**MISHNA** **And** a woman who discovers a blood stain on her body or her garment **may attribute** its existence **to any matter to which she can attribute** it:[H] If she **slaughtered a domesticated animal, an undomesticated animal, or a bird;**[N] or if she **was occupied with** the removal of blood **stains** from the garments of other women or from her own garment, from any source, such as blood that originated from a wound elsewhere on her body or even her own menstrual blood from a prior menstrual cycle; **or if she sat alongside** others **who were occupied with** removing blood stains; or if **she killed a louse;** in all of these cases, **that** woman **may attribute** the blood stain **to it.**

## NOTES

**A woman who wore three robes that had been examined by her, etc.** – לָבְשָׁה שְׁלֹשָׁה חֲלוּקוֹת הַבְּדוּקִין לָהּ וכו׳: In other words, if she passed through a marketplace of butchers or somewhere similar, she may attribute the blood to that cause even if the stain is on the robe closest to the skin and not an upper one. The early commentaries suggest several reasons for this *halakha*: An upper robe, and even two such garments, can sometimes be moved to the side, allowing blood to be sprayed on the lower one (*Tosafot* on 57b). Furthermore, the spray of the blood can come from below and thereby avoid some or even all of her clothes (Rashba).

**If she slaughtered a domesticated animal an undomesticated animal or a bird** – שָׁחֲטָה בְּהֵמָה חַיָּה וְעוֹף: It can be inferred from the mishna that a woman is fit to slaughter not only birds but domesticated and undomesticated animals as well. It is likewise stated at the beginning of tractate *Ḥullin* that everyone may slaughter an animal and their slaughter is valid, and *Tosafot* comment that this includes women. As for why that mishna does not state: Everyone slaughters, both men and women, which is the type of formulation found in the first mishna of tractate *Temura* with regard to substituting consecrated animals, it is because there is no need for such an emphasis; there is no reason to assume that women may not slaughter. Nevertheless, according to *Hilkhot Eretz Yisrael* cited by *Tosafot*, *Hilkhot Eldad HaDani* cited by other early commentaries, and Rav Shmuel ben Ḥofni Gaon, women may not slaughter because they lack fortitude and they might faint (*Smag*, positive mitzva 63; see *Yam shel Shlomo* and *Baḥ*).

*Tosafot* and many early commentaries reject this opinion in light of the *halakha* that women are fit to slaughter even sacrificial animals (see *Zevaḥim* 31b). In any case, it was very rare, at least in the lands of Ashkenaz, for women to perform ritual slaughter, and certainly not as the designated ritual slaughterer in a town. The later commentaries write that one cannot infer from the *halakha* that women are fit to slaughter sacrificial animals that they are also fit to slaughter non-sacred animals (Maharatz Ḥayyut; *Arukh HaShulḥan*, *Yoreh De'a* 1:37).

## HALAKHA

**A woman who wore three robes that had been examined by her** – לָבְשָׁה שְׁלֹשָׁה חֲלוּקוֹת הַבְּדוּקִין לָהּ: With regard to a woman who was wearing three robes, one on top of the other, if she can attribute the blood on the robe to an external source she may attribute it, even if the stain is on the robe closest to her skin. If she cannot attribute the blood to an external source, she may not attribute it and she is impure, even if the stain was on the upper robe.

If she passed through a marketplace of butchers, even if the stain was on the lower robe she may attribute it to the blood of the slaughtered animals. If she did not pass through a marketplace of butchers or any similar place, then even if the stain was on the upper robe she may not attribute the blood to an external source, and she is impure. If it is uncertain whether or not she passed by the marketplace, or if it is uncertain whether or not she was occupied with blood stains, she may not attribute the blood to that source. This ruling is in accordance with the *baraita* (Rambam *Sefer Kedusha*, *Hilkhot Issurei Bia* 9:27; *Shulḥan Arukh*, *Yoreh De'a* 190:18).

**And she may attribute its existence to any matter to which she can attribute it** – וְתוֹלָה בְּכָל דָּבָר שֶׁהִיא יְכוֹלָה לִתְלוֹת: Since the impurity of stains applies by rabbinic law, the *halakha* is lenient in that a woman may attribute a stain's existence to any matter she can attribute it to. How so? If she slaughtered a domesticated animal, an undomesticated animal, or a bird, or if she was occupied with the removal of blood stains from the garments of other women, or if she sat alongside others who were occupied with removing them, she may attribute the blood stain to these causes and she is pure (*Shulḥan Arukh*, *Yoreh De'a* 190:18; see Rambam *Sefer Kedusha*, *Hilkhot Issurei Bia* 9:27).

עד כמה תולה? רבי חנינא בן אנטיגנוס אומר: עד כגריס של פול, ואף על פי שלא הרגה. ותולה בבנה או בבעלה. אם יש בה מכה, והיא יכולה להגלע ולהוציא דם – הרי זו תולה.

How large a stain may a woman **attribute** to a louse?[H] **Rabbi Ḥanina ben Antigonus says:** It can be **up to** the area **of a split bean.**[B] **And** she may attribute the stain to a louse **even if she does not** remember that **she killed** it. **And she may attribute** the blood stain **to her son or to her husband**[H] in a case where one of them is near her and has a wound. Furthermore, **if** the woman herself **has a wound,** even if the wound scabbed over and is no longer bleeding, **but it can reopen and bleed,**[H] **that** woman **may attribute** the blood stain to that wound.

מעשה באשה אחת שבאת לפני רבי עקיבא, אמרה לו: ראיתי כתם. אמר לה: שמא מכה היתה ביך? אמרה לו: הן, וחיתה. אמר לה: שמא יכולה להגלע ולהוציא דם? אמרה לו: הן. וטהרה רבי עקיבא.

There was **an incident involving one woman who came before Rabbi Akiva.**[P] **She said to him: I saw** a blood **stain.** Rabbi Akiva **said to her: Perhaps** there **was a wound on your** body? **She said to him: Yes,** there was a wound **and it healed. He said to her:** Was it **perhaps** a wound that **could reopen and bleed? She said to him: Yes** it was. **And Rabbi Akiva deemed her ritually pure.**

ראה תלמידיו מסתכלין זה בזה, אמר להם: מה הדבר קשה בעיניכם? שלא אמרו חכמים הדבר להחמיר – אלא להקל, שנאמר: "ואשה כי תהיה זבה דם יהיה זבה בבשרה", "דם" – ולא כתם.

Rabbi Akiva **saw his students looking at each other,** wondering why he ruled leniently in this case. Rabbi Akiva **said to them: What** in this **matter is difficult in your eyes?** The reason I ruled this way is **that the Sages did not state the matter** of the impurity of blood stains in order **to be stringent; rather,** they instituted this impurity in order **to be lenient, as it is stated: "And if a woman has if a woman has an issue, and her issue in her flesh shall be blood"** (Leviticus 15:19), from which it is derived that by Torah law, **"blood"** deems her impure, **but not a stain.** Impurity from a blood stain was instituted by the Sages, and they rule leniently in any case where the stain can be attributed to another source.

עד שהוא נתון תחת הכר ונמצא עליו דם, עגול – טהור, משוך – טמא, דברי רבי אליעזר ברבי צדוק.

With regard to **an examination cloth that was placed beneath the pillow and blood was found on** the cloth, and it is unclear whether it is the blood of an examination or the blood of a louse that was crushed beneath it, if the stain is **round** the woman is **ritually pure,** as an examination to determine whether a woman is menstruating would not leave a round stain. If the stain is **elongated** the woman is **ritually impure;** this is **the statement of Rabbi Eliezer, son of Rabbi Tzadok.**

**BACKGROUND**

**Split bean** – **גריס של פול:** The bean *Vicia faba* L., which comes from the family of Fabaceae, or legumes, is primarily used as an edible vegetable. It is known today as the broad bean or fava bean. Like other legumes, its seeds grow in pods, and they are especially rich in protein. The beans can be eaten cooked, and are sometimes roasted in fire and then split into halves, at which point they are called groats [*gerisim*].

Beans were often split in two along their seams in preparation for cooking. A split bean was a convenient measure for a small area, such as that of a mark or a stain, since the interior side was smooth and could be laid down flat on the skin or a piece of cloth. Among contemporary halakhic authorities, the area of a broad bean is held to be equal to that of a circle between 19 and 21 mm in diameter.

Broad bean on a grid of 5 mm squares

Flowering broad bean plant

**HALAKHA**

**How large a stain may a woman attribute to a louse** – **עד כמה תולה:** The Sages decreed impurity only on a blood stain that is slightly larger than the size of a bean, which is the area of three lentils by three lentils. If the stain is smaller than this she may attribute it to a louse, even if she had not killed one. But if the stain is this size or larger she may not attribute it to a louse, whether the stain is square-shaped or long. This ruling is in accordance with the opinion of Rabbi Ḥanina in the mishna, and of Rav Ḥisda, stated later (Rambam *Sefer Kedusha, Hilkhot Issurei Bia* 9:23; *Shulḥan Arukh, Yoreh De'a* 190:5).

**And she may attribute the blood stain to her son or to her husband** – **ותולה בבנה או בבעלה:** If a woman's son or husband had been in contact with blood stains or had suffered an injury, she may attribute a blood stain on her clothing to them, as they frequently come into physical contact with her. But if there were no stains on them she may not attribute her stain to them, unless their activity was such that the blood would have sprayed when she was nearby, e.g., the act of slaughter (Rambam *Sefer Kedusha, Hilkhot Issurei Bia* 9:24; *Shulḥan Arukh, Yoreh De'a* 190:19).

**If the woman has a wound even if it is no longer bleeding but it can reopen and bleed** – **אם יש בה מכה והיא יכולה להגלע ולהוציא דם:** If a woman has a wound on her body she may attribute a blood stain to that wound, even if the stain is on her body, provided that the wound is in an area where blood could have dripped from it onto the place of the stain. Even after the wound has healed, if upon rubbing it may reopen and bleed again, she may attribute a stain to it despite the fact that it has scabbed over and is not bleeding (Rambam *Sefer Kedusha, Hilkhot Issurei Bia* 9:22; *Shulḥan Arukh, Yoreh De'a* 190:18).

**PERSONALITIES**

**Rabbi Akiva** – **רבי עקיבא:** Rabbi Akiva, who lived just after the destruction of the Second Temple, was one of the greatest of the *tanna'im*. Unlettered until the age of forty, Akiva was encouraged by his wife, Rachel, to devote himself to the study of Torah. After years of study under the tutelage of Rabbi Eliezer ben Hyrcanus, Rabbi Yehoshua ben Ḥananya, and others, he acquired thousands of students and established his own academy in Bnei Brak. He systematized and arranged the many oral traditions, and it was the Mishna of Rabbi Akiva as received by his disciple, Rabbi Meir, that ultimately became the basis of the six orders of the Mishna.

Rabbi Akiva was the spiritual leader of the bar Kokheva revolt. He even proclaimed bar Kokheva as the Messiah early in the struggle, but later retracted this opinion. Despite Roman decrees against disseminating Torah, the aged Rabbi Akiva continued to teach. He was ultimately arrested by the Romans, imprisoned, tried, and sentenced to death. As the Romans were torturing him to death, Rabbi Akiva recited *Shema* and explained to his students that he had now had the opportunity to fulfill the true meaning of loving God with all of one's soul (see *Berakhot* 61b). Due to his murder by the Romans, he is considered one of the ten martyrs.

גמ׳ תְּנֵינָא לְהָא דְּתָנוּ רַבָּנַן: מַעֲשֶׂה וְתָלָה רַבִּי מֵאִיר בְּקִילוֹר, וְרַבִּי תָּלָה בִּשְׂרַף שִׁקְמָה.

**GEMARA** The mishna teaches that a woman who discovers a blood stain on her body or her garment may attribute its existence to any matter to which she can attribute it. The Gemara notes: **We learn** in the mishna **that which the Sages taught** explicitly in a *baraita*: **An incident** occurred involving a blood stain found on a woman's garment, **and Rabbi Meir attributed** it **to an eye salve** [*bekilor*][L] that the woman had previously handled, **and** likewise, **Rabbi** Yehuda HaNasi **attributed** a stain **to the sap of a sycamore**[B] tree the woman had touched.

**LANGUAGE**

Eye salve [*kilor*] – קִילוֹר: From the Greek κολλύριον, *kollurion*, meaning a salve for the eyes.

״אוֹ שֶׁיָּשְׁבָה״. יָשְׁבָה – אִין, לֹא יָשְׁבָה – לָא.

§ The mishna teaches: Or if she was occupied with the removal of blood stains from the garments of other women or from her own garment, from any source, such as blood that originated from a wound elsewhere on her body or even her own menstrual blood from a prior menstrual cycle; **or if she sat** alongside others who were occupied with removing blood stains. The Gemara infers: If she knows for certain that **she sat** alongside those occupied with removing blood stains, **yes,** she may attribute blood to this source. But if she does **not** know for certain that **she sat** alongside those who were removing blood stains, but knows only that she was in the same area as they were, she may **not** attribute blood to this source.

תְּנֵינָא לְהָא דְּתָנוּ רַבָּנַן: עָבְרָה בְּשׁוּק שֶׁל טַבָּחִים, סָפֵק נִיתַּז עָלֶיהָ סָפֵק לֹא נִיתַּז עָלֶיהָ – תּוֹלָה, סָפֵק עָבְרָה סָפֵק לֹא עָבְרָה – טְמֵאָה.

Again the Gemara comments: **We learn** in the mishna **that which the Sages taught** explicitly in a *baraita*: If a woman **passed through a marketplace of butchers** and it is **uncertain whether** blood from the marketplace **sprayed on her** or **whether** it did **not spray on her, she may attribute** a stain to the butchers. But if she is **uncertain whether she passed by** the marketplace or **whether** she did **not pass by, she is** deemed **impure** and may not attribute it to that source. In this case as well, only if she is certain that she was in a circumstance to which she can attribute the blood may she attribute it to that cause.

״הָרְגָה מַאֲכוֹלֶת״. הָרְגָה – אִין, לֹא הָרְגָה – לָא. מַתְנִיתִין מַנִּי? רַבָּן שִׁמְעוֹן בֶּן גַּמְלִיאֵל הִיא, דְּתַנְיָא: הָרְגָה – תּוֹלָה, לֹא הָרְגָה – אֵינָהּ תּוֹלָה, דִּבְרֵי רַבָּן שִׁמְעוֹן בֶּן גַּמְלִיאֵל. וַחֲכָמִים אוֹמְרִים: בֵּין כָּךְ וּבֵין כָּךְ – תּוֹלָה.

§ The mishna teaches that if **she killed a louse** she may attribute the blood stain to it. The Gemara infers: If she **killed** a louse, **yes,** she may attribute blood to it, but if she **did not kill** a louse she may **not** attribute blood to it. The Gemara asks: **Whose** opinion is expressed in **the mishna?** The Gemara answers that **it is** the opinion of **Rabban Shimon ben Gamliel, as it is taught** in a *baraita*: If a woman **killed** a louse before finding blood, **she may attribute** blood to it. If **she did not kill** a louse **she may not attribute** blood to it; this is **the statement of Rabban Shimon ben Gamliel. And the Rabbis say: Both** in **this** case **and** in **that** case **she may attribute** blood to a louse.

אָמַר רַבָּן שִׁמְעוֹן בֶּן גַּמְלִיאֵל: לִדְבָרַי אֵין קֵץ, וּלְדִבְרֵי חֲבֵרַי אֵין סוֹף.

**Rabban Shimon ben Gamliel said** there is a difficulty with regard to both his opinion and that of the Rabbis: **According to my statement**, that a woman may attribute a stain only to a creature she actually killed, **there is no limit; and according to the statement of my colleagues,** who rule that she may attribute a stain to a louse even if she had not killed one, **there is no end.**

לִדְבָרַי אֵין קֵץ – שֶׁאֵין לְךָ אִשָּׁה שֶׁטְּהוֹרָה לְבַעְלָהּ, שֶׁאֵין לְךָ כׇּל מִטָּה וּמִטָּה שֶׁאֵין בָּהּ כַּמָּה טִיפֵּי דָם מַאֲכוֹלֶת.

Rabban Shimon ben Gamliel explains: **According to my statement, there is no limit** to the size of the stain she found, **as** she is impure even if it is as small as a mustard seed. Consequently, **you have no woman who is pure to her husband, as you have no bed of any sort on which there are not several drops of blood of a louse.** Since I rule that a woman may attribute blood to a louse only if she previously killed one, all women will be in a state of impurity to their husbands.

**BACKGROUND**

Sycamore – שִׁקְמָה: The sycamore, *Ficus sycomorus* L., is a tall, wide tree similar to a fig tree. Although it is possible to eat the fruits of a sycamore tree, it is usually grown for its wood, as the trunk is wide, large, and relatively light. In general, a sycamore is left to grow until it reaches a significant size, at which point it is chopped down. The remaining part of the tree grows again, and is chopped down again every few years. Sycamore trees thrive in heat and grow primarily in plains, not in mountainous regions.

HALAKHA

**She may attribute a stain to a bedbug – תּוֹלָה בְּפִשְׁפֵּשׁ:** If a woman killed a bedbug or smelled its odor, and subsequently found a blood stain on her clothing, she may attribute the stain to the bedbug if the stain is up to the width of a lupine seed, in accordance with the opinion of Rav Naḥman bar Yitzḥak. The Rashba and Rabbeinu Yeruḥam maintain that in places where bedbugs are common a woman may attribute even a stain the width of a lupine seed to them, and even if she has not killed one (*Shulḥan Arukh*, *Yoreh De'a* 190:7, and see *Shakh* there).

**If he tasted the taste of a bedbug in his mouth – שֶׁטָּעַם טַעַם פִּשְׁפֵּשׁ בְּפִיו:** One who is eating and tastes a bedbug must spit the food out of his mouth, in accordance with the mishna in tractate *Terumot* (Rambam *Sefer Zera'im*, *Hilkhot Terumot* 10:13).

לְדִבְרֵי חֲבֵרַי אֵין סוֹף – שֶׁאֵין לְךָ אִשָּׁה שֶׁאֵינָהּ טְהוֹרָה לְבַעְלָהּ, שֶׁאֵין לְךָ כָּל סָדִין וְסָדִין שֶׁאֵין בּוֹ כַּמָּה טִיפֵּי דָם.

By contrast, **according to the statement of my colleagues there is no end** to the advantage their ruling provides to women, **because** if their ruling is accepted **you have no woman who is not pure to her husband, as you have no sheet of any sort on which there are not several blood drops,** and every woman can attribute all these drops to a louse, even if she had not killed one.

אֲבָל נִרְאִין דִּבְרֵי רַבִּי חֲנִינָא בֶּן אַנְטִיגְנוֹס מִדְּבָרַי וּמִדִּבְרֵיהֶם, שֶׁהָיָה אוֹמֵר: עַד כַּמָּה הִיא תּוֹלָה – עַד כִּגְרִיס שֶׁל פּוֹל, וְלִדְבָרָיו אָנוּ מוֹדִים. וּלְרַבָּנַן דְּאָמְרִי תּוֹלָה, עַד כַּמָּה? אָמַר רַב נַחְמָן בַּר יִצְחָק: תּוֹלָה בְּפִשְׁפֵּשׁ – וְעַד כְּתוּרְמוּס.

Rabban Shimon ben Gamliel continues: **But the statement of Rabbi Ḥanina ben Antigonus appears** to be more correct **than my statement and their statement, as** Rabbi Ḥanina ben Antigonus **would say: How large** a stain may a woman **attribute** to a louse? It can be **up to** the area **of a split bean. And** therefore **we concede to** his opinion and accept **his statement.** The Gemara asks: **And according to** the opinion of **the Rabbis, who say** that a woman **may attribute** blood to a louse whether or not she killed one, **how large** can the stain be? After all, some stains are far bigger than those produced by a louse. **Rav Naḥman bar Yitzḥak says: She may attribute** a stain **to a bedbug,**[HB] which has more blood than a louse, **and** this applies to any stain whose size is **up to** the width **of a lupine** seed.[B]

תָּנוּ רַבָּנַן: פִּשְׁפֵּשׁ זֶה, אָרְכּוֹ כְּרָחְבּוֹ, וְטַעְמוֹ כְּרֵיחוֹ, בְּרִית כְּרוּתָה לוֹ – שֶׁכָּל הַמּוֹלְלוֹ מֵרִיחַ בּוֹ. אָרְכּוֹ כְּרָחְבּוֹ – לְעִנְיַן כְּתָמִים,

The Gemara continues to discuss the matter of the bedbug. **The Sages taught** in a *baraita*: **This bedbug, its length** is **equal to its width, and its taste is like its** foul **smell. A covenant is made with it,** i.e., it is a law of nature, **that anyone who squeezes it** will **smell its** foul odor. The Gemara explains with regard to which *halakhot* these characteristics of the bedbug were mentioned. The fact that **its length** is equal **to its width** was stated **with regard to the matter of stains,** i.e., if a stain is found whose length is the same as its width, one may attribute it to the blood of a bedbug even if the stain is larger than the area of a split bean.

טַעְמוֹ כְּרֵיחוֹ – לְעִנְיַן תְּרוּמָה. דִּתְנַן: אוֹ שֶׁטָּעַם טַעַם פִּשְׁפֵּשׁ בְּפִיו – הֲרֵי זֶה יִפְלוֹט. מְנָא יָדַע? טַעְמוֹ כְּרֵיחוֹ. וְאַכַּתִּי מְנָא יָדַע? בְּרִית כְּרוּתָה לוֹ, שֶׁכָּל הַמּוֹלְלוֹ מֵרִיחַ בּוֹ.

The statement that **its taste is like its** foul **smell** is applicable **with regard to the matter of** the partaking of *teruma*, the portion of the produce designated for the priest, **as we learned** in a mishna (*Terumot* 8:2): **Or if he tasted the taste of a bedbug in his mouth,**[H] which is prohibited for consumption, **this** person **must spit out** the contents of his mouth, despite the fact that it is generally prohibited to waste *teruma*. **How does he know** that there is a bedbug in his mouth? He knows because **its taste is like its** foul **smell. And still, how does he know** the smell of a bedbug? In answer to this question the *baraita* explains that one does not err with regard to the smell of the bedbug, as **a covenant is made with it that anyone who squeezes it** will **smell its** foul odor, and therefore it is a well-known smell.

BACKGROUND

**Bedbug – פִּשְׁפֵּשׁ:** This is an insect with a flattened and elliptical body, 3–5 mm in length, and reddish dark-brown in color. It has a characteristic proboscis on the front of its head that it uses for sucking. This bug is known for the foul smell it emits.

**Lupine – תּוּרְמוּס:** Lupine is the name for several plants from the legume family. The cultivated lupine, *Lupines termis*, and the yellow lupine, *L. luteus*, are particularly common. The lupine seeds grow inside pods. The seeds themselves are round, with a diameter of up to 15 mm in the cultivated lupine.

Lupine

אָמַר רַב אַשִׁי: עִיר שֶׁיֵּשׁ בָּהּ חֲזִירִים – אֵין חוֹשְׁשִׁין לִכְתָמִים. אֲמַר רַב נַחְמָן בַּר יִצְחָק: וְהָא דְּדוּקֶרֶת – כְּעִיר שֶׁיֵּשׁ בָּהּ חֲזִירִים דָּמְיָא.

The mishna teaches that a woman may attribute a blood stain as having come from another entity and remain pure. In this regard **Rav Ashi says:** In the case of **a town in which there are pigs,**[H] one need **not be concerned for stains** found on the body or clothes of a woman living there. Since pigs wander the streets and often have stains of blood on them, and their living areas attract bugs of all kinds, any blood stain found on a woman can be attributed to the pigs. **Rav Naḥman bar Yitzḥak said: And this** town **of Dukeret,**[B] where there are many slaughterhouses, garbage heaps, and bugs, **is** considered **like a town in which there are pigs.**

״עַד כַּמָּה הִיא תּוֹלָה״ וכו׳. אָמַר רַב הוּנָא: כִּגְרִיס – אֵינָהּ תּוֹלָה, פָּחוֹת מִכִּגְרִיס – תּוֹלָה. וְרַב חִסְדָּא אָמַר: כִּגְרִיס – תּוֹלָה, יָתֵר מִכִּגְרִיס – אֵינָהּ תּוֹלָה.

§ The mishna teaches: **How large** a stain may a woman **attribute** to a louse? Rabbi Ḥanina ben Antigonus says: It can be up to the area of a split bean. The Gemara notes that the meaning of the statement of Rabbi Ḥanina ben Antigonus is a matter of dispute among the Sages. **Rav Huna says:** If the stain was the size **of a split bean she may not attribute** it to the blood of a louse; if it was **less than** the size **of a split bean she may attribute** it to the blood of a louse. **And Rav Ḥisda says:** Even if it was the size **of a split bean she may** still **attribute** it to the blood of a louse; but if the stain was **more than** the size **of a split bean she may not attribute**[H] it to the blood of a louse.

לֵימָא בְּעַד וְעַד בִּכְלָל קָא מִיפַּלְגִי, דְּרַב הוּנָא סְבַר: עַד – וְלֹא עַד בִּכְלָל, וְרַב חִסְדָּא סְבַר: עַד – וְעַד בִּכְלָל.

The Gemara suggests: **Let us say** that these Sages **disagree with regard to** the matter of: **Up to and including. As Rav Huna maintains** that the term: Up to, means: **Up to** the measure **but not including** the measure, and since Rabbi Ḥanina ben Antigonus said that a stain can be up to the area of a split bean, this does not include the size of a bean itself. **And Rav Ḥisda maintains** that the term means: **Up to and including** the measure.

אֲמַר לָךְ רַב הוּנָא: אִיכָּא עַד וְעַד בִּכְלָל, וְאִיכָּא עַד וְלֹא עַד בִּכְלָל, וְהָכָא לְחוּמְרָא וְהָתָם לְחוּמְרָא.

The Gemara responds: **Rav Huna** could **say to you** that **there are** instances where the term means **up to and including** the measure, **and there are** instances where it means **up to and not including** the measure. **And** both **here,** where it means up to and not including the measure, it is intended **as a stringency,** as in the statement of Rabbi Ḥanina ben Antigonus; **and there,** where it means up to and including the measure, it is likewise intended **as a stringency.**

וְרַב חִסְדָּא אֲמַר לָךְ: בְּעָלְמָא אֵימָא לָךְ – לְחוּמְרָא אָמְרִינַן, לְקוּלָּא לָא אָמְרִינַן. וְהָכָא – כִּדְרַבִּי אַבָּהוּ, דַּאֲמַר רַבִּי אַבָּהוּ: כׇּל שִׁיעוּרֵי חֲכָמִים – לְהַחְמִיר, חוּץ מִכִּגְרִיס שֶׁל כְּתָמִים – לְהָקֵל.

**And Rav Ḥisda** could **say to you** that **in general I will say to you** that when it leads **to a stringency, we say** that the term: Up to, means up to and including the measure, whereas if it leads **to a leniency we do not say** so. **And here,** with regard to stains, I interpret the term in this manner despite the fact that it entails a leniency, **in accordance with** the opinion **of Rabbi Abbahu. As Rabbi Abbahu says: All measures of the Sages** must be interpreted **stringently, except for** the measure **of a split bean** as a standard **for stains** of blood found on a woman's clothing, which is interpreted **leniently.** Therefore, even if the stain is exactly the size of a bean the woman remains pure.

## HALAKHA

A town in which there are pigs – עִיר שֶׁיֵּשׁ בָּהּ חֲזִירִים: In a place where there are pigs, or where pigs constantly enter, a woman does not need to be concerned for a stain found on her clothing. Some authorities maintain that nowadays one may not attribute stains to pigs (*Tosafot*), but the Rashba comments that he does not know the reasoning behind this statement.

The early commentaries explain that wherever Jews live in their own neighborhood it is considered a separate town for the purposes of this *halakha*, and therefore a woman may attribute a stain to pigs only if it is clear that she was near them (*Maggid Mishne*). The later commentaries suggest this is the reason why this *halakha* is omitted by the *Shulḥan Arukh*, as repulsive creatures are uncommon in Jewish areas. In addition, any such animals owned by gentiles are kept in the gentiles' houses (Rambam *Sefer Kedusha, Hilkhot Issurei Bia* 9:28; *Arukh HaShulḥan, Yoreh De'a* 190:73; see *Tur, Yoreh De'a* 190).

More than the size of a split bean she may not attribute – יָתֵר מִכִּגְרִיס אֵינָהּ תּוֹלָה: The *halakha* is in accordance with the opinion of Rav Ḥisda, who rules that a woman may attribute a stain up to the size of a bean to the blood of a louse, even if she did not kill one. But if it is larger than a bean she may not attribute it to a louse, whether it is square-shaped or elongated (Rambam *Sefer Kedusha, Hilkhot Issurei Bia* 9:23; *Shulḥan Arukh, Yoreh De'a* 190:5).

## BACKGROUND

Dukeret – דּוּקֶרֶת: The location of this place is uncertain. Some identify it with what is now the city of Wasit, west of the Tigris River. Apparently, several important Sages, including Rav Huna and Rav Naḥman bar Yitzḥak, lived in this city or in its neighboring villages.

איכא דאמרי לה להא שמעתא באפי נפשה. רב הונא אמר: כגריס – כיתר מכגריס, ורב חסדא אמר: כגריס – כפחות מכגריס, וקמיפלגי ב״עד ועד״ דהכא, כדאמרינן. מיתיבי:

Some say this *halakha* as a distinct matter, not specifically as an explanation of the mishna: **Rav Huna says** the area **of a split bean** is considered the same **as** the area of **greater than a split bean. And Rav Ḥisda says** the area **of a split bean** is considered the same **as** the area of **less than a split bean. And** these two *amora'im* **disagree with regard to** the matter of **up to,** whether it means including or not including the measure itself, as discussed **in** this case **here,** with regard to stains. The Gemara **raises an objection:**

Perek **VIII**
Daf **59** Amud **a**

NOTES

Small [*lematta*] drops of blood and large [*lemala*] drops of blood – טיפי דמים למטה וטיפי דמים למעלה: Although the Hebrew words *lematta* and *lemala* literally mean below and above, respectively, Rashi explains that in this context the Gemara is referring to small and big drops.

היו עליה טיפי דמים למטה, וטיפי דמים למעלה – תולה בעליון עד כגריס. מאי לאו – כגרים מלמטה? לא, כגרים מלמעלה.

If **there were on** a woman's body **small drops of blood and large drops of blood,**[NH] **she may attribute** these drops to an external source, even **with regard to the largest** drop, provided that it is **up to** the size **of a split bean. What, is it not** that a drop the size **of a split bean** itself is considered **small,** like a drop that is less than the size of a bean, which contradicts the opinion of Rav Huna? The Gemara responds: **No,** it means that a drop exactly the size **of a split bean** is like **a large** drop, i.e., a drop greater than a bean.

איתמר, נמצא עליה כגריס ועוד, ואותו עוד – רצופה בו מאכולת, רבי חנינא אומר: טמאה. רבי ינאי אומר: טהורה. רבי חנינא אומר: טמאה, כי תליא – בכגרים, בכגרים ועוד – לא תליא.

It **was stated:** If a stain **was found on** a woman and it was the size **of a split bean and** slightly **more,** which is too large to be attributed to a louse, **and** in **that** area that was slightly **more** than a bean there was **a squashed louse,**[H] what is the status of that woman? **Rabbi Ḥanina says she is ritually impure,** as the stain is not attributed to a louse; **Rabbi Yannai says she is pure.** The Gemara explains their opinions: **Rabbi Ḥanina says she is impure,** in accordance with the *halakha* **that** a woman **may attribute** a stain to a louse only **with regard to** a stain whose area is up to the area **of a split bean,** whereas **with regard to** a stain the size **of a split bean and** slightly **more, she may not attribute** it to a louse.

רבי ינאי אומר: טהורה, הני מילי – היכא דלא רצופה בו מאכולת, אבל היכא דרצופה בו מאכולת – מוכחא מילתא דהאי ועוד דם מאכולת הוא. פש ליה – כגרים, כיון דבעלמא תליא, הכא נמי תליא.

By contrast, **Rabbi Yannai says she is pure,** as he maintains that **this statement** that one may not attribute a stain larger than a bean to a louse applies only **where** there is **no louse squashed** on the stain. **But** in a case **where** there is **a louse squashed** on the stain **it is apparent that this** blood that causes the stain to be slightly **more** than the size of a bean **is the blood of a louse.** Since it is visibly squashed there, there is no uncertainty in this regard. When that area is subtracted one **is left** with a stain that is the size **of a split bean,** and one may say that **since in general** a woman **attributes** a stain the size of a bean to a louse, **here too, she may attribute** the stain to another, second louse.

HALAKHA

If there were on a woman's body small drops of blood and large drops of blood – היו עליה טיפי דמים למטה וטיפי דמים למעלה: If a woman found two blood stains, one above her belt and the other below it, and she knows she did not jump backward, she is pure, as it is reasonable to assume that just as the upper stain must have come from an outside source the same is true of the lower one. This is the *halakha* only if the upper stain is larger than a bean, as it certainly came from the outside. But if it is no larger than a bean it is possible that it is from a louse, and in that case, if the lower stain is larger than a bean she is impure, in accordance with the *baraita*. It should be noted that this interpretation, according to which the terms *lematta* and *lemala* in the *baraita* mean below and above, does not follow the explanation of Rashi (*Shulḥan Arukh, Yoreh De'a* 190:17).

And in that area that was slightly more there was a squashed louse – ואותו עוד רצופה בו מאכולת: With regard to a woman who found a stain larger than a bean, the Rambam maintains she may not attribute it to a louse even if a louse was found crushed on the stain, as the blood stain of a louse would be no larger than a bean; this is in accordance with the opinion of Rabbi Ḥanina. Other commentaries rule that she is pure, in accordance with the opinion of Rabbi Yannai (Ramban; Rashba). Their reasoning is that since part of the stain was certainly caused by the louse the rest can also be attributed to a louse, because this remaining part is no larger than a bean (Rambam *Sefer Kedusha, Hilkhot Issurei Bia* 9:23; *Shulḥan Arukh, Yoreh De'a* 190:28).

בָּעֵי רַבִּי יִרְמְיָה: נִתְעַסְּקָה בִּכְגְרִיס, וְנִמְצָא עָלֶיהָ בִּכְגְרִיס וָעוֹד, מַהוּ? תִּבָּעֵי לְרַבִּי חֲנִינָא, תִּבָּעֵי לְרַבִּי יַנַּאי.

With regard to the dispute between Rabbi Ḥanina and Rabbi Yannai, **Rabbi Yirmeya raises a dilemma:** If a woman **was occupied with** an item the size **of a split bean,** e.g., the blood of a slaughtered bird, or eye salve, **and** then a stain **was found on her** the size **of a split bean and** slightly **more,**[H] **what is** the *halakha*? Rabbi Yirmeya elaborates: **The dilemma can be raised according to** the opinion of **Rabbi Ḥanina,** who maintained in the previous case that she is impure, **and** the **dilemma can be raised according to** the opinion of **Rabbi Yannai,** who ruled that she is pure.

תִּבָּעֵי לְרַבִּי חֲנִינָא – עַד כָּאן לָא קָאָמַר רַבִּי חֲנִינָא הָתָם טְמֵאָה – אֶלָּא דְּלָא נִתְעַסְּקָה, אֲבָל הָכָא דְּנִתְעַסְּקָה – תַּלְיָא? אוֹ דִּלְמָא: אֲפִילּוּ לְרַבִּי יַנַּאי דְּאָמַר טְהוֹרָה, הָנֵי מִילֵּי – הֵיכָא דִּרְצוּפָה בּוֹ מַאֲכוֹלֶת, אֲבָל הֵיכָא דְּאֵין רְצוּפָה בּוֹ מַאֲכוֹלֶת – לָא תַּלְיָא?

**The dilemma can be raised according to** the opinion of **Rabbi Ḥanina,** as perhaps **Rabbi Ḥanina states there** that **she is impure only where she was not occupied** with a louse, and there is no reason to attribute the stain to that cause. **But here, where she was occupied** with an item that can stain her, it can be claimed that **she may attribute** the stain to that source. **Or perhaps, even according to** the opinion of **Rabbi Yannai, who said** in the previous case that **she is pure, that statement** applies only **where a louse** was found **squashed on** the stain; **but** in a case **where there is no louse squashed on** the stain and there is no certainty that part of the stain came from another source, **she may not attribute** part of the stain to the item she was occupied with and part of the stain to a louse. In this situation everyone agrees she is impure.

תָּא שְׁמַע: נִתְעַסְּקָה בְּאָדוֹם – אֵין תּוֹלָה בָּהּ שָׁחוֹר, בְּמוּעָט – אֵין תּוֹלָה בּוֹ מְרוּבֶּה. הֵיכִי דָּמֵי? לָאו כִּי הַאי גַּוְונָא?

The Gemara suggests: **Come** and **hear** a resolution from a *baraita*: If a woman **was occupied with a red** item[H] **she may not attribute a black** stain **to it.** Likewise, if she was dealing **with a small** item **she may not attribute a large** stain **to it. What are the circumstances** of the second clause of this *baraita*? Is it **not** referring to **a case like this** dilemma raised by Rabbi Yirmeya where she was occupied with an item the size of a bean and a stain was found on her that was the size of a bean and slightly more? If so, the *baraita* teaches that in such a situation she may not attribute the stain to the item.

לָא, כְּגוֹן דְּנִתְעַסְּקָה בִּכְגְרִיס, וְנִמְצָא עָלֶיהָ שְׁנֵי גְּרִיסִין וָעוֹד. אִי הָכִי, מַאי לְמֵימְרָא?

The Gemara responds: **No,** the *baraita* is referring to a case **where she was occupied with** an item the size **of a split bean, and** subsequently a stain **was found on her** the size of **two split beans and** slightly **more.** In this situation she may not attribute the stain to the item she was occupied with. The Gemara asks: **If that is so, what** is the purpose **of stating** this case? Even if as much of the stain as possible is attributed to the item, a stain larger than a bean remains, and that part cannot be attributed to that source.

מַהוּ דְּתֵימָא: שְׁקוֹל כִּגְרִיס צִפּוֹר – שְׁדֵי בֵּי מִצְעֵי, זִיל הָכָא, לֵיכָּא שִׁיעוּרָא, זִיל הָכָא – לֵיכָּא שִׁיעוּרָא, קָא מַשְׁמַע לַן.

The Gemara answers that the ruling of the *baraita* is necessary **lest you say** that one should **take** the blood stain the size **of a split bean** that came from the blood of **the bird** she was previously occupied with and **cast** it **into the middle** of the stain. In other words, assume the blood from the bird is in the middle of the large stain, joining together two smaller stains. Consequently, one could say: **Go here** and measure the stain on this side, and **there is no measure** that transmits impurity, as it is less than the size of a bean, and likewise, **go there,** to the other side, and **there is no measure** that transmits impurity. Therefore, the *baraita* **teaches us** that this is not so, and in such a case she is impure.

אָמַר רָבָא: נִמְצָא עָלֶיהָ מִין אֶחָד – תּוֹלָה בּוֹ כַּמָּה מִינִין. מֵיתִיבֵי: נִתְעַסְּקָה בְּאָדוֹם – אֵין תּוֹלָה בּוֹ שָׁחוֹר! נִתְעַסְּקָה שָׁאנֵי.

**Rava says:** If **one type** of a stain **was found on** a woman, e.g., a stain from the sap of a sycamore tree or an eye salve, **she may attribute** other stains **to** that source, even if the stains are of **several types,** i.e., if they differ in color from the first stain. The Gemara **raises an objection** to the opinion of Rava from the aforementioned *baraita*: If a woman **was occupied with a red** item **she may not attribute a black** stain **to it.** The Gemara answers: A situation where she **was occupied is different** from Rava's case. Since she was occupied with a red item, there is no reason to attribute a black stain to that source. In Rava's case, by contrast, she was not occupied with any item, and therefore one can say that just as a stain of one type was sprayed upon her without her knowledge, the same occurred with regard to the other types of stains.

**HALAKHA**

**If she was occupied with an item the size of a split bean and a stain was found on her the size of a split bean and more – נִתְעַסְּקָה בִּכְגְרִיס וְנִמְצָא עָלֶיהָ בִּכְגְרִיס וָעוֹד:** If a woman was involved with blood that could not have produced a stain larger than a split bean, and she found on herself a stain as big as two split beans, some commentaries maintain that she may attribute the area of a split bean to the blood she was occupied with, and the area of the other split bean to a louse, and she is therefore pure. If the stain was larger than two split beans, however, she is impure (Rashba; Ra'ah). Others rule stringently, that she is impure even if the stain is only as large as two split beans, in accordance with the plain meaning of the *baraita* (Rosh; *Tur*). The Rema writes that one may rely on the lenient opinion, as the *halakha* is generally lenient with regard to stains (Rambam *Sefer Kedusha*, *Hilkhot Issurei Bia* 9:26; *Shulḥan Arukh*, *Yoreh De'a* 190:26).

**If a woman was occupied with a red item – נִתְעַסְּקָה בְּאָדוֹם:** In the case of a woman who was occupied with a red item and she found a black stain on herself, or the reverse, she may not attribute the stain to that source, in accordance with the ruling of the *baraita* (Rambam *Sefer Kedusha*, *Hilkhot Issurei Bia* 9:27; *Shulḥan Arukh*, *Yoreh De'a* 190:23).

אִיכָּא דְּאָמְרִי, אָמַר רָבָא: נִתְעַסְּקָה בְּמִין אֶחָד – תּוֹלָה בּוֹ כַּמָּה מִינִין. מֵיתִיבִי: נִתְעַסְּקָה בְּאָדוֹם – אֵין תּוֹלָה בּוֹ שָׁחוֹר! כִּי קָאָמַר רָבָא – דְּאִתְעַסְּקָה בְּתַרְנְגוֹלֶת, דְּאִית בָּהּ כַּמָּה מִינֵי דְּמָא.

**Some say** a different version of the above discussion. **Rava says:** If a woman **was occupied with** an item **of one type, she may attribute** stains of **several types to it.** The Gemara **raises an objection** to the opinion of Rava: If a woman **was occupied with a red** item **she may not attribute a black** stain **to it.** The Gemara answers: **When Rava said** his ruling he was referring to a situation **where she was occupied with** a slaughtered **chicken, which has several types of blood,**[H] and therefore she may attribute stains of different types to that cause.

"מַעֲשֶׂה בְּאִשָּׁה" [וכו׳]. וְהָתַנְיָא: לֹא אָמְרוּ חֲכָמִים אֶת הַדָּבָר לְהָקֵל, אֶלָּא לְהַחְמִיר!

§ The mishna teaches that there was **an incident involving** one **woman** who came before Rabbi Akiva and he deemed her pure, to the surprise of his students. He explained to them that the Sages did not state the matter of the impurity of blood stains in order to be stringent; rather, they instituted this impurity in order to be lenient. The Gemara asks: **But isn't it taught** in a *baraita* that **the Sages did not state the matter** of the impurity of blood stains **to be lenient, but** rather **to be stringent?**

אָמַר רָבִינָא: לֹא לְהָקֵל עַל דִּבְרֵי תוֹרָה – אֶלָּא לְהַחְמִיר עַל דִּבְרֵי תוֹרָה, וּכְתָמִים עַצְמָן דְּרַבָּנַן.

**Ravina says** that there is no contradiction between these two statements: The very institution of the impurity of blood stains was enacted so as **not to be** more **lenient than Torah law,** but **rather to be stringent beyond Torah law. But** since the impurity of blood **stains themselves is by rabbinic law,**[H] the Sages were lenient in specific cases.

"עַד שֶׁהוּא נָתוּן". אִיבַּעְיָא לְהוּ: מִי פְּלִיגִי רַבָּנַן עֲלֵיהּ דְּרַבִּי אֱלִיעֶזֶר בְּרַבִּי צָדוֹק, אוֹ לָא?

§ The mishna teaches with regard to **an examination cloth that was placed** beneath the pillow and blood was later found on the cloth, that Rabbi Eliezer, son of Rabbi Tzadok, maintains that if the stain is round it is ritually pure and if it is elongated it is ritually impure. Concerning this **a dilemma was raised before** the Sages: **Do the Rabbis disagree with Rabbi Eliezer, son of Rabbi Tzadok, or not?**

תָּא שְׁמַע: כֶּתֶם אָרוֹךְ – מִצְטָרֵף, טִפִּין טִפִּין – אֵין מִצְטָרְפִין. מַנִּי? אִי רַבִּי אֱלִיעֶזֶר בְּרַבִּי צָדוֹק – לָמָּה לִי צֵירוּף? הָאָמַר: מָשׁוּךְ כׇּל שֶׁהוּא – טָמֵא!

The Gemara suggests: **Come** and **hear** a resolution from a *baraita*: **An elongated stain**[H] **combines** with other elongated stains, so that if together they form the area of slightly more than a bean the woman is impure. But **a series of drops**[H] **do not combine** to constitute a stain that renders her impure. **Whose** opinion is stated in this *baraita*? **If** it is the opinion of **Rabbi Eliezer, son of Rabbi Tzadok, why do I** need **a combination** in the case of an elongated stain? **Didn't he say** that **an elongated** stain of **any** size renders her **impure?**

אֶלָּא לָאו – רַבָּנַן, שְׁמַע מִינַּהּ: פְּלִיגִי. לָא, לְעוֹלָם רַבִּי אֱלִיעֶזֶר בְּרַבִּי צָדוֹק, וְכִי אָמַר רַבִּי אֱלִיעֶזֶר בְּרַבִּי צָדוֹק – בְּעֵד, אֲבָל בְּכֶתֶם – לָא.

**Rather, is it not** the opinion of **the Rabbis,** and should one not **conclude from it** that the Rabbis **disagree** with Rabbi Eliezer, son of Rabbi Tzadok? The Gemara responds: **No, actually** the *baraita* is in accordance with the opinion of **Rabbi Eliezer, son of Rabbi Tzadok, and when Rabbi Eliezer, son of Rabbi Tzadok, said** an elongated stain is ritually impure he was referring to a stain found **on an examination cloth; but with regard to** a regular **stain** of an elongated shape, he does **not** hold it is impure regardless of its size.

תָּא שְׁמַע, דַּאֲמַר רַב יְהוּדָה, אָמַר שְׁמוּאֵל: הֲלָכָה כְּרַבִּי אֱלִיעֶזֶר בְּרַבִּי צָדוֹק. הֲלָכָה – מִכְּלָל דִּפְלִיגִי, שְׁמַע מִינַּהּ.

The Gemara suggests: **Come** and **hear, as Rav Yehuda said** that **Shmuel said:** The *halakha* is in **accordance with** the opinion of **Rabbi Eliezer, son of Rabbi Tzadok.** Since Shmuel rules that the *halakha* is in accordance with his opinion, it may be derived **by inference that** the Rabbis **disagree** with his opinion, as otherwise there would be no need for a ruling of *halakha*. The Gemara affirms: Indeed, **conclude from it** that this is correct.

הדרן עלך הרואה כתם

**HALAKHA**

Where she was occupied with a slaughtered chicken which has several types of blood – דְּאִתְעַסְּקָה בְּתַרְנְגוֹלֶת דְּאִית בָּהּ כַּמָּה מִינֵי דְּמָא: If a woman was involved with a slaughtered chicken she may attribute a stain to it if the stain is red, black, or the color of the crocus plant, as the blood that emerges from a slaughtered chicken is red, the blood of its limbs is black, and the blood of its intestines is the color of the crocus plant (Rambam *Sefer Kedusha, Hilkhot Issurei Bia* 9:27; *Shulḥan Arukh, Yoreh De'a* 190:24).

But the impurity of blood stains themselves is by rabbinic law – וּכְתָמִים עַצְמָן דְּרַבָּנַן: By Torah law a woman is rendered ritually impure and is forbidden to her husband only if she senses the emission of blood from her flesh. But the Sages decreed impurity on a stain found on her body or her clothing and deemed her forbidden to her husband even if she did not sense the emission of blood (Rambam *Sefer Kedusha, Hilkhot Issurei Bia* 9:1–2; *Shulḥan Arukh, Yoreh De'a* 190:1).

Elongated stain – כֶּתֶם אָרוֹךְ: If a stain is larger than a bean it may not be attributed to a louse, whether it is square shaped or elongated, as stated in the *baraita* (Rambam *Sefer Kedusha, Hilkhot Issurei Bia* 9:6; *Shulḥan Arukh, Yoreh De'a* 190:5).

Series of drops – טִפִּין טִפִּין: If a stain is no larger than a bean in any one place, even if there are many drops adjacent to each other that are collectively larger than a bean, the woman is pure, as each separate drop is attributed to a louse, in accordance with the ruling of the *baraita*. Some say this applies only if the stains were on her robe, but if they were on her flesh then those drops do combine to form the size of more than a bean (Rambam *Sefer Kedusha, Hilkhot Issurei Bia* 9:6, and see Ra'avad and *Maggid Mishne* there; *Shulḥan Arukh, Yoreh De'a* 190:8).

# Summary of **Perek VIII**

It was taught in Chapter Six and Chapter Seven that by Torah law a woman is not rendered ritually impure by a stain on her body or clothing, as derived from the verse: "And if a woman has an issue, and her issue in her flesh is blood" (Leviticus 15:19). This verse indicates both that she must see actual blood, not merely a stain, and that the sighting of blood must be accompanied by a physical sensation.

Nevertheless, the Sages decreed impurity even on stains. With regard to the extent of this decree, it was determined that in any situation where a stain can be attributed to an external source, e.g., if the woman passed through a place where blood is frequently sprayed from slaughtered animals, such as a butchers' marketplace, or if the blood might have come from elsewhere on her body, such as a wound, she may attribute it to that source and she is ritually pure. The same applies if she had been occupied with the removal of blood stains from the garments of other women.

It was further determined, at least according to one opinion, that the decree of the impurity of stains applies only to a stain that is found on an item that is susceptible to ritual impurity. It does not apply if the stain was discovered on an item or surface that is not susceptible to ritual impurity, such as the ground.

Likewise, if a stain was found on a woman's body or on her clothing in a place where blood from her uterus could not have reached, she is pure. But if it is possible the blood came from her uterus, she is impure. For example, if a woman has a stain on her big toe she is impure, since while she walks her toe is positioned in such a manner that blood from her uterus could drip onto it. The same reasoning applies in the case of a robe with which a woman covers herself at night: Since the position of the robe moves while she is asleep, any stain found on that robe renders her impure, as this blood could have originated in the uterus.

With regard to the size of the stain to which this decree applies, it was established that if a stain is the size of a split bean or smaller, a woman may attribute it to the blood of a squashed louse. The reason the Sages imposed this decree only on larger stains is that lice are common enough that a woman might have inadvertently squashed one and had its blood spray onto her as a result. If it sprayed onto her body, according to the Rambam she is impure no matter how small the stain, while according to others she is impure only if it is larger than a bean. If it sprayed onto her clothing she is impure only if it is larger than a bean. The principle in this regard is that the Sages did not state the matter of the impurity of blood stains in order to be stringent; rather, they instituted this impurity in order to be lenient. In other words, since the impurity of blood stains applies by rabbinic law, the Sages were lenient with regard to their status.

# Introduction to **Perek IX**

*And if a woman has an issue, and her issue in her flesh is blood, she shall be in her menstruation seven days, and whoever touches her shall be impure until the evening.*

(Leviticus 15:19)

This verse teaches that a woman is ritually impure as a menstruating woman only if blood emerges from her uterus. Normally a woman menstruates at regular intervals, and the Torah states that she becomes ritually impure when this occurs. But it can happen that a woman experiences an unusual flow of blood, e.g., while she is urinating. In such a case, it is uncertain whether the blood came from her uterus and therefore renders her impure, or whether it came from a wound elsewhere in her body and therefore does not render her impure. If she urinated into a basin where a man had also urinated, and blood is found in the basin, there is a further element of uncertainty, i.e., whether the blood came from her body or whether it came from the man.

Earlier, in Chapter Six and Chapter Eight, it was taught that a woman becomes ritually impure only when she experiences bleeding, whereas if she sees a blood stain she is not impure by Torah law. But the Sages decreed that a woman is rendered impure if she sees a blood stain. Since there are many types of common blood stains, the details of this *halakha* are complex. The Gemara discusses the extent to which the Sages were stringent with regard to blood stains. It further deals with the *halakha* in a case where one can attribute the stain to another woman or another source. For example, if two women wore the same garment or slept in the same bed and subsequently found a blood stain on it, which of them is impure?

This chapter also explains how a woman can examine a suspected blood stain with certain substances to determine whether it is indeed blood, or merely dye or some other red substance.

It was taught in the beginning of this tractate that a woman who has a fixed menstrual cycle and experiences bleeding at the expected time does not render food impure retroactively. This *halakha* applies in a case where there is a set time when she regularly menstruates. What is her status in this regard if she has a physical symptom, e.g., shivering or repeated yawning, that triggers her menstruation? In this context, the chapter discusses how a woman establishes a set pattern based on a physical sensation. It also deals with the manner in which such a pattern is displaced.

מתני׳ הָאִשָּׁה שֶׁהִיא עוֹשָׂה צְרָכֶיהָ, וְרָאֲתָה דָּם. רַבִּי מֵאִיר אוֹמֵר: אִם עוֹמֶדֶת – טְמֵאָה, וְאִם יוֹשֶׁבֶת – טְהוֹרָה. רַבִּי יוֹסֵי אוֹמֵר: בֵּין כָּךְ וּבֵין כָּךְ – טְהוֹרָה.

**MISHNA** In the case of **a woman who is urinating and saw blood**[H] intermingled with the urine, **Rabbi Meir says: If** she urinated while **standing** she is **ritually impure,**[N] as the blood could have originated in the uterus. **And if she is sitting,** she is **ritually pure,** as it is clear that the blood is from a wound. **Rabbi Yosei says: Whether** she urinates in **this** manner, i.e., standing, **or whether** she urinates in **that** manner, i.e., sitting, she is **ritually pure.**[N]

אִישׁ וְאִשָּׁה שֶׁעָשׂוּ צָרְכֵיהֶן לְתוֹךְ הַסֵּפֶל, וְנִמְצָא דָּם עַל הַמַּיִם, רַבִּי יוֹסֵי – מְטַהֵר, וְרַבִּי שִׁמְעוֹן – מְטַמֵּא, שֶׁאֵין דֶּרֶךְ הָאִישׁ לְהוֹצִיא דָּם, אֶלָּא שֶׁחֶזְקַת דָּמִים מִן הָאִשָּׁה.

In the case of **a man and a woman who urinated into a basin** [*hasefel*],[HL] **and blood is found on the water** in the basin, **Rabbi Yosei deems her ritually pure.** Even when it is clear that it is the blood of a woman who urinated, and there is only one uncertainty, Rabbi Yosei deems her ritually pure. In this case, there is a compound uncertainty: Did the blood originate with the man or with the woman, and did the blood come from the uterus or from a wound? **And Rabbi Shimon deems her ritually impure,** because there is only one uncertainty, **as it is not** the typical **manner of the man to discharge blood** with his urine; **rather, the presumptive status of the blood** is that it was discharged **from the woman.**

גמ׳ מַאי שְׁנָא עוֹמֶדֶת – דְּאָמְרִינַן מֵי רַגְלַיִם הֲדוּר לְמָקוֹר וְאַיְיתִי דָּם, יוֹשֶׁבֶת נָמֵי נֵימָא מֵי רַגְלַיִם הֲדוּר לְמָקוֹר וְאַיְיתִי דָּם!

**GEMARA** The mishna teaches that in a case where a woman finds blood in her urine Rabbi Meir distinguishes between a case where she is standing and a case where she is sitting. The Gemara asks: **What is different** about a situation where she is **standing?** The difference is **that we say** that while she was urinating the **urine returned to the uterus and brought blood** from there, which renders her impure. But if so, when she is **sitting as well, let us say** that the **urine returns to the uterus and brings blood.** Why does Rabbi Meir deem her ritually pure in that case?

אָמַר שְׁמוּאֵל: בִּמְזַנֶּקֶת. מְזַנֶּקֶת נָמֵי, דִּלְמָא בָּתַר דִּתְמוּ מַיָּא אֲתָא דָּם?

**Shmuel says,** in answer to this question: This mishna is referring specifically to a case **where** the urine **flows** in a steady stream, without the woman straining. In such a situation, when she is sitting and the urine flows in a steady stream, the stream of urine does not return to the uterus and bring blood. By contrast, if she is standing the urine does not flow in a steady stream, and she must strain to urinate. When she strains to urinate, the urine can bring blood from the uterus with it, whether she is standing or sitting. The Gemara objects: But in a case where she is sitting **as well,** when the urine **flows** in a steady stream, **perhaps after the urine has finished, blood will come** naturally from the uterus, and the flow of blood will mix with the urine?

### HALAKHA

**A woman who is urinating and saw blood – הָאִשָּׁה שֶׁהִיא עוֹשָׂה צְרָכֶיהָ וְרָאֲתָה דָּם:** If a woman sees blood in her urine, whether she urinated while standing or while sitting, she remains ritually pure. Even if she feels her body trembling she does not need to be concerned, as this is simply the sensation of the urine leaving the bladder, whereas the blood must be from a wound of some sort. The Rema writes that some say that she is ritually pure only if she was sitting while urinating (*Tur*, citing Rosh). Likewise, if she was standing and urinating in a steady stream, and she found blood in the basin into which she urinated, she remains pure. But if the urine was found on the edge of a basin, she is impure. Others claim that even when she is sitting, she is pure only if she urinates in a steady stream into a basin; while if she finds blood on the edge of the basin she is impure. Furthermore, if she was standing while urinating, she is impure in any event (Mordekhai; *Haggahot Maimoniyyot*). The Rema writes that the custom in practice is to follow the latter opinion (Rambam *Sefer Kedusha, Hilkhot Issurei Bia* 5:17; *Shulḥan Arukh, Yoreh De'a* 191:1).

**A man and a woman who urinated into a basin – אִישׁ וְאִשָּׁה שֶׁעָשׂוּ צָרְכֵיהֶן לְתוֹךְ הַסֵּפֶל:** If blood is found in a basin into which both a man and a woman have urinated, the woman remains ritually pure. The reason is that this is a compound uncertainty, as perhaps the blood came from the man, and even if it came from the woman, it is possible that it is not uterine blood (*Shulḥan Arukh, Yoreh De'a* 191:1, and *Shakh* there).

### LANGUAGE

**Basin [*sefel*] – סֵפֶל:** From the context here and in many other places it is clear that this is a large vessel into which significant quantities of liquid were poured, either for the purpose of drinking or for washing one's feet. In this context, it refers to a toilet. In modern usage this word refers to a small vessel used for drinking, but that is not the case in older sources.

### NOTES

**Rabbi Meir says, if she urinated while standing she is ritually impure – רַבִּי מֵאִיר אוֹמֵר אִם עוֹמֶדֶת טְמֵאָה:** Earlier (14b), various opinions were cited with regard to the meaning of Rabbi Meir's statement. According to Rabbi Yosei, son of Rabbi Ḥanina, Rabbi Meir deems this woman ritually impure as one who has seen a blood stain, i.e., due to uncertainty. By contrast, according to Rav Ashi, Rabbi Meir deems her impure with the definite impurity of a menstruating woman. Some commentaries write that according to the conclusion of the discussion on 14b she is certainly impure (*Tosafot* on 14b). Rabbi Meir's reasoning is explained here. He maintains that the urine will return to the uterus and bring blood from there. He evidently holds that this definitely happens, and therefore the woman is certainly impure. Others explain that Rabbi Meir agrees with those who are concerned even for the minority. If so, he does not necessarily maintain that the blood is definitely from the uterus, but since this scenario is possible, he deems the woman impure. By contrast, Rabbi Yosei rules that she is not impure, as he is not concerned for the minority of cases (Ran).

**Rabbi Yosei says, whether this or whether that she is ritually pure – רַבִּי יוֹסֵי אוֹמֵר בֵּין כָּךְ וּבֵין כָּךְ טְהוֹרָה:** The early commentaries discuss Rabbi Yosei's opinion, which is accepted as *halakha*. Some claim that Rabbi Yosei deems the woman entirely pure (*Tosafot* on 14b). Others contend that Rabbi Yosei deems her pure only with regard to the status of a menstruating woman by Torah law, but that he agrees that she is impure by rabbinic law, like a woman who finds a blood stain. In other words, Rabbi Yosei deems her impure due to uncertainty (Rabbeinu Ḥananel; *Noda BiYehuda*; *Shulḥan Arukh, Yoreh De'a* 191:1 and in the comment of Rema, and *Shakh* and *Beur HaGra* there).

אָמַר רַבִּי אַבָּא: בְּיוֹשֶׁבֶת עַל שְׂפַת הַסֵּפֶל, וּמְזַנֶּקֶת בְּתוֹךְ הַסֵּפֶל, וְנִמְצָא דָּם בְּתוֹךְ הַסֵּפֶל. דְּאִם אִיתָא דְּבָתַר דִּתְמוּ מַיָּא אֲתָא – עַל שְׂפַת הַסֵּפֶל אִיבָּעֵי לֵיהּ לְאִשְׁתַּכּוּחֵי.

**Rabbi Abba says:** This is no concern, as the mishna is referring to a case **where she is sitting on the edge of the basin and** urinates in a steady **flow**[N] **into the basin**, **and** the **blood is found** only **inside the basin. As, if it is so that after** the stream of **urine finished** the blood **came** naturally from her uterus, the blood **should have been found on the edge of the basin.** Since the blood is found only inside the basin it is clear that it came with the urine, not separately.

אָמַר שְׁמוּאֵל, וְאָמְרִי לַהּ אָמַר רַב יְהוּדָה, אָמַר שְׁמוּאֵל: הֲלָכָה כְּרַבִּי יוֹסֵי. וְכֵן אוֹרֵי לֵיהּ רַבִּי אַבָּא לְקָלָא: הֲלָכָה כְּרַבִּי יוֹסֵי.

**Shmuel said, and some say** that **Rav Yehuda said** that **Shmuel said:** The *halakha* is **in accordance with** the opinion of **Rabbi Yosei. And similarly, Rabbi Abba ruled for** a Sage called **Kala**, who inquired into this matter, that the *halakha* is **in accordance with** the opinion of **Rabbi Yosei.**

״אִישׁ וְאִשָּׁה״ [וכו׳]. אִיבַּעְיָא לְהוּ: אִישׁ וְאִשָּׁה עוֹמְדִין. מַה לִּי אָמַר רַבִּי מֵאִיר?

§ The mishna teaches: In the case of **a man and a woman** who urinated into a basin, and blood is found on the water in the basin, Rabbi Yosei deems her ritually pure. **A dilemma was raised before** the Sages: In a case where **a man and a woman were standing** and they urinated into the same basin, and blood was found in the basin, **what** would **Rabbi Meir,** who distinguishes between a woman who was sitting and a woman who was standing, **say** the *halakha* is?

כִּי אָמַר רַבִּי מֵאִיר – בְּחַד סְפֵקָא, אֲבָל בִּסְפֵק סְפֵקָא – לָא מְטַמֵּא, אוֹ דִּלְמָא לָא שְׁנָא?

The Gemara clarifies the dilemma: **When Rabbi Meir said** that a woman who sees blood in her urine while standing is impure, does this apply **when** there is only **one uncertainty,** i.e., whether the blood came from a wound or from the uterus? **Whereas** in a case **of a compound uncertainty**, i.e., whether the blood came from the man or from the woman, and even if it came from the woman, whether it came from a wound or from her uterus, perhaps Rabbi Meir **does not deem** her **impure? Or perhaps there is no difference** between the two cases according to Rabbi Meir.

אָמַר רֵישׁ לָקִישׁ: הִיא הִיא, מִמַּאי – מִדְּלָא קָתָנֵי ״רַבִּי מֵאִיר וְרַבִּי יוֹסֵי מְטַהֲרִין״.

**Reish Lakish said:** Rabbi Meir would rule in **this** case of a compound uncertainty exactly as he rules in **that** case of a single uncertainty, i.e., there is no difference between the two cases. Reish Lakish clarifies: **From where** do I know that this is Rabbi Meir's opinion? **From** the fact **that** the latter clause of the mishna **does not teach: Rabbi Meir and Rabbi Yosei deem her pure.** Instead, the mishna states merely that Rabbi Yosei deems her pure. This indicates that Rabbi Meir deems her impure even if a man and a woman both urinated into the same basin where the blood was found.

אִי הָכִי, הַשְׁתָּא רַבִּי מֵאִיר בִּסְפֵק סְפֵקָא מְטַמֵּא, בְּחַד סְפֵקָא מִיבַּעְיָא? לְהוֹדִיעֲךָ כֹּחוֹ דְּרַבִּי יוֹסֵי – דַּאֲפִילּוּ בְּחַד סְפֵקָא מְטַהֵר.

The Gemara raises a difficulty with regard to Reish Lakish's opinion: **If so**, i.e., if according to Rabbi Meir a woman is impure even when a man also urinates into the same basin, **now** that **Rabbi Meir deems her impure in** a case of **compound uncertainty, is it necessary** for the mishna to teach his opinion **in** a case of **one uncertainty?** The Gemara answers: The mishna formulated the *halakha* in that manner **to convey the far-reaching** nature of the opinion **of Rabbi Yosei,** i.e., **that he deems her pure even in** a case of **one uncertainty.**

וְאַדְּמִיפַּלְגִי בְּחַד סָפֵק – לְהוֹדִיעֲךָ כֹּחוֹ דְּרַבִּי יוֹסֵי, לִיפַּלְגוּ בִּסְפֵק סְפֵקָא – לְהוֹדִיעֲךָ כֹּחוֹ דְּרַבִּי מֵאִיר! כֹּחַ דְּהֶיתֵּרָא עָדִיף לֵיהּ.

The Gemara asks: **But** if so, **rather than** stating the **dispute in** a case of **one uncertainty,** which serves **to convey the far-reaching** nature of the opinion **of Rabbi Yosei, let** the *tanna* teach the **dispute in** a case of **compound uncertainty,** in order **to convey the far-reaching** nature of the opinion **of Rabbi Meir.** The Gemara answers: It is **preferable for the** *tanna* to teach **the strength of a lenient** ruling. If a *tanna* can formulate a dispute in a manner that emphasizes the extent of the more lenient opinion, he will do so.

**NOTES**

Where she is sitting on the edge of the basin and urinates in a steady flow – בְּיוֹשֶׁבֶת עַל שְׂפַת הַסֵּפֶל וּמְזַנֶּקֶת: The commentaries note that it is only according to the opinion of Rabbi Meir, who deems her impure if she urinates while standing, that she is impure if she urinates while sitting and strains while urinating. By contrast, according to Rabbi Yosei, who deems her pure even if she urinates while standing, she is likewise pure if she is sitting and she strains while urinating (Rosh). Others claim that even Rabbi Yosei agrees that if she urinates while sitting and strains, she is impure (*Haggahot Maimoniyyot* on Rambam *Sefer Kedusha, Hilkhot Issurei Bia* 5:17).

וְרַבִּי יוֹחָנָן אָמַר: כִּי קָאָמַר רַבִּי מֵאִיר – בְּחַד סְפֵקָא. אֲבָל בִּסְפֵק סְפֵקָא – לָא אֲמַר. אִם כֵּן, לִיתְנֵי "רַבִּי מֵאִיר וְרַבִּי יוֹסֵי מְטַהֲרִין"! אִין הָכִי נַמִי, וְאַיְּידֵי דִּסְלֵיק מֵרַבִּי יוֹסֵי – פְּתַח בְּדְרַבִּי יוֹסֵי.

**And Rabbi Yoḥanan** disagreed with Reish Lakish, and **said: When Rabbi Meir says** that the woman is impure, that applies only to a case **of one uncertainty, but** in a case **of compound uncertainty** Rabbi Meir **did not say** that she is impure. The Gemara raises a difficulty with regard to Rabbi Yoḥanan's opinion: **If so,** i.e., if Rabbi Meir deems her pure when both a man and a woman urinate into the same basin, **let** the mishna **teach: Rabbi Meir and Rabbi Yosei deem her pure.** Why does the *tanna* mention only Rabbi Yosei? The Gemara answers: **Yes, it is indeed so,** that Rabbi Meir agrees with this ruling, **but since** the mishna **left off** with the opinion **of Rabbi Yosei** at the end of the first clause of the mishna, the *tanna* **opened** the latter clause **with** the opinion **of Rabbi Yosei** as well.

וְרַבִּי יוֹסֵי, בְּחַד סְפֵקָא – מְטַהֵר, בִּסְפֵק סְפֵקָא מִיבָּעֲיָא? מַהוּ דְּתֵימָא: הָנֵי מִילֵּי – דִּיעֲבַד, אֲבָל לְכַתְּחִלָּה – לָא, קָא מַשְׁמַע לָן.

The Gemara asks: **But** as **Rabbi Yosei deems** her **pure** in a case **of one uncertainty, is it necessary** for the mishna to teach his opinion a case **of a compound uncertainty?** The Gemara answers: It is necessary for the *tanna* to state that Rabbi Yosei deems her pure in a case of compound uncertainty, **lest you say** that **this statement,** that Rabbi Yosei deems her pure, applies only **after the fact,** if the woman has already touched pure items, **but** he does **not** deem her pure ***ab initio.*** Therefore, the *tanna* **teaches us** that Rabbi Yosei deems her pure even *ab initio.*

תַּנְיָא כְּוָותֵיהּ דְּרַבִּי יוֹחָנָן: אִישׁ וְאִשָּׁה שֶׁעָשׂוּ צָרְכֵיהֶן לְתוֹךְ הַסֵּפֶל, וְנִמְצָא דָּם עַל הַמַּיִם – רַבִּי מֵאִיר וְרַבִּי יוֹסֵי מְטַהֲרִין, וְרַבִּי שִׁמְעוֹן מְטַמֵּא.

It **is taught** in a *baraita* **in accordance with** the opinion **of Rabbi Yoḥanan:** In the case of **a man and a woman who urinated into a basin, and blood is found on the water** in the basin, **Rabbi Meir and Rabbi Yosei deem her ritually pure, and Rabbi Shimon deems her ritually impure,** as there is only one uncertainty.

אִיבַּעֲיָא לְהוּ: אִשָּׁה יוֹשֶׁבֶת, מַה לִּי אֲמַר רַבִּי שִׁמְעוֹן? כִּי אֲמַר רַבִּי שִׁמְעוֹן – בְּעוֹמֶדֶת, דְּדָחֵיק לָהּ עָלְמָא, אֲבָל יוֹשֶׁבֶת – לָא. אוֹ דִּלְמָא לָא שְׁנָא?

§ The mishna teaches that Rabbi Shimon deems her ritually impure because there is only one uncertainty, as it is not the typical manner of the man to discharge blood with his urine. **A dilemma was raised before** the Sages: In a case where **a woman** was **sitting** and she urinated into a basin, and blood was found in the basin, **what** would **Rabbi Shimon say?** The Gemara explains the dilemma: **When Rabbi Shimon stated** his opinion, was he referring specifically **to** a woman who **is standing, who in general must strain** to urinate in such a position, and perhaps as a result the blood came from the uterus? **Whereas** if **she** is **sitting** without straining, in which case Rabbi Meir deems her pure, perhaps Rabbi Shimon agrees that she is **not** impure. **Or perhaps there is no difference** between the two cases according to the opinion of Rabbi Shimon.

תָּא שְׁמַע: דְּתַנְיָא, יוֹשֶׁבֶת – תּוֹלָה, עוֹמֶדֶת – אֵינָהּ תּוֹלָה, דִּבְרֵי רַבִּי מֵאִיר. רַבִּי יוֹסֵי אוֹמֵר: בֵּין כָּךְ וּבֵין כָּךְ – תּוֹלָה. רַבִּי שִׁמְעוֹן אוֹמֵר: בֵּין כָּךְ וּבֵין כָּךְ – אֵינָהּ תּוֹלָה.

The Gemara answers: **Come** and **hear, as it is taught** in a *baraita*: If a woman urinates while **sitting** and blood is found in the basin, she can **attribute** the blood to a wound and she is pure, but if she is **standing she cannot attribute** the blood to a wound, and therefore she is impure; this is **the statement of Rabbi Meir. Rabbi Yosei said: Both** in **this** case **and** in **that** case **she** can **attribute** the blood to a wound and she is pure. **Rabbi Shimon said: Both** in **this** case **and** in **that** case **she cannot attribute** the blood to a wound, and she is impure.

אִיבַּעֲיָא לְהוּ: אִישׁ וְאִשָּׁה יוֹשְׁבִין. מַה לִּי אֲמַר רַבִּי שִׁמְעוֹן? כִּי אֲמַר רַבִּי שִׁמְעוֹן עוֹמֶדֶת – דְּדָחֵיק לָהּ עָלְמָא, וְיוֹשֶׁבֶת – דְּחַד סָפֵק, אֲבָל בִּסְפֵק סְפֵקָא – לָא אֲמַר. אוֹ דִּלְמָא לָא שְׁנָא?

Another **dilemma was raised before** the Sages with regard to the opinion of Rabbi Shimon: In a case where **a man and a woman** were **sitting** and urinated into the same basin, and blood was found in the basin, **what** would **Rabbi Shimon say?** The Gemara clarifies the dilemma: **When Rabbi Shimon stated** his opinion, was he referring to a woman who **is standing, who in general must strain** to urinate in such a position and perhaps as a result the blood came from the uterus, **or** to a case where **she** alone **is sitting, which** are cases of only **one uncertainty? Whereas** in a case of **compound uncertainty,** i.e., uncertainty whether the blood came from the man or from the woman, and even if it did come from the woman, whether it was from a wound or from her uterus, perhaps **he does not say** that she is impure. **Or perhaps there is no difference** between the cases, as it is entirely atypical for a man to discharge blood.

תָּא שְׁמַע: כֵּיוָן דְּאָמַר רַבִּי שִׁמְעוֹן "חֶזְקַת דָּמִים מִן הָאִשָּׁה" – לָא שְׁנָא עוֹמְדִין, וְלָא שְׁנָא יוֹשְׁבִין.

The Gemara answers: **Come and hear** the mishna: **Since Rabbi Shimon said** that **the presumptive status of** the **blood** is that it was discharged **from the woman,** evidently there **is no difference** in his opinion whether she was **standing or** whether she was **sitting.**

מתני׳ הַשְּׁאִילָה חֲלוּקָהּ לְנׇכְרִית אוֹ לְנִדָּה – הֲרֵי זוֹ תּוֹלָה בָּהּ.

**MISHNA** In a case where a woman **lent her garment to a gentile woman or to a menstruating** Jewish **woman,**[H] and after the borrower returned the garment the owner wore it and then discovered a blood stain, she **attributes** the blood stain **to** the gentile or the menstruating woman.[N]

שָׁלֹשׁ נָשִׁים שֶׁלָּבְשׁוּ חָלוּק אֶחָד, אוֹ שֶׁיָּשְׁבוּ עַל סַפְסָל אֶחָד וְנִמְצָא עָלָיו דָּם – כּוּלָּן טְמֵאוֹת.

In a case of **three women who wore one garment**[H] **or who sat on one bench** [*safsal*],[L] one after the other, and the garment, or bench, was examined before the first of them donned it, or sat on it, and it was clean, and after the third one removed the garment, or stood up, **a blood** stain **was discovered on** the garment or on the bench, **all** the women **are ritually impure.**

יָשְׁבוּ עַל סַפְסָל שֶׁל אֶבֶן, אוֹ עַל הָאִיצְטְבָא שֶׁל מֶרְחָץ – רַבִּי נְחֶמְיָה מְטַהֵר. שֶׁהָיָה רַבִּי נְחֶמְיָה אוֹמֵר: כׇּל דָּבָר שֶׁאֵינוֹ מְקַבֵּל טוּמְאָה – אֵינוֹ מְקַבֵּל כְּתָמִים.

If **they sat on a stone bench or on the bench** [*ha'itzteva*][L] **of a bathhouse,**[B] neither of which can become ritually impure, the first because it is stone and the second because it is attached to the floor of the bathhouse, and a blood stain was found on one of those benches, **Rabbi Neḥemya deems** all three women **ritually pure, as Rabbi Neḥemya would say: Any item that is not susceptible to ritual impurity**[H] **is not susceptible to** ritual impurity due to blood **stains.** The decree of impurity due to blood stains was limited to items susceptible to ritual impurity.

גמ׳ אָמַר רַב: בְּנׇכְרִית

**GEMARA** **Rav says:** The ruling of the mishna is stated **with regard to a gentile woman**

HALAKHA

**A woman lent her garment to a gentile woman or to a menstruating Jewish woman** – הַשְּׁאִילָה חֲלוּקָהּ לְנׇכְרִית אוֹ לְנִדָּה: In a case where a woman wore a garment that she had examined and found to be free of blood stains, and after removing it she loaned it to a Jewish woman who was ritually impure due to menstruation or to a gentile woman who was old enough to menstruate, and afterward a blood stain was found on the garment, the owner of the garment is pure. The same applies if she examined the garment before loaning it to them and wore it after them, after which she discovered a blood stain. The owner may attribute the blood stain to the other woman even if she herself is counting her seven clean days. This ruling is in accordance with the Rambam's explanation of the Gemara (Rambam *Sefer Kedusha, Hilkhot Issurei Bia* 9:29; *Shulḥan Arukh, Yoreh De'a* 190:41).

**Three women who wore one garment** – שָׁלֹשׁ נָשִׁים שֶׁלָּבְשׁוּ חָלוּק אֶחָד: If three women all wore the same garment, or sat on the same bench, one after another, and a blood stain was found there, they are all ritually impure. This applies only if the bench is made of a material that is susceptible to ritual impurity, and if they all have the same likelihood of having a flow of blood. If one of them was more likely to experience bleeding than the others, e.g., one is post-menopausal, pregnant, nursing, or too young to have menstruated, the woman who is less likely to experience bleeding may attribute the blood to a woman who is more likely to experience bleeding (Rambam *Sefer Kedusha, Hilkhot Issurei Bia* 9:32; *Shulḥan Arukh, Yoreh De'a* 190:49).

**Any item that is not susceptible to ritual impurity** – כׇּל דָּבָר שֶׁאֵינוֹ מְקַבֵּל טוּמְאָה: The Sages did not render a woman ritually impure if she found a blood stain on an item that is not susceptible to ritual impurity. For example, if she examined to see that there were no blood stains on the ground or on a toilet that is not susceptible to ritual impurity (Rema), and then sat there and afterward found a blood stain, she remains pure. This *halakha* is in accordance with the opinion of Rabbi Neḥemya (Rambam *Sefer Kedusha, Hilkhot Issurei Bia* 9:7; *Shulḥan Arukh, Yoreh De'a* 190:10).

NOTES

**She attributes it to the gentile or the menstruating woman** – הֲרֵי זוֹ תּוֹלָה בָּהּ: Rashi explains that in this instance, where she attributes the stain to a gentile or an impure Jewish woman, the blood stain does not change the status of the other woman, as she is already impure. By contrast, if a ritually pure Jewish woman loans her garment to another ritually pure Jewish woman, and after both have worn it they find a blood stain, they are both ritually impure.

LANGUAGE

**Bench** [*safsal*] – סַפְסָל: From the Latin subsellium, meaning a low seat or bench.

**Bench** [*itzteva*] – אִיצְטְבָא: The primary source for this word, which appears in several different forms, is the Greek στοά, *stoa*. It has several related definitions: Column, colonnade, shed, or warehouse. The Sages used this term in different ways. In this case, the reference is to a type of bench or shelf upon which items are placed.

BACKGROUND

**Bench of a bathhouse** – אִיצְטְבָא שֶׁל מֶרְחָץ: In the Roman period, one section of a bathhouse contained an elongated vessel, similar to modern bathtubs. The lip of this vessel was wide, allowing people to sit on the edge while placing their feet in the hot water. The bench of the bathhouse is identified as this lip on the edge of the bathtub.

Roman bath with statue on the bathhouse bench, Hertfordshire, England

Perek **IX**
Daf **60** Amud **a**

הָרוֹאָה.

**who is** of age and already **seeing** a flow of menstrual blood, i.e., she has had a flow of menstrual blood.

מְמַאי? דּוּמְיָא דְּנִדָּה, מָה נִדָּה – דְּקָחָזְיָא, אַף נׇכְרִית – דְּקָא חָזְיָא.

The Gemara explains: **From where** does Rav know that this is referring to a gentile woman who once experienced a flow of blood? He infers from the mishna that the gentile woman it mentions is **similar to a menstruating woman: Just as a menstruating woman** is one **who sees,**[N] i.e., who has already experienced bleeding, **so too,** the mishna is referring to an adult **gentile woman who** already **sees** menstrual blood.

NOTES

**Just as a menstruating woman is one who sees, etc.** – מָה נִדָּה דְּקָחָזְיָא וכו׳: The commentaries explain that this does not mean that she is an actual menstruating woman; rather, it is known that she has menstruated at least once in her life. This is also the meaning in the case of the gentile woman; she has previously emitted menstrual blood (*Tosefot HaRosh*; Rashba; see Rashi).

אֲמַר רַב שֵׁשֶׁת: כִּי נַיֵּים וְשָׁכֵיב רַב אֲמָרָהּ לְהָא שְׁמַעְתָּא. דְּתַנְיָא: תּוֹלָה בְּנׇכְרִית. רַבִּי מֵאִיר אוֹמֵר: בְּנׇכְרִית הָרְאוּיָה לִרְאוֹת. וַאֲפִילּוּ רַבִּי מֵאִיר לָא קָאָמַר – אֶלָּא בִּרְאוּיָה לִרְאוֹת, אֲבָל רוֹאָה – לָא אִיצְטְרִיךְ.

**Rav Sheshet says: I say** that **when Rav was dozing or sleeping he said that** ***halakha***, i.e., it is an error. **As it is taught** in a *baraita*: If a woman loaned her garment to a gentile and subsequently found a blood stain on it, **she attributes** the stain **to the gentile woman.** This *tanna* deems it permitted for her to attribute the blood to any gentile woman, regardless of her age or her likelihood of bleeding. **Rabbi Meir** disagrees and **says:** This applies specifically **to a gentile woman who is fit to see** menstrual blood. **And** the Gemara adds that **even Rabbi Meir says only that** the gentile woman must be **fit to see** menstrual blood, **but** he too agrees that **it is not necessary** for her to be **seeing** blood at that time. She does not have to have actually experienced bleeding at some point.

אֲמַר רָבָא: וְתִסְבְּרָא רַבִּי מֵאִיר לְחוּמְרָא? רַבִּי מֵאִיר לְקוּלָּא.

**Rava said** in response to Rav Sheshet's challenge: **And** how can **you understand** that **Rabbi Meir** is coming **to be stringent?** Rav Sheshet maintains that according to the first *tanna* of the *baraita* she can attribute the blood stain to any gentile, whereas Rabbi Meir rules stringently that she may attribute it only to a gentile who is fit to experience bleeding. This is incorrect, as **Rabbi Meir** is actually coming **to be lenient.** In other words, the first *tanna* is more stringent, as he deems it permitted for her to attribute the blood stain only to a gentile woman who had experienced a menstrual flow at least once. By contrast, Rabbi Meir rules that she may attribute the stain to a gentile woman who is old enough to experience bleeding, even if she has never experienced a menstrual flow.

דְּתַנְיָא: אֵינָהּ תּוֹלָה בְּנׇכְרִית. רַבִּי מֵאִיר אוֹמֵר: תּוֹלָה. וְאֶלָּא קַשְׁיָא הָךְ! תְּרֵיץ הָכִי: וְהִיא שֶׁרוֹאָה. רַבִּי מֵאִיר אוֹמֵר – בִּרְאוּיָה לִרְאוֹת, וְאַף עַל פִּי שֶׁאֵינָהּ רוֹאָה.

The Gemara provides the reason for Rava's opinion. **As it is taught** in a *baraita*: A woman who loaned her garment to a gentile woman and subsequently finds a blood stain on it **may not attribute** the stain **to the gentile woman. Rabbi Meir says** that **she may attribute** the blood stain to the gentile woman. **But if so,** the first *baraita*, which states that according to the first *tanna* she may attribute the blood stain to any gentile woman, is **difficult.** You must **answer like this:** According to the first *tanna* she may attribute the blood to any gentile woman provided that **she sees,** i.e., that she once experienced bleeding. By contrast, **Rabbi Meir says** a more lenient opinion, **that** she may attribute it to the gentile woman provided that **she is fit to see** menstrual blood, **and** this is the *halakha* **even though she has not** actually **seen** menstrual blood yet.

תָּנוּ רַבָּנַן: תּוֹלָה בְּשׁוֹמֶרֶת יוֹם כְּנֶגֶד יוֹם בַּשֵּׁנִי שֶׁלָּהּ,

§ **The Sages taught** a *baraita* with regard to a woman who loaned her garment to another woman who was a lesser *zava*:[N] The lender **may attribute** the blood stain on the loaned garment **to a woman who observes** a clean **day for** each **day**[N] she experiences a discharge, if the blood is found **on her second** day, i.e., the day after she had a discharge, despite the fact that she does not have a presumptive status of seeing blood. It is nevertheless considered that her uterus is open and the likelihood is that she will experience bleeding.

וּבְסוֹפֶרֶת שִׁבְעָה שֶׁלֹּא טָבְלָה. לְפִיכָךְ הִיא – מְתוּקֶּנֶת. וַחֲבֶרְתָּהּ – מְקוּלְקֶלֶת, דִּבְרֵי רַבָּן שִׁמְעוֹן בֶּן גַּמְלִיאֵל. רַבִּי אוֹמֵר: אֵינָהּ תּוֹלָה, לְפִיכָךְ שְׁתֵּיהֶן מְקוּלְקָלוֹת.

**And** likewise, she may also attribute the blood stain if she loaned her garment **to a woman counting seven** clean days **who did not immerse** in a ritual bath, and who will now have to count another seven clean days. **Therefore,** the status of the one who loaned the garment **is fixed, and** the status of **the other** woman **is ruined** and she must begin her counting again; this is **the statement of Rabban Shimon ben Gamliel. Rabbi** Yehuda HaNasi **says: She may not attribute** the blood flow to either of these women. **Therefore,** the statuses of **both** the woman who loaned the garment and the one who borrowed it **are ruined,** in that both women are deemed impure.

וְשָׁוִין שֶׁתּוֹלָה בְּשׁוֹמֶרֶת יוֹם כְּנֶגֶד יוֹם בָּרִאשׁוֹן שֶׁלָּהּ,

The *baraita* continues: **And** both Rabban Shimon ben Gamliel and Rabbi Yehuda HaNasi **agree that** a woman who lends her garment **may attribute** any blood stain found on it **to a woman** who **observes a day for a day**[H] if it is **on her first** day of the discharge. In this case the status of the woman who borrowed the garment is no more ruined than it was already, as either way she can become pure on the following day.

**NOTES**

*Zava* – זָבָה: The *halakhot* of a female *zava* are not like those of a male *zav*, a man who experiences a gonorrhea-like discharge. Her impurity is not dependent on the type of discharge, but on the days on which she sees it. Even if she sees blood many times on a single day, they are all considered a single sighting.

A woman has the status of a *zava* if she experiences a blood flow not at the time of her menstrual period, but during the eleven days after her seven-day menstrual period, in accordance with the verse: "Not in the time of her impurity" (Leviticus 15:25). During the seven-day menstrual period, even if she sees blood for the entire seven days, by Torah law she may immerse on the night of the eighth day and is pure. The next eleven days are days in which it is assumed she does not experience menstrual bleeding. These are the days during which she can become a *zava*. If she sees blood on only one day during this time she is a lesser *zava*. By Torah law, she is required to wait for the passing of only one day without any discharge of blood, i.e., to observe a clean day for a day she experiences a discharge, in order to immerse and become pure. Even when she immerses in a ritual bath before the clean day is complete, if she does not experience a discharge for the rest of the day, once night comes she is considered retroactively pure from the time of her immersion. If she sees blood on two consecutive days she must observe herself on the third day and may immerse that evening or during the day. But if she sees blood on three consecutive days she becomes a greater *zava*, after which she must count seven clean days and may immerse only on the seventh day. She then brings an offering on the eighth day, after which it is permitted for her to partake of offerings.

**May attribute it to a woman who observes a clean day for each day** – **תּוֹלָה בְּשׁוֹמֶרֶת יוֹם כְּנֶגֶד יוֹם**: Some explain that this is because her uterus is open, as she saw blood the day before, and it is natural for women who have experienced a flow of blood to continue to see blood for more than one day. Although she has experienced bleeding for only one day, and therefore does not have a presumptive status of seeing blood, one can nevertheless attribute the blood stain to her as it is likely that the blood came from her. This is the *halakha* despite the fact that as a result of attributing the blood to her she will have to count an additional clean day (Rashi).

**HALAKHA**

**And they agree that she may attribute it to a woman who observes a day for a day, etc.** – **וְשָׁוִין שֶׁתּוֹלָה בְּשׁוֹמֶרֶת יוֹם כְּנֶגֶד יוֹם וכו׳**: If a woman loaned her garment to a lesser *zava* on her impure day, or to a woman who has experienced a flow of ritually pure blood, or to one experiencing hymenal bleeding, and she finds a blood stain on the garment, she may attribute it to these other women (Rambam *Sefer Kedusha, Hilkhot Issurei Bia* 9:29; *Shulḥan Arukh, Yoreh De'a* 190:42).

וּבְיוֹשֶׁבֶת עַל דַּם טוֹהַר, וּבִבְתוּלָה שֶׁדָּמֶיהָ טְהוֹרִין.

**And** they also agree **in** a case where the woman who borrowed the garment was a woman after childbirth **who is observing** the period **of** the **blood of purity.** During these days, attributing the blood to her does not ruin her status, as any blood she emits is pure and does not affect her status. **And** similarly, the lender may attribute the blood stain **to a virgin** who engages in intercourse for the first time, **as her blood is pure,** as there is an assumption that it is hymenal bleeding rather than menstrual blood.

״לְפִיכָךְ״ דְּרַבָּן שִׁמְעוֹן בֶּן גַּמְלִיאֵל לָמָּה לִי? מִשּׁוּם דְּרַבִּי.

The Gemara asks: **Why do I** need the clause starting with: **Therefore,** mentioned **by Rabban Shimon ben Gamliel?** It is obvious that the status of only one woman is ruined, so what information does this observation add? The Gemara answers that this clause does not add any new information; rather, the *baraita* taught it **because** of the use of the similar clause beginning with: Therefore, stated **by Rabbi** Yehuda HaNasi in the latter part of the *baraita*.

״לְפִיכָךְ״ דְּרַבִּי לָמָּה לִי? מַהוּ דְּתֵימָא: הַהִיא דְּאִשְׁתַּכַּח כֶּתֶם גַּבָּהּ – תִּתְקַלְקֵל, אִידָךְ – לָא תִּתְקַלְקֵל, קָמַשְׁמַע לָן.

The Gemara persists: But **why do I** need the clause starting with: **Therefore,** in the statement **of Rabbi** Yehuda HaNasi? That too is apparently superfluous. The Gemara explains: It is necessary, **lest you say** that the status of the woman **who has** the blood **stain found with her** when she is wearing the garment, should be **ruined,** whereas the status of **the other** woman should **not be ruined,** as the garment was not with her when the blood stain was discovered. Therefore, the *baraita* **teaches us** the clause beginning with: Therefore, to stress that both women are impure.

אָמַר רַב חִסְדָּא: טָמֵא וְטָהוֹר שֶׁהָלְכוּ בִּשְׁנֵי שְׁבִילִין, אֶחָד טָהוֹר וְאֶחָד טָמֵא – בָּאנוּ לְמַחֲלוֹקֶת רַבִּי וְרַבָּן שִׁמְעוֹן בֶּן גַּמְלִיאֵל.

§ With regard to the dispute between Rabban Shimon ben Gamliel and Rabbi Yehuda HaNasi, **Rav Ḥisda says:** In a case of two individuals, one of whom was **ritually impure and** the other of whom was **pure, who walked on two paths,**[H] **one** of which was **pure and** the other **one impure** due to a corpse buried there, and neither remembers which path he took, and afterward they handled items of ritual purity, e.g., the portion of produce designated for the priest [*teruma*] or consecrated items, **we have arrived at the dispute** between **Rabbi** Yehuda HaNasi **and Rabban Shimon ben Gamliel.** According to Rabban Shimon ben Gamliel, if one of the two individuals was already impure it can be assumed that he was the one who walked along the ritually impure path, and the other individual remains pure. Rabbi Yehuda HaNasi claims that there is no assumption that the one who was pure retains that state, as it is equally possible that he walked along the ritually impure path.

מַתְקִיף לַהּ רַב אַדָּא: עַד כָּאן לָא קָאָמַר רַבִּי הָתָם – אֶלָּא דְּתַרְוַיְיהוּ כִּי הֲדָדֵי נִינְהוּ, הָכָא – מַאי נָפְקָא לָן מִינַּהּ?

**Rav Adda objects to this** suggestion of Rav Ḥisda, claiming that one cannot compare the two cases. It is possible that **Rabbi** Yehuda HaNasi **states** his *halakha* **only there,** with regard to a woman who observes a day for a day, as she can immerse in a ritual bath at any time, and **therefore both** women **are like each other,** i.e., both have a presumption of ritual purity. But **here,** in the case of the two individuals walking on two paths, **what** practical **difference** does it make to the one who was previously impure if he remains ritually impure? Since there is no change of status, Rabbi Yehuda HaNasi would agree in that case that it can be assumed that the individual who was previously impure was the one who walked on the impure path.

HALAKHA

Two paths – שְׁנֵי שְׁבִילִין: In a case where there were two paths, one ritually pure and the other impure, and two people walked along them, i.e., one on each path, and one of the people was ritually pure while the other was impure, or even if the second person was impure due to uncertainty, the pure individual may attribute, i.e., he may assume that the ritually impure path was traversed by the impure individual or the one who was impure due to uncertainty. Consequently, the pure individual remains pure. This is the *halakha* even if they inquired about their status together. This ruling is in accordance with the opinion of Rabbi Yosei, son of Rabbi Ḥanina, as the *halakha* generally follows his opin on (Rambam *Sefer Tahara, Hilkhot She'ar Avot HaTumot* 19:4).

וְרַב חִסְדָּא – סוֹף סוֹף אִיהִי טְבִילָה בָּעֲיָא.

And the Gemara asks: How would **Rav Ḥisda** respond to this claim? Rav Ḥisda would answer that a woman who observes a day for a day is also not fully pure, as **ultimately she requires immersion** in a ritual bath to complete her purification, and yet Rabbi Yehuda HaNasi still rejects the attribution of the blood flow to her. Accordingly, the two cases are comparable and Rabbi Yehuda HaNasi would not assume that the individual who was already impure was the one who walked along the path that was impure.

אִיתְּמַר, אָמַר רַבִּי יוֹסֵי בְּרַבִּי חֲנִינָא: טָמֵא וְטָהוֹר, וַאֲפִילּוּ טָהוֹר וְתָלוּי, שֶׁהָלְכוּ בִּשְׁנֵי שְׁבִילִין, אֶחָד טָמֵא וְאֶחָד טָהוֹר – תּוֹלֶה טָמֵא בַּתָּלוּי, וְטָהוֹר בַּטָּהוֹר – לְדִבְרֵי הַכֹּל.

**It was stated** that **Rabbi Yosei, son of Rabbi Ḥanina, says:** In a case of two individuals, one of whom was **ritually impure and** the other of whom was **pure, or even** where one was **pure and** the other was impure due to **uncertainty, who walked on two** different **paths, one** of which was **impure and** the other **one pure,** and neither remembers which path he took, one may **attribute** by assuming that **the impure** path was the one traversed **by** the individual who was impure due to **uncertainty, and** the **pure** path was traversed **by** the one who was **ritually pure.** And **everyone agrees** with this ruling, i.e., Rabbi Yehuda HaNasi agrees with Rabban Shimon ben Gamliel in this case. This statement is in accordance with Rav Adda's objection, not in accordance with the suggestion of Rav Ḥisda.

בְּעָא מִינֵּיהּ רַבִּי יוֹחָנָן מֵרַבִּי יְהוּדָה בַּר לִיוַאי: מַהוּ לִתְלוֹת כֶּתֶם בְּכֶתֶם? אַלִּיבָּא דְּרַבִּי – לָא תִּבָּעֵי לָךְ,

§ **Rabbi Yoḥanan raised a dilemma before Rabbi Yehuda bar Livai: What is** the *halakha* **with regard to attributing** a blood **stain**[H] **to** a woman who is already impure due to having seen a blood **stain?** Rabbi Yoḥanan clarifies his question: **I am not raising** this **dilemma to you according to** the opinion **of Rabbi** Yehuda HaNasi.

הָשְׁתָּא, וּמַה הָתָם דְּקָא חַזְיָא מִגּוּפָהּ – אָמְרַתְּ אֵינָהּ תּוֹלָה, הָכָא דְּמֵעָלְמָא קָא אָתֵי – לֹא כׇּל שֶׁכֵּן?

Rabbi Yoḥanan explains why his dilemma does not apply according to the opinion of Rabbi Yehuda HaNasi: **Now, and if there,** where one loaned her garment to a woman who observes a clean day for a day, which is a case **where she sees** a discharge **from her body,** and yet **you said** that according to Rabbi Yehuda HaNasi the other woman **may not attribute** the blood stain to her, then **here,** in the case of a woman who is impure merely due to having seen a blood stain, **where** her impurity **came from** a source **external** to her, is it **not all the more so** that Rabbi Yehuda HaNasi would not permit one to attribute the blood stain to her?

כִּי תִּבָּעֵי לָךְ – אַלִּיבָּא דְּרַבָּן שִׁמְעוֹן בֶּן גַּמְלִיאֵל, הָתָם הוּא דְּקָא חַזְיָא מִגּוּפָהּ – תַּלְיָא, הָכָא דְּמֵעָלְמָא קָאָתֵי – לָא תַּלְיָא, אוֹ דִּלְמָא לָא שְׁנָא?

Rather, **when I raise** this **dilemma to you,** it is **in accordance with** the opinion **of Rabban Shimon ben Gamliel.** Rabbi Yoḥanan clarifies the dilemma: Perhaps **it is** only **there,** in the case where she loaned her garment to a woman who observes a day for a day, **where she sees** the discharge **from her body,** that the lender **may attribute** the blood stain to her, whereas **here, where** it is possible that the stain **came from** a source **external** to her, Rabban Shimon ben Gamliel would **not** permit the lender to **attribute** this new blood stain to her. **Or perhaps it is no different,** and Rabban Shimon ben Gamliel would rule leniently in both cases.

אֲמַר לֵיהּ: אֵין תּוֹלִין. מַה טַּעַם? לְפִי שֶׁאֵין תּוֹלִין.

Rabbi Yehuda bar Livai **said to** Rabbi Yoḥanan: She **may not attribute** this blood stain to a woman who was already impure due to having seen a blood stain, and both women are ritually impure. Rabbi Yoḥanan asked Rabbi Yehuda bar Livai: **What is the reason** that she may not attribute the blood stain to her? Rabbi Yehuda bar Livai answered: It is **because** in this case one **may not attribute**[N] the new blood stain to that other woman, as her previous stain might have come from an external cause.

**NOTES**

**Because one may not attribute** – לְפִי שֶׁאֵין תּוֹלִין: Some commentaries write that Rabbi Yehuda bar Livai did not answer Rabbi Yoḥanan's question and did not give a basis for his opinion. He simply responded that it is the accepted halakhic practice, and there is no need to inquire into the reason (*Arukh*). Others claim that Rabbi Yehuda bar Livai was in fact providing an explanation: Since she is not impure due to blood that certainly came from her body, but because of a blood stain found on her body or garment, which might have come from outside her body, she therefore does not have a presumptive status of seeing blood. For this reason, the blood stain found on the borrowed garment cannot be attributed to her (Rashi). The later authorities note that this form of response occurs elsewhere as well (see, e.g., *Shabbat* 21a and *Gittin* 60a).

**HALAKHA**

**What is the** ***halakha*** **with regard to attributing a blood stain, etc.** – מַהוּ לִתְלוֹת כֶּתֶם וכו׳: If a woman loaned her garment to another woman, who has seen a blood stain, whether she saw that blood stain before borrowing the garment or afterward, the new stain cannot be attributed specifically to either woman and both must be concerned for impurity. This ruling is in accordance with the opinion of Rabbi Yehuda bar Livai (Rambam *Sefer Kedusha, Hilkhot Issurei Bia* 9:29; *Shulḥan Arukh, Yoreh De'a* 190:43).

אֵיתִיבֵיהּ: אֵין תּוֹלִין כֶּתֶם בְּכֶתֶם. הִשְׁאִילָהּ חֲלוּקָהּ לְנׇכְרִית אוֹ לְיוֹשֶׁבֶת עַל הַכֶּתֶם – הֲרֵי זוֹ תּוֹלָה בָּהּ.

Rabbi Yoḥanan **raised an objection to** Rabbi Yehuda bar Livai from the following *baraita*: A woman who loans her garment to another and subsequently finds a blood stain on it **may not attribute** the blood **stain to** a woman who was impure due to having previously seen a blood **stain.** But if **she loaned her garment to a gentile woman or to** a woman who was **observing** days of impurity **due to** having seen a blood **stain, she may attribute** the blood stain found on the garment to that other woman.

הָא גּוּפָהּ קַשְׁיָא! רֵישָׁא אָמְרַתְּ אֵין תּוֹלִין, סֵיפָא אָמְרַתְּ תּוֹלִין! הָא לָא קַשְׁיָא, הָא – רַבִּי, וְהָא – רַבָּן שִׁמְעוֹן בֶּן גַּמְלִיאֵל.

Before explaining the objection, the Gemara first analyzes the *baraita*. **This** *baraita* **itself is difficult.** In **the first clause you said** that a woman who loans her garment to another and subsequently finds a blood stain on it **may not attribute** the blood stain to a woman who was impure due to having previously seen a blood stain, whereas in **the latter clause you said** that she **may attribute** the blood stain to such a woman. Rabbi Yoḥanan explains this contradiction: **This** is **not difficult. This** first clause of the *baraita* is in accordance with the opinion of **Rabbi** Yehuda HaNasi, **and that** latter clause is in accordance with the opinion of **Rabban Shimon ben Gamliel.**

אִיכָּא דְּאָמְרִי: הָא וְהָא – רַבִּי, הָא – בָּרִאשׁוֹן שֶׁלָּהּ, הָא – בַּשֵּׁנִי שֶׁלָּהּ.

**There are** those **who say** an alternative resolution of the contradiction: Both **this** clause **and that** clause are in accordance with the opinion of **Rabbi** Yehuda HaNasi. The difference is that **this** latter clause, where she may attribute the blood stain to the other woman, is referring to a case where the blood stain was found **on** that woman's **first** day, when she had just found the blood stain and is impure for that day. Since she is in any case impure for that day, she is not adversely affected by having the new stain attributed to her. The case where the blood stain may not be attributed to the other woman is a case where the blood stain in question was found **on her second** day, i.e., the day after she found the blood stain, when she is not impure but merely requires immersion. The lender may not attribute the new blood stain to her, as that would render her ritually impure for an extra day.

רַב אַשִׁי אֲמַר: הָא וְהָא – רַבָּן שִׁמְעוֹן בֶּן גַּמְלִיאֵל, וְלָא קַשְׁיָא,

**Rav Ashi said** yet another resolution of the *baraita*: Both **this** first clause **and that** latter clause are in accordance with the opinion of **Rabban Shimon ben Gamliel, and it** is **not difficult.**

Perek **IX**
Daf **60** Amud **b**

כָּאן – לְמַפְרֵעַ, כָּאן – לְהַבָּא.

**Here,** in the latter clause of the *baraita*, when she may attribute the stain to a woman who had seen a blood stain, it is referring to rendering that woman impure **retroactively** with regard to the status of pure items that she had already touched before the stain was found on the garment she borrowed. This attribution of the blood stain to the woman who was already impure due to seeing a blood stain does not harm her impure status in any way, as items she had previously touched were already considered impure. **There,** in the beginning of the *baraita*, where the ruling is that the lender may not attribute the blood stain to a woman who was already impure, it is referring to her own status **with regard to the future.**[N] With regard to the future, one may not attribute the stain to woman who had already seen a blood stain, as this attribution would ruin that woman's counting of pure days.

**NOTES**

Here retroactively, there with regard to the future – כָּאן לְמַפְרֵעַ כָּאן לְהַבָּא: According to some commentaries, Rav Ashi means that with regard to any pure items already touched by the women, impurity is ascribed to the woman who has seen a blood stain. The reason is that it does not affect her status, as even without attributing this impurity to her, she retroactively renders impure any ritually pure items she touched, since she is already impure. By contrast, with regard to the impurity of ritually pure items that the women will touch, the other woman may not attribute the blood stain to the one who was already impure due to having seen a blood stain, as this would render her status more stringent than it was beforehand (Rashi).

מִכׇּל מָקוֹם קַשְׁיָא! אָמַר רָבִינָא: לָא קַשְׁיָא, הָכִי קָאָמַר: הִשְׁאִילָה חֲלוּקָהּ לְנׇכְרִית – בַּעֲלַת כֶּתֶם הֲרֵי זוֹ תּוֹלָה בָּהּ.

The Gemara returns to the objection: The *baraita* has been resolved, but **in any case** everyone agrees that according to Rabban Shimon ben Gamliel she may attribute the stain to a woman who had previously seen a blood stain. This presents **a difficulty** to the answer of Rabbi Yehuda bar Livai, i.e., that according to Rabban Shimon ben Gamliel one may not attribute the blood stain in such a case. **Ravina said:** It is **not difficult,** as **this** is what the *baraita* **is saying** in its latter clause: If **she loaned her garment to a gentile woman,** then with regard to defining the lender as one **who had seen** a blood **stain,** the lender **may attribute** the stain **to** the gentile woman. If so, it cannot be inferred from the *baraita* that according to Rabban Shimon ben Gamliel one may attribute a blood stain to another woman who was already impure due to a blood stain.

וְהָא ״אוֹ לְיוֹשֶׁבֶת עַל הַכֶּתֶם״ קָתָנֵי! הָכִי קָאָמַר: אוֹ לְיוֹשֶׁבֶת עַל דַּם טוֹהַר – בַּעֲלַת כֶּתֶם תּוֹלָה בָּהּ.

The Gemara raises an objection: **But** the *tanna* of the *baraita* **teaches: Or to** a woman who was **observing** days of impurity **due to** having seen a blood **stain,** i.e., it mentions another woman who was already impure due to having seen a blood stain. Ravina explains that **this** is what the *tanna* **is saying:** If she loaned the garment to a gentile woman **or to** a woman after childbirth **who is observing** the period **of the blood of purity,** then with regard to defining the lender as **a woman who saw** a blood **stain, she may attribute** the stain to the gentile or to the woman observing the days of ritually pure blood, and the lender remains pure.

״שָׁלֹשׁ שֶׁלָּבְשׁוּ כו׳ שֶׁהָיָה רַבִּי נְחֶמְיָה״ כו׳: אָמַר רַב מַתָּנָה: מַאי טַעְמָא דְּרַבִּי נְחֶמְיָה – דִּכְתִיב ״וְנִקָּתָה לָאָרֶץ תֵּשֵׁב״, כֵּיוָן שֶׁיָּשְׁבָה לָאָרֶץ – נִקְּתָה.

§ The mishna teaches: In a case of **three** women **who wore** one garment, etc. If they sat on a stone bench or on the bench of a bathhouse, Rabbi Neḥemya deems all three women ritually pure, **as Rabbi Neḥemya would** say: Any item that is not susceptible to ritual impurity is not susceptible to ritual impurity due to blood stains. The Gemara clarifies the opinion of Rabbi Neḥemya. **Rav Mattana says: What is the reason** for the opinion **of Rabbi Neḥemya? As it is written:** "And her gates shall lament and mourn; **and clean she shall sit upon the ground"** (Isaiah 3:26). This teaches that **once she sits on the ground,** which is not susceptible to ritual impurity, **she shall be clean,** i.e., pure.

אָמַר רַב הוּנָא, אָמַר רַבִּי חֲנִינָא: מְטַהֵר הָיָה רַבִּי נְחֶמְיָה אֲפִילּוּ בַּאֲחוֹרֵי כְּלִי חֶרֶס. פְּשִׁיטָא!

**Rav Huna says** that **Rabbi Ḥanina says: Rabbi Neḥemya would deem her ritually pure even** if she sat **on the exterior** of an inverted **earthenware vessel.**[H] Since an earthenware vessel becomes impure only if an impure item enters its airspace, its exterior is not susceptible to ritual impurity and therefore it does not render a woman who sees a blood stain on it ritually impure. The Gemara asks: Isn't that **obvious?** Rabbi Neḥemya himself said that she does not become impure if a blood stain is found on an item that is not susceptible to ritual impurity. What does Rabbi Ḥanina add to that statement?

מַהוּ דְּתֵימָא: לִיגְזוֹר גַּבּוֹ אַטּוּ תּוֹכוֹ – קָא מַשְׁמַע לַן.

The Gemara answers: This observation is necessary, **lest you say: Let** the Sages **decree** that she becomes impure from a blood stain found on **the exterior** of an earthenware vessel, **due to** its similarity to a blood stain found on **the interior,** which would render her impure. Therefore, Rabbi Ḥanina **teaches us** that there is no such decree.

אָמַר אַבָּיֵי: מְטַהֵר הָיָה רַבִּי נְחֶמְיָה בִּמְטַלְנִיּוֹת שֶׁאֵין בָּהֶן שָׁלֹשׁ עַל שָׁלֹשׁ, דְּלָא חָזְיָין לָא לַעֲנִיִּים וְלָא לַעֲשִׁירִים.

**Abaye says: Rabbi Neḥemya would deem her ritually pure** if she saw blood stains **on small rags that do not have** an area of **three** fingerbreadths **by three** fingerbreadths,[NH] **as these rags are suitable** for use **neither for the poor nor for the wealthy.**

**NOTES**

Small rags that do not have an area of three by three fingerbreadths – מְטַלְנִיּוֹת שֶׁאֵין בָּהֶן שָׁלֹשׁ עַל שָׁלֹשׁ: The Gemara does not find it necessary to specify the unit of this measurement of three by three as it is a common expression, which refers to three by three fingerbreadths. The Sages state that any garment of at least this size is susceptible to ritual impurity, as it is suitable for use by poor people, despite the fact that wealthy people would not use it (see *Shabbat* 26b).

**HALAKHA**

On the exterior of an earthenware vessel – בַּאֲחוֹרֵי כְּלִי חֶרֶס: If a woman sat upon an overturned earthenware vessel and when she arose she found a blood spot there, she is ritually pure. The reason is that the Sages did not decree ritual impurity for any blood spot found on an item that is not susceptible to ritual impurity. This *halakha* is in accordance with the opinion of Rabbi Neḥemya (Rambam *Sefer Kedusha, Hilkhot Issurei Bia* 9:7).

Small rags that do not have an area of three by three fingerbreadths – מְטַלְנִיּוֹת שֶׁאֵין בָּהֶן שָׁלֹשׁ עַל שָׁלֹשׁ: If a woman sat on a piece of cloth that was less than three by three fingerbreadths, and she found a blood stain on it when she arose, she is ritually pure. Similarly, if she sat on the ground and found a blood spot there when she arose, she remains ritually pure, as the Sages did not decree ritual impurity for any blood stain found on an item that is not susceptible to ritual impurity (Rambam *Sefer Kedusha, Hilkhot Issurei Bia* 9:7).

דרש רב חייא בר רב מתנה משמיה דרב: הלכה כרבי נחמיה. אמר ליה רב נחמן: אבא תני מעשה בא לפני חכמים וטמאום, ואת אמרת הלכה כרבי נחמיה?!

**Rav Ḥiyya bar Rav Mattana taught in the name of Rav:** The ***halakha*** **is in accordance with** the opinion of **Rabbi Neḥemya. Rav Naḥman said** to Rav Ḥiyya bar Rav Mattana: **Father**[P] **teaches** the following *baraita*: **An incident** of this kind **came before the Sages,** involving two women who found a blood stain on an item that was not susceptible to ritual impurity, **and** the Sages **deemed** both women **ritually impure,** in accordance with the opinion of the Rabbis, who disagree with Rabbi Neḥemya. **And** yet **you say** that the ***halakha*** **is in accordance with** the opinion of **Rabbi Neḥemya?**

מאי היא? דתניא: שתי נשים שהיו טוחנות ברחיים של יד, ונמצא דם תחת הפנימית – שתיהן טמאות, תחת החיצונה – החיצונה טמאה, והפנימית טהורה, בינתים – שתיהן טמאות.

The Gemara inquires: **What is** that incident in question? **As it is taught** in a *baraita*: With regard to **two women who were grinding with a hand mill**[B] and were standing next to each other, **and blood was found beneath the** woman on the **inside,**[H] i.e., the woman standing closest to the mill, **they are both ritually impure.** The reason is that the woman standing further away pushes in to get closer to the mill, and therefore the blood stain could be from either of them. But if blood was found **beneath** the woman on **the outside,** i.e., the woman standing further from the mill, the woman on **the outside is impure and** the woman on **the inside is pure.** If the blood was found **between them, they are both impure.**

היה מעשה ונמצא דם על שפתה של אמבטי, ועל עלה של זית בשעה שמסיקות את התנור, ובא מעשה לפני חכמים – וטמאום.

The *baraita* continues: **There was an incident and blood was found on the edge of a bathtub,**[B] **and** in another case a blood stain was found **on an olive leaf at the time that** the women **were kindling the oven.**[B] **And the incident came before the Sages and** they **deemed** both women **ritually impure.** Since an olive leaf is not susceptible to ritual impurity, this *baraita* is not in accordance with the opinion of Rabbi Neḥemya.

תנאי היא, דתניא: רבי יעקב מטמא, ורבי נחמיה מטהר, והורו חכמים כרבי נחמיה.

Rabbi Ḥiyya bar Rav Mattana answered: **It is** a dispute between ***tanna'im*** whether or not the *halakha* is in accordance with the opinion of Rabbi Neḥemya. **As it is taught** in a *baraita*: If a blood stain is found on an item that is not susceptible to ritual impurity, **Rabbi Ya'akov deems her impure, but Rabbi Neḥemya deems her pure. And the Sages ruled** that the *halakha* **is in accordance with** the opinion of **Rabbi Neḥemya.**

### PERSONALITIES

**Father** – אבא: Rav Naḥman's father was called Ya'akov, and the Jerusalem Talmud always refers to Rav Naḥman as Rav Naḥman bar Ya'akov. By contrast, the Babylonian Talmud simply calls him Rav Naḥman. The Gemara in *Bava Metzia* 16b relates that Rav Naḥman's father was a scribe in Shmuel's court and would often take Rav Naḥman there when Rav Naḥman was a child. Apparently, Rav Naḥman's father taught him most of the Torah that he learned as a child, and Rav Naḥman would later cite his father as an authority (see *Beitza* 26b). Although there are no explicit statements in the Talmud citing Rav Naḥman's father, he was likely a leading scholar in his own right.

### HALAKHA

**Two women who were grinding with a hand mill and blood was found beneath the woman on the inside** – שתי נשים שהיו טוחנות ברחיים של יד ונמצא דם תחת הפנימית: If two or three women were working side by side in such a manner that at some stage they all move to the inner point, e.g., if they were all taking turns using a hand mill, and blood is found beneath the innermost woman, the two innermost women are ritually impure. If the blood is found beneath the outermost woman, she is impure and the two women on the inside remain ritually pure. This *halakha* is in accordance with the opinion expressed in the *baraita* (*Shulḥan Arukh, Yoreh De'a* 190:52).

### BACKGROUND

**Hand mill** – רחיים של יד: Hand mills were fashioned with one hole in the top stone, where the grain could be inserted, and another hole on the side for a stick, enabling the grindstone to be turned against the bottom stone. These hand mills were often used in the home. When flour was produced commercially, larger mills were used, whose stones were turned by waterpower or by animals. Such mills could, in emergencies, be turned by people as well; see, e.g., Judges 16:21.

Close-up of the two sections of a hand mill

Child using ancient hand mill

**The edge of a bathtub** – שפתה של אמבטי: Bathtubs similar to those found in modern bathrooms were in the past found only in communal bathhouses or in the homes of the very rich. Some baths had a wide ledge on which a few people could sit.

Roman bathtub

**Kindling the oven** – מסיקות את התנור: Many ovens in late antiquity were made of clay and open at the top. Fire was kindled inside to heat the oven until the fuel turned to ash. The ash was then swept away to make room for dough that had been rolled out flat, which was inserted through the hole in the top of the oven and pasted to the walls of the oven or to the heated base. Sometimes the oven had a separate fuel compartment in its base that allowed the fire to burn while the bread baked.

Remains of clay ovens such as those used in talmudic times

מתני׳ שָׁלֹשׁ נָשִׁים שֶׁהָיוּ יְשֵׁנוֹת בְּמִטָּה אַחַת, וְנִמְצָא דָּם תַּחַת אַחַת מֵהֶן – כּוּלָּן טְמֵאוֹת. בָּדְקָה אַחַת מֵהֶן וְנִמְצֵאת טְמֵאָה – הִיא טְמֵאָה וּשְׁתֵּיהֶן טְהוֹרוֹת. וְתוֹלוֹת זוֹ בָּזוֹ, וְאִם לֹא הָיוּ רְאוּיִן לִרְאוֹת – רוֹאִין אוֹתָן כְּאִילּוּ הֵן רְאוּיוֹת.

**MISHNA** In a case of **three women who were sleeping in one bed and blood was discovered beneath one of them,**[H] **all of them are ritually impure.** If when the blood was discovered **one of them examined** herself **and discovered that she was impure** due to menstruation, **she is impure and the** other **two are pure. And** if none of them examined themselves, or if all of them examined themselves and were pure, **they attribute** the blood **to each other,** i.e., if one of them is unfit to menstruate, e.g., she is pregnant, she may attribute the blood to the other women who are fit to menstruate. **And if** all three women **were not fit to see** the flow of blood, e.g., they each belonged to one of the categories listed in the mishna on 7a, **one considers them as though they were fit,** and all three are impure, because the blood must have originated from one of them.

גמ׳ אָמַר רַב יְהוּדָה, אָמַר רַב: וְהוּא שֶׁבָּדְקָה עַצְמָהּ בְּשִׁיעוּר וֶסֶת.

**GEMARA** The mishna teaches that if one of the women examined herself when the blood was discovered and found that she was impure due to menstruation, she is impure and the other two are pure. In this regard, **Rav Yehuda says** that **Rav says:** The other two women may attribute the blood to the one who examined herself only **when she examined herself within** the brief **period of time** needed for the onset of **menstruation.**[H] But if she checked herself after this time, although she is impure, the other women are also impure, due to uncertainty.

סָבַר לַהּ כְּבַר פַּדָּא, דְּאָמַר: כָּל שֶׁבַּעְלָהּ בְּחַטָּאת – טָהֳרוֹתֶיהָ טְמֵאוֹת,

The Gemara explains: Rav **holds in accordance with** the opinion of **bar Padda, who said:** There are three time periods with regard to defining a woman's ritual-purity status if she sees blood after engaging in intercourse. The shortest is the period of time required for the onset of menstruation, i.e., for menstrual bleeding to begin. The next shortest is the time it would take the woman to get out of bed after intercourse and wash her private parts. The longest period is any time longer than that. If a woman finds blood after intercourse within the period of time needed for the onset of menstruation, she must have been impure during intercourse. With regard to **any** woman **whose husband** would be liable **to** bring **a sin offering** if he had engaged in intercourse with her, because she found the blood within that short period, if she had not been engaging in intercourse, but rather had been preparing food in a state of ritual purity, and then she found blood within that short period, all the **pure items** that she touched **are ritually impure.**

בַּעְלָהּ בְּאָשָׁם תָּלוּי – טָהֳרוֹתֶיהָ תְּלוּיוֹת, בַּעְלָהּ פָּטוּר – טָהֳרוֹתֶיהָ טְהוֹרוֹת.

By contrast, with regard to any woman **whose husband** would be liable **to** bring **a provisional guilt offering**[B] if he had engaged in intercourse with her, as it is uncertain whether he violated a transgression for which he would be liable to bring a sin offering, if she had not been engaging in intercourse, but rather had been preparing food in a state of ritual purity and then found blood within that same time period, the status of all the **pure items** she touched is **suspended,** as their status is uncertain. They are not burned but they may not be eaten either. Finally, with regard to any woman **whose husband** would be **exempt** from bringing any offering, i.e., where she finds blood after a longer time period, if she had not been engaging in intercourse, but rather had been preparing food in a state of ritual purity, and then found the blood after a longer time period, all the **pure items** she touched remain **pure.**

**HALAKHA**

**Three women who were sleeping in one bed and blood was discovered beneath one of them – שָׁלֹשׁ נָשִׁים שֶׁהָיוּ יְשֵׁנוֹת בְּמִטָּה אַחַת וְנִמְצָא דָּם תַּחַת אַחַת מֵהֶן:** If three women were sleeping side by side on one bed such that their legs were entwined, and blood is found beneath one of them, they are all ritually impure. Even if their legs are not entwined, but blood is found beneath the woman in the middle, they are all impure. This is the *halakha* only if none of them had examined themselves beforehand. If one or two of the women had examined themselves and found themselves to be ritually pure, they are pure while the other one or two women, who did not check themselves, are impure (Rambam *Sefer Kedusha, Hilkhot Issurei Bia* 9:32; *Shulḥan Arukh, Yoreh De'a* 190:50–51).

**When she examined herself within the brief period of time needed for the onset of menstruation – וְהוּא שֶׁבָּדְקָה עַצְמָהּ בְּשִׁיעוּר וֶסֶת:** If three women were lying on the same bed and blood was found on the bed, and one of them examined herself and found herself to be ritually impure, the other women remain pure. If one examined and found herself pure, she is pure and the others are impure. These examinations must take place immediately after the blood is found. If the examinations were delayed by the amount of time it would take to perform an examination, i.e., the time it would take to check the folds and crevices of her vagina, this examination is ineffective and all the women are impure. This ruling is in accordance with the opinion of Rav Yehuda citing Rav (Rambam *Sefer Kedusha, Hilkhot Issurei Bia* 9:32; *Shulḥan Arukh, Yoreh De'a* 190:51).

**BACKGROUND**

**Provisional guilt offering – אָשָׁם תָּלוּי:** The provisional guilt offering appears in the Torah in Leviticus 5:17–19, and its various *halakhot* are explained in tractate *Karetot*. The standard case of a provisional guilt offering is a situation of uncertainty as to whether or not a transgression warranting a sin offering was committed. For example, if a piece of forbidden fat and a piece of permitted fat were found together and one thought they were both permitted and ate one of them, he must bring a provisional guilt offering. The offering protects him from punishment until it is determined whether or not he actually sinned. If it is discovered that he did sin, he must bring a sin offering.

וְרַבִּי אוֹשַׁעְיָא אָמַר: אֲפִילּוּ בַּעְלָהּ בְּחַטָּאת – טָהֳרוֹתֶיהָ תְּלוּיוֹת.

**And Rabbi Oshaya says:** There is no connection between her husband's obligation to bring an offering and the ritual-purity status of the items she handled. **Even** if **her husband** is liable **to** bring **a sin offering**, i.e., when she discovered the blood within the period of time needed for the onset of menstruation, the status of all the **pure items** she touched before she discovered the blood is **suspended,** as their status is uncertain.

בִּשְׁלָמָא הָתָם – אֵימַר שַׁמָּשׁ עִכְּבֵיהּ לַדָּם [אֲבָל] הָכָא – אִם אִיתָא דַּהֲוָה דָּם מַאן עִכְּבֵיהּ?

Rabbi Oshaya explains his reasoning. **Granted, there,** in the case of intercourse, where the husband must bring an offering, one can **say** that the male **organ prevented the blood** from emerging from her body, and therefore it is clear that she was impure beforehand. **But here,** in the case of preparing food in a state of ritual purity, **if it is so that there was blood** coming out of her while she was preparing the food, **what prevented** the blood from emerging from her body?

אָמַר רַבִּי יִרְמְיָה: מָשָׁל דְּרַבִּי אוֹשַׁעְיָא לְמָה הַדָּבָר דּוֹמֶה – לְיֶלֶד וְזָקֵן שֶׁהָיוּ מְהַלְּכִין בַּדֶּרֶךְ, כָּל זְמַן שֶׁהָיוּ בַּדֶּרֶךְ – יֶלֶד שׁוֹהֶא לָבֹא, נִכְנְסוּ לָעִיר – יֶלֶד מְמַהֵר לָבֹא. וְאָמַר אַבָּיֵי: מָשָׁל דְּרַבִּי אוֹשַׁעְיָא לְמָה הַדָּבָר דּוֹמֶה – לְאָדָם שֶׁנּוֹתֵן אֶצְבַּע בָּעַיִן, כָּל זְמַן שֶׁאֶצְבַּע בָּעַיִן – דִּמְעָה שׁוֹהָא לָבֹא, נָטַל הָאֶצְבַּע – דִּמְעָה מְמַהֶרֶת לָבֹא.

**Rabbi Yirmeya says a parable** in explanation **of** the opinion of **Rabbi Oshaya: To what is this matter comparable? To a child and an old man who are walking along the road. As long as they are on the road,** the **child delays his arrival,** i.e., he walks at the pace of the old man. But once **they enter the city,** the **child hastens his arrival,** and runs on ahead. Similarly, as soon as the couple has finished engaging in intercourse, the blood comes quickly, but the blood is hindered from coming out during intercourse. **And Abaye** also **says a parable** in explanation **of** the opinion of **Rabbi Oshaya: To what is this matter comparable? To a man who puts** his **finger in** his **eye. As long as** his **finger is in** his **eye,** the **tears delay their arrival** and remain in the eye. But as soon as **he** has **removed his finger** the **tears hasten their arrival.**

"וְתוֹלוֹת זוֹ בָּזוֹ". תָּנוּ רַבָּנַן: כֵּיצַד תּוֹלוֹת זוֹ בָּזוֹ. עוּבָּרָה וְשֶׁאֵינָהּ עוּבָּרָה – תּוֹלָה עוּבָּרָה בְּשֶׁאֵינָהּ עוּבָּרָה,

§ The mishna teaches: **And** with regard to three women who were sleeping in one bed and blood was discovered beneath one of them, that if one of them is unfit to menstruate **they attribute** the blood **to each other,** i.e., to the women who are fit to menstruate. In this regard, **the Sages taught** in a *baraita*: **How do they attribute** the blood to **one another?**[H] If one of the women is **pregnant and** one **is not pregnant,** the **pregnant** woman **may attribute** the blood **to the** woman **who is not pregnant.**

מֵינִיקָה וְשֶׁאֵינָהּ מֵינִיקָה – תּוֹלָה מֵינִיקָה בְּשֶׁאֵינָהּ מֵינִיקָה, זְקֵנָה וְשֶׁאֵינָהּ זְקֵנָה – תּוֹלָה זְקֵנָה בְּשֶׁאֵינָהּ זְקֵנָה, בְּתוּלָה וְשֶׁאֵינָהּ בְּתוּלָה – תּוֹלָה בְּתוּלָה בְּשֶׁאֵינָהּ בְּתוּלָה.

If one of the women is **nursing** and the other **is not nursing, the nursing** woman **may attribute** the blood **to the** woman **who is not nursing.** If one of the women is **old** and no longer experiences bleeding regularly, **and** the other one **is not old,** the **old** woman **may attribute** the blood **to** the woman **who is not old.** Likewise, if one of the women is **a virgin,** in this context, one who has not yet experienced bleeding due to her youth, **and** the other woman **is not a virgin,** in this context, one who has experienced bleeding, the **virgin may attribute** the blood **to** the woman **who is not a virgin.**

הָיוּ שְׁתֵּיהֶן עוּבָּרוֹת, שְׁתֵּיהֶן מֵינִיקוֹת, שְׁתֵּיהֶן זְקֵנוֹת, שְׁתֵּיהֶן בְּתוּלוֹת – זוֹ הִיא שֶׁשָּׁנִינוּ, לֹא הָיוּ רְאוּיוֹת לִרְאוֹת – רוֹאִין

The *baraita* continues: **If both** women **are pregnant,** or **both** women **are nursing,** or **both** women **are old,** or **both** women **are virgins,** in **this** case the *halakha* is **as we learned** in the mishna: If both women **were not fit to see** menstrual blood, and yet blood is found beneath them on the bed, **one considers** them

**HALAKHA**

**How do they attribute to one another** – **כֵּיצַד תּוֹלוֹת זוֹ בָּזוֹ:** If, in the case described in the mishna, one of the women was more likely to experience a flow of blood than the others, the ones who are less likely to experience bleeding may attribute the blood stain to the one who is more likely to experience bleeding, and they remain pure. How so? If one of two women was elderly and had passed three months without experiencing a menstrual flow, and the other was young, the elderly woman is pure and the young woman is impure. If one woman was noticeably pregnant and one was not, the pregnant woman is pure and the other is impure. If one woman was young and had never experienced a menstrual flow, and the other had experienced a menstrual flow, the one who had experienced a menstrual flow is impure, while the other woman is pure. This applies even if both women are married (*Shakh*, citing Rashi). If one woman is nursing a baby and the other is not, the one who is nursing is pure while the other is impure (Rambam *Sefer Kedusha, Hilkhot Issurei Bia* 9:33; *Shulḥan Arukh*, *Yoreh De'a* 190:52).

כְּאִילּוּ הֵן רְאוּיוֹת.

**as though they were fit,** and all three are impure, because the blood must have originated from one of them.

מתני׳ שָׁלֹשׁ נָשִׁים שֶׁהָיוּ יְשֵׁנוֹת בְּמִטָּה אַחַת, וְנִמְצָא דָּם תַּחַת הָאֶמְצָעִית – כּוּלָּן טְמֵאוֹת. תַּחַת הַפְּנִימִית – שְׁתַּיִם הַפְּנִימִיּוֹת טְמֵאוֹת, וְהַחִיצוֹנָה טְהוֹרָה. תַּחַת הַחִיצוֹנָה – שְׁתַּיִם הַחִיצוֹנוֹת טְמֵאוֹת, וְהַפְּנִימִית טְהוֹרָה.

**MISHNA** In a case of **three women who were sleeping in one bed**[N] that was located adjacent to a wall, **and blood was discovered beneath the middle** woman,[H] **all of them are ritually impure.** If the blood was discovered **beneath** the woman on **the inside,** closest to the wall, **the two innermost** women **are ritually impure and** the woman on **the outside is ritually pure.** If the blood was discovered **beneath** the woman on **the outside,** farthest from the wall, **the two outermost** women **are ritually impure and** the woman on **the inside is ritually pure.**

אֵימָתַי – בִּזְמַן שֶׁעָבְרוּ דֶּרֶךְ מַרְגְּלוֹת הַמִּטָּה, אֲבָל אִם עָבְרוּ דֶּרֶךְ עָלֶיהָ – כּוּלָּן טְמֵאוֹת. בָּדְקָה אַחַת מֵהֶן, וְנִמְצֵאת טְהוֹרָה – הִיא טְהוֹרָה, וּשְׁתַּיִם טְמֵאוֹת. בָּדְקוּ שְׁתַּיִם, וּמָצְאוּ טְהוֹרוֹת – הֵן טְהוֹרוֹת, וּשְׁלִישִׁית טְמֵאָה. שְׁלָשְׁתָּן, וּמָצְאוּ טְהוֹרוֹת – כּוּלָּן טְמֵאוֹת.

**When** is that the ruling? It is **when they passed** into their positions on the bed **via the foot of the bed; but if they passed** into their positions on the bed **via** the side of the bed, **over** the place where the blood was discovered, **all of them are ritually impure.** If immediately after the blood was discovered, **one of them examined** herself **and she was found** to be **ritually pure, she is pure and** the other **two are impure.** If **two of them examined** themselves **and found** that they were **ritually pure, they are pure and** the **third is impure.** If all **three of them examined** themselves **and found** that they were **ritually pure, all of them are ritually impure,** as the blood must have originated from one of them.

לְמָה הַדָּבָר דּוֹמֶה – לְגַל טָמֵא שֶׁנִּתְעָרֵב בֵּין שְׁנֵי גַלִּים טְהוֹרִים, וּבָדְקוּ אַחַת מֵהֶן וּמָצְאוּ טָהוֹר – הוּא טָהוֹר, וּשְׁנַיִם טְמֵאִים. שְׁנַיִם, וּמָצְאוּ טְהוֹרִין – הֵם טְהוֹרִין, וּשְׁלִישִׁי טָמֵא.

**To what** case **is this matter comparable?** It is similar **to** the case of **a ritually impure pile** of stones with an olive-bulk of a corpse beneath it, **where** this pile **was intermingled with two ritually pure piles,**[H] **and they examined one of them and found it pure. That** pile **is pure and** the other **two are impure.** If they examined **two** of them **and found** them **ritually pure, they are ritually pure and** the **third is impure.**

שְׁלָשְׁתָּן, וּמָצְאוּ טְהוֹרִין – כּוּלָּן טְמֵאִים, דִּבְרֵי רַבִּי מֵאִיר. שֶׁרַבִּי מֵאִיר אוֹמֵר: כׇּל דָּבָר שֶׁהוּא בְּחֶזְקַת טוּמְאָה – לְעוֹלָם הוּא בְּטוּמְאָתוֹ, עַד שֶׁיִּוָּדַע לְךָ טוּמְאָה הֵיכָן הִיא.

If they examined all **three of them and found** them **ritually pure, all of them are impure;** this is **the statement of Rabbi Meir, as Rabbi Meir would say:** With regard to **any item that has** the **presumptive status of ritual impurity, it forever** remains **in its** state of **ritual impurity,** even if one examined the relevant area or item and the source of impurity was not found, **until it becomes known to you where** the **ritual impurity is.** The assumption is that the impurity was not found because the examination was not conducted properly.

וַחֲכָמִים אוֹמְרִים: בּוֹדֵק עַד שֶׁמַּגִּיעַ לַסֶּלַע אוֹ לַבְּתוּלָה.

**And the Rabbis say:** One continues **searching** the relevant area **until he reaches bedrock or virgin soil,** beneath which there is certainly no ritual impurity. If no ritual impurity is found at that stage, presumably an animal dragged the olive-bulk of the corpse from beneath the pile, and the pile of rocks is pure.

**NOTES**

Three women who were sleeping in one bed – שָׁלֹשׁ נָשִׁים שֶׁהָיוּ יְשֵׁנוֹת בְּמִטָּה אַחַת: The early commentaries explain that this is referring specifically to women who were asleep. Since they move, or move each other, in their sleep, it is impossible to establish the source of the blood stain, and therefore in certain situations they are all impure. By contrast, if they were awake, they know where they have been and can credibly claim that they did not pass over the area where the stain was found. Therefore, in such a case only the woman beneath whom the stain was discovered is impure (Rosh, citing Ra'avad; Rashba).

**HALAKHA**

And blood was discovered beneath the middle woman, etc. – וְנִמְצָא דָּם תַּחַת הָאֶמְצָעִית וכו׳: If three women were lying on a bed and blood was found beneath the innermost woman, she and the middle woman are impure and the outermost woman is pure. If the blood was found beneath the outermost woman, she and the middle woman are impure and the innermost woman is pure. This is the *halakha* only when they all climbed into the bed from the foot of the bed. If they all climbed in from the side and blood is found beneath the outermost woman, they are all impure, as the blood might have been emitted even by the first woman as she climbed into the bed. Furthermore, this is the *halakha* only when the blood is found on the sheet beneath them. If the blood is found on the sheet that covers them, they are all impure, as the sheet moves around from one woman to the next (Rambam *Sefer Kedusha, Hilkhot Issurei Bia* 9:34; *Shulḥan Arukh, Yoreh De'a* 190:50).

A ritually impure pile of stones where it was intermingled with two ritually pure piles – גַּל טָמֵא שֶׁנִּתְעָרֵב בֵּין שְׁנֵי גַלִּים טְהוֹרִים: If one impure pile of items was intermingled with two other piles, and one of them was examined and found to be pure, that pile is pure and the other two are impure. If two piles were checked, they are pure and the other one is impure. If all three were examined and found to be pure, then all three are impure until they are examined thoroughly, down to the bedrock or virgin soil. If that has been done, all three are pure. This *halakha* is in accordance with the opinion of the Rabbis (Rambam *Sefer Tahara, Hilkhot Tumat Met* 9:10).

**גמ׳** מַאי שְׁנָא רֵישָׁא – דְּלָא מַפְלִיג, וּמַאי שְׁנָא סֵיפָא דְּקָמַפְלִיג? אֲמַר רַבִּי אַמִי: בִּמְשׁוּלָּבוֹת.

**GEMARA** The previous mishna taught that if blood is found beneath one of three women lying together on a bed, they are all ritually impure. By contrast, the mishna here distinguishes based on the precise location where the blood was found. The Gemara asks: **What is different in the first clause,** i.e., the previous mishna, **which did not distinguish** on the basis of where the blood was found, **and what is different in the latter clause,** i.e., this mishna, **which does distinguish** in that manner? **Rabbi Ami said** that the previous mishna is referring to a case **where** the women were lying **intertwined,** and therefore it is impossible to distinguish between the woman on the inside and the woman on the outside.

״בָּדְקָה אַחַת״ [וכו׳]. לָמָּה לֵיהּ לְמִתְנֵי ״לְמָה זֶה דּוֹמֶה״?

§ The mishna teaches: If immediately after the blood was discovered, **one of them examined** herself and she was found to be ritually pure, she is pure and the other two are impure. If two of them examined themselves and found that they were ritually pure, they are pure and the third is impure. If all three of them examined themselves and found that they were ritually pure, all of them are ritually impure. The mishna proceeds to compare this case to that of a pile of stones beneath which there is an olive-bulk of a corpse. The Gemara asks: **Why does** the *tanna* need **to teach: To what** case **is this matter comparable?** The ruling of the mishna is clear enough without this analogy.

הָכִי קָאָמַר לְהוּ רַבִּי מֵאִיר לְרַבָּנַן: מַאי שְׁנָא בְּדָם דְּלָא פְּלִיגִיתוּ, וּמַאי שְׁנָא בְּגַל דִּפְלִיגִיתוּ?

The Gemara explains that **this** is what **Rabbi Meir is saying to the Rabbis: What is different with regard to** the case of **blood, where you do not disagree** with me, as you concede that all three women are impure, **and what is different with regard to** the case of **the pile** of stones, **where you disagree** with me and maintain that all three piles of stones can be ritually pure if they are examined?

וְרַבָּנַן, בִּשְׁלָמָא הָתָם – אֵימָא עוֹרֵב נְטָלָהּ, אֶלָּא הָכָא – הַאי דָּם מֵהֵיכָא אֲתָא?!

**And the Rabbis** would counter that the two cases are different. **Granted, there,** with regard to the piles of stones, one could **say** that **a raven** or some other animal **took** away the olive-bulk of the corpse, so there is a reason to deem all the piles pure. **But here,** in the case of the three women and the blood, **from where did this blood come?** It must have come from one of them. Therefore, at least one of the women must be ritually impure, and one cannot say that all three are pure.

תַּנְיָא, אָמַר רַבִּי מֵאִיר: מַעֲשֶׂה בְּשִׁקְמָה שֶׁל כְּפַר סָבָא שֶׁהָיוּ מַחֲזִיקִין בָּהּ טוּמְאָה, וּבָדְקוּ וְלֹא מָצְאוּ, לְיָמִים נָשְׁבָה בּוֹ הָרוּחַ וַעֲקָרָתוֹ, וְנִמְצָא גּוּלְגּוֹלֶת שֶׁל מֵת תְּחוּבָה לוֹ בְּעִיקָּרוֹ. אָמְרוּ לוֹ: מִשָּׁם רְאָיָה? אֵימַר לֹא בָּדְקוּ כָּל צָרְכּוֹ.

The Gemara discusses other cases involving possible mistakes in examinations. **It is taught** in a *baraita*: **Rabbi Meir said** that there was **an incident involving a sycamore tree in Kefar Sava,**[B] **with regard to which they had a presumption of ritual impurity,** i.e., a presumption that there was a corpse buried beneath it. **And they examined** by digging in that place **and did not find** any corpse. **Some days** later, **the wind blew at it and uprooted** the sycamore tree, **and they found a skull from a corpse stuck in its roots.** This apparently indicates that in general one cannot rely upon an examination. The Sages **said to** Rabbi Meir: Do you seek to bring **a proof from there?** One can **say** that **they did not examine as much as was necessary.**

תַּנְיָא, אָמַר רַבִּי יוֹסֵי: מַעֲשֶׂה בִּמְעָרָה שֶׁל שִׁיחִין שֶׁהָיוּ מַחֲזִיקִין בָּהּ טוּמְאָה, וּבָדְקוּ עַד שֶׁהִגִּיעוּ לְקַרְקַע שֶׁהָיְתָה חֲלָקָה כַּצִּפּוֹרֶן, וְלֹא מָצְאוּ. לְיָמִים נִכְנְסוּ בָּהּ פּוֹעֲלִים מִפְּנֵי הַגְּשָׁמִים. וְנִתְּזוּ בְּקַרְדּוּמּוֹתֵיהֶן, וּמָצְאוּ מַכְתֶּשֶׁת מְלֵאָה עֲצָמוֹת. אָמְרוּ לוֹ: מִשָּׁם רְאָיָה? אֵימַר לֹא בָּדְקוּ כָּל צָרְכּוֹ.

The Gemara cites another case. **It is taught** in a *baraita*: **Rabbi Yosei said** that there was **an incident involving a cave in Shiḥin**[B] **with regard to which they had a presumption of ritual impurity** of a corpse. **And they examined** by digging inside the cave **until they reached ground that was as smooth as a fingernail, and they did not find** any corpse. **Some days** later **workers entered** the cave **because** they sought shelter from **the rain. And they dug with their shovels**[B] **and found a mortar**[B] **full of bones.** Once again, this indicates that one cannot rely upon an examination. The Sages **said to** Rabbi Yosei: Do you bring **a proof from there?** One can **say they did not examine as much as was necessary.**

**BACKGROUND**

**Kefar Sava – כְּפַר סָבָא:** The village of Kefar Sava is mentioned in the works of Josephus as a place where Alexander Yannai dug trenches to defend himself against Antiochus Dionysus. There was a Jewish presence in Kefar Sava throughout the talmudic period. Kefar Sava is listed in a mosaic found in Tel Reḥov, near Beit She'an, as one of the borders of Eretz Yisrael with regard to produce of the Sabbatical Year. This village was located in the area where the city of Kfar Saba is today.

Tel Reḥov mosaic, with Kefar Sava listed

**Shiḥin – שִׁיחִין:** Shiḥin is an abbreviated name for Kefar Shiḥin. It was a large village in the Lower Galilee, on the western side of Beit Netofa valley, and the residence of one of the twenty-four priestly watches. Together with Kefar Ḥananya on the border between the Upper and Lower Galilee, Kefar Shiḥin was known for its production of earthenware vessels.

**Shovels – קַרְדּוּמּוֹת:** Although there is no precise record of what these implements looked like in the time of the Mishna and the Gemara, it would appear from descriptions in the Gemara that they were similar to the Roman dolabra. This utensil had several functions, including cutting down trees (see Jeremiah 46:22) and digging the earth. Generally, a scythe was used for harvesting crops, but if one wanted to remove the crops and the roots it was easier to use this shovel.

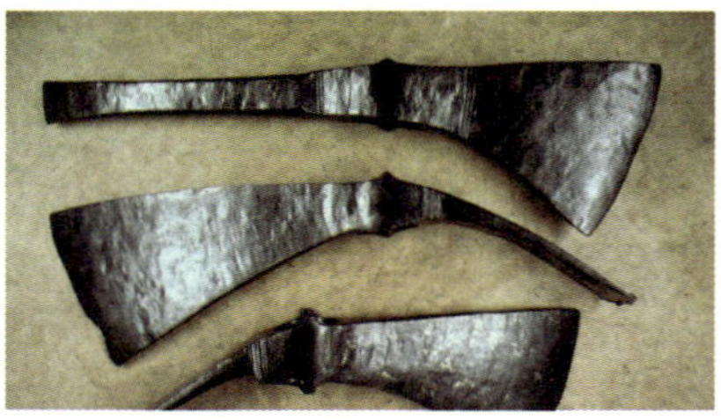

Roman dolabrae

**Mortar – מַכְתֶּשֶׁת:** During the period of the Mishna and the Talmud, extensive use was made of mortars, both to crush grain in preparation for milling, and to crush various types of legumes. Since they were designed for use with large volumes of produce, the mortars were relatively large, although there were also smaller ones for pounding seasonings and spices. Occasionally, to stabilize the mortar, it would be attached to the ground with mud, clay, or some other adhesive substance, and sometimes rocks embedded in the ground were hollowed out and turned into mortars.

Stone mortar, Khobak, India

תַּנְיָא, אַבָּא שָׁאוּל אוֹמֵר: מַעֲשֶׂה בְּסֶלַע בֵּית חוֹרוֹן שֶׁהָיוּ מַחֲזִיקִין בָּהּ טוּמְאָה, וְלֹא יָכְלוּ חֲכָמִים לִבְדּוֹק, מִפְּנֵי שֶׁהָיְתָה מְרוּבָּה. וְהָיָה שָׁם זָקֵן אֶחָד, וְרַבִּי יְהוֹשֻׁעַ בֶּן חֲנַנְיָא שְׁמוֹ, אָמַר לָהֶן: הָבִיאוּ לִי סְדִינִים! הֵבִיאוּ לוֹ סְדִינִים, וּשְׁרָאָן בַּמַּיִם, וּפְרָסָן עֲלֵיהֶם. מְקוֹם טָהֳרָה – יָבֵשׁ, מְקוֹם טוּמְאָה – לַח. וּבָדְקוּ וּמָצְאוּ בּוֹר גָּדוֹל מָלֵא עֲצָמוֹת.

The Gemara cites yet another relevant case. **It is taught** in a *baraita*: **Abba Shaul says** that there was **an incident involving bedrock in Beit Ḥoron,**[B] **with regard to which they had a presumption of ritual impurity** of a corpse. **And the Sages were unable to examine** it **because** the area of the bedrock **was too large. And there was one old man there, and his name was Rabbi Yehoshua ben Ḥananya. He said to them: Bring me sheets. They brought him sheets and he soaked them in water and spread them over** the bedrock. In every **place of ritual purity** the ground remained **dry,** and in every **place of ritual impurity** the ground became **moist.** They understood that it was not entirely bedrock, as the area where the ground was wet was actually soft earth. **And they examined** there by digging **and found a large pit filled with bones.**

תָּנָא: הוּא הַבּוֹר שֶׁמִּילֵּא יִשְׁמָעֵאל בֶּן נְתַנְיָה חֲלָלִים, דִּכְתִיב: ״וְהַבּוֹר אֲשֶׁר הִשְׁלִיךְ שָׁם יִשְׁמָעֵאל אֵת כׇּל פִּגְרֵי אֲנָשִׁים אֲשֶׁר הִכָּה בְּיַד גְּדַלְיָה״.

It is **taught: That** pit that they found is **the pit that Ishmael, son of Nethaniah, filled with corpses,**[B] **as it is written: "Now the pit where Ishmael cast all the dead bodies of the men whom he had slain by the side of Gedaliah** was that which Asa the king had made for fear of Baasa king of Israel; the same Ishmael, son of Nethaniah, filled with them that were slain" (Jeremiah 41:9).

וְכִי גְּדַלְיָה הֲרָגָן? וַהֲלֹא יִשְׁמָעֵאל הֲרָגָן! אֶלָּא מִתּוֹךְ שֶׁהָיָה לוֹ לָחוּשׁ לַעֲצַת יוֹחָנָן בֶּן קָרֵחַ וְלֹא חָשׁ – מַעֲלֶה עָלָיו הַכָּתוּב כְּאִילּוּ הֲרָגָן.

The Gemara analyzes that verse: **And did Gedaliah kill them? But didn't Ishmael kill them?** Gedaliah was one of those killed by Ishmael and his men (see Jeremiah 41:2). The Gemara answers: **Rather, since** Gedaliah **should have been concerned** and cautious based **on the advice of Johanan, son of Kareah,**[N] who warned him that Ishmael was conspiring to kill him and even offered to go and kill Ishmael in a preemptive strike (see Jeremiah 40:13–16), **but** Gedaliah **was not concerned** and he refused to listen to Johanan's advice, saying that he did not want to listen to malicious speech, **the verse ascribes him** blame **as though he** himself **killed them.**

אֲמַר רָבָא: הַאי לִישָּׁנָא בִּישָׁא, אַף עַל פִּי דִּלְקַבּוֹלֵי לָא מִבָּעֵי – מֵיחַשׁ לֵיהּ מִבָּעֵי.

§ In relation to the above comment that Gedaliah was killed after not heeding the warning of Johanan, the Gemara clarifies what is permitted when receiving such a warning. **Rava said:** With regard to **this** prohibition against listening to **malicious speech, even though one should not accept** the malicious speech as true, **one is** nevertheless **required to be concerned** about the harm that might result from ignoring it.

הָנְהוּ בְּנֵי גְּלִילָא דִּנְפַק עֲלַיְיהוּ קָלָא דִּקְטוּל נַפְשָׁא, אֲתוּ לְקַמֵּיהּ דְּרַבִּי טַרְפוֹן, אֲמַרוּ לֵיהּ: לַטְמְרִינַן מָר! אֲמַר לְהוּ: הֵיכִי נַעֲבֵיד? אִי לָא אַטְמְרִינְכוּ – חָזוּ יָתַיְיכוּ, אַטְמְרִינְכוּ – הָא אֲמוּר רַבָּנַן הַאי לִישָּׁנָא בִּישָׁא, אַף עַל גַּב דִּלְקַבּוֹלֵי לָא מִבָּעֵי – מֵיחַשׁ לֵיהּ מִבָּעֵי, זִילוּ אַתּוּן טַמְרוּ נַפְשַׁיְיכוּ.

The Gemara cites examples of people who were concerned about malicious speech. There were **these people of the Galilee about whom a rumor emerged that they had killed someone. They came before Rabbi Tarfon** and **said to him: Will the Master hide us?** Rabbi Tarfon **said to them: What should we do? If I do not hide you,** your pursuers **will see you** and kill you. If **I do hide you,** this too is problematic, as **didn't the Rabbis say:** With regard to **this** prohibition against listening to **malicious speech, even though one should not accept** the malicious speech as true, **one is required to be concerned** about the harm that might result from ignoring it? Therefore, **you** must **go** and **hide yourselves.**

BACKGROUND

**Beit Ḥoron – בֵּית חוֹרוֹן:** The city of Beit Ḥoron was divided into two adjacent towns, Upper and Lower Beit Ḥoron, located near the northern border of the tribe of Judah. These cities are mentioned in the Bible and, due to their strategic location on the main road to Jerusalem, were the site of many famous battles, including the victory of Judah Maccabee during the Great Revolt. In ancient cities such as these, which were resettled at the time of the return from the Babylonian exile, there was generally a traditionally religious community replete with Torah scholars. This incident in Beit Ḥoron teaches us about the local residents' commitment to observing mitzvot with great care.

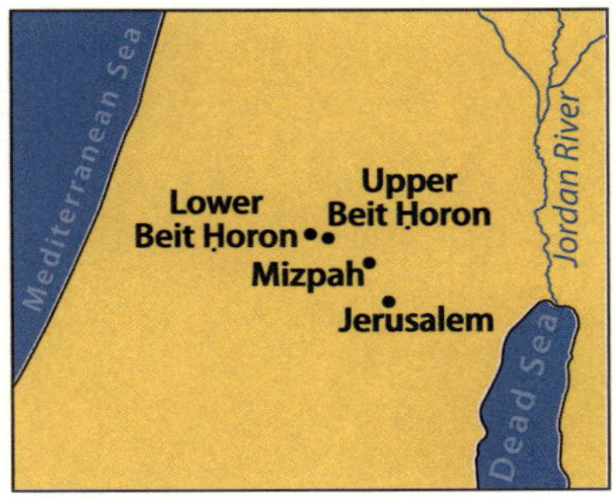


Location of Beit Ḥoron

**Pit that Ishmael son of Nethaniah filled with corpses – בּוֹר שֶׁמִּילֵּא יִשְׁמָעֵאל בֶּן נְתַנְיָה חֲלָלִים:** This is the pit into which Ishmael, son of Nethaniah, threw the corpses of his victims. Asa, king of Judah, and Baasa, king of Israel, waged war with each other throughout their reigns. In the course of one war, Asa destroyed all the buildings and fortresses that Baasa had built in the city of Ramah. Asa instructed his troops to bring the wood to Geba of Benjamin and to Mizpah, in the north of his kingdom, in order to build defensive buildings there (see I Kings 15:22). While building defenses for the Kingdom of Judah they dug a pit in which to store water or grain, as part of their preparations for a siege. This pit still existed after the destruction of the First Temple, and Ishmael threw into it the corpses of those he slew in Mizpah.

NOTES

**The advice of Johanan son of Kareah – עֲצַת יוֹחָנָן בֶּן קָרֵחַ:** This event sealed the fate of the Jews in Eretz Yisrael after the destruction of the First Temple. It is described in detail in the book of Jeremiah (chapters 40–41). After the destruction of the Temple, Gedaliah, son of Ahikam, was appointed by the king of Babylonia to govern the Jews who remained in Eretz Yisrael. Many came to Gedaliah's residence in Mizpah to accept his authority, including the prophet Jeremiah. Gedaliah issued numerous promises about the goodness they would receive from the king of Babylonia in the future if they did not rebel against him. One of those who came to visit Gedaliah was the commander of the army, Johanan, son of Kareah, and Gedaliah promised to treat him well.

Johanan knew that Baalis, king of Amon, had sent Ishmael, son of Nethaniah, to assassinate Gedaliah. Johanan secretly informed Gedaliah of this plot, but Gedaliah refused to believe him. On Rosh HaShana, Ishmael and his men rose up and slew Gedaliah, and on the following day Ishmael killed those who were loyal to Gedaliah. Eventually Ishmael fled to Amon, and Johanan went to Egypt accompanied by those loyal to him, leaving Eretz Yisrael barren and desolate. In commemoration of this tragedy the Sages established the Fast of Gedaliah on the day after Rosh HaShana.

HALAKHA

A garment in which a blood stain was lost – בֶּגֶד שֶׁאָבַד בּוֹ כֶּתֶם: If a garment had a blood stain that became lost, the garment must be washed with seven specific substances and then immersed in a ritual bath. This ruling is in accordance with the *baraita* (Rambam *Sefer Tahara, Hilkhot Metamei Mishkav UMoshav* 4:12).

״וַיֹּאמֶר ה׳ אֶל מֹשֶׁה אַל תִּירָא״ – מִכְּדִי, סִיחוֹן וְעוֹג אַחֵי הֲווּ, דְּאָמַר מָר: סִיחוֹן וְעוֹג בְּנֵי אֲחִיָּה בַּר שַׁמְחַזַאי הֲווּ. מַאי שְׁנָא מֵעוֹג – דְּקָמִסְתְּפֵי, וּמַאי שְׁנָא מִסִּיחוֹן דְּלָא קָמִסְתְּפֵי?

The Gemara cites another case of a report that caused concern. Before the battle against Og, king of Bashan, it is stated: **"And the Lord said to Moses: Do not fear** him; for I have delivered him into your hand, and all his people, and his land; and you shall do to him as you did to Sihon king of the Amorites, who dwelt at Heshbon" (Numbers 21:34). The Gemara asks: **Now, Sihon and Og were brothers, as the Master said: Sihon and Og were sons of Ahijah, son of Shamhazai.** In **what** way is Sihon **different from Og, that** God found it necessary to warn Moses not to be **afraid** of Og, **and** in **what** way **is** Og **different from Sihon, that** there was **no** need for a warning not to be **afraid** of Sihon?

אָמַר רַבִּי יוֹחָנָן, אָמַר רַבִּי שִׁמְעוֹן בֶּן יוֹחַי: מִתְּשׁוּבָתוֹ שֶׁל אוֹתוֹ צַדִּיק אַתָּה יוֹדֵעַ מָה הָיָה בְּלִבּוֹ, אָמַר: שֶׁמָּא תַּעֲמוֹד לוֹ זְכוּת שֶׁל אַבְרָהָם אָבִינוּ,

**Rabbi Yoḥanan says** that **Rabbi Shimon ben Yoḥai says: From the** answer that God gave **to that righteous** one, Moses, **you know what was in his heart,** i.e., what gave Moses cause to fear. Moses **said** to himself: **Perhaps the merit of our forefather Abraham will stand for** Og and save him. Og was the one who told Abraham that Lot had been taken captive by the four kings, enabling Abraham to rescue Lot.

שֶׁנֶּאֱמַר ״וַיָּבֹא הַפָּלִיט וַיַּגֵּד לְאַבְרָם הָעִבְרִי״, וְאָמַר רַבִּי יוֹחָנָן: זֶה עוֹג שֶׁפָּלַט מִדּוֹר הַמַּבּוּל.

The Gemara cites the source of this claim. **As it is stated: "And there came one that was saved, and told Abram the Hebrew,** now he dwelt by the terebinths of Mamre the Amorite, brother of Eshkol, and brother of Aner; and these were confederate with Abram. And when Abram heard that his brother was taken captive, he led forth his trained men, born in his house, three hundred and eighteen, and pursued as far as Dan" (Genesis 14:13–14). **And Rabbi Yoḥanan said** that the term "one that was saved" **is** referring to **Og, who was saved from** the punishment of **the generation of the flood.** For this reason, Moses was more afraid of Og.

תָּנוּ רַבָּנַן: בֶּגֶד שֶׁאָבַד בּוֹ כֶּתֶם – מַעֲבִיר עָלָיו שִׁבְעָה סַמְמָנִין וּמְבַטְּלוֹ, רַבִּי שִׁמְעוֹן בֶּן אֶלְעָזָר אוֹמֵר:

§ The Gemara cites another instance in which an impure item was lost, similar to the case discussed above involving the pile of stones. **The Sages taught** in a *baraita*: Menstrual blood is itself a source of impurity. With regard to **a garment in which** a blood **stain was lost,**[H] i.e., it is difficult to determine if the blood is still on the garment, **one applies to it,** i.e., scrubs it with, **seven** abrasive **substances** that are known to remove blood stains, **and** thereby **nullifies** the blood stain, so that the garment is pure. **Rabbi Shimon ben Elazar says:**

Perek **IX**
Daf **61** Amud **b**

NOTES

If the garment is new one examines it by a needle – חָדָשׁ בּוֹדְקוֹ בְּמַחַט: A seminal emission dries after it has left the body. When a needle is carefully passed through the garment, it will get stuck where the semen is (Rashi).

בּוֹדְקוֹ שְׁכוּנוֹת שְׁכוּנוֹת.

**He examines it section by section,** as by examining each part of the garment separately he will discover any remaining blood stain.

אָבְדָה בּוֹ שִׁכְבַת זֶרַע, חָדָשׁ – בּוֹדְקוֹ בְּמַחַט, שָׁחוּק – בּוֹדְקוֹ בַּחַמָּה. תָּנָא: אֵין שְׁכוּנָה פְּחוּתָה מִשָּׁלֹשׁ אֶצְבָּעוֹת.

In the case of a garment **in which a seminal emission,** which is also ritually impure, **was lost,**[H] i.e., it is not known where on the garment the semen is, if the garment is **new, one examines it by** sticking **a needle**[N] into every part of it. In this manner he will feel if the semen is in the garment. If the garment is **worn out, one examines it by** holding it up to **the sun,** as the sun's rays will not pass through the stained part of the garment. It was **taught** in a *baraita*: The **section** mentioned need **not** be **less than three** fingerbreadths by three **fingerbreadths** in area.

HALAKHA

A garment in which a seminal emission was lost – אָבְדָה בּוֹ שִׁכְבַת זֶרַע: With regard to a garment in which semen is lost, if it was a new garment one must examine it with a needle. If it was a worn out garment he must check it by holding it up to the sun. This ruling is in accordance with the *baraita* (Rambam *Sefer Tahara, Hilkhot Metamei Mishkav UMoshav* 4:12).

תָּנוּ רַבָּנַן: בֶּגֶד שֶׁאָבַד בּוֹ כִּלְאַיִם – הֲרֵי זֶה לֹא יִמְכְּרֶנּוּ לְגוֹי, וְלֹא יַעֲשֶׂנּוּ מַרְדַּעַת לַחֲמוֹר. אֲבָל עוֹשֶׂה מִמֶּנּוּ תַּכְרִיכִין לְמֵת. אָמַר רַב יוֹסֵף: זֹאת אוֹמֶרֶת – מִצְוֹת בְּטֵלוֹת לֶעָתִיד לָבֹא.

The Gemara cites another case of a garment in which something was lost. **The Sages taught** in a *baraita*: With regard to **a garment in which diverse kinds,**[B] a prohibited mixture of wool and linen, **was lost,**[H] i.e., it is a wool garment into which a linen thread was sewn or vice versa and it is not known where on the garment the thread is located, **one may not sell it to a gentile and one may not** even **fashion it** into **a saddlecloth for a donkey.**[B] This is prohibited lest one remove a piece of the garment and sew it onto his own clothing. **But one may fashion it** into **a shroud for a corpse,**[HN] as there is no concern that one might remove it from the dead. **Rav Yosef said: That is to say** that the **mitzvot will be nullified in the future.**[N] If this were not the case, then when the dead are resurrected they will be deriving benefit from the garment of diverse kinds in which they were buried.

אֲמַר לֵיהּ אַבָּיֵי וְאִי תֵּימָא רַב דִּימִי: וְהָא אָמַר רַבִּי מָנִי, אָמַר רַבִּי יַנַּאי, לֹא שָׁנוּ – אֶלָּא לְסָפְדוֹ, אֲבָל לְקוֹבְרוֹ – אָסוּר! אֲמַר לֵיהּ: לָאו אִיתְּמַר עֲלָהּ, אָמַר רַבִּי יוֹחָנָן אֲפִילּוּ לְקוֹבְרוֹ?

**Abaye said to** Rav Yosef, **and some say** that **Rav Dimi** said to Rav Yosef: **But didn't Rabbi Mani say** that **Rabbi Yannai said: They taught** that it is permitted to place a corpse in a shroud of diverse kinds **only** in order **to eulogize him, but it is prohibited to bury him** in a shroud of diverse kinds? Rav Yosef **said to him: Wasn't it stated with regard to that** matter that **Rabbi Yoḥanan says:** It is **even** permitted **to bury him** in a shroud of diverse kinds?

וְרַבִּי יוֹחָנָן לְטַעְמֵיהּ, דְּאָמַר רַבִּי יוֹחָנָן: מַאי דִּכְתִיב "בַּמֵּתִים חָפְשִׁי" – כֵּיוָן שֶׁמֵּת אָדָם, נַעֲשָׂה חָפְשִׁי מִן הַמִּצְוֹת.

**And Rabbi Yoḥanan** conforms **to his** standard line of **reasoning** in this regard, **as Rabbi Yoḥanan said: What** is the meaning of that **which is written: "Set apart [*ḥofshi*] among the dead,** like the slain that lie in the grave, whom You remember no more" (Psalms 88:6)? **Once a person dies, he becomes free [*ḥofshi*] from the mitzvot.**

אָמַר רַפְרָם בַּר פַּפָּא, אָמַר רַב חִסְדָּא: בֶּגֶד שֶׁאָבַד בּוֹ כִּלְאַיִם – צוֹבְעוֹ, וּמוּתָּר. אֲמַר לֵיהּ רָבָא לְרַפְרָם בַּר פַּפָּא: מְנָא לֵיהּ לְסָבָא הָא?

§ **Rafram bar Pappa says** that **Rav Ḥisda says:** With regard to **a garment in which diverse kinds was lost, one may dye it, and it is permitted**[H] to wear the garment, as wool and linen absorb dye differently, and therefore it will be easy to notice the location of the other kind of thread and remove it. **Rava said to Rafram bar Pappa: From where does the Elder,** i.e., Rav Ḥisda, derive **this** *halakha*?

אֲמַר לֵיהּ: מַתְנִיתִין הִיא, דִּתְנַן, בּוֹדֵק, עַד שֶׁמַּגִּיעַ לַסֶּלַע, וְאִי לֵיכָּא – אֵימַר עוֹרֵב נְטָלָהּ. הָכִי נַמִי: עַמְרָא וְכִיתָּנָא בַּהֲדָדֵי – לָא סָלֵיק לְהוּ צִבְעָא, וְכֵיוָן דְּלָא יְדִיעַ – אֵימַר מִנְתַּר נְתַר.

Rafram bar Pappa **said to him: It is** derived from **the mishna, as we learned:** With regard to a pile of stones that was known to have an item of ritual impurity buried beneath it, one continues **searching** beneath each of these piles **until he reaches bedrock. And if** the impure item **is not** there, i.e., if he found nothing, one can **say** that **a raven** or some other animal **took it. So too here, wool and flax,** i.e., linen, **do not absorb** the dye **in the same** manner. **And since** he dyed the garment and **he does not know** of any mixture of linen and wool within it, as the entire garment absorbed the dye in the same way, one must **say that** that thread **has fallen out,** and therefore it is permitted to wear the garment.

אֲמַר רַב אַחָא בְּרֵיהּ דְּרַב יֵיבָא מִשְּׁמֵיהּ דְּמָר זוּטְרָא: הַאי מַאן דְּרָמֵי חוּטָא דְּכִיתָּנָא בִּגְלִימֵיהּ דְּעַמְרָא וְנַתְקֵיהּ, וְלָא יָדַע אִי נְתֵיק אִי לָא נְתֵיק – שַׁפִּיר דָּמֵי.

**Rav Aḥa, son of Rav Yeiva, said in the name of Mar Zutra:** In a case of **one who put a thread of flax in a cloak of wool and it fell out, but he does not know whether it** all **fell out or** whether it **did not** all **fall out,** it is **permitted** to wear the cloak.

## NOTES

**One may fashion it into a shroud for a corpse – עוֹשֶׂה מִמֶּנּוּ תַּכְרִיכִין לְמֵת:** The early authorities ask why it is not prohibited to make shrouds from diverse kinds due to the prohibition of: "He who mocks the poor blasphemes his Creator" (Proverbs 17:5). In other words, as the deceased is incapable of fulfilling mitzvot, performing a mitzva in his presence is considered to be mocking him. For this same reason, the Sages say that one may not walk in a cemetery with ritual fringes on his garment, phylacteries on his arm, or a Torah scroll in his hand.

Some answer that the prohibition of mocking the poor does not apply to dressing a corpse in shrouds, as the prohibition derived form that verse is only due to the fact that the deceased is unable to fulfill a mitzva that a living person is performing. In the case of the shrouds, the deceased is not violating a prohibition, as he does not derive any benefit from the shrouds of diverse kinds. Likewise, if a living person has a garment of diverse kinds upon him without deriving benefit from wearing the garment he does not violate a prohibition (*Tosafot*, citing Rashbam). The commentaries further suggest that the prohibition of mocking the poor applies only to mitzvot that are considered equivalent to the entire Torah, such as wearing a garment with ritual fringes, but does not apply to other mitzvot (*Tosafot*, citing Rabbeinu Tam).

**That is to say that mitzvot will be nullified in the future – זֹאת אוֹמֶרֶת מִצְוֹת בְּטֵלוֹת לֶעָתִיד לָבֹא:** Some explain that the future referred to here is the time of the resurrection of the dead (*Tosafot*). Others maintain that it is referring to the time after death, when the deceased is no longer obligated to observe the mitzvot, but at the time of the resurrection all of the mitzvot will once again apply (Rashba).

## BACKGROUND

**Diverse kinds – כִּלְאַיִם:** The term: Diverse kinds, is referring to the prohibition by Torah law against wearing a mixture of wool and linen (see Leviticus 19:19 and Deuteronomy 22:11). One may not wear a garment into which these two materials have been spun, woven, or sewn together. Certain other combinations are prohibited by rabbinic decree. In addition, the Sages prohibited lying on a mattress that contains a mixture of wool and linen. One may manufacture, sell, and derive other benefit from these garments.

**Saddlecloth for a donkey – מַרְדַּעַת לַחֲמוֹר:** This is a type of small blanket that would be placed under the saddle on the back of a donkey or camel. It was normally made of a soft material such as woven fabric or leather, and it was designed to make the ride more comfortable for the rider or the load more comfortable for the animal. Owners of saddlecloths were not particular about their appearance and might repair a ripped saddlecloth by taking a patch from another piece of clothing of a different material, inadvertently transgressing the prohibition of *sha'atnez*. The Gemara therefore teaches that this is prohibited.

## HALAKHA

**A garment in which diverse kinds was lost – בֶּגֶד שֶׁאָבַד בּוֹ כִּלְאַיִם:** With regard to a woolen garment into which a linen thread was sewn, or vice versa, one may not sell it to a gentile lest he resell it to a Jew. Nor may one fashion it into a saddlecloth for a donkey. Since it is not noticeable, there is a concern that a Jew might find it and take part of it and sew it onto his clothing as a patch. This *halakha* is in accordance with the *baraita*, following the Rambam's version of that text (Rambam *Sefer Zera'im*, *Hilkhot Kilayim* 10:27 and *Kesef Mishne* there; *Shulḥan Arukh*, *Yoreh De'a* 301:8).

**But one may fashion it into a shroud for a corpse – אֲבָל עוֹשֶׂה מִמֶּנּוּ תַּכְרִיכִין לְמֵת:** It is permitted to fashion shrouds for the dead from fabric of diverse kinds, and even to bury the corpse in them. This ruling is in accordance with the *baraita*, in accordance with the opinion of Rabbi Yoḥanan (Rambam *Sefer Zera'im*, *Hilkhot Kilayim* 10:25; *Shulḥan Arukh*, *Yoreh De'a* 301:7).

**A garment in which diverse kinds was lost, one may dye it and it is permitted – בֶּגֶד שֶׁאָבַד בּוֹ כִּלְאַיִם צוֹבְעוֹ וּמוּתָּר:** What can be done in the case of a woolen garment that has a single thread of linen woven into it, or vice versa? It should be dyed, as wool and linen do not absorb the dye in the same manner, and therefore the thread in question will be easily identifiable and can be removed. If no thread is identifiable after dyeing, the garment is permitted, as the thread might have come out by itself. Since any prohibition due to uncertainty applies only by rabbinic law, the Sages ruled leniently in this case (Rambam *Sefer Zera'im*, *Hilkhot Kilayim* 10:27, and see Ra'avad, *Kesef Mishne*, and Radbaz there).

LANGUAGE

War [*pulmus*] – פּוּלְמוּס: From the Greek πόλεμος, *polemos*, meaning war.

Drum [*irus*] – אִירוּס: Similar terms for musical instruments are found in Arabic and other languages. Some say that the name of this instrument is derived from its use at celebrations such as engagements [*erusin*] and weddings. According to most commentaries, the *irus*, *tavla*, and *tanbura* are slightly different versions of the same instrument, a drum with skin on only one side.

מַאי טַעְמָא – מִדְּאוֹרַיְיתָא "שַׁעַטְנֵז" כְּתִיב – עַד שֶׁיְּהֵא שׁוּעַ טָווּי וְנוּז, וְרַבָּנַן הוּא דִּגְזוּר בֵּיהּ. וְכֵיוָן דְּלָא יָדַע אִי נַתְקִיהּ – שָׁרֵי.

The Gemara asks: **What is the reason** that the *halakha* is lenient in this case of uncertainty? **By Torah law,** it **is written: "Diverse kinds** [*sha'atnez*]" (Deuteronomy 22:11), and this is interpreted as an acronym indicating that the *halakha* of diverse kinds does not apply **unless** the item **is** combed **smooth** [*shua*], **spun** [*tavui*] as a thread, **and woven** [*nuz*]. Without these characteristics, the combination is not considered diverse kinds by Torah law. **And it is the Sages who decreed** that diverse kinds that are merely attached to each other are prohibited, despite the fact that they are not combed and spun together. **And** in this case, **since he does not know if it** all **fell out** it is **permitted,** as the *halakha* is lenient with regard to uncertainties involving prohibitions that are by rabbinic law.

מַתְקִיף לַהּ רַב אַשִׁי: אֵימַר – אוֹ שׁוּעַ אוֹ טָווּי אוֹ נוּז! וְהִלְכְתָא כְּמַר זוּטְרָא, מִדְּאַפְּקִינְהוּ רַחֲמָנָא בְּחֲדָא לִישָּׁנָא.

**Rav Ashi objects to this** leniency. One can **say** that by Torah law it is prohibited if the linen and wool are **either combed, or spun, or woven.** Perhaps the word *sha'atnez* does not limit the prohibition to a combination of all three activities, but to any one of them. The Gemara concludes: **And the *halakha*** is **in accordance with** the opinion of **Mar Zutra, from** the fact **that the Merciful One expresses** the prohibition in the Torah **in one word,** *sha'atnez*. Therefore, the term means all three characteristics together.

תָּנוּ רַבָּנַן: בֶּגֶד צָבוּעַ – מְטַמֵּא מִשּׁוּם כֶּתֶם, רַבִּי נָתָן בַּר יוֹסֵף אוֹמֵר: אֵינוֹ מְטַמֵּא מִשּׁוּם כֶּתֶם, שֶׁלֹּא תִּקְּנוּ בִּגְדֵי צִבְעוֹנִין לָאִשָּׁה אֶלָּא לְהָקֵל עַל כִּתְמֵיהֶן.

§ **The Sages taught** in a *baraita*: **A colored garment renders** a woman **impure due to** blood **stains** if she sees a blood stain on it. **Rabbi Natan bar Yosef says:** If she sees a blood stain on the colored garment **she is not impure due to** a blood **stain, as** the Sages **enacted** that **women** wear **colored garments,** and this decree was made **only** in order **to be lenient with regard to their** blood **stains,**[H] i.e., so that they do not become impure.

תִּקְּנוּ? מַאי תַּקְנִינְהוּ? אֶלָּא שֶׁלֹּא הוּתְּרוּ בִּגְדֵי צִבְעוֹנִין לָאִשָּׁה אֶלָּא לְהָקֵל עַל כִּתְמֵיהֶן. הוּתְּרוּ – מִכְּלָל דַּאֲסִירִי?

The Gemara questions Rabbi Natan bar Yosef's use of the word: Enacted. The Sages **enacted? What was their enactment? Rather,** Rabbi Natan bar Yosef said the reason **that** the Sages **permitted colored garments to women** was **only** in order **to be lenient with regard to her** blood **stains.** The Gemara raises an objection: From the statement that the Sages **permitted** colored garments one can conclude **by inference they were** previously **prohibited.** But was there a time when it was not permitted for women to wear colored garments?

אִין, דִּתְנַן: בְּפוּלְמוּס שֶׁל אַסְפַּסְיָנוּס גָּזְרוּ עַל עַטְרוֹת חֲתָנִים וְעַל הָאִירוּס. בִּקְּשׁוּ לִגְזוֹר עַל בִּגְדֵי צִבְעוֹנִין, אָמְרִי: הָא עֲדִיפָא – כְּדֵי לְהָקֵל עַל כִּתְמֵיהֶן.

The Gemara answers: **Yes, as we learned** in a mishna (*Sota* 49a): **In the war** [*bapulmus*][L] **of Vespasian**[B] **they decreed upon the crowns of bridegrooms,**[HB] i.e., that bridegrooms may no longer wear crowns, **and upon the drum** [*ha'irus*],[L] i.e., they also banned the playing of drums. **They** also **sought to decree with regard to colored garments,** i.e., that women may not wear such garments, but **they said: This is preferable,** that women should wear colored garments, **in order to be lenient with regard to their** blood **stains,** as a blood stain found on a colored garment does not render a woman ritually impure.

HALAKHA

Impurity of a blood stain on a colored garment – טוּמְאַת כֶּתֶם בְּבֶגֶד צָבוּעַ: If a woman finds a blood stain on a colored garment she remains ritually pure (Rambam *Sefer Kedusha*, *Hilkhot Issurei Bia* 9:7; *Shulḥan Arukh*, *Yoreh De'a* 190:10).

In the war of Vespasian they decreed upon the crowns of bridegrooms – בְּפוּלְמוּס שֶׁל אַסְפַּסְיָנוּס גָּזְרוּ עַל עַטְרוֹת חֲתָנִים: After the destruction of the Temple, the Sages of that generation decreed that a groom may not place a crown on his head for decoration. This *halakha* is in accordance with the *baraita* (Rambam *Sefer Zemanim*, *Hilkhot Ta'anit* 5:15; *Shulḥan Arukh*, *Oraḥ Ḥayyim* 560:1, 4).

BACKGROUND

War of Vespasian – פּוּלְמוּס שֶׁל אַסְפַּסְיָנוּס: This is referring to the great rebellion that led to the destruction of the Second Temple. It is named after Vespasian because he was the head of the Roman army for virtually the entirety of the war, from 67 CE until he was crowned emperor in 69 CE.

The crowns of bridegrooms – עַטְרוֹת חֲתָנִים: The Gemara in *Sota* 49b explains that the Sages wanted to permit bridegrooms to wear wreaths made from various plants and flowers, but it was accepted as *halakha* that these too are prohibited. The use of wreaths for brides was prohibited during the war of Titus, although this decree applied only to a special crown, the so-called city of gold; it was permitted to adorn brides with other kinds of crowns. The Sages also banned excessive decoration of the wedding canopy.

מתני׳ שִׁבְעָה סַמָּנִין מַעֲבִירִין עַל הַכֶּתֶם: רוֹק תָּפֵל, וּמֵי גְרִיסִין, וּמֵי רַגְלַיִם, וְנֶתֶר, וּבוֹרִית,

**MISHNA** There are **seven substances**[N] that **one applies to the stain**[H] on a garment to ascertain whether it is a blood stain or a dye, as these seven substances remove the blood. They are: **Tasteless saliva,**[B] **and liquid from split beans, and urine, and natron,**[B] **and** ***borit,***

**HALAKHA**

**Seven substances that one applies to the stain, etc.** – שִׁבְעָה סַמָּנִין מַעֲבִירִין עַל הַכֶּתֶם וכו׳: If there is uncertainty as to whether a stain on a woman's garment is menstrual blood or merely red coloring of some sort, one applies the seven abrasive substances used as laundering agents in order to test it. If it vanishes or fades, it is menstrual blood and the woman is ritually impure. If it remains the same, it is coloring and she is pure (see Ra'avad). The seven substances are tasteless saliva, liquid from split beans, urine, natron, *borit*, Cimolian earth, and potash. These seven substances must be applied in the specific order prescribed; if they are applied in the wrong order, it is as though no test of the stain has been performed. The woman must rub the garment three times with each agent, and scrub the garment between her hands after applying each one (*Maggid Mishne*, citing Rashi). The *Shulḥan Arukh* writes that nowadays one cannot rely upon this practice as the exact identities of these substances are unknown (Rambam *Sefer Kedusha, Hilkhot Issurei Bia* 9:36–37, and see Rambam *Sefer Tahara, Hilkhot Metamei Mishkav UMoshav* 4:13; *Shulḥan Arukh, Yoreh De'a* 190:31).

**BACKGROUND**

**Tasteless saliva** – רוֹק תָּפֵל: This is referring to concentrated saliva that is not mixed with liquids from food or drink. Compounds within saliva break up various other organic substances, and therefore it is useful for cleansing.

**Natron** – נֶתֶר: Some maintain that this is referring to sodium carbonate, $Na_2CO_3$, which is found in colorless clusters that crystallize from evaporating water. In nature, sodium carbonate is found in desert regions, but in ancient times it was often produced from the ash of sea algae. Also called washing soda, this compound is highly soluble in water, and when it dissolves it causes a strong basic reaction. It can dissolve many different types of fats and was therefore used as a cleaning agent as early as the biblical period.

Natural natron deposit

**NOTES**

**Seven substances** – שִׁבְעָה סַמָּנִין: Rashi in tractate *Sanhedrin* (49b) writes that the term: Substance [*sam*], refers primarily to any substance that can be used to fix something that is broken or has a defect. For example, the same term is used in reference to medicinal drugs, and it can also refer to perfume, which is used to remove foul odors. In this case too, the substances remove stains from garments.

Perek **IX**
Daf **62** Amud **a**

קָמוֹנְיָא, וְאֶשְׁלָג.

**Cimolian earth [*kamonya*],**[L] **and potash [*eshlag*].**[L]

הִטְבִּילוֹ וְעָשָׂה עַל גַּבָּיו טָהֳרוֹת, הֶעֱבִיר עָלָיו שִׁבְעָה סַמָּנִין וְלֹא עָבַר – הֲרֵי זֶה צֶבַע, הַטָּהֳרוֹת טְהוֹרוֹת וְאֵינוֹ צָרִיךְ לְהַטְבִּיל. עָבַר אוֹ שֶׁדֵּיהָה – הֲרֵי זֶה כֶּתֶם, וְהַטָּהֳרוֹת טְמֵאוֹת, וְצָרִיךְ לְהַטְבִּיל.

If **one immersed** the garment with the stain whose nature is unknown **and** then **handled ritually pure items with** the garment,[H] and then **applied** these **seven substances to** the stain **and it did not disappear, that** stain **is** presumably from **a dye, and** therefore **the ritually pure items are pure, and he need not immerse** the garment again, as there is no impurity. If the stain **disappeared or if it faded, that is** a blood **stain, and the ritually pure items** that he handled **are impure, and he must immerse** the garment again.

אֵיזֶהוּ רוֹק תָּפֵל – כָּל שֶׁלֹּא טָעַם כְּלוּם. מֵי גְרִיסִין – לְעִיסַת גְּרִיסִין שֶׁל פּוֹל חֲלוּקָה נֶפֶשׁ. מֵי רַגְלַיִם – שֶׁהֶחְמִיצוּ.

**What is tasteless saliva?**[H] It is saliva that emerges from the mouth of any person **who tasted nothing** all night, when he first awakens in the morning. **Liquid from split beans** is created through **the chewing of split beans**[H] that **divided naturally,** not by human hand, which is then applied to the stain. **The urine**[H] that is an effective detergent is specifically urine **that fermented** for three days.

**LANGUAGE**

**Cimolian earth [*kamonya*]** – קָמוֹנְיָא: Apparently from the Greek κιμωλία, *kimolia*. It refers to a white clay that was named after the Aegean island Kimolos, where it was used for washing and laundry.

**Potash [*eshlag*]** – אֶשְׁלָג: Possibly from the Persian eshgol, with the last two consonants reversed. It means a type of ash made from grasses, which was used for laundry.

**HALAKHA**

**If one immersed the garment and then handled ritually pure items with the garment** – הִטְבִּילוֹ וְעָשָׂה עַל גַּבָּיו טָהֳרוֹת: With regard to a garment that had a stain on it and that was immersed in a ritual bath and then came into contact with ritually pure items, and subsequently the stain was laundered with the seven cleansing agents and it did not disappear, one may assume that the stain is from a dye or some other color, and the pure items remain pure. The garment does not require a second immersion. If the stain disappears or lightens in color, it is a blood stain and any pure items with which it has come into contact are impure. The garment must be immersed a second time, because by trying to remove it, the person has demonstrated that he does not want the stain to remain on the garment (Rambam *Sefer Tahara, Hilkhot Metamei Mishkav UMoshav* 4:13).

**What is tasteless saliva** – אֵיזֶהוּ רוֹק תָּפֵל: Tasteless saliva is the saliva of one who has not eaten since the beginning of the night, and who slept for the second half of the night and has not yet eaten anything. Furthermore, he has not spoken a lot during the first three hours of the day. If he awoke and studied aloud a chapter of Torah in the first three hours of the day, it is no longer considered tasteless saliva, as speech nullifies the strength of the saliva and weakens it until it is like water (Rambam *Sefer Kedusha, Hilkhot Issurei Bia* 9:38).

**The chewing of split beans** – לְעִיסַת גְּרִיסִין: With regard to the cleansing agent of split beans that have been chewed, one must chew the beans until they are well mixed with a large quantity of saliva in his mouth (Rambam *Sefer Kedusha, Hilkhot Issurei Bia* 9:38).

**Urine** – מֵי רַגְלַיִם: What type of urine is considered to be one of the cleansing substances that remove a blood stain? This is urine that has become sour by being left to sit for three or more days (Rambam *Sefer Kedusha, Hilkhot Issurei Bia* 9:38).

וְצָרִיךְ לְכַסְכֵּס שָׁלֹשׁ פְּעָמִים לְכָל אֶחָד וְאֶחָד. הֶעֱבִירָן שֶׁלֹּא כְּסִדְרָן, אוֹ שֶׁהֶעֱבִיר שִׁבְעָה סַמָּנִין כְּאַחַת – לֹא עָשָׂה וְלֹא כְלוּם.

**And one must rub each and every one** of the substances **three times** over the stain, and one must apply them separately, and one must apply them in the order they are listed in the mishna. If **one applied them** in a manner that is **not in their** prescribed **order, or if one applied** all **seven substances simultaneously, he has done nothing.**[HN] One cannot determine by means of that examination whether it is blood or a dye.

גמ׳ תָּנָא: נֶתֶר אֲלֶכְסַנְדְּרִית וְלֹא נֶתֶר אַנְטִפַּטְרִית.

**GEMARA** The Gemara clarifies the identities of the seven substances that remove blood stains. With regard to natron, a Sage **taught** in a *baraita*: This is referring to **Alexandrian natron,** i.e., from the city in Egypt, **and not natron from Anpantrin,**[B] which is of a different quality.

״בּוֹרִית״. אָמַר רַב יְהוּדָה: זֶה אֲהָלָא. וְהָתַנְיָא: הַבּוֹרִית וְהָאֲהָל! אֶלָּא, מַאי בּוֹרִית – כַּבְרִיתָא.

The mishna lists *borit* as one of the seven substances. **Rav Yehuda says: This** is referring to **ice plant.**[B] The Gemara raises an objection: **But isn't it taught** in a *baraita*: ***Borit* and ice plant,** which indicates that they are two different substances? **Rather, what is *borit*? Sulfur.**

וּרְמִינְהִי: הוֹסִיפוּ עֲלֵיהֶן הַלְּבִיצִין, וְהַלְּעוּנִין, הַבּוֹרִית, וְהָאֲהָל. וְאִי בּוֹרִית כַּבְרִיתָא, מִי אִית לֵיהּ שְׁבִיעִית? וְהָתְנַן, זֶה הַכְּלָל: כָּל שֶׁיֵּשׁ לוֹ עִיקָּר – יֵשׁ לוֹ שְׁבִיעִית, וְכָל שֶׁאֵין לוֹ עִיקָּר – אֵין לוֹ שְׁבִיעִית! אֶלָּא מַאי בּוֹרִית – אֲהָלָא. וְהָתַנְיָא: הַבּוֹרִית וְהָאֲהָל? תְּרֵי גַּוְונֵי אֲהָלָא.

**And** the Gemara **raises a contradiction** from the *baraita* discussing the *halakha* of plants whose use is prohibited during the Sabbatical Year: **They added to** the list of such plants: Bulbs of **ornithogalum, and wormwood,** and **borit, and ice plant. And if it would enter your mind** to say that *borit* **is sulfur, is there sulfur** that is subject to the *halakhot* **of the Sabbatical Year? But didn't we learn** in a *baraita* that **this is the principle: Anything that has a root** and grows **is** subject to the *halakhot* of **the Sabbatical Year, and** anything **that does not have a root is not** subject to the *halakhot* of **the Sabbatical Year? Rather, what is** ***borit***? It is **ice plant. But isn't it taught** in the *baraita*: And ***borit* and ice plant?** The Gemara explains that there are **two types of ice plant,** one of which is called *borit*.

״קִמוֹנְיָא״. אָמַר רַב יְהוּדָה: שְׁלוֹף דּוֹץ. ״וְאַשְׁלָג״. אָמַר שְׁמוּאֵל: שְׁאַלְתִּינְהוּ לְנָחוֹתֵי יַמָּא, וַאֲמַרוּ: אַשְׁלְגָא שְׁמֵיהּ, וּמִשְׁתַּכַּח בֵּינֵי נִקְבֵי מַרְגָּנִיתָא, וּמַפְּקִי לַהּ בְּרַמְצָא דְּפַרְזְלָא.

With regard to the **Cimolian earth** mentioned in the mishna, **Rav Yehuda said:** This is the earth referred to as: **Pull out, stick in.**[N] **And** with regard to the ***eshlag*** mentioned in the mishna, **Shmuel said: I asked** all of **the seafarers** about the identity of *eshlag*, **and they told me it is called *ashlega*,** in Aramaic, **and can be found in the shell of the pearl, and is removed with an iron skewer.**

״הִטְבִּילוֹ וְעָשָׂה״ [כו׳]. תָּנוּ רַבָּנַן: הֶעֱבִיר עָלָיו שִׁבְעָה סַמָּנִין, וְלֹא עָבַר. צִפּוֹן, וְעָבַר – טָהֳרוֹתָיו טְמֵאוֹת.

§ The mishna teaches: If **one immersed** the garment with the stain whose nature is unknown **and** then **handled** ritually pure items with the garment, and then applied these seven substances to the stain and it did not disappear, that stain is a dye, and therefore the ritually pure items are pure, and he need not immerse the garment again, as there is no impurity. **The Sages taught** in a *baraita*: If **one applied these seven substances to** the stain **and it did not disappear,**[N] but he then applied **soap** [*tzafon*][L] **and it disappeared,**[H] any **ritually pure** items that he handled with the garment **are impure.**

## HALAKHA

**He has done nothing – לֹא עָשָׂה וְלֹא כְלוּם:** If all seven cleansing substances were used to launder the garment, but in the incorrect order, or if they were all used at the same time, the laundering is considered to be entirely ineffective. If one used the last substances first, the first ones to be applied in order are effective, and he must launder it again with the last substances in the correct order, so that all seven are used in the proper order (Rambam *Sefer Kedusha, Hilkhot Issurei Bia* 9:37).

**If one applied…soap and it disappeared – הֶעֱבִיר...צִפּוֹן וְעָבַר:** In the case of a stain that was laundered with six of the cleansing substances and did not disappear, but after one laundered it with soap it disappeared, any pure items that came into contact with the garment are impure. Although detergent removes a colored stain as well as blood, since the person did not test the stain with all seven laundering agents there is a presumption that it is a blood stain, as it is possible that if he had used the seventh agent the stain would have disappeared. This *halakha* is in accordance with the *baraita* (Rambam *Sefer Tahara, Hilkhot Metamei Mishkav UMoshav* 4:14).

## BACKGROUND

**Alexandrian natron and not natron from Anpantrin – נֶתֶר אֲלֶכְסַנְדְּרִית וְלֹא נֶתֶר אַנְטִפַּטְרִית:** The city of Alexandria in Egypt was the leading cultural and scientific center in the world, and remained as such for many generations. Alexandrian natron was considered excellent for many types of cleaning.

The city of Anpantrin was located in the north of Judea. It was built, or at least renewed and fortified, by Herod, who named it after his father, Antipater. The Greek version of the name, Ἀντίπατρος, Antipatros, appears in sources in various different forms. The city was near the springs of the Yarkon, close to modern-day Rosh HaAyin. Anpantrin had an advanced industry that manufactured a specific type of natron named after the city.

These two types of natron were different not only in the place of their production, but in the methods of their production and their quality. Alexandrian natron was manufactured from minerals in Egypt and exported to Eretz Yisrael via the port of Alexandria. Natron from Anpantrin, Eretz Yisrael, was made from plants.

**Ice plant – אֲהָלָא:** Washing soda, sodium carbonate, was used in antiquity for laundry and bathing, and was harvested from the crystalline ice plant, *Mesembryanthemum crystallinum* L., an annual plant that grows on sea-facing rocks in the Sharon region and the coastal plain in Eretz Yisrael. It is called the crystalline ice plant due to its glistening, crystal-like vesicles.

Crystalline ice plant field

## LANGUAGE

**Soap [*tzafon*] – צִפּוֹן:** From the Latin sapo, which was itself borrowed from Gallic. This word was adopted by many languages, e.g., in modern Hebrew the word for soap is *sabon*.

## NOTES

**He has done nothing [*lo asa velo kelum*] – לֹא עָשָׂה וְלֹא כְלוּם:** This phrase differs from the similar phrase used in reference to other situations where people perform a process out of order, e.g., a nazirite or leper who brought his offerings in the wrong order (*Nega'im* 14:4). There, the mishna states: He has not done anything [*lo asa kelum*]. Some explain that the use of the double negative term here indicates that the examination has no effect, both in that it does not determine whether or not the stain is pure, and in that it does not prevent the stain from imparting impurity to ritually pure items in the future (Rashi).

**Pull out, stick in [*shelof dotz*] – שְׁלוֹף דּוֹץ:** Rashi here does not explain this term. In *Sanhedrin* 49b, Rashi writes that he does not know what this is. Various explanations have been suggested. Some say that it is referring to a specific type of herb that is dried and ground and used for washing and removing dirt from one's hands (*Arukh*). Others claim that it is a type of white clay used for laundering clothes (*Musaf HeArukh*). Yet others contend that it is a type of salt with cleansing properties (Rambam's Commentary on the Mishna), or that it is referring to fine marble chips (Meiri).

**If one applied these seven substances to it and it did not disappear – הֶעֱבִיר עָלָיו שִׁבְעָה סַמָּנִין וְלֹא עָבַר:** The commentaries write that if these seven substances were not used to clean the garment, it is impure due to uncertainty (*Shulḥan Arukh, Yoreh De'a* 190:31).

צָפוֹן, צֶבַע נַמִּי מַעֲבַר! אֶלָּא: הֶעֱבִיר עָלָיו שִׁשָּׁה סַמָּנִין וְלֹא עָבַר, הֶעֱבִיר עָלָיו צָפוֹן וְעָבַר – טָהֳרוֹתָיו טְמֵאוֹת, שֶׁאִם הֶעֱבִיר שְׁבִיעִי מִתְּחִילָּה – שֶׁמָּא עָבַר.

The Gemara raises an objection with regard to this ruling: But **soap causes dye to disappear as well;** why then should one assume that the stain was blood? **Rather,** the *baraita* means that if **one applied** only **six of the** seven **substances to it and** the stain **did not disappear,** and he then **applied soap to** the stain **and it disappeared,** any **ritually pure** items that he handled with the garment **are impure.** The reason is **that if he had applied** all **seven** substances **initially, perhaps** the stain would have **disappeared,** proving that it was blood. Consequently, the garment is rendered impure due to uncertainty.

תַּנְיָא אִידָךְ: הֶעֱבִיר עָלָיו שִׁבְעָה סַמָּנִין וְלֹא עָבַר, שְׁנָאָן וְעָבַר – טָהֳרוֹתָיו טְהוֹרוֹת.

**It is taught** in **another** *baraita*: If **one applied** the **seven substances to** the stain **and it did not disappear,** indicating that it is a dye, and he then **repeated** and applied the seven substances a second time **and** the stain **disappeared,**[H] any **ritually pure** items that he handled with the garment remain **ritually pure.**

אָמַר רַבִּי זֵירָא: לֹא שָׁנוּ – אֶלָּא הַטָּהֳרוֹת שֶׁנַּעֲשׂוּ בֵּין תִּכְבּוֹסֶת רִאשׁוֹנָה לִשְׁנִיָּה, אֲבָל טָהֳרוֹת שֶׁנַּעֲשׂוּ אַחַר תִּכְבּוֹסֶת שְׁנִיָּה – טָהֳרוֹתָיו טְמֵאוֹת, שֶׁהֲרֵי הִקְפִּיד עָלָיו וְעָבַר.

In explanation of this *baraita*, **Rabbi Zeira says: They taught** that the pure items remain pure **only** with regard to **the ritually pure** items **that were handled between** the **first washing** with the seven substances **and the second** washing. **But** with regard to any **pure** items **that were handled** with the garment **after** the **second washing,** these **pure** items become **impure, as he was particular about it,** i.e., by repeating the washing procedure he showed he was concerned that it might be blood, **and** the stain **disappeared,** demonstrating that it was in fact blood.

**HALAKHA**

He repeated and it disappeared – שְׁנָאָן וְעָבַר: If one examined a stain on a garment with all seven substances and the stain remained, and he then examined the garment a second time with all seven substances and the stain disappeared, any ritually pure items that came into contact with the garment between the first and second launderings remain pure, but any ritually pure items that came into contact with the garment after the second laundering are impure. Since he has demonstrated that he is bothered by the stain and wants to remove it, the garment is impure until he removes the stain and immerses it in a ritual bath. This ruling is in accordance with the *baraita* and the opinion of Rabbi Zeira (Rambam *Sefer Tahara, Hilkhot Metamei Mishkav UMoshav* 4:14).

Perek **IX**
Daf **62** Amud **b**

אֲמַר לֵיהּ רַבִּי אַבָּא לְרַב אַשִׁי: מִידֵּי בְּקְפֵידָא תַּלְיָא מִילְּתָא?

**Rabbi Abba said to Rav Ashi,** with regard to his statement: **Does** the **matter** of purity or impurity **depend on** whether or not one is **particular** about the blood stain? If the items he handled on the garment between the first and second washings are ritually pure, then any items he handled after the second washing should likewise be pure.

אֲמַר לֵיהּ: אִין, דְּתַנְיָא, רַבִּי חִיָּיא אוֹמֵר: דַּם הַנִּדָּה וַדַּאי – מַעֲבִיר עָלָיו שִׁבְעָה סַמָּנִין וּמְבַטְּלוֹ,

Rav Ashi **said to him: Yes,** the status of purity depends upon whether or not the owner of the garment is particular about the stain. **As it is taught** in a *baraita* that **Rabbi Ḥiyya says:** If one finds **blood** on a garment that is **certainly from a menstruating woman**[H] and therefore renders the garment impure, one **may apply** the **seven substances** listed in the mishna **to it and** thereby **nullify it** from being considered a blood stain at all, even if the stain is not completely removed. And he may then immerse the garment in a ritual bath and it is ritually pure.

וְאַמַּאי? הָא דַּם נִדָּה הוּא! אַלְמָא – בִּקְפֵידָא תַּלְיָא מִילְּתָא, הָכִי נַמִּי – בִּקְפֵידָא תַּלְיָא מִילְּתָא.

Rav Ashi analyzes this ruling: **But why** is the garment pure? After all, **it** has **blood from a menstruating woman** on it. **Evidently,** the **matter** of whether or not it is ritually pure **depends upon** whether or not the owner of the garment **is particular** about the blood stain.[N] **So too** here, the **matter** of whether or not it is ritually pure **depends upon** whether or not the owner of the garment **is particular** about the blood stain.

**HALAKHA**

Blood that is certainly from a menstruating woman – דַּם הַנִּדָּה וַדַּאי: With regard to a blood stain that came from a woman who was certainly impure due to menstruation, it is nullified by being washed with the seven cleansing agents. Once the garment has been immersed in a ritual bath it may touch ritually pure items. This *halakha* is in accordance with the opinion of Rabbi Ḥiyya (Rambam *Sefer Tahara, Hilkhot Metamei Mishkav UMoshav* 4:11).

**NOTES**

Evidently the matter depends upon whether or not he is particular about the blood stain – אַלְמָא בִּקְפֵידָה תַּלְיָא מִילְּתָא: *Tosafot* ask: If so, why is there any need to use the seven substances on the garment? It should be sufficient to nullify it merely by not being particular about it. They answer that the fact that a specific individual chooses to nullify it is insufficient, due to the principle: His intention is rendered irrelevant by the opinions of all other people.

תְּנַן הָתָם: חֲרָסִין שֶׁנִּשְׁתַּמֵּשׁ בָּהֶן זָב, שֶׁבָּלְעוּ מַשְׁקִין, וְנָפְלוּ לַאֲוִיר הַתַּנּוּר, וְהוּסַּק הַתַּנּוּר – הַתַּנּוּר טָמֵא, שֶׁסּוֹף מַשְׁקֶה לָצֵאת.

§ **We learned** in a mishna **there** (see *Kelim* 9:5): In a case of **pottery,** i.e., a chamber pot, **that a man who experiences a gonorrhea-like discharge** [*zav*] **has used** and **that has absorbed** impure **liquids**[H] from the *zav*, **and** it then **fell into the air of an oven, and the oven was** subsequently **heated, the oven is impure,** as the impure **liquid will eventually emerge**[N] from the chamber pot due to the heat of the oven.

אָמַר רֵישׁ לָקִישׁ: לֹא שָׁנוּ – אֶלָּא מַשְׁקִין קַלִּים, אֲבָל מַשְׁקִין חֲמוּרִין – טָמֵא, אַף עַל פִּי שֶׁלֹּא הוּסַּק הַתַּנּוּר. רַבִּי יוֹחָנָן אָמַר: אֶחָד מַשְׁקִין קַלִּין וְאֶחָד מַשְׁקִין חֲמוּרִין, אִם הוּסַּק הַתַּנּוּר – אִין, אִי לָא – לָא.

The *amora'im* disagree with regard to the correct interpretation of this mishna. **Reish Lakish says: They taught** that the oven is impure once it is heated **only** with regard to **liquids of lesser** ritual impurity, i.e., that are not primary sources of impurity, such as the tears or urine of one who was rendered impure by contact with a corpse. **But** with regard to **liquids of greater** ritual impurity, e.g., urine of a *zav* or *zava*, the oven is **impure even though the oven was not heated. Rabbi Yoḥanan says:** With regard to **both liquids** of **lesser** ritual impurity **and liquids** of **greater** ritual impurity that fell into an oven, **if the oven was heated,** then **yes,** the oven is impure, but **if** the oven was **not** heated, it is **not** impure.

אֵיתִיבֵיהּ רַבִּי יוֹחָנָן לְרֵישׁ לָקִישׁ: הִטְבִּילוֹ וְעָשָׂה עַל גַּבָּיו טָהֳרוֹת, וְהֶעֱבִיר עָלָיו שִׁבְעָה סַמָּנִין וְלֹא עָבַר – הֲרֵי זֶה צֶבַע, וְטָהֳרוֹתָיו טְהוֹרוֹת, וְאֵין צָרִיךְ לְהַטְבִּיל!

**Rabbi Yoḥanan raised an objection to Reish Lakish** from the mishna: If **one immersed** the garment with the stain whose nature is unknown, **and** then **handled ritually pure items with** the garment, and then **applied** these **seven substances to** the stain **and it did not disappear, that** stain **is** presumably from **a dye, and** therefore **the ritually pure items are ritually pure, and he need not immerse** the garment again, as there is no impurity. Rabbi Yoḥanan understands that the stain is not definitely from a dye; even if it is from blood, such blood that is absorbed into the garment to the degree that it does not come out after this process is performed, does not impart ritual impurity. The same should apply in the case of the oven, i.e., the liquids should impart impurity only when the oven is heated and they actually emerge.

אֲמַר לֵיהּ: הַנַּח לִכְתָמִים – דְּרַבָּנַן.

Reish Lakish **said to** Rabbi Yoḥanan in response: **Leave** aside blood **stains,** i.e., one cannot cite a proof from them, as they impart impurity **by rabbinic law,** and for this reason the Sages were lenient and ruled that they do not impart impurity until they actually emerge. But with regard to liquids that are impure by Torah law, the *halakha* is different.

וְהָתָנֵי רַבִּי חִיָּיא: דַּם הַנִּדָּה וַדַּאי – מַעֲבִיר עָלָיו שִׁבְעָה סַמָּנִין, וּמְבַטְּלוֹ!

Rabbi Yoḥanan raises another objection to Reish Lakish: **But didn't Rabbi Ḥiyya teach:** If one finds **blood** on a garment that is **certainly from a menstruating woman** and therefore renders the garment impure, one **may apply** the **seven substances** listed in the mishna **to it and nullify** the stain from being considered a blood stain at all, even if the stain is not entirely removed; and he may then immerse the garment in a ritual bath and it is ritually pure?

אֲמַר לֵיהּ: רַבִּי לֹא שָׁנָה, רַבִּי חִיָּיא מְנָא לֵיהּ?

Reish Lakish **said to** Rabbi Yoḥanan in response: You cannot raise an objection to me from the *baraita* of Rabbi Ḥiyya, since if **Rabbi** Yehuda HaNasi **did not** teach this *halakha* in the Mishna, **from where** did **Rabbi Ḥiyya** learn it?[N] Rabbi Ḥiyya was a student of Rabbi Yehuda HaNasi, and therefore he could not have included a *halakha* that contradicts the Mishna. Consequently, this statement in his name must be erroneous.

**NOTES**

**As the impure liquid will eventually emerge** – **שֶׁסּוֹף מַשְׁקֶה לָצֵאת**: A liquid that is absorbed in an earthenware vessel will emerge from that vessel when it is heated in an oven. If an impure liquid is absorbed in a vessel, and that vessel is in an oven, that liquid will enter the airspace of the oven and render it ritually impure (Rashi).

**Rabbi Yehuda HaNasi did not teach this, from where did Rabbi Ḥiyya learn it** – **רַבִּי לֹא שָׁנָה רַבִּי חִיָּיא מְנָא לֵיהּ**: The early commentaries ask: Following this logic, the Gemara should never be able to challenge opinions of *amora'im* from *baraitot* that were taught in the schools of Rabbi Ḥiyya or Rabbi Oshaya, as they were both students of Rabbi Yehuda HaNasi. And yet the Gemara is filled with such objections. *Tosafot* answer that those *baraitot* of the academies of Rabbi Ḥiyya or Rabbi Oshaya that are cited as objections do not necessarily contradict the rulings of the Mishna, and they can be explained in accordance with the relevant mishna. By contrast, in this particular case it was clear to Reish Lakish that there was no source at all in the Mishna for the ruling of this *baraita*.

**HALAKHA**

**That has absorbed liquids** – **שֶׁבָּלְעוּ מַשְׁקִין**: With regard to earthenware that absorbed impure liquids and was dried and subsequently fell into the airspace of an oven, and the oven was heated, the oven is rendered ritually impure. The reason is that the liquid will eventually come out of the earthenware. This applies specifically to liquids of lesser ritual impurity. With regard to liquids of severe impurity, e.g., menstrual blood or the urine of a menstruating woman, if they could come out, and the owner of the item they are absorbed in wants them to come out, the earthenware renders the oven ritually impure even if it was not heated. If he does not necessarily want the liquid to come out of the earthenware, it renders the oven ritually impure only when it is heated and the liquid emerges. This ruling is in accordance with the opinion of Rabbi Yoḥanan, as interpreted by Rav Pappa (Rambam *Sefer Tahara*, *Hilkhot Kelim* 14:6).

אֵיתִיבֵיהּ רַבִּי יוֹחָנָן לְרֵישׁ לָקִישׁ: רְבִיעִית דָּם שֶׁנִּבְלַע בַּבַּיִת – הַבַּיִת טָמֵא. וְאָמְרִי לָהּ: הַבַּיִת טָהוֹר, וְלָא פְּלִיגִי, הָא – בְּכֵלִים דְּמֵעִיקָּרָא, הָא – בְּכֵלִים דְּבַסּוֹף.

**Rabbi Yoḥanan raised an objection to Reish Lakish** from a mishna (*Oholot* 3:2): With regard to **a quarter-*log* of blood** from a corpse **that was absorbed in** the floor of **a house,**[H] every vessel in **the house is ritually impure** by virtue of being under the same roof as the blood. The Gemara parenthetically notes: **And some say** that the mishna states that every vessel in **the house is ritually pure. And** these two statements **do not disagree,** as **this** first statement was issued **in** reference to **vessels that** were in the house **at the outset,** before the blood became absorbed; and **this** second statement was issued **in** reference to **vessels that** came into the house **at the end,** after the blood had already been absorbed.

נִבְלְעָה בִּכְסוּת, אִם מִתְכַּבֶּסֶת וְיוֹצֵא מִמֶּנָּה רְבִיעִית דָּם – טְמֵאָה, וְאִם לָאו – טְהוֹרָה!

The mishna continues: In a case where the blood **was absorbed in a garment,**[H] it is examined. **If** the garment **is washed and a quarter-*log* of blood emerges from it, it is ritually impure** and it imparts impurity to the vessels in the house as well. **But if not,** then **it is pure,** and it does not impart impurity. Apparently, only blood that can be removed from a garment is considered blood, whereas blood absorbed in the garment is insignificant. This is in accordance with the opinion that an absorbed substance does not impart ritual impurity, even if it can be removed in some manner.

אֲמַר רַב כָּהֲנָא: מִקּוּלֵּי רְבִיעִיּוֹת שָׁנוּ כָּאן, שָׁאנֵי דַּם תְּבוּסָה – דְּרַבָּנַן.

**Rav Kahana said** in response: **They taught here** a *halakha* **from** among **the leniencies** that apply to the measurement **of a quarter-*log*.** That is, this case **is different,** as the mishna is referring to **the blood of submission** discharged from a body at the time of death, and such blood is ritually impure **by rabbinic law.**[N] But in general, a ritually impure liquid that is absorbed into an item does impart impurity.

אֵיתִיבֵיהּ רֵישׁ לָקִישׁ לְרַבִּי יוֹחָנָן: כָּל הַבָּלוּעַ שֶׁאֵינוֹ יָכוֹל לָצֵאת – טָהוֹר, הָא יָכוֹל לָצֵאת – טָמֵא, וְאַף עַל גַּב דְּלָא נָפֵיק!

**Reish Lakish raised an objection to Rabbi Yoḥanan** from a mishna (*Oholot* 3:2): **Any** liquid **that is absorbed** but **that is unable to emerge is pure.** Reish Lakish infers from this mishna that if **it is able to emerge it is impure, and** that this is the *halakha* **even though it has not** yet **emerged.**

אֲמַר רַב פַּפָּא: כָּל הֵיכָא דְּאֵין יָכוֹל לָצֵאת, וְלֹא הִקְפִּיד עָלָיו – דִּבְרֵי הַכֹּל טָהוֹר, יָכוֹל לָצֵאת וְהִקְפִּיד עָלָיו – דִּבְרֵי הַכֹּל טָמֵא,

**Rav Pappa said** in defense of Rabbi Yoḥanan's opinion: **Anywhere that** the liquid **is unable to emerge and** the owner of the garment **is not particular about it,** i.e., he is not bothered that this liquid is absorbed within the garment, **everyone,** i.e., both Rabbi Yoḥanan and Reish Lakish, **agrees** that the garment **is pure.** If the liquid **is able to emerge and** the owner of the garment **is particular about it** and does not want it in his garment, **everyone agrees** that the garment **is impure.**

כִּי פְּלִיגִי – דְּיָכוֹל לָצֵאת וְלֹא הִקְפִּיד עָלָיו. מָר סָבַר: כֵּיוָן דְּיָכוֹל לָצֵאת – אַף עַל גַּב דְּלֹא הִקְפִּיד עָלָיו. וּמָר סָבַר: אַף עַל גַּב דְּיָכוֹל לָצֵאת,

**They disagree when** the liquid **is able to emerge and** the owner **is not particular about it.** One **Sage,** Reish Lakish, **holds** that **since** the liquid **is able to emerge, even though** the owner **is not particular about it,** the garment is impure. **And** one **Sage,** Rabbi Yoḥanan, **holds** that **even though** the liquid **is able to emerge,**

## NOTES

**The blood of submission [*tevusa*] is impure by rabbinic law** – דַּם תְּבוּסָה דְּרַבָּנַן: This is referring to the blood that leaves a human body just before and after death. The early commentaries write that it called by this name due to the verse: "And saw you wallowing [*mitboseset*] in your blood" (Ezekiel 16:6; see Rosh). The Sages decreed that this blood is ritually impure as a primary source of impurity, even if a full quarter-*log* did not leave the body after the person's death, and therefore it renders items impure through contact or carrying or in a tent, i.e., by being under the same roof.

## HALAKHA

**A quarter-*log* of blood that was absorbed in a house** – רְבִיעִית דָּם שֶׁנִּבְלַע בַּבַּיִת: If a quarter-*log* of blood was absorbed into the floor of a house, the house is pure from that point onward, but any item that was in the house when the blood was absorbed is ritually impure. This *halakha* is in accordance with the *baraita* (Rambam *Sefer Tahara, Hilkhot Tumat Met* 4:11).

**Was absorbed in a garment** – נִבְלְעָה בִּכְסוּת: With regard to a garment that has a quarter-*log* of blood absorbed within it, if the garment was laundered and a quarter-*log* of blood emerged, the garment renders other items ritually impure through contact, by carrying, and by the impurity of a tent. But if that amount of blood does not come out from the garment when it is laundered, it does not impart impurity in a tent. Rather, it has the status of a garment that touched a corpse. The reason is that any blood that is absorbed but cannot come out is pure. This *halakha* is in accordance with the *baraita* (Rambam *Sefer Tahara, Hilkhot Tumat Met* 4:13).

**NOTES**

**Where he passed the middle of the night and was in a state of sleep – שֶׁעָבַר עָלָיו חֲצוֹת לַיְלָה וּבְשֵׁינָה:** The reason is that sleep strengthens the saliva (Rashi; Meiri).

אִם הִקְפִּיד עָלָיו – אִין, אִי לָא – לָא.

**if he is particular** that he does not want the liquid there, then **yes,** it renders the garment impure, but **if not,** then the liquid does **not** render the garment impure.

״אֵיזֶהוּ רוֹק תָּפֵל״. תָּנָא: כָּל שֶׁלֹּא טָעַם כְּלוּם מִבָּעֶרֶב. סְבַר רַב פַּפָּא קַמֵּיהּ דְּרָבָא לְמֵימַר: כְּמַאן דַּאֲמַר לָא טְעֵים מִידֵּי בְּאוּרְתָּא. אֲמַר לֵיהּ רָבָא: מִי קָתָנֵי ״בָּעֶרֶב״ – ״מִבָּעֶרֶב״ קָתָנֵי, לְאַפּוּקֵי הֵיכָא דְּקָדֵים וְאָכֵיל.

§ The mishna teaches: **What is tasteless saliva?** A *tanna* **taught** in a *baraita*: What is the definition of tasteless saliva? **Any** saliva **where** the person **had not tasted anything since the evening. Rav Pappa,** who was sitting **before Rava, thought to say:** This **is in accordance with** the opinion of the **one who said** that **he did not eat anything** all **night** long. **Rava said to him: Is it taught:** One who had not tasted anything **in the evening,** which would indicate that it is referring only to one who did not eat since nightfall? No, the *baraita* **teaches:** Where the person had not tasted anything **since the evening,** which means even if he ate after nightfall, but did not eat for the rest of the night. This serves **to exclude** a case **where he** arose **early** in the morning **and ate,** as in such a case it is no longer tasteless saliva.

אָמַר רַבָּה בַּר בַּר חָנָה, אָמַר רַבִּי יוֹחָנָן: אֵיזֶהוּ רוֹק תָּפֵל – כָּל שֶׁעָבַר עָלָיו חֲצוֹת לַיְלָה, וּבְשֵׁינָה. לְמֵימְרָא דְּבְשֵׁינָה תַּלְיָא מִילְּתָא? וְהָתְנַן: יָשֵׁן כָּל הַיּוֹם – אֵין זֶה רוֹק תָּפֵל, נֵיעוֹר כָּל הַלַּיְלָה – הֲרֵי זֶה רוֹק תָּפֵל! הָתָם – בְּמִתְנַמְנֵם.

**Rabba bar bar Ḥana** says that **Rabbi Yoḥanan says: What is tasteless saliva? Any** saliva **where** the person did not eat any food and **he passed the middle of the night and** he was **in** a state of **sleep.**[N] The Gemara asks: Is that **to say that the matter depends on** whether or not he had **sleep? But didn't we learn** in a *baraita*: Even if **he slept the entire day, that is not tasteless saliva;** but if **he was awake the entire night, that is tasteless saliva?** This indicates that sleep is not a critical factor in producing tasteless saliva. The Gemara resolves this apparent contradiction by explaining that **there,** in the latter clause of the *baraita*, it is referring to a case **where** he was awake all night and did not sleep properly, but **was dozing** off and on.

הֵיכִי דָּמֵי מִתְנַמְנֵם? אָמַר רַב אַשִׁי: נִים וְלָא נִים, תִּיר וְלָא תִּיר, דְּקָרוּ לֵיהּ – וְעָנֵי, וְלָא יָדַע לְאַהֲדוּרֵי סְבָרָא, וְכִי מַדְכְּרוּ לֵיהּ – מִדְכַּר.

The Gemara asks: **What are the circumstances of dozing? Rav Ashi said:** It is referring to a situation in which one is **asleep and** yet **not** fully **asleep,** and **awake and** yet **not** fully **awake. If someone calls him he answers, and he is** in a mental state in which **he does not know** how **to provide** an answer that requires logical **reasoning, but when people remind him** about something when he is in that state that has happened previously **he remembers** it.

תָּנָא: הִשְׁכִּים וְשָׁנָה פִּרְקוֹ – אֵין זֶה רוֹק תָּפֵל. וְעַד כַּמָּה? אָמַר רַב יְהוּדָה בַּר שֵׁילָא, אָמַר רַב אַשִׁי, אָמַר רַבִּי אֶלְעָזָר: כָּל שֶׁיָּצָא רוֹב דִּבּוּרוֹ שֶׁל שָׁלֹשׁ שָׁעוֹת.

A *tanna* **taught** in a *baraita*: If one **rose** early in the morning **and learned** aloud **his chapter** of the Torah, **that** saliva in his mouth is **not tasteless saliva,** as speech weakens the strength of the saliva. **And how much** learning and talk removes the strength of the saliva? **Rav Yehuda bar Sheila says** that **Rav Ashi says** that **Rabbi Elazar says:** Any case **where he uttered most of his** normal amount of **speech** that he usually says **in three hours.**

״מֵי גְּרִיסִין לְעִיסַת גְּרִיסִין שֶׁל פּוֹל״ וכו׳. לֵימָא מְסַיַּיע לֵיהּ לְרֵישׁ לָקִישׁ, דַּאֲמַר רֵישׁ לָקִישׁ: רוֹק תָּפֵל צָרִיךְ שֶׁיְּהֵא עִם כָּל אֶחָד וְאֶחָד? דִּלְמָא הַבְלָא דְּפוּמָא מַעֲלֵי.

§ The mishna teaches: **Liquid from split beans** is created through **the chewing of split beans** that divided naturally, not by human hand, which are then applied to the stain. The Gemara suggests: **Let us say** that this ruling **supports** the opinion **of Reish Lakish, as Reish Lakish said: Tasteless saliva must be** mixed **with each and every one** of the other six substances in order to remove the blood stain. The Gemara answers that this is no proof, as **perhaps** it is not due to the saliva, but rather **the heat of his mouth** is what **helps** the split beans remove the stain.

מַתְנִיתִין דְּלָא כְּרַבִּי יְהוּדָה, דְּתַנְיָא, רַבִּי יְהוּדָה אוֹמֵר: מֵי גְּרִיסִין רוֹתֵחַ, וְעוֹבֵר שֶׁיִּתֵּן לְתוֹכוֹ מֶלַח.

The Gemara notes that **the mishna is not in accordance with** the opinion **of Rabbi Yehuda. As it is taught** in a *baraita* that **Rabbi Yehuda says: The liquid from split beans** is effective in removing blood stains only when it is **boiling, and before** [*over*] **one puts salt into** the pot.

מַאי מַשְׁמַע דְּהַאי "עוֹבֵר" לִישָּׁנָא דְּאַקְדּוּמֵי הוּא? אֲמַר רַב נַחְמָן בַּר יִצְחָק: דַּאֲמַר קְרָא "וַיָּרָץ אֲחִימַעַץ דֶּרֶךְ הַכִּכָּר וַיַּעֲבֹר אֶת הַכּוּשִׁי". אַבַּיֵי אֲמַר מֵהָכָא: "וְהוּא עָבַר לִפְנֵיהֶם". וְאִיבָּעֵית אֵימָא מֵהָכָא: "וַיַּעֲבֹר מַלְכָּם לִפְנֵיהֶם וַה' בְּרֹאשָׁם".

The Gemara asks: **From where may** it **be inferred that** the word *over* **is a formulation of priority? Rav Naḥman bar Yitzḥak said** that **the verse states: "And Ahimaaz ran by the way of the plain, and overran [*vayya'avor*] the Cushite"** (II Samuel 18:23), i.e., Ahimaaz overtook the Cushite. **Abaye said:** It is derived **from here: "And he passed [*avar*] before them"** (Genesis 33:3). **And if you wish, say** instead that the proof is **from here: "And their king passed [*vayya'avor*] before them and the Lord at their head"** (Micah 2:13).

"מֵי רַגְלַיִם שֶׁהֶחְמִיצוּ". תָּנָא: כַּמָּה חִימּוּצָן? שְׁלֹשָׁה יָמִים.

§ The mishna teaches: The **urine** that is an effective detergent is specifically urine **that fermented.** A *tanna* **taught** in a *baraita*: For **how** long must it be **fermented?** For **three days.**

אָמַר רַבִּי יוֹחָנָן: כָּל שִׁיעוּרֵי חֲכָמִים בִּכְתָמִים, צָרִיךְ שִׁיעוּר לְשִׁיעוּרָן. דְּיֶלֶד אוֹ דְּזָקֵן? דְּאִישׁ אוֹ דְּאִשָּׁה? מְכוּסִּים אוֹ מְגוּלִּים? בִּימוֹת הַחַמָּה אוֹ בִּימוֹת הַגְּשָׁמִים?

On the topic of the urine used to remove a blood stain, **Rabbi Yoḥanan says: All the measures of the Sages with regard to** blood **stains require a measure for their measure.** There are many types of urine, each of which has different properties, and it is unclear which is to be used. Is it urine **of a young** person **or of an old** person? Is it urine **of a man or of a woman?**[N] Is it urine that has been kept **covered or uncovered?** Is it urine **from the summer or from the rainy season?**

"וְצָרִיךְ לְכַסְכֵּס שָׁלֹשׁ פְּעָמִים". בָּעֵי רַבִּי יִרְמְיָה: אַמְטוּיֵי וְאַתּוּיֵי – חַד, אוֹ דִּלְמָא אַמְטוּיֵי וְאַתּוּיֵי – תַּרְתֵּי, מַאי? תֵּיקוּ.

§ The mishna teaches: **And one must rub** each and every one of the substances **three times. Rabbi Yirmeya raises a dilemma** with regard to this rubbing: Is the **going and coming** of the hand over the surface of the rubbed item considered **one** rubbing, **or perhaps** the **going and coming** are considered **two** actions and two distinct rubbings? **What** is the correct count? The Gemara states: The dilemma **shall stand** unresolved.[N]

"הֶעֱבִירָן שֶׁלֹּא כְּסִדְרָן". תָּנוּ רַבָּנַן: הִקְדִּים שְׁנִיִּים לָרִאשׁוֹנִים, תָּנֵי חֲדָא: שְׁנִיִּים – עָלוּ לוֹ, רִאשׁוֹנִים – לֹא עָלוּ לוֹ. וְתַנְיָא אִידָךְ: רִאשׁוֹנִים – עָלוּ לוֹ, שְׁנִיִּים – לֹא עָלוּ לוֹ.

§ The mishna further teaches: If **one applied them** in a manner that is **not in their** prescribed **order,** or if one applied all seven substances simultaneously, he has done nothing. **The Sages taught** two *baraitot* with regard to this matter. If one applied the substances from the **second** half of the list, i.e., natron, *borit*, Cimolian earth, and potash, **before the** substances from the **first** half of the list, i.e., tasteless saliva, liquid from split beans, and urine, it **is taught** in **one** *baraita*: The **second** set **count for him,** but the **first do not count for him.**[N] **And it is taught** in **another** *baraita*: The **first count for him,** but the **second do not count for him.**

אֲמַר אַבַּיֵי: אִידִי וְאִידִי – שְׁנִיִּים עָלוּ לוֹ, וְלֹא רִאשׁוֹנִים. וּמַאי "רִאשׁוֹנִים" – רִאשׁוֹנִים לְכִסְדְּרָן, וּשְׁנִיִּים לְהַעֲבָרָתָן.

**Abaye said** that there is no dispute between these two *baraitot*: Both **this** *baraita* **and that** *baraita* agree that the substances that he applied **second count for him, and not** the substances that he applied **first. And what** does the second *baraita* mean when it uses the term: **First?** It means the **first according to the order** of the mishna, which were the **second in their application.**

**NOTES**

**Of a young person or of an old person, of a man or of a woman** – דְּיֶלֶד אוֹ דְּזָקֵן דְּאִישׁ אוֹ דְּאִשָּׁה: According to Rabbi Yoḥanan there are four factors that determine the quality of urine: Age, sex, how the urine was stored, and season. Each of these can cause the urine to be strong and more effective at removing the stain, or weak and less effective. For example, the urine of a child is weaker than that of an adult, while covered urine is stronger than uncovered. Similarly, the strength of the urine is greater in the summer than in the winter (Rashi). Rashi does not explain whether urine of a man or urine of a woman is stronger, as he was uncertain about this matter (*Arukh LaNer*).

**The dilemma shall stand unresolved** – תֵּיקוּ: Although Rabbi Yirmeya's dilemma was not resolved, the early commentaries write that the reasonable conclusion is that going and coming is considered as one rubbing (Meiri).

**The second count for him but the first do not count for him** – שְׁנִיִּים עָלוּ לוֹ רִאשׁוֹנִים לֹא עָלוּ לוֹ: Since the application of the second set of three substances, i.e., saliva, liquid of split beans, and urine, is effective in that order despite the fact that it was performed after the other four, one need merely continue with the other four, i.e., natron, *borit*, Cimolian earth, and potash, for an effective test of the stain (Rashi).

מתני׳ כׇּל אִשָּׁה שֶׁיֵּשׁ לָהּ וֶסֶת – דַּיָּהּ שְׁעָתָהּ. וְאֵלּוּ הֵן הַוְּסָתוֹת: מְפַהֶקֶת, וּמְעַטֶּשֶׁת, וְחוֹשֶׁשֶׁת בְּפִי כְרֵיסָהּ וּבְשִׁפּוּלֵי מֵעֶיהָ, וְשׁוֹפַעַת, וּכְמִין צְמַרְמוֹרוֹת אוֹחֲזִין אוֹתָהּ, וְכֵן כַּיּוֹצֵא בָּהֶן. וְכׇל שֶׁקָּבְעָה לָהּ שְׁלֹשָׁה פְּעָמִים – הֲרֵי זֶה וֶסֶת.

**MISHNA** For **any woman who has** a fixed menstrual **cycle**[H] that is not time dependent, but is dependent on a physical sensation, **her time is sufficient,** i.e., she does not transmit ritual impurity retroactively, for twenty-four hours or until the last time she examined herself (see 2a). **And these are the** fixed menstrual **cycles**[N] based on sensation: When a woman menstruates after **she yawns** [*mefaheket*],[L] **or** after **she sneezes, or** after **she senses** pain **near her stomach or in her lower abdomen, or** after **she secretes** a discharge, **or** after **a type** of feverish **shuddering** [*tzemarmorot*][L] **overtakes her. And likewise** the same applies with regard to any sensation **of the like. And** in the case of **any** woman **who establishes** a pattern **for herself** by experiencing such a sensation **three times**[H] before the onset of menstruation, **that is** a fixed menstrual **cycle.**

גמ׳ תָּנֵינָא חֲדָא זִימְנָא: כׇּל אִשָּׁה שֶׁיֵּשׁ לָהּ וֶסֶת – דַּיָּהּ שְׁעָתָהּ! הָתָם – בְּוֶסֶת דְּיוֹמֵי, הָכָא – בְּוֶסֶת דְּגוּפָא.

**GEMARA** The mishna teaches that for any woman who has a fixed menstrual cycle, her time is sufficient. The Gemara objects: **We** already **learned** that her time is sufficient on **another occasion** (2a): For **any woman who has a** fixed menstrual **cycle,** and she examined herself at that time and discovered blood, **her time is sufficient,** and it is only from that moment that she transmits ritual impurity. The Gemara answers: **There,** it is referring **to a** fixed menstrual **cycle of** a certain number **of days; here,** it is referring **to a** fixed menstrual **cycle based on a physical** sensation.

כִּדְקָתָנֵי: אֵלּוּ הֵן וְסָתוֹת – הָיְתָה מְפַהֶקֶת, מְעַטֶּשֶׁת, וְחוֹשֶׁשֶׁת בְּפִי כְרֵיסָהּ, וּבְשִׁפּוּלֵי מֵעֶיהָ, וְשׁוֹפַעַת.

**As it teaches** in the continuation of the mishna: **These are the** fixed menstrual **cycles** based on sensation: When a woman menstruates after **she yawns,** or after **she sneezes, or** after **she senses** pain **near her stomach or in her lower abdomen, or** after **she secretes** a discharge. All of these are physical sensations.

שׁוֹפַעַת? הָא שָׁפְעָה וְאָזְלָא! אָמַר עוּלָּא בְּרֵיהּ דְּרַב עִילַּאי:

The mishna includes the case where **she secretes** a discharge as one of the physical sensations. The Gemara understands this as referring to a continuous discharge of blood, and therefore asks: **But** during menstruation **she is continuously discharging** blood; how can this be a signal of the onset of menstruation? **Ulla, son of Rav Ilai, said:**

בְּשׁוֹפַעַת דָּם טָמֵא מִתּוֹךְ דָּם טָהוֹר.

The mishna is referring to a case **where she discharges ritually impure blood in the midst of** discharging **ritually pure blood.**[N] For example, if she normally first discharges blood that is not red, and it therefore does not render her impure, and then she experiences a discharge of red blood.

## HALAKHA

**Any woman who has a fixed menstrual cycle – כׇּל אִשָּׁה שֶׁיֵּשׁ לָהּ וֶסֶת:** A woman who has a set pattern of menstrual bleeding, and who experienced bleeding at the expected time, is ritually impure only from that point onward. She is not impure retroactively (Rambam *Sefer Kedusha, Hilkhot Issurei Bia* 9:4).

**And these are the fixed menstrual cycles…three times, etc. – וְאֵלּוּ הֵן הַוְּסָתוֹת...שְׁלֹשָׁה פְּעָמִים וכו׳:** A woman can establish a set pattern of menstrual bleeding through certain bodily symptoms. Examples include if she yawns or has flatulence, or sneezes (according to Rambam and *Tosafot*), or experiences pain in her stomach or in her lower abdomen, or if she shivers, or if her head and limbs feel heavy. With regard to any of these symptoms, if she experiences that symptom immediately before three consecutive menstrual cycles, she has established a set pattern and must be concerned each time she experiences that symptom in the future, and it is prohibited for her to engage in intercourse when she experiences it. A solitary yawn or sneeze or the like is not considered a symptom; it is only if she yawns or sneezes involuntarily several times in a row. There is no set time for any of these symptoms; rather, each time she experiences the symptom she must assume that she will menstruate (Rambam *Sefer Tahara, Hilkhot Metamei Mishkav UMoshav* 3:6 and *Sefer Kedusha, Hilkhot Issurei Bia* 8:2 and *Maggid Mishne* on 8:1; *Shulḥan Arukh, Yoreh De'a* 189:19).

## LANGUAGE

**Yawns [*mefaheket*] – מְפַהֶקֶת:** There is a dispute among the commentaries with regard to the meaning of this term. Some maintain that it means yawn, as it does in modern Hebrew (*Tosafot*). Others explain that it refers to stretching (Rashi; Rosh).

**Shuddering [*tzemarmorot*] – צְמַרְמוֹרוֹת:** The root of this word is *tzemer*, which means to heat in Aramaic. The term, which is borrowed by Hebrew, means shivering with fever.

## NOTES

**And these are the fixed menstrual cycles – וְאֵלּוּ הֵן הַוְּסָתוֹת:** A cycle based on a physical sensation is considered fixed only after the woman experiences the same sensation before three consecutive menstrual cycles, e.g., if she yawns and experiences bleeding immediately, and this sequence happens three months in a row. But if she yawns once and experiences bleeding, then in another month sneezes and experiences bleeding, and then in a third month senses pain in her lower abdomen and experiences bleeding, she does not thereby establish a fixed menstrual cycle (Ran; Ramban; Rashba; Meiri; *Shulḥan Arukh, Yoreh De'a* 189:23).



## NOTES

**Where she discharges impure blood in the midst of pure blood – בְּשׁוֹפַעַת דָּם טָמֵא מִתּוֹךְ דָּם טָהוֹר:** In other words, she regularly sees ritually pure blood first, e.g., blood that is not red, after which she emits impure blood. In this manner she fixes a menstrual cycle: Her impure blood comes only after she discharges ritually pure blood. Therefore, every time she discharges impure blood after discharging ritually pure blood, she does not render pure items that she had touched retroactively impure (Rashi).

״וּכְמִין צְמַרְמוֹרוֹת״ וכו׳. ״וְכֵן כַּיּוֹצֵא בָּהֶן״ לְאַתוּיֵי מַאי? אֲמַר רַבָּה בַּר עוּלָּא: לְאַתוּיֵי אִשָּׁה שֶׁרֹאשָׁהּ כָּבֵד עָלֶיהָ, וְאֵבָרֶיהָ כְּבֵדִים עָלֶיהָ, וְרוֹתֶתֶת, וְגוֹסָה.

The mishna teaches: **Or a type of** feverish **shuddering** overtakes her, **and likewise** the same applies with regard to any sensation **of the like.** The Gemara asks: **What is added** by this last phrase? **Rabba bar Ulla said:** It serves **to include a woman whose head is heavy upon her or her limbs are heavy upon her, or she trembles or belches**[N] constantly.

אָמַר רַב הוּנָא בַּר חִיָּיא, אָמַר שְׁמוּאֵל: הֲרֵי אָמְרוּ לְיָמִים – שְׁנַיִם, לְוֶסָתוֹת – אַחַת, לְמַה שֶּׁלֹּא מָנוּ חֲכָמִים – שְׁלֹשָׁה.

**Rav Huna bar Ḥiyya says that Shmuel says:** The Sages **said, with regard to** establishing a set period of **days,** that **two** days are sufficient, i.e., if a woman experiences bleeding twice on the same date of the month or after the same interval, she has a fixed menstrual cycle. By contrast, **with regard to** a fixed menstrual **cycle** based on a physical sensation, it is sufficient if she experiences bleeding even **once.** But **for those** sensations **which the Sages did not include** in the mishna, she has a fixed cycle only if she experiences bleeding **three** times accompanied by one of those symptoms.

״לְמַה שֶּׁלֹּא מָנוּ חֲכָמִים״ – לְאַתוּיֵי מַאי? אֲמַר רַב יוֹסֵף: לְאַתוּיֵי רֹאשָׁהּ כָּבֵד עָלֶיהָ, וְאֵבָרֶיהָ כְּבֵדִין עָלֶיהָ, וְרוֹתֶתֶת, וְגוֹסָה. אֲמַר לֵיהּ אַבַּיֵי: מַאי קָא מַשְׁמַע לָן? מַתְנִיתִין הִיא, דְּהָא פֵּירְשָׁהּ רַבָּה בַּר עוּלָּא! אֶלָּא אֲמַר אַבַּיֵי: לְאַתוּיֵי – אָכְלָה שׁוּם וְרָאֲתָה, וְאָכְלָה בְּצָלִים וְרָאֲתָה, כָּסְסָה פִּלְפְּלִים וְרָאֲתָה.

The Gemara asks: When Shmuel said: **For those which the Sages did not include, what** did he intend **to add? Rav Yosef says:** This serves **to add** the case mentioned above, i.e., **her head is heavy upon her, or her limbs are heavy upon her, or she trembles or belches** constantly. **Abaye said** to Rav Yosef: **What is** that addition **teaching us?** In effect, **it is** already taught in **the mishna, as Rabba bar Ulla explained** above that the additional phrase: The same applies with regard to any sensation of the like, serves to include those sensations. **Rather, Abaye said:** Shmuel's phrase serves **to add** a case where **she ate garlic**[B] **and saw**[N] menstrual blood, **or ate onions**[B] **and saw** menstrual blood, or **chewed pepper**[B] **and saw**[H] menstrual blood, i.e., these triggers can give rise to a fixed cycle, but only after three occurrences.

אֲמַר רַב יוֹסֵף: לָא שְׁמִיעַ לִי הָא שְׁמַעְתָּא.

**Rav Yosef said: I did not hear this tradition** concerning the opinion of Shmuel, that with regard to days a cycle is fixed if she experiences bleeding twice, whereas for physical sensations a cycle is fixed after one occurrence. Rav Yosef had fallen ill and forgotten his studies and was therefore unable to remember that such a ruling had been issued.

**NOTES**

**Belches [*gosa*] – גּוֹסָה:** Some commentaries state that *gosa* means yawning from exhaustion (Rashi). Others explain that it refers to belching after eating, either due to the type of food eaten or the speed of eating (*Tosafot*, citing *Arukh*). Alternatively, it is referring to stretching out the arms due to tiredness (Meiri), or experiencing nausea (Rashba), or sensing a pain in her belly (*Ba'alei HaNefesh*; Meiri). In sum, the early authorities write that all of these explanations are correct. Any physical, involuntary activity that consistently precedes the emission of blood is a sign that the blood is about to emerge from her body, and she is considered to have a fixed menstrual cycle based on sensation (Rosh).

**She ate garlic and saw – אָכְלָה שׁוּם וְרָאֲתָה:** The difference between these sensations and those listed in the mishna is that here she experiences bleeding due to her intentional action of eating, whereas the mishna lists only involuntary actions.

**HALAKHA**

**She ate garlic and saw or ate onions and saw or chewed pepper and saw – אָכְלָה שׁוּם וְרָאֲתָה וְאָכְלָה בְּצָלִים וְרָאֲתָה כָּסְסָה פִּלְפְּלִים וְרָאֲתָה:** If a woman ate one of these foods and experienced bleeding, some say that she has established a fixed menstrual cycle of bleeding after eating sharp foods. In addition, some authorities claim that she is similar to a woman who experiences bleeding every time after jumping, and therefore she establishes a cycle only if she does so after a set interval of days. Others maintain that this is similar to a woman who experiences bleeding after experiencing an involuntary sensation, which means that she establishes a cycle even without a set interval of days in between.

In all cases of set cycles that are established based on bodily sensations, the woman is obligated to separate only at the time of the sensation. For example, if she normally experiences bleeding as she begins experiencing this sensation, she is prohibited to her husband for the duration of the sensation. If she typically experiences bleeding at the end of experiencing the sensation, she is prohibited only at its conclusion. This applies when she experiences bleeding only within the set time of the sensation. If her bleeding extends to after the end of the sensation, she is prohibited to her husband from the time of the sensation until the end of that day or night (Rambam *Sefer Tahara, Hilkhot Metamei Mishkav UMoshav* 3:6; *Shulḥan Arukh, Yoreh De'a* 189:24, and 189:23 in the comment of Rema).

**BACKGROUND**

**Garlic – שׁוּם:** Garlic, *Allium sativum* L., is not only used to season food; it is also believed to have health benefits. It has long been known that garlic is an anthelmintic, i.e., it kills intestinal worms. Modern studies have shown its other health benefits. About 20 percent of the dry weight of garlic is protein, and due to this large amount it is satisfying and warms the body.

Garlic flower

**Onions – בְּצָלִים:** Onions were extremely common and inexpensive, and were prepared in a variety of ways, both raw and cooked. Due to their strong flavor they were used for seasoning food. Garlic shares this property, and is often mentioned alongside onions, e.g., "We remember the fish, which we ate in Egypt for free, the cucumbers, and the melons, and the leeks, and the onions, and the garlic" (Numbers 11:5). Onions contain allyl propyl disulfide ($C_6H_{12}S_2$), which can be dangerous when ingested in large quantities.

Onion flowers

**Chewed pepper – כָּסְסָה פִּלְפְּלִים:** In the talmudic period, pepper was primarily used for spicing foods. It would be ground in a special metal spice mill. Pepper that was not ground could also be chewed.

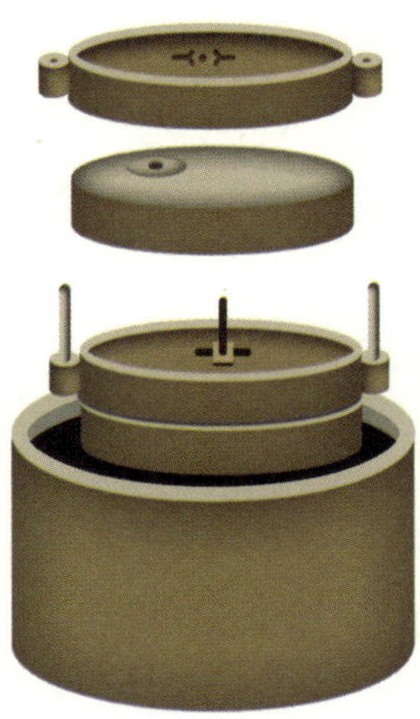

Sketch depicting a Roman-era metal spice mill

אֲמַר לֵיהּ אַבָּיֵי: אַתְּ אֲמַרִיתָהּ נִיהֲלָן, וְאַהָא אֲמַרִיתָהּ נִיהֲלָן: הָיְתָה לְמוּדָה לִהְיוֹת רוֹאָה יוֹם חֲמִשָּׁה עָשָׂר וְשִׁינְּתָה לְיוֹם עֶשְׂרִים – זֶה וָזֶה אֲסוּרִין. שָׁלֹשׁ פְּעָמִים לְיוֹם עֶשְׂרִים – הוּתַּר יוֹם חֲמִשָּׁה עָשָׂר, וְקָבְעָה לָהּ יוֹם עֶשְׂרִים, שֶׁאֵין אִשָּׁה קוֹבַעַת לָהּ וֶסֶת – עַד שֶׁתִּקְבָּעֶנָּה שָׁלֹשׁ פְּעָמִים.

His student, **Abaye, said to him: You** yourself **told us** this *halakha*, **and** it was **with regard to this** following matter that **you told** this *halakha* **to us,** taught in the mishna below: If a woman **was accustomed to see** the flow of blood on the **fifteenth day and she deviated** from the norm to see the flow of blood **on the twentieth day,** then on both **this** day, the fifteenth, **and that** day, the twentieth, it is **prohibited** for her to engage in intercourse. If she deviated from the norm to see the flow of blood **on the twentieth day three times, it becomes permitted** for her to engage in intercourse on the **fifteenth day, and she** has **established the twentieth day for herself** as the day of her fixed menstrual cycle, **as a woman establishes** a fixed menstrual **cycle only after she establishes it three times.**[H]

וְאָמְרַתְּ לָן עֲלָהּ אֲמַר רַב יְהוּדָה, אֲמַר שְׁמוּאֵל: זוֹ דִּבְרֵי רַבָּן גַּמְלִיאֵל בַּר רַבִּי שֶׁאָמַר מִשּׁוּם רַבָּן שִׁמְעוֹן בֶּן גַּמְלִיאֵל, אֲבָל חֲכָמִים אוֹמְרִים: רָאֲתָה – אֵינָהּ צְרִיכָה לֹא לִשְׁנוֹת וְלֹא לְשַׁלֵּשׁ.

Abaye continues: **And you,** Rav Yosef, **said to us with regard to this** mishna that **Rav Yehuda said** that **Shmuel said: This is the statement of Rabban Gamliel bar Rabbi** Yehuda HaNasi, **who said** it **in the name of Rabban Shimon ben Gamliel. But the Rabbis say:** If **she saw** a discharge of blood even once, she has a fixed cycle and **does not need to repeat** and experience bleeding a second time **or to repeat a third** time.

וְאָמְרִינַן לָךְ: לִשְׁנוֹת אָמְרַתְּ לָן, לְשַׁלֵּשׁ מִיבַּעְיָא? וְאָמְרַתְּ לָן: לִשְׁנוֹת – בְּוֶסֶתוֹת, לְשַׁלֵּשׁ – בְּיָמִים.

**And we said to you:** Since **you said to us** that she does not need **to repeat** a second time, **is it necessary** for you to mention that she does not need **to repeat a third** time? **And you said to us** that when you said that she does not need **to repeat** a second time, this is referring **to** a fixed menstrual **cycle** based on a physical sensation, whereas when you said she does not need **to repeat a third** time, that is referring **to** a fixed cycle of **days.**

וְנֵימָא זוֹ דִּבְרֵי רַבָּן שִׁמְעוֹן בֶּן גַּמְלִיאֵל! הָא קָא מַשְׁמַע לָן שְׁמוּאֵל: דְּרַבָּן גַּמְלִיאֵל בְּרַבִּי – כְּרַבָּן שִׁמְעוֹן בֶּן גַּמְלִיאֵל סְבִירָא לֵיהּ.

The Gemara asks: **But** why did Shmuel have to explain that the mishna is the statement of Rabban Gamliel bar Rabbi Yehuda HaNasi? **Let him say** simply that **this** mishna **is the statement of Rabban Shimon ben Gamliel,** who always requires repetition three times to establish a presumptive status. The Gemara answers that **this** is what **Shmuel teaches us: That Rabban Gamliel, son of Rabbi** Yehuda HaNasi, **holds in accordance with** the opinion of **Rabban Shimon ben Gamliel.**

**מתני׳** הָיְתָה לְמוּדָה לִהְיוֹת רוֹאָה בִּתְחִלַּת הַוְּסָתוֹת, כָּל הַטְּהָרוֹת שֶׁעָשְׂתָה בְּתוֹךְ הַוְּסָתוֹת – טְמֵאוֹת. בְּסוֹף הַוְּסָתוֹת – כָּל הַטְּהָרוֹת שֶׁעָשְׂתָה בְּתוֹךְ הַוְּסָתוֹת טְהוֹרוֹת.

**MISHNA** If a woman **was accustomed to see** the flow of blood **at the beginning of the** sensation that accompanies her **fixed** cycle, even if on one occasion she happened to experience bleeding only at the end of the sensation, **all the ritually pure items that she handled within the** duration of that sensation that accompanies her **fixed** cycle **are ritually impure.** If the woman was accustomed to experience bleeding **at the end of the** sensation that accompanies her **fixed** cycle, **all the ritually pure items that she handled within the** duration of that sensation that accompanies her **fixed** cycle **are pure.**

רַבִּי יוֹסֵי אוֹמֵר: אַף יָמִים וְשָׁעוֹת וְסָתוֹת. הָיְתָה לְמוּדָה לִהְיוֹת רוֹאָה עִם הָנֵץ הַחַמָּה – אֵינָהּ אֲסוּרָה אֶלָּא עִם הָנֵץ הַחַמָּה. רַבִּי יְהוּדָה אוֹמֵר: כָּל הַיּוֹם שֶׁלָּהּ.

**Rabbi Yosei says: Even** specific **days and** specific **hours** determine a fixed menstrual **cycle:** If a woman **was accustomed to see** the flow of blood on a certain day of the month **at sunrise,** it is **prohibited** for **her** to engage in intercourse with her husband **only at sunrise;** but during the night before and the following day, it is permitted for her to engage in intercourse. **Rabbi Yehuda says:** Once sunrise passed and she did not menstruate, **the entire day is hers** and she may engage in intercourse, in accordance with the opinion of Rabbi Yosei; but contrary to the opinion of Rabbi Yosei, intercourse the night before is prohibited.

HALAKHA

Only after she establishes it three times – עַד שֶׁתִּקְבָּעֶנָּה שָׁלֹשׁ פְּעָמִים: A woman does not establish a fixed cycle until she has experienced bleeding four times, with three equal intervals between them. For example, she experiences bleeding today, and again after twenty days, and again after another twenty days, and again after another twenty days. This is called a cycle of intervals. She must experience bleeding four times in order to have three intervals. Nevertheless, even after she experiences bleeding once after an interval, she must be concerned for that interval again. Another type of cycle is based on the days of the month. If she experiences bleeding on a certain day of the month, she must be concerned that she might again experience bleeding on the same day of the following month. Once a cycle has been repeated established, she must always be concerned for the next occurrence of that cycle, until for three consecutive times she does not experience bleeding on that day. Even after bleeding once, it is prohibited for her to engage in intercourse with her husband on the same day of the following month. After having her second menstrual period, it is prohibited for her to engage in intercourse with her husband in the third month on the day corresponding to the interval between the first two periods (Rambam *Sefer Kedusha, Hilkhot Issurei Bia* 8:4; *Shulḥan Arukh, Yoreh De'a* 189:2).

גמ׳ תָּנָא, כֵּיצַד אָמַר רַבִּי יוֹסֵי: יָמִים וְשָׁעוֹת וְסָתוֹת – הָיְתָה לְמוּדָה לִהְיוֹת רוֹאָה מִיּוֹם עֶשְׂרִים לְיוֹם עֶשְׂרִים, וּמִשֵּׁשׁ שָׁעוֹת לְשֵׁשׁ שָׁעוֹת, הִגִּיעַ יוֹם עֶשְׂרִים וְלֹא רָאֲתָה – אֲסוּרָה לְשַׁמֵּשׁ כָּל שֵׁשׁ שָׁעוֹת רִאשׁוֹנוֹת – דִּבְרֵי רַבִּי יְהוּדָה, וְרַבִּי יוֹסֵי מַתִּיר עַד שֵׁשׁ שָׁעוֹת, וְחוֹשֶׁשֶׁת בְּשֵׁשׁ שָׁעוֹת.

**GEMARA** A *tanna* **taught** in a *baraita*: **In what case did Rabbi Yosei say** that specific **days and hours** determine a fixed menstrual **cycle?** For example, if a woman **was accustomed to see** the flow of blood **on the twentieth day** and again **on the twentieth day, and in the sixth hour** of the day[N] and again **in the sixth hour** of the day the next time; if the **twentieth day arrives** a third time **and she does not see** a flow of blood, **it is prohibited for her to engage** in intercourse for **the entirety of the first six hours** of the day; **this is the statement of Rabbi Yehuda. Rabbi Yosei deems** it **permitted** for her to engage in intercourse **until the sixth hour** of the day, **and** says that she must be **concerned** only **during the sixth hour.**

עָבְרוּ שֵׁשׁ שָׁעוֹת וְלֹא רָאֲתָה – אֲסוּרָה לְשַׁמֵּשׁ כָּל הַיּוֹם כּוּלּוֹ – דִּבְרֵי רַבִּי יְהוּדָה, וְרַבִּי יוֹסֵי מַתִּיר מִן הַמִּנְחָה וּלְמַעְלָה.

The *baraita* continues: If **the sixth hour passed and she did not see**[H] a flow of blood, **it is prohibited for her to engage** in intercourse for **the entirety of the day;** this is **the statement of Rabbi Yehuda. And Rabbi Yosei deems** it **permitted** for her to engage in intercourse **from** ***minḥa*** time **onward,** i.e., from the beginning of the seventh hour.

״הָיְתָה לְמוּדָה״. וְהָתַנְיָא, רַבִּי יְהוּדָה אוֹמֵר: כָּל הַלַּיְלָה שֶׁלָּהּ!

§ The mishna teaches with regard to a woman who **was accustomed to see** the flow of blood on a certain day of the month at sunrise, that Rabbi Yehuda says: Once sunrise passed and she did not menstruate, the entire day is hers and she may engage in intercourse, but intercourse is prohibited the night before. The Gemara objects: **But isn't it taught** in a *baraita* that **Rabbi Yehuda says: The entire night is hers?** This indicates that she may engage in intercourse during the night.

לָא קַשְׁיָא, הָא – דִּרְגִילָה לִרְאוֹת בִּתְחִלַּת יְמָמָא, וְהָא – דִּרְגִילָה לִרְאוֹת בְּסוֹף לֵילְיָא.

The Gemara explains that it is **not difficult. Here,** when it is permitted for her to engage in intercourse the entire night, it is referring to a case **where she is accustomed to see** a flow of blood **at the beginning of the day,** i.e., immediately after sunrise. **And there,** in the mishna, which deems it prohibited for her to engage in intercourse all night, it is referring to a case **where she is accustomed to see** a flow of blood **at the end of the night,** i.e., just before sunrise.

תָּנֵי חֲדָא: רַבִּי יְהוּדָה אוֹסְרָהּ לִפְנֵי וִסְתָּהּ, וּמַתִּירָהּ לְאַחַר וִסְתָּהּ. וְתַנְיָא אִידַּךְ: אוֹסְרָהּ לְאַחַר וִסְתָּהּ, וּמַתִּירָהּ לִפְנֵי וִסְתָּהּ.

The Gemara cites further *baraitot* that deal with Rabbi Yehuda's opinion. It **is taught** in **one** *baraita*: **Rabbi Yehuda deems** it **prohibited for her** to engage in intercourse **before** the time of **her** fixed **cycle, but deems** it **permitted for her** to do so **after** the time of **her** fixed **cycle** if she did not experience bleeding then. **And it is taught** in **another** *baraita*: Rabbi Yehuda **deems** it **prohibited for her** to engage in intercourse **after** the time of **her** fixed **cycle but deems** it **permitted for her** to do so **before** the time of **her** fixed **cycle.**

וְלָא קַשְׁיָא, הָא – דִּרְגִילָה לְמֶחֱזֵי בְּסוֹף לֵילְיָא, הָא – דִּרְגִילָה לְמֶחֱזֵי בִּתְחִלַּת יְמָמָא.

The Gemara resolves this apparent contradiction: **And** this is **not difficult; here,** the *baraita* that rules that it is prohibited for her to engage in intercourse before the time of her fixed cycle is referring to a case **where she is accustomed to see** a flow of blood **at the end of the night.** By contrast, **there,** the *baraita* that states that it is prohibited for her to do so after the time of her fixed cycle is referring to a case **where she is accustomed to see** a flow of blood **at the beginning of the day.**

אֲמַר רָבָא: הֲלָכָה כְּרַבִּי יְהוּדָה. וּמִי אֲמַר רָבָא הָכִי? וְהָתַנְיָא: ״וְהִזַּרְתֶּם אֶת בְּנֵי יִשְׂרָאֵל מִטּוּמְאָתָם״, מִכָּאן אָמַר רַבִּי יִרְמְיָה: אַזְהָרָה לִבְנֵי יִשְׂרָאֵל שֶׁיִּפְרְשׁוּ מִנְּשׁוֹתֵיהֶן סָמוּךְ לְוִסְתָּן.

**Rava said:** The ***halakha*** is **in accordance with** the opinion of **Rabbi Yehuda.** The Gemara asks: **And did Rava** actually **say this? But isn't it taught** in a *baraita*: The verse states with regard to a menstruating woman: **"You shall separate the children of Israel from their impurity"** (Leviticus 15:31). **From here, Rabbi Yirmeya said** that there is **a warning to the children of Israel that they should separate from their wives close to** the time of **their** menstrual **cycles.**[N]

## HALAKHA

**If the sixth hour passed and she did not see – עָבְרוּ שֵׁשׁ שָׁעוֹת וְלֹא רָאֲתָה:** If the set time for a woman's menstrual cycle passed and she did not experience bleeding, she is permitted to her husband after that day or night. For example, if she usually experiences bleeding in the sixth hour of the day, she is prohibited from the beginning of the day. After the sixth hour, if she did not experience bleeding, she is prohibited to her husband until the evening. Similarly, if she typically experiences bleeding in the sixth hour of the night, she is prohibited to her husband for the entire night. This ruling is in accordance with the opinion of Rabbi Yehuda (Rambam *Sefer Kedusha, Hilkhot Issurei Bia* 4:13).

## NOTES

**And in the sixth hour of the day, etc. – וּמִשֵּׁשׁ שָׁעוֹת וכו׳:** Some commentaries maintain that Rabbi Yehuda concedes to Rabbi Yosei in a case where a woman establishes a cycle for hours and not for days, i.e., she is not obligated to separate for the entire twelve-hour period, but only for the hour in which she is accustomed to experience bleeding. Rabbi Yehuda and Rabbi Yosei disagree only in a case where she is accustomed to experience bleeding after an interval of both days and hours (*Shulḥan Arukh, Yoreh De'a* 189:3, citing Ra'avad). The early commentaries disagree with regard to the meaning of the Ra'avad's claim. Some suggest that as she has established her cycle for a certain hour and not for days, she must be concerned every single day at that hour, but she must separate only at that hour, not for the entire day (Ba'al HaMaor). Others write that she must separate at that hour one month later, on the day of the month that she experienced bleeding previously, and she is not obligated to separate the entire day (Meiri; *Ḥavvat Da'at*).

**A warning to…Israel that they should separate from their wives close to their menstrual cycles – אַזְהָרָה לְ...יִשְׂרָאֵל שֶׁיִּפְרְשׁוּ מִנְּשׁוֹתֵיהֶן סָמוּךְ לְוִסְתָּן:** The early commentaries struggle to explain how the verse: "You shall separate the children of Israel from their impurity" (Leviticus 15:31), teaches that a couple must separate close to the time of the woman's period, as there is a tradition that the entire concept of set menstrual cycles applies by rabbinic law and therefore it cannot be derived from the Torah. Therefore, some explain that this verse is not a proper source for this *halakha* but is cited as a mere support for the rabbinic law (Ra'avad). Others maintain that although the *halakha* of set periods is by rabbinic law, the requirement of separation applies by Torah law (*Ḥiddushei Rabbeinu Ḥayyim HaLevi al HaRambam* on Rambam *Sefer Kedusha, Hilkhot Issurei Bia* 4:12).

וְכַמָּה? אָמַר רָבָא: עוֹנָה. מַאי לָאו – עוֹנָה אַחֲרִיתִי? לָא, אוֹתָהּ עוֹנָה.

**And how close? Rava says: One** twelve-hour **period,** i.e., either from sunrise to sunset, or from sunset to sunrise. The Gemara explains the difficulty: **What, is it not** referring to **an additional** twelve-hour **period,** i.e., the prohibition applies to the time of her expected period itself, either day or night, as well as the previous twelve hours? This is not in accordance with the opinion of Rabbi Yehuda, who deems it prohibited for her to engage in intercourse only for the twelve hours of the expected time of her period. The Gemara answers: **No,** it is referring to **that** same twelve-hour **period.**[H]

וְתַרְתֵּי לָמָּה לִי? צְרִיכָא, דְּאִי אַשְׁמוּעִינַן הָא הֲוָה אָמִינָא: הָנֵי מִילֵּי – לְטָהֳרוֹת, אֲבָל לְבַעְלָהּ – לָא, קָא מַשְׁמַע לַן.

The Gemara asks: **And why do I** need **two** statements of Rava, i.e., both that the *halakha* is in accordance with the opinion of Rabbi Yehuda and that a woman must separate for only one twelve-hour period? The Gemara answers that both are **necessary, because if** Rava had **taught us** only **this,** that the *halakha* is in accordance with the opinion of Rabbi Yehuda in the mishna, **I would say** that **this statement** applies only **to** the handling of **pure** items, **but with regard to** engaging in intercourse with **her husband,** it does **not** apply, and with regard to intercourse, the *halakha* is in accordance with the opinion of Rabbi Yosei. Therefore, Rava **teaches us** that even with regard to intercourse, the *halakha* is in accordance with the opinion of Rabbi Yehuda.

וְאִי מֵהַהִיא – הֲוָה אָמִינָא: סָמוּךְ לְוִסְתָּהּ עוֹנָה אַחֲרִיתִי, קָא מַשְׁמַע לַן אוֹתָהּ עוֹנָה.

**And** by contrast, **if** Rava had taught us only **that** statement, that she must wait a twelve-hour period, **I would say** that she must separate **close to** the fixed time of **her** cycle for **an additional** twelve-hour **period,** as suggested above. Therefore, Rava **teaches us** that the *halakha* is in accordance with the opinion of Rabbi Yehuda, which indicates that she separates for only **that** single twelve-hour **period.**

מתני׳ הָיְתָה לְמוּדָה לִהְיוֹת רוֹאָה יוֹם חֲמִשָּׁה עָשָׂר וְשִׁינְּתָה לִהְיוֹת רוֹאָה לְיוֹם עֶשְׂרִים – זֶה וָזֶה אֲסוּרִין. שִׁינְּתָה פַּעֲמַיִם לְיוֹם עֶשְׂרִים – זֶה וָזֶה אֲסוּרִין.

**MISHNA** If the woman **was accustomed to see** the flow of blood on the **fifteenth day**[H] **and she deviated** from the norm **to see** the flow of blood **on the twentieth day,** then on both **this** day, the fifteenth, **and that** day, the twentieth, it is **prohibited** for her to engage in intercourse. If **she deviated** from the norm **twice,** then on both **this** day, the fifteenth, **and that** day, the twentieth, it is likewise **prohibited** for her to engage in intercourse.

שִׁינְּתָה שָׁלֹשׁ פְּעָמִים לְיוֹם עֶשְׂרִים – הוּתַּר חֲמִשָּׁה עָשָׂר, וְקָבְעָה לָהּ יוֹם עֶשְׂרִים, שֶׁאֵין אִשָּׁה קוֹבַעַת לָהּ וֶסֶת – עַד שֶׁתִּקְבָּעֶנָּה שָׁלֹשׁ פְּעָמִים, וְאֵינָהּ מִטַּהֶרֶת מִן הַוֶּסֶת – עַד שֶׁתֵּעָקֵר מִמֶּנָּה שָׁלֹשׁ פְּעָמִים.

If **she deviated** from the norm **to see** the flow of blood **on the twentieth day three times, it becomes permitted** for her to engage in intercourse on the **fifteenth, and she** has **established the twentieth day for herself** as the day of her fixed menstrual cycle, **as a woman establishes** a fixed menstrual **cycle only after she establishes it three times. And** a woman **is purified from the** existing fixed menstrual **cycle,** in the sense that intercourse is permitted on that day, **only when she has been displaced from** that day **three times.**

### HALAKHA

**That same twelve-hour period – אוֹתָהּ עוֹנָה:** By rabbinic law, at the expected time of a woman's menstrual cycle, she must not engage in intercourse with her husband (*Shakh*) for that day or night. She is not obligated to avoid other forms of contact with him. If her expected cycle is during the day, she must separate from him for the entire day, even if she does not anticipate the arrival of her period until the end of the day. If she does not experience bleeding, it is permitted for her to engage in intercourse immediately after nightfall. Similarly, even if she expects to experience bleeding early in the morning, she is permitted to her husband the entire night before. If she expects to experience bleeding at night, she must separate from her husband for the entire night, but is permitted during the day before and afterward. This applies whether she has established a set cycle by bleeding three consecutive times or whether she has experienced bleeding only once (Rambam *Sefer Kedusha, Hilkhot Issurei Bia* 8:3; *Shulḥan Arukh, Yoreh De'a* 184:2).

**If the woman was accustomed to see the flow of blood on the fifteenth day – הָיְתָה לְמוּדָה לִהְיוֹת רוֹאָה יוֹם חֲמִשָּׁה עָשָׂר:** If a woman was accustomed to experience bleeding on the twentieth day, and she deviated, bleeding on the twenty-third, it is prohibited for her to engage in intercourse with her husband on both the twentieth and the twenty-third days. If she again experiences bleeding on the twenty-third day, both days remain prohibited. If she experiences bleeding on the twenty-third day for a third consecutive time, the twenty-third day becomes her new accustomed time, and the twentieth day is permitted (Rambam *Sefer Kedusha, Hilkhot Issurei Bia* 8:4; *Shulḥan Arukh, Yoreh De'a* 189:14).

גמ׳ אִיתְּמַר, רָאֲתָה יוֹם חֲמִשָּׁה עָשָׂר לְחֹדֶשׁ זֶה, וְיוֹם שִׁשָּׁה עָשָׂר לְחֹדֶשׁ זֶה, וְיוֹם שִׁבְעָה עָשָׂר לְחֹדֶשׁ זֶה. רַב אָמַר: קָבְעָה לָהּ וֶסֶת לְדִילוּג. וּשְׁמוּאֵל אָמַר: עַד שֶׁתְּשַׁלֵּשׁ בְּדִילוּג.

**GEMARA** **It was stated:** If a woman **saw** menstrual blood on the **fifteenth of this month, and** on the **sixteenth of** the **month** after **that,**[H] **and** on the **seventeenth** of the **month** after **that, Rav says: She has** thereby **determined her** menstrual **cycle by skipping,**[N] i.e., as a month and a day. **And Shmuel says:** Her menstrual cycle is not determined **until she skips** a day **three times.** According to Shmuel, as the cycle is established in this case not by the date itself but by the pattern of one additional day every month, the pattern is established only when this occurs three consecutive times, i.e., when she menstruates on the fourth occasion.

נֵימָא רַב וּשְׁמוּאֵל בִּפְלוּגְתָּא דְּרַבִּי וְרַבָּן שִׁמְעוֹן בֶּן גַּמְלִיאֵל קָמִיפַּלְגִי; דְּתַנְיָא, נִיסֵּת לָרִאשׁוֹן – וּמֵת, לַשֵּׁנִי – וּמֵת, לַשְּׁלִישִׁי – לֹא תִּנָּשֵׂא, דִּבְרֵי רַבִּי. רַבָּן שִׁמְעוֹן בֶּן גַּמְלִיאֵל אוֹמֵר: לַשְּׁלִישִׁי – תִּנָּשֵׂא, לָרְבִיעִי – לֹא תִּנָּשֵׂא.

The Gemara suggests: **Shall we say that Rav and Shmuel disagree with regard to** the issue that is the subject of **the dispute between** Rabbi Yehuda HaNasi **and Rabban Shimon ben Gamliel? As it is taught** in a *baraita*: If a woman **was married to** her **first** husband **and he died,**[H] and was then married **to a second** one **and he** too **died, she may not marry a third** husband; this is **the statement of** Rabbi Yehuda HaNasi. **Rabban Shimon ben Gamliel says: She may marry a third** husband, but if he also dies **she may not marry a fourth** husband. The suggestion is that Rav and Rabbi Yehuda HaNasi hold that after two instances she has established a presumption and a pattern, whereas Shmuel and Rabban Shimon ben Gamliel maintain that the presumption is established only after three occurrences.

לָא, דְּכוּלֵּי עָלְמָא – כְּרַבָּן שִׁמְעוֹן בֶּן גַּמְלִיאֵל, וְהָכָא בְּהָא קָמִיפַּלְגִי; רַב סָבַר – חֲמִשָּׁה עָשָׂר מִמִּנְיָינָא, וּשְׁמוּאֵל סָבַר – כֵּיוָן דְּלָאו בְּדִילוּג חֲזִיתֵיהּ, לָאו מִמִּנְיָינָא הוּא.

The Gemara rejects this suggestion: **No, everyone agrees** that the *halakha* is **in accordance with** the opinion of **Rabban Shimon ben Gamliel,** that a presumption is established only after three times, **and here they disagree with regard to this** matter: **Rav holds** that when she experienced bleeding on the **fifteenth** of the month, that occasion is also one **of the number,** i.e., it counts as the first of the pattern, which therefore has three elements. **And Shmuel holds** that **since she did not see** the first time after **skipping,** i.e., after having experienced bleeding on the fourteenth of the previous month, **it is not** part of **the number,** which means that she has experienced bleeding only twice in accordance with that pattern.

אֵיתִיבֵיהּ: הָיְתָה לְמוּדָה לִהְיוֹת רוֹאָה יוֹם חֲמִשָּׁה עָשָׂר, וְשִׁינְּתָה לְיוֹם שִׁשָּׁה עָשָׂר – זֶה וָזֶה אֲסוּרִין. שִׁינְּתָה לְיוֹם שִׁבְעָה עָשָׂר – הוּתַּר שִׁשָּׁה עָשָׂר וְנֶאֱסַר חֲמִשָּׁה עָשָׂר וְשִׁבְעָה עָשָׂר.

Shmuel **raised an objection to** the opinion of Rav from a *baraita*: If a woman **was accustomed to see** a flow of blood on the **fifteenth day** of the month, **and deviated** and instead experienced bleeding **on the sixteenth day** of the month, on both **this** day, the fifteenth, **and that** day, the sixteenth, it is **prohibited** for her to engage in intercourse with her husband. If she then **deviated** and experienced bleeding **on the seventeenth day** of the following month, **the sixteenth** day becomes **permitted, and the fifteenth and seventeenth** days of the following month **are prohibited.**

## NOTES

**Rav says she has thereby determined her menstrual cycle by skipping, etc.** – רַב אָמַר קָבְעָה לָהּ וֶסֶת לְדִילוּג וכו׳: Some early commentaries maintain that the dispute between Rav and Shmuel applies only to a cycle of skipping a day each month. But with regard to a cycle on a fixed day of the month they both agree that it is established by seeing blood three times, whereas everyone concurs that a cycle of equal intervals is established by four occurrences (*Tosafot*; *Tosefot HaRosh*; Ra'avad; Rashba).

## HALAKHA

**A woman saw blood on the fifteenth of this month and the sixteenth of the month after that, etc.** – רָאֲתָה יוֹם חֲמִשָּׁה עָשָׂר לְחֹדֶשׁ זֶה וְיוֹם שִׁשָּׁה עָשָׂר לְחֹדֶשׁ זֶה וכו׳: If a woman experiences bleeding on the fifteenth of Nisan, the sixteenth of Iyyar, and the seventeenth of Sivan, she has not yet established a set cycle. The cycle is established only if she also experiences bleeding on the eighteenth of Tammuz, as the first time she experienced bleeding is not included in the count. If she already had a set cycle beforehand, and then deviated from that cycle three times to experience bleeding a month and a day later, she has established a set cycle, as even the first time she experienced bleeding was a change from her established cycle. This ruling is in accordance with the opinion of Shmuel. Although there is a principle that the *halakha* is in accordance with the opinion of Rav in ritual matters, since the Gemara concludes that the language of the *baraita* is precise and fits Shmuel's opinion, the *halakha* in this case follows his ruling. Some maintain that even if she experienced bleeding only on the fifteenth of Nisan, the sixteenth of Iyyar, and the seventeenth of Sivan, she thereby establishes a set cycle and must be concerned about the eighteenth of Tammuz, the nineteenth of Av, and so forth. This ruling is in accordance with the opinion of Rav, as the *halakha* is in accordance with his opinion in ritual matters. The *Shulḥan Arukh* adds that one should be stringent (Rambam *Sefer Kedusha, Hilkhot Issurei Bia* 8:6; *Shulḥan Arukh, Yoreh De'a* 189:5, 7).

**If a woman was married to her first husband and he died** – נִיסֵּת לָרִאשׁוֹן וּמֵת: If a woman was married, or even betrothed (*Maggid Mishne*), to two husbands, both of whom died, she may not marry a third husband, as she has a presumptive status that her husbands die. Some commentaries maintain that there is no real danger, and it is only a folk belief. Therefore, if she does marry a third husband, she is not required to divorce him. Even if they are merely betrothed, they may get married. Some rule that they must get divorced, based on the principle that a danger to one's life is treated more stringently than a prohibition, and the presumption that there is a real danger. Yet others contend that the court even forces them to divorce (Ritva). The Rema writes that this applies only if the husbands died of natural causes; but if one of them was murdered, or died in a plague or from a fall, or the like, such a death is disregarded for the purposes of this *halakha*. Consequently, many authorities are lenient in this matter, and there is no need to protest (Rambam *Sefer Kedusha, Hilkhot Issurei Bia* 21:31; *Shulḥan Arukh, Even HaEzer* 9:1, and *Beit Shmuel* there).

שִׁינְּתָה לְיוֹם שְׁמוֹנָה עָשָׂר – הוּתְּרוּ כּוּלָּן, וְאֵין אָסוּר אֶלָּא מִשְּׁמוֹנָה עָשָׂר וְאֵילָךְ. קַשְׁיָא לְרַב! אָמַר לָךְ רַב: לְמוּדָה שָׁאנֵי.

If she subsequently **deviated** and experienced bleeding **on the eighteenth day** of the following month, **all** the days **are permitted.** The fifteenth is permitted because she has now experienced bleeding three times on a different day, while the other days are permitted because she experienced bleeding only once on each day. **And** it is **prohibited** for her to engage in intercourse in the following month **only from** the **eighteenth** day **and onward,**[N] i.e., on the nineteenth day, since she has now established a pattern of bleeding after one month and one day. This **is difficult for Rav,** as he maintains that twice is sufficient to establish a pattern, whereas this *baraita* requires three instances. **Rav** could have **said to you** in response: Since she **was accustomed** to experience bleeding on the fifteenth **it is different.** In that particular case the fifteenth does not count as the beginning of a new pattern because it was already her regular established time.

וּדְקָאָרֵי לַהּ, מַאי קָאָרֵי לַהּ? לְמוּדָה אִצְטְרִיכָא לֵיהּ. מַהוּ דְּתֵימָא: כֵּיוָן דִּלְמוּדָה, וַעֲקַרְתֵּיהּ – בִּתְרֵי זִימְנֵי עָקְרָה לֵיהּ – קָא מַשְׁמַע לָן.

The Gemara expresses surprise at Shmuel's question: **And he who asked** [*udeka'arei*] **it, why did he ask it?**[L] The *baraita* clearly stresses the fact that the woman began with an established fixed menstrual cycle that was not part of the pattern. Shmuel could answer: **It was necessary** for the *baraita* to teach the case where she **was accustomed** to experience bleeding on a specific day, **lest you say** that **since she was accustomed** to experience bleeding on a specific day **and displaced** that pattern by bleeding on a different day, it should be sufficient that **with two times she displaces it.** For this reason, the *baraita* **teaches us** that an established pattern is displaced only after three occasions where she experiences bleeding on a different day. If it is not established, one displacement is enough.

מֵיתִיבֵי: רָאֲתָה יוֹם עֶשְׂרִים וְאֶחָד בְּחֹדֶשׁ זֶה, יוֹם עֶשְׂרִים וּשְׁנַיִם בְּחֹדֶשׁ זֶה, יוֹם עֶשְׂרִים וּשְׁלֹשָׁה בְּחֹדֶשׁ זֶה – קָבְעָה לָהּ וֶסֶת. סֵירְגָה לְיוֹם עֶשְׂרִים וְאַרְבָּעָה – לֹא קָבְעָה לָהּ וֶסֶת. תְּיוּבְתָּא דִּשְׁמוּאֵל!

The Gemara **raises an objection** from a *baraita*: If a woman **saw** a flow of blood on the **twenty-first day of this month,** the **twenty-second day of that month,** i.e., of the next month, and the **twenty-third day of that month,** i.e., of the third month, **she established a fixed** pattern of bleeding after one month and one day. If in the third month she instead **varied** and experienced bleeding **on the twenty-fourth day** of the month, **she has not established a fixed** pattern, as this last interval was one month and two days long. This is apparently **a conclusive refutation of** the opinion of **Shmuel,** as according to the *baraita* the pattern is established after only two equidistant intervals, whereas Shmuel requires three.

אָמַר לָךְ שְׁמוּאֵל: הָכָא בְּמַאי עָסְקִינַן – כְּגוֹן דִּרְגִילָה לְמֶחֱזֵי בְּיוֹם עֶשְׂרִים, וְשִׁינְּתָה לְיוֹם עֶשְׂרִים וְאֶחָד. דַּיְקָא נַמִי, דְּשָׁבְקִינַן לְיוֹם עֶשְׂרִים, וְנַקֵט לְיוֹם עֶשְׂרִים וְאֶחָד – שְׁמַע מִינָּהּ.

The Gemara answers that **Shmuel** could have **said to you: Here, we are dealing with** a case **where** the woman **was accustomed to see** a flow of blood **on the twentieth day** of the month, **and she deviated** and experienced bleeding **on the twenty-first day** of the month. Consequently, there were in fact a total of three equidistant intervals of one month and one day. The Gemara adds that the language of the *baraita* **is also precise,**[N] **as** for what other reason would the *baraita* **leave** aside the **twentieth day** of the month and not use that date as the example, **and** instead **take** for its example the **twenty-first day** of the month? **Learn from this** that she had an established pattern of bleeding on the twentieth of every month before the events described in the *baraita*.

**LANGUAGE**

He who asked [*deka'arei*] it why did he ask it – דְּקָאָרֵי לַהּ מַאי קָאָרֵי לַהּ: This phrase, which appears in many places in the Talmud, is read by some with a silent *alef*, i.e., *udekari*, meaning: And he who read. Others understand it as *udeka ari*, with *ari* derived from the root *yod, reish, heh*, meaning teach. The *Arukh* explains that according to the *ge'onim*, the root is *ayin, reish, alef*, which means mixed; in other words: Why did he mix distinct issues and associate them together?

**NOTES**

And it is prohibited in the following month only from the eighteenth day and onward – וְאֵין אָסוּר אֶלָּא מִשְּׁמוֹנָה עָשָׂר וְאֵילָךְ: The conclusion, according to the opinion that the average menstrual cycle is thirty days (see 9b), is that she also does not need to be concerned about experiencing bleeding on the thirtieth day, as there are either thirty-one or thirty-two days between the eighteenth day of one month and the nineteenth day of the next.

The language is also precise – דַּיְקָא נַמִי: The *tanna* should have begun his series with the twentieth of the month rather than the twenty-first, as this word is shorter, and it is the style of *tanna'im* to be brief wherever possible (Rashi).

״שֶׁאֵין הָאִשָּׁה קוֹבַעַת לָהּ וֶסֶת עַד שֶׁתִּקְבָּעֶנָּה״ וכו׳. אֲמַר רַב פַּפָּא: לָא אֲמָרָן – אֶלָּא לְמִקְבְּעָה, אֲבָל לְמֵיחַשׁ לָהּ – בַּחֲדָא זִימְנָא חָיְישָׁא.

§ The mishna teaches: **As a woman establishes a fixed** menstrual **cycle only after she establishes it** three times. **Rav Pappa says,** in explanation: **We said** that she must experience bleeding three times **only with regard to establishing** a fixed menstrual cycle, **but with regard to** being **concerned** for a pattern, even **after one time she must be concerned** that this might be the beginning of a fixed pattern.

מַאי קָא מַשְׁמַע לַן? תָּנֵינָא: הָיְתָה לְמוּדָה לִהְיוֹת רוֹאָה יוֹם חֲמִשָּׁה עָשָׂר, וְשִׁינְּתָה לְיוֹם עֶשְׂרִים – זֶה וָזֶה אֲסוּרִין!

The Gemara asks: **What is** Rav Pappa **teaching us? We learn** this in the mishna: If the woman **was accustomed to see** the flow of blood on the **fifteenth day and she deviated**[H] from the norm **to see** the flow of blood **on the twentieth day,** on both **this** day, the fifteenth, **and that** day, the twentieth, it is **prohibited** for her to engage in intercourse. This clearly demonstrates that even after bleeding only once on a certain day she must be concerned that this could be the start of a new fixed menstrual cycle.

אִי מֵהָתָם – הֲוָה אָמִינָא: הָנֵי מִילֵּי – הֵיכָא דְּקַיְימָא בְּתוֹךְ יְמֵי נִדָּתָהּ, אֲבָל הֵיכָא דְּלָא קָיְימָא בְּתוֹךְ יְמֵי נִדָּתָהּ – אֵימָא לָא, קָא מַשְׁמַע לַן.

The Gemara answers: **If** this *halakha* was derived only **from there, I would say** that **this statement** applies in a case **where** she experiences bleeding on the twentieth day while **she is standing in her days** suitable for **menstruation,**[N] i.e., the days following the eleven days after her last period, when she is most likely to menstruate. **But** in a case **where she is not standing in her days** suitable for **menstruation,** but rather during the eleven days when uterine bleeding would render her a *zava,* **I would say** that she does **not** need to be concerned that she might experience bleeding again at that time. Therefore, Rav Pappa **teaches us** that even during these eleven days she must be concerned.

״וְאֵינָהּ מִטַּהֶרֶת מִן הַוֶּסֶת״ וכו׳. אֲמַר רַב פַּפָּא: לָא אֲמָרָן, אֶלָּא דְּקַבְעֵתִּיהּ תְּלָתָא זִימְנֵי – דִּצְרִיכִי תְּלָתָא זִימְנֵי לְמֶעֱקְרֵיהּ, אֲבָל תְּרֵי זִימְנֵי – בַּחֲדָא זִימְנָא מִיעֲקַר.

§ The mishna teaches: **And** a woman **is purified from the** existing fixed menstrual **cycle,** in the sense that intercourse is permitted on that day, **only** when she has been displaced from that day three times. **Rav Pappa says,** in explanation: **We said** this **only** in the case of a set cycle **that she established** by **three times.** With regard to such a cycle, we said **that** a different **three times are necessary to displace** that cycle. **But** with regard to a cycle that is established with only **two times, it is displaced by one time** of bleeding on a different day.

מַאי קָא מַשְׁמַע לַן? תָּנֵינָא: אֵין הָאִשָּׁה קוֹבַעַת לָהּ וֶסֶת עַד שֶׁתִּקְבָּעֶנָּה שָׁלֹשׁ פְּעָמִים! מַהוּ דְּתֵימָא: חֲדָא – לְחַד, תְּרֵי – לְתַרְתֵּי, וּתְלָתָא – לִתְלָתָא, קָא מַשְׁמַע לַן.

The Gemara asks: **What is** Rav Pappa **teaching us? We learn** this in the mishna: **A woman establishes** a fixed menstrual **cycle only after she establishes it three times.** The Gemara answers that it was necessary for Rav Pappa to teach his *halakha,* **lest you say** that a cycle is displaced by bleeding **one** time on a different day **for** a cycle that was set **one** time, but by bleeding on **two** different days **for** a cycle that was established with **two** times, **and** likewise by bleeding on **three** different days **for** a cycle that was established with **three** times. Therefore, Rav Pappa **teaches us** that whether she experiences bleeding once or twice, she displaces it by bleeding once on a different day.

HALAKHA

**If the woman was accustomed to see blood on the fifteenth day and she deviated, etc.** – **הָיְתָה לְמוּדָה לִהְיוֹת רוֹאָה יוֹם חֲמִשָּׁה עָשָׂר וְשִׁינְּתָה וכו׳**: If a woman was accustomed to experience bleeding on the fifteenth of the month, and she deviated and experienced bleeding on the sixteenth, both days are prohibited. If she deviates the following month and experiences bleeding on the seventeenth, the sixteenth becomes permitted but the fifteenth remains prohibited, and the seventeenth is also prohibited. If she deviates the following month and experiences bleeding on the eighteenth, only the eighteenth is prohibited, while the other days become permitted (Rambam *Sefer Kedusha, Hilkhot Issurei Bia* 8:7, and see *Maggid Mishne* and *Kesef Mishne* there).

NOTES

**Her days suitable for menstruation** – **יְמֵי נִדָּתָהּ**: According to Torah law, there are two categories of women who experience uterine bleeding: A menstruating woman and a *zava.* A menstruating woman becomes ritually impure for seven days. On the night following the seventh, she may immerse in a ritual bath. This is the *halakha* whether her menstrual flow continues throughout those seven days or if she emitted only a single drop of blood.

A woman who experiences bleeding at a time other than her normal cycle is called a *zava.* She must wait until she experiences clean days without bleeding; only then can she purify herself by means of immersion. There are two types of *zava*: A lesser *zava,* who experiences bleeding for either one or two days, and a greater *zava,* who experiences bleeding for three days or more. A lesser *zava* is required only to observe a day for a day, whereas a greater *zava* must observe seven clean days before immersing in a ritual bath.

The early commentaries differ with regard to the timing of a woman's normal menstrual cycle. According to the Rambam, every woman has a set eighteen-day cycle: Seven days of menstruation and eleven days of *zava.* A woman begins counting from the first time she menstruates, and this cycle continues until she gives birth. After birth, the cycle starts once again. Rashi and most other commentaries rule that menstruation is considered a normal cycle whenever it occurs, and that a woman is a *zava* only if she experiences bleeding within the eleven days after the eighth day following the onset of menstruation. If she experiences bleeding at any time after those eleven days, she is considered to have begun the next cycle of menstruation.

The common practice today is to treat all incidences of uterine bleeding as the bleeding of a greater *zava,* which requires a woman to count seven clean days before immersion.

It **is taught** in a *baraita* **in accordance with** the opinion of **Rav Pappa:** If a woman **was accustomed to see** the flow of blood on the **twentieth day** after her previous flow, **and she deviated** from the norm to experience bleeding **on the thirtieth day,**[H] on both **this** day, the twentieth, **and that** day, the thirtieth, it is **prohibited** for her to engage in intercourse. If the **twentieth day arrived,** counting from the previous flow, which had occurred on day thirty, **and she did not see** a flow of blood, **it is permitted for her to engage** in intercourse **until** the **thirtieth day** after the previous flow, **and she** must be **concerned** on the **thirtieth day.**

תניא כותיה דרב פפא: היתה למודה להיות רואה יום עשרים, ושינתה ליום שלשים – זה וזה אסורין, הגיע יום עשרים ולא ראתה – מותרת לשמש עד יום שלשים, וחוששת ליום שלשים.

If the **thirtieth day arrived and she saw** a flow of blood, and then the **twentieth day** after that **arrived and she did not see** a flow of blood, **and the thirtieth day** from her previous flow **arrived and she did not see** blood on that day but saw on a later day, **and** then the **twentieth day** after her previous flow **arrived and she saw** a flow of blood, the **thirtieth day becomes permitted,** as she experienced bleeding after an interval of thirty days only twice. This is in accordance with the opinion of Rav Pappa that a cycle of bleeding that has occurred twice is displaced by a single time of not bleeding on that day.

הגיע יום שלשים וראתה, הגיע יום עשרים ולא ראתה, והגיע יום שלשים ולא ראתה, והגיע יום עשרים וראתה – הותר יום שלשים,

**HALAKHA**

**If she was accustomed to see on the twentieth day and she deviated on the thirtieth day, etc.** – היתה למודה להיות רואה יום עשרים ושינתה ליום שלשים וכו׳: With regard to a woman who has a fixed time to menstruate, on the twentieth day after her last period, and she deviates and experiences bleeding on the thirtieth day, she is prohibited to her husband on both the twentieth and the thirtieth. On the twentieth day after the thirtieth she is prohibited due to her first cycle, and if she does not experience bleeding on that day she must be concerned that she will experience bleeding on the thirtieth. If she experiences bleeding a second time on the thirtieth day, both days remain prohibited. If she experiences bleeding three times consecutively on the thirtieth day, she is no longer prohibited on the twentieth day, but only on the thirtieth. If she experiences bleeding only once or twice on the thirtieth, and then returns to experience bleeding on the twentieth, the twentieth day alone is prohibited and the thirtieth is permitted. This *halakha* is in accordance with the *baraita* (*Shulḥan Arukh, Yoreh De'a* 189:14).

Perek **IX**
Daf **64** Amud **b**

**And** she is **prohibited** on the **twentieth day, because** it is the **manner** of women that their blood flow **comes at its** usual **time.**

ונאסר יום עשרים, מפני שאורח בזמנו בָּא.

**MISHNA** **Women, with regard to** the blood that flows when **their hymens** are ruptured, **are like grapevines: There is a vine that** produces **wine** that **is red, and there is a vine that** produces **wine** that **is black; and there is a vine that** produces **wine in abundance, and there is a vine that** produces only **a meager** amount of **wine. Rabbi Yehuda says: In every vine, there are** grapes fit to produce **wine, but** any vine in **which there are no** grapes fit to produce **wine, this is a dry vine** [*durkati*].[L] Likewise, any woman who experiences bleeding is capable of giving birth, whereas one who does not experience bleeding is like a dry vine, unable to give birth.

מתני׳ נשים בבתוליהם כגפנים: יש גפן שיינה אדום, ויש גפן שיינה שחור, ויש גפן שיינה מרובה, ויש גפן שיינה מועט. רבי יהודה אומר: כל גפן יש בה יין, ושאין בה יין – הרי זה דורקטי.

**GEMARA** With regard to the term *durkati*, the Gemara explains that this means **truncated generation** [*dor katua*].[N] As **Rabbi Ḥiyya teaches: Just as leaven is good for dough, so too, blood is good for a woman.** It was likewise **taught in the name of Rabbi Meir: Any woman whose blood is plentiful, her children are plentiful.**

גמ׳ תנא: דור קטוע. תני רבי חייא: כשם שהשאור יפה לעיסה – כך דמים יפין לאשה. תנא משום רבי מאיר: כל אשה שדמיה מרובין – בניה מרובין.

הדרן עלך האשה

**LANGUAGE**

**Dry vine** [*durkati*] – דורקטי: This term is of unclear origin. Some suggest that it is from the Greek word τρύγητος, *trugētos*, meaning a vintage or harvest.

**NOTES**

**Truncated generation** [*dor katua*] – דור קטוע: Rashi explains that such women can bear children, but they do not typically have very many children. Therefore, the following generation will be less numerous than it might otherwise have been (Rashi). Others maintain that such women are incapable of having children. In Rambam's Commentary on the Mishna it states: There are some women who do not have menstrual blood or hymenal blood. Such women are unable to have children, and this is the meaning of the term *durkati*.

# Summary of **Perek IX**

There are various opinions among the Sages with regard to a woman who finds blood in a basin after urinating. Some maintain that she is ritually pure and may handle pure items *ab initio*. Others hold that she is impure, both with regard to her husband and with regard to handling pure items. Yet others distinguish between a woman who urinates while standing and one who urinates while sitting, and between urine that came out in a steady stream and urine that came out in a trickle.

The Sages also disagree with regard to a woman who urinated into a basin where a man had also urinated. Some contend that the woman is pure, as this case involves a compound uncertainty, i.e., whether the blood is from the woman or the man, and even if it is from the woman, whether it is from a wound or her uterus. Others rule that she is impure, as women are more likely to experience a flow of blood than men.

This chapter further discussed the case of a woman who lent her garment to another woman, and subsequently a blood stain was found on the garment. If the borrower was a gentile or a menstruating woman, who would not have her status affected by the blood stain, it may be attributed to her.

If several women sit or lie in the same place and a blood stain is found there, all the women are rendered impure, as the stain is equally likely to have come from any one of them. But there are other relevant factors, such as precisely where the stain was found, and whether the women examined themselves immediately after its discovery.

This chapter explained the procedure for investigating whether a stain is actually blood or merely a red substance. This examination is conducted by applying to the stain a series of cleansing agents that remove blood but do not remove other types of stains.

Another topic of discussion in this chapter was the establishment of a set pattern of menstruation based on a physical sensation, e.g., repeated sneezing, yawning, or shivering. If a woman invariably experiences the symptom immediately before emitting blood, then the symptom is established as the predictor of the onset of her menstrual cycle, and she does not retroactively render impure any items she had handled earlier. Just as a pattern of this nature is established with three repetitions, so too, it is displaced by means of three occurrences. Similarly, a pattern set by time intervals or dates of the month is displaced by three occurrences.

# Introduction to
# Perek X

*And if a woman has an issue, and her issue in her flesh is blood, she shall be in her menstruation seven days, and whoever touches her shall be impure until the evening.*

(Leviticus 15:19)

*And if a woman has an issue of her blood for many days, not in the time of her menstruation, or if she has an issue beyond the time of her menstruation; all the days of the issue [zov] of her impurity she shall be as in the days of her menstruation: She is impure.*

(Leviticus 15:25)

*But if she be purified of her ziva, then she shall count to herself seven days, and after that she shall be pure.*

(Leviticus 15:28)

*If a woman gives birth to a male, then she shall be impure for seven days; as in the days of her menstrual flow she shall be impure. And on the eighth day the flesh of his foreskin shall be circumcised. And she shall continue in the blood of purification for thirty-three days; she shall touch no consecrated item nor enter the Sanctuary until the days of her purification are fulfilled. But if she gives birth to a female, then she shall be impure for two weeks, as in her menstruation; and she shall continue in the blood of purification for sixty-six days.*

(Leviticus 12:2–5)

The Gemara derives from the verse "And if a woman has an issue, and her issue in her flesh is blood" that a woman becomes ritually impure with the impurity of menstruation only through blood that emerges from her uterus, which is the usual way for a woman to experience menstrual bleeding. There are, however, cases where a woman experiences bleeding that is not menstrual blood, e.g., blood that comes from the hymen as it is torn. The first topic of this chapter is the status of a virgin after intercourse. She will certainly experience bleeding, and might continue to do so for a few days afterward. How can she know whether the blood comes from the hymen or is menstrual blood?

There is another type of impurity for a woman who experiences bleeding: That which renders her a *zava*. A *zava* must count seven clean days and examine herself on each of those days to ensure that there is no blood, and only afterward may she immerse and purify herself. The Gemara analyzes cases where a woman does not conduct herself accordingly. For example, if she examined herself only on the first and seventh days and found that she was pure, what is her status? Can she assume that she did not discharge any blood during the days in between? Or perhaps she is considered to have counted only two clean days. It is also possible that only the last day is included, and she must count a further six days.

The Gemara also derives from the verse "And if a woman has an issue, and her issue in her flesh is blood" that menstrual blood not only renders the woman ritually impure but is itself impure and transmits impurity if it is touched or carried. The Gemara discusses the status of blood that emerges from a woman after her death, with regard to whether or not that blood has the same status as menstrual blood.

A woman after childbirth is impure, in accordance with the verse "She shall touch no consecrated item nor enter the Sanctuary until the days of her purification are fulfilled." There is a stage where she is considered ritually pure and may engage in intercourse with her husband, and yet she still has the status of one who has immersed but must wait until nightfall to complete the purification process. This woman has the status of second-degree impurity. The Gemara explores the ramifications of this *halakha*.

מתני׳ תִּינוֹקֶת שֶׁלֹּא הִגִּיעַ זְמַנָּהּ לִרְאוֹת, וְנִיסֵּת, בֵּית שַׁמַּאי אוֹמְרִים: נוֹתְנִין לָהּ אַרְבַּע לֵילוֹת, וּבֵית הִלֵּל אוֹמְרִים: עַד שֶׁתֶּחְיֶה הַמַּכָּה.

**MISHNA** In the case of **a young girl whose time to see** a menstrual flow, i.e., the age of puberty, **has not** yet **arrived,**[N] **and she married**[H] and engaged in intercourse and her hymen was torn, **Beit Shammai say:** The Sages **give her four nights** after intercourse during which the blood is attributed to the torn hymen and she remains ritually pure. Thereafter, any blood is assumed to be menstrual blood and renders her impure. **And Beit Hillel say:** The blood is attributed to the torn hymen **until the wound heals.**[NB]

הִגִּיעַ זְמַנָּהּ לִרְאוֹת וְנִיסֵּת, בֵּית שַׁמַּאי אוֹמְרִים: נוֹתְנִין לָהּ לַיְלָה הָרִאשׁוֹן, וּבֵית הִלֵּל אוֹמְרִים: עַד מוֹצָאֵי שַׁבָּת, אַרְבַּע לֵילוֹת.

In the case of a young woman **whose time to see** a menstrual flow **has arrived** but she has not yet begun to menstruate, **and she married**[H] and engaged in intercourse and her hymen was torn, **Beit Shammai say:** The Sages **give her the first night** during which the blood is attributed to the torn hymen. Thereafter, any blood is assumed to be menstrual blood. **And Beit Hillel say:** The blood is attributed to the torn hymen **until the conclusion of Shabbat,** and she may engage in intercourse with her husband for **four nights,** as it was customary for a virgin to marry on Wednesday.

רָאֲתָה וְעוֹדָהּ בְּבֵית אָבִיהָ, בֵּית שַׁמַּאי אוֹמְרִים: נוֹתְנִין לָהּ בְּעִילַת מִצְוָה, וּבֵית הִלֵּל אוֹמְרִים: כׇּל הַלַּיְלָה כּוּלָּהּ.

In the case of a young woman who **saw** menstrual blood before marriage while **she was still in her father's house,**[H] **Beit Shammai say:** The Sages **give her**[N] permission to engage only in **relations** that consummate a marriage, which are **a mitzva,**[N] after which she is ritually impure due to the blood. **And Beit Hillel say:** The husband and wife may engage even in several acts of intercourse, as any blood seen **throughout the entire night** is attributed to the torn hymen.

גמ׳ אָמַר רַב נַחְמָן בַּר יִצְחָק: וַאֲפִילּוּ רָאֲתָה. מִמַּאי – מִדְּקָא מְפַלֵּיג בְּסֵיפָא בֵּין רָאֲתָה בֵּין בְּשֶׁלֹּא רָאֲתָה, מִכְּלָל דְּרֵישָׁא – לָא שְׁנָא הָכִי וְלָא שְׁנָא הָכִי.

**GEMARA** The mishna first addresses the case of a young girl who has not yet reached puberty. **Rav Naḥman bar Yitzḥak says: And** this *halakha* applies to her **even** if **she has seen** menstrual blood. He explains his reasoning: **From where** do I derive this? I derive it **from** the fact **that** the *tanna* **distinguishes in the latter clause** of the mishna **between** a young girl who has **seen** menstrual blood **and** a young girl who has **not seen** menstrual blood. **By inference,** in **the first clause** of the mishna the *halakha* **is no different** in **this** case, where the young girl has experienced menstrual bleeding, **and** it **is no different** in **that** case, where she has not yet experienced menstrual bleeding.

**NOTES**

**A young girl whose time to see has not yet arrived – תִּינוֹקֶת שֶׁלֹּא הִגִּיעַ זְמַנָּהּ לִרְאוֹת:** The Gemara stated (5a) that the halakhically defined time for the onset of menstruation is puberty. Puberty is defined by two factors: When a girl has physical signs of puberty, i.e., two pubic hairs, and when she is old enough, i.e., twelve years old. Some commentaries say that it is sufficient for one of these factors to be present for it to be considered the time for the onset of her menstrual flow (Rashi).

**Until the wound heals – עַד שֶׁתֶּחְיֶה הַמַּכָּה:** As long as she continues to bleed due to intercourse, the wound has not yet healed (Rashi on *Ketubot* 6a).

**They give her – נוֹתְנִין לָהּ:** The early commentaries disagree as to the *halakha* in a case where she did not bleed as a result of the first act of intercourse. Some hold that even though she did not bleed, it is assumed that she is impure after completing the act of intercourse, because there is concern that there was a tiny drop of blood that was not noticed or covered by semen (Ran, citing the *ge'onim*; Rosh; Rashba; Meiri). Others hold that if she did not notice any blood she is not considered impure (Ra'avad). While the halakhic authorities rule stringently (see *Shulḥan Arukh*, *Yoreh De'a* 193), the Rema cites the lenient opinion and writes that one can rely on it in a case where they performed only the initial stage of intercourse.

**Relations that are a mitzva – בְּעִילַת מִצְוָה:** This is referring to the first act of intercourse between a husband and his virgin wife. The reason that it is called a mitzva is that the Sages said that a woman's love is directed to the one who breaks her hymen, and through this love, the husband and wife will engage in the mitzva of procreation (*Sanhedrin* 22b; *Tosafot* on *Ketubot* 4a).

**BACKGROUND**

**Until the wound heals – עַד שֶׁתֶּחְיֶה הַמַּכָּה:** The amount of time it takes for a wound to cease bleeding from the time it first forms a scab depends on several variables and also varies from person to person. Clearly, additional trauma to the wound, or even stretching the affected area, i.e., from additional acts of intercourse, could cause the wound to take longer to heal. For these reasons a specific amount of time is not given for the duration of this process, and the time the wound takes to heal depends on the circumstances of each case.

**HALAKHA**

**A young girl whose time to see has not yet arrived and she married, etc. – תִּינוֹקֶת שֶׁלֹּא הִגִּיעַ זְמַנָּהּ לִרְאוֹת וְנִיסֵּת וכו׳:** Hymenal blood is ritually pure and is not considered to be menstrual blood or *ziva* blood. It does not originate in the uterus but results from the tearing of the hymen. Technically a young girl who marries is permitted to engage in intercourse with her husband until the wound has healed and only after that time, if she subsequently bleeds, is any blood considered to be menstrual blood. This is in accordance with the opinion of Beit Hillel. Nowadays the authorities rule stringently (see *Kesef Mishne*) that one who marries a virgin may engage in intercourse only once, and after completing that act she is considered ritually impure. This applies even if the wife is young and has never menstruated, and it applies even if she examines herself afterward and does not find blood, as perhaps there was a drop of blood that she did not see because it was covered with semen. The Rema writes that some are lenient in a case where the girl had never menstruated before. He adds that the custom is to be lenient if the couple did not complete the act of intercourse and she did not bleed, but if they completed the act of intercourse she is considered impure even if she did not bleed.

Since this blood is considered impure, the wife must perform the examination marking the first step in her transition from ritual impurity to ritual purity, and she must examine herself for each of the following seven days. She may not begin to count the seven pure days until the fifth day after intercourse. All of the stringencies of a menstruating woman apply to her and her husband with the exception that a husband may lay on his wife's bed if she is not on it, which is not permitted if she has the status of a menstruating woman (Rambam *Sefer Kedusha*, *Hilkhot Issurei Bia* 5:18, 11:8; *Shulḥan Arukh*, *Yoreh De'a* 193:1 and *Even HaEzer* 63:1).

**Whose time to see has arrived and she married, etc. – הִגִּיעַ זְמַנָּהּ לִרְאוֹת וְנִיסֵּת וכו׳:** If a young woman who has never menstruated marries, she is permitted to her husband for four days and nights even though she bleeds continuously, provided that the wound has not yet healed, in accordance with the opinion of Beit Hillel (Rambam *Sefer Kedusha*, *Hilkhot Issurei Bia* 5:19).

**She saw while still in her father's house – רָאֲתָה וְעוֹדָהּ בְּבֵית אָבִיהָ:** A woman who begins menstruating before she gets married may engage in intercourse only once with her husband and then is considered ritually impure. The hymenal blood is treated as if it is ritually impure, in accordance with the opinion of Beit Shammai (Rambam *Sefer Kedusha*, *Hilkhot Issurei Bia* 5:19, and see Ra'avad there).

תַּנְיָא נַמִי הָכִי, בֵּית הִלֵּל אוֹמְרִים: עַד שֶׁתִּחְיֶה הַמַּכָּה, בֵּין רָאֲתָה בֵּין לֹא רָאֲתָה.

This explanation of Rav Naḥman bar Yitzḥak **is also taught** in a *baraita*: **Beit Hillel say:** With regard to a young girl who has not yet reached puberty, the blood she emits is attributed to the torn hymen **until the wound heals,** regardless of **whether she has seen** menstrual blood beforehand or **whether she has not** yet **seen** menstrual blood.

״עַד שֶׁתִּחְיֶה הַמַּכָּה״. עַד כַּמָּה? אָמַר רַב יְהוּדָה אָמַר רַב: כׇּל זְמַן שֶׁנּוֹחֶרֶת. כִּי אָמְרִיתָהּ קַמֵּיהּ דִּשְׁמוּאֵל, אֲמַר לִי: נְחִירָה זוֹ – אֵינִי יוֹדֵעַ מַה הִיא, אֶלָּא – כׇּל זְמַן שֶׁהָרוֹק מָצוּי בְּתוֹךְ הַפֶּה מֵחֲמַת תַּשְׁמִישׁ.

§ The mishna teaches that Beit Hillel say: The blood is attributed to the torn hymen **until the wound heals.** The Gemara clarifies: **Until when**[H] can the blood be attributed to the torn hymen? **Rav Yehuda says** that **Rav says: All the time that she is *noḥeret*.**[NL] Rav Yehuda continues: **When** I subsequently **said this** *halakha* **before Shmuel,**[B] **he said to me: This *noḥeret*, I do not know what it is,** nor do I know what Rav means by it. **Rather, all the time that the saliva is in** her **mouth due to sexual intercourse,** she may attribute the blood to the torn hymen. Shmuel is using a euphemism, i.e., as long as there is blood in her vagina resulting from sexual intercourse.

נְחִירָה דְּקָאָמַר רַב הֵיכִי דָּמֵי? אֲמַר רַב שְׁמוּאֵל בַּר רַב יִצְחָק לְדִידִי מְפָרְשָׁא לִי מִינֵּיהּ דְּרַב: עוֹמֶדֶת וְרוֹאָה, יוֹשֶׁבֶת וְאֵינָהּ רוֹאָה – בְּיָדוּעַ שֶׁלֹּא חָיְתָה הַמַּכָּה. עַל גַּבֵּי קַרְקַע וְרוֹאָה, עַל גַּבֵּי כָּרִים וּכְסָתוֹת וְאֵינָהּ רוֹאָה – בְּיָדוּעַ שֶׁלֹּא חָיְתָה הַמַּכָּה. עַל גַּבֵּי כּוּלָּם וְרוֹאָה, עַל גַּבֵּי כּוּלָּם וְאֵינָהּ רוֹאָה – בְּיָדוּעַ שֶׁחָיְתָה הַמַּכָּה.

The Gemara clarifies: This ***noḥeret* that Rav says; what is it like?** What did he mean? **Rav Shmuel bar Rav Yitzḥak said: It was explained to me by Rav** as follows: If the young girl **stands** up **and sees** blood, but she **sits and does not see** blood, **it is known that the wound has not** yet **healed,** and the blood is still attributed to the torn hymen. Similarly, if she sits **on the ground and sees** blood, but she sits **on cushions and blankets and does not see** blood, **it is known that the wound has not** yet **healed** and she may attribute the blood to the torn hymen, as the blood flows due to the strain of sitting on the ground. But if she sometimes sits **on all of them,** i.e., the ground, cushions, and blankets, **and sees** blood, and on other occasions she sits **on all of them and does not see** blood, **it is known that the wound has healed,** and this blood must now be menstrual blood.

״הִגִּיעַ זְמַנָּהּ״ וְכוּ׳. אִיתְּמַר: שִׁימְּשָׁה בַּיָּמִים, רַב אָמַר: לֹא הִפְסִידָה לֵילוֹת, וְלֵוִי אָמַר: הִפְסִידָה לֵילוֹת.

§ The mishna teaches: In the case of a young woman **whose time** to see a menstrual flow **has arrived,** Beit Hillel say: The blood is attributed to the torn hymen until the conclusion of Shabbat and she may engage in intercourse with her husband for four nights. **It was stated** that there is a dispute between *amora'im* with regard to the following case: If **she engaged in intercourse** with her husband **during the daytime,**[H] in addition to engaging in intercourse at night, **Rav says: She has not lost** her **nights,** and the blood is still attributed to the torn hymen for four nights. **Levi says: She has lost** her **nights,** since she has engaged in intercourse twice during the daytime and twice at night, and therefore she has already used up the equivalent of four nights.

רַב אָמַר: לֹא הִפְסִידָה לֵילוֹת, ״עַד מוֹצָאֵי שַׁבָּת״ תְּנַן. וְלֵוִי אָמַר: הִפְסִידָה לֵילוֹת, מַאי ״אַרְבַּע לֵילוֹת״ דְּקָתָנֵי? אַרְבָּעָה עוֹנוֹת.

The Gemara explains: **Rav says** that **she has not lost** her **nights,** as **we learned** in the mishna that the blood is attributed to the torn hymen **until the conclusion of Shabbat,** and it does not limit the number of times she may engage in intercourse during that time. **And Levi says: She has lost** her **nights,** as **what** is the meaning of the term: **Four nights, that is taught** in the mishna? It means **four** twelve-hour **periods,** either days or nights.

וּלְרַב, לָמָּה לִי לְמִיתְנָא ״אַרְבַּע לֵילוֹת״? אוֹרַח אַרְעָא קָא מַשְׁמַע לָן: דְּדַרְכָּהּ דְּבִיאָה בַּלֵּילוֹת. וּלְלֵוִי, לִיתְנֵי ״אַרְבַּע לֵילוֹת״, ״עַד מוֹצָאֵי שַׁבָּת״ לָמָּה לִי? הָא קָא מַשְׁמַע לָן: דְּשָׁרֵי לְמִבְעַל לְכַתְּחִלָּה בְּשַׁבָּת.

The Gemara asks: **And according to** the opinion of **Rav, why do I** need the mishna **to teach: Four nights?** The mishna should have stated four days, which would include both days and nights. Rav would respond that the mishna **teaches us proper conduct, as it is proper that intercourse** should be performed only **at night.**[N] The Gemara suggests: **And according to** the opinion of **Levi, let** the mishna **teach** only: **Four nights. Why do I** need the mishna to specify: **Until the conclusion of Shabbat?** Levi would answer that **this teaches us that it is permitted to engage in intercourse for the first** time **on Shabbat.**[H] Since the custom was for a virgin to marry on Wednesday, which means that one of the four first nights is Shabbat, it is permitted to engage in intercourse on that night, despite the fact that it may cause her to bleed.

**HALAKHA**

Until the wound heals, until when, etc. – עַד שֶׁתִּחְיֶה הַמַּכָּה עַד כַּמָּה וכו׳: How does a woman know when her hymenal bleeding has concluded? If she bleeds when she stands but not when she sits down, or if she bleeds when she sits on the ground but not when she sits on cushions or blankets, the wound has not yet healed. If the blood ceases whether she stands or sits, on the ground or on cushions and blankets, the wound has healed. If the blood does not stop at all, and she bleeds even when sitting on cushions and blankets, then it is no longer hymenal blood, but menstrual blood. This is in accordance with the opinion of Rav, as explained by Rav Shmuel bar Rav Yitzḥak (Rambam *Sefer Kedusha*, *Hilkhot Issurei Bia* 5:23).

If she engaged in intercourse during the daytime – שִׁימְּשָׁה בַּיָּמִים: A young woman who marries and has never experienced menstrual bleeding is permitted to engage in intercourse with her husband for four days, both day and night, even though she bleeds during intercourse, provided the wound has not yet healed, in accordance with the opinion of Rav (Rambam *Sefer Kedusha*, *Hilkhot Issurei Bia* 5:19).

That it is permitted to engage in intercourse for the first time on Shabbat – דְּשָׁרֵי לְמִבְעַל לְכַתְּחִלָּה בְּשַׁבָּת: It is permitted for a husband to engage in intercourse with his virgin wife on Shabbat. Some say that it is permitted only if the husband intends to perform the act without breaking the hymen. Some rule that since nowadays nobody is an expert in engaging in intercourse without breaking the hymen, it is forbidden to engage in intercourse with a virgin on Shabbat (*Haggahot Asheri*). Most authorities rule that it is permitted even nowadays (*Baḥ*; *Derisha*; *Taz*). The *Mishna Berura* first cites opinions that in a place where the custom is to be stringent, one may not be lenient, then cites the Taz, who writes that he heard explicitly that pious and knowledgeable people were lenient in this matter, and there is no basis to be stringent at all (*Shulḥan Arukh*, *Oraḥ Ḥayyim* 280:2 and *Even HaEzer* 63:1).

**NOTES**

All the time that she is *noḥeret* – כׇּל זְמַן שֶׁנּוֹחֶרֶת: Some explain that this term, which literally means snorts, is referring to friction in the vaginal walls, which cause the emission of blood when they rub together (Meiri). Alternatively, it is referring to the woman crying out in pain due to intercourse.

It is proper that intercourse be at night – דְּדַרְכָּהּ דְּבִיאָה בַּלֵּילוֹת: The Gemara (17a) states that one of the signs that the Jewish people are holy is that they engage in intercourse only at night.

**LANGUAGE**

Snorts [*noḥeret*] – נוֹחֶרֶת: There are several opinions with regard to the meaning of this word. Some explain that it means leaking or flowing, possibly related to the word for river, *nahar*. Others explain that it means a sound that one makes due to pain.

**BACKGROUND**

When I said this *halakha* before Shmuel – כִּי אָמְרִיתָהּ קַמֵּיהּ דִּשְׁמוּאֵל: The Rashbam explains that when Rav founded his academy in Sura, Rav Yehuda was one of his first and foremost disciples. After Rav's death, Rav Yehuda became a preeminent disciple of Shmuel in Neharde'a, and there he would teach statements that he had learned from Rav.

כִּדִשְׁמוּאֵל, דְּאָמַר שְׁמוּאֵל: פִּרְצָה דְּחוּקָה – מוּתָּר לִיכָּנֵס בָּהּ בְּשַׁבָּת, וְאַף עַל פִּי שֶׁמַּשִּׁיר צְרוֹרוֹת.

The Gemara notes that Levi's ruling is **in accordance with** the opinion **of Shmuel, as Shmuel said: It is permitted to enter into a narrow opening** in a wall **on Shabbat, and** this is the *halakha* **even though** doing so **causes pebbles to fall** from the wall. Similarly, although engaging in intercourse might cause a wound and bleeding, it is permitted on Shabbat.

אִיתְּמַר: בָּעַל וְלֹא מָצָא דָּם, וְחָזַר וּבָעַל וּמָצָא דָּם – רַבִּי חֲנִינָא אָמַר: טְמֵאָה, וְרַבִּי אַסִּי אָמַר: טְהוֹרָה.

It **was stated** that the *amora'im* engaged in a dispute: If a husband **engaged in intercourse** with a virgin **and did not find blood, and** he **went back** within the first four nights **and** again **engaged in intercourse** with her **and** this time he **found blood,**[H] **Rabbi Ḥanina says:** The wife is **ritually impure,** as this is menstruation blood. **And Rabbi Asi says: She is ritually pure,** as it is blood from the wound resulting from the act of intercourse.

רַבִּי חֲנִינָא אָמַר: טְמֵאָה, דְּאִם אִיתָא דַּהֲוָה דַּם בְּתוּלִים – מֵעִיקָּרָא הֲוֵי אָתֵי. וְרַבִּי אַסִּי אָמַר: טְהוֹרָה, דִּילְמָא אִתְרְמֵי לֵיהּ כִּדִשְׁמוּאֵל. דְּאָמַר שְׁמוּאֵל: יְכוֹלְנִי לִבְעוֹל כַּמָּה בְּעִילוֹת בְּלֹא דָּם. וְאִידָּךְ – שָׁאנֵי שְׁמוּאֵל דְּרַב גּוּבְרֵיהּ.

**Rabbi Ḥanina says: She is ritually impure, as if it is so that it is blood** from her hymen, i.e., the blood of her **virginity, it would have come at the outset,** after the first time they engaged in intercourse. **And Rabbi Asi said: She is ritually pure,** as **perhaps it happened for him** that he engaged in intercourse **like Shmuel** described. **As Shmuel said: I can engage in intercourse several times without** the appearance of **blood.** In other words, I can engage in intercourse with a virgin while leaving her hymen intact. **And the other** Sage, Rabbi Ḥanina, does not allow for that possibility, since he maintains that **Shmuel is different, as his strength** was **great.** Shmuel was particularly skilled at this, while others cannot accomplish this.

אָמַר רַב: בּוֹגֶרֶת נוֹתְנִין לָהּ לַיְלָה הָרִאשׁוֹן. וְהָנֵי מִילֵּי – שֶׁלֹּא רָאֲתָה, אֲבָל רָאֲתָה – אֵין לָהּ אֶלָּא בְּעִילַת מִצְוָה, וְתוּ לָא.

§ The mishna teaches the *halakha* of a young girl. The Gemara discusses the case of a girl who is older than twelve and a half. **Rav says:** The Sages **give a grown woman,** who engaged in intercourse on her wedding night, **the** entire **first night,**[H] during which she may engage in intercourse with her husband several times. **And this statement** applies only **if she did not see** any blood. **But if she saw** blood, **she has only the relations** that consummate a marriage, which are **a mitzva, and nothing more.**[N]

מֵיתִיבֵי: מַעֲשֶׂה וְנָתַן לָהּ רַבִּי אַרְבַּע לֵילוֹת מִתּוֹךְ שְׁנֵים עָשָׂר חֹדֶשׁ. הֵיכִי דָּמֵי? אִילֵּימָא דְּיָהֵיב לָהּ כּוּלְּהוּ בִּימֵי קַטְנוּת,

The Gemara **raises an objection** to Rav's statement from a *baraita*: There was **an incident** involving a virgin who married, **and Rabbi** Yehuda HaNasi **gave her four nights** in which to engage in intercourse **within twelve months**[H] of her wedding[N] when the blood is considered to be like blood resulting from the torn hymen. The Gemara asks: **What are the circumstances** of this case? **If we say that** Rabbi Yehuda HaNasi **gave her all of** those nights of purity **in** her **days** as **a minor,**

NOTES

**Only the relations that are a mitzva and nothing more** – אֶלָּא בְּעִילַת מִצְוָה וְתוּ לָא: Some early commentaries explain that it is permitted for the couple to engage in intercourse only once. The husband is not obligated to separate from her until he has completed the act of intercourse, even if she bleeds. Immediately after the act of intercourse, his wife has the status of a menstruating woman (Rif; Ra'avad; Rashba; Rosh).

Others explain that any bleeding due to the first act of intercourse is not considered to be impure. Therefore, even if she bleeds during that act she does not become impure, and is permitted to engage in intercourse with her husband afterward. But if she bleeds subsequently, even if still on the first night, she becomes ritually impure (Ba'al HaMaor).

**Four nights within twelve months of her wedding** – אַרְבַּע לֵילוֹת מִתּוֹךְ שְׁנֵים עָשָׂר חֹדֶשׁ: Rashi explains that she engaged in intercourse with her husband on the first night of their marriage and bled. Immediately afterward her husband left on a journey for three months. Upon his return they engaged in intercourse again and the wife bled once more. This occurred two more times.

HALAKHA

**If he engaged in intercourse and did not find blood and went back and engaged in intercourse and found blood** – בָּעַל וְלֹא מָצָא דָּם וְחָזַר וּבָעַל וּמָצָא דָּם: If a husband engaged in intercourse with his virgin wife and she did not bleed, and he again engaged in intercourse with her and she did bleed, the blood is considered to be menstrual blood even if she is a minor, because if it were hymenal blood it would have emerged the first time. This is in accordance with the opinion of Rav Ḥanina (Rambam *Sefer Kedusha, Hilkhot Issurei Bia* 5:25).

**They give a grown woman the first night** – בּוֹגֶרֶת נוֹתְנִין לָהּ לַיְלָה הָרִאשׁוֹן: A grown woman who has never menstruated is given the entire first night to engage in intercourse with her husband. The authorities add that this is only if she does not bleed as a result of the act of intercourse. If she does bleed, they are permitted to complete the act of intercourse only once to consummate the marriage (Rambam *Sefer Kedusha, Hilkhot Issurei Bia* 5:19, and see *Maggid Mishne* there).

**There was an incident and Rabbi Yehuda HaNasi gave her four nights within twelve months** – מַעֲשֶׂה וְנָתַן לָהּ רַבִּי אַרְבַּע לֵילוֹת מִתּוֹךְ שְׁנֵים עָשָׂר חֹדֶשׁ: A young woman who has never menstruated is given four nights during which the blood is considered to be pure, even if they are not consecutive nights. For example, if she engages in intercourse once, she may do so again two or three months later. This is specifically if her wound has not yet healed (Rambam *Sefer Kedusha, Hilkhot Issurei Bia* 5:22).

״עַד שֶׁתִּחְיֶה הַמַּכָּה״ תְּנַן.

in accordance with the ruling of the mishna: The Sages give her four nights, then he should have given her longer, as **we learned** in the mishna that according to Beit Hillel the blood may be attributed to the torn hymen **until the wound heals.**

אֶלָּא דְּיָהֵיב לָהּ כּוּלְּהוּ בִּימֵי נַעֲרוּת – נַעֲרוּת שְׁנֵים עָשָׂר חֹדֶשׁ מִי אִיכָּא? וְהָא אָמַר שְׁמוּאֵל: אֵין בֵּין נַעֲרוּת לְבַגְרוּת אֶלָּא שִׁשָּׁה חֳדָשִׁים בִּלְבַד! וְכִי תֵּימָא: בָּצִיר מֵהָכִי – הוּא דְּלֵיכָּא, הָא טְפֵי – אִיכָּא, הָא ״בִּלְבַד״ קָאָמַר!

**Rather,** you will say **that he gave her** these four nights **all** during her **days as a young woman. Are there twelve months** when one has the status of **a young woman? But didn't Shmuel say: The difference** in time **between** becoming **a young woman and** becoming **a grown woman is only six months?**[H] **And if you would say** that Shmuel is saying that it is in **less than** six months **that there is no** transition from young woman to grown woman status, but **there is** such a transition in **more** than six months, as women develop differently, that is not so, **as** Shmuel **said: Only,** which indicates that the period is neither less nor more than six months.

אֶלָּא דְּיָהֵיב לָהּ שְׁתַּיִם בִּימֵי קַטְנוּת וּשְׁתַּיִם בִּימֵי נַעֲרוּת – הָא בְּעָא מִינֵּיהּ רַב חִינָּנָא בַּר שֶׁלֶמְיָא מֵרַב: הִגִּיעַ זְמַנָּהּ לִרְאוֹת תַּחַת בַּעְלָהּ מַהוּ?

**Rather,** you will suggest **that** Rabbi Yehuda HaNasi **gave her two** days **during** her **days as a minor, and** he gave her **two** days **during** her **days as a young woman.** This too is difficult, as **Rav Ḥinnana bar Shelamya asked Rav:** With regard to a young girl who married before she reached puberty, and then **her time to see** menstrual blood **arrived** while she was **under** the authority of **her husband, what is the** *halakha*? Does she have the four nights when the blood is considered to be from her torn hymen?

אֲמַר לֵיהּ: כָּל בְּעִילוֹת שֶׁאַתָּה בּוֹעֵל – אֵינָן אֶלָּא אַחַת, וְהַשְּׁאָר מַשְׁלִימִין לְאַרְבָּעָה לֵילוֹת.

And Rav **said to him: All the acts of intercourse that you engage in** while she is still too young **are** considered as **only one**[H] act of intercourse, **and the remainder,** i.e., three more acts of intercourse, **complete** the total number of **four nights.** If so, Rabbi Yehuda HaNasi could not have given her two nights as a minor, since at most those acts of intercourse count as one.

אֶלָּא: דְּיָהֵיב לָהּ אַחַת בִּימֵי קַטְנוּת, וּשְׁתַּיִם בִּימֵי נַעֲרוּת, וְאַחַת בִּימֵי בַּגְרוּת – אִי אָמְרַתְּ בִּשְׁלָמָא בּוֹגֶרֶת בְּעָלְמָא יָהֲבִינַן לָהּ טְפֵי, כִּי הֵיכִי דְּאַהֲנֵי קַטְנוּת בִּימֵי נַעֲרוּת לְמִבְצַר לָהּ חֲדָא, אַהֲנֵי נַמִּי נַעֲרוּת לְבַגְרוּת לְמִבְצַר לָהּ חֲדָא.

**Rather,** you will suggest **that he gave her one** night **during her days as a minor, and two** nights **during her days as a young woman, and one** night **during her days as a grown woman.** But this is also difficult: **Granted, if you say** that **we generally give a grown woman more** than one night, then one can understand why Rabbi Yehuda HaNasi gave her one night in this case: **Just as** all the acts of intercourse she engaged in as **a minor have the effect to deduct one** night **for** her **days as a young woman,** similarly all the acts of intercourse she engaged in while **a young woman have the effect to deduct one** night **for** her days as **a grown woman,** leaving her with one.

אֶלָּא אִי אָמְרַתְּ בּוֹגֶרֶת דְּעָלְמָא לָא יָהֲבִינַן לָהּ טְפֵי, לָא לֵיתַב לָהּ אֶלָּא בְּעִילַת מִצְוָה וְתוּ לָא!

**But if you say** that **we generally do not give a grown woman more** than one night, then in this case Rabbi Yehuda HaNasi **should** have **given her** as a grown woman **only** the one act of **relations** that consummate a marriage, which are **a mitzva,** i.e., merely a single act of intercourse, **and nothing more,** as otherwise the acts of intercourse before she became a grown woman would not have affected her status.

**HALAKHA**

**The difference in time between becoming a young woman and becoming a grown woman is only six months** – אֵין בֵּין נַעֲרוּת לְבַגְרוּת אֶלָּא שִׁשָּׁה חֳדָשִׁים בִּלְבַד: There are only six months between the time when a girl becomes a young woman and the time when she becomes a grown woman, in accordance with the opinion of Shmuel (Rambam *Sefer Nashim*, *Hilkhot Ishut* 2:2; *Shulḥan Arukh*, *Yoreh De'a* 234:1).

**All the acts of intercourse that you engage in are considered as only one** – כָּל בְּעִילוֹת שֶׁאַתָּה בּוֹעֵל אֵינָן אֶלָּא אַחַת וכו׳: With regard to a minor girl who marries and becomes a young woman while she is still experiencing hymenal bleeding, all her acts of intercourse while she was a minor are considered as only one night. She may continue to engage in intercourse for another three nights during her time as a young woman to complete the four nights. Even if these three nights were not consecutive but were each spaced two months apart it is permitted, provided that the wound has not healed. This is in accordance with the opinion of Rav, as explained by the Gemara (Rambam *Sefer Kedusha*, *Hilkhot Issurei Bia* 5:22).

BACKGROUND

**Saksana – סַקְסְנָאָה:** He had this title because it is likely that he was originally from Sistan, a region in present day eastern Iran and southern Afghanistan that was an enormous province of the Sassanid Empire. Sistan was the ancient homeland of the Saka people, a Scythian tribe, and it held special significance in Zoroastrianism.

לְעוֹלָם דִּיהֵיב לָהּ אַחַת בִּימֵי קְטַנּוּת וְשָׁלֹשׁ בִּימֵי נַעֲרוּת, מִי סָבְרַתְּ כׇּל תְּלָתָא יַרְחֵי – חֲדָא עוֹנָה? כׇּל תְּרֵי יַרְחֵי – חֲדָא עוֹנָה.

The Gemara answers: **Actually,** the correct explanation is **that** Rabbi Yehuda HaNasi **gave her one** night **during her days as a minor and three** nights **during her days as a young woman.** And as for the fact that she has the status of a young woman for only exactly six months, **do you maintain** that **every three months** was counted as **one period** of the husband's absence, such that she had only two nights in six months? This is not the case. Rather, **every two months** was counted as **one period,** and therefore she had three nights during these six months when she could attribute the blood to her torn hymen.

מִנְיָמִין סַקְסְנָאָה הֲוָה שָׁקֵיל וְאָזֵיל לְאַתְרֵיהּ דִּשְׁמוּאֵל, סְבַר לְמֶעְבַּד עוּבְדָּא כְּווֹתֵיהּ דְּרַב אֲפִילּוּ רָאֲתָה. אֲמַר: לָא פְּלִיג רַב בֵּין רָאֲתָה בֵּין לֹא רָאֲתָה.

The Gemara relates that the Sage **Minyamin Saksana**[BP] **was coming and walking to the place of Shmuel. He thought** that he **would perform an action in accordance** with the opinion **of Rav,** in that he would permit a grown woman to attribute blood to her torn hymen for the entire first night, **even** though she had already **seen** menstrual blood before she was married. Minyamin mistakenly **said** to himself: **Rav does not distinguish between** a woman who **has seen** menstrual blood **and** a woman who **has not seen** menstrual blood.

קָדֵים שְׁכֵיב בְּאוֹרְחָא. קְרֵי שְׁמוּאֵל עֲלֵיהּ דְּרַב: ״לֹא יְאֻנֶּה לַצַּדִּיק כׇּל אָוֶן״.

**Before** Minyamin reached Shmuel's place, **he passed away on the road,** and he never completed the journey. Upon hearing this, **Shmuel recited** this verse **about Rav: "No mishap shall befall the righteous"** (Proverbs 12:21),[N] i.e., God does not allow prohibited acts to come from the statements of the righteous. In this case, Minyamin ruled incorrectly, based on a misunderstanding of Rav's statement.

אָמַר רַב חִינָּנָא בַּר שֶׁלֶמְיָא מִשְּׁמֵיהּ דְּרַב: כֵּיוָן שֶׁנִּתְּקוּ שִׁנָּיו שֶׁל אָדָם – נִתְמַעֲטוּ מְזוֹנוֹתָיו, שֶׁנֶּאֱמַר: ״גַּם אָנֹכִי נָתַתִּי לָךְ נִקְיוֹן שִׁנַּיִם בְּכׇל עָרֵיכֶם וְחֹסֶר לֶחֶם בְּכֹל מְקוֹמֹתֵיכֶם״.

Since the Gemara cited Rav Ḥinnana bar Shelamya, it cites another of his statements: **Rav Ḥinnana bar Shelamya said in the name of Rav: Once a person's teeth fall out** and he has difficulty eating, **his food diminishes**[N] accordingly, **as it is stated: "And I also have given you cleanness of teeth in all your cities, and lack of bread in all your places"** (Amos 4:6). The term "cleanness of teeth" is here a euphemism for having no teeth at all, which leads to a lack of bread.

״רָאֲתָה וְעוֹדָהּ״. תָּנוּ רַבָּנַן, רָאֲתָה וְעוֹדָהּ בְּבֵית אָבִיהָ, בֵּית הִלֵּל אוֹמְרִים: כׇּל הַלַּיְלָה שֶׁלָּהּ, וְנוֹתְנִין לָהּ עוֹנָה שְׁלֵמָה. וְכַמָּה עוֹנָה שְׁלֵמָה? פֵּירֵשׁ רַבָּן שִׁמְעוֹן בֶּן גַּמְלִיאֵל: לַיְלָה וַחֲצִי יוֹם.

§ The mishna teaches: In the case of a young woman who **saw** menstrual blood before marriage, while **she was still** in her father's house, Beit Hillel say: They may engage in several acts of intercourse, as any bleeding throughout the entire night is attributed to the torn hymen. **The Sages taught** in a *baraita*: In the case of a young woman who **saw** menstrual blood while **she was still in her father's house, Beit Hillel say: All the night is hers, and** the Sages **give her** one **complete period** of time during which she may attribute all bleeding to her torn hymen. **And how long is a complete period** of time in this context? **Rabban Shimon ben Gamliel explained** that it is one **night and half** of the next **day.**

PERSONALITIES

**Minyamin Saksana – מִנְיָמִין סַקְסְנָאָה:** This name appears in the Bible (II Chronicles 31:15). The name seems to be a variant of the name Binyamin, with the *bet* being replaced by another bilabial consonant, the letter *mem*, a common phenomenon.

This suggestion is supported by a parallel story that appears in the Jerusalem Talmud (*Berakhot* 2:5), where it is Binyamin Ganzakhya who attempts to apply Rav's ruling in Shmuel's community. If Minyamin Saksana'a and Binyamin Ganzakhya are one and the same, the discrepancy between their surnames must be explained.

One possibility is that this individual came from the lands of the biblical Cush, whose children include Sabtah and Sabteca (see Genesis 10:7). The Jerusalem Targum to that verse translates the name Sabteca as Zangai; in the Babylonian Talmud those names are translated by Rav Yosef as the inner Sakistan and the outer Sakistan (*Yoma* 10a). Consequently, the description Saksana used by the Babylonian Talmud may be identical with the description Ganzakhya used by the Jerusalem Talmud.

NOTES

**Shmuel recited this verse about Rav: No mishap shall befall the righteous – קְרֵי שְׁמוּאֵל עֲלֵיהּ דְּרַב לֹא יְאֻנֶּה לַצַּדִּיק כׇּל אָוֶן:** The later authorities conclude from here that there is a guarantee that no mishap will result from the ruling of a righteous person (*Da'at Torah*).

**Once a person's teeth fall out his food diminishes – כֵּיוָן שֶׁנִּתְּקוּ שִׁנָּיו שֶׁל אָדָם נִתְמַעֲטוּ מְזוֹנוֹתָיו:** The plain meaning of this statement is that when one reaches old age, which is the usual time when one's teeth fall out, and he has limited capability for chewing, his need for teeth is reduced correspondingly. Rashi states that as one earns less as his physical strength wanes, his ability to acquire food decreases as well.

## HALAKHA

**One whose winepresses or olive presses were impure and he wished to prepare his grapes and olives in ritual purity – הָיוּ גִּתָּיו וּבֵית בַּדָּיו טְמֵאוֹת וּבִקֵּשׁ לַעֲשׂוֹתָן בְּטָהֳרָה:** How does one purify the utensils from a winepress that contained grapes that were trampled by a gentile? The vessels themselves do not become impure, but they may contain impure liquids that must be removed. The planks, twigs, and troughs must be immersed in a ritual bath. If the pressing baskets are made of palm leaves or of hemp they need to be dried. If they are made of bast or of reeds they must be left unused for twelve months. If one wants to purify them immediately he must immerse them in boiling water or in water in which olives were cooked, or place them under a drainpipe or spring of running water for twelve hours. The Rambam rules like both the opinion of the first *tanna* and the opinion of Rabbi Yosei and Rabbi Shimon ben Gamliel, citing Rabbi Yosei. He holds that the latter are not disagreeing with the first *tanna* but are referring to immediate purification, and the first *tanna* is referring to purification over a longer period of time. A similar process is also used to make these utensils kosher after coming into contact with non-kosher liquids (Rambam *Sefer Tahara, Hilkhot Tumat Okhalin* 11:17 and *Sefer Kedusha, Hilkhot Ma'akhalot Assurot* 11:24 and *Kesef Mishne* and *Leḥem Mishne* there; *Shulḥan Arukh, Yoreh De'a* 138:6).

וּמִי בָּעֵינַן כּוּלֵּי הַאי? וּרְמִינְהִי: הֲרֵי שֶׁהָיוּ גִּתָּיו וּבֵית בַּדָּיו טְמֵאוֹת, וּבִקֵּשׁ לַעֲשׂוֹתָן בְּטָהֳרָה, כֵּיצַד הוּא עוֹשֶׂה, הַדַּפִּין וְהַלּוּלָבִין וְהָעֲדָשִׁין – מְדִיחָן,

The Gemara asks: **But do we require all this** time of one night and half of a day for a complete period? **And the Gemara raises a contradiction** from a *baraita*: In the case of one **whose winepresses or olive presses**[B] **were impure and he wished to prepare** his grapes and olives **in** a state of **ritual purity,**[H] **how does he act?** He should **rinse the planks**[B] used to press the grapes in the winepress, **and the palm branches**[B] used as brooms, **and the troughs,**[B]

## BACKGROUND

**His winepresses or olive presses – גִּתָּיו וּבֵית בַּדָּיו:** A winepress was typically carved into a rock into which grapes were placed and pressed. The liquid that was pressed from the grapes flowed through a channel to the lower winepress. This is seen in the verse: "For the winepress is full, the vats overflow" (Joel 4:13). Others would press their grapes in a vessel of wood or stone, which was also called a winepress.

The olive press had a wide and heavy beam for pressing the olives and producing oil, and the literal translation of the Hebrew term *bet habad* is: The building of the beam, named after its most essential element.

Olive press, Tel Hatzor, Israel

**Planks – דַּפִּין:** These are wide boards that are placed on the grapes in the press in order to split them. These boards are not particularly heavy because grapes must be pressed gently to avoid crushing the grape seeds, which can ruin the flavor of the wine.

**Palm branches – לוּלָבִין:** Rashi explains this as palm leaves used to make a broom to gather up grapes that scattered from the pile. Other commentaries say these are two pillars standing on either side of the beam that presses the olives in an olive press (see *Bava Batra* 67b) and their purpose is to stabilize the beam (Rabbeinu Gershom Meor HaGola; Ra'avad), or these are beams that were placed by the pile of grapes or olives to prevent them from falling away during the treading or crushing process (Rabbeinu Tam).

**Troughs – עֲדָשִׁין:** This is referring to the winepress itself, where the grapes are placed. It has this name because it is shaped like a trough (Rashi; Rabbeinu Gershom Meor HaGola). Some explain that it refers to the utensils of the winepress, specifically a large hollow vessel into which the wine is placed and stored until (Rashba). Alternatively, it is referring to a utensil from an olive press, i.e., the large vessel in which the olives are brought for pressing (Rosh). Rabbeinu Tam explains that it is referring to the stones or round utensils that were placed on the boards to increase the weight and press the olives. Others explain that it is referring to the stone of the upper millstone, which does not have any hollow part. The Ramban explains that it refers specifically to the lower millstone, which does have a hollow part.

Perek **X**
Daf **65** Amud **b**

## NOTES

**He should clean them – מְנַגְּבָן:** In *Avoda Zara* (74b) there is a dispute between *amora'im* as to how this cleaning was to be done. According to Rav, the press had to be cleaned with water, but according to Rabba bar bar Ḥana it was cleaned with earth. The conclusion is that they both agree that the cleaning must be done with both water and earth, but each was referring to a different type of winepress. If the winepress was wet, it must first be cleaned with earth and afterward rinsed with water. If the winepress was dry it must first be rinsed with water and afterward cleaned with earth.

## LANGUAGE

**Hemp [bitzbutz] – בִּצְבּוּץ:** The *Arukh* explains that this word is a form of the word for linen, *butz*. According to Rashi this material was hemp, which looks similar to linen.

**Bast [shifa] – שִׁיפָא:** This word may be derived from the Greek σιπύη, sipuē, meaning meal jar or flour bin.

הָעֲקָלִים שֶׁל נְצָרִים וְשֶׁל בִּצְבּוּץ – מְנַגְּבָן, שֶׁל שִׁיפָא וְשֶׁל גְּמִי – מְיַישְּׁנָן. וְכַמָּה מְיַישְּׁנָן? שְׁנֵים עָשָׂר חֹדֶשׁ. רַבָּן שִׁמְעוֹן בֶּן גַּמְלִיאֵל אוֹמֵר: מַנִּיחָן מִגַּת לְגַת וּמִבַּד לְבַד.

and he should **clean**[N] **the** pressing **baskets**[B] with ashes and water if they were made **of palm leaves or of hemp [*bitzbutz*],**[L] **or leave them dormant** if they were made **of bast [*shifa*]**[L] **or of reeds,**[B] because these absorb more of the wine. **And how long** must one **leave them dormant?** He must leave them for **twelve months. Rabban Shimon ben Gamliel says: He can lay them aside from** one **wine-pressing** season **to** the next **wine-pressing** season, **or from** one **olive-pressing** season **to** the next **olive-pressing** season.

הַיְינוּ תַּנָּא קַמָּא! אִיכָּא בֵּינַיְיהוּ חֲרָפֵי וְאַפְלֵי.

The Gemara interrupts its citation to analyze the *baraita*: Rabban Shimon ben Gamliel's statement **is the same as** that of **the first *tanna*,** as there are twelve months between one wine-pressing season and the next. The Gemara responds: The difference **between them** is the matter of the **early and late** ripening season for grapes. Rabban Shimon ben Gamliel does not require a precise measure of twelve months, as the difference in time between ripening seasons can be slightly more or less than that.

## BACKGROUND

**Baskets of an olive press – עֲקָל בֵּית הַבַּד:** The baskets were designed to keep the olives in one place and to prevent them from separating as they were being pressed by the beam. The oil would then seep through the holes in the basket into a receptacle.

**Reeds – גְּמִי:** This is referring to reeds that grow near marsh or rivers. In different kinds of reeds, beneath the husk, there is a soft inner part that can be used for a variety of purposes. One such purpose was as a bandage for wounds or fractured bones.

רַבִּי יוֹסֵי אוֹמֵר: הָרוֹצֶה לְטַהֵר מִיָּד – מְגַעִילָן בְּרוֹתְחִין, אוֹ חוֹלְטָן בְּמֵי זֵיתִים. רַבָּן שִׁמְעוֹן בֶּן גַּמְלִיאֵל אוֹמֵר מִשּׁוּם רַבִּי יוֹסֵי: מַנִּיחָן תַּחַת הַצִּינּוֹר שֶׁמֵּימָיו מְקַלְּחִין, אוֹ בְּמַעְיָין שֶׁמֵּימָיו רוֹדְפִין. וְכַמָּה? עוֹנָה. כְּדֶרֶךְ שֶׁאָמְרוּ בְּיֵין נֶסֶךְ, כָּךְ אָמְרוּ בְּטָהֳרוֹת.

The Gemara continues its citation of the *baraita*. **Rabbi Yosei says: One who wishes to purify** the baskets **immediately,** without waiting a year, **purges them in boiling water or scalds them in olive water. Rabban Shimon ben Gamliel says in the name of Rabbi Yosei: One sets them under a pipe whose water flows** constantly **or in a spring with rapid waters. And how much** time should he leave them there? He should leave them for **a period** of time. **In the** same **way that** the Sages **stated** this time frame **with regard to wine** used for **a libation** in idol worship, **so too** the Sages **stated** this time frame **with regard to matters of ritual purity.**

כְּלַפֵּי לַיָּיא? בְּטָהֳרוֹת קַיְימִינַן! אֶלָּא: כְּדֶרֶךְ שֶׁאָמְרוּ בְּטָהֳרוֹת כָּךְ אָמְרוּ בְּיֵין נֶסֶךְ.

The Gemara expresses surprise at this last clause: **Isn't it the opposite** [*kelapei layya*]?[L] **We are dealing with matters of purity** in this *baraita*. **Rather,** the *baraita* means: **In the** same **way that** the Sages **stated** this time frame **with regard to matters of ritual purity, so too** the Sages **stated** this time frame **in** the case of **wine** used for **a libation** in idol worship.

וְכַמָּה עוֹנָה? אָמַר רַבִּי חִיָּיא בַּר אַבָּא, אָמַר רַבִּי יוֹחָנָן: אוֹ יוֹם אוֹ לַיְלָה. רַבִּי חָנָה שְׁאוֹנָא, וְאָמְרִי לַהּ רַבִּי חָנָה בַּר שְׁאוֹנָא אָמַר רַבָּה בַּר בַּר חָנָה אָמַר רַבִּי יוֹחָנָן: חֲצִי יוֹם וַחֲצִי לַיְלָה.

The Gemara asks: **And how long is** the **period** of time referred to in the *baraita*? **Rabbi Ḥiyya bar Abba says** that **Rabbi Yoḥanan says: Either** the **day or the night.**[H] **Rabbi Ḥana She'ona, and some say Rabbi Ḥana bar She'ona, say** that **Rabba bar bar Ḥana says** that **Rabbi Yoḥanan says: Half a day and half a night.**

וְאָמַר רַב שְׁמוּאֵל בַּר רַב יִצְחָק: וְלָא פְּלִיגִי, הָא – בִּתְקוּפַת נִיסָן וְתִשְׁרֵי, הָא – בִּתְקוּפַת תַּמּוּז וְטֵבֵת.

**And Rav Shmuel bar Rav Yitzḥak said: And** the Sages **do not disagree.** The ruling of **this** one, who says either a day or a night, is stated **with regard to** the equinox of the **season**[B] **of Nisan or Tishrei,** when the days and night are equal; whereas the ruling of **that** one, who says half a day and half a night, is stated **with regard to** the solstice of the **season of Tammuz,** i.e., summer, **or Tevet,** i.e., winter, which have the longest day[B] or night respectively, so that half the day and half the night together amount to twelve hours. This *baraita* apparently contradicts the statement of Rabban Shimon ben Gamliel, who says that the woman may attribute the blood to her hymen for a night and half the day.

הָכָא נַמִי, אֵימָא גַּבֵּי נִדָּה: חֲצִי יוֹם וַחֲצִי לַיְלָה! וְהָא לַיְלָה וַחֲצִי יוֹם קָאָמַר! אֶלָּא: אִי לַיְלָה דְּנִיסָן וְתִשְׁרֵי, אִי חֲצִי יוֹם וַחֲצִי לַיְלָה דְּטֵבֵת וְתַמּוּז.

The Gemara answers: **Here too,** one can **say with regard to a menstruating woman** that he meant **half a day and half a night.** The Gemara raises a difficulty. **But** Rabban Shimon ben Gamliel **said a night and half a day.** The Gemara clarifies: **Rather,** this is what Rabban Shimon ben Gamliel meant: **Either a night during Nisan or Tishrei,** which is twelve hours, **or half a day and half a night during Tevet or Tammuz,** which also equals twelve hours.

וְאִיבָּעֵית אֵימָא: שָׁאנֵי כְּתוּבָּה. דְּמַגְבֵּי בַּהּ טְפֵי עַד דְּחָתְמִי.

**And if you wish, say** instead: With regard to the purity of wine, a period is twelve hours. But in the case of marriage the time frame **is different,** due to the **marriage contract,** which is signed before the marriage is consummated, **as there are those who delay for a lengthy** period **until they** complete and **sign it.**[N] Consequently, the Sages extended the period in this case to a night and half a day.

**HALAKHA**

**A period of time…either the day or the night – עוֹנָה...אוֹ יוֹם אוֹ לַיְלָה:** The utensils from a winepress in which grapes have been trampled by a gentile are considered to contain wine used for libation in idol worship. One who wishes to render them kosher immediately can place them under a pipe of running water, or in a spring, for twelve hours. Afterward they become permitted. This is in accordance with the opinion of Rabban Shimon ben Gamliel, citing Rabbi Yosei (Rambam *Sefer Kedusha, Hilkhot Ma'akhalot Assurot* 11:24 and *Sefer Tahara, Hilkhot Tumat Okhalin* 11:17; *Shulḥan Arukh, Yoreh De'a* 138:6).

**NOTES**

**It is different due to the marriage contract, as there are those who delay [*magbei*] for a lengthy period until they sign it – שָׁאנֵי כְּתוּבָּה דְּמַגְבֵּי בַּהּ טְפֵי עַד דְּחָתְמִי:** An alternative version of the text reads: A marriage contract is different because they examine [*maghei*] it thoroughly. In other words, it takes a long time to read the details of a marriage document and to check them carefully. Only afterward is the document signed and given to the wife, and only then it is permitted for her husband to be alone with her. For this reason they are given an extra half a day, as sometimes the document is signed very late at night (Rashi).

**LANGUAGE**

**Isn't it the opposite [*kelapei layya*] – כְּלַפֵּי לַיָּיא:** This expression of puzzlement is generally understood to mean: Directed to where? That is to say: Where are you facing, or more simply: How are you thinking about the given matter? The question indicates that one is looking at the matter backward. Some of the *ge'onim* understood the expression as: Facing the tail [*kelapei alya*], as if to say: You are facing the direction of the tail, like one who is riding backward on an animal. In any case, the term is understood to indicate that one is saying the opposite of what is logical.

**BACKGROUND**

**Season – תְּקוּפָה:** This refers to the equinoxes and solstices. There are four such days; see the table below.

| | | |
|---|---|---|
| Tishrei | September 23 | The day and night are equal |
| Tevet | December 22 | The shortest day of the year |
| Nisan | March 21 | The day and night are equal |
| Tammuz | June 22 | The longest day of the year |

**Longest day – הַיּוֹם הָאָרֹךְ בְּיוֹתֵר:** Since the seasons are fixed according to the solar calendar, they will not always occur on the same date in the lunar calendar. The season of Tammuz sometimes ends in Elul and sometimes continues until Tishrei. When the season of Tammuz would end a long time after Rosh HaShana, the Sages would make it a leap year, and the seasons would move earlier in the Jewish calendar.

רַב וּשְׁמוּאֵל דְּאָמְרִי תַּרְוַיְיהוּ: הֲלָכָה – בּוֹעֵל בְּעִילַת מִצְוָה, וּפוֹרֵשׁ.

§ Although the mishna provides a certain period of time for both a minor and a young woman during which they may attribute any blood to the torn hymen, nevertheless **Rav and Shmuel both say** that the ***halakha*** is that the groom **engages in relations** that consummate a marriage, which are **a mitzva, and** then he **separates**[N] from his wife.

מְתִיב רַב חִסְדָּא: מַעֲשֶׂה וְנָתַן לָהּ רַבִּי אַרְבָּעָה לֵילוֹת מִתּוֹךְ שְׁנֵים עָשָׂר חֹדֶשׁ!

**Rav Ḥisda raises an objection** from the *baraita*: There was **an incident** involving a virgin who married, **and Rabbi** Yehuda HaNasi **gave her four nights** to engage in intercourse **within twelve months** of her wedding. This indicates that the husband does not have to separate from his wife immediately after the first act of intercourse is completed.

אֲמַר לֵיהּ רָבָא: הֲדוּרֵי אַפִּירְכָא לָמָּה לִי? אוֹתֵיב מִמַּתְנִיתִין! הוּא סְבַר – מַעֲשֶׂה רַב.

**Rava said to** Rav Ḥisda: **Why do I** need **to search for a refutation** from a *baraita*, which is not necessarily known by all? One can **raise a difficulty from** an explicit statement of **the mishna,** which states that the first blood a woman sees on her wedding night is attributed to her torn hymen. The Gemara explains that Rav Ḥisda raises his objection from the *baraita*, as he **holds** that a practical **incident** ruled upon by **a Sage** is a preferable source.

מִכָּל מָקוֹם לְרַב וּשְׁמוּאֵל קַשְׁיָא! אִינְהוּ דְּעָבְדוּ כְּרַבּוֹתֵינוּ. דְּתַנְיָא, רַבּוֹתֵינוּ חָזְרוּ וְנִמְנוּ: בּוֹעֵל בְּעִילַת מִצְוָה, וּפוֹרֵשׁ.

The Gemara returns to the objection: **In any case,** this *baraita* is **difficult for Rav and Shmuel.** The Gemara answers that **they acted in accordance with** the opinion attributed to **our Sages, as it is taught** in a *baraita*: **Our Sages returned and were counted** again, i.e., they voted and decided, that the groom **engages in relations** that consummate a marriage, which are **a mitzva, and** subsequently he **separates**[H] from his wife.

אֲמַר עוּלָּא: כִּי הָווּ בָּהּ רַבִּי יוֹחָנָן וְרֵישׁ לָקִישׁ בְּתִינוֹקֶת, לָא הָווּ מַסְּקֵי מִינָּהּ אֶלָּא כִּדְמַסֵּיק תַּעֲלָא מִבֵּי כְּרָבָא, וּמְסַיְּימִי בָּהּ הָכִי: בּוֹעֵל בְּעִילַת מִצְוָה, וּפוֹרֵשׁ.

The Gemara proves that this ruling of Rav and Shmuel, based on the *baraita*, is also the opinion of Rabbi Yoḥanan and Reish Lakish. **Ulla said: When we were** learning the topic **of a young girl** who saw blood on her wedding night with **Rabbi Yoḥanan and Reish Lakish, they brought up from it only** the amount **of earth that the fox brings up from a plowed field,** i.e., they did not establish the *halakha* as stated in the mishna. **And they concluded** the discussion in **this** manner: The groom **engages in relations** that consummate a marriage, which are **a mitzva, and** then he **separates** from his wife.

אָמַר לוֹ רַבִּי אַבָּא לְרַב אַשִׁי: אֶלָּא מֵעַתָּה – בַּעַל נֶפֶשׁ לֹא יִגְמוֹר בִּיאָתוֹ! אָמַר לוֹ: אִם כֵּן, לִבּוֹ נוֹקְפוֹ וּפוֹרֵשׁ.

**Rabbi Abba said to Rav Ashi,** in light of this ruling that the groom must separate from his bride after completing the act of intercourse: **If that is so, a pious person** should **not complete his** act of **intercourse,** lest he unintentionally continue longer than is permitted. Rav Ashi **said to him** in reply: The Sages did not issue such a decree, because **if so, his heart will strike him** with fear that perhaps his wife will begin to bleed while he is engaged in the act of intercourse, **and he will separate** from his wife completely and will not consummate the marriage.

תָּנוּ רַבָּנַן: וְכוּלָּן שֶׁהָיוּ שׁוֹפְעוֹת דָּם וּבָאוֹת מִתּוֹךְ אַרְבָּעָה לֵילוֹת לְאַחַר אַרְבָּעָה לֵילוֹת, מִתּוֹךְ הַלַּיְלָה לְאַחַר הַלַּיְלָה – כּוּלָּן צְרִיכוֹת לִבְדּוֹק אֶת עַצְמָן.

§ The mishna teaches that a young girl is given four nights during which any bleeding is attributed to her torn hymen. **The Sages taught** in a *baraita*: **And** with regard to **all of them,** i.e., all the women who are given four nights, **if they were discharging blood continually, from four nights** until **after** those **four nights,** or in the case of those women who are given only one night, if they discharge blood **from that** one **night** until **after that night,** they may not attribute the blood to the torn hymen. Rather, **all of them must examine themselves,** in the manner that will be explained.

**NOTES**

**The *halakha* is that he engages in relations that are a mitzva and separates – הֲלָכָה בּוֹעֵל בְּעִילַת מִצְוָה וּפוֹרֵשׁ:** Even though the term: And separates, indicates that he must separate immediately, the early authorities write that he should wait before withdrawing from her, because withdrawing while his penis is erect also gives him pleasure. Rather, he should wait until his penis becomes flaccid and then withdraw (Rosh; Rashba; Ra'avad).

**HALAKHA**

**They returned and were counted again, that he engages in relations that are a mitzva and separates – חָזְרוּ וְנִמְנוּ בּוֹעֵל בְּעִילַת מִצְוָה וּפוֹרֵשׁ:** By Torah law one who marries a minor girl is permitted to continue to engage in intercourse with her until the hymenal bleeding has finished, regardless of whether she has ever menstruated before or not. The Sages were stringent (see *Kesef Mishne*) and ruled that one who marries a virgin may engage in the first act of intercourse and must then separate from her immediately. Even if she is so young that she is not old enough to menstruate, and even if she examined herself and did not find any blood, she is considered impure, because there may have been a tiny drop of blood that she did not notice. The Rema writes that there are some who are lenient if she did not bleed. The custom is to be lenient if they did not complete the act of intercourse and she did not bleed. Nevertheless, a pious person will not engage in intercourse with a minor. This is in accordance with the *baraita* (Rambam *Sefer Kedusha, Hilkhot Issurei Bia* 5:19; *Shulḥan Arukh, Yoreh De'a* 193:1 and *Even HaEzer* 63:1).

וּבְכוּלָּן רַבִּי מֵאִיר מַחְמִיר כְּדִבְרֵי בֵּית שַׁמַּאי.

**And with regard to all of** these women, **Rabbi Meir is stringent in accordance with the statement of Beit Shammai,** and therefore a minor girl who bleeds for more than four nights must examine herself, despite the fact that Beit Hillel say she remains ritually pure until the wound has healed. Similarly, Rabbi Meir holds that with regard to a young girl who has reached puberty, if she continues to bleed after the first night she must examine herself.

וּשְׁאָר רְאִיּוֹת שֶׁבֵּין בֵּית שַׁמַּאי וּבֵית הִלֵּל – הַלֵּךְ אַחַר מַרְאֵה דָמִים.

The *baraita* continues: **But** with regard to the **other** cases of **seeing** blood, when she does not discharge blood continuously but bleeds again the following day, concerning **which** there is a dispute **between Beit Shammai and Beit Hillel,** Rabbi Meir holds that one **follows the appearance of the blood.** In other words, he does not maintain entirely in accordance with the opinion of Beit Shammai. Beit Hillel rule that the woman is ritually pure even if the color of the blood has changed, whereas Beit Shammai hold that she is ritually impure even if the color of the blood has not changed.

שֶׁהָיָה רַבִּי מֵאִיר אוֹמֵר: מַרְאֵה דָמִים מְשׁוּנִּים הֵן זֶה מִזֶּה. כֵּיצַד: דַּם נִדָּה – אָדוֹם, דַּם בְּתוּלִים – אֵינוֹ אָדוֹם. דַּם נִדָּה – זִיהוּם, דַּם בְּתוּלִים – אֵינוֹ זִיהוּם. דַּם נִדָּה – בָּא מִן הַמָּקוֹר, דַּם בְּתוּלִים – בָּא מִן הַצְּדָדִין.

**As Rabbi Meir would say: The appearances of** impure and pure **blood differ from one another. How so?** The **blood of a menstruating woman is red,** whereas **blood** that comes from a torn hymen, indicating that she was **a virgin, is not red.** The **blood of a menstruating woman is cloudy; blood** that indicates that she was **a virgin is not cloudy.** Finally, the **blood of a menstruating woman comes from the uterus; blood** that indicates that she was **a virgin comes from the sides**[H] of the vaginal wall.

אָמַר רַבִּי יִצְחָק בַּר רַבִּי יוֹסֵי, אָמַר רַבִּי יוֹחָנָן: זוֹ דִּבְרֵי רַבִּי מֵאִיר, אֲבָל חֲכָמִים אוֹמְרִים כׇּל מַרְאֵה דָמִים – אַחַת הֵן.

**Rabbi Yitzḥak bar Rabbi Yosei says** that **Rabbi Yoḥanan says: This is the statement of Rabbi Meir.** According to Rabbi Meir, it is possible to examine the color of blood to determine whether it is menstrual blood or hymenal blood. **But the Rabbis say** that **all appearances of blood are one,** i.e., there is no distinction between the appearance of menstrual blood and blood indicating one's loss of virginity.

תָּנוּ רַבָּנַן: הָרוֹאָה דָם מֵחֲמַת תַּשְׁמִישׁ – מְשַׁמֶּשֶׁת פַּעַם רִאשׁוֹנָה וּשְׁנִיָּה וּשְׁלִישִׁית. מִכָּאן וָאֵילָךְ – לֹא תְּשַׁמֵּשׁ, עַד שֶׁתִּתְגָּרֵשׁ,

§ **The Sages taught** in a *baraita*: A woman **who sees blood due to sexual intercourse**[H] **may engage in intercourse** before the **first time** this occurs, before the **second** time this occurs, **and** before the **third** time this occurs. **From this point forward,** i.e., after three consecutive occurrences of bleeding due to intercourse, **she may not engage in intercourse until she is divorced** from her husband

**HALAKHA**

**Blood of a virgin comes from the sides – דַּם בְּתוּלִים בָּא מִן הַצְּדָדִין:** Blood resulting from the tearing of the hymen is ritually pure and is not considered to have the same status as menstrual blood or *ziva* blood, since it does not come from the uterus, in accordance with the opinion of Rabbi Meir (Rambam *Sefer Kedusha, Hilkhot Issurei Bia* 5:18).

**One who sees blood due to sexual intercourse – הָרוֹאָה דָם מֵחֲמַת תַּשְׁמִישׁ:** If a woman bleeds immediately after intercourse, i.e., within the time it takes her to extend her hand under the pillow or blanket, take an examination cloth, and wipe herself, she may engage in intercourse three times. If she bleeds each time, she is forbidden to engage in intercourse with this husband. All the more so this applies if her husband sees blood on his examination cloth each time (Rema), in which case even if he does not examine himself immediately it is still assumed that the blood came as a result of intercourse (*Shakh*). In such a case, he must divorce her and she may remarry. If she remarries and again bleeds three consecutive times due to intercourse she is forbidden to this second husband as well. He must divorce her and she may remarry. If she remarries and again bleeds three consecutive times due to intercourse she is forbidden to this third husband as well. Once he divorces her, she may not remarry, and she is forbidden to all men until she examines herself, in the manner the Gemara will explain, to determine if the blood is the result of engaging in intercourse. The Rema writes that some say that today nobody is certain of the time frame after the act of intercourse in which the blood is considered to be due to intercourse. Therefore, if she bleeds soon after intercourse three consecutive times she becomes forbidden to her husband.

If she bleeds three times after intercourse, but not consecutively, she does not become forbidden to her husband. If she bleeds three times consecutively it makes no difference whether this occurred immediately after she got married or whether some time later she started bleeding due to intercourse.

All of this applies only if she bleeds immediately after intercourse. If she does not experience bleeding immediately afterward she does not become forbidden to her husband, and she is simply rendered impure like a woman who does not have a fixed time to menstruate (Rambam *Sefer Kedusha, Hilkhot Issurei Bia* 4:20–21; *Shulḥan Arukh, Yoreh De'a* 187:1).

Perek **X**
Daf **66** Amud **a**

וְתִנָּשֵׂא לְאַחֵר.

**and is married to another** man. She is permitted to engage in intercourse with her second husband because it is possible that the bleeding was caused by engaging in intercourse with her first husband, and the issue will not reoccur when she engages in intercourse with a different man.

נִיסֵּת לְאַחֵר וְרָאֲתָה דָם מֵחֲמַת תַּשְׁמִישׁ – מְשַׁמֶּשֶׁת פַּעַם רִאשׁוֹנָה וּשְׁנִיָּה וּשְׁלִישִׁית, מִכָּאן וָאֵילָךְ – לֹא תְּשַׁמֵּשׁ, עַד שֶׁתִּתְגָּרֵשׁ וְתִנָּשֵׂא לְאַחֵר. נִיסֵּת לְאַחֵר וְרָאֲתָה דָם מֵחֲמַת תַּשְׁמִישׁ – מְשַׁמֶּשֶׁת פַּעַם רִאשׁוֹנָה וּשְׁנִיָּה וּשְׁלִישִׁית, מִכָּאן וָאֵילָךְ לֹא תְּשַׁמֵּשׁ עַד שֶׁתִּבְדּוֹק עַצְמָהּ.

**If she married another** man **and** again **saw blood due to sexual intercourse,**[N] **she may engage in intercourse** before the **first time** this occurs, before the **second** time this occurs, **and** before the **third** time this occurs. **From this point forward she may not engage in intercourse until she is divorced** from her second husband **and is married to** yet **another** man. If **she married another** man **and** again **saw blood due to sexual intercourse, she may engage in intercourse** the **first time** this occurs, the **second** time this occurs, **and** the **third** time this occurs. **From this point forward** there is a presumption that she always bleeds due to engaging in intercourse, and therefore **she may not engage in intercourse** or marry someone else **until she examines herself.**

**NOTES**

**And saw blood due to sexual intercourse – וְרָאֲתָה דָם מֵחֲמַת תַּשְׁמִישׁ:** The commentaries disagree as to the length of time in which any blood found is considered to be due to intercourse. Some say that it is the amount of time it takes a woman to climb out of bed (*Tur*). Others challenge this opinion based on Rav Ashi's statement and definition on 14b, which is rejected by the Gemara. Therefore they say that it is the time it takes her to extend her hand under the pillow or blanket to remove an examination cloth and wipe herself. This is in accordance with the opinion of Rav Ḥisda there (see *Beit Yosef* and *Shulḥan Arukh, Yoreh De'a* 187:1).

כֵּיצַד בּוֹדֶקֶת אֶת עַצְמָהּ – מְבִיאָה שְׁפוֹפֶרֶת וּבְתוֹכָהּ מִכְחוֹל, וּמוֹךְ מוּנָּח עַל רֹאשׁוֹ, אִם נִמְצָא דָּם עַל רֹאשׁ הַמּוֹךְ – בְּיָדוּעַ שֶׁמִּן הַמָּקוֹר הוּא בָּא, לֹא נִמְצָא דָּם עַל רֹאשׁוֹ – בְּיָדוּעַ שֶׁמִּן הַצְּדָדִין הוּא בָּא.

How does **she examine herself?**[H] **She brings a tube, inside of which** she places a cosmetic **brush**[E] so that it is long enough to reach deeply into her vagina, **and** an absorbent **cloth is placed on the tip** of the brush. She inserts the tube with the brush and cloth within herself and then removes it. **If blood is found on the top of the** absorbent **cloth, it is known that** the blood **comes from the uterus** and she is ritually impure. If **blood is not found on the top** of the cloth, **it is known that** the blood **comes from the sides** of the vaginal walls and she is ritually pure, and she may resume engaging in intercourse with her husband.

וְאִם יֵשׁ לָהּ מַכָּה בְּאוֹתוֹ מָקוֹם – תּוֹלָה בְּמַכָּתָהּ, וְאִם יֵשׁ לָהּ וֶסֶת – תּוֹלָה בְּוִסְתָּהּ.

**And if she has a wound in that place,** i.e., her vagina, **she attributes** the blood **to her wound,** and she is ritually pure, as it is assumed to not be uterine blood. **And if she has a** fixed menstrual **cycle,**[H] i.e., she does not bleed every time she engages in intercourse with her husband, but only at fixed times, **she attributes** the blood **to her** fixed menstrual **cycle,**[N] and she is permitted to engage in intercourse at other times.

וְאִם הָיָה דַּם מַכָּתָהּ מְשׁוּנֶּה מִדַּם רְאִיָּיתָהּ – אֵינָהּ תּוֹלָה. וְנֶאֱמֶנֶת אִשָּׁה לוֹמַר ״מַכָּה יֵשׁ לִי בַּמָּקוֹר שֶׁמִּמֶּנָּה דָּם יוֹצֵא״, דִּבְרֵי רַבִּי.

**And if the blood of her wound differed from the blood that she sees**[H] due to sexual intercourse, **she may not attribute** the blood to her wound. **And a woman is deemed credible to say: I have a wound in my uterus,**[H] **from where** the **blood is emerging.** This is **the statement of Rabbi** Yehuda HaNasi.

רַבָּן שִׁמְעוֹן בֶּן גַּמְלִיאֵל אוֹמֵר: דַּם מַכָּה הַבָּא מִן הַמָּקוֹר – טָמֵא. וְרַבּוֹתֵינוּ הֵעִידוּ עַל דַּם הַמַּכָּה הַבָּא מִן הַמָּקוֹר שֶׁהוּא טָהוֹר.

**Rabban Shimon ben Gamliel says: Blood of a wound that comes from the uterus is ritually impure** as a primary category of impurity. Although this blood does not render it prohibited for her to engage in intercourse with her husband, it does render her impure with regard to eating ritually pure food. **But our Sages testified** that they had a tradition **with regard to the blood of a wound that comes from the uterus, that it is ritually pure.**

מַאי בֵּינַיְיהוּ? אֲמַר עוּלָּא: מָקוֹר מְקוֹמוֹ טָמֵא אִיכָּא בֵּינַיְיהוּ.

The Gemara asks: **What is** the difference **between** the opinion of those Sages and the opinion of Rabban Shimon ben Gamliel? **Ulla said:** The difference **between them is** whether the **place of** a woman's **uterus is impure,** which means that any blood that passes through there is impure, even if it is blood from a wound. According to Rabban Shimon ben Gamliel, even the blood of a wound becomes impure if it passes through the uterus, whereas those Sages hold that only blood that originates in the uterus is impure.

**NOTES**

She attributes it to her fixed menstrual cycle – תּוֹלָה בְּוִסְתָּהּ: Rashi explains that she has a fixed cycle of experiencing bleeding as a result of intercourse. For example, she discharges blood due to intercourse only on certain days of the month or at certain intervals. In such cases, she may attribute the blood to that day of the month, or that interval, and it is prohibited for her to engage in intercourse with her husband on that date. At all other times she is permitted to engage in intercourse with her husband.

**BACKGROUND**

Tube inside of which she places a cosmetic brush – שְׁפוֹפֶרֶת וּבְתוֹכָהּ מִכְחוֹל: The cosmetic brush was used to apply kohl, a dark blue or black color extracted from the sulfide mineral stibnite, $SS_3$, sometimes referred to as antimonite. In antiquity, the crystals of the mineral were ground up and used by women for painting their eyelashes, eyebrows, and eyelids, thereby accenting their eyes and giving the impression that their eyes were larger than they actually were. Kohl was also used for healing the eyes. Kohl was normally kept in a thin tube and removed with a cosmetic brush. In this passage, the Gemara is probably not referring to the tube normally used to store the kohl brush, but a piece of metal folded *ad hoc* into a tube open at both ends.

Egyptian kohl tube sculpted as a monkey holding onto a palm tree

**HALAKHA**

How does she examine herself – כֵּיצַד בּוֹדֶקֶת אֶת עַצְמָהּ: How does a woman examine herself to determine whether she experiences bleeding due to intercourse or not? She takes a hollow tube of lead, or any other metal (*Shakh*), with the end folded inside to make it smooth, in accordance with the opinion of Shmuel, and she puts a cosmetic brush inside with an absorbent cloth on the end. She inserts this to the furthest point reached during intercourse, based on her assessment (*Shakh*). If there is blood on the cloth, it is clear that the blood comes from the uterus, and she is impure. If there is no blood on the cloth it is clear that the blood found after intercourse is from the vaginal walls and she is permitted to engage in intercourse with her husband. The Rema writes that even nowadays one may rely on this examination (Rambam *Sefer Kedusha, Hilkhot Issurei Bia* 4:22; *Shulḥan Arukh, Yoreh De'a* 187:2).

If she has a wound in that place…if she has a fixed menstrual cycle – אִם יֵשׁ לָהּ מַכָּה בְּאוֹתוֹ מָקוֹם...אִם יֵשׁ לָהּ וֶסֶת: The principle that a woman who experiences bleeding due to intercourse is forbidden to her husband forever applies only when she cannot attribute the blood to any other source. But if she engaged in intercourse just before the fixed time for her menstruation she may attribute the blood to menstruation. Similarly, if she has a bleeding wound and feels that it is bleeding (*Baḥ*) she may attribute it to her wound. The Rema writes that if a woman has a fixed time when her menstrual cycle usually begins, and she bleeds at a time when she is not expecting her menstrual cycle, she may attribute the bleeding to the wound even if it is not known that blood comes from this wound. He also writes that in the case of a woman who does not have a fixed time for her menstrual cycle to begin, and it is uncertain whether this blood is coming from the uterus or the vaginal walls, she may also be lenient due to the compounded uncertainty: The blood may come from the vaginal walls and it may come from the uterus, and even if it comes from the uterus it may come from the wound. At a time when she is expecting the onset of her fixed menstrual cycle, or thirty days after the onset of her previous menstruation, she may not attribute the blood to her wound, because if she does so she will never become impure. If she finds only a blood stain, she may attribute it to her wound in any event (Rambam *Sefer Kedusha, Hilkhot Issurei Bia* 4:20; *Shulḥan Arukh, Yoreh De'a* 187:4–5).

If the blood of her wound differed from the blood that she sees – הָיָה דַּם מַכָּתָהּ מְשׁוּנֶּה מִדַּם רְאִיָּיתָהּ: If the blood of her wound is different in appearance from the blood resulting from intercourse, and she sees blood that has the appearance of blood resulting from intercourse, she may not attribute it to her wound (Rambam *Sefer Kedusha, Hilkhot Issurei Bia* 4:20; *Shulḥan Arukh, Yoreh De'a* 187:5).

I have a wound in my uterus – מַכָּה יֵשׁ לִי בַּמָּקוֹר: A woman is deemed credible if she says that she has an internal wound in her uterus that is the source of the blood. She is permitted to engage in intercourse with her husband even if blood emerges from her while engaging in intercourse. This is in accordance with the *baraita*. Some authorities do not accept this *halakha*. If there is an additional possible reason to be lenient one can certainly rely upon this *halakha* (Rambam *Sefer Kedusha, Hilkhot Issurei Bia* 4:20; *Shulḥan Arukh, Yoreh De'a* 187:6 and *Pitḥei Teshuva* there).

שְׁפוֹפֶרֶת, אַפְגּוּרֵי מְפַגְּרָא לָהּ! אָמַר שְׁמוּאֵל: בִּשְׁפוֹפֶרֶת שֶׁל אֵבָר, וּפִיהָ רָצוּף לְתוֹכָהּ.

With regard to the *baraita* that states that the test for a woman who experiences bleeding due to sexual intercourse is to insert **a tube,** the Gemara asks: But won't a tube **scratch her** and cause her to bleed regardless? **Shmuel said:** The *baraita* is referring **to a tube of lead, and the mouth,** i.e., the end that is inserted, **is folded inward** so that it will not scratch her.

אֲמַר לֵיהּ רֵישׁ לָקִישׁ לְרַבִּי יוֹחָנָן: וְתִבְדּוֹק עַצְמָהּ בְּבִיאָה שְׁלִישִׁית שֶׁל בַּעַל הָרִאשׁוֹן? אֲמַר לֵיהּ: לְפִי שֶׁאֵין כָּל הָאֶצְבָּעוֹת שָׁווֹת.

The *baraita* says that if a woman experiences bleeding on three occasions due to intercourse with her husband he must divorce her. **Reish Lakish said to Rabbi Yoḥanan: But let her examine herself after the third** act of **intercourse with her first husband,**[H] so that he need not divorce her. Rabbi Yoḥanan **said to him:** It is preferable for her not to test herself and risk becoming forbidden to all men and instead to be divorced and remarry another, **because not all fingers,** i.e., penises, **are equal.** Since it is possible that sexual intercourse with her second husband might not cause her to bleed, she should not risk becoming forbidden to all men by performing the examination.

אֲמַר לֵיהּ: וְתִבְדּוֹק עַצְמָהּ בְּבִיאָה רִאשׁוֹנָה שֶׁל בַּעַל שְׁלִישִׁי? לְפִי שֶׁאֵין כָּל הַכֹּחוֹת שָׁווֹת.

Reish Lakish further **said to** Rabbi Yoḥanan: Why does she examine herself only after the third time she experiences bleeding due to sexual intercourse with her third husband? **But let her examine herself after the first** act of **intercourse with her third husband.** After the first occurrence this woman already has a presumptive status that all acts of intercourse cause her to bleed. Rabbi Yoḥanan answered: She does not perform the examination then, **because not all forces are equal.** It is possible that the manner in which the couple has intercourse causes her to bleed, and therefore it is only after three times that she has a presumptive status of bleeding after every act of intercourse.

הַהִיא דַּאֲתַאי לְקַמֵּיהּ דְּרַבִּי, אֲמַר לֵיהּ לְאַבְדָּן: זִיל בְּעָתָהּ. אֲזַל בְּעָתָהּ, וְנָפַל מִמֶּנָּה חֲרָרַת דָּם. אָמַר רַבִּי: נִתְרַפְּאָה זֹאת.

The Gemara relates: There was **a certain** woman who experienced bleeding due to sexual intercourse **who came before Rabbi** Yehuda HaNasi and asked him what she should do. Rabbi Yehuda HaNasi **said to** the Sage **Abdon,**[P] who was present at the time: **Go** and suddenly **frighten** this woman. Abdon **went** and **frightened her, and a mass** of congealed **blood fell from her**[H] vagina. **Rabbi** Yehuda HaNasi **said: This** woman is now **cured.** She will no longer experience bleeding due to sexual intercourse, as this mass of blood was the source of the blood.

הַהִיא אִתְּתָא דַּאֲתַאי לְקַמֵּיהּ דְּמָר שְׁמוּאֵל, אֲמַר לֵיהּ לְרַב דִּימִי בַּר יוֹסֵף: זִיל בְּעָתָהּ! אֲזַל בְּעָתָהּ, וְלָא נְפַל מִמֶּנָּה וְלָא מִידֵּי. אֲמַר שְׁמוּאֵל: זוֹ – מְמַלְּאָה וְנוֹפֶצֶת הִיא, וְכָל הַמְמַלְּאָה וְנוֹפֶצֶת – אֵין לָהּ תַּקָּנָה.

The Gemara relates a similar incident: There was **a certain** woman who experienced bleeding due to sexual intercourse **who came before Shmuel.** Shmuel **said to Rav Dimi bar Yosef: Go** and **frighten** this woman. Rav Dimi **went** and **frightened her, but nothing fell from her at all. Shmuel said: This** woman **is filled** with blood, **which falls** out of her during intercourse. **And any** woman who **is filled** with blood **that falls** out during intercourse **has no cure.**

**PERSONALITIES**

**Abdon – אַבְדָּן:** Also referred to as Avidan, his name is an abbreviated version of the name Abba Yudan. He was a student of Rabbi Yehuda HaNasi, with whom he had a close relationship, and Abdon often served as the one who repeated and disseminated Rabbi Yehuda HaNasi's lectures. Therefore, he was able to transmit many statements in the name of Rabbi Yehuda HaNasi of which other Sages were unaware. Considered to be one of the last *tanna'im*, Avidan was widely recognized as a wise and pious man. A series of tragic events befell him near the end of his life, when he was afflicted with leprosy and his two sons drowned. The Sages saw this as divine punishment for insulting Rabbi Yishmael, the son of Rabbi Yosei, although that too was performed in his zeal to defend his rabbi's honor. Isolated statements are cited in his name in the Talmud and midrash, and the Jerusalem Talmud cites a *halakha* in his name.

**HALAKHA**

**The third act of intercourse with her first husband – בְּבִיאָה שְׁלִישִׁית שֶׁל בַּעַל הָרִאשׁוֹן:** If a woman wishes to examine herself while still married to her first husband in order to determine whether the blood resulting from intercourse is uterine blood, she may do so, and if the examination indicates that the blood is from the vaginal walls, she remains permitted to him. If she examines herself in the required manner and finds blood from her uterus on the cloth, she is forbidden to everyone. Some say that she is forbidden to the first husband after the third time of experiencing bleeding during intercourse with him even if she examines herself. The Rema writes that one may rely on the first opinion and be lenient. If a woman feels pain during intercourse, all agree that she may rely on the examination and remain married to her first husband (*Shulḥan Arukh*, *Yoreh De'a* 187:3, and *Shakh* there).

**He frightened her and a mass of blood fell from her – בְּעָתָהּ וְנָפַל מִמֶּנָּה חֲרָרַת דָּם:** If a woman experienced bleeding due to sexual intercourse and then received a sudden fright, causing a clot of blood to come out of her, she is considered to be cured and is permitted to her husband. If she subsequently bleeds as a result of intercourse again, even once, it is clear that she has not been cured. Nowadays this cure is not relied upon, but if she did try this cure, her husband is not required to divorce her until she has engaged in intercourse once more with her husband and bleeds again (*Shulḥan Arukh*, *Yoreh De'a* 187:9).

**NOTES**

**Jewish women were stringent with themselves** – בְּנוֹת יִשְׂרָאֵל הֶחְמִירוּ עַל עַצְמָן: The early commentaries write that this was initially a custom that Jewish women accepted upon themselves; it was not based on a decree of the Sages. They wished to be stringent and add sanctity even when they were ritually pure. Once this custom was accepted, it became prohibited to transgress it, and it took on the force of Torah law (Rashba; Rivash). This is comparable to the stringency not to eat the fat adjacent to the sciatic nerve, which is technically permitted. Once the Jewish people chose to be stringent in this regard, this fat became entirely forbidden (see *Hullin* 91a).

הַהִיא דַּאֲתַאי לְקַמֵּיהּ דְּרַבִּי יוֹחָנָן, דְּכָל אֵימַת דַּהֲוַת סָלְקָא מִטְּבִילַת מִצְוָה הֲוַת קָחָזְיָא דָּמָא. אֲמַר לַהּ: שֶׁמָּא דִּימַת עִירֵיךְ עָלְתָה בֵּיךְ, לְכִי וְהִבָּעֲלִי לוֹ עַל גַּבֵּי הַנָּהָר.

The Gemara relates another incident: There was **a certain** woman **who came before Rabbi Yoḥanan** and told him **that every time she emerged from immersion** in a ritual bath, after completing the **mitzva** of purifying herself for her husband, **she would see blood** before she engaged in intercourse with him. Rabbi Yoḥanan **said to her: Perhaps the gossip** of the women **in your city,** who are jealous of the love between you and your husband, **has reached you,** and this evil eye causes you to bleed before you engage in intercourse. **Go and** immerse in the river and **engage in intercourse with** your husband **on the bank of the river,** so that the other women will not see you leaving the ritual bath and gossip about you.

אִיכָּא דְּאָמַר, אֲמַר לַהּ: תְּגַלִּי לְחַבְרוֹתַיִךְ. כִּי הֵיכִי דְּתַהֲווּ עֲלָךְ לְהַךְ גִּיסָא – נִתְהֲווּ עֲלָךְ לְהַךְ גִּיסָא. וְאִיכָּא דְּאָמַר, אֲמַר לַהּ: גַּלִּי לְחַבְרוֹתַיִךְ, כִּי הֵיכִי דְּלִבְעוּ עֲלַיִךְ רַחֲמִים. דְּתַנְיָא: ״וְטָמֵא טָמֵא יִקְרָא״ – צָרִיךְ לְהוֹדִיעַ צַעֲרוֹ לָרַבִּים, וְרַבִּים מְבַקְּשִׁים עָלָיו רַחֲמִים.

**Some say** that Rabbi Yoḥanan **said to her: Reveal** this fact **to your friends, so that** those women **who were** against **you on this side,** and gossiped about you, **will be** with **you on that side,** and be kind to you. **And some say** that Rabbi Yoḥanan **said to her: Reveal** this fact **to your friends, in order that they will pray for mercy for you, as it is taught** in a *baraita* discussing the verse: "And the leper in whom the mark is, his clothes shall be ripped and the hair of his head shall grow long and he will put a covering upon his upper lip **and will cry: Impure, impure**" (Leviticus 13:45). The leper publicizes the fact that he is ritually impure, as he **must announce his pain to the masses, and** then **the masses will pray for mercy on his** behalf.

אֲמַר רַב יוֹסֵף: הֲוָה עוּבְדָא בְּפוּמְבְּדִיתָא – וְאִתַּסִּי.

**Rav Yosef said: There was** a similar **incident in Pumbedita** of a woman who experienced bleeding immediately after immersing in a ritual bath, and she followed the advice given by Rabbi Yoḥanan **and she was cured.**

אָמַר רַב יוֹסֵף, אָמַר רַב יְהוּדָה, אָמַר רַב, הִתְקִין רַבִּי בַּשָּׂדוֹת: רָאֲתָה יוֹם אֶחָד – תֵּשֵׁב שִׁשָּׁה וְהוּא,

§ **Rav Yosef says** that **Rav Yehuda says** that **Rav says: Rabbi** Yehuda HaNasi **decreed** that **in the fields,** i.e., in those distant places where there were no Torah scholars and whose residents were not well versed in the *halakhot* of menstruating women and did not know how to distinguish between the days of menstruation and the days of *ziva*, if **she saw** blood on **one day, she must sit** and count **six** days **and that** first day. She must observe six clean days without a discharge despite the possibility that she might have experienced bleeding only in her period of *ziva*, in which case she would be impure for only one day.

שְׁנַיִם – תֵּשֵׁב שִׁשָּׁה וְהֵן, שְׁלֹשָׁה – תֵּשֵׁב שִׁבְעָה נְקִיִּים.

If she experiences bleeding for **two** days, **she must sit** and count **six** days **and** both of **those** first two days, for a total of eight days, in case the first day on which she bled was the last day of *ziva*, while the next day was the first day of her menstruation period. If she experiences bleeding for **three** days **she must sit** and count **seven clean** days, as she might be a greater *zava*, who must count seven clean days.

אָמַר רַבִּי זֵירָא: בְּנוֹת יִשְׂרָאֵל הֶחְמִירוּ עַל עַצְמָן, שֶׁאֲפִילּוּ רוֹאוֹת טִפַּת דָּם כְּחַרְדָּל – יוֹשְׁבוֹת עָלֶיהָ שִׁבְעָה נְקִיִּים.

The Gemara cites a related statement. **Rabbi Zeira says: Jewish women were stringent with themselves**[NH] to the extent **that even if they see a drop of blood** the size **of a mustard** seed, they **sit seven clean** days **for it.** By Torah law, a woman who experiences menstrual bleeding waits seven days in total before immersing, regardless of whether she experienced bleeding on those days. If she experiences bleeding during the eleven days when she is not expected to experience menstrual bleeding, she is a lesser *zava* and waits one day without bleeding and then immerses. The Jewish women accepted upon themselves the stringency that if they experience any bleeding whatsoever, they treat it as the blood of a greater *zava*, which obligates one to count seven clean days before immersing (see Leviticus 15:25).

**HALAKHA**

**Jewish women were stringent with themselves** – בְּנוֹת יִשְׂרָאֵל הֶחְמִירוּ עַל עַצְמָן: Jewish women accepted a stringency upon themselves such that if a woman sees even a tiny drop of blood the size of a mustard seed, or smaller (*Shakh*), she counts seven clean days before immersing. This applies even if she sees the blood during her days of expected menstruation. She counts seven clean days as if she were a greater *zava*. She immerses on the night after the seventh day, and only afterward is she permitted to engage in intercourse with her husband (Rambam *Sefer Kedusha, Hilkhot Issurei Bia* 11:4; *Shulḥan Arukh, Yoreh De'a* 183).

אַדְבְּרֵיהּ רָבָא לְרַב שְׁמוּאֵל וְדָרַשׁ: קָשְׁתָה שְׁנֵי יָמִים וְלַשְּׁלִישִׁי הִפִּילָה – תֵּשֵׁב שִׁבְעָה נְקִיִּים. קָסָבַר: אֵין קִשּׁוּי לִנְפָלִים, וְאִי אֶפְשָׁר לִפְתִיחַת הַקֶּבֶר בְּלֹא דָּם.

**Rava authorized**[B] **Rav Shmuel, and he taught:** If a pregnant woman experienced **labor pains** for **two days, and on the third** day **she miscarried, she must sit** and count **seven clean** days. The Gemara explains that Rava **holds** that the principle that blood that emerges while the woman experiences **labor pains** is not ritually impure does **not** apply **to miscarriages. And** Rava further maintains that **it is impossible for the womb to open without blood** emerging. Therefore, when she miscarried she must have experienced a flow of blood, even if she did not notice it.

אֲמַר לֵיהּ רַב פַּפָּא לְרָבָא: מַאי אִרְיָא, קָשְׁתָה שְׁנֵי יָמִים – אֲפִילּוּ מַשֶּׁהוּ בְּעָלְמָא! דְּהָא אָמַר רַבִּי זֵירָא: בְּנוֹת יִשְׂרָאֵל הֶחְמִירוּ עַל עַצְמָן, שֶׁאֲפִילּוּ רוֹאוֹת טִפַּת דָּם כַּחַרְדָּל – יוֹשְׁבוֹת עָלֶיהָ שִׁבְעָה נְקִיִּים!

**Rav Pappa said to Rava:** For **what** reason did you teach this *halakha* **specifically** with regard to a woman who experiences **labor pains** for **two days? Even** if she **merely** discharges **any amount** of blood she should be impure, **as Rabbi Zeira says: The Jewish women were stringent with themselves** to the extent **that even if they see a drop of blood of** the size of a **mustard** seed, that woman **sits seven clean** days **for it.** Since it is impossible for the womb to open without the emergence of blood, when this woman miscarried there must have been blood, and therefore she must count seven clean days.

אֲמַר לֵיהּ: אָמִינָא לָךְ אִיסּוּרָא, וְאַתְּ אָמְרַתְּ מִנְהָגָא? הֵיכָא דְּאַחְמוּר – אַחְמוּר, הֵיכָא דְּלָא אַחְמוּר – לָא אַחְמוּר.

Rava **said to** Rav Pappa: **I speak to you** of **a prohibition,** i.e., that by Torah law a woman who experiences difficulty in childbirth for two days and on the third miscarries must count seven clean days as a greater *zava,* **and you speak to me** of **a custom,** a mere stringency. The stringency you mention does not apply in this case. **Where** the Jewish women **were stringent, they were stringent,** i.e., if they saw a drop of blood the size of a mustard seed. **Where they were not stringent,** i.e., in a case of blood due to labor, **they were not stringent.** By contrast, in the case I described the woman is obligated to count seven clean days by Torah law.

(תְּבָעוּהָ, נֶתֶר, בְּחַמִּין, לִטְבּוֹל, קְמָטִים, עַל גַּבֵּי, נָמָל, סִימָן). אָמַר רָבָא: תְּבָעוּהָ לִינָּשֵׂא וְנִתְפַּיְּיסָה – צְרִיכָה שֶׁתֵּשֵׁב שִׁבְעָה נְקִיִּים.

The Gemara provides **a mnemonic**[B] for the following discussions: **One who proposed to her; natron; with hot** water; **to immerse; folds; on top of; a port. Rava says:** With regard to **one who proposed marriage to** a woman **and she accepted it,**[H] the emotional excitement might have caused her to have a flow of menstrual blood, which would render her ritually impure and prohibit her from engaging in intercourse. Even if she was unaware of any flow, she must consider the possibility that it occurred. Therefore, to purify herself **she must wait seven** consecutive days that are **clean** from any flow of menstrual blood and then immerse in a ritual bath. Only after that process may she marry.

רָבִינָא אִיעֲסַק לֵיהּ לִבְרֵיהּ בֵּי רַב חֲנִינָא, אֲמַר לֵיהּ: סָבַר לֵיהּ מָר לְמִכְתַּב כְּתוּבָּה לְאַרְבָּעָה יוֹם? אֲמַר לֵיהּ: אִין. כִּי מְטָא לְאַרְבָּעָה – נְטַר עַד אַרְבָּעָה אַחֲרִינָא, אִיעַכַּב שִׁבְעָה יוֹמֵי בָּתַר הַהוּא יוֹמָא.

The Gemara cites a related incident: **Ravina arranged for his son** to marry into **the family of Rav Ḥanina,** i.e., to marry Rav Ḥanina's daughter. Rav Ḥanina **said to** Ravina: **Does the Master hold** that it is appropriate **to write the marriage contract** as stating that the wedding will take place **in four days,** i.e., on Wednesday? Ravina **said: Yes. When** the **fourth** day, i.e., Wednesday **arrived, he waited until another fourth** day before marrying her, until the following Wednesday, i.e., **he delayed seven days after that day** when he had planned to marry her.

**BACKGROUND**

**Authorized – אַדְבְּרֵיהּ:** This term is used in several places in the context of the relationship between a leading Torah scholar and the Exilarch or members of his household. The *ge'onim* explain that the Sage would authorize the Exilarch to teach matters of *halakha* and homiletics in public. Rabbeinu Ḥananel adds that the Sage would assist in the preparation of the basic points of the lecture.

**Mnemonic – סִימָן:** Because the Talmud was studied orally for many generations, mnemonics were a necessary memory aid for a series of statements to remember the order in which they were taught.

**HALAKHA**

**One who proposed marriage to a woman and she accepted it – תְּבָעוּהָ לִינָּשֵׂא וְנִתְפַּיְּיסָה:** If a woman accepted an offer of marriage she must wait and count seven clean days regardless of whether she was a minor or an adult at the time. This is in accordance with the opinion of Rava. This applies even if she examined herself at the moment she accepted the offer and found herself to be pure. The concern is that due to her desire to get married there may have been a drop of blood the size of a mustard seed that she did not notice. She begins counting the seven clean days from the day after she accepted the offer of marriage, and she is not obligated to perform an examination marking the first step in her transition from ritual impurity to ritual purity. She should examine herself during the seven days, ideally every day (Rema). If she examined herself only once during the seven days it is sufficient after the fact. Some say that nowadays she requires an examination marking the first step in her transition from impurity to purity even if she is a virgin, and she also requires an examination every day (Rambam *Sefer Kedusha, Hilkhot Issurei Bia* 11:9; *Shulḥan Arukh, Yoreh De'a* 192:1, and *Shakh* and Maharshal there).

אֲמַר לֵיהּ: מַאי הַאי? אֲמַר לֵיהּ: לָא סְבַר לָהּ מָר לְהָא דְּרָבָא, דַּאֲמַר רָבָא: תְּבָעוּהָ לִינָּשֵׂא וְנִתְפַּיְּיסָה – צְרִיכָה לֵישֵׁב שִׁבְעָה נְקִיִּים. אֲמַר לֵיהּ: אֵימַר דַּאֲמַר רָבָא – בִּגְדוֹלָה דְּקָחָזְיָא דָּמָא, אֲבָל בִּקְטַנָּה דְּלָא חָזְיָא דָּמָא – מִי אֲמַר?

Rav Ḥanina **said to** Ravina: **What is this?** Why did you delay the wedding by an extra week? Ravina **said to** Rav Ḥanina: **Doesn't the Master hold in accordance with this** statement **of Rava, as Rava said:** With regard to **one who proposed marriage to** a woman **and she accepted** it, **she must wait seven** consecutive days that are **clean** from any flow of menstrual blood and then immerse in a ritual bath? Rav Ḥanina **said to** Ravina: One can **say that Rava said** this statement **with regard to an adult woman, who has seen** menstrual **blood. But did** Rava actually **say** this **with regard to a minor girl, who has not** yet **seen** menstrual **blood?**

אֲמַר לֵיהּ: בְּפֵירוּשׁ אֲמַר רָבָא לָא שְׁנָא גְּדוֹלָה לָא שְׁנָא קְטַנָּה. גְּדוֹלָה טַעְמָא מַאי? מִשּׁוּם דְּמִחַמְּדָא, קְטַנָּה נַמִי מְחַמְּדָא.

Ravina **said to** Rav Ḥanina: **Rava said explicitly** that there is **no difference** whether she is **an adult woman** and **no difference** whether she is **a minor girl. What is the reason** that **an adult woman** must wait for seven days? She must wait **because she desires** to marry her husband, and this might cause her to have a flow of blood. **A minor girl also desires** to marry her husband, which could cause a flow of blood.

אָמַר רָבָא: אִשָּׁה

§ **Rava says: A woman** who is about to immerse herself in a ritual bath for purification

Perek **X**
Daf **66** Amud **b**

לֹא תָּחוֹף לֹא בַּנֶּתֶר וְלֹא בַּחוֹל. בַּנֶּתֶר – מִשּׁוּם דְּמִקְטַף, וּבַחוֹל – מִשּׁוּם דְּמִסְרִיךְ.

**may not wash**[N] her hair **with natron or with sand.**[H] The reason she may not wash her hair **with natron** is **because** natron **pulls out** hair, and that hair may remain sitting on her head and serve as an interposition between her and the water of the ritual bath. **And** similarly, she may not wash her hair **with sand, because it sticks** to her hair and it also serves as an interposition.

וַאֲמַר אַמֵּימָר מִשְּׁמֵיהּ דְּרָבָא: אִשָּׁה לֹא תָּחוֹף אֶלָּא בְּחַמִּין, אֲבָל לֹא בְּצוֹנֵן, וַאֲפִילּוּ בְּחַמֵּי חַמָּה. צוֹנֵן מַאי טַעְמָא לָא – מִשּׁוּם דְּקָרִירִי, וּמַשְׁרוּ מַזְיָיא.

**And Ameimar said in the name of Rava: A woman washes** her hair **only with hot** water,[H] **but not with cold** water. **But** she may wash her hair **even with hot** water that was heated **in the sun.**[N] **What is the reason** that she may **not** wash her hair with **cold** water? **Because it is cold and** causes the **hair to harden,**[N] and the dirt will remain in the hair.

וְאָמַר רָבָא: לְעוֹלָם יְלַמֵּד אָדָם בְּתוֹךְ בֵּיתוֹ שֶׁתְּהֵא אִשָּׁה מְדִיחָה בֵּית קְמָטֶיהָ בַּמַּיִם. מֵיתִיבֵי: בֵּית הַקְּמָטִים וּבֵית הַסְּתָרִים אֵינָן צְרִיכִין לְבִיאַת מַיִם!

**And Rava says: A man should always teach in his house that a woman should rinse any place with creases,**[H] e.g., her armpits, **in water** before she immerses in a ritual bath, to ensure that they are clean. The Gemara **raises an objection** from a *baraita*: **Places with creases and** any **concealed part** of the body **do not require immersion in water.** In other words, the immersion is valid even if the water does not touch those parts of the body. If so, why must she rinse them before immersing?

## NOTES

**May not wash – לֹא תָּחוֹף:** Although Rava does not specify which part of the body he is referring to, Rashi explains that this is referring specifically to washing her hair. Rashi does not state whether this applies only to the hair of a woman's head or also to hair on other parts of her body. Some claim that Rashi is referring to the entire body, not only the hair (*Tosafot*, citing *Maḥzor Rabbeinu Shemariah*), while the Ritva explains that it is referring to any hair on her head or body. Others say that it means only the hair of her head (Rabbeinu Tam, cited in *Tosafot* here and in *Bava Kamma* 82a; Ramban; Rashba). The custom is for women to wash their entire body, and one must keep the prevalent custom (Ramban).

**Not with cold water but even with hot water heated in the sun – לֹא בְּצוֹנֵן וַאֲפִילּוּ בְּחַמֵּי חַמָּה:** Some explain these words to mean that she may wash in water heated in the sun, but she may not wash in cold water (*Baḥ*, Rashi). Others had a slightly different version of the text that prohibits washing in water that was heated in the sun (Rabbeinu Ḥananel, cited by the Rosh; *Tosefot HaRosh*).

**Because it is cold and causes the hair to harden – מִשּׁוּם דְּקָרִירִי, וּמַשְׁרוּ מַזְיָיא:** Some commentaries write that a woman should not wash her hair in cold water because it causes the hair to become hard and does not remove the dirt (Rashi). Others claim that cold water causes the hairs to stick to one another and become knotted. These knots are considered an interposition that invalidates the immersion (Rambam *Sefer Tahara, Hilkhot Mikvaot* 2:18; *Tur*). A practical difference between the two opinions depends on if she first washes her hair with hot water and then washes it with cold water. According to the first opinion this would be allowed, because the dirt would be removed by the hot water. According to the second opinion this would not be allowed, because the hairs will remain knotted.

## HALAKHA

**She may not wash with natron or with sand – לֹא תָּחוֹף לֹא בַּנֶּתֶר וְלֹא בַּחוֹל:** A woman may not wash her hair before immersion with natron, because it damages the hair and causes it to become tangled. Similarly, she may not wash her hair with any other substance that tangles the hair. This is in accordance with the opinion of Rava. The Rema writes that this is the *halakha ab initio*. But if she did wash her hair with natron or a similar substance and checked that her hair was not tangled or knotted, she may immerse (Rambam *Sefer Tahara, Hilkhot Mikvaot* 2:18; *Shulḥan Arukh, Yoreh De'a* 199:2).

**She washes her hair only with hot water, etc. – לֹא תָּחוֹף אֶלָּא בְּחַמִּין וכו׳:** A woman may not wash her hair in cold water before immersion because it causes her hair to become tangled. She must wash her hair in hot water, even if the water was warmed in the sun, in accordance with the opinion of Rava (Rambam *Sefer Tahara, Hilkhot Mikvaot* 2:18; *Shulḥan Arukh, Yoreh De'a* 199:2).

**Place with creases – בֵּית הַקְּמָטִים:** Women should wash any body parts with creases before immersing. Even though it is not required for the water of the ritual bath to come into contact with the internal parts of her body or those creased parts, it must be possible for the water to reach those parts. Therefore there may not be any interposition there. This is in accordance with the opinion of Rava (Rambam *Sefer Tahara, Hilkhot Mikvaot* 1:10; *Shulḥan Arukh, Yoreh De'a* 199:1).

נְהִי דְּבִיאַת מַיִם – לָא בָּעֵינַן, מָקוֹם הָרָאוּי לְבִיאַת מַיִם – בָּעֵינַן, כִּדְרַבִּי זֵירָא. דְּאָמַר רַבִּי זֵירָא: כׇּל הָרָאוּי לְבִילָּה – אֵין בִּילָּה מְעַכֶּבֶת בּוֹ, וְשֶׁאֵין רָאוּי לְבִילָּה – בִּילָּה מְעַכֶּבֶת בּוֹ.

The Gemara answers: **Granted that they do not require immersion in water,** but **we require** that they must be **a place that is suitable for immersion in water.** This is **in accordance with** the opinion **of Rabbi Zeira, as Rabbi Zeira says:** For **any** amount of flour **suitable for mingling**[H] with oil in a meal offering, **mingling is not indispensable for it,**[N] i.e., it is valid even if it is not mixed. **But** for **any** amount of flour **not suitable for mingling,** e.g., if the quantity of flour is so great that the ingredients cannot be properly mixed, **mingling is indispensable for it,** and such a meal offering is invalid. This teaches a halakhic principle: There are certain actions that prevent the fulfillment of a mitzva if they are impossible, even if the actual performance of those actions are not indispensable to the mitzva.

אָמַר רָבִין בַּר רַב אַדָּא, אָמַר רַבִּי יִצְחָק: מַעֲשֶׂה בְּשִׁפְחָתוֹ שֶׁל רַבִּי שֶׁטָּבְלָה וְעָלְתָה, וְנִמְצָא לָהּ עֶצֶם חוֹצֵץ בֵּין שִׁינֶּיהָ, וְהִצְרִיכָהּ רַבִּי טְבִילָה אַחֶרֶת.

**Ravin bar Rav Adda says** that **Rabbi Yitzḥak says:** There was **an incident involving a maidservant of Rabbi** Yehuda HaNasi[P] **who immersed** herself, **and she ascended** from her immersion **and a bone was found interposed between her teeth,**[H] **and Rabbi** Yehuda HaNasi **required her** to perform **another immersion.** This demonstrates that according to Rabbi Yehuda HaNasi one may not have a foreign object even inside one's mouth.

וְאָמַר רָבָא: טָבְלָה וְעָלְתָה וְנִמְצָא עָלֶיהָ דָּבָר חוֹצֵץ, אִם סָמוּךְ לַחֲפִיפָה טָבְלָה – אֵינָהּ צְרִיכָה לָחוֹף וְלִטְבּוֹל, וְאִם לָאו – צְרִיכָה לָחוֹף וְלִטְבּוֹל.

**And Rava says:** If a woman **immersed** in a ritual bath **and ascended** from the water, **and** she then **found on her** hair **an item that interposes** between her and the water, what is the *halakha*? **If she immersed soon** after **washing** her hair, **she does not need to wash** her hair **and immerse** in the ritual bath a second time, as it can be assumed that this item was not there when she immersed, since her hair had been cleaned. **But if** she did **not** wash her hair immediately before immersing, **she must wash** her hair **and immerse** in the ritual bath a second time.

אִיכָּא דְּאָמְרִי: אִם בְּאוֹתוֹ יוֹם שֶׁחָפְפָה טָבְלָה – אֵינָהּ צְרִיכָה לָחוֹף וְלִטְבּוֹל, וְאִם לָאו – צְרִיכָה לָחוֹף וְלִטְבּוֹל.

**There are** those **who state** a slightly different version of Rava's statement: **If she immersed on the same day that she washed** her hair,[H] **she does not need to wash** her hair **and to immerse** in a ritual bath a second time. **But if** she did **not** wash her hair on the same day that she immersed, **she must wash** her hair **and immerse** in the ritual bath a second time.

### PERSONALITIES

**A maidservant of Rabbi Yehuda HaNasi – שִׁפְחָה שֶׁל רַבִּי:** The maidservant of the household of Rabbi Yehuda HaNasi is mentioned here and in several other contexts in the Gemara. She famously used the purest, most ancient form of the Hebrew language, including words with which the Sages themselves were no longer familiar. Apparently she was an exceptional servant who was raised in the family of the *Nasi*. Her conduct and her witty and wise manner of speech are recounted in the Gemara.

### HALAKHA

**Any amount suitable for mingling – כׇּל הָרָאוּי לְבִילָּה:** One may not bring a meal offering that fills a vessel larger than sixty-tenths of an ephah, because the flour and oil cannot be mixed properly. If one vowed to bring more than sixty-tenths of an ephah of flour he must bring sixty-tenths in one vessel and the remainder in a second vessel. Although one can still fulfill his obligation without mixing, it must be possible to mix the offering, in accordance with the opinion of Rabbi Zeira (Rambam *Sefer Avoda, Hilkhot Ma'aseh HaKorbanot* 17:6).

**A bone was found interposed between her teeth – נִמְצָא לָהּ עֶצֶם חוֹצֵץ בֵּין שִׁינֶּיהָ:** If a woman immerses in a ritual bath and afterward finds an item stuck between her teeth, her immersion is not valid, in accordance with the statement of Rabbi Yehuda HaNasi (Rambam *Sefer Tahara, Hilkhot Mikvaot* 2:13; *Shulḥan Arukh, Yoreh De'a* 198:24–25).

**If she immersed on the same day that she washed her hair, etc. – אִם בְּאוֹתוֹ יוֹם שֶׁחָפְפָה טָבְלָה וכו׳:** If a woman washed her hair, checked her body, and then immersed in a ritual bath, but as she came out she noticed an interposing item on her body, if she immersed during the same day or night in which she washed her hair she does not require another immersion. If she did not immerse during the same day or night in which she washed her hair she must immerse again. The Rema writes that even if she washed her hair immediately before the immersion, but she washed it during the day and immersed at night, it is considered two periods of time and she must immerse again. He adds that according to the Rambam, if she washed and immersed within the same period of time, she immerses again without washing again (Rambam *Sefer Tahara, Hilkhot Mikvaot* 2:17, and see Ra'avad and *Kesef Mishne* there; Shulḥan *Arukh, Yoreh De'a* 199:10, and see *Beur HaGra* there).

### NOTES

**Any amount suitable for mingling, mingling is not indispensable for it – כׇּל הָרָאוּי לְבִילָּה אֵין בִּילָּה מְעַכֶּבֶת בּוֹ:** This *halakha* was stated with regard to one who brings a meal offering comprising more than sixty-tenths of an ephah of flour. The Sages require the flour to be divided into two separate offerings as it is too much to be mixed together in one receptacle. In this context, Rabbi Zeira says that although there is no requirement to actually mix the flour and oil, as an offering that has not been mixed is valid, it must be fit to be mixed thoroughly. If it is impossible in practice to mix the meal offering, it is not valid. This principle is subsequently applied to other areas of *halakha* in that there are cases in which part of a mitzva must be potentially feasible despite the fact that this procedure is not indispensable to the rite. The reasoning is that if it is impossible to perform part of the mitzva, it is as though one actively eliminated that aspect of the mitzva.

מאי בינייהו? איכא בינייהו: למסמך לחפיפה טבילה, למיחף ביממא ולמטבל בליליא.

The Gemara asks: **What** is the practical difference **between** these two versions of Rava's statement? The Gemara answers: The practical difference **between them** is **with regard to washing** her hair **close to immersion.**[N] According to the first version of Rava's statement, she must wash her hair immediately before immersing, whereas according to the second version she has more time. Another difference between the two versions is **with regard to washing** her hair **during the day and immersing at night** immediately afterward. According to the first version of Rava's statement, provided that she washed her hair immediately before immersing, it makes no difference whether or not she washed and immersed on the same day. Conversely, according to the second version she must wash her hair on the same day or night as her immersion.

אמר רבא: אשה לא תעמוד על גבי כלי חרס ותטבול. סבר רב כהנא למימר: טעמא מאי – משום גזירת מרחצאות, הא על גבי סילתא – שפיר דמי.

§ **Rava says: A woman may not stand on top of earthenware utensils** that are submerged in the ritual bath **and immerse.**[H] **Rav Kahana thought to say: What is the reason** for this? It is **because** the Sages issued **a decree** against immersing in this manner, as it appears like immersing in **bathhouses,**[N] i.e., the purpose of the decree is to prevent women from thinking that it is permitted to immerse in a bathhouse, which contains drawn water and is not valid as a ritual bath. It can be inferred from this reasoning that it is **permitted** for a woman to stand **on top of a plank of wood** that is in the ritual bath.

אמר ליה רב חנן מנהרדעא: התם טעמא מאי – משום דבעית, סילתא נמי בעיתא.

**Rav Ḥanan from Neharde'a said to** Rav Kahana that this is not the reason for Rava's statement. Rather, **there,** in the case of submerged earthenware utensils, **what is the reason** that she may not immerse? She may not immerse **because she** will be **afraid** that she might fall off, and consequently she will not immerse herself properly. By the same logic, **she** will **also** be **afraid** when she is standing on top of **a plank of wood,** and therefore this is also prohibited.

אמר רב שמואל בר רב יצחק: אשה לא תטבול

**Rav Shmuel bar Rav Yitzhak says: A woman may not immerse** herself

**NOTES**

**Washing her hair close to immersion – למסמך לחפיפה טבילה:** Some commentaries hold that according to everyone the immersion should be performed immediately after the washing *ab initio*. The Gemara is referring to a case where an interposing item was found on her after she immersed, and the dispute is about in what circumstances can one assume that the interposing item was not on her body during her immersion (*Tosafot*; *Tosefot HaRosh*). Others write that this very issue, whether or not the immersion should be performed immediately after the washing *ab initio*, is in dispute here (Rashba; *Eizehu Mekoman*; see Rashi).

**Because of a decree against immersing that appears like immersing in bathhouses – משום גזירת מרחצאות:** The early commentaries explain that this is based on a mishna (*Mikvaot* 5:2) that prohibits immersing while standing on a bench, due to a decree lest she immerse in a bathhouse. They explain that Rav Kahana is concerned lest a woman come to immerse in drawn water in a bathhouse. He holds that just as the Sages prohibited immersing while standing on a bench, due to the fact that people would sit on benches in the bathhouse, they also prohibited immersion while standing on any other earthenware utensil. Rav Ḥanan of Neharde'a holds that there is no reason to prohibit immersion while standing on any other earthenware utensil, because there is no chance of confusing it with a bathhouse bench. Therefore the reason that it is prohibited for a woman to immerse while standing on an earthenware utensil is that she may be afraid of falling and will therefore not immerse herself properly (*Tosefot HaRosh*).

**HALAKHA**

**She may not stand on top of earthenware utensils and immerse – לא תעמוד על גבי כלי חרס ותטבול:** A woman may not stand on earthenware vessels or a plank of wood when she immerses. This is because the Sages were concerned that she may not immerse properly due to a fear of falling off. If she did immerse while standing on earthenware vessels or a plank of wood, the immersion is valid. This is in accordance with the opinion of Rava, as explained by Rav Ḥanan of Neharde'a (Rambam *Sefer Tahara*, *Hilkhot Mikvaot* 1:11; *Shulḥan Arukh*, *Yoreh De'a* 198:31).

Perek **X**
Daf **67** Amud **a**

בנמל, אף על גב דהשתא ליכא – אימר ברדיוני נפל.

in a port [*banamal*],[LN] where the boats are drawn up onto shore, as there is a lot of mud there, which can stick to her and interpose between her and the water. **Even though now,** after the immersion, **there is no** mud stuck to her feet or body, one can **say** that perhaps **while she walked** back after immersing the mud **fell** off. Since one cannot be certain that there was no mud stuck to her body while she immersed, she may not immerse in a port.

**LANGUAGE**

**Port [*namal*] – נמל:** In some variant readings, this word appears as *lamen*, which is similar to the Greek λιμήν, *limēn*, meaning a port or a place on the shore for boats to anchor, as well as a beach and a border.

**NOTES**

**In a port – בנמל:** There are different versions of the text of the Gemara here and it has various explanations. Some say that it is prohibited to immerse in a port due to the people present there. A woman who immerses in such a place will be concerned that others might see her, which will lead her to immerse hastily and perhaps incorrectly. They explain that the mats placed by Shmuel's father around the site of immersion served as a partition so that nobody could see his daughters immersing (*Tosafot*, citing Rabbeinu Ḥananel).

אֲבוּה דִּשְׁמוּאֵל עֲבַד לִבְנָתֵיהּ מִקְוָואוֹת בְּיוֹמֵי נִיסָן, וּמַפְצֵי בְּיוֹמֵי תִּשְׁרֵי.

The Gemara relates that **Shmuel's father**[P] **prepared ritual baths for his daughters in the days of Nisan,** by digging holes and letting them fill with natural rainwater, **and** he placed **mats**[B] in the Euphrates River **in the days of Tishrei.**[NH] Since the water was shallow and the riverbed was muddy, he placed mats on the riverbed so that they could immerse without getting dirty.

אָמַר רַב גִּידֵּל אָמַר רַב: נָתְנָה תַּבְשִׁיל לִבְנָהּ וְטָבְלָה וְעָלְתָה – לֹא עָלְתָה לָהּ טְבִילָה, אַף עַל גַּב דְּהָשְׁתָּא לֵיכָּא – אֵימַר בִּרְדִיּוֹנֵי נְפַל.

The Gemara cites a similar *halakha* involving the interposition of an item during immersion. **Rav Giddel says** that **Rav says:** If a woman **gave a cooked** dish **to her son, and** afterward she **immersed**[H] in a ritual bath **and ascended** from the ritual bath, the **immersion is ineffective for her.** The reason is that **even though now,** after the immersion, **there is no** food stuck to her body, one can **say** that perhaps **as she walked** back after immersing the food **fell** off. Since one cannot be certain that there was no food stuck to her body while she immersed, she should not handle food immediately before immersing.

אָמַר רָמִי בַּר אַבָּא: הָנֵי רַבְדֵי דְּכוּסִילְתָּא, עַד תְּלָתָא יוֹמֵי – לָא חָיְיצִי, מִכָּאן וְאֵילָךְ – חָיְיצִי.

**Rami bar Abba said:** With regard to **these bloodletting incisions** [*ravdei dekhusilta*],[HL] **until three days** have passed since the bloodletting, when they have not yet formed a hard scab, they do **not interpose** and invalidate an immersion. **From this** point **forward they interpose,** as the scab is too hard for the water to penetrate.

אָמַר מָר עוּקְבָא: לִפְלוּף שֶׁבָּעַיִן, לַח – אֵינוֹ חוֹצֵץ, יָבֵשׁ – חוֹצֵץ. אֵימָתַי נִקְרָא יָבֵשׁ – מִשָּׁעָה שֶׁמַּתְחִיל לְירַק.

**Mar Ukva said:** With regard to **mucus that is in the eye,**[H] if it is **moist, it does not interpose** and invalidate an immersion. But if the mucus is **dry** and hard **it interposes. When is it called dry?** It is called dry **from the time that it begins to turn yellow.**

אָמַר שְׁמוּאֵל: כָּחוֹל שֶׁבְּתוֹךְ הָעַיִן – אֵינוֹ חוֹצֵץ. וְשֶׁעַל גַּבֵּי הָעַיִן – חוֹצֵץ. אִם הָיוּ עֵינֶיהָ פּוֹרְחוֹת – אֲפִילּוּ עַל גַּבֵּי הָעַיִן אֵינוֹ חוֹצֵץ.

**Shmuel says: Eye shadow that is in the eye**[H] **does not interpose**[N] and invalidate an immersion. **But** eye shadow **that is on** or around **the eye interposes.** And **if** the woman's **eyes were** constantly **blinking,** then **even** eye shadow **that is on** or around **the eye does not interpose,** as the constant blinking removes the eye shadow.

## PERSONALITIES

**Shmuel's father – אֲבוּה דִּשְׁמוּאֵל:** Shmuel's father was the *amora* Rabbi Abba bar Abba the Priest, one of the first generation of *amora'im*. In the Babylonian Talmud he is often referred to as the father of his famous son, since the name Abba was very common. In the Jerusalem Talmud he is referred to as Rabbi Ba bar Va.

The Sages of Eretz Yisrael considered him very important, and even after he returned to Babylonia they would send him their halakhic questions. He was especially close to Levi ben Sisi, who came from Eretz Yisrael to Babylonia and was his closest friend. In addition to his great Torah knowledge, Abba bar Abba was wealthy and owned many fields. His became wealthy though trading in silk. In addition to Shmuel he had a son who was a Torah scholar known as Rabbi Pineḥas.

## BACKGROUND

**Mats – מַפְּצֵי:** This is referring to a type of woven reed mat. It seems that whereas a regular mat was woven from whole reeds, this type of mat was made from pieces of reeds. For this reason it was softer than a regular reed mat. It was harder than a leather surface and for this reason leather was the preferred surface for sitting on.

## NOTES

**Ritual baths…in the days of Nisan and mats in the days of Tishrei – מִקְוָואוֹת בְּיוֹמֵי נִיסָן וּמַפְצֵי בְּיוֹמֵי תִּשְׁרֵי:** The Torah mentions two types of purifying waters (see Leviticus 11:36): A spring and a pit, i.e., a ritual bath. There are many halakhic differences between these two, one of which is that the water of a ritual bath must be gathered in a single place, whereas a spring is comprised of flowing water. In Nisan, Shmuel's father was concerned that the river might contain rainwater, which renders one pure only when it is gathered, and therefore he fashioned a ritual bath for his daughters adjacent to the river, to avoid the risk of an invalid immersion in flowing rainwater. In Tishrei it is possible to immerse in the river because there is very little rain during the summer months. For this reason, during that period Shmuel's father prepared mats for his daughters to immerse in the river.

**Eye shadow that is in the eye does not interpose – כָּחוֹל שֶׁבְּתוֹךְ הָעַיִן אֵינוֹ חוֹצֵץ:** Some explain that since eye shadow placed in the eye must be kept moist to prevent damage to the eye, it is not considered an interposition (*Or Zarua*, citing Rashbam).

## LANGUAGE

**Bloodletting incision [*rivda dekhusilta*] – רִיבְדָא דְּכוּסִילְתָּא:** *Rivda* refers to a puncture or an incision. *Khusilta* is the Aramaic term for bloodletting or the wound created in the process of bloodletting.

## HALAKHA

**Ritual baths…in the days of Nisan and mats in the days of Tishrei – מִקְוָואוֹת בְּיוֹמֵי נִיסָן וּמַפְצֵי בְּיוֹמֵי תִּשְׁרֵי:** Immersion in running spring water is valid. By contrast, immersion in rainwater is valid only if the water is collected in one place (*Beit Yosef*). If flowing spring water is mixed with a small amount of rainwater it is considered as a spring. But if the rainwater constitutes the majority of a spring or of a river, it does not render pure one who immerses in it while the water is flowing; rather, such water is effective only if gathered in one place. Therefore, if a river is mostly rainwater, one must place reed mats or something similar to form an enclosure to gather the water before immersion.

The Rema writes that one should be stringent and rule in accordance with this opinion. He adds that there are some who permit immersion in rivers all year long, even when much of the water is from rainwater and melted snow, because most water in a river comes from the river's source. He writes that the custom in most places without a ritual bath is to immerse in the river, and one should not object to those who act leniently. Nevertheless, one must be careful not to immerse in a river that is comprised entirely of rainwater and dries up when there is no rain. Even though all the other rivers contribute water to it when it rains, since it dries completely when there is no rain it is prohibited to immerse there unless the water is gathered in one place. A river that does not dry up, even if it spreads over its banks during the rainy season, may be used for immersion. This is in accordance the lenient opinion and based on custom (Rambam *Sefer Tahara, Hilkhot Mikvaot* 9:13; *Shulḥan Arukh, Yoreh De'a* 201:2).

**If a woman gave a cooked dish to her son and immersed – נָתְנָה תַּבְשִׁיל לִבְנָהּ וְטָבְלָה:** If a woman feeds her child and then immerses, the immersion is invalid because she may have dirt or grease on her hands. This is in accordance with the opinion of Rav Giddel, citing Rav (Rambam *Sefer Tahara, Hilkhot Mikvaot* 2:19; *Shulḥan Arukh, Yoreh De'a* 199:6).

**These bloodletting incisions, etc. – הָנֵי רַבְדֵי דְּכוּסִילְתָּא וכו׳:** Dried blood on a wound is an interposition. The pus within it is not an interposition. If the pus oozes out, within the first three days of being wounded it is liquid and is not an interposition, but after that time it is considered to be dry and is an interposition. Therefore, a woman who has many scratches on her body must soak in water until the scabs become soft. This is in accordance with the opinion of Rami bar Abba (Rambam *Sefer Tahara, Hilkhot Mikvaot* 2:20; *Shulḥan Arukh, Yoreh De'a* 198:9).

**Mucus that is in the eye – לִפְלוּף שֶׁבָּעַיִן:** Mucus around the eye is an interposition even if it is soft. The *Beit Yosef* writes, citing the Ra'avad, that in the case of hard mucus in the eye it is only when one immerses in order to handle or eat ritually pure food that it is an interposition, but if she is immersing herself only in order to become permitted to her husband it is not considered an interposition (Rambam *Sefer Tahara, Hilkhot Mikvaot* 2:1; *Shulḥan Arukh, Yoreh De'a* 198:7, and see *Shakh* there).

**Eye shadow that is in the eye – כָּחוֹל שֶׁבְּתוֹךְ הָעַיִן:** Eye shadow within the eye does not interpose, but that which is outside the eye does interpose. If a woman constantly opens and closes her eyes, then even the eye shadow outside the eye does not interpose. This is in accordance with the opinion of Shmuel (Rambam *Sefer Tahara, Hilkhot Mikvaot* 2:21; *Shulḥan Arukh, Yoreh De'a* 198:8).

אָמַר רַבִּי יוֹחָנָן: פָּתְחָה עֵינֶיהָ בְּיוֹתֵר, אוֹ עָצְמָה עֵינֶיהָ בְּיוֹתֵר – לֹא עָלְתָה לָהּ טְבִילָה.

**Rabbi Yoḥanan says:** If a woman **opened her eyes very** wide **or closed her eyes very** tightly[H] while immersing, this **immersion is ineffective for her.** Such open or closed eyelids prevent the water from reaching the creases around the eyes.

אָמַר רֵישׁ לָקִישׁ: הָאִשָּׁה לֹא תִּטְבּוֹל אֶלָּא דֶּרֶךְ גְּדִילָתָהּ. כִּדְתְנַן: הָאִישׁ נִרְאֶה כְּעוֹדֵר וּמוֹסֵק זֵיתִים, אִשָּׁה נִרְאֵת כְּאוֹרֶגֶת וּכְמֵנִיקָה אֶת בְּנָהּ.

**Reish Lakish says: A woman may immerse** herself in a ritual bath **only in the manner that she grows,** i.e., she may not force her arms to her sides or close her legs tightly. She is not obligated to spread her limbs widely, but simply stand in her normal manner. **As we learned** in a mishna (*Nega'im* 2:4): When **a man** has a leprous mark between his legs and stands before a priest for inspection, he should **appear like** one who is **hoeing,** i.e., with his legs slightly apart, **and** if it is under his arm, he should appear like one who is **harvesting olives,** with his arms slightly raised. If the mark is not visible when he is standing in that manner, it is not impure. By contrast, **a woman** with a leprous mark between her legs should **appear like** one who is **weaving, and** if the mark is beneath her breast she should appear **like** a woman who is **nursing her son.**[H]

אָמַר רַבָּה בַּר רַב הוּנָא: נִימָא אַחַת קְשׁוּרָה – חוֹצֶצֶת,

**Rabba bar Rav Huna says: A single hair tied**[H] in a knot **interposes** and invalidates an immersion.

**HALAKHA**

**If she opened her eyes very wide or closed her eyes very tightly – פָּתְחָה עֵינֶיהָ בְּיוֹתֵר אוֹ עָצְמָה עֵינֶיהָ בְּיוֹתֵר:** A woman should not close her eyes too tight while immersing nor open them too wide. If she did so there is a dispute between the authorities as to whether the immersion was valid or not (Rambam *Sefer Tahara, Hilkhot Mikvaot* 2:22; *Shulḥan Arukh, Yoreh De'a* 198:39).

**And like a woman who is nursing her son – וּכְמֵנִיקָה אֶת בְּנָהּ:** A woman immersing for purity in a ritual bath should not stand fully upright, nor bend in half, but should stoop forward slightly, as she stands when setting up a loom. The underside of her breasts should be visible as they are when she nurses a baby, and her armpits should be visible as they are when she weaves while standing. She is not obligated to separate her legs too far, nor separate her arms from her body, but keeps them in the manner in which she walks. If she bends over too far or stands too straight the immersion is nevertheless valid, although there are some who say it is invalid (Rambam *Sefer Tahara, Hilkhot Mikvaot* 1:10; *Shulḥan Arukh, Yoreh De'a* 198:35).

**A single hair tied – נִימָא אַחַת קְשׁוּרָה:** A single knotted hair interposes and invalidates an immersion. This is only if the woman is particular that it should not be knotted, but if the woman is not particular the immersion is valid. If the majority of her hair is knotted, each hair by itself, the Rambam writes, citing the *ge'onim*, that the immersion is invalid. The Rambam himself holds that the head is not treated as an independent entity in evaluating whether the interposition covers most of the area that has to be immersed, and the immersion is not valid only if the water is unable to reach the majority of the entire body. The Ra'avad agrees with the opinion of the *ge'onim* (Rambam *Sefer Tahara, Hilkhot Mikvaot* 2:15; *Shulḥan Arukh, Yoreh De'a* 198:5, and *Beur HaGra* there).

Perek **X**
Daf **67** Amud **b**

שָׁלֹשׁ – אֵינָן חוֹצְצוֹת, שְׁתַּיִם – אֵינִי יוֹדֵעַ. וְרַבִּי יוֹחָנָן אָמַר: אָנוּ אֵין לָנוּ אֶלָּא אַחַת.

**Three** hairs tied together in a knot **do not interpose,** as three hairs cannot be tied so tightly that water cannot penetrate them. With regard to **two** hairs tied together in a knot, **I do not know**[N] the *halakha*. **And Rabbi Yoḥanan says: We have** a tradition that **only one**[N] hair interposes, but two or more do not prevent the water from reaching the body.

**NOTES**

**Two I do not know – שְׁתַּיִם אֵינִי יוֹדֵעַ:** There is a dispute between the early authorities as to the status of two hairs tied together. Some write that two hairs do not interpose (Rambam *Sefer Tahara, Hilkhot Mikvaot* 2:15; *Smag*; Rosh). According to them there is a dispute in the Gemara between Rabba bar Rav Huna and Rabbi Yoḥanan, and the *halakha* is in accordance with the opinion of Rabbi Yoḥanan, who says that only one knotted hair interposes. Others write that it is uncertain whether two hairs tied together interpose or not (Ran; Rashba; Rabbeinu Yeruḥam) because they hold that Rabbi Yoḥanan does not disagree with Rabba bar Rav Huna concerning this, but all agree that the *halakha* of two knotted hairs is uncertain (*Beit Yosef*).

**We have only one – אָנוּ אֵין לָנוּ אֶלָּא אַחַת:** The early authorities write that this is referring to a case where the majority of the hairs on a woman's head are each knotted individually (Rosh). The Rambam writes (*Sefer Tahara, Hilkhot Mikvaot* 2:15) that although this is the ruling of the *ge'onim* (see also Ra'avad), he holds that the head is part of the body with regard to defining a majority in immersion, and therefore even if all of the hairs are knotted individually it does not interpose, provided that she is not particular about it. But if she has other substances interposing between her body and the water, her hair combines with them to potentially form a majority, which interposes even if she is not particular about her hair.

אָמַר רַבִּי יִצְחָק, דְּבַר תּוֹרָה: רוּבּוֹ הַמַּקְפִּיד עָלָיו – חוֹצֵץ, רוּבּוֹ וְאֵינוֹ מַקְפִּיד עָלָיו – אֵינוֹ חוֹצֵץ. וְגָזְרוּ עַל רוּבּוֹ שֶׁאֵינוֹ מַקְפִּיד – מִשּׁוּם רוּבּוֹ הַמַּקְפִּיד, וְגָזְרוּ עַל מִיעוּטוֹ הַמַּקְפִּיד – מִשּׁוּם רוּבּוֹ הַמַּקְפִּיד.

§ **Rabbi Yitzḥak says: By Torah law,**[N] if there is an interposition between a person and the water, and it covers **the majority of his** body, and **he is particular**[NH] and wants the interposing substance removed, **it interposes** and invalidates an immersion in a ritual bath. But if it covers the **majority of his body but he is not particular**[N] **about** that substance, **it does not interpose. But** the Sages **issued a decree** prohibiting substances covering **the majority** of **his** body with regard to **which he is not particular, due to** substances covering **the majority** of **his** body about **which he is particular. And** likewise, they issued a decree against substances covering **the minority** of **his** body with regard to which he is **particular, due to** substances covering **the majority** of **his** body about which he is **particular.**

וְלִגְזוֹר נַמִי עַל מִיעוּטוֹ שֶׁאֵינוֹ מַקְפִּיד, מִשּׁוּם מִיעוּטוֹ הַמַּקְפִּיד! הִיא גּוּפָהּ גְּזֵרָה, וַאֲנַן נֵיקוּם וְנִגְזוֹר גְּזֵרָה לִגְזֵרָה?!

The Gemara raises a difficulty: **But let them also issue a decree** prohibiting substances covering **the minority** of **his** body with regard to **which he is not particular, due to** substances covering **the minority** of **his** body about which he is **particular.** The Gemara answers: The Sages did not issue such a decree, as that prohibition **is itself** a rabbinic **decree, and will we arise and issue a decree to** prevent the violation of another **decree?**

אָמַר רַב: נִדָּה בִּזְמַנָּהּ – אֵינָהּ טוֹבֶלֶת אֶלָּא בַּלַּיְלָה, וְשֶׁלֹּא בִּזְמַנָּהּ – טוֹבֶלֶת בֵּין בַּיּוֹם בֵּין בַּלַּיְלָה. רַבִּי יוֹחָנָן אָמַר: בֵּין בִּזְמַנָּהּ בֵּין שֶׁלֹּא בִּזְמַנָּהּ – אֵינָהּ טוֹבֶלֶת אֶלָּא בַּלַּיְלָה, מִשּׁוּם סְרָךְ בִּתָּהּ.

§ The Gemara returns to discuss the issue of the correct time for immersion. **Rav says: A menstruating woman** who wishes to immerse to complete her purification process **at her time,** i.e., at the end of seven days, **may immerse only at night,**[H] i.e., on the night after the seventh day, the night of the eighth day. **But** a woman who wishes to immerse **not at her time,** i.e., on the eighth day or afterward, **may immerse either during the day or at night. Rabbi Yoḥanan says: Whether** she is immersing **at her time or not at her time,** she **may immerse only at night.** This is **because her daughter** might **follow** her example when she is old enough, and also immerse in the daytime, but she may do so on the seventh day, when immersion is not valid.

וְאַף רַב הֲדַר בֵּיהּ, דְּאָמַר רַבִּי חִיָּיא בַּר אָשֵׁי, אָמַר רַב: נִדָּה, בֵּין בִּזְמַנָּהּ בֵּין שֶׁלֹּא בִּזְמַנָּהּ – אֵינָהּ טוֹבֶלֶת אֶלָּא בַּלַּיְלָה, מִשּׁוּם סְרָךְ בִּתָּהּ.

**And even Rav retracted** his opinion and ruled that a woman who is immersing after menstruation may never do so during the day. **As Rabbi Ḥiyya bar Ashi said** that **Rav said: A menstruating woman** who wishes to immerse to complete her purification process, **whether at her time** or **whether not at her time, may immerse only at night, because her daughter** might **follow** her example and immerse during the daytime of the seventh day.

## NOTES

**By Torah law** – **דְּבַר תּוֹרָה**: Rabbi Yitzḥak stated his ruling concerning a case where the material that interposes covers only the majority of the body, but a substance that covers the person entirely is considered to interpose by Torah law, even if he is not particular to remove it, as explained in *Yevamot* 78b.

**If it covers the majority of his body and he is particular** – **רוּבּוֹ הַמַּקְפִּיד עָלָיו**: Rabbi Yitzḥak does not explain the meaning of the term majority. Some explain that this refers only to hair, and only with regard to hair is there a distinction between the majority and the minority. But with regard to the body, even a small interposition that covers only a minority of the body interposes (Rashi). Many early authorities disagree with this opinion and explain that Rabbi Yitzḥak holds that the immersion is not valid only if there is an interposition covering the majority of the body (*Tosafot*; *Tosefot HaRosh*).

**If it covers the majority but he is not particular** – **רוּבּוֹ וְאֵינוֹ מַקְפִּיד עָלָיו**: Some early authorities explain that since this individual is not particular about the interposing substance, it will not be removed, and therefore it is nullified as part of his body, and for this reason it does not interpose (Rashi on *Sukka* 6b).

## HALAKHA

**If it covers the majority of his body and he is particular** – **רוּבּוֹ הַמַּקְפִּיד עָלָיו**: By Torah law if there was a substance covering the majority of a person who was about to immerse, or the majority of a utensil that is being immersed, the immersion is not valid. This applies only if the person is particular about the presence of the substance and would want to remove it, but a substance about which a person is not particular does not invalidate the immersion even if it covers the majority of his body. Similarly, a substance that covers less than the majority of the body, even if the person is particular about it, does not invalidate the immersion.

By rabbinic law any substance about which one is particular invalidates the immersion, even if covers only a small amount of the body or utensil. This is a decree, lest one immerse where there is a substance that covers the majority of the body or utensil. Similarly, any substance that covers the majority of the body or utensil invalidates the immersion by rabbinic law, even if one is not particular about it, least one immerse where there is a substance about which one is particular. This is in accordance with the opinion of Rabbi Yitzḥak (Rambam *Sefer Tahara, Hilkhot Mikvaot* 1:12; *Shulḥan Arukh Yoreh De'a* 198:1).

**May immerse only at night** – **אֵינָהּ טוֹבֶלֶת אֶלָּא בַּלַּיְלָה**: A woman may not immerse to render herself pure from impurity due to menstruation on the seventh day, but only on the night afterward. If she does not immerse at the correct time she may also not immerse during the daytime on the eighth or ninth day because her daughter will notice and may eventually immerse on the seventh day. This is in accordance with the opinion of Rabbi Yoḥanan (Rambam *Sefer Kedusha, Hilkhot Issurei Bia* 4:7; *Shulḥan Arukh, Yoreh De'a* 197:3).

אַתְקֵין רַב אִידִי בְּנֶרֶשׁ לְמִטְבַּל בְּיוֹמָא דִּתְמָנְיָא, מִשּׁוּם אַרְיָוָתָא, רַב אַחָא בַּר יַעֲקֹב בְּפַפּוּנְיָא – מִשּׁוּם גַּנָּבֵי,

The Gemara cites examples of Sages who permitted immersion on the eighth day due to exceptional circumstances. **Rav Idi decreed in Neresh**[B] **that** the women **may immerse** during the daytime **on the eighth day**[H] **due to the lions** that roamed the area at night and posed a threat to women who immersed at that time. **Rav Aḥa bar Yaakov** decreed **in Pappunya**[B] that the women should immerse during the daytime on the eighth day **due to thieves** who posed a threat to women who immersed at that night.

רַב יְהוּדָה בְּפוּמְבְּדִיתָא – מִשּׁוּם צִנָּה, רָבָא בִּמְחוֹזָא – מִשּׁוּם אַבּוּלָאֵי.

Similarly, **Rav Yehuda** decreed **in Pumbedita**[B] that the women should immerse in the daytime on the eighth day **due to** the **cold** of the night. **Rava** decreed **in Meḥoza**[B] that the women should immerse in the daytime on the eighth day **due to** the **gatekeepers** [*abula'ei*],[L] who were untrustworthy and might hurt the women on their way to and from immersion.

אֲמַר לֵיהּ רַב פָּפָּא לְרָבָא וּלְאַבָּיֵי: מִכְּדֵי הָאִידָּנָא כּוּלְּהוּ סְפֵק זָבוֹת שַׁוְּינְהוּ רַבָּנַן, לִיטְבְּלִינְהוּ בְּיוֹמָא דִּשְׁבִיעָאָה?

§ **Rav Pappa said to Rava and to Abaye: Since nowadays the Sages have given** all women who menstruate the status of **an uncertain** greater ***zava*****, may they immerse on the seventh day** during the daytime? A greater *zava*, after counting seven clean days, may immerse on the seventh day. Since all women who menstruate now count seven clean days after the bleeding ceases, more than seven days from the onset of her menstruating have passed by the seventh clean day.

מִשּׁוּם דְּרַבִּי שִׁמְעוֹן, דְּתַנְיָא: ״אַחַר תִּטְהָר״ – אַחַר אַחַר לְכוּלָּן, שֶׁלֹּא תְּהֵא טוּמְאָה מַפְסֶקֶת בֵּינֵיהֶן. רַבִּי שִׁמְעוֹן אוֹמֵר: ״אַחַר תִּטְהָר״ – אַחַר מַעֲשֶׂה תִּטְהָר.

Rava and Abaye replied that they may nevertheless not immerse on the seventh day, **due to** the statement **of Rabbi Shimon. As it is taught** in a *baraita*: The verse states: "But if she be purified of her *ziva*, then she shall count to herself seven days, **and after that she shall be pure**" (Leviticus 15:28). The purification of a *zava* must be **after** the seven days, i.e., **after all of the** days, which must be consecutive so **that there are no** days of **impurity separating between** the seven clean days. **Rabbi Shimon says** that the phrase **"And after that she shall be pure"** teaches that **after the action** of counting seven clean days **she shall be pure.** In other words, once she has examined herself at the beginning of the seventh day she may immerse on that day.

אֲבָל אָמְרוּ חֲכָמִים: אָסוּר לַעֲשׂוֹת כֵּן, שֶׁמָּא תָּבֹא לִידֵי סָפֵק.

Rabbi Shimon continues: **But the Sages said: It is prohibited to do so,** i.e., to immerse on the seventh day, **lest she come to** a case of **uncertainty.** If she were to engage in intercourse with her husband on that seventh day after immersion, and afterward on the same day she experiences bleeding, it would retroactively nullify her entire seven clean days, which would mean that she engaged in intercourse with her husband while she was impure, rendering them both liable to receive the punishment of *karet*.

אָמַר רַב הוּנָא: אִשָּׁה חוֹפֶפֶת בְּאֶחָד בְּשַׁבָּת וְטוֹבֶלֶת בִּשְׁלִישִׁי בְּשַׁבָּת – שֶׁכֵּן אִשָּׁה חוֹפֶפֶת בְּעֶרֶב שַׁבָּת וְטוֹבֶלֶת בְּמוֹצָאֵי שַׁבָּת.

§ **Rav Huna says: A woman may wash** her hair[N] **on the first** day **of the week,** Sunday, **and immerse on the third** day **of the week,** i.e., Monday night. The proof of this is **that** sometimes **a woman washes** her hair **on the eve of Shabbat, but** she does not **immerse** until **the conclusion of Shabbat,** which is the same interval as from Sunday to Monday night.

**BACKGROUND**

Neresh – נֶרֶשׁ: Neresh was a Babylonian city near the Neresh River, south of Sura. It was an important agricultural and commercial center that was home to a large number of date-palm farmers and producers of alcoholic beverages. Straddling the desert, its inhabitants were considered uncultured. Regardless, it was home to a Jewish community for many generations, producing no small number of Sages. At one point the prominent *amora* Rav Pappa was the head of the academy in Neresh.

Pappunya – פַּפּוּנְיָא: The city of Pappunya was built between Pumbedita and Meḥoza, on the banks of the Pappa River, after which it was named. Among the Rabbis of this city were Rav Aḥa bar Yaakov and Rav Mattana.

Pumbedita – פּוּמְבְּדִיתָא: Pumbedita, a town on the Euphrates River northwest of Neharde'a, was an important center of the Babylonian Jewish community for many generations. As early as the Second Temple period, Pumbedita was referred to simply as: The Diaspora. After the destruction of Neharde'a, its academy moved to Pumbedita, and Torah study continued there uninterrupted until the end of the geonic period.

Meḥoza – מְחוֹזָא: Meḥoza was a city on the Tigris River located near the Malka River. It was a large commercial city, most of whose inhabitants were Jews. Unlike the case in most other Jewish communities, the Jews in Meḥoza generally earned their living from commerce. Many Jews in Meḥoza were converts or immigrants from several other countries. After Neharde'a was destroyed in 259 CE, many of the scholars from its academy relocated to Meḥoza, which became the Torah center of leading scholars such as Rav Naḥman; Rav Sheshet; Rava, who later became head of the academy in Meḥoza; Ameimar; and Rav Kahana, who was Rav Ashi's teacher. After Abaye's death in approximately 338 CE, the academy in Pumbedita, then headed by Rava, also moved to Meḥoza for a period of time.

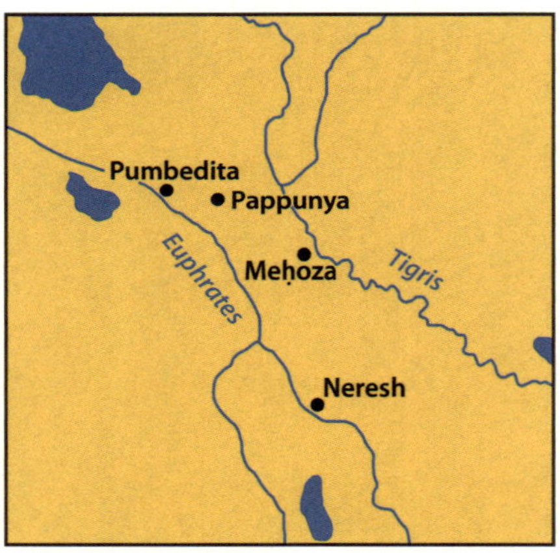


Location of Pumbedita, Pappunya, Meḥoza, and Neresh

**LANGUAGE**

Gatekeepers [*abula'ei*] – אַבּוּלָאֵי: This word appears to derive from the Greek βουλή, *boulē*, meaning a council or group of officials. Some explain that it refers to the city guards who patrolled the walls.

**HALAKHA**

Rav Idi decreed in Neresh that women may immerse on the eighth day – אַתְקֵין רַב אִידִי בְּנֶרֶשׁ לְמִטְבַּל בְּיוֹמָא דִּתְמָנְיָא: Even though the Sages said that a woman may immerse only at night, when there are exigent circumstances she may immerse on the eighth day, in accordance with the decree of Rav Idi. Examples include if a woman is afraid to immerse at night due to the cold or thieves, or if the city gates are closed at nightfall (Rambam *Sefer Kedusha, Hilkhot Issurei Bia* 4:8; *Shulḥan Arukh, Yoreh De'a* 197:4).

**NOTES**

A woman may wash her hair – אִשָּׁה חוֹפֶפֶת: The requirement to wash one's hair before immersion is a decree of Ezra. The Gemara (*Bava Kamma* 82a) explains that the verse: "And he shall wash [*et*] his flesh in water, and he shall be pure" (Leviticus 14:9), teaches that no item may interpose between one's body and the water. The word *et* serves to include one's hair in this *halakha*. This is referring only to the requirement to examine whether there are knots or dirt; there is no obligation to wash one's hair by Torah law. Ezra decreed that washing hair is a requirement.

אִשָּׁה חוֹפֶפֶת בְּאֶחָד בַּשַּׁבָּת וְטוֹבֶלֶת בָּרְבִיעִי בַּשַּׁבָּת – שֶׁכֵּן אִשָּׁה חוֹפֶפֶת בְּעֶרֶב שַׁבָּת וְטוֹבֶלֶת בְּמוֹצָאֵי יוֹם טוֹב שֶׁחָל לִהְיוֹת אַחַר הַשַּׁבָּת.

Similarly, **a woman may wash** her hair **on the first** day **of the week,** Sunday, **and immerse on the fourth** day **of the week,** Tuesday night. The proof of this is **that** sometimes **a woman washes** her hair **on the eve of Shabbat, but** she does not **immerse** until **the conclusion of the Festival that occurs after Shabbat,** which is the same interval as from Sunday to Tuesday night.

אִשָּׁה חוֹפֶפֶת בְּאֶחָד בַּשַּׁבָּת וְטוֹבֶלֶת בַּחֲמִישִׁי בַּשַּׁבָּת – שֶׁכֵּן אִשָּׁה חוֹפֶפֶת בְּעֶרֶב שַׁבָּת וְטוֹבֶלֶת בְּמוֹצָאֵי שְׁנֵי יָמִים טוֹבִים שֶׁל רֹאשׁ הַשָּׁנָה שֶׁחָל לִהְיוֹת אַחַר הַשַּׁבָּת.

Furthermore, **a woman may wash** her hair **on the first** day **of the week,** Sunday, **and immerse on the fifth** day **of the week,** Wednesday night. The proof of this is **that** sometimes **a woman washes** her hair **on the eve of Shabbat, but** she does not **immerse** until **the conclusion of two days of Rosh HaShana that occurs after Shabbat,**[B] which is the same interval as from Sunday to Wednesday night.

וְרַב חִסְדָּא אֲמַר: כּוּלְּהוּ – אָמְרִינַן, ״שֶׁכֵּן״ – לָא אָמְרִינַן, הֵיכָא דְּאֶפְשָׁר – אֶפְשָׁר, הֵיכָא דְּלָא אֶפְשָׁר – לָא אֶפְשָׁר.

**But Rav Ḥisda said: We say** that **all of these** long gaps between a woman washing her hair and immersing are permitted. But **we do not say** as proof **that**[H] since a woman washes her hair before Shabbat and immerses only several days later, she may do so during a regular week as well. One cannot learn this *halakha* from those situations involving Shabbat, as one cannot derive cases where alternatives are possible from those cases where alternatives are not possible. **Where it is possible** for a woman to wash her hair and immerse immediately, **it is possible,** and she is not allowed to do so any earlier. But **where it is not possible** for a woman to wash her hair immediately before immersion, e.g., when she must immerse after the conclusion of Shabbat or a festival, **it is impossible,** and for this reason she is permitted to wash her hair in advance.

וְרַב יֵימָר אֲמַר: אֲפִילּוּ ״שֶׁכֵּן״ – נַמִי אָמְרִינַן, לְבַר מֵאִשָּׁה חוֹפֶפֶת בְּאֶחָד בַּשַּׁבָּת וְטוֹבֶלֶת בַּחֲמִישִׁי בַּשַּׁבָּת, דִּלְמוֹצָאֵי שְׁנֵי יָמִים טוֹבִים שֶׁל רֹאשׁ הַשָּׁנָה שֶׁלְּאַחַר הַשַּׁבָּת לֵיתָא, דְּאֶפְשָׁר דְּחוֹפֶפֶת בַּלַּיְלָה וְטוֹבֶלֶת בַּלַּיְלָה.

**And Rav Yeimar said: We even say** the proof **that** since a woman washes her hair before Shabbat and immerses only several days later, she may do so during a regular week as well. Rav Yeimar agrees with Rav Huna in all cases **apart from** that of **a woman who washes** her hair **on the first** day **of the week,** Sunday, **and immerses on the fifth** day **of the week,** Wednesday night. He maintains that Rav Huna's proof **from the conclusion of two days of Rosh HaShana that is after Shabbat is not** a sufficient proof, **as** even in such a case a woman may not wait so long. Rather, **it is possible** for her **to wash** her hair **at night** after the conclusion of Rosh HaShana **and immerse** on **that** same **night,** so that she should not have such a long gap between washing her hair and immersing.

דָּרַשׁ מָרֵימָר: הִלְכְתָא כְּרַב חִסְדָּא, וּכְדִמְתָרֵץ רַב יֵימָר.

**Mareimar taught: The** ***halakha*** **is in accordance with** the opinion of **Rav Ḥisda,** that a woman should not wash her hair many days before immersing except when there is no other possibility. **And** the *halakha* is also **in accordance with** the manner in **which Rav Yeimar explains** that if Rosh HaShana occurs after Shabbat a woman should wash her hair on the night of her immersion.

אִיבַּעְיָא לְהוּ: אִשָּׁה מַהוּ שֶׁתָּחוֹף בַּלַּיְלָה וְתִטְבּוֹל בַּלַּיְלָה? מָר זוּטְרָא אוֹסֵר, וְרַב חִינָּנָא מִסּוּרָא שָׁרֵי.

§ **A dilemma was raised before** the Sages: **What is** the *halakha* with regard to whether **a woman may wash** her hair **at night and immerse on** that same **night? Mar Zutra deems it prohibited** for her to do so. Since she will be in a hurry to immerse and return to her husband, there is a concern that she will not wash and examine her hair thoroughly. **And Rav Ḥinnana from Sura deems it permitted** for a woman to wash her hair on the night of her immersion.

**BACKGROUND**

**Two days of Rosh HaShana that occurs after Shabbat – שְׁנֵי יָמִים טוֹבִים שֶׁל רֹאשׁ הַשָּׁנָה שֶׁחָל לִהְיוֹת אַחַר הַשַּׁבָּת:** Such a scenario does not occur nowadays since Rosh HaShana cannot occur on a Sunday according to the fixed Hebrew calendar. When Rav Huna, who lived in the third century CE, presented this statement, such a situation could have occurred.

For an extended period in antiquity the Hebrew calendar was established by the court based on the testimony of people who witnessed the appearance of the new moon. Various persecutions under Roman rule in the years following the destruction of the Second Temple made it more and more difficult to establish months using this system and to ensure that all Jewish communities in Eretz Yisrael and the Diaspora were celebrating the holidays on the same day. Since the fourth century CE the Jewish calendar has operated on a fixed astronomical system in which, with few exceptions, months of twenty-nine days alternate with those of thirty days. Among the *halakhot* upon which the fixed calendar was based is the principle that Rosh HaShana can never occur on a Sunday, Wednesday, or Friday. This was established in order to ensure that Yom Kippur never occurs immediately before or after Shabbat and that Hoshana Rabba never comes out on Shabbat.

**HALAKHA**

**We do not say that – שֶׁכֵּן לָא אָמְרִינַן:** If the night of immersion occurs at the conclusion of a Shabbat that is also a festival, the woman must wash her hair before Shabbat. Similarly, if a two-day festival occurs on Thursday and Friday and her time of immersion is at the onset of Shabbat, she must wash her hair on Wednesday and keep her hair tied so that it will not become dirty. When she immerses she must check her entire body and hair carefully for any item that interposes. This is in accordance with the opinion of Rav Ḥisda, who rules stringently (Rambam *Sefer Tahara*, *Hilkhot Mikvaot* 2:16, and *Kesef Mishne* there; *Shulḥan Arukh*, *Yoreh De'a* 199:6, and *Beur HaGra* there).

### PERSONALITIES

Rav Naḥman bar Yitzḥak – רַב נַחְמָן בַּר יִצְחָק: Rav Naḥman bar Yitzḥak belonged to the fourth generation of Babylonian *amora'im*. He studied under Rav Naḥman and Rav Ḥisda. He learned with Rava and after Rava's death became the head of the academy in Pumbedita, a position he held from 352–357 CE. He was well known for his piety in observance of mitzvot, as well as for his refined character traits. His respect for others manifested itself in his kind manner and gentle speech. Furthermore, he advocated for dedication to intense Torah study.

אֲמַר לֵיהּ רַב אַדָּא לְרַב חִינָּנָא מִסּוּרָא: לָאו הָכִי הֲוָה עוּבְדָּא בִּדְבֵיתְהוּ דְּאַבָּא מָרִי רֵישׁ גָּלוּתָא דְּאֵיקוּט, אֲזַל רַב נַחְמָן בַּר יִצְחָק לְפַיּוֹסָהּ. וְאָמְרָה לֵיהּ: מַאי אִיתֵיהּ הָשְׁתָּא?

**Rav Adda said to Rav Ḥinnana from Sura: Was there not an incident** like **this involving the wife of Abba Mari, the Exilarch, who quarreled** with her husband, and as a result she did not want to immerse in a ritual bath to become permitted to him; and **Rav Naḥman bar Yitzḥak**[P] **went to appease her** and to persuade her to immerse, **and she said to him: What is there** that can be done **now?** There is no reason for me to hurry and immerse now.

Perek **X**
Daf **68** Amud **a**

### NOTES

Are you lacking kettles – דּוּדֵי חָסְרַת: The early commentaries disagree as to the purpose of these kettles. Some say that they were used to heat water for washing hair (*Arukh*). Others explain that hot water would be added into the cold water of the ritual bath so that the women could immerse in warm water (Rosh, citing Rabbeinu Ḥananel). According to this explanation, the Gemara here states explicitly that it is permitted to add hot water to a ritual bath. This *halakha* is a matter of dispute (Ra'avya; Riva; *Sefer HaAgudda*).

### BACKGROUND

His letter – אִגַּרְתֵּיהּ: Due to the great distances between Jewish communities, not only between Eretz Yisrael and Babylonia but also between other communities in distant lands, and due to the dangers of journeying from one to another, there was great dependence on letters sent from one community to another. Sages of Eretz Yisrael sent many letters to the Sages of Babylonia. These were sent for many reasons, either to warn or notify the people about their observance of certain mitzvot, or to notify them of the New Month. This dependence on letters lasted for many centuries. Ravin was one of those who wrote many letters.

תִּסְגֵּי אַיְיתֵי לְמָחָר. וְיָדַע מַאי קָאָמְרָה לֵיהּ. אֲמַר: דּוּדֵי חָסְרַת, טַשְׁטְקֵי חָסְרַת, עַבְדֵי חָסְרַת?

Rather, **it is sufficient if you come** back again **tomorrow** and speak with me then about this matter. **And** Rav Naḥman bar Yitzḥak **knew what she was saying to him.** She was alluding to the fact that she had not washed her hair while it was still daylight, and therefore she could not immerse that evening. Rav Naḥman bar Yitzḥak **said** to her: **Are you lacking kettles** [*dudei*][NL] to heat water to wash your hair? **Are you lacking buckets** [*tashtekei*][L] to bring the water to wash your hair? **Are you lacking servants,** who can help you prepare to wash your hair? It can be inferred from this story that Rav Naḥman bar Yitzḥak holds that it is permitted for a woman to wash her hair and immerse on the same night.

דָּרַשׁ רָבָא: אִשָּׁה חוֹפֶפֶת בְּעֶרֶב שַׁבָּת וְטוֹבֶלֶת בְּמוֹצָאֵי שַׁבָּת. אֲמַר לֵיהּ רַב פַּפָּא לְרָבָא: וְהָא שְׁלַח רָבִין בְּאִגַּרְתֵּיהּ, אִשָּׁה לֹא תָּחוֹף בְּעֶרֶב שַׁבָּת וְתִטְבּוֹל בְּמוֹצָאֵי שַׁבָּת.

§ **Rava taught: A woman may wash** her hair **on the eve of Shabbat and immerse at the conclusion of Shabbat. Rav Pappa said to Rava: But didn't Ravin send** the following *halakha* **in his letter:**[B] **A woman may not wash** her hair **on the eve of Shabbat and immerse at the conclusion of Shabbat?** Instead, she should wash her hair after the conclusion of Shabbat immediately before she immerses.

וּתְמַהּ עַל עַצְמְךָ הֵיאָךְ חוֹפֶפֶת בַּיּוֹם וְטוֹבֶלֶת בַּלַּיְלָה – הָא בָּעֵינַן "תֵּיכֶף לַחֲפִיפָה טְבִילָה", וְלֵיכָּא!

**And** furthermore, you should **be astounded with yourself: How** did the Sages deem it permitted for a woman on a weekday to **wash** her hair **during the day and immerse at night? Don't we require** that her **immersion** must be **immediately** after **washing** her hair? **And** if she washes her hair during the day, this requirement will **not** be fulfilled. The Sages reluctantly permitted a woman to wash her hair during the day, and they permitted this only due to the concern that she might not wash her hair properly if she would wait until night. Consequently, with regard to an immersion on the conclusion of Shabbat, she should avoid washing her hair a day or more in advance.

### LANGUAGE

Kettle [*dud*] – דּוּד: This word refers to large cauldrons that were placed on the fire to heat water. They were used primarily for cooking. The word is used in the verse: "And they roasted the Paschal offering with fire according to the law; and they cooked the sanctified offerings in pots, and in cauldrons [*uvadevadim*], and in pans, and carried them quickly to all the children of the people" (II Chronicles 35:13). Onkelos translates the verse: "When we sat by the fleshpots" (Exodus 16:3), as: By the pots [*dudei*] of meat.

The word is also used to refer to a large vessel that is used for storing produce, like a large basket, as in the verse: "And behold two baskets [*duda'ei*] of figs" (Jeremiah 24:1).

Buckets [*tashtekei*] – טַשְׁטְקֵי: From the Latin word testa, which means earthenware. It refers to a pot or a deep bowl.

Earthenware pot from the talmudic era

הֲדַר אוֹקֵי רָבָא אָמוֹרָא עֲלֵיהּ וְדָרַשׁ: דְּבָרִים שֶׁאָמַרְתִּי לִפְנֵיכֶם טָעוּת הֵן בְּיָדִי, בְּרַם כָּךְ אָמְרוּ מִשְּׁמֵיהּ דְּרַבִּי יוֹחָנָן אִשָּׁה לֹא תָּחוֹף בְּעֶרֶב שַׁבָּת וְתִטְבּוֹל בְּמוֹצָאֵי שַׁבָּת, וּתְמַהּ עַל עַצְמְךָ הֵיאַךְ חוֹפֶפֶת בַּיּוֹם וְטוֹבֶלֶת בַּלַּיְלָה – הָא בָּעֵינַן ״סָמוּךְ לַחֲפִיפָה טְבִילָה״ וְלֵיכָּא!

As a result of Rav Pappa's comments, **Rava then appointed an interpreter**[B] **before him** to publicize his retraction, **and he taught: The statement I said to you was a mistake of mine. But** in fact **this** is what the Sages **said in the name of Rabbi Yoḥanan: A woman may not wash** her hair **on the eve of Shabbat and immerse after the conclusion of Shabbat. And** furthermore you should **be astounded with yourself. How** can a woman **wash** her hair **during the day and immerse at night? Don't we require:** Her **immersion** must be **immediately** after **washing** her hair? **And** if she washes her hair on the eve of Shabbat, this principle will **not** be fulfilled.

וְהִלְכְתָא: אִשָּׁה חוֹפֶפֶת בַּיּוֹם וְטוֹבֶלֶת בַּלַּיְלָה. וְהִלְכְתָא: אִשָּׁה לֹא תָּחוֹף אֶלָּא בַּלַּיְלָה. (אֶלָּא) קַשְׁיָא הִלְכְתָא אַהִלְכְתָא!

The Gemara concludes: **And the *halakha*** is that **a woman may wash** her hair **during the day and immerse at night.**[H] **And the *halakha*** is that **a woman may wash** her hair **only at night.** The Gemara comments: This is **difficult,** as one ***halakha*** contradicts **the** other ***halakha*.**

לָא קַשְׁיָא, הָא – דְּאֶפְשָׁר, הָא – דְּלָא אֶפְשָׁר.

The Gemara answers: It is **not difficult. This** ruling that she may wash her hair during the day is referring to a case **where it is possible,** e.g., when she immerses on a weeknight and can wash her hair shortly beforehand during the daytime. **That** ruling that she is permitted to wash her hair only at night is referring to a case **where it is not possible,**[N] e.g., when her time for immersion is after the conclusion of Shabbat. Since she may not wash her hair on the eve of Shabbat for an immersion after the conclusion of Shabbat, she must wash her hair at night, after Shabbat has ended, immediately before she immerses.

מתני׳ נִדָּה שֶׁבָּדְקָה עַצְמָהּ יוֹם שְׁבִיעִי שַׁחֲרִית וּמָצְאָה טְהוֹרָה, וּבֵין הַשְּׁמָשׁוֹת לֹא הִפְרִישָׁה, וּלְאַחַר יָמִים בָּדְקָה וּמָצְאָה טְמֵאָה – הֲרֵי הִיא בְּחֶזְקַת טְהוֹרָה.

**MISHNA** In the case of **a menstruating woman who examined herself** on the **seventh day** of menstruation in **the morning and found** that **she is ritually pure** and eligible to immerse in a ritual bath that evening, **but** during **twilight** of the seventh day she **did not** perform an examination that marks the **transition** between the days when she has a flow of blood and the days when she no longer has a flow of blood but immersed despite not having performed the examination, **and after** several **days she examined** herself and **found** that **she is ritually impure, the presumptive status of that** woman is one of **ritual purity** from the time of her immersion until her examination, and all ritually pure items that she handled in the interim remain pure.

בָּדְקָה עַצְמָהּ בְּיוֹם שְׁבִיעִי שַׁחֲרִית וּמָצְאָה טְמֵאָה, וּבֵין הַשְּׁמָשׁוֹת לֹא הִפְרִישָׁה, וּלְאַחַר זְמַן בָּדְקָה וּמָצְאָה טְהוֹרָה – הֲרֵי זוֹ בְּחֶזְקַת טְמֵאָה.

If **she examined herself on** the **seventh day** of menstruation in **the morning and found** that **she is ritually impure,** i.e., her menstrual flow continued, **and** during **twilight** of the seventh day she **did not** perform an examination to confirm the **transition** from ritual impurity to ritual purity but immersed nonetheless, **and after** several **days she examined** herself and **found** that **she is ritually pure, the presumptive status of that** woman is one of **ritual impurity** from the time of her immersion until her examination, and all ritually pure items that she handled in the interim are impure. Since she found blood during her last examination in her days of menstruation, the concern is that the flow of blood continued during the days that followed, and therefore her immersion on the eve of the eighth day was ineffective.

וּמְטַמְּאָה מֵעֵת לְעֵת וּמִפְּקִידָה לִפְקִידָה. וְאִם יֵשׁ לָהּ וֶסֶת – דַּיָּהּ שְׁעָתָהּ.

In a case where there was no blood found during the examination on the seventh morning and she did not examine herself during twilight, and several days later she discovered blood, where the mishna says that a woman's presumptive status is one of ritual purity, that is the *halakha* only for the days following immersion. **But she transmits ritual impurity** to the ritually pure items that she handled before the examination in which she found blood **for a** twenty-four-hour **period and from examination to examination,** in accordance with the *halakha* of a woman who experiences bleeding (see 2a). **And if she has** a fixed menstrual **cycle,** on the day that she examined herself and found blood, **her time is sufficient,** i.e., it is assumed that the bleeding began then, and she does not transmit impurity retroactively.

**BACKGROUND**

**Interpreter – אָמוֹרָא:** The word interpreter [*amora*] has the same meaning as the word disseminator [*meturgeman*] used in the Mishna. This interpreter of the Sages' statements was often a scholar himself, sometimes even an important Sage, whose role was to translate the exposition from Hebrew to Aramaic and to project it so that it could be heard by everyone. Sometimes there was more than one disseminator if the speech needed to be projected to a large group. Often, the disseminator would not only translate but also explain the exposition, as the Sage would state the most basic ideas and the disseminator would expand and develop them. For this reason, the Sages of the talmudic period describe themselves as *amora'im*, as they saw their role as being similar to that of these interpreters for the Sages of the Mishna.

**HALAKHA**

**A woman may wash her hair during the day and immerse at night – אִשָּׁה חוֹפֶפֶת בַּיּוֹם וְטוֹבֶלֶת בַּלַּיְלָה:** A woman must wash her hair immediately before immersion *ab initio*. The best practice is for her to begin washing her hair while it is still daytime, continue washing until it is dark, and then immerse. The best practice is to also comb her hair immediately before immersing, even though she has already washed her hair. The Rema writes that in exigent circumstances, when she must wash her hair during the day, or when she is unable to wash her hair during the day and must do so at night, it is permitted for her to do so. This is provided that she is not rushing to get home to her husband and she takes care to wash her hair properly (Rambam *Sefer Tahara*, *Hilkhot Mikvaot* 2:16, and *Kesef Mishne* there; *Shulḥan Arukh*, *Yoreh De'a* 199:3–4 and *Beur HaGra* there).

**NOTES**

**This is where it is possible, that is where it is not possible – הָא דְּאֶפְשָׁר הָא דְּלָא אֶפְשָׁר:** The Gemara does not specify which is the possible case and which is the case where it is not possible. It also does not explain which *halakha* applies in each case. Some commentaries maintain that the case referred to as possible is one where a woman is able to wash her hair during the day. This applies on weekdays, before she immerses at night. The case referred to as not possible is one where a woman must immerse at the conclusion of Shabbat and she is therefore unable to wash her hair during the day, as it is Shabbat. In such a case, since it is impossible she must wash her hair at night (Rashi).

Others contend that the case referred to as possible is one where a woman is able to wash her hair at night, as in the usual case of immersion, whether during the week or at the conclusion of Shabbat. The case referred to as not possible is one when a Festival occurs immediately after Shabbat and she is unable to wash her hair that night or during the day. In this case she must wash her hair before Shabbat (*She'iltot* of Rav Aḥai; Rambam; Rashbam).

**HALAKHA**

**Even on the second day of her menstruation, etc. – אֲפִילּוּ בַּשֵּׁנִי לְנִדָּתָהּ וכו׳:** With regard to a menstruating woman who examined herself during her days of menstruation and found that the flow of blood had stopped, even if it stopped on the second of her seven days, and she did not examine herself again until after her days of menstruation concluded; and when she examined herself she found that she was impure, there is no assumption that she saw blood during the intermediate days such that she would be a *zava*. Rather, she has a presumptive status of purity during those days (Rambam *Sefer Kedusha, Hilkhot Issurei Bia* 6:20).

**A menstruating woman who examined herself on the seventh day in the morning – נִדָּה שֶׁבָּדְקָה עַצְמָהּ בַּיּוֹם הַשְּׁבִיעִי שַׁחֲרִית:** If a menstruating woman examined herself on the morning of the seventh day and found that she was impure, and during twilight she did not perform the examination to confirm her transition from impurity to purity but several days later she examined herself and found that she was ritually pure, she is considered to be an uncertain *zava*. If she finds herself to be impure she is a definite *zava*. Since she was impure at the outset and when she examined herself, she has a presumptive status that the flow of blood did not cease. This is in accordance with the opinion of Rav. Rav disagrees with Levi only when she examines herself and finds herself to be impure, but if she finds herself to be pure Rav concedes to Levi that she is not a definite *zava* but an uncertain *zava* (Rambam *Sefer Kedusha, Hilkhot Issurei Bia* 6:20).

וְרַבִּי יְהוּדָה אוֹמֵר: כׇּל שֶׁלֹּא הִפְרִישָׁה בְּטׇהֳרָה מִן הַמִּנְחָה וּלְמַעְלָה – הֲרֵי זוֹ בְּחֶזְקַת טְמֵאָה. וַחֲכָמִים אוֹמְרִים: אֲפִילּוּ בַּשֵּׁנִי לְנִדָּתָהּ בָּדְקָה וּמָצְאָה טְהוֹרָה, וּבֵין הַשְּׁמָשׁוֹת לֹא הִפְרִישָׁה, וּלְאַחַר זְמַן בָּדְקָה וּמָצְאָה טְמֵאָה – הֲרֵי זוֹ בְּחֶזְקַת טְהוֹרָה.

**And Rabbi Yehuda says:** With regard to **any** woman **who did not** perform the examination marking her **transition** from ritual impurity to ritual purity on the seventh day **from *minḥa* time onward,**[N] even if she performed an examination and found no blood that morning, **the presumptive status of that** woman is one of **ritual impurity. And the Rabbis say: Even if on the second day of her menstruation**[H] **she performed the examination and found** that **she is ritually pure, and** she **did not** perform the examination marking her **transition** from ritual impurity to ritual purity on the seventh day **during twilight, and after** several **days she examined** herself **and found** that **she is ritually impure, the presumptive status of that** woman is one of **ritual purity** from the time of her immersion until her examination.

גמ׳ אִיתְּמַר, רַב אָמַר: זָבָה וַדַּאי, וְלֵוִי אָמַר: זָבָה סָפֵק.

**GEMARA** The Gemara cites a dispute between *amora'im* with regard to a case where a woman did not perform an examination indicating her transition from ritual impurity to ritual purity, and three days passed in which it is possible that she received the status of a *zava*, and then she found that she was ritually impure. It **was stated** that **Rav says:** This woman is **a definite** greater ***zava*****. And Levi says:** She is **an uncertain** greater ***zava*****.**

אַהַיָּיא? אִילֵימָא אַרֵישָׁא – ״הֲרֵי זוֹ בְּחֶזְקַת טְהוֹרָה״ קָתָנֵי.

The Gemara asks: **To which** clause of the mishna does this dispute apply? **If we say** that Rav and Levi are referring **to the first clause,** i.e., a woman who examined herself on the morning of the seventh day and found herself to be ritually pure, but she did not examine herself at twilight, and several days later she examined herself and found herself to be impure, this cannot be correct, as the mishna **teaches: The presumptive status of that woman** is one of **ritual purity.** She is not a *zava* at all.

אֶלָּא אַסֵּיפָא. בִּשְׁלָמָא סְפֵק זָבָה – אָמְרִינַן, אֶלָּא זָבָה וַדַּאי נַמִי? הֲרֵי בָּדְקָה וּמָצְאָה טְהוֹרָה!

**Rather,** say that they are referring **to the latter clause** of the mishna, when she examined herself on the morning of the seventh day and found herself to be ritually impure. If so, **granted** Levi's opinion is reasonable, as **we say** that this woman is **an uncertain** greater ***zava*****. But** how can one explain Rav's opinion that she is **even a definite** greater ***zava*****?** After all, **she examined** herself **and found** that **she is ritually pure.** If so, how can she be a definite *zava*?

אֶלָּא כִּי אִיתְּמַר דְּרַב וְלֵוִי – שְׁמַעְתָּא בְּאַפֵּי נַפְשָׁהּ אִיתְּמַר: נִדָּה שֶׁבָּדְקָה עַצְמָהּ בַּיּוֹם הַשְּׁבִיעִי שַׁחֲרִית וּמָצְאָה טְמֵאָה, וּבֵין הַשְּׁמָשׁוֹת לֹא הִפְרִישָׁה, וּלְאַחַר יָמִים בָּדְקָה וּמָצְאָה טְמֵאָה, רַב אָמַר – זָבָה וַדַּאי, וְלֵוִי אָמַר – זָבָה סָפֵק.

**Rather, when** the dispute **of Rav and Levi was stated,** it **was stated** as **a distinct *halakha*** unrelated to the mishna, as follows: With regard to **a menstruating woman who examined herself on the seventh day** in **the morning**[H] **and found** that she was **ritually impure, and** at **twilight** of the seventh day she **did not** perform an examination to confirm her **transition** from ritual impurity to ritual purity, **and after** several **days she examined** herself **and found** that **she is ritually impure, Rav says:** This woman is **a definite** greater ***zava*****. And Levi says:** She is **an uncertain** greater ***zava*****.**

רַב אָמַר: זָבָה וַדַּאי, כֵּיוָן דְּמֵעִיקָּרָא נִמְצֵאת טְמֵאָה, וְעַכְשָׁיו נִמְצֵאת טְמֵאָה – טְמֵאָה וַדַּאי. וְלֵוִי אָמַר: סְפֵק זָבָה, אֵימַר, פָּסְקָה בֵּינֵי וּבֵינֵי.

The Gemara explains their opinions. **Rav says:** This woman is **a definite** greater ***zava*****, since from the outset she found** herself to be **ritually impure, and now she found** herself to also be **ritually impure.** Consequently, she is **definitely impure. And Levi says:** This woman is **an uncertain** greater ***zava*****,** as one can **say** that perhaps **she stopped** experiencing bleeding **in between** the morning of her seventh day of menstruation when she first found herself to be impure and several days later, on the second occasion that she found herself to be impure.

**NOTES**

**From *minḥa* time onward – מִן הַמִּנְחָה וּלְמַעְלָה:** The early commentaries disagree with regard to the exact definition of this time. Some say that it is referring to twilight (Rashi; Rabbi Betzalel Ronsburg), and the phrase: From *minḥa* time onward, means the conclusion of the time for reciting the *minḥa* prayer. Others hold that this is referring to the time known as *minḥa ketana*, which begins approximately two and a half hours before sunset.

וְכֵן תָּנָא לֵוִי בְּמַתְנִיתָא: אַחַר הַיָּמִים, בֵּין בָּדְקָה וּמָצְאָה טְהוֹרָה, בֵּין בָּדְקָה וּמָצְאָה טְמֵאָה – הֲרֵי זוֹ סְפֵק זָבָה.

**And Levi taught similarly in a *baraita*:**[P] If a woman examined herself on the seventh day of menstruation and found herself to be impure, and she did not perform the examination to confirm her transition from ritual impurity to ritual purity, and **after** several **days** she examined herself, **whether she examined** herself **and found** herself to be **ritually pure** or **whether she examined** herself **and found** herself to be **ritually impure, she is an uncertain** greater ***zava*.**

״וּמְטַמְּאָה מֵעֵת לְעֵת״. לֵימָא תֶּהֱוֵי תְּיוּבְתָּא דְּרָבָא! דְּאָמַר רָבָא: לוֹמַר שֶׁאֵין הָאִשָּׁה מְטַמְּאָה מֵעֵת לְעֵת בְּתוֹךְ יְמֵי זִיבָתָהּ!

§ The mishna teaches: **But she transmits ritual impurity** to the ritually pure items that she handled before the examination in which she found blood **for** a twenty-four-hour **period.** The Gemara suggests: **Let us say that it is a conclusive refutation** of the opinion **of Rava, as Rava said,** with regard to the statement in the mishna on 38b that a woman has a presumptive status of ritual purity during the eleven days of potential *ziva*: This serves **to say that a woman does not transmit ritual impurity for** a twenty-four-hour **period** before experiencing bleeding **during her days of *ziva*.**

וְלָאו אוֹתְבִינֵיהּ לְרָבָא חֲדָא זִימְנָא! הָכִי קָאָמְרִינַן: לֵימָא תֶּהֱוֵי תְּיוּבְתָּא דְּרָבָא נַמִי מֵהָא!

The Gemara asks: **But didn't** the Gemara already cite **a conclusive refutation** of the opinion **of Rava one time,** on 39a? The Gemara explains that **this is** what **we are saying: Let us say that** there **is a conclusive refutation** of the opinion **of Rava from this** mishna **as well.**

אָמַר לָךְ רָבָא: כִּי קָתָנֵי ״מְטַמְּאָה מֵעֵת לְעֵת״ – אַרֵישׁ פִּרְקִין קָאֵי, אַ״רָאֲתָה וְעוֹדָהּ בְּבֵית אָבִיהָ״.

The Gemara responds that **Rava** could have **said to you** that **when** the mishna **teaches: She transmits ritual impurity for** a twenty-four-hour **period,** it is **referring to the beginning of our chapter.** Specifically, it is speaking **of** the mishna on 64b, which discusses the case of a young woman who **saw** menstrual blood before marriage while **she was still in her father's house.** According to Beit Hillel she may engage in intercourse only the first night, during which the blood is considered the blood from the torn hymen rather than the blood of menstruation. This mishna is teaching that from that point onward, when she experiences bleeding she renders items impure retroactively for a twenty-four-hour period, like other women.

סָלְקָא דַּעְתָּךְ אָמִינָא – כֵּיוָן דְּמִפְסְקִי לְהוּ יָמִים טְהוֹרִין – כִּתְחִלַּת נִדָּתָהּ דָּמְיָא, וְלָא תְּטַמֵּא מֵעֵת לְעֵת, קָא מַשְׁמַע לָן.

The Gemara explains that this ruling is necessary, as it might **enter your mind to say** that **since** her cycle of menstruation and *ziva* is **interrupted** by **days** when any blood she discharges is considered to be **ritually pure,** she now reverts back as though it is **considered like the beginning of her** days of **menstruation, and she does not transmit ritual impurity** retroactively **for** a twenty-four-hour **period.** Therefore, this mishna **teaches us** that she does transmit impurity retroactively.

״אִם יֵשׁ לָהּ וֶסֶת״. נֵימָא תֶּהֱוֵי תְּיוּבְתָּא דְּרַב הוּנָא בַּר חִיָּיא אָמַר שְׁמוּאֵל, דְּאָמַר רַב הוּנָא בַּר חִיָּיא אָמַר שְׁמוּאֵל: לוֹמַר שֶׁאֵין הָאִשָּׁה קוֹבַעַת לָהּ וֶסֶת בִּימֵי זִיבָתָהּ.

§ The mishna teaches: And **if she has a fixed** menstrual **cycle** on the day that she examined herself and found blood, her time is sufficient and she does not transmit impurity retroactively. The Gemara asks: **Shall we say** that this **is a conclusive refutation** of the opinion **of Rav Huna bar Ḥiyya,** with regard to the ruling he says that **Shmuel says? As Rav Huna bar Ḥiyya says** that **Shmuel says,** with regard to the mishna on 38b that teaches that a woman has a presumptive status of ritual purity during the eleven days of potential *ziva*: This serves **to say that a woman does not establish a fixed** menstrual **cycle during her days of *ziva*.**

**PERSONALITIES**

Levi taught similarly in a *baraita* – כֵּן תָּנָא לֵוִי בְּמַתְנִיתָא: This is referring to Levi ben Sisi, one of the Sages in Eretz Yisrael in the transitional generation between the *tanna'im* and the *amora'im*. He was the preeminent disciple of Rabbi Yehuda HaNasi, the redactor of the Mishna. Levi also collected and compiled *baraitot*. When a *baraita* from this collection is cited by the Gemara it is introduced with the words: Levi taught in a *baraita*.

אֲמַר לָךְ רַב הוּנָא בַּר חִיָּיא: כִּי אָמְרִינַן אֵין אִשָּׁה קוֹבַעַת לָהּ וֶסֶת בִּימֵי זִיבָתָהּ – דְּלָא בָּעֲיָא תְּלָתָא זִימְנֵי לְמִיעֲקַר. דְּאָמְרִינַן דָּמֶיהָ מְסוּלָּקִין, וְכֵיוָן דְּדָמֶיהָ מְסוּלָּקִין – דַּיָּהּ שְׁעָתָהּ.

The Gemara answers that **Rav Huna bar Ḥiyya** could have **said to you: When we say** that **a woman does not establish** a fixed menstrual **cycle during her days of** ***ziva***, we meant this only as a leniency, **that** she does **not require three times to uproot**[H] any such cycle. Rather, she uproots it after one time when she does not experience bleeding in accordance with that cycle. **As we say** that **her** menstrual **blood is removed** during her days of *ziva*, and she is unlikely to discharge menstrual blood during that time. **And since her blood is removed,** if she established a fixed menstrual cycle it **is sufficient for her** to be deemed impure from the **hour** that she saw the menstrual flow. There is no decree of retroactive impurity on items that she previously touched due to the concern that the blood flow might have started earlier.

״רַבִּי יְהוּדָה אוֹמֵר״. תַּנְיָא, אָמְרוּ לוֹ לְרַבִּי יְהוּדָה: אִלְמָלֵי יָדֶיהָ מוּנָּחוֹת בְּעֵינֶיהָ כָּל בֵּין הַשְּׁמָשׁוֹת – יָפֶה אַתָּה אוֹמֵר,

§ The mishna teaches that **Rabbi Yehuda says:** With regard to any woman who did not perform the examination indicating her transition from ritual impurity to ritual purity on the seventh day from *minḥa* time onward, even if she performed an examination and found no blood that morning, the presumptive status of that woman is one of ritual impurity. It **is taught** in a *baraita* that the Rabbis **said to Rabbi Yehuda:** If the *halakha* **had** been that a woman who will immerse must keep her **hands placed in her eyes,** a euphemism for her vagina, for **the entire twilight** period, what **you say is fine.** It would be reasonable to assume that since she did not examine herself at the end of the day she has a presumptive status of ritual impurity.

עַכְשָׁיו – אֵימַר עִם סִלּוּק יָדֶיהָ רָאֲתָה, מַה לִּי הַפְרִישָׁה בְּטָהֳרָה בַּשְּׁבִיעִי מִן הַמִּנְחָה וּלְמַעְלָה – מַה לִּי הַפְרִישָׁה בְּטָהֳרָה בָּרִאשׁוֹן.

But **now** that you say that it is insufficient to examine herself in the morning, what is your reasoning? Evidently, you **say** that **when she removed her hand** from examining herself perhaps **she saw** blood and is impure. If so, **what** difference is it **to me** if she performed the examination indicating her **transition** from ritual impurity **to ritual purity on the seventh** day **from** ***minḥa*** time **onward,** and **what** difference is it **to me** if she performed the examination indicating her **transition** from ritual impurity **to ritual purity on the first** day of her counting?

בָּרִאשׁוֹן – מִי אִיכָּא לְמַאן דַּאֲמַר?

The Gemara asks: Why do the Rabbis mention an examination **on the first** day of her counting? **Is there one who said**[H] that if a woman examines herself only on the first day that is sufficient?

אִין, וְהָתַנְיָא, אָמַר רַבִּי: שָׁאַלְתִּי אֶת רַבִּי יוֹסֵי וְרַבִּי שִׁמְעוֹן כְּשֶׁהָיוּ מְהַלְּכִים בַּדֶּרֶךְ, נִדָּה שֶׁבָּדְקָה עַצְמָהּ יוֹם שְׁבִיעִי שַׁחֲרִית וּמָצְאָה טְהוֹרָה, וּבֵין הַשְּׁמָשׁוֹת לֹא הִפְרִישָׁה, וּלְאַחַר הַיָּמִים בָּדְקָה וּמָצְאָה טְמֵאָה, מַהוּ?

The Gemara answers: **Yes,** there is such an opinion, **as it is taught** in a *baraita* that **Rabbi** Yehuda HaNasi **says: I asked Rabbi Yosei and Rabbi Shimon** the following question **when they were walking on the road:** With regard to **a menstruating woman who examined herself** on the **seventh day** in **the morning and found** herself to be **ritually pure, but at twilight** she did **not** perform the examination indicating her **transition** from ritual impurity to ritual purity, **and after** several **days she examined** herself **and found** herself to be **ritually impure, what is** the *halakha*?

אָמְרוּ לוֹ: הֲרֵי זוֹ בְּחֶזְקַת טָהֳרָה. שִׁשִּׁי, חֲמִישִׁי, רְבִיעִי, שְׁלִישִׁי, שֵׁנִי, מַאי? אָמְרוּ לוֹ: לָא שְׁנָא.

Rabbi Yosei and Rabbi Shimon **said to him: She has a presumptive status of ritual purity** up until the moment that she discovered that she was impure. Rabbi Yehuda HaNasi asked them additional questions: If she examined herself on the **sixth** day, or the **fifth** day, or the **fourth** day, or the **third** day, or even the **second** day, **what** is the *halakha*? Rabbi Yosei and Rabbi Shimon **said to him:** The *halakha* **is no different.** In all of these cases she has a presumptive status of ritual purity until she discovers that she is impure.

**HALAKHA**

That she does not require three times to uproot – דְּלָא בָּעֲיָא תְּלָתָא זִימְנֵי לְמִיעֲקַר: If a woman establishes a fixed menstrual cycle during her days of *ziva* it is uprooted after one time of her not experiencing menstrual bleeding at that time, because she has a presumptive status of not experiencing bleeding during her *ziva* days. This is in accordance with the Gemara's explanation of Rav Huna bar Ḥiyya's statement (Rambam *Sefer Kedusha, Hilkhot Issurei Bia* 8:9).

Is there one who said – מִי אִיכָּא לְמַאן דַּאֲמַר: In the case of a menstruating woman who examined herself on the first day of her days of menstruation, even though she finds herself ritually pure she is considered to be ritually impure, because for the entire first day she has a presumptive status that her uterus is open and discharging blood. This is in accordance with the Rambam's explanation of the Gemara (Rambam *Sefer Kedusha, Hilkhot Issurei Bia* 6:20, and see *Maggid Mishne* there).

בְּרִאשׁוֹן לֹא שָׁאַלְתִּי, וְטָעִיתִי שֶׁלֹּא שָׁאַלְתִּי. אַטּוּ כּוּלְּהוּ לָאו בְּחֶזְקַת טוּמְאָה קָיְימִי? וְכֵיוָן דִּפְסַק – פְּסַק, רִאשׁוֹן נַמִי, כֵּיוָן דִּפְסַק – פְּסַק.

Rabbi Yehuda HaNasi comments: **I did not ask** about a woman who examined herself **on the first** day, **and I erred** in **that I did not ask** them. If I would have asked them they would have told me that even if she examined herself only on the first day, she still has a presumptive status of ritual purity. Rabbi Yehuda HaNasi explains his reasoning: **Is that to say** that on **all** of these other days **she was not standing with a presumptive** status **of ritual impurity? And** nevertheless, **once** she performed the examination and her blood is found to have **stopped,** it is considered to have **stopped,** and she now has the presumptive status of a woman whose bleeding has stopped. If so, on the **first** day **too, once** she performed the examination and her blood is found to have **stopped,** it is considered to have **stopped,** and she now has a presumptive status of a woman whose bleeding has stopped.

וּמֵעִיקָּרָא מַאי סְבַר? הוֹאִיל וְהוּחְזַק מַעְיָן פָּתוּחַ.

The Gemara asks: **And initially, what** did Rabbi Yehuda HaNasi **hold?** Why didn't he ask them about a woman who examined herself only on the first day? The Gemara answers that he held that **since she has a presumptive status** that her **spring,** i.e., her uterus, **is open,** as she had just begun experiencing bleeding, an examination conducted on that day is ineffective. In any event, this *baraita* teaches that there is an opinion that even if a woman examined herself only on the first day, she has a presumptive status of ritual purity.

**מתני׳** הַזָּב וְהַזָּבָה שֶׁבָּדְקוּ עַצְמָן בְּיוֹם רִאשׁוֹן וּמָצְאוּ טָהוֹר, וּבְיוֹם הַשְּׁבִיעִי וּמָצְאוּ טָהוֹר, וּשְׁאָר יָמִים שֶׁבֵּינְתַיִים לֹא בָּדְקוּ, רַבִּי אֱלִיעֶזֶר אוֹמֵר: הֲרֵי הֵן בְּחֶזְקַת טָהֳרָה. רַבִּי יְהוֹשֻׁעַ אוֹמֵר: אֵין לָהֶם אֶלָּא יוֹם רִאשׁוֹן וְיוֹם שְׁבִיעִי בִּלְבַד. רַבִּי עֲקִיבָא אוֹמֵר: אֵין לָהֶם אֶלָּא יוֹם שְׁבִיעִי בִּלְבַד.

**MISHNA** With regard to a *zav*[B] **and a** *zava*,[B] who are required to count and examine themselves on each of seven clean days before purification in a ritual bath, **who examined themselves on** the **first day and found** themselves **ritually pure,** i.e., with no blood, **and** they examined themselves **on the seventh day and found** themselves **ritually pure, and on the rest of the intervening days they did not examine** themselves, **Rabbi Eliezer says: The presumptive status of** the *zav* and the *zava* is one of **ritual purity. Rabbi Yehoshua says:** In that case, the *zav* and the *zava* **have** counted **only the first day and the seventh day,** two of the seven clean days, and they must count another five days to complete the tally. **Rabbi Akiva says:** The *zav* and the *zava* **have** counted **only** the **seventh day,**[N] and they must count another six days to complete the tally.

**גמ׳** תַּנְיָא, אָמַר לוֹ רַבִּי אֱלִיעֶזֶר לְרַבִּי יְהוֹשֻׁעַ: לִדְבָרֶיךָ אַתָּה מוֹנֶה בְּסֵירוּגִין, וְהַתּוֹרָה אָמְרָה ״אַחַר תִּטְהָר״ – אַחַר אַחַר לְכוּלָּן, שֶׁלֹּא תְּהֵא טוּמְאָה מַפְסֶקֶת בֵּינֵיהֶן!

**GEMARA** It is taught in a *baraita* that **Rabbi Eliezer said to Rabbi Yehoshua: According to your statement,** that the first day is included in her count of seven, **you are counting at intervals,** i.e., with days in-between that do not count, **and the Torah states:** "But if she be purified of her *ziva*, then she shall count to herself seven days, **and after that she shall be pure**" (Leviticus 15:28). This teaches that the purification of a *zava* must be **after** the seven days, i.e., **after all of the** days, which must be consecutive so **that there are no days of impurity separating between** the seven clean days.

**BACKGROUND**

*Zav* – **זָב**: The *halakhot* relating to the stringent ritual impurity caused by this condition appear in Leviticus, chapter 15, and in tractate *Zavim*. The *zav* becomes ritually impure as a result of discharging a white, pus-like substance. A man who experiences this discharge on one occasion becomes ritually impure for one day, similar to a man who experiences a seminal emission. If one experiences a second discharge on the same day or the following day, or if the initial discharge is prolonged, he contracts the more severe ritual impurity of a *zav*, which lasts seven days. One who experiences a third discharge on that day or the next day is obligated to bring an offering as part of his purification process. Not only does he become ritually impure, he also imparts ritual impurity through contact with vessels or people, by being moved by them, by moving them, and by lying or sitting on them. He also imparts impurity to items under a very heavy stone by sitting on the stone, although the stone itself does not thereby become impure. The fluids of a *zav*, i.e., his saliva, urine, and semen, impart ritual impurity, and the surfaces on which he sits or lies become primary sources of ritual impurity and can themselves impart ritual impurity to other articles.

*Zava* – **זָבָה**: A *zava* is a woman who experiences a flow of menstrual-type blood during a time of the month when she is not due to experience menstrual bleeding. The first discharge makes her ritually impure, but until the third discharge she is a lesser *zava* and she observes a clean day for a day she experiences a discharge. After experiencing bleeding on the third day, the woman is considered a greater *zava*. A *zava* imparts ritual impurity in the same way as a *zav*, through contact with vessels or people, by being moved by them, by moving them, and by lying or sitting on them. In addition, a man who engages in sexual intercourse with her becomes a primary source of ritual impurity and imparts ritual impurity to others. A greater *zava* is purified through immersion in a ritual bath following seven clean days without bleeding. The immersion of a *zava* may take place during the day on the last day of her purification or any time thereafter. A greater *zava* is also obligated to bring an offering as part of her purification process.

**NOTES**

**Rabbi Akiva says, they have counted only the seventh day – רַבִּי עֲקִיבָא אוֹמֵר אֵין לָהֶם אֶלָּא יוֹם שְׁבִיעִי בִּלְבַד:** Since it is possible that they experienced a discharge on any of the intermediate days, which would overturn the counting of the previous days, they count the seventh day as their first day (Rashi).

אָמַר לוֹ רַבִּי יְהוֹשֻׁעַ: וְאַתָּה, אִי אַתָּה מוֹדֶה בְּזָב שֶׁרָאָה קֶרִי, וּבְנָזִיר שֶׁהִילֵּךְ סְכָכוֹת וּפְרָעוֹת, שֶׁמּוֹנֶה בְּסֵירוּגִין? וְהַתּוֹרָה אָמְרָה "וְהַיָּמִים הָרִאשֹׁנִים יִפְּלוּ".

**Rabbi Yehoshua says: And you** too, **do you not concede with regard to a *zav* who experienced a seminal emission** during his count of seven clean days, **and with regard to a nazirite who walked** under **overhanging boughs and protrusions** that have items whose status of impurity is uncertain beneath them, **that** they **count at intervals,** as both are impure for one day before resuming their counting? **And** yet **the Torah states** with regard to a nazirite who definitely contracted ritual impurity from a corpse: **"But the former days shall be void,** because his consecration was defiled" (Numbers 6:12). This indicates that even in cases where the Torah says that one must count consecutively, it is permitted to count with intervals in between countings.

וְרַבִּי אֱלִיעֶזֶר; בִּשְׁלָמָא הָתָם – "לְטָמְאָה בָהּ" אָמַר רַחֲמָנָא – שֶׁאֵינָהּ סוֹתֶרֶת אֶלָּא יוֹמָהּ, וְאִי מִשּׁוּם אִיחְלוּפֵי – זָב בְּבַעַל קֶרִי לָא מִיחֲלַף.

**And** how would **Rabbi Eliezer** respond to Rabbi Yehoshua's claim? He would say: **Granted, there** in the cases of the *zav* and the nazirite, **the Merciful One states:** "This is the law of him that has an issue, and of him from whom an emission of semen goes out, **so that he is thereby impure"** (Leviticus 15:32). This teaches **that** when a *zav* experiences a seminal emission it **overturns** the counting of **only that** one **day. And if** one would claim that the Sages should issue a decree **due to** the concern that one might **confuse** the *halakha* of one who had an emission of *ziva* during the seven clean days with a *zav* who had a seminal emission during the seven clean days, that is not a concern. The reason is that an emission of a ***ziva*** will **not be confused with** the case of **one who experienced a seminal emission.**

נָזִיר שֶׁהִילֵּךְ עַל גַּבֵּי סְכָכוֹת וּפְרָעוֹת נַמִי מִדְּאוֹרַיְיתָא אֹהֶל מְעַלְּיָא בָּעֵינַן, וְרַבָּנַן הוּא דִּגְזוּר – וְרַבָּנַן בִּדְאוֹרַיְיתָא לָא מִיחֲלַף.

Similarly, Rabbi Eliezer would say that in the case of **a nazirite who walked under overhanging boughs and protrusions** that have items whose status of impurity is uncertain beneath them, there is **also** no need to overturn all the previous days of counting, as **by Torah law we require a full-fledged tent** over a corpse, **and** it was **the Sages who decreed** that one who walks under overhanging boughs and protrusions is ritually impure. **And** a *halakha* that applies **by rabbinic law will not be confused** with a *halakha* that is mandated **by Torah law.**

אֲבָל הָכָא, אִי חָיְישִׁינַן דִּלְמָא חֲזַאי בְּסָפֵק, אָתֵי לְאִיחְלוּפֵי בְּוַדַּאי.

**But here,** in the case of a *zava* who counts only the first and seventh day, **if we are concerned** that as she did not count the five intermediate days **perhaps she saw** blood during those days, and since what occurred on those days is **uncertain,** only the first day counts for her, then one might **come to confuse** this situation **with** a case where she is **certain** that she saw blood during the intermediate days. One might mistakenly think that even if she definitely experiences bleeding during the intermediate days she can still count the first day as one of her seven clean days before immersing.

תָּנֵי, רַבִּי יוֹסֵי וְרַבִּי שִׁמְעוֹן אָמְרִי: נִרְאִין דִּבְרֵי רַבִּי אֱלִיעֶזֶר מִדִּבְרֵי רַבִּי יְהוֹשֻׁעַ, וְדִבְרֵי רַבִּי עֲקִיבָא מִדִּבְרֵי כּוּלָּן, אֲבָל הֲלָכָה כְּרַבִּי אֱלִיעֶזֶר.

It **is taught** in a *baraita* that **Rabbi Yosei and Rabbi Shimon say: The statement of Rabbi Eliezer appears** more correct **than the statement of Rabbi Yehoshua, and the statement of Rabbi Akiva** appears more correct **than the statement of all of them. But** nevertheless, the ***halakha*** is **in accordance with** the opinion of **Rabbi Eliezer.**[H]

אִיבַּעְיָא לְהוּ: הַזָּב וְהַזָּבָה שֶׁבָּדְקוּ עַצְמָן יוֹם רִאשׁוֹן וְיוֹם שְׁמִינִי וּמָצְאוּ טָהוֹר, וּשְׁאָר הַיָּמִים לֹא בָּדְקוּ,

§ **A dilemma was raised before** the Sages: With regard to **a *zav* and a *zava* who examined themselves** on the **first day** of their seven clean days and found themselves to be pure, **and** they examined themselves again on the **eighth day and found** themselves to be **pure, but** they did **not examine** themselves on **the remainder of the days,**

**HALAKHA**

**But the *halakha* is in accordance with the opinion of Rabbi Eliezer – אֲבָל הֲלָכָה כְּרַבִּי אֱלִיעֶזֶר:** If a *zava* only examined herself once during her seven clean days, whether on the first day or seventh day or any of the other days, since she finds herself to be ritually pure before the seventh day, she has fulfilled her obligation. This is in accordance with the opinion of Rav cited later in the Gemara. The same applies to a *zav*. Others hold that she must examine herself on both the first and seventh days, and one may not be lenient (Rambam *Sefer Kedusha, Hilkhot Issurei Bia* 6:22, and *Haggahot Maimoniyyot* there; *Shulḥan Arukh, Yoreh De'a* 196:4).

לְרַבִּי אֱלִיעֶזֶר מַהוּ? תְּחִלָּתָן וְסוֹפָן בָּעֵינַן, וְהָכָא – תְּחִלָּתָן אִיכָּא, סוֹפָן לֵיכָּא. אוֹ דִילְמָא – תְּחִלָּתָן אַף עַל גַּב שֶׁאֵין סוֹפָן?

**according to** the opinion of **Rabbi Eliezer,** that if they examined themselves on the first and seventh days they are considered to be pure during the intermediate days as well, **what is the** *halakha*?[N] **Do we require the first and last** days **of** the seven, **and** if so, **here there is** an examination on the **first** day, and yet **there is no** examination on the **last** day, but only on the eighth day? **Or perhaps** Rabbi Eliezer requires an examination only on the **first of** the days, and this is sufficient **even though there is no** examination on the **last** of the seven days.

אֲמַר רַב: הִיא הִיא, תְּחִלָּתָן אַף עַל פִּי שֶׁאֵין סוֹפָן. וְרַבִּי חֲנִינָא אֲמַר: תְּחִלָּתָן וְסוֹפָן בָּעֵינַן, הָכָא – תְּחִלָּתָן אִיכָּא, סוֹפָן לֵיכָּא.

**Rav said: This** case of examining on the first and eighth days **is** the same as **that** of examining on the first and seventh days, i.e., Rabbi Eliezer requires an examination only on the **first of** the days, and this examination is sufficient **even though there is no** examination on the **last of** the days. **And Rabbi Ḥanina said: We require** an examination on **the first and last** days **of** the seven, and **here there is** an examination on the **first** day but **there is no** examination on the **last** day. Consequently, Rabbi Eliezer would not permit a *zav* or a *zava* to count any of the days in this case.

מֵיתִיבֵי: וְשָׁוִין בְּזָב וּבְזָבָה שֶׁבָּדְקוּ עַצְמָן יוֹם רִאשׁוֹן וְיוֹם שְׁמִינִי וּמָצְאוּ טָהוֹר – שֶׁאֵין לָהֶם אֶלָּא שְׁמִינִי בִּלְבַד. מַאן "שָׁוִין"? לָאו רַבִּי אֱלִיעֶזֶר וְרַבִּי יְהוֹשֻׁעַ?

The Gemara **raises an objection** to the opinion of Rav from a *baraita*: **And** the Sages **agree with regard to a** *zav* **and a** *zava* **who examined themselves** on the **first day and** on the **eighth day and found** themselves to be **ritually pure, that they have only** the **eighth** day as part of their count. The Gemara asks: **Who** are the Sages who **agree** to this? Are they **not Rabbi Eliezer and Rabbi Yehoshua?** These two Sages, who disagree in a case where the *zav* and *zava* examined themselves on the first and seventh days, are evidently the ones who agree in the case of a woman who performed an examination on the first and the eighth days. This seems to contradict Rav's opinion.

לָא, רַבִּי יְהוֹשֻׁעַ וְרַבִּי עֲקִיבָא.

The Gemara rejects this suggestion: **No,** the Sages referred to here are **Rabbi Yehoshua and Rabbi Akiva.** Both of them agree that in this case the first day is not included in the count. Conversely, Rabbi Eliezer would say that the first seven days are included in the count and the eighth day is unnecessary, as there is a presumptive status of ritual purity from her examination on the first day.

אָמַר רַב שֵׁשֶׁת, אָמַר רַב יִרְמְיָה בַּר אַבָּא, אָמַר רַב: נִדָּה שֶׁהִפְרִישָׁה בְּטָהֳרָה בַּשְּׁלִישִׁי שֶׁלָּהּ – סוֹפַרְתּוֹ לְמִנְיַן שִׁבְעָה נְקִיִּים.

§ The Gemara cites another discussion with regard to which days are included in the count of seven clean days. **Rav Sheshet says** that **Rav Yirmeya bar Abba says** that **Rav says: A menstruating woman who** performed the examination marking the first step in her **transition** from ritual impurity **to ritual purity on her third** day **counts** that day as part **of the number of seven clean** days.

נִדָּה, סְפִירָה לָמָּה לָהּ? אֶלָּא אֵימָא: זָבָה שֶׁהִפְרִישָׁה בְּטָהֳרָה בַּשְּׁלִישִׁי שֶׁלָּהּ – סוֹפַרְתּוֹ לְמִנְיַן שִׁבְעָה נְקִיִּים.

The Gemara asks: **Why does a menstruating woman** require any kind of **counting?** If this is during her days when she is expected to menstruate she may immerse after the conclusion of seven days, whether or not those days were clean. **Rather, say** that Rav meant as follows: **A** *zava* **who** performed the examination marking the first step in her **transition** from ritual impurity to **ritual purity on her third** day[H] **counts** that day as part **of the number of seven clean** days.

**NOTES**

**According to the opinion of Rabbi Eliezer what is the *halakha* – לְרַבִּי אֱלִיעֶזֶר מַהוּ:** The question with regard to an examination on the first and eighth days applies only according to the opinion of Rabbi Eliezer. According to the opinion of Rabbi Yehoshua, although she may count days that are not consecutive, they must be days that can combine with each other. An examination on the eighth day cannot combine with the examination on the first day, as it is too distant. It is therefore clear that in his opinion the woman has verified there is no blood only for the eighth day in such a case. Similarly, according to the opinion of Rabbi Akiva, who is concerned that she might experience bleeding between the examination on the first day and the examination on the seventh day, the same applies if she examines herself on the eighth day. Therefore he too agrees that she verified there is no blood only for the eighth day in this case (Rashi).

**HALAKHA**

**A *zava* who performed her transition to ritual purity on her third day – זָבָה שֶׁהִפְרִישָׁה בְּטָהֳרָה בַּשְּׁלִישִׁי שֶׁלָּהּ:** If a woman performs an examination on the third day of her *ziva* and finds that the bleeding has ceased, and she did not examine herself on the first of her seven days but on the seventh day she examined herself and found herself to be pure, she has a presumptive status of not having experienced bleeding for the entire time. This is in accordance with the statement of Rav Yirmeya bar Abba, citing Rav (Rambam *Sefer Kedusha, Hilkhot Issurei Bia* 6:22; *Shulḥan Arukh, Yoreh De'a* 196:4).

אֲמַר לֵיהּ רַב שֵׁשֶׁת לְרַב יִרְמְיָה בַּר אַבָּא: רַב כְּכוּתָאֵי אֲמָרָהּ לִשְׁמַעְתֵּיהּ, דְּאָמְרִי יוֹם שֶׁפּוֹסֶקֶת בּוֹ סוֹפֶרֶתוֹ לְמִנְיַן שִׁבְעָה!

**Rav Sheshet said to Rav Yirmeya bar Abba:** Did **Rav say his** *halakha* **in accordance with** the opinion of **the Samaritans, who say** that **the day on which** a *zava* **ceases** to experience the emission of *ziva* **counts toward** the **number** of **seven** clean days, and she does not need to count seven complete days?

כִּי קָאָמַר רַב, לְבַר מִשְּׁלִישִׁי. בַּר מִשְּׁלִישִׁי, פְּשִׁיטָא! לָא צְרִיכָא, כְּגוֹן דְּלָא בָּדְקָה עַד שְׁבִיעִי,

Rav Yirmeya bar Abba replied: **When Rav says** his *halakha*, he meant **apart from** the **third** day. Rav Sheshet challenged: If Rav meant **apart from** the **third** day, that is **obvious;** there is no need for him to issue such a statement at all. Rav Yirmeya bar Abba replied: **No,** the statement that she begins counting immediately after the third day is **necessary** for a case **where** once she saw that she was clean after the third day of her *ziva* emissions **she did not examine** herself again **until** the **seventh** day.

וְאַשְׁמוּעִינַן הָתָם – תְּחִלָּתָן אַף עַל פִּי שֶׁאֵין סוֹפָן, וְהָכָא קָא מַשְׁמַע לָן – סוֹפָן אַף עַל פִּי שֶׁאֵין תְּחִלָּתָן.

**And** Rav is **teaching us** two *halakhot*. **There,** in the previous discussion with regard to the opinion of Rabbi Eliezer, Rav stated that an examination **at the beginning** is sufficient, **even though there is no** examination at the **end** of the seven days. **And here he teaches us** that an examination at the **end of** the seven days is sufficient, **even though there is no** examination at the **beginning of** the seven days, but only on the day when she ceased experiencing bleeding.

דְּמַהוּ דְּתֵימָא: תְּחִלָּתָן אַף עַל פִּי שֶׁאֵין סוֹפָן הוּא דְּאָמְרִינַן, דְּאוֹקְמִינְהוּ אַחֶזְקַיְיהוּ, אֲבָל סוֹפָן אַף עַל פִּי שֶׁאֵין תְּחִלָּתָן – לָא, קָא מַשְׁמַע לָן.

Rav Yirmeya adds **that** it is necessary to teach both *halakhot*, **lest you say** that **we say** that an examination **at the beginning** is sufficient **even though there is no** examination at the **end of** the seven days, **as we establish** the clean days **in** accordance with **their presumptive status. But** one might have thought that Rav would **not** permit her to consider all the days to have been clean in a case of an examination at the **end of** the seven days **even though there is no** examination at the **beginning of** the seven days, where no presumptive status was established. Therefore, this second statement of Rav **teaches us** that even if she only examined herself at the end of the seven clean days it is sufficient.

אִינִי, וְהָא כִּי אֲתָא רָבִין אֲמַר: מְתִיב רַבִּי יוֹסֵי בְּרַבִּי חֲנִינָא "טוֹעָה".

The Gemara raises a difficulty with regard to Rav Yirmeya's explanation. **Is that so? But when Ravin came** from Eretz Yisrael **he said: Rabbi Yosei, son of Rabbi Ḥanina, raised an objection** to the opinion of Rabbi Yehoshua ben Levi, that a woman who is uncertain whether or not she miscarried an actual fetus must bring an offering (see 29a). The reason is that the majority of pregnant women carry actual fetuses. Rabbi Yosef objected to this from the case of a woman who was **forgetful,**[N] i.e., a woman who left town when she was pregnant, and later returned no longer pregnant. It is unknown whether she miscarried an actual fetus, and if it was a fetus, whether it was male or female. The conclusion there was that she does not have any days when blood she discharges is considered ritually pure, which is the *halakha* following a birth, as her miscarriage might not have been a fetus at all. Apparently, here one does not follow the principle that the majority of pregnant women carry actual fetuses.

NOTES

A woman who was forgetful – טוֹעָה: The main discussion of a woman who is forgetful is on 29b. A *baraita* there teaches: A woman left home for an extended period of time while she was full, i.e., pregnant, and came back when she was empty, as she miscarried the fetus, but it is unknown exactly when and what she miscarried; she spent three weeks in our presence during which she was pure, i.e., she did not experience any bleeding, and for the following ten weeks she alternated between one impure week, in which she experienced bleeding every day, and one pure week, in which she did not experience bleeding at all. In such a case, the woman may engage in intercourse with her husband at the end of the fifth week following her return, on the eve of the thirty-fifth day, after which she is again prohibited from engaging in intercourse with him.

There is a dispute between *tanna'im* as to how many times she must immerse. Beit Shammai hold that she must immerse ninety-five times, whereas Beit Hillel hold that she needs to immerse thirty-five times, and Rabbi Yosei bar Yehuda holds that she must immerse only once.

וְלָא יָדַעְנָא מַאי תְּיוּבְתֵּיהּ. דְּקַיְימָא לַן, שָׁבוּעַ קַמָּא דְּאָתְיָא לְקַמָּן – בְּלֵילְוָתָא מַטְבְּלִינַן לָהּ, בִּימָמָא לָא מַטְבְּלִינַן לָהּ.

Ravin continues: **And I do not know what his objection is,** as the reason that she does not have any days when blood she discharges is considered ritually pure is not only due to the uncertainty as to whether or not she miscarried a fetus, but because it is also unknown when that miscarriage occurred, i.e., even if she miscarried a fetus, perhaps the days when blood she discharges is considered ritually pure had already been completed. **As we maintain** that the **first week that she comes before us,** when the court is uncertain with regard to her impurity, **we** tell **her** to **immerse** every **night** of that week, in the manner of a woman purifying herself after menstruation or childbirth, but **we do not** tell **her** to **immerse during the daytime,** as she has not counted seven clean days (see 29b).

וְאִי סָלְקָא דַּעְתָּךְ לָא בָּעֵינַן סְפוּרִין לְפָנֵינוּ – בִּימָמָא נַמִי נַטְבְּלִינָהּ, דִּילְמָא יוֹלֶדֶת זָכָר בְּזוֹב הִיא, וַעֲבָדָה לָהּ סְפוּרִין! אֶלָּא לָאו שְׁמַע מִינָּהּ – בָּעֵינַן סְפוּרִין בְּפָנֵינוּ!

The Gemara explains how this discussion apparently contradicts Rav Yirmeya's explanation. **And if it enters your mind** that **we do not require** all seven clean days to be **counted before us,** i.e., if an examination on the seventh day is sufficient, **let us** tell her to **immerse also** during **the daytime,** as **perhaps she gave birth to a male** baby **during** her days **of** ***ziva*****, and** already **performed her** seven days of **counting** before she came before the court. The Gemara concludes: **Rather,** must one **not conclude from** this statement of Ravin that **we require** that her seven clean days be **counted before us,** which is why the court does not instruct her to immerse during the daytime.

וְלָאו מִי אוֹקִימְנָא כְּרַבִּי עֲקִיבָא דְּאָמַר בָּעֵינַן סְפוּרִין לְפָנֵינוּ?!

The Gemara rejects this contention. **But didn't we interpret** that the *baraita* is **in accordance with** the opinion of **Rabbi Akiva, who said** that **we require** her seven clean days to be **counted before us?** By contrast, Rav's statement was in accordance with the opinion of Rabbi Eliezer, who holds that the days do not need to be counted before us.

וּמְנָא תֵּימְרָא דִּלְרַבָּנַן לָא בָּעֵינַן סְפוּרִין לְפָנֵינוּ – דִּתְנַן: טוֹעָה שֶׁאָמְרָה "יוֹם אֶחָד טָמֵא רָאִיתִי" – מַטְבִּילִין אוֹתָהּ תֵּשַׁע טְבִילוֹת,

§ The Gemara stated earlier that according to the opinion of the Rabbis, the seven clean days do not need to be counted before us. The Gemara analyzes their opinion: **And from where do you say that according to** the opinion of **the Rabbis we do not require** that the seven days be **counted before us?** This is **as we learned** in a *baraita*: With regard to a woman who was **forgetful** and does not know whether she is now in her days of menstruation or days of *ziva*, **who said: I saw** blood on **one day of impurity,**[N] the court instructs **her to immerse nine immersions.**

שֶׁבַע לְנִדָּה וּתְרֵי לְזִיבָה. "בֵּין הַשְּׁמָשׁוֹת טָמֵא רָאִיתִי" – מַטְבִּילִין אוֹתָהּ אַחַת עֶשְׂרֵה טְבִילוֹת.

The *baraita* clarifies: Since there is no way of knowing whether she is a woman purifying herself after menstruation or after *ziva*, she must immerse **seven** immersions on the following seven nights, **for** purification from **menstruation,** as each of these days might be the last of the seven days of menstruation. **And** she must also immerse during **two** days as purification **from** ***ziva*****,** i.e., on the day that she arrives, in case she experienced bleeding the day before, and on the following day, as perhaps she experienced bleeding on the day of her arrival. But if this woman says: **I saw** blood **at twilight** that renders me **impure,** the court instructs **her** to **immerse eleven immersions.**

אַחַת עֶשְׂרֵה מַאי עֲבִידְתַּיְיהוּ? אֲמַר רַב יִרְמְיָה מִדִּפְתִּי: כְּגוֹן שֶׁבָּאת לְפָנֵינוּ בֵּין הַשְּׁמָשׁוֹת,

The Gemara asks: These **eleven** days, **what is their purpose?** If she would normally require nine immersions, why does she require an extra two immersions if she experienced bleeding at twilight? **Rav Yirmeya of Difti said:** The *baraita* is referring specifically to a case **where she came before us at twilight** and says that she also experienced bleeding at twilight, but it is not clear whether she experienced bleeding on a previous day at twilight, or today at twilight.

NOTES

A woman who was forgetful who said, I saw blood on one day of impurity – טוֹעָה שֶׁאָמְרָה יוֹם אֶחָד טָמֵא רָאִיתִי: Some explain that this refers to a woman who is certain that she performed an examination marking the beginning of her transition from ritual impurity to ritual purity after she stopped experiencing bleeding. If she does not know whether she has performed this examination she may not immerse at all (Ramban; Ran). Others write that even if she is uncertain about this it does not prevent her from immersing because this examination is a stringency, and immersing at the first possible time is its own mitzva (*Tosefot HaRosh*).

BACKGROUND

Galaḥi – גַּלְּחִי: Rashi explains that this was the custom in a place named Galaḥi. The later commentaries explain that the word Galaḥi is either another name for the city of Sodom (*Arukh LaNer*), or it refers to a specific neighborhood within Sodom (*Arukh*). In *Sanhedrin* (109a–b) there are many stories about the wickedness of the people of Sodom, and the story of the orphan slaughtering the oxen is included among them (Ya'avetz).

LANGUAGE

Widow [*armelata*] – אַרְמַלְתָּא: This Aramaic word is phonetically related to, and has the same meaning as, the Hebrew word for widow, *almana*.

וְהָוְיָין תְּמָנֵי לְנִדָּה וּתְלָת לְזִיבָה.

Rav Yirmeya explains: Therefore, she requires **eight** immersions to purify herself **from menstruation,** seven in case each of the following nights is the night after the seventh day of menstruation, and the eighth in case she experienced bleeding during twilight of the day she arrived, and this occurred in a time which was actually part of the next day, such that she needs to immerse also on the eighth night from her arrival, **and three** additional immersions during the day to purify herself **from *ziva*.** She must immerse during the day three times: She must immerse immediately, because if she experienced bleeding on the previous day during twilight it may have still been day, and right now, at twilight, it might still be day; she must immerse on the next day, because if she experienced bleeding on the previous day during twilight it may have already been night; and she must immerse during the day following the next day, because perhaps she experienced bleeding this twilight after it was night.

״לֹא רָאִיתִי כָּל עִיקָּר״ – מַטְבִּילִין אוֹתָהּ חָמֵשׁ עֶשְׂרֵה טְבִילוֹת. אָמַר רָבָא: הַאי דִּינָא דְּלָא דִּינָא, דַּיְינֵי בְּגַלְּחִי, דְּאִית לֵיהּ תּוֹרָא – לִירְעֵי חַד יוֹמָא, דְּלֵית לֵיהּ תּוֹרָא – לִירְעֵי תְּרֵי יוֹמֵי.

If this woman who is forgetful with regard to her cycle of menstruation and *ziva* says: **I have not seen any** blood **at all,** the court instructs **her to immerse fifteen immersions. Rava said,** in reference to this final *halakha* in the *baraita*: **This *halakha*** is **not** a logical ***halakha*.** Rather, it is like the *halakha* that **they judge in** a place named **Galaḥi.**[B] In that place they follow the behavior of Sodom, and say that with regard to one **who has** one **ox,**[N] **he must shepherd** the local flocks **one day,** and one **who does not have an ox must shepherd** the local flocks for **two days.** It is not logical that a woman who has not experienced a flow of blood must immerse more times than one who has experienced a flow of blood.

אִתְרְמֵי לְהוּ יַתְמָא בַּר אַרְמַלְתָּא, יָהֲבִי לֵיהּ תּוֹרֵי, אֲזַל נַכְסִינְהוּ. אֲמַר לְהוּ: דְּאִית לֵיהּ תּוֹרָא – לִשְׁקוֹל חַד מַשְׁכָּא, דְּלֵית לֵיהּ תּוֹרָא – לִשְׁקוֹל תְּרֵי מַשְׁכֵי. אָמְרִי לֵיהּ: מַאי הַאי דְּקָאָמְרַתְּ? אֲמַר לְהוּ: סוֹף דִּינָא כִּתְחִלַּת דִּינָא. תְּחִלַּת דִּינָא לָאו מַאן דְּלֵית לֵיהּ עָדִיף? סוֹף דִּינָא נַמִי – מַאן דְּלֵית לֵיהּ עָדִיף!

Apropos the mention of Galaḥi, the Gemara relates an incident that occurred in that place. **There was an orphan** in that town, **the son of a widow** [*armelata*],[L] who had no oxen of his own. The people of that town **gave him their oxen** to shepherd. This orphan **went and slaughtered** all of the oxen. **He said** to the townspeople: Whoever **has an ox should take one skin,** while one **who does not have an ox should take two skins.** The people of Galaḥi **said to** the orphan: **What is this that you are saying,** i.e., what is the reason? **He said to them: The end of the law is like the beginning of the law: Isn't the beginning of the law** that one **who has no** ox **is preferred,** and must shepherd the oxen for two days? So too, with regard to **the end of the law,** one **who has no** ox **is preferred** and should receive two hides.

הָכָא נַמִי, וּמָה הֵיכָא דְּאָמְרָה ״רָאִיתִי״ – סָגֵי לָהּ אִי בְּתֵשַׁע טְבִילוֹת אִי בְּאַחַת עֶשְׂרֵה טְבִילוֹת, הֵיכָא דְּקָאָמְרָה אִיהִי ״לֹא רָאִיתִי״ בָּעֲיָא חָמֵשׁ עֶשְׂרֵה טְבִילוֹת?!

The Gemara returns to discuss Rava's comment with regard to the ruling of the *baraita*: **Here too** one can claim: **And if** in a case **where she says: I saw** blood, **it is sufficient for her** to immerse **either nine immersions or eleven immersions,** so too, in a case **where she says: I did not see** any flow of blood at all, is it logical that **she requires fifteen immersions?**

אֶלָּא אֵימָא הָכִי: ״רָאִיתִי וְאֵינִי יוֹדַעַת כַּמָּה רָאִיתִי, אִי בִּימֵי נִדָּה רָאִיתִי אוֹ בִּימֵי זִיבָה רָאִיתִי״ – מַטְבִּילִין אוֹתָהּ חָמֵשׁ עֶשְׂרֵה טְבִילוֹת. אֲתַאי קַמַּן בִּימָמָא – יָהֲבִינַן לָהּ שֶׁבַע לְנִדָּה,

**Rather, say** that **this** is what the *baraita* means: If a woman says: **I saw** a flow of blood **but I do not know how many** days **I saw** blood, and likewise I do not know **whether I saw** the flow **during the days of menstruation or** if **I saw** the flow **during the days of *ziva*,** in such a case, the court instructs **her to immerse fifteen immersions.** The reason for these immersions is as follows: If **she comes before us during the daytime, we give her seven** immersions, beginning from that night, to remove the impurity **of menstruation.** Any of those seven nights might be the night after the last of her days of menstruation.

NOTES

**One who has one ox, etc.** – דְּאִית לֵיהּ תּוֹרָא וכו׳: The early commentaries explain why this ruling is illogical. It requires very little extra work for one who owns an ox that he must look after to look after oxen belonging to others at the same time (see *Bava Metzia* 69a). Conversely, one who has no oxen and therefore would not normally be tending to an animal at all should not be required to do so, as that would prevent him from performing another task. Certainly, there is no reason for him to have to watch the oxen for two days (*Yad Ramah*).

וּתְמָנֵי לְזִיבָה, אֲתַאי קַמָּן בְּלֵילְוָתָא – יָהֲבִינַן לָהּ תְּמָנֵי לְנִדָּה וְשַׁב לְזִיבָה.

**And** she requires **eight** immersions during the day to purify her **from** her ***ziva***, as it is possible that she experienced bleeding for three consecutive days, rendering her a greater *zava*, and one of those was on this day that she came before the court, and it is also possible that the day she arrived she did not experience bleeding, and she was a *zava* during her last clean day and had to immerse that day. If **she comes before us at night, we give her eight** immersions to purify herself **from her menstruation,** including one on the night that she comes before the court, **and seven** immersions during the day to purify herself **from** her ***ziva***.

זִיבָה – תְּמָנֵי בָּעֲיָא! אֶלָּא, אִידִי וְאִידִי שַׁב לְנִדָּה וּתְמָנֵי לְזִיבָה.

The Gemara raises a difficulty: With regard to her ***ziva***, she still **requires eight** immersions. Since it is possible that she experienced bleeding for the third day on the day before coming to the court, she might be a greater *zava*, who starts her clean days only the day after she arrived. In addition, any of the first seven days may be the last clean day, on which she has to immerse herself. The Gemara answers: **Rather,** in both **this** case **and that** case she requires **seven** immersions to purify herself **from** the impurity of **menstruation, and eight** immersions to purify herself **from** the impurity of ***ziva***.

בְּלֵילְוָתָא, תְּמָנֵי לְנִדָּה בָּעֵי!

The Gemara raises a further difficulty: If the woman comes **at night** to the court, she **requires eight** immersions to purify herself **from** her impurity of **menstruation.** Why does the *baraita* require her to immerse a total of only fifteen times when there are cases where she must immerse sixteen times?

זִיבָה דִּפְסִיקָא לֵיהּ, דְּלָא שְׁנָא כִּי אָתְיָא קַמָּן בִּימָמָא, לָא שְׁנָא כִּי אָתְיָא קַמָּן בְּלֵילְיָא – חָשֵׁיב לָהּ. נִדָּה דְּלָא פְּסִיקָא לֵיהּ, דְּכִי אָתְיָא קַמָּן בְּלֵילְוָתָא – בָּעֵי תְּמָנֵי, בִּימָמָא – לָא קָבָעֵי תְּמָנֵי, לָא קָחָשֵׁיב לָהּ.

The Gemara answers: With regard to purifying herself from the impurity of ***ziva*, which** can be taught in **a distinct** manner, **as there is no difference whether she comes before us during the day** and **there is no difference whether she comes before us at night,** the *baraita* **counts** the fixed amount of eight immersions. By contrast, with regard to purifying herself from **menstruation, which** the *tanna* **cannot** teach in **a distinct** manner, **as when she comes before us at night she requires eight** immersions but if she comes before us **during the day** she does **not require eight** immersions, the *tanna* **did not count** both options, but mentioned only seven immersions, which is the minimum number required.

וְאִי סָלְקָא דַּעְתָּךְ סְפוּרִין לְפָנֵינוּ בָּעֵינַן – כָּל הָנֵי טְבִילוֹת לָמָּה לִי? תִּסְפּוֹר שַׁב וַהֲדַר תִּטְבּוֹל! אֶלָּא לָאו שְׁמַע מִינָּהּ – רַבָּנַן הִיא, דְּאָמְרִי לָא בָּעֵינַן סְפוּרִין לְפָנֵינוּ.

The Gemara returns to the initial purpose of this discussion, which was to indicate that the Rabbis do not require all seven days of counting before the court. **And if it enters your mind** that **we require** seven days of **counting before us, why do I need all of these immersions? She** should **count seven** clean days **and** only **afterward immerse. Rather,** must one **not conclude from this** that the *baraita* **is** in accordance with the opinion of **the Rabbis,** who disagree with Rabbi Akiva and **who say** that **we do not require** seven days of **counting before us?**

אֲמַר לֵיהּ רַב אַחָא בְּרֵיהּ דְּרַב יוֹסֵף לְרַב אַשִׁי: לָאו תֵּרוּצֵי קְמְתָרְצִינַן לָהּ?! תְּרֵיץ וְאֵימָא הָכִי – ״סָפַרְתִּי וְאֵינִי יוֹדַעַת כַּמָּה סָפַרְתִּי, אִם בִּימֵי נִדָּה סָפַרְתִּי וְאִם בִּימֵי זִיבָה סָפַרְתִּי״ – מַטְבִּילִין אוֹתָהּ חֲמֵשׁ עֶשְׂרֵה טְבִילוֹת.

**Rav Aḥa, son of Rav Yosef, said to Rav Ashi,** in rejection of this proof: But **didn't you resolve** a difficulty in the *baraita*? Since you admit that the *baraita* in any event requires revision, **resolve** this difficulty too, **and say this:** If a woman comes and says: **I counted**[N] clean days **but I do not know how many** days **I counted,**[N] and I do not know **whether I counted during the days of menstruation or whether I counted during the days of *ziva***, the court instructs **her to immerse fifteen immersions.** If so, there is no proof that the Rabbis hold that the counting does not need to be before the court.

**NOTES**

**I counted** – סָפַרְתִּי: The term: I counted, refers to a specific act performed by the woman. Therefore some explain that when she says: I counted, she means: I examined myself (Rashi). There is no requirement for her to actually count aloud. Others explain that proper practice is for a woman to count verbally each of her days (*Shela*, cited by *Minḥat Ḥinnukh*).

**But I do not know how many I counted** – וְאֵינִי יוֹדַעַת כַּמָּה סָפַרְתִּי: She does not know if she examined herself during some of her clean days or on all of them (Rashi).

"סְפַרְתִּי וְאֵינִי יוֹדַעַת כַּמָּה סָפַרְתִּי" – חַד יוֹמָא מִיהָא אִי אֶפְשָׁר דְּלָא סָפְרָה, חַסְרָה לָהּ טְבִילָה!

The Gemara raises a difficulty with regard to this interpretation of the *baraita*: If it is referring to a case where the woman said: **I counted** clean days **but I do not know how many days I counted, it is impossible that she did not count at least one** clean **day.** If so, she should not be required to immerse on the eighth day, in which case **she is lacking** one **immersion,** as the *baraita* rules that she must immerse fifteen times.

אֶלָּא אֵימָא: "אֵינִי יוֹדַעַת אִם סָפַרְתִּי אִם לֹא סָפַרְתִּי".

The Gemara answers: **Rather, say** that she claims: **I do not know if I counted** any clean days **or I did not count** any clean days. Likewise, she does not know whether she saw the blood during her days of menstruation or during her days of *ziva*. Therefore, she must immerse fifteen times, as it is possible that she has not yet counted at all.

מתני׳ הַזָּב, וְהַזָּבָה, וְהַנִּדָּה, וְהַיּוֹלֶדֶת, וְהַמְּצוֹרָע שֶׁמֵּתוּ – מְטַמְּאִין בְּמַשָּׂא, עַד שֶׁיִּמּוֹק הַבָּשָׂר. גּוֹי שֶׁמֵּת – טָהוֹר מִלְּטַמֵּא.

**MISHNA** The corpses of **a** ***zav*****, and a** ***zava*****, and a menstruating woman, and a woman after childbirth, and a leper, who died,**[H] **transmit ritual impurity by carrying** their corpses, **until the flesh decays.** With regard to the corpse of **a gentile who died,**[H] although when alive he transmits impurity like a *zav*, once he dies he is **ritually pure** and is prevented **from transmitting impurity.**

בֵּית שַׁמַּאי אוֹמְרִים: כׇּל הַנָּשִׁים מֵתוֹת נִדּוֹת. וּבֵית הִלֵּל אוֹמְרִים: אֵין נִדָּה אֶלָּא שֶׁמֵּתָה נִדָּה.

**Beit Shammai say:** The status of **all women** when they **die** is as though they were **menstruating women** at the time of death. Therefore, the garments that they were wearing before they died are impure and require immersion. **And Beit Hillel say: Only** a woman **who died** with the impurity of **a menstruating woman** has the status of **a menstruating woman** after death.

גמ׳ מַאי "בְּמַשָּׂא"? אִילֵימָא בְּמַשָּׂא מַמָּשׁ – אַטּוּ כׇּל מֵת מִי לָא מְטַמֵּא בְּמַשָּׂא!

**GEMARA** The mishna teaches that the corpse of one of these impure people transmits ritual impurity by carrying. The Gemara asks: **What** does the mishna mean by the term: **By carrying? If we say** that it **literally** means **by carrying,** that is difficult: **Is that to say** that **every** other **corpse does not impart ritual impurity by carrying?** Since every corpse imparts impurity through carrying, why does the mishna need to specify this *halakha* in these specific cases?

אֶלָּא: מַאי "בְּמַשָּׂא"? בְּאֶבֶן מְסָמָא,

**Rather, what** does the mishna mean when it states: **By carrying** [***bemassa***]?[N] It means imparting impurity **through a very heavy stone** [***even mesama***].[N] There is a unique *halakha* with regard to the ritual impurity of a *zav* and a menstruating woman. If they sit on an item, even one that cannot become ritually impure, and beneath that item there is a vessel, although the weight of the *zav* or the menstruating woman has no physical effect on the vessel, it becomes ritually impure.

דִּכְתִיב: "וְהֵיתָיִת אֶבֶן חֲדָא וְשֻׂמַת עַל פֻּם גֻּבָּא".

The Gemara notes that the word *mesama* is based on a verse, **as it is written: "And a stone was brought and placed** [***vesumat***] **upon the mouth of the den;** and the king sealed it with his own signet and with the signet of his lords, that nothing might be changed concerning Daniel" (Daniel 6:18). Accordingly, the mishna is teaching that although a corpse does not normally impart ritual impurity to vessels under a heavy stone, these specific types of corpses do transmit impurity in this manner.

### HALAKHA

A *zav* and a *zava* and a menstruating woman and a woman after childbirth and a leper, who died – הַזָּב וְהַזָּבָה וְהַנִּדָּה וְהַיּוֹלֶדֶת וְהַמְּצוֹרָע שֶׁמֵּתוּ: If a *zav*, a *zava*, a menstruating woman, a woman after childbirth, or a leper, die, they transmit ritual impurity through lying or sitting after their death just as they did while alive. Until when does the body transmit this impurity? Until the flesh has decayed. This impurity is by rabbinic law, due to the possibility that one of these people first fainted and appeared dead, though still alive. Any surface which one of these sat or lay on after death becomes a primary source of ritual impurity by rabbinic law. This is in accordance with Rav's explanation of the mishna (Rambam *Sefer Tahara*, *Hilkhot Metamei Mishkav UMoshav* 6:4).

A gentile who died – גּוֹי שֶׁמֵּת: The corpse of a gentile does not transmit impurity through lying or sitting because when he was alive his impurity was by rabbinic law, in accordance with Rabbi Yehuda HaNasi's explanation of the mishna (Rambam *Sefer Tahara*, *Hilkhot Metamei Mishkav UMoshav* 6:4).

### NOTES

What does the mishna mean when it states: By carrying – מַאי בְּמַשָּׂא: The wording of the Gemara teaches that the impurity of a heavy stone is due to ritual impurity imparted by carrying, i.e., a *zav* who sits on a heavy stone transmits impurity to any pure items underneath the stone as if he carried them.

Through a very heavy stone [*even mesama*] – בְּאֶבֶן מְסָמָא: There are different explanations of this matter. The book of Daniel describes how the king placed a rock at the entrance to the lion's den after throwing Daniel inside: "And a stone was brought and placed [*vesumat*] upon the mouth of the den; and the king sealed it with his own signet and with the signet of his lords, that nothing might be changed concerning Daniel" (Daniel 6:18). This indicates that the stone was very heavy and bigger than a single person could move. This stone is meant to remain in one place, which is why it is called *even mesama*, which is related to the word *hasama*, meaning placed.

מַאי טַעֲמָא? אֲמַר רַב: גְּזֵרָה שֶׁמָּא יִתְעַלְּפָה.

The Gemara asks: **What is the reason** that the Sages decreed that these specific types of corpses impart ritual impurity through a heavy stone? **Rav said:** It is **a decree** due to the possibility that **perhaps** one of these people might **faint** while sitting on the heavy stone, and it might be mistakenly thought they are dead and do not impart impurity to the vessels beneath.

תָּנָא, מִשּׁוּם רַבִּי אֱלִיעֶזֶר אָמְרוּ: עַד שֶׁיִּבָּקַע כְּרֵיסוֹ.

A *tanna* **taught** in a *baraita* that the Sages **said in the name of Rabbi Eliezer:** All of these types of corpses listed in the mishna impart ritual impurity through a heavy stone **until the belly** of the corpse **bursts.** The Sages imposed their decree only in cases where the corpse resembles a person who has fainted. Once the corpse is clearly no longer alive, it no longer imparts ritual impurity through a heavy stone.

״גּוֹי שֶׁמֵּת״ [כו׳]. תַּנְיָא, אָמַר רַבִּי: מִפְּנֵי מָה אָמְרוּ גּוֹי שֶׁמֵּת טָהוֹר מִלְּטַמֵּא בְּמַשָּׂא – לְפִי שֶׁאֵין טוּמְאָתוֹ מֵחַיִּים מִדִּבְרֵי תוֹרָה, אֶלָּא מִדִּבְרֵי סוֹפְרִים.

§ The mishna teaches: With regard to the corpse of **a gentile who died,** although when alive he transmits impurity like a *zav*, once he dies he is ritually pure and is prevented from transmitting impurity. **It is taught** in a *baraita* that **Rabbi** Yehuda HaNasi **said: For what** reason **did** the Sages **say** that the corpse of **a gentile who died is ritually pure** and is prevented **from transmitting impurity by carrying? Because his impurity** that he transmits even **when alive is not by Torah law, but by rabbinic law.** The Sages decreed that every living gentile imparts ritual impurity in the manner of a *zav*; they did not extend their decree to include the corpse of a gentile in the manner of the corpse of a *zav*.

תָּנוּ רַבָּנַן: שְׁנֵים עָשָׂר דְּבָרִים שָׁאֲלוּ אַנְשֵׁי אֲלֶכְּסַנְדְּרִיָּא אֶת רַבִּי יְהוֹשֻׁעַ בֶּן חִינַּנְיָא: שְׁלֹשָׁה דִּבְרֵי חָכְמָה, שְׁלֹשָׁה דִּבְרֵי הַגָּדָה, שְׁלֹשָׁה דִּבְרֵי בוּרוּת, שְׁלֹשָׁה דִּבְרֵי דֶּרֶךְ אֶרֶץ.

§ **The Sages taught: The** wise **people of Alexandria asked twelve matters of Rabbi Yehoshua ben Ḥinnana.**[P] **Three** of them were **matters of wisdom,**[N] **three** were **matters of *aggada*, three** were **matters of ignorance,** and **three** were **matters of behavior.**

שְׁלֹשָׁה דִּבְרֵי חָכְמָה: הַזָּב וְהַזָּבָה וְהַנִּדָּה וְהַיּוֹלֶדֶת וְהַמְּצוֹרָע שֶׁמֵּתוּ, עַד מָתַי מְטַמְּאִין בְּמַשָּׂא? אָמַר לָהֶן: עַד שֶׁיִּמּוֹק הַבָּשָׂר.

The Gemara lists the questions. **Three** were **matters of wisdom:** The first question was with regard to **a *zav* and a *zava* and a menstruating woman and a woman after childbirth and the leper, who died: Until when do they transmit ritual impurity by carrying?** Rabbi Yehoshua **said to them: Until the flesh decays.** This is the *halakha* taught in the mishna.

בַּת מְשׁוּלַּחַת, מַה הִיא לְכֹהֵן?

The second question referred to the **daughter** of a wife who had been **sent away** by her husband, i.e., divorced, who then married another, but after her divorce from her second husband or his death she returned and remarried her first husband, to whom she is forbidden (see Deuteronomy 24:1–4), and a daughter was born from this marriage. **What is her**, i.e., the daughter's, status **with regard to** marrying **a priest?**[H]

מִי אָמְרִינַן קַל וָחוֹמֶר: וּמָה אַלְמָנָה לְכֹהֵן גָּדוֹל, שֶׁאֵין אִיסּוּרָהּ שָׁוֶה בַּכֹּל – בְּנָהּ פָּגוּם, זוֹ שֶׁאִיסּוּרָהּ שָׁוֶה בַּכֹּל – אֵינוֹ דִּין שֶׁבְּנָהּ פָּגוּם? אוֹ דִּילְמָא: מַה לְאַלְמָנָה לְכֹהֵן גָּדוֹל – שֶׁהִיא עַצְמָהּ מִתְחַלֶּלֶת?

**Do we say an *a fortiori* inference: And if** in the case of **a widow** married **to a High Priest, whose prohibition does not apply to all,** i.e., it is prohibited for her only to marry a High Priest (see Leviticus 21:13–15), and yet the lineage of **her son is flawed,** as he is disqualified from the priesthood, then in the case of **this** daughter of a remarried divorcée, **whose prohibition applies equally to all** men, **is it not right that her son** should be of **flawed** lineage? **Or perhaps** this comparison can be refuted: **What** is notable **about a widow married to a High Priest?** It is notable in **that she herself is disqualified** from the priesthood, i.e., if a High Priest engages in intercourse with her she is disqualified from partaking of *teruma*, whereas a remarried divorcée is not disqualified from partaking of *teruma*.

אָמַר לָהֶן:

Rabbi Yehoshua **said to them:**

**PERSONALITIES**

Rabbi Yehoshua ben Ḥinnana – רַבִּי יְהוֹשֻׁעַ בֶּן חִינַּנְיָא: Rabbi Yehoshua ben Ḥinnana, sometimes referred to as Rabbi Yehoshua ben Ḥananya or often simply as Rabbi Yehoshua, was one of the greatest Sages in the generation following the destruction of the Temple. He served as an important leader of the people during this time of transition. Rabbi Yehoshua was well known by both Jews and gentiles not only for his brilliance in Torah knowledge, but also for his knowledge of science and the natural world, from astronomy to zoology. Many stories are told of his encounters with the Roman emperor, apparently Hadrian, as well as with the sages of other nations. Stories are told of his encounters with the sages of Athens and of Alexandria, which were two world centers of knowledge at that time.

**NOTES**

Three matters of wisdom – שְׁלֹשָׁה דִּבְרֵי חָכְמָה: Some explain that the term matters of wisdom means matters of *halakha* (Rashi).

**HALAKHA**

The daughter of a wife who had been sent away, what is her status with regard to a priest – בַּת מְשׁוּלַּחַת מַה הִיא לְכֹהֵן: If a man remarries his divorced wife after she had been married to another in the interim, the offspring is of unflawed lineage, in accordance with Rabbi Yehoshua ben Ḥinnana's reply to the wise people of Alexandria (Rambam *Sefer Kedusha*, *Hilkhot Issurei Bia* 15:2).

היא תּוֹעֵבָה, וְאֵין בָּנֶיהָ תּוֹעֵבִין.

With regard to one who remarries his divorced wife, the Torah states: "Her former husband, who sent her away, may not take her again to be his wife, after she is defiled, for that is an abomination before the Lord; and you shall not cause the land to sin, which the Lord your God gives you for an inheritance" (Deuteronomy 24:4). By inference, **she,** the divorced wife, **is an abomination, but her children are not abominations.** In other words, if he transgressed the prohibition and remarried this woman, the daughters from that marriage are not disqualified from marrying priests.

שְׁנֵי מְצוֹרָעִין שֶׁנִּתְעָרְבוּ קָרְבְּנוֹתֵיהֶן זֶה בָּזֶה, וְקָרַב קָרְבָּנוֹ שֶׁל אֶחָד מֵהֶן, וּמֵת אֶחָד מֵהֶן, הַשֵּׁנִי מַה תְּהֵא עָלָיו?

The third question was as follows: **Two** wealthy people who were **lepers** came to purify themselves and each brought a sin offering, a guilt offering, and a burnt offering. **Their offerings**[B] **became intermingled**[H] **with each other, and the offering of one of them was sacrificed, and** subsequently **one of them died. What shall be with the second** individual, i.e., how can he complete his purification process? If the other one had not died, they could both bring the remaining offering with the stipulation that it should be sacrificed on behalf of whoever is the owner. But now that one is dead, the other person may not bring the remaining animal, as one may not sacrifice a sin offering for one who is dead. He may also not bring another animal instead, as the animal that was already sacrificed might have been his, and one may not bring a second sin offering.

אָמַר לָהֶן: כּוֹתֵב נְכָסָיו לַאֲחֵרִים – וְהָוֵי עָנִי, וּמֵבִיא חַטַּאת הָעוֹף הַבָּא עַל הַסָּפֵק.

Rabbi Yehoshua **said to them:** The solution is for him to **write** a contract giving all **his possessions to others,** whom he trusts to return them as a gift later, **and he is** then considered to be **destitute. And** as a poor leper, he **brings a bird sin offering,** which can be **brought** even **in** a case of **uncertainty.**

וְהָאִיכָּא אָשָׁם! אָמַר שְׁמוּאֵל: כְּשֶׁקָּרַב אֲשָׁמוֹ.

The Gemara challenges: **But there is** the **guilt offering** that a leper must bring, and this must be an animal not a bird, and may not be brought in a case of uncertainty. How can this leper bring his guilt offering? **Shmuel says:** Rabbi Yehoshua was referring specifically to a case **where his guilt offering** had already been **sacrificed,** before the animals became intermingled.

אֲמַר רַב שֵׁשֶׁת: גַּבְרָא רַבָּה כִּשְׁמוּאֵל לֵימָא כִּי הַאי מִילְּתָא. כְּמַאן, אִי כְּרַבִּי יְהוּדָה דַּאֲמַר אָשָׁם קָבְעָה – וְכֵיוָן דְּקָבְעָה לָהּ אָשָׁם בַּעֲשִׁירוּת, לָא מָצֵי מַיְיתֵי חַטָּאת בְּדַלּוּת.

**Rav Sheshet said:** Is it possible that **a great man like Shmuel would say a statement like this? In accordance with whose** opinion does this solution apply? **If it is in accordance with** the opinion of **Rabbi Yehuda, who says** that if the leper was wealthy when he sacrificed his **guilt offering** he **has** thereby **fixed** his manner of atonement, and must bring animals as his other two offerings, it is difficult: **And once he fixed his guilt offering** as an animal **while he was wealthy, he may not bring** a bird **sin offering when he is destitute.**

דִּתְנַן: מְצוֹרָע שֶׁהֵבִיא קָרְבַּן עָנִי וְהֶעֱשִׁיר, אוֹ עָשִׁיר וְהֶעֱנִי – הַכֹּל הוֹלֵךְ אַחַר חַטָּאת, דִּבְרֵי רַבִּי שִׁמְעוֹן.

**As we learned** in a mishna (*Nega'im* 14:11): With regard to **a leper who brought an offering**[N] **of a destitute person and** thereafter **he became wealthy, or** if he brought an offering of **a wealthy person and** thereafter **he became destitute,**[H] **everything follows after** the **sin offering;** this is **the statement of Rabbi Shimon.** If he was wealthy when he brought the sin offering, he brings the burnt offering of the wealthy; if he was destitute at that time, he brings the burnt offering of the destitute.

**BACKGROUND**

**Offering of a leper** – קָרְבַּן מְצוֹרָע: The *halakhot* of *tzara'at*, traditionally rendered as leprosy but not necessarily identified medically with that illness, are recorded in the Torah in Leviticus (see chapters 13–14). They are detailed in tractate *Nega'im*, which deals exclusively with the different types of leprosy. The *halakhot* of the purification of a leper after he has been healed from his affliction are also stated in the Torah (see Leviticus 14:1–32). Part of the procedure is performed outside the Temple, e.g., shaving his hair. The leper brings to the Temple a lamb for a guilt offering and a *log* of oil, which are waved by the priest. After the sacrifice of the guilt offering, the priest applies some of the animal's blood to the earlobe of the leper, his right thumb, and his right big toe. Next, the priest takes some of the oil in his hand and sprinkles it seven times. Some of the remaining oil is placed on the leper's earlobe, thumb, and big toe. Finally, some of the leftover oil is placed on the leper's head. When all this has been done, the leper sacrifices a lamb, or a bird if he is poor, as a sin offering, and a second lamb, or bird if he is poor, as a burnt offering.

**HALAKHA**

**Two lepers, their offerings became intermingled, etc.** – שְׁנֵי מְצוֹרָעִין שֶׁנִּתְעָרְבוּ קָרְבְּנוֹתֵיהֶן וכו׳: If the offerings of two lepers became intermingled and one of the sin offerings is slaughtered and its blood sprinkled, and then one of the lepers dies, what should the remaining leper do? He may not offer the second sin offering, since the first one may have been his and one may not bring two sin offerings for one sin. He may also not bring another animal in its place, because one does not bring a sin offering in a case of uncertainty. He may not bring a bird offering instead because a wealthy person may not bring the offering of a poor person. He must give all his possessions to another, so that he becomes poor, and then he may bring a bird as his sin offering, but it may not be eaten (Rambam *Sefer Korbanot*, *Hilkhot Meḥusrei Kappara* 5:10, and *Kesef Mishne* and *Leḥem Mishne* there).

**Who brought an offering of a destitute person and he became wealthy or an offering of a wealthy person and he became destitute** – שֶׁהֵבִיא קָרְבַּן עָנִי וְהֶעֱשִׁיר אוֹ עָשִׁיר וְהֶעֱנִי: If a leper brings the offering of a poor person and then becomes wealthy, or vice versa, his status is defined based on his situation at the time his guilt offering was sacrificed. If he was wealthy at that time he must bring the other offerings of a wealthy person, and if he was poor at that time he brings the offerings of a poor person. This is in accordance with the opinion of Rabbi Yehuda (Rambam *Sefer Korbanot*, *Hilkhot Meḥusrei Kappara* 5:9).

**NOTES**

**A leper who brought an offering** – מְצוֹרָע שֶׁהֵבִיא קָרְבָּן: Once a leper is healed, he must bring two birds as the first stage of his purification process. Afterward it is permitted for him to shave and enter the Israelite camp. Seven days later he brings three sheep, one as a guilt offering, one as a burnt offering, and one as a sin offering, as well as a meal offering and a *log* of oil. If the leper is poor he brings a sheep as his guilt offering and two doves or pigeons as his burnt offering and sin offering. The animals are sacrificed in the following order: Guilt offering, sin offering, then burnt offering.

וְרַבִּי יְהוּדָה אוֹמֵר: הַכֹּל הוֹלֵךְ אַחַר אָשָׁם. רַבִּי אֱלִיעֶזֶר בֶּן יַעֲקֹב אוֹמֵר: הַכֹּל הוֹלֵךְ אַחַר צִפּוֹרִים.

**And Rabbi Yehuda says: Everything,** i.e., the sin offering and the burnt offering, **follows after** his status at the time that his **guilt offering** was brought. **Rabbi Eliezer ben Ya'akov says: Everything follows after** the offering of the **birds,**[N] brought seven days earlier, at the start of his purification process.

וְאִי כְּרַבִּי שִׁמְעוֹן דַּאֲמַר חַטָּאת קָבְעָה – אַף עַל גַּב דְּלָא קָרַב אָשָׁם, נֵיתֵי אַחֵר. דְּהָא שָׁמְעִינַן לֵיהּ לְרַבִּי שִׁמְעוֹן דַּאֲמַר לַיְיתֵי וְלִתְנֵי.

Rav Sheshet continues: **And if** Rabbi Yehoshua's statement is **in accordance with** the opinion of **Rabbi Shimon, who said** that the **sin offering fixed** the status of the remaining offerings, it is difficult: Why did Shmuel state that the case is where his guilt offering had already been sacrificed? **Even if the guilt offering had not been sacrificed** before the animals became intermingled, **let him bring another** animal as his guilt offering, and stipulate that if the guilt offering that was already slaughtered was his, this animal should be a peace offering. **As we have heard that Rabbi Shimon said: Let him bring** another animal **and stipulate** with regard to it.

דְּתַנְיָא, אָמַר רַבִּי שִׁמְעוֹן: לְמָחֳרַת מֵבִיא אֲשָׁמוֹ וְלוּגּוֹ עִמּוֹ, וּמַעֲמִידוֹ בְּשַׁעַר נִקָּנוֹר, וּמַתְנֶה עָלָיו וְאוֹמֵר ״אִם מְצוֹרָע הוּא – הֲרֵי אֲשָׁמוֹ וְלוּגּוֹ עִמּוֹ. וְאִם לָאו – אָשָׁם זֶה יְהֵא שַׁלְמֵי נְדָבָה״.

**As it is taught** in a *baraita* that **Rabbi Shimon says,** with regard to a leper of uncertain status who must bring a guilt offering and a *log* of oil for his purification: **The following day,** on the eighth day of his purification, he **brings his guilt offering and his** ***log*** of oil **with it,**[N] and the priest **stands him at the Gate of Nicanor,**[B] **and the** leper **stipulates with regard to** the offering **and says: If this** person, i.e., I, was **a leper, this is his guilt offering and** this is **his** ***log*** of oil **with it. And if not, this** animal that I brought for **a guilt offering shall be a voluntary peace offering,** as the two offerings are sacrificed in the same manner.

וְאוֹתוֹ אָשָׁם טָעוּן

**And that guilt offering** of uncertain status **requires**

BACKGROUND

**Gate of Nicanor – שַׁעַר נִקָּנוֹר:** The Gate of Nicanor, which was situated by the main entrance to the Temple courtyard, was used when it was necessary for someone to be as close as possible to the courtyard without actually entering it.

Gate of Nicanor

NOTES

**Everything follows after the sin offering…after his guilt offering…after the birds – הַכֹּל הוֹלֵךְ אַחַר חַטָּאת...אַחַר אָשָׁם...אַחַר צִפּוֹרִים:** The Gemara (*Arakhin* 17b) explains their dispute. They all derive from the verse: "This is the law of one who has the mark of leprosy, whose means do not suffice for his purification" (Leviticus 14:32). Rabbi Shimon holds that his status as a wealthy or poor individual is contingent upon the offering that atones and purifies him from sin, i.e., the sin offering.

**The following day he brings his guilt offering and his** ***log*** **with it – לְמָחֳרַת מֵבִיא אֲשָׁמוֹ וְלוּגּוֹ עִמּוֹ:** The Gemara does not explain the context of Rabbi Shimon's statement. Rashi explains that it refers to one who is a leper of uncertain status, who must bring a guilt offering and a *log* of oil on the eighth day for his purification. Therefore the term: The next day, refers to the day following the seventh day of his purification.

Perek **X**
Daf **70** Amud **b**

שְׁחִיטָתוֹ בַּצָּפוֹן, וְטָעוּן מַתְּנַת בְּהוֹנוֹת, וּסְמִיכָה, וּנְסָכִים, וּתְנוּפָה, וְחָזֶה וְשׁוֹק, וְנֶאֱכָל לְזִכְרֵי כְהוּנָּה לְיוֹם וְלַיְלָה.

that **its slaughter** must be performed **in the north**[N] of the Temple courtyard, as in the case of a guilt offering, **and** it **requires placement** of the blood on the right **thumb and** right **big toe**[N] and right earlobe of the leper, as described in Leviticus 14:14, **and** it requires **placing hands** on the head of the animal, **and** the accompanying wine **libations and waving of the breast and thigh,** like a peace offering. **And it is eaten by males of the priesthood for** one **day and** the following **night,** like a guilt offering, rather than for two days, like a peace offering.

NOTES

**Its slaughter is in the north – שְׁחִיטָתוֹ בַּצָּפוֹן:** The requirement that offerings of the most sacred order be slaughtered in the north of the Temple courtyard is specified with regard to the burnt offering: "And he shall slaughter it on the side of the altar northward before the Lord; and Aaron's sons, the priests, shall sprinkle its blood against the altar round about" (Leviticus 1:11). This principle is also applied to all other offerings of the most sacred order.

Northern part of the Temple courtyard

**And requires placement on the thumb and big toe – וְטָעוּן מַתְּנַת בְּהוֹנוֹת:** Part of the purification process of a leper on his eighth day is that after he has shaved his hair and immersed on the previous day, a priest places the blood of his guilt offering on his right thumb, big toe, and earlobe. The priest also places some of the oil on these three places.

NOTES

Because he thereby brings sacrificial animals to… disqualification – שֶׁמֵּבִיא קָדָשִׁים לְבֵית הַפְּסוּל: In bringing this offering he reduces the permitted time for eating the offering. A peace offering may be eaten for two days and a night, whereas due to uncertainty he may eat this offering only for a single day and a night, and any meat that is left over to the second day has to be burned (Rashi).

Three matters of ignorance [*burot*] – שְׁלֹשָׁה דִּבְרֵי בוּרוֹת: There is a dispute with regard to the meaning of the term *burot*. Some write that it means ignorance (Rashi). Others contend that it is referring to matters related to creation (Maharsha). Yet others claim that it means matters of the dead, who lie in the ground, and that the term should be written as pits [*borot*] (*Hokhmat Betzalel*).

וְלֹא הוֹדוּ לוֹ חֲכָמִים לְרַבִּי שִׁמְעוֹן, מִפְּנֵי שֶׁמֵּבִיא קָדָשִׁים לְבֵית הַפְּסוּל!

**But the Rabbis did not concede to Rabbi Shimon, because** they hold that he thereby **brings sacrificial** animals **to a situation** where the time that they may be eaten is restricted, thereby increasing **the** likelihood of **disqualification,**[N] as it might be a peace offering, which may be eaten for two days and one night.

שְׁמוּאֵל סָבַר לָהּ כְּרַבִּי שִׁמְעוֹן בַּחֲדָא, וּפְלִיג עֲלֵיהּ בַּחֲדָא.

The Gemara answers that **Shmuel holds in accordance with** the opinion of **Rabbi Shimon with regard to one** *halakha*, i.e., that it is not the guilt offering that fixes whether the leper must bring the offerings of a wealthy person or a destitute person, **but he disagrees with him with regard to one** other *halakha*, as he does not permit such a stipulation in the case of a guilt offering.

שְׁלֹשָׁה דִּבְרֵי אַגָּדָה: כְּתוּב אֶחָד אוֹמֵר ״כִּי לֹא אֶחְפֹּץ בְּמוֹת הַמֵּת״, וְכָתוּב אֶחָד אוֹמֵר ״כִּי חָפֵץ ה׳ לַהֲמִיתָם״! כָּאן – בְּעוֹשִׂין תְּשׁוּבָה, כָּאן – בְּשֶׁאֵין עוֹשִׂין תְּשׁוּבָה.

The Gemara details the **three matters of *aggada*** that the sages of Alexandria asked Rabbi Yehoshua. **One verse states: "For I have no pleasure in the death of him that dies,** says the Lord God; but turn yourselves, and live" (Ezekiel 18:32). **And one verse states,** with regard to the sons of Eli the High Priest, who did not pay attention to the reproof of their father: "If one man sins against another, God shall judge him; but if a man sins against the Lord, who shall pray for him? But they did not listen to the voice of their father, **because the Lord desired to kill them"** (I Samuel 2:25). Rabbi Yehoshua replied to them: **Here,** the verse in Ezekiel is referring to a case **where** the sinners **repent,** whereas **there,** the verse in Samuel is speaking of a case **where** the sinners **do not repent.**

כְּתוּב אֶחָד אוֹמֵר ״כִּי…לֹא יִשָּׂא פָנִים וְלֹא יִקַּח שֹׁחַד״, וְכָתוּב אֶחָד אוֹמֵר ״יִשָּׂא ה׳ פָּנָיו אֵלֶיךָ״! כָּאן – קוֹדֶם גְּזַר דִּין, כָּאן – לְאַחַר גְּזַר דִּין.

The sages of Alexandria also asked the following: **One verse states: "For** the Lord your God, He is God of gods, and Lord of lords, the great God, the mighty, and the awful, **Who shows no favor nor takes graft"** (Deuteronomy 10:17), **and one verse states: "The Lord shall show favor to you** and give you peace" (Numbers 6:26). How can this contradiction be resolved? Rabbi Yehoshua replied to them: **Here,** the verse in Numbers is dealing with the time **before** one's **sentence** is issued, when God shows favor and forgives; **there,** the verse in Deuteronomy is referring to **after** the **sentence** has been issued, when He no longer forgives.

כְּתוּב אֶחָד אוֹמֵר ״כִּי בָחַר ה׳ בְּצִיּוֹן״, וְכָתוּב אֶחָד אוֹמֵר ״כִּי עַל אַפִּי וְעַל חֲמָתִי הָיְתָה הָעִיר הַזֹּאת לְמִן הַיּוֹם אֲשֶׁר בָּנוּ אוֹתָהּ עַד הַיּוֹם הַזֶּה״! כָּאן – קוֹדֶם שֶׁנָּשָׂא שְׁלֹמֹה אֶת בַּת פַּרְעֹה, כָּאן – לְאַחַר שֶׁנָּשָׂא שְׁלֹמֹה אֶת בַּת פַּרְעֹה.

The sages of Alexandria further asked: **One verse states: "For the Lord has chosen Zion;** He has desired it for His dwelling place" (Psalms 132:13), **and one verse states: "For this city has been to Me a provocation of My anger and of My fury from the day that they built it until this day,** so that I should remove it from before My face" (Jeremiah 32:31). Rabbi Yehoshua replied to them: **Here,** the verse in Psalms is referring to the time **before Solomon married Pharaoh's daughter** (see I Kings 3:1), whereas **there,** the verse in Jeremiah is speaking of the time **after Solomon married Pharaoh's daughter.**

שְׁלֹשָׁה דִּבְרֵי בוּרוֹת: אִשְׁתּוֹ שֶׁל לוֹט מַהוּ שֶׁתְּטַמֵּא? אָמַר לָהֶם: מֵת מְטַמֵּא, וְאֵין נְצִיב מֶלַח מְטַמֵּא.

The Gemara lists the **three matters of ignorance**[N] that the sages of Alexandria asked Rabbi Yehoshua. **What is** the *halakha* with regard to **the wife of Lot,** who was turned into a pillar of salt as she fled from the city of Sodom (Genesis 19:26), in terms of whether **she transmits ritual impurity** as a corpse? Rabbi Yehoshua **said to them: A corpse transmits ritual impurity, but a pillar of salt,** even if it was formerly a person, **does not impart ritual impurity.**

בֶּן שׁוּנַמִּית מַהוּ שֶׁיְּטַמֵּא? אָמַר לָהֶן: מֵת מְטַמֵּא, וְאֵין חַי מְטַמֵּא.

The sages of Alexandria also asked Rabbi Yehoshua: **What is** the *halakha* with regard to **the son of the Shunammite** woman, who died and was brought to life by Elisha (II Kings 4:33–36), in terms of whether **he transmits ritual impurity** as a corpse? Rabbi Yehoshua **said to them: A corpse transmits ritual impurity, but a living** person **does not transmit ritual impurity,** even if he had been dead temporarily.

מֵתִים לֶעָתִיד לָבֹא, צְרִיכִין הַזָּאָה שְׁלִישִׁי וּשְׁבִיעִי, אוֹ אֵין צְרִיכִין? אָמַר לָהֶן: לִכְשֶׁיִּחְיוּ, נִחְכַּם לָהֶן. אִיכָּא דְּאָמְרִי: לִכְשֶׁיָּבֹא מֹשֶׁה רַבֵּינוּ עִמָּהֶם.

The sages of Alexandria also asked Rabbi Yehoshua: With regard to **the dead** who will be resurrected **in the future,** will they **require sprinkling** with ashes of the red heifer on the **third and seventh** days, like one who is purified after coming into contact with a corpse, **or** will **they not require** that sprinkling? Rabbi Yehoshua **said to them: When they come to life, we will be clever for them** and clarify the *halakha*. **There are** those **who say** that Rabbi Yehoshua said to them: **When Moses our teacher comes with them,** he will tell us the correct *halakha*.

שְׁלֹשָׁה דִּבְרֵי דֶרֶךְ אֶרֶץ: מַה יַּעֲשֶׂה אָדָם וְיֶחְכַּם? אָמַר לָהֶן: יַרְבֶּה בִּישִׁיבָה, וִימַעֵט בִּסְחוֹרָה. אָמְרוּ: הַרְבֵּה עָשׂוּ כֵּן, וְלֹא הוֹעִיל לָהֶם! אֶלָּא: יְבַקְשׁוּ רַחֲמִים מִמִּי שֶׁהַחָכְמָה שֶׁלּוֹ, שֶׁנֶּאֱמַר ״כִּי ה׳ יִתֵּן חָכְמָה מִפִּיו דַּעַת וּתְבוּנָה״.

The sages of Alexandria also asked Rabbi Yehoshua **three matters of behavior: What** should **a person do to become wise?** Rabbi Yehoshua **said to them:** He should **increase** his time spent **sitting** in the study house **and minimize** his dealings **in merchandise.** The sages of Alexandria **said** to Rabbi Yehoshua: **Many** people **have done so, and** it **did not help them** to acquire wisdom. Rabbi Yehoshua responded: **Rather, they should pray for mercy** to receive wisdom **from the One to Whom wisdom belongs, as it is stated: "For the Lord gives wisdom; out of His mouth comes knowledge and discernment"** (Proverbs 2:6).

תָּנֵי רַבִּי חִיָּיא: מָשָׁל לְמֶלֶךְ בָּשָׂר וָדָם שֶׁעָשָׂה סְעוּדָה לַעֲבָדָיו, וּמְשַׁגֵּר לְאוֹהֲבָיו מִמַּה שֶּׁלְּפָנָיו.

With regard to the subject of wisdom, **Rabbi Ḥiyya teaches a parable of a flesh-and-blood king who prepared a feast for his servants.** The servants eat the food placed before them, **but** in addition **he sends** some **of** the food **that is before him to those he loves.** Similarly, God sends some of His wisdom to those He loves, as the verse states: "For the Lord gives wisdom."

מַאי קָא מַשְׁמַע לַן? דְּהָא בְּלָא הָא, לָא סַגְיָא.

The Gemara asks: Since the path to wisdom is through prayer, **what** is Rabbi Yehoshua **teaching us** when he says that one should increase his time spent sitting and studying? The Gemara answers that Rabbi Yehoshua is teaching **that this,** prayer, **without that,** sitting and learning, **does not suffice.**

מַה יַּעֲשֶׂה אָדָם וְיִתְעַשֵּׁר? אָמַר לָהֶן: יַרְבֶּה בִּסְחוֹרָה, וְיִשָּׂא וְיִתֵּן בֶּאֱמוּנָה. אָמְרוּ לוֹ: הַרְבֵּה עָשׂוּ כֵּן וְלֹא הוֹעִילוּ! אֶלָּא: יְבַקֵּשׁ רַחֲמִים מִמִּי שֶׁהָעוֹשֶׁר שֶׁלּוֹ. שֶׁנֶּאֱמַר ״לִי הַכֶּסֶף וְלִי הַזָּהָב״.

The sages of Alexandria asked: **What** should **a person do to become wealthy?** Rabbi Yehoshua **said to them:** He should **increase** his time involved in **merchandise and conduct his business faithfully.** The sages of Alexandria **said** to Rabbi Yehoshua: **Many** people **have done so, and** it **did not help them** become rich. Rabbi Yehoshua replied: **Rather, they should pray for mercy** to receive wisdom **from the One to Whom wealth belongs, as it is stated: "Mine is the silver, and Mine the gold,** says the Lord of hosts" (Haggai 2:8).

מַאי קָא מַשְׁמַע לַן? דְּהָא בְּלָא הָא לָא סַגִּי,

The Gemara asks: Since the path to wealth is through prayer, **what is** Rabbi Yehoshua **teaching us** when he says that one should increase his time spent involved in merchandise and conduct his business faithfully? Once again, the Gemara answers: Rabbi Yehoshua is teaching **that this,** prayer, **without that,** being involved in honest business, **does not suffice.**

מַה יַּעֲשֶׂה אָדָם וְיִהְיוּ לוֹ בָּנִים זְכָרִים? אָמַר לָהֶם: יִשָּׂא אִשָּׁה הַהוֹגֶנֶת לוֹ,

The sages of Alexandria further asked: **What** should **a person do to have male children?** Rabbi Yehoshua **said to them:** He should **marry a woman who is fit for him**

Perek **X**
Daf **71** Amud **a**

וְיִקַדֵּשׁ עַצְמוֹ בִּשְׁעַת תַּשְׁמִישׁ.

**and sanctify himself** by acting modestly **at the time of sexual intercourse.**[N]

אָמְרוּ: הַרְבֵּה עָשׂוּ כֵּן, וְלֹא הוֹעִילוּ! אֶלָּא: יְבַקֵּשׁ רַחֲמִים מִמִּי שֶׁהַבָּנִים שֶׁלּוֹ, שֶׁנֶּאֱמַר: ״הִנֵּה נַחֲלַת ה׳ בָּנִים שָׂכָר פְּרִי הַבָּטֶן״.

The sages of Alexandria **said** to Rabbi Yehoshua: **Many** people **have done so, and** it **did not help them.** Rabbi Yehoshua said: **Rather, they should pray** to receive sons **from the One to Whom sons belong, as it is stated: "Behold, children are a heritage of the Lord; the fruit of the womb is a reward"** (Psalms 127:3).

מַאי קָא מַשְׁמַע לַן – דְּהָא בְּלָא הָא לָא סַגִּי.

The Gemara again asks: Since the path to sons is through prayer, **what** is Rabbi Yehoshua **teaching us** when he said that one should marry an appropriate woman and conduct himself with modesty during intercourse? The Gemara answers: Rabbi Yehoshua is teaching **that this,** prayer, **without that,** marrying an appropriate woman and being modest, **does not suffice.**

**NOTES**

**And sanctify himself by acting modestly at the time of sexual intercourse – וְיִקַדֵּשׁ עַצְמוֹ בִּשְׁעַת תַּשְׁמִישׁ:** Even though the Gemara here does not specify how he sanctifies himself during intercourse, Rashi explains that it refers to engaging in modest conduct during that act.

## BACKGROUND

**Quarter-*log* of blood – רְבִיעִית דָּם:** A quarter-*log* serves as the basis for measures of liquid volume. It is approximately 80–150 ml, according to the varying opinions of the halakhic authorities. It is halakhically considered to be the minimum amount of blood required to sustain a person. There are various opinions as to how the Sages arrived at this measurement. One holds that they estimated the amount of blood in a newborn baby, or the minimum amount a newborn needs to survive.

It is interesting to note that this amount is approximately the quantity of blood pumped by the heart with every heartbeat.

## HALAKHA

**A woman who died and a quarter-*log* of blood emerged from her body – הָאִשָּׁה שֶׁמֵּתָה וְיָצְאָה מִמֶּנָּה רְבִיעִית דָּם:** If a woman dies and blood emerges from her body, it transmits impurity as a blood spot, since any uterine blood is impure. Even if the blood emerged after her death and she was not a menstruating woman, since it emerged from an impure source it transmits impurity. If there is a quarter-*log* of blood it also transmits impurity in a tent. This is in accordance with the opinion of the first *tanna* of the mishna and Rabbi Ze'eiri's explanation (Rambam *Sefer Tahara, Hilkhot Metamei Mishkav UMoshav* 4:15).

מַאי ״שָׂכָר פְּרִי הַבָּטֶן״? אָמַר רַבִּי חָמָא בְּרַבִּי חֲנִינָא: בִּשְׂכַר שֶׁמַּשְׁהִין עַצְמָן בַּבֶּטֶן כְּדֵי שֶׁתַּזְרִיעַ אִשְׁתּוֹ תְּחִילָּה – נוֹתֵן לוֹ הַקָּדוֹשׁ בָּרוּךְ הוּא שְׂכַר פְּרִי הַבָּטֶן.

With regard to the verse from Psalms, the Gemara asks: **What** is the meaning of the phrase: **"The fruit of the womb is a reward"** (Psalms 127:3)? What act is rewarded here? **Rabbi Ḥama, son of Rabbi Ḥanina, says: In reward for** men **withholding their** semen **in their belly in order** to allow **their wives to emit seed first, the Holy One, Blessed be He, gives him the reward of the fruit of the womb,** i.e., sons.

״בֵּית שַׁמַּאי אוֹמְרִים״ [וכו׳]. מַאי טַעֲמַיְיהוּ דְּבֵית שַׁמַּאי? אִי נֵימָא מִשּׁוּם דִּכְתִיב ״וַתִּתְחַלְחַל הַמַּלְכָּה״, וַאֲמַר רַב: מְלַמֵּד שֶׁפֵּירְסָה נִדָּה, הָכָא נַמִי – אַגַּב בִּיעֲתוּתָא דְּמַלְאֲכָא דְּמוֹתָא חַזְיָא. וְהָאֲנַן תְּנַן: שֶׁחֲרָדָה מְסַלֶּקֶת אֶת הַדָּמִים! הָא לָא קַשְׁיָא, פַּחֲדָא – צָמֵית, בִּיעֲתוּתָא – מְרַפְיָא.

§ The mishna teaches that **Beit Shammai say:** The status of all women when they die is as though they were menstruating women. The Gemara asks: **What is the reason** for the opinion **of Beit Shammai? If we say** that their opinion is **due to** that **which is written: "Then the queen was exceedingly distressed** [*vatitḥalḥal*]" (Esther 4:4), this is difficult. The Gemara first explains the derivation. **And Rav said:** This **teaches that she began to menstruate** out of fear, as the cavities [*ḥalalim*] of her body opened. **Here too,** when a woman is about to die, **due to the fear of the Angel of Death she sees** blood. This is difficult, as **didn't we learn** in a mishna (39a) **that trepidation eliminates** the flow of menstrual **blood?** The Gemara answers: **This** is **not difficult. Anxiety** generated by extended worry **contracts** the muscles and prevents the blood from flowing, but sudden **fear relaxes** the muscles and causes the blood to flow.

אֶלָּא, הָא דִּתְנַן, בֵּית שַׁמַּאי אוֹמְרִים: כָּל הָאֲנָשִׁים מֵתִים זָבִין, וּבֵית הִלֵּל אוֹמְרִים: אֵין זָב אֶלָּא מִי שֶׁמֵּת זָב.

**But** if the reason Beit Shammai hold that all women who die have the status of menstruating women is due to fear, then what about **that which we learned** in a *baraita*: **Beit Shammai say:** The status of **all men** when they **die** is as though they were *zavim*; **and Beit Hillel say: Only** a man **who died** with the impurity of **a** *zav* has the status of **a** *zav*. If the reason that Beit Shammai maintain that all women who die have the status of menstruating women is due to fear of the Angel of Death, presumably they also should consider all men who die to have the status of a *zav* for the same reason.

אִקְרִי כָּאן ״מִבְּשָׂרוֹ״ – וְלֹא מֵחֲמַת אוֹנְסוֹ!

But this is difficult, as **I will apply here** the principle stated with regard to a *zav*: "An issue **out of his flesh**" (Leviticus 15:2) renders a man impure, **but not** an issue **due to circumstances beyond his control.** If a man has a discharge of *ziva* due to an illness or some accident, he does not become impure. Consequently, if he has a discharge due to fear after seeing the Angel of Death, he would not become ritually impure.

אֶלָּא, טַעֲמָא דְּבֵית שַׁמַּאי כִּדְתַנְיָא: בָּרִאשׁוֹנָה הָיוּ מַטְבִּילִין כֵּלִים עַל גַּבֵּי נִדּוֹת מֵתוֹת, וְהָיוּ נִדּוֹת חַיּוֹת מִתְבַּיְּישׁוֹת. הִתְקִינוּ שֶׁיְּהוּ מַטְבִּילִין עַל גַּבֵּי כָּל הַנָּשִׁים, מִפְּנֵי כְּבוֹדָן שֶׁל נִדּוֹת חַיּוֹת.

**Rather, the reason** for the opinion **of Beit Shammai** is **as it is taught** in a *baraita*: **At first they would** ritually **immerse** all the **utensils** that had been used **by** women who **died** while **menstruating,** which had thereby contracted ritual impurity even if the utensils did not touch the women after their death. **And** as a result, **the living menstruating women were embarrassed,** as they saw that the status of a menstruating woman is so severe that it remains even after death. The Sages therefore **instituted that one must immerse** the utensils which had been used **by all** dying **women, due to the honor of living menstruating women.**

בָּרִאשׁוֹנָה הָיוּ מַטְבִּילִין עַל גַּבֵּי זָבִין מֵתִין, וְהָיוּ זָבִין חַיִּין מִתְבַּיְּישִׁין. הִתְקִינוּ שֶׁיְּהוּ מַטְבִּילִין עַל גַּבֵּי כָּל הָאֲנָשִׁים, מִפְּנֵי כְּבוֹדָן שֶׁל זָבִין חַיִּים.

Similarly, **at first they would immerse** all the utensils that had been used by ***zavin***, men suffering from gonorrhea, **who died,** as the utensils had thereby contracted ritual impurity even if the utensils did not touch the men after their death. **And** as a result, **the living *zavin* were embarrassed.** Therefore, the Sages **instituted that one must immerse** the utensils that had been used **by all** dying men, **due to the honor of the living *zavin*.**

מתני׳ הָאִשָּׁה שֶׁמֵּתָה וְיָצְאָה מִמֶּנָּה רְבִיעִית דָּם – מְטַמְּאָה מִשּׁוּם כֶּתֶם, וּמְטַמְּאָה בְּאֹהֶל.

**MISHNA** With regard to **a woman who died, and** after her death **a quarter-*log* of blood**[B] **emerged from her** body,[H] although the blood emerged after death, it **transmits ritual impurity** by touching and carrying, **due to** the impurity of the **spot** of blood of a menstruating woman. This impurity as blood of menstruation applies to any amount of blood she emits, despite the *halakha* that generally, the blood of a corpse transmits impurity only if it is at least a quarter-*log* in volume. **And** as it is a quarter-*log* of blood, **it transmits impurity in a tent,** as it is the blood of a corpse.

רַבִּי יְהוּדָה אוֹמֵר: אֵינָהּ מְטַמְּאָה מִשּׁוּם כֶּתֶם, מִפְּנֵי שֶׁנֶּעֱקַר מִשֶּׁמֵּתָה. וּמוֹדֶה רַבִּי יְהוּדָה בְּיוֹשֶׁבֶת עַל מַשְׁבֵּר וּמֵתָה, וְיָצְאָה מִמֶּנָּה רְבִיעִית דָּם – שֶׁהִיא מְטַמְּאָה מִשּׁוּם כֶּתֶם. אָמַר רַבִּי יוֹסֵי: לְפִיכָךְ אֵינָהּ מְטַמְּאָה בְּאֹהֶל.

**Rabbi Yehuda says:** That quarter-*log* of blood **does not transmit impurity due to** the impurity of the **spot** of blood of a menstruating woman, **because that** blood **was displaced after she died. And Rabbi Yehuda concedes in** the case of a woman who is **sitting** in childbirth **on the travailing chair** [*mashber*][L] **and she died, and a quarter-*log* of blood emerged from her** body, **that** this blood **transmits ritual impurity due to** the impurity of the **spot** of blood of a menstruating woman. In that case, the blood was displaced while she was still alive. **Rabbi Yosei said: For that** reason, that quarter-*log* of blood **does not transmit impurity in a tent**, as it did not come from a corpse.

גמ׳ מִכְּלָל דְּתַנָּא קַמָּא סָבַר: אַף עַל גַּב דְּנֶעֱקַר דָּם מִשֶּׁמֵּתָה – מְטַמְּאָה מִשּׁוּם כֶּתֶם?

**GEMARA** The mishna teaches that according to Rabbi Yehuda a quarter-*log* of blood that emerges from a woman after death does not transmit impurity due to the impurity of a spot of blood of a menstruating woman, despite the fact that it came from the uterus. The Gemara raises a difficulty: **By inference** one might think **that the first *tanna* holds** that **even though the blood was displaced after she died, it renders** one **ritually impure due to** the impurity of a blood **spot.** This is not reasonable, as a dead woman cannot attain the status of a menstruating woman.

אָמַר רַבִּי זְעֵירִי: מָקוֹר מְקוֹמוֹ טָמֵא אִיכָּא בֵּינַיְיהוּ.

**Rabbi Ze'eiri said:** Even the first *tanna* agrees that blood from the uterus which leaves the body after death does not impart impurity as a spot. Rather, the difference **between** the opinions of the first *tanna* and Rabbi Yehuda is whether the **place of** a woman's **source,** i.e., her uterus, **is impure,** and therefore any blood that passes through there is impure, even if it left her body after death. The first *tanna* maintains that even blood that appears after her death transmits impurity like the blood of menstruation, as it passed through the uterus when she was still alive, whereas Rabbi Yehuda holds that this blood does not transmit impurity as blood of menstruation, despite the fact that it passed through her uterus.

״וּמוֹדֶה רַבִּי יְהוּדָה״.

§ The mishna teaches: **And Rabbi Yehuda concedes** in the case of a woman who was sitting in childbirth when she died, that the quarter-*log* of blood which emerged from her body transmits the ritual impurity of the spot of the blood of a menstruating woman. And Rabbi Yosei said: For that reason, that quarter-*log* of blood does not transmit impurity in a tent.

מִכְּלָל דְּתַנָּא קַמָּא סָבַר בְּאֹהֶל נַמִי מְטַמֵּא? אָמַר רַב יְהוּדָה: דַּם תְּבוּסָה אִיכָּא בֵּינַיְיהוּ.

The Gemara asks: **By inference,** one might conclude **that the first *tanna*,** i.e., Rabbi Yehuda, **holds** that the blood which emerges from a woman who died during childbirth **also transmits impurity in a tent.** This cannot be correct, as the blood left her while she was still alive. **Rav Yehuda said:** The difference **between** Rabbi Yehuda and Rabbi Yosei is with regard to **blood of submission** discharged from a body at the time of death, which contains a mixture of blood that leaves a person when he is still alive and blood that emerges after his death. Rabbi Yehuda holds that the blood which emerges from a woman who dies during childbirth is blood of submission, which transmits impurity in a tent by rabbinic law. Rabbi Yosei maintains that it is clear that this blood emerged from her body before she died, and therefore it is not blood of submission.

דְּתַנְיָא, אֵיזֶהוּ דַּם תְּבוּסָה? פֵּירֵשׁ רַבִּי אֶלְעָזָר בְּרַבִּי יְהוּדָה: הָרוּג שֶׁיָּצָא מִמֶּנּוּ דָּם בֵּין בְּחַיָּיו בֵּין בְּמוֹתוֹ, סָפֵק בְּחַיָּיו יָצָא סָפֵק בְּמוֹתוֹ יָצָא, סָפֵק בְּחַיָּיו וּבְמוֹתוֹ – זֶהוּ דַּם תְּבוּסָה.

**As it is taught** in a *baraita*: **What is blood of submission,**[N] which imparts ritual impurity (see 62b)? **Rabbi Elazar, son of Rabbi Yehuda, explained:** The case is one of a person who was **killed, from whom** a quarter-*log* of **blood emerged,** a flow which began **while he was alive and** continued **after his death,** and it is **uncertain** whether a full quarter-*log* **emerged while he was alive**[H] and therefore does not transmit ritual impurity, and it is **uncertain** whether **it emerged** out **after his death,** in which case it imparts ritual impurity by Torah law, and it is **uncertain** whether the quarter-*log* emerged partly **while he was alive and** partly **after his death.**[H] **That is blood of submission.**

**LANGUAGE**

**Travailing chair [*mashber*] – מַשְׁבֵּר:** This is a term for the place where a woman sits when giving birth. There is a similar word in Aramaic, *metavra*. The term appears in the verse: "And they said to him: Consequently says Hezekiah: This day is a day of trouble, and of rebuke, and of scorn; for the children are come to the birth [*mashber*], and there is not strength to bring forth" (II Kings 19:3). Some explain that it is called this because that is where the pain of childbirth breaks [*meshaber*] a woman.

**NOTES**

**The blood of submission [*tevusa*] – דַּם תְּבוּסָה:** This is referring to the blood which leaves a human body just before and just after his death. Some commentaries explain that the term *tevusa* is based on the verse: "And saw you wallowing [*mitboseset*] in your blood" (Ezekiel 16:6). The Sages decreed that this blood is ritually impure as a primary source of impurity, and therefore it renders items impure through contact or carrying or by a tent, i.e., by being under the same roof.

**HALAKHA**

**Uncertain whether a quarter-*log* emerged while he was alive – סָפֵק בְּחַיָּיו יָצָא:** In the case of a corpse that was on a bed and a quarter-*log* of blood emerged from it, and it is uncertain whether some of the blood emerged while the person was alive or all of it emerged after his death, the *halakha* is like other cases of uncertain impurity. Any person or item that touches this blood in a private domain is rendered ritually impure, but a person or item that touches the blood in a public domain is pure. This is in accordance with the opinion of the Rabbis (Rambam *Sefer Tahara*, *Hilkhot Tumat Met* 2:14).

**Uncertain whether partly while he was alive and partly after his death – סָפֵק בְּחַיָּיו וּבְמוֹתוֹ:** In the case of blood which emerged from a person before his death that is mixed with blood that emerged after his death, where the total amount of blood is at least a quarter-*log*, but it is not known how much blood emerged while he was alive and how much after his death, this blood is called: Blood of submission. This blood transmits ritual impurity through carrying or touching, and in a tent. The impurity is by rabbinic law. This is in accordance with the opinion of the Rabbis (Rambam *Sefer Tahara*, *Hilkhot Tumat Met* 2:13).

**NOTES**

**And has still not stopped** – וַעֲדַיִין לֹא פָּסַק: The meaning of this phrase is unclear. Some commentaries explain that the Sages decreed that since the blood is still coming out, a quarter-*log* may emerge after death. But if the blood stopped flowing, and less than a quarter-*log* emerged after death, the Sages did not decree impurity (*Tosafot*, citing Rabbeinu Yitzḥak of Dampierre).

**HALAKHA**

**And his blood was dripping into a hole** – וְדָמוֹ מְטַפְטֵף לְגוּמָּא: In the case of blood that emerges from a person while he is alive, where it runs down into a hole, and blood continues to drip into that hole after his death, all of the blood is ritually pure, because each drip is nullified by the blood that emerged during his lifetime (Rambam *Sefer Tahara*, *Hilkhot Tumat Met* 2:14).

וַחֲכָמִים אוֹמְרִים: בִּרְשׁוּת הַיָּחִיד – סְפֵקוֹ טָמֵא, בִּרְשׁוּת הָרַבִּים – סְפֵקוֹ טָהוֹר.

**And the Rabbis say** that this is not blood of submission, but a case of uncertain ritual impurity by Torah law, as it might all have emerged after death. Therefore, one applies the principle that **in a private domain** a case of **uncertainty** is considered to be **ritually impure,** whereas **in a public domain** a case of **uncertainty** is considered to be **ritually pure.**

אֶלָּא אֵיזֶהוּ דַּם תְּבוּסָה – הָרוּג שֶׁיָּצָא הֵימֶנּוּ רְבִיעִית דָּם בְּחַיָּיו וּבְמוֹתוֹ, וַעֲדַיִין לֹא פָּסַק, סָפֵק רוּבּוֹ בְּחַיָּיו וּמִיעוּטוֹ בְּמוֹתוֹ, סָפֵק מִיעוּטוֹ בְּחַיָּיו וְרוּבּוֹ בְּמוֹתוֹ – זֶהוּ דַּם תְּבוּסָה.

**Rather, what is blood of submission?** The case is one of a person who has been **killed from whom a quarter-*log* of blood emerged while he was alive and** continued emerging **after his death and has still not stopped**[N] coming out. It is clear that a full quarter-*log* did not emerge after his death, but it is **uncertain** whether **the majority** emerged **while he was alive and the minority after his death,** and equally **uncertain** whether **the minority** emerged **while he was alive and the majority after his death. That is blood of submission.**

רַבִּי יְהוּדָה אוֹמֵר: הָרוּג שֶׁיָּצָא מִמֶּנּוּ רְבִיעִית דָּם, וְהָיָה מוּטָל בְּמִטָּה וְדָמוֹ מְטַפְטֵף לְגוּמָּא – טָמֵא, מִפְּנֵי שֶׁהַטִּפָּה שֶׁל מִיתָה מְעוֹרֶבֶת בּוֹ. וַחֲכָמִים מְטַהֲרִין, מִפְּנֵי

**Rabbi Yehuda says:** In the case of one who has been **killed from whom a quarter-*log* of blood emerged, and he was lying in a bed and his blood was dripping into a hole**[H] in the ground, the blood in the ground **is ritually impure, because the drop of death is mixed with it. And the Rabbis deem it ritually pure, because**

Perek **X**
Daf **71** Amud **b**

**BACKGROUND**

**Crucified** – צָלוּב: Execution by crucifixion was one of the typical Roman forms of capital punishment. This torturous form of execution was routinely used to punish slaves, captives, and rebels. The act of crucifixion, nailing the prisoner's hands and feet to a wooden cross, was not enough to kill the crucified person. Ultimately, the prisoner would die from blood loss and dehydration; therefore, there were cases where people were removed from the cross and managed to recuperate. Until his death, the blood of the prisoner would drip continually onto the ground beneath him, and would continue to drip even after his death.

שֶׁרִאשׁוֹן רִאשׁוֹן נִפְסָק. שַׁפִּיר קָאָמְרִי לֵיהּ רַבָּנַן לְרַבִּי יְהוּדָה! רַבִּי יְהוּדָה לְטַעְמֵיהּ, דַּאֲמַר אֵין דָּם מְבַטֵּל דָּם.

each **first** drop and every other **first** drop is **separated** from the other drops of blood, i.e., it did not flow in a steady stream. Since the blood initially emerged while he was alive and is pure, every drop of blood which emerged after his death is nullified when it falls into that blood, and therefore the entire puddle of blood is ritually pure. The Gemara asks: **The Rabbis are saying well to Rabbi Yehuda;** how does he respond to their claim? The Gemara answers that **Rabbi Yehuda** conforms **to his** line of **reasoning, as he said: Blood does not nullify blood.**[N]

רַבִּי שִׁמְעוֹן אוֹמֵר: צָלוּב עַל הָעֵץ, שֶׁדָּמוֹ שׁוֹתֵת לָאָרֶץ, וְנִמְצָא תַּחְתָּיו רְבִיעִית דָּם – טָמֵא. רַבִּי יְהוּדָה מְטַהֵר, שֶׁאֲנִי אוֹמֵר טִפָּה שֶׁל מִיתָה עוֹמֶדֶת לוֹ עַל גַּב הָעֵץ.

**Rabbi Shimon says:** In the case of one who is **crucified**[B] **on wood, whose blood** does not drip but runs down the wood **to the earth, and a quarter-*log* of blood is found underneath him,** the blood is **ritually impure. Rabbi Yehuda deems** the blood **ritually pure.** He explains his reasoning: **As I say** that the quarter-*log* of blood found underneath the body came out while he was still alive, and **the drop of** blood that came out after his **death remains on the wood.**

וְרַבִּי יְהוּדָה נֵימָא אִיהוּ לְנַפְשֵׁיהּ: שֶׁאֲנִי אוֹמֵר טִפָּה שֶׁל מִיתָה עוֹמֶדֶת עַל גַּב הַמִּטָּה! שָׁאנֵי בְּמִטָּה דִּמְחַלְחֲלָה.

The Gemara raises a difficulty with regard to the opinion of Rabbi Yehuda. **And Rabbi Yehuda, let him say to himself** with regard to one who was killed on a bed and his blood is dripping into a hole in the ground: **As I say** that all the blood found underneath the body emerged while he was still alive and **the drop of** blood that came out after his **death remains on the bed.** Why does Rabbi Yehuda deem the blood ritually impure in such a case? The Gemara answers: The case **of the bed is different,** as the blood **seeps** through the bed onto the floor, whereas in the case of one who is crucified some of the blood may remain on the tree.

**NOTES**

**Blood does not nullify blood** – אֵין דָּם מְבַטֵּל דָּם: There is a dispute between *tanna'im* (*Zevaḥim* 77b) with regard to the blood of an offering which becomes mixed with water. The Rabbis hold that as long as it has the appearance of blood, the mixture may be presented on the altar, even if there is more water than blood. Similarly, if the blood of an offering becomes mixed with wine or the blood of a non-consecrated animal, the wine or blood is viewed as if it were water, and if blood mixed with that amount of water would have the appearance of blood it may be presented on the altar. By contrast, Rabbi Yehuda holds that one type of item is not nullified by something of the same type. Therefore, blood is not nullified when it is mixed with other blood. Consequently, if even one drop of blood of a consecrated animal becomes mixed with blood of a non-consecrated animal, the blood of the consecrated animal is not nullified and the mixture may be presented on the altar.

מתני׳ בָּרִאשׁוֹנָה הָיוּ אוֹמְרִים: הַיּוֹשֶׁבֶת עַל דַּם טָהוֹר – הָיְתָה מְעָרָה מַיִם לַפֶּסַח.

**MISHNA** **Initially** the Sages **would say,** with regard to a woman who gave birth and observed the seven or fourteen days of impurity for a male or female child, respectively, and then immersed in a ritual bath and **who is observing** the period **of the blood of purity,**[NH] that **she would pour water** from a vessel in her hands **to** rinse **the Paschal offering.**[N] Although it is permitted for such a woman to engage in intercourse with her husband, her halakhic status is like that of one who immersed that day and the sun has not yet set. She therefore assumes second-degree ritual impurity and confers third-degree ritual impurity upon *teruma* with which she comes into contact. Consequently, she may touch the vessel, as second-degree ritual impurity does not render a vessel impure. She may not touch the water, as it is designated for rinsing the Paschal offering and therefore it is treated with the sanctity of sacrificial food, which is rendered impure by second-degree ritual impurity.

חָזְרוּ לוֹמַר: הֲרֵי הִיא כְּמַגַּע טְמֵא מֵת לְקָדָשִׁים – כְּדִבְרֵי בֵית הִלֵּל, בֵּית שַׁמַּאי אוֹמְרִים: אַף כִּטְמֵא מֵת.

The Sages **then said:** Her status **is like** that of one who came into **contact with one impure** with impurity imparted by **a corpse,** i.e., one with first-degree ritual impurity, who renders **consecrated** items impure. But with regard to all non-sacred items, even non-sacred items treated with the sanctity of sacrificial food, such as the water used to rinse the Paschal offering, she has second-degree ritual impurity. Consequently, it is permitted for her to touch not only the vessel, but the water inside it as well, **in accordance with the statement of Beit Hillel. Beit Shammai say:** The status of the woman is **even like** that of one who is **impure** due to contact with **a corpse,** who is a primary source of ritual impurity and renders even a non-sacred vessel impure.

גמ׳ מְעָרָה – אִין, נוֹגַעַת – לָא, אַלְמָא: חוּלִּין שֶׁנַּעֲשׂוּ עַל טָהֳרַת הַקֹּדֶשׁ – כְּקֹדֶשׁ דָּמוּ.

**GEMARA** The mishna teaches: A woman who gave birth, observed the days of impurity, immersed in a ritual bath, and who is now observing the period of the blood of purity **would pour** water from a vessel in her hands to rinse the Paschal offering. The Gemara infers: Pouring from a vessel, **yes,** this is permitted, but she may **not touch** the water itself. **Apparently, non-sacred** produce, e.g., even liquid such as the water for rinsing the Paschal offering, **that was prepared according to** the level of **ritual purity** required **for sacrificial** food,[NH] i.e., with the same stringencies as required for sacrificial food, **is considered like sacrificial** food.

אֵימָא סֵיפָא: חָזְרוּ לוֹמַר הֲרֵי הִיא כְּמַגַּע טְמֵא מֵת לְקָדָשִׁים, לְקָדָשִׁים – אִין, לְחוּלִּין – לָא, אַלְמָא: חוּלִּין שֶׁנַּעֲשׂוּ עַל טָהֳרַת הַקֹּדֶשׁ לָאו כְּקֹדֶשׁ דָּמוּ!

But now **say the latter clause** of the mishna: The Sages **then said:** Her status **is like** that of one who came into **contact with one impure** with impurity imparted by **a corpse,** i.e., one with first-degree ritual impurity, who renders **consecrated** items impure. This indicates that **with regard to consecrated** items, **yes,** she renders them impure, but **with regard to non-sacred** items, e.g., the water used to rinse the Paschal offering, she does **not** render them impure. **Apparently, non-sacred** produce **that was prepared according to** the level of **ritual purity** required **for sacrificial** food **is not considered like sacrificial** food.

NOTES

**One who is observing the period of the blood of purity – הַיּוֹשֶׁבֶת עַל דַּם טָהוֹר:** If a woman gives birth to a boy, she is impure for seven days; if she gives birth to a girl she is impure for fourteen days. After that she immerses, and then any blood she discharges during the following thirty-three days after giving birth to a son, or sixty-six days after a daughter, is ritually pure. In other words, she is permitted by Torah law to engage in intercourse with her husband during that time, even if she experiences bleeding. With regard to touching items, she has the status of one who immersed that day and is waiting for nightfall for the purification process to be completed. Accordingly, she is considered to have second-degree impurity, and she may not partake of *teruma* during these days of purity. The Gemara refers to her as one who has immersed and is waiting for the end of a long day, as the verse states: "And she shall continue in the blood of purification thirty-three days; she shall touch no sacred item, nor enter the Sanctuary, until the days of her purification be completed" (Leviticus 12:4).

**She would pour water to rinse the Paschal offering – הָיְתָה מְעָרָה מַיִם לַפֶּסַח:** There are several opinions as to why she would be pouring water for a Paschal offering. Rashi writes that she fills the vessel which will be used to rinse the meat of the offering before it is roasted. She does not pour the water directly onto the offering, which is not yet present.

**Non-sacred produce that was prepared according to the level of ritual purity for sacrificial food – חוּלִּין שֶׁנַּעֲשׂוּ עַל טָהֳרַת הַקֹּדֶשׁ:** Some people had the custom of eating their non-consecrated food while maintaining the level of ritual purity required for sacred food, in order that their family members should not come to consume sacred food accidentally in a state of ritual impurity.

HALAKHA

**One who is observing the period of the blood of purity, etc. – הַיּוֹשֶׁבֶת עַל דַּם טָהוֹר וכו׳:** A woman who has immersed seven days after giving birth to a son or fourteen days after giving birth to a daughter is considered to have first-degree ritual impurity with regard to sacred items and food. She becomes pure with regard to sacred items and food only once she has completed her days of purity (*Kesef Mishne*; see Ra'avad). The Rambam adds that since she is impure with regard to sacred items and food she requires another immersion at the conclusion of her days of purity, and only afterward may she touch them. This is in accordance with the ruling of the mishna (Rambam *Sefer Tahara, Hilkhot Metamei Mishkav UMoshav* 5:4).

**Non-sacred produce that was prepared according to the level of ritual purity for sacrificial food – חוּלִּין שֶׁנַּעֲשׂוּ עַל טָהֳרַת הַקֹּדֶשׁ:** Non-sacred food that was prepared as if it had the purity of sacrificial food, which then comes into contact with third-degree impurity remains pure, like other non-sacred food. This is in accordance with the opinion of the first *tanna* of the *baraita*. The Ra'avad writes that this is a minority opinion of Rav Naḥman, but that the discussion in the Gemara and the unattributed *baraita* (see *Ḥagiga* 20a) hold that non-sacred food that was prepared as if it had the sanctity of sacrificial food has the same status as sacrificial food (Rambam *Sefer Tahara, Hilkhot She'ar Avot HaTumot* 12:16, and see *Kesef Mishne* there).

The Gemara explains: **Whose** opinion is expressed in the latter clause of **the mishna? It is** the opinion of **Abba Shaul, as it is taught** in a *baraita* that **Abba Shaul says:** With regard to **one** who was ritually impure **who immersed that day** and is waiting for nightfall for the purification process to be completed, he has the status of one who is impure with **first**-degree impurity **with regard to sacrificial** food,[N] in **that** he **renders two** items of sacrificial food **impure, and disqualifies one** additional item. In other words, the first item of sacrificial food that he touches assumes the status of second-degree impurity. A second item that comes into contact with the first item assumes third-degree impurity. A third item that comes into contact with the second assumes fourth-degree impurity and is therefore disqualified from being eaten, but it does not impart impurity to other items.

מַתְנִיתִין מַנִּי – אַבָּא שָׁאוּל הִיא, דְּתַנְיָא, אַבָּא שָׁאוּל אוֹמֵר: טְבוּל יוֹם תְּחִילָּה לַקֹּדֶשׁ, לְטַמֵּא שְׁנַיִם, וְלִפְסוֹל אֶחָד.

**MISHNA** **And** Beit Shammai **concede** to Beit Hillel that a woman observing the days of purity **partakes of** second-**tithe**[H] produce, as it is permitted for one who immersed that day to eat second-tithe produce. **And she separates** part of **her** dough as ***ḥalla*, and she draws** the vessel with the part of the dough that she separated **near** the rest of the dough, **and she designates it** with the **name** of *ḥalla*.

מתני׳ וּמוֹדִים שֶׁהִיא אוֹכֶלֶת בְּמַעֲשֵׂר, וְקוֹצָה לָהּ חַלָּה, וּמַקֶּפֶת וְקוֹרָא לָהּ שֵׁם,

**And** Beit Shammai further concede to Beit Hillel **that if** a drop **from her saliva or from the blood of purity fell onto a loaf of *teruma*,**[H] the loaf **is ritually pure,** as any liquid discharged from the body of one who immersed that day is ritually pure.

וְאִם נָפַל מֵרוּקָּהּ וּמִדַּם טׇהֳרָהּ עַל כִּכַּר שֶׁל תְּרוּמָה – שֶׁהוּא טָהוֹר.

There is another dispute between the *tanna'im* with regard to a woman who completed her days of purity. **Beit Shammai say:** Her immersion at the end of the days of impurity does not render it permitted for her to enter the Temple or to partake of *teruma*; rather, **she requires immersion** even **at the conclusion** of the days of purity. **And Beit Hillel say: She does not require immersion at the conclusion**[HN] of the days of purity to render it permitted for her to partake of *teruma*, as the immersion at the end of the days of impurity is sufficient.

בֵּית שַׁמַּאי אוֹמְרִים: צְרִיכָה טְבִילָה בָּאַחֲרוֹנָה, וּבֵית הִלֵּל אוֹמְרִים: אֵינָהּ צְרִיכָה טְבִילָה בָּאַחֲרוֹנָה.

**GEMARA** The mishna teaches that Beit Shammai concede to Beit Hillel that the woman observing the days of purity partakes of second-tithe produce. The Gemara explains that the reason is **as the Master said:** When the period of ritual impurity of a *zav* or leper has been completed, and he **immersed** during the day **and ascended** from the ritual bath, he **may partake of** second **tithe**[H] immediately.

גמ׳ דְּאָמַר מָר: טָבַל וְעָלָה – אוֹכֵל בְּמַעֲשֵׂר.

The mishna teaches: **And she separates** part of **her** dough as ***ḥalla*.**[H] The Gemara explains that **non-consecrated** food that is **untithed produce with regard to *ḥalla*,** as it has not had *ḥalla* separated from it, e.g., this dough from which a piece has been set aside for the future separation of *ḥalla*, **is not considered like *ḥalla*,** and therefore is not rendered impure by the contact of a woman observing the days of purity.

״וְקוֹצָה לָהּ חַלָּה״. חוּלִּין הַטְּבוּלִין לְחַלָּה – לָאו כְּחַלָּה דָּמוּ.

## HALAKHA

**Partakes of second tithe – אוֹכֶלֶת בְּמַעֲשֵׂר:** During her days of purity a woman who has given birth is considered like one who has immersed during the day but is waiting for nightfall with regard to *teruma* and tithes. Therefore she may partake of tithes, but disqualifies *teruma*, in accordance with the ruling of the mishna (Rambam *Sefer Tahara, Hilkhot Metamei Mishkav UMoshav* 5:4).

**A drop from her saliva or from the blood of purity fell onto a loaf of *teruma* – נָפַל מֵרוּקָּהּ וּמִדַּם טׇהֳרָהּ עַל כִּכַּר שֶׁל תְּרוּמָה:** If saliva or blood falls from a woman after childbirth during her days of purity onto a loaf of *teruma* bread, the bread remains ritually pure. This is in accordance with the mishna (Rambam *Sefer Tahara, Hilkhot Metamei Mishkav UMoshav* 5:4).

**Immersion at the conclusion – טְבִילָה בָּאַחֲרוֹנָה:** A woman does not require another immersion at the end of her days of purity before she may partake of *teruma*, in accordance with the opinion of Beit Hillel (Rambam *Sefer Tahara, Hilkhot Metamei Mishkav UMoshav* 5:4).

**He immersed and ascended, he may partake of second tithe – טָבַל וְעָלָה אוֹכֵל בְּמַעֲשֵׂר:** One who was ritually impure and immersed in a ritual bath may partake of second tithe even before nightfall, in accordance with the mishna in tractate *Nega'im* 14:3 (Rambam *Sefer Zera'im, Hilkhot Ma'aser Sheni* 3:4).

**And she separates part of her dough as *ḥalla* – וְקוֹצָה לָהּ חַלָּה:** A woman who is impure due to menstruation may separate *ḥalla* outside of Eretz Yisrael, since it is prohibited for her only to eat it, but not to touch it (Rambam *Sefer Zera'im, Hilkhot Terumot* 12:1).

## NOTES

**One who immersed that day is impure with first-degree impurity with regard to sacrificial food – טְבוּל יוֹם תְּחִילָּה לַקֹּדֶשׁ:** By Torah law one who was ritually impure and immersed that day and is waiting for nightfall does not transmit impurity to sacred food, but he does disqualify it. By rabbinic law he also renders it impure to the degree that it renders other sacred food ritually impure.

**She does not require immersion at the conclusion – אֵינָהּ צְרִיכָה טְבִילָה בָּאַחֲרוֹנָה:** The early commentaries write that even according to the opinion of Beit Hillel she must immerse before she may partake of sacred food, and she may partake of offerings of lesser sanctity only after she has brought the atonement offerings and immersed. The reason she must immerse at the end is that it has been a long time since her initial immersion and she will have taken her mind off sanctified food, and *teruma* as well, according to the opinion of Beit Shammai (Rashi).

״וּמַקֶּפֶת״. דְּאָמַר מָר: מִצְוָה לִתְרוֹם מִן הַמּוּקָף.

The mishna also teaches that she **draws** the vessel with the part of the dough that she separated **near** the rest of the dough. The Gemara explains that this is **as the Master said:** It is **a mitzva to separate** *teruma* **from** produce that is situated **nearby**[NH] the produce it comes to exempt, *ab initio*.

״וְקוֹרָא לָהּ שֵׁם״. סָלְקָא דַּעְתָּךְ אָמֵינָא נִגְזוֹר דִּלְמָא אָתֵי לְמִנְגַּע בָּהּ מֵאַבְּרַאי – קָא מַשְׁמַע לַן.

The mishna states: **And she designates it** with the **name** of *ḥalla*. The Gemara explains that it is necessary for the *tanna* to teach this *halakha*, as it might **enter your mind to say: Let us decree lest she comes to touch** the *ḥalla* **from the outside.**[N] Therefore, the mishna **teaches us** that there is no such decree.

״וְאִם נָפַל מֵרוּקָּה״. דִּתְנַן: מַשְׁקֶה טְבוּל יוֹם (מַשְׁקִין הַיּוֹצְאִין מִמֶּנּוּ) כְּמַשְׁקִין הַנּוֹגֵעַ בָּהֶם, וְאֵלּוּ וָאֵלּוּ אֵינָן מְטַמְּאִין, חוּץ מִמַּשְׁקֵה הַזָּב – שֶׁהוּא אַב הַטּוּמְאָה.

The mishna teaches: **And** Beit Shammai concede to Beit Hillel that **if** a drop **from her saliva** or from the blood of purity fell onto a loaf of *teruma*, that the loaf is ritually pure, as any liquid discharged from the body of one who immersed that day is ritually pure. The Gemara explains that the reason is **as we learned** in a mishna (*Tevul Yom* 2:1): The *halakha* with regard to **liquids** that emerge **from one who immersed himself that day** from his state of ritual impurity **is like** that of **liquids that he touches.**[H] **And** both **these and those,** the liquids that emanated from him and the liquids that he touched, **do not transmit ritual impurity.** This is the *halakha* **except for liquids** that come **from a** *zav*, **who is a primary source of ritual impurity.**

״בֵּית שַׁמַּאי״. מַאי בֵּינַיְיהוּ? אָמַר רַב קְטִינָא: טְבוּל יוֹם אָרוֹךְ אִיכָּא בֵּינַיְיהוּ.

The mishna teaches that **Beit Shammai** say: Her immersion at the end of the days of impurity does not render her permitted; rather, she requires immersion even at the end of the days of purity. And Beit Hillel say: The immersion at the end of the days of impurity is sufficient. The Gemara asks: **What is** the difference **between them,** i.e., what is the basis of their dispute? **Rav Ketina said:** The difference **between them** is with regard to the status of **one who immersed that day,** i.e., at the end of his time of impurity, and **a long** time has passed since the immersion. Beit Shammai hold that as a long time has passed, i.e., thirty-three days after the birth of a boy or sixty-six days after the birth of a girl, she may not rely on that immersion. Beit Hillel maintain that she may still rely on that initial immersion.

**מתני׳** הָרוֹאָה יוֹם אַחַד עָשָׂר, וְטָבְלָה לָעֶרֶב וּמְשַׁמְּשָׁה

**MISHNA** There is a dispute with regard to a woman **who sees** blood on the **eleventh day,** which is the final day of the period fit for the flow of a *zava*. It is permitted for her to engage in intercourse with her husband after observing one clean day corresponding to the one day that she saw blood, but in this case, she failed to observe one clean day. Rather, **she immersed** in a ritual bath that **evening,** the eve of the twelfth day, **and** then **engaged in intercourse**[H] with her husband.

בֵּית שַׁמַּאי אוֹמֵר: מְטַמְּאִין מִשְׁכָּב וּמוֹשָׁב, וְחַיָּיבִין בְּקָרְבָּן.

**Beit Shammai say:** Since she did not observe that corresponding clean day, she retains the status of a *zava*. Therefore both she, the *zava*, and her husband, who engaged in intercourse with a *zava*, **transmit impurity** to items designated for **lying or sitting,** to the extent that these transmit impurity to food and drink that came in contact with them, and in her case, to people as well. **And** each of them is **liable** to bring a sin offering for participating in intercourse involving a *zava*.

## NOTES

**It is a mitzva to separate *teruma* from produce that is nearby – מִצְוָה לִתְרוֹם מִן הַמּוּקָף:** *Teruma* must be separated from produce that is all in one place. One may not set aside *teruma* on behalf of produce that is elsewhere. This is a decree in case the produce that is meant to be *teruma* was actually lost at the time when it was designated as such, which would mean that *teruma* was not separated at all. Others maintain that it is a Torah edict, not based on logical reasoning, that one may not separate *teruma* or tithes from produce that is not nearby (*Tosefot HaRosh*).

**From the outside – מֵאַבְּרַאי:** According to most manuscript versions of the Talmud, this term belongs with the previous sentence, not here. The Gemara should read as follows: And she designates it with the name of *ḥalla* from the outside. In other words, she designates it without placing her hand inside the container of the dough.

## HALAKHA

**It is a mitzva to separate *teruma* from produce that is nearby – מִצְוָה לִתְרוֹם מִן הַמּוּקָף:** One may separate *teruma* only from produce that is gathered in one place. For example, if one has fifty *se'a* of produce in one location and fifty *se'a* in another location, he may not separate two *se'a* from one location for the entire one hundred *se'a*. If one did separate *teruma* from another location, the separation is valid. This is in accordance with the mishna (*Ḥalla* 1:9). This is provided that the separated *teruma* is protected. But if one has wine or oil barrels that are breaking or leaking, he may not say: These are *teruma* on behalf of the produce in my home. If he does so it has no effect. This is in accordance with a *baraita* cited in *Bava Kamma* 115b (Rambam *Sefer Zera'im*, *Hilkhot Terumot* 3:17).

**Like that of liquids that he touches – כְּמַשְׁקִין הַנּוֹגֵעַ בָּהֶם:** Liquids that emerge from one who immersed himself that day and is waiting for nightfall have the status of liquids that he himself touched. For instance, if the liquids touched non-sacred liquid, the non-sacred liquid is considered ritually pure. If they touched a liquid of *teruma*, it assumes third-degree impurity. If they touched a liquid that was consecrated, the liquid assumes fourth-degree impurity (Rambam *Sefer Tahara*, *Hilkhot She'ar Avot HaTumot* 10:4).

**She immersed that evening and then engaged in intercourse – טָבְלָה לָעֶרֶב וּמְשַׁמְּשָׁה:** If a woman experiences bleeding on the eleventh day of *ziva* and immerses that night, she transmits ritual impurity to items designated for lying or sitting even though she cannot become a greater *zava* (Rambam *Sefer Kedusha*, *Hilkhot Issurei Bia* 6:17).

וּבֵית הִלֵּל אוֹמְרִים: פְּטוּרִים מִן הַקָּרְבָּן.

**And Beit Hillel say:** Although they transmit impurity to items designated for lying or sitting, **they are exempt from** bringing **the** sin **offering.** Since the twelfth day is unfit for the flow of a *zava*, and even if she were to experience bleeding on the eleventh, twelfth, and thirteenth days she would not become a greater *zava*, one who experiences bleeding on the eleventh does not need to observe a corresponding clean day.

טָבְלָה בַּיּוֹם שֶׁל אַחֲרָיו וְשִׁמְּשָׁה אֶת בֵּיתָהּ, וְאַחַר כָּךְ רָאֲתָה – בֵּית שַׁמַּאי אוֹמְרִים: מְטַמְּאִין מִשְׁכָּב וּמוֹשָׁב, וּפְטוּרִין מִן הַקָּרְבָּן.

If the woman **immersed on the day following** the eleventh day **and she engaged in intercourse with** the man of **her house,** i.e., her husband, on that twelfth day **and then saw** blood, **Beit Shammai say: They transmit impurity** to items designated for **lying or sitting** by rabbinic law, as the Sages issued a decree of impurity in the case when the second day is the twelfth day, due to a case when the second day is within the eleven days fit for the flow of a *zava*. **And they are exempt from** bringing **the** sin **offering,** as she observed part of the twelfth day, and the bleeding she experienced after engaging in intercourse, which occurred during her period of menstruation, is not fit to be appended to the discharge of the *zava* on the eleventh day.

וּבֵית הִלֵּל אוֹמְרִים: הֲרֵי זֶה גַּרְגְּרָן. וּמוֹדִים בְּרוֹאָה בְּתוֹךְ אַחַד עָשָׂר יוֹם, וְטָבְלָה לָעֶרֶב וְשִׁמְּשָׁה – שֶׁמְּטַמְּאִין מִשְׁכָּב וּמוֹשָׁב. וְחַיָּיבִין בְּקָרְבָּן.

**And Beit Hillel say:**[N] **That** husband **is a glutton,**[N] as he could not wait for the conclusion of the twelfth day before engaging in intercourse. Nevertheless, the Sages did not issue a decree of impurity. **And Beit** Hillel **concede** to Beit Shammai **in** a case where the woman **sees** blood **in the midst of the eleven-day** period, **and she immersed in the evening and engaged in intercourse** with her husband without observing a corresponding clean day, **that they transmit impurity** to items designated for **lying or sitting. And** each of them is **liable to** bring a sin **offering** for participating in intercourse involving a *zava*.

טָבְלָה בַּיּוֹם שֶׁל אַחֲרָיו וְשִׁמְּשָׁה – הֲרֵי זֶה תַּרְבּוּת רָעָה, וּמַגָּעָן וּבְעִילָתָן תְּלוּיִין.

If she saw blood in the midst of the eleven days and observed part of a corresponding clean day and **immersed on the day following** the day that she saw blood **and engaged in intercourse**[H] with her husband, **that is wayward conduct,** as the possibility exists that she will experience bleeding after intercourse that will be appended to the bleeding of the previous day, rendering her a *zava* and disqualifying the immersion. **And** the status of ritually impure items with which **they came into contact and** the status of **their intercourse is contingent** upon whether she experiences bleeding on the day of her immersion, in which case the ritually pure items become impure and they are liable to bring a sin offering, or whether she does not experience bleeding that day, in which case the ritually pure items remain pure and the woman and man are exempt from bringing a sin offering.

**גמ׳** תָּנוּ רַבָּנַן: וְשָׁוִין בְּטוֹבֶלֶת לַיְלָה לְזָבָה – שֶׁאֵינָהּ טְבִילָה. וְשָׁוִין בְּרוֹאָה בְּתוֹךְ אַחַד עָשָׂר יוֹם, וְטָבְלָה לָעֶרֶב וְשִׁמְּשָׁה – שֶׁמְּטַמְּאָה מִשְׁכָּב וּמוֹשָׁב, וְחַיָּיבִין בְּקָרְבָּן.

**GEMARA** **The Sages taught** in a *baraita*: **And** Beit Shammai and Beit Hillel **agree with regard to** a woman who **immersed** at **night to** purify herself after having been a lesser ***zava***,[H] **that it is not** a valid **immersion. And** Beit Shammai and Beit Hillel also **agree with regard to** a woman **who sees** blood **in the midst of** her **eleven days** of *ziva*,[N] rendering her a lesser *zava* who must wait one clean day and immerse the day after, **but** she **immersed in the** first **evening** without waiting one clean day **and engaged in intercourse** with her husband, **that she transmits impurity** to items designated for **lying or sitting** that came in contact with the couple, **and** she and her husband **are liable to** bring a sin **offering.**

**NOTES**

**And Beit Hillel say** – וּבֵית הִלֵּל אוֹמְרִים: This discussion is cited on 54a, and the *amora'im* disagree as to its meaning. Rav Sheshet holds that it is forbidden to be a glutton, whereas Rav Ashi holds that it is inappropriate behavior but does not transgress any prohibition.

**That husband is a glutton** – הֲרֵי זֶה גַּרְגְּרָן: Although according to Beit Hillel there is no sin, as she observed some time of the day, nevertheless Rav Ashi understands that it is behavior that can lead to transgression: If a husband is accustomed to engage in intercourse with his wife on the twelfth day of her days of *ziva*, he might also come to engage in intercourse with her in the midst of the eleven days, on the day after she experienced bleeding (Rashi).

**They agree with regard to one who sees blood in the midst of her eleven days of *ziva*** – שָׁוִין בְּרוֹאָה בְּתוֹךְ אַחַד עָשָׂר יוֹם: Since the *baraita* began by saying that Beit Hillel and Beit Shammai agree that an immersion at night for *ziva* is not a valid immersion, why does the *baraita* later repeat that Beit Hillel agree with Beit Shammai in such a case that the *zava* and her husband are impure and must bring an offering? Rashi explains that the *baraita* starts by mentioning a general *halakha* with regard to a *zava* who immersed, and then proceeds to explain the circumstances of this specific case.

**HALAKHA**

**Immersed on the day following the day she saw blood and engaged in intercourse** – טָבְלָה בַּיּוֹם שֶׁל אַחֲרָיו וְשִׁמְּשָׁה: A lesser *zava* who immersed on the day she was observing a clean day is conditionally pure. If she completes the day without experiencing any bleeding, anything she touched remains pure, as does her husband if she engaged in intercourse with him. Nevertheless, her behavior is improper, since had she experienced further bleeding they would be ritually impure (Rambam *Sefer Kedusha*, *Hilkhot Issurei Bia* 6:13).

**Immersed at night to purify herself after having been a lesser *zava*** – בְּטוֹבֶלֶת לַיְלָה לְזָבָה: A greater or lesser *zava* who immerses herself on the night of the day she is observing as a clean day is considered like one who has not immersed at all, and she transmits ritual impurity to items designated for lying or sitting (Rambam *Sefer Kedusha*, *Hilkhot Issurei Bia* 6:12).

לֹא נֶחְלְקוּ אֶלָּא בְּיוֹם אַחַד עָשָׂר יוֹם, שֶׁבֵּית שַׁמַּאי אוֹמְרִים: מְטַמְּאִין מִשְׁכָּב וּמוֹשָׁב, וְחַיָּיבִין בְּקָרְבָּן. וּבֵית הִלֵּל – פּוֹטְרִין מִקָּרְבָּן.

**They disagree only in** the case of a woman who sees blood on the **eleventh day** of her days of *ziva*, and immersed that evening, and engaged in intercourse with her husband. **As Beit Shammai say: They transmit impurity** to items designated for **lying or sitting and are liable to** bring a sin **offering, and Beit Hillel deem** them **exempt from** bringing a sin **offering.**

אָמְרוּ לָהֶן בֵּית שַׁמַּאי לְבֵית הִלֵּל: מַאי שְׁנָא יוֹם אַחַד עָשָׂר מִיּוֹם תּוֹךְ אַחַד עָשָׂר? אִם שִׁיוָּה לוֹ לְטוּמְאָה, לֹא יְשַׁוֶּה לוֹ לְקָרְבָּן?

The *baraita* continues: **Beit Shammai said to Beit Hillel: What the difference** between the **eleventh day** itself and another **day in the midst of** the **eleven** days of *ziva*? **If you equate** the eleventh day to the other days **with regard to ritual impurity,** will you **not equate it with regard to** liability to bring **an offering?**

אָמְרוּ לָהֶן בֵּית הִלֵּל לְבֵית שַׁמַּאי: לֹא אִם אֲמַרְתָּ בְּתוֹךְ אַחַד עָשָׂר יוֹם – שֶׁכֵּן יוֹם שֶׁלְּאַחֲרָיו מִצְטָרֵף עִמּוֹ לְזִיבָה, תֹּאמְרוּ בְּיוֹם אַחַד עָשָׂר – שֶׁאֵין יוֹם שֶׁלְּאַחֲרָיו שֶׁנִּצְטָרֵף עִמּוֹ לְזִיבָה!

**Beit Hillel said to Beit Shammai: No, if you say** that she is liable to bring an offering if she experiences bleeding **in the midst of the eleven days,** that is **because the following day combines with it** as a day **of** *ziva*. **Will you say** the same **with regard to the eleventh day, when the following day does not combine with it** as a day **of** *ziva*?

אָמְרוּ לָהֶם בֵּית שַׁמַּאי: הַשְׁווּ מִדּוֹתֵיכֶם, אִם שִׁיוָּה לוֹ לְטוּמְאָה – יְשַׁוֶּה לוֹ לְקָרְבָּן, וְאִם לֹא שִׁיוָּה לוֹ לְקָרְבָּן – לֹא יְשַׁוֶּה לוֹ לְטוּמְאָה.

**Beit Shammai said to** Beit Hillel: **Apply your method equally. If you equate** the two cases, bleeding on the eleventh day and bleeding on one of the other days of *ziva*, **with regard to ritual impurity, equate** them also **with regard to** liability to bring **an offering. And if** you **do not equate** them **with regard to** liability to bring **an offering, do not equate** them **with regard to ritual impurity** either.

אָמְרוּ לָהֶם בֵּית הִלֵּל: אִם הֱבִיאֲנוּהוּ לִידֵי טוּמְאָה – לְהַחְמִיר, לֹא נְבִיאֵהוּ לִידֵי קָרְבָּן – לְהָקֵל.

**Beit Hillel said to** Beit Shammai: Even **if we have brought** a woman who experiences bleeding on the eleventh day and the man who engages in intercourse with her **to ritual impurity,** due to a decree **to be stringent,** so that people should not confuse one who experiences bleeding on the eleventh day with one who experiences bleeding during the other days with regard to ritual impurity, **we will not bring** them **to** the liability of bringing **an offering, to be lenient.** It would be a leniency to permit them to bring an unnecessary and therefore a non-sacred animal into the Temple courtyard.

וְעוֹד, מִדִּבְרֵיכֶם אַתֶּם נוֹשְׁכִין, שֶׁאַתֶּם אוֹמְרִין, טָבְלָה יוֹם שֶׁלְּאַחֲרָיו וְשִׁמְּשָׁה, וְאַחַר כָּךְ רָאֲתָה – מְטַמֵּא מִשְׁכָּב וּמוֹשָׁב, וּפְטוּרָה מִן הַקָּרְבָּן אַף אַתֶּם הַשְׁווּ מִדּוֹתֵיכֶם – אִם שִׁיוָּה לוֹ לְטוּמְאָה – יְשַׁוֶּה לוֹ לְקָרְבָּן,

**And furthermore, from your** own **statement you are refuted, as you say** that if **she immersed on the following day and engaged in intercourse, and afterward she saw blood, she transmits impurity** to items designated for **lying or sitting, but she is exempt from** bringing **the offering. You too** should **apply your method equally. If you equate** a *zava* who immersed on the twelfth day with one who immersed on the night after the eleventh day **with regard to ritual impurity, equate** these cases also **with regard to** liability to bring **an offering.**

וְאִם לֹא שִׁיוָּה לוֹ לְקָרְבָּן – לֹא יְשַׁוֶּה לוֹ לְטוּמְאָה! אֶלָּא – לְהַחְמִיר וְלֹא לְהָקֵל, הָכָא נַמִי – לְהַחְמִיר וְלֹא לְהָקֵל.

**And if** you **do not equate** them **with regard to** liability to bring **an offering, do not equate** them **with regard to ritual impurity** either. Beit Hillel continued: **Rather,** you agree with us that the two are equated **to be stringent, but not to be lenient.** We say that **here too,** the two should be equated **to be stringent but not to be lenient.**

אָמַר רַב הוּנָא: מִשְׁכָּבָהּ וּמוֹשָׁבָהּ שֶׁבַּשֵּׁנִי – בֵּית שַׁמַּאי מְטַמְּאִין, אַף עַל פִּי שֶׁטָּבְלָה, אַף עַל פִּי שֶׁלֹּא רָאֲתָה. מַאי טַעְמָא? כֵּיוָן דְּאִילּוּ חַזְיָא – מְטַמְּאָה, הַשְׁתָּא נַמִי מְטַמְּיָא.

§ **Rav Huna says,** in further clarification of Beit Shammai's opinion: If a woman experiences bleeding during the eleven days of *ziva* and must observe one clean day, but did not wait until the conclusion of that second day before immersing, with regard to **her** items designated for **lying or sitting, on the second** day, **Beit Shammai render** them **impure** by rabbinic law. This is the *halakha* **even though she has immersed** in a ritual bath and **even though she did not see** any blood after her immersion. **What is the reason? Since if she would see** blood **she** would **render** these surfaces **ritually impure** by Torah law, **now too she renders** them **ritually impure** by rabbinic law.

HALAKHA

And she engaged in intercourse with the man of her house and then saw blood – וְשִׁמְּשָׁה אֶת בֵּיתָהּ וְאַחַר כָּךְ רָאֲתָה: A woman who immerses herself on the twelfth day after sunrise is forbidden to her husband until the evening, and she has the status of a lesser *zava*. If they transgressed and engaged in intercourse, they are both exempt from punishment. Even if she sees a drop of blood on the twelfth day after they have engaged in intercourse, it is blood of menstruation and does not combine with the blood she saw on the previous day (Rambam *Sefer Kedusha*, *Hilkhot Issurei Bia* 6:18 and *Maggid Mishne* there; *Sefer Tahara*, *Hilkhot Metamei Mishkav UMoshav* 5:8, and Ra'avad and *Kesef Mishne* there).

If a man sees one sighting of *ziva* – הָרוֹאֶה רְאִיָּיה אַחַת שֶׁל זוֹב: A man who sees one sighting of *ziva* has the same halakhic status as one who sees a seminal emission, in accordance with the opinion of Beit Hillel (Rambam *Sefer Korbanot*, *Hilkhot Meḥusrei Kappara* 2:6).

אָמַר רַב יוֹסֵף: מַאי קָא מַשְׁמַע לַן? תְּנֵינָא: טָבְלָה יוֹם שֶׁלְּאַחֲרָיו וְשִׁמְּשָׁה אֶת בֵּיתָהּ, וְאַחַר כָּךְ רָאֲתָה. בֵּית שַׁמַּאי אוֹמְרִים: מְטַמְּאָה מִשְׁכָּבוֹת וּמוֹשָׁבוֹת וּפְטוּרָה מִן הַקָּרְבָּן!

**Rav Yosef said: What is** Rav Huna **teaching us? We** already **learn** in the mishna: If the woman **immersed on the day following** the eleventh day **and she engaged in intercourse with** the man of **her house** on that twelfth day **and then saw** blood,[H] **Beit Shammai say: They transmit impurity** to items designated for **lying or sitting** by rabbinic law. **And they are exempt from** bringing **the sin offering.** Her impurity applies by rabbinic law, lest this case be confused with one where she experiences bleeding during the eleven days when she would be impure by Torah law. By inference, if she experienced bleeding on one of her eleven days and immersed on the following day, she would likewise render items designated for lying or sitting ritually impure by rabbinic law.

אָמַר רַב כָּהֲנָא: רָאֲתָה שָׁאנֵי.

**Rav Kahana said:** Rav Huna is teaching that Beit Shammai render her ritually impure even if she does not experience bleeding. Based on the mishna alone, one might have thought that the case where **she saw** blood **is different,** and it is only in this situation that Beit Shammai render her impure by rabbinic law.

אָמַר רַב יוֹסֵף: וְכִי רָאֲתָה מַאי הָוֵי? רְאִיָּיה דְּנִדָּה הִיא!

**Rav Yosef said,** in refutation of Rav Kahana's claim: **And if she saw** blood on the twelfth day, **what of it?** A discharge of blood on the twelfth day **is a sighting of a menstruating woman,** which does not render her a *zava* by Torah law. Therefore, it is comparable to a case where she experienced bleeding on one day during her eleven days of *ziva* and immersed on the following day, and she does not experience bleeding on that following day at all.

אָמַר לֵיהּ אַבַּיֵי לְרַב יוֹסֵף: רַב כָּהֲנָא הָכִי קָא קַשְׁיָא לֵיהּ, בִּשְׁלָמָא הֵיכָא דְּרָאֲתָה – גָּזְרִינַן רְאִיָּיה דְּנִדָּה אַטּוּ רְאִיָּיה דְּזָבָה, אֶלָּא הֵיכָא דְּלָא רָאֲתָה – מַאי נִגְזוֹר בַּהּ?

**Abaye said to Rav Yosef: This is what** is **difficult for Rav Kahana: Granted,** in a case **where she saw** blood on the twelfth day, it stands to reason that **we decree** impurity with regard to **a sighting of a menstruating woman due to a sighting of a *zava*. But** in a case **where she did not see** any blood at all, for **what** reason should the Sages **decree** impurity **upon her?**

וְעוֹד: תְּנַן, הָרוֹאֶה רְאִיָּיה אַחַת שֶׁל זוֹב – בֵּית שַׁמַּאי אוֹמְרִים: כְּשׁוֹמֶרֶת יוֹם כְּנֶגֶד יוֹם, וּבֵית הִלֵּל אוֹמְרִים: כְּבַעַל קֶרִי.

Abaye continues: **And furthermore, we learned** in a mishna (*Zavim* 1:1): If a man **sees one sighting of *ziva*** (see 35b),[H] **Beit Shammai say:** His status on the following day is **like** that of **a woman who observes** a clean **day for a day** she experiences a discharge. In other words, he must immerse and observe that day in purity, and if he touches tithes their status is suspended, since if he sees another discharge on that day, they are retroactively impure. **And Beit Hillel say:** His status is **like** that of a man **who experiences a seminal emission,** who is purified by his immersion, and therefore any tithes this man touches on the second day remain pure even if he later experiences a second discharge.



NOTES

Beit Shammai say it is contingent, etc. – בֵּית שַׁמַּאי אוֹמְרִים תּוֹלִין וכו׳: Rashi explains that this is referring to a ritually pure individual who moves the first drop of *ziva* seen by a *zav*, and afterward that person touched ritually pure items. The status of those items is contingent on whether or not the *zav* sees a second discharge. If he does, he becomes a full-fledged *zav* retroactively, and both the person who moved the first drop and the items he touched become ritually impure.

וְתַנְיָא הַמֵּסִיט אֶת הָרְאִיָּיה – בֵּית שַׁמַּאי אוֹמְרִים: תּוֹלִין, וּבֵית הִלֵּל מְטַהֲרִין.

**And it is taught** in a *baraita*: If one **moves the** discharge **seen** by a *zav* on the first day, **Beit Shammai say:** Due to the uncertainty, his status of ritual purity is **contingent**[N] upon whether he sees another emission. If the *zav* sees a discharge a second time he will retroactively have been a full-fledged *zav* and his discharge renders one who moves it impure. But if he does not see another discharge he will remain like one who experienced a seminal emission, which means that his discharge does not render one who moves it impure. **And Beit Hillel deem** him **pure.** The discharge has the status of a seminal emission and does not transmit impurity to one who moves it.

מִשְׁכָּבוֹת וּמוֹשָׁבוֹת שֶׁבֵּין רְאִיָּיה רִאשׁוֹנָה לִרְאִיָּיה שְׁנִיָּיה – בֵּית שַׁמַּאי תּוֹלִין, וּבֵית הִלֵּל מְטַהֲרִין.

The *baraita* continues: With regard to items designated for **lying or sitting** and their status **between the first sighting and the second sighting,**[H] **Beit Shammai** say: Due to the uncertainty their status of ritual purity is **contingent** upon whether he sees another emission, **and Beit Hillel deem** them **pure.**

וְקָתָנֵי רֵישָׁא: הָרוֹאֶה רְאִיָּיה אַחַת שֶׁל זוֹב – בֵּית שַׁמַּאי אוֹמְרִים: כְּשׁוֹמֶרֶת יוֹם כְּנֶגֶד יוֹם. אַלְמָא: שׁוֹמֶרֶת יוֹם כְּנֶגֶד יוֹם, לְבֵית שַׁמַּאי תּוֹלִין!

Abaye explains Rav Kahana's difficulty with Rav Huna's opinion: It **is taught in the first clause** of the *baraita* that if a man **sees one sighting of *ziva*, Beit Shammai say:** His status is **like** that of **a woman who observes** a clean **day for a day**[N] she experiences a discharge. **Apparently, according to** the opinion of **Beit Shammai** the ritual purity status of **a woman who observes** a clean **day for a day** she experiences a discharge is **contingent** upon whether she experiences an emission of blood. This is difficult for Rav Huna, who explains that Beit Shammai hold that a woman who observes a clean day for each day of discharge is definitely impure, by rabbinic law.

לָא תֵּימָא ״שׁוֹמֶרֶת יוֹם כְּנֶגֶד יוֹם״, אֶלָּא אֵימָא ״כְּבוֹעֵל שׁוֹמֶרֶת יוֹם כְּנֶגֶד יוֹם״.

The Gemara answers that Rav Huna would explain: **Do not say** that his status is like that of **a woman who observes** a clean **day for a day. Rather, say** that he is **like one who engages in intercourse with a woman who observes** a clean **day for a day** after she has immersed. Rav Huna agrees that items designated for lying or sitting that this man sits or lies on is ritually impure only if she experiences bleeding before the end of the day.

מַאי שְׁנָא אִיהוּ דְּלָא מְטַמֵּא מִשְׁכָּב וּמוֹשָׁב, וּמַאי שְׁנָא אִיהִי דִּמְטַמְּיָא לֵיהּ?

The Gemara asks: **What is different** with regard to **him,** a man who engages in intercourse with a woman who is observing a clean day for a day, **that he does not transmit impurity** to items designated for **lying or sitting, and what is different** with regard to **her,** that woman herself, **that she** does **transmit impurity to** items designated for lying or sitting?

אִיהוּ דְּלָא שְׁכִיחִי בֵּיהּ דָּמִים – לָא גְּזוּר בֵּיהּ רַבָּנַן, אִיהִי דִּשְׁכִיחִי בָּהּ דָּמִים – גְּזוּר בָּהּ רַבָּנַן.

The Gemara explains: With regard to **him, as he does not frequently** see **blood, the Sages did not issue a decree** rendering **him** impure to such an extent, if the woman has not seen blood on the second day. Whereas with regard to **her, as she does frequently** see **blood, the Sages did issue a decree** rendering her definitely impure to this degree.

וּמַאי שְׁנָא מִשְׁכָּב וּמוֹשָׁב דִּמְטַמְּיָא לֵיהּ, וּמַאי שְׁנָא בּוֹעֵל דְּלָא מְטַמְּיָא לֵיהּ?

The Gemara further inquires: **And** since a decree was applied to her, as she commonly sees blood, **what is different** with regard to items designated for **lying or sitting, that she transmits impurity to them, and what is different** with regard to the **one who engages in intercourse** with her, **that she does not render him impure?**

מִשְׁכָּב וּמוֹשָׁב דִּשְׁכִיחַ – מְטַמְּיָא לֵיהּ, בּוֹעֵל דְּלָא שְׁכִיחַ – לָא מְטַמְּיָא.

The Gemara answers: With regard to items designated for **lying or sitting, she renders them ritually impure because she frequently** sits or lies on them, whereas with regard to **one who engages in intercourse** with her, **which is not** nearly as **frequent,** she does **not render him ritually impure.**

תְּנַן: טָבְלָה יוֹם שֶׁלְּאַחֲרָיו וְשִׁמְּשָׁה – הֲרֵי זוֹ תַּרְבּוּת רָעָה,

The Gemara raises another difficulty with regard to Rav Huna's opinion. **We learned** in the mishna: If she saw blood on the eleventh day and observed part of a corresponding clean day and **immersed** on **the day following** the day that she saw blood **and engaged in intercourse** with her husband, **that is wayward conduct,** as the possibility exists that she will experience bleeding after intercourse that will be appended to the bleeding of the previous day, rendering her a *zava* and disqualifying the immersion.

מַגָּעָן וּבְעִילָתָן תְּלוּיִין. מַאי לָאו, דִּבְרֵי הַכֹּל הִיא?

The mishna adds: And the status of ritually impure items with which **they came into contact and** the status of **their intercourse is contingent** upon whether she experiences bleeding on the day of her immersion. The Gemara explains the difficulty. **What, is it not** correct to say that **all,** i.e., Beit Shammai and Beit Hillel, **agree** with this clause of the mishna? If so, Beit Shammai concur that this woman renders items impure only due to uncertainty. This is not in accordance with the statement of Rav Huna.

**HALAKHA**

**Lying or sitting between the first sighting and the second sighting – מִשְׁכָּבוֹת וּמוֹשָׁבוֹת שֶׁבֵּין רְאִיָּיה רִאשׁוֹנָה לִרְאִיָּיה שְׁנִיָּיה:** Any item designated for lying or sitting that a man sits or lies on after one discharge of *ziva* remains pure, because he does not become a *zav* until he has experienced two discharges of *ziva*. This is in accordance with the opinion of Beit Hillel (Rambam *Sefer Tahara, Hilkhot Metamei Mishkav UMoshav* 1:12).

**NOTES**

**Like a woman who observes a clean day for a day – כְּשׁוֹמֶרֶת יוֹם כְּנֶגֶד יוֹם:** The *halakhot* governing a female *zava* are dissimilar to those of a male *zav*. Her impurity is not dependent on the number of discharges, but on the days in which she experiences them. Even if she experiences bleeding many times on a single day, all of them are considered as one. Furthermore, a woman is a *zava* only if she experiences a blood flow not at the time of her menstrual period, as it is stated: "Not in the time of her menstruation" (Leviticus 15:25). The period of *ziva* is the eleven days after her seven-day menstrual period. If she experiences bleeding on only one day during this time she has the status of a lesser *zava*. By Torah law, she is obligated to wait one day without any discharge of blood, i.e., she observes a day for a day, in order to become ritually pure. If she experiences bleeding on two consecutive days she must observe the third day, and immerses, and is pure that evening. If she experiences bleeding on three consecutive days she becomes a greater *zava*. She must therefore count seven clean days and may immerse only on the seventh day. Finally, she must bring an offering on the eighth day, after which it is permitted for her to eat consecrated foods.

לָא, בֵּית הִלֵּל הִיא. דְּתַנְיָא, אָמַר לָהֶם רַבִּי יְהוּדָה לְבֵית הִלֵּל: וְכִי לָזוֹ אַתֶּם קוֹרִין ״תַּרְבּוּת רָעָה״? וַהֲלֹא לֹא נִתְכַּוֵּין זֶה אֶלָּא לִבְעוֹל אֶת הַנִּדָּה! נִדָּה סָלְקָא דַּעְתָּךְ?

The Gemara answers: **No, this** clause of the mishna **is** only in accordance with the opinion of **Beit Hillel. As it is taught** in a *baraita* that **Rabbi Yehuda said to Beit Hillel:**[N] **Do you call this** type of behavior **wayward conduct? But he intended only to engage in intercourse with a menstruating woman.** The Gemara questions the meaning of Rabbi Yehuda's statement. Can it **enter your mind** that he intended to engage in intercourse with **a menstruating woman?** The mishna and *baraita* are not referring to a man who engages in intercourse with a menstruating woman.

אֶלָּא אֵימָא ״לִבְעוֹל אֶת הַזָּבָה״. זָבָה סָלְקָא דַּעְתָּךְ? אֶלָּא אֵימָא ״לִבְעוֹל שׁוֹמֶרֶת יוֹם כְּנֶגֶד יוֹם״.

**Rather, say** that Rabbi Yehuda meant that this man intended only **to engage in intercourse with a** *zava*. The Gemara rejects this formulation as well: Can it **enter your mind** that Rabbi Yehuda said he intended to engage in intercourse with **a** *zava*? The mishna and *baraita* are not referring to a man who engages in intercourse with a *zava* either. **Rather, say** that Rabbi Yehuda meant that this man intended **to engage in intercourse with a woman who observes** a clean **day for a day** she experiences a discharge. This *baraita* indicates that the latter clause of the mishna is only according to the opinion of Beit Hillel, as Rabbi Yehuda directed his comments specifically to them.

אִיתְּמַר: עֲשִׂירִי – רַבִּי יוֹחָנָן אָמַר: עֲשִׂירִי כִּתְשִׁיעִי, מַה תְּשִׁיעִי – בָּעֵי שִׁימּוּר, אַף עֲשִׂירִי – בָּעֵי שִׁימּוּר.

§ The Gemara cites another discussion concerning a woman who experiences bleeding toward the end of her eleven days of *ziva*. **It was stated** with regard to a woman who experiences bleeding on the **tenth** day of her eleven days of *ziva*, that **Rav Yoḥanan says:** The **tenth** day is considered **like the ninth,**[H] i.e., **just as the ninth** day **requires** the **observance** of a day clean from discharges on the following day, **so too does the tenth** day **require observance** of a day in case she experiences bleeding on the eleventh day.

רֵישׁ לָקִישׁ אָמַר: עֲשִׂירִי כְּאַחַד עָשָׂר, מָה אַחַד עָשָׂר – לָא בָּעֵי שִׁימּוּר, אַף עֲשִׂירִי – לָא בָּעֵי שִׁימּוּר.

**Reish Lakish says:** The **tenth** day is considered **like** the **eleventh** day, as in such a case it is impossible for her to experience bleeding for the three consecutive days within the eleven days of *ziva*. **Just as** the **eleventh** day **does not require** the **observance** of a day clean from discharges, **so too** the **tenth** day **does not require** the **observance** of a day clean from discharges, since even if she experiences bleeding on both the eleventh and the twelfth days, the last of the three consecutive days was already the start of her days of menstruation, and therefore she does not become a greater *zava*.

אִיכָּא דְּמַתְנֵי לָהּ אַהָא, אָמַר לוֹ רַבִּי אֶלְעָזָר בֶּן עֲזַרְיָה לְרַבִּי עֲקִיבָא: אֲפִילּוּ אַתָּה מַרְבֶּה ״בְּשֶׁמֶן״ [״בְּשֶׁמֶן״] כָּל הַיּוֹם כּוּלּוֹ – אֵינִי שׁוֹמֵעַ לְךָ! אֶלָּא, חֲצִי לוֹג שֶׁמֶן לְתוֹדָה, וּרְבִיעִית יַיִן לְנָזִיר, וְאַחַד עָשָׂר יוֹם שֶׁבֵּין נִדָּה לְנִדָּה – הֲלָכָה לְמֹשֶׁה מִסִּינַי.

**There are** those **who teach** the dispute between Rabbi Yoḥanan and Reish Lakish **with regard to this** case: **Rabbi Elazar ben Azarya**[P] **said to Rabbi Akiva: Even** if **you** were to **amplify** and derive *halakhot* from the repeated terms **"in oil," "in oil,"** stated with regard to the thanks offering (see Leviticus 7:12) **for the entire day, I would not listen to you**[N] and accept your claim. **Rather,** the *halakha* that **one-half of a** ***log*** is the requisite amount of **oil for the thanks offering, and** the *halakha* that **one-quarter** of a *log* is the amount of **wine for a nazirite, and** the *halakha* that a woman who experiences an emission of blood during the **eleven days that are between** one period of **menstruation and** the next period of **menstruation**[H] is a *zava*, each of these is **a** ***halakha*** transmitted **to Moses from Sinai.** None of the *halakhot* are derived from verses.

מַאי ״הֲלָכָה״? רַבִּי יוֹחָנָן אָמַר: הֲלָכָה אַחַד עָשָׂר. רֵישׁ לָקִישׁ אוֹמֵר: הִלְכוֹת אַחַד עָשָׂר.

The Gemara asks: **What** is the ***halakha*** mentioned here with regard to the eleven days between one period of menstruation and the next? **Rabbi Yoḥanan says:** It is referring to the ***halakha*** that distinguishes the first ten days from the **eleventh** day. **Reish Lakish says:** It is referring to two *halakhot* that distinguish the first ten days from the **eleventh.**

**NOTES**

**Rabbi Yehuda said to Beit Hillel – אָמַר לָהֶם רַבִּי יְהוּדָה לְבֵית הִלֵּל:** Some commentaries have a version that reads: Beit Shammai said to Beit Hillel (Gra).

**I would not listen to you – אֵינִי שׁוֹמֵעַ לְךָ:** Some explain that the phrase: I would not listen to you, means that I do not accept that this *halakha* is derived from verses, but rather it is a *halakha* transmitted to Moses at Sinai. Rabbi Elazar ben Azarya and Rabbi Akiva agree with regard to the actual *halakha*, and disagree only as to its source (Rashi).

**HALAKHA**

**The tenth is like the ninth – עֲשִׂירִי כִּתְשִׁיעִי:** If a woman experiences bleeding on the tenth of her days of *ziva* she immerses on the eleventh day and observes that as a clean day. If she experiences bleeding after her immersion any food that she touched becomes impure retroactively, as does her husband if they engaged in intercourse. This is the *halakha* even though she cannot become a greater *zava* in this time. This is in accordance with the opinion of Rabbi Yoḥanan (Rambam *Sefer Tahara, Hilkhot Metamei Mishkav UMoshav* 5:8).

**Eleven days…between one period of menstruation and the next period of menstruation – אַחַד עָשָׂר יוֹם שֶׁבֵּין נִדָּה לְנִדָּה:** Any blood that a woman discharges not during her days of menstruation is blood of *ziva*. There is a *halakha* transmitted to Moses from Sinai that there are eleven days between the days of menstruation (Rambam *Sefer Kedusha, Hilkhot Issurei Bia* 6:3).

**PERSONALITIES**

**Rabbi Elazar ben Azarya – רַבִּי אֶלְעָזָר בֶּן עֲזַרְיָה:** One of the most significant *tanna'im* in the generation following the destruction of the Temple, Rabbi Elazar ben Azarya descended from a family blessed with great wisdom, distinguished lineage, and wealth. His father, Azarya, was also a Torah scholar and an extremely wealthy man. Azarya supported his brother Shimon, one of the Sages, who is therefore referred to as Shimon, brother of Azarya. Rabbi Elazar ben Azarya was from a family of priests descended from Ezra the Scribe, and there are traditions that draw parallels between them. The Gemara describes how his knowledge, wealth, and family lineage led to his being chosen by the Sages to replace Rabban Gamliel as *Nasi* when the latter was removed from his position of leadership after repeatedly and publicly humiliating Rabbi Yehoshua (see *Berakhot* 27b).

רַבִּי יוֹחָנָן אָמַר: הֲלָכָה אַחַד עָשָׂר, אַחַד עָשָׂר הוּא דְּלָא בָּעֵי שִׁימּוּר – הָא לְאַחֲרִינֵי עָבֵיד שִׁימּוּר. וְרֵישׁ לָקִישׁ אָמַר: הִלְכוֹת אַחַד עָשָׂר, לָא אַחַד עָשָׂר בָּעֵי שִׁימּוּר, וְלָא שִׁימּוּר לַעֲשִׂירִי הָוֵי.

The Gemara elaborates: **Rabbi Yoḥanan says** that this is referring to the ***halakha*** which distinguishes the first ten days from the **eleventh. It is** the **eleventh that does not require** the **observance** of a day clean from discharges, **but for the other** ten days she must **perform observance. And Reish Lakish says:** It is referring to two ***halakhot*** that distinguish the first ten days from the **eleventh.** The **eleventh** day **does not require observance, and it does not** serve as a day of **observance for the tenth** day, i.e., the tenth day also does not require observance. The tenth day does not require observing since day eleven is excluded from being a day of observation for the previous day.

הָנֵי הֲלָכוֹת נִינְהוּ? הָנֵי קְרָאֵי נִינְהוּ! דְּתַנְיָא: יָכוֹל הָרוֹאָה שְׁלֹשָׁה יָמִים בִּתְחִילַּת נִדָּה רְצוּפִים תְּהֵא זָבָה.

The Gemara raises a difficulty with regard to Rabbi Elazar ben Azarya's claim that the eleven days of *ziva* is a *halakha* transmitted to Moses from Sinai. Are **these *halakhot*** transmitted to Moses from Sinai? Not so; rather, **these are** derived from **verses. As it is taught** in a *baraita*: One **might** have thought that **one who sees** blood for **three consecutive days**[NH] **at the beginning of** the days of **menstruation will be a *zava*** and is required to count seven clean days and to bring an offering afterward (see Leviticus 15:28–30).

וּמָה אֲנִי מְקַיֵּים "אִשָּׁה כִּי תִהְיֶה זָבָה דָּם יִהְיֶה זֹבָהּ" – בְּרוֹאָה יוֹם אֶחָד (אֲבָל הָרוֹאָה שְׁלֹשָׁה יָמִים בַּתְּחִילָּה תִּהְיֶה זָבָה)? תַּלְמוּד לוֹמַר:

**And** if so, **how do I realize** the meaning of the verse: "And **if a woman has a flow, and her flow on her flesh be blood,** she shall be in her impurity seven days; and whoever touches her shall be impure until the evening" (Leviticus 15:19)? This is referring **to** one **who sees** blood on only **one day.** But perhaps one who sees blood for three days at the beginning of her days of menstruation should become a *zava*? **The verse states:**

Perek **X**
Daf **73** Amud **a**

"בְּלֹא עֶת נִדָּתָהּ" (עַל נִדָּתָהּ) סָמוּךְ לְנִדָּתָהּ.

"And if a woman has a discharge of her *ziva* blood for many days **not in the time of her menstruation,** or if she has a discharge beyond the time of her menstruation, all the days of the issue of her *ziva* she shall be as in the days of her menstruation: She is impure" (Leviticus 15:25). This verse teaches that a woman becomes a *zava* only if she experiences bleeding **close to** her days of **menstruation,** i.e., on the day following her days of menstruation, but not during her days of menstruation.

וְאֵין לִי אֶלָּא סָמוּךְ לְנִדָּתָהּ, מוּפְלָג לְנִדָּתָהּ יוֹם אֶחָד מִנַּיִן? תַּלְמוּד לוֹמַר "אוֹ כִּי תָזוּב".

The *baraita* continues: **And I have** derived **only** that she is a *zava* in a case where she experiences bleeding **close to** her time of **menstruation. From where** do I derive that if she experiences bleeding **one day separated from** her days of **menstruation** she is also a *zava*? **The verse states: "Or if she has a discharge** beyond the time of her menstruation" (Leviticus 15:25).

אֵין לִי אֶלָּא יוֹם אֶחָד, מִנַּיִן לְרַבּוֹת מוּפְלָג שְׁנַיִם, שְׁלֹשָׁה, אַרְבָּעָה, חֲמִשָּׁה, שִׁשָּׁה, וְשִׁבְעָה, שְׁמוֹנָה, תִּשְׁעָה, עֲשָׂרָה, מִנַּיִן?

The *baraita* further states: **I have** derived **only** that she is a *zava* in a case where she experiences bleeding **one day** away from her time of menstruation. **From where** is it derived **to include** a case when she experiences bleeding **two, three, four, five, six, seven, eight, nine,** or **ten** days **separated from** her days of menstruation that she is also a *zava*? **From where** is this derived?

אָמַרְתָּ: מַה מָּצִינוּ בָּרְבִיעִי – שֶׁרָאוּי לִסְפִירָה וְרָאוּי לְזִיבָה, אַף אֲנִי אָבִיא הָעֲשִׂירִי – שֶׁרָאוּי לִסְפִירָה וְרָאוּי לְזִיבָה.

**You say** as follows: **Just as we find** with regard to a woman who experiences bleeding **on the fourth** day of her days of *ziva*, **that** it **is fit for counting,** i.e., if she experiences bleeding for the first time on that day she must count one clean day for the one day that she experienced bleeding, **and** it **is fit for *ziva*,** i.e., if it is the last of three consecutive days of sightings that she becomes a greater *zava*, **so too I will bring** and include **the tenth** day, **as** it **is fit for counting** if she experiences bleeding for the first time on that day, **and fit for *ziva*** if she experiences bleeding for the third consecutive day on the tenth day.

NOTES

**One who sees for three consecutive days** – הָרוֹאָה שְׁלֹשָׁה יָמִים...רְצוּפִים: The early commentaries write that a woman becomes a greater *zava* and has to count seven clean days only if she experiences bleeding on three consecutive days during her days of *ziva*. This is also the ruling of the Rambam (*Sefer Kedusha, Hilkhot Issurei Bia* 6:7).

HALAKHA

**One who sees for three consecutive days** – הָרוֹאָה שְׁלֹשָׁה יָמִים...רְצוּפִים: If a woman experiences bleeding on the tenth, eleventh, and twelfth days of her days of *ziva*, she does not become a greater *zava* but goes from being a lesser *zava* to having the status of a menstruating woman, since the twelfth day is the first of her days of menstruation. This is in accordance with the *baraita* (Rambam *Sefer Kedusha, Hilkhot Issurei Bia* 6:16).

וּמִנַּיִן לְרַבּוֹת אַחַד עָשָׂר? תַּלְמוּד לוֹמַר "בְּלֹא עֶת נִדָּתָהּ". יָכוֹל שֶׁאֲנִי מְרַבֶּה אַף שְׁנֵים עָשָׂר? אָמַרְתָּ: לָאו.

The *baraita* continues: **And from where** is it derived **to include** a case where she experiences bleeding on the **eleventh** day after her days of menstruation? **The verse states: "Not in the time of her menstruation"** (Leviticus 15:25). One **might** have thought **that I include even** the **twelfth** day after her period of menstruation. **You** must **say: No,** as that is no longer within her days of *ziva*.

וּמָה רָאִיתָ לְרַבּוֹת אַחַד עָשָׂר וּלְהוֹצִיא שְׁנֵים עָשָׂר? מְרַבֶּה אֲנִי אַחַד עָשָׂר – שֶׁרָאוּי לִסְפִירַת "אוֹ כִּי תָזוּב". וּמוֹצִיא אֲנִי שְׁנֵים עָשָׂר – שֶׁאֵין רָאוּי לִסְפִירַת "אוֹ כִּי תָזוּב".

The *baraita* further states: **And what did you see to include** the **eleventh** day **and to exclude** the **twelfth** day? **I include** the **eleventh** day **as it is fit for counting** the seven clean days that follow sightings on three consecutive days which ended on the fourth day, as derived from the verse: **"Or if she has a discharge** beyond the time of her menstruation" (Leviticus 15:25), as explained; **and I exclude** the **twelfth** day **as it is not fit for counting** the seven clean days after the fourth day, a requirement derived from the same verse: **"Or if she has a discharge** beyond the time of her menstruation."

וְאֵין לִי אֶלָּא שְׁלֹשָׁה יָמִים, שְׁנֵי יָמִים מִנַּיִן? תַּלְמוּד לוֹמַר "יְמֵי". יוֹם אֶחָד מִנַּיִן? תַּלְמוּד לוֹמַר "כָּל יְמֵי".

The *baraita* continues: **And I have** derived **only** that a woman is impure as a *zava* if she experiences bleeding for **three** consecutive **days. From where** do I derive that she is impure if she experiences bleeding for **two** consecutive **days?** The continuation of **the verse states:** "All the **days** of the issue of her *ziva* she shall be as in the days of her menstruation: She is impure" (Leviticus 15:25). The plural "days" indicates two days. **From where** is it derived that she is impure if she experiences bleeding on only **one day? The verse states: "All the days** of the issue of her *ziva* she shall be as in the days of her menstruation: She is impure."

"טְמֵאָה" – מְלַמֵּד שֶׁמְּטַמְּאָה אֶת בּוֹעֲלָהּ כְּנִדָּה. "הִיא" – הִיא מְטַמְּאָה אֶת בּוֹעֲלָהּ, וְאֵין הַזָּב מְטַמֵּא מַה שֶּׁהוּא בּוֹעֵל.

The *baraita* further explains that the word **"impure"** in that verse **teaches that** a *zava* **renders one who engages in intercourse with her impure,** just **like a menstruating woman**[H] does. The term: **"She** is impure," indicates that **she,** a *zava,* **renders** a man **who engages in intercourse with her impure, but a *zav* does not render** a woman **whom he engages in intercourse** with **ritually impure.**[H]

וַהֲלֹא דִּין הוּא: וּמַה הִיא שֶׁאֵינָהּ מְטַמְּאָה בִּרְאִיּוֹת כְּבְיָמִים – מְטַמְּאָה אֶת בּוֹעֲלָהּ, הוּא שֶׁמְּטַמֵּא בִּרְאִיּוֹת כְּבְיָמִים – אֵינוֹ דִּין שֶׁמְּטַמֵּא מַה שֶּׁהוּא בּוֹעֵל? תַּלְמוּד לוֹמַר "הִיא" – הִיא מְטַמְּאָה אֶת בּוֹעֲלָהּ, וְאֵין הַזָּב מְטַמֵּא מַה שֶּׁהוּא בּוֹעֵל.

One might have thought that one who engages in intercourse with a *zav* has the same status as one who engages in intercourse with a *zava*. Could **this not** be derived through an *a fortiori* **inference? And if** a *zava,* **who does not become impure through** three **sightings like** she becomes impure if she experiences bleeding **for** three consecutive **days,** and yet she **renders** a man **who engages in intercourse with her impure,** then with regard to a *zav,* **who becomes impure through** three **sightings** even on a single day **like** he becomes impure by seeing a discharge for three consecutive **days, isn't it logical that he** should **render** a women **whom he engages in intercourse** with **ritually impure?** Therefore, **the verse states:** "**She** shall be impure." This teaches that a *zava* **renders** a man **who engages in intercourse with her impure, but a *zav* does not render** a woman **whom he engages in intercourse** with **ritually impure.**

וּמִנַּיִן שֶׁהוּא עוֹשֶׂה מִשְׁכָּב וּמוֹשָׁב? תַּלְמוּד לוֹמַר "כְּמִשְׁכַּב נִדָּתָהּ".

**And from where** is it derived **that** a *zava* **transmits impurity** to items designated for **lying or sitting? The verse states:** "Every bed which she lies on all the days of her discharge shall be for her **like the bed of her menstruation;** and everything that she sits on shall be impure, as the impurity of her menstruation" (Leviticus 15:26).

HALAKHA

**She renders one who engages in intercourse with her impure like a menstruating woman** – שֶׁמְּטַמְּאָה אֶת בּוֹעֲלָהּ כְּנִדָּה: One who engages in intercourse with a menstruating woman has the status of the woman herself with regard to ritual impurity, and becomes a primary category of ritual impurity. Therefore he renders vessels impure through contact; renders any person impure through carrying, touching, or moving; and renders items impure through lying or riding on them like a menstruating woman. This is in accordance with the *baraita* (Rambam *Sefer Tahara, Hilkhot Metamei Mishkav UMoshav* 3:1).

**But a *zav* does not render a woman whom he engages in intercourse with ritually impure** – וְאֵין הַזָּב מְטַמֵּא מַה שֶּׁהוּא בּוֹעֵל: A woman who engages in intercourse with a *zav* has the ritual impurity status of one who touched a *zav* (Rambam *Sefer Tahara, Hilkhot Metamei Mishkav UMoshav* 3:3).

וְאֵין לִי אֶלָּא שְׁלֹשָׁה יָמִים, שְׁנֵי יָמִים מִנַּיִן? תַּלְמוּד לוֹמַר "יְמֵי". יוֹם אֶחָד מִנַּיִן? תַּלְמוּד לוֹמַר "כָּל יְמֵי".

**And I have** derived **only** that she transmits impurity to items designated for lying or sitting if she experiences bleeding for **three** consecutive **days** and is a greater *zava*. **From where** do I derive that she transmits impurity to items designated for lying or sitting if she experiences bleeding for **two** consecutive **days** and is only a lesser *zava*? **The verse states "days."** And **from where** do I derive that she transmits impurity to items designated for lying or sitting even if she experiences bleeding on only **one day?**[H] **The verse states: "All the days** of her discharge."

וּמִנַּיִן שֶׁסּוֹפֶרֶת אֶחָד לְאֶחָד? תַּלְמוּד לוֹמַר "יִהְיֶה לָהּ". יָכוֹל תִּסְפּוֹר שִׁבְעָה לִשְׁנַיִם, וְדִין הוּא: וּמָה הוּא שֶׁאֵין סוֹפֵר אֶחָד לְאֶחָד – סוֹפֵר שִׁבְעָה לִשְׁנַיִם, הִיא שֶׁסּוֹפֶרֶת אֶחָד לְאֶחָד – אֵינוֹ דִּין שֶׁתִּסְפּוֹר שִׁבְעָה לִשְׁנַיִם? תַּלְמוּד לוֹמַר "יִהְיֶה לָהּ" – אֵינָהּ סוֹפֶרֶת אֶלָּא יוֹמָהּ.

The *baraita* continues: **And from where** is it derived **that she counts one** clean day **for** experiencing bleeding on **one** day? **The verse states:** "All the days of her discharge **shall be for her."** One **might** have thought that she **must count seven** clean days **for** experiencing bleeding on **two** consecutive days. **And this is a logical inference: Just as** a *zav*, **who does not count one** clean day if he sees a discharge **on one** day, nevertheless **must count seven** clean days if he sees a discharge **on two days,** then with regard to a *zava*, **who counts one** clean day if she experiences bleeding **on one** day, **isn't it logical that** she should **count seven** clean days if she experiences bleeding **on two** consecutive days? **The verse states:** "All the days of her discharge **shall be for her,"** which teaches that **she counts only her** one **day**[H] even if she experiences bleeding for two consecutive days.

אַלְמָא קְרָאֵי נִינְהוּ! לְרַבִּי עֲקִיבָא – קְרָאֵי, לְרַבִּי אֶלְעָזָר בֶּן עֲזַרְיָה – הִלְכְתָא.

The Gemara explains the difficulty from this *baraita*: **Evidently,** the *halakhot* of the eleven days of *ziva* **are** derived from **verses** and are not a *halakha* transmitted to Moses from Sinai. The Gemara answers: **According to** the opinion of **Rabbi Akiva** these *halakhot* are derived from **verses. According to** the opinion of **Rabbi Elazar ben Azarya** they are a ***halakha*** transmitted to Moses from Sinai.

אֲמַר לֵיהּ רַב שְׁמַעְיָה לְרַבִּי אַבָּא: אֵימָא, בִּימָמָא – תֶּהֱוֵי זָבָה, בְּלֵילְיָא – תֶּהֱוֵי נִדָּה! אֲמַר לֵיהּ: עֲלָךְ אֲמַר קְרָא "עַל נִדָּתָהּ" – סָמוּךְ לְנִדָּתָהּ, סָמוּךְ לְנִדָּתָהּ אֵימַת הָוֵי? בְּלֵילְיָא, וְקָא קָרֵי לָהּ "זָבָה".

With regard to the verse discussing the days of *ziva*, **Rav Shemaya said to Rabbi Abba:** But one can **say** that if she experiences bleeding **during the daytime she shall be a *zava*,** but if she experiences bleeding **at night she shall be a menstruating woman,** as the verse specifies "days." Rabbi Abba **said to him: With regard to your claim, the verse states: "Beyond the time of her menstruation"** (Leviticus 15:25), which teaches that she becomes a *zava* if she experiences bleeding **close to her** days of **menstruation. When is** the time **close to her** days of **menstruation? At night. And** with regard to an emission during this time **the** verse **calls her a *zava*.**

תָּנָא דְּבֵי אֵלִיָּהוּ: כָּל הַשּׁוֹנֶה הֲלָכוֹת בְּכָל יוֹם – מוּבְטָח לוֹ שֶׁהוּא בֶּן הָעוֹלָם הַבָּא, שֶׁנֶּאֱמַר "הֲלִיכוֹת עוֹלָם לוֹ" – אַל תִּקְרֵי "הֲלִיכוֹת" אֶלָּא "הֲלָכוֹת".

The Gemara concludes the tractate with a general statement with regard to Torah study. **The school of Elijah taught:**[B] **Anyone who studies *halakhot* every day is guaranteed that he is destined for the World-to-Come, as it is stated: "His ways [*halikhot*] are eternal"** (Habakkuk 3:6).[N] **Do not read** the verse as *halikhot*; **rather,** read it as ***halakhot*.**[N] The verse indicates that the study of *halakhot* brings one to eternal life in the future world.

הדרן עלך תינוקת
וסליקא לה מסכת נדה

**HALAKHA**

From where do I derive one day – יוֹם אֶחָד מִנַּיִן: If a woman experiences bleeding for only one or two days during her days of *ziva* she is a lesser *zava*. She must observe one clean day corresponding to one of the days that she experienced bleeding, and during that time she has the same status as a greater *zava* (Rambam *Sefer Kedusha*, *Hilkhot Issurei Bia* 6:7–8).

She counts only her one day – אֵינָהּ סוֹפֶרֶת אֶלָּא יוֹמָהּ: A lesser *zava* must count only one clean day. This is in accordance with the *baraita* (Rambam *Sefer Kedusha*, *Hilkhot Issurei Bia* 6:8–10).

**NOTES**

His ways are eternal – הֲלִיכוֹת עוֹלָם לוֹ: In the Jerusalem Talmud (*Megilla* 1:5), this verse is cited to derive the principle that the *halakhot* will not be nullified in the future time to come. It says in this verse that the *halakhot* are eternal. The later authorities add that the word "His" [*lo*] has the numerical value of 36, which alludes to the 36 tractates of the Babylonian Talmud. This is an additional reason why this statement is cited here, at the completion of the Babylonian Talmud (*Hatam Sofer*).

Rather as *halakhot* – אֶלָּא הֲלָכוֹת: The word *halakhot* completes the tractate and the entire Babylonian Talmud. Rashi writes that this term includes the study of Mishna, *baraitot*, and *halakhot* transmitted to Moses at Sinai.

**BACKGROUND**

The school of Elijah taught – תָּנָא דְּבֵי אֵלִיָּהוּ: In many places in the Talmud and the midrash, Elijah the prophet appears to people, especially to Sages, and resolves their dilemmas. As it is stated in the Prophets (II Kings 2:11), Elijah did not die, and he continues to serve as an emissary of God. The verse describes how a letter arrived for King Jehoram from Elijah the prophet many years after Elijah's time on earth (II Chronicles 21:12).

The midrash named *Tanna deVei Eliyahu* or *Seder Eliyahu* comprises two parts: *Seder Eliyahu Rabba*, which has thirty-one chapters, and *Seder Eliyahu Zuta*, which has fifteen chapters, though there are some editions which have a different numbering system. The entire work is written in Hebrew and contains biblical commentary, events of Jewish history, and first-person stories of Elijah the prophet. Some of these stories begin with the phrase: Father Elijah said.

The Talmud often quotes *Tanna deVei Eliyahu*, and the final paragraph of the Gemara is from *Seder Eliyahu Zuta*, chapter 2. Some hold that *Tanna deVei Eliyahu* and the school of Eliyahu are not references to Elijah the prophet; rather, they are named for one of the *tanna'im* who lived during the Second Temple period (*Be'er Sheva*).

# Summary of **Perek X**

The Sages distinguish between the hymenal blood of a girl who is a minor, less than twelve years old, and that of a young woman, who is over twelve. They also distinguish with regard to the blood of a young woman, between the ages of twelve and twelve and a half, who has previously menstruated, and one who has not yet menstruated. There are disputes relating to the ritual purity and impurity of each of these women.

Concerning a minor, some Sages hold that any blood that emerges during the first four nights of her marriage is attributed to the torn hymen, and she remains ritually pure. Others hold that the blood is considered to be pure as long as the wound has not healed. There is an opinion that blood that emerges only when she is standing but not when she is sitting, or only when she sits on a coarse item but not when she sits on a soft one, is considered to be from the hymen.

With regard to a young girl who has never previously menstruated, some rule that only blood that emerges during the first night is considered pure, whereas any blood that emerges after that time is menstrual blood and is impure. Others maintain that any blood that emerges during the first four nights is ritually pure.

According to some Sages, it is permitted for a young girl who has previously menstruated to engage in intercourse only once, after which she is impure until she completes her purification process. Others hold that any blood she discharges for the entire first night is considered pure blood.

The *halakhot* stated in the mishna with regard to pure blood seen by a virgin are in accordance with the basic *halakha*. In practice, anyone who marries a virgin may engage in intercourse with her only once, after which she becomes impure and forbidden to him until she has waited a certain amount of time and immersed in a ritual bath. According to some early commentaries this is the conclusion of the Gemara as stated by Rav and Shmuel, and Rabbi Yoḥanan and Reish Lakish. According to other early commentaries it is a custom that became universally accepted during the time of the *ge'onim*.

A greater *zava* must count seven clean days and examine herself on each of those days. There is a dispute with regard to her status if she examined herself only on the first and seventh days. Some contend that as she examined herself at the beginning and the end of the period, she may consider herself to have remained clean during the intermediate days. Others maintain that the two days that she examined herself are counted, but she must count another five clean days. Yet others hold that only the examination on the last day counts, and therefore she must count another six clean days. There is an additional dispute concerning the *halakha* if a woman checked herself only on the first or seventh day.

With regard to the status of blood that emerges from a woman after her death, there are different opinions. Everybody agrees that the blood is treated as blood which flowed from a corpse and as such imparts the impurity of a dead person only if there is a quarter-*log*. With regard to the question of whether the blood imparts impurity in any amount, there are different opinions. Some rule that the blood is impure, as although it emerged only after her death, it originated in the uterus, and any blood that originates in the uterus is impure even if it is not menstrual blood. Others claim that blood from the uterus which is not menstrual blood is pure, and therefore the blood only has the impurity of any other blood that flowed from a woman after her death.

This chapter also discussed the status of a woman after childbirth, during her days of pure blood, with regard to consecrated items and *teruma*.

# Common **Acronyms**

Since the publication of the first volume of the *Koren Talmud Bavli* we have employed some transliterated acronyms, such as Rambam, to give the translation a more authentic flavor. These acronyms are used throughout this volume where they are well known and where the acronym helps readers easily identify the author in question. The following chart provides the full name of each author or work alongside its common acronym.

| Acronym | Full Name |
|---|---|
| HaAri | Rabbi Yitzḥak Luria |
| Ba'al HaMaor | Rabbi Zeraḥya HaLevi |
| *Baḥ* | *Bayit Ḥadash* |
| *Beur HaGra* | Commentary of Rabbi Eliyahu of Vilna on the *Shulḥan Arukh* |
| *Derashot Mahari Mintz* | Homilies of Rabbi Yehuda Mintz |
| *Derashot Ra'anaḥ* | Homilies of Rabbi Eliyahu ben Ḥayyim |
| Geranat | Rabbi Naftali Trop |
| *Gilyon Maharsha* | Marginalia of Rabbi Shlomo Eiger |
| Gra | Rabbi Eliyahu of Vilna, the Vilna Gaon |
| Graḥ | Rabbi Ḥayyim Soloveitchik |
| Grib | Rabbi Yehuda Bakhrakh |
| Griz | Rabbi Yitzḥak Ze'ev Soloveitchik |
| *Haggahot HaGra* | Comments of Rabbi Eliyahu of Vilna on the Talmud |
| *Haggahot Maharsha* | Comments of Rabbi Shmuel Eliezer Eidels |
| *Hassagot HaRa'avad* | Comments of Rabbi Avraham ben David on the Rambam's *Mishne Torah* |
| Ḥida | Rabbi Ḥayyim David Azulai |
| *Ḥiddushei Aggadot LaMaharal* | *Ḥiddushei Aggadot* by Rabbi Yehuda Loew of Prague |
| *Ḥiddushei Aggadot LaRashba* | *Ḥiddushei Aggadot* by Rabbi Shlomo ben Adderet |
| *Ḥiddushei HaGeranat* | *Ḥiddushei* Rabbi Naftali Trop |
| *Ḥiddushei HaGriz* | *Ḥiddushei* Rabbi Yitzḥak Ze'ev Soloveitchik |
| *Ḥiddushei HaRim* | *Ḥiddushei* Rabbi Yitzḥak Meir of Gur |
| *Ḥiddushei Ri Ḥaver* | *Ḥiddushei* Rabbi Yitzḥak Isaac Ḥaver |
| *Kitzur Piskei HaRosh* | Abridged Halakhic Rulings of Rabbeinu Asher ben Rabbi Yeḥiel |
| Mabit | Rabbi Moshe ben Yosef di Trani |

| Acronym | Full Name |
|---|---|
| Maharal | Rabbi Yehuda Loew of Prague |
| Maharam Alashkar | Rabbi Moshe Alashkar |
| Maharam Brisk | Rabbi Mordekhai Brisk |
| Maharam Ḥalawa | Rabbi Moshe Ḥalawa |
| Maharam Lublin | Rabbi Meir of Lublin |
| Maharam Mintz | Rabbi Moshe Mintz |
| Maharam of Rothenburg | Rabbi Meir of Rothenburg |
| Maharam Padua | Rabbi Meir of Padua |
| Maharam Schick | Rabbi Moshe Schick |
| Maharam Schiff | Rabbi Meir Schiff |
| Maharatz Ḥayyut | Rabbi Tzvi Hirsch Chajes |
| Mahari Abuhav | Rabbi Yitzḥak Abuhav |
| Mahari Bassan | Rabbi Yeḥiel Bassan |
| Mahari Beirav | Rabbi Ya'akov Beirav |
| Mahari ben Lev | Rabbi Yosef ben Lev |
| Mahari ben Malkitzedek | Rabbi Yitzḥak ben Malkitzedek |
| Mahari Berona | Rabbi Yisrael Berona |
| Mahari Kurkus | Rabbi Yosef Kurkus |
| Mahari Mintz | Rabbi Yehuda Mintz |
| Mahari Weil | Rabbi Ya'akov Weil |
| Mahariḥ | Rabbi Yeḥezkia ben Ya'akov of Magdeburg |
| Maharik | Rabbi Yosef Colon |
| Maharikash | Rabbi Ya'akov Castro |
| Maharil | Rabbi Ya'akov HaLevi Molin |
| Maharit | Rabbi Yosef di Trani |
| Maharit Algazi | Rabbi Yom Tov Algazi |
| Maharsha | Rabbi Shmuel Eliezer Eidels |
| Maharshal | Rabbi Shlomo Luria |
| Malbim | Rabbi Meir Leibush ben Yeḥiel Michel Wisser |
| Netziv | Rabbi Naftali Tzvi Yehuda Berlin |
| *Nimmukei HaGrib* | Comments of Rabbi Yehuda Bakhrakh on the Maharsha |
| *Piskei HaRid* | Halakhic Rulings of Rabbi Yeshaya di Trani the Elder |
| *Piskei Riaz* | Halakhic Rulings of Rabbi Yeshaya di Trani the Younger |
| Ra'ah | Rabbi Aharon HaLevi |
| Ra'anaḥ | Rabbi Eliyahu ben Ḥayyim |
| Ra'avad | Rabbi Avraham ben David |
| Ra'avan | Rabbi Eliezer ben Natan |
| Ra'avya | Rabbi Eliezer ben Yoel HaLevi |
| Rabbi Avraham ben HaRambam | Rabbi Avraham, son of the Rambam |

| Acronym | Full Name |
|---|---|
| Rabbi Shlomo ben Rashbatz | Rabbi Shlomo, son of Rabbi Shimon ben Tzemaḥ Duran |
| Radak | Rabbi David Kimḥi |
| Radbaz | Rabbi David ben Zimra |
| Ralbag | Rabbi Levi ben Gershon |
| Ramah | Rabbi Meir HaLevi |
| Rambam | Rabbi Moshe ben Maimon |
| Ramban | Rabbi Moshe ben Naḥman |
| Ran | Rabbeinu Nissim ben Reuven of Gerona |
| Rashash | Rabbi Shmuel Strashun |
| Rashba | Rabbi Shlomo ben Adderet |
| Rashbam | Rabbi Shmuel ben Meir |
| Rashbatz | Rabbi Shimon ben Tzemaḥ Duran |
| Rashi | Rabbi Shlomo Yitzḥaki |
| Re'em Horowitz | Rabbi Elazar Moshe Horowitz |
| Rema | Rabbi Moshe Isserles |
| Ri HaLavan | Rabbeinu Yitzḥak ben Ya'akov of Prague |
| Ri Ḥaver | Rabbi Yitzḥak Isaac Ḥaver |
| Ri Migash | Rabbi Yosef Migash |
| Riaf | Rabbi Yoshiya Pinto |
| Riaz | Rabbi Yeshaya di Trani the Younger |
| Rid | Rabbi Yeshaya di Trani the Elder |
| Ridvaz | Rabbi Ya'akov David ben Ze'ev Wilovsky |
| Rif | Rabbi Yitzḥak Alfasi |
| Rim | Rabbi Yitzḥak Meir of Gur |
| Ritva | Rabbi Yom Tov ben Avraham Asevilli (of Seville) |
| Riva | Rabbeinu Yitzḥak ben Asher |
| Rivam | Rabbi Yitzḥak ben Meir |
| Rivan | Rabbi Yehuda bar Natan |
| Rivash | Rabbi Yitzḥak ben Sheshet |
| Rosh | Rabbeinu Asher ben Rabbi Yeḥiel |
| *Shakh* | *Siftei Kohen* by Rabbi Shabtai Cohen Rappaport |
| *Shas* | The Six Orders of the Mishna |
| *She'elat Ya'avetz* | Responsa of Rabbi Ya'akov Emden |
| *Shela* | *Shenei Luḥot HaBerit* by Rabbi Yeshaya HaLevi Horowitz |
| *Siddur Rashi* | Siddur compiled by Rashi's students |
| *Sma* | *Sefer Meirat Einayim* by Rabbi Yehoshua Falk |
| *Smag* | *Sefer Mitzvot Gadol* by Rabbi Moshe of Coucy |
| *Smak* | *Sefer Mitzvot Katan* by Rabbi Yitzḥak ben Yosef of Corbeil |
| *Talmid HaRa'ah* | A student of Rabbi Aharon HaLevi |

| Acronym | Full Name |
|---|---|
| *Talmid HaRashba* | A student of Rabbi Shlomo ben Adderet |
| *Tashbetz* | Responsa of Rabbi Shimon ben Tzemaḥ Duran |
| *Taz* | *Turei Zahav* by Rabbi David HaLevi |
| *Tosefot HaRosh* | *Tosefot* of Rabbeinu Asher ben Rabbi Yeḥiel |
| *Tosefot Ri HaLavan* | *Tosefot* of Rabbeinu Yitzḥak ben Ya'akov of Prague |
| *Tosefot Rid* | *Tosefot* of Rabbi Yeshaya di Trani the Elder |
| *Tur* | *Sefer HaTurim* by Rabbi Ya'akov ben Asher |
| *Tzlaḥ* | *Tziyyun LeNefesh Ḥayya* by Rabbi Yeḥezkel Landau |
| Ya'avetz | Rabbi Ya'akov Emden |

# Index of **Background**

# Index of Background

# Index of **Background**



# Index of **Language**

# Index of **Language**

# Index of **Personalities**



# Image **Credits**

All images are copyright © Koren Publishers Jerusalem Ltd., except:

**p10** © Marie-Lan Nguyen; **p11** © udi Steinwell; **p22** © Rama; **p29** top image © Matt Tilghman, www.shutterstock.com; **p29** bottom image © Marilyn barbone, www.shutterstock.com; **p45** © Catalin Voicu, www.shutterstock.com; **p46** © Nick Thompson; **p47** left image © Vera Buhl; **p47** middle top image © Samira; **p47** middle bottom image © Teresa Ling; **p47** right image © Mahmoud burnat; **p50** top image © NoahHafra; **p50** bottom image © Atamari; **p86** © courtesy of the Temple Institute; **p99** top image © Rav Natan Slifkin; **p99** bottom left image © H. Zell; **p99** bottom right image © Dr. Shamshad Alam; **p101** © Shirley Singer; **p106** © Jeanne Michelle Smith; **p107** © Ken Fairfax and Nyetta; **p108** © Hanay; **p110** © Mentnafunangann; **p117** top image © Velela; **p117** bottom image © Niranjan Gaikwad, www.shutterstock.com; **p125** top image © Marie-Lan Nguyen; **p125** bottom image © Grand Canyon National Park; **p128** top image © Bukvoed; **p128** bottom image © Ori~; **p130** © Молли; **p153** first image © Pablo Dodda; **p153** second image © Carlos Delgado; **p153** third image © Arturo Nikolai; **p153** fourth image © Andrew Stawarz; **p158** © Clint – Bitfire Inc; **p160** © Hodgkin T, Adams W.; **p164** © Ariel Palmon; **p169** top image © Professor Zohar Amar, Bar Ilan University; **p169** bottom image © Daniel P. Diffendale; **p170** © jome jome; **p173** top left image © Ian sane; **p173** bottom left image © Alvesgaspar; **p173** top right image © Janie Easterman; **p173** bottom right image © Pentocelo; **p174** © Malte; **p179** top image © Deror avi; **p179** bottom image © Bukvoed; **p203** © Sallie; **p206** © Daderot; **p217** © Limor Sidi; **p252** © Lazaregagnidze; **p279** © HaRav Menachem Makover, courtesy of Ve*Harenu Bevinyano*; **p299** top image © Jess Van Dyke; **p299** bottom image © Michael N Maggs; **p304** © Klaram; **p308** © Marie-Lan Nguyen; **p322** top image © Jamain; **p322** middle image © Archives et jardin personnels; **p322** bottom image © Kadri Damla; **p337** © Linda Spashett; **p342** © Wilhelmy; **p346** left image © José María Escolano; **p346** bottom middle image © Pseudoanas; **p346** right image © Jamain; **p347** top image © Philip Pikart; **p347** bottom image © Frits van der Meer; **p348** © Ian Scott; **p351** top image © Eitan f; **p351** bottom image © Denis Barthel; **p353** © Bff; **p354** top left image © Hans Hillewaert; **p354** bottom left image ©Wibowo Djatmiko; **p354** top right image © Patrice78500; **p354** bottom right image © YuvalR; **p356** © Rosser1954; **p382** © Electron Microscopy Unit, AAHL, CSIRO; **p395** © Menachem Brody, photo@shechem.org; **p396** © Los Angeles County Museum of Art; **p411** top image © Sarefo; **p411** bottom image © Sergej Razvodovskij, www.shutterstock.com; **p414** top image © Sarefo; **p414** bottom image © Honeyhuyue; **p416** © Gideon Pisanty (Gidip); **p428** © Legis; **p434** left image © MatthiasKabel; **p434** top middle image © Purrrpl Haze; **p434** bottom middle image © Wknight94; **p434** right image © Inu, www.shutterstock.com; **p438** top image © Daniel Ventura; **p438** middle image © Dr. K. Grote; **p438** bottom image © Ezralalsim10; **p443** © Dr. Stefan P. Peter; **p444** © Tamara Kulikova; **p451** top image © Alexander Prokopenko; **p451** bottom image © Balajijagadesh; **p468** © Almog; **p472** © Rama; **p484** © Rogers Fund, 1934; **p499** top image © courtesy of the Temple Institute; **p499** bottom image © HaRav Menachem Makover, courtesy of Ve*Harenu Bevinyano*.

# תלמוד בבלי

## — מהדורת נאה —

### נדה

Steinsaltz Center

ירושלים

KOREN

# תלמוד בבלי

הוצאת קורן ירושלים

— מהדורת נאה —

## נדה


COMMENTARY BY

Rabbi Adin Even-Israel Steinsaltz

EDITOR-IN-CHIEF

Rabbi Dr Tzvi Hersh Weinreb

EXECUTIVE EDITOR

Rabbi Joshua Schreier



STEINSALTZ CENTER

KOREN PUBLISHERS JERUSALEM

Please note that the number ranges that appear at the bottom of each daf of the Vilna pages indicate the corresponding pages of the Koren Talmud Bavli translation and commentary.

# שמאי

*שמאי אומר: כל הנשים דיין שעתן. הלל אומר: מפקידה לפקידה, ואפילו לימים הרבה. וחכ"א לא כדברי זה ולא כדברי זה, אאלא מעת לעת – ממעטת על יד מפקידה לפקידה, ומפקידה לפקידה – ממעטת על יד מעת לעת.* בכל אשה שיש לה וסת – דיה שעתה. גוהמשמשת בעדים – הרי זו כפקידה, וממעטת על יד מעת לעת ועל יד מפקידה לפקידה. כיצד דיה שעתה? היתה יושבת במטה ועסוקה בטהרות, ופרשה וראתה – היא טמאה והן טהורות. אע"פ שאמרו: מטמאה מעת לעת – דאינה מונה אלא משעה שראתה.§ **גמ'** מאי טעמיה דשמאי? קסבר: העמד אשה על חזקתה, ואשה בחזקת טהורה עומדת. והלל, כי אמר העמד דבר על חזקתו – היכא דלית ליה ריעותא מגופיה, אבל איתתא כיון

**שמאי** אומר כל הנשים דיין שעתן. אם ראתה דם, די לנו אם תטמא תרומה וטהרות שתגע בהן משעת ראייה ואילך. ולא אמרי': כי היכי דהשתא אישתכח דם בבית החיצון, אי הות בדקה נמי מקמי הכי הוה אישתכח, וכותלי בית הרחם העמידוהו, וקיימא לן בפ' "יוצא דופן" (לקמן דף מ.) כל הנשים מטמאות בבית החיצון. **מפקידה לפקידה.** בודקה עצמה באחד בשבת ומצאתה טהורה, וליום רביעי בדקה ומצאתה טמאה – חיישינן, ומטמאה מספק כל הטהרות שנתעסקה בהן משעת בדיקת אחד בשבת. דשמא עם סילוק ידיה ראתה, וכותלי בית הרחם העמידוהו. **ואפי' לימים הרבה.** בין בדיקה ראשונה לשניה – מטמאינן כל הטהרות שנתעסקה בהן בינתיים, אבל הנך דמקמי בדיקה קמייתא – טהורות, דהא כשבדקה עצמה מצאתה טהורה. **לא כדברי זה.** שהחמיר יותר מדאי, דודאי כולי האי ימים רבים לא מוקמי ליה כותלי בית הרחם. **ולא כדברי זה.** שמיקל יותר מדאי. **אלא מעת לעת ממעטת על יד מפקידה לפקידה.** שאם יש ימים הרבה בין פקידה לפקידה – לא מטמאינן להו לכולהו טהרות דביני וביני, אלא אותם שנתעסקה בהם מאתמול בשעה הזאת. וטעמייהו דרבנן מפרש לקמן בגמרא. נמצא מעת לעת ממעטת זמן מפקידה לפקידה. **ומפקידה לפקידה ממעטת על יד מעת לעת.** שאם היה זמן מפקידה לפקידה מועט מזמן מעת לעת – הולכין אחריו להקל. כגון בדקה עצמה שחרית ומצאתה טהורה, וחזרה ובדקה ערבית ומצאתה טמאה, דאמרי' לקמן במתני' (דף יא.): פעמים צריכה להיות בודקת שחרית ובין השמשות – לא מטמאינן טהרות של ליל אמש. דהא בדקה שחרית ומצאתה טהורה, וליכא למימר דהוי דם מאתמול בהאי שעתא. אלא הנך טהרות דמבדיקת שחרית ואילך מטמאינן, דהיינו "מפקידה לפקידה". **על יד.** על כח מפקידה לפקידה הוא בא, וממעטו. כמו: "פוסל על ידו" דיבמות (דף לו.) וכן הרבה. **כל אשה שיש לה וסת.** קבוע ג' פעמים ובדקה בשעת וסתה ומצאתה טמאה. **דיה שעתה.** וליכא למימר דמעיקרא הוה התם דודאי אורח בזמנו בא. **המשמשת בעדים.** שבודקה עצמה בעד דהיינו בסדין קודם תשמיש ולאחר תשמיש. **הרי זו כפקידה וממעטת על יד כו'.** ואם ראתה דם אחר כך בבדיקת ערבית, והיא שמשה בצהרים בעדים – לא מטמאינן טהרות דמבדיקת שחרית עד תשמיש, שהרי קודם תשמיש בדקה ומצאתה טהורה, וליכא למימר: מקמי הכי הוה, אלא הנך דמתשמיש ואילך טמאות. **אף על פי שאמרו כו'.** אשאין לה וסת קאי. **אינה מונה.** ימי נדה אלא משעה כו'. **גמ' העמד אשה על חזקתה.** שהרי מספק אתה בא לטמאותה, לענין טהרות דקודם ראייה ספק הוה לה דם מקודם לכן ספק לא הוה, הלכך העמד אשה על חזקתה שהיתה קודם ראייה כשנתעסקה בטהרות אלו. **כגון ספק לא נגע.** ל"ג. דהתם לאו משום חזקה הוא, דהא ספק טומאה ברשות הרבים – טהור, דהיינו "ספק נגע, הלכתא גמירי לה".

**מעת** לעת. (א) מפרש בגמ' דתולין, לא אוכלין ולא שורפין. ודוקא לקדשים או לתרומה, אבל לחולין לכ"ע דיה שעתה, דאוקמא לה בחזקת טהורה. וא"ת: מאי שנא מכל ספק טומאה, דברה"י טמא ודאי אף לחולין, ולא מוקמינן בחזקת טהרה, משום דילפי' (לקמן דף ג.) מסוטה, מדפריך בגמרא לר"ש: אי מה סוטה טמאה ודאי ברה"י, אף הכא טמאה ודאי? ומשני: שאני סוטה דאיכא רגלים לדבר. משמע דלרבנן, דאמרי: ברה"י טמאות, אתי שפיר. וטעם דתרתי לריעותא לא הוצרך אלא לטמא אפילו בר"ה! וי"ל: דלא ילפינן מסוטה לטמאה למפרע, ולכך בטומאה דמעת לעת מוקמינן לה אחזקתה. וא"ת: במעת לעת דקיל טפי משאר טומאות כדפרישית, אמאי החמירו בו לטמאה אף בר"ה, ובכל שאר טומאות אמרינן: בר"ה – ספקו טהור, כדמוכח בשמעתין דקאמר: והלל כי קאמר אוקי מילתא אחזקתה – כגון ספק נגע ספק לא נגע, אבל במעל"ע כו'. ולא אמרינן: אוקי מילתא אחזקתה אלא בר"ה, אלמא במעת לעת אף בר"ה טמא! וכן לקמן (דף ה:) מוקי מתני': כשנושאין אותה חברותיה במטה, א"כ הוו להו תלתא, והוי ר"ה כדמוכח בריש "שני נזירים" (נזיר נז.) ואפ"ה המטה טמאה! ואע"ג דיש לדחות: כגון שהכילה מפסקת בין נדה לחברותיה, אין נראה, דבהדיא יש בירושל' דמגעה בר"ה מטמא במעת לעת! וי"ל: דאף בר"ה לא נטהר בקדשים משום חזקת טהרה, כיון דאיכא ריעותא מגופה. ואע"ג דמסוטה ילפינן לטהר בר"ה, אפי' היכא דליכא חזקה, (ב) כמו שאפרש לקמן, הכא לא ילפינן מסוטה משום שהאשה שראתה השתא ודאי טמאה היא. ולא גמרינן מסוטה לטהר בר"ה, אלא כמו ספק נגע ספק לא נגע – שגם עתה בספק, דומיא דסוטה. ומיהו בדבר שאין בו דעת לישאל – טהור במעת לעת, דלקמן מקשינן אמתני': דבר שאין בו דעת לישאל הוא? ומוקמינן: בשחברותיה נושאות אותה במטה. והיינו, משום דדבר שאין בו דעת לישאל לא גמרינן מסוטה. *אלא גמרינן לטהר מדרב גידל, דאמר רב גידל (סוטה דף כט.): כתיב "והבשר אשר יגע בכל טמא לא יאכל", הא ספק – טהור, וכתיב "כל טהור יאכל בשר", הא ספק – טמא? אלא, כאן – שאין בו דעת לישאל, כאן – שיש בו דעת לישאל. ובטומאת בשר קדש שייך למפרע כמו להבא. ועוד י"ל: דלא גמרינן מסוטה אלא טומאת מגע, ולא טומאת ראייה. לכך מטמא אף ברה"ר. אבל דבר שאין בו דעת לישאל – טהור, דבטומאת בשר קדש שייך טומאה ע"י ראיית הזב או הזבה או הנדה, (ג) דאסרינן לאכול בשר קדש, והוי בכלל "כל טהור יאכל בשר" (ויקרא ז) וא"ת: מאי שנא דבנגע באחד בלילה (לקמן דף ד.) דמטמאין רבנן אף בר"ה, כדמוכח בתוספתא היכא דלא ראהו חי מבערב, משום דכל הטומאות כשעת מציאתן. ואשה נמי אמרינן (לקמן דף ד.): כיון דשכיחי בה דמים – כאינה בדוקה דמיא, ואמאי מטהרינן לחולין אף ברה"י? וי"ל: דלקמן [נמי] בנגע באחד בלילה איירי בקדשים, וכן קופה (לקמן דף ג:) דפריך הלל לשמאי איירי בקדשים, דאי לאו הכי תקשה ליה לנפשיה. וכן פלוגתא דחזקיה ור' יוחנן (שם): (ד) המדלה י' דליים מים, איירי במים שנעשו על טהרת הקדש ללוש בהן עיסת מנחות או להדיח בהן בשר קדש, דכקדש דמו. וא"ת: ומ"ש דאמרינן בנגע באחד לשרוף, ובמעת לעת אמרינן תולין, דאשה נמי מיקריא "במקום מציאתה", דכל מקום שהיא – טומאתה עמה. דאי לאו הכי, תקשי אשה לחזקיה דמטהר בקופה ממקום למקום! וי"ל: משום דלבו נוקפו ויבטל מפריה ורביה, דסבור דשכיחא טומאה, כיון ששורפין עליה תרומה, ופריש. דכה"ג, אמרינן לקמן (דף ג:). והא דפריך הלל לשמאי, היינו משום דלבו נוקפו – לא היה לו לטהר לגמרי. *אך קשה: לפ"ז, מאי פריך להלל ממקוה, נימא: משום דלבו נוקפו? וא"ת: אמאי מטהר שמאי טפי באשה מבקופה ונגע באחד, אע"ג דמשני שמאי דאשה אין לה שוליים, היינו להאי לישנא דאי הוה דם מעיקרא הוה אתי, אבל לשאר לישני לית לן האי טעמא? וי"ל: דטעמא דשמאי – משום דאשה בדוקה היא. והא דקאמר: כיון דשכיחי בה דמים – "כאינה בדוקה דמיא, היינו להלל. וא"ת: לר"מ, אמאי מטהר בנגע באחד ובאשה תולין? וי"ל: משום (ה) דמוקמה אחזקתה, ואשה – משום דאיכא ריעותא מגופה. **והלל כי אמר דמוקי מילתא אחזקתיה.** כגון ספק נגע ספק לא נגע, היינו בר"ה, כדפרישית. אבל ברה"י – לא מוקמינן אחזקתיה, והוי טומאה ודאי, (ו) ילפינן מסוטה. ודוקא ספק נגע ספק לא נגע הוי ודאי טמא, אבל טמא שנגע באחד מן החביות ואינו יודע באיזה מהם נגע – הוו שניהם טמאים מספק, ואין טמאין שניהם בודאי. דלא גמרינן מסוטה אלא דבר שיכול להיות, והכא האחד טהור בודאי. וכן משמע בריש "שני נזירים" (נזיר נז.) דקתני: אמר להם אחד "ראיתי אחד מכם שנטמא, ואיני יודע איזה מכם" – מביאין קרבן טומאה וקרבן טהרה. ולא מייתי כל אחד קרבן טומאה, משום דלא גמרינן מסוטה אלא דבר שיכול להיות. והא דפריך התם: אמאי מייתו קרבן טומאה? לייתו תרווייהו קרבן טהרה! דאחד שאמר לשנים, הוו להו ג', והוי ר"ה, וספקו טהור. אע"ג דאין יכול להיות שיהו שניהם טהורין, דהאחד ודאי טמא. וכן גבי "שני שבילים" בפ"ק דפסחים (דף י.) מטהרינן שניהם, בבאו לישאל זה אחר זה, אע"ג שבודאי נטמא האחד? התם, לאו מסוטה גמרינן, אלא דמוקמינן כל אחד בחזקת טהרה, כדאיתא הכא דהוי טעמא משום דמוקמינן מילתא אחזקתיה. *ומיהו היכא דליכא חזקה לטהרה – מטהרינן בר"ה מסוטה, כמו מקוה שנמדד ונמצא חסר דמטהר ר"ש בר"ה, דגמרינן מסוטה, אע"ג דליכא למימר "העמד מקוה על חזקתו", דאדרבה "העמד טמא על חזקתו". ואם תאמר: והיכי ילפינן מסוטה לטהר ברשות הרבים אפילו ליכא חזקה, הא סוטה אית לה חזקת טהרה? ויש לומר: כיון דקינא לה ונסתרה – איתרע חזקתה. ואע"ג דאין סתירה בר"ה, מכל מקום איתרע חזקתה, דשייך קנאת סתירה באפילה ובלילה

אף על גב דר"ש מטהר במקוה שנמדד מסוטה. גי':

אך קשה דמטהר אף ברה"י ובקופה *) מטהר ר' יוחנן ברה"י וכן בנגע בא' בלילה אפילו ראוהו חי לכך נראה דטעמא דשמאי משום ביטול פריה ורביה ולהכי לא עבדינן סייג ברה"י אפי' אי לא כבדוק דמיא. גי': *[צ"ל: *מטמא]

ומיירי כעין ב' נזירים דליכא למילף מסוטה ולריכי טעמא דחזקה. גי':

## תוספי הרא"ש

בכ"י נחסרו הרבה תבות מפירוש הדף הזה והגיהם הרב בעל חשק שלמה והוסיפסע"פדעתוהרחבה לפי המסך דברי פירוש רבינו והתיבות שהוסיף מוקפות בחצאי רבוע.

**כל** הנשים דיין שעתן. [האי] כל לאו דוקא דמודה שמאי בשוטה לשינויא דש"ס דמרגשת בעצמה ולשינויא דאם איתא דהוה דם מעיקרא הוה אתי מודה למשמשת במוך ותנא כל לאפוקי מדרבי אליעזר דאמר [בד"ז ע"א] (דוכן) ארבעה נשים [דיין שעתן] ותו לא: [דיין שעתן]. לאו דוקא דאפי' שעה אחת אינה מטמאה למפרע כדאמרי' לקמן [דף ט"ו ע"א] אחר זמן בועלה נכנס להיכל ומקטיר קטורת ואמרינן דסבר לה כשמאי [ומיהו אם ראתה בתוך שיעור וסת] מודה דבועלה חייב חטאת דהיינו שעת ראיה ממש [וכן אם ראתה אחר זמן בתוך שיעור אשם תלוי] אבל ראתה אחר [אותו] זמן לית ליה לב"ש. וא"ת מה שייך למתני לשון דיין כיון [דאינה מטמאה רק משעת ראיה ואילך פשיטא דטמאה והו"ל] למימר דכל הנשים מטמאות מראייתן ואילך דאשכחן דדייק [כה"ג התם בפ' הזהב [דף נג ע"ב] גבי דיו שיאמר הוא וחומשו ובסוטה פ' היה מביא [דף יד ע"ב] גבי מנחה [מגישה בקרן מערבית דרומית] ודיו וי"ל דנקט דיין שלא תאמר מעל"ע [כחכמים] או מפקידה לפקידה [כהלל] ואע"ג דשמאי פתח ברישא מ"מ הוה מסתבר למעבד סייג וקאתי [לאפוקי מזה וכן בסוטה שם. דאמר דיו משו'] דסד"א תיבעי הגש' מנחה גופה וכן ההוא דפרק בתרא [דמכילתין דף ס"ה מניחן תחת] הצינור שמימיו מקלחין ודיו א) וכן ההיא דשלהי מסכת טהרות [אם נתנן בשיבולת הנהר דיו] וכן ההיא [דפ"ד] דמעשר שני הפודה מעשר שני ולא קרא עליו שם [ר"מ אומר דיו וכן ההיא דלקמן דף ל'] דיו לטבילה שתהא באחרונה **ואפי'** לימים הרבה. הא [דהוצרך לפרש זה] דלא תימא מפקידה לפקידה דנקט היינו בסתם [פקידה דשחרית או ערבית קא מיירי] כדלקמן [דף ד' ע"ב]: **על** יד. [על כח מפקידה לפקידה כמו פוסל על ידו דפרק האשה רבה דף צ"ו] א"נ [על יד היינו אחר מפקידה] כמו על ידו החזיק [בעזרא ג'] [מ"ט] דשמאי הכי נמי מצי למיבעי מ"ט דהלל המטהר [בחולין דהא מעל"ע שבנדה אינו אלא לקודש] ואיכא למ"ד אף לתרומה אבל בחולין לד"ה טהור אבל [נקט טפי לפרש טעמא דשמאי] משום דמטהר לגמרי א"נ ה"ק מ"מ מ"ט [דשמאי שלא עשה סייג לדבריו ומשני דאזלינן] בתר חזקה הלכך אפי' סייג לא בעי [והלל קסבר כיון דאית לה ריעותא מגופה תו ליכא כאן חזקה] והלכך ראוי לעשות סייג: **קסבר** העמד אשה. [תימה דמ"ש מכל ספק טומאה דברה"י טמא ולא אהני הך חזקה ועוד דאף לחולין לטמא] דאף דאיכא חזקה דטהרה דהא ילפינן מסוטה [ועוד דאמאי אמרי' דבמעל"ע שבנדה תולין והא כל ספק טומאה ילפינן מסוטה דברה"י טמא ודאי וכמו גבי מקוה שנמדד (לקמן ע"ב) דאמרי' דלמדו מסוטה] ופריך אי מה סוטה ברה"י טמא ודאי וכו' הרי דילפינן מסוטה ועוד אמרינן בפ"ק דשבת (דף ט"ו) גבי כלי זכוכית דמשו"ה אינו אלא תולין משום דהוי טומאה דרבנן ב)הא בדאורייתא שורפין וי"ל דלא ילפינן ספק טומאה מסוטה אלא כעין [סוטה] שנולד הספק בשעת המעשה דבשעת

סתירה איכא למיחש שמא נבעלה [לבועל וכה"ג לענין טהרות שהיו] מונחים אצל שרץ ספק נגעו ספק לא נגעו אבל במעת לעת שבנדה דבעת שנגעה [בטהרות עדיין] לא היה ראוי להסתפק שמא היא טמאה מחמת טומאה שנמצאת אחרי כן כה"ג [ליכא] למילף מסוט' וקש' מהא דאמרינן לקמן נגע באחד בלילה ואינו יודע אם חי אם מת [ולמחר השכים] ומצאו מת ר"מ מטהר וקתני בתוספתא דטהרות (פ"ו) שזה ספק טומאה [ברה"ר] וקתני תו התם ישב על גבי אבן ולמחר מצא עליה שרץ או רוק ר"מ מטהר [שזה ספק] טומאה ברה"ר ומודים חכמים שאם ראוה נקיה מבערב שהוא טהור שזה ספק טומאה ברה"ר ומדפליג בין רה"י לרה"ר ש"מ דלמפרע נמי ילפינן מסוטה [ונראה דוודאי לא] ילפינן למפרע מסוטה אלא חומרא בעלמא דאחמור רבנן ברה"י מרה"ר [התם] והאי דקאמרינן שזה ספק טומאה ברשות הרבים ה"ק כיון דאפי' היכא דמדאורייתא מטמא [ברה"י] מטהר ברה"ר כ"ש הכא דאפי' ברה"י טהור מדאורייתא וא"ת א"כ מעת לעת שבנדה נמי דהוי למפרע וטמא מדרבנן נטהר ברה"ר ולקמן משמע דמעל"ע אפי' ברה"ר טמא גבי היתה יושבת במטה ועוסקת בטהרות דמוקמינן ליה בשחברותיה נושאות אותה במטה וכיון דאיכא תלתא עם האשה היושבת חשיב ברה"ר כדמוכח בריש פ' שני נזירים דילפינן מסוטה [דכל בי] תלתא הוי רה"ר וכן מוכח בשמעתין דקאמר והלל כי אמר [העמד דבר על חזקתו] היכא דלית ליה ריעותא מגופה [כגון] ספק נגע ספק לא נגע [אבל איתתא] דאיכא ריעותא מגופה טמא ומשמע אפי' ברה"ר והכי איתא בירוש' [כאן בפירקין בסוף הלכה ה' דטומאת מעת לעת טמא אפי' ברה"ר] וי"ל דגבי מעל"ע לא שייך לחלק [בין רה"ר לרה"י] שאין ספיקתה ראוי להתגלות יותר מחמת רבים [כמו בנגע באחד בלילה ולכל שאר ספק טומאה שראוי הספק להגלות] ברה"ר יותר מרה"י. ומה"ט ניחא דלא [השוו טומאות מעל"ע לשאר טומאות וגזור] אפי' ברה"ר ומ"ש בדבר שאין בו [דעת לשאול דלא גזור במעל"ע וכדאמר] לקמן [דף ה] גבי היתה יושבת במטה ועוסקת בטהרות [והיינו משום] דרה"ר אינו שייך למעל"ע כלל וכדפרישנא אבל חלוק [בין דבר שיש בו דעת לשאול לאין בו שייך שפיר גם בטומאת מעל"ע] שראוי ספיקתה להתברר בשיש בו דעת לישאל טפי כדכתיבנא התם ומה"ט ניחא הא דאחמירו רבנן במעת לעת טפי לענין רה"ר דבטהרות טהור וכאן תולין ולענין רה"י הקילו דבעלמא [ק"ל דברה"י שורפין והכא תולין] וק"ל לפי מה דפריך מנגע בא' בלילה אמעל"ע תקש' לי' אמקוה דקאמ' ושניהן לא למדוה אלא מסוטה הא לא דמי לסוטה דהוי טומאה למפרע הלכך י"ל דדוקא מעל"ע לא דמי לסוטה דרא"א כלל

## עין משפט נר מצוה

א א מיי' פ"ג מהלכות מטמאי משכב ומושב הלכה ד ופ"ט מהלכות איסורי ביאה הלכה ג סמג לאוין קיא:

ב ב מיי' פ"ט מהלכות איסורי ביאה הלכה ד ופ"ג מהלכות משכב ומושב הלכה ה סמג שם:

ג ג מיי' פ"ג מהלכות משכב ומושב הלכ' ד:

ד ד מיי' פ"ט מהלכות איסורי ביאה הלכה ג:

א) לפנינו שם ליתא לתיבת דיו וכן בתוספתא לטהרות ליתא. וצ"ע: ב) לכאורה נ"ע דלא מיירי שם בטומאת ספק רק בודאי ומשום דעשו הכירה בטומאה דרבנן.

**הגהות הב"ח** (א) תוס' ד"ה מעת לעת מפרש בגמ'. נ"ב בדף ו' ע"א: (ב) בא"ד כמו שאפרש לקמן. נ"ב בד"ה והלל: (ג) בא"ד או הנדה דאסורים לאכול בשר: (ד) בא"ד ור' יוחנן וכן המדלה י' דליים: (ה) בא"ד וי"ל משום דמוקמה אחזקתיה ואשה משום: (ו) ד"ה והלל וכו' ודאי דילפי' מסוטה:

**גליון הש"ס** **מתני'** דיין שעתן. עי' מנחות יט ע"ב תד"ה כנגד: **תוס'** ד"ה מעת לעת וכו' הוו להו תלתא והוי רה"ר. עי' סוטה כח ע"ב תד"ה ברה"ר: **בא"ד** וי"ל דאף ברה"ר לא נטהר בקדשים וכו'. עי' טהרות פ"ה מ"ז בר"ש: **בא"ד** אלא טומאת מגע ולא טומאת ראייה. עי' לקמן יז ע"ב תד"ה ואין שורפין. ולקמן כח ע"א תד"ה ורבנן: **בא"ד** כאינה בדוקה דמיא היינו להלל. כאן שייך הגליון אך קשה וכו': **תוס'** ד"ה והלל וכו' לא מסוטה גמרינן אלא דמוקמינן כל א' בחזקת טהרה וכו'. עי' לקמן ס ע"א תד"ה כאנו:

ה א מיי' פ"ג מהלכות מקוואות הלכה ו סמג עשין רמח טוש"ע י"ד סימן רא סעיף נח:
ו ב מיי' פ"ה מהלכות תרומות הלכה כד:

כֵּיוָן דְּמִגּוּפָהּ קָחָזְיָא — לָא אָמְרִינַן אוֹקְמָהּ אַחֶזְקָתָהּ. וּמַאי שְׁנָא מִמִּקְוֶה? *דִּתְנַן: א מִקְוֶה שֶׁנִּמְדַּד וְנִמְצָא חָסֵר — כָּל טָהֳרוֹת שֶׁנַּעֲשׂוּ עַל גַּבָּיו לְמַפְרֵעַ, בֵּין בִּרְשׁוּת הָרַבִּים בֵּין בִּרְשׁוּת הַיָּחִיד טְמֵאוֹת. לְשַׁמַּאי — קַשְׁיָא לְמַפְרֵעַ. לְהִלֵּל קַשְׁיָא וַדַּאי, דְּאִילּוּ מֵעֵת לְעֵת שֶׁבְּנִדָּה תּוֹלִין, לֹא אוֹכְלִין וְלֹא שׂוֹרְפִין, וְאִילּוּ הָכָא — טוּמְאָה וַדַּאי! הָתָם מִשּׁוּם דְּאִיכָּא לְמֵימַר: הַעֲמֵד טָמֵא עַל חֶזְקָתוֹ, וְאֵימָא לֹא טָבַל. אַדְּרַבָּה, הַעֲמֵד מִקְוֶה עַל חֶזְקָתוֹ וְאֵימָא לֹא חָסַר! הֲרֵי חָסֵר לְפָנֶיךָ! הָכָא נַמִי: הֲרֵי דָּם לְפָנֶיךָ! הַשְׁתָּא הוּא דַּחֲזַאי. הָכָא נַמִי: הַשְׁתָּא הוּא דְּחָסַר! הָכִי הַשְׁתָּא? הָתָם — אִיכָּא לְמֵימַר חֲסַר וַאֲתָא חָסֵר וַאֲתָא, הָכָא — מִי אִיכָּא לְמֵימַר חֲזַאי וַאֲתָא חֲזַאי וַאֲתָא? וּמַאי קוּשְׁיָא? דִּלְמָא הַגַּם הַגַּם חֲזִיתֵיהּ? הָתָם — אִיכָּא תַּרְתֵּי לְרֵיעוּתָא, הָכָא — אִיכָּא חֲדָא לְרֵיעוּתָא. וּמַאי שְׁנָא מֵחָבִית? *דִּתְנַן: ב הָיָה בּוֹדֵק אֶת הֶחָבִית לִהְיוֹת מַפְרִישׁ עָלֶיהָ תְּרוּמָה וְהוֹלֵךְ, וְאַחַ"כ נִמְצָא חוֹמֶץ, כָּל ג' יָמִים (הָרִאשׁוֹנִים) — וַדַּאי, מִכָּאן וְאֵילָךְ — סָפֵק. קַשְׁיָא לְשַׁמַּאי! הָתָם, מִשּׁוּם דְּאִיכָּא לְמֵימַר: הַעֲמֵד טֶבֶל עַל חֶזְקָתוֹ, וְאֵימַר לֹא נִתְקַן. אַדְּרַבָּה, הַעֲמֵד יַיִן עַל חֶזְקָתוֹ וְאֵימַר לֹא הֶחְמִיץ! הֲרֵי הֶחְמִיץ לְפָנֶיךָ! הָכָא נַמִי, הֲרֵי דָּם לְפָנֶיךָ! הַשְׁתָּא הוּא דַּחֲזַאי. הָתָם נַמִי, הַשְׁתָּא הוּא דְּהֶחְמִיץ! הָכִי הַשְׁתָּא? הָתָם — אִיכָּא לְמֵימַר: הֶחְמִיץ וַאֲתָא הֶחְמִיץ וַאֲתָא, הָכָא — מִי אִיכָּא לְמֵימַר: חֲזַאי וַאֲתָא חֲזַאי וַאֲתָא? וּמַאי קוּשְׁיָא, דִּלְמָא הַגַּם הַגַּם חֲזִיתֵיהּ? הָתָם אִיכָּא תַּרְתֵּי לְרֵיעוּתָא, הָכָא — אִיכָּא חֲדָא לְרֵיעוּתָא. וְרָמֵי חָבִית אַמִּקְוֶה: מַאי שְׁנָא הָכָא — וַדַּאי, וּמ"ש הָכָא — סָפֵק? א"ר חֲנִינָא מִסּוּרָא: מַאן תַּנָּא חָבִית — ר"ש הִיא, דִּלְגַבֵּי מִקְוֶה נַמִי סְפֵקָא מַשְׁוֵי לֵיהּ. *דִּתְנַן: א) מִקְוֶה שֶׁנִּמְדַּד וְנִמְצָא חָסֵר. כָּל הַטָּהֳרוֹת שֶׁנַּעֲשׂוּ עַל גַּבָּיו לְמַפְרֵעַ, בֵּין בִּרְשׁוּת הָרַבִּים בֵּין בִּרְשׁוּת הַיָּחִיד — טְמֵאוֹת. *ר"ש אוֹמֵר: בִּרְשׁוּת הָרַבִּים — טְהוֹרוֹת, בִּרְשׁוּת הַיָּחִיד תּוֹלִין.

וּשְׁנֵיהֶם

קדושין עט. ב"ב צו. (חולין י) [תוספתא דתרומות פ"ד] [צ"ל דתניא]

א) גיטין לא: מקוואות פ"ב מ"ב קדושין עט.

**רש"י**

כֵּיוָן דְּמִגּוּפָהּ קָחָזְיָא. מוּעֶדֶת *(וַעֲלוּלָה) הִיא לְכָךְ אֵין לָהּ חֶזְקַת טָהֳרָה. וּמַאי שְׁנָא מִמִּקְוֶה. לְתַרְוַיְיהוּ פָּרֵיךְ. שֶׁנַּעֲשׂוּ עַל גַּבָּיו. טָהֳרוֹת שֶׁנִּשְׁתַּמְּשׁוּ בְּכֵלִים שֶׁטָּבְלוּ בּוֹ. בֵּין בִּר"ה בֵּין בִּרה"י. בֵּין שֶׁהַמִּקְוֶה עוֹמֵד בִּר"ה דְּקַיְימָא לָן: סְפֵק טוּמְאָה בִּר"ה — סְפֵקוֹ טָהוֹר, הָכָא — טָמֵא, דְּלָאו סָפֵק הוּא אֶלָּא וַדַּאי, כִּדְמְפָרֵשׁ טַעֲמָא לְקַמָּן בִּשְׁמַעְתִּין. לְשַׁמַּאי קַשְׁיָא לְמַפְרֵעַ. דְּהָא מְטַמְּאִינַן טָהֳרוֹת לְמַפְרֵעַ, וְלָא אָמְרִינַן: הַעֲמֵד מִקְוֶה עַל חֶזְקָתוֹ. דְּאִילּוּ מֵעֵת לְעֵת. טָהֳרוֹת דְּמְטַמְּאִין לְהוּ מִשּׁוּם סְפֵקָא דְּמֵעֵת לְעֵת לְרַבָּנַן, וְה"ה מִפְּקִידָה לִפְקִידָה דְּהִלֵּל. תּוֹלִין. אִם תְּרוּמָה הֵן. וְלֹא שׂוֹרְפִין. כִּדְקָתָנֵי בְּבָרַיְיתָא דְּ"הָרוֹאָה כֶּתֶם", (א) לְקַמָּן בְּפִירְקִין (דף ו.). וְאִילּוּ הָכָא. בְּמִקְוֶה. טוּמְאָה וַדָּאִית. מְטַמְּאִינַן לְהוּ לְמַפְרֵעַ, וְשׂוֹרְפִין אֶת הַתְּרוּמָה. מִדְּקָתָנֵי "בִּר"ה טָמֵא", אַלְמָא כְּוַדַּאי מְשַׁוֵּי לֵיהּ. לֹא טָבַל. טְבִילָה הוֹגֶנֶת, הִלְכָּךְ טוּמְאָה וַדָּאִית יֵשׁ. חָסֵר וַאֲתָא חָסֵר וַאֲתָא. וְאִיתְרַע לָהּ לַחֲזָקָה מִקַּמֵּי הָכִי טוּבָא, וְלָא יָדְעִינַן מֵאֵימַת, הִלְכָּךְ רִיעַ טְפֵי מֵאִשָּׁה. הָכָא מִי אִיכָּא לְמֵימַר כו'. הִלְכָּךְ עַד שְׁעַת מְלִיאַת דָּם לָא אִיתְרְעִי חֲזָקָה, וְהַךְ דְּאִישְׁתַּכַּח הַשְׁתָּא אִיכָּא לְמֵימַר דְּהַשְׁתָּא הוּא דַּחֲזַאי. הַגַּם הַגַּם. לְשׁוֹן רְבִיָּה, שֶׁהַדָּם הוֹלֵךְ וְגָדֵל. וְדוֹמֶה לוֹ בְּמַסֶּכֶת שְׁבִיעִית בְּפ"ד: בָּרִאשׁוֹנָה הָיוּ אוֹמְרִים מְלַקֵּט אָדָם מִתּוֹךְ שָׂדֵהוּ עֵצִים וַעֲשָׂבִים הַגַּם הַגַּם, כְּדֶרֶךְ שֶׁמְּלַקֵּט מִשֶּׁל חֲבֵירוֹ כו'. כְּלוֹמַר, ע"י שֶׁיִּהְיֶה הַדָּם רָבֶה בַּמָּקוֹר, יוֹצֵא מִמֶּנּוּ מְעַט מְעַט כְּחַרְדָּל מַה שֶּׁאֵין הַמָּקוֹר יָכוֹל לְהַחֲזִיקוֹ, וְיוֹצֵא מְעַט לַבַּיִת הַחִיצוֹן, וְזֶה כַּמָּה יָמִים הִתְחִיל. וְהִיא נִטְמֵאת מִטִּיפַּת דָּם כְּחַרְדָּל, כִּדְלְקַמָּן (דף מ.). תַּרְתֵּי לְרֵיעוּתָא. הַעֲמֵד טָמֵא עַל חֶזְקַת טוּמְאָה, וּבְחֶזְקַת טָהֳרָה דְּמִקְוֶה אִיכָּא רֵיעוּתָא שֶׁהֲרֵי חָסֵר לְפָנֶיךָ. אֲבָל בְּאִשָּׁה, בְּדִידָהּ הוּא דְּאִיכָּא רֵיעוּתָא, שֶׁהוּרַע חֶזְקַת טָהֳרָתָהּ קְצָת, שֶׁהֲרֵי דָּם לְפָנֶיךָ. וּמִשּׁוּם הַךְ רֵיעוּתָא לְחוּדָהּ לָא מַרְעִינַן לָהּ, הוֹאִיל וּבְטָהֳרוֹת לָא מַשְׁכַּחַת רֵיעוּתָא אַחֲרִיתָא, דְּכִי אָמְרַתְּ: הַעֲמִידֵם עַל חֶזְקָתָם — בְּחֶזְקַת טָהֳרָתָם הֵם. וּמַאי שְׁנָא מֵחָבִית. לְב"ש פָּרֵיךְ.

הָיָה בּוֹדֵק אֶת הֶחָבִית. טוֹעֲמָהּ אִם הִיא בְּחֶזְקָתָהּ שֶׁלֹּא הֶחֱמִיצָה. לִהְיוֹת מַפְרִישׁ עָלֶיהָ. כְּלוֹמַר, לִהְיוֹת סוֹמֵךְ עָלֶיהָ, וְהוֹלֵךְ וְשׁוֹתֶה שְׁאָר חָבִיּוֹת, וְנוֹתֵן עֵינָיו בְּזוֹ לְהַפְרִישׁ מִמֶּנָּה עֲלֵיהֶם לְאַחַר זְמַן, שֶׁהַתְּרוּמָה נִיטֶּלֶת בְּמַחֲשָׁבָה. כָּל ג' יָמִים וַדַּאי. פְּלוּגְתָּא דְּר' יוֹחָנָן וְר' יְהוֹשֻׁעַ בֶּן לֵוִי בְּבָבָא בַּתְרָא בְּפֶ' "הַמּוֹכֵר פֵּירוֹת" (דף צו.) ר' יוֹחָנָן אוֹמֵר: כָּל ג' יָמִים לְאַחַר בְּדִיקָה רִאשׁוֹנָה שֶׁמְּצָאָהּ בְּחֶזְקָתָהּ — וַדַּאי יַיִן, וְאִם אָמַר בְּתוֹךְ ג' יָמִים "הֲרֵי זוֹ תְּרוּמָה עַל אֵלּוּ הַסְּמוּכִין לָהּ" — כּוּלָּם מְתוּקָּנוֹת. מִכָּאן וְאֵילָךְ — סָפֵק, וּתְרוּמָה הִיא, וְיַחֲזוֹר וְיִתְרוֹם. וְר' יְהוֹשֻׁעַ בֶּן לֵוִי אוֹמֵר: כָּל ג' יָמִים קוֹדֶם בְּדִיקָה אַחֲרוֹנָה שֶׁנִּמְצֵאת חוֹמֶץ — וַדַּאי חוֹמֶץ, דְּכֵיוָן דְּעַכְשָׁיו חוֹמֶץ גָּמוּר הוּא, וַדַּאי אֵין פָּחוֹת מִג' יָמִים שֶׁהִתְחִיל לְהַחְמִיץ. וְאִם עֲשָׂאוֹ בְּתוֹךְ אוֹתָן ג' יָמִים תְּרוּמָה עַל מָקוֹם אַחֵר — אֵינוֹ תְּרוּמָה, אַלִּיבָּא דְּרַבִּי דְּאָמַר בְּ"הַמּוֹכֵר אֶת הַסְּפִינָה" (ב"ב פד:) יַיִן וְחוֹמֶץ שְׁנֵי מִינִין הֵן. דְּאִי לְרַבָּנַן, הָא קַיְימָא לָן (תרומות פ"ב מ"ו) תּוֹרֵם מִן הָרָעָה עַל הַיָּפָה — תְּרוּמָתוֹ תְּרוּמָה. מִכָּאן וְאֵילָךְ לְמַפְרֵעַ — סָפֵק, וְהָוְיָא זוֹ תְּרוּמָה, וְיַחֲזוֹר וְיִתְרוֹם. אַלְמָא בֵּין לְמָר בֵּין לְמָר מְסַפְּקִינַן רֵיעוּתָא לְמַפְרֵעַ! וְרָמֵי חָבִית אַמִּקְוֶה. דְּהָא תַּרְוַיְיהוּ אִיכָּא תַּרְתֵּי לְרֵיעוּתָא. מַאי שְׁנָא. בְּמִקְוֶה דְּמַחְזְקִינַן לְמַפְרֵעַ טוּמְאַת וַדַּאי, וּמ"ש בְּחָבִית דְּקָאָמַר סָפֵק. בִּרה"י תּוֹלִין. טַעֲמָא מְפָרֵשׁ לְקַמָּן. *)מִסּוֹטָה. דִּכְתִיב (במדבר ה): "וְהִיא נִטְמָאָה", אִיתְקַשׁ טוּמְאָה לְסוֹטָה.

*) שייך לקמן

וַעֲשָׂאוּהָ

**תוספות**

*ובעת שאין בני אדם מצויין. וא"ת: א"כ, היכי ילפינן מסוטה דברה"י ספקו טמא אפי' היכא חזקה, הא בסוטה איתרע חזקה, וקרא ד"ונטמאה" לאייתר לאגמורי בעלמא טומאה מסוטה, אימא: דוקא היכא דליכא חזקה, ואיצטריך קרא לאשמועינן דהוי טמא ודאי, אע"ג שאינו אלא ספק וגם לטהר בר"ה, אע"ג דליכא חזקה? וי"ל: דילפינן מסוטה, שעשאה הכתוב ודאי טמאה, אע"ג דאית לה חזקה שאינה טמאה ודאי, ולא איתרע אלא חזקת טהרה ודאית. **דאיכא** ריעותא מגופה. אבל אי לאו האי טעמא, הוה מוקמינן לה אחזקת טהרה, אע"ג דהשתא ודאי טמאה. כמו בנגע באחד, דמטהרים אף רבנן בראהו חי מבערב, אע"ג דהשתא הוא מת, וליכא עוד חזקת חיות. *ומ"מ אם עשו מבהמה גבינות, ושחטוה, ונמצאת טרפה — אין להתיר הגבינות מטעם "אוקי בהמ' בחזק' שלא היתה טרפה מתחלה", כיון דמעולם לא היתה אותה שעה מבוררת — לא חשיבה חזקה, כדמוכח ב"הכל שוחטין" (חולין יא:) דקאמר: אתיא(א) ממכה אביו ומפרה אדומה, דאזלינן בתר רובא. והיכי מוכח, דלמא משום דמוקי לה (ב) בחזקת שאינה טרפה? אלא לא חשיב אותה חזקה. כדפרישית. ול"ע להתיר הגבינות. **להלל** קשה ודאי. דמדקאמר ר' שמעון בסיפא "ברה"י תולין", מכלל ד"טמאות" דקאמרי רבנן ברישא היינו ודאי. **השתא** הוא דחזאי. ורב דאמר בפ' "י' יוחסין" (קידושין עט.): הרי היא בוגרת לפנינו, גבי "קדשה אבי' בדרך, וקדשה עצמה בעיר", ושניהם ביומא דמשלים ו' חדשים שבין נערות לבגרות, ולא קאמר: השתא הוא דבגרה? היינו משום דרגילות שערות לבא מלפרא. וכי פריך התם לשמואל ממקוה וחבית, ה"נ מצי למיפרך לרב, דדוקא בשערות קאמר רב, אלא דפריך לשמואל טפי בפשיטות. והא דקאמר התם: לימא רב דאמר כר' נתן, דאמר: אם בריא הוא — עליו להביא ראיה ששכיב מרע היה, אע"ג דרב דוקא בשערות קאמר? התם נמי רוב העולם בריאים, ואית לן למימר דבריא היה, כמו שהוא עכשיו. **התם** תרתי לריעותא. תימה דבפ"ק דחולין (דף י, ושם) אמרינן: שחטה, ונמצא הסכין פגום, ושבר בו עצמות אחרי כן. רב חסדא אמר: כשרה, משום דעצם ודאי פוגם (ג) כו'. ופריך ליה מטבל ועלה, ונמצא עליו דבר חוצץ אע"פ שנתעסק באותו המין כל היום כולו, לא עלתה לו טבילה. ומשני: סכין — איתרעי, בהמה — לא איתרעי. והשתא הא איכא תרתי לריעותא: דהרי פגום לפניך, והעמד בהמה בחזקת איסור, כדאמר הכא. דה"נ איתרעי מקוה, ואדם לא איתרעי, ואפ"ה מטמאינן? וי"ל: דהתם משום דעצם ודאי פוגם, כדאמר התם. א"נ: אין סברא לחלק בין מקוה איתרעי לאדם איתרעי. והתם ה"פ: סכין איתרעי, ואיכא ספיקי טובא: שמא בעצם נפגם; ואפי' בעור נפגם, שמא נפגם במיעוט בתרא; ואת"ל נפגם במיעוט קמא, שמא לא שחט כנגד הפגימה. אך קשה, דאמר התם: מנלן דאזלינן בתר חזקה? דכתיב: "ויצא הכהן מן הבית", ודילמא אדנפיק ואתי בציר ליה שיעורא? אלא אוקמי' אחזקה. וקשה: (ד) התם, משום דליכא ריעותא, ואכתי היכא דאיכא ריעותא מנלן דאזלינן בתר חזקה? וי"ל: דמוכח היכא דבא כהן בסוף שבוע, וראה והנה כהה הנגע, ואיתרע חזקה (ה) — מטמאינן אדם הנכנס שם באותו שבוע, וחייב קרבן אם נכנס בעזרה. וקשה: אדרבה, נימא התם: הרי חסר הנגע לפניך, ואוקי גברא בחזקת טהרה, כדאמר הכא גבי מקוה לטמא בודאי? וי"ל: דגבי מקוה, רגילות להתחסר מעט מעט, ולכך איכא למימר דמעיקרא חסר. אבל הנגע, רגילות להתחסר בבת אחת פחות מכגרים, לכך אמרינן התם: השתא הוא דחסר, ואוקי הנגע בחזקת שלם דיציאת כהן מן הבית. וכשטימא הכהן את הבית, אפי' נתחסר הנגע אחרי כן קודם שנכנס זה, גזירת הכתוב הוא שהבית טמא, עד שיראה הכהן בסוף שבוע, ויטהרנו. **היה** בודק את החבית. אפי' לרבנן, דאית להו ב"המוכר את הספינה" (ב"ב פד.) יין וחומץ — מין אחד הוא, היינו כשמתכוין לתרום מן החומץ. והכא מיירי שנתכוין לתרום מן היין, ונמצא חומץ, דהוה ליה תרומה בטעות, כדמשמע בתוספתא דתרומות פרק(ב) "התודה והמעשר".

מיהו בירושלמי דסוטה משמע דאפילה ולילה הוי רה"י גמור. גי':

והא דאמרי פ"ק דחולין (דף ט.) גבי בא זאב ונטל בני מעיים התם גמרינן מסוטה דבר"ה ספיקו טהור היינו לפי סברת דברי המקשה דמדמי איסור לסכנתא אבל מסקנא דשני לן בין איסורא לסכנתא לא ילפי' מסוטה. גי':

ושניהם

א) [צ"ל עדים זוממין בתוס' לחולין. יא. ד"ה אתיא מפרה אדומה] ב) [צ"ל התורס]

**הגהות הב"ח**

(א) רש"י ד"ה ולא שורפין וכו' לקמן בפירקין. נ"ב בדף ו ע"א [illegible] (ב) תוס' ד"ה דאיכא וכו' בחזקת שאינה טרפה. [illegible] (ג) ד"ה התם וכו' דעצם ודאי פוגם ועוד ספק פוגם וכו' ופריך: (ד) בא"ד וקשה לאלמא התם משום: (ה) בא"ד ואיתרע חזקה ואפ"ה מטמאינן אדם:

**גליון הש"ס**

גמ' ומ"ש מחבית. עי' רפ"ג דתרומות ובר"ש שם:

**תוספי הרא"ש**

[illegible] מתחלת ברייתה היא טרפה ואע"ג דטרפה אינה חיה רוב טרפות קאמר או אם הוגלד פי המכה יש לאסור הגבינות [שנעשה בתוך] שלשת ימים קודם השחיטה:

**ואילו** הכא טמאה ודאי. משמע מתוך פרש"י ז"ל דמלשון טמאה קא דייק וקשה דהא בסוף קדושין גבי תינוק שנמצא בצד העיסה דקתני וחכמים מטמאין ואמר ר' יוחנן אין זו חזקה ששורפין עליה את התרומה ועוד לקמן גבי קופה שנשתמשו בה טהרות ואמר ר' יוחנן טמאות בעי למימר דלתלות קאמר ונראה לפרש דהא דדייק דטמאות ודאי משום דתני בסיפא ר' שמעון אומר ברה"י תולין: **אדרבה** העמד מקוה על חזקתו ואימר לא חסר. משמע דפריך אפילו (לב"ש) [לב"ה] דהוה לן לטהר לגמרי משום חזקה דמקוה אע"ג דאיכא נמי חזקה דטמא מ"מ חזקת מקוה עדיף שהרי הטמא טבל לפנינו אלא שאנו אומרים שמא לא טבל טבילה הוגנת כי שמא היה חסר המקוה וכיון דאמרת העמד מקוה על חזקתו נסתלקה חזקת הטמא כנ"ל: **ה"נ** הרי דם לפניך. ואיתרעאי חזקת האשה ואע"ג דלא איתרע חזקת הטהרות ס"ד השתא כיון דטומאה דידהו משום לתא דידה לא מוקמינן להו אחזקתייהו עד דמשני הכא חדא הוא דאיכא לריעותא התם איכא תרתי לריעותא. וא"ת כיון דודאי טבל לא הוה לן למימר העמד טמא על חזקתו לרב חסדא דמכשר השוחט בסכין ונמצאת פגומה

**תוספי הרא"ש**

[illegible] אם תמצא חומץ וכן מוכח בתוספתא דתרומות פרק התורם והמעשר בשבת דתאני התם [פ"ד] התורם חבית של יין ונמצאת של חומץ אם ידוע שהיתה של חומץ עד שלא תרמה אינה תרומה ואם משנתרמה ידע שהחמיץ זה תרומה ואם ספק תרומה ויחזור ויתרום דברי רבי שרבי אומר יין וחומץ שני מינין הן וחכמים אומרים מין אחד הם. היה בלבו לתרום מן היין על היין ומה שבידו חומץ אין תרומתו תרומה וקתני בתר הכי היה בודק את החבית כו' כדאיתא בשמעתין אלמא מוכח בהדיא דמודו בה רבנן. והא דפליגי ברישא משום שהיתה בלבו שתהיה תרומה בכל ענין בין תמצא יין בין תמצא חומץ. וא"ת מאי שנא מתורם מחומץ על יין לרבנן מתורם מן הטמא על הטהור ומקישות המרה על המתוקה דמשמע בהאשה רבה דבשוגג תרומתו תרומה ובמזיד אין תרומתו תרומה. ומחומץ על היין אמרי' דבמזיד תרומתו תרומה ובשוגג אין תרומתו תרומה וי"ל דשאני טמא וקישות [ונמצא] מרה דלא חזו לאכילה הלכך תקינו רבנן שלא תהיה תרומתו במזיד ויש כח ביד חכמים לעקור דבר מן התורה כדקאמר התם בפרק האשה רבה או כמ"ד לא עשה ולא כלום לתקן השירים אבל חומץ חזי לאכילה ואיכא מאן דניחא ליה בחלא הלכך בכל ענין תרומתו תרומה חוץ ממי שהיה בלבו לתרום מיין על יין דהוי כמפרש שלא תהא תרומה אם תמצא חומץ:

מה

א) אינו מובן דמאי ריעותא אית לה לבהמה דהא אין עלולה לטרוף כלל ואולי דר"ל דאיתרע לה החזקה דהרי טרפה לפנינו וכ"ה בתוס' ד"ה דאיכא. ב) ר"ל הלכך דאי לאו דאתיליד ריעותא בטמא גופיה הו"א דאין ספק תלויה מוציא מידי ודאי טבילה אבל הכא לאו וודאי טבל מקריא וכ"ה בתוס' חולין דף ו ע"ש.

וּשְׁנֵיהֶם לֹא לְמָדוּהָ אֶלָּא מִסּוֹטָה. *רַבָּנַן סָבְרִי: כִּי סוֹטָה, מַה סוֹטָה — סָפֵק הִיא וַעֲשָׂאוּהָ כְּוַדַּאי, הָכָא נַמִי — סָפֵק וַעֲשָׂאוּהָ כְּוַדַּאי. אִי מִסּוֹטָה, אֵימָא כִּי סוֹטָה, מַה סוֹטָה בִּרה"ר טָהוֹר, הָכָא נַמִי בִּרה"ר טָהוֹר! הָכִי הַשְׁתָּא! הָתָם — מִשּׁוּם סְתִירָה הוּא, וּסְתִירָה בִּרה"ר לֵיכָּא, הָכָא — מִשּׁוּם חָסֵר הוּא, מַה לִּי חָסֵר בִּרה"ר מַה לִּי חָסֵר בִּרה"י. וְכִי תֵּימָא: הָא כָּל סְפֵק טוּמְאָה בִּרה"ר טָהוֹר! כֵּיוָן דְּאִיכָּא תַּרְתֵּי לְרֵיעוּתָא — כְּוַדַּאי טוּמְאָה דָּמֵי. וְרַבִּי שִׁמְעוֹן סָבַר: כִּי סוֹטָה, מַה סוֹטָה בִּרה"ר טָהוֹר, הָכָא נַמִי בִּרה"ר טָהוֹר. אִי מִסּוֹטָה, אֵימָא כִּי סוֹטָה, מַה סוֹטָה בִּרה"י טְמֵאָה וַדַּאי, הָכָא נַמִי בִּרה"י טְמֵאָה וַדַּאי! הָכִי הַשְׁתָּא! הָתָם — יֵשׁ רַגְלַיִם לַדָּבָר, שֶׁהֲרֵי קִינֵּא לָהּ וְנִסְתְּרָה. הָכָא — מַאי רַגְלַיִם לַדָּבָר אִיכָּא? וְאִי בָּעֵית אֵימָא, הַיְינוּ טַעֲמָא דְּרַבִּי שִׁמְעוֹן: גָּמַר סוֹף טוּמְאָה מִתְּחִלַּת טוּמְאָה. מַה תְּחִלַּת טוּמְאָה, סָפֵק נָגַע סָפֵק לֹא נָגַע בִּרה"ר טָהוֹר, אַף סוֹף טוּמְאָה, סָפֵק טָבַל סָפֵק לֹא טָבַל בִּרה"ר טָהוֹר. וְרַבָּנַן — הָכִי הַשְׁתָּא! הָתָם — גַּבְרָא בְּחֶזְקַת טָהֳרָה קָאֵי, מִסְּפֵקָא לָא מַחְתִּינַן לֵיהּ לְטוּמְאָה. הָכָא — גַּבְרָא בְּחֶזְקַת טוּמְאָה קָאֵי, מִסְּפֵקָא לָא מַפְקִינַן לֵיהּ מִטּוּמְאָתוֹ. וּמַאי שְׁנָא מִמָּבוֹי? *דִּתְנַן: הַשֶּׁרֶץ שֶׁנִּמְצָא בְּמָבוֹי — מְטַמֵּא לְמַפְרֵעַ, עַד שֶׁיֹּאמַר "בָּדַקְתִּי אֶת הַמָּבוֹי הַזֶּה, וְלֹא הָיָה בּוֹ שֶׁרֶץ", אוֹ עַד שְׁעַת הַכִּיבּוּד! הָתָם נַמִי, כֵּיוָן דְּאִיכָּא שְׁרָצִים דְּגוּפֵיהּ, וּשְׁרָצִים דְּאָתוּ מֵעָלְמָא — כְּתַרְתֵּי לְרֵיעוּתָא דָּמֵי. וְאב"א, הַיְינוּ טַעֲמָא דְּשַׁמַּאי: הוֹאִיל וְאִשָּׁה מַרְגֶּשֶׁת בְּעַצְמָהּ. וְהִלֵּל — כִּסְבוּרָה הַרְגָּשַׁת מֵי רַגְלַיִם הִיא. וּלְשַׁמַּאי, הָאִיכָּא יְשֵׁנָה? יְשֵׁנָה נַמִי, אַגַּב צַעֲרָהּ מִיתְעֲרָא, מִידֵּי דַּהֲוָה אַהַרְגָּשַׁת מֵי רַגְלַיִם. וְהָאִיכָּא שׁוֹטָה? מוֹדֶה שַׁמַּאי בְּשׁוֹטָה. הָא "כָּל הַנָּשִׁים" קָתָנֵי? כָּל הַנָּשִׁים פִּקְחוֹת. וְלִיתְנֵי "נָשִׁים"? לְאַפּוּקֵי מִדְּרַבִּי אֱלִיעֶזֶר, דְּא"ר אֱלִיעֶזֶר: *אַרְבַּע נָשִׁים, וְתוּ לָא. [לקמן ז.] קמ"ל — כָּל הַנָּשִׁים. וְהָאִיכָּא כְּתָמִים, לֵימָא תְּנַן כְּתָמִים דְּלָא כְּשַׁמַּאי! אָמַר אַבַּיֵי: מוֹדֶה שַׁמַּאי בִּכְתָמִים, מ"ט — בְּצִפּוֹר לֹא נִתְעַסְּקָה, בְּשׁוּק שֶׁל טַבָּחִים לֹא עָבְרָה, הַאי דָּם מֵהֵיכָא אָתֵי? (א) אִי בָּעֵית אֵימָא, הַיְינוּ טַעֲמֵיהּ דְּשַׁמַּאי: דְּאִם אִיתָא דַּהֲוָה דָּם — מֵעִיקָּרָא הֲוָה אָתֵי. וְהִלֵּל — כּוֹתְלֵי בֵית הָרֶחֶם הֶעֱמִידוּהוּ. וְשַׁמַּאי — כּוֹתְלֵי בֵית הָרֶחֶם לָא מוֹקְמֵי דָּם. (א) מְשַׁמֶּשֶׁת בְּמוֹךְ מַאי אִיכָּא לְמֵימַר? אָמַר אַבַּיֵי: מוֹדֶה שַׁמַּאי בִּמְשַׁמֶּשֶׁת בְּמוֹךְ. רָבָא אָמַר: מוֹךְ נַמִי, אַגַּב זֵיעָה מִכְוִיץ כָּוִיץ. וּמוֹדֶה רָבָא בְּמוֹךְ דָּחוּק. וּמַאי אִיכָּא בֵּין הָנֵי לִישָּׁנֵי לְהָאֵיךְ לִישָּׁנָא?

אִיכָּא

א) [עי' תוס' כתובות לט. ד"ה שלא וכו']

---

**רש"י**

וַעֲשָׂאוּהָ כְּוַדַּאי. שֶׁאֲסוּרָה לְבַעְלָהּ עַד שֶׁתִּשְׁתֶּה. סוֹטָה בִּרְשׁוּת הָרַבִּים טְהוֹרָה. אֵין רְשׁוּת הָרַבִּים מְקוֹם סְתִירָה. רַגְלַיִם לַדָּבָר. סִימַן טוּמְאָה אִיכָּא. שֶׁהֲרֵי קִינֵּא לָהּ וְנִסְתְּרָה. הִתְרָה בָּהּ: "אַל תִּסָּתְרִי עִמּוֹ", וְנִסְתְּרָה. מַאי רַגְלַיִם לַדָּבָר אִיכָּא. דְּלֶיהֱוֵי חָסֵר מִקּוֹדֶם לָכֵן, דִּילְמָא הַשְׁתָּא הוּא דְּחָסֵר. וש"מ דְּקָסָבַר ר' שִׁמְעוֹן בִּשְׁאָר סְפֵק טוּמְאָה דְּעָלְמָא נַמִי בִּרה"י תּוֹלִין, דְּהָא אֵין רַגְלַיִם לַדָּבָר. וְאִיבָּעֵית אֵימָא. אִי מִסּוֹטָה גָּמְרֵי רַבָּנַן, הֲוָה לְהוּ לְמֵימַר: בִּרה"ר — טָהוֹר. אֶלָּא לָאו מִסּוֹטָה מָלֵינַן לְמִגְמַר, דִּתְחִלַּת טוּמְאָה אִיתְקַשׁ לְסוֹטָה, סוֹף טוּמְאָה לָא אִיתְקַשׁ, וְאִם כֵּן מַאי טַעֲמָא דְּרַבִּי שִׁמְעוֹן דִּמְטַהֵר בִּרה"ר. גָּמַר סוֹף טוּמְאָה. דְּהַיְינוּ טְבִילָה, מִתְּחִלַּת מַגַּע הַטּוּמְאָה. וּמַאי שְׁנָא מִמָּבוֹי. לְשַׁמַּאי פָּרֵיךְ. מְטַמֵּא לְמַפְרֵעַ. כָּל טָהֳרוֹת שֶׁנַּעֲשׂוּ בַּמָּבוֹי. עַד שֶׁיֹּאמַר. עָלָיו אָדָם: "בְּאוֹתוֹ הַיּוֹם בָּדַקְתִּי", וְשׁוּב אֵינוֹ מְטַמֵּא מֵאוֹתוֹ הַיּוֹם וּלְמַפְרֵעַ, אֲבָל עַד אוֹתוֹ יוֹם הוּא מְטַמֵּא. אוֹ עַד שְׁעַת הַכִּיבּוּד. אֲבָל טָהֳרוֹת דְּקוֹדֶם כִּיבּוּד — טְהוֹרִין, דְּחֶזְקַת יִשְׂרָאֵל בּוֹדְקִין מְבוֹאוֹתֵיהֶן בִּשְׁעַת כִּיבּוּדֵיהֶן, וְאִי הֲוָה בְּהַהִיא שַׁעְתָּא, הֲוָה מִישְׁתַּכַּח. אֲבָל טָהֳרוֹת דִּלְאַחַר כִּיבּוּד — טְמֵאוֹת מִסָּפֵק, שֶׁמָּא לְאַחַר כִּיבּוּד מִיָּד נָפַל. מַרְגֶּשֶׁת. שנט"ר בְּלַעַ"ז כְּלוֹמַר, יוֹדַעַת בְּעַצְמָהּ כְּשֶׁיּוֹצֵא דָּם מִמֶּנָּה. וְהָא, מִדְּלָא אַרְגְּשָׁה מֵאֶתְמוֹל, וַדַּאי הַשְׁתָּא בִּבְדִיקַת עֵד נְפַק. וְהָא אִיכָּא שׁוֹטָה. שֶׁאֵינָהּ מְבִינָה לְהַרְגִּישׁ. לְאַפּוּקֵי מִדְּר' אֱלִיעֶזֶר. בְּמַתְנִי' הִיא לְקַמָּן (דף ז.). וְהָא אִיכָּא כְּתָמִים. הָרוֹאָה כֶּתֶם, דְּקַיְימָא לָן לְקַמָּן (דף נו.) מְטַמְּאָה לְמַפְרֵעַ, עַד שֶׁתֹּאמַר "בָּדַקְתִּי חָלוּק זֶה, וְלֹא הָיָה בּוֹ כֶּתֶם", אוֹ עַד שְׁעַת כִּבּוּס. וְלָא אָמְרִינַן: אִי נָפֵיק מִגּוּפָהּ, הֲוָה מַרְגֶּשֶׁת. לֵימָא. תְּנַן "כְּתָמִים" דְּלָא כְּשַׁמַּאי, דְּכֵיוָן דְּאָמַר: אִשָּׁה מַרְגֶּשֶׁת, אַמַּאי טְמֵאָה? לֵימָא: לָאו מִגּוּפָהּ הֲוָה, הוֹאִיל וְלָא אַרְגְּשָׁה! בְּצִפּוֹר לֹא נִתְעַסְּקָה. דְּנֵימָא: מִדַּם צִפּוֹר הֲוָה, דְּאָמַר הָתָם: תּוֹלָה בְּכָל דָּבָר שֶׁהִיא יְכוֹלָה לִתְלוֹת, בְּפֶ' "הָרוֹאָה כֶּתֶם" (לקמן נח.). מְשַׁמֶּשֶׁת בְּמוֹךְ. מְמַלְּאָה אִשָּׁה אוֹתוֹ מָקוֹם מוֹכִין, לִשְׁאוֹב אֶת הַזֶּרַע, שֶׁלֹּא תִּתְעַבֵּר, וְאֵינָהּ נוֹטַלְתּוֹ מִשָּׁם אֶלָּא בִּשְׁעַת הַצּוֹרֶךְ. וְשֶׁמָּא מוֹךְ הֶעֱמִיד אֶת הַדָּם. ג' נָשִׁים *מְשַׁמְּשׁוֹת בְּמוֹךְ: קְטַנָּה, מְעוּבֶּרֶת, וּמֵנִיקָה. [לקמן מה.] מִכְוִיץ כָּוִיץ. וְיֵשׁ מְקוֹמוֹת לַדָּם לָצֵאת. כָּוִיץ. דשריי"ט בְּלַעַ"ז. בֵּין הָנֵי לִישָּׁנֵי. "אִשָּׁה מַרְגֶּשֶׁת" וּ"מֵעִיקָּרָא הֲוָה אָתֵי". לְהָאֵיךְ לִישָּׁנָא. "הַעֲמֵד אִשָּׁה עַל חֶזְקָתָהּ".

לְאַבַּיֵי

מסורת הש"ס: [לקמן ז.] · לקמן נו. · [לקמן מה.]

---

**תוספות**

**ושניהם** לא למדוה אלא מסוטה. תימה: דהא רבנן מטמאין אף ברה"ר, משום דהוי תרתי לריעותא, אם כן לא הוי ספק, ולא שייך זה לסוטה מידי! וכן בחבית, דהוי ודאי טבל לרבנן דומיא דמקוה, הא לא גמרינן מסוטה אלא טומאה. ורבי שמעון נמי, דגמר חבית מטומאה, הא לא שייך מידי לסוטה! ואומר ר"ת: דלא קאמר הכי אלא לפרש דלא תקשי להו מסוטה, *וטעמא דרבנן: משום דהוי תרתי לריעותא, והוי ודאי ולא ספק. ולרבי שמעון הוי ספק, דלית ליה טעמא ד"הרי חסר לפניך", דהשתא הוא דחסר, וכנגד "העמד מקוה בחזקת שלם" איכא למימר: "העמד טמא על חזקתו". ולכך ברה"י תולין מדינא, ואע"ג דלא ילפינן מסוטה. ולכך בחבית נמי ספק, אבל ברה"ר מטהר, אע"ג דליכא חזקה, דמסוטה ילפינן. כדפי' לעיל. (ג) ובכל ספק טומאה אית ליה ברה"י תולין.

*__גמר__ סוף טומאה מתחלת טומאה. – תימה: דשפיר קאמרי רבנן, דהתם איכא חזקת טהרה? וי"ל: דגמר מתחלת טומאה היכא דליכא חזקת טהרה, כגון ההיא דתנוק, דפ' בתרא דקדושין (ג) (דף פ.) דאיכא רוב תינוקות מטפחין כנגד חזקת העיסה, ואינו רוב גמור, והוי פלגא כנגד החזקה. ואילו היה בה דעת לישאל מן התורה היה ברה"י – טמא גמור, וברה"ר – טהור גמור, דגמרינן מסוטה. ורבנן, התם איכא חזקת טהרה פי' כנגד רוב טיפוח, והוי ספק, וגמרי מסוטה לטהר ברה"ר. אבל הכא גברא בחזקת טומאה, והוי תרתי לריעותא, והוי ודאי.

**השרץ** שנמצא במבוי. לשמאי פריך, דמטהר לגמרי.

**ושרצים** דמעלמא. וא"ת: סיפא דקתני התם: כתם שנמצא בחלוקה – מטמא למפרע, עד שתאמר "בדקתי את החלוק, ולא היה בו כתם", או עד שעת הכבוס, מאי איכא למימר? דהתם ליכא למימר: דאיכא דם מגופה, ומעלמא – דמשום דם דמעלמא אינו טמא אלא חלוק. ולקמן בפרקין (דף ו.) נמי אמרינן: הרואה כתם – מקולקלת למנינה! וי"ל: דהואיל ואם הכתם יבש הוא ע"כ טמאה למפרע, ופעמים נמי אף כשהוא לח, מוכיח דלא אתא השתא אלא על ידי שהייה או ע"י ריקוד. כדאמר ב"הרואה כתם" (לקמן נז:) לא פלוג רבנן בכתמים.

**ואיבעית** אימא טעמא דשמאי הואיל ואשה מרגשת בעצמה. נראה דלהאי לישנא נמי צריך טעמא ד"העמד אשה על חזקתה", דאל"כ, כי קאמר "מודה שמאי בשוטה" וכן "מודה שמאי במוך", וכי יטמאנה למפרע, אף לחולין? והלא כל הנשים דיין שעתן לחולין, אף להלל! אלא הני טעמי לא איצטריך אלא כי היכי דלא נעבד סייג בקדשים*.

**מרגשת** בעצמה. פי': כשנעקר דם מן המקור. ומדלא הרגישה עד עכשיו, השתא הוא דחזאי. וא"ת: וכי בדקה עצמה ומצאה טמאה, ולא הרגישה, מאי [טעמא דשמאי, נימא: כמו שלא הרגישה עכשיו, כך נימא: שמא נעקר מאתמול ולא הרגישה] וי"ל: דלא פלוג רבנן, הואיל ורוב פעמים מרגשת. דהא לטעמא דאם איתא דהוה דם מעיקרא הוה אתי, שוכבת אפרקיד מאי איכא למימר? אלא, לא פלוג רבנן. והא דקאמר "מודה שמאי בשוטה ובמוך" – משום דהנהו חלוקות משאר נשים, ולא שייך למימר בהו: לא פלוג רבנן. ורש"י פירש: מה שעכשיו לא הרגישה, כסבורה הרגשת עד הוא. וקשה: מאתמול נמי נימא: הא דלא הרגישה אם שמשה, כסבורה הרגשת שמש הוא, ואמאי מטהרין למפרע? אלא שמאי אית ליה דלעולם אשה מרגשת, ואינה חוששת בהרגשת עד ושמש, כמו שאינה חוששת בהרגשת מי רגלים.

**מודה** שמאי בשוטה. ואם תאמר: והא אין בו דעת לישאל? וי"ל: כגון אדם שנגע בה, ורוצה לעסוק בקדשים, ואותו אדם יש בו דעת לישאל.

**והא** איכא בתמים. פירוש: לשמאי דאית ליה טעמא דהרגשה לטהר אף בקדשים, היה לנו לטהר כתמים אפי' מכאן ולהבא, דאית לן למימר: כיון דלא הרגישה – ודאי מעלמא אתי. כדאמר (לקמן דף ה.) גבי "תינוקת שלא הגיע זמנה לראות": אפילו סדינין שלה מלוכלכין בדם – אין חוששין לה, אימר: בשוק של טבחים עברה, ולאו אדעתה. אבל להלל לא קשה, כיון דאינו ברור לו טעמא דהרגשה לטהר בקדשים, אין לנו לתלות בכתמים ולומר דמעלמא אתי אפילו לחולין, דרגלים לדבר הוא דמגופה אתי, אפילו למפרע.

איכא

ומיהו לפי זה לא א"ש הא דאמר לקמן עשה סייג לדבריך כיון דאיכא טעמא דאם איתא דהוה דם כו' לא הוה אלא סייג ושמא טעמא דהרגשה אהני אף בשוטה לחולין. גי':

---

**תוספי הרא"ש**

**מה** סוטה ספק היא ועשאוה כודאי. לאוסרה על בעלה עד שתשתה אע"ג דמן הדין מותרת לבעלה דאוקמה בחזקת צדקת ואע"ג דנסתרה לא נבעלה אלא גזירת הכתוב להוציאה מחזקתה ולאוסרה מספק: **אי** מה סוטה ברשות היחיד ודאי טמאה [illegible]

[illegible]

**תוספי הרא"ש**

כודאי. טבל אע"ג דלא שייך ביה למילף מסוטה. ור' שמעון נמי דמשוי חבית ומקוה ספק אין זה מכח ספק סוטה

טהרה דלמא שאני סוטה דאית לה חזקת טהרה. וברשות היחיד דוקא הוא דגלי לן קרא דטמאה ולא אזלינן בתר חזקה ומינה ילפינן בעלמא ספק טומאה ברשות היחיד אבל ברשות הרבים אוקמה אדינא וכיון דליכא [illegible] אדינא לטמאות מספק וכי תימא דברשות הרבים נמי איתרע (קינא) [חזקתה] שהרי קינא לה ונסתרה. הא אמרינן לקמן בשמעתין דסתירה ברשות הרבים ליכא. וי"ל דברשות הרבים נמי איתא סתירה [illegible] קרן זוית. ואפי' הכי לא אסר רחמנא אלא ברשות היחיד. שדרך הוא ליסתר שם אלמא [illegible] דאיתרעאי חזקתה שריא. וא"ת כיון דחשבינן סוטה כפלגא ופלגא משום דאיכא רגלים [illegible] טומאה ברשות היחיד נוקמה אחזקה לטהר ולא נילף מסוטה אלא היכא דאיכא רגלים [illegible] רגלים לדבר והוו כמו פלגא ופלגא מ"מ אית לה חזקת היתר ואפקה קרא מחזקתה [illegible] לספק טומאה מפקינן ליה מחזקתיה אע"ג דליכא רגלים לדבר ומ"מ ספק טומאה [ברה"ר] [illegible] אי לאו דילפינן מסוטה לטהר הוה מטמינן כיון דהחמיר קרא ברשות היחיד לטמאות [illegible] חזקת טהרה הוה מטמינן ברשות הרבים היכא דהוה פלגא ופלגא: **הכא** מאי רגלים [illegible] האי דקאמר ושניהן לא למדוה אלא מסוטה הא לא ילפינן מסוטה מידי דהא רבנן [illegible] הרבים ומשום דאיכא תרתי לריעותא חשיבי ליה כודאי טומאה וכן בחבית חשיב ליה כודאי

אלא מסברא דחשיב תרתי לריעותא ספק דחבית לא שייך למילף מסוטה ומפרש ר"ת דשניהם לא למדוה אלא מסוטה לאו מילף ממש קאמר אלא דלא קשיא להו דין סוטה. ומי' ר' שמעון ודאי יליף רשות הרבים מסוטה כיון דחשיב ליה ספק יליף מסוטה לטהר ברשות הרבים אבל רשות היחיד לא יליף מסוטה לטמא ודאי משום דשאני סוטה משום דאיכא רגלים לדבר. ולישנא דחיק. וי"ל דאיצטריך למילף חבית ומקוה מסוטה דאי לאו דאשכחן בשום דוכתא דעשה הכתוב ספק כודאי לא הייתי מיקל לשרוף ברשות היחיד ובחבית לבטל התרומה לגמרי משום תרתי לריעותא ור' שמעון נמי לא היה מטהר ברשות הרבים דאיכא חזקה כנגד חזקה אי לאו דיליף מסוטה: **הכא** מאי רגלים לדבר איכא. פרש"י דבר ר' שמעון בשאר ספק טומאות דעלמא נמי ברשות היחיד תולין תימה דלא משתמיט לן בכוליה תלמודא דפליג ר' שמעון בתחלת טומאה. ויש מפרשים דבתחלת טומאה מודה ר' שמעון דהלכתא גמירי לה כדאיתא בפ"ק דחולין [דף ט ע"ב] וכי תימא השתא בתחלת טומאה שורפין בסוף טומאה לא כ"ש הא קי"ל דאין דנין ק"ו מהלכה הלכך בסוף טומאה אמר ר"ש תולין כיון דאיכא לתלות להקל כמו להחמיר דהרי חסר לפניך לר' שמעון ריעותא ולא יתכן האי פירוש' דע"כ הלכתא גמירי לה לאו דוקא שיהא הלכה למשה מסיני דהא בסוטה בפ' כשם יליף לה מק"ו. ונ"ל דהאי ק"ו פריכא הוא דקאמר התם ומה סוטה שלא עשה בה שגג כמזיד

---

**הגהות הב"ח**

(א) גמ' ואיבעית אימא היינו טעמיה: (ב) תוס' ד"ה ושניהם וכו' כדפרישית לעיל. נ"ב בד"ה והלל: (ג) ד"ה גמר וכו' דפרק בתרא דקידושין. נ"ב בדף פ' וע"ש בתוס' בד"ה סמוך [illegible]:

[ועי' תוס' קדושין פ. ד"ה וכהנים]

**גליון הש"ס**

**תוס'** ד"ה גמר וכו' וי"ל דגמר מתחלת טומאה וכו' כגון ההיא דתינוק וכו' [illegible]

[ואיבעית אימא היינו טעמא דר"ש גמר סוף טומאה מתחלת טומאה [illegible]]

אִיכָּא בֵּינַיְיהוּ: לְמִרְמֵי חָבִית וּמִקְוֶה וּמָבוֹי. לְהָאֵיךְ לִישָּׁנָא — אִיכָּא לְמִרְמִינְהוּ, לְהָנֵי לִישְׁנֵי — לֵיכָּא לְמִרְמֵי. וּמַאי אִיכָּא בֵּין הַאי לִישָּׁנָא לְהָאֵיךְ לִישָּׁנָא? לְאַבַּיֵי — אִיכָּא מוֹךְ, לְרָבָא — אִיכָּא מוֹךְ דָּחוּק. תַּנְיָא כִּי הַאי לִישָּׁנָא דְּאִם אִיתָא דַּהֲוָה דָּם מֵעִיקָּרָא הֲוָה אָתֵי, אָמַר לוֹ הִלֵּל לְשַׁמַּאי: אִי אַתָּה מוֹדֶה בְּקוּפָּה שֶׁנִּשְׁתַּמְּשׁוּ בָּהּ טְהָרוֹת בְּזָוִית זוֹ, וְנִמְצָא שֶׁרֶץ בְּזָוִית אַחֶרֶת — שֶׁטְּהָרוֹת הָרִאשׁוֹנוֹת טְמֵאוֹת? אָמַר לוֹ: אֲבָל! וּמָה הֶפְרֵשׁ בֵּין זוֹ לָזוֹ? לָזוֹ יֵשׁ לָהּ שׁוּלַיִם, לָזוֹ — אֵין לָהּ שׁוּלַיִם. רָבָא אָמַר: טַעֲמָא דְּשַׁמַּאי מִשּׁוּם בִּטּוּל פְּרִיָּה וּרְבִיָּה. תַּנְיָא נַמִּי הָכִי, אָמַר לוֹ שַׁמַּאי לְהִלֵּל: א"כ בִּטַּלְתָּ בְּנוֹת יִשְׂרָאֵל מִפְּרִיָּה וּרְבִיָּה. וּמַאן דְּתָנֵי הַאי לִישָּׁנָא, הָא תַּנְיָא כִּי הָאֵיךְ לִישָּׁנָא דְּאִם אִיתָא דַּהֲוָה דָּם — מֵעִיקָּרָא הֲוָה אָתֵי! הָתָם, הִלֵּל הוּא דְּקָטָעֵי, הוּא סָבַר: טַעֲמָא דְּשַׁמַּאי דְּאִם אִיתָא דַּהֲוָה דָּם — מֵעִיקָּרָא הֲוָה אָתֵי, וְקָא מַקְשֵׁי לֵיהּ קוּפָּה. וַאֲמַר לֵיהּ שַׁמַּאי: טַעֲמָא דִּידִי — מִשּׁוּם בִּטּוּל פְּרִיָּה וּרְבִיָּה, וּלְמַאי דְּקָטָעֵית נַמִּי, דְּקָמַקְשִׁית קוּפָּה — לָזוֹ יֵשׁ לָהּ שׁוּלַיִם, וְלָזוֹ אֵין לָהּ שׁוּלַיִם. וּלְמַאן דְּתָנֵי הַאי לִישָּׁנָא, הָא תַּנְיָא כִּי הָאֵיךְ לִישָּׁנָא מִשּׁוּם בִּטּוּל פְּרִיָּה וּרְבִיָּה! הָכִי קָאָמַר לֵיהּ הִלֵּל לְשַׁמַּאי: אִין, טַעֲמָא קָאָמְרַתְּ דְּאִם אִיתָא דַּהֲוָה דָּם מֵעִיקָּרָא הֲוָה אָתֵי, וּמִיהוּ — עֲשֵׂה סְיָיג לִדְבָרֶיךָ, דְּמַאי שְׁנָא מִכָּל הַתּוֹרָה כּוּלָּהּ דְּעָבְדִינַן סְיָיג? אָמַר לֵיהּ: א"כ בִּטַּלְתָּ בְּנוֹת יִשְׂרָאֵל מִפְּרִיָּה וּרְבִיָּה! וְהִלֵּל — מִפְּרִיָּה וּרְבִיָּה מִי קָאָמִינָא? לְטָהֳרוֹת הוּא דְּקָאָמִינָא! וְשַׁמַּאי — לְטָהֳרוֹת נַמִּי לָא, דְּאִם כֵּן *לִבּוֹ נוֹקְפוֹ וּפוֹרֵשׁ. (שולי"ם, בדוקי"ן, מכוסי"ן בזוי"ת, סימ"ן) אִיתְּמַר: קוּפָּה שֶׁנִּשְׁתַּמְּשׁוּ בָּהּ טְהָרוֹת בְּזָוִית זוֹ, וְנִמְצָא שֶׁרֶץ בְּזָוִית אַחֶרֶת. [לקמן יח. סה:] חִזְקִיָּה אָמַר: טְהָרוֹת הָרִאשׁוֹנוֹת טְהוֹרוֹת. רַבִּי יוֹחָנָן אָמַר: [א]טְהָרוֹת הָרִאשׁוֹנוֹת טְמֵאוֹת. וְהָא (א) (בֵּית) שַׁמַּאי וְהִלֵּל מוֹדוּ בְּקוּפָּה דִּטְהָרוֹת הָרִאשׁוֹנוֹת טְמֵאוֹת! כִּי מוֹדוּ שַׁמַּאי וְהִלֵּל — בְּקוּפָּה שֶׁיֵּשׁ לָהּ שׁוּלַיִם, כִּי פְּלִיגֵי חִזְקִיָּה וְרַבִּי יוֹחָנָן — [ב]בְּקוּפָּה שֶׁאֵין לָהּ שׁוּלַיִם. אֵין לָהּ שׁוּלַיִם מ"ט דְּר' יוֹחָנָן? אֵין לָהּ שׁוּלַיִם [ג]וְיֵשׁ לָהּ אוֹגְנַיִם. (ב) וְהָתַנְיָא: [ד]הַמְדַלֶּה עֲשָׂרָה דְּלָיִים מַיִם בְּזֶה אַחַר זֶה וְנִמְצָא שֶׁרֶץ בְּאֶחָד מֵהֶן — הוּא טָמֵא וְכוּלָּן טְהוֹרִין. וְאָמַר רֵישׁ לָקִישׁ מִשּׁוּם רַבִּי יַנַּאי: לֹא שָׁנוּ אֶלָּא שֶׁאֵין לָהּ אוֹגְנַיִם, [ה]אֲבָל יֵשׁ לָהּ אוֹגְנַיִם — כּוּלָּן טְמֵאִין. לֵימָא חִזְקִיָּה לֵית לֵיהּ דְּר' יַנַּאי! מַיָּא — שָׁרְקִי, פֵּירֵי — לָא שָׁרְקִי. אִי נַמִּי: מַיָּא — לָא קָפֵיד עֲלַיְיהוּ, פֵּירֵי — קָפֵיד עֲלַיְיהוּ. וְאִי בָּעֵית אֵימָא: כִּי מוֹדוּ שַׁמַּאי וְהִלֵּל — בְּקוּפָּה שֶׁאֵינָהּ בְּדוּקָה, כִּי

לְאַבַּיֵי אִיכָּא מוֹךְ. לְלִישָּׁנָא דְּ"אִשָּׁה מַרְגֶּשֶׁת", אֲפִי' מְשַׁמֶּשֶׁת בְּמוֹךְ נַמִּי דַּיָּהּ שַׁעְתָּהּ. וּלְלִישָּׁנָא דְּ"מֵעִיקָּרָא הֲוָה אָתֵי", מְשַׁמֶּשֶׁת בְּמוֹךְ מְטַמְּאָה לְמַפְרֵעַ. וְנִמְצָא בָּהּ שֶׁרֶץ בְּזָוִית אַחֶרֶת. לְאַחַר שֶׁנִּיטְּלוּ טְהָרוֹת מִן הַקּוּפָּה. שֶׁטְּהָרוֹת הָרִאשׁוֹנוֹת טְמֵאוֹת לְמַפְרֵעַ. וְדַוְקָא בְּזָוִית אַחֶרֶת, כְּגוֹן קוּפָּה אֲרוּכָּה אַמָּתַיִם וְג' אַמּוֹת, דְּאִיכָּא לְמֵימַר: קוֹדֶם שֶׁנִּיטְּלוּ הַטְּהָרוֹת הֲוָה הָתָם, וְנִטְמָא הַכְּלִי מֵחֲמַת הַשֶּׁרֶץ, וּטְהָרוֹת מֵחֲמַת הַכְּלִי, וְאִיהוּ הוּא דְּלָא נִתְעַסֵּק בְּאוֹתוֹ זָוִית, וְלָא אַשְׁכְּחֵיהּ. אֲבָל בְּאוֹתוֹ זָוִית – לָא, דְּוַדַּאי בָּתַר הָכִי נְפַל, דְּאִי הֲוָה הָתָם בִּשְׁעַת טְהָרוֹת, הֲוָה חָזֵי לֵיהּ כְּשֶׁהוֹלִיכָן. אֲבָל. כֵּן הַדָּבָר. וּמָה הֶפְרֵשׁ בֵּין זוֹ לָזוֹ. וְהָא טוּמְאָה דִּלְמַפְרֵעַ הוּא. שׁוּלַיִם. פונ"ך בְּלַעַ"ז וְעִכְּבוּ הַשּׁוּלַיִם אֶת הַשֶּׁרֶץ מִלָּצֵאת, וְהוּא הוֹצִיא טְהָרוֹת דֶּרֶךְ פִּיהָ מִלְמַעְלָה, וְהַשֶּׁרֶץ שֶׁבְּזָוִית אַחֶרֶת לֹא רָאָה. וְלָזוֹ אֵין לָהּ שׁוּלַיִם. וְאִי הֲוָה דָּם מֵאֶתְמוֹל בְּבֵית הַחִיצוֹן, הֲוָה נָפֵיק וְנָפֵיל. מִפְּרִיָּה וּרְבִיָּה. דְּכֵיוָן דְּחָיְישִׁינַן לְדָם בְּבֵית הַחִיצוֹן, לִבּוֹ נוֹקְפוֹ, וּפוֹרֵשׁ מִן הָאִשָּׁה. וְקָא מַקְשֵׁי לֵיהּ קוּפָּה. הֲרֵי קוּפָּה דְּלָא אָמַר: אִם אִיתָא דַּהֲוָה שֶׁרֶץ, מֵעִיקָּרָא הֲוָה נָפֵיק עִם הַטְּהָרוֹת, כְּשֶׁעֵירָה אֶת הַקּוּפָּה. סְיָיג. חִזּוּק וְגָדֵר מִדְּרַבָּנַן לְטַמֵּא לְמַפְרֵעַ. וְה"ה דְּמָצֵי לְמִיפְרַךְ הָנֵי מַתְנִי' אַהָנָךְ לִישָּׁנָא דִּלְעֵיל, וּלְתָרוּצֵי כִּי הַאי גַּוְונָא: הִלֵּל טָעֵי וְסָבַר טַעֲמָא דְּשַׁמַּאי אִם אִיתָא כו', וְקַשְׁיָא לֵיהּ קוּפָּה, וְקָאָמַר לֵיהּ שַׁמַּאי: טַעֲמָא דִּידִי מִשּׁוּם הַעֲמֵד אִשָּׁה עַל חֶזְקָתָהּ, אִי מִשּׁוּם אִשָּׁה מַרְגֶּשֶׁת. וּלְמַאי דְּקָא טָעֵית נַמִּי, דְּקָא מַקְשַׁתְּ לִי קוּפָּה, זוֹ יֵשׁ לָהּ שׁוּלַיִם כו'. שֶׁיֵּשׁ לָהּ שׁוּלַיִם. וְהוּא הוֹצִיאָן דֶּרֶךְ הַפֶּה, הִלְכָּךְ אִם שֶׁרֶץ הָיָה בָּהּ, לֹא רָאָהוּ וְלֹא יָצָא. שֶׁאֵין לָהּ שׁוּלַיִם. כְּגוֹן חָבִית שֶׁל עֵץ שֶׁנִּיטְּלוּ שׁוּלֶיהָ, וְיָכוֹל לְהִשְׁתַּמֵּשׁ בְּאוֹרֶךְ חֲלָלָן כְּשֶׁהֵן מוּטָּלוֹת בַּקַּרְקַע. וּכְשֶׁהוּא מְעָרֶה אוֹתָן, הוּא מַגְבִּיהַּ רֹאשׁ הָאֶחָד וּמְעָרֶה, וְהַכֹּל יוֹצֵא מִמֶּנָּה. מַאי טַעְמָא דְּר' יוֹחָנָן. הָא וַדַּאי אִילּוּ הֲוָה הָתָם בִּשְׁעַת טְהָרוֹת, הֲוָה נָפֵיק בַּהֲדַיְיהוּ. אוֹגְנִים. בִּמְקוֹם הַשּׁוּלַיִים יֵשׁ אוֹגָנִים, שֶׁכְּפוּפִין רָאשֵׁי הַנְּסָרִים כְּלַפֵּי פְּנִים. וּכְשֶׁהוּא מְעָרֶה, אִיכָּא לְמֵימַר: אוֹגָנִים עִכְּבוּ. עֲשָׂרָה דְּלָיִים. י' פְּעָמִים בִּדְלִי אֶחָד, וּמְעָרֶה בִּכְלִי גָּדוֹל. וְכוּלָּן טְהוֹרִין. דְּאָמַר: הָשְׁתָּא הוּא דְּנָפַל, דְּהוֹאִיל שֶׁלֹּא מָצָא קוֹדֶם שֶׁעֵירָה הַדְּלִי בַּפַּעַם הַזֹּאת לְתוֹךְ הַכְּלִי — טְהוֹרִין. שֶׁאֵין לוֹ אוֹגְנִים. לַדְּלִי, דְּהָשְׁתָּא וַדַּאי אִם אִיתָא דַּהֲוָה הָתָם בִּזְמַנָּא קַמָּאֵי, הֲוָה נָפֵיל מִן הַדְּלִי עִם הַמַּיִם. מַיָּא שָׁרְקִי. וְאֵין צָרִיךְ לַהֲפוֹךְ הַדְּלִי עַל פָּנָיו כְּשֶׁהוּא מְעָרֶה, הִלְכָּךְ אִיכָּא לְמֵימַר: אוֹגָנִים עִכְּבוּהוּ לַשֶּׁרֶץ. אֲבָל פֵּירֵי לָא שָׁרְקִי, וּכְשֶׁעֵירָה טְהָרוֹת מִמֶּנָּה, הֲפָכָהּ כּוּלָּהּ עַל פָּנֶיהָ, לְפִי שֶׁאֵין פֵּירוֹת נוֹחִין לִישָּׁרֵק וְלָצֵאת. הִלְכָּךְ, אִי הֲוָה שֶׁרֶץ עִם הַטְּהָרוֹת, הֲוָה שָׁרֵיק וְנָפֵיל בַּהֲדַיְיהוּ. לָא קָפֵיד עֲלַיְיהוּ. אִי מְשַׁיֵּיר מִינַּיְיהוּ לְתוֹךְ הַדְּלִי. הִלְכָּךְ, אֵינוֹ שׁוֹפֵךְ כָּל הַדְּלִי עַל פָּנָיו, וּמָלוּ אוֹגָנִים לְעַכּוּבֵי שֶׁרֶץ. קָפֵיד עֲלַיְיהוּ. לְאַפּוּקִינְהוּ כּוּלְּהוּ. וְהוֹפֵךְ קוּפָּה עַל פִּיהָ, וְלָא מְשַׁיֵּיר מִידֵּי. וְאִם אִיתָא דַּהֲוָה שֶׁרֶץ, הָכִי נַמִּי דְּלָא אִישְׁתַּיֵּיר. בְּקוּפָּה שֶׁאֵינָהּ בְּדוּקָה. שֶׁלֹּא בְּדָקָהּ בִּשְׁעַת שֶׁנָּתַן טְהָרוֹת לְתוֹכָהּ. הִלְכָּךְ, אֵין לְהַעֲמִידָהּ עַל חֶזְקַת טָהֳרָה. וְהָא

**איכא** בינייהו למרמי חבית ומקוה. וא"ת: להני טעמי נמי איכא למרמי, דהא מודה שמאי בשוטה דלא מרגשת, דלמפרע תולין, ובמקוה שורפין. וכן להלל, דלית ליה הני טעמי, צריך לשנויי כדמשני דהתם תרתי לריעותא? וי"ל: דטעמא דהרגשה מהני להלל שלא לטמא ודאי, ולשמאי מהני אף בשוטה שלא לטמאותה בודאי. א"נ יש לומר: דידע טעמא דתרתי לריעותא לשרוף, אבל תולין, אע"ג דליכא תרתי לריעותא. ועיקר פירכא דלעיל לשמאי, דמשום דליכא באשה תרתי לריעותא, מ"מ לא היה לו לטהר לגמרי. וא"ת: אכתי איכא למירמי, דבמקוה מטמאין אף ברה"ר, ובנגע באחד בלילה מטהרים חכמים ברה"ר ברואהו חי מבערב! אלא ע"כ היינו טעמא, משום דבמקוה איכא תרתי לריעותא? וי"ל: דלא קשה ליה לעיל, אלא בשאי דמטהר שמאי אף ברשות היחיד. **לאביי** איכא מוך. ה"מ למימר נמי דאיכא בינייהו שוטה, דללישנא קמא דאשה מרגשת – מודה שמאי בשוטה. ואין לומר דללישנא דאי הוה דם מעיקרא הוה אתי, מודה נמי שמאי בשוטה, דשמא דם אחר נפל קודם בדיקה, משום דמשמע דעל דם שנמצא עכשיו קאמר. **כי** פליגי חזקיה ור' יוחנן בקופה שאין לה שולים. שאז משתמשין בה כשהיא מושכבת. וקופה היא מרובעת, ומשתמשין בה לרחבה, ונמצאו טהרות בימין ושרץ בשמאל. ופליגי, דלחזקיה אית ליה: טהרות האחרונות – טמאות, אבל הראשונות – טהורות, דשרץ בתר הכי נפל. דאילו הוה התם מעיקר', כשהגביה הקופה לערות ממנה הטהרות היה נופל גם השרץ. ור' יוחנן אמר: דטהרות הראשונות נמי טמאות, שהאוגנים עכבו השרץ מליפול בארץ. ולכך לא ראהו, לפי שהטהרות נפלו לצד ימין, ולצד שמאל שהשרץ שם, לא ראה. אבל אם היתה הקופה עגולה, מודה רבי יוחנן דהראשונות טהורות, דאז נופלין השרץ והטהרות במקום אחד. ואע"פ שהאוגנים מעכבין מליפול בארץ, מ"מ אי הוה השרץ התם, היה רואהו. ולכך נקט דוקא "נמצא בזוית אחרת". וכן מוכח בפ"ק דשבת (דף ח.) דסתם קופה מרובעת, גבי כוורת נקט "רחבה ששה", לפי שהיא עגולה וצריך להיות בה ד' מרובעים. ובקופה נקט "רחבה ד' [לפי שהיא מרובעת]. ודליים, אפי' הם עגולים, אתי שפיר, דרגילות הוא לערות המים מהר, ואין רואין אם נשאר שרץ בכלים. ולר' יוחנן, קופה דשמאי ה"ה דמצי למנקט אפילו באין לה שולים אך יש לה אוגנים. א)**והתניא** המדלה י' דליים כו' – הקשה הר"ר מנחם: אמאי לא מייתי מתניתין דטהרות פ"ד (מ"ד) דתנן: המדלה י' דליים, ונמצא שרץ בא' מהן – הוא טמא, וכולן טהורין? וי"ל: דהתם לא קתני "זה אחר זה", ואיכא למימר דמיירי כשמדלה שם י' דליים, והם כולם יחד בבור, והעשירי שהגביה נמצא בו שרץ. ולא ידעינן כשהיה השרץ על המים בבור, אם בשאר דליים נגע בעודן בבור והוי ספק טומאה צפה על פני המים, דטהור אף ב) ברה"ר, כדאיתא בסוף נזיר (דף סד.) ואין חילוק בין יש לה אוגנים בין אין לה אוגנים. אי נמי: לא קתני "מים" במתניתין, ואיכא למימר דמיירי בבור שיש בו יין ושמן. וקמ"ל דט' דליים הראשונים טהורים, ולא אמרינן שהשרץ היה תחלה בבור וטימא הכל, אלא אמרינן דדלי זה אחרון נפל תחלה בעודו ריקן. וכשדלאו לבור לבסוף – הוא טמא ומטמא כל מה שבבור, אבל שאר דליים הראשונים – טהורים.

כי

א) עיין מהר"ס ב) נ"ל ברה"י

ז א ב ג מיי' פי"ז מהל' שאר אבות הטומאה הלכה ב:

ח ד ה מיי' שם הלכה א:

## תוספי הרא"ש

כמזיד ואונס כרצון עשה בה ספק כודאי שרץ שעשה בו שוגג כמזיד ואונס כרצון אינו דין שיעשה בו ספק כודאי. ואיכא לאקשויי מה לטומאת שרץ שכן יש לה טהרה במקוה. הלכך נקל עליהן שלא לטמאן מספק ועוד איכא למימר נזקי אדם יוכיחו שעשה בהן שוגג כמזיד ואונס כרצון [ולא] עשה בהם ספק כודאי אלא נקט ק"ו לרווחא דמילתא דהלכה למשה מסיני היא כדקאמר סתמא דתלמודא בחולין הלכך לא חש לאקשויי: **ואיבעית** אימא היינו טעמא דר' שמעון. כלומר ודאי מסוטה לא ילפינן סוף טומאה דתחלת טומאה דוקא איתקש לסוטה הלכך לרבנן כיון דאיכא תרתי לריעותא בודאי חשיב ליה. ור' שמעון אע"ג דלא חשיב ליה תרתי לריעותא מ"מ כיון דאיכא חזקה בנגד חזקה מאי טעמיה דמטהר ברה"ר גמר סוף טומאה מתחלת טומאה וא"ת והיאך יליף סוף טומאה דאיכא חזקת טומאה מתחלת טומאה דאיכא חזקת טהרה וי"ל דיליף מתחלת טומאה כי ההיא דפ' כסוי הדם דהוי פלגא ופלגא דמטהרים ברשות הרבים אפי' במקום הראוי להיות ספק וה"ה סוף טומאה אפי' במקום חזקה ורבנן אמרי התם איכא חזקת טהרה דכנגד ריעותא דטיפוח איכא חזקת טהרה ומיעוטא דאין מטפחין והוה ליה ספק וגמרי' מסוטה לטהר ברשות הרבים אבל הכא גברא בחזקת טומאה כלומר איכא תרתי לריעותא והוי כודאי. והאי דקאמר [ר"ש] ברשה"י תולין משום דתחלת טומאה נמי ס"ל ברשות היחיד תולין. ומיהו להך פירו' דפרי' דר' שמעון ס"ל בספק טומאה בעלמא שורפין א"כ א)לר' שמעון משום דאכתי איכא למיפרך אי מה תחלת טומאה ברשות היחיד טמא ודאי אף סוף טומאה כן וי"ל דלטהר ברשות הרבים ילפינן שפיר מתחלת טומאה דגלויי מלתא בעלמא הוא לטהר כיון דהוי פלגא ופלגא כי היכי דמטהרינן בתחלת טומאה אבל לטמאות ודאי ברשות היחיד לא ילפינן מהלכה: **ושרצים** דאתו לה מעלמא כו'. [וא"ת] תיקשי ליה מסיפא דתנן פ' דם הנדה וכן הכתם שנמצא בחלוק מטמא למפרע וכי תימא דאיכא דמים דאשה זו ודמים דנשים דעלמא התינח חלוק אלא אשה אמאי מקולקלת למנינה כדתנן לקמן בפרקין. וי"ל דשאני התם דאיכא כתם דממה נפשך מטמא לפרע היכא דהכתם יבש או במקום שאין דם זה ראוי לבא בחלוק אלא א"כ שיחתה או איזדקרא דאיכא למימר למפרע שיחתה או איזדקרא ולאו אדעתה הלכך לא פליג בכולהו: **הואיל** ואשה מרגשת בעצמה. וא"ת חזאי בלא הרגשה מאי איכא למימר ופרש"י האי דלא ארגשה עכשיו משום דסבורה הרגשת העד הואי וכי האי גונא אמרינן בריש הרואה כתם. וק' דא"כ היכא דשמשה תטמא דסבור הרגשת שמש הואי כדאמרי' נמי התם וי"ל דכי חזאי בלא הרגשה מלתא דלא שכיח הוא ולא עבוד רבנן חיזוק דכשמרגשת בודקת לאלתר אבל שינה ושוטה וכתמים שכיחי הלכך פריך מינייהו: **מודה** שמאי בשוטה. ודוקא בטהרות שנגעה והם בידי אדם אבל מונח על גבי קרקע הוי שוטה דבר שאין בו דעת לשאל ומטהרים ליה מעת לעת כדמוכח לקמן ג)כיון דמודה שמאי להלל בשוטה והלל לא קאמר דטמא בחולין א"כ מאי טעמא דשמאי דקא מטהר בחולין בשוטה אלא מטעם חזקה והשתא צריכינן לטעמא דחזקה מדלא אסרינן בשוטה אפי' בחולין אלא דאתא לפרושי מאי טעמא לא עבוד סייג וכן כל הנך טעמי דלקמן כדמפרש על טעמא דביטול פריה ורביה: **לימא** תנן כתמים דלא כשמאי. דכיון דלא ארגשה ודאי לאו מגופה אתא ואפי' מכאן ולהבא לא תטמא אבל הך לא פריך שלא תטמא למפרע. אלא מכאן ולהבא דהא השתא נמי אשכחא ולא מרגשא. ועוד כדפ"ל דגזסור בכולהו משום דפעמים ראוי לטמאות למפרע ממה נפשך. ועוד מאי קשיא ליה אי שמאי מטהר כתמים למפרע הא אשכחן נמי ר' שמעון בן אלעזר בסוף בא סימן דמטהר כתמים למפרע אבל מכאן ולהבא ליכא מאן דמטהר: **משמשת** במוך. אע"ג דנקט משמשת במוך לא שנותנין המוך בשעת תשמיש דהא ודאי אסור אפי' לג' נשים דמשמשות במוך משום השחתת זרע האיש דהוי כזורע על העצים ועל האבנים אלא נותנהו לאחר תשמיש כדי

(א) גמ' והא שמאי והלל מודו כו"ל תיבת בית נמחק: (ב) שם והתניא המדלה עשרה דליים. נ"ב משנה היא פ"ד דטהרות משנה ד':

## תוספי הרא"ש

כדי שתשאוב הזרע שלא תתעבר*): **להני** לישני ליכא למירמי. ונפקא מינה דלא נצטרך לחלק בעלמא בין חדא לריעותא לתרתי לריעותא. וא"ת להני לישני נמי איכא למירמי להלל. וי"ל דהלל נמי אית ליה הני טעמי לענין לתלות יהא דלא פריך לימא (למימר) תנן כתמים דלא כהלל משום דלא חשיב להני טעמא לטהר אלא לענין דתלינן ולא שרפינן. וא"ת מ"מ איכא למירמי משום שוטה ומוך דחוק דמודי בהו שמאי. ומסתמא הוו כמו שאר מעת לעת דתולין ומאי שנא מחבית מקוה ומבוי וי"ל דהא לא קשיא ליה דמשום הני תרתי לא עבוד רבנן תקנתא לשרוף בחדא לריעותא דסגי בהכי דלא מטהרינן להו לגברי וא"ת אכתי צריכי הני תרי לישני לטעמא דחדא לריעותא ותרתי לריעותא כי היכי דלא תיקשי ממקוה אנגע באחד בלילה דאפי' רבנן מודו בראוהו חי מבערב שטהור ברשות הרבים כדתניא בתוספתא וי"ל דלא קשיא ליה אלא הא דמטהרין ברשות היחיד אבל הא דמטהרינן ברשות הרבים לא קשה כולי האי ובקל נוכל למצוא טעם לזה ולא נצטרך לחלק בין חדא ותרתי לריעותא: **לאביי** איכא מוך. הוה מצי למימר בין לאביי בין לרבא איכא בינייהו שוטה: **אמר** הלל לשמאי אי אתה מודה בקופה כו'. וא"ת ולימא ליה הלל לנפשיה דההיא אפי' לחולין ובמעת לעת דוקא בקדשים או לתרומה למאן דאית ליה ולפי מאי דמפרש לקמן דכל המומאות כשעת מציאתן היינו דוקא לקדשים או לתרומה ניחא וכי תימא אכתי לימא לנפשיה דהכא לשרוף ובמעת לעת דוקא לתלות וי"ל דלגבי האי איר ליה לב"ה נמי טעם דפריה ורביה שלא רצו לדחמיר לשרוף שלא יהא לבו נוקפו ופורש. וא"ת א"כ לעיל דפריך להלל ממקוה דאילו מעת לעת שבנדה תולין והכא טמאות. לישני משום שלא יהא לבו נוקפו ופורש. וי"ל דודאי מקדשים לקדשים איכא לשנויי הכי דבעלמא החמירו לשרוף קדשים והכא לא רצו להחמיר כדי שלא יהא לבו נוקפו ופורש אבל אי בעלמא מטמאינן אפילו חולין לא מכתבר למימר דהכא תולין משום שלא יהא לבו נוקפו ופורש: **התם** הלל הוא דקא טעי. והכא נמי צריך לשנויי לאינך לישני דמרגשת או דחזקה וא"ת וללישנא דחזקה אמאי לא מקשי ליה הלל מקופה דאמאי טמאות נימא העמד קופה על חזקתה כמו גבי אשה. וי"ל דמיירי בקופה שאינה בדוקה. אבל אשה בדוקה היא ולא כהך לישנא דאמרי' לקמן דכיון דשכיחי בה דמים כשאינה בדוקה היא. או א"נ אע"ג דשכיחי בה דמים מ"מ חזקת טהרה אית לה: והקשה ה"ר שמשון מקוצי להאי טעמא דחזקה מניין לו (חזקה לשמאי) דהלל טעה בסברתו וסבר דאם איתא דהוה דם כו' והלא מקופה קשה נמי ללישנא דחזקה כמו ללישנא דאם איתא דהוה דם מעיקרא וכו' כדפרישנא דבשלמא לאידך לישני דמרגשת או דפריה ורביה לא שייך כלל למיפרך מקופה הלכך ידע שטעה אבל ללישנא דחזקה לא טעה ומאי קא משני ליה לזו יש לה שוליים ולזו אין לה שוליים. ותירץ דהוה פשיטא ליה לשמאי דאילו היה הלל יודע דטעם דידיה משום חזקה לא היה מקשה לו מקופה לפי שדבר פשוט הוא לחלק בין קופה שאינה בדוקה לאשה בדוקה: **ה"ק** ליה הלל לשמאי אין טעמא קאמ' ומיהו עשה סייג לדבריך הק' הר' משה מאיברא דהא פרישנא לעיל בריש מכילתין דהאי דבעי מאי טעמא דשמאי היינו משום דלא עביד סייג והא קא משני דמשום חזקה לא בעי למעבד סייג. א"כ מאי תו קאמר ליה הלל לשמאי מיהו עשה סייג לדבריך. וכן טעמא דמרגשת נמי פרשי' לעיל משום סייג ושמאי נמי השיבו לפי דבריו דלדידך נמי משום טעמא דפריה ורביה ראוי למנוע שלא לעשות סייג: **טהרות** הראשונות קרי להו ראשונות לפי שכשנמצא השרץ כבר ניטלו הטהרות. ודוקא נמצא השרץ בזוית אחרת וטעמא דר' יוחנן משום דאיפשר שהיה שם שרץ ולא ראהו. וכגון שהקופה הרבה רחבה אבל בקופה קטנה מודה ר' יוחנן דטהורות. אע"ג דלקמן בדלי שהוא קטן ולא אמרינן אם איתא דהוה ביה שרץ מעיקרא הוה חזי ליה. משום דבשעה ששופך המים מן הדלי לא אסיק אדעתיה שיעלה שרץ עם המים אבל כשמשתמש טהרות עם הקופה נזהר יפה לראות שלא יהא

*) עד כאן שייך לע"א

א) נראה דצ"ל א"כ אכתי איכא למיפרך לר"ש אי מה תחילת טומאה. ב) נראה דחסר כאן וצ"ל ונראה דלהאי לישנא נמי צריך טעמא דהעמד אשה על חזקתה.

כי פליגי חזקיה ור' יוחנן — בקופה בדוקה. מר סבר: הא בדקה. ומר סבר: אאימור, עם סילוק ידו נפל. והא דומיא דאשה קתני, ואשה בדוקה היא! כיון דשכיחי בה דמים — כשאינה בדוקה דמיא. ואיבעית אימא: כי מודו שמאי והלל — בקופה שאינה מכוסה, כי פליגי חזקיה ורבי יוחנן — בבקופה מכוסה. מכוסה, היכי נפל? כגון שתשמישה ע"י כסוי. והא דומיא דאשה קתני, ואשה מכוסה היא! כיון דשכיחי בה דמים — כשאין מכוסה דמיא. ואיבעית אימא: כי מודו שמאי והלל — בזוית קופה, כי פליגי חזקיה ורבי יוחנן — בזוית בית. והא קופה קאמר! גה"ק: קופה שנשתמשו בה טהרות בזוית בית זו, וטלטלוה בזוית אחרת, ונמצא שרץ בזוית אחרת. חזקיה סבר: לא מחזקינן טומאה ממקום למקום, ורבי יוחנן סבר: דמחזקינן. ומי מחזקינן? והתנן: *נגע באחד בלילה, ואינו יודע אם חי אם מת, ולמחר השכים ומצאו מת — ר"מ מטהר, וחכמים המטמאין, שכל הטמאות כשעת מציאתן. ותני עלה: וכשעת מציאתן, ובמקום מציאתן! וכי תימא: הני מילי — לשרוף, אבל לתלות — זתלינן. ומי תלינן? והתנן: *חמחט שנמצאת מלאה חלודה או שבורה — טהורה, שכל הטמאות כשעת מציאתן. ואמאי? לימא: האי מעיקרא — מחט מעלייתא היא, והשתא הוא דהעלה חלודה! ועוד, *תנן: טמצא שרץ שרוף על גבי הזיתים, וכן מטלית *המהומהם — טהור, שכל הטמאות כשעת מציאתן! וכי תימא: כשעת מציאתן — בין לקולא בין לחומרא ובמקום מציאתן. אבל שלא במקום מציאתן — משרף לא שרפינן, מתלא תלינן, *והתנן: *) יככר ע"ג הדף, ומדף טמא מונח תחתיו, אע"פ שאם נפלה א"א אלא א"כ נגעה — טהורה, שאני אומר: אדם טהור נכנס לשם ונטלה, עד שיאמר: "ברי לי שלא נכנס אדם שם", וא"ר אלעזר: כלא נצרכה אלא למקום מדרון! התם כדקתני טעמא, שאני

[נ"ל ודחו]

*) תוספתא לטהרות (דף תשעז פ"א) פ"ד

**רש"י**

והא דומיא דאשה קתני. בההיא דהלל ושמאי דקתני "מה הפרש בין זו לזו". ואשה בדוקה היא. מקודם לכן, דהא כל שחרית וערבית היא בודקת, אפ"ה טהרות דקופה טמאות, וקשיא לחזקיה. כשאינה בדוקה דמיא. וקופה נמי, כשאינה בדוקה עסקינן. ואיבעית אימא. הא והא בבדוקה, אלא דשמאי והלל כשאינה מכוסה, ופיה מלמעלה. הלכך, איכא למימר: עם סילוק ידיו נפלו. וחזקיה במכוסה, מש"ה מטהר. מכוסה. בתמיה: היכי נפל האי שרץ, והיכי איסתפק בה השתא? שתשמישה ע"י כסוי. כשהוא רוצה להכניס לתוכה ולהוציא מתוכה, מגלה ומכסה אותה. הלכך, חזקיה סבר: כל זמן שהטהרות בתוכה, נזהר בה וכסה. והשתא, לאחר שניטלו ממנה, הסיח דעתו משמירתה, ולא נזהר לכסותה, ונפל. ור' יוחנן סבר: חיישינן שמא כשגילה להשתמש בה, בעוד שהטהרות בתוכה נפל. מכוסה היא. דלא נפיל בה דם מעלמא, וקופה דכוותה במכוסה עסקי' ואפ"ה טמאה, וקשיא לחזקיה. בזוית בית. כדמפרש ואזיל: שטלטלה לקופה בזוית אחרת, לאחר שניטלו טהרות ממנה. ממקום למקום. דלא אמרינן: מאידך זוית הוה בה שרץ עם הטהרות, אלא אמרינן: לאחר שהביאה כאן נפל בה. ובמקום מציאתן. אם מצאו שחרית מת באותו מקום שנגע בו בלילה — טמא, אבל מצאו במקום אחר מת — טהור, ולא אמרינן: כי היכי דהכא מת, התם נמי הוה מת במקומו הראשון. לשרוף. דלא מחזקינן טומאה ודאית ממקום למקום לשרוף עליה תרומה. אבל מתלא תלינן. דהרי משמע במקום מציאתן הוא, דחכמים מטמאין טומאה ודאי. אבל שלא במקום מציאתן, טומאתן הוה ספק. ור' יוחנן נמי, לתלות קאמר. חלודה. רדולי"א. או שבורה. (א) ע"ג טהרות, ומכיר בה שהיא טמאה. טהורה מלטמא. טהרות שנמצאת עליהן. ולא אמרינן: שלמה נפלה עליהם, וטמאתם, ואח"כ נשברה. אלא אמרינן: שבורה או חלודה, כאשר (ג) היתה עתה, נפלה עליהם. אלמ' כל הטמאות כשעת מציאתן מחזקי' להו, ואפי' תלייה ליכא, דקתני "טהורה". וקס"ד דה"ה נמי למקום מציאתן דמחזקינן להו בטומאה, ולא מספקינן לה במקום אחר אפילו לתלות, וקשיא לר' יוחנן. נמצא שרוף. השרץ. מטלית. טלית של זב היתה. *)(המהומהם). הבלויה. מצאה בלויה ע"ג זיתים. טהורה. מלטמא הזיתים, דאמרינן: הכי נפלה עלייהו לאחר שבלתה וטהרה מטומאתה. אלמא, לא מחזקינן טומאה משעה לשעה אפי' לתלות, דקתני "טהורה", וה"ה ממקום למקום. וכי תימא לא דמי. דהכא משום הכי טהור, משום דשעת מציאתה ומקום מציאתה בטהרה הואי. דבתר שעת מציאתן אזלינן בין לקולא בין לחומרא. בין לקולא — כי הכא, גבי מחט ומטלית לאחזוקי בטהורה ודאי. בין לחומרא — כגון נגע באחד בלילה, לאחזוקי בטומאה ודאית. ושלא במקום מציאתן. דליכא רגלים לדבר כולי האי — משרף לא שרפינן, מתלא תלינן. הדף. קרש מונח על גבי יתדות בכותל. ומדף טמא. בגד טמא מונח תחת הדף בקרקע. בת"כ קרי "מדף" לעליונו של זב. ומדף — לשון טומאה קלה הוא, כדלקמן. וס"ד השתא, שהוא עליונו של זב דטמא מדאורייתא. ומיהו טומאתו קלה משל מדרס, דלא הוי אב הטומאה לטמא אדם וכלים. ובא ומצא את הככר ע"ג הקרקע מן הבגד והלאה. ונטלה. ולא נפלה על גבי המדף, שנטלו מעל הדף והניחה לארץ. לא נצרכה. האי "שאני אומר". אלא למקום מדרון. שאע"פ שהדף שהככר עליה מקום מדרון, וראויה הככר ליפול, ואם נפלה — נגעה בבגד, אפילו הכי טהורה, שאני אומר כו'. אלמא, לא מחזקינן טומאה ממקום למקום, דנימא: מעל הדף נפל ונתגלגל לכאן. שאני

*) [נ"ל המהוהא]

**תוספות**

כי פליגי חזקיה ור' יוחנן בקופה בדוקה. וא"ת: דבנגע באחד בלילה אמרו חכמים: אם ראוהו חי מבערב — טהור, שספק טומאה ברה"ר — ספקו טהור. משמע דברה"י, אפילו ראוהו חי — טמא. והשתא הך קופה, היכי *דמיא? אי ברה"ר — מאי טעמא דרבי יוחנן דמטמא? ואי ברה"י — מ"ט דחזקיה דמטהר? וי"ל: דברה"י איירי וחזקיה יפרש הברייתא דבראוהו חי מבערב — טהור אפילו ברה"י, וספק טומאה ברה"ר טהור דקאמר, היינו דהוי כאילו הוא ספק טומאה ברה"ר, כיון שהיא בדוקה תחלה. ואגב דרישא נקט האי לישנא במילתיה דר"מ, היכא דלא ראוהו חי מבערב מתחלה, דקתני בתוספתא "ר"מ מטהר ברה"ר", נקט נמי במילתייהו דחכמים בסיפא "רה"ר".

והא אשה מכוסה היא. פי' רש"י: דלא נפל בה דם מעלמא. וקשה: דכ"ש שהיא טמאה, דאין לתלות בדם אחר אלא בא מגופה! לכך י"ל: "מכוסה היא" — שהמקום סתום, וכשהדם יוצא — נפתח, והיה לה להרגיש. וא"ת: והא בקופה בדוקה פליגי, דאי לאו הכי מאי מועיל כשהיא מכוסה. וא"כ, מאי פריך "והא אשה מכוסה", מאי מועיל כסוי, כיון דלאו כבדוקה דמיא? וי"ל: שרוצה ליישב אפי' אי חשיב לה כבדוקה.

שכל הטמאות כשעת מציאתן. לעיל(א) פי' דהיינו דוקא לקדשים. והא דמחט שנמצאת מלאה חלודה דטהורה, דכל הטמאות כשעת מציאתן אפילו להקל, לאו משום דהוי כשעת מציאתן דאורייתא, אלא משום דמוקי הטהרות אחזקתייהו. וא"ת: מאי פריך מככר הנתונה על גבי דף, דלמא בככר של חולין איירי? וי"ל: דאפילו בחולין לא היה לנו לעשות כל כך, לתלות באדם טהור, שהנפילה נראית יותר. והיה לנו לטמא ממקום למקום, כיון דלא אפשר ליפול אלא אם כן נגע, אי בשום מקום אנו מחמירין אפילו בקדשים.

ומי תלינן והא אנן תנן כו' וא"ת: והיא הנותנת, משום דאזלינן בתר שעת מציאתה לגמרי אפילו ממקום למקום לתלות לכך מחט שנמצאת מלאה חלודה טהורה לגמרי ואע"ג דמצינן למימר דהיינו דקאמר וכ"ת כשעת מציאתן לגמרי בין לקולא בין לחומרא מ"מ מאי ס"ד דמקשה? וי"ל: דס"ד כיון דמחמיר כל כך בטומאה לתלות אפי' ממקום למקום(ג) [ע"כ אינו טעם גמור דדוקא בקדשים הוא ומשום חומרא] א"כ במחט לא היה לו לטהר לגמרי משום שעת מציאתה אלא הוה ליה למימר השתא הוא דעלתה חלודה. ככר הנתונה על גבי דף. וא"ת: שאני התם, שאין בו דעת לישאל, כדאמר בסמוך? וי"ל: דפריך אי בשום מקום אנו מחמירין ממקום למקום, אפילו בקדשים לא היה לנו לעשות ספק ולתלות באדם טהור, דיותר יש לתלות בנפילה. שאני אומר אדם טהור. וא"ת: דהכא תלינן באדם טהור, ובפ"ק דחולין (דף ט:) גבי "צלוחית שהניחה מכוסה ובא ומצאה מגולה" תלינן באדם טמא, וכן פ"ק דפסחים (דף י:) גבי "קורדום"? ותירץ ר"ת: דגבי כלים הנמצאין דווקא גזרינן טומאה, משום דאית להו טהרה במקוה, וליכא פסידא. אבל באוכלין, דאיכא פסידא, דלית להו טהרה במקוה — לא החמירו. אי נמי: הכא מוכחא מילתא דאדם טהור הסירה בכוונה, כדי שלא תפול על מדף טמא. אבל בעלמא — טמאין, בין באוכלין בין בכלים, דליכא למימר: אדם בכוונה עשה לתקנתא.

ג)הכא נמי נימא עורב אתא ושדא. אף על גב דאדם שנשתמש בקופה יש בו דעת לישאל, מכל מקום פריך: כיון דעל ידי תליית אדם טהור, אין אתה חושבו ספק, אף על גב שהנפילה נראה יותר. אם כן, הרבה מצוי הוא, שאדם טהור בא לשם, הכא נמי נימא: אתא עורב ושדא, ולא הוי ספק.

לא נצרכה אלא למקום מדרון. פירוש: כשהמדף במקום מדרון, דאפילו נפל הככר על גבי מדף — לא נשאר לשם. אבל אם המדף בקרקע שוה — פשיטא דטהור.

א) בריש מכילתין ד"ה מעל"ע. ב) נ"י כ"י ג) דבור זה שייך לע"ב

ואיבעית

**תוספי הרא"ש**

דאשה בדוקה והוי כראוה חי חדא כיון דשכיחי בה דמים לאו בדוקה היא כדאמרינן לעיל בשמעתין. ועוד אפי' בראוהו חי מטמאינן ברשות היחיד לכל דבר. ונ"ל דהך דכל הטמאות כשעת מציאתן הוי כמו מעת לעת דדוקא לקדשים או לתרומה למאן דאית ליה וכן פלוגתא דחזקיה ור' יוחנן דמייתי' עלה הא דהלל ושמאי וכן המדלה עשרה [דליים מים] שצריך לאותן מים להדחת בשר קדשים או לבשל או ללוש מנחות וכמ"ד חולין שנעשו על טהרת הקדש כקדש דמו. וכי תימא אכתי תקשי מאי שנא הכא דשורפין ומעת לעת דוקא לתלות. וי"ל דמשום פריה ורביה לא רצו להחמיר לשרוף. וכן שמאי אע"ג דאית ליה כשעת מציאתן מדמקשה ליה הלל מקופה מטהר לגמרי במעת לעת משום בטול פריה ורביה וכ"ת והיכי מקילין לתלות היכא דאימ' למה לי טומאה מטעם שעת מציאתן והא שעת מציאתן דאורייתא הוא תדע דתולין בו בין להקל בין להחמיר י"ל דהא דאמר והא דאמרינן בשעת מציאתן אפי' להקל גבי מחט ושרץ שרוף לאו משום דשעת מציאתן דאוריית' אלא משום דמוקמינן טהרות אחזקתן: ותני עלה בשעת מציאתן ובמקום מציאתן. תמיה לי מאי קא פריך שאני הכא דרגלים לדבר דכיון שלא מצאו במקומו שחי היה במקום שנגע בו ובא לזה המקום ומת שם. ושמא משמע ליה דדוקא ובמקום מציאתן אפי' ידוע שעל ידי אדם או ד"א ניטלטל ובא לכאן: (נכתב על הגליון) דמהוהה. פר"ח כגון טלית שנשרפה משני צדדיה ונשארה כגון קורי עכביש (ע"כ) והתנן ככר כו'. תי' לפי מאי דפרישית בשעת מציאתן היינו דוקא לקדשים או לתרומה מאי פריך דלמא הכא מיירי בככר של חולין וי"ל מ"מ דייק שפיר מדמטהרינן הכא אפי' במקום מדרון שהיה ראוי להחמיר ש"מ

דבעלמא לא מחזקי טומאה ממקום למקום אפילו בקדשים וא"ת אכתי מאי קשיא ליה האי דמטהרי' הכא היינו משום שאין בו דעת לישאל כדמסקינן וי"ל דלכולהו לישני דאוקימנא פלוגתייהו בשאינה בדוקה מטמא ר' יוחנן אפי' ברשות הרבים תדע מדפריך (לנ"ב) מכל הטומאות בשעת מציאתן ותני עלה ובמקום מציאתן הא שלא במקום מציאתן לא. ומאי קושיא דלמא משום דאיירי ברשות הרבים כדקתני בתוספתא מוקי לה דוקא במקום מציאתן אלא ודאי אפילו ברשות הרבים מטמא ר' יוחנן אפילו שלא במקום מציאתן וא"כ ה"ה נמי בדבר שאין בו דעת לישאל: שאני אומר אדם. הכא תלינן באדם טהור. וכן פרק כיסוי הדם גבי רוב תינוקות מטפחין לפי המפ' מטפחין בעיסה המיעוט שאין מטפחין תלינן שאדם טהור נתן לו הבצק וקשה דבפרק קמא דפסחים גבי קרדרום שאבד בבית אמרי' שאני אומר אדם טמא נכנס לשם ונטלו. וכן פ"ק דחולין גבי צלוחית שהניחה מגולה ומצאה מכוסה טמאה שאני אומר אדם טמא נכנס לשם וכיסה. ותירץ ר"ת דגבי כלים החמירו משום דגזרו אספק כלים הנמצאים ואחמור בספק כלים יותר מבספק אוכלין משום

**תוספי הרא"ש**

יהא שם שרץ במקום שנשתמשו: המדלה עשרה דלאים. תימה דשבק מתני' ומייתי ברייתא דיש משנה כיוצא בה בפרק [ד' מ"ד] דמסכת טהרות המדלה עשרה דלאין ונמצא שרץ באחד מהן הוא טמא וכולן טהורין. וי"ל דהתם לא קתני בזה אחר זה ומיירי במדלה עשרה דליין בבת אחת וקמ"ל דלא חיישינן שמא נגעו זה בזה דלאין בשרץ ונטמאו שאר משום דהוי ספק טומאה צפה על פני המים ואפי' ברשות היחיד טהור כדאיתא בסוטה ובנזיר ואהך מתני' לא שייך למימר ר' ינאי במילתיה א"נ במסכת כלים מבור של יין דלא קתני התם מים. ולא קתני נמי המדלה בברייתא ולא חיישינן שמא היה השרץ בכלי ראשון ולהך שנויא קשה למה נקט י' דליים אפילו בדלי אחת הוה מצי לאשמועינן דלא חיישינן א)שמא היה השרץ בבור ונטמא הוייז: כי פליגי חזקיה ור' יוחנן בקופה בדוקה. קשה לר"י אי ברשות הרבים מאי טעמא דרבי יוחנן דמטמא ואי ברשות היחיד מאי טעמא דחזקיה דמטהר הא תנא גבי נגע באחד בלילה דמודים חכמים בראוהו חי מבערב דטהור מפני שזה ספק רשות הרבים משמע הא רשות היחיד טמא וי"ל דהיינו טעמא דחזקיה דמטהר אפילו ברשות היחיד בקופה בדוקה משום דאיכא נמי למיתלי אם איתא דהוה שרץ מעיקרא הוה חזי ליה ומיהו טעם גמור לא הוי לטהר מגופה אתא וי"ל מהאי טעמא: ואשה מכוסה היא. פרש"י ולא נפיל דמים מעלמא וקשה דכ"ש דאמרינן דמכוסה היא שהמקור סתום ובית החיצון כמכוסה דמי שאין רגיל ליכנס בו דם מן המקור אם לא שתרגיש: וחכמים מטמאין שכל הטמאות בשעת מציאתן וא"ת מאי שנא מעת לעת שבגדה דלא אמרינן כל הטמאות בשעת מציאתן כמו שעתה נמצא הדם בבית החיצון גם קודם לכן היה בבית החיצון אם היתה בודקת עצמה ותטמא אפי' חולין ואפי' לשרוף כדמטמאינן הכא. וכי תימא משום דאשה

א) עי' כתוס סד"ה והתניא ב) ע"כ שייך לעמוד הקודם.

**עין משפט נר מצוה**

ט א ב ג ד מיי' פי"ז מהלכות שאר אבות הטומאה הלכה ב:
י ה מיי' שם פי"ח הלכ' יז:
נ"ל רמ"ה
יא ו מיי' שם ופט"ז הלכה ו הלכה ג:
יב ז מיי' שם פי"ג הלכ' ב:
יג ח ט מיי' שם פט"ז הלכה ה:
יד י כ מיי' פט"ו שם הלכה ז:

**מסורת הש"ס**

עירובין לה: טהרות פ"ה מ"ז

טהרות פ"ג מ"ה

שם פ"ט מ"ט [לקמן נו.]

[נ"ל המהוהא מלשון תוהו ובהו ר"ל דבר שאין בו ממש תי"ט פכ"ד דכלים משנה י"ג בשם הערוך ובכ"מ... עיין פי' הר"ש טהרות ... לקמן נו. איתא המהוהא]

**הגהות הב"ח**

(א) רש"י ד"ה או שבורה על גבי. נ"ב ובמשנה ה' פ"ג דטהרות פי' הברטנורה שאינה מכירה ואינה מונחת ע"ג טהרות ונ"מ היא אם חוזר לטומאה ישנה: (ב) ד"ה טהורה מלטמא וכו' כאשר היא עתה נפלה וכו' מספקינן להו במקום:

**גליון הש"ס**

גמ' ור"י סבר מחזקינן. עי' טהרות פ"ט מ"ט נמצא בגג המעטן טהור. וצ"ע:

שאני אומר: "אדם טהור נכנס לשם, ונטלה". הכא נמי – נימא: "עורב אתא, ושדא"! אדם דבכוונה – אמרינן, עורב דשלא בכוונה – לא אמרינן. מכדי, האי ככר – ספק טומאה ברה"י הוא, [א]וכל ספק טומאה ברה"י – ספקה טמא! משום דהוי דבר שאין בו דעת לישאל, *[ב]וכל דבר שאין בו דעת לישאל, בין ברה"ר בין ברשות היחיד – ספקו טהור. ואב"א: הכא בטומאה דרבנן. [ג]דיקא נמי, דקתני "מדף", כדכתיב °"עלה נדף". § "וחכ"א לא כדברי זה" כו'. § ת"ר: וחכ"א לא כדברי זה ולא כדברי זה. לא כדברי שמאי – שלא עשה סייג לדבריו, ולא כדברי הלל – שהפריז על מדותיו. אלא: מעת לעת ממעטת על יד מפקידה לפקידה, ומפקידה לפקידה – ממעטת על יד מעת לעת. מעת לעת ממעטת על יד מפקידה לפקידה, [ד]כיצד? בדקה עצמה באחד בשבת ומצאת טהורה, וישבה שני ושלישי ולא בדקה, ולרביעי בדקה ומצאה טמאה – אין אומרים: תטמא מפקידה לפקידה, אלא מעת לעת. ומפקידה לפקידה ממעטת על יד מעת לעת, כיצד? בדקה עצמה בשעה ראשונה ומצאת טהורה, וישבה לה שניה ושלישית ולא בדקה, ולרביעית בדקה ומצאה טמאה – אין אומרים: תטמא מעת לעת, אלא מפקידה לפקידה. פשיטא, כיון דבדקה עצמה בשעה ראשונה ומצאת טהורה – לא מטמינן לה מעת לעת! איידי דתנא "מעל"ע ממעטת על יד מפקידה לפקידה", תנא נמי "מפקידה לפקידה ממעטת על יד מעת לעת". אמר רבה: מאי טעמייהו דרבנן – אשה מרגשת בעצמה. א"ל אביי: אם כן, תהא דיה שעתה! ורבה – *לחדודי לאביי הוא דבעי. אלא מאי טעמייהו דרבנן? כי הא דאמר רב יהודה, אמר שמואל: [ה]חכמים תקנו להן לבנות ישראל שיהו בודקות עצמן שחרית וערבית. שחרית – להכשיר טהרות של לילה, וערבית – להכשיר טהרות של יום. וזו הואיל ולא בדקה – הפסידה עונה. מאי "עונה"? עונה יתירה. א"ל רב פפא לרבא: והא זימנין משכחת לה ג' עונות במעת לעת! השוו חכמים מדותיהן, שלא תחלוק במעת לעת. (א) איבעית אימא: *שלא יהא חוטא נשכר. מאי בינייהו? איכא בינייהו: דאתניסה ולא בדקה. § "כל אשה שיש לה וסת" [וכו']. § לימא מתני' ר' דוסא היא ולא רבנן, *) דתניא, *ר"א אומר: ארבע נשים דיין שעתן, בתולה, מעוברת, מניקה, וזקנה. *ר' דוסא אומר: כל אשה שיש לה וסת – דיה שעתה! אפילו תימא רבנן, עד כאן לא פליגי רבנן עליה דר' דוסא – אלא שלא בשעת וסתה, אבל בשעת וסתה – מודו ליה, ומתניתין בשעת וסתה – ודברי הכל. מכלל דר' דוסא – אפילו שלא בשעת וסתה אמר. מאן תנא להא דת"ר: אשה שיש לה וסת כתמה טמא למפרע, שאם תראה שלא בשעת וסתה – מטמאה מעת לעת, נימא רבנן היא ולא רבי דוסא? אפילו תימא רבי דוסא, ע"כ לא פליג רבי דוסא עלייהו דרבנן – אלא בשעת וסתה, אבל שלא בשעת וסתה – מודי להו. ומתניתין – בשעת וסתה, ור' דוסא היא, וברייתא

*) [משום פלוגתא דר' דוסא ליתא במשנה שפיר גרסי' דתניא]

תורה אור: °ויקרא כו

**רש"י**

שאני אומר כו'. אבל בקופה, הא נמצא שרץ לתוכה, ושעת מליאתה טמאה היא. עורב איתי ושדא. לאחר שטלטל הקופה לזוית אחרת, ובזוית הראשונה לא היה. מכדי האי ככר ספק טומאה הוא. ספק נגע ספק לא נגע. אבל אקופה לא פריך, דהא לא איתחזיק טומאה בזוית של בית הראשון. וכי היכי דפריך אככר, מצי למיפרך אמחט ואמטלית, ולשנויי כדמשני. שאין בו דעת לישאל. אם נגע אם לא נגע. ספקו טהור. דהא (ב) קיימא לן: ספקו – טמא ברה"י משום דגמרינן מסוטה, שסוטה יש בה דעת לישאל אם נטמאה אם לאו. בטומאה דרבנן. כגון הנך מעלות ד"חומר בקדש" (חגיגה כ.) בגדי פרושין – מדרס לאוכלי תרומה (שם יח.) ומש"ה אפילו ברה"י – ספקו טהור. עלה נדף. דבר הקל. ה"נ טומאה קלה. אית דאמרי: "מדף" – עליונו של זב, ושבוש הוא. דעליונו של זב מטמא כבר מן התורה, בפרק "בנות כותים" (לקמן דף לג.) נתקו הכתוב מטומאה חמורה לטומאה קלה, לומר לך דאינו מטמא אלא אוכלין ומשקין. ומעיקרא כי אותביניה, הכי הוה ס"ד דעליונו של זב הוא. שהפריז. שהגדיל והרחיב מדתו, (ג) שמטמאה למפרע מפקידה לפקידה. איידי דתנא מעת לעת ממעטת על יד מפקידה לפקידה. דאיצטריך למיתניה, דלא תימא: עם סילוק ידיה ראתה באחד בשבת, תנא נמי כו'. מאי טעמא דרבנן. מאי האי שיעורא דמעת לעת. דבשלמא מפקידה לפקידה דהלל ניחא, דשמא עם סילוק ידיה ראתה, אלא מעת לעת מאי שיעורא הוא? אשה מרגשת בעצמה. ואם איתא דעם סילוק ידיה ראתה – הות מרגשת. אם כן. דאשה מרגשת. תהא דיה שעתה. ואפילו מעת לעת אמאי מטמא למפרע. חכמים תקנו להן וכו'. מתני' היא (לקמן יא.): פעמים היא צריכה להיות בודקת כו'. שחרית. להכשיר טהרות של לילה, להוציא מכלל ספק טומאה, שאם תמצא טהורה – תדע שלא ראתה בלילה. ולכשתמצא ערבית טמאה – יצאו אלו מספק. וזו. שבדקה עכשיו ומצאה טמאה, והרי ימים רבים שלא בדקה. הפסידה עונה. כל טהרות שנתעסקה בהן בעונה הזאת הפסידתה. מאי עונה. הרי שתי עונות הן, היום והלילה, דהיינו מעת לעת. כגון אם מצאה ערבית טמאה – הפסידתה כל טהרות של יום ושל אמש. ומשני: עונה יתירה. הפסידתה משום קנס, שהרי הפסידתה טהרות של אמש משום קנס. אבל טהרות של יום – לאו קנס הוא, דאי נמי בדקה שחרית ומצאתה טהורה, וערבית ומצאתה טמאה – הפסידה טהרות של יום, דהיינו "מפקידה לפקידה ממעטת על יד מעת לעת". ג' עונות. כגון אם לא בדקה ימים רבים, ובדקה בצהרים – דמטמאין לה מעת לעת, דהוה להו ג' עונות: היום, אמש, ואתמול למפרע עד צהרים. והשתא קנסינן לה שתי עונות, ורבנן: חדא הוא דקנסו, ותו לא. ומשני: חכמים השוו מדותיהם. שלא תחלוק במעת לעת, זמן קבוע וחלוט נתנו לה למפרע. ואפילו עשתה אותו זמן מג' עונות, כגון שבדקה בצהרים, ולא בדקה שחרית ואמש – לא רצו לגרוע ולמעט זמנה הקבוע לה, אלא פסקו דבריהם, שלא תתן דברים לשיעורין. אב"א. להכי מטמינן לה מצהרים דאתמול, דאי אמרת לא נקנס אלא עונה יתירה – נמצא חוטא נשכר. דאילו זו שלא בדקה עצמה ימים רבים, ובדקה לה היום שחרית – היתה נקנסת מעת לעת שלם. ומפני שאיחרה עד הצהרים, והוסיפה לחטוא – לא תפסיד אלא לילה וחצי יום. דאיתניסה. שנאנסה שחרית ולא בדקה. ללישנא ד"חוטא נשכר" – ליכא, דהא נאנסה. ללישנא ד"לא תחלוק" – איכא. ד' נשים דיין שעתן. מפני שדמיהן מסולקים, ואין דם מצוי בהן. בתולה. בתולת דמים, שלא ראתה דם מימיה, ואפילו היא נשואה קרי לה "בתולה". והכי מפרש במתני' וכולה מפרש במתני'. רבי דוסא אומר כו'. ופליגי רבנן בעלמא עליה. אלא שלא בשעת וסתה. דכיון דראתה שלא בזמנה, איכא למיחש דלמא מקמי הכי הוה, דהא ליכא למימר: אורח בזמנו בא. כתמה טמא למפרע. עד שעת הכבוס, אף על גב דבראייתה – דייה שעתה, מטמאינן כתמה למפרע. דהא אשכחינן בראייה טומאה למפרע, שאם תראה שלא בשעת וסתה – מטמאה למפרע. לימא רבנן היא. דאמרי: שלא בשעת וסתה – מטמאה למפרע. ולוקמא

**תוספות**

ואיבעית אימא בטומאה דרבנן. לא בא לתרץ דאפילו אי הוי דבר שיש בו דעת לישאל דאתי שפיר, דמה לו לתרץ זה, כיון דאמת הוא דככר ומדף אין בהם דעת לישאל. אלא מתרץ: אפי' אין לתלות באדם טהור כמו בנפילה, לפי שהנפילה קרובה לודאי, כמו שסובר המקשה, אתי שפיר. דאיירי בטומאה דרבנן, ואיירי בבגדי עם הארץ לפרושים. ורש"י דפי' בבגדי פרושים, דהוי מדרס לאוכלי תרומה, נראה שסובר שעתה בא לתרץ אפי' בשיש בו דעת לישאל. ולכך לא רצה לפרש בבגדי ע"ה, לפרושים, משום דהתם לא היינו מקילין. כדאמרינן בשבת פ"ק (דף טו:) דעל ו' ספיקות שורפין את התרומה, וחשיב בגדי ע"ה, דעל ודאי מגען – שורפין, ועל ספק מגען – תולין. (וחשיב בגדי ע"ה). [ולפי שיטתו היה יכול לפרש דס"ד דמקשה ד"מדף" היינו בגדי עם הארץ. ושמא לא פירש כן, משום דבת"כ איקרי "מדף" עליונו של זב. וכן במסכת זבין פ"ה [מ"ב] ובעדיות פ"ו [מ"ג].

*כל אשה שיש לה וסת דיה שעתה. – תימה: למה הפסיק ושנה "המשמשת בעדים"? ה"ל למיתני מיד "כיצד דיה שעתה"? וי"ל: דקמ"ל, אע"ג דיש לה וסת – צריכה לשמש בעדים, כדאמר בגמרא. אע"ג דתנן לקמן (דף יא.): "אע"ג שאמרו דיה שעתה – צריכה להיות בודקת", (ד) הכא תנא ליה לאשמועינן: דאותה בדיקה חשובה היא למעט מעת לעת, דהוי חדוש, כדאמרי' בגמרא. ולקמן, היינו בד' נשים דדיין שעתן. והא דמשמע הכא דאפי' אותן דדיין שעתן צריכין בדיקה, ובשילהי "בנות כותים" (לקמן דף לח:) תנן דכל י"א שבין נדה לנדה הרי היא בחזקת טהרה, ומפרש בגמרא: דאינה צריכה בדיקה, ואפ"ה קאמר התם דמטמאה מעל"ע, בע"ה (ה) אפרש לשם.

וברייתא

**עין משפט נר מצוה**

טו א מיי' פט"ו מהל' שאר אבות הטומאה הלכה ח:

טז ב מיי' שם פט"ז הלכה ב:

יז ג מיי' פ"ו מהלכות משכב ומושב הלכה ג ע"ש בכ"מ וכפי' רש"י בשם אית דאמרי:

יח ד מיי' שם פ"ג הלכה ד:

יט ה מיי' פ"ד מהלכות משכב ומושב הלכה ז סמג לאוין קיא:

[שייך במשנה לעיל ב.]

**מסורת הש"ס**

[לקמן ה: סוטה כח:]

[ברכות לג: וש"נ]

[יבמות לב: וש"נ]

לקמן ז.

[לקמן טו:]

## תוספי הרא"ש

משום דכלים ליכא פסידא כולי האי שיש להם טהרה במקוה. ועי"ל דכל הני ניחא דאיכא למיתלי בטמא כמו בטהור כגון סתם עם הארץ אבל תינוק והך דהכא בשלמא טהור חשש שלא יטמא הככר והעיסה אלא טמא אמאי: **בטומאה** דרבנן. פרש"י כגון הנך מעלות דחומר בקדש בגדי פרושים מדרס לאוכלי תרומה ומה שלא פירש בגדי עם הארץ מדרס לפרושי' משום דבההיא שרפי' תרומה כדאמרי' פ"ק דשבת על ו' ספיקות שורפין את התרומה. על ספק בגדי עם הארץ וכיון דשרפינן עלייהו תרומה לא מקילינן בה לתלות באדם טהור ולפי סברא זו לא היה צריך רש"י לפרש בתחלת הסוגיא דס"ד דמדף הוי עליונו של זב דטמא מדאורייתא שהיה יכול לומר דס"ד דהיינו בגדי עם הארץ ושמא לא פי' כן אלא משום דבת"כ קרי לעליונו של זב מדף. ותנן נמי במס' זבין פ"ה והמדף מלמעלן ובמס' עדיות פ"ו שהחי עושה משכב ומושב מתחתיו לטמא אדם לטמא בגדים ועל גביו מדף לטמאות אוכלין ומשקין: **שהפריז.** בזיי"ן כמו פרזות תשב ירושלים ואי גרס הפרין בנו"ן יש לפרשו לשון גידול כמו מפרין על שדהו באיזהו נשך וכמו פורנא ליתמי: **מ"ט** דרבנן במעת לעת. והא דתניא המניח פירות מפריש עליהן תרומות ומעשרות מעות להיות מפריש עליהן מעשר שני מפריש עליהן בחזקת שהן קיימין ואם אבדו הרי זה חושש מעת לעת בין למ"ד בגמ' מעת לעת של בדיקה בין למ"ד מעת לעת של הנחה לא שייך למיפרך מ"ט. דעם סילוק ידו לא שכיח דמיתבדי הלכך הוצרכו חכמים ליתן שיעור כפי הנראה בעיניהן: **כל** אשה שיש לה וסת דייה שעתה. סדר המשנה ק"ק דמעיקרא הוה ליה למיתני המשמשת והדר כיצד ולההוא לישנא דמפרש בגמ' ומשמשת ניחא דקאי אכל אשה שיש לה וסת אי נמי תכף לדברי חכמים בעי לאשמועינן דלא איירי אלא באשה שאין לה וסת:

## הגהות הב"ח

(א) גמ' ואיבעית אימא שלא יהא חוטא: (ב) רש"י ד"ה ספקו טהור דהא דקיי"ל: (ג) ד"ה שהפריז וכו' מדתו שתטמא למפרע: (ד) תום' ד"ה כל אשה וכו' להיות בודקת כו' הכא: (ה) בסה"ד אפרש לשם. נ"ב בדף לט בד"ה והיולדת:

## גליון הש"ס

**רש"י** ד"ה שהפריז שהגדיל והרחיב. כמו פרזות תשב ירושלים (זכריה ב') רש"י בב"מ סט: **ד"ה** מפרין:

וברייתא

וּבָרַיְיתָא — דִּבְרֵי הַכֹּל. וְלוֹקְמָא אִיפְּכָא! כֵּיוָן דְּאִיכָּא לְאוֹקוּמֵי לְקוּלָּא וּלְחוּמְרָא — לְחוּמְרָא מוֹקְמִינַן. קָתָנֵי: "שֶׁאִם תִּרְאֶה שֶׁלֹּא בְּשַׁעַת וְסָתָהּ — מְטַמְּאָה מֵעֵת לְעֵת", טַעְמָא — דְּאִשָּׁה שֶׁיֵּשׁ לָהּ וֶסֶת הוּא, דִּפְלִיגִי רַבָּנַן בֵּין כִּתְמָהּ לִרְאִיָּיתָהּ, הָא שְׁאָר נָשִׁים שֶׁאָמְרוּ חֲכָמִים דַּיָּין שְׁעָתָן — כִּתְמָן כִּרְאִיָּיתָן. מַנִּי? רַבִּי חֲנִינָא בֶּן אַנְטִיגְנוֹס הִיא. דְּאָמַר רַב יְהוּדָה, אָמַר שְׁמוּאֵל מִשּׁוּם רַבִּי חֲנִינָא בֶּן אַנְטִיגְנוֹס: [א]כָּל הַנָּשִׁים — כִּתְמָן טָמֵא לְמַפְרֵעַ. [ב]וְנָשִׁים שֶׁאָמְרוּ חֲכָמִים דַּיָּין שְׁעָתָן — כִּתְמָן כִּרְאִיָּיתָן, חוּץ מִתִּינוֹקֶת שֶׁלֹּא הִגִּיעַ זְמַנָּהּ לִרְאוֹת שֶׁאֲפִילּוּ סְדִינִין שֶׁלָּהּ מְלוּכְלָכִין בְּדָם, אֵין חוֹשְׁשִׁין לָהּ. וּמִי אִית לֵיהּ לְרַבִּי חֲנִינָא כֶּתֶם כְּלָל? וְהַתַּנְיָא: כָּל הַנָּשִׁים כִּתְמָן טָמֵא, וְנָשִׁים שֶׁאָמְרוּ חֲכָמִים דַּיָּין שְׁעָתָן — כִּתְמָן טָמֵא. ר' חֲנִינָא בֶּן אַנְטִיגְנוֹס אוֹמֵר: נָשִׁים שֶׁאָמְרוּ חֲכָמִים דַּיָּין שְׁעָתָן — אֵין לָהֶן כֶּתֶם. מַאי לָאו: אֵין לָהֶן כֶּתֶם כְּלָל לֹא, אֵין לָהֶן כֶּתֶם לְמַפְרֵעַ, אֲבָל יֵשׁ לָהֶן כֶּתֶם מִכָּאן וּלְהַבָּא. מִכְּלָל דְּתַנָּא קַמָּא סָבַר: אֲפִי' לְמַפְרֵעַ? אִין, ר"מ הִיא, דְּמַחְמִיר גַּבֵּי כְּתָמִים. דְּתַנְיָא: כָּל הַנָּשִׁים — כִּתְמָן טָמֵא לְמַפְרֵעַ, וְנָשִׁים שֶׁאָמְרוּ חֲכָמִים דַּיָּין שְׁעָתָן — כִּתְמָן טָמֵא לְמַפְרֵעַ, דר"מ. רַבִּי חֲנִינָא בֶּן אַנְטִיגְנוֹס אוֹמֵר: נָשִׁים שֶׁאָמְרוּ חֲכָמִים דַּיָּין שְׁעָתָן — כִּתְמָן כִּרְאִיָּיתָן. וְתִינוֹקֶת שֶׁהִגִּיעַ זְמַנָּהּ לִרְאוֹת — יֵשׁ לָהּ כֶּתֶם, [ג]וְשֶׁלֹּא הִגִּיעַ זְמַנָּהּ לִרְאוֹת — אֵין לָהּ כֶּתֶם. וְאֵימָתַי הִגִּיעַ זְמַנָּהּ לִרְאוֹת? — [ד]מִשֶּׁהִגִּיעוּ יְמֵי הַנְּעוּרִים.§ "וְהַמְשַׁמֶּשֶׁת בְּעֵדִים" כו'.§ אָמַר רַב יְהוּדָה, אָמַר שְׁמוּאֵל: [ה]עֵד שֶׁלִּפְנֵי תַשְׁמִישׁ — אֵינוֹ מְמַעֵט כַּפְּקִידָה. מ"ט? אָמַר רַב קְטִינָא: מִתּוֹךְ שֶׁמְּהוּמָּה לְבֵיתָהּ. וְכִי מְהוּמָּה לְבֵיתָהּ, מַאי הָוֵי? מִתּוֹךְ שֶׁמְּהוּמָּה לְבֵיתָהּ — אֵינָהּ מַכְנֶסֶת לְחוֹרִין וְלִסְדָקִין. תְּנַן: הַמְשַׁמֶּשֶׁת בְּעֵדִים — הֲרֵי זוֹ כִּפְקִידָה, מַאי לָאו: חַד לִפְנֵי תַשְׁמִישׁ, וְחַד לְאַחַר תַּשְׁמִישׁ? לָא, אִידִי וְאִידִי — לְאַחַר תַּשְׁמִישׁ, וְאֶחָד לוֹ וְאֶחָד לָהּ. כִּדְתְנַן: *דֶּרֶךְ בְּנוֹת יִשְׂרָאֵל מְשַׁמְּשׁוֹת בִּשְׁנֵי עֵדִים, אֶחָד לוֹ וְאֶחָד לָהּ. הַאי מַאי? אִי אָמְרַתְּ בִּשְׁלָמָא חַד לִפְנֵי תַשְׁמִישׁ וְחַד לְאַחַר תַּשְׁמִישׁ — אִיצְטְרִיךְ, סד"א: מִתּוֹךְ שֶׁמְּהוּמָּה לְבֵיתָהּ — לָא בָּדְקָה שַׁפִּיר, קמ"ל הֲרֵי זוֹ כִּפְקִידָה. אֶלָּא אִי אָמְרַתְּ: אִידִי וְאִידִי לְאַחַר תַּשְׁמִישׁ — פְּשִׁיטָא! מַהוּ דְּתֵימָא: שֶׁמָּא תִּרְאֶה טִפַּת דָּם כְּחַרְדָּל, וְתַחְפֶּנָּה שִׁכְבַת זֶרַע — קמ"ל וְאִיבָּעֵית אֵימָא: [ו]שְׁתֵּי בְדִיקוֹת אַצְרְכוּהָ רַבָּנַן, חַד — לִפְנֵי תַשְׁמִישׁ, וְחַד — לְאַחַר תַּשְׁמִישׁ, וְכִי קָתָנֵי "הֲרֵי זוֹ כִּפְקִידָה" — אַלְּאַחַר תַּשְׁמִישׁ. וְהָא "הַמְשַׁמֶּשֶׁת" קָתָנֵי! תְּנֵי: "וּמְשַׁמֶּשֶׁת".§ "מְמַעֶטֶת עַל יַד מֵעֵת לְעֵת".§ הַשְׁתָּא מֵעֵת לְעֵת מְמַעֶטֶת, מִפְּקִידָה

**רש"י**

וְלוֹקְמָא אִיפְּכָא. כִּדְאוֹקְמֵיהּ מֵעִיקָּרָא, ומ"ט (א) הָדְרִי בָּהּ, הָא שַׁפִּיר מָצֵי לְאוֹקְמֵי מַתְנִי' — דִּבְרֵי הַכֹּל, וּבָרַיְיתָא — רַבָּנַן. לְקוּלָּא וּלְחוּמְרָא. מֵעִיקָּרָא אוֹקִימְנָא לְקוּלָּא, דְּבִשְׁעַת וְסָתָהּ — דִּבְרֵי הַכֹּל דַּיָּהּ שְׁעָתָהּ, וּבְשֶׁלֹּא בִּשְׁעַת וְסָתָהּ — פְּלִיגִי. וְהַשְׁתָּא אוֹקִימְנָא פְּלוּגְתָּא — בִּשְׁעַת וְסָתָהּ, וְאִיכָּא דְּמַחְמִיר וּמְטַמֵּא לָהּ לְמַפְרֵעַ. וְשֶׁלֹּא בִּשְׁעַת וְסָתָהּ ד"ה מְטַמְּאָה לְמַפְרֵעַ. קָתָנֵי שֶׁאִם תִּרְאֶה. כְּמוֹ "אָמַר מָר". שֶׁאִם תִּרְאֶה כו'. אַלְמָא דְּטַעַם דְּכִתְמָהּ מְטַמֵּא לְמַפְרֵעַ, מִשּׁוּם דְּאַשְׁכְּחַן בְּהוּ רְאִיָּיה טְמֵאָה לְמַפְרֵעַ, דְּהַשְׁתָּא לָא הֲוָה כִּתְמָהּ חָמוּר מֵרְאִיָּיתָהּ. וש"מ דְּאִשָּׁה דְּיֵשׁ לָהּ וֶסֶת, הוּא דִּפְלוּג רַבָּנַן בֵּין כִּתְמָהּ לִרְאִיָּיתָהּ: דְּכִתְמָהּ מְטַמֵּא לְמַפְרֵעַ, וּבִרְאִיָּיתָהּ דַּיָּהּ שְׁעָתָהּ, מִשּׁוּם דְּבִרְאִיָּיתָהּ שֶׁלֹּא בִּשְׁעַת וְסָתָהּ אַשְׁכַּחַן טוּמְאָה לְמַפְרֵעַ. הָא שְׁאָר נָשִׁים שֶׁאָמְרוּ חֲכָמִים דַּיָּין שְׁעָתָן. כְּגוֹן אַרְבַּע נָשִׁים, דְּלָא אַשְׁכְּחַן בְּהוּ רְאִיָּיה טְמֵאָ' לְמַפְרֵעַ, כִּתְמָן נַמִי אֵינוֹ טָמֵא לְמַפְרֵעַ. כִּתְמָן כִּרְאִיָּיתָן. מִכָּאן וְאֵילָךְ טְמֵאוֹת. חוּץ מִתִּינוֹקֶת כו'. דַּאֲפִילּוּ מִכָּאן וּלְהַבָּא, נַמִי לָא. וְהָא דְּאָמַר: בְּתוּלַת דָּמִים כִּתְמָן כִּרְאִיָּיתָן, דְּמִכָּאן וּלְהַבָּא מִיהָא טְמֵאָה, הַיְינוּ כְּשֶׁהִגִּיעַ זְמַנָּהּ לִרְאוֹת וְלֹא רָאֲתָה. מְלוּכְלָכִין בְּדָם. וְלָא יָדְעָה אִי אָתֵי מִגּוּפָהּ אִי לָא. אֵין חוֹשְׁשִׁין לָהּ. וַאֲפִילּוּ אֵין לָהּ בַּמֶּה לִתְלוֹת, דִּבְשׁוּק שֶׁל טַבָּחִים לֹא עָבְרָה, אִיכָּא לְמֵימַר: עָבְרָה, וְלָאו אַדַּעְתָּהּ. דְּהָא בְּגוּפָהּ אֵין לִתְלוֹת כָּל עִיקָּר, דִּכְתָמִין דְּרַבָּנַן נִינְהוּ, וְכִי גְּזוּר רַבָּנַן — בְּהִגִּיעַ זְמַנָּהּ, דְּדָם מָצוּי בָּהּ. אֲבָל בְּהָא — לָא גְּזוּר, הוֹאִיל וְאֵין בָּהּ דָּמִים. וּלְקַמָּן מְפָרֵשׁ אֵיזֶה הוּא זְמַנָּהּ, מִשֶּׁיַּגִּיעוּ יְמֵי הַנְּעוּרִים, שֶׁהֵבִיאָה שְׁתֵּי שְׂעָרוֹת, אוֹ בַּת י"ב שָׁנָה וְיוֹם אֶחָד וְאַע"פ שֶׁלֹּא הֵבִיאָה שְׁתֵּי שְׂעָרוֹת. וּמִי אִית לֵיהּ לְרַבִּי חֲנִינָא כֶּתֶם כְּלָל. בְּאַרְבַּע נָשִׁים, וַאֲפִילּוּ מִכָּאן וּלְהַבָּא. דְּמַחְמִיר בִּכְתָמִים. טְפֵי מִבִּרְאִיָּיתָהּ. דִּרְאִיַּית אַרְבַּע נָשִׁים, הוֹאִיל וְאֵין דָּם מָצוּי בָּהֶן, אָמְרִינַן: הַשְׁתָּא אָתֵי, וּמִכִּי אָתֵי חֲזִיתֵיהּ. אֲבָל בְּכֶתֶם אִיכָּא לְמֵימַר: אִי בָּדְקָה לְחָלוּק, מֵעִיקָּרָא הֲוָה אִישְׁתַּכַּח. רַבִּי חֲנִינָא בֶּן אַנְטִיגְנוֹס אוֹמֵר נָשִׁים שֶׁאָמְרוּ חֲכָמִים דַּיָּין שְׁעָתָן כִּתְמָן כִּרְאִיָּיתָן. כְּלוֹמַר, נָשִׁים שֶׁאָמְרוּ חֲכָמִים דַּיָּין שְׁעָתָן, כִּתְמָן כִּרְאִיָּיתָן לְטַמְּאָהּ מִכָּאן וּלְהַבָּא. יֵשׁ לָהּ כֶּתֶם. מִכָּאן וּלְהַבָּא, אַע"פ שֶׁלֹּא רָאֲתָה מִיָּמֶיהָ. אֵינוֹ מְמַעֵט. עַל יַד מֵעֵת לְעֵת וְעַל יַד מִפְּקִידָה לִפְקִידָה. שֶׁמְּהוּמָּה לְבֵיתָהּ. מְמַהֶרֶת לְשַׁמֵּשׁ. אֶחָד לוֹ. שֶׁמְּקַנֵּחַ בּוֹ בְּעַצְמוֹ. וְתַחְפֶּנָּה שִׁכְבַת זֶרַע. וַאֲפִי' דִּלְאַחַר תַּשְׁמִישׁ נַמִי לָא לֶיהֱוֵי כִּפְקִידָה, קמ"ל. וְאִי בָּעֵית אֵימָא. לְעוֹלָם חַד לִפְנֵי תַשְׁמִישׁ וְחַד לְאַחַר תַּשְׁמִישׁ, וְאפ"ה "הֲרֵי זוֹ כִּפְקִידָה" אַלְּאַחַר תַּשְׁמִישׁ קָאֵי. וְא"ת: עֵד שֶׁלִּפְנֵי תַשְׁמִישׁ לָמָּה הוּזְכַּר? מַתְנִיתִין תַּרְתֵּי קָתָנֵי, וְאַשְׁמוּעִינַן תַּנָּא דְּמַתְנִיתִין דִּשְׁנֵי בְדִיקוֹת אַצְרְכוּהָ רַבָּנַן. וְה"ק: "וּמְשַׁמֶּשֶׁת בְּעֵדִים" — כְּלוֹמַר: מְצֻוָּה עָלֶיהָ לְשַׁמֵּשׁ בְּעֵדִים, וְאַע"פ שֶׁיֵּשׁ לָהּ וֶסֶת. "הֲרֵי זוֹ כִּפְקִידָה" — הַהוּא דִּלְאַחַר תַּשְׁמִישׁ. וְהָא הַמְשַׁמֶּשֶׁת קָתָנֵי. דְּלָאו לָשׁוֹן חוֹבָה הוּא, אַלְמָא חֲדָא קָתָנֵי, וּמִשּׁוּם "הֲרֵי זוֹ כִּפְקִידָה" נָקַט לָהּ. וְה"ק: וְאִשָּׁה הַמְשַׁמֶּשֶׁת בְּעֵדִים — הֲרֵי זוֹ כִּפְקִידָה, וְאַקַּמָּא נַמִי קָאֵי. דְּאִי אַסֵּיפָא לְחוּדָהּ, רִאשׁוֹן לָמָּה הוּזְכַּר. תְּנֵי וּמְשַׁמֶּשֶׁת. וְתַרְתֵּי מִילֵּי נִינְהוּ, וְה"ק: מְצֻוָּה עָלֶיהָ לְשַׁמֵּשׁ בְּעֵדִים, וַהֲרֵי (ב) כִּפְקִידָה — אַסֵּיפָא. וְקַמָּא לָא נָקַט לֵיהּ אֶלָּא לְאַשְׁמוּעִינַן דִּמְצֻוָּה לִבְדּוֹק קוֹדֶם תַּשְׁמִישׁ. הַשְׁתָּא מֵעֵת לְעֵת. דְּאֶתְמוֹל דִּזְמַן אָרוֹךְ הוּא, מְמַעֶטֶת פְּקִידָה זוֹ דְּעֵדִים.

**תוספות**

וּבָרַיְיתָא דברי הכל. דשלא בשעת וסתה — מטמא למפרע. אבל לגמרי לא אתי כרבנן, דלדידהו אפי' בשעת וסתה נמי. וא"ת: מעיקרא מאי סבר, דאמרי' איפכא, ולא אמרי' לחומרא? ויש לומר: דמעיקרא בעי לאוקומי מתניתין ככ"ע, אבל כשהביא הברייתא — לא מצי לאוקומי ככ"ע, הדר ביה, וקאמר לחומרא. **הָא** שאר נשים שאמרו חכמים דיין שעתן כתמן כראייתן. משמע שיש להחמיר ביש לה וסת טפי מבד' נשים, א"כ ר' דוסא דאמר ביש לה וסת דיה שעתה, כל שכן דאית ליה בד' נשים. וקשה: דא"כ לקמן (דף ז:) דפסיק כרבי אליעזר בד' אמאי חשיב הך בהדייהו? כיון דרבי דוסא סבר כותיה, לא ה"ל למיחשב! דכה"ג אמרינן (ג) לקמן. וי"ל: הא דיש לה וסת כתמה טמא למפרע, לאו משום דחמיר טפי מד' נשים, אלא משום דגזור בשעת וסתה אטו שלא בשעת וסתה, אע"ג דבראייה לא גזרינן. **ר"מ** היא דמחמיר בכתמים. פירש"י: דמחמיר בכתמים טפי מבראייה. ואין נראה, דא"כ, מה לו להתלמוד להאריך ולומר דמחמיר בכתמים? הוה ליה למימר: "ר"מ, היא דתניא" וכו', ולא יותר! ועו, דבסמוך (ד) תניא: הרואה כתם — מקולקלת למנינה, ורואה דם — אינה מקולקלת למנינה. אלמא שאר תנאים נמי אחמירו טפי בכתמים מבראייה! ואע"ג דהך ברייתא כר"מ, דקתני: "מטמאה את בועלה למפרע", ובפרק "כל היד" (לקמן דף טו.) אמרינן: דוקא לר"מ מטמאה בועלה למפרע. מכל מקום, הא דמקולקלת למנינה, מיהו אתי ככ"ע. וכן שילהי "בא סימן" (לקמן נג:) תניא: הרואה כתם — מטמאה עצמה (ה) למפרע בקדשים. והיינו, לענין שמקולקלת למנינה, כמו שאפרש שם בע"ה. ונראה לפרש: "רבי מאיר היא דמחמיר בכתמים" — שהוא רגיל להחמיר בכתמים טפי מרבנן, כדתנן פרק "בא סימן" (שם נג:) הרואה כתם (ו) — חוששין משום זוב, דברי ר"מ. וחכמים אומרים: אין בכתמים משום זוב. ואמרי' התם: מאן חכמים? ר' חנינא בן אנטיגנוס, דמיקל יותר בכתמים, כדאמרינן הכא. ובכמה דוכתי מחמיר ר"מ כדאמרינן לקמן (דף נט:) גבי "אשה שעושה צרכיה", ובפרק "כל היד" (לקמן דף יד.) אמרינן: בדקה בעד [שאין] בדוק לה, והניחה בקופסא, ולמחר מצאה עליו דם ר"מ מטמא, וחכמים מטהרין. ולכך קאמר הכא: "ר"מ דמחמיר בכתמים". ואע"ג דבפ' "האשה" (לקמן דף נט:) תניא: השאילה חלוקה לנכרית — אינה תולה בנכרית. ר"מ אומר: תולה בנכרית. אלמא מיקל טפי מרבנן! מ"מ ברוב מקומות מחמיר. **כָּל** הנשים כתמן טמא למפרע ונשים שאמרו כו' — לא זו אף זו קתני. **תְּנִי** ומשמשת. אף על פי שאמרו דיה שעתה. **הַשְׁתָּא** מעת לעת ממעטת. — פירוש: השתא מעת לעת, דפשעה ולא בדקה שחרית, כי בדקה ערבית ומצאה טמאה, בדיקה של צהרים דלאחר תשמיש — מיעטה, דלא מטמאה מעת לעת. כל שכן כשבדקה שחרית, ולא פשעה כלום — דממעטת, דלא מטמאה משחרית.

מסייע

**תוספי הרא"ש**

**וּבָרַיְיתָא** דברי הכל. כלומר אף ר' דוסא מודה דשלא בשעת וסתה מטמאה מעת לעת וכ"ש דהא אפי' בשעת וסתה מטמאה מעת לעת מי' פשיטא דברייתא לא אתיא אלא כר' דוסא מדקתני שאם תראה שלא בשעת וסתה מטמאה מעת לעת מכלל דבשעת וסתה דיה שעתה. וללישנא קמא קי"ל כרבנן כסתמא דמתני' וללישנא בתרא קי"ל כר' דוסא. וסתמא דמתני' ור' דוסא (וקתני) ות"ק לא פליגי דהא לקמן פסקי' כר' אליעזר דאמר ד' נשים דיין שעתן: **לְחוּמְרָא** מוקמינן. וא"ת ומעיקרא אמאי לא אוקמיה לחומרא. וי"ל מקמי דשמיע ליה ניחא ליה לאוקומא לקולא ותהיה מתני' דברי הכל אבל השתא דשמיע ליה ברייתא דממה נפשך חד מינייהו דברי הכל [לא ניחא ליה] לאוקומי לקולא א)ומתני' דברי הכל וברייתא כיחידאה: **רַבִּי** מאיר היא דמחמיר בכתמים. פרש"י טפי מבראיה וקשה דרבנן נמי אשכחן דמחמרי דרואה אע"ג דמטמאה מעת לעת אינה מקולקלת למנינה ורואה כתם מקולקלת כדאיתא לקמן בשמעתין. וי"ל דההיא ר' מאיר היא מדקתני ברואה כתם מטמאה בועלה למפרע והיינו דוקא לר' מאיר כדאמרי' לקמן פרק כל היד. ומיהו קשה דלא הוה ליה למימר דמחמיר בכתמים אלא ר"מ היא דתניא וכו' הלכך נראה לפרש דמחמיר בכתמים בעלמא טפי מדרבנן כדתניא בפ' בא סימן הרואה כתם הרי זו מקולקלת וחוששת משום זוב דברי ר' מאיר וחכמים אומרים אין בכתמים משום זוב והתם נמי אמרינן בגמ' מאן חכמים ר' חנינא בן אנטיגנוס ולהכי מיקיל נמי הכא כדתניא כו' וכן משמע בירושלמי דערלה פרק התרומה דקאמר ר' מאיר מחמיר בדבריהן ומייתי מהך דחוששת משום זוב: אין מכניסתו לחורין ולסדקין הלכך לא הוי בדיקה. מכאן משמע דכל בדיקת נשים שצריך להכנים לחורין ולסדקין. ובענין אחר לא מיקרי בדיקה אלא קינוח וכן מוכח לקמן בסוף פירקין גבי אשה מהו שתבדוק עצמה כשיעור וסת לחייב בעלה חטאת: **הַשְׁתָּא** מעת לעת ממעטת. אע"פ שפשעה ולא בדקה כראוי לא [מטמאה למפרע] מפקידה לפקידה שלא הפסיקה בבדיקות מיבעיא:

הא

א) אינו מובן דאם נוקמי לקולא הברייתא אתיא כרבנן ואינו כיחידאה והדבר צ"ע.

**עין משפט נר מצוה**

כ א מיי' פ"ט מהלכות איסורי ביאה הלכה ג ופ"ג מהלכות משכב ומושב הלכה ז:
כא ב מיי' פ"ט מהלכות איסורי ביאה הלכה ה ופ"ג מהל' משכב ומושב הלכה ח:
כב ג מיי' פ"ט מהל' איסורי ביאה הלכה ה סמג לאוין קיא טוש"ע י"ד סימן קצ סעיף ב:
כג ד מיי' שם ופ"ב מהלכות איסות הלכה א סמג שם טוש"ע שם וסימן קפט סעיף כז:
כד ה מיי' פ"ג מהל' משכב ומושב הלכ' ד:
כה ו מיי' פ"ד מהלכות איסורי ביאה הלכה טז סמג לאוין קיא טוש"ע י"ד סימן קצ סעיף א ב:

**מסורת הש"ס**

לקמן יד.

**הגהות הב"ח**

(א) רש"י ד"ה ולוקמא וכו' ומ"ט הדרית בך הא: (ב) ד"ה תני וכו' והרי זו כפקידה: (ג) תוס' ד"ה הא שאר וכו' דכה"ג אמרינן לקמן. נ"ב בדף ח: (ד) ד"ה ר"מ וכו' דבסמוך נ"ב דף: (ה) בא"ד מטמאה עצמה וקדשים למפרע והיינו לענין מקולקלת כנ"ל: (ו) בא"ד הרואה כתם חוששת משום:

**גליון הש"ס**

**תוס'** ד"ה ר"מ היא כו' ונראה לפרש ר"מ היא. עי' בר"ש רפ"ב דערלה:

מִפְּקִידָה לִפְקִידָה מִיבָּעֲיָא! מַהוּ דְּתֵימָא: מֵעֵת לְעֵת – חָשׁוּ בָּהּ רַבָּנַן לִפְסֵידָא דְּטָהֳרוֹת, אֲבָל מִפְּקִידָה לִפְקִידָה – לָא, קמ"ל. § "כֵּיצַד דַּיָּהּ שְׁעָתָהּ" וכו'. § לָמָּה לִי לְמִיתְנֵי "הָיְתָה יוֹשֶׁבֶת בַּמִּטָּה, (א) וַעֲסוּקָה בְּטָהֳרוֹת"? לִיתְנֵי "הָיְתָה עֲסוּקָה בְּטָהֳרוֹת וּפָרְשָׁה וְרָאֲתָה"! הָא קמ"ל: טַעֲמָא – דְּדַיָּהּ שְׁעָתָהּ, הָא מֵעֵת לְעֵת – מִטָּה נַמִי מְטַמְּיָא. מְסַיֵּיעַ לֵיהּ לִזְעִירִי, דְּאָמַר זְעִירִי: [א]מֵעֵת לְעֵת שֶׁבְּנִדָּה – עוֹשָׂה מִשְׁכָּב וּמוֹשָׁב לְטַמֵּא אָדָם לְטַמֵּא בְּגָדִים. מִכְּדִי הַאי מִטָּה דָּבָר שֶׁאֵין בּוֹ דַּעַת לִישָּׁאֵל הוּא, *וְכָל דָּבָר שֶׁאֵין בּוֹ דַּעַת לִישָּׁאֵל – סְפֵקוֹ טָהוֹר! תַּרְגְּמָהּ זְעִירִי: כְּשֶׁחַבְרוֹתֶיהָ נוֹשְׂאוֹת אוֹתָהּ בַּמִּטָּה, דְּהָוְיָא לֵיהּ יַד חַבְרוֹתֶיהָ. *וְהַשְׁתָּא דְּא"ר יוֹחָנָן: [ב]סְפֵק טוּמְאָה הַבָּאָה בִּידֵי אָדָם – נִשְׁאָלִין עָלֶיהָ, אֲפִי' בִּכְלִי מוּנָּח ע"ג קַרְקַע, כְּמִי שֶׁיֵּשׁ בּוֹ דַּעַת לִישָּׁאֵל – אע"פ שֶׁאֵין חַבְרוֹתֶיהָ נוֹשְׂאוֹת אוֹתָהּ בַּמִּטָּה. גּוּפָא, א"ר יוֹחָנָן: סְפֵק טוּמְאָה הַבָּאָה בִּידֵי אָדָם – נִשְׁאָלִים עָלֶיהָ אֲפִי' בִּכְלִי הַמּוּנָּח עַל גַּבֵּי קַרְקַע – כְּמִי שֶׁיֵּשׁ בּוֹ דַּעַת לִישָּׁאֵל. מֵיתִיבֵי, *[ג]הָיָה מִתְעַטֵּף בְּטַלִּיתוֹ וְטָהֳרוֹת וְטוּמְאוֹת בְּצִדּוֹ, וְטָהֳרוֹת וְטוּמְאוֹת לְמַעְלָה מֵרֹאשׁוֹ, סָפֵק נָגַע סָפֵק לֹא נָגַע – טָהוֹר. וְאִם אִי אֶפְשָׁר אא"כ נָגַע – טָמֵא. *רשב"ג אוֹמֵר: אוֹמְרִים לוֹ "שְׁנֵה", וְשׁוֹנֶה. אָמְרוּ לוֹ: *אֵין שׁוֹנִים בְּטָהֳרוֹת, [לקמן נח:] אַמַּאי? הָא סְפֵק טוּמְאָה הַבָּאָה בִּידֵי אָדָם הוּא! בַּר מִינַּהּ דְּהַהִיא, דְּתָנֵי רַב הוֹשַׁעְיָא: [ד]בִּרְשׁוּת הַיָּחִיד – סְפֵקוֹ טָמֵא, בִּרְשׁוּת הָרַבִּים – טָהוֹר. גּוּפָא, אָמַר זְעִירִי: מֵעֵת לְעֵת שֶׁבְּנִדָּה – עוֹשָׂה מִשְׁכָּב וּמוֹשָׁב לְטַמֵּא אָדָם לְטַמֵּא בְּגָדִים. אִינִי, וְהָא כִּי אֲתָא אֲבִימִי מִבֵּי חוֹזָאֵי, אֲתָא וְאַיְיתֵי מַתְנִיתָא בִּידֵיהּ: מֵעֵת לְעֵת שֶׁבְּנִדָּה – מִשְׁכָּבָהּ וּמוֹשָׁבָהּ כְּמַגָּעָהּ. מַאי לָאו: מָה מַגָּעָהּ לֹא מְטַמֵּא אָדָם – אַף מִשְׁכָּבָהּ לֹא מְטַמֵּא אָדָם! אָמַר רָבָא: וְתִסְבְּרָא? קַל וָחוֹמֶר הוּא, וּמָה כְּלִי חֶרֶס הַמּוּקָּף צָמִיד פָּתִיל, *[ה]הַנִּיצּוֹל בְּאֹהֶל הַמֵּת – [ו]אֵינוֹ נִיצּוֹל בְּמֵעֵת לְעֵת שֶׁבְּנִדָּה. מִשְׁכָּבוֹת וּמוֹשָׁבוֹת, שֶׁאֵינָן נִיצּוֹלִין בְּאֹהֶל הַמֵּת – אֵינוֹ דִּין שֶׁאֵין נִיצּוֹלִין בְּמֵעֵת לְעֵת שֶׁבְּנִדָּה? וְהָא אֲבִימִי מִבֵּי חוֹזָאֵי מַתְנִיתָא קָאָמַר! אֵימָא: מִשְׁכָּבָהּ וּמוֹשָׁבָהּ

כְּמַגַּע

**רש"י**

**מִפְּקִידָה לִפְקִידָה.** דְּשַׁחֲרִית הַיּוֹם, דִּזְמַן מוּעָט מִבָּעֲיָא. **טַעְמָא** (ב) מִשּׁוּם דַּיָּהּ שְׁעָתָהּ. מִשּׁוּם דְּיֵשׁ לָהּ וֶסֶת. הָא אִם אֵין לָהּ וֶסֶת, דִּמְטַמְּיָא מֵעֵת לְעֵת – מִטָּה נַמִי טְמֵאָה, כְּמִשְׁכַּב נִדָּה עַצְמָהּ שֶׁמְּטַמֵּא אָדָם הַנּוֹגֵעַ בּוֹ טוּמְאָה חֲמוּרָה לְטַמֵּא בְּגָדִים שֶׁעָלָיו, דִּכְתִיב (ויקרא טו): "וְכָל *אֲשֶׁר יִגַּע בְּמִשְׁכָּבָהּ יְכַבֵּס בְּגָדָיו". ה"ג **לְטַמֵּא אָדָם לְטַמֵּא בְּגָדִים.** שֶׁהָאָדָם מְטַמֵּא בְּגָדִים שֶׁעָלָיו, וְאַע"פ שֶׁלֹּא נָגְעוּ בְּגָדִים בַּמִּטָּה. **מִכְּדֵי הַךְ מִטָּה דָּבָר שֶׁאֵין בּוֹ דַּעַת לִישָּׁאֵל הוּא.** וּמֵעֵת לְעֵת – סְפֵק טוּמְאָה הוּא, וְכָל שֶׁאֵין בּוֹ דַּעַת לִישָּׁאֵל כו'. דִּבְשְׁלָמָא אַטָּהֳרוֹת בְּלֹא מִטָּה – נִיחָא, דְּכֵיוָן דְּהִיא עֲסוּקָה בָּהֶן וְאוֹחַזְתָּן בְּיָדָהּ, הָווּ לְהוּ כְּיָדָהּ, וְהִיא יֵשׁ בָּהּ דַּעַת לִישָּׁאֵל. אֶלָּא מִטָּה, כֵּיוָן דְּע"ג קַרְקַע מוּנַּחַת, דְּלָאו בְּיָדָהּ הוּא, וּסְפֵקוֹ טָהוֹר. דְּכָל סְפֵק טוּמְאָה לְטַמֵּא, מִסּוֹטָה גָּמְרִינַן לָהּ, וְסוֹטָה יֵשׁ בָּהּ דַּעַת לִישָּׁאֵל. **כְּשֶׁחַבְרוֹתֶיהָ נוֹשְׂאוֹת אוֹתָהּ בַּמִּטָּה.** בְּאוֹתוֹ מֵעֵת לְעֵת, דְּהָוְיָא לֵיהּ הַךְ מִטָּה (ג) בְּיַד חַבְרוֹתֶיהָ שֶׁיֵּשׁ בָּהּ דַּעַת לִישָּׁאֵל, הִלְכָּךְ טְמֵאָה. **הַבָּאָה בִּידֵי אָדָם.** כְּגוֹן זוֹ, דְּטוּמְאָה עַל יָדָהּ בָּאָה. וּכְגוֹן נוֹשֵׂא שֶׁרֶץ בְּיָדוֹ, סָפֵק נָגַע בִּכְלִי הַמּוּנָּח ע"ג קַרְקַע סָפֵק לֹא נָגַע. וְאַע"פ שֶׁאָדָם לֹא הָיָה עָסוּק בַּכְּלִי (ד) הַמִּיטַּמֵּא, הוֹאִיל וְהַטּוּמְאָה בָּאָה ע"י אָדָם, סָפֵק נָגְעָה הַטּוּמְאָה בַּכְּלִי סָפֵק לֹא נָגְעָה – חָשְׁבִינַן לָהּ כְּמוֹ שֶׁיֵּשׁ בָּהּ דַּעַת לִישָּׁאֵל, וּבִרְה"י סְפֵקוֹ טָמֵא. **נִשְׁאָלִין.** כְּלוֹמַר, טָמֵא. **כְּמִי שֶׁיֵּשׁ בּוֹ דַּעַת לִישָּׁאֵל.** וְכִי אָמְרִינַן: דָּבָר שֶׁאֵין בּוֹ דַּעַת לִישָּׁאֵל – סְפֵקוֹ טָהוֹר, כְּגוֹן שֶׁרֶץ הַמּוּטָּל אֵצֶל כְּלִי ע"ג קַרְקַע סָפֵק נָגַע סָפֵק לֹא נָגַע. **הָיָה מִתְעַטֵּף בְּטַלִּיתוֹ וְטָהֳרוֹת בְּצִדּוֹ.** וְהוּא הָיָה טָמֵא. סָפֵק טִימֵּא טְהָרוֹת בַּטַּלִּית כְּשֶׁהִגְבִּיהוֹ עַל כְּתֵפוֹ, סָפֵק לֹא נָגַע. אוֹ טֻמְאוֹת בְּצִדּוֹ, כְּגוֹן שֶׁרֶץ, וְהוּא טָהוֹר. סָפֵק נִטְמָא טַלִּיתוֹ, סָפֵק לֹא נִטְמָא. **טָהוֹר.** קס"ד דַּאֲפִילּוּ בִּרְה"י מִשּׁוּם דַּהֲוֵי דָּבָר שֶׁאֵין בּוֹ דַּעַת לִישָּׁאֵל. וְאַע"ג דְּבָאָה בִּידֵי אָדָם, הוֹאִיל וְטָהֳרוֹת מוּנָּחוֹת עַל גַּבֵּי קַרְקַע וְאֵין אוֹחֲזָן בְּיָדוֹ, אֵין נִשְׁאָלִין עֲלֵיהֶם. **שְׁנֵה.** פַּעַם אַחֶרֶת, אִם יִגַּע עַכְשָׁיו – בְּיָדוּעַ שֶׁנָּגַע בַּתְּחִלָּה. **אֵין שׁוֹנִין.** שֶׁמָּא עַכְשָׁיו נָגַע וְקוֹדֶם לָכֵן לֹא נָגַע, אוֹ חִילּוּף. **כְּמַגָּעָהּ.** *בִּכְלִי שֶׁנָּגְעָה בּוֹ נִדָּה, שֶׁאֵינוֹ מְטַמֵּא אָדָם, שֶׁהֲרֵי רִאשׁוֹן הוּא, וְאֵינוֹ מְטַמֵּא אָדָם אֶלָּא אַב הַטּוּמְאָה. **אַף מִשְׁכָּבָהּ לֹא מְטַמֵּא אָדָם.** וְקַשְׁיָא לִזְעִירִי, דְּאָמַר: מִשְׁכָּבָהּ וּמוֹשָׁבָהּ מְטַמֵּא אָדָם אַף לְטַמֵּא בְּגָדִים. **כְּלִי חֶרֶס. נִיצּוֹל בְּאֹהֶל הַמֵּת,** דִּכְתִיב (במדבר יט): "וְכֹל כְּלִי פָתוּחַ אֲשֶׁר אֵין צָמִיד פָּתִיל עָלָיו טָמֵא" הָא יֵשׁ צָמִיד פָּתִיל עָלָיו – טָהוֹר. **אֵינוֹ נִיצּוֹל.** אִם הֵסִיט בְּתוֹךְ מֵעֵת לְעֵת – טָמֵא כְּאִילּוּ הֱסִיטָתָהּ לְאַחַר רְאִיָּיתָהּ, כִּדְתַנְיָא בַּבָּרַיְיתָא לְקַמָּן. **אֵינוֹ דִּין שֶׁאֵינָן נִיצּוֹלִין בְּמֵעֵת לְעֵת.** (ה). שֶׁיְּטַמְּאוּ כְּמִשְׁכַּב נִדָּה עַצְמָהּ, אָדָם וּבְגָדִים שֶׁעָלָיו.

כְּמַגַּע

**תוספות**

**מסייע** ליה לזעירי. תימה: דממתני' לא שמעינן לטמא אדם ובגדים? **מכדי** מטה אין בו דעת לישאל. מטהרות לא פריך, דכיון שעסוקין בהן – מיקרי שפיר "יש בו דעת לישאל", כדפירש הקונטרס. **כשחברותיה** נושאות אותה במטה. משמע הכא: דפשיטא דכיון דחברותיה נושאות אותה במטה – דמקרי מטה "דבר שיש בו דעת לישאל". ותימה לריצ"א: דבסוף פ"ק דפסחים (דף יט.) קאמר: ועל המחט שנמצא בבשר – שהסכין והידים טהורות. ומוקי לה: במחט טמא מת, וטהורות – משום דעזרה רה"ר הוא. אבל אי הוה רה"י – הוה טמא. ופריך: אמאי? והא אין בו דעת לישאל! הוא דאמר כרבי יוחנן, דאמר: ספק טומאה הבאה בידי אדם – נשאלין עליה. והשתא, מאי מקשה התם, ומה צריך לאתויי הך דרבי יוחנן, דכיון דאדם תופס את הסכין – חשוב "דבר שיש בו דעת לישאל" אפילו בלא רבי יוחנן, כדמשמע הכא? וי"ל: דהכא חשיב טפי "דבר שיש בו דעת לישאל" כשחברותיה נושאות אותה במטה, משום דנדה נמי המטמאה יש בה דעת לישאל. אי נמי: משום שגם חברותיה הנושאות, גם הם טמאות במשא הנדה. אבל התם, אין האדם טמא, אלא הסכין שנגע במחט. והשתא נמי אתי שפיר דפריך בסמוך לרבי יוחנן מ"היה מתעטף בטליתו", ולא פריך נמי לזעירי – משום דהאדם התופס הטלית, לא דמי לחברותיה שגם הן טמאות, ויש בהן דעת לישאל*. [או משום שהנדה המטמאה יש בה דעת לישאל] **ספק** טומאה הבאה בידי אדם נשאלין עליה ואפילו בבלי המונח ע"ג קרקע. וא"ת: מאי קמ"ל רבי יוחנן? מתני' היא (טהרות פ"ג מ"ח) תינוק שנמצא בצד העיסה כו'. דחכמים מטמאין, משום דעשו לתינוק כ"יש בו דעת לישאל", אע"פ שהעיסה אין בה דעת לישאל. ובמס' טהרות פ"ד (מ"ט) תנן: טמא שפשט רגלו לבין המשקין, ספק נגע ספק לא נגע – טמא ברה"י. עוד תנן התם בסיפא: היה מקל בידו, ובראשו (ו) מלאה משקין טמאין, וזרקה לבין הככרות, ספק נגע בו – טהור. וטעמא, משום דטומאת משקין לטמא אחרים לאו דאורייתא, וה"ל ספק [לטמא אחרים] דרבנן, כדמפרש התם. הא לאו הכי – ספקו טמא! וי"ל: דמצי למימר שהעיסה והמשקין והככרות בידי אדם, וקמ"ל רבי יוחנן: אפילו מונחים ע"ג קרקע, או טהרות ביד טהור וטומאה מונחת ע"ג קרקע.

**היה** מתעטף בטליתו. פירוש: טליתו טמא וטהרות בצדו, או טליתו טהור וטמאות בצדו, כגון שרץ ואינו יודע אם נגע בו. או טומאה וטהרות לפניו, וטליתו טהור, ואינו יודע אם נגע לטומאה ואח"כ לטהרות. וקמ"ל, דלא הוי ספק ספקא: שמא לא נגע הטלית בשרץ, ואפילו נגע – ספק לא נגע בטהרות. דאם נגע בשרץ – כמו כן נגע בטהרות. **ואם** אי אפשר אא"כ נגע טמא. וא"ת: פשיטא, כיון דאי אפשר – ודאי נגע! וי"ל: דלאו "א"א כלל" קאמר, אלא כלומר, "קרוב לודאי". ובתוספתא) נמי תניא: אם אי אפשר אא"כ נגע – ספקו טמא. מדקאמר "ספקו טמא", משמע דלא הוי ודאי נגע. וכן מדקאמר רבן שמעון בן גמליאל: אומרים לו "שנה", דליכא למימר דארישא קאי, דקאמר "ספקו טהור", וקאמר איהו "אומרים לו שנה", ואם נגע – טמא. דא"כ, לא הוי פליגי רבנן לומר: אין שונין בטהרות, דבפרק "הרואה" (לקמן נח.) אמרינן דדוקא להקל אין שונין, אבל להחמיר שונין. וכן בריש שחיטת חולין (דף ג:) אמרינן: אי אמר "ברי לי שלא נגעתי", לאו דוקא "ברי", דעזרה רה"ר כדאמרינן בפסחים (דף)ב). **ומה** כלי חרס שהוא מוקף צמיד פתיל. וא"ת: ונימא, דיו כמשכבות דאהל המת, דלא מטמא אדם ובגדים. או דיו ככלי חרס, דמעת לעת? ועוד, נימא: פכין קטנים יוכיחו, דטמאים במת וטהורים במעת לעת שבנדה, דלא אתו לכלל מגע, אף משכבות כמו כן! ומיהו רש"י פי' דהכי עביד ק"ו: ומה כלי חרס, שטהור באהל המת, טמא במעת לעת שבנדה כמו בנדה עצמה – משכבות ומושבות, דטמאים באהל המת, אינו דין שיטמאו במעת לעת שבנדה כנדה עצמה?! ומיהו אכתי קשה: מה לכלי חרס, שכן אין לו טהרה במקוה!ג) *כדפריך בפ' "כשם" (סוטה כט:) או, שכן מטמא מאוירו! וי"ל: טהרות דשאר כלים יוכיחו, שאין להם טומאת אויר, ויש להם טהרה במקוה, וטמאין במעת לעת שבנדה כבנדה עצמה, שהם ראשונים. דהא פשיטא ליה דאפילו משכבות טמאין במעת לעת, כדאמר בברייתא. ועביד ק"ו לטמא אדם ובגדים, ולא מצי למיעבד הכי ק"ו: ומה כלי חרס, שאינו מטמא מגבו בכל טמאות, טמא תוכו במעת לעת שבנדה כנדה עצמה – משכבות, לא כל שכן! כדאמר בפרק "בהמה המקשה" (חולין עא:) אטו מגבו קאמרינן, מתוכו קאמרינן. והתם מפורש הפשט.

[ה"ג הניצול באהל המת כו' - תימה: הא דאינו ניצול במעת לעת היינו בהיסט, דחשיב כאילו נגע בתוכו, דמריבויא דמגע אתי. ובמגע אהל המת, נמי טמא, דכך נ"לא] (כר"ע) דקאמר: מה פכין קטנים, שטהורים בזב - טמא באהל המת, מפך, שטמא בזב א"ד שיטמא באהל המת! נימא: כלי חרס המוקף צמיד פתיל יוכיח! אלא כדפירש' וי"ל: דהתם עביד ק"ו ממדרס, והשתא אין לומר מוקף צמיד פתיל יוכיח, דהא טהור מן המדרס].

א) [דטהרות פ"ד] ב) יט: וע' תוס' חולין ב: ד"ה דליתיה קמן וכו' האי ספק לא דמי לשאר ספק וכו' ולע"ק] ג) נ"ל או שכן מטמא מאוירו כדפריך בפרק כשם

**עין משפט נר מצוה**

כו א מיי' פ"ג מהלכות משכב ומושב הלכה ח:

כז ב ג ד מיי' פט"ז מהלכות שאר אבות הטומאות הלכה ו:

כח ה מיי' פ"ה ופכ"א מהל' טומאת מת הלכה ח:

כט ו מיי' פ"ג מהלכות משכב ומושב הלכה ח:

**הגהות הב"ח**

(א) גמ' במטה ועסוקה בטהרות: (ב) רש"י ד"ה טעמא דדיה שעתה כצ"ל ותיבת משום נמחק: (ג) ד"ה כשחברותיה וכו' הך מטה ביד חברותיה: (ד) ד"ה הבאה וכו' בכלי הטמא כצ"ל ותיבת המי נמחק: (ה) ד"ה אינו דין וכו' במעת לעת כמשכב נדה עצמה לטמא אדם ובגדים שעליו כצ"ל ותיבת שיטמאו נמחק: (ו) תוס' ד"ה ספק וכו' ובראשו משקין כצ"ל ותיבת מלאה נמחק:

[לעיל ז: סוטה כח:]

פסחים יט:

**גליון הש"ס**

גמ' הניצול באהל המת. עי' חגיגה כב ע"א תד"ה אין שונין: תוס' ד"ה ואם א"א כו' וי"ל דלאו כלל. עי' בחידושי ריטב"א מכות דף ז ע"א ד"ה וא"ר:

תוספתא דטהרות פ"ד ע"ש

[בתוספתא אי' רבי דוסא אומר אומרין לו כו' אמרו לו אין שונין כו' רשב"ג אומר עתים שהוא שונה]

**תוספי הרא"ש**

**הא** מעת לעת מטה נמי מטמיא. וא"ת ולא ליתני אלא מטה לחודה טהרות למה לי למיתני. וי"ל דאי לא תנא אלא מטה דיה שעתה שלא לעשות משכב ומושב הא טהרות מיטמאי הלכך תנא טהרות לגופא ומטה לדיוקא ...

... עזרה רשות הרבים היא ופריך האי מחט דבר שאין בו דעת לישאל הוא ... דהוי ספק טומאה הבאה בידי אדם ... דעת לישאל ... טומאה מונחת על גבי קרקע. ע"כ הך לאו דר' יוחנן היא דפשיטא דהיכא דאיכא דעת נוגע לא בעי' דעת מגיע דכיון דטהרה יש בה דעת לישראל לא חיישינן לטומאה דתנן בפ"ה דמסכת טהרות כזית מן המת בפי עורב ספק האהיל על האדם ועל הכלים ברשות היחיד ספק אדם טמא ספק כלים טהור. וטובא תנן במסכת טהרות כי האי גונא. וי"ל דמהתם לא שמעינן אלא שהאדם עצמו מקבל טומאה דהוי דומיא דסוטה דהיא עצמה נאסרת אבל לטמאות כלים שבידו והטומאה מונחת על גבי קרקע לא שמעינן אלא מהך דר' יוחנן והא דפריך התם מכדי האי מחט דבר שאין בו דעת לישאל הוא אסכין קא פריך ואהא מייתי הא דר' יוחנן. ואע"ג דאיכא למימר דדייק עזרה ברשות הרבים מידים טהורות משמע ליה דמכולהו מילתא קא דייקא. והא דזעירי לא מצי לאיתויי בפסחים משום דבטומאה נמי יש דעת לישאל ומיהו הוה מצי לאיתויי מההיא דקופה שנשתמשו בה טהרות דא"ל הלל לשמאי דהתם שרץ מונח על גבי קרקע והטהרות הם בידי אדם אלא דמלתיה דר' יוחנן מיפרשא טפי. ומיהו קשה מאי קמ"ל דר' יוחנן הא שמעינן ליה מתינוק שנמצא בצד העיסה ס"פ בתרא דקדושין דחכמים

**תוספי הרא"ש**

דחכמים מטמאין לפי שעשו התינוק כמי שיש בו דעת לישאל. והתם העיסה מונחת על גבי קרקע ותנן נמי במס' טהרות רגלו לבין משקין טהורים ספק נגע ספק לא נגע טמא ולזעירי קשה טפי דבעי חברותיה נושאות אותה במטה. ותיקשי ליה הך דמטמאין אפי' בטהרות המונחות על גבי קרקע ... ולמאי דפירשתי לעיל דאיכא לפלוגי בין לטמאות האדם עצמו או לטמאות הטהרות בידו ניחא לפירוש רש"י דלא דמיא אלא להא דר' יוחנן: **ואם** אי אפשר אלא א"כ נגע טמא. ברוב ספרים גרסינן ספיקו טמא וכן בתוס' גרס אי אי איפשר לכוין ספיקו טמא כלומר דאיכא למיתלי טפי בנגע מבלא נגע דאי דוקא קתני דאי אפשר בלא נגיעה פשיטא דטמא. ועוד מדקתני סיפא אומר לו שנה דע"כ אסיפא קאי. ורשב"ג שנה להקל קאמר דאי ארישא דקאמר ת"ק טהור ואמר איהו אומר לו שנה בההיא הוו מודו רבנן. דהא אמרינן בפ' הרואה כתם אין שונין בטהרות להקל אלא להחמיר ומי' למאי דמסקי' לקמן דבריש' ברשות היחיד ספיקו טמא מצי קאי ארשות (היחיד) [הרבים] דרישא וכמו שפירשתי (דאיכא) [והיכא] דקרוב לטומאה טפי מלטהרה מטמאינן אפי' ברשות (היחיד) [הרבים] כן מוכח נמי בשמעתתא קמייתא דחולין דקאמר התם אי אמר ברי לי שלא נגעתי שחיטתה כשרה ולמה לי ברי הא אמרינן בפ"ק דפסחים דעזרה רשות הרבים היא אלא לפי שאינו מצוי שישחוט אדם ולא יגע בבשר בעינן ברי לי הכא נמי כיון שבטורח יכול להתעטף שלא יגע מטמאינן. ואפי' לטהר ברשות היחיד מטהרין בספק הרגיל כדאמרינן בפרק קמא דפסחים כל מקום שחזיר וחולדה יכולין להלך

**הגהות מהר"ב רנשבורג** א] תוס' ד"ה ה"ג הניצול באוהל המת וכו' ובמגע אהל המת נמי טמא דכך נ"ל בפרק ר' עקיבא (שבת דף פ"ד ע"ב) דקאמר וכו' כנ"ל:

כְּמַגַּע עַצְמָהּ, מַה מַּגַּע עַצְמָהּ — מְטַמֵּא אָדָם לְטַמֵּא בְּגָדִים, אַף מִשְׁכָּבָהּ וּמוֹשָׁבָהּ — מְטַמֵּא אָדָם לְטַמֵּא בְּגָדִים. תַּנְיָא כְּוָותֵיהּ דְּרָבָא: [א]הָרוֹאָה (א) דָּם — מְטַמְּאָה מֵעֵת לְעֵת. וּמַה הִיא מְטַמְּאָה? — מִשְׁכָּבוֹת וּמוֹשָׁבוֹת, אוֹכָלִין וּמַשְׁקִין, וּכְלִי חֶרֶס הַמּוּקָּף צָמִיד פָּתִיל, וְאֵינָהּ מְקוּלְקֶלֶת לְמִנְיָנָהּ, [ב]וְאֵינָהּ מְטַמְּאָה אֶת בּוֹעֲלָהּ לְמַפְרֵעַ. *ר' עֲקִיבָא אוֹמֵר: מְטַמְּאָה אֶת בּוֹעֲלָהּ. וְאֵינָהּ מוֹנָה אֶלָּא מִשָּׁעָה שֶׁרָאֲתָה. [ג]הָרוֹאָה כֶּתֶם מְטַמְּאָה לְמַפְרֵעַ, וּמַה הִיא מְטַמְּאָה? — אוֹכָלִין וּמַשְׁקִין, מִשְׁכָּבוֹת וּמוֹשָׁבוֹת, וּכְלִי חֶרֶס הַמּוּקָּף צָמִיד פָּתִיל, [ד]וּמְקוּלְקֶלֶת לְמִנְיָנָהּ, וּמְטַמְּאָה אֶת בּוֹעֲלָהּ, וְאֵינָהּ מוֹנָה אֶלָּא מִשָּׁעָה שֶׁרָאֲתָה. [ה]וְזֶה וָזֶה תּוֹלִין, לֹא אוֹכְלִין וְלֹא שׂוֹרְפִין. וְרָבָא, אִי שְׁמִיעַ לֵיהּ מַתְנִיתָא — לֵימָא מַתְנִיתָא! וְאִי לָא שְׁמִיעַ לֵיהּ מַתְנִיתָא — קַל וָחוֹמֶר מְנָא לֵיהּ? לְעוֹלָם שְׁמִיעַ לֵיהּ מַתְנִיתָא, וְאִי מִמַּתְנִיתָא הֲוָה אָמֵינָא: אוֹ אָדָם אוֹ בְּגָדִים, אֲבָל אָדָם וּבְגָדִים — לָא, מִשּׁוּם הָכִי קָאָמַר ק"ו. אָמַר רַב הוּנָא: מֵעֵת לְעֵת שֶׁבְּנִדָּה לַקֹּדֶשׁ אֲבָל לֹא לִתְרוּמָה. אִי הָכִי, לִיתְנֵי גַּבֵּי מַעֲלוֹת! כִּי קָתָנֵי — הֵיכָא דְּאִית לֵיהּ דְּרָרָא דְּטוּמְאָה, אֲבָל הֵיכָא דְּלֵית לֵיהּ דְּרָרָא דְּטוּמְאָה — לָא קָתָנֵי. מֵיתִיבֵי: מַה הִיא מְטַמְּאָה — אוֹכָלִין וּמַשְׁקִין. מַאי לָאו: בֵּין דְּקֹדֶשׁ בֵּין דִּתְרוּמָה! לָא, דְּקֹדֶשׁ. תָּא שְׁמַע, *רַבִּי יְהוּדָה אוֹמֵר: אַף בִּשְׁעַת עֲבֵרָתָן מִלֶּאֱכוֹל בִּתְרוּמָה. וְהָוֵינַן בָּהּ: מַאי דַּהֲוָה הֲוָה! אָמַר רַב חִסְדָּא: לֹא נִצְרְכָה אֶלָּא לְתַקֵּן שִׁירַיִם שֶׁבְּפָנֶיהָ! רַב הוּנָא מַתְנֵי: לִישְׂרוֹף שִׁירַיִם שֶׁבְּיָדֶיהָ. שֶׁבָּדְקָה עַצְמָהּ כְּשִׁיעוּר וֶסֶת. ת"ש: (א) מַעֲשֶׂה וְעָשָׂה רַבִּי כְּר"א, לְאַחַר שֶׁנִּזְכַּר אָמַר: כְּדַי הוּא ר"א (ג) לִסְמוֹךְ עָלָיו בִּשְׁעַת

א) לקמן ט: עירובין מו. ב) [ברכות ט. וש"נ]

---

**רש"י**

כְּמַגַּע עַצְמָהּ. כִּנְגִיעַת עַצְמָהּ. כְּלוֹמַר, אָדָם הַנּוֹגֵעַ בְּמִשְׁכָּבָהּ בְּתוֹךְ מֵעֵת לְעֵת, כְּאִילּוּ נוֹגֵעַ בִּבְשַׂר נִדָּה עַצְמָהּ, שֶׁהוּא וּבְגָדִים שֶׁעָלָיו טְמֵאִים. דִּכְתִיב (ויקרא טו): "וְכָל הַנּוֹגֵעַ בָּהּ יִטְמָא", וְתַנְיָא בְּתוֹרַת כֹּהֲנִים: יָכוֹל לֹא יְהֵא הַנּוֹגֵעַ בָּהּ מְטַמֵּא בְּגָדִים בְּמַגָּע? קַל וָחוֹמֶר: אִם מִשְׁכָּבָהּ — מְטַמֵּא אָדָם לְטַמֵּא בְּגָדִים, הִיא עַצְמָהּ — לֹא כָּל שֶׁכֵּן! אִם כֵּן, לָמָּה נֶאֱמַר "כָּל הַנּוֹגֵעַ בָּהּ יִטְמָא" — שֶׁאֵינוֹ חוֹזֵר וּמְטַמֵּא אָדָם וּכְלֵי חֶרֶס. אַף מִשְׁכָּבָהּ. בְּתוֹךְ מֵעֵת לְעֵת. הָרוֹאָה כֶּתֶם מְטַמְּאָה לְמַפְרֵעַ. עַד שְׁעַת כִּיבּוּסוֹ שֶׁל חָלוּק זֶה שֶׁכִּבְּסָה קוֹדֶם לְבִישָׁה זוֹ. וּכְלֵי חֶרֶס הַמּוּקָּף כו'. כְּלוֹמַר, אֲפִילּוּ הוּא מוּקָּף צָמִיד פָּתִיל, שֶׁאִי אֶפְשָׁר לִיגַּע בְּתוֹכוֹ — מְטַמְּאָה אוֹתוֹ בְּהֶיסֵּט. שֶׁהַזָּב וְהַנִּדָּה מְטַמְּאִין כְּלֵי חֶרֶס בְּהֶיסֵּט, מַה שֶּׁאֵין כֵּן בִּשְׁאָר טְמֵאִין, דִּכְתִיב (שם): "וּכְלִי חֶרֶס אֲשֶׁר יִגַּע בּוֹ הַזָּב יִשָּׁבֵר". וְתַנְיָא בְּתוֹרַת כֹּהֲנִים: יָכוֹל יְטַמֵּא הַזָּב כְּלִי חֶרֶס מֵאֲחוֹרָיו בְּמַגָּע? נֶאֱמַר כָּאן "בּוֹ", וְנֶאֱמַר לְהַלָּן "וּכְלִי חֶרֶס אֲשֶׁר תְּבוּשַּׁל בּוֹ יִשָּׁבֵר". מַה לְּהַלָּן — מֵאֲוִירוֹ, אַף כָּאן — מֵאֲוִירוֹ. אִם כֵּן, מַה ת"ל "אֲשֶׁר יִגַּע בּוֹ", וַהֲלֹא אֲוִיר כְּלִי חֶרֶס טָמֵא בְּלֹא נְגִיעָה, כִּדְקַיְימָא לָן בְּ"הַכֹּל שׁוֹחֲטִין" (חולין כד.) תּוֹכוֹ, אע"פ שֶׁלֹּא נָגַע בּוֹ. אֶלָּא אֵיזֶהוּ מַגָּעוֹ שֶׁהוּא כְּכוּלּוֹ? — הֱוֵי אוֹמֵר: זֶה הֶיסֵּטוֹ. מְקוּלְקֶלֶת לְמִנְיָנָהּ. אַבְּדָה פֶּתַח נִדּוּתָהּ. שֶׁאִילּוּ הָיְתָה יוֹדַעַת יוֹם רְאִיָּיתָהּ, תְּהֵא סוֹפֶרֶת. (ג) אִם תִּרְאֶה לְאַחַר שִׁבְעָה — שׁוֹמֶרֶת יוֹם כְּנֶגֶד יוֹם, וְאִם תִּרְאֶה ג' — תְּהֵא זָבָה. אֲבָל עַכְשָׁיו שֶׁאֵינָהּ יוֹדַעַת יוֹם רְאִיָּיתָהּ — אֵינָהּ יוֹדַעַת אֵימָתַי הִיא בְּתוֹךְ י"א יוֹם שֶׁבֵּין נִדָּה לְנִדָּה, וַהֲרֵי הִיא טוֹעָה. וְאֵינָהּ מְקוּלְקֶלֶת לְמִנְיָנָהּ. דְּהָא וַדַּאי מֵהַשְׁתָּא הָוְיָא פֶּתַח נִדּוּתָהּ, וְלַיּוֹם שְׁמִינִי לִרְאִיָּיתָהּ יַתְחִילוּ י"א יוֹם שֶׁבֵּין נִדָּה לְנִדָּה. וְרַבָּנַן לָא גְּזוּר מֵעֵת לְעֵת אֶלָּא לְטָהֳרוֹת, אֲבָל גַּבֵּי כְּתָמִים לָא יָדְעִינַן אֵימַת נָפֵיק מִינָּהּ, וְאֵינָהּ מוֹנָה שִׁבְעָה יָמִים דְּקוֹדֶם טְבִילָה אֶלָּא מִשָּׁעָה שֶׁרָאֲתָה. וְכֵן בְּכֶתֶם, לְסוֹף ז' יָמִים טוֹבֶלֶת וּטְהוֹרָה. אֲבָל פֶּתַח נִדּוּתָהּ, לֵידַע אֵימַת מַתְחִילִין יְמֵי זִיבָה אָבְדָה (א) עַד שֶׁתֵּשֵׁב ז' נְקִיִּים, כִּדְתַנְיָא בַּעֲרָכִין (דף ח.). וְרָבָא. דִּפְשִׁיטָא לֵיהּ בִּכְלֵי חֶרֶס לְעֵיל, וְגָמַר מִשְׁכָּבוֹת מִכְּלֵי חֶרֶס, מַאי שְׁנָא דִּפְשִׁיטָא לֵיהּ בִּכְלֵי חֶרֶס טְפֵי מִמִּשְׁכָּב? אִי שְׁמִיעַ לֵיהּ הָא מַתְנִיתָא. דְּקָתָנֵי "כְּלֵי חֶרֶס", לֵימָא מַתְנִיתָא, וְלִיפְשׁוֹט מִינָּהּ מִשְׁכָּבָהּ לְהֶדְיָא. וְאִי לָא שְׁמִיעַ לֵיהּ מַתְנִיתָא קַל וָחוֹמֶר מְנָא לֵיהּ. מִכְּלֵי חֶרֶס, הָא כְּלֵי חֶרֶס גּוּפֵיהּ לָא קָאָמַר לֵיהּ? אִי מִמַּתְנִיתָא. הֲוֵי אָמֵינָא: לְמִשְׁכָּבוֹת דְּקָתָנֵי: לְטַמֵּא אָדָם אוֹ בְּגָדִים. אֲבָל אָדָם וּבְגָדִים. שֶׁהָאָדָם יְטַמֵּא בְּגָדָיו שֶׁלֹּא נָגְעוּ בַּמִּשְׁכָּבוֹת, אֵימָא לָא, קמ"ל קַל וָחוֹמֶר מִכְּלֵי חֶרֶס. וְה"ק: וּמַה כְּלֵי חֶרֶס, שֶׁנִּיצּוֹל בְּאֹהֶל הַמֵּת — אֵינוֹ נִיצּוֹל בְּמֵעֵת לְעֵת שֶׁבְּנִדָּה מִלְּטַמֵּא בְּהֶיסֵּט, כְּאִילּוּ נִיסַּט מִנִּדָּה עַצְמָהּ. מִשְׁכָּבוֹת, שֶׁאֵין נִיצּוֹלִין בְּאֹהֶל הַמֵּת — אֵינוֹ דִּין שֶׁאֵין נִיצּוֹלִין בְּמֵעֵת לְעֵת שֶׁבְּנִדָּה מִלְּטַמֵּא כְּמִשְׁכַּב נִדָּה גְּמוּרָה! גַּבֵּי מַעֲלוֹת. בְּפֶרֶק "חוֹמֶר בַּקֹּדֶשׁ" (חגיגה כ.). מֵעֵת לְעֵת. לֵיכָּא דְּרָרָא דְּטוּמְאָה, דְּהַשְׁתָּא הוּא דַּחֲזַאי, אֶלָּא גְּזֵירָה בְּעָלְמָא הוּא. מַה הִיא מְטַמְּאָה. הַיְינוּ בָּרַיְיתָא דִּלְעֵיל. לֹא דְּקֹדֶשׁ. כְּגוֹן: שֶׁמֶן דִּמְנָחוֹת וְיֵין דִּנְסָכִים. אַף בִּשְׁעַת עֲבֵרָתָן. מַתְנִיתִין הִיא (לקמן ד' יא.) אַף בְּשָׁעָה שֶׁהֵם מְסַלְּקוֹת וּמִתְעַסְּקוֹת לֶאֱכוֹל תְּרוּמָה, צְרִיכוֹת לִבְדּוֹק. לְתַקֵּן שִׁירַיִם שֶׁבְּפָנֶיהָ. שֶׁנָּגְעָה בָּהֶם. וּמְהַנְיָא לָהּ הַךְ בְּדִיקָה, שֶׁאִם תִּמָּצֵא עַכְשָׁיו טְהוֹרָה, לִכְשֶׁתִּבְדּוֹק עַרְבִית כְּמִשְׁפָּטָהּ וְתִמָּצֵא טְמֵאָה — לֹא תְּטַמֵּא לְמַפְרֵעַ אֶלָּא עַד שְׁעַת בְּדִיקָתָהּ. וְלֹא תְּהֵא הַתְּרוּמָה בִּכְלַל טוּמְאָה דְּמַפְרֵעַ, שֶׁהֲרֵי בָּדְקָה לְאַחַר הָעֲבָרָתָהּ. אַלְמָא, טוּמְאַת מַפְרֵעַ לִתְרוּמָה נַמִּי גְּזוּר. לְתַקֵּן. דּוּמְיָא דִּלְהַכְשִׁיר דְּאָמַר לְעֵיל: שַׁחֲרִית — לְהַכְשִׁיר טָהֳרוֹת שֶׁל לַיְלָה כו'. וּמְשַׁנֵּינַן: רַב הוּנָא מַתְנֵי. לְהָא דְּרַבִּי יְהוּדָה, שֶׁבְּדִיקָה זוֹ בָּאָה לִשְׂרוֹף שִׁירַיִם שֶׁבְּיָדֶיהָ, אִם תִּמָּצֵא טְמֵאָה — תִּשָּׂרֵף, וּכְגוֹן שֶׁבּוֹדֶקֶת עַצְמָהּ לְאַחַר עֲבֵרָתָהּ לְאַלְתַּר. כְּשִׁיעוּר וֶסֶת. מִיָּד סָמוּךְ לִנְגִיעָה בְּדִיקָה, דְּאִם תִּמָּצֵא טְמֵאָה — וַדַּאי בִּשְׁעַת נְגִיעָה נַמִּי טְמֵאָה הָיְתָה, דַּאֲפִילּוּ חוּלִּין נַמִּי מְטַמּוּ. וּמַצְרִיךְ לָהּ ר' יְהוּדָה בְּדִיקָה לִתְרוּמָה כְּשִׁיעוּר וֶסֶת, כִּי הֵיכִי דְּלָא תֵּיכוּל תְּרוּמָה טְמֵאָה לְאַחַר זְמַן. אֲבָל לְתַקֵּן, לָא סְבִירָא לֵיהּ לְרַב הוּנָא. דְּכָל כַּמָּה דְּלָא בָּדְקָה — מִיתַּקְנָא וְקַיְימָא, דְּטוּמְאַת מַפְרֵעַ לָא גְּזוּר בֵּיהּ רַבָּנַן. [כְּשִׁיעוּר] וֶסֶת. מְפָרֵשׁ בְּפ"ב (לקמן יד:) מָשָׁל לְשַׁמָּשׁ וְעֵד שֶׁעוֹמְדִין בְּצַד הַמַּשְׁקוֹף, בִּיצִיאַת הַשַּׁמָּשׁ נִכְנָס הָעֵד, וּלְשׁוֹן "וֶסֶת" הַיְינוּ: מִיָּד. מַעֲשֶׂה וְעָשָׂה רַבִּי כְּר' אֱלִיעֶזֶר. בְּאִשָּׁה יַלְדָּה שֶׁעָבְרוּ עָלֶיהָ שָׁלֹשׁ עוֹנוֹת שֶׁל שְׁלֹשִׁים יוֹם שֶׁלֹּא רָאֲתָה, וְאָמַר רַבִּי אֱלִיעֶזֶר בְּמַתְנִיתִין (לקמן ז.): כָּל אִשָּׁה שֶׁעָבְרוּ עָלֶיהָ שָׁלֹשׁ עוֹנוֹת — דַּיָּהּ שַׁעְתָּהּ. וּפְלִיגִי רַבָּנַן עֲלֵיהּ, דְּאֵין דַּיָּהּ שַׁעְתָּהּ אֶלָּא שֶׁעָבְרוּ עָלֶיהָ ג' עוֹנוֹת מֵחֲמַת זִקְנָה סָמוּךְ לְזִקְנָתָהּ. לְאַחַר שֶׁנִּזְכַּר. שֶׁלֹּא יָפֶה עָשָׂה. בִּשְׁעַת

א) גי' רש"א עד שתשב שבעה עשר נקיים ע"ש

---

**תוספות**

ואינה מונה אלא משעה שראתה. תימה: פשיטא, כיון דמקולקלת למנינה משעת כיבוס, ואינה יודעת מתי ראתה, אם כן לא תוכל לספור ז' ימים ולטבול, אלא מיום מציאת הכתם! וי"ל: דמיירי שראתה יום אחד או ב' ימים אחר מציאת הכתם, וקמ"ל: דאינה מונה מיום מציאת הכתם, אלא מיום שראתה.

[ואי ממתניתא ה"א או אדם או בגדים. הקשה הר"ר: היכי מצי למימר "או אדם או בגדים", והא ברייתא דקתני, אדימי קתני: משכבה ומושבה כמגעה.א] והשתא מגעה לא מטמא, לא אדם ולא בגדים. ואי במגע עצמה, מטמאה אדם ובגדים. גי'].

אבל היכא דליכא דררא דטומאה לא קתני. וא"ת: ליתני ליה במעלות אחרונות, דאמרינן התם (חגיגה דף כא:) חמש קמייתא, (ג) אית להו דררא דטומאה דאורייתא — איתנהו בין בקדש ובין בחולין שנעשו על טהרת קדש. בתרייתא, דלית להו דררא דטומאה דאורייתא — איתנהו בקדש כו' *ופי' "דאית להו דררא דטומאה דאורייתא": כלומר, שייכי בטומאה הנוהגת בחולין דאורייתא. אבל בתרייתא — לא שייכי כלל בטומאה דאורייתא הנוהגת בחולין. אבל אין לפרש: דרישא קתני טומאה דאורייתא, וסיפא טומאה דרבנן — דהא קתני בקמייתא "בגדי אוכלי תרומה מדרס לאוכלי קדש", דהוי דרבנן. ובבתרייתא נמי קתני צירוף ורביעי בקדש, דהוי דאורייתא. וי"ל: דמעת לעת לית ליה אפילו דררא דטומאה דרבנן. וא"ת: והא מעת לעת אפילו בחולין טמא, כשנעשו על טהרת הקדש, כדאמר בסמוך: קבלה מיניה רב שמואל ברבי יצחק — בחולין שנעשו על טהרת הקדש. והנך בתרייתא ליתנהו בחולין שנעשו על טהרת הקדש, ואית להו דררא דטומאה טפי, כדפרישית! וי"ל: לפי שרגילות הוא קצת שנעקר הדם לפני ראייתה, לכך גזרו רבנן אף בחולין שנעשו על טהרת הקדש, ואף לתרומה לאיכא דאמרי. ומכל מקום לית להו דררא דטומאה, משום דבשעה שעוסקין בטהרות אין שם ספק טומאה, ואין לה להניח ולפרוש מלעסוק בטהרות, שאינה יודעת מתי תראה אחרי כן.

מאי לאו בין דקדש בין דתרומה. וא"ת: ואמאי לא פריך ממתני' דמטמאה מעת לעת, ונימא: מאי לאו בין דקדש בין דתרומה? וי"ל: דפריך מהכא, משום דנחית לפרושי אוכלין ומשקין, והוה ליה לפרושי גם דקדש. ואם תאמר: ואמאי לא מייתי סייעתא מדתניא בפרק "בא סימן" (לקמן נג:) דמטמאה עצמה וקדשים למפרע, דמשמע: קדשים — ולא תרומה, וקשה לאיכא דאמרי אף לתרומה? וי"ל: דנקט התם קדשים — משום דרשב"א פליג התם אף בקדשים.

כשבדקה עצמה כשיעור וסת. לאו בדיקה לגמרי קאמר, דבדיקה הויא לחורין ולסדקין, כדאמר פרק "כל היד" (לקמן דף יד:) דהויא טפי משיעור וסת. אלא כלומר, קנחה עצמה. והוה מצי למימר בדיקה ממש, לתלות, דאפילו אחר זמן הוי ספיקא דאורייתא, דמחייב לקמן ב"כל היד" (שם) אשם תלוי. ואפילו למאן דפטר, היינו משום דבעי חתיכה משתי חתיכות, אבל ספיקא דאורייתא מיהו הוי לה. אלא דניחא ליה למנקט שיעור וסת, ולשרוף (הג"ה: אף ברה"ר. דבשמעתין של פרוזדור מוכיח דאין חילוק בין רה"ר לרה"י לטומאה דאתא מגופה) אבל לאחר זמן, אע"ג דהוה ספק דאורייתא — אין שורפין, כדאמר בשמעתין ד"פרוזדור", ולקמן בפרק "האשה" (דף ס:) אמרינן: כל שבעלה באשם תלוי — טהרותיו תלויות וכל שבעלה בחטאת — טהרותיו טמאות, ואיכא דאמרי: כל שבעלה בחטאת — טהרותיו תלויות, אבל טמאות — לא הוו.

בשעת

---

**עין משפט נר מצוה**

ל א מיי' פ"ג מהלכות משכב ומושב הלכה ח:

לא ב ג מיי' שם ופ"ט מהלכות איסורי ביאה הלכה ג:

לב ד מיי' פ"ט מהלכות איסורי ביאה הלכה ג:

לג ה מיי' פ"ג מהלכות משכב ומושב הלכה ט:

**הגהות הב"ח**

**הגהות מהר"ב רנשבורג**

**תוספי הרא"ש**

---

בועלה לא שכיח דאמרו אסור לעשות כן שמא תבא לידי ספק וצ"ל דהכא נמי לא שכיח כמו משכבות ומושבות: *)תניא כותיה דרבא. דפשטא דברייתא משמע דמשכבות ומושבות אף לטמא אדם וכלים אף על דחי לה או אדם או בגדים: ואינה מונה אלא משעה שראתה. אע"ג דת"ק אינה מקולקלת ר' עקיבא איצטריך דאמר מטמאה את בועלה וס"ד נמי דמקולקלת: ומטמאה את בועלה. גר' דלקמן פ"ב תנן ומודים חכמים לר' עקיבא ברואה כתם שמטמאה את בועלה ופליגי בגמרא רב למפרע אי להבא ומסתמא רבנן דהכא היינו רבנן דהתם: ואינה מונה אלא משעה שראתה. מקולקלת למנינה לחומרא מ"מ ימי נדותה אינה מונה אלא משעה שראתה ומילתא דפשיטא היא: ...תא קאמר משכבה ומושבה כמגעה וממה נפשך לא מצי למימר או אדם או בגדים דאי כמגעה לא אוכלין ומשקין ואי כמגע עצמה אדם ובגדים ליטמא. ותירץ רבינו מאיר דסד"א דהא דקאמר דהוי אב הטומאה כמגע עצמה ולא ראשון. ומי' לאו לגמרי כמגע עצמה דאילו התם לטמא בגדים. ואילו הכא או אדם או בגדים. דאין סברא להחמיר כל כך במעת לעת כמשכב נדה גמורה: דלית ליה דררא דטומאה לא קתני. תימה דהא אמרינן בפרק חומר בקודש דעשר מעלות שנו כאן

דטומאה ג)מעת לעת חשיב דררא דטומאה טפי מה' בתרייתא הלכך הוו כחולין שנעשו על טהרת הקודש: מאי לאו בין דקודש בין דתרומה. תימה תיקשי ליה מתני' דמטמאה מעת לעת מאי לאו בתרומה. וי"ל משום דהך ברייתא נחתא לפרושי טפי דקת' אוכלין ומשקין וגם משכבות ומושבות וס"ד דאי לא איירי אלא בקודש הוה ליה לפרושי. וא"ת אמאי לא מייתי ליה סייעתא מדתניא מטמאה עצמה וקדשים למפרע פי' עצמה שמקולקלת למנינה וקאמר דדוקא קדשים מטמא לקמן עצמה לטהרות ולישנא דעצמה לא משמע כפירושו. ועוד דלפי' תיקשי מהך ברייתא דאמר אבל לא לתרומה. וי"ל לא נקט דוקא קדשים אלא משום רבותא דר' שמעון בן אלעזר דפליג אף בקדשים: שבדקה עצמה כשיעור אותיום. בשלהי פירקין גבי הא דבעי מיניה הונא אשה מהו שתבדוק עצמה כשיעור אותיום. לחייב בעלה חטאת. ופריך מי שיעור אותיום והתניא איזהו שיעור אותיום כו' אלא מהו שתקנה. ה"ה הכא מצי הכי. א"נ התם גבי תשמיש דמסתמא לא פירש בקושי. וקיימא לן בסוף פ"ב דשבועות בעריות פטור ולא מחייבינן ליה אלא אשעת קישוי הלכך אחר פירשתו באבר מת הוי

*) ע"ב שייך לדף ה'

א) נראה דחסר כאן וצ"ל הוה אמינא או אדם או בגדים. ותימה הא מתניתא קאמר וכו'. ב) נראה דצ"ל דטומאה טפי מעל"ע ומיהו מעל"ע חשיב וכו'.

בְּשָׁעַת הַדְּחָק. וְהָוֵינַן בָּהּ: *מַאי "לְאַחַר שֶׁנִּזְכַּר"? אִילֵימָא לְאַחַר שֶׁנִּזְכַּר דְּאֵין הֲלָכָה כְּרַבִּי אֱלִיעֶזֶר אֶלָּא כְּרַבָּנַן, בִּשְׁעַת הַדְּחָק הֵיכִי עָבֵיד כְּוָותֵיהּ? אֶלָּא (לָאו) דְּלָא אִיתְמַר הִלְכְתָא לָא כְּמַר וְלָא כְּמַר, וְכֵיוָן שֶׁנִּזְכַּר — דְּלָאו יָחִיד פָּלֵיג עֲלֵיהּ אֶלָּא רַבִּים פְּלִיגִי עֲלֵיהּ, אָמַר "כְּדַי הוּא רַבִּי אֱלִיעֶזֶר *לִסְמוֹךְ עָלָיו בִּשְׁעַת הַדְּחָק". אִי אָמְרַתְּ בִּשְׁלָמָא לִתְרוּמָה — הַיְינוּ דַּהֲוַאי תְּרוּמָה בִּימֵי רַבִּי, אֶלָּא אִי אָמְרַתְּ לְקֹדֶשׁ — °קֹדֶשׁ בִּימֵי רַבִּי מִי הֲוַאי? כִּדְעוּלָּא, *דְּאָמַר עוּלָּא: חַבְרַיָּא מַדְכַן בְּגָלִילָא, הָכָא נַמִּי בִּימֵי רַבִּי. ת"ש: מַעֲשֶׂה בְּשִׁפְחָתוֹ שֶׁל רַבָּן גַּמְלִיאֵל שֶׁהָיְתָה אוֹפָה כִּכָּרוֹת שֶׁל תְּרוּמָה, וּבֵין כָּל אַחַת וְאַחַת מְדִיחָה יָדֶיהָ בַּמַּיִם וּבוֹדֶקֶת. בָּאַחֲרוֹנָה בָּדְקָה וּמָצְאָה טְמֵאָה, וּבָאת וְשָׁאֲלָה אֶת רַבָּן גַּמְלִיאֵל וְאָמַר לָהּ: כּוּלָּן טְמֵאוֹת. אָמְרָה לוֹ: רַבִּי, וַהֲלֹא בְּדִיקָה הָיְתָה לִי בֵּין כָּל אַחַת וְאַחַת? אָמַר לָהּ: א"כ הִיא טְמֵאָה וְכוּלָּן טְהוֹרוֹת. קָתָנֵי מִיהַת "כִּכָּרוֹת שֶׁל תְּרוּמָה"! א] מַאי "תְּרוּמָה"? — תְּרוּמַת לַחְמֵי תוֹדָה. תְּרוּמַת לַחְמֵי תוֹדָה בַּאֲפִיָּה מַאי בָּעֲיָא? דְּאַפְרְשִׁינְהוּ בְּלִישַׁיְיהוּ. וְכִי הָא דְּאָמַר רַב טוֹבִי *בַּר רַב קְטִינָא: אלַחְמֵי תוֹדָה שֶׁאֲפָאָן ד' חַלּוֹת — יָצָא. וְהָוֵינַן בָּהּ: וְהָא בָּעֵינַן אַרְבָּעִים? בלְמִצְוָה. וְהָא בָּעֵינַן אַפְרוּשֵׁי תְּרוּמָה מִינַּיְיהוּ? וְכִי תֵּימָא דְּמַפְרִישׁ פְּרוּסָה מִכָּל חַד וְחַד — *"אֶחָד" אָמַר רַחֲמָנָא — גשֶׁלֹּא יִטּוֹל פְּרוּסָה! וְאָמְרִינַן: דדְּאַפְרְשִׁינְהוּ בְּלִישַׁיְיהוּ, הָכָא נַמִּי — דְּאַפְרְשִׁינְהוּ בְּלִישַׁיְיהוּ. ת"ש: שׁוּב מַעֲשֶׂה בְּשִׁפְחָה שֶׁל רַבָּן גַּמְלִיאֵל שֶׁהָיְתָה גָּפָה חָבִיּוֹת שֶׁל יַיִן, וּבֵין כָּל אַחַת וְאַחַת מְדִיחָה יָדֶיהָ בַּמַּיִם וּבוֹדֶקֶת. וּבָאַחֲרוֹנָה בָּדְקָה וּמָצְאָה טְמֵאָה, וּבָאת וְשָׁאֲלָה לְרַבָּן גַּמְלִיאֵל וְאָמַר לָהּ: כּוּלָּן טְמֵאוֹת. אָמְרָה לוֹ: וַהֲלֹא בְּדִיקָה הָיְתָה לִי בֵּין כָּל אַחַת וְאַחַת? אָמַר לָהּ: אִם כֵּן, הִיא טְמֵאָה וְכוּלָּן טְהוֹרוֹת. אִי אָמְרַתְּ בִּשְׁלָמָא חֲדָא דְּקֹדֶשׁ וַחֲדָא דִּתְרוּמָה הִיא, הַיְינוּ דְּהַדְרָה וְשָׁיְילָה, אֶלָּא אִי אָמְרַתְּ אִידִי וְאִידִי דְּקֹדֶשׁ, לָמָּה לָהּ לְמֶהְדַּר וּלְשַׁיְילֵיהּ? מַעֲשֶׂה שֶׁהָיָה — בִּשְׁתֵּי שְׁפָחוֹת הָיָה. לִישָּׁנָא אַחֲרִינָא אָמְרִי לָהּ: אָמַר רַב הוּנָא מֵעֵת לְעֵת שֶׁבְּנִדָּה — *המְטַמְּאָה בֵּין לְקֹדֶשׁ וּבֵין לִתְרוּמָה, מִמַּאי? — מִדְּלָא קָתָנֵי לָהּ גַּבֵּי מַעֲלוֹת. א"ל רַב נַחְמָן: וְהָא תָּנֵי תַּנָּא "לְקֹדֶשׁ אֲבָל לֹא לִתְרוּמָה"! *קַבְּלָהּ מִינֵּיהּ רַב שְׁמוּאֵל בַּר רַב יִצְחָק: ובְּחוּלִּין שֶׁנַּעֲשׂוּ עַל טׇהֳרַת קֹדֶשׁ, וְלֹא בְּחוּלִּין שֶׁנַּעֲשׂוּ עַל טׇהֳרַת תְּרוּמָה. *תְּנַן הָתָם: זנוֹלַד לָהּ סְפֵק טוּמְאָה, עַד שֶׁלֹּא גִּלְגְּלָה — תֵּעָשֶׂה בְּטוּמְאָה, מִשֶּׁגִּלְגְּלָה — תֵּעָשֶׂה בְּטׇהֳרָה. עַד שֶׁלֹּא גִּלְגְּלָה — תֵּעָשֶׂה בְּטוּמְאָה, חוּלִּין נִינְהוּ, *חוּמוּתָּר לִגְרוֹם טוּמְאָה לְחוּלִּין שֶׁבְּאֶרֶץ יִשְׂרָאֵל. מִשֶּׁגִּלְגְּלָה — תֵּעָשֶׂה בְּטׇהֳרָה, חוּלִּין הַטְּבוּלִין לְחַלָּה — כְּחַלָּה דָּמוּ, *וְאָסוּר לִגְרוֹם טוּמְאָה לְחַלָּה. טתָּנָא: וַחֲלָתָהּ

בְּשָׁעַת הַדְּחָק. שְׁנֵי בַּצּוֹרֶת הָיוּ, וְלֹא רָצָה לְהַפְסִיד טָהֳרוֹת. אֶלָּא רַבִּים פְּלִיגֵי עֲלֵיהּ. וּבְטֵלִין דִּבְרֵי הַיָּחִיד, וְהִתְחִיל לְהִתְחָרֵט, וְאָמַר "כְּדַי הוּא" כו'. קֹדֶשׁ בִּימֵי רַבִּי מִי הֲוָה. כַּמָּה שָׁנִים הָיָה אַחַר הַחוּרְבָּן, בְּסוֹף הַתַּנָּאִים. חַבְרַיָּא מַדְכַן בְּגָלִילָא. חֲבֵרִים שֶׁבַּגָּלִיל מְטַהֲרִים יֵינָם לִנְסָכִים, וְשַׁמְנָן לִמְנָחוֹת, שֶׁמָּא יִבָּנֶה בהמ"ק בִּימֵיהֶם, וּלְעוֹלָם קֹדֶשׁ הָווּ. כָּךְ שָׁמַעְתִּי בְּ"חוֹמֶר בַּקֹּדֶשׁ", וְכָךְ הִיא שְׁנוּיָה. (א). כּוּלָּן טְמֵאוֹת. מִשּׁוּם מֵעֵת לְעֵת שֶׁבְּנִדָּה. הִיא טְמֵאָה. מִשּׁוּם פְּקִידָה לִפְקִידָה. תְּרוּמַת לַחְמֵי תוֹדָה. אַרְבַּע חַלּוֹת מִד' מִינִין שֶׁבַּתּוֹדָה נוֹתְנִין לַכֹּהֵן, דִּכְתִיב (ויקרא ז): "וְהִקְרִיב מִמֶּנּוּ אֶחָד מִכָּל קׇרְבָּן תְּרוּמָה" וגו'. בַּאֲפִיָּה מַאי בָּעֲיָא. הָא מ' חַלּוֹת בָּעֵי לָהּ לְמֵיפָא, וַהֲדַר אַפְרוּשֵׁי ד' לִתְרוּמָה, וְאַרְבָּעִין לָא מִיקְרוּ "תְּרוּמָה". וּמְשַׁנֵּי דְּאַפְרְשִׁינְהוּ בְּלִישַׁיְיהוּ. לְעוֹלָם מַאי "תְּרוּמָה" — תְּרוּמַת לַחְמֵי תוֹדָה, וּדְקָאָמַר: בַּאֲפִיָּה מַאי בָּעֲיָא — כְּגוֹן שֶׁהִפְרִישׁ לְד' מֵהָאַרְבָּעִים חַלּוֹת בְּעִיסָּתָן, וּלְאַחַר אֲפִיַּית כּוּלָּן שָׁחַט תּוֹדָה עֲלֵיהֶן. שֶׁאֲפָאָן ד' חַלּוֹת. עֶשֶׂר עֶשְׂרוֹנִים שֶׁל חָמֵץ אֲפָאָן כּוּלָּן בְּחַלָּה אַחַת, וְג' עֶשְׂרוֹנוֹת וּשְׁלִישׁ שֶׁבְּחַלּוֹת מַצָּה אֲפָאָן בְּחַלָּה אַחַת, וְכֵן שֶׁל רְקִיקִין, וְכֵן שֶׁל רְבוּכָה. הָא בָּעֵינַן מ'. בִּמְנָחוֹת יָלְפִינַן לָהּ בְּפֶרֶק "הַתּוֹדָה" (דף עו.) וְאַמַּאי יָצָא? וּמְשַׁנֵּי: לְמִצְוָה. אֲבָל עִיכּוּבָא — לֵיכָּא. וְהָא בָּעֵי אַפְרוּשֵׁי תְּרוּמָה. אַחַת מִכָּל מִין, דְּהַיְינוּ א' מֵעֶשֶׂר, וְכֵיוָן דְּלֵיכָּא עֶשֶׂר — הֵיאַךְ יַפְרִישׁ? וְכ"ת דְּמַפְרִישׁ פְּרוּסָה. מִכָּל חַלָּה מְעַט לַכֹּהֵן. אֶחָד אָמַר רַחֲמָנָא. "וְהִקְרִיב מִמֶּנּוּ אֶחָד מִכָּל קׇרְבָּן" וגו' וְדָרְשִׁינַן בִּמְנָחוֹת (דף עז.) שֶׁלֹּא יִטּוֹל פְּרוּסָה לִתְרוּמַת כֹּהֵן. דְּאַפְרְשִׁינְהוּ בְּלִישַׁיְיהוּ. נָטַל אֶחָד מֵעֶשֶׂר לִתְרוּמָה, וְתֵשַׁע הַנּוֹתָרִים לַבְּעָלִים, מִכָּל מִין וּמִין אָפָה בְּחַלָּה אַחַת. גָּפָה. סוֹתֶמֶת בְּטִיט בְּיָדֶיהָ, וּמְדִיחָה יָדֶיהָ מִן הַטִּיט. קִבְּלָהּ מִינֵּיהּ רַב שְׁמוּאֵל. לְהַךְ תְּיוּבְתָּא מֵרַב נַחְמָן, וְאוֹקְמָא לְהָא דְּקָתָנֵי: "לְקֹדֶשׁ אֲבָל לֹא לִתְרוּמָה", הָכִי קָאָמַר: בְּחוּלִּין שֶׁנַּעֲשׂוּ עַל טׇהֳרַת קֹדֶשׁ כו' אֲבָל בִּתְרוּמָה מַמָּשׁ — נָהֲגָא. נוֹלַד לָהּ. גָּרְסִי'. נוֹלַד בָּעִיסָּה סְפֵק טוּמְאָה. גִּלְגּוּל בְּחוּלִּין. זֶהוּ גְּמַר מְלָאכָה לְחַלָּה. תֵּעָשֶׂה בְּטוּמְאָה. אִם יִרְצֶה — יְטַמְּאֶנָּה בַּיָּד, דְּסוֹף סוֹף חַלַּת סָפֵק הִיא, וְלֹא תֵּאָכֵל. תֵּעָשֶׂה בְּטׇהֳרָה. בְּכֵלִים טְהוֹרִים, וְאַל יְטַמְּאֶנָּה בַּיָּד. וְאַע"פ דְּסוֹף סוֹף חַלָּתָהּ אֲסוּרָה — אָסוּר לְטַמְּאָהּ בַּיָּד. הוֹאִיל וְנִגְמְרָה מְלַאכְתָּהּ לְחַלָּה, אָסוּר לִגְרוֹם לָהּ טוּמְאָה וַדָּאִית, דִּכְתִיב: "וַאֲנִי נָתַתִּי לְךָ אֶת מִשְׁמֶרֶת תְּרוּמוֹתָי", וְדָרְשִׁינַן בִּבְכוֹרוֹת (דף לד.) שְׁתֵּי תְרוּמוֹת בְּמַשְׁמַע, טְהוֹרָה וּתְלוּיָה, וְאָמַר קְרָא: שׁוֹמְרֶנָּה. וַחֲלָתָהּ

**בשעת** הדחק. פירש רש"י: בשני בצורת. ולא דק, דבפירקין (לקמן דף ט:) אמר דאפי' רבנן מודו בשני בצורת. וי"ל: דהאי "בשעת הדחק" היינו אדם שנגע במעת לעת שבנדה, ועשה מעט טהרות לפני ראייתה, ואחר הוראתו עסק בטהרות הרבה. ולא דמי לשני בצורת, כיון דמקודם לכן לא היתה שעת הדחק, ואפיש בטהרות ע"י הוראת טעות. ועוד י"ל: "שעת הדחק" — שהשואל הלך לו, והיה טורח גדול לרדוף אחריו, כדאמר בפרק "אע"פ" (כתובות דף ס:) רהטו אבתריה תלתא *מילי בחלא, ולא אדרכיה.

**דאפרשינהו** בלישייהו. אף על גב דאין הלחם קדוש אלא משקרמו פניו בתנור, ונשחט עליו הזבח (מנחות עח:) מ"מ קרי להו "תרומה" — לפי שיחדו אותה לקרות לה שם תרומה לאחר אפייה ושחיטת הזבח, והיתה מופרשת בלישייהו. ולא לאחר אפייה, משום דבעודה עיסה יכול לעשותה עבות ונאות. ונראה דקדושת (*הפת) איכא עלייהו, ואסור לשנותה בחלות אחרות. כדמשמע סוף פרק קמא דנדרים (דף יב.) "כחלת אהרן ובניו וכתרומתו" — מותרין, ודייק: הא "כתרומת לחמי תודה" — אסור! ומוקי: דאפרשינהו בלישייהו. ומדאסר הככר שהתפיס בלחמי תודה, משמע דאיכא עליה קדושת *הפת בעודה עיסה.

**בשפחתו** של ר"ג. פירש רשב"ס דהיינו ר"ג הזקן, דאמרינן בשילהי פ"ק דשבת (ד' טו.) הלל ושמעון, גמליאל ושמעון, נהגו נשיאותן *לפני הבית ק' שנה. ומיהו אין רגילות להזכיר סתם ר"ג אלא ר"ג הזקן. ויכול להיות שזהו ר"ג דיבנה, חבירו של רבי אליעזר ורבי יהושע. **נולד** לה ספק טומאה עד שלא גלגלה. פירוש: נולד לה ספק טומאה, הנוהגת אף בחולין, קודם גלגול — יכול לגרום לה טומאה ודאית. ואין לאסור משום "משמרת תרומותי", דקודם גלגול אכתי לא פתיכא ביה חלה. כמו המפריש חלתו קמח — דלא עשה ולא כלום. והפסד כהן נמי ליכא — כיון דנולד לה ספק טומאה כבר משגלגלה. "תעשה בטהרה" — פירוש: אם לאחר גלגול נולד לה ספק טומאה, דלא שייך בחולין אלא בחלה — תעשה בטהרה. אע"ג דחלתה תלויה, וליכא הפסד כהן — אסור לגרום לה טומאה, משום "משמרת תרומותי". וה"ה דאפי' נולד לה ספק טומאה דשייכא אף לחולין, דאסור לגרום טומאה. אלא דמפרש בברייתא: איזה ספק אמרו, בספק חלה, דאפילו בספק טומאה דלא שייכא בחולין — חלתה תלויה. ואשמועינן: חולין הטבולין לחלה — כחלה דמו. אבל אין לפרש: דרישא נמי, שנולד לה ספק טומאה עד שלא גלגלה, איירי נמי בספק חלה, דהיינו בטומאה דלא שייכא בחולין, ואע"ג דעדיין טהורה גמורה היא — תעשה בטומאה ודאית. דקודם גלגול, אכתי לא איקרי "טבולה לחלה", ולא אסור משום "משמרת תרומותי". והפסד כהן נמי ליכא, שיפריש עליה ממקום אחר. דאין נראה דקרי "ספק טומאה" קודם גלגול, כיון שטהורה גמורה היא. ואם תאמר: דאמר בעבודה זרה פ' "רבי ישמעאל" (דף נו. ושם) אין בוצרין עם ישראל העושה פירותיו בטומאה. ויש פירוש שפירש רש"י בהם: משום דאסור לגרום טומאה לתרומה, משום "משמרת תרומותי". והשתא, הלא אין קבע למעשר, אלא עד שיקפה, או עד שישלה. והכא אמר: עד שלא גלגלה — תעשה בטומאה? וי"ל: דהתם, אם הפריש אפילו קודם שיקפה או שישלה — הוי תרומה, כמו שהקדימו בשבלין. אבל הכא, אם הפריש חלה קודם גלגול, הוי כמו הפריש חלתו קמח, דאמר ב"האיש מקדש" (קדושין דף מו:) דלא עשה ולא כלום. ולכך לא מיקריא "טבולה לחלה" (ועל פירוש הקונטרס קשה: דבתוספתא דחלה מסיים בה הכי: "וכן פירות, עד שלא נגמרה מלאכתן — יעשו בטומאה, משנגמרה מלאכתן — יעשו בטהרה". גי') אי נמי: יש לפרש: דהתם נמי לא אסור משום "משמרת תרומותי" כפירש"י, כיון דאכתי לא הוקבע לתרום. אלא משום הפסד כהן אסר לה. אבל הכא, כבר נולד לה ספק, וליכא הפסד כהן.

לד א ב ג ד מיי' פי"ט מהל' מעשה קרבנות הלכה כב:
לה ה ו מיי' פ"ג מהל' משכב ומושב הלכ' ט:
לו ז מיי' פ"ח מהלכות בכורים הלכה י סמג עשין קמא:
לז ח מיי' שם ופי"ז הלכה יב ופט"ז מהל' טומאת אוכלין הלכה ט:
[נ"ל פרסין]
לח ט מיי' פ"ח מהלכות בכורים הלכה י ופי"א מהלכות שאר אבות הטומאות הלכה טז:
ס"א הפה נמי איכא

[לקמן ט: עירובין מו.]
ס"א ל"ג
[ברכות ט. וש"נ]
חגיגה כה.
[נדרים יב: ע"ש מנחות עו.] וכס איתא בר רב קיטנא]
מנחות עז: [פסחים לז. נדרים יב:]
חלה פ"ג מ"ב
[לקמן ז.]
[סוטה לג.]
[סוטה שם גיטין נג.]

### הגהות הב"ח
(א) רש"י ד"ה חבריא וכו' היא שנויה. נ"ב בקף כה:

### גליון הש"ס
גמ' קודש בימי רבי מי הוה. [illegible] אבל פ"ג הלכה א' [illegible] שם מטמאה בין לקודש ובין לתרומה. [illegible] לט ע"ב [illegible]

### תוספי הרא"ש
לקינוח ולא לבדיקה. אבל אי הוי משמש מת בעריות חייב או שפירש בקישוי הוי שפיר שיעור אותיום לבדיקה כ"ש לענין אוכלת בתרומה: **בשעת** הדחק. פרש"י שנת בצורת. וליתא דהא רבנן מודו לקמן בפירקין בשנת בצורת או היכא דאפיש טהרות. אלא לא הוה כולי האי שעת הדחק כמו הנך דלקמן: **והוינן** בה מאי לאחר שנזכר. הוה מצי למפשט בלא והוינן בה אלא משום דמילתא דתמיהא היא אם אין הלכה כר' אליעזר למה סמך עליו בשעת הדחק הלכך נחת לפרושי: **דאפרישינהו** בלישייהו. לא שקרא עליה שם דהא בקרימת התנור ובשחיטת הזבח הוא דקדשי ובתר הכי כתי' והרים אלא שיחדם לשם תרומה ולעשותם יפים ונאים לכבוד המצוה ואפשר אע"פ שיחדם יכול לשנותם דאכתי לא קדשי: **הכא** נמי דאפרישינהו בלישייהו. ולא הוו אלא חולין שנעשו על טהרת הקדש דאכתי לא קדשי. אי נמי לאחר שקרמו פניהם בתנור ונשחט עליהם הזבח ונטמאו כשהוציאתן מן התנור: **מעשה** שהיה בשתי שפחות היה. הקשה ה"ר שמשון מקוצי לישני חדא בקדש וחדא בחולין שנעשו על טהרת הקדש דהוה ניחא טפי דהשתא קשה אפי' את"ל דשתי שפחו' היה אמאי הוצרך לשנות אלו שני המעשים כיון דהכל איירי בענין אחד. ותירץ ר"מ אי הוה מוקמינן להו הכי הוה צריכינן לאוקומי ההיא דהיתה גפה חביות בחולין שנעשו על טהרת הקדש. וכיון דהיין היה עדיין בחביות א"כ לא נתקדש עדיין בכלי ולא הוי אלא חולין שנעשו על טהרת הקדש. וההוא עובדא דחביות היה באחרונה מדקתני בברייתא ושוב מעשה בשפחה. וא"כ הוה קשה כיון דאמר לה גבי קדש דכולן טהורות כ"ש בחולין שנעשו על טהרות הקדש. ולמה לה למהדר ולשיולי וליכא למימר דהוצרכה לישאל משום האחרונה דלא היתה יודעת כלל אם יש טומאה למפרע בחולין שנעשו על טהרת הקדש. מ"מ כי אמר לה גבי חביות דכולן טמאות למה לה למהדר ולימא ליה והלא בדיקה היתה לי בין כל אחת ואחת כיון דאפי' בקדש קאמר לה כולן טהורות כ"ש בחולין שנעשו על טהרת הקדש. אבל אי קמייתא הואי בתרומה ובתרייתא בחולין שנעשו על טהרת הקדש א) מטמאה מעת לעת ולא מהניא בדיקה שבנתיים ולפי מאי דפירשתי לעיל דלא משכחת לה לחמי תודה דהוו קדש אלא בשחט עליהן הזבח בעודם בתנור ניחא דלא בעי לשנויי הכי דלכתחלה אין שוחטין את התודה אם לא יהיה הלחם בעזרה דלא פליגי ר' יוחנן ור"ל בפרק התודה אלא בשוחט את התודה בדיעבד ולחמה חוץ לחומה ור' יוחנן מכשיר ור"ל פוסל. אבל לכתחלה אין שוחטין את התודה עד שיהא הלחם בעזרה. ואשה בעזרה מניין הלכך הך דלחמי תודה נמי לא איירי אלא בחולין שנעשה על טהרת הקדש: **תנן** התם במסכת חלה נולד לה ספק טומאה עד שלא גלגלה תעשה בטומאה. פרש"י דבלאו הכי לא אכיל לה כהן כיון דנולד לה ספק טומאה משמע הא אם לא נולד בה ספק טומאה תיעשה בטהרה. ואין לפרש דה"ה נמי לא נולד לה ספק טומאה ומשום רבותא דסיפא נקטיה דאע"ג דמטמאת בספק תיעשה בטהרה. דהא בפרק הניזקין תנן גבי אשת חבר שמסייעת לאשת עם הארץ משתטיל מים לא תגע בה משום מסייע ידי עוברי עברה ואפי' קודם גלגול ואין לומר משום דקסבר אסור לגרום טומאה לחולין שבארץ ישראל ומשתטיל מים והוכשרו לא תגע. דהא אמרינן התם רישא בטומאת חולין וסיפא בטומאת חלה ואמרי' נמי בירושלמי כלה דמתני' דע"ז דאין בוצרין עם ישראל העושה פירותיו בטומאה משום דמסייע ידי עוברי עברה ומפרש טעמא דכתיב ונתתם ממנו את תרומת ה' לאהרן הכהן. עשה שינתנו לאהרן בכיהונו אלמא דאסור לטמאות החולין כדי להפסיד התרומה לכהן:
שלא

א) נראה דל"ל שפיר הוות בעיא למשאל דשמא מטמאה מעל"ע וכו'.

### הגהות מהר"ב רנשבורג
א] גמ' מאי תרומה תרומת לחמי תודה. נ"ב עי' ספר ברכת הזבח למס' מנחות דף עו ע"ב בד"ה ההיא פליגא וכו' ודו"ק:

*וחלתה תלויה, לא אוכלין ולא שורפין. באיזה ספק אמרו? – בספק חלה. מאי "ספק חלה"? אביי ורבא דאמרי תרוייהו: שלא תאמר בהוכחות שנינו כמו שני שבילין, דהתם – חולין גרידא נמי מטמו, אלא בנשען. *דתנן: אזב וטהור שהיו פורקין מן החמור, או טוענין. בזמן שמשאן כבד – טמא, משאן קל – טהור, וכולן טהורין לבני הכנסת, בוטמאין לתרומה. וחולין הטבולין לחלה כחלה דמו? *והתניא: *גאשה שהיא טבולת יום – לשה את העיסה, וקוצה הימנה חלתה, °ומניחתה בכפישה או באנחותא, ומקפת וקורא לה שם, מפני שהוא שלישי, דושלישי טהור בחולין. ואי אמרת חולין הטבולין לחלה כחלה דמו – הא טמיתנהו! אמר אביי: הכל שודאי מטמא חולין – גזרו על ספקו משום חולין הטבולין לחלה. והאי טבול יום, כיון דלא מטמא ודאי חולין – לא גזרו עליו משום חולין הטבולין לחלה. והא מעת לעת שבנדה, דודאי מטמא חולין – ולא גזרו על ספקה משום חולין הטבולין לחלה! דאמר מר: *קבלה מיניה רב שמואל בר רב יצחק בחולין שנעשו על טהרת קדש, ולא בחולין שנעשו על טהרת תרומה! התם – לא פתיכא בהו תרומה, הכא – פתיכא בהו תרומה. ואיבעית אימא: הנח מעת לעת – ודרבנן. § מתני' *רבי אליעזר אומר, זארבע נשים דיין שעתן: בתולה מעוברת מניקה וזקינה. אמר רבי יהושע: אני לא שמעתי אלא בתולה, אבל

**רש"י**

וחלתה תלויה. כשעשאה בטהרה, משום ספק הנולד לה ראשון. באיזה ספק אמרו. כלומר: באיזה ספק הוזכרו לומר "חלתה תלויה". בספק חלה. בספק טומאה הנוהגת בחלה ואינה נוהגת בחולין, כגון נשען, כדמפרש בסמוך דטהור לבני הכנסת ואסור לתרומה. ואיצטריך לאשמועינן, דאע"ג דלא נהגא בחולין גרידא, הכא כיון דטבולין לחלה – נהגא בהן. מאי ספק חלה. כלומר: מאי קאמר? שלא תאמר בהוכחות שנינו. בספק טומאה מוכחת. כגון שני שבילין. אחד טמא ואחד טהור, ספק הלך בטמא ספק הלך בטהור. והא ספקא היא דמהניא בחולין הטבולין לחלה, אבל טומאה שאינה מוכחת – לא. דהא לא איצטריך לאשמועינן דאפילו לחולין גרידא נמי מהני לאוכל חולין בטהרה, הלכך מהניא נמי הכא. אלא אפילו בנשען. דהוי ספק טומאה שאינה מוכחת, הואיל ותנן לקמן דמהניא לתרומה, מהניא נמי לחולין הטבולין לחלה. פורקין. משאוי. טמא. דשמא מתוך כובד המשא נשען זב על הטהור, ונמלא טהור מסיטו, או טהור ניסט עליו, וכתיב במרכב הזב (ויקרא טו): "והנושא אותם", וכ"ש זב בעצמו. וכולן. אפי' משא כבד. טהורין לבני הכנסת. אוכלין חוליהן בטהרה, שאין זה היסט גמור, וכל שכן שספק הוא. וטמאין לתרומה. מדרבנן, ואפי' בספק. וחולין הטבולין לחלה כחלה דמו. דמהני בהו ספק נשען, כחלה גמורה. וקוצה לה חלה. שכל זמן שלא קראה שם עליה, הרי היא כחולין, וטבול יום דינו כשני, ואינו עושה שלישי בחולין. וכשהיא קוצה, לא תקרא לה שם. אלא מניחתה לחלה בכפישה או באנחותא, הם כלים שאין להם בית קיבול, כגון נסרים, ואין מקבלין טומאה. ואצרכוה רבנן הני, משום היכרא, שלא תגע בה שוב מאחר שקראה לה שם. ודכוותה אמר בסוף פ' "הניזקין" (גיטין סא.) ובתשובת רב האי ראיתי: "אנחותא" – נסרים, לווחין שמנסרין הנגרים ומשפין הלווחין. ומקפת. מקרבתה לכלי אצל העיסה, וקוראה לה שם, שמלוה לתרום מן המוקף. "מוקף" – סמוך, כמו "מקיפין שתי חביות" במס' ביצה (דף לג.) וכמו "אין מקיפין בבועי" (חולין מו.) – שמקיפין זו לזו, לראות אם דומים הם בנקביהן. שודאי מטמא חולין. כמו משא הזב. דודאי. נדה ממש. ספקה. מעת לעת. ולא בחולין שנעשו על טהרת תרומה. וקס"ד הוא הדין לחולין הטבולין לחלה, דהם נמי נעשין בטהרת חלה המעורבת בהן. ומשנינן: חולין הטבולין לחלה חמירי. מחולין שנעשו על טהרת תרומה, דהכא – עריבא בהו חלה, אבל התם – נטירותא יתירתא קביל עליה. פתיכא. מעורבת.
מתני'

**תוספות**

כהן. ועוד דאפילו לא נולד לה ספק – שרי לטמאותה, וליכא הפסד כהן, דחבר הוא, ויפריש עליה ממקום אחר. אבל התם איירי בעם הארץ, שלא יפריש ממקום אחר. וא"ת: דבפרק "הניזקין" (גיטין דף סא.) תנן: משאלת אשה לחברתה החשודה על השביעית נפה וכברה כו', אבל לא תבור ותטחון עמה. משאלת אשת חבר לאשת ע"ה נפה וכברה, ובוררת וטוחנת עמה. אבל משתטיל למים – לא תגע בהם. ובעי בגמרא: מ"ש רישא ומ"ש סיפא? אמר אביי: בדמאי הקילו. ומשתטיל למים, דהוכשרו – לא תגע בהם, אף קודם לישה. רבא אמר: בעם הארץ דר"מ, וטומאה וטהרה דרבנן. ופריך: והא מדקתני סיפא "משתטיל למים", מכלל דרישא איירי בלא הכשר, ומאי טומאה וטהרה איכא? ומשני: אידי ואידי בהוכשר, ורישא – בטומאת חולין, וסיפא – בטומאת חלה, ו"משתטיל למים" – היינו, לישה וגלגול. אלמא אוסר אביי ליגע, כי הוכשר לברור ולטחון, אף קודם גלגול ולישה, אע"ג דאם הפריש קודם לישה וגלגול – לא עשה ולא כלום! (וי"ל) ולדידיה נמי צריך לתרץ: דהתם אסור משום הפסד כהן, ובשמעתין ליכא הפסד כהן, כדפרישית. ולרבא, דשרי לגרום טומאה קודם גלגול, אע"ג דאיכא הפסד כהן, צריך לתרץ אההיא דפרק "רבי ישמעאל" (ע"ז דף נו.) כתירוץ ראשון: דהתם אסור, משום "משמרת תרומותי". אבל בעיסה, קודם גלגול לא מיקריא "טבלה לחלה", כיון דאם הפריש חלת קמח – לא עשה ולא כלום. אי נמי: כמו שתירץ ר"ת שם: דהתם בגיטין ליכא כי אם חשדא בעלמא, אבל ההיא ד"אין בוצרין" מיירי בודאי עושה פירותיו בטומאה. ושם יש להאריך.

**שלא** תאמר בהוכחות שנינו. פירש"י: כגון שני שבילים, ספק הלך בטהור. ולדבריו צריך לומר: שבאו לשאול בבת אחת, דאי בזה אחר זה – טהורין. ונראה לפרש כי ההיא דתניא בתוספתא דטהרות (פ"ו) ב' שבילין, אחד טמא ואחד טהור, והלך באחד מהם, ועשה טהרות.א) והלך בשני, ועשה טהרות – אלו ואלו מוכיחים. פירוש: מוכיחים לטומאה, דאיזה מהם נטהר? ומשום לישנא ד"מוכיחים" קאמר הכא: "בהוכחות שנינו". **וכולן** טהורים לבני הכנסת. פירש"י: דקאי א"משאן כבד". ואין נראה, דבמשאן כבד נראה דטמא אף לחולין, דאי אפשר שלא יסוט זה את זה. אלא א"משאן קל" קאי. וכן משמע במס' זבין (פ"ג מ"ג) דקתני התם: משאן קל – טהורין לבני הכנסת, וטמאין – לתרומה. והא דקתני הכא: כולן טהורין לבני הכנסת – אכל עינא דטהרה דהתם קאי. וא"ת: דהכא קרי ליה "בני הכנסת" לחברים האוכלין חולין בטהרה, ובפרק "פסולי המוקדשין" (בכורות לו:) גבי "מומי בכור" קאמר דהתרתם על פי ג' בני הכנסת, והתם אפילו ג' הדיוטות כשרים! וי"ל: דהכא נמי מוזכר "בני הכנסת" לגריעותא, כלומר: שאינם אוכלין תרומה.

**ומקפת** וקורא לה שם. הכא משמע דאפילו (א) בשעת קריאת שם צריך הקפה. וקשה: דאמר בסוטה פרק "כשם" (דף ל.) רבי אליעזר אומר: חלה ניטלת מן המוקף מן הטהור על הטמא. כילד? ב' עיסות, אחת טמאה ואחת טהורה – נוטל שיעור חלה מעיסה שלא הורמה חלתה, ונותן פחות מכביצה מעיסה טהורה באמצע, בין שיעור חלה לעיסה טמאה, כדי ליטול מן המוקף. והתניא: "כבילה"? ומשני: הך ברייתא סברה: חולין הטבולין לחלה – לאו כחלה דמו, ולהכי לא אתי כבילה, דהוי שני ומטמא לשיעור חלה. והשתא, מ"מ קשה: כשיקרא לה שם "חלה", יהיה שלישי? אלא משמע דבשעת קריאת שם, ירחיק מעט שיעור חלה, שלא יגע בכבילה. ותשיב שפיר "מוקף", כיון דלפני קריאת שם היתה מחוברת! וי"ל: דהתם מיירי כשיש הרבה מעיסה טהורה, ולא שיעור חלה גרידא. כדקתני: ב' עיסות, אחת טהורה ואחת טמאה. ורוצה להפריש קצת מן הטהורה, כדי לתקן עצמה ואף הטמאה. הלכך, כיון דחולין הטבולין לחלה – לאו כחלה דמו, לאו האי בילה דהוא שני מטמא העיסה הטהורה. וכי יפריש ממנה חלה, ויקיף לה – אין בכך כלום. *והא דפסקינן לקמן כר' אליעזר דאמר: הסל מצרפן לחלה, ולא בעי נגיעה – היינו להתחייב בחלה, אם לש פחות מכשיעור. דהכי תנא במסכת חלה (פ"ב מ"ד) העושה עיסתו קביים, ונגעו זה בזה – פטורין מן החלה, עד שישוכו. ר"א אומר: אף הרודה ונותן לסל – הסל מצרפן. וכן משמע ב"אלו עוברין" (פסחים מח.) והשתא אתי שפיר, דר"א גופיה מצריך נגיעה בשעת קריאת שם, בפרק "כשם" (סוטה דף ל.) וכגון דפסח להגיע כל המצות (בסל) כשמפרישין אחת על כולן, דאין הסל מצרפן לכך. ואע"ג דאמרינן בפ"ק דבילה (דף ט.) ובבכורות בפרק "עד כמה" (דף כז.) (ב) אמרינן: תרומת חוצה לארץ אוכל והולך, ואח"כ מפריש. אע"ג דאין מוקף למה שאכל כבר, היינו בעיסה שנילושה יחד והיתה כבר מחוברת, הקילו בתרומת חוצה לארץ. ול"ע אי חשוב מוקף בנגיעה גרידא, בלא צירוף הכלי או בלא נשיכה. ד"נותן פחות מכבילה באמצע" מצינן למימר: דהיינו נשיכה.

ועי"ל דאפילו [בלא] מוקף אפשר שיועיל צירוף סל ובפרק כשם דבעי ר' אליעזר נגיעה משום דמקפיד על נגיעתו משום טומאה אין מועיל צירוף כלי וכן משמע קצת בירושלמי דאמר במסכת חלה בפ"ב דבר שהוא מקפיד על [חבורו] אין הבית מצטרף (נראה במקום בית גרסינן כלי) אינו מקפיד על תערובתו הכלי מצרף עיסה טהורה ועיסה טמאה עשו אותם כדבר שמקפיד על תערובתו. גי':

**והאי** טבול יום כיון דודאי לא מטמא חולין לא גזרו עליו משום חולין הטבולין. ותימה: דהכא משמע דאין שני פוסל בחולין הטבולין לחלה. ובברייתא נמי קתני: (ג) ובשלישי טהור בחולין, משמע דכ"ש דאין שני פוסל בחולין שנעשו על טהרת תרומה, כדאמר בסמוך, דמשמע דקילי מחולין הטבולין לחלה. ובפרק שני דחולין (דף לג:) אמרינן: דשלישי נוהג בחולין שנעשו על טהרת תרומה, ובפרק "כשם" (סוטה דף ל.) שהבאתי לעיל מוכח דשני עושה שלישי בחולין הטבולין לחלה, למ"ד כחלה דמו? וי"ל: דטבול יום קיל טפי, דאין צריך רק הערב שמש. והא דתניא בברייתא דשלישי דטבול יום. אי נמי, ה"פ: כיון דשלישי טהור בחולין דעלמא, לא גזרו חכמים בחולין הטבולין לחלה ליטמא מטבול יום. ולכך פריך מיניה טפי א"נשען", ולא פריך מיניה אכל שלישי דנוהג בחולין הטבולין לחלה – משום דנשען נמי טומאה קלישא הוא, ומטמא אפילו משא קל. כדפרישית לעיל.

**הנח** מעת לעת דרבנן. אע"ג דנשען נמי דרבנן – טומאת מעת לעת קיל טפי, שאין שום ספק טומאה בשעה שעוסקת בטהרות.

שמותי

א) מיהו בתוספתא שלפנינו גרסי' והלך חבירו ועשה טהרות אלו ואלו מוכיחות כו' והיינו כפי' רש"י וע' רש"א

**עין משפט נר מצוה**

לט א מיי' פ"ח מהלכות משכב ומושב הלכה ט:
מ ב מיי' פט"ז מהלכות טומאת אוכלים הלכה ח סמג עשין רעו:
מא ג מיי' פ"ח מהל' טומאת אוכלים הלכ' היז:
מב ד מיי' פי"א מהל' שאר אבות הטומאה הלכה ב:
מג ה מיי' שם הלכה טז ופ"ח מהלכות בכורים הלכה י:
מד ו מיי' פ"ג מהלכות משכב ומושב הלכה ט:
מה ז מיי' שם פ"ד הלכה א ופ"ט מהל' איסורי ביאה הלכה ד סמג לאוין קיא:

**מסורת הש"ס**

[תוספתא דחלה פ"א]
[זבין פ"ג מ"ב]
[ג"ל והתנן]
[טבול יום פ"ד מ"ב]
[לעיל ו:]

**הגהות הב"ח**

(א) תוס' ד"ה ומקפת וכו' לאפילו לענין קריאת שם: (ב) בא"ד בפרק עד כמה נמי אמרינן: (ג) ד"ה והאי וכו' ובברייתא נמי קתני ובשלישי טהור:

**גליון הש"ס**

גמ' ומניחתה בכפישה. ע"ל עא ע"ב במתני' דלא קתני להא וצ"ע:

**תוספי הרא"ש**

**שלא** תאמר בהוכחות שנו. פרש"י כגון שני שבילין ספק הלך בטומאה דאפי' בחולין נמי טמא וקשה דבכל דוכתי מייתי שני שבילין לענין טהרה מיהו לפעמים דאפי' ברשות הרבים טמא לכ"ע כגון אם באו לישאל בבת אחת כדמפרש בפ"ק דפסחים (דחולין). ונראה דמיירי בההיא דתוספתא דטהרות שני שבילין אחד טמא ואחד טהור והלך באחד מהן ועשה טהרות ובא חברו והלך בשני ועשה טהרות אם אלו ואלו קיימות הרי אלו מוכיחות לטומאה ואפי' באו לישאל בזה אחר זה דחיישינן שמא יבא אחד ויאכל את שתיהם ומשום דקתני התם הרי אלו מוכיחות קרי ליה הכא בהוכחות: **אלא** בנשען. כלומר אף בספק נשען שהוא ספק חלה אמרינן חלתה תלויה ולא אמרינן כיון דבשעה שנולד ספק זה היתה חולין ונשען טהור לחולין טהורה היא. אלא כל העיסה כחלה חשבינן לה דחולין הטבולין לחלה כחלה דמו. וכ"ש בספק הנוהג בחולין דחלה תלויה. ומי' מתני' ע"כ בהוכחות איירי דאי בנשען ברישא דעד שלא גלגלה לא ניטמאת בספק נשען דאכתי לא חל עליו חלה ואמאי תיעשה בטומאה הא קא מפסיד חלת כהן. אלא ודאי בהוכחות קא איירי הלכך שרי לטמאותה קודם גלגול. אבל אם המתין מלטמא אותה עד לאחר גלגול אע"פ שנולד בה ספק קודם גלגול אסור לטמאותה. ואפי' לר' יהושע דאמר גבי חבית של תרומה שנולד בה ספק טומאה יניחנה במקום התורפה. הא אמרינן ספ"ק דפסחים גרמא אין בידים לא ואביי ורבא הוא דקאמרי הדך דסיפא לאו דוקא בהוכחות אלא ה"ה נמי בנשען: **משאן** כבד טמאין. משום דאי אפשר שלא יהא ניסט הזב על הטהור או הטהור על הזב. ואם הטמא הסיט את הטהור טמא כדמוכח בשבת פרק אמר ר' עקיבא עובד כוכבים ועובדת כוכבים בין שהסיטו אחרים בין אחרים שהסיטו אותם טמאין. וכן טהור שהסיט את הטמא טמא כדמוכח נמי התם ולקמן בפרק יוצא דופן דאמר' קנה בקומטו של טהור והסיט בו את הזב טמא. ופרש"י משום דכתיב במשכב הזב והנושא אותם וכ"ש זב עצמו. והאי טעמא פריכא הוא כדאמרינן לקמן פ' בנות כותיים שעיר המשתלח יוכיחו שגורם טומאה לאחרים והוא עצמו טהור. אלא מהיקשא נפקא לן כדאמרינן בפרק רבי עקיבא מקיש משכבו לו. ועוד יש לומר ק"ו ומה משכב שאינו עושה משכב מטמא במשא. זב שעושה משכב לא כ"ש: **וכולם** טהורים. פרש"י אמשאן כבד קאי. ויש ספרים דגרסי בפ"ג דמסכת זבין משאן קל טהורים לבני הכנסת ול"ג וכולן: **לבני** הכנסת. היינו אוכלי חוליהן בטהרה. ובבכורות בפ' כל הפסולין גבי בכור שיש לו מום מובהק אמרינן דהתרתו על פי ג' בני הכנסת. כלומר הדיוטות שאינן מומחין והכא קרי להו בני הכנסת לפי שאינן אוכלי תרומה: **מקפת** וקוראה לה שם. משמע הכא דאע"פ שהפרישתה לקרות לה שם לא חשיב מוקף כיון דבשעת קריאת שם לאו מוקף הוא. וקשה מהא דאמרינן בסוטה פרק כשם גבי חלה ניטלת מן הטהורה על הטמאה כיצד שתי עיסות אחת טמאה ואחת טהורה נוטל כדי חלה מעיסה שלא הורמה חלתה ונותן פחות מכביצה באמצע. ואיכא מאן דתאני התם בביצה וקסבר אין שני עושה שלישי בחולין ומותר לגרום טומאה לחולין שבארץ ישראל הלכך העיסה ראשונה והביצה שניה ואינו חוזר ומטמא אותו כדי חלה כל זמן שאין שם חלה עליו דחולין הטבולין לחלה לאו כחלה דמו. והשתא מ"מ כשיקרא לה שם תיטמא החלה אלא ודאי יפרידה תחלה ואח"כ יקרא לה שם וקרינא ביה מוקף כיון שהיתה מוקפת לדעת שיקרא שם לאלתר אחר כך. וי"ל דלעולם צריך לקרות שם בשעה שהוא מוקף אלא שיאמר שתהא שם תרומה חל עליה לכשיפרישנה ועוד י"ל דהכא נמי חשיב מוקף אם היתה קוצה חלה ומניחתה בכפישה וקורא שם אלא חיישינן שמא תשכחנה בידה ותקרא לה שם קודם הנחתה בכפישה הלכך הזקיקוה לחזור ולהקיפה אחר שתנתן בכפישה להיכירא. א"נ הכא דמפסיק מנא לא חשיב מוקף אע"פ שהפרישתה מתחילתה לשם כך: **התם** לא פתיכא בהו תרומה. משמע הכא דחולין שנעשו על טהרת הקודש קילי מחולין הטבולים לחלה. ותימה דלעיל קתני מפני שהוא שלישי ושלישי טהור בחולין. ובפ"ק דחולין משמע דחולין שנעשו על טהרת הקודש יש בהן שלישי. וי"ל דשאני טבול יום (דשאני) דקלישא טומאתו דשמשא ממילא ערבא והאי דקאמר ושלישי טהור בחולין. בשלישי כזה קאמר. והא דפריך מינה לעיל אההיא דנשען (דמעשה) [דחומרא] יתירא הוא הא דמטמאינן נשען בתרומה הלכך מסתבר ליה שאין להחמיר ולטמאות נשען בחולין הטבולין לחלה טפי מבשלישי דטבול יום: **הנח** מעת לעת דרבנן. פי' טומאה קלה משאר טומאות דרבנן:
ר'

אבל הלכה כרבי אליעזר. איזו היא בתולה — [א]כל שלא ראתה דם מימיה, אע"פ שנשואה. מעוברת — [ב]משיודע עוברה. מניקה — [ג]עד שתגמול את בנה. נתנה בנה למניקה, גמלתו, או מת, ר"מ אומר: מטמאה מעת לעת, וחכ"א [ד]דיה שעתה. איזוהי זקנה — [ה]כל שעברו עליה שלש עונות סמוך לזקנתה. *רבי אליעזר אומר: כל אשה שעברו עליה שלש עונות — דיה שעתה. רבי יוסי אומר: מעוברת ומניקה שעברו עליהן שלש עונות — דיין שעתן. [ו]ובמה (א) אמר דיה שעתה — בראייה ראשונה, אבל בשנייה — מטמאה מעת לעת. ואם ראתה הראשונה מאונס — אף השנייה דיה שעתה.§ **גמ'** תניא, אמר לו רבי אליעזר לרבי יהושע: אתה לא שמעת, (ב) אני שמעתי. אתה לא שמעת אלא אחת, ואני שמעתי הרבה. אין אומרים למי שלא ראה את החדש: יבא ויעיד, אלא למי שראהו. כל ימיו של רבי אליעזר היו עושין כרבי יהושע, לאחר פטירתו של רבי אליעזר החזיר רבי יהושע את הדבר ליושנו. כרבי אליעזר בחייו מ"ט לא? *משום דרבי אליעזר שמותי הוא, וסבר: אי עבדינן כוותיה בחדא — עבדינן כוותיה באחרנייתא, ומשום כבודו דר"א לא מצינן מחינן בהו. לאחר פטירתו של ר"א דמצינו מחינן בהו, החזיר את הדבר ליושנו. אמר רב יהודה, אמר שמואל: הלכה כרבי אליעזר בארבע. חדא — דאמרן. ואידך: *המקשה כמה תשפה ותהא זבה — מעת לעת, דברי ר"א והלכה כדבריו. ואידך: *הזב והזבה שבדקו עצמן יום ראשון — ומצאו טהור, יום שביעי — ומצאו טהור, ושאר הימים לא בדקו, רבי אליעזר אומר: הרי אלו בחזקת טהרה. רבי יהושע אומר: אין להן אלא יום הראשון ויום השביעי בלבד. רבי עקיבא אומר: אין להם אלא יום שביעי בלבד. ותניא, *ר"ש ורבי יוסי אומרים: נראין דברי רבי אליעזר מדברי רבי יהושע, ודברי ר"ע מדברי כולן, אבל הלכה כר' אליעזר. ואידך, *דתנן: אחורי כלים שנטמאו במשקין, ר' אליעזר אומר: מטמאין את המשקין ואין פוסלין את האוכלין, [ז]מטמאין את המשקין — ואפילו דחולין, [ח]ואין פוסלין את האוכלין — ואפילו דתרומה. רבי יהושע אומר: מטמאין את המשקין ופוסלין את האוכלין. א"ר יהושע: ק"ו ומה טבול יום, שאין מטמא משקה חולין — פוסל אוכלי תרומה, אחורי כלים, שמטמא משקה חולין — אינו דין שפוסל אוכלי תרומה? ורבי אליעזר — אחורי כלים דרבנן, וטבול יום דאורייתא, ורבנן — מדאורייתא לא עבדינן קל וחומר. דמדאורייתא [ט]אין אוכל מטמא כלי, ואין משקה מטמא כלי, [י]ורבנן הוא דגזור גזרה משום משקין דזב וזבה. [כ]משקין דעלולין לקבל טומאה — גזרו בהו רבנן, אוכלין דאין עלולין לקבל טומאה — לא גזרו בהו רבנן. [ל]ומאי שנא אחורי כלים דנקט — משום דקילי, (א) דתנן: [מ]כלי שנטמא מאחוריו במשקין — אחוריו טמא, תוכו, אזנו, אוגנו, ידיו — טהורין. [נ]נטמא תוכו — כולו טמא. מאי קמ"ל שמואל? בכולהו תנן הלכתא! וכי תימא: אחורי כלים קמ"ל דלא תנן; ולימא הלכה כר"א באחורי כלים א] אלא, הא קמ"ל ב) שאין למדין הלכה מפי תלמוד. ותו ליכא? והאיכא דתנן, ג) ר"א אומר: מלמדין

א) ברכות נב. בכורות לח. חגיגה כב: כלים פכ"ה מ"ו ב) ב"ב ק"ל: ע"ש ג) [יבמות קט.]

**מתני'** וחכ"א דיה שעתה. עד כ"ד חדש, שהוא זמן הנקת התינוק. ובגמרא מפרש טעמא. שעברו עליה. שלא ראתה. שלש עונות. מפרש לה בגמרא. סמוך לזקנתה. מפרש בגמרא. כל אשה. וה"ה ילדה. מעוברת ומניקה כו'. אבל לא עברו עליה — לא. ופליג אדרבי אליעזר ואת"ק דקאמר לעיל: מעוברת דיה שעתה — משיודע העובר, ומניקה — משנולד. בראייה ראשונה. שראתה הבתולה או המעוברת או הזקנה לאחר שלש עונות. אבל בשנייה מטמאה מעת לעת. שהרי חזרה לקדמותה להיות דמים מצויים בה. **גמ'** אין אומרים למי שלא ראה את החדש שיבא ויעיד. שראה. שמותי. לשון שמתא, שהרי ברכוהו, כדאמרינן ב"הזהב" (ב"מ דף נט:) הלכך לא עבדינן כוותיה באחרנייתא. דמצינן מחינן בהו. אי עבדי כוותיה באחרנייתא. המקשה. מחמת ולד בתוך אחד עשר יום שבין נדה לנדה, וקשתה שלשה ימים רצופין, ובכל יום ראתה דם. וקי"ל דאינה זבה מחמת שלשה ימי קישוי, ליטען שבעה נקיים וקרבן, דכתיב: "כי יזוב זוב דמה", ודרשינן ב"בנות כותים":* דמה — מחמת עצמה, ולא מחמת ולד. ואם שפתה מן הצער, שעמדה בלא צער לאחר השלשה ימים, וילדה — נתגלה הדבר למפרע שלא בא הדם מחמת הולד, והרי היא יולדת בזוב, וצריכה שבעה נקיים לבד ימי טומאת לידה. וצריכה שני קרבנות: אחד לזוב, ואחד ללידה. וכמה תשפה. תעמוד ותנוח מצערה לאחר השלשה של קושי, ותהא זבה למפרע מחמת הקושי. מעת לעת. אם שפתה מחלות היום זה עד כעת מחר, איכא למימר דלאו משום ולד הוה, וקרינן ביה "כי יזוב זוב דמה". ופליג ר' יהושע עליה בפרק "בנות כותים"*. שבדקו עצמן. כשפסקו מזובן, הוצרכו לספור שבעה נקיים בלא ראייה, כדכתיב: "וספר לו" וגו'. ובדקו עצמן ראשון ושביעי, ושאר חמשה ימים שבינתיים לא בדקו. בחזקת טהרה. הואיל ותחלתו וסופו בטהרה, וטובל לערב של שביעי. **אלא** ראשון ושביעי. וצריכין למנות עוד חמשה ימים, דחוששים שמא ראו בינתיים. ומיהו אי הוה ידעה בודאי שראתה בינתיים — סתרה לנקיות הראשון, דרחמנא אמר (ויקרא טו) "ואחר תטהר", "אחר" — אחר לכולן, שלא תהא טומאה מפסקת בינתיים. אבל השתא, חששא היא, ומונה לסירוגין. **אלא** יום שביעי בלבד. דשמא ראתה ימים שבינתיים, וסתרה את טהרת יום הראשון. דכולהו נקיים בעינן, דכתיב: "ואחר תטהר", "אחר" — אחר לכולן, שלא תהא טומאה מפסקת בינתיים. מדברי ר' יהושע. שר"א השוה מדותיו, דקסבר: כיון דתחלתן וסופן בטהרה — מחזקינן נמי לאמצעיים בטהרה. אבל רבי יהושע, כיון דאמצעיים חייש לטומאה — נסתרה טהרת יום ראשון. **אחורי** כלים. דאמרינן לקמן: אחוריים — טמאין, ותוכו — טהור. וטומאת משקין לטמא כלים דרבנן, והכי הוא דגזור שלא יטמא תוכו בנגיעת אחוריו. וטעמא מפרש בבכורות: עבדו רבנן היכרא בהך טומאה, דלידעו אינשי דמדרבנן היא, ולא נשרוף עליה תרומה וקדשים. שנטמאו במשקין. ומשקין בשרץ, והוו ראשונים. ולא מטמאו כלים מדאורייתא אלא אב הטומאה, ורבנן הוא דגזור. מטמאין **את** המשקין. מדרבנן, דכיון דעלולין לקבל טומאה — מיטמו בכל דהו, להיות ראשונים, ויפסלו את השני בחולין. ואין פוסלין **את** האוכלין. רבותא קתני: דאפילו מפסל לא פסלי, כדמפרש טעמא ואזיל. טבול יום שני הוא. ואינו מטמא משקה חולין, דקי"ל כל הפוסל את התרומה — מטמא משקה להיות תחלה, חוץ מטבול יום. וטעמא מפרש (א) בפ"ק דשבת (דף יד.). **אחורי** כלים. בטומאת משקין דרבנן. דכלי אינו מקבל טומאה מדאורייתא אלא מאב הטומאה, בפ"ק דפסחים (דף יח.). **וטבול** יום. לפסול אוכלי תרומה דאורייתא, כדקיימא לן: טבל ועלה — אוכל במעשר כו'. ומקרא נפקא לן ביבמות (דף עד.) ואפילו בנגיעה. **משום** משקה זב וזבה. רוקו ומימי רגליו, שהן אבות הטומאה, כדכתיב (ויקרא טו): "וכי ירוק הזב" וגו'. ומ"ש **אחורי** כלים דנקט. לינקוט "תוכי כלים", וכגון דנגעו משקין טמאין לתוכו, והוו נמי דרבנן. משום דקילי. אבל תוכי כלים, כיון דאחמירו בהו רבנן, כדקתני "נטמא תוכו — כולו טמא", מודה רבי אליעזר שפוסלין את האוכלין. **הא** קמ"ל. מדאיצטריך למימר להו הלכה, שמע מינה דאין למדין הלכה מפי תלמוד, מתוך המשנה וברייתא ששנויה בהן "הלכה כפלוני" — אין למדין מהן. שהאמוראים האחרונים דקדקו בטעמי התנאים, והעמידו הלכה על בוריה. אבל הראשונים לא דקדקו איש בדברי חבירו, אלא כל אחד מה ששמע מרבו מלמדה לתלמידו שמועה כמו שהיא. והיא היתה נקרא "משנה" ו"ברייתא" והיה נותן לבו לתת טעם לשמועתו, זה נותן טעם לדבריו, וזה נותן בה טעם אחר. כדאמר (שבת דף סג.): ליגמר איניש, והדר ליסבר. ואותה סברא היתה נקראת "תלמוד" בימי התנאים, ומשנה ששנויה בה פסק הלכה, מסברת תלמוד שלהן ניתנית, ואין למדין הימנה. מלמדין

א) [נ"ל בפ"ק דפסחים]

**שמותי** הוא. פירש"י: שברכוהו. וקשה: דמסתמא לא היה מזכיר לשון שמתא. ובמעשה גופיה דפרק "הזהב" (ב"מ דף נט:) אינו מזכיר אלא לשון ברכה. ופירש ר"ת ורשב"ס ד"שמותי הוא": היינו, דהוה מתלמידי שמאי. וכן איתא בירושלמי *פרק קמא דתרומות, דתנן: סאה של תרומה טמאה, שנפלה לתוך מאה של תרומה טהורה ב"ש אוסרין, ובית הלל מתירין. לאחר שהודו, א"ר אליעזר: תירום ותשרף. מי הודה למי? וקאמר: ב"ש לב"ה. א"ר אסי: מתניתין אמרה כן, לאחר שהודו אמר ר' אליעזר: יתרום ותרום ותשרף. ורבי אליעזר לאו שמותי הוה? בתמיה. וכן מפרש באלפא ביתא דרבי מכיר*. **רבי** אליעזר אומר הרי היא בחזקת טהרה. מכאן משמע: אשה שספרה ז' נקיים, ובדקה יום ראשון ויום ז' ומצאה טהורה — דחשיב ספירה. רק שבדקה עצמה יום שפסקה בו לערב, והפסיקה בטהרה. ודוקא יום ז' אבל יום ח' — לא. ומיהו לכתחלה [לא מועיל] וצריכה לבדוק בכל יום. **משום** דקילי. אבל תוך כלי פוסל אוכלין דתרומה, משום דהוי מי"ח דבר (שבת יג:) האוכלין והכלים שנטמאו במשקין. ועל

הקשה הר' ראבי"ה דהאלו מגלחין (דף טו.) איבעיא לן מנודה מהו בתפילין תיקו ור' אליעזר היה מניח תפילין כדאמר בסוף פ' ד' מיתות (דף סח.) ואין לומר דלא חש לנידוי דהא חלץ מנעליו. *) פסק. גי':

## תוספי הרא"ש

ר' אליעזר שמותי הוא. פירש"י ברכוהו ול"נ להזכיר עליו לשון שמתא דבשעת מעשה לא קאמר אלא ברכוהו. ועוד ניחא הכא דלא בעי למיעבד כוותיה משום דאיירי בטהרות ועל עסק טהרות ברכוהו וחייש דלמא אתי למיעבד כוותיה באחרנייתא דטהרות. אבל בריש רבי אליעזר דמילה גבי מכשירי מילה דקאמר רבי אליעזר שדוחין את השבת וקאמר התם פעם אחת שכחו ולא הביאו כו' ופריך והיכי עביד כר' אליעזר חדא דר' אליעזר שמותי הוא ומה בכך וכי בשביל זה לא יהא הלכה כמותו בשום מקום. ונראה כפי' הערוך דשמותי מתלמידי בית שמאי כדאיתא בירושלמי פ"ה דמסכת תרומה גבי סאה תרומה טמאה שנפלה למאה סאה תרומה טהורה דמוכח משום דהודו ב"ש לב"ה משום דרבי אליעזר שמותי הוא וקתני דר' אליעזר אומר תירום ותישרף כדברי ב"ה. והכי איתא נמי במסכתא יו"ט דירושלמי פ"ב ואע"פ שהיה מתלמידי ריב"ז כדאיתא במסכת אבות ורבן יוחנן [בן זכאי] מתלמידי ב"ה היה כדאיתא פרק יש נוחלין קים ליה לתלמודא דבכל דבריו קאי כב"ש וא"ת מאי נפקא ליה מינה לר' יהושע אי עביד כוותיה באחרנייתא הא איהו דקאמר אין משגיחין בבת קול. ואמרינן סוף פ"ק דיבמות דלמ"ד אין משגיחין בבת קול הרוצה לעשות כבית שמאי עושה. וי"ל דמ"מ קסבר ר' יהושע הלכה כבית הלל משום דבית הלל רובא. אע"ג דב"ש מחדדי טפי: **חדא** הא. ואע"ג דר' יהושע לא פליג עליה אצטריך למיפסק הלכתא כוותיה לאפוקי מר' דוסא דפליג עליה ואמר כל אשה שיש לה ווסת דיה שעתה ומוכח לעיל דפליגי. ומיהו קשה דבכולי פרקין ופרק כל היד מוכח דהלכה כר' דוסא. ונראה דאתא לאפוקי מדר' אליעזר דמתני' דאמר כל האשה שעברו עליה ג' עונות דייה שעתה. ור' יוסי דמתני' דאמר מעוברת ומניקה שעברו עליה ג' עונות דיין שעתה. ואפשר ר' דוסא ות"ק דידיה לא פליגי דת"ק איירי בר' נשים דמחמת סילוק דמים דיין שעתן אף שלא בשעת וסתן ולא פליג אהא דאורח בזמנו בא. ומר אמר חדא ומר אמר חדא ולא פליגי והא דקאמר לעיל דרבנן פליגי עליה דר' דוסא. רבנן אחריתי נינהו דכיון דקתני בברייתא ר' דוסא אומר מכלל דרבנן פליגי עליה: **המקשה** כמה תשפה ותהא זבה. מתני' דפ' בנות כותיים הוה מצי לאיתויי אלא דניחא ליה לאיתויי ברייתא משום דקתני בה והלכה כדבריו. כבאחרנייתא: **הזב** והזבה שבדקו עצמן כו' הרי אלו בחזקת טהרה. והלכה כדבריו. ולקמן פליגי בה רב ור' חנינא אי אמרינן תחלתן אע"פ שאין סופן. סופן אע"פ שאין תחלתן. ומיהו לכתחלה צריך בדיקה כל שבעה. ולא מיקריא בדיקה אלא בהכנסת חורין וסדקין. ואידך מיקרי קנוח כדפירשתי לעיל. והנשים שסומכות על שמעיינות בחלוקיהן ואין מוצאות בו כתם לאו שפיר עבידן: **רבי** יהושע אומר אין להם אלא יום ראשון ויום שביעי. ונראה דר' יהושע סבר כר' אליעזר דלא בעי ספורי' לפנינו ומדרבנן קאמר מדאוקמי לקמן בפ' המפלת שמעתתא דטועה כר' עקיבא. דסבר דבעינן ספורים לפנינו ולא מוקי לה כר' יהושע: **ורבנן** מדאורייתא לא אמרינן ק"ו. וא"ת ונילף ק"ו ממעת לעת דהוי נמי דרבנן. לההוא לישנא דאמרי' לעיל אפילו לתרומה. ואין לומר מה למעת לעת שכן עושה משכב ומושב איכא למימר תוכי כלים יוכיחו דאין עושין משכב ופוסל אוכלי תרומה. ואפשר לומר דמעת לעת נמי מטמא משקה חולין משום דקי"ל כל הפוסל את התרומה מטמא משקין להיות תחלה. ור"מ תירץ דאיכא למפרך מה למעת לעת דאיכא ספק טומאה דאורייתא דדלמא אתא דם לבית החיצון ונראה לי דלא קשה דכי היכי דאין למדין דברי סופרים מדברי תורה הכי נמי אין למדין דברי [סופרים] (תורה) מדברי סופרים והכי תנן במסכת ידים בפ' ג' היד מטמאה את חברתה דברי ר' יהושע וחכמים אומרים אין שני עושה שני. אמר להן והלא כתבי הקדש מטמאין את הידים אמר לו אין דנין דברי תורה מדברי סופרים ולא דברי סופרים מדברי תורה ולא דברי סופרים מדברי סופרים. וכן כתב ר"מ דמילי דרבנן ממילי דרבנן לא ילפינן מק"ו דאם לא כן לא תמצא שום חלוק בדבריהם דליכא למיפרך משום דאמרינן היא גופה גזירה דכי פרכת מה לדברי פלוני יצא בו דין איכא למימר היא גופה תיתי מק"ו אבל בכל דבר גזרו לפי הנראה בעיניהם לצורך סייג ואין ללמוד זה מזה אע"ג דבפ"ק דעירובין קאמר ומה חצר שאינה ניתרת בלחי וקורה ניתרת בעומד מרובה על הפרוץ כו' אע"ג דכולהו מדרבנן. י"ל דהתם מספקא ליה לתלמודא היכי תקון מעיקרא עבוד שפיר ק"ו דהכי והכי תקון מכח ק"ו אבל ר' אליעזר היה מקובל דהכי תקון הלכך כי היכי דבדאורייתא מדאורייתא לא עבדינן ק"ו הכי נמי מדרבנן אדרבנן לא עבדי ק"ו לסתור קבלתו: **ומאי** שנא אחורי לא עבדינן ק"ו הכי נמי מדרבנן. כלים דנקט משום דקילי אבל תוך כלים דחמירי מודו כ"ע דפוסל אוכלי תרומה דמי"ח דבר הוא בפ"ק דשבת האוכלים והכלים שנטמאו במשקין:

בסדר

**הגהות מהר"ב רנשבורג** א] גמ' אלא הא קמ"ל שאין למדין הלכה מפי תלמוד. נ"ב וכתב הרשב"א בתשובה סי' של"ה דהיינו דווקא כשהוא נגד הכלל שבידינו אבל כשאינו סותר כללים האמור בגמרא אז למידין הלכה מפי משנה וברייתא:

*) [ועי' תוס' ב"מ נט: ד"ה וקרע ובתוס' מועד קטן טו: ד"ה לא אשארא]

מו א מיי' פ"ט מהל' איסורי ביאה הלכה ה ופ"ד מהל' משכב ומושב הלכה א סמג לאוין קיא:

[נ"ל פ"ה]

מז ב מיי' פ"ט מהלכות איסורי ביאה הלכה ד ופ"ד מהל' משכב ומושב הלכה א סמג שם טוש"ע י"ד סי' קפט סעיף לג:

מח ג ד מיי' שם סמג שם טוש"ע י"ד שם:

[ועי' תוס' שבת קל: ד"ה דר"א כו' וכן ברש"י שם ד"ה שמותי]

מט ה מיי' פ"ט מהל' איסורי ביאה הלכה ה ופ"ד מהל' משכב ומושב הלכה א סמג שם טוש"ע י"ד שם סעיף כח:

נ ו מיי' פ"ד מהלכות משכב ומושב הלכה א והלכה ה ועי' בהשגות ובכ"מ:

נא ז מיי' פ"ז מהלכות שאר אבות הטומאות הלכה ה:

נב ח מיי' שם הלכה ו:

נג ט מיי' שם הלכה א והלכה ז:

[לקמן לו:]

נד י כ מיי' שם הלכה א והלכה ב:

נה ל מיי' בכ"מ שם הלכה ה:

נו מ נ מיי' שם הלכה ג:

טהרות פ"ח מ"ז

עירובין מו. [וכן הגירסא רבי אליעזר וכן עיקר וכן נ"ל בהסוגיא להלן]

### הגהות הב"ח

(א) במשנה ובמה אמרו דיה שעתה: (ב) גמ' ואני שמעתי אתה לא שמעת אלא אחת ואני שמעתי (הרבה) תא"מ וג"כ ס"א ארבע:

[לקמן דף לו:]

שבת קל:

[לקמן סח:] [לקמן לו:] [לקמן סח.]

אמְלַמְּדִין אֶת הַקְּטַנָּה שֶׁתְּמָאֵן בּוֹ, *וְאָמַר רַב יְהוּדָה אָמַר שְׁמוּאֵל: הֲלָכָה כְּר' אֱלִיעֶזֶר! כִּי אָמַר שְׁמוּאֵל, הֲלָכָה כְּר' אֱלִיעֶזֶר בְּד' — בְּסֵדֶר טְהָרוֹת, אֲבָל בִּשְׁאָר סְדָרִים — אִיכָּא טוּבָא. וְה"נ מִסְתַּבְּרָא, *דִּתְנַן, ר' אֱלִיעֶזֶר אוֹמֵר: אַף הָרוֹדֶה וְנוֹתֵן לַסַּל — בהַסַּל מְצָרְפָן לְחַלָּה. וְאָמַר רַב יְהוּדָה אָמַר שְׁמוּאֵל: הֲלָכָה כְּר"א, ש"מ. וּמַאי אוּלְמֵיהּ דְּהַאי מֵהַאי? מִשּׁוּם דְּקָאֵי רַבִּי אֶלְעָזָר כְּוָתֵיהּ. *דִּתְנַן, רַבִּי אֶלְעָזָר אוֹמֵר: מְלַמְּדִין אֶת הַקְּטַנָּה שֶׁתְּמָאֵן בּוֹ. וּמִי קָאֵי? וְהָא *אַצְרְכוּ מַצְרְכִינַן לְהוּ, וְלָא דָּמְיָין לַהֲדָדֵי! אֶלָּא מִשּׁוּם דְּקָאֵי רַבִּי יְהוּדָה בֶּן בָּבָא כְּוָתֵיהּ. *דְּתַנְיָא, רַבִּי יְהוּדָה בֶּן בָּבָא הֵעִיד ה' דְּבָרִים: גשֶׁמְּמָאֲנִים אֶת הַקְּטַנּוֹת, דוְשֶׁמַּשִּׂיאִין אֶת הָאִשָּׁה ע"פ עֵד אֶחָד, הוְשֶׁנִּסְקַל תַּרְנְגוֹל בִּירוּשָׁלַיִם עַל שֶׁהָרַג אֶת הַנֶּפֶשׁ, ווְעַל יַיִן בֶּן מ' יוֹם שֶׁנִּתְנַסֵּךְ ע"ג הַמִּזְבֵּחַ, זוְעַל תָּמִיד שֶׁל שַׁחַר שֶׁקָּרַב בְּד' שָׁעוֹת. מַאי "קְטַנּוֹת" — לָאו חֲדָא דְּר' אֶלְעָזָר וְחַד דְּר' אֱלִיעֶזֶר? לָא, מַאי "קְטַנּוֹת" — קְטַנּוֹת דְּעָלְמָא. אִי הָכִי, גַּבֵּי אִשָּׁה נַמִי, נִתְנֵי "נָשִׁים", וְנֵימָא נָשִׁים דְּעָלְמָא! אֶלָּא, מִדְּהָכָא קָתָנֵי "אִשָּׁה", וְהָכָא קָתָנֵי "קְטַנּוֹת", ש"מ דַּוְקָא קָתָנֵי, ש"מ. וְכֵן *א"ר אֶלְעָזָר: הֲלָכָה כְּר"א בְּד'. וְתוּ לֵיכָּא? וְהָתְנַן רַבִּי אֱלִיעֶזֶר אוֹמֵר: מְלַמְּדִין אֶת הַקְּטַנָּה שֶׁתְּמָאֵן בּוֹ, *וְא"ר אֶלְעָזָר: הֲלָכָה כְּר"א. וְכִי תֵּימָא: כִּי א"ר אֶלְעָזָר הֲלָכָה כְּר"א בְּד' — בְּסֵדֶר טְהָרוֹת, אֲבָל בִּשְׁאָר סִדְרֵי — אִיכָּא, וּמִי אִיכָּא? *וְהָתְנַן: חהַוֶּרֶד וְהַכּוֹפֶר וְהַלָּטוֹם וְהַקֶּטֶף — יֵשׁ לָהֶן שְׁבִיעִית, וְלִדְמֵיהֶן שְׁבִיעִית, *יֵשׁ לָהֶן בִּיעוּר וְלִדְמֵיהֶן בִּיעוּר. וְא"ר פְּדָת: מַאן תְּנָא קְטָפָא פֵּירָא — ר"א. וְא"ר זֵירָא: חֲזֵי דְּמִינָּךְ וּמֵאֲבוּךְ קַשְׁרִיתוּ קְטָפָא לְעָלְמָא! אַתְּ אָמְרַתְּ מַאן תְּנָא קְטָפָא פֵּירָא ר"א, וַאֲבוּךְ אָמַר הֲלָכָה כְּר"א בְּד'. וְאִם אִיתָא, לֵימָא לֵיהּ: כִּי אָמַר אַבָּא הֲלָכָה כְּר"א בְּד' — בְּסֵדֶר טְהָרוֹת, אֲבָל בִּשְׁאָר סִדְרֵי — אִיכָּא. אֶלָּא קַשְׁיָא הַהִיא! מִשּׁוּם דְּקָאֵי רַבִּי אֶלְעָזָר כְּוָתֵיהּ, דִּתְנַן רַבִּי אֶלְעָזָר אוֹמֵר: מְלַמְּדִים אֶת הַקְּטַנָּה שֶׁתְּמָאֵן בּוֹ. וּמִי קָאֵי? וְהָא אַצְרוּכֵי מַצְרְכִינַן לְהוּ, וְלָא דָּמְיָין לַהֲדָדֵי! אֶלָּא מִשּׁוּם דְּקָאֵי רַבִּי יְהוּדָה בֶּן בָּבָא כְּוָותֵיהּ. וְתוּ לֵיכָּא? *וְהָתְנַן, ר"ע אוֹמֵר: אוֹמְרָהּ בְּרָכָה רְבִיעִית בִּפְנֵי עַצְמָהּ, ר' אֱלִיעֶזֶר אוֹמֵר: אוֹמְרָהּ בְּהוֹדָאָה. וְא"ר אֶלְעָזָר: הֲלָכָה כְּר"א! א"ר אַבָּא: הַהוּא — דְּאָמַר מִשּׁוּם רַבִּי חֲנִינָא בֶּן גַּמְלִיאֵל, דְּתַנְיָא, רַבִּי עֲקִיבָא אוֹמֵר: אוֹמְרָהּ בְּרָכָה רְבִיעִית בִּפְנֵי עַצְמָהּ, רַבִּי חֲנִינָא בֶּן גַּמְלִיאֵל אוֹמֵר: אוֹמְרָהּ בְּהוֹדָאָה. וְהָא

---

מְלַמְּדִין אֶת הַקְּטַנָּה. בְּפֶרֶק "בֵּית שַׁמַּאי" בִּיבָמוֹת: *ב' אַחִין נְשׂוּאִין ב' אֲחָיוֹת יְתוֹמוֹת, אַחַת גְּדוֹלָה וְאַחַת קְטַנָּה. מֵת בַּעְלָהּ שֶׁל גְּדוֹלָה וְנִמְצֵאת זְקוּקָה לְיַבֵּם בַּעַל הַקְּטַנָּה, וְדוֹחָה זִיקָתָהּ נִישּׂוּאֵי אֲחוֹתָהּ הַקְּטַנָּה, וְאוֹסַרְתָּהּ עָלָיו, שֶׁאֵין נִישּׂוּאֵי קְטַנָּה כְּלוּם. וְאִם יְגָרְשֶׁנָּה לַקְּטַנָּה בְּגֵט — שׁוּב אֵינוֹ יָכוֹל לְיַבֵּם אֶת הַגְּדוֹלָה, שֶׁאֲחוֹת גְּרוּשָׁתוֹ הִיא. אֶלָּא מְלַמְּדִין אֶת הַקְּטַנָּה שֶׁתְּמָאֵן בּוֹ, וּמֵיאוּן עוֹקֵר נִישּׂוּאִין הָרִאשׁוֹנִים, וּמוּתָּר לְיַבֵּם הַגְּדוֹלָה. הָרוֹדֶה וְנוֹתֵן לַסַּל. כְּגוֹן שֶׁהָיָה לָשׁ אֶת עִיסָּתוֹ פָּחוֹת פָּחוֹת מֵחֲמֵשֶׁת רְבָעִים, לְפוֹטְרוֹ מִן הַחַלָּה. הַסַּל מְצָרְפָן. כְּשֶׁרוֹדָן מִן הַתַּנּוּר. מַאי אוּלְמֵיהּ דְּהַאי. דְּחַלָּה מֵהַהִיא דְּמֵיאוּן, דְּפָשְׁטַת לָהּ מִינָּהּ, דְּאָמְרַתְּ: ה"נ מִסְתַּבְּרָא? הָא שָׁמְעִינַן מֵהַהִיא דְּמֵיאוּן דְּבִשְׁאָר סִדְרֵי אִיכָּא הֲלָכָה כְּר"א. וּמְשַׁנֵּי. מֵהַהִיא דְּמֵיאוּן לֵיכָּא לְמִשְׁמַע מִינָּהּ דְּבִשְׁאָר סְדָרִים אִיכָּא, דְּהָתָם מִשּׁוּם דְּקָאֵי ר' אֶלְעָזָר כְּר"א וְאִיכָּא לְמֵימַר: מִשּׁוּם דִּמְסַיֵּיעַ ר' אֶלְעָזָר לְר"א מִש"ה הֲלָכָה כְּמוֹתוֹ בְּהָא, אֲבָל מִשּׁוּם דִּידֵיהּ לְחוּדֵיהּ — לָא. מְלַמְּדִין אֶת הַקְּטַנָּה. בְּמִילְּתָא אַחֲרִיתִי הִיא, בְּפ' ב"ש. וּמִי קָאֵי וְהָא אַצְרוּכֵי מַצְרְכִינַן לֵיהּ. הָתָם דְּאָמַר שְׁמוּאֵל בְּקַמַּיְיתָא הֲלָכָה כְּר"א וּבְאִידָךְ נַמִי הֲלָכָה כְּר' אֶלְעָזָר, וְאָמְרִי' צְרִיכָא, דְּאִי אַשְׁמוּעִינַן כו'. אַלְמָא ר' אֶלְעָזָר וְר"א לָאו חַד טַעֲמָא קָאָמְרִי, מִדְּאִיצְטְרִיךְ לִשְׁמוּאֵל לְמֵימַר בְּתַרְוַיְיהוּ הֲלָכָה. שֶׁמְּמָאֲנִין אֶת הַקְּטַנּוֹת. מְבַקְּשִׁין מֵהֶן שֶׁיְּמָאֲנוּ, כְּגוֹן הָנָךְ דְּרַבִּי אֶלְעָזָר וְר"א כְּדֵי לְקַיֵּים מִצְוַת יִבּוּם. וְשֶׁמַּשִּׂיאִין אִשָּׁה. שֶׁהָלַךְ בַּעְלָהּ לִמְדִינַת הַיָּם, וְשָׁמְעָה מִפִּי עֵד אֶחָד שֶׁמֵּת — מַשִּׂיאִין אוֹתָהּ לְאַחֵר. וְשֶׁנִּסְקַל תַּרְנְגוֹל. כִּדְכְתִיב (שמות כא): "וְהֵמִית אִישׁ אוֹ אִשָּׁה הַשּׁוֹר יִסָּקֵל", וְהוּא הַדִּין לְכָל חַיָּה וְעוֹף, כִּדְאוֹקִימְנָא בְּ"שׁוֹר שֶׁנָּגַח אֶת הַפָּרָה" (ב"ק דף נד:) דְּיָלֵיף "שׁוֹר" "שׁוֹר" מִשַּׁבָּת, אֶלָּא שֶׁדִּבֵּר הַכָּתוּב בַּהוֹוֶה. בֶּן מ' יוֹם. וּמַקְמֵי הָכִי — פָּסוּל, דְּה"ל יַיִן מִגִּתּוֹ. קְטַנּוֹת דְּעָלְמָא. וּלְעוֹלָם עֵדוּת בֶּן בָּבָא אַדְּר' אֶלְעָזָר קָאֵי. וְלָא אַדְּר"א. וְה"ק: כָּל קְטַנּוֹת שֶׁיָּבֹאוּ לְמָאֵן לְפָנֵינוּ, כִּי הַהִיא דְּר"א — מְלַמְּדִין אוֹתָן לְמָאֵן. לִיתְנֵי נָשִׁים. שֶׁמַּשִּׂיאִין נָשִׁים ע"פ עֵד אֶחָד. וְנֵימָא מַאי נָשִׁים נָשִׁים דְּעָלְמָא. כִּי הֵיכִי דְּאָמַר "מַאי קְטַנּוֹת — קְטַנּוֹת דְּעָלְמָא". דַּוְקָא קָתָנֵי. קְטַנּוֹת, שְׁתַּיִם: אַחַת דְּר' אֶלְעָזָר, וְאַחַת דְּר' אֱלִיעֶזֶר, וְאִשָּׁה דְּלֵיכָּא לְמֵימַר הָכִי, נְסָבָהּ בִּלְשׁוֹן יָחִיד. וְכֵן אָמַר ר' אֶלְעָזָר. אַדִּשְׁמוּאֵל קָאֵי וַאֲמוֹרָא הוּא, וְהוּא ר' אֶלְעָזָר בֶּן פְּדָת. וְרַבִּי אֶלְעָזָר דְּמֵיאוּן תַּנָּא הוּא, וְהוּא ר' אֶלְעָזָר בֶּן שַׁמּוּעַ. הַוֶּרֶד וְהַכּוֹפֶר. מִין בְּשָׂמִים הֵן. קֶטֶף. מִין אִילָן, וְאֵין עוֹשֶׂה פְּרִי אֶלָּא שְׂרָף (יוֹצֵא וְנוֹטֵף מֵהֶן) וְזֶהוּ פִּרְיוֹ. יֵשׁ לָהֶן שְׁבִיעִית. שֶׁצָּרִיךְ לְהַפְקִירָם, וְאָסוּר לַעֲשׂוֹת בָּהֶן סְחוֹרָה, וְלָא אָמְרִי' עֵצִים בְּעָלְמָא נִינְהוּ, וּשְׁבִיעִית אֵינָהּ נוֹהֶגֶת בְּעֵצִים, כִּדְאָמְרִי' בְּ"לוּלָב הַגָּזוּל" (סוכה דף מ.). בִּיעוּר. כְּשֶׁכָּלָה לַחַיָּה מִן הַשָּׂדֶה. וְאע"ג דְּיֵשׁ לָהֶן שְׁבִיעִית, אִיצְטְרִיךְ לְמֵימַר יֵשׁ לָהֶן בִּיעוּר, דְּיֵשׁ שֶׁיֵּשׁ לוֹ שְׁבִיעִית לֵיאָסֵר בִּסְחוֹרָה *וּמְלוּגְמָא, וְאֵין לוֹ בִּיעוּר. כְּגוֹן דָּבָר הַמִּתְקַיֵּים בָּאָרֶץ כָּל יְמֵי הַחוֹרֶף, שֶׁאֵינָהּ כָּלָה לַחַיָּה מִן הַשָּׂדֶה. אֲבָל כָּל דָּבָר שֶׁיֵּשׁ לוֹ בִּיעוּר — יֵשׁ לוֹ שְׁבִיעִית. וְא"ר פְּדָת. בְּרֵיהּ דְּר"א בֶּן פְּדָת. מַאן תְּנָא. לְהָא דְּקָתָנֵי "יֵשׁ לָהֶן שְׁבִיעִית" דְּקָסָבַר קְטָפָא פֵּירָא — ר' אֱלִיעֶזֶר, כִּדְאָמַר לְקַמָּן, ר"א אוֹמֵר: הַמַּעֲמִיד בִּשְׂרַף הָעָרְלָה — אָסוּר. שָׁרִיתוּ קִטְפָא. בַּשְּׁבִיעִית. כְּר"א בְּד'. וְתוּ לָא, אַלְמָא בִּקְטָפָא פֵּירָא לָא עָבֵיד כְּוָותֵיהּ לְחוּמְרָא. אוֹמְרָהּ בְּרָכָה רְבִיעִית. לְהַבְדָּלָה בְּמוֹצָאֵי שַׁבָּתוֹת, וְאֵינוֹ כּוֹלְלָהּ בְּ"חוֹנֵן הַדָּעַת". וְאָמַר רַבִּי אֶלְעָזָר הֲלָכָה כְּרַבִּי אֱלִיעֶזֶר. בִּבְרָכוֹת יְרוּשַׁלְמִי. וְהָא

---

**ועל** היין בן מ' יום. פרש"י: דקודם לכן הוי "יין מגתו." אע"ג דאמרי' ב"המוכר פירות" (ב"ב דף צז.) יין מגתו אם הביא – כשר, בן מ' יום – לכתחילה נמי יביא, אפילו יש הרבה מיין אחר. **יש** להן ביעור ולדמיהם ביעור. אע"ג דשביעית תופסת דמיה, יש חילוק בביעור בין דמיה לעצמה. כדתנן (א) בפ"ב דשביעית, ר' מאיר: אומר דמיה מתבערים עד ר"ה, אבל הן מתבערין עד הפסח.

**קטף**. פירש רש"י: שם העץ. וכן בברייתא פ"ק דכריתות (דף ו.) *רשב"ג אומר: הצרי אינו אלא שרף מעצי הקטף. ושרף עצמו נקרא "קטף", על שם העץ. כדאמר הכא, דיש בו שביעית. ובסמוך נמי אמר: דקטפו זהו פריו. "וצרי ולוט" (בראשית לז) – מתרגמינן: קטף ולוטא. ומה שפירש"י דאינו עושה פירות, אלא שרף נוטף ממנו, וזהו פריו – אינו לטעמי דמוקי ליה ר' זירא בסמוך: בקטפא דפירא. ונראה דרש"י פירש כן לשינויא בתרא, גי'.

**ואמר** רבי פדת מאן תנא כו' – ואם תאמר: דבפרק קמא דברכות (דף ה:) אמר ליה ר' יוחנן לרבי אלעזר: אי משום בני – דין גרמא דעשיראה ביר, משמע דלרבי אלעזר לא היו לו בנים! ויש לומר: שאחרי כן נולד לו, או היו לו בנים הרבה ומתו מקצתם, ואמר ליה רבי יוחנן כך כדי לנחמו. **מאן** תנא דאמר קטפא פירא ר' אליעזר. ואם תאמר: במאי פליגי, אי ביעורו והנאתו שוה – מאי טעמא דרבנן, דאפי' עצים הוו אסירי בשביעית אי לאו דאין הנאתו וביעורו שוה. ואי אין הנאתו וביעורו שוה – לא אסור בשביעית? ואין סברא לומר: דפליגי אי הנאתו וביעורו שוה אי לאו. ויש לומר: דודאי הנאתו וביעורו שוה, ולפי שאינו כי אם לחלוחי העץ – שרו רבנן, דבטל אגב העץ. ורבי אליעזר סבר דהנאתו חשיבא, והוי פירי*.

**ואבוך** אמר הלכה כר"א בד'. אע"ג דר' יוסי קאי כוותיה, דב"הגוזל קמא" (ב"ק דף קא.) אית *להו דשביעית נוהגת בעצים, וא"כ כ"ש קטפא. ומשום דרבי יוסי קאי כותיה, לא חשיב ליה עם הנך. (ב) דטעמא דר' יוסי, משום דלא בעי הנאתו וביעורו שוה, ולא קיימא לן כוותיה. אלא אין שביעית נוהגת בעצים. דר' יוסי נמי מודה דקטפא לאו פירא הוא לענין ערלה.

[**משום** דקאי רבי יהודה בן בבא כותיה. אע"ג דבמתני' נמי חזר בו ר' יהושע וקאי כוותיה, ואפ"ה מני לה בד'? וי"ל: דשמא ר' יהושע סבר כר' יוסי דמצריך ג' עונות במעוברת ומניקה, דפליג ארבי אליעזר. ולא הדר ביה אלא ממה שאמר "אני לא שמעתי אלא בתולה". גי':

א) **ומי** קאי. הר"מ ז"ל אמר: דלא פריך מברייתא אברייתא, משום דה"א דהדר ביה מההיא דהודאה ב) (אחרינא שמע) מרבותיו אבל השתא דקאמר דקאי בשיטתיה משמע דלא הדר ביה דאל"כ אכתי תיקשי ותו ליכא לכך פריך שפיר ומי קאי. גי'.]

א) **מפני** שצריך לומר הבדלה בחונן הדעת. הקשה הר"ר יעקב מאורלינ"ש: ונכלליה מכלל, דהכי פריך פרק (ג) "תפלת השחר" (ברכות דף כט.) אהא דאמר שמואל: כל השנה מתפלל "הביננו", חוץ ממוצאי שבת, מפני שצ"ל הבדלה ב"חונן הדעת". ופריך: ונכלליה מכלל! וי"ל: דהתם פריך, משום דלא ישנה אדם משום הבדלה מכמו שהוא מתפלל כל השנה, [כיון דסבר דכל השנה מתפלל "הביננו"] אלא יכלול ב"הביננו" והכא קאמר ר' חנינא ג) [כיון דס"ל דכל השנה אינו מתפלל "הביננו" א"כ]: במוצאי יוה"כ, מפני טורח תענית, לא ישנה מכמו שהוא מתפלל כל השנה, כדי שיאמר הבדלה ב"חונן הדעת".

א) שייך לע"ב ב) [נ"ל אחר ששמע] ג) כ"י כ"י

והא

## תוספי הרא"ש

**בסדר** טהרות. בפ' בתרא דע"ז גבי הנהו גנבי בעובדא דנהרדעא ואמר שמואל חמרא שרי ואמרינן כמאן כר' אליעז' דאמר ספק ביאה טהור. קשה לפי גירסת ר"ת דמפר' כמאן כר' אליעזר בניחותא דהכא אמר שמואל דבסדר טהרות אין הלכה כר' אליעזר אלא בארבע. והתם נמי מספקא ליה לרב דימי הא דשרא ר' אלעזר אי משום דס"ל כר' אליעז' דאמר ספק ביאה טהור אי משום דקסבר רוב גנבי ישראל נינהו ובשמעתין קאמר ר' אלעזר נמי הלכה כר' אליעזר בד' ותו לא ואי הוה גרס בההיא דספק ביאה ר' אלעזר ניחא א"נ במס' טהרות גבי כל מקום שאתה יכול לרבות ספיקות גרס ר' אלעזר מטהר דכיון דקאי ר' אלעזר כותיה אפשר דהלכה כמותו דכי האי גוונא משנינן לקמן. וכן יש לפרש ההיא דפ' כל הגט דאמר ר' אלעזר שמאל ולילה פסולין ופוסלין והיינו כר' אליעזר דפרק מצות חליצה. אלא דאיכא תנאי התם דקיימי כותיה: ר' אליעזר אומר הרודה ונותן לסל וכו'. משנה היא במסכת חלה וקתני רישא העושה עיסתו קבים פטורים מן החלה עד שישוכו ר' אליעזר אומר אף הרודה כו' משמע דר' אליעזר לא בעי נשיכה. וקשה דבפ' אלו עוברין קאמר ר' יהושע בן לוי עלה דההיא דר' אליעזר לא שנו אלא ככרות של בעל הבית שנושכות זו את זו אבל כעכין לא. ואם לא גרס אף במילתיה דר' אליעזר ניחא דאיכא למימר דר' אליעזר בעי תרתי צירוף סל עם נשיכה. ואי גרס אף יש לפרש דת"ק בעי נשיכה בעודו עיסה לפי שראוין להתחבר ולהעשות ככר אחד אבל עשה שתי ככרות ונתנן בתנור או בסל עד שנשכו זה בזה לא סגי בהכי לת"ק. ולר' אליעזר מהני ובירושלמי פליגי תנאי אית תנוי תני הסל מצרף ואין התנור מצרף ואית תני תנור מצרף ואין הסל מצרף ומסיק נשכו כאן וכאן מצטרף לא נשכו כאן וכאן אין מצטרף אלמא שייך נשיכה בתנור ובסל ומסיק באלו עוברין דאפי' כעכין לא בעי ר' אליעזר (שכיחא) נשיכה ונראה אע"ג דמהני צירוף סל להתחייב בחלה היכא דלש פחות מכשיעור. מ"מ לענין מוקף לא מהני צירוף סל דהא ר' אליעזר גופיה הוא דאמר פרק כשם דחלה ניטלת מן הטהור על הטמא כגון דנוטל כדי חלה מעיסה שלא הורמה חלתה ונותן פחות מכביצה באמצע כדי ליטול מן המוקף. ולמה דוחק לעשות כן יניח אותו כדי חלה בבלי שהעיסה טמאה בתוכו ולא יגע. אלא ודאי לא השיב מוקף בהכי אע"פ שמצרף להתחייב. ועי"ל דאפי' להתחייב לא מצרף אלא א"כ נגע ולא אתא ר' אליעזר לאפוקי אלא דלא בעי' נשיכה. וכן משמע לישנא דמתני' דקתני העושה עיסתו קבים ונגעו זה בזה פטורין עד שישוכו ר' אליעזר אומר אף הרודה כו' משמע דאתי לאפוקי נשיכה אבל נגיעה בסל בעי. ועי"ל דאפי' אם תמצא לומר דלענין מוקף מועיל צירוף סל בלא נגיעה לא היה יכול לעשות כן בפרק כשם בטמאה וטהורה דכיון דקפיד עלייהו שלא יגעו זה בזה אין מועיל צירוף כלי כדמוכח בירושלמי בפ"ב דחלה דאמרינן התם דבר שמקפיד על תערובתו אין הכלי מצרף עיסה טהורה ועיסה טמאה עשו אותו כדבר שמקפיד על תערובתו בעיסה תחלה אבל בעיסה שניה אין לשני מגע אצל הטבל: **ושנסקל** תרנגול בירושלים כו'. הא דתנן בפ' שור שנגח את הפרה ואחד כל הבהמה לנפילת הבור כו' ולא חשיב להורג את הנפש משום דכיון דתנא חסימה דאתיא שור שור משבת ה"ה הא. והא דתנא התם לכלאים לאו משום כלאים דהנהגה איצטריך דמשור שור משבת נפקא. אלא משום כלאים דהרבעה דאתי בהמתך בהמתך משבת: **ועל** יין בן ארבעים יום. פי' רש"י דמקמי הכי פסול דהוה ליה יין מגתו אע"ג דאמרי' בפ"ק דתענית גבי ט' באב דבג' ימים נפיק ליה מכלל יין מגתו לגבי ניסוך בעינן מן המובחר וגם יש דינין חלוקים כדאיתא בפרק בן סורר ומורה: **יש** להן שביעית ולדמיהן שביעית. אע"ג דשביעית תופסת דמיה איצטריך למיתני הן ודמיהן לפי שיש דברים שחלוקין כי ההיא דתנן בפ"ז דמסכת שביעית גבי עיקר הלוף שוטה כו' ר' מאיר אומר דמיהן מתבערין עד ר"ה משמע אבל לא הן: **מאן** תנא קיטפא פירא ר' אליעזר. תימה אי קיטפא הנאתו וביעורו שוה מ"ט דרבנן ואי הנאתו אחר ביעורו מ"ט דר' אליעזר דבעינן דומיא דאכילה שהנאתו וביעורו שוה כדאיתא בהגוזל קמא ובמסכת סוכה דפטרי' עצים מדין שביעית משום דהנאתו אחר ביעורו וי"ל דקטף הנאתו וביעורו שוה ואפי' הכי פטרי ליה רבנן משום דבטל אגב העץ כיון דלא חשיב ליה פירא: **ואביך** אמר הלכה כר' אליעזר בארבע. וא"ת לימא בהא הלכה כר' אליעזר משום דקאי ר' יוסי כותיה דקסבר שביעית נוהגת בעצים בהגוזל קמא א"כ יש לקטף שביעית וי"ל דאין זה מטעם קיטפא פירא דמודה ר' יוסי בהעלה. ועוד דבהא אין הלכה כר' יוסי דקיימא לן אין שביעית נוהג בעצים: **ואמר** ר' אלעזר הלכה כר' אליעזר. פרש"י בברכות ירושלמי איתא ובתלמוד שלנו ליתא. ואיכא דפסיק כותיה פ' אין עומדין ביום טוב שחל להיות אחר השבת ואנן קי"ל השתא כמרגניתא דתקין רב ושמואל ותודיענו כדמסיק התם:

והא

הגהות הב"ח

(א) תוס' ד"ה יין לכן וכו' כדתנן בפ' שביעי דשביעית: (ב) ד"ה ואבוך וכו' עם הנך מכל מקום טעמא דר' יוסי: (ג) ד"ה מפני וכו' פרק תפלת השחר נ"ב כדכן כעי פריך הכי ואסיקנא בקשיא.

עין משפט נר מצוה

סה א מיי' פ"ב מהל' תפלה הל"י טוש"ע א"ח סי' תריט עד סי' תרכב:

סו ב מיי' שם פ"ב הלכה ג יב טוש"ע או"ח סי' תרכב סעיף א:

סז ג ד ה מיי' פ"ו מהל' שמיטין הל"ט וה"י ופט"ו מהל' מאכלות אסורות הל' כו:

סח ו מיי' פ"ט מהל' איסורי ביאה הל"ה ופ"ד מהל' מטכב ומושב הל"א סמג לאוין קיא:

סט ז מיי' פ"ח מהל' שמיטין הל' כא כב:

ע ח מיי' פ"ט מהל' איסורי ביאה הל"ה ופ"ד מהל' מטכב ומושב הל"א סמג לאוין קיא טוש"ע יו"ד סי' קפט סעיף לג:

עא ט מיי' פ"ד מהל' מטכב ומושב הל"א:

עב י מיי' פ"ט מהל' איסורי ביאה הל"א סמג לאוין קיא ועשין רמג:

[ואין זה במשנה אלא מדברי ת"ק התם משמע הכין]

מסורת הש"ס

יומא פז: פסחים ג.

ע"ז לה: [ערלה פ"א מ"ז]

ע"ז שם ערלה פ"א מ"ז

שביעית פ"ו מ"ו [וכסו איתא ר"ש אומר אין לקטף שביעית מפני שאינו פרי]

[ערכין כט. וש"נ]

[תוספתא שביעית פ"ג ע"ש]

[פסחים נג.]

שביעית פ"ד מ"ה ב"ב פ:

כתובות י: [לקמן סד:]

[תוספתא פ"א]

ישעיהו כו

בראשית לח

גמרא

וְהָא קַשִּׁישׁ מִינֵּיהּ טוּבָא! אֶלָּא: מִשּׁוּם דְּקָאֵי רַבִּי חֲנִינָא בֶּן גַּמְלִיאֵל בְּשִׁיטָתֵיהּ. וּמִי קָאֵי? *וְהַתַּנְיָא: אאוֹר יוה"כ — מִתְפַּלֵּל שֶׁבַע וּמִתְוַדֶּה, שַׁחֲרִית — מִתְפַּלֵּל שֶׁבַע וּמִתְוַדֶּה, מוּסָף — מִתְפַּלֵּל שֶׁבַע וּמִתְוַדֶּה, מִנְחָה — מִתְפַּלֵּל שֶׁבַע וּמִתְוַדֶּה, בִּנְעִילָה — מִתְפַּלֵּל שֶׁבַע וּמִתְוַדֶּה, בְּעַרְבִית — מִתְפַּלֵּל שֶׁבַע מֵעֵין שְׁמוֹנֶה עֶשְׂרֵה. רַבִּי חֲנִינָא בֶּן גַּמְלִיאֵל מִשּׁוּם אֲבוֹתָיו אוֹמֵר: במִתְפַּלֵּל שְׁמוֹנֶה עֶשְׂרֵה, מִפְּנֵי שֶׁצ"ל הַבְדָּלָה בְּ"חוֹנֵן הַדַּעַת". אָמַר ר"נ בַּר יִצְחָק: אִיהוּ אָמַר מִשּׁוּם אֲבוֹתָיו, וְלֵיהּ לָא ס"ל. א"ל ר' יִרְמְיָה לְר' זֵירָא: וְאַתְּ לָא תִּסְבְּרָא דְּמַאן תְּנָא קִטְפָא פֵּירָא ר"א הוּא? *וְהָתְנַן, ר"א אוֹמֵר: הַמַּעֲמִיד בִּשְׂרַף עָרְלָה — אָסוּר! אֲפִילּוּ תֵּימָא רַבָּנַן, געַ"כ לָא פְּלִיגִי רַבָּנַן עֲלֵיהּ דְּר"א אֶלָּא בְּקִטְפָא דְּגַוְוזָא, אֲבָל בְּקִטְפָא דְּפֵירָא — מוֹדוּ לֵיהּ. *דִּתְנַן, דא"ר יְהוֹשֻׁעַ: שָׁמַעְתִּי בְּפֵירוּשׁ שֶׁהַמַּעֲמִיד בִּשְׂרַף הֶעָלִין, בִּשְׂרַף הָעִיקָּרִין — מוּתָּר, בִּשְׂרַף הַפַּגִּין — אָסוּר, מִפְּנֵי שֶׁהוּא פְּרִי. וְאִיבָּעֵית אֵימָא: הכִּי פְּלִיגִי רַבָּנַן עֲלֵיהּ דְּר"א — בְּאִילָן הָעוֹשֶׂה פֵּירוֹת, אֲבָל בְּאִילָן שֶׁאֵינוֹ עוֹשֶׂה פֵּירוֹת — מוֹדוּ דְּקִטְפּוֹ זֶהוּ פִּרְיוֹ. דִּתְנַן, *ר"ש אוֹמֵר: אֵין לְקֶטֶף שְׁבִיעִית, *וַחכ"א יֵשׁ לַקֶּטֶף שְׁבִיעִית, מִפְּנֵי שֶׁקִּטְפּוֹ זֶהוּ פִּרְיוֹ. מַאן חֲכָמִים? לָאו רַבָּנַן דִּפְלִיגִי עֲלֵיהּ דְּר"א? א"ל הַהוּא סָבָא, הָכִי א"ר יוֹחָנָן: *מַאן חֲכָמִים — ר"א דְּאָמַר קִטְפּוֹ זֶהוּ פִּרְיוֹ. אִי ר"א, מַאי אִירְיָא אִילָן שֶׁאֵינוֹ עוֹשֶׂה פְּרִי? אֲפִילּוּ אִילָן הָעוֹשֶׂה פְּרִי — קִטְפּוֹ זֶהוּ פִּרְיוֹ! לְדִבְרֵיהֶם דְּרַבָּנַן קָאָמַר לְהוּ, לְדִידִי אֲפִי' אִילָן הָעוֹשֶׂה פֵּירוֹת נַמִי קִטְפּוֹ זֶהוּ פִּרְיוֹ, לְדִידְכוּ — אוֹדוּ לִי מִיהַת בְּאִילָן שֶׁאֵינוֹ עוֹשֶׂה פֵּירוֹת דְּקִטְפּוֹ זֶהוּ פִּרְיוֹ, וְרַבָּנַן אָמְרִי לֵיהּ: לָא שְׁנָא. § "אֵיזוֹ הִיא בְּתוּלָה — כָּל שֶׁלֹּא רָאֲתָה" כו'. § ת"ר ינִשֵּׂאת וְרָאֲתָה דָּם מֵחֲמַת נִישּׂוּאִין, יָלְדָה וְרָאֲתָה דָּם מֵחֲמַת לֵידָה — עֲדַיִין אֲנִי קוֹרֵא לָהּ "בְּתוּלָה", שֶׁהֲרֵי בְּתוּלָה שֶׁאָמְרוּ — בְּתוּלַת דָּמִים, וְלֹא בְּתוּלַת בְּתוּלִים. אִינִי, וְהָאָמַר רַב כָּהֲנָא, *תָּנָא, ג' בְּתוּלוֹת הֵן: בְּתוּלַת אָדָם, בְּתוּלַת קַרְקַע, בְּתוּלַת שִׁקְמָה. בְּתוּלַת אָדָם — כָּל זְמַן שֶׁלֹּא נִבְעֲלָה, נָפְקָא מִינַּהּ — לְכ"ג, א"נ — לִכְתוּבָּתָהּ מָאתַיִם. בְּתוּלַת קַרְקַע — כ"ז שֶׁלֹּא נֶעֶבְדָה, *נָפְקָא מִינַּהּ — לְנַחַל אֵיתָן, א"נ — לְמִקָּח וּמִמְכָּר. בְּתוּלַת שִׁקְמָה — כ"ז שֶׁלֹּא נִקְצְצָה, נָפְקָא מִינַּהּ — לְמִקָּח וּמִמְכָּר, אִי נַמִי — לְמִקְצְצָהּ בַּשְּׁבִיעִית, כְּדִתְנַן: *זאֵין קוֹצְצִין בְּתוּלַת שִׁקְמָה בַּשְּׁבִיעִית, מִפְּנֵי שֶׁהִיא עֲבוֹדָה. וְאִם אִיתָא, לִיתְנֵי נַמִי הָא! אָמַר ר"נ בַּר יִצְחָק: כִּי קָתָנֵי — מִידֵי דְּלֵית לֵיהּ שֵׁם לְוַוי, אֲבָל מִידֵי דְּאִית לֵיהּ שֵׁם לְוַוי — לָא קָתָנֵי. רַב שֵׁשֶׁת בְּרֵיהּ דְּרַב אִידִי אָמַר: כִּי קָתָנֵי — מִידֵי דְּתָלֵי בְּמַעֲשֶׂה, מִידֵי דְּלָא תָּלֵי בְּמַעֲשֶׂה — לָא קָתָנֵי. רַבִּי חֲנִינָא בְּרֵיהּ דְּרַב אִיקָא אָמַר: כִּי קָתָנֵי — מִידֵי דְּלָא הָדַר לִבְרִיָּיתוֹ, מִידֵי דְּהָדַר לִבְרִיָּיתוֹ — לָא קָתָנֵי. רָבִינָא אָמַר: כִּי קָתָנֵי — מִידֵי דְּקָפֵיד עֲלֵיהּ זְבִינָא, מִידֵי דְּלָא קָפֵיד עֲלֵיהּ זְבִינָא — לָא קָתָנֵי. וְלָא קָפְדִי? *וְהַתַּנְיָא, רַבִּי חִיָּיא אוֹמֵר: כְּשֵׁם שֶׁהַשְּׂאוֹר יָפֶה לְעִיסָּה — כָּךְ דָּמִים יָפִין לָאִשָּׁה, וְתַנְיָא מִשּׁוּם ר"מ: כָּל אִשָּׁה שֶׁדָּמֶיהָ מְרוּבִּין — בָּנֶיהָ מְרוּבִּין! אֶלָּא כִּי קָתָנֵי — מִידֵי דְּקָפֵיץ עֲלֵיהּ זְבִינָא, מִידֵי דְּלָא קָפֵיץ עֲלֵיהּ זְבִינָא — לָא קָתָנֵי. ת"ר: אֵיזוֹהִי בְּתוּלַת קַרְקַע — כָּל שֶׁמַּעֲלָה רְשׁוֹשִׁין וְאֵין עֲפָרָהּ תִּיחוֹחַ, נִמְצָא בָּהּ חֶרֶס — בְּיָדוּעַ שֶׁנֶּעֶבְדָה, צוּנְמָא — הֲרֵי זוֹ בְּתוּלַת קַרְקַע. § "מְעוּבֶּרֶת מִשֶּׁיִּוָּדַע עוּבָּרָהּ". § וְכַמָּה הַכָּרַת הָעוּבָּר? סוּמְכוֹס אוֹמֵר מִשּׁוּם רַבִּי מֵאִיר: חשְׁלֹשָׁה חֳדָשִׁים. וְאע"פ שֶׁאֵין רְאָיָה לַדָּבָר — זֵכֶר לַדָּבָר, שֶׁנֶּאֱמַר: °"וַיְהִי כְּמִשְׁלֹשׁ חֳדָשִׁים" וְגוֹמֵר. "זֵכֶר לַדָּבָר"? קְרָא כְּתִיב, וּרְאָיָה גְּדוֹלָה הִיא! מִשּׁוּם דְּאִיכָּא דְּיָלְדָה לְט' וְאִיכָּא דְּיָלְדָה לְשִׁבְעָה. ת"ר *טהֲרֵי שֶׁהָיְתָה בְּחֶזְקַת מְעוּבֶּרֶת וְרָאֲתָה דָּם, וְאח"כ הִפִּילָה רוּחַ אוֹ כָּל דָּבָר שֶׁאֵינוֹ שֶׁל קַיָּימָא — הֲרֵי הִיא בְּחֶזְקָתָהּ, וְדַיָּהּ שְׁעָתָהּ. וְאע"ג שֶׁאֵין רְאָיָה לַדָּבָר — זֵכֶר לַדָּבָר, שֶׁנֶּאֱמַר: °"הָרִינוּ חַלְנוּ כְּמוֹ יָלַדְנוּ רוּחַ". מַאי "זֵכֶר לַדָּבָר"? הֲרֵי רְאָיָה גְּדוֹלָה הִיא! כִּי כְּתִיב הַאי קְרָא — בִּזְכָרִים כְּתִיב. וּרְמִינְהִי: יקָשְׁתָה שְׁנַיִם, וְלַשְּׁלִישִׁי הִפִּילָה רוּחַ אוֹ כָּל דָּבָר שֶׁאֵינוֹ שֶׁל קַיָּימָא — הֲרֵי זוֹ יוֹלֶדֶת בְּזוֹב. וְאִי אָמְרַתְּ לֵידָה מְעַלְּיָיתָא הִיא, קוּשְׁי

רש"י

וְהָא קַשִּׁישׁ מִינֵּיהּ טוּבָא. דְּהָא ר' אֱלִיעֶזֶר הָיָה בִּימֵי ר"ג בְּנוֹ שֶׁל ר"ש הַנֶּהֱרָג בַּהֲרוּגֵי מַלְכוּת, וּבַעַל אֲחוֹתוֹ הָיָה, כִּדְאָמְרִי' בְּ"הַזָּהָב" (ב"מ דף נט.). וְר' חֲנִינָא — בְּנוֹ שֶׁל ר"ג הָיָה. אוֹר. לֵיל כְּנִיסָתוֹ. מֵעֵין שְׁמוֹנֶה עֶשְׂרֵה. שֶׁאוֹמֵר בְּשִׁבְעָה בְּרָכוֹת מֵעֵין שְׁמוֹנֶה עֶשְׂרֵה, כְּגוֹן ג' רִאשׁוֹנוֹת וְג' אַחֲרוֹנוֹת כְּתִקְנָן, וְאוֹמֵר "הֲבִינֵנוּ" בָּאֶמְצַע, וּמְסַיֵּים בְּ"שׁוֹמֵעַ תְּפִלָּה", כִּדְאָמְרִינַן בִּבְרָכוֹת (דף כט.) וְיֵשׁ בָּהּ מֵעֵין כּוּלָּם. הַמַּעֲמִיד. חֲלֵב בְּהֵמָה לַעֲשׂוֹת גְּבִינָה. בְּקִטְפָא דְּגַוְוזָא. בִּשְׂרָף הַנּוֹטֵף מִן הָעֵץ, דְּכְעֵץ בְּעָלְמָא הָוֵי. אֲבָל קֶטֶף הָוֵי שְׂרַף הַפַּגִּין, וּמוֹדוּ בְּהוּ רַבָּנַן. לָאו רַבָּנַן דִּפְלִיגִי עֲלֵיהּ דְּר"א. בִּשְׁאָר אִילָנוֹת, וְחָזִינַן דְּבִקְטָף סְבִירָא לְהוּ כְּוָותֵיהּ. בְּתוּלַת דָּמִים. דְּמֵי נִדָּה וְלֹא דְּמֵי בְּתוּלִים, דַּאֲפִילּוּ נִבְעֲלָה — עֲדַיִין הִיא בְּתוּלַת דָּמִים. לְכֹהֵן גָּדוֹל. שֶׁמְּצֻוֶּה (א) לִיקַּח בְּתוּלָה. לִכְתוּבָּתָהּ מָאתַיִם. דְּאִם נִבְעֲלָה — תּוּ לָא מִיקְרֵי "בְּתוּלָה", וּכְתוּבָּתָהּ מָנֶה. לְמִקָּח וּמִמְכָּר. שֶׁאִם אָמַר לוֹ: "קַרְקַע בְּתוּלָה אֲנִי מוֹכֵר לְךָ" — נוֹתֵן לוֹ קַרְקַע שֶׁלֹּא נֶעֶבְדָה, לְפִי שֶׁעוֹשָׂה פֵּירוֹת מְרוּבִּין וּשְׁמֵנִים. שֶׁלֹּא נִקְצְצָה. כֵּן מִנְהָג לְקוֹצְצָהּ, כְּדֵי שֶׁיִּרְבֶּה עוֹבְיוֹ וְיוֹצִיא עֲנָפִים הַרְבֵּה בִּמְקוֹם הַחֲתָךְ, וְנִקְרָא "סַדַּן שִׁקְמָה". לְמִקָּח וּמִמְכָּר. לְפִי שֶׁנּוֹחַ לוֹ בִּבְתוּלָה, שֶׁיַּלְדָּה הִיא, וְיִקְלְעֶנָּה וּמִתְעַבָּה. לִיתְנֵי נַמִי הָא. וְנֵימָא: "אַרְבַּע בְּתוּלוֹת הֵן". שֵׁם לְוַוי. כְּגוֹן בְּתוּלָה דְּמַתְנִיתִין לָאו "בְּתוּלָה" סְתָם מִיקַּרְיָא, אֶלָּא "בְּתוּלַת דָּמִים". דִּסְתָם "בְּתוּלָה" בְּנָשִׁים הַיְינוּ בְּתוּלַת בְּתוּלִים. וְכֵן קַרְקַע בְּתוּלָה, וְכֵן שִׁקְמָה בְּתוּלָה, לָא בָּעֵי שֵׁם לְוַוי. דְּתָלֵי בְּמַעֲשֶׂה. שֶׁאֵינוֹ מְאַבֵּד שְׁמוֹ אֶלָּא ע"י מַעֲשֶׂה, אֲבָל רְאִיַּית דָּם — מֵאֵילֶיהָ בָּאָה, וְאָבְדָה שֵׁם "בְּתוּלָה". דְּהָדַר לִבְרִיָּיתוֹ. כְּגוֹן זְקֵנָה, שֶׁמִּסְתַּלְּקִין דָּמֶיהָ. דְּקָפֵיד עֲלֵיהּ זְבִינָא. נוֹתֵן עֵינָיו בְּכָךְ, כְּגוֹן בְּתוּלָה נוֹחָה לִינָּשֵׂא מִבְּעוּלָה, וְכֵן קַרְקַע וְשִׁקְמָה. אֲבָל בְּתוּלַת דָּמִים — אֵין אָדָם נוֹתֵן עֵינָיו בְּדָמִים, דְּלָא חָיֵישׁ אִי חַזְיָא אִי לָא חַזְיָא. דְּקָפֵיץ עֲלֵיהּ. שֶׁנּוֹחָה בְּתוּלָה לַלָּקוֹחוֹת, כְּגוֹן בְּתוּלַת בְּתוּלִים וְקַרְקַע וְשִׁקְמָה. אֲבָל בְּתוּלַת דָּמִים, כָּל כַּמָּה דְּחָזְיָא — נִיחָא לֵיהּ טְפֵי, כִּדְאָמְרִינַן. רְשׁוֹשִׁין. אֲבָנִים דַּקִּין שֶׁקּוֹרִין פרדוי"א. לָשׁוֹן אַחֵר: רִגְבֵי אֲדָמָה קָשִׁין, שֶׁאֵין עֲפָרָהּ מִתְפַּזֵּר. חֶרֶס. מְכִיתַּת חֲרָסִים. בְּיָדוּעַ שֶׁנֶּעֶבְדָה. דְּאִי לֹא נֶעֶבְדָה, חֶרֶס זֶה מֵאַיִן בָּא לְתוֹכָהּ? צוּנְמָא. סֶלַע. דְּיָלְדָה לְז'. (ב) שֶׁמָּא נִיכַּר עוּבָּרָהּ לִשְׁלִישׁ יָמֶיהָ, דְּהַיְינוּ שְׁנֵי חֳדָשִׁים וּשְׁלִישׁ, קמ"ל דְּאָזְלִינַן בָּתַר רוֹב נָשִׁים. דַּיָּהּ שְׁעָתָהּ. לָא אָמְרִינַן: אִיגַּלַּאי מִילְּתָא לְמַפְרֵעַ דְּלָאו הֵרָיוֹן הוּא, וְנִטְמְאוּ טְהָרוֹת דְּמֵעֵת לְעֵת שֶׁל רְאִיָּיה. זֵכֶר לַדָּבָר. דְּהֵרָיוֹן רוּחַ שְׁמֵיהּ הֵרָיוֹן. קָשְׁתָה שְׁנֵי יָמִים. בְּתוֹךְ אַחַד עָשָׂר יְמֵי זוֹב, וְלַשְּׁלִישִׁי נַמִי רָאֲתָה, וְאח"כ הִפִּילָה רוּחַ בּוֹ בַּיּוֹם, וְלֹא שָׁפְתָה מִן הַצַּעַר — הֲרֵי לֵידָה זוֹ בְּזוֹב. וּצְרִיכָה שִׁבְעָה נְקִיִּים, וְקָרְבָּן לְזִיבָתָהּ, דְּכֵיוָן דְּלָאו וָלָד הוּא — הָוְיָא זָבָה מַעַלְיָא.

תוספות

והא קשיש מיניה טובא. ר"א מרבי חנינא. פרש"י: שר' חנינא היה בנו של ר"ג דיבנה. וכ"נ, דבפרק "המפלת" (לקמן דף כג.) א"ר חנינא בן גמליאל: נראין דברי ר"מ בבהמה ובחיה. וא"ת: והא בת"כ (פ' אמור) גבי "פנחס איש הסתת שעלה גורלו להיות כ"ג" כו' אמר ר' חנינא בן רבן גמליאל: וכי סתת היה, והלא חתנינו היה, ותורש היה?! ואי בן ר"ג דיבנה היה, היאך היה לו חתן כ"ג, והלא היה אחר החורבן? וי"ל: דלאו חתנינו ממש קאמר, אלא חתן אבותיו. וכן משמע, דלא אמר "חתני" אלא "חתנינו היה".

בקטפא דפירא מודו ליה דתנן א"ר יהושע כו' וא"ת: [א"כ] אמאי אוקי רבי פדת מתניתין כר"א, כיון דרבנן מודו בקטפא דפירא? ואי משום דבעי לאוקומי בכל מיני קטף, אפי' בדגווזא, מ"מ היכי קאמר ליה ר' זירא: חזי דמשתריא קטפא לעלמא, הא ודאי אמת הוא דקטפא דגווזא שרי! דאף ר' זירא מודה דאין הלכה כר"א אלא בד' וליכא למימר: דאתי למטעי ולמשרי אף קטפא דפירא, מדלא מוקי רבי פדת מתני' בקטפא דפירא ודברי הכל, מכלל דסבר אף בקטפא דפירא רבנן הוא דשרו — הא לא אתי למטעי, דהא חזינן במשנה שאוסר רבי יהושע שרף הפגים! וי"ל: שיטעו ויסברו שרבי יהושע "שמעתי" קאמר, וליה לא ס"ל, מדלא מוקי ר' פדת מתני' כוותיה, ובקטפא דפירא. ואפשר דר' פדת סבר דקטפא דפירא שרי, ור' [יהושע] קאמר "שמעתי" וליה לא סבירא ליה. מאן חכמים (א"ר יוחנן) ר"א. אע"ג דתנא בלשון "חכמים", ניחא ליה לאוקומי כר"א, ולא לימא ג' מחלוקות בדבר.

תוספי הרא"ש

והא קשיש מיניה. פרש"י ר' חנינא בנו של ר"ג דיבנה הוה חבירו של ר' אליעזר ור' אליעזר [בעל אחותו] דר"ג [היה] כדאיתא בפרק הזהב והך לאו ראיה דאפשר דלא דהוה קשיש הרבה אע"ג דר' (אליעזר) [גמליאל] היה נשוי אחות אביו אלא לקמן בהמפלת משמע שהיה בימי ר' מאיר או אחריו דקאמר ר' (מאיר) חנינא בן גמליאל נראין דברי ר' מאיר. ובקדושין הוא בר פלוגתיה דר' מאיר בתנאי כפול. ותימה דבת"כ גבי פנחס שעלה גורלו להיות כ"ג אמר ר' חנינא בן גמליאל והלא חתנינו היה משמע דקודם חורבן הוה. וי"ל דחתן בית אבא קאמר מדלא קתני חתני. וא"ת הא בסוף מסכת סוטה אמר רשב"ג אלף ילדים היו בבית אבא ולא נשתייר מהם אלא אני כאן ובן אחי אבא בעסיא. אני למדתי תורה ובן אחי אבא למד חכמת יונית. אלמא לא היו לו אחים והכא משמע שר' חנינא היה אחיו. וי"ל דבבית אבי אבא קאמר כשנהרג (ר"ג) [רשב"ג] הזקן. תדע מדקאמר בן אחי אבא וכשאמר דבר זה עדיין היה ר' חנינא אחיו קטן: ומי קאי כוותיה והתניא כו'. הקשה הר' שמשון מקוצי מאי קשיא ליה השתא טפי משום דקאי ר' אליעזר כוותיה בלאו הכי תקשי מדידיה אדידיה. וי"ל דמדידיה אדידיה לא קשה דאיכא למימר הא דלעיל איירי במוצאי שבת ליום טוב והכא איירי במוצאי שבת לחול. אבל השתא דקאמר דר' אליעזר קאי כוותיה ע"כ קאי במוצאי שבת לחול דבהכי איירי ר' אליעזר: מפני שצריך לומר הבדלה בחונן הדעת. וא"ת ונכלליה מכלל דהכי נמי פריך בפרק תפלת השחר למ"ד אין מתפללין במוצאי שבת הבינו. וי"ל דהתם פריך שפיר כיון דקאמרת דכל השנה כולה מתפלל אדם הבינו במוצאי שבת נמי לא ישנה מנהגו ויכלול הבדלה בהבינו עם שאר הברכות שהוא כולל אבל הכא דסבר דכל השנה מתפלל י"ח שלימות ליכא למיפרך ונכלליה לשנות מנהגו של כל השנה: אבל בקיטפא דפירא מודו ליה. אמאי דקאמר ר' זירא לעיל חזי דמינך ומאבוך קשריתו קיטפא לעלמא קמתמה. ותימה ור' פדת באיזו קיטפא איירי אי בקיטפא דפירא אפי' ר' יהושע מודה דאסור ואמאי קאמר ליה קיטפא לעלמא כדתנן שרף הפגין אסור ואי בקיטפא דגווזא אמאי קפיד ר' זירא ודאי קיטפא דגווזא שרי וי"ל דר' פדת איירי בקיטפא דפירא וסבר דר' יהושע נמי סבר דקיטפא לאו פירא הוא ושרי ודאסר בשרף הפגין בערלה משום דכתיב וערלתם ערלתו את פריו ומרבינן את הטפל לפריו אפי' מידי דלא פירא כגון קילפין רמונים ואגוזים אבל שרף העלין ושרף העיקרין דלאו פירא הוא שרי דלא הוי השרף טפל לפרי. ור' זירא סבר דכי היכי דסבר ר' יהושע גבי ערלה קיטפא דפירא פירא הוא ה"נ גבי שביעית קיטפא פירא הוא ואסור ומשום הכי קפיד ולשינויא אחרינא איירי ר' פדת בקיטפא דגווזא באילן שאינו עושה פירות והיה סובר כההוא סבא דסבירא דר' אליעזר אוסר וחכמין מתירין וקא שרי לעיל. ור' זירא הקפיד כי הוא סובר דרבנן מודו באילן שאינו עושה פירות דקטפו זהו פריו: נפקא מינה לכ"ג. משמע דלא אסירא ליה אלא בעולת אדם. תימה הרי בוגרת ומוכת עץ דאמרינן פרק הבא על יבמתו לא ישא ומדאורייתא כדמוכח התם. וי"ל דבדיעבד אם נשא נשוי כדאיתא התם אבל בעולת אדם אם נשא יוציא א"נ ה"ק נפקא מינה לכ"ג אם היא בעולת איש ועדיין היא בתולה כגון שבעל בהטייה אפי' הכי אסורה כדאיתא פ' אין דורשין ועדיין היא בתולה גבי בתולה שעיברה. וא"ת אמאי לא קאמר נפקא מינה לענין אונס ומפתה. וי"ל דהתם אימעיט בעולת אע"פ שהיא בתולת אדם: מידי דקפיץ עליה זבינא. ת' הרי בתולת השקמה דסדן השקמה עדיף כדתנן בהמוכר את הבית המוכר את השדה מכר בתולת השקמה אבל לא בתולת סדן השקמה ושמא התם לפי שיש לו שם לווי ולא משום דעדיף. ומי' לעיל משמע דעדיף דקאמר אין קוצצין דשביעית מפני שהוא עבודה אלמא שהוא מיתקן ומשביח מן הקציצה כמו זימור בכרמים. וי"ל דהאי דעדיף היינו משום הגדול ועב מבתולת השקמה והלוקח מחברו אילן של שקמה גדול ניחא ליה טפי שתהא בתולה משיקצוץ הענפים ואחר כך ישביח ואם היה סדן אם יקצוץ אין גזען מחליף:

הגהות הב"ח

(א) רש"י ד"ה לכהן גדול שמצווה ליקח בתולה: (ב) ד"ה דילדה לשבעה טמאה:

גליון הש"ס

גמ' ואח"כ הפילה רוח. עי' לקמן ט ע"ב רש"י ד"ה הרי היא ככל הנשים וכו'. וכ"ת תגלי מילתא למפרע וכו' וכו' ולע"ע: רש"י ד"ה דילדה לשבעה וכו' לאזלינן בתר רוב נשים. עיין סנהדרין סט ע"א:

קושי סמוך ללידה רחמנא טהריה! אמר רב פפי: *הנח מעת לעת — דרבנן. רב פפא אמר: מידי הוא טעמא — אלא משום דראשה כבד עליה ואבריה כבדין עליה, הכא נמי — ראשה ואבריה כבדין עליה. בעא מיניה רבי ירמיה מרבי זירא: ראתה ואח"כ הוכר עוברה, מהו? כיון דבעידנא דחזאי לא הוכר עוברה — [א]מטמיא, או דלמא: כיון דסמוך לה חזאי לא מטמיא? א"ל: מידי הוא טעמא — אלא משום דראשה כבד עליה ואבריה כבדין עליה, *בעידנא דחזאי — אין ראשה כבד עליה ואין אבריה כבדין עליה. בעא מיניה ההוא סבא מר' יוחנן: הגיע עת וסתה בימי עבורה ולא בדקה, מהו? קא מיבעיא לי אליבא דמ"ד *וסתות דאורייתא. מאי! כיון דוסתות דאורייתא — בעיא בדיקה, או דלמא: כיון דדמיה מסולקין, לא בעיא בדיקה? א"ל, תניתוה: *רבי מאיר אומר, [ב]אם היתה במחבא והגיע שעת וסתה ולא בדקה — טהורה, שחרדה מסלקת את הדמים. טעמא — דאיכא חרדה, הא ליכא חרדה והגיע וסתה ולא בדקה — טמאה, אלמא: וסתות דאורייתא. וכיון דאיכא חרדה — דמיה מסולקין, ולא בעיא בדיקה. [ג]הכא נמי — דמיה מסולקין ולא בעיא בדיקה. § "מניקה עד שתגמול" וכו'. ת"ר: *מניקה שמת בנה בתוך עשרים וארבע חדש — הרי היא ככל הנשים, ומטמאה מעת לעת ומפקידה לפקידה. לפיכך, אם היתה מניקתו והולכת ארבע או חמש שנים — דיה שעתה, דברי ר"מ. *רבי יהודה ורבי יוסי ורבי שמעון אומרים: [ד]דיין שעתן כל עשרים וארבע חדש, לפיכך, [ה]אם היתה מניקתו ארבע וחמש שנים — מטמאה מעת לעת ומפקידה לפקידה. כשתמצא לומר, לדברי ר"מ — *דם נעכר ונעשה חלב, לדברי רבי יוסי ורבי יהודה ורבי שמעון — *אבריה מתפרקין, ואין נפשה חוזרת עד עשרים וארבע חדש. "לפיכך" דר"מ למה לי — משום "לפיכך" דרבי יוסי. ולפיכך דרבי יוסי למה לי? מהו דתימא: רבי יוסי תרתי אית ליה, קמ"ל תניא נמי הכי: *דם נעכר ונעשה חלב, דברי ר"מ. רבי יוסי אומר: אבריה מתפרקין, ואין נפשה חוזרת עליה עד עשרים וארבע חדש. א"ר אלעאי: מאי טעמא דר"מ — דכתיב: °"מי יתן טהור מטמא לא אחד". ורבנן — א"ר יוחנן: זו שכבת זרע, שהוא — טמא, ואדם הנוצר ממנו — טהור. ור"א אומר: *אלו מי הנדה, [ו]שהמזה ומזין עליו — טהור, ונוגע — טמא. ומזה טהור? והכתיב: °"ומזה מי הנדה יכבס בגדיו"! מאי "מזה" — נוגע. והכתיב "מזה", והכתיב "נוגע"? ועוד, מזה — בעי כבוס, [ז]נוגע — לא בעי כבוס! אלא: מאי "מזה" — נושא. וליכתוב "נושא"! [ח]קמ"ל דעד דהוי כשיעור הזאה. הניחא למ"ד *הזאה צריכה שיעור, אלא למ"ד אין צריכה שיעור, מאי איכא למימר? אפילו למ"ד אינה צריכה שיעור, [ט]ה"מ — אגבא דגברא, אבל במנא — בעינא שיעור. *כדתנן: כמה יהיו במים ויהא בהן כדי הזאה — כדי שיטבול ראשי גבעולין ויזה. והיינו דאמר שלמה: "אמרתי אחכמה והיא רחוקה ממני". § "איזו היא זקנה כל שעברו עליה שלש עונות" [סמוך לזקנתה]. היכי דמי "סמוך לזקנתה"? אמר רב יהודה: כל שחברותיה אומרות עליה "זקנה היא". *ורבי שמעון אומר: כל

**רש"י**

קושי סמוך ללידה. שלא שפתה בינתים, ודם הקושי מחמת הולד הוא בא. רחמנא טהריה. מזיבה בתוך י"א יום, בפרק "בנות כותים" (לקמן לז.). אמר רב פפי. אין, ודאי דלאו לידה היא, אבל לענין דייה שעתה חשיב ולד, דמעת לעת דרבנן. רב פפא אמר. אף על גב דלאו ולד הוא, אפילו הכי דייה שעתה. דטעמא דמעוברת דייה שעתה — משום דראשה ואבריה כבדין מחמת חולי, ולפיכך דמיה מסולקין, הלכך בהריון של רוח נמי ראשה ואבריה כבדין. ואח"כ הוכר עוברה. סמוך לראייתה מיד. וסתות דאורייתא. אותה בדיקה שהצריכוה לאשה להבדק בשעת וסתה — דבר תורה הוא, הלכה למשה מסיני. דאורח בזמנו בא, ואם בא יום וסתה, ולא בדקה — מחזקינן לה טמאה, לקמן בפרק "כל היד" (דף טז.). וקא מבעיא לן: אם לא בדקה ביום וסתה, בימי עיבורה מהו. אם היתה במחבא. מחמת פחד גרכום (א) או ליסטין. ה"ג: אלמא וסתות דאורייתא. וכיון דאיכא חרדה כו'. ה"נ. במעוברת, הואיל ודמיה מסולקין — טהורה. ומטמאה מעת לעת. שאין הדבר תלוי אלא בהנקת התינוק, לפי שהדם נעכר ונעשה חלב, וכיון שמת — חוזר הדם לקדמותו. לפיכך. כיון דבינקה תליא מילתא, אם היתה מניקתו כו'. דיה שעתה. אע"פ שמת. שאין הטעם תלוי בינקת הולד, אלא מתוך צער לידה אבריה מתפרקין, ודמה מסתלק, ואינו חוזר עד כ"ד חדש. הלכך לא שנא מת, לא שנא חי. לפיכך. כיון דלאו בתינוק תליא מילתא, אם היתה מניקתו כו', שהרי לסוף כ"ד חדש חוזר הדם. נפשה. דמה. למה לי. כיון דאמר: "הרי היא ככל הנשים", אלמא בתינוק תליא מילתא, פשיטא דאם מניקתו לעולם דדיה שעתה! מהו דתימא רבי יוסי תרתי אית ליה. דם נעכר, ואבריה מתפרקין. והיכא דמת בתוך כ"ד חדש — דיה שעתה, משום דעדיין לא חזר דמה. והיכא דמניקתו חמש שנים — נמי דיה שעתה, אף על פי שחוזר נפשה לסוף כ"ד חדש, הנקת תינוק עוכרת לדם ונעשה חלב. קמ"ל. "לפיכך", דדוקא קאמר רבי יוסי. שאין הטעם תלוי אלא בפירוק אברים, בין יונק בין שאינו יונק — דיה שעתה כ"ד חדש, לא פחות ולא יותר. אבל "לפיכך" דר"מ לא איצטריך. דלר"מ אין סילוק דמים תוך כ"ד חדש טפי מלאחר כ"ד חדש. דאי יש סילוק, אמאי אמרינן דכי מת תוך כ"ד חדש מטמאה מעת לעת? וכיון דאין סילוק — אין חזרה. והלכך כי מניקתו לעולם, על כרחך דיה שעתה. מ"ט דר"מ. כלומר, מנ"ל לר"מ דדם נעכר ונעשה חלב. טהור מטמא. חלב מדם. לא אחד. בתמיה. כלומר, יחידו של עולם. ורבנן אמר רבי יוחנן. כלומר, ורבנן האי קרא מאי עבדי ליה — לכדרבי יוחנן כו'. ועוד נוגע לא בעי כבוס. דכתיב: "ומזה מי הנדה יכבס בגדיו והנוגע במי הנדה יטמא עד הערב". הניחא למאן דאמר כו'. פלוגתא היא במסכת זבחים בפ' "כל הזבחים שנתערבו" (דף פ.). כדי שיטבול ראשי גבעולין. של אזוב, ולא (ג) שיספוג בקינוח. אמרתי אחכמה. בטעם זה: למה מזה ומזין עליו — טהור, ונוגע — טמא. והיא רחוקה ממני.

**תוספות**

קושי סמוך ללידה רחמנא טהריה. וא"ת: דבפרק "בנות כותים" (לקמן לו:) *אמר: דמה מחמת עצמה, ולא מחמת ולד. ופריך, ונימא: דמה מחמת עצמה, ולא מחמת אונס? ומשני: מטהר אני בולד, שכן יש לו טהרה אחרי כן, מה שאין כן באונס. והשתא, והא בלידת רוח אין טהרה! ויש לומר: *דפריך א"ואי בעית אימא" דקאמר התם: ולד — אין לך אונס גדול מזה.

אי נמי: הואיל ואיכא לידה, דיש טהרה אחרי כן - איכא לאוקמיה קרא בכל ענין לידה, אפילו בלידת רוח שאין טהרה אחרי כן, בשפיר שאינו מרוקם, אע"ג דאין טהרה אלא בשפיר מרוקם. גליון.

הא ליבא חרדה ולא בדקה טמאה אלמא וסתות דאורייתא. [כי הגיע שעת וסתה] וא"ת: ודלמא לעולם וסתות דרבנן, ומיירי דהשתא בדקה עצמה ומצאה טמאה. וכי איכא חרדה — טהורה למפרע ולא מטמאינן, אלא משעה שמצאה טמאה ואילך. הא ליכא חרדה, ובדקה אחרי כן ומצאה טמאה — טמאה משעת וסתה? דהכי אמרינן פרק "כל היד" (לקמן דף טו.) למ"ד וסתות דרבנן, [בדקה אחרי כן] ומצאה טמאה — טמאה, טהורה — טהורה. ולמ"ד וסתות דאורייתא, אפילו בדקה ומצאה טהור — טמא, דאורח בזמנו בא. *(וי"ל: דסמיך ארישא דתנא פ' "בנות כותים" (לקמן לט.) הגיע שעת וסתה ולא בדקה — טמאה. אלמא וסתות דאורייתא. ומיהו קשה: דבפרק "כל היד" (שם דף טז.) מוכיח מהכא דסבר רבי מאיר וסתות דאורייתא, ואיכא מאן דלא מפרש (ג) התם רישא כר' מאיר, ואם כן דלמא ר"מ פליג ארישא) וי"ל: דדייק מדקתני "מסלקת הדמים", משמע: הדמים הידועים בה והמנוררים לבא, אלמא וסתות דאורייתא.

לפיכך דרבי מאיר למה לי. השתא לא בעי לשנויי: [מהו דתימא] דתרתי בעי רבי מאיר, קמ"ל "לפיכך" דבחד סגי — דאין סברא שלא תהא מסולקת בדמים אלא ע"י שני דברים. אבל על ר' יוסי ס"ד שתהא מסולקת באחד מב' דברים או בזה או בזה.

ונוגע טמא. וא"ת: והלא מזין עליו נמי בעי טבילה והערב שמש, כמו נוגע? וי"ל: דמ"מ הוי חדוש, שזה בא לו טומאה על ידי הזאה, וזה בא לו טהרה ע"י הזאה. א"נ: בטהור שמזין עליו בחנם קאמר הכא, וכדתנן דפ"ק דיומא (דף יד.) דתניא: טהור שנפל עליו הזאה — טמאתו, דברי רבי עקיבא. ורבנן אמרי: ק"ו, על הטמא — טהור, על הטהור — לא כ"ש!

מאי מזה נושא. וא"ת: ומנ"ל לאפוקי קרא ממשמעותיה? וי"ל: מדכתיב "והזה הטהור על הטמא" משמע שהוא טהור לעולם. ואע"ג דדרשינן נמי (ביומא דף מג.) "הטהור" — מכלל שהוא טמא, לימד על טבול יום שטהור בפרה. תרתי ש"מ. [ה"ג: א"נ, כיון דלורך מלוה הוא, נוגע סברא הוא דטהור.*) (בא' מזין עליו) ע"כ ודוחק] (א"נ). נוגע ונושא דטמא — היינו בחנם, אבל כדי להזות על הטמא — לא. ועוד מזה בעי כבוס. בפ' "יוצא דופן" (לקמן דף מג:) מפורש מה שמקשים על זה מנבלת בהמה טמאה.

*) צריך תקון והגהה

עין משפט
נר מצוה

פא א ב מיי' פ"ט מהל' איסורי ביאה הל"ה ופ"ד מהל' משכב ומושב הל"א סמג לאוין קא טוש"ע יו"ד סי' קפט סעי' כט:
פב ג טוש"ע יו"ד סי' קפט סעי' א:
פג ד ה מיי' פ"ד מהל' משכב ומושב הל"א וע"ש בכ"מ ובטוש"ע יו"ד סי' קפט סעי' כז וסעי' ל:
פד ו מיי' שם הל"ג סמג שם טוש"ע יו"ד סי' קפט סעי' כז והכל שם:
פה ז מיי' שם הל"ד סמג שם:

**כל** שקורין לה **אמא אמא** ואינה בושה. ובירושלמי פריך: וכי בדעתה תלויה הדבר? ומשני: כל שראויה לקרותה "אמא".

**ימי** טומאה וימי טהרה. פרש"י: שבעה ימי נדות, ושלשה ימי זיבה. אך קצת דוחק דקרי לאחד עשר יום "ימי טומאה", ולקמן תנן בפרק "בנות כותים" (דף לח:) כל י"א יום – בחזקת טהרה. וקרא נמי קרי להו "בלא עת נדתה". ור"ח גריס, אמר רבא אמר רב חסדא: כ"ג.

**זקנה** שעברו עליה שלש עונות. פירוש: סמוך לזקנתה, ועוד עברו עליה שלש עונות – דיה שעתה. והא דתנן (לעיל דף ז.) במה אמרו "דיה שעתה" – בראשונה, אבל בשניה – מטמאה מעת לעת, היינו כי ראתה בשניה בסוף שלשים.

**פיחתה** והותירה. פרש"י: כגון לנ"א, לנ"ב, ולנ"ג. לאו דוקא בענין זה, דהא לקמן בפרק "האשה" (דף סד.) פליגי בה רב ושמואל, בראתה בט"ו לחדש זה, וט"ז לחודש זה, וי"ז לחדש זה, אי קבעה וסת לדילוג. ומיהו למאי דפריש התם: דדוקא ברואה לדילוג לחדש, אבל ראתה היום, ואחר ט"ז יום, ואחר י"ז ימים – לא קבעה וסת לדילוג, אתי שפיר.

קמזיא

א כָּל שֶׁקּוֹרִין לָהּ "אִמָּא, *אִמָּא" וְאֵינָהּ בּוֹשָׁה. ר' זֵירָא וְר' שְׁמוּאֵל בַּר רַב יִצְחָק, חַד אָמַר: ב כָּל שֶׁאֵינָהּ מַקְפֶּדֶת, וְחַד אָמַר: כָּל שֶׁאֵינָהּ בּוֹשָׁה. מַאי בֵּינַיְיהוּ? אִיכָּא בֵּינַיְיהוּ: בּוֹשָׁה וְאֵינָהּ מַקְפֶּדֶת. וְכַמָּה עוֹנָה? אָמַר רֵישׁ לָקִישׁ מִשּׁוּם רַבִּי יְהוּדָה נְשִׂיאָה: ג עוֹנָה בֵּינוֹנִית, שְׁלֹשִׁים יוֹם. וְרָבָא אָמַר רַב חִסְדָּא: עֶשְׂרִים יוֹם. וְלָא פְּלִיגִי, מַר קָחָשֵׁיב יְמֵי טוּמְאָה וִימֵי טָהֳרָה, וּמַר לָא חָשֵׁיב יְמֵי טוּמְאָה. ת"ר ד זְקֵנָה שֶׁעָבְרוּ עָלֶיהָ שָׁלֹשׁ עוֹנוֹת וְרָאֲתָה – דַּיָּהּ שְׁעָתָהּ, וְעוֹד עָבְרוּ עָלֶיהָ שָׁלֹשׁ עוֹנוֹת וְרָאֲתָה – דַּיָּהּ שְׁעָתָהּ, וְעוֹד עָבְרוּ עָלֶיהָ שָׁלֹשׁ עוֹנוֹת וְרָאֲתָה – הֲרֵי הִיא כְּכָל הַנָּשִׁים, וּמְטַמְּאָה מֵעֵת לְעֵת וּמִפְּקִידָה לִפְקִידָה. וְלָא (*מִיבָּעְיָא) שֶׁכִּוְּונָה, אֶלָּא אֲפִי' פִּיחֲתָה (וַאֲפִילּוּ) וְהוֹתִירָה. אֲפִי' פִּיחֲתָה, וְלָא מִבָּעְיָא כִּוְּונָה? אַדְּרַבָּה, כִּי כִּוְּונָה – קָבְעָה לָהּ וֶסֶת, וְדַיָּהּ שְׁעָתָהּ! וְכִי תֵּימָא: רַבָּנַן הִיא, דִּפְלִיגִי עֲלֵיהּ *דְּרַבִּי דּוֹסָא, דְּאָמְרִי אִשָּׁה שֶׁיֵּשׁ לָהּ וֶסֶת – מְטַמְּאָה מֵעֵת לְעֵת, אִיפְּכָא מִבָּעֵי לֵיהּ, וְלֵימָא: וְלֹא שֶׁפִּיחֲתָה וְהוֹתִירָה, אֶלָּא אֲפִי' כִּוְּונָה! ה תְּנֵי: לֹא שֶׁפִּיחֲתָה וְהוֹתִירָה אֶלָּא אֲפִי' כִּוְּונָה. וְאִיבָּעֵית אֵימָא, ה"ק: וְלֹא שֶׁכִּוְּונָה אֶלָּא שֶׁפִּיחֲתָה וְהוֹתִירָה, אֲבָל כִּוְּונָה – קָבְעָה לָהּ וֶסֶת וְדַיָּהּ שְׁעָתָהּ, וּמַנִּי – רַבִּי דּוֹסָא הִיא.§ ר"א אוֹמֵר: כָּל אִשָּׁה שֶׁעָבְרוּ עָלֶיהָ" וכו'.§ תַּנְיָא, אָמַר לָהֶם רַבִּי אֱלִיעֶזֶר לַחֲכָמִים: מַעֲשֶׂה בְּרִיבָה אַחַת בְּהִיתְלוֹ שֶׁהִפְסִיקָה שָׁלֹשׁ עוֹנוֹת, וּבָא מַעֲשֶׂה לִפְנֵי חֲכָמִים וְאָמְרוּ דַּיָּהּ שְׁעָתָהּ. אָמְרוּ לוֹ: אֵין שְׁעַת הַדְּחָק רְאָיָה. מַאי "שְׁעַת הַדְּחָק"? אִיכָּא דְּאָמְרִי: שְׁנֵי בַצּוֹרֶת הֲווּ, אִיכָּא דְּאָמְרִי: טְהָרוֹת אַפֵּישׁ לַעֲבִידָא, וְחָשׁוּ רַבָּנַן לְהֶפְסֵד דְּטָהֳרוֹת. ת"ר: *מַעֲשֶׂה וְעָשָׂה רַבִּי כְּר' אֱלִיעֶזֶר, לְאַחַר שֶׁנִּזְכַּר אָמַר: *כְּדַי הוּא ר' אֱלִיעֶזֶר לִסְמוֹךְ עָלָיו בִּשְׁעַת הַדְּחָק. מַאי "לְאַחַר שֶׁנִּזְכַּר"? אִילֵימָא – לְאַחַר שֶׁנִּזְכַּר דְּאֵין הֲלָכָה כְּר' אֱלִיעֶזֶר אֶלָּא כְּרַבָּנַן, בִּשְׁעַת הַדְּחָק הֵיכִי עָבֵיד כְּוָותֵיהּ? אֶלָּא – דְּלָא אִיתְּמַר הִילְכְתָא לָא כְּמַר וְלָא כְּמַר, וּמַאי "לְאַחַר שֶׁנִּזְכַּר" – לְאַחַר שֶׁנִּזְכַּר דְּלָאו יָחִיד פָּלֵיג עֲלֵיהּ, אֶלָּא רַבִּים פְּלִיגִי עֲלֵיהּ, אָמַר: כְּדַי הוּא ר' אֱלִיעֶזֶר לִסְמוֹךְ עָלָיו בִּשְׁעַת הַדְּחָק. ת"ר: ו תִּינוֹקֶת שֶׁלֹּא הִגִּיעַ זְמַנָּהּ לִרְאוֹת וְרָאֲתָה, פַּעַם רִאשׁוֹנָה – דַּיָּהּ שְׁעָתָהּ, שְׁנִיָּה – דַּיָּהּ שְׁעָתָהּ, שְׁלִישִׁית – הֲרֵי הִיא כְּכָל הַנָּשִׁים, וּמְטַמְּאָה מֵעֵת לְעֵת וּמִפְּקִידָה לִפְקִידָה. עָבְרוּ עָלֶיהָ שָׁלֹשׁ עוֹנוֹת וְרָאֲתָה – דַּיָּהּ שְׁעָתָהּ, וְעוֹד עָבְרוּ עָלֶיהָ שָׁלֹשׁ עוֹנוֹת וְרָאֲתָה – דַּיָּהּ שְׁעָתָהּ, וְעוֹד עָבְרוּ עָלֶיהָ שָׁלֹשׁ עוֹנוֹת וְרָאֲתָה – הֲרֵי הִיא כְּכָל הַנָּשִׁים, וּמְטַמְּאָה מֵעֵת לְעֵת וּמִפְּקִידָה לִפְקִידָה. ז וּכְשֶׁהִגִּיעַ זְמַנָּהּ לִרְאוֹת, פַּעַם רִאשׁוֹנָה – דַּיָּהּ שְׁעָתָהּ, שְׁנִיָּה – מְטַמְּאָה מֵעֵת לְעֵת וּמִפְּקִידָה לִפְקִידָה, עָבְרוּ עָלֶיהָ שָׁלֹשׁ עוֹנוֹת וְרָאֲתָה – דַּיָּהּ שְׁעָתָהּ. אָמַר מָר: עָבְרוּ עָלֶיהָ שָׁלֹשׁ עוֹנוֹת – דַּיָּהּ שְׁעָתָהּ,

הדר

יְמֵי טוּמְאָה וִימֵי טָהֳרָה. מֵרְאִיָּיה וְעַד רְאִיָּיה שְׁלֹשִׁים יוֹם. יְמֵי טוּמְאָה עֲשָׂרָה: שִׁבְעָה לְנִדָּה וּשְׁלֹשָׁה לְזִיבָה, וְעֶשְׂרִים יְמֵי טָהֳרָה. הֲרֵי הִיא כְּכָל הַנָּשִׁים. דְּכֵיוָן דְּעָשְׂתָה כָּךְ שָׁלֹשׁ פְּעָמִים, אֵין זֶה סִילּוּק דָּמִים אֶלָּא שִׁינּוּי וֶסֶת. וְכִי תֵּימָא: תִּיגַּלֵּי מִלְּתָא לְמַפְרֵעַ שֶׁאַף בָּרִאשׁוֹנָה מִתּוֹךְ שֶׁדָּמִים מְלוּיִין בָּהּ רָאֲתָה, וְנִטְמָא טָהֳרוֹת לְמַפְרֵעַ! לָא אַחְמוּר רַבָּנַן כּוּלֵּי הַאי בְּמֵעֵת לְעֵת. בְּשֶׁכִּוְּונָה. שֶׁרָאֲתָה שָׁלֹשׁ רְאִיּוֹת הַלָּלוּ בְּתִשְׁעִים יוֹם אוֹ בְּיוֹם תִּשְׁעִים וְאֶחָד. אֶלָּא אֲפִילּוּ פִּיחֲתָה. כְּגוֹן רִאשׁוֹנָה לְתִשְׁעִים וּשְׁלֹשָׁה, וּשְׁנִיָּה לְסוֹף תִּשְׁעִים וּשְׁנַיִם, וּשְׁלִישִׁית לְתִשְׁעִים וְאֶחָד. אוֹ הוֹתִירָה, כְּגוֹן רִאשׁוֹנָה לְנ"א יוֹם, וּשְׁנִיָּה לְנ"ב, וּשְׁלִישִׁית לְנ"ג – אֲפִילּוּ הָכִי מְטַמְּאָה מֵעֵת לְעֵת. וּלְקַמָּן פָּרֵיךְ: מַאי "אֲפִילּוּ", הָא וַדַּאי הָכִי הוּא דִּמְטַמְּאָה מֵעֵת לְעֵת, דְּכֵיוָן שֶׁפִּיחֲתָה אוֹ הוֹתִירָה, בַּמֶּה נִטְהַר? וֶסֶת אֵין כָּאן, סִילּוּק דָּמִים אֵין כָּאן! אֲבָל אִם כִּוְּונָה, יֵשׁ כָּאן וֶסֶת, וְדַיָּהּ שְׁעָתָהּ. אִיפְּכָא מִיבָּעֵי לֵיהּ. וְלָא כְּשֶׁפִּיחֲתָה אוֹ הוֹתִירָה בִּלְבַד אָמְרוּ חֲכָמִים שֶׁתְּטַמֵּא מֵעֵת לְעֵת. אֶלָּא אֲפִילּוּ כִּוְּונָה. דְּאִיכָּא לְמֵימַר: יֵשׁ כָּאן קְבִיעוּת וֶסֶת, וְדַיָּהּ שְׁעָתָהּ – אֲפִילּוּ הָכִי מְטַמְּאָה מֵעֵת לְעֵת, כְּרַבָּנַן דִּפְלִיגִי עֲלֵיהּ דְּרַבִּי דּוֹסָא. וְאִיבָּעֵית אֵימָא. סַמֵּי מִכָּאן "אֲפִילּוּ", וְרַבִּי דּוֹסָא הִיא, וְהָכִי קָאָמַר: וְלֹא כְּשֶׁכִּוְּונָה, דְּאִי כִּוְּונָה – קָבְעָה וֶסֶת וְדַיָּהּ שְׁעָתָהּ, אֶלָּא שֶׁפִּיחֲתָה וְהוֹתִירָה. בְּהִיתְלוֹ. שֵׁם מָקוֹם. שְׁנֵי בַצּוֹרֶת הֲווּ. וְאִיכָּא הֶפְסֵד מְרוּבֶּה, חָשְׁשׁוּ. לְאַחַר שֶׁנִּזְכַּר. שֶׁלֹּא יָפֶה הוֹרָה. שְׁנִיָּה דַּיָּהּ שְׁעָתָהּ. שֶׁבִּרְאִיָּיה רִאשׁוֹנָה לֹא הוּחְזְקָה בְּדָמִים, הוֹאִיל וְלֹא הִגִּיעַ זְמַנָּהּ לִרְאוֹת, עַד שֶׁתִּתְחַזֵּק כִּשְׁאָר חֲזָקוֹת. שְׁלִישִׁית מְטַמְּאָה מֵעֵת לְעֵת. וּכְדְאָמַר לְקַמָּן, דְּהָא מַתְנִיתִין רַבִּי הִיא, דְּאָמַר בִּתְרֵי זִימְנֵי הָוֵי חֲזָקָה. הִלְכָּךְ בִּשְׁנֵי רְאִיּוֹת הוּחְזְקָה לִהְיוֹת דָּמִים מְלוּיִין בָּהּ, וּמִשֶּׁהוּחְזְקָה וְאֵילָךְ גּוֹזֵר בָּהּ רַבָּנַן מֵעֵת לְעֵת. עָבְרוּ עָלֶיהָ שָׁלֹשׁ עוֹנוֹת וְרָאֲתָה. סִילּוּק דָּמִים הוּא זֶה, וַאֲפִילּוּ בְּהִגִּיעַ זְמַנָּהּ לִרְאוֹת אִית לֵיהּ לְהַאי תַּנָּא דְּעָבְרוּ עָלֶיהָ שָׁלֹשׁ עוֹנוֹת דַּיָּהּ שְׁעָתָהּ, כִּדְקָתָנֵי סֵיפָא. וְר' אֱלִיעֶזֶר הִיא, דְּאָמַר בְּמַתְנִיתִין: כָּל אִשָּׁה שֶׁעָבְרוּ עָלֶיהָ ג' עוֹנוֹת – דַּיָּהּ שְׁעָתָהּ, כִּדְלְקַמָּן. בס"א אֵינוֹ. ה"ג: ת"ר תִּינוֹקֶת **שֶׁלֹּא הִגִּיעַ זְמַנָּהּ לִרְאוֹת, וְרָאֲתָה פַּעַם רִאשׁוֹנָה** – דַּיָּהּ שְׁעָתָהּ, שְׁנִיָּה – דַּיָּהּ שְׁעָתָהּ, שְׁלִישִׁית – הֲרֵי הִיא כְּכָל הַנָּשִׁים. וְאַע"ג דִּלְגַבֵּי בְּתוּלַת דָּמִים בְּמַתְנִי' תְּנַן: בַּמֶּה אָמְרוּ דַּיָּין שְׁעָתָן – בִּרְאִיָּיה רִאשׁוֹנָה, אֲבָל בַּשְּׁנִיָּה – מְטַמְּאָה מֵעֵת לְעֵת. הָנֵי מִילֵּי בְּהִגִּיעַ זְמַנָּהּ לִרְאוֹת (א) דָּמִים, דְּדָמִים מְלוּיִין בָּהּ, וּבַחֲדָא זִימְנָא אִיתַּחְזְקָה. אֲבָל זוֹ שֶׁאֵינָהּ רְאוּיָה לִרְאוֹת צְרִיכָה שֶׁתִּתְחַזֵּק בַּחֲזָקָה גְּמוּרָה, וּבִתְרֵי זִימְנֵי הָוְיָא חֲזָקָה, דְּהָא מַתְנִיתִין רַבִּי הִיא, וְכִדְמוֹקְמִינַן לֵיהּ לְקַמָּן. הִילְכָּךְ בִּשְׁתֵּי רְאִיּוֹת הָוְיָא חֲזָקָה, וּבַשְּׁלִישִׁית מְטַמְּאָה מֵעֵת לְעֵת. וּבְהַהִיא רְאִיָּיה דְּאִיתַּחְזַק בָּהּ לָא גָּזְרוּ רַבָּנַן טוּמְאָה לְמַפְרֵעַ, כִּי הֵיכִי דִּבְתוּלָה דְּמַתְנִי' דְּהִגִּיעַ זְמַנָּהּ לִרְאוֹת, דְּמִיחְזְקָה בַּחֲדָא רְאִיָּיה, וְאָמְרוּ רַבָּנַן: דַּיָּהּ שְׁעָתָהּ בְּאוֹתָהּ רְאִיָּיה. אַף זֹאת הַמּוּחְזֶקֶת בִּרְאִיָּיה שְׁנִיָּה, דַּיָּהּ שְׁעָתָהּ, עַד שֶׁתִּרְאֶה אֶת הַשְּׁלִישִׁית. עָבְרוּ עָלֶיהָ שָׁלֹשׁ עוֹנוֹת. לְאַחַר שֶׁהוּחְזְקָה וְרָאֲתָה. דַּיָּהּ שְׁעָתָהּ. כְּרַבִּי אֱלִיעֶזֶר אוֹקְמִינַן לָהּ לְקַמָּן, דְּאָמַר: כָּל אִשָּׁה שֶׁעָבְרוּ עָלֶיהָ שָׁלֹשׁ עוֹנוֹת דַּיָּהּ שְׁעָתָהּ, כִּדְקָתָנֵי סֵיפָא אַף בְּהִגִּיעַ זְמַנָּהּ וְרָאֲתָה, עָבְרוּ עָלֶיהָ שָׁלֹשׁ עוֹנוֹת וְרָאֲתָה דַּיָּהּ שְׁעָתָהּ, אַלְמָא ר"א הִיא. וְעוֹד עָבְרוּ עָלֶיהָ שָׁלֹשׁ עוֹנוֹת וְרָאֲתָה דַּיָּהּ שְׁעָתָהּ. לְקַמָּן בָּעֵי גְּמָרָא: דְּאִי לָא עָבְרוּ עָלֶיהָ שְׁלֹשָׁה עוֹנוֹת שְׁנִיּוֹת, אֶלָּא לְסוֹף עוֹנָה חָזַאי כִּשְׁאָר נָשִׁים מַאי? לְפִי שֶׁיֵּשׁ לִנְטוֹת הַדָּבָר לִשְׁנֵי צְדָדִים, כִּדְבָעֵי לְפָרוּשֵׁי (ב) בְּסֵיפָא. וְעוֹד עָבְרוּ עָלֶיהָ ג' עוֹנוֹת וְרָאֲתָה. מְטַמְּאָה מֵעֵת לְעֵת. דְּאִיגַּלַּאי מִילְּתָא דְּהָנָךְ הַפְסָקוֹת לָאו סִילּוּק דָּמִים הֵם, אֶלָּא שִׁינּוּי וֶסֶת. וְלֹא שֶׁכִּוְּונָה אֶלָּא שֶׁפִּיחֲתָה וְהוֹתִירָה, כִּדְאָמְרִינַן לְעֵיל. וְאַף עַל גַּב דִּלְרַבִּי הָוֵי חֲזָקָה בִּתְרֵי זִימְנֵי, וְהוֹכָחָה (ג) דְּשִׁינּוּי וֶסֶת לְדִילּוּגוֹ לָאו סִילּוּק דָּמִים הֵן, אֲפִילּוּ הָכִי לָא מְטַמְּאִינַן לָהּ בַּשְּׁנִיָּה מֵעֵת לְעֵת. דְּכֵיוָן דְּלֹא הִגִּיעַ זְמַנָּהּ לִרְאוֹת הָוְיָא הַפְסָקָה רִאשׁוֹנָה, מַחְזְקִינַן לָהּ בְּחוֹזֶרֶת לְקַדְמוּתָהּ שֶׁלֹּא יְהוּ עוֹד דָּמִים מְלוּיִין בָּהּ, וּצְרִיכָה שֶׁתִּתְחַזֵּק כְּבַתְּחִלָּה, וּפַעַם רִאשׁוֹנָה וּשְׁנִיָּה – דַּיָּהּ שְׁעָתָהּ, וּשְׁלִישִׁית – מְטַמְּאָה מֵעֵת לְעֵת. הִלְכָּךְ רְאִיָּיה הַסְּמוּכָה לָהּ לְשָׁלֹשׁ עוֹנוֹת קַמָּאֵי – הִיא רִאשׁוֹנָה, וְהַסְּמוּכָה לַשְּׁנִיָּה – הִיא הַשְּׁנִיָּה, וּבַשְּׁלִישִׁית – תְּטַמֵּא מֵעֵת לְעֵת. וְאַף עַל גַּב דְּבְהַפְסָקָה חֲזִיתָהּ – שִׁינּוּי וֶסֶת הוּא, וְלֹא סִילּוּק דָּמִים. ע"כ. **וּכְשֶׁהִגִּיעַ זְמַנָּהּ לִרְאוֹת פַּעַם רִאשׁוֹנָה דַּיָּהּ שְׁעָתָהּ שְׁנִיָּה מְטַמְּאָה מֵעֵת לְעֵת.** דְּהַיְינוּ בְּתוּלָה דְּמַתְנִיתִין, דִּתְנַן בָּהּ: "בַּמֶּה אָמְרוּ דַּיָּהּ שְׁעָתָהּ – בִּרְאִיָּיה רִאשׁוֹנָה, אֲבָל בַּשְּׁנִיָּה – מְטַמְּאָה מֵעֵת לְעֵת". עָבְרוּ עָלֶיהָ כו'. רַבִּי אֱלִיעֶזֶר הִיא, דְּאָמַר: אֲפִילּוּ יַלְדָּה שֶׁעָבְרוּ עָלֶיהָ שָׁלֹשׁ עוֹנוֹת – דַּיָּהּ שְׁעָתָהּ. **אָמַר מָר**. גַּבֵּי תִּינוֹקֶת שֶׁלֹּא הִגִּיעַ זְמַנָּהּ לִרְאוֹת, וְרָאֲתָה שָׁלֹשׁ פְּעָמִים, וְאַחַר כָּךְ עָבְרוּ עָלֶיהָ שָׁלֹשׁ עוֹנוֹת וְרָאֲתָה – דַּיָּהּ שְׁעָתָהּ.

הדר

מסורת הש"ס

[מלה זו נראה כמיותרת וע' סוכה כח: ובעירובין פב. וכן בהרמב"ם ובטוש"ע ליתא]

ר"מ מוחק כ"ז וע"ש

[לעיל ז:]

[לעיל ו. עירובין מו:]

[ברכות ט. וש"נ]

הגהות הב"ח

(א) רש"י ד"ה ה"ג וכו' זמנה לראות דדמים מלויין כצ"ל ותיבת דמים נמחק: (ב) ד"ה ועוד עברו וכו' כדבעי לפרושי לקמן כצ"ל ותיבת בסיפא נמחק: (ג) ד"ה ועוד עברו וכו' והוכחה דשינתה וסת לדילוג ולאו סילוק וכו' לראות היא הפסקה:

תוספי הרא"ש

בעי טבילה. כדאיתא בפ"ק דמגילה. וי"ל דמ"מ ההזאה גורמת לה הטהרה דאם לא היו מזין עליו לא היה טהור לעולם. ומזה טהור לגמרי כדכתיב והזה הטהור על הטמא והיינו חדושיה אע"ג דנושא טמא ומזה נמי קא דרי שיעור הזאה טמא טהור: **ועוד** מזה בעי כיבום נוגע לא בעי כיבום. וכיון דכתיב במזה כיבום בגדים ובנוגע לא כתיב ביה כיבום בגדים לית לן למימר דמזה היינו נוגע ותימה והא גבי נבלת בהמה כתיב והאוכל מנבלתה יכבס את בגדיו ודרשי' ליה לשיעור לנוגע כאוכל. אבל האוכל עצמו לא מטמא דממעטינן ליה מבה דכתיב גבי נבלת העוף דדרשי' בה בה ולא באחרת. ונוגע לא בעי כיבום הכא נמי נימא דמזה היינו נוגע אע"ג דבמזה כתיב ביה כיבום ונוגע לא בעי כיבום. וי"ל דמילף ילפינן ליתן לו שיעור אוכל. אבל לא אמרינן דמזה היינו נוגע כיון דמזה כתיב ביה כיבום ונוגע לא בעי כיבום. וא"ת הכא נמי ליתן לנוגע כשיעור הזאה ואמאי אמרינן מזה היינו נושא ולא מוקמינן ליה ליתן לנוגע שיעור הזאה. י"ל כיון דכתיב במזה כיבום ונוגע לא (היה) בעי כיבום לא מוקמינן ליה לשיעורא דנוגע אלא מוקמינן ליה בנושא דלא כתיב ביה כלל. אע"פ דבהאוכל נבלה כתיב ביה כיבום ומוקמי' ליתן שיעור דלא בעי כיבום. שאני התם דילפינן נמי שיעור' לנושא דבעי כיבום אבל הכא אי לא (בעי) אתי למילף כי אם הנוגע לא הוה למיכתב במזה כיבום ועוד כיבום דאוכל נבלה אצטריך למיכתב דאי לא כתיב ביה כיבום לא הוה ממעטינן מיניה אלא שאינו טעון כיבום כנבלת עוף טהור אבל טמויי מטמא אבל השתא דכתיב ביה כיבום איתמעיט לגמרי. וי"מ ועוד מזה בעי כיבום ונוגע לא בעי כיבום כלומר אי אפשר לומר דמזה היינו נוגע דבמזה בעי כיבום ואילו נוגע קי"ל דלא בעי כיבום כדמוכחי כמה משניות ואי אמרינן דמזה היינו נוגע א"כ ליבעי נוגע כיבום אלא ע"כ צריך לפרושי דכיון דכתיב במזה כיבום ובנוגע לא כתיב כיבום לא אמרינן דמזה היינו נוגע ור"מ הקשה מ"ט הדר ביה ממאי דאמר מזה היינו נוגע אי משום דקשיא ליה והא כתיב מזה והא כתיב נוגע. ועוד מזה בעי כיבום נוגע לא בעי כיבום לישני ליה דהיכא דלא נגע כשיעור הזאה לא בעי כיבום ומזה אתי לאורויי אנוגע כבשיעור הזאה דבעי כיבום ותירץ דלא ניחא ליה לאוקומי קרא בנוגע להטעינו כיבום ובמשא יהיה טהור לגמרי דלא אשכחן טומאה דלא מטמאה אלא במגע וטעון כבוס בגדים להכי אוקמה במשא וטעון כיבום ובמגע לא בעי כיבום דאשכחן טומאה כיוצא בה דנבלה מטמאה אדם ולא בעי כיבום ובמשא בעי כיבום. וכן מרכב הזב חמור משאו ממגעו ועוד מיסתבר ליה לאוקומיה טפי בנושא מבנוגע דלשון מזה משמע לשון הזייה והתזה דהיינו נושא. אבל אין במשמעותו לשון נוגע כלל ושמעתי דהמזה מי הנדה הוא כמו הזיית מי הנדה כלומר יש בהזיית מי הנדה טומאה ואיכא לאוקומי בנוגע ובנושא. כדכתיב וישב יורם להתרפא ביזרעאל מן המכים אשר יכוהו ארמים. וכמו דאת אמר ממכת מכים והמכה מכים. אמרינן נמי מהמזאה מזה: [ע"כ שייך לעמוד הקודם] **רבא** אמר עשרים יום. ר"ח גרים כ"ג דלא חשיב ג' ימי זיבות ימי טומאה דאמרינן לקמן כל י"א יום בחזקת טהרה שדמיה מסולקין: **ולא** שכוונה אלא שפיחתה והותירה. פרש"י כגון שראתה לצ"ג יום ולצ"ב מהו דוקא דכי האי גוונא נמי קבעה לה ווסת כשתראה יום צ"ד תהא דיה שעתה אלא לא דלגה הימים בכוון: **שניה** דיה שעתה. פי' רש"י אע"ג דבהגיע זמנה תנן בשניה מטמאה מעת לעת היינו משום דמצויין בה דמים ואינה צריכה שתתחזק ובחדא זימנא חשבינן לה מוחזקת אבל בזו בעינן חזקה גמורה. ואתיא כרבי דאמר בתרי זמני הויא חזקה ובראייה שמוחזקת בה דייה שעתה מי' לקמן לא משמע הכי דגרסינן תינוקת שהגיע זמנה

תוספי הרא"ש

לראות כו' כמו אמר מר ועלה קאי מני ר' היא ומשמע דבהגיע זמנה בעינן שתתחזק חזקה גמורה. ובראייה שמתחזקת בה מטמאה מעת לעת. הא דאמרינן הכא דשניה דיה שעתה. י"ל דבהגיע זמנה דוקא אמרינן בראייה שמתחזקת בה מטמאה מעת לעת אבל בלא הגיע בעינן שתתחזק תחלה. ולרשב"ג כשהגיע מטמא' בשלישי' וכשלא הגיע ברביעית וקשה דא"כ מתני' דתנן במה אמרו דיה שעתה בראשונה אבל בראייה שניה מטמאה מעת לעת היינו כר'. ובסוף הבא על יבמתו אמרי' ווסתות סתם לן תנא כרשב"ג דתנן אין האשה קובעת לה ווסת עד שתקבענה ג' פעמים והא סתם לן נמי כר' במתני' וי"ל דסתמא בתרייתא עיקר. ומי' קשה דהא דאמר רב כהנא לעיל ג' בתולות הן ופריך ליתני בתולת דמים. ומאי פריך דלמא כרשב"ג ס"ל דכוותיה קי"ל בווסתות כדאמרינן ביבמות. והלכך לא מצי למיתני דכל הני דחשיב בפעם ראשונה לא מיקרי עוד בתולה אבל בתולת דמים מפעם ראשונה עדיין בתולה היא וכן בשניה ואפי' אי ס"ל כר' ניחא דפעם ראשונה עדיין מיקרא בתולה עד שניה. אלא שבראייה שמתחזקת בה מטמאה על כן נראה כדפרש"י. וברוב ספרים ל"ג לקמן הגיע זמנה לראות. אלא ה"ג מני רבי היא ואלא הגיע זמנה קאי: **עברו** עליה ג' עונות דיה שעתה. פרש"י כר' אליעזר כדקתני סיפא אף בהגיע זמנה ובתוספתא לא משמע כדקתני בהך דלא הגיע זמנה דיה שעתה וגבי הגיע זמנה קתני מטמאה מעת לעת ופליג עלה ר' אליעזר אלמא רבנן מודו בלא הגיע זמנה ואע"ג דהוחזקה בראיות כיון דלא הגיע זמנה בהפסקות מדמו לה למעוברת ומניקה אליבא דר' יוסי במתני': **ועוד** עברו עליה ג' עונות. פרש"י בתשובה אע"ג דלר' בתרי זמני הויא חזקה אינה מתחזקת עד הפסקה שלישית דבהפסקה ראשונה חזרה לקדמותה והוי כאילו לא ראתה מעולם וצריכה שתתחזק כבתחלה בשתי ראיות ובשלישית תטמא דהיינו ראייה ראשונה דאחר הפסקה ראשונה ושניה שלאחר הפסקה שניה. ובשלישית תטמא מעת לעת וכיון דחשיב לה כהפסקה ראשונה בחזרה לקדמותה אינה כמנין שתי הפסקות שלאחר כך ונמצא שאין אחר ראיה ראשונה שלה אלא שתי הפסקות ולאותה הפסקה שהיא מתחזקת לקביעות וסת מטמאה מעת לעת. וזה דחקו דלא קתני גם הגיע זמנה ועוד עברו ג' עונות דייה שעתה מכלל דבהגיע ועברו ג' פעמים מטמאה מעת לעת כיון שקובעת ראייה באותה וסת. אע"ג דפירש"י לעיל דבראייה שמתחזקת בה דייה שעתה יש לחלק בחזקה זו משום דאיגלאי מלתא שלא נסתלקה מן הדמים מעולם ומיהו באותן שקודם זו דיין שעתן אע"ג דאיגלאי מלתא כיון שבאותה שעה לא נודע עדיין כמו שמצינו לעיל גבי היתה בחזקת טהרה מעוברת ולפי פירושו הא דתנן לעיל גבי זקנה ועוד עברו עליה שלש עונות דייה שעתה אתיא כרשב"ג דבתולה וזקנה שוות:

הדר קחזיא בעונות מאי? אמר רב גידל, אמר רב: פעם ראשונה ושניה — דיה שעתה, שלישית — מטמאה מעת לעת ומפקידה לפקידה. ועוד, עברו עליה ג' עונות וראתה — דיה שעתה, הדר קחזיא בעונות מאי? אמר רב כהנא, אמר רב גידל אמר רב: פעם ראשונה — דיה שעתה, שניה — מטמאה מעת לעת ומפקידה לפקידה. מני? רבי היא, דאמר: *בתרי זימני הוי חזקה. אימא סיפא: עברו עליה ג' עונות וראתה — דיה שעתה, אתאן לר"א! וכי תימא: רבי היא, ובעונות סבר לה כר"א, ומי סבר לה? והא "לאחר שנזכר" קאמר! אלא: ר"א היא, ובוסתות סבר לה כרבי. כתם שבין ראשונה ושניה — טהור. שבין שניה ושלישית — חזקיה אמר: טמא, רבי יוחנן אמר: [א]טהור. חזקיה אמר: טמא, כיון דאילו חזיא — מטמאה, כתמה נמי — טמא. ורבי יוחנן אמר: טהור, כיון דלא אתחזקה בדם — כתמה נמי לא מטמינן לה.

מתקיף

הדר קא חזיא בעונות. אחר ראיה זו. מאי. דיה שעתה או מטמאה מעת לעת? מי אמרינן: הא דקתני בתרה "ועוד עברו עליה ג' עונות", דוקא קתני "עברו", דאי חזאי לסוף עונה – מטמאה מעת לעת. דאע"ג דלא הגיע זמנה, כיון דהוחזקה רואה קודם הפסקת ג' עונות ראשונות הרי היא כהגיע זמנה, וכי הפסיקה בראשונות וראתה, דיה שעתה בההיא ראיה, כר"א וכי חזיא תו לסוף עונה מטמאה מעת לעת, ככל אשה שעברו עליה ג' עונות, דאין דיה שעתה אלא בראשונה. אבל היכא דחזרו ועברו ג' (א) שניות וראתה, דיה שעתה בההיא ראיה, כר"א. ואע"ג דלא חזינן דקמיירי רבי אליעזר. אלא בהעברה ראשונה, מיהו מודה דדיה שעתה בשניות עד דתתחזק, או כרבי או כרשב"ג. ואע"ג דרישא רבי היא, סיפא כרשב"ג. דאי כרבי כיון דחזאי בעונות הוה מדמינן לה להגיע זמנה, כי חזאי בהפסקה נמי, כיון דתרי זימני חזאי בהפסקה איגלאי מילתא למפרע דשינוי וסת הוא ולא סילוק דמים, ובשניה מטמאה מעת לעת, שאין זו צריכה להתחזק בדמים. או דילמא, אי חזאי לסוף עונה נמי כ"ש דדיה שעתה, דמוכח מילתא דהפסקה ראשונה זו סילוק דמים היתה ולא שינוי וסת, ויש לומר: חזרה לקדמותה, וצריכה להתחזק עוד אחר ההפסקה בשתי ראיות כבתחלה. והאי דנקט "ועוד עברו וראתה דיה שעתה" – רבותא אשמעינן: אע"ג דתרי זימני חזאי בהפסקה, לא אמרינן: איגלאי מילתא דשינוי וסת הוא ולא סילוק דמים, ותטמא בשניה מעת לעת. אלא אפילו לרבי דיה שעתה, דהפסקה קמייתא לעולם בחוזרת לקדמותה נדון אותה, ולא דמיא להגיע זמנה, וצריכה שתתחזק בשתי ראיות, ובג' תטמא מעת לעת, כדקתני ואזיל. *אמר רב גידל פעם ראשונה. היא הראיה הסמוכה להפסקה ראשונה. ושניה. היא הראיה שתראה לסוף עונה – דיה שעתה. ושלישית. אם תראה עוד לסוף עונה. מטמאה מעת לעת. והאי דנקט תנא "ועוד עברו עליה ג' עונות" – רבותא הוא דנקט, כדפי' דכל שכן אי חזאי בעונות, דמוכחא מילתא דהפסקה קמייתא סילוק הואי, וכולה רבי היא. ועוד עברו עליה ג' עונות וראתה דיה שעתה הדר קחזיא בעונות. אחר ראיה זו. מאי. דיה שעתה או מטמאה מעת לעת? מי אמרינן: הא דהדר תנא בתרא ראיה שלישית בהפסקה, דוקא נקט, דהכא הוא דמטמאה מעת לעת, דאיגלאי מילתא דשינוי וסת הואי הפסקותיה לראות בדילוג, שהרי הוחזקה בהפסקות, וא"נ לא חשבת להפסקה קמייתא בהדייהו – הא מחזקא בתרתי בתרייתא. אבל אי חזיא לסוף עונה – הרי היא דיה שעתה, דלא אתחזק בדילוג, ואמרינן: הפסקה שניה נמי חוזרת לקדמותה, וכל דמיה מסולקין, וצריכה להתחזק בשתי ראיות, אחת הסמוכה להפסקה שניה, והשניה היא שתראה לסוף עונה, ובשלישית תטמא מעת לעת. או דילמא, כולי האי לא אמרינן דחזרה לקדמותה, ובהפסקה שניה דיינינן לה כהגיע זמנה, והפסיקה וראתה. דבההיא ראיה לחודה הוא דדיה שעתה, אבל בשניה תטמא מעת לעת. והאי דנקט תנא בשלישית: "ועוד עברו עליה וראתה מטמאה מעת לעת" – הוא הדין נמי אם לא עברו, ורבותא אשמועינן: דלא תימא כל ראיה הסמוכה להפסקה דיה שעתה, אלא כיון דאיתחזק בדילוג, אמרינן: שינוי וסת הוא ולא סילוק דמים. אמר רב גידל אמר רב. ראשונה לסדר ראיות הללו שאנו עסוקין בהן לישאל קא חזיא בעונות, מאי היא הראיה הסמוכה להפסקה שניה דעלה קיימינן דיה שעתה, ושניה היא הראיה שתראה לסוף עונה מטמאה מעת לעת. והא דתנא הפסקה שלישית גבי מעת לעת – לרבותא הוא דנקט, כדפרישית, דלא תימא: כל ראיה שלאחר הפסקה תהא דיה שעתה. מני רבי היא. דהא בין רישא בין סיפא כרבי שנינן לה. אימא סיפא. דהגיע זמנה לראות, אתאן לר"א דאמר: כל אשה שעברו עליה ג' עונות דיה שעתה. ומרישא דאיירי בלא הגיע זמנה לא מצי למיפרך ליה, דאיכא למימר: בההיא אפילו רבנן מודו דחוזרת לקדמותה היא. ובעונות סבר לה כרבי אליעזר. בהפסקת שלש עונות סבר לה כרבי אליעזר. והא לאחר שנזכר קאמר. למדנו שהוקשה בעיניו על שעשה כמותו. ובוסתות סבר לה כרבי. דאמר: בתרי זימני הויא חזקה לכל דבר. כתם שבין ראשונה לשניה. שנמצא בבגדה של תינוקת שלא הגיע זמנה – ודאי טהור, דהכתי לאו בחזקת דמים היא, ואמרינן לעיל (דף ה.) תינוקת שלא הגיע זמנה לראות, אפילו סדינין שלה כו'. חזקיה אמר טמא. דהא בתרי זימני איתחזקה בדמים והויא חזקה, דאילו הדרא חזיא – מטמיא למפרע, אלמא בחזקת דמים הוחזקה. ורבי יוחנן אמר טהור כיון דלא אתחזקה בדם. כלומר, כל זמן שלא נהגנו בה עדיין תורת מוחזקת בדמים לטמאה למפרע, לא גזרו על כתמה.

מתקיף

**קחזיא** בעונות מאי. פרש"י: דמבעיא ליה אי חזיא לסוף ל' שלאחר הפסקת ג' עונות ראשונות, אם מטמאה מעת לעת. דכיון דהוחזקה לרואה קודם הפסקת ג' עונות ראשונות – הרי היא כהגיע זמנה לראות, וככל אשה שעברו עליה ג' עונות דאין דיה שעתה אלא בראשונה. ודוקא בחזרו ועברו עליה שלש עונות שניות דיה שעתה, כר"א. ואע"ג דלא חזינן דמיירי ר"א בעונות שניות אלא בעונות ראשונות, מיהו מודה דדיה שעתה בשניות [עד שתתחזק] או כרבי או כרשב"ג. ואע"ג דרישא רבי היא, סיפא רשב"ג. דלרבי, *כי חזיא לסוף עונות שאחר הפסקת שלש עונות (ראשונות) – מטמאה מעת לעת, ודמיא להגיע זמנה לראות. וכי חזרו ועברו עליה שלש עונות שניות – נמי מטמאה מעת לעת. דכיון דתרתי זימני חזיא בהפסקה, איגלאי מילתא לרבי דשינוי וסת הוא, ולא סילוק דמים, שאין זו צריכה להתחזק בדמים. ולפי' זה הא דתניא (לעיל דף ז:) זקנה שעברו עליה שלש עונות שניות, דדיה שעתה, אתיא דלא כרבי. דלרבי, מטמאה מעת לעת כאילו חזיא לסוף עונה. וכן *פי' רשב"ס בפרק אחרון (דף סח.). ואין נראה, דלא היה להתלמוד להסתפק בזה, והיה לו (ב) לפסוק: מדרישא רבי, סיפא נמי רבי. ובחזיא לסוף עונה – נמי דיה שעתה, כמו בחזרו ועברו עליה שלש עונות. לכך נראה דאפילו מטמאה מעת לעת, כי חזיא לסוף עונה שלאחר הפסקת שלש עונות ראשונות, כהפסקת שלש עונות שניות, דהויא מסולקת בדמים – דיה שעתה, אפילו לרבי, כיון שלא הגיע זמנה לראות. [ואין חילוק בין לא הגיע זמנה לראות לזקנה] והויא ברייתא דזקנה, נמי רבי היא. ול"ע בהגיע זמנה לראות, ועברו עליה שלש עונות שניות לר"א מי אמרינן דיה שעתה כמו בזקנה לרבנן. ומדלא אשמעינן בהגיע זמנה לראות, דהוי דיה שעתה עד הפסקת שלש עונות שלישיות, דהויא רבותא טפי מבלא הגיע זמנה לראות – אין להוכיח דאפילו ראתה סוף שלש עונות שניות מטמאה מעת לעת, דמצינו למימר: דמשום הכי אשמעינן בלא הגיע זמנה לראות, דאפילו הכי מטמאה בשלישית מעת לעת.

**ברוב** ספרים גרסינן: "וכשהגיע זמנה לראות, פעם ראשונה דיה שעתה, שניה מטמאה מעת לעת מני רבי היא" – ושבוש הוא, ולא גרסינן ליה. אלא ה"ג: "מני רבי היא". ומוכח מרישא, מתינוקת שלא הגיע זמנה לראות, דקתני: שלישית הרי היא ככל הנשים, והיינו משום דבתרי זימני הוי חזקה, ובההיא דמיתחזקא לא מטמאה מעת לעת. דאילו לרשב"ג, עד ראיה רביעית לא הויא ככל הנשים. אבל סיפא דהגיע זמנה לראות, דשניה מטמאה מעת לעת – אתי ככולי עלמא, דבראייתה ראשונה הוחזקה, כדתנן: במה אמרו דיה שעתה בראיה ראשונה כו'. ומתניתין ע"כ אתיא כרשב"ג, דבפרק "הבא על יבמתו" (יבמות דף סד:) אמרינן: וסתות ושור המועד – סתם לן תנא כרשב"ג, אבל כרבי לא סתם לן תנא. ועוד: אי מסיפא דייק, ורישא כרשב"ג, תקשי: רישא רשב"ג, וסיפא – רבי? וא"ת: דהכא אמר דבההיא ראיה דמחזקינן לה לא מטמאה מעת לעת, ובפרק "אלו הנשרפין" (סנהדרין דף פא:) גבי "מי שלקה ושנה" אמר *דאין עבירות מחזקות, אחר שעבר שתי עבירות – מיד כונסין אותו לכיפה, אליבא דרבי? וי"ל: דהתם, כיון שהוחזק לעבירה, מה לנו להמתין עד שיעבור פעם שלישית. אבל הכא, חכמים תקנו מעת לעת אם תראה אחר שהוחזקה לראות. **רבי** יוחנן אמר טהור. משמע: הא כתם שאחר שלישי – טמא, דהיינו כרבי. ובשלהי פרק "הבא על יבמתו" (יבמות דף סד:) אמר ר' יצחק בר' יוסי אמר רבי יוחנן גבי "מלה בנה ראשון" כו' כרבן שמעון בן גמליאל? וי"ל: דהתם מסיק דר' יצחק סומקא לאו בר סמכא הוא. אי נמי: כל הך סוגיא קיימא אברייתא דלעיל, דאתא כרבי.

וכי

עין משפט נר מצוה: פו א מיי' פ"ט מהלכות איסורי ביאה הל' ה סמג לאוין קיא:

נ"ל כיון דאי חזיא לסוף כו' ר"מ

נ"ל שניות

נ"י כ"י פי' רשב"ס לעיל בפירושו אחרון

נ"י כ"י

[לעיל דף ז:]

מסורת הש"ס: לקמן סז. כתובות מג: יבמות כו: סד: [עירובין לז. סנהדרין פא: ב"מ קו:]

ע' רש"א שפי' פי' אחר דלא כפי' רש"י

### הגהות הב"ח

(א) רש"י ד"ה מאי דיה וכו' אבל היכא דחזרו ועברו ג' עונות שניות: (ב) תום' ד"ה קחזיא וכו' והיה לו לפשוט מדרישא:

### תוספי הרא"ש

**קא** חזיא בעונות מאי. [פירש"י] מי אמרינן דדוקא נקט שלשה עונות אבל ראתה אחר עונה מטמאה מעת לעת דאע"ג דלא הגיע זמנה כיון שראתה שלשה פעמים חשבינן לה כהגיע זמנה הלכך אם ראתה אחר ג' עונות דייה שעתה כר' אלעזר אבל אם ראתה אחר עונה מטמאה מעת לעת אע"ג דלר' אלעזר לא אמר אלא בהעברה ראשונה ה"ה נמי דדייה שעתה אף בשניה עד שתתחזק או כר' או כרשב"ג ואע"ג דרישא ר' היא [סיפא] כרשב"ג דאי כר' כיון דאילו חזאי בעונה הוה מדמה לה להגיע זמנה כי חזאי בהפסקה נמי כיון דתרי זמני חזאי בהפסקה איגלאי מילתא לר' דשנוי וסת הוי ולא סילוק ובשניה מטמאה מעת לעת שאין זו צריכה להתחזק בדמיה או דלמא הדרה לקדמותה וצריכה להתחזק אחר הפסקה בשתי ראיות כבתחלה והאי דנקט ג' עונות לרבותא נקט דאע"ג דראתה ב' פעמים לג' עונות לא הויא חזקה לר' וזהו דוחק גדול מאי מספקא ליה לתלמודא אמאי תיסוק אדעתין למימר רישא ר' וסיפא רשב"ג הלכך נראה לפרש דאתיא רישא וסיפא כר' ובכל מקום שצריכה חזקה באותה ראיה שהיא מתחזקת בה דייה שעתה בראייה דהפסקות כמו בראיות ראשונות ואינה מטמאה מעת לעת עד שתתחזק והפסקה ראשונה בכלל ההפסקות היא. וה"ה דהוה מצי למיתני בהגיע זמנה ועוד עברו: **כתם** שבין שניה לשלישית. תי' דפליגי אליבא דר' דלית הלכתא כוותיה דהוה להו לפלוגי אליבא דרשב"ג בין שלישית לרביעית ושמא משום דשמעתין כר' נקט בין שניה לשלישית ונפקא מינה לרשב"ג בין שלישית לרביעית:

מתקיף לה ר' אלעאי: וכי מה בין זו לבתולה שדמיה טהורין? א"ל ר' זירא: זו — *שירפה מצוי, וזו — אין שירפה מצוי. אמר עולא, א"ר יוחנן משום ר"ש בן יהוצדק: [א]תינוקת שלא הגיע זמנה לראות וראתה, פעם ראשונה ושניה — רוקה ומדרסה בשוק טהור, כתמה נמי טהור, ולא ידענא אם דידיה אם דרביה. למאי נפקא מינה? למיהוי דבריו של אחד במקום שנים. כי אתא רבין וכל נחותי ימא אמרוה כר"ש בן יהוצדק. אמר רב חלקיה בר טובי: תינוקת שלא הגיע זמנה לראות, אפילו שופעת כל ז' — אינה אלא ראיה אחת. אפילו שופעת — ולא מבעיא פוסקת? אדרבה, פוסקת הויא לה כשתי ראיות! [ב]אלא: תינוקת שלא הגיע זמנה לראות, ושופעת כל ז' — אינה אלא ראיה אחת. אמר רב שימי בר חייא: מדלפת אינה כרואה. והא קחזיא! אימא: אינה כשופעת אלא כפוסקת. מכלל דשופעת (נמי) — כי נהרא? אלא אימא: [ג]אינה אלא כשופעת. תנו רבנן: [ד]חזקה, בנות ישראל עד שלא הגיעו לפרקן — הרי הן בחזקת טהרה, ואין הנשים בודקות אותן. משהגיעו לפרקן — הרי הן בחזקת טומאה, ונשים בודקות אותן. רבי יהודה אומר: אין בודקין אותן ביד — מפני שמעוותות אותן, אלא סכות אותן בשמן מבפנים ומקנחות אותן מבחוץ, והן נבדקות מאיליהן. § "רבי יוסי אומר מעוברת" וכו'. § תני תנא קמיה דר' אלעזר: רבי יוסי אומר מעוברת ומניקה שעברו עליה ג' עונות — דיה שעתה, א"ל: פתחת בתרי וסיימת בחדא! דלמא מעוברת והיא מניקה קאמרת, ומילתא אגב אורחיה קמ"ל — דימי עיבורה עולין לה לימי מניקותה וימי מניקותה עולין לה לימי עיבורה. כדתניא: *ימי עיבורה עולין לה לימי מניקותה, וימי מניקותה עולין לה לימי עיבורה; כיצד, הפסיקה שתים בימי עיבורה ואחת בימי מניקותה, שתים בימי מניקותה ואחת בימי עיבורה, אחת ומחצה בימי עיבורה ואחת ומחצה בימי מניקותה — מצטרפות לג' עונות. בשלמא ימי עיבורה עולין לה לימי מניקותה משכחת לה — דקמניקה ואזלא ומיעברה, אלא ימי מניקותה עולין לה לימי עיבורה היכי משכחת לה? איבעית אימא: בלידה יבשתא, ואיבעית אימא: דם נדה לחוד ודם לידה לחוד, ואיבעית אימא: תני חדא. § "במה אמרו דיה שעתה" וכו'. § אמר רב: [ה]אכולהו, ושמואל אמר: ל"ש אלא בתולה וזקנה, אבל מעוברת ומניקה — דיין כל ימי עיבורן, דיין כל ימי מניקותן. וכן אמר ר' שמעון בן לקיש: אכולהו, ורבי יוחנן אמר: לא שנו אלא בתולה וזקנה, אבל מעוברת ומניקה — דיין כל ימי עיבורן, דיין כל ימי מניקותן. כתנאי, מעוברת ומניקה שהיו

שופעות

## רש"י

מתקיף לה רבי אלעאי. לחזקיה: מה בין זו לבתולה שדמיה טהורין? בתולה שנשאת יש שדמיה טהורין עד שתחיה המכה דתלינן בבתולים, ויש שדמיה טהורין ד' לילות, ויש שדמיה טהורין כל לילה הראשונה, כדאמרינן פרק בתרא (לקמן דף סד.). (א) וכולהו קי"ל דכל זמן שדמיה טהורין — אין לה כתם, דקתני בפ' "האשה" (לקמן דף ס.): ושוין שתולה בשומרת יום כנגד יום בראשון שלה ובבתולה שדמיה טהורים. (ב) מהתם שמעינן דאין לה כתם, ואע"ג דראתה פעם אחת. דלא מפלגינן בין הגיע זמנה ללא הגיע, בין שראתה פעם אחת בבית אביה, שהיא אחת מן הבתולות שדמיה טהורין. והא הכא, דאילו חזת בשינוי מראה דמיה מטמאה מעת לעת, דהגיע זמנה לראות וראתה בבית אביה, אפילו הכי לא מטמאינן כתמה, ומ"ש הך מהא. זו שירפה מצוי. בתולה שדמיה טהורין שרף שלה מצוי מחמת בתולים, הילכך כתמה טהור, דתלינן בדם בתולין. וזו אין שירפה מצוי. לטהרה, ולתלות בו. רוקה ומדרסה בשוק טהור. כגון שנמצא רוקה בשוק, וקים לן שקודם לכן ראתה ב' פעמים, ואין אנו יודעים אם נדה היא אם לאו — מספיקא לא מחזקינן לה כספק הרוקין, הואיל ולא הוחזקה רואה. ולא ידענא כו'. עולא הוא דקאמר: לא ידענא אי א"ר יוחנן מסקנא דהא מילתא דקאמר: "כתמה נמי טהור" מדעתיה, או משמיה דר"ש בן יהוצדק כרוקה ומדרסה. דבריו של אחד במקום שנים. אי אמר להא "וכתמה נמי טהור" משמיה דרביה, הוי חזקיה דאמר לעיל טמא — אחד במקום שנים, דהא פליג עליה ר' יוחנן לעיל מלביה, וחזינן דקאי ר"ש כוותיה. ה"ג: אמרוה כר"ש בן יהוצדק. כשמו של ר"ש בן יהוצדק, וה"ל חזקיה אחד במקום ב', וש"מ הלכה כר' יוחנן. אינה אלא ראיה אחת. לאחזוקה כרואה, ודיה שעתה עד שתפסוק ותחזור ותראה שתי ראיות. ולא מבעיא פוסקת. וחוזרת ורואה. ושופעת כל שבעה. סמי מכאן "אפילו". מדלפת. טיף אחר טיף. אינה כרואה. דמשמע, דאפילו כראיה אחת אינה חשובה. אלא כפוסקת. והוו להו ראיות טובא, והוחזקה רואה, ולכשתפסוק ותחזור ותראה — מטמאה מעת לעת. ופרכינן: מכלל דשופעת דאמר לעיל, אינה אלא ראיה אחת, היינו דשופעת כי נהרא? בתמיה. כיון דמדלפת אינה חשובה שופעת, וא"א להיות שופעת כמעין כל שבעה, וקיה. בחזקת טומאה. כלומר, בחזקת דמים מלוכלכים הם. שמעוותות אותן. כלומר, מסקרין לה בגלוון, ומייתו לה לידי ראיה. מבפנים. שסיכת שמן מגיה הדם אם זמנו הוא. פתחת בתרתי. מעוברת ומניקה. וסיימת בחדא. דקאמר "דיה שעתה", "דיין שעתן" מיבעי ליה! מעוברת והיא מניקה. שנולד עוברה ומניקתו. א"נ: מניקה ונתעברה. והוא הדין למעוברת גרידתא, והא דנקט "מעוברת והיא מניקה" לומר לך שמצטרפין ימי מניקה לימי עיבורה לג' עונות, כגון שהפסיקה שתים בימי עיבורה ואחת בימי מניקתה, או חלוף. דהכי משמע "מעוברת והיא מניקה" בתוך הפסקת העונות הללו. ימי עיבורה עולין לה לימי מניקתה. כגון אם היתה מניקה ונתעברה, והפסיקה תחלת עונה קצת בימי מניקתה, והשלימה בימי עיבורה. אלא ימי מניקתה עולין לה לימי עיבורה היכי משכחת לה. דילדה ולא חזאי, הא ראתה דם בלידתה, ונמצא שלא עברו עליה ג' עונות! תני חדא. "ימי עיבורה עולין לה לימי מניקתה", ולא תיתני "ימי מניקתה עולים לה לימי עיבורה". אכולהו. ד' נשים כולהו קתני לה, דבשניה מטמאה מעל"ע. בתולה וזקנה. בתולה כיון דראתה פעם ראשונה ושניה — הוחזקה רואה, זקנה נמי כיון דאיתחזקא תרי זימני אחר ג' עונות — איתפתח דלאו סילוק דמים הוא אלא דילוג וסת. אבל מעוברת ומניקה. ודאי דמיה מסולקין, ואפילו לא נסתלקו מתחלתן, מסתלקין והולכין הן תדיר. ברוך.

שופעות.

## תוספות

וכי מה בין זו לבתולה שדמיה טהורין. דאם נשתנו מראה דמיה למחרת מראיית שעת תשמיש — טמאה, ואילו מצאה כתם לאחר תשמיש — טהורה, כדאי' בפ' "האשה" (לקמן דף ס.) תולה בבתולה שדמיה טהורין, ומדלא מפליג משמע: אפילו הדם משונה — טהור? ומשני: הכא, אין שירפה של טהרה מצוי, דאם הכתם בא מגופה — טמאה ודאי. אבל התם, שירפה של טהרה מצוי. לכך טהורה, דאיכא למימר: האי כתם מעלמא בא, ואפילו אי אתא מגופה — איכא למימר: דם בתולים הוא, (ואיכא למימר) ולא חיתה עדיין המכה.

אמר רבי יוחנן משום רבי שמעון בן יהוצדק. משמע שהיה רבו, ובפרק "זה בורר" (סנהדרין דף כו.) קרי ליה ר"ל לר"ש בן יהוצדק "רועי בקר", ולא היה מוחה ר' יוחנן על כבוד רבו! ואומר ר"ת: דתרי הוו*.

רוקה בשוק טהור. פי' בשוק, שאין ידוע אם ראתה אם לאו — אין להחזיקה כרואה, כיון שלא הגיע זמנה לראות ולא ראתה שלשה פעמים. ומיירי אפילו בבת ע"ה. אבל בבית, ידוע אם ראתה אם לאו.

למהוי דבריו של אחד במקום שנים. וא"ת: ודילמא ר"ש בן יהוצדק סבר לה כרשב"ג דבג' זימני הוי חזקה, וחזקיה נמי מודה דלרשב"ג כתמה טהור? וי"ל: דרוקה ומדרסה קיל טפי מבכתמה מדמספקא ליה בכתם אי טמא אם לאו. וכיון דקיל טפי, אי ס"ל כרשב"ג, ה"ל לטהר רוקה ומדרסה עד פעם רביעית.

הרי הן בחזקת טהרה. וא"ת: במתני' דקתני "צריכה להיות בודקת חוץ מן הנדה" כו' אמאי לא מפקא מי שלא הגיע זמנה, וההוא ד"בנות כותים" (לקמן דף לב:) דכל י"א בחזקת טהרה, ומפרש בגמרא לענין שאינה צריכה בדיקה? וי"ל: דלא מפרש במתני' אלא הנהו דאינן צריכים בדיקה מחמת דאין קפידא בראייתם, דנדה — בלאו הכי טמאה, ויושבת על דם טוהר — אפילו אם תראה לעולם טהור. אבל לא הגיע זמנה לראות *וי"א, דאינה צריכה בדיקה מחמת דמסולקין בדמים, לא קתני.

פתחת בתרי וסיימת בחדא. וא"ת: והא במתני' נמי "ד' נשים" קתני "במה אמרו דיה שעתה"? וי"ל: דהתם ליכא למיטעי, אבל הכא איכא למיטעי ולומר: מעוברת והיא מניקה.

דהויא מניקה ואיעברה. וא"ת: והיכי איעברה בלא ראיה, והא אמרינן בשלהי "המפלת" (לקמן לח:) דאין אשה מתעברת אלא סמוך לטבילתה או לוסתה? וי"ל: דרוב פעמים כך הוא, וזימנין דמיתרמי ומיעברה. א"נ: בימים שהיא רגילה לראות אין מתעברת אלא סמוך לטבילתה או סמוך לוסתה.

דיין כל ימי עיבורן. משמע: אפילו רואה כמה פעמים. ואף על פי דבלא הגיע זמנה לראות אמר לעיל: שלישית מטמאה מעת לעת — היינו משום דכיון שהוחזקה לראות, בטל הסילוק. אבל הכא, מעוברת ומניקה המסתלקין עדיין קיימים. ואפילו לא נסתלקו בתחלה, מסתלקין והולכין בסוף. וא"ת: מ"ש דלא הגיע זמנה לראות לא בעיא בדיקה, ומעוברת ומניקה בעיא בדיקה, כדקתני במתניתין "צריכה להיות בודקת" אכולהו? וי"ל: דכל זמן שלא הוחזקה, היא מסולקת בדמים יותר מכולן. אלא

[נ"ל וי"א יום]

## תוספי הרא"ש

לבתולה שדמיה טהורין. ותנן לקמן נשתנו מראה דמים שלה טמאה ובכתמה טהור ואפילו מצא הכתם בשינוי מראה דהא אמרינן לקמן בפרק האשה תולה בבתולה שדמיה טהורין ותנן לקמן נשתנו מראה דמים שלה ומשמע בכל ענין אפילו מראה הכתם משונה והיינו טעמא דהא דנשתנו מראה דמים שלה טמאה לאו טומאה ודאי אלא מספק שמא דם נדה הוא ובכתם דאיכא לספוקי נמי אימר מעלמא אתי עברה בשוק של טבחים ולאו אדעתה מקילינן כיון דא"נ מגופה הוי שמא טהור הוא: רוקה ומדרסה בשוק טהור. רוקה ניחא דבאשה אחרת היא רוקה טמא דאע"ג דספק טומאה ברשות הרבים טהור גזרו על ספק רוקין הנמצאין דאפילו שוטה אחת בעיר או נכרית תנן בפ"ה דמס' טהרות דכל הרוקין שבעיר טמאין אבל מדרסה קשה דאפילו אשה אחרת נמי טהור מדרסה ברשות הרבים. וי"ל משום דבאשה אחרת תנן בפ"ה במס' טהרות מי שדרסה אשה על בגדיו או שישבה עמו בספינה אם מכירתו שאוכלת בתרומה כלים טהורים ואם לאו ישאלנה ובדך דשלא הגיע זמנה ואינה מכירתו אינו צריך לישאל. ועוד נראה דאפילו בבנות עם הארץ איירי ואע"פ שגזרו על ציגורא דעם הארץ שהוא רגיל בטומאה הכא לא גזור הואיל ואינה רגילה לראות והא דנקט בשוק לאו דוקא דאפילו בבית נמי טהור אלא אורחא דמלתא נקט דבבית אם היא טהורה אם לאו: למיהוי דבריו של אחד במקום שנים. וא"ת דלמא רבי שמעון בן יהוצדק כרשב"ג ס"ל אבל אליבא דר' הוי טמא בחזקה וי"ל דאם איתא דס"ל בחזקה הוה ליה למימר בין שניה לשלישית טמא אלא ודאי כר' ס"ל והיכי כתמה שבין שניה לשלישית טהור: ואין הנשים בודקות אותן. והא דלא תני ליה במתני' גבי נדה ויושבת על דם טוהר לפי שזאת פשוטה היא. ומי' קשה דלא קתני במתני' י"א שבין נדה לנדה. דאיכא למ"ד בפ' בנות כותים דאין צריכה בדיקה. וי"ל דלא קתני מתני' אלא הנך דאין נפקותן בראייתן. נדה בלאו הכי טמאה. ויושבת על דם טוהר אפילו תראה טהורה: פתחת בתרתי וסיימת בחדא. מתני' לא קשיא ליה דקתני ד' נשים וקאמר עלה במה אמרו דייה שעתה ומסיק בגמרא דקאי אכולהו או אתרי. משום דבבא אחריתי היא. וברישא קתני דיין שעתן. א"נ משום דהכא איכא למימר דאיירי בחדא איתתא משום

## עין משפט נר מצוה

פז א מיי' פ"ט מהלכות איסורי ביאה הל' ה ועי' כמ"מ טוש"ע י"ד סימן קצ סעיף ג ד:

פח ב ג מיי' פ"ד מהל' משכב ומושב הל' ב' סמג לאוין קיא טוש"ע י"ד סימן קצ סעיף ג:

פט ד מיי' שם הל' ח:

צ ה מיי' פ"ד מהלכות משכב ומושב הל' ה:

[ועי' תוס' סוכה יח: ד"ה דברי ותוס' נט. ד"ה דאמר ובגמ' יומא מג: אפילו לרביה לא נייח לא"ר יוחנן משום ר"ש בן יהוצדק ובגמ' ר"ה לד: הא דרביה]

## מסורת הש"ס

[פי' כבר התחילה לראות דם טמא והוחזקו מן הטעמא והבתולה אין שירפה מצוי. ערוך ערך שרף ג']

רש"ל מ"ז

לקמן לו.

## הגהות הב"ח

(א) רש"י ד"ה מתקיף וכו' וכולהו קי"ל: (ב) בא"ד שדמיה טהורים שמעינן כצ"ל ותיבת מהתם נמחק:

## גליון הש"ס

תוס' ד"ה דהוא וכו' וי"ל דרוב פעמים. עי' סוטה כז ע"א תד"ה אליבא:

שופעות דם ובאות – דיין כל ימי עיבורן, ודיין כל ימי מניקותן, דברי ר"מ רבי יוסי ור' יהודה ורבי שמעון אומרים: לא אמרו דיין שעתן אלא בראייה ראשונה, אבל בשניה – מטמאה מעת לעת ומפקידה לפקידה.§ "ואם ראתה ראשונה" וכו'.§ א"ר הונא: קפצה וראתה, קפצה וראתה, קפצה וראתה – קבעה לה וסת. למאי? אילימא לימים – הא כל יומא דלא קפיץ לא חזאי! אלא לקפיצות, והתניא: [א]כל שתקבענה מחמת אונס – אפילו כמה פעמים לא קבעה וסת! מאי לאו – לא קבעה וסת כלל! לא, לא קבעה וסת לימים לחודייהו ולקפיצות לחודייהו, [ב]אבל קבעה לה וסת לימים ולקפיצות. לימים לחודייהו פשיטא! אמר רב אשי: כגון דקפיץ בחד בשבת וחזאי, וקפיץ בחד בשבת וחזאי, [ובשבת קפצה ולא חזאי,] ולחד בשבת חזאי בלא קפיצה. מהו דתימא: איגלאי מילתא למפרע דיומא הוא דקגרים ולא קפיצה, קמ"ל דקפיצה נמי דאתמול גרמא, והאי דלא חזאי – משום דאכתי לא מטא זמן קפיצה. לישנא אחרינא, א"ר הונא: [ג]קפצה וראתה, קפצה וראתה, קפצה וראתה – קבעה לה וסת לימים ולא לקפיצות. היכי דמי? [ד]א"ר אשי: דקפיץ בחד בשבת וחזאי, וקפיץ בחד בשבת וחזאי, [א](ובשבת קפצה ולא חזאי,) ולחד בשבת (אחרינא) חזאי בלא קפיצה, דהתם איגלאי מילתא דיומא הוא דקא גרים.§ **מתני'** אע"פ שאמרו דיה שעתה – [ה]צריכה להיות בודקת, חוץ מן הנדה והיושבת על דם טוהר. [ו]ומשמשת בעדים – חוץ מיושבת על דם טוהר, ובתולה שדמיה טהורים. [ז]ופעמים צריכה להיות בודקת – שחרית ובין השמשות, [ח]ובשעה שהיא עוברת לשמש את ביתה. יתירות עליהן כהנות [ט]בשעה שהן אוכלות בתרומה. *רבי יהודה אומר: אף בשעת עברתן מלאכול בתרומה.§ **גמ'** "חוץ מן הנדה". דבתוך ימי נדתה לא בעי בדיקה. *הניחא לרבי שמעון בן לקיש דאמר אשה קובעת לה וסת בתוך ימי זיבתה, ואין אשה קובעת לה וסת בתוך ימי נדתה – שפיר; אלא לרבי יוחנן דאמר [י]אשה קובעת לה וסת בתוך ימי נדתה – תבדוק, דילמא קבעה לה וסת! אמר לך רבי יוחנן: [כ]כי אמינא אנא – היכא דחזיתיה ממעין סתום, אבל חזיתיה ממעין פתוח – לא אמרי.§ "והיושבת על דם טוהר".§ קס"ד: מבקשת לישב על דם טוהר. הניחא לרב דאמר *[ל]מעין אחד הוא, התורה טמאתו והתורה טהרתו – שפיר, אלא ללוי דאמר שני מעינות הם – תבדוק, דילמא אכתי לא פסק ההוא מעין טמא! אמר לך לוי: הא מני

בית

---

**רש"י**

שופעות. לאו דוקא. קפצה. הוי אונס. קפצה וראתה. ג' פעמים קבעה לה וסת, כדמפרש ואזיל. אילימא לימים. כגון קפצה באחד בשבת וראתה, וקפצה באחד בשבת וראתה, וכן שלישית – קבעה לה וסת באחד בשבת. וכל זמן שתראה עוד באחד בשבת, ואפילו בלא קפיצה – דיה שעתה. ואם הגיע אחד בשבת, ולא בדקה עצמה – טמאה מספק, דאורח בזמנו הוא בא, כל יומא באחד בשבת. דלא קפיץ לא חזאי. אלמא לאו וסתה הוא. אלא לקפיצות. כיון דראתה שלש פעמים על ידי קפיצה, הורגלה לראיית קפיצה, ובכל יום שתקפוץ מחזיקינן לה ברואה. ואם לא בדקה – טמאה, ואפילו שאר ימות שבת. לימים ולקפיצות. כל אחד בשבת שתקפוץ – מחזיקינן לה ברואה, דזמנה הוא לראות באחד בשבת על ידי קפיצה. לימים לחודייהו פשיטא. דלא קבעה. דיומא הוא דקא גרים. ויהא באחד בשבת וסתה, אפילו בלא קפיצה. קמ"ל. הא דאמר דלא קבעה וסת לימים, דקפיצה דאתמול גרמה לראייה דהאידנא. ואין לה וסת באחד בשבת בלא קפיצה, ולא לקפיצה בלא אחד בשבת, מדלא חזיא מאתמול. מתני' אע"פ שאמרו דיה שעתה. באשה שיש לה וסת. צריכה להיות בודקת. בכל יום שחרית וערבית, כשאר נשים. חוץ מן הנדה. משראתה יום אחד – טמאה שבעה, ואינה צריכה בדיקה כל שבעה, שהרי בלא ראייה היא טמאה. והיושבת על דם טוהר. דלמה לה בדיקה, אפילו תראה דם – טהורה היא! ומשמשת בעדים. אע"פ שיש לה וסת צריכה לשמש בעדים ולבדוק לפני תשמיש ולאחר תשמיש. ובתולה שדמיה טהורין. ד' לילות. דהיא אינה צריכה לשמש בעדים, שהרי דמה טהור, ואפילו נשתנו מראה דמיה, הואיל ושמשה אמרינן: דמשום תשמיש נשתנה. אבל שחרית וערבית, היכא דלא שמשה (א) אחר בעילה ראשונה, צריכה בדיקה, כדמפרש בגמרא: שמא נשתנו מראה דמים שלה. ופעמים צריכה להיות בודקת. כל אשה. שחרית ובין השמשות. שחרית – להכשיר טהרות של לילה, ערבית – להכשיר טהרות של יום, כדאמרינן טעמא בריש פירקין. לשמש את ביתה. עם בעלה. גמ' מתוך ימי זיבתה. כגון ראתה בראש חודש, וחזרה וראתה בט"ו לחודש, כשעומדת בימים שהיא ראויה לזיבה דהיינו י"א יום שבין נדה לנדה. וחזרה וראתה בראש חודש, ובט"ו לחודש. וחזרה וראתה בט"ו לחודש, ולא ראתה בראש חודש שלפניו – שקבעה לה וסת לט"ו בחודש, ומצטרפין תרתי ראיות דימי זיבה להך ראייה לקביעות וסת. ואין אשה קובעת לה וסת בימי נדתה. כגון ראתה בראש חודש, וחזרה וראתה בחמישי בחודש דהיינו בימי נדות, וחזרה וראתה עוד פעמים בחמישי בחודש – לא קבעה וסת. שאין ראיית ימי נדה ראייה לקבוע, שהיא עלולה לראות בימי נדותה. שפיר. קתני במתניתין דלא בעיא בדיקה, דאי לטמויי – טמאה היא, ואי לקבוע וסת ולידע אם תשנה וסת שלשה פעמים ליום אחר שאינה למודה עד עכשיו – הא אמרת דלא קבעה. ממעין סתום. כדמפרש אליבא דר' יוחנן בשילהי פ' "בנות כותים" (לקמן דף לט.) כגון דחזאי ריש ירחא, וריש ירחא, ועשרים וחמשה, וריש ירחא – דהוה ראייה בתרייתא בימי נדותה, דאפילו הכי הוה קביעות וסת בריש ירחא. כדמפרש התם, דאמר: וסתה בריש ירחא קבעה, והא דאקדים וחזאי – דמים יתירי איתוספו בה. דהא ודאי קבעה, משום דתחילת הוסת הוחזק ממעין סתום וגם ראייה אחרונה חשבינן לה כמעין סתום, כדאמר: הא דאקדים וחזאי – תוספת דמים הוא. אבל ממעין פתוח, כגון שהראיות הראשונות של וסת (ב) יהו בתוך ימי נדה כי מתניתין *) (דלא מיירי בתחלת נדה, דהא לא מפליג בה מידי, אלא סתמא קתני "חוץ מן הנדה") הילכך לא בעיא בדיקה בימי נדות, שהרי נפתח מעינה, ואפילו היא רואה – לא תקבע וסת. לישנא אחרינא: ממעין סתום – שראתה היום, ופסקה, וחזרה וראתה ברביעי או בחמישי לנדתה. אבל ממעין פתוח – כגון שלא פסקה, וראתה א' ב' ג' ד' לחודש, וראתה פעם שניה בד' בחודש, וכן שלישית – לא מהניא ראייה דרביעי בחודש דנדות קמא למיקבע, ומתניתין במעיין פתוח. (ג) וראשון ישר בעיני. מבקשת לישב. כשכלין ימי לידה, כגון בשביעי לזכר או יום י"ד לנקבה – לא בעיא בדיקה, דהא אפילו אינה רואה היא טמאה. הניחא לרב דאמר. בפרק "בנות כותים" (לקמן דף לה.). מעין אחד הוא. דם הבא בתוך ז' של לידה ודם הבא לאחר שבעה – ממעין אחד הוא. התורה טמאתו. תוך שבעה לזכר וי"ד לנקבה. והתורה טהרתו. כל ימי הטוהר. שפיר. קתני מתניתין דלא בעיא בדיקה, דהא בין פסקה ובין לא פסקה, טמאה היום וטהורה למחר. אלא ללוי. דאמר: שני מעיינות הן, נפתח הטמא כל ימי הלידה ונסתם הטהור, ולסוף שבעה לזכר וי"ד לנקבה – נסתם הטמא ונפתח הטהור. ואוקימנא התם דשופעת מתוך שבעה לאחר שבעה, ס"ל ללוי דאפילו בשמיני לעולם היא טמאה, עד שתפסוק, דהא לא נסתם הטמא – תבדוק בשביעי דילמא וכו'.

*) רש"ל מ"ז ועיין רש"א [בשם מורינו ורבינו הרב הגאון המפורסם מוהר"ר שאול נר"ו אב"ד דק"ק אמשטרדם וז"ל הגאון נר"ו. ע' במהרש"א שהאריך לקיים הנוסחא הישנה בפירוש דחוק ואולי דברי הגאונים יש לקיים הנוסחא הישנה בפשיטות דודאי פירוש תחלת נדה דקאמר רש"י היינו תחלת וסת והוצרך לפרש דלא תקשי היכי קתני נדה אינה צריכה בדיקה הא זמנין דצריכה לבדוק כגון בתחלת וסת שהיא רוצה לקבוע וסת ותחזי ריש ירחא וה' בירחא וריש ירחא דצריכה בדיקה בה' בה' בירחא שמא תראה פעם ג' בה' בירחא לחוד וכמ"ש התוס'. לכך פי' רש"י דודאי תנא דמתני' לא מיירי בתחלת וסת דהא סתמא קתני חוץ מן הנדה וקאי אדלעיל דקתני אע"פ שאמרו דיה שעתה והיינו אשה שיש לה וסת כדפירש"י ואהא קתני צריכה להיות בודקת חוץ מן הנדה וכיון דלא מפליג תנא מידי מסתמא הך דחוץ מן הנדה קאי אהך דדיה שעתה דלעיל דמיירי שיש לה וסת קבוע א"כ ודאי מיירי תנא דמתני' במעין פתוח מש"ה אינה צריכה בדיקה דלא אהני לה מידי ובהכי אתו דברי רש"י כפשוטן בלי שום גמגום וק"ל ע"כ דברי הרב הגאון נר"ו ודברים ברורים הם למבין]:

---

**תוספות**

**אלא** לקפיצות והתניא כו'. פרש"י: לקפילות לחודייהו. וקשה: דאם כן, לישני בסמוך: לא קבעה וסת לימים אלא לקפילות לחודייהו, ולמה חוזר מסברתו? ובסמוך נמי, דפריך: לימים פשיטא? לישני: דלא קבעה וסת לקפילות לחודיה, כדקס"ד מעיקרא? ונראה לפרש: "אלא לקפילות" – אף לקפילות, דהיינו לימים עם קפילות, אבל קפילות לחודייהו – פשיטא להתלמוד דלא קבעה.

**קפצה** וראתה. (ד) ג' זימני גרסי' כדאמרינן [ב"הבא על יבמתו"] (יבמות דף סד.) דבוסתות סתם לן תנא כרשב"ג, לקמן פרק "האשה" (דף סג.) דתנן: אין האשה קובעת וסת, עד שתקבענו ג' פעמים.

**ממעין** סתום. פירש רש"י: כגון דחזאי ריש ירחא, וריש ירחא, וכ"ה בירחא, וריש ירחא. ומעין פתוח – כגון שהראיות הראשונות של וסת היו בתוך ימי נדה, (או כ"ה בירחא, וריש ירחא) או ריש ירחא, וה' בירחא, וכן בשניה ובשלישית חזאי חמש בירחא, ולא חזאי ריש ירחא. וא"ת: ולרב פפא דמפרש (ה) שילהי "בנות כותים" (לקמן דף לט:) ריש ירחא וחמש בירחא – תרי זימני, ובשלישי – חמש בירחא ולא חזאי ריש ירחא, דקבעה לה וסת בה' בירחא ברביעית, קשה אליביה מתניתין לרבי יוחנן! וי"ל: דאיהו יפרש "מעין פתוח" – דחזאי שלשה זימני ריש ירחא וחמש בירחא. ולמאי (ו) דפריש לקמן דר"פ איירי דחזאי ג' זימנין ריש ירחא וחמש בירחא, דהאי נמי מקרי "מעין סתום", יפרש מתני' "מעין פתוח" כפירוש אחר דרש"י, דפירש: שראתה א' ב' ג' ד' רצופים בג' חדשים ראשונים.

אלא

---

**עין משפט נר מצוה**

**צא** א מיי' פ"ח מהל' איסורי ביאה הלכה ה סמג לאוין קיח טוש"ע י"ד סימן קפט סעיף יז:

**צב** ב מיי' שם ועי"ש בהשגות ובמ"מ טוש"ע שם סעיף יח:

**צג** ג ד מיי' שם ועי"ש במ"מ טוש"ע שם סעיף יז:

**צד** ה מיי' פ"ד מהל' מטמאי משכב ומושב הל' ו סמג לאוין קיא:

**צה** ו מיי' שם הלכה ז ופ"ד מהל' איסורי ביאה הל' טז ועי"ש סמג שם טוש"ע י"ד סי' קפד סעיף א וסימן קפו סעיף א:

**צו** ז מיי' פ"ד מהלכות משכב ומושב הל' ז טוש"ע י"ד סימן קצו סעיף ד:

**צז** ח ט מיי' שם הל' ז:

**צח** י כ מיי' פ"ח מהל' איסורי ביאה הל' ט ועי"ש במ"מ סמג שם טור י"ד סי' קפט:

**צט** ל מיי' שם פ"י הלכה א:

---

**תוספי הרא"ש**

משום הכי קא דייק: **אלא** לקפיצות. פרש"י לקפיצות לחודייהו. וקשה לפירושו א"כ מאי פריך בתר ימים לחודייהו פשיטא לישני ליה דאתא לאשמועינן דלקפיצות לחודייהו לא קבעה לה וסת כדהוה ס"ד מעיקרא. וע"ק כיון דלא קאי האי דקאמר מעיקרא אלא לקפיצות הוה ליה לשנויי בתר דפריך ליה מברייתא אלא לקפיצות ולימים הלכך נ"ל הא דקאמר לקפיצות היינו לקפיצות עם הימים אבל לקפיצות לחודייהו הוה פשיטא ליה דלא קבעה מידי דהוה אימים לחודייהו: **אע"פ** שאמרו דיה שעתה צריכה להיות בודקת. הקשה הר' יעקב מאורלינש דהכא אמרינן דאע"פ דדייה שעתה צריכה להיות בודקת. וגבי י"א יום שבין נדה לנדה אשכחן איפכא דתנן פרק בנות כותים כל י"א יום בחזקת טהרה ואמרינן בגמרא למאי הלכתא אמר רב יהודה לומר שאינה צריכה בדיקה. ותניא התם בשומרת יום מטמאה מעת לעת וי"ל דהנך מהכא מן הדין כיון דדיין שעתן כ"ש דלא בעו בדיקה אלא משום שלא תשתכח תורת בדיקה. אבל גבי י"א יום אם לא תבדוק עכשיו תבדוק לאחר מכאן: **תבדוק** דלמא קבעה לה וסת. תמיה לי דבדיקה כזו לא אשכחן שתקנו חכמים שתהא אשה צריכה לבדוק שמא קבע לה וסת דא"כ אפילו אשה שאינה עסוקה בטהרות תבדוק בכל יום שמא תקבע לה וסת וצ"ע: הלכך לשון שני עיקר:

עד

---

**הגהות הב"ח**

(א) רש"י ד"ה ובתולה שדמיה וכו' אחר בעילה ראשונה. נ"ב ללשון ראשון שפירש"י בגמ' לאו דוקא שלא שמשה כלל אחר בעילה ראשונה דאפילו שמשה אלא שהיום לא שמשה ועסקה בטהרות וק"ל: (ב) ד"ה ממעין וכו' של וסת הוו בתוך ימי נדה: (ג) בא"ד וראשון ישר. נ"ב וכן מוכח לקמן דף לט ע"ב ע"ש: (ד) תוס' ד"ה קפלה וראתה ג' זימני. נ"ב ע"ל בסוף פ' בנות כותים דף לט ע"ב כתבו התוס' בד"ה אלמא דהתלמוד לא חש להזכיר תלתא זימני: (ה) ד"ה ממעין וכו' שילהי בנות. נ"ב עיין בתוס' בד"ה אלמא: (ו) בא"ד ולמאי דפרישית לקמן דרב פפא:

ר"מ מ"ז

רש"ל מ"ז

לעיל ו.

[לקמן לט:]

[לקמן לה: וש"נ]

**הגהות הגר"א**

[א] גמ' ובשבת קפלה ולא חזאי. נ"ב ל"ג לה וכן הוא בכל הפוסקים ואף הרמב"ם שמפרש דפליג אלישנא קמא מפרש דמיירי כך ועיין במגיד משנה:

**גליון הש"ס**

**תום'** ד"ה קפלה וראתה ג' זימני גרסינן וכו'. ע"ל לט ע"ב תוספות ד"ה אלמא:

---

**ממעין** פתוח לא אמרי. לאותו לשון שפרש"י כשהראיות ראשונות בימי נדה היינו פתוח קשה למאי דבעי למימר בסוף בנות כותים דאפילו כי האי גונא אמר רבי יוחנן א"כ תקשי ליה מתני'

קך א מיי' פ"ט מהלכות איסורי ביאה הל' יח סמג לאוין קיא טוש"ע י"ד סימן קצג סעיף ה:
[לעיל ז:]
קכא ב מיי' שם הל' כ טוש"ע י"ד סימן קפז סעיף יג:
[שייך לעיל במשנה]
קכב ג מיי' פ"ד מהלכות מטמא משכב ומושב הל' ז:
קכג ד מיי' שם הלכה ז ועיין בהשגות ובכ"מ ופ"ד מהל' איסורי ביאה הלכה ט סמג לאוין קיא ועשין רמג וטוש"ע י"ד סימן קפו סעיף א:
קכד ה מיי' פ"ד מהל' מטמא משכב ומושב הל' ז:
קכה ו מיי' פ"ד מהל' איסורי ביאה הל' ט סמג שם טוש"ע י"ד סימן קפד סעיף יא ועיין בטור וכו':

*בֵּית שַׁמַּאי הִיא, דְּאָמְרִי מַעְיָן אֶחָד הוּא. וְסָתַם לָן תַּנָּא כְּב"ש? סְתָם וְאַחַר כָּךְ מַחֲלוֹקֶת הוּא, וְכָל *סְתָם וְאח"כ מַחֲלוֹקֶת – אֵין הֲלָכָה כִּסְתָם. וְאבע"א מִי קָתָנֵי "מְבַקֶּשֶׁת לֵישֵׁב"? "יוֹשֶׁבֶת" קָתָנֵי. אִי יוֹשֶׁבֶת, מַאי לְמֵימְרָא? מַהוּ דְּתֵימָא: תִּיבְדּוֹק, דְּדִילְמָא קָבְעָה לָהּ וֶסֶת, קמ"ל דְּמַעְיָן טָהוֹר לְמַעְיָן טָמֵא לָא קָבְעָה. הָנִיחָא לְלֵוִי דְּאָמַר שְׁנֵי מַעְיָנוֹת הֵם, אֶלָּא לְרַב דְּאָמַר מַעְיָן אֶחָד הוּא – תִּבְדּוֹק, דִּילְמָא קָבְעָה לָהּ וֶסֶת! אֲפִילּוּ הָכִי, מִימֵי טָהֳרָה לִימֵי טוּמְאָה – לָא קָבְעָה.§ "וּמְשַׁמֶּשֶׁת בְּעֵדִים" וכו'.§ תְּנַן הָתָם: *תִּינוֹקֶת שֶׁלֹּא הִגִּיעַ זְמַנָּהּ לִרְאוֹת וְנִשֵּׂאת, ב"ש אוֹמְרִים: נוֹתְנִין לָהּ אַרְבַּע לֵילוֹת. וב"ה אוֹמְרִים: [א]עַד שֶׁתֶּחְיֶה הַמַּכָּה. אָמַר רַב גִּידֵּל, אָמַר שְׁמוּאֵל: לֹא שָׁנוּ אֶלָּא שֶׁלֹּא פָּסְקָה מֵחֲמַת תַּשְׁמִישׁ, וְרָאֲתָה שֶׁלֹּא מֵחֲמַת תַּשְׁמִישׁ. [ב]אֲבָל פָּסְקָה מֵחֲמַת תַּשְׁמִישׁ וְרָאֲתָה – טְמֵאָה. עָבַר לַיְלָה אַחַת בְּלֹא תַּשְׁמִישׁ וְרָאֲתָה – טְמֵאָה. נִשְׁתַּנּוּ מַרְאֵה דָּמִים שֶׁלָּהּ – טְמֵאָה. מְתִיב ר' יוֹנָה: וּבְתוּלָה שֶׁדָּמֶיהָ טְהוֹרִים, אַמַּאי? תְּשַׁמֵּשׁ בְּעֵדִים, דְּדִילְמָא נִשְׁתַּנּוּ מַרְאֵה דָּמִים שֶׁלָּהּ! אָמַר רָבָא, אֵימָא רֵישָׁא: חוּץ מִן הַנִּדָּה וְהַיּוֹשֶׁבֶת עַל דַּם טוֹהַר – הוּא דְּלָא בָּעֲיָא בְּדִיקָה, אֲבָל בְּתוּלָה שֶׁדָּמֶיהָ טְהוֹרִין – בָּעֲיָא בְּדִיקָה. אֶלָּא קַשְׁיָין אַהֲדָדֵי! כָּאן – שֶׁשִּׁמְּשָׁה, דְּאֵימָא שַׁמָּשׁ עֲכָרָן, כָּאן – שֶׁלֹּא שִׁמְּשָׁה. תַּנְיָא נַמִי הָכִי: בד"א שֶׁלֹּא פָּסְקָה מֵחֲמַת תַּשְׁמִישׁ וְרָאֲתָה שֶׁלֹּא מֵחֲמַת תַּשְׁמִישׁ, אֲבָל פָּסְקָה מֵחֲמַת תַּשְׁמִישׁ וְרָאֲתָה – טְמֵאָה, עָבַר לַיְלָה אַחַת בְּלֹא תַּשְׁמִישׁ וְרָאֲתָה – טְמֵאָה, נִשְׁתַּנּוּ מַרְאֵה דָּמִים שֶׁלָּהּ – טְמֵאָה.§ "פְּעָמִים הִיא צְרִיכָה" וכו'.§ א"ר יְהוּדָה אָמַר שְׁמוּאֵל: לֹא שָׁנוּ אֶלָּא לְטָהֳרוֹת, אֲבָל לְבַעְלָהּ – מוּתֶּרֶת. פְּשִׁיטָא, "שַׁחֲרִית" תְּנַן! אֶלָּא, אִי אִתְּמַר – אַסֵּיפָא אִתְּמַר: וּבְשָׁעָה שֶׁהִיא עוֹבֶרֶת לְשַׁמֵּשׁ אֶת בֵּיתָהּ. א"ר יְהוּדָה אָמַר שְׁמוּאֵל: לֹא שָׁנוּ [ג]אֶלָּא בְּאִשָּׁה עֲסוּקָה בְּטָהֳרוֹת, דְּמִגּוֹ דְּבָעֲיָא בְּדִיקָה לְטָהֳרוֹת – בָּעֲיָא נַמִי בְּדִיקָה לְבַעְלָהּ. אֲבָל אֵינָהּ עֲסוּקָה בְּטָהֳרוֹת – לָא בָּעֲיָא בְּדִיקָה. מַאי קמ"ל? תְּנֵינָא: *[ד]כָּל הַנָּשִׁים בְּחֶזְקַת טָהֳרָה לְבַעֲלֵיהֶן! [לקמן טו:] אִי מִמַּתְנִי' – הֲוָה אָמֵינָא: הָנֵי מִילֵּי – בְּאִשָּׁה שֶׁיֵּשׁ לָהּ וֶסֶת, אֲבָל אִשָּׁה שֶׁאֵין לָהּ וֶסֶת – בָּעֲיָא בְּדִיקָה. וְהָא מַתְנִי' בְּאִשָּׁה שֶׁיֵּשׁ לָהּ וֶסֶת עָסְקִינַן! מַתְנִי' – בֵּין שֶׁיֵּשׁ לָהּ וֶסֶת בֵּין אֵין לָהּ וֶסֶת, וְהָא קמ"ל דְּאע"ג דְּיֵשׁ לָהּ וֶסֶת, [ה]מִגּוֹ דְּבָעֲיָא בְּדִיקָה לְטָהֳרוֹת – בָּעֲיָא נַמִי בְּדִיקָה לְבַעְלָהּ. וְהָא אֲמַרָהּ שְׁמוּאֵל חֲדָא זִימְנָא! *דְּאָמַר רַבִּי זֵירָא, [לקמן יב:] אָמַר רַבִּי אַבָּא בַּר יִרְמְיָה, אָמַר שְׁמוּאֵל: אִשָּׁה שֶׁאֵין לָהּ וֶסֶת – אֲסוּרָה לְשַׁמֵּשׁ עַד שֶׁתִּבְדּוֹק. וְאוֹקִימְנָא: *בַּעֲסוּקָה בְּטָהֳרוֹת! [לקמן טז.] *חֲדָא מִכְּלַל חֲבֶרְתָּהּ אִתְּמַר. *) [מגילה כב: וש"נ] תַּנְיָא נַמִי הָכִי: בד"א – לְטָהֳרוֹת, אֲבָל לְבַעְלָהּ – מוּתֶּרֶת. [ו]בד"א – שֶׁהִנִּיחָהּ בְּחֶזְקַת טְהוֹרָה, אֲבָל הִנִּיחָהּ בְּחֶזְקַת טְמֵאָה לְעוֹלָם הִיא בְּטוּמְאָתָהּ, עַד שֶׁתֹּאמַר לוֹ "טְהוֹרָה אֲנִי".

*) לקמן טז:

בְּעָא

**רש"י**

ב"ש הִיא דְּאָמְרִי. בְּפֶרֶק "בְּנוֹת כּוּתִים"* [לקמן לה:] מַעְיָן אֶחָד הוּא. יוֹשֶׁבֶת קָתָנֵי. שֶׁכְּבָר נִכְנְסוּ יְמֵי טוֹהַר. דִּילְמָא קָבְעָה לָהּ וֶסֶת. תּוֹךְ שְׁמוֹנִים דִּנְקֵבָה, ג' רְאִיּוֹת מֵעֶשְׂרִים לְעֶשְׂרִים – לְרשב"ג, וּלְרַבִּי – ג' רְאִיּוֹת מִשְּׁלֹשִׁים לִשְׁלֹשִׁים, שֶׁכְּשֶׁיִּכְלוּ יְמֵי טוֹהַר ה"ל וֶסֶת לְעֶשְׂרִים. הַמַּכָּה. מַכַּת בְּעִילָה, דְּכָל זְמַן שֶׁתְּהֵא רוֹאָה דָּם מֵחֲמַת תַּשְׁמִישׁ – דַּם בְּתוּלִים הוּא. [לקמן לה:] לֹא שָׁנוּ. אַבֵּית הִלֵּל קָאֵי. שֶׁלֹּא פָּסְקָה. מִמַּרְאוֹת דָּם. מֵחֲמַת תַּשְׁמִישׁ. דְּכָל זְמַן שֶׁשִּׁמְּשָׁה, רָאֲתָה. [יבמות מב.] וְרָאֲתָה שֶׁלֹּא מֵחֲמַת תַּשְׁמִישׁ. כְּלוֹמַר, אֲפִילּוּ חָזְרָה וְרָאֲתָה בַּיּוֹם שֶׁלֹּא מֵחֲמַת תַּשְׁמִישׁ – מַחְזְקִינַן לָהּ בְּדַם בְּתוּלִים, הוֹאִיל וּמֵחֲמַת תַּשְׁמִישׁ לֹא פָּסְקָה. אֲבָל פָּסְקָה מֵחֲמַת תַּשְׁמִישׁ. שֶׁשִּׁמְּשָׁה פַּעַם אַחַת וְלֹא רָאֲתָה, וְאַחֲרֵי כֵן רָאֲתָה, בֵּין שֶׁרָאֲתָה מֵחֲמַת תַּשְׁמִישׁ בֵּין שֶׁלֹּא רָאֲתָה מֵחֲמַת תַּשְׁמִישׁ – טְמֵאָה. דְּאָמְרִינַן: כֵּיוָן דְּבִשְׁעַת תַּשְׁמִישׁ פָּסְקָה פַּעַם אַחַת, רַגְלַיִם לַדָּבָר שֶׁהַבְּתוּלִים כָּלוּ כְּבָר, וְזֶה מִמָּקוֹם טָמֵא יָרַד. [כתובות ו. לקמן סד:] נִשְׁתַּנּוּ מַרְאֵה דָּמִים. מִמַּרְאֵה דַּם בְּעִילָה רִאשׁוֹנָה. תְּשַׁמֵּשׁ בְּעֵדִים. אֶחָד לִפְנֵי תַּשְׁמִישׁ וְאֶחָד לְאַחַר תַּשְׁמִישׁ. כָּאן שֶׁשִּׁמְּשָׁה. הָא דְּקָתָנֵי שֶׁאֵינָהּ מְשַׁמֶּשֶׁת בְּעֵדִים, מִשּׁוּם דְּשִׁמְּשָׁה עַכְשָׁיו, דְּאִי נַמִי חָזְיָא לְאַחַר תַּשְׁמִישׁ וְנִשְׁתַּנּוּ מַרְאֵה הַדָּם – טְהוֹרִין. דְּאֵימוּר שַׁמָּשׁ עֲכָרָן. אֵבֶר הַתַּשְׁמִישׁ. כָּאן שֶׁלֹּא שִׁמְּשָׁה. הָא דְּאָמַר "נִשְׁתַּנּוּ מַרְאֵה דָּמִים שֶׁלָּהּ, טְמֵאָה" – שֶׁלֹּא שִׁמְּשָׁה הַיּוֹם, אֶלָּא בְּטָהֳרוֹת עֲסוּקָה סָמוּךְ לִבְדִיקָה. הִילְכָּךְ, לְעִנְיַן טָהֳרוֹת שַׁחֲרִית וְעַרְבִית בָּעֲיָא בְּדִיקָה. וְלִפְנֵי תַּשְׁמִישׁ הַיְינוּ טַעְמָא דְּלָא בָּעֲיָא בְּדִיקָה: דְּכֵיוָן דִּלְאַחַר תַּשְׁמִישׁ לָא בָּעֲיָא בְּדִיקָה, לִפְנֵי תַּשְׁמִישׁ נַמִי לָא אַצְרְכוּהָ רַבָּנַן. דְּאָמְרִינַן לְקַמָּן: כָּל לְבַעְלָהּ – לָא בָּעֲיָא בְּדִיקָה, אֶלָּא מִגּוֹ דְּבָעֲיָא בְּדִיקָה לְאַחַר תַּשְׁמִישׁ לְטָהֳרוֹת בָּעֲיָא נַמִי בְּדִיקָה לִפְנֵי תַּשְׁמִישׁ לְבַעְלָהּ, וְהָכָא לֵיכָּא מִגּוֹ. לִישָּׁנָא אַחֲרִינָא: כָּאן שֶׁשִּׁמְּשָׁה לְאַחַר תַּשְׁמִישׁ רִאשׁוֹן – לָא בָּעֲיָא בְּדִיקָה, וַאֲפִילּוּ שַׁחֲרִית וְעַרְבִית, וַאֲפִילּוּ נִשְׁתַּנּוּ – אֵימוּר: שַׁמָּשׁ עֲכָרָן. וְהָא דְּתָנֵי נִשְׁתַּנּוּ טְמֵאִין – כְּשֶׁלֹּא שִׁמְּשָׁה לְאַחַר לַיְלָה הָרִאשׁוֹן. וְלָאו טַעֲמָא הוּא, דְּא"כ אֲפִילּוּ לֹא נִשְׁתַּנּוּ – נַמִי טְמֵאָה, דְּהָא עָבְרָה עָלֶיהָ לַיְלָה אַחַת בְּלֹא תַּשְׁמִישׁ אָמְרִינַן לְעֵיל דִּטְמֵאָה. לֹא שָׁנוּ. הָא דִּתְנַן שַׁחֲרִית וְעַרְבִית בּוֹדֶקֶת. אֲבָל לְבַעְלָהּ מוּתֶּרֶת. בְּלֹא בְּדִיקָה. פְּשִׁיטָא שַׁחֲרִית תְּנַן. דְּטָהֳרוֹת הוּא, דְּהָא אֵין מְשַׁמְּשִׁין מִטָּה בַּיּוֹם. מִגּוֹ דְּבָעֲיָא בְּדִיקָה לְטָהֳרוֹת. לְאַחַר תַּשְׁמִישׁ, שֶׁמָּא רָאֲתָה לְאַחַר תַּשְׁמִישׁ מֵחֲמַת תַּשְׁמִישׁ. בָּעֲיָא נַמִי בְּדִיקָה לְבַעְלָהּ. לִפְנֵי תַּשְׁמִישׁ. הָא נַמִי תְּנֵינָא. בְּמַתְנִי' פ"ב (לקמן טו.). בְּחֶזְקַת טָהֳרָה. לְבַעֲלֵיהֶן, וּמַתְנִיתִין דְּקָתָנֵי דְּבָעֵינַן בְּדִיקָה עַל כָּרְחָךְ הָכִי מִתְפָּרְשָׁא לָהּ מַתְנִיתִין: דְּהָכָא בַּעֲסוּקָה בְּטָהֳרוֹת, וְהָתָם בְּשֶׁאֵינָהּ עֲסוּקָה בְּטָהֳרוֹת. וְהָא מַתְנִי' דְּהָכָא בְּיֵשׁ לָהּ וֶסֶת עָסְקִינַן. דְּקָתָנֵי: "וְאַעַ"פ שֶׁאָמְרוּ דַּיָּהּ שַׁעְתָּהּ" וכו', וְהָא וַדַּאי בְּשֶׁיֵּשׁ לָהּ וֶסֶת, וַעֲלָהּ מַיְירֵי שְׁמוּאֵל וְאָמַר: אֲבָל לְבַעְלָהּ מוּתֶּרֶת, אֲבָל אֵין לָהּ וֶסֶת – לָא קָאָמַר. בֵּין יֵשׁ לָהּ בֵּין אֵין לָהּ. דְּכֵיוָן דְּאָמַר: יֵשׁ לָהּ וֶסֶת בָּעֲיָא בְּדִיקָה, כ"ש דְּאֵין לָהּ וֶסֶת, וְאַכּוּלְּהוּ קָאָמַר שְׁמוּאֵל, אֲבָל לְבַעְלָהּ מוּתֶּרֶת. וְהָא דְּאַיְירֵי מַתְנִיתִין בְּיֵשׁ לָהּ וֶסֶת, הָא קָא מַשְׁמַע לָן דְּאַף עַל גַּב כו'. וְהָאָמַר שְׁמוּאֵל חֲדָא זִימְנָא. דַּאֲפִילּוּ אֵין לָהּ וֶסֶת לָא בָּעֲיָא בְּדִיקָה לְבַעְלָהּ, אֶלָּא אִם כֵּן רְגִילָה לַעֲשׂוֹת טָהֳרוֹת. וְאוֹקִימְנָא. לְקַמָּן. בַּמֶּה דְּבָרִים אֲמוּרִים. דְּבָעֲיָא בְּדִיקָה. לְטָהֳרוֹת. כְּלוֹמַר, בַּעֲסוּקָה בְּטָהֳרוֹת, אֲבָל לְבַעְלָהּ גְּרֵידָא שֶׁאֵינָהּ עֲסוּקָה בְּטָהֳרוֹת – לָא.

כְּשִׁיעוּר

בעי

**תוספות**

**אלא** לרב דאמר מעין אחד הוא תבדוק. הוה מלי לשנויי: דרב מוקי במבקשת לישב, אלא דניחא ליה לשנויי אליבא דתרווייהו מתני' בענין אחד. **אפילו** הכי מימי טהרה לימי טומאה לא קבעה. – ואין להקשות: לר"א דאמר,* כל אשה שעברו עליה ג' עונות כו', [לעיל ז:] תבדוק בימי טוהר, שמא תפסוק ג' עונות – דהכי נמי מימי טהרה לימי טומאה, לא מקרי הפסקה.

*[שייך לעיל במשנה] **ומשמשת** בעדים. א"ארבע נשים" וא"אשה שיש לה וסת" קאי. **שלא** פסקה מחמת תשמיש. דכל פעם שמשמשת רואה, אפילו תשמיש מופלג מחבירו חדש או שלשה חדשים – הוי דם תשמיש, וטהור. כדאמר בפ' בתרא (לקמן סה,) מעשה ונתן לה רבי ד' לילות מתוך שנים עשר חדש. וכי שמשה בלילה וראתה למחרתו, או בלילה שלאחר כך בלא תשמיש – טהורה. אבל אם ראתה יום שני לשמושה – טמאה. כדקאמר "עבר עליה לילה אחת בלא תשמיש" כו'. וביום תשמיש נמי, אם נשתנו מראה דמים שלה משל אמש – טמאה. ואם פסקה מחמת תשמיש, וראתה אחרי כן, אפילו באותו יום בין בתשמיש בין בלא תשמיש – טמאה. דודאי חיתה המכה, וכלו בביאה ראשונה כל דמי בתולים. ואפילו *לרב אסי דאמר בפרק בתרא (שם סד:) [נ"ל לרב אסי] בעל ולא מצא דם, וחזר ובעל ומצא דם – טהורה, היינו משום דאימא: בביאה ראשונה בעל בהטייה, כשמואל. אבל הכא, דבביאה ראשונה מצא דם ובשניה לא מצא דם – ודאי חיתה המכה.

**כל** הנשים בחזקת טהרה לבעליהן. – פירשתי לקמן פ"ב (דף טו.).

**חדא** מכלל חברתה איתמר. פי' רשב"ם: דהך דהכא איתמר מכלל ההיא דלקמן. ואין נראה, דבההיא לא – פירש שמואל דאיירי בעסוקה בטהרות, אלא רבא דייק בפירקין מדלא מפליג ליה רבי ירמיה בר אבא לרבי זירא: ביש לה וסת – לטהרות בעיא בדיקה, לבעלה – לא בעיא בדיקה. אין לה וסת – לבעלה נמי בעיא בדיקה, ש"מ קסבר שמואל: כל לבעלה לא בעיא בדיקה. לכך נראה לפרש: דההיא איתמר מכלל הך דהכא, ומשום דרבי ירמיה בר אבא הוה ידע מהך דהכא דאף אין לה וסת לא בעיא בדיקה לבעלה, לא מפליג לרבי זירא הכי.

**תניא** נמי הכי כו' – אבל לבעלה מותרת. וא"ת: ודילמא דוקא ביש לה וסת איירי? וי"ל: מדתני סיפא "אבל הניחה בחזקת טמאה", מכלל דמיירי באין לה וסת. דאי ביש לה וסת דוקא, ה"ל לפלוגי בדידה: אפילו אם הניחה בחזקת טהורה, אם אין לה וסת כו'. אלא משום דאף באין לה וסת לא משכחת טמאה לבעלה, אלא בהניחה בחזקת טמאה. ובסמוך בברייתא דחמרין ופועלין כו', דקתני נמי: אבל הניחה בחזקת טמאה, אע"ג דביש לה וסת מיירי – היינו משום דבהניחה בחזקת טמאה אשמועינן: אפילו ערה – טמאה, עד שתאמר "טהורה אני". אבל הניחה בחזקת טהורה, באין לה וסת, היכא דערה – לא בעיא בדיקה. דכיון דבא מן הדרך, מסתמא תובעה. ואמרינן לקמן (דף יב.) כיון שתבעה, אין לך בדיקה גדולה מזו. וה"ר יהודה בן הר"ר י"ט כתב: דרישא דברייתא זו הכי שנויה בתוספתא: מעוברת ומניקה – בועלה טהור, פירוש: אפילו לרבי עקיבא, דאמר לעיל ברואה דם דמטמאה בועלה למפרע. וכל אשה שיש לה וסת, וכן שאר כל הנשים פי' דאין להן וסת. דאין סברא לפרש: בתולה וזקנה – דאם כן, הוה תני להו בהדי מעוברת ומניקה דרישא. מטמאות במגע – פירוש: לטהרות, וטהורות לבעליהן. אלמא ברייתא מיירי דאין לה וסת.

**תוספי הרא"ש**

**עד** שתחיה המכה. אין לפרש דאתוך ד' לילות קאי אבל לאחר ד' לילות אפילו לא חיתה טמאה דא"כ ליתנייה בעדיות גבי קולי ב"ש וחומרי ב"ה. וליכא נמי לפרושי דבחיתה תליא מילתא בין תוך ד' לילות בין לאחר ד' מדתנן לקמן בפרק בת' הגיע זמנה לראות ב"ה אומרים עד מוצאי שבת ד' לילות ולא מפליג בין חיתה ללא חיתה. הלכך נ"ל דשיעור דחיתה לאחר ארבע לילות אבל תוך ד' אפילו חיתה טהורה ועוד נראה לדקדק מדתנן בתולה שדמיה טהורין ואמאי תבדוק דלמא חיתה אלא ודאי בתוך ד' טהורה בכל ענין ומתני' בתוך ד' לילות איירי והא דפריך בסמוך מנשתנו מראה דמים שלה משום דבנשתנו אין סברא לחלק: **אבל** פסקה מחמת תשמיש וראתה טמאה. תימה לי מאי קמ"ל היינו עד שתחיה המכה דהכי מפרש שמואל לקמן כל זמן שהרוק מצוי בתוך הפה. וצ"ל דאגב דבעי למימר מילי אחרנייתא נקטיה נמי להך אע"ג דשמעינן לה מאידך דשמואל ואפילו למ"ד בריש תינוקת בעל ולא מצא דם (טהור') וחזר ובעל ומצא דם טהורה שאני התם דמעיקרא לא מצא דם ואיכא למימר בעל בהטייה ולא צד בתוליה הלכך כשחזר ובעל ומצא דם תלינן בדם בתולים. אבל הכא דמעיקרא מצא דם השתא דלא מצא בביאה זו אמרינן דחיתה המכה. וא"ת הכא בלא הגיע זמנה איירי וכל לילות שבימי קטנות אינן חשובות אלא כלילה אחת ונותנין לה עוד שלשה לילות בימי נערות כדאיתא לקמן בפרק בתרא. ולעיל פירש' דבכל ד' לילות אפילו חיתה טהורה. וי"ל דהא דחשבינן כל ימי קטנות אחת היינו בשלא פסקה מחמת תשמיש ועי"ל דהא דקאמרי ב"ה עד שתחיה המכה היינו בין תוך ד' לילות בין לאחר ד' לילות. והא דתנן לקמן גבי הגיע זמנה ב"ה אומרים עד מוצאי שבת ד' לילות היינו בשלא חיתה המכה. וא"ת א"כ תבדוק שמא פסקה מחמת תשמיש וי"ל דלא מצינו בדיקה כזאת דלא מהניא לטמאותה עכשיו אלא שאם תראה אחרי כן שתהיה טמאה. אע"ג דלעיל מצרכינן בדיקה משום וסת לא דמי דהתם הוא לקבוע לה וסת כל ימיה כל זמן שלא תעקרנו: **עברה** עליה לילה אחת בלא תשמיש וראתה טמאה ודוקא בו ביום שאין בו תשמיש אבל שמשה ביום של אחריו כל ראיות של אותו היום טהורות אם לא פסקה מחמת תשמיש כדאמרינן

כדאמרינן בפרק בתרא שנתן לה ד' ד' לילות מתוך י"ב חדש וה"פ דברייתא דשמשה ולא פסקה מחמת תשמיש כל ראיות של אותו יום טהורות אפילו שלא מחמת תשמיש אבל ראיות של מחרת לא: **אמאי** תשמש בעדים. דלמא נשתנו מראה דמים שלה אע"ג דאיירינן בשלא הגיע זמנה והך לא בעיא בדיקה דהא תניא לעיל דעד שלא הגיע פרקה הרי היא בחזקת טהורה ואין הנשים בודקות אותן מ"מ אמתני' קא פריך דאיירי בהגיע זמנה: **אימור** שמש עכרן. ואין לומר תבדוק אימור נשתנית עכירה זאת מעכירה אחרת שאינו עוכר לעולם בשוה ובכל ענין שעכרו טהור: **פשיטא** שחרית. טהרות היא ועדיפא מינה הוה מצי למפרך דכיון דקתני בשעת שהיא עוברת לשמש את ביתה למה לה שתבדוק שחרית לשמש כל היום וערבית לשמש כל הלילה בבדיקה זו סגיא אלא משום דאיכא למימר לא סמכינן על ההיא בדיקה (שלי דאי) משום דאמרינן לעיל דאינה מכניסתו לחורין ולסדקין: **אלא** אי איתמר אסיפא איתמר. ובשעה שהיא עוברת לשמש את ביתה. מכאן נראה הא דקתני מתני' ומשמשת בעדים היינו לאחר תשמיש אחד לו ואחד לה כמתני' דפ' כל היד ולא כפי' רש"י שפירש אחד לפני תשמיש ואחד לאחר תשמיש דאם כן הוה ליה למימר אלא אי איתמר ארישא איתמר ומשמשת בעדים ועוד מאי כי קאמר ובשעה שהיא עוברת לשמש את ביתה היינו משמשת בעדים: **אי** מתני' ה"א ה"מ באשה שיש לה וסת והא דקתני כל הנשים היינו בין ערות בין ישנות: **ואוקימנא** בעסוקה בטהרות. וא"ת והלא לא פירש שמואל בדבריו בהדיא דאיירי בעסוקה בטהרות אלא דר' אבא הוא דאוקים ליה דשמואל איירי בהכי י"ל דהיינו דקא משני חדא מכלל חברתה אתמר דר' אבא גופיה לא קים ליה אלא מהך דהכא א"נ ר' אבא קים ליה שפיר [פירש] בדבריו בעסוקה בטהרות: **בד"א** בטהרות. תימה מאי תניא נמי הכי דילמא באשה שיש לה וסת איירי וי"ל דסמיך ארישא דברייתא השנויה בתוספתא מעוברת ומניקה בועלה טהור. וכל אשה שיש לה וסת ושאר כל הנשים מטמאות במגע וטהורות לבעליהן בד"א שהניחה בחזקת טהרה פי' בועלה טהור אפילו לר' עקיבא דאמר לעיל דרואה מעת לעת מטמאה את בועלה. וכל אשה שיש לה וסת ושאר כל הנשים. פי' אפילו אין להם וסת מטמאות במגע לטהרות וטהורות לבעליהן כלומר מותרות לבעליהן בלא בדיקה:

כדי

בְּעָא מִינֵּיהּ רַבִּי זֵירָא מֵרַב יְהוּדָה: אִשָּׁה מַהוּ שֶׁתִּבְדּוֹק עַצְמָהּ לְבַעְלָהּ? אָמַר לֵיהּ: [א]לֹא תִבְדּוֹק. וְתִבְדּוֹק, וּמַה בְּכָךְ? א] * [ב]אִם כֵּן — לִבּוֹ נוֹקְפוֹ וּפוֹרֵשׁ. בְּעָא מִינֵּיהּ רַבִּי אַבָּא מֵרַב הוּנָא: אִשָּׁה מַהוּ שֶׁתִּבְדּוֹק עַצְמָהּ כְּשִׁיעוּר וֶסֶת, כְּדֵי לְחַיֵּיב בַּעְלָהּ חַטָּאת? א"ל: מִי מַשְׁכַּחַת לָהּ לִבְדִיקָה כְּשִׁיעוּר וֶסֶת? וְהָתַנְיָא: *אֵיזֶהוּ שִׁיעוּר וֶסֶת — מָשָׁל לְשַׁמָּשׁ וְעֵד שֶׁעוֹמְדִים בְּצַד הַמַּשְׁקוֹף, בִּיצִיאוֹת הַשַּׁמָּשׁ — נִכְנָס עֵד, הֲוֵי: וֶסֶת שֶׁאָמְרוּ לְקִנּוּחַ וְלֹא לִבְדִיקָה. אֶלָּא: מַהוּ שֶׁתְּקַנֵּחַ? אִיכָּא דְּאָמְרִי, הָכִי בְּעָא מִינֵּיהּ: אִשָּׁה מַהוּ שֶׁתִּבְדּוֹק עַצְמָהּ, כְּדֵי לְחַיֵּיב בַּעְלָהּ אָשָׁם תָּלוּי? אָמַר לוֹ: לֹא תִבְדּוֹק. וְתִבְדּוֹק, וּמַה בְּכָךְ? א"כ לִבּוֹ נוֹקְפוֹ וּפוֹרֵשׁ.§ "וּבְשָׁעָה שֶׁהִיא עוֹבֶרֶת" וכו'.§ אָמַר ר' אַמִּי אָמַר רַבִּי יַנַּאי: [ג]וְזֶהוּ *עֵדֶן שֶׁל צְנוּעוֹת. א"ל רַבִּי אַבָּא בַּר מָמֵל לר' אַמִּי: תַּנָּא תָּנֵי "צְרִיכוֹת" וְאַתְּ תָּנֵי "צְנוּעוֹת"! אָמַר לֵיהּ: שֶׁאֲנִי אוֹמֵר כָּל הַמְקַיֵּים דִּבְרֵי חֲכָמִים נִקְרָא "צָנוּעַ". אָמַר רָבָא: וְשֶׁאֵינוֹ מְקַיֵּים דִּבְרֵי חֲכָמִים, "צָנוּעַ" הוּא דְּלָא מִקְרֵי, הָא "רָשָׁע" לָא מִקְרֵי? אֶלָּא אָמַר רָבָא: צְנוּעוֹת, עֵד שֶׁבָּדְקוּ בּוֹ עַצְמָן לִפְנֵי תַּשְׁמִישׁ זֶה — אֵין בּוֹדְקוֹת בּוֹ לִפְנֵי תַּשְׁמִישׁ אַחֵר; וְשֶׁאֵינָן צְנוּעוֹת — בּוֹדְקוֹת וְלֹא אִיכְפַּת לְהֶן. גּוּפָא, אָמַר רַבִּי זֵירָא, אָמַר רַבִּי אַבָּא בַּר יִרְמְיָה, אָמַר שְׁמוּאֵל: [ד]אִשָּׁה שֶׁאֵין לָהּ וֶסֶת — אֲסוּרָה לְשַׁמֵּשׁ עַד שֶׁתִּבְדּוֹק. אָמַר לֵיהּ ר' זֵירָא לְרַבִּי אַבָּא בַּר יִרְמְיָה: אֵין לָהּ וֶסֶת — בָּעֲיָא בְּדִיקָה, יֵשׁ לָהּ וֶסֶת — לָא בָּעֲיָא בְּדִיקָה? א"ל: יֵשׁ לָהּ וֶסֶת, עֵרָה — בָּעֲיָא בְּדִיקָה, יְשֵׁנָה — לָא בָּעֲיָא בְּדִיקָה. אֵין לָהּ וֶסֶת; בֵּין עֵרָה בֵּין יְשֵׁנָה — בָּעֲיָא בְּדִיקָה. אָמַר רָבָא, וְלֵימָא לֵיהּ: יֵשׁ לָהּ וֶסֶת, לְטָהֳרוֹת — בָּעֲיָא בְּדִיקָה, לְבַעְלָהּ — לָא בָּעֲיָא בְּדִיקָה, אֵין לָהּ וֶסֶת — אֲפִילּוּ לְבַעְלָהּ נַמִי בָּעֲיָא בְּדִיקָה; וּמִדְּלָא א"ל הָכִי, ש"מ קָסָבַר שְׁמוּאֵל: [ה]כָּל לְבַעְלָהּ — לָא בָּעֲיָא בְּדִיקָה. ת"ר: [ו]חַמָּרִין וּפוֹעֲלִין וְהַבָּאִין מִבֵּית הָאֵבֶל וּמִבֵּית הַמִּשְׁתֶּה — נְשֵׁיהֶם לָהֶם בְּחֶזְקַת טָהֳרָה, וּבָאִין וְשׁוֹהִין עִמָּהֶם, בֵּין יְשֵׁנוֹת בֵּין עֵרוֹת. [ז]בד"א — שֶׁהִנִּיחָן בְּחֶזְקַת טָהֳרָה, אֲבָל הִנִּיחָן בְּחֶזְקַת טוּמְאָה — לְעוֹלָם הִיא טְמֵאָה, עַד שֶׁתֹּאמַר לוֹ "טְהוֹרָה אֲנִי". וְהָא, שְׁמוּאֵל בְּמַאי מוֹקֵי לָהּ? אִי בְּשֶׁיֵּשׁ לָהּ וֶסֶת — קַשְׁיָא עֵרָה! וְאִי בְּשֶׁאֵין לָהּ וֶסֶת — קַשְׁיָא בֵּין עֵרָה בֵּין יְשֵׁנָה! לְעוֹלָם בְּשֶׁיֵּשׁ לָהּ וֶסֶת, וְכֵיוָן שֶׁתְּבָעָהּ — אֵין לְךָ בְּדִיקָה גְּדוֹלָה מִזּוֹ. אֲמַר לֵיהּ רַב פַּפָּא לְרָבָא: מַהוּ לְמֶעְבַּד כִּי הָא מַתְנִיתָא? א"ל

**רש"י**

כְּשִׁיעוּר וֶסֶת. מִיָּד לְאַחַר בְּעִילָה, בְּחַטָּאת, דְּאָמְרִינַן לְקַמָּן בְּפ"ב (דף יד.) נִמְצָא עַל סָדִין שֶׁלָּהּ אוֹתִיּוֹם, כְּלוֹמַר, מִיָּד לְאַחַר בְּעִילָה – חַיָּיבִין בְּקָרְבָּן, דְּוַדַּאי דָּם הֲוָה בִּשְׁעַת בִּיאָה. לִבְדִיקָה. לְחוֹרִין וְלִסְדָקִין. הִילְכָּךְ, כְּשִׁיעוּר וֶסֶת לָא מַשְׁכַּחַת לָהּ. לְשַׁמָּשׁ. אֵבֶר. וְעֵד. סָדִין שֶׁמְּקַנַּחַת בּוֹ. לְקִינּוּחַ. מִבַּחוּץ. אִם בְּקִינּוּחַ מָצְאָה דָּם בְּכַשִּׁיעוּר הַזֶּה – חַיָּיבִין חַטָּאת, אֲבָל אִם בִּבְדִיקָתָהּ מָצְאָה – כְּבָר אָרַךְ הַשִּׁיעוּר, שֶׁהֲרֵי לֹא בְּצַד הַמַּשְׁקוֹף עוֹמֵד אֶלָּא בְּיָדָהּ אוֹחַזְתּוֹ, וְיֵשׁ כָּאן שִׁיעוּר עוֹדֵף כְּדֵי הֲבָאָה מִיָּדָהּ לַמַּשְׁקוֹף, וְאָשָׁם תָּלוּי אִיכָּא וְלֹא חַטָּאת. מַהוּ שֶׁתְּקַנֵּחַ. אִשָּׁה שֶׁאֵינָהּ עֲסוּקָה בְּטָהֳרוֹת מִי בָּעֲיָא קִינּוּחַ לְאַחַר תַּשְׁמִישׁ כְּשִׁיעוּר וֶסֶת, לֵידַע אִם תִּמְצָא דָּם, וִיהֵא בַּעְלָהּ חַיָּיב חַטָּאת. מַהוּ שֶׁתִּבְדּוֹק. בְּדִיקָה מַמָּשׁ. בְּאָשָׁם תָּלוּי. דְּאָמְרִינַן לְקַמָּן (שם.): נִמְצָא עַל שֶׁלָּהּ לְאַחַר זְמַן יוֹתֵר מִכַּשִּׁיעוּר וֶסֶת – חַיָּיבִין בְּאָשָׁם תָּלוּי, דְּסָפֵק הֲוָה דָּם בִּשְׁעַת בִּיאָה סָפֵק בָּא לְאַחַר מִכָּאן. א"כ. שֶׁמַּצְרִיכָהּ לִבְדּוֹק אַחַר בִּיאָה. לִבּוֹ נוֹקְפוֹ. קוֹדֶם בִּיאָה, וְהָא דִּתְנַן לְקַמָּן (שם.): דֶּרֶךְ בְּנוֹת יִשְׂרָאֵל מְשַׁמְּשׁוֹת בִּשְׁנֵי עֵדִים – בָּעֲסוּקוֹת בְּטָהֳרוֹת. וְזֶהוּ עֵדֶן שֶׁל צְנוּעוֹת. כְּלוֹמַר, מִדַּת חֲסִידוּת שָׁנוּ כָּאן, וְלָאו חִיּוּבָא הוּא, דְּאָמְרִינַן בְּפֶרֶק שֵׁנִי (שם.): הַצְּנוּעוֹת מְתַקְּנוֹת לָהֶן שְׁלִישִׁי לְתַקֵּן אֶת הַבַּיִת, זֶהוּ עֵדֶן, אַלִּפְנֵי תַּשְׁמִישׁ קָאֵי. אֵין בּוֹדֶקֶת בּוֹ. לִפְנֵי תַּשְׁמִישׁ אַחֵר, לְפִי שֶׁמְּטוּנָּף וְכֵהֶה מַרְאִית לִיבּוּנוֹ בִּבְדִיקָה רִאשׁוֹנָה, וְשׁוּב אֵין נִרְאֵית בּוֹ טִיפָּה כְּחַרְדָּל. יֵשׁ לָהּ וֶסֶת לָא בָּעֲיָא בְּדִיקָה. בִּתְמִיָּה. וְהָא קָתָנֵי מַתְנִיתִין בְּיֵשׁ לָהּ וֶסֶת, דְּבָעֲיָא בְּדִיקָה, כֵּיוָן דַּעֲסוּקָה בְּטָהֳרוֹת. וּלְקַמָּן פָּרֵיךְ: לִישַׁנֵּי לֵיהּ, הָא בְּשֶׁאֵינָהּ עֲסוּקָה בְּטָהֳרוֹת? וּמְשַׁנֵּי: קָסָבַר שְׁמוּאֵל כִּי אֵינָהּ עֲסוּקָה, אֲפִילּוּ אֵין לָהּ וֶסֶת – לָא בָּעֲיָא בְּדִיקָה לְבַעְלָהּ, הוֹאִיל וְאֵינָהּ עֲסוּקָה בְּטָהֳרוֹת. עֵרָה. דַּחֲזְיָא לַעֲסוּקֵי בְּטָהֳרוֹת, בָּעֲיָא בְּדִיקָה לְבַעְלָהּ. אִי נַמִי: דְּלֵיכָּא טִירְחָא לְעוּרָהּ, אֲבָל יְשֵׁנָה – אִיכָּא לְעָרָא, וְלָא אַטְרְחוּהָ רַבָּנַן. אִי נַמִי: יְשֵׁנָה, דְּלָא חֲזְיָא לְטָהֳרוֹת, אֲפִילּוּ רְגִילָה לַעֲסוֹק בְּטָהֳרוֹת – לָא בָּעֲיָא בְּדִיקָה. לְטָהֳרוֹת בָּעֲיָא בְּדִיקָה. כְּלוֹמַר, הָעֲסוּקָה בְּטָהֳרוֹת בָּעֲיָא בְּדִיקָה, אֲפִילּוּ לְבַעְלָהּ. לְבַעְלָהּ לָא בָּעֲיָא בְּדִיקָה. הֵיכָא דְּאֵינָהּ עֲסוּקָה. אֵין לָהּ וֶסֶת אֲפִילּוּ לְבַעְלָהּ. גְּרֵידָא, דְּאֵינָהּ עֲסוּקָה בְּטָהֳרוֹת – בָּעֲיָא בְּדִיקָה. כָּל לְבַעְלָהּ. בְּלָא טָהֳרוֹת. לָא בָּעֲיָא בְּדִיקָה. אֲפִילּוּ אֵין לָהּ וֶסֶת. הִילְכָּךְ, הָא דְּאָמַר שְׁמוּאֵל: אֲסוּרָה לְשַׁמֵּשׁ עַד שֶׁתִּבְדּוֹק – בָּעֲסוּקָה [בְּטָהֳרוֹת] קָאֵי, וְהַיְינוּ דְּאָמַר לְעֵיל וְאוֹקִימְנָא בָּעֲסוּקָה בְּטָהֳרוֹת. כֵּיוָן שֶׁתְּבָעָהּ. לְתַשְׁמִישׁ. אֵין לְךָ בְּדִיקָה גְּדוֹלָה מִזּוֹ. דְּאִי לָא קִים לָהּ דִּטְהוֹרָה הִיא, הֲוָה בָּדְקָה. וּבְדִיקָה דְּקָאָמַר שְׁמוּאֵל לְעֵיל, בִּתְבִיעָה סַגִּי. וְלִבִּי מְגַמְגֵּם. כִּי הָא מַתְנִיתָא. (א) בָּעֲיָא בְּדִיקָה, אוֹ תְּבִיעָה. סוֹדָנִי.

**תוספות**

בעי ר' זירא אשה מהו שתבדוק. פי': לפני תשמיש. לבו נוקפו ופורש. פר"ח: כיון דרואה אשתו בודקת, מחשב שאם לא הרגישה – לא היתה בודקת, לפי שיודעת שחכמים לא תקנו לבדוק. כדי לחייב בעלה חטאת. הכא נמי הוה מצי למיבעי: מהו שתבדוק קודם תשמיש, ותניח העד עד הבקר, כדי לחייב בעלה חטאת. אלא דכבר השיב לו: שאם תבדוק לפני תשמיש, לבו נוקפו ופורש. צנוע לא מיקרי רשע לא מיקרי. בתמיה. וא"ת: בריש כתובות (דף ג:) דאמר: משום צנועות ומשום פרוצות, כיון דקרי להו "צנועות", הנהו דלא עבדי הכי, אמאי קרי להו "פרוצות"? וי"ל: דהתם קרי להו "צנועות" – כדאמרינן התם: זמנין דלא אניס, וסברה דאניס. ואע"ג שבדין היה לה לתלות שאין אניס, דרוב העולם אינן אנוסים. ופרוצות – משום דזימנין דאנוס, פירוש: פעמים דיודעת שהוא אנוס, ואמרה דלא אנוס. ול"ג התם "וסברה". אשה שאין לה וסת אסורה לשמש עד שתבדוק. ובעסוקה בטהרות איירי. וא"ת: מאי קמ"ל, מתניתין היא (לעיל יא.) ובשעה שהיא עוברת לשמש את ביתה! וליכא למימר: דאתא לאשמועינן דאע"ג דאין לה וסת, דמותר לקיימה על ידי בדיקה כר"ח בן אנטיגנוס. וכן פירש רש"י לקמן, דהלשון משמע דלא בא להשמיענו היתרא, אלא להשמיענו שצריכה בדיקה? וי"ל: דקמ"ל באין לה וסת, דאפילו ישנה – צריכה בדיקה. בין ישנות. פי': דליכא איסור נדות, אבל אסור לבא על הישנה, כדאמר בנדרים ,ב] *(כ:) א"נ: הכא לא לגמרי בישנה איירי, אלא אינה ערה כל כך שתדע להשיב אם היא טהורה אם לאו. שמואל במאי מוקי לה. וא"ת: ולוקמה באינה עסוקה בטהרות? ויש לומר: דדייק מלישנא יתירא דקתני "נשיהם להם בחזקת טהרה", ואמאי איצטריך תו למיתני "ובאין ושוהים עמהם", אלא לגלויי דאיירי דעסוקה בטהרות. ובפ"ב (לקמן דף טו.) דקתני "כל הנשים בחזקת טהרה", וקתני בתר הכי "והבאין מן הדרך נשיהם להם בחזקת טהרה", וקתני תרתי, אע"ג דאינה עסוקה בטהרות איירי, התם אשמועינן: דאין לחלק בין באין מן הדרך לבני העיר. וא"ת: בלא שמואל תקשי מתניתין דמצרכת בדיקה בעסוקה בטהרות אברייתא דהכא! וי"ל: דפריך לשמואל אפילו בישנה, באין לה וסת, אבל מתני' לא מיירי בישנה. וכן פי' רשב"ם. [א"נ: ממתני' ה"מ לחוקי ולאוקומי באין לה וסת ודיה שעתה לא קאי אלא אצריכה להיות בודקת ותו לא, אע"ג דפשטא דמתניתין ביש לה וסת, כדפריך לעיל: והא מתניתין ביש לה וסת עסקינן]. כיון שתבעה. פירוש: כיון שבא מן הדרך, מפייסה ותובעה לתשמיש, ואי חזיא כבר – רמיא אנפשה שהרגישה בשעת ראייה, וזוכרת. אבל אם לא בא מן הדרך – אסור בערה, לפי שאינו מאריך בפיוס של תשמיש, אלא בא עליה מיד, ולא רמיא אנפשה לאזכורי שהרגישה. מהו למעבד כי הא מתניתא. פי' רש"י: כי הא מתניתא דבעיא בדיקה או תביעה. וקשה: דבערה דוקא מצריך בדיקה, ואם כן מאי קא מהדר ליה: דמגניא באפיה, דבתביעה לא מגניא באפיה? ועוד: אי לבעלה גרידא קבעי, כדמשמע דלגבי בעל היה שואל, הא פשיטא, דאמר לעיל (דף יא:) כל לבעלה – לא בעיא בדיקה. וגם אין להחמיר לבדוק, דא"כ לבו נוקפו ופורש, כדאמר לעיל. ואי בעסוקה בטהרות קבעי, פשיטא שצריכה בדיקה, כדתנן "ובשעה שהיא עוברת לשמש ביתה" כו'. ותו: למה תולה בעייתו בברייתא זו, כיון דמתניתין נמי מצרכה בדיקה לטהרות? ונראה לפרש: "מהו למעבד כי הא מתניתא" דלא מצרכה מידי בישנה, דשמא אף לבעלה גרידא צריך להקילה ולתובעה. והא דאמרינן לעיל, דאפילו באין לה וסת לא בעיא בדיקה לבעלה א) בישנה, מ"מ דילמא תביעה בעיא. אי נמי: לעיל איירי כשהוא בעיר, דאם איתא דהיתה טמאה – הוה אמרה ליה קודם לכן. אבל בבא מן הדרך, איכא למיחש. ומתני' דפ"ב (לקמן טו.) דבאין מן הדרך נשיהם להם בחזקת טהרה, איכא נמי למימר דהיינו דלא בעו בדיקה, אבל בעו תביעה. אי נמי: בערות דווקא. אי נמי: ביש לה וסת.

א) גי' רש"י אפילו וע"ש

אמר

**תוספי הרא"ש**

כדי לחייב בעלה חטאת. ע"כ סמוך לוסתה איירי דשלא בסמוך לוסתה לא מיחייב חטאת דאנוס הוא כדאמרינן בפ"ב דשבועות. וא"כ תימה מאי קא מהדר ליה א"כ לבו נוקפו ופורש והלא חייב הוא לפרוש סמוך לוסתה כדאיתא התם. ודוחק לומר שמתוך כך יפרוש שלא בשעת וסתה. ונ"ל דלאו דוקא קאמר לחייב בעלה חטאת. אלא כלומר להיות (באונס) [באיסור] חטאת היכא דלא אניס: עד שבודקות בו לפני תשמיש זה כו'. אין זה צנועות דתנן לקמן פרק כל היד והצנועות מתקנות להן עד שלישי לתקן את הבית אלא צניעות אחרת וגדול מהך דלקמן דאילו צנועות דהכא עד שבודקות בו לפני תשמיש זה אין בודקות בו לפני תשמיש אחר וצנועות דלקמן היינו שנזהרות דוקא א) במעת דלאחר תשמיש דעד שבודקות בו לאחר תשמיש לפי שמלוכלך בשכבת זרע אבל עד שלפני תשמיש זה בודקות בו לפני תשמיש אחר ולא איכפת להו. ותי' לי אמאי אמר ר' ינאי זו היא עידן של צנועות אמתני' דבשעה שהיא עוברת לשמש את ביתה הוה מצי למימר נמי אבדיקות שחרית וערבית. צנועות עד שבודקות בו שחרית אין בודקת בו ערבית. ואיכא למימר דאפילו צנועות לא איכפת להו בהם אבל בעד שלפני תשמיש איכא למיחש שמחמת חימוד רוב התאוה הוריעה כבר ומלוכלך קצת: גופא אמר רבי זירא. ל"ג גופא דהא מפסיק במתני' ובשעה שהיא עוברת לשמש את ביתה: אי בשיש לה וסת קשיא ערה. תי' מאי קא קשיא ליה דלמא הך ברייתא איירי באינה עסוקה בטהרות. ותי' ר"ת מדקתני חמריו ופועליו הבאין מבית האבל ומבית המשתה ואלו רגילין לעסוק בטהרות. חמרים שרגילין להוליך תבואה מעיר לעיר. ופועלין העושין בטהרות אצל בעלי בתים. הבאים מבית האבל להברותו. ומבית המשתה של חתן שמסובין שם אוכלי טהרות. ומי' קשה אדפריך לשמואל מהך ברייתא תיקשי ממתני' אהך ברייתא דקתני ובשעה שהיא עוברת לשמש את ביתה אלמא דערה בעיא בדיקה. וי"ל דלמתני' ניחא דלא תני לא ערה ולא ישנה שמעינן מינה דלא שייך לחלק לגבי טהרות בין ערה לישנה הלכך איכא לאוקומי מתני' בעסוקה בטהרות וברייתא בשאינה עסוקה אבל שמואל שהזכיר לענין טהרות ערה וישנה משמע דאיירי [הברייתא] לענין טהרות כלומר בין ערה הראויה לעסוק בטהרות בין ישנה שאינה ראויה לעסוק בטהרות. ודלא כאותם המפרשים דישינה לא אטרחוה רבנן: כיון שתבעה אין לך בדיקה גדולה מזו. שכן דרכו לבא מן הדרך לתבוע ולרצות ולפיים ורמיא אנפשה ואי חזיא ארגשה והויא כמו בדיקה. אבל בשאין לה וסת אפילו ישנה בעיא בדיקה וישנה לא שייך תביעה הלכך אוקמה בשיש לה וסת. ותימה כיון דתביעה הויא כבדיקה א"כ בסיפא דהניחה בחזקת טמאה תביעה נמי הויא כמו אמרה לו טהורה אני א"כ מאי איכא בין רישא לסיפא. וצ"ל בסיפא אישנות קאי: מהו למיעבד כי הא מתניתא. תי' מאי קא בעי הא ליכא מאן דפליג אהך ברייתא. וי"ל דמיבעיא ליה לענין בעלה ובאינה עסוקה בטהרות דהא רב פפא ורבא ורב כהנא בבבל היו עומדין שאינן עסוקין בטהרות ומיבעיא ליה אם יש להחמיר ולהצריכה תביעה דנהי דאינה יכולה לבדוק כדאמרינן לעיל דא"כ לבו נוקפו ופורש. מיהו אם יוכל להחמיר להצריך תביעה וא"ל לא דאי מצרכינן לה תביעה א"כ מיגניא

א) נראה דצ"ל היינו שנזהרות דוקא בעד שלאחר תשמיש שלא לבדוק בו ג"כ קודם תשמיש לפי שעד שלאחר תשמיש הוא מלוכלך בשכבת זרע וכו'.

**עין משפט נר מצוה**

קו א ב מיי' פ"ד מהל' איסורי ביאה הל' ט' ועי' בהשגות סמג לאוין קיא טוש"ע י"ד סימן קפד סעיף א ובהג"ה וסימן קפו סעיף א:

קז ג מיי' שם סמג שם טוש"ע י"ד סימן קפד סעיף א ובהג"ה וסימן קפו סעיף א לדעת הרמב"ם:

קח ד מיי' פ"ד מהלכות איסורי ביאה הלכה טז וע"ש ופ"ח שם הל' ג סמג שם טור ש"ע שם סעיף ב:

קט ה מיי' שם הלכה טז וע' בהשגות ובפ"ד מהלכות מטמאי משכב ומושב הלכה ז ובהשגות שם ובכ"מ סמג שם טוש"ע י"ד סי' קפו סעיף ב:

קי ו מיי' פ"ד מהלכות איסורי ביאה הל' ט סמג שם טוש"ע י"ד סימן קפד סעיף א [וברב אלפס שבועות פ"ב דף רנ:]

קיא ז מיי' שם:

[אין זה בנדרים ולא בשאר דוכתי בש"ס רק במס' כלה איתא עשרה הם כממזרים בני אימה בני שיכורה וכו' וי"א אף בני ישינה והרמב"ם בהל' דעות פ"ה הל' ד כתב ולא תהי' ישינה ע"ש ומהתימה שלא נזכר דין זה בש"ע א"ח סימן ר"מ ובאה"ע סי' כ"ה וגם האחרונים העלימו עין בסימנים האלו מאזהרה זו והנה הב"י על טור י"ד סימן קפ"ד והב"ח והש"ך העתיקו דברי תוס' זו ככתבם וכלשונם כדאמר בנדרים ותקפו משנתם עליהם במחילה מכבודם הגשא ומה דאי' בנדרים כ: איגו ענין על הישינה כלל ע"ש]

**מסורת הש"ס**

לעיל ג: ע"ש [לקמן לה:]

[לקמן יד:]

[בערוך ערך עדן כ' פי' לשון עת וזמן לפי שמצאה בגי' עידן בו"ה אבל לפי גי' הספרים שלנו הוא לשון עד שבודקו' בו ועי' רש"ל]

**הגהות הב"ח**

(א) רש"י ד"ה כי הא מתני' אישנות קאי מי בעיא כצ"ל ונ"ב ס"א:

**הגהות מהר"ב רנשבורג**

א] גמ' א"כ לבו נוקפו ופורש. נ"ב עיין סדרי טהרה סימן קצ ס"ק ס"ז דף לו ע"ב בד"ה וע"פ הדברים האלה וכו' ושם מבואר מה שיל"ד בזה יעוש"ה ודו"ק: ב] תוס' ד"ה בין ישנות וכו' כדאמרינן בנדרים דף כ ע"ב. נ"ב יעו"ש בנדרים דף כ ע"ב דחשיב תשע בני מדות וכן קתני להו במסכת כלה ומוסיף התם וי"א אף בני ישינה יעוש"ה ואולי בגמרא דנדרים שלפני התוספות היה כתוב נמי הך ויש אומרים אף בני ישינה:

קיב א מיי' פ"ד מהל' איסורי ביאה הל' טז וע' בהשגות ובמ"מ סמג לאוין קיא ועשין רמג טוש"ע י"ד סימן קפו סעיף ב:

קיג ב ג עי' במיי' פ"ד מהל' איסורי ביאה הלכה טז ובהשגות ובפ"ד מהל' מטמאי משכב ומושב הלכה ז ובהשגות ובמ"מ ובכ"מ טוש"ע י"ד סי' קפו סעיף ב:

א"ל: *סודני, לא, דמגניא באפיה. אמר רב כהנא: שאלתינהו לאינשי ביתיה דרב פפא ודרב הונא בריה דרב יהושע, כי אתו רבנן מבי רב מצרכי לכו בדיקה? ואמרו לי: לא. ולישיילינהו לדידהו! דילמא אינהו קא מחמירי אנפשייהו. ת"ר: אשה שאין לה וסת – אסורה לשמש, ואין לה לא כתובה ולא פירות ולא מזונות ולא בלאות, ויוציא ולא מחזיר עולמית, *דברי ר"מ. רבי חנינא בן אנטיגנוס אומר: [א]משמשת בשני עדים, הן עותה הן תקנתה. משום אבא חנן אמרו: אוי לו לבעלה. אסורה לשמש – דילמא מקלקלת ליה. ואין לה כתובה – כיון דלא חזיא לביאה לית לה כתובה, ולא פירות, ולא מזונות, ולא בלאות – תנאי כתובה ככתובה דמו. "ויוציא ולא יחזיר עולמית" פשיטא! לא צריכא – דהדרה ואתקנה, מהו דתימא ליהדרה, קמ"ל דזימנין דאזלא ומנסבא ומתקנא, ואמר: "אילו הייתי יודע שכך היה – אפילו הייתם נותנין לי מאה מנה לא הייתי מגרשה", ונמצא גט בטל ובניה ממזרין. "משום אבא חנן אמרו: אוי לו לבעלה". איכא דאמרי: לר"מ אמר ליה – דבעי לאגבויה כתובתה. איכא דאמרי: לרבי חנינא בן אנטיגנוס קא"ל – דמקלקלת ליה. אמר רב יהודה, אמר שמואל: הלכה כר' חנינא בן אנטיגנוס. ובמאי? אי בעסוקה בטהרות – הא אמרה שמואל חדא זימנא! ואי בשאינה עסוקה בטהרות – הא אמר: כל לבעלה – לא בעיא בדיקה, *דא"ר זירא, א"ר אבא בר ירמיה, אמר שמואל: [ב]אשה שאין לה וסת – אסורה לשמש עד שתבדוק, ואוקימנא לה – [ג]בעסוקה בטהרות! מאן דמתני הא, לא מתני הא.§

## הדרן עלך שמאי אומר

סודני. תלמיד חכם, על שם (תהלים כה) "סוד ה' ליראיו". לא בעיא בדיקה. דכי מצטרכא לה בדיקה – מיגניא באפיה. *ל"א: מהו למעבד כי הא מתניתא, דלא בעיא בדיקה. דאיהו ס"ל דאין מן הדרך לאו דוקא, וכ"ש יושב בביתו. אמר ליה: סודני. רב פפא מטיל שכר הוה כדאמר ב"איזהו נשך" (ב"מ דף סה.): שיכרא לא פסיד, ומטיל שכר נקרא "סודני", כדאמרינן ב"ערבי פסחים" (פסחים דף קיג.): תמרי *בחלוזך, לבי סודנא רהוט. לא מיגניא באפיה. בתמיה. אם אתה מצריכה בדיקה, והלא תמאס ותתגנה בפניו! דלמא אינהו מחמירי אנפשייהו. ומצריכים בדיקה לנשותיהן, ומורים לאחרים היתר כהילכתא דאוקימנא דלא בעיא בדיקה. לפיכך שאל לנשותיהן, דאיהו נמי בעי לאחמורי כוותייהו. לישנא אחרינא: אינהו מחמירי אנפשייהו, ומורים דצריכה בדיקה להחמיר, והם אין מצריכין נשותיהן לבדוק. ושיבוש הוא, דלאו היינו מחמירי אנפשייהו אלא מקילי אנפשייהו ומחמירי לאחרים, וחלילה לעשות כן. ולא פירות. שאוכל בעלה מנכסי מלוג שלה, ולא אמרינן: כיון דאין לה כתובה הימנו, אישתכח דלאו אשתו היא, וליהדר לה פירי דאכל. ולא מזונות. אם הלך למדינת הים קודם שגירשה, אין בית דין פוסקים לה מזונות מנכסיו. ולא בלאות. כגון, אם הכניסה לו בגדים בשומת כתובתה, ואמרינן בכתובות (דף עט.) עיילא ליה גלימא – מכסי בה ואזיל עד דבלי. וזו כשמגרשה, אע"ג שקלת הבלאות קיימין – אין מחזירין לה. בשני עדים. סדינין. עותה. אי חזאי. תקנתה. אי לא חזאי. אוי לבעלה. כדמפרש לקמן. מזונות. תנאי כתובה הן: "את תהא יתבא בביתי, ומיתזנא מנכסי". ובלאות נמי משומת כתובה הן, ששמו לה מה שהיא מכנסת, והוא מקבלן עליו לשלם לכשיימות או לכשיגרשנה. כמו שאנו כותבין: "ודין נדוניא דהנעלת ליה" וכו'. ובניה ממזרים. הילכך, אומרים לו: "הוי יודע שהמגרש את אשתו משום וסת – לא יחזיר, ואפילו היא חוזרת וקובעת", ותו לא מצי למימר: "אילו הייתי יודע שכך" כו', שהרי התרו בו, וגמר בדעתו וגרשה. והכי נמי אמרינן גבי מוציא את אשתו משום שם רע או משום נדר, במס' גיטין (דף מו.). דבעי לאגבויה כתובתה. והכי קאמר ליה: "את אמרת: אין לה כתובה. ואנא סבירא לי: אוי לו לבעלה, שנחסר ממונו, דודאי יש לה כתובה". דמקלקלה ליה. את אמרת: משמשת בעדים אוי לבעלה, דדילמא לא חזיא לפני תשמיש, וחזיא בשעת תשמיש. הא אמר שמואל חדא זימנא. כדמותיב ואזיל מדר' אבא בר ירמיה, ומינה שמעינן דס"ל לשמואל דעסוקה בטהרות – בעיא בדיקה לבעלה, ושאינה עסוקה בטהרות – לא בעיא בדיקה. מאן דמתני הא לא מתני הא. לעולם בעסוקה, ודקשיא לך: תרתי למה לי? – רב יהודה דמתני הא משמיה דשמואל לא מתני הא דר' אבא, ורבי אבא לא מתני הא דרב יהודה. ואי קשיא: הא רב יהודה נמי אמרה, דאמר רב יהודה לעיל גבי מתני' דקתני לעיל: "ובשעה שהיא עוברת לשמש את ביתה", ואמר רב יהודה אמר שמואל: "לא שנו אלא בעסוקה" כו' – לאו פירכא היא, דרב יהודה לא אשמועינן התם בעסוקה מידי. דממתני' הוה שמעינן בין עסוקה בין אינה עסוקה, ואתא רב יהודה למימר ואשמועינן משמיה דשמואל דשאינה עסוקה לא בעיא בדיקה, והכא אשמועינן דהלכה כר"ח וכאותה משנה דעסוקה בטהרות בעיא בדיקה, והכא עיקר. ואית דמפרשי כי האי לישנא: והאמר שמואל חדא זימנא, לעיל [א] דאוקימנא למתני' דקתני: "משמשת בעדים" בעסוקה בטהרות! מאן דמתני הא כו' לעולם בשאינה עסוקה, ודקשיא לך דרבי אבא בר ירמיה אהא דרב יהודה, לא תקשי, אמוראי נינהו אליבא דשמואל. וטועין בדבר, דא"כ קשיא דרב יהודה אדרב יהודה, דהא איהו גופיה אמר דשאינה עסוקה לא בעיא בדיקה.

## הדרן עלך שמאי אומר

אמר ליה מגניא באפיה. פירוש: אם צריך להקילה עד שתתיישב דעתה להשיב אם טהורה היא אם לאו. מי מצריכי לכו בדיקה. פירוש: להקיץ אתכם עד שתתיישב דעתכם להשיב אם טהורה היא, וכגון שהיו באין מדי שבת או מדי חדש, אבל לא לזמן מרובה, כדאמר לקמן (דף טו.) והוא שבא תוך ימי עונתה, אבל יותר – יש לחוש שמא ראתה בינתיים. לא פירות. נכסי מלוג שאכל, ולא דין פירות, דהיינו: פרקונה. ואיירי בין הכיר בה ובין לא הכיר בה. דבלא הכיר בה – הוי מקח טעות, ומחלה ליה, דניחא לה דניפוק עלה שמא דאישות, כדאמרינן גבי אילונית בפרק "איזהו נשך" (ב"מ דף סז.) ובהכיר בה נמי אין לה כלום, כדאמר ב"יש מותרות" (יבמו' פה:) בשניו' לעריות: שהיא *מרגילתו, משום דזרעה כשר. כיון דלא חזיא לביאה לית לה כתובה. אע"ג דאיכא מאן דאמר בפ' "בנות כותים" (לקמן דף לט.) אפילו לר"מ: אשה שאין לה וסת מותרת לשמש בי"א שבין נדה לנדה, לפי שהיא מסולקת מדמים, מ"מ צריך לגרשה, דילמא מקלקלת ליה בשאר יומי. וכיון דאסור לקיימה, אין לה כתובה. וכל זמן שלא גרשה, מותר לשמש באותן י"א יום. ולאבא חנן, דאית לה כתובה, היינו משום דמותרת לשמש בי"א יום, כיון דחזיא לביאה, אע"פ שגזרו חכמים עליו לגרשה – לא תפסיד בכך כתובתה. אילו הייתי יודע שכך הוא. וא"ת: והא כיון דאינה תובעת כתובתה, לא מצי להוציא לעז, כדאמר בפרק "הבא על יבמתו" (יבמות דף סה.) גבי "נשאת לשלישי ולא היו לה בנים, ונשאת לרביעי והיו לה בנים" כו'. וקאמר: אומרים לה "שתיקותיך יפה ליך מדבוריך", שלא יוציא לעז ויאמר "אילו הייתי יודע" כו'. ופריך: אי איהי שתקה, אנן מי שתקינן? ומשני: השתא הוא דבריאת. וי"ל: דהכא בקל ע"י סממנים תחזיר לוסתה, ואיכא לעז טפי. ולא דמי לעקרה, דאין לה רפואה בקל לבא לידי בנים, ומשמיא הוא דמסו לה. והר"ר שלמה מדריו"ש תירץ: דהכא איכא למיחש דמתקנא וקבעה לה וסת, כמו שהיה סמוך לגרושין, דאיגלאי מילתא דבעוד שהיא תחתיו איברית ולא השתא. והכא לא שייך למיפרך: "אנן מי שתקינן?", כיון דלא שייך כאן לומר: "השתא הוא דאיברית", דכיון שאומרים לו: "הוי יודע" כו', תו ליכא לעז. וכן לר"י ב"השולח" (גיטין דף מו: ושם) גבי אילונית, לא שייך למפרך, אע"ג דאינו כ"א חשש אילונית. דודאי אילונית אין לה רפואה, ולא שייך "השתא הוא דאיברית", דכיון שאומרים לו: "הוי יודע" – מגרשה לגמרי. [אבל אם תובעת כתובתה, יכול לומר: "אדעתא דהכי לא גירשתיך"] וגבי נשאת לרביעי, אין נ"ל "הוי יודע", דאינו יכול להוציא לעז, דאיכא למימר: "השתא הוא דאיברית". ואי לאו טעמא ד"השתא הוא דאיברית", אפילו לרבנן (ב) לא חיישינן לקלקול גבי אילונית, לא הוה שתקינן. משום דכיון דכבר גרשה ראשון ושני – ניכר שגם השלישי שגרשה, משום בנים מגרשה, ואיכא לעז, אי לאו טעמא ד"השתא הוא דאיברית". דמתני הא לא מתני הא. פירש רש"י: רב יהודה דפסיק הלכה כר"ח דאיירי בעסוקה בטהרות, לא מתני ההיא דר' אבא בר' ירמיה. והקשה רש"י: הא רב יהודה גופיה אמר משמיה דשמואל: לא שנו אלא לטהרות! ותירץ: דהתם, לא אשמועינן רב יהודה אלא דלבעלה לא בעיא בדיקה. וא"ת: והא מתני' ביש לה וסת, אבל אין לה וסת – איכא למימר דאסורה כר"מ, א"כ שמואל דאוקמא אפילו באין לה וסת, משמע דסבר כר"ח בן אנטיגנוס! וי"ל: דמתני' משמע שפיר גם באין לה וסת, וה"ק: אפילו אותה שדיה שעתה משמשת בעדים, וכ"ש שאין לה וסת. וא"ת: ואמאי לא משני הכא, דחדא מכלל חברתה איתמר, כדלעיל? וי"ל: דלעיל אינו בפירוש בדברי רבי אבא בר ירמיה דלבעלה לא בעיא בדיקה, ואף רבי אבא לא חילק לר' זירא בין יש לה וסת לאין לה וסת בין טהרות לבעלה, משום דשמיע לה מכלל דרב יהודה דלבעלה לא בעיא בדיקה. אבל הכא פירש בהדיא משמיה דשמואל דאין לה וסת מותר לקיימה אם תבדוק. וכן בפסקא דהלכה כר"ח אין להקשות: דמה צריך לפסוק כר"ח, כיון דבעסוקה בטהרות איירי, וכי הילכתא למשיחא? דהא בא"י לעולם היו עסוקים בטהרות, כדאמר לעיל (דף ו.) חבריא מדכן בגלילא. הדרן עלך שמאי אומר

### תוספי הרא"ש

מיגניא באפיה שיזכור דם נדותה שהוא דבר מגונה לאשה כדאמרינן היא מליאה דם והכל רצין אחריה: ולא פירות. פרש"י פירות שאכל לא ישלם לה ומדקאמר בתר הכי ולא פירות משום דתנאי כתובה ככתובה דמי משמע דפירות היינו פרקונה שהוא תחת פירות שהוא תנאי כתובה אם אישתבאי אפרוקינך: ולא בלאות פרש"י בלאותיה שהן קיימין. וקשה דהוה ליה למימר ולא בלאות קיימין כדאמרינן בסוף אלמנה ניזונת ועוד תנן התם הממאנת והשניה כו' ולא בלאות ודייק בגמ' אי דאיתנהו אידי ואידי שקלא אלמא בלאות סתם אינן קיימין: ולא מזונות תנאי כתובה ככתובה דמי. פרש"י את יתבת בביתי ומיתזנת מנכסי ולא הוה ליה לפרושי הכי דהרי במזונות אלמנה קאי. אלא ואנא אפלח ואוקיר ואיזון ואפרנס כו': ונמצא גט בטל. לאו דוקא גט בטל דהא לא אתני על מנת אני מגרשיך שאין לך וסת ואם תתרפת (לא) יהא בטל הגט. אלא חיישינן שמא יוציא לעז על הגט דאי הוה מצי לאהדורה הוה יוציא לעז על הגט שלא גרשה אלא בשביל שלא היה לה וסת ויהיה סבור שמותר להחזירה אע"פ שנשאת דלא הוי אלא כזנות בעלמא לפי שהגט אינו גט הלכך אומר' לו שהמוציא את אשתו משום שאין לה וסת אינו יכול להחזירה וכיון שאינו יכול להחזירה לא יוציא לעז על הגט: ונמצא גט בטל. תימה היאך יוכל להוציא לעז נימא השתא הוא דברית כדמסיק בסוף הבא על יבמתו גבי נשאת לרביעי והיו לה בנים. י"ל דהתם באילונית אינו מצוי שתתרפא ולא היה מכנים עצמו לאותו ספק מלהניח מלגרש שמא תתרפא [א]לפי שאינו יכול להוציא לעז על הגט ולומר אילו הייתי יודע שעתידה להתרפאות לא הייתי מגרשה. אבל הכא רגילות הוא שתתרפא ולחזור ולקבוע לה וסת הלכך היה יכול להוציא לעז ולומר אילו הייתי יודע שתתרפי כל כך במהרה לא הייתי מגרשך: דבעי לאגבויי כתובה כיון דחזיא לביאה מדאורייתא. א"כ משום דחזיא בימי זיבה דאיכא מאן דסבירא ליה הכי בסוף בנות כותים אפילו לרבי מאיר: הדרן עלך שמאי אומר

### הגהות הב"ח

(א) רש"י ד"ה מאן דמתני וכו' לעיל דאוקי למתני': (ב) תוס' ד"ה אילו וכו' אפילו לרבנן דלא חיישי לקלקול גבי:

עיין רש"ל שכתב דהאי ל"א אינו מלשון רש"י

[ברכות מד: מנחות עא. פסחים קיג.]

פירוש כלי שנותנין בו תמרים. רש"ל

[לקמן לט.]

[לעיל יא:]

[פי' הסיתו לעבירה]

א) נראה דצ"ל ולפיכך אינו יכול וכו'.

כל היד המרבה לבדוק, בנשים — משובחת, ובאנשים — תקצץ. § **גמ'** מ"ש נשים ומאי שנא אנשים? נשים לאו בנות הרגשה נינהו — משובחות, אנשים דבני הרגשה נינהו — תקצץ. אי הכי, מאי איריא מרבה? כי לא מרבה נמי! כי קתני "מרבה" — אנשים. תנא: בד"א — לענין שכבת זרע, אבל לענין זוב — אף הוא משובח כנשים. ואפי' לענין שכבת זרע, אם בא לבדוק בצרור או בחרס — בודק. ובמטלית לא? והתניא: בודק עצמו במטלית ובכל דבר שרוצה! כדאמר אביי: במטלית עבה, הכא נמי — במטלית עבה. והיכא איתמר דאביי? אהא, דתנן: היה אוכל בתרומה והרגיש שנזדעזעו איבריו — אוחז באמתו ובולע את התרומה. אוחז? והתניא, רבי אליעזר אומר: כל האוחז באמתו ומשתין — כאילו מביא מבול לעולם! אמר אביי: במטלית עבה. רבא אמר: אפילו תימא במטלית רכה, כיון דעקר — עקר. ואביי — חייש דלמא אתי לאוסופי, ורבא לא חייש דלמא אתי לאוסופי. ולא? והתניא: הא למה זה דומה — לנותן אצבע בעין, שכל זמן שאצבע בעין — עין מדמעת וחוזרת ומדמעת! ורבא — כל אחמומי והדר אחמומי, בשעתיה — לא שכיח. גופא, ר"א אומר: כל האוחז באמה ומשתין — כאילו מביא מבול לעולם. אמרו לו לרבי אליעזר: והלא נצוצות נתזין על רגליו, ונראה ככרות שפכה, ונמצא מוציא לעז על בניו שהן ממזרים! אמר להן: מוטב שיוציא לעז על בניו שהן ממזרים, ואל יעשה עצמו רשע שעה אחת לפני המקום. תניא אידך, אמר להן רבי אליעזר לחכמים: אפשר, יעמוד אדם במקום גבוה וישתין, או ישתין בעפר תיחוח, ואל יעשה עצמו רשע שעה אחת לפני המקום. הי אמר להו ברישא? אילימא קמייתא אמר להו ברישא, בתר דאמר להו איסורא הדר אמר להו תקנתא?! אלא, הא אמר להו ברישא. ואמרו ליה: אין לו מקום גבוה ועפר תיחוח מאי? אמר להן: מוטב שיוציא לעז על בניו, ואל יעשה עצמו רשע שעה אחת לפני המקום, וכל כך למה? מפני שמוציא שכבת זרע לבטלה. דא"ר יוחנן: כל המוציא שכבת זרע לבטלה — חייב מיתה, שנאמר: "וירע בעיני ה' (את) אשר עשה וימת גם אותו". רבי יצחק ורבי אמי אמרי: כאילו שופך דמים, שנאמר: "הנחמים באלים תחת כל עץ רענן שוחטי הילדים בנחלים תחת סעיפי הסלעים", אל תקרי "שוחטי" אלא "סוחטי". רב אסי אמר: כאילו עובד עבודה זרה, כתיב הכא: "תחת כל עץ רענן", וכתיב התם: "על ההרים הרמים ותחת כל עץ רענן". רב יהודה ושמואל הוו קיימי אאיגרא דבי כנישתא (א) דשף ויתיב בנהרדעא. אמר ליה רב יהודה לשמואל: צריך אני להשתין. א"ל שיננא, אחוז באמתך והשתן לחוץ. היכי עביד הכי? והתניא, ר"א אומר: כל האוחז באמתו ומשתין — כאילו מביא מבול לעולם! אמר אביי: עשאו כבולשת. דתנן: בולשת שנכנסה לעיר. בשעת שלום, חביות פתוחות — אסורות, סתומות — מותרות. בשעת מלחמה — אלו ואלו מותרות, לפי שאין להן פנאי לנסך. אלמא: דכיון דבעיתי — לא אתי לנסוכי, הכא נמי — כיון דבעיתי לא אתי להרהורי. והכא מאי ביעתותא איכא? איבעית אימא: ביעתותא דליליא ודאיגרא. ואיבעית אימא: ביעתותא דרביה. ואב"א: ביעתותא דשכינה. ואיבעית אימא: אימתא דמריה עליה, דקרי שמואל עליה: אין זה ילוד אשה. ואיבעית אימא: נשוי הוה, דאמר רב נחמן: אם היה נשוי — מותר. ואיבעית אימא: כי הא אורי ליה, דתני אבא בריה דרבי בנימין בר חייא: אבל מסייע בביצים מלמטה. ואיבעית אימא: כי הא אורי ליה, דאמר רבי אבהו, אמר רבי יוחנן: גבול יש לו, מעטרה ולמטה — מותר, מעטרה

**רש"י**

**כל** היד המרבה לבדוק. שבודקת תמיד שמא ראתה. בנשים משובחת. שמתוך כך לא אתי לידי ספק טומאה, ובעלה לא אתי לידי איסורא. ובאנשים. שבודק עצמו תדיר באמתו שמא יצא ממנו קרי. תקצץ. שמתחמם ומרגיש כשממשמש באמה, ומוליא שכבת זרע לבטלה. **גמ'** הרגשה. שמזדעזעין אבריו כשמתחמם, ורואה קרי. אנשים. "משובחת" דקתני קאי "מרבה", אבל אי"תקצץ" דאנשים — אפילו חדא זימנא. לענין זיבה. שיצא זוב ממנו, ורוצה לבדוק כדי למנות ראיותיו: שתים — לטומאה, ושלש — לקרבן. זוב דומה למי בצק של שעורים, ובא מבשר המת. ושכבת זרע בא מבשר החי, וקשורה כלובן ביצה שאינה מוזרת. בצרור. דבר קשה, אינו מחמם. במטלית עבה. קשה היא, ואינה מחממת. שנזדעזעו אבריו. שנעקר זרע מגופו. אוחז באמה. שלא יצא הזרע עד שיבלע את התרומה שבפיו. דתנן לקמן בפ' "יוצא דופן" (דף מ.): הזב ובעל קרי אין מטמאין עד שתצא טומאתן לחוץ. כאילו מביא מבול. שעבירה זו היתה בידם, דכתיב (בראשית ו): "כי השחית כל בשר", ואמרו: ברותחין קלקלו. כיון דעקר עקר. ומשום חמום דהשתא לא נפיק מידי. לא שכיח. וכי קתני "למה זה דומה" (ב) דתחילתו לא יצא אלא ע"י משמוש האבר, שאינו נעקר יחד, אלא כשהוא ממשמש יוצא מעט מעט והולך. אבל היכא דיצא מהרגשה ונעקר כולו כאחד, תו לא מוסיף. ניצוצות ניתזין. שאינו אוחז, ואינו מטיל למרחוק. כרות שפכה. סריס אין מימי רגליו עושים כיפה. איסורא. אסור לאחוז, ואפילו אי אפשר לו בענין אחר, אע"פ שמוליא לעז, כדקתני: מוטב שיוליא לעז כו'. תקנתא. ישתין על גבי עפר תיחוח, דמשמע דאי ליכא הני יאחוז באמה. הנחמים באלים. שמתחממים בעלי אילנות במדורות גדולים, כלומר, בעלי הנאות. באלים. כמו (שם לה) "תחת האלה". דשף ויתיב. שם מקום (ג) המובלע במלכות נהרדעא. מפי מורי הזקן. אחוז באמה. שלא יפלו מים על הגג. עשאוהו. לאו דרב יהודה. כבולשת. "בולשת" — חיל שמחפשין ובוזזין, כדמתרגמינן (שם לא) "ויחפש": "ובלש". דליליא. ומתיירא שמא יפול. דרביה. שמואל. דשכינה. שורה בבית הכנסת. אימתא דמריה. הקב"ה. ואפי' במקום אחר נמי שרי לדידיה. עטרה. שפה גבוהה המקפת את ראש הגיד.

**תוספות**

**כל** היד. באנשים תקצץ. ואם צריך לבדוק, יבדוק בצרור או בחרס, כדאמר בגמ' וא"ת: הא לקמן אמר דלמטה מעטרה מותר, והיינו בפי האמה, ושם הוא בודק עצמו! וי"ל: דגם למעלה לצד הגוף צריך לבדוק, שמא הלך שם טפת קרי. א"נ: אפי' מעטרה ולמטה לא שרי, אלא להשתין משום ניצוצות או משום בית הכנסת, אבל כדי לבדוק עצמו — לא.

**[נשים** דלאו בנות הרגשה נינהו. לר"ת דמפרש (יבמות יב:) "ג' נשים משמשות במוך" – היינו: צריכות, ושאר נשים מותרות משום [דלא] מיפקדא אפריה ורביה, י"ל: כיון דלאו בנות איסור הרגשה נינהו, אפילו הוו מרגישות. לפי' ר"ת קשה לר' יוחנן בן ברוקה, דתניא (שם דף סה:) על שניהם נאמר "פרו ורבו"! ועוד: נהי נמי דלא מפקדו אפ"ו, להשחית זרע הוקשו לאיש לכל עונשין שבתורה! וי"ל: דהיינו טעמא, שהנשים לעולם מזריעות בפנים, ושם הוא דרך להזריע, אבל אנשים מזריעים בחוץ, ואין דרך להזריע שם. ג"י].

**אוחז** והתניא רבי אליעזר אומר כו' – ואם תאמר: לימא הא דקאמר "אוחז ובולע" היינו למטה מעטרה, דשרי? וי"ל: אם יניח הזרע לבא עד פי האמה, שוב לא יוכל לעכבו. אי נמי: כיון שאוחז באמה בדוחק שלא יצא זרע, יש הרהור אפי' למטה מעטרה. וא"ת: ומאי פריך מר' אליעזר, והלא רבנן פליגי עליה ושרו! וכן לקמן מאי פריך אדרב יהודה מרבי אליעזר? וי"ל: דרבנן לא שרו אלא במשתין משום לעז ממזרות, אבל לצורך ד"א – אסרי. ורב יהודה נמי היה עומד במקום גבוה, דליכא ניצוצות, ולא היה אוחז אלא כדי שלא יפול מי רגלים על הכותל, ובהא לא שרו רבנן. אי נמי: לסוף הודו חכמים לדברי ר' אליעזר, מדאמר בפרק "כיצד מברכין" (ברכות דף מ.) אין מי רגלים כלין אלא בישיבה או בעפר תיחוח או במקום גבוה, והיינו כרבי אליעזר. אבל אוחז באמה לא קאמר, אע"ג דמסתמא כמו כן כלין. ולקמן בפירקין (דף טז.) שלש שנאתי, וחשיב "אוחז באמה ומשתין", ולא הוזכר שם רבי אליעזר*.

**והלא** ניצוצות ניתזין. וא"ת: וישפשף בידו, כדאמרי' בפ' "אמר להם הממונה" (יומא ל.) דמצוה לשפשף! וי"ל: דכשאין אוחז איכא רוב ניצוצות, ולא סגי בשפשוף. אבל באוחז ליכא אלא מעט, וסגי בשפשוף. דאי הוה סגי בשפשוף אף כשאינו אוחז, גם רבנן לא הוו שרו.

**ויעמוד** במקום גבוה. ואפילו בקרקע קשה. והא דאמר בפרק "מומין אלו" (בכורות דף מד:) לא ישתין לא על גבי מקום קשה ולא על גבי כלי, דאמר רב: הני מודרי דבבל מהדרי מיא לעין עיטם? וי"ל: דהתם מיירי סמוך לפרת, שהיא גבוה מכל הנהרות, כדאמרינן (בכורות דף נה.) כל הנהרות למטה משלש נהרות, ושלש נהרות למטה מפרת, ומפרת שהוא גבוה מכולם יורד לעין עיטם שהוא גבוה, כדאמרי' (זבחים דף נד:) סבור למבנייה בעין עיטם, דמדלי טפי. אבל רחוק מפרת, או אפילו לתוך שאר נהרות – שרי.

**אם** היה נשוי מותר. ופי' "כל כתבי" (שבת דף קיח:) דקאמר דקרי ליה לרבי "רבינו הקדוש" – שלא הניח ידו למטה מאבנטו, היינו רבותא: שהיה נשוי, והיה מחמיר על עצמו.

**תוספי הרא"ש**

**מתני'** כל היד המרבה וכו' ובאנשים תקצץ. באותו ענין שהוא מתחמם אבל מעטרה ולמטה או בצרור או במטלית עבה אם בא לבדוק בודק: **נשים** דלאו בנות הרגשה נינהו. פרש"י שאינן מתחממות ורואות קרי מחמת מישמוש. משמע הא אם מתחממות אסור אלמא נשים מוזהרות על השחתת זרע. וכן משמע מתוך פר"ח שפי' נשים דלאו בנות הרגשה נינהו שרואות דם בלא הרגשה ומשמע שר"ל אע"ג דמפקות זרע לבטלה טוב לה שתבדוק כדי להפריש מטומאת טהרות ולשמש עם בעלה בטומאה. אבל אנשים שאינן רואין קרי ולא הרגישו למה יבדקו אבל אם היו רואים בלא הרגש מיקרי משובח כשבודק אע"פ שמוציא זרע מידי דהוה אזב. ועוד י"ל דלאו בני איסור הרגשה נינהו אע"פ שמתחממות ורואות קרי וא"ת ומ"ט וכ"ת משום דלא מיפקרי אפריה ורביה אנשים נמי לאחר שקיימו לא ליסרו. ומי' י"ל אנשים לעולם מיפקדי משום דכתיב בבקר זרע את זרעך ולערב אל תנח ידיך כדאיתא בפרק הבא על יבמתו ומיהו קשה לר' יוחנן בן ברוקה דאמר התם על שניהם הוא אומר פרו ורבו ליתסרין. וי"ל דהיינו טעמא דאנשים מיפקדי לפי שמזריע מבחוץ אבל אשה מזרעת מבפנים. והא דאמרי' ג' נשים משמשות במוך דמשמע הא שאר נשים אסירי וי"ל לפר"ח ולרש"י ניחא דאסירי משום השחתת זרע ולאידך פירושא נמי איכא למימר דאסירי משום שמשחיתות זרע האיש. א"נ איכא לפרושי צריכות לשמש במוך: **אי** הכי מאי איריא מרבה כי לא מרבה נמי. פי' אא"ב מתני' לענין זוב איירי ואע"ג דבזוב ליכא למיחש מ"מ גזרה לענין זוב אטו שמא יבדוק לענין שכבת זרע וכי גזור רבנן דוקא במרבה אבל בלא מרבה לא גזור כיון דאינו אסור אלא משום גזירה בעלמא ועוד דלא מצי למיגזר אפי' בלא מרבה שהרי צריך הוא לבדוק כדי לידע מנין ראיותיו ולספור ז' נקיים אלא כיון דמוקמת מתני' משום דאנשים בני הרגשה נינהו אלמא בשכבת זרע מוקמת לה דאי בזוב ומשום גזרה הכי הוה לך למימר אנשים דאתי לידי הרגשה בשכבת זרע. א"ה אפי' לא מרבה נמי. א"נ י"ל אא"ב מתני' בבודק בצרור או בחרס או במטלית עבה דלא אתי לידי חימום. ומי' במרבה גזור שמא ישכח ויבדוק במטלית רכה אלא כיון דאמרת אנשים דבני הרגשה נינהו אלמא דבמטלית רכה מוקמת לה דאי במטלית עבה ומשום גזירה הכי הוה לך למימר אנשים דאיכא למיגזר בהו משום הרגשה: **והתניא** רבי אליעזר אומר. אע"ג דרבנן פליגי עליה. פריך מר' אליעזר וכן לקמן פריך מיניה עליה דשמואל דנראה שגזרו חכמים והודו לר' אליעזר ולאו מחלוקת גמור הוא אלא ששאלו לו מה יעשו לניצוצות וכן משמע סתמא דתלמודא ביומא בפרק אמר להם הממונה גבי כל המטיל מים טעון (כבוס) קידוש ידים ורגלים ודייק בגמרא בשלמא רגלים משום דאיכא ניצוצות ומדאיכא ניצוצות אלמא משמע דאסור לאחוז באמה וכן בפ' כיצד מברכין דקאמר ואי ליכא עפר תיחוח יעמוד במקום גבוה וישתין במקום מדרון: **והלא** ניצוצות ניתזין. תימה אמאי לא מהדר שמשפשף כדמשמע ביומא או יסייע מביצים ולמטה או מעטרה ולמטה:

**עין משפט נר מצוה**

א א מיי' פ"ד מהלכות משכב ומושב הלכה ו וס"ח מהל' איסורי ביאה הל' יא סמג לאוין קיא טוש"ע י"ד סי' קפד סעי' א' וסי' קנו סעיף ט [וברב אלפס שבת פרק י"ד דף מב.]:
ב ב מיי' פכ"א מהל' איסורי ביאה הל' כ סמג לאוין קכו טוש"ע אה"ע סימן כג סעיף ד:
ג ג מיי' פ"ז מהלכות תרומות הלכה ד:
ד ד מיי' פכ"א מהל' איסורי ביאה הל' כג סמג שם טוש"ע א"ח סי' ג סעיף יד וטוש"ע אה"ע סימן כג סעי' ד:
ה ה מיי' פ"ד מהלכות תפילין הל' יח וע"ש טוש"ע א"ח סי' ג סעי' יג:
ו ו מיי' פכ"א מהלכות איסורי ביאה הל' יח סמג לאוין קכו טוש"ע אה"ע סי' כג סעיף א:
ז ז מיי' שם הלכה יח טוש"ע שם סעיף ב:
ח ח מיי' פי"ב מהלכות מאכלות אסורות הל' כד סמג לאוין קמח טוש"ע י"ד סימן קכט סעיף יב:
ט ט מיי' פרק כא מהל' איסורי ביאה הל' כג סמג לאוין קכו טוש"ע א"ח סי' ג סעיף יד וטוש"ע אה"ע סימן כג סעיף ד:
י י טוש"ע א"ח סי' ג סעיף טו:
יא כ טוש"ע שם סעי' יד:

**מסורת הש"ס**

[לקמן ל"ה:] — לקמן מ. — שבת מא. לקמן מג. — [ר"ה יב.] — [לקמן מג.] — [וע"ע פרש"י ב"ה כז: ובמגילה כט. ובע"ז מג:] — בראשית לח — ישעיהו נז — דברים יב — [ברכות לו. וש"נ ועמ"ש בס"ד על הגליון חגיגה טו: פירושו של שינגא] — ע"ז ע: [כתובות כז. שבת מח.] — [וע"ע תוס' יומא ל. ד"ה מנוה]

**הגהות הב"ח**

(א) גמ' כנישתא דשף ויתיב. נ"ב עי' בפרש"י פ' בני העיר וס"פ אם אין מכירין: (ב) רש"י ד"ה לא שכיח וכו' דומה דתחילתו: (ג) ד"ה דשף וכו' המובלע נ"ב פירוש הנשמט בתוך תחום של נהרדעא:

המקשה

מֵעֲטָרָה וּלְמַעְלָה — אָסוּר. אָמַר רַב: אהַמַּקְשֶׁה עַצְמוֹ לָדַעַת — יְהֵא בְּנִדּוּי. וְלֵימָא "אָסוּר"! דְּקָמְגָרֵי יצה"ר אַנַּפְשֵׁיהּ. וְרַבִּי אַמִי אָמַר: נִקְרָא "עֲבַרְיָין", *שֶׁכָּךְ אוּמָּנָתוֹ שֶׁל יֵצֶר הָרָע, הַיּוֹם אוֹמֵר לוֹ: "עֲשֵׂה כָּךְ", וּלְמָחָר אוֹמֵר לוֹ: "עֲשֵׂה כָּךְ", וּלְמָחָר אוֹמֵר לוֹ: "לֵךְ עֲבוֹד עֲבוֹדָה זָרָה", וְהוֹלֵךְ וְעוֹבֵד. אִיכָּא דְּאָמְרִי, אָמַר רַבִּי אַמִי: בכָּל הַמֵּבִיא עַצְמוֹ לִידֵי הִרְהוּר — אֵין מַכְנִיסִין אוֹתוֹ בִּמְחִיצָתוֹ שֶׁל הקב"ה, כְּתִיב הָכָא: °"וַיֵּרַע בְּעֵינֵי ה'", וּכְתִיב הָתָם: °"כִּי לֹא אֵל חָפֵץ רֶשַׁע אָתָּה* לֹא יְגוּרְךָ רָע". (א) וְאָמַר ר' אֶלְעָזָר: מַאי דִּכְתִיב °"יְדֵיכֶם דָּמִים מָלֵאוּ" — גאֵלּוּ הַמְנָאֲפִים בַּיָּד. תָּנָא דְּבֵי רַבִּי יִשְׁמָעֵאל: °"לֹא תִנְאָף" — לֹא תְהֵא בְךָ נִיאוּף, בֵּין בַּיָּד בֵּין בָּרֶגֶל. ת"ר: הַגֵּרִים וְהַמְשַׂחֲקִין בְּתִינוֹקוֹת — מְעַכְּבִין אֶת הַמָּשִׁיחַ. בִּשְׁלָמָא גֵּרִים — כְּדְר' חֶלְבּוֹ, *דא"ר חֶלְבּוֹ, דקָשִׁין גֵּרִים לְיִשְׂרָאֵל כְּסַפַּחַת. אֶלָּא מְשַׂחֲקִין בְּתִינוֹקוֹת מַאי הִיא? אִילֵימָא מִשְׁכַּב זָכוּר — בְּנֵי סְקִילָה נִינְהוּ! אֶלָּא דֶּרֶךְ אֵבָרִים — בְּנֵי מַבּוּל נִינְהוּ! אֶלָּא הדְּנָסְבִי קְטַנּוֹת, דְּלָאו בְּנוֹת אוֹלוּדֵי נִינְהוּ. *דא"ר יוֹסֵי: *אֵין בֶּן דָּוִד בָּא עַד שֶׁיִּכְלוּ כָּל הַנְּשָׁמוֹת שֶׁבַּגּוּף, שֶׁנֶּאֱמַר: °"כִּי רוּחַ מִלְּפָנַי יַעֲטוֹף וּנְשָׁמוֹת אֲנִי עָשִׂיתִי". § "בָּאֲנָשִׁים תִּקָּצֵץ". § אִיבַּעְיָא לְהוּ: דִּינָא תְּנַן, אוֹ לְטוּתָא תְּנַן? דִּינָא תְּנַן — כִּי הָא *דְּרַב הוּנָא קָץ יְדָא, אוֹ לְטוּתָא תְּנַן? ת"ש: דְּתַנְיָא, רַבִּי טַרְפוֹן אוֹמֵר: יָד לָאַמָּה — תִּקָּצֵץ יָדוֹ עַל טַבּוּרוֹ. אָמְרוּ לוֹ: (יָשַׁב לוֹ קוֹץ בִּכְרֵיסוֹ לֹא יִטְּלֶנּוּ? א"ל: לֹא.) וַהֲלֹא כְּרֵיסוֹ נִבְקַעַת! אָמַר לָהֶן: מוּטָב תִּבָּקַע כְּרֵיסוֹ, וְאַל יֵרֵד לִבְאֵר שַׁחַת. אִי אָמְרַתְּ בִּשְׁלָמָא דִּינָא תְּנַן — הַיְינוּ דְּאָמְרִי "וַהֲלֹא כְּרֵיסוֹ נִבְקַעַת", אֶלָּא אִי אָמְרַתְּ לְטוּתָא תְּנַן — מַאי "כְּרֵיסוֹ נִבְקַעַת"? אֶלָּא מַאי — דִּינָא תְּנַן? לָא סַגִּי דְּלָאו עַל טַבּוּרוֹ? אֶלָּא, ה"ק רַבִּי טַרְפוֹן: יכָּל הַמַּכְנִיס יָדוֹ לְמַטָּה מִטַּבּוּרוֹ — תִּקָּצֵץ, אָמְרוּ לוֹ לְרַבִּי טַרְפוֹן: יָשַׁב לוֹ קוֹץ בִּכְרֵיסוֹ, לֹא יִטְּלֶנּוּ? אָמַר לָהֶן: לֹא. וַהֲלֹא כְּרֵיסוֹ נִבְקַעַת! אָמַר לָהֶן: מוּטָב תִּבָּקַע כְּרֵיסוֹ, וְאַל יֵרֵד לִבְאֵר שַׁחַת. §

**מתני'** *יהַחֵרֶשֶׁת וְהַשּׁוֹטָה וְהַסּוּמָא וְשֶׁנִּטְרְפָה דַּעְתָּהּ, אִם יֵשׁ לָהּ פִּקְחוֹת — מְתַקְּנוֹת אוֹתָן, וְהֵן אוֹכְלוֹת בִּתְרוּמָה. §

**גמ'** "חֵרֶשֶׁת". אִיהִי תִּבְדּוֹק לְנַפְשָׁהּ! דְּתַנְיָא, אָמַר רַבִּי: חֵרֶשֶׁת הָיְתָה בִּשְׁכוּנָתֵינוּ, לֹא דַּיָּהּ שֶׁבּוֹדֶקֶת לְעַצְמָהּ — אֶלָּא שֶׁחַבְרוֹתֶיהָ רוֹאוֹת וּמַרְאוֹת לָהּ! חהָתָם — בִּמְדַבֶּרֶת וְאֵינָהּ שׁוֹמַעַת, הָכָא — בְּשֶׁאֵינָהּ מְדַבֶּרֶת וְאֵינָהּ שׁוֹמַעַת. *כִּדְתְנַן: טחֵרֵשׁ שֶׁדִּבְּרוּ חֲכָמִים בְּכָל מָקוֹם — אֵינוֹ שׁוֹמֵעַ וְאֵינוֹ מְדַבֵּר. § "הַסּוּמָא". § יאִיהִי תִּבְדּוֹק לְנַפְשָׁהּ וְתֵיחֱזֵי לַחֲבֶרְתָּהּ! א"ר יוֹסֵי בְּרַבִּי חֲנִינָא: סוּמָא אֵינָהּ מִשְׁנָה. § "וְשֶׁנִּטְרְפָה דַּעְתָּהּ". § הַיְינוּ שׁוֹטָה! כשֶׁנִּטְרְפָה דַּעְתָּהּ מֵחֲמַת חוֹלִי. תָּנוּ רַבָּנַן: *לכֹּהֵן שׁוֹטֶה מַטְבִּילִין אוֹתוֹ וּמַאֲכִילִין אוֹתוֹ תְּרוּמָה לָעֶרֶב, וּמְשַׁמְּרִין אוֹתוֹ שֶׁלֹּא יִישַׁן, יָשַׁן — טָמֵא, לֹא יָשַׁן — טָהוֹר. רַבִּי אֱלִיעֶזֶר בְּרַבִּי צָדוֹק אוֹמֵר: עוֹשִׂין לוֹ כִּיס שֶׁל עוֹר. אָמְרוּ לוֹ: כָּל שֶׁכֵּן שֶׁמֵּבִיא לִידֵי חִימּוּם! אָמַר לָהֶן: לְדִבְרֵיכֶם שׁוֹטֶה אֵין לוֹ תַּקָּנָה! אָמְרוּ לוֹ: לְדִבְרֵינוּ, יָשַׁן — טָמֵא, לֹא יָשַׁן — טָהוֹר, לִדְבָרֶיךָ — שֶׁמָּא יִרְאֶה טִפָּה כְּחַרְדָּל וְתִבָּלַע בַּכִּיס! תָּנָא, מִשּׁוּם רַבִּי אֶלְעָזָר אָמְרוּ: עוֹשִׂין לוֹ כִּיס שֶׁל מַתֶּכֶת. אָמַר אַבַּיֵי: מוְשֶׁל נְחֹשֶׁת. *כִּדְתַנְיָא, *רַבִּי יְהוּדָה אוֹמֵר: רוֹאִין אוֹתָן גִּבְעוֹלִין שֶׁל אֵזוֹב כְּאִילּוּ הֵן שֶׁל נְחֹשֶׁת. אָמַר רַב פַּפָּא: שְׁמַע מִינַּהּ — נמִכְנָסַיִם אֲסוּרִים. וְהָכְתִיב: °"וַעֲשֵׂה לָהֶם מִכְנְסֵי בָד לְכַסּוֹת בְּשַׂר עֶרְוָה"! הַהוּא — כִּדְתַנְיָא: מִכְנְסֵי כֹהֲנִים לְמָה הֵן דּוֹמִין? סכְּמִין פֶּמַלַנְיָא שֶׁל פָּרָשִׁים. לְמַעְלָה — עַד מָתְנַיִם, לְמַטָּה — עַד יְרֵכַיִם, וְיֵשׁ לָהֶם שְׁנָצִים, וְאֵין לָהֶם לֹא בֵּית הַנֶּקֶב וְלֹא בֵּית הָעֶרְוָה. אָמַר אַבַּיֵי:

רוֹכְבֵי

תורה אור: בראשית לח; תהלים ה; ישעיהו א; שמות כ; ישעיהו נז; שמות כח.

[נ"ל מ"ז] [נ"ל כדתנן]

---

**רש"י**

מֵעֲטָרָה וּלְמַעְלָה. לְצַד הַגּוּף. וַיֵּרַע. אַלְמָא מִיקְרֵי רַע. וּכְתִיב לֹא יְגוּרְךָ. לֹא יָגוּר עִמְּךָ רַע. בַּיָּד. מוֹצִיא זֶרַע לְבַטָּלָה. כְּסַפַּחַת. דִּכְתִיב בַּגֵּרִים (ישעיה יד): "וְנִלְוָה הַגֵּר עֲלֵיהֶם וְנִסְפְּחוּ עַל בֵּית יַעֲקֹב", לְשׁוֹן סַפַּחַת. שֶׁקָּשִׁים לְיִשְׂרָאֵל כְּסַפַּחַת, שֶׁאֵין בְּקִיאִים בְּמִצְוֹת, וּמְבִיאִין פּוּרְעָנוּת. וְעוֹד, שֶׁמָּא לְמֵדִים יִשְׂרָאֵל מִמַּעֲשֵׂיהֶן. מִפִּי מוֹרִי הַזָּקֵן. וְיֵשׁ אוֹמֵר: שֶׁכָּל יִשְׂרָאֵל עֲרֵבִים זֶה בָּזֶה. וְלָאו מִילְּתָא הִיא, שֶׁלֹּא נִתְעָרְבוּ בִּשְׁבִיל הַגֵּרִים, דְּאָמְרִינַן בְּמַס' סוֹטָה (דף לז.): נִמְצָא לְכָל אֶחָד מִיִּשְׂרָאֵל שֵׁשׁ מֵאוֹת אֶלֶף וּשְׁלֹשֶׁת אֲלָפִים וְתק"ן בְּרִיתוֹת, שֶׁכּוּלָּן נִתְעָרְבוּ זֶה בָּזֶה. אַלְמָא לֹא נִתְעָרְבוּ עַל הַגֵּרִים. בְּנֵי סְקִילָה נִינְהוּ. וְאַתְּ אָמְרַתְּ "מְעַכְּבִים אֶת הַמָּשִׁיחַ" וְתוּ לָא, הֲלֹא בְּמִיתָה הֵן נִידוֹנִים! דֶּרֶךְ אֵבָרִים. הַיְינוּ שִׁכְבַת זֶרַע לְבַטָּלָה, וְאֵינוֹ מִשְׁכַּב זָכוּר, דְּבְמִשְׁכַּב זָכוּר כְּתִיב (ויקרא כ) "מִשְׁכְּבֵי אִשָּׁה". דְּנָסְבִי קְטַנּוֹת. וְהוּא רָאוּי לְהוֹלִיד, נִמְצָא בָּטֵל מִפְּרִיָּה וּרְבִיָּה כָּל יְמֵי קַטְנוּתָהּ. שֶׁבַּגּוּף. חֶדֶר כִּי גּוּף — שֵׁם מָקוֹם הַמְיוּחָד לַנְּשָׁמוֹת הָעֲתִידִים לִהְיוֹת נוֹלָדִים. כִּי רוּחַ. הָרוּחוֹת שֶׁלְּפָנַי — שֶׁגָּזַרְתִּי לִהְיוֹת נוֹלָדִים קוֹדֶם, "יַעֲטוֹף" מְעַכֵּב אֶת הַגְּאוּלָּה. דִּקְרָא בַּגְּאוּלָּה כְּתִיב: "כִּי לֹא לְעוֹלָם אָרִיב וְלֹא לָנֶצַח אֶקְצוֹף" וגו', (ב) נְשָׁמוֹת שֶׁאֲנִי עָשִׂיתִי יַעֲטוֹף. וּמְסֵיפֵיהּ לְרֵישֵׁיהּ מִדְרֵישׁ. "יַעֲטוֹף", כְּמוֹ (בראשית ל) "וְהָעֲטוּפִים לְלָבָן". קָץ יְדָא. דְּאָמְרִינַן בְּסַנְהֶדְרִין: כָּל הַמֵּרִים יָדוֹ עַל חֲבֵירוֹ — תִּקָּצֵץ, דִּכְתִיב: "וּזְרוֹעַ רָמָה תִּשָּׁבֵר". רַב הוּנָא קָץ יָדָא. אַלְמָא "תִּקָּצֵץ" — דִּינָא הוּא. תִּקָּצֵץ יָדוֹ עַל טַבּוּרוֹ. קס"ד טַבּוּרוֹ מַמָּשׁ, וְהַיְינוּ דְּאָמְרִי לֵיהּ: וַהֲלֹא כְּרֵיסוֹ נִבְקַעַת כְּשֶׁקּוֹצְצִין שָׁם אֶת יָדוֹ. לְמַטָּה מִטַּבּוּרוֹ. וְהָכִי קָאָמַר: תִּקָּצֵץ עַל שֶׁהִכְנִיסָהּ לְמַטָּה מִטַּבּוּרוֹ. וַהֲלֹא כְּרֵיסוֹ נִבְקַעַת. מִפְּנֵי הַקּוֹץ. **מתני'** מְתַקְּנוֹת אוֹתָן. בּוֹדְקוֹת אוֹתָן וּמַטְבִּילִין אוֹתָן. **גמ'** וּמַרְאוֹת לָהּ. שֶׁהָיְתָה בְּקִיאָה בְּמַרְאֵה דָּם טָמֵא וְדָם טָהוֹר. מְדַבֶּרֶת וְאֵינָהּ שׁוֹמַעַת. כְּבָר שָׁמְעָה וְלָמְדָה לְדַבֵּר, וְאַחַר כֵּן נִתְחָרְשָׁה. בְּכָל מָקוֹם. לְהוֹצִיא מִכְּלַל בֶּן דַּעַת. שֶׁלֹּא יִישַׁן. כְּדֵי שֶׁלֹּא יִתְחַמֵּם וְיִרְאֶה. כִּים שֶׁל עוֹר. וּכְשֶׁיִּרְצוּ לְהַאֲכִילוֹ, יִבְדְּקוּ בַּכִּים. וְתִבָּלַע בַּכִּים. וְקָאָכֵיל תְּרוּמָה בְּטוּמְאַת הַגּוּף, וְהָוֵי בְּמִיתָה, דִּכְתִיב (ויקרא כב): "וּמֵתוּ בוֹ כִּי יְחַלְּלֻהוּ". רוֹאִין אוֹתָן. לְעִנְיַן מֵי חַטָּאת קָאָמַר לְטַמֵּא בְּמַשָּׂא דְּבָעֵי' עַד דְּהָוֵי כְּשִׁיעוּר הַזָּאָה, כִּדְאָמַר בְּפ"ק (לעיל ט.): כַּמָּה יְהוּ בַּמַּיִם וְיִהְיֶה בָּהֶם כְּדֵי הַזָּאָה — כְּדֵי שֶׁיִּטְבּוֹל רָאשֵׁי גִבְעוֹלִין וְיַזֶּה, כְּלוֹמַר, כְּדֵי שֶׁיְּהֵא בָּהֶם כְּדֵי לְהַזּוֹת לְבַד מַה שֶּׁהָאֵזוֹב בּוֹלֵעַ. רַבִּי יְהוּדָה אוֹמֵר כו' שֶׁל נְחֹשֶׁת. אַלְמָא שֶׁל נְחֹשֶׁת לֹא בָּלַע. שְׁמַע מִינָּהּ. מִדְּקָתָנֵי: כָּל שֶׁכֵּן שֶׁאַתָּה מְבִיאוֹ לִידֵי חִימּוּם, אַלְמָא מִכְנָסַיִם אֲסוּרִין. פֶּמַלַנְיָא. סִינָר, פורליינ"ט, חֲלָלוֹ תָּלוּי לְמַטָּה בְּרוֹחַב שֶׁלֹּא יִתְעַטֵּף הָאֵבֶר וְיִתְחַמֵּם. שֶׁל פְּרוּשִׁים. לְנוּעִים. ל"א שֶׁל פָּרָשִׁים. שְׁנָצִים. אשרלט"ש, כְּעֵין שֶׁלָּנוּ. וְאֵין לָהֶם לֹא בֵּית הַנֶּקֶב וְלֹא בֵּית הָעֶרְוָה. כְּלוֹמַר, חֲלָלוֹ רָחָב וְתָלוּי לְמַטָּה, וְלֹא הָיָה תִּיק בֵּין הַיְּרֵכַיִם לִהְיוֹת הָאֵבֶר מִתְעַטֵּף בּוֹ שֶׁלֹּא יָבֹא (הָאֵבֶר) לִידֵי הִרְהוּר, וְהַיְינוּ "בֵּית הָעֶרְוָה". וּבֵית הַנֶּקֶב כְּשֶׁהֵן קְצָרוֹת כְּנֶגֶד נֶקֶב הָרְעִי כְּתַבְנִית אָדָם נִכְנָסוֹת בֵּין עַגְבוֹתָיו וּמְלוּכְלָכוֹת בְּזֵיעָה, וּגְנַאי הוּא לְבִגְדֵי קֹדֶשׁ בְּכָךְ. לִישָּׁנָא אַחֲרִינָא: בֵּית הַנֶּקֶב וּבֵית הָעֶרְוָה — דַּרְכָּן הָיָה לַעֲשׂוֹת נְקָבִים בַּמִּכְנָסַיִם כְּנֶגֶד בֵּית הָעֶרְוָה לְהַשְׁתִּין מַיִם לַחוּץ דֶּרֶךְ שָׁם, וְכֵן כְּנֶגֶד בֵּית הָרְעִי, וּכְשֶׁגּוֹמֵר קוֹשֵׁר הַנֶּקֶב בִּרְצוּעָה וְסוֹתְמוֹ.

רוֹכְבֵי

---

**תוספות**

**המקשה** עצמו לדעת יהא בנדוי. אינו מנודה מעצמו, אלא כלומר: חייבים לנדותו. כדאמרי' בפ"ק דקדושין (דף כח:) עד היכן הוא גלגול שבועה? עד שיאמר "השבע לי שאין עבדי אתה". ההוא שמותי משמתינן ליה! דתניא: הקורא לחברו "עבד" – יהא בנדוי. משמע ד"יהא בנדוי" היינו: דמשמתינן ליה. **בין** ביד בין ברגל. היינו: דמספסף מילתו ביד או ברגל. **קשים** גרים לישראל כספחת. מה שמקשה רש"י דלא חשיב בסוטה ערבות דערב רב, י"ל: לפי שלא ידע חשבונן. מיהו במכילתא אמר דערב רב היו כפלים כיוצאי מצרים. (ג) ור"י מפרש: דלפיכך קשים, שמטמעים בישראל, ואמר בפ' "עשרה יוחסין" (קדושין דף ע:) אין שכינה שורה אלא על משפחות המיוחסות שבישראל. וכן נראה, דהתם על ההיא מילתא מייתי דר' חלבו. [וע"ע תוס' יבמות מז, ותוס' קדושין ע, ד"ה "קשים"]. **עד** שיכלו כל הנשמות שבגוף. והא דאמר (שבת דף קיח:) אילמלי שמרו ישראל ב' שבתות – מיד היו נגאלים! וי"ל: דהרבה היו יולדות בכרס אחד. **דינא** תנן. ובשבת (דף קח:) דאמרי' "יד לפה – תקצץ", אינו לא דינא ולא לטותא, אלא כלומר: טוב לו לקוץ ידו קודם שיגע למקומות הללו, משום בת מלך. **אלמא** דינא תנן. השתא סבור דתקצץ ממש, והיינו דקאמר "כריסו נבקעת", ומשני: ה"ק, תקצץ ידו על טבורו, פי' על שנגע על טבורו, ולעולם לטותא הוא. והא דקתני "כריסו נבקעת" לא קאי א"תקצץ" אלא על "ישב לו קוץ", דאם לא יסיר הקוץ – תבקע כריסו. וקשה: דמאי ס"ד מעיקרא, דהא בהדיא קתני "והלא כריסו נבקעת" אחר "ישב לו קוץ"? ומיהו בתוספתא גריס "והלא כריסו נבקעת" ברישא, והשתא אתי שפיר. ומ"מ משני: דה"ק, אם אסור לעולם ליגע, פעמים שכריסו נבקעת, כגון אם ישב לו קוץ.

רוכבי

---

**עין משפט נר מצוה**

יב א ב מיי' פכ"א מהל' איסורי ביאה הל' יט סמג לאוין קכו טוש"ע אה"ע סי' כג סעיף ג [וברב אלפס שבת פי"ד דף מב:]

יג מיי' שם הל' יח טוש"ע שם סעיף ב:

יד ד מיי' פי"ג מהל' איסורי ביאה הל' יח:

טו ה מיי' שם פכ"א הלכה יח סמג שם טוש"ע אה"ע סימן כג סעיף א:

טז ו מיי' שם הלכה כג סמג שם טוש"ע שם סעיף ז:

יז ז ח מיי' שם פ"ח הל' טו ופ"ד מהל' משכב ומושב הלכה ט סמג לאוין קיא טוש"ע י"ד סי' קצו סעיף ח:

יח ט מיי' פ"ב מהל' אישות הלכה כו:

יט י מיי' פ"ח מהלכות איסורי ביאה הל' טו סמג לאוין קיא טוש"ע י"ד סימן קצו סעיף ז:

כ כ מיי' פ"ד מהלכות משכב ומושב הל' ט סמג שם טוש"ע שם סעיף ח:

[נ"ל דאמר רב אסי כ"א ביבמות]

כא ל מ מיי' פ"ז מהל' תרומות הלכה ה:

כב נ טוש"ע אה"ע סי' כג סעיף ו בהגה"ה:

כג ס מיי' פ"ח מהל' כלי המקדש הל' יח:

---

**תוספי הרא"ש**

**המקשה** עצמו לדעת יהא בנדוי. מפרש ר"ת ראוי שינדוהו חכמי הדור. אבל רב לא נדה אותו. וכן ההיא דאמרי' בנדרים השומע הזכרה מפי חברו חייב לנדותו ואם לא נדהו יהא בנדוי היינו דמשמתינן ליה דאי לא תימא הכי חמור השומע שהוא מנודה מפי האמורא ממי שמוציא ההזכרה מפיו ועוד ראיה מהא דאמרי' פ"ק דקידושין עד היכן גלגול שבועה עד שיאמר לו השבע שאין עבדי אתה. ופריך ההוא שמותי משמתינן ליה דתניא הקורא לחברו עבד יהא בנדוי אלמא כל היכא דאמרי' יהא בנדוי היינו שחכמי הדור חייבין לנדותו: **קשים** גרים לישראל כספחת. רבי' יצחק הקשה לההוא פי' דכל ישראל ערבים זה לזה מהא דלא חשיב בסוטה אלא ערבות דישראל ואילו ערבות דערב רב לא קא חשיב ולאו פירכא היא דמשום שלא היה חשבונם ידוע לא קא חשיב להו ואע"ג דאיכא למ"ד במכלתין שהיו כפלים כישראל. מ"מ במקרא לא הוזכר חשבונם וי"מ לפי שאין שכינה שורה אלא על משפחות המיוחסות שבישראל כדאמרינן בפ"ק דקדושין וכן משמע הכא דמייתי הא דר' חלבו אהא דהגרים מעכבין את המשיח דמשמע שע"י שהגרים מעורבין מתרחקת שכינה ומשיח מתעכב: **עד** שיכלו כל נשמות שבגוף. והא דאמרינן בפ' כל כתבי אלמלי שומרים ישראל שתי שבתות מיד נגאלין שמא אותה גזירה דעד שיכלו היתה בטלה בזכות שהיו שומרים שתי שבתות כהלכתן א"נ היו יולדות הנשים ששה בכרס אחד. כדי למהר לכלות הנשמות: **היינו** דאמרי ליה כריסו נבקעת. ס"ד דקאי אתקצץ ידו על טיבורו וסמיך אהא דתניא בתוספתא ר' טרפון אומר תקצץ ידו על טיבורו אמרו לו והלא כריסו נבקעת: ועל האזוב של נחשת. וא"ת והיאך יזה והאמרינן לעיל בפ"ק דשיעור הזאה כדי שיטבול ראשי גבעולין ויזה ואי בליעת הכלי הוי בכלל שיעור זה א"כ לא ישאר כדי לטבול ראשי גבעולין ואיך יוכל להזות. וי"ל נהי דלא ישאר כדי טבילת ראשי גבעולין יטביל ראשי העלין שבראש האזוב:

רוכבי

---

**מסורת הש"ס**

שבת קח:

[נ"ל לא יגורך רע א"ר אלעזר מאי לא יגורך רע לא יגור במגורך רע וא"ר אלעזר מאי דכתיב ידיכם כו' כך איתא בכל אלפס לשבת פי"ד]

יבמות מז: ודף קט: קדושין ע:

ע"ז ה. יבמות סב. סג.

סנהדרין נח:

חולין לח.

חגיגה כ: [תרומות פ"א מ"ב]

[תוספתא פ"ב]

[פרה פי"ב מ"ה ע"ש ותוספתא פרה פי"א וסיים כל שאינו בולע]

בהגה"ה

**הגהות הב"ח**

(א) גמ' אמר ר' אלעזר מאי דכתיב כצ"ל ואות ו' נמחק: (ב) רש"י ד"ה כי רוח וכו' וגו' ונשמות שאני: (ג) תוס' ד"ה קשים וכו' ור"י מפרש כ"ב ועי' בתוס' פרק החולץ ופ' עשרה יוחסין פי' בע"ה:

ארוכבי גמלים אסורין לאכול בתרומה. *תניא נמי הכי: רוכבי גמלים – כולם רשעים, הספנים – כולם צדיקים, החמרים – מהן רשעים מהן צדיקים. איכא דאמרי: הא – דמכף, הא – דלא מכף, ואיכא דאמרי: הא – *דמטרטין, הא – דלא מטרטין. ריב"ל *בלייט אמאן דגני אפרקיד. איני, והאמר רב יוסף: *גפרקדן לא יקרא קרית שמע, קרית שמע הוא דלא יקרא, הא מגנא – שפיר דמי! דלענין מגנא – כי מצלי שפיר דמי, הלענין ק"ש – כי מצלי אסור. והא ר' יוחנן מצלי וקרי ק"ש! ושאני רבי יוחנן דבעל בשר הוה.§ **מתני'** *זדרך בנות ישראל משמשות בשני עדים, אחד לו ואחד לה. חוהצנועות מתקנות שלישי, לתקן את הבית. *טנמצא על שלו – טמאין, וחייבין קרבן. ינמצא על שלה *אותיום – טמאין, וחייבין בקרבן. נמצא על שלה לאחר זמן – כטמאין מספק, לופטורים מן הקרבן. איזהו "אחר זמן"? מכדי שתרד מן המטה ותדיח פניה, ואח"כ מטמאה מעת לעת, נואינה מטמאה את בועלה. *ר"ע אומר: אף מטמאה את בועלה. סמודים חכמים לרבי עקיבא ברואה כתם שמטמאה את בועלה.§ **גמ'** וניחוש דלמא דם מאכולת הוא! אמר רבי זירא: אותו מקום בדוק הוא אצל מאכולת, ואיכא דאמרי: דחוק הוא אצל מאכולת. מאי בינייהו? איכא בינייהו – עדאשתכח מאכולת רצופה, להך לישנא דאמר בדוק הוא – פהא מעלמא אתאי, להך לישנא דאמר דחוק הוא – אימא שמש רצפה. איתמר, בדקה בעד הבדוק לה, וטחתו בירכה, ולמחר מצאה עליה דם, אמר רב: צטמאה נדה. א"ל רב שימי בר חייא: והא חוששת אמרת לן! איתמר נמי, אמר שמואל: טמאה נדה. וכן מורין בי מדרשא: טמאה נדה. איתמר, בדקה בעד שאינו בדוק לה והניחתו בקופסא, ולמחר מצאה עליו דם, א"ר יוסף: כל ימיו של ר' חייא טימא, ולעת זקנתו טיהר. איבעיא להו: היכי קאמר? כל ימיו טימא משום נדה, ולעת זקנתו – טיהר משום נדה וטימא משום כתם. או דלמא: כל ימיו טימא משום כתם, ולעת זקנתו טיהר מולא כלום? תא שמע, דתניא: בדקה בעד שאינו בדוק לה והניחתו בקופסא, ולמחר מצאה עליו דם, רבי אומר: קטמאה משום נדה, ורבי חייא אמר: טמאה משום כתם.

אמר

---

רוכבי גמלים. אבריהם מתחממים בבשר הגמל, ומוציאים זרע. כולם רשעים. כדאמר. כולם צדיקים. שדרים בסכנה, ולבם לאביהם שבשמים. דמכף. לשון אוכף של חמור. אם יש לו אוכף – האבר אינו מתחמם, שהעץ קשה הוא. ואם אין לו אוכף – מתחמם בבשר החמור. אבל דרך גמלים לרכוב בלא אוכף, אלא במרדעת, ומתחמם. דמטרטין. ירך מכאן וירך מכאן, ואברו מתחמם. דלא מטרטין. רוכב כאשה. מטרטין. לשון מאזנים, כדאמרי' במנחות (דף פז.) וכי טורטני יכניס. אפרקיד. פניו למעלה. וגנות הוא, שפעמים שיתקשה אבר תוך שינתו, ויתגלה. ועוד: שידיו מונחות לו על אברו, ומתחמם. מצלי. מוטה מעט על צדו. כי מצלי נמי אסור. אא"כ יושב או שוכב כולו על צדו. **מתני'** אחד לו ואחד לה. לקנח לאחר תשמיש. לתקן את הבית. כלומר: לבדוק לפני תשמיש, ולהכין עצמה לבעלה. וה"ה לכל הנשים, כדתנן בפ"ק (לעיל יא.), ובשעה שהיא עוברת לשמש את ביתה. והא דנקט "צנועות" – כדמפרש בפ"ק: צנועות, עד שבודקת בו לפני תשמיש זה, אין בודקת בו לפני תשמיש אחר. נמצא דם על שלו. ואפילו לאחר זמן, ששהה לאחר בעילה זמן ארוך קודם קינוח – בידוע שהיה דם בשעת תשמיש. טמאים. שניהם טומאת שבעה, כדין בועל נדה, כדכתיב (ויקרא טו): "ותהי נדתה עליו". *אותיום. מיד לאחר בעילה. לאחר זמן. לאחר אותיום – טמאים מספק שניהם שבעה ימים. ומיהו טומאת ספק הוא, לתלות אבל לא לשרוף. את פניה. פניה שלמטה. ואח"כ. כלומר: שהשתא יותר מכשיעור הזה "אחר אחר" הוא זה. מטמאות מעת לעת. טהרות ואדם במגע טומאת ערב, ומדרבנן כדין מעת לעת, דאמר בפ"ק: ומה היא מטמאה – משכבה ומושבה. וכיון דעושה משכב ומושב לטמא אדם, כל שכן דהיא עצמה מטמאה אדם. ואינה מטמאה את בועלה. טומאת שבעה ימים. ר"ע אומר אף מטמאה את בועלה. ר"ע לטעמיה, דאמר: כל מעת לעת מטמאה את בועלה מספק טומאת שבעה, בפ"ק (לעיל ו.). **גמ'** מאכולת. כינה. ואמאי טמאין ודאי לשרוף תרומה ולהתחייב בקרבן ודאי? להוי ספק, לתלות תרומה ולהביא אשם תלוי ולא חטאת! דדלמא דם מאכולת הוא, שהיה באותו מקום באשה, וכשבעל – נדבק בו. בדוק. דודאי אין שם מאכולת, ודם ודאי מגופה אתיא. דחוק הוא. שאין מאכולת יכולה ליכנס שם. רצופה. מעוכה על העד רחוק מן הדם קצת. ללישנא דבדוק – כיון דקים להו לרבנן דאין שם מאכולת, ודאי דם מגופה הוא, שהרי העד היה בדוק לה קודם הקינוח, ומאכולת *(מעלמא הואי קאתי בעד שהיא רצופה). וללישנא דדחוק – איכא לספוקי שמא האי דם ממאכולת, ומתוך שדחוק הוא, מיעכה השמש בשעת תשמיש. ולמחר מצאה עליה דם. על הירך. טמאה נדה. טומאה ודאית, דכיון דהעד בדוק לה שלא היה בו דם קודם בדיקה, ודאי מגופה אתאי על העד, ומשם הוטח בירכה. ולא אמרינן: דלמא מעלמא אתא על ירכה, וספק טומאה היא. ולמחר מצאה עליו דם. על העד, ואיכא לספוקי: דלמא מקמי הכי הוה ביה. להכי לא נקט הכא "טחתו בירכה", דא"כ הוו להו תרי ספיקי לקולא: חדא, דלמא לאו מן העד הוטח על ירכה. ואפילו את"ל מן העד אתא, דלמא כיון דאינו בדוק – מקמי הכי הוה. משום נדה. טומאה ודאית, דכיון דחזקת דמים שם, לא מספקינן במקמי הכי. משום כתם. כלומר: טומאת ספק, ותולין.

שבירכה

---

רוכבי גמלים אסורין לאכול בתרומה. ואע"ג דאמר שמואל בפ' "יוצא דופן" (לקמן דף מג.) כל שכבת זרע שאין כל גופו מרגיש – אינו מטמא! הכא דלמא הרגיש כל גופו, ולאו אדעתיה. **רוכבי** גמלים כולם רשעים החמרים מהן רשעים מהן צדיקים. וא"ת: דאמרינן בפרק "עשרה יוחסין" (קדושין דף פב.) גמלים – רובן כשרים, חמרים – רובן ליסטין? וי"ל: דהכא איירי ברוכבים ומשום הרהור, והתם לא איירי ברוכבים אלא בנותנין סחורה על הגמלים והם הולכים ברגל רחוק במקום סכנה. וחמרין *[שהם ליסטים, משום דבשעה שקונים] עושין רמאות במשא ובמתן.

**אפרקיד.** פי' הקונטרס: פניו למעלה. וכן משמע ב"המוכר את הספינה" (ב"ב דף עד,) גבי מתי מדבר דגנו אפרקיד, וחליף טייעא תותי ברכייהו ורומחא בידיה. ולשון "אפרקיד": אפורייאה קדל *(קדקדא) ולא כפירוש הערוך דפי' פניו מטה, ולשון "אפרקיד": אפוי קיד. ועוד קשה רי"ש ד"אפרקיד" למה לי?! [וע"ע תוספות פסחים קח, ד"ה "פרקדן"]. **לייט** אמאן דגני אפרקיד. פי' בקונטרס: שידיו מונחות על מילתו, ומתחמם. ורשב"ם פירש: שבגדיו נופלין על אמתו, ומתחמם. ומה שפי' עוד: שפעמים [מתקשה ומתגלה] לא נראה, דבבית סגור או אפל מאי א"ל. ועוד שמעתי: כששוכב אפרקיד מתחמם השדרה, ומחממת זה יתקשה האבר, ויבא לידי קרי. גליון.

**ק"ש** כי מצלי אסור. היינו כשהוא קצת אפרקיד, אבל על צדו לגמרי – שרי, כדאמר בפ' "מי שמתו" (ברכות דף כד.) שנים שהן ישנים במטה – זה הופך פניו לכאן וזה הופך פניו לכאן, וקורין ק"ש. **וליחוש** דלמא דם מאכולת הוא. אבל על בדיקות דמטמאינן לה אם מצא דם לא פריך, דדלמא חומרא היא. אבל הכא פריך אמאי חייבין בקרבן, דלמא מייתי חולין בעזרה. ועוד נראה, וכן פר"ת, דפריך א"נמצא על שלו", כי לא נמצא על שלה אמאי מטמאין, כיון דאיכא הוכחה דלא אתי מגופה. **דחוק** הוא אצל מאכולת. אין לפרש: שאינה יכולה ליכנס אלא בדוחק ולפעמים נכנסת, דא"כ הוה ליה למימר בסמוך ללישנא דדחוק הוא: אימר איתרמויי איתרמי, ולמה צריך להזכיר דשמש רצפה. לכך י"ל: בדוק הוא – שאינה באה כלל סמוך לרחם מפני הזוהמא שיוכל השמש להכניס, ודחוק הוא אצל מאכולת, היינו דאינה נכנסת בשום פנים מאליה, אלא שפעמים שמתקרבת לרחם כ"כ עד שהשמש מכניסה ומרצפה.

**וטחתו** בירכה. פירוש: במקום (א) שאין דם המקור יכול ליפול שם. **ולמחר** מצאה עליה דם. ה"ג רש"י פי' על ירכה, וקאמר דטמאה נדה, דאיכא למימר דמן העד נתלכלך ירכה ולא מעלמא. וא"ת: ותבדוק העד! וי"ל: שנאבד העד. א"נ: שמא דם העד עצמו בא מדם ירכה, כיון שנמצא על העד רק במקום שנגע בירכה וכגון שיש כגרים ועוד, דליכא חששא דמאכולת. *ודוקא בעד הבדוק לה, אבל בשאינו בדוק לה – הוי ספק ספקא, כדפי' רש"י. ודוקא טחתו בירכה, אבל הניחתו בקופסא – פשיטא דטמאה. ור"ח גרס: "ומצאה עליו" – פירוש: על העד, וטחתו בירכה – היינו בגלוי, שלא הניחתו בקופסא. דבהניחתו בקופסא פשיטא דטמאה. ופריך: והא "חוששין" אמרת לן, דאימר מעלמא אתי. **אמר** שמואל טמאה נדה. אפי' ר' חייא דמטהר בסמוך מודה הכא, דהא ר' חייא כר' יוסי ס"ל, ושמואל גופיה פסיק ב"האשה" (לקמן נט:) כרבי יוסי, והכא קאמר דטמאה נדה.

או שמא כיון שנמצא על ירכה במקום שנגע בעד מוכח מילתא שמחמת העד הוא וטמאה. גליון:

בעד

---

## תוספי הרא"ש

**רוכבי** גמלים אסורים לאכול בתרומה. דוקא בשעה שהן רוכבין שמא יראה קרי בעוד התרומה בפיו אבל לאחר שירד מותר דלא חיישינן שמא ראה קרי ושכח דאמרי' לקמן פרק יוצא דופן כל שכבת זרע שאין גופו מרגיש בה אינה מטמאה: **רוכבי** גמלים כולם רשעים. והא דאמרי' בסוף קדושין הגמלים כולן כשרים בבעלי סחורה מיירי והולכין ברגל ומשאן על הגמלים והולכין לארץ מרחקים לסחורה בדרך מדבריות במקום גדודי חיות ולסטים ומכוונים לבם לשמים ומשאן ומתנן באמונה. והחמרין שאינן מתרחקין כל כך משאם ומתנם ברמאות: **לייט** אמאן דגני אפרקיד. פי' שוכב על גביו כי עגבותיו מתחממין על המטה ובא לידי קרי כדאמרינן בפרק הערל מייתינן מיא חמימא דשערי ומנחינן ליה אבי פיקרי ומיקרי בי פיקרי היינו עגבותיו כשמניח עליהם דבר חם מתחמם ובא לידי קרי: **וליחוש** דלמא דם מאכולת הוא. אבל בדיקה שבדקה ומצאה א) טמא לא קפדי דמצי למימר דמטמאינן להו מספיקא אבל מתני' דקתני חייבין בקרבן אלמא ודאי מגופה אתי ועוד כיון שמצא על שלו ולא על שלה מסתברא כי דם מאכולת הוא: **אימור** שמש רצפה. וא"ת כיון דאיכא למיחש לצריפת שמש א"כ משתכחא מאכולת התם א"כ אפי' ליכא מאכולת רצופה נמי ניחוש דרצפו שמש ודם מאכולת הוא ואע"ג דמאכולת ליתא קמן דלמא נאבדה המאכולת ונשאר הדם. וי"ל דרציפה של שמש לא שכיח לא תלינן בה אלא היכא דמוכחא מלתא דאשתכח מאכולת רצופה: **וטחתו** בירכה ולמחר מצאה עליה דם. פרש"י על הירך ותימה ונבדוק בעד עצמו שאי אפשר שלא יהא ניכר רושם על העד וצ"ל דמיירי שאבד העד. ור"ח גרס ומצאה עליו כלומר על העד וקמ"ל דלא חיישינן שמא בא מן הירך על העד: **והא** חוששת אמרת לן. תימה דאמרי' בריש הרואה כתם על בשרה ודאי טמא דאם איתא דמעלמא אתי על חלוקה איבעי ליה לאישתכוחי וא"כ ה"נ אפי' הדם על הירך טמאה ודאי וכ"ת הך דלקמן לפי מסקנא דשמעתין מ"מ קשה דמשמע דרב גופיה לא קאמר אלא דוקא טחתו אבל אם לא טחתו לא. ומצי' למימר דה"ה לא טחתו והאי דנקט טחתו לאשמועינן דוקא בדוק אבל אינו בדוק לא ועוד מצינו למימר דמיירי הכא כשיש לה מכה ואי לאו דטחתו הוה תלינן בדם המכה: **ולעת** זקנתו טהר מכלום. תימה היכא מצינו למימר טהר מכלום והא אמרינן לקמן בריש הרואה כתם על חלוקה ודאי טהור דאי איתא דמגופה אתא על בשרה איבעי ליה לאישתכוחי ומשמע הא על בשרה ועל חלוקה דליכא הוכחה הוי ספיקא והכא כעל בשרה ועל חלוקה דמי דמהכא נמי ליכא הוכחה. וי"ל דהא דלקמן היינו לפי המסקנא דהכא ומיהו [אכתי] קשה דהא תנן לקמן פ' האשה ג' נשים שלבשו חלוק אחד ונמצא עליו דם כולם טמאין וה"נ כשבדקה בעד שאינו בדוק לה הוי כאילו קינחה בו אשה אחרת קודם דטמאה מספק והיכי הוה בעי למימר דטהר מכלום דא"כ תיקשי ליה מהך מתני' וי"ל דשאני התם דממה נפשך צריך לטמאות אחת מהן הדדמי לבאו לשאול בבת אחת גבי שני שבילין והוי מינייהו מפקת. אבל הכא תלינן שמא הדם היה על העד קודם לכן והתם נמי אילו היתה אחת מהן שומרת יום כנגד יום או בתולה שדמיה טהורין היו שתים האחרות תולות בה:

ור'

א) נראה שצ"ל שבדקה ומצאה דם על העד דמטמאינן אותה לא קשיא לן דשמא דם מאכולת הוא דמצי למימר וכו':

---

### עין משפט נר מצוה

כד א מיי' פ"ז מהל' תרומות הלכה ו טוש"ע אה"ע סי' כג סעיף ו:

כה ב מיי' פכ"א מהל' איסורי ביאה הלכה יט סמג לאוין קיא טוש"ע שם סעי' ב:

כו ג מיי' פ"ב מהל' ק"ש הלכה ב ועי' בהשגות ובכ"מ סמג עשין יח טוש"ע א"ח סי' סג סעי' א:

כז ד מיי' פכ"א מהל' איסורי ביאה הלכה יט סמג לאוין קכו טוש"ע אה"ע סי' כג סעיף ג:

כח ה ו מיי' פ"ב מהל' ק"ש הלכה ב סמג עשין יח טוש"ע א"ח סימן סג סעיף א:

רש"ל מ"ז וגי' רש"א או קדקדא

כט ז מיי' פ"ד מהלכות איסורי ביאה הלכה יד וע"ש סמג לאוין קיא טוש"ע י"ד סי' קפו סעי' ב וע"ש:

ל ח מיי' שם הלכה טז סמג שם טוש"ע שם סעיף א:

יומא ו. [לעיל ו.]

לא ט י מיי' פ"ה מהל' שגגות הל' ו:

לב כ מיי' שם (ופ"ד מהלכות איסורי ביאה) סמג לאוין קיא טוש"ע י"ד סימן קצ סעי' לג:

לג ל מ מיי' פ"ה מהל' שגגות הל' ו:

לד נ מיי' שם (ופ"ד מהל' משכב ומושב הלכה ח):

לה ס מיי' פ"ג מהל' מטמאי משכב ומושב הל' ח:

לו ע פ מיי' פ"ד מהל' איסורי ביאה הלכה יח ועי' במ"מ סמג לאוין קיא טוש"ע י"ד סי' קצ סעי' לה:

לז צ מיי' שם הלכה יט ועי' במ"מ סמג שם טוש"ע שם סעי' לה:

לח ק טוש"ע שם סעי' לג:

### מסורת הש"ס

קדושין פב. [ע"ש]

[כמו מאזנים שמשקל אחד מכאן ומשקל אחד מכאן]

קדושין לג: וש"נ ברכות יג:

[לעיל ה.]

[לקמן נז: שבועות יח. כריתות יז:]

[גי' הערוך אותיאום ע"ש וכתב שם דלשון יוני הוא ועי' פרש"י ביומא ו. ובכריתות יז: אותיום מיד בלשון יוני ויתכן לומר דעדות הערוך ועדותו של רש"י נכונים ע"פ מ"ש תוס' ב"ק פג. ד"ה לשון ע"ש]

[לשון יון הוא כן פרש"י בריש יומא]

ס"א לאחר בעילה לאחר על אברו

### הגהות הב"ח

(א) תוס' ד"ה וטחתו וכו' שאין דם נ"ב עיין ר"פ הרואה כתם:

אָמַר לוֹ ר' חִיָּיא: אִי אַתָּה מוֹדֶה שֶׁצְּרִיכָה כִּגְרִים וְעוֹד? א"ל: אֲבָל. אָמַר לוֹ: א"כ (אַתָּה) אַף אַתָּה עֲשִׂיתוֹ כֶּתֶם. וְרַבִּי סָבַר: אבָּעֵינַן כִּגְרִים וְעוֹד – לְאַפּוּקֵי מִדַּם מַאֲכוֹלֶת, וְכֵיוָן דִּנְפַק לָהּ מִדַּם מַאֲכוֹלֶת – וַדַּאי מִגּוּפָהּ אֲתָא. מַאי לָאו בְּזִקְנוּתוֹ קָאֵי? הָא בְּיַלְדוּתוֹ – טִימֵּא מִשּׁוּם נִדָּה! שְׁמַע מִינָּהּ. מִשְׁתַּבַּח לֵיהּ רַבִּי לְרַבִּי יִשְׁמָעֵאל בְּרַבִּי יוֹסֵי בְּרַבִּי חָמָא בַּר בִּיסָא דְּאָדָם גָּדוֹל הוּא. אָמַר לוֹ: לִכְשֶׁיָּבֹא לְיָדְךָ, הֲבִיאֵהוּ לְיָדִי. כִּי אֲתָא, א"ל: בְּעֵי מִינַּאי מִילְּתָא. בְּעָא מִינֵּיהּ: בָּדְקָה בְּעֵד שֶׁאֵינוֹ בָּדוּק לָהּ, וְהִנִּיחַתּוּ בְּקוּפְסָא, וּלְמָחָר מָצְאָה עָלָיו דָּם, מַהוּ? אָמַר לוֹ: כְּדִבְרֵי אַבָּא אֵימָא לָךְ, אוֹ כְּדִבְרֵי רַבִּי אֵימָא לָךְ? א"ל: כְּדִבְרֵי רַבִּי אֵימָא לִי. אָמַר רַבִּי יִשְׁמָעֵאל: זֶהוּ שֶׁאוֹמְרִין עָלָיו דְּאָדָם גָּדוֹל הוּא?! הֵיאַךְ מַנִּיחִין *דִּבְרֵי הָרַב וְשׁוֹמְעִין דִּבְרֵי הַתַּלְמִיד?! וְר' חָמָא בַּר בִּיסָא סָבַר: רַבִּי – רֵישׁ מְתִיבְתָּא הוּא, וּשְׁכִיחִי רַבָּנַן קַמֵּיהּ, וּמְחַדְּדִי שְׁמַעְתָּתֵיהּ. מַאי רַבִּי וּמַאי רַבִּי יוֹסֵי? אָמַר רַב אַדָּא בַּר מַתְנָא, תָּנָא: רַבִּי – מְטַמֵּא, וְרַבִּי יוֹסֵי – מְטַהֵר. וְאָמַר רַבִּי זֵירָא: כְּשֶׁטִּימֵּא רַבִּי – כְּר"מ, וּכְשֶׁטִּיהֵר רַבִּי יוֹסֵי – לְעַצְמוֹ טִיהֵר. *דְּתַנְיָא, *הָאִשָּׁה שֶׁהָיְתָה עוֹשָׂה צְרָכֶיהָ וְרָאֲתָה דָּם, ר"מ אוֹמֵר: אִם עוֹמֶדֶת – טְמֵאָה, אִם יוֹשֶׁבֶת – טְהוֹרָה. רַבִּי יוֹסֵי אוֹמֵר: בֵּין כָּךְ וּבֵין כָּךְ טְהוֹרָה. א"ל רַב אַחָא בְּרֵיהּ דְּרָבָא לְרַב אַשִׁי: וְהָא א"ר יוֹסֵי בְּר' חֲנִינָא: כְּשֶׁטִּימֵּא ר"מ – לֹא טִימֵּא אֶלָּא מִשּׁוּם כֶּתֶם, וְאִילּוּ רַבִּי מִשּׁוּם נִדָּה קָאָמַר! א"ל: אֲנַן הָכִי קָאָמְרִינַן: כִּי אִיתְּמַר הַהִיא – מִשּׁוּם נִדָּה אִיתְּמַר.§ "נִמְצָא עַל שֶׁלָּהּ אוֹתִיּוֹם טְמֵאִין" וכו'.§ ת"ר *אֵיזֶהוּ שִׁיעוּר וֶסֶת? – מָשָׁל לְשַׁמָּשׁ וְעֵד שֶׁעוֹמְדִין בְּצַד הַמַּשְׁקוֹף, בִּיצִיאַת שַׁמָּשׁ נִכְנָס עֵד, הֲוֵי: וֶסֶת שֶׁאָמְרוּ – לְקִינּוּחַ, אֲבָל לֹא לִבְדִיקָה.§ "נִמְצָא עַל שֶׁלָּהּ לְאַחַר זְמַן" וכו'.§ תָּנָא: *וְחַיָּיבִין אָשָׁם תָּלוּי. וְתַנָּא דִּידָן מ"ט – בבָּעֵינַן חֲתִיכָה מִשְׁתֵּי חֲתִיכוֹת.§ "אֵיזֶהוּ אַחַר זְמַן" וכו'.§ וּרְמִינְהִי, אֵיזֶהוּ "אַחַר זְמַן"? פֵּירֵשׁ ר' (א) אֱלִיעֶזֶר בְּרַבִּי צָדוֹק: כְּדֵי שֶׁתּוֹשִׁיט יָדָהּ תַּחַת הַכַּר אוֹ תַּחַת הַכֶּסֶת וְתִטּוֹל עֵד וְתִבְדּוֹק בּוֹ! אָמַר רַב חִסְדָּא: מַאי "אַחַר" – אַחַר (ב) אַחַר. וְהָא קָתָנֵי עֲלָהּ: "נִמְצָא עַל שֶׁלָּהּ לְאַחַר זְמַן – טְמֵאִין מִסָּפֵק וּפְטוּרִין מִן הַקָּרְבָּן. אֵיזֶהוּ "אַחַר זְמַן" – כְּדֵי שֶׁתֵּרֵד מִן הַמִּטָּה וְתָדִיחַ פָּנֶיהָ"! גה"ק: אֵיזֶהוּ "אַחַר זְמַן"? – כְּדֵי שֶׁתּוֹשִׁיט יָדָהּ לְתַחַת הַכַּר אוֹ לְתַחַת הַכֶּסֶת וְתִטּוֹל עֵד וְתִבְדּוֹק בּוֹ, וּכְדֵי שֶׁתֵּרֵד מִן הַמִּטָּה וְתָדִיחַ אֶת פָּנֶיהָ – מַחֲלוֹקֶת ר"ע וַחֲכָמִים. וְהָא אח"כ קָתָנֵי! ה"ק: וְזֶהוּ אח"כ שֶׁנֶּחְלְקוּ ר"ע וַחֲכָמִים. רַב אַשִׁי אָמַר: אִידִי וְאִידִי חַד שִׁיעוּרָא הוּא, עַד בְּיָדָהּ – כְּדֵי שֶׁתֵּרֵד מִן הַמִּטָּה וְתָדִיחַ אֶת פָּנֶיהָ, אֵין עַד בְּיָדָהּ – כְּדֵי שֶׁתּוֹשִׁיט יָדָהּ לְתַחַת הַכַּר אוֹ לְתַחַת הַכֶּסֶת וְתִטּוֹל עֵד וְתִבְדּוֹק בּוֹ. מֵיתִיבִי: אֵיזֶהוּ "אַחַר זְמַן"? דָּבָר זֶה שָׁאַל רַבִּי אֶלְעָזָר בְּרַבִּי צָדוֹק לִפְנֵי חֲכָמִים בְּאוּשָׁא, וְאָמַר לָהֶם:

שֶׁמָּא

רש"י

שֶׁצְּרִיכָה כִּגְרִים וְעוֹד. כְּשִׁיעוּר שְׁאָר כְּתָמִים שֶׁאֵין מְטַמְּאִין אֶלָּא בִּכְגְרִים וְעוֹד, כִּדְאָמְרִינַן בְּ"הָרוֹאָה כֶּתֶם" (לקמן דף נח.) דְּעַד כִּגְרִים יְכוֹלָה לִתְלוֹת וְלוֹמַר "דַּם מַאֲכוֹלֶת הוּא". אֲבָל. הֵן בֶּאֱמֶת. אָמַר לוֹ. ר' חִיָּיא. אַף אַתָּה עֲשִׂיתוֹ כֶּתֶם. נוֹהֵג אַתָּה בּוֹ דִּין כֶּתֶם דְּשִׁיעוּרוֹ כִּגְרִים וְעוֹד, וּבְפָחוֹת מִכָּאן – לָאו כְּלוּם. הִלְכָּךְ, טוּמְאָתוֹ נַמִי סָפֵק, דְּאִי וַדַּאי רְאִיָּה הֲוַאי מִגּוּפָהּ כִּדְקָאָמְרַתְּ, הָאָמַר בְּפֶ' "יוֹצֵא דוֹפֶן" (לקמן דף מ.): אֲפִי' כְּעֵין הַחַרְדָּל וּבְפָחוֹת מִכֵּן. לְאַפּוּקֵי מִדַּם מַאֲכוֹלֶת. דְּכֵיוָן דְּאֵינוֹ בָּדוּק לָהּ כָּל כַּמָּה דְּלֵיכָּא כִּגְרִים וְעוֹד, הֲוָה לָהּ לְסַפּוּקֵי בְּדַם מַאֲכוֹלֶת קוֹדֶם בְּדִיקָה. מַאי לָאו בְּזִקְנוּתוֹ קָאֵי. מִדְּפָלֵיג עֲלֵיהּ דְּרַבִּי רַבֵּיהּ. אֲמַר לֵיהּ. רַבִּי יִשְׁמָעֵאל לְרַבִּי חָמָא: בְּעֵי מִינַּאי מִילְּתָא. כְּדִבְרֵי אַבָּא. רַבִּי יוֹסֵי אוֹ כְּדִבְרֵי רַבִּי, וּלְקַמָּן תָּנֵי פְּלוּגְתַּיְיהוּ בִּשְׁמַעְתִּין. לְעַצְמוֹ טִיהֵר. לְטַעֲמֵיהּ אָזֵיל, דְּקָאָמַר נַמִי הָכִי בְּדוּכְתָּא אַחֲרִיתֵי (לקמן דף נט.). צְרָכֶיהָ. מַטִּילָה מַיִם. עוֹמֶדֶת טְמֵאָה. דְּכֵיוָן דִּדְחוּקָה הִיא – הַדּוֹר מֵי רַגְלַיִם לַמָּקוֹר, וְאַיְיתֵי דָּם. וְהָכִי מְפָרֵשׁ בְּפֶ' "הָאִשָּׁה" (שם). יוֹשֶׁבֶת טְהוֹרָה. דִּמְּמְקוֹם מֵי רַגְלַיִם הוּא בָּא וְאֵין טָמֵא אֶלָּא דַּם הַמָּקוֹר. וּמִדְּקָאָמַר רַבִּי מֵאִיר: עוֹמֶדֶת – טְמֵאָה, וְאַף עַל גַּב דְּאִיכָּא לְסַפּוּקִינְהוּ בִּמְקוֹם מֵי רַגְלַיִם, כֵּיוָן דְּרַגְלַיִם לַדָּבָר דְּדָחֵיק לָהּ עָלְמָא וְחֶזְקַת דָּמִים מִן הַמָּקוֹר מִיטַּמְּיָא – ה"נ מִיטַּמְּיָא. מִשּׁוּם כֶּתֶם. טוּמְאַת סָפֵק לִתְלוֹת, וְאִילּוּ רַבִּי לְעֵיל טִימֵּא מִשּׁוּם נִדָּה, דְּקָתָנֵי: "רַבִּי אוֹמֵר: טְמֵאָה נִדָּה". כִּי אִיתְּמַר. הַהִיא דְּר' יוֹסֵי בַּר חֲנִינָא. הֲוֵי וֶסֶת שֶׁאָמְרוּ. לְחַיְּיבָהּ בְּחַטָּאת. לְקִינּוּחַ. מִבַּחוּץ וְלֹא לִבְדִיקָה מִבִּפְנִים, דְּאִ"כ שָׁהֲתָה יוֹתֵר מִכַּשִּׁיעוּר, וְאֵין כָּאן אֶלָּא טוּמְאַת סָפֵק וְאָשָׁם תָּלוּי. תָּנָא וְחַיָּיבִין בְּאָשָׁם תָּלוּי. אַ"נִמְצָא לְאַחַר אוֹתִיּוֹם" קָאֵי, דְּקָתָנֵי בְּמַתְנִיתִין: "וּפְטוּרִין מִן הַקָּרְבָּן". בָּעֵינַן חֲתִיכָה מִשְׁתֵּי חֲתִיכוֹת. דִּכְתִיב בְּאָשָׁם תָּלוּי (ויקרא ה): "אַחַת מִכָּל מִצְוֹת ה'" וְקָסָבַר: יֵשׁ אֵם לַמִּקְרָא "מִצְוֹת" קָרֵינַן. הִילְכָּךְ, בָּעֵינַן שְׁתַּיִם: אַחַת שֶׁל אִיסּוּר, וְאַחַת שֶׁל הֶיתֵּר, וְאָכַל אַחַת וְאֵינוֹ יוֹדֵעַ אֵיזֶהוּ אָכַל. אִשְׁתּוֹ וַאֲחוֹתוֹ עִמּוֹ בַּבַּיִת, וּבָא עַל אַחַת מֵהֶן, כְּסָבוּר: אִשְׁתּוֹ הִיא, וְנוֹדַע שֶׁשְּׁתֵּיהֶן הָיוּ בַּמִּטָּה, וְאֵינוֹ יוֹדֵעַ עַל אֵיזֶהוּ מֵהֶן בָּא. אֲבָל הָכָא, חֲדָא חֲתִיכָה הִיא: סָפֵק שַׁרְיָא סָפֵק אֲסוּרָה. וְתַנָּא בְּרָא סָבַר: יֵשׁ אֵם לַמָּסוֹרֶת. וְהָכִי פְּלִיגִי בְּמַסֶּכֶת כְּרֵיתוֹת (דף יז.). שֶׁתּוֹשִׁיט. וְעוֹדָהּ בַּמִּטָּה, הָא "כְּדֵי שֶׁתֵּרֵד" – שִׁיעוּרָא רַבָּה, (ג) וְאֵינָהּ מְטַמְּאָה אֶת בּוֹעֲלָהּ אֶלָּא כִּשְׁאָר מַגָּע מֵעֵת לְעֵת. מַאי אַחַר. דְּקָתָנֵי בְּמַתְנִי' "אֵיזֶהוּ אַחַר זְמַן כְּדֵי שֶׁתֵּרֵד" – לָאו אַ"אַחַר אוֹתִיּוֹם" קָאֵי, דִּמְטַמְּאִים מִסָּפֵק, אֶלָּא אֵיזֶהוּ "אַחַר זְמַן" שֶׁהוּא אַחַר אוֹתוֹ שֶׁלְּאַחַר אוֹתִיּוֹם, שֶׁאֵינָהּ מְטַמְּאָה אֶת בּוֹעֲלָהּ לְרַבָּנַן אֶלָּא לְר"ע – כְּדֵי שֶׁתֵּרֵד כו'. וְהָא עֲלָהּ קָתָנֵי כו'. אַלְמָא אַ"טְמֵאִין מִסָּפֵק" קָאֵי, מִשּׁוּם שֶׁמְּטַמְּאָה אֶת בּוֹעֲלָהּ אֲפִי' לְרַבָּנַן. הָכִי קָאָמַר. חַסּוּרֵי מִחַסְּרָא וְהָכִי קָתָנֵי: אֵיזֶהוּ אַחַר זְמַן שֶׁהֵן טְמֵאִין מִסָּפֵק – כְּדֵי שֶׁתּוֹשִׁיט. אֲבָל שָׁהֲתָה כְּדֵי שֶׁתֵּרֵד – מְטַמְּאָה מֵעֵת לְעֵת, וְאֵינָהּ מְטַמְּאָה אֶת בּוֹעֲלָהּ. רַבִּי עֲקִיבָא אוֹמֵר: מְטַמְּאָה אֶת בּוֹעֲלָהּ, וַאֲפִילּוּ כָּל מֵעֵת לְעֵת. וְהָא אח"כ קָתָנֵי. דְּקָתָנֵי בְּמַתְנִי': "וְאח"כ מְטַמְּאָה מֵעֵת לְעֵת וְאֵינָהּ מְטַמְּאָה" כו', אַלְמָא כְּשֶׁשָּׁהֲתָה יוֹתֵר מִכְּדֵי שֶׁתֵּרֵד הוּא דִּפְלִיגִי, אֲבָל בִּכְדֵי שֶׁתֵּרֵד – *טוּמְאָה אֲפִילּוּ לְרַבָּה, וְקַשְׁיָא בָּרַיְיתָא דִּ"כְדֵי שֶׁתּוֹשִׁיט". וְזֶהוּ אח"כ. הַאי שִׁיעוּרָא דִּ"כְדֵי שֶׁתֵּרֵד" זֶהוּ "אח"כ" שֶׁנֶּחְלְקוּ בּוֹ ר"ע וַחֲכָמִים. עַד בְּיָדָהּ. שֶׁאֵינָהּ צְרִיכָה לְהוֹשִׁיט יָדָהּ תַּחַת הַכַּר, הָוֵי שִׁיעוּרָא בִּכְדֵי שֶׁתֵּרֵד וְתַדִּיחַ בְּאוֹתוֹ עֵד. אֵין עַד בְּיָדָהּ. דְּבָעֲיָא לְהוֹשִׁיט יָדָהּ תַּחַת הַכַּר. בִּכְדֵי שֶׁתּוֹשִׁיט. וְתִבְדּוֹק וְעוֹדָהּ בַּמִּטָּה. וּלְרַב חִסְדָּא אֲפִי' עַד בְּיָדָהּ, נָפֵישׁ "כְּדֵי שֶׁתֵּרֵד" מִ"כְּדֵי שֶׁתּוֹשִׁיט", הִילְכָּךְ "אַחַר אַחַר" הוּא.

שֶׁמָּא

תוספות

בעד שאינו בדוק לה. נראה לפרש: דידעה שהיה נקי לפני יום או יומים, ועתה בשעת בדיקה נטלתו ממקום המוצנע, ולא בדקה העד. אבל אין נראה לפרש: שלא היה בדוק מעולם, דבהא לא היה רבי מחזיק טומאה ודאי. מאי לאו בזקנותו. פרש"י: מדפליג על רבי. ואין נראה, דמצינו הרבה תלמידים שחולקים על רבם בילדותם! ורשב"ם פירש: דרבי חייא תחילה למד בבבל, ולעת זקנתו עלה ולמד לפני רבי, כדאמרינן (סוכה דף כ.) חזרה ונשתכחה – עלו רבי חייא ובניו, ויסדוה. ועי"ל: מדקאמר רבי חייא "אף אתה עשיתו כתם", ולא קאמר "אף אתה רבי", ש"מ דבזקנותו היה, דהוה תלמיד חבר, כדאמר בשילהי "מי שמת" (ב"ב דף קנח:) בן עזאי – תלמיד חבר של רבי עקיבא, דאמר ליה (*"שב אתה", ולא קאמר "שב מר"). האיך מניחין דברי הרב. משמע דר' יוסי היה רבו של רבי. וקשה: דאמר בפ' (ד) "זה בורר" (סנהדרין כד.) כמה מחבבים זה את זה, דאילו ר' יוסי קיים, הוה כפוף ויושב לפני רבי, ואמר "כבר הורה זקן". ורש"י פי' התם: *שהיה כפוף, מחמת כבוד נשיאותו של רבי. ואין נראה, דא"כ היכי מוכיח דמחבבין זה את זה, וכי בשביל נשיאות לא היה לו לפסוק כרבו? ואור"ת: *דבבחרותו של רבי היה ר' יוסי גדול יותר, ובזקנותו [מחמת התלמידים] נתחכם רבי יותר, כדאמר נמי הכא: הואיל ושכיחי רבנן קמיה – מחדדין שמעתתיה. ורבי יוסי מטהר. נראה דלגמרי מטהר, מדקאמר "לעצמו טיהר". כמו גבי "אשה שעשתה צרכיה", דהתם נראה דלגמרי מטהר. דאין נראה לפרש "לעצמו טיהר", דמדמטהר גבי אשה שעשתה צרכיה לגמרי, הכא בעד שאינו בדוק – יטהר לכל הפחות מנדה ויעשנה כמו כתם, דא"כ, מאי פריך בסמוך: האמר ר' יוסי בר' חנינא לא טימא ר"מ כו', מאי קושיא? והלא יש להחמיר בעד שאינו בדוק לה טפי מבאשה שעושה צרכיה! מיהו ר"ח פירש: דר' יוסי לאו לגמרי מטהר באשה שעושה צרכיה, וכמסקנא דר"מ משום נדה איתמר. ולפי' זה הא דתנן בפ' "האשה" (לקמן דף נט:) איש ואשה שעשו צרכיהן בספל ונמצא דם, דר' יוסי מטהר, ופריך בגמרא: למה לי הן בבא? ומשני: אי מרישא, ה"א דיעבד קמ"ל סיפא, דאף לכתחלה. לפי' ר"ח לא קאי אף לכתחלה ארישא, אלא אסיפא דוקא.

בעינן חתיכה מב' חתיכות. וא"ת: ברים פ' "ספק אכל" (כריתות דף יז,) דפריך לר' חייא בר רב דבעי חתיכה מב' חתיכות מברייתא דהכא, ומשני: רבי אליעזר היא, דאמר: כוי חייבין על חלבו אשם תלוי. אדמקשה מברייתא, לסייעיה ממתני' דהכא דפטרה מקרבן? *וי"ל: דשמא מתניתין לא פטריה אלא מחטאת, ולא פליג אברייתא. והא דקאמר "ותנא דידן", ה"ק: את"ל דמתניתין פוטר אף מאשם תלוי, היינו טעמא דסבר בעינן חתיכה מב' חתיכות. מאי אחר אחר אחר. ותימה: כיון דתנא "כדי שתושיט ידה ותטול עד תחת הכר", דהוי טמא בועלה שבעה, וחייב אשם תלוי, ממילא ידעינן דאם תשהה יותר עד שתרד מן המטה ד"אחר אחר" הוא, ואינה מטמאה בועלה טומאת שבעה! [עיין ברשב"א].

לא

[בכריתות איתא זה בקושיא]

רבנן קמיה דמחדדן שמעתתיה כדאמרינן נמי בעלמא הרבה למדתי מרבותי ומתלמידי יותר מכולם: מאי אחר אחר אחר. תימה למה לי שיעורא דאחר אחר דכיון דאשמעינן זמן דאחר ממילא ידעינן דטפי פורתא הוי אחר אחר. וי"ל כדי להבחין ולידע זמן שלאחר דטפי פורתא הוי אחר אחר:

עד

תוספי הרא"ש

ור' קסבר בעינן כגרים ועוד לאפוקי מדם מאכולת. ולר' האי דקתני בדקה בעד שאינו בדוק לה היינו בחלוקה או בסדינה דאילו באחד מכל הבגדים ליכא למיחש לדם מאכולת: בזקנותו קאי. פרש"י ז"ל מדפליג עליה דרבי ומיהו בכמה מקומות בתלמוד מצינו שנחלק התלמיד עם הרב ונראה לפרש דדייק מדא"ל אף אתה עשיתו כתם. ולא קאמר אף אתה רבי עשאו כתם משמע דבזקנותו היה. שאז היה לו תלמיד חבר כדאמרינן בפ' מי שמת דבן עזאי תלמיד חבר דר' עקיבא מדקא"ל שבאת ולא קאמר שבא ר'. אבל אין לפרש דדייק משום דלית לן לאוקמי לפלוגתייהו בג' דיינין חלוקין שר' טימא משום נדה ור' חייא בילדותו משום כתם ובזקנותו טיהר מכלום א"נ שלא להפליג כ"כ בין סברת ר' לסברת ר' חייא דע"כ ר' יוסי מטהר לגמרי בהך דלקמן דמייתי עלה הך ר' יוסי אומר בין כך ובין כך טהורים והיינו לגמרי כדמפרש לקמן בפרק האשה. ומיהו ר"ח פירש דטהורים דר' יוסי לאו דוקא: מניחין דברי הרב. תימה והאמרינן בפ' זה בורר אילו היה ר' יוסי קיים כפוף ויושב לפני רבי מפרש רשב"ם מפני כבוד נשיאותו. ור"ת מפרש דלסוף נתחכם רבי ביותר כשנעשה ראש ישיבה מרוב התלמידים כדאמרינן הכא דשכיחי

עין משפט נר מצוה

לט א מיי' פ"ד מהל' איסורי ביאה הלכה יט וע"ש במ"מ סמג לאוין קכו טוש"ע י"ד סימן קצ סעיף לג:

מ ב מיי' פ"ח מהלכות שגגות הל' ב סמג עשין ריב:

מא ג מיי' שם פ"ה הל' ו טור י"ד סימן קפז:

[נ"ל שבאת ולא קאמר שבא מר]

[ובשבת נא.]

[וע"ע בתוס' לשבת נא. ד"ה אילו היה וכו']

מסורת הש"ס

סנהדרין כט. קדושין מב:

נ"ל דתנן

לקמן נז: נט:

[לעיל יב.]

[כריתות יז:]

נ"ל מטמאה אפי' לרבנן וקשיא כו'

הגהות הב"ח

(א) גמ' פי' ר' אלעזר בר' צדוק: (ב) שם מאי אחר אחר דאחר וכו': (ג) רש"י ד"ה שתושיט וכו' רבה הוא ואינה: (ד) תוס' ד"ה היאך וכו' בפ' זה בורר כ"ד בדף כ"ד וכן בדף כ"ה כמה טומנין בדף נח. ולכן פי' רש"י כפוף מפני כבוד הנשיאות כו':

גליון הש"ס

גמ' משתבח ליה כו'. כעין זה ברכות לה ע"ח ובשבת שם אמר רב חסדא מאי אחר אחר וכו'. כעין זה נזיר קף טו ע"ב: רש"י ד"ה בעינן וכו' אבל שההה כדי שתרד וכו'. עי' רש"י לקמן דף ע"ב ד"ה בעלה באשם תלוי וכו' וטומאת לדף ז ע"ב ברש"י ד"ה אלא לאחר:

שֶׁמָּא כְּרַבִּי עֲקִיבָא אַתֶּם אוֹמְרִים, שֶׁמְּטַמְּאָה אֶת בּוֹעֲלָהּ? אָמְרוּ לוֹ: לֹא שְׁמַעְנוּ. אָמַר לָהֶם, כָּךְ פֵּרְשׁוּ חֲכָמִים בְּיַבְנֶה: [א]לֹא שֶׁהָתָה כְּדֵי שֶׁתֵּרֵד מִן הַמִּטָּה וְתַדִּיחַ אֶת פָּנֶיהָ — תּוֹךְ זְמַן הוּא זֶה, וּטְמֵאִין מִסָּפֵק, וּפְטוּרִין מִקָּרְבָּן, וְחַיָּיבִין בְּאָשָׁם תָּלוּי. שֶׁהָתָה כְּדֵי שֶׁתֵּרֵד מִן הַמִּטָּה וְתַדִּיחַ אֶת פָּנֶיהָ — אַחַר הַזְּמַן הוּא זֶה. וְכֵן כְּשֶׁשָּׁהֲתָה מֵעֵת לְעֵת וּמִפְּקִידָה לִפְקִידָה — [ב]בּוֹעֲלָהּ מְטַמֵּא מִשּׁוּם מַגָּע, וְאֵינוֹ מְטַמֵּא מִשּׁוּם בּוֹעֵל. רַבִּי עֲקִיבָא אוֹמֵר: אַף מְטַמֵּא מִשּׁוּם בּוֹעֵל. רַבִּי יְהוּדָה בְּנוֹ שֶׁל רַבָּן יוֹחָנָן בֶּן זַכַּאי אוֹמֵר: בַּעְלָהּ נִכְנָס לַהֵיכָל וּמַקְטִיר קְטוֹרֶת. בִּשְׁלָמָא לְרַב חִסְדָּא — הַיְינוּ דִּמְטַהֲרִי רַבָּנָן. אֶלָּא לְרַב אַשִׁי — אַמַּאי מְטַהֲרִי רַבָּנָן? וְכִי תֵּימָא: דְּאֵין עֵד בְּיָדָהּ, הַאי "עֵד בְּיָדָהּ" וְ"אֵין עֵד בְּיָדָהּ" מִיבְּעֵי לֵיהּ! קַשְׁיָא.§ "רַבִּי יְהוּדָה בְּנוֹ שֶׁל רַבָּן יוֹחָנָן בֶּן זַכַּאי אוֹמֵר: בַּעְלָהּ נִכְנָס לַהֵיכָל וּמַקְטִיר קְטוֹרֶת". וְתִיפּוֹק לֵיהּ דַּהֲוָה נוֹגֵעַ בְּמֵעֵת לְעֵת שֶׁבְּנִדָּה! הוּא דְּאָמַר כְּשַׁמַּאי, דְּאָמַר: *כָּל הַנָּשִׁים דַּיָּין שְׁעָתָן. וְתִיפּוֹק לֵיהּ דַּהֲוָה בַּעַל קֶרִי! בְּשֶׁלֹּא גָּמַר בִּיאָתוֹ.§ "וּמוֹדִים חֲכָמִים לְרַבִּי עֲקִיבָא בְּרוֹאָה כֶּתֶם".§ אָמַר רַב: לְמַפְרֵעַ, וְרַבִּי מֵאִיר הִיא. וּשְׁמוּאֵל אָמַר: [ג]מִכָּאן וּלְהַבָּא, וְרַבָּנָן הִיא. מִכָּאן וּלְהַבָּא, פְּשִׁיטָא! מַהוּ דְּתֵימָא: הוֹאִיל *וּמֵעֵת לְעֵת דְּרַבָּנָן, וּכְתָמִים דְּרַבָּנָן, מַה מֵּעֵת לְעֵת — לֹא מְטַמְּאָה אֶת בּוֹעֲלָהּ, אַף כְּתָמִים לֹא מְטַמְּאָה אֶת בּוֹעֲלָהּ, קָא מַשְׁמַע לַן. וְאֵימָא הָכִי נַמִי! הָתָם — אֵין שׁוֹר שָׁחוּט לְפָנֶיךָ, הָכָא — יֵשׁ שׁוֹר שָׁחוּט לְפָנֶיךָ. וְכֵן אָמַר רֵישׁ לָקִישׁ: לְמַפְרֵעַ, וְרַבִּי מֵאִיר הִיא. רַבִּי יוֹחָנָן אָמַר: מִכָּאן וּלְהַבָּא, וְרַבָּנָן הִיא.§

**מתני'** *[ד]כָּל הַנָּשִׁים בְּחֶזְקַת טָהֳרָה לְבַעֲלֵיהֶן. [ה]הַבָּאִין מִן הַדֶּרֶךְ — נְשֵׁיהֶן לָהֶן בְּחֶזְקַת טָהֳרָה.§

**גמ'** לָמָּה לֵיהּ לְמִתְנֵי "הַבָּאִין מִן הַדֶּרֶךְ"? סד"א: הָנֵי מִילֵּי — הֵיכָא דְּאִיתֵיהּ בְּמָתָא, דְּרַמְיָא אַנַּפְשָׁהּ וּבָדְקָה, אֲבָל הֵיכָא דְּלֵיתָא בְּמָתָא — דְּלָא רַמְיָא אַנַּפְשָׁהּ — לָא, קָא מַשְׁמַע לַן. אָמַר רֵישׁ לָקִישׁ מִשּׁוּם רַבִּי יְהוּדָה נְשִׂיאָה: [ו]וְהוּא שֶׁבָּא וּמְצָאָהּ בְּתוֹךְ יְמֵי עוֹנָתָהּ. אָמַר רַב הוּנָא: לֹא שָׁנוּ אֶלָּא שֶׁאֵין לָהּ וֶסֶת, אֲבָל יֵשׁ לָהּ וֶסֶת — אָסוּר לְשַׁמֵּשׁ. כְּלַפֵּי לְיָיא? אַדְּרַבָּה, אִיפְּכָא מִסְתַּבְּרָא! אֵין לָהּ וֶסֶת — אֵימָא חֲזַאי, יֵשׁ לָהּ וֶסֶת — וֶסֶת קָבִיעַ לָהּ! אֶלָּא, אִי אִיתְּמַר — הָכִי אִיתְּמַר, אָמַר רַב הוּנָא: [ז]לֹא שָׁנוּ אֶלָּא שֶׁלֹּא הִגִּיעַ שְׁעַת וְסְתָּהּ, אֲבָל הִגִּיעַ שְׁעַת וְסְתָּהּ — אֲסוּרָה. קָסָבַר: *וְסָתוֹת דְּאוֹרַיְיתָא. רַבָּה בַּר בַּר חָנָה אָמַר: אֲפִילּוּ הִגִּיעַ שְׁעַת וְסְתָּהּ — נַמִי מוּתֶּרֶת, קָסָבַר: [ח]וְסָתוֹת דְּרַבָּנַן. רַב אַשִׁי מַתְנֵי הָכִי, אָמַר רַב הוּנָא: לא

---

**רש"י**

שֶׁמָּא כְּר"ע אַתֶּם אוֹמְרִים שֶׁמְּטַמְּאָה אֶת בּוֹעֲלָהּ. כָּל מֵעֵת לְעֵת, וְאֵין לָכֶם שִׁיעוּר בַּדָּבָר אֶלָּא מֵעֵת לְעֵת. לֹא שְׁמַעְנוּ. אֶת שִׁיעוּרוֹ, (וּכְר"א) לָא סְבִירָא לַן. לֹא שֶׁהָתָה כְּדֵי שֶׁתֵּרֵד. אֶלָּא כְּדֵי שֶׁתֵּשֵׁב וְתִבְדּוֹק וְעוֹדָהּ בַּמִּטָּה – טְמֵאִין מִסָּפֵק, דְּהַיְינוּ אַחַר אוֹתִיּוֹס, כְּרַב חִסְדָּא. שֶׁהָתָה כְּדֵי שֶׁתֵּרֵד. דְּנָפֵישׁ שִׁיעוּרֵיהּ. אַחַר הַזְּמַן הוּא זֶה. כְּלוֹמַר: אַחַר אַחַר הוּא זֶה. וְכֵן מֵעֵת לְעֵת. כְּלוֹמַר: כַּשִּׁיעוּר הַזֶּה, וּמִכָּאן וּלְהַלָּן כָּל מֵעֵת לְעֵת שֶׁל בְּעִילָה אִם בָּדְקָה וּמְצָאָתָהּ טְמֵאָה – בּוֹעֲלָהּ מְטַמְּאָה מִשּׁוּם נוֹגֵעַ בְּמֵעֵת לְעֵת בְּנִדָּה טוּמְאַת עֶרֶב, וְסָפֵק מִדְּרַבָּנַן לִתְלוֹת. וְאֵינוֹ מְטַמֵּא מִשּׁוּם בּוֹעֵל נִדָּה טוּמְאַת שִׁבְעָה, וַאֲפִילּוּ לִתְלוֹת. נִכְנָס לַהֵיכָל. לְקַמָּן מְפָרֵשׁ לָהּ. בִּשְׁלָמָא לְרַב חִסְדָּא. דְּאָמַר: כְּדֵי שֶׁתֵּרֵד "אַחַר אַחַר" הוּא, הַיְינוּ דִּמְטַהֲרִי רַבָּנַן. וְכִי תֵימָא דְּאֵין עֵד בְּיָדָהּ. דְּאַחַר שֶׁתֵּרֵד הוּצְרְכָה לְהוֹשִׁיט, דַּהֲוָה לְהוּ תְּרֵי שִׁיעוּרֵי, א"כ אִיבָּעֵי לֵיהּ לְמִיתְנֵי וּלְפַלּוּגֵי בֵּין עֵד בְּיָדָהּ לְאֵין עֵד בְּיָדָהּ, דְּלָא תֵּיפּוֹק חוּרְבָּה מִינֵּיהּ. דְּהַשְׁתָּא מַשְׁמַע: דַּאֲפִילּוּ עֵד בְּיָדָהּ, דְּלֹא שָׁהֲתָה אֶלָּא כְּדֵי שֶׁתֵּרֵד, מְטַהֲרִי רַבָּנַן. וּמִדְּלָא מַפְלִיג, ש"מ דְּוַדַּאי מְטַהֲרִי רַבָּנַן בִּכְדֵי שֶׁתֵּרֵד לְחוּדֵיהּ. בְּשֶׁלֹּא גָּמַר בִּיאָתוֹ. וַאֲפִילּוּ הָכִי לְר"ע מְטַמְּאָה אֶת בּוֹעֲלָהּ, דְּהַעֲרָאָה בְּנִדָּה – כִּגְמַר בִּיאָה, דִּכְתִיב (ויקרא כ): "אֶת מְקוֹרָהּ הֶעֱרָה", אֲבָל לְעִנְיַן קֶרִי – עַד שֶׁיַּזְרִיעַ. וְר"מ הִיא. דְּמַחְמִיר בִּכְתָמִים, כִּדְאָמַר בְּפ"ק (לעיל ה.) וּלְקַמָּן בְּפֶרֶק "בָּא סִימָן" (דף נב.). פְּשִׁיטָא. מַאי מוֹדֵי, הָא בִּלְמַפְרֵעַ פְּלִיגִי לְגַבֵּי מֵעֵת לְעֵת, וְלָא בְּמִכָּאן וּלְהַבָּא? וּכְתָמִים דְּרַבָּנַן. אֲפִי' מִכָּאן וּלְהַבָּא. אֵין שׁוֹר שָׁחוּט. דְּאֶתְמוֹל לָא חֲזַאי, אֶלָּא סְיָיג בְּעָלְמָא הוּא. הָכָא הֲרֵי שׁוֹר שָׁחוּט לְפָנֶיךָ. דִּבְלִפּוּר לָא נִתְעַסְּקָה, וּבְשׁוּק שֶׁל טַבָּחִים לֹא עָבְרָה, וּמִיּוֹם שֶׁלְּבָשַׁתּוּ הָיָה בְּסָפֵק זֶה. **מתני'** כָּל הַנָּשִׁים בְּחֶזְקַת טָהֳרָה לְבַעֲלֵיהֶן. בְּלָא בְּדִיקָה, שֶׁלֹּא הוּזְכְּרָה בְּדִיקָה אֶלָּא לַעֲסוּקָה בְּטָהֳרוֹת. **גמ'** בְּתוֹךְ יְמֵי עוֹנָתָהּ. ל' יוֹם לִרְאִיָּיה, אֲבָל לְאַחַר ל' – בָּעְיָא בְּדִיקָה, הוֹאִיל וּסְתָם נָשִׁים חָזְיָין לְסוֹף עוֹנָה. לֹא שָׁנוּ. דְּכִי מְצָאָהּ תּוֹךְ יְמֵי עוֹנָתָהּ לָא בָּעְיָא בְּדִיקָה. אֶלָּא שֶׁלֹּא הִגִּיעַ עֵת וְסְתָּהּ. בְּתוֹךְ אוֹתָן יָמִים שֶׁהָיָה בַּדֶּרֶךְ, כְּגוֹן אִשָּׁה שֶׁיֵּשׁ לָהּ וֶסֶת, וְלֹא הִגִּיעַ בְּתוֹךְ אוֹתָן הַיָּמִים. אֲבָל הִגִּיעַ עֵת וְסְתָּהּ. קוֹדֶם בִּיאָתוֹ מִן הַדֶּרֶךְ. אֲסוּרָה. דְּאוֹרַח בִּזְמַנּוֹ בָּא. דְּאוֹרַיְיתָא. הִלְכָּךְ מַחְזְקִינַן לָהּ בְּטוּמְאַת סָפֵק. וְסָתוֹת דְּרַבָּנַן. הִצְרִיכוּהָ חֲכָמִים לִבְדּוֹק בְּיוֹם וְסְתָּהּ, שֶׁמָּא תִּרְאֶה. וּמִיהוּ הֵיכָא דְּלָא הֲוָה בָּעִיר, וְלָא יָדְעִינַן אִי בָּדְקָה אִי לָא בָּדְקָה – לָא מְסַפְּקִינַן לָהּ בְּטוּמְאָה. לא

---

**תוספות**

**לא** שהתה כדי שתרד מן המטה מטמאה את בועלה [וחייבת באשם תלוי] שהתה כדי שתרד כו' ר"ע אומר מטמאה בועלה. תימה: אי ר"ע מודה ברישא, כדמשמע דלא פליג אלא אסיפא, א"כ סבר: יש אם למסורת. ובפ"ק דסנהדרין (דף ד.) אית ליה לר"ע יש אם למקרא, גבי "רביעית דם הבא משני מתים". דקאמר "נפשות" קרינן! וליכא למימר: דהכא פליג נמי ברישא, דהתנן פ' "דם שחיטה" (כריתות דף כב:) בחתיכה של קודש וחתיכה של חולין, אכל אחד את הראשונה ובא אחר ואכל את השניה – זה מביא אשם תלוי, וזה מביא אשם תלוי, דברי ר"ע. ואמאי חייב השני, הא בשעה שאכל לא היו לפניו ב' חתיכות, ולמאן דבעי ב' חתיכות פטור בכה"ג, כדאמר התם בסוף פרקין. ורבי נמי אית ליה בפ' "ספק אכל" (שם דף יח.) היכא דאכל את הראשונה במזיד והשניה בשוגג, דחייב אשם תלוי על השניה, ורבי סבר בפ"ק דסנהדרין (דף ד.) יש אם למקרא! וי"ל: דיש שום חילוק בין מקרא למסורת זה למקרא ומסורת דעלמא. דחייא בר רב דבעי ב' חתיכות, סבר: דכ"ע סברי הכא דיש אם למקרא, ורב אסי דפליג עליה סבר: דכ"ע סברי יש אם למסורת, *כמו שמצינו (ב"מ דף כב:) גבי "יותן" דומיא ד"יתן" ו"עובד" דומיא ד"עבד" (פסחים דף כו:) ו"עוני" דומיא ד"עני" (שם לו.) ו"כפות" דומיא ד"כפת" (סוכה דף לב.) והתם יש טעמא אחרינא. ותדע: דכי פריך התם תובא לחייא בר רב, ומשני: ר"א היא דמחייב אשם תלוי על חלב כוי, והא כמה תנאי פליגי במקרא ובמסורת, ואמאי נקט טפי ר"א דשמותי הוא? וגם המקשה, וכי לא הוה ידע דטובא תנאי פליגי במקרא ובמסורת? אלא כדפרישית. ועוד י"ל: דר"ע ורבי איירו דהראשון לא אכל כל החתיכה, אלא חציה, וכשאכל השניה – היו עדיין ב' החתיכות לפניו. וכענין זה מתרץ הירושלמי ב"האשה רבה"*. **האי** עד בידה ואין עד בידה מיבעי ליה. פרש"י: דה"ל לפלוגי הכל בשהתה. וקשה: דלמא מפליג בדידה באין עד בידה, בין שהתה ללא שהתה? ונראה לפרש: דה"ל לפרושי בברייתא באין עד בידה, כיון דמתניתין איירי ביש עד בידה. **כשמאי** דאמר דיה שעתה. ומ"מ מודה שמאי בחד "אחר" דטמא שבעה, כיון דחייב אשם תלוי. **אמר** רב למפרע ור"מ היא. וא"ת: דבפ"ק דיומא (דף ב.) תנן: מפרישין כ"ג מביתו ז' ימים דשמא יבא על אשתו *ספק נדה, וקאמר: *כמאן כר"ע דאמר: אף מטמאה את בועלה. וקאמר רב חסדא: דאתי אפילו כרבנן, ובחד "אחר" מודו דבועלה טמא ז' אמאי לא משני: שמא תמצא כתם? דהא מודים חכמים לר"ע ברואה כתם! וי"ל: משום שמואל דאמר הכא: מכאן ולהבא. ועוד י"ל: דהיא תבדוק חלוקה קודם פרישתו, ואז לא נטמא הכהן קודם בדיקה. וא"ת: אמאי קאמר "שמא תמצא אשתו ספק נדה", לימא "ודאי נדה" אם תבדוק שיעור וסת סמוך לבעילה? וי"ל: דהא לא שכיחא. **הכי** איתמר לא שנו אלא שלא הגיע שעת וסתה. לא היה לו לחזור ממה שאמר תחלה "לא שנו אלא שאין לה וסת", דאמת הוא דהיא בחזקת טהרה, כדאמרינן בפ"ק (לעיל יב.) כל לבעלה לא בעיא בדיקה, אפילו אין לה וסת. והיה יכול להוסיף: ויש לה וסת נמי, כשלא הגיע שעת וסתה כו'. אלא מיישב הלשון שאמר תחלה בלא תוספת. **אפי'** הגיע זמן וסתה מותרת. תימה: היאך מותרת, הא אמרינן בשבועות פ"ב (דף יח:) ולקמן פרק "האשה" (דף סג:) אזהרה לבני ישראל שיפרשו מנשותיהן סמוך לוסתן! וי"ל: כששהתה אחר וסתה שבעה ימים, שיכולה לטבול איירי, דספק טבילה מוציאה מידי ספק ראתה, כההוא דר' יוחנן דבסמוך. ולמ"ד וסתות דאורייתא, אפילו ששהתה כשיעור זמן טבילה – אסורה, דודאי ראתה חשבינן לה, ומתוך כך יש לדקדק דס"ל לרבי יוחנן דבסמוך (א) וסתות דרבנן. אפילו

---

**עין משפט נר מצוה**

מב א מיי' פ"ה מהל' שגגות הל' ו:

מג ב ג מיי' פ"ג מהל' מטמאי משכב ומושב הלכה ח:

מד ד מיי' פ"ד מהל' איסורי ביאה הל' ט ופ"ד מהל' משכב ומושב הל' ז סמג לאוין קיא:

מה ה ו מיי' פ"ד מהל' איסורי ביאה הל' ט סמג שם:

מו ז מיי' שם הלכה ט ועי' במ"מ סמג שם טוש"ע י"ד סי' קפד סעיף א:

מז ח מיי' פ"ג מהלכות משכב ומושב הל' ט:

---

**מסורת הש"ס**

[צ"ל וכר"ע]

[לעיל ב.]

[לעיל ט.]

[לעיל יא:]

[לעיל ט. וש"נ]

[יומא ח.]

עיין רש"א

[וע"ע תוס' סוכה ו: ד"ה ר"ש ותוס' שם לב. ד"ה כפת ותוספות סנהדרין ד"ה כולהו ותוס' זבחים מ. ד"ה לא נצרכא]

[שם ו.]

---

**הגהות הב"ח**

(א) תוס' ד"ה אפי' וכו' דבסמוך וסתות דרבנן כ"ב כלומר דהשתא דרבי יוחנן נמי ס"ל וסתות דרבנן וכדסבירא ליה לרב אליבא דר"ה בר יצחק הכי נקטינן וכדכתבו התוס' בדף טז בד"ה ור"ה בר יצחק וכן כתב בהשר"י:

---

**תוספי הרא"ש**

**עד** בידה ואין עד בידה מיבעי ליה. פרש"י א"כ איבעי ליה למתני' לפלוגי בין עד בידה לאין עד בידה דלא תיפוק מיניה חורבא דהשתא משמע דאפי' עד בידה ולא שהה אלא כדי שתרד מטהרי רבנן. וקשה לפי' דהא מתני' אוקימנא בעד בידה ואע"ג דלא קתני עד בידה ולא חיישינן דלמא נפיק מיניה חורבא. ועוד אמאי קאמר עד בידה ואין עד בידה מיבעי ליה לא הוה ליה למימר אלא אין עד בידה מיבעי ליה הלכך נראה לפרש דה"ק אע"ג דאוקימנא מתני' בעד בידה מ"מ כי נוקי ברייתא באין עד בידה אכתי תקשי לך א"כ נתני בהדיא במתני' עד בידה ואין עד בידה כברייתא אלא ש"מ מדתנן סתם בחד ענינא איירי: **סד"א** ה"מ היכא דאיתיה במתא רמיא אנפשה ובדקה. תי' והא לעיל בפ"ק אמרינן איפכא דהבאים מן הדרך נשיהן להם בחזקת טהרה טפי מאינך וי"ל דהכא ודאי לענין בדיקה היכי דאיתיה במתא בדקה טפי מהיכא דליתיה במתא אבל לעיל דאיירי לענין תביעה אורחא דמילתא הבא מן הדרך דרכו לפיים ולרצות: **אפי'** הגיע עת וסתה מותרת וסתות דרבנן. ומ"מ היאך מותרת הא אמרינן בספ"ב דשבועות אזהרה לבני ישראל שיפרשו מנשותיהן שעה אחת סמוך לווסתן כ"ש שאם עבר וסתן שיש לספק שמא ראתה. וי"ל דמיירי כגון ששהתה אחר וסתה כשיעור שיכולה לטבול כההיא דר' יוחנן דלקמן דאמר בעלה מחשב ימי וסתה ובא עליה ומ"ד וסתות דאורייתא אפי' שהתה כשיעור זמן טבילה אסור דודאי ראתה חשבינן לה ומתוך זה יש לדקדק דס"ל לר' יוחנן לקמן וסתות דרבנן:

א"ר

<sup></sup>

אלא שנו אלא שאין לה וסת לימים אלא יש לה וסת לימים ולקפיצות, כיון דבמעשה תליא מילתא — אימא לא קפיץ ולא חזאי. אבל יש לה וסת לימים — אסורה לשמש, קסבר — וסתות דאורייתא. רבה בר בר חנה אמר: אפילו יש לה וסת לימים — מותרת, קסבר — וסתות דרבנן. אמר רב שמואל משמיה דרבי יוחנן: באשה שיש לה וסת — בעלה מחשב ימי וסתה ובא עליה. אמר ליה רב שמואל בר ייבא לרבי אבא: אמר רבי יוחנן אפילו ילדה, *דבזיזא למטבל? אמר ליה: אטו ודאי ראתה מי אמר רבי יוחנן? אימר דאמר רבי יוחנן — ספק ראתה ספק לא ראתה, ואם תמצא לומר ראתה — אימא טבלה, אבל ודאי ראתה — מי יימר דטבלה? הוה ליה ספק וודאי, *ואין ספק מוציא מידי ודאי. ולא? *והתניא: גחבר שמת והניח מגורה מלאה פירות, אפילו הן בני יומן — הרי הן בחזקת מתוקנין. והא הכא, ודאי טבל, ספק מעושר ספק אינו מעושר, וקאתי ספק ומוציא מידי ודאי! התם ודאי וודאי הוא, כדרב חנינא חוזאה. דאמר רב חנינא חוזאה: דחזקה על חבר שאינו מוציא מתחת ידו דבר שאינו מתוקן. ואיבעית אימא: ספק וספק הוא, וכדרבי אושעיא. *דא"ר אושעיא: המערים אדם על תבואתו ומכניסה במוץ שלה, כדי שתהא בהמתו אוכלת ופטורה מן המעשר. ואכתי, אין ספק מוציא מידי ודאי? *) והתניא: מעשה בשפחתו של מסיק אחד ברימון, שהטילה נפל לבור, ובא כהן והציץ בו לידע אם זכר אם נקבה, ובא מעשה לפני חכמים וטהרוהו, מפני שחולדה וברדלס מצויים שם. והא הכא — דוודאי הטילה נפל, ספק גררוהו ספק לא גררוהו, וקאתי ספק ומוציא מידי ודאי! לא תימא "הטילה נפל לבור", יאלא אימא כמין

*) פסחים ט. ע"ז מא: [תוספתא דאהלות פט"ז]

[פסחים ד: ע. ע"ז מא:]

לא שנו. הא דתנן "בחזקת טהרה", דמשמע אפילו הגיע עת וסתה. אלא באין לה וסת לימים. לחודייהו בלא קפיצה, אלא לקפיצה ולימים. מחשב ימי וסתה. אם שהה בדרך שבעה ימים אחר וסתה, דעכשיו עומדת בימים שיכולה להטהר, אפילו הגיע וסתה אמרינן: טבלה ואין צריך לשואלה. דבזיזא. בושה היא לטבול, עד שיפייסנה. ודאי ראתה מי א"ר יוחנן. שלא יהא צריך לשואלה, ואפילו היא זקנה. אימר טבלה. וכיון דטעמא דר' יוחנן משום ספיקא הוא, לא שנא ילדה לא שנא זקנה. הוי ספק. להיתר. ודאי. לאיסור. ואין ספק מוציא. את הדבר מידי ודאי שלו. והא הכא דוודאי טבל. דהא חזינן שנגמרה מלאכתן וממורחין הן. איבעית אימא ספק וספק הוא. דכי היכי דמספקא לן אי מעשרי אי לא, ה"נ מספקא לן דלמא לא טביל ולא איחייב במעשר, דאימא כרבי אושעיא עיילה ומכניסה במוץ שלה. דאין טבל מתחייב במעשר אלא בראיית פני הבית, כשרואה את הפתח. וכיון דבשעת ראיית פני הבית לא נגמרה מלאכתו למעשר, תו לא מיחייבא, אע"פ שהוא דשה וממרחה לאחר שהכניסה. מידי דהוה אמכניס פירות דרך גגו וקרפיפו לבית, אפילו היא ממורחת, דקיימא לן דפטורה מן המעשר הואיל ולא ראתה את הפתח. כדי שתהא בהמתו אוכלת. אפי' לאחר מירוח. ולהכי נקט "בהמתו", דאילו אמאכל אדם לא מצי למימר הכי, דאי נמי לא מחייב מדאורייתא — רבנן גזור על אכילת קבע, אפי' בדבר שלא נגמרה מלאכתו. אבל מאכל בהמה — קבע שלה, עראי חשיב לה, דתנן במסכת פאה (פ"א מ"ו) מאכיל לבהמה לעופות ולחיות, עד שימרח. הילכך כל כמה דלא חל עליה שם טבל דאורייתא — מאכיל לבהמתו. והכא כיון דאיכא למימר דעביד להו כרבי אושעיא — מותרין לאדם, דלגבי איסורא דרבנן מהניא חזקת חבר. אם זכר הוא כו'. כהן חכם היה, ומורה הוראות, ומתכוין להורות לה ימי טומאה וטהרה. אי נמי: שגורה אצלו בבית, ונוגעת בתרומתו, ורוצה להזהר ממנה כל ימי טומאתה. וי"א: לידע אימתי יהא זמן הבאת קרבנה, אם יארע במשמרתו אם לאו. ולא סבירא לי, דבשביל (א) תור עולה חטאת לכולה משמרה — לא עייל האי כהן נפשיה להכי. ועוד: שהרי היא יכולה לאחר קרבנה כל זמן שתרצה. וגם לשון ראשון אינו נראה, דאי חכם הוא — כלום הוא בא להאהיל ולעבור על לאו דטומאת מת? אלא כהן עם הארץ היה, או קטן, ושגרתו אשה להציץ ולראות. וטהרוהו. מאהל המת. כמין

אפילו ילדה דבזיזא למיטבל. פ"ה אפי' נערה שבושה לטבול. ומשני: ודאי ראתה מי א"ר יוחנן הך נמי, כיון שלא ראתה בודאי שרי רבי יוחנן. ואינו מיושב. ור"ח מפרש, וכן ר"ת: אפי' ילדה דבזיזא למיטבל פי' שהולידה, ומפחדת לטבול תוך ל' כדאמר בפ' "מפנין" (שבת דף קכט.) דבת רב חסדא טבלה תוך שלשים ללידה וחלתה, ואמטיה רבא *לערסא, ואיתסיאת. והשתא אתי שפיר דא"ל: ודאי ראתה מי א"ר יוחנן, א"כ יולדת אפילו לא היתה דואגת לטבול לא יתיר רבי יוחנן דספק טבילה אינו מוציאה מידי ודאי ראתה. ו"בזיז" – לשון פחד, כההיא דפ"ב דיבמות (דף כו.): לא מיבעיא אביו דבזיז בריה מיניה. מיהו בפ' "אלו דברים" (פסחים דף עב.) משמע שהוא לשון בושת, גבי "יבמתו בזיזה מיניה", ובפ' "ב"ש" (יבמות דף קיב.) "מבזו בזיז מיניה". מיהו גם יש לפרש לשון פחד. ובערוך *פי' לשון בושת. חבר שמת והניח מגורה מלאה פירות כו' בפ"ק דחולין (דף י.) גבי "שחט ונמצא סכין פגומה" קאמר נמי: אין ספק מוציא מידי ודאי, ולא מייתי מהך דחבר ושפחה, משום דהכא הוי ספק טוב ורגיל, ואפי' לקולא מוציא מידי ודאי. וה"נ לא שייך לאתויי ההיא דהתם ד"טבל ועלה" דאתי ספק ומוציא מידי ודאי, דהתם היינו משום דהוי לחומרא.

בהמתו אוכלת. דוקא בהמתו, כדפ"ה: דכל מה שהיא אוכלת – מיקרי עראי, אבל אדם אסור מדרבנן לאכול אכילת קבע. וכן משמע בתוספתא, ומייתי לה בפ"ק דביצה (דף יג.) הכניס לבית שבלים לעשות מהן עיסה – אוכל מהן עראי, ופטור. וכן משמע נמי מדנקט "בהמתו". והא דפריך במנחות בפרק "רבי ישמעאל" (דף סז.) אמאי דקאמר "מירוח הגוי אינו פוטר, משום בעלי כיסים", פירוש: עשירים שמוכרין תבואתן לגוים קודם מירוח וחוזרין וקונין אחר מירוח, אפשר דעבד כר' אושעיא – פירוש: שיוכל להערים ולפטור, שיכניס התבואה במוץ שלה, ומה הועילו חכמים בתקנתם? משמע דלגמרי פטור! ה"פ: עביד ליה כרבי אושעיא, ובמידי דמאכל בהמה מה הועילו חכמים בתקנתם. מיהו אי מירוח הגוי אינו פוטר רק ערלי, כמו שהיה קודם מירוח, אתי שפיר. אך ק"ע בשילהי פ"ק דבכורות (דף יא:) והשתא קשה: כיון דהוי ודאי טבל לענין אכילת קבע, אפילו הכניסה במוץ כדפרישית, היכי אתי ספק ומוציא מידי ודאי דחשבינן להו בחזקת מתוקנים? וליכא למימר: דספק מוציא מידי ודאי דרבנן, דהא בפרק קמא דפסחים (דף ט.) פריך מיניה אהא דקאמר התם "כל מקום שחולדה וברדלס מצויין שם – אין צריך בדיקה", הא ודאי חמץ – צריך בדיקה, דספק אכל אין מוציא מידי ודאי, ופריך מהך דחבר, ומשני: ספק וספק הוא, כדרבי אושעיא. והשתא מ"מ תזינא הכא דמוציא מידי ודאי דרבנן, ובדיקת חמץ נמי הוי דרבנן, דמדאורייתא בבטול בעלמא סגי! ואומר ר"י: דמתניתי' דהתם איירי שלא בטלו, דהוי ודאי דאורייתא. ועוד אומר ר"י: דהא דקאמר הכא דהוו בחזקת מתוקנים, היינו בהנך דלא חזו אלא לבהמה. כדי שתהא בהמתו אוכלת. משמע דטבל שראה פני הבית, אפילו בהמתו נמי לא אכלה. ותימה לר"י: מ"ש משאר הנאות דשרו, דלא מצינו טבל שיהיה אסור בהנאה? וי"ל: דדרשינן ב"במה מדליקין" (שבת דף כו.) גבי "אין מדליקין בטבל טמא, משום דכתיב "את משמרת תרומותי" – בשתי תרומות הכתוב מדבר, אחת טהורה ואחת טמאה, מה טהורה אין לך בה פי' אכילתה, אלא משעת הרמה ואילך, אף טמאה כן, דהיינו הדלקה. והדר גמר טהורה מטמאה, דמיתסרה בהדלקה קודם הרמה, וה"ה למאכיל לבהמתו וכל שאר הנאה של כילוי. ומהכא נמי שמעינן דאין ישראל מאכיל לבהמתו כרשיני תרומה. [וע"ע תוס' פסחים לד, ד"ה "מחמין לו"]. בשפחתו של מסיק. משמע דשפחה מטמאה בלידה, וכן מוכח בפ' "רבי אליעזר דמילה" (שבת דף קלה:) דקאמר: לקח שפחה ונתעברה אצלו – זהו "יליד בית" שנימול לשמונה. והתם קאמר: כל שאין אמו טמאה לידה – אינו נימול לשמונה. ובת"כ תניא נמי בהדיא: אין לי אלא בני ישראל, גיורת ושפחה בין משוחררת ובין שאינה משוחררת מנין? ת"ל: "אשה". ונראה דהא דיליף לאינה משוחררת מ"אשה", אסמכתא בעלמא הוא, ואגב אחריני נקט לה. דבפ"ק דכריתות (דף ז.) משמע מג"ש ד"לה" "לה" אתיא, ובפ' "הערל" (יבמות דף עד:) לא יליף מ"אשה" אלא גיורת ומשוחררת, ושאינה משוחררת אינו מזכיר שם*). ובא כהן והציץ. אומר ר"ת: דכהן שוטה היה, דאפילו אם נאמר דשל גבירתה היה, לא היה לו לטמאות. דאמר בת"כ דאין כהנים מטמאין לנפלים, דבעינן דומיא ד"אביו ואמו". ועוד, דכאן לא היה לצורך המת. ספק גררוהו ההיא שעתא כו' וא"ת: והאי בור היכא קאי, אי ברה"ר – אפילו בספקא אחת טהור, אי ברה"י – מאי משני: שהטילה כמין נפל לבור, **)והתניא דברה"י כל ספקות שאתה יכול להרבות טמא? וי"ל: דגרירת חולדה וברדלס הוי ספק הרגיל, וקרוב לודאי. ותדע דאפילו מידי ודאי בעי למימר שמוציא זה הספק. ואומר ר"י: דצריך לומר דרגלי הכהן היו ברה"ר, דאי רגליו היו ברה"י – ניחוש דלמא גררוהו כנגד רגליו, וטומאה בוקעת ועולה. דע"כ ליכא בחוריהן פותח טפח, דכי איכא – מאי מועלת גרירה, והא בפותח טפח מביא הטומאה. ועוד י"ל: דרגלי הכהן ברשות היחיד, וגררוהו ואכלוהו הוי ספק הרגיל. מסיק. בסמ"ך גרס, שהיה מוסק זיתים.

*) [ועי' תוס' יבמות עד: ד"ה ושפחה מנין] **) [נ"ל והתנן טהרות פ"ו מ"ד]

וחוששת

# תוספי הרא"ש

א"ר יוחנן אפי' ילדה דבזיזא למטבל. פרש"י אשה בחורה שבושה לטבול. וקשה מאי קאמר אטו ודאי ראתה מי קאמר ר' יוחנן וכי אשה בחורה ודאי ראתה. לכן נראה לפרש אפי' ילדה כלומר אם ילדה אשתו ולד ושהתה כדי טבילה שיראה לטבול כדאמרינן בסוף מפנין גבי ברתיה דרב חסדא דאמטיוה לערסא בתריה דרבא. ומי' גם לרש"י ניחא דה"פ אטו ודאי ראתה אפי' בזקינה מי א"ר יוחנן וכיון דרבי יוחנן לא איירי אלא בספק ראתה משום דהוי ספק ספיקא בילדה נמי הוי ספק ספיקא ואין ספק מוציא מידי ודאי. דבר פשוט הוא שאין לו לספק להוציא מידי ודאי אלא הכא מיירי בספק הרגיל וקרוב לודאי וכן ההיא דפ"ק דפסחים ובע"ז פ' כל הצלמים. והאי ספק וודאי דהכא לא שייך לההוא דפ"ק דחולין דעור ספק פגים ועצם ודאי פגים ואין ספק מוציא מידי ודאי ומייתי עלה ההיא דטבל ועלה ונמצא עליו דבר חוצץ דהתם אין ספק כל כך רגיל כי הנך דהכא הלכך לא מייתי הנך דהכא התם והך דטבל ועלה לא שייך הכא דהתם לחומרא הספק מוציא מידי ודאי: והתניא חבר שמת. למאי דלא ידע טעמא דחזקת חבר. נראה דנקט חבר משום דהוי ספק הרגיל דדרך חבר שמת או שהלך למדינת הים להודיע לבני ביתו אם הניח דבר שאינו מתוקן א"נ ס"ד דוקא חבר משום דאפי' הן בני יומן: שתהא בהמתו אוכלת דאי לאו הכי לא הוה מצי למיכל דאסור להאכילה טבל כדאמרי' בפרק במה מדליקין אין מדליקין בטבל טמא ופרש"י וכ"ש בטהור וטעמא כדדריש התם מה תרומה טהורה אין לך בה פי' אכילתה אלא משעת הרמה ואילך אף טמאה אין לך בה דהיינו הסקה אלא משעת הרמה והדר ילפי' טהורה מטמאה דאין לך בה הדלקה אלא משעת הרמה ואילך וה"ה אכילת בהמה דכל הנאה של כילוי אסור: ופטורה מן המעשר. ופרש"י ואכתי תיקשי לך דספק מוציא מידי ודאי דאפי' עבד כרבי אושעיא לענין אכילה דידיה ודאי טבל הוי [ותירץ] דלגבי איסורא דרבנן מהניא חזקת חבר והכא ניחא אבל בסוף פ"ק דפסחים לא מצי לשנויי הכי דמייתי לה על בדיקת חמץ גבי הא דתנן אין חוששין שמא גררה חולדה מבית לבית דחיק טעמא דלא חזינן הא חזינן דשקל חוששין כו' ואין ספק מוציא מידי וודאי ובדיקת חמץ מדרבנן היא דמדאורייתא בביטול בעלמא סגי וא"כ צריכין לתירוצא קמא דחזקת חבר. ופי' רבי' אפרים דבהמתו לאו דוקא דאפי' הוא עצמו שרי לאכול ממנו קבע אע"ג דקודם ראיית פני הבית אסור לאכול אכילת קבע מדרבנן. שאני התם דמצי אתי לידי חיוב דאורייתא כשיראה פני הבית אבל כשמרחו בבית דתו לא אתי לידי חיוב ולהכי שרי אפי' אכילת קבע שריא. והאי דנקט בהמתו משום דכל זמן שהיא במוץ [אינה] מוכנת אלא לבהמה ולא לאדם א"נ משום שתולה ההערמה בשביל בהמתו ומייתי ראיה מההיא דמנחות פרק ר' ישמעאל גלגול העובד כוכבים פוטר מירוח דעובד כוכבים אינו פוטר גזירה משום בעלי כיסין ופריך גלגול נמי ומשני אפשר דאפיה לה פחות מה' רבעים מירוח נמי אפשר דעביד ליה כר' אושעיא ואי לבהמתו דוקא קאמר ר' אושעיא מאי פריך ניחא ליה טפי למיעבד ע"י עובד כוכבים כדי לפטרה לגמרי. וקשה לפי' דבפ"ק דיו"ט תניא הכנים שבלים לעשות עיסה אוכל מהן עראי ופטור וסתמא הכנים לבית קאמר ובתוספתא קתני בהדיא המכנים שבלים לבית והכנים שבלים היינו במוץ וקתני אוכל עראי דוקא וע"ק לפי' למ"ד בהשוכר את הפועלים דחטין ושעורין דבני גורן נינהו בגורן תלינהו רחמנא ואם עשאן גורן בשדה נתחייבו במעשר אפילו בלא ראיית פני הבית א"כ ה"נ אם עשאן גורן בבית אחר שהכניסן במוץ מיחייבי דלא גרע עשאן גורן בבית מעשאן גורן בשדה. וא"כ אכתי יכולין לבא לידי חיוב ואמאי שרו באכילת קבע [ולכן] נ"ל דאכילת קבע אסירא וההיא דפ' ר' ישמעאל ע"כ ה"פ תרומה נמי במידי דמאכל בהמה אפשר דעביד כרבי אושעיא ואמאי אין מירוח עובד כוכבים פוטר. א"נ אפי' אי אמרינן מירוח העובד כוכבים פוטר אינו פוטר אלא מאכילת בהמתו אבל אכילת עצמו לא. והשתא פריך שפיר אמאי אינו פוטר להתירו מאכילת עראי אפשר דעביד לה כר' אושעיא. אע"ג דגלגול העובד כוכבים פוטר לגמרי ומותר אפילו אכילת קבע היינו טעמא שאנו עושין אחר גלגול כמו קודם גלגול אבל קודם מירוח היה אסור באכילת קבע וההיא דפסחים אע"ג דבדיקת חמץ מדרבנן חמור בחמץ כדבדאורייתא א"נ מיירי כשלא בטלו הלכך הוי ודאי דאורייתא: מעשה בשפחה של מסיק כו' משמע הכא דשפחה טמאה לידה דלא מיסתבר לומר שהולד היה של הגברת דאם כן למה הוזכרה השפחה. וקשה מהא דאמרינן ביבמות פרק הערל דבר אל בני ישראל אין לי אלא בנות ישראל גיורת ושפחה משוחררת מנין ת"ל אשה. משמע דוקא משוחררת דומיא דגיורת ועוד דפריך בנות מיכל תרומה נינהו ואינה משוחררת בת מיכל תרומה אם היא שפחת כהן. וי"ל דע"כ שפחה טמאה לידה כדמשמע בפ' ר' אליעזר דמילה דקאמר התם לקח שפחה ונתעברה אצלו זהו יליד בית שנימול לח' ולעיל מיניה קאמר אמר רבא אמר רב אשי כל שאין אמו טמאה לידה אינו נימול לח' ובפ"ק דכריתות תנן וכן שפחה שהפילה מביאה קרבן ונאכל. ובת"כ אמרינן בהדיא דבר אל בני ישראל אין לי אלא בנות ישראל מנין לרבות את הגיורת ואת השפחה בין משוחררת בין שאינה משוחררת והאי דקאמר ביבמות משוחררת לאו למעוטי אינה משוחררת אלא קיצר הברייתא לפי שלא הוצרך אלא למשוחררת דפריך גיורת ושפחה בנות מיכל תרומה נינהו: ובא כהן והציץ. שוטה היה דאפי' אי הוה טמא מוהר אפי' בו ביום שנטמא מידי דהוה אנזיר פ"ג מינין ואפי' אם היה קרובו חדא דשלא לצורך המת ועוד דבעי' בני קיימא דומיא דאביו ואמו: והא הכא דודאי נפל ספק גררוהו. תימה האי בור היכי דמי אי רה"ר הוא מאי פריך [הא שפיר] טהרוהו דספק טומאה ברשות הרבים ספיקו טהור ואי רשות היחיד הוא מאי קאמר שהטילה כמין נפל הא אפי' ספק ספיקא נמי טמא דתנן במס' טהרות כל מקום שאתה יכול לרבות ספיקות וספק ספיקות ברשות היחיד טמא. וי"ל דשאני הכא דגרירת חולדה וברדלס ספק הרגיל הוא הלכך מטהרינן בספק ספיקא. ואכתי קשה אי ברה"י אפי' ודאי גררוהו ניחוש שמא גררוהו תחתיו וטומאה בוקעת ועולה ואין לומר דסתם חור שלהם פותח טפח דא"כ מביא טומאה לבור ולא אהני מה שגררוהו. ואין לומר דסתם חור שלהם הוא רחב מבפנים אבל פתחו לבור אינו רחב טפח דאכתי טומאה בוקעת ועולה. כדתנן בפ' אהלות בית שהוא קמור תחת הבור. יש בו פותח טפח ואין ביציאתו פותח טפח טומאה בתוכו הבית טמא. י"ל דהבור רה"י וסביב הבור רה"ר (א):

ה) ועי' בתוס' כאן ד"ה ספק:

חוששת

מח א טוש"ע י"ד סי' קפד סעיף יא וסעיף יב:
מט ב שם סעיף יב:
נ ג מיי' פ"ט מהלכות מעשר הלכה ב סמג עשין קלה:
פי' בשימוש
נא ד מיי' שם הל' י:
[ולעיל ע. וש"נ]
נב ה מיי' פ"ט הל' ו סמג שם טוש"ע י"ד סימן שלא סעיף פד:
נג ו מיי' פ"ו מהלכות טומאת מת הל' יא:
[ערוך כז ע"ש דגרים בכל הענו לעיל כזין בבקף]
חולין י. פסחים ט. וש"נ

**הגהות הב"ח** (א) רש"י ד"ה אם זכר וכו' דבשביל תור עולה אחת:

**הגהות מהר"ב רנשבורג** א] רש"י ד"ה אם זכר הוא וכו' דבשביל תור עולה וכו'. תיבת עולה נמחק וצ"ב חטאת:

כמין נפל. הלכך ספק וספק הוא, דדלמא מעיקרא לאו נפל הוא. ודאי גררוהו. הלכך ודאי וודאי הוא. וסתות דאורייתא או דרבנן. הא דקיימא לן דבעי בדיקה בשעת וסתה – דאורייתא היא, דאם לא בדקה – טמאה, ואפילו בדקה אחר זמן ומצאתה טהורה, דאורח בזמנו בא, ודם חזאי ונפל לקרקע. או דרבנן הוא דאצרכוה, ואם לא בדקה – טהורה. ולבסוף ראתה. בבדיקה ראשונה שבדקה עצמה לאחר זמן, ומצאתה טמאה. חוששת לוסתה וחוששת לראייתה. אם זמן וסתה קודם מעת לעת של ראייתה – מטמאינן טהרות (א) דוסתה ואילך, דלמא בזמנו בא. ואם מעת לעת של ראייתה קודם לוסתה, דלא שהתה משעת וסתה עד ראייתה מעת לעת – אזלינן בתר ראייה, וטמאה מעת לעת. וקס"ד דה"ה נמי אם בדקה ומצאתה טהורה דחוששת לוסתה, והא דנקט ראתה – משום דבעי למימר "וחוששת לראייתה". טעמא דראתה. דכיון דבבדיקה ראשונה מצאתה טמאה, אם בדקה נמי בשעת וסתה הוה משכחה. דכ"ע. אפי' רב מודה דוסתות דאורייתא, והא דקאמר דבמצאתה טהורה – טהורה, כשבדקה בשיעור וסת של וסתה, דודאי אי הוה דם הוה משכחה. ושמואל סבר: אפי' הכי טמאה, דאורח בזמנו בא, הואיל ולא בדקה בשעת וסת ממש. וכאן שלא בדקה עצמה כו'. הא דקאמר לעיל וסתות דאורייתא, וטמאה אפילו לרב – בשלא בדקה עצמה בשיעור וסת, ואח"כ בדקה ומצאתה טהורה – טמאה. *ואיכא דאמרי: דמר אמר חדא ומר אמר חדא, ולא פליגי. טמאה נדה. אם הגיע וסתה ולא בדקה, קסבר: וסתות דאורייתא. תבדק. לאחר וסתה מצאתה טמאה – טמאה משעת וסתה, טהורה – טהורה. אף אנן נמי תנינא. דלרבי מאיר וסתות דאורייתא. במחבא. מחמת פחד ליסטין וגולשת. הרואה דם מחמת מכה. שיש לה במעיה. אפי' בתוך ימי נדתה. כלומר, בימים שהיא למודה לראות, דהיינו שעת עונתה או שעת וסתה. טהורה. דתלינן במכה שבאותו מקום. אם יש לה וסת חוששת לוסתה. כלומר, כשאין לה וסת קבוע מודינא לך שאף על פי שעברה עונתה – תולה במכה. אבל אם יש לה וסת קבוע, וראתה ביום וסתה, אפי' מחמת מכה – חיישינן שמא טיפת נדה מעורבת בו. מקומו טמא. וכל דם הבא דרך שם, ואפילו אינו דם נדה – הוי אב הטומאה, לטמא אדם טומאת ערב, ואם נגעה בטהרות – טמאים. וקאמר ליה רבי כו'. ולהקל על דבריו בא, וה"ק: אם יש לה וסת, כלומר אם אתה אומר לטמאה מפני וסתה – חוששת לוסתה, כלומר, יש לך לטמאה טומאת שבעה. והואיל ואינך חושש לכך, שהרי אתה אומר טהורה משום נדה, שוב אין לה טומאה. מתני' שני עדים. חדשים על כל תשמיש, אחד לפניו ואחד לאחריו, ולמחר תעיין בהם. או תשמש לאור הנר. ותבדוק לאחר תשמיש עד שתקנחה בו. דיה בשני עדים כל הלילה. אחד לפני תשמיש ראשון, ואחד לאחר תשמיש אחרון. ואע"ג דמשמשת, ולא ידעה אי חזאי ביני וביני – בין לבית שמאי בין לבית הלל לא איכפת לן, דלא הוצרכו לבדוק אלא לחומר טהרות.

[גי' הרא"ש בעא מיניה רבא מר"נ]
[לעיל ע. וש"נ]

כמין נפל. והא "לידע אם זכר אם נקבה" קתני! ה"ק: ובא כהן והציץ בו לידע אם נפל הפילה אם רוח הפילה, ואת"ל נפל הפילה – לידע אם זכר אם נקבה. ואיבעית אימא: כיון דחולדה וברדלס מצויים שם – ודאי גררוהו. *בעו מיניה מרב נחמן: וסתות דאורייתא או דרבנן? אמר להו: מדאמר הונא חברין משמיה דרב, אשה שיש לה וסת, והגיע שעת וסתה ולא בדקה, ולבסוף ראתה – [א]חוששת לוסתה וחוששת לראייתה, אלמא – *וסתות דאורייתא. איכא דאמרי, הכי קא"ל: טעמא – דראתה, הא לא ראתה – אין חוששין, אלמא – וסתות דרבנן. איתמר: אשה שיש לה וסת, והגיע שעת וסתה ולא בדקה, ולבסוף בדקה. אמר רב: [ב]בדקה ומצאת טמאה – טמאה, טהורה – טהורה. ושמואל אמר: אפילו בדקה ומצאת טהורה – נמי טמאה, מפני *שאורח בזמנו בא. לימא בוסתות קמיפלגי, דמ"ס – דאורייתא, ומ"ס – דרבנן! אמר ר' זירא דכ"ע – וסתות דאורייתא, כאן – שבדקה עצמה כשיעור וסת, כאן – שלא בדקה עצמה כשיעור וסת. ר"נ בר יצחק אמר: בוסתות גופייהו קמיפלגי, דמ"ס – וסתות דאורייתא, ומר סבר – וסתות דרבנן. אמר רב ששת: כתנאי, ר' אליעזר אומר טמאה נדה, ורבי יהושע אומר תבדק. והני תנאי כי הני תנאי, דתניא, רבי מאיר אומר: טמאה נדה, וחכ"א תבדק. אמר אביי: אף אנן נמי תנינא, *דתנן, ר"מ אומר: [ג]אם היתה במחבא, והגיע שעת וסתה ולא בדקה – טהורה, *שחרדה מסלקת את הדמים. טעמא – דאיכא חרדה, הא ליכא חרדה – טמאה, אלמא – וסתות דאורייתא. לימא הני תנאי בהא נמי פליגי, דתניא: [ד]הרואה דם מחמת מכה – אפילו בתוך ימי נדתה, טהורה, דברי רשב"ג. רבי אומר: אם יש לה וסת – חוששת לוסתה. מאי לאו, בהא קמיפלגי, דמר סבר – וסתות דאורייתא, ומר סבר – וסתות דרבנן! אמר רבינא: לא, דכ"ע – [ה]וסתות דרבנן, והכא *במקור מקומו טמא קמיפלגי. רשב"ג סבר: אשה – טהורה, ודם טמא – דקאתי דרך מקור. ואמר ליה רבי: אי חיישת לוסת – אשה נמי טמאה, ואי לא חיישת לוסת – מקור מקומו טהור הוא.§ **מתני'** בית שמאי אומרים: צריכה ב' עדים על כל תשמיש ותשמיש, או תשמש לאור הנר. בית הלל אומרים: [ו]דיה בשני עדים כל הלילה.§

גמ'

[לקמן נו: נח. סד:]

**וחוששת** לראייתה. פרש"י: לענין מעת לעת. אע"ג דקי"ל כרבי דוסא, דאשה שיש לה וסת דיה שעתה – שלא בשעת וסת מודה דמטמא למפרע. ועוד י"ל: דהכא מיירי לענין שתהא מקולקלת למניינה. **אלמא** וסתות דאורייתא. השתא סבר: הא דנקט "ראתה" – לאשמועינן דחוששת לראייתה, ולא חשבינן לה כאילו ודאי ראתה מזמן הוסת. וה"ה דכי לא ראתה – חוששת. ואם תאמר: היאך רוצה להוכיח דוסתות דאורייתא, והלא אפי' אי וסתות דרבנן, כיון דראתה עכשיו – טמאה גם מזמן הוסת מספק? וי"ל: הני מילי לטהרות, אבל מקולקלת למניינה לא הויא.

**אלמא** וסתות דרבנן. וא"ת: דלעיל (דף טו.) אמר רב הונא: לא שנו אלא שלא הגיע שעת וסתה כו', אלמא וסתות דאורייתא! וי"ל: דהכא קאמר משמיה דרב, וליה לא ס"ל, ואליבא דרב איכא לקמן ב' לשונות. אי נמי: לעיל אתי כלישנא קמא דהכא. **ורב** נחמן בר יצחק אמר בוסתות גופייהו פליגי. – נראה דהלכה דוסתות דרבנן, דהא רב נחמן בר יצחק דהוא בתראה אית ליה דלרב וסתות דרבנן,[א] ובפ' "יש בכור" (בכורות דף מט:) פסיק כרב באיסורי. ועוד: דקיימא לן כר' יהושע דבסמוך לגבי רבי אליעזר, וכחכמים לגבי ר' מאיר. ואע"ג דתנן בפ' "בנות כותים" (לקמן דף לט.) ברישא דהיתה במחבא, הגיע שעת וסתה ולא בדקה – טמאה, מ"מ נראה דהלכה הוי וסתות דרבנן, כדפרישית. ועוד: דאיכא דמוקי לה בפרק "בנות כותים" (שם) כרבי מאיר. וכן פסק בשאלתות דרב אחאי* ור"ח הילכך אשה שיש לה וסת, ולא בדקה בשעת וסתה, ואח"כ בדקה ומצאתה טהורה – טהורה לבעלה. ומיהו נראה לכתחלה צריכה לבדוק בשעת הוסת. **ומר** סבר וסתות דרבנן. נראה דדוקא במרגשת שבא דם זה מן המכה, ואפ"ה אם זמן וסת הוא, אי וסתות דאורייתא – חיישינן שמא גם מן המקור בא הדם. אבל אם אינה מרגשת יציאת דם מן המכה – טמאה לכ"ע, אם הוא זמן וסתה. דאי לאו הכי, וכי לעולם לא תהא נדה, והלא קודם מכה הוה לה וסת. **במקור** מקומו טמא קמיפלגי. ורשב"ג לטעמיה בריש "תינוקת" (לקמן דף סו.) ואע"ג דטומאת בית הסתרים היא, ובפרק "דם הנדה" (לקמן נה.) אמר נמי דדם בעי רביעית, והכא קאמר טמא אע"ג דליכא רביעית, כדאמרינן בפ' "יוצא דופן" (לקמן דף מא:) מקור שהזיע כב' טיפי מרגליות – טמאה. שמא הכא הלמ"מ הוא. תדע, שהמקור – טמא, והאשה – טהורה. **ב"ש** אומרים צריכה ב' עדים על כל תשמיש. פרש"י: ב' עדים חדשים, א' – לפני תשמיש, ואחד – לאחר תשמיש, ומצנעת עד הבקר. ובה"א דיה בב' עדים כל הלילה, אחד – לפני תשמיש ראשון, ואחד – לאחר תשמיש אחרון.* וקשה: דלפני תשמיש לא בעו חדשים אלא מנועות? ועוד קשה מה שפירש לב"ה דלא מצרכי לבדוק בכל תשמיש, דלעיל* אמר דאינן צנועות – עד שבודקות בו לפני תשמיש זה, בודקות בו לפני תשמיש אחר, משמע דבכל תשמיש בודקות! מיהו הא י"ל: בודקות בתשמיש אחר, שבלילה שניה. ועוד קשה: מה יודעת מתי שימש באחרונה, שתבדוק אחריו? ואם היתה בודקת בשחר, כשהיא עומדת, א"כ אינה בודקת סמוך לתשמיש לידע אם בועל בנדות לטמא בועלה ז' ועוד קשה: דקאמר ב"ש "שמא תתפנה שכבת זרע בביאה שניה", היה לו לומר "בביאה אחרונה", כיון דלב"ה אינה בודקת עד לאחר תשמיש אחרון! ועוד: דב"ה נקט "נימוק", וב"ש נקט לישנא אחרינא "שמא תתפנה", היה לו לב"ש נמי למינקט "נימוק", כיון דקאי על דם שברחם ולא על הדם שעל העד, דהא בית הלל לא מצרכי בדיקה אחר תשמיש ראשון! ועוד:

*[ועוד דמשמע או תשמש לאור הנר אם רוצה להקל כב"ה ואפילו תשמש לאור הנר צריכה לב"ש בדיקה בכל תשמיש אבל לפירוש [ב] רש"י ולפירוש ר"י א"ש תשמש לאור הנר פי' שבודקת מיד מסתמא אם היתה שם טיפת חרדל היתה רואה אפי' על עד ישן. ולפירוש ר"י קיימא שפיר ב"ש אדם שעל העד [ג] אבל לעולם קיימא אדם שבתוך הפה דלישנא בתוך הפה הכי משמע גי"]

[לקמן סד:]
[פ' מנורע סי' פט]
[לקמן עח. סוטה כ.]

כמתני' דהיתה במחבא. ואע"ג דקתני רישא הגיע שעת וסתה ולא בדקה טמאה הא אמרי' לקמן פ' בנות כותים כולה ר"מ היא ועל זה יש לסמוך באשה שיש לה וסת ולא בדקה בשעת וסתה ואח"כ בדקה ומצאה טהורה דטהורה ודאי: **מאי** לאו בהא קא מיפלגי דמר סבר וסתות דאורייתא ומר סבר וסתות דרבנן הלכך תולין בהדם דמחמת מכה בא. תימה לי אם יש לה מכה זמן ארוך וכי כל הדמים שתראה יהיו טהורין וכי בשביל הכאה נסתלקו דמי המקור. וצ"ע: **במקור** מקומו טמא קא מיפלגי. ורשב"ג לטעמיה דאמר לקמן בריש תינוקת דם טמא דאתי דרך מקור ואין לדמותו לטומאת בית הסתרים דשמא הלכה למשה מסיני תדע דהמקור טמא אע"ג דהאשה נמי טהורה: **ב"ש** אומרים צריכה שני עדים. פי' שניהם לאחר תשמיש אחד לו ואחד לה כותיה דמתני' דלעיל דרך בנות ישראל לשמש בשני עדים ופליגי ב"ש וב"ה בהנך שני עדים ב"ש סברי צריך לעיין בהן בכל תשמיש ותשמיש. וב"ה סברי יבדקו בהן בכל תשמיש ותשמיש ואין צריך לראותם עד אור הבוקר ובעד דלפני תשמיש לא איירי בהו. ורבי' שמשון פי' לב"ה אחד לפני תשמיש ראשון ואחד לפני תשמיש אחרון. וקשה לפי' מה היא יודעת כמה פעמים תשמש בלילה אלא בקומה בשחרית תבדוק ואנן בדיקה דלאחר תשמיש בעי' אולי ראתה מחמת תשמיש וליכא לאקשויי לפי' רבינו שמשון לב"ש (דהך) דהא דרך צנעות להצריך עדים חדשים בכל פעם דהא מודו ב"ש דאי משמשת לאור הנר אינה צריכה עדים חדשים:

## תוספי הרא"ש

**חוששת** לוסתה וחוששת לראייתה. אע"ג דקי"ל כר' דוסא דכל אשה שיש לה וסת דיה שעתה הא מסקינן לעיל דשלא בשעת וסתה מודי להו. ועוד י"ל דלענין שתהא מקולקלת למנינה איירי הכא: **אלמא** וסתות דרבנן. הא דס"ל לרב הונא לעיל דוסתות דאורייתא לא קשה דהכא משמיה דרב קאמר ואליבא דרב מסיק בסמוך שתי לשונות: **ורב** נחמן בר יצחק אמר בוסתות גופייהו קא מיפלגי. כותיה קי"ל דהוא בתרא והלכתא כרב באיסורי כדאיתא בבכורות פרק יש בכור הלכך כותיה קי"ל דוסתות דרבנן וכן סבר ר' יוחנן לעיל וכן פסק בשאלתות דרב אחאי ור"ח. ועוד דקי"ל כר' יהושע לגבי ר' אליעזר וכמו חכמים לגבי רבי מאיר אע"ג דפליגי לקמן רשב"ג ור' וקי"ל הלכה כר' מחבירו הא פליגי נמי אחריני בהנך ברייתות. ועוד דהא דחיק רבינא דהוא בתראה למימר דכ"ע וסתות דרבנן ולא קי"ל

**נד** א ב מיי' פ"ג מהל' משכב ומושב הל' ה ופ"ח מהל' איסורי ביאה הל' יג ועי' במ"מ וטוש"ע י"ד סי' קפד סעיף ט:
**נה** ג טוש"ע שם סעיף ח:
**נו** ד מיי' פ"ח מהלכות איסורי ביאה הל' י סמג לאוין קיא טוש"ע י"ד סי' קפז סעיף ה וסעיף ו ובהגה"ה:
**נז** ה מיי' שם הל' יד ופ"ג מהלכות משכב ומושב הלכה ט:
**נח** ו מיי' פ"ד מהלכות איסורי ביאה הל' יז סמג שם טוש"ע י"ד סי' קפו סעיף ב בהגה"ה:

## הגהות הב"ח

(א) רש"י ד"ה חוששת וכו' טהרות למוסתה ואילך:

הא' לישנא איכא דאמרי אינו מלשון רש"י אבל הוא נשמט מנוסחת התלמוד וכ"ה בגמרא ישנה רש"א

[לעיל ט.] לקמן לט.

## הגהות מהר"ב רנשבורג

א] תוס' ד"ה ורב נחמן בר יצחק וכו' ובפרק יש בכור. נ"ב עי' מעדני י"ט בפ"ק סי' א' בד"ה וקי"ל הלכתא וכו': ב] ד"ה ב"ש אומרים צריכה וכו' בהגי' בדיקה בכל תשמיש אבל לפי' רשב"ם כצ"ל: ג] בא"ד בהגה"ה אבל לב"ה קיימא וכו' כצ"ל:

## גליון הש"ס

**תוס'** ד"ה אלמא כו' אפי' אי וסתות דרבנן וכו'. עי' לעיל ט ע"א תד"ה הא וכו' דהוכיחו כן מסוגיא דהכא והיינו ללישנא בתרא דרב סבר וסתות דרבנן ואפ"ה ס"ל דמצאה טמאה חוששת לוסתה וא"כ מה הקשו דלמא הלישנא קמא ס"ל דאי היה וסתות דרבנן לא מטמאינן למפרע לחוש לוסתה ובהא פליגי הנך ב' לישני וכמו דצ"ל לתירוצם דפליגי באם וסתות דרבנן אם מקולקלת למניינה:

שמא

נט א מיי' פ"ד מהל' איסורי ביאה הלכה ט סמג לאוין קיח:
ס ב מיי' שם הלכה יז סמג שם טור וש"ע י"ד סי' קפו סעיף ב בהגה"ה:
סא ג מיי' פכ"א מהל' איסורי ביאה הל' י סמג לאוין קנו טוש"ע אה"ע סימן כה סעיף ה טוש"ע א"ח סימן רמ סעיף יא:
סב ד מיי' פ"ה מהל' תשובה כל הפרק:

תורה אור

**גמ'** ת"ר אע"פ שֶׁאָמְרוּ "הַמְשַׁמֵּשׁ מִטָּתוֹ לְאוֹר הַנֵּר – הֲרֵי זֶה מְגוּנֶּה", בש"א: צְרִיכָה שְׁנֵי עֵדִים עַל כָּל תַּשְׁמִישׁ, אוֹ תְּשַׁמֵּשׁ לְאוֹר הַנֵּר. וּבה"א: דַּיָּהּ בִּשְׁנֵי עֵדִים כָּל הַלַּיְלָה. תַּנְיָא, אָמְרוּ לָהֶם ב"ש לב"ה: לְדִבְרֵיכֶם לֵיחוּשׁ שֶׁמָּא תִּרְאֶה טִיפַּת דָּם כְּחַרְדָּל בְּבִיאָה רִאשׁוֹנָה, וּתְחַפֶּנָּה שִׁכְבַת זֶרַע בְּבִיאָה שְׁנִיָּה! א"ל ב"ה: אַף לְדִבְרֵיכֶם – לֵיחוּשׁ עַד שֶׁהָרוֹק בְּתוֹךְ הַפֶּה שֶׁמָּא נִימּוֹק וְהוֹלֵךְ לוֹ! אָמְרוּ לָהֶם: לְפִי שֶׁאֵינוֹ דּוֹמֶה נִימּוֹק פַּעַם אַחַת לְנִימּוֹק שְׁתֵּי פְּעָמִים. תַּנְיָא, א"ר יְהוֹשֻׁעַ: רוֹאֶה אֲנִי אֶת דִּבְרֵי ב"ש. אָמְרוּ לוֹ תַּלְמִידָיו: רַבִּי, כַּמָּה הֶאֱרַכְתָּ עָלֵינוּ! אָמַר לָהֶם: מוּטָב שֶׁאַאֲרִיךְ עֲלֵיכֶם בְּעוה"ז כְּדֵי שֶׁיַּאֲרִיכוּ יְמֵיכֶם לְעוה"ב. אָמַר ר' זֵירָא: מִדִּבְרֵי כּוּלָּם נִלְמַד בַּעַל נֶפֶשׁ לֹא יִבְעוֹל וְיִשְׁנֶה. רָבָא אָמַר: *בּוֹעֵל וְשׁוֹנֶה, כִּי תַּנְיָא הַהִיא – לְטָהֳרוֹת. תַּנְיָא נַמִי הָכִי: *בד"א – לְטָהֳרוֹת, אֲבָל לְבַעְלָהּ – מוּתֶּרֶת. אוּבד"א – שֶׁהִנִּיחָהּ בְּחֶזְקַת טָהֳרָה, אֲבָל הִנִּיחָהּ בְּחֶזְקַת טְמֵאָה – לְעוֹלָם הִיא בְּחֶזְקָתָהּ עַד שֶׁתֹּאמַר לוֹ "טְהוֹרָה אֲנִי". א"ר אַבָּא, א"ר חִיָּיא בַּר אַשִׁי, אָמַר רַב: בבָּדְקָה בְּעֵד, וְאָבַד – אֲסוּרָה לְשַׁמֵּשׁ עַד שֶׁתִּבְדּוֹק. מַתְקִיף לָהּ ר' אִילָא: אִילּוּ אִיתָא מִי לָא מְשַׁמְּשָׁה וְאע"ג דְּלָא יָדְעָה? הַשְׁתָּא נַמִי – תְּשַׁמֵּשׁ! א"ל רָבָא: זוֹ – מוֹכִיחָהּ קַיָּים, וְזוֹ – אֵין מוֹכִיחָהּ קַיָּים. *א"ר יוֹחָנָן: *גאָסוּר לְאָדָם שֶׁיְּשַׁמֵּשׁ מִטָּתוֹ בַּיּוֹם. (אָמַר רַב הַמְנוּנָא) מַאי קְרָא? שֶׁנֶּאֱמַר: °"יֹאבַד יוֹם אִוָּלֶד בּוֹ וְהַלַּיְלָה אָמַר הוֹרָה גָבֶר" לַיְלָה נִיתָּן לְהֵרָיוֹן, וְיוֹם לֹא נִיתָּן לְהֵרָיוֹן. ר"ל אָמַר מֵהָכָא: °"בּוֹזֵה דְרָכָיו יָמוּת". וְר"ל הַאי קְרָא דְּר' יוֹחָנָן מַאי דָּרֵישׁ בֵּיהּ? מִבָּעֵי לֵיהּ לִכְדְדָרֵישׁ רַבִּי חֲנִינָא בַּר פַּפָּא. דְּדָרֵישׁ ר' חֲנִינָא בַּר פַּפָּא: א] אוֹתוֹ מַלְאָךְ הַמְּמוּנֶּה עַל הַהֵרָיוֹן, "לַיְלָה" שְׁמוֹ, וְנוֹטֵל טִפָּה וּמַעֲמִידָהּ לִפְנֵי הקב"ה וְאוֹמֵר לְפָנָיו: רבש"ע טִפָּה זוֹ מַה תְּהֵא עָלֶיהָ? גִּבּוֹר אוֹ חַלָּשׁ, חָכָם אוֹ טִיפֵּשׁ, עָשִׁיר אוֹ עָנִי? וְאִילּוּ "רָשָׁע אוֹ צַדִּיק" – לָא קָאָמַר, כִּדְר' חֲנִינָא. *דא"ר חֲנִינָא: הַכֹּל בִּידֵי שָׁמַיִם – דחוּץ מִיִּרְאַת שָׁמַיִם, שֶׁנֶּאֱמַר: °"וְעַתָּה יִשְׂרָאֵל מָה ה' אֱלֹהֶיךָ שׁוֹאֵל מֵעִמָּךְ כִּי אִם לְיִרְאָה" וגו'. וְר' יוֹחָנָן: א"כ נִכְתּוֹב קְרָא "גָּבֶר הוֹרָה", מַאי "הוֹרָה גָבֶר"? לַיְלָה נִיתָּן לְהֵרָיוֹן, וְיוֹם לֹא נִיתָּן לְהֵרָיוֹן. וְר' יוֹחָנָן, הַאי קְרָא דְּר"ל מַאי דָּרֵישׁ בֵּיהּ? מִבָּעֵי לֵיהּ לִכְדִכְתִיב בְּסֵפֶר בֶּן סִירָא: "שְׁלֹשָׁה שָׂנֵאתִי, וְאַרְבָּעָה לֹא אֲהַבְתִּי: שַׂר הַנִּרְגָּל בְּבֵית הַמִּשְׁתָּאוֹת, וְאָמְרִי לָהּ: שַׂר הַנִּרְגָּן (וְאָמְרִי לָהּ: שַׂר הַנִּרְגָּז,) וְהַמּוֹשִׁיב שֶׁבֶת בִּמְרוֹמֵי קֶרֶת, וְהָאוֹחֵז בְּאַמָּה וּמַשְׁתִּין מַיִם. *וְהַנִּכְנָס לְבֵית חֲבֵירוֹ פִּתְאוֹם. אָמַר רַבִּי יוֹחָנָן: וַאֲפִילּוּ לְבֵיתוֹ. אָמַר רַבִּי שִׁמְעוֹן בֶּן יוֹחַאי: אַרְבָּעָה דְּבָרִים הקב"ה שׂוֹנְאָן וַאֲנִי אֵינִי אוֹהֲבָן: הַנִּכְנָס לְבֵיתוֹ פִּתְאוֹם, וְאצ"ל – לְבֵית חֲבֵירוֹ. *וְהָאוֹחֵז בְּאַמָּה וּמַשְׁתִּין מַיִם,

וּמַשְׁתִּין

איוב ג | משלי יט | דברים י

**גמ'** מְגוּנֶּה. טַעֲמָא מְפָרֵשׁ לְקַמָּן. **שֶׁמָּא** תִּרְאֶה. בְּבִיאָה רִאשׁוֹנָה, וְיַעֲמִידוּהוּ כּוֹתְלֵי בֵּית הָרֶחֶם. וְכֵיוָן דְּלָא מַצְרִיכִיתוּ בְּדִיקָה בֵּין תַּשְׁמִישׁ לְתַשְׁמִישׁ, כִּי הָדַר מְשַׁמֵּשׁ – תְּחַפֶּנָּה שִׁכְבַת זֶרַע בְּבִיאָה שְׁנִיָּה, וְכִי בָּדְקָה לְאַחַר תַּשְׁמִישׁ אַחֲרוֹן לָא מִינְכַּר לְמָחָר. וּנְהִי נַמִי דִּלְדִידַן (א) מְשַׁמְּשָׁא לְאַחַר קִינּוּחַ, וְאע"ג דְּלָא יָדְעִינַן עַד לְמָחָר, מִיהוּ בָּעֵינַן מוֹכִיחָהּ קַיָּים. דְּאִי לָאו הָכִי, מַה הוֹעִילוּ חֲכָמִים בְּתַקָּנָתָם. עַד שֶׁהָרוֹק בְּתוֹךְ הַפֶּה כו'. "רוֹק" – דָּם, "פֶּה" – אוֹתוֹ מָקוֹם. כְּלוֹמַר, אֲפִילּוּ כְּשֶׁהָיְתָה בּוֹדֶקֶת לְאַחַר תַּשְׁמִישׁ, שֶׁמָּא רָאֲתָה טִפָּה כְּחַרְדָּל וְחִפְּתָה שִׁכְבַת זֶרַע בְּאוֹתָהּ בִּיאָה עַצְמָהּ. הֶאֱרַכְתָּ. הֶחֱמַרְתָּ. בַּעַל נֶפֶשׁ. חָסִיד. לֹא יִבְעוֹל וְיִשְׁנֶה. בְּלָא בְּדִיקָה בֵּינְתַיִם, דַּאֲפִילּוּ ב"ה מַצְרְכִי בְּדִיקָה לְסוֹף תַּשְׁמִישׁ. אַלְמָא חָיְישִׁינַן לְשֶׁמָּא רָאֲתָה דָּם מֵחֲמַת תַּשְׁמִישׁ, אַלְמָא מִי שֶׁהוּא יָרֵא וּפוֹרֵשׁ מִסְּפֵק אִיסּוּר – לֹא יִבְעוֹל וְיִשְׁנֶה. בד"א. דְּבָעֲיָא בְּדִיקָה. בָּדְקָה בְּעֵד. בַּלַּיְלָה לִפְנֵי תַּשְׁמִישׁ. וְאע"ג דְּלֹא יָדְעָה. דְּהָא לב"ה עַד לְמָחָר לָא בָּדְקָה. וַאֲפִי' לב"ש נַמִי, אִם יֵשׁ לָהּ ב' עֵדִים לְכָל תַּשְׁמִישׁ, מְשַׁמֶּשֶׁת בְּלָא נֵר, אַף ע"ג דְּלָא יָדְעָה אִי אִיכָּא דָּם בָּעֵדִים שֶׁל תַּשְׁמִישׁ רִאשׁוֹן. זוֹ מוֹכִיחָהּ קַיָּים. הֲרֵי הָעֵד לְפָנֵינוּ, וּלְמָחָר תִּרְאֶה בּוֹ, וּמְהַנֵּי לָהּ לְטָהֳרוֹת. דְּכִי אַצְרְכוּהָ רַבָּנַן לְשַׁמֵּשׁ בְּעֵדִים – מִשּׁוּם טָהֳרוֹת הוּא, וְגַם אִם יִמָּצֵא דָּם בְּאוֹתוֹ שֶׁלִּפְנֵי תַּשְׁמִישׁ – תָּבִיא חַטָּאת כַּפָּרָתָהּ. וְזוֹ. שֶׁאָבַד עֵדָהּ אֵין מוֹכִיחָהּ קַיָּים, וְאִי אָמְרַתְּ תְּשַׁמֵּשׁ – מַה תַּקָּנַת חֲכָמִים יֵשׁ כָּאן, דַּהֲרֵי הִיא כְּמוֹ שֶׁלֹּא בָּדְקָה. בּוֹזֵה דְּרָכָיו. תַּשְׁמִישׁ. כְּמוֹ (משלי ל) "דֶּרֶךְ גֶּבֶר בְּעַלְמָה". וְהַמְשַׁמֵּשׁ בַּיּוֹם – בָּא לִידֵי בִּזָּיוֹן, שֶׁמָּא יִרְאֶה בָּהּ דָּבָר מְגוּנֶּה, וְתִתְגַּנֶּה עָלָיו. הַכֹּל בִּידֵי שָׁמַיִם. כָּל מִדּוֹתָיו וְקוֹרוֹתָיו שֶׁל אָדָם בָּאִין לוֹ בִּגְזֵרַת מֶלֶךְ, חוּץ מִזּוֹ. כִּי אִם לְיִרְאָה. דָּבָר זֶה לְבַדּוֹ הוּא שׁוֹאֵל מִמְּךָ, לְפִי שֶׁהַכֹּל בְּיָדוֹ, וְזֶה בְּיָדְךָ. מַאי הוֹרָה גָּבֶר. מִדְּסָמַךְ הֵרָיוֹן לְלַיְלָה, ש"מ לְמִדְרַשׁ הָכִי: לַיְלָה נִיתָּן לְהֵרָיוֹן, וְלֹא יוֹם. מִדְּאַסְמְכֵיהּ קְרָא – שָׁמְעִינַן לִדְר' יוֹחָנָן, וּמִגּוּפָהּ דִּקְרָא – שָׁמְעִינַן לְהָא דְּר' חֲנִינָא בַּר פַּפָּא. מִיבָּעֵי לֵיהּ כו'. וְהַיְינוּ "בּוֹזֵה דְרָכָיו" – שֶׁמְּגַנֶּה עַצְמוֹ, שֶׁמַּלְעִיזִין עָלָיו בְּנֵי הַמְּדִינָה בְּמִנְהָגוֹ. שַׂר. תַּלְמִיד חָכָם. הַנִּרְגָּל. רָגִיל. נִרְגָּן. מַרְבֶּה דְּבָרִים. וְאָמְרִי לָהּ נִרְגָּז. כּוֹעֵס, דְּנִרְאֶה כְּנָבָל וּמִשְׁתַּכֵּר. וְהַמּוֹשִׁיב שֶׁבֶת. לַתַּלְמִידִים בִּמְרוֹמֵי קֶרֶת אַחַת, שֶׁנִּרְאֶה מִגַּסֵּי הָרוּחַ. וְעוֹד: שֶׁמַּפְסִיקִין אוֹתָן עוֹבְרֵי דְרָכִים. וַאֲפִילּוּ לְבֵיתוֹ. דִּלְמָא עָבְדִי מִידֵי דִּצְנִיעוּתָא.

מְקַרְקֵשׁ

ועוד: דקאמר "מדברי כולן נלמד בעל נפש לא יבעול וישנה" – פירוש: בלא בדיקה בינתים, אפילו לבעלה גרידא, הא לב"ה אף לטהרות לא צריכה בדיקה! ונראה לר"י כפירוש רשב"ם: דלב"ש צריכה ב' עדים חדשים אחר תשמיש: אחד – לו, ואחד – לה. והא דקתני "צריכה" – היינו, כלומר, שהיא מכינה, כדתנן: בנות ישראל משמשות בב' עדים, אחד – לו ואחד – לה. אע"ג דלפני תשמיש אינה צריכה חדש, אלא נגועות – היינו לפי שאין העד מלוכלך כ"כ אבל לאחר תשמיש, שמלוכלך בשכבת זרע – צריכות בכל פעם חדש. וב"ה אומרים: דיה בב' עדים כל הלילה, מודים שצריכה בדיקה אחר כל תשמיש, אך דלא מצרכי חדש. וטעמא, משום דלאחר תשמיש איכא רוב לכלוך משכבת זרע, ואין ריוח בעד חדש. ואפשר דאפילו נגועות לא בעו חדש לאחר תשמיש. והשתא אתי שפיר הכל. **לא** יבעול וישנה. פירוש: אם לא יבדוק, דשמא מחמת חימוד תשמיש ראשון ראתה. ודוקא בעל נפש, דר' זירא ידע נמי דלבעלה לא בעיא בדיקה. ורבא אמר: אפי' בעל נפש לא, דלמא לבו נוקפו ופורש. וא"ת: ומאי מייתי "תניא נמי הכי", דלמא ברייתא לא איירי בבעל נפש, אלא בסתם בני אדם או בביאה ראשונה? וי"ל: ד"אבל לבעלה מותרת" משמע היתר גמור לכל העולם ואפי' בביאה שניה. **בדקה** ואבד העד. לפירוש רשב"ם ה"פ: בדקה לפני תשמיש ואבד העד לפני תשמיש – אסורה לשמש עד שתבדוק פעם שניה, אבל לאחר תשמיש אפילו לא אבד העד, צריכה לעולם בדיקה לפני תשמיש. ור"א פריך ממתני' שפיר, אע"ג דמתני' לא איירי בעד שלפני תשמיש, אלא בשל אחר תשמיש. א"נ מיירי הכא בעד שאחר תשמיש, אם אבד אסורה לשמש עד שתבדוק, אפי' אם רוצה לשמש מיד אחר תשמיש ראשון. אבל אם לא אבד – מותרת. כי למה תבדוק ג' פעמים מיד זה אחר זה. **מלאך** הממונה על ההריון. אבל על הלידה אין שום מלאך ממונה, כדאמר בריש תענית (דף ב.) ג' מפתחות בידו של הקב"ה של חיה ושל גשמים ושל תחיית המתים. והנהו שלש מפתחות נמי פעמים מוסרין לשליח לפי שעה, שהרי אליהו *היה בידו מפתח של גשמים, והחייה המת, וכן אלישע וכמה צדיקים, ואף ברי (*אותת) (איוב לז) שהוא שר מטר אין עושה אלא ברשות הקב"ה. **הכל** בידי שמים חוץ מיראת שמים. וב"אלו נערות" (כתובות ל.) דאמר: הכל בידי שמים חוץ מצינים ופחים – הכא איירי בתולדות האדם ובמדותיו, והתם מיירי במאורעות כגון צנים ופורעניות, דהכל נגזר עליו ואינו יכול ליזהר. כדאמר בחולין (דף ז:) אין אדם נוקף אצבעו מלמטה אא"כ מכריזין עליו מלמעלה, חוץ מצינים ופחים – שיכול לשמור עצמו. וא"ת: והא חזקיה חזא דהוו ליה בני דלא מעלו (ברכות י.) אלמא דנגזר קודם לידה שלא יהיו יראי שמים! וי"ל: דהראהו מה שעתיד להיות. ועוד: דהרבה דברים תלוי במזל, כדאמר בשילהי שבת (דף קנו.) מאן דאיתיליד בצדק – יהא צדקן במצות, דאיתיליד בשבת – מתקרי קדישא. וכן הא דאמרי כלדאי לאמיה דרב נחמן בר יצחק: בריך, גנבא ליהוי (שם:) *)ועוד: דאין זה בידי שמים, כי אין הקב"ה רוצה לשנות הילוך המזלות. **שר** ב] הנרגל. פירש בערוך: שמתרעמים עליו בבית המשתאות.

*) כך היא גי' רש"ל וגי' ר"מ נ"ל גנבא ליהוי ואין זה בידי שמים כו' וע"ש

ומשתין

שבת פז. כתובות סה.
[לשיטתיה לקמן לח: ובעירובין ק:] [לעיל יח:]
ברכות לג: מגילה כה.
[עי' סנהדרין דף קיג.]
[נ"ל יטריח עב]
[מס' ד"א פ"ה ועי' פסחים קיב.]
[עי' תוס' לעיל יג. סד"ה אוחז]

[ואסור לשמש מטתו ביום שנאמר והלילה אמר הורה גבר ר"ל אמר מהכא בוזה דרכיו ימות כך היא גי' הערוך בערך שמש א' ומעתה תבין מאי דכסמוך דקאמר ור"ל האי קרא דר' יוחנן וכו' ור"י א"כ נכתוב וכו' ור"ל האי קרא דר"ל מאי דריש ביה וכו']

## הגהות הב"ח

(א) רש"י ד"ה שמא וכו' לדלידן משמשת:

## הגהות מהר"ב רנשבורג

א] גמ' אותו מלאך הממונה על ההריון. ע"ב עי' דרשת מהרש"א דף לו ע"ג ודף לד ע"א: ב] תוס' ד"ה שר הנרגל. כצ"ל לפי מ"ש מהרש"א בח"א:

## תוספי הרא"ש

**שמא** תראה טפת דם כחרדל בביאה ראשונה ותחפנו שכבת זרע בביאה שניה. פרש"י וישאר בבית הרחם ויעמידו כותלי בית הרחם הדם בביאה ראשונה ובביאה שניה תחפנו שכבת זרע ולא יראה על העד ול"נ דלא משמע דאיירי שיהא נימוק בתוך הפה אלא בתשובת ב"ה ולאידך פי' שפירשתי שבודקת בכל תשמיש ותשמיש ניחא דה"פ שמא תראה טפת דם כחרדל על העד בביאה ראשונה ותחפנה שכבת זרע על העד בביאה שניה: **מדברי** כולם נלמוד בעל נפש לא יבעול וישנה. ואף לב"ה נמי צריכה בדיקה לאחר תשמיש אחרון אלמא חיישינן שמא תראה מחמת תשמיש וכ"ש לפירושינו דלב"ה נמי צריכה בדיקה על כל תשמיש ותשמיש: **בדקה** בעד אחד ואבד אסורה לשמש עד שתבדוק. לפרש"י ניחא דאיירי בבדיקה דקודם תשמיש. ואם אבד אותו עד לא תשמש עד שתבדוק אבל לפי מה דפרישנא דאיירי בבדיקה דלאחר תשמיש מאי קאמר בדקה בעד ואבד אפי' לא אבד נמי צריכה לבדוק לפני תשמיש ודוחק לפרש אסורה לשמש עד שתבדוק בדיקה אחרת אחר תשמיש זה מלבד בדיקה שלפני תשמיש אחר א"נ לא קאי אבדיקות דמתניתין אלא בדיקת עד שלפני תשמיש ומשום דבעי לאותובי עלה ממתניתין דבודקת בכל תשמיש ותשמיש אע"ג דלא ידעה מייתי לה הכא: **מלאך** הממונה על ההריון. והא דאמרינן בריש תענית ג' מפתחות לא נמסרו ביד שליח של חיה ושל גשמים ושל תחיית המתים י"ל דהקב"ה נותן לאשה הריון ואח"כ מתעסק בה המלאך: **הכל** בידי שמים חוץ מיראת שמים. הא דאמרינן בפ' אלו נערות הכל בידי שמים חוץ מצינים פחים במאורעות הבאים לאדם בכל יום ויום אבל הכא בדברים הנגזרים על האדם להתנהג בהן כל ימי חייו והא דאמרינן בסוף מס' שבת האי מאן דמתייליד בצדק יהיה צדקן במצות ואמרינן נמי התם דאמרו ליה כלדאי לאימיה דר"נ בריך גנבא להוי אלמא צדיק ורשע תלוי (במצות) במזל. י"ל (איפשר) [שאף] שמזלו נוטה באחד מן הדרכים מ"מ בידו הוא להתחזק על יצרו:

מקרקיש

וּמַשְׁתִּין מַיִם עָרוֹם לִפְנֵי מִטָּתוֹ, וְהַמְשַׁמֵּשׁ מִטָּתוֹ בִּפְנֵי כָּל חַי. אָמַר לֵיהּ רַב יְהוּדָה לִשְׁמוּאֵל: וַאֲפִי' לִפְנֵי עַכְבָּרִים? א"ל *שִׁינָּנָא, לָא, אאֶלָּא כְּגוֹן שֶׁל בֵּית פְּלוֹנִי – שֶׁמְּשַׁמְּשִׁין מִטּוֹתֵיהֶן בִּפְנֵי עַבְדֵיהֶם וְשִׁפְחוֹתֵיהֶם. וְאִינְהוּ מַאי דְּרוּשׁ? °"שְׁבוּ לָכֶם פֹּה עִם הַחֲמוֹר" *עַם הַדּוֹמֶה לַחֲמוֹר. רַבָּה בַּר רַב הוּנָא מְקַרְקֵשׁ זָגֵי דְּכִילְתָא, אַבַּיֵי בָּאלִי דִּידְבֵי, *רָבָא בָּאלִי פְּרוּחֵי. אָמַר ר"ש בֶּן יוֹחַי: ה' דְּבָרִים הֵן שֶׁהָעוֹשֶׂה אוֹתָן מִתְחַיֵּיב בְּנַפְשׁוֹ וְדָמוֹ בְּרֹאשׁוֹ: *הָאוֹכֵל שׁוּם קָלוּף, וּבָצָל קָלוּף, וּבֵיצָה קְלוּפָה, וְהַשּׁוֹתֶה מַשְׁקִין מְזוּגִין שֶׁעָבַר עֲלֵיהֶן הַלַּיְלָה, וְהַלָּן בְּבֵית הַקְּבָרוֹת, וְהַנּוֹטֵל צִפָּרְנָיו וְזוֹרְקָן לִרְה"ר בוְהַמַּקִּיז דָּם וּמְשַׁמֵּשׁ מִטָּתוֹ.§ הָאוֹכֵל שׁוּם קָלוּף" כו'.§ וְאע"ג דְּמַנְחִי בְּסִילְתָא, וּמְצַיְּירֵי וַחֲתִימֵי – רוּחַ רָעָה שׁוֹרָה עֲלֵיהֶן. וְלָא אֲמַרַן אֶלָּא דְּלָא שַׁיֵּיר בָּהֶן עִיקָּרָן אוֹ קְלִיפָּתָן, אֲבָל שַׁיֵּיר בָּהֶן עִיקָּרָן אוֹ קְלִיפָּתָן לֵית לָן בָּהּ.§ "וְהַשּׁוֹתֶה מַשְׁקִין מְזוּגִין שֶׁעָבַר עֲלֵיהֶן הַלַּיְלָה".§ אָמַר רַב יְהוּדָה אָמַר שְׁמוּאֵל: וְהוּא שֶׁלָּנוּ בִּכְלֵי מַתָּכוֹת. אָמַר רַב פַּפָּא: וּכְלֵי נֶתֶר כִּכְלֵי מַתָּכוֹת דָּמוּ. וְכֵן אָמַר רַבִּי יוֹחָנָן: וְהוּא שֶׁלָּנוּ בִּכְלֵי מַתָּכוֹת, וּכְלֵי נֶתֶר כִּכְלֵי מַתָּכוֹת דָּמוּ.§ "וְהַלָּן בְּבֵית הַקְּבָרוֹת".§ *כְּדֵי שֶׁתִּשְׁרֶה עָלָיו רוּחַ טוּמְאָה – זִימְנִין דְּמִסַּכְּנִין לֵיהּ.§ "וְהַנּוֹטֵל צִפָּרְנָיו וְזוֹרְקָן לִרְשׁוּת הָרַבִּים"§ מִפְּנֵי שֶׁאִשָּׁה מְעוּבֶּרֶת עוֹבֶרֶת עֲלֵיהֶן וּמַפֶּלֶת. וְלָא אֲמַרַן אֶלָּא דְּשָׁקֵיל בִּגְנוּסְטְרֵי. וְלָא אֲמַרַן אֶלָּא דְּשָׁקֵיל דִּידֵיהּ וְדִכְרָעֵיהּ. וְלָא אֲמַרַן אֶלָּא דְּלָא גָּז מִידֵי בַּתְרַיְיהוּ, אֲבָל גָּז מִידֵי בַּתְרַיְיהוּ – לֵית לָן בָּהּ. וְלָא הִיא, לְכוּלְּהוּ מִילְּתָא חָיְישִׁינַן. ת"ר: *ג' דְּבָרִים נֶאֶמְרוּ בַּצִּפָּרְנַיִם: א) שׂוֹרְפָן – חָסִיד, קוֹבְרָן – צַדִּיק, זוֹרְקָן – רָשָׁע.§ "וְהַמַּקִּיז דָּם וּמְשַׁמֵּשׁ מִטָּתוֹ".§ *דְּאָמַר מָר: מַקִּיז דָּם וּמְשַׁמֵּשׁ מִטָּתוֹ – הָוְיָין לוֹ בָּנִים וִיתָקִין. הִקִּיזוּ שְׁנֵיהֶם וְשִׁמְּשׁוּ – הָוְיָין לוֹ בָּנִים בַּעֲלֵי רָאתָן. אָמַר רַב: וְלָא אֲמַרַן אֶלָּא דְּלָא טָעֵים מִידֵי, אֲבָל טָעֵים מִידֵי – לֵית לָן בָּהּ. אָמַר רַב חִסְדָּא: אָסוּר לוֹ לְאָדָם שֶׁיְּשַׁמֵּשׁ מִטָּתוֹ בַּיּוֹם, שֶׁנֶּאֱמַר: °"וְאָהַבְתָּ לְרֵעֲךָ כָּמוֹךָ". מַאי מַשְׁמַע? אָמַר אַבַּיֵי: *שֶׁמָּא יִרְאֶה בָּהּ דָּבָר מְגוּנֶּה, וְתִתְגַּנֶּה עָלָיו. אָמַר רַב הוּנָא: *יִשְׂרָאֵל קְדוֹשִׁים הֵם, וְאֵין מְשַׁמְּשִׁין מִטּוֹתֵיהֶן בַּיּוֹם. אָמַר רָבָא: גוְאִם הָיָה בֵּית אָפֵל – מוּתָּר. דוְת"ח – מַאֲפִיל בִּכְסוּתוֹ וּמְשַׁמֵּשׁ. תְּנַן: אוֹ תְּשַׁמֵּשׁ לְאוֹר הַנֵּר! אֵימָא: תִּבְדּוֹק לְאוֹר הַנֵּר. ת"ש: אע"פ שֶׁאָמְרוּ הַמְשַׁמֵּשׁ מִטָּתוֹ *לְאוֹר הַנֵּר הֲרֵי זֶה מְגוּנֶּה! אֵימָא: "הַבּוֹדֵק מִטָּתוֹ לְאוֹר הַנֵּר הֲרֵי זֶה מְגוּנֶּה". תָּא שְׁמַע: וְשֶׁל בֵּית מוּנְבַּז הַמֶּלֶךְ הָיוּ עוֹשִׂין ג' דְּבָרִים וּמַזְכִּירִין אוֹתָן לְשֶׁבַח. הָיוּ מְשַׁמְּשִׁין מִטּוֹתֵיהֶם בַּיּוֹם, וּבוֹדְקִין מִטּוֹתֵיהֶם בְּמֵילָא פַּרְהָבָא, וְנוֹהֲגִין טוּמְאָה וְטָהֳרָה בִּשְׁלָגִים. קָתָנֵי מִיהָא "מְשַׁמְּשִׁין מִטּוֹתֵיהֶן בַּיּוֹם"! אֵימָא: "בּוֹדְקִין מִטּוֹתֵיהֶם בַּיּוֹם". הָכִי נַמִי מִסְתַּבְּרָא, דְּאִי ס"ד מְשַׁמְּשִׁין – מַזְכִּירִין אוֹתָן לְשֶׁבַח? אִין ה"נ – דְּאַגַּב דְּאִיכָּא אוֹנֶס שֵׁינָה מִגַּנְיָא בְּאַפֵּיהּ. "וּבוֹדְקִין מִטּוֹתֵיהֶן בְּמֵילָא פַּרְהָבָא". מְסַיַּיע לֵיהּ לִשְׁמוּאֵל, דַּאֲמַר שְׁמוּאֵל: האֵין בּוֹדְקִין אֶת הַמִּטָּה אֶלָּא בְּפָקוֹלִין, אוֹ בְּצֶמֶר נָקִי וְרַךְ. אֲמַר רַב: הַיְינוּ דְּכִי הֲוַאי הָתָם בְּעַרְבֵי שַׁבָּתוֹת הָווּ אָמְרִי "מַאן בָּעֵי פָּקוֹלֵי *בְּנַהֲמָא", וְלָא יָדַעְנָא מַאי קָאָמְרִי. אָמַר רָבָא: הָנֵי שָׁחְקֵי דְּכִיתָּנָא מַעֲלֵי לִבְדִיקָה. אִינִי, וְהָא תָּנָא דְּבֵי מְנַשֶּׁה: ואֵין בּוֹדְקִין אֶת הַמִּטָּה לֹא בְּעֵד אָדוֹם, וְלֹא בְּעֵד שָׁחוֹר, וְלֹא בְּפִשְׁתָּן, אֶלָּא בְּפָקוֹלִין אוֹ בְּצֶמֶר נָקִי וְרַךְ! לָא קַשְׁיָא, הָא – בְּכִיתָּנָא, הָא – בְּמָאנֵי דְּכִיתָּנָא. וְאִיבָּעֵית אֵימָא: הָא וְהָא בְּמָאנֵי דְּכִיתָּנָא, הָא – בַּחֲדַתֵּי, הָא – בְּשַׁחֲקֵי. "נוֹהֲגִין טוּמְאָה וְטָהֳרָה בִּשְׁלָגִין". *תְּנַן הָתָם: זשֶׁלֶג אֵינוֹ לֹא אוֹכֶל וְלֹא מַשְׁקֶה. חִישֵּׁב עָלָיו לַאֲכִילָה – אֵינוֹ מְטַמֵּא טוּמְאַת אוֹכָלִין, לְמַשְׁקֶה – מְטַמֵּא טוּמְאַת מַשְׁקִין. נִטְמָא מִקְצָתוֹ – לֹא נִטְמָא כּוּלּוֹ, א] נִטְהַר מִקְצָתוֹ – נִטְהַר כּוּלּוֹ. הָא גוּפָא קַשְׁיָא, אָמַרְתְּ נִטְמָא מִקְצָתוֹ – לֹא נִטְמָא כּוּלּוֹ, וַהֲדַר תָּנֵי נִטְהַר מִקְצָתוֹ – נִטְהַר כּוּלּוֹ, לְמֵימְרָא דְּנִטְמָא כּוּלּוֹ! אָמַר אַבַּיֵי: חכְּגוֹן שֶׁהֶעֱבִירוֹ עַל אֲוִיר תַּנּוּר, *דְּהַתּוֹרָה הֵעִידָה עַל כְּלִי חֶרֶס אֲפִילּוּ

א) [במ"ק יח. איתא הקוברן צדיק שורפן חסיד זורקן וכו' וכן יתכן להיות ודע דגי' הערוך ערך שלש זורקן רשע שורפן חסיד קוברן צדיק]

מְקַרְקֵשׁ זָגֵי. פַּעֲמוֹנִים הַתְּלוּיִים בַּכִּילָּה שֶׁסָּבִיב מִטָּתוֹ מְקַשְׁקְשָׁן בְּעֵת תַּשְׁמִישׁ, לָסוּר בְּנֵי בֵיתוֹ מִשָּׁם. בָּאלִי דִּידְבֵי. מְגָרֵשׁ הַזְּבוּבִים, שֶׁלֹּא לְשַׁמֵּשׁ מִטָּתוֹ בִּפְנֵי כָּל חַי. פְּרוּחֵי. יַתּוּשִׁים. דָּמוֹ בְּרֹאשׁוֹ. נֶעֱנָשׁ עַל עַצְמוֹ, וְחוֹבַת דָּמוֹ נִדְרֶשֶׁת מִמֶּנּוּ לְאַחַר מִיתָתוֹ. וּרְאָיָה לַדָּבָר: "וְדָמוֹ בְרֹאשֵׁנוּ" דִּמְרַגְּלִים (יהושע ב) – חוֹבַת דָּמוֹ יְהֵא מוּטָּל בְּרֹאשֵׁנוּ. (א). וּמִתְחַיֵּיב בְּנַפְשׁוֹ. כְּלוֹמַר, הוּא גּוֹרֵם לְעַצְמוֹ. שֶׁעָבַר עֲלֵיהֶם הַלַּיְלָה. אַכּוּלְּהוּ קָאֵי, אַשּׁוּם וּבָצָל וּמַשְׁקִין. בְּסִילְתָא. סַל. עִיקָּרָן. שְׂעָרוֹת שֶׁבְּרֹאשׁ הַשּׁוּם וְהַבָּצָל. רוּחַ טוּמְאָה. כְּמִדַּת הַלַּיִלִּים, שֶׁקּוֹרִין גרמנטי"ר, הָאוֹחֲזִים אֶת הָעֵינַיִם. בִּגְנוּסְטְרֵי. מִסְפָּרַיִם. חָסִיד. עָדִיף מִצַּדִּיק, כְּשֶׁקּוֹבְרָן אִיכָּא לְמֵיחַשׁ דְּהָדְרִי וּמִגַּלּוּ. וִיתָקִין. חַלָּשִׁים. בַּעֲלֵי רָאתָן. חַלָּשִׁים יוֹתֵר מִדַּאי, שֶׁיֵּשׁ לָהֶם שֶׁרֶץ בְּמוֹחָם, כִּדְאָמַר בִּכְתוּבּוֹת. תַּלְמִיד חָכָם. דְּיָדַע לְאִצְטְנוּעֵי נַפְשֵׁיהּ. אַף עַל פִּי שֶׁאָמְרוּ הַמְשַׁמֵּשׁ מִטָּתוֹ כו'. כִּדְאִיתָא בַּבָּרַיְיתָא דִּלְעֵיל בְּרֵישׁ שְׁמַעְתִּין, וּמַסְקָנָא: "אוֹ תְּשַׁמֵּשׁ לְאוֹר הַנֵּר" – אַלְמָא מְגוּנֶּה הוּא דְּהָוֵי, אֲבָל אִיסּוּרָא לֵיכָּא, מִדְּקָתָנֵי "אוֹ תְּשַׁמֵּשׁ". וְהַשְׁתָּא לֵיכָּא לְמֵימַר: תִּבְדּוֹק, דְּא"כ מַאי "אע"פ שֶׁאָמְרוּ" כו'. אֵימָא הַבּוֹדֵק מִטָּתוֹ לְאוֹר הַנֵּר כו'. מִשּׁוּם דְּלָא מִיבְדִּיק שַׁפִּיר, אפ"ה אוֹ תָּבִיא שְׁנֵי עֵדִים לְכָל תַּשְׁמִישׁ, אוֹ תִּבְדּוֹק לְאוֹר הַנֵּר. מֵילָא פַּרְהָבָא. קוטו"ן. מִתּוֹךְ שֶׁהוּא לָבָן, נִרְאֵית בּוֹ טִיפָּה כְּחַרְדָּל. לִישָּׁנָא אַחֲרִינָא: צֶמֶר נָקִי וְרַךְ. וּמַזְכִּירִין חֲכָמִים אוֹתָן לְשֶׁבַח. בִּתְמִיָּה. וְהִי אִי הֲוָה מוּתָּר בְּעָלְמָא הֲוָה תְּמִיהַּ לָן, וְכ"ש שֶׁמַּזְכִּירִין לְשֶׁבַח, וּמַה הוּא שִׁבְחָן? אוֹנֶס שֵׁינָה. מִתּוֹךְ שֶׁהוּא נֶאֱנָס בְּשֵׁינָה אֵינוֹ מִתְאַוֶּה לָהּ כָּל כָּךְ, וּמְשַׁמֵּשׁ לְקִיּוּם מִצְוַת עוֹנָה בְּעָלְמָא אוֹ לִרְצוֹתָהּ, וְלִבּוֹ קָץ בָּהּ. וְהוּא מִבְּנֵי תֵּשַׁע מִדּוֹת דְּאָמְרוּ בִּנְדָרִי' (דף כ.). °פָּקוֹלִין. קוטו"ן. דְּכִי הֲוַאי הָתָם. בְּאֶרֶץ יִשְׂרָאֵל. בְּעַרְבֵי שַׁבָּתוֹת. זְמַן עוֹנַת פְּרוּשִׁים וְתַלְמִידֵי חֲכָמִים מֵעֶרֶב שַׁבָּת לְעֶרֶב שַׁבָּת. שָׁחְקֵי דְּכִיתָּנָא. בְּגָדִים בְּלוּיִין שֶׁל פִּשְׁתָּן. וְלֹא בְּפִשְׁתָּן. שֶׁאֵינוֹ לָבָן, וְאֵין דָּם נִיכָּר יָפֶה אֶלָּא בְּעֵד לָבָן. שְׁחָקִים. לְבָנִים יוֹתֵר מִן הַחֲדָשִׁים. חִישֵּׁב עָלָיו וכו'. דְּקָרוֹב הוּא לִהְיוֹת מַשְׁקֶה יוֹתֵר מֵאוֹכֶל. לֹא נִטְמָא כו'. דְּאֵינוֹ חִבּוּר, אֶלָּא כָּל קוֹרֶט בִּפְנֵי עַצְמוֹ חָשׁוּב, וְאֵינוֹ טָמֵא אֶלָּא מְקוֹם מַגַּע טוּמְאָה. נִטְהַר מִקְצָתוֹ. כְּגוֹן חִישֵּׁב עָלָיו לְמַשְׁקֶה, וְנִטְמָא טוּמְאַת מַשְׁקִין – סָלְקָא לֵיהּ הַשָּׁקָה בְּמִקְוֶה כִּשְׁאָר מַיִם. וְלֹא מִשּׁוּם טְבִילָה, דְּאֵין אוֹכֶל וּמַשְׁקֶה נִטְהָרִין בְּמִקְוֶה, דְּלָא כְּתִיב טְבִילָה אֶלָּא בְּאָדָם וּכְלִי. אֲבָל יַיִן וְלֹא שׁוּם מַשְׁקֶה – אֵין לָהֶם טָהֳרָה אֶלָּא (ב) מַיִם, וּמִשּׁוּם זְרִיעָה – דְּכִי מַשִּׁיק לְהוּ, הָווּ לְהוּ חִבּוּר מַיִם שֶׁבִּכְלִי עִם מֵי הַמִּקְוֶה, וּבְטֵילוּ לְהוּ גַּבַּיְיהוּ. כִּדְתְנַן (תרומות פ"ט מ"ז) שְׁתִילֵי תְרוּמָה שֶׁנִּטְמְאוּ וּשְׁתָלָן – טָהֲרוּ מִלְּטַמֵּא, אַלְמָא מְטַהֲרָא לְהוּ זְרִיעָה, וּמַיִם בְּמַיִם זוֹ הִיא זְרִיעָתָן. נִטְהַר מִקְצָתוֹ. שֶׁלֹּא נָגְעוּ הַמַּיִם אֶלָּא בְּפִי הַכְּלִי. נִטְהַר כּוּלּוֹ. וּמִדְּקָתָנֵי "נִטְהַר כּוּלּוֹ" מִכְּלָל דְּטָמֵא כּוּלּוֹ, וְהֵיכִי מַשְׁכַּחַת לָהּ דְּנָגְעָה טוּמְאָה בְּכוּלּוֹ. שֶׁהֶעֱבִירוֹ. לַשֶּׁלֶג. עַל אֲוִיר תַּנּוּר. וְשֶׁרֶץ בְּתוֹכוֹ דְּנִטְמָא מֵאֲוִיר כְּלִי חֶרֶס. דְּהַתּוֹרָה הֵעִידָה. "כֹּל אֲשֶׁר בְּתוֹכוֹ יִטְמָא" (ויקרא יא). וַאֲפִילּוּ

**ומשתין** מים ערום לפני מטתו. דאמר בשבת (דף סב:) דקשה לעניותא. ויש ספרים דגרסי הכא: "משמש מטתו ערום", וכן הוא בויקרא רבה. וטעמא, שיש לו להיות צנוע בשעת תשמיש, כדאמרינן בנדרים (דף כ.). **מקרקש** זגי. פ"ה: פעמונים התלוים בכילה, להוציא ממנו בני ביתו. וקשה לר"ת: דאין זה מדת צניעות! ונראה לו כגירסת ר"ח והערוך [ערך גזא'] "מקרקש גזי זבובים", דאמר בבכורות (דף ז:) דבש הגזין והצירעין. והוי דומיא דאביי דבלי דידבי ורבא דבלי פרוחי. **שמשמשין** מטותיהן בפני עבדיהן. ומיירי בלילה או במקום אפל, דבמקום אורה, אפי' בלא לפני עבדיהם אסור. **שורפן** חסיד.ב] – דליכא למיחש שמא יתגלו. ובערוך [ערך "שלש"] פירש: ששרפת צפורן מזקת לאדם, וכן כל דבר הבא מן האדם, כדאמר בס"פ "כלל גדול" (שבת דף עה:) גבי דם הנדה: איידי דחלשא, לא מנכעה לשורא. ולכך הוא חסיד – שמחמיר לשורפן, אע"ג שמזיק לו. **אימא** בודקין מטותיהן ביום. ולכן מזכירין לשבח, דאע"ג דאמרו ב"ש צריכה ב' עדים על כל תשמיש ותשמיש, ולב"ה דיה בב' עדים כל הלילה ומעיינא בהו למחר, מ"מ מודו דאם רוצה לעיין בלילה לאור הנר – הרשות בידה. **הא** בחדתי הא בשחקי. תימה: דפ"ק דשבועות (דף ו:) גבי "שאת – כצמר לבן, שניה לה – כקרום ביצה", ומפרש: כמו גלימא דכיתנא ושחקיה, משמע שהחדש לבן מן הישן! וי"ל: דהתם – בגלימא שאין רגילות לכבס, והכא – בחלוק וכיוצא בו שמכבסין תדיר. ועוד י"ל: דהתם לענין חשיבות מיירי, כי הנך דלעיל, כגון שבור מלכא וריש גלותא*).

*) [ועי' תוס' שבועות ו: ד"ה גלימא]

## תוספי הרא"ש

**מקרקיש** זגי בכלתיה. פרש"י ז"ל פעמונים התלויים בכילה להשמיע קול שיפרשו ממנו ול"נ לר"ת דאין זה צניעות להודיע לבני ביתו שהוא רוצה לשמש ונראה לו כפי' הערוך דגרסי' גזי שהוא מין זבובים דאמרינן במס' (טהרות) בכורות הגזין והצרעין דומיא דרב פפא ואביי דבלו דידבי ופרוחי אלא שכל אחד מוסיף צניעות (להכריע) [להבריח] עוד הקטנים יותר: **הנוטל** צפרניו וזורקן לרה"ר. בפ"ג דמו"ק אמרינן דשלא במקומן לא מזקי: שורפן חסיד. פי' הערוך משום דשריפת צפרנים או כל דבר שהוא מגופו מזיק לו וגם מסריח לו בשעת שריפה הלכך מיקרי חסיד: **הא** בחדתי הא בעתיקי. תימה דאמרינן בפ"ק דשבועות גבי שאת כצמר לבן שניה לה כקרום ביצה מפ' כמו גלימא דכיתנא ושחקיה משמע דהחדש לבן מן הישן וי"ל דהא דשמעתין עדיפי עתיקי משום הרכות ולא משום הלבנונית ועי"ל דלשם מיירי לענין חשיבות דומיא דהנך דלעיל שבור מלכא וריש גלותא: (מכאן ואילך שייך לע"ב) **ואפי'** מלא חרדל. לאו דוקא דאין אוכל מקבל טומאה פחות מכביצה: **דם** העלייה טהור. תימה מנא לן דטהור וכ"ת משום דלקמן נפקא לן מקרא ה' דמים ודם העלייה לאו מאותו המראה א"כ דם הנמצא בפרוזדור למה הוי ספק וי"ל דהיינו טעמא דטהור דכתיב בקרא ממקור דמיה ולא טמא הכתוב אלא דם המקור והיינו החדר שמצויין שם רוב דמים שהוא כמו מקור נובע ועי"ל דכיון דנפקא לן מקרא ה' דמים א"כ לא טמא הכתוב אלא במקום שכולן מצויין וקים להו דבעלייה לא משתכחי כולהו: **והא** אנן תנן שחזקתו מן המקור. ותימה והא מתני' נמי קתני ספקו טמא ומפרשינן ליה ספיקו ודאי טמא וי"ל דרבה הוה ידע דאינהו לא קאמרי הכי עי"ל דמתני' אין לחוש כיון דקתני בהדיא שחזקתו מן המקור ורש"י דייק דספיקו טמא ולא ודאי מדתנן מן הלול ולחוץ ספיקו טהור דאי סבירא להו מן הלול ולפנים ודאי טמא הוה להו לטמויי מספק מן הלול ולחוץ וליכא למימר דסבירא להו כלישני דבתר חזקה אזלת דא"כ לא הוה להו למימר ספיקו טהור דלהך לישנא ליכא ספיקא והא דאמרינן דספיקו

סג א טוש"ע א"ח סי' רמ סעיף ו:
סד ב מיי' פ"ד מהל' דעות הלכה יט:
סה ג מיי' פכ"א מהל' איסורי ביאה. דין זה לא הזכירו הרמב"ם ועי' במ"מ הל' י סמג לאוין קכו טוש"ע א"ח סימן רמ סעיף יא [וברב אלפס עירובין פ"י דף קכד. אמר רבא ואם היה בית אפל מותר ואמר רבא ואיתימא רב פפא ותלמיד חכם מאפיל בכסותו ומשמש]:
סו ד מיי' שם הלכה י טוש"ע שם בהגה"ה [וברב אלפס שם]:
סז ה ו מיי' פ"ד שם הלכה טו סמג לאוין קיא טוש"ע י"ד סי' קצו סעיף ו:
סח ז ח מיי' פ"א מהל' טומאת אוכלין הלכה כב:

[ברכות נו. וש"נ ועמ"ש בס"ד חגיגה טו: פירושו של מלת שיננא]
קדושין סח. יבמות סב. ב"ק מט. כתובות קיא.
מס' ד"א פי"א
[סנהדרין סה: ע"ש פרש"י]
[מ"ק יח.]
כתובות עז: גיטין ע.
קדושין מא.
שבת פו. ע"ש כתובות נו. סה.
[היינו תשמיש בלשון נקיה כדכתיב כי אם הלחם אשר הוא אוכל ערוך ערך פקל ב']
תוספתא דטהרות פ"ב [ועמ"ש בס"ד על הגליון דחולין פז: ועי' הר"ש סוף מ"ב פ"ג דטהרות]
[חולין כד:]

## הגהות הב"ח

(א) רש"י ד"ה דמו וד"ה ומתחייב הד"א: (ב) ד"ה נטהר וכו' אלא במים ומשום:

## גליון הש"ס

**רש"י** ד"ה פקולין קוטו"ן. עי' מגילה יז ע"ב ברש"י ד"ה הפקולי ועי' בערוך ערך פקל ולע"ק:

## הגהות מהר"ב רנשבורג

גמ' א] נטהר מקצתו נטהר כולו. נ"ב עי' ר"ש פ"ג דטהרות סוף משנה ב': ב] תוס' ד"ה שורפן חסיד וכו'. נ"ב עי' דרשת מהרא"נ"ח דף נט ע"ד:

עין משפט
נר מצוה

[וע"ע תוס' שבת לה. ד"ה אי לענין]

סט א ב מיי' פ"ה מהל' איסורי ביאה הלכה ג סמג לאוין קיא טוש"ע י"ד סי' קפג סעיף א:

ע ג מיי' שם הלכה ג והלכה ז:

עא ד ה מיי' שם הל' ה ובזמן הזה שאין אנו בקיאין בכל טמא מגיד משנה בשם הרמב"ן שם:

מסורת הש"ס

אֲפִילּוּ מָלֵא חַרְדָּל.§ **מתני'** אמָשָׁל מָשְׁלוּ חֲכָמִים בָּאִשָּׁה: הַחֶדֶר וְהַפְּרוֹזְדוֹר וְהָעֲלִיָּיה. בדַּם הַחֶדֶר – טָמֵא, דַּם הָעֲלִיָּיה – טָהוֹר, *נִמְצָא בַּפְּרוֹזְדוֹר – סְפֵקוֹ טָמֵא, לְפִי שֶׁחֶזְקָתוֹ מִן הַמָּקוֹר.§ **גמ'** רָמִי בַּר שְׁמוּאֵל וְרַב יִצְחָק בְּרֵיהּ דְּרַב יְהוּדָה תָּנוּ נִדָּה בֵּי רַב הוּנָא. אַשְׁכַּחִינְהוּ רַבָּה בַּר רַב הוּנָא דְּיָתְבִי וְקָאָמְרִי: גהַחֶדֶר מִבִּפְנִים, וְהַפְּרוֹזְדוֹר מִבַּחוּץ, וַעֲלִיָּיה בְּנוּיָה עַל שְׁתֵּיהֶן, וְלוּל פָּתוּחַ בֵּין עֲלִיָּיה לַפְּרוֹזְדוֹר. נִמְצָא מִן הַלּוּל וְלִפְנִים – סְפֵקוֹ טָמֵא, מִן הַלּוּל וְלַחוּץ – סְפֵקוֹ טָהוֹר. אֲתָא וַאֲמַר לֵיהּ לַאֲבוּהּ: סְפֵקוֹ טָמֵא אָמְרַתְּ לָן מָר? וְהָא אֲנַן "שֶׁחֶזְקָתוֹ מִן הַמָּקוֹר" תְּנַן! א"ל, אֲנָא הָכִי קָאָמִינָא: דמִן הַלּוּל וְלִפְנִים – וַדַּאי טָמֵא, מִן הַלּוּל וְלַחוּץ – סְפֵקוֹ טָמֵא. אָמַר אַבַּיֵי: מַאי שְׁנָא מִן הַלּוּל וְלַחוּץ דִּסְפֵקוֹ טָמֵא – דִּדְלְמָא שָׁחֲתָה, וּמֵחֶדֶר אֲתָא; מִן הַלּוּל וְלִפְנִים נַמִי, אֵימָא אִזְדַּקְרָה – וּמֵעֲלִיָּיה אֲתָא! אֶלָּא אָמַר אַבַּיֵי: אִי בָּתַר חֲשָׁשָׁא אָזְלַתְּ – אִידִי וְאִידִי סָפֵק הוּא, וְאִי בָּתַר חֲזָקָה אָזְלַתְּ – מִן הַלּוּל וְלִפְנִים – וַדַּאי טָמֵא, מִן הַלּוּל וְלַחוּץ – וַדַּאי טָהוֹר. [ב"ב כד.] *תָּנֵי רַבִּי חִיָּיא: הדָּם הַנִּמְצָא בַּפְּרוֹזְדוֹר – חַיָּיבִין עָלָיו עַל בִּיאַת מִקְדָּשׁ, וְשׂוֹרְפִין עָלָיו אֶת הַתְּרוּמָה. וְרַב קְטִינָא אָמַר: אֵין חַיָּיבִין עָלָיו עַל בִּיאַת מִקְדָּשׁ, וְאֵין שׂוֹרְפִין עָלָיו אֶת הַתְּרוּמָה. לְהָךְ לִישָּׁנָא דְּאָמַר אַבַּיֵי אִי בָּתַר חֲשָׁשָׁא אָזְלַתְּ – מְסַיַּיע לֵיהּ לְרַב קְטִינָא וּפְלִיגָא דְּרַבִּי חִיָּיא, לְהָךְ לִישָּׁנָא דְּאָמְרַתְּ אִי בָּתַר חֲזָקָה אָזְלַתְּ – מְסַיַּיע לֵיהּ לְרַבִּי חִיָּיא, וּפְלִיגָא

---

**רש"י**

**ואפילו מלא חרדל.** שאין נוגע בתנור אלא גרגרין שאצל הדפנות, ואפ"ה כולו טמא מן האויר. **מתני'** החדר והפרוזדור. בגמ' מפרש היכי קיימי. **דם החדר טמא.** והיינו מקור. **ספקו טמא.** מספק טמא טומאה ודאית. **שחזקתו כו'.** במקור מחזקינן ליה, ולא אמרינן: מעלייה אתא, ודמים דעלייה טהורין. דמפרוזדור לא אתי דם, אלא דמי חדר ודמי עלייה פעמים שהן נכנסין לפרוזדור. **גמ'** חדר מבפנים ופרוזדור מבחוץ. שניהם זה אצל זה בעובי גופה: חדר – לצד אחוריה, ופרוזדור – לפניה, וכותלי רחם – למטה באמצע פרוזדור, ודרך שם דמים יוצאים. **ולול פתוח כו'.** ודמי עלייה באין לפרוזדור דרך הלול. **נמצא בפרוזדור.** מן הלול ולפנים, לצד החדר. **ספקו טמא.** דאי מעלייה אתא – מן הלול ולחוץ איבעי ליה לאשתכוחי. דהא כי נחית מן הלול לפרוזדור – כלפי חוץ הוא יורד ויוצא דרך יליאה, ואינו חוזר לצד אחוריה. ולקמן פריך: ודאי טמא הוי, ואמאי קתני "ספקו טמא"? **ספקו טמא.** ולא ודאי, מדקתני: "מן הלול ולחוץ – ספקו טהור". **והא אנן שחזקתו מן המקור תנן.** מדקתני "חזקתו", מכלל דטומאה ודאית קאמר. ובמאי מוקמת לה? לא מן הלול ולפנים, ולא מן הלול ולחוץ, דלדידך ליכא טומאה ודאית. **מן הלול ולפנים.** ודאי טמא, ומתניתין – מן הלול ולפנים. **ספקו טמא.** לתלות, שהרי שני דמים יוצאין דרך שם: דמי החדר ודמי העלייה, ולא ידעינן מהי אתא. ואע"ג דאיכא לאחזוקי בדם עלייה, דאי מחדר אתא – לא הוה אזיל בפרוזדור עד מן הלול ולחוץ, דהוה נפיק ליה ונחית דרך יליאת פתח פרוזדור, אפ"ה מטמאינן לה מספקא: דילמא שחתה ונפלה על פניה, ונשתרבב הדם בכל הפרוזדור, ובא מצד אחוריה לצד פניה כשיצא מן החדר. **דספקו טמא.** ולא אמרינן: ודאי טהור. **אזדקרה.** נזקפה לצד אחוריה, כגון פרקדנית שקורין שובינ"א, ואיכא למימר: מעלייה נחית לפרוזדור, והא דלא נפיק ונחית מפרוזדור דרך פתח בית הרחם וחזר לצד החדר – משום זקיפה הוא. וכיון דאיכא לאחזוקי הכי והכי – הוי ספק ולא ודאי. **אי בתר חששא אזלת.** דלא מחזקת ליה לדם כמנהגו והילוכו, אלא באת לחוש לקורות הנולדות כגון שחתה. **אידי ואידי ספקא הוי.** דכי היכי דמספקא מן הלול ולחוץ – דלמא שחתה, איכא לספוקי נמי מן הלול ולפנים – דלמא אזדקרה. **ואי בתר חזקה אזלת.** דמחזקת ליה לדם כמנהג הילוכו, ולא חיישינן לאימור שחתה ולאימור אזדקרה. **מן הלול ולפנים ודאי טמא.** דודאי מחדר אתא, דאי מעלייה אתא – מן הלול ולחוץ איבעי ליה לאשתכוחי, ומתניתין דקתני "שחזקתו מן המקור" נמי מן הלול ולפנים. **מן הלול ולחוץ ודאי טהור.** ולא אמרינן: אימור שחתה, והוה ליה ספק לתלות, אלא כמנהגו מחזקינן ליה ודאי טהור. **חייבין עליו.** אם נכנסה למקדש, דודאי טמאה. ולקמן מפרש אי מן הלול ולפנים אי לחוץ. **אין חייבין.** אבל איסורא – איכא, אלמא ספק הוא. **להך לישנא.** דאי בתר חששא – אידי ואידי ספקא הוא. **מסייע ליה לרב קטינא.** דאמר: ספקא הוא, ומוקמינן בין מן הלול ולפנים בין מן הלול ולחוץ, ופליגא דר' חייא אדאביי, דהא על כרחיך לאביי להאי לישנא ליכא טומאה ודאי, לא שנא לפנים לא שנא לחוץ לא שנא בגג לא שנא בקרקעית, דכיון דתלי טעמא בחששא – בכולהו איכא לספוקי הכי והכי. **להך לישנא.** דבתר חזקה, מסייע ליה לר' חייא, ומתוקמא במן הלול ולפנים. **ופליגא**

כאן

---

**תוספות**

**אפילו מלא חרדל.** למאי דמפרש ר"ת דאין פחות מכביצה מקבל טומאה, לאו דוקא "מלא חרדל" אלא "מלא ביצים". אלא משום דמדרבנן מקבל טומאה, נקט ליה*. **פרוזדור.** "פרוז" בלשון יון: לפני, "דור" – לשון דירה. אית דגרס "פרוזדוד" בדל"ת. **ודם העלייה.** – משמע דדם העלייה טהור, אפי' הוא ממראה דמים טמאים. דאי אין בעלייה מד' מיני דמים טמאים – אם כן, דם שבפרוזדור אמאי הוי ספק? נחזי אי הוי מד' מיני דמים אי לאו! ודוחק לומר: דאיירי בנאבד, והיינו טעמא דטהור: דכתיב "ממקור דמיה" – דוקא דמי מקור, דהיינו חדר. אי נמי: "דמיה" כתיב – מקום שמצויין שם הרבה דמים, ובעלייה ליכא אלא מין אחד. **והתנן** שחזקתו מן המקור. ואע"ג דבמתני' קתני נמי "ספקו טמא" – היינו ספקו ודאי טמא, כדקתני בהדיא "שחזקתו מן המקור". והוה מצי לשנויי: כגון שנמצא בקרקע פרוזדור, כדמשני בסמוך אר' חייא. א"נ: שמא קרקע פרוזדור, לא הוה קרי ליה "ספק". **מן** הלול ולפנים נמי כו'. פירוש: לדבריך, שאתה חושש לשינוי, אמאי ודאי טמא? ניחוש נמי דלמא איזדקרה ומעלייה אתא! ותימה: דאדרבה, כיון דמן הלול ולחוץ, אע"פ שמן העלייה הוא בא שם כדרכו, חיישינן לדם החדר שהוא רחוק, ואין יכול לבא אלא ע"י שחייה, משום דרוב דמים מן המקור אתו מש"ה יש לטמא בודאי מן הלול ולפנים, ולתלות בדמי החדר המרובים והקרובים יותר מדמי העלייה! וע"ק: דבפרק "לא יחפור" (ב"ב דף כג.), א"ר חנינא: רוב וקרוב – הלך אחר הרוב. ומוכח התם דרבי חנינא מיירי, אפילו בקורבא דמוכח. ואמר אביי: אף אנן נמי תנינא כר' חנינא, נמצא בפרוזדור – ספקו טמא, שחזקתו מן המקור. ואע"ג דאיכא עלייה דמקרבה טפי. ומאי ראייה מייתי? דהא ללישנא דבתר חששא *אזלת, לא אזלינן, בתר רובא כלל טפי מקורבא. אלא אידי ואידי ספקא הוי, ואפילו מן הלול ולפנים. שדמי החדר רוב, וגם באין משם בלא שינוי – חיישינן לדמי העלייה שהם מעטים ואינם יכולין לבא שם, אא"כ נזדקרה. וללישנא דבתר חזקה אזלת, מטהר מן הלול ולחוץ, ולא חייש לרובא דדמי החדר. והא דמטמא מן הלול ולפנים – לאו משום רובא גרידא, אלא משום דבא נמי מן החדר בלא שינוי. וקורבא דעלייה לא מוכח כלל, דלא חיישינן לאיזדקרה. ונראה לפרש: דכל אמוראי דשמעתין איירי בגג פרוזדור. וכן הענין, דגג פרוזדור מן הלול ולפנים, גבוה ומשתפע ועולה. ואינו יכול לבא שם מן העלייה, אלא א"כ נזדקרה. ומן החדר אינו יכול לבא לגג פרוזדור, אפילו מן הלול ולפנים, אלא א"כ שחתה ביותר. והוא שינוי גדול מדיקור של עלייה. כי הלול שדמי החדר יוצאים לפרוזדור. הוא לצד קרקע פרוזדור. אבל מן הלול ולחוץ, משתפע ויורד ובא שם מן העלייה כדרכו, ומן החדר בא שם בשינוי גדול יותר ממן הלול ולפנים. והשתא פריך שפיר: מ"ש מן הלול ולחוץ דספק, אף על גב דמן החדר אינו בא שם אלא בשינוי גדול מאד, ומן העלייה בא שם כדרכו, אלא משום דשחתה רגילות הוא. דאי לא רגילות הוא, הוי ודאי טהור. ואפילו הכי לא בעי למיזל בתר רובא שיהא ודאי טמא, מן הלול לפנים נמי אימור איזדקרה. דכיון דשחתה רגילות הוא, איזדקרה נמי רגילות. ואמאי ודאי טמא? ואע"ג דרוב דמים מן המקור, אין ללכת אחר הרוב, כמו מן הלול ולחוץ דלא הוי טמא ודאי, אף ע"ג דשחתה הוי רגילות. אלא אמר אביי: אי בתר חששא אזלת, משום דשחתה רגילות הוא, כדפרישית – אידי ואידי ספקא. ואי בתר חזקה אזלת, ולא בתר חששא דשחתה לאו רגילות הוא – מן הלול ולחוץ ודאי טהור. ומ"מ מן הלול ולפנים, אע"ג דשחתה לאו רגילות הוא – הוי ודאי טמא. דממה נפשך: על ידי שינוי בא, או שחתה או איזדקרה. ואית לן למימר: דמן החדר אתא, משום דחזקת דמים מן המקור באין. ומוכח שפיר ב"לא יחפור" מהא לישנא, דבתר חזקה דהוי עיקר, כדמשמע לישנא "שחזקתו מן המקור", דרוב וקרוב – הלך אחר הרוב, אפילו בקורבא דמוכחא. דמן הלול ולפנים – ודאי טמא, דאזלינן אחר רוב דמים שמן המקור, אע"ג דהעלייה מקרבא ומוכח. דהא מעלייה בא בשינוי מועט יותר ממן החדר, כדפרישית. **ואין** שורפין עליו את התרומה. תימה: כיון דהוי ספק טומאה ברה"ר טהור ודאי, וברה"י – טמא ודאי, ושורפין! וי"ל: כדפירשתי לעיל (דף ג.) דמסוטה לא ילפינן טומאה דאתיא ע"י ראיית גופה. לכן בכל מקום ספק. ול"ע במכילתין (דף עא.) גבי דם תבוסה, דמשמע דספק יצא מחיים ספק לאחר מיתה, ברשות היחיד – ספקו טמא, ברשות הרבים – ספקו טהור. ואם תאמר: וכיון דלא ילפינן מסוטה, נוקי אשה בחזקתה, ונטהר אפילו ברשות היחיד? ויש לומר: משום דדמי החדר מצויין ביותר, כדאמר ב"לא יחפור" (ב"ב דף כג.) רוב ומצוי קאמרת? ולא חשיב חזקה וקורבא לגבי רובא אלא כפלגא ופלגא.

*וללישנא דבתר חששא אזלינן שחזקתו מן המקור היינו אפילו מן הלול ולחוץ יש לחוש שמא מן המקור בא משום דהשתא הוי רגילות ולא בא אלא ליתן טעם אמאי ספיקו טמא מבחוץ ולעולם אידי ואידי ספיקא הוי. גליון

---

**גליון הש"ס**

**מתני'** נמצא בפרוזדור. עי' לקמן מב ע"ב תוד"ה שהולכת.

---

**תוספי הרא"ש**

דספיקו טמא לישנא דמתני' נקט: **אימר** שחתה ומחדר אתא. תימה אמאי לא נטהר מן הלול ולחוץ מספק ספיקא דאימר לא שחתה ואת"ל שחתה אימור מעלייה אתא כלומר יותר רגיל בלא שחייה מעל ידי שחייה וכן מן הלול ולפנים [הו"ל לומר] דטמא ודאי דאימור לא נזדקרה ומחדר אתא ואת"ל מזדקרא אכתי איכא למתלי בחדר ואמאי אמר אביי דספיקא הוי. ועוד תימה דמשמע דמההוא טעמא דמטמינן מן הלול ולחוץ אית לן לתלות לטהר מן הלול ולפנים אדרבה מההוא טעמא דמהדרינן מן הלול ולחוץ ולתלות בדם החדר ואע"פ שהוא רחוק משום דרוב הדמים מן המקור מההוא טעמא גופיה יש לנו לטמאות מן הלול ולפנים ודאי ולתלות בדם החדר המרובין והקרובים יותר מדמי העלייה ועוד תימה דבפ' לא יחפור דייק אביי דרוב וקרוב הולכין אחר הרוב ממתני' דקתני ספיקו טמא שחזקתו מן המקור ואף ע"ג דאיכא עלייה דמיקרבא והיכי דייק מינה והא ללישנא דבתר חששא לא אזיל בתר רובא כלל טפי מבתר קורבה דאידי ואידי ספיקא הוי וללישנא דבתר חששא לא אזיל [אלא בתר] חזקה מטהר מן הלול ולחוץ ולא חייש לרוב דמי החדר והא דמטמאי מן הלול ולפנים לאו משו' דלא אזל בתר רובא אלא משום דלא איזדקרא. ועוד תימה מאי קאמר התם אע"ג דאיכא עלייה דמיקרבא גם לחדר הם קרובים דביציאתן מן החדר בא לפרוזדור ונראה לפרש שכן הוא הענין שגג פרוזדור מן הלול ולפנים גבוה הרבה ואינו יכול לבא דם מן העלייה שם אלא א"כ נזדקרה ומן החדר אינו יכול לבא לגג פרוזדור אלא אם כן שחתה אבל מן הלול ולחוץ אין גג פרוזדור כל כך גבוה ויכול לבא שם מן העלייה כי אורחיה בלי שינוי ומן החדר אינו יכול לבא שם אלא על ידי שחייה מרובה והכי פריך מאי שנא מן הלול ולחוץ דמשוית ליה ספיקא אע"ג דמן העלייה יכול לבא שם כדרכו ומן החדר אינו יכול לבא שם אלא בשחייה מרובה משום דאימור שחתה ומן החדר אתא. ועו"כ כיון דחיישינן לשחתה רגילות הוא דאם לא היה רגילות ומצוי (זה בזה) הוי ודאי טהור ואע"ג דרגילות הוא לא בעי למימר שיהיה ודאי טמא אע"ג שרוב דמים מן החדר אלא חשבינן ליה ספק. מן הלול ולפנים נמי אימור איזדקרא ומעלייה אתא ואמאי אמרינן דודאי טמא דמדשחתה רגילות כמו כן איזדקרא רגילות. ואע"ג דרוב דמים מן המקור לא הוה לן למימר דודאי טמא כמו מן הלול ולחוץ דלא בעית לטמויי ודאי אע"ג דשחתה רגילות הוא: אלא אמר אביי אי בתר חששא קא אזלת. כלומר דחשבת לשחתה רגילות ואפ"ה לא הוי ודאי טמא מן הלול ולחוץ. אידי ואידי ספיקא הוא כלומר מן הלול ולפנים נמי ספיקו הוי כיון דלא אזלת בתר רוב דמי המקור ואי בתר חזקה אזלת כלומר בתר חזקת רוב דמים מן המקור מן הלול ולפנים ודאי טמא מן הלול ולחוץ ודאי טהור דשחתה לאו רגילות הוא ומ"מ מן הלול ולפנים ודאי טמא דממה נפשך ע"י שינוי בא שם ע"י שחייה או ע"י זקירה ויש לן לומר דע"י שחייה בא דמשום חזקת דמים מן המקור והשתא אביי לא אזיל בתר חששא אלא אביי פריך ליה לרבה דמשוי ליה מן הלול ולפנים ודאי טמא ומן הלול ולחוץ ספיקו טמא דאי בתר חששא אזיל אידי ואידי ספיקא הוי והכי לא מצינן למימר דמתני' קתני שחזקתו מן המקור אלמא יש כאן טומאה ודאית אלמא מתני' סברא דבתר חזקה אזלינן ומן הלול ולפנים ודאי טמא ומן הלול ולחוץ ודאי טהור הילכך מייתי ראיה מהך מתני' דרוב וקרוב הולכין אחר הרוב אע"ג דאיכא עלייה דמיקרבא שהרי נמצא בגג פרוזדור שהוא קרוב לעלייה והכי מוכחא הסוגיא דכל הני אמוראי איירי בשנמצא בגג פרוזדור: **ואין** שורפין עליו את התרומה. ותימה כיון דחשיב ליה ספק ברשות היחיד יהיה ודאי טמא וברה"ר יהיה ודאי טהור וי"ל כדפרשינן לעיל בריש מכלתין דלא שייך לחלק בין רה"ר לרה"י אלא במקום שע"י שהן רבים ראוי הספק להתברר. ותימה אמאי לא מטהרינן לגמרי ונוקי אשה בחזקת טהרה וי"ל משום דדמי החדר מצויין ביותר כדאמרינן בפ' לא יחפור רוב ומצוי קאמרינן ולא חשבינן קורבה וחזקה לגבי רובא אלא כפלגא ופלגא:

ופליגא דרב קטינא. לרב הונא – לא פליגי, אכאן – מן הלול ולפנים, כאן – מן הלול ולחוץ. אלא לרמי בר שמואל ולרב יצחק בריה דרב יהודה, דאמרי מן הלול ולחוץ – ספקו טהור, מן הלול ולפנים – ספקו טמא הני במאי מתוקמא – מן הלול ולפנים, לימא פליגא דרבי חייא! לא קשיא, כאן – כשנמצא בקרקע פרוזדור, וכאן – שנמצא בגג פרוזדור. אמר רבי יוחנן: בשלשה מקומות הלכו בו חכמים אחר הרוב ועשאום כודאי: מקור, שליא, חתיכה. מקור – הא דאמרן, שליא – *דתנן: בשליא בבית – הבית טמא, גולא שהשליא ולד, אלא שאין שליא בלא ולד. ר"ש אומר: נמוק הולד עד שלא יצא. חתיכה – *דתנן: *דהמפלת יד חתוכה ורגל חתוכה – אמו טמאה לידה, ואין חוששין שמא מגוף אטום באת. ותו ליכא? והאיכא תשע חנויות! דתניא: *התשע חנויות כולן מוכרות בשר שחוטה, ואחת מוכרת בשר נבלה, ולקח מאחת מהן ואינו יודע מאיזה מהן לקח – ספקו אסור, ובנמצא – הלך אחר הרוב. טומאה – קאמרינן, איסור – לא קאמרינן. והאיכא, *זתשע צפרדעין ושרץ אחד ביניהם, ונגע באחד מהן ואינו יודע באיזה מהן נגע, ברה"י – ספקו טמא, ברה"ר – ספקו טהור, ובנמצא – הלך אחר הרוב! טומאה דאשה – קאמרינן, טומאה בעלמא – לא קאמרינן. והאיכא הא *דאמר רבי יהושע בן לוי: חעברה בנהר והפילה

**רש"י**

ופליגא דרב קטינא. אהך לישנא דאביי. דהא להאי לישנא ליכא טומאת ספק, דכיון דתלי טעמא בחזקה לא שנא גג, לא שנא קרקע: מן הלול ולפנים – טמא ודאי, מן הלול ולחוץ – טהור ודאי. לרב הונא. דאמר ליה לבריה: מן הלול ולפנים – ודאי, מן הלול ולחוץ – ספקא. לא פליגי. לא דר' חייא ולא דרב קטינא עליה, ואהדדי נמי לא פליגי. כאן מן הלול ולפנים. דר' חייא. כאן מן הלול ולחוץ. דרב קטינא. אלא לרמי בר שמואל ולרב יצחק. דאמרי: מן הלול ולחוץ – ספק טהור, על כרחך הני מתני' דר' חייא ודרב קטינא במאי מיתוקמי – במן הלול ולפנים. דהא מן הלול ולחוץ – אפילו ספקא ליכא, דהא "טהור" קאמרינן, ודרב קטינא קיימא כוותייהו. אלא רבי חייא דאמר טומאה ודאית, לימא פליגא עלייהו, דלדידהו ליכא טומאה ודאית. ומשנינן. לא פליגי, הא דרבי חייא דאמר ודאי – במן הלול ולפנים. בקרקע פרוזדור. דהיינו כדרך יציאתו מן החדר. ודרמי ורב יצחק דאמרי ספק טמא – בגג פרוזדור, שקרוב לעלייה. ולעולם בתר חזקה אזלי, ומודו בקרקע פרוזדור במתני' וכדרבי חייא. אבל בגגו, במן הלול ולפנים, על כרחך יצא זה ממנהג הילוכו. דהבא מן החדר – היה לו לימצא בקרקע פרוזדור, שהחדר נמוך ושוה לפרוזדור, ואם מן העלייה בא – הוה לו לימצא מן הלול ולחוץ. הלכך איכא למיתליה בתרי ספיקי: דילמא מעלייה אתא לפרוזדור, ואזדקרה. או מחדר אתא לפרוזדור, וע"י שנזדקרה (א) עלה הדם מלמטה למעלה. (ב) כיון דרמי ורב יצחק לא יהבי טעמא למילתייהו, איכא לאוקמי בשינוי. אבל לאביי, ללישנא דבתר חששא, ליכא לשנויי הכי, ופליג דר' חייא עליה. דכיון דאביי תלי טעמא בחששא, וכל היכא דאיכא למיחש להאי ולהאי משוי ליה ספק, אפילו בקרקע פרוזדור איכא לספוקי בחדר (ג) ובעלייה, הילכך דרבי חייא פליג עליה. ועשאום כודאי. משום דאזלינן בתר רובא. הא דאמרינן. במתניתין שחזקתו לא בא אלא מן המקור, וכדתני רבי חייא, אלמא כיון דרוב דמים התם שכיחי – מחזקינן ליה מן המקור. הבית טמא. אף אם אין ולד נראה – הבית טמא משום אהל המת. שאין שליא בלא ולד. ושורפין עליה את התרומה. אלמא, כיון דרוב שליות אינן בלא ולד מחזקינן לה בטומאה ודאית. נימוק הולד. ונעשה דם ונתערב בדם הלידה ובטל ברוב. והכי מפרש טעמא לקמן בפ' "המפלת" (דף כז.). יד חתוכה. מחותכת בצורתה בחיתוך אצבעות. אמו טמאה לידה. ותשב חומר זכר לימי טוהר וחומר נקבה לענין טומאה דמחזקינן לה בלידה ודאית ליתן לה ימי טומאה וימי טהרה, דאמרינן: הלך אחר הרוב, ורוב נשים ולד מעליא ילדן, אלא שנימוק. ואין חוששין. לומר: לא יהיו לה ימי טוהר, שמא אינו ולד, דדילמא מגוף אטום הוא בא, וקיימא לן ב"המפלת" (לקמן דף כד.) דאינו ולד. והיינו כודאי, מדיהבינן לה ימי טוהר, הואיל ורוב נשים לאו גוף אטום ילדן. ספקו אסור. דכל קבוע – כמחצה על מחצה דמיא. וכיון שלקחה ממקום הקביעות – מחזקינן לה כמחצה על מחצה. ובנמצא. בקרקע, דה"ל מופרש מהן, ולא לקחו ממקום הקביעות. הלך אחר הרוב. ומותר. דכל דפריש – מרובא פריש. ברשות היחיד כו'. דהוה ליה ספק, ואע"ג דרובא לצפרדעים ואין להם טומאה, כיון דשרץ קבוע ביניהם – הוה ליה מחצה על מחצה. ובנמצא. שפירש אחד מהן למקום אחר, ונגע בו אדם שם – טהור, דהשתא לאו קבוע הוי, ואמרינן: כל דפריש – מרובא פריש, ולצפרדע הוא. והפילה.

**תוספות**

כאן שנמצא בקרקע פרוזדור. פ"ה: דלעיל אליבא דבתר חששא אזלינן, דקאמר דפליגא דר' חייא, לא מצי לשנויי הכי – דכיון דתלי אביי טעמא בחששא, איכא למיחש אפילו בקרקע פרוזדור לדם עלייה. וקשה לפירושו: דנמצא על שלה או על שלו, אמאי חייבין בקרבן, מי עדיף מנמצא מן הלול ולפנים דלא הויא אלא ספק, אפי' בקרקע פרוזדור? ונראה לפרש: דלאביי ליכא לאוקמי דר' חייא בקרקע פרוזדור, דכיון דאפי' מן הלול ולחוץ, דבא מן העלייה כדרכו וקרוב, חייש לדם המקור, אם כן מן הלול ולפנים בקרקע פרוזדור – מילתא דפשיטא היא, דמן החדר אתא, ולא הוה צריך רבי חייא לאשמועינן.

שליא בבית כו'. פ"ה: דרוב שליות יש להם ולד. וקשה: דתנן בפ' "בהמה המקשה" (חולין דף עז.) שליא שיצתה מקצתה – אסורה באכילה. ואי יש שליא בלא ולד, הוה לן למשרי, משום דסמוך מיעוטא דאין בה ולד לפלגא שלא יצא רוב הולד, וה"ל מחצה שיש בה רוב ולד – מיעוטא. דסתם שליא שיצתה מקצתה ויש בה ולד – מחצה יש בהן רוב ולד, ומחצה אין בהן רוב ולד, כדמוכח בפ"ק דב"ק (דף יא.). וכה"ג אמר התם: *סמוך מיעוטא דנדמה למחצה דנקבות, וכן (ד) *בפ"ק דבכורות (דף כ:) סמוך מיעוטא דמפילות למחצה דנקבות! ויש ליישב פ"ה: דהתם מיירי בשליא שיצתה מקצתה, ונמצא ולד תוך השליא. ונראה לפרש: דאין שליא כלל בלא ולד, אך מיעוטא נימוק, ורובן אין נימוקים עד שילא לבית החיצון, כדאמר בפ' "המפלת" (לקמן כז.) וא"ת: ואמאי לא מייתי הכא מרישא דתנן ב"המפלת" (שם דף כד:) המפלת סנדל או שליא – תשב לזכר ולנקבה, אלמא דרובן אין נימוקין קודס יליאה! וי"ל: דאפי' נמוקין מצינן למימר דטמאה לידה, דקאמר קרא: "אשה כי תזריע" אפי' לא ילדה, אלא כעין שהזריעה אמו, טמאה לידה. ואע"ג דההיא דרשא – כרבי שמעון, בריש "יוצא דופן" (לקמן דף מ.) ורבנן דרשו לה: עד שתלד ממקום שמזריע! י"ל: דתרתי ש"מ. א"נ י"ל: מרישא לא מייתי, דהו"א דטעמא דרבנן משום שאין שום שליא בלא ולד, ואין שום ולד נימוק אפילו מיעוט. לכך מייתי סיפא דאמר ר' שמעון: נימוק הולד, אע"פ שלא יצא. וכיון דסבר רבי שמעון דרובן נימוקין, ולרבנן אינם נימוקין אלא מיעוטן. דאין סברא לומר דלר"ש רובן נימוקין, ולרבנן אפילו מיעוטן אין נימוקין. וקלת נראה, דאדרבה ארישא סמיך וסיפא לא מייתי אלא משום דמינה מוכיח דטעמא דרבנן משום רובא, כדפרישית. דאי משליא בבית גופה מייתי, מאי איריא משום רוב אפי' מחצה על מחצה שורפין, דהוה ליה ספק טומאה ברה"י דטמא. המפלת יד חתוכה. הא דלא מייתי מתני' ד"המפלת" (לקמן דף כח.) המפלת ואין ידוע מהו, ובהמפלת חתיכה מיירי, כדמוכח התם בגמרא (דשליא בבית) משום דהכא מפרש בהדיא: אין חוששין שמא מגוף אטום באה, דמשמע דהוי מטעם דהולכים בתר רובא. ותו ליכא. וא"ת: והא איכא הא דתנן לקמן בפ' "האשה" (דף נט:) איש ואשה שעשו צרכיהם בספל, ונמצא בו דם, רבי שמעון מטמא, שחזקת דמים מן האשה! ואי משום דרבי שמעון קתני לה, הא קאמר שליא, אע"ג דרבי מאיר קתני לה, כדאמר ב"המפלת" (לקמן דף כז.) וכ"ת דאין שורפין על אותו רוב תרומה, א"כ לקמן דדחיק לאשכוחי למעוטי מאי, לימא: למעוטי רובא דר' שמעון! וי"ל: דהתם מסייע חזקת האדם לרוב. וא"ת: וליחשוב נמי הא דתנן ב"הרואה" (לקמן דף נז:) נמצאת אתה אומר שלש ספקות באשה, ובמגעות ובהסיטות – הלך אחר רוב. ואי אין שורפין עליו תרומה, לימא: למעוטי הא! ויש לומר: דשורפין, והוי טעמא משום דרוב דמים באין מן המקור, דחשיב בג' דברים. ספקו אסור. בשילהי פ"ק דכתובות (דף טו.) נפקא לן קבוע מ"וארב לו". וא"ת: לר"ש דדריש מ"וארב לו" – עד שיתכוין לו, קבוע מנא ליה? וי"ל: דמסקינן בפ' "הנשרפין" (סנהדרין דף עט.) דסבר רבי שמעון כרבי, ד"ונתת נפש תחת נפש" – ממון, א"כ מהתם שמעינן עד שיתכוין לו, ואייתר "וארב לו" – לקבוע. אך לתנא דבי חזקיה דדריש "מכה אדם" "ומכה בהמה" דשאינו מתכוין פטור ממיתה וממון, ולא דריש "ונתת נפש תחת נפש" לממון, וע"כ עד שיתכוין לו נפקא ליה מ"וארב לו", קשה: קבוע מנא ליה?*. הלך אחר הרוב. משמע: אפי' נמלא קרוב לחנות המוכרת נבלה. וא"ת: א"כ, מאי קמ"ל, ר' חנינא(א) דרוב וקרוב – הלך אחר הרוב? וי"ל דקמ"ל, אפי' בקורבה דמוכחא. מיהו קשה מקושיא דרבי זירא, דהתם תקשי ליה מתני' ד"ט' חנויות"(ב). אחר הרוב. הכא איכא חזקה כנגד הרוב, דבהמה בחזקת איסור עומדת. וגבי ט' לפרדעים נמי קאמר הלך אחר הרוב, ואם רוב שרצים (ה) טמאים אע"ג דאיכא חזקת טהרה, דאי לא הוי חזקה כנגד הרוב לא הוה פריך מידי, דמצינן למימר דרבי יוחנן לא חשיב אלא היכא דאיכא חזקה כנגד הרוב.

א) [ב"ב כג:]. ב) [ועי' תוס' ב"ב כג: ד"ה מתיב וכו' כתבו ישוב על זה]

אלא

**תוספי הרא"ש**

כאן שנמצא בגג פרוזדור. פרש"י ז"ל אבל אביי ללישנא דבתר חששא ליכא לשנויי הכי דכיון דתלי אביי טעמא בחששא כל היכא דאיכא למיחש משוינן ליה ספק לא שנא גג ולא שנא קרקע איכא לספוקי בחדר ובעלייה. וקשה לפי' דא"כ להך לישנא לא משכחת לעולם אשה ודאי טמאה ואמאי נמצא על שלו חייבין בקרבן דמי עדיף מן הלול ולפנים מקרקע פרוזדור דהוי נמי ספיקא. ונראה לפרש דלהך לישנא נמי שני ליה בין גג לקרקע והאי דלא שני הכי משום דר' חייא ע"כ לית ליה לישנא דחששא אפי' בגג פרוזדור דאי הוה סבר הכי כיון דמחמיר כולי האי דחייש לדם המקור מן הלול ולחוץ אע"פ שדם העלייה בא שם כדרכו בלא שנוי וגם קרוב לעלייה מילתא דפשיטא הוא דטמא ודאי בקרקע פרוזדור ולא אצטריך למתנייה אלא ודאי סבר מן הלול ולחוץ ודאי טהור הלכך אצטריך לאשמועינן דמן הלול ולפנים שורפין: הלכו חכמים אחר הרוב. אפי' איכא מיעוטא וחזקה דלא מרעי לרובא ואפי' ר' מאיר דחייש למיעוטא הכא מודי ולא אמרינן סמוך מיעוטא לחזקה דהעמד אשה בחזקת טהרה משום מיעוטא דלא שכיח הוא כמו מקור שרוב דמי מקור מצויין: שליא דתנן פרש"י רוב שליא יש לה ולד ומיעוטא אין בה ולד וקשה לפי' דאי מהאי טעמא חשיב ליה רוב א"כ מרישא ה"ל לאתויי המפלת סנדל או שליא תשב לזכר ולנקבה ומדיהבינן ליה ימי טוהר דזכר אלמא חשבינן להך רוב כודאי ועוד דלישנא דאין שליא שאין עמה ולד משמע דאין כאן ספיקא אלא כל שליא יש עמה ולד וכן משמע מהא דתנן פרק בהמה המקשה שליא (אסורה) שיצתה מקצתה אסורה באכילה ואם יש שליא בלא ולד הו"ל למישריה דסתם שליא דיצתה מקצתה מחצה יש באותו מקצת רוב ולד ומחצה אין בו רוב ולד כמו שמוכיח פ"ק דבב"ק וסמוך מיעוטא דיש שליא בלא וולד למחצה דאותם נמי דיש בה ולד אין במקצתה רוב ולד והוה להו מחצה שיש בה רוב ולד מיעוטא דכה"ג אמרינן פ' בהמה המקשה גבי המבכרת שהפילה שליא סמוך מיעוטא דנדמה למחצה דנקבות וכן פ"ג דבכורות סמוך מיעוטא דמפילות למחצה נקבות וכן בפ' בתרא דיבמות ויש ליישב פרש"י ז"ל בדוחק כגון שמצינו ולד בזאת השליא ויש לפרש דרובא דשמעתין היינו שאנו תולין שלא נימוק הולד בשעת יציאתו כדאמרינן לקמן פ' המפלת אמרו לו לר' מאיר אי אתה מודה שאם הוציאוהו בספל בבית החיצון שהוא טהור אמר להם אינו דומה נימוק פעם אחת לנימוק שתי פעמים ורוב זה שאינו נימוק בבית הפנימי חשיב ליה כודאי אע"ג דאיכא למימר העמד בית בחזקת טהור. וא"ת אכתי תיקשי לך לידוק מרישא מדקתני תשב לזכר ולנקבה אלמא דרובא אינן נימוקין קודם יציאה וי"ל דאפי' היה נימוק מ"מ היתה טמאה לידה כדדרשינן לקמן בפ' המפלת אשה כי תזריע אפי' לא ילדה אלא כעין שהזריעה אמו טמא לידה. ואע"ג דר' שמעון הוא דדריש ליה הכי ורבנן הוו דרשי מיניה עד שתלד במקום שמזרעת למעוטי יוצא דופן איכא למימר תרוייהו ש"מ. א"נ היינו דלא מייתי רישא משום דאי לאו סיפא ה"א דאין שום ולד נימוק בפנים אבל מדקאמר ר' שמעון בסיפא נימוק הולד עד שלא יצא משמע דלת"ק מיעוטא נימוקין: תשע צפרדעים כו' הלך אחר הרוב כו'. ה"נ איכא חזקה דמשמע אם רוב שרצים טמא אע"ג דאיכא (מיעוטא) חזקת טהרה: טומאה דאשה קאמרינן ותימה והאיכא נמי הא דתנן לקמן איש ואשה שעשו צרכיהם לתוך הספל חזקת דמים מן האשה ואי משום דר"ש קתני לה הא קתני נמי שליא אע"ג דר"מ קתני לה כדאיתא בפ' המפלת וכ"ת דאין שורפין על אותו רוב תרומה א"כ הא דדיק לאשכוחי למעוטי מאי לימא למעוטי רובא דר"ש וי"ל שאני התם דאיכא חזקת אדם שהוא בחזקת שאינו רואה דם ומסייע לחזקת רוב דמים מן האשה ומילתא דפשיטא היא ולא אצטריך למחשביה:
מאי

**הגהות הב"ח**

(א) רש"י ד"ה בקרקע פרוזדור וכו' ועל ידי שנזדקרה נ"ב ס"א שנתהפך: (ב) בא"ד וכיון דרמי: (ג) בא"ד בחדר ובעלייה: (ד) תוס' ד"ה שליא וכו' וכן בפ"ג דבכורות: (ה) ד"ה אחר וכו' רוב שרצים טמא אף על גב:

**גליון הש"ס**

רש"י ד"ה אמו טמאה לידה וכו' ליתן לה ימי טומאה וימי טהרה. ע"ל דף כח ע"א וצ"ע:

**עין משפט נר מצוה**

עב א מיי' פ"ה מהל' איסורי ביאה הל' ה:
עג ב מיי' פ"ב מהל' טומאת מת הל' י:
עד ג מיי' שם ופ"י מהל' איסורי ביאה הל' יד:
עה ד מיי' פ"י מהל' איסורי ביאה הלכה יא סמג לאוין קיא ועשין רמב:
עו ה מיי' פ"ח מהל' מאכלות אסורות הל' יא וע"ש כמ"מ סמג לאוין קמא טוש"ע י"ד סי' קי סעיף ג:
עז ו מיי' שם ופי"ז מהל' אבות הטומאות הל' ח:
עח ז מיי' פי"ח מהל' שאר אבות הטומאה הלכה ב:
עט ח מיי' פ"י מהל' איסורי ביאה הלכה יט ופ"א מהל' מחוסרי כפרה הל' ו ז טוש"ע י"ד סימן קלד סעיף טו:

**מסורת הש"ס**

לקמן כז. [בכורות כב.]
פסחים ט. כתובות טו. חולין לה.
[כתובות טו. ע"ש תוספתא טהרות פ"ו]
[לקמן כט.]
נ"ל דתניא
לקמן כז. [ודף כח.]
[חולין עז:]
[נ"ל בפ"ג]
[ועי' תוס' כתובות טו. ד"ה פרט ותוס' ב"ק מד: ד"ה כל ותוס' סנהדרין עט. ד"ה וכל]

וְהִפִּילָה — מְבִיאָה קָרְבָּן וְנֶאֱכָל, הַלֵּךְ אַחַר רוֹב נָשִׁים, וְרוֹב נָשִׁים וָלָד מְעַלְּיָא יָלְדָן. מַתְנִיתִין קָאָמְרִינַן, שְׁמַעְתָּתָא — לָא קָאָמְרִינַן. וְהָא *כִּי אֲתָא רָבִין אֲמַר: מְתִיב רַבִּי יוֹסֵי בַּר רַבִּי חֲנִינָא טוֹעֶה, וְלָא יָדַעְנָא מַאי תְּיוּבְתֵּיהּ, מַאי לָאו: לָא תְּיוּבְתָּא אֶלָּא סַיְיעָתָא? לָא, דִּלְמָא: לָא תְּיוּבְתָּא וְלָא סַיְיעָתָא. לְמַעוּטֵי מַאי? אִילֵימָא לְמַעוּטֵי רוּבָּא דְּאִיכָּא חֲזָקָה בַּהֲדֵיהּ, דְּלָא שָׂרְפִינַן עֲלֵיהּ אֶת הַתְּרוּמָה — וְהָא אֲמָרָהּ ר' יוֹחָנָן חֲדָא זִימְנָא! *דִּתְנַן: תִּינוֹק הַנִּמְצָא בְּצַד הָעִיסָּה וּבָצֵק בְּיָדוֹ — רַבִּי מֵאִיר מְטַהֵר, וַחֲכָמִים [א]מְטַמְּאִין, שֶׁדַּרְכּוֹ שֶׁל תִּינוֹק לְטַפֵּחַ. וְאָמְרִינַן: מַאי טַעֲמָא דְּר"מ — קָסָבַר: רוֹב תִּינוֹקוֹת מְטַפְּחִין, וּמִיעוּט אֵין מְטַפְּחִין, וְעִיסָּה זוֹ בְּחֶזְקַת טְהוֹרָה עוֹמֶדֶת, *סְמוֹךְ מִיעוּטָא לַחֲזָקָה — וְאִיתְרַע לֵיהּ רוּבָּא. וְרַבָּנַן — מִיעוּטָא — כְּמַאן דְּלֵיתֵיהּ דָּמֵי, וְרוּבָּא וַחֲזָקָה — רוּבָּא עָדִיף. *וְאָמַר רֵישׁ לָקִישׁ מִשּׁוּם רַבִּי אוֹשַׁעְיָא: זוֹ הִיא חֲזָקָה שֶׁשּׂוֹרְפִין עָלֶיהָ אֶת הַתְּרוּמָה, וְרַבִּי יוֹחָנָן אָמַר: [ב]אֵין זוֹ חֲזָקָה שֶׁשּׂוֹרְפִין עָלֶיהָ אֶת הַתְּרוּמָה! אֶלָּא לְמַעוּטֵי רוּבָּא דְּרַבִּי יְהוּדָה. *דִּתְנַן, [ג]הַמַּפֶּלֶת חֲתִיכָה, אִם יֵשׁ עִמָּהּ דָּם — טְמֵאָה, וְאִם לָאו — טְהוֹרָה. רַבִּי יְהוּדָה אוֹמֵר: בֵּין כָּךְ וּבֵין כָּךְ טְמֵאָה. *וְאָמַר רַב יְהוּדָה, אָמַר שְׁמוּאֵל: לֹא טִימֵּא רַבִּי יְהוּדָה אֶלָּא בַּחֲתִיכָה שֶׁל אַרְבַּע מִינֵי דָמִים, אֲבָל (א) שְׁאָר מִינֵי דָמִים — טְהוֹרָה. וְרַבִּי יוֹחָנָן אָמַר: שֶׁל אַרְבַּע מִינֵי דָמִים — דִּבְרֵי הַכֹּל טְמֵאָה, וְשֶׁל שְׁאָר דָּמִים — דִּבְרֵי הַכֹּל טְהוֹרָה. לֹא נֶחְלְקוּ אֶלָּא כְּשֶׁהִפִּילָה וְאֵינָהּ

והפילה. ואין ידוע אם ולד הוא. ונאכל. חטאת העוף שלה נאכלת, ולא אמרינן: על הספק באה, ואינה נאכלת דדלמא לאו ולד הוא, וחולין מלוקין הן, ומליקת חולין נבלה. שמעתתא. ר' יהושע בן לוי – אמורא הוא, ו"שלשה מקומות" דאמר ר' יוחנן – משנה או ברייתא הן. והא כי אתא רבין אמר. בפ' "המפלת" (לקמן דף כט.). מתיב רבי יוסי ברבי חנינא. אדרבי יהושע בן לוי מתני' חדא דמיירי באשה טועה שלא ידעה אימתי ילדה. והתם קתני לה, וקאמר רבין: לא ידענא מאי תיובתא דרבי יוסי, דלאו תיובתא היא. והתם מפרש טעמא. מאי לאו. ה"ק רבין: דהא מתני' לאו תיובתא היא דרבי יהושע, אלא סייעתא, אלמא מתני' אמרה כרבי יהושע, ואשכחן ארבעה מקומות בטומאת נשים במתני' שהלכו אחר הרוב, וקשיא לר' יוחנן דלא קחשיב אלא תלת. למעוטי מאי. "ג' מקומות" דקאמר רבי יוחנן דמשמע הני ותו לא למעוטי מאי? דמשום רובא לא נשוייה ודאי. אילימא למעוטי רובא. בטומאת אשה. דאיכא חזקה בהדיה. כלומר: כנגדה, דמרעא לה חזקה לרובא, וקאתי מיניה למעוטי דלא אזלינן בתר ההוא רובא לשוויה מילתא ודאי, ולא שורפין תרומה עלה דההיא טומאה. הא אמרה רבי יוחנן חדא זימנא. בשאר טומאות, דהיכא דסתרה חזקה לרובא דלא אזלינן בתר רובא לשוייה ודאי, וממילא שמעינן לטומאת אשה. לטפח. בשרים. סמוך מיעוטא לחזקה. והוו להו לטהר תרי ורובא לחודיה לטמא, ואין א' עומד במקום שנים. זו היא חזקה כו'. חזקה זו שאנו מחזיקין סתם רוב תינוקות מטפחין – חזקה גמורה החזיקוה, לעשותה ודאי ולשרוף עליה תרומה. אלא למעוטי רובא דרבי יהודה. דאע"ג דאמר "זיל בתר רובא", הכי גמר לה ר' יוחנן דטמא דקאמר רבי יהודה – לתלות קאמר, ולא לשרוף. חתיכה. בלא צורה. אם יש עמה דם טמאה. האשה טמאה כשאר נדה, ולא משום לידה, דלאו ולד הוא. של ארבע כו'. שהחתיכה מארבע מראות דם טמא השנויין במתני'. ואע"ג ד"חמשה" תנן, שחור – אדום הוא, אלא שלקה. דכיון דמראה דם טמא יש בה – אמרינן: כולו דם הוא, וטמאה נדה. ורבנן סברי: אין זה דם, אלא בשר. של שאר מיני דמים. כגון ירוק ולבן, שטהורין הן. ואינה

**אלא** סייעתא. דקתני התם: (ב) כשהביאה ג' שבועות טהורים ועשרה שבועות אחד טמא ואחד טהור, וקאמר דלא משמשת עד אור ל"ה ואי ליתא לדרבי יהושע אמאי והא ספק ספיקא הוא אימר רוח הפילה ואת"ל: נפל הפילה אימא הרחיקה לידתה ואע"ג דבלאו הכי איכא כמה ספקות אימא זכר ואת"ל נקבה: אימא לא ילדה בזוב ואפילו יולדת נקבה בזוב אימא הרחיקה לידתה מ"מ אי ליתא לדרבי יהושע איכא ספק אחר יותר דאימא לא ילדה כלל והוה לן למישרי. ומשני: לא, דלמא לא תיובתא ולא סייעתא, דבלאו הכי איכא ספיקי טובא, ואסרינן. ה"ה אי ליתא דר' יהושע, נמי אסרינן.

**למעוטי** רובא דאיכא חזקה בהדיה. פירוש: כנגד הרוב. ואם תאמר: הלא גם בהני שלשה דברים איכא חזקה דטהרה, ושורפין משום רוב! ויש לומר: דרוב תינוקות מטפחין אינו רוב גמור, כמו שאפרש, ובהני ג' דברים הוי רוב גמור. אי נמי: בהני שלשה נמי לא הוי רוב גמור, ואשמועינן רבי יוחנן דאפילו הכי שורפין, כיון דהריעותא באה מגופה. ושליא נמי קרי לה טומאת אשה, משום שע"י אשה טומאה באה לבית. ולפי זה אפי' אשכחנא גבי אשה שום מתני' דשורפין על הרוב את התרומה, הא דלא חשיב לה רבי יוחנן, משום דהתם שמא הוא רוב חשוב, ולא הוי שום חדוש. ומיהו לפירוש זה לא מייתי לעיל אלא מסיפא משליא בבית, דאיכא למימר דרוב דאינם נימוקין אינו רוב גמור. דרישא דמפלת שליא חשב לזכר ולנקבה, על כרחך הוי רוב חשוב, מדלא קתני נמי "ולנדה", כדדייק ב"המפלת" (לקמן דף כח.) ואם רוב אינן נימוקין אינו רוב גמור, הא דקתני לעיל "מביאה קרבן ונאכל" אינו מטעם רוב, אלא אפי' נימוק – הויא טמאה לידה.

**האמר** ר' יוחנן חדא זימנא. תימה: אפי' לא אמר, [°]היכי מלינן למעוטי? (ג) הא טומאת אשה דוקא קאמר! ומיהו לר"ת דמפרש דהא דתינוק טמא משום דנשים נדות מגפפות אותו, ניחא קצת, דגם תינוק הוי טומאת אשה. **רוב** תינוקות מטפחין. פ"ה: מטפחין באשפה שיש בה שרצים, אבל ודאי נגע בעיסה, שהרי בצק בידו. ור"ת מפרש: רוב תינוקות מטפחין בעיסה, דטיפוח שייך באוכל ומשקה, כדאמר בפ' "רבי ישמעאל" (ע"ז דף ס:) או שהיה מטפח על פי החבית מרותחת. ובירושלמי איכא: מפני שדרכו של תינוק לטפח בעיסה. ובתוספתא (פ"ג דטהרות) נמי משמע שאין ידוע אם התינוק נגע בעיסה, דקתני אההיא דתינוק, א"ר יוסי: אם יכול לפשוט ידו וליקח – טמא, ואם לאו – טהור. אבל התינוק, אומר ר"ת: דודאי טמא, כדקתני בתוספתא (שם) לפי שנשים נדות מגפפות ומנשקות אותו. והא דאמר בפ"ג דטהרות (מ"ז) תינוק בצד הקברות ושושנים בידו, אע"פ שאין השושנים אלא ממקום טומאה – התינוק טהור. שאני אומר: אדם טהור כו' – היינו טהור מטומאת מת, שאינו צריך הזאה ג' וז' אבל טומאת ערב טמא, כדין נוגע בנדה. א"נ בידוע שהוא בודאי טהור. א"נ כשהתינוק מלוכלך, כדקתני בתוספתא (שם) תינוק שהניחתו אמו, ומצאתו כמו שהוא – טהור. בד"א שהניחתו מלוכלך, אבל הניחתו נקי – טמא, מפני שנשים נדות מגפפות אותו. **סמוך** מיעוטא לחזקה ואיתרע ליה רובא. קשה: דבפ' בתרא דיבמות (דף קיט:) אמר: סמוך מיעוטא לחזקה, והוה ליה פלגא ופלגא! ויש לומר: דלהכי איתרע הכא רובא, משום דתינוק הוי דבר שאין בו דעת לישאל, [כמו בפ' "י' יוחסין", ולא גמרינן מסוטה אלא ביש בו דעת לישאל] ולהכי, כי הוי פלגא ופלגא – טהור, מדרב גידל. *וא"ש מהאי טעמא הא דאמר: ספק נגע ברה"י – טמא, ולא אמר: סמוך פלגא דלא נגע לחזקת טהרה, ואיתרע לה פלגא דנגע. דאפילו רבנן דלית להו סמוך מיעוטא לחזקה, מודו דסמכינן פלגא לחזקה. אלא כיון שיש בו דעת לישאל – גזרת הכתוב הוא דגמרינן מסוטה לטמא ברה"י אפי' איכא חזקת טהרה. אבל בשאין בו דעת לישאל, אזלינן בתר רובא, ובפלגא ופלגא – טהור, מדרב גידל.

**מיעוטא** כמאן דליתא דמי. אע"ג דאמרינן בפ' "י' יוחסין" (קדושין פ:) דעשו התינוק כמי שיש בו דעת לישאל – איצטריך הכא למימר לרבנן: מיעוטא כמאן דליתיה דמי, לטמא אף ברה"ר אך קשה: כיון דמיעוטא כמאן דליתיה דמי, ורובא וחזקה – רובא עדיף, אמאי עשאוהו כמי שיש בו דעת לישאל? אפילו אין בו דעת לישאל – טמא אף ברה"ר ועוד: דאמאי אין שורפין עליו את התרומה? ואומר ר"ת: דרוב תינוקות אינו רוב גמור, ולא הוי כנגד חזקה אלא כפלגא ופלגא. ומן התורה טהור אף ברה"י כיון דאין בו דעת לישאל. והא דקאמר התם: עשאוהו כאילו יש בו דעת לישאל – היינו כלומר: עשאוהו כאילו הוא רוב גמור, לפי שנראה לעולם שהוא רוב, אע"פ שאינו רוב גמור, ולכך אין שורפין עליו את התרומה. אבל ליכא למימר: כיש בו דעת לישאל ממש, דאמאי עשאוהו טפי הכא מבחולדה המהלכת ע"ג ככרות, דטהור? ואפי' אם תמצי לומר: דגזרו אטו תינוק גדול שיש בו דעת לישאל, אכתי מ"מ ברה"ר אמאי טמא? אלא נראה, דעשאוהו כאילו הוא רוב גמור, כדפרישית. ולר"מ טהור, ואע"פ שעשאוהו כרוב גמור – משום סמוך מיעוטא לחזקה, ואיתרע ליה רובא. וא"ת: לר"מ ל"ל סמוך מיעוטא לחזקה? אפי' בלא חזקה יטהר, כיון דחייש למיעוטא – הוי ספק, ואין בו דעת לישאל – טהור מדרב גידל! ואומר ר"י: דנקט חזקה בהדי מיעוטא, לאשמועינן דהחזקה אינה מסייעה לרוב. דאי הוה חזקה מסייעה לרוב, הוי כמו מיעוטא דמיעוטא, דלא חייש ר"מ [והא דר"מ דחייש למיעוטא, אי הוה דאורייתא או דרבנן, אין להאריך כאן]. **למעוטי** רוב דרבי יהודה. הוי מצי למיפרך: הניחא ללישנא דמפרש רבי יוחנן טעמא דרבי יהודה משום דרוב חתיכות של ד' מיני דמים הן, אלא ללישנא אחרינא דהמפלת (לקמן דף כח:) דאמר רבי יוחנן, טעמא דרבי יהודה: דאי אפשר לפתיחת הקבר בלא דם ולא משום רוב, למעוטי מאי? דכעין זה פריך לקמן (כב:) בגמ' ד"המפלת מין דגים", דליכא למימר דה"ק: רוב פתיחת הקבר אינו בלא דם, ולא שורפין עליה תרומה, דהא קאמר התם לרבי יהושע דאמר: אי אפשר לפתיחת קבר בלא דם, דמביאה קרבן ונאכל, אם כן טמא ודאי הוא ושורפין עליו את התרומה.

אמר

פ א ב מיי' פט"ז מהל' שאר אבות הטומאה הלכה ג:
פב ג מיי' פ"ה מהל' איסורי ביאה הל' יג סמג לאוין קיא ועשין רמג טור י"ד סימן קפח וסימן קלד:

### תוספי הרא"ש

**מאי** לאו תיובתיה אלא סייעתיה. דלקמן מוכח דמתוך תשובתו שהשיב לא ידענא מאי תיובתיה אימור הרחיקה לידתה משמע דהוי סייעתיה ולקמן נדקדק בו בע"ה: **הא** אמרה ר' יוחנן חדא זימנא. תימה אפי' לא אמרה רבי יוחנן היכי מצי למעוטי והאמרינן טומאה דאשה דוקא קאמר ולפי' ר"ת שפי' פ' כיסוי הדם דלטפח קאי אעיסה ושייך טפוח באוכלין ומשקין כדתנן בע"ז בפ' ר' ישמעאל או שהיה מטפח על פי החבית המרותחת וסתם תינוק טמא כדתניא בתוספתא דמס' טהרות תינוק שהניחתו אמו ומצאתו כמו שהוא טהור. בד"א שהניחתו מלוכלך אבל הניחתו נקי טמא מפני שהנשים נדות מנשקות אותו ומגפפות אותו השתא ניחא דבטומאת אשה מיירי: **למעוטי** רובא דר' יהודה. כלישנא קמא דהמפלת אתיא הך שמעתא והוה מצי למיפרך להך לישנא דאמר ר' יוחנן דבאפשר לפתיחת קבר בלא דם קא מיפלגי למעוטי מאי כה"ג פריך לקמן גבי מפלת מין דגים ואיכא למימר האי דלא פריך ליה הכי סמיך אהא דאיכא למימר דאתא למעוטי רובא דר' שמעון הך דאיש ואשה שעשו צרכיהן לתוך הספל ואין שורפין אליו את התרומה:

לקמן כט. סט.
טהרות פ"ג מ"ה קדושין פ. חולין פו.
שם יבמות קיט.
[קדושין פ.]
לקמן כח.
[שם]

### הגהות הב"ח

(א) גמ' אבל של שאר מיני: (ב) תום' ד"ה אלא וכו' התם והביאה ג': (ג) ד"ה האמר וכו' למעוטי הא הא טומאה:

נ"י כ"י
[סוטה כט.]

### גליון הש"ס

**תום'** ד"ה האמר וכו' היכי מלינן למעוטי וכו'. יסוד זה כתבו תוס' ג"כ גיטין ה ע"א ד"ה כשניסת:

נ"י כ"י

ואינה יודעת מה הפילה. *רבי יהודה סבר: זיל בתר רוב חתיכות, ורוב חתיכות של ארבע מיני דמים הויין. ורבנן סברי: "זיל בתר רוב חתיכות" לא אמרינן. § **מתני'** חמשה דמים טמאים באשה: האדום, והשחור, וכקרן כרכום, וכמימי אדמה, וכמזוג. בש"א: אף כמימי תלתן, וכמימי בשר צלי, וב"ה מטהרים. *הירוק, עקביא בן מהללאל מטמא, וחכמים מטהרין. אמר רבי מאיר: אם אינו מטמא משום כתם – מטמא משום משקה. רבי יוסי אומר: לא כך ולא כך. איזהו אדום – כדם המכה. שחור – כחרת. עמוק מכן – טמא, דיהה מכן – טהור. וכקרן כרכום – כברור שבו. וכמימי אדמה – מבקעת בית כרם, ומציף מים, *וכמזוג – שני חלקים מים ואחד יין, מן היין השרוני. § **גמ'** מנלן דאיכא דם טהור באשה? דלמא כל דם דאתי מינה טמא! אמר רבי חמא בר יוסף *אמר רבי אושעיא, אמר קרא: (דברים יז) "כי יפלא ממך דבר למשפט בין דם לדם" – בין דם טהור לדם טמא. אלא מעתה "בין נגע לנגע", הכי נמי בין נגע טמא לנגע טהור? א] וכי תימא: ה"נ – נגע טהור מי איכא? וכי תימא: (ויקרא יג) "כולו הפך לבן טהור הוא" – ההוא "בוהק" מקרי! אלא: בין נגעי אדם לנגעי בתים ולנגעי בגדים – וכולן טמאין, הכא נמי – בין דם נדה לדם זיבה – וכולן טמאין! האי מאי? בשלמא התם – איכא לאפלוגי בנגעי אדם, ובפלוגתא דרבי יהושע ורבנן, *דתנן, אם בהרת קודם לשער לבן – טמא, ואם שער לבן קודם לבהרת – טהור, ספק – טמא, ורבי יהושע אומר: כהה. ואמר רבה: כהה וטהור. בנגעי בתים – כי הא פלוגתא דר"א בר"ש ורבנן, *דתנן, ר"א בר"ש אומר: לעולם אין הבית טמא עד שיראה כשני גריסין על שני אבנים, בשני כותלים, בקרן זוית, ארכו כשני גריסין ורחבו כגריס. מ"ט דר"א בר"ש? כתיב: (שם יד) "קיר" וכתיב: "קירות", איזהו קיר שהוא כשני קירות – הוי אומר: זה קרן זוית. בנגעי בגדים – בפלוגתא דר' יונתן בן אבטולמוס ורבנן. *דתניא, ר' יונתן בן אבטולמוס אומר: מנין לפריחת בגדים שהיא טהורה – נאמר (שם יג) "קרחת" ו"גבחת" בבגדים, ונאמר "קרחת" ו"גבחת" באדם, מה להלן – פרח בכולו טהור, אף כאן נמי – פרח בכולו טהור. אלא הכא, אי דם טהור ליכא במאי פליגי? וממאי דהני טהורין והני טמאין? אמר רבי אבהו, *דאמר קרא: (מלכים ב ג) "ויראו מואב את המים אדומים כדם". למימרא דדם אדום הוא, אימא אדום ותו לא! א"ר אבהו: אמר קרא (ויקרא יב) "דמיה" (שם כ) "דמיה" – הרי כאן ארבעה. והא אנן "חמשה" תנן! *אמר רבי חנינא: שחור – אדום הוא, אלא שלקה. תניא נמי הכי: *שחור – כחרת, עמוק מכן – טמא, דיהה אפי' ככחול – טהור. ושחור זה, לא מתחלתו הוא משחיר, אלא כשנעקר הוא משחיר, משל לדם מכה – לכשנעקר הוא משחיר. § בש"א אף כמימי תלתן". § ולית להו לב"ש "דמיה" "דמיה" הרי כאן ארבעה? אב"א: לית להו. ואב"א: אית להו, מי לא א"ר חנינא שחור – אדום הוא, אלא שלקה, ה"נ מלקא הוא דלקי. § וב"ה מטהרין". § היינו תנא קמא! איכא בינייהו לתלות.

---

ואינה יודעת מה הפילה. שאבדה החתיכה קודם שבאה לפנינו. לא אמרינן זיל בתר רוב חתיכות כו'. דלא סבירא להו: רוב חתיכות – של ד' מיני דמים, ואשמועינן רבי יוחנן לעיל: בג' מקומות הלכו אחר הרוב, ותו לא – למעוטי הא רובא דר' יהודה. דלר' יהודה דאזיל בתר רובא, לא כודאי משוית ליה לשרוף על מגעה את התרומה. **מתני'** וכקרן כרכום. כזוית גן שכרכום גדל בו. וכמימי אדמה. לקמן מפרש לה לכולהו במתניתין. ל"א: "כקרן כרכום" – כנוגה זיו כרכום, כמו (שמות לד) "כי קרן עור פניו". וכמזוג. כיין אדום המזוג במים, ואע"ג דקליש אדמימות דיליה – טמא. תלתן. פנגרי"ג. וכמימי בשר צלי. מוהל היוצא ממנו. אם אינו מטמא משום כתם כו'. מפרש בגמרא. כדם המכה. מפרש בגמ'. כחרת. איידרמינ"ט. עמוק מכן. שעמוק במראה שחרורית, כלומר: שחור יותר מחרת – טמא. דיהה. פלד"ש, שנדחית מראיתו. כברור שבו. שיש עלין בירורין במראה אדמומית יותר מחבריהן. ובגמרא מפרש להו. בית כרם. מקום, ומשם מביא אדמה ונותנה בכלי. ומציף עליה מים. כלומר, נותן שם מים עד שיהו המים צפין על האדמה. וכמזוג. כיצד? כגון שני חלקים מים כו'. **גמ'** אלא מעתה כו'. עד "וכולן טמאין", לשון קושיא הוא. בוהק. לשון לובן, שנראה באנשים בחורים טפות לבנות מאד בפניהם. בשלמא התם. גבי נגעים, אע"ג דכולהו לטמא איכא לאוקומי קרא דאיירי בפלוגתא דזקן ממרא וסנהדרין שבדורו, דכתיב (דברים יז): "והאיש אשר יעשה בזדון", כגון דמפלגי בנגעי אדם, ובפלוגתא דרבי יהושע כו', דקאמר זקן ממרא כחד מינייהו וסנהדרין כחד מינייהו. אם בהרת קודמת לשער לבן טמא. דשער לבן – מסימני טומאה, וכגון שקדמתו בהרת, דכתיב (ויקרא יג): "והנה נהפך שער לבן בבהרת". כהה טהור. הרי הוא כנגע שכהה מראיתו בשבוע של הסגר, שהוא סימן טהרה, דכתיב (שם): "והנה כהה הנגע" וגו'. ובשם רבי משה הדרשן שמעתי: "קיהה" – כלומר, קיהה בדבר ונחלק עליו. וכן מצאתי בת"כ: ר' יהושע קיהה וטיהר. שיעור נגע בגרים. לאורך ולרוחב. כשני גריסין על שני אבנים שבקרן זוית. אחד בכותל זה ואחד בכותל זה. ארכו כשני גריסין ורחבו כגרים. דכשהוא מוטל ארכו על ב' אבנים, נמצא בכל אבן גרים על גרים כשיעור נגע. ושתי אבנים בעינן, דכתיב (שם יד): "וחלצו את האבנים". כתיב "קיר". "ומראיהן שפל מן הקיר" (שם). פריחה. פרחה צרעת בכולהו. שהיא טהורה. ואע"פ שלא נאמר אלא באדם (שם יג): "ואם פרוח תפרח" וגו'. למימרא דדם אדום הוא. ואלו כולם אדומין הן. ואימא אדום ותו לא. האדום שבאדומים, דהיינו "כדם המכה" דמתניתין. דמיה דמיה. "והיא גלתה את מקור דמיה" (שם כ) "וטהרה ממקור דמיה" (שם יב) – הרי ד' מיני אדמומית טמאה בה, אבל שלמטה מהן – לאו דם הוא. דיהה מכן. אפילו הוא שחור ככחול – טהור, הואיל ואינו שחור כחרת. לכשנעקר. מן הגוף לוקה, ומשחיר. לתלות.

---

**אמר** רבה כיהה וטהור. נראה דרבה גרס, דבפרק "הפועלים" (ב"מ דף פו:) אמר: מאן מוכח – רבה בר נחמני, ואמר: טהור. פ"ה: כיהה – שיש לו דין כיהה. וקשה: דבשלהי נזיר (דף סה:) פריך: ודלמא כיהה, וטמא, והיכי מצי למימר הכי, והא "כיהה" משמע: טהור! *ועוד: דא"כ ר' יהושע לא פליג את"ק: ובדוחק י"ל: דאדרבי יהושע פריך, ומנליה דטהור? *(ורבינו תם) גרים: ור' יהושע קיהה" – פירוש: עמד למנין, דקיהה לשון אסיפה, כמו (יבמות דף קי:) מקהו אקהייתא בשוקא. והשתא פריך התם: אימא עמד למנין, והביא ראיה לדברי ת"ק מיהו דוחק הוא, דא"כ מאי משני: אמר קרא "לטהרו", היכי מוכח מהאי קרא שטיהר, דלמא כי היכי דדרשי ליה רבנן, דריש נמי רבי יהושע. **רבי** יהושע אומר כיהה. הקשה ר"ת: דמאי טעמייהו דרבנן דמטמאי מספיקא? נוקי גברא אחזקיה, כדקי"ל בפ"ק דחולין (דף י:) דמדאורייתא אזלינן בתר חזקה! ורבי יהושע נמי, אמאי צריך קרא? ובפרק "המדיר" (כתובות דף עה:) נמי, דקאמר: לא תימא דלא אזיל רבי יהושע בתר חזקה דגופה כלל – פירוש: דקאמר התם גבי "משארסתני נאנסתי": לא מפיה אנו חיין. אלא הני מילי היכא דאיכא חזקה דממונא, אבל היכא דליכא חזקה דממונא – אזיל, דתנן: אם בהרת כו'. והשתא מה צריך ראיה על זה דאזיל בתר חזקה? ועוד: דשאני גבי נגעים, דגלי קרא! וי"ל: דדרך השער להתלבן מחמת הנגע, לפיכך נראין הדברים דבהרת קדמה. וכן מוכח בתוספתא בפרק "יש נוהלין" בשער לבן, דקתני, אמר להן: אף שער שחור – סוף שבהרתו הפכתו. אלמא דדרך השער ללקות מן הבהרת. וב"המדיר" (שם) דקאמר: היכא דליכא חזקה דממונא, אזיל רבי יהושע בתר חזקה דגופה. היינו אפילו דאיכא ריעותא, דאי לא אזיל, לא הוה מוקי קרא דלטהרו אספק בהרת קדמה, דשכיח הרבה ואיכא ריעותא טפי, אלא הוה מוקי לה לדרשה אחריתי כרבנן. אי נמי: מהתם יליף דאזיל בתר חזקת הגוף, אע"ג דאיכא ריעותא. ור"ת מפרש בע"א ואין להאריך כאן. **מה** להלן פרחה בכולו טהור. מדמדמה פריחה דאדם לפריחת בגדים. הא דכתיב (ויקרא יג) "וכסתה הצרעת את כל עור הנגע מראשו ועד רגליו" – אגופו של אדם קאי,ב] אע"ג דפשטיה דקרא משמע דאנגע קאי. דאיירי לעיל בנגע שנטמא על ידי שיש בו מחיית בשר חי, ועליה קאי "וכסתה הצרעת את כל עור הנגע מראשו של נגע עד רגליו" – כלומר: עד סופו. אבל הכא משמע דקאי אאדם דומיא דבגד. וכן מוכח בכמה מקומות בת"כ ובריש "איזהו מקומן" (זבחים מט:).

הירוק

---

## תוספי הרא"ש

**רבי** יהושע אומר כהה. כך גרש"י ופי' דין נגע כהה יש לו וקשה מהא דפריך בסוף נזיר אימא כיהה וטימא והיכי מצי למימר הכי הא כהה טהור הוא. ור"ת גר' ר' יהושע קיהה בקו"ף לשון אסיפה כמו מקהו אקהייתא בשוקא דנהרדעא לשון אסיפה כלומר אסף התלמידים ועמד למנין והשיב תשובות והשתא פריך התם שפיר ואימא עמד למנין והביא ראיה לדברי ת"ק מיהו שינויא דהתם דחיק מאי קא משני אמר קרא לטהרו או לטמאו היכי מוכח מהאי קרא שטיהר דילמא לעולם הביא ראיה לדברי ת"ק וכי היכי דדריש אינהו להאי קרא דריש ליה נמי איהו. הקשה ר"ת מאי טעמא דת"ק דמטמי מספקא נוקי גברא אחזקיה דאמרינן פ"ק דחולין דמוקמי' גברא אחזקתיה ועוד רבנן דפליגי עליה דר' יהושע מאן ניהו ר"ג ור' אליעזר דאשכחן דפליגי עליה לענין חזקות בפ"ק דכתובות גבי ראוה מעוברת וגבי משארסתני נאנסתי ואמרי' עלה בפ' המדיר לא תימא לא אזיל רבי יהושע בתר חזקה כלל אלא כי לא אזיל רבי יהושע בתר חזקה דגופא היכא דאיכא חזקה דממונא אבל ליכא חזקה דממונא אזיל בתר חזקה דגופא כדתנן אם בהרת קדמה וכו' והשתא י"ל התם דאיכא חזקה דממונא דמרעא לחזקה דגופא אזיל ר' אליעזר בתר חזקה דגופא הכא דליכא דמרע ליה לכ"ש ועוד ר' יהושע אמאי אצטריך קרא בשילהי נזיר לאשמועינן דטהור תיפוק לי בתר חזקה ואע"ג דאיכא ריעותא דהרי בהרת לפניך הך ריעותא לא חשבינן מדאורייתא אלא מדרבנן להחמיר בקדשים ולתלות במעת לעת. ואומר ר"ת דהכא מיירי בשנזקק לטומאה שמתחלה הוה מצורע מוחלט ונולד בו ספק זה ואח"כ נתרפא מן הראשון דרבנן לא דרשי לקרא ומטמאין מספק כיון דאיכא תרי חזקי דסתרי אהדדי העמד אדם בחזקת טומאה וטמא או העמידנו בחזקת שלא היה בו נגע זה וטהור אבל לר' יהושע דדריש ליה לקרא מטהר אפי' כשנזקק לטומאה. ותימה היכי דייק בפרק המדיר מהכא דר' יהושע אזיל בתר חזקה דגופא היכא דליכא חזקה דממונא שאני הכא דגלי קרא וי"ל דאת"ל דלא אזיל בעלמא בתר חזקה דגופא הוה מוקמינן בדדמי טפי בלא נזקק לטומאה אבל השתא דאזיל בתר חזקה דגופא תו לא צריך קרא אלא היכא דנזקק לטומאה. וקשה לפי' דלא מצינו חזקה כיוצא בזה לטמויי גברא ע"י נגע שנולד בו מספק משום דמוקמינן ליה בחזקת טומאה מן הנגע שנתרפא דאטו אם א)הטבילה נדה כל טמא בתוך מעת לעת וכי יעמידנו לטמאות חולין ולשרוף קדשים לא מיסתבר כלל למימר הכי כיון שנטהר בודאי מטומאה ראשונה. ועוד מוכיח בהדיא במס' נגעים דבלא נזקקה לטומאה פליגי דקתני גבי פלוגתא דר' יהושע ורבנן כל ספק נגעים טהור חוץ מזה ועוד אחר ואיזה זה מי שהיתה בו בהרת כגרים והסגירו ובסוף שבוע היה בו כסלע ספק שהיא היא ספק שהיא אחרת הבאה תחתיה טמא אלמא דבלא נזקק לטומאה איירי כיון דכיוצא בו טהור בעלמא ועוד דומיא דההיא דהיתה בו בהרת כגרים והסגירו דבשלא נזקק לטומאה איירי שהרי לא הוחלט מעולם הילכך נר' לפרש דבלא נזקק לטומאה איירי והא דמטמו רבנן מספק ולא מוקמי ליה בחזקת טהרה לפי שדרך השער להתלבן מחמת הנגעים כדמוכח בתוספתא פ' יש בשער לבן דקתני אף בשער שחור סוף שהבהרת הופכתו לפי שמחמת החולי ותשות הכח יבש המעיין ונהפך השער לדבר וסימן ללבן שער שיבה הלכך מוכח' מילתא שהבהרת קדמה והא דדייק בכתובות מהכא דר' יהושע אזיל בתר חזקת הגוף צריך לפרש אפי' היכא דאיכא ריעותא כי הכא: **מה** להלן פרח בכולו טהור. מדמדמי פריחת אדם לפריחת בגדים יש להוכיח דהא דכתיב וכסתה הצרעת את כל עור הנגע מראשו ועד רגליו אבל גופו של כל אדם קאי אע"פ שמשמע מראשו ורגליו אנגע קאי דמיירי לעיל מיניה בנגע שנטמא על ידי שהיה בו מחית בשר חי ומשמע דעליה קאי שאם הלכה לה המחיה וכסתה הצרעת את כל הנגע מראשו של נגע ועד סופו אבל אי אפשר לומר כן כדמוכח בשמעתין דבנגעי בגדים לא שייך מחייה: **אלא** הכא אי דם טהור ליכא במאי פליגי. הק' ה"ר יהודה והא משכחת לה דפליגי בדם לידה בפלוגתא דרב ולוי אם שני מעיינות הם או מעיין אחד ובדם זיבה בפלוגתא דר' אליעזר ור' יהושע בזב ובזבה שבדקו עצמן יום ראשון ויום שביעי וי"ל משום דמשמע ליה דקרא דבין דם לדם איירי בג' דמים שחלוקין בו זקן ממרא וחכמים וכן בין נגע לנגע וכן בין דין לדין כדאיתא בפרק הנחנקין דאי לא הוו רק ב' דמים בבין דם סגי ומדכתיב לדם משמע עוד שלישי ואי ליכא דם טהור לא משכחת פלוגתא בדם נדה: **אבע"א** לית להו. פי' לית להו ד' דמים דוקא אלא נפקי להו טפי מקראי דאי לית להו כלל דמיה א"כ תיקשי להו לימא אדום ותו לא:

א) הלשון משובש בכאן ונראה דצ"ל דאטו אם נדה וכל טמא שנפל ספק אם נגעו במת או לא ואח"כ טבלו מטומאה הראשונה הכי נעמידם בחזקת טומאה ודאית לטמאות כו'.

הירוק

---

[לקמן כח.]

עדיות פ"ה מ"ו סנהדרין פז:

שבת עז.

סנהדרין פז:

### הגהות מהר"ב רנשבורג

א] גמ' וכי תימא הכי נמי נגע טהור. נ"ב עי' שבת דף קלב ע"ב תוס' ד"ה [illegible]. ב] תוס' ד"ה מה להלן וכו' ואע"ג דפשטיה דקרא. נ"ב עי' ערכין יח [illegible] ודו"ק:

נגעים פ"ד מ"ג סנהדרין עח. פז: (ודף קיג)

סנהדרין פז: זבחים מט: [וכס איתא ר' נתן]

[שבת קח.]

[לקמן כ. חולין מז: סוכה לג:]

[תוספתא פ"ג]

---

וע"ש בתוס' דשם פירשו בענין אחר שיתיישב הך קושיא

נ"ל ורבינו חננאל כך כתבו תוס' ביבמות ובכתובות ובסנהדרין וכתבו בסנהדרין עוד דר"ח לא גריס אומר אלא ר' יהושע קיהה כלומר ר"י הקשה ודקדק בדבר כו' ע"ש

**פב** א ב מיי' פ"ה מהל' איסורי ביאה הל' ז סמג עשין קיא טוש"ע י"ד סימן קפח סעיף א ועי' בטור [וברב אלפס שבועות פ"ב דף רפח:]:

**פג** ג מיי' שם הל' ו ופ"א מהל' משכב ומושב הל' ח סמג שם טוש"ע שם:

**פד** ד מיי' פ"ה מהל' איסורי ביאה הל"ח:

**פה** ה ו מיי' שם הל' ט:

**פו** ז מיי' שם הל' ח:

**פז** ח מיי' שם הל' י:

**פח** ט מיי' פ"ב מהל' טומאת צרעת הל' ו:

**פט** י מיי' שם הל' ט:

**צ** כ מיי' פי"ד מהלכות טומאת צרעת הלכה ז:

**צא** ל מיי' שם פי"ב הלכה ח' סמ"ג עשין רל"ד:

נגעים פ"ד מי"א כתובות עה: ב"מ פו. סנהדרין פז: נזיר סה: ע"ש

[שייך למשנה לעיל]
צב א מיי' פ"ח מהל' מטמאי משכב ומושב הלכה ח:
צג ב מיי' פ"ט מהל' איסורי ביאה הל' כג סמג לאוין קיא טוש"ע י"ד סי' קפח סעיף ז וסעיף כו:
צד ג מיי' שם הל' כד טוש"ע שם סעי' יט:
צה ד מיי' שם פ"ה הלכה ח:

לְתִלוֹת.§ הַיָּרוֹק עֲקַבְיָא בֶּן מַהֲלַלְאֵל מְטַמֵּא.§ וְלֵית לֵיהּ לַעֲקַבְיָא "דָּמֶיהָ" "דָּמֶיהָ" הֲרֵי כָּאן אַרְבָּעָה? אב"א: לֵית לֵיהּ, וְאב"א: אִית לֵיהּ, מִי לָא א"ר חֲנִינָא שָׁחוֹר — אָדוֹם הוּא אֶלָּא שֶׁלָּקָה, הָכָא נַמִי — מִלְקָא הוּא דְּלָקֵי.§ "וַחֲכָמִים מְטַהֲרִין".§ הַיְינוּ ת"ק! אִיכָּא בֵּינַיְיהוּ לְתִלוֹת.§ א"ר מֵאִיר: אִם אֵינוֹ מְטַמֵּא מִשּׁוּם כֶּתֶם" כו'.§ א"ר יוֹחָנָן: יָרַד ר"מ לְשִׁיטַת עֲקַבְיָא בֶּן מַהֲלַלְאֵל, וְטִימֵּא. וְה"ק לְהוּ לְרַבָּנַן: נְהִי דְּהֵיכָא דְּקָא מַשְׁכַּחַת כֶּתֶם יָרוֹק אַמָּנָא לָא מְטַמְּאִיתוּ, הֵיכָא דְּקָחָזְיָא דָּם יָרוֹק מִגּוּפָהּ — תְּטַמֵּא. אִי הָכִי, "אִם אֵינוֹ מְטַמֵּא מִשּׁוּם כֶּתֶם, מְטַמֵּא מִשּׁוּם מַשְׁקֶה", "מִשּׁוּם רוֹאָה" מִבָּעֲיָא לֵיהּ! אֶלָּא ה"ק לְהוּ: נְהִי הֵיכָא דְּקָא חַזְיָא דָּם יָרוֹק מֵעִיקָּרָא לָא מְטַמְּאִיתוּ, הֵיכָא דְּחַזְיָא דָּם אָדוֹם וַהֲדַר חַזְיָא דָּם יָרוֹק — תְּטַמֵּא, מִידֵּי דַּהֲוָה אַמַּשְׁקֵה זָב וְזָבָה. וְרַבָּנַן — *[א]דּוּמְיָא דְּרוֹק, מָה רוֹק שֶׁמִּתְעַגֵּל וְיוֹצֵא, אַף כֹּל שֶׁמִּתְעַגֵּל וְיוֹצֵא, לְאַפּוּקֵי הַאי — דְּאֵין מִתְעַגֵּל וְיוֹצֵא. אִי הָכִי — שַׁפִּיר קָאָמְרִי לֵיהּ רַבָּנַן לר' מֵאִיר! אֶלָּא ה"ק לְהוּ: לֶהֱוֵי כְּמַשְׁקֶה לְהַכְשִׁיר אֶת הַזְּרָעִים. וְרַבָּנַן — בָּעֵי °"דַּם חֲלָלִים" וְלֵיכָּא. אִי הָכִי, שַׁפִּיר קָאָמְרִי לֵיהּ רַבָּנַן לר' מֵאִיר! אֶלָּא הָכִי קָאָמַר לְהוּ — *אַלְפוּהָ בְּג"ש, כְּתִיב הָכָא: °"שְׁלָחַיִךְ פַּרְדֵּס רִמּוֹנִים" וּכְתִיב הָתָם: °"וְשֹׁלֵחַ מַיִם עַל פְּנֵי חוּצוֹת". וְרַבָּנַן — אָדָם דָּן ק"ו מֵעַצְמוֹ, *וְאֵין אָדָם דָּן ג"ש מֵעַצְמוֹ.§ "רַבִּי יוֹסֵי אוֹמֵר לֹא כָּךְ" וכו'.§ הַיְינוּ ת"ק! *הָא קמ"ל: מַאן ת"ק — רַבִּי יוֹסֵי, וְכָל הָאוֹמֵר דָּבָר בְּשֵׁם אוֹמְרוֹ *מֵבִיא גְּאוּלָּה לָעוֹלָם.§ "אֵיזֶהוּ אָדוֹם כְּדַם הַמַּכָּה".§ מַאי "כְּדַם הַמַּכָּה"? אָמַר רַב יְהוּדָה, אָמַר שְׁמוּאֵל: כְּדַם שׁוֹר שָׁחוּט. וְלֵימָא: כְּדַם שְׁחִיטָה! אִי אָמַר כְּדַם שְׁחִיטָה — הֲוָה אָמִינָא כְּכוּלָּהּ שְׁחִיטָה, קמ"ל כְּדַם הַמַּכָּה — כִּתְחִילַּת הַכָּאָה שֶׁל סַכִּין. עוּלָּא אָמַר: כְּדַם צִפּוֹר חַיָּה. אִיבַּעְיָא לְהוּ: חַיָּה — לְאַפּוּקֵי שָׁחוּט, אוֹ דִּלְמָא לְאַפּוּקֵי כָּחוּשׁ? תֵּיקוּ. זְעִירִי, אָמַר רַבִּי חֲנִינָא: כְּדַם מַאֲכוֹלֶת שֶׁל רֹאשׁ. מֵיתִיבֵי: *[ב]הָרְגָה מַאֲכוֹלֶת — הֲרֵי זֶה תּוֹלָה בָּהּ, מַאי לָאו — דְּכוּלֵּיהּ גּוּפָהּ! לָא, דְּרֹאשָׁהּ. אַמֵּי וַרְדִּינָאָה, א"ר אַבָּהוּ: כְּדַם אֶצְבַּע קְטַנָּה שֶׁל יָד, שֶׁנִּגְפָּה וְחָיְיתָה וְחָזְרָה וְנִגְפָּה, וְלֹא שֶׁל כָּל אָדָם אֶלָּא שֶׁל בָּחוּר שֶׁלֹּא נָשָׂא אִשָּׁה. וְעַד כַּמָּה? — עַד בֶּן עֶשְׂרִים. מֵיתִיבֵי: *[ג]תּוֹלָה בִּבְנָהּ וּבְבַעְלָהּ, בִּשְׁלָמָא בִּבְנָהּ — מַשְׁכַּחַת לָהּ, אֶלָּא בַּעְלָהּ — הֵיכִי מַשְׁכַּחַת לָהּ? אָמַר ר"נ בַּר יִצְחָק: כְּגוֹן שֶׁנִּכְנְסָה לַחוּפָּה וְלֹא נִבְעֲלָה. ר"נ אָמַר: [ד]כְּדַם הַקָּזָה. מֵיתִיבֵי: *מַעֲשֶׂה וְתָלָה ר"מ בְּקִילוֹר

(במדבר כג; שיר ד; איוב ה)

**רש"י**

לְתִלוֹת. ת"ק סָבַר: ה' דָּמִים – טְמֵאִין וַדַּאי, וְאִידָךְ – סְפֵיקָא, וּלְב"ה – טְהוֹרִין מַמָּשׁ. הַיְינוּ ת"ק. דְּקָאמַר: ה' דָּמִים, וְתוּ לָא. יָרַד ר' מֵאִיר כו'. וּמְטַמֵּא דַּם יָרוֹק מִשּׁוּם נִדָּה. אַמָּנָא. עַל בִּגְדָהּ. לָא מְטַמְּאִיתוּ. דְּכֵיוָן דְּיָרוֹק הוּא, מִסְתַּמָּא לָאו מִגּוּפָהּ אָתָא, דְּלָא שְׁכִיחַ, וְלָא תָּלֵינַן בָּהּ אֶלָּא הֵיכָא דְּחַזְיָא מִגּוּפָהּ דָּם הוּא. נְהִי דְּהֵיכָא. דַּחֲזִיתֵיהּ דָּם יָרוֹק מֵעִיקָּרָא לָא מְטַמְּאִיתוּ מִשּׁוּם רוֹאָה, דְּלָאו דָּם הוּא, וְהַיְינוּ "מִשּׁוּם כֶּתֶם", כְּלוֹמַר, כִּשְׁאָר דָּם שֶׁכִּתְמוֹ טָמֵא. תְּטַמֵּא מִשּׁוּם מַשְׁקֶה. כְּרוּקָהּ וּכְמֵי רַגְלֶיהָ, אִם נוֹגְעִין בּוֹ אָדָם וְכֵלִים וְטָהֳרוֹת בְּאוֹתוֹ דַּם יָרוֹק שֶׁרָאֲתָה בִּימֵי נִדּוּתָהּ שֶׁהָיְתָה נִדָּה מִדַּם אָדוֹם, וְאַמַּאי מְטַהֲרִיתוּ לְגַמְרֵי. שֶׁמִּתְעַגֵּל וְיוֹצֵא. שֶׁמִּתְחַסֵּף תְּחִלָּה וְאַחַ"כ יוֹצֵא, לְאַפּוּקֵי דָּם, בֵּין טָמֵא בֵּין טָהוֹר, כְּשֶׁהוּא בָּא – נוֹטֵף וְיוֹצֵא רִאשׁוֹן רִאשׁוֹן. לֶהֱוֵי כְּמַשְׁקֶה. לְהַכְשִׁיר זְרָעִים, שֶׁאִם יִגַּע שֶׁרֶץ בָּהֶן – יִטְמָא, וְאַמַּאי מְטַהֲרִיתוּ לְגַמְרֵי? דַּם חֲלָלִים יִשְׁתֶּה. דָּם שֶׁהַנֶּפֶשׁ יוֹצְאָה בּוֹ קָרוּי "מַשְׁקֶה". וּלְעִנְיַן הֶכְשֵׁר בָּעֵינַן מַשְׁקֶה, כִּדִכְתִיב (ויקרא יא): "וַאֲשֶׁר יָבֹא עָלָיו מַיִם יִטְמָא וְכָל מַשְׁקֶה אֲשֶׁר יִשָּׁתֶה", כְּלוֹמַר: אוֹכֶל וּמַשְׁקֶה אֲשֶׁר יִשָּׁתֶה יָבֹא עַל הָאוֹכֶל, וְהָכִי מוֹקְמִינַן לָהּ בִּפְסָחִים (דף טז.). אַלְפוּהָ בְּג"ש. לְהַכְשִׁיר אֶת הַזְּרָעִים. שְׁלָחַיִךְ. דַּם נִדּוּת הַשָּׁלוּחַ מִן הָאִשָּׁה. פַּרְדֵּס רִמּוֹנִים. כְּפַרְדֵּס זֶה שֶׁהוּא נָעוּל לְהִשְׁתַּמֵּר, כָּךְ בְּנוֹת יִשְׂרָאֵל נוֹעֲלוֹת פִּתְחֵיהֶן בִּימֵי נִדּוּתָן מֵהִיזָּקֵק לְבַעֲלֵיהֶן. "עִם פְּרִי מְגָדִים" – הַיְינוּ בָּנִים. וּכְתִיב "שִׁילּוּחַ" בְּמַיִם, מַה מַּיִם – מַכְשִׁירִין, אַף דַּם נִדּוּת – מַכְשִׁיר. אֵין אָדָם דָּן ג"ש מֵעַצְמוֹ. אֶלָּא אִם כֵּן קִבְּלָהּ מֵרַבּוֹ הֲלָ"מ. דִּדְלָמָא קְרָא לְמִילְּתָא אַחֲרִיתֵי אִיצְטְרִיךְ. שׁוֹר. דָּמוֹ אָדוֹם, כִּדְאָמַר בְּסֵדֶר יוֹמָא (דף נו.) הַאי חִיוָּר, וְהַאי סוּמָק. דַּם שְׁחִיטָה. מִשְׁתַּנֶּה וְהוֹלֵךְ. צִפּוֹר חַיָּה. דָּם הַיּוֹצֵא מִצִּפּוֹר חַי ע"י מַכָּה. אוֹ דִלְמָא לְאַפּוּקֵי כָּחוּשׁ. וְהַאי "חַיָּה" – לְשׁוֹן בְּרִיאָה הוּא. הָרְגָה מַאֲכוֹלֶת. אִשָּׁה הָרוֹאָה כֶּתֶם בְּבִגְדָהּ, אִם הָרְגָה מַאֲכוֹלֶת – תּוֹלָה בָּהּ. וְאִי קַשְׁיָא: הָא שִׁיעוּר כֶּתֶם – כִּגְרִיס וְעוֹד, וּמַאֲכוֹלֶת כּוּלֵּי הַאי לָא הָוֵי, כִּדְאָמַר בְּפִירְקִין: *בָּעֵינַן כִּגְרִיס וְעוֹד, לְאַפּוּקֵי מִדַּם מַאֲכוֹלֶת! לָא קַשְׁיָא, הַהִיא לְר' חֲנִינָא בֶּן אַנְטִיגְנוֹס, הָא – לְרַבָּנַן בְּפֶרֶק "הָרוֹאָה כֶּתֶם" (לקמן דף נח.) דְּלָא בָּעֵי הַאי שִׁיעוּר. מַאי לָאו מַאֲכוֹלֶת דְּכוּלָּהּ גּוּפָהּ. אַלְמָא, כָּל מַאֲכוֹלֶת דּוֹמָה לְדַם נִדּוּת, וְאַתְּ אָמַרְתְּ: דַּם מַאֲכוֹלֶת שֶׁל רֹאשׁ הוּא דְּדָמֵי לְדַם נִדּוּת, אֲבָל דִּשְׁאָר הַגּוּף – לָא. אַמֵּי וַרְדִּינָאָה. נָאֶה כְּוֶרֶד, וּבְגִיטִּין (דף מח.) קָרֵי לֵיהּ "אַמֵּי שַׁפִּיר נָאֶה". ל"א: "וַרְדִּינָאָה" – מָקוֹם הוּא שֶׁשְּׁמוֹ וַרְדִּינָא, בְּעֵירוּבִין (דף מט.). תּוֹלָה. כִּתְמָהּ. בִּבְנָהּ וּבְבַעְלָהּ. אִם יֵשׁ בָּהֶן מַכָּה, שֶׁמָּא נָטַף עָלֶיהָ כְּשֶׁשּׁוֹכְבִין יַחַד. אַלְמָא דַּם בְּנָהּ וּבַעְלָהּ דּוֹמֶה לְדַם נִדּוּת. בִּשְׁלָמָא בְּנָהּ מַשְׁכַּחַת לָהּ. שֶׁלֹּא נָשָׂא. אֶלָּא בַּעְלָהּ. הָא נָשׂוּי הוּא. רַב נַחְמָן. אַמַּתְנִי' קָאֵי. וְתָלָה רַבִּי מֵאִיר. כֶּתֶם. בְּקִילוֹר.

**תוספות**

*הירוק עקביא בן מהללאל מטמא. האי "ירוק" היינו כאתרוג, ולא ירוק ככרתי, דאין זה נוטה לאדמומית. וסתם "ירוק" כן הוא, כדאמר ב"לולב הגזול" (סוכה דף לד: ושם) ירוק – ככרתי, מכלל דסתם "ירוק" – לאו הכי הוא. א] לית ליה. פירוש: לית ליה ד' דווקא, אלא נפקא ליה החמישי מקרא אחרינא. ירד רבי מאיר לשיטת עקביא בן מהללאל וטימא. – תימה: והא לקמן בפ' "בנות כותים" (לג.) גבי "כותי מטמא משכב התחתון כעליון" מפרש ר' מאיר: לפי שמשלימות דם אדום לדם ירוק, אלמא אית ליה דטהור! ונראה, דהכא איירי מדרבנן. וכן מוכח מדקאמר: נהי דכי משכחת כתם אמנא – לא מטמא, היכי דחזיא ירוק מגופה – תטמא. ויש לדחות: דלעולם כי חזיא מגופה – מטמא מדאורייתא, ומ"מ כי משכחת אמנא – לא מטמא, דאין רגילות לצאת דם ירוק מגופה, ויש לתלות דמעלמא אתא. או שמא דם ירוק לאו דווקא נקט, אלא כלומר: דם שהוא טהור, לכ"ע משלימות לדם אדום. אי נמי: עיקר טעמא דר"מ כטעמא אחרינא דקאמר: יום שפוסקת בו – סופרת למנין שבעה, וטעמא קמא נקט לרבנן.

כתיב הכא "שלחיך פרדס" וא"ת: ה"מ דם שהאשה טמאה בו, כדמשמע קרא כפרדס שהוא נעול – כך בנות ישראל נועלות פתחיהן מליזקק לבעליהן בימי נדותן,ב] אבל דם ירוק שהוא טהור – לא! ותו: דמשמע דלא פליגי אלא בדם ירוק,ג] אבל בדם נדה מודו כ"ע דמכשיר, וכיון דרבנן לית להו ג"ש דם נדה מנא להו? וי"ל: דדם נדה נפקא להו בתוספתא דשבת פ' *("הזורק") דקתני: מנין *לדם שהוא משקה? נאמר כאן: "וטהרה ממקור דמיה", ונאמר להלן: "ביום ההוא יהיה מקור נפתח לבית דוד וליושבי ירושלם לחטאת ולנדה". ויש לתמוה: דהכא משמע דלכ"ע דם הנדה לא הוה בכלל "דם חללים", ובשבת פרק "חבית" (דף קמג:) משמע דחלב האשה טמא משום דם מגפתה. דקתני: לא אם אמרת בחלב האשה שמכשיר שלא לרצון, שכן דם מגפתה מכשיר. ומפרש רש"י: דחלב היה דם תחלה, כדאמרינן (לעיל דף ט.) דם נעכר ונעשה חלב. והכא אמרינן דאפי' דם נדה לא הוי בכלל "דם חללים" כ"ש חלב! ודוחק לומר: דחלב בא מעיקר דם שבגוף כמו דם מגפתה, אבל דם נדה – לא. ומיהו בלאו הכי קשה התם: דמאי קמהדר להו רבי עקיבא לרבנן: מחמיר אני בחלב מבדם, שהחולב לרפואה – טמא, ומקיז לרפואה – טהור? ועוד: למה לי קרא בפ' "דם הנדה" (לקמן נה:) דחלב האשה חשיב משקה, מדכתיב: "ותפתח את נאד החלב ותשקהו", תיפוק ליה מטעמא דדם נעכר ונעשה חלב! ומיהו סוגיא דלקמן איכא למימר דלא סבר לה (א) כרבי מאיר דדם נעכר כו'. לכך נראה דה"פ התם: לא אם אמרת בחלב האשה שמכשיר כו'. כלומר: כיוןד] דאיכא קרא לקמן בחלב שמכשיר לכל הפחות לרצון, דין הוא שיכשיר גם שלא לרצון, כיון דחזינן גבי אשה בשום מקום דמכשיר שלא לרצון, כמו דם מגפתה. אבל בהמה, אע"ג דחלבה מכשיר לרצון מ"ותפתח את נאד החלב", בשביל כך לא תכשיר שלא לרצון, כיון דלא אשכחן בבהמה מידי דמכשיר שלא לרצון, שדם מגפתה טהור. אמר להם: מחמיר אני בחלב יותר מבדם, שהחולב לרפואה כו'. כלומר, חלב דמכשיר לאו בחומרא דדם מגפתה תליא מילתא, שהרי מקיז לרפואה טהור, דהיינו לרצון. ולא אמרינן: כשם שחלבה לרצון טמא, כך דמה לרפואה טמא. אלא ודאי חלב האשה דמטמא משום דמשקה גמור הוא, וכ"ש חלב בהמה דליהוי טפי משקה, דמיוחד לקטנים ולגדולים. אמרו לו: סלי זיתים וענבים יוכיחו, דמיוחדים לקטנים ולגדולים, ושלא לרצון – טהור. והשתא לא קשה מדם הנדה, דפשיטא דלא הוי בכלל "דם חללים". ולקמן בעז"ה נפרש דקראי דפרק "דם הנדה" אסמכתא בעלמא נינהו.

[נ"ל הגוזז פ"ט] [נ"ל לדם נדה] [חולין קד: מגילה טו. אבות פ"ו מ"ו]

**תוספי הרא"ש**

הירוק עקביא בן מהללאל מטמא. מכאן משמע דסתם ירוק הוא צבע הדומה לחלמון של ביצה או לזהב שנוטה לאדמומית. וכן משמע באלו טרפות גבי מראות הריאה דקאמר כבשותא וכמוריקא וכביצה טריפה אלא ירוקה דכשרה היכי דמי ככרתי ובפ' לולב נמי אמרינן ירוק ככרתי מכלל דסתם ירוק לא הוי ככרתי ואמרי' בב"ר גבי וירק את חניכיו שהוריקן בזהב. וכה"א ואברותיה בירקרק חרוץ אלמא סתם ירוק הוא צבע הנוטה לאדמימות כזהב: ירד ר"מ לשיטתו של עקביא בן מהללאל וטימא. ותימה והא אמרינן לקמן בפ' בנות כותים גבי כותים מטמאין משכב תחתון כעליון ומפ' ר' מאיר טעמא משום שרואות דם אדום ומשלימות לדם ירוק אלמא קסבר דדם ירוק טהור הוא. וי"ל דמדרבנן איירי הכא:

כתיב הכא שלחיך פרדס רמונים. פרש"י שלחיך דם נדות שהאשה שולחת מגופה פרדס רמונים כפרדס הזה שהוא נעול מליכנס בו כך הן נועלות פתחיהן בימי נדותן מליזקק לבעליהן וקשה דא"כ היכי יליף מהכא דם ירוק שהוא מכשיר כיון דקראי איירי בדם נדות שהאשה טמאה בו. וע"ק דמשמע דלא פליגי אלא בדם ירוק אבל דם נדה מודו כ"ע דמכשר וכיון דרבנן לית להו ג"ש דם נדה מנא להו. וי"ל דדם נדות נפקא בתוספתא דשבת מג"ש דמקור מקור דתניא התם בפ' הבונה מנין לדם נדה שהוא משקה שנאמר וטהרה ממקור דמיה ואומר ביום ההוא יהיה מקור נפתח לבית דוד וליושבי ירושלם לחטאת ולנדה וסבירא ליה לר' מאיר דהאי שלחיך אם אינו ענין לדם נדות דנפקא ממקור מקור תנהו ענין לדם ירוק: מאי לאו דכולי גופא. יש שרוצין לדקדק דבזמן הזה דאין אנו בקיאין במראה דמים אין לנו לתלות אפי' עברה בשוק של טבחים ולא בשום דבר שיכולה לתלות בו כיון דאם היינו בקיאין הוו מכירין שאינו דומה לו כדמשמע הכא שאינה תולה בדם מאכולת דכולי גופא משום דלא דמי. וליתא דהא אמרינן לקמן עברה בשוק של טבחים הרי זו תולה ולא קאמר תראה לחכם אלא היא עצמה תולה וסתם אשה אינה בקיאה בדמים והכא מיירי בחכם הבקי במראה דמים אבל בזמן הזה שאין אנו בקיאין תולה בכל מה שיכולה לתלות וכן עמא דבר:

**הגהות הב"ח**

(א) תוס' ד"ה כתיב וכו' דלא סבר לה כר"מ. נ"ב לעיל דף יט ע"א:

**הגהות מהר"ב רנשבורג**

א] תוס' ד"ה לית ליה. נ"ב עי' רש"י לעיל... ב] ד"ה כתיב הכא וכו' אבל דם ירוק שהוא טהור. נ"ב עי' חידושי רמב"ן ורשב"א ור"ן... ג] בא"ד אבל בדם נדה מודו. נ"ב עי' הרמב"ם פ"י מהל' טומאת אוכלין... ד] בא"ד דאיכא קרא לקמן בחלב שמכשיר. נ"ב עיין פי' הר"ש במכשירין פ"ו משנה ח:

[לקמן נו.] [עי' רשב"א ור"ן] [פסחים טז.] [חולין קד: ע"ש פירש"י ודוגמתו בשבת קנ. ר' יוסי ובחולין לז. ע"ש כריתות כג. ע"ש] [בדף יז:] [לקמן נח.] [שם] [שם]

פלי

בְּקִילוֹר וְרַבִּי תָּלָה בִּשְׂרַף שִׁקְמָה. מַאי לָאו — אַאָדוֹם? לָא, אַשְּׁאָר דָּמִים. אַמֵּימָר וּמָר זוּטְרָא וְרַב אַשִׁי הֲווּ יָתְבִי קַמֵּיהּ אוּמָּנָא, אשָׁקְלֵי לֵיהּ קַרְנָא קַמַּיְיתָא לְאַמֵּימָר, חַזְיֵיהּ, אֲמַר לְהוּ: אָדוֹם דִּתְנַן — כִּי הַאי. שָׁקְלֵי לֵיהּ אַחֲרִיתִי, אֲמַר לְהוּ: אִשְׁתַּנִּי. אָמַר רַב אַשִׁי: כְּגוֹן אֲנָא, דְּלָא יָדַעְנָא בֵּין הַאי לְהַאי — לָא מִבָּעֵי לִי לְמֶחֱזֵי דָּמָא. § "שָׁחוֹר כְּחֶרֶת". אָמַר רַבָּה בַּר רַב הוּנָא: בחֶרֶת שֶׁאָמְרוּ — דְּיוֹ. תַּנְיָא נַמִי הָכִי: שָׁחוֹר — כְּחֶרֶת, וְשָׁחוֹר שֶׁאָמְרוּ — דְּיוֹ. וְלֵימָא דְּיוֹ! אִי אָמַר דְּיוֹ — הֲוָה אָמִינָא: כִּי פַּכְחוּתָא דִּדְיוֹתָא, קמ"ל — כִּי חָרוּתָא דִּדְיוֹתָא. אִיבַּעְיָא לְהוּ: בְּלַחָה אוֹ בִּיבֵשְׁתָּא? גתָּא שְׁמַע: דְּרַבִּי אַמִּי פָּלֵי קוֹרְטָא דִּדְיוֹתָא וּבָדֵיק בָּהּ. אָמַר רַב יְהוּדָה, אָמַר שְׁמוּאֵל: דכְּקִיר, כִּדְיוֹ, וּכְעֵנָב — טְמֵאָה, וְזוֹהִי שֶׁשָּׁנִינוּ "עָמוֹק מִכֵּן — טְמֵאָה". אָמַר רַבִּי אֶלְעָזָר: הכְּזַיִת, כְּזֶפֶת, וּכְעוֹרֵב — טָהוֹר, וְזוֹהִי שֶׁשָּׁנִינוּ "דֵּיהֶה מִכֵּן — טָהוֹר". עוּלָּא אָמַר: כִּלְבוּשָׁא סִיוָאָה. עוּלָּא אִקְלַע לְפוּמְבְּדִיתָא, חַזְיֵיהּ לְהַהוּא טַיָּיעָא דִּלְבוּשׁ לְבוּשָׁא אוּכָּמָא. אֲמַר לְהוּ: "שָׁחוֹר" דִּתְנַן — כִּי הַאי. מָרְטוּ מִינֵּיהּ פּוּרְתָּא פּוּרְתָּא, יָהֲבוּ בֵּיהּ אַרְבַּע מְאָה זוּזֵי. רַבִּי יוֹחָנָן אָמַר: *אֵלּוּ כֵּלִים הָאוֹלְיָירִין הַבָּאִים מִמְּדִינַת הַיָּם. לְמֵימְרָא דְּאוּכָּמֵי נִינְהוּ? *וְהָאָמַר לְהוּ רַבִּי יַנַּאי לְבָנָיו: בָּנַי, אַל תִּקְבְּרוּנִי לֹא בְּכֵלִים שְׁחוֹרִים וְלֹא בְּכֵלִים לְבָנִים. שְׁחוֹרִים — שֶׁמָּא אֶזְכֶּה, וְאֶהְיֶה כְּאָבֵל בֵּין הַחֲתָנִים, לְבָנִים — שֶׁמָּא לֹא אֶזְכֶּה, וְאֶהְיֶה כְּחָתָן בֵּין הָאֲבֵלִים, אֶלָּא בְּכֵלִים הָאוֹלְיָירִין הַבָּאִים מִמְּדִינַת הַיָּם. אַלְמָא — לָאו אוּכָּמֵי נִינְהוּ! לָא קַשְׁיָא, הָא — בִּגְלִימָא, הָא — בִּפְתוֹרָא. אָמַר רַב יְהוּדָה, אָמַר שְׁמוּאֵל: ווְכוּלָּם אֵין בּוֹדְקִין אֶלָּא עַל גַּבֵּי מַטְלִית לְבָנָה. אָמַר רַב יִצְחָק בַּר אֲבוּדִימִי: וְשָׁחוֹר — עַל גַּבֵּי אָדוֹם. אָמַר רַב יִרְמְיָה מִדִּפְתִּי: וְלָא פְּלִיגִי, הָא — בְּשָׁחוֹר, הָא — בִּשְׁאָר דָּמִים. מַתְקִיף לָהּ רַב אַשִׁי: אִי הָכִי, לֵימָא שְׁמוּאֵל "חוּץ מִשָּׁחוֹר"! אֶלָּא אָמַר רַב אַשִׁי: בְּשָׁחוֹר גּוּפֵיהּ קָמִיפַּלְגִי. אָמַר עוּלָּא: כּוּלָּן — עָמוֹק מִכֵּן — טָמֵא, דֵּיהֶה מִכֵּן — טָהוֹר, כְּשָׁחוֹר. וְאֶלָּא מַאי שְׁנָא שָׁחוֹר דְּנָקַט? סד"א: הוֹאִיל *וְאָמַר רַבִּי חֲנִינָא שָׁחוֹר — אָדוֹם הוּא, אֶלָּא שֶׁלָּקָה, הִילְכָּךְ — אֲפִילּוּ דֵּיהֶה מִכֵּן נַמִי לִיטַמֵּא, קָמַשְׁמַע לָן. רַבִּי אַמִּי בַּר אַבָּא אָמַר: וְכוּלָּן, עָמוֹק מִכֵּן — טָמֵא, דֵּיהֶה מִכֵּן — נַמִי טָמֵא, חוּץ מִשָּׁחוֹר. אֶלָּא מַאי אַהֲנֵי שִׁיעוּרֵיהּ דְּרַבָּנַן? לְאַפּוֹקֵי דֵּיהֶה דְּדֵיהֶה. וְאִיכָּא דְּאָמְרִי, רָמִי בַּר אַבָּא אָמַר: וְכוּלָּן עָמוֹק מִכֵּן — טָהוֹר, דֵּיהֶה מִכֵּן — טָהוֹר, חוּץ מִשָּׁחוֹר. וּלְהָכִי מְהַנֵּי שִׁיעוּרֵיהּ דְּרַבָּנַן. בַּר קַפָּרָא אָמַר: זוְכוּלָּן, עָמוֹק מִכֵּן — טָמֵא, דֵּיהֶה מִכֵּן — טָהוֹר. חחוּץ מִמֶּזֶג, שֶׁעָמוֹק מִכֵּן — טָהוֹר, דֵּיהֶה מִכֵּן — טָהוֹר. בַּר קַפָּרָא אֲדִיהוּ לֵיהּ — וְדַכֵּי, אַעֲמִיקוּ לֵיהּ — וְדַכֵּי. אָמַר רַבִּי חֲנִינָא: כַּמָּה נָפִישׁ גַּבְרָא *דִּלְבֵּיהּ כְּמִשְׁמַעְתֵּיהּ! § "וּכְקֶרֶן כַּרְכּוֹם". תָּנָא: *לַח וְלֹא יָבֵשׁ. תָּנֵי חֲדָא: כַּתַּחְתּוֹן וְלֹא כָּעֶלְיוֹן, וְתַנְיָא אִידָךְ: *כָּעֶלְיוֹן וְלֹא כַּתַּחְתּוֹן, וְתַנְיָא אִידָךְ: כָּעֶלְיוֹן, וְכָל שֶׁכֵּן כַּתַּחְתּוֹן, וְתַנְיָא אִידָךְ: כַּתַּחְתּוֹן, וְכָל שֶׁכֵּן כָּעֶלְיוֹן. אָמַר אַבַּיֵי: טתְּלָתָא דָּרֵי וּתְלָתָא טַרְפָּן הָוְיָין, נְקוֹט דָּרָא מְצִיעָאָה וְטַרְפָּא מְצִיעֲתָא בִּידָךְ. כִּי אָתוּ לְקַמֵּיהּ דְּרַבִּי אַבָּהוּ, אֲמַר לְהוּ: יבְּגוּשַׁיְיהוּ שָׁנִינוּ. § "וּכְמֵימֵי אֲדָמָה". תָּנוּ רַבָּנַן: *כְּמֵימֵי אֲדָמָה — מֵבִיא אֲדָמָה שְׁמֵנָה מִבִּקְעַת בֵּית כֶּרֶם, וּמֵצִיף עָלֶיהָ מַיִם, דִּבְרֵי רַבִּי מֵאִיר. [א] רַבִּי עֲקִיבָא אוֹמֵר: מִבִּקְעַת יוֹדְפַת. רַבִּי יוֹסֵי אוֹמֵר: כמִבִּקְעַת סִכְנִי. רַבִּי שִׁמְעוֹן אוֹמֵר: אַף מִבִּקְעַת גִּנּוֹסַר וְכַיּוֹצֵא בָּהֶן. תַּנְיָא אִידָךְ: וּכְמֵימֵי אֲדָמָה — מֵבִיא אֲדָמָה שְׁמֵנָה מִבִּקְעַת בֵּית כֶּרֶם, לוּמֵצִיף עָלֶיהָ מַיִם כִּקְלִיפַּת הַשּׁוּם, וְאֵין שִׁיעוּר לַמַּיִם — מִשּׁוּם דְּאֵין שִׁיעוּר לֶעָפָר. וְאֵין בּוֹדְקִין אוֹתָן צְלוּלִין אֶלָּא עֲכוּרִין. צָלְלוּ — חוֹזֵר וְעוֹכְרָן. וּכְשֶׁהוּא עוֹכְרָן — אֵין עוֹכְרָן בַּיָּד מאֶלָּא בִּכְלִי. אִיבַּעְיָא לְהוּ: אֵין עוֹכְרִין אוֹתָן בַּיָּד אֶלָּא בִּכְלִי — דְּלָא לִרְמְיֵיהּ בִּידֵיהּ וְלַעֲכְרִינְהוּ, אֲבָל בְּמָנָא, כִּי עָכַר לֵיהּ בִּידֵיהּ — שַׁפִּיר דָּמֵי, אוֹ דִּלְמָא: דְּלָא לְעַכְרִינְהוּ בִּידֵיהּ, אֶלָּא בְּמָנָא? ת"ש: כְּשֶׁהוּא בּוֹדְקָן — אֵין בּוֹדְקָן אֶלָּא בַּכּוֹס. וַעֲדַיִין תִּבְּעֵי לָךְ: בְּדִיקָה — בַּכּוֹס, עֲכִירָה בְּמַאי? תֵּיקוּ. כִּי אָתוּ לְקַמֵּיהּ דְּרַבָּה בַּר אֲבוּהּ, אֲמַר לְהוּ: נבִּמְקוֹמָהּ שָׁנִינוּ. רַבִּי חֲנִינָא פָּלֵי קוֹרְטָא דְּגַרְגִּשְׁתָּא וּבָדֵיק בֵּיהּ, *לֵיִיט עֲלֵיהּ רַבִּי יִשְׁמָעֵאל בְּרַבִּי יוֹסֵי בְּאַסְכָּרָה. רַבִּי

בְּקִילוֹר. אִנְפְּלַסְטְ"ר, וְאָדוֹם הוּא, וְנִתְעַסְּקָה בּוֹ. אַלְמָא קִילוֹר דּוֹמֶה לְדַם נִדּוּת, וְאַע"ג דְּלָא הָוֵי סוּמָּק כּוּלֵּי הַאי, וְקַשְׁיָא לְכוּלְּהוּ דְּדָיְיקֵי בֵּין דַּם בָּחוּר לְדַם נָשׂוּי מִשּׁוּם דְּסוּמָּק טְפֵי, וּבֵין דַּם מַאֲכוֹלֶת שֶׁל רֹאשׁ לִשְׁאָר דַּם מַאֲכוֹלֶת. אוּמָּנָא. מַקִּיז דָּם בְּקֶרֶן. בֵּין הַאי לְהַאי. בֵּין קַמָּא לְבַתְרָא. חֶרֶת שֶׁאָמְרוּ דְּיוֹ. כְּלוֹמַר: לֹא כְּשַׁחְרוּרִית חֶרֶת הַנִּיתָּךְ בַּמַּיִם, אֶלָּא שַׁחְרוּרִית חֶרֶת הַנִּיתָּךְ בִּדְיוֹ. כִּי פַּכְחוּתָא דִּדְיוֹתָא. קְלִישׁוּת הַדְּיוֹ. כְּשֶׁהַכְּלִי מָלֵא, יוֹרֵד שַׁחְרוּרִית הַחֶרֶת לְמַטָּה, וּמִלְמַעְלָה הוּא בָּרוּר וְאֵינוֹ שָׁחוֹר כׇּל כָּךְ. בְּלַחָה. כִּדְיוֹ לַחָה, כִּדְמְפָרֵשׁ. אוֹ בִּיבֵשְׁתָּא. שֶׁכֵּן דֶּרֶךְ שֶׁנּוֹתְנִין חֶרֶת בִּדְיוֹ, כְּשֶׁשּׁוֹלְקִים קְלִיפּוֹת הַקּוֹלְרִים, וְהוּא מִתְיַיבֵּשׁ. פָּלֵי קוֹרְטָא דִּדְיוֹתָא. מְבַקֵּעַ חֲתִיכוֹת דְּיוֹ יָבֵשׁ. וּבוֹדֵק בּוֹ. מַרְאִית דָּם שָׁחוֹר. כְּקִיר. שַׁעֲוָה שְׁחוֹרָה. כַּעֲנָבָה. עֲנָבִים שְׁחוֹרִים. ל"א: "קִיר" — שֵׁם עֵשֶׂב שָׁחוֹר. עוּלָּא אַשָּׁחוֹר דְּמַתְנִיתִין קָאֵי, דְּקָתָנֵי: טָמֵא. סִיוָאָה. שֵׁם מָקוֹם, וְעוֹשִׂין שָׁם מַלְבּוּשִׁים שְׁחוֹרִים. אוֹלְיָירִין. בַּלָּנִים מְחַמְּמֵי מֶרְחֲצָאוֹת. לָשׁוֹן אַחֵר: שֵׁם מָקוֹם. שֶׁמָּא אֶזְכֶּה. לְגַן עֵדֶן, וְהַצַּדִּיקִים מְלוּבָּשִׁים לְבָנִים. גְּלִימֵי אוֹלְיָירִין. הֲווּ סוּמָּקֵי, אֲבָל פָּתוּרֵי, כְּגוֹן מַפָּה וְסָדִין אוֹלְיָירִין, הָווּ שְׁחוֹרִין. וְכוּלָּן. חֲמִשָּׁה דָּמִים. מַטְלִית לְבָנָה. מַרְאוֹת הַדָּמִים נִיכָּרִים בָּהּ. וְשָׁחוֹר. דָּם שָׁחוֹר נִבְדָּקָה מַרְאִיתוֹ אִם שָׁחוֹר הִיא כְּחֶרֶת אוֹ דֵּיהָה מִכֵּן עַל גַּבֵּי בֶּגֶד אָדוֹם. כּוּלָּם. הַדָּמִים. עָמוֹק מִכֵּן. מֵאוֹתוֹ שִׁיעוּר הַשָּׁנוּי בְּמַתְנִיתִין לְכָל אֶחָד, אִי הֲוָה סוּמָּק טְפֵי — טָמֵא. דֵּיהָה מִכֵּן טָהוֹר. כְּשָׁחוֹר. וְאַע"פ דְּלָא תְּנַן בְּמַתְנִיתִין "דֵּיהָה מִכֵּן טָהוֹר" אֶלָּא גַּבֵּי שָׁחוֹר, הוּא הַדִּין לְכוּלְּהוּ. אֲפִי' דֵּיהָה מִכֵּן לִיטַמֵּא. דְּהַאי אָדוֹם הֲוָה, וְע"י לְקוּתָא הוּשְׁחַר. קָא מַשְׁמַע לָן. דְּאֵין דֶּרֶךְ דָּם אָדוֹם הַמַּשְׁחִיר עַל יְדֵי לְקוּתָא לִהְיוֹת דֵּיהֶה. דֵּיהֶה דְּדֵיהֶה. שֶׁנִּדְהָה מַרְאִיתוֹ יוֹתֵר מִדַּאי. עָמוֹק מִכֵּן טָהוֹר. אִם מֵאוֹתוֹ מַרְאֶה הוּא, אֲבָל אִם הֶאֱדִים הַרְבֵּה עַד שֶׁבָּא לִכְלַל אֶחָד מִשְּׁאָר הַמַּרְאוֹת שֶׁל מַעְלָה הֵימֶנּוּ — הֲרֵי בָּא לַחֲדָא מֵהָנָךְ דְּמַתְנִי'. אֲדִיהוּ לֵיהּ. דָּם הַדּוֹמֶה לְמָזְגָא. כַּתַּחְתּוֹן. עָלֶה תַּחְתּוֹן. תְּלָתָא דָּרֵי. דְּעָלִין הָווּ זוֹ לְמַעְלָה מִזּוֹ. נְקוֹט דָּרָא מְצִיעָא. לִבְדּוֹק בָּהּ אֶת הַדָּם. וְטַרְפָּא מְצִיעָא. דְּהַהוּא מְשׁוּבָּח לִבְדּוֹק מִכּוּלָּן, וּמִיהוּ כּוּלֵּיהּ דָּרָא כְּשֵׁרָה לִבְדּוֹק, וְהָא דְּקָתָנֵי "כַּתַּחְתּוֹן וְלֹא כָּעֶלְיוֹן" הָכִי קָאָמַר: כְּשׁוּרָה אֶמְצָעִית וְלֹא כָּעֶלְיוֹנָה הֵימֶנָּה, וְהָא דְּקָתָנֵי "כָּעֶלְיוֹן וְלֹא כַּתַּחְתּוֹן" כְּשׁוּרָה אֶמְצָעִית וְלֹא כַּתַּחְתּוֹנָה הֵימֶנָּה, דְּאֵין כָּשֵׁר לִבְדּוֹק אֶלָּא בְּדָרָא אֶמְצָעִית. וְהָא דְּתַנְיָא: "כַּתַּחְתּוֹן וְכ"ש כָּעֶלְיוֹן", דְּמַשְׁמַע דְּתַרְוַיְיהוּ כְּשֵׁרִין לִבְדּוֹק אֶלָּא שֶׁהָעֶלְיוֹן מְשׁוּבָּח — לָאו אַדָּרֵי קָאֵי, אֶלָּא אַעָלִין דְּדָרָא מְצִיעָא, וְה"ק: בְּעָלֶה תַּחְתּוֹן שֶׁהוּא בָּרוּר, וְכ"ש בָּעֶלְיוֹן הֵימֶנּוּ, דְּהַיְינוּ אֶמְצָעִי שֶׁהוּא בָּרוּר מְאֹד. וְהָא דְּתַנְיָא "כָּעֶלְיוֹן וְכ"ש כַּתַּחְתּוֹן" — הָכִי קָאָמַר: "כָּעֶלְיוֹן" — כְּעָלֶה עֶלְיוֹן, וְכ"ש כַּתַּחְתּוֹן כְּעָלֶה הָאֶמְצָעִי. בְּגוּשַׁיְיהוּ שָׁנִינוּ. לִבְדּוֹק בָּהֶן, וְלֹא לְאַחַר כְּתִישָׁתָן. וְאֵין שִׁיעוּר לַמַּיִם. מִשּׁוּם דְּאֵין שִׁיעוּר לֶעָפָר, אֶלָּא יָבִיא עָפָר כְּמוֹ שֶׁיִּרְצֶה, אִם רַב אִם מְעַט, וְיָצִיף עַל מַיִם כְּעוֹבִי קְלִיפַּת הַשּׁוּם לְמַעְלָה מִן הֶעָפָר. אֶלָּא עֲכוּרִין. שֶׁתְּהֵא מַרְאִית אֲדָמָה נִכְנֶסֶת בַּמַּיִם. וּכְשֶׁהוּא עוֹכְרָן. הַמַּיִם בֶּעָפָר. לָא לִרְמְיֵיהּ בִּידֵיהּ. לֹא יִתֵּן הֶעָפָר אֶל תּוֹךְ יָדוֹ וְיַעֲכוֹר הַמַּיִם בֶּעָפָר שֶׁבְּיָדוֹ, אַע"פ שֶׁחוֹזֵר וְנוֹתְנוֹ בִּכְלִי לְאַחַר עֲכִירָה. אֲבָל. אִם הֶעָפָר בִּכְלִי, כִּי עָכַר לְהוּ בִּידֵיהּ בְּאֶצְבַּע — שַׁפִּיר דָּמֵי. אוֹ דִּלְמָא לָא לְעַכְרִינְהוּ בִּידֵיהּ. כְּשֶׁהַמַּיִם בַּסֵּפֶל — לֹא יַעֲכְרֵם בְּאֶצְבָּעוֹ, אֶלָּא בְּבָזָךְ אוֹ בִּכְלִי אַחֵר. אֶלָּא בְּכוֹס שֶׁל זְכוּכִית. אַלְמָא לָא לִירְמֵי עָפָר וּמַיִם בְּכַפּוֹ וְיִבְדּוֹק. אֲמַר לְהוּ בִּמְקוֹמָהּ שָׁנִינוּ. שֶׁאֵין הָאֲדָמָה דּוֹמָה לְדָם אֶלָּא בִּמְקוֹמָהּ, אֲבָל הֵבִיאָהּ בְּמָקוֹם אַחֵר — נִשְׁתַּנָּה מַרְאִיתָהּ. פָּלֵי. מְבַקֵּעַ. וּבָדֵיק לָהּ. בְּלֹא מַיִם. לֵיִיט עֲלֵיהּ ר' יִשְׁמָעֵאל. לְאַחַר שֶׁיַּעֲשֶׂה כֵּן, בְּאַסְכָּרָה. דְּרַבִּי

פלי קורטא דדיותא. מכאן משמע שדיו שלנו הוא קרוי "דיו", מדקאמר "קורטא דדיותא", משמע שהוא יבש. ואוסר ר"ת לכתוב ס"ת בדיו של עפצים, לפי שהוא לעולם לח. ובפ' [שני] דגיטין (דף יט.) מפורש. והא

כשחור. תימה דדיהה מאדום עדיין הוא אדום יותר מקרן כרכום וכן דיהה מקרן כרכום אדום ממימי אדמה וכן למ"ד עמוק מכן טהור לפרש"י עמוק ממזג הוא כמימי אדמה וצ"ל דאלו ד' מראות טמאים אבל שאר מראות שביניהן טהורין אע"פ שיש מראה שהוא דיהה מהן והוא טמא והיינו טעמא דמדמיה דמיה נפקא לן ד' מראות דמים וקים להו לרבנן דהני ד' מראות דמים שכיחי בנשים וכל שאינו דומה לאלו המראות טהור אע"פ שיש מראה למטה ממנו שהוא דיהה יותר וטמא: לאפוקי דיהה דדיהה. לפרש"י נמי הוה מצי למימר לאפוקי עמוק דעמוק:

גליון הש"ס

גמ' נקוט דרא מציעתא. כעין זה תענית יד ע"א:

הגהות הגר"א

[א] גמ' ר"ע אומר נמתקת וכ"ב רבי יהודה אומר:

תוספי הרא"ש

שחור כחרת עמוק מכן טמא. פרש"י ז"ל שחור מיכן אע"ג דגבי נגע אמרינן דעמוק היינו לבן כמראה חמה שעמוקה מן הצל יש לחלק דגבי נגע שהוא לבן קרי לנגע שהוא לבן יותר עמוק וגבי דם שחור קרי למה שהוא שחור יותר. ור"ח פי' עמוק מיכן לבן ממנו מעט ודיהה מיכן מה שהוא לבן יותר: כקיר כדיו כענבא טמא. וזו היא ששנינו עמוק מכאן טמא. וא"ת מה שייך לומר גבי דיו עמוק מכאן [הא] אמרינן שחור כחרת היינו דיו. וי"ל דמיירי הכא בדיו שאין בו חרת כפר"ח דעמוק מכן הוא לבן יותר. ולפירש"י צ"ל דעמוק מכן לא קאי אדיו: וכולן עמוק מכן טמא דיהה מכן טהור

והא

עין משפט נר מצוה

צו א ב ג מיי' פ"ה מהל' איסורי ביאה הלכה ח:
צז ד ה מיי' שם הל' ט:
צח ו מיי' שם הל' יב:
צט ז מיי' שם הלכה י:
ק ח מיי' שם הלכה ז:
קא ט י כ ל מ נ מיי' שם הלכה ח:

שבת קיד. | שם | [לעיל יט. סוכה לג: חולין מז:] | ס"א דעביד כשמעתיה רש"א | [תוס' פ"ג] | [תוספתא שם] | [תוספתא שם פ"ג] | [לעיל יד. וש"נ]

עין משפט נר מצוה

קב א טוש"ע י"ד סי' רמב סעיף לא בהג"ה:
קג ב מיי' פ"ה מהל' איסורי ביאה הל' י סמג עשין קיא טוש"ע י"ד סימן קפח סעיף ב:
קד ג טוש"ע שם ולא איפסיקא ולחומרא:
קה ד מיי' שם הל' יב:

רבי חנינא הוא דחכים, כולי עלמא – לאו חכימי הכי. אמר רבי יוחנן: חכמתא דרבי חנינא גרמא לי דלא אחזי דמא, מטמינא – מטהר, מטהרנא – מטמא. אמר רבי אלעזר: ענוותנותא דרבי חנינא גרמא לי דחזאי דמא, ומה רבי חנינא דענותן הוא – מחית נפשיה לספק וחזי, אנא לא אחזי? אמר רבי זירא: טבעא דבבל גרמא לי דלא חזאי דמא, דאמינא: בטבעא לא ידענא, בדמא ידענא? למימרא דבטבעא תליא מלתא, והא *רבה הוא דידע בטבעא ולא ידע בדמא! כל שכן קאמר, ומה רבה דידע בטבעא – לא חזא דמא, ואנא אחזי? עולא אקלע לפומבדיתא, אייתו לקמיה דמא ולא חזא. אמר: ומה *רבי אלעזר דמרא דארעא דישראל הוה, כי מקלע לאתרא דר' יהודה – לא חזי דמא, אנא אחזי? ואמאי קרו ליה "מרא דארעא דישראל"? – דההיא אתתא דאייתא דמא לקמיה דרבי אלעזר, הוה יתיב רבי אמי קמיה. ארחיה, אמר לה: האי דם חימוד הוא. בתר דנפקה אטפל לה רבי אמי. א"ל: בעלי היה בדרך וחמדתיו. קרי עליה: °"סוד ה' ליראיו". *אפרא הורמיז אמיה דשבור מלכא שדרה דמא לקמיה דרבא, הוה יתיב רב עובדיה קמיה, ארחיה, אמר לה: האי דם חימוד הוא. אמרה ליה *לבריה: תא חזי כמה חכימי יהודאי! א"ל: *דלמא כסומא בארובה? הדר שדרה ליה שתין מיני דמא, וכולהו אמרינהו. ההוא בתרא דם כנים הוה, ולא ידע, אסתייע מילתא ושדר לה סריקותא דמקטלא *כלמי. אמרה: יהודאי, בתווני דלבא יתביתו! אמר רב יהודה: מרישא הוה חזינא דמא, כיון דאמרה לי אמיה דיצחק ברי: האי טיפתא קמייתא לא מייתינן לה קמייהו דרבנן, משום דזהימא – לא חזינא, בין טמאה לטהורה ודאי חזינא. ילתא אייתא דמא לקמיה דרבה בר בר חנה – וטמי לה, הדר אייתא לקמיה דרב יצחק בריה דרב יהודה – ודכי לה. והיכי עביד הכי? *והתניא: אחכם שטימא – אין חבירו רשאי לטהר, אסר – אין חבירו רשאי להתיר! מעיקרא טמויי הוה מטמי לה, כיון דא"ל: דכל יומא הוה מדכי לי כי האי גונא, והאידנא הוא דחש בעיניה – דכי לה. ומי מהימני? אין. והתניא: בנאמנת אשה לומר "כזה ראיתי ואבדתיו". גאיבעיא להו: "כזה טיהר איש פלוני חכם" מהו? תא שמע: נאמנת אשה לומר "כזה ראיתי ואבדתיו". שאני התם – דליתיה לקמה. תא שמע: דילתא אייתא דמא לקמיה דרבה בר בר חנה – וטמי לה. (א) לקמיה דרב יצחק בריה דרב יהודה – ודכי לה. והיכי עביד הכי? והתניא: חכם שטימא אין חבירו רשאי לטהר וכו', ואמרינן: טמויי הוה מטמי לה, כיון דאמרה ליה דכל יומא מדכי לה כי האי גונא, והאידנא הוא דחש בעיניה – הדר דכי לה, אלמא: מהימנא לה! רב יצחק בר יהודה – אגמריה סמך. רבי ראה דם בלילה – וטימא, ראה ביום – וטיהר, המתין שעה אחת – חזר וטימא, אמר: אוי לי שמא טעיתי! "שמא טעיתי"!? ודאי טעה! דתניא: לא יאמר חכם "אילו היה לח היה ודאי טמא", אלא אמר: *אין לו לדיין אלא מה שעיניו רואות. מעיקרא אחזקיה בטמא, כיון דחזא לצפרא דאשתני אמר *(ליה) ודאי טהור הוה, ובליליה הוא דלא אתחזי שפיר. כיון דחזא דהדר אשתני, אמר: האי – טמא הוא, ומפכח הוא דקא מפכח ואזיל. רבי בדיק לאור הנר, רבי ישמעאל ברבי *יוסף בדיק ביום המעונן ביני עמודי. אמר רב אמי בר שמואל: דוכולן אין בודקין אותן אלא בין חמה לצל. רב נחמן אמר רבה בר אבוה: בחמה, ובצל ידו.§ "וכמזוג שני חלקים" כו'.§ תנא: השרוני

תהלים כה

ע"ב פ"ז מ"ן

תורה אור

דרבי חנינא הוא דחכים. ומאי בדיק כה"ג. דמרא דארעא דישראל. בקי במראות דם מכל חכמי ארץ ישראל, כדמפרש לקמן. פומבדיתא. אתריה דרב יהודה, כשילהי פ"ק דסנהדרין (דף יז:) "סבי דפומבדיתא" – רב יהודה ורב עינא. ולא חזא. משום כבודו דרב יהודה. ארחיה. הריח בו. חימוד. שנתאוית לבעלה, וראתה הדם מחמת תאוה. איפרא הורמיז. נכרית היתה, וכן שמה. ואעפ"כ היתה משמרת עצמה מנדות, וקרובה להתגייר, ואף קרבנות היתה שולחת.* ולשון יוני: "איפרא" – חן, כמו "אפריון נמטייה לרבי שמעון" (ב"מ דף קיט.). הורמיז. כמו (ב"ב דף עג.) "הורמיז בר ליליתא", כלומר: יופי שדים היה לה. ארחיה כו'. ואע"ג דאמר לעיל: רבא לא ידע בדמא – ניסא איתרחיש ליה. שלח לה. משום דורון. סריקותא. מסרק נאה. מקטלא כלמי. שהורגין עליה כנים, וסברה: ודאי הבין, ומשום הכי שלח לי האי. כלמי. כנים, כדמתרגמינן "כנים": קלמתא. (ב) בתווני לבא. בחדרי הלב אתם יושבים. *"מחדרים" מתרגמי': מתווניא. כלומר: כל חכמה מצויה בכם. לא חזינא. דדילמא אשתני, ואע"ג דמראה דם טהור יש לה – דלמא אי אייתא טיפתא קמייתא, הוה מיחזי טמא. בין טמאה לטהורה. כשכלין ימי טוהר של זכר או של נקבה, וראתה ביום ארבעים ואחד או ביום שמונים ואחד. חזינא להוא דמא. אי דם טמא – מטמינא, ואי לאו מחמשה דמים הוא – מטהרינא, דההוא ודאי טיפתא קמייתא מייתא, דלא מזהמא. דעד השתא חזאי ואתא דם טוהר, שכל מ' לזכר ופ' לנקבה – מעין פתוח. ואפי' פסקה יום או יומים, הואיל ומוחזקת היא בדמים – לא זהמא ומייתא טיפתא קמייתא. מעיקרא טמויי טמי לה. רב יצחק משום כבודו דרבה בר בר חנה. כזה ראיתי. מביאה דם אחר או שלה או של חברתה, ואומרת: "כזה ראיתי ואבדתיו". אם דם זה טהור – לא מספקינן ליה בטומאה משום דם האבוד, דמהימנא למימר "כזה ראיתי". כזה טיהר לי פלוני כו'. מהו שתסמוך עליה חברתה שהראתה דמה לזו, ואמרה לה: "כדם זה שלך הראיתי גם אני לפלוני חכם, וטיהר". נאמנת אשה כו'. אלמא קים לה במראה דמים. דליתיה קמן. אבל הכא דאיתיה קמן – ניחזי אנן. אגמריה סמך. דפשיטא ליה דטהור, והאי דהוה מטמא מעיקרא – משום כבודו דרבה בר בר חנה. אבל אי הוה מספקא ליה – לא הוה סמיך עלה. ראה ביום. לאותו דם עצמו. חזר וטימא. קס"ד דלא חזר וראהו, אלא מאליו חזר בו וטימא, דסבר: שמא אמש טמא הוה ועכשיו שייבש נשתנה ממראיתו ממה שהיה לו אמש, ואילו הוה לח כמתחלתו – הוה נראה טמא, לפיכך חזר בו ממה שטיהר. שמא טעיתי. במה שחזרתי וטימאתי הואיל ומראיהו עכשיו טהור. מעיקרא אחזקיה בטומאה. כלומר: אמש לא מספק טימא, אלא שפיר חזייה ואחזיק בטומאה, דאמרי' לקמן: רבי בדק לאור הנר. דאישתני. הלבין. דהדר אישתני. עוד יותר. מפכח. מראה אדמומיתו עוברת, הילכך הדר למילתיה קמייתא וטימא. והא דאמרינן: אין לו לדיין אלא מה שעיניו רואות – היכא דלא אחזיה כשהוא לח, ולא אידמי ליה כטמא. בין העמודים. היכא דגרסי, ואע"ג דליכא נהורא כולי האי. ובצל ידו. נותן ידו כנגד חמה על הדם, ומעיין. השרוני.

והא רבא דידע. "רבה" גרס. דרבא היה בקי, כדמוכח בסמוך גבי דאפרא הורמיז. ורש"י פירש בסמוך: דאיתרחיש ליה ניסא. ואין נראה, דדוקא בסוף הוא דאיתרחיש ליה ניסא, כדמוכח בסמוך.

טיפתא קמייתא. ושאר חכמים שהיו רואין לא היו מחמירין כ"כ או שהיו בקיאין ביותר.

כל יומא הוה מטהר לי כה"ג. – משמע שלא היתה רגילה להראות לרב נחמן בעלה, ושמא לא היה בקי. והא דאמר ר"נ לעיל (דף יט:) בדם הקזה – קבלה היתה בידו. אי נמי: היתה חוששת שמא היה מחמיר על עצמו להיות לבו נוקפו, ופורש, ולא יסמוך על חכמתו. אי נמי: שלא תתגנה בפניו. אבל אין לומר דאסור לראות דמי אשתו, דהא במס' נגעים (פ"ב מ"ה) תנן: כל הנגעים אדם רואה, חוץ מנגעי עצמו. ר"מ אומר: אף לא נגעי קרוביו. כל הנדרים אדם מתיר, חוץ מנדרי עצמו. ר' יהושע אומר: אף לא נדרי אשתו. ואילו "כל הדמים אדם רואה, חוץ מדמי אשתו" לא קתני.

אגמריה סמך. לפי הפשט משמע דלכך האמין לדבריה, אבל בענין אחר [פירוש: בלא דבריה] לא היה מתיר, אע"ג דאגמריה סמך. וקשה: דבפ' "אלו טרפות" (חולין מט.) אמרו גבי "ההיא מחטא דאישתכח בסימפונא דכבדא", הונא מר בריה דרב אידי – טריף, ורב אחא בר מניומי – מכשיר! לכך נראה לפרש: דהשתא הדר ביה משינויא קמא, והיכא דאגמריה סמיך – רשאי להתיר, אע"ג דחכם כבר אסר. ויש מקשה על ילתא: היכי עבדה הכי, הא אמרינן בפ"ק דמס' ע"ז (דף ז.): הנשאל לחכם וטימא, לא ישאל לחכם ויטהר וי"ל: דקפידא לא הויא אשואל, אלא אחכם. אבל השואל, ישאל כל מה שירצה, דמתוך כך ידקדקו בדבר. ופעמים שהראשון טועה, ויצא הדבר לאורה. [ועי' תוס' ע"ז, ז. ד"ה "הנשאל" ותוס' חולין מד, ד"ה "היכי"].

## הדרן עלך כל היד

## תוספי הרא"ש

והא רבה דידע בטיבעא ולא ידע בדמא. רבה גרס אבל רבא היה בקי. כדמוכח לקמן גבי היפרא אורמיז ולא כמו שפרש"י דאיתרחיש ליה ניסא דלא משמע הכי דוקא בדם כנים הוא דאיתרחיש ליה ניסא ועוד דרבא לא חזי דמא בשני דרבי זירא: ארחיה אמר האי דם חימוד הוא. פי' וטמא כדאמרינן תבועה לינשא ונתפייסה צריכה לישב ז' נקיים שמא מחמת חימוד ראתה דם ולהראות חכמתו הוא דאמר הכי: טיפתא קמייתא לא מייתי קמייהו דרבנן. שאר החכמים שהיו רואין לא היו מחמירין כל כך (כלומר) או שמא היו בקיאין יותר ורואין היו בזה שמביאין לפניהם אי זה מראות דם ראתה אף בטיפה קמייתא: ילתא אייתי דמא קמיה דרבה בר בר חנה. מה שלא הראתה לרב נחמן בעלה שמא לא היה בקי והא דאמר רב נחמן לעיל דדם הקזה קבלה היתה בידו. אי נמי היתה יראה שלא יחמיר על עצמו להיות לבו נוקפו ופורש ולא יסמוך על חכמתו. אי נמי שלא תתגנה בפניו א)ואין לומר דלפי מעשה שלא היה רב נחמן בעיר דמדקאמרה כל יומא הוה מטהר לי כה"ג משמע שהיתה רגילה להראות לו. ואין לומר דאין אדם רואה דמי אשתו דהא תנן במס' נגעים כל הנגעים אדם רואה חוץ מנגעי אשתו ר' מאיר אומר אף לא נגעי קרוביו. כל הנדרים אדם מתיר חוץ מנדרי עצמו ר' יהודה אומר אף לא נדרי אשתו ואילו כל הדמים אדם רואה חוץ מדמי אשתו לא קתני: אגמריה סמיך. והשתא הדר ביה משינוייא קמא דמעיקרא טמויי טמי לה דכיון דאגמריה סמיך מצי שפיר לטהר מה שאסר הראשון דהא דאמרי' אין חבירו רשאי לטהר היינו טעמא דוקא מסברא אבל אין לפרש דאגמריה סמיך ולפיכך האמין לדבריה ולעולם צריכין לשנוייא קמא דא"כ קשה מההיא דאמרינן פרק אלו טריפות ההיא מחטא דאישתכח בסימפונא רבא דכבדא מר הונא בריה דרב אידי טריף רב אדא בר מניומי מכשיר ותימה ילתא היכי עבדה הכי והא אמרינן פ"ק דע"ז הנשאל לחכם וטימא לא ישאל לחכם ויטהר וי"ל דקפידא דהתם לאו אשואל קאי אלא אחכם. כלומר שלא יתיר חכם מה שאסר חבירו אבל השואל יכול לישאל מה שירצה ובלבד שיאמר פלוני טימא לי ואם יראה לשני שטעה הראשון ישא ויתן עמו עד שיחזירנו ובהכי ניחא נמי הא דפריך לעיל והיכי עביד הכי והתניא חכם שטימא כו' ומאי קא פריך דלמא איהי לא קאמרה ליה שרבה בר בר חנה טימא לה אלא ודאי לא היתה שואלת לו אם לא שהיתה אומרת לו שכבר טימא לה רבה בר בר חנה: סליק פרק כל היד

א) נראה דצ"ל ואין לומר דבאותו זמן שבאתה לשאול לרבה בר בר חנה לא היה רב נחמן בעיר.

[יומא ט: גיטין יט:]

[עי' תוס' גיטין יח. ד"ה הורמין וכו' חולקים אפרש"י דהכא]

[בערוך ערך סרק ב' איתא קלמי ודע דבכל התרגומים שלפנינו תרגום כנים קלמתא וכ"כ המתורגמן ודברי רש"י ד"ה כלמי וכו' וכן רש"י ברכות נח: ד"ה ומסמרטוטי וכו' נע"ק]

מסורת הש"ס

[כלאיתא בזבחים קטז:]

[לפמ"ש רש"י ד"ה ארחיה וכו' מוכח דגרסתו היה רבא ועי' תוס' ד"ה והא רבה וכו']

(דברים לב)

### הגהות הב"ח

(א) גמ' ת"ש דילתא וכו' וטמי לה הדר אייתא לקמיה דר' יצחק: (ב) רש"י ד"ה בתווני. נ"ב עי' בע"ז דף כח ע"ב פי' תוספות באוכמתא בבי"ת ע"ש:

לברה כצ"ל יעב"ץ

[ב"ב יב:]

חולין מד: ע"ז ז. ע"ש ברכות סג:

ב"ב קלג. סנהדרין ו:

[נ"ל יוסי]

*הַשָּׁרוֹנִי נִידּוֹן כַּכַּרְמְלִי, חַי — אוְלֹא מָזוּג, חָדָשׁ — וְלֹא יָשָׁן. אָמַר רַב יִצְחָק בַּר אֲבוּדִימִי: וְכוּלָּן אֵין בּוֹדְקִין אוֹתָן אֶלָּא בְּכוֹס טִבֶּרְיָא פָּשׁוּט. מַאי טַעְמָא? אָמַר אַבַּיֵי: שֶׁל כָּל הָעוֹלָם כּוּלּוֹ, מַחֲזִיק לוֹג — עוֹשִׂין אוֹתוֹ מִמָּנֶה, שְׁנֵי לוּגִּין — עוֹשִׂין אוֹתוֹ מִמָּאתַיִם. כּוֹס טִבֶּרְיָא פָּשׁוּט, אֲפִי' מַחֲזִיק שְׁנֵי לוּגִּין — עוֹשִׂין אוֹתוֹ מִמָּנֶה, וְאַיְּידֵי דְּקָלִישׁ — יָדִיעַ בֵּיהּ טְפֵי.§

# הדרן עלך כל היד

*הַמַּפֶּלֶת בחֲתִיכָה, אִם יֵשׁ עִמָּהּ דָּם — טְמֵאָה, וְאִם לָאו — טְהוֹרָה. ר' יְהוּדָה אוֹמֵר: בֵּין כָּךְ וּבֵין כָּךְ — טְמֵאָה. *גהַמַּפֶּלֶת כְּמִין קְלִיפָּה, כְּמִין שְׂעָרָה, כְּמִין עָפָר, כְּמִין יַבְחוּשִׁין אֲדוּמִּים — תַּטִּיל לַמַּיִם, אִם נִמּוֹחוּ — טְמֵאָה, וְאִם לָאו — טְהוֹרָה. דהַמַּפֶּלֶת כְּמִין דָּגִים, חֲגָבִים, שְׁקָצִים וּרְמָשִׂים, אִם יֵשׁ עִמָּהֶם דָּם — טְמֵאָה, וְאִם לָאו — טְהוֹרָה. *הַמַּפֶּלֶת מִין בְּהֵמָה חַיָּה וְעוֹף, בֵּין טְמֵאִין בֵּין טְהוֹרִין, האִם זָכָר — תֵּשֵׁב לְזָכָר, וְאִם נְקֵבָה — תֵּשֵׁב לִנְקֵבָה, וְאִם אֵין יָדוּעַ — תֵּשֵׁב לְזָכָר וְלִנְקֵבָה, דִּבְרֵי רַבִּי מֵאִיר. וַחֲכָמִים אוֹמְרִים: וכָּל שֶׁאֵין בּוֹ מִצּוּרַת אָדָם — אֵינוֹ וָלָד.§

**גמ'** *אָמַר רַב יְהוּדָה, אָמַר שְׁמוּאֵל: לֹא טִימֵּא רַבִּי יְהוּדָה אֶלָּא בַּחֲתִיכָה שֶׁל אַרְבַּעַת מִינֵי דָמִים, אֲבָל שֶׁל שְׁאָר מִינֵי דָמִים — טְהוֹרָה. וְר' יוֹחָנָן אָמַר: שֶׁל אַרְבַּעַת מִינֵי דָמִים — דִּבְרֵי הַכֹּל טְמֵאָה, שֶׁל שְׁאָר מִינֵי דָמִים — דִּבְרֵי הַכֹּל טְהוֹרָה. לֹא נֶחְלְקוּ אֶלָּא שֶׁהִפִּילָה וְאֵינָהּ יוֹדַעַת מַה הִפִּילָה. *רַבִּי יְהוּדָה סָבַר: זִיל בָּתַר רוֹב חֲתִיכוֹת, וְרוֹב חֲתִיכוֹת שֶׁל (מִינֵי) אַרְבַּעַת מִינֵי דָמִים הָוְיָין. וְרַבָּנַן סָבְרִי: לָא אָמְרִינַן רוֹב חֲתִיכוֹת שֶׁל אַרְבַּעַת מִינֵי דָמִים. אִינִי, וְהָא כִּי אֲתָא רַב הוֹשַׁעְיָא מִנְּהַרְדְּעָא, אֲתָא וְאַיְיתֵי מַתְנִיתָא בִּידֵיהּ: הַמַּפֶּלֶת חֲתִיכָה זאֲדוּמָּה, שְׁחוֹרָה, יְרוּקָּה, וּלְבָנָה, אִם יֵשׁ עִמָּהּ דָּם — טְמֵאָה, וְאִם לָאו — טְהוֹרָה. רַבִּי יְהוּדָה אוֹמֵר: בֵּין כָּךְ וּבֵין כָּךְ טְמֵאָה — קַשְׁיָא לִשְׁמוּאֵל בַּחֲדָא, וּלְרַבִּי יוֹחָנָן בְּתַרְתֵּי. לִשְׁמוּאֵל בַּחֲדָא — דְּאָמַר שְׁמוּאֵל: לֹא טִימֵּא רַבִּי יְהוּדָה אֶלָּא בַּחֲתִיכָה שֶׁל אַרְבַּעַת מִינֵי דָמִים, וְהָא קָתָנֵי יְרוּקָּה וּלְבָנָה, וּפָלֵיג רַבִּי יְהוּדָה! וְכִי תֵּימָא: כִּי פָּלֵיג רַבִּי יְהוּדָה — אַאֲדוּמָּה וּשְׁחוֹרָה, וְאַיְרוּקָּה וּלְבָנָה — לָא, אֶלָּא יְרוּקָּה וּלְבָנָה לְמַאן קָתָנֵי לָהּ? אִילֵימָא רַבָּנַן — הַשְׁתָּא אֲדוּמָּה וּשְׁחוֹרָה מְטַהֲרִי רַבָּנַן, יְרוּקָּה וּלְבָנָה מִיבַּעְיָא? אֶלָּא לָאו — לְרַבִּי יְהוּדָה, וּפָלֵיג! וְתוּ, לְרַבִּי יוֹחָנָן דְּאָמַר: שֶׁל אַרְבַּעַת מִינֵי דָמִים — דִּבְרֵי הַכֹּל טְמֵאָה, הָא קָתָנֵי אֲדוּמָּה וּשְׁחוֹרָה, וּפְלִיגִי רַבָּנַן! וְכִי תֵּימָא: כִּי פְּלִיגִי רַבָּנַן — אַיְרוּקָּה וּלְבָנָה, אֲבָל אַאֲדוּמָּה וּשְׁחוֹרָה — לָא, אֶלָּא אֲדוּמָּה וּשְׁחוֹרָה לְמַאן קָתָנֵי לָהּ? אִילֵימָא רַבִּי יְהוּדָה — הַשְׁתָּא יְרוּקָּה וּלְבָנָה טְמֵאָה, אֲדוּמָּה וּשְׁחוֹרָה מִיבַּעְיָא? אֶלָּא לָאו — רַבָּנַן, וּפְלִיגִי! אֶלָּא אָמַר רַב נַחְמָן בַּר יִצְחָק: *בְּאֶפְשָׁר לִפְתִיחַת הַקֶּבֶר בְּלֹא דָם קָמִיפַּלְגִי, וּבִפְלוּגְתָּא דְּהָנֵי תַּנָּאֵי, דְּתַנְיָא: חקָשְׁתָה שְׁנַיִם וְלַשְּׁלִישִׁי הִפִּילָה, וְאֵינָהּ יוֹדַעַת מַה הִפִּילָה, הֲרֵי

[כריתות י. לקמן כב: לח. סו.]

רש"י

הַשָּׁרוֹנִי. מָזוּג. נִידּוֹן כַּכַּרְמְלִי חַי. דְּהָכִי נַמִּי בָּדְקִי בְּכַרְמְלִי חַי. וְאִית דְּגָרְסִי: כַּשָּׁרוֹנִי נִידּוֹן הַכַּרְמְלִי. בְּכוֹס טִבֶּרְיָא שֶׁל זְכוּכִית פָּשׁוּט. טנג"ש. וְאַיְּידֵי דְּקָלִישׁ, נִרְאֶה בּוֹ אַדְמוּמִית הַיַּיִן. **הדרן עלך כל היד**

**הַמַּפֶּלֶת** חֲתִיכָה אִם יֵשׁ עִמָּהּ דָּם טְמֵאָה. מִשּׁוּם נִדָּה. וְאִם לָאו טְהוֹרָה. דְּלָאו לֵידָה הִיא. דְּאִי לֵידָה הָוְיָא, בְּלֹא דָם נַמִּי טְמֵאָה, דִּכְתִיב (ויקרא יב): "כִּימֵי נִדַּת דְּוֹתָהּ תִּטְמָא". ר' יְהוּדָה **אוֹמֵר** כו'. מְפָרֵשׁ בַּגְּמָרָא. כְּמִין שְׂעָרָה. שֵׂעָר. יַבְחוּשִׁין. יַתּוּשִׁין. **אִם** נִימּוֹחוּ טְמֵאָה. מִשּׁוּם נִדָּה, דְּדָם הוּא. מִין דָּגִים. נַמִּי לָאו וָלָד הוּא, וְטַעֲמָא מְפָרֵשׁ בַּגְּמָרָא. הִלְכָּךְ אִי אִיכָּא דָּם טְמֵאָה — נִדָּה, וְאִם לָאו — טְהוֹרָה. תֵּשֵׁב לְזָכָר. יְמֵי טוּמְאַת שִׁבְעָה וִימֵי טָהֳרָהּ. ל"ג: "וְכָל דָּמִים שֶׁתִּרְאֶה בָּהֶן טְהוֹרִין". לְזָכָר וְלִנְקֵבָה. לְחוּמְרָא: יְמֵי טוּמְאָה דִּנְקֵבָה שְׁבוּעַיִם, וִימֵי טוֹהַר כָּלִים לְסוֹף אַרְבָּעִים יוֹם כְּזָכָר, וְלֹא פ' כִּנְקֵבָה. וּבַגְּמָרָא מְפָרֵשׁ מַאי שְׁנָא דְּלַחַיָּה וְעוֹף קָרֵי "וָלָד" יוֹתֵר מִדָּגִים. **גמ'** שֶׁל ד' מִינֵי דָמִים. דְּקָסָבַר: הִיא גּוּפָהּ דָּם, הִלְכָּךְ טְמֵאָה נִדָּה, אֲבָל וָלָד לָא הָוֵי. יְרוּקָּה וּלְבָנָה. לָאו מֵאַרְבַּע מִינֵי דָמִים הֵן, אֶלָּא: אָדוֹם, וּכְמֵימֵי אֲדָמָה, וּכְקֶרֶן כַּרְכּוֹם, וּכְמָזוּג. וְשָׁחוֹר לָא קָא חָשֵׁיב, דְּהַיְינוּ אָדוֹם אֶלָּא שֶׁלָּקָה. **לָא אָמְרִינַן** כו'. דְּקָסָבְרִי: אֵין רוֹב חֲתִיכוֹת שֶׁל אַרְבַּע מִינֵי דָמִים, דְּלָא אִתַּחְזַק לָן הַאי רוּבָּא. לְמַאן קָתָנֵי לָהּ. כְּלוֹמַר, לְהוֹדִיעַ דְּבָרָיו שֶׁל מִי בָּא. **אֶלָּא** לְר' יְהוּדָה. לְהוֹדִיעַ דְּאַיְרוּקָּה וּלְבָנָה נַמִּי פָּלֵיג. וְתוּ לְרַבִּי יוֹחָנָן וכו'. כְּלוֹמַר, הַךְ קוּשְׁיָא דִּירוּקָּה וּלְבָנָה לָא אִיבָּעֵי לָן לְפָרוּשֵׁי. דְּכִי הֵיכִי דְּקַשְׁיָא לֵיהּ לִשְׁמוּאֵל, קַשְׁיָא לֵיהּ לְרַבִּי יוֹחָנָן. דְּהָא רַבִּי יוֹחָנָן נַמִּי אָמַר עַל שְׁאָר מִינִין לְרַבִּי יְהוּדָה טְהוֹרָה, וְהָכָא קָתָנֵי יְרוּקָּה וּלְבָנָה, וּפָלֵיג רַבִּי יְהוּדָה! וְתוּ קַשְׁיָא אַחֲרִיתִי לְר' יוֹחָנָן, דְּאָמַר: שֶׁל אַרְבַּעַת מִינֵי דָמִים דִּבְרֵי הַכֹּל כו'. הָכִי גָּרְסִינַן: וְכִי תֵּימָא. כִּי פְּלִיגִי רַבָּנַן אַיְרוּקָּה וּלְבָנָה, אֶלָּא אֲדוּמָּה וּשְׁחוֹרָה לְמַאן קָתָנֵי לָהּ כו', אֶלָּא לָאו רַבָּנַן, וּפְלִיגִי. פְּתִיחַת הַקֶּבֶר. הָרֶחֶם. **בְּלֹא** דָם. דַּם לֵידָה. הִלְכָּךְ לְרַבָּנַן כִּי לֵיכָּא דָּם — טְהוֹרָה, וַאֲפִילּוּ הַחֲתִיכָה שֶׁל אַרְבַּע מִינֵי דָמִים. דַּחֲתִיכָה לָאו דָּם הוּא, אֶלָּא בָּשָׂר. וְלָא אָמַר דָּם אַחֵר אִיכָּא, וַאֲנַן הוּא דְּלָא חָזֵינַן, דְּקָסָבְרִי רַבָּנַן: אֶפְשָׁר לִפְתִיחַת הַקֶּבֶר בְּלֹא דָם. (א) לְר' יְהוּדָה, אֲפִילּוּ יְרוּקָּה וּלְבָנָה טְמֵאָה, דְּוַדַּאי דָּם אַחֵר הֲוָה, וַאֲנַן הוּא דְּלָא חָזֵינַן, דְּאִי אֶפְשָׁר לִפְתִיחַת הַקֶּבֶר בְּלֹא דָם. קָשְׁתָה שְׁנַיִם. בְּתוֹךְ י"א יוֹם שֶׁבֵּין נִדָּה לְנִדָּה, וְרָאֲתָה דָּם מֵחֲמַת קוֹשִׁי. וְלַשְּׁלִישִׁי הִפִּילָה. וְאֵינָהּ יוֹדַעַת אִם רָאֲתָה דָּם בְּאוֹתָהּ לֵידָה, אִם לָאו. (ג) וְאֵינָהּ יוֹדַעַת. אִם נֵפֶל הוּא, וְאִם רוּחַ בְּעָלְמָא הוּא. הֲרֵי

[לעיל יח:] [לקמן כב. כד:] חולין עא. [כריתות ז: בכורות מ.] [לעיל יח:] [שם יט.]

תוספות

**אלא** בחתיכה של ד' מיני דמים. דקסבר ר' יהודה: דם נדות הוא, ונקרש ונעשה חתיכה, כדאמר לקמן גבי "מפלת מין דגים". ורבנן סברי: מקור מגדל חתיכה, ולא דם נדות הוא. **ורבנן** סברי **לא אמרינן** רוב חתיכות. תימה: ונימא דהוה פלגא ופלגא, ויהא ודאי טמא ברה"י, אע"ג דאיכא חזקת טהרה! וי"ל: דאמרי' לעיל (דף יח:) דאפילו לרבי יהודה לא הוי רוב גמור, ואין שורפין עליו את התרומה, ולרבנן אפילו פלגא לא הוי, ואדרבה רוב החתיכות לאו של ד' מיני דמים הם. **לרבי** יוחנן **אדומה** ושחורה למאן קתני לה **אי** לרבי יהודה. וה"פ: המפלת אדומה ושחורה דינו כדמפרש ר' יהודה בסיפא: השתא ירוקה כו'. ומתוך פי' ר"ח משמע דל"ג ו"כ"ת כי פליגי רבנן אירוקה ולבנה", וכן נראה, דהא בהדיא קתני במילתייהו שחורה ואדומה, ואין זו סוגיית התלמוד.

*__ואינו__ נאכל. דאימא: לא ראתה ולא ילדה, וב' קרבנות אין צריכה להביא, משום דאימא ראתה וילדה דא"כ קושי סמוך ללידה הוא, וטהורה, כיון דלא שפתה מעת לעת, דיש קושי לנפלים. וכן צ"ל לרבי יהושע, דסבר: יש קושי לנפלים. דאי אין קושי, היה לה להביא שני קרבנות: של זיבה דהוי ודאי — נאכל, ושל לידה דהוי ספק — אינו נאכל. דלזיבה וללידה לא סגי בקרבן חד, מידי דהוי אחלב ודם, כדאמרינן בפ"ב דכריתות (דף ט:) ולקמן בפ' "יוצא דופן" (דף מ.).

באפשר

שייך לע"ב

הגהות הב"ח

(א) רש"י ד"ה בלא דם וכו' ולרבי יהודה אפילו: (ג) ד"ה ולשלישי וד"ה ואינה הד"א:

והרמב"ם וסמ"ג כתבו חלק א' מן יין השרוני של א"י חי חדש וב' חלקי מים כו' ועי' רש"א

עין משפט נר מצוה

קו א מיי' פ"ה מהלכות איסורי ביאה הל' י:

א ב מיי' פ"ה מהלכות איסורי ביאה הל' יג טור י"ד סי' קפח וסי' קלד עי' בהשגות ובמ"מ ובכ"ע:

ב ג ד מיי' שם פ"ה הל' יד והל' טו ועי' בהשגות ובמ"מ סמג לאוין קיא טוש"ע י"ד סי' קפח סעיף ד:

ג ה ו מיי' שם פ"י הל' ח סמג שם טוש"ע שם סי' קלד סעיף ג:

ד ז מיי' שם פ"ה הל' יג:

ה ח מיי' פ"ז מהלכות איסורי ביאה הל' ד:

הרי זו ספק לידה ספק זיבה, מביאה קרבן ואינו נאכל. רבי יהושע אומר: מביאה קרבן ונאכל, *אשאי אפשר לפתיחת הקבר בלא דם. לישנא אחרינא אמרי לה, אמר רב יהודה, אמר שמואל: לא טימא רבי יהודה אלא בחתיכה של ארבעה מיני דמים, אבל של שאר מיני דמים – טהורה. איני, והא כי אתא רב הושעיא מנהרדעא, אתא ואייתי מתניתא בידיה: המפלת חתיכה אדומה ושחורה ירוקה ולבנה, אם יש עמה דם – טמאה, ואם לאו – טהורה. ורבי יהודה אומר: בין כך ובין כך – טמאה. קתני "אדומה ושחורה ירוקה ולבנה" – ופליג ר' יהודה! וכי תימא: כי פליג ר' יהודה – אאדומה ושחורה, אבל ירוקה ולבנה – לא, אלא ירוקה ולבנה (א) מאן קתני לה? אילימא לרבנן – השתא אדומה ושחורה קא מטהרי רבנן, ירוקה ולבנה מיבעיא? אלא לאו לר' יהודה, ופליג! אלא אמר (רב יהודה:) *באפשר לפתיחת הקבר בלא דם קמיפלגי, ובפלוגתא דהני תנאי, דתניא: קשתה שנים ולשלישי הפילה, ואינה יודעת מה הפילה – הרי זו ספק לידה ספק זיבה, מביאה קרבן ואינו נאכל. רבי יהושע אומר: מביאה קרבן ונאכל, לפי שאי אפשר לפתיחת הקבר בלא דם. ת"ר: המפלת חתיכה, °סומכוס אומר משום רבי מאיר, וכן היה רבי שמעון בן מנסיא אומר כדבריו: קורעה, אם יש דם בתוכה – טמאה, ואם לאו – טהורה. כרבנן, ועדיפא מדרבנן, כרבנן – דאמרי אפשר לפתיחת הקבר בלא דם, ועדיפא מדרבנן – דאינהו סברי עמה – אין, בבתוכה – לא, וסומכוס סבר: אפילו בתוכה. ותניא אידך, המפלת חתיכה, ר' אחא אומר: קורעה, אם תוכה מאדים – טמאה, ואם לאו – טהורה. כסומכוס, ועדיפא מסומכוס. ותניא אידך, המפלת חתיכה, רבי בנימין אומר: קורעה, אם יש בה עצם – אמו טמאה לידה. אמר רב חסדא: ובחתיכה לבנה. וכן כי אתא *זוגא דמן חדייב, אתא ואייתי מתניתא בידיה: גהמפלת חתיכה לבנה – קורעה, אם יש בה עצם – אמו טמאה לידה. אמר רבי יוחנן משום רבי שמעון בן יוחי: דהמפלת חתיכה – קורעה, אם יש בה דם אגור – טמאה, ואם לאו – טהורה. כסומכוס וקילא מכולהו. בעא מיניה רבי ירמיה מרבי זירא: הרואה דם בשפופרת מהו? °"בבשרה" אמר רחמנא – ולא בשפופרת, או דלמא: האי *"בבשרה" מיבעי ליה – שמטמאה מבפנים כבחוץ? אמר ליה: ה"בבשרה" אמר רחמנא – ולא בשפופרת. דאי "בבשרה" מבעי ליה שמטמאה מבפנים כבחוץ, *א"כ נימא קרא (*"בבשר",) מאי "בבשרה" – שמע מינה תרתי. והא"ר יוחנן משום רבי שמעון בן יוחי: המפלת חתיכה – קורעה, אם יש בה דם אגור – טמאה, ואם לאו – טהורה! הכי השתא? התם – דרכה של אשה לראות דם בחתיכה, הכא – אין דרכה של אשה לראות דם בשפופרת. לימא שפופרת תנאי היא. דתניא: המפלת חתיכה, אף על פי שמלאה דם, אם יש עמה דם – טמאה, ואם לאו – טהורה. רבי אליעזר אומר: "בבשרה" – ולא בשפיר, ולא בחתיכה. ר' אליעזר היינו תנא קמא! אימא: שרבי אליעזר אומר "בבשרה" – ולא בשפיר ולא בחתיכה, וחכמים אומרים: אין זה דם נדה אלא דם חתיכה. תנא קמא נמי מטהרי מטהר! אלא דפלי פלויי איכא בינייהו, תנא קמא סבר: "בבשרה" – ולא בשפיר ולא בחתיכה, והוא הדין לשפופרת. והני מילי – היכא דשיעא, אבל פלי פלויי – טמאה, מאי טעמיה – "בבשרה" קרינא ביה. ואתו רבנן למימר: ואף על גב דפלי פלויי – אין זה דם נדה אלא דם חתיכה. הא דם נדה – ודאי טמא, ואפילו בשפופרת נמי! אמר אביי: בשפופרת כולי עלמא לא פליגי דטהורה,

כי

תורה אור

ויקרא טו

הרי זו ספק לידה וספק זיבה. ספק אם זיבה היא, וחייבת בקרבן זיבה. ספק אם לידה היא, וחייבת בקרבן לידה. ספק אינה לא לידה ולא זיבה, ואין עליה קרבן. כיצד? אם ילדה בשלישי ולד גמור – הרי כאן לידה ולא זיבה. ואפי' ראתה דם עם לידתה להשלים ג' ראיות, דקושי סמוך ללידה רחמנא טהרה, לקמן בפ' "בנות כותים" (דף לו.) "כי יזוב זוב דמה" – דמה מחמת עצמה, ולא מחמת ולד. ואם לא היה ולד, וראתה דם עם לידתה – הרי כאן זיבה גמורה. דהשתא לאו קושי סמוך ללידה הוא, דאין כאן לידה. ואם לא היה ולד, ולא ראתה דם – אין כאן לא לידה ולא זיבה, דשני ימים הוא דחזאי. הלכך מביאה קרבן אחד לאכול בקדשים – דשמא יולדת או זבה היא. ואינו נאכל חטאת העוף שלה – דשמא אינה לא יולדת ולא זבה. דאפשר לפתיחת הקבר בלא דם, ובשלישי לא חזאי, וולד נמי לא הואי – והאי קרבן מליקת חולין היא, ונבלה. שאי אפשר. הלכך, מה נפשך: אם ולד הוא – הרי כאן לידה, ואם אינו ולד – הרי כאן זיבה, דבשלישי חזאי. ועדיפא. חמירא. אם תוכה מאדים. הבשר מאדים, ואפי' אין שם דם ממש. כסומכוס. דאמר: תוכה כעמה. ועדיפא מדסומכוס, דאיהו בעי דם ממש. טמאה לידה. ויש לה ימי טוהר, ותשב לזכר ולנקבה ימי טומאה דנקבה וימי טוהר דזכר. לבנה. דהוא מין בשר. זוגא דמן חדייב. שני תלמידי חכמים מאותו מקום. אגור. דם הרבה. כסומכוס. דאמר: דם שבתוכו מטמא אותה משום נדה. וקילא מכולהון. מדסומכוס – דלא בעי אגור, ומדר' אחא – דאמר אפילו אין תוכה אלא מאדים. בשפופרת. הכניסה קנה חלול באותו מקום, ונמצא בתוכו דם. בבשרה. "דם יהיה זובה בבשרה" – שיצא דרך כותלי בית הרחם, ואין מפסיק. והאי קרא בנדה כתיב, ופרשה שניה נאמרה בזבה (ויקרא טו): "ואשה כי יזוב זוב דמה" וגו'. שמטמאה בפנים כבחוץ. מאחר שיצא מן המקור לפרוזדור, והעמידו כותליה – מיד היא מטמאה. משא"כ בזב ובעל קרי, דאין מטמאין עד שתצא טומאתן לחוץ. אם יש בה דם אגור כו'. ומאי שנא משפופרת? דרכה של אשה לראות דם בחתיכה. הלכך "בבשרה" קרינא ביה, דמין במינו – לא חייץ. שפיר. עור הולד קודם שנברא בתוכו גידים ועצמות ובשר. דפלי פלויי. שיש בה שורות שורות ביקועים מבחוץ, והדם שם. (ב) דת"ק. לא מטהר לה אלא מגזרת הכתוב, סבר: האי דם טהור הוא, ומשום חלילה היא טהורה, ומשום גזרת הכתוב. וה"ה לשפופרת, כיון דטעמא משום חלילה הוא. וה"מ דשיעא. חתיכה, והדם בתוכה לא נגע. אבל היכא דפלי פלויי. והדם שם ונוגע ברחם. טמאה. דקרינן "בבשרה". והיינו דקאמרי: אם יש עמה דם, דפלי פלויי – טמאה, ואם לאו – טהורה. ורבנן בתראי לא דייקי לישנא דקרא, והאי דמטהרי: משום דלאו דם נדה הוא. הלכך לא שנא בתוכה כי שיעא, ולא שנא פלי פלויי דנגע ברחם – טהורה. אבל שפופרת, דם נדה היא – טמאה. דלא דרשינן "בבשרה" אלא לטמאה בפנים כבחוץ. כולי עלמא לא פליגי (דטהורה. דאין דרך הרואה בכך).

כי

**באפשר** לפתיחת הקבר בלא דם קמיפלגי. להך לישנא תימה: ד"ג' מקומות" דקאמר ר' יוחנן לעיל (דף יח.) דהלכו חכמים אחר הרוב, למעוטי מאי?*. **בתוכה** מאדים. ואע"ג דלא האדים מבחוץ. ונראה דאם האדים מבחוץ, עדיף טפי, אפילו לא האדים מבפנים. כמו דםא] אגור, דבפנים אינו מועיל אלא לסומכוס, ומבחוץ – אפילו לרבנן. **זוזא**. פירש בערוך: שם חכם. **אם** יש בה עצם טמאה לידה. – והא דתנן הך קודם הא דדם אגור דמיירי נמי בנדה ולא בלידה – משום דתני כל דברייתא ברישא. **והאמר** רבי שמעון בן יוחי. וא"ת: וליסייעיה ממתני' דבעי עמה דם! וי"ל: היינו משום דקסבר דאינו דם נדות. **הא** דם נדה טמאה אפילו בשפופרת. וא"ת: מנליה הא, אימא הא דדם נדה טמאה משום דפלי פלויי, וקרינן ביה "בבשרה", כדמשני אביי לפירש"י? וי"ל: דנראה לו למקשה דרבנן פליגי אמאי דקאמר ר' אליעזר בהדיא "בבשרה" ולא בשפיר ולא בחתיכה. ואתו רבנן למימר: דלא מטעם "בבשרה" טהור, אלא משום דאינו דם נדות. הא אם היה דם נדות – טמאה, אפילו בשפופרת. דאי דם נדות טהור בשפופרת – אם כן, לא הוו פליגי רבנן אמאי דקאמר רבי אליעזר בהדיא.

[עי' תוס' לעיל יח: ד"ה למעוטי כו' כתבו ביתר ביאור]

ו א טוש"ע י"ד סי' קפח סעיף ג ועי' בהשגות בפ"ה מהל' איסורי ביאה הל' יג ובהגהות מיי' ריש פ"י:

ז ב מיי' פ"ה מהלכות איסורי ביאה הל' יג:

ח ג מיי' שם פ"י הל' ד סמג לאוין קיא טוש"ע י"ד סי' קצד סעיף ג:

ט ד מיי' שם פ"ה הל' יד סמג שם טור ש"ע י"ד סי' קפח סעיף ה:

י ה ו מיי' שם הל' יג ועי' בהשגות ובכ"מ ובכ"מ סמג שם טוש"ע י"ד סי' קפח סעיף ג:

גליון הש"ס

**גמ'** סומכוס אומר משום ר"מ. לקמן כה ע"א:

נ"ל זוזא וכ"ה בתוס' ועי' רש"א [וכ"ג הערוך זוזא ופי' שם אדם ולא כרש"י דגרס זוגא ופי' שני ת"ח וכו' ולפירושו מלת אתא ואייתי בידיה ק"ק דאתו ואייתי בידייהו הל"ל]

[לקמן מ: מא: נז:]

[לקמן נז:] ס"א בשרה

הגהות מהר"ב רנשבורג

א] תוס' ד"ה בתוכה מאדים וכו' לא האדים מבפנים כמו דם אגור מלת אגור נמחק:

רש"ל מ"ז וגרס לדייקין לישנא דקרא

[לקמן כב: לח. סו. כריתות י.]

נ"ל ר' יוחנן רש"ל [לקמן כב:]

הגהות הב"ח

(א) גמ' למאן קתני לה: (ב) רש"י ד"ה דפלי וד"ה דת"ק וכו' סבר האי דם טמא הוא כצ"ל והד"א:

## תוספי הרא"ש

**המפלת** חתיכה. הרי זו ספק לידה ספק זיבה אי סבירא ליה יש קושי לנפלים ניחא דאינה מביאה אלא קרבן אחד אבל אי סבר דאין קושי לנפלים צריכה להביא שני קרבנות דדילמא הויא זבה ויולדת וקרבן לידה וקרבן זיבה לא שריכי אהדדי ליפטר בקרבן אחד כדאיתא בפ"ב דכריתות ולקמן ביוצא דופן מידי דהוה אאכל חלב ודם ואיכא לפרש הא דקאמר מביאה קרבן ואינו נאכל מביאה על כל ספק שלה קרבן ואין אחד מהן נאכל. ור' יהושע סבר דאחד מן הקרבנות נאכל דודאי זבה היא אבל ספק לידה היא לפיכך אינו נאכל: **מאי** בבשרה ש"מ תרתי. ולקמן בריש הרואה כתם פריך דמיבעי ליה בבשר עד שתרגיש בבשרה וכשני תרתי ש"מ וצ"ל דכולה שמעינן מיניה ממיעוט דה"א שמעינן למעוטי שפופרת ומבי"ת שמעינן שמטמא בפנים כבחוץ דמשמע בעודו בבשר טמאה וממשמעות דבשר שמעינן שתרגיש בבשרה: הא דם נדה ודאי טמא אפילו בשפופרת דס"ד השתא דאין חילוק בין חתיכה לשפופרת כמו דאמרינן בחתיכה א' הוי דם א)נדה טמא משום דפלא אפלויי ובבשרה קרינא ביה וי"ל דתלמודא דייק מתוך דבריהם דהכי סבירא להו משום דפליגי באיזה טעם נטהר היכא דשיע דר' אליעזר מטהר מדרשא דקרא ומשמע ליה דאתו רבנן למימר דלאו מן השם הוא זה אלא משמע דאין זה דם נדה אלא דם חתיכה. הילכך לר' אליעזר דמטהר מדרשא דקרא משום חציצה היכא דפלא אפלויי קרינא ביה בבשרה וטמאה ולרבנן דלא דרשי למעט היכא דלא נגע בבשרה ומטהרי משום דאין זה דם נדה ושפופרת טמאה דלא בעי' שיגע בבשרה ובבשרה דרשי ליה לטמאות בפנים כבחוץ ולא מפליג השתא בין חתיכה לשפופרת: ב)**אין** דרכה של אשה לראות דם בחתיכה ואפילו דפלא אפלויי משום דאין זה דם נדה אלא דם חתיכה וקשה דהשתא לא הוי הך דאין דרכה של אשה לראות דם בחתיכה כמו אין דרכה של אשה לראות דם בשפופרת דההוא הוי מטעם הפסקה והכא משום דאין זה דם נדה. וע"ק דא"כ הו"ל למימר לרבנן דאין זה דם נדה כדקאמרינן מעיקרא. וע"ק כיון דאביי לא בא לחדש בדבריו אלא לחלק בין שפופרת לחתיכה ופליגי בחתיכה כדפליגי מעיקרא א"כ לא הו"ל למימר אלא בשפופרת כ"ע לא פליגי כו' כי פליגי בחתיכה. ופי' השר מקוצי דבהא פליגי ר' אליעזר ורבנן דר' אליעזר סבר דרכה של אשה לראות כו' וכיון שרואה כדרך שהנשים רואות טמאה ורבנן סברי אין דרכה של אשה לראות דם בחתיכה ואע"ג דפלי אפלויי וכיון שלא ראתה כדרך שהנשים דרכן לראות טהורה אע"ג דהוי דם נדה וגם נוגע בבשרה ופליגי ר' אליעזר ורבנן בקרא דדרשינן בבשרה ולא בשפופרת דר' אליעזר סבר דממעטינן שפופרת משום הפסקה וכן חתיכה היכא שאין הדם נוגע בבשר אבל אי פלי איפלויי קרינא שפיר בבשרה ורבנן סברי דטעמא דשפופרת משום שאין דרכה של אשה לראות כך וכן בחתיכה נמי אפילו אי אפלאי אפלויי ולפי שאין דרך הנשים לראות כך והאי דקאמרי אין זה דם נדה הכי קאמרי אין דם נדה רגיל לבא בזה הענין וכן עשה מעשה השר מקוצי באשה שנעקר מקור שלה וכמין חתיכת בשר נפל לה בבית החיצון ולא היתה פוסקת לראות כל זמן שאותה חתיכה היתה בבית החיצון וטיהר אותה לבעלה כיון דאין דרך נשים לראות כן:

א) חסר כאן בדברי רבינו וכן נ"ל אי הוי דם נדה טמא ה"נ בשפופרת וא"ת מנליה הא אימא הא דדם נדה טמאה משום דפלי פלויי וקרינן ביה בבשרה וי"ל וכו'. ב) שייך לדף שאח"ז

כִּי פְּלִיגֵי בַּחֲתִיכָה. מָר סָבַר דַּרְכָּהּ שֶׁל אִשָּׁה לִרְאוֹת דָּם בַּחֲתִיכָה, וּמָר סָבַר אֵין דַּרְכָּהּ שֶׁל אִשָּׁה לִרְאוֹת דָּם בַּחֲתִיכָה. רָבָא אָמַר: דְּכוּלֵּי עָלְמָא אֵין דַּרְכָּהּ שֶׁל אִשָּׁה לִרְאוֹת דָּם בַּחֲתִיכָה, וְהָכָא בְּאִשָּׁה טְהוֹרָה *וּמָקוֹר מְקוֹמוֹ טָמֵא קָמִיפַּלְגִי. דְּר' אֱלִיעֶזֶר סָבַר: אִשָּׁה טְהוֹרָה, וְדָם טָמֵא דְּהָא אָתֵי דֶּרֶךְ מָקוֹר. וְרַבָּנַן סָבְרִי: אִשָּׁה טְהוֹרָה, וּמָקוֹר מְקוֹמוֹ טָהוֹר. בְּעָא מִינֵּיהּ רַבָּה מֵרַב הוּנָא: הָרוֹאֶה קֶרִי בְּקֵיסָם מַהוּ? °"מִמֶּנּוּ" אָמַר רַחֲמָנָא עַד דְּנָפֵיק מִבְּשָׂרוֹ וְלֹא בְּקֵיסָם. אוֹ דִּלְמָא הַאי "מִמֶּנּוּ" עַד שֶׁתֵּצֵא טוּמְאָתוֹ לַחוּץ, [א]וַאֲפִי' בְּקֵיסָם נַמִי? אֲמַר לֵיהּ: תֵּיפּוֹק לֵיהּ דְּהוּא עַצְמוֹ אֵינוֹ מְטַמֵּא אֶלָּא *[ב]בַּחֲתִימַת פִּי הָאַמָּה. לְמֵימְרָא דְּנוֹגֵעַ הָוֵי? אֶלָּא מֵעַתָּה — אַל יִסְתּוֹר בְּזִיבָה! אַלְמָה תַּנְיָא: °"זֹאת תּוֹרַת הַזָּב וַאֲשֶׁר תֵּצֵא מִמֶּנּוּ שִׁכְבַת זֶרַע" מַה זִּיבָה סוֹתֶרֶת — [ג]אַף שִׁכְבַת זֶרַע נַמִי סוֹתֵר? אֲמַר לֵיהּ: סְתִירָה, הַיְינוּ טַעְמָא דְּסוֹתֵר — *לְפִי שֶׁאִי אֶפְשָׁר לָהּ בְּלֹא צַחְצוּחֵי זִיבָה. אֶלָּא מֵעַתָּה תִּסְתּוֹר כָּל ז'! אַלְמָה תַּנְיָא: "זֹאת תּוֹרַת הַזָּב" וגו' מַה זִּיבָה סוֹתֶרֶת — אַף שִׁכְבַת זֶרַע סוֹתֵר, אִי מַה זִּיבָה סוֹתֶרֶת כָּל ז', אַף שִׁכְבַת זֶרַע נַמִי סוֹתֵר כָּל ז'? ת"ל °"לְטָמְאָה בָהּ" — אֵין לְךָ בָּהּ אֶלָּא מַה שֶּׁאָמוּר בָּהּ — [ד]סוֹתֶרֶת יוֹם אֶחָד? אֲמַר לֵיהּ: גְּזֵירַת הַכָּתוּב הִיא, זִיבָה גְּמוּרָה דְּלָא עָרְבָה בָּהּ שִׁכְבַת זֶרַע — סוֹתֶרֶת כָּל שִׁבְעָה, צַחְצוּחֵי זִיבָה דְּעָרְבָה בָּהּ שִׁכְבַת זֶרַע — לֹא סוֹתֶרֶת אֶלָּא יוֹם אֶחָד. בְּעָא מִינֵּיהּ ר' יוֹסֵי בְּרַבִּי חֲנִינָא מֵרַבִּי אֶלְעָזָר: דָּם יָבֵשׁ מַהוּ? °"כִּי יָזוּב זוֹב דָּמָהּ" אָמַר רַחֲמָנָא — עַד דְּמִידַּב דָּיֵיב לֵיהּ, לַח — אִין, יָבֵשׁ — לָא, אוֹ דִּלְמָא: הַאי "כִּי יָזוּב זוֹב דָּמָהּ" — אוֹרְחָא דְּמִילְּתָא הִיא, [ה]וּלְעוֹלָם אֲפִילּוּ יָבֵשׁ נַמִי? א"ל: תְּנֵיתוּהָ, *[ו]דַּם הַנִּדָּה [ז]וּבְשַׂר הַמֵּת — מְטַמְּאִין לַחִים וִיבֵשִׁים. אֲמַר לֵיהּ: לַח וְנַעֲשָׂה יָבֵשׁ לָא קָא מִיבָּעֲיָא לִי, כִּי מִיבָּעֲיָא לִי — יָבֵשׁ מֵעִיקָּרָא. [ח]הָא נַמִי תְּנֵיתוּהָ: *)הַמַּפֶּלֶת כְּמִין קְלִיפָּה, כְּמִין שְׂעָרָה, כְּמִין עָפָר, כְּמִין יַבְחוּשִׁין אֲדוּמִּין — תַּטִּיל לַמַּיִם, אִם

*) [לעיל כח. לקמן נז:]

תורה אור: ויקרא טו; שם; שם; שם
[לקמן נד:]

---

**רש"י**

כִּי פְּלִיגֵי בַּחֲתִיכָה. וּדְפָלֵי פַּלּוּיֵי. דְּת"ק סָבַר: "בִּבְשָׂרָהּ" – לְמַעוּטֵי תּוֹךְ חֲתִיכָה, אֲבָל דָּם הַנִּרְאֶה בַּבְּקָעִים – טָמֵא, דְּהָא "בִּבְשָׂרָהּ" קָרֵינַן בֵּיהּ. וְרַבָּנַן בַּתְרָאֵי סָבְרִי: אֲפִי' פָּלֵי פַּלּוּיֵי – טְהוֹרָה, דְּאֵין זֶה דַּם נִדָּה, דְּאֵין דַּרְכָּהּ שֶׁל אִשָּׁה לִרְאוֹת דָּם בַּחֲתִיכָה. אִשָּׁה טְהוֹרָה. דְּלָאו רְאִיָּיה הִיא. וּמִיהוּ טִיפַּת דָּם מְטַמְּאָה טְהָרוֹת אִם נָגְעָה בָּהֶן, וְאֶת הָאִשָּׁה טוּמְאַת עֶרֶב – מִשּׁוּם דְּנָגְעָה בַּמָּקוֹר. דִּקְרָא מְתוֹרַת רְאִיָּיה מְעַטֵיהּ, וְלָאו מְטוּמְאָה. וְרַבָּנַן סָבְרִי. דָּם נַמִי טָהוֹר. וְהָכִי קָאָמַר: אֵין זֶה דַּם נִדָּה (שֶׁתִּתֵּן שׁוּם טוּמְאָה עָלָיו) שֶׁאִילּוּ הָיָה דָּם – הָיָה לוֹ לְטַמְּאָה כְּנִדָּה, וְעַכְשָׁיו אֵין לוֹ שׁוּם טוּמְאָה אֶלָּא כַּחֲתִיכַת בָּשָׂר בְּעָלְמָא. הָרוֹאֶה קֶרִי בְּקֵיסָם. הִכְנִיס קֵיסָם בְּפִי אַמָּה, וְהוֹצִיא בּוֹ זַרְעוֹ. מִמֶּנּוּ. "אֲשֶׁר תֵּצֵא מִמֶּנּוּ שִׁכְבַת זֶרַע". הוּא עַצְמוֹ. וַאֲפִילּוּ בְּלֹא קֵיסָם. אֵינוֹ מְטַמֵּא אֶלָּא בַּחֲתִימַת פִּי הָאַמָּה. עַד שֶׁיֵּצֵא מִמֶּנּוּ כְּדֵי חֲתִימַת פִּי אַמָּתוֹ. וְהָכָא כֵּיוָן דְּהִכְנִיס לֵיהּ קֵיסָם – בָּצַר לֵיהּ שִׁיעוּרָא כְּדֵי קֵיסָם. לְמֵימְרָא דְּנוֹגֵעַ הָוֵי. מִדְּיָהֵיב שִׁיעוּרָא, מִכְּלָל דְּטוּמְאַת קֶרִי לָאו מִשּׁוּם רְאִיָּיה הִיא, אֶלָּא מִשּׁוּם דְּבָשָׂר הָאֵבֶר נוֹגֵעַ בְּשִׁכְבַת זֶרַע הַיּוֹצֵא מִמֶּנּוּ. וּמִשּׁוּם הָכִי בָּעֵי שִׁיעוּרָא, כְּטוּמְאַת כָּל מַגָּעוֹת דְּבָעֵי שִׁיעוּרָא, כְּגוֹן שֶׁרֶץ וּנְבֵלָה וָמֵת. דְּאִי רְאִיָּיה חֲשִׁיבָא לֵיהּ בְּטוּמְאַת רְאִיָּיה – לָא בָּעֵיָא שִׁיעוּרָא, דְּהָא נִדָּה רוֹאָה הִיא, וְלָא בָּעֵיָא שִׁיעוּרָא. אַל יִסְתּוֹר בְּזִיבָה. זָב שֶׁפָּסַק וְהִתְחִיל לִמְנוֹת ז' יְמֵי סְפִירוֹ, וְרָאָה קֶרִי – אַל יִסְתּוֹר אֶת מִנְיָנוֹ, כִּי הֵיכִי דְּאִי נָגַע בְּשֶׁרֶץ – לָא סָתַר לִסְפִירַת זִיבָתוֹ. אַלְמָה תַּנְיָא זֹאת תּוֹרַת הַזָּב. הִקִּישׁ הַכָּתוּב שִׁכְבַת זֶרַע לְזִיבָה. מַה זִּיבָה סוֹתֶרֶת. דִּכְתִיב: "וְסָפְרָה לָּהּ וְאַחַר תִּטְהָר" – אַחַר אַחַר לְכוּלָּן, שֶׁלֹּא תְּהֵא טוּמְאָה מַפְסֶקֶת בֵּינֵיהֶם, אַף שִׁכְבַת זֶרַע – סוֹתֵר. לְפִי שֶׁאִי אֶפְשָׁר. לִרְאוֹת שִׁכְבַת זֶרַע הַבָּאָה מִן הַזָּב בְּלֹא טִיפַּת נִתְלוֹתֵי זִיבָה, דְּהַשְׁתָּא קָלַת זִיבָה דְּאִית בֵּיהּ קָא סָתַר. כָּל ז'. אִם רָאָה בַּשְּׁבִיעִי – סוֹתֵר כָּל אוֹתָן יָמִים שֶׁסָּפַר. אֶלָּא מַה שֶּׁאָמוּר בָּהּ. בְּשִׁכְבַת זֶרַע לְעִנְיַן טוּמְאָה. מַה טוּמְאָתָהּ – יוֹם אֶחָד, אַף סְתִירָתָהּ – אֵינָהּ סוֹתֶרֶת אֶלָּא אוֹתוֹ יוֹם, וְאִם רָאָה בַּז' – אֵין צָרִיךְ לִסְפּוֹר עוֹד אֶלָּא יוֹם א'. דָּם יָבֵשׁ. כְּגוֹן שֶׁיָּצָא מְגוּפָהּ חֲתִיכָה שֶׁל דָּם יָבֵשׁ. זוֹב דָּמָהּ. מַשְׁמַע: לַח, שֶׁהֲרֵי אֵין דַּרְכּוֹ לָזוּב אֶלָּא לַח. לַח וְנַעֲשָׂה יָבֵשׁ. דְּהָא א] קָתָנֵי: "מְטַמְּאִין יְבֵשִׁין" כְּנָפַל דָּם לַח עַל הַבֶּגֶד, וְיָבֵשׁ, וְאַחַר כָּךְ נָגַע הַדָּם בִּטְהָרוֹת. דּוּמְיָא דְּיָבֵשׁ בְּשַׂר הַמֵּת, דְּיָבֵשׁ מֵעִיקָּרָא בְּשַׂר הַמֵּת לֵיכָּא. אִם

---

**תוספות**

כי פליגי בחתיכה. פ"ה: ודפלי פלויי. וקשה: דא"כ השתא "אין דרך לראות דם בחתיכה" פירוש: שאינו דם נדות, לא הוי כההוא ד"אין דרכה לראות בשפופרת". דהתם הוי דם נדות מן המקור, אלא שאין דרכה לראות באותו ענין! ויש *לומר: דפליגי בחתיכה העשויה כמין שפופרת, והוי אגילה בין דם לבשר. דת"ק מטמא – דדרכה לצאת בענין זה, ורבנן סברי: אע"ג דדם נדות הוא, אין דרכה לראות בענין זה, ואין זה "דם נדות" דקאמרי רבנן ה"פ: אין זה דם נדות שטימאה הכתוב. אבל בפלי פלויי – גם רבנן מטמאין, כיון דדם נדות הוא ונוגע בבשרה. **אלא** בחתימת פי האמה. אין לפרש דבעי שיעור חתימת פי האמה כר"ש דפ' "אלו דברים" (פסחים סז:) דסבר כר' נתן דבעי חתימת פי האמה בזב, דכתיב (ויקרא טו) "או החתים בשרו מזובו", ואיתקש בעל קרי לזב. דא"כ מאי פריך למימרא דנוגע הוי אלא מעתה לא יסתור בזיבה, הא כיון דאיתקש לזב – שפיר יסתור! והיכי דייק מינה דנוגע הוי? [ועוד: אי סבר כר' שמעון, מאי פריך רב הונא: ותיפוק ליה דהוא עצמו כו' והלא דרך קיסם יכול לראות הרבה מחתימת פי האמה] אלא נראה לפרש: דסבר כדתנן לקמן בפרק "יוצא דופן" (דף מ.) דזוב וקרי מטמאין בכל שהוא. והכי קאמר: צריך שיגע בחתימת פי האמה, משום דטומאת בית הסתרים לא מטמאה. לכך פריך: כיון דנוגע הוי, דקא מטהרת בקיסם עד שיגע בפי האמה, מעתה לא יסתור בזיבה.

(**למימרא** דנוגע הוי). וא"ת: ומנליה למקשה דרב הונא לא מצריך שיעור חתימת פי האמה כרבי שמעון? וי"ל: מדקאמר "ותיפוק ליה דהוא עצמו אינו מטמא אלא בחתימת פי האמה" ולא קאמר "כשיעור חתימה", ולא קאמר נמי דאיתקש לזב – שמע מינה דלא לשיעור נקטיה, אלא משום נגיעה. ועוד: אי סבר כרבי שמעון, מאי פריך רב הונא "ותיפוק ליה דהוא עצמו" כו', והלא דרך קיסם יכול לראות קרי הרבה יותר מחתימת פי האמה! וא"ת: ואם נוגע הוי, א"כ למ"ד בפרק "יוצא דופן" (לקמן דף מג:) לרואה ולנוגע בכל שהוא, למה לי דכתב רחמנא רואה? וי"ל: דעל ידי שנכתב רואה, הא דדרשינן בפרק "אלו דברים" (דף סו:) "זב" "וכל זב" – לרבות בעל קרי שמשתלח חוץ לב' מחנות, מוקמינן ברואה ולא בנוגע. ונפקא מינה הא דאמר הכא, דאפי' רואה אינו טמא אלא משום נוגע, שאינו טמא אלא בנגיעה מבחוץ. וא"ת: ומנלן דנוגע הוי, נגמר מדאחמיר ביה רחמנא לענין שילוח מחנות, אלמא רואה הוי! וכה"ג בעי למימר פרק "יוצא דופן" (לקמן דף מג.) גבי פולטת שכבת זרע דרואה הוי, מדאזהיר רחמנא על בעלי קריין בסיני. וי"ל: דילפינן דנוגע הוי, מדאיתקש לנוגע, דנוגע מרבינן א) מ"איש איש" בפ' "יוצא דופן" (שם דף מג.) ועוד: דבההוא קרא גופיה איתקש נמי לשרץ. וא"ת: ונוגע דכתב רחמנא למה לי, תיפוק ליה מ"והבגד אשר יהיה עליו שכבת זרע"? וי"ל: דאדם מבגד לא ילפינן, שהרי נושא נבלת בהמה מטמא בגדים שעליו אפילו אם אינו לבוש בהן, אבל אדם לא מטמא אפילו הוא עליו. והכי איתא בפרק קמא דבבא בתרא (דף ט:) גבי עולא משגש אורחא דאימיה. וא"ת: דלקמן בפרק "יוצא דופן" (דף מב.) אמרינן לרבנן דרבי שמעון, דאפילו פולטת שכבת זרע רואה הויא, ולכך מטמא בפנים כבחוץ. ור' שמעון נמי לא פליג אלא בפולטת שכבת זרע דלא מטמא בפנים כבחוץ, אבל בבעל קרי משמע דרואה הוי, דלא אשכחן דפליגי! וי"ל: דרב הונא סבר כרבי שמעון, דלדידיה אפי' בעל קרי נוגע הוי, דאי רואה הוי – אף בפולטת הוה דריש לטמא בפנים כבחוץ. ואפילו לרבנן נמי אפשר דדוקא פולטת רואה הויא ומטמא בפנים כבחוץ, משום דאשכחן בטומאת נדות וזיבות דמטמאה בפנים כבחוץ. אבל בועלה, דלא אשכחן ביה טומאה בפנים כבחוץ, לא הוי רואה. ומיהו ההיא דר' אליעזר ברבי שמעון פליגא, דאמר בפרק "יוצא דופן" (שם דף מג.) שכבת זרע, לרואה – במשהו, ולנוגע – בכעדשה. מדמפליג, משמע דסבר דרואה הוי. אי נמי: שאני התם דגמר טעמא מקרא. **אלא** מעתה לא יסתור בזיבה. תימה: תקשה ליה אמתני' דמסכת כלים (פ"א מ"א) דתנן: אבות הטומאה: השרץ והשכבת זרע, ולא חשיב בעל קרי! ותנן נמי בשלהי מסכת זבין: בעל קרי – כמגע שרץ, אלמא נוגע הוי, מדלא הוי אלא ראשון! ושמא אפי' רואה נמי לא הוי אב הטומאה משום דרשא. ומהאי טעמא מטמא ר' יהושע קרי של זב במשא. והא דלא מצריך קרא התם כי הכא, מפרש ר"ת: דהתם מיירי בשרואה זיבות בו ביום, דאז יש בו רוב זיבות, וסבר ר' יהושע דלא אפשר בלא נתלותי זיבה בעין. ורבי אליעזר דפליג עליה ב"כיצד הרגל" (ב"ק דף כה.) ואמר דאינו מטמא במשא, מודה דאי אפשר בלא ניתלותי זיבה, ואפילו הכי לא מטמא במשא, דכיון דפתיכא ביה שכבת זרע. והכא נמי אי לאו קרא, לא הוה סותר אפילו יום אחד.

א) [נ"ל מאו איש]

---

**תוספי הרא"ש**

**ודם** טמא דקא אתי דרך מקור. פי' חתיכה ודם שבתוכה טמא משום שנגע במקור אע"ג שאין עליה לא תורת אוכל ולא תורת משקה מידי דהוה אמקור שהזיע כשני טיפי מרגליות דא"ר יוחנן לקמן בפ' יוצא דופן דטמאין משום דמקור מקומו טמא ואע"ג דלא חשיבי משקה דלא עדיף מדם ירוק דאמרינן לעיל בסוף כל היד דלא הוי משקה לרבנן. ודבר תימה הוא אפילו יהבת להו תורת אוכל או תורת משקה היאך חוזרין ומטמאין את האשה לטומאת ערב כדאיתא פרק יוצא דופן והלא אינו אלא ראשון בעלמא מחמת נגיעת המקור וצ"ל דהלכות מקור הל"מ הם: **בעא** מיניה רבה מרב הונא ול"ג רבא שלא ראה רב הונא מעולם דביום שמת רב יהודה נולד רבא. וכתוב בכתב רב שרירא דרב יהודה מלך אחר רב הונא ב' שנים. וכן יש להביא ראיה מההיא דאמרינן בפ' בתרא דמועד קטן גברא רבה כרב יהודה ליתא דלישרי לך זיל גבי נשיאה ורב הונא היה גדול מרב יהודה כדאמרינן ריש פרק בתרא דקידושין ובפ' בתרא דגיטין תנן בעא מיניה שמואל מרב הונא: **הרואה** קרי בקיסם חלול ולא נקט שפופרת משום דפי האמה דחוק הוא ותיפוק לי דהוא עצמו אינו מטמא אלא בחתימת פי האמה דבעינן שיצא בדוחק כדי שיגע בראש פי האמה בגלוי דלא ליהוי מגע בית הסתרים והא דתנן לקמן פרק יוצא דופן ומטמאין בכל שהן מוקי לה רב הונא בנוגע בה ולא בעי לשנויי דמתניתין דלקמן ורב הונא דהכא כר' נתן דאמר התם בגמרא דזב צריך בחתימת פי האמה ואמרינן בפסחים דה"ה לבעל קרי דאיתקש לזב דא"כ היכי דייק הכא למימר דנוגע הוי דהא דבעי ר' נתן בחתימת פי האמה לאו משום דנוגע הוי אלא משום דבעי שיעור כחתימת פי האמה ואכתי תיקשי לך היכי דייק מינה דנוגע הוי דילמא הא דבעי בחתימת פי האמה היינו משום דס"ל כר' נתן וי"ל דא"כ מאי קא"ל רב הונא לרבה ותיפוק לי וכו' והלא דרך קיסם יכול לראות קרי הרבה יותר מחתימת פי האמה: **למימרא** דנוגע הוי ותימה למה לי דכתב רחמנא רואה כלל הא הוי בכלל נוגע בקרא וי"ל משום שיש דברים שרואה חמור מנוגע כגון לענין שילוח מחנות דבעל קרי משולח הוא לשתי מחנות כדאיתא פרק אלו דברים וע"י שנכתב מרבינן ליה מוזב וכל זב לרבות בעל קרי וא"ת הא דדרשינן לקרא בפ' יוצא דופן או איש לרבות את הנוגע למה לי תיפוק לי מוהבגד אשר יהיה עליו שכבת זרע וי"ל דאדם מבגדים לא ילפי' כדאיתא בפ"א דב"ב ובהכי מיתרצא נמי פירכא קמייתא. וא"ת וניגמר מדאחמור רחמנא בבעלי קריין לענין שילוח מחנות אלמא רואה הוי דהא גבי פולטת שכבת זרע משמע בפ' יוצא דופן דהוה אמרינן דרואה הויא מדאחמור רחמנא אבעלי קריין בסיני אי לאו משום דסיני חידוש הוא דהא זבין ומצורעין חמירי ולא חמיר בהו רחמנא וי"ל דמ"מ הואיל מדאחמור לענין בעל קרי. וא"ה לא אמרינן דפולטת רואה הויא גם לענין שאר בעל קרי אם החמיר עליו שלא יכנס במקום קדוש לא גמרינן מיניה דרואה הויא ועי"ל דילפינן בעל קרי דנוגע הוי משום דאיתקש לנוגע דמרבינן נוגע מדכתיב או איש ועוד דאיתקש נמי לשרץ בההוא קרא גופיה: **אלא** מעתה אל יסתור בזיבה. תימה תיקשי ליה מתניתין טובא דקסבר דנוגע הוי דתנן בריש מס' כלים אבות הטומאות השרץ וש"ז ולא חשיב בעל קרי ועוד תנן במס' זבין ומייתי לה בפ' אלו דברים בעל קרי כמגע שרץ אלמא נוגע הוי מדלא הוי אלא ראשון וצ"ל דאפילו אי אמרינן רואה הוי לא הוי אב הטומאה ונפקא מינה דרואה הוי דמטמא מבפנים בלא נגיעה מבחוץ. ומיהו קשה דאפילו פולטת ש"ז אמרינן לקמן פ' יוצא דופן לרבנן דר' שמעון דמטמאה בפנים כבחוץ משום דרואה הויא ואפילו ר' שמעון לא פליג אלא בפולטת אבל בבעל קרי לא אשכחן דפליגי וי"ל דאפילו לרבנן דוקא פולטת דמרבי לה מקרא כדאיתא לקמן בבשרה מלמד שמטמאה בפנים כבחוץ אין לי אלא נדה זבה מנין ת"ל זובה ופולטת ש"ז מנין ת"ל יהיה אבל בעל קרי אפילו לרבנן נוגע הוי כיון דאינו מטמא אלא בחוץ והא דאמר ר' אלעזר בר' שמעון בפ' יוצא דופן לרואה במשהו ולנוגע בכעדשה אע"ג דקא מפליג בין נוגע לרואה א"ה בעל קרי לא הוי רואה אלא נוגע והא דמטמא במשהו מקרא יליף לה התם: **אף** ש"ז נמי סותרת. משמע דאי לאו קרא לא סתרא אע"ג דלא אפשר לה בלא צחצוחי זיבה וקשה דבסוף כיצד הרגל א"ר יהושע ש"ז של זב מטמא במשא לפי שאי אפשר לה בלא צחצוחי זיבה ואמאי לא מצרכינן התם קרא כי הכא וליכא למימר דמהכא ילפינן דאי אפשר בלא צחצוחי זיבה מדסתרא כמו זיבה דהא מילתא דתליא בסברא הוא ולא בעיא קרא כדאמרינן בבעל קרי שלא הטיל מים וביבמה שרקקה דם. וא"ה בעי קרא דסתרא בזיבה לענין משא אמאי לא מצריך קרא ור"ת תירץ דמיירי התם ביום שראתה זיבה ראה קרי מטמא במשא לפי שיש רוב זיבות בעין הלכך לא בעי קרא וכיוצא בזה מצינן בתחילת מס' זבין ברואה קרי בשני ובשלישי לספירתו ב"ש אומרים סתר הימים שלפניו ובה"א לא סתר אלא יומו ומודים ברואה ברביעי שלא סתר אלא יומו והיינו טעמא דב"ש דבשני ובשלישי אי אפשר בלא זיבות הרבה בעין ועי"ל דהכא לא איצטריך קרא אלא למימר דאינה סותרת כל ז' ואי לאו קרא היה סותר כל ז' משום דאי אפשר בלא צחצוחי זיבה

---

**מסורת הש"ס**

לעיל טז. וש"נ
[לקמן מג: פסחים סז:]
[נזיר סו. ב"ק כה.]

**גליון הש"ס**

**רש"י** ד"ה מה זיבה וכו' ואחר תטהר אחר וכו'. לקמן לג ע"ב ודף סז ע"ב: **ד"ה** אלא מה כו' אלא יום א'. עי' ברא"ש במכילתין פ"ד סי' א':

**הגהות מהר"ב רנשבורג**

א] רש"י ד"ה לח ונעשה יבש דהא דקתני מטמאין וכו' כצ"ל:

**עין משפט נר מצוה**

יא א ב מיי' פ"ה מהל' שאר אבות הטומאות הלכה א ועי' כס"מ:
נ"א לפרש
יב ג ד מיי' פ"ג מהל' מחוסרי כפרה הלכה א ב:
יג ה מיי' פ"ה מהלכות איסורי ביאה הלכה יד סמג לאוין קיא טוש"ע י"ד סימן קפח סעיף ד:
יד ו מיי' פ"ב מהלכות מטמאי משכב ומושב הלכה א סמג עשין רמג:
טו ז מיי' פ"ב מהלכות טומאת המת הלכה א:
טז ח מיי' פ"ה מהל' איסורי ביאה הלכה יד סמג לאוין קיא טוש"ע י"ד סימן קפח סעיף ד:
נ"י כ"י
ר"מ מ"ז והכל ד"א

יז א ב ג מיי' פ"ה מהל' איסורי ביאה הלכה יד ועי' בכ"מ סמג לאוין קיא טוש"ע י"ד סימן קפח סעיף ד:

אִם נְמוֹחוּ — טְמֵאָה. [א] אִי הָכִי — בְּלֹא נְמוֹחוּ נַמִּי! אָמַר רַבָּה: כִּי לֹא נְמוֹחוּ — בְּרִיָּה בִּפְנֵי עַצְמָהּ הִיא. וּמִי אִיכָּא כִּי הַאי גַּוְונָא? אִין, וְהָתַנְיָא, *א"ר אֶלְעָזָר בְּר' צָדוֹק, שְׁנֵי מַעֲשִׂים הֶעֱלָה אַבָּא מִטִּבְעִין לְיַבְנֶה: מַעֲשֶׂה בְּאִשָּׁה שֶׁהָיְתָה מַפֶּלֶת כְּמִין קְלִיפּוֹת אֲדוּמּוֹת, וּבָאוּ וְשָׁאֲלוּ אֶת אַבָּא, וְאַבָּא שָׁאַל לַחֲכָמִים, וַחֲכָמִים שָׁאֲלוּ לָרוֹפְאִים, וְאָמְרוּ לָהֶם: אִשָּׁה זוֹ מַכָּה יֵשׁ לָהּ בְּתוֹךְ מֵעֶיהָ שֶׁמִּמֶּנָּה מַפֶּלֶת כְּמִין קְלִיפּוֹת, תַּטִּיל לַמַּיִם, אִם נְמוֹחוּ — טְמֵאָה. וְשׁוּב מַעֲשֶׂה בְּאִשָּׁה שֶׁהָיְתָה מַפֶּלֶת כְּמִין שְׂעָרוֹת אֲדוּמּוֹת, וּבָאָה וְשָׁאֲלָה אֶת אַבָּא, וְאַבָּא שָׁאַל לַחֲכָמִים, וַחֲכָמִים לָרוֹפְאִים, וְאָמְרוּ לָהֶם: שׁוּמָא יֵשׁ לָהּ בְּתוֹךְ מֵעֶיהָ, שֶׁמִּמֶּנָּה מַפֶּלֶת כְּמִין שְׂעָרוֹת אֲדוּמּוֹת, תַּטִּיל לַמַּיִם, אִם נְמוֹחוּ — טְמֵאָה. אָמַר רֵישׁ לָקִישׁ: [א]וּבְפוֹשְׁרִין. תַּנְיָא נַמִּי הָכִי: תַּטִּיל לַמַּיִם, וּבְפוֹשְׁרִין. רשב"ג אוֹמֵר: מְמַעַכְתּוֹ בְּרוֹק עַל גַּבֵּי הַצִּפּוֹרֶן. מַאי בֵּינַיְיהוּ? אָמַר רָבִינָא: [ב]מָעוּךְ עַל יְדֵי הַדְּחָק אִיכָּא בֵּינַיְיהוּ. הָתָם תְּנַן: *כַּמָּה הִיא שְׁרִיָּיתָן בְּפוֹשְׁרִין — מֵעֵת לְעֵת, הָכָא מַאי? מִי בָּעֵינָא מֵעֵת לְעֵת, אוֹ לָא? שֶׁרֶץ וּנְבֵלָה דְּאַקּוּשֵׁי — בָּעֵינַן מֵעֵת לְעֵת, אֲבָל דָּם דְּרַכִּיךְ — לָא, אוֹ דִּלְמָא לָא שְׁנָא? [ג]תֵּיקוּ. § "הַמַּפֶּלֶת כְּמִין דָּגִים". § וְלִיפְלוֹג נַמִּי רַבִּי יְהוּדָה בְּהָא! אָמַר רֵישׁ לָקִישׁ: בְּמַחֲלוֹקֶת שְׁנוּיָה, וְרַבָּנַן הִיא. וְרַבִּי יוֹחָנָן אָמַר: אֲפִילּוּ תֵּימָא רַבִּי יְהוּדָה. עַד כָּאן לָא קָאָמַר רַבִּי יְהוּדָה הָתָם אֶלָּא גַּבֵּי חֲתִיכָה — דְּעָבֵיד דָּם דְּקָרֵישׁ וְהָוֵי חֲתִיכָה, אֲבָל בְּרִיָּה — לָא הָוֵי. וּלְהַךְ לִישָּׁנָא דְּא"ר *יוֹחָנָן: בְּאִי אֶפְשָׁר לִפְתִיחַת הַקֶּבֶר בְּלֹא דָּם קָמִיפַּלְגִי, לִפְלוֹג נַמִּי ר' יְהוּדָה בְּהָא! מַאן דְּמַתְנֵי הַךְ לִישָּׁנָא מַתְנֵי הָכִי: רַבִּי יוֹחָנָן וְרֵישׁ לָקִישׁ דְּאָמְרִי תַּרְוַיְיהוּ בְּמַחֲלוֹקֶת שְׁנוּיָה, וְרַבָּנַן הִיא. § "הַמַּפֶּלֶת כְּמִין בְּהֵמָה" [וכו']. § אָמַר רַב יְהוּדָה, אָמַר שְׁמוּאֵל: מ"ט דְּר' מֵאִיר — הוֹאִיל וְנֶאֶמְרָה בּוֹ יְצִירָה כְּאָדָם. אֶלָּא מֵעַתָּה, הַמַּפֶּלֶת דְּמוּת תַּנִּין תְּהֵא אִמּוֹ טְמֵאָה לֵידָה הוֹאִיל וְנֶאֱמַר בּוֹ יְצִירָה כְּאָדָם, שֶׁנֶּאֱמַר: °"וַיִּבְרָא אֱלֹהִים אֶת הַתַּנִּינִם הַגְּדוֹלִים"! אָמְרִי: דָּנִין יְצִירָה מִיצִירָה, וְאֵין דָּנִין בְּרִיאָה מִיצִירָה. מַאי נָפְקָא מִינָּהּ? הָא *תָּנָא דְּבֵי רַבִּי יִשְׁמָעֵאל: °"וְשָׁב הַכֹּהֵן" °"וּבָא הַכֹּהֵן" זוֹ הִיא שִׁיבָה זוֹ הִיא בִּיאָה! וְעוֹד: נִגְמַר בְּרִיאָה מִבְּרִיאָה, דִּכְתִיב °"וַיִּבְרָא אֱלֹהִים אֶת הָאָדָם בְּצַלְמוֹ"! אָמְרִי: "וַיִּבְרָא" — לְגוּפֵיהּ, "וַיִּיצֶר" לְאַפְנוּיֵי, וְדָנִין יְצִירָה מִיצִירָה. אַדְּרַבָּה: "וַיִּיצֶר" — לְגוּפֵיהּ, "וַיִּבְרָא" לְאַפְנוּיֵי, וְדָנִין בְּרִיאָה מִבְּרִיאָה! אֶלָּא "וַיִּיצֶר" מוּפְנֶה מִשְּׁנֵי צְדָדִין, מוּפְנֶה גַּבֵּי אָדָם וּמוּפְנֶה גַּבֵּי בְּהֵמָה. "וַיִּבְרָא" — גַּבֵּי אָדָם מוּפְנֶה, גַּבֵּי תַּנִּינִים אֵינוֹ מוּפְנֶה. מַאי מוּפְנֶה גַּבֵּי בְּהֵמָה? אִילֵימָא מִדִּכְתִיב: °"וַיַּעַשׂ אֱלֹהִים אֶת חַיַּת הָאָרֶץ", וּכְתִיב: °"וַיִּצֶר [ה'] אֱלֹהִים מִן הָאֲדָמָה כָּל חַיַּת הַשָּׂדֶה" — גַּבֵּי תַּנִּין נַמִּי אַפְנוּיֵי מוּפְנֶה, דִּכְתִיב: °"וְאֵת כָּל רֶמֶשׂ הָאֲדָמָה", וּכְתִיב: °"וַיִּבְרָא אֱלֹהִים אֶת הַתַּנִּינִם הַגְּדוֹלִים"! "רֶמֶשׂ" דִּכְתִיב הָתָם — דְּיַבָּשָׁה הוּא. וּמַאי נָפְקָא מִינָּהּ בֵּין מוּפְנֶה מִצַּד אֶחָד לְמוּפְנֶה מִשְּׁנֵי צְדָדִין? נָפְקָא מִינָּהּ דְּאָמַר רַב יְהוּדָה אָמַר שְׁמוּאֵל *מִשּׁוּם רַבִּי יִשְׁמָעֵאל: כָּל גְּזֵרָה שָׁוָה שֶׁאֵינָהּ מוּפְנָה כָּל עִיקָּר — אֵין לְמֵדִין הֵימֶנָּה. מוּפְנָה מִצַּד אֶחָד, °לְרַבִּי יִשְׁמָעֵאל — *לְמֵדִין וְאֵין מוֹשִׁיבִין, לְרַבָּנַן — לְמֵדִין וּמְשִׁיבִין. מוּפְנָה מִשְּׁנֵי צְדָדִין, דִּבְרֵי הַכֹּל — לְמֵדִין וְאֵין מְשִׁיבִין. וְרַבִּי יִשְׁמָעֵאל, מַאי אִיכָּא בֵּין מוּפְנֶה מִצַּד אֶחָד לְמוּפְנֶה מִשְּׁנֵי צְדָדִין? נָפְקָא מִינָּהּ דְּהֵיכָא דְּאִיכָּא מוּפְנֶה מִצַּד אֶחָד וּמוּפְנֶה מִשְּׁנֵי צְדָדִין, שָׁבְקִינַן מוּפְנֶה מִצַּד אֶחָד וְיָלְפִינַן

תורה אור: בראשית א | ויקרא יד | שם | בראשית א | שם | שם ב | שם א | שם

**רש"י**

אם נמוחו טמאין. דדם הוא. אלמא, אע"ג דכי חזיתיה יבש היה כעפר. בריה בפני עצמה. ולא דם. כי האי גוונא. מפלת כמין שערות וקליפות. מטבעין. שם העיר. קליפות. גלדי המכה. דרך שומא. להיות בה שער. ובפושרין. דאי בדק בצונן, ולא נימוח — לא מטהרינן לה בהכי, דדילמא אי הוה בפושרין הוה נימוח. מאי ביניהו. מאי פלוגתייהו? ע"י הדחק. לת"ק, אי נימוח מאליו — הוא דהוי דם, אבל נימוח על ידי מיעוך — לאו דם הוא. ולרבן שמעון, אפילו נימוח ע"י מיעוך — נמי דם הוא. כמה היא שרייתן. בפ' "דם הנדה": השרץ והנבלה מטמאין לחין, ואין מטמאין יבשין. ואם יכולין להשרות ולחזור לכמות שהיו — טמאין. וכמה היא שרייתן כו'. דאקושי. קשים. לא. בעינן מעת לעת, אלא או יום או לילה, ואם לא נמוחו — טהורים. וליפלוג נמי ר' יהודה בהא. ולימא: בין כך ובין כך — טמאה. דהא טעמא דר' יהודה אוקמינן דאי אפשר לפתיחת הקבר בלא דם! במחלוקת שנויה. משנה זו שנויה במחלוקת, דלאו סתמא ודברי הכל היא, אלא ר' יהודה פליג. והוי חתיכה. דטעמא לאו משום פתיחת הקבר בלא דם הוא, אלא בחתיכה עצמה סבירא ליה דהויא דם, וכגון שהיא מארבעה מיני דמים. ולהך לישנא כו'. כדאמרן לעיל בשמעתין. יצירה. "וייצר ה' אלהים *(את) חית השדה ואת עוף" וגו', וכתיב באדם: "וייצר ה' אלהים את האדם עפר מן האדמה". ורבנן לית להו גזירה שוה. תנין. דג גדול, ואמאי תנן: המפלת מין דגים — טהורה? זו היא שיבה זו היא ביאה. כלומר, ילפינן גזירה שוה משיבה לביאה, כמו דהוו תרוייהו שיבה או תרוייהו ביאה. מה שיבה — חולץ וקוצה וטח כו'. ועוד גבי אדם נמי כתיב בריאה. דכתיב: "ויברא אלהים את האדם בצלמו", ונילף בריאת דגים מבריאת אדם? ויברא. דאדם לגופיה. וייצר לאפנויי. לגזירה שוה, ודנין ג"ש לחיה ולעוף, דכתיב בהו יצירה, דדמי מדדמי. מופנה. גבי אדם, דהא כתיב "ויברא". ומופנה גבי בהמה. כדמפרש, דהא כתיב: "ויעש אלהים את חית" (השדה) וגו'. גבי אדם מופנה. דהא כתיב "וייצר". גבי תנין לאו מופנה. דלא כתיב קרא אחרינא. ופרכינן: גבי תנין נמי מופנה הוא. דכתיב בקרא דויעש: "ואת כל רמש האדמה". ומאי נפקא מינה. דניחא לך למילף משני צדדין טפי? כל ג"ש שאינה מופנה כל עיקר אין למדין הימנה. ואפילו אין להשיב. אין משיבין. ואפי' יש להשיב. לרבנן למדין הימנה. אם אין להשיב, ואם יש להשיב — משיבין. והך פלוגתא דרבי ישמעאל ורבנן, שמואל גמרא גמיר ליה מרביה, וכאן הוא מקומה, ואינה לא במשנה ולא בברייתא.

להכי

**תוספות**

**אם** נמוחו טמאה. וא"ת: והא לא מיקרי "יבש", דהא הנך דתנן בפ' "דם הנדה" (לקמן דף נד:) דמטמאין לחים ואין מטמאין יבשים, תני התם: אם יכולים לשרות ולחזור לכמות שהיו — מטמאין, כדאמר התם? ויש לומר: דמכל מקום פשיט שפיר דלא אמר "כי יזוב זוב דמה" דמידב דייב. אי נמי: התם איירי בלחים ונתייבשו. ולהכי, אע"ג דנתייבשו, כיון שיכולין לחזור לכמות שהיו — מטמאין. אבל הכא בלחים ונתייבשו לא קמיבעיא ליה, אלא ביבש מעיקרו, ואפילו אם יכול להיות נימוח במים.

**אבל** דם דרכיך לא. וא"ת: והא דם הנדה נמי, קתני לקמן בהדי אידך דפרק "דם הנדה" (דף נד:) וי"ל: דהתם מיירי בדם הנדה שנפל על הבגד ונתייבש ביותר, אבל דם הנדה באפי נפשיה — הוי רכיך. וע"ק: דהתם קתני "רוק וזוב וניעו", דרכיכי? וי"ל: דמ"מ אקושי נינהו טפי מדם. דאינהו התחילו ליבש זה כמה ימים, דרגילין להתייבש קודם יציאתם. אבל דם אינו רגיל להתייבש קודם יציאתו מן הרחם. **או** דלמא לא שנא. תימה: דבפרק "דם הנדה" (לקמן דף נו.) תניא, רשב"ג אומר: בפושרין מעת לעת. ואמאי לא אשמועינן רבותא טפי, דאפי' לא יחזור ע"י פושרין מעת לעת, אלא על ידי מיעוך — טמא, לרשב"ג דהא אפי' לגבי דם חשיב מיעוך, כל שכן בנבלה ושרץ דאקושי. דע"כ ע"י מיעוך נימוח טפי מפושרין, דהא אפילו את"ל דרבנן בעו מעת לעת, במיעוך ע"י הדחק לא חשיב דם לרבנן!

**ליפלוג** נמי רבי יהודה בהא. אשערה וקליפה לא פריך, דליפלוג רבי יהודה — דמועטין נינהו, ולא שייך בהו פתיחת קבר. **הואיל** ונאמרה בהו יצירה. אף על גב דבבהמה לא כתיב בה יצירה, הא אמרי' ב"בהמה המקשה" (חולין דף עא.) דבהמה טהורה בכלל חיה טהורה ליצירה. **המפלת** דמות תנין. הוה מצי למנקט "דגים" סתמא, דבקרא ד"ויברא את התנינים" כתיב נמי "כל נפש חיה הרומשת אשר שרצו המים". אלא נקט "תנין" — לפי שהוא סמוך ל"ויברא". **זו** היא שיבה זו היא ביאה. וא"ת: אמאי לא משני, ה"מ היכא דליכא דדמי ליה כו'. וליכא למימר דה"פ: דלילף תרוייהו יצירה ובריאה לטמא בהמה ודגים, דע"כ לא נתקבלה ג"ש אלא חדא מינייהו. מדקאמר לקמן: שבקינן מופנה מצד אחד וילפינן ממופנה מב' צדדים? וי"ל: דעיקר קושיא א"ועוד" סמיך*). **התם** ביבשה כתיב. תימה: וכי לא ידע דביבשה כתיב, דקרא דתנינים כתיב בחמישי, והאי בששי?

*) [ועי' תוס' יומא ב: ד"ה הנ"מ ותוס' מנחות ז. ד"ה מאי נ"מ]

**תוספי הרא"ש**

זיבה ודוקא לענין סתיר' מיטמיעה קרא אבל לשאר דברים הוי כצחצוחי זיבה גמורה תדע מדאמרינן בבעל קרי שלא הטיל מים לבשיטול מים טמא לפי שאי אפשר בלא צחצוחי קרי אלמא חשיבי צחצוחין כאילו היה בעין. עוד אמרינן בפ' מצות חליצה יבמה שרקקה דם תחלוץ לפי שאי אפשר בלא צחצוחי הרוק אלמא חשיבי צחצוחין כרוק בלא ריבוי דקרא: **הרואה** דם יבש מהו. הא דלא פשיטא ליה ממתניתין דהמפלת חתיכה כדא"ר יהודה בין כך ובין כך טמאה משום דאיכא דמוקי לה דפליגי בדאיפשר לפתיחת הקבר בלא דם: **הא** נמי תנינא כו'. אם נימוחו טמאה. תימה הא לאו יבש מעיקרא הוא דאפי' הנך דתנן לקמן בפ' דם הנדה שרץ ונבלה מטמאין לחין ולא יבשים. התם אם יכולין לשרות ולחזור כמות שהן מטמאין ביבשן וכ"ת התם במעת לעת הכא במעת לעת והא מיבעיא לן בשמעתין אי אמרינן בהא מעת לעת או לא ... **אמרו** אשה זו מכה יש לה בתוך מעיה כו'. לא שהיה ברור לרופאים שהיה לה מכה בתוך מעיה דא"כ אפילו אם נימוחו טהורה כדאמרינן לעיל הרואה דם מחמת מכה אפילו בתוך ימי נדתה טהורה. אלא אמרו הרופאים אולי אשה זו מכה יש לה בתוך מעיה ויבדק הדבר ע"י הטלת מים אם נימוחו דם נדה הוא ולא בא מחמת מכה וכן ההוא עובדא דשומא: **שרץ** ונבלה דאקושי בעינן מעת לעת. ותימה והא דם נדה נמי קתני לקמן בהדי אינך דפ' דם הנדה דלא מיקרו יבשים אלא במעת לעת וי"ל דהתם מיירי בדם הנדה שעל הבגד שנתייבש הרבה אבל דם באנפי נפשיה הוי רכיך. ומיהו תימה דלקמן נמי קתני רוק וזוב וניעו דרכיכי נינהו וי"ל דמ"מ אקושי נינהו טפי מאינך דהכא דהנהו התחילו להתייבש זה כמה ימים אבל דם דהכא שיצא יבש מן הרחם אינו רגיל להתייבש זמן גדול קודם צאתו: **וניפלוג** נמי ר' יהודה בהא. אדגים וחגבים פריך אבל בקליפה ושערה לא שייך ביה פתיחת הרחם אבל משינויא דר' יוחנן נ"ל דקאי אפילו ארישא דקליפה ושערה דהא ברישא מטמא ר' יהודה בכל ענין ולא קאמר תטיל למים וקליפה שערה ועפר כולהו בריה דלא עביד דם דקריש והוי כי הני: **הואיל** ונאמר בהם יצירה כאדם. ותימה בהמה דלא נאמר בה יצירה מא"ל וי"ל הא אמרינן בפ' המקשה בהמה טהורה בכלל חיה טהורה ליצירה והתם דפריך הניחא לר' מאיר אלא לרבנן מ"מ למיפרך נמי לר' מאיר הניחא לרב יהודה אלא לר' יוחנן ולר' (מאיר) [ינאי] דמפרשי טעמא אחרינא לקמן לר' מאיר מא"ל: **הואיל** ונאמר בו בריאה כאדם. אע"ג דג"ש דיצירה ניתנה ודבריאה לא ניתנה זו היא שיבה זו היא ביאה והא תנא דבי ר' ישמעאל וליכא למימר ה"מ היכא דליכא דדמי ליה אבל היכא דאיכא דדמי ליה מדדמי ליה ילפינן כדאמר בפ' כיסוי הדם דשאני התם משום שאי אפשר לקיים את שניהם דאי גמרינן שחיטה משחיטה הוי שחיטה שאינה ראויה שמה שחיטה ואי גמרינן שחיטה מטביחה לא הוי שמה שחיטה הלכך שבקינן טביחה וילפינן משחיטה אבל הכא איכא למיגמר תרווייהו: **ניגמר** בריאה מבריאה. כלומר ליתא להא דר' ישמעאל לגבי הא משום דאית ליה למיגמר מדדמי ליה אע"ג דלא סתרי אהדדי לגבי הא ודאי אית לן למימר דכשנאמרה למשה מסיני יצירה מיצירה ה"ה בריאה מבריאה כיון דמשמעות בריאה ויצירה שוין: **אמרי** ויברא לגופיה. לפי שנאמר תחילה. אדרבה ויצר לגופיה מיהא כיון דנתקבלה ג"ש יצירה יצירה וכי שבקינן יצירה ונילף בריאה בריאה כיון דאפשר לומר (או) הכי מסתברא למימר יצירה יצירה שנאמרה למשה מסיני וי"ל דמיסתבר ליה טפי למימר יצירה לגופיה שהיא מפרש עיקר היצירה: **ולרבי** ישמעאל מאי איכא למופנה מצד אחד למופנה משני צדדין דבשלמא לרבנן ניחא דילפינן יצירה מיצירה מופנה משני צדדין דאין משיבין אלא לר' ישמעאל כיון דתרווייהו אין משיבין מאי איכא בין מופנה מצד אחד למופנה משני צדדין ומשני דלהכי אפנייה רחמנא לבהמה משני צדדין כי היכי דלא תיגמר ממופנה מצד אחד ואי לאו דאפנייה לבהמה כ"א מצד אחד דלא ליכתוב גבי אדם אלא או יצירה או בריאה דהשתא הוי ג"ש דבהמה מופנה מצד אחד ודתנין לא הוי מופנה כלל וי"ל דאי לא לא מופנה גבי אדם הוה ילפינן בריאה דתנין מיצירה

**מסורת הש"ס**

[תוספתא פ"ד]

לקמן נד: נו.

[נ"ל מן האדמה כל חית]

[לעיל כה: נדפס בלוידו בשם רש"ל לר' יוחנן]

עירובין נא. יומא נז: מכות יג: יבמות יז: נזיר כה: הוריות ח: מנחות ז. וקף מה: בכורות לב. חולין פה.

[שלשה תיבות הללו משום ר' ישמעאל נריכים תיקון]

[שבת סד.]

**גליון הש"ס**

גמ' לר' ישמעאל למדין כו'. מדברי תוס' נזיר מח ע"ב ד"ה ולאחותו מבואר דהיה לפם הגי' כאן בהיפוך דר"י ס"ל למדין ומשיבין.

**הגהות מהר"ב רנשבורג**

א] גמ' אם נמוחו טמאה א"ה. עי' ש"ך סי' קפח ס"ק יז ודוק ועי' בהשגות הרז"ה לבעל המאור בשער הפרישה אות ג':

וְיָלְפִינַן מוּפְנֶה מִשְּׁנֵי צְדָדִין. וּלְהָכִי אַפְנְיֵיהּ רַחֲמָנָא לִבְהֵמָה מִשְּׁנֵי צְדָדִין, כִּי הֵיכִי דְּלָא נִגְמַר מִן מוּפְנֶה מִצַּד אֶחָד. רַב אַחָא בְּרֵיהּ דְּרָבָא מַתְנֵי לָהּ מִשְּׁמֵיהּ דְּרַבִּי אֶלְעָזָר לְקוּלָּא: כָּל גְּזֵרָה שָׁוָה שֶׁאֵינָהּ מוּפְנָה כָּל עִיקָּר — לְמֵידִין וּמְשִׁיבִין. מוּפְנָה מִצַּד אֶחָד, לְרַבִּי יִשְׁמָעֵאל לְמֵידִין וְאֵין מְשִׁיבִין, לְרַבָּנַן — לְמֵידִין וּמְשִׁיבִין. מוּפְנָה מִשְּׁנֵי צְדָדִין, דִּבְרֵי הַכֹּל לְמֵידִין וְאֵין מְשִׁיבִין. וּלְרַבָּנַן, מַאי אִיכָּא בֵּין מוּפְנָה מִצַּד אֶחָד לְשֶׁאֵינָהּ מוּפְנָה כָּל עִיקָּר? נ"מ הֵיכָא דְּמַשְׁכַּחַת לָהּ מוּפְנָה מִצַּד אֶחָד וְשֶׁאֵינָהּ מוּפְנָה כָּל עִיקָּר, וְלָאו לְהַאי אִית לֵיהּ פִּירְכָא, וְלָאו לְהַאי אִית לֵיהּ פִּירְכָא — שָׁבְקִינַן שֶׁאֵינָהּ מוּפְנָה כָּל עִיקָּר, וְגָמְרִינַן מִמּוּפְנָה מִצַּד אֶחָד. וְהָכָא מַאי פִּירְכָא אִיכָּא? מִשּׁוּם דְּאִיכָּא לְמִיפְרַךְ: מַה לְּאָדָם — שֶׁכֵּן מְטַמֵּא מֵחַיִּים. וְכֵן א"ר חִיָּיא בַּר אַבָּא, א"ר יוֹחָנָן: הַיְינוּ טַעֲמָא דְּר"מ — הוֹאִיל וְנֶאֶמְרָה בּוֹ "יְצִירָה" כְּאָדָם. א"ל רַבִּי אַמִי: אֶלָּא מֵעַתָּה, הַמַּפֶּלֶת דְּמוּת הַר, אִמּוֹ טְמֵאָה לֵידָה — שֶׁנֶּאֱמַר: °"כִּי הִנֵּה יוֹצֵר הָרִים וּבוֹרֵא רוּחַ"! אֲמַר לֵיהּ: הַר מִי קָא מַפֶּלֶת? אֶבֶן הִיא דְּקָא מַפֶּלֶת, הַהוּא "גּוּשׁ" אִיקְרֵי. אֶלָּא מֵעַתָּה, הַמַּפֶּלֶת רוּחַ, תְּהֵא אִמּוֹ טְמֵאָה לֵידָה הוֹאִיל וְנֶאֶמְרָה בּוֹ "בְּרִיאָה" כְּאָדָם, דִּכְתִיב: °"וּבוֹרֵא רוּחַ"! וְכִי תֵּימָא: לָא מוּפְנֶה — מִדַּהֲוָה לֵיהּ לְמִכְתַּב "יוֹצֵר הָרִים וְרוּחַ", וּכְתִיב "וּבוֹרֵא רוּחַ" ש"מ לְאַפְנוּיֵי! א"ל: דָּנִין דִּבְרֵי תוֹרָה מִדִּבְרֵי תוֹרָה, *וְאֵין דָּנִין דִּבְרֵי תוֹרָה מִדִּבְרֵי קַבָּלָה. (אָמַר) רַבָּה בַּר בַּר חָנָה, אָמַר רַבִּי יוֹחָנָן: הַיְינוּ טַעֲמָא דְּר"מ — הוֹאִיל וְעֵינֵיהֶם דּוֹמוֹת כְּשֶׁל אָדָם. אֶלָּא מֵעַתָּה [א]הַמַּפֶּלֶת דְּמוּת נָחָשׁ, תְּהֵא אִמּוֹ טְמֵאָה לֵידָה — *הוֹאִיל וְגַלְגַּל עֵינוֹ עֲגוּלָּה כְּשֶׁל אָדָם! וְכִי תֵּימָא: הָכִי נַמִי — לִיתְנֵי נָחָשׁ! אִי תָּנָא נָחָשׁ, הֲוָה אָמֵינָא: בְּנָחָשׁ הוּא דִּפְלִיגִי רַבָּנַן עֲלֵיהּ דְּר"מ — דְּלָא כְּתִיב בֵּיהּ "יְצִירָה", אֲבָל בְּהֵמָה וְחַיָּה — לָא פְּלִיגִי, דִּכְתִיבָא בֵּיהּ "יְצִירָה". וְהָא גַּבֵּי מוּמִין קָתָנֵי לָהּ *[ב]אֶת שֶׁגַּלְגַּל עֵינוֹ עָגוֹל כְּשֶׁל אָדָם! לָא קַשְׁיָא, הָא — בְּאוּכָּמָא, הָא — *בְּצִירְיָא. רַבִּי יַנַּאי אָמַר: הַיְינוּ טַעֲמָא דְּר"מ — הוֹאִיל וְעֵינֵיהֶם הוֹלְכוֹת לְפָנֵיהֶם כְּשֶׁל אָדָם. וַהֲרֵי עוֹף, דְּאֵין עֵינָיו הוֹלְכוֹת לְפָנָיו, וְקָאָמַר ר"מ דְּטָמֵא! אָמַר אַבָּיֵי: **בְּקָרְיָא וְקִיפּוֹפָא, וּבִשְׁאָר עוֹפוֹת — לָא. מֵיתִיבֵי: ר' חֲנִינָא בֶּן (אַנְטִיגְנוֹס) אוֹמֵר: נִרְאִין דִּבְרֵי ר"מ בִּבְהֵמָה וְחַיָּה, וְדִבְרֵי חֲכָמִים בְּעוֹפוֹת, מַאי עוֹפוֹת? אִילֵימָא בְּקָרְיָא וְקִיפּוֹפָא, מ"ש בְּהֵמָה וְחַיָּה — דְּעֵינֵיהֶן הוֹלְכוֹת לִפְנֵיהֶן כְּשֶׁל אָדָם, קָרְיָא וְקִיפּוֹפָא — נַמִי! אֶלָּא פְּשִׁיטָא — בִּשְׁאָר עוֹפוֹת, מִכְּלָל דְּר"מ פָּלֵיג בִּשְׁאָר עוֹפוֹת! חַסּוּרֵי מִיחַסְּרָא וְהָכִי קָתָנֵי, ר' חֲנִינָא בֶּן (אַנְטִיגְנוֹס) אוֹמֵר: נִרְאִין דִּבְרֵי ר"מ בִּבְהֵמָה וְחַיָּה, וְהוּא הַדִּין לְקָרְיָא וְקִיפּוֹפָא, וְדִבְרֵי חֲכָמִים בִּשְׁאָר עוֹפוֹת, שֶׁאַף ר"מ לֹא נֶחֱלַק עִמָּהֶם אֶלָּא בְּקָרְיָא וְקִיפּוֹפָא, אֲבָל בִּשְׁאָר עוֹפוֹת מוֹדֵי לְהוּ. וְהַתַּנְיָא, א"ר אֶלְעָזָר בְּר' צָדוֹק: הַמַּפֶּלֶת מִין בְּהֵמָה וְחַיָּה, לְדִבְרֵי ר"מ — וָלָד, וּלְדִבְרֵי חֲכָמִים — אֵינוֹ וָלָד, וּבְעוֹפוֹת — תִּיבָּדֵק. לְמַאן, תִּיבָּדֵק? לָאו לְדִבְרֵי ר"מ דְּאָמַר קָרְיָא וְקִיפּוֹפָא — אִין, שְׁאָר עוֹפוֹת — לָא? אָמַר רַב אַחָא בְּרֵיהּ דְּרַב אִיקָא: לָא, תִּיבָּדֵק לְרַבָּנַן, דְּאָמְרִי קָרְיָא וְקִיפּוֹפָא — אִין, שְׁאָר עוֹפוֹת — לָא. ומ"ש קָרְיָא וְקִיפּוֹפָא מִבְּהֵמָה וְחַיָּה? הוֹאִיל וְיֵשׁ לָהֶן לְסָתוֹת כְּאָדָם. בְּעָא מִינֵּיהּ רַבִּי יִרְמְיָה מֵר' זֵירָא: לְר"מ דְּאָמַר בְּהֵמָה בִּמְעֵי אִשָּׁה וָלָד מְעַלְּיָא הוּא, קִבֵּל בָּהּ אָבִיהָ קִידּוּשִׁין מַהוּ? לְמַאי נָפְקָא מִינָּהּ — לְאִיתְסוּרֵי בַּאֲחוֹתָהּ. לְמֵימְרָא דְּחַיֵּי? וְהָאָמַר רַב יְהוּדָה, אָמַר רַב: לֹא אֲמָרָהּ ר"מ אֶלָּא הוֹאִיל וּבְמִינוֹ מִתְקַיֵּים! אָמַר רַב אַחָא בַּר יַעֲקֹב: עַד כָּאן הֵבִיאוֹ רַבִּי יִרְמְיָה לְר' זֵירָא לִידֵי *גִּיחוּךְ וְלָא גָּחֵיךְ. גּוּפָא, אָמַר רַב יְהוּדָה, אָמַר רַב: לֹא אֲמָרָהּ רַבִּי מֵאִיר אֶלָּא הוֹאִיל וּבְמִינוֹ מִתְקַיֵּים. אָמַר רַב יִרְמְיָה מִדִּפְתִּי:

אַף

עמוס ד

שם

**רש"י**

לְהָכִי **אַפְנְיֵיהּ רַחֲמָנָא** כו'. כְּרַבָּנַן. **דְּלָא** תִּגְמַר מִמּוּפְנֶה מִצַּד אֶחָד. מִשּׁוּם דִּמְשִׁיבִין, וְכָאן יֵשׁ לְהָשִׁיב: מַה לְּאִישׁ שֶׁכֵּן מְטַמֵּא מֵחַיִּים, כִּדְלְקַמֵּיהּ. **לְקוּלָּא**. דְּלָא בָּעֵינַן מוּפְנֶה כּוּלֵּי הַאי. לְרַבָּנַן. כֵּיוָן דִּלְמוּפְנֶה מִצַּד אֶחָד לְמֵדִין וּמְשִׁיבִין, וְלְשֶׁאֵינוֹ מוּפְנֶה כָּל עִיקָּר אָמְרִינַן דִּבְרֵי הַכֹּל לְמֵדִין וּמְשִׁיבִין, מַאי אִיכָּא בֵּין מוּפְנֶה מִצַּד אֶחָד לְשֶׁאֵינָהּ מוּפְנָה כָּל עִיקָּר? **וְהָכָא מַאי פִּירְכָא אִיכָּא**. כְּלוֹמַר, וְהָכָא בְּגז"ש דְּתָנֵי אָדָם, מַה תְּשׁוּבָה אִיכָּא, דְּקָאָמְרַתְּ דְּנִיחָא לָךְ לְמִיגְמַר מֵחַיָּה, דַּהֲוֵי מוּפְנֶה מִשְּׁנֵי צְדָדִין, מִשּׁוּם דְּאֵין מְשִׁיבִין, וְלָא נִגְמַר בְּרִיאָה בְּרִיאָה מִתַּנִּין, מִשּׁוּם דְּמוּפְנֶה מִצַּד אֶחָד הוּא וּמְשִׁיבִין, וּמַאי אִית לָךְ לְאוֹתוּבֵי? **שֶׁכֵּן מְטַמֵּא מֵחַיִּים**. מְקַבֵּל טוּמְאָה בְּחַיָּיו מִשֶּׁרֶץ אוֹ מִשְּׁאָר טוּמְאוֹת — דִּין הוּא שֶׁתְּהֵא יוֹלַדְתּוֹ טְמֵאָה לֵידָה, תֹּאמַר בְּאֵלּוּ. הִלְכָּךְ גַּבֵּי דָּגִים פָּרְכִינַן לֵיהּ, דְּמוּפְנֶה מִצַּד אֶחָד הוּא. אֲבָל גַּבֵּי בְּהֵמָה, אע"ג דְּפִירְכָא הִיא, לָא פָּרְכִינַן לָהּ הוֹאִיל וּמוּפְנָה הִיא מִשְּׁנֵי צְדָדִין. **וְכֵן אָמַר רַבִּי חִיָּיא** כו'. אַדְּרַב יְהוּדָה אָמַר שְׁמוּאֵל קָאֵי. הַר מִי קָמַפֶּלֶת. מִי מַפֶּלֶת גֶּפֶל גָּדוֹל כְּהַר? **דְּמוּת אֶבֶן הוּא** דְּמַפֶּלֶת. חֲתִיכַת בָּשָׂר דְּמוּת אֶבֶן גּוּשׁ בְּעָלְמָא מִיקְרֵי, וְלָא כְּתִיבָא בֵּיהּ יְצִירָה. **גּוּשׁ**. כְּמוֹ (איוב ז) "גּוּשׁ עָפָר". **הוֹאִיל וְעֵינֵיהֶן**. שֶׁל חַיָּה וּבְהֵמָה. **דּוֹמוֹת לְשֶׁל אָדָם**. שָׁחוֹר שֶׁבָּעַיִן הָוֵה עָגוֹל בִּבְהֵמָה, כְּשֶׁל אָדָם. אֲבָל דְּדָגִים, לָאו עָגוֹל הוּא. **וְהָא** גַּבֵּי מוּמִין תָּנֵי לָהּ. כְּלוֹמַר, הֵיכִי אָמְרַתְּ דְּעֵין בְּהֵמָה דּוֹמֶה לְאָדָם, וְהָא גַּבֵּי מוּמֵי הַבְּכוֹר קָתָנֵי לָהּ בִּבְכוֹרוֹת (דף מ.) וְשֶׁגַּלְגַּל עֵינוֹ הָוֵי מוּם. וּמִדְּחָשֵׁיב לֵיהּ מוּם, נִמְצָא שֶׁאֵין דֶּרֶךְ בְּהֵמָה לִהְיוֹת עֵינֶיהָ כְּאָדָם. **בְּאוּכָּמָא**. שָׁחוֹר שֶׁבָּעַיִן הָוֵי עָגוֹל בִּבְהֵמָה כְּאָדָם, וְהָא דְּתָנֵי דַּהֲוֵי מוּם — בְּצִירְיָא, מְקוֹם מוֹשַׁב כָּל הָעַיִן, לָא הָוֵי עָגוֹל בִּבְהֵמָה כְּאָדָם. וְאִי הָוֵי עָגוֹל — הָוֵי מוּם. דְּכָל בּוֹר שֶׁל מוֹשַׁב הָעַיִן קָרוּי "גַּלְגַּל", כִּדְאָמְרִי' לְקַמָּן (דף כד.): וְעָמַדְתִּי בְּגַלְגַּל עֵינוֹ שֶׁל מֵת עַד חוֹטְמִי. וּמִפְּנֵי שֶׁהוּא עָגוֹל כְּגַלְגַּל. **לִפְנֵיהֶם**. לְאַפּוּקֵי דָּגִים דְּעֵינֵיהֶם בְּצִדֵּיהֶם, וְכֵן נָחָשׁ. **קָרְיָא וְקִיפּוֹפָא**. עוֹף הַצּוֹעֵק בַּלַּיְלָה, וּפָנָיו דּוֹמֶה לְחָתוּל, וְעֵינָיו לְפָנָיו. **חַסּוּרֵי מִיחַסְּרָא וְהָכִי קָתָנֵי**. נִרְאִין דִּבְרֵי ר"מ בִּבְהֵמָה וּבְחַיָּה, וְהוּא הַדִּין לְקָרְיָא וְקִיפּוֹפָא דְּעֵינָיו הוֹלְכוֹ' לְפָנָיו, וְאע"פ דִּפְלִיגִי רַבָּנַן עֲלֵיהּ. **וְדִבְרֵי חֲכָמִים**. נִרְאִין לְר"מ בִּשְׁאָר עוֹפוֹת, דְּר"מ נַמִי מוֹדֶה לְהוּ. **וְהַתַּנְיָא**. בִּנְיחוּתָא. **וּמַאי שְׁנָא קָרְיָא וְקִיפּוֹפָא**. דְּקָאָמַר לְרַבָּנַן דַּהֲוֵי וָלָד טְפֵי מִשְּׁאָר עוֹפוֹת? אִי מִשּׁוּם דְּעֵינֵיהֶם הוֹלְכוֹת לִפְנֵיהֶם — הֲרֵי חַיָּה וּבְהֵמָה נַמִי דְּעֵינֵיהֶן הוֹלְכוֹת לִפְנֵיהֶם, וּפְלִיגֵי רַבָּנַן. **לְסָתוֹת**. לְחָיַיִם וְקוּפִין כְּאָדָם, מַה שֶּׁאֵין כֵּן בִּבְהֵמָה וּבְחַיָּה. **לְמֵימְרָא דְּחַיֵּי**. הָא אֲחוֹתָהּ לָא מִיתַּסְרָא אֶלָּא בְּחַיֶּיהָ, דְּאֵין אִיסּוּר אֲחוֹת אִשָּׁה אֶלָּא בְּחַיֶּיהָ. **וּבְמִינוֹ**. כְּגוֹן בְּהֵמָה גְּמוּרָה מִתְקַיֶּימֶת, וּבְמִינוֹ הוּא דְּמִתְקַיֵּים אֲבָל אִיהוּ — לָא. **לִידֵי גִּיחוּךְ**. שְׂחוֹק. בְּכָל תַּחְבּוּלוֹת הַלָּלוּ עָסַק ר' יִרְמְיָה לְהָבִיא ר' זֵירָא לִידֵי שְׂחוֹק, וְלֹא שָׂחַק — דְּאָסוּר לָאָדָם שֶׁיְּמַלֵּא פִּיו שְׂחוֹק, *) וְר' זֵירָא מַחְמִיר טְפֵי.

*) [ברכות לא.]

אַף

**תוספות**

**ויָלפינן** ממופנה משני צדדין. תימה: ולשתוק מהפנאה דאדם, דהשתא תנין לא מופנה כלל ובהמה מופנה בצד אחד, ואין משיבין? **יוצר** הרים. ומופנה הוא, כדקאמר בסמוך. **ליתני** נחש. ואע"ג דקתני "חיה", ונחש בכלל חיה, כדכתיב (בראשית ג) "והנחש היה ערום מכל חית השדה" — לאחר שנקצצו רגליו לא מיקרי "חיה" סתם, אלא "חיה הרומשת", ולא הוי בכלל "חיה" דמתניתין.

**קריא** וקיפופא. ג' מיני קיפוף יש: "הכוס והינשוף" (ויקרא יא) מתרגמינן: קריא וקיפופא, והתנשמת נמי אמר ב"אלו טריפות" (חולין דף סג.) זה בזות שבעופות, ואמר אביי: בזות שבעופות — קיפוף. ועוד: קיפוף — מין חיה, כדאמר ב"הרואה" (ברכות נז:) כל מיני חיה יפין לחלום, חוץ מן הקוף והקיפוף*. **לאיתסורי באחותה**. — לענין גופה לא בעי אם הבא עליה חייב משום אשת איש או אם חייב ההורגה, דפשיטא ליה דאינה חיה ג' שנים שתהא בת ביאה, ולא שנה שלא תהא טרפה. ומיהו הוה מצי למבעי אם הרובע חייב סקילה כדין הבא על הבהמה. **הואיל** ובמינו מתקיים. אע"פ דדריש ג"ש דיצירה בעי טעמא, הואיל ובמינו מתקיים. דאפילו בולד גמור בעינן מתקיים, למעוטי נולד חתיכה או חסרה. וא"ת: והא גופו תייש ופניו אדם דאינו מתקיים, ואמרינן בסמוך דכ"ע אדם הוי! וי"ל: דאע"ג דלא חיי לא בבהמה ולא באשה, מ"מ גופו תייש כתיקונו ופניו אדם כתיקונו, ואינו חסר מאומה.

ומלא

**תוספי הרא"ש**

מיצירה דבהמה דהוי מופנה מצד אחד אבל השתא אייתר ליה הפנאה דאדם למעוטי דלא תלמוד תנין כלל מהך גז"ש **והכא** מאי פירכא איכא וא"ת אפילו אי ליכא פירכא נימא לרבנן נמי כמו לר' ישמעאל (לא) דשבקינן מופנה מצד אחד וילפינן ממופנה משני צדדין. וי"ל דלר' ישמעאל הוא דאמרי' הכי משום דהפנאה של צד השני שלא לצורך הוא דלאו הכי אין משיבין הלכך לא באה אלא כדי לדחות מופנה מצד אחד אבל לרבנן דהפנאה של צד השני לצורך הוא כדי שלא נשיב אם יש להשיב [א]הלכך לא אמרינן מטמאה מחיים שבאתה לדחות מופנה מצד אחד: **מה** לאדם שכן מטמא מחיים. ותימה בהמה תוכיח דלא מטמאה מחיים וטמאה לידה וא"כ ניליף תנין בגז"ש מיצירה דבהמה וליכא למיפרך שמטמא מחיים. וי"ל דאיכא למיפרך מה לבהמה שכן מטמאה לאחר מיתה ותימה וניליף מעוף טהור וי"ל מה לעוף שכן מטמא בגדים אבית הבליעה. וקשה ניליף מעוף טמא וי"ל דאיכא למיפרך מה לעוף טמא שכן עושין ממנו דבר המקבל טומאה כגון מהעצמות או מהעורות משא"כ בדגי הים כדתנן בפ' י"ח דמס' כלים כל שבים טהור: דכתיב כי הנה יוצר הרים ובורא רוח ומופנה מדמצי למיכתב בורא רוח והרים: **ואין** דנין דברי תורה מדברי קבלה. וא"ת האמרי' לעיל דבתוספתא דבשבת יליף מקור מקור את מקורה הערה והנה מקור נפתח לבית דוד דהיינו דברי תורה מדברי קבלה וי"ל דשאני הכא דמצי למילף דברי תורה מדברי תורה הלכך לא ילפינן מדברי קבלה: **ליתני** נחש. ותימה והא קתני חיה ונחש בכלל חיה כדאמר בסנהדרין (וכל) [ואת כל נפש] החיה הרומשת לרבות הנחש וי"ל דלא הוי נחש בכלל חיה. והתם דריש לרבות את הנחש מחיה הרומשת על הארץ דמשמע דחיה שנעשית רומשת והיינו נחש שהלך בקומה זקופה ונעשה הולך על גחון אבל סתם חיה לא הוי נחש בכלל: **ליתני** נחש. פי' ליתני נחש לחודיה דאין לפרש ליתני נחש בהדי בהמה וחיה דא"כ היכי קאמר אי תנא נחש ה"א בנחש הוא דפליגי דא"כ בהמה וחיה ועוף למאן קתני לה אי לר' מאיר דהשתא נחש דלא כתיב ביה יצירה קאמר ר' דהוי ולד בהמה וחיה ועוף דכתיב בהו יצירה מיבעיא. מיהו קשה ליתני נחש בהדייהו ולא הוה מצי למיפרך מידי וי"ל דלא ניחא ליה למיתני נחש בהדיה חיה דלמא אתי למיטעי ולמימר דנחש לא הוי בכלל חיה. והתם דרשינן וכל חיה הרומשת זה נחש: הא באוכמא הא בציירא בירושלמי גרס גלגלי אדם עגולים גלגלי בהמה ארוכין א"ר יוסי בר אבין באדם הלבן רבה על השחור ובהמה שחור רבה על הלבן: **קריא** וקיפופא. כוס וינשוף מתרגמינן קריא וקיפופא עוד יש קיפוף אחד בעופות ובפ' אלו טרפות תניא תנשמת זו בזואת שבעופות ואמר אביי בזואת שבעופות קיפוף שמו: **לאיתסורי** באחותה. הא דלא קאמר לענין גופה לחייב הבא עליה משום אשת איש או להתחייב ההורגה דמילתא דפשיטא היא דלא חיי כולי האי שתהא ראויה לביאה או לצאת מידי טרפה: **למימרא** דחיה. פרש"י דאין איסור אחות אשה אלא בחייה וקשה לפירושו דמצי לאוקומי בעיא דר' ירמיה לאסור חמותה ואליבא דמ"ד חמותו לאחר מיתה בשריפה וגם לכ"ע איסורא איכא הלכך נראה לפרש למימרא דחיי ... נפק מידי נפל דתפסי בה קידושין והא לא מצי למיבעי אם כזית ממנו מטמא באהל ועצם כשעורה אם מטמא דמילתא דפשיטא הוא כיון דאמו טמאה לידה טמא כמו נפל: **לא** אמרה ר' מאיר אלא הואיל ובמינו מתקיים. ותימה והא פירשנו לעיל טעמי מקרא דגמר יצירה יצירה וי"ל דמ"מ (ק"ו) צריך טעמא להתקיים דאפי' באדם בדבר שאין מתקיים לא חשיב לידה כדאמרינן כדי שינטל מן החי וימות. ותימה מאי קפריך לימא הא דקאמר הואיל ובמינו מתקיים היינו שמתקיים י"ב חדש אבל זה אינו מתקיים י"ב חדש אבל פחות מתקיים והוי כטריפה וי"ל דא"כ הו"ל למימר הואיל ובמינו חי אבל מדנקט מתקיים משמע דאין מתקיים כלל. ותימה לקמן דאמר הואיל וגופו תייש ופניו אדם הא לא מתקיים בשום מקום כה"ג וי"ל דמ"מ מה שיש בו מאדם ומתייש הוי כל אחד כתקנו. מיהו בירושלמי משמע דהוא עצמו חי דגרסינן התם רבנן מקשו על דר' מאיר הפילה דמות עורב עומד בראש דקל אומר לו בא חלוץ בא יבם והדר קאמר אדאת מקשה לר' מאיר תיקשי לרבנן דאמר ר' יוחנן כולו אדם ופניו בהמה אינו ולד כולו בהמה ופניו אדם ולד כולו אדם ופניו בהמה עומד וקורא

א) נראה דצ"ל אם יש להשיב כמו דפרכינן מה לאדם שכן מטמא בחיים הלכך לא אמרינן שבאתה לדחות וכו'.

**עין משפט נר מצוה**

יח א מיי' פ"ו מהלכות איסורי ביאה הלכה י:

יט ב מיי' פ"ב מהלכות איסורי מזבח הלכה ב:

[לפנינו איתא והקפוד וכו' פרש"י שם אמנם איתא כל מיני עופות יפין לחלום חוץ מן קריא וקפופא וכן הגי' בערוך ע"ש בערך קריא וצע"ק]

**מסורת הש"ס**

תורה אור

[חגיגה י: ב"ק כ:]

[לקמן כד:]

בכורות מ.

ס"א גמליאל

**גליון הש"ס**

**גמ'** בקריא וקיפופא. בויקרא י"א ואת הכוס ואת השלך ואת הינשוף התרגום וקריי' ושלינונא וקיפופא:

תורה אור

אף אנן נמי תנינא: *המפלת כמין בהמה חיה ועוף *(ולד מעליא הוא), דברי ר"מ. וחכ"א עד שיהא בו מצורת אדם. והמפלת סנדל, או שליא, או שפיר מרוקם, והיוצא מחותך – אהבא אחריו בכור לנחלה בואינו בכור לכהן. ואי ס"ד דחיי, הבא אחריו בכור לנחלה מי הוי? אמר רבא: לעולם – דחיי, ושאני התם דאמר קרא °"ראשית אונו" – *מי שלבו דוה עליו, יצא זה שאין לבו דוה עליו. (דברים כא) א] בעא מיניה רב אדא בר אהבה מאביי: לרבי מאיר דאמר בהמה במעי אשה – ולד מעליא הוא, אדם במעי בהמה מאי? למאי נפקא מיניה – לאשתרויי באכילה. ותפשוט ליה מהא דר' יוחנן, *דא"ר יוחנן: גהשוחט את הבהמה ומצא בה דמות יונה – אסורה באכילה! הכי השתא? התם – לא פרסות איכא ולא פרסה איכא, הכא – נהי דפרסות ליכא, פרסה מיהא איכא.§ וחכ"א כל שאין בו" כו'.§ אמר רב ירמיה בר אבא, אמר רב: הכל מודים, גופו תייש ופניו אדם – אדם, גופו אדם ופניו תייש – ולא כלום, לא נחלקו אלא שפניו אדם ונברא בעין אחת כבהמה. שרבי מאיר אומר: מצורת אדם. וחכ"א: כל צורת אדם. *אמר לו לרב ירמיה בר אבא: והא איפכא תניא, ר"מ אומר: "כל צורת", וחכ"א "מצורת"! אמר להו: *אי תניא – תניא. אמר ר' ירמיה בר אבא, אמר רבי יוחנן: דמצח, והגבינים, והעינים, והלסתות, וגבות הזקן – עד שיהו כולם כאחד. רבא אמר חסא: מצח, והגבן, והעין, והלסת, וגבת הזקן – עד שיהו כולם כאחת. ולא פליגי, הא כמ"ד "כל צורת", הא כמ"ד "מצורת". מיתיבי: *צורת פנים שאמרו – אפילו פרצוף אחד מן הפרצופין, חוץ מן האוזן. למימרא *דמחד נמי סגי! אמר אביי: כי תניא ההיא – לעכב תניא, וכמ"ד "כל צורת". ואיבעית אימא: לעולם כמ"ד "מצורת", ומאי "אחד" – אחד אחד. אמר רבא: הנברא בעין אחת ובירך אחד, מן הצד – אמו טמאה, באמצע – אמו טהורה. אמר רבא: ושטו נקוב – אמו טמאה, ושטו אטום – אמו טהורה. ת"ר: זהמפלת גוף אטום – אין אמו טמאה לידה. ואיזהו גוף אטום? רבי אומר: כדי שינטל מן החי וימות. וכמה ינטל מן החי וימות? רבי זכאי אומר:

עד

---

**אף אנן נמי תנינא.** דלא חיי. **דברי ר"מ.** רישא במסכת בכורות (דף מו.), והכי קתני: יש בכור לנחלה ואין בכור לכהן, וקא חשיב ואזיל: המפלת מין בהמה וחיה ועוף (א), הבא אחריו – בכור לנחלה. דהאי, לאו בכור הוא לגבי נחלה, דלא חיי. *אין בכור לכהן. שהרי זה פטר את הרחם. **וחכ"א עד שיהיה בו מצורת אדם.** אינו פוטר את הבא אחריו מבכורת כהן. **סנדל.** צורה פחותה, שאין צורת פניו ניכרת. שאין סנדל בלא ולד אחר, ומתוך דוחק חבירו הוא נמעך, כדמפרש בפירקין (לקמן דף כה.) משל לאדם שסטר את חבירו, והחזיר צורתו לאחוריו. ואם יוצא סנדל ראשון – פוטר את אחיו מפדיון כהן. **או שליא.** דאין שליא בלא ולד, ופוטר את הבא אחריו לאחר זמן. **שפיר.** עור דפוס הולד. **מרוקם.** שכבר אבריו ניכרין קצת, ולקמן בפירקין (שם.) מפרש לה. **הבא אחריו.** אחר כל אלה. **בכור לנחלה.** דהני לאו בני נחלה נינהו, דלא חיי. **מי שלבו דוה עליו.** לב אביו מתאבל על מותו, הוא דחשיב לענין נחלה. **אדם במעי בהמה.** שחטה, ומצא בה דמות אדם, מהו? מי אמרינן: כי היכי דאזיל ר"מ בתר אימיה, הכי נמי זיל בתר בהמה, ושרי לאכילה. **עוף** אין לו פרסה. אבל אדם, נהי דפרסות ליכא, שאין פרסותיו סדוקות, שאין לו שני עקבים כמו לבהמה. **פרסה מיהא איכא.** וכתיב (ויקרא יא): "כל מפרסת פרסה בבהמה תאכלו", דאם נמצא תוך מעי בהמה קלוט, כל זמן שלא יצא לאויר העולם, אע"ג דאין לו אלא פרסה – אוכלו. ואפילו לר"ש דאמר: קלוט בן פרה – אסור, מודה הוא דאם נשחטה אמו ונמצא במעיה – דמותר. והכי מפרש בפרק "בהמה המקשה" (חולין סח.). **גופו תייש ופניו אדם אדם הוא.** דבתר צורת פנים אזלינן. **בעין אחד** כבהמה. אחת מעיניו דומה לבהמה. ה"ג: **רבי מאיר אומר מצורת וחכ"א כל צורת.** שרבי מאיר אומר: כיון שיש בו מצורת אדם – הוי ולד, ואע"ג דאין כל צורתו כצורת אדם. **והא איפכא תניא.** שר"מ אומר: כל צורת. והאי "כל צורת" דר"מ הכי קאמר: כל שהוא צורת אדם שבו – הוי ולד, ואפילו כל פניו תייש, אלא שנבראה בעין אחת או בלסת אחת הדומה לאדם. **וחכ"א מצורת.** עד שיהיה בו מקצת צורה ניכרת, כגון חצי הפרצוף דומה לאדם. **אי תניא תניא.** שמעתי אני מרב מה שאמרתי, אבל אתם, הואיל ויש משנה בידכם – לכו אחריה. **הגבינים.** גבות עינים, סורצי"ל, וגבות הזקן סנטר, שקורין מנטו"ן. **עד שיהיו כולם כאחד.** לרבנן, כדמפרש בסמוך דר' ירמיה כרבנן, וכדפירשה רב לפלוגתא. דרב תנא הוא, ופליג. ולא הדר ביה מהאי דאמר לרבנן דבעו כל צורת האדם. והא דקחשיב ר' ירמיה ואזיל, הא קמ"ל דאפילו לרבנן האזנים לא קפדינן. והא דחסא נמי כרבנן, ואליבא דתנא דברייתא דאמר לא בעי אלא "מצורת", וקמ"ל דבחד לא בעי צורות שלמות, והאוזן לא קא קפיד. **אפילו פרצוף אחד.** אבר אחד, כגון עינו או מצחו או לסת אחד דדומה לאדם – הוי ולד. **חוץ מן האזנים.** אזניו כשל אדם ושאר צורתו כבהמה – לא חשיב פרצוף, אלמא למ"ד "מצורת" בחד סגי, וקשיא לרבא דאמר חסא. **אמר אביי כי תניא ההיא לעכב תניא.** כלומר, צורת פנים שאמרו חכמים דמעכבים, אפילו אבר אחד כבהמה מעכבא, חוץ מן האוזן דלא מעכבא. וכמ"ד לרבנן "כל צורת" מתוקמא. ואע"ג דמצי לאוקמי כדאיתא, וכדר"מ דאמר "כל דהו צורת" – ניחא ליה לאוקומי כרבנן. **ואיבעית אימא לעולם כמ"ד מצורת.** ולא קשיא לחסא. **ומאי אחד אחד אחד.** כלומר, מכל ראשי איברים יהיה אחד דומה לאדם כחסא, דאמר: העין והלסת כו' וכמ"ד "מצורת". **מן הצד.** שעינו בצדו ויריכו בצדו, כשאר בני אדם. קסבר: **אמו טמאה.** **ושטו נקוב.** קסבר: טרפה חיה. **ושטו אטום.** סתום.

עד

---

**ומצא** בה דמות יונה. וא"ת: ודילמא לרבנן, ולא לר"מ? וי"ל: דא"כ, ה"ל לר' יוחנן למימר "לרבנן מלא בה דמות יונה" כו'. א"נ י"ל: דלא מיבעיא ליה אלא לר"מ דבדבר קל עושהו ולד בהמה במעי אדם, ואדם במעי בהמה נמי קרוי ולד או לא? אבל לרבנן, פשיטא ליה דשרי, דלא מיקרי ולד אלא אדם במעי אשה. ומייתי ראיה מר' יוחנן דאמר אסורה אפילו לרבנן וכ"ש לרבי מאיר. **שר"מ** אומר מצורת. פי' בקונטרס: מקצת כל צורת עין ולסת וגבת וזקן. וחכ"א: "כל צורת" – משני לדדים, ב' עינים כו'. ואע"ג דלר' מאיר כי לא דמי כלל לאדם טמאה לידה, משום דכתיב בהם "ילידה", כי דמי לאדם בעי שיהא דומה לו במקצת כל היצירה. והא פלוגתא דייק מדתנן "וחכ"א: כל שאין בו מצורת אדם", ולא קתני "וחכ"א: אינו ולד" – מכלל דפליגי נמי בולד שמקצתו אדם ומקצתו בהמה. דלר"מ במקצת כל צורתו קרוי ולד, ולרבנן בעיא כל הצורה. והא דקתני במתני' "מצורת" לר"מ קאמר. לדידן, בעינן "כל צורת". לדידך, אודי לן מיהא ד"מקצת צורה" בעינן.

**והתניא** איפכא ר"מ אומר כל צורה. פ"ה: כל שהוא, אפילו עין אחד בלא לסת וגבינין. וחכ"א: "מצורת" – כל חצי הצורה. וקשה לפירושו: ד"כל צורה" דרב ודברייתא אינן שוין! ועוד: דהא תניא איפכא, לא הוה איפכא ממש! ועוד: דרב ור' יוחנן דבסמוך פליגי אברייתא, וארבי יוחנן ליכא למימר "תנא הוא ופליג", כמו ארב, כדמשמע פ"ק דכתובות (דף ח.) גבי (אין ברכת) חתנים מן המנין! ועוד קשה לפירושו: דרבא אמר חסא כרבנן דברייתא, וא"כ: כי פריך ליה מברייתא ד"צורת פנים שאמרו, אפילו פרצוף אחד", לישני ליה: דאתא כר"מ דברייתא, כיון דס"ל כברייתא, דהשתא כי משני ליה אביי: כי תניא ההיא לעכב מוקי לה כרב, והוא לא ס"ל הכי! ונראה לפרש: והתניא איפכא ממש, שר"מ אומר "כל צורה" – דבעיא ב' עינים ולסתות, דגרוע מכולה בהמה, דהתם "ילידה" כתיב. ורבנן אמרי: "מצורת" – חצי צורה. והשתא רבי יוחנן דאמר: המצח והגבינים והעינים כר"מ דברייתא, ורבא אמר חסא – כרבנן. ופריך ליה מברייתא, ואוקי לה כר"מ ור"ח גרים בדברי רב "ר"מ אומר כל צורת, וחכ"א מצורת", כמו במתניתין, ובברייתא איפכא. **אמר** רבא ושטו נקוב אמו טמאה לידה. קסבר: טרפה חיה. וכן בפ"ק דתמורה (דף יא:) גבי "רגל של זו עולה (או) כולה עולה", דקאמר רב חסדא דבדבר שעושה אותה טרפה – כולה עולה, דטרפה אינה חיה. ורבא אמר: דוקא דבר שעושה אותה נבלה – כולה עולה, דטרפה חיה. ובפ"ק דבכורות (דף ג.) פלוגתא איפכא *) גבי מקלת לגוי, מקלתה להפקיע מן הבכורה. דרב חסדא אמר: דבר שעושה אותה נבלה, דטרפה חיה. ורבא אמר: דבר שעושה אותה נמי טריפה, דטרפה אינה חיה. ואומר ר"ת: דהוי כאיכא דאמרי*.

*) נ"ל גבי מקנה לעובד כוכבים מקלת כו'. רש"א

עד

---

**עין משפט נר מצוה**

כ א מיי' פ"ב מהלכות נחלות הלכה י סמג עשין צו טוש"ע ח"מ סימן רעז סעיף ו:

כא ב מיי' פי"א מהל' בכורים הלכה טו סמג עשין קמד טוש"ע י"ד סי' שה סעיף כב:

כב ג מיי' פ"א מהלכות מאכלות אסורות הלכה ז סמג לאוין קלב טוש"ע י"ד סימן יג סעיף ה:

כג ד מיי' פ"י מהל' איסורי ביאה הלכה ט סמג לאוין קיא טור י"ד סימן קצד:

כד ה מיי' שם הלכה י:

כה ו ז מיי' שם הלכה יא סמג שם טור שם:

---

**תוספי הרא"ש**

וקורא בתורה אומר לו בא לשוחטך כולו בהמה ופניו אדם עומד וחורש בשדה ואומר לו בא חלוץ בא יבם: **אף** אנן נמי תנינא המפלת מין בהמה חיה ועוף. בספרי' כתוב ולד [מעליא] הוא דברי ר"מ ול"ג ליה דלית' במתני' דבכורות ואבא אחריו קאי דלא הוי בכור לכהן: **לר'** מאיר דאמר בהמה במעי אשה כו' לרבנן לא קא מבעיא ליה דכי היכי דבהמה במעי אשה בהמה הוי הכי נמי אדם במעי בהמה [אדם] הוי אבל לרבי מאיר דאמר בהמה במעי אשה הוי ולד אדם במעי [בהמה] איכא למיבעי מי אזלינן בתר סברא ואדם הוי או דלמא בתר אימא שדינן ליה כמו בהמה במעי אשה והא דקא"ל ותיפשוט ליה מדרבי יוחנן הוה מצי לשנויי דההיא כרבנן ואנן אליבא דר"מ קא מיבעי' לן אלא דעדיפא מינה קא משני: **ונברא** בעין אחד כבהמה שר' מאיר אומר מצורת וחכמים אומרים כל צורת. ה"ג רש"י וקשה דמנא ליה לרב לומר דחכמים אומרים כל צורת הא קתני במתניתין וחכמים אומרים עד שיהא בו מצורת אדם. ועוד גרים רש"י והא איפכא תניא שר' מאיר אומר כל צורת וחכמים אומרים מצורת ופי' כל צורת כל דהו צורת וקשה דהאי כל צורת לא הוי פירושו בכל צורה שאמר רב ועוד דלא הוי איפכא שאף לדברי הברייתא בעו חכמים טפי צורת אדם מר' מאיר ועוד דבבל דוכתא דאמרינן אי תניא תניא פי' והדרי בי ועו"ק דתנחה לרב אלא

---

[דיבור זה שייך למטה אחר ד"ה בכור לנחלה]

בכורות מו.

[שלש תיבות הללו ליתא במשנה דבכורות]

[ב"ב קיח:]

חולין סט.

[נ"ל אמרו לו]

[שבת קטו: וש"נ]

[תוספתא פ"ד]

[נ"ל דבחד]

**הגהות הב"ח**

(א) רש"י ד"ה המפלת וכו' ועוף ולד מעליא הוא דברי ר"מ כצ"ל וכל"א עם ד"ה ואין בכור:

**הגהות מהר"ב רנשבורג**

א] גמ' בעא מיניה רב אדא בר אהבה מאביי לרבי מאיר. נ"ב עיין תבואות שור:

---

לר' יוחנן תיקשי ליה הברייתא דלאו תנא הוא כדמוכח פ"ק דכתובות ועוד כי פריך מברייתא מצורת פנים שאמרו כו' א)(פ"ל שר' מאיר סבר או כולו אדם או כולו בהמה) לישני דכרבי מאיד אתיא דאמר כל דהו צורה ופר"ת הא דפליגי בגופו אדם ופניו תייש פלוגתא אחרת היא והפכו סברת ר"מ ורבנן דלרבנן חשיב בקל ולד טפי מלרבי מאיר וה"פ לא נחלקו אלא שפניו אדם ונברא בעין אחד בבהמה כלומר כל צדו אחד בבהמה כדאמרינן לקמן המצח והגבין והלסת ועין עד שיהו כלן כאחד וה"ק שר' מאיר אומר כל צורת וחכמים אומרים מצורת כלומר לר' מאיר לא הוי ולד עד שיהא בו כל צורת אדם ולרבנן אפי' במקצת צורה ודייק לה רב ממתניתין דקתני וחכמים אומרים [illegible] אלא משום דאיכא פלוגתא אחריתי באותו שדומה במקצת לאדם ובמקצת לבהמה אע"ג דבהך פלוגתא [illegible] [illegible]

א) אין מקומו כאן רק להלן [illegible] ב) נראה דצ"ל [illegible]

עַד הָאַרְכּוּבָה. רַבִּי יַנַּאי אוֹמֵר עַד לִנְקָבָיו. ר' יוֹחָנָן אוֹמֵר מִשּׁוּם רַבִּי יוֹסֵי בֶּן יְהוֹשֻׁעַ: עַד [א]מְקוֹם טַבּוּרוֹ. בֵּין רַבִּי זַכַּאי לְרַבִּי יַנַּאי אִיכָּא בֵּינַיְיהוּ *טְרֵפָה חָיָה, מָר סָבַר: טְרֵפָה חָיָה, וּמָר סָבַר: [ב]טְרֵפָה אֵינָהּ חָיָה. [א] בֵּין ר' יַנַּאי לְר' יוֹחָנָן אִיכָּא בֵּינַיְיהוּ דְּר"א, *דְּאָמַר רַבִּי אֶלְעָזָר: נִיטַּל יָרֵךְ וְחָלָל שֶׁלָּהּ — נְבֵלָה. אָמַר רַב פָּפָּא: מַחֲלוֹקֶת מִלְּמַטָּה לְמַעְלָה, אֲבָל מִלְּמַעְלָה לְמַטָּה אֲפִי' כָּל דְּהוּ טְהוֹרָה. וְכֵן אָמַר רַב גִּידֵּל, אָמַר רַבִּי יוֹחָנָן: [ד]הַמַּפֶּלֶת אֶת שֶׁגּוּלְגָּלְתּוֹ אֲטוּמָה — אִמּוֹ טְהוֹרָה. וְאָמַר רַב גִּידֵּל, אָמַר רַבִּי יוֹחָנָן: הַמַּפֶּלֶת כְּמִין אַפַּקְתָּא דְּדִיקְלָא — אִמּוֹ טְהוֹרָה. אִיתְמַר, הַמַּפֶּלֶת מִי שֶׁפָּנָיו מוּסְמָסִים. רַבִּי יוֹחָנָן אָמַר: אִמּוֹ טְמֵאָה, ר"ל אָמַר: אִמּוֹ טְהוֹרָה. אֵיתִיבֵיהּ ר' יוֹחָנָן לְרֵישׁ לָקִישׁ: *הַמַּפֶּלֶת יָד חֲתוּכָה וְרֶגֶל חֲתוּכָה — אִמּוֹ טְמֵאָה לֵידָה, וְאֵין חוֹשְׁשִׁין שֶׁמָּא מִגּוּף אָטוּם בָּאתָה. וְאִם אִיתָא — לִיתְנֵי שֶׁמָּא מִגּוּף אָטוּם אוֹ מִמִּי שֶׁפָּנָיו מוּסְמָסִין! אָמַר רַב פַּפִּי: בְּפָנָיו מוּסְמָסִין — כּוּלֵּי עָלְמָא לָא פְּלִיגֵי דִּטְמֵאָה, כִּי פְּלִיגֵי — [ה]בְּפָנָיו טוּחוֹת, וְאִיפְּכָא אִיתְמַר, רַבִּי יוֹחָנָן אָמַר: [ו]אִמּוֹ טְהוֹרָה, וְרֵישׁ לָקִישׁ אָמַר: אִמּוֹ טְמֵאָה. וְלוֹתְבֵיהּ ר"ל לְרַבִּי יוֹחָנָן מֵהָא! מִשּׁוּם דְּשָׁנֵי לֵיהּ: הַיְינוּ גּוּף אָטוּם, הַיְינוּ מִי שֶׁפָּנָיו טוּחוֹת. *בְּנֵי רַבִּי חִיָּיא נְפִיק לְקִרְיָיתָא, אֲתוּ לְקַמֵּיהּ דַּאֲבוּהוֹן, אָמַר לָהֶם: כְּלוּם בָּא מַעֲשֶׂה לְיֶדְכֶם? אָמְרוּ לוֹ: פָּנִים טוּחוֹת בָּא לְיָדֵינוּ, וְטִימֵּאנוּהָ. אָמַר לָהֶם: צְאוּ וְטַהֲרוּ מַה שֶּׁטִּמֵּאתֶם. מַאי דַּעֲתַיְיכוּ — לְחוּמְרָא, חוּמְרָא דְּאָתְיָא לִידֵי קוּלָּא הִיא, דְּקָיְהָבִיתוּ לָהּ יְמֵי טוֹהַר. *אִיתְמַר, [ז]הַמַּפֶּלֶת בְּרִיָּה שֶׁיֵּשׁ לָהּ ב' גַּבִּים וּב' שִׁדְרָאוֹת. אָמַר רַב: בְּאִשָּׁה — אֵינוֹ וָלָד, [ח]בִּבְהֵמָה — אָסוּר בַּאֲכִילָה. וּשְׁמוּאֵל אָמַר: בְּאִשָּׁה — וָלָד, בִּבְהֵמָה — מוּתָּר בַּאֲכִילָה. בְּמַאי קָמִיפַּלְגִי? בִּדְרַב חָנִין בַּר אַבָּא, *דְּאָמַר רַב חָנִין בַּר אַבָּא: [ט]"הַשְּׁסוּעָה" — בְּרִיָּה שֶׁיֵּשׁ לָהּ ב' גַּבִּין וּב' שִׁדְרָאוֹת. רַב אָמַר: בְּרִיָּה בְּעָלְמָא — לֵיתָא, וְכִי אַגְמְרֵיהּ רַחֲמָנָא לְמֹשֶׁה — בִּמְעֵי אִמָּהּ אַגְמְרֵיהּ. וּשְׁמוּאֵל אָמַר: בְּרִיָּה בְּעָלְמָא — אִיתָא, וְכִי אַגְמְרֵיהּ רַחֲמָנָא לְמֹשֶׁה — בְּעָלְמָא אַגְמְרֵיהּ, אֲבָל בִּמְעֵי אִמָּהּ — שַׁרְיָא. אֵיתִיבֵיהּ רַב שִׁימִי בַּר חִיָּיא לְרַב: *רַבִּי חֲנִינָא בֶּן אַנְטִיגְנוֹס אוֹמֵר, כָּל שֶׁיֵּשׁ לוֹ ב' גַּבִּין וּשְׁנֵי שִׁדְרָאוֹת — *פָּסוּל לַעֲבוֹדָה, אַלְמָא דְּחַיֵּי! *(וְקַשְׁיָא לְרַב.) *א"ל: שִׁימִי אַתְּ! [י]שֶׁשִּׁדְרָתוֹ עֲקוּמָּה. מֵיתִיבֵי: [כ]יֵשׁ בְּעוּבָּרִין שֶׁהֵן אֲסוּרִין. בֶּן אַרְבָּעָה — לְדַקָּה, בֶּן שְׁמֹנָה — לְגַסָּה, הֵימֶנּוּ וּלְמַטָּה — אָסוּר. יָצָא מִי שֶׁיֵּשׁ לוֹ שְׁנֵי גַּבִּין וּשְׁנֵי שִׁדְרָאוֹת. מַאי "יָצָא"? לָאו, יָצָא מִכְּלַל עוּבָּרִין שֶׁאֲפִילּוּ בִּמְעֵי אִמָּן אֲסוּרִין? רַב מְתָרֵץ לְטַעֲמֵיהּ, וּשְׁמוּאֵל מְתָרֵץ לְטַעֲמֵיהּ. רַב מְתָרֵץ לְטַעֲמֵיהּ: בֶּן אַרְבָּעָה — לְדַקָּה, בֶּן ח' — לְגַסָּה, הֵימֶנּוּ וּלְמַטָּה — אָסוּר. בַּמֶּה דְּבָרִים אֲמוּרִים — כְּשֶׁיָּצָא לַאֲוִיר הָעוֹלָם, [ל]אֲבָל בִּמְעֵי אִמּוֹ — שָׁרֵי, יָצָא מִי שֶׁיֵּשׁ לוֹ שְׁנֵי גַּבִּין וּשְׁנֵי שִׁדְרָאוֹת, דַּאֲפִילּוּ בִּמְעֵי אִמּוֹ נַמִי אָסוּר. וּשְׁמוּאֵל

**רש"י**

עַד הָאַרְכּוּבָה, שֶׁנֶּחְתְּכוּ רַגְלֶיהָ עַד לְמַעְלָה מִן הָאַרְכּוּבָה שֶׁהִיא טְרֵפָה. וְקָסָבַר: טְרֵפָה אֵינָהּ חָיָה. עַד לִנְקָבָיו. וּנְקָבָיו בִּכְלָל. קָסָבַר: טְרֵפָה חָיָה, הִלְכָּךְ עַד לָאַרְכּוּבָה — הָוֵי וָלָד, אֲבָל עַד לִנְקָבָיו — הָוֵי נְבֵלָה. כְּר' אֶלְעָזָר דְּאָמַר: נִיטַּל הַיָּרֵךְ וְחָלָל שֶׁלָּהּ — נְבֵלָה, וַאֲפִי' בְּחַיֶּיהָ מְטַמְּאָה, הִלְכָּךְ לָא חָיָה. וּבִשְׁחִיטַת חוּלִּין (דף כא.) מְפָרֵשׁ: הֵיכִי דָּמֵי חָלָל שֶׁלָּהּ? כָּל שֶׁרְבוּלָּהּ וְנִרְאֵית חֲסֵרָה. עַד טַבּוּרוֹ. אֲבָל עַד נְקָבָיו — לָא, דְּלֵית לֵיהּ דְּרַבִּי אֶלְעָזָר. וְאִי מִשּׁוּם טְרֵפָה — קָסָבַר: טְרֵפָה חָיָה. בֵּין ר' יַנַּאי לְרַבִּי יוֹחָנָן אִיכָּא בֵּינַיְיהוּ דְּר' אֶלְעָזָר. וְתַרְוַויְהוּ אִית לְהוּ טְרֵפָה חָיָה. מִלְמַעְלָה. שֶׁנֶּחְתַּךְ מִגּוּלְגָּלְתּוֹ. אֲטוּמָה. חֲסֵרָה. כְּמִין אַפַּקְתָּא דְּדִיקְלָא. שֶׁהַדֶּקֶל לְמַטָּה יָחִיד, וּמִתְפַּצֵּל מִלְמַעְלָה. כָּךְ הָיוּ יָדָיו וְרַגְלָיו עַל כְּתֵפוֹ, וּמִלְּמַטָּה הוּא בְּלֹא צוּרָה. מוּסְמָסִין. מְעוּכִין קְצָת, וְלֹא כָּל כָּךְ כְּפָנָיו טוּחוֹת. כִּי פְּלִיגֵי בְּפָנָיו טוּחוֹת. שֶׁאֵין צוּרָה בָּהֶן נִיכֶּרֶת לְגַמְרֵי. וְאִיפְּכָא אִיתְמַר. וְלֹא מִשּׁוּם צוֹרֶךְ (*מַפִּיק) לָהּ, אֶלָּא הָכִי גְּמַר לָהּ מֵרַבֵּיהּ. לוֹתְבֵיהּ רֵישׁ לָקִישׁ לְר' יוֹחָנָן מֵהָא. דְּאִם אִיתָא, לִיתְנֵי "אוֹ מִמִּי שֶׁפָּנָיו טוּחוֹת". הַיְינוּ פָּנָיו טוּחוֹת. אֲבָל בְּפָנָיו מוּסְמָסִין לֵיכָּא לְשַׁנּוּיֵי הָכִי, דְּהָא נִיכֶּרֶת בָּהֶן הַצּוּרָה. וְלָאו אָטוּם הוּא, דְּאָטוּם הַיְינוּ חָסֵר לְגַמְרֵי. לְחוּמְרָא. שֶׁטִּמֵּאתֶם אוֹתָהּ שְׁבוּעַיִם, מִשּׁוּם סְפֵק נְקֵבָה. חוּמְרָא דְּאָתֵי לִידֵי קוּלָּא הוּא. דְּכֵיוָן דְּוָלָד הוּא, יְהַבִיתוּ לָהּ יְמֵי טוֹהַר. מִיהָא ל"ג דְּזָכָר, וּמְטַהֲרִיתוּ לְדַם רְאִיָּיתָהּ שֶׁלֹּא כַּדִּין, דִּטְמֵאָה נִדָּה הִיא, דְּלָאו וָלָד הוּא. בִּבְהֵמָה אָסוּר בַּאֲכִילָה. אִם נִשְׁחֲטָה אִמּוֹ וְנִמְצָא בִּמְעֶיהָ, וְכָל שֶׁכֵּן יָצָא לַאֲוִיר הָעוֹלָם, דְּנֵפֶל הוּא, וּנְבֵלָה. מוּתָּר בַּאֲכִילָה. דִּכְתִיב (ויקרא יא): "כֹּל בַּבְּהֵמָה תֹּאכֵלוּ" — כָּל הַנִּמְצָא בַּבְּהֵמָה תֹּאכְלוּ, וּבִלְבַד שֶׁיִּהְיוּ לוֹ פַּרְסוֹת אוֹ פַּרְסָה, כִּדְאָמַר בִּ"בְהֵמָה הַמַּקְשָׁה לֵילֵד" (חולין סט.). הַשְּׁסוּעָה. רַחֲמָנָא אַסְרָהּ, דִּכְתִיב (דברים יד): "אֶת זֶה לֹא תֹאכְלוּ וגו' הַשְּׁסוּעָה". רַב סָבַר. הַאי דְּאָסַר רַחֲמָנָא — כְּשֶׁנִּמְצֵאת בִּמְעֵי בְּהֵמָה אֲסוּרָה, דְּהָא בְּרִיָּה בְּעָלְמָא בִּפְנֵי עַצְמָהּ לֵיתָא. בְּעָלְמָא אַגְמְרֵיהּ. אוֹתוֹ הַמִּין אָסַר, אֲבָל אִם נִמְצֵאת בִּמְעֵי פָּרָה — מוּתָּר. ר' חֲנִינָא בֶּן אַנְטִיגְנוֹס. בִּבְכוֹר קָאֵי, וְקָאָמַר דְּהָוֵי מוּם. וּמִדְּפָסַל לֵיהּ לְקָרְבָּן, מִכְּלָל דִּלְהֶדְיוֹט — שָׁרֵי. וְקַשְׁיָא לְתַרְוַויְהוּ, דְּהָא אֲפִי' יָצָא לַאֲוִיר הָעוֹלָם — שָׁרֵי, וּשְׁמוּאֵל לָא שָׁרֵי אֶלָּא בִּמְעֵי אִמּוֹ. וְהָא דְּאַקְשֵׁי רַב שִׁימִי טְפֵי לְרַב מִדִּשְׁמוּאֵל — מִשּׁוּם דְּגַבֵּיהּ הֲוָה קָאֵי, וּבַר בְּרֵיהּ הֲוָה, כִּדְאָמַר בְּפֶרֶק "כָּל הַבָּשָׂר" (שם קיא.): רַב אִקְלַע לְבֵי רַב שִׁימִי בַּר חִיָּיא בַּר בְּרֵיהּ. שִׁימִי אַתְּ. בְּכַמָּה דּוּכְתִּין אַשְׁכַּחַן דְּמִהַדַּר לֵיהּ רַב הָכִי: "שִׁימִי אַתְּ". וְנִרְאֶה בְּעֵינַי מִשּׁוּם דְּבַר בְּרֵיהּ הֲוָה, וְקָאָמַר לֵיהּ הָכִי — מִשּׁוּם חֲבִיבוּתֵיהּ. כְּלוֹמַר, אַתָּה יוֹדֵעַ לַהֲשִׁיבֵנִי. וַאֲנִי שָׁמַעְתִּי: שֶׁמִּדַּת צְנִיעוּת הָיָה בּוֹ בְּרַב, שֶׁלֹּא הָיָה זוֹקֵף עֵינָיו לְמַעְלָה, הִלְכָּךְ לֹא הָיָה מַכִּירוֹ. וְלָא נִהְרָא לִי: שֶׁהֲרֵי לֹא מָצִינוּ שֶׁאָמַר רַב כָּךְ לְשׁוּם אָדָם, אֶלָּא לָזֶה אָמַר כֵּן בְּכַמָּה מְקוֹמוֹת, כָּאן וּבִמְנָחוֹת (דף קי.). וְעוֹד שָׁמַעְתִּי: מִשּׁוּם דְּחָרִיף הֲוָה וְדָחִיק לֵיהּ, כִּי הַהִיא דְּאָמַר *(בְּמוֹעֵד קָטָן (דף כט)) רַחֲמָנָא לִישֵׁזְבָן מִכִּיסּוּפֵיהּ דְּרַב שִׁימִי. וְלָאו הִיא, דְּהָתָם רַב שִׁימִי בַּר אַשִׁי הֲוָה דְּדָחִיק לֵיהּ לְרַב פַּפָּא. שֶׁשִּׁדְרָתוֹ עֲקוּמָּה. הָא דְּרַבִּי חֲנִינָא, דְּמַשְׁמַע דְּחַיֵּי — לָאו שְׁנֵי גַּבִּין מַמָּשׁ, אֶלָּא שֶׁשִּׁדְרָתוֹ עֲקוּמָּה (כָּזֶה) וְנִרְאִין כִּשְׁתַּיִם. יֵשׁ בְּעוּבָּרִין. שֶׁיָּצְאוּ לַאֲוִיר הָעוֹלָם שֶׁאֲסוּרִין מִשּׁוּם נְבֵלָה. לָאו יָצָא מִכְּלַל עוּבָּרִין. דְּהָנֵי, אַע"ג דְּלֹא כָּלוּ חֳדָשֵׁיהֶן, כִּי נִמְצְאוּ בִּמְעֵי אִמָּן — שָׁרוּ. אֲבָל הַאי, אֲפִי' בִּמְעֵי אִמָּן — אָסוּר. וְקַשְׁיָא לִשְׁמוּאֵל. רַב מְתָרֵץ לְטַעֲמֵיהּ. דְּרַב לֹא צָרִיךְ לְתָרוּצֵי, אֶלָּא מִשּׁוּם הִיא גּוּפָהּ דְּלָא מִשְׁתַּמַּע שַׁפִּיר. דְּהָא רֵישָׁא — כְּשֶׁיָּצְאוּ לַאֲוִיר הָעוֹלָם מַיְירֵי, וְסֵיפָא דְּקָתָנֵי "יָצָא" — מַשְׁמַע דַּעֲלָהּ קָאֵי, וּכְשֶׁיָּצָא לַאֲוִיר הָעוֹלָם — מַשְׁמַע דְּמוּתָּר. וְאִי אֶפְשָׁר לוֹמַר כֵּן, הִלְכָּךְ צָרִיךְ לְהוֹסִיף עָלֶיהָ: "אֲבָל בִּמְעֵי אִמּוֹ שָׁרֵי", דִּכְתִיב: "כֹּל בַּבְּהֵמָה תֹּאכֵלוּ". בְּפֶרֶק "בְּהֵמָה הַמַּקְשָׁה" (חולין סט.). יָצָא מִי שֶׁיֵּשׁ לוֹ שְׁנֵי גַּבִּין וכו'. דְּכִי כָּתַב רַחֲמָנָא "הַשְּׁסוּעָה" — לְמֵיסַר בִּמְעֵי אִמּוֹ אֲסָרָהּ, דְּהָא מִין בִּפְנֵי עַצְמָהּ לֵיתָא. וּשְׁמוּאֵל

**תוספות**

**עד** הארכובה. והארכובה בכלל, דהיינו מן הארכובה ולמעלה. ואין שייך להביא זה גבי "כל שיעורי חכמים להחמיר, לענין עד ועד בכלל, ב"אלו טרפות" (חולין נה.) ואע"ג דתנינן יד אמרי' בפרקין דטמאה לידה — היינו, כשניכר שהמותר נמחה כשפירש. א"נ: כאן מיירי דניכר היטב שלא נברא יותר, כגון במקום החסרון יש עור נקרס.

**ליתני** שמא מגוף אטום באת או ממי שפניו כו' וא"ת: והא איכא טובא דלא תני, כגון פניו טייח (ופניו) אטום ואפקותא דדיקלא? וי"ל: דפניו מוסמסין דומה לגוף אטום, והויא ליה למיתני בהדיה טפי מאחריני.

**אמר** רב פפא בפניו מוסמסין כ"ע לא פליגי. והא דקאמר איתיביה ר' יוחנן לר"ל — לא היו דברים מעולם. [ב]וכענין זה יש בריש חולין (דף ד)*.

**רבי** חנינא בן אנטיגנוס אומר כל שיש כו' פ"ה: מדהוי מום לקרבן, מכלל דלהדיוט — שרי. וקשה לתרוייהו, דהא אפי' יצא לאויר העולם — שרי, ושמואל לא שרי ליה אלא במעי אמו. וקשה לר"ת דבפ' *"אלו מומין" (דף מג:) תנא ליה גבי מומי כהן, ולא גבי מומי בהמה. והתם נמי פריך מרב, ולא מייתי משמואל מידי! ונראה לר"ת: דארב דוקא פריך, דאמר: באשה אינו ולד — אלמא, אינו מתקיים. והא חשיב ליה גבי מומי כהן — אלמא, חי! אבל לשמואל, דאמר: באשה ולד מתקיים — לא פריך מידי. ובבהמה נמי אר"ת דמתקיים לשמואל. והא דאמר בסמוך, דכי יצא לאויר העולם, אסור — היינו משום "שסועה" דאסר רחמנא. ורש"י פירש בסמוך לפי שיטתו דאסור משום נפל, ושסועה דאסר רחמנא — היינו מין בהמה דעלמא, שיש לאם ולולד שני גבין וכן ב' שדראות. אבל הנולד מבהמה שאין לה אלא גב אחד ושדרה אחת — לא איצטריך קרא למיסר, דנפל גמור הוי. ובאשה מיהא מתקיים, אף לפירושו, מדקאמר "באשה ולד". ולישנא דבעלמא אגמריה משמע כפירושו. וא"ת: בפרק "אלו טרפות" (חולין ס:) דפריך גבי שסועה שיש לה ב' גבין: וכי משה קניגי היה? והשתא לפ"ה: אתי שפיר, דשסועה מין בעלמא הוא לשמואל ואינה מצויה אלא ביער. לכך קאמר: וכי קניגי היה. אבל לפי' ר"ת: שאף לשמואל אינו מין בפני עצמו אלא שכך נולד מן הבהמה, מה ענין זה אצל קניגי? וי"ל: דאף לפירוש ר"ת: אם לא היה קניגי, ורגיל לראות ומכיר בהמות משונות, לא היה מכיר בהמה זו שיש לה ב' גבין, אע"פ שגם נולד מבהמות של ישוב, שאינה רגילה להוליד מבהמה שאינה משונה. מי

**מסורת הש"ס**

[חולין מב. וש"נ] | חולין כא. לב: [תמורה יח:] | [נ"ל מפיד] | [לקמן כח. לעיל יח.] | ביצה ט: | בכורות מג: | חולין ס: וע"ש | [בכורות מג:] | ע"ש בבכורות דל"ג פסול לעבודה | [מנחות כט. קי. וע"ש פרש"י בכורות שם וע"ש פירש"י] | [נ"ל בתענית ט:]

**גליון הש"ס**

**גמ'** בפניו טוחות ואיפכא. כעין זה שבת עו ע"א וזבחים לד ע"א: **תום'** ד"ה אמר וכו' וכענין זה יש בריש חולין. נ"ל דל"ל בריש החולץ וכן בעירובין מ ע"א וב"ב קנד ע"ב ובכורות ז ע"ב:

**הגהות מהר"ב רנשבורג**

א] גמ' בין ר' ינאי לר' יוחנן איכא בינייהו דר"א. נ"ב עיין חולין נז ע"א תוס' ד"ה דלמא וכו' שכתבו דליכא מאן דפליג אר"א והכא פליג ר' יוחנן ובתמורה יא ע"ב פליג רב ששת וצ"ע ועיין כרו"פ סי' כ' ס"ק ב' מ"ש בזה ודבריו צ"ע: ב] תום' ד"ה אמר רב פפא וכו' וכענין זה פריש החולץ ל"ה ע"ב כצ"ל לענ"ד יעוי"ש תוס' ד"ה כולי עלמא וכו' ועיין שיטה מקובצת ביצה דף לט ע"ב מבואר כדברי יעוש"ה:

**עין משפט נר מצוה**

כו א מיי' פ"י מהלכות איסורי ביאה הלכה יא:

כז ב מיי' פי"א מהלכות שחיטה הלכה א [ופ"ד מהלכות מאכלות אסורות הלכה ט] סמג לאוין קלב טוש"ע י"ד סי' נז סעיף יח [ועוד בטוי"ד סימן כט]:

רש"א וטעו

כח ג מיי' שם פ"ג הלכה יט ופ"ב מהלכות אבות הטומאה הלכה א:

[ועי' תוספות יבמות לה: ד"ה כולי עלמא]

כט ד ה ו ז מיי' פ"י מהל' איסורי ביאה הלכה יא טור י"ד סי' קצד [וברב אלפס חולין פ"ד דף רפב]:

[נ"ל מומין אלו]

ל ח מיי' פ"א מהלכות מאכלות אסורות הלכ' ו סמג עשין סב טוש"ע י"ד סי' יג סעיף ו:

לא ט מיי' שם הלכה ו:

לב י מיי' פ"ח מהלכות ביאת מקדש הלכה י:

לג כ מיי' פ"ד מהלכות מאכלות אסורות הלכה ד סמג לאוין קלב טוש"ע י"ד סי' טו סעי' ב:

לד ל מיי' שם פ"ה הלכה יד סמג שם טוש"ע י"ד סי' יג סעיף ב:

**תוספי הרא"ש**

(בשביל) [בשכל] גופו תייש וראשו אדם כיון שכל גופו תייש: **ליתני** שמא מגוף אטום בא או ממי שפניו מוסמסין אע"ג דאיכא טובא דלא קתני כגון ושטו אטום ואפקתא דדיקלא י"ל דכל הני בכלל גוף אטום איתנהו אבל אי פניו מוסמסין הוי כמו גוף אטום ה"ל למיתני בהדיא וכ"ש גוף אטום: ר' חנינא בן אנטיגנוס אומר מי שיש לו שני גבין ושתי שדראות. פרש"י דגבי מומי בהמה מיתניא וליתיה דלגבי מומי אדם מיתניא בפ' אלו מומין ואהך דאמר רב באשה אינו ולד פריך:

[צריך תיקון ובפרט לפי' רש"י ד"ה ר' חנינא וכו' וקשיא לתרוייהו וכו' צריך תיקון וכן בילקוט רמז תתל"א ליתא]

לה א ב מיי' פ"י מהל' איסורי ביאה הלכה יא טור י"ד סי' קלד:
לו ג ד מיי' שם הלכה י:
לז ה מיי' שם הלכה ד סמג לאוין קיא טוש"ע י"ד סי' קלד סעיף ג ועכשיו הכל אמו טמאה שאין אנו בקיאין בצורות:
לח ו מיי' שם הלכה ב:
לט ז מיי' שם הלכה יב סמג שם טור ש"ע שם:

ושמואל מתרץ לטעמיה. רישא וסיפא, בשיצא לאויר העולם. דאע"ג דכלו לו חדשיו. נפל הוא, דלא חיי, ונבלה הואי. שאינו חתוך. כולו שלם כעין דף, ואין בו חיתוך אברים וצורה, אלא חלק כעין עיגול. וטמאה שבעת ימים וביום השמיני ימול. משמע, מי שהוא ראוי לחיות שמנה ימים – אמו טמאה לידה, ומי שאינו ראוי לחיות שמנה לברית – לא. א"ל רב. לתנא: סיים בה נמי הכי, ואימא "יצאו אלו מי שיש לו שני גבין" וכו'. כוותיה דשמואל. בשני גבין, דולד הוא, וקאמר: טמאה אפילו בלידה יבשתא, דולד הוא. הרי אמרו אשה יולדת לט' ויולדת לז'. ואנא נמי אמינא: כי היכי דבהמה לט' כדאמרי' לעיל "בן ח' לגסה – נפל", הכא נמי יולדת לז' – נפל, או לאו נפל הוא, ומותר. הימנו ולמטה. בברייתא דלעיל תניא. מאי לאו אגסה. נמי קאי, דקתני: בן ח' לגסה, והימנו ולמטה, כגון בר ז' – אסור. אדקה. בן ד' לדקה, והימנו ולמטה, כגון בר תלתא – אסור. אלא אי אמרת אדקה פשיטא. הואיל ובר תלתא הוא – לא חיי. כל בציר תרי ירחי. מכדרכו – חיי, כי היכי דבאשה ובבהמה גסה בר ז' חיי, דהוי תרי ירחי בציר מכי אורחיה, הכי נמי בר תלתא לדקה – חיי, אע"ג דבר ד' – לא חיי. קמ"ל. דלא חיי. דמות לילית. שידה. שד יש לו פרצוף אדם, ויש לו כנפים. הנהג בן אחיך ובא. כלומר, הבא בן אחיך ובא עמו. ה"ג: בהליכתן יצתה כלת חנינא לקראת רבי יהושע. [בכורות מט:]

מתני' מלא גנונים. גוונים. המפלת סנדל. אין סנדל בלא ולד אחר. ובשביל סנדל תשב לזכר ולנקבה, דספק זכר ספק נקבה הוא. ואם הולד אחר נקבה – אין הסנדל לא מעלה ולא מוריד, ולא תשב אלא לנקבה ימי טומאה וימי טהרה. שאפי' הוא זכר, הואיל ונקבה בהדיה – לא בלירי ימי טומאתה וימי טהרה דנקבה. שהרי של זכר מובלעין בתוך של נקבה. [שם ח.] וכי אצטריך "תשב לזכר ולנקבה" – כגון שהולד השני זכר, דיהבינן לה חומרת טומאה דנקבה – בשביל הסנדל, וימי טוהר לזכר – לחומרא. גמ' שמא ולד היה ונימוח. כיון דלאו דם הוא, ולאו מים נינהו, איכא למיחש לולד. [נ"ל לרבי] כמה יין חי כו'. לשון גוזמא. ה"ג: [ברש"י ליתא וכן נ"ל] רבא אמר. "מלא" תנן. סכויין. שחורין שמעתי. ל"א: סכויין בלא מוח [לעיל כג.] ומשיחה אלא יבשה. מזוג. יותר מדאי. קולית. עצם הירך. דיילא. (א) שמש דרבנן, ואדא שמו.

פרשתבינא.

תורה אור

ושמואל מתרץ לטעמיה: בן ארבעה לדקה, בן שמנה לגסה, הימנו ולמטה – אסור. במה דברים אמורים – בשלא כלו לו חדשיו, אבל כלו לו חדשיו – מותר. יצא מי שיש לו ב' גבין וב' שדראות, דאע"ג דכלו לו חדשיו, אם יצא לאויר העולם – אסור, במעי אמו – שרי. תני תנא קמיה דרב: המפלת בריית גוף שאינו חתוך, ובריית ראש שאינו חתוך, יכול תהא אמו טמאה לידה – ת"ל: °"אשה כי תזריע וילדה זכר וגו' וביום השמיני ימול" וגו' – מי שראוי לברית שמנה [א]יצאו אלו שאינן ראויין לברית שמנה. א"ל רב, וסיים בה הכי: [ב]ושיש לו שני גבין ושני שדראות. רבי ירמיה בר אבא סבר למעבד עובדא כוותיה דשמואל, אמר ליה רב הונא: מאי דעתיך – לחומרא? חומרא דאתי לידי קולא הוא, דקיהבת לה דמי טוהר. עביד מיהא כותיה דרב, *דקיימא לן: הלכתא כרב באיסורי, בין לקולא בין לחומרא. אמר רבא: הרי אמרו אשה יולדת לתשעה ויולדת לשבעה, *בהמה גסה יולדת לתשעה יולדת לשבעה או לא ילדה? אמר רב נחמן בר יצחק, ת"ש: הימנו ולמטה – אסור, מאי לאו אגסה? לא, אדקה. האי מאי? אי אמרת בשלמא אגסה – אצטריך, סלקא דעתך אמינא: הואיל ובאשה חיי – בבהמה נמי חיי, קמ"ל דלא חיי. אלא אי אמרת אדקה איתמר, פשיטא! בת תלתא ירחי מי קא חיי?! אצטריך, סד"א: כל בציר תרי ירחי חיי, קמ"ל. אמר רב יהודה, אמר שמואל: [ג]המפלת דמות לילית – אמו טמאה לידה. ולד הוא, אלא שיש לו כנפים. תנ"ה, א"ר יוסי: מעשה בסימוני באחת שהפילה דמות לילית, ובא מעשה לפני חכמים, ואמרו ולד הוא אלא שיש לו כנפים. המפלת דמות נחש, הורה חנינא בן אחיו של רבי יהושע: [ד]אמו טמאה לידה. הלך ר' יוסף וספר דברים לפני ר"ג. שלח לו: *רבי יהושע, הנהג בן אחיך ובא. בהליכתן יצתה כלת *(ר') חנינא לקראתו, אמרה לו: רבי, המפלת כמין נחש מהו? אמר לה: אמו טהורה. אמרה לו: והלא משמך אמרה לי חמותי אמו טמאה? ואמר לה מאיזה טעם *הואיל וגלגל עינו עגול כשל אדם! מתוך דבריה נזכר רבי יהושע, שלח לו לרבן גמליאל: מפי הורה חנינא. אמר אביי, ש"מ: צורבא מרבנן דאמר מילתא, לימא בה טעמא, דכי מדכרו ליה – מדכר.§

ויקרא יב

מתני' [ה]המפלת שפיר מלא מים, מלא דם, מלא גנונים – אינה חוששת לולד, [ו]ואם היה מרוקם – תשב לזכר ולנקבה. *[ז]המפלת סנדל או שליא – תשב לזכר ולנקבה.§ גמ' בשלמא דם ומים – לא כלום היא, אלא גנונים – ניחוש שמא ולד הוה ונימוח? אמר אביי: כמה יין חי שתת אמו של זה שנמוח עוברה בתוך מעיה? רבא אמר: "מלא" תנן, ואם איתא דאתמוחי אתמח – מחסר חסר. רב אדא בר אהבה אמר: "גוונים" תנן, ואם איתא דאתמוחי אתמח – כולה בחד גוונא הוי קאי. *תניא, אבא שאול אומר: קובר מתים הייתי והייתי מסתכל בעצמות של מתים. השותה יין חי – עצמותיו שרופין, מזוג – עצמותיו סכויין, כראוי – עצמותיו משוחין. וכל מי ששתייתו מרובה מאכילתו – עצמותיו שרופין, אכילתו מרובה משתייתו – עצמותיו סכויין, כראוי – עצמותיו משוחין. [א] תניא, אבא שאול אומר, ואיתימא רבי יוחנן: קובר מתים הייתי, פעם אחת רצתי אחר צבי, ונכנסתי בקולית של מת, ורצתי אחריו שלש פרסאות, וצבי לא הגעתי וקולית לא כלתה. כשחזרתי לאחורי אמרו לי: של עוג מלך הבשן היתה. תניא, אבא שאול אומר: קובר מתים הייתי, פעם אחת נפתחה מערה תחתי, ועמדתי בגלגל עינו של מת עד חוטמי. כשחזרתי לאחורי אמרו: עין של אבשלום היתה. ושמא תאמר: אבא שאול ננס הוה – אבא שאול ארוך בדורו הוה ורבי טרפון מגיע לכתפו, ור' טרפון ארוך בדורו הוה ור"מ מגיע לכתפו, רבי מאיר ארוך בדורו הוה ורבי מגיע לכתפו, רבי ארוך בדורו הוה ורבי חייא מגיע לכתפו, ורבי חייא ארוך בדורו הוה ורב מגיע לכתפו, רב ארוך בדורו הוה ורב יהודה מגיע לכתפו, ורב יהודה ארוך בדורו הוה ואדא דיילא מגיע לכתפו,

פרשתבינא

[עי' תוספות לקמן כה: ד"ה המפלת]
[מו"ק כ:]

מי שראוי לבריאת נשמה. ולית דגרס "לברית שמנה".

המפלת דמות לילית אמו טמאה לידה. וא"ת: פשיטא, מי גרע מגופו תיש ופניו אדם, דהוי ולד לכ"ע וי"ל: דהתם יצא מתורת בהמה והוי אדם, והכא לא יצא כלל מתורת לילית. אך ק"ק דאמרי' לעיל (כג.) בעופות תבדק, לרבנן דקריא וקיפופא הוי ולד, אף על גב דלסתות לא מפיק ליה כלל מתורת כוס וינשוף? וי"ל: שמואל דהכא יפרש לעיל, תבדק לר"מ.

אכילתו מרובה משתייתו. פי': יותר מדאי מרובה על השתיה. דהא דרך אכילה להיות מרובה על השתיה, כדאמרי' בפ"ק דמגילה (דף יב.) "והשתיה כדת אין אונס" – כדת של תורה, דאכילה מרובה משתייה, דקרבנות יש יותר מנסכים. [לא נמצא שם] והא דאמרי' *ב"ערבי פסחים" (דף קי.) ובגיטין (דף ע.) אכול שליש ושתה שליש והנח שליש. לכשתכעוס, תעמוד על מילואך – לאו דוקא, אלא שבין אכילה ושתיה יהיו שני שלישים.

פרשתבינא

## הגהות הב"ח

(א) רש"י ד"ה דיילא שמש. נ"ב ובסוף פ' חבית איתא דאדא דיילא שמש דרב יהודה הוה וע"ש:

## הגהות מהר"ב רנשבורג

א] גמ' תניא אבא שאול אומר ואיתימא ר' יוחנן. נ"ב עיין כתובות ח ע"א תוס' ד"ה רב וכו' דאיכא ר' יוחנן שהוא תנא:

## תוספי הרא"ש

ואע"ג דכלו לו חדשיו אם יצא לאויר העולם אסור. פרש"י משום דנפל הוא ואינו מתקיים והוי כנבלה. ולא רצה לפרש משום דאגמריה רחמנא למשה דשסועה בעלמא אסירא דא"כ לא הוי ליה לתנא למיתנייה באיסור' בהדי עוברין דאסירי משום נפל. וצ"ל אע"ג דאמר שמואל באשה ולד ומתקיים בבהמה אינו מתקיים. והא דאמר שמואל בריה בעלמא איתא היינו מין אחד שכולן יש להן שני גבין ושני שדראות. אבל אם נמצא במעי בהמה אינו מתקיים. וי"מ בבהמה נמי מתקיים ויצא לאויר העולם אסור משום קרא דהשסועה והא דאמר שמואל בריה בעלמא הוא לאו מין בפני עצמו קאמר אלא הכי אגמריה רחמנא למשה דאם נולד מבהמה ויצא לאויר העולם אסור דאילו הוי מין בפני עצמו אם ולד במעי בהמה אמאי ליתסר כיון דשסועה לאו מסימני טומאה דבהמה אלא דרחמנא אסר אותו מין ולאו משום דסימן טומאה הוי. וקשה להך פי' מהא דקאמר בפ' אלו טרפות על הך דקאמר בריה בעלמא היא שיש לה שני גבין ושני שדראות וכי משה רבינו קניגי היה או בלסטרי היה מכאן תשובה לאומרים אין תורה מן השמים ואי לא הוה מין בפני עצמו אלא שכך נולד מן הבהמה מה ענין זה אצל קניגי או בלסטרי. וי"ל דמי שהוא קניגי או בלסטרי ומכיר בכל מיני חיות לפעמים מזדמן לידו שהוא מוצא במיני בהמה ולד כזה: המפלת דמות לילית אמו טמאה לידה. וא"ת פשיטא ומי גרע מגופו תייש ופניו אדם דהוי ולד ואפ' לרבנן דלית להו דרשא דיצירה יצירה וי"ל דלא דמי התם פניו אדם מוציאין אותו מתורת תייש הלכך חשיב אדם אבל הכא מה שכל גופו אדם אין מוציאין אותו מתורת לילית. כלומר שהרי לילית זו היא צורתה משא"כ תייש שאין צורתו כפני אדם. ומיהו קשה מהא דאמרינן לעיל ובעופות תבדק לרבנן דאי קריא וקיפוף אין שאר עופות לא אלמא קריא וקיפוף הוי ולד משום שדומה לאדם שיש לו לסתות אע"ג דמה שיש לו לסתות אין מוציא אותו מתורת קריא וקיפוף א"כ הכא נמי פשיטא וי"ל דרב יהודה אמר שמואל דהכא ס"ל תבדק לר' מאיר. והקשה ר"מ דהא רב יהודה אמר שמואל אמר לעיל דטעמא דר"מ משום יצירה וא"כ לר' מאיר בכל העופות מיחשב ליה לידה ותירץ דלרב יהודה אמר שמואל פליג ר' אלעזר בר צדוק אתנא דמתניתין דסבר דטעמא דר"מ משום יצירה ולא שנא קריא וקיפוף ול"ש שאר עופות ולר' אלעזר בר צדוק דאמר תיבדק לר"מ סבר דטעמא דר"מ משום דעיניהם הולכות לפניהם ודוקא קריא וקיפוף: עצמותיו סבואין כמו זולל וסובא ותשוש. ותימה והלא ראוי לעשות כן כדאמרינן והשתיה כדת אין אונס כדתה של תורה אכילה מרובה משתיה כדאשכחן גבי נסכים. וי"ל דהכא מיירי באכילה מרובה משתיה יותר מדאי וממה שראוי לו וכן מזוג היינו יותר מדאי והא דאמרינן בגיטין אכול שליש ושתה שליש לכשתכעום

*פרשתבינא דפומבדיתא קאי ליה לאדא דיילא עד פלגיה, וכולי עלמא קאי לפרשתבינא דפומבדיתא עד חרציה. שאלו לפני רבי: המפלת שפיר מלא בשר, מהו? אמר להם: לא שמעתי. אמר לפניו ר' ישמעאל בר' יוסי, כך אמר אבא: מלא דם — טמאה נדה, מלא בשר — טמאה לידה. א"ל: אילמלי דבר חדש אמרת לנו משום אביך — שמענוך, עכשיו מדהא קמייתא כיחידאה קאמר — כסומכוס שאמר משום ר"מ הא נמי — שמא כרבי יהושע אמרה, ואין הלכה כר' יהושע. דתניא, המפלת שפיר שאינו מרוקם — ר' יהושע אומר: ולד, וחכ"א: [א]אינו ולד. אמר ר"ש בן לקיש משום ר' אושעיא: מחלוקת — בעכור, אבל בצלול — דברי הכל אינו ולד. ור' יהושע בן לוי אמר: בצלול מחלוקת. איבעיא להו: בצלול מחלוקת — אבל בעכור דברי הכל ולד, או דלמא — בין בזה ובין בזה מחלוקת? תיקו. מיתיבי, את זו דרש ר' יהושע בן חנניא: °"ויעש ה' אלהים לאדם ולאשתו כתנות עור וילבישם" — מלמד שאין הקב"ה עושה עור לאדם אלא א"כ נוצר. אלמא בעור תליא מילתא, לא שנא עכור ול"ש צלול. אי אמרת בשלמא בצלול מחלוקת — היינו דאיצטריך קרא, אלא אי אמרת בעכור מחלוקת — למה לי קרא? סברא בעלמא הוא! אלא שמע מינה: בצלול מחלוקת, *שמע מינה. וכן אמר ר"נ אמר רבה בר אבוה: מחלוקת בעכור, אבל בצלול — דברי הכל אינו ולד. איתיביה רבא לר"נ: *אלא אמרו, [ב]סימן ולד בבהמה דקה — טינוף, בגסה — שליא, [ג]באשה — שפיר ושליא. ואילו שפיר בבהמה — לא פטר. אי אמרת בשלמא בצלול מחלוקת — משום הכי: אשה דרבי בה קרא — פטר בה שפיר, בבהמה דלא רבי קרא — לא פטר בה שפיר. אלא אי אמרת בעכור מחלוקת, מכדי סברא הוא, מאי שנא אשה ומאי שנא בהמה? מי סברת, רבי יהושע מפשט פשיט ליה? רבי יהושע ספוקי מספקא ליה, ואזיל הכא לחומרא, והכא לחומרא. גבי אשה דממונא הוא — ספק ממונא לקולא. גבי בהמה דאיסורא הוא, דאיכא לגבי גיזה ועבודה — ספק איסורא לחומרא. ה"נ גבי אשה — ספק טומאה לחומרא. ומי מספקא ליה? והא קרא קאמר! מדרבנן, וקרא — אסמכתא בעלמא הוא. א"ל רב חנינא בר שלמיא לרב: הא רבי, הא ר' ישמעאל בר' יוסי, והא רבי אושעיא, והא רבי יהושע בן לוי, מר כמאן ס"ל? א"ל: אני אומר, אחד זה ואחד זה — אינה חוששת. ושמואל אמר: אחד זה ואחד זה — חוששת. ואזדא שמואל לטעמיה, דכי אתא רב דימי אמר: מעולם לא דכו שפיר בנהרדעא, לבר מההוא שפירא דאתא לקמיה דשמואל, דמנח עליה חוט השערה מהאי גיסא וחזיא מהאי גיסא, אמר: אם איתא דולד הואי — לא הוה זיג כולי האי. § "ואם היה מרוקם" וכו'. § תנו רבנן, *איזהו שפיר מרוקם? אבא שאול אומר: [ד]תחלת ברייתו *מראשו, ושתי עיניו כשתי טיפין של זבוב. תני רבי חייא: [ה]מרוחקין זה מזה. שני חוטמין — כשתי טיפים של זבוב. תני רבי חייא: [ו]ומקורבין זה לזה. ופיו מתוח כחוט השערה, וגויתו כעדשה, ואם היתה נקבה — *נדונה כשעורה לארכה. וחתוך ידים ורגלים אין לו, ועליו מפורש בקבלה: °"הלא כחלב תתיכני וכגבינה תקפיאני. עור ובשר תלבישני ועצמות וגידים תסוככני. חיים וחסד עשית עמדי ופקודתך שמרה רוחי". [ז]ואין בודקין אותו במים — שהמים עזין

וטורדין

בראשית ג | איוב י

**רש"י**

**פרשתבינא.** שם איש. **כסומכוס.** בריש פירקין, דם שבתוך החתיכה – מטמא משום נדה, ויחידאה היא. **כר' יהושע אמרה.** דמשום עור שפיר לחודיה מטמא [משום לידה, ויחידאה היא. דדילמא אפילו במלא בשר פליגי, כיון דאינו מרוקם – מעולם לא היה ולד. ואע"ג דפליג רבי יהושע בשפיר לחודיה, תורה אור במלא דם מודה דלאו ולד הוא, דדם מוכיח עליו]. **בעכור.** מה שבתוכו עכור, דאיכא למימר: ולד היה, ונימוח. **בצלול.** שהוא מלא מים צלולין. **היינו דאיצטריך קרא.** לרבי יהושע, דמשום עור לחודיה הוי ולד. **אלא אי אמרת.** טעמא דרבי יהושע משום דעכור הוא, ואיכא למימר נימוח ולאו משום עור, קרא ל"ל? **אלא** לאו בצלול מחלוקת. ותיובתא דר"ל. **אלא אמרו.** רישא בבכורות פרק "הלוקח בהמה מן הגוי" (דף יט.) לענין לפטור את שבא אחריו מתורת בכור. **טינוף.** לאחר שקבלה מן הזכר ונוצר הולד, נימוח וזב הימנו ויוצא והולך. ואותו טינוף פוטרתה מן הבכורה. **שפיר ושליא.** או שפיר או שליא. **ספוקי מספקא ליה.** בעכור גופיה אי ולד הוא אם לאו. **הכא לחומרא והכא לחומרא.** גבי בכורת בהמה אמר: דלאו ולד הוא, ולא פטר את הבא אחריו. דאי אמרת פטר – קא גזיז ועביד ביה עבודה, ודילמא לאו ולד הוא ההוא קמא, וקאתי לידי תקלה. וגבי טומאת ולד אזיל לחומרא, דקאמר: ולד הוא, וטמאה שבועיים, וימי טוהר לא ס"ל דניתיב לה. וגבי בכור אדם דקולא היא, דקאמר: פטר את הבא אחריו, ולא איכפת לן – דאין קדושה בבכור אדם אלא ממון כהן ה' סלעים, וספק ממונא לקולא, דכהן הוי "מוציא מחבירו עליו הראיה". **הא רבי.** דאמר לעיל: לא שמעתי. **והא רבי ישמעאל.** דאמר: מלא בשר טמאה לידה. **והא רבי אושעיא.** דאמר: בעכור מחלוקת. **והא רבי יהושע בן לוי.** דאמר: בצלול מחלוקת. **אחד זה ואחד זה.** אחד עכור ואחד צלול. **חוששת.** ויושבת ימי טומאה, ואין לה ימי טוהר – דספק ולד הוא ולא ודאי. **לא דכו שפיר.** לא טיהרו את המפלת שפיר משבועים, ואפי' בלידה יבשתא. **נהרדעא.** אתריה דשמואל. **זיג.** צלול. **טיפין של זבוב.** עיני זבוב. **ופיו מתוח כחוט השערה.** סדק קטן, ונראה כאילו חוט השערה מתוח שם. **גויתו.** גיד אבר הזכר. והא דתנן: "תשב לזכר ולנקבה", אלמא מספקא לן אם זכר אם נקבה – כשאין ניכר בו האבר מיירי. **כשעורה.** היא סדוקה לארכה. **וחיתוך ידים ורגלים.** עדיין אין נראין, כדאמרינן: תחלת ברייתו מראשו. **כחלב.** זהו שכבת זרע, שהוא ניתך וקלוש מתחלה בשעת יציאתו כחלב, ואח"כ נעשה קפוי.

וטורדין

**תוספות**

**פרשתבינא.** פ"ה: שם איש, וכן בערוך.* ואינו כן, דאם כן ה"ל למימר "מפומבדיתא". אלא פרשב"ם: לשון פרנסות וממשלה. **מלא** בשר מהו. ממתני' דקתני "מלא דם ומלא מים" ליכא למפשט, דדילמא הא מלא בשר – חוששת, אבל ודאי ולד – לא הוי. א"נ: הא דלא חשיב, משום דבפלוגתא לא מיירי. **שמא** כר' יהושע. אע"ג דבעי למימר בסמוך: "מחלוקת בצלול, אבל בעכור דברי הכל ולד", רבי נמי מסופק היה בהא, דהא קאמר: שמא.

(לעיל) **כסומכוס.** וא"ת: ואם שפיר מלא דם הוי כחתיכה שבתוכה דם – שפיר מלא בשר נמי להוי כחתיכה של בשר, דאמר בפירקין דאינה טמאה לידה כשאין בה עצם? ויש לומר: דשפיר דמיא לולד טפי מחתיכה, וטמא אפילו אין בה עצם, אע"ג דבמלא דם שניהם שוים. **מחלוקת** בצלול. פ"ה: מלא מים, וכן משמע. וקשה: וכי עדיף ממלאה דם, דאמר לעיל דטמאה נדה ולא לידה אפי' לרבי יהושע? לכך נראה לפרש: דצלול ועכור – היינו בשר עכור ובשר צלול. **שאין** הקב"ה עושה עור כו' ד"כתנות עור" בעור אדם מיירי, כדמתרגמינן: על משך בשריהון. **סימן** ולד בבהמה דקה טינוף. האי "טינוף" הוא ולד עצמו. ולא דמי ל"טינוף" דלקמן, דרוב בהמות מטנפות" – דהתם, טינוף של אחר יצירת הולד. **גבי** בהמה לחומרא. ואע"ג דקולא הוא שמוציאין ממון מרשות ישראל, היינו משום דאי לא יהיב לכהן – אתי למשרי בגיזה ועבודה. **אינה** חוששת. וקסבר רב: דבעכור מחלוקת [ר"י] ורבנן. **תחלת** ברייתו מראשו. תימה דבפ' בתרא דסוטה (דף מה:) קסבר אבא שאול: תחלת ברייתו מטיבורו, ומשלח שרשיו אילך ואילך? ונראה לר"ת: דגרס *"ברשון", וכן פר"ח: ובתוספתא פירש: כעין חגב, ד"סלעם" מתרגמינן: רשון, וכן משמע דמיירי בשיעור האברים*. **עור** ובשר תלבישני ועצמות וגידים תסוככני. ברישא "עור ובשר", והדר – "עצמות וגידים". ובתחיית המתים דיחזקאל (סימן לז) איפכא – גידין, והדר בשר. ומפרש במדרש:* למה הדבר דומה? לאדם שפושט, וחוזר ולובש. *מה שפושט ראשון – לובש אחרון. אבל בתחלת בריית הולד – עור ובשר תחלה, ואח"כ עצמות וגידין.

לידע

**עין משפט נר מצוה**

[ערך פשתיכנא]

**מ** א מיי' פ"י מהלכות איסורי ביאה הלכה ד:

**מא** ב מיי' פ"ד מהלכות בכורות הלכה י סמג עשין ריא טוש"ע י"ד סימן שטו סעיף ז:

**מב** ג מיי' פי"א מהלכות בכורות הלכה יד ופ"י מהלכות איסורי ביאה הלכה ב והלכה יד סמג עשין קמד טוש"ע י"ד סימן שה סעיף כג:

**מג** ד ה ו ז מיי' פ"י מהלכות איסורי ביאה הלכה ג סמג לאוין קיא:

**מסורת הש"ס**

רש"ל

[גי' הערוך פשתיכנא וכ"א בע"י וגם איתא ג"כ עד חרציה קודם עד פלגיה]

[עי' תוס' ע"ז נג סוף ד"ה או דילמא וגם סח. בתוס' ד"ה תיקו]

בכורות יט.

[תוספתא פ"ד]

[נ"ל ברשון פי' חגב. כך גי' הילקוט]

[בע"י הגי' נקבה נכרת כשיעורה סדוקה לארכה]

[נ"ל כרשון וכן איתא בערוך ערך רשון]

[עי' תוס' יומא פה. ד"ה אבא שאול]

[ריש פרשת תזריע]

נ"ל מה שפושט אחרון לובש ראשון אבל כו'. רש"ל וכן הוא ברש"י דיחזקאל ועי' ר"מ ורש"א שגורסין גירסא שלפנינו והכל אחד

**תוספי הרא"ש**

לכשתכעוס תעמוד במילואך לאו דוקא שיהו אכילה ושתיה שוין אלא בין אכילה ושתיה יהיו שני שלישים: **פושתיכנא** דפום בדיתא. פרש"י שכך שמו וקשה דה"ל למימר מפום בדיתא אלא לשון ממשלה ופרנסות היא: **שפיר** מלא בשר מהו. ממתניתין דקתני מלא דם ומלא מים ליכא למיפשט דמשמע הא מלא בשר טמאה לידה משום דאיכא למימר הא מלא בשר חוששת אבל ודאי לא או א"נ אפילו חוששת אינה והאי דלא חשיב ליה משום דבפלוגתא לא קא מיירי: **הא** נמי שמא ר' יהושע אמרה. אע"ג דאיכא מ"ד בסמוך מחלוקת בצלול ומיבעיא ליה אי בעכור ד"ה ולד גם ר' מסופק בדבר דהא שמא קאמר. ותימה אי כר' יהושע אפילו מלא דם נמי תהא טמאה לידה. כלומר דהא בצלול קאמר דהוי ולד ומלא דם לא גרע מצלול ואי הוה מפרשי' דעכור וצלול דהיינו ממראה בשר הוה ניחא אבל רש"י פי' צלול כמו מים צלולין: **שאין** הקב"ה עושה עור לאדם כו'. דכתנות עור מתרגמינן על משך בשריהון ובעור אדם איירי קרא ש"מ דעיקר יצירת אדם בעור קאי מדתלי כתנות בעור האדם: **סימן** לולד בבהמה דקה טינוף. האי טינוף הוי מיחוי הולד עצמו ולאו כי האי טינוף דאמרינן לקמן רוב היולדות מטנפות דהתם בטינוף שקודם הולד קאמר: **גבי** בהמה דאיסורא הוא כו'. ואף לכהן צריך ליתנו ולא אמרינן ספק ממונא לקולא משום דאי לא יהיב ליה אתי למשרייה בגזה ועבודה: **תחלת** ברייתו מראשו. ר"ח גרס ברשון וכן ר"ת והכי נמי איתא בתוספתא כלומר כעין חגב דסלעם מתרגמינן רשונא ולפי הספר דגרסינן מראשו קשה דהא שמעינן לאבא שאול גופיה בפ' בתרא דסוטה שהולד נולד מטיבורו ומשלח שרשיו אילך ואילך: **עור** ובשר תלבישני כו'. גבי תחיית המתים דיחזקאל כתיב ברישא גידין והדר בשר והדר עור ומפרש במדרש מלבוש שלובש ראשון פושט אחרון:

סנדל

וְטוֹרְדִין אוֹתוֹ, אֶלָּא בּוֹדְקִין אוֹתוֹ בְּשֶׁמֶן — שֶׁהַשֶּׁמֶן רַךְ וּמְצַחְצְחוֹ. וְאֵין רוֹאִין אֶלָּא בַּחַמָּה. כֵּיצַד בּוֹדְקִין אוֹתוֹ? כֵּיצַד בּוֹדְקִין אוֹתוֹ? כִּדְאָמְרִינַן! אֶלָּא: בַּמֶּה בּוֹדְקִין אוֹתוֹ לֵידַע אִם זָכָר הוּא אִם נְקֵבָה הִיא? אַבָּא שָׁאוּל בַּר נָשׁ, וְאָמְרִי לָהּ אַבָּא שָׁאוּל בַּר רְמָשׁ אוֹמֵר: [א]מֵבִיא קֵיסָם שֶׁרֹאשׁוֹ חָלָק וּמְנַעְנֵעַ בְּאוֹתוֹ מָקוֹם. אִם מְסַכְסֵךְ — בְּיָדוּעַ שֶׁזָּכָר הוּא, וְאִם לָאו — בְּיָדוּעַ שֶׁנְּקֵבָה הִיא. א"ר נַחְמָן אָמַר רַבָּה בַּר אֲבוּהּ: [ב]ל"ש אֶלָּא מִלְּמַטָּה לְמַעְלָה, אֲבָל מִן הַצְּדָדִין — אֵימָא: כּוֹתְלֵי בֵית הָרֶחֶם נִינְהוּ. א"ר אַדָּא בַּר אַהֲבָה: [ג]תָּנָא, אִם הָיְתָה נְקֵבָה — נִדּוֹנָה כִּשְׂעוֹרָה סְדוּקָה. מַתְקִיף לָהּ ר"נ: וְדִילְמָא חוּט שֶׁל בֵּיצִים נִינְהוּ? אָמַר אַבַּיֵי: הַשְׁתָּא בֵּיצִים גּוּפַיְיהוּ — לָא יְדִיעִי, חוּט שֶׁל בֵּיצִים — יְדִיעַ?! א"ר עַמְרָם, תָּנָא: ב' יַרְכוֹתָיו כְּב' חוּטִין שֶׁל זְהוֹרִית. וְא"ר עַמְרָם עֲלָהּ: כְּשֶׁל עֵרֶב. וּשְׁנֵי זְרוֹעוֹתָיו כְּב' חוּטִין שֶׁל זְהוֹרִית, וְא"ר עַמְרָם עֲלָהּ: כְּשֶׁל שְׁתִי. א"ל שְׁמוּאֵל לְרַב יְהוּדָה: *שִׁינָּנָא, [ד]לָא תַּעֲבֵיד עוּבְדָא עַד שֶׁיְּשַׂעֵיר. וּמִי אָמַר שְׁמוּאֵל הָכִי? וְהָאָמַר שְׁמוּאֵל: אַחַת זוֹ וְאַחַת זוֹ — חוֹשֶׁשֶׁת! אָמַר רַב אַמִּי בַּר שְׁמוּאֵל, לְדִידִי מְפָרְשָׁא לִי מִינֵּיהּ דְּמָר שְׁמוּאֵל: לָחוּשׁ — חוֹשֶׁשֶׁת, יְמֵי טָהֳרָה — [ה]לָא יָהֲבִינַן לָהּ עַד שֶׁיְּשַׂעֵיר. לְמֵימְרָא דְּמִסַּפְקָא לֵיהּ לִשְׁמוּאֵל? וְהָא הַהוּא שַׁפִּירָא דַּאֲתַאי לְקַמֵּיהּ דְּמָר שְׁמוּאֵל. אֲמַר: הָא בַּר אַרְבְּעִין וְחַד יוֹמָא, וְחָשֵׁיב מִיּוֹמָא *דְּאָזְלָא לִטְבִילָה עַד הַהוּא יוֹמָא, וְלָא הֲוָה אֶלָּא אַרְבְּעִין יוֹמִין, וַאֲמַר לְהוּ: הַאי בְּנִדָּה בָּעַל. כְּפַתֵיהּ — וְאוֹדִי! *שָׁאנֵי שְׁמוּאֵל דְּרַב גּוּבְרֵיהּ.§ "הַמַּפֶּלֶת סַנְדָּל" וכו'.§ ת"ר: *סַנְדָּל דּוֹמֶה לְדָג שֶׁל יָם, מִתְּחִלָּתוֹ וָלָד הוּא אֶלָּא שֶׁנִּרְצַף. רשב"ג אוֹמֵר: [ו]סַנְדָּל דּוֹמֶה לְלָשׁוֹן שֶׁל שׁוֹר הַגָּדוֹל. מִשּׁוּם רַבּוֹתֵינוּ הֵעִידוּ: סַנְדָּל צָרִיךְ צוּרַת פָּנִים. א"ר יְהוּדָה, אָמַר שְׁמוּאֵל: הֲלָכָה — סַנְדָּל צָרִיךְ צוּרַת פָּנִים. א"ר אַדָּא, א"ר יוֹסֵף, א"ר יִצְחָק: סַנְדָּל צָרִיךְ צוּרַת פָּנִים, וַאֲפִי' מֵאֲחוֹרָיו. מָשָׁל לְאָדָם שֶׁסָּטַר אֶת חֲבֵירוֹ, וְהֶחֱזִיר פָּנָיו לַאֲחוֹרָיו. בִּימֵי רַבִּי יַנַּאי בִּקְּשׁוּ לְטַהֵר אֶת הַסַּנְדָּל שֶׁאֵין לוֹ צוּרַת פָּנִים, אָמַר לָהֶם ר' יַנַּאי: [ז]טִיהַרְתֶּם אֶת הַוְּולָדוֹת! וְהָתַנְיָא, מִשּׁוּם רַבּוֹתֵינוּ הֵעִידוּ: סַנְדָּל צָרִיךְ צוּרַת פָּנִים! אָמַר רַב בֵּיבָי בַּר אַבַּיֵי אָמַר רַבִּי יוֹחָנָן: מֵעֵדוּתוֹ שֶׁל רַבִּי נְחוּנְיָא נִשְׁנֵית מִשְׁנָה זוֹ. אָמַר רַבִּי זְעִירָא: זָכָה בָּהּ רַב בֵּיבָי בִּשְׁמַעְתֵּיהּ, דַּאֲנָא וְהוּא הֲוֵינָא יָתְבִינַן קַמֵּיהּ דְּרַבִּי יוֹחָנָן כִּי אַמְרַהּ לְהָא שְׁמַעְתָּא, וְקָדַם אִיהוּ וַאֲמַר וְזָכָה בָּהּ. *לָמָּה הִזְכִּירוּ סַנְדָּל, [ח]וַהֲלֹא אֵין סַנְדָּל שֶׁאֵין עִמּוֹ וָלָד? אִי דְּאִתְיְלִידָא נְקֵבָה בַּהֲדֵיהּ — ה"נ, הָכָא בְּמַאי עָסְקִינַן — [ט]דְּאִתְיְלִיד זָכָר בַּהֲדֵיהּ. מַהוּ דְּתֵימָא, הוֹאִיל *וְאָמַר רַב יִצְחָק בַּר אַמִּי: אִשָּׁה מַזְרַעַת תְּחִלָּה — יוֹלֶדֶת זָכָר, אִישׁ מַזְרִיעַ תְּחִלָּה — יוֹלֶדֶת נְקֵבָה, מִדְּהָא זָכָר — הָא נַמִּי זָכָר, קמ"ל: אֵימָא שְׁנֵיהֶם הִזְרִיעוּ בְּבַת אַחַת, הַאי זָכָר וְהַאי נְקֵבָה. דָּבָר אַחֵר: שֶׁאִם תֵּלֵד נְקֵבָה לִפְנֵי שְׁקִיעַת הַחַמָּה, וְסַנְדָּל לְאַחַר שְׁקִיעַת הַחַמָּה, מוֹנָה תְּחִלַּת נִדָּה לָרִאשׁוֹן וּתְחִלַּת נִדָּה לָאַחֲרוֹן. סַנְדָּל דִּתְנַן

גַּבֵּי

**רש"י**

וְטוֹרְדִין אוֹתוֹ. מְמַחִין. בַּר רְמָשׁ. וּמְנַעְנֵעַ. בְּאוֹתוֹ מָקוֹם מִלְּמַטָּה לְמַעְלָה, כִּדְאָמַר בְּסָמוּךְ. אִם מְסַכְסֵךְ. הַקֵּיסָם, שֶׁיֵּשׁ דָּבָר הַמְעַכֵּב — הַיְינוּ גִּיד, דְּאִי נְקֵבָה — לֵיכָּא עִיכּוּבָא. מִלְּמַטָּה לְמַעְלָה. שֶׁהֲרֵי בְּסֶדֶק הַשְּׂעוֹרָה אֵין עִיכּוּב לָאָרְכָּהּ. תָּנָא אִם הָיְתָה נְקֵבָה נִידּוֹנֵת כִּשְׂעוֹרָה סְדוּקָה. לְאוֹסוּפֵי וּלְפָרוּשֵׁי אֲתָא, דִּלְעֵיל תָּנֵי "נִידּוֹנֵת כִּשְׂעוֹרָה", וְלָא תָּנֵי "סְדוּקָה". חוּט מַבְדִּיל. מִלְּמַטָּה לְמַעְלָה בֵּין ב' הַבֵּיצִים, וְנִרְאֶה עָמוֹק כְּסֶדֶק. לָא יְדִיעִי. אֵין נִיכָּרִין מֵחֲמַת קָטְנָן. שְׁתֵּי יַרְכוֹתָיו. כְּשֶׁהוּא מַתְחִיל לְהִבָּרְאוֹת בְּחִיתּוּךְ יָדַיִם וְרַגְלַיִם. עֵרֶב. עָבֶה מִשְּׁתִי. לָא תַּעֲבֵיד עוּבְדָא. לַעֲשׂוֹתוֹ וָלָד, עַד שֶׁיְּהֵא לוֹ שְׂעָרוֹת בְּרֹאשׁוֹ. לָחוּשׁ חוֹשֶׁשֶׁת. לְהַחְמִיר וְלֵישֵׁב שְׁבוּעַיִם. כְּפַתֵיהּ וְאוֹדִי. אַלְמָא הָיָה בָּקִי בִּילִירַת הַוָּלָד! דְּרַב גּוּבְרֵיהּ. הוּא בָּקִי, וְאֵין כּוּלָּן בְּקִיאִין. דָּג שֶׁל יָם. דָּג יֵשׁ בַּיָּם וּשְׁמוֹ "סַנְדָּל". אֶלָּא שֶׁנִּרְצַף. נִמְעַךְ. [לָשׁוֹן שֶׁל שׁוֹר הַגָּדוֹל. דְּהַיְינוּ פָּנָיו טוּחוֹת. וְאַע"ג דְּאוֹקְמִינַן לְעֵיל: פָּנָיו טוּחוֹת — אֵין אִמּוֹ טְמֵאָה, גַּבֵּי סַנְדָּל וַדַּאי אִמּוֹ טְמֵאָה לֵידָה, (סַנְדָּל) דְּוָלָד שֶׁעִמּוֹ מוֹכִיחַ עָלָיו דְּוָלָד הוּא, אֶלָּא שֶׁנִּימּוֹק ע"י חֲבֵרוֹ שֶׁדְּחָקוֹ]. צָרִיךְ צוּרַת פָּנִים אֲפִי' מֵאֲחוֹרָיו. כְּלוֹמַר, אֲפִי' אֵינוֹ אֶלָּא מֵאֲחוֹרָיו הָוֵי וָלָד. שֶׁסָּטַר. הִכָּהוּ עַל לְחָיוֹ. מִשְׁנָה זוֹ. דְּקָתָנֵי "צָרִיךְ צוּרַת פָּנִים", מֵעֵדוּתוֹ שֶׁל רַבִּי נְחוּנְיָא נִשְׁנֵית. הוּא הֵעִיד עָלֶיהָ בְּבֵית הַמִּדְרָשׁ, וִיחִידָאָה הִיא. זָכָה בָּהּ רַב בֵּיבָי בִּשְׁמַעְתֵּיהּ. מַזָּלוֹ גָּרַם לוֹמַר שְׁמוּעָה זוֹ, וְקַדְמַנִי. שֶׁגַּם אֲנִי שְׁמַעְתִּיהָ מֵר' יוֹחָנָן, דְּמֵעֵדוּתוֹ שֶׁל רַבִּי נְחוּנְיָא נִשְׁנֵית, וְלֹא זָכִיתִי לְאוֹמְרָהּ. וַהֲלֹא אֵין סַנְדָּל שֶׁאֵין עִמּוֹ וָלָד. וּבְלָא סַנְדָּל נַמִּי הָוְיָא טְמֵאָה לֵידָה? אִי דְּאִיתְיְלִיד נְקֵבָה בַּהֲדֵיהּ ה"נ. דְּלֹא הָיָה צָרִיךְ לְהַזְכִּירוֹ, דְּיֵשׁ לָהּ יְמֵי טוּמְאָה וְטָהֳרָה דִּנְקֵבָה. שֶׁאֲפִילּוּ הוּא זָכָר גָּמוּר, כִּי אִיכָּא נְקֵבָה בַּהֲדֵיהּ — יוֹשֶׁבֶת לִנְקֵבָה יְמֵי טוּמְאָה וְטָהֳרָה, וְשֶׁל זָכָר מוּבְלָעִים בְּתוֹכָן. דְּאִיתְיְלִיד זָכָר בַּהֲדֵיהּ. וּמְסַפְּקִי' לְסַנְדָּל בִּנְקֵבָה, וְיוֹשֶׁבֶת שְׁבוּעַיִם לְטוּמְאָה. אֲבָל טָהֳרָה דִּנְקֵבָה לָא יָהֲבִינַן לָהּ, דְּדִילְמָא זָכָר הוּא. הַאי נַמִּי זָכָר. וְלֹא תֵּשֵׁב אֶלָּא לְזָכָר. קמ"ל כו'. ד"א. אֲפִי' יָלְדָה עִמּוֹ נְקֵבָה, צָרִיךְ לְהַזְכִּיר סָפֵק סַנְדָּל (א). שֶׁאִם תַּפִּיל שְׁנַיִם אֶחָד לִפְנֵי שְׁקִיעַת הַחַמָּה וְאֶחָד לְאַחַר שְׁקִיעַת הַחַמָּה מוֹנָה תְּחִלַּת נִדָּה לָרִאשׁוֹן וּתְחִלַּת נִדָּה לָאַחֲרוֹן. וְה"ג לָהּ בַּתּוֹסֶפְתָּא, וְה"פ: שֶׁאִם תַּפִּיל שְׁנֵיהֶם, נְקֵבָה לִפְנֵי שְׁקִיעַת הַחַמָּה וְסַנְדָּל לְאַחַר שְׁקִיעָה — מוֹנָה לְאַחַר שֶׁיִּכְלוּ יְמֵי טוֹהַר לָרִאשׁוֹן תְּחִלַּת נִדָּה, וְכֵן לָאַחֲרוֹן. כְּגוֹן אִם תִּרְאֶה בְּיוֹם שְׁמוֹנִים וְאֶחָד לָרִאשׁוֹן — הָוְיָא תְּחִלַּת נִדָּה. דְּדִילְמָא סַנְדָּל שֶׁנּוֹלַד לְאַחַר שְׁקִיעָה זָכָר הוּא, וְכָלוּ יְמֵי טוֹהַר שֶׁלּוֹ לְסוֹף מ' וְלָא מָשְׁכִי בָּתַר פ"א דִּנְקֵבָה. וּכְשֶׁתַּחֲזוֹר וְתִרְאֶה בַּפ' לִרְאִיָּיתָהּ, וְתִרְצֶה לִהְיוֹת סוֹפֶרֶת יוֹם כְּנֶגֶד יוֹם — אָמְרִינַן דִּלְמָא סַנְדָּל נְקֵבָה הֲוָה, וּמָשׁוּךְ יְמֵי טוֹהַר שֶׁלּוֹ עַד פ"א לָרִאשׁוֹן. וּמַה שֶּׁרָאֲתָה בְּיוֹם פ"א לָרִאשׁוֹן — דַּם טוֹהַר הוּא, א] וְעַכְשָׁיו מַה שֶּׁהִיא רוֹאָה בְּיוֹם פ"א — תְּחִלַּת נִדָּה הוּא. וְהַיְינוּ "תְּחִלַּת נִדָּה לָאַחֲרוֹן". וּבְהָכִי הָוְיָא מְקוּלְקֶלֶת, דְּלָא יָדְעִינַן בְּהָךְ רְאִיָּה בַּתְרַיְיתָא: אִי נִדָּה הִיא, אִי שׁוֹמֶרֶת יוֹם כְּנֶגֶד יוֹם. לִישָּׁנָא אַחֲרִינָא גָּרְסִי': "שֶׁאִם תֵּלֵד נְקֵבָה לִפְנֵי שְׁקִיעָה, וְסַנְדָּל לְאַחַר שְׁקִיעָה — מוֹנָה תְּחִלַּת לֵידָה מִן הָאַחֲרוֹן, וְסוֹף לֵידָה מִן הָרִאשׁוֹן", וְה"פ: אֲפִילּוּ הֵיכָא דְּאִיתְיְלִיד נְקֵבָה בַּהֲדֵיהּ, הוּצְרַךְ "סַנְדָּל". שֶׁאִם תֵּלֵד נְקֵבָה לִפְנֵי שְׁקִיעָה, וְהַסַּנְדָּל שֶׁהוּא סָפֵק זָכָר לְאַחַר שְׁקִיעָה "מוֹנָה תְּחִלַּת לֵידָה", דְּהַיְינוּ יְמֵי טוּמְאָה מִן הָאַחֲרוֹן. דְּדִילְמָא סַנְדָּל נַמִּי נְקֵבָה הִיא, וּמָנֵינַן מִינֵּיהּ י"ד שֶׁהוּא ט"ו לָרִאשׁוֹן. "וְסוֹף לֵידָה", דְּהַיְינוּ יְמֵי טוֹהַר, מָנֵינַן מִן הָרִאשׁוֹן לְהַחְמִיר. שֶׁאִם תִּרְאֶה בְּיוֹם פ"א, דְּהַיְינוּ פ' לָאַחֲרוֹן — מְטַמֵּינַן לָהּ מִשּׁוּם נִדָּה. דְּאָמְרִי': סַנְדָּל זָכָר הֲוָה, וַהֲרֵי אַרְבָּעִים יְמֵי טוֹהַר שֶׁלּוֹ. וְדִנְקֵבָה קַמַּיְיתָא נַמִּי הַשְׁתָּא כָּלוּ לְהוּ. וְהַיְינוּ צוֹרֶךְ — דְּאִי לָאו "סַנְדָּל", הֲוֵי מְנְיָנָהּ נַמִּי יְמֵי טוּמְאָה לָרִאשׁוֹן, וְלָא מְטַמְּאָה אֶלָּא י"ד וְהַשְׁתָּא יָתְבָה ט"ו וְאִי הֲוָה פְּשִׁיטָא לָן שֶׁהַסַּנְדָּל נְקֵבָה הִיא — לָא הָוְיָא תְּחִלַּת נִדָּה עַד פ"ב לָרִאשׁוֹן, דְּבָתַר וָלָד אַחֲרוֹן אָזְלִינַן.

גַּבֵּי

**תוספות**

לידע אם זכר הוא. הא דאמר "גויתו בכעדשה" — לא שמקומו בולט, אלא שמקומו ניכר בכעדשה. *המפלת סנדל או שליא תשב לזכר ולנקבה. וא"ת: בשליא ליתני נמי "ולנדה", דאימא: הרחיקה לידתה, וכבר כלו ימי טוהר, כדאיתא לקמן בפירקין (דף כח.) גבי המפלת יד חתוכה. אע"ג דאמר בסמוך: אין תולין השליא בולד יותר מג' ימים — להחמיר חוששין יותר מג' ימים? וי"ל: דלא דמו. דבהמפלת יד חתוכה — איכא למימר דהראש או רוב הגוף כבר ילדה מקודם, וכלו ימי טוהר. אבל שליא — אימא: הולד בתוכה, או שלם או נימוק. ועוד י"ל: דאי הוה תני "ולנדה" ה"א מביאה קרבן ואינו נאכל, דספק לידה היא. קמ"ל מביאה קרבן ונאכל. והכי נמי קאמר לקמן. קא משמע לן אימא שניהם הזריעו בבת אחת. לר"ת שפירש דאין (ב) מתעברת וחוזרת ומתעברת, ואפילו נפל, אתי שפיר, וצ"ל שהזריעו בבת אחת. אבל לפרש"י שפירש* גבי ג' נשים משמשות במוך, מעוברת — שמא תעשה עוברה סנדל, שולד אחרון ממעך צורה הראשונה. והא דאין אשה חוזרת ומתעברת[ב] — היינו בן קיימא (*דאין) נפל חוזרת ומתעברת, לא הוה צ"ל הכא "אימא שניהם הזריעו בבת אחת", והל"ל "בביאה ראשונה הזריעה היא תחלה, ובביאה שניה הזריע הוא תחלה"! ומיהו י"ל: דבענין זה בב' ביאות אין חדוש למתני "תשב לזכר ולנקבה", דפשיטא, דפעמים הוא מזריע תחלה ופעמים היא. ולא אמר "מדהאי זכר, האי נמי זכר". אבל בביאה אחת, סד"א: מדהאי זכר, האי נמי זכר קמ"ל: "אימא שניהם הזריעו בבת אחת". ומיהו קשה: מנלן דלא אמרינן בביאה אחת "מדהאי זכר, האי נמי זכר"? אימא: לעולם אמרי' ומתני' בב' ביאות, ואשמועינן מתני' דסנדל הוי ולד אף בלא צורת פנים, ולאפוקי מעדותו של רבי נחוניא. ואע"ג דכבר אשמעינן בבכורות ובכריתות דמייתי בסמוך דסנדל הוא ולד, מ"מ איצטריך נמי לאשמועינן דהוי ולד לענין לידה? וי"ל: דהיינו דקמשני בלשון שני. ומיהו תימה גם לפר"ת: דלקמן (דף כח.) גבי זכר וטומטום, משני נמי: "שהזריעו שניהם בבת אחת", ותרתי למה לי? ואי אתא לאשמועינן דהוי ולד — והא כבר תנא בהדיא ברישא "טומטום או אנדרוגינוס תשב לזכר ולנקבה"! סנדל

[דף כח.]

**עין משפט נר מצוה**

[שייך לעיל במשנה כז:]

מד א ב ג ד ה מיי' פ"י מהל' איסורי ביאה הלכה ג סמג לאוין קיא:

מה ו ז ח ט מיי' שם הלכה יב:

**תוספי הרא"ש**

סנדל או שליא תשב לזכר ולנקבה. ותימה מפלת שליא תשב נמי לנדה דאמר הרחיקה לידתה וי"ל דבשליא לא שייך למימר הרחיקה לידתה דאין מיהו הולד יוצא בלא השליא ואפילו את"ל דחיישינן י"ל דלהכי לא תנא לנדה דלא תימא מביאה קרבן ואינו נאכל דבה"ג משני לקמן בפירקין: אמר להם טהרתם את הולדות. אפילו בלא צורה נמי הוי ולד ואע"ג דבפניו טוחות קאמר ר' יוחנן לעיל דלא הוי ולד שאני סנדל (שרכמו) [שדחקו] חבירו דמעיקרא הוה ליה צורת פנים: קמ"ל שניהן הזריעו בבת אחת. מכאן משמע דאפילו שלא ירצה אין אשה מתעברת חוזרת ומתעברת והא דאמרינן ג' נשים משמשות במוך מעוברת שמא תעשה עוברה סנדל לאו משום דחיישינן שמא תתעבר פעם אחרת אלא חיישינן שמא מעוברת היא תאומים ואם היתה משמשת כדרכה נכנס הזרע בין הולדות ודוחקן ונעשה האחד סנדל ובפרישות לקמן פרק יוצא דופן: סנדל דתנן

**מסורת הש"ס**

[יבמות ק. וע' כריתות יב: ותוס' שם ד"ה שמא]

נ"ל דאי

גי' רש"ל

[בכורות לו. וש"נ]

[עי' תוס' סוטה כז. ד"ה אליבא]

[לקמן סד:]

[תוספתא פ"ד]

[תוספתא פ"ד ע"ש]

[לקמן כח. ע"ש לח. ע"ש ברכות ס. ע"ש]

**הגהות הב"ח**

(א) רש"י ד"ה ש"א אפי' וד"ה שאם הכ"א: (ב) תוס' ד"ה קמ"ל וכו' דאין אשה מתעברת וחוזרת וכו' שפיר שנ"ל:

**הגהות מהר"ב רנשבורג**

א] רש"י ד"ה שאם תפיל שנים וכו' ועכשיו מה שהיא רואה ביום פ"א. נמחק ד"ה קמ"ל וכו'. היינו בן קיימא דאין נפל חוזרת ומתעברת וכו' כצ"ל:

*גַּבֵּי בְּכוֹרוֹת לְמַאי הִלְכְתָא? לַבָּא אַחֲרָיו – אבְּכוֹר לְנַחֲלָה בוְאֵין בְּכוֹר לְכֹהֵן. סַנְדָּל דִּתְנַן גַּבֵּי כְּרֵיתוּת לְמַאי הִלְכְתָא? שֶׁאִם תֵּלֵד וָלָד דֶּרֶךְ דּוֹפֶן, וְסַנְדָּל דֶּרֶךְ רֶחֶם – גדְּמַיְיתָא קָרְבָּן אַסַּנְדָּל. וּלְרַבִּי שִׁמְעוֹן דְּאָמַר: *יוֹצֵא דֶּרֶךְ דּוֹפֶן – וָלָד מְעַלְּיָא הוּא מַאי אִיכָּא לְמֵימַר? אָמַר רַבִּי יִרְמְיָה: שֶׁאִם תֵּלֵד וָלָד בִּהְיוֹתָהּ גּוֹיָה, וְסַנְדָּל לְאַחַר שֶׁנִּתְגַּיְּירָה – דְּמַיְיתָא קָרְבָּן אַסַּנְדָּל. אֲמַרוּהָ רַבָּנַן קַמֵּיהּ דְּרַב פַּפָּא: וּמִי אִיתְנְהוּ לְהָנֵי שִׁינּוּיֵי? וְהָא תַּנְיָא: כְּשֶׁהֵן יוֹצְאִין – אֵין יוֹצְאִין אֶלָּא כְּרוּכִין! אָמַר רַב פַּפָּא: שְׁמַע מִינַּהּ מִכְרַךְ כָּרֵיךְ לֵיהּ וָלָד לְסַנְדָּל אַפַּלְגֵּיהּ, וּמְשַׁלְחִיף לֵיהּ כְּלַפֵּי רֵישֵׁיהּ. גַּבֵּי בְּכוֹרוֹת – כְּגוֹן שֶׁיָּצְאוּ דֶּרֶךְ רָאשֵׁיהֶם, דְּסַנְדָּל קָדֵים וְנָפֵיק. גַּבֵּי כְּרֵיתוּת – שֶׁיָּצְאוּ דֶּרֶךְ מַרְגְּלוֹתֵיהֶם, דְּוָלָד קָדֵים וְנָפֵיק. רַב הוּנָא בַּר תַּחֲלִיפָא מִשְּׁמֵיהּ דְּרָבָא אָמַר: אֲפִילּוּ תֵּימָא מְצוּמְצָמִין, וְאֵיפוּךְ שְׁמַעְתָּא, גַּבֵּי בְּכוֹרוֹת – שֶׁיָּצְאוּ דֶּרֶךְ מַרְגְּלוֹתֵיהֶם, וָלָד דְּאִית בֵּיהּ חִיּוּתָא – סָרֵיךְ וְלָא נָפֵיק, סַנְדָּל דְּלֵית בֵּיהּ חִיּוּתָא – שָׁרֵיק וְנָפֵיק. גַּבֵּי כְּרֵיתוּת – שֶׁיָּצְאוּ דֶּרֶךְ רָאשֵׁיהֶן, וָלָד דְּאִית בֵּיהּ חִיּוּתָא – מִדְּנָפֵיק רֵישֵׁיהּ הָוְיָא לֵידָה, סַנְדָּל – עַד דְּנָפֵיק רוּבֵּיהּ.§ **מתני'** *דשִׁלְיָא בַּבַּיִת – הַבַּיִת טָמֵא. הלֹא שֶׁהַשִּׁלְיָא וָלָד, אֶלָּא שֶׁאֵין שִׁלְיָא בְּלֹא וָלָד. רַבִּי שִׁמְעוֹן אוֹמֵר: נִימּוֹק הַוָּלָד עַד שֶׁלֹּא יָצָא.§ **גמ'** תָּנוּ רַבָּנַן: *ושִׁלְיָא תְּחִלָּתָהּ דּוֹמָה לְחוּט שֶׁל עֵרֶב, וְסוֹפָהּ דּוֹמָה כְּתוּרְמוֹס, וַחֲלוּלָה כַּחֲצוֹצֶרֶת, וְאֵין שִׁלְיָא פְּחוּתָה מִטֶּפַח. רַבִּי שִׁמְעוֹן בֶּן גַּמְלִיאֵל אוֹמֵר: זשִׁלְיָא דּוֹמָה לְקוּרְקְבָן שֶׁל תַּרְנְגוֹלִין, שֶׁהַדַּקִּין יוֹצְאִין מִמֶּנָּה. תַּנְיָא, רַבִּי *אוֹשַׁעְיָא זְעִירָא דְּמִן חַבְרַיָּא: חֲמִשָּׁה שִׁיעוּרָן טֶפַח, וְאֵלּוּ הֵן: שִׁלְיָא, שׁוֹפָר, שִׁדְרָה, דּוֹפֶן סוּכָּה, וְהָאֵזוֹב. שִׁלְיָא – הָא דַּאֲמַרַן. שׁוֹפָר – דְּתַנְיָא, *כַּמָּה יְהֵא שִׁיעוּר שׁוֹפָר? חפֵּירֵשׁ רַבִּי שִׁמְעוֹן בֶּן גַּמְלִיאֵל: כְּדֵי שֶׁיֹּאחֲזֶנּוּ בְּיָדוֹ וְיֵרָאֶה לְכָאן וּלְכָאן טֶפַח. שִׁדְרָה מַה הִיא? *דְּא"ר פַּרְנָךְ, אָמַר רַבִּי יוֹחָנָן: טשִׁדְרוֹ שֶׁל לוּלָב צָרִיךְ שֶׁיְּהֵא יוֹצֵא מִן הַהֲדַס טֶפַח. דּוֹפֶן סוּכָּה – *דְּתַנְיָא: ישְׁתַּיִם כְּהִלְכָתָן, שְׁלִישִׁית – אֲפִילּוּ טֶפַח. אֵזוֹב – דְּתָנֵי רַבִּי חִיָּיא: כאֵזוֹב – טֶפַח. אָמַר רַבִּי חֲנִינָא בַּר פַּפָּא, דָּרֵישׁ שֵׁילָא אִישׁ כְּפַר תְּמַרְתָּא: תְּלָת מַתְנִיתָא וְתַרְתֵּי שְׁמַעְתָּתָא – שִׁיעוּרָא טֶפַח. תַּרְתֵּי? חֲדָא הִיא! אָמַר אַבַּיֵי: אֵימָא אָמַר רַבִּי חִיָּיא אֵזוֹב טֶפַח. וְתוּ לֵיכָּא? וְהָאִיכָּא: *לטֶפַח עַל טֶפַח עַל רוּם טֶפַח מְרוּבָּע – מֵבִיא אֶת הַטּוּמְאָה וְחוֹצֵץ בִּפְנֵי הַטּוּמְאָה! טֶפַח – קָאָמְרִינַן, טֶפַח עַל טֶפַח לָא קָאָמְרִינַן. וְהָא אִיכָּא: *מאֶבֶן הַיּוֹצֵא מִן הַתַּנּוּר טֶפַח וּמִן הַכִּירָה שָׁלֹשׁ אֶצְבָּעוֹת – חִבּוּר! כִּי קָאָמְרִינַן – הֵיכָא דִּבְצִיר מִטֶּפַח לָא חֲזֵי, אֲבָל הָכָא – כ"ש דִּבְצִיר מִטֶּפַח יַד תַּנּוּר הוּא. וְהָאִיכָּא

תַּנּוּרֵי

**רש"י**

גַּבֵּי בְּכוֹרוֹת. דְּקָתָנֵי (בכורות דף מו.): הַמַּפֶּלֶת סַנְדָּל – הַבָּא אַחֲרָיו בְּכוֹר לְנַחֲלָה, וְאֵין בְּכוֹר לְכֹהֵן. לְמַאי הִלְכְתָא. קס"ד לַבָּא אַחֲרָיו לְסוֹף שָׁנָה אוֹ לְסוֹף שְׁנָתַיִם קָמַיְירֵי. וְל"ל סַנְדָּל, וַהֲלֹא בְּלֹא סַנְדָּל פָּטַר וָלָד דְּבַהֲדֵיהּ אֶת הַבָּא אַחֲרָיו? וּמְשַׁנֵּי: לַבָּא אַחֲרָיו, כְּלוֹמַר לְכָךְ הוּזְכַּר סַנְדָּל אִם יָצָא וָלָד שֶׁעִמּוֹ אַחֲרָיו הָוֵי בְּכוֹר לְנַחֲלָה וְלֹא בְּכוֹר לְכֹהֵן. גַּבֵּי כְּרֵיתוּת. בְּפ"ק (לעיל דף ז.) לְעִנְיַן חִיּוּב קָרְבָּן. לְמַאי הִלְכְתָא. תֵּיפוֹק לֵיהּ דְּמִשּׁוּם וָלָד שֶׁעִמּוֹ תָּבִיא קָרְבָּן. וָלָד יוֹצֵא דֶּרֶךְ דּוֹפֶן. ע"י סַם לָא מִיחַיְּיבָא קָרְבָּן דִּכְתִיב גַּבֵּי קָרְבָּן (ויקרא יב): "אִשָּׁה כִּי תַזְרִיעַ וְיָלְדָה זָכָר" – עַד שֶׁתֵּלֵד מִמָּקוֹם שֶׁמַּזְרַעַת. וּלְר' שִׁמְעוֹן כו'. לְקַמָּן בְּפֶ' "יוֹצֵא דוֹפֶן" (דף מ.). כְּשֶׁהֵן יוֹצְאִין. סַנְדָּל וְוָלָד שֶׁעִמּוֹ. כְּרוּכִין. דְּבוּקִין זֶה בָּזֶה וְלֹא דְּבוּקִין מַמָּשׁ. וּמִדְּיוֹצְאִין יַחַד אִי אֶפְשָׁר שֶׁתִּתְגַּיֵּיר בֵּינְתַיִים. שְׁמַע מִינַּהּ. מִדְּהוּזְכַּר סַנְדָּל גַּבֵּי כְּרֵיתוּת מִשּׁוּם גֵּירוּת, וּכְגוֹן שֶׁיָּצָא וָלָד תְּחִלָּה וְאַחַר כֵּן סַנְדָּל, וְגַבֵּי בְּכוֹרוֹת כְּגוֹן שֶׁיָּצָא סַנְדָּל תְּחִלָּה, כִּדְאוֹקְמִינַן לְעֵיל דְּפוֹטֵר וָלָד מֵחָמֵשׁ סְלָעִים וְתַנְיָא דִּבְבַת אַחַת יוֹצְאִין – שְׁמַע מִינַּהּ אֵין שׁוֹכְבִין זֶה אֵצֶל זֶה, דְּא"כ, לֹא מַשְׁכַּחַתְּ לַהּ שֶׁיָּצָא זֶה קוֹדֶם זֶה. אֶלָּא הַאי "כְּרוּכִין" דְּקָתָנֵי הָכִי הוּא: מִכְרַךְ כָּרֵיךְ לֵיהּ וָלָד לְסַנְדָּל אַפַּלְגֵּיהּ דְּרֹאשׁ הַוָּלָד תָּחוּב כְּנֶגֶד טִיבּוּרוֹ שֶׁל סַנְדָּל. וּמְשַׁלְחִיף לֵיהּ כְּלַפֵּי רֵישֵׁיהּ. כְּלוֹמַר דְּחָפוֹ וָלָד בְּרֹאשׁוֹ לְסַנְדָּל כְּלַפֵּי חוּץ. גַּבֵּי בְּכוֹרוֹת. דְּבָעֵינַן שֶׁיֵּצֵא הַסַּנְדָּל תְּחִלָּה, כְּגוֹן שֶׁיָּצְאוּ דֶּרֶךְ רָאשֵׁיהֶן כו'. מְצוּמְצָמִין. שׁוֹכְבִין זֶה אֵצֶל זֶה. וְאֵיפוּךְ שְׁמַעְתָּא. מֵימְרָא דְּרַב פַּפָּא דְּאָמַר בִּבְכוֹרוֹת שֶׁיָּצְאוּ דֶּרֶךְ רָאשֵׁיהֶן. סָרֵיךְ. אוֹחֵז בְּיָדָיו לְמַעְלָה וְאֵינוֹ מְמַהֵר לָצֵאת, וְסַנְדָּל מַחֲלִיק וְיוֹצֵא קוֹדֶם. שָׁרֵיק. מַחֲלִיק. הָוְיָא לֵידָה. דְּקַיְימָא לָן בְּהַאי פִּירְקָא (דף כח.): יָצָא רֹאשׁוֹ – הֲרֵי הוּא כַּיָּלוּד. אֲבָל סַנְדָּל – עַד דְּנָפֵיק רוּבָּא, דְּאֵין רֹאשׁ נֵפֶל חָשׁוּב, דְּהָכִי אָמְרִינַן בִּבְכוֹרוֹת (דף מו.): אֵין הָרֹאשׁ פּוֹטֵר בִּנְפָלִים, וְאַדְּנָפֵיק סַנְדָּל – נִתְגַּיְּירָה וְטָבְלָה. **מתני'** הַבַּיִת טָמֵא. מִשּׁוּם אֹהֶל הַמֵּת, דְּוָלָד הָוֵה בָּהּ וּמֵת. נִימּוֹק הַוָּלָד. וְנַעֲשָׂה דָּם, וְנִתְעָרֵב בְּדַם הַלֵּידָה וּבָטֵל בָּרוֹב. **גמ'** וְסוֹפָהּ. כְּשֶׁהִיא הוֹלֶכֶת וְרוֹוַחַת – הָוְיָא רְחָבָה כְּתוּרְמוּס. לִישָּׁנָא אַחֲרִינָא גָּרְסִינַן בַּתּוֹסֶפְתָּא: וְרֹאשָׁהּ דּוֹמֶה כְּתוּרְמוּס. שֶׁיֹּאחֲזֶנּוּ בְּיָדוֹ. אֲחִיזָה (א) אִית בָּהּ טֶפַח, שֶׁהַטֶּפַח אַרְבַּע אֶצְבָּעוֹת בְּגוּדָל. שִׁדְרוֹ שֶׁל לוּלָב צָרִיךְ שֶׁיְּהֵא יוֹצֵא מִן הַהֲדַס טֶפַח. לְבַד אוֹרֶךְ הֶעָלִין. "שִׁדְרָה" קָרֵי כָּל זְמַן שֶׁהֶעָלִין הוֹלְכִין וּמִתְחַבְּרִין וּמוֹסִיפִין, וְאַחַר שֶׁכָּלְתָה הַשִּׁדְרָה גְּבוֹהִין אוֹרֶךְ הֶעָלִין לְמַעְלָה. חֲדָא הִיא. דְּלֵיכָּא שְׁמַעְתָּא אֶלָּא הַאי דְּשִׁדְרָה דְּאָמַר ר' יוֹחָנָן. אָמַר אַבַּיֵי. לָא תֵּימָא: "תָּנֵי ר' חִיָּיא אֵזוֹב טֶפַח", דְּמַשְׁמַע מַתְנִי' הִיא. אֶלָּא אֵימָא: "אָמַר רַבִּי חִיָּיא", וּמִנַּפְשֵׁיהּ קָאָמְרָהּ. וְרַבִּי חִיָּיא – תַּנָּא וַאֲמוֹרָא הוּא, וְהֵיכָא דְּאָמַר מִנַּפְשֵׁיהּ בִּלְשׁוֹן מֵימְרָא, הָוְיָא שְׁמַעְתָּא. טֶפַח עַל טֶפַח עַל רוּם טֶפַח. אֹהֶל קָטָן שֶׁהוּא טֶפַח אוֹרֶךְ וְטֶפַח רוֹחַב וְרוּם חֲלָלוֹ טֶפַח. מֵבִיא הַטּוּמְאָה. אִם כַּזַּיִת מִן הַמֵּת בְּצַד זֶה וּכְלִי בְּצַד זֶה – הָוֵה טָמֵא כְּלִי, מֵחֲמַת אֹהֶל הַמֵּת. וְחוֹצֵץ בִּפְנֵי הַטּוּמְאָה. אִם טוּמְאָה תַּחְתָּיו וּכְלִי עַל גַּבָּיו – הַכְּלִי טָהוֹר. וּלְהָכִי נָקַט "עַל רוּם טֶפַח", דְּאִי הָוֵה חָלָל רוּמוֹ פָּחוּת מִטֶּפַח – הָוְיָא טוּמְאָה רְצוּצָה, וּכְנֶגְדּוֹ לְמַעְלָה עַד לָרָקִיעַ – טָמֵא, כִּדְאָמְרִי' בְּ"הָעוֹר וְהָרוֹטֶב" (חולין קכו.). וּלְעִנְיַן אָהֳלֵי טוּמְאָה, נָמֵי לָא מַיְירֵי – דְּלָאו אֹהֶל הוּא. תַּנּוּר. מְקוֹם שְׁפִיתַת שְׁתֵּי קְדֵרוֹת, כִּירָה *– מְקוֹם שְׁפִיתַת קְדֵרָה אַחַת. חִבּוּר. וּכְתַנּוּר דָּמֵי, מִפְּנֵי שֶׁצְּרִיכָה לַתַּנּוּר לִהְיוֹת לוֹ יָד. שֶׁאִם נִטְמָא הַתַּנּוּר – פַּת שֶׁעָלֶיהָ טָמֵא. שֶׁהַתַּנּוּר אע"פ שֶׁאֵינוֹ מְקַבֵּל טוּמְאָה מִגַּבּוֹ – מְטַמֵּא הוּא אֶת אֲחֵרִים מִגַּבּוֹ, כִּדְאָמַר בְּתוֹרַת כֹּהֲנִים. הִלְכָּךְ יָדוֹ, אע"ג דְּלֵית לֵיהּ אֲוִיר – מְטַמְּאָה. אֲבָל יוֹתֵר מִטֶּפַח – עוֹמֶדֶת לִינָּטֵל, שֶׁהִיא גְּדוֹלָה יוֹתֵר מִדַּאי, וְלָא הָוְיָא יָד.

**תוספות**

**סנדל**. דלית ליה חיותא – עד שילא רובו, אבל ראשו – לא. אע"ג דשמואל דאמר: אין הראש פוטר בנפלים איתותב בפ' "יש בכור" (בכורות דף מו:) – נפל דאית ליה צורת פנים עדיף מסנדל. והא דקאמר: ולד דאית ליה חיותא מדנפיק רישיה, לאו דוקא דאית ביה חיותא, דהא אפי' לית ביה חיותא, כיון דאיתותב שמואל. ועוד: דמשמע בירושלמי דולד שעם הסנדל אינו מתקיים. אלא כלומר: שראוי לחיות, דהיינו שנגמר בצורת פנים. ור"ח גריס: "ולד דאית ביה חיותא מדנפיק רובי' סנדל דלית ביה חיותא מדנפיק כוליה". פי' "רוביה" – רוב הראש, "כוליה" – כל הראש. אבל כל הגוף פשיטא דלא צריך, דרובו ככולו. **שדרה** טפח. וא"ת: תקשי הך ברייתא לרב יהודה אמר שמואל דאמר* צריך שילא לולב מן ההדס טפח ולא מצריך שדרה ופליג על ר' פרנך! וי"ל: דלא מתניא בי ר' חייא ובי ר' אושעיא. אי נמי: בברייתא לא תני שדרה אלא שהתלמוד קבע בברייתא שדרה, משום דקים לן הכי. ואם תאמר: דטפח זה קטן, דמפרש התם אמה בת ה' טפחים עשה אותה בת ו' לא מהם ג' להדס ואחד ללולב! ויש לומר: דמכל מקום כיון דאיכא שם טפח עליה, חשיב ליה הכא עם שאר טפחים. אי נמי: טפח דלולב לא קאי אטפחים קטנים, ולא קאי קטנים כ"א אטפחים של הדס. **ותו** ליכא. ואם תאמר: והא איתא ב"המוכר את הספינה" (ב"ב דף פט.) קנה של מאזנים – טפח, וב"העור והרוטב" (חולין דף קכג.) בכדי אחיזה – טפח, גם בטרפות יש דשיעורו טפח? ולפי המסקנא דלא איירי בדרבנן אלא בדכתיב ולא מפורש שיעורייהו, אתי שפיר. **מן** התנור טפח. היינו להוציא הטומאה, שאם נטמא התנור מתוכו – נטמא היד, דחשיב כגוף התנור. דאף על גב דאין התנור מקבל טומאה מגבו, אם נטמא תוכו – גבו נמי טמא, כדאמר פ' "אלו דברים" (ברכות דף נב.) דנטמא תוכו – כולן טמאין. ובת"כ נמי אמר: מרובה מדת לטמא ממדת ליטמא, שמטמא אחרים מגבו ואינו מיטמא מגבו. ויד, דין גב יש לה. ואם נגע השרץ ליד – לא נטמא התנור, כדאמרינן בתוספתא (ב"ק דכלים פ"ו) אין טומאה לכלי חרס אלא מתוכו והיסטו בלבד, ולא קתני על ידו. וב"העור והרוטב" (חולין דף קיח.) דבעי למימר יד להכניס, יעמיד התוספתא בתנור שאין לו יד.

אבל

**תוספי הרא"ש**

גבי בכורות למה לי. קס"ד הא דקתני לבא אחריו היינו בלידה אחרת מדלא קתני הבא עמו: ולר' שמעון דאמר יוצא דופן כו' ולא מצי למימר שאם ילדה ולד קודם שקיעה וסנדל לאחר שקיעה שאין מביאה קרבן עד פ"א לסנדל דלא לענין הכי מיתניא דקתני התם המפלת סנדל מביאה קרבן ונאכל משמע דחיוב הקרבן אתא לאשמועינן דלא תימא שהיא פטורה לגמרי: **ולד** דאית ביה חיותא סריך. אע"ג דאמרינן בירושלמי אין סנדל אלא שרצמו חי ואינו יוצא עם החי אלא עם המת היינו שמת בשעת יציאה מתוך הדחק שדוחקין זה את זה אבל עם היציאה הוא חי וסריך ולא נפיק עד שיצא מקצת הסנדל: ולד דאית ביה חיותא מדנפיק רישיה הו"ל לידה סנדל עד דנפיק רוביה. הכי גרים רש"י ופי' דסבר כשמואל דאמר אין הראש פוטר בנפלים ולא חשיב כילוד עד דנפיק רוב הוולד. וקשה דהא איתותב שמואל בפ' יש בכור וצ"ל דבסנדל לא חשיב ראש אפילו יש בו צורת פנים דכיון דנרצם לא חשיב כשאר נפל. והא דקאמר ולד דאית ביה חיותא לאו דוקא אלא ראוי לחיות קאמר וי"ס דגרסי ולד מכי נפיק רוביה דרישיה הו"ל לידה סנדל עד דנפיק כוליה דהיינו כל הראש. דולד סגיא ברוב ראשו אע"פ שהוא נפל כדקאמר ר' יוסי לקמן משיצא כתקנו לחיים ובנפל איירי ומפרש התם דהיינו רוב ראשו ולת"ק דבעי ראש שלם בנפלים ולמתני' דבכורות דמשמע דולד הבא עמו חי ואינו בכור לכהן אי אפשר ליישב לפי הירושלמי: **שדרה**. מפרש לקמן בשדרו של לולב. ותימה הך ברייתא תיקשי לרב יהודה אמר שמואל דפליג על ר' פרנך בלולב הגזול ואמר שצריך שיצא לולב מן ההדס טפח ושמא לשון שדרה אינו שנוי בברייתא. א"נ לא מיתנייא בי רבי חייא ובי ר' אושעיא דאושעיא זעירא קתני לה: **שיאחזנו** בידו ויראה לכאן ולכאן. והיינו שיעור טפח שהוא ד' אצבעות בגודל ונקטינן בהאי לישנא כדי לפרש הטעם: **ותו** ליכא. תימה ואכתי איכא טובא דתנן במס' כלים יד הפרגול טפח. ובפ' המוכר את הספינה גבי קנה מאזנים. וטפח לבית אחיזה גבי המפשיט בהעור והרוטב. ובאלו טריפות קתני מילי טובא דשיעורן טפח גבי טריפות. ובפ' לא יחפור ובכירה טפח. ולפי המסקנא ניחא כולהו דלא מיירי אלא בדכתיבן ולא מפרשי שיעורייהו והני אין שמות הטרפות ולא שמות הכלים כתובין: **אבן** היוצא מן התנור טפח. לאו להכנים לו הטומאה מיירי דלא עדיפא ידו מגבו אלא להוציא את הטומאה והכי תניא בתוספתא דאין טומאה לכלי חרס אלא מאוירו והסיטו ואילו יד לא קא חשיב ואמרינן נמי הא יש צמיד פתיל עליו טהור מי לא עסקינן אפי' יש בו יד ואי הוה יד מכנים טומאה לא הוה מציל בצמיד פתיל כדאמר בשבת פרק ר' עקיבא נמי מי לא עסקינן דיחדנהו לאשתו נדה ומוכח מהכא דכלי חרס אינו מטמא מדרס ואע"ג דבריש סוגיא דהעור והרוטב משמע דסבר תלמודא דיש יד לתנור להכניס ולהוציא ועדיף מגבו במסקנא לא צריך למימר הכי: **ובכירה** ג' אצבעות. פרש"י דכירה הוא מקום שפיתת קדרה אחת. וליתא דבפ' כירה אמרינן שהוא מקום שפיתת שתי קדרות אבל כופה הוא מקום שפיתת קדרה אחת:

אבל

**מסורת הש"ס**

[בכורות מו.]

[לקמן מ.]

[לעיל יח. בכורות כב.]

[תוספתא פ"ד]

[עי' פרש"י ותוס' חולין יב: ד"ה דמן חבריא וע"ע פרש"י בחולין לא. ד"ה זעירא]

ר"ה כז: ע"ש

סוכה לב:

סוכה ו: [סנהדרין ד.]

אהלות פ"ג מ"ז [סוכה י.]

כלים פ"ה מ"ב

[עי' תוס' ע"ב סוף ד"ה בפלוגתא]

**הגהות הב"ח**

(א) רש"י ד"ה שיאחזנו בידו אחיזה אין בה:

**עין משפט נר מצוה**

מו א מיי' פ"ב מהלכות נחלות הל' י סמג עשין לז טוש"ע ח"מ סי' רעז סעיף ו:

מז ב מיי' פי"א מהלכות בכורים הל' טו סמג עשין קמד טוש"ע י"ד סימן שס סעיף כב:

מח ג מיי' פ"י מהלכות איסורי ביאה הלכה יב ופ"א מהל' מחוסרי כפרה הלכה ו:

מט ד מיי' פכ"ו מהל' טומאת מת הל' י:

נ ה מיי' פ"י מהלכות איסורי ביאה הל' יד:

[סוכה לב:]

נא ו ז מיי' שם הל' יג:

נב ח מיי' פ"א מהלכות שופר הלכה ה וע"ש סמג עשין מה טוש"ע א"ח סימן תקפו סעיף ט:

נג ט מיי' פ"ז מהלכות לולב הלכה ח וע"ש סמג עשין מד טוש"ע א"ח סי' תרנ סעיף א:

נד י מיי' פ"ד מהלכות סוכה הל' ב וע"ש סמג עשין מג טוש"ע א"ח סי' תרל סעיף ב:

נה כ מיי' פי"א מהלכות טומאת צרעת הל' א ופ"ג מהל' פרה אדומה הלכה ב:

נו ל מיי' פי"ג מהלכות טומאת מת הלכה א:

נז מ מיי' פי"ז מהלכות כלים הלכה א:

נח א מיי' פט"ו מהל' כלים הלכה ב:
נט ב מיי' שם פרק ט"ז הלכה א:
ס ג מיי' שם פט"ו הל"א:
סא ד מיי' פ"י מהל' איסורי ביאה הל' יד סמג לאוין קיא טוש"ע י"ד סי' קצ"ד סעיף ד:
סב ה מיי' שם הלכה טז טוש"ע שם סעיף ז:

תנורי בנות, *דתניא: *תנור — תחלתו ארבעה ושיריו ד', דברי רבי מאיר. וחכמים אומרים: אבמה דברים אמורים — בגדול, אבל בקטן — תחלתו כל שהוא. משתגמר מלאכתו, בושיריו ברובו. *וכמה "כל שהוא"? אמר רבי ינאי: גטפח, שכן עושין תנורי בנות טפח! בפלוגתא לא קמיירי. השתא דאתית להכי — הא נמי פלוגתא היא. דקתני סיפא: אמר ר' יהודה, לא אמרו טפח — אלא מן התנור ולכותל. והאיכא מסגרת טפח! בדכתיבן לא קא מיירי. והאיכא *כפורת טפח! בקדשים לא קמיירי. והאיכא: *דיה לקורה שהיא רחבה טפח! בדרבנן לא קמיירי, אלא בדכתיבן ולא מפרשי שיעורייהו. יתיב רב יצחק בר שמואל בר מרתא קמיה דרב כהנא ויתיב וקאמר, אמר רב יהודה, אמר רב: כל שלשה ימים הראשונים — תולין את השליא בולד, מכאן ואילך — חוששין לולד אחר. אמר ליה: ומי אמר רב הכי? והאמר רב: אין הולד מתעכב אחר חבירו כלום! אישתיק. אמר ליה: דלמא כאן — בנפל, כאן — בבן קיימא? אמר ליה: את אמרת לשמעתיה דרב? בפירוש אמר רב הכי: הפילה נפל, ואחר כך הפילה שליא — כל שלשה ימים תולין את השליא בולד, מכאן ואילך — חוששין לולד אחר. ילדה ואח"כ הפילה שליא — אפילו מכאן ועד עשרה ימים אין חוששין לולד אחר. שמואל ותלמידי דרב ורב יהודה הוו יתבי. חליף ואזיל רב יוסף בריה דרב מנשיא מדויל לאפייהו, באלי ואתי, אמר: אתי לן גברא דרמינן ליה בגילא דחטתא, ומרמי ומדחי. אדהכי אתא. אמר ליה שמואל: מאי אמר רב בשליא? א"ל: הכי אמר רב: דאין תולין את השליא אלא בדבר של קיימא. שיילינהו שמואל לכל תלמידי דרב ואמרי ליה הכי, הדר חזייה לרב יהודה בישות. בעא מיניה רבי יוסי בן שאול מרבי: המפלת דמות עורב ושליא מהו? אמר ליה: אין תולין אלא בדבר שיש במינו שליא. קשורה בו מהו? אמר ליה: דבר שאינו שאלת. איתיביה: *ההמפלת מין בהמה חיה ועוף ושליא עמהן, בזמן שהשליא קשורה עמהן — אין חוששין לולד אחר, אין שליא קשורה עמהן — חוששין לולד אחר, הריני מטיל עליהן חומר

חומר

**רש"י**

תנורי בנות. נערות קטנות עושין תנורין לשחוק. תחלתו ארבעה. תנור בן ד' טפחים מקבל טומאה, אם נגמרה מלאכתו. ושיריו ד'. נטמא תנור גדול ושברו, ונשתיירו ד' טפחים — עדיין טמא. ה"ג: תחלתו כל שהוא, משתגמר מלאכתו, ושיריו ברובו. ומקשה בה"העור והרוטב": רובו דטפח למאי חזי? ומשני: האי "ושיריו" — אגדול קאי, וה"ק: שירי גדול — ברובו. ומותבינן: בגדול, והא קאמר "שיריו ד'"? ומשנינן: ההוא — בתנור בר ז', דד' הוי רובו, והא — בתנור בר ט'. בפלוגתא. כגון הכא, דלר"מ לא הוי שיעורא בטפח. לא אמרו טפח אלא בין תנור ולכותל. דאם יותר מטפח עומדת ליקלך, מפני שמעכב את התנור מלקרבו לכותל, ודוחקת את הכותל. הילכך יותר מטפח, עומדת ליטל היא. אבל לצד הבית, אפי' גדולה הרבה — יד הוא לתנור. בדכתיבן. ששיעורו מפורש מן התורה. דיה לקורה. לגבי מבוי. מדרבנן. כגון מבוי, דכל מצותו מדברי סופרים. כל ג' ימים. כגון ילדה ולד תחלה, ושליא אחריו, בתוך ג' ימים. תולין השליא. בו, ואין חוששין לאחר, דתוך הזמן הזה עשויה השליא להתעכב אחר הולד שהיתה ממנו, טפי — לא. ואם זה זכר — תשב לזכר בלבד, ולא אמרינן: שליא אחרת היתה עם ולד זה, ונימוח, ושליא זו דולד אחר היא. דדרך שליא לשהות אחר ולד ג' ימים. מכאן ואילך חוששין. שמא ולד אחר היה עמו, ונקבה היה, ותשב ימי טומאה דנקבה. ואי נמי הוי האי ולד נקבה — אכתי מהניא ספק דשליא, דמניא ימי טוהר לחומרא. שאם תראה ליום פ"א לולד, ופסקה עד יום שמיני, וראתה — לא הויא שומרת יום כנגד יום. *דאמר בהדיא שליא נקבה הואי, ומה שראתה ביום פ"א — דם טוהר הוה. דמשליא מנינן, והשתא הוא דהויא תחלת נדה, והיא נקראת טועה. בנפלים. מתעכב. את אמרת לשמעתיה דרב. בתמיה. כלומר, את אתית לפרושי מדידך? בפירוש. פירשה רב הכי. ילדה. בן קיימא. באלי ואתי. שהיה ממהר לבא, כמו (לעיל דף יז.): באלי דידבי, פי': מגרש. מדויל. שם מקום. בגילא דחיטתא. כלומר, בשאלות מועטות. מירמי ומידחי. כלומר, להקשותו ולדחותו, שלא ידע להשיב. אלא בדבר של קיימא. שכיוצא בו מתקיים אם היום היו חדשיו כלו. למעוטי שאם הפילה דבר שאין ראוי לבריית נשמה, כגון בירך אחד באמצע, או גוף אטום או מפלת מין בהמה וחיה ועוף ואח"כ הפילה שליא — אפי' בתוך ג' חוששת לולד אחר. חזייה לרב יהודה בישות. דשמעה, ולא אמרה ניהליה. המפלת עורב ושליא מהו. מי תלינן שליא בעורב, ולא ניחוש לולד אחר. או לא תלינן? שיש במינו. כגון אדם ובהמה וחיה, אבל עוף — לא.

חומר

**תוספות**

אבל בקטן תחלתו כל שהוא. וא"ת: וגדול שאין לו ד' טפחים, אמאי טהור? והלא אף בקטן טפי טמא! וי"ל: דגדול וקטן היינו ברוחב, והרוחב הרבה צריך גובה ד' להחזיק חומו. אבל קטן שהוא צר, די בגובה טפח. תחלתו כל שהוא. משתגמר מלאכתו, שיריו ברובו. במשניות גרסינן: תחלתו כל שהוא, שיריו ברובו, משתגמר מלאכתו. ואיזהו גמר מלאכתו וכו'. ודרך התלמוד שמהפך פעמים מסדר המשנה, לפי הצורך. משום דבפ' "העור והרוטב" (חולין דף קכד.) בעי: רובו דטפח למאי חזי? ומשני: אגדול תני ליה בסוף. ופריך: והא שיריו ד' קאמר? ומשני: לא קשיא, הא — בתנור בר ט' הא — בתנור בר ז' ומפרש התם רש"י: דבתנור ט' — סגי בארבעה, אע"ג דלא הוי רובא. ותנור ז' אע"ג דלא הוי ד' — סגי ברובא. וקשה לר"ת: לא יהיה סופו חמור מתחלתו, דהא תחלתו ד' ונראה כפירש"י שפירש כאן דתנור בר ז' (א) וד' הוי רובא. ותנור בר תשעה — ברובא. וקשה: דלמה ליה למנקט בר ט' הוה ליה למנקט בר ח' ושיריו ברובו? ולפרש"יא] דהתם ניחא: דנקט ט' אע"ג דהוי ד' מיעוטא. ומה שהקשה ר"ת לא קשה מידי. דהעושה כלי חרס — אינו עושה אלא דבר חשוב. אבל כלי שנתמעט, כל זמן שראוי — אינו מתבטל. כמו *גרדומי ציצית, דבשירים סגי. וכן משמע מדפריך: שיריו טפח למאי חזי? משמע: דאי הוה חזי — הוה ניחא ליה, אע"ג דבציר מתחלתו*. כל שהוא טפח. פר"ת: ב"לא יחפור" (ב"ב דף יט) דפעמים כל שהוא בציר מטפח, ופעמים טפי מטפח*. בפלוגתא לא קמיירי. ואע"ג דפליגי בדופן סוכה דר"ש אומר דרביעית טפח, מ"מ טפח לדופן אחד צריך לכ"ע אבל לתנור, אע"ג דבין התנור ולכותל לכ"ע טפח, מ"מ בסתם תנור פליגי. והא דפרש"י דכירה מקום שפיתת קדרה אחת — לא דק, דבפ' "כירה" (שבת דף לח:) אמר דכירה זהו מקום שפיתת ב' קדרות. את אמרת שמעתיה דרב. כלומר, כוונת מעצמך, ומתחלה שכחת, ולכך שתק. ולפ"ה: שפי' בתמיה, צריך לומר דמתחלה לא חש להשיבו. ילדה ואח"כ הפילה שליא אפי' עד י' ימים אין חוששין לולד אחר. אע"ג דאמר לקמן דנשתהא הולד שלשה חדשים, מ"מ לא שכיח, וכל כמה דלא חזינן — לא חיישינן. המפלת חיה ועוף כו' — דוקא נקט חיה ועוף, דאי בתחלה ולד ואח"כ שליא, עד ג' ימים תולין, ואין חוששין לולד אחר. ולכאורה נראה הטעם: דחיה ועוף אין דרכן של נשים להפיל, ולכך איכא לספוקי שהשליא אינה מהם. וקשה: דבפרק "בהמה המקשה" (חולין דף עז:) אהא דתנן: שליא שיצתה מקצתה — אסורה באכילה. ומסיק: אר"א לא שנו אלא שאינה קשורה בולד פי' שיש לה ולד אחר. וכיון דאינה קשורה בו, חוששין לולד אחר בשליא, ולכך אסורה. ומייתי: תניא נמי הכי, מהך דהמפלת חיה ועוף. והיכי מייתי, הא אדרבה משמע הכא דוקא חיה ועוף דלאו אורחיה, אבל נפל דאורחיה תולין כל שלשה ימים, ובבן קיימא אפי' כמה ימים? וי"ל דאין הדבר תלוי באורחיה ולא אורחיה, אלא קים ליה להתלמוד ב]דאמר צורת אדם — רגילה השליא להתעכב, אבל לאחר בהמה חיה ועוף — אינה רגילה להפרד השליא מן הולד, אפי' במעי האשה כמו במעי הבהמה. וא"ת וכי אינה קשורה בולד, אמאי קאמר ר"א דאסורה באכילה? הא אמרינן הכא דלא הוי אלא ספק, ולא ודאי ולד אחר. מדקתני: הריני מטיל עליה חומר שני ולדות, שמא נימוח שפיר של שליא זו. וא"כ הוי ספק ספיקא! דלמא אין כאן ולד אחר, ואפי' איכא — שמא לא יצא לא ראשו ולא רובו. ובפ"ק דב"ק (דף יא.) גבי שליא שיצתה מקצתה ביום ראשון, משמע דספק ספיקא שרי. דפריך: מאי קמ"ל דאין מקצת שליא בלא ולד — תנינא: שליא שיצתה מקצתה אסורה! פי' ואם יש מקצת שליא בלא ולד — הוה ליה ספק ספיקא, ושרי! וי"ל דברייתא דקתני, שמא איירי בשליא שאחר הולד, ור"א איירי בשליא שיצתה קודם הולד, דודאי יש שם ולד אחר כשאינה קשורה בו. כדאמרינן בשמעתין: לא אמרו תולין השליא בולד אלא בשליא שבאה אחר הולד. והתם מייתי ראיה דבאינה קשורה חוששין לולד אחר, לאפוקי מדר' יוחנן דהתם. אי נמי: אפילו בספק ספיקא אסרה ר"א דגזרינן מקצתה אטו רובה, או אטו אין עמה ולד אחר, דיטעו העולם ויסברו: הא דשרינן מה שבפנים — לאו משום ספק ספיקא, אלא משום כל בבהמה, וגזרת הכתוב הוא דאפי' יצא רובו שרי מיעוטו שבפנים. כיון דחזו דשרינן ביצתה מקצתה, ואפשר דיצא הראש באותו מקצת, והוי כיוצא רובו. ולא יעלו על לבם דמשום ספק ספיקא שרי.

חומר

**תוספי הרא"ש**

אבל בקטן תחלתו כל שהוא. ותימה אמאי אמרינן בגדול שתחלתו ד' אפי' פחות מד' יהא תורת קטן עליו שתחלתו טפח וי"ל דגדול ניכר בדפוס שלו שסופו להיות גדול ולא חשיב כלי עד שיהא גבוה ד' דבפחות מכאן אינו מחזיק את חומו: תחלתו כל שהיא משתגמר מלאכתו. הגרש"י ובפ"ה דכלים לא תני הכי אלא הכי מיתניא אבל בקטן תחלתו כל שהוא ושיריו ברובו משתגמר מלאכתו ואי זו היא גמר משיסיקנו לאפות בו סופגנין אלמא קאי על שיריו ברובו דקטן אין אופין בו סופגנין: ושיריו ברובו. פרש"י דפריך בהעור והרוטב רובו דטפח למאי חזי ומשני דאגדול קאי גדול הא אמרינן ושיריו ד' ומשני הא בתנור שבעה דשיריו בארבעה אבל ברובו לא מטמינן ליה דלא חמירי שיריו מתחלתו דהא מתחלתו כשהוא שלם לא הוי תנור בציר מד'. והא דקתני רובו (בתנור) בתנור ט' אע"ג דבחציו איכא ד' לא מטמינן עד דאיכא רובא. כך פי' בפרק העור והרוטב. ונראה לפרש איפכא דבתנור ט' כי היכי דמחמרינן בתחלתו דמטמא בד' מחמרינן נמי בשיריו ברובו ובר שבעה שיריו ברובו ואין זה דוחק אם סופו חמור מתחלתו דכיון שכבר היה כלי בראיות מעט נשאר שם כלי עליו וכיוצא בזה אשכחן בלולב הגזול דגרדומי אזוב כשרין וכן גרדומי ציצית בריש התכלת. ועוד דכי פריך התם רובו דטפח למאי חזי לא קשה ליה אלא משום דהוי יותר מדאי דבר מועט ולא חזי למידי אבל במאי דס"ד דסופו חמור מתחלתו לא קשה ליה ולא מידי ועוד למה לי למנקט תנור בר ט' בתנור בר ח' סגיא אבל אי אמרינן דבר ט' בד' ניחא הא דנקט בר ט' לרבותא אע"ג דד' הוי מיעוטא אפ"ה טמא ובר ז' ברובו אע"ג דלא הוי אלא ג' טפחים וחצי ומשהו טמא: וכמה כל שהוא אמרי דבי ר' ינאי טפח. תימה דבפ' מי שמת גבי שייר כל שהוא משמע דכל שהוא ר"ל דוקא כל שהוא וכן פ"ק דקידושין גבי קרקע כל שהוא חייב בפאה ובבכורים ולכתוב עליו פרוזבול ולקנות נכסים שאין עמהן אחריות דמוקי לה במחט ותלו בה מרגניתא וי"ל הא דקרי הכא לטפח כל שהוא משום דמעיקרא תנא שיעורא רבה. וגבי חבית של (שותפין) שיתופי מבואות דאמרינן בפ' חלון צריך שיגביה כל שהוא ומפרש כל שהוא טפח התם נמי קרי ליה כל שהוא משום דבעלמא לא קנה הגבהה פחות מג' טפחים. ומיהו לר"ת דמפרש דכל הגבהה סגיא בטפח קשה ויש לחלק דשמא לגבי קרקע לא קרי כל שהוא אלא אם כן הוי דוקא: בפלוגתא לא קא מיירי. אע"ג דבין תנור לכותל מיהא מודה רבי יהודה מ"מ בסתם תנור פליגי: את אמרת לשמעתיה דרב. לשון שבח הוא ששבחו ובא זה והזכירו כדאמרינן רבי טרפון שמע ושכח רבי עקיבא דורש ומסכים: ילדה ואח"כ הפילה אפילו מכאן ועד עשרה ימים אין חוששין לולד אחר. לא דמי להאי דאמרינן לקמן ששהה ולד אחר חבירו ג' חדשים דמילתא דלא שכיחא הוא א"נ היכא דילדה ולד קיימא אח"כ אפשר ששוהה ולד אחר חבירו אבל היכא שאחרון נפל אין דרכו להשתהות אחר הראשון: אין תולין את השליא אלא בדבר של קיימא. פרש"י שכיוצא בו מתקיים אם היו חדשיו כלו לאפוקי שאם הפילה דבר שאינו לבריית נשמה כגון אם נברא בירך אחד באמצעו או גוף אטום וחזי ביה ברב יהודה בישות דאמר לעיל שתולין את השליא בולד ולא פי' באיזה ולד תולין כך פ"ה אבל לא רצה לפרש אין תולין את השליא אלא בולד של קיימא אבל לא בנפל דא"כ הוה מפליג אהא דאמר רב לעיל וגם אהא דבעא מיניה ר' יוסי בן שאול מר' המפלת עורב ושליא מהו דע"כ לא קא מיבעי ליה אלא בדבר שאין במינו שליא אבל במינו שליא פשיטא ליה דתולין וכן הך ברייתא דהמפלת כמין בהמה חיה ועוף ועוד דהו"ל למימר אין תולין את השליא אלא בולד של קיימא אבל מדקאמר בדבר של קיימא משמע שכיוצא בו מתקיים במקום אחר:
מ"ט

כלים פ"ה מ"א חולין קכד.
[חולין שם ע"ש עירובין יד: וש"נ]
שבת לג: סוכה ד:
[עירובין יג:]
[נ"ל דתנן]
[מנחות לט.]
[ועי' היטב תוס' חולין קכד. ד"ה הא בתנורא וכן ברש"י שם]
[ועי' תוס' ב"ב קו. ד"ה וכל היכא ועוד שם כז: ד"ה בחיטה ועוד קדושין כו. ד"ה קרקע]
דאימר בהדי שליא
חולין עז.

**הגהות הב"ח**

(א) תום' ד"ה תחלתו וכו' ז' הוי כל"ל ואות ו' נמחק:

**הגהות מהר"ב רנשבורג**

א] תוס' ד"ה תחילתו כל שהוא וכו' הוה ליה למינקט בר שמנה ושיריו ברובו ולפרש"י. נ"ב עי' בפ"ה דכלים משנה א' בפי' הרא"ש ובהגה"ה שם: ב] ד"ה המפלת וכו' אלא קים ליה להש"ס דאמר צורת אדם וכו' כצ"ל:

חוֹמֶר שְׁנֵי וְלָדוֹת, *שֶׁאֲנִי אוֹמֵר: שֶׁמָּא נִמּוֹחַ שָׁפִיר שֶׁל שִׁלְיָא, וְנִמּוֹחַ שִׁלְיָא שֶׁל שָׁפִיר! תְּיוּבְתָּא. אָמַר רַבָּה בַּר שֵׁילָא, אָמַר רַב מַתְּנָה, אָמַר שְׁמוּאֵל: מַעֲשֶׂה וְתָלוּ אֶת הַשִּׁלְיָא בְּוָלָד עַד עֲשָׂרָה יָמִים, בוְלֹא אָמְרוּ תּוֹלִין — אֶלָּא בְּשִׁלְיָא הַבָּאָה אַחַר הַוָּלָד. אָמַר רַבָּה בַּר בַּר חָנָה, אָמַר רַבִּי יוֹחָנָן: גמַעֲשֶׂה וְתָלוּ אֶת הַשִּׁלְיָא בְּוָלָד עַד כ"ג יָמִים. אֲמַר לֵיהּ רַב יוֹסֵף — עַד כ"ד אֲמַרְתְּ לָן. אָמַר רַב אַחָא בְּרֵיהּ דְּרַב עֲוִירָא, (א) א"ר יִצְחָק: מַעֲשֶׂה וְנִשְׁתַּהָה הַוָּלָד אַחַר חֲבֵירוֹ ל"ג יוֹם. א"ל רַב יוֹסֵף: ל"ד אֲמַרְתְּ לָן. הָנִיחָא *לְמַאן דְּאָמַר יוֹלֶדֶת לְתִשְׁעָה יוֹלֶדֶת לְמִקּוּטָּעִין — מַשְׁכַּחַת לָהּ: אֶחָד נִגְמְרָה צוּרָתוֹ לְסוֹף שִׁבְעָה, וְאֶחָד נִגְמְרָה צוּרָתוֹ לִתְחִלַּת תִּשְׁעָה. אֶלָּא לְמ"ד יוֹלֶדֶת לְתִשְׁעָה אֵינָהּ יוֹלֶדֶת לְמִקּוּטָּעִין, מַאי אִיכָּא לְמֵימַר? אֵיפוֹךְ שְׁמַעְתְּתָא: ל"ג — לְשִׁלְיָא, כ"ג — לְוָלָד. א"ר אָבִין בַּר רַב אַדָּא, אָמַר רַב מְנַחֵם אִישׁ כְּפַר שְׁעָרִים, וְאָמְרִי לָהּ בֵּית שְׁעָרִים: מַעֲשֶׂה וְנִשְׁתַּהָה וָלָד אֶחָד אַחַר חֲבֵירוֹ ג' חֳדָשִׁים, וַהֲרֵי הֵם יוֹשְׁבִים לְפָנֵינוּ בְּבֵית הַמִּדְרָשׁ. וּמַאן נִינְהוּ? *יְהוּדָה וְחִזְקִיָּה בְּנֵי רַבִּי חִיָּיא. וְהָא אָמַר מָר: אֵין אִשָּׁה מִתְעַבֶּרֶת, וְחוֹזֶרֶת וּמִתְעַבֶּרֶת! אָמַר אַבַּיֵי: טִיפָּה אַחַת הָיְתָה וְנִתְחַלְּקָה לִשְׁתַּיִם, *אֶחָד נִגְמְרָה צוּרָתוֹ בִּתְחִלַּת ז' וְאֶחָד בְּסוֹף ט'. § "שִׁלְיָא בַּבַּיִת הַבַּיִת טָמֵא". § תָּנוּ רַבָּנַן: *שִׁלְיָא בַּבַּיִת — הַבַּיִת טָמֵא. לֹא שֶׁהַשִּׁלְיָא וָלָד, אֶלָּא שֶׁאֵין שִׁלְיָא שֶׁאֵין וָלָד עִמָּהּ, דִּבְרֵי רַבִּי מֵאִיר. רַבִּי יוֹסֵי וְרַבִּי יְהוּדָה וְרַבִּי שִׁמְעוֹן מְטַהֲרִין. אָמְרוּ לוֹ לְרַבִּי מֵאִיר: אִי אַתָּה מוֹדֶה שֶׁאִם הוֹצִיאוּהוּ בְּסֵפֶל לְבֵית הַחִיצוֹן שֶׁהוּא טָהוֹר? אָמַר לָהֶן: *אֲבָל! וְלָמָּה — לְפִי שֶׁאֵינוֹ. אָמְרוּ לוֹ: כְּשֵׁם שֶׁאֵינוֹ בְּבֵית הַחִיצוֹן — כָּךְ אֵינוֹ בְּבַיִת הַפְּנִימִי! °אָמַר לָהֶן: אֵינוֹ דּוֹמֶה נִמּוֹק פַּעַם אַחַת לְנִמּוֹק ב' פְּעָמִים. יָתֵיב רַב פַּפָּא אֲחוֹרֵי דְּרַב בֵּיבַי קַמֵּיהּ דְּרַב הַמְנוּנָא, וְיָתֵיב וְקָאָמַר: מַאי טַעְמָא דְּרַבִּי שִׁמְעוֹן — קָסָבַר כָּל טוּמְאָה שֶׁנִּתְעָרֵב בָּהּ מִמִּין אַחֵר — בָּטְלָה. אֲמַר לְהוּ רַב פַּפָּא: הַיְינוּ נַמִי טַעֲמַיְיהוּ דְּרַבִּי יְהוּדָה וְרַבִּי יוֹסֵי. אַחִיכוּ עֲלֵיהּ: מַאי שְׁנָא? פְּשִׁיטָא! אָמַר רַב פַּפָּא: אֲפִילּוּ כִּי הָא מִילְּתָא לֵימָא אִינִישׁ וְלָא נִשְׁתּוֹק קַמֵּיהּ רַבֵּיהּ, מִשּׁוּם שֶׁנֶּאֱמַר *°"אִם נָבַלְתָּ בְהִתְנַשֵּׂא וְאִם זַמּוֹתָ יָד לְפֶה". וְאָזְדָא רַבִּי שִׁמְעוֹן לְטַעֲמֵיהּ, דְּתַנְיָא: דמְלֹא תַרְוָד רָקָב שֶׁנָּפַל לְתוֹכוֹ עָפָר כָּל שֶׁהוּ — טָמֵא, וְרַבִּי שִׁמְעוֹן מְטַהֵר. מַאי טַעְמָא דְּרַבִּי שִׁמְעוֹן? אָמַר (ב) רַבָּה, אַשְׁכַּחְתִּינְהוּ לְרַבָּנַן דְּבֵי רַב דְּיָתְבִי וְקָאָמְרִי: אִי אֶפְשָׁר שֶׁלֹּא יִרְבּוּ שְׁתֵּי פְרִידוֹת עָפָר עַל פְּרִידָה אַחַת שֶׁל רָקָב, וְחָסֵיר לֵיהּ. וְאָמֵינָא לְהוּ: אַדְּרַבָּה, א"א שֶׁלֹּא יִרְבּוּ שְׁתֵּי פְרִידוֹת רָקָב עַל

פְּרִידָה

חוֹמֶר שְׁנֵי וְלָדוֹת. אִם זֶה זָכָר — חָיְישִׁינַן דִּלְמָא נְקֵבָה הָוֵה הַהוּא דְּשִׁלְיָא, וְתֵשֵׁב לְזָכָר וְלִנְקֵבָה. וּלְרַבָּנַן דְּאָמְרִי: הַמַּפֶּלֶת חַיָּה וְעוֹף — אֵינוֹ וָלָד, מַאי חוּמְרָא אִיכָּא בְּהַאי וָלָד? מַחְמְרִינַן עֲלָהּ לְמֵימַר: לֵיכָּא שׁוּם וָלָד, וְאֵין לָהּ דַּם טוֹהַר, וְהַיְינוּ חוּמְרָא דִּילֵיהּ, וּמִשּׁוּם שִׁלְיָא מְטַמֵּינַן לָהּ שְׁבוּעַיִם. שֶׁאֲנִי אוֹמֵר. וָלָד הָוֵה עִם הַשִּׁלְיָא וְנִימּוֹחַ הַשָּׁפִיר שֶׁל שִׁלְיָא. שָׁפִיר. וָלָד. וְשֶׁמָּא נִימּוֹחָה שִׁלְיָיתוֹ שֶׁל שָׁפִיר. כְּלוֹמַר וְשִׁלְיָיתוֹ שֶׁל זֶה שֶׁלְּפָנֵינוּ נִימּוֹחַ, וְזוֹ אֵינָהּ שֶׁלּוֹ הוֹאִיל וְאֵינָהּ קְשׁוּרָה בּוֹ. קָתָנֵי מִיהָא "בִּזְמַן שֶׁקְּשׁוּרָה עִמָּהֶן". תְּיוּבְתָּא דְּרַבִּי. דְּאָמַר: "דָּבָר שֶׁאֵינוֹ שָׁלֵם". אַחַר הַוָּלָד. אֲבָל יָצְתָה שִׁלְיָא קוֹדֶם — חוֹשְׁשִׁין לְאַחֵר. הָנִיחָא לְמ"ד כו'. פְּלוּגְתַּיְיהוּ לְקַמָּן בְּפ' "בְּנוֹת כּוּתִים" (דף לח.). לְסוֹף ז'. יוֹם אוֹ יוֹמַיִם (ג) בְּתוֹךְ חֹדֶשׁ ז' בְּסוֹפוֹ, דְּחַיֵּי. וְאֶחָד לִתְחִלַּת תִּשְׁעָה. יוֹם אֶחָד בַּחֹדֶשׁ. "דְּהָווּ לְהוּ" ל"ג. אֶלָּא לְמ"ד אֵינָהּ יוֹלֶדֶת לְמִקּוּטָּעִים הֵיכִי מַשְׁכַּחַת לָהּ. תַּרְוַיְיהוּ בַּחֹדֶשׁ הַשְּׁבִיעִי — לֵיכָּא לְמֵימַר, דְּחֹדֶשׁ כּוּלֵּי הַאי לָא הָוֵי. וְאִם זֶה לְסוֹף ז' וְזֶה לְסוֹף ט' — טְפֵי אִיכָּא. וְאִם זֶה בְּז' וְזֶה בְּח' — לָא חַיֵּי. וּמִדְּקָרֵי לְהוּ "וָלָד" וְלָא "נֵפֶל" — מִכְּלָל דִּבְנֵי קְיָימָא נִינְהוּ. אֵיפוֹךְ. שְׁמַעֲתָא דְּר' יוֹחָנָן. כ"ג. לְוָלָד, מַשְׁכַּחַת לָהּ דְּאֶחָד נִגְמְרָה צוּרָתוֹ לִתְחִלַּת ז' וְאֶחָד לְסוֹף ז', °דִּלְכוּ"ע יוֹלֶדֶת לְז' יוֹלֶדֶת לְמִקּוּטָּעִין. הָאָמַר מָר כו'. קס"ד: בְּג' חֳדָשִׁים לָא מַשְׁכַּחַת לָהּ, אא"כ נִתְעַבְּרָה זֶה אַחַר זֶה. לְבֵית הַחִיצוֹן. לְבַיִת אַחֵר, שֶׁהַבַּיִת טָהוֹר. אֲבָל. הֵן. אָמְרוּ לוֹ לָמָּה. מַאי שְׁנָא בַּיִת רִאשׁוֹן דִּמְטַמֵּית לֵיהּ? אֲמַר לְהוּ: לְפִי שֶׁאֵינוֹ, הוֹאִיל וְטִלְטְלוּהוּ נִמּוֹק. מ"ט דְּר"ש. נְהִי דְּנִמּוֹק, מ"מ כָּל גּוּפוֹ שֶׁל מֵת כָּאן הֲוָה, וְה"ל כְּרָקָב וּכְנֶגֶל, [כְּבַשַׂר הַמֵּת שֶׁנִּימּוֹחַ וְנַעֲשָׂה לֵיחָה סְרוּחָה]. מִמִּין אַחֵר. אֲפִי' מִמִּין טוּמְאָה, אִם אֵינָהּ שָׁוָה לָהּ — בְּטֵלָה. אַחִיכוּ עֲלֵיהּ. אֲמַרוּ לֵיהּ: פְּשִׁיטָא, מַאי שְׁנָא טַעֲמַיְיהוּ מִטַּעֲמֵיהּ, כּוּלָּהּ חֲדָא מִילְּתָא אָמְרִי! אֲפִי' כִּי הַאי מִילְּתָא. דְּאָתְיָא לִידֵי חוּכָא. לֵימָא אִינִישׁ. דִּלְמָא מִתּוֹךְ דְּבָרָיו אָמְרִי לֵיהּ טַעְמָא. וְלָא לִישְׁתּוֹק. וְלֵימָא: מְסַבְּרָנָא לֵיהּ. אִם נָבַלְתָּ. עַלְמָךְ עַל ד"ת, סוֹפְךָ לְהִתְנַשֵּׂא. וְאִם זַמּוֹתָ. וְשָׁתַקְתָּ, סוֹפְךָ לָשׂוּם יָד עַל פֶּה — שֶׁלֹּא תֵּדַע לְהָשִׁיב לַשּׁוֹאֲלִין. מְלֹא תַרְוָד. כַּף. רָקָב. רִקְבוּבִית שֶׁל מֵת. וְזֶה שִׁיעוּרוֹ לְטַמֵּא בְּאֹהֶל הֲלָכָה לְמֹשֶׁה מִסִּינַי. א"א. אַף עַל גַּב דְּרוּבָּא רָקָב, אִי אֶפְשָׁר לְמָקוֹם שֶׁנָּפַל הֶעָפָר שֶׁלֹּא תְּהֵא גַּרְגֵּר שֶׁל רָקָב בֵּין שְׁנֵי גַרְגְּרִים שֶׁל עָפָר, וּבָטֵל הָרָקָב, וּבָצִיר לוֹ שִׁיעוּרָא דְּתַרְוָד.

פְּרִידָה

חומר שני ולדות. פי' הקונטרס: לר"מ דבחיה ועוף טמאה לידה, הוי חומר ב' ולדות. אם חיה ועוף הם זכר — יהבינן לה חומר שליא, דמספקינן בנקבה לטומאה. וחומר חיה ועוף לטהרה, דשמא אין ולד בשליא. וקשה לר"מ אי חיה ועוף זכר, אמאי מספקא שליא בנקבה? הא הוי ספק ספיקא: דשמא אין בשליא ולד, ואפילו יש — שמא זכר הוא! ולכך י"ל "חומר ב' ולדות" דקאמר, היינו לענין שהפילה שליא בשני אחר חיה ועוף. ולרבנן דאמרי דאין טומאת לידה בחיה ועוף — לית לה ימי טוהר כלל, דשמא אין ולד בשליא. ומשום שליא נותנין לה חומרא דזכר ונקבה. וא"ת: לרבנן נימא שלא תשב רק ז' לטומאת לידה, דאימור: אין ולד בשליא. ואפי' יש — שמא זכר הוא? וי"ל: דא"כ אם תראה ביום ל"ד ותחזור ותראה ביום מ"א איכא למימר נמי: אימור לא ילדה כלל, והויא במ"א שומרת יום כנגד יום. ואפי' איכא ולד, אימור: נקבה היא, ושתי ראיות דם טוהר הוא, א"א בתרוייהו למיזל לקולא, *דסתרו אהדדי, אזלינן בתרווייהו לחומרא. וכן נ"ל: אמתניתין,* דקתני "המפלת ואין ידוע אם ולד הוא תשב לזכר ולנקבה ולנדה", אע"ג דאיכא ספק ספיקא: שמא לא ילדה, ואפי' ילדה — שמא זכר הוא, ואמאי תשב לנקבה? אלא ודאי כדפרישית. אלא למ"ד אינה יולדת למקוטעין מאי איכא למימר. וא"ת: ונימא דנגמר צורתו, ואשתהי עד שמיני. דהכי אית ליה לרבה תוספאה בפ' "הערל" (יבמות דף פ:) דעבד עובדא באשה שהלך בעלה למדינת הים וילדה לי"ב חדש, ואכשריה? °ויש לומר: דרוב אמוראים לית להו דרבה תוספאה. מ"ט דר"ש. משום דבמתניתין אינו מזכיר כי אם ר"ש, קאמר מ"ט דר"ש. פ"ה: נהי דנימוק, מ"מ כל הגוף של המת כאן, וה"ל כרקב של מת *וכנגל. וקשה: דא"כ מאי משני: כל טומאה שנתערב בה מין אחר בטלה, והיכי בעי למימר דבטל הולד, משום דדם הלידה מבטל משהו מן הולד כמו מלא תרוד דמייתי התם. ודאי דשיעורו מלומלם, כי יתבטל ממנו משהו, בציר ליה שיעורא מן התרוד. אבל כי יתבטל מעט מן הולד, אכתי ישאר יותר מכזית או ממלא תרוד! לכך נראה לר"י דנפל שבשליא אין עליו תורת נגל ורקב, כיון שאינו נגמר. ואינו בשר לטמא בכזית, אלא מטעם מת שלם. וה"פ: מ"ט דר"ש, הרי יש כאן מת שלם? ומשני: (ד) כל טומאות שנתערבה כו'. ומהאי טעמא כי נתבטל ממנו משהו — טהור. והשתא מייתי שפיר ממלא תרוד רקב, ופריך: אדרבה כו', וה"נ השפיר מבטל משהו של מין אחר! ומשני רבי יוחנן: משום בטול ברוב נגעו בה. שדם הלידה והליחה רבה על כל השפיר, (ה) ומשבטל כולו — בטל אף בבית ראשון. ור"ל סבר: דאפילו בלא בטול ברוב — טהור, משום בלבול צורה, שנטרף במימיו ונתבלבל צורתו לר"ש אף בבית הראשון. ומדר"ל נמי יש להוכיח דלא מטמא משום רקב ונגל. דא"כ לא הוה מטהרינן משום בלבול, אלא ודאי טמא מטעם מת שלם. ובעי נמי ר"ל: שלם בצורתו. ושאר אמוראי פליגי עליה בבלבול צורה, אך בעי שיהא שלם. וא"ת: לסאי דס"ד דרבי שמעון מטהר אף בבית הפנימי, משום בטול משהו, היכי קתני בברייתא "כשם שאינו בבית החיצון, כך אינו בבית הפנימי משום בטול משהו", הלא גם לרבי שמעון לא נתבטל כולו בבית הפנימי כמו בבית החיצון, אלא דמטהר משום בטול משהו? ויש לומר: דה"ק: כשם שאתה מודה בבית החיצון שנימוק, כך יש לטהר בבית הפנימי משום בטול משהו, דאין כאן מת שלם. ואם תאמר: בנזיר פרק "כ"ג" (דף נ.) דפריך: על המת ועל כזית מן המת, נזיר מגלח על כזית מן המת, מגלח על המת לא כ"ש ומשני: לא נצרכה אלא למת שאין בו כזית בשר, ולא נתקשרו אבריו בגידין. אמאי לא משני: בשליא שאינה מטמאה אלא שלם? וי"ל: דשליא לא מקריא "מת". א"נ: היינו הא דמשני התם.

גלגילון

## תוספי הרא"ש

מ"ט דר' שמעון. ה"ה דה"מ למימר מ"ט דרבנן בבית החיצון אלא משום דר' שמעון איירי בטהרה במתני' אבל רבנן דמתניתין לא איירי לענין טהרה. פרש"י ז"ל מ"ט דר"ש נהי נמי דנימוק מ"מ גופו של מת כאן הוא והו"ל כרקב וכנצל. וקשה לפי' מהא דאמרי' בסמוך ואזדא ר"ש לטעמיה דמטהר מלא תרווד רקב שנפל לתוכו עפר כל שהו לפי שאי אפשר שלא ירבו שני פרידי עפר על פרידא אחת. (נצל) [של] רקב וחסר ליה. והיכי מדמי ליה להך דהכא דע"כ לא מטהר ר"ש אלא כמלא תרווד מצומצם דחסר ליה כשרבה שני פרידי עפר על פרידא אחת של רקב אבל בשני תרוודין של רקב לא היה מטהר בשביל עפר כל שהו שנפל לתוכו והכא מי לא עסקינן דאיכא בהאי שפיר כמה זתים דכי מבטלי מי לידה כל שהו ממנו אכתי נשתייר בו כזית נצל ונצל שיעורו בכזית כדאמרינן בנזיר פרק כ"ג ואכתי לא אסיק אדעתיה שיהא הטעם משום ביטול ברוב הילכך נ"ל דאין (למיחוי) [על] השיליא לא תורת בשר ולא תורת עצמות ולא תורת נצל דהוא מוהל שקרש כדאמרינן בנזיר אלא מטעם שכל המת ישנו שם מטמינן ליה כדאמרינן בנזיר פרק כ"ג דקתני מגלח על המת ועל כזית מן המת ופריך על כזית ממנו מגלח על כלו לא כל שכן ומשני לא נצרכה אלא למת שאין עליו כזית בשר או לנפל שלא נתקשרו איבריו בגידין אלמא אע"ג דלא בא לכלל אדם כיון דישנו למת שלם מטמא וכן משמע לקמן בשמעתין דקאמר ריש לקיש שפיר שטרפוהו מימיו נעשה כמת שנתבלבלה צורתו וטהור ולית ליה לריש לקיש שיהא בטל ברוב מדמטהר מטעם בלבול צורה אלמא לא מטמי ר"ל מטעם בשר ונצל דאי הוה עליה (דאית ביה) תורת בשר ונצל לא היה טהור בבלבול צורה אלא מטעם מת שלם בעלמא מטמא ומדר"ל נשמע לר' יוחנן דבהא לא פליגי והשתא דמי להך דמלא תרווד רקב דכיון שנתבטל ממנו כל שהוא ואינו מת שלם בצר ליה שיעוריה ור' מאיר פליג עליה בהא דסבר דאינו טהור משום דנתבטל ממנו כל שהו אבל בבית החיצון נימוק כולו או רובו ומתבטל ור' שמעון קמ"ל כמו שיש לטהר בבית החיצון מחמת שנתבטל כולו כך יכול לטהר בבית הפנימי מחמת שנתבטל ממנו משהו: **מלא** תרווד רקב. פרש"י דמשו"ה לא מטמא במגע משום דאין נוגע וחוזר ונוגע. וקשה דא"כ באהל המת נמי לא ליטמי למ"ד בהעור והרוטב דאין מאהיל וחוזר ומאהיל והתם אמרינן דמלא תרווד מטמא במשא ובאהל אבל לא במגע אלא כך הלכה למשה מסיני:

מלא

---

ר"ה יא. יבמות מב. [לקמן לח: בכורות כ.]

[לקמן מ. יבמות סה:]

[יבמות סה:]

רש"ל

[תוספתא פ"ד ע"ש]

[פי' כן הדבר]

משלי ל

[ברכות סג:]

ע"י רש"ל ורש"א

[לקמן כט.]

[פי' נגל הוא המת שנקרש ועי' בערוך ערך נגל]

סג א מיי' פ"י מה' איסורי ביאה הט"ז סמג לאוין קיא:

סד ב ג מיי' שם הי"ד סמג שם טוש"ע י"ד סי' קצד ס"ד:

סה ד מיי' פ"ג מה' טומאת מת ה"ד:

## הגהות הב"ח

(א) גמ' דרב עולא אמר ר' יוחנן מעשה: (ב) שם אמר רבא אשכחתינהו: (ג) רש"י ד"ה לסוף ז' יום או יומים בסוף חדש: (ד) תוס' ד"ה מאי טעמא וכו' ומשני כל טומאה וכו': (ה) בא"ד על כל השפיר ונתבטל כולו:

## גליון הש"ס

גמ' אמר להן אינו דומה כו'. לעיל ע"ב: רש"י ד"ה כ"ג וכו' לדכולי עלמא כו'. לקמן לח ע"ב: תוס' ד"ה אלא כו' וי"ל כו'. עי' לקמן לח ע"א תוד"ה שיפורא:

[בערך גלגל ע']

סו א ב מיי' פ"ג מה' טומאת מת ה"ד:
סז ג מיי' שם פ"ד ה"י:
סח ד מיי' שם פ"ג ה"ח:
סט ה מיי' פ"ד מה' בכורות הי"ב ועי' כ"מ סמג עשין ריא טוש"ע י"ד סי' שטו ס"ז:
ע ו מיי' פ"א מה' שאר אבות הטומאה הט"ז:
עא ז מיי' פ"ד מה' בכורות הי"ב סמג עשין ריא טוש"ע י"ד סי' שטו ס"ז:
עב ח ט י מיי' פ"ג מה' טומאת מת ה"ט:

פרידה אחת (א) עפר *(ונפיל) ליה שיעורא! אלא אמר רבה: היינו טעמא דרבי שמעון, סופו כתחלתו, מה תחלתו — נעשה לו דבר אחר גנגילון, אף סופו — נעשה לו דבר אחר גנגילון. מאי היא? דתניא: איזהו *מת שיש לו רקב ואיזהו מת שאין לו רקב: [א]נקבר ערום בארון של שיש, או ע"ג רצפה של אבנים — זהו מת שיש לו רקב, ואיזהו מת שאין לו רקב — נקבר בכסותו, או בארון של עץ, או ע"ג רצפה של לבנים — זהו מת שאין לו רקב. [ב]ולא אמרו רקב — אלא למת בלבד, למעוטי הרוג — דלא. גופא: מלא תרוד רקב שנפל לתוכו עפר כל שהוא — טמא, ור' שמעון מטהר. *[ג]מלא תרוד רקב שנתפזר בבית — הבית טמא, ורבי שמעון מטהר. וצריכא. דאי אשמעינן קמייתא — בההיא קאמרי רבנן — משום דמכניף, אבל נתפזר — אימא מודו לו לרבי שמעון דאין מאהיל וחוזר ומאהיל. ואי אשמעינן בהא — בהא אמר רבי שמעון דאין מאהיל וחוזר ומאהיל, אבל בהא — אימא מודה להו לרבנן, צריכא. *תניא אידך: *[ד]מלא תרוד ועוד עפר בית הקברות — טמא. ורבי שמעון מטהר. מאי טעמייהו דרבנן? לפי שא"א למלא תרוד ועוד עפר בית הקברות שאין בו מלא תרוד רקב. השתא דאמרת טעמא דרבי שמעון משום סופו כתחלתו, גבי שליא מאי טעמא? אמר רבי יוחנן: משום בטול ברוב נגעו בה. *ואזדא רבי יוחנן לטעמיה, דאמר רבי יוחנן: רבי שמעון ור"א בן יעקב אמרו דבר אחד. רבי שמעון — הא דאמרן. רבי אליעזר — *דתניא, *רבי אליעזר בן יעקב אומר: [ה]בהמה גסה ששפעה חררת דם — הרי זו תקבר, ופטורה מן הבכורה. *ותני רבי חייא עלה: [ו]אינה מטמאה לא במגע ולא במשא. ומאחר שאינה מטמאה לא במגע ולא במשא, אמאי תקבר? [ז]כדי לפרסמה שהיא פטורה מן הבכורה. אלמא ולד מעליא הוא, ואמאי תני רבי חייא אינה מטמאה לא במגע ולא במשא? אמר רבי יוחנן: משום בטול ברוב נגעו בה. א"ר אמי, אמר רבי יוחנן: ומודה רבי שמעון שאמו טמאה לידה. אמר ההוא סבא לרבי אמי: אסברא לך טעמא דרבי יוחנן, דאמר קרא: °"אשה כי תזריע וילדה זכר" וגו' (ויקרא יב) — *אפילו לא ילדה אלא כעין שהזריעה — טמאה לידה. ריש לקיש אמר: [ח]שפיר שטרפוהו במימיו — נעשה כמת שנתבלבלה צורתו. אמר ליה רבי יוחנן לריש לקיש: [ט]מת שנתבלבלה צורתו מנלן דטהור? אילימא מהא דאמר רבי שבתאי אמר ר' יצחק מגדלאה, ואמרי לה א"ר יצחק מגדלאה א"ר שבתאי: [י]מת שנשרף ושלדו קיימת טמא, מעשה היה וטמאו לו פתחים גדולים, וטהרו

וטהרו

פרידה. גרגיר. סופו. של רקב כתחלתו. מה תחלתו. כשנקבר, אם יש דבר הראוי לירקב ולעשות רקב (ב) של מת. גנגילון. בטול. שאותו דבר אחר – מבטלו. אף סופו, לאחר שנעשה רקב כשנקבר כהלכתו – ד"א המתערבת בו מבטלו. ולשון "גנגילון" – דבר העומד כנגדו לבטלו ולקלקלו. ולקמן פריך: הואיל וטעמא דר"ש ברקב כדאמר השתא, גבי שליא דליכא למימר הכי, מ"ט? מאי היא. דאמר: תחלתו – ד"א נעשה לו גנגילון. שאין לו רקב. שאין רקב שלו מטמא. ערום בארון של שיש או ע"ג רצפה של אבנים. דהשתא אין תערובת ברקבוביתו. נקבר בכסותו. דאיכא רקבובית, או אפילו ערום בארון של עץ דאיכא רקבובית. או ע"ג רצפה של לבנים. שעפרן נמחה. שאין לו רקב. מפני דבר אחר המעורב בו. לאפוקי הרוג דלא. לפי שיצא דמו וחסר, וקיימא לן במס' נזיר (דף נא.) מת שחסר – אין לו רקב. שנתפזר בתוך הבית [הבית] טמא. משום אהל. דאין מאהיל וחוזר ומאהיל. גג שכנגד זה מאהיל על חצי שיעור, ושכנגד זה מאהיל על חצי שיעור, ושני אהלות הן, ואין מצטרפין. מלא תרוד ועוד. יותר ממלא תרוד עפר בית הקברות. *ל"א: רקב ממש של מת. אלא כגון שנקבר בכסותו או בקרקע בלא ארון של שיש, ויש כאן מלא תרוד ועוד מאותו עפר, דהוו מעורבין רקב ועפר. בטל ברוב. שדם הלידה נתרבה על מיחוי הולד, ומבטלו. אמרו דבר אחד. ולקמן מוקמינן דר"א בן יעקב משום בטול ברוב. בהמה גסה. שלא היה לה ולד מעולם. תקבר. החררה, שהוא מיחוי של בכור. ופטורה מן הבכורה. שאם תלד עוד – אין ולדה לכהן. אינה מטמאה. אותה חררה. ומאחר דאינה מטמאה. אלמא, לא חיישינן לולד, אמאי תקבר? ומשני: כדי לפרסמה. שנפטרה מן הבכורה, שידעו הכל שזה פטר רחם. ופרכינן: מדפטורה מן הבכורה, אלמא ולד מעליא היא, אמאי אינה מטמאה? בטול ברוב. מיחוי הנפל בטל בדם. ומודה ר"ש. במתני' בשליא, אע"ג שהבית טהור, אמו טמאה לידה. כעין שהזריעה. כלומר, דנימוח כזרע. שטרפוהו. כמו (חולין סד.): ביצים טרופות בקערה, שמחקוהו ובלבלוהו. במימיו. שהדיחוהו בהן. א"נ: במי הלידה והטינוף שיוצא עמו. שנתבלבלה. נמחק כולו, כמו שרוף שנתפזר ואין שלדו קיימת. ושלדו קיימת. גופו קיים, שלא נתפזר האפר, ועדיין נראה כשלם. פתחים גדולים. של ארבעה טפחים.

[נ"ל ונפיש] נזיר כח. [תוספתא אהלות פ"ב] [אהלות פ"ג מ"ב] [נ"ל לא] אהלות פ"ב מ"ב ועי' רש"ל [בכורות כב.] בכורות כא. שם [לקמן מ.]

גלגילון. פירש בערוך:* דבר הנגלל עמו. למעוטי הרוג. דמחוסר דם. והא דאמר עולא בפ' "כ"ג" (נזיר נא.) אין רקב למת, אלא לבא מן הבשר מן הגידין ומן העצמות. א"כ משמע דאין רקב טמא, אא"כ בא משלשתן יחד. אבל רקב מדם – לא בעי! מ"מ אם חסר מדמו בשעה שנקבר – אין לו דין רקב. מלא תרוד ועוד. פ"ה: כגון שנקבר בכסותו. ואין נראה לרשב"ם דבתחלה מודו כ"ע דדבר אחר נעשה לו גלגילון. ונראה לרשב"ם דהכא מיירי בנקבר ערום. ודרכן היה לטוח כוכין בסיד, ומיד שנתרקב היה התרוד ממנו טמא. ואח"כ נפל מן הסיד, ונתערבה עם הרקב שכבר היה טמא. ומהך לא עביד צריכותא, דקמ"ל משום דא"א שלא יהא תרוד מרקב קודם שנתערב בו עפר. כדי לפרסמה שפטורה. הא דתנן בפ' "בהמה המקשה" (חולין דף עז.) מבכרת שהפילה שליא – ישליכנה לכלבים. התם א"צ פרסום, דהכל יודעים שיש ולד בשליא. משום בטול ברוב נגעו בה. וא"ת דבבכורות פרק "הלוקח בהמה" (כג.) גבי נבלה בטלה בשחוטה, וקאמר: אין מטמאה במגע, אבל מטמאה במשא דטומאה, כמאן דאיתא דמיא. ופריך מחררת דם דאינה מטמאה, לא במגע ולא במשא, משום בטול ברוב. אלמא דכמאן דליתיה דמיא! ומשני: משום דה"ל טומאה סרוחה. ופריך: הניחא לבר פדא, דדריש: עד לגר. [נ"ל תנן וג"ע] אלא *לר' דדריש: עד לכלב, קשיא! [נ"ל לר' יוחנן] ואמאי לא מקשה מהך, דשפיר דאינו מטמא באהל משום בטול ברוב, אלמא כמאן דליתיה דמי! והשתא לא מצי לשנויי: משום דהוי טומאה סרוחה, דאפילו מת סרוח מטמא! וי"ל: משום דאיכא למדחי דטעמא משום בילבול צורה, כדר"ל ולא משום בטול ברוב. אי נמי: כיון דטעמא דשפיר משום מת שלם, אע"ג דטומאה כמאן דאיתיה דמי, אין להחשיבו שלם, כיון שנתבטל ברוב לגמרי.

מת שנתבלבלה צורתו מנלן דטהור. [נ"ל דתנן] – וקשה: מאי פריך ליה ר' יוחנן, האמר בסמוך דר' יוחנן כר"א, וא"כ ר"ל ניחא טפי, דקאי כרבנן, דקתני במסכת אהלות: וחכמים מטהרים! וי"ל: דר"י ור"ל, אליבא דרבנן פליגי. דר"ל סבר דלרבנן דמטהרי ברובע, ה"נ דמטהרי אפילו בשלם בשאין שלדו קיימת ונתבלבל צורתו. אבל שלדו קיימת – טמאה מדרבי יצחק דאתיא כרבנן. דאי כר"א אפי' אין שלדו קיימת טמא, דהא מטמא ר"א ברובע של אפר. וא"ל *לר' [נ"ל ר"י] יוחנן: מנלן הא דרבנן מטהרו משום בלבול צורה, דלמא טעמא דרבנן דכשנשרף אין עוד שם מת עליו, אפילו כולו שלם ושלדו קיימת. אבל שפיר שם מת עליו וטמא, אי לאו משום דבטל ברוב. ומילתא דרבי יצחק לא אתיא כרבנן אלא כר"א דמטמא מת שרוף, וחסר ושלדו קיימת נקט לטהר פתחים קטנים. א"נ קסבר ר' יוחנן °דרבנן לא מטהרי אלא ברובע דחסר. אבל אם העפר שלם, אפי' אין שלדו קיימת – טמא. והשתא אתי שפיר, שא"צ לחלק בין שפיר ושליא למת שנשרף ואין שלדו קיימת, דשניהם שוין לר"ל ולר' יוחנן. ובירושלמי איכא: שפיר *שנתבלבל [ס"א שנתקלקל] צורתו, מהו? ר' יוחנן אמר: טמא, ר"ל אמר: טהור. איתיביה ר"ל לר' יוחנן מרבי יצחק מגדלאה, ומשני: דבר תורה אפילו שלדו קיימת טהורה, מפני מה אמרו טמא? מפני כבודו. פירוש: מפני כבודו של מת הוא דלא בטל. וזהו כפירוש ראשון, דאף בשלדו קיימת טהור, דבר תורה. וחולק על הגמרא שלנו דמוקי לה כר"א מילתא דרבי יצחק, והתם מוקי לה כרבנן.

שנשרף

## הגהות הב"ח

(א) גמ' פרידה אחת של עפר: (ב) רש"י ד"ה מה תחלתו וכו' ולעשות רקב נעשה לו לרקב של מת:

## גליון הש"ס

תוס' ד"ה מת שנתבלבלה כו' דרבנן לא מטהרי כו'. עי' בר"ש פ"ב דאהלות מ"א:

## תוספי הרא"ש

מלא תרווד. ועוד רקב עפר בית הקברות פרש"י כגון שנקבר בכסותו ול"נ דהא משמע לעי' דכ"ע מודו שתחלתו ד"א נעשה לו גלגילון וכדאמרינן בנ"ר פרק כ"ג אלא מיירי שנקבר ערום בארון של שיש או בארון טוח בסיד שהמת נעשה רקב קודם שנרקב הקבר ומיהו לבסוף נרקב ונתערב בו ורבנן לטעמיהו דלא בעינן סופו ור"ש לטעמיה דאמר סופו כתחלתו: ר' שמעון ור' אליעזר בן יעקב אמרו דבר אחד. היינו ד"א שמתבטל ברוב מיד בלא הוצאת ספל לבית חיצון: וכי מאחר דלא מטמאה כו' ותימה כי ההוי ולד נמי תיקש ליה אמאי תקבר דסמוך מיעוטא דנדמה למחצה דנקבות והוו להו זכרים מיעוטא כדאיתא פרק בהמה המקשה וי"ל דלאלומי פירכיה נקט הכי: כדי לפרסמה שהיא פטורה מן הבכורה. והא דתנן פרק בהמה המקשה המבכרת שהפילה שיליא ישליכנה לכלבים ולא אמרינן תקבר כדי לפרסמה שהיא פטורה מן הבכורה וי"ל דבשיליא אין צריך פרסום דהכל יודעים שאין שליא בלא וולד: כעין שהזריעה כו' אליבא דר"ש הוא דבעי' האי טעמא אבל רבנן דאפילו באהל נמי מטמא משום דאינו נימוח בשעת לידה לא צריך האי טעמא וכן מוכח לקמן בריש יוצא דופן: מת שנתבלבלה צורתו מנא לן דטהור. ותימה מאי (קאמר ניחא ליה לר') [פריך ליה ר'] יוחנן אדרבה לר"ל ניחא טפי דקאי כרבנן ור' יוחנן כר' אליעזר כדאמר בסמוך וי"ל דהא דקאמר לקמן דר' יוחנן כר' אליעזר לאו דוקא כר' אליעזר אלא משום דר' אליעזר מטמא באפר שרופין נקט ר' אליעזר ש"מ דלא חייש לבלבול צורה ואפילו רבנן דמטהרי משום דבעינן שיהא שם שלם של מת אבל לבילבול צורה לא חיישי ור"ל סבר טעמא דרבנן משום בלבול צורה ואפילו יש שם כל אפרו של מת ודייק מדר' שבתאי והאי דנקט רובע משום רבות' כלומר לאו למימרא דרבנן דפליגי עליה דר"א מטמאין ביותר מרובע אע"ג דליכא מת שלם דרבנן מת שלם בעינן והא דנקט רובע משום רבותא דר' אליעזר נקט"ה:

אנדרוגינוס

תורה אור

וּמְטַהֲרוּ לוֹ פְּתָחִים קְטַנִּים. וְקָא דָּיְיקַתְּ מִינַּהּ: טַמְאָה — דְּשִׁלְדּוֹ קַיֶּימֶת, הָא לָאו הָכִי — טָהוֹר. אַדְּרַבָּה, דּוּק מִינַּהּ לְהַאי גִּיסָא: שִׁלְדּוֹ קַיֶּימֶת — הוּא דְּמְטַהֲרוּ לוֹ פְּתָחִים קְטַנִּים, הָא לָאו הָכִי — פְּתָחִים קְטַנִּים נַמִי טְמֵאִין, דְּכָל חַד וְחַד חָזֵי לְאַפּוּקֵי חַד חַד אֵבֶר! א"ל רָבִינָא לְרַב אַשִׁי: ר' יוֹחָנָן דְּאָמַר כְּמַאן כְּר' אֱלִיעֶזֶר. *דִּתְנַן, אֵפֶר שְׂרוּפִין, ר"א אוֹמֵר: שִׁיעוּר' בְּרוֹבַע. הֵיכִי דָּמֵי מֵת שֶׁנִּשְׂרַף וְשִׁלְדּוֹ קַיֶּימֶת? אָמַר אַבַּיֵּי: כְּגוֹן שֶׁשְּׂרָפוֹ עַל גַּבֵּי קַטַבְלָא. רָבָא אָמַר: כְּגוֹן שֶׁשְּׂרָפוֹ עַל גַּבֵּי אַפּוּדְרִים. רָבִינָא אָמַר: אכְּגוֹן דְּאִיחָרְכֵי אַחְרוּכֵי. ת"ר: *בהַמַּפֶּלֶת יָד חֲתוּכָה וְרֶגֶל חֲתוּכָה — אִמּוֹ טְמֵאָה לֵידָה, וְאֵין חוֹשְׁשִׁין שֶׁמָּא מִגּוּף אָטוּם בָּאוּ. רַב חִסְדָּא וְרַבָּה בַּר רַב הוּנָא דְּאָמְרִי תַּרְוַיְיהוּ: אֵין נוֹתְנִין לָהּ יְמֵי טוֹהַר, מ"ט — אֵימָא הִרְחִיקָה לֵידָתָהּ. מְתִיב רַב יוֹסֵף: *גהַמַּפֶּלֶת וְאֵין יָדוּעַ מַה הִפִּילָה — תֵּשֵׁב לְזָכָר וְלִנְקֵבָה. וְאִי ס"ד כָּל כְּהַאי גַּוְונָא אֵימָא הִרְחִיקָה לֵידָתָהּ — לִתְנֵי וּלְנִדָּה! אָמַר אַבַּיֵּי: אִי תָּנָא לְנִדָּה, הֲוָה אָמִינָא — מְבִיאָה קָרְבָּן וְאֵינוֹ נֶאֱכָל, קמ"ל דדְּנֶאֱכָל. אָמַר רַב הוּנָא: ההוֹצִיא עוּבָּר אֶת יָדוֹ וְהֶחֱזִירָהּ — אִמּוֹ טְמֵאָה לֵידָה. שֶׁנֶּאֱמַר: °"וַיְהִי בְלִדְתָּהּ וַיִּתֶּן יָד". מְתִיב רַב יְהוּדָה: הוֹצִיא עוּבָּר אֶת יָדוֹ — אֵין אִמּוֹ חוֹשֶׁשֶׁת לְכָל דָּבָר! אָמַר רַב נַחְמָן: ולְדִידִי מִיפָּרְשָׁא לִי מִינֵּיהּ דְּרַב הוּנָא, לָחוּשׁ — חוֹשֶׁשֶׁת, יְמֵי טוֹהַר — לָא יָהֲבִינַן לָהּ עַד דְּנָפֵיק רוּבֵּיהּ. וְהָא "אֵין אִמּוֹ חוֹשֶׁשֶׁת לְכָל דָּבָר" קָאָמַר! אָמַר אַבַּיֵּי: אֵינָהּ חוֹשֶׁשֶׁת לְכָל דָּבָר — מִדְּאוֹרַיְיתָא, אֲבָל זמִדְּרַבָּנַן — חוֹשֶׁשֶׁת. וְהָא קְרָא קָאָמַר! מִדְּרַבָּנַן, וּקְרָא — אַסְמַכְתָּא בְּעָלְמָא.§

**מתני'** *חהַמַּפֶּלֶת טוּמְטוּם וְאַנְדְּרוֹגִינוֹס — תֵּשֵׁב לְזָכָר וְלִנְקֵבָה. טוּמְטוּם וְזָכָר, אַנְדְּרוֹגִינוֹס וְזָכָר — תֵּשֵׁב לְזָכָר וְלִנְקֵבָה. טוּמְטוּם וּנְקֵבָה, אַנְדְּרוֹגִינוֹס וּנְקֵבָה — תֵּשֵׁב לִנְקֵבָה בִּלְבַד. טיָצָא מְחוּתָּךְ אוֹ מְסוּרָס, מִשֶּׁיָּצָא רוּבּוֹ — הֲרֵי הוּא כְּיָלוּד. *יָצָא כְּדַרְכּוֹ — עַד שֶׁיֵּצֵא רוֹב רֹאשׁוֹ. וְאֵיזֶהוּ רוֹב רֹאשׁוֹ — מִשֶּׁיֵּצֵא פַּדַּחְתּוֹ.§

**גמ'** הַשְׁתָּא טוּמְטוּם לְחוּדֵיהּ וְאַנְדְּרוֹגִינוֹס לְחוּדֵיהּ אָמַר תֵּשֵׁב לְזָכָר וְלִנְקֵבָה, טוּמְטוּם וְזָכָר אַנְדְּרוֹגִינוֹס וְזָכָר מִיבַּעְיָא?! אִיצְטְרִיךְ, מַהוּ דְּתֵימָ', הוֹאִיל וְא"ר יִצְחָק: *אִשָּׁה מַזְרַעַת תְּחִלָּ' — יוֹלֶדֶת זָכָר, אִישׁ מַזְרִיעַ תְּחִלָּה — יוֹלֶדֶת נְקֵבָה, אֵימָא: מִדְּהַאי זָכָר — הַאי נַמִי זָכָר, קמ"ל — אֵימָא שְׁנֵיהֶם הִזְרִיעוּ בְּבַת אַחַת, זוֹ זָכָר וְזֶה נְקֵבָה. אָמַר ר"נ אָמַר רַב: יטוּמְטוּם וְאַנְדְּרוֹגִינוֹס שֶׁרָאוּ לוֹבֶן אוֹ אוֹדֶם — אֵין חַיָּיבִין עַל בִּיאַת מִקְדָּשׁ, וְאֵין שׂוֹרְפִין עֲלֵיהֶם אֶת הַתְּרוּמָה. כרָאוּ לוֹבֶן וְאוֹדֶם כְּאֶחָד — אֵין חַיָּיבִין עַל בִּיאַת מִקְדָּשׁ, אֲבָל שׂוֹרְפִין עֲלֵיהֶם אֶת הַתְּרוּמָה, שֶׁנֶּאֱמַר: °"מִזָּכָר וְעַד נְקֵבָה תְּשַׁלֵּחוּ

תשלחו

**רש"י**

וּמְטַהֲרוּ לוֹ פְּתָחִים קְטַנִּים. הַפְּתוּחִים מֵאַרְבָּעָה, כִּשְׁאָר מֵתִים שְׁלֵמִים שֶׁהַגְּדוֹלִים מַצִּילִין עַל הַקְּטַנִּים. דְּקיי"ל: מֵת – פִּתְחוֹ בְּאַרְבָּעָה. אִם הוּא בַּבַּיִת – כָּל הַפְּתָחִים טְמֵאִים, וְאִם פָּתַח פָּתוּחַ מֵאַרְבָּעָה – טָהוֹר. וְהָנֵי מִילֵּי – לְהַצִּיל אֶת שְׁאָר פְּתָחִים, אֲבָל לְהוֹצִיא – הָא אָמְרִי': פּוֹתֵחַ טֶפַח מוֹצִיא הַטּוּמְאָה לְצַד שֵׁנִי. וְהָכִי אָמְרִי' בְּמַסֶּ' אֳהָלוֹת: (פ"ג מ"ו) הַמֵּת – פִּתְחוֹ בְּאַרְבָּעָה. בד"א? לְהַצִּיל אֶת הַפְּתָחִים, אֲבָל לְהוֹצִיא אֶת הַטּוּמְאָה – בְּפוֹתֵחַ טֶפַח. ר' יוֹחָנָן. דִּפְלִיג עֲלֵיהּ דְּרֵישׁ לָקִישׁ, דְּבָעֵי לְמֵימַר דְּמֵת שֶׁנִּתְבַּלְבְּלָה צוּרָתוֹ – טָמֵא, דְּאָמַר כְּמַאן? כְּר' אֱלִיעֶזֶר. בְּרוֹבַע. רוֹבַע הַקַּב. קַטַבְלָא. עוֹר שָׁלוּק וְקָשֶׁה, וְאֵינָהּ נִשְׂרֶפֶת עִם הַמֵּת. אַפּוּדְרָא. אֶבֶן שַׁיִשׁ. וְתַרְוַיְיהוּ, כְּגוֹן שֶׁעֲשׂוּיוֹת בֵּית קִיבּוּל וּמְחִילוֹת, שֶׁאֵין הֶעָפָר יָכוֹל לְהִתְפַּזֵּר. דְּאִיחָרַךְ אִיחָרוּכֵי. הַמֵּת, וְלֹא נַעֲשָׂה אֵפֶר. אֵין נוֹתְנִין לָהּ יְמֵי טוֹהַר. דְּאע"ג דִּפְשִׁיטָא לָן דְּוָלָד הוּא. אֵימַר הִרְחִיקָה לֵידָתָהּ. הֲרֵי כַּמָּה יָמִים שֶׁיָּצָא רוֹב הַוָּלָד לַאֲבָרִים, וּכְבָר עָבְרוּ יְמֵי טוֹהַר שֶׁלָּהּ, וְלָא יָדְעִינַן מֵאֵימַת נִמְנֵי. נִיתְנֵי וּלְנִדָּה. שֶׁכָּל דָּמִים שֶׁתִּרְאֶה יִהְיוּ טְמֵאִים, שֶׁלֹּא יִהְיוּ לָהּ יְמֵי טוֹהַר. וְהָכִי אִיבָּעֵי לֵיהּ לְמִיתְנֵי: "תֵּשֵׁב לְזָכָר וְלִנְקֵבָה וּלְנִדָּה", כְּלוֹמַר שְׁבוּעַיִים, דִּנְקֵבָה מְטַמְּאָה בְּלֹא שׁוּם רְאִיָּיה, דְּדִלְמָא נְקֵבָה הֲוַאי. וִימֵי טוֹהַר לֹא יִהְיֶה לָהּ, שֶׁהֲרֵי כַּמָּה יָמִים שֶׁהִתְחִילָה לֵילֵד וְיָצָא הָרוֹב, וְהַיְינוּ "לְנִדָּה". וּלְקַמָּן בְּהַאי פִּירְקָא (דף ל.) מְפָרֵשׁ לָמָּה הוּזְכַּר זָכָר – שֶׁאִם תִּרְאֶה לְסוֹף ל"ד וְתַחֲזוֹר וְתִרְאֶה לְיוֹם מ"א – תְּהֵא מְקוּלְקֶלֶת עַד יוֹם מ"ח. הֲוָה אָמִינָא מְבִיאָה קָרְבָּן וְאֵינוֹ נֶאֱכָל. דְּכֵיוָן דְּתָנֵי "לְנִדָּה", מַשְׁמַע: דְּמִסַּפְּקָא לֵיהּ אִי וָלָד הוּא אִי לָא, קמ"ל מִדְּלָא תָּנֵי "לְנִדָּה", אֶלָּא "לְזָכָר וְלִנְקֵבָה" דְּוַדַּאי פְּשִׁיטָא לָן דְּוָלָד הוּא, וּמְבִיאָה קָרְבָּן וְנֶאֱכָל. וּמִיהוּ יְמֵי טוֹהַר לֵית לָהּ, אֵימַר: הִרְחִיקָה לֵידָתָהּ. וַיִּתֶּן יָד. אַלְמָא: לֵידַת יָד קְרוּיָה לֵידָה. וְהָא קְרָא קָאָמַר. רַב הוּנָא, אַלְמָא: לֵידָה דְּאוֹרַיְיתָא קָרֵי לֵיהּ. מתני' לְזָכָר וְלִנְקֵבָה. יְמֵי טוֹהַר לְזָכָר וִימֵי טוּמְאָה דִּנְקֵבָה. תֵּשֵׁב לִנְקֵבָה בִּלְבַד. אֲפִי' הָוֵי טוּמְטוּם זָכָר – בָּתַר נְקֵבוֹת אָזְלִינַן, דְּכָל יְמֵי זָכָר, בֵּין לְטוּמְאָה בֵּין לְטָהֳרָה, מוּבְלָעִים תּוֹךְ שֶׁל נְקֵבָה. מְסוֹרָס. דֶּרֶךְ מַרְגְּלוֹתָיו, וּלְשׁוֹן הִיפּוּךְ הוּא, כְּמוֹ: *"סָרֵס הַמִּקְרָא וְדָרְשֵׁהוּ". גמ' אִיצְטְרִיךְ. אע"ג דְּטוּמְטוּם לְחוּדֵיהּ מְסַפְּקִינַן בְּזָכָר וּבִנְקֵבָה, הֵיכָא דְּאִיתְיְלִיד זָכָר בַּהֲדֵיהּ נֵימָא: זָכָר הוּא, דְּמוֹכְחָא מִילְּתָא דְּהִיא הִזְרִיעָה תְּחִילָּה, קמ"ל. לוֹבֶן. דּוֹמֶה לְקֶרִי. אוֹדֶם. דּוֹמֶה לְדַם נִדּוּת. אֵין חַיָּיבִין עַל בִּיאַת מִקְדָּשׁ. דִּלְמָא טָהוֹר הוּא, וְקָמַיְיתֵי חוּלִּין בָּעֲזָרָה. דְּאֵין זָכָר מְטַמֵּא בְּאוֹדֶם, וְאֵין נְקֵבָה מְטַמְּאָה בְּלוֹבֶן. וְאֵין שׂוֹרְפִין עֲלֵיהֶם תְּרוּמָה. אֶלָּא תּוֹלִין, כִּי חָזַאי אוֹדֶם – אִיכָּא לְמֵימַר: זָכָר הוּא, וְאֵין אוֹדֶם מְטַמֵּא בּוֹ. וְאִי חָזַאי לוֹבֶן – אִיכָּא לְמֵימַר נְקֵבָה הִיא, וְאֵין לוֹבֶן מְטַמֵּא בָּהּ, הִילְכָּךְ תּוֹלִין. רָאוּ אוֹדֶם וְלוֹבֶן כְּאֶחָד. דְּמִמ"נ טָמֵא, אפ"ה לְעִנְיַן טוּמְאַת בִּיאַת מִקְדָּשׁ – פְּטִירֵי מִקָּרְבָּן, כִּדְמְפָרֵשׁ טַעֲמָא.

תשלחו.

**תוספות**

**שנשרף** על גבי קטבלא. פי' עור שלוק. היה בעור דפוס של אדם וצורתו, דכי נמי נשרף עליו – צורתו ותוך אברים ניכרים.

**אמר** רב נחמן אמר רב טומטום ואנדרוגינוס כו' – קסבר רב דאנדרוגינוס ספק זכר ספק נקבה הוא. דאי בריה הוא – לא יטמא לא בלובן ולא באודם! אלא ודאי סבר ספקא הוא. והא דפסיק רב בפרק "הערל" (יבמות דף פג.) כר' יוסי באנדרוגינוס – לא כר' יוסי דמתני' דהתם, דאמר: מאכיל בחזה ושוק, דזכר ודאי הוי, אלא כרבי יוסי דברייתא דקאמר התם: אנדרוגינוס – בריה בפני עצמו הוא, ולא הכריעו בו חכמים לידע אם זכר אם נקבה. ולאו בריה בעלמא הוא, אלא כלומר: ספקא. וכן משמע לישנא ד"לא הכריעו", והיינו כמו שסובר רב בשמעתין ובפ' בתרא דיומא (ד' עד.) דקאמר: "כל חלב" – לרבות כוי וחצי שיעור. ופריך: אילטריך קרא לרבויי ספקא? ומשני: דכוי – בריה הוי. (א) האי "בריה הוי" – בריה ממש, ולא ספקא. והקשה רבינו שמואל בחור: דתניא בתוספתא דמס' בכורי' [פ"ב] "הריני נזיר שזה איש או אשה" – הרי הוא נזיר. ר' יוסי אומר: אנדרוגינוס – בריה בפני עצמו הוא, ולא יכלו חכמים להכריע אם איש או אשה. אבל טומטום – אינו כן, אלא ספק איש או אשה. ואי לר' יוסי אנדרוגינוס נמי ספק, במאי פליגי ת"ק והוא? ועוד: מאי "אבל טומטום אינו כן"? וי"ל: דלעולם ספק הוא. ולא דמי לספק טומטום, דבטומטום לא שייך למיתני ביה "ולא הכריעו חכמים" – דאין כולן שוין, דלפעמים כשנקרע נמצא זכר ולפעמי' – נקבה, וספק שלו יכול להתברר. אבל אנדרוגינוס כולם – או זכר או נקבה, אבל לא הכריעו חכמים איזהו. ונפקא מינה: אם קידש טומטום אשה, או נתקדשה, ונקרע. וגם לענין שופר אמרי' (ר"ה דף כט.) אנדרוגינוס – מוציא את מינו, טומטום – אינו מוציא לא מינו ולא שאינו מינו. ולא פליג ר' יוסי את"ק, אלא מפרש מילתיה דת"ק או כולה ר' יוסי היא. אי נמי: פליגי, וקאמר: כיון דלא הכריעו חכמים – אינו נזיר, דלא היה בדעתו להיות נזיר אא"כ הוי זכר ודאי או נקבה ודאית, וכיון דלא הכריעו – הוי לעולם ספק.

**שנאמר** מזכר ועד נקבה זכר ודאי כו'. תימה: בשלמא טומטום אילטריך למעוטי, כיון שיש טומטום שהוא זכר ויש טומטום שהוא נקבה, ופטרו הכתוב כל זמן שהוא ספק, כדממעט (א) במעשר בהמה בקפץ אחד מן המנוין לתוכו – עשירי ודאי אמר רחמנא, ולא עשירי ספק. ולעיל (ב) גבי ספק בהרת קדמה לשער לבן, דדריש לה מקראי בשלהי נזיר (דף סה:) אבל אנדרוגינוס, למה צריך למעוטי, כיון דסבר רב דספק הוי וכולן שוין, קמי שמיא גליא אם זכר אם נקבה, ואמאי ממעט ליה? והכי פריך בבכורות בפ' "על אלו מומין" (דף מא: ושם) בסופו גבי הא דתניא: כשהוא אומר למטה "הזכר", שאין ת"ל – להוציא טומטום ואנדרוגינוס. ופריך: מני? אילימא ת"ק קסבר: אנדרוגינוס ספקא הוא – אלטריך קרא למעוטי ספקא? וי"ל: דהתם פריך שפיר, דממעט אנדרוגינו' מ"הזכר" יתירא דכתיב גבי עולה, ולהכי פריך: אלטריך קרא למעוטי ספקא, דכיון דקמי שמיא גליא אם נקבה הוי – אמאי צריך למעוטי? ואם זכר הוא (ג) – בא למעוטי משום דמשונה משאר זכרים. א"כ ש"מ דזכר הוא, ולא ספק. אבל הכא דכתיב: "מזכר ועד נקבה" איכא למימר דממעט לה מטעם שהוא משונה. והוי ספק, משום דלא ידענא אי מזכר ממעט ליה, והוי זכר, או מנקבה ממעט ליה, והוי נקבה? ונראה לומר: דתרי מיעוטי נינהו, דהוי מצי למכתב "מזכר ועד אדם" או "מנקבה ועד אדם", ואתא חד לאנדרוגינוס וחד לטומטום. אי נמי: מההיא מיעוטא דממעטינן אנדרוגינוס, ממעטינן נמי טומטום, ולא נימא דתרי מיעוטי נינהו. ואי מזכר ממעטינן להו אילטריך למכתב "נקבה" – דלא נימא: "זכר" למעוטי נקבה אתא, או איפכא.

אמר

א) [ב"מ ו: ז.] ב) [דף יט.]

**מסורת הש"ס**

אהלות פ"ב מ"ב

[לעיל יח. כז.]

[לקמן כט.]

[ב"ב קכז.]

[בכורות מו:]

ברכות ס. ע"ש [לעיל כה: לקמן לא. ע"ש]

**הגהות הב"ח**

(א) תד"ה אמר וכו' דכוי בריה הוי האי בריה: (ב) ד"ה שנאמר וכו' וזכר הוא ובא למעוטי:

**עין משפט נר מצוה**

עג א מיי' פ"ג מהל' טומאת מת הל"ג:

עד ב מיי' פ"י מהל' איסורי ביאה הל"ח סמג לאוין קיא טוש"ע יו"ד סי' קצד ועי' כמ"מ:

עה ג מיי' שם הל"ט סמג שם טוש"ע שם סעי' ט וע' כמ"מ הל"א שהגיה להרמב"ם בל"ע שלא הביא דין הרחיקה לידתה:

עו ד מיי' פ"א מהל' מחוסרי כפרה הל' ו ז:

עז ה מיי' פ"י מהל' איסורי ביאה הל"ז סמג לאוין קיא טוש"ע יו"ד סי' קצד סעי' יא:

עח ו ז מיי' שם הל"ג:

עט ח מיי' שם הל"ח סמג שם טוש"ע שם סעיף ח:

פ ט מיי' שם הל"ג טוש"ע שם סעי' ג:

פא י ב מיי' פ"ז מהל' מטמאי משכב ומושב הלכה ז:

**פירוש רב האי גאון**

פדחתו. פי' מצח בלשון מקרא ופדחת בלשון חכמים:

**תוספי הרא"ש**

אנדרוגינוס וזכר מיבעיא איצטריך סד"א כו'. והאי טעמא לא שייך אלא באנדרוגינוס אבל טומטום אינו זוכר: קמ"ל שניהם הזריעו בבת אחת. אע"ג דהך מילתא שמעינן בבר לעיל ממתניתין דפסדל היאיכא [לעיל] שיניא אחריא שאם תלד נקבה קודם שקיעת החמה כו' דמונין תחלת נדה מן הראשון ותחלת נדה מן האחרון: ראו לובן ואודם כאחת כו'. וסבירא ליה דספק זכר ספק נקבה הוי. הלכך שורפין עליו את התרומה דממה נפשך טמא הוא אי זכר או אבל אי בריה הוא אינו טמא לא בלובן ולא באודם ותימה דבפ' הערל משמ' דסבר רב דבריה הוי דתנן התם ר' יוסי ור"ש אומרים אנדרוגינוס כהן שנשא בת ישראל מאכילה בתרומה וקאמר רב ליתא למתניתין מקמי ברייתא דתניא ר' יוסי אומר אנדרוגינוס בריה בפני עצמה ולא הכריעו בו [חכמים] אם זכר אם נקבה ופשיט התם דהילכתא כר' יוסי באנדרוגינוס ומסתמא פסק כר' יוסי דברייתא דחשיבא ליה עיקר וי"ל דהא דקאמר התם ר' יוסי דאנדרוגינוס בריה הוא לא שיהא בריה בפני עצמו לא זכר ולא נקבה דא"כ מאי לא הכריעו בו חכמים אלא ודאי ספיקא בעלמא הוא והא דקאמר התם רב אנדרוגינוס חייבין עליו סקילה משני מקומות שנאמר ואת זכר לא תשכב משכבי אשה איזהו זכר שיש לו שני משכבות הוי אומר זה אנדרוגינוס לא בשביל דחשיב ליה זכר ודאי אלא גזירת הכתוב הוא. וכן בפ' אותו ואת בנו דקאמר ר' יוסי כוי בריה בפני עצמו הוא ולא הכריעו בו חכמים אם חיה אם בהמה הוי נמי ספיקא מדקאמר בפ' כסוי הדם כוי אין שוחטין אותו ביו"ט ואם שחטו אין מכסין את דמו ואי בריה ממש קאמר שאינו לא חיה ולא בהמה א"כ לא שייך ביה כסוי אלא ודאי ספיקא הוי וכן מוכח לשון הכריעו אבל בריה דפ' בתרא דיומא הוי בריה ממש דקאמר התם כל חלב לרבות כוי ופריך כוי ספיקא הוי איצטריך קרא למעוטי ספיקא. ומשני קסבר האי תנא כוי בריה בפני עצמו הוא. וכן בפ"ק דחגיגה דקאמר כל זכורך להוציא טומטום ואנדרוגינוס וקאמר בשלמא אנדרוגינוס בריה בפני עצמו הוא אלא טומטום ספיקא

**תוספי הרא"ש**

הוי מכלל דבריה דקאמ' בריה ממש ולא כמו בריה דר' יוסי. ומיהו בתוספתא דמס' ביכורים משמע דר' יוסי סבר דאנדרוגינוס הוי בריה ממש דקתני ר' יוסי אומר אנדרוגינוס בריה בפני עצמה הוא ולא יכלו חכמים לעמוד עליו ולהכריע אם איש אם אשה אבל טומטום אינו כן אלא או ספק איש או ספק אשה מכלל דאנדרוגינוס לאו ספיקא הוא אלא דאין ספיקו הוא וי"ל לדעולם ספיקא כעין ספיקא דטומטום דאנדרוגינוס אין בו הכרעה לידע אם איש או אשה לפי שכולם שוין אבל טומטום יש שהוא זכר ויש שהוא נקבה וספיקא יכול להתברר שאם יקרע ימצא זכר או נקבה ונפקא מינה אם קדש אשה או נתקדש ונקרע ונפקא מינה נ"ב לגבי שופר ויוצא בו כדאמרי' אנדרוגינוס מוציא את מינו טומטום אינו מוציא לא את מינו ולא את שאינו מינו: שנאמר מזכר ועד נקבה זכר ודאי ונקבה ודאית ולא טומטום ואנדרוגינוס. ותימה כיון דאנדרוגינוס ספיקא הוי איצטריך קרא למעוטי ספיקא דהכי פריך בפ' אלו מומין בבכורות גבי אנדרוגינוס ופ' בתרא דיומא גבי כוי ובכריתות פרק דם שחיטה ובפ"ק דחולין גבי תחלת הציהוב שבזה ושבזה בשלמא טומטום איצטריך שיש מהן זכר ויש מהן נקבה ופטרו הכתוב כשהוא ספק אפילו אם יקרע אח"כ ויתברר ספיקו למפרע וכן גבי קפץ אחד מן המנויין לתוכו כולן פטורין דממעט עשיר ספק ולעיל גבי קדמה בהרת לשער לבן דדריש ליה מקרא בסוף נזיר איצטריך קרא לאורויי לן בספק הנארע מה יהא דינו אבל באנדרוגינוס אין בו שום ספיקא שכולן שוין וגבי שמיא גליא אם הוא זכר אם נקבה וי"ל דהא דמיעטיה הכא לאו משום ספיקא דספיקא קמי שמיא ליכא אלא משום דהוי זכר משונה או נקבה משונה ולדידן הוא דמספקא לן משום דתרי מיעוטי כתיבי זכר ונקבה ואתא חד מינייהו לטומטום למעוטי טומטום וחד מינייהו למעוטי אנדרוגינוס ולא ידענא אם אנדרוגינוס הוא זכר ומיעטיה מזכר ונקבה למעוטי טומטום או נקבה הוי ומיעטיה מנקבה וזכר למעוטי טומטום והא דפריך בפ' אלו מומין גבי אנדרוגינוס איצטריך קרא למעוטי ספיקא ולא אמרינן דמיעטיה משום דהוי זכר משונה י"ל דהתם פריך שפיר משום דמיעטיה מהזכר יתירה דכתיב גבי עולה ופריך מני אילימא ת"ק ספיקא הוי איצטריך קרא למעוטי ספיקא ואי מיעטיה משום דזכר משונה הוי א"כ תיפשוט דזכר הוי ולא ספיקא א"נ י"ל דבלאו טומטום איצטריכי הני תרי מיעוטי לאנדרוגינוס דאי הוה כתיב זכר לחודיה לא הוה ממעטינן מיניה אנדרוגינוס משום דמספקא לן דילמא נקבה הוא וזכר הוה מוקמינן לדרשא אחריתי וכן נמי אי הוה כתיב נקבה לחודה אבל השתא דכתיב תרוייהו ממה נפשך נתמעט אנדרוגינוס בין שהוא זכר בין שהוא נקבה ועי"ל דלטומטום לחודיה צריכי תרוייהו למעוטי ספיקא דידיה מדין זכר אם אח"כ נמצא זכר (או נקבה) או מדין נקבה אם אח"כ נמצא נקבה וסבר רב הונא דשקולין הן ואתו

תְּשַׁלֵּחוּ" זָכָר וַדַּאי, נְקֵבָה וַדָּאִית, וְלֹא טוּמְטוּם וְאַנְדְּרוֹגִינוּס. לֵימָא מְסַיַּיע לֵיהּ: טוּמְטוּם וְאַנְדְּרוֹגִינוּס שֶׁרָאוּ לוֹבֶן אוֹ אוֹדֶם — אֵין חַיָּיבִין עַל בִּיאַת מִקְדָּשׁ, וְאֵין שׂוֹרְפִין עֲלֵיהֶם אֶת הַתְּרוּמָה. רָאוּ לוֹבֶן וְאוֹדֶם כְּאַחַת — אֵין חַיָּיבִין עַל בִּיאַת מִקְדָּשׁ, אֲבָל שׂוֹרְפִין עֲלֵיהֶם אֶת הַתְּרוּמָה. מ"ט? לָאו מִשּׁוּם שֶׁנֶּאֱמַר: °"מִזָּכָר וְעַד נְקֵבָה תְּשַׁלֵּחוּ" — זָכָר וַדַּאי, נְקֵבָה וַדָּאִית, וְלֹא טוּמְטוּם וְאַנְדְּרוֹגִינוּס? אָמַר עוּלָּא: לָא, הָא מַנִּי — ר' אֱלִיעֶזֶר הִיא. *דִּתְנַן, רַבִּי אֱלִיעֶזֶר אוֹמֵר: "הַשֶּׁרֶץ °וְנֶעְלַם מִמֶּנּוּ" — עַל הֶעְלֵם שֶׁרֶץ הוּא חַיָּיב, וְאֵינוֹ חַיָּיב עַל הֶעְלֵם מִקְדָּשׁ. רַבִּי עֲקִיבָא אוֹמֵר: "וְנֶעְלַם מִמֶּנּוּ וְהוּא טָמֵא" — עַל הֶעְלֵם טוּמְאָה הוּא חַיָּיב, וְאֵינוֹ חַיָּיב עַל הֶעְלֵם מִקְדָּשׁ. *וְאָמְרִינַן: מַאי בֵּינַיְיהוּ? וְאָמַר חִזְקִיָּה: שֶׁרֶץ וּנְבֵלָה אִיכָּא בֵּינַיְיהוּ, דְּרַבִּי אֱלִיעֶזֶר סָבַר בָּעֵינַן עַד דְּיָדַע אִי בְּשֶׁרֶץ אִיטַּמֵּי אִי בִּנְבֵילָה אִיטַּמֵּי, וְר' עֲקִיבָא סָבַר [א]לָא בָּעֵינַן. לָאו אָמַר רַבִּי אֱלִיעֶזֶר הָתָם בָּעֵינַן דְּיָדַע אִי בְּשֶׁרֶץ אִיטַּמֵּי אִי בִּנְבֵלָה אִיטַּמֵּי, הָכָא נַמִּי — בָּעֵינַן דְּיָדַע אִי בְּלוֹבֶן אִיטַּמֵּי, אִי בְּאוֹדֶם אִיטַּמֵּי. אֲבָל לְרַבִּי עֲקִיבָא, דְּאָמַר מִשּׁוּם טוּמְאָה מִיחַיַּיב, הָכָא נַמִּי — מִשּׁוּם טוּמְאָה מִיחַיַּיב. וְרַב, מַאי שְׁנָא בִּיאַת מִקְדָּשׁ דְּלָא — דִּכְתִיב: "מִזָּכָר וְעַד נְקֵבָה תְּשַׁלֵּחוּ" — זָכָר וַדַּאי, נְקֵבָה וַדָּאִית, וְלֹא טוּמְטוּם וְאַנְדְּרוֹגִינוּס. אִי הָכִי — תְּרוּמָה נַמִּי לָא נִשְׂרוֹף, דִּכְתִיב: °"וְהַזָּב אֶת זוֹבוֹ לַזָּכָר וְלַנְּקֵבָה" — זָכָר וַדַּאי, נְקֵבָה וַדָּאִית, וְלֹא טוּמְטוּם וְאַנְדְּרוֹגִינוּס! הַהוּא מִבְּעֵי לֵיהּ לְכִדְרַבִּי יִצְחָק, דְּאָמַר רַבִּי יִצְחָק: *"לַזָּכָר" — לְרַבּוֹת אֶת הַמְּצוֹרָע לְמַעְיְנוֹתָיו, "וְלַנְּקֵבָה" — לְרַבּוֹת אֶת הַמְּצוֹרַעַת לְמַעְיְנוֹתֶיהָ. הַאי נַמִּי מִבְּעֵי לֵיהּ *בְּמִי שֶׁיֵּשׁ לוֹ טָהֳרָה בְּמִקְוֶה, פְּרָט לִכְלִי חֶרֶס — דִּבְרֵי רַבִּי יוֹסֵי! אִם כֵּן — נִכְתּוֹב רַחֲמָנָא "אָדָם", וְכִי תֵּימָא אִי כְּתַב רַחֲמָנָא "אָדָם" הֲוָה אָמִינָא — כְּלֵי מַתָּכוֹת לָא, מִ"כָּל טָמֵא לָנֶפֶשׁ" נָפְקָא! "זָכָר וּנְקֵבָה" לָמָּה לִי — לְכִדְרַב. וְאֵימָא: כּוּלֵּיהּ לְכִדְרַב הוּא דַּאֲתָא! אִם כֵּן, נִכְתּוֹב "זָכָר וּנְקֵבָה", מַאי "מִזָּכָר וְעַד נְקֵבָה" — עַד כָּל דָּבָר שֶׁיֵּשׁ לוֹ טָהֳרָה בְּמִקְוֶה. אִי הָכִי, כִּי אִיטַּמֵּי בִּשְׁאָר טוּמְאוֹת — לָא לִישַׁלְּחוּ! אָמַר קְרָא: "מִזָּכָר" — מִטּוּמְאָה הַפּוֹרֶשֶׁת מִן הַזָּכָר. וְכָל הֵיכָא דִּכְתִיב "מִזָּכָר עַד נְקֵבָה" לְמַעוֹטֵי טוּמְטוּם וְאַנְדְּרוֹגִינוּס הוּא דַּאֲתָא? וְהָא גַּבֵּי עֲרָכִין, דִּכְתִיב °"הַזָּכָר", *וְתַנְיָא: [ב]"הַזָּכָר" — וְלֹא טוּמְטוּם וְאַנְדְּרוֹגִינוּס, יָכוֹל לֹא יְהֵא בְּעֵרֶךְ אִישׁ אֲבָל יְהֵא בְּעֵרֶךְ אִשָּׁה — תַּלְמוּד לוֹמַר: "הַזָּכָר וְאִם נְקֵבָה" — [ג]זָכָר וַדַּאי, נְקֵבָה וַדָּאִית, וְלֹא טוּמְטוּם וְאַנְדְּרוֹגִינוּס. טַעְמָא — דִּכְתִיב "הַזָּכָר וְאִם נְקֵבָה", הָא "מִזָּכָר וּנְקֵבָה" לָא מְמַעֵט! הַהוּא מִבְּעֵי לֵיהּ לְחַלֵּק

תורה אור: במדבר ה | ויקרא ה | שם טו | ויקרא כז

---

תשלחו. היינו שילוח טמאים ממקדש. רבי אליעזר היא. דבעי לענין קרבן טומאה עד דידע במאי איטמי. אבל לרבנן, דלא בעו בשאר טומאות עד דידע במאי איטמי, הכא נמי מחייבי, דלא דרשינן "זכר ודאי, נקבה ודאית". השרץ ונעלם. "או בנבלת שרץ ונעלם ממנו". על העלם שרץ. שנטמא וידע, ובשעה שנכנס נעלם ממנו טומאה — חייב. ואינו חייב על העלם מקדש. אם כשנכנס למקדש זכור לטומאה, ונעלם ממנו מקדש ונכנס, שאינו סבור שזה מקדש, וכשיצא נזכר — פטור. שרץ ונבלה. לפניו, וידע שנגע באחד מהם, ואינו יודע באיזה מהם נגע, וכשבא למקדש שכח אותו, ומשיצא נזכר. ר' אליעזר. דאזכר שם שרץ, סבר: דבעינן עד דידע אם בשרץ איטמי כו'. הזב את זובו לזכר ולנקבה. ולדרוש נמי: זכר ודאי נקבה ודאית מטמא בזיבה, ולא טומטום. לזכר לרבות מצורע. שהוא מוקש לזב, להיות מעינותיו אב הטומאה לטמא אדם וכלים כזב, דכתיב ביה (ויקרא טו): "וכי ירוק הזב" וגו'. פרט לכלי חרס טמא. שאין טעון שילוח מן העזרה. הוה אמינא כלי מתכות לא. טעון שילוח, ולהכי שני בדיבוריה למדרש: כל שיש לו דין הנוהג בזכר ובנקבה, דהיינו טהרה במקוה. מוכל טמא נפקא. דאף כלי מתכות בעי שילוח, ועל כרחין הוה דרשינן: אדם ודמי ליה, ולא כלי חרס שאין לו טהרה. עד נקבה. משמע: כל מי שיש לו דין שהוא מזכר עד נקבה, שיש להן טהרה. אי הכי. לעיל קאי, כיון דאמר רב לענין שילוח: זכר ודאי ולא טומטום, בשאר טומאות נמי כגון טומטום שנטמא במת או בשרץ ונכנס למקדש — יפטר. הזכר. "והיה ערכך הזכר". תלמוד לומר הזכר. ה"א דריש. אם נקבה. "אם" קדריש. ההוא מיבעי ליה. למכתב "זכר ונקבה". לחלק.

---

אמר עולא הא מני ר' אליעזר היא. והא דתנן בלהי "הערל" (יבמות פג.) רבי אליעזר אומר: אנדרוגינוס חייבין עליו סקילה כזכר — הא אמרינן התם: לא לכל אמר רבי אליעזר אנדרוגינוס חייבין עליו. אי נמי: י"ל: דהכא הכי קאמר: האי תנא דאמר אין חייבין על ביאת מקדש, דריש "השרץ" כרבי אליעזר. פרט לכלי חרס גרסי'. ותו לא. ולא גרס "שאין לו טהרה במקוה", דבשלהי "המוצא תפילין" (עירובין קד:) בעי למימר: משום דאינו נעשה אב הטומאה. ואין צריך למוחקו, דאף ע"ג דאינו מן הברייתא נקטיה התלמוד משום דמסיק התם: דה"ה שרץ, אע"ג דאב הטומאה הוא. וא"ת: דאמר *בפ"ק דסוטה (דף ט) ובפרק "אלו דברים" (פסחים סז.) אפי' מת מותר ליכנס במחנה לויה, שנאמר: "ויקח משה את עצמות יוסף עמו" וגו', מאי אפי' — אדרבה מת קיל טפי, דאין לו טהרה במקוה, ואפילו במחנה שכינה נמי! ויש לומר: דאיכא למ"ד בשלהי עירובין (דף קד:) דמחייב מכניס שרץ למקדש, אע"ג דאין לו טהרה במקוה, וה"ה מת. אי נמי: מת מחייב טפי, משום דיש במינו טהרה במקוה, כגון אדם חי. הוה אמינא כלי מתכות לא. הוי מצי למנקט "כלי שטף", אלא נקט "כלי מתכות" משום דחמיר, דחרב הרי הוא כחלל. עד כל דבר שיש לו טהרה במקוה. מלשון "עד" דריש, כדפ"ה. דמשמע: כל מי שיש לו דין שמזכר עד נקבה, דהיינו שיש לו טהרה במקוה. וא"ת: "כל טמא לנפש" אם כן למאי אתא? ויש לומר: דדריש "אלו דברים" בפסחים (דף סו:) דריש ליה שפיר. אי הכי בשאר טומאות נמי. פירוש: כיון דדריש "מזכר ועד נקבה" למי שיש לו טהרה במקוה, אם כן מוקמינן קרא גם בשאר טומאות דלאו לובן ואודם דשייכו בכלים, ואם כן דטומאת מת ושרץ נמי לא לישלחו טומטום ואנדרוגינוס. תלמוד לומר הזכר. ה"א ד"הזכר" דריש. ותימה: דבפ' "על אלו מומין" (בכורות דף מא.) אמרינן: שאני הכא, דכתיב: "הזכר הזכרים", משמע: משום דכתיב "הזכרים", אבל ה"א ד"הזכר" לא חשיב יתור למעט אנדרוגינוס? ושמא איכא שום דרשא התם דדריש מה"א.

הא מזכר לחודיה לא ממעט. הך ברייתא אתיא כרבי יהודה, כדמוכח במסכת שבת בפרק "ר"א דמילה" (דף קלו:) על הא דקאמר רבי יהודה: אנדרוגינוס דוחה שבת. דקאמר רב חסדא: לא לכל אמר ר' יהודה זכר הוא, שאם אתה אומר כן — בערכין יערך, ותניא: "הזכר" – ולא טומטום כו'. פירוש: סתם ספרא רבי יהודה. וקאמר רב נחמן בר יצחק: אף אנן נמי תנינא: אנדרוגינוס פסול לקדוש מי חטאת, דברי רבי יהודה. ופריך: מאי שנא גבי מילה? ומשני: משום דכתיב "המול לכם כל זכר". והשתא תימה: דהכא גבי ערכין צריך יתורא למעט טומטום ואנדרוגינוס, ולא ממעט להו מלשון "זכר" ו"נקבה" וגבי מילה אדרבה צריך יתורא לרבות! וגבי קדוש ממעט ליה, אף ע"ג דליכא יתורא אחרינא לאנדרוגינוס, אלא משום דכתיב "ונתן" ולא כתיב "ונתנה" – למעוטי אשה. והנה מצינו למימר: דכיון דגלי בערכין דלא הוי בכלל זכר, ילפינן קדוש מערכין. ומילה נמי הוה ילפינן, אי לאו דגלי קרא ד"כל זכר". והא דלא ילפינן קדוש ממילה – משום דטפי אית לן למילף מערכין לחומרא. והכא דפריך: וכל היכא דכתיב "זכר" למעט טומטום ואנדרוגינוס? והא גבי ערכין כו', לא מצי לשנויי דמערכין ילפינן – דאדרבה, ממילה אית לן למילף דהוי בכלל זכר, כדי להטעינו שילוח, ולא מערכין לקולא. ובפרק "על אלו מומין" (בכורות מא:) דמצריך קרא יתירא למעט טומטום ואנדרוגינוס, דקאמר: כשהוא אומר "הזכר" למטה שאין ת"ל, ולא ילפינן מערכין לחומרא שלא להכשירו לעולה ולהצריך קרבן אחר – התם אצטריך קרא לקרבן נדבה, כגון שאמר "הרי זו עולה", והוי קולא שאינו קדוש, דלא הוה ילפינן מערכין לקולא אלא ממילה לחומרא, ולהכי אצטריך קרא. אך קשה דבפ' "הערל" (יבמות עב:) משמע דלא פסיל ליה ר' יהודה לענין קדוש אלא משום דהוי ספק איש ספק אשה. דתנן התם, ר' יהודה אומר: אנדרוגינוס שקדש – קדושיו פסולין, משום שהוא ספק אשה, ואשה פסולה לקדש? וי"ל: דלגבי ערך אף ע"ג דהוא זכר או נקבה, ממעטו הכתוב מערך איש ואשה, לפי שהוא משונה. ואי הוה מיעוטא דזכר לחודיה, הוה אמינא: דאפקיה רחמנא מערך זכר ואוקמיה בערך נקבה אפילו הוא זכר, וכן איפכא. וגבי מילה, אי נקבה היא – הא איצטריך קרא לרבויי, ואי זכר הוא, שמא איכא שום דרשא דהוה ממעטינן ליה, אי לאו דריבהו הכתוב. והיא דבכורות (דף מא:) ד"הזכר" – ולא טומטום ואנדרוגינוס, איכא למימר דלא אתיא כר' יהודה, דכיון דספק הוא לא אצטריך קרא למעוטי ספקא. ואף ע"ג דסתם ספרא ר' יהודה היא, היינו בסתמא אחרינא אבל הא ע"כ לאו רבי יהודה היא.

ה"ג

---

## תוספי הרא"ש

ואתו תרוייהו: **אמר** עולא הא מני ר' אליעזר הוא. ותימה הא תנן בסוף הערל ר' אליעזר אומר אנדרוגינוס חייבין עליו סקילה כזכר וי"ל דהא אמרינן התם לא לכל אמר ר' אליעזר אנדרוגינוס זכר מעליא ועי"ל הא דקאמר הכא סבר לה כר' אליעזר היינו בפלוגתא דהשרץ ונעלם: **פרט** לכלי חרס גרס. ול"ג שאין לו טהרה במקוה דאינו מן הברייתא כדמוכח בסוף המוצא תפילין דבעינן למימר לפי שאינו נעשה אב הטומאה ומיהו אין צריך למחקו אע"ג שאינו מן הברייתא והאי דנקט ליה תלמודא משום דמסקינן התם דבשרץ (נמי) פליגי נמי תנאי והיינו ע"כ משום שאין לו טהרה במקוה: **ה"א** כלי מתכות לא. ה"ה דהוה מצי למימר כל כלי שטף לא [אלא] נקט כלי מתכות לרבותא דאע"ג דחמירי דחרב הרי הוא כחלל: **עד** כל דבר שיש לו טהרה במקוה. והשתא לא איצטריך כל טמא לנפש לכלי מתכות ובריש אלו דברים בפסחים דריש ליה לדרשא אחרינא: **אי** הכי נטמאו בשאר טומאות נמי לא לשלחו. אא"ב דכולהו לכדרב (הונא) הוא דאתא ניחא דאמרי' מזכר מטומאה הפורשת מזכר אבל כיון דאמרת דעד אתא לרבויי כל דבר שיש לו טהרה במקוה ואינהו אפילו בשאר טומאות נשתלחו א"כ טומטום ואנדרוגינו' נמי [לא לישלחו אפי' בטומאת מת ושרץ] ומשני דאפילו הכי דרשינן מזכר מטומאה הפורשת מן הזכר:

---

עין משפט נר מצוה:
פב א מיי' פי"א מהל' שגגות הל"ב:
פג ב ג מיי' פ"א מהל' ערכין הל"ה סמג עשין קכח:

מסורת הש"ס:
[נ"ל בפ"ג דסוטה כ:]
שבועות יד:
שם יח:
[לקמן לד:]
[עירובין קד: ע"ש]
ערכין ד: שבת קלו: בכורות מב.

לְחַלֵּק בֵּין עֵרֶךְ אִישׁ לְעֵרֶךְ אִשָּׁה.§ "יָצָא מְחוּתָּךְ אוֹ מְסוֹרָס" וכו'.§ א"ר אֶלְעָזָר: אֲפִילּוּ הָרֹאשׁ עִמָּהֶן. וְר' יוֹחָנָן אָמַר: לֹא שָׁנוּ אֶלָּא שֶׁאֵין הָרֹאשׁ עִמָּהֶן, אֲבָל הָרֹאשׁ עִמָּהֶן – *(הָרֹאשׁ פּוֹטֵר.) לֵימָא בִּדְשְׁמוּאֵל קָמִיפַּלְגִי, *דְּאָמַר שְׁמוּאֵל: אֵין הָרֹאשׁ פּוֹטֵר בִּנְפָלִים בְּשָׁלֵם – דְּכוּלֵּי עָלְמָא לָא פְּלִיגִי, כִּי פְּלִיגִי – בִּמְחוּתָּךְ. דְּמָר סָבַר: בְּשָׁלֵם הוּא דְּקָחָשֵׁיב, בִּמְחוּתָּךְ לָא קָחָשֵׁיב. וּמָר סָבַר: בִּמְחוּתָּךְ נַמִי חָשֵׁיב. (לִישָּׁנָא אַחֲרִינָא: טַעְמָא – דְּיָצָא מְחוּתָּךְ אוֹ מְסוֹרָס, הָא כְּתִקְנוֹ – הָרֹאשׁ פּוֹטֵר, תַּרְוַיְיהוּ לֵית לְהוּ דִּשְׁמוּאֵל, דְּאָמַר שְׁמוּאֵל: אֵין הָרֹאשׁ פּוֹטֵר בִּנְפָלִים.) אִיכָּא דְּמַתְנֵי לָהּ לְהָא שְׁמַעְתָּא בְּאַפֵּי נַפְשָׁהּ, א"ר אֶלְעָזָר: אֵין הָרֹאשׁ כְּרוֹב אֵבָרִים, וְרַבִּי יוֹחָנָן אָמַר: [א]הָרֹאשׁ כְּרוֹב אֵבָרִים. וְקָמִיפַּלְגִי בִּדְשְׁמוּאֵל. תְּנַן: יָצָא מְחוּתָּךְ אוֹ מְסוֹרָס, מִשֶּׁיֵּצֵא רוּבּוֹ – הֲרֵי הוּא כְּיָלוּד. מִדְּקָאָמַר (א) מְסוֹרָס, מִכְּלָל דִּמְחוּתָּךְ – כְּתִקְנוֹ, וְקָאָמַר מִשֶּׁיֵּצֵא רוּבּוֹ – הֲרֵי זֶה כְּיָלוּד. קַשְׁיָא לְרַבִּי יוֹחָנָן! אָמַר לָךְ רַבִּי יוֹחָנָן: אֵימָא "יָצָא מְחוּתָּךְ וּמְסוֹרָס". וְהָא "אוֹ" קָתָנֵי! הָכִי קָאָמַר: יָצָא מְחוּתָּךְ אוֹ שָׁלֵם, וְזֶה וָזֶה מְסוֹרָס – מִשֶּׁיֵּצֵא רוּבּוֹ הֲרֵי זֶה כְּיָלוּד. אָמַר רַב פַּפָּא: כְּתַנָּאֵי. יָצָא מְחוּתָּךְ אוֹ מְסוֹרָס – מִשֶּׁיֵּצֵא רוּבּוֹ הֲרֵי הוּא כְּיָלוּד, רַבִּי יוֹסֵי אוֹמֵר: מִשֶּׁיֵּצֵא כְּתִקְנוֹ. מַאי קָאָמַר? אָמַר רַב פַּפָּא, הָכִי קָאָמַר: יָצָא מְחוּתָּךְ וּמְסוֹרָס – מִשֶּׁיֵּצֵא רוּבּוֹ הֲרֵי הוּא כְּיָלוּד, הָא כְּתִקְנוֹ – הָרֹאשׁ פּוֹטֵר. רַבִּי יוֹסֵי אוֹמֵר – מִשֶּׁיֵּצֵא רוּבּוֹ כְּתִקְנוֹ. מַתְקִיף לָהּ רַב זְבִיד: מִכְּלָל דִּבִמְסוֹרָס – רוּבּוֹ נַמִי לֹא פּוֹטֵר, הָא קי"ל *[ב]דְּרוּבּוֹ כְּכוּלּוֹ! אֶלָּא אָמַר רַב זְבִיד, הָכִי קָאָמַר: יָצָא מְחוּתָּךְ וּמְסוֹרָס – מִשֶּׁיֵּצֵא רוּבּוֹ הֲרֵי זֶה כְּיָלוּד, הָא כְּתִקְנוֹ – הָרֹאשׁ פּוֹטֵר. רַבִּי יוֹסֵי אוֹמֵר: מִשֶּׁיֵּצֵא כְּתִקְנוֹ לְחַיִּים. תַּנְיָא נַמִי הָכִי: יָצָא מְחוּתָּךְ (אוֹ) מְסוֹרָס – מִשֶּׁיֵּצֵא רוּבּוֹ הֲרֵי זֶה כְּיָלוּד, הָא כְּתִקְנוֹ – הָרֹאשׁ פּוֹטֵר. ר' יוֹסֵי אוֹמֵר: מִשֶּׁיֵּצֵא כְּתִקְנוֹ לְחַיִּים. וְאֵיזֶהוּ כְּתִקְנוֹ לְחַיִּים – מִשֶּׁיֵּצֵא רוֹב רֹאשׁוֹ. וְאֵיזֶהוּ רוֹב רֹאשׁוֹ? ר' יוֹסֵי אוֹמֵר: מִשֶּׁיֵּצְאוּ צְדָעָיו, אַבָּא חָנָן מִשּׁוּם ר' יְהוֹשֻׁעַ אוֹמֵר: [ג]מִשֶּׁיֵּצֵא פַּדַּחְתּוֹ, וְי"א: מִשֶּׁיֵּרָאוּ קַרְנֵי רֹאשׁוֹ.§

**מתני'** *[ד]הַמַּפֶּלֶת וְאֵין יָדוּעַ מַהוּ – תֵּשֵׁב לְזָכָר וְלִנְקֵבָה, אֵין יָדוּעַ אִם וָלָד הָיָה אִם לָאו – תֵּשֵׁב לְזָכָר וְלִנְקֵבָה וּלְנִדָּה.§

**גמ'** *א"ר יְהוֹשֻׁעַ בֶּן לֵוִי: [ה]עָבְרָה נָהָר וְהִפִּילָה – מְבִיאָה קָרְבָּן וְנֶאֱכָל, הַלֵּךְ אַחַר רוֹב נָשִׁים, וְרוֹב נָשִׁים וָלָד מְעַלְּיָא יָלְדָן. תְּנַן: אֵין יָדוּעַ אִם וָלָד הָיָה – תֵּשֵׁב לְזָכָר וְלִנְקֵבָה וּלְנִדָּה. אַמַּאי תֵּשֵׁב לְנִדָּה? לֵימָא: הַלֵּךְ אַחַר רוֹב נָשִׁים, וְרוֹב נָשִׁים וָלָד מְעַלְּיָא יָלְדָן! [ו]מַתְנִי' – בְּשֶׁלֹּא הוּחְזְקָה עוּבָּרָה, וְכִי קָאָמַר ריב"ל – [ז]כְּשֶׁהוּחְזְקָה עוּבָּרָה. ת"ש: [ח]בְּהֵמָה שֶׁיָּצְאָה מְלֵאָה וּבָאָה רֵיקָנִית – הַבָּא אַחֲרָיו בְּכוֹר מִסָּפֵק. וְאַמַּאי? הַלֵּךְ אַחַר רוֹב בְּהֵמוֹת, וְרוֹב בְּהֵמוֹת וָלָד מְעַלְּיָא יָלְדָן, וְהַאי – פָּשׁוּט הוּא! אָמַר רָבִינָא: מִשּׁוּם דְּאִיכָּא לְמֵימַר, רוֹב בְּהֵמוֹת יוֹלְדוֹת דָּבָר הַפּוֹטֵר מִבְּכוֹרָה, וּמִיעוּטָן יוֹלְדוֹת דָּבָר שֶׁאֵינוֹ פּוֹטֵר מִבְּכוֹרָה, וְכָל הַיּוֹלְדוֹת – מְטַנְּפוֹת, וְזוֹ הוֹאִיל וְלֹא טִינְּפָה – אִתְרַע לָהּ רוּבָּא. אִי כָּל הַיּוֹלְדוֹת מְטַנְּפוֹת, הָא – מִדְּלָא מְטַנְּפָה – בְּכוֹר מְעַלְּיָא הוּא! אֶלָּא אֵימָא: רוֹב יוֹלְדוֹת מְטַנְּפוֹת, וְזוֹ הוֹאִיל וְלֹא טִינְּפָה – אִתְרַע לָהּ רוּבָּא. *כִּי אֲתָא רָבִין אֲמַר: מְתִיב רַבִּי יוֹסֵי בְּרַבִּי חֲנִינָא טוֹעָה, וְלָא יָדְעָנָא מַאי תְּיוּבְתָּא. מַאי הִיא? דְּתַנְיָא, אִשָּׁה

---

**רש"י**

לְחַלֵּק. הִילְכָּךְ, אִי לָאו הֵ"א – "וְאִם" לָא מְמַעֵט טוּמְטוּם. אֲבָל הָכָא, מִדַּה"ל לְמִכְתַּב "אָדָם תְּשַׁלְּחוּ", וּכְתִיב "זָכָר וּנְקֵבָה" – ש"מ לִדְרָשָׁה. וַאֲפִילּוּ הָרֹאשׁ עִמָּהֶם. אַמְּחוּתָּךְ קָאֵי, דְּהֵיכָא דְּיָצָא מְחוּתָּךְ, אֲפִי' יָצָא הָרֹאשׁ – אֵין חָשׁוּב וָלָד, עַד שֶׁיֵּצֵא רוּבּוֹ. אֵין הָרֹאשׁ פּוֹטֵר בִּנְפָלִים. יָצָא רֹאשׁ הַנֵּפֶל, כְּגוֹן יוֹלֶדֶת תְּאוֹמִים לִשְׁבִעָה. אֶחָד נִגְמְרָה צוּרָתוֹ, וְאֶחָד לֹא נִגְמְרָה צוּרָתוֹ. וְיָצָא רֹאשׁ הַנֵּפֶל, וְהֶחֱזִירוֹ, וְאח"כ יָצָא אָחִיו – הָוֵי בְּכוֹר לְכֹהֵן. שֶׁאֵין רֹאשׁ הַנֵּפֶל פּוֹטֵר אֶת הַבָּא אַחֲרָיו מִן הַבְּכוֹרָה. וְרַבִּי אֶלְעָזָר אִית לֵיהּ דִּשְׁמוּאֵל. בְּאַנְפֵּי נַפְשֵׁיהּ. וְלָא אַמַּתְנִיתִין. וְאִיכָּא בֵּינַיְיהוּ: מַאן דְּמַתְנֵי לָהּ אַמַּתְנִיתִין – מַשְׁמַע דְּאַמְּחוּתָּךְ קָא פְּלִיגִי, וְאִיכָּא לְמֵימַר כְּדַאֲמַרַן, דִּבְשָׁלֵם אֲפִי' ר' אֶלְעָזָר מוֹדֶה, דְּלֵית לֵיהּ דִּשְׁמוּאֵל. וּמַאן דְּמַתְנֵי לָהּ בְּאַנְפֵּי נַפְשֵׁיהּ מַשְׁמַע: דְּאַשָּׁלֵם נַמִי פְּלִיגִי, וּבִדְשְׁמוּאֵל. אֵין הָרֹאשׁ כְּרוֹב אֵבָרִים. יָצָא הָרֹאשׁ – אֵינוֹ כְּיָלוּד. וּבְנֵפֶל קָאֵי, דְּאִי בְּבֶן קַיְּימָא – לֵיכָּא לְמ"ד, דְּהָא מַתְנִיתִין הִיא: "יָצָא כְּדַרְכּוֹ – מִשֶּׁיֵּצֵא רוֹב רֹאשׁוֹ". כְּתִקְנוֹ. רֹאשׁ יָצָא תְּחִלָּה, וְקָאָמַר דְּבָעֵינַן רוּבָּא, וְקַשְׁיָא לְר' יוֹחָנָן. מַאי קָאָמַר. רַבִּי יוֹסֵי "מִשֶּׁיֵּצֵא כְּתִקְנוֹ", ס"ד דִּמְסוֹרָס בְּרוּבָּא לָאו יָלוּד הוּא. מְחוּתָּךְ וּמְסוֹרָס. מְחוּתָּךְ וְדֶרֶךְ מַרְגְּלוֹתָיו. הָא כְּתִקְנוֹ. דֶּרֶךְ רֹאשׁוֹ, אֲפִי' מְחוּתָּךְ – הָרֹאשׁ פּוֹטֵר. רוּבּוֹ כְּתִקְנוֹ. תַּרְוַיְיהוּ בָּעֵינַן בִּמְחוּתָּךְ. מַתְקִיף לָהּ רַב זְבִיד. לְתֵירוּצָא דְּמִתָּרְצִינַן אַלִּיבָּא דְּרַבִּי יוֹסֵי. מִכְּלָל דִּמְסוֹרָס רוּבּוֹ נַמִי לֹא פָּטַר. בִּתְמִיָּה. כֵּיוָן דְּרַבִּי יוֹסֵי לָאו אַדִּיוּקָא קָאֵי, אֶלָּא אַדְּקָתָנֵי בְּגוּפֵיהּ "יָצָא מְחוּתָּךְ וּמְסוֹרָס מִשֶּׁיֵּצֵא רוּבּוֹ", וַעֲלָהּ קָאֵי דְּרַבִּי יוֹסֵי וְאָמַר: אע"ג דְּנָפֵיק רוּבּוֹ – בָּעֵינַן נַמִי כְּתִקְנוֹ, מִכְּלָל דִּמְסוֹרָס רוּבּוֹ נַמִי לֹא פָּטַר? בִּתְמִיָּה. אֶלָּא אָמַר רַב זְבִיד. רַבִּי יוֹסֵי אַדִּיוּקָא דְּת"ק קָאֵי, דְּאָמַר: הָא כְּתִקְנוֹ הָרֹאשׁ פּוֹטֵר וְאע"ג דִּמְחוּתָּךְ. וְקָאָמַר ר' יוֹסֵי: אֵין הָרֹאשׁ פּוֹטֵר אֶלָּא שֶׁיָּצָא כְּתִקְנוֹ וּכְשֵׁאָר וְלָדוֹת שֶׁיּוֹצְאִין לְחַיִּים, אֲבָל מְחוּתָּךְ – אֲפִילּוּ כְּתִקְנוֹ אֵין הָרֹאשׁ פּוֹטֵר. כְּתִקְנוֹ. אֲפִי' מְחוּתָּךְ הָרֹאשׁ פּוֹטֵר. *מִי שֶׁיָּצָא כְּתִקְנוֹ לְחַיִּים. הוּא דְּרֹאשׁ פּוֹטֵר. אֲבָל מְחוּתָּךְ, אֲפִילּוּ כְּתִקְנוֹ – בָּעֵינַן רוּבּוֹ. צְדָעָיו. טנפל"ש. קַרְנֵי רֹאשׁוֹ. גּוֹבַהּ רֹאשׁוֹ שֶׁאֵצֶל הָעוֹרֶף. **מתני'** וְאֵין יָדוּעַ מַהוּ. אִם זָכָר אִם נְקֵבָה, אֲבָל יוֹדַעַת הִיא שֶׁהוּא וָלָד. לְזָכָר וְלִנְקֵבָה. יְמֵי טוֹהַר דְּזָכָר וִימֵי טוּמְאָה דִּנְקֵבָה. אֵין יָדוּעַ אִם וָלָד הָיָה אִם לָאו תֵּשֵׁב לְזָכָר וְלִנְקֵבָה וּלְנִדָּה. כְּלוֹמַר, כְּשֶׁתִּרְאֶה – תְּהֵא נִדָּה, שֶׁאֵין לָהּ יְמֵי טוֹהַר, דְּשֶׁמָּא לָאו וָלָד הוּא. וּבַגְּמָרָא* מְפָרֵשׁ לָמָּה הוּזְכַּר זָכָר הוֹאִיל וְאֵין לָהּ דַּם טוֹהַר, דְּאִי מִשּׁוּם טוּמְאַת לֵידָה – הָא קָתָנֵי "נְקֵבָה". **גמ'** וְהִפִּילָה. וְאֵינָהּ יוֹדַעַת מַה: אִם נֵפֶל, אִם רוּחַ, שֶׁהֲרֵי נָפַל לַמַּיִם. אַמַּאי תֵּשֵׁב לְנִדָּה. נֵיתִיב לָהּ מִיהָא יְמֵי טוֹהַר דְּזָכָר. שֶׁיָּצְאָה מְלֵאָה. כְּשֶׁהָיְתָה מְעוּבֶּרֶת יָצְתָה לַחֲפַר. וּבָאָה. בּוֹ בַּיּוֹם רֵיקָנִית. בְּכוֹר מִסָּפֵק. שֶׁמָּא זֶה הָיָה וָלָד – וְהַבָּא אַחֲרָיו אֵינוֹ בְּכוֹר, אוֹ שֶׁמָּא רוּחַ הִפִּילָה – וְהַבָּא אַחֲרָיו בְּכוֹר מְעַלְּיָא הוּא. הִילְכָּךְ סָפֵק הוּא, וְיֵאָכֵל בְּמוּמוֹ לַבְּעָלִים וְלֹא לַכֹּהֵן, דְּהַמּוֹצִיא מֵחֲבֵירוֹ עָלָיו הָרְאָיָה. וְהַאי פָּשׁוּט הוּא. וְיֵאָכֵל בְּלֹא מוּם. מְטַנְּפוֹת. יוֹם אֶחָד קוֹדֶם לֵידָה, כְּעֵין גלייר"א. מְתִיב רַבִּי יוֹסֵי. אַדְּר' יְהוֹשֻׁעַ בֶּן לֵוִי. טוֹעָה. מִמַּתְנִיתָא דְּמַיְירֵי בְּאִשָּׁה טוֹעָה שֶׁלֹּא יָדְעָה עֵת לֵידָתָהּ. הָאִשָּׁה

---

**תוספות**

ה"ג: אמר רב פפא כתנאי יצא מחותך או מסורס כו' מאי קאמר. – דאין סברא דברוב שלם ומסורס או ברוב כתקנו ומחותך לא הוי לרבי יוסי כילוד. וקאמר רב פפא דגרסינן בברייתא "מחותך ומסורס", הא מחותך ויצא כתקנו – הראש פוטר, ולרבי יוסי אין הראש פוטר, והיינו פלוגתייהו דרבי יוחנן ורבי אלעזר. **מכלל** דבמסורס רובו נמי לא פוטר. וא"ת: ודלמא ר' יוסי אתא למימר דאפי' כתקנו בעינן רוב, ואין הראש פוטר, וה"ה דבמסורס נמי סגי ברוב? וי"ל: דא"כ הוה ליה לרבי יוסי למימר: "אפילו כתקנו עד שיצא רובו", והוה משמע שבא להחמיר. לכך משני רב זביד: מדקאמר *"משיצא רובו כתקנו", ולא קאמר "עד שיצא" – משמע דרבי יוסי בא להקל. וה"ק: יצא מחותך מסורס – עד שיצא רובו, הא כתקנו – הראש פוטר. ור' יוסי מקיל וקאמר: (או עד שיצא) כתקנו לחיים. פירוש: מה שחשוב חיים, דהיינו רוב ראשו, כדמפרש בברייתא בסמוך, ר' יוסי אומר: משיצא רוב ראשו. ורבינו חננאל פירש: "לחיים" – בר קיימא, דדוקא בר קיימא הראש פוטר, אבל לא בנפלים. וקשה: א"כ אמאי איתותב שמואל פרק "יש בכור" (בכורות דף מז:) כיון דרבי יוסי קאי כוותיה.

**תשב** לזכר ולנקבה ולנדה. אע"ג דהוי ספק ספיקא – תשב לנקבה, דאי מטהרת לה מטומאת נקבה משום ספק ספיקא. הכי נמי נטהרנה אם ראתה בל"ד ומ"א מספק ספיקא, ולא ניחוש לזכר, והוי תרי קולי דסתרן אהדדי, א] כדפרשינן לעיל (ב) (ד' כד:) ומיהו בטועה בגמ' מחמרינן, אע"ג דאיכא כמה ספיקי.

**וזו** הואיל ולא טנפה. וכגון שלא שהתה הבהמה בחוץ, דאם שהתה, אימור: טנפה וילדה. אימר

שפר"ח מחיים בר קיימא אבל בנפל אין הראש פוטר דלפי [זה] אמאי איתותב שמואל בבכורות דקאמר אין הראש פוטר בנפלים בפ' יש בכור הא איכא ר' יוסי הכא דקאי כוותיה: **תשב** לזכר ולנקבה ולנדה. ותימה אמאי תשב שבועים לנקבה והא ספק ספיקא הוא דשמא לא ילדה ואת"ל ילדה אימור זכר הואי ובפ"ק דב"ק משמע שיש לנו להקל בספק ספיקא גבי שליא שיצתה מקצתה ביום הראשון וי"ל דא"כ אם תראה ביום ל"ד תחזור ותראה ביום מ"א אמרינן בגמרא דמשום חששא דזכר מקולקלת עד יום מ"ח ואמאי (לא) תהא מקולקלת דשמא לא ילדה כלל ואת"ל ילדה אימור נקבה הואי אלא ודאי לא אמרינן הכא תרי קולי דסתרי אהדדי אלא מוקמינן כל חד וחד אדיניה וטמאה שבועים משום חומרא דנקבה ומקולקלת למנינה משום חומרא דזכר. ואע"ג דבשמעתא דטועה מחמירינן אע"ג דאיכא כמה ספיקות יש לחלק היכא דנחתא כבר לתורת טומאה: **רוב** היולדות מטנפות. האי טינוף הוי קודם לידה ולא כמו טינוף דלעיל דהוי מיהוי הולד עצמו. ומיירי בשלא שהתה בחוץ כ"א מעט דאם שהתה הרבה אימור טינפה וילדה:

---

**תוספי הרא"ש**

ר' יוסי אומר משיצא כתקנו מאי קאמר. פרש"י וכי ס"ד דמסורס ברובא לאו ילוד הוא ומפרש רב פפא ר' יוסי אדיוקא דת"ק קאי הא דקאמר הא כתקנו הראש פוטר וקאמר ר' יוסי משיצא רובו כתקנו דאפילו כתקנו בעי' רובא ומיהו גם במסורס נמי הוי כילוד ברובו ורב זביד פריך ליה לרב פפא דמשמע ליה (כלומר דלפי דברי רב פפא ר' יוסי לא קאי אדיוקא) דע"כ ר' יוסי לא קאי אדיוקא דת"ק דא"כ הו"ל למימר אפי' כתקנו עד שיצא רובו אבל מדקאמר משיצא משמע שבא להקל דבקל הוי לידה טפי מלת"ק. ותימה אי קאי אמאי דקאמר ת"ק יצא מחותך מסורס משיצא רובו (כלומר אלא) [כמו] דס"ד מעיקרא מקמי דדייק רב פפא וקאמר ר' יוסי משיצא כתקנו אז מהני רוב אבל מסורס לא מהני רוב א"כ אז לא בא ר' יוסי להקל והו"ל למימר עד שיצא רובו כתקנו. וי"ל דהא לא קשה ליה משום דר' יוסי לא קאי אמאי דקאמר הת"ק (כלומר) לפי פשט הברייתא מקמי דאיירי רב פפא דת"ק איירי במחותך [או] מסורס משיצא רובו הרי זה כילוד וקאמר ר' יוסי אני אומר דוקא משיצא רובו כתקנו אבל רב פפא שמגיה בדברי ת"ק הא כתקנו הראש פוטר אי איתא דר' יוסי (אתא) [עלה] קאי הו"ל למימר עד שיצא רובו כתקנו הילכך משני רב זביד דר' יוסי אמר משיצא כתקנו לחיים דהיינו משיצא רוב ראשו ומיקל ר' יוסי וחשיב ליה בקל ילוד טפי מת"ק. ולא כמו

---

**עין משפט נר מצוה**

פד א ב ג מיי' פ"י מהל' איסורי ביאה הל"ו וע"ש סמג לאוין קיא טוש"ע יו"ד סי' קלד סעיף י:

פה ד מיי' שם הלי"ט סמג שם טוש"ע שם סעיף ט:

פו ה מיי' פ"א מהל' מחוסרי כפרה הל' ו ז:

פז ו מיי' פ"י מהל' איסורי ביאה הלי"ט:

פח ז מיי' פ"א מהל' מחוסרי כפרה הל"ו ז:

נ"ל משיצא כתקנו כו' עד שיצא רובו הא כתקנו כו' ור"י מקי"ל וקאמר משיצא כתקנו כו' רש"א

פט ח מיי' פ"ד מהל' בכורות הלי"ג וע' בהשגות וע"ש סמג עשין ריא טוש"ע יו"ד סימן שטו סעיף ז:

---

**מסורת הש"ס**

ס"א הרי הוא כילוד

[בכורות מו:]

ס"א ל"ג

[נזיר מב. חולין ע. הוריות ג:]

נ"א ל"ג

נ"ל משיצא

[לעיל כח.]

[לעיל יח.]

[לקמן ל.]

[לעיל יח: לקמן סט.]

**הגהות הב"ח**

(א) גמ' מדקאמר או מסורס וכו' הרי הוא כילוד: (ב) תד"ה תשב כו' לעיל נ"ב בדף כז ריש ע"א:

**גליון הש"ס**

גמ' אריב"ל עברה נהר וכו'. לעיל יח ע"א: שם אי כל היולדות. כעין זה כתובות עז ע"א:

**הגהות מהר"ב רנשבורג**

א] תוד"ה תשב וכו' דסתרן אהדדי כדפרי' לעיל דף כז ע"א כצ"ל:

אשה שיצתה מלאה ובאה ריקנית, והביאה לפנינו שלשה שבועין טהורין, ועשרה שבועות אחד טמא ואחד טהור — משמשת לאור שלשים וחמש, ומטבילין אותה תשעים וחמש טבילות, דברי ב"ש. וב"ה אומרים: שלשים וחמש. *רבי יוסי בר' יהודה אומר: דיה לטבילה שתהא באחרונה. בשלמא שבוע ראשון לא משמשת — אימר: יולדת זכר היא, שבוע שני — אימר: יולדת נקבה היא, שבוע שלישי — אימר: יולדת נקבה בזוב היא, אלא שבוע רביעי — אע"ג דקא חזיא דם — תשמש, דהא דם טהור הוא! לאו משום דלא אזלינן בתר רובא? אלא מאי "לא ידענא מאי תיובתא"? אימר: הרחיקה לידתה. הך שבוע חמישי דטהור הוא, תשמש! הך שבוע רביעי, כל יומא ויומא מספקין בסוף לידה ובתחלת נדה. ועשרין ותמניא גופיה, אימר: תחלת נדה היא, ובעיא למיתב שבעה לנדתה. בעשרים וחד תשמש! רבי שמעון היא, דאמר: *אסור לעשות כן, שמא תבא לידי ספק. לאורתא תשמש! כשראתה בערב. "ומטבילין אותה תשעים וחמש טבילות". שבוע קמא מטבילין אותה בלילותא — אימר: יולדת זכר היא. שבוע שני מטבילין אותה (א) בלילותא — אימר: יולדת נקבה היא, בימאמא — אימר: יולדת זכר בזוב היא. שבוע שלישי מטבילין לה בימאמא — אימר: יולדת נקבה בזוב היא, בלילותא — ב"ש לטעמייהו, דאמרי: *טבולת יום ארוך בעי טבילה. מכדי

**אימר** הרחיקה לידתה. תימה: דרבי יוסי ברבי חנינא לא אסיק אדעתיה האי שינויא, וברייתא לא מפרש כלל בענין אחר. **ר"ש** היא. תימה: דכ"ש דאתיא כרבנן דאסרי בפ' בתרא (לקמן סז:) לשמש דאורייתא! ועוד קשה: דהכא משמע דר"ש לא אסר טבילה אלא תשמיש דוקא, ובפרק בתרא (שם סז:) משמע דאסורה לטבול! וי"ל: דטבילה, האמוראין אסרוה. ולקמן (שם ד"ה "אבל") נפרש בע"ה.

**כשראתה** מבערב. וא"ת: כיון דראתה מבערב, אמאי מטבילינן לה לב"ש בלילותא משום טבולת יום ארוך? וי"ל: דלאו דוקא מבערב, אלא כלומר בשעה או בחצי שעה בלילה, וטובלת בתחלת הלילה, ורואה מיד אחר הטבילה. ואם היתה באה לשמש קודם טבילה — הרשות בידה.

**בשבוע** קמא מטבילין לה בלילותא אימור יולדת זכר היא. זה האריכות אינו צריך אלא לב"ה, דלב"ש מטבילין לה כל פ' לילות משום טבולת יום ארוך. והאי שבוע קמא דלילותא אינו כמו שבועים דיממא, אלא ו' לילות משבוע קמא, וליל תחלת שבוע שניה. ושבוע שניה נמי, בלילותא היינו ו' לילות משבוע שניה, וליל תחלת שבוע שלישי. ושבוע שני ושלישי דיממא אינו כענין זה.

עשרים

האשה שיצאה מלאה וחזרה ריקנית. לסוף זמן מרובה, ואינה יודעת אימת יצא הריונה. והביאה לפנינו. כלומר: משבאה לפנינו ישבה לה שלשה שבועים טהורים מכל וכל, עם יום בואה. ולא דק כולי האי, דיום זה ספק טמא, דשמא ראתה בו ביום קודם שבאתה לפנינו, ואפ"ה קרי ליה "טהור", דקאי אמכאן ולהבא. דקס"ד השתא: שבאתה לפנינו ביום, ומשבאתה לפנינו — לא ראתה. ועשרה שבועים אחד טמא ואחד טהור. אחד טמא — שהיתה רואה בכל יום, ואחד טהור — שכל הימים של אותו שבוע היו טהורין. משמשת לאור שלשים וחמש. שהוא ליל סוף שבוע חמישי, והוא ליל כניסת שלשים וחמש ויציאת יום ל"ד ושוב אינה משמשת. וטעמא דכולן מפרש לקמן ואמאי נקט הכי י"ג שבועים. ומטבילין אותה צ"ה טבילות. משום דטבילה בזמנה מצוה. וכולהו מפרש לקמן. ומשום הני ל"ה טבילות נקט י"ג שבועים, דספק זמן הטבילות משוך י"א שבועים, ופלגא די"ב, ואיידי דצריך לפלגא נקט כולה. ואיידי דתנא "שבוע טמא", דהיינו י"ב, תנא נמי "שבוע י"ג טהור". והכי מפרש לקמיה. וב"ה סברי ל"ה. וטעמייהו מפרש לקמן. ותרוייהו סבירי להו: טבילה בזמנה מצוה. באחרונה. כשתפסוק לגמרי ותטהר, דלית ליה טבילה בזמנה מצוה. בשלמא שבוע ראשון כו'. השתא מפרש תיובתא. אימר יולדת זכר היא. וכל יומא ויומא דשבוע ראשון איכא לספוקי: דלמא ביום שבאתה ילדה שעה אחת קודם שבאה לפנינו, וכל שבעת הימים האלו הוו שבעת ימי לידה. שבוע ראשון. יומא דאתיא לקמן קחשיב בכלל שבוע ראשון. אימר יולדת נקבה היא. וביום שבאת לפנינו ילדה, ומשכי ימי לידה הנך תרתי שבועי. בזוב. שמא מתוך י"א יום דימי זיבה ילדה, וראתה ג' רצופין, ובלא צער דהוה שופי סמוך ללידה — ובעיא שבעה נקיים לזיבתה. ואע"ג דקא יתבה י"ד נקיים, הואיל ואיכא לספוקינהו בימי לידה — לא סלקא לה. דקסבר: ימי לידה שאינה רואה בהן — אין עולין לה לספירת זיבתה. אלא שבוע רביעי. אי אמרינן רוב נשים ולד מעליא ילדן, האי ולד הוא, שהרי הוחזקה עוברה. תשמש. ואע"ג דהך שבוע קא חזיא, שהרי ראשון הוא לשבועים שעוברים עליה אחד טמא ואחד טהור. האי דם טוהר הוא. דאכתי משכי מ' יום דזכר. לאו משום דלא אזלינן בתר רובא. ומספקינן לה בלא ולד ולית לה דם טוהר, וקשה לריב"ל. אימר הרחיקה לידתה. האי דלא יהבינן לה ימי טוהר, לאו משום ספק דלאו ולד הוא, אלא אימר: הרי ימים רבים קודם שבאת לפנינו ילדה, וכלו לה ימי טהרתה. אבל לענין קרבן מביאה קרבן ונאכל, בין קרבה ובין הרחיקה — בת קרבן היא, מאחר *דקפדינן ארובא. שבוע חמישי דטהור הוא תשמש (ב) כו'. ואמאי לא משמשת עד ליל שביעי? ומשנינן: שבוע רביעי. שראתה בכל יום, כל יומא איכא לספוקי לסוף לידה סוף ימי טוהר. כלומר, אתמול כלו ימי טוהר, והיום היא תחלת נדה. הילכך יום כ"ח, שהוא סוף שבוע רביעי, מספקינן לה בתחלת נדה. ובעיא למימני משבוע חמישי ששה ימים, להשלים שבעת ימי נדות. ובליל שביעי טובלת ומשמשת, שהוא אור לשלשים וחמש משבאת לפנינו. וליל שמיני, שהוא תחלת שבוע ששי, נמי לא משמשת — שהשבוע ששי טמא הוא, דמוקמינן לה לקמן שהיא רואה מבערב בכל ימי ראייתה. מכאן ואילך לא משמשת לעולם, דדילמא שבוע רביעי תחלת נדה היא, והששי בימי זיבה, והרי היא זבה. ושבוע שביעי שהוא טהור, תספור לנקיים. ואם לא שרואה מבערב, היתה משמשת ליל תחלת שבוע שמינית. ואע"ג דיכולה לטבול ביום שביעי, שמקצת היום ככולו לענין ספירה, אפ"ה לא משמשת ביום, דמוקמינן לה כר"ש דאסר. וכן לעולם י"ל בכל שבועים טמאים שלה: זהו בימי זיבה, וצריכה ז' נקיים. וכל שבוע טהור, תספור לנקיים. אבל שבוע רביעית — ממ"נ אין אתה יכול לספקו בזיבה, שאין זיבה אלא לאחר נדות, והרי זו ישבה ג' שבועים טהורים, והרביעי הוא דראתה. הילכך בתחלת נדה הוא דאיכא לספוקי, ולא בעיא למיתב בשבוע חמישי אלא ששה ימים משום ספק יום אחרון של רביעי, דמספקינן לה בתחלת נדה. בעשרים וחד. שהוא סוף שבוע שלישית תשמש. דהא אפי' קרבה לידתה ליל, בו ביום שבאת לפנינו — כבר כלו ימי טומאה, והיום שביעי לנקיים של ספירה. וקי"ל דטבילת זב וזבה ביום, בפ"ק דיומא (דף ו.) דמקצת היום ככולו. הילכך ביום כ"א תשמש. ר"ש היא דאמר. בת"כ: אסור לעשות כן, לשמש זבה ביום טבילתה. שמא תבא לידי ספק. שמא תראה לאחר תשמיש, ונמצא שסתרה כל מנייניה, דהא לא הוו נקיים כל שבעה, ונמצא משמשת זבה. לאורתא תשמש. בליל תחלת שבוע רביעית. דקס"ד השתא, שאינה רואה אלא ביום. ואף ע"ג דהאי שבוע רביעי טמא הוא, מיהו בליל תחלת שבוע אכתי טהורה היא, ותשמש הלילה. ומשני: כשראתה מבערב. וכן היא נוהגה לראות בכל שבוע טמא מבערב. בלילותא. בכל לילה ולילה. דבכל לילה מספקינן לה [שמא] השתא סוף שבעה ללידתה הוא, וטבילה בזמנה מצוה. אימר יולדת זכר בזוב היא. ויום ראשון דשבוע שני אמרינן: שמא *שבעת ימים קודם שבאת לפנינו ילדה, ושבוע ראשון הוה ספירה לנקיים, ולמחר ביום תחלת שבוע שני תהא טבילת זיבתה. וכן כל ימי שבוע שני, כל יומא ויומא איכא לספוקי: דלמא קלת משבוע ראשון הוי בכלל ימי לידה, והשתא כלין ימי הספירה. אבל שבוע ראשון לא טבלה ביום, ואף ע"ג דבכל יום איכא לספוקי שמא הרחיקה לידתה, והשתא כלין ימי הספירה. משום דבעינן שבעת ימי הנקיים לפנינו ודאין, והני דקודם לכן ספק הוו נקיים ספק לא הוו. והכי מפרש לקמן. ויום אחרון דשבוע קמא הוה בעיא טבילה, משום ספקא דהשתא כלין ימי הספירה ואיכא ז' ספורין לפנינו. ולקמן מתרצין: דטבילה חדא בשבוע לא קחשיב. בלילותא אימור יולדת נקבה הואי. וכל לילה איכא לספוקי: האידנא סוף שבועים, וליל אחרון מספקינן: שמא ביום שבאתה ילדה, והשתא כלין. שבוע שלישי מטבלינן לה בימאמא. אימר: יולדת נקבה בזוב היא, וכל יומא איכא לספוקי: השתא כלין ימי ספירה. יום ראשון — דלמא ששה ימים קודם שבאת לפנינו ילדה, ושבועים הרי עשרים יום, והיום הוי כ"א, שסוף ספירה הוא. ולמחר אמרי': ה' ימים קודם ביאתה ילדה, והיום כלים. ויום אחרון אימר: ביום שבאתה ילדה, והיום כלים. בלילותא. דשבוע שלישי מטבילין לה, ואף ע"ג דליכא לספוקי בשבוע שלישי בסוף לידת נקבה. ב"ש לטעמייהו. דאמרי בפ' אחרון (לקמן דף עא.): טבולת יום ארוך, דהיינו יולדת שהיא טבולת יום כל ששים וששה, שהרי לסוף שבועים היא טובלת, ואינה אוכלת בתרומה עד שיכלו ימי טוהר, כדכתיב: "בכל קדש לא תגע". וקאמרי ב"ש שצריכה לטבול לאור שמונים ואחד, שהוא סוף שמונים. הילכך כל ליליא איכא לספוקי: השתא כלים (עד) שמונים יום מיום שבאת לפנינו. ושבוע קמא נמי איכא לספוקי בהכי, אלא לא איכפת לן — משום דסוף סוף הא קא טבלה בכל ליליא.
מכדי

**אימור** הרחיקה לידתה. והיינו הא דאמרינן לעיל מאי לאו לא תיובותיה אלא סייעתיה משום דמשמע דאי ליתא דלר' יהושע לא הוה מחמירין בה כל אלו החומרות משום דהוי ספק ספיקא שמא רוח הפילה ואת"ל נפל הפילה אימור הרחיקה לידתה אע"ג דבלאו הכי איכא כמה ספיקות אימור זכר ואת"ל נקבה אימור לא ילדה בזוב ואת"ל ילדה נקבה בזוב אימור הרחיקה לידתה משמע אי ליתא לדר' יהושע ניתוספא עוד ספיקא אחרת ואימור לא ילדה כלל והוה לן למשרייה ומשני לא תיובתיה ולא סייעתיה דכיון דבלאו הכי איכא ספיקא טובא אפילו ניתוספא עוד ספיקא אחרת אסרינן לה ועי"ל מדאיצטריך לאשמועי' דלא משמשא בשבוע רביעי אע"ג דחזיא ביה א"כ חשיבא יולדת ודאי דאי ספק יולדת חשיבא ליה לא הוה צריך לאשמועינן דלא משמשת והיינו דקאמר מאי לאו לא תיובתיה אלא סייעתיה דמתוך שהקשה לו שבוע רביעי אע"ג דחזיא ביה דם תשמש אלמא הוי חדוש שאינה משמשת ברביעי ואי ספק יולדת חשבת ליה לא הוי שום חדוש ומשני לא תיובתיה ולא סייעתיה דלא אתא לאשמועינן הא דאינה משמשת ברביעי אלא (אומרי') [מילי] אחרינא דמחמרי בה אשמועינן: **ר"ש** הוא דאמר אבל אמרו חכמים כו'. תימה כ"ש רבנן היא דמשמע לקמן פ' בתרא דרבנן אסרי מדאורייתא לשמש וצ"ע לקמן. תי' דהכא משמע דתשמיש דוקא אמר ר' שמעון אבל טבילה שרי ביומא דז' ובפ' בתרא משמע דאסור לטבול ביומי דז' משום דר' שמעון וי"ל דאמוראי בתראי החמירו בטבילה: **בשראתה** מבערב. ותימה והלא טובלת בשבוע רביעי לב"ש בלילות משום ספיקת טבולת יום ארוך ואם היא רואה מבערב רואה היא א"כ כבר נדה היא ולמה תטבול וי"ל דדרכה לטבול מיד בתחלת הלילה והיא ראתה מיד אחר הטבילה קודם שתלך לישן: **בשבוע** קמא מטבילינן לה בלילות אימור יולדת זכר כו' ולא היה [צריך] כל זה משום ב"ש דמיד היא זקוקה לטבול משום טבולת יום ארוך אבל לב"ה איצטריך: אימור יולדת זכר בזוב הואי. אימור נקבה הוה סגיא אלא אפילו משום ספק זכר צריכה לטבול:

[לקמן ל. שבת קכח. יומא פח.]

[לקמן ל. סז:]

[לקמן עח:]

נ"ל דסמכינן

ס"א ששה

הגהות הב"ח

(א) גמ' שבוע שני מטבילין אותה בימאמא אימר יולדת זכר בזוב היא בלילותא כו' נקבה היא שבוע שלישי כו"ל: (ב) רש"י ד"ה שבוע חמישי דטהור הוא תשמש כוליה ומאי:

מכדי ימי טהרה כמה הוו – שתין ושיתא, דל שבוע ג' דאטבלינן לה – פשו להו שתין נכי חדא, שתין נכי חדא ותלתין וה' – תשעין וד' הויין, תשעין וחמש מאי עבידתייהו? אמר רב ירמיה מדפתי: כגון שבאת לפנינו בין השמשות, דיהבינן לה טבילה יתירתא. ולב"ה *דאמרי טבולת יום ארוך – לא בעי טבילה, ל"ה מאי עבידתייהו? עשרים ותמניא – כדאמרן, הך שבוע ה' מטבלינן כל ליליא ליליא, אימר סוף נדה היא. י' שבועין למה לי? בתמניא ופלגא סגי! איידי דתנא פלגא דשבוע – מסיק ליה, *ואיידי דתנא שבוע טמא – תנא נמי שבוע טהור. והאיכא טבילת זבה! דלפני תשמיש – קחשיב, דלאחר תשמיש – לא קחשיב. ולב"ש דחשיב דלאחר תשמיש – ניחשוב נמי טבילת זבה! בלידה – קמיירי, בזיבה – לא קמיירי. והאיכא יולדת בזוב! יולדת בזוב – קחשיב, זיבה גרידתא – לא קחשיב. שבועתא קמא דאתיא לקמן ליטבלה ביומא, דילמא כל יומא ויומא שלימו לה ספורים דידה! הא מני – *ר"ע היא, דאמר: בעינן ספורים בפנינו. סוף שבוע קמא ליטבלה! חד בשבוע לא קמיירי. יומא קמא דאתיא לקמן ליטבלה, דילמא שומרת יום כנגד יום היא! בזבה גדולה – קמיירי, בזבה קטנה – לא קמיירי. ש"מ תלת, ש"מ: ר"ע היא, דאמר: בעינן ספורים בפנינו. וש"מ: *ר"ש היא, דאמר: אבל אמרו חכמים אסור לעשות כן, שמא תבא לידי ספק. וש"מ: טבילה בזמנה מצוה. *ורבי יוסי בר' יהודה אומר: דיה לטבילה באחרונה, ולא אמרינן טבילה בזמנה מצוה.§

**מתני'** [א]המפלת ליום מ' – אינה חוששת לולד, *ליום מ"א – תשב לזכר ולנקבה ולנדה. *רבי ישמעאל אומר: יום מ"א – תשב לזכר ולנדה, יום פ"א – תשב לזכר ולנקבה ולנדה, שהזכר נגמר למ"א והנקבה לפ"א. וחכ"א: [ב]אחד בריית הזכר ואחד בריית הנקבה – זה וזה מ"א.§ **גמ'** למה הוזכר זכר? אי לימי טומאה – הא קתני נקבה, ואי לימי טהרה – הא

מכדי ימי טוהר כמה. משכה ספקא דידהו לבתר שבועים קמאי? שתין ושיתא. ושבועים – הרי פ'. ומהני ס"ו טבילות, כבר טבלה מהן ז' בלילי שבוע שלישי, משום הך ספקא דטבולת יום ארוך. דל הני ז' פשו להו שתין נכי חדא. שעדיין צריכה לטבול משום הך ספק בתוך י' שבועים הבאים, ול"ה שטבלה בתוך ג' השבועים הראשונים, שבעה בראשונה וכ"ח בשתים אחרונות – הרי ל"ה ושתין נכי חדא – הרי צ"ד. טבילה יתירתא. עד השתא הוה ס"ד. דבאת לפנינו ביום, כגון ביום ר"ח ניסן, ואטבלוה לאורתא. ומשכו פ' דילה ל' מניסן וכ"ט דאייר וכ"א דסיון כלים פ' יום – הרי פ' טבילות בלילות, וי"ד ביממים של ב' שבועות הראשונות – הרי צ"ד. והשתא מוקמינן שבאת לפנינו בין השמשות לילה שהוא ר"ח. ואטבלה בההיא ליליא משום ספק סוף טומאה, ומשכי נמי פ' שלה עד כ"א בסיון כאילו באתה ביום ראש חדש, דאיכא לספוקי דילמא באותו בין השמשות ילדה והוא מר"ח והאי טבילה דליל ראש חדש איתוספא לה. נמצאו לה ח' טבילות בשבוע ראשונה, וכ"ח דב' וג' – הרי ל"ו. וקשיא לי: אמאי נקט בין השמשות, ה"ל לאוקמא שבאת לפנינו בלילה? ומסתברא דלהכי נקט בין השמשות, דדק בלישנא דמתני' דנקט "ג' שבועים טהורים", הילכך כי איכא בין השמשות – איכא למיקרי יום זה טהור, דשמא בין השמשות יממא הוא, ומיום שעבר הוא, והיום הזה כולו טהור. ומיהו טבילותיה משכי עד שמונים לבד מהך, משום דבין השמשות ספק ליליא. ל"ה. דקאמרי ב"ה מאי עבידתייהו? ומשני: עשרין ותמניא הויין. כדאמר. י"ד ביממים וי"ד בלילות, וכולן משום ספק סוף ימי טומאה. והוא הדין דלב"ה הוו להו עשרין ותשע, דכיון דאוקמינן שבאה בין השמשות, איכא (א) ט"ו טבילות בלילה משום ספק בין השמשות. והאי דלא מותבינן ליה לקמיה, משום דאותבינן אחריתי, ומשנינן: חד בשבוע לא קמיירי, והך נמי חדא בשבוע היא. האי שבוע ה'. שאינה רואה בו כל יומא איכא לספוקי בסוף נדה ומטבלינן לה בכל לילות. דשבוע ד' ראתה בכל יום, ויום ראשון – דילמא תחלת נדה היא וטובלת לסוף שבעה שהוא ליל ראשון של שבוע ה', וליל שני נמי טבלה – דילמא יום ראשון של שבוע רביעי מימי טוהר הוא ויום ב' הואי תחלת נדה והאידנא הוי ליל טבילתה, וכן כולהו, והוו להו שבעה טבילות. והוא הדין נמי דכל לילות של שבועים טהורים איכא לספוקי סוף נדה משום שבוע טמא שלפניה, אלא ב"ה טבילות דלאחר ל"ה דהוא ליל תשמיש לא קחשיב. דכל טבילות דב"ה – קודם תשמיש נינהו, והכי אמר לקמן. בתמניא ופלגא סגיא. לבד הג' שבועות דטהורה, דהא כלין ימי טבילה בסוף שמונים, והוא באמצע שבוע תשיעי של י' שבועים. שבוע. תשיעי טמא הוא. טבילת זבה. דכל שבוע טמא איכא לספוקי בזיבה, לבד משבוע רביעי שאי אתה יכול לספקו בכך, כדפרישית לעיל, שאין זבה אלא לאחר נדות, וזו לא ראתה כלום עד הרביעי. וכל שבוע טהור איכא לספוקי בימי ספירת זיבתה, ובעיא למטבל ביום ז' של כל שבוע טהור. ר"ע. דפרק אחרון (לקמן דף סט.). סוף שבוע ראשון. ביום השביעי ליטבלה ביום, דילמא בין השמשות יום הוא, ויום ראשון שבאתה לפנינו טהור, ואיכא ז' ספורים לפנינו. וה"ה דהוה לן לאותובי לב"ה דליחשוב עוד טבילה יתירתא לטבילות הלילות של ספק לידה, הואיל ובין השמשות באתה, אלא האי שינויא גופיה אית ביה דחדא בשבוע לא קמיירי, הילכך לא פריך. **מתני'** המפלת. שליא. ליום מ'. לטבילתה. אינה חוששת לולד. שלא נגמר יצירתו עד שיכלו כל מ' יום. ולנדה. דילמא ליכא ולד. ובגמ' מפרש למה הוזכר זכר. תשב לזכר. ז' ימי טומאה, ואפילו בלידה יבשתא. אבל שבועים דנקבה ליכא לספוקי, כדקתני טעמא: שיצירת נקבה לפ"א. **גמ'** הא קתני נקבה. דה"ל שבועים, ויש בכלל מאתים מנה. אי לימי טוהר. להחמיר שלא יהא לה אלא ימי טוהר דזכר. הא

**עשרים** ותמניא כדאמרן. אף על גב דכ"ט הויין עם טבילה יתירתא דבין השמשות שבאתה לפנינו, פ"ה דההיא טבילה יתירתא דהויא חדא בשבוע לא קחשיב. ואין נראה, דהא ב"ש חשבי לה אלא ודאי לא חשיב טבילה יתירתא חדא בשבוע כיון שלא היתה בפנינו אלא עכשיו ונראה כמו שפי' רש"י בתשובתו דב"ה לא חשיב טבילה דליל תחלת שבוע ג' דכיון דתו לא מטבלינן א] להנדה לא מיקריא חדא בשבוע אבל לב"ש דמטבילין לה בלילות לא הוי חדא בשבוע.

**והאיכא** טבילת זבה. עדיפא הוה מצי למיפרך: דכל שבועים טהורים ניטבל לה בלילותא משום נדה, דהשתא לא פריך אלא חדא בשבוע. ונראה כגירסת ר"ח דגרים: "אי הכי כל שבועים טהורים נמי", והיינו הך פירכא (ב) דפריך, ומשני: דלפני תשמיש קחשיב. **יומא** קמא דאתיא לקמן נטבלה דילמא שומרת יום היא. וא"ת והא אמר דחד בשבוע לא קמיירי? וי"ל: דהשתא לא הויא חד בשבוע, דהא איכא נמי טבילה בסוף שבוע. ועוד: דמשום חששא דשומרת יום טובלת גם ביום שני, דשמא עכשיו ראתה כשבאת לפנינו. ועוד: מטעמא דשומרת יום נטבלה כל שבוע קמא, דכל יומא מספקא בסוף לידה, ולא סלקא לשימור, דאין ימי לידה עולים לימי ספירת זיבתה. ומיהו קשה: דהוה מצי למיפרך מכל שבוע, כדפרישית, ולא פריך אלא מיומא קמא.

**שמע** מינה תלת. הוה מצי למינקט: שמע מינה דימי לידה שאינה רואה בהן אין עולין לספירת זיבתה. אלא אר"ת: דפשיטא ליה להתלמוד שאין עולין, דקי"ל כאביי בסוף פרק "בנות כותים" (לקמן לז.) והוא למ"ד מיע"ל קג"ס. ולקמן נפרש בע"ה. ותימה: דהך ברייתא סברה דלב"ש וב"ה אין עולין, ובפרק "בנות כותים" (שם לה:) גבי פלוגתא דרב ולוי אי שתי מעיינות הן או מעיין אחד, איכא ברייתא דלב"ש ולב"ה עולין? וי"ל: דתרי תנאי (ג) הוא אליבייהו.

**ושמע** מינה טבילה בזמנה מצוה. – כך פסק ר"ת דהלכה כב"ש וב"ה. ותימה: דפשיטא דר' יוסי בר' יהודה יאמר דלא פליגי עליה ב"ש וב"ה ומעשים בכל יום שאין לך אשה טובלת בזמן טבילת נדה ולא בזמן טבילת שומרת יום כנגד יום וזבה. ובפ' בתרא (לקמן דף סז:) נמי אמר: מכדי האידנא כולהו ספק זבות שוינהו, ניטבלינהו ביממא דז' משמע: שלא היו טובלין ביום בשום פעס. *ורבינו אליהו הזקן שיסד באזהרות טבילה בזמנה על ד' גדילים כולו, יסד דלא כהילכתא. דה"נ יסד כר"א (סנהדרין דף מה.) דאמר: כל נסקלין נתלין, דדריש ריבוי ומיעוט, וקי"ל דדרשינן כללי ופרטי, דהא קיימא לן דקרקע אינה נגזלת. שומר

לקמן עא:
[יבמות ג. וש"נ]
[לקמן סט.]
[לעיל כט: לקמן סז:]
[שבת קכא: לעיל כט: יומא פח.]
[בכורות כא.]
[כריתות י.]
[וע"ע תוס' יומא ד"ה דכ"ע]

צ א מיי' פ"י מהל' איסורי ביאה הל"ב סמג לאוין קיא טוש"ע יו"ד סי' קצז סעי' ב:
צא ב מיי' שם הל"א:

### הגהות הב"ח

(א) רש"י ד"ה כדאמר י"ד וכו' איכא שמונה טבילות בלילה: (ב) תד"ה והאיכא כו' הך פירכא דפרישית ומשני: (ג) ד"ה שמע וכו' תנאי הוו אליבייהו:

### הגהות מהר"ב רנשבורג

א] תוד"ה עשרים ותמניא וכו' לא מטבלינן להנדה לא. תיבות להנדה לא ימחקו. וכ"ב לה לב"ש כל"ל:

### תוספי הרא"ש

**תשעים** וד' הוו. תימה דלקמן פריך דהוו טבילי יתרי והכא פריך (דס"ד) [דחסר] ליה: **יומא** קמא דאתיא לקמן נטבלה בימא דילמא שומרת יום כנגד יום היא. ולא מצי לשנויי חדא בשבוע לא קא מיירי דהשתא הוי תרי בשבוע חד בתחלת שבוע וחד בסוף שבוע. ועוד שגם יום שני צריכה טבילה משום חששא זו דשמא עכשיו ראתה כשבאתה ועוד דמטעם שומרת יום צריכה לטבול שבוע קמא בכל יום דבכל יומא מספקינן לה שמא עכשיו שלמי שבוע לזכר וספירה דובה קטנה. ומיהו תימה הוא אם היה יכול להקשות בכל יום ולא הקשה אלא מיומא קמא וגם בשבוע שני צריכה לטבול בכל יום משום חששא זו: **ש"מ** תלת. מדלא קאמר ש"מ דיומי לידה שאינה רואה בהן אין עולין לה לספירתה מדקדק ר"ת דפשוט היה לתלמוד ולא חש לומר ש"מ אע"ג דבסוף בנות כותים פליגי אביי ורבא. וקאמר רבא דעולין אין הלכה בהא כרבא אלא כאביי והיינו למ"ד דיע"ל קג"מ. ותימה דהא ברייתא סוברת דלב"ש ולב"ה אין עולין ולקמן בפ' בנות כותים גבי פלוגתא דרב ולוי שני מעיינות הן או מעין אחד הוא משני ההיא ברייתא דקתני יולדת בזוב ששפרה ולא טבלה הלכו ב"ש לשיטתן וב"ה לשיטתן דקסברי ימי לידה שאינה רואה בהן עולין לספירת זיבתה צ"ל דתרי תנאי נינהו אליבא דב"ש וב"ה: ה"מ ר' עקיבא היא אין הלכה כמותו בזה דלעיל פסקינן הלכה כר' אליעזר בארבע: וש"מ דטבילה בזמנה מצוה. אין הלכה כן אלא כר' יוסי בר' יהודה דאמר לאו מצוה וכן מעשים בכל יום שאין לך אשה טובלת בזמנה טבילה של נדה ושל זבה ושל שומרת יום. ולקמן בפ' בתרא נמי אמרינן מכדי האידנא כולהו ספק זיבות נינהו נטבול בימא דשמבעה משמע שלא היו טובלות בשום פעם ביום ור"ח פסק דהלכה כב"ש וב"ה דאמרי טבילה בזמנה מצוה ואינה ראיה דפשיטא דר' יוסי בר יהודה לא פליג עלייהו אלא סבר לא נחלקו ב"ש וב"ה בדבר זה: **ולמה** הוזכר זכר. תימה דלא פריך ארישא דאין ידוע אם ולד הוא וצ"ל דנטר עד סיפא ופריך אתרוייהו:

הָא קָתָנֵי נִדָּה! [א]שֶׁאִם תִּרְאֶה יוֹם ל"ד וְתַחֲזוֹר וְתִרְאֶה יוֹם מ' וְאֶחָד – תְּהֵא מְקוּלְקֶלֶת עַד מ"ח. [ב]וְכֵן לְעִנְיַן נְקֵבָה, שֶׁאִם תִּרְאֶה יוֹם ע"ד וְתַחֲזוֹר וְתִרְאֶה יוֹם פ"א תְּהֵא מְקוּלְקֶלֶת עַד פ"ח.§ "רַבִּי יִשְׁמָעֵאל אוֹמֵר יוֹם מ"א תֵּשֵׁב לְזָכָר וּלְנִדָּה" כו'.§ תַּנְיָא, רַבִּי יִשְׁמָעֵאל אוֹמֵר: טִימֵּא וְטִיהֵר בְּזָכָר, וְטִימֵּא וְטִיהֵר בִּנְקֵבָה, מַה כְּשֶׁטִּימֵּא וְטִיהֵר בְּזָכָר – יְצִירָתוֹ כַּיּוֹצֵא בּוֹ, אַף כְּשֶׁטִּימֵּא וְטִיהֵר בִּנְקֵבָה – יְצִירָתָהּ כַּיּוֹצֵא בָּהּ. אָמְרוּ לוֹ: אֵין לְמֵדִין יְצִירָה מִטּוּמְאָה. אָמְרוּ לוֹ לְר' יִשְׁמָעֵאל: מַעֲשֶׂה בְּקְלֵיאוֹפַּטְרָא מַלְכַּת אֲלֶכְּסַנְדְּרוֹס שֶׁנִּתְחַיְּיבוּ שִׁפְחוֹתֶיהָ הֲרִיגָה לַמַּלְכוּת, וּבְדָקָן וּמְצָאָן זֶה וָזֶה לְמ"א! אָמַר לָהֶן: אֲנִי מֵבִיא לָכֶם רְאָיָה מִן הַתּוֹרָה, וְאַתֶּם מְבִיאִין לִי רְאָיָה מִן הַשּׁוֹטִים?! מַאי רְאָיָה מִן הַתּוֹרָה? אִילֵימָא "טִימֵּא וְטִיהֵר בְּזָכָר וְטִימֵּא וְטִיהֵר בִּנְקֵבָה" כו' – הָא קָאָמְרִי לֵיהּ: אֵין דָּנִין יְצִירָה מִטּוּמְאָה! אָמַר קְרָא "תֵּלֵד" – הוֹסִיף לָהּ הַכָּתוּב לֵידָה אַחֶרֶת בִּנְקֵבָה. וּמַאי "רְאָיָה מִן הַשּׁוֹטִים"? אֵימַר: נְקֵבָה קָדֵים וְאִיעַבּוּר אַרְבְּעִין יוֹמִין קַמֵּי זָכָר. וְרַבָּנַן – סַמָּא דְּנַפְצָא אַשְׁקִינְהוּ. וְר' יִשְׁמָעֵאל – אִיכָּא גּוּפָא דְּלָא מְקַבֵּל סַמָּא. *אָמַר לָהֶם ר' יִשְׁמָעֵאל: מַעֲשֶׂה בְּקְלַפַּטְרָא מַלְכַּת יְוָונִית שֶׁנִּתְחַיְּיבוּ שִׁפְחוֹתֶיהָ הֲרִיגָה לַמַּלְכוּת, וּבְדָקָן וּמְצָאָן זָכָר לְאַרְבָּעִים וְאֶחָד, וּנְקֵבָה לְפ"א! אָמְרוּ לוֹ: *אֵין מְבִיאִין רְאָיָה מִן הַשּׁוֹטִים? מַאי טַעְמָא? הַךְ דִּנְקֵבָה (א) אִיעַתְּרָה אַרְבְּעִין יוֹמִין, וַהֲדַר אִיעַבַּר. וְרַבִּי יִשְׁמָעֵאל – לְשׁוֹמֵר מָסְרִינְהוּ, וְרַבָּנַן *אֵין אַפּוֹטְרוֹפּוֹס לַעֲרָיוֹת, אֵימָא שׁוֹמֵר גּוּפֵיהּ בָּא עָלֶיהָ. וְדִילְמָא אִי קְרָעוּהוּ לְהַךְ דִּנְקֵבָה בְּאַרְבְּעִין וְחַד הֲוָה מִשְׁתַּכְחָא כְּזָכָר? אָמַר אַבַּיֵי: בְּסִימָנֵיהוֹן שָׁוִין.§ "וַחֲכ"א: אֶחָד בְּרִיַּית זָכָר וְאֶחָד בְּרִיַּית נְקֵבָה" וכו'.§ חֲכָמִים הַיְינוּ ת"ק! וְכִי תֵּימָא: *לְמִסְתְּמָא רֵישָׁא כְּרַבָּנַן, וְיָחִיד וְרַבִּים *הֲלָכָה כְּרַבִּים, פְּשִׁיטָא! מַהוּ דְּתֵימָא: מִסְתַּבְּרָא טַעְמָא דְּרַבִּי יִשְׁמָעֵאל, דְּקָמְסַיֵּיעַ לֵיהּ קְרָאֵי, קמ"ל. דָּרַשׁ רַבִּי שַׂמְלַאי: לְמָה הַוָּלָד דּוֹמֶה בִּמְעֵי אִמּוֹ – לְפִנְקָס שֶׁמְּקוּפָּל וּמוּנָּח. יָדָיו עַל שְׁתֵּי צְדָעָיו, שְׁתֵּי אַצִּילָיו עַל ב' אַרְכּוּבוֹתָיו, וּב' עֲקֵבָיו עַל ב' עַגְבוֹתָיו, וְרֹאשׁוֹ מוּנָּח לוֹ בֵּין בִּרְכָּיו, וּפִיו סָתוּם וְטַבּוּרוֹ פָּתוּחַ, וְאוֹכֵל מִמַּה שֶּׁאִמּוֹ אוֹכֶלֶת, וְשׁוֹתֶה מִמַּה שֶּׁאִמּוֹ שׁוֹתָה, וְאֵינוֹ מוֹצִיא רְעִי שֶׁמָּא יַהֲרוֹג אֶת אִמּוֹ. *וְכֵיוָן שֶׁיָּצָא לַאֲוִיר הָעוֹלָם – נִפְתַּח הַסָּתוּם וְנִסְתַּם הַפָּתוּחַ, שֶׁאִלְמָלֵא כֵּן אֵינוֹ יָכוֹל לִחְיוֹת אֲפִילּוּ שָׁעָה אַחַת. וְנֵר דָּלוּק לוֹ עַל רֹאשׁוֹ וְצוֹפֶה וּמַבִּיט מִסּוֹף הָעוֹלָם וְעַד סוֹפוֹ, שֶׁנֶּאֱמַר: °"בְּהִלּוֹ נֵרוֹ עֲלֵי רֹאשִׁי לְאוֹרוֹ אֵלֶךְ חֹשֶׁךְ". וְאַל תִּתְמַהּ, שֶׁהֲרֵי אָדָם יָשֵׁן כָּאן וְרוֹאֶה חֲלוֹם בְּאַסְפַּמְיָא. וְאֵין לְךָ יָמִים שֶׁאָדָם שָׁרוּי בְּטוֹבָה יוֹתֵר מֵאוֹתָן הַיָּמִים, שֶׁנֶּאֱמַר: °"מִי יִתְּנֵנִי כְיַרְחֵי קֶדֶם כִּימֵי אֱלוֹהַּ יִשְׁמְרֵנִי", וְאֵיזֶהוּ יָמִים שֶׁיֵּשׁ בָּהֶם יְרָחִים וְאֵין בָּהֶם שָׁנִים – הֱוֵי אוֹמֵר: אֵלּוּ יַרְחֵי לֵידָה. וּמְלַמְּדִין אוֹתוֹ כָּל הַתּוֹרָה כּוּלָּהּ, שֶׁנֶּאֱמַר: °"וַיֹּרֵנִי וַיֹּאמֶר לִי יִתְמָךְ דְּבָרַי לִבֶּךָ שְׁמֹר מִצְוֹתַי וֶחְיֵה", וְאוֹמֵר: °"בְּסוֹד אֱלוֹהַּ עֲלֵי אָהֳלִי". מַאי "וְאוֹמֵר"? וְכִי תֵּימָא נָבִיא הוּא דְּקָאָמַר – ת"ש: "בְּסוֹד אֱלוֹהַּ עֲלֵי אָהֳלִי". וְכֵיוָן שֶׁבָּא לַאֲוִיר הָעוֹלָם – בָּא מַלְאָךְ וְסְטָרוֹ עַל פִּיו, וּמְשַׁכְּחוֹ כָּל הַתּוֹרָה כּוּלָּהּ, שֶׁנֶּאֱמַר: °"לַפֶּתַח חַטָּאת רוֹבֵץ". וְאֵינוֹ יוֹצֵא מִשָּׁם עַד שֶׁמַּשְׁבִּיעִין אוֹתוֹ, שֶׁנֶּאֱמַר: °"כִּי לִי תִּכְרַע כָּל בֶּרֶךְ תִּשָּׁבַע כָּל לָשׁוֹן", "כִּי לִי תִּכְרַע כָּל בֶּרֶךְ" – זֶה יוֹם הַמִּיתָה, שֶׁנֶּאֱמַר: °"לְפָנָיו יִכְרְעוּ כָּל יוֹרְדֵי עָפָר", "תִּשָּׁבַע כָּל לָשׁוֹן" – זֶה יוֹם הַלֵּידָה, שֶׁנֶּאֱמַר: °"נְקִי כַפַּיִם וּבַר לֵבָב אֲשֶׁר לֹא נָשָׂא לַשָּׁוְא נַפְשִׁי וְלֹא נִשְׁבַּע לְמִרְמָה", וּמַה הִיא הַשְּׁבוּעָה שֶׁמַּשְׁבִּיעִין אוֹתוֹ – תְּהִי צַדִּיק וְאַל תְּהִי רָשָׁע, וַאֲפִילּוּ כָּל הָעוֹלָם כּוּלּוֹ אוֹמְרִים לְךָ צַדִּיק אַתָּה – הֱיֵה בְּעֵינֶיךָ כְּרָשָׁע. [א] וֶהֱוֵי יוֹדֵעַ שֶׁהקב"ה טָהוֹר וּמְשָׁרְתָיו טְהוֹרִים, וּנְשָׁמָה שֶׁנָּתַן בְּךָ טְהוֹרָה הִיא, אִם אַתָּה מְשַׁמְּרָהּ בְּטָהֳרָה – מוּטָב, וְאִם לָאו – הֲרֵינִי נוֹטְלָהּ מִמְּךָ. תָּנָא דְּבֵי ר' יִשְׁמָעֵאל: מָשָׁל לְכֹהֵן שֶׁמָּסַר תְּרוּמָה לְעַם הָאָרֶץ, וְאָמַר לוֹ: אִם אַתָּה מְשַׁמְּרָהּ בְּטָהֳרָה – מוּטָב, וְאִם לָאו – הֲרֵינִי שׂוֹרְפָהּ לְפָנֶיךָ. א"ר אֶלְעָזָר: מַאי

---

**שומר** גופיה בא עליה. ואפילו היה סריס או אשה, אפשר שהניח אחרים לבא. *וכי **תימא** למיסתמא כרבנן. ואע"ג דרישא נמי סתמא קתני – לא חשיב סתמא, כיון דפליג עליה רבי ישמעאל, והוי אדרבה סתם ואח"כ מחלוקת, כדאמרינן ב"החולץ" (יבמות מב:).

**שני** אציליו על שני ארכובותיו. פ"ה איישילי"ש. ור"ת פירש: דאציל היינו קוד"א. דאמר בפ' "האומר משקלי" (ערכין יט:) משקל ידי עלי, משקל רגלי עלי כו' ומכניס ידו עד האציל, ורגלו עד הארכובה. וקוד"א ביד הוא, כנגד הארכובה ברגל. ועוד: דהתם משמע דאציל הוא מרפק, ובאהלות (פ"א מ"ח) משמע שמנה לפי סדרי אברי האדם, דמרפק היינו קוד"א. ועוד אמר בפ"ב דזבחים (דף יח:) "לא יחגרו ביזע" – שאין חוגרין אלא כנגד אצילי ידיהם, והיינו כנגד הקוד"א, שדרך העולם לחגור. ובבית השחי, אדרבה שם הוא מקום זיעה*.

*) **שתום** העין. "שתום" הוא לשון גילוי ופתיחה, כדמתרגם: "דשפיר חזי". וכן בלשון משנה במסכת ע"ז (דף סט,) הוי לשון פתיחה: כדי שישתום ויסתום ויגוב. והכא דייק שנסתמה עינו, מדכתיב "שתום העין" לשון יחיד. והא דכתיב (במדבר כד) "וגלוי עינים" – היינו לפי מה שהיה בתחלה.

*) שייך לדף לא

---

הָא קָתָנֵי נִדָּה. דְּכָל דָּמִים שֶׁתִּרְאֶה טְמֵאִים! וּמְשַׁנֵּי: לְכָךְ הוּזְכַּר זָכָר – שֶׁאִם תִּרְאֶה לְיוֹם ל"ד וְתַחֲזוֹר וְתִרְאֶה לְיוֹם מ"א, תְּהֵא מְקוּלְקֶלֶת עַד מ"ח. שֶׁכְּשֶׁרָאֲתָה לְיוֹם ל"ד לְלֵידָתָהּ, אָמְרִינַן: טְמֵאָה. אע"ג דְּאַכַּתִּי מָשְׁכִי יְמֵי טוֹהַר, דְּזָכָר מְסַפְּקִינַן לָהּ דִּלְאו וָלָד, וְתֵשֵׁב לְנִדָּה. וְכִי הֲדַר חָזְיָא לְיוֹם מ"א שֶׁהוּא ח' לִרְאִיָּיתָהּ, וְתִרְאֶה לִהְיוֹת שׁוֹמֶרֶת יוֹם כְּנֶגֶד יוֹם, אָמְרִינַן: וָלָד הָיָה, וְזָכָר הָיָה, וּרְאִיָּיה דְּיוֹם ל"ד – דַּם טוֹהַר הִיא, וְהַשְׁתָּא הוּא דְּהָוְיָא תְּחִלַּת נִדָּה. וְהַשְׁתָּא מְקַלְקְלִינַן לָהּ, דְּלָא טָבְלָה עַד מ"ח, שֶׁהוּא ח' לִרְאִיָּיה אַחֲרוֹנָה. וְאִי לָאו מִשּׁוּם סְפֵקָא דְּזָכָר, הֲוָה טָבְלָה לְמָחָר לְיוֹם מ"ב, מִמ"נ: אִי לָאו וָלָד הוּא – הֲרֵי שׁוֹמֶרֶת יוֹם כְּנֶגֶד יוֹם הִיא, וְאִי וָלָד הוּא וּנְקֵבָה הִיא – אַכַּתִּי הֲוָה דַּם טוֹהַר עַד שְׁמוֹנִים. וּסְפֵקָא דְּזָכָר מְקַלְקְלָא לָהּ. וְכֵן לְעִנְיַן נְקֵבָה. כְּלוֹמַר, וּסְפֵקָא דִּנְקֵבָה נַמִּי מְקַלְקְלָא לָהּ הַאי קִלְקוּלָא. עַד פ"ח. דְּלָא טָבְלָה עַד פ"ח. דְּאִי הֲוָה פְּשִׁיטָא לָן דְּלָאו וָלָד הוּא – הֲוַאי טָבְלָה לְמָחָר, בְּיוֹם פ"ב. דִּרְאִיַּית פ"א בְּאַחַד עָשָׂר יוֹם שֶׁבֵּין נִדָּה לְנִדָּה הִיא. וּמִשּׁוּם דִּמְסַפְּקָא לָן דִּילְמָא וָלָד הֲוָה, וּרְאִיָּיה דְּיוֹם ע"ד דַּם טָהוֹר הֲוָה, וְהַשְׁתָּא הָוְיָא תְּחִלַּת נִדָּה – לָא טָבְלָה עַד פ"ח. **טִימֵּא** וְטִיהֵר בְּזָכָר. מ' יוֹם בֵּין שְׁתֵּיהֶן, ז' לְטוּמְאָה וְל"ג יוֹם לִימֵי טוֹהַר. נִתְחַיְּיבוּ הֲרִיגָה. וּמִתּוֹךְ שֶׁעוֹמְדוֹת לֵיהָרֵג, נִיסּוּ בָּהֶם וְיִחֲדוּם לְבִיאָה. וְקָרְעוּ שְׁתֵּיהֶם לְסוֹף מ', וְנִמְצָא אֶחָד זָכָר וְאֶחָד נְקֵבָה. תֵּלֵד. דְּ"אִם נְקֵבָה תֵּלֵד" (ויקרא יב) קְרָא יְתֵירָא הוּא, דְּמָצֵי לְמִכְתַּב "וְאִם נְקֵבָה וְטָמְאָה שְׁבוּעַיִם", דְּהָא כְּתִיב לְעֵיל "וְיָלְדָה זָכָר". מִקַּמֵּי זָכָר. וְאַף ע"ג שֶׁיִּחֲדוּם לִבְעוֹל בְּיוֹם אֶחָד, שֶׁמָּא מְעוּבֶּרֶת הָיְתָה קוֹדֶם לָכֵן. סַמָּא **דְּנַפְצָא**. סַם שֶׁמַּפֶּלֶת בּוֹ וּמְנַפְּלָא כָּל זֶרַע שֶׁבַּמֵּעַיִם קוֹדֶם לָכֵן. לְשׁוֹמֵר מָסְרִינְהוּ. שֶׁלֹּא בָּא אָדָם עֲלֵיהֶן אֶלָּא אוֹתוֹ הַיּוֹם. **וְדִילְמָא** אִי קְרָעוּהָ כו'. לְרַבִּי יִשְׁמָעֵאל פָּרֵיךְ: נְהִי נַמִּי דִּלְשׁוֹמֵר מָסְרִינְהוּ, אֶפָּ"ה מְנָלַן שֶׁלֹּא נוֹצְרָה נְקֵבָה עַד פ"א, דִּילְמָא אִי קְרָעוּהָ לְהַךְ לְיוֹם מ"א הֲוָה מִשְׁתַּכְחָא? בְּסִימָנֵיהוֹן שָׁוִין. נְקֵבָה שֶׁנִּמְצֵאת לְיוֹם פ"א לֹא הָיוּ אֵבָרֶיהָ וּשְׂעָרָהּ וְצִפּוֹרְנֶיהָ אֶלָּא כְּשִׁיעוּר שֶׁל זָכָר לְיוֹם מ"א. הַיְינוּ ת"ק. דְּתָנָא לְעֵיל: "לְיוֹם מ"א – תֵּשֵׁב לְזָכָר וְלִנְקֵבָה וּלְנִדָּה", אַלְמָא בְּרִיַּית נְקֵבָה לְיוֹם מ"א. וְכִי תֵּימָא **רֵישָׁא**. לְהָכִי תְּנָא לֵיהּ: לְאַשְׁמוּעִינַן סְתָמָא דְּמַתְנִיתִין כְּרַבָּנַן, וְנִשְׁמַע מִינָּהּ דְּהִלְכְתָא כְּוָותַיְיהוּ. וְלָא נְהִירָא לִי גִּירְסָא וּפֵירוּשָׁהּ: דְּה"ל "סְתָם וְאַח"כ מַחֲלוֹקֶת", וְאֵין הֲלָכָה כִּסְתָם! וְנ"ל דְּהָכִי גָּרַס: "וְכִי תֵּימָא לְמִסְתְּמָא כְּרַבָּנַן, וְיָחִיד וְרַבִּים הֲלָכָה כְּרַבִּים – פְּשִׁיטָא! מַהוּ דְּתֵימָא" כו'. וְהָכִי פֵּירוּשָׁהּ: וְכִי תֵּימָא תָּנָא הַךְ סֵיפָא, לְאַשְׁמְעִינַן דִּסְתָמָא דִּלְעֵיל סְתָמָא דְּרַבָּנַן הִיא, וְיָחִיד וְרַבִּים הֲלָכָה כְּרַבִּים – פְּשִׁיטָא דִּסְתָמָא דְּרַבִּים הִיא, הוֹאִיל וּסְתָמָא, תָּנְיֵיהּ רַבִּי, וְלָא אַשְׁכַּחַן יְחִידָאָה דְּאָמַר הָכִי, דְּנֵימָא: פְּלוֹנִי הִיא. מַהוּ **דְּתֵימָא** כו'. קָמַשְׁמַע לָן מִדְּמַהְדַּר רַבִּי וּשְׁנָאָהּ בִּלְשׁוֹן חֲכָמִים, שְׁמַע מִינָּהּ דַּהֲלָכָה כִּסְתָם רִאשׁוֹן, וְאַף עַל פִּי שֶׁמַּחֲלוֹקֶת ר' יִשְׁמָעֵאל בְּלְּדוֹ. **פִּנְקָס**. לוּחִין שֶׁכּוֹתְבִין בָּהֶן הַגַּלָּחִים. **אַצִּילָיו**. *איישיל"ש. **נִפְתָּח הַסָּתוּם**. פִּיו. **וְנִסְתַּם הַפָּתוּחַ**. טַבּוּר. **שֶׁמָּא יַהֲרוֹג אֶת אִמּוֹ**. שֶׁבֵּית הָרֶחֶם אֵינוֹ רָחָב לְהוֹצִיא רְעִי הַנֶּאֱסָף בּוֹ. ת"ש **בְּסוֹד אֱלוֹהַּ עֲלֵי אָהֳלִי**. וְהָא אוֹקְמֵיהּ בְּיַרְחֵי לֵידָה, מִדִּכְתִיב: "כְּיַרְחֵי קֶדֶם". **וְלֹא נִשְׁבַּע לְמִרְמָה**. שֶׁקִּיֵּים שְׁבוּעָתוֹ לִשְׁמוֹר אֶת הַתּוֹרָה. דְּאִי בִּשְׁבוּעָה בְּעָלְמָא – הַאי מִשּׁוּם דְּ"לֹא נִשְׁבַּע לְמִרְמָה", חָשֵׁיב לְהוּ בְּעוֹלִין בְּהַר ה'? מַאי

---

תורה אור

לפי התוס' היו גורסין גירסא אחרת בגמ' וה"ג וכ"ת למסתמא כרבנן פשיטא יחיד ורבים הלכה כרבים וע' מהר"מ

**צב** א ב מיי' פ"י מהל' איסורי ביאה הל' כא:

[ויתר ביאור בתוס' מנחות לז. ד"ה קיבורת ותוס' חולין קו: ד"ה אמר רב וע' תוס' שבת לב. ד"ה במרפקו ותוס' ערכין יט. ד"ה במרפקו]

[תוספתא פ"ד]

[שבת קד: חולין מט:]

[חולין יא: כתובות יג:]

[לקמן מט. ע"ש הגי' אחרת וע' בפירש"י דהכא]

[ברכות ט. וש"נ]

יבמות עח:

### תוספי הרא"ש

**שומר** גופיה בא עליהן. ואם הוה אשה או סריס אפשר שהניח אחרים לבא עליהם: **וכ"ת** למיסתמא. אע"ג דברישא נמי קתני סתמא לא חשיב סתמא דהא קא פליג עליה ר' (שמעון) [ישמעאל] והוי סתם ואח"כ מחלוקת כדמוכח בפרק (הערל) [החולץ] (יבמות דף מב):

### הגהות הב"ח

(א) גמ' הך דנקבה איתרא ארבעין יומין:

### גליון הש"ס

**גמ'** וכ"ת למסתמא. עי' מנחו' יב ע"א תד"ה וחכ"א:

### הגהות מהר"ב רנשבורג

א] גמ' והוי ודע שהקב"ה טהור. נ"ב עיין דרשת מהרא"ח דף מה ע"ב:

פי' תחת זרועותיו רש"ל

מַאי קְרָא? °"מִמְּעֵי אִמִּי אַתָּה גוֹזִי". מַאי מַשְׁמַע דְּהַאי "גּוֹזִי" לִישָּׁנָא דְּאִשְׁתַּבּוּעֵי הוּא? דִּכְתִיב: °"גָּזִּי נִזְרֵךְ וְהַשְׁלִיכִי". וְאָמַר רַבִּי אֶלְעָזָר: לְמָה וָלָד דּוֹמֶה בִּמְעֵי אִמּוֹ? לֶאֱגוֹז מוּנָּח בְּסֵפֶל שֶׁל מַיִם, אָדָם נוֹתֵן אֶצְבָּעוֹ עָלָיו – שׁוֹקֵעַ לְכָאן וּלְכָאן. תָּנוּ רַבָּנַן: שְׁלֹשָׁה חֳדָשִׁים הָרִאשׁוֹנִים – וָלָד דָּר בַּמָּדוֹר הַתַּחְתּוֹן, אֶמְצָעִיִּים – וָלָד דָּר בַּמָּדוֹר הָאֶמְצָעִי, אַחֲרוֹנִים – וָלָד דָּר בַּמָּדוֹר הָעֶלְיוֹן. וְכֵיוָן שֶׁהִגִּיעַ זְמַנּוֹ לָצֵאת – מִתְהַפֵּךְ וְיוֹצֵא, וְזֶהוּ חֶבְלֵי אִשָּׁה. וְהַיְינוּ *דִּתְנַן: חֶבְלֵי שֶׁל נְקֵבָה מְרוּבִּין מִשֶּׁל זָכָר. וְאָמַר רַבִּי אֶלְעָזָר: מַאי קְרָא? °"אֲשֶׁר עֻשֵּׂיתִי בַסֵּתֶר רֻקַּמְתִּי בְּתַחְתִּיּוֹת אָרֶץ". "דַּרְתִּי" לֹא נֶאֱמַר, אֶלָּא "רֻקַּמְתִּי", מַאי שְׁנָא? חֶבְלֵי נְקֵבָה מְרוּבִּין מִשֶּׁל זָכָר. זֶה בָּא כְּדֶרֶךְ תַּשְׁמִישׁוֹ וְזֶה בָּא כְּדֶרֶךְ תַּשְׁמִישׁוֹ, זוֹ הוֹפֶכֶת פָּנֶיהָ וְזֶה אֵין הוֹפֵךְ פָּנָיו. תָּנוּ רַבָּנַן: שְׁלֹשָׁה חֳדָשִׁים הָרִאשׁוֹנִים – תַּשְׁמִישׁ קָשֶׁה לָאִשָּׁה וְגַם קָשֶׁה לַוָּלָד, אֶמְצָעִיִּים – קָשֶׁה לָאִשָּׁה וְיָפֶה לַוָּלָד, אַחֲרוֹנִים – יָפֶה לָאִשָּׁה וְיָפֶה לַוָּלָד, שֶׁמִּתּוֹךְ כָּךְ נִמְצָא הַוָּלָד מְלוּבָּן וּמְזוֹרָז. תָּנָא: הַמְשַׁמֵּשׁ מִטָּתוֹ לְיוֹם תִּשְׁעִים – כְּאִילּוּ שׁוֹפֵךְ דָּמִים. מְנָא יָדַע? אֶלָּא אָמַר אַבָּיֵי: ◦מְשַׁמֵּשׁ וְהוֹלֵךְ, °וְ"שׁוֹמֵר פְּתָאִים ה'". תָּנוּ רַבָּנַן: *שְׁלֹשָׁה שׁוּתָּפִין יֵשׁ בָּאָדָם, הקב"ה וְאָבִיו וְאִמּוֹ. אָבִיו – מַזְרִיעַ הַלּוֹבֶן, שֶׁמִּמֶּנּוּ עֲצָמוֹת וְגִידִים וְצִפָּרְנַיִם וּמוֹחַ שֶׁבְּרֹאשׁוֹ וְלוֹבֶן שֶׁבָּעַיִן. אִמּוֹ – מַזְרַעַת אוֹדֶם, שֶׁמִּמֶּנּוּ *עוֹר וּבָשָׂר [א] וּשְׂעָרוֹת וְשָׁחוֹר שֶׁבָּעַיִן. וְהקב"ה נוֹתֵן בּוֹ רוּחַ וּנְשָׁמָה *וּקְלַסְתֵּר פָּנִים וּרְאִיַּית הָעַיִן וּשְׁמִיעַת הָאוֹזֶן וְדִבּוּר פֶּה וְהִלּוּךְ רַגְלַיִם *וּבִינָה וְהַשְׂכֵּל. וְכֵיוָן שֶׁהִגִּיעַ זְמַנּוֹ לְהִפָּטֵר מִן הָעוֹלָם, הקב"ה נוֹטֵל חֶלְקוֹ, וְחֵלֶק אָבִיו וְאִמּוֹ מַנִּיחַ לִפְנֵיהֶם. אָמַר רַב פַּפָּא: הַיְינוּ דְּאָמְרִי אֱינָשֵׁי "פּוּץ מִילְחָא, וּשְׁדִי בִּשְׂרָא לְכַלְבָּא". דָּרַשׁ רַב חִינָּנָא בַּר פַּפָּא: מַאי דִּכְתִיב °"עוֹשֶׂה גְדוֹלוֹת עַד אֵין חֵקֶר וְנִפְלָאוֹת עַד אֵין מִסְפָּר" – בֹּא וּרְאֵה שֶׁלֹּא כְּמִדַּת הקב"ה מִדַּת בָּשָׂר וָדָם. מִדַּת בָּשָׂר וָדָם – נוֹתֵן חֵפֶץ בְּחֵמֶת צְרוּרָה וּפִיהָ לְמַעְלָה, סָפֵק מִשְׁתַּמֵּר, סָפֵק אֵין מִשְׁתַּמֵּר. וְאִילּוּ הקב"ה – צָר הָעוּבָּר בִּמְעֵי אִשָּׁה פְּתוּחָה, וּפִיהָ לְמַטָּה, וּמִשְׁתַּמֵּר. דָּבָר אַחֵר: אָדָם נוֹתֵן חֲפָצָיו לְכַף מֹאזְנַיִם – כָּל זְמַן שֶׁמַּכְבִּיד, יוֹרֵד לְמַטָּה. וְאִילּוּ הקב"ה – כָּל זְמַן שֶׁמַּכְבִּיד הַוָּלָד, עוֹלֶה לְמַעְלָה. דָּרַשׁ רַבִּי יוֹסֵי הַגְּלִילִי: מַאי דִּכְתִיב °"אוֹדְךָ (ה') עַל כִּי נוֹרָאוֹת נִפְלֵיתִי נִפְלָאִים מַעֲשֶׂיךָ וְנַפְשִׁי יוֹדַעַת מְאֹד"? – בֹּא וּרְאֵה, שֶׁלֹּא כְּמִדַּת הקב"ה מִדַּת בָּשָׂר וָדָם. מִדַּת בָּשָׂר וָדָם – אָדָם נוֹתֵן זֵרְעוֹנִים בַּעֲרוּגָה, כָּל אַחַת וְאַחַת עוֹלָה בְּמִינוֹ. וְאִילּוּ הקב"ה – צָר הָעוּבָּר בִּמְעֵי אִשָּׁה, וְכוּלָּם עוֹלִין לְמִין אֶחָד. דָּבָר אַחֵר: צַבָּע נוֹתֵן סַמְמָנִין לְיוֹרָה – כּוּלָּן עוֹלִין לְצֶבַע אֶחָד. וְאִילּוּ הקב"ה צָר הָעוּבָּר בִּמְעֵי אִשָּׁה – כָּל אַחַת וְאַחַת עוֹלָה לְמִינוֹ. דָּרַשׁ רַב יוֹסֵף: מַאי דִּכְתִיב °"אוֹדְךָ ה' כִּי אָנַפְתָּ בִּי יָשֹׁב אַפְּךָ וּתְנַחֲמֵנִי", בַּמֶּה הַכָּתוּב מְדַבֵּר? – בִּשְׁנֵי בְּנֵי אָדָם שֶׁיָּצְאוּ לִסְחוֹרָה. יָשַׁב לוֹ קוֹץ לְאֶחָד מֵהֶן, הִתְחִיל מְחָרֵף וּמְגַדֵּף. לְיָמִים שָׁמַע שֶׁטָּבְעָה סְפִינָתוֹ שֶׁל חֲבֵירוֹ בַּיָּם, הִתְחִיל מוֹדֶה וּמְשַׁבֵּחַ. לְכָךְ נֶאֱמַר "יָשֹׁב אַפְּךָ וּתְנַחֲמֵנִי". וְהַיְינוּ דְּאָמַר רַבִּי אֶלְעָזָר: מַאי דִּכְתִיב °"עוֹשֶׂה נִפְלָאוֹת (גְּדוֹלוֹת) לְבַדּוֹ. וּבָרוּךְ שֵׁם כְּבוֹדוֹ לְעוֹלָם"? אֲפִילּוּ בַּעַל הַנֵּס אֵינוֹ מַכִּיר בְּנִסּוֹ. דָּרֵישׁ רַבִּי חֲנִינָא בַּר פַּפָּא: מַאי דִּכְתִיב °"אָרְחִי וְרִבְעִי זֵרִיתָ וְכָל דְּרָכַי הִסְכַּנְתָּה"? מְלַמֵּד שֶׁלֹּא נוֹצָר אָדָם מִן כָּל הַטִּפָּה, אֶלָּא מִן הַבָּרוּר שֶׁבָּהּ. תָּנָא דְּבֵי רַבִּי יִשְׁמָעֵאל: מָשָׁל לְאָדָם שֶׁזּוֹרֶה בְּבֵית הַגְּרָנוֹת, נוֹטֵל אֶת הָאוֹכֶל וּמַנִּיחַ אֶת הַפְּסוֹלֶת. כִּדְרַבִּי אַבָּהוּ, *דְּרַבִּי אַבָּהוּ רָמֵי: כְּתִיב °"וַתַּזְרֵנִי חַיִל", וּכְתִיב °"הָאֵל הַמְאַזְּרֵנִי חָיִל" – אָמַר דָּוִד לִפְנֵי הקב"ה: רבש"ע, זֵירִיתַנִי וְזֵרַזְתַּנִי. דָּרַשׁ רַבִּי אַבָּהוּ: מַאי דִּכְתִיב °"מִי מָנָה עֲפַר יַעֲקֹב וּמִסְפָּר אֶת רֹבַע יִשְׂרָאֵל"? מְלַמֵּד שֶׁהקב"ה יוֹשֵׁב וְסוֹפֵר אֶת רְבִיעִיּוֹתֵיהֶם שֶׁל יִשְׂרָאֵל, מָתַי תָּבֹא טִיפָּה שֶׁהַצַּדִּיק נוֹצָר הֵימֶנָּה. וְעַל דָּבָר זֶה נִסְמֵית עֵינוֹ שֶׁל בִּלְעָם הָרָשָׁע. אָמַר: מִי שֶׁהוּא טָהוֹר וְקָדוֹשׁ, וּמְשָׁרְתָיו טְהוֹרִים וּקְדוֹשִׁים, יָצִיץ בְּדָבָר זֶה?! מִיָּד נִסְמֵית עֵינוֹ, דִּכְתִיב: °"נְאֻם הַגֶּבֶר שְׁתֻם הָעָיִן". וְהַיְינוּ דְּאָמַר רַבִּי יוֹחָנָן: מַאי דִּכְתִיב °"וַיִּשְׁכַּב עִמָּהּ בַּלַּיְלָה הוּא"? – מְלַמֵּד שֶׁהקב"ה סִיֵּיעַ בְּאוֹתוֹ מַעֲשֶׂה, שֶׁנֶּאֱמַר: °"יִשָּׂשכָר חֲמֹר גָּרֶם" – ◦חֲמוֹר גָּרַם לוֹ לְיִשָּׂשכָר. *אָמַר רַבִּי יִצְחָק, אָמַר רַבִּי *אַמִי: אִשָּׁה מַזְרַעַת תְּחִילָּה – יוֹלֶדֶת זָכָר, אִישׁ מַזְרִיעַ תְּחִילָּה – יוֹלֶדֶת נְקֵבָה. שֶׁנֶּאֱמַר: °"אִשָּׁה כִּי תַזְרִיעַ וְיָלְדָה זָכָר". תָּנוּ רַבָּנַן: בָּרִאשׁוֹנָה הָיוּ אוֹמְרִים, אִשָּׁה מַזְרַעַת תְּחִילָּה – יוֹלֶדֶת זָכָר, אִישׁ מַזְרִיעַ תְּחִילָּה – יוֹלֶדֶת נְקֵבָה, וְלֹא פֵּירְשׁוּ חֲכָמִים אֶת הַדָּבָר. עַד שֶׁבָּא רַבִּי צָדוֹק וּפֵירְשׁוֹ: °"אֵלֶּה בְּנֵי לֵאָה אֲשֶׁר יָלְדָה לְיַעֲקֹב בְּפַדַּן אֲרָם וְאֵת דִּינָה בִתּוֹ" – תָּלָה הַזְּכָרִים בַּנְּקֵבוֹת וּנְקֵבוֹת בַּזְּכָרִים. °"וַיִּהְיוּ בְנֵי אוּלָם אֲנָשִׁים גִּבּוֹרֵי חַיִל דֹּרְכֵי קֶשֶׁת וּמַרְבִּים בָּנִים וּבְנֵי בָנִים" – וְכִי בְּיָדוֹ שֶׁל אָדָם לְהַרְבּוֹת בָּנִים וּבְנֵי בָנִים? אֶלָּא מִתּוֹךְ

שֶׁמַּשְׁהִין

**רש"י**

**מַאי קְרָא.** דְּמַשְׁבִּיעִין אוֹתוֹ בְּיוֹם הַלֵּידָה? **נִזְרֵךְ.** לְשׁוֹן נְזִירוּת, דְּהַיְינוּ נֶדֶר דְּדָמֵי לִשְׁבוּעָה. **לְמָה. וָלָד דּוֹמֶה.** **חֶבְלֵי.** צַעֲרָהּ. **רֻקַּמְתִּי.** הַיְינוּ יְצִירָה רִאשׁוֹנָה, וּכְתִיב "בְּתַחְתִּיּוֹת" – דְּהַיְינוּ, מָדוֹר תַּחְתּוֹן. **דֶּרֶךְ תַּשְׁמִישָׁן.** הָאִישׁ פָּנָיו לְמַטָּה, כֵּן זָכָר נוֹלָד פָּנָיו לְמַטָּה. וּנְקֵבָה – פָּנֶיהָ לְמַעְלָה, הִילְכָּךְ נְקֵבָה צְרִיכָה לְהִתְהַפֵּךְ. דְּהָא כְּשֶׁהִיא בִּמְעֵי אִמָּהּ פָּנֶיהָ לְמַטָּה, כִּדְאָמְרִינַן (א) לְעֵיל ["רֹאשׁוֹ לוֹ בֵּין בִּרְכָּיו"] אֲבָל זָכָר – אֵין צָרִיךְ לְהִתְהַפֵּךְ. **קָשֶׁה לָאִשָּׁה וְקָשֶׁה לַוָּלָד.** מִפְּנֵי שֶׁדָּר בַּמָּדוֹר הַתַּחְתּוֹן. **קָשֶׁה לָאִשָּׁה** – לָא יָדַעְנָא לָמָּאי. **זָרִיז.** מְלַבֵּן אֶת הַוָּלָד מִגִּיעוּלָיו. **מְזוֹרָז.** חָזָק וּבָרִיא. **לְיוֹם תִּשְׁעִים.** לִשְׁלֹשָׁה יָמִים הָוֵי סִיּוּתוֹ. **מְנָא יָדַע.** הָא לָא יָדַע אֵימַת מְעוּבֶּרֶת? **קְלַסְתֵּר.** זִיו. **מַרְאֵה הָעַיִן.** שֶׁאַע"פ שֶׁנִּבְרֵאת הָעַיִן מִן הָאָב וְהָאֵם, אֵינוֹ רוֹאֶה. תֵּדַע שֶׁהֲרֵי הַמֵּת יֵשׁ לוֹ עֵינַיִם וְיֵשׁ לוֹ שְׂפָתַיִם וְיֵשׁ לוֹ אָזְנַיִם – וְאֵינוֹ רוֹאֶה וְלֹא שׁוֹמֵעַ וְלֹא מְדַבֵּר. **פּוּץ מִילְחָא.** הַשְׁלֵךְ הַמֶּלַח מִן הַבָּשָׂר, וְשׁוּב אֵינוֹ רָאוּי אֶלָּא לִכְלָבִים. כָּךְ הַנְּשָׁמָה הִיא מֶלַח לַגּוּף לְקַיְּימוֹ, כֵּיוָן שֶׁהָלְכָה, אָז מַסְרִיחַ הַגּוּף. **עוֹלֶה לְמַעְלָה.** כִּדְתָנֵי לְעֵיל: אַחֲרוֹנִים, דָּר בַּמָּדוֹר הָעֶלְיוֹן. **כּוּלָּן עוֹלִין לְמִין אֶחָד.** זֶרַע הָאָב וְהָאֵם נַעֲשִׂין בְּרִיָּה אַחַת. **צֶבַע.** כַּמָּה סַמְמָנִין צָרִיךְ לְצֶבַע שָׁחוֹר: קְלִיפַּת עֵץ, וּטְחִינַת רֵיחַיִים שֶׁל נַפָּחִים, וְכַמָּה דְּבָרִים, וְכוּלָּן נַעֲשִׂין שָׁחוֹר. וְאֵינוֹ יָכוֹל לְצוֹבְעוֹ בְּיוֹרָה אַחַת מִשְּׁנַיִם וּשְׁלֹשָׁה גְּוָונִים, בִּשְׁנַיִם וּשְׁלֹשָׁה מְקוֹמוֹת. **כָּל אֶחָד וְאֶחָד עוֹלֶה לְמִינוֹ.** לוֹבֶן מִן הָאִישׁ וְשָׁחוֹר מִן הָאִשָּׁה. **כִּי אָנַפְתָּ בִּי.** מִפְּנֵי שֶׁכָּעַסְתָּ עָלַי, אֲנִי מוֹדֶה לְךָ, שֶׁלְּטוֹבָתִי הָיָה. **יָשַׁב לוֹ קוֹץ בְּרַגְלוֹ.** לְאֶחָד מֵהֶם, וְלֹא יָכוֹל לָצֵאת. **לְבַדּוֹ.** הוּא לְבַדּוֹ יוֹדֵעַ שֶׁהוּא נֵס, אֲבָל בַּעַל הַנֵּס – אֵינוֹ מַכִּירוֹ. **אָרְחִי.** תַּשְׁמִישׁ, כְּמוֹ "דֶּרֶךְ גֶּבֶר בְּעַלְמָה" (משלי ל). **וְרִבְעִי.** תַּשְׁמִישׁ, לְשׁוֹן "לְרִבְעָה". **זֵרִיתָ.** בֵּירַרְתָּ בְּנָפָה, שֶׁקּוֹרִין ווּ"ן, כְּמוֹ (ישעיה ל) "בְּרַחַת וּבַמִּזְרֶה". **הַבָּרוּר.** קלי"ר בְּלַעַ"ז. **וַתַּזְרֵנִי.** חָסֵר א', *לְשׁוֹן "מִזְרֶה". **וַתְּאַזְּרֵנִי.** לְשׁוֹן חֲגִירַת כֹּחַ בְּמָתְנַיִם. **זֵירִיתַנִי.** מִן הַבָּרוּר, וְאַח"כ זֵירַזְתַּנִי. **רְבִיעִיּוֹתֵיהֶם.** עוֹנַת תַּשְׁמִישָׁן. **הוּא.** קוּדְשָׁא בְּרִיךְ הוּא סִיְּיעָהּ, שֶׁנָּטָה חֲמוֹרוֹ שֶׁל יַעֲקֹב לְאֹהֶל לֵאָה, וְאוֹתוֹ הַלַּיְלָה שֶׁל הָאַחֲרוֹת הָיָה. **וְלֹא פֵּירְשׁוּ.** אֶת הַדָּבָר מְנָלַן. **זְכָרִים בַּנְּקֵבוֹת.** בְּנֵי לֵאָה. **נְקֵבוֹת בַּזְּכָרִים.** "וְאֵת דִּינָה בִתּוֹ", מִשּׁוּם הַךְ דְּרָשָׁה: אִישׁ מַזְרִיעַ תְּחִלָּה – יוֹלֶדֶת נְקֵבָה.

שֶׁמַּשְׁהִין

**הגהות הגר"א**

[א] גמ' ושערות. נ"ב ודם כו' ובינה. נ"ב ודעה:

**הגהות הב"ח**

(א) רש"י ד"ה דרך כו' לעיל נ"ב נראה דהיינו מדאמר ורֹאשו על ברכיו כו':

כאן מתחיל הדבור זירתני מן הבור ואח"כ זיריתני לשון מזרה זירזתני ותאזרני לשון כו' כצ"ל רש"ל

**תוספי הרא"ש**

**שתום** העין. הוא לשון גילוי עין ולשון משנה הוא לשון גילוי ופתיחה במס' ע"ז כדי שישתום ויסתום ויגוף והא דדייק דנסתם עינו היינו משום דכתיב סתום לשון יחיד:

**גליון הש"ס**

**גמ'** משמש והולך. יבמות יב ע"ב: **שם** חמור גרם לו ליששכר. בערוך ערך חמרא כתב כלומר כשחזר יעקב מן השדה נהק החמור ושמעה לאה ויצאה לקראתו וקראתו:

[נ"ל ודעת ובינה והשכל כך איתא בע"י ונע"ק בתוס' דב"ק כה. ובתוס' דב"ב קיא. ובתוס' דזבחים סט: ד"ה ק"ו אכן ברור שהיה לתוס' כנוסחת השאלתות שהעתקתי שהאם מזרעת אודם שממנו עור ובשר ודם וכו' וא"כ גבי חלק האם נמי הוה חמשה וזה ברור בכוונת תוס' בב"ק כה. ובשאר דוכתי]

**מסורת הש"ס**

תהלים עא | ירמיהו ז | רש"ל | תהלים קלט | [נ"ל דתניא] | תהלים קטז | [קדושין ל:] | [בשאלתות פרשת יתרו סי' נו איתא עור ובשר ודם ושערות וכו'] | *[בערוך מביאו בערך קלסטר בטי"ת] | איוב ט | תהלים קלט | ישעיהו יב | תהלים עב | שם קלט | יומא מז. | שמואל ב כב | תהלים יח | במדבר כג | שם כד | בראשית ל | שם מט | ברכות ס: ע"ש לעיל כה: [ודף כח. ע"ש] | בע"י אי' אסי | ויקרא יב | בראשית מו | דה"א ח

עין משפט נר מצוה

א א מיי' פ"ב מהל' מטמאי משכב ומושב הלכה י:

שֶׁמַּשְׁהִין עַצְמָן. מִלְּהַזְרִיעַ. יְכוֹלְנִי. שֶׁיִּשְׁהֶא עַצְמוֹ מִלְּהַזְרִיעַ. יִבְעוֹל וְיִשְׁנֶה. שֶׁמִּתּוֹךְ תַּאֲוַת בְּעִילָה רִאשׁוֹנָה, תְּהֵא מַזְרַעַת. וּגְהִי נַמִּי דְּתַזְרִיעַ אַחֲרָיו, תִּקְדּוֹס הַזְרָעָתָהּ בִּבְעִילָה שְׁנִיָּה. בְּעָוֹן. עַל יְדֵי דַּם נִדָּה, שֶׁהוּא סִימָן לְהֵרָיוֹן, כִּדְקַיְימָא לָן (כתובות דף י.): כָּל אִשָּׁה שֶׁדָּמֶיהָ מְרוּבִּין – בָּנֶיהָ מְרוּבִּין. וְהוּא מְבִיאוֹ לִידֵי עָוֹן. וְקָדַיֵיק ר' יִצְחָק: "בְּעָוֹן" – שֶׁסָּמוּךְ לַעֲוֹן נִדּוֹת, שֶׁהוּא מוּזְהָר לִפְרוֹשׁ הֵימֶנָּה. וּבְחֵטְא. לְשׁוֹן טְבִילָה וְטָהֳרָה, כִּדְמְפָרֵשׁ. וְה"ק: עַל יְדֵי דַּם נִדּוֹת, שֶׁהוּא מֵבִיא לִידֵי עָוֹן, "חוֹלָלְתִּי" – שֶׁהוּא גָּרַם לִי שֶׁנִּבְרֵאתִי, וּכְשֶׁנִּתְחַטְּאָה אִמִּי מִמֶּנּוּ יֶחֱמַתְנִי. כַּר. מִנְחָה, דְּהַיְינוּ סִימַן שָׁלוֹם. נְקִיָּה. חֲסֵרָה, כְּמוֹ (ב"ק דף מא.): יָצָא פְּלוֹנִי נָקִי מִנְּכָסָיו. עַד דְּאָמְרָה מְזוֹנֵי. שֶׁיּוֹדַעַת לְהִתְפַּלֵּל. נְקֵבָה. כְּשֶׁתִּנָּקוֹב וְתִפָרֵשׁ שְׂכָרְךָ וְאֶתֵּנָה, וּנְקֵבָה נַמִּי הָכִי דָּרְשִׁינַן. לְפִיכָךְ תָּבִיא קָרְבָּן. שְׁבוּעַת בִּיטּוּי חַטָּאת. מְזִידָה הִיא. וְאֵין כָּאן קָרְבָּן, דְּהָא "וְנֶעְלַם" כְּתִיב בִּשְׁבוּעַת בִּיטּוּי. וּבַחֲרָטָה תַּלְיָא. לִפְתּוֹחַ לָהּ בַּחֲרָטָה, וְיַתִּיר לָהּ חָכָם שְׁבוּעָתָהּ. אֲבָל קָרְבָּן אֵינוֹ עוֹקֵר וּמַתִּיר שְׁבוּעָתָהּ. וְעוֹד קָרְבַּן שְׁבוּעָה בָּעֵי אִתּוּיֵי. כִּשְׂבָּה אוֹ שְׂעִירָה, וְהַאי עוֹף הוּא! מִתְחָרֶטֶת לְשִׁבְעָה. וּמִתְאַוָּה לְתַשְׁמִישׁ בַּעְלָהּ, כְּדֵי שֶׁתַּחְזוֹר וְתִתְעַבֵּר זָכָר. מִפְּנֵי מָה מִילָה לִשְׁמוֹנָה. וְלֹא לְשִׁבְעָה? שֶׁלֹּא יִהְיוּ הַכֹּל שְׂמֵחִין. שֶׁאוֹכְלִין וְשׁוֹתִין בַּסְּעוּדָה, וְאָבִיו וְאִמּוֹ עֲצֵבִים, שֶׁאֲסוּרִין בְּתַשְׁמִישׁ. נִדָּה שִׁבְעָה. לָאו בְּיוֹלֶדֶת קָאֵי. מִפְּנֵי שֶׁאָדָם רָגִיל בְּאִשְׁתּוֹ. כָּל שָׁעָה שֶׁיִּרְצֶה. קָץ בָּהּ. מְאוּסָה עָלָיו. אָמְרָה תּוֹרָה: כָּל שָׁעָה שֶׁתִּרְאֶה – תְּהֵא טְמֵאָה שִׁבְעָה, כְּדֵי שֶׁלֹּא יְהֵא רָגִיל בָּהּ, וְתִתְחַבֵּב עָלָיו. מְחַזֵּר עַל הָאִשָּׁה. אָדָם פָּנוּי מְבַקֵּשׁ וּמְחַזֵּר, עַד שֶׁנּוֹשֵׂא. פָּנָיו לְמַטָּה. בִּשְׁעַת תַּשְׁמִישׁ. זֶהוּ מִמָּקוֹם שֶׁנִּבְרָא. מִסְתַּכֵּל בָּאֲדָמָה, שֶׁנּוֹצַר מִמֶּנָּה. וְהִיא מִסְתַּכֶּלֶת בּוֹ, שֶׁנּוֹצְרָה הֵימֶנּוּ. מְקַבֵּל פִּיּוּס. נוֹחַ לִרְצוֹת. זֶה מִמָּקוֹם שֶׁנִּבְרָא. אֲדָמָה, עָפָר תִּיחוּחַ, נוֹחַ לִיבָּטֵל. אֲבָל בָּשָׂר וַעֲצָמוֹת – קָשִׁין. עֶצֶם. כְּשֶׁמַּכִּין בּוֹ, קוֹלוֹ נִשְׁמָע. אֲבָל קַרְקַע כְּשֶׁמַּכִּין בּוֹ, אֵין קוֹלוֹ נִשְׁמָע.

## הדרן עלך המפלת

בְּנוֹת כּוּתִים נִדּוֹת מֵעֲרִיסָתָן. מִקַּטְנוּתָן, וּבַגְּמָרָא מְפָרֵשׁ טַעֲמָא. תַּחְתּוֹן כָּעֶלְיוֹן. מְפָרֵשׁ בַּגְּמָ'. וְהֵן יוֹשְׁבוֹת עַל כָּל דָּם וָדָם. כְּלוֹמַר, לְהָכִי הָווּ בּוֹעֲלֵי נִדּוֹת, מִשּׁוּם דְּכָל דָּם שֶׁרוֹאוֹת, בֵּין אָדוֹם בֵּין יָרוֹק, יוֹשְׁבוֹת עָלָיו יְמֵי נִדּוּת. וְזוֹ תַּקָּלָה הִיא לָהֶם, שֶׁאִם רוֹאָה דַּם יָרוֹק הַיּוֹם – מַתְחֶלֶת לִמְנוֹת שִׁשָּׁה וְהוּא, אִם תִּרְאֶה בְּאוֹתָם יְמֵי נִדּוּת דַּם אָדוֹם – אֵינָהּ מוֹנָה אֶלָּא מִיּוֹם רְאִיָּיה רִאשׁוֹנָה, וְאוֹתוֹ דַּם יָרוֹק – טָהוֹר הָיָה, וּמֵרְאִיָּיה שְׁנִיָּה הִיא צְרִיכָה לִמְנוֹת. אֵין חַיָּיבִין עָלֶיהָ. הַלּוֹבֵשׁ אוֹ מִתְכַּסֶּה בְּאוֹתָן בְּגָדִים וְנִכְנַס לַמִּקְדָּשׁ – פָּטוּר מִקָּרְבָּן, אוֹ אִם נָגְעוּ אוֹתָן בְּגָדִים שֶׁל מִשְׁכָּב בִּתְרוּמָה – תּוֹלִין, דְּלָא יָדְעִינַן אִי נִדָּה הִיא אִי לָא. וְהָא דְּקָאָמַר דְּמִסְתַּמָּא טְמֵאוֹת – גְּזֵירָה דְּרַבָּנַן הִיא. גְּמ' אֲפִילּוּ דִּידָן נַמִּי. אִי חַזְיָא בַּעֲרִיסָתָן – טְמֵאָה, דְּתַנְיָא לְקַמָּן (דף לב.): בַּת יוֹם אֶחָד לְנִדָּה מִנַּיִן? תַּלְמוּד לוֹמַר: "וְאִשָּׁה". דְּאִיכָּא מִיעוּטָא דְּחָזְיָין. בְּקַטְנוּתָן. חָיְישִׁינַן לְמִיעוּטָא. וּמְטַמְּאִינַן לְכוּלְּהוּ מֵעֲרִיסָתָן, מִשּׁוּם דְּדִילְמָא חַזְיָא. אִיש

כִּי קוֹלֵךְ עָרֵב.ד] אבל היא אינה מקלסתו בקול ערב, אלא ב"צח ואדום".

## הדרן עלך המפלת

בנות כותים. והן יושבות על כל דם ודם. ואם תאמר: ותיפוק ליה שהן נדות מעריסתן? ויש לומר: דהיינו דוקא בקטנותן – דלא דרשי "ואשה", כדאמר בגמרא. אבל גדולות, דמפרשי להו וטבלי – לא מטמו אלא משום דיושבות על כל דם ודם. תחתון כעליון. מפרש בגמרא: תחתונו של בועל נדה כעליונו של זב, דלא מטמא אלא אוכלין ומשקין. ו"עליונו של זב" מפרש רשב"ם: שהכריע הזב בכף מאזנים את האוכלין ומשקין שבכף שניה. ולא נהירא, דבפ' "ר"ע" (שבת דף פג.) קרי ליה "היסט" מה שהכריע הזב בכף מאזנים, והיסט נפקא לן מ"אשר יגע בהם הזב", ועליונו של זב נפקא לן בשמעתין מקרא אחרינא? ונראה ד"עליונו של זב" – היינו בגד שמקלתו על הזב ומקלתו נגרר על הארץ. ולאו היינו היסט אלא כשמסיטו כולו, כדאמר: איזהו מגעו שהוא ככולו? הוי אומר, זה היסטו.

*שֶׁמַּשְׁהִין עַצְמָן בַּבֶּטֶן, כְּדֵי שֶׁיַּזְרִיעוּ נְשׁוֹתֵיהֶן תְּחִלָּה, שֶׁיִּהוּ בְּנֵיהֶם זְכָרִים – מַעֲלֶה עֲלֵיהֶן הַכָּתוּב כְּאִילּוּ הֵם מַרְבִּים בָּנִים וּבְנֵי בָנִים. וְהַיְינוּ דְּאָמַר רַב קְטִינָא: יְכוֹלְנִי לַעֲשׂוֹת כָּל בָּנַי זְכָרִים. *אָמַר רָבָא: הָרוֹצֶה לַעֲשׂוֹת כָּל בָּנָיו זְכָרִים – יִבְעוֹל וְיִשְׁנֶה. וְאָמַר רַבִּי יִצְחָק, אָמַר רַבִּי *אַמִי: **אֵין אִשָּׁה מִתְעַבֶּרֶת אֶלָּא *סָמוּךְ לְוִסְתָּהּ, שֶׁנֶּאֱמַר: °"הֵן בְּעָוֹן חוֹלָלְתִּי". א] וְרַבִּי יוֹחָנָן אָמַר: *סָמוּךְ לִטְבִילָה, שֶׁנֶּאֱמַר: °"וּבְחֵטְא יֶחֱמַתְנִי אִמִּי". *מַאי מַשְׁמַע דְּהַאי "חֵטְא" לִישָּׁנָא דְּדִכּוּיֵי הוּא? – דִּכְתִיב: °"וְחִטֵּא אֶת הַבַּיִת", וּמְתַרְגְּמִינַן: וִידַכֵּי יָת בֵּיתָא. וְאִי בָּעֵית אֵימָא מֵהָכָא °"תְּחַטְּאֵנִי בְאֵזוֹב וְאֶטְהָר". וְאָמַר רַבִּי יִצְחָק אָמַר רַבִּי אַמִי: ב] כֵּיוָן שֶׁבָּא זָכָר בָּעוֹלָם – בָּא שָׁלוֹם בָּעוֹלָם, שֶׁנֶּאֱמַר: °"שִׁלְחוּ כַר מוֹשֵׁל אֶרֶץ", "זָכָר" – זֶה כַּר. וְאָמַר ר' יִצְחָק *דְּבֵי רַבִּי אַמִי: בָּא זָכָר בָּעוֹלָם – בָּא כִּכָּרוֹ בְיָדוֹ. "זָכָר" – זֶה כַּר, דִּכְתִיב: °"וַיִּכְרֶה לָהֶם *כֵּירָה גְדוֹלָה". נְקֵבָה – אֵין עִמָּהּ כְּלוּם, "נְקֵבָה" – נְקִיָּיה בָּאָה. עַד דְּאָמְרָה "מְזוֹנֵי" – לָא יָהֲבִי לָהּ, דִּכְתִיב: °"נָקְבָה שְׂכָרְךָ עָלַי וְאֶתֵּנָה". שָׁאֲלוּ תַּלְמִידָיו אֶת רַבִּי שִׁמְעוֹן בֶּן יוֹחַי: מִפְּנֵי מָה אָמְרָה תּוֹרָה יוֹלֶדֶת מְבִיאָה קָרְבָּן? אָמַר לָהֶן: *בְּשָׁעָה שֶׁכּוֹרַעַת לֵילֵד – קוֹפֶצֶת וְנִשְׁבַּעַת שֶׁלֹּא תִּזָּקֵק לְבַעְלָהּ. לְפִיכָךְ אָמְרָה תּוֹרָה: תָּבִיא קָרְבָּן. מַתְקִיף לָהּ רַב יוֹסֵף: וְהָא מְזִידָה הִיא, וּבַחֲרָטָה תַּלְיָא מִילְּתָא! וְעוֹד, קָרְבַּן שְׁבוּעָה בָּעֵי אִיתּוּיֵי. וּמִפְּנֵי מָה אָמְרָה תּוֹרָה זָכָר לְשִׁבְעָה וּנְקֵבָה לְאַרְבָּעָה עָשָׂר? זָכָר, שֶׁהַכֹּל שְׂמֵחִים בּוֹ – מִתְחָרֶטֶת לְשִׁבְעָה. נְקֵבָה, שֶׁהַכֹּל עֲצֵבִים בָּהּ – מִתְחָרֶטֶת לְאַרְבָּעָה עָשָׂר. ג] וּמִפְּנֵי מָה אָמְרָה תּוֹרָה מִילָה לִשְׁמוֹנָה? שֶׁלֹּא יְהוּ כּוּלָּם שְׂמֵחִים וְאָבִיו וְאִמּוֹ עֲצֵבִים. תַּנְיָא, הָיָה ר"מ אוֹמֵר: מִפְּנֵי מָה אָמְרָה תּוֹרָה נִדָּה לְשִׁבְעָה? מִפְּנֵי שֶׁרָגִיל בָּהּ וְקָץ בָּהּ. אָמְרָה תּוֹרָה: תְּהֵא טְמֵאָה שִׁבְעָה יָמִים, כְּדֵי שֶׁתְּהֵא חֲבִיבָה עַל בַּעְלָהּ כִּשְׁעַת כְּנִיסָתָהּ לַחוּפָּה. שָׁאֲלוּ תַּלְמִידָיו אֶת רַבִּי דּוֹסְתַּאי בְּרַבִּי יַנַּאי: *מִפְּנֵי מָה אִישׁ מְחַזֵּר עַל אִשָּׁה, וְאֵין אִשָּׁה מְחַזֶּרֶת עַל אִישׁ? מָשָׁל לְאָדָם שֶׁאָבַד לוֹ אֲבֵידָה, מִי מְחַזֵּר עַל מִי? בַּעַל אֲבֵידָה מְחַזֵּיר עַל אֲבֵידָתוֹ. וּמִפְּנֵי מָה אִישׁ פָּנָיו לְמַטָּה, וְאִשָּׁה פָּנֶיהָ לְמַעְלָה כְּלַפֵּי הָאִישׁ? זֶה מִמָּקוֹם שֶׁנִּבְרָא וְזוֹ מִמָּקוֹם שֶׁנִּבְרֵאת. וּמִפְּנֵי מָה הָאִישׁ מְקַבֵּל פִּיּוּס, וְאֵין אִשָּׁה מְקַבֶּלֶת פִּיּוּס? זֶה מִמָּקוֹם שֶׁנִּבְרָא וְזוֹ מִמָּקוֹם שֶׁנִּבְרֵאת. מִפְּנֵי מָה אִשָּׁה קוֹלָהּ עָרֵב, וְאֵין אִישׁ קוֹלוֹ עָרֵב? זֶה מִמָּקוֹם שֶׁנִּבְרָא וְזוֹ מִמָּקוֹם שֶׁנִּבְרֵאת. שֶׁנֶּאֱמַר °"כִּי קוֹלֵךְ עָרֵב וּמַרְאֵךְ נָאוֶה".§

## הדרן עלך המפלת חתיכה

**בְּנוֹת** *כּוּתִים נִדּוֹת מֵעֲרִיסָתָן. וְהַכּוּתִים מְטַמְּאִים מִשְׁכָּב תַּחְתּוֹן כָּעֶלְיוֹן, מִפְּנֵי שֶׁהֵן בּוֹעֲלֵי נִדּוֹת, וְהֵן יוֹשְׁבוֹת עַל כָּל דָּם וָדָם. אוְאֵין חַיָּיבִין עֲלֵיהֶן עַל בִּיאַת מִקְדָּשׁ, וְאֵין שׂוֹרְפִין עֲלֵיהֶם אֶת הַתְּרוּמָה, מִפְּנֵי שֶׁטּוּמְאָתָן סָפֵק.§ **גְּמ'** ה"ד. אִי דְּקָא חָזְיָין – אֲפִילּוּ דִּידָן נַמִּי, וְאִי דְּלָא קָחָזְיָין דִּידְהוּ נַמִּי לָא! אָמַר רָבָא בְּרֵיהּ דְּרַב אַחָא בַּר רַב הוּנָא אָמַר רַב שֵׁשֶׁת: הָכָא בְּמַאי עָסְקִינַן בִּסְתָמָא, דְּכֵיוָן דְּאִיכָּא מִיעוּטָא דְּחָזְיָין חָיְישִׁינַן. וּמַאן תַּנָּא *דְּחָיֵישׁ לְמִיעוּטָא – ר"מ

גליון הש"ס

גמ' אין אשה מתעברת אלא סמוך לוסתה. פ' לעיל י ע"ב תד"ה דהויא: תוס' ד"ה תחתון כו' והיסט נפקא לן מאשר יגע בהם הזב. לקמן מג ע"א כל אשר יגע בו הזב כל"ל:

תוספי הרא"ש

שנאמר כי קולך ערב. אבל היא אינה מקלסתו בקול ערב אלא בצח ואדום:

סליק פירקא

בנות כותים נדות מעריסתן. הקשה ר"ת לרבינא דאמר בפ' אין מעמידין דתינוקת גויה בת ג' שנים ויום אחד הואיל וראויה לביאה מטמאה בזיבה מאי שנא מבנות כותים דהחמירו אפילו מעריסותיהן מיהו ממשנה זו לא קשה דסברה גרי אמת הן דקתני מפני שטומאתן בספק דכיון דאי חזיא טמאה מדאורייתא החמירו בהן יותר מבגוים אבל קשה מדר' יוסי דאמר ר' אליביה בפ"ק דשבת אף בנות כותים נדות מעריסתן בו ביום גזרו ושמעינן ליה לר' יוסי במנחות בפרק ר' ישמעאל דסבר כותים גרי אריות הן דקאמר תורמין משל גוים על של כותים ואומר ר"ת דחמירו בהם לפי שהן מצויין אצל ישראל וכדי שלא יטמעו בהן. ומיהו יש דברים שהקילו בהם יותר מבגוים דתינוק גוי מטמא בזיבה דגזרו עליהם שיהו כזבין לכל הכותים לא גזרו אלא משום חששא דבועלי נדות כמו דתניא מתני' ואע"ג דמתני' קא סברה גרי אמת הן מסתברא דה"ה למ"ד גרי אריות הם דלא אשכחן תנא דפליג בהא למימר שעשו כותים כזבים וכן לענין יין נסך לא גזרו על יין של כותים עד שבא ר' מאיר וגזר כדאיתא בפ"ק דחולין ואע"ג דר' מאיר סבר גרי אמת הן כדמוכח בשור שנגח ד' וה' מ"מ לא מצינו אדם שאסר יינם תחלה אפילו מאן דאית ליה גרי אריות הן: והן יושבות על כל דם ודם. ותימה למה לי למימר שהן יושבות על דם ודם כיון שגזרו עליהן שהן נדות מעריסותיהן וי"ל משום דלא תימא דוקא בקטנות גזרו משום דכי חזיין לא מפרשי להו כדאיתא בגמרא אבל בגדולות לא (ילפינן) [גזרינן] הוצרך טעם בגדולות: אי דקא חזיין כו'. אין לפרש אי דקא חזיין אם רגילות קטנות לראות דא"כ מאי קאמר רב ששת הב"ע בסתמא ואי אין רגילות לראות אמאי מטמינן בסתמא לכך פרש"י דמיירי שראתה ותימה מאי קשה ליה א"כ אפילו לא חזיין נמי דילמא גזרו עליהן כמו שגזרו על גוים אע"ג דדם גויה כדם בהמה הילכך בכותים נמי אע"ג דלא חזיין גזרו בהו. וי"ל משום דסברה כותים גרי אמת מדקתני ואין חייבין עליהן על ביאת מקדש מפני שטומאתן בספק הילכך לא מסתבר ליה למימר שגזרו עליהם כמו על גוים: חיישינן למיעוטא. ותימה הא דאמרינן בפ"ק דשבת הגזירה מי"ח דבר היא ומה הוצרכו לגזרו והלא בכל מקום חייש ר' מאיר למיעוטא וי"ל דמתחלה היו סבורים דכותים דרשי אשה ואשה וכי חזו מפרשי להו ושוב בדקו ומצאו דכי חזו לא מפרשי להו והודיעו לכל שהן נדות מעריסותיהן ומיהו תימה כיון דחיישינן למיעוט אפילו בדידן נמי ניחוש ואמאי אמרינן בפ"ק תינוקת שלא הגיע זמנה לראות פעם ראשונה ושניה רוקה ומדרסה בשוק טהור. וכ"ת היינו דקא משני לקמן אנן דכי חזיין מפרשי להו לא גזרו בהו רבנן משום דלא שכיח כלל שלא ימצא דם בבגדה אם ראתה מ"מ ניחוש שמא סמוך ללידתה בשעה שנולדה ראתה בעוד שהיתה מלוכלכת בדם הלידה וי"ל דהך מיעוטא לא שכיח כלל אע"ג דקרי ליה בסמוך מיעוטא דשכיח שהטבילה קודם לאמה מ"מ בשעת הלידה לא שכיח כלל ותימה כיון דמטעמא דחיישינן למיעוטא גזרינן היכי קאמר בפ"ק דשבת אליבא דר' יוסי אף בנות כותים נדות מעריסתן בו ביום גזרו וי"ל חדא דאשכחן לר' יוסי דחייש למיעוטא ביבמות ריש פרק אלמנה ועוד דר' יוסי דאית ליה כותים גרי אריות וגזרו עליהן כדי שלא יטמעו בהם כדרך שגזרו על גוים והא דצריכי' לטעמא דחייש למיעוטא משום דר' יוסי דסבר גרי אמת הן והא דאמר ר' יוסי טעם מעשה (בעינבל) [בעין בול] כו' לסייע לדברי ר"מ קאמר (או) א"נ איצטריך לאשמועינן דלא תימא היאך גזרו עליהן נדות כדי שלא יטמאו בהן כיון דאין נמצא בם היינו לת"ק דמתני' אשמועינן דזימנין דאיכא כי היכי דלא ליהוו מילי דרבנן כי חוכא ואטלולא ואפילו משכח תנא דסבירא ליה כותים גרי אמת הן ולא חייש למיעוטא אומר ר"ת דאפשר דאית ליה בנות כותים נדות מעריסתן נדות בכל לפי שהיו מקולקלין במעשיהם הרחיקום כדי שלא יטמעו בהם והא דאיצטריך לומר הכא טעמא משום דחיישינן למיעוטא משום דמתני' מוכחת דבהכי תליא טעמא משום דכי חזיין לא מיפרשי ולא משום טימוע מדאיצטריך לן לפרושי

הגהות מהר"ב רנשבורג א] גמ' ור"י אמר סמוך לטבילה. נ"ב עי' סוטה דף כז ע"א ותוס' שם ד"ה אליבא ובתוס' כנסת יחזקאל סי' לג ובשו"ת אבן השהם סי' יד לא עיינו שם כל צרכם דוק ותשכח גם על מהרש"א בח"א כאן יפלא דא"כ איך אמר הש"ס התם כי תיבעי לך אליבא דמ"ד וכו' סמוך לטבילה ומאי בעיא הא סמוך לוסתה לא מצי מנטר לה ודו"ק: ב] שם כיון שבא זכר בעולם בא שלום בעולם שנאמר וכו' נ"ב עי' דרשת מהרלנ"ח דף ח ע"ב: ג] שם ומפני מה אמרה תורה מילה לשמנה. נ"ב עיין מהרלנ"ח הנ"ל דף ט ע"ג: ד] תוד"ה כי קולך ערב. נ"ב עיין לעוף אהבה:

ר"מ הִיא. *דְּתַנְיָא, קָטָן וּקְטַנָּה – לֹא חוֹלְצִין וְלֹא מְיַבְּמִין, דִּבְרֵי ר"מ. אָמְרוּ לוֹ לְר"מ: אׅיָפֶה אָמַרְתָּ שֶׁאֵין חוֹלְצִין – "אִישׁ" כָּתוּב בַּפָּרָשָׁה, וּמַקְשִׁינַן אִשָּׁה לְאִישׁ, וּמַה טַּעַם אֵין מְיַבְּמִין? אָמַר לָהֶן: קָטָן – שֶׁמָּא יִמָּצֵא סָרִיס, קְטַנָּה – שֶׁמָּא תִּמָּצֵא אַיְלוֹנִית, וְנִמְצְאוּ פּוֹגְעִין בָּעֶרְוָה שֶׁלֹּא בִּמְקוֹם מִצְוָה. וְרַבָּנַן: בזִיל בָּתַר רוּבָּא דִּקְטַנִּים – וְרוֹב קְטַנִּים לָאו סָרִיסִים נִינְהוּ, זִיל בָּתַר רוּבָּא דִּקְטַנּוֹת – וְרוֹב קְטַנּוֹת לָאו אַיְלוֹנִית נִינְהוּ. אֵימַר דְּשָׁמְעַתְּ לֵיהּ לְר"מ מִיעוּטָא דִּשְׁכִיחַ, אֲבָל מִיעוּטָא דְּלָא שְׁכִיחַ מִי שָׁמְעַתְּ לֵיהּ? °הָא נַמִי מִיעוּטָא דִּשְׁכִיחַ הוּא. דְּתַנְיָא, א"ר יוֹסֵי: *מַעֲשֶׂה בְּעֵין בּוֹל – וְהִטְבִּילוּהָ קוֹדֶם לְאִמָּהּ. וְאָמַר רַבִּי: מַעֲשֶׂה בְּבֵית שְׁעָרִים – וְהִטְבִּילוּהָ קוֹדֶם לְאִמָּהּ. וְא"ר יוֹסֵף: מַעֲשֶׂה בְּפוּמְבְּדִיתָא – וְהִטְבִּילוּהָ קוֹדֶם לְאִמָּהּ. בִּשְׁלָמָא דְּר' יוֹסֵי וּדְרַבִּי – מִשּׁוּם תְּרוּמַת א"י, אֶלָּא דְּרַב יוֹסֵף לָמָּה לִי? וְהָא *אָמַר שְׁמוּאֵל: גאֵין תְּרוּמַת חו"ל אֲסוּרָה – אֶלָּא בְּמִי שֶׁטּוּמְאָה יוֹצְאָה מִגּוּפוֹ, וְהָנֵי מִילֵּי – בַּאֲכִילָה, אֲבָל בִּנְגִיעָה – לָא! אָמַר מָר זוּטְרָא: לֹא נִצְרְכָה אֶלָּא לְסוּכָה שֶׁמֶן שֶׁל תְּרוּמָה. דְּתַנְיָא: °"וְלֹא יְחַלְּלוּ אֶת קָדְשֵׁי בְּנֵי יִשְׂרָאֵל *אֲשֶׁר יָרִימוּ לַה'" – לְרַבּוֹת אֶת הַסָּךְ וְאֶת הַשּׁוֹתֶה. שׁוֹתֶה לָמָּה לִי קְרָא? *שְׁתִיָּה בִּכְלַל אֲכִילָה! אֶלָּא, לְרַבּוֹת דאֶת הַסָּךְ *כְּשׁוֹתֶה. וְאִיבָּעֵית אֵימָא מֵהָכָא: °"וַתָּבֹא כַמַּיִם בְּקִרְבּוֹ וְכַשֶּׁמֶן בְּעַצְמוֹתָיו". אִי הָכִי – דִּידָן נַמִי! אֲנַן דְּדָרְשִׁינַן "אִשָּׁה" "וְאִשָּׁה", וְכִי חַזְיָין מַפְרְשִׁי לְהוּ – לָא גָּזְרוּ בְּהוּ רַבָּנַן. אִינְהוּ דְּלָא דָּרְשִׁי "אִשָּׁה" "וְאִשָּׁה", וְכִי חַזְיָין לָא מַפְרְשִׁי לְהוּ – גָּזְרוּ בְּהוּ רַבָּנַן. מַאי "אִשָּׁה" "וְאִשָּׁה"? דְּתַנְיָא: *"אִשָּׁה" – אֵין לִי אֶלָּא אִשָּׁה, התִּינוֹקֶת בַּת יוֹם אֶחָד לְנִדָּה מִנַּיִן? ת"ל: "וְאִשָּׁה". אַלְמָא, כִּי מַרְבֵּי קְרָא – בַּת יוֹם אֶחָד מַרְבֵּי, וּרְמִינְהוּ: "אִשָּׁה" – אֵין לִי אֶלָּא אִשָּׁה, ותִּינוֹקֶת בַּת ג' שָׁנִים וְיוֹם אֶחָד לְבִיאָה מִנַּיִן? ת"ל: "וְאִשָּׁה"! אָמַר רָבָא: הִלְכְתָא נִינְהוּ, וְאַסְמְכִינְהוּ רַבָּנַן אַקְּרָאֵי. הֵי קְרָא וְהֵי הִלְכְתָא? אִילֵימָא בַּת יוֹם אֶחָד – הִלְכְתָא, בַּת שָׁלֹשׁ שָׁנִים וְיוֹם אֶחָד – קְרָא, קְרָא סְתָמָא כְּתִיב! אֶלָּא, בַּת ג' שָׁנִים וְיוֹם אֶחָד – הִלְכְתָא, בַּת יוֹם אֶחָד – קְרָא. וּמֵאַחַר דְּהִלְכְתָא, קְרָא ל"ל? לְמַעוּטֵי

(ויקרא כב) (תהלים קט)

**רש"י**

אִישׁ כָּתוּב בַּפָּרָשָׁה. (דברים כה): "וְאִם לֹא יַחְפּוֹץ הָאִישׁ" אִישׁ פּוֹטְרָהּ בַּחֲלִיצָה, וְלֹא קָטָן. אֶלָּא מַה טַּעַם אֵין מְיַבְּמִין, וְיִגְדְּלוּ יַחַד? סָרִים. לָאו בַּר הֲקָמַת שֵׁם הוּא, וְאֵינוֹ מְצוּוֶּה לְיַבֵּם, וְכֵן אַיְלוֹנִית. וְכֵיוָן דְּמְיַיבֵּם בְּלֹא מִצְוָה – נוֹשֵׂא אֵשֶׁת אָחִיו בְּחִנָּם, וְעֶרְוָה הִיא, וּבְכָרֵת. בְּעֵין בּוֹל. מָקוֹם. קוֹדֶם לְאִמָּהּ. יוֹלֶדֶת נְקֵבָה טוֹבֶלֶת לְי"ד, וּבִתָּהּ רְאָתָה לְיוֹם אוֹ לְיוֹמַיִם שֶׁנּוֹלְדָה, וְהִטְבִּילוּהָ קוֹדֶם לְאִמָּהּ מִשּׁוּם מַגַּע תְּרוּמָה. עֵין בּוֹל וּבֵית שְׁעָרִים מֵא"י פּוּמְבְּדִיתָא – חוּץ לָאָרֶץ. מִשּׁוּם תְּרוּמַת א"י. דְּמִיפַּסְלָא בִּנְגִיעָה. יוֹצְאָה מִגּוּפוֹ. כְּגוֹן זָב וְזָבָה וְנִדָּה. וְהָנֵי מִילֵּי בַּאֲכִילָה. כּוּלָּהּ שְׁמוּאֵל אֲמָרָהּ, בִּבְכוֹרוֹת בְּפֶ' "הַלּוֹקֵחַ בְּהֵמָה" (דף כז.) וַאֲפִי' זָב וְנִדָּה לָא פָּסְלֵי לָהּ בִּנְגִיעָה. לְסוּכָה שֶׁמֶן שֶׁל תְּרוּמָה. דְּסִיכָה כַּאֲכִילָה, וּבַאֲכִילָה קָאָמְרִינַן דִּתְרוּמַת חו"ל אֲסוּרָה לְנִדָּה. דְּתַנְיָא. דְּסִיכָה כַּאֲכִילָה. וְלֹא יְחַלְּלוּ. בְּפָרָשַׁת אַזְהָרַת טְמֵאִים בִּתְרוּמָה כְּתִיב. לְרַבּוֹת אֶת הַסָּךְ. בִּכְלַל "בַּקֳּדָשִׁים לֹא יֹאכַל עַד אֲשֶׁר יִטְהָר". שְׁתִיָּה בִּכְלַל אֲכִילָה, דִּכְתִיב (דברים יד): "וְאָכַלְתָּ מַעְשַׂר דְּגָנְךָ" וגו', "תִּירוֹשׁ" – חַמְרָא הוּא, וְקָרֵי לֵיהּ אֲכִילָה. וַתָּבֹא כַמַּיִם וגו'. בִּקְלָלָה גַּבֵּי רָשָׁע קָאֵי. א"ה. דְּחָיֵישׁ לְמִיעוּטָא. דִּידָן נַמִי. לִיטַמּוּ כּוּלְּהוּ מֵעֲרִיסָתָן. אִשָּׁה וְאִשָּׁה. לְרַבּוֹת קְטַנָּה, כִּדְמְפָרֵשׁ. מַפְרְשִׁי לְהוּ. מִמַּגַּע קָדָשִׁים. וְאִשָּׁה כִּי תִהְיֶה זָבָה וגו'. בְּנִדָּה מִשְׁתָּעֵי קְרָא, דִּכְתִיב (ויקרא טו): "שִׁבְעַת יָמִים תִּהְיֶה בְנִדָּתָהּ". וּרְמִינְהוּ אִשָּׁה. "וְאִשָּׁה אֲשֶׁר יִשְׁכַּב אִישׁ אוֹתָהּ שִׁכְבַת זָרַע". לְבִיאָה. שֶׁמִּטַּמְּאָה בְּבִיאַת אָדָם מִגְּזֵרַת הַכָּתוּב, דִּכְתִיב "וְטָמְאוּ". וְלֹא מִשּׁוּם נוֹגַעַת בְּשִׁכְבַת זֶרַע הוּא, שֶׁהֲרֵי מַגַּע בֵּית הַסְּתָרִים הוּא וְאֵינוֹ מְטַמֵּא. הִלְכְתָא נִינְהוּ. לְעִנְיַן נִדָּה בַּת יוֹם אֶחָד וּלְעִנְיַן בִּיאָה בַּת ג'. דְּבָרִים הַלָּלוּ הֲלָכָה לְמֹשֶׁה מִסִּינַי הֵם, כִּדְמְפָרֵשׁ וְאָזֵיל דַּחֲדָא מִינַּיְיהוּ הִלְכְתָא. הֵי קְרָא וְהֵי הִלְכְתָא. כְּלוֹמַר, מִכְּדֵי קְרָא חֲדָא מִינַּיְיהוּ מִשְׁתַּמַּע, הֵי מִינַּיְיהוּ מִשְׁתַּמַּע מִקְּרָא בְּלָא הִלְכְתָא וְהֵי מִינַּיְיהוּ אִצְטְרִיךְ הִלְכְתָא? קְרָא סְתָמָא כְּתִיב. כֵּיוָן דְּוָי"ו לְרַבּוּיֵי אֲתָא כָּל שֶׁהוּא אִשָּׁה, מַשְׁמַע בַּת יוֹם אֶחָד. אֲבָל בַּת ג' לָא מַשְׁמַע מִינֵּיהּ טְפֵי מִבַּת ב' אוֹ בַּת ד'. אֶלָּא בַּת ג'. לְעִנְיַן בִּיאָה הִלְכְתָא, דְּמִקְּרָא לָא מִשְׁתַּמַּע, וְרַבָּנַן אַסְמַכְתָּא בְּעָלְמָא אַסְמְכוּהָ. וּבַת יוֹם א' לְנִדָּה – מִשְׁתַּמְּעָא מִקְּרָא. וּמֵאַחַר. דְּבִיאָה בַּת ג' הֲלָכָה לְמֹשֶׁה מִסִּינַי הִיא, וּמִקְּרָא לָא מִשְׁתַּמַּע, עִיקַּר קְרָא דְּוָי"ו יְתֵירָא לְמַאי אֲתָא? לְמַעוּטֵי

**תוספות**

**רבי** מאיר היא. תימה: דמשמע דמתני' (לעיל דף לא:) דבנות כותים נדות מעריסתן לא אתיא כרבנן, אלא כרבי מאיר דחייש למיעוטא, וסבר דכותים גרי אמת הן, כדמוכח פ' "שור שנגח ד' וה'" (ב"ק לח:) אבל לרבנן, דלא חיישי למיעוטא – לא הוו נדות מעריסתן. ולא לר' יוסי, אע"ג דחייש למיעוטא בפרק "אלמנה" (יבמות דף*) כיון דקסבר כותים גרי אריות הן, כדמוכח במנחות בפרק "רבי ישמעאל" (דף סו:) דקאמר: תורמין משל (*ישראל) על של גוים – ואם כן, כותים לא מטמאו בנדות, כדאמר לקמן: בנות ישראל מטמאין בזיבה, ואין גוים מטמאים בזיבה. ותימה: והא בנות כותים דהוו נדות מעריסתן, *הוו מי"ח דבר, ובפ"ק דשבת (דף יג:) משמע דליכא מאן דפליג על י"ח דבר, ומשמע התם (דף יז:) דהוי מי"ח דבר לכ"ע! וי"ל: דאפי' רבנן דלא חיישי למיעוטא, ואפילו גרי אריות הן – שוינהו רבנן נדות מעריסתן, וגזרו עליהם טומאה כדי שלא יטמעו בהן, כמו שגזרו על בת גוי. וא"ת: אם כן, אמאי מוקי לה כר"מ ומשום דחייש למיעוטא, לוקמיה ככ"ע ומשום טימוע. דר"מ נמי אית ליה טעמא דטימוע, דאמר בפ' "ד' וה'" (ב"ק דף לח:): קנסא דקניס ר"מ בממונא – כדי שלא יטמעו בהן! וי"ל: משום דע"כ מתני' לית ליה טעמא דטימוע, אלא משום חשש ראיה, כדקתני "לפי שיושבות על כל דם ודם". והא דא"כ יוסי "מעשה בעין בול, והטבילוה קודם לאמה", אע"ג דטעמא דרבי יוסי משום טימוע – הוצרך להביא ראיה דשכיח הוא שרואות הן בקטנותן. דאי לאו הכי, הוי כחוכא ואטלולא למיגזר בהן נדות. וא"ת: לר"מ דחייש למיעוטא, וקסבר דכותים גרי אמת הן, א"כ הוו נדות מעריסתן מן התורה, ולמה מני לה מי"ח דבר? וי"ל: דמסתמא לא ראתה מיד אחר ההולדה רגע אחד, א"כ אוקמה בחזקת שלא ראתה, וסמוך רובא דלא חזו לחזקה שלא ראתה, °והוו הנך דחזו מיעוטא דמיעוטא ולא מטמו מדאורייתא, אלא מדרבנן הוא דגזרו עליהם מי"ח דבר. וא"ת: ולר' יוסי דגרי אריות הן, אמאי גזרו בכותים דהוו נדות מעריסתן, ובבת גוי לא גזרו עד בת ג' שנים, כדאמרינן התם? ויש לומר: דהחמירו בכותים דעבדי קצת מצות, ולא בדילי ישראל מינייהו, וגזרו עליהם מעריסתן – דלא ליתי וליטמעו בהן. אבל מגוים הוו בדילי טובא, ולא גזרו עלייהו עד דליהוי ראויות לביאה.

**שמא** תמצא אילונית. וא"ת: ותתיבם ממה נפשך, דאם אילונית היא – הוי קידושי אחיו (א) טעות, כדתנן (יבמות דף ב:) וכולן שנמצאו אילונית – צרותיהן מותרות, משום דלא הויא צרת ערוה! ותירץ ר"ת: דהכא איירי בדקבל עלויה אחיו. וכי האי גוונא משני בריש "בן סורר ומורה" (סנהדרין דף סט:) ואין להאריך כאן יותר. וא"ת: ובקטן אמאי חיישינן שמא ימצא סריס – ונידבדקיה אם עושה כיפה כשמשתין, או אחד משאר סימנין דאמר ב"הערל" (יבמות דף פ:) ואיכא למ"ד התם דלא הוי סריס עד שיהו בו כל סימני סריס! וי"ל: דאין מועלת הבדיקה עד שהוא גדול בשנים. **והטבילוה** קודם לאמה. ומשום שראתה. דאי משום שנגעה באמה שטמאה לידה, א"כ מאי אשמעינן? כל ולדות נמי טמאין! *ובפרק "עד כמה" (בכורות דף כז.) דקאמר גבי חלה דמאכילתו לכהן קטן ה"ה לכהן גדול שטבל, כדמשמע הכא. **שתיה** בכלל אכילה. וא"ת: בפרק "העור והרוטב" (חולין דף קכ.) גבי חֵלֶב, למה לי "כל נפש" לרבות שותה? ויש לומר: דאשמעינן דחלב מהותך שמיה חלב*. **וכשמן** בעצמותיו. ואם תאמר: דמעיקרא מייתי מן התורה, והדר מייתי אסמכתא?! דבפרק "ר"ע" (שבת דף פו.) תנן דסיכה ביוה"כ אסור, אע"ג שאין ראיה לדבר, זכר לדבר – שנאמר: "ותבא כמים בקרבו". ואומר רבינו תם: דקרא ד"לא יחללו" נמי אסמכתא הוא, דבפרק "הנשרפין" (סנהדרין דף פג.) דרשינן מיניה דטבל במיתה, ובפרק קמא דזבחים (דף ג:) מידרש לדרשא אחריתי. ומדאורייתא לא הוי סך כשותה, וכן לענין יוה"כ ותדע: דאין חייבין כרת אלא אוכל ושותה בלבד. ואמר נמי בפרק בתרא דיומא (דף עז:) מי שיש לו חטטין בראשו – סך כדרכו, ואינו חושש. ועוד אומר ר"ת: דדוקא סיכת שמן אסמכוה רבנן אקרא, ואסור מדרבנן. אבל סיכה של שומן חזיר ושל חֵלֶב – שריא. ובפרק "כל שעה" (פסחים דף כד:) אמר: המניח חלב של שור הנסקל ע"ג מכתו – פטור אבל אסור הוא, משום דאסור בהנאה. משמע: אבל חלב דעלמא – אפילו איסורא ליכא*. **אי** גרס הלכתא הוא א"ש דלא הוי הלכתא אלא חדא. ומיהו ברוב ספרים גרס "נינהו" – היינו, לפי שלא פירש רבא הי קרא והי הלכתא, כלומר, אחד מן הפסוקים, וא"נ לפרש משום דקאי נמי אקרא דזכרים דלקמן. ובסוף "הישן" (סוכה דף כח.) גבי "אזרח" להוציא את הנשים, קאמר: "הלכתא נינהו", אע"ג דליכא אלא חדא. (שייך לע"ב) **לנקבה** כל שהיא בין גדולה בין קטנה. – וקרא ד"ואשה" דזבה אתי לדרשה אחרינא. ומעיינות דמצורע ומצורעת – צריך לומר דמפיק ליה מקרא אחרינא. דליכא למימר דתרווייהו משמעתי מחדא קרא, דהא לקמן אמר אביי: מדקאמר ר' יוסי "זאת תורת הזב" – בין גדול בין קטן, איתור "לזכר" – לרבות מעיינות. למעוטי

**עין משפט נר מצוה**

ב א מיי' פ"א מהלכות יבום הלכה טו יז סמג עשין נב טוש"ע אה"ע סימן קסז סעיף ג ד:
ג ב מיי' שם טוש"ע שם סעיף ה:
[וס"ז: עי' תוס' בד"ה אין תופסין]
[וכותים]
ד ג מיי' פ"ז מהלכות תרומות הל' ח [וברב אלפס פסחים פ"ג דף קמו.]:
[ועי' תוס' שבת עז: ד"ה אף בנות]
ה ד מיי' שם פ"ט הלכ' ב:
ו ה ו מיי' פ"ו מהלכות איסורי ביאה הלכה ה ופ"א מהלכות מטמאי משכב ומושב הלכה ג:

**תוספי הרא"ש**

לפרושי והן יושבות על כל דם ודם ואי אית לן טעמא דטימוע אפילו בודאי לא חזו גזרו עליהם: **והטבילות** קודם לאמה. ותימה דילמא משמע דנגעה באמה וי"ל דא"כ כולהו נמי א"נ למה לטבול משום מגע א"א שלא תינק מאמה: **אין** תרומת חוצה לארץ. משמע הכא דשייך תרומה בחוצה לארץ וכן מוכח במה דוכתי וקשה מהא דאמרינן בפ"ק דחולין דר' מאיר אכל עלה של ירק בבית שאן וע"י כן התיר רבי כל בית שאן אלמא דאין תרומה נוהגת בחוצה לארץ וי"ל דהתם בדמאי שאינו נוהג בחוצה לארץ וכן ההיא דבצר לאו היינו בצרה בפ' בתרא דע"ז: **ואיבעית** אימא מהכא ותבא כמים בקרבו כו'. לאו דרשא גמורה היא אלא אסמכתא בעלמא דבשבת פרק ר' עקיבא קאמר עלה אף על פי שאין ראיה לדבר זכר לדבר משום דברחיצה משתעי קרא כדאמרינן בפ' בתרא דיומא מה שמן מאבראי כו' תימה דבתר דמייתי קרא מדאורייתא מייתי קרא דאסמכתא ואומר ר"ת דקרא (קרא) נמי אסמכתא הוא דלכמה דרשות דרשינן ליה בפ"ק דזבחים דרשינן מיניה דאין חולין מחללין קדשים ועוד ילפינן מיניה דטבל לבמיתה ומדאוריית' לא הוי סך כשותה והא דתנן במס' תרומות דסך שמן של תרומה משלם קרן וחומש היינו מדרבנן וכן לענין יום הכיפורים אמרינן דאינו חייב כרת אלא אוכל ושותה ואמרינן נמי בפ' בתרא דיומא דמי שיש לו חטטין בראשו סך כדרכו ואינו חושש ואי הויא סיכה מדאורייתא לא הוה מקילינן ביה כולי האי וכל קראי דיום הכפורים אסמכתא בעלמא ניהו ואומר עוד ר"ת דוקא סיכה של שמן אסמכוה אקרא ואסרוה אבל סיכה של שומן חזיר או חלב שריא. הלכתא ניהו גרס ואי גרס ניהנו לפי שלא פי' הי הלכתא והי קרא שייך לומר ניהנו כלומר מאחד מאלו השנים: למעוטי

**מסורת הש"ס**

יבמות סא: קיט. בכורות יט:
[תוספתא פ"ה]
בכורות כז.
ג"ל את אשר
[שבועות כב: יומא עו.] [שבת פו.]
יומא עו: [שבת פו.]
[לקמן מד.]
הוא ענין בפני עצמו. רש"ל ועיין ר"מ
[ועי' היטב תוס' חולין סה ד"ה לרבות]
[וע"ע תוס' יומא עו: ד"ה דתנן וכו']

**הגהות הב"ח**

(א) תוס' ד"ה שמא וכו' קידושי אחיו קידושי טעות:

**גליון הש"ס**

גמ' הא נמי מיעוטא דשכיח הוא. עי' שבת סה ע"א ברש"י ד"ה ואפילו: תוס' ד"ה ר"מ וכו' והוו הנך דחזו מיעוטא למיעוטא וכו'. כדאמרי' יבמות קיט:

לְמַעוּטֵי [א]אִישׁ מֵאוֹדֶם. וְהָא דְּתַנְיָא: "אִשָּׁה" — אֵין לִי אֶלָּא אִשָּׁה, [ב]בַּת י' יָמִים לְזִיבָה מִנַּיִן — ת"ל: "וְאִשָּׁה". לָמָּה לִי? לִיגְמַר מִנִּדָּה! צְרִיכָא, דְּאִי כְּתַב רַחֲמָנָא בְּנִדָּה — הֲוָה אָמִינָא: נִדָּה — מִשּׁוּם דְּכִי חֲזַאי חַד יוֹמָא, בָּעֲיָא לְמֵיתַב ז', אֲבָל זָבָה, דְּאִי חֲזַאי חַד יוֹמָא — בְּשׁוֹמֶרֶת יוֹם כְּנֶגֶד יוֹם סַגִּי לָהּ, אֵימָא: לָא, צְרִיכָא. וְלִיכְתּוֹב רַחֲמָנָא בְּזָבָה, וְלָא בָּעֵי בְּנִדָּה, וַאֲנָא יָדַעְנָא דְּאֵין זָבָה בְּלֹא נִדָּה! אִין ה"נ. וְאֶלָּא קְרָא לָמָּה לִי? לְמַעוּטֵי אִישׁ מֵאוֹדֶם. הָא מִיעַטְתֵּיהּ חֲדָא זִימְנָא? חַד — לְמַעוּטֵי מִשִּׁכְבַת זֶרַע, וְחַד — לְמַעוּטֵי מִדָּם. וְכֵן לְעִנְיַן זְכָרִים. *דְּתַנְיָא: °"אִישׁ אִישׁ", מַה ת"ל [ויקרא טו] "אִישׁ אִישׁ"? — *לְרַבּוֹת [ג]תִּינוֹק בֶּן יוֹם אֶחָד, שֶׁהוּא מְטַמֵּא בְּזִיבָה, דִּבְרֵי רַבִּי יְהוּדָה. רַבִּי יִשְׁמָעֵאל בְּנוֹ שֶׁל ר' יוֹחָנָן בֶּן בְּרוֹקָה אוֹמֵר: אֵין צָרִיךְ, הֲרֵי הוּא אוֹמֵר: °"לַזָּכָר וְלַנְּקֵבָה" [שם], "לַזָּכָר" — כָּל שֶׁהוּא זָכָר, בֵּין שֶׁהוּא גָּדוֹל בֵּין שֶׁהוּא קָטָן. "וְלַנְּקֵבָה" — כָּל שֶׁהִיא נְקֵבָה, בֵּין גְּדוֹלָה בֵּין קְטַנָּה. א"כ, מַה ת"ל "אִישׁ אִישׁ"? *דִּבְּרָה תוֹרָה כִּלְשׁוֹן בְּנֵי אָדָם. אַלְמָא, כִּי מְרַבֵּי קְרָא — בֶּן יוֹם אֶחָד מְרַבֵּי. וּרְמִינְהוּ: "אִישׁ" — אֵין לִי אֶלָּא אִישׁ, [ד]בֶּן תֵּשַׁע שָׁנִים וְיוֹם אֶחָד מִנַּיִן? ת"ל: °"וְאִישׁ"! [שם] אָמַר רָבָא: *הִלְכְתָא נִינְהוּ, וְאַסְמְכִינְהוּ רַבָּנַן אַקְּרָאֵי. הֵי הִלְכְתָא וְהֵי קְרָא? אִילֵימָא בֶּן יוֹם אֶחָד — הִלְכְתָא, וּבֶן ט' שָׁנִים וְיוֹם אֶחָד — קְרָא, קְרָא סְתָמָא כְּתִיב! אֶלָּא בֶּן ט' שָׁנִים וְיוֹם אֶחָד — הִלְכְתָא, וּבֶן יוֹם א' — קְרָא. וְכִי מֵאַחַר דְּהִלְכְתָא הִיא, קְרָא לָמָּה לִי? לְמַעוּטֵי [ה]אִשָּׁה מִלּוֹבֶן. לָמָּה לִי לְמִכְתַּב בִּזְכָרִים, וְלָמָּה לִי לְמִכְתַּב בִּנְקֵבוֹת? צְרִיכִי, דְּאִי כְּתַב רַחֲמָנָא בִּזְכָרִים — מִשּׁוּם [ו]דְּמִטַּמְּאוּ בִּרְאִיּוֹת כְּבְיָמִים, אֲבָל נְקֵבוֹת דְּלָא מִטַּמְּאוּ בִּרְאִיּוֹת כְּבְיָמִים — אֵימָא לָא. וְאִי כְּתַב רַחֲמָנָא בִּנְקֵבוֹת — מִשּׁוּם [ז]דְּקָמִטַּמְּאוּ בְּאוֹנֶס, אֲבָל זְכָרִים דְּלָא מִטַּמְּאוּ בְּאוֹנֶס — אֵימָא: לָא, צְרִיכָא. § "הַכּוּתִים מְטַמְּאִין מִשְׁכָּב תַּחְתּוֹן כָּעֶלְיוֹן". § מַאי "מִשְׁכָּב תַּחְתּוֹן כָּעֶלְיוֹן"? אִילֵימָא דְּאִי אִיכָּא י' מַצָּעוֹת וְיָתֵיב עֲלַיְיהוּ — מִטַּמּוּ לְהוּ, פְּשִׁיטָא, דְּהָא דָּרַס לְהוּ! אֶלָּא [ח]שֶׁיְּהֵא תַּחְתּוֹנוֹ שֶׁל בּוֹעֵל נִדָּה כְּעֶלְיוֹנוֹ שֶׁל זָב, מָה עֶלְיוֹנוֹ שֶׁל זָב — אֵינוֹ מְטַמֵּא אֶלָּא אוֹכָלִין וּמַשְׁקִין, אַף תַּחְתּוֹנוֹ שֶׁל בּוֹעֵל נִדָּה — אֵינוֹ מְטַמֵּא אֶלָּא אוֹכָלִין וּמַשְׁקִין. עֶלְיוֹנוֹ שֶׁל זָב מְנָלַן? דִּכְתִיב: °"וְכָל הַנּוֹגֵעַ בְּכֹל אֲשֶׁר יִהְיֶה תַחְתָּיו יִטְמָא" [שם], מַאי "תַּחְתָּיו"? אִילֵימָא

**רש"י**

לְמַעוּטֵי אִישׁ מֵאוֹדֶם. וְאע"ג דִּקְרָא לָאו בְּאוֹדֶם מַיְירֵי – עַל כָּרְחֵיךְ, כֵּיוָן דִּקְרָא יְתֵירָא הוּא, לִדְרָשָׁא אָתָא. וּמַה שֶּׁיֵּשׁ לְךָ לִדְרוֹשׁ דָּבָר הַקָּרוֹב לָעִנְיָן, דְּרוֹשׁ בּוֹ. וְה"ק: אִשָּׁה טְמֵאָה בְּדָבָר הָאָמוּר בָּהּ, דְּהַיְינוּ אוֹדֶם, וְאֵין אִישׁ טָמֵא בְּדָבָר הָאָמוּר בְּאִשָּׁה. וְאִי קַשְׁיָא: ה"ל לְמִיכְתַּב לְהַךְ דְּרָשָׁה גַּבֵּי נִדָּה? אִין ה"נ, דִּלְגַבֵּי נִדָּה נַמִי קְרָא אַחֲרִינָא כְּתִיב, דְּדָרְשִׁינַן לֵהּ לְקַמָּן הָכִי. וּמִיהוּ תַּרְוַיְיהוּ צְרִיכִי, כִּדְקָאָמַר לְקַמָּן: הַהוּא דְּגַבֵּי נִדָּה – לְמַעוּטֵי אִישׁ מִדָּם מַמָּשׁ, שֶׁאֵין דָּם הַיּוֹצֵא מִפִּי הָאַמָּה מְטַמֵּא בְּזִיבָה. וְהַאי – לְמַעוּטֵי שִׁכְבַת זֶרַע אָדוֹם. הַאי – בְּמַאי דְּאִישְׁתַּעֵי בֵּיהּ, וְהַאי – בְּמַאי דְּאִישְׁתַּעֵי בֵּיהּ. וְהָא דְּתַנְיָא אִשָּׁה. לְעִנְיַן זָבָה כְּתִיב: "וְאִשָּׁה כִּי יָזוּב זוֹב דָּמָהּ יָמִים רַבִּים". "יָמִים" ב' "רַבִּים" ג'. בַּת י' יָמִים. דִּבְצִיר מֵהָכִי לֵיכָּא זִיבָה: ז' יְמֵי נִדָּה וְג' יְמֵי זִיבָה, שֶׁאֵין זִיבָה אֶלָּא לְאַחַר נִדּוּת, כִּדְמְפָרֵשׁ בְּשַׁמַּעְתָּא בַּתְרַיְיתָא דִּמְכִילְתִּין. לִגְמַר מִנִּדָּה. כֵּיוָן דְּבַת יוֹם אֶחָד מְטַמְּאָה בְּנִדָּה, בַּת י' נַמִי מִטַּמְּאָה בְּזִיבָה, דְּאֵין זִיבָה בְּלֹא נִדָּה, שֶׁאֵינָהּ אֶלָּא לְאַחַר נִדּוּת. וְאֶלָּא קְרָא. "וְאִשָּׁה" דִּכְתִיב גַּבֵּי נִדָּה, לָמָּה לִי? לְמַעוּטֵי אִישׁ מֵאוֹדֶם. דְּהָכִי מַשְׁמַע: אִשָּׁה מִטַּמְּאָה בְּנִדָּה, וְלֹא אִישׁ. וְהָא מִיעַטְתֵּיהּ. לְעֵיל. חַד לְמַעוּטֵי מִשִּׁכְבַת זֶרַע. אָדוֹם, אִם יִרְאֶה שִׁכְבַת זֶרַע אָדוֹם. וְכֵן לְעִנְיַן זְכָרִים. מְרַבֵּי בֶּן יוֹם אֶחָד. אִישׁ אִישׁ. "כִּי יִהְיֶה זָב". אִישׁ אֵין לִי אֶלָּא אִישׁ. "וְאִישׁ כִּי תֵצֵא מִמֶּנּוּ שִׁכְבַת זָרַע". ה"נ גָּרְסִינַן: "וּמֵאַחַר דְּהִלְכְתָא, קְרָא לָמָּה לִי". וְהַבֶּן תִּשְׁעָה לְשִׁכְבַת זֶרַע קָמְהַדַּר. לָמָּה לִי לְמִיכְתַּב בִּזְכָרִים. "אִישׁ אִישׁ" לְרַבּוֹת קָטָן בֶּן יוֹמוֹ, וְלָמָּה לִי לְמִיכְתַּב בִּנְקֵבוֹת "וְאִשָּׁה" לְרַבּוֹת בַּת יוֹם אֶחָד לְנִדָּה וּבַת י' לְזִיבָה? בִּרְאִיּוֹת כְּבְיָמִים. בֵּין שֶׁרוֹאֶה ג' בְּיוֹם אֶחָד, בֵּין שֶׁרוֹאָה שָׁלֹשׁ בִּשְׁלֹשָׁה יָמִים רְצוּפִין – הָוֵי זָב, כִּדְיָלְפִינַן בְּב"ק בְּפֶרֶק "כֵּיצַד" (דף כד.) "לַזָּכָר וְלַנְּקֵבָה" – מַה נְּקֵבָה בְּיָמִים, אַף זָכָר בְּיָמִים. וּרְאִיּוֹת בְּגוּפֵיהּ כְּתִיב, מָנָה הַכָּתוּב שָׁלֹשׁ, וּקְרָאוֹ "טָמֵא". אֲבָל זָבָה שֶׁרָאֲתָה שָׁלֹשׁ בְּיוֹם אֶחָד – לָא הָוְיָא זָבָה. זָב לָא מִיטַּמֵּא בְּאוֹנֶס. דִּכְתִיב: "מִבְּשָׂרוֹ" – וְלֹא מֵחֲמַת אוֹנְסוֹ. זָבָה מִיטַּמְּאָה בְּאוֹנֶס, בְּהַאי פִּירְקָא (לקמן דף לו.): כְּשֶׁהוּא אוֹמֵר "כִּי יָזוּב זוֹב דָּמָהּ" – הֲרֵי אוֹנֶס אָמוּר. מִשְׁכַּב הַזָּב וְהַנִּדָּה מְטַמֵּא אָדָם. דִּכְתִיב (ויקרא טו): "וְאִישׁ אֲשֶׁר יִגַּע בְּמִשְׁכָּבוֹ", וּכְתִיב (שם): "וְכָל הַנּוֹגֵעַ בְּמִשְׁכָּבָהּ" וגו'. כְּעֶלְיוֹנוֹ שֶׁל זָב. וְלֹא כְּתַחְתּוֹנוֹ שֶׁמְּטַמֵּא אָדָם. אִילֵימָא

**תוספות**

**למעוטי** אשה מלובן. אע"ג דבכל דוכתין דורשין וי"ו לרבות, והכא דורשין למעוטי. פרש"י: כיון דלא אצטריך לרבות, מיפרשי לקרא דלכך אייתר, לומר: דדוקא איש אמרתי לך, ולא אשה. וכן גבי אשה – אשה אמרתי לך, ולא איש. הקשה הריב"ן: למה לי למעוטי אשה מלובן, הא ממעטינן לעיל בפ"ב (דף יט.) מ"דמיה" "דמיה" דד' דמים טמאים באשה, ותו לא? ותירץ: דמ"מ ה"א דאתי בק"ו מאיש, דלא מיטמא באודם – מיטמא בלובן. אשה – לא כ"ש! ואע"ג דאיכא למיפרך: מה לאיש, שכן מיטמא בראיות כבימים! איכא למימר: גילוי מילתא בעלמא הוא.

**צריכי** דאי כתב רחמנא זכר כו'. תימה: הא פרשב"ס בפ' "דם הנדה" (לקמן דף נד:) דאיתקש זב לנדה, מדכתיב "והדוה בנדתה" וגו' לטמא אדם לטמא בגדים, אם נשא משכבה ומושבה. וכן פי' בסמוך גבי כלי חרס, דמטמא בהיסט. וכן משמע ב"יוצא דופן" (לקמן דף מא:) דמצריך קרא גבי נדה דמיטמאה בפנים כבחוץ, מדכתיב "בבשרה". וגבי זב צריך קרא דלא מיטמא בפנים כבחוץ, "כי יהיה זב מבשרו" – עד שתצא מבשרו, משמע דאיצטריך קרא דלא נגמר מנדה.*

**עליונו** של זב מנלן. זאת היתה גירסת רש"י: דכתיב "וכל הנוגע בכל אשר יהיה תחתיו יטמא". מאי "תחתיו"? אילימא תחתיו דזב מ"אשר יגע במשכבו" נפקא! אלא כל אשר יהיה הזב תחתיו. והיה כתוב בספרים: ומאי ניהו? נושא. מאי טעמא? "והנשא" כתיב. ולא גרים רש"י: דהא כבר נפקא מתחתיו, ועוד: *דכתיב "והנושא", כתיב כבוס בגדים. וחזר בו רש"י מגירסא זו. דהיכי מוקי האי קרא בעליונו של זב? הא בהדיא בת"כ מוקי לה במרכב! ועוד: היכי הוה בעי לאוקומי במשכב, הא במשכב כתיב כבוס בגדים בנוגע בו, והכא לא כתיב כבוס בגדים! וכי ה"ג פרכינן בפ"ק (לעיל דף ט.) גבי "מזה מי נדה", ועוד: היכי מוקי ליה בעליונו של זב דאינו מטמא אלא אוכלין ומשקין, הלא אין להם טהרה במקוה, וקרא כתיב "יטמא עד הערב"! ונראה דרש"י ל"ג מאי "תחתיו" אילימא כו', אלא גרים: "כל הנוגע בכל אשר יהיה תחתיו יטמא עד הערב", והנושא נמי יטמא, ומאי ניהו? נישא. מאי טעמא? "והנשא" כתיב – נתקו הכתוב מטומאה כו'. וה"פ: "והנוגע בכל אשר יהיה תחתיו" במרכב איירי, כדמוקי לה בת"כ, דהאי קרא אחר מרכב כתיב. וחלק בין מגעו למשאו, דמגעו – מטמא אדם ולא בגדים, דהכא לא כתיב כבוס בגדים. ובמשאו – מטמא אדם לטמא בגדים, כדקמסיים קרא "והנושא אותם יכבס בגדיו", וקאי על כל מה דכתיב בענין: מעיינותיו, ומרכבו, ומושבו. ועליונו של זב דרשינן הכא מדכתיב "והנשא" חסר בלא וי"ו, קאי ארישא דקרא דמרכב, דכתיב ביה "יטמא", ולא כתיב ביה כבוס בגדים. והכי קאמר: הנוגע במרכב הזב יטמא, וכן הנושא, דהיינו עליונו של זב נתקו הכתוב מטומאה שלאחריו. דע"כ "והנישא" ארישא דקרא קאי ולא אסיפא, דהא כתיב "אותם" וגבי נישא לא שייך "אותם". אלא "אותם" קאי אמאי דקרינן "נושא", והמסורת קאי ארישא דקרא. ופריך: אימא דנתקו מטומאה חמורה לטמא אדם לטמא בגדים, אבל אדם או בגדים ליטמא כמו מרכב! ומשני: ד"יטמא" – טומאה קלה משמע, דהנושא סמוך לנוגע במרכב, ובגד שנגע במרכב לא מטמא אלא אוכלין ומשקין. ומיהו יש ליישב גירסא ראשונה דדריש מ"תחתיו" ואף על גב דקרא איירי במרכב, מכל מקום תיבה ד"תחתיו" לא איירי במרכב אלא בתחתיו. דאמר בת"כ, ומייתי לה בפרק "בכל מערבין" (עירובין דף כז.) האוכף – טמא מושב, והתפוס – טמא מרכב. אלמא מה שתחתיו, לא אקרי מרכב אלא מושב. ולהכי קאמר (א) דבעי "תחתיו", במאי מיירי: אי במשכב מ"אשר יגע" כו'. והוה מצי למפרך: דבמשכב כתיב כבוס בגדים, והכא לא כתיב. אלא דעדיפא מיניה פריך. א"נ, מש"ה לא כתיב כבוס בגדים – משום דעיקר קרא במרכב כתיב, דלא בעי כבוס בגדים. ומפרש: אלא שהזב "תחתיו" – דהיינו, עליונו של זב דלא מטמא אלא אוכלין ומשקין וטומאת ערב דכתיב בקרא – משום מרכב, דמרכב מטמא אדם או בגדים. וגרס שפיר: מאי טעמא? "והנשא" כתיב, ד"מתחתיו" גרידא לא הוה מוקמינן בעליונו של זב, דלא הייתי בודים טומאה מלבנו, אלא הוה מוקמינן לה במרכב. ואי לאו נמי "תחתיו", מ"נושא" לא הוה מוקמינן ליה לטומאה קלה דאוכלין ומשקין בנשא, כיון דכתיב ביה כבוס בגדים, וה"א דנתקו לטמא אדם או בגדים קמ"ל "תחתיו" דאיירי בעליונו של זב, ונכתב גבי מרכב דליכא כבוס בגדים, וכתיב ביה "יטמא" דמשמע טומאה קלה. ועוד, דע"כ גרסינן: "והנשא" כתיב. דאי לא דרשינן עליונו של זב אלא מתחתיו, היכי פריך "אימא נתקו מטומאה חמורה?" היכא כתיב ביה טומאה חמורה, דקאמר "נתקו"? והנשא

**תוספי הרא"ש**

**למעוטי** אשה מלובן. אע"ג דקרא איירי בשכבת זרע של איש ממעטינן מיניה זיבה דאשה דלא שייכא טומאת קרי באשה והא דדרשינן בכל מקום וי"ו לרבות ובשמעתין דרשינן למעט חשיב רש"י דכיון דלא איצטרכי לריבויא כדקאמ' תלמודא מפרשינן לקראי הכי דלכך יתיר הוא"ו לומר דוקא אשה אמרתי לך ולא איש וכן נמי גבי איש ותימה ולמה לי למעט אשה מלובן הא אמרינן ד' דמים טמאים באשה ותו לא. והשיב רש"י דהא דאמרינן ד' דמים טמאים באשה היינו למעוטי שאר מראות שנוטין לאדמימות כגון במימי תלתן ובמימי בשר צלי וירוק טהורין מטומאת שבעה אבל לובן דהכא לאו ממראה דם הוא והוה מטמינן ליה באשה טומאת ערב מק"ו דאיש שאינו מטמא באודם מטמא בלובן אי לאו דמיעטיה קרא: **צריכי** דאי כתב בזכרים. ותימה והא איתקש זב ונדה כדמפרש בגמרא בריש דם הנדה דהא דנדה מטמא (עושה) משכב ומושב לטמא אדם לטמא בגדים משום דהוקשה לזב דכתיב והזבה בנדתה והזב את זובו וכן פי' בשמעתין לקמן דהא דזבה ונדה מטמו כלי חרס בהיסט משום דאיתקוש לזב דכתיב ביה וכלי חרס אשר יגע בו הזב דרשינן מיניה איזהו מגעו שהוא ככולו הוי אומר זה היסטו וכן מוכח לקמן דאיתקוש בריש פרק יוצא דופן דדרשינן גבי נדה שמטמאה בפנים כבחוץ מדכתיב בבשרה וגבי זב מיבעי לן קרא דאינו מטמא בפנים כבחוץ מדכתיב איש כי יהיה זב מבשרו עד שתצא מבשרו ואי איתקש זב לנדה דאיצטריך קרא דלא ניגמר מנדה ומיהו גבי בעל קרי אע"ג דלא איתקוש מיבעי ליה קרא לקמן דאינו מטמא בפנים כבחוץ מדכתיב איש כי תצא ממנו שכבת זרע עד שתצא טומאתו לחוץ אלא ודאי לא צריך היקשא לכך דה"א גילוי מילתא בעלמא דכל מי שטומאה יוצאה מגופו שיטמא בפנים כבחוץ כיון שנעקר ופירכא קמייתא איכא לשנויי דהיקשא אתיא לסוף טומאה דכל מה שטמא בזה טמא בזה אבל לעיקר טומאה לטמות בו יום אחד לא הוקשו כג"ל: **בעליונו** של זב. פרש"י כגון זב בכף מאזנים ואדם או כלים בכף שניה וכרע הזב וקשה דהאי היסט הוא כדאמרינן בשבת בסוף פרק ר"ע דכל טומאות המסיטות טהורות חוץ מזב המסיט ומסיק זב וכל דדמי ליה כגון ע"ז שהסיטה אחרים כגון שכרעה בכף מאזנים והיסט נפקא לן מקרא אחרינא. וי"ל דעליונו של זב כגון בגד מקצתו מונח על ראשו ומקצתו מונח בארץ דמטעם היסט אינו טמא עד שיסיט את כולו כדאמרינן איזהו מגעו שהוא ככולו הוי אומר זה היסטו. א"נ שאצבעו של זב תחת הנדבך ואוכלים ומשקין על גביו ואין הזב מסיטן ומטמאין משום עליונו של זב: **ועליונו של** זב מנא לן. ה"ג רש"י כפירושי' דכתיב והנוגע בכל אשר יהיה תחתיו טמא מאי

**עין משפט נר מצוה**

ז א מיי' פ"א מהלכות מטמאי משכב ומושב הלכה ו ומיי' פ"ה מהל' שאר אבות הטומאות הלכה ג:
ח ב מיי' פ"ד מהלכות איסורי ביאה הלכה א ופ"א מהלכות מטמאי משכב ומושב הלכה ג:
ט ג מיי' פ"א מהלכות מטמאי משכב ומושב הלכה ד ופ"ג מהלכות מחוסרי כפרה הלכה ו:
י ד מיי' פ"ה מהלכות אבות הטומאות הלכה ב:
יא ה מיי' פ"א מהלכות מטמאי משכב ומושב הלכה ו:
יב ו מיי' פ"ב מהלכות מחוסרי כפרה הלכה ו:
יג ז מיי' פ"ה מהלכות איסורי ביאה הלכה א:
יד ח מיי' פ"ג מהלכות מטמאי משכב ומושב הלכה ב:

ערכין ג. [כריתות ח] לקמן מד.
[וע' תוס' לקמן מג: ד"ה עד שילא]
נ"ל דכתב

**מסורת הש"ס**

[דהוה כעין מיעוט אחר מיעוט שהוא לרבות תוי"ט רפ"ב דזבים]
[לקמן מד. וש"נ]
[עי' תוס' סוכה כח. ד"ה הלכתא וע"ע קדושין ט. ד"ה הלכתא]

**הגהות הב"ח**

(א) תוס' ד"ה עליונו וכו' ולהכי קאמר דבעי תחתיו במאי מיירי:

אילימא תחתיו דזב — מ"ואיש אשר יגע במשכבו" נפקא, אלא הנוגע בכל אשר יהיה הזב תחתיו, ומאי ניהו — עליון של זב (והנושא נמי יטמא, ומאי ניהו — נישא, מ"ט? "והנשא" כתיב.) א נתקו הכתוב מטומאה חמורה והביאו לידי טומאה קלה, לומר לך שאינו מטמא אלא אוכלין ומשקין. אימר: נתקו הכתוב מטומאה חמורה — דלא מטמא אדם לטמא בגדים, אבל אדם או בגדים ליטמא! אמר קרא "יטמא" — טומאה קלה משמע. ותחתונו של בועל נדה, מנלן? דתניא ° "ותהי נדתה עליו", יכול יעלה לרגלה? ת"ל: *"יטמא ז' ימים". ומה ת"ל "ותהי נדתה עליו"? שיכול לא יטמא אדם וכלי חרס, ת"ל: "ותהי נדתה עליו", מה היא ב מטמאה אדם וכלי חרס — ג אף הוא מטמא אדם וכלי חרס. אי מה היא ד עושה משכב ומושב לטמא אדם לטמא בגדים, אף הוא עושה משכב ומושב לטמא אדם לטמא בגדים? ת"ל: "וכל המשכב אשר ישכב עליו יטמא". שאין ת"ל "וכל המשכב אשר ישכב עליו יטמא", ומה ת"ל "וכל המשכב אשר" וגו' — ה נתקו הכתוב מטומאה חמורה והביאו לידי טומאה קלה, לומר לך שאינו מטמא אלא אוכלין ומשקין. *פריך רב אחאי: אימא נתקו הכתוב מטומאה חמורה והביאו לטומאה קלה — דלא ליטמא אדם לטמויי בגדים, אבל אדם ובגדים ליטמא! אמר רב אסי: "יטמא" — טומאה קלה משמע. אימא: "ותהי נדתה עליו" — כלל, "וכל המשכב" — פרט, כלל ופרט — אין בכלל אלא מה שבפרט: משכב ומושב — אין, מידי אחרינא — לא! אמר אביי: "יטמא ז' ימים" מפסיק הענין, הוי כלל ופרט המרוחקין זה מזה, *וכל כלל ופרט המרוחקין זה מזה — אין דנין אותו בכלל ופרט. רבא אמר: לעולם דנין, "וכל" — ריבויא הוא. מתקיף לה רבי יעקב: אימא כהיא, מה היא — לא חלקת בה בין מגעה למשכבה לטמא אדם ולטמא בגדים לחומרא, אף הוא — לא תחלוק בו בין מגעו למשכבו לטמא אדם ולטמא בגדים לקולא! *אמר רבא: "עליו" — להטעינו משמע. § "מפני שהן בועלי נדות" וכו'. § אטו כולהו בועלי נדות נינהו? א"ר יצחק מגדלאה: בנשואות שנו. § "והן יושבות על דם" וכו'. § תניא, אר"מ: אם הן יושבות על כל דם ודם — תקנה גדולה היא להן, אלא — שרואות דם אדום ומשלימות אותו לדם ירוק. דבר אחר: * ו יום שפוסקת בו, סופרתו למנין שבעה. מתקיף לה רמי בר חמא: ותספרנו, ואנן נמי ניספריה, דקיימא לן *מקצת היום ככולו! אמר רבא: אם כן שכבת זרע דסתר בזיבה היכי משכחת לה? והא מקצת היום ככולו! אי דחזאי בפלגא דיומא — ה"נ, הכא במאי עסקינן (א) — דחזאי סמוך לשקיעת החמה. וליקום וליימא ליה לקרא: כי כתיבא סמוך לשקיעת החמה כתיבא? אין, על ברחך *שבקיה לקרא, דאיהו דחיק ומוקי אנפשיה. בעי רמי בר חמא: *פולטת שכבת זרע, מהו שתסתור בזיבה? ז רואה היתה — וסותרת, או

תורה אור: ויקרא טו | שם

**רש"י**

אילימא תחתיו דזב. דהוא מדרס הזב. ומאי ניהו נישא. בגד הנישא על הזב, מאי טעמא? "והנושא" "והנישא" כתיב. לא ידענא מאי היא, ונראה בעיני שהוא פי' משובש. נתקו הכתוב מטומאה חמורה. מדכתיב: "וכל הנוגע בכל אשר יהיה תחתיו יטמא והנושא אותם יכבס בגדיו". ומדלא ערבינהו וניכתוב: "וכל הנוגע בכל אשר יהיה תחתיו והנושא אותם יכבס בגדיו", ואפסקינהו ב"יטמא" – מכלל דהאי "יטמא" לאו באדם ובגדים קמיירי, אלא באוכלין ומשקין. "והנושא אותם" נדרש בתורת כהנים לנושא משכבו ומושבו של זב. אימא. להכי אפסקינהו קרא: דלא יטמא אדם לטמא בגדים שעליו, להכי כתב "יטמא" – דאדם לחודיה טמא. או אם נגעו בגדים – יהו בגדים טמאים, ולא הוא. יעלה לרגלה. יעלה לסופה. כגון בא עליה בששי שלה – יטבול בליל המחרת כמותה. ז' ימים. ואפילו בא עליה בשביעי. מה היא מטמאה אדם לטמא בגדים. שעליו, דאתי בקל וחומר ממשכבה, אף הוא מטמא אדם לטמא בגדים שעליו. וכלי חרס בהיסט. ואע"ג דאין כלי חרס מקבל טומאה אלא מאוירו, בהיסט זב וזבה – מיטמא, כדכתיב (ויקרא טו): "(*כל כלי) חרס אשר יגע בו הזב", ואמרי' במכילתין: איזהו מגעו שהוא ככולו? הוי אומר: זה היסטו. שאין ת"ל וכל המשכב אשר ישכב עליו יטמא. שהרי כבר נאמר: "ותהי נדתה עליו", ובדידה כתיב: "וכל הנוגע במשכבה יכבס בגדיו". מטומאה חמורה. שלא יהיה משכבו חמור כמשכבה לטמא אדם ובגדים שעליו. אבל אדם ובגדים. או אדם אם תגע בו, או בגדים אם תגע בהם. מידי אחרינא לא. כגון אדם וכלי חרס. וכל המשכב. ריבויא הוא, ולאו פרטא. אימא כהיא. בועלה כמותה, דהא אקשינהו קרא. לחומרא. ששניהן מטמאין אדם לטמא בגדים. אף הוא לא תחלוק בין מגעו למשכבו. ולקולא, ששניהם לא יטמאו. דהא במשכבו – פשיטא לן שנתקו הכתוב, הלכך במגעו נמי – שאם נגע באדם, לא יטמאנו לטמא בגדים. דהא כתיב: "ותהי נדתה עליו", דהוקשו הוא והיא בהאי קרא. עליו. להחמיר משמע, ולא להקל. אטו כולהו בועלי נדות נינהו. והא איכא פנויים? אם הן יושבות על כל דם ודם. שהן רואות, בין טמא בין טהור – יושבת עליו ז' ימי נדתה, שהתחיל מנינה משנשתנה מראה דם, ותמנה ז' ימים. תקנה גדולה היא להם. אבל אינן עושות כן, אינן מונות אלא מראייה ראשונה כשאר נשים. וזהו קלקולה: שרואה דם אדום, ומשלימתו לדם ירוק. כגון ראתה ירוק תחלה, סבורה היא: שהיא טמאה, ומונה ממנו ז' ימים. וכשרואה בחמישי שלה דם אדום – אינה משמרת אלא שני ימים, להשלים ז' לראייתה הראשונה. והיא צריכה למנות מראייה שניה. יום שפוסקת בו. כשהיא רואה ג' רצופים לאחר ז' ימי הנדה, והויא זבה, ופוסקת באמצע היום – סופרת אותו קצת היום שעד הערב למנין שבעה נקיים. ואנן ז' נקיים שלמים בעינן לזבה. א"כ. דלענין נקיים מקצת היום ככולו, זב שפסק והתחיל לספור וראה קרי, וקיי"ל דסותר אותו היום ותו לא, ב"המפלת" בשמעתא קמייתא (לעיל דף כב.), ואי מקצת היום ככולו – מאי סותר? הא איכא קצת היום לבא. אי דחזאי בפלגא דיומא כו'. קושיא היא, ומשני: וליימא ליה לקרא כו' בתמיה. וקא מהדר לאוקמי אתקפתיה אין על ברחך שבקיה לקרא כו'. דכיון דקיי"ל בכל דוכתי "מקצת היום ככולו", איהו דחיק ומוקים אנפשיה בסמוך לשקיעת החמה. פולטת. כגון ששמשה בזוב, ופסקה, והתחילה למנות, ופלטה. מהו שתסתור מניינה? הא דקי"ל דפולטת טמאה – משום רואה היא, וסתרה. או

**תוספות**

והנשא כתיב. חסר וי"ו, תימה: דבמסורת הוא מלא? מיהו מלינו שהמסורת הוא חולק על התלמוד במסכת שבת (דף נה:) גבי בני עלי "מעבירים" כתיב, ובמקראות שלנו כתיב "מעבירים" מלא. מה היא מטמאה אדם וכלי חרס. משום דב"השותפין" (ב"ב ט:) גבי נושא נבלה ומדרס *אע"ג דמטמא שאר בגדים שעליו אינו מטמא אדם וכלי חרס לכך נקטינהו הכא. כלל ופרט המרוחקין זה מזה. מפורש בפ' "החובל" (ב"ק פה.). תניא א"ר מאיר וכו' – לרבי יוחנן דאמר בפ' "כל היד" (לעיל יט:) ירד ר"מ לשיטת עקביא בן מהללאל, וטימא דם ירוק, יפרש "דם ירוק" דהכא – לאו ירוק ממש כי ההיא דלעיל, אלא דיהה ממנו. וכן לעקביא: מטמאה כותית דם ירוק דיהה, מדם ירוק שהוא טמא. ולעיל פי' בע"א. סופרתו למנין ז'. וא"ת: א] ודאמר ב"כילד צולין"* [ובמס' נזיר] (דף טו:) מקצת היום ככולו, וזבה גדולה אמר התם דמשכחת אלידיה ברואה בין השמשות, וכי ככותים סוברי? דהכי פריך לקמן (דף סט.) לרב, דאמר: יום שפוסקת בו עולה למנין שבעה, "ורב, ככותאי אמרה לשמעתיה?". וי"ל: דר' יוסי לית ליה מקצת היום ככולו אלא בסוף ספירה, כמו שומרת יום. אבל בתחלה, כמו שאומרים כותים – מודה דלא אמרינן. ומה שקשה מפ"ק דר"ה (דף י.) נפרש בסוף *מכילתין* בע"ה *. דאיהו דחיק ומוקי אנפשיה. אין האמת כן, מדפריך בפ' בתרא (לקמן דף סט.) ורב, ככותאי אמרה לשמעתיה? רואה הויא וסתרה. אור"י: דמשכחת בשמשה, בהיתר שתסתור ע"י פליטה אחר ראיית ג' ימים רצופין דקי"ל כרבנן, בפ' "ר' עקיבא" (שבת פו:) דבעינן שש עונות שלמות. א"נ: אחר ראייה אחת, ואחר תיקון רבי זירא* דסופרת שבעה נקיים על טיפת דם כחרדל. דמסתמא צריך נמי נקיים מזרע, דכעין דאורייתא תקון. ומכאן, אשה ששמשה, וראתה מיד – אין לה להתחיל לספור נקיים עד אחר יום ד' דבעינן ו' עונות שלמות. וכן פסק ר"ת. ואפילו רבא דפליג הכא ארמי בר חמא, נראה דחזר בו, מדלא הסיעו.

**תוספי הרא"ש**

מאי תחתיו אילימא תחתיו דזב מאיש אשר יגע במשכבו נפקא אלא כל הנוגע בכל אשר יהיה הזב תחתיו טמא נתקו הכתוב מטומאה חמורה וכו' ופי' מדכתיב בכל אשר יהיה תחתיו יטמא והנושא אותם יכבס בגדיו ולא ערבינהו וניכתוב וכל הנוגע בכל אשר יהיה תחתיו והנושא אותם יכבס בגדיו ואפסקינהו ביטמא מכלל דהאי יטמא לאו באדם ובגדים קאי אלא באוכלין ומשקין ובספרים כתוב מאי ניהו נישא ומ"ט והנושא והנישא כתיב וכתב רש"י לא ידענא מאי היא ונראה בעיני שהוא פי' משובש ובתשובה כתב דה"ג דכתיב וכל הנוגע בכל אשר יהיה תחתיו יטמא עד הערב והנושא נמי יטמא ומאי ניהו נישא מ"ט והנישא כתיב נתקו הכתוב כו' וה"פ והנוגע בכל אשר יהיה תחתיו דזב בא הכתוב ולימד על המרכב שיטמא במגע דהאי קרא בתר מרכב כתיב וחלק משאו ממגעו שמגעו מטמא אדם ולא בגדים ומשאו מטמא אדם לטמא בגדים כדמסיים ביה קרא והנושא אותם יכבס בגדיו וקאי אכל האמור דכתיב ביה יטמא עד הערב

**הגהות הב"ח**

(א) גמ' במאי עסקינן דחזאי. נ"ב עיין בנזיר דף טז:

**הגהות מהר"ב רנשבורג**

א] תוד"ה סופרתו למנין ז' וא"ת הא דאמר ר' יוסי כו'. כנ"ל:

בענין זב עצמו ומעיינותיו ומושבו ומרכבו כולן מטמאין במשא את האדם לטמא בגדים והכא דרשינן דהאי דכתיב והנושא חסר וא"ו למידרשיה אנישא לעליונו של זב דקאי ארישיה דקרא דכתיב ביה יטמא עד הערב טומאה קלה ונתקו הכתוב מטומאה חמורה שלאחריו וה"ק הנוגע במרכב הזב יטמא טומאה קלה לטמא אוכלין ומשקין וכן הנישא על הזב דע"כ דרשא דנישא אטומאה דרישא קאי ולא אטומאה דסיפא דטומאה דסיפא כתיב ביה אותם וגבי נישא לא שייך אותם אלא אותם אמקרא קאי דקרינן נושא ודרשא דמסורת ארישא דקרא על גירס' הספ' שכתוב בפ' מאי תחתיו אילימא תחתיו דזב מאיש אשר יגע במשכבו נפקא הקש' דהאי קרא לאו במשכבו כתיב אלא במרכב מוקי לה בת"כ. ועוד הו"ל לאקשויי דגבי משכב כתיב יכבס בגדיו והכא כתיב יטמא עד הערב ועוד היכי מוקמינן לה באוכלין ומשקין הנוגעים בעליונו הא אין להם טהרה במקוה והכא כתיב יטמא עד הערב: ופריך אימא ניתקו הכתוב מטומאה חמורה כו' כלומר ממאי דהנישא יש לו דין של נוגע במרכב הזב דלמא דמטמא אדם או בגדים: והנשא כתיב חסר וא"ו. תימה דבמסורת משמע שהוא מלא (שכתוב בו לית מלא) ומיהו מצינו בכמה מקומות שהתלמוד חולק על מסורת הספרים בשבת בפ' במה בהמה אמר רב הונא בריה דרב יהושע מעבירם כתיב ובכל הספרים שלנו כתיב מעבירים: מה היא מטמאה אדם וכלי חרס. פרש"י אדם לטמא בגדים שעליו וכלי חרס בהיסט אף בועל נדה כן והקשה השר מקוצי דבסוף זבין תנן בועל נדה כטמא מת אלא שחמור ממנו בועל נדה שמטמא משכב תחתון בעליון. ולפרש"י ליתני נמי שמטמא אדם לטמא בגדים וכלי חרס בהיסט ותירץ הוא דאדם וכלי חרס דנקט היינו דוקא אדם ולא בגדים שעליו וכלי חרס במגע ולא בהיסטו. ותימה א"כ אמאי נקט כלי חרס וי"ל משום שמצינו בטומאות שמטמאין בגדים וכלי שטף ואין מטמאין אדם וכלי חרס כדתנן בפ' בתרא דזבים כל המטמא בגדים בשעת מגעו מטמא כלי שטף במגע אבל לא אדם וכלי חרס. (או בת"כ) [ובתו"כ] דריש ליה מקרא בפרש' ויהי ביום השמיני מנין לעשות שאר כלים כבגדים ת"ל יטמא אי יטמא יכול יטמא אדם וכלי חרס ת"ל בגד בגד מטמא ואינו מטמא אדם וכלי חרס. והא דאמרינן בסמוך עליו להטעינו משמע לאו להחמיר עליו לגמרי כמו בנדה. אלא במקצת לטמא אדם וכלים במגע. וכן פי' רבינו שמשון במס' כלים. והביא ראיה מהך ברייתא דת"כ דתאני התם בתר דקאמר ניתקו הכתוב מטומאה חמורה לקלה גבי משכב נמצאת אומר משכבו כמגעו מה מגעו מטמא אחד ופוסל אחד אף משכבו מטמא אחד ופוסל אחד. ונ"ל דלאו ראיה היא אדרבה משמע משכבו כמגעו היינו במה שנגע בבועל נדה כדאמר לעיל בפ"ק מעת לעת משכבה ומושבה כמגעה מאי לאו מה מגעה לא מטמא אף משכבה לא מטמא אלמא לכאורה משמע דמגעה היינו שנגע בנדה אע"ג דלבתר הכי דחי ליה. אימא משכבה כמגע עצמה ועוד דלפום ריהטא דתלמודא משמע שאין בועל נדה קל מנדה לענין משכב ומושב [illegible] נתקו הכתוב מטומאה חמורה אבל כל שאר חומרות שבנדה ישנן בבועל נדה והאי דקאמר מה היא מטמאה אדם היינו במשא ובמגע ובמעיינותיו. ומה שהקשה השר מקוצי [illegible] תנא ושייר [illegible] מעיינות וכל שאר טומאות של נדה [illegible]: אם הן יושבות על כל דם ודם תקנה גדולה היא להם. פי' אם רואות דם אדום [illegible] דם ירוק יושבות [illegible] ז' נקיים [illegible] תקנה גדולה היא להם

[ג"ל וטמא] | [ג"ל וכלי] | כתובות מז. יבמות כד. מו. קדושין יג. [בכורות ע.] [שבועות מח: זבחים יב. חולין סה:] | [פסחים ו: ב"ק פה. מנחות נה:] | [בס"י איתא אמר קרא עליו] | [תוספתא פ"ה לקמן סט.] | [פסחים ז. וש"נ] | [פסחים נט: קדושין סח.] | [לקמן מב.] | [פסחים דף פא: וש"נ] | [דף עא: כד"ה הרואה] | [ועיין תוס' פסחים פא. ד"ה אי נמי]

טו א מיי' פ"ו מהלכות מטמאי משכב ומושב הלכה ג:
גי' מהר"מ אע"ג דמטמא בגדים שעליו ושאר בגדים אינו מטמא אדם וכלי חרס כו' כצ"ל
טז ב מיי' שם פ"ו הלכה ה:
יז ג מיי' שם פ"ו הל' [illegible]:
יח ה מיי' שם פ"ג הלכה [illegible]:
כ ו טוש"ע י"ד סי' קצו סעיף א:
כא ז מיי' פ"ו מהלכות איסורי ביאה הלכה טז:

או דילמא, נוגעת היתה – ולא סתרה? אמר רבא: *לפום חורפא שבשתא, נהי נמי דסתרה, כמה תסתור? תסתור שבעה – דיה כבועלה. תסתור יום אחד – °"ואחר תטהר" אמר רחמנא (ויקרא טו) *"אחר" – אחר לכולן, שלא תהא טומאה מפסקת ביניהם. וליטעמיך, זב גופיה היכי סתר? "לטהרתו" אמר רחמנא – שלא תהא טומאה מפסקת ביניהן! אלא מאי אית לך למימר – שלא תהא טומאת זיבה מפסקת ביניהן, הכא נמי – שלא תהא טומאת זיבה מפסקת ביניהן.§ "ואין חייבין עליהן על ביאת מקדש" וכו'.§ רב פפא איקלע לתואך. אמר: אי איכא צורבא מרבנן הכא, איזיל אקביל אפיה. אמרה ליה ההיא סבתא: איכא הכא צורבא מרבנן, ורב שמואל שמיה, ותני מתניתא, יהא רעוא דתהוי כוותיה! אמר: מדקמברכי לי בגוויה – ש"מ ירא שמים הוא. אזל לגביה. רמא ליה תורא, רמא ליה מתני' אהדדי. תנן: אין חייבין עליהן על ביאת מקדש, ואין שורפין עליהן את התרומה, מפני שטומאתה ספק. אלמא – מספיקא לא שרפינן תרומה, ורמינהי: *אעל ששה ספקות שורפין את התרומה, על ספק בגדי עם הארץ! אמר רב פפא: יהא רעוא דלתאכיל האי תורא לשלמא, הכא במאי עסקינן בכותי חבר. כותי חבר בועל נדה משוית ליה? שבקיה, ואתא לקמיה דרב שימי בר אשי. אמר ליה: מאי טעמא לא משנית ליה; בכותי שטבל ועלה, ודרס על בגדי חבר, ואזלו בגדי חבר ונגעו בתרומה. דאי משום טומאת עם הארץ – הא טביל ליה, ואי משום בועל נדה – ספק בעל בקרוב ספק לא בעל בקרוב. ואם תמצי לומר בעל בקרוב – ספק השלימתו ירוק ספק לא השלימתו, והוי ספק ספיקא, בואספק ספיקא לא שרפינן תרומה. ותיפוק ליה משום בגדי עם הארץ, *דאמר מר: גבגדי עם הארץ מדרס לפרושין! אמר ליה: בכותי ערום.§ **מתני'** בנות צדוקין, בזמן שנהגו ללכת בדרכי אבותיהן – הרי הן ככותיות, פרשו ללכת בדרכי ישראל – הרי הן כישראלית. רבי יוסי אומר: לעולם הן כישראלית, עד שיפרשו ללכת בדרכי אבותיהן.§ **גמ'** איבעיא להו: סתמא מאי? ת"ש: בנות צדוקין, בזמן שנוהגות ללכת בדרכי אבותיהן – הרי הן ככותיות, הא סתמא – כישראלית. אימא סיפא: פרשו ללכת בדרכי ישראל – הרי הן כישראלית, הא סתמא – ככותיות! *אלא מהא ליכא למשמע מיניה. ת"ש: דתנן, ר' יוסי אומר: לעולם הן כישראלית עד שיפרשו ללכת בדרכי אבותיהן. מכלל דת"ק סבר: סתמא ככותיות, ש"מ. תנו רבנן: *מעשה בצדוקי אחד שספר עם כהן גדול בשוק, ונתזה צנורא מפיו ונפלה לכהן גדול על בגדיו, והוריקו פניו של כהן גדול וקדם אצל אשתו. אמרה לו: אף על פי שנשי צדוקים הן – מתיראות מן הפרושים, ומראות דם לחכמים. אמר רבי יוסי: בקיאין אנו בהן יותר מן הכל, והן מראות דם לחכמים, חוץ מאשה אחת שהיתה בשכונתינו, שלא הראת דם לחכמים ומתה. ותיפוק ליה משום צנורא דעם הארץ! אמר אביי: בצדוקי חבר. אמר רבא: צדוקי חבר, בועל נדה משוית ליה? אלא אמר רבא:

רגל

**רש"י**

או משום נוגעת. ונוגע – לא סותר. דיה כבועלה. זב המונה וראה קרי – אינו סותר אלא יום אחד. תסתור יום אחד. אם כן, לא הוו רצופין, ורחמנא אמר "ואחר תטהר" – אחר אחר לכולן. כלומר, זמן אחד לכולן, שיהו רצופין טהרתן. לטהרתו אמר רחמנא. "שבעת ימים לטהרתו" – משמע: טהרה אחת, שלא תהא הפסקה ביניהם. והיכי סתר קרי יום א' ולא הוו רצופין? אלא מאי אית לך למימר שלא תהא טומאת זיבה מפסקת ביניהן. שאם רואה זוב – סותר את כל מה שמנה, אבל קרי – לא הויא הפסקה. לתואך. מקום. רמא ליה תורא. רב שמואל שחט שור לכבוד רב פפא. על ספק בגדי עם הארץ. כלומר, על בגדי עם הארץ אם נגעו בה – נשרפת, משום שמא טמא היה. והאי כותי נמי, תיפוק ליה אם נגע משכבו בתרומה – דתהא נשרפת, משום דעם הארץ הוא, והוה ליה בגדי עם הארץ. שבקיה. רב פפא לאושפיזיה, משום דכספיה, ואזל לגבי רב שימי. מאי טעמא. לא תשני ליה: מתני' דתנן "אין שורפין על תחתונו של כותי את התרומה" – בכותי שטבל ועלה ודרס על בגדי חבר, דהיינו במשכבו, ונגע ההוא מדרס בתרומה. לא בעל בקרוב. כבר עברו ימי טומאתו, וסלקא ליה טבילה. משום בגדי עם הארץ מדרס לפרושים. כלומר, כשם שמדרס מטמא אדם ובגדים, כך בגדי עם הארץ מדרס לפרושים. סתמא מאי. לתנא קמא דאמר: נהגו ללכת בדרכי אבותיהן – הרי אלו ככותיות, פרשו ללכת בדרכי ישראלית – הרי אלו כישראלית, סתמא – מאי? עד שיפרשו. אבל סתמא – כישראלית, מכלל דלת"ק סתמא – ככותיות. והוריקו פניו. חרה לו שנטמאו בגדיו, וקדם כהן גדול אצל אשתו של צדוקי לשואלה אם השלימה לדם ירוק או לא. בקיאין אנו בהן. אני מכיר בנשי צדוקים, ששכן היה להן. ותיפוק ליה. דאפילו עם הארץ ישראל, דאינו בועל נדה, קי"ל: צינורא דע"ה מטמאה, כל זמן שהיא לחה.

**תוספות**

השיבו וכולהו אמוראי סברי פרק "יוצא דופן" (לקמן דף מב.) דרואה הויא, וסתרה אף לר"ש וכ"ש לרבנן. והא דקאמר רבא לקמן (דף לז.) "ואחר תטהר" – שלא תהא טומאה מפסקת ביניהם, אביי אומר: שלא תהא זיבה מפסקת ביניהם. משם אין להוכיח דרבא לא חזר בו, דהתם איירי בטומאת לידה שטמאה ז' ועושה משכב ומושב כמו נדה – ולכך קאמר שלא תהא מפסקת. אבל קרי, דלא סותר אלא יום א' – לא מפסיק.

*לטהרתו אמר רחמנא. ורבא סבר: דלא משמע מלטהרתו – שלא תהא טומאה מפסקת.

ורמינהו על ו' ספקות שורפין את התרומה. משום דכותי דמתני' ע"ה הוא, קפריך: מדמספקי' ליה בבועל נדה, והא קתני דעל ספק בגדי עם הארץ שורפין. *אבל פשיטא דאיכא ספקי טובא שאין שורפין עליהם את התרומה, °כגון טומטום בלובן או באודם, וכיוצא בו. ובמסקנא דאמר: ספק בועל ברחוק ספק בועל בקרוב, ואפילו בועל בקרוב – שמא לא השלימתו לדם ירוק, לא היה צריך לעשות ספק ספיקא, כדפירשנו. או שמא נראה להחמיר בזה כמו בספק בגדי ע"ה לכך משכח ביה ספק ספיקא. ומכאן קשה על מה שפירש"י בפ"ק דשבת (דף טו.) על הן (*ברייתא) דעל ו' ספקות כו' על ספק מי רגלי אדם שכנגד מי רגלי בהמה, ופירש: דהשתא יש להסתפק שמא של בהמה הן, ואפילו של אדם הן – שמא של חבר הן. והכא משמע דעל ספק ספיקא אין שורפין! ומיהו אין להשוות גזירת חכמים, דפעמים נראה להם להחמיר, אפילו בספק ספיקא. ור"ת פי' התם: דכיון דהם כנגד מי רגלי בהמה – ודאי דגוי הם, דישראל – היה נפנה לצדדין, כדאמר *ב"הניזקין" (דף סד) וקשה: דאפילו ודאי הם דישראל – שורפין, משום דשמא דע"ה הן, כדשרפינן על ספק הרוקין הנמצאים, בההיא (*ברייתא) ועוד דאטומאה דגוי – לא שרפינן תרומה, כדאמר לקמן (דף לד.) עבדו רבנן היכרא, דלא לישרוף עליה תרומה וקדשים! ונראה לפרש: דלהכי נקט "כנגד מי רגלי בהמה" – דאז ניכר שאינה של בהמה, שאינן דומין לאותן שכנגדן, וליכא אלא ספיקא אחת. אבל אם היה להסתפק בשל בהמה – לא הוי שרפי, דהוי ליה ספק ספיקא.

שדרס על בגדי חבר. והם נגעו בתרומה. והא דלא אוקי: כגון שנגע הכותי בתרומה – משום דמתניתין לא איירי בהכי.

בכותי ערום. והא דלא אוקי: כגון שדרס ברגלו יחף – משום דאי היה לבוש בגדים שישבה עליהן אשתו נדה, אע"ג דטבל – הוי אב הטומאה, כדאמר בת"כ: והנושא את המדרס – הרי הוא מטמא שנים ופוסל אחד. לכך מוקי בערום, דכשפירש מן המדרס – לא היה אלא ראשון, כדאמרינן בת"כ, *ואינו מטמא כלי. והוה מצי למימר: כשהטביל גם הבגדים, או שלבש בגדי חבר.

*בועל נדה משוית ליה. ואיהו סבר: שהוא חבר למילי דעלמא, ובזאת סבר לעשות בטוב, וכן אביי דסמוך. ותיפוק ליה משום צינורא דע"ה. – דוקא לענין צינורא עשאוהו כזב, שאפשר ליזהר ויכולין לעמוד בה. אבל חומרא יתירא, כגון משכב ומושב והיסט – לא עשאוהו כזב. דבשילהי "הניזקין" (גיטין סא:) פריך: וליחוש שמא תסיטם אשתו נדה. אבל להיסט דנפשיה – לא איכפת לן. ושמעתין נמי מוכח דאין לו טומאת מדרס, דאי אית ליה – לעיל דפריך על ו' ספיקות כו', למאי דחשיב כותי כע"ה הוה ליה לאקשויי מתני' גופה: אמאי קתני מטמא משכב התחתון כעליון, הא תחתונו של ע"ה הוי כתחתונו של זב! אלא ודאי אין לו טומאת מדרס. והא דמשני: בכותי שטבל ועלה ודרס כו', דאי משום טומאת ע"ה הא טביל ליה – היינו משום דאי

לא

**עין משפט נר מצוה**

כב א ב מיי' פי"ג מהל' שאר אבות הטומאה הלכה יג:

כג ג מיי' פ"ו מהלכות משכב ומושב הלכה ח:

עיין מהר"ם

נ"ל דלא גרסי' התוס' בגמ' אלמא מספיקא לא שרפינן תרומה ורמינהו וכו' דמלשון זה משמע דרמי הספיקות אהדדי. מהר"מ

[נ"ל מתני']

[נ"ל בסנהדרין דף קה:]

[נ"ל מתני']

**מסורת הש"ס**

[עירובין ג. כ"מ נו: כ"ב קטו:]

[לקמן לו. סז: ע"ש סח:]

טהרות פ"ד מ"ה שבת טו:

חגיגה יח: (וש"נ)

[ברכות כט. וש"נ ועיין נדרים עב.]

[תוספתא פ"ה]

**גליון הש"ס**

תוס' ד"ה ורמינהו וכו' כגון טומטום בלובן. לעיל כח ע"ב:

עיין רש"ל

[שייך לעיל קודם ד"ה שדרס]

**תוספי הרא"ש**

להם אבל פשיטא שלא היו יושבות שבעה על דם ירוק שרואות אחר דם אדום דדם אדום הוא ודאי טמא ודם ירוק מספקינן להו שאם היו יושבות ז' נמי על דם (אדום) ירוק א)שאחר דם אדום לא היתה זאת תקנה להם שהיו טועות בין נדה לזיבה אלא שרואות דם אדום ומשלימתו לדם ירוק דלא מספקא להו בדם ירוק כלל אלא מחשבי ליה טמא כמו דם אדום: **שבקיה** לקרא דהוא דחיק ומוקי אנפשיה. דיחויא בעלמא הוא דדייק רמי בר חמא לאוקומי לתיובתיה ולאו עיקר הוא ואיהו גופיה לא סביר להו הכי אלא דמקשה אנן נמי ניספריני' ולא היה יודע טעמו של התנא למה אינה סופרת יום שפוסקת בו ולקמן נמי בפ' בתרא אמרינן אטו רב ככותאי אמרה לשמעתיה דאמרי יום שפוסקת בו סופרתו למנין ז' ומיהו ר' יוסי אית ליה הכי בפ' כיצד צולין דקאמר זבה תחלת היום עולה לה בסופה וכיון שתחלת היום עולה לה בסופה א"כ כ"ש שסוף היום עולה לה בתחלתה ק"ו מנדה שאין תחלת היום עולה לה בסופה סוף היום עולה לה בתחלתה כ"ש זבה כיון שתחלת היום עולה לה בסופה שסוף היום עולה בתחלתה: **פולטת** שכבת זרע מהו שתסתור בזיבה. פרש"י ששימשה באיסור דפולטת לאחר ג' ימים אינה טמאה משום שכבר מסרחת ומשכחת לה נמי לרבנן דאמרי שש עונות שלימות בעי' כגון ששמשה ביום א' וראתה אח"כ וכן נמי ביום ב' וביום ג' ופלטה ביום ד' קודם שעברו על זה שש עונות או א"נ כגון שספרה ז' נקיים וביום הז' טבלה וטהור' כדאמר לקמן אחר מעשה תטהר אלא שאמרו חכמים אסור לעשות כן שמא תבא לידי ספק: **וליטעמיך** זב גופיה היכי סתר. נראה שדברי רבא נדחו כי אין להשיב על זה הלכך יש להחמיר בפולטת כיון דלא איפשיטא הבעיא וסותרת יום אחד דאימור רואה הויא וכן לקמן בפ' יוצא דופן סברי כולהו אמוראי דרואה הויא ואפילו לרבי שמעון ולרבנן פשיטא להו דרואה הויא ונראה דרבא גופיה הדר ביה כיון שהקשו על דבריו ולא מצא תשובה ואע"ג דלקמן בפירקין גבי ימי לידה דקאמר רבא אינה סותרת ועולה ודייק לה מדתניא ואחר תטהר שלא תהא טומאה מפסקת ביניהן ואם אינה עולה איפסיק ליה לידה משמע דלית ליה שלא תהא טומאת זיבה מפסקת ביניהן איכא למימר דטומאת לידה חשיב ליה כעין זיבה משום דמטמאה ז' ימים אבל מטומאת קרי אפשר שחזר בו הלכך צריכה כל אשה ליזהר שלא תתחיל ימי ליבונה עד יום חמישי לשימושה כגון אם שמשה ביום ראשון יהא יום חמישי תחלת ספירתה שמא לא תוכל לזהר שלא תפלוט וקי"ל כרבנן דאמרי שש עונות שלימות בעינן בשבת פרק ר' עקיבא: **ודרס** על בגדי חבר. מדלא נקט נגע משמע דאי לאו דטבל הוה מטמא מדרס כמו זב והא דאמרינן בפ' הניזקין שמא תשב עליהן אשתו נדה לא קאי אלא אבגדי פרושים מדרס לאוכלי תרומה אבל עם הארץ עצמו עושה מדרס בלא חשש אשתו וכן צינורא שלו טמאה כדאמרינן לקמן בשמעתין משום דעשאוהו לגמרי כזב ותימה אמאי אינו מטמא בהיסט נמי כזב. ובפ' הניזקין משמע שאינו מטמא בהיסט דקאמר התם גבי מוקף צמיד פתיל שמא הסיטתם אשתו נדה וקאמר נמי התם גבי חלה שבכפישה כשבא עם הארץ ליטול נוטל את שניהם אלמא שאינו מטמא אותה בהיסט וכן בפ"ב דע"ז ובפ' אין דורשין גבי היו חמריו ופועליו טעונין טהרות דמוקי לה במטהר חמריו ופועליו לכך משום חשד מגע דאין אדם משמר מה שביד חבירו אבל משום היסט דעם הארץ לא איכפת ליה. ואומר ר"ת דלכך לא גזרו עליה טומאת היסט משום דאין לך אדם מעביר חבית ממקום למקום. ומיהו במס' טהרות משמע דאפילו טומאת מדרס אין לו דתנן התם בפ"ז הגנבים שנכנסו לבית אין טמא אלא מקום רגלי הגנבים ומה הם מטמאין את האוכלין ואת המשקין וכלי חרס הפתוחים אבל לא משכבות ומושבות וכלי חרס המוקפין צמיד פתיל ואם יש עמהם עובד כוכבים או אשה הכל טמא ומתוך שמעתי' נמי יש לדקדק דאין מדרס לעם הארץ מדאיצטריך ליה למיפרך מההיא דעל ספק בגדי ע"ה תיקשי ליה מתני' גופה דלפי מאי דחשיב כותי כעם הארץ אמאי תנן שמטמא משכב תחתון כעליון הא תחתונו של ע"ה כתחתונו של זב. אלא ודאי אינו מטמא מדרס ומה שחלקו בטומאת ע"ה לפי שאין גוזרין על הצבור אלא א"כ רוב הצבור יכולין לעמוד בה ובמגעו ובצינורא שלו איפשר ליזהר אבל במשכב ומושב והיסט לא רצו להחמיר. והא דקאמר אי משום ע"ה הא קא טביל ליה היינו משום דאי לא טביל הוה מטמא במגע את מה שדרס עליו משום דאוקי לה בכותי ערום והאי דנקט ודרס ולא נקט ונגע משום דבעי ב)דלהוי בגדי חבר תחתונו של כותי דאיירי ביה מתני' שמטמאין משכב תחתון כעליון. ותימה ולוקמה בלא טבל וכגון שיש דבר מפסיק בין בגדי חבר לרגלו של כותי (פ"ל ג)כיון דמשום מגע הוא ולא משום מדרס דאי הוה משום מדרס אפילו יש דבר מפסיק הוא טמא) וי"ל דע"כ צריך לאוקמי בטבל כי היכי ד)

קרויו

א) נראה דל"ל על דם אדום שאחר דם ירוק זאת תקנה להם שלא היו טועות בין נדה לזיבה אלא שרואות וכו'. ב) נראה דל"ל משום דבעי לומר דהוו בגדי חבר תחתונו של כותי וכו'. ג) נראה דמתיבת פ"ל עד תיבת הוא טמא הג"ה על דברי רבינו שנכתב מן הצד. ד) חסר כאן בכתבי התוספי הרא"ש.

רגל הוה וטומאת עם הארץ. דלאו לדוקי, דדרך אשתו להראות דם. כטהרה שוינהו רבנן. ברגל. אבל לדוקי, דסתמא בועל נדה הוא, נהי נמי דטומאת עם הארץ – ליכא, טומאת בועל נדה – איכא. ויאסף וגו'. בפלגש בגבעה כתיב, ומיניה שמעינן: בכל זמן שישראל נאספים למקום אחד – קרי להו "חברים", ורגל היינו אסיפה. **מתני'** בית שמאי מטהרין. בדם גויה. אע"ג דברוקה ובמימי רגליה מודו דחכמים גזרו עליהם להיות כזבין לכל דבריהם, אפי' הכי דמה טהור. וטעמא מפרש בגמרא: דשיירו בה רבנן, למיהוי היכרא דטומאתה מדרבנן. ודם טוהר של מצורעת. ואע"ג דמעיינות מצורעת, כגון רוקה ומימי רגליה, הוי אב הטומאה, כדאמר ב"המפלת" (לעיל דף כח.) "לזכר" – לרבות מצורע שמעיינותיו טמאים כשל זב, דכתיב ביה: "וכי ירוק הזב בטהור", אפילו הכי דם טוהר שלה טהור, דלאו מעיין הוא. דדומיא דרוק בעינן, שמתעגל ויוצא, כדאמרינן בפ"ב (לעיל דף יט:) גבי דם הירוק. וב"ה אומרים כרוקה וכמימי רגליה. שמטמאין לחין ואין מטמאין יבשין, גבי דם גויה מטמא מדרבנן, שגזרו עליהן שיהו כזבין לכל דבריהם. והך היכרא הוא דעבוד בה, דאילו דישראלית – מטמא לח ויבש, ודגויה – לח ולא יבש. כרוקה וכמימי רגליה, דאמר לקמן בפרק "דם הנדה"* דאין מטמאין יבשין. ודם טוהר של מצורעת נמי, אע"ג דדם לאו מעיין הוא – דין מעיין אית ליה, דרחמנא רבייה, כדאמר בגמרא. דם היולדת. שעברו ימי טומאת לידה, ולא טבלה. בית שמאי אומרים כרוקה וכמימי רגליה. מטמא לח, ואינו מטמא יבש. והכי תני לה בהדיא בתוספתא דעדיות, דנדה כל זמן שלא טבלה – הרי היא בנדתה לכל דבריה. הלכך רוקה ומימי רגליה – בטומאתן. ולקמן בפרק "דם הנדה" (נו.) ילפינן מקראי דאין רוק של זב מטמא יבש. ודמה נמי, אף על גב דדם טוהר הוא לבית שמאי, כדאמר בגמרא דביומי תליא רחמנא, והא מלו. ומשום מעיין נמי ליכא לטמויי, דהא אין מתעגל ויוצא, אפילו הכי רבנן גזור עליה, הואיל וטמאה היא, גזרה לאחר ז' אטו תוך ז'. ומיהו לא גזור עליה שיטמא לח ויבש כלפני ז', דעבוד בה היכרא דלידעו דטומאתה מדרבנן, ולא נשרוף עליה תרומה וקדשים. ואע"ג דגבי דם גויה לא אמרי בית שמאי הכי, אלא מטהרי לגמרי, והיינו טעמא, כדאמר בגמרא: משום דחיישינן דלמא אתי לחלק בשל תורה, ולמימר מטמא לח ולא יבש. התם הוא דכל טומאת גוי – דרבנן, כדי שלא יהו ישראל רגילין אצלן במשכב זכור.* וכיון דטמאו מגען ורוקן ומימי רגליהן, ואיכא הרחקה טובא, הלכך טהרו את דמה לגמרי להיכרא, דלידעו דטומאת רוקה ומימי רגליה דרבנן, דלא נשרוף תרומה עלייהו. ולא חלקו בדמה, דילמא אתי לחלק בשל תורה. אבל הכא – אין כאן מדרבנן אלא דם לבדו, שהוא דם טוהר, הלכך גזור ושיור בה להיכרא, דליכא למיחש דלמא אתי לחלוקי בשל תורה, דהכל יודעין דכיון דעברו ימי לידתה דדם טוהר הוא. ובית הלל אומרים מטמא לח ויבש. דטומאתן מן התורה כל זמן שלא טבלה, דקסברי: ביומי וטבילה תלא רחמנא. **גמ'** גזרו עליהן שיהו כזבין לכל דבריהן. משום שלא יהא תינוק ישראל רגיל אצלו במשכב זכור. עשיתו כשל תורה. דכיון דליכא היכרא, אתי למשרף עליה תרומה וקדשים. ליטמא לח ולא יבש. כדקאמריתו. חלקת בשל תורה. אתי לחלק בדם ישראלית שהוא של תורה ולמימר: דמטמא לח ולא יבש. הילכך שיירוה, ולא גזור בה שום טומאה, כי היכי דניהוי היכרא לטומאת גוים דמדרבנן היא, ולא נשרוף עליה תרומה. אי הכי רוקה ומימי רגליה נמי. דלגבי ישראלית לח ולא יבש, כי מטמית להו בגויה, עשיתו כשל תורה דקיי"ל בפ' "דם הנדה" (לקמן דף נה:): רוקו וניעו – מטמאין לחין ולא יבשין, ונעביד היכרא ברוקה דגויה ומימי רגליה לטהרן לגמרי. דם. לגבי רוק לא שכיח חשיב ליה. זובו. של גוי. טמא אפילו לבית שמאי. דמקילי בדם האשה בזוב של זכר, מודו שהטיפה מטמא אחרים במגע. קריו טהור אפילו לבית הלל. עבדי ביה היכרא, דלידעו דטומאת גוים דרבנן. דב"ה נמי היכרא בעו, כדאמרינן בדם הגויה (ג) ברוקה ובמימי רגליה, ולא טמאוהו לח ויבש כישראלית. וגבי זב, דגבי ישראל נמי כל טומאותיו לחין ולא יבשין, אי לא מטהרי חדא מינייהו לגמרי – ליכא היכרא. קריו תלוי במעשה. אין קרי בא אלא ע"י הימום. גויה שפלטה כו' טמאה. השכבת זרע, אבל בגויה לא שייכא בה טומאה כבהמה דעלמא. טהורה. הטיפה *(אלא) קריו טהור. ואפילו

---

רגל הוה, *[א]וטומאת עם הארץ ברגל – כטהרה שוינהו רבנן, דכתיב: "ויאסף כל איש ישראל אל העיר כאיש אחד חברים" – הכתוב עשאן כולן חברים.§ **מתני'** *דם גויה ודם טהרה של מצורעת, ב"ש מטהרים, ובית הלל אומרים: [ב]כרוקה וכמימי רגליה. *דם היולדת שלא טבלה, ב"ש אומרים: כרוקה וכמימי רגליה, וב"ה אומרים: [ג]מטמא לח ויבש. [ד]ומודים ביולדת בזוב – שהיא מטמאה לח ויבש.§ **גמ'** ולית להו לב"ש *"דבר אל בני ישראל *ואמרת אליהם איש איש כי יהיה זב" *בני ישראל מטמאין בזיבה, ואין *הגוים מטמאין בזיבה, [ה]אבל גזרו עליהן שיהו כזבין לכל דבריהם? אמרי לך ב"ש: (ההוא בזכרים איתמר, דאי בנקבות) היכי לעביד? ליטמא לח ויבש – עשיתו כשל תורה, ליטמי לח ולא ליטמי יבש – חלקת בשל תורה. אי הכי, רוקה ומימי רגליה נמי! כיון דעבדינן היכרא בדמה – מידע ידיע דרוקה ומימי רגליה דרבנן. ולעביד היכרא ברוקה ומימי רגליה, ולטמויי לדמה! רוקה ומימי רגליה דשכיחי – גזרו בהו רבנן, דמה *דלא שכיחא – לא גזרו ביה רבנן. אמר רבא: [ו]זובו טמא – אפילו לב"ש, [ז]קריו טהור – אפילו לב"ה. זובו טמא אפילו לב"ש – דהא איכא למעבד היכרא בקריו, קריו טהור אפי' לב"ה – [ח]עבוד ביה רבנן היכרא, כי היכי [א] דלא לשרוף עליה תרומה וקדשים. ולעביד היכרא בזובו ולטמויי לקריו! זובו דלא תלי במעשה – גזרו ביה רבנן, קריו דתלי במעשה – לא גזרו ביה רבנן. לימא מסייע ליה: *[ט]גויה שפלטה שכבת זרע מישראל – טמאה, [י]ובת ישראל שפלטה שכבת זרע מן הגוי – טהורה. מאי לאו טהורה גמורה? לא, טהורה – מדאורייתא, (א) טמאה – מדרבנן. ת"ש, נמצאת אומר: שכבת זרע של ישראל – טמאה בכל מקום, ואפילו

---

לא טביל, היה טמא מטעם מגעו, דהא מוקי ליה בכותי ערום. והא דנקט "ודרס", ולא נקט "ונגע" – משום דמתניתין איירי בתחתונו. ואין להקשות: ולוקמה דלא טבל, וכגון שיש דבר מפסיק בין בגדי חבר לרגליו של כותי – דהא ע"כ איצטריך לאוקמי בטבל, כי היכי דליהוי ספק ספקא. דאי לא טבל – מה לי בועל בקרוב, מה לי ברחוק. וכן משמע בפרק (ג) ד' דמסכת טהרות, דתנן: הגנבים שנכנסו בבית – אין טמא אלא מקום רגלי הגנבים. ומה הם מטמאין? אוכלין ומשקין וכלי חרס פתוחים. אבל משכבות ומושבות וכלי חרס המוקף צמיד פתיל – טהורים. ואם יש עמהם גוי או אשה – הכל טמאין. משמע דאין עם הארץ עושה משכב ומושב, ואין מטמא בהיסט. והא דקתני (שם פ"ח מ"א) הדר עם עם הארץ בחצר, ושכח כלים בחצר אפי' חביות המוקפות צמיד פתיל, הרי אלו טמאין. היינו משום אשתו. וכן הא דתנן בתוספתא דחגיגה (פ"ג) ספק רשות עם הארץ, מדרסו והיסטו – טהורין לחולין, וטמאין לתרומה. היינו נמי משום חששא דאשתו. ומיירי ההיא דטהרות נמי לתרומה. והא דבגדי עם הארץ מדרס נמי לפרושים, היינו משום דחיישינן שמא ישבה עליהם אשתו נדה. והר"ר משה מפונטויי"ז היה מפרש: דלאשום דבר לא עשו עם הארץ כזב, ואינו מטמא אלא משום בגדיו שישבה עליהן אשתו נדה, והרי הוא נושא את המדרס. וצינורא שלו טמא – לפי שנגעה בשפתיו, ולא משום מעיין. ולא נראה: דאם כן, למה ליה למימר לעיל "אי משום טומאת עם הארץ, הא טביל ליה", דכיון דעל כרחך איירי בערום כדפי' לעיל, אפילו אי לא טביל ליה – לא מטמא, כיון שפירש מן המדרס, כדתנא בתורת כהנים שהבאתי לעיל! ועוד: גבי לדוקי דהכא, דפריך: "תיפוק ליה משום צינורא דעם הארץ", פירוש: ומה הרויח במה שקדם אצל אשתו? והא אם בועל נדה הוא – נטמא הוא ובגדיו כנושא רוקו של זב, ואי משום צינורא דעם הארץ – לא נטמא אלא הבגד לחוד משום משקה שמטמא כלי מדרבנן*. **ליטמא** לח ולא יבש חילקת בשל תורה. אע"ג דדם יולדת שלא טבלה דטהורה מן התורה, אמרי ב"ש דמטמא לח ולא יבש – התם ידעי, כיון שעברו ימי לידה, דאין דמה [טמא] מן התורה. אבל גויה שעשאוה כנדה, שהרי הם כזבין, אם נחלק בדמה – אתי לחלק בשל ישראל. ודם טהרה של מצורעת, שטהור לגמרי – אין לחוש, שלא החמירו בה, כיון דכבר טבלה, ודם טהור הוא.

**וזובו** טמא דעבדי היכרא בקריו. וא"ת: ואמאי לא שרפינן? הא שרפינן על ספק רוקו דעם הארץ, פרק קמא דשבת (טו:) כל שכן בזובו של גוי! ויש לומר: דבעם הארץ שורפין – משום דאית ביה דררא דטומאה דאורייתא, אם הוא זב או בועל נדה. אבל גוי אין לו שום טומאה דאורייתא.

כי

---

## תוספי הרא"ש

**קרויו** טהור אפילו לב"ה עבוד רבנן היכירא דלא לישרף עליה תרומה וקדשים. והא דאמרינן פ"ק דשבת על ששה ספיקות שורפים את התרומה וקא חשיב ספק מי רגלי אדם לאו משום שמא של עובד כוכבים הם אלא משום של ע"ה אע"פ שהחמירו בעובד כוכבים יותר מע"ה לענין משכב ומושב והיסט לא החמירו בו לשרוף תרומה על טומאתו וקשה מהא דאמרינן בת"כ בני ישראל מטמאין בזיבה ואין העובדי כוכבים מטמאין בזיבה ואע"פ שאינן מטמאין בזיבה טמאין בזוב ושורפין עליהן את התרומה וצ"ל דשוב החמירו עליהן לשרוף: **קרויו** דתלי במעשה לא גזרו ביה רבנן. דכיון דאפשר למנוע עצמו שלא יבא לידי קרי חשיב כלא שכיח:

---

**מסורת הש"ס:** חגיגה כו. | שופטים כ | עדיות פ"ה מ"א | [עדיות פ"ה מ"ד לקמן לה:] | [נ"ל דברו] | ויקרא טו | נ"ל ואמרתם | רש"א מ"ז וכ"ה בספרים ישנים | [דף נ"ד] | [עירובין סג. וש"נ] | מקוואות פ"ח מ"ד | [שבת יז:]

**עין משפט נר מצוה:**
כד א מיי' פי"א מהל' מטמאי משכב ומושב הל"ט:
כה ב מיי' פ"ב מהל' מטמאי משכב ומושב הל' י ופ"ה שם הלכה:
כו ג מיי' שם פ"ה הל"ב:
כז ד מיי' שם פ"ב הל"א:
כח ה מיי' שם הל' י ופ"ד מהל' איסורי ביאה הל' ז:
כט ו ז ח מיי' פ"ב מהל' מטמאי משכב ומושב הל' י ופ"ה מהל' שאר אבות הטומאה הלכה יז:
ל ט מיי' פ"ה מהל' שאר אבות הטומאה הל' טז:
לא י מיי' שם הלכה יז:

שבת פג.
[עי' תוס' סוכה כח: ד"ה לרבות ותוס' סנהדרין פו. ד"ה בני ותוס' מנחות סח: ד"ה אין]

**הגהות הב"ח**
(א) גמ' וטמאה מדרבנן: (ב) רש"י ד"ה קריו טהור וכו' בדם הגויה כרוקה וכמימי רגליה: (ג) תד"ה (בדף הקודם) ותיפוק וכו' וכן משמע בפ' שביעי [מ"ו] דמס' טהרות:

ועיין ר"ש פ"ז דטהרות מ"ה באורך

**גליון הש"ס**
**מתני'** כרוקה וכו'. ע"ל נו ע"ב תד"ה מבין הגוים: **גמ'** ואין הגוים מטמאין בזיבה. עי' ב"ב כ ע"א תד"ה וגוי:

**הגהות הגר"א**
[א] גמ' דלא לשרוף עליה תרומה וקדשים נמחק. ונ"ב דלא לחייב עליה על טומאת מקדש וקדשיו:

נ"ל אלמא

וַאֲפִי' בִּמְעֵי גוֹיָה. וְשֶׁל גּוֹי טָהוֹר' בְּכָל מָקוֹם וַאֲפִי' בִּמְעֵי יִשְׂרְאֵלִית, [א]חוּץ מִמֵּי רַגְלַיִם שֶׁבָּהּ. וְכִי תֵּימָא ה"נ טָהוֹר' מִדְּאוֹרַיְיתָ', אֲבָל טְמֵאָה מִדְּרַבָּנַן, אַטּוּ מֵי רַגְלֶיהָ מִדְּאוֹרַיְיתָא מִי מְטַמְּאוּ? אֶלָּא ש"מ: טְהוֹרָה אֲפִילּוּ [ב]מִדְּרַבָּנַן, ש"מ. אָמַר מָר: שִׁכְבַת זֶרַע שֶׁל יִשְׂרָאֵל – טְמֵאָה בְּכ"מ, אֲפִי' בִּמְעֵי גוֹיָה. תִּפְשׁוֹט דְּבָעֵי רַב פַּפָּא. *דְּבָעֵי רַב פַּפָּא: שִׁכְבַת זֶרַע שֶׁל יִשְׂרָאֵל בִּמְעֵי גוֹיָה מַהוּ? בְּתוֹךְ ג' – לָא קָמִיבָּעֲיָא לֵיהּ לְרַב פַּפָּא, כִּי קָמִיבָּעֲיָא לֵיהּ – לְאַחַר ג' מַאי? יִשְׂרָאֵל דְּדָיְיגֵי בְּמִצְוֹת – חֲבִיל גּוּפַיְיהוּ וּמַסְרִיחַ, גּוֹיִם דְּלָא דָּיְיגֵי בְּמִצְוֹת – לָא חֲבִיל גּוּפַיְיהוּ וְלָא מַסְרִיחַ. אוֹ דִּילְמָא: *כֵּיוָן דְּאָכְלִי שְׁקָצִים וּרְמָשִׂים – חֲבִיל גּוּפַיְיהוּ, וּמַסְרִיחַ? תֵּיקוּ. § "דַּם טָהֳרָה שֶׁל מְצוֹרַעַת ב"ש" כו'. § מַאי טַעֲמָא דְּב"ה? אָמַר ר' יִצְחָק:* "לַזָּכָר" – לְרַבּוֹת מְצוֹרָע לְמַעְיְנוֹתָיו, "וְלַנְּקֵבָה" – לְרַבּוֹת מְצוֹרַעַת לְמַעְיְנוֹתֶיהָ. מַאי "מַעְיְנוֹתֶיהָ"? אִילֵימָא שְׁאָר מַעְיְנוֹתֶיהָ – מִזָּכָר נָפְקָא, אֶלָּא לְדָמָהּ – לְטַמֵּא דַּם טָהֳרָה שֶׁלָּהּ. וּב"ש – נְקֵבָה מִזָּכָר לָא אָתְיָא, דְּאִיכָּא לְמִיפְרַךְ: מַה לְּזָכָר – שֶׁכֵּן טָעוּן פְּרִיעָה וּפְרִימָה, וְאָסוּר בְּתַשְׁמִישׁ הַמִּטָּה, תֹּאמַר בִּנְקֵבָה – דְּלָא. וּב"ה? לִכְתּוֹב רַחֲמָנָא בִּנְקֵבָה, וְלָא בָּעֵי זָכָר. וַאֲנָא אָמִינָא: וּמַה נְּקֵבָה שֶׁאֵינָהּ טְעוּנָה פְּרִיעָה וּפְרִימָה, וְאֵינָהּ אֲסוּרָה בְּתַשְׁמִישׁ הַמִּטָּה – רַבֵּי רַחֲמָנָא מַעְיְנוֹתֶיהָ. זָכָר – לֹא כ"שׁ! אִם אֵינוֹ עִנְיָן לְזָכָר – תְּנֵהוּ עִנְיָן לִנְקֵבָה, וְאִם אֵינוֹ עִנְיָן לְמַעְיְנוֹתֶיהָ – תְּנֵהוּ עִנְיָן לְדָמָהּ, לְטַמֵּא דַּם טָהֳרָה שֶׁלָּהּ. וּב"ש – זָכָר מִנְּקֵבָה לָא אָתְיָא, דְּאִיכָּא לְמִיפְרַךְ: מַה לִּנְקֵבָה – שֶׁכֵּן מְטַמְּאָה *מֵאוֹנֶס, תֹּאמַר בְּזָכָר דְּלָא. וּב"ה? קָיְימִי בִּמְצוֹרָע וּפָרְכִי מִילֵּי דְּזָב? וּב"ש? שׁוּם טוּמְאָה פָּרְכִי. וְאִיבָּעֵית אֵימָא, אָמְרִי לָךְ ב"ש: הַאי "לַזָּכָר" מִיבָּעֵי לֵיהּ, "לַזָּכָר" – כָּל שֶׁהוּא זָכָר, (הַאי) בֵּין גָּדוֹל בֵּין קָטָן. וּבֵית הִלֵּל? נָפְקָא לְהוּ מִ"זֹּאת תּוֹרַת *הַזָּב" – בֵּין גָּדוֹל בֵּין קָטָן. אָמַר רַב יוֹסֵף, כִּי פָּשֵׁיט רַבִּי שִׁמְעוֹן בֶּן לָקִישׁ בְּזָב, בָּעֵי הָכִי: רְאִיָּה רִאשׁוֹנָה שֶׁל זָב קָטָן, מַהוּ שֶׁתְּטַמֵּא בְּמַגָּע? °"זֹאת תּוֹרַת הַזָּב וַאֲשֶׁר תֵּצֵא מִמֶּנּוּ שִׁכְבַת זֶרַע" אָמַר רַחֲמָנָא, כָּל שֶׁשִּׁכְבַת זֶרַע שֶׁלּוֹ מְטַמֵּא – רְאִיָּה רִאשׁוֹנָה שֶׁלּוֹ מְטַמְּאָה, וְהַאי – כֵּיוָן דְּשִׁכְבַת זֶרַע שֶׁלּוֹ לָא מְטַמְּאָה – רְאִיָּה רִאשׁוֹנָה נַמִּי לָא תְּטַמֵּא. אוֹ דִּילְמָא: כֵּיוָן דְּאִילּוּ אִיהוּ חָזֵי תַּרְתֵּי – מִצְטָרְפָא, מְטַמְּיָא? אָמַר רָבָא, ת"ש: "זֹאת תּוֹרַת הַזָּב" – [ג]בֵּין גָּדוֹל בֵּין קָטָן, מַה גָּדוֹל – רְאִיָּה רִאשׁוֹנָה שֶׁלּוֹ מְטַמֵּא, אַף קָטָן – רְאִיָּה רִאשׁוֹנָה נַמִּי מְטַמֵּא. בָּעֵי רַב יוֹסֵף: *רְאִיָּה רִאשׁוֹנָה שֶׁל מְצוֹרָע מַהוּ שֶׁתְּטַמֵּא בְּמַשָּׂא? מְקוֹם זִיבָה מַעְיָן הוּא – וּמְטַמֵּא, אוֹ דִּילְמָא לָאו מַעְיָן הוּא? אָמַר רָבָא, ת"ש: *°"זוֹבוֹ טָמֵא הוּא" לִימֵּד עַל הַזּוֹב שֶׁהוּא טָמֵא. בְּמַאי? אִילֵימָא בְּזָב גְּרִידָא לַאֲחֵרִים

תורה אור: ויקרא טו | שם

---

**רש"י**

וַאֲפִי' בִּמְעֵי גוֹיָה. שֶׁאִם תִּפְלְטֶנּוּ עַל הַבֶּגֶד, תְּטַמְּאֶנּוּ. חוּץ מִמֵּימֵי רַגְלֶיהָ שֶׁבָּהּ. דְּאִי פָּתִיכִי בְּמֵימֵי רַגְלֶיהָ – טְמֵאִים, כִּדְאָמְרִינַן לְעֵיל: גָּזְרוּ עֲלֵיהֶם שֶׁיְּהוּ כְּזָבִים. אֲבָל קִרְיוֹ – טָהוֹר, כִּדְאָמְרִינַן: עֲבַדוּ בֵּיהּ רַבָּנַן הֶיכֵּרָא. כִּי מִבָּעְיָא לֵיהּ לְאַחַר ג'. דִּלְגַבֵּי יִשְׂרְאֵלִית – טְהוֹרָה, כִּדְאָמַר בְּמַסֶּכֶת שַׁבָּת בְּפֶרֶק ר"ע. דְּדָיְיגֵי. יְרֵאִים וַחֲרֵדִים בְּמִצְוֹת, וּמִתּוֹךְ דַּאֲגָתָן – מִתְחַמְּמִין. חֲבִיל. חַם. שְׁאָר מַעְיְינוֹתֶיהָ. כְּגוֹן רוּקָהּ וּמֵימֵי רַגְלֶיהָ דְּאָתוּ מִזָּב, דִּכְתִיב בֵּיהּ (ויקרא טו) "וְכִי יָרוֹק הַזָּב", וּמִינֵּיהּ נָפְקִי שְׁאָר מַעְיָינוֹת. מִזָּכָר נָפְקָא. כֵּיוָן דְּאִתְרַבֵּי מְצוֹרָע לְמַעְיְינוֹתָיו, אִתְרַבֵּי מְצוֹרַעַת לְכָל מַעְיְינוֹתֶיהָ דְּאִיכָּא דִּכְוָותַיְיהוּ בְּזָכָר. אֶלָּא לְדָמָהּ. דְּלֵיתֵיהּ בְּזָכָר. וְאָסוּר בְּתַשְׁמִישׁ הַמִּטָּה. בְּשִׁבְעַת יְמֵי סְפִירוֹ, דִּכְתִיב: "וְיָשַׁב מִחוּץ לְאָהֳלוֹ", וְאֵין "אָהֳלוֹ" אֶלָּא אִשְׁתּוֹ, שֶׁנֶּאֱמַר (דברים ה): "שׁוּבוּ לָכֶם לְאָהֳלֵיכֶם". תֹּאמַר בִּנְקֵבָה מְצוֹרַעַת דְּלֵיתָא בְּכָל הָנֵי. בִּכְרֵיתוּת בְּפֶרֶק "ד' מְחוּסְּרֵי כַפָּרָה" (דף ח.) אִישׁ פּוֹרֵעַ וּפוֹרֵם, וְאֵין אִשָּׁה פּוֹרַעַת וּפוֹרֶמֶת. וְגַבֵּי תַּשְׁמִישׁ נַמִּי "מִחוּץ לְאָהֳלוֹ" כְּתִיב – וְלֹא מִחוּץ לְאָהֳלָהּ. הִילְכָּךְ לָא אָתְיָא מִזָּכָר וְאִיצְטְרִיךְ לִנְקֵבָה לְגוּפָהּ, וּלְעוֹלָם לִשְׁאָר מַעְיָנוֹת. וּמֵהֵיכָא דְּנָפְקִי שְׁאָר מַעְיָנוֹת, לֵיכָּא לְמֵימַר דְּיָלְפִינַן לְדָם – דִּשְׁאָר מַעְיָנוֹת יָלְפִינַן מֵרוֹק, מָה רוֹק שֶׁמִּתְעַגֵּל וְיוֹצֵא, הוּא מִתְאַסֵּף תְּחִלָּה יַחַד וְאַחַר כָּךְ יוֹצֵא, וְדָם – לָאו מִתְעַגֵּל וְיוֹצֵא הוּא. וְאִם אֵינוֹ עִנְיָן לִשְׁאָר מַעְיְינוֹתֶיהָ. דְּנָפְקִי מִ"לַּנְּקֵבָה". שֶׁכֵּן מְטַמְּאָה בְּאוֹנֶס. לְגַבֵּי זִיבָה. וּפָרְכִי: מִילֵּי דְּזָב. בִּתְמִיָּה. ה"ג: וְאִי בָּעֵית אֵימָא, אָמְרִי לָךְ ב"ש הַאי "לַזָּכָר" מִיבָּעֵי לֵיהּ כָּל שֶׁהוּא זָכָר כו'. ול"ג: "נְקֵבָה – כָּל שֶׁהִיא נְקֵבָה" כו'. דְּא"כ מַעְיָינוֹת לִמְצוֹרָע מְנָא לְהוּ? אֶלָּא "לַנְּקֵבָה" – לְרַבּוֹת מְצוֹרַעַת לְמַעְיְינוֹתֶיהָ, וְיָלֵיף זָכָר מִנְּקֵבָה לְמַעְיָינוֹת, וְהַאי "לַזָּכָר" דְּמִיַּיתַּר לְהוּ לְב"ה, דָּרְשִׁי לֵיהּ ב"ש לְזָב קָטָן שֶׁמְּטַמֵּא בְּזִיבָה בֶּן יוֹמוֹ. וְלָא נָפְקָא לְהוּ מֵ"אִישׁ אִישׁ" – דִּסְבִירָא לְהוּ: דִּבְּרָה תּוֹרָה כִּלְשׁוֹן בְּנֵי אָדָם. וְתִינוֹקֶת קְטַנָּה נָפְקָא לְהוּ מֵ"אִשָּׁה" "וְאִשָּׁה", כִּדְיָלְפִינַן בְּרֵישׁ פִּירְקָא. וְאִייַּתַּר לְהוּ "לַנְּקֵבָה" דְּהָכָא – לְרַבּוֹת מְצוֹרַעַת לְמַעְיְינוֹתֶיהָ. וּב"ה נַמִּי לָא דָּרְשִׁי "אִישׁ אִישׁ", מִיהוּ נָפְקָא לְהוּ מִ"זֹּאת תּוֹרַת הַזָּב" – בֵּין גָּדוֹל בֵּין קָטָן מְטַמֵּא בְּזִיבָה. כִּי פָּשִׁיט. כִּי דָּרֵישׁ. מַהוּ שֶׁתְּטַמֵּא. שְׁנִיָּה לָא מִיבַּעְיָא לָן, דְּהָא מְרַבִּינַן לָהּ מִ"לַּזָּכָר" – כָּל שֶׁהוּא זָכָר. וְהָתָם, תַּרְתֵּי רְאִיּוֹת כְּתִיבֵי "וְהַזָּב אֶת זוֹבוֹ". וְרִאשׁוֹן שֶׁל זָב גָּדוֹל נָפְקָא לָן מֵהַאי קְרָא: "זֹאת תּוֹרַת הַזָּב" דְּהַיְינוּ חֲדָא רְאִיָּה, דַּחֲדָא זִיבָה כְּתִיב בִּקְרָא (ויקרא טו): "וַאֲשֶׁר תֵּצֵא מִמֶּנּוּ שִׁכְבַת זֶרַע" אִיתְקַשׁ רְאִיָּה רִאשׁוֹנָה לְקֶרִי. אֲבָל דְּקָטָן, מַאי? מִי אָמְרִינַן כֵּיוָן דִּלְקֶרִי אִיתְקַשׁ – לָא מַשְׁכַּחַת לַהּ אֶלָּא בְּגָדוֹל דְּאִיתֵיהּ בְּקֶרִי, אֲבָל קָטָן דְּלֵיתֵיהּ בְּקֶרִי – לֵיתֵיהּ בִּרְאִיָּה רִאשׁוֹנָה. אוֹ דִּילְמָא, כֵּיוָן דְּאִילּוּ חָזֵי קָטָן רְאִיָּה אַחֲרִיתִי מִצְטָרֶפֶת לְקַמַּיְיתָא, טוּמְאַת שִׁבְעָה כְּדִין זָב בַּעַל שְׁתֵּי רְאִיּוֹת. מְטַמֵּא. נַמִּי כְּשֶׁל גָּדוֹל טוּמְאַת עֶרֶב בְּקֶרִי. רְאִיָּה רִאשׁוֹנָה שֶׁל מְצוֹרָע מַהוּ שֶׁתְּטַמֵּא בְּמַשָּׂא. שֶׁל אִישׁ טָהוֹר לָא תִּבָּעֵי לָךְ, דְּוַדַּאי לָא מְטַמֵּא בְּמַשָּׂא, דְּאִיתְקַשׁ לְקֶרִי, וְקֶרִי לָא מְטַמֵּא בְּמַשָּׂא, כְּדִתְנַן בְּפ"ק דְּמַסֶּכֶת כֵּלִים. וּשְׁנִיָּה נַמִּי לָא תִּבָּעֵי לָךְ, דַּאֲפִילּוּ בְּאָדָם טָהוֹר מְטַמְּיָא בְּמַשָּׂא, כִּדְאָמַר לְקַמָּן בְּפֶרֶק "דַּם הַנִּדָּה" (דף נה.) זוֹב מְטַמֵּא בְּמַשָּׂא, וְיָלֵיף לַהּ מִ"זּוֹבוֹ טָמֵא הוּא". וְהַהוּא בִּרְאִיָּה שְׁנִיָּה כְּתִיב, דְּמָנָה הַכָּתוּב שְׁתַּיִם, וְזָב בַּעַל שְׁתֵּי רְאִיּוֹת – זָב גָּמוּר הוּא לְטוּמְאָה, אֶלָּא שֶׁאֵין טָעוּן קָרְבָּן. כִּי תִּיבָּעֵי לָן רִאשׁוֹנָה, דִּבְאָדָם דְּעָלְמָא – לָא מְטַמְּיָא אֶלָּא בְּמַגָּע, הָכָא בִּמְצוֹרָע מַאי? מְקוֹם זִיבָה מַעְיָן הוּא, וְאִיתְרַבֵּי מִ"לַּזָּכָר" – לְרַבּוֹת מְצוֹרָע לְמַעְיְינוֹתָיו, וּמַעְיָינוֹת מְטַמְּאוֹ בְּמַשָּׂא, כִּדְאָמַר בְּפֶרֶק "דַּם הַנִּדָּה" (לקמן דף נה.): "וְכִי יָרוֹק הַזָּב בַּטָּהוֹר" – בְּמַה שֶׁבַּיָּד טָהוֹר. אוֹ לָאו מַעְיָן הוּא. וַהֲוָיָא כִּשְׁאָר רְאִיָּה רִאשׁוֹנָה שֶׁל כָּל אָדָם, דִּבְמַגָּע מְטַמְּיָא. זוֹבוֹ טָמֵא. הַיְינוּ רְאִיָּה שְׁנִיָּה, שֶׁהֲרֵי מָנָה הַכָּתוּב שְׁתַּיִם: "זָב מִבְּשָׂרוֹ זוֹבוֹ טָמֵא". לִימֵּד עַל הַזּוֹב שֶׁהוּא טָמֵא. וְאָמַר בְּ"דַם הַנִּדָּה" (שם דף נה.) דְּהַאי קְרָא לְרַבּוֹת לְמַגָּע, לָא אִיצְטְרִיךְ, דְּלָא גָּרַע מִשִּׁכְבַת זֶרַע, אֶלָּא לְמַשָּׂא. אִילֵימָא בְּזָב גְּרִידָא. דְּלָאו מְצוֹרָע, לָמָּה לִי קְרָא לְטִיפָּה עַצְמָהּ, פְּשִׁיטָא? לַאֲחֵרִים

[שבת פו:] [ע"ז לו:] [לעיל כח:] [נ"ל באונס] [נדרים לה:] [לקמן נה.]

---

**תוספות**

כִּי קמיבעיא ליה לאחר ג'. אע"פ שהתלמוד קבעו בדברי רב פפא בשבת פרק "ר"ע" (דף פו:) אינו מדברי רב פפא, כדמשמע הכא. וכי האי גוונא אשכחן פ' "המקבל" (ב"מ דף קיב.) דבעו מרב ששת: קבלן עובר ב"בל תלין" או לא? אומן קונה בשבח כלי, והלוואה היא. או אינו קונה, ושכירות היא. אמר להו: עובר. וב"הגוזל" קמא" (ב"ק דף לט.) מוקי לה ההיא בעיא בשליח לאגרת, דלא שייך אומן קונה בשבח כלי. *א"נ י"ל: דהכל מדברי רב פפא, והכא סבר המקשה דרב פפא בעי בין תוך ג' בין לאחר ג' מי אמרינן דכיון דאכלי שקצים ורמשים – אף בתוך ג' מסריח, וטהור. או דלמא כיון דלא דייגי במצות – אף אחר ג' טמא. **אם** אינו ענין לזכר תנהו ענין לנקבה. וא"ת: ולוקי ליה בדם מגפתו או יוצא מפיו או מנחיריו ושאר משקין שבו שאינו מעין, דמטהר לקמן בפרק "דם הנדה" (דף נה.) בזב? וי"ל: דלא בעי לאוקמיה בהו, משום דלא אשכחן בהו טומאה בשום מקום. אבל דם טוהר דמי לדם נדה, אפילו למ"ד ב' מעינות הן. **ובית** הלל נפקא להו מזאת תורת הזב. הוה מצי למימר מ"איש איש", אלא דבעי לאוקמי בית הלל אפי' כמ"ד דברה תורה כלשון בני אדם. **מקום** זיבה מעין הוא או לא. וא"ת: דבפ' "דם הנדה" (לקמן דף נו.) משמע דזוב לאו מעין הוא, דאמר: ונילף מ"זובו" שאינו מתעגל? וי"ל: דהתם קאמר ונילף מ"זובו" אי לאו מעין הוא. א"נ: אף על גב דאינו מתעגל, כדקאמר התם, מ"מ בעי ליה הכא אי כמעין הוא, ורבינן ליה במצורע מקרא ד"לזכר" כמו שאר מעינות, כיון דבזב אית ליה לזוב טומאה חמורה כמו ברוקו ומימי רגליו. **אילימא** בזב גרידא לאחרים גורם טומאה. תימה: וכי לא ידע רבא *סיפא דברייתא, דקתני בה בהדיא, לקמן בפרק "דם הנדה" (דף נה.) שעיר המשתלח יוכיח? לאחרים

---

## תוספי הרא"ש

**כי** קא מיבעיא לי' לאחר ג'. אע"פ שהתלמוד קבעו בדברי רב פפא בפרק ר' עקיבא אינו מדברי רב פפא אלא שהתלמוד פי' שם הסוגי' כפי המסקנא דהכא וכי האי גוונא אשכחן בפ' המקבל גבי קבלנות עובר משום בל תלין או לא: **אם** אינו ענין לזכר כו'. ותימה ולוקמה בזכר לטמא דם היוצא מפיו ומפי האמה ושאר השקין שבו שאינו מעין דמטהר לקמן בפ' דם הנדה וי"ל דלא מסתבר ליה לאוקומי אלא במידי דאשכחן ליה טומאה במקום אחר ודם טהרה שייכא ביה טומאה בלא ימי טוהר ואפי' למ"ד שני מעיינות הן מ"מ דמי לדם נדה דאתי מן המקור. ותימה ולוקמה לטמא קרויו של זב במשא וי"ל דלא מסתבר כיון שלא מצינו בקרי טומאת משא בשום מקום: **לזכר** כל שהוא זכר בין גדול בין קטן. רש"י ל"ג לנקבה כל שהיא נקבה בין גדולה בין קטנה דלנקבה אצטריך לרבות מעיינות מצורע ולפירושיו קאי ואבע"א אהא דאמרי' וב"ש אין שום טומאה פריך ואתא למימר דלא פרכינן שום טומאה. ונראה דקאי ואבע"א ארישא דמילתא דמפר' ר' יצחק דטעמ' דב"ה משום דדריש לזכר לרבות מצורע למעיינותיו וב"ש מוקמי לה לרבות קטן וקטנה ולא מוקמי ליה למעיינות כלל כר' ישמעאל בנו של ר' יוחנן בן ברוקה בריש פרקין ומעיינות נפקא להו מקרא אחרינא וכן לקמן בשמעתין דמאן דמוקי ליה לרבות קטן לא מוקי ליה למעיינות כלל מדקאמר על רב יוסף הא איהו דאמר זאת תורת הזב בין גדול בין קטן ואייתר ליה לזכר למעיינותיו: **ראיה** ראשונה של זב מהו שתטמא. פרש"י שניה לא קא מיבעי' לן דהא מרבינן לה מלזכר כל שהוא זכר והתם תרתי ראיות כתיבי משמע דאי הוי נפיק ליה קטן מזאת תורת הזב לא קא מיבעי' ליה דפשיטא ליה דמטמא כיון דחדא ראיה כתיב בקרא א)א"כ מאי פשיטא ליה לרב יוסף אמר קרא זאת תורת הזב בין גדול בין קטן הא איהו נמי פשיטא ליה דמאן דדריש קטן מהך קרא דראיה ראשונה שלו טמאה. ועוד הקשה רבי' מאיר דא"כ דריש לקיש מיבעיא ליה אליבא דב"ש דלא כהלכתה ופי' דמיבעי' אליבא דב"ה וה"ק מהו שתטמא מי אמרינן דוקא זב בעל שתי ראיית הוא דמרבינן מזאת תורת הזב אע"ג דבקרא לא כתיב אלא זב פעם אחת קאי נמי אזב בעל שתי ראיות דהא טובא קראי דלא כתיב אלא זב פעם אחת ואינן נוהגין בזב בעל ראיה אחת כגון כל המשכב אשר ישכב עליו הזב וכל כלי אשר ישב עליו הזב וגו' וה"נ זאת תורת הזב קיימי אראיות דכתיבי דלעיל הילכך אמרינן דריבויא דזאת תורת דמרבינן מינה בין גדול בין קטן בראיה שניה ושלישית איירי אבל בראיה אחת לחודה לא מרבינן קטן כיון דאיתקש לבעל קרי הילכך לא מטמאה ראיה ראשונה כי היכי דשכבת זרע לא מטמאה או דילמא כיון דחזאי תרתי כו': **מקום** זיבה מעיין הוא. תימה דהכא מיבעא ליה אי הוי מעיין או לא ובפ' דם הנדה פשיט ליה דזוב אינו מתעגל וחוזר ויוצא ונבלע: **אילימא** בזב גרידא לאחרים

א) נראה דל"ל וקשה לי דא"כ מאי פשיט ליה רבא לרב יוסף מברייתא דזאת תורת הזב וכו'

---

**עין משפט נר מצוה**

לב א מיי' פ"ב מהל' מטמאי משכב ומושב הל' ו והל' ז:

לג ב מיי' פ"ה מהל' אבות הטומאה הל' יז:

לד ג מיי' פ"א מהל' מטמאי משכב ומושב הל' יב:

[ע"ע תוס' ב"ק יט. ד"ה רב אשי ותוס' יומא מ: ד"ה ועשהו ותוס' שבועות כה. ד"ה ושמואל]

[עמ"ש על הגליון בתוס' פסחים נז. ד"ה אלא לאו]

[עי' תוס' ב"ק כה. ד"ה אלא]

לה א מיי' פ"א מהל' מטמאי משכב ומושב הל' יג:

לו ב ג מיי' פ"ב מהל' מחוסרי כפרה הל' ב והל' ו סמג עשין רמז:

לַאֲחֵרִים גּוֹרֵם טוּמְאָה, לְעַצְמוֹ לֹא כׇּל שֶׁכֵּן? אֶלָּא פְּשִׁיטָא — בְּזָב מְצוֹרָע, וּמִדְּאִיצְטְרִיךְ קְרָא לְרַבּוֹיֵי בִּרְאִיָּיה שְׁנִיָּה — שְׁמַע מִינָּהּ: מְקוֹם זִיבָה לָאו מַעְיָן הוּא. אֲמַר לֵיהּ רַב יְהוּדָה מִדִּסְקַרְתָּא לְרָבָא: מִמַּאי? דִּילְמָא לְעוֹלָם אֵימָא לָךְ — בְּזָב גְּרֵידָא, וּדְקָאָמְרַתְּ לַאֲחֵרִים גּוֹרֵם טוּמְאָה, לְעַצְמוֹ לֹא כׇּל שֶׁכֵּן — *שָׂעִיר הַמִּשְׁתַּלֵּחַ יוֹכִיחַ, שֶׁגּוֹרֵם טוּמְאָה לַאֲחֵרִים — וְהוּא עַצְמוֹ טָהוֹר! אָמַר אַבָּיֵי: מַאי תִּבְּעֵי לֵיהּ? וְהָא הוּא דְּאָמַר: "זֹאת תּוֹרַת הַזָּב" — בֵּין גָּדוֹל בֵּין קָטָן, וְכֵיוָן דְּנָפְקָא לֵיהּ מֵהָתָם — אִיַּיתַּר לֵיהּ "לַזָּכָר" לְרַבּוֹת מְצוֹרָע לְמַעְיָנוֹתָיו, "נְקֵבָה" — לְרַבּוֹת מְצוֹרַעַת לְמַעְיְנוֹתֶיהָ, וְאַקְּשֵׁיהּ רַחֲמָנָא מְצוֹרָע לְזָב גָּמוּר, מָה זָב גָּמוּר — מְטַמֵּא בְּמַשָּׂא, אאַף רְאִיָּיה רִאשׁוֹנָה שֶׁל מְצוֹרָע — מְטַמְּאָה בְּמַשָּׂא. *א"ר הוּנָא: ברְאִיָּיה רִאשׁוֹנָה שֶׁל זָב מְטַמְּאָה בְּאוֹנֶס, שֶׁנֶּאֱמַר: "זֹאת תּוֹרַת הַזָּב וַאֲשֶׁר תֵּצֵא מִמֶּנּוּ שִׁכְבַת זָרַע", מַה שִּׁכְבַת זֶרַע — מְטַמֵּא בְּאוֹנֶס, אַף רְאִיָּיה רִאשׁוֹנָה שֶׁל זָב — מְטַמְּאָה בְּאוֹנֶס. תָּא שְׁמַע: *רָאָה רְאִיָּיה רִאשׁוֹנָה — בּוֹדְקִין אוֹתוֹ. מַאי לָאו — לְטוּמְאָה? גלָא, לְקׇרְבָּן. ת"ש: בַּשְּׁנִיָּה בּוֹדְקִין אוֹתוֹ. לְמַאי? אִילֵימָא לְקׇרְבָּן, אֲבָל לְטוּמְאָה לָא, *אִקְרִי כָּאן "מִבְּשָׂרוֹ" וְלֹא מֵחֲמַת אוֹנְסוֹ, אֶלָּא לָאו — לְטוּמְאָה, וּמִדְּסֵיפָא לְטוּמְאָה — רֵישָׁא נַמִי לְטוּמְאָה! מִידֵּי אִירְיָא? הָא — כִּדְאִיתָא, וְהָא — כִּדְאִיתָא. תָּא שְׁמַע, *רַבִּי אֱלִיעֶזֶר אוֹמֵר: אַף בַּשְּׁלִישִׁי בּוֹדְקִין אוֹתוֹ מִפְּנֵי הַקׇּרְבָּן. מִכְּלָל דְּתַנָּא קַמָּא — מִפְּנֵי הַטּוּמְאָה קָאָמַר! לָא, דְּכוּלֵּי עָלְמָא לְקׇרְבָּן, וְהָכָא *בְּ"אֶתִים" קָא מִיפַּלְגִי, דרַבָּנַן *לָא דָּרְשִׁי "אֶתִים", וְרַבִּי אֱלִיעֶזֶר דָּרֵישׁ "אֶתִים". רַבָּנַן לָא דָּרְשִׁי "אֶתִים": ה"הַזָּב" — חֲדָא, "זוֹבוֹ" — תַּרְתֵּי, "לַזָּכָר" — בַּשְּׁלִישִׁי אַקְּשֵׁיהּ רַחֲמָנָא לִנְקֵבָה. וְרַבִּי אֱלִיעֶזֶר דָּרֵישׁ "אֶתִים": "הַזָּב" — חֲדָא, "אֶת" — תַּרְתֵּי, "זוֹבוֹ" — תְּלָת, בָּרְבִיעִי אַקְּשֵׁיהּ רַחֲמָנָא לִנְקֵבָה. תָּא שְׁמַע, רַבִּי יִצְחָק אוֹמֵר: וַהֲלֹא זָב בִּכְלַל בַּעַל קֶרִי הָיָה, וְלָמָּה יָצָא — לְהָקֵל עָלָיו וּלְהַחְמִיר עָלָיו. לְהָקֵל עָלָיו — שֶׁאֵין מְטַמֵּא בְּאוֹנֶס, וּלְהַחְמִיר עָלָיו

שֶׁהוּא

**לַאֲחֵרִים גּוֹרֵם טוּמְאָה.** כְּלוֹמַר, טִיפָּה זוֹ גּוֹרֶמֶת לְבַעְלָהּ שֶׁמְּטַמֵּא בְּמַשָּׂא, כִּדְכְתִיב (ויקרא טו) "וְכֹל* אֲשֶׁר יִהְיֶה תַּחְתָּיו", וְאוֹקְמִינַן בְּעֶלְיוֹנוֹ שֶׁל זָב, הִיא עַצְמָהּ – לֹא כׇּל שֶׁכֵּן! **אֶלָּא בְּזָב** מְצוֹרָע. אִיצְטְרִיךְ, דְּלָא אָתֵי בְּקַל וָחוֹמֶר, דְּלֹא גָּרְמָה לוֹ טוּמְאָה, שֶׁהֲרֵי מֵחֲמַת נִגְעוֹ הָיָה מְטַמֵּא בְּמַשָּׂא, וַאֲפִילּוּ בְּאֹהֶל. **וּמִדְּאִיצְטְרִיךְ** קְרָא לְרַבּוֹיֵי לַשְּׁנִיָּה ש"מ בָּרִאשׁוֹנָה. דְּלָאו מַעְיָין הוּא, דְּאִי מַעְיָן הוּא – רִאשׁוֹנָה מְטַמְּאָה, שְׁנִיָּה – לֹא כׇּל שֶׁכֵּן! **לְעוֹלָם אֵימָא** לָךְ **בְּזָב גְּרֵידָא.** דְּאִי בִּמְצוֹרָע – לָא אִיצְטְרִיךְ קְרָא לְרַבּוֹיֵי, דַּאֲפִילּוּ רִאשׁוֹנָה מְטַמֵּא מִשּׁוּם מַעְיָין. **וּדְקָאָמְרַתְּ** כו' שָׂעִיר הַמִּשְׁתַּלֵּחַ יוֹכִיחַ **שֶׁגּוֹרֵם טוּמְאָה.** לִמְשַׁלְּחוֹ, כִּדְכְתִיב (ויקרא טז): "וְהַמְשַׁלֵּחַ אֶת הַשָּׂעִיר" וגו'. וְהוּא עַצְמוֹ טָהוֹר, שֶׁאֵין בְּהֵמָה מְטַמְּאָה מֵחַיִּים. **מַאי תִּיבְּעֵי לֵיהּ.** לְרַב יוֹסֵף. **הָא אִיהוּ אָמַר כו'.** בֵּין קָטָן בֵּין גָּדוֹל לְזִיבָה, וְלָא אִיצְטְרִיךְ "וְהַזָּב אֶת זוֹבוֹ לַזָּכָר" לְרַבּוֹת קָטָן, דְּהָא מִ"זֹּאת תּוֹרַת הַזָּב" נָפְקָא, וְאִיַּיתַּר "לַזָּכָר" לְרַבּוֹת מְצוֹרָע. **וְאִיתַּקַּשׁ** מְצוֹרָע לְזָב גָּמוּר. בַּעַל שְׁתֵּי רְאִיּוֹת, דְּהָא בְּהַאי קְרָא דְּהֶיקֵּשָׁא דִּמְצוֹרָע תַּרְתֵּי כְּתִיבֵי: "וְהַזָּב אֶת זוֹבוֹ" – הֲרֵי שְׁתַּיִם, וּכְתִיב בֵּיהּ "לַזָּכָר" – לְרַבּוֹת מְצוֹרָע כְּדִין זָב גָּמוּר. מַה זָּב גָּמוּר – זוֹבוֹ מְטַמֵּא בְּמַשָּׂא, אַף מְצוֹרָע – זוֹבוֹ מְטַמֵּא בְּמַשָּׂא, וַאֲפִילּוּ רִאשׁוֹנָה. דְּבִשְׁלָמָא אִי מַפֵּיק לֵיהּ הַאי "לַזָּכָר" לְזָב קָטָן, וְיָלֵיף מְצוֹרָע זָכָר מִמְּצוֹרַעַת נְקֵבָה – אִיכָּא לְמִבְּעֵי רְאִיָּיה רִאשׁוֹנָה מַהוּ: מִי הָוֵי מִתְעַגֵּל וְיוֹצֵא וּמִתְרַבֵּי עִם שְׁאָר מַעְיָינוֹת. אוֹ לָאו, דִּבִנְקֵבָה לֵיכָּא זוֹב לוֹכַן לְמִילְפֵיהּ מֵהֶיקֵּשָׁא דְּזָב גָּמוּר אִי לָאו מַעְיָין הָוֵי. אֲבָל הַשְׁתָּא דִּמְצוֹרָע זָכָר אִיתַּקַּשׁ לְזָב גָּמוּר – לָא צָרִיךְ תּוּ לְמִבְּעֵי. וְאִית דִּמְפָרְשִׁי בַּעְיָא דְּרַב יוֹסֵף הָכִי: רְאִיָּיה רִאשׁוֹנָה שֶׁל מְצוֹרָע מַהוּ שֶׁתְּטַמֵּא בְּמַשָּׂא? בְּזָב גְּרֵידָא לָא תִּבְּעֵי לָךְ – דְּוַדַּאי מְטַמֵּא, כִּדְאָמַר לְקַמָּן: "לִימֵּד עַל הַזּוֹב שֶׁהוּא טָמֵא", וּמוֹקְמִינַן בְּ"דַם הַנִּדָּה", דִּקְרָא לְמַשָּׂא אָתָא. כִּי תִּבְּעֵי לָךְ בִּמְצוֹרָע: דְּאִיכָּא לְמֵימַר בְּזָב גְּרֵידָא הוּא דִּמְטַמֵּא, מִשּׁוּם דְּגוֹרֶמֶת לוֹ טוּמְאָה. אֲבָל בִּמְצוֹרָע, כְּבָר טָמֵא הוּא, וְאֵינָהּ גּוֹרֶמֶת לוֹ טוּמְאָה – לָא מְטַמְּיָא הַטִּיפָּה. אִי לָא אָמְרִינַן מַעְיָין הוּא כְּרוּקוֹ אוֹ מֵימֵי רַגְלָיו, מַאי? מַעְיָין הוּא אוֹ לָא. לִימֵּד עַל הַזּוֹב, וּמוֹקְמִינַן לָהּ בִּרְאִיָּיה רִאשׁוֹנָה. וְהָכִי מַשְׁמַע: "כִּי יִהְיֶה זָב מִבְּשָׂרוֹ" – אוֹתוֹ הַזָּב טָמֵא לַאֲחֵרִים, לְבַעְלָהּ. וּמִדְּאִיצְטְרִיךְ לְרַבּוֹיֵי לִרְאִיָּיה רִאשׁוֹנָה – ש"מ: לָאו מַעְיָן הוּא. וְשִׁיבּוּשׁ הוּא, מִפְּנֵי כַּמָּה תְּשׁוּבוֹת: חֲדָא, דְּקָא פָּשֵׁיט לֵיהּ מְקוֹם זִיבָה לָאו מַעְיָין הוּא, וְהָא לְמַשָּׂא רַבְּיֵיהּ קְרָא! כִּדְאָמַר בְּ"דַם הַנִּדָּה": מַה לִּי מַעְיָין וּמַה לִּי לָאו מַעְיָין. וְעוֹד: מִי אִיכָּא לְאוֹקְמֵי לְהַאי קְרָא בִּרְאִיָּיה רִאשׁוֹנָה? וְהָא מֵהָכָא נָפְקָא לָן בְּכׇל דּוּכְתֵּי: מָנָה הַכָּתוּב שְׁתַּיִם וּקְרָאוֹ "טָמֵא"! וְעוֹד: מִי אִיכָּא לְמֵימַר בִּרְאִיָּיה רִאשׁוֹנָה בְּזָב גְּרֵידָא לַאֲחֵרִים גּוֹרֵם טוּמְאַת מַשָּׂא? הָא זָב בַּעַל רְאִיָּיה אַחַת אֵינוֹ אֶלָּא כְּרוֹאֶה קֶרִי, כִּדְאָמַר בְּכַמָּה מְקוֹמוֹת: שְׁתַּיִם לְטוּמְאַת זִיבָה וְשָׁלֹשׁ לְקׇרְבָּן! וְעוֹד: רְאִיָּיה רִאשׁוֹנָה, הָא אַקְּשֵׁיהּ לְעֵיל לְקֶרִי, וְקֶרִי לָא מְטַמֵּא בְּמַשָּׂא! וּמִשּׁוּם שֶׁכָּתוּב בַּסְּפָרִים: "מִדְּאִיצְטְרִיךְ קְרָא בִּרְאִיָּיה רִאשׁוֹנָה" מְפָרְשִׁי לֵיהּ הָכִי, וְלָאו מִילְּתָא הִיא. דְּהַאי "בִּרְאִיָּיה רִאשׁוֹנָה" (א) פֵּירוּשׁ הָיָה בַּסְּפָרִים, וּלְקַמֵּיהּ קָאֵי. וְהָכִי קָאָמַר: מִדְּאִיצְטְרִיךְ קְרָא לְרַבּוֹיֵי לַשְּׁנִיָּה, ש"מ: רִאשׁוֹנָה מְקוֹם זִיבָה לָאו מַעְיָין הוּא. וה"ג בִּשְׁלְהֵי שְׁמַעְתָּא: מַה זָּב גָּמוּר מְטַמֵּא זוֹבוֹ בְּמַשָּׂא, אַף מְצוֹרָע כו'. אַלְמָא, זָב גָּמוּר הוּא, דִּמְטַמֵּא טִיפַּת זוֹבוֹ בְּמַשָּׂא. אֲבָל זָב בַּעַל רְאִיָּיה אַחַת – לָא. **מְטַמֵּא בְּאוֹנֶס.** אוֹתָהּ טוּמְאָה קַלָּה הָאֲמוּרָה בָּהּ מַגָּע וְטוּמְאַת עֶרֶב בְּקֶרִי, וּלְהִצְטָרֵף לַשְּׁנִיָּה לְטַמֵּא כְּזָב גָּמוּר. וְהָא דִּכְתִיב: "מִבְּשָׂרוֹ" וְלֹא מֵחֲמַת אוֹנְסוֹ – עַל כׇּרְחָךְ אַרְאִיָּיה שְׁנִיָּה דִּכְתִיב בַּתְרָהּ קָאֵי, וְלָא אַרִאשׁוֹנָה. דְּהָא אִיתַּקַּשׁ לְשִׁכְבַת זֶרַע, וְשִׁכְבַת זֶרַע כׇּל עַצְמוֹ מֵחֲמַת אוֹנֶס חִימּוּם בָּא. **בּוֹדְקִין אוֹתוֹ.** בְּשִׁבְעָה דְּרָכִים: בְּמַאֲכָל, בְּמִשְׁתֶּה, בִּקְפִיצָה, וּבְמַשָּׂאוֹי כו'. **מַאי לָאו לְטוּמְאָה.** דְּאִי בְּאוֹנֶס הוּא – הָוֵי טָהוֹר לְגַמְרֵי. **לֹא לְקׇרְבָּן.** דְּאִי קַמַּיְיתָא בְּאוֹנֶס – לָא מִצְטָרְפָא לְשָׁלֹשׁ לְחַיְּיבוֹ קׇרְבָּן. **אִילֵימָא לְקׇרְבָּן אֲבָל לְטוּמְאָה.** הָאֲמוּרָה בּוֹ, דְּהַיְינוּ טוּמְאָה חֲמוּרָה – לָא בָּעֵי בְּדִיקָה. (ב) קְרִי כָּאן מִבְּשָׂרוֹ וְלֹא מֵחֲמַת אוֹנְסוֹ. וְהַאי "מִבְּשָׂרוֹ" – בִּקְרָא דִּשְׁתֵּי רְאִיּוֹת כְּתִיב. **אֶתִים.** (ויקרא טו) "וְהַזָּב אֶת זוֹבוֹ לַזָּכָר וְלַנְּקֵבָה". **זָב חֲדָא** זוֹבוֹ תַּרְתֵּי לַזָּכָר. כְּלוֹמַר, עַד כָּאן יֵשׁ לוֹ דִּין זָכָר, שֶׁאֵינוֹ מְטַמֵּא בְּאוֹנֶס. מִכָּאן וְאֵילָךְ, דְּהַיְינוּ שְׁלִישִׁית, "לַנְּקֵבָה" כְּתִיב – כְּלוֹמַר, יֵשׁ לוֹ דִּין נְקֵבָה שֶׁמְּטַמְּאָה בְּאוֹנֶס, כְּדִילְפִינַן בְּפִירְקִין (לקמן דף לו.) מִ"כִּי יָזוּב זוֹב", וְאִיהִי נַמִי מַיְיתָא לֵיהּ לִידֵי קׇרְבָּן. **בָּרְבִיעִית.** אָז אַקְּשֵׁיהּ רַחֲמָנָא לִנְקֵבָה, דַּאֲפִילּוּ בְּאוֹנֶס. וְלָא לְעִנְיַן טוּמְאָה – דְּהָא מִכִּי חַזְיָא תַּרְתֵּי אִיטַּמֵּי לֵיהּ, וּלְקׇרְבָּן נַמִי לָא – דְּמִשְּׁלֹשָׁה אִיחַיַּיב לֵיהּ, אֶלָּא לִסְתִירָה. כְּגוֹן דְּפָסַק וְהִתְחִיל לִסְפּוֹר שִׁבְעָה נְקִיִּים, וְרָאָה רְאִיָּיה רְבִיעִית, אֲפִילּוּ בְּאוֹנֶס – סוֹתֵר. **וַהֲלֹא** זָב בִּכְלַל בַּעַל קֶרִי הָיָה. כִּדְמְפָרֵשׁ לְקַמֵּיהּ וְאָזֵיל דְּאִיתְּקוּשׁ לְשִׁכְבַת זֶרַע. **וְלָמָּה יָצָא.** בְּפָרָשַׁת זָבִין לְהִכָּתֵב לְעַצְמוֹ? לְהָקֵל עָלָיו. שֶׁלֹּא יְטַמֵּא בְּאוֹנֶס, דְּהָא קֶרִי מְטַמֵּא בְּאוֹנֶס.

שהוא

**לאחרים** גורם טומאה. פירש רש"י: לזב עצמו גורם טומאת משא, כדכתיב "וכל* אשר יהיה תחתיו", ואוקמינן ליה בעליונו של זב. ואין נראה, דעליונו של זב אינו קרוי משא, ואינו מטמא אלא אוכלין ומשקין! ועוד: דבזוב כי האי גוונא לא אשכחן אלא כשהטיפה בכף מאזנים וכרעה לכף שניה! לכן נראה לפרש: לזב עצמו גורם טומאת משא, שהנושא הזב – טמא, הנושא הזוב – לא כל שכן דטמא! ובשאר טומאות דלאו משא, כגון משכב ומושב, אין לפרש, דהא למצורע נמי גורם טומאה. דאילו מצורע גרידא, אינו עושה משכב ומושב אלא לטמא אוכלין ומשקין, כדפרישית בפרק "אלו דברים" (פסחים סו.) ואם זב הוא – מטמא משכבו אדם ובגדים. **לעולם** אימא לך בזב גרידא. תימה: דמכל מקום תפשוט דלאו מעיין הוא. דאי מעיין הוא – למה לי קרא לטמא בזוב? דהא מיד שראה משהו של ראייה שניה – מיד נעשה זב, למ"ד זוב מטמא במשהו, דלא בעי כחתימת פי האמה ומשהו שני לטמא כדין מעיין, דאי אפשר לטיפה שלא תתחלק שני משהויין! ושמא כמו שמשהו ראשון שבו נעשה זב אינו מטמא במשא, הוא הדין כל מה שנקרא ראייה אחת, דהיינו (ג) *)כמו גריון לשילה (זבים פ"א מ"ה) דלא מטמא במשא, אע"ג דרוקו ומימי רגליו טמאין מיד אחר ראיית זוב משהו ראשון. **אף** ראייה ראשונה של מצורע מטמאה במשא. תימה: אם כן, לעיל מגליה לאוקומי קרא בדם טהרה של מצורעת? הא איצטריך קרא לכדהכא! **מאי** לאו לטומאה. וא"ת: מאי קושיא, דילמא הא דאמר רב הונא מטמא באונס – היינו טומאת ערב כבעל קרי, והכא מיירי להצטרף לשניה לטמא טומאה חמורה לעשותו זב, והוי השתא שפיר רישא דומיא דסיפא? וי"ל: מדלא נקט "הרואה ראייה אחת של זיבה", אלא נקט "ראייה ראשונה של זב", משמע דאיירי באותו שראה שתי ראיות, והראשונה היתה באונס. ד"זב" אינו קרוי עד שיראה שתי ראיות. ויליף מהיקשא ד"זאת תורת" דאיירי בזב גמור, ומקיש ראשונה של השתים לשכבת זרע. **מכלל** דתנא קמא לטומאה. לאו מן הלשון מדקדק, מדאצטריך ר' אליעזר להזכיר קרבן, מכלל דת"ק איירי לטומאה דא"כ לא הוה משני מידי. אלא הכי דייק: מכלל דתנא קמא לא מצריך בדיקה משום קרבן אלא משום טומאה. דאי משום קרבן – הוה ליה לאצרוכי נמי בדיקה בשלישי, כרבי אליעזר. וקשה: דהא בלאו מילתיה דרבי אליעזר הוה מצי למפרך, מדקתני במס' זבים (פרק ב' מ"ב) בהדיא במילתיה דרבנן גופייהו "בשלישי אין בודקין אותו"? ושמא מייתי מרבי אליעזר, משום דבעי לפרושי במאי פליגי. אי

*) רש"ל גדיון לשילוח פי' גדיון שם מקום ושילוח הוא הנהר כמו מי השילוח כן פי' הרמב"ם בפ"ק דזבים וע' בר"ש

לז א מיי' פ"ב מהל' מחוסרי כפרה הל' א:
לח ב ג מיי' פ"ה מהל' משכב ומושב הל' א ובפ"ז מהל' איסורי ביאה הל' ז והל"ח סמג לאוין קיא ועשין רמג:
לט ד מיי' פ"ו מהל' איסורי ביאה הל"א סמג לאוין קיא ועשין רמג:
מ ה מיי' שם פ"ז הל' ז:
מא ו מיי' פ"ה מהל' משכב ומושב הל"ב:
מב ז מיי' פ"ז מהל' איסורי ביאה הל' ז:
מג ח מיי' פ"ג מהל' משכב ומושב הל"א:
ס"א לאחר מ' הוו ב"ה כו'. מהר"ס
מד ט מיי' פ"ז מהל' איסורי ביאה הל"ה:
נ"ל ואפילו ביולדת בזוב מטהרין ב"ש וב"ה מטמאי משום דמעין א' כו'. מהר"מ

שֶׁהוּא עוֹשֶׂה מִשְׁכָּב וּמוֹשָׁב. אֵימַת? אִילֵימָא בִּרְאִיָּיה שְׁנִיָּה — הֵיכָא הֲוָה בִּכְלַל בַּעַל קֶרִי? אֶלָּא פְּשִׁיטָא — בִּרְאִיָּיה רִאשׁוֹנָה, וְקָתָנֵי "לְהָקֵל עָלָיו שֶׁאֵינוֹ מְטַמֵּא בְּאוֹנֶס"! וְתִסְבְּרָא "לְהַחְמִיר עָלָיו שֶׁהוּא עוֹשֶׂה מִשְׁכָּב וּמוֹשָׁב", בִּרְאִיָּיה רִאשׁוֹנָה בַּר מִשְׁכָּב וּמוֹשָׁב הוּא? אֶלָּא הָכִי קָאָמַר, רַבִּי יִצְחָק אוֹמֵר: וַהֲלֹא זָב בִּכְלַל בַּעַל קֶרִי הָיָה בִּרְאִיָּיה רִאשׁוֹנָה, וְלָמָּה יָצָא בִּרְאִיָּיה שְׁנִיָּיה — לְהָקֵל עָלָיו וּלְהַחְמִיר עָלָיו, לְהָקֵל עָלָיו — שֶׁאֵינוֹ מְטַמֵּא בְּאוֹנֶס, וּלְהַחְמִיר עָלָיו — שֶׁהוּא עוֹשֶׂה מִשְׁכָּב וּמוֹשָׁב. אָמַר רַב הוּנָא: [א]זוֹב דּוֹמֶה לְמֵי בָצֵק שֶׁל שְׂעוֹרִים, זוֹב בָּא מִבְּשַׂר הַמֵּת, שִׁכְבַת זֶרַע בָּא מִבְּשַׂר הַחַי. זוֹב — דֵּיהָה, וְדוֹמֶה לְלוֹבֶן בֵּיצָה הַמּוּזֶרֶת, שִׁכְבַת זֶרַע — קְשׁוּרָה, וְדוֹמָה לְלוֹבֶן בֵּיצָה שֶׁאֵינָהּ מוּזֶרֶת.§ "דַּם הַיּוֹלֶדֶת שֶׁלֹּא טָבְלָה" וכו'.§ תַּנְיָא, אָמְרוּ לָהֶן בֵּית הִלֵּל לְבֵית שַׁמַּאי: אִי אַתֶּם מוֹדִים בְּנִדָּה שֶׁלֹּא טָבְלָה וְרָאֲתָה דָּם, שֶׁהִיא טְמֵאָה? אָמְרוּ לָהֶם בֵּית שַׁמַּאי: לֹא אִם אֲמַרְתֶּם בְּנִדָּה — שֶׁאֲפִילּוּ טָבְלָה וְרָאֲתָה, טְמֵאָה. תֹּאמְרוּ בְּיוֹלֶדֶת — שֶׁאִם טָבְלָה וְרָאֲתָה, שֶׁהִיא טְהוֹרָה. אָמְרוּ לָהֶם: יוֹלֶדֶת בְּזוֹב תּוֹכִיחַ, שֶׁאִם טָבְלָה וְרָאֲתָה לְאַחַר יְמֵי סְפִירָה — טְהוֹרָה, [ב]לֹא טָבְלָה וְרָאֲתָה — טְמֵאָה! אָמְרוּ לָהֶם: הוּא הַדִּין, וְהִיא הַתְּשׁוּבָה. לְמֵימְרָא דִּפְלִיגִי? וְהָתְנַן: וּמוֹדִים בְּיוֹלֶדֶת בְּזוֹב שֶׁהִיא מְטַמְּאָה לַח וְיָבֵשׁ! לָא קַשְׁיָא, [ג]כָּאן — שֶׁסָּפְרָה, כָּאן — שֶׁלֹּא סָפְרָה. וְהָתַנְיָא: *יוֹלֶדֶת בְּזוֹב שֶׁסָּפְרָה וְלֹא טָבְלָה וְרָאֲתָה, הָלְכוּ בֵּית שַׁמַּאי לְשִׁיטָתָן וּב"ה לְשִׁיטָתָן. *אִיתְּמַר, רַב אָמַר: [ד]מַעְיָן אֶחָד הוּא, הַתּוֹרָה טִמְּאַתּוּ וְהַתּוֹרָה טִהֲרַתּוֹ. וְלֵוִי אָמַר: שְׁנֵי מַעְיָנוֹת הֵם, נִסְתַּם הַטָּמֵא — נִפְתַּח הַטָּהוֹר, נִסְתַּם הַטָּהוֹר — נִפְתַּח הַטָּמֵא. מַאי בֵּינַיְיהוּ? אִיכָּא בֵּינַיְיהוּ: שׁוֹפַעַת מִתּוֹךְ שִׁבְעָה לְאַחַר שִׁבְעָה, וּמִתּוֹךְ אַרְבָּעָה עָשָׂר לְאַחַר אַרְבָּעָה עָשָׂר, וּמִתּוֹךְ אַרְבָּעִים לְאַחַר אַרְבָּעִים, וּמִתּוֹךְ שְׁמוֹנִים לְאַחַר שְׁמוֹנִים, [ה]לְרַב — רֵישָׁא לְקוּלָּא וְסֵיפָא לְחוּמְרָא, לְלֵוִי — רֵישָׁא לְחוּמְרָא וְסֵיפָא לְקוּלָּא. מֵיתִיבִי, דַּם הַיּוֹלֶדֶת שֶׁלֹּא טָבְלָה, בֵּית שַׁמַּאי אוֹמְרִים: כְּרוּקָּהּ וּכְמֵימֵי רַגְלֶיהָ, וּב"ה אוֹמְרִים: מְטַמֵּא לַח וְיָבֵשׁ. קָא ס"ד דִּפְסָקָה, בִּשְׁלָמָא לְרַב דְּאָמַר מַעְיָן אֶחָד הוּא — מִשּׁוּם הָכִי מְטַמֵּא לַח וְיָבֵשׁ, אֶלָּא לְלֵוִי, דְּאָמַר שְׁנֵי מַעְיָנוֹת הֵן, אַמַּאי מְטַמֵּא לַח וְיָבֵשׁ? אָמַר לָךְ לֵוִי: הָכָא בְּמַאי עָסְקִינַן — בְּשׁוֹפַעַת. אִי בְּשׁוֹפַעַת — מ"ט דְּב"ש? קָסָבְרִי ב"ש: מַעְיָן אֶחָד הוּא. בִּשְׁלָמָא לְלֵוִי — הַיְינוּ דְּאִיכָּא בֵּין ב"ש וּב"ה, אֶלָּא לְרַב מַאי בֵּינַיְיהוּ? אִיכָּא בֵּינַיְיהוּ יוֹמֵי וּטְבִילָה, דְּבֵית שַׁמַּאי סָבְרִי בְּיוֹמֵי תָּלָה רַחֲמָנָא, וּב"ה סָבְרִי [ו]בְּיוֹמֵי וּטְבִילָה. ת"ש: וּמוֹדִים בְּיוֹלֶדֶת בְּזוֹב שֶׁהִיא מְטַמְּאָה לַח וְיָבֵשׁ. ס"ד הָכָא נַמִי דִּפְסָקָה, בִּשְׁלָמָא לְרַב דְּאָמַר מַעְיָן אֶחָד הוּא — מִשּׁוּם הָכִי מְטַמֵּא לַח וְיָבֵשׁ, אֶלָּא לְלֵוִי דַּאֲמַר שְׁנֵי מַעְיָנוֹת הֵן, אַמַּאי מְטַמֵּא לַח וְיָבֵשׁ? אָמַר לָךְ: הָכָא נַמִי בְּשׁוֹפַעַת. אִי בְּשׁוֹפַעַת — לְמַאי אִיצְטְרִיךְ? לְב"ש אִיצְטְרִיךְ, אַף עַל גַּב דְּקָאָמְרִי בֵּית שַׁמַּאי מַעְיָן אֶחָד הוּא וּבְיוֹמֵי תָּלָה רַחֲמָנָא, הָנֵי מִילֵּי — בְּיוֹלֶדֶת גְּרֵידְתָּא, דִּשְׁלִימוּ לְהוּ יוֹמֵי, [ז]אֲבָל יוֹלֶדֶת בְּזוֹב דְּבָעֵי סְפִירָה — לָא. תָּא שְׁמַע: *°"דָּוֹתָהּ תִּטְמָא" — [ח]לְרַבּוֹת אֶת בּוֹעֲלָהּ, "דָּוֹתָהּ תִּטְמָא" — לְרַבּוֹת הַלֵּילוֹת, "דָּוֹתָהּ תִּטְמָא" — [ט]לְרַבּוֹת הַיּוֹלֶדֶת בְּזוֹב שֶׁצְּרִיכָה שֶׁתֵּשֵׁב שִׁבְעָה יָמִים נְקִיִּים. בִּשְׁלָמָא לְרַב דְּאָמַר מַעְיָן אֶחָד הוּא — מִשּׁוּם הָכִי בָּעֲיָא שִׁבְעָה יָמִים נְקִיִּים, אֶלָּא

תורה אור: ויקרא יב

סנהדרין פז: [לעיל יח:]

שֶׁהוּא עוֹשֶׂה מִשְׁכָּב וּמוֹשָׁב. אָב הַטּוּמְאָה, מַה שֶּׁאֵין כֵּן בְּקֶרִי. אֶלָּא פְּשִׁיטָא בִּרְאִיָּיה רִאשׁוֹנָה. דַּהֲוֵי בִּכְלַל קֶרִי, כִּדְאַקְשִׁינַן לְעֵיל: "הַזָּב וַאֲשֶׁר תֵּצֵא מִמֶּנּוּ" וכו'. דֵּיהָה. כְּלוֹמַר, מִתְמַקְמֵק וְנִפְרָד, וְאֵינוֹ קָשׁוּר. מוּזֶרֶת. שֶׁאֵינָהּ מַשְׁרֶצֶת אֶפְרוֹחַ תַּחַת תַּרְנְגוֹלֶת. יוֹלֶדֶת בְּזוֹב תּוֹכִיחַ שֶׁאִם טָבְלָה. לְאַחַר שֶׁמָּנְתָה ז' נְקִיִּים לְבַד יְמֵי טוּמְאַת לֵידָה. וְרָאֲתָה טְהוֹרָה הִיא. דְּדָם טָהוֹר הוּא, וְכִי לֹא טָבְלָה וְרָאֲתָה — טָמֵא. אָמְרוּ לָהֶם בֵּית שַׁמַּאי הוּא הַדִּין כו'. כְּלוֹמַר, כִּי הֵיכִי דְּאָמְרִינַן בְּיוֹלֶדֶת גְּמוּרָה גְּרֵידָא שֶׁלֹּא טָבְלָה וְרָאֲתָה — טְהוֹרָה, כָּךְ יוֹלֶדֶת בְּזוֹב שֶׁעָבְרוּ עָלֶיהָ יְמֵי לֵידָה וְשִׁבְעָה נְקִיִּים, וְלֹא טָבְלָה, וְרָאֲתָה — טְהוֹרָה. כָּאן שֶׁסָּפְרָה. א] בִּרְאִיּוֹתָהּ בְּסָפְרָה ז' נְקִיִּים. מַתְנִיתִין דְּמוֹדוּ בֵּית שַׁמַּאי — כְּשֶׁעָבְרוּ יְמֵי לֵידָה, וַעֲדַיִין לֹא סָפְרָה אַחֲרֵיהֶם שִׁבְעָה נְקִיִּים. וְהָכִי קָאָמַר: אַף עַל גַּב דְּאָמְרִי בֵּית שַׁמַּאי בְּיוֹלֶדֶת גְּרֵידְתָּא כְּרוּקָּהּ וּכְמֵימֵי רַגְלֶיהָ, מוֹדִים בְּיוֹלֶדֶת בְּזוֹב שֶׁלֹּא סָפְרָה, דְּכָל זְמַן שֶׁלֹּא סָפְרָה — זָבָה הִיא. וְאִם רָאֲתָה — לָא הָוֵי כְּרוּקָּהּ וּכְמֵימֵי רַגְלֶיהָ. דְּאִילּוּ רוֹק — מְטַמֵּא לַח וְלֹא יָבֵשׁ, כִּדְאָמַר בְּ"דַם הַנִּדָּה" (לקמן נו.): "וְכִי יָרוֹק" — כְּעֵין רְקִיקָה. דְּהַיְינוּ לַח, אֲבָל דָּמָהּ — מְטַמֵּא לַח וְיָבֵשׁ, כִּשְׁאָר דַּם הַנִּדָּה, כְּדִילְפִינַן בְּ"דַם הַנִּדָּה" (שם דף נד.). וְהָתַנְיָא. בְּנִיחוּתָא. בֵּית שַׁמַּאי לְשִׁיטָתָן. כִּי הֵיכִי דִּמְטַהֲרִי בְּיוֹלֶדֶת גְּרֵידְתָּא, מְטַהֲרִי בְּהַךְ. דְּקָסָבְרִי: בְּיוֹמֵי תָּלָה רַחֲמָנָא, וְהָא מָלוּ לָהּ כָּל יָמִים שֶׁלָּהּ. וּבֵית הִלֵּל לְשִׁיטָתָן. דְּקָסָבְרִי: בְּיוֹמֵי וּטְבִילָה תָּלָה רַחֲמָנָא, וְכֵיוָן דְּלֹא טָבְלָה — הָוֵי דָּמָהּ טָמֵא כְּטוּמְאַת לֵידָה דַּהֲוֵי אָב הַטּוּמְאָה. מַעְיָן אֶחָד הוּא. דַּם הַבָּא בִּימֵי לֵידָה וְדַם הַבָּא בִּימֵי טוֹהַר — מִמַּעְיָן אֶחָד הֵן בָּאִין. הַתּוֹרָה טִמְּאַתּוּ. כָּל שִׁבְעָה לְזָכָר וי"ד לִנְקֵבָה. וְהַתּוֹרָה טִהֲרַתּוֹ. אַחַר מִכֵּן. נִסְתַּם הַטָּמֵא. לְאַחַר שְׁבוּעַיִם, וְנִפְתָּח הַטָּהוֹר. נִסְתַּם הַטָּהוֹר. לְאַחַר שְׁמוֹנִים, וְנִפְתָּח הַטָּמֵא. לְרַב רֵישָׁא. דְּשׁוֹפַעַת מִתּוֹךְ יְמֵי טוּמְאָה לִימֵי טָהֳרָה — לְקוּלָּא, וּטְהוֹרָה, וְאַף עַל גַּב דְּלֹא פָּסַק, דְּהָא הַתּוֹרָה טִהֲרַתּוֹ. וְסֵיפָא. דְּשָׁפְעָה מִתּוֹךְ מ' לְאַחַר מ' וּמִתּוֹךְ פ' לְאַחַר שְׁמוֹנִים — לְחוּמְרָא, וּטְמֵאָה לְאַחַר שְׁמוֹנִים, דְּהַתּוֹרָה טִמְּאַתּוּ. לְלֵוִי רֵישָׁא לְחוּמְרָא. כֵּיוָן דְּלֹא פָּסְקָה, לֹא נִסְתַּם מַעְיָן טָמֵא. וְסֵיפָא לְקוּלָּא. דְּכֵיוָן דְּלֹא פָּסְקָה, לֹא נִסְתַּם מַעְיָן טָהוֹר. קס"ד דִּפָסְקָה יוֹם אוֹ שְׁנַיִם. לְאַחַר שְׁבוּעַיִם, וּמִשּׁוּם הָכִי מְטַמֵּא לַח וְיָבֵשׁ, דְּמִמַּעְיָן טָמֵא בָּא, וְהַתּוֹרָה לֹא טִהֲרַתּוֹ לְב"ה אֶלָּא בְּיוֹמֵי וּטְבִילָה. אֶלָּא לְלֵוִי. הָא מִמַּעְיָן טָהוֹר אָתָא, דְּכִי פָּסְקָה נִסְתַּם הַטָּמֵא? בְּשׁוֹפַעַת. מִתּוֹךְ יְמֵי טוּמְאָה לִימֵי טָהֳרָה, וְלֹא פָּסְקָה. בִּשְׁלָמָא לְלֵוִי. דְּאָמַר: לְב"ה ב' מַעְיָנוֹת הֵן. הַיְינוּ דְּאִיכָּא בֵּין בֵּית שַׁמַּאי וּבֵית הִלֵּל. דִּלְבֵית הִלֵּל שְׁנֵי מַעְיָנוֹת הֵן, וְכֵיוָן דְּלֹא פָּסַק, טְמֵאָה דְּלֹא נִסְתַּם הַטָּמֵא. וּלְבֵית שַׁמַּאי מַעְיָן אֶחָד הוּא, וְהַתּוֹרָה טִהֲרַתּוֹ אַחַר שְׁבוּעַיִם. אֶלָּא לְרַב. דְּאָמַר: מַעְיָן אֶחָד הוּא, אִי בֵּית הִלֵּל קַיְימֵי כְּוָתֵיהּ. מַאי אִיכָּא כו'. כְּלוֹמַר, בְּמַאי קָמִיפַּלְגִי, וּמַאי טַעֲמָא דְּבֵית הִלֵּל דִּמְטַמְּאִין? בְּיוֹמֵי וּטְבִילָה. לָא שְׁנָא שׁוֹפַעַת לָא שְׁנָא פּוֹסֶקֶת, כָּל זְמַן שֶׁלֹּא טָבְלָה — הָוֵי דָּמָהּ טָמֵא בִּימֵי לֵידָתָהּ. וּמוֹדִים בְּיוֹלֶדֶת בְּזוֹב שֶׁמְּטַמְּאָה. וְאוֹקִימְנָא: כְּשֶׁעָבְרוּ יְמֵי לֵידָתָהּ וְלֹא סָפְרָה אַחֲרֵיהֶן ז' נְקִיִּים. וְקס"ד: הָכָא נַמִי דְּפָסְקָה אַחַר שְׁבוּעַיִם, וּמִשּׁוּם הָכִי מְטַמְּאָה, דְּמִמַּעְיָן טָמֵא אָתוּ, וְהַתּוֹרָה לֹא טִהֲרַתּוֹ עַד שֶׁתֵּשֵׁב ז' נְקִיִּים כְּדִין זָבָה. אַמַּאי מְטַמְּאָה. דְּהָא מִמָּקוֹם טָהוֹר הוּא בָּא, וַהֲרֵי הוּא כְּדַם מַגֵּפָתָהּ וּכְרוּקָּהּ שֶׁמְּטַמֵּא לַח מִשּׁוּם מַעְיָן הַזָּב וְלֹא יָבֵשׁ? לְב"ש אִצְטְרִיךְ. דְּקָאָמַר מַעְיָן אֶחָד הוּא, וּמְטַהֲרֵי לָהּ בְּיוֹלֶדֶת גְּרֵידְתָּא אַחַר יְמֵי לֵידָתָהּ מִיָּד, דְּבְיוֹמֵי תָּלָה רַחֲמָנָא, אִצְטְרִיךְ בְּיוֹלֶדֶת בְּזוֹב לְאַשְׁמוֹעִינַן דִּמְטַמְּאָה. (א) דְּהָנֵי מִילֵּי. דַּהֲוֵי דַּם טוֹהַר לְאַחַר יְמֵי לֵידָה — בְּיוֹלֶדֶת גְּרֵידְתָּא, אֲבָל בְּיוֹלֶדֶת בְּזוֹב, דְּבָעְיָא סְפוּרִים — כָּל זְמַן שֶׁלֹּא סָפְרָה, הָוֵי דָּמָהּ כְּדַם זִיבָה, דְּהָא מֵחַד מַעְיָן אָתֵי, וְתוֹרָה לֹא טִהֲרַתּוֹ עַד שֶׁתִּסְפּוֹר, כִּדְכְתִיב: "וְאַחַר תִּטְהָר" אַחַר אַחַר לְכוּלָּן. דָּוֹתָהּ תִּטְמָא. קְרָא יְתֵירָא הוּא, דַּה"ל לְמִכְתַּב: "וְטָמְאָה ז' יָמִים כִּימֵי נִדָּהּ" וְלִשְׁתּוֹק. לְרַבּוֹת שֶׁמְּטַמְּאָה אֶת בּוֹעֲלָהּ בְּנִדָּה. וּלְרַבּוֹת אֶת הַלֵּילוֹת כַּיָּמִים, דְּלָא תֵּימָא: "יָמִים" כְּתִיב. מִשּׁוּם הָכִי בָּעֲיָא. הַפְסָקָה שִׁבְעָה נְקִיִּים, דְּמִמַּעְיָן דָּמִים טְמֵאִים אָתֵי, וְהַתּוֹרָה לֹא טִהֲרַתּוֹ עַד שֶׁתִּסְפּוֹר שִׁבְעָה נְקִיִּים, כִּדְכְתִיב: "דָּוֹתָהּ תִּטְמָא".
אֶלָּא

[לקמן לו.]

[לקמן לז:]

**אי** אתם מודים בנדה. תימה: מאי קסברי בית הלל, דקמייתי מנדה, דפשיטא כדמהדר להו בית שמאי? וי"ל: דמייתי, משום דאיתקש לידה לנדה, דכתיב "כימי נדת דותה", וכתיב "וטמאה שבועים כנדתה".
**איכא** בינייהו שופעת מתוך שבעה כו' — איכא בינייהו טובא, כל הני דפריך בסמוך, אלא דפשוט יותר נקט.
**בשופעת**. והשתא אפי' בטבלה יטמאו בית הלל לח ויבש. ומתניתין דנקט "ולא טבלה" — משום בית שמאי. וא"ת: דבעדיות קתני הך דיולדת גבי קולי בית שמאי וחומרי בית הלל, הלא בשופעת מתוך מ' (*למה) הוו בית הלל לקולא? וי"ל: דכי אתשיל, בתחלת לידה אתשיל.
**אי** בשופעת למאי איצטריך. וא"ת: מכל מקום משום בית שמאי איצטריך, כדמשני. ומאי סלקא דעתיה דמקשה, דהא לרב נמי לא אצטריך סיפא אלא לאשמועינן דמודו בית שמאי דמטמא לח ויבש משום דלא ספרה? ויש לומר: דלרב איצטריך לאשמועינן דמודו בית שמאי ביולדת בזוב משום דמעיין אחד הוא. דאי מרישא, הוה אמינא דטעמייהו משום דקסברי ב' מעיינות הן, *ואפילו ביולדת בזוב מטהרין, ובית הלל סברי דמעיין אחד הוא. לכך אצטריך סיפא. אלא ללוי דמוקי רישא בשופעת, וסברי ב"ש מעיין אחד הוא, סיפא מאי קא משמע לן?
ושוין

הגהות הב"ח
(א) רש"י ד"ה לב"ש אילטריך וד"ה דהני מילי הד"א:

הגהות מהר"ב רנשבורג
א] רש"י ד"ה כאן שספרה בראיותה. מלת בראיותה נמחק ונ"ב ברייתא:

## תוספי הרא"ש
**אי** אתם מודים בנדה כו' ותימה מאי קסברי ב"ה דמייתי ראיה מנדה דשפיר קא מהדרו ב"ש וי"ל משום דיולדת ילפינן מנדה דאיתקש דכתיב כימי נדת דותה תטמא וכתיב וטמאה שבועים כנדתה ואמרינן לקמן בפרקין כימי נדתה כך ימי לידתה: **אי** בשופעת למאי איצטריך לב"ש איצטריך. תימה מאי קסבר הא לרב נמי לב"ש איצטריך ומטעם דמפרש וי"ל דלרב איצטריך לב"ש מטעם אחרינא דלא תימא במעיין אחד ובשתי מעיינות פליגי ב"ש וב"ה ולכ"ע ביומי וטבילה תלה רחמנא וביולדת בזוב בלא שופעת אין מטמא לח ויבש וכיון דתנא דמודו ב"ש ביולדת בזוב שמטמאה לח ויבש לא ס"ל דשני מעיינות הן:

אלא ללוי דאמר שני מעינות הן, למה לי שבעה? במשהו סגיא! הכי קאמר: צריכה שתפסוק משהו, שיעלו לה לשבעה נקיים. ת"ש: *ימי עיבורה עולים לה לימי מניקותה, וימי מניקותה עולים לה לימי עיבורה. כיצד? הפסיקה שתים בימי עיבורה ואחת בימי מניקותה, שתים בימי מניקותה ואחת בימי עיבורה, אחת ומחצה בימי עיבורה ואחת ומחצה בימי מניקותה – עולין לה לג' עונות. בשלמא לרב דאמר מעין אחד הוא – משום הכי בעי הפסק שלש עונות, אלא ללוי דאמר שני מעינות הן – למה לי הפסק שלש עונות? במשהו סגי! הכי קאמר: °צריכה שתפסוק משהו, כדי שיעלו לה לשלש עונות. ת"ש: ושוין [א]ברואה אחר דם טוהר שדיה שעתה. בשלמא ללוי דאמר שני מעינות הן – משום הכי דיה שעתה, אלא לרב דאמר מעין אחד הוא אמאי דיה שעתה? תטמא מעת לעת! [ב]דליכא שהות. ותטמא מפקידה לפקידה! כיון דמעת לעת ליכא, מפקידה לפקידה נמי לא גזרו בה רבנן. תא שמע: *יולדת בזוב שספרה ולא טבלה וראתה, הלכו ב"ש לשיטתן ובית הלל לשיטתן. בשלמא לרב דאמר מעין אחד הוא – משום הכי מטמא לח ויבש, אלא ללוי דאמר שני מעינות הן אמאי מטמא לח ויבש? אמר לך לוי: אנא דאמרי – כתנא דשוין. ואיבעית אימא: בשופעת. והא "ספרה" קתני! הכא ביולדת נקבה בזוב עסקינן, דשבוע קמא פסקה, שבוע בתרא לא פסקה, [ג]וקסבר: ימי לידתה שאין רואה בהן – עולין לה לספירת זיבתה. אמר ליה רבינא לרב אשי, אמר לן רב שמן מסברא, אקלע מר זוטרא לאתרין ודרש: הילכתא כוותיה דרב לחומרא, והלכתא כוותיה דלוי לחומרא. רב אשי אמר: הלכתא כוותיה דרב, בין לקולא בין לחומרא. דריש מרימר: הלכתא כוותיה דרב, בין לקולא בין לחומרא. [ד]והלכתא כוותיה דרב בין לקולא בין לחומרא. §

מתני'

**אלא** ללוי במשהו סגי. ותפסוק משהו לאחר שבועים דנסתם הטמא, ותמתין שבעה ותטבול. ואפי' תראה כל שבעה – יעלו לה בנקיים, דהא לאו דם טמא הוא. שתפסוק משהו. לאחר שבועים דנקבה, דאי בתוך שבועים – לאו הפסק היא, דכיון דחוזרת ורואה בתוך שבועים – חזר הטמא להפתח. ימי עיבורה עולין לה. בפ"ק (לעיל דף י.) אמרי': מעוברת ומניקה שעברו עליה ג' עונות, וראתה – דיה שעתה. עולין לה. כלומר, מצטרפים לימי מניקותה. כגון היתה מניקה, והתחילה לפסוק, ונתעברה, והשלימה ג' עונות – מצטרפין ימי עיבורה לימי מניקותה. **בשלמא** לרב. דאמר: מעין אחד הוא – משום הכי מעוברת שהתחילה להפסיק וילדה צריכה להשלים ג' עונות, שלא תראה אחר לידה כלום. ודם לידה לא מפסיק לשלש עונות, כדתלינן בפ"ק: *דם נדה לחוד, ודם לידה לחוד. אבל אחר לידה, אי חזאי – לא השלימה ג' עונות, ומטמאה מעת לעת, שאין דמיה מסולקין. **אלא** ללוי. אפי' אי חזיא לאחר שבועים – הא לאו ממעין טמא אתי, ויעלו לה להשלמת שלש עונות, דהוי כאילו דם מחוטמה אתא. במשהו סגיא. שתפסוק אחר ימי לידה משהו, דנימא: נסתם הטמא. שיעלו לה. ימי טהרה. לשלש עונות. ואפי' תראה. ושוין. שמאי והלל דפליגי במעת לעת. **ברואה אחר** דם טוהר שדיה שעתה. קס"ד: אפי' לזמן מרובה, כגון שלא ראתה עד יום שמונים וארבע או תשעים. **בשלמא** ללוי דאמר שני מעינות הן משום הכי דיה שעתה. שהרי דמיה מסולקין, שכמה ימים שעברו ולא ראתה דם ממעין זה, והויא לה ראייה ראשונה, ודיה שעתה. ומניקה – מארבע נשים היא, דדיין שעתן בראייה ראשונה. **אלא** לרב דאמר מעין **אחד הוא**. לאו ראייה ראשונה היא, והרי הוחזקה בדמים. **דליכא** שהות. כגון שראתה ביום שמונים ואחד מיד, דליכא למימר: מעת לעת, דאפי' הוה מאתמול כי הידנא בבית החיצון – דם טהור הוא. **ותטמא** מפקידה לפקידה. כגון אם בדקה שחרית ומצאתה טמאה – תטמא טהרות של ערבית. והכא ליכא למימר: דליכא שהות, דאי אפילו מפקידה לפקידה ליכא – צריכא למימר דדיה שעתה? וב"ה לשיטתן. דכל זמן שלא טבלה מטמא לח ויבש, והא כיון דספרה אחר ימי לידה – ודאי פסק, וקשיא ללוי. **כתנא** דשוין. דאמר לעיל: ושוין ברואה אחר דם טוהר, שדיה שעתה. ואנא אוקימנא: בדאיכא שהות, ואפ"ה דיה שעתה – אלמא, שני מעיינות הן. ***והא** ספרה קתני. ואי לא פסק, היכי ספרה? ומשני: לעולם בשופעת מימי טומאה לימי טוהר, וספירה הכי הואי: כגון שהיתה יולדת נקבה בזוב, וימי טומאת לידה שני שבועים, ופסקה שבוע קמא. וזו היא ספירתה, דקסבר: ימי לידתה שאינה רואה בהן – עולין לה לספירת זיבתה. ושבוע שני לא פסקה, וחזר ונפתח מעין טמא, ושופעת מתוכו בתוך שבוע שלישי. ומש"ה מטמא לח ויבש לב"ה, דהא ממעין טמא אתא, ותורה לא טהרתו אלא ביומי וטבילה. ולב"ש טהור – דביומי תליא רחמנא, והא שלמו להו. ולהכי נקט "יולדת נקבה", דאי ילדה זכר – אי אפשר לה לספור שבעה שלא תפסוק משהו אחר ימי לידה, דלא הוו אלא שבעה. **כוותיה** דרב **לחומרא**. בשופעת מתוך שמונים לאחר שמונים, דמטמאה, ולא אמרי' ממעין טהור אתא. **והלכתא** כוותיה דלוי **לחומרא**. בשופעת מתוך י"ד לאחר י"ד, דאמר: ב' מעיינות הן וכיון דלא נסתם הטמא – לא הוי דם טוהר. **בין** לקולא. כגון שופעת מתוך י"ד לאחר י"ד, דהוה ליה רב לקולא, דאמר: מעין אחד הוא, והתורה טהרתו, ולא בעי הפסקה.

מתני'

**ושוין** ברואה אחר דם טוהר שדיה שעתה. וא"ת: לרבי יוסי דאמר בפ"ק (לעיל דף ז.): מעוברת ומניקה צריכות שלש עונות, ומפרש דמצטרפי ג' עונות דעיבורה ואחת דמניקתה, למה לי עונה דמניקתה? הא אמר הכא דאחר דם טוהר דיה שעתה! וי"ל: הא, דלא כר' יוסי. אי נמי: בהפסיקה ג' עונות וראתה ראשונה מאונס – אף שניה דיה שעתה, כדאמר בפ"ק (שם:). אבל אחר דם טוהר – אין דיה שעתה אלא בראייה ראשונה, אבל שניה – לא, אפי' היתה הראשונה מאונס, כיון שנפתח מעין טמא. וא"ת: לר"מ ולאידך תנאי דאית להו בפ"ק (שם:) מניקה דיה שעתה, תיפוק ליה דהוה אחר דם טוהר! ומיהו לתירוץ שני אתי שפיר. וי"ל: דמטעם שהוא אחר דם טוהר, אין דיה שעתה אלא לראייה ראשונה. אבל מטעם מניקה, דיה שעתה כל ימי מניקותה, כר"מ דפ"ק (שם דף יא.). וא"ת: והכא למה לי משום דם טוהר? תיפוק ליה דמניקה היא! וי"ל: דנ"מ להיכא דמת בנה או גמלתו, לרבי מאיר דאמר לעיל: הרי היא ככל הנשים. (א) ולרבי יוסי נמי, דאמר בפ"ק: אפי' גמלתו או נתנה בנה למניקה, דיה שעתה – נפקא מינה לאחר דם טוהר, להיכא דלא ראתה עד לאחר כ"ד חדש, וטעמא דמניקה איצטריך לראייתה הראשונה באונס, דאף השניה דיה שעתה, כדפרישית.

**דליכא** שהות. אבל איכא שהות – מטמאה מעת לעת, לרב דאמר מעין אחד הוא. ואע"ג דדיה שעתה כל ימי מניקותה, הכא מיירי במת בנה או בהפילה, כדפרישית. וא"ת: דבפרק "אלו נערות" (כתובות דף לז.) אמר: הגיורת שראתה דם בתוך מעת לעת – דיה שעתה. רבי יוסי אומר: הרי היא ככל הנשים? וי"ל: סוגיא דהכא לא אתיא כר' יוסי דהתם. א"נ התם היתה בת טומאה, אם היתה מתגיירת מקודם. או משום דאיתא בגוה טומאה דרבנן.

**ואיבעית** אימא בשופעת והא ספרה קתני. וא"ת: מאי קאמר ב"ה לעיל: יולדת בזוב תוכית, שאם טבלה וראתה – טהורה? והא כיון דשופעת, אפי' טבלה – טמאה, ללוי דאמר שני מעיינות הן, דהא מעין טמא הוא! וי"ל: דלדברי ב"ש קאמרי להו, דאית להו מעין אחד הוא.

**שבוע** בתרא לא פסקה. מכאן אומר ר"ת דיולדת בזוב, או בזמן הזה דכולהו נשים חשבינהו כיולדת בזוב, שסופרין אחר ימי טומאת הלידה שבעה נקיים. וראתה בימי טוהר קודם טבילה – אינה סותרת, דהא אמר הכא דכי ראתה שבוע שלישי דלא סתרה, אע"ג דדם טמא הוא. כ"ש דראיית דם טוהר אינה סותרת, דאפי' ב"ה דמטמאין לח ויבש, מודו דעלתה לה ספירתה. ומכאן אין להוכיח על זבה שאינה יולדת שספרה ז' נקיים וראתה, שלא תסתור – דאיכא למימר: דהכא דוקא לא סתרה, משום דראייה זו אינה גורמת לה טומאה, דכל שבועים טמאים בלאו הכי. ואע"ג דבשבוע ג' גורם לה טומאה, מ"מ אינה נעשית בה נדה ולא זבה, וכשתפסק – טהורה מיד. ומ"מ נראה דאשה דעלמא – נמי לא סתרה. דמסתברא דאין סתירה מועלת אלא בתוך החשבון, כדאמר "ואחר תטהר" – שלא תהא טומאה מפסקת ביניהם. אבל לאחר ספירה – לא. מיהו לדידן דאית לן חומרא דרבי זירא, פשיטא דסותרת, דהא אפי' טבלה וראתה, צריכה ז' נקיים.

**הלכתא** כרב לחומרא. ואם תאמר: הא תרי חומרי דסתרי אהדדי נינהו? וי"ל: דהכא דמספקא לן – פסיק כמר להחמיר וכמר להחמיר, וכי האי גוונא איכא שלהי "יוצא דופן" (לקמן דף מז:) הלכה כדברי כולן להחמיר, גבי סימני בגרות וחצר צורית. הקשה הרב רבי מרדכי בר יצחק: ללוי, דאמר שני מעיינות הן, הא דתניא בפרק "יש בכור" (בכורות דף מו:) גיורת שילא פדחת ולדה בהיותה גויה, ואחר כך נתגיירה – אין נותנין לה ימי טומאה וימי טהרה. ואי שני מעיינות הן, אמאי אין נותנין לה ימי טהרה? הלא מעין טמא סתום! ובריש "יוצא דופן" (לקמן דף מ:) נמי תנן, דאין יושבין עליו ימי טומאה וימי טהרה. ומההיא ברייתא דבכורות (דף מו:) לא קשה כל כך ללוי, דמוקי (ב) כב"ש דאמר מעין

**מסורת הש"ס**

[לעיל י:]

[שם דף י:]

[לעיל לה:]

ע' רש"א ור"מ

**עין משפט נר מצוה**

**מה** א ב מיי' פ"ד מהל' משכב ומושב הלכה ו:

**מו** ג מיי' פ"ז מהל' איסורי ביאה הל' א ועי' בכ"מ סמג לאוין קיא טוש"ע יו"ד סי' קצ סעיף א:

**מז** ד מיי' שם פ"ו הל' א סמג שם טוש"ע יו"ד סימן קצד:

## תוספי הרא"ש

**ושוין** ברואה אחר דם טוהר שדיה שעתה. ותימה לעיל דקאמר ר' יוסי מעוברת ומניקה שעברו עליה ג' עונות דיה שעתה ומפרש דמצטרפי שתים בימי עיבורה ואחד בימי מניקותה למה לי אותה שבימי מניקותה תיפוק לי דרואה אחר דם טוהר הוא. וי"ל דהך דלא כר' יוסי אליבא דלוי ותימה אליבא דלוי למה לי לדרואה אחר דם טוהר תיפוק לי משום שהיא מניקה וי"ל דאתיא כר' מאיר דאמר בפירקין דאם גמלתו ומת הרי היא ככל הנשים ובלאו הכי לא אתיא כר' יוסי אליבא דרב דמפרש דליכא שהות דהא ר' יוסי לא חייש להכי בפ' אלו נערות גבי גיורת שנתגיירה וראתה בתוך מעת לעת. ומיהו יש לחלק משום דהתם היתה בת טומאה אם היתה מתגיירת מקודם או משום דשייכא טומאה בנכרית מדרבנן: **ואיבעית** אימא בשופעת. תימה היכי קאמר לעיל יולדת בזוב תוכיח שאם טבלה וראתה טהורה לא טבלה טמאה והא כיון דמוקי לה לוי בשופעת אפי' טבלה טמאה לב"ה דקסברי שני מעיינות הן אליבא דלוי וי"ל דלדברי ב"ש דקסברי מעין אחד הן קאמר יולדת בזוב תוכיח: **בשבוע** קמא פסק בשבוע בתרא לא פסק. וקסברי ימי לידה שאינה רואה בהן עולין לה לספירת זיבתה ואע"פ שראתה בשבוע שני קודם הטבילה לא סתרה מניינה מכאן מדקדק ר"ת דאשה שילדה בזוב או בזמן הזה דחשיבי כולהו נשי יולדת בזוב אם ספרה ז' נקיים בימי טוהר אפי' ראתה אחרי כן קודם טבילה אינה סותרה אע"ג דלב"ה מטמא לח ויבש מודו דאינה סותרת מניינה ויש ליתן טעם הא דאין ראיית שבוע שני סותרת משום דראייה זו אינה גורמת לה טומאת נדות ולא טומאת זיבות אבל זבה דעלמא דספרה ז' נקיים ואח"כ ראתה ראויה לסתור לפי שע"י אותה ראייה היא נעשית נדה ומיהו מיסתבר למימר דלא שייך סתירה אלא בימי ספירתה משום דאמרי' ואחר תטהר אחר אחר לכולן שלא תהא טומאת זיבה מפסקת ביניהן אבל אם שלמו ימי ספירה בלא הפסקת טומאה כבר אין שום זבה עליה ולא שייך בה סתירה: **והלכתא** כותיה דרב לחומרא וכותיה דלוי לחומרא. ותימה והא אמרי' בפ"ק דעירובין ובפרק אלו טריפות דעביד כתרי חומרי דסתרי אהדדי עליו הכתוב אומר הכסיל בחושך הולך. י"ל הכא משום דמספקא לן פסיק כמר לחומרא וכמר לחומרא. וכה"ג אמרינן לקמן בפ' יוצא דופן הלכה כדברי כולם להחמיר גבי סימני בגרות וחצר צורית. הק' ה"ר יום טוב בר' יצחק. ללוי דאמר שני מעיינות הן קשה מהא דתניא בפ' יש בכור גיורת שיצתה פדחת ולדה בגיותה אין נותנין לה ימי טומאה וימי טהרה ואי שתי מעיינות הן אמאי לא יהבינן לה ימי טהרה. וכן יש להקשות דממתניתין דאמרי' לקמן יוצא דופן אין יושבין עליו ימי טומאה וימי טהרה י"ל דהא מני ב"ש היא דאמרי מעין אחד הוא אי נמי כדמשני הכא אנא דאמרי כתנא דשווין אבל ק' ליה מסתם מתני' דיוצא דופן ועוד דלעיל בפ"ק פריך לוי וסתם לן תנא כב"ש וקאמר סתם וח"כ מחלוקת ואח"כ סתם וי"ל דאין נותנין לה ימי טהרה דקאמר איכא לאוקמי לענין זה שאם ראתה ביום ז' לזכר או י"ד לנקבה הויא נדה על ידי ראיה ואין לה תורת טומאת לידה דפקעי כשנכנסין ימי טוהר. א"נ אע"ג דשני מעיינות הן יש לטמאות הדם משום דמן המקור קא אתי אלא דוקא במקום שהתורה טהרתו:

## הגהות הב"ח

(א) תוס' ד"ה ושוין וכו' ולר' יוסי נמי כ"כ נ"ל דס"ל להתוס' דפליגי תנאי אליבא דר' יוסי דתנא דברייתא ס"ל אליבא דר' יוסי דמניקה ד"ה שעתה בראייה ראשון אע"ג [דלא עברו] ג' עונות ופליג אמתניתין אליבא דר' יוסי [דמצריך] ג' עונות ע"ל דף ז' ע"ב ובראש דף יא: (ב) ד"ה הילכתא וכו' ללוי דמוקי לה כב"ש:

## גליון הש"ס

**גמ'** צריכה שתפסוק משהו. הך משהו אינו מובן לכאורה דהא ע"כ בלא ראתה כל ימי לידה דאל"כ הך ראייה גופא הוי הפסק בתוך ג' עונות דלוקא דבלידה אמרי' לעיל דם [illegible]

ר'

**מתני'** המקשה – נדה. קשתה שלשה ימים בתוך י"א יום, ושפתה מעת לעת, וילדה – הרי זו יולדת בזוב, דברי רבי אליעזר. רבי יהושע אומר: לילה ויום, כלילי שבת ויומו. ששפתה מן הצער, ולא מן הדם. כמה היא קישויה? ר' מאיר אומר: אפילו ארבעים וחמשים יום. רבי יהודה אומר: דיה חדשה. ר' יוסי ור' שמעון אומרים: אין קישוי יותר משתי שבתות.§

**גמ'** אטו כל המקשה נדה היא? אמר רב: נדה ליומא. ושמואל אמר: חיישינן שמא תשפה. ור' יצחק אמר: המקשה אינה כלום. והקתני "המקשה – נדה"! אמר רבא: בימי נדה – נדה, בימי זיבה – טהורה. והתניא, המקשה בימי נדה – נדה, בימי זיבה – טהורה. כיצד, קשתה יום אחד ושפתה שנים, או שקשתה שנים ושפתה יום אחד, או ששפתה וקשתה וחזרה ושפתה – הרי זו יולדת בזוב. אבל שפתה יום אחד וקשתה שנים, או ששפתה שנים וקשתה יום אחד, או שקשתה ושפתה וחזרה וקשתה – אין זו יולדת בזוב. כללו של דבר: קושי סמוך ללידה – אין זו יולדת בזוב, שופי סמוך ללידה – הרי זו יולדת בזוב. חנניא בן אחי ר' יהושע אומר: כל שחל קישויה בשלישי שלה, אפילו כל היום כולו בשופי – אין זו יולדת בזוב. "כללו של דבר" לאתויי מאי? לאתויי דחנניא. מה"מ? דת"ר: "דמה" – דמה מחמת עצמה ולא מחמת ולד. אתה אומר מחמת ולד, או אינו אלא מחמת אונס? כשהוא אומר: "ואשה כי יזוב זוב דמה" – הרי אונס אמור, הא מה אני מקיים "דמה"? – דמה מחמת עצמה ולא מחמת ולד. ומה ראית לטהר את הולד ולטמא באונס? מטהר אני בולד – שיש טהרה אחריו, ומטמא אני באונס – שאין טהרה אחריו. אדרבה, מטהר אני באונס – שכן אונס בזב טהור! השתא מיהא באשה קיימינן, ואונס באשה לא אשכחן. ואיבעית אימא: מאי דעתיך – לטהורי באונס ולטמויי בולד? אין לך אונס גדול מזה! אי הכי, נדה נמי נימא "זובה" – זובה מחמת עצמה ולא מחמת ולד. אתה אומר ולד, או אינו אלא אונס? כשהוא אומר: "ואשה כי תהיה זבה" – הרי אונס אמור, הא מה אני מקיים "זובה" – זובה מחמת עצמה, ולא מחמת ולד! אמר ר"ל: אמר קרא "תשב" – יש לך ישיבה אחרת שהיא כזו, ואיזו זו – זו קושי בימי זיבה. ואימא: זו קושי בימי נדה! אלא אמר אבוה דשמואל: אמר קרא "וטמאה שבועים כנדתה" – ולא כזיבתה, מכלל דזיבתה טהור, ואיזו זו – זו קושי בימי זיבה. והשתא דכתיב "וטמאה שבועים כנדתה", "דמה" למה לי? אי לאו "דמה" הוה אמינא כנדתה ולא כזיבתה, ואפילו בשופי, קמ"ל. שילא בר אבינא עבד עובדא כוותיה דרב. כי קא נח נפשיה דרב, א"ל לרב אסי: זיל צנעיה, ואי לא צייתא – גרייה. הוא סבר "גדייה" א"ל. בתר דנח נפשיה דרב, א"ל: הדר בך! דהדר ביה רב. א"ל: אם איתא דהדר ביה – לדידי הוה אמר לי. לא צייתא. גדייה. א"ל: ולא מסתפי מר מדליקתא? א"ל: אנא איסי בן יהודה, דהוא איסי בן גור אריה, דהוא איסי בן גמליאל, דהוא איסי בן מהללאל – אסיתא דנחשא, דלא שליט ביה רקבא. א"ל: ואנא שילא בר אבינא – בוכנא דפרזלא, דמתבר אסיתא דנחשא. חלש רב אסי. עיילוה בחמימי אפקוה מקרירי, עיילוה בקרירי אפקוה מחמימי, נח נפשיה דרב אסי. אזל

תורה אור: ויקרא טו | שם | שם יב

**מתני' המקשה.** ורואה דם, הרי זו נדה. ובגמרא פריך ומתרץ לה. **קשתה.** מחמת ולד. **ג' ימים.** בתוך אחד עשר יום שבין נדה לנדה, ורואה כל שלשתן הימים רצופין. **ושפתה.** מצערה. **מעת לעת.** ברביעי. **וילדה.** איגלאי מילתא דדמים שראתה, לא באו מחמת ולד, הלכך הרי זו יולדת בזוב. אבל אם לא שפתה סמוך ללידתה – כל דמים שראתה, מחמת ולד הוא, ורחמנא טהרינהו מזיבה, דכתיב: "זוב דמה" – דמה מחמת עצמה, ולא דמה מחמת ולד. **לילה ויום.** דאם שפתה בחצי יום שלישי, וילדה יום רביעי, דשפתה מעת לעת – אין זו שופי, אלא אם כן שפתה לילה ויום שלאחר הלילה, כלילי שבת ויומו. **ששפתה מן הצער ולא מן הדם.** דאע"ג דחזיא דם – הוי שופי. **כמה הוא קישויה.** דלא אתיא לידי זיבה בכל דמים שתראה? **אפילו ארבעים או חמשים יום.** אם לא שפתה יום אחד סמוך ללידה, לא אתיא לידי זיבה, ולא הויא יולדת בזוב. **דיה חדשה.** דיה אם נטהר את הקושי חדש אחד, היינו תשיעי. אבל קשתה שלשה בתוך י"א ימי זיבה בחדש השמיני, ואפי' מקשה והולכת כל תשיעי – הרי זו יולדת בזוב, מחמת שלשה ימים של שמיני. **גמ' אטו** כל המקשה נדה היא. אילו קשתה בימי זיבה, מי הויא נדה? והא אין נדות בימי זוב! **אמר רב נדה ליומא.** וה"ק: המקשה ורואה דם בימי זיבה, אע"ג דלא אתיא ביה לידי זיבה – מיהו באותו היום אסורה לשמש. אבל לערב טובלת, ואינה צריכה לשמור יום כנגד יום, דרחמנא טהריה לדם קושי. **ושמואל אמר.** אף צריכה לשמור יום כנגד יום, מדרבנן. דחיישינן שמא תשפה, ונמצא שלא היה דם קושי מחמת ולד, ונמצא משמש עם זבה קטנה דאורייתא, וענוש כרת. **אינה כלום.** ואפילו באותו היום משמשת. **בימי נדה.** בימים הראוים לנדות. **נדה.** דקושי לא טהריה רחמנא אלא מזיבה, אבל מנדה – לא טהריה, כדאמרי' לקמן. **בימי זיבה.** בתוך אחד עשר יום, טהורה. **והתניא.** בניחותא. **ושפתה.** שנים מן הצער, ולא מן הדם. הרי זו יולדת בזוב. אם ראתה כל שלש, הואיל ושופי סמוך ללידה, נמצא דם הקושי שלא מחמת ולד. **כל שחל קישויה.** לאו לשון התחלה הוא, אלא הכי קאמר: כל שקשתה בשלישי, אפי' שעה אחת בליל כניסת שלישי, אפילו כל היום כולו בשופי ושפתה מליל ד' שעה אחת להשלמת מעת לעת – אין זו יולדת בזוב, דבעינן שופי כל יום ג' המביאה לידי זבה. **וכי יזוב זוב.** "זוב" משמע זוב מ"מ, ואפי' באונס. **שיש טהרה אחריו.** דם טוהר. **ואונס באשה לא אשכחן.** דטהור. **זובה.** "דם יהיה זובה", ובנדה משתעי, דפרשה ראשונה נאמרה בנדה, ושניה בזבה, כדכתיב בשניה "בלא עת נדתה". **ולא מחמת ולד.** אלמה אמרינן לעיל "בימי נדה נדה". **תשב** על דמי טהרה. דהוה ליה למכתב "וששים יום וששת ימים דמי טהרה". **שהיא כזו.** שדמיה טהורים. **ואיזו זו.** כלומר, היכא משכחת זיבה טהורה? זו קושי בימי זיבה. דסמיך אדכתיב "דמה" מחמת עצמה, ולא מחמת ולד. **ואפי' בשופי.** ואפי' הפסיק שופי בין קושי ללידה, נימא: טהורה, הואיל ודם בקושי בא. **כוותיה דרב.** נדה ליומא. **צנעיה.** הסתר אותו דבר, אמור לו שיחזור בו דטהור לגמרי. **גרייה.** ברי"ש. כלומר, גרור ומשוך אותו בדברי טעם וראיות שיחזור בו. **גדייה.** הכריתו בשמתא, כמו (דניאל ד) "גודו אילנא". **לדידי הוה אמר לי.** דתלמידיה אנא. **גדייה.** שמתיה. **מדליקתא.** שמא תכוה בגחלתי. **אסיתא.** משום דשמיה הכי, דריש לשמיה הכי. **עיילוה בחמימי.** חולי הוא. **קרירי.** חולי צונן. אזל

**מעין** אחד הוא. א"נ: כדמשני הכא, אנא דאמר כתנא דשוין אבל סתם מתניתין ד"יוצא דופן" קשה. וי"ל: דאין נותנין לה ימי טוהר" איכא לאוקמי לענין שאם ראתה ביום ז' לזכר או ביום י"ד לנקבה, דהויא תחלת נדה, דאין טומאת לידה עליה. אי נמי: אע"ג דשני מעינות הן, יש לטמא הדם דמן המקור קאתי, אלא דוקא במקום שהתורה מטהרתו.

**כלילי** שבת ויומו. קים ליה לרבי יהושע דאם לא שפתה לילה ויום, אע"פ ששפתה מעת לעת – מחמת ולד היה. **נדה** ליומא. נראה דאף לבעלה לא חיישינן שמא תשפה, דאזלינן בתר רוב נשים מקשות דאינן שפות לילה ויום. דהא עובדא דשילא בר אבינא נראה דלבעלה הוי, ולא לטהרות. **או** ששפתה וקשתה וחזרה ושפתה. כדי נסבה, דהא מרישא שמעינן לה, דקתני: קשתה שנים ושפתה יום אחד, וכ"ש הא, דטמאה. וכן בסיפא לא היה צריך למתני "קשתה ושפתה וקשתה", כיון דתנא "שפתה שנים וקשתה יום אחד" דטהורה. אי נמי: אתא לאשמועינן, אע"ג דלא קשתה כל יום הסמוך ללידה אלא מקצתו. וכן ברישא בכי האי גוונא. **ואימא** קושי בימי נדה. ור"ל: ס"ד דמסתבר טפי לאוקומיה בזיבה, משום דאשכחן זב אונס דטהור הוא. **גדייה.** פרש"י: דרב אסי טעה בין רי"ש לדלי"ת, (א) ואין נראה. אלא נראה דאיהו אמר ליה גדייה בדלי"ת רפה, כלומר משכהו בדברי טעם עד שיחזור, כמו (שמות יב) "משכו", דמתרגמינן: נגודו. וכמו (ב"ב דף יג.) "גוד או איגוד". והוא סבר: "גדייה" בדגש, כמו "גודו אילנא". **איסי** בן מהללאל. ב"ערבי פסחים" (פסחים דף קיג.) יש תנא דיש לו כל השמות הללו, ועוד קרי ליה התם "הוא יוסף הבבלי הוא יוסף איש הוצל". ולא תנא אחר הוא, כמו שיש מפרשין שם, דהא בפרק "הוציאו לו" (יומא דף נג:) פריך מאיסי בן יהודה ליוסף איש הוצל. והכא לא מייתי אלא שמות דאיסי דדמי לרב אסי.

דבר

**מח** א ב ג ד מיי' פ"ו מהל' איסורי ביאה הלכה א:
**מט** ה ו מיי' שם הל"ג:
**נ** ז מיי' שם הלכה ד וע' במ"מ:
**נא** ח מיי' שם הל"א:
**נב** ט מיי' שם פ"ה הל' א סמג לאוין קיא טוש"ע יו"ד סי' קפג סעיף א:

## תוספי הרא"ש

ר' (יוסי) [יהושע] אומר לילה ויום. ונראה דבסברא פליגי ע"י בקיאין בתולדות דמעיין: **חיישינן** שמא תשפה. ומאן דלא חייש משום מילתא דלא שכיח הוא כיון שנפתח הקבר ושופעת דם שתשפה קודם לידה: **או** ששפתה יום אחד וקשתה וחזרה ושפתה. כדי נסבה דמרישא שמעינן ליה דקתני קשתה שנים ושפתה יום וכ"ש זו אלא אגב סיפא נקטיה דקתני קשתה יום אחד ושפתה יום אחד וחזרה וקשתה סד"א שהשופים שבינתים מוכיח על הקושי דלאו מחמת ולד הואי: **ואימא** זו קושי שבימי נדה. ונראה דטעמא דריש לקיש משום דמשמע ליה דטפי איכא לאוקומי בזיבה משום דאשכחן אונס בזב טהור וישיבה אחת מיעט קרא ולא יותר ותלמודא לא חייש לסברא דיליה כיון דאונס האשה מיהא לא אשכחן: **הוא** סבר גדייה א"ל בדלי"ת דגושה והוא א"ל בדלי"ת רפויה כלומר משוך אותו בדברים כמו משכו דמתרגמינן נגודו: **אנא** איסי בן יהודה דהוא איסי בן גור אריה כו'. תנא אחד הוא שיש לו ה' שמות הללו בערבי פסחים וביומא פ' הוציאו לו ועוד חשיב התם יוסף הבבלי ויוסף איש הוצל ולא חשיב להו הכא משום דאין נופלין על שם רב אסי:

## הגהות הב"ח

(א) תוס' ד"ה גדייה וכו' ואין נראה וכו'. נ"ב נ"ל שאפשר לומר דטעותו היה בתיבת לנעיה דאיתא בקידושין דף כה דהוא לשון נידוי ע"כ היה סבר דאמר ליה שיגדיה היינו שינדוהו וק"ל וכן נר' שהוא דעת רש"י כי רש"י ז"ל לא כתב זה כלל שטעה בין ר' לד':

[סנהדרין פז: לעיל ז:] [יבמות פג.] [לקמן לז:] [לקמן לח:] [לקמן לח:] [עיין ערוך ערך גנע ב] [עי' תוס' יומא נג: ד"ה הוא]

אזל שילא אמר לדביתהו: צבית לי זוודתא, דלא ליזיל ולימא ליה לרב מילי עילואי. צביתה ליה זוודתא, נח נפשיה דשילא. חזו דפרחא אסא מהאי פוריא להאי פוריא, אמרי: ש"מ עבדו רבנן פייסא. בעי רבא: קושי מהו שתסתור בזיבה? דבר המטמא סותר – והאי נמי מטמא כימי נדה הוא, או דילמא: דבר הגורם – סותר, והאי – לאו גורם הוא? א"ל אביי: אונס בזיבה יוכיח, שאינו גורם – וסותר! אמר ליה: לאיי, האי נמי גורם הוא. *דתנן, [א]ראה ראייה ראשונה – בודקין אותו, שניה – בודקין אותו, שלישית – אין בודקין אותו. ולרבי אליעזר, דאמר אף בשלישי בודקין אותו, ה"נ כיון דלא גרים לא סתר? אמר ליה: לרבי אליעזר, ה"נ. ת"ש, *רבי אליעזר אומר: אף בשלישית בודקין אותו, ברביעית – אין בודקין אותו. מאי לאו – לסתירה? לא, לטמויה להויא טיפה במשא. ת"ש, בשלישית, רבי אליעזר אומר: בודקין אותו, ברביעית – אין בודקין אותו, לקרבן אמרתי ולא לסתירה. אלא לר"א, תפשוט דדבר שאינו גורם – סותר, לרבנן מאי? ת"ש, דתני אבוה דרבי אבין: מה גרם לו זובו – שבעה, לפיכך – סותר שבעה, מה גרם לו קריו – יום אחד, לפיכך – סותר יום אחד. מאי "שבעה"? אילימא דמטמא שבעה – האי "מה זובו טמא שבעה" מבעי ליה, אלא לאו: דבר הגורם – סותר, דבר שאינו גורם – אינו סותר, ש"מ. אמר אביי: *[ב]נקטינן, אין קושי סותר בזיבה. ואי משכחת תנא דאמר סותר – ההוא ר"א היא. תניא, רבי מרינוס אומר: [ג]אין לידה סותרת בזיבה. *איבעיא להו: מהו שתעלה? אביי אמר: אינה סותרת ואינה עולה. רבא אמר: [ד]אינה סותרת ועולה. אמר רבא: מנא אמינא לה – דתניא, °"ואחר תטהר" – *אחר אחר לכולן, שלא תהא טומאה מפסקת ביניהם. אי אמרת בשלמא עולה – היינו דלא מפסקת טומאה, אלא אי אמרת אינה עולה – °אפסיק ליה לידה! ואביי אמר לך: שלא תהא טומאת זיבה מפסקת ביניהם. אמר רבא: מנא אמינא לה – דתניא, *[ה]"מזובה" מזובה ולא מנגעה, מזובה – ולא מלידתה. ואביי אמר לך: תני חדא "מזובה ולא מנגעה", ולא תתני "ולא מלידתה". ורבא – האי מאי? אי אמרת בשלמא "מזובה ולא מלידתה", אידי דאצטריך ליה לידה – תנא נגעה אטו לידה, אלא אי אמרת "מזובה ולא מנגעה" – האי °מ"וכי יטהר הזב מזובו" נפקא – *מזובו ולא מנגעו! ואביי – חד בזב וחד בזבה. וצריכי, דאי כתב רחמנא בזב

**רש"י**

אזל שילא אמר לדביתהו צבית לי זוודתא. תכריכין. מילי. שלא ילבשין עלי בפני רב. דקא פרח אסא. רגילין היו להניח הדס על המטה, וההדס של אלו פורח היה והולך ממטה למטה. פייסא. שלום. קושי מהו שתסתור בזיבה. כל מה שספרה. דבר הגורם. לידי זיבה אם ראתה שלש, והאי – לאו גורם הוא, דלא אתיא בה לידי זיבה. ואי קשיא: והרי קרי שאינו גורם, כדקי"ל, וסותר? ההיא לאו סתירה היא, דחד יומא הוא דסותר, וכי קא בעי רבא – לסתור הכל. שאינו גורם. כדקי"ל: ולא מחמת אונסו. וסותר. כדאמר בפירקין: ברביעית – אין בודקין אותו. לאיי. בחמת אונס נמי גורם הוא לידי זוב, שאם ראה שתים שלא באונס ושלישית באונס – מצטרפין לקרבן. דתנן: שלישית – אין בודקין אותו. לקרבן אמרתי. דבעי בדיקה, ולא לסתירה. אלא. לא תוקי כדתרצת, לטמויי במשא, אלא ודאי – לסתירה, ובעיין לא תפשוט. דאנן לרבנן בעינן, ואת פשטת מדר"א. ש"מ. מדנקט לשון "גרמא", מכלל דקיימא ליה: דבר הגורם – סותר. רבי אליעזר היא. דאמר: אונס סותר, ואינו גורם. מהו שתעלה. אם ילדה בזוב, ובימי לידתה לא ראתה – מהו שיעלה לה לנקיים, ולא תצטרך לספור אחריהן? אינה סותרת. אם היתה זבה, ופסקה, והתחילה לספור, וילדה – אינה סותרת. וימי לידתה, אפי' אינה רואה בהן – אין משלימין לספירתה, אלא משלמת אחריהן *אם טהרה. מזובה. "וספרה לה מזובה". ולא מנגעה. כיון שטהרה מזובה, סופרת מיד, °ותביא קרבן לזיבתה, ואז תטהר מלטמא בועלה, ואפילו מנוגעת. ולא צריכה להמתין עד שתטהר אף מנגעה. ולא מלידתה. כיון שטהרה מזובה, סופרת מיד, ואינה צריכה להמתין עד שיעברו ימי לידתה. אלמא, ילדה בימי ספירה – אינה סותרת, ועולה. זב.

**תוספות**

**דבר** הגורם סותר כו' וא"ת: יולדת בזוב תוכיח, דסותרת לרב דאמר מעין אחד הוא, אע"ג דדם טוהר אינו גורם שום טומאה! וי"ל: דדם טוהר חשיב גורם טפי, כיון שאם לא ילדה הויא זבה או נדה, לרב דאמר מעין אחד הוא. ולא דמי לקושי, דלעולם דם שתראה מחמת קושי לידה אינו גורם זיבה. **נקטינן** דאין קושי סותר. מכאן משמע דלא דרשי "אתים", אם לא שנפרש לעיל (דף לה.) "ורבנן אתים לא דרשי" – היינו להך דרשא. אך משמע דלא דרשי כלל*. **אביי** אמר אינה סותרת ואינה עולה. כתב רש"י בתשובה אחת דאביי מודה דימי לידה שאינה רואה בהן, עולים לספירת זיבתה. דהכי מוכח פרק "בא סימן" (לקמן דף נד:) מן הברייתא, והכא – אליבא דר' מרינוס קיימין. תדע דאין רגילות למיבעי חדא מילתא בתרי דוכתי, דבעי לה הכא, ובשילהי פ' "בא סימן" (שם) ותו: היאך חולק אביי אברייתא דהתם? ותו: דמה להם לאביי ורבא להזכיר סתירה? לא היה להם להזכיר אלא עלייה דפליגי בה! אלא אליבא דר' מרינוס בעי מהו שתעלה, דמדנקט "אין לידה סותרת", ולא קאמר נמי דעולה, מכלל דסבירא ליה דאינה עולה. או דלמא: הא בהא תליא, כיון דאינה סותרת, ע"כ עולה, מ"ואחר תטהר" שלא תהא טומאה מפסקת ביניהן. ומייתי רבא: מנא אמינא לה – דמסתמא רבי מרינוס לא פליג אקרא. ואביי מייתי מנא אמינא לה – דאיכא תנא דפליג אברייתא ד"בא סימן" (שם) ואיכא למימר דר' מרינוס סבירא ליה נמי הכי, מדלא קאמר ר' מרינוס "אינה סותרת ועולה". וה"ה דהוה מצי אביי לאתויי ברייתא דטועה, ב"המפלת" (לעיל דף כח:) דסברה דאין עולה. אלא דרבא הוה מוקי לה כר' אליעזר, כדמוקי ברייתא דבסמוך. כן פרש"י. ומה שפירש דמייתי רבא "מנא אמינא לה", דמסתמא לא פליג ר' מרינוס אקרא, קשה: דהא ע"כ ר"א פליג! וי"ל: דהוה מצי למימר "וליטעמיך", אלא בלאו הכי דחי ליה אביי שפיר. ומה שפירש ברייתא ד"המפלת" (שם דף כח:) מוקי לה רבא כרבי אליעזר – דוקא בהא הויא כרבי אליעזר, דאין עולין לה. אבל לגמרי לא הויא כר' אליעזר, דהא מוקי לה כר"ע דבעי ספורים בפניהו, ור"א פליג עליה בפ"ק (לעיל דף ז:) ור"ת מפרש: דהלכתא כאביי, דאין עולין, וכברייתא ד"המפלת" (שם דף כט:) ומדקדק: מדלא קאמר עלה (לעיל ל.) ש"מ ארבע, דימי לידה אין עולין. לאפוקי מן הברייתא דלעיל ללוי לאחד שינויא, ומברייתא ד"בא סימן" (לקמן דף נד:) דסברי דעולין. אלא אינו מונה אלא דברים של חדוש, אבל הא פשיטא לן דאין עולין. ועוד אומר ר"ת: דברייתא ד"בא סימן" איכא למימר כדמפרש ליה רב פפא, משום דאימא ילדה זכר, להכי עולה שבוע שני לספירת זיבתה. ודבריו נראה טפי, מדקתני "ואין קרבנו נאכל", א"כ איכא למימר: אימר לא ילדה, ואפי' ילדה – אימא ילדה זכר. ותדע דלא קיבל דברי רב הונא דהתם, ולא הדר ביה, אלא סבר דאין עולין: מדקאמר בשמעתין "רב פפא אמר: ע"כ הקישן הכתוב", ואי סבר עולין א"כ ע"כ צריך לאוקמי כר"א כדמוקי רבא, ואמאי דחיק לאוקמי כרבנן דר"א דאמרי אין דנין אפשר משאי אפשר, כיון דבלאו הכי צריך לאוקמי כר"א דאמר אין עולין! אלא ודאי לא הדר ביה. ומיהו אי גרסינן לעיל דאמר סותר "רבי אלעזר", והכא "רבי אליעזר" – אין להוכיח כלום. ודברי רב פפא דלקמן, איכא למימר דאינו עיקר, אע"פ דהוי ספק ספיקא, [(א)] שבוע שני אינו עולה לספירת זיבתה. דאיכא למיחש דילמא נקבה היא, כדאמר רב הונא התם. משום דאיכא נמי ספק ספיקא בסוף ימי טוהר דסתרה לה, כדפרישית לעיל גבי "המפלת חיה ועוף" (דף כז. סד"ה "חומר") ומיהו כיון דאין קרבנה נאכל, איכא בלאו הכי ספק ספיקא: שמא לא ראתה, ואפילו ראתה – שמא לא ילדה. ואומר ר"ת: דימי לידה שאינה רואה בהן, הוא למ"ד מיע"ל קג"ס, ולא "לחי העומד מאליו" בפ"ק דעירובין (דף טו.) ורב סעדיה כתב דנשים שלנו דחשבינן להו כיולדות בזוב, אם עברו ימי טומאת ז' לזכר או י"ד לנקבה, וספרה שבעה נקיים בימי טוהר או אפילו בימי טומאה – מותרת לבעלה עד מ' לזכר ופ' לנקבה. אע"פ שרואה דם – הכתוב קראו "דם טוהר", שכן שנו חכמים: ימי לידה שאינה רואה בהן עולים לה לימי ספירת זיבתה, הרי בהדיא חולק על ר"ת. והא דלא קאמר ב"המפלת" (שם דף ל.) ש"מ ד' – איכא למימר משום דלא קאמר אלא היכא דמצי למימר "הא מני? פלוני היא", כדקאמר: ש"מ ר"ע היא, ש"מ ר"ש היא, ש"מ טבילה בזמנה מצוה, לאפוקי מדר' יוסי בר' יהודה. אבל בהא דאין עולין – לא מצי למימר "הא מני רבי אליעזר היא", דלאביי לכ"ע אין עולין.

**רבא** אמר אינה סותרת. וא"ת: והא *רב סובר בפ"ג (דף טו) דאי אפשר לפתיחת הקבר בלא דם, וא"כ – תסתור, דהכא בעינן שבעה נקיים מדם! וי"ל: *דרב אליבא דר' מרינוס קאמר כדפרישית, וסבר דאפשר לפתיחת הקבר בלא דם, דהא קאמר דאינה סותרת.

מה

**תורה אור**

ויקרא טו — ואחר תטהר

ויקרא טו — וכי יטהר הזב מזובו

**מסורת הש"ס**

[לעיל לה.] זבים פ"ב מ"ב

[נזיר סה: ע"ש לעיל לה. ע"ש]

מן אם כו' עד לה הד"א ואח"כ מה"ד מזובה ולא כו'. כל"ל

[ע' פירש"י עירובין ה. ד"ה והא"ר נקטינן]

[לקמן נד.]

[לעיל לג: לקמן מז: סח:]

[שם]

[מגילה ח.]

[נ"ל והא רבא סובר כפ' בתרא (סו.)] [נ"ל דרבא]

**עין משפט נר מצוה**

נג א מיי' פ"ב מהל' מחוסרי כפרה הל"ה:

נד ב ג מיי' פ"ז מהל' איסורי ביאה הל"י:

נה ד ה מיי' שם טוש"ע סימן קצד:

[וע"ע תוס' בכורות ו. ד"ה ור"ש]

**גליון הש"ס**

גמ' אפסיק ליה לידה: ע"ל לג ע"א תד"ה רואה: רש"י ד"ה ולא מנגעה וכו' ותביא קרבן לזיבתה. ע' טורי אבן מגילה ח ע"א ד"ה מזובו:

**הגהות הב"ח**

(א) תוס' ד"ה אביי וכו' אע"פ דהוי ספק ספיקא אפילו הכי שבוע שני אינו:

**תוספי הרא"ש**

**או** דילמא דבר הגורם סותר. אע"ג דקרי סותר היינו יום אחד וכן הוא גורם טומאה יום אחד. ותימה והרי דם טוהר דאינו גורם טומאה וסותר לרב דאמר מעיין אחד הוא כדאמר לעיל דיולדת בזוב צריכה שתשב ז' נקיים וי"ל דדם טוהר לרב חשיב גורם טפי שאם תראה בזה העניו בימים הראויין לזיבה תהא בו זבה ולא דמי לקושי משום דם שיראה בקושי לעולם לא יגרום זיבות: **אמר** ליה אביי אונס בזוב יוכיח שאינו גורם וסותר. אביי לית ליה הא דאמר רב הונא לעיל ראיה ראשונ' של זב מטמאה באונס: **איבעיא** להו מהו שתעלה. כתב רש"י בתשובה דהך בעיא אליבא דר' מרינוס הוא דמיבעיא לן ולאו תלמודא באפי נפשיה הוא דמיבעיא ליה משום דלקמן פ' בא סימן מיבעיא ליה לתלמודא ימי לידה שאינה רואה בהן מהו שיעלו לספירת זיבתה. ומייתי עלה ת"ש ואין שיטת התלמוד לישאל בעי' אחת לפעמי' ולישא וליתן בה אלא הכא לר' מרינוס הוא דקבעי דנקט לישנא דסותרת ומיבעיא ליה מאי סבירא ליה בעליה מי אמרי' מדלא קאמר ימי לידה עולין לספירת זיבתה אינה עולה אית ליה או דילמא הא בהא תליא כיון דאינה סותרת ע"כ עולה דאם לא כן לא מניא רצופין ורחמנא אמר אחר אחר לכולן. אביי אמר אינה סותרת דוקא קאמר ואינם עולין ואפי' אינה רואה בהן אלא משלמת ספירתה לאחר שבועיים וה"מ דלא חזיא דם אבל אי חזיא דם לא אחר אחר הוא דאע"ג דלאו טומאת זיבה הוא מ"מ מדם בעי' נקיים דהא אפי' דם טהור סותר לרב דאמר מעין אחד הוא כ"ש דם דימי טומאה ורבא אמר אינה סותרת ועולה דהא בהא תליא: **אמר** רבא. מנא אמינא לה. דכל דאית ליה דאינה סותרת אית ליה דעולה דדתניא ואחר תטהר כו' וע"כ ר' מרינוס לא פליג אקרא וכן מייתי מקרא דוטהרה מזובה דע"כ ר' מרינוס לא פליג אקרא. מי' ק' דהא ע"כ ר' אליעזר פליג אחך קרא דוטהרה מזובה דאיהו נמי אמר דמסתר נמי סתרה. וכ"ש דאינה עולה. והכי משנ' רבא גופיה לקמן וי"ל דאה"נ דהוה מצי למימר אביי ולטעמי':

נו א מיי' פ"ז מהל' איסורי ביאה הל"א וע' במ"מ:

בְּזָב – מִשּׁוּם דְּלָא מְטַמֵּא בְּאוֹנֶס, אֲבָל זָבָה דְּמִטַּמְּיָא בְּאוֹנֶס – אֵימָא לָא, צְרִיכָא. וְאִי כָּתַב רַחֲמָנָא בְּזָבָה – מִשּׁוּם דְּלָא מְטַמְּיָא בִּרְאִיּוֹת כְּבְיָמִים, אֲבָל זָב דִּמְטַמֵּא בִּרְאִיּוֹת כְּבְיָמִים – אֵימָא לָא, צְרִיכָא. אָמַר אַבַּיֵי: מְנָא אָמִינָא לָהּ – דְּתַנְיָא: °"דְּוֹתָהּ תִּטְמָא" – *לְרַבּוֹת אֶת בּוֹעֲלָהּ, "דְּוֹתָהּ תִּטְמָא" – לְרַבּוֹת אֶת הַלֵּילוֹת, "דְּוֹתָהּ תִּטְמָא" לְרַבּוֹת אֶת הַיּוֹלֶדֶת בְּזוֹב שֶׁצְּרִיכָה שֶׁתֵּשֵׁב שִׁבְעָה נְקִיִּים. מַאי לָאו נְקִיִּים מִלֵּידָה? לָא, מִדָּם. וְאָמַר אַבַּיֵי: מְנָא אָמִינָא לָהּ – דְּתַנְיָא: כִּימֵי נִדָּתָהּ כָּךְ יְמֵי לֵידָתָהּ, °מַה יְמֵי נִדָּתָהּ – אֵין רְאוּיִן לְזִיבָה וְאֵין סְפִירַת שִׁבְעָה עוֹלָה מֵהֶן, אַף יְמֵי לֵידָתָהּ שֶׁאֵין רְאוּיִן לְזִיבָה – אֵין סְפִירַת שִׁבְעָה עוֹלָה מֵהֶן. וְרָבָא – הָא מַנִּי רַבִּי אֱלִיעֶזֶר הִיא, דְּאָמַר מִסְתַּר נַמִּי סָתְרָה. וְכִי דָּנִין אֶפְשָׁר מִשֶּׁאִי אֶפְשָׁר? אָמַר רַב אַחַדְבוֹי בַּר אַמִּי: ר' אֱלִיעֶזֶר הִיא, *דְּאָמַר דָּנִין אֶפְשָׁר מִשֶּׁאִי אֶפְשָׁר. וְרַב שֵׁשֶׁת אָמַר: עַל כָּרְחָךְ הִקִּישָׁן הַכָּתוּב. אִיכָּא דְּאָמְרִי, אָמַר רַב אַחַדְבוֹי בַּר אַמִּי אָמַר רַב שֵׁשֶׁת: רַבִּי אֱלִיעֶזֶר הִיא, דְּאָמַר דָּנִין אֶפְשָׁר מִשֶּׁאִי אֶפְשָׁר, וְרַב פַּפָּא אָמַר: עַל כָּרְחָךְ הִקִּישָׁן הַכָּתוּב.§ "קָשְׁתָה שְׁלֹשָׁה יָמִים" וכו'.§ אִיבַּעְיָא לְהוּ: שָׁפְתָה מִזֶּה וּמִזֶּה מַהוּ? רַב חִסְדָּא אָמַר: אטְמֵאָה, רַבִּי חֲנִינָא אָמַר: טְהוֹרָה. א"ר חֲנִינָא: מָשָׁל לְמֶלֶךְ שֶׁיָּצָא וְחַיָּילוֹתָיו לְפָנָיו, בְּיָדוּעַ שֶׁחַיָּילוֹתָיו שֶׁל מֶלֶךְ הֵן. וְרַב חִסְדָּא אָמַר: כָּל שֶׁכֵּן דְּבָעֵי נָפֵישׁ חַיָּילוֹת טְפֵי. תְּנַן, רַבִּי יְהוֹשֻׁעַ אוֹמֵר: לַיְלָה וְיוֹם כְּלֵילֵי שַׁבָּת וְיוֹמוֹ, שֶׁשָּׁפְתָה מִן הַצַּעַר וְלֹא מִן הַדָּם. טַעְמָא – דְּמִן הַצַּעַר וְלֹא מִן הַדָּם, הָא מִזֶּה וּמִזֶּה – טְהוֹרָה. תְּיוּבְתָּא דְּרַב חִסְדָּא? אָמַר לָךְ רַב חִסְדָּא: לָא מִבַּעְיָא מִזֶּה וּמִזֶּה – דִּטְמֵאָה, דְּפָסְקִי לְהוּ חַיָּילוֹת לְגַמְרֵי, אֲבָל מִן הַצַּעַר וְלֹא מִן הַדָּם, אֵימָא: כִּי הֵיכִי דְּמִדָּם לָא פָּסְקָה – מִקּוֹשִׁי נַמִּי לָא פָּסְקָה, וְהָא – תּוּנְבָּא בְּעָלְמָא הוּא דְּנָקַט לָהּ, קמ"ל. תְּנַן: קָשְׁתָה שְׁלֹשָׁה יָמִים בְּתוֹךְ אַחַד עָשָׂר יוֹם, וְשָׁפְתָה מֵעֵת לְעֵת וְיָלְדָה – הֲרֵי זוֹ יוֹלֶדֶת בְּזוֹב. הֵיכִי דָּמֵי? אִילֵימָא כִּדְקָתָנֵי – לָמָּה לִי שָׁלֹשׁ? בִּתְרֵי בְּקוֹשִׁי וְחַד בְּשׁוֹפִי סַגִּי! אֶלָּא לָאו הָכִי קָאָמַר: קָשְׁתָה שְׁלֹשָׁה וְשָׁפְתָה מִזֶּה וּמִזֶּה, אוֹ שֶׁקָּשְׁתָה שְׁנַיִם וְשָׁפְתָה מֵעֵת לְעֵת – הֲרֵי זוֹ יוֹלֶדֶת בְּזוֹב, וּתְיוּבְתָּא דְּר' חֲנִינָא! אָמַר לָךְ רַבִּי חֲנִינָא: לָא, לְעוֹלָם כִּדְקָתָנֵי, וְהָא קָא מַשְׁמַע לָן: דְּאע"ג *דְּמַתְחִיל קִישּׁוּי בַּשְּׁלִישִׁי, וְשָׁפְתָה מֵעֵת לְעֵת – טְמֵאָה, לְאַפּוּקֵי מֵרַבִּי חֲנִינָא.§ "כַּמָּה הִיא קְשׁוּיָהּ ר"מ אוֹמֵר" וכו'.§ הַשְׁתָּא חֲמִשִּׁים מַקַּשְׁיָא, אַרְבָּעִים מִיבַּעְיָא? אָמַר רַב חִסְדָּא: ל"ק, כָּאן – לַחוֹלָה, כָּאן – לַבְּרִיאָה. א"ר לֵוִי: אֵין הַוָּלָד מְטַהֵר אֶלָּא יָמִים הָרְאוּיִין לִהְיוֹת בָּהֶן זָבָה, וְרַב אָמַר: אֲפִי' בְּיָמִים הָרְאוּיִין לִסְפִירַת זָבָה. אָמַר רַב אַדָּא בַּר אַהֲבָה: וּלְטַעְמֵיהּ דְּרַב אֲפִי'

תורה אור: ויקרא יב

---

**רש"י**

זָב מְטַמֵּא בֵּין בְּשָׁלֹשׁ רְאִיּוֹת בְּיוֹם אֶחָד, בֵּין בְּשָׁלֹשׁ רְאִיּוֹת בְּג' יָמִים רְצוּפִין. אֲבָל זָבָה אֵינָהּ מְטַמְּאָה אֶלָּא בִּשְׁלֹשָׁה יָמִים, כִּדְכְתִיב בָּהּ "יָמִים". בְּב"ק (דף כד.) מְרַבִּינַן זָב לְיָמִים. נְקִיִּים מִלֵּידָה. שֶׁלֹּא תְּהֵא לֵידָה בֵּינֵיהֶם, דְּאע"ג דְּלָא חַזְיָא – כְּמַאן דְּחַזְיָא דָּמֵי, דְּהָא יְמֵי לֵידָה טְמֵאִין בְּלֹא דָּם. מַה יְמֵי נִדָּתָהּ אֵין רְאוּיִין לְזִיבָה. דְּאֵין זָבָה אֶלָּא אַחַר נִדָּה, וְאֵין סְפִירַת שִׁבְעָה לְזִיבָה עוֹלָה מֵהֶן. דְּהָא מִכִּי הָוְיָא זָבָה – לָא חָיְילָא יְמֵי נִדָּה לְעוֹלָם, עַד שֶׁתֵּשֵׁב שִׁבְעָה נְקִיִּים. וְכָל דָּם שֶׁרוֹאָה – אֵינָהּ אֶלָּא סוֹתֶרֶת, אֲבָל נִדָּה לָא הָוְיָא. הִילְכָּךְ לָא מַשְׁכַּחַת יְמֵי סְפִירָה בִּימֵי נִדָּה, וְלָא יְמֵי נִדָּה בִּימֵי סְפִירָה. אַף יְמֵי לֵידָה. הוֹאִיל וְדָמוּ לְנִדָּה, וְאֵין רְאוּיִין לְזִיבָה, כִּדְאָמַר: וְלֹא דָּמָהּ מֵחֲמַת וָלָד. הָכִי נַמִּי לְעִנְיַן סְפִירָה מְדַמִּינַן לְהוּ לְנִדָּה, וְלֹא תַּעֲלֶה בָּהֶן סְפִירַת שִׁבְעָה, כְּגוֹן אִם יָלְדָה בִּימֵי סְפִירָה. הָכִי גָּרְסִינַן: אַף יְמֵי לֵידָתָהּ שֶׁאֵין רְאוּיִין לְזִיבָה, אֵין סְפִירַת שִׁבְעָה עוֹלָה מֵהֶן. מִסְתַּר נַמִּי סָתְרָה. וְכ"ש דְּלָא סָלְקָא, כִּי הֵיכִי דְּס"ל בְּאוֹנֶס בְּזָב, שֶׁאֵינוֹ גּוֹרֵם וְסוֹתֵר. יְמֵי לֵידָה נַמִּי, אע"ג דְּלָא גָּרְמִי, סָתְרִי. וְכִי קָאָמֵינָא אֲנָא לְרַבָּנַן דְּאָמְרִי דָּבָר שֶׁאֵינוֹ גּוֹרֵם אֵינוֹ סוֹתֵר, אֵינָהּ סוֹתֶרֶת וְעוֹלָה. וְכִי דָּנִין אֶפְשָׁר. כְּגוֹן לֵידָה, דְּאֶפְשָׁר לָהּ לָלֶדֶת בִּימֵי סְפִירָה. מִשֶּׁאִי אֶפְשָׁר. מִימֵי נִדָּה, דְּלֹא אֶפְשָׁר לִהְיוֹת נִדָּה בִּימֵי סְפִירָה? ר' אֱלִיעֶזֶר הִיא. בְּמַסֶּכֶת מְנָחוֹת בְּפ' "הַתּוֹדָה", דְּיָלֵיף פֶּסַח דּוֹרוֹת מִפֶּסַח מִצְרַיִם, שֶׁלֹּא יָבִיא אֶלָּא מִן הַחוּלִּין. אָמַר לוֹ ר"ע: וְכִי דָּנִין אֶפְשָׁר מִשֶּׁאִי אֶפְשָׁר? בְּמִצְרַיִם אַכַּתִּי לָא הֲוָה מַעֲשֵׂר, אֲבָל לְדוֹרוֹת דְּאִיכָּא מָעוֹת מַעֲשֵׂר שֵׁנִי – נַיְיתֵי מִנַּיְיהוּ! אָמַר לוֹ: אַף ע"פ שֶׁאִי אֶפְשָׁר, רְאָיָה גְּדוֹלָה הִיא, וְנִלְמַד הֵימֶנָּה. הִקִּישָׁן הַכָּתוּב. וַאֲפִי' לר"ע, הָנֵי מִילֵּי דְּאֵין דָּנִין, כְּגוֹן גְּזֵרָה שָׁוָה. אֲבָל הֶקֵּישָׁא – אֵין מְשִׁיבִין עַל הַהֶקֵּשׁ. רַב חִסְדָּא אָמַר טְמֵאָה. דְּהָא אִיכָּא שׁוֹפִי. רַבִּי חֲנִינָא אָמַר טְהוֹרָה. כֵּיוָן דְּשָׁפְתָה אַף מִן הַדָּם – אִיגַּלַּאי מִילְּתָא דְּדַם הַקּוֹשִׁי מֵחֲמַת וָלָד אָתָא. אֲבָל כִּי שָׁפְתָה מִן הַצַּעַר וְרוֹאָה דָּם – אִיגַּלַּאי מִילְּתָא דְּמִקַּמֵּי הָכִי הֲוֵי חָזְיָא נַמִּי בְּלֹא קוֹשִׁי. לְפָנָיו. יוֹם אֶחָד אוֹ שְׁנַיִם קוֹדֶם בִּיאָתוֹ. דְּמַפֵּישׁ חַיָּילוֹת טְפֵי. סָמוּךְ לְבִיאָתוֹ. דְּפָסְקוּ לְהוּ חַיָּילוֹת לְגַמְרֵי. דְּהַשְׁתָּא וַדַּאי קַמַּאי לָא מֵחֲמָתֵיהּ אָתוּ, דְּאִי מֵחֲמָתֵיהּ אָתוּ – כָּל שֶׁכֵּן דְּמַפֵּישׁ חַיָּילוֹת. תּוּנְבָּא. אשטורדישו"ן, שֶׁאֵינָהּ מַרְגֶּשֶׁת בְּצַעֲרָהּ, מֵחֲמַת שַׁעֲמוּמִית הַחוֹלִי. (א). אִי נַמִּי כִּי קָתָנֵי. שְׁלֹשָׁה בְּקוֹשִׁי וְא' בְּשׁוֹפִי וּבְכוּלָּן רָאֲתָה, לָמָּה לִי כּוּלֵּי הַאי? אוֹ שֶׁקָּשְׁתָה שְׁנַיִם וְשָׁפְתָה מֵעֵת לְעֵת. בַּשְּׁלִישִׁי מִן הַצַּעַר וְלֹא מִן הַדָּם, כִּדְקָתָנֵי "שְׁלֹשָׁה בְּקוֹשִׁי", וּמִקְצָת שְׁלִישִׁי וּמִקְצָת רְבִיעִי – בְּשׁוֹפִי. הָא קמ"ל דְּאע"ג. דְּקָשְׁתָה בְּקְצָת שְׁלִישִׁי וְלֹא שָׁפְתָה לַיְלָה וְיוֹם כְּלֵילֵי שַׁבָּת וְיוֹמוֹ, אֶלָּא לַיְלָה *וּשְׁנֵי חֲלָאֵי יוֹם טְמֵאָה. וּלְאַפּוּקֵי מִדְּר' חֲנִינָא בֶּן אֲחִי רַבִּי יְהוֹשֻׁעַ. דְּאָמַר לְעֵיל (דף לו.): כָּל שֶׁאֵל קִישּׁוּיָהּ לִהְיוֹת בַּשְּׁלִישִׁי שֶׁלָּהּ כו'. בְּרִיאָה. אַרְבָּעִים. אֵין הַוָּלָד מְטַהֵר אֶלָּא יָמִים הָרְאוּיִין לִהְיוֹת בָּהּ זָבָה. דְּהַיְינוּ י"א יוֹם שֶׁבֵּין נִדָּה לְנִדָּה. אֲבָל רָאֲתָה אַחֲרֵיהֶן – טְמֵאָה נִדָּה, כִּדְאָמַר לְעֵיל: בִּימֵי נִדָּה נִדָּה. אַף יָמִים הָרְאוּיִין לִסְפִירַת זִיבָה. כְּגוֹן הִתְחִיל הַקּוֹשִׁי בִּימֵי הַזִּיבָה – טְהוֹרִין כָּל יְמֵי זִיבָה וְשִׁבְעָה אַחֲרֵיהֶם, דְּהָא בָּתַר זָבָה שַׁיְּיכִי. וְכִי כָּתַב רַחֲמָנָא (ב) "כְּנִדָּתָהּ" וְלֹא כְּזִיבָתָהּ, דְּזִיבָתָהּ טְהוֹרָה – אַהָנֵי נַמִּי קָאֵי. אֲבָל אַחַר שִׁבְעָה אִם יַאֲרִיךְ – טְמֵאָה נִדָּה. וּלְטַעְמֵיהּ דְּרַב. כֵּיוָן דְּאָמַר רַב בְּהָנָךְ יָמִים דְּשַׁיְּיכִי בָּתַר זִיבָה טַהֲרִינְהוּ רַחֲמָנָא לְעִנְיַן קוֹשִׁי. אַף

[לעיל לה:]

מנחות פב: יט. [סוכה נ: וש"נ]

גי' רש"ל דחל

עיין רש"א

---

**תוספות**

מה ימי נדותה דאין ראוין לזיבה. וא"ת: דבשילהי "בא סימן" (לקמן דף נד.) אמר: ימי נדותה שאינה רואה בהן – עולין לספירת זיבתה! וי"ל: דהתם מיירי בזבה קטנה שרואה יום י"א דיום י"ב הויא ביה תחלת נדה, ועולה לה. על כרחך הקישן הכתוב. ואין משיבין על ההיקש. וא"ת: והא בפ' "התודה" (מנחות דף פ.) פריך ר"ע לר' אליעזר: וכי דנין אפשר משאי אפשר, אע"ג דטעמא דרבי אליעזר דדריש היקשא מ"ועבדת" שיהו כל העבודות שוות. ור"ע: נמי אית ליה היקשא ד"ועבדת", בפרק "מי שהיה טמא" (פסחים דף לו.) וי"ל: דהתם לא מצי למימר "על כרחך הקישן הכתוב", דאיצטריך היקשא להנהו דרשות דפסחים (דף לו.). ארבעים מיבעיא. בסוכה *לא פריך כי האי גוונא ארבי יהודה דמכשיר עד ארבעים וחמשים אמה התם – משום דקים ליה דלאו דוקא, אלא "ארבעים וחמשים" כדאמרי אינשי, ואפילו טובא. אבל הכא הוי דוקא חמשים, כדקתני בסמוך: וחמשים שהולד מטהר. ובפרק "מפנין" (שבת דף קכו:) דפריך: השתא ה' קופות, ד' מיבעיא? – המקשה סבר דדוקא נקט. ומשני: דלאו דוקא נקט, אלא ד' וה' כדאמרי אינשי. ועוד משני: דהוה דוקא, ד' – מאוצר קטן, וה' – מאוצר גדול. ובפרק "אע"פ" (כתובות דף ס.) תינוק יונק אפי' ד' וה' שנים – נמי לא דייק התם, משום דלאו דוקא ה' אלא לפי צרכו, כדקאמר התם: ואפילו חבילתו על כתפו. ובפרק "הזרוע" (חולין דף קלג:) דאמר: כהן טבח ב' וג' שבתות – פטור מן המתנות, מכאן ואילך – חייב במתנות. התם נקט ב' – לרבי, דאמר *בתרי זימני הוה חזקה. ולרשב"ג – ג'*. ורב אדא בר אהבה אמר אף ימים הראויים לספירת סתירת זיבתה. וא"ת: מה הוסיף על דברי רב, הא לרב נמי הראוין לספירה היינו ז' ימים אחר י"א יום, ואז מתחילות י"א אחרים, שהם ימי זיבה. וא"כ לדידיה נמי לעולם קושי מטהר? וי"ל: דאינה נדה עד שיעברו שבעה ימי הספירה אחר י"א ואם ראתה אז, אף בקושי – טמאה לרב, ולרב אדא – טהורה, דראויין לספירת סתירת זיבתה. ור"ת פי' דלוי אינו מטהר אלא תשעה ימים הראוין ליעשות בהן זבה. אבל י' וי"א דאינם ראויין ליעשות בהן זבה, דאפילו ראתה אפי' גם בי"ב – אינה אלא נדה. ורב מוסיף ימים הראויין לספירה, כגון עשירי וי"א וחמשה ימים אחרי כן. אבל שני ימים משבעה ימים אחרונים אם ראתה בהן – טמאה לרב. ורב אדא מוסיף אף אותם שני ימים, ונמצא כולן טהורין.

[דף כ: וש"נ]

[יבמות סד:]

[וע"ע תוס' שבת דף ס: ד"ה הספק]

---

**תוספי הרא"ש**

אמר אביי מנא אמינא לה דתניא דותה תטמא כו'. הכי מייתי אביי ראיה לר' מרינוס דכיון דאשכחן תנא דפליג אברייתא דבא סימן דסבר עולין אית לן למימר דר' מרינוס נמי סבר הכי מדלא קאמר בהדיא עולין וה"ה דהוה מצי אביי לאיתויי ההיא דיצאה מליאה ובאה ריקנית דלעיל דאית ליה דאין עולין אלא דאי הוה מייתי לה הוה מוקי לה רבא נמי כר' אליעזר כך פרש"י בתשובה. ולפי פי' בין אביי בין רבא מצו סברי כמסקנא בסוף בא סימן ואליבא דר' מרינוס הוא דפליגי. ור"ת פי' דאדעתא דנפשייהו פליגי דהלכת' כותיה דאביי דאמר אין עולין ומדקדק מהא דאמר לעיל אהך ברייתא' דיצאה מליאה ש"מ תלת ולא קאמר ש"מ אין עולין לאפוקי מברייתא דלעיל דסברא עולין ללוי אליבא דחד שינויא דשני בשופעת וכו' ולפי המסקנא עולין לה וכו' ולאפוקי מברייתא דסוף בא סימן. אלא אינו מונה אלא דברים של חידוש הך דר' עקיבא ודר' שמעון וטבילה בזמנה אלא הא פשיטא ליה דאין עולין ויש לדחות דלא חשיב אלא הנך ג' דאיכא פלוגתא דתנאי. אבל בהא דאין עולין לא הוה מצי למימר ש"מ ר' אליעזר היא דהא לאביי אתיא אפי' כמאן דפליג על ר' אליעזר כדקאמר אביי הכא דלר' מרינוס דאמר אינה סותרת אין עולין. ועוד אומר ר"ת דהא דאמרינן בסוף בא סימן דעולין היינו רב הונא בריה דרב יהושע דמסיק לה התם אבל רב פפא דחי לה התם ולא קבל תשובתו של רב הונא ולא הדר ביה אלא סובר כאביי דאמר אין עולין מדפריך בסוף סוגיין וכי דנין איפשר משאי אפשר. רב פפא אמר ע"כ הקישן הכתוב ולמה ליה לרב פפא למימר הכי הא בלאו הכי אוקמה רבא כר' אליעזר אלא ש"מ דרב פפא לטעמיה דאמר אין עולין ואומר ר"ת דהיא הלמד של יע"ל קג"ם ולא כאותם המפרשים דהיינו למד של לחי העומד מאיליו דעירובין: מה ימי נדה שאינן ראויין לזיבה ואין ספירת ז' עולה מהן. משום דכל זיבה זמן שהזיבה מושכת אין מתחיל פתח נדותה והא דאמרינן בסוף בא סימן זאת אומרת ימי נדה שאינה רואה בהן עולין לספירת זיבתה בזיבה קטנה בשומרת יום כנגד יום איירי: הג"ה רש"י אף ימי לידתה שאינן ראוין לזיבה אין ספירת ז' עולה מהן ופי' דאין ראויין לזיבה כדדרשינן דמה מחמת עצמה ולא מחמת וולד. וקשה לי דמהך קרא לא ממעיטנא אלא דם הקושי שאינו טמא בזיבה אבל ימי לידה לא ממעיטנא מהתם הלכך נראה הגירסת הספרים אף ימי לידתה אין ראויין לזיבה ואין ספירת ז' עולה מהן וכולה מילתא יליף לה מהיקישא. ע"כ הקישן הכתוב. וכ"ע מודו הכא. וקשה דבפ' התודה גבי ר' אליעזר דיליף פסח דורות מפסח מצרים דאינו בא אלא מן החולין ויליף לה ר' אליעזר מועבדת שיהיו כל עבודות של חדש זה כזה ואפ"ה קאמר ר"ע וכי דנין איפשר משאי איפשר ואין לומר דלית ליה לר' עקיבא ההוא היקישא דהא בפסחים בפ' מי שהיה טמא מקיש להו אהדדי לכמה דברים וי"ל כיון דאיצטריך היקישא לשאר דברים לא שייך התם למימר ע"כ הקישן הכתוב לענין איפשר משאי איפשר: ור' חנינא אמר טהור. מסתברא דר' חנינא אמתניתין דוקא קאי ששפתה מעת לעת אבל טפי לא מסתבר שיקדימו כל כך חיילות לפני המלך: השתא נ' מקשיא מ' מיבעיא. בריש סוכה דקאמר ר' יהודה מכשיר עד מ' או נ' אמה לא דייק הכי משום דקים ליה התם דלאו דוקא אלא מ' ונ' כדאמרי' אינשי וה"ה לטובא כדמשני בשבת בריש מפנין ומאן דמשני התם ד' מאוצר קטן וחמש מאוצר גדול קסבר דוקא קתני דלאו מיסתבר ליה לפנות כל כך בשבת וה"נ קים ליה דדוקא הוא דלא מיסתבר לטהר הקישוי לעולם. ועוד דקתני בשמעתין וחמשים שהוולד מטהר וכן גבי סנדל המסומר דייק הכי בפ' במה אשה גבי ארבע וחמש ובפ' אע"פ דכתובות גבי יונק תינוק והולך ד' או ה' שנים לא דייק משום דפשיטא ליה דלאו דוקא ה' אלא כל לפי צורך הוולד. וכן בריש אע"פ בכתובות אבל חכמים אומרים משהה אדם את אשתו אפי' ד' או ה' שנים בלא כתובה התם נמי לאו דוקא דפשיטא ליה ד' וה' כדאמרי' אינשי ואפי' טובא. וקשה מהא דאמרינן בחולין פ' הזרוע כהן טבח שתים ושלש שבתות פטור מן המתנות מכאן ואילך חייב אמאי לא דייק התם. וי"ל דנקט שנים לר' דאמר בתרי זימני הויא חזקה ושלש לרשב"ג: הראויין

---

**הגהות הב"ח**

(א) רש"י ד"ה תונבא וכו' החולי הס"ד ואח"כ מ"ה אילימא כדקתני שלשה: (ב) ד"ה אף ימים וכו' כתב רחמנא כנדתה ולא כזיבתה:

**גליון הש"ס**

גמ' מה ימי נדתה. בחדושי הרשב"א גיטין דף ט ד"ה הא דקתני היה הגי' כאן הקיש ימי נדתה לימי לידתה מה ימי נדתה וכו':

אפי' ימים הראויין לספירת סתירת זבה. תנן, כמה הוא קשויה? ר"מ אומר: ארבעים וחמשים יום. בשלמא לרב – משכחת לה כרב אדא בר אהבה, אלא ללוי קשיא! אמר לך לוי: מי קתני "טהורה בכולן"? בימי נדה – נדה, בימי זיבה – טהורה. לישנא אחרינא אמרי, א"ר לוי: אין הולד מטהר אלא ימים הראויין להיות בהן זבה גדולה, מ"ט? °"דמה ימים רבים" כתיב. א] אבא שאול משמיה דרב אמר: אפילו ימים הראויין להיות בהן זבה קטנה, מ"ט? "ימי" ו"כל ימי" התם כתיבי. תנן, כמה הוא קשויה? ר"מ אומר: אפי' ארבעים וחמשים יום, קשיא לתרוייהו! מי קתני "טהורה בכולן"? קשתה בימי נדתה – נדה, בימי זיבתה – טהורה. תניא, היה ר"מ אומר: יש מקשה ק"נ יום ואין זיבה עולה בהן. כיצד, שנים בלא עת, ושבעה נדה, ושנים של אחר הנדה, וחמשים שהולד מטהר, ושמונים של נקבה, ושבעה נדה, ושנים של אחר הנדה. אמרו לו: א"כ יש מקשה כל ימיה ואין זיבה עולה בהן! אמר להן: מאי דעתייכו – משום נפלים, ב אין קושי לנפלים. ת"ר: ג יש רואה מאה יום ואין זיבה עולה בהן. כיצד, שנים בלא עת, ושבעה נדה, ושנים של אחר הנדה, ושמונים של נקבה, ושבעה נדה, ושנים של אחר הנדה. מאי קמ"ל? לאפוקי ממ"ד: *אי אפשר לפתיחת הקבר בלא דם, קמ"ל דאפשר לפתיחת הקבר בלא דם. § ר' יהודה אומר "דיה" וכו'. § תניא, רבי יהודה אומר משום רבי טרפון: דיה חדשה, ויש בדבר להקל ולהחמיר. כיצד, קשתה שנים בסוף שמיני ואחד בתחלת תשיעי, ואפילו בתחלת תשיעי ילדה – הרי זו יולדת בזוב. אבל קשתה יום אחד בסוף שמיני ושתים בתחלת תשיעי, ואפילו בסוף תשיעי ילדה – אין זו יולדת בזוב. אמר רב אדא בר אהבה: ש"מ, קסבר רבי יהודה שיפורא גרים. איני, והא אמר שמואל: אין אשה מתעברת ויולדת ב] אלא למאתים ושבעים ואחד יום, או למאתים ושבעים ושנים יום, °או למאתים ושבעים ושלשה! הוא דאמר כחסידים הראשונים, דתניא: חסידים הראשונים לא היו משמשין מטותיהן אלא ברביעי בשבת, שלא יבואו נשותיהן לידי

תורה אור: ויקרא טו

---

**רש"י**

אף ימים הראויין לספירת סתירת זבה. בימי זיבה. דלעולם היא טהורה עד שתפשה, שהרי כל ימיה ראויין לכך: שאם תספור ששה ותראה – סותרת הכל, ונמצאו הימים הבאין ראויין לספירה. והא דתנאן: "בימי נדה נדה" – היכא דהתחיל קושי מימי נדה, אבל התחיל בימי זיבה – כל מה שנמשך הקושי, טהורה. (א) ועוד ארבעים וחמשים יום. קס"ד: לגמרי מטהר לה ר"מ מזוב ומנדות. בימי נדה נדה. וק"ק ר"מ: כמה הוא קשויה שלא תבא להתחייב בקרבן ולספירת נקיים? ארבעים וחמשים יום. ומיהו בכל הני ארבעים, כי שלמי ימי זוב ומטו ימי נדות – טמאה נדה. וכי הדרי שלמי ז' ימי נדות, ומטו ימי זוב – טהורה. זבה גדולה. דאתא שלשה רצופין בתוך י"א יום – טהורה מספירת נקיים ומקרבן. אבל לא ראתה אלא יום אחד – צריכה לשמור יום כנגד יום. דהי כתיב "דמה", דדרשינן: ולא מחמת ולד – בזבה גדולה כתיב, דכתיב בההוא קרא "ימים רבים". ואם משך קשויה יותר מאחד עשר יום, שנכנסה לימים שראויים לנדה – טמאה. ימי וכל ימי זוב טומאתה וגו'. ומינייהו נפקא לן זבה קטנה, בשילהי מכילתין במסכת בבריתא. קשיא לתרוייהו. דקאמרי: זבה גדולה וקטנה הוא דמטהר ולד, אבל אם יצאה אחריהן – טמאה. בימי זיבה. למר כדאית ליה, ולמר כדאית ליה. יש מקשה. שהיא רואה. ק"נ יום. רצופין. ואין זבה עולה בהן. ולא שתהא מקשה כל ק"נ יום. כיצד ראתה ב' בלא עת. בלא עת נדתה הרי י"א ימים שלאחר נדתה, שהן ימי זיבה ואינה זבה עד שתראה בהן ג' רצופין. ואם ראתה שנים בסופן, כשתראה למחר – הוי פתח של נדותה, ואינו מצטרף לה לזיבה, אלא תחלת נדה הויא. וכל שבעה תהיה נדה – הרי ט' ימים רצופין. ושנים שלאחר הנדה, שהן מן י"א של ימי זוב. וכל כמה דלא חזיא ג' בימי זיבה, לא הויא זבה – הרי י"א רצופין. וקשתה חמשים והיא חולה, ואמרינן לעיל בחולה חמשים – הרי ס"א. וביום ס"א ילדה נקבה, ואפילו רואה כל שמונים אינה זבה, ואחד ושמונים הוי תחילת נדה, ואם תראה ז' – הרי מאה ומ"ח. ושנים שלאחר הנדה ותפסוק – הרי ראתה ק"נ רצופין, ואינה זבה. אבל אם תראה יותר – הויא זבה, דהוו להו ג' לאחר הנדה. וחמשים שהולד מטהר. הנך חמשים של קושי לפני השמונים. א"כ. דקחשבת שמונים של נקבה. יש מקשה לעולם. ואינה זבה, כגון טולדת לי"ד של נקבה, ומתעברת, ולסוף שמונים שבעה לנדה, ושנים לאחר הנדה, ומקשה חמשים, וחוזרת ומפלת נקבה. וכן לעולם. אמר להן. ר"מ: מאי דעתייכו? משום נפלים, כדפרשינן. אין הנפל מטהר קישויו. ואנן – בולד דאית ליה קושי קמיירינן. יש רואה. בלא קושי. קמ"ל דאפשר לפתיחת הקבר בלא דם. דאי לא אפשר – הויא לה זבה כשילדה אחר שנים שלאחר הנדה, דהוי ליה יום לידה שלישי. ואי הויא חזיא קודם לידה בפתיחת הקבר – הרי היא זבה, הואיל ובלא קושי ראתה. להקל ולהחמיר. פעמים שאינו מטהר כלום, פעמים שהוא מטהר חדש ויום אחד. הרי זו יולדת בזוב. הואיל ורוב זיבה בשמיני הואי, שאין הולד מטהר – שדינן חד יומא בתר תרין, והרי היא זבה. ואף בסוף תשיעי ילדה. ואע"ג דתשיעי כולו בשופי, חוץ משני ימים – אין זו יולדת בזוב בלבד שלא תראה דם בימי השופי. ולא אמרינן: כיון דשופי סמוך ללידה, נסמכינהו לדם הקושי – דקסבר ר' יהודה: שיפורא גרים. כלומר, החדש של תשיעי גורמת לידת הולד. דמשנכנס החדש, הוה זמן לידה. הילכך כל הדמים שרואה בו בקושי, אינו אלא מחמת הולד, ואע"ג דאיכא שופי בתרייהו, ואפי' בתחלת תשיעי הוי מחמת ולד, דקסבר: יולדת לט', יולדת למקוטעין. שיפורא. שופר שתוקעין בו ב"ד בקידוש החדש. דהוו להו ט' חדשים שלמים של שלשים, וביום ראשון של עשירי יולדת. או למאתים ושבעים ואחד. או לרע"ב. כלומר, אם לא קלטה הזרע יום ראשון, קולטת בשני. ומיום קליטתו הוי התחלת העיבור. או לרע"ג. שאם לא קלטה בשני, קולטת בשלישי. אבל אם לא קלטה בשלישי – שוב אינו קולט, דקי"ל דעד שלישי הוי ראוי להזריע, מכאן ואילך – מסריח, במסכת שבת (דף פו.) בפולטת שכבת זרע ביום השלישי, בפרק "ר' עקיבא". אלמא, לא ילדה למקוטעין. [הוא]. שמואל דאמר כחסידים. לידי

---

**תוספות**

להיות בהן זבה גדולה. *רש"י פירש: לאפוקי י' וי"א דאינה ראויה להתחיל בהן זבה גדולה. ור"ח פירש: לאפוקי יום ראשון ויום שני של י"א דאינה ראויה עדיין להיות זבה גדולה אם לא תראה יום ג'.

מאי דעתיך משום נפלים. תימה: דבלאו נפלים מלינן לאשכוחי יותר מק"נ כגון *יהודה וחזקיה, ואחר הולד השני תספור שמונים לנקבה ושבעה ימים לנדה ושני ימים אחרי כן! וי"ל: דלא שכיח. וא"ת: והלא בלא קושי משכחת כל ימיה שלא תהא זבה, כגון שהפילה אחר פ' לנקבה וז' לנדה וב' ימים אחר נדה. ובשלמא בסמוך גבי "יש רואה ק' ימים", איכא למימר דבחד ולד מיירי. אי נמי: בבן קיימא, אבל הכא מיירי בנפלים, מדקאמר "אין קושי לנפלים"? ויש לומר: דלא מיירי ביולדת בלא קשוי.

שיפורא גרים. פירוש: שופר שתוקעין בר"ח בקדוש החדש תשיעי של עיבורה. ואם תאמר: והיכי מוכח דחדש לבנה גרים, דילמא חדש תשיעי של אחר ח' חדשים של שלשים יום להריונה גרים, אפי' הוא מתחיל באמצע חדש הלבנה? וי"ל: דאם כן, הו"ל למימר "דיה חדש אחרון", אבל "חדשה" משמע: חדש המבורר, דהיינו חדש הלבנה. וקאי ש"מ אמתני' כמו אברייתא. א"נ משום דברייתא מוכחא דיולדת למקוטעים, כדקתני "אפילו בתחלת ט' ילדה", וליום אחד לא הוה קרי "חדשה". אבל חדש לבנה קרי שפיר "חדשה", אפי' יום אחד (כו'). אי נמי: מסיפא דברייתא מוכח, דע"כ חדש לבנה גרים, דקתני: אבל קשתה יום אחד בסוף שמיני, ושנים בתחלת תשיעי, ואפי' ילדה בסוף ט' כו' כו'. והיאך יכולה לידע דקשתה שנים בט' אי לא דמיירי בחידושה של לבנה?! דנהי דהיכא דילדה בסוף ט' יכולה לידע, כגון שילדה לרע"ג ימים לשמושה, דאז מתחיל תשיעי שלה שלשים יום לפני לידתה, דהזרע לא נקלט עד יום ג' לשמושה. דאי נקלט יום ראשון, היתה יולדת לרע"א לשמושה, דאין הולד משתהה יותר, °דלא קי"ל כרבה תוספאה דפרק "הערל" (יבמות דף פ:) מ"מ מדקאמר אפי' ילדה בסוף ט' משמע נמי שילדה באמצע תשיעי, ואז אי אפשר לדעת אם קשתה ב' ימים בט' בצמצום. דאי קשתה בר"מ, וברמ"א, וברמ"ב משמושה – שמא לא נקלט הזרע עד מחרת התשמיש, וא"כ לא קשתה אלא יום אחד בחדש ט'. ואם קשתה ברמ"א, ורמ"ב, ורמ"ג, שנקלט הזרע ביום התשמיש – א"כ ג' ימים קשתה בחדש ט'. אלא ודאי שיפורא גרים ונראה דלרבי יהודה שיפורא דט' חדשים גרים, ואם נתעברה בסוף החדש – יולדת בתחלת תשיעי. דאי בעינן שמונה הראשונים שלמים, א"כ כי נתעברה בסוף החדש שיפורא דט' – הוה ליה עשירי, אא"כ נתעברה בתחלת החדש. והא

---

**תוספי הרא"ש**

הראויין להיות בהן זבה גדולה. פר"ח לאפוקי עשירי וי"א דאין ראויין להתחיל בהן זבה גדולה א"נ לאפוקי יום ראשון ויום שני של י"א דאין ראויין להיות בהן זבה גדולה ולשון ראויין משמע כפירושו: מאי דעתיכו משום נפלים וכו'. ותימה בלא נפלים נמי משכחת לה (נמי) יותר מק"נ ימים כגון יהודה וחזקיה שנשתהו ג' חדשים זה אחר זה וי"ל דלא מילתא דלא שכיח הוא א"נ כשנתעברה תאומים לא קא מיירי: יש רואה ק' יום. ותימה כל ימיה משכחת לה דאחר שמונים של נקבה הפילה נקבה אחרת וי"ל דבחד ולד איירי א"נ היינו האי דפריך מאי קמ"ל דאי חידוש של ק' יום הא משכחת לה אפי' טובא ולר' מאיר משכחת לה כל ימיה כה"ג אלא אדר' מאיר קאי בלידת קושי: ש"מ קסבר ר' יהודה שיפורא גרים. שופר שתוקעין ב"ד בקידוש החדש דחד החדש של עיבור הוא לפי חידוש הלבנה ותימה דלמא דיה חדשה דקאמר היינו ל' יום האחרונים שהוא חדש תשיעי וי"ל דא"כ ה"ל למימר דיה חדש אחרון אבל חדשה משמע חדש המבורר דהיינו חדש הלבנה וקאי [ש"מ] אמתני' כמו אבריתא אלא שנקבע בתלמוד אחר הברייתא א"נ משום דברייתא מוכחא דיולדת למקוטעין מדקתני אפי' בתחלת תשיעי ילדה ולא מיקרי חדש לענין חדש העיבור כיון דאין בו אלא יום אחד וכו' שייך עליה למימר כמתניתין דיה חדשה. ונראה דר' יהודה בחדש ראשון של עיבור נמי שיפורא גרים ואם עיברה ביום אחרון של אדר יולדת בתחלת מרחשון כדקתני סוף ח' ותחלת ט' משמע דמילתא דפסיקא היא דאי אמרת דבעיא ח' חדשים הראשוני' שלימי' א"כ לא משכחת לה דשיפורא דט' גרים אלא א"כ נתעברה בתחלת החדש וא"כ לר' יהודה משכחת לה דאשה יולדת (לח) [לז] חדשים ובו' ימים: והאמר שמואל אין אשה מתעברת. לא הוה מצי למימר דר' יהודה איירי בנפלים מדנקט שמיני ותשיעי ולא נקט שלישי ורביעי:

---

**עין משפט נר מצוה**

לא נמצא זה בפירש"י שלפנינו

נז א מיי' פ"ה מהל' איסורי ביאה הל' ה':

[לעיל כז.]

נח ב מיי' שם הל' ח':

נט ג מיי' שם הל' ט' ועי' כס"מ:

**מסורת הש"ס**

[לעיל כה. וש"נ]

**הגהות הב"ח**

(א) רש"י ד"ה עד ארבעי':

**גליון הש"ס**

גמ' או למאתים ושבעים ושלשה. בירושלמי פ' החולץ אי' או לרע"ד וע' ביפה מראה שם: תוס' ד"ה שיפורא וכו' דלא קי"ל כרבה תוספאה. ע' לעיל כז ע"א תוס' ד"ה אלא:

**הגהות מהר"ב רנשבורג**

א] גמ' אבא שאול משמיה דרב אמר. נ"ב בסה"ד ד' קמט ע"ד לא ידעתי מי הוא ולפעמים אבא שאול משמיה דרבי וכו' פסחים קף פו ע"א לאבא שאול גבל בית רבי הוה: ב] שם אלא למאתים ושבעים וכו'. נ"ב ע' תבואת שור:

עין משפט
נר מצוה

ס א מיי' פ"ז מהל' איסורי ביאה הל"ט:
סא ב מיי' שם פ"ח הלי"א סמג לאוין קיא:

לידי חילול שבת. ברביעי ותו לא? אימא: מרביעי ואילך. אמר מר זוטרא: מאי טעמייהו דחסידים הראשונים – דכתיב: °"ויתן [ה'] לה הריון" "הריון" בגימטריא מאתן ושבעים וחד הוו. אמר מר זוטרא: אפי' למ"ד *יולדת לתשעה – אינה יולדת למקוטעים, יולדת לשבעה – יולדת למקוטעים, שנאמר: °"ויהי לתקופות הימים *ותהר חנה ותלד בן", מיעוט "תקופות" – שנים, מיעוט "ימים" – שנים.§ "רבי יוסי ור"ש אומרים אין קושי יותר מב' שבתות".§ אמר שמואל: מאי טעמייהו דרבנן – דכתיב: °"וטמאה שבועים כנדתה" – כנדתה ולא כזיבתה, מכלל – דזיבתה טהורה, וכמה – שבועים. ת"ר: יש מקשה עשרים וחמשה יום ואין זיבה עולה בהן. כיצד, שנים בלא עת, ושבעה נדה, וב' שלאחר נדה, וארבעה עשר שהולד מטהר. ואי אפשר שתתקשה עשרים וששה יום בלא ולד, ולא תהא יולדת בזוב. "בלא ולד"? בתלתא נמי סגי! אמר רב ששת, אימא: במקום שיש ולד. אמר ליה רבא: והא "בלא ולד" קתני! אלא אמר רבא, הכי קאמר: אי אפשר שתתקשה עשרים וששה יום במקום שיש ולד ולא תהא יולדת בזוב, ובמקום שאין ולד אלא נפל – בתלתא נמי הויא זבה, מ"ט? אין קושי לנפלים.§ **מתני'** [א]המקשה בתוך שמונים של נקבה – כל דמים שהיא רואה טהורין, עד שיצא הולד, ורבי אליעזר מטמא. אמרו לו לרבי אליעזר: ומה במקום שהחמיר בדם השופי – היקל בדם הקושי, מקום שהיקל בדם השופי – אינו דין שנקל בדם הקושי? אמר להן: דיו לבא מן הדין להיות כנדון, ממה היקל עליה – מטומאת זיבה, אבל טמאה טומאת נדה.§ **גמ'** תנו רבנן: "תשב" – לרבות המקשה בתוך שמונים של נקבה, שכל דמים שהיא רואה טהורין, עד שיצא הולד. ור"א מטמא. אמרו לו לר"א: ומה במקום שהחמיר בשופי שלפני הולד – היקל בשופי שלאחר הולד. מקום שהיקל בקושי שלפני הולד – אינו דין שנקל בקושי שלאחר הולד? אמר להם: דיו לבא מן הדין להיות כנדון, ממה היקל עליה – מטומאת זיבה, אבל מטמאה טומאת נדה. אמרו לו: °הרי אנו משיבין לך לשון אחר, ומה במקום שהחמיר בשופי שלפני הולד – היקל בקושי שעמו. מקום שהיקל בשופי שלאחר הולד – אינו דין שנקל בקושי שעמו? אמר להם: אפילו אתם משיבין כל היום כולו – דיו לבא מן הדין להיות כנדון, ממה היקל עליה – מטומאת זיבה, אבל מטמאה טומאת נדה. אמר רבא: בהא זכינהו ר"א לרבנן, לאו אמריתו "דמה" – דמה *מחמת עצמה ולא מחמת ולד, ה"נ – °"וטהרה ממקור דמיה" – דמיה מחמת עצמה ולא מחמת ולד. אימא: בימי נדה – נדה, בימי זיבה – טהורה! אמר קרא: "תשב" – ישיבה אחת לכולן.§ **מתני'** [ב]כל אחד עשר יום בחזקת טהרה: ישבה

תורה אור: רות ד; שמואל א א; ויקרא יב; שם

**דין** לבא מן הדין להיות כנדון. וא"ת: ובלא ק"ו נמי אמאי מטמא? תיפוק ליה דקושי לא גרע משופי, ולמה בשביל קישוי יש לה להיות טמאה? וי"ל: דטעמא דרבי אליעזר, כדמפרש רבא בגמרא, "דמיה" – מחמת עצמה, ולא מחמת ולד. ולכך צריך להו לרבנן ק"ו ומחמת ק"ו אית לן למדרש קרא דדמיה למילתא אחריתי. וליכא לאוקמי קרא אפי' בימי נדה, דליכא ק"ו דרבנן נמי דרשי "תשב" – ישיבה אחת לכולן. ורבי אליעזר סבר: דכיון דאיכא לאוקומי קרא בימי נדה, אפי' אי נימא ק"ו משום "דיו" אין לך לטהר אלא בימי זיבה, אבל בימי נדה – טמאה. ולדידיה אף בימי זיבה טמאה, משום "תשב" – ישיבה אחת לכולן, כדאמר בגמ'.
**אימא** בימי זיבה טהורה בימי נדה טמאה. פי' הקונטרס: ארבי אליעזר פריך, דמטמא אף בימי זיבה. מדקאמר ת"ק "כל דמים שהיא רואה – טהורה", ועלה קא"ר אליעזר דטמאה, ולא מפליג – משמע דאף בימי זיבה דטמאה. ו"דיו" דקא"ר אליעזר – לדבריהם דרבנן קאמר להו. והר"ר מנחם מפרש: דרבי אליעזר לא מטמא אלא בימי נדה, כדקאמר "דיו". והא דקפריך "ואימא בימי זיבה טהורה" – הוי סיום מילתא דרבא, דאמר: בהא זכינהו רבי אליעזר לרבנן, דהא מקרא ד"דמיה" הוו להו לרבנן לטמא בימי נדה, ולטהר בימי זיבה! ומשני: "תשב" – ישיבה אחת לכולן, וכיון דמק"ו מטהרין בימי זיבה, אית לן לטהר מקרא ד"תשב" אף בימי נדה, דהא משמע ישיבה אחת לכולן, ואין לחלק בהן, ואם כן קרא ד"דמיה" אתא למילתא אחריתי. והכי דרשינן לעיל בברייתא לרבנן מ"תשב" שכל דמיה טהורים. ואם תאמר: וכיון דאי לאו קרא ד"תשב" אף רבנן הוו מטמאין מקרא ד"דמיה", א"כ היכי בעו למעבד ק"ו דאף בימי נדה טהורה, דקאמרי "הרי אנו משיבין אותך בלשון אחר"? *וי"ל: דפרכינן ליה, כיון דמק"ו מוכיח דטהורה אף בימי נדה, אית לן למימר "דמיה" לדרשא אחריתי.

גי' רש"א וכו' במקום וי"ל וכ"ל בלשון אחר וכו' דפרכינן ליה כיון דמק"ו מוכח כו' וע"ש

לידי חילול שבת. שלא תלד בשבת, ויצטרך לחלל עליה את השבת. אלא מרביעי ואילך. אבל ליל שלישי וליל שני ומוצאי שבת – לא. דאי מתעברה למוצאי שבת – שמא תלד לרע"ג דמטי בשבת, ונמצא שבת מתחלל, שניתן רשות לחללו מפני סכנת גופה. והיכי דמי? עשה מרע"ג ימים שבועים, מאה ימים – הוו שבועים שווין, בר מתרי יומי. וכן לק' ימים האחרים שני ימים – הרי ארבע ימים עודפים על השבועים, וע' ימים – כולן שוים, וג' ימים תן על ד' העודפים – הרי שבוע. וכיון שהתחילו במוצאי שבת – נמצאו כלים בשבת. ואם נתעברה בשני – דלמא ילדה לרע"ב דמטי בשבת. ואם נתעברה בשלישי – דלמא ילדה לרע"א דמטי בשבת. אבל בד', אי ילדה לרע"א – מטי בחד בשבא, ואי לרע"ב – מטי בתרי בשבא, ואי לרע"ג – מטי בתלתא בשבא. אלמא כשמואל סבירי להו. (א) ברביעי ותו לא. כל שכן דאי מעברא בה' או בו' או בשבת, דלא מטי יום לידה בשבת. לתקופות הימים. כתיב. מיעוט ימים שנים. דכל מקום שנאמר "ימים" ולא נאמר כמה – תפוס המועט בידך, ולא המרובה. שאם אתה אומר: ימים שלשה או ארבעה – אני אומר: עשרה או ק'. כך שנו חכמים (סוכה דף ה.): כל שמשמעו מרובה ומשמעו מועטת, תפסת מרובה – לא תפסת, תפסת מועט – תפסת. הלכך, כאן שנאמר "ימים" – מכיון שנכנסו שני ימים בחדש שביעי, ילדה. מכלל דזיבתה טהורה. ומהכא גמרינן לעיל קושי בימי זיבה. יש מקשה. שרואה כ"ה יום בין קושי ובין שופי. שנים בלא עת וז' דנדה וב' לאחר נדה. בלא קושי. וי"ד בקושי. לרבי יוסי ולר"ש. והכא לא חשיב אלא קודם לידה, ואי אפשר למקשה כ"ו יום שלא תהא זבה – שהולד אינו מטהר אלא י"ד יום הסמוכים ללידה, ופשו להו ג' בין נדות לקושי, ובהנהו שלשה הויא זיבה. בלא ולד. לקמן פריך: משמע שאין שם ולד, א"כ לאו קושי הוא, ולמה לי כ"ו, בתלתא לאחר הנדה סגי? **מתני'** המקשה תוך שמונים. שנתעברה בימי טוהר, או שנשתהה ולד אחר חבירו ב' חדשים ואלי. אחד נגמרה צורתו באמצע שביעי, ואחד נגמרה צורתו לסוף תשיעי, כמעשה דיהודה וחזקיה בני ר' חייא (לעיל דף כז.). טהורין. דכל תוך מלאת הוי דם טוהר. ורבי אליעזר מטמא. נדה, דכיון דבקושי בא – לאו דם טוהר הוא, אלא מחמת ולד שבמעיה, ומזיבה הוא דטהור, אבל בימי נדה – נדה. שהחמיר בדם השופי. כגון שאר יולדת שרואה ג' בשופי, וילדה – הרי זו יולדת בזוב. היקל בדם הקושי. לטהרה מזובה. מקום שהיקל בדם השופי. לטהרה מכל טומאה, כגון תוך מלאת. אינו דין שנקל בדם הקושי. לטהרה מכל טומאה, ואפי' מנדות. דיו לבא מן הדין. כגון קושי של תוך מלאת, שאתם למדין מקושי דעלמא. להיות כנדון. כקושי דעלמא. **גמ'** תשב. "על דמי טהרה". עד שיצא הולד. יצא הולד – טמאה לידה. הרי אנו משיבין אותך לשון אחר. שלא נלמד קושי שלאחר (ב) מקושי שלפני, כדאמרי' לעיל: מקום שהיקל בקושי שלפני הולד, אינו דין שנקל בקושי שלאחריו. דהכא הוא דאיכא למימר: דיו לקושי שלאחריו להיות כקושי שלפניו, שהרי ממנו אנו למדים. אלא הכי גמרינן: מקום שהיקל בשופי שלאחריו, אינו דין שנקל בקושי שעמו, שעם השופי. דהשתא ילפינן קושי של אחריו דטהור לגמרי, וליכא למימר: ממה היקל מטומאת זיבה, כדקאמר. דיו לבא כו'. שהרי ק"ו אינו נידון אלא מכח קושי שלפניו, כדקתני: ומה במקום שהחמיר בשופי שלפני הולד, היקל בקושי שעמו. זכינהו. תשובה נצחת יכול להשיבן. אימא בימי נדה נדה. לר"א פריך: כיון דאית ליה "דיו", לודי מיהא דבימי זיבה טהורה כקושי שלפניו. כגון ראתה בקושי שבעה ימים ראשונים – תהא טמאה, ואם ראתה יותר – יהא הדם טהור, ותטבול לאחר שבעה ראשונים של קושי. ישיבה אחת לכולן. או כולן טהורין, או כולן טמאין. **מתני'** כל אחד עשר יום. אחר הנדות אשה עומדת בחזקת טהרה, ובגמרא מפרש למאי הלכתא. ישבה

מסורת הש"ס

[לעיל כז. בכורות כ.] ר"ה יא. יבמות מב.

[ולכאורה הטענין פליאה וכבן דע דז"ל הרד"ק לתקופת הימים ימי העיבור כתרגומו לזמן משלם יומיא ופירוש ותהר חנה שהרתה כבר כלאחר כלאה משילה ידעה אלקנה בעלה והרתה כמו שאמר ויזכרה ה' לתקופת הימים זהו כשהשלים ימי ההריון ילדה בן ויש ווין מורות לשעבר וכו']

[לעיל לו:]

הגהות הב"ח

(א) רש"י ד"ה ברביעי נ"ל קודם ד"ה אלא מרביעי: (ב) ד"ה הרי אנו וכו' קושי שלאחר הולד מקושי שלפני הולד כדאמרי' לעיל מקום שהיקל בקושי:

גליון הש"ס

**גמ'** הרי אנו משיבין לך. כזה במתני' דב"ק כה ע"א: **תום'** ד"ה והא וכו' אי נמי מדקתני ילדה וכו'. כדמשמע לעיל כו ע"ב הפילה נפל וכו' ילדה וכו':

תוספי הרא"ש

**אמר** להן דיו. ותימה דל ק"ו מהכא מנין לטמאו' אטו משום קישוי מיגרע גרע וי"ל דטעמא דר' אליעזר כדמפרש בגמ' וטהרה ממקור דמיה מחמת עצמה ולא מחמת ולד וטעמא דרבנן מתשב. ותימה כיון דטעמא דר' אליעזר מקרא מאי קאמרי לה ק"ו וי"ל דה"ק דמיסתבר למדרש קרא כדדרשי' אנן משום ק"ו ור' אליעזר השיבם דאפי' דרשיתו ק"ו אין לכם לטהר אלא בימי זיבה ומשום דיו אבל בימי נדה טמאה ומיהו ר' אליעזר אליבא דנפשיה ס"ל דאפי' בימי נדה טמאה כדפרשי' בגמ' ואימא בימי נדה נדה בימי זיבה טהורה ופרש"י דלר' אליעזר קפריך והא דפשיטא ליה לתלמודא דר' אליעזר מטמא אפי' בימי זיבה מדקתני סתמא ר' אליעזר מטמא ושמע דאיירי אפי' בימי זיבה דומיא דקישוי דאייר ביה בבבא קמייתא. ועוד כיון דדריש ליה מקרא משמע ליה דבכל ענין טמא. וה"ר מנחם פי' דר' אליעזר דוקא בימי נדה מטמא כדמוכח מדיו והא דאמר ואימא בימי נדה נדה בימי זיבה טהורה לאו לר' אליעזר קא פריך אלא מסקנא דמילתא דרבא היא דקאמר בהא זכנהו ר' אליעזר לרבנן ומפרש ואזיל היכי זכנהו ואע"ג דאית להו ק"ו יש לכם לטמאות בימי נדה מדכתיב דמיה ומשני אליבא דרבנן אמר קרא תשב ישיבה אחת לכולן וכיון דמטהרינן בימי זיבה ה"ה בימי נדה וכפר"ח ואסיקנא לרבנן ישיבה אחת לכולן:

**ישבה לה ולא בדקה** טמאה מפני שחזקת נשים רואות... 

א ישבה לה ולא בדקה, שגגה, נאנסה, הזידה ולא בדקה טהורה. הגיע שעת וסתה ולא בדקה הרי זו טמאה. *ר"מ אומר: ב אם היתה במחבא, והגיע שעת וסתה ולא בדקה – הרי זו טהורה, מפני *שחרדה מסלקת את הדמים. ג אבל ימי הזב והזבה, ושומרת יום כנגד יום הרי אלו בחזקת טומאה.§ **גמ'** למאי הלכתא? אמר רב יהודה: לומר שאינה צריכה בדיקה. והא מדקתני סיפא "ישבה ולא בדקה" מכלל דלכתחלה בעיא בדיקה! סיפא אתאן לימי נדה, ד וה"ק: כל י"א בחזקת טהרה ולא בעיא בדיקה, אבל בימי נדתה בעיא בדיקה. ישבה ולא בדקה, שגגה, נאנסה, הזידה ולא בדקה – טהורה. רב חסדא אמר: לא צריכא אלא לר"מ, דאמר: *אשה שאין לה וסת אסורה לשמש, ה"מ – בימי נדתה, אבל בימי זיבתה בחזקת טהרה קיימא. א"ה, אמאי א"ר מאיר: יוציא ולא יחזיר עולמית? דלמא אתיא לקלקולא בימי נדה. הא מדקתני סיפא "הגיע שעת וסתה ולא בדקה" מכלל דבאשה שיש לה וסת עסקינן! חסורי מחסרא והכי קתני: כל י"א בחזקת טהרה ושריא לבעלה, ובימי נדה אסורה. בד"א – באשה שאין לה וסת, אבל יש לה וסת מותרת, וצריכה בדיקה. ישבה ולא בדקה, שגגה, נאנסה, הזידה ולא בדקה – טהורה, הגיע שעת וסתה ולא בדקה טמאה. הא מדסיפא ר"מ – רישא לאו ר"מ! כולה ר"מ היא, וה"ק: אם לא היתה במחבא, והגיע שעת וסתה ולא בדקה טמאה, שר"מ אומר, אם היתה במחבא והגיע שעת וסתה ולא בדקה טהורה, שחרדה מסלקת את הדמים. *רבא אמר: לומר שאינה מטמאה מעת לעת. מיתיבי: ה הנדה, והזבה, והשומרת יום כנגד יום, והיולדת – כולן מטמאות מעת לעת. תיובתא. *רב *הונא בר חייא אמר שמואל: לומר ו שאינה קובעת לה וסת בתוך ימי זיבתה. *אמר רב יוסף: לא שמיע לי הא שמעתתא. א"ל אביי: את אמרת ניהלן ואהא אמרת לן, *ז היתה למודה להיות רואה יום ט"ו (יום) ושינתה ליום כ' – זה וזה אסורין לשמש. שינתה פעמים ליום כ' – זה וזה אסורין. ואמרת לן עלה אמר רב יהודה אמר שמואל: ל"ש אלא ט"ו לטבילתה שהן כ"ב לראייתה, דהתם בימי נדתה קאי לה, אבל ט"ו לראייתה, דבימי זיבתה קאי – לא קבעה. אמר רב פפא, אמריתא לשמעתא קמיה רב יהודה מדסקרתא: מקבע לא קבעה, מיחש מהו דניחוש לה? אישתיק ולא א"ל ולא מידי. אמר רב פפא: נחזי אנן, היתה למודה להיות רואה ליום ט"ו ושינתה ליום כ' – זה וזה אסורין. ואמר

**רש"י**

ישבה לה ולא בדקה. אכל נשים קאי, ולאו לעיל מהדר. טמאה. דאורח בזמנו בא. במחבא. מחמת ליסטין או (א) כרכום. ימי הזב. ימי ספירו. ושומרת יום. כיון שנפתח מעיינה וראתה היום, אע"ג דבתוך י"א היא, הויא למחר בחזקת טמאה. **גמ'** לומר שאינה צריכה בדיקה. שחרית וערבית, ומשעברו – צריכה לבדוק, כדאיתא בפ"ק (לעיל דף יא.). והא מדקתני סיפא ישבה. דמשמע דיעבד, מכלל כו'. והאי דפריך (ב) הכי, דס"ד דהאי "ישבה" – אתוך י"א קאי. לימי נדה. לימים שראויין לנדה, כגון אחר י"א שבין נדה לנדה. בחזקת טהרה. שנסתלקו דמיה בנדותה ואזלו. בימי נדה. לאחר שעברו י"א וראויים לבא ימי נדה. בעיא בדיקה. לכתחלה, אבל ישבה ולא בדקה – דיעבד טהורה. ואם הגיע וסת הקבוע לה, ולא בדקה – הויא ודאי טמאה. לא נצרכא. הא דקתני "כל י"א בחזקת טהרה" – אלא לר"מ, בסוף פרק ראשון בגמרא. אמאי יוציא. תשמש כל י"א? דלמא אתיא לקלקולא בימי נדה. בימים הראויים לנדה אסורה לשמש, שמא תקלקלנו. רבא אמר. מתני' דקתני "כל י"א בחזקת טהרה". לומר. שאם תראה בהם – אינה מטמאה מעת לעת, לפי שמסולקין דמיה. הנדה. כלומר, אשה שרואה דם – מטמאה מעת לעת בראיית תחלת נדותה. והזבה ושומרת יום. כלומר, והרואה בתוך י"א, בין שרואה ג' ימים דהויא זבה, בין שרואה יום אחד דהויא שומרת יום – מטמאה מעת לעת בראייה ראשונה. היולדת. שיצא דם בפתיחת הקבר – מטמאה מעת לעת בראייה ראשונה. חייא בר רב הונא. פי' אמתני' מהדר. בתוך ימי זיבתה. כגון ראתה ג' פעמים מט"ו לט"ו – אין זה וסת לענין דיה שעתה או לענין שאם לא בדקה תהיה טמאה, דמט"ו לט"ו הוו ימי זיבה. וכן כל הימים משישלמו ז' ימי נדות עד י"א, דשלמי ימי זיבה בהדי נדות. לא שמיע לי הא שמעתתא. דרב יוסף תלמידו דרב יהודה, שהוא תלמיד של רב ושמואל. וחלה רב יוסף, ונעקר תלמודו. וכשהיה שומע מימרא דרב ושמואל ואינו נזכר לאותה שמועה, מתמיה: ולאו תלמידו של רב יהודה אני? ולא אמר לי שמועה זו! ואביי תלמידו מזכירו (נדרים דף מא.). את אמרת ניהלן. קודם חולייך. ה"ג: ואהא אמרת ניהלן. על משנה זו אמרת לנו משמיה, דאין אשה קובעת לה וסת בימי זיבה. למודה. רגילה. יום ט"ו. לקמן מפרש: ליום ט"ו לטבילתה. ושינתה לה וסת. ליום כ' פעם אחת. זה וזה אסורין. אין צ"ל ט"ו שעבר שאסור – שהרי כל היום המתינה שמא תראה, דקי"ל דחייב אדם לפרוש מאשתו סמוך לוסתה. ואין צ"ל יום כ' שראתה בו – שהרי נדה היא. אלא ה"ק: כשיחזור ויגיע ט"ו – אסורה לשמש, שהרי יום וסתה הוא, ועדיין לא דילגתו אלא פעם אחת, ואין וסת נעקר בפחות מג"פ. וכשיגיע יום כ' לראייה של כ' – אסורה לשמש, שמא תקבע וסת מכ' לכ', שהרי שינתה פעם אחת ליום כ'. וכן פעמים ליום כ' זה וזה אסורין, יום ט"ו ויום כ' הבא. אבל ג' פעמים ליום כ' – הותר יום ט"ו ונאסר יום כ'. לא שנו. דליום ט"ו הוי וסת קבוע, דליבעי תלתא זימני למיעקריה. אלא שהיתה רגילה לראות יום ט"ו לטבילתה. לסוף ז' ימי נדה, ורואה ליום ט"ו שהוא יום כ"ב לראייתה. דכבר שלמו ימי זוב לסוף י"א, והרי ד' ימים שהגיעו ימים שראויה להיות בהם נדה. מקבע לא קבעה. בתוך ימי זיבה, דתבעי ג' זימני למיעקריה, דבחדא זימנא הוא דעקר לה, ואם ישבה ולא בדקה – טהורה. מיחש מהו דניחוש לה. אם היתה רגילה מט"ו לט"ו, דהיינו תוך ימי זוב, מי בעיא למיחש ולא תשמש ליום ט"ו קודם ראייה, שמא תראה? ואמר

[לעיל ט. טז.] [לקמן עה. סוטה כ:] [לעיל יב:] [לקמן סח:] [בס"י הגי' חייא בר ר"ה וכ"ג רש"י] [עירובין י. וש"נ] לקמן סג.

**תוספות**

**לא צריכא** (ג) לר"מ. ומועיל מה שהיא בחזקת טהרה, שמותרת לשמש כל זמן שלא גירשה. א"נ: אינו חייב לגרשה, עד שעברו י"א יום. **והיולדת** כולן מטמאות מעת לעת. אע"ג דמעוברת דיה שעתה – היינו בשאר דם שרואה כשהיא מעוברת, ולא בראיית דם לידה שרואה מחמת פתיחת הקבר. וי"מ דהכא כרבי יוסי, דבעי ג' עונות. א"נ: כגון שקודם כבר ראתה פעם אחת, וקסבר דבשני מטמאה מעת לעת, ולית ליה דיין שעתן כל ימי עיבורן. ואשמעינן: אע"ג דראייה שניה זו מחמת אונס לידה ראתה, אפ"ה מטמא מעת לעת. הקשה הר"ר יעקב מאורלייני"ש: דהכא תני זבה ושומרת יום מטמאה מעת לעת, ואפ"ה מפרש רב יהודה לעיל דכל י"א יום אינה צריכה בדיקה. ובפ"ק (לעיל דף יא.) אמרי' דאשה שיש לה וסת, וד' נשים, ואשה שעברו עליה ג' עונות – דיין שעתן, ותנא התם: אע"פ שאמרו "דיין שעתן", צריכות להיות בודקות! וי"ל: דיש לה וסת, איכא למימר, כיון דאורח בזמנו בא – צריכה בדיקה בשעת וסתה. והנך נמי איכא למימר דצריכה בדיקה, שלא תשתכח תורת בדיקה מהן. בתולת דמים – כשתראה, ומעוברת ומניקה – לכשיעברו ימי עיבורה ומניקותה, לפי שהורגלו זמן מרובה בלא בדיקה. וזקנה, אע"ג דלא אתיא תו לידי בדיקה, וליכא למיגזר בה מידי מ"מ גזר לה, אטו אחריני. אבל תוך י"א יום – אינה צריכה בדיקה, דזמן מועט הוא, ולא תשתכח תורת בדיקה, דאחר י"א יום תבדוק, וכן זמן מועט יש משבדקה. **רב** הונא בר חייא אמר שמואל לומר שאינה קובעת וסת בימי זיבתה. ולא מיבעיא בימי ספירת זיבה ממש דאינה קובעת, אלא משמע דאפי' בימים הראוים לזיבה, אע"ג דאינה זבה ומעיינה סתום – אינה קובעת. כגון שרואה פעם אחת תוך י"א יום. ופליג ארבי יוחנן ור"ל: דאמרי בסמוך: אשה קובעת לה וסת תוך ימי זיבתה ממש, דהיינו באמצע ספירת זיבתה דומיא דתוך ימי נדותה, וכ"ש דקובעת בימים הראויים לזיבה. וקי"ל כרבי יוחנן לגבי שמואל, כדאמר פרק "מי שהוציאוהו" (עירובין דף מז:).

**מקבע** לא קבעה ע"י ראייה זו. – של תוך ימי זיבה, לא קבעה וסתה, שתצטרך לעוקרו על ידי שלש פעמים כאילו קבעה וסת בימי נדה. אבל מהו שתחוש ע"י קביעות של ימי נדה לאסור פעם רביעי, אפי' בא הוסת בימי זיבה? והא מייתי שפיר דחיישינן. אלמא

[לקמן סח:]

**עין משפט נר מצוה**

סב א מיי' פ"ח מהל' איסורי ביאה הלי"ב ופ"ג מהל' מטמאי משכב ומושב הל"ה סמג לאוין קיא טוש"ע יו"ד סימן קצו סעי' ד:

סג ב (מיי' שם) סמג שם טוש"ע שם סי' קפד סעיף ח:

סד ג עי' במיי' שם פ"ז הל' כא כב:

סה ד מיי' שם פ"ח הלכה יא:

סו ה מיי' פ"ג מהל' משכב ומושב הל"ד:

סז ו מיי' פ"ח מהל' איסורי ביאה הל"ט סמג לאוין קיא טור יו"ד סימן קפט:

סח ז מיי' שם הל"ח סמג שם טוש"ע יו"ד סי' קפט סעי' ב וסעי' יד:

**הגהות הב"ח**

(א) רש"י ד"ה במחבא וכו' ככרכוס. נ"ב משנה דכתובות דף סה ושם מבואר: (ב) ד"ה והא מדקתני וכו' דפריך הכי קס"ד דהאי: (ג) תוס' ד"ה לא צריכא אלא לר"מ:

**תוספי הרא"ש**

**לא** צריכא לר' מאיר כו'. ותימה וכיון דצריך להוציא משום דילמא אתי לקלקולא בימי נדה מאי נפקא מינה דאחד עשר בחזקת טהרה וי"ל דנפקא מינה דמותרת לשמש כל זמן שלא גירשה. א"נ דלא אתי חיוב לגרשה עד שיעברו י"א יום: **והיולדת** כולן מטמאות מעת לעת. אע"ג דמעוברת דייה שעתה הכא שיצא דם לפתיחת הקבר שאני אי נמי כר' יוסי דבעי הפסקה ג' עונות א"נ כגון שראתה פעם אחת ולית ליה הדיין כל ימי עיבורן: **לומר** שאינה קובעת וסת בתוך ימי זיבתה. ה"פ דמתני' כל י"א יום בחזקת טהרה כלומר היא בחזקת שאינה רואה והיא מסולקת מדמים הילכך אפי' אירע שראתה ג' פעמים בתוך ימי זיבתה מקרה בעלמא הוא ולא הוי קביעות וסת: מיחש מהו דתיחוש ליה. פירש"י אם היתה למודה לראות מט"ו לט"ו מהו שתחוש לפרוש מבעלה כשיגיע זמן וסתה ופשיט ליה רב פפא מהא דאמרינן היכא דשינתה לכ"ז דכי הדדי אתו כ"ב קיימא בתוך ימי זיבתה וקתני זה וזה אסור וכי היכי דחוששת כשיגיע זמן וסתה בתוך ימי זיבתה לוסת שקבעה חוץ לימי זיבה ה"ה חוששת לוסת שקבעה בתוך ימי זיבתה. וניחא טפי לפרושי הכי מיקבע לא קבעה בימי זיבתה מיחש מהו שתחוש בתוך ימי זיבתה לוסת שקבעה חוץ לימי זיבתה מי אמרינן כי היכי דלא קבעי לה וסת בתוך ימי זיבתה משום שהיא מסולקת דמים. הכי נמי אינה צריכה לפרוש כשיגיע זמן וסתה בתוך ימי זיבתה:

וְאָמַר רַב יְהוּדָה אָמַר שְׁמוּאֵל, ל"ש אֶלָּא ט"ו לִטְבִילָתָהּ שֶׁהֵן כ"ב לִרְאִיָּיתָהּ, וְשִׁינְּתָה לְיוֹם כ"ז דְּכִי הָדְרִי וְאָתוּ עֶשְׂרִין וְתַרְתֵּי — קַיְימָא לָהּ בְּתוֹךְ יְמֵי זִיבָתָהּ, וְקָתָנֵי "זֶה וְזֶה אֲסוּרִין" — אַלְמָא [א]דְּחָיְישִׁינַן לָהּ. וְקָסָבַר רַב פַּפָּא: עֶשְׂרִין וְתַרְתֵּין — מֵעֶשְׂרִין וְתַרְתֵּין מָנֵינַן, נִדָּה וּפִתְחָה — מֵעֶשְׂרִין וְז' מָנֵינַן. א"ל רַב הוּנָא בְּרֵיהּ דְּרַב יְהוֹשֻׁעַ לְרַב פַּפָּא: מִמַּאי? דִּלְמָא עֶשְׂרִין וְתַרְתֵּין נַמִי מֵעֶשְׂרִין וְז' מָנֵינַן, דְּכִי הָדְרִי וְאָתוּ עֶשְׂרִין וְתַרְתֵּין — קַיְימָא לָהּ בְּתוֹךְ יְמֵי נִדּוּתָהּ. וה"נ מִסְתַּבְּרָא. דְּאִי לָא תֵּימָא הָכִי, הַאי תַּרְנְגוֹלְתָּא דְּרָמְיָא יוֹמָא וְכָבְשָׁה יוֹמָא, וְרָמְיָא יוֹמָא וְכָבְשָׁה יוֹמָא, וְכָבְשָׁה תְּרֵי יוֹמֵי וְרָמְיָא חַד יוֹמָא, כִּי הָדְרָה נָקְטָה — כִּדְלְקַמֵּיהּ נָקְטָה אוֹ כִּדְמֵעִיקָּרָא נָקְטָה? עַל כָּרְחָךְ כִּדְלְקַמֵּיהּ נָקְטָה! א"ל רַב פַּפָּא, אֶלָּא הָא דְּאָמַר ר"ל: *אִשָּׁה קוֹבַעַת לָהּ וֶסֶת בְּתוֹךְ יְמֵי זִיבָתָהּ, וְאֵין אִשָּׁה קוֹבַעַת לָהּ וֶסֶת בְּתוֹךְ יְמֵי נִדּוּתָהּ. וְרַבִּי יוֹחָנָן אָמַר: אִשָּׁה קוֹבַעַת לָהּ וֶסֶת בְּתוֹךְ יְמֵי נִדּוּתָהּ, ה"ד? לָאו כְּגוֹן דַּחֲזַאי רֵישׁ יַרְחָא, וְחַמְשָׁא בְּיַרְחָא, וְרֵישׁ יַרְחָא, וְחַמְשָׁא בְּיַרְחָא, וְהָשְׁתָּא חֲזַאי בְּחַמְשָׁא בְּיַרְחָא, וּבְרֵישׁ יַרְחָא לָא חֲזַאי, וְקָאָמַר: אִשָּׁה קוֹבַעַת לָהּ וֶסֶת בְּתוֹךְ יְמֵי נִדּוּתָהּ — אַלְמָא, מֵרֵישׁ יַרְחָא מָנֵינָא! א"ל: לָא, הָכִי א"ר יוֹחָנָן: [ב]כְּגוֹן דַּחֲזַאי רֵישׁ יַרְחָא, וְרֵישׁ יַרְחָא, וְעֶשְׂרִין וַחֲמִשָּׁה בְּיַרְחָא, וְרֵישׁ יַרְחָא, דְּאָמְרִינַן דְּמֵי יְתֵירֵי הוּא דְּאִתּוֹסְפוּ בָּהּ. וְכֵן כִּי אֲתָא רָבִין וְכָל נָחוֹתֵי יַמָּא, [ג]אֲמָרוּהָ כְּרַב הוּנָא בְּרֵיהּ דְּרַב יְהוֹשֻׁעַ.§

## הדרן עלך בנות כותים

וְאָמַר רַב יְהוּדָה. דְּהַאי ט"ו הַיְינוּ לִטְבִילָה, שֶׁהוּא כ"ב לִרְאִיָּיתָהּ, וְשִׁינְּתָה לְכ"ז. וְקָתָנֵי: דְּכִי מָטֵי יוֹם כ"ב – אֲסוּרָה לְשַׁמֵּשׁ. וְקס"ד דְּהַאי כ"ב לָאו לִרְאִיַּית הַדִּילּוּג קָאָמַר, אֶלָּא כ"ב לְאוֹתוֹ יוֹם שֶׁהָיְתָה רְאוּיָה לִרְאוֹת בּוֹ וְדִילַּגְתּוֹ, דְּהָוֵי יוֹם י"ז לִרְאִיָּיתָהּ, וּבְתוֹךְ יְמֵי זִיבָה הִיא לִרְאִיַּית כ"ז. (א) וְקָתָנֵי אֲסוּרָה. דְּכִי הָדַר אָתוּ כ"ב לְחֶשְׁבּוֹן יוֹם שֶׁהָיְתָה רְאוּיָה לִרְאוֹת בּוֹ כְּשֶׁדִּילְּגָה בָּהּ, קַיְימָא לָהּ בִּימֵי זִיבָה לְחֶשְׁבּוֹן רְאִיָּיתָהּ, כִּדְפָרֵישִׁית. וְקָסָבַר רַב פַּפָּא: יוֹם עֶשְׂרִין וְתַרְתֵּין דְּאָסְרִינַן עֲלָהּ – מִיּוֹם כ"ב מָנֵינַן. כְּלוֹמַר לָאו כ"ב לִרְאִיַּית דִּילּוּגָהּ שֶׁהָיָה בְּכ"ז, אֶלָּא כ"ב מִיּוֹם שֶׁהָיְתָה רְאוּיָה לִרְאוֹת לִימּוּדָהּ. וּמִדְּקָרֵי לְהוּ רַב פַּפָּא "יְמֵי זִיבָה", קָסָבַר: נִדָּה וּפִתְחָהּ יְמֵי נִדּוּתָהּ וְזוּבָהּ, מֵעֶשְׂרִין וְז' מָנֵינַן. דְּהַיְינוּ, מִיּוֹם רְאִיַּית דִּילּוּגָהּ, וּמִיּוֹם רְאִיַּית כ"ז עַד הַשְׁתָּא, לָא הָווּ *(לָהּ) י"ז. דְּאִי לְיוֹם שֶׁרְאוּיָה לִרְאוֹת כְּשֶׁדִּילְּגָה מָנֵינַן יְמֵי נִדּוּת וְזוֹב, לָא הֲוָה קָרֵי לְהוּ "יְמֵי זוֹבָהּ", דְּהָא חָלְפוּ לְהוּ כ"ב מֵהַהוּא יוֹמָא. פִּתְחָה. קָרֵי חֶשְׁבּוֹן הַנִּדָּה לִימֵי הַנִּדָּה וְזוֹב. מִמַּאי. דְּהַאי יוֹם כ"ב דְּאָסְרִינַן לֵיהּ מָנֵינַן מִיּוֹם כ"ב שֶׁהָיְתָה רְאוּיָה לִרְאוֹת כְּשֶׁדִּילְּגָה, דְּמָטֵי לֵיהּ בִּימֵי זִיבָה לְחֶשְׁבּוֹן רְאִיָּיה שֶׁרָאֲתָה בְּכ"ז. דִּלְמָא. הַאי יוֹם כ"ב דְּאָסְרִינַן עֲלָהּ, מָנֵינַן מִיּוֹם רְאִיָּיתָהּ, שֶׁכְּבָר שָׁלְמוּ יְמֵי זוֹב, כִּי הָדְרִי אָתוּ הָנָךְ כ"ב וְקַיְימָא לָהּ ד' יָמִים בַּיָּמִים הָרְאוּיִם לְנִדּוּת. (ב) וְהָכִי מִסְתַּבְּרָא. דְּהָא מִשּׁוּם דְּחָיְישִׁינַן שֶׁמָּא תַּחְזוֹר לְקַדְמוּתָהּ לִרְאוֹת מִכ"ב לְכ"ב אָסְרִינַן לָהּ, דְּהַשְׁתָּא הָוֵי כ"ב לִרְאִיָּיה. אֲבָל לְיוֹם כ"ב לְחֶשְׁבּוֹן יוֹם שֶׁהָיְתָה רְאוּיָה לִרְאוֹת – לָא מָצֵי אָסְרִינַן מִשּׁוּם הָא חֲשָׁשָׁא. דַּאֲפִי' חוֹזֶרֶת לְקַדְמוּתָהּ, לֹא תִּרְאֶה הַיּוֹם שֶׁהוּא י"ז לִרְאִיָּיתָהּ – דְּהַהִיא לֹא הָיְתָה לְמוּדָה לִרְאוֹת אֶלָּא לְכ"ב לִרְאִיָּיה. וְאִי מִשּׁוּם שֶׁהוּא כ"ב לַיּוֹם הָרָאוּי לָהּ – אֵין זֶה דֶּרֶךְ הַחוֹזֶרֶת לְוִסְתָּהּ, לְקַצֵּר יְמֵי טָהֳרָתָהּ וּלְמַהֵר יְמֵי רְאִיָּיתָהּ, כְּדֵי שֶׁיָּבֹא לְפִי חֶשְׁבּוֹן שֶׁל תְּחִלָּה, אֶלָּא חוֹזֶרֶת וְקוֹבַעַת כ"ב לַיּוֹם שֶׁרָאֲתָה. דְּאִלת"ה הַאי תַּרְנְגוֹלְתָּא דְּרָמְיָא יוֹמָא וְכָבְשָׁה יוֹמָא וְרָמְיָא יוֹמָא וְכָבְשָׁה תְּרֵי יוֹמֵי וְרָמְיָא יוֹמָא כִּי הָדְרָה נָקְטָה (ג) כִּדְלְקַמָּן נָקְטָה כו'. כְּלוֹמַר, תַּרְנְגוֹלֶת הָרְגִילָה לְהַטִּיל בֵּיצָה הַיּוֹם, וְלַעֲמוֹד לְמָחָר, וּלְהַטִּיל יוֹם ג' וְלַעֲמוֹד יוֹם ד'. וְשִׁינְּתָה וִסְתָּהּ, וְעָמְדָה מִלֶּדֶת יוֹם ה' עִם יוֹם ד', דְּהָווּ לְהוּ תְּרֵי יוֹמֵי, וְרָמְיָא יוֹם שִׁשִּׁי "כִּי הָדְרָה נָקְטָה", אִם הִיא חוֹזֶרֶת לְמִנְהָגָהּ לְהַטִּיל יוֹם וְלַעֲמוֹד יוֹם. כִּדְלְקַמֵּיהּ נָקְטָה. מֵעַכְשָׁיו הִיא חוֹזֶרֶת לִמְנוֹת, כְּגוֹן שֶׁעוֹמֶדֶת יוֹם ז' שֶׁאַחַר יוֹם ו' שֶׁהֵטִילָה, וּמַטֶּלֶת יוֹם שְׁמִינִי. אוֹ כִּדְמֵעִיקָּרָא נָקְטָה. לְפִי חֶשְׁבּוֹן שֶׁהָיְתָה רְאוּיָה לְהַטִּיל מִתְּחִלָּה, שֶׁהָיְתָה רְאוּיָה לֵילֵד בְּה', וְלַעֲמוֹד בְּו', וּלְהַטִּיל בְּז', וְלַעֲמוֹד בְּח', הַשְׁתָּא מַטִּילָה יוֹם ז' עִם ו' כְּנֶגֶד ב' יָמִים שֶׁעָמְדָה, כְּדֵי שֶׁתַּעֲמוֹד בְּיוֹם ח' כְּפִי שֶׁהָיְתָה רְאוּיָה לַחֶשְׁבּוֹן הָרִאשׁוֹן. עַל כָּרְחָךְ כִּדְלְקַמֵּיהּ נָקְטָה. וְהָא אִשָּׁה נַמִי, כְּשֶׁחוֹזֶרֶת לְוִסְתָּהּ לִרְאוֹת לְיוֹם כ"ב – לָאו לְפִי חֶשְׁבּוֹן הָרִאשׁוֹן, אֶלָּא לְיוֹם כ"ב לִרְאִיָּיתָהּ. הִלְכָּךְ, הַאי יוֹמָא הוּא דְּאָסְרִינַן. א"ל רַב פַּפָּא אֶלָּא הָא דְּאָמַר כו' אֵין אִשָּׁה קוֹבַעַת לָהּ וֶסֶת תּוֹךְ יְמֵי נִדּוּתָהּ. בַּיָּמִים שֶׁהִיא נִדָּה, כִּדְבָעֵינַן לְפָרוּשֵׁי מִילְּתָא דְּרַבִּי יוֹחָנָן: דַּחֲזַאי רֵישׁ יַרְחָא, וְה' בְּיַרְחָא, וְרֵישׁ יַרְחָא, וְה' בְּיַרְחָא. וְהַשְׁתָּא חֲזַאי בְּה' בְּיַרְחָא – דְּהָווּ לְהוּ ג' זִימְנֵי בְּה' בְּיַרְחָא, וּמֵעַכְשָׁיו יִהְיֶה לָהּ וֶסֶת בְּה' בַּחֹדֶשׁ. לְרֵישׁ לָקִישׁ לָא הֲוָה וֶסֶת – דְּהָא תְּרֵי זִימְנֵי קַמָּאֵי דְּה' בְּיַרְחָא הָוֵי תּוֹךְ יְמֵי נִדּוּתָהּ מַמָּשׁ, דְּהָא נִדָּה הָוְיָא מֵרֵישׁ יַרְחָא. וּפַעַם ג' הֲוָה יְמֵי נִדָּה, לְפִי חֶשְׁבּוֹן הָרָאוּי שֶׁהָיְתָה רְאוּיָה לִרְאוֹת רֵישׁ יַרְחָא. וּמִדְּקָרֵי לְפַעַם ג' "תּוֹךְ יְמֵי נִדָּה" – אַלְמָא לְפִי חֶשְׁבּוֹן הָרָאוּי מָנֵינַן. א"ל לֹא אֶלָּא הָכִי א"ר יוֹחָנָן. כְּגוֹן דְּחָזְיָא תְּרֵי זִימְנֵי בְּרֵישׁ יַרְחָא, וּפַעַם שְׁלִישִׁית בְּכ"ה, וּרְבִיעִית בְּר"ח, דְּה"ל הָךְ רְאִיָּיתָהּ בַּתְרַיְיתָא שֶׁהִיא שְׁלִישִׁית לִרְאִיָּיה שֶׁל ר"ח בְּתוֹךְ יְמֵי נִדּוּתָהּ מַמָּשׁ, שֶׁהִיא נִדָּה מִיּוֹם כ"ה. וּמש"ה קָרֵי לְהוּ "תּוֹךְ יְמֵי נִדּוּתָהּ", דְּהָא נִדָּה הִיא. וְטַעְמָא מַאי הָוֵי קְבִיעוּת, הָא אוֹרְחָהּ בְּהָכִי שֶׁנִּפְתַּח מַעְיָינָהּ – מִשּׁוּם דְּקָאָמַר: הָךְ רְאִיָּיה דְּרֹאשׁ חֹדֶשׁ, רְאִיַּית וִסְתָּהּ הִיא, וְהַיּוֹם זְמַנָּהּ. וְהַאי דְּאַקְדִּים וַחֲזַאי בְּכ"ה – דָּמִים יְתֵירֵי אִיתּוֹסְפוּ בָּהּ. אֲמָרוּהָ. לְהָא דְּרַבִּי יוֹחָנָן. כְּרַב הוּנָא. וּכְדִמְתָרְצִינַן.

## הדרן עלך בנות כותים

**אלמא** מריש ירחא מנינן. וא"ת: דילמא משום ראיה ראשונה קרי ליה "תוך ימי נדה"? *ופרש"י: דדייק מדקאמר "קובעת תוך ימי נדותה" משמע דפעם ג' דהוא הקביעות, (ד) הוי כימי נדתה. אלמא חשיב כאילו ראתה ריש ירחא. והקשה לו ריב"א: דלמה לא תירץ לו כגון שראתה ריש ירחא וה' בירחא שלשה זימני, דהשתא הוי ממש תוך ימי נדתה, וקבעה וסת ודיה שעתה אם תראה בחמשה בירחא של חדש ד' או שצריכה לפרוש מבעלה כל ה' בירחא עד שתעקור וסתה ג' פעמים? והשיבו רש"י: משום דבפ"ק (לעיל דף יא.) מוקמינן דר' יוחנן במעיין סתום משום דפריך אמתניתין דהתם דקתני דבימי נדתה אינה צריכה בדיקה ולבדוק דלמא קבעה לה וסת כרבי יוחנן ולכך המקשה אוקי הכא מילתיה דר' יוחנן במעיין סתום שראתה בג' ה' בירחא ולא בריש ירחא דראייה שלישית היא ממעיין סתום ומתניתין דפ"ק (שם דף יא.) כגון שראתה תרי זימני ריש ירחא וה' בירחא ובשלישית כי ראתה ריש ירחא לא תבדוק בה' בירחא שאפילו תראה לא קבעי' לה וסת, דמעיין פתוח הוא. אבל פעם ראשונה ושניה בודקת בימי נדה שמא תראה בג' בה' בירחא ולא בריש ירחא. ולהכי לא הוה מצי לשנויי כגון דראתה ג' זימני ריש ירחא וה' בירחא, דא"כ הוה ליה מעיין פתוח. אלא משני כגון שראתה תרי זימני ריש ירחא לחוד, דהוי מעיין סתום, ובג' נמי אע"ג דכבר ראתה בכ"ה מה שראתה בריש ירחא חשיב מעיין סתום כדמשני דהא דחזאי בכ"ה דמים יתרים הוא דאתוספו בה. ועוד נראה לפרש דהכא דייק דחשיב כאילו ראתה בג' בריש ירחא. דאי לאו הכי, אמאי קבעה לה וסת, הלא ראיה זו אינה מעין האחרות שבאו בימי נדותה. ומיהו תימה לומר *כיון כדמעיקרא נקטה וחשיב כאילו ראתה ריש ירחא, כיון דאכתי לא קבעה לה וסת בריש ירחא. דלא דמי לההיא דלעיל, דכבר קביע לה וסת לכ"ב כדקאמר "היתה למודה לראות". ונראה לפרש: דמיירי כגון שראתה ג' זמני בריש ירחא וה' בירחא. ואין לחוש אם אין התלמוד מזכיר תלתא זימני, דה"נ בפ"ק (שם דף יא.) לא קאמר תלתא זימני גבי "קפצה וראתה". והא דנקט והשתא חזאי בה' בירחא ובריש ירחא לא חזאי – לאו משום דע"י ראייה זו השתא קבעה לה וסת, דהא קבעה לה כבר מג' זימני קמאי. אלא לומר לך שדיה שעתה בראייה זו, כדרבי דוסא דאמר בפ"ק (לעיל דף ד:) דאין דיה שעתה אלא בשעת וסת דוקא. ומיהו אף בלא ראתה השתא הוה מצי למימר דקבעה לה וסת לענין שאסורה בה' בירחא עד שתעקור הוסת ג' פעמים. והשתא מוכח אע"ג דברביעי לא חזאי ריש ירחא קבעה לה וסת בה' בירחא משום דכיון שראתה ג' זימנין ה' בירחא גם בחדש ד' חשוב כאילו ראתה ריש ירחא, וה"נ כ"ב מכ"ב מנינן. והוי מצי למימר: וליטעמיך דאוקמית מילתיה דר' יוחנן במעין פתוח, א"כ תקשה מתני' דפ"ק (שם דף יא.) דקתני דאינה בודקת בימי נדה. א"נ הא חשיב מעיין סתום, ומעיין פתוח יפרש כמו שפירש"י בלשון שני בפ"ק (שם יא.) שראתה אבג"ד, ובהכי איירי מתני' דהתם, דבהכי לא קבעה לה וסתה.

## הדרן עלך בנות כותים

עין משפט נר מצוה

סט א מיי' פ"ח מהל' איסורי ביאה הל"ט סמג שם טוש"ע יו"ד סי' קפט סעי' יד:

ע ב טור יו"ד סי' קפט:

עא ג טוש"ע יו"ד סי' קפט סעיף יד:

לא נמצא זה בפירש"י שלפנינו

גי' רש"א כאן

### תוספי הרא"ש

**אלא** הא דאמר ריש לקיש כו'. בין ריש לקיש בין ר' יוחנן מודו דקובעת וסת בתוך ימי זיבתה ופליגי אשמואל דאמר אין אשה קובעת לה וסת בתוך ימי זיבתה. ולשמואל לא מיבעיא בימי זיבה ממש דאינה קובעת אלא אפי' בימים הראויין לזיבה אינה קובעת כדמוכח לעיל. ולר' יוחנן לא מיבעיא בדמים הראויים לזיבה אלא אפי' בימי זיבה קובעת דבהכי איירי הכא דומיא דתוך ימי נדתה: **אלמא מריש** ירחא מנינן. ותימה דילמא משום ראיות ראשונות קרי להו תוך ימי נדתה וי"ל אי לאו משום מריש ירחא מנינן לא הוה קובעת וסת כיון שאין השלישי מעין האחרים שהיו בימי נדה. א"נ א) משמע ליה דקביעות וסת חל בתוך ימי נדתה דהיינו ראייה שלישית שבן נקבעה הוסת. ומי' תימה לומר הכי דכל דמעיקרא נקט וחשיבא כאילו ראתה בריש ירחא מאחר דאכתי לא קבעה לה וסת בריש ירחא דלא דמי לההיא דלעיל דכבר קבעה לה וסת בהכי וי"ל דמיירי הכא כגון דחזאי ג' זימני בריש ירחא וחמשא בירחא אלא שהתלמוד לא חש להאריך כמו קפצה וראתה קפצה וראתה דלעיל לא נקט אלא תרי זימני ולפי זה הא דנקט והשתא חזאי בחמשא בירחא ובריש ירחא לא חזאי לא נקיט ליה משום דהוי השתא קביעות וסת דידה אלא לומר שדיה שעתה בראיה זו ואליבא דמ"ד בפ"ק דלא אמרינן דיה שעתה אלא בשעת וסתה ואי לא דחשבי' לה כאילו ראתה בריש ירחא לא הוה חמשא בירחא זמן וסתה דלא קבעה לה וסת אלא בתוך ימי נדתה. ולפי דברי רב פפא קשה מתני' דפ"ק לר' יוחנן דכולן צריכין להיות בודקת חוץ מן הנדה דתיבדוק דילמא קבעה לה וסת דליכא לשנויי כי קאמר ר' יוחנן דחזאי ממעיין סתום דכה"ג קרי מעין פתוח כשראיות הראשונות בימי נדה כדפרי' התם רש"י מתוך כך נראה כלשון אחרון דפי' שם רש"י: **סליק פרק בנות כותים בס"ד**

[נ"ל אלא]

[לעיל יא.]

### הגהות הב"ח

(א) רש"י ד"ה ואמר ר' יהודה וד"ה וקתני הד"א: (ב) ד"ה והכי נמי מסתבר': (ג) ד"ה דאי לא תימא וכו' הדרה נקטה כד לקמיה נקטה: (ד) תוס' ד"ה אלמא וכו' הקביעות הויא בימי נדתה:

א) נ"ל דמשמע ליה דהא דקאמר דקביעות וכו' ראיה שלישית שבה נקבעת.

## משנה וגמרא

תורה אור

**יוצא** [א]דופן – אין יושבין עליו ימי טומאה וימי טהרה, ואין חייבין עליו קרבן. *ר"ש אומר: הרי זה כילוד. [ב]כל הנשים מטמאות בבית החיצון, שנאמר: °"דם יהיה זובה בבשרה" (ויקרא טו). אבל הזב ובעל קרי – [ג]אינן מטמאין, עד שתצא טומאתן לחוץ. *[ד]היה אוכל בתרומה, והרגיש שנזדעזעו אבריו – אוחז באמה, ובולע את התרומה. [ה]ומטמאין בכל שהוא, אפילו כעין החרדל ובפחות מכן.§ **גמ'** א"ר מני בר פטיש: מאי טעמייהו דרבנן, אמר קרא: °"אשה כי תזריע וילדה זכר" (שם יב) – עד שתלד במקום שהיא מזרעת. ור"ש – ההיא, דאפילו *לא ילדה אלא כעין שהזריעה, אמו טמאה לידה. *ור"ש מאי טעמיה? אמר ר"ל, אמר קרא: "תלד" – *לרבות יוצא דופן. ורבנן – האי מבעי ליה לרבות טומטום ואנדרוגינוס. דסלקא דעתך אמינא: "זכר" ונקבה כתיב – זכר ודאי, נקבה ודאית, ולא טומטום ואנדרוגינוס, קמ"ל. ורבי שמעון – נפקא ליה מדתני בר ליואי. דתני בר ליואי: "לבן" – לבן מכל מקום, "לבת" – לבת מ"מ. ורבנן – האי מבעי ליה לחייב על כל בן ובן, ולחייב על כל בת ובת. ורבי שמעון – נפקא ליה מדתני *תנא קמיה דרב ששת: °"זאת תורת היולדת" (שם) – [ו]מלמד שמביאה קרבן אחד על ולדות הרבה. יכול תביא על לידה ועל זיבה כאחת? אלא יולדת דאכלה דם, ויולדת דאכלה חלב – בחד קרבן תסגי לה?! אלא: יכול תביא על לידה שלפני מלאת ועל לידה שלאחר מלאת כאחת – [ז]ת"ל: "זאת". ורבנן – אע"ג דכתיב "זאת", איצטריך "לבן או לבת", סד"א: ה"מ בתרי עיבורי (רש"ל מ"ז) (דחד הוי נפל) אבל בחד עבורא, כגון *יהודה וחזקיה בני ר' חייא, אימר בחד קרבן סגי לה, קמ"ל. *א"ר יוחנן: ומודה רבי שמעון בקדשים – [ח]שאינו קדוש. מאי טעמא, גמר לידה לידה מבכור, מה התם – פטר רחם, אף כאן – פטר רחם. ולגמר לידה מאדם, מה התם – יוצא דופן, אף כאן – יוצא דופן? מסתברא, מבכור הוה ליה למילף שכן "אמו" מ"אמו". אדרבה, מאדם הוה ליה למילף, שכן פשוט מפשוט! אלא, מבכור הוה ליה למילף, שכן: אם, בהמת קדשים, פגול, נותר, וטמא. אדרבה, מאדם הוה ליה למילף, שכן: פשוט, זכר, קדוש, במתנה! הנך נפישן. אמר רב חייא בריה דרב הונא משמיה דרבא: תניא דמסייע ליה לר' יוחנן, *ר' יהודה אומר: °"זאת תורת העולה היא העולה" (שם ו) – הרי אלו ג' מיעוטין, פרט

## רש"י

**יוצא** דופן. על ידי סם נפתחו מעיה, והוציאו את העובר לחוץ, ונתרפאת. כל הנשים. לענין נדה. מטמאות. מכי אתא דם לבית החיצון, אע"ג דהעמידוהו כותלי רחמה. בבשרה. משמע: בתוך בשרה. לחוץ. בגמרא יליף לה. שנזדעזעו אבריו. נעקר שכבת זרע מגופו. **גמ'** אלא כעין שהזריעה. כגון נימוק הולד, כדאמר ב"המפלת" (לעיל כו.): שליא בבית – הבית טמא כו'. רבי שמעון אומר: הולד נימוק. ואמר בגמרא: מודה רבי שמעון שאמו טמאה לידה, ויליף טעמא מהכא. אבל רבנן לא צריך להו קרא להכי, דהא לדידהו כיון דאמרי הבית טמא, לית להו נימוק, ופשיטא דאמו טמאה לידה. תלד. "ואם נקבה תלד", דמצי למכתב "ואם נקבה וטמאה שבועים". לחייב על כל בן ובן. שאם טבלה לאחר י"ד לנקבה, ושמשה ונתעברה וילדה לאחר שמונים – מביאה שני קרבנות. תורת היולדת. משמע: תורה אחת ליולדת ולדות הרבה. שלפני מלאת. ילדה עכשיו, וילדה לאחר שמונים. קמא הוי "לפני מלאת", ובתרא הוי "לאחר מלאת". זאת. משמע כמו שמפורש בענין: קרבן אחד לולד אחד. הני מילי. דאין מביאה על שלפני מלאת ולאחר מלאת קרבן אחד. בתרי עיבורי. שילדה, וחזרה ונתעברה בתוך ימי טוהר, וילדה לאחר שמונים. כגון יהודה וחזקיה. דאמרינן ב"המפלת" (לעיל כז.) שנשתהה אחרון אחר הראשון ג' חדשים. מודה ר"ש. ביוצא דופן. שאינו קדוש. קדושת הגוף, אלא כשאר קדשים שקדם מומן להקדשן – דלא קדשי אלא כעלים וכחבנים לדמיהם, ויוצאין לחולין ליגזז וליעבד. לידה לידה. כתיב בקדשים (ויקרא כב): "שור או כשב או עז כי יולד", וכתיב בבכור (דברים טו): "אשר יולד". מאדם. לענין טומאה וטהרה, דכתיב: "וילדה זכר". אמו מאמו. בבכור כתיב (שמות כב): "שבעת ימים יהיה עם אמו", ובקדשים כתיב (ויקרא כב): "והיה שבעת ימים תחת אמו". שכן אם בהמת קדשים פיגול נותר וטמא. אם – בתרוייהו כתיב "אמו". ותרוייהו בהמת קדשים, ופיגול ונותר וטמא נוהג בהם. לאפוקי אדם, דליתיה בכל הני. פשוט. אדם משתעי בין בפשוט בין בבכור, וכן קדשים הוו פשוטים. ובין באדם ובין בקדשים לא משתעו בזכרים לחודייהו טפי מבנקבות, לאפוקי בכור דליתיה אלא בזכרים. ותרוייהו, בין אדם בין קדשים, לא הוו קדושין מאליהם, אבל בכור קדושתו מאליו. ובין קדשים ובין אדם לא הוו מתנות כהונה, כגון שלמים לבעלים הן, לאפוקי בכור דהוי ממתנות כהונה. דמסייע ליה לרבי יוחנן. דאמר דמודה ר"ש ביוצא דופן דקדשים. זאת תורת העולה היא העולה. ומהאי קרא נפקא לן בזבחים (דף כז.) פסולין, שאם עלו – לא ירדו. דכתיב "על מוקדה" – משעלה תוקד. וכתב רחמנא "זאת", דמשמע מיעוטא, כלומר: זאת אם עלתה – לא תרד, אבל אחרת, אע"פ שעלתה – תרד. וכתיב "היא", דמשמע מיעוטא. וכתיב "העולה", דמשמע: "העולה" – עולה כשרה, ולא פסולה. והני תלתא מיעוטי ממעטי הני תלתא פסולי. שנשחטה

## תוספות

**יוצא** דופן. ממקום שמזורעת. ואם תאמר: למה לי קרא, נילף לידה לידה מבכור, כדילפינן לענין קדשים בסמוך? וי"ל: דאי לאו קרא, הוה דרשינן מ"תלד" – לרבות יוצא דופן, כדדריש ר"ש. **כעין** שהזריעה. פרש"י: ולרבנן לא צריך קרא, דהא סברי ב"המפלת" (לעיל כו.) דרובן אינם נימוקים. ומיהו איצטריך להיכא דהושיטה חיה ידה במעי אשה *ומעכב את הולד, דטמאה לרבנן! וי"ל: דתרתי ש"מ*.

**מודה** ר"ש בקדשים שאינו קדוש. בפ' בתרא דבכורות (דף מז:) גבי ר"א ברבי יהודה דאית ליה יוצא דופן קדוש, אמר: סבר לה כר"ש דאמר יוצא דופן ולד מעליא הוא. ותימה: דהא ר"ש מודה דבקדשים אינו קדוש, כדאמר רבי יוחנן הכא, וכדמוכח נמי בברייתא דמייתי בסמוך? וי"ל: דסבר כר"ש ועדיפא מדר"ש דאפילו בקדשים קאמר דקדוש. **גמר** לידה לידה מבכור. בפ' "ולד חטאת" (דף יג.) במעילה, גבי ולד המעושרת לא ינק *מן המעושרת, יליף "אמו" "אמו" מבכור, והכל אחד, כדמוכח בשמעתין. וא"ת: דבפרק "מרובה" (ב"ק דף עז:) אמר: כל מקום שנאמר "שה" – אינו אלא להוציא את הכלאים. וקאמר: למעוטי מאי? אי למעוטי קדשים – בהדיא כתיב בהו "או כשב", פרט לכלאים. אם למעשר "תחת" "תחת" יליף מקדשים. ואי לבכור – "העברה" "העברה" יליף ממעשר. והשתא אמאי אצטריך למילף בכור ממעשר, ומעשר גופיה ילפינן מקדשים, הוה ליה למימר דנילף בכור "לידה" "לידה", או "אמו" "אמו" מקדשים! וי"ל: דלא ילפינן "לידה" "לידה" או "אמו" "אמו" אלא כגון הכא דאיירי בלידה, או במעילה דאיירי בענין אמהות. וא"ת: ובשמעתין, אמאי צריך ג"ש ד"לידה" "לידה" או "אמו" "אמו", נילף פסול יוצא דופן בקדשים מג"ש ד"תחת" ממעשר, ומעשר מג"ש: ד"העברה" מבכור? וי"ל: דג"ש ד"לידה" וד"אמו" צריך לשום דרשה אחריתי. **הנך** נפישין. וא"ת: דבפרק "יש בכור" (בכורות דף מז:) אר"ש דיוצא דופן בכור לנחלה הוי, דיליף מ"וילדו לו בנים" לידה מאשה, דאית ליה הכא דהוי ולד. והשתא לילף מבכור בהמה, שכן בכור זכר (מתנות) וי"ל: דאדם מאדם עדיף, שכן אין שייך בהו פגול נותר וטמא דאינו קדשים, ושייך בהו טומאה וטהרה. ובפרק "ראשית הגז" (חולין דף קלז.) דקאמר פשוט מפשוט עדיף, אע"ג דהנהו נפישי – התם משום דהוי בהמה מבהמה. אבל הכא, דבהמה מאדם – לא. **זאת** היא העולה. הכי כתיב קרא "זאת תורת העולה היא העולה" – הרי ג' מיעוטי: "זאת" ו"היא" וה' ד"העולה" תנינא.א] ד"העולה" קמא דריש רבא ב"תמיד נשחט" (פסחים נח:) "העולה" – עולה ראשונה. מהני ג' מיעוטי ממעט הנך, ומ"תורת" מרבינן אינך פסולין, דאם עלו – לא ירדו, כר"ש. וא"ת: והא ר' יהודה סברב] *בפ"ק דזבחים (דף כד) דרצפה מקדשת כמזבח, ואם כן כולם יעלו, והיכי משכחת פסול בכל הנהו, לבר מהני ג' כיון דאם עלו – לא ירדו? וי"ל: כגון שיש הפסק בין הבהמה לרצפת עזרה. ואם תאמר: והיכי ממעט הני ג' פסולי, הא צריך חד מיעוט לרובע ונרבע ולכל הנהו דמודה רבי שמעון בהו דאם עלו – ירדו? וי"ל: דנשחטה בלילה ויצא דמה, ממעט תרוייהו מחד מיעוטא, דשקולים הם. וא"ת: קדשי קדשים ששחטן בדרום, דאמר בריש מעילה (דף ג:) דאליבא דר' יהודה כ"ע ל"פ דתרד, אמאי? הא ליכא מיעוטא רביעית! ולר"ש נמי, לרבא דאמר תרד, הא "פסולן בקדש" הוא, דהא אית ליה הכשר בקדשים קלים דכשרים בדרום. כמו שאפרש, דהיכא דאית ליה הכשר בעלמא, איקרו "פסולן בקדש"? וי"ל: דשחיטה בדרום הוי כעין שחיטת חוץ, וכמו דחנקינהו דמי, כדקאמר התם לר"ש.

פרט

## עין משפט נר מצוה

א א מיי' פ"י מהל' איסורי ביאה הל"ה סמג עשין רמב ולאוין קיא טוש"ע יו"ד סי' קלד סעי' יד:

נ"ל ומיעכב

[ועי' תוס' לעיל יח. ד"ה שליא]

ב ב מיי' שם פ"ה הל"ב סמג שם טוש"ע יו"ד סי' קפג סעי' א:

ג ג מיי' פ"ה מהל' אבות הטומאה הל"א:

ד ד מיי' פ"ז מהל' תרומות הל"ד:

ה ה מיי' פ"ה מהל' איסורי ביאה הל"א ופ"א מהל' משכב ומושב הל"ח סמג לאוין קיא טוש"ע יו"ד סי' קפג סעיף א:

גי' מהר"מ מן המעושרת וכן ולד קדשים מן המקודשת יליף שם קדשים מבכור מג"ש דאמו כנ"ל

ו ו ז מיי' פ"א מהל' מחוסרי כפרה הל"א:

ז ח מיי' פ"ג מהל' איסורי מזבח הל"ד והלכה יא:

## תוספי הרא"ש

**שתלד** ממקום שמזרע'. ותימה בלא כי תזריע נמי לשון תלד משמע למעוטי יוצא דופן כדדרשינן גבי קדשים כי יולד פרט ליוצא דופן ובפ' יש בכור נמי ממעטינן יוצא דופן מוילדו לו. וי"ל דהתם לאו מלשון לידה קא ממעט אלא דגמרינן לידה מבכור כדגמרינן לקמן גבי קדשים ותימה אכתי תיקשי לך הכא נמי ניגמר לידה מבכור. וי"ל דאי לאו כי תזריע הוה מיסתבר למידרש טפי לכדדריש ליה ר' שמעון: **ר' שמעון** מ"ט. כלומר אמאי לא דריש קרא כדדרשי ליה רבנן: **סד"א** זכר ודאי. אע"פ דבפ' המפלת משמע דלא דרשינן ליה בהכי אלא היכא דמייתר שאני הכא דכתיבי טובא בן ובת הלכך זכר ונקבה מייתר: **זאת** וגו' היא העולה. הרי אלו ג' מיעוטין זאת והיא וה"א דהעולה שני אבל העולה קמא דריש מיניה העולה עולה ראשונה בפ' תמיד נשחט. ובכל אינך דמפרש ר' שמעון מודה ר' יהודה [דאם עלו לא ירדו] כדמפרש טעמא בזבחים. ותימה והא ר' יהודה סבר א) בפ"ק דזבחים דרצפה מקדשת כמזבח א"כ כולם יעלו א"כ היכי משוי לה פסול פיגול נותר טמא וכל אינך לבר הני ג'. וי"ל כגון שיש הפסק בינו ובין רצפת העזרה:

א) נ"ל בזבחים בפ' ק"ק (דף נט)

## מסורת הש"ס

[לעיל כו.] [לעיל יג.] [לעיל כז:] [כריתות ז:] [בכורות מז:] [כריתות ט:] לעיל כז. [חולין נח. ע"ז כג:] הוריות ב: זבחים כז: פד. ע"ש

## גליון הש"ס

**מתני'** וימי טהרה. ע"ל לו ע"א תד"ה הילכתא: **שם** היה אוכל בתרומה. ע"ל יג ע"א:

## הגהות מהר"ב רנשבורג

א] תוס' ד"ה זאת כו'. דהעולה תנינא דהעולה. נ"ב עי' זבחים דף פד ע"א תוס' ד"ה זאת כו' ומה שתמה שם עליהם בעל טהרות הקדש והנ"ק ויעו"ש בס' חק נתן ודו"ק: ב] בא"ד בפ"ק דזבחים דף כז. נ"ל יד ויעו"ש בתוס' ד"ה הג"ה:

ח א מיי' פ"ג מהל' פסולי המוקדשין הל"ו:
ט ב מיי' שם הל"ז:
י ג מיי' שם הל"ה:

תורה אור

אפרט לנשחטה בלילה, ושנשפך דמה, ושיצא דמה חוץ לקלעים – שאם עלתה תרד. רבי שמעון אומר: עולה – אין לי אלא עולה כשרה, מנין לרבות שנשחטה בלילה, ושנשפך דמה, ושיצא דמה חוץ לקלעים, בוהלן, והיוצא, והטמא, והנותר, ושנשחט חוץ לזמנו וחוץ למקומו, ושקבלו פסולין וזרקו את (א) דמן, והנתנין למעלה שנתנן למטה, והנתנין למטה שנתנן למעלה, והנתנין בחוץ שנתנן בפנים, והנתנין בפנים שנתנן בחוץ, והפסח והחטאת ששחטן שלא לשמן, מנין? ת"ל: °"זאת תורת העולה". ויקרא ו ריבה תורה אחת לכל העולין – שאם עלו לא ירדו. יכול שאני מרבה את הרובע, והנרבע, והמוקצה, והנעבד, ואתנן, והמחיר, והכלאים, והטרפה, ויוצא דופן. גת"ל: "זאת". ומה ראית לרבות את אלו ולהוציא את אלו? אחר

שנשחטה בלילה ושנשפך דמה. לארץ ולא נזרק. ושיצא דמה חוץ לקלעים. אבל כל הנך פסולי אחריני דמכשר בהו רבי שמעון, כגון לן, ויוצא שיצא הבשר קודם זריקת דם, וטמא, ושנשחט לאוכלו חוץ לזמנו וחוץ למקומו – כולן מודה נמי רבי יהודה דלא ירדו. וטעמא מפרש רבי יהודה במסכת זבחים בפרק "המזבח מקדש" (דף פד.): מפני מה אמרו לן בדם – כשר? שהרי לן כשר בבשר, וכן כולן. והלן. דם הלן. והיוצא. בשר עולה שיצא, והכניסו והעלה. והנותר. בשר שנותר חוץ לזמנו, והקטירו. ושנשחט. על מנת לאוכלו חוץ לזמנו, דהוי פיגול. ושקבלו פסולין את דמו וזרקוהו. כגון בעל מום או שאר פסולין. ולהכי נקט "קבלו פסולין", ולא נקט "ששחטוהו פסולין" – שהשחיטה כשרה בפסולין, כדתנן (זבחים דף לא.): כל הפסולין ששחטו – שחיטתן כשרה. והנתנין למעלה. מחוט הסיקרא דקי"ל: חטאת בהמה – למעלה, דכתיב בה קרנות, ועולה – למטה. הנתנין בפנים. על מזבח הפנימי, כגון פר העלם דבר ופר כהן משיח. (ב). והחטאת ששחטו שלא לשמן. להכי נקט פסח והחטאת – דקיימא לן (שם דף ב.): כל הזבחים שנזבחו שלא לשמן – כשרין, חוץ מפסח וחטאת. הרובע והנרבע מוקצה ונעבד. פסולין ליקרב, כדיליף לקמן בשמעתין. מוקצה. שיחדו לנורך תקרובת עבודה זרה. ונעבד. שהשתחוה לו. כלאים. פסולין לקרבן, שנאמר (ויקרא כב): "שור או כשב" – פרט לכלאים. אחר

פרט לנשחטה בלילה. בפרק "המזבח מקדש" (זבחים דף פד:) מפרש טעמא אמאי מודה רבי יהודה בהנך דלא ירדו טפי מהני ג' וקאמר: לן בדם כשר – שכן לן באימורין א] (ג) כשר. שהרי לן כשר בבשר לכתחלה, דנאכל לשני ימים ולילה אחד. יוצא כשר – שהרי יוצא כשר בבמה. וטמא – דחזי לעבודת צבור. חוץ לזמנו – שהרי מרצה בפגולו. חוץ למקומו – איתקש לחוץ לזמנו. קבלו פסולין וזרקו (ד) – בהנך פסולים דחזו לעבודת צבור. ואם תאמר: נשחטה בלילה ויצא דמה, נמי ליתכשרו, דאין לילה ויוצא פסול בבמה, כדאמר בפרק "פרת חטאת" (זבחים דף קכ.) וכן קבלו פסולין דלא מכשר אלא בהנך דחזו לעבודת צבור אבל זר – לא, דהא כשר בבמה. וכן חוץ למקומו, מה צריך לטעמא דאיתקש לחוץ לזמנו, תיפוק ליה דכשר בבמה? מיהו רש"י פי' ב"המזבח מקדש" (שם פד:) דיוצא (ה) *דכשר הוא, דילפינן מבמה, אבל הכשר דם דחמיר – לא ילפינן מבמה, אם לא נמצא לן הכשר בפנים. אך קשה: אמאי אצטריך למילף לן בדם מאימורין, ואימורין מלן דבשר, ופשיט מיניה ב"איזהו מקומן" (שם דף נו) דגמרי בנין אב מבנין אב. לילף חד בנין אב: לן בדם מלן דבשר? וכ"ת: דלא בעי למילף דם מבשר שאינו קרב, אלא ילפינן מאימורין דקרבי, ואימורין מבשר, משום דהוי בשר מבשר, מכל מקום תימה: דנילף לן דמה שנפסל בשקיעת החמה דאם עלו לא ירדו מאימורין שלנו בלא מזבח בשקיעת החמה דלא מיפסלי בשקיעת החמה דמלותן כל הלילה, וכיון דלן דם בשקיעת החמה, אע"ג דמיפסל – לא ירד, מעתה גם לן בעמוד השחר – לא ירד, דאין חילוק. ותדע דהא לן שתי לילות – לא ירד, אע"ג דאין כיוצא בו כשר, ואפילו בבשר! על כן י"ל: דפסול דם לא ילפינן מאימורין שכשרים לכתחלה כל הלילה, משום דאיכא תרתי: חדא, דהוי דם מבשר. ועוד, דהוי פסול מהכשרו בכך. ולהכי נמי גבי דם לא ילפינן מבמה, דאיכא נמי תרי שנויי: פנים מחוץ, ופסול מהכשרו בכך. אבל יוצא דבשר לא חמיר, וילפינן מבמה (ו) דמים הנתנין למטה שנתנן למעלה או איפכא, וכן הנתנין בפנים שנתנן בחוץ, כיון דכל אחד כשר בחבירו – לא תרד, דדם מדם בפנים ילפינן [פסול] מהכשרו. ומיהו תימה: יצא דמה חוץ לקלעים, אמאי תרד לר"י נילף יצא דם מאימורין שיצאו, ואימורים שיצאו מבמה או מבשר שלמים שיצא חוץ לקלעים דכשר, וכיון דיצא חוץ לקלעים – לא ירד, הוא הדין אפילו חוץ לחומה, דאין חילוק כדפירשתי לעיל. וא"ת: דבפרק "חטאת העוף" (זבחים דף סח:) גבי זר וסכין מטמאין בגדים בבית הבליעה, פריך: מאי שנא שמאל – דהכשירו ביום הכפורים, ולילה – באברין ופדרים, זר נמי – נילף מבמה, דתניא: מנין ליוצא שהוא כשר, שהרי כשר בבמה. ומאי פריך, הא דווקא בשר ילפינן מבמה להאי תנא, ולא דם כדפרישית? ותו, בשמאל ולילה דהוא עבודת דם היכי יליף מהכשרו בכך? *וי"ל: דההיא סוגיא כר"ש דמכשיר אפילו נשחטה בלילה ויצא דמה, ואפילו דם יליף מהכשרו מבמה ומבשר ונשפך דמה, לפי שכבר נעשה השחיטה בהכשר, או גם הקבלה כמו שאפרש. ותדע דההיא כרבי שמעון, דבמשנה דהתם קאמר: "כל שפסולו בקדש – אין מטמא בגדים בבית הבליעה, וכל שאין פסולו בקדש – מטמא", ורבי שמעון נמי בשמעתין קאמר: כל שפסולו בקדש – אם עלו לא ירדו. והכי פריך: והתניא, יוצא כשר שהרי כשר בבמה, וכמו דיליף ר' יהודה אימורין מבמה ה"נ ליליף לר"ש פסול דם מבמה. ומיהו לר"ת (ז) דגרסינן פ"ב דזבחים (דף כד:) והתניא, מלק בשמאל – פסול, ול"ג: זרק בשמאל, דלא מצינו משנה זו בשום מקום. ומשני: פליגי בברייתא ור"ש מכשיר, ההיא דפ' "חטאת העוף" (שם דף סח:) לא אתיא כר"ש, דלדידיה מלק בשמאל – כשר, אלא תנא אחר הוא, וסבר לה כר' שמעון, ובמלק בשמאל לא סבר ליה כוותיה. ושנשפך דמה. נראה דלרבי יהודה תרד, אפילו נתקבלה ואח"כ נשפך, דומיא דיצא דמה, דהוי אפילו נתקבל. דאי ביצא קודם שנתקבל, כגון שיצא מן הצואר לחוץ, אם כן היינו נשפך דמה, דאין כלי שרת מקדש אלא בפנים, כדאמר ב"המזבח מקדש" (שם פח.). חוץ למקומו. ור' יהודה נמי לא פליג אלא בג' דלעיל. וקשה: דבפרק "התודה" (מנחות דף עט.) אמרינן: חטאת ששחטה חוץ למקומה, *רבא אומר: תרד. רבה אומר: לא תרד. והדר ביה רבה לגבי רבא. והתם אתי כרבי יהודה, דקתני התם, אמר רבי יהודה: לא נחלקו על חוץ לזמנו, שקדש הלחם. על מה נחלקו, על חוץ למקומו. רבי אליעזר אומר: קדש. רבי יהושע אומר: לא קדש. והדר ביה רבי אליעזר לגבי רבי יהושע! ויש לומר: דהתם רבי יהודה אליבא דרבי יהושע קאמר, דלא מקיש חוץ למקומו לחוץ לזמנו, אבל רבי יהודה גופיה מקיש, דקאמר ב"המזבח מקדש" (זבחים פד:) טעמא דחוץ למקומו דלא ירדו, משום דאיתקש לחוץ לזמנו. *הלן. היינו לן דדם, והנותר היינו לן דאימורין. דאילו בשר, אפילו אינו נותר – ירד, דכל שממנו לאשים הרי הוא ב"בל תקטירו". והנתנין למעלה שנתנן למטה. אפילו רבי יהודה מודה דלא ירדו, דדם מדם בפנים יליף שפיר מהכשרו בכך, כדפירשתי לעיל. והכי נמי אמר בפ"ב דזבחים (דף כז:) קתני מיהא "הנתנין למעלה שנתנן למטה", ולא פליג רבי יהודה. וקשה: דאמר בריש מעילה: קדשי קדשים ששחטן בדרום מהו שירדו? אליבא דר' יהודה פשיטא דירדו, כי תבעי לך אליבא דר' שמעון, מאי? רב יוסף אמר: לא ירדו, רבה אמר: עד כאן לא קאמר ר"ש התם דלא ירדו אלא בנתנין למטה שנתנן למעלה, למעלה שנתנן למטה, ולעולם ששחטן למטה, אבל הכא ששחטן בדרום וקבל דמן בצפון – אף ר"ש מודה דירדו, דכתנקינהו דמי. והשתא אמאי נקט "הנתנין למעלה שנתנן למטה" טפי מאחריני, אדרבה הוה ליה למנקט "נשחטין בלילה, ונשפך דמה", אע"ג דפליג אדרבי יהודה ואמר דלא ירדו, היינו משום ששחטן בצפון? אלא יש לומר: דנקט "הנתנים למעלה שנתנן למטה" משום דמינה מייתי רב יוסף. ד"נתנין למעלה" משמע ליה דהוי בכלל עולת העוף, שדינה למעלה, ומלקה, ומצה דמה למטה. וכי היכי דהתם לא ירדו, אע"פ שהמליקה לא היתה במקומה, הכי נמי קדשי קדשים שנשחטו בדרום. ורבה אומר "הנתנין למעלה שנתנן למטה", איירי דווקא בזבחים, ולכך לא ירדו, ששחיטה וקבלה היתה כדינה בצפון. אבל שחיטת דרום, וכן מליקת עולת העוף למטה – לא. אם כן לרב יוסף, דהוי בכלל הנתנים למעלה עולת העוף, פליג רבי יהודה כדאמר התם דבשחיטת דרום אליבא דרבי יהודה פשיטא דירדו. ובפ"ב דזבחים (דף כז:) אמר דלא פליג רבי יהודה? וי"ל: דכיון דבזבחים מיהא מודה רבי יהודה דלא ירדו, שייך שפיר למימר: לא פליג רבי יהודה. כמו בקבלו פסולין וזרקו, דקאמר נמי התם דלא פליג, אע"ג דרבי יהודה לא מודה אלא בהנך דחזו לעבודת צבור, ור"ש אפילו בהנך דלא חזו לעבודת צבור קאמר דלא ירדו, דלא גרע מנשפך דמה שלא נזרק כלל דלא ירדו לר"ש ומיהו אין ראיה, דמצינן למימר דאף לרבי שמעון בהנך דלא חזו לעבודת צבור, כגון זר, אם קיבל דם – ירדו, כיון דלא מצינו בעלמא הכשר בפנים. ומבמה לא ילפינן עבודת דם אף לר"ש ונשחטה בלילה, דלא ירד לרבי שמעון, היינו משום דילפינן מאימורין. ונשפך הדם נמי, דלא ירד לרבי שמעון, דווקא שנשפך אחר שכבר נתקבל, אבל נשפך מן הצואר – ירד, דמשום שחיטה לבדה שנעשית בהכשר לא מיקרי "פסולו בקדש". וקבלו פסולין, בהנך דווקא דחזו לעבודת ציבור, אף לר"ש ולא הוי פירוש: קבלו או זרקו, דאם כן פליג אר' יהודה, דהא לרבי שמעון אפילו זרקו הנך דלא חזו לעבודת צבור – לא ירדו, דלא גרע מנשפך. אלא פי' קבלו וזרקו אותו דם עצמו, מכל מקום בלא ראיה יש לומר: דשייך שפיר דלא פליג רבי יהודה, כיון דמודה בזבחים. וכן משמע

גי' מהר"ם דבשר כו'

עי' במס' זבחים פד: בתוס' ד"ה ומוליא שכתוב שם בשם הג"ה ובע"כ צ"ל כן דאל"כ דברי תוס' סתרי אהדדי דבד"ה והניתנים כתבו הכא וז"ל ומיהו אין ראיה וע"ש ועיין מהר"מ

מהר"מ

עיין מהר"מ

(שייך קודם ד"ה הלן)

הגהות הב"ח

(א) גמ' וזרקו את דמו והנתנין: (ב) רש"י ד"ה הנתנין וכו' משיח הס"ד ואח"כ מ"ה והפסח והחטאת ששחטן שלא: (ג) תוס' ד"ה פרט וכו' לן בדם כשר שכן לן באימורין כשר לן באימורין כשר שהרי לן כשר בבשר וכו' בבמה וטמא דחזי לעבודת צבור וכו' שהרי מרצה לפיגולו נ"ב עיין פירושו בריש מעילה בדף ב ע"ב בפרש"י והעיקר בפ' שני דזבחים ריש דף כט: (ד) בא"ד קבלו פסולין וזרקו את דמו בהנך דחזו לעבודות: (ה) בא"ד דיוצא דבשר הוא וכו' לא נמצא לו הכשר בפנים: (ו) בא"ד וילפינן מבמה מיהו הנתנין למטה וכו' דדם מדם בפנים ילפינן מהכשירו בכך ומיהו כצ"ל: (ז) בא"ד ומיהו לר"ת דגרס פ"ב דזבחים:

הגהות מהר"ב רנשבורג

א] תוס' ד"ה פרט כו' שכן לן באימורין כשר ולן באימורין כשר שהרי לן כשר כו'. כצ"ל:

**עין משפט נר מצוה**

יא א ב ג ד מיי' פ"ג מהל' איסורי מזבח הלכה ו:
יב ה מיי' שם הל"ד:
יג ו מיי' שם הל"ה:
יד ז מיי' פ"י מהל' איסורי ביאה הל"ה סמג עשין רמג:
טו ח מיי' שם ופ"ח מהל' משכב ומושב הלכה טו:

**מסורת הש"ס**

[זבחים לח. קיד. מנחות פג. חולין ג. תמורה כה. כריתות כג:]

ב"ק מ: תמורה כח. בכורות מא. [זבחים פה:]

חולין לח: ב"ק עז: בכורות יב. יז. כז.

תורה אור

אַחַר שֶׁרִיבָּה הַכָּתוּב וּמִיעֵט! אָמַרְתָּ: מְרַבֶּה אֲנִי אֶת אֵלּוּ — שֶׁהָיָה פְּסוּלָן בַּקֹּדֶשׁ, וּמוֹצִיא אֲנִי אֶת אֵלּוּ — שֶׁלֹּא הָיָה פְּסוּלָן בַּקֹּדֶשׁ. קָתָנֵי מִיהַת יוֹצֵא דוֹפֶן דְּלָא, מַאי לָאו — יוֹצֵא דוֹפֶן דְּקָדָשִׁים? אָמַר רַב הוּנָא בְּרֵיהּ דְּרַב נָתָן: לֹא, יוֹצֵא דוֹפֶן דִּבְכוֹר. בְּכוֹר מִ"פֶּטֶר רֶחֶם" נָפְקָא! אֶלָּא מַאי, דְּקָדָשִׁים? מֵ"אִמּוֹ" "אִמּוֹ" נָפְקָא! הַאי מַאי, אִי אָמְרַתְּ בִּשְׁלָמָא דְּקָדָשִׁים — הַיְינוּ דְּאַצְרִיכֵי תְּרֵי קְרָאֵי, חַד — לִבְהֵמַת חוּלִּין דְּאוֹלִיד דֶּרֶךְ דּוֹפֶן וְאַקְדְּשָׁהּ, וְחַד — לִבְהֵמַת קָדָשִׁים דְּאוֹלִיד דֶּרֶךְ דּוֹפֶן, וְקָסָבַר *וַלְדוֹת קָדָשִׁים בַּהֲוָיָיתָן הֵן קְדוֹשִׁים. אֶלָּא אִי אָמְרַתְּ דִּבְכוֹר — מִ"פֶּטֶר רֶחֶם" נָפְקָא! הָכִי נַמִי מִסְתַּבְּרָא, מִדְּקָתָנֵי: "הָרוֹבֵעַ וְהַנִּרְבָּע וְהַמּוּקְצֶה וְהַנֶּעֱבָד וְהַכִּלְאַיִם" הָנֵי מֵהָכָא נָפְקָא? מֵהָתָם נָפְקָא! ויקרא א °"מִן הַבְּהֵמָה" — *[א]לְהוֹצִיא הָרוֹבֵעַ וְהַנִּרְבָּע. "מִן הַבָּקָר" — [ב]לְהוֹצִיא אֶת הַנֶּעֱבָד. "מִן הַצֹּאן" [ג]לְהוֹצִיא אֶת הַמּוּקְצֶה. "וּמִן הַצֹּאן" — [ד]לְהוֹצִיא אֶת הַנּוֹגֵחַ. וְתוּ, כִּלְאַיִם, מֵהָכָא נָפְקָא? מֵהָתָם נָפְקָא — שם כב °"שׁוֹר אוֹ כֶשֶׂב אוֹ עֵז". "שׁוֹר" — *[ה]פְּרָט לְכִלְאַיִם, "אוֹ עֵז" — [ו]פְּרָט לְנִדְמֶה! אֶלָּא: אִצְטְרִיכוּ תְּרֵי קְרָאֵי, חַד — לִבְהֵמַת חוּלִּין, וְחַד — לִבְהֵמַת קָדָשִׁים, הָכָא נַמִי — אִיצְטְרִיךְ תְּרֵי קְרָאֵי. ת"ר: [ז]הַמַּקְשָׁה שְׁלֹשָׁה יָמִים, וְיָצָא וָלָד דֶּרֶךְ דּוֹפֶן הֲרֵי זוֹ יוֹלֶדֶת בְּזוֹב, וְרַבִּי שִׁמְעוֹן אוֹמֵר: אֵין זוֹ יוֹלֶדֶת בְּזוֹב. [ח]וְדָם הַיּוֹצֵא מִשָּׁם — טָמֵא, וְרַבִּי שִׁמְעוֹן מְטַהֵר. בִּשְׁלָמָא רֵישָׁא — רַבִּי שִׁמְעוֹן לְטַעְמֵיהּ, וְרַבָּנַן לְטַעֲמַיְיהוּ, אֶלָּא סֵיפָא — בְּמַאי פְּלִיגֵי? אָמַר רָבִינָא: כְּגוֹן שֶׁיָּצָא וָלָד דֶּרֶךְ דּוֹפֶן, וְדָם

**רש"י**

אַחַר שֶׁרִיבָּה הַכָּתוּב וּמִיעֵט אָמַרְתָּ כו'. הוֹאִיל וְכָתוּב אֶחָד רִיבָּה, וְכָתוּב אֶחָד מִיעֵט, מֵעַתָּה יֵשׁ לְךָ לֵילֵךְ אַחַר אוֹמֶד הַדַּעַת. **מְרַבֶּה אֲנִי אֶת אֵלּוּ שֶׁהָיָה פְּסוּלָן בַּקֹּדֶשׁ.** שֶׁלְּאַחַר שֶׁבָּאוּ לָעֲזָרָה אֵירַע פְּסוּלָן. **מִפֶּטֶר רֶחֶם נָפְקָא.** דְּלָא קָדֵישׁ, וְכֵיוָן דְּחוּלִּין הוּא, לָמָּה לִי לְמַעוּטֵי? פְּשִׁיטָא, אִם עָלָה יֵרֵד! **מֵאִמּוֹ אִמּוֹ נָפְקָא.** נַמִי דְּלָא קָדֵישׁ, דְּגָמַר מִבְּכוֹר. **תְּרֵי קְרָאֵי.** "אִמּוֹ" "אִמּוֹ" וְ"זֹאת". חַד לִבְהֵמָה דְּחוּלִּין. וְאוֹלִיד דֶּרֶךְ דּוֹפֶן וְאַקְדְּשֵׁיהּ, וְשָׁמְעִינַן מֵ"אִמּוֹ" "אִמּוֹ" דְּלָא קָדֵישׁ. וְחַד, לִבְהֵמָה דְּקָדָשִׁים. דְּעַל כָּרְחָךְ וָלָד הַיּוֹצֵא מִמֶּנָּה קָדוֹשׁ מֵאֵלָיו, וְאִיצְטְרִיךְ לְמַעוּטֵי מִ"זֹּאת" דְּאַע"ג דְּקָדֵישׁ, אִם עָלָה יֵרֵד, הוֹאִיל וְלֹא הָיָה פְּסוּלוֹ בַּקֹּדֶשׁ. וְקָסָבַר וַלְדוֹת קָדָשִׁים בַּהֲוָיָיתָן הֵן קְדוֹשִׁין. נִרְאֶה בְּעֵינַי דְּלָא גָּרְסִי' לֵיהּ, וּפֵירוּשׁ מְשׁוּבָּשׁ הוּא. דְּכָל שֶׁכֵּן לְמַאן דְּאָמַר מִשְּׁעַת יְצִירָה הֵן קְדוֹשִׁים, דְּהַיְינוּ בִּמְעֵי אִמּוֹ, דְּאִיצְטְרִיךְ לְמַעוּטֵי מִ"זֹּאת". **הָכִי נַמִי מִסְתַּבְּרָא.** דְּכָל הָנֵי פְּסוּלִין דְּהָכָא, בִּבְהֵמוֹת קָדָשִׁים קָאָמַר. וְרוֹבֵעַ וְנִרְבָּע — כְּגוֹן שֶׁהִקְדִּישָׁן, וּלְבַסּוֹף נִרְבְּעוּ. וּמוּקְצֶה וְנֶעֱבָד — נַמִי בְּקָדָשִׁים קַלִּים, וְאַלִּיבָּא דְּרַבִּי יוֹסֵי הַגְּלִילִי דְּאָמַר: מָמוֹן בְּעָלִים הֵן, וְיָכוֹל לְאוֹסְרָן. וְהָכִי נַמִי מוֹקְמִינַן בְּפֶרֶק בַּתְרָא דִּזְבָחִים (דף קיד.). וְאֶתְנַן וּמְחִיר — כְּשֶׁנָּתַן לָהּ עוּבָּר בֶּהֱמַת קָדָשִׁים קַלִּים בְּאֶתְנָן. וְקָסָבַר: בַּהֲוָיָיתָן הֵם קְדוֹשִׁים, וְלֹא קוֹדֶם לָכֵן. לְפִיכָךְ, אִיסּוּר אֶתְנָן וּמְחִיר — חָל עֲלֵיהֶם, וּקְדוּשָּׁה דְּמִמֵּילָא — נַמִי חָיְילָא עֲלַיְיהוּ, וַהֲרֵי הֵם קְדוֹשִׁים. וְכִלְאַיִם וּטְרֵפָה וְיוֹצֵא דוֹפֶן — נַמִי בְּוַלְדוֹת קָדָשִׁים. **הָכִי נַמִי מִסְתַּבְּרָא.** דִּבְקָדָשִׁים קָאֵי, וּתְרֵי קְרָאֵי אִיצְטְרִיכָא לֵיהּ, כִּדְאָמַר: מִדְּקָתָנֵי הָרוֹבֵעַ וְהַנִּרְבָּע וְקָא מְמַעֵט לְהוּ מֵהַאי קְרָא, וְכִי מֵהָכָא נָפְקָא? מֵהָתָם נָפְקָא! מִן הַבְּהֵמָה. "אָדָם כִּי יַקְרִיב מִכֶּם מִן הַבְּהֵמָה" — וְלֹא כָּל בְּהֵמָה, לְהוֹצִיא אֶת הָרוֹבֵעַ וְהַנִּרְבָּע. **נוֹגֵחַ.** שֶׁהֵמִית אֶת הָאָדָם. וְהַאי "רוֹבֵעַ וְנִרְבָּע וְנוֹגֵחַ" דְּקָתָנֵי, כְּגוֹן עַל פִּי עֵד אֶחָד, אוֹ עַל פִּי הַבְּעָלִים דְּמוֹדֶה בִּקְנָס פָּטוּר. הִלְכָּךְ, לְהֶדְיוֹט — שָׁרֵי, וּלְגָבוֹהַּ — אָסוּר. אֲבָל ע"פ שְׁנֵי עֵדִים — בִּסְקִילָה הוּא, וּלְהֶדְיוֹט נַמִי אָסוּר. **כִּלְאַיִם.** מִן הָעֵז וּמִן הַכֶּבֶשׂ. **נִדְמֶה.** אָבִיו וְאִמּוֹ מִן הָעֵז, וְהוּא כֶּבֶשׂ. וְכֵיוָן דְּנָפְקֵי מֵהָתָם דְּלָא קָדֵשׁ, לָמָּה לִי לְמַעוּטֵי מֵהָכָא דְּיֵרְדוּ, הָא חוּלִּין נִינְהוּ? לִבְהֵמָה דְּחוּלִּין. וְאַקְדְּשֵׁהּ. **הַמַּקְשָׁה ג' יָמִים.** בִּימֵי זִיבָה, וְרָאֲתָה דָּם כָּל שְׁלֹשָׁה דֶּרֶךְ רֶחֶם. **וְיָצָא וָלָד דֶּרֶךְ דּוֹפֶן הֲרֵי זוֹ יוֹלֶדֶת בְּזוֹב.** כְּלוֹמַר, זָבָה הִיא. דְּכִי טִיהֵר רַחֲמָנָא מִזִּיבָה דַּם הַקּוֹשִׁי, הָנֵי מִילֵּי בְּלֵידָה מַעַלְיָיתָא, אֲבָל דֶּרֶךְ דּוֹפֶן — לָאו לֵידָה הִיא. **אֵין זוֹ יוֹלֶדֶת בְּזוֹב.** וְר"ש לְטַעֲמֵיהּ, דְּאָמַר: יוֹצֵא דוֹפֶן — וָלָד מַעַלְיָא הוּא, וּמְטַהֵר אֶת קִישּׁוּיוֹ. **וְדָם הַיּוֹצֵא מִשָּׁם.** לְקַמָּן מְפָרֵשׁ מַאי קָאָמַר. **ר"ש לְטַעְמֵיהּ.** דְּאָמַר בְּמַתְנִיתִין "יוֹשֶׁבֶת עָלָיו יְמֵי טוּמְאָה" אֲפִילּוּ בְּלֵידָה יְבֵשָׁה, וִימֵי טָהֳרָה. אַלְמָא, וָלָד הוּא. הִלְכָּךְ לְעִנְיַן קוֹשִׁי נַמִי וָלָד הוּא, וּמְטַהֵר אֶת קִישּׁוּיוֹ. **אֶלָּא סֵיפָא בְּמַאי פְּלִיגֵי.** הָא לֵיכָּא לְמֵימַר: דָּם הַיּוֹצֵא עִמּוֹ דֶּרֶךְ דּוֹפֶן — יְהֵא טָמֵא כְּדַם הַלֵּידָה. דְּאִם כֵּן, אִיפְּכָא מִבָּעֵי לֵיהּ: רַבִּי שִׁמְעוֹן מְטַמֵּא, דְּאָמַר: וָלָד הוּא. וַחֲכָמִים מְטַהֲרִים! אֶלָּא וַדַּאי אֲפִי' לְרַבִּי שִׁמְעוֹן לָא הָוֵי אֶלָּא כְּדַם הַמַּכָּה. וְהָא דְּאָמַר רַבִּי שִׁמְעוֹן בְּמַתְנִיתִין: "יוֹשֶׁבֶת עָלָיו יְמֵי טוּמְאָה" — מִשּׁוּם וָלָד קָאָמַר, וְלֹא מִשּׁוּם דָּם. וְדָם

**תוספות**

משמע בריש מעילה דמשום שחיטה לבדה שנעשה בהכשר, לא חשיב "פסולו בקדש", אף לרבי שמעון. דפריך רב יוסף לרבה מדתניא בפרק (א) "דם חטאת העוף" בזבחים (דף סו:) וכולן אין מטמאין (ב) בבית הבליעה, וקתני לעיל: עולת העוף שעשאה כמעשה החטאת, ותנן התם (דף סח:) כל שפסולו בקדש – אינו מטמא, וה"ה דלא ירדו! ומאי פריך? הא התם מוכח בזבחים דעולת העוף שעשאה כמעשה חטאת, היינו שהמילוי עשה למטה, אבל המליקה היתה במקומה! אלא ודאי רבה דאמר: ירדו, אפילו שחט בצפון וקבל בדרום, דמשום שחיטה גרידא לא מקרי "פסולו בקדש" אף לרבי שמעון. ומיהו יש לדחות: דבשחט בצפון מודה רבה דלא ירדו, ופריך ליה רב יוסף, משום שהמילוי הוי כמו השחיטה, שממצה ומוציא דם מן העוף כמו שעושה בשחיטה, ואע"פ שמלק למעלה, כיון שמילה למטה, הוי כשחט בדרום. **שהיה** פסולן בקדש. שאין פסולן יכול להיות עד אחר שהוקדש, אבל רובע ונרבע מצי להיות בעודן חולין. וקשה דאמרינן בזבחים פ' "חטאת העוף" (דף סח:) זר וסכין מטמאין, (ג) אלמא חשיב "אין פסולן בקדש" אע"ג דלא שייכי עד לאחר שהוקדש. ושמאל ולילה נמי הוה מטמאין, אי לאו דאית להו הכשר במקום אחר, כדאמר התם. ודוקין שבעין, קאמר רבי עקיבא דאם עלו לא ירדו, משום דכשר בעוף. אלמא חשיב "פסולו בקודש" אע"ג דיכול להיות קודם הקדש! ונראה לפרש: דהיכא דכיוצא בו כשר במקום אחר, קרי "פסולו בקדש". ונשחט בלילה – אית ליה הכשר באברים ופדרים, ויוצא דמה שכן כשר באימורים, ואימורים – שכן כשר בבמה, ונשפך דמה – כיון שקבלה היתה בהכשר, מיקרי "פסולו בקדש". ולשון "פסולו בקדש" היינו שאין כאן פסול גמור, אלא נפסל בקדושתו. וכן משמע, דפריך התם: מ"ש שמאל – דאית ליה הכשר ביום הכיפורים, ולילה – באברים ופדרין, ולכך אין מטמאין, דהוי "פסולן בקדש". **היינו** דאיצטריך תרי קראי. וא"ת: וליבעי ג' קראי בכל הפסולין, כמו בטרפה דחשיב הכא בהדייהו. דבפרק קמא דמנחות (דף ו.) מצריך ג' קראי בטרפה: חד, לנטרפה קודם הקדשה, וחד, לנטרפה לאחר הקדשה. ואפילו הכי איצטריך הכא למעוטי מ"זאת" דאם עלתה תרד, וה"נ בשאר פסולין ליבעי תרי קראי, בלא קרא ד"זאת" – חד, לקודם הקדש. וחד, לאחר הקדש, דלא יעלו. וקרא ד"זאת" לירדו. ויש לומר: כיון דגלי לן קרא בטרפה, ה"ה לשאר פסולים. **קסבר** ולדות קדשים בהויתן הן קדושים. פרש"י: דל"ג ליה, דהא כ"ש למ"ד במעי אמן הן קדושים, דאיצטריך למעוטי מ"זאת" ונראה דגרס ליה, ולרבותא נקטיה: דאע"ג דבהויתן הן קדושים, ולא קדם הקדשן לפסולן, אצטריך קרא למעוטי, כיון דהפסול לא בא תחלה אלא בבת אחת. אבל לא מצי למגרס "קסבר במעי אמן הן קדושים", דהא בסוף פרק "דם שחיטה" (כריתות דף כג:) קאמר דקסבר ר"ש בהויתן הן קדושים. וכן מוכח משמעתין, דמוקי קרא ד"זאת" לבהמת קדשים. ואתנן ומחיר לא אשכחן אחר הקדש, אפי' לרבי יוסי הגלילי דאמר: קדשים קלים ממון הדיוט הוא, דאמר בפרק "מי שהיה טמא" (פסחים דף צ.) "לכל נדר" – פרט לנדור, שאין אתנן חל עלייהו. ולא משכחת אלא בולדות קדשים, וכמ"ד בהויתן הן קדושים, ונתנם לזונה בעודם בבטן. והכי מוקי לה בפ' "פרת חטאת" (זבחים דף קיד.) וכן פ"ה. וא"ת: דבשילהי תמורה (דף לג:) תנן: אלו הן הנקברים – קדשים שהפילו, וחולין שנשחטו בעזרה. ור"ש אומר: חולין שנשחטו בעזרה – ישרפו. משמע דלא פליג אקדשים שהפילו, וכיון דבהוייתן הן קדושים – אמאי יקברו? והלא אין קדושה חלה עלייהו, כדתנן פרק "כילד מערימין" (שם דף כד:), רשב"ג אומר: ילדה טומטום ואנדרוגינוס – אין קדושה חלה עלייהו, וקאמר: דקסבר דבהויתן הן קדושים, ואפילו קדושת דמים אין חלה עלייהו. דאי חלה, הא אמר בפרק "אלו קדשים" (שם דף יט:) מגו דנחתא קדושת דמים, נחתא נמי קדושת הגוף. ואם כן, קדשים שהפילו, דאסורים בהנאה לרבי שמעון, אמאי? ויש לומר: דפליג גם ארישא, אלא דלא נחת לפלוגי אלא בחולין שנשחטו בעזרה. תדע, דהא חשיב התם נמי בשר בחלב – בקבורה, ולרבי שמעון – שרי בהנאה, בפ"ק דבכורות (דף י.) א"נ י"ל: דנפל קדושה חלה עליה טפי מטומטום ואנדרוגינוס, משום דאי הוה בר קיימא, היה ראוי לקרבן. וא"ת: כיון דסבר בהויתן הן קדושים, היאך קדושה חלה על יוצא דופן וכלאים, דמ"ש מטומטום ואנדרוגינוס? וי"ל: דמיירי כגון שהקדישן בפה קודם שנולדו, דאע"ג דאין קדושת אמן חלה עליהם, קדושת פה – חלה עליהם. מיהו מתני' ד"כילד מערימין" (תמורה דף כד:) משמע דאפילו בקדושת פה – אין קדושה חלה עליהם. ועוד, דבשילהי פ"ב דתמורה (דף יז.) קאמר: אי אתה מוצא אלא בולדות קדשים, ואליבא דרבי יהודה. ואמאי לא משכחת בהקדישו בפה? ושמא י"ל: דדווקא טומטום ואנדרוגינוס אין קדושה חלה עליהם. **ורבנן** לטעמייהו. וא"ת: אע"ג דלא מטמאי לידה, מ"מ ליטהר דם קישויה. דאפי' בהפילה רוח פריך בפ"ק (לעיל דף ח:): שיהא קישויה טהור, אע"ג דאין נותנין לה ימי טומאה וימי טהרה! ויש לומר: דהתם משום דבעי למימר דמיקרי לידה, כדמייתי קרא "כמו ילדנו רוח", אבל הכא מיעטיה קרא מדין ולד. ואזדא

**תוספי הרא"ש**

**שהיה** פסולן בקדש. פרש"י לאחר שבאו לעזרה אירע פסולן. וקשה לפירושו דא"כ רובע ונרבע בעזרה נמי הוה לן למימר אם עלו לא ירדו. וע"ק דבזבחים פ' חטאת העוף חשיב ר' יוחנן מליקה א) ודלא הייתה פסולן בקדש ושמאל ולילה לא חשיב להו פסולן בקדש אי לאו דמשכח להו הכשירא במקום אחר כדאיתא התם הלכך נראה לפרש דפסול שבא ע"י דבר שכשר במקום אחר כביוצא בו קרי פיסולו בקדש כלומר פסול זה קדוש וכשר במקום אחר: **היינו** דאיצטריך תרי קראי חד לבהמה דחולין כו'. ותימה וליבעי ג' קראי בכל הני כמו טריפה דחשיב הכא בהדי שאר פסולין כדאשכחן בפ"ק דמנחות דמצריך תרי קראי לטריפה חד לטריפה קודם הקדש וחד לטריפה לאחר הקדש וא"ה איצטריך רבא למיעוטי מזאת דאם עלתה תרד ובשאר פסולין נמי ליבעי תלתא קראי חד ליפסל קודם הקדש וחד ליפסל לאחר הקדש דלא יעלו לכתחלה וקרא שלישי דאם עלו ירדו וי"ל דכיון דגלי רחמנא בטריפה ה"ה לכל שאר פסולין. תדע דמטריפה ילפינן בעלמא דהא אכתי מצריך התם קרא לטריפה היכא דהויתה לה שעת הכושר ומשמע התם דממשקה ישראל לא הוה שמעינן אלא היכא דלא הוה לה שעת הכושר ובכל דוכתי איתי ממשקה ישראל אפי' על דבר שהיתה לו שעת הכושר בפ' כל האסורים גבי נעבד דקאמר מדאסר רחמנא נעבד לגבוה. ובפ' אלו עוברין גבי מוקצה ובפ' כל הבשר גבי אותו ואת בנו ותלמודא לא נחת לפרושי הכא אלא תרי קראי דאיירי בהו בשמעתין וסמך אהא דילפינן מטריפה דאסורה אף להדיוט: **חד** לבהמת קדשים ואוליד דרך דופן ה"ה דהוה מצי למימ' למקדיש וולד ויצא דרך דופן כדאיתא בספ"ב דתמורה ומאחר דאין קדושין מהיכן מקדישין: אי אתה מוצא אלא במקדיש וולד ויצא דרך דופן וסבר וולדות קדשים בהווייתן הן קדושים. פרש"י דל"ג ופי' משובש הוא דכ"ש למ"ד במעי אמן הן קדושים משעת יצירה איצטריך למעוטי מזאת ונראה דגרס ליה שפיר ולרבותא נקטיה אע"ג דקסבר בהווייתן הן קדושים איצטריך למעוטי כיון דלא קדם פיסולן להקדשן אבל אי אפשר לומר במעי אמן הן קדושים בהדדיא מוכח פרק דם שחיטה דסבר ר' שמעון בהווייתן הם קדושים להההוא תנא דאמר לר' שמעון דאין איסור חל על איסור אפי' בקדשים דמוקי כל חלב בוולדות קדשים וקסבר בהווייתן הן קדושים והוי איסור בת אחת. והך שמעתא גופה. מוכח הכי דצריך לאוקומי הנך פסולי בבהמה דקדשים שלא קדם הפסול להקדש ואתנן ומחיר לא משכחת לה אלא כמ"ד בהווייתן הן קדושים ונתן לה ולד קדשים באתננה ואי במעי אמן קדושים לא משכחת לה שיהא (לא) אתנן ומחיר חל עליהן כדמוכח פ' בתרא דזבחים וכן פרש"י. ותימה וכיון דקסבר בהווייתן הן קדושים היאך קדושה חל על יוצא דופן כלאים הא משמע בפ' כיצד מערימין דטומטום ואנדרוגינוס אין קדושה חלה עליהן למ"ד בהווייתן הם קדושים וצריך לחלק בין טומטום ואנדרוגינוס ליוצא דופן וכלאים משום דניכר פיסול בגופן:

**הגהות הב"ח**

(א) תוס' ד"ה (בעמוד הקודם) וכיוצא בו וכו' מדתניא בפ' חטאת העוף כצ"ל ותיבת דם נמחק: (ב) בא"ד אין מטמאין בגדים בבית הבליעה וקתני לעיל עולת העוף שעשה כמעשה החטאת ותנן התם כל שפסולו בקדש אינו מטמא בגדים אבית הבליעה וה"ה דלא ירדו: (ג) ד"ה שהיה וכו' זר וסכין מטמאין בגדים אבית הבליעה אלמא חשיב:

א) נ"ל מליקה זר וסכין דמטמאה בגדים אבית הבליעה והלא וכו'.

ודם דרך רחם, ואזדא ר' שמעון לטעמיה ורבנן לטעמייהו. מתקיף לה רב יוסף: חדא – דהיינו רישא, ועוד, "משם" – מקום ולד משמע! אלא אמר רב יוסף: [א]כגון שיצא ולד ודם דרך דופן, *ובמקור מקומו טמא קמיפלגי, מר סבר – [ב]מקור מקומו טמא, ומ"ס מקור מקומו טהור. אמר ר"ל: לדברי המטמא בדם – מטמא באשה, לדברי המטהר בדם – מטהר באשה. ור' יוחנן אמר: אף [ג]לדברי המטמא בדם – מטהר באשה. ואזדא ר' יוחנן לטעמיה, *דאמר רבי יוחנן משום ר"ש בן יוחי: מנין שאין אשה טמאה עד שיצא מדוה דרך ערותה, שנאמר: °"ואיש אשר ישכב את אשה דוה וגלה את ערותה את מקורה הערה" – [ד]מלמד שאין אשה טמאה עד שיצא מדוה דרך ערותה. אמר ריש לקיש משום רבי יהודה נשיאה: מקור שנעקר ונפל לארץ – טמאה, שנאמר: °"יען השפך נחושתך ותגלי ערותך". למאי? אילימא לטומאת שבעה "דם" אמר רחמנא, ולא חתיכה! אלא לטומאת ערב. אמר רבי יוחנן: [ה]מקור שהזיע כשתי טיפי מרגליות – טמאה. למאי? אילימא לטומאת שבעה – חמשה דמים טמאין באשה, ותו לא! [ו]אלא לטומאת ערב. [ז]ודווקא תרתי, אבל חדא – אימא מעלמא אתיא. § "כל הנשים מטמאין בבית החיצון". § הי ניהו "בית החיצון"? אמר ריש לקיש: כל שתינוקת יושבת ונראת. א"ל רבי יוחנן: אותו מקום – גלוי הוא אצל שרץ! אלא אמר רבי יוחנן: [ח]עד בין השינים. איבעיא להו: בין השינים. כלפנים או כלחוץ? ת"ש, דתני רבי זכאי: עד בין השינים, [ט]בין השינים עצמן – כלפנים. במתניתא תנא: מקום דישה. מאי "מקום דישה"? אמר רב יהודה: [י]מקום שהשמש דש. תנו רבנן: *"בבשרה" – מלמד שמטמאה בפנים כבחוץ. ואין לי אלא נדה, זבה מנין? ת"ל: "זובה בבשרה". [כ]פולטת ש"ז מנין? ת"ל: "יהיה". ור' שמעון אומר: דיה כבועלה, מה בועלה – אינו מטמא עד שתצא טומאה לחוץ, אף היא – אינה מטמאה עד שתצא טומאתה לחוץ. וסבר רבי שמעון דיה כבועלה? והתניא, °"ורחצו במים וטמאו עד הערב". אמר ר' שמעון: וכי מה בא זה ללמדנו? אם לענין נוגע בשכבת זרע – הרי כבר נאמר למטה "או איש", *אלא מפני שטומאת בית הסתרים היא, [ל]וטומאת בית הסתרים אינה מטמאה, [מ]אלא שגזרת הכתוב הוא! לא קשיא, כאן – במשמשת, כאן – בפולטת. פולטת – תיפוק ליה דהא שמשה! בשטבלה לשמושה. למימרא דמשמשת בטומאת ערב סגי לה? והא אמר רבא: [נ]משמשת – כל שלשה ימים אסורה לאכול בתרומה, שאי אפשר לה שלא תפלוט! הכא במאי עסקינן – שהטבילוה במטה. מכלל דכי קאמר רבא – דאזלה איהי בכרעה וטבלה, דילמא בהדי דקאזלה שדיתא?

וכי

תורה אור: ויקרא כ; יחזקאל טז; ויקרא טו

**רש"י**

ודם דרך רחם. בשלשת ימי הקושי קודם לידה, ואמור רבנן דזיבה היא, דלא מטהר לה ולד, דלאו לידה היא, ורבי שמעון מטהר. (א) לטמא, הואיל וימי זיבה הן, ודם קושי בימי זיבה – רחמנא טהריה. שיצא ולד ודם דרך דופן. ופלוגתא אחריתי היא, ולאו אקושי קאי, דרישא איירי כשיצא דם דרך רחם קודם לידה. רבנן סברי מקור מקומו טמא. הלכך טיפת דם מטמאה, ואע"ג דדרך דופן לאו ראייה היא לטמא את האשה טומאת שבעה, מיהו טיפה עצמה מטמאה במגע משום דנגע במקור ומקור מקומו טמא. ורבי שמעון סבר: מקור מקומו טהור מלטמא טיפה הנוגעת בו, הלכך כי אתא דם דרך דופן, טהור מלטמא וכדם מכה דמי, וכי אתא נמי דרך רחם, טהור כל ימי זיבה, היכא דליכא שופי סמוך ללידה דולד מטהרו ואע"ג דולד דרך דופן נפק. מטמא באשה טומאת שבעה. משום ראיית נדה, ואע"ג דבא דרך דופן. שנעקר. חתיכת בשר. נחושתך. שולייך והיינו מקור, וכתיב "ותגלי ערותך" אלמא נעקר ונשפך לארץ קרי ליה ערוה כאילו הוא במקומו, הילכך טמא. נחושתך – שולים, כדאמר במסכת שבת (דף מא.): מפני שנחושתה מחממתה. ובטהרות נמי בכמה דוכתין: נחושתו של תנור (כלים פ"ח מ"ג). לטומאת ערב. מפני שנגעה בו בילידתה. טיפי מרגליות. דם לבן וצלול. לטומאת ערב. מפני שנגע במקור ונוגע בה. מעלמא. מן הצדדין. כשהתינוקת יושבת. נפתח רחמה קצת. א"ר יוחנן. לשון קושיא הוא. אותו מקום. מי קרי "בבשרה" כולו חוץ הוא, ואפי' אגב מגע שרץ דקיימא לן אין מגע בית הסתרים מטמא – גלוי הוא אם נגע שם שרץ. טומאת בית הסתרים. לקמן יליף מ"וידיו לא שטף במים" (ויקרא טו) דלאו בר טמויי הוא, ובתורת כהנים נמי: מיניה נפקא לן. כמין שינים. יש בתוך הרחם תלתולי בשר. שהשמש. אבר. תלמוד לומר זובה בבשרה. ואע"ג דבנדה כתיב מדאפקיה בלשון זובה ילפינן זיבה. יהיה. זובה בבשרה. בועלה. בעל קרי אינו מטמא עד שתצא טומאתו לחוץ, כדכתיב (שם טו): "ואשר תצא ממנו שכבת זרע". ה"ג בתורת כהנים: מה בא זה ללמדנו אם לענין הנוגע בשכבת זרע הרי כבר אמור למטה אלא מפני כו'. (ב) מה בא זה ללמדנו. הא משום טבילה דידיה לא איצטריך דהא כתיב לעיל: "ואיש כי תצא ממנו שכבת זרע", ואם ללמד עליה שצריכה טבילה אם נגע בשרה מבחוץ בשכבת זרע כשיצאתה ממנו, הרי כבר אמור למטה בפרשת "אמור אל הכהנים" (ויקרא כב): "או איש אשר תצא", ואמר לקמן בפרקין (דף מג.): מנין לנוגע בש"ז? ת"ל: "או איש", אלמא: מיניה נפקא לן. אלא. בא ללמדנו שאפי' לא נגע בשרה מבחוץ בקרי – טמאה מפני טיפת תשמיש. והוצרך להשמיענו שטמא, דאי לא אשמעי' לא הוה (ג) קיימא לן, מפני שהיא טומאת בית הסתרים, ואינה מטמאה, אלא מפני שגזרת הכתוב הוא. אלמא, לא אמרינן דדיה כבועלה. במשמשת. גזרת הכתוב, ולא בפולטת. פולטת. תיפוק ליה דקודם יציאתו חוץ טמאה היא, דהא שמשה. בשטבלה לשמושה. ולמחר פלטה, וקאמר לך ר' שמעון בה: דיה כבועלה. כל שלשה כו'. וכיון דכל שלשה אסורה משום תשמישה, דיה כבועלה היכי משכחת לה? אי לאחר שלשה אפי' יצא נמי, טהורה, דהא שכבת זרע מסרחת היא! הכא במאי עסקינן. הא דקאמר ר"ש דטהורה, בטבלה לתשמישה – שהטבילוה במטה, דכיון דלא זזה ממקומה, אפשר לה בלא פליטה. מכלל. דהא דרבא, כגון דאזלא איהי בכרעה, א"כ מאי "אי אפשר שלא תפלוט כל שלשה", דמשמע טמאה ודאית, הא בחזקת טהורה היא טפי, דאיכא למימר: בהדי דאזלא ומסגייא בכרעה, שדיתיה לכוליה קודם טבילה!

**תוספות**

ואזדא ר' יוחנן לטעמיה. וא"ת: והא משמיה דר"ש קאמר, ור"ל נמי מודה דר' שמעון מטהר באשה, דקאמר: לדברי המטהר בדם – מטהר באשה! וי"ל: דה"פ מילתיה דר"ל לדברי המטמא בדם – מטמא באשה משום ראייה, ומיירי כגון שילא הולד והדם דרך דופן, ובקושי, דלאו קושי דולד הוא. ורבי שמעון דמטהר בדם – מטהר באשה, דולד הוה, וקושי סמוך ללידה רחמנא טהריה. אבל אי לאו ולד הוא, אף לרבי שמעון טמאה, דלא בעינן שילא דרך ערותה לכ"ע ור' יוחנן אמר דאף רבנן מטהרי באשה, דבעינן שילא דרך ערותה לכ"ע והשתא קאמר שפיר "ואזדא רבי יוחנן לטעמיה", אע"ג דמשמיה דרבי שמעון קאמר, דמדרבי שמעון נשמע לרבנן.

וסבר ר"ש דיה כבועלה והתניא וכו' אע"ג דקרא במשמשת איירי, סבר המקשה דמטעם משמשת לא היתה טמאה, אי לאו משום שהזרע נפלט לבית החיצון. וא"ת: לרבנן נמי תקשה, דאמאי איצטריך קרא, תיפוק ליה מ"יהיה" ויש לומר: אף דרבי שמעון אדרבי שמעון פריך, וכי משני "כאן בפולטת, כאן במשמשת" אתי נמי שפיר אף לרבנן. ואיצטריך קרא למשמשת, אע"פ שנכנס הזרע מתחלה לבית הפנימי ולא יצא לבית החיצון, דאי יצא – תיפוק ליה משום פליטת הזרע. ואפילו למ"ד לעיל "במקום שהשמש דש הוי בית החיצון", היינו באדם בינוני, וכן באשה בינונית, אבל בגדול וקטנה – משכחת לה שפיר שהזרע נכנס לבית הפנימי מתחלה. אי נמי: שמא לרבנן לא מטמא משום פליטת זרע, אלא כשהיה הזרע בבית הפנימי ונפלט לחיצון. אבל כשעומד הזרע בחיצון במקומו, ולא נפלט שם ממקום אחר – לא מטמא אלא משום משמשת.

פולטת תיפוק ליה דהא שמשה. היה יודע דליסני ליה "כשטבלה לשימושה", דהא כתיב "וטמאה עד הערב", אלא משום דבעי למפרך מרבא דאמר: כל שלשה לא מהני לה טבילה. ואם תאמר: בלאו הכי מצי לאקשויי מרבא אקרא! ויש לומר: דקרא איכא לאוקומי דאזלא איהי בכרעה. אי נמי: כשקנחה עצמה יפה, דאפשר לכבד הבית שלא ישתייר כלום. דתנן במס' מקוואות (פ"ח מ"ד) האשה ששמשה את ביתה, וירדה וטבלה, ולא כבדה את הבית – כאילו לא טבלה. אבל השתא אמאי דמשני "כאן בפולטת, כאן במשמשת" פריך שפיר: דאי איתא דכבדה הבית, אם כן תיפוק ליה דהרי פלטה!

מסתברא

**עין משפט נר מצוה**

טז א ב ג ד מיי' פ"ו מהל' איסורי ביאה הל"ה ופ"א מהל' משכב ומושב הל"ט:
יז ה ו מיי' פ"א מהל' משכב ומושב הל"י:
יח ז מיי' שם הלי"א:
יט ח ט י מיי' פ"ה מהל' איסורי ביאה הל"ב טור יו"ד סי' קפג:
כ כ מיי' פ"ה מהל' אבות הטומאה הלי"א:
כא ל מיי' פ"ה מהל' אבות הטומאה הל"ט ופ"א מהל' טומאת מת הלכה ג:
כב מ מיי' פ"ה מהל' אבות הטומאה הל"ט:
כג נ מיי' פ"ז מהל' תרומות הל"ז:

**תוספי הרא"ש**

כגון שיצא ולד דרך דופן ודם דרך רחם וברישא פליגי באשה אם היא זבה ובסיפא פליגי בדם אם הוא טמא ופריך ליה רב יוסף חדא דהיינו רישא והא בהא תליא וחד טעמא הוא: ואזדא ר' יוחנן לטעמיה וקשה דהא ר' יוחנן משום רשב"י קאמר לה ומודה ר"ל דלר' שמעון בעי' שיצא מדוה דרך ערותה ונראה לפ' דר"ל קאי אברייתא לשנויי שינויא אחרינא כגון שיצא ולד ודם דרך דופן. וה"ק לדברי המטמא בדם מטמא באשה כלומר מי שמטמא בדם היינו משום שמטמא באשה דלא חשיב ליה לידה ויולדת בזוב היא אע"פ שלא יצא מדוה דרך ערותה היא טמאה וגם הדם טמא ולדברי המטהר בדם היינו משום דמטהר באשה דחשיב ליה לידה ומקושי מטהר הלכך היא טהורה והדם טהור ודוקא בקושי אבל בשופי טמא אע"ג דקאתי דרך דופן דר' שמעון לא בעי שיצא מדוה דרך ערותה. ורישא איירי ביצא ולד דרך דופן ודם דרך רחם וסיפא דיצא ולד ודם דרך דופן וקמ"ל דלא בעינן שיצא מדוה דרך ערותה. ור' יוחנן אמר אף לדברי המטמא בדם מטהר באשה ולכ"ע בעי' שיצא מדוה דרך ערותה ורבנן לא מטמו בדם אלא משום דנגע במקור: וסבר ר' שמעון דיה כבועלה והתניא כו'. תימה כיון דמדמי משמשת לפולטת לרבנן נמי תיקשי למה לי מיהיה תיפוק לי מורחצו. וליכא למימר דהא דמטמא קרא משמשת כשיצא לחוץ ונגע בה מאבראי דא"כ מאו איש נפקא. וי"ל דלרבנן ניחא ליה דאיצטריך יהיה ליה למימר דרואה הויא לכל דבר מדרבי ליה קרא דאיירי בנדה וזבה ואי לא כתיב אלא קרא דורחצו הוה נפקא לן מיניה דמטמאה בפנים כבחוץ אבל לא ידעי' דרואה הויא ותימה לרבנן למה להו קרא דורחצו דהך קרא דיהיה שמעינן שפיר דרואה הויא ומטמאה בפנים כבחוץ. וי"ל דאי לאו קרא דורחצו דש"מ טומאה באשה ששמשה שטמאה מחמת ש"ז לא הוה דרשי' יהיה לפולטת ש"ז כיון דלא אשכחן בשום דוכתא דאשה טמאה מחמת ש"ז: כאן בפולטת כאן במשמשת. תימה היכא טעי תלמודא לדמויי משמשת לפולטת דהא קרא במשמשת כתיב דכתיב ואשה אשר ישכב איש אותה וי"ל דהוה טעי בלישנא דברייתא דקתני מפני שטומאת בית הסתרים היא דמשמע דה"ק דאע"ג דגבי טומאות בעלמא בית הסתרים לא מטמו במגע הכא גזירת הכתוב הוא דמטמא כאילו נגע בה בגלוי ומאחר דמשום מגע מטמא ליה כאלו נגע בה בגלוי ס"ד דה"ה בפולטת ומ"מ משני ליה כאן במשמשת וה"ק גזירת הכתוב דמשמשת טמאה בכל ענין אפי' בבית הסתרים ולהך מסקנא ניחא נמי לרבנן דאיצטריך קרא דיהיה דלא שמעינן דפולטת מטמא בפנים כמשמשת. ותימה כיון דשמעינן דפולטת מטמאה בפנים למה לי קרא דורחצו תיפוק לי שדרך תשמיש נגע ש"ז בבשרה. וי"ל אינה מטמאה אלא בבית החיצון ומשמשת טמא הכתוב אפי' נכנס הזרע לבית הפנימי ולא נגע כלל בחיצון: למימרא דמשמשת בטומאת ערב סגי לה והאמר רבא. תימה דמשמע דלא קשה מהא מילתיה דרבא אלא לפי סוגיא דשמעתין ואמאי דבלא סוגיא דשמעתין הוה מצי לאקשויי מקרא לרבא דבקרא משמע דלית ליה אלא טומאת ערב דכתיב ורחצו במים וטמאו עד הערב. וע"ק מאי פריך מהא דקאמר בטומאת ערב סגי לה. לימא דמיירי כגון בקנחה יפה יפה עצמה או רחצה בחמין דע"כ אפשר לה לכבד את הבית יפה שלא ישתייר בה ש"ז כדאמרינן ביבמות ס"פ אלמנה גבי משמשת טובלת ואוכלת בתרומה לערב וכן פ' ב"ש ובהאשה רבה עומדת מחיקו וטובלת ואוכלת בתרומה. ועוד תנן בפ' ח' דמס' מקואות האשה ששימשה את ביתה וירדה וטבלה ולא כבדה את ביתה כאילו לא טבלה. וי"ל דמהך פירכא מיתרצא פירכא קמייתא דמקרא לא מצי לאקשויי לרבא דאיכא לאוקומי כשכבדה את ביתה אבל השתא דמוקי הך קרא דורחצו במשמשת ע"כ מיירי דלא כבדה את הבית דאי כבדה תיפוק לי דטמאה משום דנגע ש"ז בבשרה מבחוץ דהרי פלטה:

**מסורת הש"ס**

[לעיל עז. וש"נ]
מכות יז:
[לעיל כח: וש"נ]
לקמן מב:

**הגהות הב"ח**

(א) רש"י ד"ה ודם וכו' ור' שמעון מטהר מלטמא: (ב) ד"ה מה בא זה וכו' ה"ג אלא ה"ק ובהך לא מחייב ממנו ש"ז והחך במים ואם ללמד וכו' ואחרי' לקמן בפירקין נ"ב כדך מג ע"ב ובתוס' לשם מפורש אמאי איצטריך או איש ולפינן ליה מוכל בגד וכל עור אשר יהיה עליו ש"ז וכבס במים וגו': (ג) בא"ד לא אשמועי' לא הוה ידעינן ליה מפני שהיא:

**גליון הש"ס**

גמ' שאי אפשר לה שלא תפלוט. ע' יבמות לד ע"ב תד"ה התורה:

וְכִי תֵּימָא: דִּילְמָא אִשְׁתַּיֵּיר, אִי הָכִי "חָיְישִׁינַן שֶׁמָּא נִשְׁתַּיֵּיר" מִבָּעֵי לֵיהּ! אֶלָּא לְרָבָא נַמִי – שֶׁהִטְבִּילוּהָ בְּמִטָּה, וְלָא קַשְׁיָא, כָּאן – בְּמִתְהַפֶּכֶת, כָּאן – בְּשֶׁאֵינָהּ מִתְהַפֶּכֶת. וְרָבָא אַקְּרָא קָאֵי, וְהָכִי קָאָמַר: [א]כִּי כָּתַב רַחֲמָנָא "וְרָחֲצוּ בַמַּיִם וְטָמְאוּ עַד הָעָרֶב" – בְּשֶׁאֵינָהּ מִתְהַפֶּכֶת, אֲבָל בְּמִתְהַפֶּכֶת – כָּל שְׁלֹשָׁה יָמִים אֲסוּרָה לֶאֱכוֹל בִּתְרוּמָה, שֶׁאִי אֶפְשָׁר לָהּ שֶׁלֹּא תִּפְלוֹט. בְּעָא מִינֵּיהּ רַב שְׁמוּאֵל בַּר בִּיסְנָא מֵאַבָּיֵי: *פּוֹלֶטֶת שִׁכְבַת זֶרַע, רוֹאָה הָוְיָא אוֹ נוֹגַעַת הָוְיָא? נָפְקָא מִינַּהּ: לִסְתּוֹר וּלְטַמֵּא בְּמַשֶּׁהוּ, וּלְטַמֵּא בִּפְנִים כְּבַחוּץ. מַה נַּפְשָׁךְ, אִי שְׁמִיעַ לֵיהּ *מַתְנִיתִין, לְרַבָּנַן – רוֹאָה הָוְיָא, וּלְר' שִׁמְעוֹן – נוֹגַעַת הָוְיָא. וְאִי לָא שְׁמִיעַ לֵיהּ *מַתְנִיתִין, מִסְתַּבְּרָא – נוֹגַעַת הָוְיָא! לְעוֹלָם שְׁמִיעַ לֵיהּ *מַתְנִיתִין, וְאַלִּיבָּא דְּרַבָּנַן – לָא קָמִיבַּעְיָא לֵיהּ, כִּי קָא מִיבַּעְיָא לֵיהּ – אַלִּיבָּא דְּר"ש. וּלְטַמֵּא בִּפְנִים כְּבַחוּץ לָא קָמִיבַּעְיָא לֵיהּ, כִּי קָמִיבַּעְיָא לֵיהּ – לִסְתּוֹר וּלְטַמֵּא בְּכָל שֶׁהוּא, מַאי? כִּי קָאָמַר רַבִּי שִׁמְעוֹן דַּיָּהּ כְּבוֹעֲלָהּ – הָנֵי מִילֵּי לְטַמּוּיֵי בִּפְנִים כְּבַחוּץ, אֲבָל לִסְתּוֹר וּלְטַמֵּא בְּכָל שֶׁהוּא – רוֹאָה הָוְיָא, אוֹ דִּילְמָא – לָא שְׁנָא? אִיכָּא דְּאָמְרִי: לְעוֹלָם לָא שְׁמִיעַ לֵיהּ מַתְנִיתָא, וְהָכִי קָמִיבַּעְיָא לֵיהּ, מִדְּאַחְמִיר רַחֲמָנָא אַבַּעֲלֵי קְרָיִין בְּסִינַי – רוֹאָה הָוְיָא. אוֹ דִּילְמָא: לָא גָּמְרִינַן מִסִּינַי, דְּחִידּוּשׁ הוּא, דְּהָא זָבִין וּמְצוֹרָעִים דַּחֲמִירִי – וְלָא אַחְמִיר בְּהוּ רַחֲמָנָא? א"ל: [ב]רוֹאָה הָוְיָא. אֲתָא שַׁיְילֵיהּ (א) לְרָבָא, א"ל: רוֹאָה הָוְיָא. אֲתָא לְקַמֵּיהּ דְּרַב יוֹסֵף, א"ל: רוֹאָה הָוְיָא. הֲדַר אֲתָא לְקַמֵּיהּ דְּאַבָּיֵי, א"ל: *כּוּלְּכוּ בְּרוּקָא חֲדָא תְּפִיתוּ. אֲמַר לֵיהּ: שַׁפִּיר אָמְרִי לָךְ, עַד כָּאן לָא קָאָמַר ר"ש דַּיָּהּ כְּבוֹעֲלָהּ – אֶלָּא לְטַמֵּא בִּפְנִים כְּבַחוּץ, אֲבָל לִסְתּוֹר וּלְטַמֵּא בְּכָל שֶׁהוּא – רוֹאָה הָוְיָא.§ ת"ר: [א] [ג]הַנִּדָּה, וְהַזָּבָה, וְהַשּׁוֹמֶרֶת יוֹם כְּנֶגֶד יוֹם, וְהַיּוֹלֶדֶת – כּוּלָּן מְטַמְּאוֹת בִּפְנִים כְּבַחוּץ. בִּשְׁלָמָא כּוּלְּהוּ – לְחַיֵּי, אֶלָּא יוֹלֶדֶת, [ב] אִי בִּימֵי נִדָּה – נִדָּה, אִי בִּימֵי זִיבָה – זִיבָה! לָא צְרִיכָא – שֶׁיָּרְדָה לִטְבּוֹל מְטוּמְאָה לְטָהֳרָה. וְכִי הָא דְּאָמַר רַבִּי זֵירָא א"ר חִיָּיא בַּר אַשִׁי, אָמַר רַב: [ד]יוֹלֶדֶת שֶׁיָּרְדָה לִטְבּוֹל מְטוּמְאָה לְטָהֳרָה, וְנֶעֱקַר מִמֶּנָּה דָּם, בִּירִידָה – טְמֵאָה, בַּעֲלִיָּיה – טְהוֹרָה. א"ל רַבִּי יִרְמְיָה לְר' זֵירָא: בִּירִידָה אַמַּאי טְמֵאָה? טוּמְאָה בְּלוּעָה הִיא! א"ל: *זִיל שַׁיְילֵיהּ לְרַבִּי אָבִין, דְּאַסְבְּרִית נִיהֲלֵיהּ, וְכַרְכִּישׁ לִי בְּרֵישֵׁיהּ בֵּי מִדְרְשָׁא. אֲזַל שַׁיְילֵיהּ, א"ל: עֲשָׂאוּהָ כְּנִבְלַת עוֹף טָהוֹר, [ה]שֶׁמְּטַמְּאָה בְּגָדִים בְּבֵית הַבְּלִיעָה. מִי דָּמֵי? הָתָם

וְכִי תֵּימָא חָיְישִׁי' שֶׁמָּא נִשְׁתַּיֵּיר בָּהּ. וּמִסְּפֵיקָא קָא מְטַמְּאָה, א"כ מַאי "אִי אֶפְשָׁר", "חָיְישִׁינַן" מִיבָּעֵי לֵיהּ! אֶלָּא לְרָבָא נַמִי. דְּלָא אָזְלָה, הִילְכָּךְ כָּל שָׁעָה פּוֹלֶטֶת, וְהָא דְּר' שִׁמְעוֹן דִּיכוֹלָה לִטְבּוֹל לְשִׁמּוּשָׁהּ, כְּגוֹן שֶׁלֹּא נִתְהַפְּכָה לְאַחַר הַטְּבִילָה, וּדְרָבָא – בְּמִתְהַפֶּכֶת. וְרָבָא. לְפָרוּשֵׁי לָן קְרָא אֲתָא: דְּכִי כְּתִיב "וְרָחֲצוּ בַמַּיִם", דְּמַשְׁמַע דִּיכוֹלָה לִטְבּוֹל בּוֹ בַּיּוֹם – כְּשֶׁאֵינָהּ מִתְהַפֶּכֶת. ל"א: מִתְהַפֶּכֶת בִּשְׁעַת תַּשְׁמִישׁ, וְאֵין הַזֶּרַע נִקְלָט בָּרֶחֶם יַחַד – הִילְכָּךְ פּוֹלֶטֶת וְהוֹלֶכֶת מְעַט מְעַט. אֵינָהּ מִתְהַפֶּכֶת בִּשְׁעַת תַּשְׁמִישׁ – נִקְלָט הַזֶּרַע יַחַד, וְיוֹצֵא בְּבַת אַחַת. רוֹאָה הָוְיָא. מִשּׁוּם רְאִיָּיה טַמְּיֵיהּ קְרָא, *וּמִשּׁוּם נוֹגַעַת בְּשִׁכְבַת זֶרַע. דְּעַד הַשְׁתָּא הָוְיָא נְגִיעַת בֵּית הַסְּתָרִים, וְלָא הָוְיָא טְמֵאָה אֶלָּא בְּיוֹם תַּשְׁמִישׁ, וּמִגְּזֵרַת הַכָּתוּב, וְכִי פָּלְטָה – נָגְעָה לְבָרַאי, וּמְטַמְּיָא. לִסְתּוֹר. בְּזִיבָה בִּימֵי סְפִירָה, אִי רוֹאָה הָוְיָא – סוֹתֶרֶת, אֲבָל נוֹגַעַת – לָא, שֶׁאִם נָגְעָה בְּשׁוּם טוּמְאָה – אֵינָהּ סוֹתֶרֶת, דְּהָא "וְסָפְרָה לָּהּ" כְּתִיב, וְהָאִיכָּא! וּלְטַמֵּא בְּמַשֶּׁהוּ. לִרְאִיָּיה לָא בָּעֵינַן שִׁיעוּרָא, כִּדְאָמְרִי' בְּמַתְנִי': לְדַם נִדָּה וּלְזִיבָה וּלְקֶרִי – מְטַמְּאִין בְּכָל שֶׁהוּא, אֲבָל נוֹגֵעַ – בָּעֵי שִׁיעוּרָא, כִּדְאָמַר בְּפִירְקִין (לקמן דף מג.): אִיכָּא לְמ"ד כָּעֲדָשָׁה, וְאִיכָּא לְמ"ד כַּחֲתִימַת פִּי הָאַמָּה. אִי שְׁמִיעַ לֵיהּ. לְרַב שְׁמוּאֵל. מַתְנִיתָא. דִּפְלִיגִי רַבָּנַן וְר"ש לְעֵיל, דְּקָאָמְרִי רַבָּנַן: פּוֹלֶטֶת שִׁכְבַת זֶרַע מְטַמְּאָה בִּפְנִים כְּבַחוּץ, וּלְר"ש דְּדַיָּהּ כְּבוֹעֲלָהּ. לְרַבָּנַן רוֹאָה הָוְיָא. לְעִנְיַן לְטַמֵּא בִּפְנִים כְּבַחוּץ, וּלְר"ש – נוֹגַעַת הָוְיָא. וְאִי לָא שְׁמִיעַ לֵיהּ. אַמַּאי מְסַפְּקָא לֵיהּ? מִסְּבָרָא נוֹגַעַת הָוְיָא, דְּהָא לָא מִגּוּפָהּ חָזְיָא, אֶלָּא מַה שֶּׁקִּבְּלָה הִיא פּוֹלֶטֶת. וְאַלִּיבָּא דְּרַבָּנַן לָא קָמִיבַּעְיָא לֵיהּ. דְּכֵיוָן דִּלְרַבָּנַן מְטַמְּיָא בִּפְנִים כְּבַחוּץ, אַלְמָא רוֹאָה הָוְיָא, וְכ"ש דִּמְטַמְּאָה בְּמַשֶּׁהוּ. וּלְעִנְיַן סְתִירָה נַמִי סָתְרָה, דְּהָא בְּתוֹרַת זִיבָה מְרַבֵּי לֵיהּ מִ"יִּהְיֶה (ג) זוֹבוֹ". כִּי קָא מִיבָּעֵי לֵיהּ אַלִּיבָּא דְּר"ש. וּלְטַמֵּא בִּפְנִים לָא מִיבָּעֵי לֵיהּ, דְּהָא שָׁמְעִינַן לְר"ש דְּלָא מְטַמְּיָא. כִּי קָא מִבַּעְיָא לֵיהּ לִסְתּוֹר וּלְטַמֵּא בְּמַשֶּׁהוּ. מַהוּ, מִי אָמְרִי' כִּי אָמַר ר' שִׁמְעוֹן דַּיָּהּ כְּבוֹעֲלָהּ לְטַמֵּא בִּפְנִים כְּבַחוּץ, מַה בּוֹעֲלָהּ – לָא מְטַמֵּא, אִיהִי נַמִי – לָא מְטַמְּאָה, אֲבָל לִסְתּוֹר וּלְטַמֵּא בְּמַשֶּׁהוּ – לָא מְשַׁוֵּי לָהּ כְּנוֹגַעַת, דְּהָא א"כ אָמַר דַּיָּהּ כְּבוֹעֲלָהּ – סָתְרָה וּמְטַמְּאָה בְּמַשֶּׁהוּ, כְּבוֹעֲלָהּ. אוֹ דִּילְמָא, לָא שְׁנָא, דְּכִי הֵיכִי דִּלְעִנְיַן טוּמְאַת פְּנִים מְשַׁוֵּי לָהּ נוֹגַעַת, לְעִנְיַן מַשֶּׁהוּ וּסְתִירָה – נַמִי מְשַׁוֵּי לָהּ נוֹגַעַת. לְעוֹלָם לָא שְׁמִיעַ לֵיהּ. מַתְנִי', וּדְקָאָמְרִינַן: מִסְּבָרָא נוֹגַעַת הָוְיָא, לָא הִיא. מִסְּבָרָא לָא מִיפְשַׁט לָן, דְּאִיכָּא לְמֵימַר: מִדְּאַחְמִיר רַחֲמָנָא בְּבַעֲלֵי קְרָיִין בְּסִינַי, דִּכְתִיב (שמות יט): "אַל תִּגְּשׁוּ אֶל אִשָּׁה", וְלָא הִזְהִיר עַל טְמֵא שֶׁרֶץ – רוֹאָה הָוְיָא. כּוּלְּכוּ בְּרוּקָא חֲדָא תְּפִיתוּ. כּוּלְּכֶם שְׁמוּעָה אַחַת. "תְּפִיתוּ" – לְשׁוֹן רוֹק, וַחֲבֵירוֹ בִּכְתוּבּוֹת: "תּוּף שְׁדֵי", בְּפֶרֶק "אַף עַל פִּי" (דף סא.). אָמַר לֵיהּ. אַבָּיֵי: שַׁפִּיר אָמַר לָךְ. אֲבָל לִסְתּוֹר וּלְטַמֵּא בְּמַשֶּׁהוּ רוֹאָה הָוְיָא. דְּאִי נַמִי דַּיָּהּ כְּבוֹעֲלָהּ, מְטַמְּיָא כְּבוֹעֲלָהּ בְּמַשֶּׁהוּ וְסָתְרָה כְּבוֹעֲלָהּ. כּוּלָּן מְטַמְּאִין בִּפְנִים כְּבַחוּץ. בִּרְאִיָּיה רִאשׁוֹנָה, אֲבָל בִּשְׁנִיָּיה לֵיכָּא לְמֵימַר, דְּהָא בְּלָא רְאִיָּיה טְמֵאָה הִיא. וְהַיּוֹלֶדֶת. לְקַמָּן מְפָרֵשׁ. הַזָּבָה וְשׁוֹמֶרֶת יוֹם. הָכִי קָאָמַר: בֵּין שֶׁרָאֲתָה ג' יָמִים, בֵּין שֶׁרָאֲתָה יוֹם אֶחָד – מְטַמְּאָה בְּבֵית הַחִיצוֹן בִּרְאִיָּיה רִאשׁוֹנָה. אִי בִּימֵי נִדָּה. יָלְדָה וְרָאֲתָה – הָא תָּנֵי לֵיהּ, וְאִי בִּימֵי זִיבָה – הָא תָּנֵי לֵיהּ לְזִיבָה. לְאַחַר שְׁבוּעַיִם וְקַיְימָא לָן כְּבֵית הִלֵּל דְּאָמְרִי בִּ"בְנוֹת כּוּתִים" (לעיל דף לה.) בְּיוֹמֵי וּטְבִילָה תָּלָא רַחֲמָנָא, דְּלָא הָוֵי דַּם טוֹהַר אֶלָּא לְאַחַר טְבִילָה. וְנֶעֱקַר דָּם. לְבֵית הַחִיצוֹן, וְעָמַד שָׁם יוֹם אוֹ יוֹמַיִם. טְמֵאָה. כָּל זְמַן שֶׁהוּא בָּהּ, וּכְשֶׁיָּצָא – בָּעְיָא טְבִילָה אַחֲרִיתִי, דְּלָא טִהֲרָתָהּ טְבִילָה. וְהַיְינוּ דְּתַנְיָא: יוֹלֶדֶת מְטַמְּיָא בְּבֵית הַחִיצוֹן. טוּמְאָה בְּלוּעָה הִיא. וְקַיְימָא לָן בְּפֶרֶק "בְּהֵמָה הַמַּקְשָׁה" (חולין דף עא.): טוּמְאָה בְּלוּעָה – אֵינָהּ מְטַמְּאָה, לֹא בְּמַגָּע וְלֹא בְּמַשָּׂא. וְהָכָא, הָא טוּמְאָה בְּלוּעָה הִיא. וְלָא דָּמְיָא לְכָל הַנָּשִׁים שֶׁמְּטַמְּאוֹת בְּבֵית הַחִיצוֹן, דְּהָתָם מִשּׁוּם רְאִיָּיה (ג) דְּמֵאֶתְמוֹל הִיא, וְטוּמְאַת שִׁבְעָה, וְרַחֲמָנָא אָמַר "בִּבְשָׂרָהּ" – מִכִּי אָתָא בְּבֵית הַחִיצוֹן הָוְיָא רְאִיָּיה. אֲבָל הָכָא, מִשּׁוּם מַשָּׂא וּנְגִיעָה הִיא, וְטוּמְאַת עֶרֶב. דְּאִי מִשּׁוּם רְאִיָּיה מֵאֶתְמוֹל אִיעֲקַר, וּמֵאֶתְמוֹל הָוְיָא רְאִיָּיה, וּרְאִיָּיה דְּמֵאֶתְמוֹל לָא מְהַנְּיָא לָהּ הָאִידָּנָא. דְּמֵאֶתְמוֹל הֲוָה לְהוּ יְמֵי טוּמְאָה, וְהַשְׁתָּא הָווּ לְהוּ יְמֵי טוֹהַר, וְטוּמְאָה בְּלוּעָה לָא מְטַמְּיָא בְּמַגָּע וּבְמַשָּׂא. אַסְבְּרִית נִיהֲלֵיהּ. פֵּירַשְׁתִּי לוֹ טַעְמָא. וְכַרְכִּישׁ לִי בְּרֵישֵׁיהּ. הוֹדָה לִדְבָרַי וְנִעְנַע בְּרֹאשׁוֹ. בְּגָדִים בְּבֵית הַבְּלִיעָה. בְּגָדִים שֶׁהוּא לָבוּשׁ בָּהֶן בְּשָׁעָה שֶׁנּוֹגֵעַ בָּהּ אֵינָן טְמֵאִין, שֶׁאֵין לָהֶן טוּמְאַת מַגָּע, דְּאָמַר רַחֲמָנָא "לֹא יֹאכַל לְטָמְאָה בָהּ" (ויקרא כב) – אֵין לְךָ אֶלָּא מַה שֶּׁאָמוּר בָּהּ, אֲכִילָה וְלֹא מַגָּע. וּמַה הִיא מְטַמְּאָה – בְּגָדִים שֶׁהוּא לָבוּשׁ בִּשְׁעַת בְּלִיעָה, כִּדְכְתִיב (שם יז): "[וְכָל] נֶפֶשׁ אֲשֶׁר תֹּאכַל נְבֵלָה וּטְרֵפָה בָּאֶזְרָח וּבַגֵּר וְכִבֶּס בְּגָדָיו וְטָהֵר". וּבְנִבְלַת עוֹף טָהוֹר כְּתִיב, דְּנִבְלַת בְּהֵמָה לָא מְטַמְּאָה בְּבֵית הַבְּלִיעָה, כִּדְאָמַר בִּשְׁמַעְתִּין. וְנִבְלַת עוֹף טָמֵא נַמִי לָא מְטַמְּאָה, כִּדְאָמַר בְּתוֹרַת כֹּהֲנִים: מִי שֶׁאִיסּוּרוֹ מִשּׁוּם "בַּל תֹּאכַל נְבֵלָה" – יָצָא עוֹף טָמֵא, שֶׁאֵין אִיסּוּרוֹ מִשּׁוּם "בַּל תֹּאכַל נְבֵלָה", אֶלָּא מִשּׁוּם "בַּל תֹּאכַל טָמֵא". הָתָם

[נ"ל או משום]
[לעיל לג.]
[נ"ל מתניתא]
[נ"ל מתניתא]
[נ"ל מתניתא]
[שבת לט:]
[ב"ב קמב:]

**מסתברא** דנוגע הויא. ומסיני לא גמרינן, דחדוש הוא. ולהכי לרבנן נמי איצטריך "יהיה", דלא גמרינן מסיני, אע"ג דבסמוך בעי למימר דאף לר"ש רואה הויא וסתרה.
**מדאחמיר** רחמנא אבעלי קריין בסיני. מאיש לא מוכח, דפשיטא דרואה הוי. אלא מאשה, דמשום פולטת הזהיר רחמנא ג' ימים "אל תגשו אל אשה". **דהא** זבין ומצורעים דחמירי. אף ע"ג דאכתי לא נאמרה פרשת טומאה ושילוח טמאים, מ"מ ראוי להחמיר בהן יותר מבפולטת. **עד** כאן לא קאמר ר' שמעון כו'. אבל לטמא במשהו – רואה הויא. וא"ת: והא אמר בפסחים פרק "אלו דברים" (דף סז:) דר' שמעון סבר כר' נתן דזב בעי שיעור כחתימת פי האמה, ויליף בעל קרי מזב. וא"כ אמאי מטמא במשהו, נימא: "דיה כבועלה"! וי"ל: דרבי שמעון ודאי לא מטמא במשהו, והכא ה"ק: אפי' למאן דאית ליה כר' שמעון דפולטת ולא מטמאה בפנים כבחוץ, מ"מ מטמאה במשהו אי סבר דאיש מטמא במשהו.
**בירידה** טמאה. הדם טמא, דביומי וטבילה תליא רחמנא, וטמאה האשה – משום נוגע טומאת ערב. **אמאי** טומאה בלועה היא. לאביי דאמר בסמוך: אותו מקום של אשה בלוע הוי, ניחא דקרי ליה "טומאה בלועה". ולרבא נמי דאמר: בית הסתרים הוי, י"ל: דמיירי בשנעקר הדם מן המקור ולא יצא לבית החיצון. והא דמסיק "שיצא לחוץ" – לרבא לא צריך שיצא לחוץ לגמרי, אלא שיצא לבית החיצון דהוי בית הסתרים, וטמא במשא. ומיהו "עשאוה כנבלת עוף טהור" משמע דסבר כאביי, דלרבא אמר לקמן דמקום נבלת עוף טהור – בית הסתרים הוי.
**עשאוה** כנבלת עוף טהור. אע"ג דבעלמא לא החמירו בטומאה בלועה, הכא גזרו רבנן טפי, כדי שלא יבא לטעות ולטהרו על ידי טבילה אפילו כשיצא לחוץ. וכי משני "הכא נמי כשיצא לחוץ", סבר דלא גזרו.
שהוציא

**כד** א מיי' פ"ז מהל' תרומות הל"ז:
**כה** ב מיי' פ"ה מהל' אבות הטומאה הל"ט והלכה יא:
**כו** ג מיי' פ"ה מהל' איסורי ביאה הל"ב:
**כז** ד מיי' פ"ה מהל' משכב ומושב הל"ג סמג לאוין קיא:
**כח** ה מיי' פ"ג מהל' שאר אבות הטומאה הלכה א:

## תוספי הרא"ש

**מדאחמיר** רחמנא אבעלי קריין בסיני. לאו מאיש גמר דא"כ יגמר ממקדש דאחמיר רחמנא לשלח בעל קרי חוץ לב' מחנות כמו זב והתם לאו חידוש הוא אלא גמר אשה מאשה דמטעם פולטת החמיר הכתוב (דבעלי קריין) בסיני שיפרשו ג' ימים מנשותיהן: **דהא** זבין ומצורעין דחמירי. פי' שעתיד להחמיר עליהן יותר מבעלי קריין. ע"כ לא קאמר ר' שמעון דייה כבועלה כו' אבל לטמא במשהו רואה הויא וק' מהא דאמרינן בפסחים פ' אלו דברים דר' שמעון סבר כר' נתן דאיצטריך כחתימת פי האמה ויליף בעל קרי מזב וא"כ דייה כבועלה ולא תטמא במשהו וי"ל דלר' שמעון ודאי אינה מטמא' במשהו והכא ה"ק דאפי' סבירא לן כר' שמעון הא דאית ליה לעיל שאינה מטמאה בפנים כבחוץ מ"מ איפשר דס"ל דמטמאה במשהו: **הנדה** והזבה ושומרת יום כנגד יום כולם מטמאות בפנים כבחוץ. פרש"י בראיה ראשונה אבל בשניה ליכא למימר דהא בלא ראיה טמאה היא והה"ק הזבה והשומר' יום כלומר בין שראתה ג' ימים בין שראתה יום אחד מטמאה בבית החיצון בראיה ראשונה. ונ"ל דבתנ' דחק דמשכח' לה שפיר נפקותא בזבה דמטמאה בפנים כבחוץ אע"ג דכבר טמאה היא כגון שראתה ביום ראשון וביום שני ונעקר הדם ביום ג' ויצא לבית החיצון ולא יצא לחוץ עד יום ד' דאי לאו דמטמאה בפנים כבחוץ לא הויא זבה שלא ראתה ג' ימים רצופין: **אמאי** טומאה בלועה היא. אליבא דאביי קא פריך דאית ליה לקמן דאותו מקום של אשה בלוע הוא. ומי' לרבא נמי איכא למימר דקרי ליה טומאה בלועה משום דאיירי שנעקר מהמקור ולא יצא עדיין לבית החיצון והא דמסיק הכא נמי בשיצא לחוץ לרבא אע"ג דלא יצא לחוץ לגמרי אלא שיצא לבית החיצון לגמרי. ומי' מדקאמר עשאוה כנבלת עוף טהור משמע דס"ל כאביי דלרבא אמרינן לקמן דמקום נבלת עוף טהור בית הסרים הוי: **עשאוה** כנבלת עוף טהור. ואע"פ שלא החמירו בשאר טמאות בלועות דעלמא הכא גזרו טפי שלא יבא לטהרה ע"י טבילה זו אפי' נגע בה כשיצא לחוץ:
שהוציא

## הגהות הב"ח

(א) גמ' אתא שיילה לרבה. נ"ב רבה גרסי' ועי' במ"ש התוס' בפ' בנות כותים דף לג ד"ה רואה: (ב) רש"י ד"ה ואליבא וכו' מיהוא זבה: (ג) ד"ה טומאה בלועה וכו' מקום ראייה היא כנ"ל ותיבת דמאתמול נמחק:

## הגהות מהר"ב רנשבורג

א] גמ' ת"ר הנדה והזבה. נ"ב עיין סד"ט סי' קלד ס"ק כ"ו: ב] שם אי בימי נדה נדה. נ"ב יעו"ש בסי' הנ"ל ס"ק ב' בד"ה אך מ"ש הב"ח: בעין משפט אות ד'. נ"ל מיי' פ"ה מהל' איסורי ביאה:

**כט** א עי' בהגהות מיי' ריש פ"ו מהל' איסורי ביאה:

ר"מ מ"ז

**ל** ב מיי' פ"א מהל' מילה הלכ"ט סמג עשין כח טוש"ע יו"ד סי' רסב סעי' ד:

**לא** ג ד מיי' פ"א מהל' טומאת מת הל"ג וכל"ח:

**לב** ה ו ז מיי' פ"ג מהל' אבות הטומאות הלכה ח:

**לג** ח מיי' פ"ח מהל' טומאת מת הל"ג והלכה ח:

**לד** ט מיי' פ"ד מהל' כלים הל"ה:

הָתָם – אֵין לָהּ טוּמְאָה בַּחוּץ, הָכָא – כִּי נָפֵיק לְבָרַאי לִיטַּמֵּי! הָכָא נַמִי – כְּשֶׁיָּצָא לַחוּץ. אִי יָצָא לַחוּץ – מַאי לְמֵימְרָא? מַהוּ דְּתֵימָא: מִגּוֹ דְּמַהֲנֵי טְבִילָה לַדָּם דְּאִיכָּא גַּוַּאי – תְּהַנֵּי נַמִי לְהַאי, קמ"ל. שְׁמַעְתִּין – אִיפְּרִיק, אֶלָּא יוֹלֶדֶת, אִי בִּימֵי נִדָּה – נִדָּה, אִי בִּימֵי זִיבָה – זִיבָה! הָכָא בְּמַאי עָסְקִינַן – אבְּלֵידָה יְבֶשְׁתָּא. לֵידָה יְבֶשְׁתָּא מַאי "מְטַמֵּא בִּפְנִים כְּבַחוּץ" אִיכָּא? כְּגוֹן שֶׁהוֹצִיא וָלָד רֹאשׁוֹ חוּץ לַפְּרוֹזְדוֹר, וּכְדְרַב אוֹשַׁעְיָא. *דְּאָמַר רַב אוֹשַׁעְיָא: גְּזֵרָה שֶׁמָּא יוֹצִיא הַוָּלָד רֹאשׁוֹ חוּץ לַפְּרוֹזְדוֹר. וְכִי הַהוּא דַּאֲתָא לְקַמֵּיהּ דְּרָבָא, אֲמַר לֵיהּ: א] מַהוּ לְמִמְהַל בְּשַׁבְּתָא? אֲמַר לֵיהּ: שַׁפִּיר דָּמֵי. בָּתַר דִּנְפַק, אֲמַר רָבָא: ס"ד דְּהַהוּא גַּבְרָא לָא יָדַע דְּשָׁרֵי לְמִמְהַל בְּשַׁבְּתָא?! אֲזַל בָּתְרֵיהּ, אֲמַר לֵיהּ: אֵימָא לִי אִיזִי, גּוּפָא דְּעוּבְדָא הֵיכִי הֲוָה? אֲמַר לֵיהּ: שְׁמָעִית וָלָד דְּצָוַיץ אַפַּנְיָא דְּמַעֲלֵי שַׁבְּתָא, וְלָא אִתְיְלִיד עַד שַׁבְּתָא. אֲמַר לֵיהּ: בהַאי – *הוֹצִיא רֹאשׁוֹ חוּץ לַפְּרוֹזְדוֹר הוּא, וַהֲוֵי מִילָה שֶׁלֹּא בִּזְמַנָּהּ, וְכָל מִילָה שֶׁלֹּא בִּזְמַנָּהּ – אֵין מְחַלְּלִין עָלֶיהָ אֶת הַשַּׁבָּת. אִיבַּעְיָא לְהוּ: אוֹתוֹ מָקוֹם שֶׁל אִשָּׁה, בָּלוּעַ הָוֵי אוֹ בֵּית הַסְּתָרִים הָוֵי? לְמַאי נָפְקָא מִינַּהּ – כְּגוֹן שֶׁתָּחֲבָה לָהּ חֲבֶירְתָּהּ כְּזַיִת נְבֵלָה בְּאוֹתוֹ מָקוֹם. אִי אָמְרַתְּ בָּלוּעַ הָוֵי – טוּמְאָה בְּלוּעָה לָא מְטַמְּאָה, וְאִי אָמְרַתְּ בֵּית הַסְּתָרִים הָוֵי – נְהִי דִּבְמַגָּע לָא מְטַמְּיָא, בְּמַשָּׂא מִיהָא מְטַמְּיָא! אַבָּיֵי אָמַר: בָּלוּעַ הָוֵי. רָבָא אָמַר: גבֵּית הַסְּתָרִים הָוֵי. אָמַר רָבָא: מְנָא אָמִינָא לָהּ – דְּתַנְיָא, *אֶלָּא מִפְּנֵי שֶׁטּוּמְאַת בֵּית הַסְּתָרִים הִיא, וְטוּמְאַת בֵּית הַסְּתָרִים לֹא מְטַמְּאָה, אֶלָּא שֶׁגְּזֵרַת הַכָּתוּב הִיא. וְאַבָּיֵי – חֲדָא וְעוֹד קָאָמַר, חֲדָא – דְּטוּמְאָה בְּלוּעָה הִיא, וְעוֹד – אֲפִילּוּ אִם תִּמְצֵי לוֹמַר טוּמְאַת בֵּית הַסְּתָרִים הִיא – אֵינָהּ מְטַמְּאָה, אֶלָּא שֶׁגְּזֵרַת הַכָּתוּב הִיא. אִיבַּעְיָא לְהוּ: מְקוֹם נִבְלַת עוֹף טָהוֹר, בָּלוּעַ הָוֵי אוֹ בֵּית הַסְּתָרִים הָוֵי? לְמַאי נָפְקָא מִינַּהּ – כְּגוֹן שֶׁתָּחַב לוֹ חֲבֵירוֹ כְּזַיִת נְבֵלָה לְתוֹךְ פִּיו. אִי אָמְרַתְּ בָּלוּעַ הָוֵי – טוּמְאָה בְּלוּעָה לָא מְטַמְּיָא. *(אֶלָּא אִי) אָמְרַתְּ בֵּית הַסְּתָרִים הָוֵי – נְהִי נַמִי דִּבְמַגָּע לָא מְטַמֵּא, בְּמַשָּׂא מִיהָא מְטַמֵּא, אַבָּיֵי אָמַר: בָּלוּעַ הָוֵי, וְרָבָא אָמַר: דבֵּית הַסְּתָרִים הָוֵי. אָמַר אַבָּיֵי: מְנָא אָמִינָא לָהּ – דְּתַנְיָא, *יָכוֹל תְּהֵא נִבְלַת בְּהֵמָה מְטַמְּאָה בְּגָדִים אַבֵּית הַבְּלִיעָה – ת"ל: (ויקרא כב) °"נְבֵלָה וּטְרֵפָה לֹא יֹאכַל לְטָמְאָה בָהּ" – מִי שֶׁאֵין לָהּ טוּמְאָה אֶלָּא אֲכִילָתָהּ, היָצְתָה זוֹ שֶׁמְּטַמְּאָה קוֹדֶם שֶׁיֹּאכְלֶנָּה. וְתֵיתֵי בְּק"ו מִנִּבְלַת עוֹף טָהוֹר: וּמַה נִּבְלַת עוֹף טָהוֹר, שֶׁאֵין לָהּ טוּמְאָה בַּחוּץ – וְיֵשׁ לָהּ טוּמְאָה בִּפְנִים, זוֹ שֶׁיֵּשׁ לָהּ טוּמְאָה בַּחוּץ – אֵינוֹ דִּין שֶׁיֵּשׁ לָהּ טוּמְאָה בִּפְנִים? אָמַר קְרָא "בָּהּ" – בָּהּ וְלֹא בְּאַחֶרֶת. אִם כֵּן מַה תַּלְמוּד לוֹמַר (שם יא) °"וְהָאוֹכֵל"? זלִיתֵּן שִׁיעוּר לַנּוֹגֵעַ וְלַנּוֹשֵׂא כְּאוֹכֵל, מָה אוֹכֵל – בִּכְזַיִת, אַף נוֹגֵעַ וְנוֹשֵׂא – בִּכְזַיִת. אָמַר רָבָא: שֶׁרֶץ בְּקוּמְטוֹ – טָהוֹר, נְבֵלָה בְּקוּמְטוֹ – טָמֵא. שֶׁרֶץ בְּקוּמְטוֹ טָהוֹר – שֶׁרֶץ בִּנְגִיעָה הוּא דִּמְטַמֵּא, וּבֵית הַסְּתָרִים לָאו בַּר מַגָּע הוּא. נְבֵלָה בְּקוּמְטוֹ – טָמֵא, חנְהִי דִּבְמַגָּע לָא מְטַמֵּא – בְּמַשָּׂא מִיהָא מְטַמֵּא. טשֶׁרֶץ בְּקוּמְטוֹ, וְהִכְנִיסוֹ לַאֲוִיר הַתַּנּוּר – טָמֵא. פְּשִׁיטָא! מַהוּ דְּתֵימָא: "תּוֹכוֹ" אָמַר רַחֲמָנָא, וְלֹא

**רש"י**

הָתָם אֵין לָהּ טוּמְאָה בַּחוּץ. כִּדְפָרֵישִׁית: "לְטָמְאָה בָהּ" – אֵין לְךָ בָּהּ אֶלָּא מַה שֶּׁאָמוּר בָּהּ, וְהַךְ הוּא דִּגְזוֹר בָּהּ רַחֲמָנָא. הָכָא כִּי נָפֵיק לְבָרַאי תִּיטַּמֵּי. וְכֵיוָן דְּמִטַּמְּאָה בַּחוּץ, הָוְיָא כִּשְׁאָר טוּמְאוֹת דְּלָא מְטַמְּאוֹת בְּלוּעוֹת. הָכָא נַמִי כְּשֶׁיָּצָא לַחוּץ. לִכְשֶׁיֵּצֵא לַחוּץ מְטַמֵּא אוֹתָהּ אִם נֶעֱקַר קוֹדֶם טְבִילָה, וְאִם טָבְלָה – טְהוֹרָה כָּל זְמַן שֶׁהוּא שָׁם, וְלִכְשֶׁיֵּצֵא וְיִגַּע בָּהּ – יְטַמְּאֶנָּה. מַאי לְמֵימְרָא. הָא דָּם טָמֵא הוּא, דְּקוֹדֶם טְבִילָה נֶעֱקַר. שְׁמַעְתִּין. דְּרַבִּי זֵירָא, דַּהֲוָה קַשְׁיָא לָן: טוּמְאָה בְּלוּעָה הִיא. אִיפְּרִיק. דְּלִכְשֶׁיֵּצֵא לַחוּץ הוּא דְּקָאָמַר, וְהָשְׁתָּא לָא מִתּוֹקְמָא בָּרַיְיתָא דְּקָתָנֵי "יוֹלֶדֶת מְטַמְּאָה בְּבַיִת הַחִיצוֹן" כְּדְרַבִּי זֵירָא, דְּהָא לְרַבִּי זֵירָא לָא מְטַמְּיָא עַד הָשְׁתָּא שֶׁיֵּצֵא, וְהָדְרָא קוּשְׁיָא לְדוּכְתִּין. בְּלֵידָה יְבֵישְׁתָּא. דְּלֵיכָּא לֹא נִדָּה וְלֹא זִיבָה. אִי בִּיבֶשְׁתָּא. מַאי מְטַמְּיָא בִּפְנִים אִיכָּא? כְּגוֹן שֶׁהוֹצִיא וָלָד רֹאשׁוֹ חוּץ לַפְּרוֹזְדוֹר. וְאוֹלִיד, וְקָאָמַר: דְּאַע"ג דַּאֲכַתִּי רֹאשׁוֹ בִּפְנִים הוּא, דְּהַיְינוּ בַּבַּיִת הַחִיצוֹן – הָוֵי כַּיָּלוּד, וּטְמֵאָה לֵידָה, וּכְרַב אוֹשַׁעְיָא דְּאָמַר: חוּץ לַפְּרוֹזְדוֹר – וָלָד הָוֵי. דְּאָמַר רַב אוֹשַׁעְיָא. בְּפֶרֶק "בְּהֵמָה הַמַּקְשָׁה" (חולין דף עב.) אַהָא דִּתְנַן:* "אִשָּׁה שֶׁמֵּת עוּבָּרָהּ בְּתוֹךְ מֵעֶיהָ, וּפָשְׁטָה חַיָּה אֶת יָדָהּ וְנָגְעָה בּוֹ – הַחַיָּה טְמֵאָה טוּמְאַת שִׁבְעָה, וְהָאִשָּׁה טְהוֹרָה עַד שֶׁיֵּצֵא הַוָּלָד", וְהָוֵינַן בָּהּ: חַיָּה, אַמַּאי טְמֵאָה? טוּמְאָה בְּלוּעָה הִיא! וְאָמַר רַב אוֹשַׁעְיָא: הַךְ טוּמְאַת חַיָּה – מִדְּרַבָּנַן, גְּזֵרָה שֶׁמָּא יוֹצִיא וָלָד אֶת רֹאשׁוֹ חוּץ לַפְּרוֹזְדוֹר וְתִגַּע בּוֹ, דְּמִכִּי נָפַק – הֲוָה לֵיהּ יָלוּד, וְלָא הָוֵי בְּלוּעָה, וְטָמֵא מִדְּאוֹרַיְיתָא מִשּׁוּם נוֹגֵעַ בְּמֵת. אַלְמָא חוּץ לַפְּרוֹזְדוֹר – יָלוּד הוּא, הִילְכָּךְ לְעִנְיָן לְטַמֵּא אֶת אִמּוֹ טוּמְאַת לֵידָה – נַמִי יָלוּד הוּא. וְכִי הַהוּא דַּאֲתָא כו'. כְּלוֹמַר, מִדְּרָבָא נַמִי שָׁמְעִינַן דְּרֹאשׁוֹ חוּץ לַפְּרוֹזְדוֹר הָוֵי כַּיָּלוּד. ס"ד. כְּלוֹמַר, אֶפְשָׁר שֶׁאֵין זֶה הָאִישׁ יוֹדֵעַ שֶׁמִּילָה בְּשַׁבָּת מוּתֶּרֶת, אֶלָּא וַדַּאי דָּבָר סָפֵק אֵירַע בּוֹ. דִּצְוַיץ. שָׁמַעְתִּי אֶת הַוָּלָד נוֹעֵק בְּתוֹךְ הַמֵּעַיִים מִבְּעוֹד יוֹם שֶׁל עֶרֶב שַׁבָּת. טוּמְאָה בְּלוּעָה לֹא מְטַמְּאָה. דַּהֲרֵי הִיא כְּמִי שֶׁאֵינָהּ, וְאֵין בָּהּ לֹא מַגָּע וְלֹא מַשָּׂא, וּטְהוֹרָה אִשָּׁה זוֹ. וְאִי אָמְרַתְּ בֵּית הַסְּתָרִים הָוֵי. כִּשְׁאָר בֵּית הַקְּמָטִים – טוּמְאָה לֹא בָּטְלָה. וּנְהִי דִּבְמַגָּע לָא מְטַמְּיָא, דְּלָא מְטַמֵּא בֵּית הַסְּתָרִים בִּנְגִיעָה, בְּמַשָּׂא מִיהָא מְטַמְּאָה, וּטְמֵאָה אִשָּׁה זוֹ שֶׁהֲרֵי נוֹשֵׂאת אֶת הַנְּבֵלָה. מְקוֹם נִבְלַת עוֹף טָהוֹר. בֵּית הַבְּלִיעָה שֶׁל אָדָם, שֶׁאֵין לְנִבְלַת עוֹף טָהוֹר טוּמְאָה אֶלָּא שָׁם. שֶׁתָּחַב לוֹ חֲבֵירוֹ. דְּאִי תָּחַב הוּא לְעַצְמוֹ – אִיטַּמֵּי לֵיהּ בְּמַגָּע. בָּהּ. בְּגָדִים טְמֵאִים בְּבֵית הַבְּלִיעָה, וְלֹא בְּאַחֶרֶת. קוּמְטוֹ. כְּגוֹן בֵּין אַצִּילָיו, אוֹ שְׁאָר קְמָטִים פרונ"ש בְּלַעַ"ז.

קמ"ל

**תוספות**

**שהוציא** ולד ראשו חוץ לפרוזדור. אבל בפרוזדור עצמו – טהורה, דלא חשוב כבחוץ. ואם תאמר: והא אמר לעיל בפ"ק (דף יז:) דם הנמצא בפרוזדור – ספקו טמא! ויש לומר: התם ספקו טמא, כשילא לחוץ. ועוד: יש לחלק בין (דם) לידה לדם נדה. וא"ת: דבריש "בהמה המקשה" (חולין דף סח.) ובפרק "יש בכור" (בכורות דף מו:) עביד צריכותא הא דתניא ד"ראשו כילוד באדם ובבהמה": דאי תנא בהמה – משום דלית לה פרוזדור, אבל אשה דאית לה פרוזדור – אימא לא. ומאי נפקא מינה במאי דאית לה פרוזדור? כיון דבעינן שיוציא ולד ראשו חוץ לפרוזדור, כדמשמע הכא! ויש לומר: דפרוזדור דהתם לא הוי כי האי דהכא, דהתם – קרי "פרוזדור" לעובי הירכים שמתכסה בהן ראשו של ולד, וה"א דלא חשיב כילוד. וכן פירש שם בקונטרס.

**וכדרב** אושעיא כו'. דילא ראשו חוץ לפרוזדור הוי כילוד, ומלתיה דרב אושעיא איתמר אהא דפריך ב"בהמה המקשה" (חולין עב. ושם) גבי "אשה שמת עוברה בתוך מעיה ונגעה חיה בעובר – טמאה": ואמאי טמאה, הא טומאה בלועה היא! ומשני רב אושעיא כו'. תימה: אמאי נקט "ראשו" למשום דהוי כילוד, כדמשמע הכא אפילו הוליא ידו – נמי טמאה החיה שנגעה בו או הסיטתו, דהא תו לאו טומאה בלועה היא! ויש לומר: דגזרת הכתוב הוא, דלא מטמא עד שיהא כילוד, כדדריש התם רבי ישמעאל: "על פני השדה" – להוליא עובר שבמעי אמו. והשתא ניחא (א) דבעי התם: מאי טעמא דרבי ישמעאל, אע"פ שטעמו פשוט, דהא טומאה בלועה היא! אלא קים ליה דמטהר עד שילא כל כך דמקרי לידה.

**יצתה** זו שטמאה כו'. לאו מיעוטא הוא, דא"כ מאי קאמר דתיתי בק"ו אלא "ילתה זו" – היינו, שאינו בכלל פסוק זה. וא"ת: ומאי יתרץ רבא מן הברייתא? וי"ל: דמיירי כגון שבית הבליעה רחב כ"כ שלא יסיט נבלה שתחב לו חבירו.

**מה** ת"ל והאוכל ליתן שיעור אבילה לנוגע ולנושא. תימה: כיון דבאכילה כתיב כבוס בגדים, ובנוגע לא כתיב – לית לן לאוקמא שיעור אכילה לנוגע, אלא בנושא, דכתיב ביה כבוס בגדים! כדאשכחן לעיל בפ"ק (דף ט.) ובפ"ק דיומא (דף יד.) דאמר: "ומזה מי הנדה יכבס בגדיו" – היינו נושא, ואפקה רחמנא בלשון הזאה, ליתן שיעור הזאה כנושא ולא כנוגע, משום דלא כתיב ביה כבוס בגדים! ויש לומר: דהתם לא כתיב נושא בהדיא, אבל הכא אי לא קאי "והאוכל" אלא אנושא גרידא, א"כ לא נכתוב נושא, וממילא נימא דמאי "אוכל" – נושא. כמו התם דלא כתיב נושא, ואמרינן מאי "מזה" – נושא. ומיהו תימה: כבוס בגדים דכתב רחמנא באוכל למה לי? וכ"ת: דאי לא הוה כתיב ביה כבוס בגדים, הוה מוקמינן ליה בנוגע ולא בנושא דבעי כבוס בגדים א"כ לא לכתוב נוגע כלל! ושמא לשום דרשא איצטריך. ואם תאמר: דבפרק "בהמה המקשה" (חולין דף עא.) מפיק טומאה בלועה מהאי קרא ד"והאוכל מנבלתה יכבס בגדיו וטמא עד הערב" מי לא עסקינן דאכל סמוך לשקיעת החמה, והשתא הא (ב) דקאמר הכא האי "אוכל" לא אכילה ממש הוא אלא ליתן שיעור אכילה לנוגע ולנושא! ויש לומר: דהתם מפיק, משום דאין מקרא יוצא מידי פשוטו.

למימרא

**תוספי הרא"ש**

**שהוציא** הולד ראשו חוץ לפרוזדור אבל בפרוזדור עצמו טהור דלא חשיב כבחוץ והא דאמר לעיל פ"ב דם הנמצא בפרוזדור ספיקו טמא י"ל דיש חילוק בין דם ללידה ועוד דהתם ספיקו טמא כשהוציאו לחוץ קאמר. וקשה מהא דאמרינן בריש בהמה המקשה ובפ' יש בכור לנחלה דאיצטריך למיתני באדם ובהמה דלידת ראש הוא לידה דאי תנא באדם ה"א משום דחשיב פרצוף דידיה ואי תנא בהמה ה"א משום דאין לה פרוזדור אימא לא וכיון דבעינן שיוציא ולד ראשו חוץ לפרוזדור כדמשמע הכא למה לי פרוזדור למנוע לידת ראש שלא תחשב לידה כיון שהוציא ראשו חוץ לפרוזדור וי"ל דפרוזדור דהכא לאו כפרוזדור דהתם אלא עובי הירכים קרי פרוזדור שמתכסה בהן ראש הולד הילכך הוה ס"ד דלא הוי כילוד וכפרש"י התם: **דאמר** רב אושעיא גזירה שמא יוציא ראשו חוץ לפרוזדור ומילתא דרב אושעיא איתמר אהא דאמרינן בפ' בהמה המקשה גבי אשה שמת עוברה בתוך מעיה דחיה טמאה טומאת ז' והאשה טהורה עד שיצא הולד ופריך אמאי טומאה בלועה היא וקאמר רב אושעיא גזירה שמא יוציא ראשו וכו' ומדמייתי הכא הא דרב אושעיא לומר דחשוב כילוד בהוצאת הראש חוץ לפרוזדור משמע דרב אושעיא נקט דוקא ראשו ותימה אמאי נקט ראשו אפי' הוציא ידו חוץ לפרוזדור טמאה החיה שנגעה בה דתו לא הוי טומאה בלועה וי"ל דגזירת הכתו' היא דעד שתהא כילוד לא מטמא כדדריש ר' ישמעאל בפ' בהמה המקשה על פני השדה להוציא עובר שבמעי אשה: **יצתה** זו שטומאתה קודם שיאכלנה. לאו מיעוטא הוא דא"כ מאי פריך תיתי בק"ו אלא ה"פ יצתה זו כלומר לא איירי קרא בההיא. ותימה רבא מאי קא משני מהך ברייתא וי"ל דסבר דבית הבליעה רחב ואפשר שלא יסיט הנבילה שתחב לו חבירו. א"נ כי קאמר רבא דבית הסתרים הוי היינו בהתחלת בית הבליעה אבל בסופו מודה דבלוע הוי והכא מיירי כגון שתחב לו בעומק בית הבליעה: **מה** אכילה בכזית אף נוגע ונושא בכזית. ותימה כיון דבקרא דהאוכל כתיב כיבוס בגדים ובנוגע לא כתיב כיבוס בגדים הוה לן לאוקומי שיעור אכילה לנושא דוקא דכתיב ביה כיבוס בגדים אבל לא גבי נוגע דלא כתיב ביה כיבוס כדאמרינן לעיל גבי מזה וי"ל דאי לא קאי אלא אנושא לא הו"ל למיכתב נושא כלל וממילא הוה אמינא מאי אוכל נושא כיון דאי אפשר לטמא אוכל ממש כמו גבי מזה דלא כתיב נושא ואמרינן מאי מזה נושא. ומיהו תימה כיבוס בגדים דכתיב באוכל למה לי וכ"ת דאי לא כתיב כיבוס הוה מוקמינן ליה בנוגע ולא בנושא דכתיב ביה כיבוס בגדים הא ליתא דא"כ לא ניכתוב נוגע כלל. ולעיל בפ"ק כתבתי תירוץ בשם הר' יחיאל:

תורה אור

ויקרא כב

שם יא

חולין עב. ע"ש

[דף עא.]

[פי' דאילו לא הוליא ראשו לא הוה מגיע לכל כמה דאיתא בממי אמו פיו סתום. כ"ז לשון שאלתות פרשת לך לך סי' ט]

[לעיל מב:]

[נ"ל מאי אמרת]

[ע' זבחים סט: ובחולין ק:]

**הגהות הב"ח**

(א) תוס' ד"ה וכדרב אושעיא וכו' והשתא ניחא דמצריך התם רבי ישמעאל טעמא מקרא אע"פ שטעמו פשוט כצ"ל: (ב) ד"ה מה ת"ל והאוכל וכו' והשתא הא דקאמר הכא דהאי אוכל כצ"ל:

**הגהות מהר"ב רנשבורג**

א] גמ' א"ל מהו לממהל בשבתא. נ"ב עיין דרשת מהרלנ"ח דף מו ע"ד:

ולא תוך תוכו, קמ"ל. אמר ר"ל: אקנה בקומטו של זב, והסיט בו את הטהור – טהור. קנה בקומטו של טהור, והסיט בו את הזב – טמא. מאי טעמא – דאמר קרא: °"וכל אשר יגע בו הזב וידיו לא שטף במים" זהו הסיטו של זב, *שלא מצינו לו טומאה בכל התורה כולה. ואפקיה רחמנא בלשון נגיעה, למימרא דהיסט ונגיעה כידיו, מה התם – מאבראי, אף הכא – מאבראי. § "אבל הזב ובעל קרי אינן מטמאין" וכו'. § זב – דכתיב: °"כי יהיה זב מבשרו", עד שיצא זובו מבשרו. בעל קרי – דכתיב: °"ואיש כי תצא ממנו שכבת זרע". § "היה אוכל בתרומה והרגיש" וכו'. אוחז? *והתניא, ר"א אומר: כל האוחז באמה ומשתין, כאילו מביא מבול לעולם! אמר אביי: במטלית עבה. רבא אמר: אפילו תימא במטלית רכה, כיון דעקר – עקר. ואביי – חייש דילמא אתי לאוסופי, ורבא – לאוסופי לא חייש. (א) *והתניא: למה זה דומה – לנותן אצבע בעין, שכל זמן שאצבע בעין – מדמעת וחוזרת ומדמעת! ורבא – כל אחמומי והדר אחמומי בשעתא – לא שכיח. אמר שמואל: *בכל שכבת זרע שאין כל גופו מרגיש בה – אינה מטמאה. מ"ט? "שכבת זרע" אמר רחמנא – בראויה להזריע. מיתיבי: *גהיה מהרהר בלילה, ועמד ומצא בשרו חם – טמא! תרגמא רב הונא: דבמשמש מטתו בחלומו, דאי אפשר לשמש בלא הרגשה. לישנא אחרינא, אמר שמואל: כל שכבת זרע שאינו יורה כחץ – אינה מטמאה. מאי איכא בין האי לישנא להאי לישנא? איכא בינייהו: הנעקרה בהרגשה, ויצאה שלא בהרגשה. מילתא דפשיטא ליה לשמואל מיבעיא ליה לרבא. דבעי רבא: נעקרה בהרגשה, ויצתה שלא בהרגשה, מהו? ת"ש: *ובעל קרי שטבל ולא הטיל מים, לכשיטיל מים טמא. שאני התם דרובה בהרגשה נפק. לישנא אחרינא, אמרי לה *אמר שמואל: כל שכבת זרע שאינו יורה כחץ – אינה מזרעת, אזרועי הוא זדלא מזרעא, הא טמויי – מטמיא, שנאמר: °"כי יהיה בך איש אשר לא יהיה טהור מקרה" – אפילו קרי בעולם. בעי רבא: גוי שהרהר, וירד וטבל, מהו? אם תמצי לומר בתר עקירה אזלינן, הני מילי – לחומרא, אבל הכא דלקולא – לא אמרינן, או דילמא לא שנא? זתיקו. בעי רבא: זבה שנעקרו מימי רגליה וירדה וטבלה, מהו? אם תמצא לומר בתר עקירה אזלינן, הני מילי שכבת זרע, דלא מצי נקיט לה, אבל מימי רגליה דמצי נקיט לה – לא, או דילמא לא שנא? חתיקו. בעי רבא: גויה זבה שנעקרו מימי רגליה, וירדה

(ויקרא טו; שם; שם; דברים כג)

**רש"י**

קמ"ל. דהאי לא "תוך תוכו" הוא, אלא כגון כלי בתוך התנור ופיו למעלה מפי התנור. והסיט בו את הטהור טהור. כדמפרש טעמא לקמן. בקומטו של טהור והסיט בו את הזב טמא. הטהור. שהרי נשא את הזב, וזב מטמא במשא, דכתיב במשכב (ויקרא טו): "והנושא אותם", וק"ו לזב עצמו. מאי טעמא. טהור הניסט בקנה של קומטו של זב טהור? דכתיב וכל אשר יגע בו הזב וגו'. והאי קרא לאו למגע איצטריך, דהא כתיב: "והנוגע בבשר הזב", אלא זה הסיטו של זב. מכאן למדנו: זב שהסיט את הטהור – טמא, שלא מצינו בכל התורה טומאה המסטת טהרה שתטמא, אלא אם כן נשא טהור את הטמא, והכא בזב הוא דגלי רחמנא. וכתב "וידיו" – דדרשינן הכי: היכא דהסיט בו הזב בידיו, כלומר, בגלוי (ב). לא שטף במים. מילתא אחריתי היא: למילף לנטילת ידים לאכילה מהכא. אלמא הסיט זב את הטהור – אינו טמא, אלא א"כ הסיטו בגלוי בידיו. ומדאפקיה בלשון נגיעה ילפינן נמי לכל נגיעות, דאין מגע בית הסתרים מטמא. אבל טהור שהסיט את הזב, דנפקא לן מקרא אחרינא דלא כתיב ביה "ידיו" – טמא אפילו הסיטו בקנה שבקומטו, מידי דהוה אנבלה בקומטו שהיא מטמאה במשא, דהא מ"מ הרי הוא נושא את הטומאה. ל"א: קנה בקומטו של טהור והסיט את הזב – להכי טמא, שנגע הקנה בגילוי של זב, ונטמא הקנה מחמת הזב, וחוזר ומטמא את הטהור. ואע"ג דטהור קמוט, דגילויא גבי זב הוא דבעינן. אבל קנה בקומטו של זב, והסיט את הטהור – טהור, הואיל וזב קמוט, וגבי זב כתיב "וידיו". ושיבוש הוא, מפני כמה דברים: חדא, דקנה פשוטי כלי עץ הוא, ואינו מקבל טומאה. וא"ת: בקנה חלול, נהי נמי דמקבל טומאה, אפ"ה אין חוזר ומטמא הטהור, שהרי אין מגע של זב חוזר ומטמא אדם, שאין לך נוגע בטומאה מטמא אדם חוץ מן הנוגע במת. ועוד, אי טומאת הטהור משום נגיעת קנה היא, והרי בקומטו הוא דנגע, ובית הסתרים לאו בר מגע הוא, דהא אמרינן לעיל "שרץ בקומטו טהור". ועוד, לשון "הסיט" אמאי נקט? ועוד, הסיט טהור את הזב – מי נפק מהאי קרא? "וכל אשר יגע בו הזב" כתיב, והיינו אשר יסיטנו הזב, ולא כתיב "כל אשר יגע בזב"! כאילו מביא מבול. שמחמם את אבריו, ומביא לידי קרי. וזהו קלקול דור המבול, שנאמר (בראשית ו): "כי השחית כל בשר". במטלית עבה. שאינה מחממת. לא שכיח. והא דתניא: "כל זמן שאצבע בעין מדמעת" ה"מ היכא דמתחלה ממשמש וחימם את עצמו, ויוצא כל שעה מעט. אבל זה שנזדעזעו אבריו – נעקר כל הזרע ביחד, ושוב אינו חוזר ומתחמם לעקור עוד מיד בשעה אחת. בשרו חם. אברו. טמא. שמא יצא ממנו קרי, ואמאי? והא לא ארגיש! במשמש מטתו בחלומו. דאי נפק – ודאי ארגיש. ויצתה בלא הרגשה. דאינו יורה כחץ. לכשיטיל מים טמא. דנשתייר מן הקרי ויוצא עכשיו, ואע"ג דלא נפיק בהרגשה, הואיל ומעיקרא איעקר בהרגשה. גוי שהרהר. ונעקר ולא יצא. וירד וטבל. לשם גירות, ואח"כ יצא קריו. מהו. אפי' אם תמצי לומר לגבי ישראל דכי נעקר בהרגשה ויצא שלא בהרגשה – טמא, דאזלינן בתר עקירה, הכא לא ניזיל בתר עקירה דהיינו קולא, הואיל וכשהוא גוי נעקר – וטהור, דאמר ב"בנות כותים": *קריו טהור, אפילו לב"ה. או דילמא לא שנא. לחומרא כגון לגבי עקירה דהרגשה דישראל, ולא שנא לקולא כי הכא – אזלינן בתר עקירה. שנעקרו מימי רגליה. דהוי מעין אב הטומאה. וירדה וטבלה. וטהרה מזובה, ואח"כ הטילתו, מהו? מי אזלינן בתר עקירה ומטמאו, או לא. דלא מצי נקיט לה. מלאכת, הילכך מכי עקר חשיב ליה לורך יציאה. [גויה]. סתם גויה מי רגליה מטמאין, דחכמים גזרו עליהן שיהו כזבין לכל דבריהם. וירדה

**תוספות**

למימרא דהיסט ונגיעה בידיו. פרש"י: דמהכא ילפינן לכל נגיעות, כגון שרץ ונבלה שנגעו בסתרו של טהור. וקשה: דאי מזב ילפינן, כי היכי דבעינן גלוי הזב ה"נ בעינן שיגע בגלוי של טהור. לענין היסט נמי נילף דנבעי שיסיט הטהור בגילוי, כדבעינן בגילוי הזב, והכא אמרינן דקנה בקומטו של טהור והסיט בו את הזב – טמא, ואמר נמי דבית הסתרים מטמא במשא! אלא נראה לפרש: דזב ושרץ ונבלה שנגעו בסתרו של טהור, דטהור – לאו מזב ילפינן, אלא ילפינן מלשון נגיעה דכתיב בכולהו. וטהור הנוגע בזב – נמי כתיב "הנוגע בבשר הזב", ולשון נגיעה משמע מאבראי, שיגע הטהור בגלוי בטומאה. וכן משמע פ"ק דקדושין (דף כה.) דאמר עולא: הכל מודים דלשון גלוי הוא אצל שרץ, "וכי יגע" אמר רחמנא, והאי – בר נגיעה הוא. משמע, דמלשון נגיעה דכתיב בשרץ הוא דריש, דלא מייתי קרא ד"ידיו" דכתיב בזב. ומיהו רש"י גריס התם: "אשר יגע בו", והיינו קרא דכתיב גבי זב. והא דאצטריך הכא למדרש מ"ידיו" ולא נפקא ליה מנגיעה דכתיב בזב – משום דההיא נגיעה, בהיסט איירי, ולא משמע גילוי כמו נגיעה ממש. לכך דריש לה מ"ידיו" דבעינן גילוי הזב בין בהיסט בין במגע מדאפקיה בלשון נגיעה. א"נ: מנגיעה דהכא דכתיב גבי "ידיו" מינה ילפינן לכל נגיעות דהוו מאבראי. **בראויה** להזריע. ואפי' יצאה בלא הרגשה איירי, כדמוכח בסמוך. ותימה: דא"כ משמע דראוי להזריע אע"פ שאינו יורה כחץ, ובשילהי נדרים (דף צא.) וכן ביבמות (דף סה.) אמר: איהי קים לה ביורה כחץ, משמע דאי אין יורה כחץ – אינו ראוי להזריע! וי"ל: דלהא לישנא דהכא לא מצריך רק שבתחלת עקירת שכבת זרע תהא ראויה להזריע, אע"ג דלסוף יציאתה היא בענין שאינו ראוי להזריע. א"נ ראוי להזריע הוא, אלא שאינה ראויה להתעבר לפי שאינו יורה כחץ, ואינו נכנס לתוך גופה אלא שותת ויוצא לחוץ. **הא** טמויי מטמיא. פירוש: ואפילו נעקרה בלא הרגשה. דאם לא כן, היינו לישנא קמא. **זבה** שנעקרו מימי רגליה. וכן בעי מגויה. שאל ריב"א מרש"י: אמאי לא בעי מזכר זב וגוי? והשיב: דנראה לו לפי שבאשה מתעגלין כל [מימי] רגליה בבת אחת לפתחה, מה שאין כן באיש.

**עין משפט נר מצוה**

לה א מיי' פ"ח מהל' מטמאי משכב ומושב הלכה ה:
לו ב מיי' פ"ה מהל' שאר אבות הטומאה הל"ד סמג עשין רמו:
לז ג ד מיי' שם הל"ה:
לח ה מיי' שם הל"ו:
לט ו מיי' שם הל"ז:
מ ז מיי' שם הל"ח:
מא ח מיי' פ"ב מהל' מטמאי משכב ומושב הלכה ט:

**תוספי הרא"ש**

למימרא דהיסט ונגיעה בידיו. פרש"י (דמתני') דמהכא ילפינן לכל הנגיעות דאין מגע בית הסתרים מטמא מדאפקיה רחמנא בלשון נגיעה ללמד על כל נגיעה דכתיבא גבי טומאה שתהא [בגלוי] והיינו דאמרי' בפ"ק דקדושין אמר עולא הכל מודים דלשון גלוי הוא אצל השרץ כי יגע אמר רחמנא והאי בר נגיעה הוא ומיהו פשיטא ליה דבעי' שיהא גלוי אלא דסמיך אנגיעה דהכא דאיתקש לידיו:
אוחז ס"ד והתניא ר' אליעזר אומר כל האוחז ומשתין כו'. פירכא זו תמוהה בעיני כיון דכתיב בקרא משמרת תרומותי וצוה הכתוב לשמור אותה שלא תטמא וכי בשביל חכמי' שאמרו כאילו מביא מבול לעולם לא ימנע למטמאות את התרומה א)וצ"ע:
שכבת זרע אמר רחמנ' בראויה להזריע. אפי' באין יורה כחץ איירי כדמפרש בסמוך וראוייה להזריע כיון שנעקר בהרגשה. ותי' דאמרינן בסוף נדרים איהי קים לה ביורה כחץ וכיון שאומרת שאינו יורה כחץ יוציא ויתן כתובה ומאי נפקא לן אם אינו יורה כחץ מ"מ ראוי הוא להזריע וי"ל דלעולם בשאינו יורה כחץ אינו ראוי להזריע ובהא פליגי הני לישני דהכא דלישנא קמא סבר כיון שנעקר מתחלה באותו ענין שראויה להזריע מטמאה או א"נ ראויה היא להזריע אלא שאינה יכולה להתעבר בשאינה יורה כחץ לפי שאינו נכנס עד מקום ההריון אלא שותת ויורה לחוץ:
אזרועי הוא דלא מזרעא הא טמויי מטמאה. אפי' נעקר בלא הרגשה דאי לאו הכי היינו לישנא קמא: זבה שנעקרו מימי רגליה. פרש"י בתשובה דלהכי בעי בזבה ולא בעי בזב לפי שבאשה מתעגלין כל מימי רגליה בבת אחת לפתחה משא"כ באיש:

א) ולפי מש"כ בב"י בא"ע בר"ס כ"ג בשם הזוה"ק וכ"כ בשו"ע שם דעון זה חמור מכל עבירות בתורה נתיישב זה ובלא"ה י"ל דשב וא"ת עדיף וכמש"כ ביבמות דף צ ע"ב ודו"ק.

**מסורת הש"ס**

[שבת פג: וש"נ]
שבת מה. לעיל יג.
[לעיל יג.]
מקואות פ"ח מ"ג
מקואות פ"ח מ"ג חולין כד:
[חגיגה טו.]
[לקמן דף לז.]

**הגהות הב"ח**

(א) גמ' לא חייש ולא והתניא: (ב) רש"י ד"ה דכתיב וד"ה לא שטף הס"ד:

**גליון הש"ס**

גמ' אמר שמואל כל ש"ז וכו'. ע' לעיל יד ע"א תד"ה רוכבי: שם דלא מזרעא הא טמויי מטמיא. ע' לקמן נו ע"א תד"ה שן: רש"י ד"ה לא שטף וכו' למילף לנטילת ידים וכו'. חולין קו ע"א ד"ה מגוה וע"ע בתוס' שם ד"ה מגוה וע' רש"י קדושין כה ע"א ד"ה לענין טומאה:

תורה אור

וְיָרְדָה וְטָבְלָה, מַהוּ? אִם תִּמְצֵי לוֹמַר בָּתַר עֲקִירָה אָזְלִינַן אע"ג דְּמָצֵי נָקִיט לְהוּ, ה"מ – יִשְׂרְאֵלִית דִּטְמֵאָה דְּאוֹרַיְיתָא, אֲבָל גּוֹיָה זָבָה, דִּטְמֵאָה דְּרַבָּנַן – לָא, אוֹ דִּילְמָא – לָא שְׁנָא? [א]תֵּיקוּ.§ "וּמְטַמְּאִין בְּכָל שֶׁהֵן".§ אָמַר שְׁמוּאֵל: זָב צָרִיךְ כַּחֲתִימַת פִּי הָאַמָּה, שֶׁנֶּאֱמַר: °"אוֹ הֶחְתִּים בְּשָׂרוֹ מִזּוֹבוֹ". וְהָאֲנַן תְּנַן: מְטַמְּאִין בְּכָל שֶׁהֵן! הוּא דְּאָמַר כְּרַבִּי נָתָן. *דְּתַנְיָא, רַבִּי נָתָן אוֹמֵר מִשּׁוּם רַבִּי יִשְׁמָעֵאל: זָב *צָרִיךְ כַּחֲתִימַת פִּי הָאַמָּה, [ב]וְלֹא הוֹדוּ לוֹ. מ"ט דְּרַבִּי יִשְׁמָעֵאל? – דְּאָמַר קְרָא: "אוֹ הֶחְתִּים בְּשָׂרוֹ מִזּוֹבוֹ". וְרַבָּנַן? – הַהוּא מִבָּעֵי לֵיהּ [ג]לַח מְטַמֵּא, וְאֵינוֹ מְטַמֵּא יָבֵשׁ. וְרַבִּי יִשְׁמָעֵאל? – הַהוּא מֵ"רָר" נָפְקָא. וְרַבָּנַן? – הַהוּא לְמִנְיָנָא הוּא דַּאֲתָא: (א) "זוֹבוֹ" חֲדָא, "רָר בְּשָׂרוֹ" – תְּרֵי, "אֶת זוֹבוֹ" – תְּלָת, [ד]לִימֵּד עַל זָב בַּעַל שָׁלֹשׁ רְאִיּוֹת שֶׁחַיָּיב בְּקָרְבָּן. "אוֹ הֶחְתִּים בְּשָׂרוֹ מִזּוֹבוֹ טָמֵא" – מִקְצָת זוֹבוֹ טָמֵא, לִימֵּד עַל זָב בַּעַל שְׁתֵּי רְאִיּוֹת שֶׁמְּטַמֵּא מִשְׁכָּב וּמוֹשָׁב. וְרַבִּי יִשְׁמָעֵאל מִנְיָנָא מְנָא לֵיהּ? נָפְקָא לֵיהּ מִדְּרַבִּי סִימַאי, *דְּתַנְיָא, רַבִּי סִימַאי אוֹמֵר: מָנָה הַכָּתוּב שְׁתַּיִם – וּקְרָאוֹ "טָמֵא", שָׁלֹשׁ – וּקְרָאוֹ "טָמֵא". הָא כֵּיצַד? [ה]שְׁתַּיִם – לְטוּמְאָה, וְשָׁלֹשׁ – לְקָרְבָּן. וּלְמַאן דְּנָפְקָא לֵיהּ תַּרְוַיְיהוּ °מִ"זֹּאת תִּהְיֶה טוּמְאָתוֹ בְּזוֹבוֹ", °"אִישׁ אִישׁ כִּי יִהְיֶה זָב מִבְּשָׂרוֹ" מַאי עָבֵיד לֵיהּ? מִבָּעֵי לֵיהּ – עַד שֶׁיֵּצֵא מִבְּשָׂרוֹ. "זוֹבוֹ טָמֵא" לָמָּה לִי? [ו]לִימֵּד עַל הַזּוֹב שֶׁהוּא טָמֵא. אָמַר רַב חֲנִילָאִי מִשּׁוּם ר"א בְּר"ש: [ז]שִׁכְבַת זֶרַע, לָרוֹאֶה – בְּמַשֶּׁהוּ, לַנּוֹגֵעַ – בְּכַעֲדָשָׁה. וְהָאֲנַן "מְטַמְּאִין בְּכָל שֶׁהֵן" תְּנַן! מַאי לָאו – לַנּוֹגֵעַ? לָא, לָרוֹאֶה. ת"ש: *חוֹמֶר בְּשִׁכְבַת זֶרַע מִבְּשֶׁרֶץ, וְחוֹמֶר בְּשֶׁרֶץ מִבְּשִׁכְבַת זֶרַע. חוֹמֶר בְּשֶׁרֶץ – שֶׁהַשֶּׁרֶץ אֵין חֲלוּקָה טוּמְאָתוֹ, מַה שֶּׁאֵין כֵּן בְּשִׁכְבַת זֶרַע. חוֹמֶר בְּשִׁכְבַת זֶרַע – שֶׁהַשִּׁכְבַת זֶרַע מְטַמֵּא בְּכָל שֶׁהוּא, מַה שֶּׁאֵין כֵּן בְּשֶׁרֶץ. מַאי לָאו – לַנּוֹגֵעַ? לָא, לָרוֹאֶה. וְהָא דּוּמְיָא דְּשֶׁרֶץ קָתָנֵי, מַה שֶּׁרֶץ – בִּנְגִיעָה, אַף שִׁכְבַת זֶרַע – בִּנְגִיעָה! אָמַר רַב אַדָּא בַּר אַהֲבָה: שׁוּם שֶׁרֶץ קָתָנֵי, וְשׁוּם שִׁכְבַת זֶרַע קָתָנֵי. וְשֶׁרֶץ לֹא מְטַמֵּא בְּמַשֶּׁהוּ? וְהָא אֲנַן תְּנַן: *[ח]הָאֵבָרִים אֵין לָהֶם שִׁיעוּר. פָּחוֹת מִכַּזַּיִת בְּשַׂר הַמֵּת, וּפָחוֹת מִכַּזַּיִת בְּשַׂר נְבֵלָה, וּפָחוֹת מִכַּעֲדָשָׁה מִן הַשֶּׁרֶץ! שָׁאנֵי אֵבֶר – דְּכוּלֵּיהּ בִּמְקוֹם עֲדָשָׁה קָאֵי, דְּהָא אִילּוּ חָסֵר פּוּרְתָּא – אֵבֶר [ט]מִי קָמְטַמְּיָא? שִׁכְבַת זֶרַע דַּחֲלוּקָה טוּמְאָתוֹ מַאי הִיא? *אִילֵימָא בֵּין יִשְׂרָאֵל [י]לְדָגוּים – ה"נ אִיכָּא [כ]עַכְבָּר דְּיָם וְעַכְבָּר דְּיַבָּשָׁה! [ל]אֶלָּא – בֵּין קָטָן לְגָדוֹל. אָמַר רַב פַּפָּא: כְּתַנָּאֵי, מִנַּיִן לְרַבּוֹת נוֹגֵעַ בְּשׁ"ז – ת"ל: °"אוֹ אִישׁ". וּפְלִיגִי תַּנָּאֵי בְּעָלְמָא, דְּאִיכָּא דְּאָמְרִי *דּוֹן מִינָּהּ וּמִינָּהּ, וְאִיכָּא דְּאָמְרִי דּוֹן מִינָּהּ וְאוֹקֵי בְּאַתְרָא. לְמ"ד דּוֹן מִינָּהּ וּמִינָּהּ: מַה שֶּׁרֶץ – בִּנְגִיעָה, אַף שִׁכְבַת זֶרַע – בִּנְגִיעָה. וּמִינָּהּ, מַה שֶּׁרֶץ – בְּכַעֲדָשָׁה, אַף ש"ז – בְּכַעֲדָשָׁה. וּלְמ"ד דּוֹן מִינָּהּ וְאוֹקֵי בְּאַתְרָא: מַה שֶּׁרֶץ – בִּנְגִיעָה, אַף ש"ז – בִּנְגִיעָה. וְאוֹקֵי בְּאַתְרָא: מַה ש"ז לָרוֹאֶה – בְּמַשֶּׁהוּ, אַף לַנּוֹגֵעַ – בְּמַשֶּׁהוּ. א"ל רַב הוּנָא בְּרֵיהּ דְּרַב נָתָן לְרַב פַּפָּא: מִמַּאי דְּמֵ"אוֹ אִישׁ" דְּשֶׁרֶץ קָמְרַבֵּי לֵיהּ, דִּילְמָא מֵ"אוֹ אִישׁ אֲשֶׁר תֵּצֵא מִמֶּנּוּ שִׁכְבַת זָרַע" קָמְרַבֵּי לֵיהּ. וּדְכ"ע דּוֹן מִינָּהּ וּמִינָּהּ? שַׁיְילִינְהוּ לְתַנָּאֵי, אִיכָּא דְּתָנֵי כְּרַב פַּפָּא, וְאִיכָּא דְּתָנֵי כְּרַב הוּנָא בְּרֵיהּ דְּרַב נָתָן.§ **מתני'** [מ]תִּינוֹקֶת בַּת יוֹם אֶחָד – מִטַּמְּאָה בְּנִדָּה, בַּת י' יָמִים – מִטַּמְּאָה בְּזִיבָה. *[נ]תִּינוֹק בֶּן יוֹם אֶחָד – מְטַמֵּא בְּזִיבָה, [ס]וּמְטַמֵּא בִּנְגָעִים, [ע]וּמְטַמֵּא בְּטָמֵא מֵת, [פ]וְזוֹקֵק לְיִבּוּם, [צ]וּפוֹטֵר מִן הַיִּבּוּם, [ק]וּמַאֲכִיל בִּתְרוּמָה, [ר]וּפוֹסֵל (אֶת) [מִן] הַתְּרוּמָה,

וְנוֹחֵל

**רש"י**

וְיָרְדָה וְטָבְלָה. לְשֵׁם יְהוּדִית. אִם תִּמְצֵי לוֹמַר בְּזָבָה נֶעֶקְרוּ מֵימֵי רַגְלֶיהָ וְיָרְדָה וְטָבְלָה, אָזְלִינַן בָּתַר עֲקִירָה – ה"מ בְּיִשְׂרָאֵל, דְּטוּמְאָתוֹ מִדְּאוֹרַיְיתָא. לַח מְטַמֵּא. דְּ"הֶחְתִּים" מַשְׁמַע לַח, שֶׁהַיָּבֵשׁ אֵינוֹ חוֹתֵם פִּי הָאַמָּה, דְּנָפֵיל. רָר. מַשְׁמַע לַח, כְּמוֹ (שמואל א כא) "וַיּוֹרֶד רִירוֹ". בְּזוֹבוֹ חֲדָא. "זֹאת תִּהְיֶה טוּמְאָתוֹ בְּזוֹבוֹ" – חֲדָא, "רָר" – תְּרֵי, "אֶת זוֹבוֹ" – תְּלָת, לְקָרְבָּן. אוֹ הֶחְתִּים. לַח. מִזּוֹבוֹ. "טוּמְאָתוֹ הִיא" – מִקְצָת זוֹבוֹ אִית בֵּיהּ טוּמְאַת זִיבָה. שְׁתַּיִם וּקְרָאוֹ טָמֵא. "כִּי יִהְיֶה זָב מִבְּשָׂרוֹ" – חֲדָא, "זוֹבוֹ טָמֵא" – תְּרֵי, "טָמֵא". שָׁלֹשׁ וּקְרָאוֹ טָמֵא. "זֹאת תִּהְיֶה טוּמְאָתוֹ בְּזוֹבוֹ" – חֲדָא, "רָר בְּשָׂרוֹ אֶת זוֹבוֹ" – תְּרֵי, "אוֹ הֶחְתִּים בְּשָׂרוֹ מִזּוֹבוֹ" – תְּלָת, "טוּמְאָתוֹ הִיא". עַל הַזּוֹב. שֶׁהַטִּיפָּה עַצְמָהּ טְמֵאָה. לַנּוֹגֵעַ בְּכַעֲדָשָׁה. דִּמְנְּגִיעָה דְּשֶׁרֶץ נָפְקָא לָן נְגִיעָה דְּש"ז, לְקַמָּן מֵ"אוֹ אִישׁ אֲשֶׁר יִגַּע" וגו'. אֵין לוֹ חֲלוּקַת טוּמְאָה. דְּשֶׁרֶץ קָטָן מְטַמֵּא כְּגָדוֹל, אֲבָל קָטָן פָּחוֹת מִבֶּן ט' אֵין לוֹ קֶרִי. שׁוּם שֶׁרֶץ קָתָנֵי. אֵין לְךָ שֶׁרֶץ מְטַמֵּא בְּמַשֶּׁהוּ, אֲבָל ש"ז יֵשׁ מְטַמֵּא בְּמַשֶּׁהוּ, כְּגוֹן לָרוֹאֶה. דְּכוּלֵּיהּ בִּמְקוֹם כַּעֲדָשָׁה קָאֵי. כְּלוֹמַר, מִתּוֹךְ חֲשִׁיבוּתֵיהּ שֶׁהוּא אֵבֶר הָוֵי חָשׁוּב בִּמְקוֹם כַּעֲדָשָׁה. תֵּדַע. דְּמִשּׁוּם חֲשִׁיבוּתָא דְּאֵבֶר הוּא, דְּהָא אִילּוּ חָסֵר פּוּרְתָּא מִן הָאֵבֶר דְּהָוֵי בְּצִיר מִכַּעֲדָשָׁה, מִי מְטַמֵּא? עַכְבָּר דְּיָם. אֵינוֹ מְטַמֵּא, כְּדְתַנְיָא בְּ"הָעוֹר וְהָרוֹטֵב" (חולין דף קכו.) דְּ"עַל הָאָרֶץ" כְּתִיב. כְּתַנָּאֵי. נוֹגֵעַ, אִי בְּמַשֶּׁהוּ אִי בְּכַעֲדָשָׁה. ת"ל אוֹ אִישׁ. קס"ד מֵ"אוֹ אִישׁ אֲשֶׁר יִגַּע בְּכָל שֶׁרֶץ אֲשֶׁר יִטְמָא" יָלְפִי'. וְשָׁמְעִי' בְּעָלְמָא. תַּנָּאֵי דִּפְלִיגִי בְּכַמָּה דּוּכְתֵּי בְּדוֹן מִינָּהּ וּמִינָּהּ, וּבְדוֹן מִינָּהּ וְאוֹקֵי בְּאַתְרָא. הִילְכָּךְ הָנָךְ תַּנָּאֵי עַל כָּרְחָךְ פְּלִיגִי בְּנוֹגֵעַ בְּקֶרִי: לְמ"ד דּוֹן מִינָּהּ וּמִינָּהּ – דּוֹן ש"ז מִשֶּׁרֶץ, דְּהָא מִקְּרָא דְּשֶׁרֶץ יָלְפִינַן לָהּ, דְּמַה שֶּׁרֶץ מְטַמֵּא בִּנְגִיעָה, אַף ש"ז בִּנְגִיעָה. וּמִינָּהּ – מַה שֶּׁרֶץ בְּכַעֲדָשָׁה כו'. וְאוֹקֵי בְּאַתְרָא. הַנַּח ש"ז בִּמְקוֹמָהּ, כִּדְאַשְׁכַּחַן בִּרְאִיָּיה דִּבְמַשֶּׁהוּ. דִּילְמָא מֵאוֹ אִישׁ אֲשֶׁר תֵּצֵא מִמֶּנּוּ כו'. יָלְפִינַן לָהּ, וַאֲפִי' לְמ"ד דּוֹן מִינָּהּ וּמִינָּהּ הָוֵה בְּמַשֶּׁהוּ, דְּהָא נְגִיעָה מֵרְאִיָּיה יָלֵיף, וּדְכ"ע דּוֹן מִינָּהּ וּמִינָּהּ הָוֵה, דְּהָכָא לֵיכָּא פְּלוּגְתָּא דְּאוֹקֵי בְּאַתְרָא, דְּהָא מִינֵּיהּ וּבֵיהּ יָלֵיף. אִיכָּא דְּתָנֵי כְּרַב פַּפָּא. מֵ"אוֹ אִישׁ אֲשֶׁר יִגַּע בְּכָל שֶׁרֶץ". **מתני'** וְזוֹקֵק לְיִבּוּם. אִם נוֹלַד יוֹם אֶחָד קוֹדֶם מִיתַת אָחִיו. אֲבָל נוֹלַד לְאַחַר מִיתַת אָחִיו – אֵינוֹ זוֹקֵק, דִּכְתִיב (דברים כה): "כִּי יֵשְׁבוּ אַחִים יַחְדָּו". וּפוֹטֵר מִן הַיִּבּוּם. אִם נוֹלַד לְאַחַר מִיתַת אָבִיו, וְחָיָה שָׁעָה אַחַת, וּמֵת. אֲבָל כָּל זְמַן שֶׁמְּעוּבֶּרֶת – אֵינוֹ מַתִּירָהּ לְיַבֵּם. וּמַאֲכִיל בִּתְרוּמָה. בַּת יִשְׂרָאֵל שֶׁנִּישֵּׂאת לְכֹהֵן, וּמֵת, וְנוֹלַד לָהּ בֵּן לְאַחַר מִיתָתוֹ – אוֹכֶלֶת בִּשְׁבִילוֹ בִּתְרוּמָה בּוֹ בַּיּוֹם שֶׁנּוֹלַד, כִּדְכְתִיב (ויקרא כב): "וִילִיד בֵּיתוֹ הֵם יֹאכְלוּ בְלַחְמוֹ", וְדָרְשִׁינַן: יַאֲכִילוּ אֶת אִמָּם. אֲבָל הִנִּיחָהּ מְעוּבֶּרֶת – אֵינָהּ אוֹכֶלֶת בִּשְׁבִילוֹ עַד שֶׁיִּוָּלֵד. וּפוֹסֵל (אֶת) [מִן] הַתְּרוּמָה. קס"ד: כְּגוֹן בַּת כֹּהֵן שֶׁנִּישֵּׂאת לְיִשְׂרָאֵל, וּמֵת, וְהִנִּיחַ בֵּן יוֹם אֶחָד – פְּסָלָהּ מִתְּרוּמַת בֵּית אָבִיהָ כָּל יְמֵי חַיָּיו, דִּכְתִיב (שם): "וְזֶרַע אֵין לָהּ וְשָׁבָה אֶל בֵּית אָבִיהָ", וְהָא – יֵשׁ לָהּ זֶרַע. וּבַגְּמָרָא פָּרֵיךְ: אֲפִילּוּ עוּבָּר נַמִי פּוֹסֵל!

וְנוֹחֵל

**תוספות**

**את** זובו תלת. לא דריש אתין. אי נמי: אתי לדרשא אחריתי. **עד** שיצא מבשרו. ובפרק "בנות כותים" (לעיל דף לה.) דדריש מ"בשרו" ולא מחמת אונסו – תרתי שמעת מינה. וא"ת: ול"ל קרא עד שילא מבשרו, מהיכא תיתי שיטמא בפנים כבחוץ? דאי מנדה וזבה – הא בריש "בנות כותים" (שם דף לג:) מצריך קרא לרבות קטן לזב ולנדה ולזבה, ולא ילפינן מהדדי. וי"ל: דהוה ילפינן מנדה וזבה ופולטת במה הצד לר"ש *נמי י"ל: כיון דגלי לן קרא ששוין הן זב וזבה לענין קטנים, גם לענין פנים כבחוץ היינו משוין אותם, אי לאו "מבשרו". **והתנן** האברים אין להם שעור. וא"ת: וכי לא ידע דאבר שלם דוקא קאמר? וי"ל: דפריך אמאי דמשני דשום שכבת זרע קתני, דשום שרץ נמי אשכחן, כגון אברים! ומשני: דלאו היינו כל שהוא, דאי חסר ליה – טהור. **מנין** לרבות נוגע בשכבת זרע ת"ל או איש. מ"והבגד אשר יהיה עליו שכבת זרע" לא מצי למילף, דבגד חמור מאדם, דנושא הנבלה מטמא בגדים בחבורו ולא אדם, כדאמר בפ"ק דבבא בתרא (דף ט:). וא"ת: מ"ט דריש מ"או איש" דשרץ, ושביק "או איש" דכתיב בש"ז גופיה? וי"ל: דמסתבר ליה טפי לרבות נוגע מקרא דנוגע, ולא מההיא דש"ז דמיירי ברואה. וא"ת: ול"ל יתורא ד"או איש", תיפוק ליה מדאיתקש ש"ז לשרץ. דמהאי טעמא ילפינן בשרץ בגד ועור משכבת זרע, בפ' "במה אשה" (שבת דף סד.) ובפרק "כילד הרגל" (ב"ק דף כה:) וי"ל: דאי לאו "או איש", הוה אמינא דלא הוקשה אלא מ"ש בפירוש, כגון נוגע דשרץ לרואה דש"ז ומצי למימר דרב פפא דמרבה נוגע מ"או איש" דשרץ הא דאמר התם דאיתקש אהדדי, היינו משום דקרא דשרץ איירי בש"ז ומ"או איש" דשרץ נמי לא הוה מוקמינן לנוגע בש"ז אי לאו דאסמכינהו בהדיא. **ומטמא** בנגעים. משום דבנגעים כתיב (ויקרא יג) "איש או אשה", ובטומאת מת נמי כתיב (במדבר יט) "ואיש אשר יטמא ולא יתחטא", איצטריך קרא בהו לרבויי. אבל לענין זוקק ליבום ופוטר מן היבום ומאכיל תרומה – לא כתיב "איש", ולא איצטריך קרא אלא למעוטי עובר.

כנעוריה

דדלילמא בגד חמור דנושא את הנבלה מטמא בגדים בחיבורין ולא אדם. והכי אמרינן בפ"ק דב"ב. ותימה מ"ט דריש מאו איש דכתיב גבי שרץ ושביק או איש דכתיב גבי ש"ז וי"ל משום דבנוגע מסתבר למילף מנוגע ולא מאו איש דש"ז דמיירי ברואה. ותימא תיפוק לי מדאיתקשא ש"ז לשרץ דמהך היקישא ילפינן להו מהדדי לענין בגד ועור פ' במה אשה ופ' כיצד הרגל וי"ל רב פפא דמרבי נוגע מאו איש דשרץ סבר דאיצטריך גם ההיקש דאי לאו היקישא לא הוה מרבינן מאו איש דשרץ נוגע בשכבת זרע ומהאי היקישא דש"ז לחודה לא הוה שמעינן נוגע דרואה קרי הוא דאיתקש לנוגע בשרץ. והא דילפי' היקישא לענין מגע בגד ועור היינו בתר דמרבי' מאו איש דשרץ נוגע בש"ז אמרינן נמי לענין מגע נמי איתקוש ורב הונא בריה דרבי נתן דמרבי מגע מאו איש דש"ז דאי לאו הכי לא משכחת לה דאיתקש נוגע בשרץ לנוגע וכו' אלא לרב הונא בריה דרב נתן הא דנקט התם לשון היקישא לאו דוקא אלא סמוכין דבתרי קראי כתיבי אבל לרב פפא היקש ממש הוא דמאו איש דכתיב גבי שרץ מרבינן נוגע בש"ז: וממטמא בנגעים. דכתיב אדם ולהכי איצטריך לרבויי משום דכתיב בנגעים איש או אשה ובטומאת מת נמי כתיב ואיש אשר יטמא אבל לענין לזוקק לייבום ולהאכיל בתרומה לא כתיב איש ולא איצטריך מתניתין להשמיענו יום אחד אלא למעוטי עובר א"נ שלא נצריך ל' יום להוציאו מתורת נפל:

**תוספי הרא"ש**

**רר** תרי זובו תלת. רבנן לא דרשי אתים דלמאן דדריש אתים חשיב את למניינא בפרק בנות כותים גבי והזב את זובו וכי קא בעי ר' ישמעאל מניינא למה לי הוה מצי למימר דסבר כמאן דדריש אתים. א"נ קים ליה לתלמודא דהאי את אתא לדרש' אחריתי: **ורבי** ישמעאל מנינא למה לי. פי' מנין שתים לטומאה ושלש לקרבן: **(כי)** עד שיצא מבשרו. בפ' בנות כותים דרשינן מבשרו ולא מחמת אונסו ותרוייהו ש"מ: **והתנן** האיברים אין להן שיעור כו'. תימה מאי ס"ד של המקשה וכי לא ידע דאבר שלם דוקא קאמר וי"ל דקשיא ליה הא דאמרינן דשום ש"ז קתני הילכך פרי' שהשרץ נמי אשכחן כל שהו באיברים א"כ מה חילוק יש ביניהן ומשני דלאו היינו כל שהו דכיון דאי חסר ביה טהור: **נוגע** בש"ז ת"ל אי איש. מהבגד אשר עליו ש"ז לא נפיק

**עין משפט נר מצוה**

מב א מיי' פ"ב מהל' מטמאי משכב ומושב הלכה ט:

מג ב מיי' פ"ב מהל' מחוסרי כפרה הל"ט ועיין מ"ש בזה הכ"מ בפ"ה מהל' אבות הטומא' הלכה א:

מד ג מיי' פ"ב מהל' מטמאי משכב ומושב הלכה א:

[לעיל מא.]

מה ד ה מיי' פ"ב מהל' מחוסרי כפרה הל"ו:

מו ו מיי' פ"א מהל' משכב ומושב הלכה יב:

מז ז מיי' פ"ה מהל' אבות הטומאה הל"א:

מח ח ט מיי' פ"ב מהל' טומאת המת הל"ג ופ"ב מהל' אבות הטומא' הל"ג ופ"ד שם הל"ג:

מט י מיי' פ"ב מהל' משכב ומושב הל"י ופ"ה מהל' אבות הטומאה הלכה יז:

נ כ מיי' פ"א מהל' כלים הלכה ג:

נא ל מיי' פ"ה מהל' שאר אבות הטומאה הלכה ב:

נב מ מיי' פ"ד מהל' איסורי ביאה הל"א ופ"א מהל' משכב ומושב הל"ג:

נג נ מיי' פ"א מהל' משכב ומושב הלכה ד:

נד ס מיי' פ"ט מהל' טומאת צרעת הל"א:

נה ע מיי' פ"א מהל' טומאת מת הלי"ד:

נו פ מיי' פ"א מהל' יבום וחליצה הל"ו סמג עשין כב טוש"ע אה"ע סי' קנו סעי' א:

נז צ מיי' שם הל"ה סמג שם טוש"ע שם סי' קנו סעיף ה:

נח ק מיי' פ"ו מהל' תרומות הלכה יב [וברב אלפס יבמות פ"ה דף כה ע"ב]:

נט ר מיי' שם הל"ג:

**מסורת הש"ס**

פסחים סז:

[לעיל כב.]

מגילה ח.

[תוספתא דכלים ריש פ"א]

[אהלות פ"א מ"ז מעילה טז: ע"ש]

[עי' תוס' ב"ב כ. ד"ה ועובד כוכבים שושבן]

[יבמות עח: ב"ק כה: שבועות לג. זבחים לא. מנחות סב. קז. חולין קכ:]

[חולין נח.]

**הגהות הב"ח**

(א) גמ' דלתא בזובו חדא:

**גליון הש"ס**

גמ' לימד על הזוב שהוא טמא. לעיל לד ע"ב:

*[א]ונוחל ומנחיל, [ב]והההורגו חייב, *והרי הוא לאביו ולאמו ולכל קרוביו כחתן שלם.§ **גמ'** מנהני מילי? דת"ר: *"אשה" אין לי אלא אשה, בת יום אחד לנדה מנין? ת"ל: "ואשה".§ "בת י' ימים לזיבה".§ מנא ה"מ? דת"ר: "אשה" – אין לי אלא אשה, בת י' ימים לזיבה מנין? ת"ל: "ואשה".§ "תינוק בן יום אחד" כו'.§ מנא הני מילי? דת"ר: °"איש איש". מה ת"ל *"איש איש"? – לרבות בן יום אחד שמטמא בזיבה, דברי רבי יהודה. רבי ישמעאל בנו של רבי יוחנן בן ברוקא אומר: אינו צריך, הרי הוא אומר °"והזב את זובו לזכר ולנקבה". "לזכר" – כל שהוא, בין גדול בין קטן. "לנקבה" – כל שהיא, בין גדולה בין קטנה. אם כן מה ת"ל "איש איש"? *דברה תורה כלשון בני אדם.§ "ומטמא בנגעים".§ דכתיב: °"אדם כי יהיה בעור בשרו" – *אדם כל שהו.§ "ומטמא בטמא מת".§ דכתיב: °"ועל הנפשות אשר היו שם" – נפש כל דהו.§ "וזוקק ליבום".§ דכתיב: °"כי ישבו אחים יחדיו" – אחים שהיה להם ישיבה אחת בעולם.§ "ופוטר מן היבום".§ °"ובן אין לו" אמר רחמנא – והא אית ליה.§ "ומאכיל בתרומה".§ דכתיב: °"ויליד ביתו הם יאכלו בלחמו", קרי ביה: "יאכילו בלחמו".§ "ופוסל מן התרומה".§ °"וזרע אין לה" אמר רחמנא – והא אית לה. מאי איריא זרע? אפילו עובר נמי, דכתיב: "כנעוריה" *[ג]פרט למעוברת! וצריכי, דאי כתב רחמנא "וזרע אין לה" משום דמעיקרא חד גופא והשתא תרי גופי, אבל הכא – דמעיקרא חד גופא והשתא חד גופא – אימא תיכול, כתב רחמנא "כנעוריה". ואי כתב רחמנא "כנעוריה" – משום דמעיקרא גופה סריקא והשתא גופה מליא, אבל הכא – דמעיקרא גופה סריקא והשתא גופה סריקא – אימא תיכול, צריכא. קראי אתרוץ, אלא מתניתין, מאי איריא בן יום אחד – אפי' עובר נמי! אמר רב ששת: הב"ע – בכהן שיש לו שתי נשים אחת גרושה ואחת שאינה גרושה, ויש לו בנים משאינה גרושה, ויש לו בן יום אחד מן הגרושה – [ד]דפוסל בעבדי אביו מלאכול בתרומה. ולאפוקי מדר' יוסי *דאמר עובר נמי פוסל, קמ"ל: בן יום אחד – אין, עובר – לא.§ "נוחל ומנחיל".§ נוחל ממאן? – מאביו, ומנחיל למאן? – לאחיו מאביו, אי בעי – מאבוה לירתי ואי בעי – מיניה לירתי! *אמר רב ששת: [ה]נוחל בנכסי האם, להנחיל לאחיו מן האב. [ו]ודוקא בן יום אחד, אבל עובר – לא. מ"ט – דהוא מיית ברישא, [ז]ואין הבן יורש את אמו בקבר

## רש"י

ונוחל ומנחיל. מפרש בגמרא. כחתן שלם. מפרש בגמרא. **גמ'** אשה. "ואשה כי תהיה זבה" וגו', והאי קרא בנדה משתעי. בת עשרה ימים כו'. "ואשה כי תזוב זוב דמה" קרא דריש. אדם. משמע כל שהוא מין אדם, אפילו קטן, כדכתיב (במדבר לא): "ונפש אדם מן הנשים" וגו', ובקטנות משתעי קרא. נפשות. כל שיש בו נפש. כנעוריה. "ושבה אל בית אביה כנעוריה". כלומר, אם דומה לימי נעורים "ושבה", ואם לאו – לא תשוב. קראי אתרוץ. דתרוייהו צריכי. אלא מתניתין. מדנקט "יום אחד", ולא נקט "עובר", דוקא נקט. אמר רב ששת. האי "פוסל" לאו א"אמו" קאי, אלא א"עבדיו" קאי, והכא בכהן שהיו לו שתי נשים וכו'. אחת גרושה. שהיתה גרושה, ועבר ונשאה. ויש לו בנים. משאינה גרושה, והן כהנים כשרים. ועבדים שנפלו להן בירושה – אוכלין בתרומה בשבילן, דכתיב (ויקרא כב): "וכהן כי יקנה נפש קנין כספו" וגו'. ויש לו בן יום אחד מן הגרושה. והוא חלל, ואינו ראוי לכהונה, ויש לו חלק בעבדים – ופוסל את כולן מן התרומה, שאין אנו יודעין לברור מי מגיע לחלקו. ודוקא בן יום אחד, דראוי לירושה, אבל כל זמן שלא נולד – אוכלין כולן, דאין זכייה לעובר. ולאפוקי מדר' יוסי. דאמר במסכת יבמות בפרק "אלמנה לכהן גדול" (דף סז.): יש לו זכייה, ואפילו הוא במעי אשה זרה הכשרה לכהונה – פוסלה, דקסבר: כל זמן שהוא במעי זרה – זר הוא, וכל שכן האי דבמעי גרושה הוא, דאפילו כשיולד לא יהא ראוי. לאחיו מן האב. דהא אין ירושה אלא לקרובי האב. אי בעי מאבוה לירת. אפי' חשיבנא ליה כמאן דליתיה – ירתי לאחר מיתת אביהם, ואיהו מאי אהני? נוחל בנכסי האם. אם מתה אמו ביום שנולד – הרי הוא יורשה, וכשמת הוא – באין אחיו מאביו ויורשין הימנו נכסי אמו. דאי לאו איהו – הוו שקלי ליה קרובי האם, דבן נוחל את אמו. אבל האם – אינה נוחלת את בנה, וכל שכן קרובי האם – שאין נוחלין אותו, דכתיב (במדבר א): "למשפחותם לבית אבותם" – משפחת האם אינה קרויה "משפחה". אבל עובר. שבמעיה, אם מתה מעוברת – אינו נוחל להנחיל את קרוביו מן האב. בקבר.

## תוספות

**בנעוריה** פרט למעוברת. ואם תאמר: תיפוק ליה מ"וזרע אין לה" – עיין עליה, כי היכי דפסלינן בריש "החולץ" (יבמות לה:) חלילת מעוברת מ"אין לו" – עיין עליו? וי"ל: דהתם לא קאמר אלא "עיין והמתן אם יהיה ולד של קיימא", אבל לא מיפטרא מן היבום משום דכתיב "אין לו". וה"נ לא מיפסלא מן התרומה בהכי. **אמר** רב ששת הכא במאי עסקינן בכהן שיש לו ב' נשים. וא"ת: למה לי ב' נשים, לוקמה באשה אחת גרושה, ויש לו בן אחד ממנה. דדוקא בן יום אחד פוסל, ולא עובר, ואכלי העבדים בשביל כל המשפחה כולה לרבנן דר' יוסי, כדאמר ביבמות בפרק "אלמנה" (דף סז.) ועוד הקשה ה"ר אפרים: דבפרק "מי שמת" (ב"ב דף קמב.) אמר רב ששת: אחד זה ואחד זה קנה, בין מזכה לעובר בין לכשתלד. ופריך ליה ממתני' ד"בן יום אחד נוחל, אבל עובר – לא"! ומשני: דהתם משום דאיהו מיית ברישא. והשתא ליפרוך מרישא ד"בן יום אחד פוסל, אבל עובר – לא", משום דעובר לית ליה זכייה כדמפרש הכא רב ששת גופיה. ולא ה"מ לשנויי מידי! *וי"ל: דסבר רב ששת דלרבנן דר' יוסי נמי עובר אית ליה זכייה, וטעמא דעובר אינו פוסל – משום סמוך מיעוטא דמפילות למחצה דנקבות, והוה ליה זכרים מיעוטא, ולמיעוטא לא חיישינן כדחייש רבי יוסי. ולהכי אוקי הכא בכהן שיש לו ב' נשים, ויש לו בנים משאינה גרושה – דכיון דיש לו בנים, לא פסיל עובר אף ע"ג דיש לו זכייה, דלא חיישינן למיעוט הזכרים כדפי' אבל אם אין לו בנים – פוסל עובר גם לרבנן, דאית ליה זכייה, דבין הוא זכר בין היא נקבה הרי הן שלה. ופליג רב ששת אשמואל דאמר בפרק "אלמנה" (יבמות דף סז.) דלרבנן אוכלין בשביל כל המשפחה כולה, דסבר שמואל דלרבנן לית ליה זכייה לעובר. והשתא ניחא הא דקאמר התם *רב ששת "מנא אמינא לה, דתניא גר שמת" כו', ולא דחי ליה: דהך ברייתא כר' יוסי, דרבנן נמי לא פליגי, אלא דלא חיישי למיעוטא כדפי'. ואם תאמר: דבפרק "מי שמת" (ב"ב דף קמב.) גבי "גר שמת ובזבזו ישראל נכסיו, והיתה אשתו מעוברת – לא קנו. שמעו אחרי כן שהפילה אשתו – המחזיק בשניה קנה, בראשונה – לא קנה", אמאי לא קנה המחזיק בראשונה, כיון דלבסוף הפילה, הא בפ' "אלמנה" (יבמות סז:) אמרינן דזכרים הוו מיעוטא, משום מיעוטא דמפילות, ואין לעובר שסופו להיות נפל חלק בעבדים? וי"ל: דהתם משום דתלינן שמא כבר בשעת אכילת העבדים מת העובר בבטן, ולית ליה זכייה. **ואי** בעי מיניה לירות כו'. וא"ת: דבפרק "מי שמת" (ב"ב קמב.) דפריך לרב ששת מהך ד"בן יום א' נוחל ומנחיל, אבל עובר – לא", ומשני: נוחל את האם להנחיל לאחים מן האב. והשתא מה היתה סברת המקשה, דע"כ צריך לומר כדמשני רב ששת, דאי לאו הכי תקשה ליה: אי בעי – מיניה לירות, אי בעי – מאבוה לירות, כדמקשה הכא! וי"ל: דיפרש כמר בריה דרב יוסף, שממעט בחלק בכורה, אבל עובר – לא. ולאו משום "וילדו לו", אלא משום דעובר לית ליה זכייה. א"נ: ידע שפיר, כדמשני רב ששת, נוחל את האם להנחיל לאחיו מן האב, אך היה סבור דאיהי מייתא ברישא, וקאמר "עובר – לא", משום דלא קנה. ובשילהי פ"ק דערכין (דף ז.) דאמר שמואל: אשה שיצתה ליהרג – מכין אותה כנגד הריון שלה, כדי שימות הולד תחלה. הא לאו הכי – הולד מת לבסוף, ופריך ליה מהא ד"בן יום אחד נוחל" – אלמא ולד מת תחלה! הוה מצי לשנויי: "אבל עובר – לא" לומר שממעט בחלק בכור, כדאמר בשמעתין. אלא דניחא ליה לאוקמי מילתא דרב ששת, דאמר הכא "איהו מיית ברישא", אליבא דשמואל ולחלק האמת, שיש חילוק בין מתה לנהרגה.

**איהו** מיית ברישא. והא דתנן בפ' "בהמה המקשה" (חולין דף עד.) השוחט את הבהמה ומצא בה בן ט' חי – יש חילוק בין מתה לנהרגה, כדאמר בערכין (דף ז.). והא דאמר נמי ב"השוחט" *במתה אמה והדר ילידתיה – היינו נמי כשנהרגה. אי נמי: כגון דמתה אמו מחמת לידה, דכיון דעקר הולד לצאת, אז לא מיית. כדאמר שמואל שילהי פ"ק דערכין (דף ז.) ישבה על המשבר ומתה – מחתכין אותה בשבת, ומוציאין הולד. וא"ת: אם כן, עובר נוחל ומנחיל בישבה על המשבר ומתה תחלה? י"ל: דאין הכי נמי, ונקט "בן יום אחד" – משום דפסיקא ליה דנוחל ומנחיל, אבל עובר – לא פסיקא ליה. ומיהא, "בן יום אחד – ההורגו חייב" דקתני, אבל עובר, לא – היינו אפילו נהרגה או ישבה על המשבר עד שילא ראשו, כדתנן במסכת אהלות פ"ז (משנה ו) ומייתי לה בפרק "בן סורר ומורה" (סנהדרין דף עב:) אשה המקשה – חותך אבר

## תוספי הרא"ש

**בנעוריה** פרט למעוברת. ותימה תיפוק לי מוזרע אין לה עיין עליה כי היכי דפסלינן בריש החולץ חליצת מעוברת מואין לו עיין עליו וי"ל דהתם לא קאמ' אלא עיין והמתן אם יבא הוולד לידי בן קיימא. אבל לא פטר ליה מן שהיא מעוברת הכא נמי הוה אמרי' שתמתין מלאכול עד שתראה אם הוולד יהיה בן קיימא אבל לא מיפסלא מתרומה ללקות עליה כמו זר: **בכהן** שיש לו שתי נשים. תימה כיון דאתיא כרבנן דסברי דעובר אין לו זכיה כדקאמרינן לאפוקי מר' יוסי א"כ למה לי ב' נשים הוה מצי למימר באשה אחת גרושה ואין לו בנים ממנה דדוקא בן יום אחד פוסל ולא עובר אלא אוכל בשביל כל המשפחה לרבנן כדאיתא ביבמות פ' אלמנה ועוד הקשה ה"ר אפרים דבפ' מי שמת פריך לרב ששת דאמר המזכה לעובר קנה ממתניתין דבן יום אחד נוחל ומנחיל אבל לא עובר ומשני דהוא מיית ברישא כדמשני הכא. והכא אדפריך מסיפא הו"ל למיפרך מהך רישא ולא הוה מצי לשנויי הכי ובהך פירכא אחריתי מיתרצא פירכא קמייתא דרב ששת דמוקי לה בכהן שיש לו שתי נשים לטעמיה דאית ליה דעובר אית ליה זכייה. והא דאמרי רבנן דעובר אינו פוסל משום דהוו להו זכרים מיעוטא ור' יוסי דקאמר דעובר פוסל דחייש למיעוט והשתא איצטריך לאוקומי בכהן שיש לו שתי נשים ויש לו בנים משאינה גרושה דאי אין לו אלא אשה אחת גרושה אפי' עובר פוסל דבין הוא זכר בין היא נקבה זכה בנכסים ואין למשפחה זכות בנכסים כיון דעובר אית ליה זכיה: **אמר** רב ששת נוחל בנכסי האם. בפ' מי שמת פריך לרב ששת דאמר המזכה לעובר [קנה] ממתניתין דקתני בן יום אחד אבל עובר לא ומתרץ רב ששת התם דפירושא דמתניתין כדמתרץ הכא. ותימה מה היתה שם סברת המקשה דבלאו רב ששת תיקשי פי' דמתני' כדפריך הכא אי בעי מיניה לירתו אי בעי' מאבוה לירתו וי"ל דמשמע ליה לפרושי מתניתין כגון שהקנה נכסיו לאחר אם לא יהיה לו יורש בשעת מיתה וקמ"ל דבן יום אחד הוי יורש. אבל עובר לא דלא קנה ופירושא דמנחיל הוי כמו דמפרש הכא דמנחיל לאחיו מן האב נכסי אמו אבל עובר לא משום דלא קנה ורב ששת משני דנוחל ומנחיל חדא מילתא היא. א"נ ס"ד כדמפרש רב יוסף לומר שממעט בחלק בבורה אבל עובר לא בלאו טעמא דוילדו לו אלא משום דאין לו זכיה. א"נ הוה ידע שפיר כמו שמפרש רב ששת נוחל מאחי האם להנחיל לאחים מן האב והו מפרש ליה משום דעובר אין לו זכיה:
מ"ט

## עין משפט נר מצוה

ם א מיי' פ"א מהל' נחלות הל' ג ועי"ש סמג עשין לו טוש"ע חו"מ סי' רעו סעיף ה:
סא ב מיי' פ"ב מהל' רוצח הלכה ו:
[שמחות פ"ג]
סב ג מיי' פ"ח מהל' תרומות הל"ב:
סג ד מיי' שם הל"ד [וברב אלפס פ"ח דב"ב דף ריא]:
סד ה מיי' פ"א מהל' נחלות הלי"ג ועי' בהשגות ובמ"מ סמג עשין לו טוש"ע חו"מ סי' רעו סעיף ה [וברב אלפס שם]:
סה ו שם בהג"ה:
סו ז מיי' שם הלי"ג סמג שם טוש"ע שם [וברב אלפס שם]:

## מסורת הש"ס

[ב"ב קמב. ערכין ז.] [לעיל לב.] [לעיל לב: ערכין ג.] ב"מ לה: ודף לג: נדרים ג. סנהדרין נו. סה: מכות יב. (ר"ה ח) כתובות סז: גיטין מא: יבמות עא. קדושין יז: [ברכות לא: ע"ז כז. כריתות יא. זבחים קח:] יבמות פז. יבמות סז. ב"ב קמב. [ערכין ז.] [עי' ערכין ג.] [עי' מהר"ם] [ובב"ב קמב.] [חולין לח:]

עין משפט נר מצוה

סז א ב מיי' פ"ב מהל' נחלות הל' יג סמג עשין צו טוש"ע חו"מ סי' רעז סעיף ה:

סח ג מיי' שם הל' ב טוש"ע שם סעי' ג:

סט ד ה ו מיי' פ"ב מהל' אבל הל' א וה' סמג עשין מד טוש"ע יו"ד סי' שעד סעי' ח:

ע ז מיי' פ"ג מהל' איסורי ביאה הל' יד טוש"ע אה"ע סי' קסז סעי' ד:

עא ח טוש"ע אה"ע סי' קסז סעי' ה:

עב ט מיי' פ"ג מהל' איסורי ביאה הל"ב:

עג י מיי' פ"ג מהל' מטמאי משכב ומושב הלכה ג:

עד כ מיי' פ"ו מהל' תרומות הל"ג:

עה ל מיי' פ"א מהל' איסורי ביאה הל"ג ופ"ט שם הל"ג טוש"ע אה"ע סי' ו סעי' א וסי' כ סעי' א:

עו מ מיי' פ"א מהל' איסורי ביאה הל"ג:

[עי' תוס' סנהדרין פד: ד"ה כ"ג]

[דשבת פט"ז]

בקבר להנחיל לאחיו מן האב. איני, והא הוה *עובדא ופרכס עד תלת פרכוסי! אמר מר בריה דרב אשי: *מידי דהוה אזנב הלטאה דמפרכסת. מר בריה דרב יוסף משמיה דרבא אמר: [א]לומר שממעט בחלק בכורה. ואמר מר בריה דרב יוסף משמיה דרבא: [ב]בן שנולד אחר מיתת האב – אינו ממעט בחלק בכורה, מאי טעמא – "וילדו לו" בעינן. (דברים כא) בסורא מתנו הכי. בפומבדיתא מתנו הכי: אמר מר בריה דרב יוסף משמיה דרבא, [ג]בכור שנולד לאחר מיתת אביו – אינו נוטל פי שנים, מאי טעמא – "יכיר" (שם) בעינן, והא ליכא. והלכתא בכל הני לישני דמר בריה דרב יוסף משמיה דרבא. § "וההורגו חייב". § דכתיב: "ואיש כי יכה כל נפש" (ויקרא כד) – מ"מ. § "והרי הוא לאביו ולאמו ולכל קרוביו כחתן שלם". § למאי הלכתא? אמר רב פפא: [ד]לענין אבלות. כמאן? דלא כרשב"ג, *דאמר: [ה]כל ששהה שלשים יום באדם – אינו נפל, הא לא שהה – ספק הוי! הכא במאי עסקינן – [ו]דקים ליה שכלו לו חדשיו. § **מתני'** [ז]בת *שלש שנים ויום אחד מתקדשת בביאה. [ח]ואם בא עליה יבם קנאה, *[ט]וחייבין עליה משום אשת איש, [י]ומטמאה את בועלה לטמא משכב תחתון כעליון. [כ]נשאת לכהן תאכל בתרומה. [ל]בא עליה אחד מן הפסולין פסלה מן הכהונה. [מ]בא עליה אחד מכל העריות האמורות בתורה מומתין *עליה, והיא פטורה. *פחות מכן כנותן אצבע בעין. § **גמ'** ת"ר: בת ג' שנים מתקדשת בביאה, דברי רבי מאיר. וחכ"א: בת ג' שנים ויום אחד. מאי בינייהו? אמרי דבי רבי ינאי: ערב ראש השנה איכא בינייהו. ור' יוחנן אמר: *ל' יום בשנה חשובין שנה איכא בינייהו. מיתיבי, בת ג' שנים, ואפי' בת שתי שנים ויום אחד מתקדשת בביאה, דברי רבי מאיר. וחכמים אומרים: בת שלשה שנים ויום אחד.

בשלמא

**רש"י**

בקבר. כי מת הוא קודם לה. ופרכס. עובר שבמעי אמו אחר מיתתה תלתא פרכוסי, אלמא היא מייתה ברישא. לומר שממעט כו'. מתניתין דקתני "נוחל ומנחיל", לומר: שממעט בחלק בכורה. כגון אם היה בן יום אחד כשמת אביו, והיה לו אח בכור ואח פשוט, ומת הוא אחר אביו – נוחל הוא מאביו את חלק רביעי שבנכסיו, ומנחילו לשני אחיו, וחולקין הבכור והפשוט את חלקו של זה בשוה. ונמצא ממעט בחלק הבכור. דאי לאו איהו – הוה שקיל בכור תרי תילתי, כגון משׂשה זהובים ארבעה, ופשוט נוטל ב' זהובים. ועכשיו – נוטל הבכור ג' זהובים כנגד שני אחין, ומחלקו של זה ג' רבעי זהוב. נמצאו ביד בכור ד' זהובים חסר רביע, וביד פשוט ב' זהובים ורביע. ודוקא בן יום א', אבל עובר – אינו ממעט, כדאמר לקמן: בן שנולד לאחר מיתת אביו – אינו ממעט בחלק הבכורה, ונוטל הבכור שליש בכורתו, ובין שלשתן יחלקו ב' שלישים. מאי טעמא. אמרינן בן יום אחד דממעט, אבל עובר לא? וילדו לו בעינן. משמע: בחייו. בכור שנולד אחר מיתת אביו. כגון מת אביו, והאשה מעוברת תאומים – אין היוצא ראשון נוטל פי שנים. דלאו תאומים לא משכחת לה, דכיון דבכור לא נולד עד מות אביו, פשוט מהיכן בא? אי נמי: שהניח ב' נשים מעוברות. כמאן דלא כר' שמעון. אכולה מתני' קאי, דקא חשיב בן יום אחד בן קיימא. באדם. דאילו בבהמה שמונה ימים לא הוי נפל. **מתני'** בת ג' שנים. ביאתה ביאה לכל דבר. מתקדשת. אם מסרה אביה לכך. אם בא עליה יבם קנאה. וזכה בנכסי אחיו ליורשה ולטמא לה. וחייבין עליה. אם קבל בה אביה קדושין מזה, ובא אחר עליה – נהרג, דביאתה ביאה. ומטמאה את בועלה. אם היא נדה. אבל פחות מכן, אע"ג שמטמאה במגע – אינה מטמאה את בועלה משום בועל נדה לטומאת ז', אלא משום נוגע ולטומאת ערב. תחתון. של בועל נדה. כעליונו. של זב. מן הפסולין. כגון חלל, נתין וממזר ועבד וגוי. פסלה. מתרומת אביה אם היא בת כהן, כדתניא בגמרא ד"אלמנה לכהן גדול" ביבמות (דף סח.): מנין לכהנת, לויה וישראלית שבא עליהן? כו' ת"ל: "כי תהיה לאיש זר" – כיון שנבעלה לפסול לה, פסלה. מכל העריות. כגון אביה או חמיה. והיא פטורה. מפני שהיא קטנה, ולאו בת עונשין. **גמ'** ערב ראש השנה. של שנה רביעית. לרבי מאיר גופיה לא הוי בת ביאה עד יום אחרון של שלישית, דהוא ערב ראש השנה. ולרבנן – עד למחר, דמיקלע יום ראשון ברביעית. שלשים יום איכא בינייהו. לרבי מאיר – מכי איקלע שלשים יום בשנה שלישית הויא בת ביאה, ולרבנן – עד דמיקלע שנה רביעית. ואיכא בינייהו טובא.

בשלמא

**תוספות**

אבר, יצא ראשו – אין דוחין נפש מפני נפש. ומיהו אפשר דדוקא היכא דאמו חיה לא מיחייב ההורגו עד שיצא ראשו, שתלוי קצת בחיות אמו. אבל היכא דמתה – חייב, משום דכמונח בקופסא דמי. וא"ת: אם תמצי לומר דמותר להורגו בבטן אפי' מתה אמו, ולא הוי כמונח בקופסא, אמאי מחללין עליו את השבת, שמביאין סכין דרך ר"ה לקרוע האם, כדמוכח בפ' קמא דערכין (דף ז:)? וי"ל: דמכל מקום משום פקוח נפש מחללין עליו את השבת, אף ע"ג דמותר להרגו. דהא גוסס בידי אדם – ההורגו פטור, כדאמר פרק "הנשרפין" (סנהדרין עח.) דרוב גוססים למיתה, ומחללין את השבת עליו, כדאמר פרק בתרא דיומא (ד' פד:) דאין מהלכין בפקוח נפש אחר הרוב. **מאי** טעמא וילדו לו בעינן. למ"ד: המוכה לעובר לא קנה, לא איצטריך למדרש מ"וילדו" כדאמר בפ' "מי שמת" (ב"ב דף קמב:). **איש** כי יכה כל נפש אפילו כל דהו. האי קרא כתיב ב"אמור אל הכהנים". ותימה: דבריש "הנחנקין" (סנהדרין דף פד:) דריש מקרא אחרינא דכתיב ב"אלה מסעי": "כל מכה נפש".*. **הא** לא שהה ספקא הוי. משמע הכא דלרבנן הוי טפי בר קיימא מלרשב"ג, דאפילו בן יום א' הוי לדידהו בן קיימא, וכן בפ' "החולץ" (יבמות דף לו.) ואילו בתוספתא *מתניא פלוגתייהו על בן ח' דלרבנן אפילו שהה שלשים יום – הוי נפל, ואתא רשב"ג למימר דאם שהה ל' יום – הוי בר קיימא, דאמר: בן ז' הוא, ואישתהויי אשתהי. וכן בפרק "הערל" (יבמות דף פ:) ויש לומר: דבתרתי פליגי. ודייק מדלא קאמר רשב"ג "אם שהה ל' יום – אינו נפל", כיון דקאי ארבנן דאמרי בבר ח' דהוי נפל. ומדנקט "כל ששהה" – משמע דבכל ולדות בעי רשב"ג יום ל' ואם כן שמעינהו לרבנן, דלאו בל' תלוי, אלא בחדשי ההריון.

**דקים** ליה דכלו לו חדשיו. הא לא קים ליה – ספקא הוי. ובנפל מן הגג או אכלו ארי איירי, דבפיהק ומת – אפילו לרבנן הוי נפל, כדאמר פרק "רבי אליעזר אם לא הביא" (שבת קלו.). ואם תאמר: אם כן, מאי טעמא דרשב"ג כיון דליכא ריעותא אמאי אינו מתאבל עליו, דניזיל אחר רוב ולדות דהוו בני קיימא ובפ' "רבי אליעזר אם לא הביא" (שם) דאסר ההוא עגלה דאשתחיט ביומא דשביעאה, משום דהתם פסיק הלכה כרשב"ג, אמאי לא אזלינן בתר רובא? וי"ל: דנפלין הוי מיעוט דשכיח, ודבר ההווה הוא, ולכך החמירו חכמים, ולענין אבלות הקילו. וגדולה מזאת מצינו דאמר בפרק "יש בכור" (בכורות דף מט.) דיום ל' כשלפניו לענין אבלות, אע"ג דקי"ל ב"החולץ" (יבמות לו:) דמת ביום ל', ועמדה ונתקדשה, אם אשת כהן היא – אינה חולצת, דחשיב בר קיימא. וא"ת: דהכא אמר דבלא שהה ספקא הוא, ואינו מתאבל עליו, ובמסכת שמחות (פ"ד ה"ג) תנן: ספק אחיו ספק אינו אחיו – מתאבל עליו. וי"ל: דשאני התם, כיון דבר קיימא הוא, אי אין מתאבל עליו – סברי עלמא דאין מתאבלין על אחין. א"נ: בספק בן ט' לראשון או בן ז' לאחרון, דמה נפשך חד מינייהו חייב, וגנאי הדבר לפטור שניהם. **שלשים** יום איכא בינייהו. הא דלא קאמר: יום אחד בשנה חשוב שנה איכא בינייהו, דלרבי מאיר בב' שנים ויום אחד סגי, ולא הוי פליג אברייתא דבסמוך – היינו משום דבשנת ג' בשביל יום אחד לא הוה קרי ליה "שלש שנים". וא"ת: ולימא דיום ראשון של שנה רביעית איכא בינייהו, דלרבי מאיר במקצת היום סגי, ולרבנן בעינן מעת לעת עד שעה שנולדה, כדאמר פ"ב דזבחים (דף כה:) דשעות פוסלות בקדשים? וי"ל: דקים ליה דרבנן לא בעו מעת לעת. ועוד: דאם כן, אף לר' מאיר הוה ליה למתני "ג' שנים ויום אחד", והוה ליה לפרושי דלא בעינן מעת לעת. והא דתנן בפרק "אלו נערות" (כתובות דף כט.) הגיורת שנתגיירה פחותה מבת ג' שנים ויום אחד יש לה קנס, לא אתיא כרבי מאיר, מדמצריך יום אחד אחר שלש שנים. ואם תאמר: והיכי מוכח התם דרישא כרבי מאיר, דקאמר פרק "אלו נערות": נערה – אין, קטנה – לא, והתם ע"כ אסיפא דמתני' סמיך, דקתני (א) "כל מקום שיש מכר – אין קנס". דמנערות איכא למימר דלא אתי למעוטי קטנות, אלא בוגרות. דבפרק "ארבע מיתות" (סנהדרין דף סו:) תנן: אין חייב הבא על נערה המאורסה, עד שתהא נערה. ודייק התם: דאתא לאפוקי קטנה, דאי לאפוקי בוגרת אלא "על נערה" מבעי ליה. אלמא "נערה" – אפילו קטנה משמע. אלא אסיפא סמיך, כדפרישית, והיכי דייק מסיפא דמתני' דרישא נמי ר"מ כיון דמליעתא לא אתיא כוותיה? וי"ל: דלאו ממש ר"מ היא קאמר, אלא דדייק דתנא דההוא פירקא סבר דקטנה אין לה קנס, כדקתני בסיפא. וא"כ "נערות" נקט – לאפוקי קטנות. ורבא דפריך בפ"ק דכתובות (דף יא.) הגיורת יש לה קנס, יהבינן לה קנס דאזלה ואכלה בהיותה נכרית? אלמא סבר דמתני' סבר דקטנה יש לה קנס – היינו משום דסבר כיון דהך בבא דגיורת לא אתיא כר' מאיר במאי דנקט שלש שנים ויום אחד, אם כן גם לענין דקטנה יש לה קנס אתיא כרבנן. (ב) וה"ה דפריך בפ' "ד' וה'" (ב"ק לח:) ממתני' ד"אלו נערות" (דף כט.) דקתני: כותית – יש לה קנס, לרבי מאיר, אע"ג דההיא דגיורת לא אתיא כר"מ מ"מ כיון דסתם מתני' ר"מ היא – מאי דמצינן לאוקומי כוותיה, מוקמינן.

אחר

**תוספי הרא"ש**

מ"ט וילדו לו בעינן. למ"ד המוכה לעובר לא קנה לא איצטריך וילדו לו כדפרשי' לעיל והו"ג אמרינן בפרק מי שמת: **איש** כי יכה כל נפש אפי' כל דהו האי אדם קרא כתיב באמור אל הכהנים ותימה דבריש אלו הן הנחנקין דריש ליה מקרא אחרינא דכתיב באלה מסעי כל מכה נפש לפי עדים: **הא** לא שהה ספיקא הוי משמע הכא דחשיב בן קיימא לרבנן טפי מלרשב"ג. ותימה דבפ' הערל משמע איפכא דבן שמונה אמר רבנן דבר שהה ל' יום הוי נפל ולרשב"ג לא הוי נפל אלא אמרינן דבר ז' הוא ואישתהויי אישתהי וי"ל דבתרתי פליגי דבבן ח' פליגי דהדי מיתנא פלוגתייהו בתוספתא והא דאמרינן הכא דפליגי בסתם ולדות דייק תלמודא מדקתני לרשב"ג כל ששהה ל' יום באדם אינו נפל דאי לא פליגי אלא בבן ח' כדרשב"ג בתוספתא ה"ל למימר אינו נפל ומדנקט האי לישנא כל ששהה ל' יום באדם אינו נפל משמע דשמעינהו לרבנן דמקילי בסתם ולדות לומר שיצאו לאלתר מידי נפל. וקאמר רשב"ג דוקא אם שהה ל' יום באדם אינו נפל ולא מפליג רשב"ג בין סתם ולדות לבן ח' להכי אמר כל ששהה שכולל כל הולדות. ותימה האיך ניחא ליה מתניתין אליבא דרבנן והא בפיהק ומת אפי' רבנן מודו ואמאי חייב באבילות וי"ל דמיתוקמא מתני' בנפל מן הגג ואכלו ארי ותימה בנפל מן הגג דליכא ריעותא מ"ט דרשב"ג ניזיל בתר רוב נשים דוולד מעליא ילדן וע"ק דבפ' ר"א דמילה פסקינן כרשב"ג ואסרי' עגלא תליתאה דאישתחיט ביומא דשבעה וי"ל כיון דמיעוטא דנפלים מצוי והוה חיישינן למיעוטא כזה כדאמרינן גבי מים שאין להם סוף כיון דמיעוט ניצולין [חיישינן] ליה. ולענין אבלות נמי כיון דנפלים מצויין הן לא אזלינן בתר רובא להחמיר דלענין אבילות הקילו חכמים וגדולה מזו בפ' יש בכור כדאמרינן יום ל' כיום שלפניו לענין אבילות משום דקי"ל דהלכה כדברי המקיל באבל אע"ג דקי"ל בפ' החולץ דאם (ילדה) [מת] בתוך ל' ועמדה ונתקדשה עם אשת כהן היא אינה חולצת דחשיב בר קיימא והיינו כקולי דמר וכקולי דמר לא חשו באבילות דרבנן. ותימה הכא אמרינן דהיכא דאינו שהה דאינו מתאבל על הספק ובמס' שמחות תנן הספיקות מתאבלין עליהן וי"ל דהתם אמרי' בספק בן ט' לראשון ובן ז' לאחרון דממה נפשך חד מינייהו חייב להתאבל וגנאי הדבר לפטור שניהן: **וחייבין** עליה משום אשת איש. פרש"י אם קבל בה אביה קדושין ובא עליה נהרג דביאתו ביאה וק' לפי' למה לי למיתני הך בבא היינו אם בא עליה אחד מן העריות האמורות בתורה מומתין על ידיה. ונראה לפרש דקאי אהא דקאמר אם בא עליה יבם קנאה דלא תימא לא קנאה אלא מדרבנן מידי דהוה אביאת בן ט' קמ"ל דקנאה מדאורייתא וחייבין עליה משום אשת איש: **ערב** ראש השנה איכא בינייהו. לר' מאיר סגי ליה בערב ראש השנה לרבנן צריך שתכנס לשנה רביעית: **שלשים** יום בשנה חשובין שנה איכא בינייהו ותימא לימא שנה שלישית איכא בינייהו לבר יום אחד דלר' מאיר בשתי שנים ויום א' סגי דיום אחד בשנה חשוב שנה ולא הוה פליג אברייתא דבסמוך וי"ל דמשום יום אחד לא הוה קרי לה בת ג' שנים. ותימא ולימא יום ראשון של רביעית איכא בינייהו דלר' מאיר בתחלת שנה רביעית סגי ולרבנן בעי' מעת לעת עד שעה שנולדה כדאמר לקמן בפירקין לענין קדשים. וי"ל דקים ליה דלרבנן לא בעי מעת לעת ועוד דא"כ גם לר' מאיר ה"ל למיתני בת ג' שנים ויום אחד ולפרושי דלא בעינן מעת לעת:

מסורת הש"ס

ב"ב קמב:

[שם: ערכין ז. חולין כח.]

שבת קלו. יבמות לו: וקף פ: [תוספתא דשבת פט"ז]

סנהדרין נה: סוטה: קדושין י. יבמות נז.

[אריכות תו' במשנה זו ע' ביבמות נז: וקדושין י. ובסנהדרין נה: פירשו תוס' כל בבי מתניתין הכא]

[במשנ' שבמשניו' על ידה כתובות]

[לקמן מה. ר"ה י: מכות ג:]

הגהות הב"ח

(א) תוס' ד"ה שלשים וכו' דקתני כ"מ. נ"ב בדף מ ע"ב: (ב) בא"ד כרבנן והא דפריך:

בְּשְׁלָמָא לְר' יוֹחָנָן, כִּי הֵיכִי דְּאִיכָּא תַּנָּא דְּקָאָמַר: *יוֹם אֶחָד בַּשָּׁנָה חָשׁוּב שָׁנָה, הָכִי נַמִּי אִיכָּא תַּנָּא דְּאָמַר: *ל' יוֹם בַּשָּׁנָה חֲשׁוּבִין שָׁנָה. אֶלָּא לְר' יַנַּאי קַשְׁיָא! קַשְׁיָא. § "פָּחוֹת מִכָּאן כְּנוֹתֵן אֶצְבַּע בָּעַיִן". § אִיבַּעְיָא לְהוּ: הָנֵי בְּתוּלִין מֵיזַל אָזְלִי וְאָתוּ, אוֹ דִּלְמָא אִתְצוּדֵי הוּא דְּלָא מִתְצְדִי עַד לְאַחַר ג'? לְמַאי נָפְקָא מִינָּהּ? — כְּגוֹן שֶׁבָּעַל בְּתוֹךְ ג' וּמָצָא דָּם, וּבָעַל לְאַחַר שָׁלֹשׁ וְלֹא מָצָא דָּם. אִי אָמְרַתְּ מֵיזַל אָזְלִי וְאָתוּ — שָׁהוּת הוּא דְּלָא הָוְיָא לְהוּ, אֶלָּא אִי אָמְרַתְּ אִתְצוּדֵי הוּא דְּלָא מִתְצְדִי עַד לְאַחַר ג', הָא — אַחֵר בָּא עָלֶיהָ, מַאי? מַתְקִיף לָהּ רַב חִיָּיא בְּרֵיהּ דְּרַב אִיקָא: וּמַאן לֵימָא לָן דְּמַכָּה שֶׁבְּתוֹךְ ג' אֵינָהּ חוֹזֶרֶת לְאַלְתַּר שֶׁמָּא חוֹזֶרֶת לְאַלְתַּר, וְהָא — אַחֵר בָּא עָלֶיהָ! אֶלָּא נָפְקָא מִינָּהּ: כְּגוֹן שֶׁבָּעַל בְּתוֹךְ ג' וּמָצָא דָּם, וּבָעַל לְאַחַר ג' וּמָצָא דָּם. אִי אָמְרַתְּ מֵיזַל אָזְלִי וְאָתוּ — הַאי דַּם בְּתוּלִין הוּא, אֶלָּא אִי אָמְרַתְּ אִתְצוּדֵי הוּא דְּלָא מִתְצְדִי אֶלָּא עַד לְאַחַר ג' — הַאי דַּם נִדָּה הוּא, מַאי? אָמַר רַב חִסְדָּא, ת"ש: פָּחוֹת מִכָּאן — כְּנוֹתֵן אֶצְבַּע בָּעַיִן, לָמָּה לִי לְמִתְנֵי "כְּנוֹתֵן אֶצְבַּע בָּעַיִן"? לִתְנֵי "פָּחוֹת מִכָּאן — וְלֹא כְלוּם", מַאי לָאו — הָא קמ"ל: [א]מָה עַיִן — מְדַמַּעַת וְחוֹזֶרֶת וּמְדַמַּעַת, אַף בְּתוּלִין מֵיזַל אָזְלִי וְאָתוּ. ת"ר: מַעֲשֶׂה בְּיוּסְטְנִי בִּתּוֹ שֶׁל אַסְוִירוּס בֶּן אַנְטְנִינוּס שֶׁבָּאת לִפְנֵי רַבִּי. אָמְרָה לוֹ: רַבִּי, אִשָּׁה בְּכַמָּה נִיסֵּת? אָמַר לָהּ: בַּת ג' שָׁנִים וְיוֹם אֶחָד. וּבְכַמָּה מִתְעַבֶּרֶת? אָמַר לָהּ: בַּת י"ב שָׁנָה וְיוֹם אֶחָד. אָמְרָה לוֹ: אֲנִי נִשֵּׂאתִי בְּשֵׁשׁ וְיָלַדְתִּי בְּשֶׁבַע, אוֹי לְשָׁלֹשׁ שָׁנִים שֶׁאִבַּדְתִּי בְּבֵית אַבָּא! וּמִי מִעַבְּרָה? *וְהָתָנֵי רַב בֵּיבָי קַמֵּיהּ דְּרַב נַחְמָן: ג' נָשִׁים מְשַׁמְּשׁוֹת בְּמוֹךְ, קְטַנָּה מְעוּבֶּרֶת וּמֵנִיקָה. קְטַנָּה — שֶׁמָּא תִּתְעַבֵּר וְתָמוּת, מְעוּבֶּרֶת — שֶׁמָּא תַּעֲשֶׂה עוּבָּרָהּ סַנְדָּל, מֵנִיקָה — שֶׁמָּא תִּגְמוֹל אֶת בְּנָהּ וְיָמוּת. וְאֵיזוֹהִי קְטַנָּה — מִבַּת י"א שָׁנָה וְיוֹם אֶחָד וְעַד י"ב שָׁנָה וְיוֹם אֶחָד. פָּחוֹת מִכָּאן, אוֹ יָתֵר עַל כֵּן — מְשַׁמֶּשֶׁת וְהוֹלֶכֶת — דִּבְרֵי ר"מ. וַחכ"א: אַחַת זוֹ וְאַחַת זוֹ — מְשַׁמֶּשֶׁת כְּדַרְכָּהּ וְהוֹלֶכֶת, וּמִן הַשָּׁמַיִם יְרַחֲמוּ, שֶׁנֶּאֱמַר: °"שׁוֹמֵר פְּתָאִים ה'" (תהלים קטז). אִיבָּעֵית אֵימָא: °"אֲשֶׁר בְּשַׂר חֲמוֹרִים בְּשָׂרָם" (יחזקאל כג). וְאִיבָּעֵית אֵימָא: °"אֲשֶׁר פִּיהֶם דִּבֶּר שָׁוְא וִימִינָם יְמִין שָׁקֶר" (תהלים קמד). ת"ר: מַעֲשֶׂה בְּאִשָּׁה אַחַת שֶׁבָּאת לִפְנֵי ר"ע. אָמְרָה לוֹ: ר', נִבְעַלְתִּי בְּתוֹךְ שָׁלֹשׁ שָׁנִים, מָה אֲנִי לִכְהוּנָּה? אָמַר לָהּ: [ב]כְּשֵׁרָה אַתְּ לִכְהוּנָּה. אָמְרָה לוֹ: רַבִּי, אֶמְשׁוֹל לְךָ מָשָׁל, לְמָה הַדָּבָר דּוֹמֶה — לְתִינוֹק שֶׁטָּמְנוּ לוֹ אֶצְבָּעוֹ בִּדְבַשׁ. פַּעַם רִאשׁוֹנָה וּשְׁנִיָּה — גּוֹעֵר *בָּהּ, שְׁלִישִׁית — מְצָצָהּ. אָמַר לָהּ: אִם כֵּן — פְּסוּלָה אַתְּ לִכְהוּנָּה. *רָאָה הַתַּלְמִידִים מִסְתַּכְּלִים זֶה בָּזֶה. אָמַר לָהֶם: לָמָּה הַדָּבָר קָשֶׁה בְּעֵינֵיכֶם? *[אָמְרוּ לֵיהּ] כְּשֵׁם שֶׁכָּל הַתּוֹרָה הֲלָכָה לְמֹשֶׁה מִסִּינַי, כָּךְ פְּחוּתָה מִבַּת שָׁלֹשׁ שָׁנִים — כְּשֵׁרָה לִכְהוּנָּה הֲלָכָה לְמֹשֶׁה מִסִּינַי. וְאַף רַבִּי עֲקִיבָא לֹא אֲמָרָהּ אֶלָּא *לְחַדֵּד בָּהּ אֶת הַתַּלְמִידִים. §

**מתני'** *) [ג]בֶּן תֵּשַׁע שָׁנִים וְיוֹם אֶחָד שֶׁבָּא עַל יְבִמְתּוֹ — קְנָאָהּ, וְאֵין נוֹתֵן גֵּט עַד שֶׁיַּגְדִּיל. [ד]וּמְטַמֵּא בְּנִדָּה לְטַמֵּא מִשְׁכָּב תַּחְתּוֹן כָּעֶלְיוֹן. [ה]וּפוֹסֵל וְאֵינוֹ מַאֲכִיל בִּתְרוּמָה, [ו]וּפוֹסֵל אֶת הַבְּהֵמָה מֵעַ"ג הַמִּזְבֵּחַ, [ז]וְנִסְקֶלֶת עַל יָדוֹ. [ח]וְאִם בָּא עַל אַחַת מִכָּל הָעֲרָיוֹת הָאֲמוּרוֹת בַּתּוֹרָה — מוּמָתִין עַל יָדוֹ, וְהוּא פָּטוּר. §

**גמ'** וְלִכְשֶׁיַּגְדִּיל, בְּגֵט סַגִּי לָהּ? *וְהָתַנְיָא: [ט]עָשׂוּ בִּיאַת בֶּן ט' כְּמַאֲמָר בְּגָדוֹל, מַה מַּאֲמָר בְּגָדוֹל צָרִיךְ גֵּט לְמַאֲמָרוֹ וַחֲלִיצָה לְזִיקָתוֹ, אַף בִּיאַת בֶּן ט' — צָרִיךְ גֵּט *לְמַאֲמָרוֹ וַחֲלִיצָה לְזִיקָתוֹ! אָמַר רַב, הָכִי קָאָמַר, לִכְשֶׁיַּגְדִּיל

*) ב"ב קנו. סנהדרין נה:

---

**רש"י**

בְּשְׁלָמָא לְרַבִּי יוֹחָנָן. דְּאָמַר: מִכִּי אִיקְלַע תְּשִׁיבוּת שָׁנָה בְּשָׁנָה שְׁלִישִׁית, לְרַבִּי מֵאִיר הָוְיָא בַּת בִּיאָה, נִיחָא. וְאַע"ג דְּאָמַר רַבִּי יוֹחָנָן: ל' יוֹם, וְהָכָא קָתָנֵי "יוֹם אֶחָד" — תַּנָּאֵי הִיא, בְּפֶרֶק "אַרְבָּעָה רָאשֵׁי שָׁנִים" (ר"ה דף י.), דְּאִיכָּא לְמ"ד יוֹם אֶחָד בַּשָּׁנָה חָשׁוּב שָׁנָה, וְאִיכָּא לְמַאן דְּאָמַר כו'. אֶלָּא לְרַבִּי יַנַּאי. דְּאָמַר: לְר"מ, עַד סוֹף שָׁנָה שְׁלִישִׁית לָאו בַּת בִּיאָה הִיא, קַשְׁיָא. הָנֵי בְּתוּלִין. בְּתוֹךְ ג' שָׁנִים. [ר"ה ב: וש"נ] אִיתְצוּד. לְשׁוֹן צֵידָה, כְּלוֹמַר, אֵינָן נִיטָּלִין עַל יְדֵי בִּיאָה, וְאֵינוֹ דַּם בְּתוּלִין עַד ג' שָׁנִים וְיוֹם אֶחָד. [שם י: מכות ג: לעיל מד:] אִי אָמְרַתְּ מֵיזַל אָזְלִי. בְּבִיאָה בְּתוֹךְ ג' לְגַמְרֵי, וְהָדַר אָתוּ — לָא מַחְזְקִינַן לָהּ כְּזוֹנָה. דְּהָא דְּלָא הָדוּר — שָׁהוּת הוּא דְּלָא הָוְיָא לְהוּ, מִתּוֹךְ בְּעִילָה שֶׁבָּעַל תָּדִיר. אֶלָּא אִי אָמְרַתְּ. לָא אָזְלֵי בְּבִיאָה תּוֹךְ ג' הֲוָה לֵיהּ לְמֵיתֵי דָּם לְאַחַר ג'. וְכֵיוָן דְּלָא חָזְיָא — אַחֵר בָּא עָלֶיהָ לְאַחַר ג' וְזוֹנָה הִיא, וּפְסוּלָה לִכְהוּנָּה. וּמַאן לֵימָא לָן. כְּלוֹמַר, אֲפִי' אִם תִּמְצֵי לוֹמַר: מֵיזַל אָזְלֵי בְּבִיאָה תּוֹךְ ג', מִי אִיכָּא לְמֵימַר שָׁהוּת לָא הֲוָה לְהוּ, מַאן לֵימָא לָן דְּלָא הָדְרֵי לְאַלְתַּר. הַאי דַּם נִדָּה הוּא. הַאי דְּתוֹךְ ג'. יוּסְטְנִי. אוֹי לְשָׁלֹשׁ שָׁנִים שֶׁאִבַּדְתִּי. מִשֶּׁנִּרְאֵיתִי לְבִיאָה. מְשַׁמְּשׁוֹת בְּמוֹךְ. תַּקָּנָתָן הֲוָה לְשַׁמֵּשׁ בְּמוֹךְ, שֶׁלֹּא יִתְעַבְּרוּ. סַנְדָּל. כְּשֶׁמִּתְעַבֶּרֶת תְּאוֹמִים, פְּעָמִים שֶׁאֶחָד דּוֹחֵק אֶת חֲבֵירוֹ וּפוֹחֵת אֶת צוּרָתוֹ, כִּדְאָמְרִינַן בִּמְכִילְתִּין: *אֵין [לעיל כה:] סַנְדָּל שֶׁאֵין עִמּוֹ וָלָד. תִּגְמוֹל. תַּפְרִישׁ אֶת בְּנָהּ מִלְּהָנִיק, מֵחֲמַת עִיבּוּרָהּ. פָּחוֹת מִכֵּן. אֵינָהּ צְרִיכָה לְשַׁמֵּשׁ בְּמוֹךְ, דְּוַדַּאי לֹא תִתְעַבֵּר. יָתֵר עַל כֵּן. אִם תִּתְעַבֵּר — לֹא תָמוּת. מְצָצָהּ. כְּלוֹמַר, אַף אֲנִי טָעַמְתִּי טַעַם זְנוּת. לֹא אֲמָרָהּ. הָא דְּקָאָמַר "פְּסוּלָה לִכְהוּנָּה" אֶלָּא לְחַדֵּד.

**מתני'** קְנָאָהּ. וְזָכָה בְּנִכְסֵי אָחִיו, וְאַע"ג שֶׁאֵין קִנְיָן לְקָטָן, הֲרֵי קְנוּיָה לוֹ וְעוֹמֶדֶת. [יבמות יב: ק: כתובות לט: נדרים לה. ותוספתא פ"ב] וְאֵינוֹ נוֹתֵן גֵּט עַד שֶׁיַּגְדִּיל. אִם בָּא לְגָרְשָׁהּ, דְּקִידּוּשֵׁי אָחִיו — קִידּוּשִׁין גְּמוּרִין, וְגֵירוּשִׁין שֶׁל זֶה — אֵינָם גֵּירוּשִׁין גְּמוּרִין, דְּאֵינוֹ בֶּן דַּעַת. וּמְטַמֵּא בְּנִדָּה. אִם בָּא עָלֶיהָ, דְּבִיאָתוֹ בִּיאָה לְכָל דָּבָר. וּפוֹסֵל. כְּגוֹן בֶּן ט' שָׁנִים כּוּתִי אוֹ מַמְזֵר שֶׁבָּא עַל הַכֹּהֶנֶת — פְּסָלָהּ מִתְּרוּמַת אָבִיהָ, אֲבָל בְּבֶן תֵּשַׁע יִשְׂרָאֵל שֶׁבָּא עַל בַּת כֹּהֵן, לֵיכָּא לְמֵימַר דְּפוֹסֵל מִן הַתְּרוּמָה, דְּאִי מִשּׁוּם בִּיאַת זְנוּת — לֹא פְּסָלָהּ זְנוּת, דְּכָשֵׁר מִן הַתְּרוּמָה. וְאִי מִשּׁוּם קִדּוּשִׁין, לְמֶהֱוֵי בַּת כֹּהֵן לְיִשְׂרָאֵל — לָאו קִדּוּשִׁין נִינְהוּ, דְּקָטָן דְּקָדֵישׁ — אֵין קִדּוּשָׁיו קִדּוּשִׁין. וְאֵינוֹ מַאֲכִיל. כְּגוֹן יָבָם בֶּן ט' כֹּהֵן הַבָּא עַל יְבִמְתּוֹ, אַע"ג דְּקָנֵי לָהּ בְּהַךְ בִּיאָה לֹא אָכְלָה בִּתְרוּמָה. וּפוֹסֵל אֶת הַבְּהֵמָה. אִם רְבָעָהּ ע"פ עֵד אֶחָד אוֹ ע"פ הַבְּעָלִים, אֲבָל סְקִילָה — לֹא, דְּמוֹדֶה בִּקְנָס פָּטוּר. [בס ר"מ] וְנִסְקֶלֶת עַל יָדוֹ. אִם יֵשׁ עֵדִים. [לקמן נח:]

**גמ'** בְּגֵט סַגְיָא לָהּ. בִּתְמִיָּה, אִם בָּא לְגָרְשָׁהּ. מַאֲמָר. [גי' מהר"ם וע"ש] קִידּוּשֵׁי יְבָמָה. וַחֲלִיצָה לְזִיקָתוֹ. דְּאֵין קִדּוּשִׁין גּוֹמְרִין בִּיבָמָה לִהְיוֹת כְּאִשְׁתּוֹ לָצֵאת בְּגֵט בְּלֹא חֲלִיצָה, אֲבָל בִּיאָה גּוֹמֶרֶת בָּהּ כְּדִכְתִי' (דברים כה): "יָבֹא עָלֶיהָ". [ברכות לג: וש"נ] בִּיאַת בֶּן תֵּשַׁע. בִּיבִמְתּוֹ. [יבמות נו. ורב אלפס גרס לביאתו] לִכְשֶׁיַּגְדִּיל

---

**תוספות**

**אחר** בא עליה. ואם אשת כהן היא — אסורה, אבל אשת ישראל — לא, דפיתוי קטנה — אונס הוא. ואם תאמר: אמאי דחיק לאשכוחי נפקותא שבא עליה אחר לגבי זנות, לימא בפשיטות: כגון שבעל תוך שלשה ומצא דם, דאי לא מיתלדו — האי דם נדות הוא, כדאמר בסמוך? וי"ל: דניחא ליה לאשכוחי לענין זנות, דהויא כל ימיה אסורה לבעלה. ותו דלענין אי הוה דם נדות או דם בתולין לא נפקא מינה האידנא מידי, דאפילו הוא דם בתולים, הא תקון דבועל בעילת מצוה ופורש.

**האי** דם נדה הוא. פירוש: הך דתוך ג' דהך דלאחר ג' לכ"ע הוי דם בתולין. ותימה: דאמאי נקט כלל שבעל אחר ג' כיון דלא נפקא מינה מידי? ופירש ר"ת: משום דנקטיה לעיל, נקטיה נמי הכא. ומיהו י"ל: אף דם שלאחר ג' יש להסתפק בדם נדה אי אמרינן איתצודי הוא דלא מיתצוד, כיון דבתוך ג' ראתה ודאי דם נדות, אם כן דרכה לראות מחמת חימוד בעילה. אם כן גם אחר ג' יש להסתפק בדם נדה? ובתשובה אחת פרש"י: ד"איתצודי הוא דלא מיתצוד" דקאמר, היינו דלא שכיח הוא דמיתצוד, אבל כי איתצודי — תו לא הדרי. וקאמר דנפקא מינה דבעל תוך ג' ומצא דם, ואחר ג' לא מצא, דאי לא איתצוד — האי אחר בא עליה, דליכא אלא ספיקא אחת: דאי דם בתולין היה תוך ג' מותרת, ואם דם נדה היה — הרי היא זונה. והדר קאמר שבעל ומצא דם תוך ג' ואחר ג' דאיכא לספוקי בתרווייהו בדם נדה: דאי בתוך ג' דם בתולין, אחר ג' דם נדה, דהא לא הדרי. ואי תוך ג' דם נדה הוא, אחר ג' דם בתולין. וקשה לפי זה: דאמאי לא אשכחן לענין זנות דמצא דם תוך ג' ושוב לא בעל עד י"ב שנים ולא מצא דם, דאי מיזל ואתו — האי אחר בא עליה. אע"ג דספק בא עליה אחר בקטנות או בגדלות, כיון דספקא אחת היא — אסורה אף לבעלה ישראל. ואי אתצודי לא מיתצוד — שריא לבעלה ישראל, דאימור: דם דתוך ג' דם בתולין הוה, ואפי' אי הוה דם נדות — אימר: אחר בא עליה בקטנות, ואונס הוה? וי"ל: דאין רגילות שישהא עד י"ב שנה מלבא על אשתו.

**בת** י"ג שנים ויום א'. תימה: דלקמן תניא, אלו דברי רבי אמתני' דקתני "בת י"ב ויום אחד נדרה נדר". ויש ספרים דגרסי: "בת י"ב ויום אחד", ואי גרסינן "בת *י"ד שנה" בלא "יום אחד" אתי שפיר. ו"מתעברת וילדת" קאמר, ושנת י"ג אין צריך להיות שלם. [א"ה קמ"ש]

**מה** אני לכהונה. שנבעלה לפסול לה. קודם

---

**תוספי הרא"ש**

**אחר** בא עליה ואם אשת כהן אסורה אבל אשת ישראל לא דפיתוי קטנה אונס הוא. ותימה למה האריך כל כך לוקמה כפשטה לענין דם נדות דאי לא מיתצדי האי דם נדות הוא. וי"ל דניחא ליה השתא לאשכוחי איסור והיתר לבעלה ואי לענין דם נדה לא נפקא מינה מידי לבעלה דאפי' אם דם בתולים הוא א)הא תקון רבנן דבועל בעילת מצוה ופורש. אלא נפקא מינה כגון שבעל בתוך ג' ומצא דם ובעל לאחר ג' ולא מצא דם כו'. אי אמרת איתצודי הוא דלא מיתצדי עד לאחר ג' האי דם נדה הוא פי' אותו דם שמצא בתוך ג' ודאי דם נדה הוא דדם בתולים לא מיתצדי בתוך ג' וקשה לפירושו למה הזכיר בעילה דלאחר ג' כיון דליכא לספוקי בהך בעילה דלאחר ג' דודאי דם בתולים הוי כיון דלא מיתצדי בתוך ג'. לכ"נ כמו שפרש"י בתשובה איתצודי הוא דלא מיתצדי דקאמר היינו דלא שכיח דמיתצדי אבל כי מיתצדי לא הדרי והאי דקאמר האי דם נדה הוא בין תוך ג' בין אחר שלשה דבתוך ג' מספקינן דילמא לא איתצוד ודם נדה הוא והך דלאחר ג' אמרינן דילמא בתוך ג' איתצוד והשתא דם נדה הוא א"נ כגון שבעל בתוך ג' ולאחר ג' ולא טבלה בנתיים והשתא הויא ודאי [נדה] או מקמא או מבתרא. ותימה כיון דאמרינן דזימנין דמיתצדי היכי קאמר לעיל דאחד בא עליה והא זימנין דמיתצדי. וי"ל כיון דמיתצדי תלינן באשת כהן לחומרא. והשתא ניחא דפריך דילמא מכה שבתוך ג' חוזרת לאלתר והא ודאי בא עליה אחר משום דכי היכי דאסרה לה מספק כי אסרת לה מטעם איתצודי הוא דלא מיתצדי הכי נמי יש לאוסרה מספק כי אמרת מיזל אזלי ואתו משום דילמא חוזרת לאלתר: **אמר** לה בת י"ג שנה ויום אחד. תימה דלקמן אמתניתין דבת י"ב שנה ויום אחד נדריה (נדר) [קיימין] תניא אלו דברי ר'. וי"ס דגרסינן הכי בת י"ב שנה ויום אחד ואי גרס הכא י"ג סתם ניחא דמתעברת ויולדת בתוך שנת י"ג: **מה** אני לכהונה. שנבעלה לפסול לה:

א) עי' לקמן דף ס"ה ע"ב אלא מעתה בעל לא יגמור ביאתו א"ל א"כ לבו נוקפו ופורש ויש לייישב ודו"ק.

---

**עין משפט נר מצוה**

עז א מיי' פ"ה מהל' איסורי ביאה הל' כה:

עח ב מיי' שם פי"ח הל' ו סמג לאוין קפא טוש"ע אה"ע סי' ו סעי' ט:

עט ג מיי' פ"א מהל' יבום הלט"ז ופ"ה שם הלי"ח סמג עשין נב טוש"ע אה"ע סימן קסז סעיף ב [וברב אלפס יבמות פ"י דף לה הכי קאמר עד שיגדיל ויבעול ויתן גט]:

פ ד מיי' פ"ג מהל' מטמאי משכב ומושב הלכה ג:

פא ה מיי' פ"ח מהל' תרומות הלי"ח:

פב ו מיי' פ"ד מהל' איסורי מזבח הל"ג:

פג ז מיי' שם הל"ב:

פד ח מיי' פ"א מהל' איסורי ביאה הלי"ג:

פה ט מיי' פ"ה מהל' יבום הלי"ח סמג עשין נב טוש"ע אה"ע סי' קסז סעי' א:

אלִכְשֶׁיַּגְדִּיל יִבְעוֹל וְיִתֵּן גֵּט.§ **מתני'** בבַּת אַחַת עֶשְׂרֵה שָׁנָה וְיוֹם א' – נְדָרֶיהָ נִבְדָּקִין, בַּת שְׁתֵּים עֶשְׂרֵה שָׁנָה וְיוֹם א' – נְדָרֶיהָ קַיָּימִין, וּבוֹדְקִין כָּל שְׁתֵּים עֶשְׂרֵה. בֶּן שְׁתֵּים עֶשְׂרֵה שָׁנָה וְיוֹם אֶחָד – נְדָרָיו נִבְדָּקִין, בֶּן י"ג שָׁנָה וְיוֹם אֶחָד – נְדָרָיו קַיָּימִין, וּבוֹדְקִין כָּל שְׁלֹשׁ עֶשְׂרֵה. קוֹדֶם לַזְּמַן הַזֶּה, אע"פ שֶׁאָמְרוּ "יוֹדְעִין אָנוּ לְשֵׁם מִי נָדַרְנוּ, לְשֵׁם מִי הִקְדַּשְׁנוּ" – אֵין נִדְרֵיהֶם נֶדֶר, וְאֵין הֶקְדֵּשָׁן הֶקְדֵּשׁ. לְאַחַר הַזְּמַן הַזֶּה, אע"פ שֶׁאָמְרוּ "אֵין אָנוּ יוֹדְעִין לְשֵׁם מִי נָדַרְנוּ, לְשֵׁם מִי הִקְדַּשְׁנוּ" – נִדְרָן נֶדֶר וְהֶקְדֵּשָׁן הֶקְדֵּשׁ.§ **גמ'** וְכֵיוָן דְּתָנָא "בַּת אַחַת עֶשְׂרֵה שָׁנָה וְיוֹם א' – נְדָרֶיהָ נִבְדָּקִין", "בַּת י"ב שָׁנָה וְיוֹם א' – נְדָרֶיהָ קַיָּימִין" לָמָּה לִי? סד"א: בּוֹדְקִין לְעוֹלָם, קמ"ל. וְכֵיוָן דְּתָנֵי "בַּת י"ב שָׁנָה וְיוֹם אֶחָד – נְדָרֶיהָ קַיָּימִין", "בּוֹדְקִין כָּל שְׁתֵּים עֶשְׂרֵה" לָמָּה לִי? סָלְקָא דַּעְתָּךְ אָמִינָא: הוֹאִיל וְאָמַר מָר: *ל' יוֹם בַּשָּׁנָה חֲשׁוּבִים שָׁנָה, הֵיכָא דְּבָדַקְנָא ל' וְלֹא יָדְעָה לְהַפְלוֹת – אֵימָא: תּוּ לָא לִיבְדּוֹק, קמ"ל. וְלִתְנֵי הָנֵי תַּרְתֵּי בָּבֵי: "בַּת י"ב שָׁנָה וְיוֹם א' – נְדָרֶיהָ קַיָּימִין, וּבוֹדְקִין כָּל י"ב", "בַּת אַחַת עֶשְׂרֵה וְיוֹם א' – נְדָרֶיהָ נִבְדָּקִין" לָמָּה לִי? אִיצְטְרִיךְ, סד"א סְתָמָא – בִּשְׁתֵּים עֶשְׂרֵה בָּעֲיָא בְּדִיקָה, בְּאַחַת עֶשְׂרֵה לָא בָּעֲיָא בְּדִיקָה. וְהֵיכָא דְּחָזֵינַן לָהּ דַּחֲרִיפָא טְפֵי – מִיבְּדְקָה בְּאַחַת עֶשְׂרֵה, קמ"ל. "קוֹדֶם הַזְּמַן הַזֶּה" וְאַחַר הַזְּמַן הַזֶּה" לָמָּה לִי? סד"א: הנ"מ – הֵיכָא דְּלָא קָאָמְרִי אִינְהוּ, אֲבָל הֵיכָא דְּקָאָמְרִי אִינְהוּ – נִסְמוֹךְ עֲלַיְיהוּ, קמ"ל. ת"ר: אֵלּוּ דִּבְרֵי רַבִּי. ר"ש בֶּן אֶלְעָזָר אוֹמֵר: דְּבָרִים הָאֲמוּרִים בְּתִינוֹקֶת – בְּתִינוֹק אֲמוּרִים, דְּבָרִים הָאֲמוּרִים בְּתִינוֹק – בְּתִינוֹקֶת אֲמוּרִים. א"ר חִסְדָּא: מ"ט דְּרַבִּי? דִּכְתִיב: °"וַיִּבֶן ה' [אֱלֹהִים] אֶת הַצֵּלָע" (בראשית ב) – מְלַמֵּד שֶׁנָּתַן הקב"ה בִּינָה יְתֵירָה בָּאִשָּׁה יוֹתֵר מִבָּאִישׁ. וְאִידָּךְ – הַהוּא מִבָּעֵי לֵיהּ לִכְדְרֵישׁ לָקִישׁ, *דְּאָמַר רֵישׁ לָקִישׁ מִשּׁוּם ר"ש בֶּן מְנַסְיָא: "וַיִּבֶן ה' [אֱלֹהִים] אֶת הַצֵּלָע אֲשֶׁר לָקַח מִן הָאָדָם לְאִשָּׁה וַיְבִאֶהָ אֶל הָאָדָם" מְלַמֵּד שֶׁקִּלְּעָהּ הקב"ה לְחַוָּה וְהֱבִיאָהּ אֵצֶל אָדָם הָרִאשׁוֹן, שֶׁכֵּן בִּכְרַכֵּי הַיָּם קוֹרִין לְקַלְּעִיתָא – בְּנְיָיתָא. וְר"ש בֶּן אֶלְעָזָר מ"ט? אָמַר רַב שְׁמוּאֵל בַּר רַב יִצְחָק: מִתּוֹךְ שֶׁהַתִּינוֹק מָצוּי בְּבֵית רַבּוֹ, נִכְנֶסֶת בּוֹ עַרְמוּמִית תְּחִלָּה. *אִיבַּעְיָא לְהוּ: תּוֹךְ זְמַן, כְּלִפְנֵי זְמַן אוֹ כִּלְאַחַר זְמַן? לְמַאי הִלְכְתָא? אִי לִנְדָרִים – לָאו כְּלִפְנֵי זְמַן דָּמְיָא, וְלָאו כִּלְאַחַר זְמַן דָּמְיָא. אֶלָּא, לְעוֹנָשִׁין מַאי? רַב וְר' (א) חֲנִינָא דְּאָמְרִי תַּרְוַיְיהוּ: תּוֹךְ זְמַן – כְּלִפְנֵי זְמַן, ר' יוֹחָנָן וְר' יְהוֹשֻׁעַ בֶּן לֵוִי דְּאָמְרִי תַּרְוַיְיהוּ: תּוֹךְ זְמַן – כִּלְאַחַר זְמַן. אָמַר רַב נַחְמָן בַּר יִצְחָק, א] וְסִימָנָיךְ: °"וְזֹאת לְפָנִים בְּיִשְׂרָאֵל" (רות ד). מְתִיב רַב הַמְנוּנָא: אַחַר זְמַן הַזֶּה, אע"פ שֶׁאָמְרוּ "אֵין אָנוּ יוֹדְעִים לְשֵׁם מִי נָדַרְנוּ, לְשֵׁם מִי הִקְדַּשְׁנוּ" – נִדְרֵיהֶם נֶדֶר וְהֶקְדֵּשָׁן הֶקְדֵּשׁ, הָא תּוֹךְ זְמַן – כְּלִפְנֵי זְמַן! אֲמַר לֵיהּ רָבָא: אֵימָא רֵישָׁא, קוֹדֶם הַזְּמַן הַזֶּה, אע"פ שֶׁאָמְרוּ "יוֹדְעִים אָנוּ לְשֵׁם מִי נָדַרְנוּ, לְשֵׁם מִי הִקְדַּשְׁנוּ" – אֵין נִדְרֵיהֶם נֶדֶר, וְאֵין הֶקְדֵּשָׁן הֶקְדֵּשׁ, הָא תּוֹךְ זְמַן – כִּלְאַחַר זְמַן! וְלָא הִיא, רָבָא קָטָעֵי. הוּא סָבַר: רַב הַמְנוּנָא מִמִּשְׁנָה יְתֵירָה קָדָיֵיק, וְאַדְּדָיֵיק מִסֵּיפָא – לִידוֹק מֵרֵישָׁא. וְלָא הִיא, רַב הַמְנוּנָא מִגּוּפָא דְּמַתְנִיתִין קָא דָּיֵיק, הָא לְאַחַר זְמַן הֵיכִי דָּמֵי? אִי דְּלָא אַיְיתֵי שְׁתֵּי שְׂעָרוֹת – קָטָן הוּא, אֶלָּא לָאו – דְּאַיְיתֵי שְׁתֵּי שְׂעָרוֹת,

וְטַעְמָא

---

**לכשיגדיל יבעול.** וְהַךְ בִּיאָה הָוֵי קִנְיָן גָּמוּר, וְאִם בָּא לְגָרְשָׁהּ – אֵינָהּ צְרִיכָה חֲלִיצָה, דִּכְתִיב (דברים כה): "וּלְקָחָהּ לוֹ לְאִשָּׁה" – כֵּיוָן שֶׁלְּקָחָהּ נַעֲשֵׂית כְּאִשְׁתּוֹ לְכָל דָּבָר*. **מתני' נבדקין.** אִם יָדְעָה לְשֵׁם מִי נָדְרָה וּלְשֵׁם מִי הִקְדִּישָׁה. **קודם הזמן הזה.** כְּגוֹן בְּתִינוֹקֶת קוֹדֶם שֶׁיָּבֹא רֹאשׁ הַשָּׁנָה שֶׁל שְׁתֵּים עֶשְׂרֵה, וּבְתִינוֹק – קוֹדֶם רֹאשׁ הַשָּׁנָה שֶׁל שְׁלֹשׁ עֶשְׂרֵה. **אין נדריהן נדר.** דִּקְטַנִּים הֵן. **אחר הזמן הזה.** בְּתִינוֹקֶת – מִבַּת שְׁתֵּים עֶשְׂרֵה וְיוֹם אֶחָד וּלְמַעְלָה, בְּתִינוֹק מִי"ג שָׁנָה וְיוֹם אֶחָד וּלְמַעְלָה. **אפילו אמרו אין אנו יודעין כו'.** גְּדוֹלִים הֵם, וּבִכְלַל שׁוֹטֶה נַמִי לָא מַחְזְקִינַן לְהוּ – דְּסוֹפוֹ לָבֹא לִכְלַל דַּעַת, וְאֵין שׁוֹטֶה אֶלָּא הַמְקָרֵעַ כְּסוּתוֹ וְהַלָּן בְּבֵית הַקְּבָרוֹת וְהַיּוֹצֵא יְחִידִי בַּלַּיְלָה. *אֲבָל תּוֹךְ הַזְּמַן הַזֶּה, אִם יוֹדֵעַ לְשֵׁם מִי נָדַר – הָוֵי נֶדֶר, וְאִם לָאו – לָא הָוֵי נֶדֶר, דְּקָטָן הוּא. וּבַגְּמָרָא מְפָרֵשׁ כּוּלָּהּ מִילְּתָא. **גמ' למה לי.** מִמֵּילָא יָדְעִנָא דְּמִכָּאן וְאֵילָךְ לָא בָּעֵי בְּדִיקָה. **סד"א בודקין לעולם.** וְהַאי דְּקָתָנֵי "בַּת אַחַת עֶשְׂרֵה נִבְדָּקִין" לְמַעוּטֵי קוֹדֶם זְמַן הַזֶּה דְּלָא בָּדְקִינַן לֵיהּ, דַּאֲפִילּוּ יָדַע, קָטָן הוּא, קמ"ל דִּלְמַעוּטֵי אַחַר זְמַן נַמִי אָתָא. **בודקין כל י"ב למה לי.** הָא תָּנָא דְּמִיּוֹם א' בִּשְׁתֵּים עֶשְׂרֵה מַתְחִילִין לִבְדּוֹק, וְאֵינָן קַיָּימִין בְּלֹא בְּדִיקָה עַד יוֹם אֶחָד בְּי"ג, אַלְמָא כָּל י"ב הָוֵי זְמַן בְּדִיקָה. **היכא דבדקנא ל' יום.** קַמַּאי דִּשְׁתֵּים עֶשְׂרֵה. **ולא ידעה להפלות.** לְפָרֵשׁ לְשֵׁם מִי נָדְרָה. וְלִישָּׁנָא דִּקְרָא נָקַט "כִּי יַפְלִיא לִנְדּוֹר". **תו לא נבדוק.** וְלֶיחְזְקָהּ בִּקְטַנָּה. **בת י"א כו' למה לי.** (ב) מִדְּתָנֵן לֵיהּ "בּוֹדְקִין כָּל י"ב" שָׁמְעִינַן: דְּמִקַּמֵּי הָכִי – לָא. **הָנֵי מִילֵּי.** דְּמִקַּמֵּי הָכִי מוּחְזָקִין קְטַנִּים, וּלְאַחַר זְמַן מוּחְזָקִין גְּדוֹלִים. **היכא דלא קאמרי אינהו.** קוֹדֶם הַזְּמַן "יוֹדְעִין אָנוּ", וּלְאַחַר זְמַן "אֵין אָנוּ יוֹדְעִין". **דברים האמורים כו'.** דְּתִינוֹק מְמַהֵר לְהִתְחַכֵּם יוֹתֵר מִתִּינוֹקֶת. **לעונשין.** וּכְגוֹן דְּאַיְיתֵי שְׁתֵּי שְׂעָרוֹת תּוֹךְ הַזְּמַן. דְּאִי לָא אַיְיתֵי – אֲפִילּוּ לְאַחַר זְמַן לָאו בַּר עוֹנָשִׁין הוּא. וּלְאַחַר זְמַן אִי אַיְיתֵי ב' שְׂעָרוֹת – הָוֵי גָּדוֹל וּבַר עוֹנָשִׁין. **כלפני הזמן.** וְלָא עָנְשִׁינַן לֵיהּ, וּשְׁתֵּי שְׂעָרוֹת הָוְיָא לְהוּ שׁוּמָא. **וזאת לפנים.** "וְזֹאת" לְשׁוֹן נְקֵבָה, כְּלוֹמַר, רַב חֲנִינָא דִּשְׁמֵיהּ לְשׁוֹן נְקֵבָה אָמַר "לְפָנִים" – כְּלוֹמַר, לִפְנֵי זְמַן, וְלֹא תִּטְעֶה לְהַחֲלִיף דִּבְרֵיהֶם. ל"א: שְׁמוֹ (ג) שֶׁל רַב דְּאָמַר כְּלִפְנֵי הַזְּמַן מוּבְלָע בְּתֵיבַת "בְּיִשְׂרָאֵל". **מתיב רב המנונא.** קס"ד כִּדְאָמַר לְקַמָּן: דְּרַב הַמְנוּנָא מִשְּׁנָה יְתֵירָה דָּיֵיק, דְּלָא אִיצְטְרִיךְ לְמִתְנְיֵיהּ, כִּדְפָרְכִינַן לְעֵיל. וְהָא דְּתָנֵי לֵיהּ תַּנָּא דְּמַתְנִי' – לְמֵידַק מִינָּהּ לְעִנְיַן עוֹנָשִׁין: הָא תּוֹךְ הַזְּמַן כְּלִפְנֵי הַזְּמַן, דְּאִי לְעִנְיַן נְדָרִים – לָא כְּלִפְנֵי זְמַן וְלָא כִּלְאַחַר זְמַן. **מגופא דמתני' דייק.** דְּלָא מִתּוֹקְמָא אֶלָּא כְּשֶׁהֵבִיא שְׁתֵּי שְׂעָרוֹת, וַאֲפ"ה לָא חָשֵׁיב לֵיהּ גָּדוֹל עַד לְאַחַר זְמַן. וְהַשְׁתָּא לֵיכָּא לְמִיפְרַךְ: לִידוֹק מֵרֵישָׁא, דְּהָא לָא דָּיֵיק מִידֵּי, דְּבֵין רֵישָׁא וּבֵין סֵיפָא לְגוּפָא אִיצְטְרִיךְ לְעִנְיַן נְדָרִים, דְּלָא תֵּימָא: הָנֵי מִילֵּי הֵיכָא דְּלָא קָאָמְרִי אִינְהוּ, אֲבָל הֵיכָא דְּקָאָמְרִי אִינְהוּ כו', כִּדְאָמַר לְעֵיל. וּמֵיהוּ מִגּוּפָא דְּסֵיפָא שָׁמְעִינַן, דְּעַד דְּמָטוּ לְאַחַר זְמַן – בָּעֵינַן יוֹדֵעַ לְהַפְלוֹת, וְאִם אֵינוֹ יוֹדֵעַ לְהַפְלוֹת, (ד) וַאֲפִילּוּ הֵבִיא ב' שְׂעָרוֹת – לָאו אִישׁ הוּא, דְּנֶיהֱוֵי נִדְרוֹ נֶדֶר מֵחֲמַת אִישׁוּת בְּלֹא הַפְלָאָה. **קטן הוא.** וְאַמַּאי נִדְרוֹ נֶדֶר? הָא לָאו בְּחֶזְקַת גָּדוֹל הוּא כָּל זְמַן שֶׁלֹּא הֵבִיא ב' שְׂעָרוֹת! וּמוּפְלָא סָמוּךְ לְאִישׁ, נַמִי לָא הָוֵי, דְּהָא אֵינוֹ יוֹדֵעַ לְשֵׁם מִי נָדַר, וּמֵהֵיכָא תֵּיתֵי דְּנִדְרוֹ נֶדֶר? **אלא לאו בשהביא.** וּמִשּׁוּם הָכִי נִדְרוֹ נֶדֶר, אע"ג דְּאֵין יוֹדֵעַ לְהַפְלוֹת, דְּהָא גָּדוֹל הוּא.

וְטַעְמָא.

---

**קודם** הזמן הזה למה לי סד"א כו' וא"ת: ובת י"א שנה למה ליה למימר דאילו חריפא לא בדקינן לה, דהיינו "קודם הזמן"? ויש לומר: דזו אף זו קתני, דלא מיבעיא דלא אמרי, אלא אפילו אמרי – לא מהני. **אלו** דברי רבי. נראה דהלכה כרבי, דלקמן בפירקין אמרי': כל י"ב שנה ממאנת, ומכאן ואילך – אינה ממאנת, ובפ' "נערה שנתפתתה" (כתובות ד' נא.) אמר דהלכה כרבי לגבי רשב"א לבד מלגבי מילתא דהתם. ובי"ש נוחלין" (ב"ב דף קכד:) נמי פסיק הלכה כרבי מחבירו. **שהתינוק** מצוי בבית רבו. ואפילו אין לו רב – רגיל לצאת ולבא, ומתפקח יותר. **אילימא** לנדרים. ובלא הביא ב' שערות, ואפ"ה נדרו נדר אם ידע למי נדר, כיון שהוא שנה לפני גדלות, דמסתמא יביא ב' שערות כשיהיה בן י"ג ויום אחד, כדאמר רבא לקמן: חזקה הביאה שערות. **אלא** לענין עונשין. וכגון שהביא ב' שערות תוך הזמן. מי חשיב גדול, כמו לאחר זמן, לענין חליצה, וקדושין, ונדרים – לקיים נדרו אפי' אינו יודע למי נדר, כיון שהביא ב' שערות. ומיבעיא ליה: אי הוי שומא, אי לאו.

בן

---

**פו** א מיי' פ"ה מהל' יבום הל' כא סמג עשין נב טוש"ע אה"ע סי' קסז סעי' ב:
**פז** ב מיי' פי"א מהל' נדרים הל' א ב ג סמג לאוין רמא טוש"ע יו"ד סי' רלג [וברב אלפס יבמות פי"ג דף מד]

תורה אור

[יבמות כ.] [חגיגה ג:] [לעיל ע"א וש"נ] ברכות סא. ע"ש שבת לג. ע"ש עירובין יח. ע"ש ב"ב קנה.

## תוספי הרא"ש

**אלו** דברי ר' כוותיה קי"ל בפרק מי שמת גבי בת י"ד שנה שמכרה בנכסי אביה. ופריך תלמודא ולישלח ליה בת י"ב שנה ויום אחד ולקמן נמי בשמעתין קאמר רבא כל י"ב ממאנת והולכת לה ובפרק אע"פ ובפ' יש נוחלין אמרינן הלכה כר' מחבירו: **מלמד** שנתן הקב"ה בינה יתירה באשה יותר מבאיש. פירוש הקדים בה בינה יותר מבאיש: שהתינוק מצוי וכו'. ואפי' אין לו רב רגיל לבוא ולצאת עם בני אדם ומתפקח יותר ואפי' אין רגיל כלל אין תולדתו משתנית מאבותיו ואבות אבותיו: **תוך** זמן כלאחר זמן. ומופלא סמוך לאיש הוי לעולם שנה אחת סמוכה לגדלות בין מיהר להביא בין איחר להביא: **וזאת** לפנים בישראל. פי' ריב"ל היה לוי כדאמרינן בפ' כל הבשר [דף קו ע"ב] ר' מיאשא בריה דר' יהושע בן לוי לוי הוה. כלומר אותם שהם ישראל אמרו לפנים:

## הגהות הב"ח

(א) גמ' רב ור' חנינה: (ב) רש"י ד"ה בת י"א וכו' מדתני ליה: (ג) ד"ה וזאת לפנים וכו' ל"א שמו של רב נ"ב ולי נראה ר"ב ורב"י חנינ"ה בגימטר' בישרא"ל. יואל: (ד) ד"ה מגופא וכו' להפלות אפי':

## הגהות מהר"ב רנשבורג

א] גמ' וסימניך וזאת לפנים בישראל. עיין דרשת מהרא"נ"ח דף יז ע"א:

פח א ב ג ד מיי' פ"ב מהל' אישות הלי"ח סמג עשין כ טוש"ע אה"ע סימן קנה סעי' יד:
פט ה מיי' שם הל"ח ופי"א מהל' גירושין הל"א סמג שם טוש"ע שם סעיף יב [וברב אלפס יבמות פי"ג דף מד]:
צ ו ז ח מיי' פי"א מהל' גירושין הל"ד סמג עשין נ טוש"ע אה"ע סי' קנה סעיף יט [וברב אלפס שם]:
צא ט מיי' שם הל"ה טוש"ע שם סעי' כ [וברב אלפס שם]:

**וטעמא.** דחשיבי להו שערות, דלאחר זמן הוא דגמרו למלתיה, בין בשערות בין בשנים. הא תוך הזמן – חשבינן להו שומא, דקטן הוא, ולא מלית לרבויי מאיש. **בן ט' שנים שהביא שערות שומא.** ואפי' לר' יוסי ברבי יהודה, ומבן ט' ועד בן י"ב ויום אחד – פלוגתא. **שומא.** ורוא"ה בלע"ז, ודרכה ליגדל שער בה.

**הא י"ג גופיה סימן.** ואפי' לרבנן, והדר תני כו'. **מאי לאו תנאי היא.** ואליבא דרבנן י"ג הוי תוך זמן לתינוק, כדקתני במתני'. **ורישא.** דמשוית י"ג סימן. **רבי היא.** דאמר: בתינוקת הויא י"ג לאחר זמן. **וסיפא.** דמשמע שומא. **ר"ש בן אלעזר.** (א). דאמר: י"ג בתינוקת הוי תוך זמן. בכל הנך תירוצי מוקמינן תוך זמן כלפני זמן. **והוא שעודן בו.** כשהגדיל, אבל נשרו בינתיים – איגלאי מילתא דשומא הוי. **מתני לשמעתא דרבא בהאי לישנא.** דשמעת מיניה נמי: תוך זמן כלפני זמן. **ממאנת והולכת.** ואין חוששין שמא הביאה ב' שערות, דאפילו הביאה – שומא נינהו, והיינו תוך זמן כלפני זמן. **אינה ממאנת.** שמא הביאה, ועכשיו הוי סימן, דהא לאחר זמן הוא. ואם יבמה היא – לא חשבינן לה גדולה לענין חליצה, ואינה חולצת. **גדולה היא.** אם הביאה. **וכי תימא מספקא ליה.** אם הביאה אם לא הביאה, הלכך מיאון, לא – דלמא הביאה. וחליצה, נמי לא – שמא לא הביאה. **והא מיפשט פשיטא ליה לרבא.** דכיון דהגיעה לכלל שנותיה, דודאי הביאה. **ה"מ לענין** (ב). דאי אתיא למיחלץ לאחר זמן, ובדקנו ולא אשכחן א](*ליה) – חיישינן למימר: גדולה היא, ותחלוץ, שהסימנין נשרו. אבל לענין מיאון חיישינן. שמא נשרו, לחומרא, וקנאה בביאה ובעיא גט. **והא חיישינן קאמר.** ולא "ודאי נשרו", וחיישינן – לחומרא משמע. **אלא לעולם.** "אינה ממאנת" דרבא – בדלא בדקנוה, הלכך מסתמא אמרינן: כיון שהגיעה לכלל שנותיה – ודאי אית לה, ואינה צריכה בדיקה, ובעיא גט. **ולענין חליצה חיישינן.** גרסינן. כלומר, ולענין חליצה. משום הכי אינה חולצת, דחיישינן: שמא לא הביאה סימנין. ודקשיא לך: האמר רבא, חזקה הביאה סימנין? ל"ק: כי אמר רבא חזקה – למיאון, דלא ממאנת מסתמא, אבל לחליצה – בעיא בדיקה. **חוששין שמא נשרו.** ואם הגיעה לכלל שנותיה, ובדקו ולא אשכחו – לא ממאנת. **דקידשה תוך זמן.** יתומה מדעת אמה ואחיה, לדעתה. **ובעל אחר זמן.** דאיכא ספיקא דאשת איש דאורייתא, דבשעת בעילה דלאחר זמן – שמא הביאה, והויא לה ביאה זו קדושין גמורין, דהא גדלה, ושוב אינה יוצאה במיאון. **אבל מעיקרא.** דמכי עברה שעתא דתרתי סרי, ולא בעל – לא חיישינן שמא נשרו, דהא לא הוו בה קדושין גמורין, דאין מעשה קטנה כלום אא"כ קבל אביה קידושין. הלכך מספיקא לא מחמרינן עלה, היכא דלא אשכחן. אבל הביאה ודאי סימנין, אע"ג דקידושי קמאי לא הוו קדושין אלא מדרבנן – לא תקנו רבנן מיאון בגדולה, דלמא אתיא למאן הנבעלת לאחר שגדלה, דהאיך הויא אשת איש, דביאה שבא עליה משגדלה מקדשה לה. **הקדיש.** תוך הזמן תינוק היודע להפליא. **ואכל.** את הקדשו. **לוקה.** ואע"ג דמילתא אחריתי לאו בר עונשין הוא. **כי יפליא.** מיניה מרבינן מופלא סמוך לאיש. "מופלא" – יודע לפרש לשם מי נדר, "סמוך לאיש" – שהוא סמוך לבא לכלל גדול, דהיינו שנה אחת קודם זמן שהוא ראוי להביא שערות, והיינו בתינוקת – כל י"ב, ובתינוק – כל י"ג. **ולא יחל.** אע"ג דבהאי קרא לא כתיב "כי יפליא", מ"מ, כיון דנפקא לן מיניה דיודע להפלות הוי נדרו נדר, קאי בבל יחל. דהא כתיב "איש כי ידור נדר" וגו', ומופלא סמוך לאיש – בכלל "איש", וסמיך ליה ו"לא יחל דברו".

לפי

תורה אור

וטעמא דלאחר זמן הוא, דגמר' לה למילתיה, הא תוך זמן – כלפני זמן. ועוד, מתיב רבי זירא: °"איש כי יפליא לנדור נדר" מה ת"ל "איש" – לרבות בן י"ג שנה ויום אחד, שאע"פ שאינו יודע להפליא – נדריו קיימין. ה"ד? אי דלא אייתי שתי שערות – קטן הוא. אלא לאו דאייתי שתי שערות, וטעמא – דבן י"ג ויום אחד הוא דהוה ליה "איש", הא תוך זמן – כלפני זמן! תיובתא. אמר ר"נ: כתנאי, *[א]בן ט' שנים שהביא ב' שערות – שומא, [ב]מבן ט' ועד י"ב שנה ויום אחד – שומא. רבי יוסי ברבי יהודה אומר: סימן. בן י"ג שנה ויום אחד – דברי הכל סימן. הא גופא קשיא, אמרת: מבן ט' ועד י"ב שנה ויום אחד – שומא, הא י"ג שנה גופא – סימן. והדר תני: [ג]בן י"ג שנה ויום אחד – סימן, הא י"ג שנה גופא – שומא! מאי לאו – תנאי היא, דמר סבר: תוך זמן – כלאחר זמן, ומר סבר: תוך זמן – כלפני זמן! לא, דכ"ע תוך זמן כלפני זמן, ואידי ואידי בתינוקת. ורישא – רבי, וסיפא ר"ש בן אלעזר. ואיבעית אימא: הא והא בתינוק, ורישא ר"ש בן אלעזר, וסיפא – רבי. ואיבעית אימא: הא והא רבי, הא – בתינוק, הא – בתינוקת. ואב"א: הא והא ר"ש בן אלעזר, הא – בתינוק, הא – בתינוקת. רבי יוסי ברבי יהודה אומר: סימן. א"ר כרוספדאי בריה דרבי שבתאי: והוא שעודן בו. תניא נמי הכי, בן ט' שנים ויום אחד שהביא ב' שערות – שומא, מבן ט' ועד י"ב שנה ויום אחד [ד]ועודן בו – שומא. ר' יוסי בר' יהודה אומר: סימן. אמר רבא: הילכתא תוך זמן – כלפני זמן. רב שמואל בר זוטרא מתני לה לשמעתא דרבא בהאי לישנא, אמר רבא: [ה]קטנה, כל י"ב שנה – ממאנת והולכת, מכאן ואילך – אינה ממאנת ואינה חולצת. הא גופא קשיא, אמרת אינה ממאנת – אלמא גדולה היא, אי גדולה היא – תחלוץ! וכי תימא – מספקא ליה, ומי מספקא ליה? והאמר רבא: *[ו]קטנה שהגיעה לכלל שנותיה – אינה צריכה בדיקה, חזקה הביאה סימנין! ה"מ בסתמא, [ז]אבל הכא דבדקו ולא אשכחו – לא. אי הכי, תמאן! חוששין שמא נשרו. *הניחא למ"ד חוששין, אלא למ"ד אין חוששין, מאי איכא למימר? דאיתמר, רב *פפא אמר: אין חוששין שמא נשרו, רב פפי אמר: חוששין. הני מילי – לענין חליצה, אבל לענין מיאון – חוששין. מכלל דמ"ד חוששין – חולצת? והא "חוששין" בעלמא קאמר? אלא, לעולם – דלא בדקה, ולענין חליצה – חיישינן, [ח]וכי קאמר רבא חזקה – למיאון, אבל לחליצה – בעיא בדיקה. אמר רב דימי מנהרדעא: [ט]הלכתא, חוששין שמא נשרו. והני מילי – היכא דקדשה בתוך זמן ובעל לאחר זמן, דאיכא ספיקא דאורייתא, °אבל מעיקרא – לא. אמר רב הונא: הקדיש ואכל – לוקה, שנאמר: °"איש כי יפליא לנדור" °"ולא יחל דברו", כל שישנו בהפלאה – ישנו בבל יחל, וכל שאינו בהפלאה – אינו בבל יחל. מתיב רב הונא בר יהודה (*לרבא) לסיועי לרב הונא:

במדבר ו | קדושין טז: ע"ש | [נ"ל לה] | [לקמן מח:] | [יבמות יג.] | [נ"ל רב כהנא] | שם ל | רש"א מ"ז וע"ש

**בן** ט' שנים שהביא ב' שערות שומא. אי ל"ג "ויום אחד", אתי שפיר, דאתיא אף כרבי יוסי. ואי גרסינן "ויום אחד", איירי באין עודן בו בשנת י"ג דמודה רבי יוסי בנשרו. **קטנה** כל י"ב שנה ממאנת. להך לישנא אין להוכיח דתוך זמן כלפני זמן, דהא "ממאנת" היינו: דבדקו ולא אשכחו. או כמו שמעמיד במסקנא, דלא בדקו. אבל היכא דאיכא שערות – מצינו למימר דהוי כלאחר זמן, ואינה ממאנת. ומ"מ נראה דהלכה דתוך זמן כלפני זמן, דמ"ד כלאחר זמן איתותב לעיל, ור"נ דאמר לעיל נמי כתנאי, דחי ליה התלמוד וגם בלישנא קמא פסיק רבא בהדיא דתוך זמן כלפני זמן. **אבל** לחליצה בעיא בדיקה. תימה: דרבא סבר הכא דאינה חולצת עד שתהא גדולה, ובפ' "התקבל" (גיטין דף סה.) אמר רבא: ג' מדות בקטן: הגיע לעונת נדרים – נדרו נדר, וכנגדו בקטנה – חולצת. משמע, דקטנה בהגעת לעונת נדרים דידה – חולצת, דהיינו בת י"א ויום אחד. ואפי' מיירי התם בהביאה, הא אמר הכא דתוך זמן כלפני זמן! ורשב"ם פירש: "כנגדו בקטנה" – היינו, בת י"ב שנה ויום אחד, דהוי עונת נדרים דקטן. ולא נהירא. ומפרש ר"ת: דהתם רבה אליבא דר' יוסי, דקאמר: קטנה חולצת, וקמ"ל דדוקא כשהגיעה לעונת נדרים. וכן משמע בפרק "מצות חליצה" (יבמות דף קה:) דאמר: מדברי ר' יוסי נלמד, קטנה חולצת בפעוטות, כבת שית וכבת שבע, דאז היא בת כוונה לחליצה. ורבא אמר: עד שתגיע לעונת נדרים – פירוש: לרבי יוסי. והילכתא: עד שתביא ב' שערות, וכל זה מדברי רבא. ועוד י"ל: דהתם בפ' "התקבל" (גיטין דף סה.) גרסינן: רבה. דהא קאמר התם: ולמכור בנכסי אביו – עד שיהא בן כ' שנה, ואילו רבא אית ליה בפרק "מי שמת" (ב"ב דף קנה.) דלמכור בנכסי אביו – עד שיהא בן י"ח וכן צריך להיות שם בספרים, ולא כספרים דגרסי התם איפכא, כדמוכח סוגיא דהתם*.

אי

[בב"ב קנה. ד"ה איתמר וכו' האריכו בביאור יותר]

## הגהות הב"ח

(א) רש"י ד"ה ר' שמעון בן אלעזר היא דאמר: (ב) ד"ה הני מילי לענין חליצה דאי:

## גליון הש"ס

גמ' אבל מעיקרא לא. ע' לקמן נב ע"ב תד"ה הלכה:

## הגהות מהר"ב רנשבורג

א] רש"י ד"ה הני מילי וכו' ולא אשכחן ליה לא חיישינן וכו'. כצ"ל וכ"ה ברש"י סביב הרי"ף ביבמות סוף פרק ב"ש:

## תוספי הרא"ש

**כי יפליא מה ת"ל איש.** כלומר אי הוה כתיב כי יפליא בלא איש ה"א כל מי שיודע להפלות אפי' קטן הרבה ת"ל איש איש וש"מ דהאי דמרבינן קטן מכי יפליא היינו סמוך לאיש מכלל דכשהוא איש לא בעי' שיהא יודע להפלות ולא מיסתבר ליה למידרש קרא כפשטיה איש כי יפליא משמע דבעינן שיהא איש ויודע להפלות משום שמילתא דפשיטא היא דכיון שהוא בן י"ג ולא הוחזק כשוטה שנדרו נדר והקדשו הקדש כנ"ל: **בן** ט' שנים שהביא שתי שערות כו'. אי ל"ג בן יום א' ניחא דתנא הך בבא משום דמודה בה ר' יוסי ואי גרס ויום א' י"ל דמיירי דאין עודן בו בשנת י"ג דבהא מודה ר' יוסי בר' יהודה דלקמן: אי הכי תמאן. חוששין שמא נשרו אבל כל שנת י"ב ממאנת אפי' הוי תוך זמן כלאחר שזמן ואין חוששין שמא נשרו: **אבל** לחליצה בעיא בדיקה. משמע הכא לרבנן דקטנה לאו בת חליצה היא. ותימה דפ' התקבל אמר רבא ג' מדות בקטן הגיע לעונת נדרים נדריו נבדקין וכנגדו בקטנה חולצת אלמא בת חליצה היא כל שנת י"ב. ופי' רבי' שמואל וכנגדו בקטנה לאו שהגיעה היא לעונת נדרים קאמר אלא אזמן הגעת נדרים של קטן קאי דהיינו שכשהוא בן י"ב שנה ויום אחד וק' לר"ת דבההיא קאמר רבה פ' מצות חליצה דקטנה שהגיעה לעונת נדרים חולצת ותלמודא פסיק הכא והילכתא עד שתביא ב' שערות. ואומר ר"ת דאליבא דר' יוסי דאמר דקטנה בת חליצה היא איירי רבא וכן מוכח בההיא סוגיא דפ' מצות חליצה דקאמר התם מדברי ר' יוסי נלמוד קטנה חולצת בפעוטות דבעי' שתהיה קצת בת בינה דחליצה צריכה כוונה וקאמר רבא עד שתגיע לעונת נדרים. ועי"ל דבההיא דבפ' התקבל גרס רבה משום דקאמר אחרי כין למכור בנכסי אביו עד שיהא בן כ' ואמרינן בפ' מי שמת אמר רבא אמר רב נחמן בן י"ח מוכר בנכסי אביו ולא מיסתבר לומר הא דידיה הא דרביה דהא מסיק התם דמכללא איתמר ומתוך מעשה שבא לפניו:

לְפִי שֶׁמָּצִינוּ שֶׁהִשְׁוָה הַכָּתוּב הַקָּטָן כְּגָדוֹל לְזָדוֹן שְׁבוּעָה, וּלְאִיסָּר, וּלְבַל יַחֵל, יָכוֹל יְהֵא חַיָּיב עַל הֶקְדֵּשׁוֹ קָרְבָּן? ת"ל: °"זֶה הַדָּבָר". קָתָנֵי מִיהַת לְאִיסָּר וּלְבַל יַחֵל — חַיָּיב. אֵימָא: לְאִיסּוּר בַּל יַחֵל. אִיסּוּר בַּל יַחֵל, מַה נַּפְשָׁךְ, אִי מוּפְלָא סָמוּךְ לְאִישׁ דְּאוֹרַיְיתָא — מִילְקָא נַמִי לִילְקֵי, וְאִי מוּפְלָא סָמוּךְ לְאִישׁ לָאו דְּאוֹרַיְיתָא — אִיסּוּר נַמִי לֵיכָּא! לְאוֹתָן הַמּוּזְהָרִים עָלָיו. *שְׁמַע מִינָּהּ: קָטָן אוֹכֵל נְבֵלוֹת — ב"ד מְצוּוִּין עָלָיו לְהַפְרִישׁוֹ! הָכָא בְּמַאי עָסְקִינַן — אכְּגוֹן °שֶׁהִקְדִּישׁ הוּא וְאָכְלוּ אֲחֵרִים. הָנִיחָא לְמ"ד הִקְדִּישׁ הוּא וְאָכְלוּ אֲחֵרִים — לוֹקִין, אֶלָּא לְמ"ד אֵין לוֹקִין מַאי אִיכָּא לְמֵימַר? דְּאִיתְּמַר, הִקְדִּישׁ הוּא וְאָכְלוּ אֲחֵרִים, רַב כָּהֲנָא אָמַר: אֵין לוֹקִין, רַבִּי יוֹחָנָן וְר"ל דְּאָמְרִי תַּרְוַיְיהוּ: בלוֹקִין! מִדְּרַבָּנַן, וּקְרָא אַסְמַכְתָּא בְּעָלְמָא. גּוּפָא, הִקְדִּישׁ וְאָכְלוּ אֲחֵרִים. רַב כָּהֲנָא אָמַר: אֵין לוֹקִין, רַבִּי יוֹחָנָן וְר"ל דְּאָמְרִי תַּרְוַיְיהוּ: לוֹקִין. בְּמַאי קָמִיפַּלְגִי? מָר סָבַר: *גמוּפְלָא סָמוּךְ לְאִישׁ — דְּאוֹרַיְיתָא, וּמָר סָבַר: מוּפְלָא סָמוּךְ לְאִישׁ — מִדְּרַבָּנַן. מְתִיב רַב יִרְמְיָה: יְתוֹמָה שֶׁנָּדְרָה — בַּעְלָהּ מֵפֵר לָהּ. אִי אָמְרַתְּ בִּשְׁלָמָא מוּפְלָא סָמוּךְ לְאִישׁ דְּרַבָּנַן, אָתוּ נִשּׂוּאִין דְּרַבָּנַן — וּמְבַטְּלֵי נִדְרָא דְּרַבָּנַן. אֶלָּא אִי אָמְרַתְּ דְּאוֹרַיְיתָא — אָתוּ נִשּׂוּאִין דְּרַבָּנַן וּמְבַטְּלֵי נִדְרָא דְּאוֹרַיְיתָא?! אָמַר רַב יְהוּדָה, אָמַר שְׁמוּאֵל: בַּעְלָהּ מֵפֵר לָהּ מִמָּה נַפְשָׁךְ, אִי דְּרַבָּנַן — דְּרַבָּנַן הוּא, אִי דְּאוֹרַיְיתָא *קָטָן אוֹכֵל נְבֵלוֹת הוּא, דוְאֵין ב"ד מְצוּוִּין עָלָיו לְהַפְרִישׁוֹ. וְהָא כִּי גָּדְלָה, אָכְלָה בַּהֲפָרָה קַמַּיְיתָא! אָמַר רַבָּה בַּר לִיוַאי: בַּעְלָהּ מֵפֵר לָהּ כָּל שָׁעָה וְשָׁעָה, וְהוּא שֶׁבָּעַל. וְהָא הֵאֵין בַּעַל מֵפֵר בְּקוֹדְמִין! *כִּדְרַב פִּנְחָס מִשְּׁמֵיהּ דְּרָבָא, דְּאָמַר רַב פִּנְחָס מִשְּׁמֵיהּ דְּרָבָא: כָּל הַנּוֹדֶרֶת — עַל דַּעַת בַּעְלָהּ הִיא נוֹדֶרֶת. אָמַר אַבַּיֵי ת"ש: *קָטָן שֶׁלֹּא הֵבִיא ב' שְׂעָרוֹת, רַבִּי יְהוּדָה אוֹמֵר: *אֵין תְּרוּמָתוֹ תְּרוּמָה, רַבִּי יוֹסֵי אוֹמֵר: ועַד שֶׁלֹּא בָּא לְעוֹנַת נְדָרִים — אֵין תְּרוּמָתוֹ תְּרוּמָה, מִשֶּׁבָּא לְעוֹנַת נְדָרִים — תְּרוּמָתוֹ תְּרוּמָה. סַבְרוּהָ: קָסָבַר ר' יוֹסֵי זתְּרוּמָה בַּזְּמַן הַזֶּה — דְּאוֹרַיְיתָא. אִי אָמְרַתְּ בִּשְׁלָמָא מוּפְלָא סָמוּךְ לְאִישׁ, דְּאוֹרַיְיתָא — אָתֵי גַּבְרָא דְּאוֹרַיְיתָא וּמְתַקֵּן טַבְלָא דְּאוֹרַיְיתָא. אֶלָּא אִי אָמְרַתְּ דְּרַבָּנַן — אָתֵי גַּבְרָא דְּרַבָּנַן וּמְתַקֵּן טַבְלָא דְּאוֹרַיְיתָא?! לָא, קָסָבַר רַבִּי יוֹסֵי תְּרוּמָה בַּזְּמַן הַזֶּה דְּרַבָּנַן. וְסָבַר ר' יוֹסֵי חתְּרוּמָה בַּזְּמַן הַזֶּה דְּרַבָּנַן? *וְהָתַנְיָא בְּסֵדֶר עוֹלָם: °"אֲשֶׁר יָרְשׁוּ אֲבוֹתֶיךָ וִירִשְׁתָּהּ", יְרוּשָּׁה רִאשׁוֹנָה וּשְׁנִיָּה — יֵשׁ לָהֶן, שְׁלִישִׁית — אֵין לָהֶן. *וְא"ר יוֹחָנָן: מַאן תְּנָא סֵדֶר עוֹלָם — ר' יוֹסֵי! *) ר' יוֹסֵי *תְּנֵי (א) לָהּ, וְלָא סָבַר לָהּ. ה"נ מִסְתַּבְּרָא, דְּתַנְיָא: עִיסָּה שֶׁנִּדְמְעָה אוֹ שֶׁנִּתְחַמְּצָה בִּשְׂאוֹר שֶׁל תְּרוּמָה

חַיֶּיבֶת

*) [ע' תוס' עירובין ט: ד"ה אי לא]

במדבר ל | דברים ל | תורה אור

---

**אי** מופלא הסמוך לאיש דאורייתא מילקא נמי לילקי. וא"ת: ואמאי פריך בפשיטות דלילקי, הא איכא אמוראי דאמרי דנדרו נדר — לענין שאם אכלו אחרים שלוקין, אבל הוא לא לקי, דקטן הוא לעונשין! וי"ל: דהכי פריך, אי מופלא הסמוך לאיש דאורייתא, ואית ליה איסורא לקטן, מילקא נמי לילקי.

**לאותן** המוזהרין עליו. תימה: א"כ היכי ס"ד דליחייבו קרבן, לפי שמניחין לו לעבור על נדרו? וי"ל: דהוה מצי למימר "ולטעמיך", אלא דבלאו הכי פריך שפיר.

**כגון** שהקדיש הוא ואכלו אחרים. וא"ת: ואמאי לא מוקי, כגון שאכל הוא בעצמו לכשהגדיל. והוה ניחא טפי, דזדון שבועה לא מתוקמא אלא כשאכל בעצמו. דאפי' נשבע שלא יאכלו אחרים, אין בכך כלום, כל זמן שלא אסר עליהם בקונם דהוי כהקדש? וי"ל: דניחא ליה לאוקומי כשאכלו אחרים מיד סמוך לנדרו.

**רבי** יוחנן ור"ל דאמרי תרוייהו לוקין. וא"ת: והא סבר ר"ל, התראת ספק לא שמה התראה ב"התערובות" (זבחים עח.) גבי "נותר ופגול שבללן זה בזה", והכא התראת ספק הוא, דשמא לא יביא ב' שערות עד ב' שנים או ג' ונמצא דאכתי לא הוי מופלא סמוך לאיש! ואי איירי שאכלו אחרים לאחר שהגדיל, א"כ הל"ל: כשאכלו הוא בעצמו. וכשהביא שתי שערות נמי לא איירי, דא"כ הוא עצמו אם יאכלנו — ילקה, דרבי יוחנן אית ליה לעיל, דתוך זמן כלאחר זמן! וי"ל: דאזלינן בתר רוב שמביאין שתי שערות בזמנן, דהיינו בני י"ג ויום א'.

**אין** ב"ד מצווין להפרישו. וא"ת: לרב הונא דאמר שהוא עצמו לוקה, מה מועיל הפרתו? ותו: מה משני, הא בעי רבי יוחנן למימר בפרק "חרש" (יבמות דף קיד.) דב"ד מצווין להפרישו! וי"ל: דלמסקנא דקאמר דעל דעת בעלה נודרת, אתי שפיר, והוה מצי למימר השתא: וליטעמיך, הא סבר ר' יוחנן דב"ד מצווין להפרישו, אלא דבלא"ה פריך שפיר.

**כדרב** פנחס דאמר על דעת בעלה היא נודרת. והוי כמו "אלא", אע"ג דלא כתוב בספרים "אלא". וכעין זה יש בפ' "אע"פ" (כתובות דף נט.) *אמר רב הונא בריה דרב יהושע: באומר "יקדשו ידיך לעושיהם", דאין בספרים "אלא". ובנדרים (דף *יג) יש בספרים "אלא". וא"ת: א"כ אמאי נכתב בפרשת נדרים דבעל מפר לאשתו, אפי' אינה אשתו כגון הכא, הבעל מפר, דעל דעתו נודרת? וי"ל: דאיצטריך לענין שאם אמר "קיים ליכי" — שאינו יכול להפר. א"נ משום דאמר רחמנא בעל מפר, קאמר לעולם על דעתו היא נודרת. ואע"ג דהכא לא הוו אלא נישואין דרבנן, ולא אמרה תורה שיפר מ"מ היא סבורה שבידו להפר, כמו בשאר נשים, ונודרת על דעתו. **אי** אמרת בשלמא מופלא הסמוך לאיש דאורייתא. וא"ת: אדפריך מרבי יוסי, לסיועי מדרבי יהודה דאמר: אין תרומתו תרומה — אלמא סבר דמופלא הסמוך לאיש דרבנן, ולכך לא מתקן טבל דאורייתא! וי"ל: דר' יהודה נמי אית ליה דמופלא סמוך לאיש דאורייתא, ולהכל לתקן טבל — לא איתרבי להיות כגדול. ואינה

---

לְפִי שֶׁמָּצִינוּ שֶׁהִשְׁוָה הַכָּתוּב. מִ"כִּי יַפְלִיא", דְּמַשְׁמַע: יוֹדֵעַ לְהַפְלוֹת, סָמוּךְ לְאִישׁ, דַּאֲכַתִּי קָטָן הוּא כָּל שָׁנָה זוֹ. זֶה הַדָּבָר אֲשֶׁר צִוָּה וגו'. כְּלוֹמַר, לְאִיסָּר וְ"לֹא יַחֵל" אָמַרְתִּי שֶׁיְּהֵא אִיסָּרוֹ אִיסָּר וְנִדְרוֹ בְּבַל יַחֵל, וְלֹא לְקָרְבַּן מְעִילָה וּבַל יַחֵל, הַיְינוּ מַלְקוּת, וּמְסַיֵּיעַ לֵיהּ לְרַב הוּנָא. אֵימָא לְאִיסּוּר בַּל יַחֵל. כְּלוֹמַר, אִיסּוּרָא בְּעָלְמָא וְלֹא מַלְקוּת. אִי מוּפְלָא סָמוּךְ לְאִישׁ דְּאוֹרַיְיתָא. מִ"כִּי יַפְלִיא לִנְדּוֹר נֶדֶר". מִילְקָא נַמִי לִילְקֵי. דְּהָא כָּל זְמַן דְּנִדְרוֹ נֶדֶר קָאֵי עֲלֵיהּ בְּבַל יַחֵל. אִיסּוּרָא נַמִי לֵיכָּא. עָלָיו, אִם אֲכָלוֹ. דְּהָא אִי אָתוּ רַבָּנַן לְתַקּוּנֵי, הָכִי תַּקּוּן: שֶׁלֹּא יֹאכְלוּ אֲחֵרִים אֶת הֶקְדֵּשׁוֹ, אוֹ הוּא לִכְשֶׁיַּגְדִּיל. אֲבָל בְּקַטְנוּתוֹ — לֹא בָּאוּ לֶאֱסוֹר עָלָיו, דְּקָטָן לָאו בַּר קַבּוֹלֵי עֲלֵיהּ תַּקַּנְתָּא דְּרַבָּנַן הוּא. וּמְשַׁנֵּי: לְעוֹלָם דְּרַבָּנַן. וְאִיסּוּרָא אַמַּאן קָאֵי — עַל אוֹתָן הַמּוּזְהָרִים עָלָיו לְהַפְרִישׁוֹ מֵאִיסּוּרָא. ש"מ כו'. פְּלוּגְתָּא הִיא בְּפֶרֶק "חֵרֵשׁ שֶׁנָּשָׂא פִּקַּחַת" בִּיבָמוֹת (דף קיד.). אֶלָּא הָכָא בְּמַאי עָסְקִינַן כו'. וּלְעוֹלָם כִּדְקָתָנֵי, וְלְאִיסָּר וּלְבַל יַחֵל דַּהֲוֵי מַלְקוּת גָּמוּר. וְאַפ"ה לָא תְּסַיְּיעֵיהּ לְרַב הוּנָא מֵהָא, דְּהָא דְּקָתָנֵי מַלְקוּת אַהֶקְדֵּשׁ קָטָן — לָאו לְדִידֵיהּ קָאָמַר, אֶלָּא לַאֲחֵרִים שֶׁאָכְלוּ אֶת הֶקְדֵּשׁוֹ. מִדְּרַבָּנַן. כְּלוֹמַר, מ"ד אֵין לוֹקִין, מוֹקִים לְהָא דְּקָתָנֵי "לְאִיסָּר וּלְבַל יַחֵל" כִּדְאוֹקְמִינַן: לְאִיסּוּר בַּל יַחֵל אִיסּוּרָא בְּעָלְמָא, וּמִדְּרַבָּנַן, וּמִקְּרָא דְּ"כִי יַפְלִיא" דְּקָתָנֵי שֶׁהִשְׁוָה הַכָּתוּב — אַסְמַכְתָּא בְּעָלְמָא. יְתוֹמָה. שֶׁהִשִּׂיאַתָּהּ אִמָּהּ, דְּבַת מֵיאוּן הִיא, דְּנִשּׂוּאִין דִּידַהּ מִדְּרַבָּנַן. בַּעְלָהּ מֵפֵר נִדְרָהּ. וְלָא קָרֵי לָהּ "יְתוֹמָה" אֶלָּא בְּקַטְנוּתָהּ, כָּל זְמַן שֶׁרְאוּיָה לְמֵיאוּן. אִי אָמְרַתְּ בִּשְׁלָמָא מוּפְלָא סָמוּךְ לְאִישׁ. לָא הָוֵי נִדְרוֹ נֶדֶר אֶלָּא מִדְּרַבָּנַן, מִשּׁ"ה בַּעְלָהּ מֵפֵר לָהּ, דְּאָתוּ נִשּׂוּאִין דְּרַבָּנַן כו'. וְהָא לְכִי גָּדְלָה אָכְלָה. בְּהַהִיא הֲפָרָה, דְּלָאו הֲפָרָה הִיא, וְנִמְצָא גָּדוֹל אוֹכֵל נְבֵלוֹת. כָּל שָׁעָה. וַאֲפִילּוּ מִשֶּׁגָּדְלָה. וְהוּא שֶׁבָּעַל. לְאַחַר שֶׁגָּדְלָה, דַּהֲוְיָא לַהּ בְּעִילָה קִדּוּשִׁין גְּמוּרִין דְּאוֹרַיְיתָא, דְּמַעֲשֶׂה גְּדוֹלָה — מַעֲשֶׂה. הִלְכָּךְ אָתוּ נִישּׂוּאִין דְּאוֹרַיְיתָא, וּמְבַטְּלִין נִדְרָא דְּאוֹרַיְיתָא. אֵין הַבַּעַל מֵפֵר. נְדָרִים הַקּוֹדְמִין לְנִישּׂוּאִין, בְּמַסֶּכֶת נְדָרִים, וְהַאי נֶדֶר קָדַם לְהַךְ בְּעִילָה דְּאוֹרַיְיתָא. עַל דַּעַת בַּעְלָהּ. וְהַךְ קְטַנָּה, עַל דַּעְתּוֹ שֶׁל זֶה נָדְרָה, וְכִי אָמְרִינַן: אֵין הַבַּעַל מֵפֵר בְּקוֹדְמִין — הֵיכָא דְּלֵית לָהּ בַּעַל בִּשְׁעַת נֶדֶר כְּלָל. כִּדְרַב פִּנְחָס. כְּלוֹמַר, לָא תּוֹקֵי לָהּ לְבָרַיְיתָא כְּשֶׁהַבַּעַל מֵפֵר לָהּ כָּל שָׁעָה וְשָׁעָה, (ב) לְעוֹלָם נִדְרָהּ דְּאוֹרַיְיתָא, וּדְקַשְׁיָא לָךְ: אָתוּ נִשּׂוּאִין דְּרַבָּנַן וּמְבַטְּלִין נִדְרָא דְּאוֹרַיְיתָא? אַהָכִי מְבַטְּלַת, דְּכָל הַנּוֹדֶרֶת כו'. לְעוֹנַת נְדָרִים. הַיְינוּ מוּפְלָא הַסָּמוּךְ לָאִישׁ, שֶׁנְּדָרָיו נִבְדָּקִין. סַבְרוּהָ. רַבָּנַן בְּנֵי הַיְשִׁיבָה, דְּבָעוּ לְאוֹתוּבֵי לְרַב כָּהֲנָא מֵהָכָא. תְּרוּמָה דְּאוֹרַיְיתָא. וְקָאָמַר: מִשֶּׁבָּא לְעוֹנַת נְדָרִים תְּרוּמָתוֹ תְּרוּמָה, וּתְרוּמָה וְהֶקְדֵּשׁ וְנֶדֶר — חֲדָא הִיא, דְּמִקְדְּשָׁהּ בְּדִבּוּרוֹ שֶׁקּוֹרֵא עָלֶיהָ שֵׁם. יְרוּשָּׁה רִאשׁוֹנָה. שֶׁל יְהוֹשֻׁעַ. וּשְׁנִיָּה. בִּימֵי עֶזְרָא. יֵשׁ לָהֶן. כְּלוֹמַר, בְּגָלוּת נְבוּכַדְנֶצַּר בָּטְלָה קְדוּשַּׁת הָאָרֶץ, וְנִצְטָרְכוּ לְיוֹרְשָׁהּ וּלְקַדְּשָׁהּ בַּשְּׁנִיָּה. אֲבָל שְׁלִישִׁית. לֶעָתִיד לָבֹא. אֵין לָהֶם. כְּלוֹמַר, אֵינָהּ יְרוּשָּׁה, דְּלֹא יִצְטָרְכוּ לְרִשְׁתָּהּ וּלְקַדְּשָׁהּ — דְּלֹא בָּטְלָה קְדוּשָּׁתָהּ, מִגְּזֵרַת הַכָּתוּב. וְאָמַר רַבִּי יוֹחָנָן. בְּעָלְמָא. מַאן תַּנָּא סֵדֶר עוֹלָם רַבִּי יוֹסֵי. דְּהוּא סְתָמָא, כִּי הֵיכִי דִּסְתָם מַתְנִיתִין ר"מ. תָּנֵי (ג) וְלָא סָבַר לָהּ. לְהָא דְּרָשָׁא דְּקָתָנֵי "שְׁלִישִׁית אֵין לָהֶן", אֶלָּא וַדַּאי בָּטְלָה קְדוּשַּׁת הָאָרֶץ, וּתְרוּמָתָהּ דְּהָשְׁתָּא — דְּרַבָּנַן. עִיסַּת חוּלִּין שֶׁנִּדְמְעָה. כְּגוֹן שֶׁנָּפַל סְאָה שֶׁל תְּרוּמָה לְתוֹךְ פָּחוֹת מִמֵּאָה שֶׁל חוּלִּין.

חַיֶּיבֶת

---

שבת קמה. יבמות קיד. [גיטין נה.]

[נזיר כט: סב.]

[שבת קמה. וש"נ]

גיטין פב: נדרים עג: שבת מו: יבמות כט:

תרומות פ"א מ"ג

[וכסדר המשנה שלפנינו ר' יהודה אומר תרומתו תרומה וע"ש בפי' הר"ש]

יבמות פב:

[שם:]

[עירובין לח:]

---

צב א ב מיי' פי"א מהל' נדרים הל"ה:

צג ג מיי' שם הל"ד:

צד ד מיי' פי"ז מהל' מאכלות אסורות הל' כז סמג לאוין קמא טוש"ע או"ח סי' שמג וטוש"ע יו"ד סי' שעג סעי' א בהג"ה:

צה ה מיי' פי"א מהל' נדרים הל"כ סמג לאוין רמא טוש"ע יו"ד סי' רלד סעי' ב וסעי' לה:

צו ו ז מיי' פ"ד מהל' תרומות הל"ה:

צז ח מיי' פ"א שם הל' כו:

### הגהות הב"ח

(א) גמ' תני לה ולא סבר לה נ"ב ל"ע מן עירובין דף נו ושבת דף קלו וסנהדרין דף פו ושבועות פ"ק ובכמה מקומות: (ב) רש"י ד"ה כדרב פנחס וכו' לעולם וכו' אהכי מבטלין: (ג) ד"ה תני לה ולא סבר:

### גליון הש"ס

גמ' שהקדיש הוא ואכלו אחרים. ע' נדרים טו ע"א בר"ן שם:

[בגמ' שלפנינו איתא אלא]

נ"ל פה

### תוספי הרא"ש

ש"מ קטן אוכל נבלות כו'. תי' כי ב"ד מצווין נמי להפרישו ומי ניחא הא קתני יכול יהא חייב על הקדשו קרבן. וי"ל שהיה יכול לומר ולטעמיך: הקדיש הוא ואכלו אחרים. הכי נמי הוה מצי למימר שגדל הוא עצמו ואכל א"נ לא רצה לומר לפי ששנה כבר לזדון שבועה ולכך מיתוקמא בהקדיש הוא כו' כדי שתהא איירי בתרוייהו ולא משכחת זדון שבועה באחרים הילכך בעי לאוקומי סיפא באחרים: וקרא אסמכתא בעלמא הוא. והא דקא אמר יכול יהא חייב על הקדשו קרבן לפי האסמכתא הולך ודורש הפסוק: ר' יוחנן ור"ל דאמרי תרוייהו לוקין. תימה הא שמעינן לר"ל דאמר התראת ספק לא שמה התראה בפרק התערובות גבי הפיגול והנותר והטמא שבללן זה בזה וכל מופלא סמוך לאיש התראת ספק היא דשמא לא יביא שערות ונמצא דאכתי לא הוי שנה שלפני גדול וכשהביא שתי שערות לא איירי דא"כ הוא עצמו אם אכל ילקה לר' יוחנן דאמר לעיל תוך זמן כלאחר זמן וי"ל דאזלינן בתר רובן שמביאין שערות בזמנן: אי דאורייתא קטן אוכל נבילות כו'. תי' הוה מצי למיפרך והא בעי ר' יוחנן בפ' חרש דב"ד מצווין להפרישו אלא בלאו הכי פריך שפיר (ולהכי) [ולפי] המסקנא דרב פינחס בלא"ה ניחא: כרב פנחס כו'. פרש"י ולהכי מיפר בקודמין הואיל שנדרה על דעת בעלה ודחק לפ' משום דאין כתוב אלא בספרים אחרים ומצינו בפ' אע"פ דאמר רב הונא בריה דרב יהושע באומרת יקדשו ידי לעושיהן ואין כתוב בספרים אלא אעפ"כ הוי פירושו כמו אלא. ובנדרים בסוגיא זו כתוב אלא בכל הספרים הילכך נראה לפ' דאדלעיל קאי דפריך אתי נישואין דרבנן ומבטלי נדרה דאורייתא ומשני אין כדר' פינחס דכיון דנודרת על דעת בעלה יכול להפר אפי' הוי נישואין דרבנן. ותימה א"כ למה נכתבה הפרת הבעל כלל כיון דכל אשה נודרת על דעת בעלה י"ל דכיון דאמר קיים ליכי שוב אין הבעל יכול להפר אפי' הוי נישואין דרבנן א"נ אפי' פירשה בהדיא שנדרה שלא לדעתו בעלה מיפר לה בעל ברחה. א"נ משום דנתנה תורה רשות לבעל להפר הוא דאמרינן דנודרת על דעתו לפי שנראה לה שבידו להפר כמו בשאר נשים הילכך כיון שנדרה על דעתו וסמוכה על שולחנו כל עיקרו על דעתו נדרה ויכול להפר: סברוה קסבר תרומה בזמן הזה דאורייתא ובעי לאיתויי סייעתא לר"ל. ותימה דהא ר"ל סבר בפרק הערל תרומה בזמן הזה דרבנן וי"ל דהוה מצי למימר ולטעמיך: אתי גברא דרבנן ומתקן טבל דאורייתא. ותימה אדפריך מדר' יוסי ליסייעיה מדר' יהודה דאמר אין תרומתו תרומה וי"ל דר' יהודה שפיר מצי סבר דמופלא סמוך לאיש דאורייתא ואפ"ה אין תרומתו תרומה דדוקא להקדיש ולאסור הוי מופלא סמוך לאיש כגדול אבל לתקן הכרי לא חשיב כגדול הילכך אין תרומתו תרומה:

תורה אור

חַיֶּיבֶת בְּחַלָּה, [א]וְאֵינָהּ נִפְסֶלֶת בִּטְבוּל יוֹם, דִּבְרֵי ר"מ וְר' יְהוּדָה. ר' יוֹסֵי וְר"ש [ב]פּוֹטְרִין מִן הַחַלָּה. סַבְרוּהָ: מַאן דְּאָמַר תְּרוּמָה דְּאוֹרַיְיתָא – חַלָּה דְּאוֹרַיְיתָא, מַאן דְּאָמַר תְּרוּמָה דְּרַבָּנַן – חַלָּה דְּרַבָּנַן. אִי אָמְרַתְּ בִּשְׁלָמָא, קָסָבַר רַבִּי יוֹסֵי חַלָּה בַּזְּמַן הַזֶּה דְּרַבָּנַן – אָתֵי דִּמּוּעַ דְּרַבָּנַן וּמַפְקַע חַלָּה דְּרַבָּנַן. אֶלָּא אִי אָמְרַתְּ חַלָּה דְּאוֹרַיְיתָא – אָתֵי דִּמּוּעַ דְּרַבָּנַן וּמַפְקַע חַלָּה דְּאוֹרַיְיתָא?! וְדִלְמָא קָסָבַר רַבִּי יוֹסֵי תְּרוּמָה בַּזְּמַן הַזֶּה – דְּאוֹרַיְיתָא, וְחַלָּה – דְּרַבָּנַן? *וְכִדְאַהֲדַר רַב הוּנָא בְּרֵיהּ דְּרַב יְהוֹשֻׁעַ. דְּאָמַר רַב הוּנָא בְּרֵיהּ דְּרַב יְהוֹשֻׁעַ, אַשְׁכַּחְתִּינְהוּ לְרַבָּנַן דְּבֵי רַב דְּיָתְבִי וְקָאָמְרִי: אֲפִילּוּ לְמ"ד תְּרוּמָה בַּזְּמַן הַזֶּה דְּרַבָּנַן חַלָּה דְּאוֹרַיְיתָא, שֶׁהֲרֵי *שֶׁבַע שֶׁכִּבְּשׁוּ וְשֶׁבַע שֶׁחִלְּקוּ – נִתְחַיְּיבוּ בְּחַלָּה וְלֹא נִתְחַיְּיבוּ *בְּמַעֲשֵׂר. וְאָמִינָא לְהוּ אֲנָא: אֲפִילּוּ לְמ"ד תְּרוּמָה בַּזְּמַן הַזֶּה דְּאוֹרַיְיתָא – [ג]חַלָּה דְּרַבָּנַן. *דְּתַנְיָא: אִי "בְּבוֹאֲכֶם", יָכוֹל מִשֶּׁנִּכְנְסוּ לָהּ שְׁנַיִם וּשְׁלֹשָׁה מְרַגְּלִים? ת"ל: "בְּבוֹאֲכֶם" [ד]בְּבִיאַת כּוּלְּכֶם אָמַרְתִּי, וְלֹא בְּבִיאַת מִקְצָתְכֶם, וְכִי אַסְּקִינְהוּ עֶזְרָא – לָא כּוּלְּהוּ סְלוּק.§ **מתני'** מָשָׁל מָשְׁלוּ חֲכָמִים בָּאִשָּׁה: פַּגָּה, בּוֹחַל, וְצֶמֶל. פַּגָּה – עוֹדָהּ תִּינוֹקֶת, בּוֹחַל – אֵלּוּ יְמֵי נְעוּרֶיהָ. בָּזוֹ וּבָזוֹ *אָמְרוּ: *[ה]אָבִיהָ זַכַּאי בִּמְצִיאָתָהּ, וּבְמַעֲשֵׂה יָדֶיהָ, [ו]וּבַהֲפָרַת נְדָרֶיהָ. צֶמֶל – כֵּיוָן שֶׁבָּגְרָה, שׁוּב אֵין לְאָבִיהָ רְשׁוּת בָּהּ. אֵיזֶהוּ סִימָנֶיהָ? ר' יוֹסֵי הַגְּלִילִי אוֹמֵר: [ז]מִשֶּׁיַּעֲלֶה הַקֶּמֶט תַּחַת הַדַּד. ר"ע אוֹמֵר: [ח]מִשֶּׁיִּטּוּ הַדַּדִּים. בֶּן עַזַּאי אוֹמֵר: [ט]מִשֶּׁיַּשְׁחִיר הַפִּטּוּמֶת. רַבִּי יוֹסֵי אוֹמֵר: [י]כְּדֵי שֶׁיְּהֵא נוֹתֵן יָדוֹ עַל הָעוֹקֶץ, וְהוּא שׁוֹקֵעַ וְשׁוֹהֵא לַחֲזוֹר.§ **גמ'** פַּגָּה – עוֹדָהּ תִּינוֹקֶת, כְּדִכְתִיב °"הַתְּאֵנָה חָנְטָה פַגֶּיהָ". בּוֹחַל – אֵלּוּ יְמֵי הַנְּעוּרִים, *כְּדִתְנַן: [כ]הַתְּאֵנִים – מִשֶּׁיַּבְחִילוּ, וְאָמַר רַבָּה בַּר בַּר חָנָה, אָמַר רַב: מִשֶּׁיַּלְבִּין רָאשֵׁיהֶן. וְאִיבָּעֵית אֵימָא מֵהָכָא: °"וַתִּקְצַר נַפְשִׁי בָּהֶם וְגַם נַפְשָׁם בָּחֲלָה בִי". צֶמֶל – כְּמ"ד: יָצְתָה מְלֵאָה.§ וְאֵיזֶהוּ סִימָנִים? ר' יוֹסֵי הַגְּלִילִי אוֹמֵר: מִשֶּׁיַּעֲלֶה הַקֶּמֶט.§ אָמַר שְׁמוּאֵל: לֹא מִשֶּׁיַּעֲלֶה הַקֶּמֶט מַמָּשׁ, [ל]אֶלָּא כְּדֵי שֶׁתַּחֲזִיר יָדֶיהָ לַאֲחוֹרֶיהָ, וְנִרְאֵית כְּמִי שֶׁיַּעֲלֶה הַקֶּמֶט תַּחַת הַדַּד. שְׁמוּאֵל בָּדַק בְּאַמְתֵיהּ, וִיהַב לָהּ ד' זוּזֵי דְּמֵי בּוֹשְׁתָּהּ. שְׁמוּאֵל לְטַעְמֵיהּ, דְּאָמַר שְׁמוּאֵל: °"לְעוֹלָם בָּהֶם תַּעֲבוֹדוּ" – [מ]לַעֲבוֹדָה נְתַתִּים וְלֹא לְבוּשָׁה. שְׁמוּאֵל מְיַיחֵד לְהֶן, רַב נַחְמָן מַחְלִיף לְהֶן, רַב שֵׁשֶׁת מָסַר לְהֶן לַעֲרָבִי, וַאֲמַר לְהֶן: אִזְדַּהֲרוּ מִיִּשְׂרָאֵל.§ "רַבִּי יוֹסֵי אוֹמֵר" כו'.§ מַאי "עוֹקֶץ"? אָמַר שְׁמוּאֵל: [נ]עוּקְצוֹ שֶׁל דַּד. ת"ר: *אֵלּוּ הֵן סִימָנֵי בַגְרוּת? ר"א בְּר' צָדוֹק אוֹמֵר: [ס]מִשֶּׁיִּתְקַשְׁקְשׁוּ הַדַּדִּין. ר' יוֹחָנָן בֶּן בְּרוֹקָה אוֹמֵר: מִשֶּׁיַּכְסִיף רֹאשׁ הַחוֹטֶם. מִשֶּׁיַּכְסִיף? אַזְקוּנָה לָהּ! אֶלָּא א"ר אַשִׁי: [ע]מִשֶּׁיַּפְצִיל *רֹאשׁ הַחוֹטֶם. ר' יוֹסֵי אוֹמֵר: מִשֶּׁתַּקִּיף [פ]הָעֲטָרָה, ר"ש אוֹמֵר: [צ]מִשֶּׁנִּתְמַעֵךְ הַכַּף

שיר ב · זכריה יא · ויקרא כה · [ע"ן פי' קטנה]

---

**רש"י**

חַיֶּיבֶת בְּחַלָּה. וְלָא אָמְרִינַן דִּתְרוּמָה פּוֹטֶרֶת לָהּ, וְאַע"ג דִּתְרוּמָה אֵינָהּ חַיֶּיבֶת בְּחַלָּה, מְדוּמָּע – חַיָּיב בְּחַלָּה, מ"ט? דְּדִימּוּעַ דְּרַבָּנַן הוּא, דְּמִדְּאוֹרַיְיתָא – חַד בִּתְרֵי בָּטֵיל, דִּכְתִיב (שמות כג): "אַחֲרֵי רַבִּים לְהַטּוֹת", וְרַבָּנַן הוּא דְּאַצְרוּךְ אֶחָד וּמֵאָה. הִלְכָּךְ, לָא אָתֵי דִּימּוּעַ דְּרַבָּנַן, וּמַפְקַע חַלָּה אֲפִילּוּ בַּזְּמַן הַזֶּה, דְּקָסָבְרִי ר"מ וְרַבִּי יְהוּדָה: חַלָּה בַּזְּמַן הַזֶּה – דְּאוֹרַיְיתָא. פּוֹטְרִין מִן הַחַלָּה. כִּדְמְפָרֵשׁ לְקַמָּן, דְּקָסָבְרִי: חַלָּה בַּזְּמַן הַזֶּה – דְּרַבָּנַן, וְאָתֵי דִּימּוּעַ דְּרַבָּנַן, וּמַפְקַע חַלָּה דְּרַבָּנַן. וְהַיְינוּ דַּאֲמַרַן לְעֵיל: תָּנֵי וְלָא סָבַר לָהּ, דְּהָא חָזֵינַן דִּלְרַבִּי יוֹסֵי חַלָּה בַּזְּמַן הַזֶּה דְּרַבָּנַן. וְסַבְרוּהָ הָנָךְ רַבָּנַן דְּמַיְיתֵי רְאָיָיה מֵהָכָא, דְּכִי הֵיכִי דְּקָאָמַר ר' יוֹסֵי חַלָּה בַּזְּמַן הַזֶּה דְּרַבָּנַן, הוּא הַדִּין לִתְרוּמָה. וְדִלְמָא. אַע"ג דְּקָא חָזֵית מֵהָכָא לְר' יוֹסֵי חַלָּה דְּרַבָּנַן, אפ"ה סְבִירָא לֵיהּ: תְּרוּמָה דְּאוֹרַיְיתָא, וְלֵיכָּא הָכִי נַמִי מִסְתַּבְּרָא, דְּקָא בָּעֵית לְאַתּוֹיֵי. נִתְחַיְּיבוּ בְּחַלָּה. דִּכְתִיב בְּחַלָּה (במדבר טו): "בְּבוֹאֲכֶם אֶל הָאָרֶץ", וַהֲרֵי בָּאוּ. וְלֹא נִתְחַיְּיבוּ בְּמַעֲשֵׂר. *דִּבְמַעֲשֵׂר כְּתִיב (דברים יד): "תְּבוּאַת זַרְעֶךָ" – עַד שֶׁיַּכִּיר כָּל אֶחָד וְאֶחָד אֶת שֶׁלּוֹ. **מתני'** פַּגָּה. סְמָדָר. כָּךְ בְּאִשָּׁה, עוֹדָהּ תִּינוֹקֶת – קָרוּ לָהּ "פַּגָּה" כָּל זְמַן שֶׁאֵין לָהּ סִימָן, לֹא בְּדַדִּים וְלֹא בִּשְׂעָרוֹת. בּוֹחַל. כְּשֶׁהַפֵּרִי גָּדֵל קְצָת, כִּדְתָנֵי בַּגְּמָרָא: "הַתְּאֵנִים מִשֶּׁיַּבְחִילוּ". כָּךְ כְּשֶׁיֵּשׁ לָהּ סִימָן דַּדִּין קְצָת – כְּיָדוּעַ שֶׁהֵבִיאָה שְׁתֵּי שְׂעָרוֹת, וְנַעֲרָה הִיא. צֶמֶל. בַּגְּמָ' מְפָרֵשׁ לָהּ לְשׁוֹן נוֹטָרִיקוֹן: יָצְתָה מְלֵאָה, שֶׁיֵּשׁ לָהּ סִימָן מוּבְהָק בְּדַדֶּיהָ, וּלְקַמָּן מְפָרֵשׁ סִימָנִין בְּמַתְנִי'. וְהִיא בּוֹגֶרֶת. בָּזוֹ וּבָזוֹ. אֲפִי' כְּשֶׁהִיא נַעֲרָה, אָבִיהָ זַכַּאי כו', דִּכְתִיב (במדבר ל): "בִּנְעוּרֶיהָ בֵּית אָבִיהָ" – כָּל שֶׁבַח נְעוּרֶיהָ לְאָבִיהָ. אֵיזוֹ הִיא סִימָנִין. אַצֶּמֶל קָאֵי. קֶמֶט. פרונצ"ש. שֶׁגָּדְלוּ דַּדֶּיהָ, עַד שֶׁכָּפוּל מְעַט עַל הֶחָזֶה, וְיֵרָאֶה כְּקֶמֶט. מִשֶּׁיִּטּוּ. גְּדוֹלִים יוֹתֵר. הַפִּטּוּמֶת. רֹאשׁ הַדַּד, כְּמוֹ (סוכה דף לד.) נִיטְּלָה פִּטְמָתוֹ. עוֹקֶץ. כְּמוֹ "עוּקְצֵי הָאֲגָסִים" (עוקצין פ"א מ"ו). פוכיל"ש בְּלַעַ"ז. חוּדּוֹ שֶׁל דַּד שֶׁהַתִּינוֹק יוֹנֵק, וּפִטּוּמֶת הַיְינוּ סְבִיבוֹת עוֹקֶץ. **גמ'** מִשֶּׁיַּבְחִלוּ. חַיָּיבִין בְּמַעֲשֵׂר. מִשֶּׁיַּלְבִּין רָאשֵׁיהֶן. שֶׁמִּשְׁתַּנִּין כְּשֶׁמַּגְדִּילִין. הָכָא נַמִי, מִשֶּׁיִּשְׁתַּנֶּה הַדַּד וְיֵרָאֶה בּוֹ סִימָן שֶׁמַּגְדִּיל. בָּחֲלָה בִי. גָּדְלָה עָלַי. אָדָם הַקָּץ בְּדָבָר נִרְאֶה לוֹ כְּגָדוֹל. אנקייסנ"ן בְּלַעַ"ז. מְיַיחֵד לְהוּ. שִׁפְחוֹתָיו מְיַיחֵד לַאֲנָשִׁים עֲבָדָיו, וְאֵינוֹ מַפְקִירָן מִשּׁוּם בּוֹשֶׁת. מַחְלִיף לְהֶן. אֶת שֶׁל זֶה בָּזֶה, וְאֵינוֹ מַקְפִּיד עַל בּוֹשְׁתָּן. לַעֲרָבִי. מַפְקִיר שִׁפְחוֹתָיו לַעֲרָבִיִּים, וְנוֹהֵג בָּהֶן מִנְהַג הֶפְקֵר. מִשֶּׁיִּתְקַשְׁקְשׁוּ. כְּמוֹ (סוטה דף ט.) "מְקַשְׁקֶשֶׁת לְפָנָיו כְּזוֹג". בטנ"ט בְּלַעַ"ז. כְּלוֹמַר גְּדוֹלִים הַרְבֵּה. חוֹטֶם. *סָפֵק. מִשֶּׁיַּפְצִיל. *סָפֵק. מִשְׁתַּקִּיף עֲטָרָה. שֶׁגָּדוֹל הָעוֹקֶץ וְעָב, וּמוּקָּף עֲטָרָה. וְהַיְינוּ שִׁיעוּרָא דְּא"ר יוֹסֵי נַמִי בְּמַתְנִי': שֶׁיְּהֵא נוֹתֵן יָדוֹ עַל הָעוֹקֶץ וְשׁוֹקֵעַ וְשׁוֹהֶא לַחֲזוֹר. הַכַּף.

כתובות כח. · [עי' רש"י בכתובות כח. וב"מ פט. ובכל דוכתא מפרש טעם אחר] · כתובות כח. · [בסדר המשנה ל"ג אמרו] · [כתובות מו:] · מעשרות פ"א מ"ב · [עי' תוס' ד"ה ראש] · [נ"ל פסק וכן גי' רש"ל] · [פי' משיתחיל ליגקב שנרא' כמפולל ערוך ערך פלל]

---

**תוספות**

**ואינה** נפסלת בטבול יום. וא"ת: ב"אלו עוברין" (פסחים דף מד.) גבי "מקפה של חולין ושום ושמן של תרומה" קאמר דאם נגע טבול יום במקצתו *– דפסל כולו במגעו! וי"ל: דהתם מיירי בשעשאו גוש בקערה. **אתי** דימוע דרבנן ומפקע חלה דרבנן. מכאן מביא ריב"א ראיה דתרומה בטלה ברוב דאורייתא. והא דדרשינן בסיפרא מ"את מקדשו ממנו" דעולה בק"א – אסמכתא בעלמא הוא. וכן הא דקאמר התם, דערלה וכלאי הכרם דכפל איסורו ליאסר בהנאה כפל בעלייתו, שצריך אחד ומאתים. ומיהו ראייה דהכא יש לדחות: דלעולם מדאורייתא הכל נאסר לזרים, מטעם תערובת התרומה שאינה ניכר. אבל מה שגם החולין נחשבו כתרומה, ליפטר מן החלה כאילו הכל תרומה – זה אינו אלא מדרבנן. ומיהו יש להביא ראיה גבי "נפלו אגוזים ונתפצעו" ב"הניזקין" (גיטין דף נד:) דיש ספרים דגרסי "והא הכא דמדאוריית' ברובו בטלה", ובשלהי "הערל" (יבמות דף פב.) גבי "שתי קופות, אחת של חולין ואחת של תרומה, ולפניהן שתי סאות" כו' דקא"ר *יוחנן: והוא שרבו חולין על התרומה פי' דשרי מדאורייתא. ולהכי אמר "שאני אומר". ובריש ההוא פירקא (דף עג:) נמי קאמר: תרומה חמורה ממעשר שכן מחפ"ז, ולא חשיב ק"א. **ל"ג** אילו נאמר כי תבואו הייתי אומר משנכנסו ב' או ג' מרגלים – דהא רישא דברייתא הכי איתא בספרי (פרשת שלח) (ובספ"ק דקדושין מייתי לה) משונה ביאה זו של חלה, דבעלמא כתיב "כי תבואו", "כי יביאך", וכאן כתיב "בבואכם" – לומר: מיד כשנכנסו, קודם כבוש וחילוק. אלמא משמע ד"כי תבואו" משמע ביאה חשובה, דהיינו לאחר כבוש וחילוק. והיכי מצי למימר: אפי' ב' או ג' מרגלים? אלא הכי גרסינן: אי "בבואכם" – יכול אפי' ב' או ג' מרגלים. וקאי אדלעיל מיניה. **לא** כולהו סלוק. ואם תאמר: והלא "כל יושביה עליה" קרינן לענין יובל, לפי שמקצת כל השבטים עלו, לפר"ת דאמר דיובל נהג בבית שני מהאי טעמא? וי"ל: דבבואכם משמע טפי בביאת כולכם. ואם תאמר: היכי ס"ד מעיקרא דתרומה בזמן הזה דאורייתא לרבי יוסי, והוי סייעתא לר"ל דלעיל, הא ר"ל גופיה סבר דלר' יוסי תרומה בזמן הזה דרבנן, בפרק "הערל" (יבמות ד' פא.) וי"ל: דהוי מצי למימר "וליטעמיך". **איזהו** סימניה. פ"ה סימני בגרות. ורבי יוסי דאמר בגמרא "משתקיף העטרה", היינו נמי דקאמר הכא "משיתן ידו על העוקץ". וקשה: דאי חד שיעורא הוא, למה שינה רבי יוסי לשונו? ותו: דכל תנאי דגמרא, שום אחד מהם אינו מזכיר משיעורא דמתניתין! ועוד: דאם כן, בבוחל לא נתן שום סימן, ובגמרא קאמר: בוחל מלמעלה – בידוע שהביאה ב' שערות, הא לא שמעינן סימני דבוחל? לכך פר"ת: ד"איזהו סימניה" דקאמר הכא, א"בוחל" קאי. ולפירוש זה אתי שפיר הא דקאמר בגמרא: הלכה כדברי כולן להחמיר, לענין מיאון. **בדק** באמתיה ויהיב ד' זוזי דמי בושתה. להנצל מעונש היה נותן לה, דהא ר' יהודה אמר ב"החובל" (ב"ק דף פז.) אין לעבדים בושת. ואפילו למ"ד: יש לעבדים בושת – הוי לרבו. **ראש** החוטם. פ"ה: ספק, דלא אתפרש. ובפרק "לולב הגזול" (סוכה דף לה:*) גבי אתרוג, מזכיר "פיטומא, ועוקץ, וחוטם", ומתוך כך משמע דשלשתן באתרוג לצד ראשו, ואין אחד מהם לצד זנבו, דומיא דדד. דגבי דד ליכא לפרושי הכי כמו שפירש באתרוג. ***מסר** להו לערבי. משמע מכאן דשפחה כנענית מותרת בגוי, וה"ה דעבד כנעני מותר בגויה, ולא גזרו עליו משום *) נשג"ז. אע"ג דאיסור נדה ואשת איש דאורייתא שייך שפיר בעבד. וא"כ בשלהי מסכת ע"ז (דף עו:) דא"ל שבור מלכא לבטי: אדכר לך מה דעבדת באורתא, שקבל גויה זונה שמסר לו אושפיזו, (*ורב) יהודה לא קבל גויה זונה – לא עשה בטי איסורא, דמותר הוה בה, דהא עבד הוה, כדקאמר בפרק "עשרה יוחסין" (קדושין דף ע:) דבטי בר טבי ברמות רוחיה לא קבל גיטא דחירותא.

הלכה

*) נ"ל משום נשג"א רש"א

[ועס לו. ד"ה נטלה] · שייך לעיל · [נ"ל ומר]

---

**תוספי הרא"ש**

**ואינה** נפסלת בטבול יום. והא דאמרינן בפ' אלו עוברין המקפה של חולין והשום והשמן של תרומה אם נגע טבול יום במקצתו פסל מקום מגעו והכא אמרינן דלא פסל כלל וי"ל דהתם מיירי שהן גוש בקערה וניכרין בפני עצמן: **אתי** דימוע דרבנן ומפקע חלה דרבנן. מכאן משמע דתרומה בטל ברוב מדאורייתא והא דדריש ליה בסיפרי את מקדשו ממנו מה שאתה מרים ממנו מקדשו אסמכתא היא וכן מוכח בסוף פ' הערל גבי שתי קופות אחת של חולין ואחת של תרומה ולפניהן שתי סאין א' של חולין וא' של תרומה ונפלו אלו לתוך אלו מותרין שאני אומר חולין לתוך חולין נפלו ותרומה לתוך תרומה נפלה וקא"ר יוחנן והוא שרבו חולין על התרומה פי' שאז הן מותרין מן התורה הלכך [הולכין בהם] להקל אלמא ברבייה שרי מן התורה: **אלו** נאמר כי תבואו הייתי אומר משנכנסו שנים או שלשה מרגלים. א) רק בתוס' הגירסא בס"פ ול"ג גירסא זו דאדרבה כי תבואו משמע ביאת כולם כדמשמע בפ"ק דקידושין דקאמר התם הואיל ונאמרו ביאות בתורה סתם ופרט לך הכתוב באחת מהן לאחר ירושה וישיבה אף כל לאחר ירושה וישיבה ואע"ג דאיכא מ"ד לשם דבעי ביאה ומושב מ"מ לא אשכחן כי תבואו דמשמע לאחר בכניסת שנים ושלשה מרגלים קודם שיכנסו כולם. אלא ה"ג אי בבא הייתי אומר משעה שנכנסו בה שנים שלשה מרגלים דמשמע תחלת ביאה מדלא כתיב כי תבואו והכי תניא בסיפרי בפ' שלח לך א"ר ישמעאל שנה הכתוב ביאה זו מכל ביאות שבתורה שבכל מקום הוא אומר והיה כי תבוא והיה כי יביאך וכאן ואמר בבואכם ללמדך כיון שנכנסו לארץ מיד נתחייבו בחלה והיינו דקאמר הכא אילו נאמר בבא ולא כתיב כם הייתי אומר דתחילת ביאה כיון דמשונה ביאה זו ת"ל בבואכם דמשמע ביאת כולכם: **לאו** כולהו סלוק. ותימה והא כל יושביה עליה קרינן ביה לענין יובל כיון שהיו שם מכל השבטים לפר"ת שפי' דיובל נוהג בבית שני מהאי טעמא וי"ל דבבואכם משמע טפי ביאת כולכם ואע"פ שהיו שם מכל השבטים לא מיקרי ביאת כולכם: **אי** זהו סימניה. פרש"י דאצמל קאי ומתוך זה הוצרך לפ' הא דקא"ר יוסי [בברייתא] משתקיף העטרה היינו נמי שיעורא דמשיתן ידו על העוקץ והוא שוקע. וקשה לפי' דלמה שינה ר' יוסי לשונו ועוד דבכולהו תנאי בגמרא לא אמר אחד מהן שיעורא דמתניתין ועוד א"כ ליה יהיב תנא סימנא אבוחל ולקמן תנן בא סימן התחתון עד שלא בא העליון והיינו סימני בוחל. ומפר"ת דאי זהו סימניה דאבוחל קאי ותנאי דגמ' מפרשי סימני בגרות: **משתשחיר** הפיטומת. פרש"י ראש הדד כמו ניטלה פיטמתו דאתרוג. ועוקץ פי' חודו של דד מלמעלה. ובפ' לולב הגזול פרש"י ב' פירושים. ונראה דשניהן הן במקום אחד אלא האחד בצד ראשו והאחד בצד זנבו דגבי דד ליכא לפרושי הכי ומסתמא פיטמת ועוקץ דהתם דומיא דהך דהכא: ויהיב לה ד' זוזי דמי בושתה להנצל מן העונש היה עושה כן דהא אין לעבדים בושת דאמרינן בפ' החובל ואפי' למ"ד יש להם בושת יתנן הכל לרב: **ומסר** להו לערבאי. מכאן משמע דשפחה כנענית מותרת לעובד כוכבים וה"ה דעבד מותר בעובדת כוכבים ולא גזרו עליהן משום נשג"ז ואע"ג דאיסור נדה ואשת איש שייך בעבד מן התורה ושלהי ע"ז דא"ל שבור מלכא לבטי אידכר מה דעבדת באורתא ופרש"י ז"ל ששלחו לו זונה כדרך הערביים וקבלה אומר ר"ת אין צריך לומר שהיה רשע דמותר היה בה כי עבד היה כדאמרינן בקדושין בטי בר טבי ברמות רוחיה לא קביל גיטא דחירותא: **משיפציל** ראש החוטם. פרש"י ספק וגבי אתרוג נמי מזכיר פיטמת ועוקץ וחוטם ונראה לפ' כמו חוטם דהתם דהיינו מקום שמתחיל לשפע על פי העוקץ וכן הכא למעלה מן הפיטומת מתחיל לשפע כלפי הדד וחריצין כמין פיצולין נראה בהם:

א) נראה דל"ל כך הגירסא כתובה בספרים רק בתוס' כתבו דלא נהירא וכו'.

---

**עין משפט נר מצוה**

צח א מיי' פ"ח מהל' טומאת אוכלין הלט"ו: ס"א פוסל מקום מגעו

צט ב מיי' פ"ו מהל' בכורים הל"ד:

ק ג ד מיי' פ"ה שם הל"ה סמג עשין קמא טוש"ע יו"ד סימן שכב סעיף ב:

קא ה מיי' פי"ז מהל' אבידה הלי"ג ופ"ג מהל' אישות הלי"א סמג עשין מח ועד טוש"ע חו"מ סי' עד סעי' ב וטוש"ע אה"ע סי' לז סעיף א:

קב ו מיי' פי"א מהל' נדרים הל"ו סמג לאוין רמב טוש"ע יו"ד סימן רלד סעיף א:

קג ז ח ט י מיי' פ"ב מהל' אישות הל"ז:

קד כ מיי' פ"ב מהל' מעשר הל"ה:

[כתובות כה. ב"מ פט.]

[בכתובות איתא ולא נתחייבו בתרומה וע' ברש"י שם דגרים תרווייהו]

קה ל מיי' פ"ב מהל' אישות הל"ז:

קו מ מיי' פ"ט מהל' עבדים הל"ח:

קז נ ס ע פ צ מיי' פ"ב מהל' אישות הל"ז [וברב אלפס יבמות פי"ג דף מה.]

עין משפט נר מצוה

קח א ב מיי' פ"ב מהל' אישות הל"ז ח [וברב אלפס יבמות מה]:

קט ג מיי' פ"ד מהל' מעשר הל"ח והל"י:

קי ד מיי' פ"ב מהל' אישות הל"ה סמג עשין נא טוש"ע אה"ע סי' קנה סעי' יב [וברב אלפס שם]:

קיא ה מיי' שם הלי"א וע' בהשגות ובמ"מ ובל"מ סמג שם טוש"ע שם וסי' קעב סעי' ו:

קיב ו מיי' הל' שם וע' בהג"ל וסמג שם טוש"ע שם סי' קנה סעי' יג [וברב אלפס שם]:

קיג ז מיי' הל' שם טוש"ע שם סעיף יב:

[המעיין יראה דטעות הוא מלת צורית וגם במשנ' ליתא]

קיד ח עי' במיי' פ"ב מהל' אישות הל' כא:

[נ"ל בפ' בתרא דערכין דף לא.]

[גי' הרי"ף והרא"ש להחמי' ר' יוחנן וסבי אמרי הלכה כדברי כולן להחמיר]

תורה אור

הכף. וכן היה רבי שמעון *(בן יוחי) אומר: שלשה סימנין נתנו חכמים באשה מלמטה, וכנגדן מלמעלה. פגה מלמעלה – בידוע שלא הביאה שתי שערות. בוחל מלמעלה – בידוע שהביאה שתי שערות. צמל מלמעלה – בידוע שנתמעך הכף. מאי "כף"? אמר רב הונא: [א]מקום תפוח יש למעלה מאותו מקום, כיון שמגדלת מתמעך והולך. שאלו את רבי: הלכה כדברי מי? שלח להו: [ב]כדברי כולן *להחמיר. רב פפא ורב חיננא בריה דרב איקא, חד מתני – אהא, וחד מתני – אחצר צורית. דתנן, *איזוהי חצר *צורית שחייבת במעשר? *ר"ש אומר: חצר הצורית, שהכלים נשמרים בתוכה. מאי "חצר הצורית"? אמר רבה בר בר חנה, א"ר יוחנן: שכן בצור מושיבין שומר על פתח החצר. *ר"ע אומר: כל שאחד פותח ואחד נועל – פטורה. ר' נחמיה אומר: כל שאין אדם בוש לאכול בתוכה – חייבת. רבי יוסי אומר: כל שנכנסים לה, ואין אומרים לו "מה אתה מבקש" – פטורה. ר' יהודה אומר: שתי חצרות זו לפנים מזו, הפנימית – חייבת, והחיצונה – פטורה. שאלו את רבי: הלכה כדברי מי? אמר להו: [ג]הלכה כדברי כולן *להחמיר.§ **מתני'** *[ד]בת עשרים שנה שלא הביאה שתי שערות, תביא ראיה שהיא בת עשרים שנה – והיא איילונית, לא חולצת ולא מתיבמת. *בן עשרים שנה שלא הביא שתי שערות, יביאו ראיה שהוא בן עשרים שנה – והוא סרים, לא חולץ ולא מיבם, אלו דברי בית הלל. בית שמאי אומרים: זה וזה – *בן שמונה עשרה. ר' אליעזר אומר: הזכר – כדברי בית הלל, והנקבה – כדברי בית שמאי, שהאשה ממהרת לבא לפני האיש.§ **גמ'** ורמינהי: *אחד לי בן תשע שנים ויום אחד, ואחד לי בן עשרים שלא הביא שתי שערות! *אמר רב שמואל בר רב יצחק, אמר רב: [ה]והוא שנולדו בו סימני סרים. אמר רבא: דיקא נמי, דקתני "והוא סרים", ש"מ. וכי לא נולדו לו סימני סרים, עד כמה? *תני ר' חייא: [ו]עד רוב שנותיו. כי אתו לקמיה דרבי *חייא, אי כחיש, אמר להו: אבריוה. אי בריא, אמר להו: אכחשוה, דהני סימנים – זימנין דאתו מחמת כחישותא, זימנין דאתו מחמת בריאותא. *אמר רב: הלכתא בכולי פרקא – מעת לעת. ועולא אמר: דתנן – תנן, ודלא תנן – לא תנן. בשלמא לעולא, היינו דקתני הכא "יום אחד" והכא לא קתני. אלא לרב, ליתני! ועוד, תני, רבי יוסי בן כיפר אומר משום רבי אליעזר: [ז]שנת עשרים שיצאו ממנה שלשים יום – הרי היא כשנת עשרים לכל דבריה. וכן הורה רבי בלוד: שנת שמונה עשרה שיצאו ממנה שלשים יום – הרי היא כשנת שמונה עשרה לכל דבריה. בשלמא דרבי ודרבי יוסי בן כיפר לא קשיא, הא – כבית שמאי, הא – כבית הילל, אלא לרב קשיא! תנאי היא, דתניא: *[ח]שנה האמורה בקדשים, שנה האמורה בבתי ערי חומה, שתי שנים שבשדה אחוזה, שש שנים שבעבד עברי, וכן שבבן ושבבת – כולן מעת לעת. שנה האמורה בקדשים מנא לן? *אמר רב אחא בר יעקב: אמר קרא °"כבש בן שנתו" (ויקרא יב) – שנתו שלו, ולא שנה של מנין עולם. שנה האמורה בבתי ערי חומה מנלן? אמר קרא: °"עד תום שנת ממכרו" (שם כה) – ממכרו שלו, ולא שנת של מנין עולם. שתי שנים שבשדה אחוזה מנלן? אמר קרא: °"במספר (שם) שני

**רש"י**

הכף. מלמטה הוא על בית הרחם, כמין תפוח גבוה, כדמפרש לקמן. מלמעלה. בדדין. להחמיר. איזה מאלו שתביא – שוב אין אביה מפר נדריה, דמחזקינן לה בוגרת. נתקשקשו ואע"ג דלא הכסיף, הכסיף אע"ג דלא התקשקשו, וכן כולם. אית דאמרי: "להחמיר" – אינה ממאנת, משעה שנראה בה אחד מן הסימנין הללו. ואינה חולצת, עד שיהו כולם. ולאו מילתא היא. דאפילו לא הביאה אחד מהן – גדולה היא, ואינה ממאנת וחולצת. שהרי כל הסימנים הללו – בבגרות נאמרו, ומימי נערות היא גדולה למיאון ולחליצה, שהרי הביאה שתי שערות. ל"א: "הלכה כדברי כולן להחמיר" – הביאה אחד מן הסימנים הללו, ואפילו הקודם שבכולן, ולא הביאה את כולן – בוגרת ואינה בוגרת. ואם קבל אביה בה קדושין, וקדשה היא את עצמה לאחר – צריכה גט משניהם. דכיון שהביאה אחד מן הסימנין הללו, יצתה לה במקצת מרשות אביה, דאיכא למימר: בוגרת הויא, ואין כח בקדושי אביה להפקיע קדושין שלה. וגם בה אין כח להפקיע קדושי אביה, עד שתביא את כולם. שחייבת במעשר. שקובעת תבואה למעשר, דקי"ל: חצר קובעת, במסכת ביצה (דף לד.). שאחד פותח ואחד נועל. שאין השומר קבוע לפתוח ולנעול, אלא זה פותח וזה נועל – לאו בת שימור היא, ופטורה, דלאו שמה "חצר". כל שנכנסין לה כו' פטורה. ואע"ג דאין אדם בוש לאכול בתוכה. כדברי כולן להחמיר. דאם יש בה אחד מכל אלו – חייבת. אם יש שם שומר – חייבת, כר' (א) ישמעאל, אע"ג דאחד פותח ואחד נועל. ואי ליכא פותח ונועל – חייבת, כר"ע. ואע"ג דליכא שומר. ואי אין אדם בוש לאכול בתוכה – חייבת, ואע"ג דליכא שומר, ואיכא פותח ונועל. ואם אמר לו "מה אתה מבקש" – חייבת, ואפי' לית בה חד מכל הני. ל"א: "הלכה כדברי כולן להחמיר" – כיון שאין אדם בוש לאכול בתוכה, קובעת למעשר, שאין אוכלין מפירות הנכנסים לה עד שיתעשרו. ולהפריש מהן על טבל אחר – אסור, עד שיהיה לה שומר קבוע. **מתני'** לא חולצת ולא מתיבמת. ונשאת לכל (ב) שתרצה, דרחמנא פטרה, דכתיב (דברים כה): "והיה הבכור אשר תלד" – פרט לאילונית, שאינה יולדת. סרים. לאו בר חליצה הוא, דכתיב (שם כה): "להקים לאחיו שם בישראל", והאי לאו בר הכי הוא. ה"ג: יביאו ראיה שהוא בן עשרים. קרובי האשה יביאו ראיה. **גמ'** ורמינהי אחד לי בן תשע שנים וכו'. שניהם דין אחד להם, וביאתו – כמאמר בגדול, כדאמרינן לעיל, אלמא קטן הוא, ובעיא אמתוני. אמר רב שמואל. מתני' כגון שנולדו בו סימני סרים המפורשים ב"הערל": כל שאין בשרו מוליא הבל כשהוא רוחץ, ושערו לקוי, ובשרו מחליק. כי אתו לקמיה דר' חייא. בן עשרים שנה שלא הביא. בכוליה פרקא מעת לעת. חשבינן לה שנה, ולא בתר מנין עולם, שיהא יום אחד של שנת עשרים חשוב שנה. דאף על גב דלא תנן במתניתין "בן עשרים שנה ויום אחד" – כמאן דתנן "יום אחד" דמי, וצריך להשלים את כולה. דתנן תנן. היכא דתנן "יום אחד", כגון "בת שלשה שנים ויום אחד" וכולהי דמתני' בר מסיפא דקתני "בת עשרים שלא הביאה שתי שערות" – דהתם לא בעינן עשרים שלמים, אלא משנכנס יום אחד בשנת עשרים. בשלמא דרבי ודר' יוסי בן כיפר לא קשיין. אהדדי למהוי מתני' משבשתא, דמר כב"ש ודמר כב"ה דמתני'. בקדשים. היכא דכתיב "כבש בן שנתו". מעת לעת. מיום ליום, ולא אמרינן: למנין עולם, שתכלה שנתו ערב ר"ה. שבבן ושבבת. קסבר: היינו "בן עשרים שנה" ו"בת עשרים שנה" דמתני', אלמא מעת לעת בעינן הלכתא דהאי תנא. והנך דלעיל סברי לה כעולא. שתי שנים שבשדה אחוזה. המוכר שדה אחוזה לחבירו – אינו מותר לגואלה בפחות משתי שנים, שיאכלנה לוקח שתי שנים, כדכתיב (ויקרא כה): "במספר שני תבואות ימכר לך". ומכאן ואילך, אם בא לגאול – גואל, ומחשב לו פירות של שתי שנים, לפי חשבון הדמים שמכרה לו, לפי שנים הבאים עד היובל. שהלוקח שדה מחבירו, יודע שיחזירנו לו ביובל. ואם היו עד היובל עשר שנים, ומכרה לו בעשרה ליטרין – נמצא קונה פירות של כל שנה בליטרא. שני

**תוספות**

**הלכה** כדברי כולן להחמיר. מספק פוסק כמר לחומרא וכמר לחומרא, כדפרישי' בפרק "בנות כותים" (לעיל דף לו.).

**איזהו** חצר (צורית) כו'. קשה לר"ת: דבפרק "השוכר את הפועלים" (ב"מ דף פח.) א"ר ינאי: אין הטבל חייב במעשר עד שיראה פני הבית! ותירץ: דמדרבנן – חצר קובעת למעשר, ומדאורייתא – בעינן ראיית פני הבית.

**בת** עשרים כו' יביאו ראיה. פירוש: קרובי האשה. ואי גרסינן "תביא" – היינו, היא בעצמה. ואי גרסינן "יביא" – קאי אבעל, שיביא ראיה שזו היא אילונית, והוו קדושי טעות אם רוצה לישא אחותה.

**דברי** ב"ה. תימה דבפ' "הערל" (יבמות דף פ.) איתמר: אכל חלב מבן י"ב שנה עד י"ח שנה, ונולדו בו סימני סרים. אמאי שביק דברי ב"ה דאמר כ' שנה, ונקט דברי ב"ש ואפי' לר' אליעזר, הזכר כדברי ב"ה והתם איירי בזכר? וי"ל: דהתם נקט כרבי, שהורה בסמוך עד י"ח.

**עד** רוב שנותיו. ומכאן ואילך גדול הוא, והוי ודאי סרים.

**זימנין** דאתו מחמת כו'. יש ספרים דגרסי: "זימנין דנתרן". [ע' תוס' ב"ב קנה, ד"ה "הכי גרס ר"ת"].

**כולן** מעת לעת. בפרק שני דזבחים (דף כה:) אמר: דשעות פוסלות בקדשים, וכן בבתי ערי חומה, כדמשמע *(פ"ב דזבחים) ולא דמי לאחריני כדאמרינן דלא בעינן בהן מעת לעת לשעות, כדפרישית לעיל (דף מד:) גבי "ל' יום איכא בינייהו". [ועי' תוספות ערכין לא, ד"ה "מיום"].

ובשביעית

**מסורת הש"ס**

[ליתא בתוספתא] [גי' רי"ף ורא"ש להחמיר ר' יוחנן וסבי אמרי הל' כדברי כולן להחמיר] מעשרות פ"ג מ"ה [במשנה איתא ר' ישמעאל אמר חצר הצורית וכו'] [שם] יבמות פ. וקף לז: [יבמות פ. לז.] ב"ב קנה: [בסדר המשנה בנין] [יבמות נו:] [יבמות לז. ב"ב קנה:] [עי' תוס' יבמות פ: ד"ה עד שיהא] [ביבמות שם איתא לקמיה דרבא] [ערכין יח:] [תוספתא דנגעים פ"ט ערכין יח: כל הענין] [בכורות כז:]

**הגהות הב"ח**

(א) רש"י ד"ה כדברי כולן וכו' חייבת כר' שמעון וכו' אע"ג דאחד וכו' ואם אומרין לו מה וכו': (ב) ד"ה לא חולצת וכו' לכל מי שתרצה:

**תוספי הרא"ש**

**הלכה** כדברי כולם להחמיר. מספק פוסק כחומרי דמר וכחומרי דמר כדפרישית בפרק בנות כותים: **איזהו** חצר צורית. הקשה ר"ת מהך מתני' מר' ינאי דאמר בפ' השוכר את הפועלים אין הטבל מתחייב במעשר עד שיראה פני הבית. ותירץ דחצר קובעת מדרבנן אבל מדאורייתא עד שיראה פני הבית: **בת** עשרים שנה כו'. יביאו ראיה פי' קרובי האשה ואי גרסינן תביא פי' היא עצמה ואי גרסינן יביא ראיה פי' הבעל אם רוצה לישא אמה או אחותה יביא שזאת היא אילונית והיו קידושיה קידושי טעות: **שנה** האמורה בקדשי'. בפ"ב דזבחים איכא למ"ד שעות פוסלות בקדשים דדריש שה תמים זכר בן שנה יהיה שיהו כל הוויותיו תם ובן שנה ופריך מי איכא מידי דבשעת שחיטה בן שנה בקבלה והולכה בן שתי שנים. אמר רבא זאת אומרת ששעות פוסלות בקדשי' והשתא מעת לעת של קדשים אינו שוה לאחרים דלא בעינן בהו מעת לעת בשעות כדפי' לעיל גבי ל' יום איכא בינייהו ושנה נמי דבתי ערי חומה משמע נמי בפ' בתרא דערכין דבעי' מעת לעת אף לשעות דדריש התם עד תום שנת ממכרו שנה שלו ולא שנת של מנין עולם והדר דריש מימים דבעי' מעת לעת. והקשה ר"מ מאי איצטריך האי קרא גבי קדשים מההוא קרא דדריש בזבחים בן שנה יהיה דשעות פוסלות ידעינן דלשנתו מנינן דאי מנינן למנין עולם לא משכחת לה דבשחיטה היה בן שנה ובזריקה היה בן שתים שאם שחטו סמוך לבין השמשות וזרקו בלילה תיפוק לי משום פסול לילה. ואם זרקו למחר תיפוק לי משום לן. ותירץ דאיצטריך ההוא קרא לאשמועינן דפסול משום עברה זמנו ואם עלה ירד כדאמרינן בפ' בתרא דזבחים גבי בני יונה שעבר זמנן שאם עלו ירדו. וסד"א כיון דבשעת שחיטה היה בן שנה וזרקו לא ירד קמ"ל קרא כיון דבשעה שהיתה הקבלה היה יותר מבן שנה אם עלה ירד. ונ"ל דאי לא דידעינן מהבא דבתר שנה דידיה אזלינן לא הוה דרשינן מיהיה דשעות פוסלות וכן גבי בתי ערי חומה איכא תרי קראי: **שנתו** שלו ולא שנה של מנין עולם. ותימה תיפוק לי מדאמרה תורה להקריב בראש השנה לתמיד אלמא בתר שנתו אזלינן דאי לשנת מנין עולם הו"ל בן שתי שנים שכבר נולד ז' ימים לפני ראש השנה דאם לא כן הו"ל מחוסר זמן. וי"ל דאפ' אזלינן בתר שנות עולם לא מנינן ליה שנה א)אלא משעת הרצאה ואם נולד ז' ימים לפני ראש השנה מתחלת שנתו בראש השנה:

א) וכלאותא בר"ה [דף ו ע"ב] ע"ש.

"שני תבואות ימכר לך" – פעמים שאתה מוכר שלשה תבואות בשתי שנים. שש שנה
שמות כא שבעבד עברי מנלן? אמר קרא: °"שש שנים יעבוד ובשביעית" – ובשביעית נמי יעבוד. שבבן ושבבת למאי הלכתא? אמר רב גידל, אמר רב: לענין ערכין. ורב יוסף אמר: לפרקין ד"יוצא דופן". א"ל אביי: מי פליגת? א"ל: לא, הוא אמר חדא, ואנא אמינא חדא, ולא פליגינן. והכי נמי מסתברא, דאי ס"ד פליגי, מאן דאמר לערכין לא אמר ליוצא דופן? והאמר רב: הלכתא בכולהו פרקין מעת לעת! אלא למ"ד לערכין, מ"ט לא אמר ל"יוצא דופן"? דומיא דהנך, מה הנך דכתיבן, אף הני נמי – דכתיבן. ואידך – האי "שבבן ושבבת", "שבזכר ושבנקבה" מבעי ליה! אמר רב יצחק בר נחמני, א"ר אלעזר: הלכה כר' יוסי בן כיפר שאמר משום ר' אליעזר. א"ר זירא: *איזבה ואיסק ואגמר לשמעתא מפומיה דמרא! כי סליק אשכחיה לר' אלעזר, אמר ליה: אמרת הלכה כרבי יוסי בן כיפר? אמר ליה: מסתברא אמרי, מדכולהו פירקין תני "יום אחד", והכא לא קתני – שמע מינה מסתברא כותיה.§

# הדרן עלך יוצא דופן

**בא סימן** [א] התחתון עד שלא בא העליון – או חולצת או מתיבמת. בא העליון עד שלא בא התחתון, אף על פי שאי אפשר, ר' מאיר אומר: לא חולצת ולא מתיבמת, וחכ"א: [ב] או חולצת או מתיבמת. מפני שאמרו, אפשר לתחתון לבא עד שלא בא העליון, אבל אי אפשר לעליון לבא עד שלא בא התחתון.§

**גמ'** "אע"פ שאי אפשר", והלא בא! "בא" לר' מאיר, "אע"פ שאי אפשר" – לרבנן. וליתני "בא העליון, ר"מ אומר: לא חולצת ולא מתיבמת. וחכ"א: או חולצת או מתיבמת", ואנא ידענא (א) משום דאי אפשר הוא! אי לא תנא "אע"פ שאי אפשר", הוה אמינא: רוב נשים – תחתון אתי ברישא, ומיעוט – עליון אתי ברישא. ורבי מאיר *לטעמיה – דחייש למיעוטא, ורבנן לטעמייהו – דלא חיישי למיעוטא. והני מילי – בסתמא, אבל היכא דבדקן ולא אשכחן – אימר מודו ליה רבנן לר"מ דעליון קדים, קמ"ל דאי אפשר. (ב) ודאי אתי,
יחזקאל טז ומנתר הוא דנתר. בשלמא לר"מ – היינו דכתיב: °"שדים נכונו ושערך צמח", אלא לרבנן – איפכא מבעי ליה! ה"ק: כיון ש"שדים נכונו" – בידוע ש"שערך צמח".
שם כג בשלמא לר"מ – היינו דכתיב: °"בעשות ממצרים דדיך למען שדי נעוריך", אלא לרבנן – איפכא מבעי ליה! ה"ק: כיון שבאו דדיך – בידוע שבאו נעוריך. ואיבעית אימא: מאי "שדי" – כולה בדדי כתיב, וה"ק הקב"ה לישראל:
איכרפו

---

שני תבואות. מיעוט "שני" שנים. וכתיב "תבואות", ומשמע כל תבואות של שתי שנים – להביא תבואה שלישית. ושלש תבואות לא משכחת לה בשתי שנים, אלא מעט לעת. כגון מכרה לו באלול מלאה פירות – נמצא אוכלן, ואוכל תבואה עד שיחזור ויקצור קודם אלול הבא – הרי שתי תבואות בשנה אחת. ועוד יאכל תבואה תורה אור השנית, שהיא שנה השלישית לפי מנין העולם. בשביעית נמי יעבוד. כגון נמכר בניסן, וכשיגיע תשרי של שביעית – עברו שש למנין עולם, והוא יעבוד עד ניסן. לערכין. דהיכא דכתיב (ויקרא כז): "מבן ששים שנה ומעלה" פשיטא לן דשנת ששים כלמטה, דהא "ומעלה" כתיב. אבל בן חמש שנים, דלא כתיב (שם) אלא "מבן חמש שנים ועד בן עשרים שנה", ולא כתיב "מבן חמש שנים ומעלה" – אי לא אשמועינן הכא מעט לעת, הוה אמינא: שנת חמש כלמעלה. להכי אשמועינן הכא דבעינן ה' שנים מלאים בכלל ערך הראשון שהוא מועט. לפרקין דיוצא דופן. להיכא דלא תנן "ויום אחד", כגון בן עשרים ובת עשרים. מ"ט לא אמר ליוצא דופן. הואיל וס"ל נמי בהנך מעט לעת. [ביצה כז. מ"ק כב. חולין נ.] דומיא דהנך. כלומר, אף על גב דבהנך ד"יוצא דופן" הוי נמי מעט לעת, מיהו האי "שבבן ושבבת" דמתניתין לא איירי בהן כלל. דהא דומיא דקדשים וערי חומה ועבד עברי קתני, דכתיבן. הלכך ערכין נמי כתיבן. אבל שנת עשרים לענין שערות לא כתיבי באורייתא, אלא הלכתא היא. שבזכר ושבנקבה מיבעי ליה. לישנא דקרא, דכתיב (שם): "ולנקבה עשרת שקלים", אלא "בן ובת" לישנא דמתניתין היא: בן עשרים ובת עשרים. אזבה ואיסק. לארעא דישראל לאתריה דרבי אלעזר בן פדת. ואגמר שמעתא. דרבי יצחק בר נחמני. מפומיה דמרא. רבי אלעזר.

## הדרן עלך יוצא דופן

**בא** סימן התחתון. שתי שערות סימן נערות. העליון. בושל. או חולצת. גדולה היא שהשערות סימן מובהק ועליהן סמכינן, ולקמן מפרש טעמא. אע"פ שאי אפשר. פרכינן בגמרא: והלא בא. אבל אי אפשר כו'. דהא ודאי מדאתא עליון תחתון נמי אתא אלא שנשרו. גמ' בא לר"מ. דכיון דאמר ר"מ לא חולצת, דקטנה היא, מכלל דס"ל אפשר לעליון לבא קודם לתחתון. וליתני בא העליון. עד שלא יבא התחתון, ולא ליתני "אע"פ שאי אפשר". רוב נשים תחתון אתי ברישא ומיעוט עליון. והאי דקאמר ר"מ: קטנה היא, משום דחייש למיעוטא שהעליון בא בקטנותה. ורבנן אזלו בתר רובא, הלכך מכי אתא עליון – לא בעיא בדיקה, דמסתמא תחתון אתא. וכיון דטעמייהו דרבנן משום רובא הוא, ה"מ בסתמא היכא דלא בדקו. אבל היכא דבדקו ולא אשכחו. תחתון. אימא מודו. דקטנה היא, וממיעוטא היא, קמ"ל כו'. שדים נכונו. והדר "ושערך צמח", אלמא עליון זימנין דקדים. בעשות ממצרים דדיך. שהיו מצרים משחקים בך, וממעכין דדיך. למען שדי נעוריך. כדי להתחנף ולזנות בך, כשתהיה ראויה לאשה ותבואי לימי נערות. "שדי" – לשון השלכה. כלומר, עדיין היו שערות נעוריך עומדים להתפלח ולנאת. אלמא, דדים קדמי. ומאי שדי. דמשמע, דעדיין היו לנאת. כולה בדדי כתיב. והאי "שדי" – לשון שדים.
איכרפו.

---

**ובשביעית** נמי יעבוד. *וא"ת: הא תינח שנת ששית, אלא בתחלה אימא: ל' יום לפני ראש השנה – יהיו חשובים שנה, ומשם ואילך ה' שנים שלמים? וי"ל: כיון דגלי קרא דששית הויא שנה שלמה, הוא הדין דראשונה בעינן שלמה. **רב** גידל אמר רב לערכין. וא"ת: כיון דבערכין מוקי לה, א"כ הדרא קושיא לדוכתין, דלרב גידל לא משכח רב תנא כוותיה! וי"ל: דקסבר, רב תנא הוא, ופליג. **אמר** ר"א הלכה כר' יוסי בן כיפר. וא"ת: והא רבי אלעזר גופיה פסיק בפ"ק (לעיל ח.) כרבי אליעזר בד' ותו לא? וכ"ת דהך דהכא לא חשיב, משום דר' יוסי בן כיפר קאי כוותיה, הא חשיב נמי התם ההיא דד' נשים, אע"ג דרבי יהושע קאי כוותיה! אלא משום דרבי יהושע מרבי אליעזר קבלה, הכא נמי רבי יוסי משמיה דרבי אליעזר קאמר לה! וי"ל: משום דהכא קאי רבי כוותיה, כדקאמר "וכן הורה רבי בלוד", ולא מכח רבי אליעזר פסיק. א"נ דוקא במשניות אמר בפ"ק דהלכתא כוותיה בארבע.

## הדרן עלך יוצא דופן

**בא** סימן. ר"מ אומר לא חולצת ולא מתיבמת. וא"ת: ולר' מאיר, למה הוזכר סימן העליון, כיון דלא סמכינן עליה. ולעיל נמי, דתנא "איזהו סימנים", ומפרש ר"ת: דאבוחל קאי? וי"ל: דאיצטריך לענין עונשים וקידושין ומילי טובא, דרוב פעמים תחתון אתי ברישא, כדקאמר בגמרא. וא"נ, אי חזינן עליון – מסתמא כבר בא התחתון, וגדולה היא, וצריכה גט לקדושין, וגם אסור באחותה. **וחכ"א** או חולצת או מתיבמת. אפילו היא קטנה [יבמות קה:] מתיבמת לרבנן דר"מ דלא חיישי למיעוטא גבי *ההיא ד"קטן וקטנה לא חולצין" כו'. אבל לחליצה – בעינן שתהא גדולה, כדאמר נמי התם: יפה אמרת שאין חולצין, "איש" כתיב בפרשה, ומקשינן אשה לאיש, ולית להו דרבי יוסי דאמר בפרק "מצות חליצה" (שם דף קה:) אשה בין גדולה בין קטנה.
רבן

---

ע' רש"א

א א מיי' פ"ב מהל' אישות הל"א סמג עשין נ טוש"ע אה"ע סי' קנה סעיף יב [וברב אלפס יבמות פי"ג דף מה]:

ב ב מיי' שם הל"ה:

### תוספי הרא"ש

**ובשביעית** נמי יעבוד. ותימה תינח שנה ששית א) דילפינן מהכא דבעינן שתמשך עבודתו עד שנה תחלת שביעית ולא אמרינן ל' יום ראש השנה חשוב שנה אבל בשנה ראשונה דלמא ל' יום לפני ר"ה חשוב שנה וי"ל כיון דגלי קרא דשנה ששית שלימה הה"נ שנה ראשונה: **אמר** רב גידל אמר רב לערכין. אי לערכין דוקא קאמר צ"ל דס"ל רב תנא הוא ופליג: א"ר אלעזר הלכה כר' יוסי בן כיפר. ותימה הא ר' אלעזר גופיה הוא דאמר דאין הלכה כר' אליעזר אלא בד' וכ"ת משום דאיכא ר' יוסי בן כיפר דקאי כותיה לא קא חשיב ליה הא ליתא דהא ההיא דד' נשים ר' יהושע קאי כותיה אלא משום דר' יהושע מר' אליעזר קבלה הכא נמי ר' יוסי בן כיפר משום ר' אליעזר אמרו וי"ל דהכא נמי איכא ר' דקאי כותיה כדאמרינן לעיל וכן הורה בלוד ולא מכח ר' אליעזר הורה א"נ דוקא במשניות הוא דאמר ר' אלעזר בפ"ק הלכה כר' אליעזר בארבע:

סליק פירקא

**ר"מ** אומר לא חולצת ולא מתייבמת. ותימה לר"מ למה הוזכר סימן העליון כיון דלא סמכינן עליה כלל. וי"ל דודאי סמכינן עליה לענין עונשין וקידושין כיון דרוב פעמים תחתון אתי ברישא כדאיתא בגמ' ור' מאיר הוא דחייש למיעוט להחמיר הילכך אינה חולצת ואינה מתייבמת עד שתביא סימן התחתון: **וחכ"א** [או] חולצת או מתייבמת. ה"ה דאפי' קטנה מתייבמת לרבנן דר"מ דלא חיישי למיעוט אבל לחליצה בעי גדולה כדאמרי ליה יפה אמרת שאין חולצין איש כתוב בפרשה:

א) נראה דצ"ל דילפינן מהכא שיהיה שנה שלמה ולפעמים נמשך עבודתו בתוך שנת השביעית ולא אמרינן וכו'.

### הגהות הב"ח

(א) גמ' ואנא ידענא דמשום: (ב) שם קמ"ל דאי אפשר אלא ודאי תחתון אתי ומנתר:

ג א מיי' פ"ב מהל' אישות הל"ח:
ד ב ג ד מיי' שם הל"כ וע' במ"מ וכ"מ וכל"מ סמג עשין טוש"ע אה"ע סי' קנה סעיף טו [וכרב אלפס יבמות פי"ג דף מה]:

איכרפו דדיך – לא הדרת בך, אישתדו דדיך – נמי לא הדרת בך. דכולי עלמא מיהא – אתחתון סמכינן, מנלן? אמר רב יהודה, אמר רב, וכן *תנא דבי ר' ישמעאל: אמר קרא °"איש או אשה כי יעשו מכל חטאות האדם" (במדבר ה) – השוה הכתוב אשה לאיש לכל עונשין שבתורה, מה איש – בסימן אחד, אף אשה – בסימן אחד. ואימא: או האי או האי! כאיש, מה איש – תחתון ולא עליון, אף אשה – תחתון ולא עליון. תניא נמי הכי, א"ר אליעזר בר' צדוק, כך היו מפרשין ביבנה, ואמרו: אכיון שבא תחתון – שוב אין משגיחין על עליון. תניא, רשב"ג אומר: בנות כרכים – תחתון ממהר לבא, מפני שרגילות במרחצאות. בנות כפרים – עליון ממהר לבא, מפני שטוחנות ברחים. ר"ש בן אלעזר אומר: בנות עשירים – צד ימין ממהר לבא, שנישוף באפקריסותן. בנות עניים – צד שמאל ממהר לבא, מפני ששואבות כדי מים עליהן, ואיבעית אימא: מפני שנושאין אחיהן על גססיהן. ת"ר: צד שמאל קודם לצד ימין, רבי חנינא בן אחי ר' יהושע אומר: מעולם לא קדם צד שמאל לצד ימין, חוץ מאחת שהיתה בשכונתי, שקדם צד שמאל לצד ימין, וחזר לאיתנו. ת"ר: בכל הנבדקות – נבדקות על פי נשים, גוכן היה רבי אליעזר מוסר לאשתו, ורבי ישמעאל מוסר לאמו. רבי יהודה אומר: לפני הפרק ולאחר הפרק – נשים בודקות אותן, תוך הפרק – אין נשים בודקות אותן, שאין משיאין ספקות על פי נשים. ר"ש אומר: דאף תוך הפרק – נשים בודקות אותן. ונאמנת אשה להחמיר אבל לא להקל. כיצד, "גדולה היא" – שלא תמאן, "קטנה היא" – שלא תחלוץ. אבל אין נאמנת לומר "קטנה היא" – שתמאן, ו"גדולה היא" – שתחלוץ. אמר מר, רבי יהודה אומר: לפני הפרק ולאחר הפרק – נשים בודקות אותן. בשלמא לפני הפרק – בעי בדיקה, דאי משתכחי לאחר הפרק – שומא נינהו. אלא לאחר הפרק למה לי בדיקה? והאמר רבא: *קטנה שהגיעה לכלל שנותיה – אינה צריכה בדיקה, חזקה הביאה סימנין! כי אמר רבא חזקה – למיאון אבל לחליצה – בעיא בדיקה. תוך הפרק אין נשים בודקות אותן, קסבר: תוך הפרק כלאחר הפרק (דמי), ולאחר הפרק דאיכא חזקה דרבא – סמכינן אנשים ובדקי, (א) תוך הפרק דליכא חזקה דרבא – לא סמכינן אנשים, ולא בדקי נשים. ר"ש אומר: אף תוך הפרק נשים בודקות אותן, קסבר: תוך הפרק – כלפני הפרק, ובעיא בדיקה, דאי משתכחי לאחר הפרק – שומא נינהו. ונאמנת אשה להחמיר אבל לא להקל. האי מאן קתני לה? איבעית אימא: רבי יהודה – ואתוך הפרק, ואיבעית

---

**רש"י**

איכרפו. כשהתחילו לגדל ולעקוץ. אישתדו. גדולות כל צרכן כשדים גמורים. לשון אחר: איכרפו – נפחו ממיעוך מלרים, כלומר: לקית על ידם. "אישתדו" יבשו. זאת מצאתי. איש. אין בו סימן עליון, שאין בו סימן דדים משפנים. תניא נמי הכי. דאתחתון סמכינן. שטוחנות ברחים. ומתוך שמנידות זרועותיהן תדיר, מתפשטים דדיהן. שנישוף. פריי"ד בלע"ז. כמו (יומא דף ל.): מלוה לשפשף. אפקריסותן. מעפורת, והוא סודר ותולה על דד הימין. אבל בנות עניים אין להן מעפורת. על גססיהן. על לדיהן. "על לד תנשאו" מתרגמינן: על גססיהן תתנטלון (ישעיה סו). לפני הפרק. קודם עונת נדרים. שאפילו הביאה – שומא נינהו, וקטנה היא. נשים בודקות אותן. דבין אמרו "איתנהו", בין אמרו "ליתנהו" – בקטנה מחזקינן לה, ולאו עלייהו סמכינן. ובדיקתן להכי מהניא, דאי משתכחי בה הני גופייהו לאחר הפרק – אמרינן: שומא נינהו, כדמפרש לקמן. ולאחר הפרק נמי, אי אמרי "איתנהו" – מהימני, וחלצה, דהא אורחא הוא למיהוי לה. ואי אמרי "ליתנהו" – לא ממאנת, דחיישינן שמא נשרו. הלכך אנשים לא סמכינן. תוך הפרק. דמספקא לאו גדולה היא, ואי משתכחי – מחזקינן לה בגדולה. אין נשים בודקות אותן. שאין נשים כדאי לסמוך עלייהו, להתיר ספקות על פיהן, ולומר: גדולה היא, שתחלוץ. וס"ל לרבי יהודה: הביאה שתי שערות תוך הפרק – סימן הוא כלאחר הפרק. הלכך, לא מהימנן. והכי מפרש לה לקמן. ר"ש אומר כו'. מפרש לקמן. דאי משתכחי. השתא אמרינן נמי לאחר הפרק: שומא נינהו, ולא חלצה, אי לא אתו בה אחריני. ולהכי הוא דמהימני (ב) למיאון, להחמיר שלא תמאן. אבל לחליצה בעיא בדיקה. והאשה נאמנת עליה, הואיל ולאחר הפרק הוה, ואורחא למיהוי לה. כדפרשינן לקמן לאחר הפרק, דאיכא חזקה דרבא, סמכינן אנשים. ה"ג: קסבר תוך הפרק כלאחר הפרק (דמי) ולאחר הפרק דאיכא חזקה כו'. והכי פירושא: תוך הפרק להכי לא מהימנא, דקסבר רבי יהודה: תוך הפרק אם הביאה – אמרינן: סימן הם, וגדולה היא. הלכך, אתי למשרי מידי דלאו אורחא ע"פ נשים דלאו כהלכתא. דאע"ג שנאמנות הן לאחר הפרק – התם הוא דאיכא חזקה דרבא, אבל תוך הפרק כו'. ר"ש אומר כלפני הפרק דמי. ושומא נינהו, הלכך לאו עלייהו סמכינן, למימר: גדולה היא או קטנה היא. ולהכי הוא דמהני – דאי משתכחי לאחר הפרק, שומא נינהו. הא מאן קתני לה. דהא (ג) אדר"ש – לא מתוקמא, דכיון דאמר: תוך הפרק – כלפני הפרק, אי בדקו לה תוך הפרק, מאי "גדולה היא שלא תמאן" איכא? והא אמרת: אפי' משתכחי – שומא נינהו! אי בעית אימא רבי יהודה. ואתוך הפרק דקאמר אין הנשים בודקות אותן, דתוך הפרק – כלאחר הפרק דמי, ואי לא בדקו שפיר – אתי למימר אקטנה דגדולה היא. וקמ"ל דלהחמיר – מהימנא. אבל לפני הפרק – ליכא למימר: גדולה שלא תמאן, דהא אפילו הביאה – דברי הכל, שומא נינהו. ולאחר הפרק – אפילו להקל קאמר רבי יהודה: מהימנא. ואיבעית

---

**תוספות**

רבן שמעון בן גמליאל אומר בנות כפרים כו'. פליג אדרבנן דאמרי: בכולהון ממהר לבא התחתון. ואדר"מ נמי פליג, דהא ר' מאיר לא מפליג בין כרכים לכפרים. בשלמא לפני הפרק כו' דאי משתכחי לאחר הפרק שומא נינהו. פירש בקונט' ולא תחלוץ. והדין עמו, א] דליכא לפרושי: שומא נינהו ותמאן, דהא קתני בסיפא דאינה נאמנת לומר "קטנה היא", ותמאן. וא"ת: אמאי בודקין אותה? לא תבדוק, ותחלוץ לאחר הפרק! דהא השתא סבר המקשן ד"חזקה דהביאה סימנין" דקאמר רבא, דהויא לחליצה. ולמאי דמשני נמי, דבחליצה בעי בדיקה, נבדוק אחר הפרק, ותו לא. דליכא למיחש שמא מלפני הפרק באו, והוו שומא, דהא דוקא כי ראו אותם לפני הפרק קאמר הכא דשומא נינהו, אבל אם לא ראו אותם מקודם – משמע דאין לנו לחוש. ובשלהי "מצות חליצה" (יבמות דף קה:) נמי דאמר ליה רבי לאבדן: זיל בדקה, מסתמא לא בדקוה לפני הפרק. וכן משמע בפרק "מי שמת" (ב"ב דף קנה.) גבי בני ברק, דקאמר: מהו לבודקו. אלמא אי משתכחי בהו סימנים, לא אמרינן דלפני הפרק באו! וי"ל: דהא דקאמר דבודקין אותן, היינו לכתחילה. א"נ "בודקין" לאו דוקא, אלא כלומר: דאם בדקו – דמהני בדיקתן קאמר. וא"ת: אמאי פריך, אלא לאחר הפרק למה לי בדיקה, הא נפקא מינה: שאם בדקו ולא מצאו שום שערות, או שמצאו אותן שערות עצמן – דאינה חולצת! כמו שאנו מפרשים בדיקה דלפני הפרק. ויש לומר: דהך בדיקה דלאחר הפרק, משמע ליה דהיינו להחזיקה כגדולה. דאי להחזיקה כקטנה א"כ תוך הפרק אמאי אינן נאמנות? השתא אחר הפרק – נאמנות, כ"ש – תוך הפרק! ולכך פריך: דבלא בדיקה נמי מחזקינן לה כגדולה.

איבעית אימא רבי יהודה ואתוך הפרק ואי בעית אימא ר' שמעון כו'. וא"ת: ומאי קאמר דנאמנת לומר "גדולה היא", שלא תמאן, מה צריך לנאמנות? הא בלאו הכי לא ממאנת! ואפילו אמרה "קטנה היא" – אינה נאמנת, כדקתני סיפא: אבל אינה נאמנת לומר "קטנה היא" ותמאן. וי"ל: דנפקא מינה, שאם בדקו אנשים אחר בדיקתה, ולא מצאו שערות אפ"ה לא תמאן. ואי לאו נשים – הוה ממאנת שפיר, דאפילו למ"ד חוששים שמא נשרו, היינו דוקא לאחר הפרק לר' יהודה, משום דרבא דחזקה שהביאה סימנין. אבל תוך הזמן, לרבי יהודה, דליכא חזקה, או אחר זמן, לר"ש ב] דלית ליה חזקה דרבא – אין חוששין שמא נשרו. והשתא שאמרו הנשים שהיו שערות – נאמנות, ולא תמאן. ואע"ג דאפילו תוך הזמן לר' יהודה דליכא חזקה, או אחר זמן לר"ש אינה ממאנת – אהני חזקה דרבא, לבדקו ולא מצאו שערות, דמשום חזקה אמרינן דנשרו, כדפסיק לעיל: והילכתא, חוששין שמא נשרו, והוא שבעל לאחר זמן. וא"ת: ונאמנת לומר "קטנה היא" שלא תחלוץ, מאי אהני נאמנת, הלא אפילו אמרה "יש שערות" – אינה נאמנת, כדקתני סיפא: אינה נאמנת לומר "גדולה היא" כו'! °וי"ל: דנאמנת לומר שאותן שערות היו קודם הפרק. דאי לאו האשה, הוה אמינא: אחר הפרק באו, ותלנה, *) כדפריך לעיל.

ואיבעית

*) נ"ל כדפריכית

---

**תוספי הרא"ש**

ר"ג אומר בנות כפרים עליון ממהר לבא. פליג אדרבנן דקאמרי אי אפשר ולא קא מפליגי ופליג נמי אדר' מאיר דאמר אפשר ולא מפליג בין כרכין לכפרים: כיצד גדולה היא שלא תמאן. תימה אמאי אהני נאמנות דידה דבלא בדיקה דידה לא ממאנה דחיישינן שמא הביאה סימנין לר' יהודה תוך הפרק ולר' שמעון אחר הפרק ותו אפי' אי אמרה ליכא שערות לא מהימנא כדקתני סיפא ואינה נאמנת לומר קטנה היא שתמאן כ"ש דאם אמרה דאיכא שערות. שלא תמאן וי"ל דנפקא מינה דאי אמרה איכא שערות ואח"כ בדקוה אנשים ואמרו דליכא שערות ואימר נשרו ולא תמאן אבל אי לאו דיבורה הויא ממאנת אפי' למ"ד חוששין שמא נשרו ה"מ לאחר הפרק דאיכא חזקה דרבא אבל תוך הפרק לא: וקטנה היא שלא תחלוץ. תימה אמאי אהני נאמנות דידה ממילא לא חלצה. ועוד אפי' אומרת דיש שערות לא חלצה כדקתני סיפא אינה נאמנת לומר גדולה היא שתחלוץ כ"ש שאם אמרה קטנה היא שלא תחלוץ. וי"ל דאהני נאמנות דידה לומר דהני שערות היו קודם הפרק ולא תחלוץ ואי לאו דיבורה ה"א לאחר הפר' באו וחולצת. ותימה תוך הפרק אמאי אין נאמנת לר' יהודה לומר קטנה שתמאן. ועוד אפי' בסתמא נמי תמאן דהא כי אמר רבא חזקה הביאה סימנין ולא תמאן בסתמא היינו לאחר הפרק שכבר הגיעה לכלל אבל תוך הפרק תמאן בסתמא כ"ש אם בדקוה נשים ואמרו אין לה שערות שתמאן וכן לר' שמעון אחר הפרק תמאן אפי' בסתמא כיון דלית ליה חזקה דרבא וכ"ש על פי נשים וי"ל דלעולם לא ממאנת בסתמא כיון דלית ליה חזקה והה"נ על פי נשים. והא דאמר רבא דדוקא הגיעה לכלל שנותיה אמרינן חזקה הביאה סימנין אבל קודם לכן לא היינו כשבעל דאפי' בדקוה אנשים ולא מצאו שערות אינה ממאנת דאמרינן חזקה הביאה שערות ונשרו אבל תוך הפרק אפי' בעל ובדקוה אנשים ולא מצאו שערות ממאנ' ולא חיישינן שמא נשרו:

---

בשלמא לפני הפרק בעי' בדיקה כו'. הא דקאמר בעי' בדיקה לאו דוקא דכי נמי לא בדקוה לפני הפרק ובדקו לאחר הפרק ומצאו סימנין אין לנו לחוש שמא לפני הפרק היו ושומא נינהו וכן מוכח בהדיא דקאמר דאי משתכחי לאחר הפרק שומא נינהו דמשמע דוקא משום דראו אותם שהיו באין לפני הפרק ולכך אינה חולצת הא לא ראו אותם קודם אין לחוש. וכן בשילהי פ' מצות חליצה דא"ל ר' לאבדן זיל בדקה ומסתמא לא בדקוה לפני הפרק וכן בפרק מי שמת גבי בני ברק דקאמר מהו לבודקו אלמא אי אשכחן ביה סימנין לא אמרינן לפני הפרק באו ובעיא בדיקה דקאמר הכא היינו דמהניא בדיקתה ומיהו דבר פשוט אם תמצא לומר דחיישינן שמא לפני הפרק באו היכא דחזינן ריבוי שערות הרבה לא חיישינן שמא כולם לפני הפרק באו: **אלא** לאחר הפרק למה לי כו'. תימה מאי ק' ליה לימא (דאם) נפקא מינה דאם אומרת שאין שערות דאינה חולצת כעין שאנו מפרשים בדיקה דלפני הפרק דאינה צריכה אלא דאי מתרמי הכי וי"ל דמשמע ליה דנשים בודקות אותן דנאמנות להעיד שיש שערות דאי להחזיקה בקטנה אפי' תוך הפרק נמי הילך צריך למצוא נפקותא באמירת הנשים יותר מאם היו שותקות א) הייתי אומר דלאחר הפרק באו אבל לאחר הפרק דל עדותן מהכא הא סמכינן אחזקה דרבא: **ר'** שמעון אומר אף תוך הפרק כו'. אומר ר"ח דהלכה כר' שמעון כדמוכח לעיל פ' יוצא דופן דמסיק תיובתא למ"ד תוך זמן כלאחר זמן ואין חושש לומר דתנא דשמעתין דאמר תוך הפרק כלאחר הפרק ומתוך כך פסק דאין הלכה כרבא דאמר חזקה הביאה סימנין דהא ר' שמעון דהילכתא כוותיה קאמר דלית ליה חזקה דרבא. ועוד אמרינן בפ' מי שמת אמר רב נחמן בודקין לחליצה ולמיאונין ולגירושין ואין נראה ראיה מזה (הפסק) [לפסוק] דלא כרבא דאע"ג דקי"ל כר' שמעון בהא דתוך הפרק כלפני הפרק אין הלכה כמותו בהא דלית ליה דרבא דתרי מילי נינהו. ורבא גופיה הוא דפסיק לעיל הלכתא תוך זמן כלפני זמן. והקשה ר"ת על פרש"י דפי' דתוך הפרק ותוך הזמן חדא מילתא היא דאמאי קרי ליה לעיל זמן והכא קרי ליה פרק. ועוד דפרק משמע סמוך לגדלות ממש כי ההיא דשבת פרק המוציא בנות ישראל שהגיעו לפירקן. וביבמות פ' הבא על יבמתו ומשיאן סמוך לפירקן. ועוד אמאי איתותב לעיל מ"ד תוך זמן כלאחר זמן כיון דפליגי הכא תנאי. (ועוד) ומפרש ר"ת דפליגי ביום אחרון של שנת י"ב לנקבה וי"ג לזכר ואותו יום קרוי תוך הפרק ולר' יהודה הוי זמן הבאת שערות מתחלת היום ולר' שמעון מסופו. וכה"ג אשכחן פלוגתא בעשרה יוחסין גבי קדשה אביה בדרך והיא עצמה בעיר ביומא דמישלם שית והלכה כר' (יוסי) [יהודה] לגבי ר' שמעון כדאיתא בפ' מי שהוציאוהו:

א) נראה דחסר כאן וצ"ל בשלמא לפני הפרק בעי בדיקה דאי משתכחי וכו' שומא ננהו דאי לאו עדותן הייתי אומר וכו'.

---

**מסורת הש"ס**

יבמות פב: כ"ק טו. תמורה ב: קדושין לה. פסחים מג. סוכה כח:

[לעיל מו.]

**הגהות הב"ח**

(א) גמ' סמכינן אנשים ובדקי נשים תוך: (ב) רש"י ד"ה דאי משתכחי וכו' הוא דמהמני הס"ד: (ג) ד"ה הא מאן קתני לה דהא כדר"ש:

**גליון הש"ס**

תוס' ד"ה איבעית וכו' וי"ל דנאמנת לומר שאותן שערות. תמוה לי הא בזה מתרלא גם קושייתם הראשונה וכפשוטו דבאמת בלאו חזקה דרבא ממאנת והכל מיירי בחד ענין דכמו לענין חליצה במה דאמרי' נאמנת לומר קטנה שלא תחלוץ היינו בבדקו ומצאו ב' שערות נאמנת שהם שומא שלא תחלוץ והיא דאינה נאמנת שתחלוץ היינו דלא נבדקה ע"י אנשים א"נ לומר שהביאו ב' שערות שתחלוץ וה"נ מפרשה הכי למיאון והכל בחד גוונא. דהיינו בבדקו ומצאו ב' שערות וכן אומרים שהם שומא נאמנות לחומרא שלא תחלוץ וא"נ לומר שתמאן והיכא דלא בדקו אותה וכן אומרות שהביאו ב' שערות נאמנות לחומרא שלא תמאן אבל לא להקל שתחלוץ ומכוון שמעתא טובא:

**הגהות מהר"ב רנשבורג**

א] תוס' ד"ה בשלמא וכו' דליכא לפרושי שומא נינהו ותמאן. נ"ב עיין מהרלב"ח ח"א סי' כו ובב"ש סי' קנה ס"ק כט: ב] ד"ה איבעית אימא וכו' דלית ליה חזקה דרבא אין חוששין. נ"ב עיין שו"ת הריב"ש סי' קפב:

ה א ב מיי' פ"ו מהל' פרה אדומה הל"ז ופי"ט מהל' כלים הל"א והל"ב:

ו ג מיי' פי"ט מהל' כלים הלכה א:

וְאִיבָּעֵית אֵימָא: רַבִּי שִׁמְעוֹן, (א) וּלְאַחַר הַפֶּרֶק, וְלֵית לֵיהּ חֲזָקָה דְּרָבָא.§ "מִפְּנֵי שֶׁאָמְרוּ אֶפְשָׁר" כו'.§ הָא תּוּ לָמָּה לִי? הָא תָּנָא לֵיהּ רֵישָׁא! *וְכִי תֵּימָא: מִשּׁוּם דְּקָא בָּעֵי לְמִסְתְּמָה כְּרַבָּנַן – פְּשִׁיטָא, *יָחִיד וְרַבִּים הֲלָכָה כְּרַבִּים! מַהוּ דְּתֵימָא: מִסְתַּבְּרָא טַעֲמָא דְּר"מ דְּקָא מְסַיֵּיעַ לֵיהּ קְרָאֵי, קמ"ל. וְאִיבָּעֵית אֵימָא: מִשּׁוּם דְּקָא בָּעֵי לְמִתְנֵי "כַּיּוֹצֵא בּוֹ".§ **מתני'** כַּיּוֹצֵא בּוֹ: כָּל כְּלִי חֶרֶס שֶׁהוּא מַכְנִיס – מוֹצִיא, וְיֵשׁ שֶׁמּוֹצִיא וְאֵינוֹ מַכְנִיס. כָּל אֵבֶר שֶׁיֵּשׁ בּוֹ צִפּוֹרֶן – יֵשׁ בּוֹ עֶצֶם, וְיֵשׁ שֶׁיֵּשׁ בּוֹ עֶצֶם וְאֵין בּוֹ צִפּוֹרֶן. *כָּל הַמְטַמֵּא מִדְרָס – מְטַמֵּא טְמֵא מֵת, וְיֵשׁ שֶׁמְּטַמֵּא טְמֵא מֵת וְאֵינוֹ מְטַמֵּא מִדְרָס.§ **גמ'** [א]מַכְנִיס – פָּסוּל לְמֵי חַטָּאת, וּפָסוּל מִשּׁוּם גַּסְטְרָא, מוֹצִיא – כָּשֵׁר לְמֵי חַטָּאת, וּפָסוּל מִשּׁוּם גַּסְטְרָא. *אָמַר רַב אַסִי, [ב]שׁוֹנִין: כְּלִי חֶרֶס – שִׁיעוּרוֹ בְּכוֹנֵס מַשְׁקֶה, וְלֹא אָמְרוּ "מוֹצִיא מַשְׁקֶה" – אֶלָּא לְעִנְיַן גַּסְטְרָא בִּלְבַד. מַאי טַעְמָא? אָמַר מָר זוּטְרָא בְּרֵיהּ דְּרַב נַחְמָן: לְפִי שֶׁאֵין אוֹמְרִים "הָבֵא גַּסְטְרָא לְגַסְטְרָא". תָּנוּ רַבָּנַן: [ג]כֵּיצַד בּוֹדְקִין כְּלִי חֶרֶס לֵידַע אִם נִיקַּב בְּכוֹנֵס מַשְׁקֶה אִם לָאו? יָבִיא עֲרֵיבָה מְלֵאָה מַיִם וְנוֹתֵן קְדֵרָה לְתוֹכָהּ, אִם כָּנְסָה – בְּיָדוּעַ שֶׁכּוֹנֵס מַשְׁקֶה, וְאִם לָאו – בְּיָדוּעַ שֶׁמּוֹצִיא מַשְׁקֶה. רַבִּי

[לעיל ל:] [ברכות ט. וש"נ] סוכה כ. [לעיל מג:] [שבת נו.]

### רש"י

וְאִיבָּעֵית אֵימָא ר"ש (ב) וּלְאַחַר הַפֶּרֶק. קָאֵי, דְּקָאָמַר ר"ש: תּוֹךְ הַפֶּרֶק בּוֹדְקוֹת וְלָא חָיְישִׁינַן לְמִסְמַךְ עֲלַיְיהוּ לַחֲלִיצָה וּלְמֵיאוּן, דְּהָא אֲפִי' מִשְׁתַּכְחִי – כִּלְפְנֵי הַפֶּרֶק דָּמֵי, וּקְטַנָּה הִיא. אֲבָל לְאַחַר הַפֶּרֶק, דְּאִי מִשְׁתַּכְחִי, סִימָן נִינְהוּ, וְשָׁרֵינַן לָהּ – לָא מְהֵימְנִי אֶלָּא לְהַחְמִיר, דְּלֵית לֵיהּ חֲזָקָה דְּרָבָא. לְמִסְתְּמָה כְּרַבָּנַן. דְּהָא "מִפְּנֵי שֶׁאָמְרוּ" סְתָמָא הִיא, וְקמ"ל סְתָם מִשְׁנָה כְּרַבָּנַן דְּאָמְרִי "אִי אֶפְשָׁר". קְרָאֵי. "שָׁדַיִם נָכוֹנוּ", "בַּעְשׂוֹת מִמִּצְרַיִם דַּדָּיִךְ". **מתני'** שֶׁהוּא מַכְנִיס. מַשְׁקֶה, כְּשֶׁמַּנִּיחוֹ עַל הַמַּיִם. יֵשׁ בּוֹ נֶקֶב גָּדוֹל, שֶׁהַמַּיִם נִכְנָסִין לְתוֹכוֹ. מוֹצִיא. כָּל שֶׁכֵּן אִם נוֹתֵן הַמַּיִם לְתוֹכוֹ – יוֹצֵא הַמַּשְׁקֶה לַחוּץ. וְיֵשׁ. נֶקֶב קָטָן, שֶׁמּוֹצִיא וְאֵינוֹ מַכְנִיס. וּבַגְּמָרָא מְפָרֵשׁ מַאי נָפְקָא מִינָּהּ. כָּל אֵבֶר. אֶצְבַּע יְתֵרָה. שֶׁיֵּשׁ בּוֹ צִפּוֹרֶן יֵשׁ בּוֹ עֶצֶם. וְהָוֵי אֵבֶר חָשׁוּב. וּמְטַמֵּא בְּאֹהֶל, אֲפִי' אֵין בּוֹ שִׁיעוּר. דְּקַיְימָא לָן: *הָאֵבָרִים אֵין לָהֶם שִׁיעוּר, אֲפִי' פָּחוֹת מִכַּזַּיִת מִן הַמֵּת. וְיֵשׁ שֶׁיֵּשׁ בּוֹ עֶצֶם כו'. לָא הָוֵי אֵבֶר אִם יְתֶרֶת הִיא, אֲבָל אֵינָהּ שֶׁל יְתֶרֶת אֲפִי' אֵין בּוֹ צִפּוֹרֶן, אֵבֶר הוּא, וּמְטַמֵּא. כָּל הַמְטַמֵּא בְּמִדְרַס הַזָּב מְטַמֵּא בְּמֵת. כִּדְמְפָרֵשׁ בַּגְּמָרָא: שֶׁאֵין לְךָ כְּלִי הָרָאוּי לְמוֹשַׁב הַזָּב שֶׁאֵין שֵׁם כְּלִי עָלָיו, וְרָאוּי לְקַבֵּל כָּל טוּמְאוֹת. וְהָא דְּנָקַט טְמֵא מֵת – מִשּׁוּם דּוּמְיָא דְּמִדְרָס הוּא, דְּאָב הַטּוּמְאָה הוּא. וְהָכִי קָאָמַר: כָּל הָרָאוּי לִהְיוֹת אָב הַטּוּמְאָה בְּמִדְרַס הַזָּב – רָאוּי לִהְיוֹת אָב הַטּוּמְאָה, אִם נָגַע בְּמֵת אוֹ נִטְמָא בְּאֹהֶל הַמֵּת. וְיֵשׁ. שֶׁהוּא כְּלִי גָּמוּר לְקַבֵּל כָּל טוּמְאוֹת, וְנַעֲשֶׂה אָב הַטּוּמְאָה עַל יְדֵי מֵת, וְאֵינוֹ נַעֲשֶׂה אָב הַטּוּמְאָה עַל יְדֵי הַזָּב בְּמִדְרָס, כִּדְמְפָרֵשׁ בַּגְּמָרָא. **גמ'** לְמֵי חַטָּאת. לְקַדֵּשׁ בּוֹ מֵי חַטָּאת. דְּרַחֲמָנָא אָמַר (במדבר יט): "מַיִם חַיִּים אֶל כֶּלִי", וְהַאי לָאו "כְּלִי" הוּא. וּפָסוּל מִשּׁוּם גַּסְטְרָא. כְּלוֹמַר, כָּל שֶׁכֵּן אִם נִקְּבָה גַּסְטְרָא בְּכוֹנֵס מַשְׁקֶה – בָּטֵיל לָהּ מִתּוֹרַת גַּסְטְרָא, וּטְהוֹרָה מִכָּל טוּמְאָה. דְּהָא אֲפִי' כְּלִי שָׁלֵם, מִכִּי נָקֵיב כְּכוֹנֵס מַשְׁקֶה – בָּטֵיל לֵיהּ. גַּסְטְרָא. הַיְינוּ שִׁבְרֵי כְּלִי חֶרֶס הָרְאוּיִין לִמְלָאכָה, וַעֲדַיִין מְקַבְּלִין טוּמְאָה, כִּדְתַנְיָא בַּגְּמָרָא ב"אֵלּוּ טְרֵפוֹת" (חולין דף נד:): הַדַּקִּין שֶׁבִּכְלֵי חֶרֶס, הֵן וְקַרְקְרוֹתֵיהֶן וְדוּפְנוֹתֵיהֶן יוֹשְׁבִין שֶׁלֹּא מְסוּמָּכִין, שִׁיעוּרָן – כְּדֵי סִיכַת קָטָן עַד לוֹג. וּמִלּוֹג עַד סְאָה – בִּרְבִיעִית כו'. מוֹצִיא. דְּנֶקֶב קָטָן הוּא. כָּשֵׁר לְמֵי חַטָּאת. דִּכְלִי שָׁלֵם בְּנֶקֶב קָטָן כּוּלֵּי הַאי – לָא בָּטֵיל. וּפָסוּל מִשּׁוּם גַּסְטְרָא. גַּסְטְרָא שֶׁנִּקְּבָה, אֲפִילּוּ כְּמוֹצִיא מַשְׁקֶה – בָּטְלָה לָהּ. שׁוֹנִין. הֲלָכָה לְמֹשֶׁה מִסִּינַי. שִׁיעוּרוֹ בְּכוֹנֵס מַשְׁקֶה. פָּחוֹת שֶׁל שִׁיעוּרִים הַמְבַטְּלִים אוֹתוֹ מִהְיוֹת כְּלִי. "כּוֹנֵס מַשְׁקֶה" הוּא שִׁיעוּר הָרִאשׁוֹן שֶׁהוּא מְבַטְּלוֹ מִהְיוֹת כְּלִי, לְמֵי חַטָּאת. כִּדְאָמַר בְּמַסֶּכֶת שַׁבָּת (דף צה.), חָמֵשׁ מִדּוֹת בִּכְלֵי חֶרֶס: [נִיקַּב כְּמוֹצִיא מַשְׁקֶה – טָהוֹר מִלְּטַמֵּא גַּסְטְרָא, וַעֲדַיִין כְּלִי הוּא לְקַדֵּשׁ בּוֹ מֵי חַטָּאת] נִיקַּב כְּכוֹנֵס מַשְׁקֶה – פָּסוּל לְקַדֵּשׁ בּוֹ מֵי חַטָּאת, וַעֲדַיִין כְּלִי הוּא לְכָל שְׁאָר דְּבָרִים; נִיקַּב כְּשׁוֹרֶשׁ קָטָן – טָהוֹר לְהַכְשִׁיר זְרָעִים, וַעֲדַיִין כְּלִי הוּא לְטוּמְאָה, שֶׁהֲרֵי רָאוּי לְקַבֵּל בּוֹ זֵיתִים; נִיקַּב כְּמוֹצִיא זַיִת – טָהוֹר מִטּוּמְאָה שֶׁקִּבֵּל, עַד שֶׁיְּיַחֲדֶנּוּ לְרִמּוֹנִים. נִיקַּב כְּמוֹצִיא רִמּוֹן – טָהוֹר מִכְּלוּם. נִמְצָא כּוֹנֵס מַשְׁקֶה הוּא שִׁיעוּר הָרִאשׁוֹן, אֲבָל כְּמוֹצִיא מַשְׁקֶה – לָא בָּטֵיל. וְלֹא אָמְרוּ מוֹצִיא מַשְׁקֶה. בָּטֵיל אֶלָּא לְעִנְיַן גַּסְטְרָא בִּלְבָד, אע"פ שֶׁאֵינוֹ מַכְנִיס. לְפִי שֶׁאֵין אוֹמְרִים "הָבֵא גַּסְטְרָא לְגַסְטְרָא", כְּשֶׁנִּיקְּבָה כְּמוֹצִיא מַשְׁקֶה – שׁוּב אֵין חָס עָלֶיהָ, וְאֵינוֹ מִשְׁתַּמֵּשׁ בָּהּ. שֶׁאֵין אוֹמֵר: "הָבֵא גַּסְטְרָא אַחֶרֶת, וְנַנִּיחַ תַּחַת גַּסְטְרָא זוֹ, לְקַבֵּל מַשְׁקֶה הַיּוֹצֵא". אֲבָל בִּכְלִי שָׁלֵם שֶׁנִּקַּב כְּמוֹצִיא מַשְׁקֶה – לָא בָּטֵיל מִכְּלוּם, לְפִי שֶׁהוּא חָס עָלָיו, וְאֵינוֹ שׁוֹבְרוֹ, וּמִשְׁתַּמֵּשׁ בּוֹ. וּמֵבִיא גַּסְטְרָא, וּמַנִּיחַ תַּחְתָּיו לְקַבֵּל מַשְׁקֶה הַיּוֹצֵא. אם כָּנְסָה. אִם נִכְנַס מַשְׁקֶה לְתוֹכָהּ.

ר'

### תוספות

**ואיבעית** אימא רבי שמעון ולאחר הפרק ולית ליה חזקה דרבא. ר"ח פוסק: דהלכה כרבי שמעון, דתוך הפרק כלפני הפרק, כדמסקינן שלהי "יוצא דופן" (לעיל דף מו.) וההוא דאית ליה דתוך הזמן כלאחר זמן איתותב לעיל. °ומתוך כך פסק נמי דאין הלכה כרבא, דאמר: חזקה הביאה סימנין. דהא ר' שמעון, דפסקינן כוותיה, לית ליה דרבא. ועוד: בפרק "מי שמת" (ב"ב דף קנו.) אמר רב נחמן: בודקין לחליצה ולמיאונים. ואין נראה, דאפילו יהיה הלכה כר' שמעון בהא דתוך הפרק כלפני הפרק, אין הלכה כמותו בהא דלית ליה חזקה דרבא, דלאו הא בהא תליא. ורבא גופיה פסיק לעיל דתוך הזמן כלפני זמן. והא דמוקי התלמוד ברייתא כרבי שמעון ולית ליה דרבא, אע"ג דאתי שפיר כרבי יהודה וכרבא, אין זו ראייה מן התלמוד (ג)דמיישב הברייתא בכל ענין. ודרב נחמן נמי ליתא מקמי רבא, דהוי בתרא. ועוד: דרבא נמי איכא לאוקומי מילתיה דרב נחמן דאמר "בודקין למיאונין" היינו תוך הפרק, דליכא חזקה. אי נמי: אחר הפרק, ובודקין אם לא ימלאו שערות – תמאן, דאין חוששין שמא נשרו אלא כשבעל אחר זמן. ורבא איירי בשבעל. ומעשים בכל יום דסמכינן אבדיקת נשים לאחר הפרק, והיינו דלא כר"ש. ואפי' בתוך הפרק כלפני הפרק, אומר רבי דאין הלכה כרבי שמעון. דעל כרחך "תוך הזמן" ו"תוך הפרק" לאו חדא מילתא הוא. דאי חדא מילתא הוא, א"כ אמאי איתותבו לעיל רבי יוחנן ורבי יהושע בן לוי, דאמרי תוך הזמן כלאחר הזמן, כיון דפליגי הכא תנאי? ועוד: דלעיל קרי ליה "זמן", והכא קרי ליה "פרק". ועוד: "פרק" משמע גדלות, כמו (יבמות דף סב:) המשיאן סמוך לפרקן, ובפרק "המוליא יין" (שבת דף פ:) בנות ישראל שהגיעו לפרקן. ו"לא הגיעו" – פירוש: הביאו ב' שערות, ולא הגיעו לכלל שנים. ומפרש רבינו תם: דפליגי הכא ביום אחרון של שנת י"ב ויום אחד לנקבה, או ביום שנת י"ג ויום אחד לזכר. ואותו יום אקרי "תוך הפרק" דלר' יהודה הוי זמן הבאת שערות מתחלת היום, ולרבי שמעון בסופו. וקי"ל כרבי יהודה לגבי רבי שמעון, בפרק "מי שהוציאוהו" (עירובין דף מו:) והשתא יבם קטן, או יבמה קטנה, שבאו לחלוץ – טוב לכתחלה לבודקם לפני הפרק אם יש להם שערות, וכן לאחר הפרק. ואם הן אותן שהיו קודם – נמתין עד שיביאו שערות אחרות. אבל יבם גדול ויבמה גדולה, דלא אפשר עוד לברר – חולצין שפיר אם יש להם שערות, ואין לחוש שמא לפני הפרק באו, כדפירשתי לעיל. ואם יש ליבמה דדים גדולים – אין צריך לבדוק אחר השערות, דהא אמרינן לעיל: אי אפשר שיבא העליון עד שיבא התחתון. **כשר** למי חטאת. והא דאמרינן (יומא דף ב.) שכל מעשיה בכלי גללים, בכלי אבנים, בכלי אדמה – היינו בזמן שמזין על כהן השורפה, שהחמירו שם, לפי שהקילו לטמאותה לשחטה בטבול יום להוציא מלבן של צדוקים א). **אלא** לענין גסטרא. פירש ר"ח: ב)"גסטרא" הוא שבר בלשון יון. ונראה דאין שבר כלי חרס טמא משום גסטרא, אלא א"כ יחדו. דהא אפילו שלם, כשניקב בכונס משקה – טהור, עד שייחדנו לאוכלין. כ"ש אם נשבר לגמרי, דבעו השברים יחוד. וא"ת: והא דתנן ג) ומייתי לה בפרק "אלו טרפות" (חולין דף נד:) הדקין שבכלי חרס, הן וקרקרותיהן ודופנותיהן – שיעורן בכדי סיכת קטן עד לוג, ומלוג עד סאה ברביעית כו', כיון דאיירי ע"י יחוד, אפילו שבר מכלי גדול יהא שיעורו בכדי סיכת קטן! וי"ל: דאין דרך לייחד שבר קטן הבא מכלי גדול, ובטלה דעתו אצל כל בני אדם. ואם תאמר: הא דתניא בתוספתא דכלים ס"פ "מחט וטבעת": ושולי המחלין וקרקעות הכלים – אין ממלאים, ואין מקדשין בהם. שפאן ועשאן כלי – מקדשין בהן כו', דברי ר"מ. וחכ"א: כלי שטהר שעה אחת – אין לו טומאה עולמית. *ואין לומר: דכשצריך תקון – תו לא נחית ליה טומאה, דהתנן במסכת כלים (פ"ה מ"ה) חתכו חוליות פחות מד' טפחים – טהור, מרחו בטיט – מקבל טומאה משיסיקנו לאפות בו סופגנין. אלמא מהני בה תיקון, ולא מסתברא דאתיא כר"מ ולא כרבנן! וי"ל: דמה שאין לו טומאה לעולם – היינו בשברים הפחותים משיעור המפורש בחולין (דף נה.) ומחמת גריעותם לא מהני תקון בהן, אבל הך דתנור – מיירי דע"י תקון הוא כבתחלה. **אם** כנסה בידוע שהוא כבונס משקה. והא דאמר בפרק "כל הבשר" (חולין דף קז.) אי בזיע דוולא ככונס משקה – מילף לייפי, ומטבילין בו הידים דהוו מחוברין לנהר, לאו היינו ככונס משקה דהכא. דהתם איירי כשהנקב כל כך גדול, עד שהמים מקלחין, והוי חבור ע"י נצוק לידים, דאע"ג דלענין טבילה, לא הוי חבור. וכונס משקה דהכא – שיורד טיף טיף, כדאמר בסמוך. מיהו אפשר דההוא כונס משקה הוי כדהכא, דהתם נמי מייתי האי כונס משקה דהכא, דאמר רבא: כלי שניקב בכונס משקה – אין נוטלין הימנו לידים. משמע דשוין. ואע"ג דלא הוי נצוק, דבדבר מועט הוי חבור לענין טבילת ידים. וגם רש"י לא הזכיר שם נצוק. ואע"ג דבכולי שמעתין במתניתין ובברייתא לא קאמר כונס משקה אלא בכלי חרס, ובסוף "המצניע" (שבת דף צה:) נמי קאמר: ה' מדות בכלי חרס, משמע דדווקא בכלי חרס הן כל אותם מדות ולא בכלי עץ מ"מ הא דרבא דאמר בפ' "כל הבשר": כלי שנקב בכונס משקה – אין נוטלין הימנו לידים, יש להחמיר בכל הכלים שניקבו ככונס משקה שלא ליטול מהם, כיון שלא הזכיר שם כלי חרס, אלא קאמר "כלי" סתם.

יש

א) [וע"ע תוס' חגיגה כג. ד"ה שפופרת] ב) [עי' בערוך גסטר א'] ג) [כלים פ"ב מ"ב]

### תוספי הרא"ש

**בשר** למי חטאת. והא דאמרינן כל מעשיה בכלי גללים כלי אדמה נעשית היינו בז' ימים שמזין כל כהן השורף את הפרה והחמירו שם לפי שהקילו לטמאותו להוציא מלבן של צדוקין: **אלא** לענין גסטרא מפ' ר"ח זהו שבר בלשון יון ונראה שאין שבר כלי חרס מטמא משום גסטרא אלא א"כ יחדו לאוכלין א)כ"ש נשבר לגמרי שהשבר צריך יחוד (ותימה) [וא"ת] והא דתנן במס' כלים ומייתי לה בפרק אלו טריפות הדקין שבכלי חרס הן ודפנותיהן שיעורן בכדי סיכת קטן. ועד לוג ומלוג עד סאה ברביעית. וכיון דאיירי ע"י יחוד אפי' הגדול שבהן יהא שיעורו כדי סיכת קטן וי"ל כיון דאין דרך לייחד שבר כלי גדול כשהן קטנים כל כך בטלה דעתו. ומיהו קשה מהא דתניא בתוספתא דכלים גבי קרקרו' הכלי ודופנותיהן שיפן ועשאן כלי מקבלין טומאה מכאן ולהבא דברי ר' מאיר וחכ"א כל כלי חרס שטהור שעה אחת שוב אין לו טומאה עולמית. והכא אמרינן אע"ג דטהור לגמרי יש לו טומאה ע"י יחוד וכן בניקב כמוציא זית טהור מלקבל זיתים ועדיין כלי הוא לקבל רמונים ופרש"י דאם יחדו לרמונים מקבל טומאה מכאן ולהבא. וי"ל דודאי כשאינו צריך תיקון נחתא לידי טומאה ע"י יחוד וההיא תוספ' דאין לו טומאה לעולם היינו כשצריך (טומאה) תיקון. ותימה הא דתנן במס' כלים חתכו חוליות פחות מד' טפחים טהור מירחו בטיט מקבל טומאה משיסיקנו לאפות בו סופגנין אלמא מועיל בו תיקון ולא מיסתבר לאוקומי כר' מאיר אלא כרבנן וי"ל דהא דאמרי רבנן דאין לו טומאה לעולם היינו בשברים קטנים פחותים משיעור המפורש בחולין דמחמת גריעותן לא מהני בהו תיקון אבל הך דתנור מיירי שהוא כלי חשוב כמתחלה ע"י תיקונו: **ביצד** בודקין כלי חרס לידע אם ניקב בכונס משקה. כולי שמעתי' מדבר כלי חרס לענין כונס משקה וכן בפ' המצניע דקאמר רבא חמש מדות בכלי חרס ניקב בכונס משקה דדוקא כלי חרס מתבטל מתורת כלי שניקב בכונס משקה אבל של עץ ושל מתכת לא והא דאמר רבא בפ' כל הבשר כלי שניקב בכונס משקה אין נוטלים ממנו לידים היינו דוקא כלי חרס אבל משאר כלים נוטלין אע"פ שניקב בכונס משקה מ"מ צריך להחמיר כיון דנקט התם כלי סתם:

### הגהות הב"ח

(א) גמ' רבי שמעון ולאחר הפרק: (ב) רש"י ד"ה ואיבעית אימא ר"ש ולאחר הפרק: (ג) תוס' ד"ה ואיבעית וכו' אין זו ראייה מן הש"ס שהש"ס מיישב וכו' ועוד דלרבא נמי:

### גליון הש"ס

**תום'** ד"ה ואיבעית וכו' ומתוך כך פסק נמי. וכעין זה כתבו תוס' בשם ר"ת כתובות פח ע"ב ד"ה לאפוקי:

רש"ל

[ע' בתוס' פ' אלו טריפות בשם מסודרים בדברים יפה]

א) נראה דחסר וצ"ל דהא אפי' שלם כשניקב בכונס משקה טהור עד שיחדנו לאוכלין כ"ש וכו'.

רַבִּי יְהוּדָה אוֹמֵר: כּוֹפֵף אָזְנֵי קְדֵרָה לְתוֹכָהּ, וּמֵצִיף עָלֶיהָ מַיִם, וְאִם כּוֹנֵס — בְּיָדוּעַ שֶׁכּוֹנֵס מַשְׁקֶה, וְאִם לָאו — בְּיָדוּעַ שֶׁמּוֹצִיא מַשְׁקֶה. אוֹ שׁוֹפְתָהּ עַל גַּבֵּי הָאוּר, אִם הָאוּר מַעֲמִידָהּ — בְּיָדוּעַ שֶׁמּוֹצִיא מַשְׁקֶה, וְאִם לָאו — בְּיָדוּעַ שֶׁמַּכְנִיס מַשְׁקֶה. ר' יוֹסֵי אוֹמֵר: אַף לֹא שׁוֹפְתָהּ עַל גַּבֵּי הָאוּר — מִפְּנֵי שֶׁהָאוּר מַעֲמִידָהּ, אֶלָּא שׁוֹפְתָהּ עַל גַּבֵּי הָרֶמֶץ. אִם רֶמֶץ מַעֲמִידָהּ — בְּיָדוּעַ שֶׁמּוֹצִיא מַשְׁקֶה, וְאִם לָאו — בְּיָדוּעַ שֶׁכּוֹנֵס מַשְׁקֶה. הָיָה טוֹרֵד טִיפָּה אַחַר טִיפָּה — בְּיָדוּעַ שֶׁכּוֹנֵס מַשְׁקֶה. מַאי אִיכָּא בֵּין ת"ק לְר' יְהוּדָה? אָמַר עוּלָּא: כִּינּוּס עַל יְדֵי הַדְּחָק אִיכָּא בֵּינַיְיהוּ.§ "כָּל אֵבֶר שֶׁיֵּשׁ בּוֹ צִפּוֹרֶן" וכו'.§ איֵשׁ בּוֹ צִפּוֹרֶן — מְטַמֵּא בְּמַגָּע וּבְמַשָּׂא וּבְאֹהֶל, יֵשׁ בּוֹ עֶצֶם וְאֵין בּוֹ צִפּוֹרֶן — מְטַמֵּא בְּמַגָּע וּבְמַשָּׂא, וְאֵינוֹ מְטַמֵּא בְּאֹהֶל. *אָמַר רַב חִסְדָּא, דָּבָר זֶה רַבֵּינוּ הַגָּדוֹל אֲמָרוֹ, הַמָּקוֹם יִהְיֶה בְּעֶזְרוֹ: אֶצְבַּע יְתֵרָה שֶׁיֵּשׁ בּוֹ עֶצֶם וְאֵין בּוֹ צִפּוֹרֶן — מְטַמֵּא בְּמַגָּע וּבְמַשָּׂא, וְאֵינוֹ מְטַמֵּא בְּאֹהֶל. אָמַר רַבָּה בַּר בַּר חָנָה א"ר יוֹחָנָן: בוּכְשֶׁאֵינָהּ נִסְפֶּרֶת עַל גַּב הַיָּד.§ "כָּל הַמְטַמֵּא מִדְרָס" וכו'.§ גכָּל דַּחֲזֵי לְמִדְרָס — מְטַמֵּא טְמֵא מֵת. "וְיֵשׁ שֶׁמְּטַמֵּא טְמֵא מֵת — וְאֵין מְטַמֵּא מִדְרָס", לְאַתּוּיֵי מַאי? לְאַתּוּיֵי סְאָה וְתַרְקַב, *דְּתַנְיָא: °"וְהַיּוֹשֵׁב עַל הַכְּלִי", יָכוֹל כָּפָה סְאָה וְיָשַׁב עָלֶיהָ, אוֹ תַּרְקַב וְיָשַׁב עָלָיו יְהֵא טָמֵא — ת"ל: °"אֲשֶׁר יֵשֵׁב עָלָיו הַזָּב" — דמִי שֶׁמְּיוּחָד לִישִׁיבָה, יָצָא זֶה שֶׁאוֹמְרִים לוֹ "עֲמוֹד וְנַעֲשֶׂה מְלַאכְתֵּנוּ".§

מתני' *הכָּל הָרָאוּי לָדוּן דִּינֵי נְפָשׁוֹת — רָאוּי לָדוּן דִּינֵי מָמוֹנוֹת, וְיֵשׁ שֶׁרָאוּי לָדוּן דִּינֵי מָמוֹנוֹת וְאֵינוֹ רָאוּי לָדוּן דִּינֵי נְפָשׁוֹת.§

גמ' אָמַר רַב יְהוּדָה: ולְאַתּוּיֵי מַמְזֵר. תְּנֵינָא חֲדָא זִימְנָא: *הַכֹּל כְּשֵׁרִין לָדוּן דִּינֵי מָמוֹנוֹת, וְאֵין הַכֹּל כְּשֵׁרִין לָדוּן דִּינֵי נְפָשׁוֹת. וְהָוֵינַן בָּהּ: לְאַתּוּיֵי מַאי? וְאָמַר רַב יְהוּדָה: לְאַתּוּיֵי מַמְזֵר! חֲדָא — זלְאַתּוּיֵי גֵּר, וַחֲדָא — לְאַתּוּיֵי מַמְזֵר. וּצְרִיכִי, דְּאִי אַשְׁמְעִינַן גֵּר — מִשּׁוּם דְּרָאוּי לָבֹא בַּקָּהָל, אֲבָל מַמְזֵר דְּאֵין רָאוּי לָבֹא בַּקָּהָל — אֵימָא לָא. וְאִי אַשְׁמְעִינַן מַמְזֵר — מִשּׁוּם דְּקָאָתֵי מִטִּפָּה כְּשֵׁרָה, אֲבָל גֵּר דְּקָאָתֵי מִטִּפָּה פְּסוּלָה — אֵימָא לָא, צְרִיכָא.§

מתני' *כָּל הַכָּשֵׁר לָדוּן — כָּשֵׁר לְהָעִיד, וְיֵשׁ שֶׁכָּשֵׁר לְהָעִיד וְאֵינוֹ כָּשֵׁר לָדוּן.§

גמ' לְאַתּוּיֵי מַאי? א"ר יוֹחָנָן: לְאַתּוּיֵי סוּמָא בְּאַחַת מֵעֵינָיו. וּמַנִּי?

רַבִּי

[לקמן נ.] [לקמן נא:] [קדושין עו: סנהדרין לו:] ויקרא טו שם

**רש"י**

ר' יְהוּדָה אוֹמֵר. לֹא כָּךְ בּוֹדְקִין אוֹתָהּ, דְּהָא קוּלָּא הוּא, דְּאַיְּידֵי דְּדָחֵיק לְהוּ לְשׁוּלַיִם – אֵימָא: עָיְילִי מַיָּא לְגַוָּהּ, אֲפִילּוּ בְּנֶקֶב קָטָן. אֶלָּא הָכִי בָּדְקִינַן לָהּ: כּוֹפֶה פִּי הַקְּדֵרָה לְתוֹךְ הָעֲרֵיבָה, קוֹדֶם שֶׁיִּתֵּן הַמַּיִם, וְאַח"כ נוֹתֵן מַיִם בָּעֲרֵיבָה עַד שֶׁיְּהוּ מַיִם צָפִין עַל שׁוּלֶיהָ. אִם כְּנָסָהּ – בְּיָדוּעַ כו'. אִם הָאוּר מַעֲמִידָהּ. שֶׁלֹּא יֵצֵא הַמַּשְׁקֶה – בְּיָדוּעַ שֶׁנֶּקֶב קָטָן הוּא, וְאֵינוֹ רָאוּי לְהַכְנִיס מַשְׁקֶה. שֶׁהָאוּר מַעֲמִיד. אֲפִילּוּ נֶקֶב גָּדוֹל. רֶמֶץ. גֶּחָלִים וְאֵפֶר בּוֹעֲרִים. הָיָה טוֹרֵד טִיפָּה אַחַר טִיפָּה. כְּלוֹמַר, וְזוֹ נַמִּי בְּדִיקָה: אִם נָתַן לְתוֹכוֹ מַיִם, וְהֵן יוֹצְאִין טִיף אַחַר טִיף – בְּיָדוּעַ שֶׁכּוֹנֵס מַשְׁקֶה. ה"ג: מַאי אִיכָּא בֵּין תַּנָּא קַמָּא לְר' יְהוּדָה כִּינּוּס ע"י הַדְּחָק אִיכָּא בֵּינַיְיהוּ. לְת"ק הָוֵי כִּינּוּס, כִּדְפְרִישִׁית. יֵשׁ בּוֹ צִפּוֹרֶן. וַאֲפִי' הִיא יְתֵרָה, כְּגוֹן אֶצְבַּע שִׁשִּׁית. מְטַמֵּא בְּמַגָּע וּבְמַשָּׂא וּבְאֹהֶל. דְּהָוֵי אֵבֶר חָשׁוּב, וַאֲפִי' לֵיכָּא כַּזַּיִת – בָּשָׂר מְטַמֵּא בְּאֹהֶל, דְּקי"ל: הָאֵבָרִים – אֵין לָהֶן שִׁיעוּר, בְּפ' "יוֹצֵא דוֹפֶן" (לעיל דף מג.), אֵין בּוֹ צִפּוֹרֶן – לָא הָוֵי אֵבֶר, וּמִיהוּ מְטַמֵּא בְּמַגָּע וּבְמַשָּׂא, כְּדִין עֶצֶם כִּשְׂעוֹרָה, שֶׁהֲרֵי יֵשׁ בּוֹ עֶצֶם. וְאֵינוֹ מְטַמֵּא בְּאֹהֶל. עַד דְּאִיכָּא כַּזַּיִת בָּשָׂר. דְּקַיְימָא לָן: עֶצֶם כִּשְׂעוֹרָה – מְטַמֵּא בְּמַגָּע וּבְמַשָּׂא, וְלֹא בְּאֹהֶל. וְאִי אִיכָּא כַּזַּיִת בָּשָׂר – וַדַּאי מְטַמֵּא, דְּהָא אִיכָּא כַּזַּיִת מִן הַמֵּת. וְאִי לָאו יְתֵרָה הִיא – וַדַּאי מְטַמֵּא מִשּׁוּם אֵבֶר בְּאֹהֶל. וְאַע"ג דְּלֵיכָּא כַּזַּיִת בָּשָׂר, דַּאֲפִילּוּ יְתֵרָה אָמְרִי' לְקַמָּן דְּאִי נִסְפֶּרֶת עַל גַּב הַיָּד הָוְיָא אֵבֶר. רַבֵּינוּ הַגָּדוֹל. רַב. עַל גַּב הַיָּד. שֶׁאֵינָהּ עוֹמֶדֶת בְּשׁוּרַת הָאֶצְבָּעוֹת. לְאַתּוּיֵי סְאָה וְתַרְקַב. שֶׁאֵינָן מִדְרָס הַזָּב לְטַמֵּא אָדָם וְכֵלִים, אֲבָל טְמֵאִין הֵם טוּמְאַת מַגַּע הַזָּב לִהְיוֹת רִאשׁוֹנִים, וּבְמֵת נַעֲשִׂין אַב הַטּוּמְאָה. מִי שֶׁמְּיוּחָד לִישִׁיבָה. הוּא דְּהָוֵי אַב הַטּוּמְאָה, דִּכְתִיב: "וִכַבֵּס בְּגָדָיו" וגו'. מתני' כָּל הָרָאוּי לָדוּן דִּינֵי נְפָשׁוֹת. כ"ש שֶׁהוּא כָּשֵׁר לְדִינֵי מָמוֹנוֹת. גמ' לְאַתּוּיֵי מַמְזֵר. דְּכָשֵׁר לְדִינֵי מָמוֹנוֹת, וּפָסוּל לְדִינֵי נְפָשׁוֹת. *כִּדְכְתִי' (בסנהדרין דף לו.): "כּוּלָּךְ יָפָה רַעְיָתִי". גֵּר. נַמִּי כָּשֵׁר לְדִינֵי מָמוֹנוֹת. לְאַתּוּיֵי סוּמָא בְּאַחַת מֵעֵינָיו. דְּכָשֵׁר לְהָעִיד, וְאֵינוֹ כָּשֵׁר לָדוּן. אֲבָל בִּשְׁתֵּי עֵינָיו – אֲפִילּוּ לְעֵדוּת, פָּסוּל, דִּכְתִיב (ויקרא ה): "אוֹ רָאָה".

רַבִּי

**תוספות**

יש בו עצם ואין בו צפורן מטמא במגע ובמשא אבל לא באהל. בפ' *"אלו מומין" (בכורות מה.) אית דמפרש טעמא: גזרה שאינה נספרת על גב היד אטו נספרת. אבל באהל המת לא גזרו, דעבדי היכרא דלא לישרוף עליה תרומה וקדשים. ואית דאמר: משום דעצם כשעורה נגע בה. ותימה להאי טעמא, אמאי מטמא במגע כשנוגע בבשר ואינו נוגע בעצם, דאי משום דבשר הוי יד ושומר לעצם – האמר רב בפרק "העור והרוטב" (חולין דף קיח:) דאין יד לפחות מכזית, ואין שומר לפחות מכפול, ו"רבינו הגדול" דהכא היינו רב! ויש לומר: דגזרו חכמים אטו לפעמים דיש בעצם כפול. אי נמי: נגיעת בשר אטו נגיעת עצם. או גזרו מגע אטו משא. כל המטמא מדרס. היינו מק"ו דפכין קטנים. ובפ' "כילד הרגל" (ב"ק דף כה:) פירשנו.

תנינא חדא זימנא. תימה: מאי קושיא, הא כמה כללות תנא במתני' אע"ג דתנא להו בדוכתא אחריתי. דקתני *"כל שהוא חייב בפאה – חייב במעשר" כו', ושמעינן לה ממתני' במסכת פאה (פ"א מ"ד) דקתני: לקיטתו כאחד ומכניסו לקיום, ובמעשר לא תני ליה. וכן *"כל שחייב בראשית הגז חייב – במתנות", ושמעינן לה ממתניתין ד"ראשית הגז", וכל שיש לו ביעור – יש לו שביעית" שמעינן נמי ממתני' דשביעית! וי"ל: דלא פריך אלא אדרב יהודה, דמאי הוצרך למימר לאתויי ממזר הכא והתם. *והשתא אתי שפיר דלא קאמר: דההיא דסנהדרין (דף לו:) לאתויי חלל דכשר לדיני ממונות ופסול לדיני נפשות, כדתנן התם:* (א) אין כשר לדיני נפשות אלא מן המשיאין לכהונה. אלא לא פריך אמתני' כי אם על רב יהודה, ואדרב יהודה לא מצי לשנויי: דהדא לאתויי חלל – דמלישנא דסיפא ד"אחד דיני ממונות", דקתני דאין כשר לדיני נפשות אלא מן המשיאין לכהונה משמע: אבל כשר לדיני ממונות, ולכל הפחות מוקמינן אחלל דכשר. וצ"ל: דרב יהודה אתא לאשמועינן דגר וממזר כשרים לדיני ממונות, דפסולין לדיני נפשות שמעינן ממתני' דהתם. וגרסינן הכא, כמו שיש ספרים דגרסי בסנהדרין (דף לו:): אי אשמועינן גר – משום דראוי לבא בקהל כו', ואי אשמועינן ממזר – דבא מטפה כשרה, להכי כשר לדיני ממונות, אבל גר – אימא לא. ול"ג איפכא, כמו שהיה בספרים: אי אשמועינן גר – משום דבא מטיפה פסולה, ולכך פסול לדיני נפשות, דרב יהודה לא אתא לאשמועי' הא דפסול לדיני נפשות, כדפרישנא. לאתויי ממזר. וא"ת: ואמאי לא קאמר "לאתויי בעל מום דפסול בדיני נפשות" ומפיק לה בפרק "אחד דיני ממונות" (סנהדרין דף לו:) ובריש "מצות חליצה" (יבמות דף קא.) כשם שבית דין מנוקין בצדק, כך מנוקין מכל מום. וי"ל: דלא איירי אלא בפסול יוחסין, וה"נ איתא בפ' "זה בורר" (סנהדרין דף כז:) דפריך: והא עד זומם דדיני ממונות, דכשר לדיני נפשות ופסול לדיני ממונות. ומשני: בפסול יוחסין קמיירי. חדא לאתויי גר. משמע: דכשר, אע"ג דאין אמו מישראל. ותימה דבפ' "החולץ" (יבמות דף מה:) אמרי' דרבא אכשר לרב מרי בר רחל ומנייה בפורסי דבבל, דכיון דאמו מישראל "מקרב אחיך" קרינא ביה! וי"ל: דהכא מיירי לדון גר חבירו, כדאמר בפרק "מצות חליצה" (שם דף קב.) גר – דן חבירו דבר תורה, ואם היתה אמו מישראל – דן אפילו ישראל. ולא כמו שפירש שם בקונט' דלענין דיני נפשות איירי הא ד"דן את חברו", אבל בדיני ממונות – דן אפי' ישראל. וא"ת: דבפרק "עשרה יוחסין" (קדושין דף עו:) על גמרא ד"מי שהוחזקו אבותיו" כו' דפריך: למימרא דלא אוקמינן פסולין, ורמינהי "הכל כשרין"! כו', ואמר רב יהודה: לאתויי ממזר. ומאי קושיא? לישני: דהיינו דוקא לדון ממזר כיוצא בו, דומיא דגר! ואם נאמר: דהכא מיירי בגר שאמו מישראל – הוה אתי שפיר. וי"ל: דשאני ממזר, דכיון דאביו ואמו מישראל "מקרב אחיך" קרינן ביה. תדע, דהא (ג) דדרשינן "עליך" הוא דבעינן "מקרב אחיך", וממזר מקרי שפיר "עליך" – דבא מזרע ישראל. ואם ממזר פסול לדון את ישראל – מיפסיל נמי לדון את ממזר חברו. והא דתניא בתוספתא: אין מעמידין מלך אלא מן המשיאין לכהונה – היינו מדרבנן, דמדאורייתא אפי' ממזר חשיב "מקרב אחיך". והא דעביד צריכותא בין גר לממזר, אע"ג דחלוקין זה מזה, כדפי' נקט צריכותא – לפי שהמשנה שנויה סתם, ואין חלוק זה מפורש בה. וא"ת בפ': "מצות חליצה" (יבמות דף קא:) דא"ל רב שמואל בר יהודה לרב יהודה: תנינן, בב"ד של ישראל, ולא בב"ד של גרים. ורגיל ר"ת לומר דאותו רב שמואל, היינו בנו של רב יהודה הינדואה, דאמר בפ"ק דקידושין (דף כב:) דגר שאין לו יורשין הוה, ונתגייר הוא ובנו. וכן משמע הלשון, דקאמר "ואנא גר" "אנא" משמע דהוא עצמו נתגייר. וכיון דלא היתה אמו מישראל – לשאר דינין נמי מיפסיל, ואמאי הוצרך להביא קרא דחליצה? וגם רב יהודה, היאך בררו לדיין? וי"ל: דקבלו עליהם החולץ והחולצת, דבדיני ממונות הוי כשר, ולחליצה – מיפסיל, כדאמר התם. אי נמי: התם לחליצת גרים איירי. ואין להאריך כאן יותר.

כל

**עין משפט נר מצוה**

נ"ל מומין אלו

ז א ב מיי' פ"ב מהל' טומאת מת הל"ז:

ח ג ד מיי' פכ"ז מהל' כלים הלט"ז:

ט ה מיי' פי"א מהל' סנהדרין הלי"א ופ"ב שם הלכה ט:

י ו מיי' פ"ב שם הל"ט סמג עשין צז טוש"ע חו"מ סי' ז סעי' ב:

יא ז מיי' שם סמג שם טוש"ע שם סעי' א:

**תוספי הרא"ש**

יש בו עצם ואין בו ציפורן מטמא במגע ובמשא אבל לא באהל. ותימה דבפ' אלו מומין (דף מה) [אית דאמר] דמשום עצם כשעורה נגעו בה אמאי טמא כשנוגע בבשר ואינו נוגע בעצם. וכ"ת משום יד או שומר דהא דאמרינן אין שומר לטומאה חמורה היינו להצטרף אבל להוציא טומאה יש שומר הא רב הוא דאמר בפ' העור והרוטב דאין יד לפחות מכזית ואין שומר לפחות מכפול. ורבינו הגדול דהכא היינו רב וי"ל דגזרו חכמים פחות מכשיעור אטו פול דפעמים יש בעצם כפול והבשר מכסהו. א"נ גזרינן נגיעת בשר אטו נגיעת עצם א"נ גזרינן מגע אטו משא: כל המטמא מדרס מטמא טמא מת. ואפי' הוא פשוטי כלי עץ דאינו ראוי לקבל טומאה כיון דחזי למדרס מקבל טומאה דילפינן ליה מפכין קטנים שטהורים בזב דלמגע לא חזו שאינו יכול ליגע לתוכן ובהיסט נמי לא מטמא דהיסטו (בע"י) [ילפינן] מקרא דאשר יגע בו הזב ומה שאינו בא לכלל מגע אינו בא לכלל משא אע"ג דראוי לנגיעת שער הזב. בת"כ ילפינן דשער הזב דמטמא מהנוגע בבשר הזב וכיון שאינו ראוי לנגיעת בשר אינו מטמא בשער. ותימה כלי חרס המוקף צמיד פתיל אם לא יטמא בהיסט דאינו ראוי לנגיעה. ולעיל בפ"ק אמרינן שמטמאה מעת לעת שבבנדה ואר"ת דצמיד פתיל חשוב בא לכלל מגע לפי שעומד ליפתח אע"ג דבכי קולית בבילה אמרינן מחוסר נקיבה כמחוסר מעשה ואע"ג דחשב עליו לנקבו אינו מטמא במשא שאני התם דמסתמא אינו עומד לינקב אלא ע"י מחשבה אבל צמיד פתיל סתמא עומד לינקב וה"ה דמצי למיעבד ק"ו מסאה ותרקב ופכין גדולים דלא מטמו מדרס ומטמו טמא מת אלא דניחא ליה למינקט פכין קטנים שטהורין בכל טומאת הזב ואע"ג דמטמאין במעיינות הזב נהי דבשער הזב לא מטמו משום דבעינן ראוי לנגיעת בשר מ"מ רוקו דכתיב בהדיא וכי ירוק הזב בטהור פשיטא ליה דלא בעינן בהו ראוי לנגיעת בשר מ"מ טהורים מכל טומאות המחוברות לזב: מפץ שמטמא בזב אינו דין שיהא טמא במת. ותימה כלי חרס המוקף צמיד פתיל יוכיח שטמא בזב וטהור במת. ואומר ר"ת דלא שייך לעשות יוכיח מצמיד פתיל דכה"ג שהוא טמא בזב היה טמא במת דמה שהוא טמא בהיסט היינו משום דהוי כאילו נגע זב בתוכו דאי זהו מגעו שהוא ככולו הוי אומר זה היסטו ובמת נמי אם היה מת בתוכו היה טמא: לאיתויי ממזר. תימה אמאי לא קאמר לאיתויי בעל מום שפסול לדיני נפשות משום ונשאו אתך בדומין לך כדאיתא בפ' עשרה יוחסין ובפ' אחד דיני ממונות מפיק ליה מכשם שב"ד מנוקין בצדק כך מנוקים מכל מום. ולימא נמי לאיתויי אשה שכשירה לדיני ממונות כמו שמפרש לקמן ופסולה לדיני נפשות משום ונשאו אתך וי"ל דלא מיירי אלא בפסול יוחסין והכי נמי אמרינן בפ' זה בורר דפריך התם והאיכא עד זומם דכשר לדיני ממונות ופסול לדיני נפשות ומשני בפסול יוחסין קא מיירי: תנינא חדא זימנא. [illegible]

**הגהות הב"ח**

(א) תוס' ד"ה תנינא וכו' כדתנן התם ואין הכל כשרים לדון דיני נפשות וכו' דקתני ואין הכל כשרים לדון דיני נפשות: (ג) ד"ה חדא וכו' דהא דדרשינן עליך:

[בכורות מה:] שבת נג. חגיגה כג: סנהדרין כז: ודף לו: סנהדרין לב. לו: קדושין עו: (הוריות ד:) [נ"ל כלמייתי]

**תוספי הרא"ש**

דלא קאמר דאצטריך מתניתין דסנהדרין משו' חלל דכשר לדיני ממונות ופסול לדיני נפשות כדתנן התם אין כשר לדיני נפשות אלא שמשיאין לכהונה משום שלא פריך אלא לרב יהודה ותימה אמאי לא קאמר לאיתויי חלל וי"ל משום דשמעינן ליה מלישנא דמתני' דקתני בסיפא אין כשר לדיני נפשות אלא כהני' לוים וישראלי' המשיאין לכהונה ומיהו ק' דממזר וגר נמי שמעינן מהתם. וי"ש דגר' בסנהדרין איפכא ואי שמעינן גר משום דראוי לבא בקהל אבל ממזר אימא לא ואי אשמועינן ממזר משום דבא מטפה כשרה אבל גר אימא לא והשתא הוי חדוש דרב יהודה מה שהן כשרין לדיני ממונות והשתא לא שמעינן לה מלישנא דמתניתין משום דאיירי בדיני נפשות: חדא לאיתויי גר וחדא לאיתויי ממזר. כלומר תני בחדא זימנא במילתא דרב יהודה (חדא) לאיתויי גר משמע הכא דגר כשר אע"ג דאין אמו מישראל. ותימה דבפ' החולץ אמרינן רבא אכשריה לרב מרי בר רחל ומנייה אפורסיה דבבל דכיון דאמו מישראל מקרב אחיך קרי' ביה וי"ל דהכא איירי לדון גר חבירו כדאמרינן בפ' מצות חליצה גר דן את חבירו דבר תורה ואם היתה אמו מישראל דן אפי' ישראל ולא כמו שפרש"י שם דבדיני נפשות איירי דן את חבירו ולא ישראל אאבל לדיני ממונות כשר. ועוד דמייתי התם קרא דמקרב אחיך ואילו בדיני נפשות ממעטינן מונשאו אתך בסנהדרין ובקידושין. ותי' הא דאמרינן בעשרה יוחסין מי שהוחזקו אבותיו משוטרי הרבים וכו' למימרא דלא מוקמינן פסולין לדינא והתנן הכל כשרין לדון כו'. ואמר רב יהודה לאיתויי ממזר. ומאי קשה ליה היינו דוקא לדון חבירו כדאמרינן גבי גר וי"ל דגבי ממזר לא שייך לפלוגי בין ישראל כשר לממזר דמקרב אחיך קרינן ביה כיון דאביו ואמו מישראל ואי מיפסל לישראל כשר מיפסיל נמי לחבירו. והא דקאמר בגר וממזר דצריכי אע"פ שהן חלוקין [illegible]

א) מזה משמע דגר' רבינו כאן כו' ואי אשמעינן גר משום דקאתי מטפה פסולה ומשו"ה פסול לד"נ אבל ממזר וכו'.

רַבִּי מֵאִיר הִיא. *דְּתַנְיָא, הָיָה רַבִּי מֵאִיר אוֹמֵר: מַה ת"ל °"עַל פִּיהֶם יִהְיֶה כָּל רִיב וְכָל נָגַע" וְכִי מָה עִנְיַן רִיבִים אֵצֶל נְגָעִים? *מַקִּישׁ רִיבִים לִנְגָעִים: מַה נְּגָעִים [א]בַּיּוֹם, דִּכְתִיב: °"וּבְיוֹם הֵרָאוֹת בּוֹ" — [ב]אַף רִיבִים בַּיּוֹם. וּמַה נְּגָעִים שֶׁלֹּא בְּסוּמָא, דִּכְתִיב: °"לְכָל מַרְאֵה עֵינֵי הַכֹּהֵן" — אַף רִיבִים שֶׁלֹּא בְּסוּמָא. וּמַקִּישׁ נְגָעִים לְרִיבִים, מָה רִיבִים — שֶׁלֹּא בִּקְרוֹבִים, אַף נְגָעִים — שֶׁלֹּא בִּקְרוֹבִים. אִי מָה רִיבִים — בִּשְׁלֹשָׁה, אַף נְגָעִים — בִּשְׁלֹשָׁה? וְדִין הוּא, מָמוֹנוֹ — בִּשְׁלֹשָׁה, גּוּפוֹ — לֹא כ"ש! ת"ל: °"וְהוּבָא אֶל אַהֲרֹן הַכֹּהֵן אוֹ אֶל אַחַד מִבָּנָיו הַכֹּהֲנִים" — הָא לָמַדְתָּ, [ג]שֶׁאֲפִילּוּ כֹּהֵן אֶחָד רוֹאֶה אֶת הַנְּגָעִים. *הַהוּא סָמְיָא דַּהֲוָה בְּשִׁבָבוּתֵיהּ דְּרַבִּי יוֹחָנָן, דַּהֲוָה *קָדַיֵּין דִּינָא, [ד]וְלָא קָאָמַר לֵיהּ וְלָא מִידִי. הֵיכִי עָבֵיד הָכִי? *וְהָאָמַר רַבִּי יוֹחָנָן: הֲלָכָה כִּסְתָם מִשְׁנָה, וּתְנַן: כָּל הַכָּשֵׁר לָדוּן — כָּשֵׁר לְהָעִיד, וְיֵשׁ כָּשֵׁר לְהָעִיד וְאֵין כָּשֵׁר לָדוּן. וְאָמְרִינַן: לְאַתּוֹיֵי מַאי? וְאָמַר רַבִּי יוֹחָנָן: לְאַתּוֹיֵי סוּמָא בְּאַחַת מֵעֵינָיו! רַבִּי יוֹחָנָן סְתָמָא אַחֲרִינָא אַשְׁכַּח, דִּתְנַן: *[ה]דִּינֵי מָמוֹנוֹת דָּנִין בַּיּוֹם וְגוֹמְרִין בַּלַּיְלָה. וּמַאי אוּלְמֵיהּ דְּהַאי סְתָמָא מֵהַאי סְתָמָא? אִיבָּעֵית אֵימָא: סְתָמָא דְּרַבִּים עָדִיף, וְאִיבָּעֵית אֵימָא: מִשּׁוּם דְּקָתָנֵי לַהּ גַּבֵּי הִלְכְתָא דְּדַיָּינֵי.§ **מתני'** כָּל שֶׁחַיָּיב בְּמַעַשְׂרוֹת — מְטַמֵּא טוּמְאַת אוֹכָלִין, וְיֵשׁ שֶׁמְּטַמֵּא טוּמְאַת אוֹכָלִין וְאֵינוֹ חַיָּיב בְּמַעַשְׂרוֹת.§ **גמ'** לְאַתּוֹיֵי מַאי? לְאַתּוֹיֵי [ו]בָּשָׂר וְדָגִים וּבֵיצִים.§ **מתני'** כָּל שֶׁחַיָּיב בְּפֵאָה — חַיָּיב בְּמַעַשְׂרוֹת, וְיֵשׁ שֶׁחַיָּיב בְּמַעַשְׂרוֹת וְאֵינוֹ חַיָּיב בְּפֵאָה.§ **גמ'** לְאַתּוֹיֵי מַאי? לְאַתּוֹיֵי תְּאֵנָה, וְיָרָק שֶׁאֵינוֹ חַיָּיב בְּפֵאָה. דִּתְנַן, *כְּלָל אָמְרוּ בְּפֵאָה: [ז]כָּל שֶׁהוּא אוֹכֶל, וְנִשְׁמָר, וְגִידּוּלוֹ מִן הָאָרֶץ, וּלְקִיטָתוֹ כְּאֶחָד, וּמַכְנִיסוֹ לְקִיּוּם — חַיָּיב בְּפֵאָה. אוֹכֶל — לְמַעוּטֵי סְפִיחֵי סְטִים וְקוֹצָה, וְנִשְׁמָר — לְמַעוּטֵי הֶפְקֵר, וְגִידּוּלוֹ מִן הָאָרֶץ — לְמַעוּטֵי כְּמֵהִים וּפִטְרִיּוֹת, וּלְקִיטָתוֹ כְּאֶחָד — לְמַעוּטֵי תְּאֵנָה, וּמַכְנִיסוֹ לְקִיּוּם — לְמַעוּטֵי יָרָק. וְאִילּוּ גַּבֵּי מַעֲשֵׂר *תְּנַן: [ח]כָּל שֶׁהוּא אוֹכֶל, וְנִשְׁמָר, וְגִידּוּלוֹ מִן הָאָרֶץ — חַיָּיב בְּמַעַשְׂרוֹת, וְאִילּוּ "לְקִיטָתוֹ כְּאֶחָד, וּמַכְנִיסוֹ לְקִיּוּם" לָא קָתָנֵי. (א) אִם הָיוּ בָּהֶם שׁוּמִים וּבְצָלִין — חַיָּיבִין, דִּתְנַן, *מַלְבְּנוֹת בְּצָלִים שֶׁבֵּין הַיָּרָק, ר' יוֹסֵי אוֹמֵר: פֵּאָה מִכָּל אַחַת וְאַחַת, וַחכ"א [ט]מֵאַחַת עַל הַכֹּל. אָמַר רַבָּה בַּר בַּר חָנָה, א"ר יוֹחָנָן: עוֹלְשִׁין שֶׁזְּרָעָן מִתְּחִילָּה לִבְהֵמָה, וְנִמְלַךְ עֲלֵיהֶן לְאָדָם צְרִיכוֹת

## רש"י

רַבִּי מֵאִיר הִיא. דְּפָסֵיל סוּמָא בְּאַחַת מֵעֵינָיו לָדוּן. שֶׁלֹּא בְּסוּמִין. אֲפִילּוּ סוּמָא בְּאַחַת מֵעֵינָיו. דִּכְתִיב לְכָל מַרְאֵה עֵינֵי הַכֹּהֵן. עַד דְּאִיכָּא כּוּלּוֹ "מַרְאֶה". וּמָה רִיבִים שֶׁלֹּא בִּקְרוֹבִים. דְּנָפְקָא לָן מִ"לֹא יוּמְתוּ אָבוֹת עַל בָּנִים" (דברים כד): אַף נְגָעִים, אֵין כֹּהֵן רוֹאֶה נֶגַע קְרוֹבוֹ. וְגוֹמְרִין בַּלַּיְלָה. אַלְמָא, לָא מַקְשִׁינַן רִיבִים לִנְגָעִים, דִּכְתִיב: "וּבְיוֹם הֵרָאוֹת בּוֹ בָּשָׂר", וְכִי הֵיכִי דִּלְעִנְיַן לַיְלָה לָא מַקִּישׁ — לְעִנְיַן סוּמָא נַמִי לָא מַקִּישׁ. סְתָמָא דְּרַבִּים עָדִיף. הַהִיא דִּלְעֵיל אוֹקְמִינַן כְּר"מ, דְּיָחִיד הוּא. דְּקָתָנֵי לַהּ גַּבֵּי הִלְכְתָא דְּדַיָּינֵי. בְּסַנְהֶדְרִין, דְּהָא מַיְירֵי כּוּלֵּיהּ מַסֶּכְתָּא בְּדִינִין, הִילְכָּךְ עִיקָּר הִיא. אֲבָל הַךְ, לָא תְּנַן לַהּ הָכָא גַּבֵּי נִדָּה אֶלָּא אַגַּב גְּרָרָא דְּנָקֵט כַּיּוֹצֵא בּוֹ. **מתני'** כָּל שֶׁחַיָּיב בְּמַעַשְׂרוֹת מְטַמֵּא טוּמְאַת אוֹכָלִין. דְּאֵין חַיָּיב לָךְ בְּמַעֲשֵׂר אֶלָּא אוֹכֶל. **גמ'** בְּפֵאָה. כְּתִיב (ויקרא יט): "וּבְקוּצְרְכֶם אֶת קְצִיר" וגו', דּוּמְיָא דְּקָצִיר — דְּמַכְנִיסוֹ לְקִיּוּם, וְאִיכָּא כָּל הָנֵי. מַכְנִיסוֹ לְקִיּוּם. שֶׁאָדָם יָכוֹל לְאוֹצְרוֹ. לְמַעוּטֵי סְפִיחֵי סְטִים וְקוֹצָה. דְּאֵין אוֹכֶל אֶלָּא מִין צֶבַע. סְטִים. קרו"ג. קוֹצָה. גויטר"א. וְלָא יָדַעְנָא אַמַּאי נָקַט סְפִיחִים. וְכִמְדוּמֶּה לִי, שֶׁהָרִאשׁוֹנִים רְאוּיִם לַאֲכִילָה. תְּאֵנָה. אֵינָהּ (ג) מִתְבַּשֶּׁלֶת כְּאֶחָד. וְאִילּוּ לְקִיטָתוֹ כְּאֶחָד. דִּמְמַעֵט תְּאֵנָה וּמַכְנִיסוֹ לְקִיּוּם, דִּמְמַעֵט יָרָק. לָא קָתָנֵי. אַלְמָא תְּאֵנָה וְיָרָק חַיָּיבִין בְּמַעֲשֵׂר מִדְּרַבָּנַן, דְּמִדְּאוֹרַיְיתָא לָא מִיחַיֵּיב אֶלָּא דָּגָן וְתִירוֹשׁ וְיִצְהָר. שׁוּמִים וּבְצָלִים. מַכְנִיסָן לְקִיּוּם, לְפִיכָךְ חַיָּיבִים בְּפֵאָה. מַלְבְּנוֹת. שׁוּרוֹת. מִכָּל אֶחָד וְאֶחָד. דְּיָרָק הַזָּרוּעַ בֵּין שׁוּרָה לְשׁוּרָה מַפְסִיק לְהוּ. עוֹלְשִׁין. עֵשֶׂב וּשְׁמוֹ קרישפל"א.

## תוספות

*כל הכשר לדון כשר להעיד. וא"ת: והרי אשה, דכשרה לדון, כדכתיב בדבורה "והיא שופטה את ישראל בעת ההיא", ובשלהי פ"ק דב"ק (דף טו.) דרשינן: "אשר תשים לפניהם" — השוה הכתוב אשה לאיש לכל עונשין שבתורה. וכי היכי דהאי קרא מיירי בנדונין מיירי נמי בדיינין. כדדרשינן ב"המגרש" (גיטין פח:) "לפניהם" — ולא לפני גוים. ואשה פסולה להעיד, כדאמר בפרק "שבועת העדות" (שבועות דף ל.)! וי"ל: ה"ק, כל איש הכשר לדון — כשר להעיד. אי נמי: נהי דבנידונין הוי אשה בכלל, מ"מ בדיינים אין אשה בכלל. ודבורה היתה דנה ע"פ הדיבור. אי נמי: לא היתה דנה, אלא מלמדת להם הדינים. ובירושלמי פוסל אשה לדון. *אית דילפי מ"ועמדו שני אנשים", (ג): שני מ"על פי שנים עדים", ואית דילפי מ"וישארו שני אנשים במחנה"*).

**ורבי** מאיר היא. וא"ת: אמאי קאמר "לאתויי סומא", ופליג מתניתין אסתמא דסנהדרין (דף לב.) לימא "לאתויי אוהב ושונא", דכשרין להעיד ופסולין לדון, כדאמר בפרק "זה בורר" (שם כז:) לרבנן דרבי יהודה? וי"ל: דלא פסיקא ליה, שהרי לכל העולם כשרין. א"נ מתניתין ע"כ לא מיתוקמא כרבנן, דהא קתני "כל הכשר לדון — כשר להעיד", והרי סומא בשתי עיניו, לרבנן, דכשר לדון, דהא לא מקשינן ריבים לנגעים, ואילו להעיד — פסול מ"או ראה". ואפילו במה שראה קודם שנסתמא — פסול להעיד, כדאמר ב"יש נוחלין" (ב"ב קכח.) היה יודע לו עדות קודם שנסתמא, ונסתמא — פסול. וא"ת: בפרק "חזקת הבתים" (שם דף מג.) דפריך: וליסלקו בי תרי מינייהו ולידיינו, הא בפ' "יש נוחלין" שהבאתי, פוסל תחלתו בפסול וסופו בכשרות! וכי תימא: לדון — כשר טפי, והתנן "כל הכשר לדון — כשר להעיד"! וי"ל: דמתניתין מיירי בלהבא, כל הכשר לדון להבא — כשר להעיד מה שיראה מכאן ולהבא*.

**כל** שחייב במעשר מטמא טומאת אוכלין. וא"ת: הא אמרינן בפ"ק דחולין (דף ו.) אינו חושש לשאור ותבלין שבה, לא משום מעשר, ולא משום שביעית. משמע, דמעשר נוהג בתבלין. וא"כ מטמא טומאת אוכלין. ובפרק "העור והרוטב" (שם דף קיז:) תנן: והקיפה מצטרפין לטומאת אוכלין, ומפרש בגמרא (שם דף קכ.) מאי "קיפה"? — תבלין, אלמא אין להם טומאת אוכלין אלא ע"י צירוף! וי"ל: דאיכא ב' מיני תבלין, דהנהו דאין ראויין אלא לטעמא — לא מטמו טומאת אוכלין, ואין חייבין במעשר. אבל תבלין דראויין נמי בפני עצמן, ועבידן נמי לטעמא, כגון שומים ובצלים — חייבין במעשר, ומטמאים טומאת אוכלין. אי נמי: ההיא דפ"ק דחולין (דף ו.) לצדדין קתני, ולא קאי "מעשר" אתבלין אלא אשאור גרידא. ושביעית קאי אף אתבלין דאף במאכל בהמה נוהגא, כדתנן במס' שביעית. עוד הקשה הרב ר"ש מטוי"ל דלקמן (דף נא:) אמרינן דנמנו וגמרו דאין פלפלין מטמאין טומאת אוכלין, ובפ' "בכל מערבין" (עירובין כח:) אמר: זרע הגרגיר למאי חזי? וקאמר: שכן ראשונים שלא היה להם פלפלין, היו שוחקין אותו, ומטבילין בו את הצלי, וכ"ש דפלפלין מתעשרין מהאי טעמא! וי"ל: דזרע גרגיר, כי שוחקין אותו להטביל בו — חזי אף בעינו, אלא דאין רגילות לשוחקן כדי לאוכלן בלא טיבול, לפי שע"י טיבול עדיף טפי. אבל פלפלין — לאחר שנשחקו, לא חזו בעינייהו אלא ע"י טיבול*. **ספיחי** סטים. פי' בקונטרס: דדוקא נקט ספיחים, אבל תחלתן — ראויין לאכילה. אי נמי: ספיחים ראויין יותר, וס"ד דחייב בפאה, קמ"ל.

**וגידולו** מן הארץ למעוטי כמהין ופטריות. בפרק "כיצד מברכין" (ברכות דף מ:) פריך, והא *תנן: אם אמר "כל גידולי קרקע עלי קונס" — אסור בכמהים ופטריות? ומשני: מירבא — רבו מארעא, מינק — לא ינקי מארעא. והא "כל דבר שאין גידולו מן הארץ" קתני! תני: *"וכל דבר שאין יונק מן הארץ". א"כ נמי בשמעתין צריך למיתני "יונק מן הארץ". **למעוטי** תאנה. תימה: מאי שנא דתאנה וירק חייבין במעשר, ופטורים מן הפאה, דמן התורה אין נוהג פאה ומעשר אלא בדגן תירוש ויצהר בלבד. ומאי שנא דחייבו חכמים טפי במעשר מבפאה? ואומר ר"ת: משום דתאנה אין לקיטתה כאחד, הלכך לא גזרו חכמים פאה בה, שלא יצפו עניים מתי יגמור בעל הבית לקיטתו, ויפסידו יותר במקום אחר ממה שירויחו בפאה זאת. וירק נמי, אין הפאה חשובה ואינה שוה כ"א מעט, ואם ימתינו אחריה עד הערב — יפסידו יותר. **שזרען** מתחלה לבהמה. משמע, דסתמא — לאדם קיימי, או לתרוייהו, ואפ"ה, כי זרען לבהמה — פקע שם אוכל מינייהו, (ד) אף על גב דאמר (כריתות דף*) כל המיוחד לאוכל אדם — טמא, עד שיפסל מלאכול לכלב, דכיון שזרען לבהמה — אין עליה שם אוכל, ולא היה *שני גידולים מעולם לאדם. והא דאמר ב"העור והרוטב" (חולין קכח.) עולשין שלקטן והדיחם לבהמה, ונמלך עליהן לאדם — צריכות הכשר שני. קשה: כיון דסתמן לאדם, משום דהדיחן לבהמה — לא פקעי מינייהו שם אוכל, (ה) שיפסל מלאכול לכלב, ואמאי לא הוכשרו? וי"ל: דמיירי שהיו מתחלה מיוחדים לבהמה. אי נמי: שמא אין הכשר מועיל אף באוכל אדם, אי הוי הכשר לצורך בהמה. מחשבת

## תוספי הרא"ש

ר"מ היא. תימה אמאי קאמר לאיתויי סומא ופליגא אסתם מתניתין דסנהדרין לימא לאיתויי אוהב ושונא דכשרין להעיד ואין כשרין לדון לר' יהודה כדאיתא בפ' זה בורר וי"ל דלא פסיקא ליה משום דלשאר אנשים כשרין לדון א"נ ע"כ מתניתין לא מיתוקמא כרבנן דהא קתני כל הכשר לדון כשר להעיד והרי סומא בשתי עיניו דכשר לדון דלא מקשינן ריבים לנגעים וההוא סומא דהוה בשיבבותיה דר' יוחנן מסתמא סומא בשתי עיניו היה ופסול להעיד דאו ראה כתיב ואפי' במה שראה קודם שנסתמא פסול להעיד כדאמרינן ביש נוחלין היה יודע עדות וקודם שנסתמ' ונסתמא פסול: **כל שחייב** במעשר מטמא טומאת אוכלין.

קשה מהא דאמרינן (ביש נוחלין) [בפ"ק דחולין] אינו חושש לשאור ולתבלין שבה משום מעשר ומשום שביעית. ובפ' העור והרוטב תנן הקיפה מצטרף לטמא טומאת אוכלין וקאמר בגמרא מאי קיפה תבלין אלמא תבילין אין לו טומאת אוכלין אלא על ידי צירוף אע"ג דחייב במעשר וי"ל דיש מיני תבלין שאינן ראויין אלא לטעמא והני לית להו טומאה ולא מיחייבי במעשר. ויש מיני תבלין שראויין בפני עצמן וגם עבידי לטעמא כגון שומים ובצלים ואותם יש להם (טומאה) וגם חייבין במעשר. א"נ הך דקיפה שאני שכבר נתן טעם בקדירה כדאמרינן גבי שבת משנתן טעם בקדירה אינו מטמא טומאת אוכלין א"נ משום מעשר דקאמר (ביש נוחלין) [בחולין] לא קאי אתבלין אלא אשאור אבל שביעית קאי אף אתבלין דהא במאכל בהמה נמי נהגא שביעית: ספיחי סטים. פרש"י דוקא נקט ספיחין אבל תחלתו ראוי לאכילה. ועי"ל דספיחין ראויין יותר וסד"א דליחייבו בפאה: **גידולו** מן הארץ למעוטי כמהין ופטריות. בפ' כיצד מברכין ובפרק הנודר מן הירק פריך והתנן אם אמר גידולי קרקע עלי אסור בכמהין ופטריות. ומשני מירבא רבו מארעא מינק לא ינקי מארעא. והא דבר שאין גידולו מן הארץ קתני תני על דבר שאינו יונק מן הארץ. ובשמעתין נמי צריך למיתני יונק מן הארץ למעוטי כמהין ופטריות: **למעוטי** תאנה. פרש"י טעמא דתאנה וירק פטורין מן הפאה וחייבין במעשר משום דבספרי מיחייב מן התורה כל מילי דפאה בר מתאנה וירק ובשביל הני תרתי לא רצו חכמים לגזור אבל במעשר לא מחייב אלא [בדגן תירוש ויצהר] וגזרו על כל שאר דברים. וקשה לר"ת דהכי נמי דריש בסיפרי מקרא חיוב מעשר בכל מילי אע"ג דפשיטא דמעשר פירות מדרבנן. אלא הנך דרשות אסמכתא בעלמא נינהו גבי מעשר [וגם] גבי פאה דפאה נמי לא מצינו אלא א)בכרם זית וכן כל הנך דתנן במס' ביצה אין עולין באילן משום שבות כו' וכן דריש בסיפרי משבתון שבות אלא כל הנך דרשות דסיפרי אסמכתות בעלמא נינהו ותו דמדרבנן נמי (בז') ב)אילנות אין חייבין בפאה אלא ה' מיני אילנות דחשיב במס' פאה האוג והחרובין כו'. והא דקאמר למעוטי תאנה לאו דוקא אלא כל תאנה דדמי ליה. ואומר ר"ת דהיינו טעמא דלא תקנו פאה בדבר שאין לקיטתו כאחד משום הפסד עניים שהיו מצפין בכל יום מתי יגמור לקיטתו ומתבטלין ובירק נמי דאין מכניסו לקיום יש ריוח מועט לעניים שממתינין עד הערב ומפסידין במקום אחר: **שזרען** מתחלה לבהמה משמע דסתמא לאדם קאי או לתרווייהו ואפ"ה כי זרען לבהמה פקע שם אוכל מינייהו ואע"ג דאמרינן כל המיוחד לאוכל אדם טמאין עד שיפסל מלאכול לכלב כיון דהני גידולין לא היו מעולם לאדם דהא זרען לבהמה ליכא עלייהו שם אוכל:

א) נראה דצ"ל אלא בתבואה ובכרם וזתים וכן כל הנך וכו'. ב) נ"ל בכל האילנות אין חייבין וכו'.

בא א ב מיי' פ"ג מהל' טומאת אוכלין הל"ג:
בב ג מיי' שם הל"י:
בג ד ה מיי' שם הל"ג:
בד ו מיי' שם ומיי' פ"ג מהל' שאר אבות הטומאות הל"ח:

צריכות מחשבה לכשיתלשו. קסבר: מחשבת חבור לא שמה מחשבה. אמר רבא: אף אנן נמי תנינא, *י"ג דברים נאמרו בנבלת עוף טהור, וזה אחד מהן – צריכה מחשבה ואינה צריכה הכשר. אלמא: מחשבת חיים – לא שמה מחשבה, הכא נמי – מחשבת חבור לא שמה מחשבה. רבי זירא אמר: הכא בגוזל שנפל מן הרום עסקינן, דלא הוה קמן דלחשוב עליה. א"ל אביי: תרנגולת שביבנה, מאי איכא למימר? א"ל: תרנגול ברא הוה. אחיכו עליה: תרנגול ברא – עוף טמא הוא, ועוף טמא מי קמטמא? אמר להו אביי: *גברא רבה אמר מילתא לא תחיכו עליה, בתרנגולת שמרדה, ומאי ברא – דאיבראי ממרה. רב פפא אמר: תרנגולתא דאגמא הואי. רב פפא לטעמיה, *דאמר רב פפא: תרנגול דאגמא – אסור, תרנגולתא דאגמא – שריא, וסימניך: עמוני ולא עמונית. דרש מרימר: תרנגולתא דאגמא – אסירא. חזיוה רבנן דדרסה ואכלה, והיינו גירותא. ת"ר: *גוזל שנפל לגת, וחשב עליו להעלותו לכותי – טמא, לכלב – טהור. ר' יוחנן בן נורי אומר: אף לכלב – טמא. א"ר יוחנן בן נורי: ק"ו, אם מטמא טומאה חמורה שלא במחשבה, לא יטמא טומאה קלה שלא במחשבה? אמרו לו: לא, אם אמרת בטומאה חמורה – שכן אינה יורדת לכך, תאמר בטומאה קלה – שכן יורדת לכך! אמר להן: תרנגולת שביבנה תוכיח, שיורדת לכך – וטמאוה שלא במחשבה. אמרו לו: *משם ראיה? כותים היו שם, וחשבו עליה לאכילה. במאי עסקינן? אילימא בכרכים – למה לה מחשבה? והתנן: *נבלת בהמה טהורה בכל מקום, ונבלת עוף טהור והחלב בכרכים – אין צריכין לא מחשבה ולא הכשר! אלא בכפרים, ומי איכא למ"ד דלא בעיא מחשבה? *והתנן: נבלת בהמה טמאה בכל מקום, ונבלת עוף טהור בכפרים – צריכה מחשבה, ואינה צריכה הכשר! א"ר זעירא בר חנינא: לעולם – בכרך, וגתו מאסתו ועשאתו ככפר. א"ר יוחנן בן נורי: קל וחומר, אם מטמאה טומאה חמורה שלא במחשבה – לא תטמא טומאה קלה שלא במחשבה? אמרו לו: לא, אם אמרת בטומאה חמורה – שכן אינה יורדת לכך. מאי "אינה יורדת לכך"? אמר רבא, הכי קאמרי ליה: לא, אם אמרת
בטומאה

**רש"י**

צריכות מחשבה. לאכילה, ושוב תטמא טומאת אוכלין, שיחשב עליהן לאחר תלישתן לאוכלן, ואע"ג דכבר חשב בחבורן, שהרי נמלך עליהן לאדם. צריכות מחשבה. לאכילה, ושוב תטמא מאיליה, ותחזור ותטמא אוכלין במגע, דהא מאיליה קודם מחשבה אין לה טומאה אלא בבית הבליעה. ואינה צריכה הכשר. כדיליף לקמן בשמעתין: כל שסופו לטמא טומאה חמורה – אין צריך הכשר, לא שום הכשר ירידת טומאה, לא הכשר מים, ולא הכשר שרץ, אלא מאיליה בלא שום נגיעה. אלמא מחשבת חיים. דהא מחיים – סתמא לאכילה, ואפ"ה לא מהניא ההיא מחשבה לטומאה, דבעינן מחשבה בשעה שראוי לקבל טומאה, ומחיים – לאו בר קבולי טומאה הוא. הכא נמי מחשבת חבור. הואיל ומחובר לאו בר קבולי טומאה, לא שמה מחשבה. מן הרום. עוף הבר פורח באויר, דלא הוה קמן מחיים דליחשביה. תרנגולת שביבנה. דאמרינן לקמן: כותים היו שם, וחשבו עליה. והא תרנגולת עוף מזומן הוה, והויא קמן מחיים, ואפילו הכי בעי מחשבה לטומאת מגע. עוף טמא מי מטמא בבית הבליעה. והא קיימא לן (חולין דף ק.) מי שאיסורו משום "בל תאכל נבלה", יצא זה שאיסורו משום "בל תאכל טמא" – לא. ותרנגולת שביבנה מטמיא, בבית הבליעה הואי, מדקא מייתי לה רבי יוחנן בן נורי לקמן סייעתא למילתיה דפליג בגוזל שנפלה בגת, אלמא דומיא דגוזל הוא. שמרדה. שברחה ונעשית מדברית לאדוניה, ושם גדלה אפרוחין. ומהן נפל אחד כאן, דלא היתה בו מחשבה מעולם. ומאי ברא. דקאמר לכו. דאיבראי ממרה. הנעשה מדברית לאדוניה. תרנגולתא. נקבה דאגמא הואי, דההוא עוף טהור הוא אליבא דרב פפא. חזיוה רבנן דדרסה. מקבלת ברגליה מה שאוכלת. ואני אומר, שדורסת על מאכלה ברגליה לאחוז שלא יבא כולו לפיה, ואין עוף טהור עושה כן. והיינו גירותא. דקיימא לן, גירותא – עוף טמא הוא, דאמר בפרק "כל הבשר" (חולין דף קט:): כל מה דאסר לן רחמנא – שרא לן לקבליה, אסר לן דמא – שרא לן כבדא, אסר לן גירותא – שרא לן לישנא דכוורא. גוזל. טהור. שנפל לגת. ומת. וחשב עליו. להעלותו לכותים להאכילו. טמא. טומאת אוכלין, ומטמא אוכלין אחרים במגע. דמעצמו באה עליו טומאה משחשב עליו, כדיליף לקמן: הואיל וסופו מטמא אדם, כגון האוכלו, מטמא בגדים בבית הבליעה. לענין טומאה קלה נמי, לא בעי הכשר מים, ולא הכשר נגיעת שרץ. "הכשר" – היינו, דבר שמכשירו לטומאה, כגון שרץ ומים. אף לכלב טמא. טומאת אוכלין. ולאו משום דאכילת כלב מחשבה היא, אלא לר' יוחנן בן נורי לא בעי מחשבה. טומאה חמורה. כגון האוכלה, מטמא בגדים בבית הבליעה. ואפילו לא חשב עליו, כגון שלא ידע שזה הוא. טומאה קלה. אוכלין ומשקין. אינה יורדת לכך. אינה יורדת לדין מחשבה. ולקמן מפרש מה היא. תרנגולת שביבנה תוכיח. שמתה תרנגולת ביבנה, ובא מעשה לפני חכמים, וטמאוה שלא במחשבה. ואף על פי שיורדת לכך, כלומר, דלטומאה קלה טמאוה שלא במחשבה, ובטומאה קלה אמרת יורדת לכך. בכל מקום. ואפילו בכפרים, דליכא אוכלין מרובין, סתמא – לאכילה. ונבלת עוף טהור בכרכים. דאיכא עם רב, ואוכלין הכל. וכן חלב בהמה דכרכים – אין צריכין מחשבה, אבל בכפרים – בעי מחשבה. נבלת בהמה טמאה בכל מקום. סתמא לאו לאכילה, הלכך בעיא מחשבה. ונהי דאי איכא כזית בלא מחשבה – מטמיא אפילו אדם וכלים, וכל שכן אוכלין ומשקין. אלא להכי מהניא מחשבתה: דאי איכא פחות מכביצה שאר אוכלין, ופחות מכזית נבלה משלים לכביצה, אי חשיב (א) ליה – מצטרפא בהדייהו, ומקבלת טומאה במגע שרץ, ואי לא – לא. ואינה צריכה הכשר. דסופה לטמא טומאה חמורה. לעולם בכרך. והיינו טעמא דלרבנן בעיא מחשבה, דגת שנפל לתוכה מאסתו, ואינו הגון לאכילה כל כך.
טומאה

**תוספות**

מחשבת חיים לא שמה מחשבה. דמחיים לא חשב לאוכלה עד אחר שחיטה, והרי מתה. אבל אי שמה מחשבה – לא פקע שם אוכל מינה, במה שנתנבלה, עד שתפסל מאכילת כלב. תרנגולתא דאגמא. הזכר אסור, לפי שאין לו סימני טהרה. ולא שרי מטעם "כל היוצא מן הטהור – טהור", שהרי האם לא ילדה האפרוח, אלא ביצים הטילה, והאפרוח מעפרא קא גדיל, ונאסר ממילא ע"י סימני טומאה. ונקבה נמי אין לאוסרה, למאן דאסר זה וזה גורם, דהא אפרוח לא יצא אלא מן הביצה, ומעפרא קגדיל, כדפרישית. ומיהו נראה עיקר: ששני מינים הן, והמין שקורין "תרנגולתא דאגמא" – שרי הזכר והנקבה, דיש להן סימני טהרה. והמין שקורין "תרנגול דאגמא" – אסור הזכר והנקבה, דאין נראה שמין אחד חלוק הזכר מהנקבה. ועוד: כיון דלא הוי מעופות טמאין הכתובין, דבההו בכל מין יש זכר ונקבה, משום סימני טומאה אין לאסור, עד שיהא בו כל ד' סימנים דמנשר ילפינן*.

אלא בכפרים. תימה דע"כ רבי יוחנן בן נורי לא בעי מחשבה אפילו בכפרים, מדעביד ק"ו וא"כ מאי פריך? ויש לומר: דה"פ, [אלא] בכפרים, ומי איכא כו', וא"כ בלא נפל לגת נמי לרבנן צריך מחשבה. ואע"ג דמקשה אסיק אדעתיה הא דנקט "נפל לגת", מכל מקום פריך מעיקרא: אילימא בכרכים כו', דסבר דמחמת נפילה לגת לא מימאס כולי האי, עד שיעשה ככפר, עד דמשני רבי זירא. ל"ג גבי כפרים "והחלב" – דחלב דמאי? אי דבהמה טהורה, וצריכה מחשבה בכפרים, דאין דרך לאכול חלב – אם כן אמאי אין צריך הכשר? דחלב נבלת בהמה טהורה אין סופה לטמא טומאה חמורה, כדאמרינן ב"כל שעה" (פסחים כג.) מ"חלב נבלה וחלב טרפה יעשה לכל מלאכה"! ואי בחלב שחוטה – הא דם שחיטה לא מכשר, כיון דקאמר צריך מחשבה, וליכא אכתי שם אוכל עליו עד שחישב, דהכשר אינו מועיל עד שיהא אוכל, כדאמר ב"העור והרוטב" (חולין קכח.) גבי "עולשין שהדיחן לבהמה". ובחלב בהמה טמאה – פשיטא דחלב צריך מחשבה, דמ"ש מבשרה? וגבי "כרכים" גרסינן ליה, ומיירי בחלב שחוטה, דכיון דאין צריך מחשבה – הוי אוכל, ומתכשר בדם שחיטה.
שום

**מסורת הש"ס**

זבחים קה: טהרות פ"א מ"א בכורות י. [שקלים ח.]
[ברכות ט: גיטין נה:]
חולין סב:
[טהרות פ"ח מ"ו]
[שבת כט: וש"נ]
עוקצין פ"ג מ"ג בכורות י. כריתות כא.
עוקצין פ"ג מ"ג בכורות שם כריתות שם
[וע' תוס' חולין סב:]

**תוספי הרא"ש**

מחשבת חיים לא שמה מחשבה א). ואע"ג דלא חשיב לאוכלו מחיים כיון דמיוחד לאוכל אדם לא פקע שם אוכל מיניה במה שנתנבלה עד שיפסל מלאכול לכלב אי מחשבת חיים שמה מחשבה: דאיבראי ממרה וילדה אפרוחין במדבר שלא היתה עליהם מחשבה מעולם: תרנגולתא דאגמא שריא. שני מינין הם אותו מין שנקראין בלשון זכר אסירי הזכר והנקבה אבל אין לפרש שיהא מין אחד חלוק הזכר מן הנקבה: אלא בכפרים מי איכא למ"ד דלא בעי מחשבה. תימה מאי פריך דילמא ר' יוחנן בן נורי פליג אהך מתני' וכי משני גתו מאסתו ועשאו כפר. צ"ל דר' יוחנן בן נורי פליג עלה. ומי' מצי למימר דר' יוחנן בן נורי סבר דלא נפסלה מחמת הגת וי"ל דלרבנן פריך משום דס"ל דלא על חנם נקט נפל לגת הלכך פריך אילימא בכפרים בלא נפל נמי צריך מחשבה ומעיקרא דפריך אילימא בכרכים משמע ליה דמחמת נפילה בגת לא נמאס כולי האי שיעשה כפר עד דמשני ר' זירא גיתו מאסתו כו': ל"ג גבי כפרים והחלב דאי בחלב שחוטה כיון דקאמר צריך מחשבה ולא הוה עליה תורת אוכל בשעת שחיטה לא מכשר ליה דם שחיטה כדמוכח בהעור והרוטב מההיא דעולשין שהדיחן דהכשר אינו מועיל עד שיהא עליו תורת אוכל וא"כ אמאי אינו צריך הכשר ואי בחלב דנבלת בהמה טהורה אמאי אין צריך הכשר הלא אין לנו שום טומאה כדאמרינן בפ' כל שעה מחלב נבלה וחלב טרפה יעשה לכל מלאכה ואי בחלב בהמה טמאה פשיטא דצריך מחשבה כמו הבשר אבל גבי כרכין גרס והחלב ומיירי בחלב שחוטה:

**הגהות הב"ח**

(א) רש"י ד"ה נבלת בהמה וכו' אי חשיב עליה מצטרפא:

א) נראה דצ"ל דאי שמה מחשבה אע"ג דלא חשיב לאוכלו וכו'. וכן בתוס' צריך להגיה ולסרס דבריהם וצ"ל אבל אי שמה מחשבה אע"ג דמחיים לא חשב לאכלה וכו' והרי מתה לא פקע וכו'.

תורה אור

בטומאה חמורה – שכן אינה עושה כיוצא בה, תאמר בטומאה קלה – שעושה כיוצא בה. אמר ליה אביי: כל דכן הוא, ומה טומאה חמורה דקילא – דאינה עושה כיוצא בה – מטמאה שלא במחשבה. טומאה קלה דחמירא, דעושה כיוצא בה – אינו דין שמטמאה שלא במחשבה? אלא אמר רב ששת, הכי קאמר: לא אם אמרת בטומאה חמורה – שכן אינה צריכה הכשר, תאמר בטומאה קלה – שצריכה הכשר. ומי צריכה הכשר? והתנן, *שלשה דברים נאמרו בנבלת עוף טהור: צריכה מחשבה, [א]ואינה מטמאה אלא בבית הבליעה, [ב]ואינה צריכה הכשר! נהי דהכשר שרץ לא בעיא, הכשר מים בעיא. מאי שנא הכשר שרץ דלא בעיא, כדתנא דבי רבי ישמעאל, הכשר מים נמי לא תבעי, כדתנא דבי רבי ישמעאל! *דתנא דבי רבי ישמעאל: °"על כל זרע זרוע אשר יזרע", מה זרעים שאין סופן לטמא טומאה חמורה – צריכין הכשר, [ג]אף כל שאין סופן לטמא טומאה חמורה – צריכין הכשר, [ד]יצתה נבלת עוף טהור שסופה לטמא טומאה חמורה – שאין צריך הכשר. אלא אמר רבא ואיתימא רב פפא: שום טומאה חמורה בעולם, שום טומאה קלה בעולם. אמר רבא: ומודה רבי יוחנן לענין מעשר, דמחשבת חיבור – שמה מחשבה. אמר רבא: מנא אמינא לה – *דתנן, [ה]הסיאה והאזוב והקורנית שבחצר, אם היו נשמרין – חייבין. היכי דמי? אילימא דזרעינהו מתחלה לאדם – צריכא למימר? אלא לאו דזרעינהו מתחלה לבהמה, וקתני: "אם היו נשמרין – חייבין". אמר רב אשי: [ו]הכא בחצר שעלו מאיליהן עסקינן, וסתמא – לאדם קיימי. והכי קאמר: [ז]אם החצר משמרת פירותיה – חייבין, ואם לאו – פטורין. מתיב רב אשי: *כל שחייבין במעשרות – מטמאין טומאת אוכלין. ואם איתא, הא איכא הני – דקחייבין במעשר ואין מטמאין טומאת אוכלין! אמר רבא, הכי קאמר: כל מין שחייב במעשר – מטמא טומאת אוכלין. ה"נ מסתברא, מדקתני סיפא: *כל שחייב בראשית הגז – חייב במתנות, ויש שחייב במתנות ואין חייב בראשית הגז. ואם איתא, האיכא טרפה – [ח]דחייבת בראשית הגז, [ט]ואינה חייבת במתנות! אמר רבינא: הא מני – רבי שמעון היא, *דתנן: *ר"ש פוטר את הטרפה מראשית הגז. אמר רב שימי בר אשי, תא שמע: *[י]המפקיר את כרמו, והשכים בבקר ובצרו – חייב בפרט, ובעוללות, ובשכחה, ובפאה, ופטור מן המעשר. והא אנן תנן: כל שחייב בפאה – חייב במעשרות! אלא לאו שמע מינה: מין קתני, שמע מינה. *תנן התם: [כ]מודים חכמים לר' עקיבא *בזורע שבת או חרדל בשנים ושלשה מקומות, שנותן פאה מכל אחד ואחד. והא

(ויקרא יא) [חולין קלו:] חולין קלז:

**רש"י**

טומאה חמורה אינה עושה כיוצא בה. מאחר שמטמאה נבלה את האדם, אין אותו אדם חוזר ומטמא אדם. שאין מטמא אדם אלא אב הטומאה. אבל אוכל, חוזר ומטמא אוכל, מדרבנן. הכשר שרץ. שיכשירו ארץ להביאו לידי טומאה. שאין סופן לטמא טומאה חמורה. אין לך אוכל מטמא אדם. שום טומאה חמורה שום טומאה קלה. לא אם אמרת בטומאה חמורה, דין הוא שמטמא בלא מחשבה. שלא מצינו שום טומאה שמטמא טומאה חמורה, שתהא צריכה הכשר. תאמר בטומאה קלה דאוכלין, שאע"פ שזו אינה צריכה הכשר – הרי כל אוכלין יש עליהם שום טומאה קלה, וצריכין הכשר, הלכך הכא נמי בעיא מחשבה. לענין מעשר. דהואיל ונמלך עליהן לאדם, הויא מחשבה, וחייבין במעשר. הסיאה. פוליו"ל. והקורנית. סדריא"ה. נשמרין. ס"ד אם היו נשמרין לאכילת אדם. אלא לאו דזרען לבהמה. וקתני: אם חזר ושמרן לאדם – חייבין. לאדם קיימי. וכיון דסתמייהו לאדם, מאי "אם היו נשמרין"? הכי קאמר: אם החצר משמרת פירותיה, דלא הוי הפקר – חייבין. מתיב רב אשי. לרבא. ואם איתא. דלענין מעשר הויא מחשבה, הא איכא עולשין שזרען לבהמה, ונמלך עליהם לאדם – דחייבין במעשר, ואינן מטמאין. דהא לענין טומאה אמרת: לאו מחשבה היא. ראשית הגז. הגוזז צאנו חייב ליתן בכל שנה מן הגז מעט לכהן, וב"שחיטת חולין" מפרש שיעורא. במתנות. זרוע, לחיים והקיבה. ויש שחייב במתנות. כגון בקר, ואינו חייב בראשית הגז. ת"ש. דמין קתני במתני'. ופטור מן המעשר. דהפקר פטור מן המעשר. ובפרט ובפאה להכי מחייב, כדאמרינן ב"הגוזל" בבא קמא *משום "תעזוב" יתירא. דכתיב במשנה תורה "לא תפאר אחריך", ואמר מר (חולין דף קלא.): לא תטול תפארתו ממנו, והיינו פאה. ודרשינן בספרי: "אחריך" – זו שכחה, וכתיב: "לגר ליתום ולאלמנה יהיה", וכתיב בתריה: "כי תבצור כרמך לא תעולל אחריך לגר ליתום ולאלמנה יהיה" – הרי פאה ושכחה ועוללות. ל"ל למהדר ומכתב בפרשה "קדושים" בכולהו "לעני ולגר תעזוב אותם" – לרבות הפקר כי האי גוונא, אבל הפקר גמור – פטור מכולם, כדתנן לעיל: ונשמר – פרט להפקר. תנן התם כו'. האי דנקט לה הכא, משום דאותיב עלה מתני' ודר' יוחנן נמי עולשין שזרען כו' משום דאותיב עליה מתני' נקט לה הכא. מודים חכמים לרבי עקיבא. אע"פ דפליגי במנמר שדהו ושייר קלחים לחים. "מנמר" טיי"ר בלע"ז, שמלקט כאן את המבושלים כל צרכן, ומניח את הלחים שלא בשלו, וחוזר ומלקט במקום אחר, דהוה ליה מנומר. וקאמר ר' עקיבא: כשהוא חוזר ולוקט – נותן פאה מכל אחד ואחד שהקליר שביניתים מפסיק. וחכמים אומרים: פאה מאחת על הכל. ומודים חכמים לרבי עקיבא בזורע שבת או חרדל כו'. להכי נקט הני, שאין דרכן לעשות מהן ערוגה אלא זורען לתבלין בעלמא בשנים ושלשה מקומות. "שבת" אני"ט. והא

**תוספות**

שום טומאה חמורה בעולם כו' – תימה: דיפרש הא דקתני "דאינה יולדת לכך" המחשבה גופה, דלא מצינו טומאה חמורה שצריכה מחשבה בשום מקום. דהא דאמרינן דנבלת בהמה ועוף טהור צריכין מחשבה, היינו לטומאת אוכלין לצרף פחות מכזית ופחות מכביצה אוכלין, אבל כזית מהם – מטמא אדם וכלים בלא מחשבה, כדפרישית. אבל טומאה קלה צריכה מחשבה בעלמא. ומיהו נבלה נמי בעינן שתהא ראויה לגר, לבר פדא*.

אלא דזרעינהו לבהמה. והא דנקט "שבחצר", לפי מאי דמסיק שעלו מאיליהן – אתי שפיר, משום דבחצר אין דרך לזרוע אלא בגינה. ועוד: דבחצר – סתמא לאדם, לפי שרואה ויודע מתי ללוקטן עד שלא יתקשו. ולפי מאי דס"ד השתא, יש לפרש: דנקט "חצר", לפי שדרך התנא למנקט "חצר", דגם בשאר דבר תני "חצר". דקתני התם: תאנה (א) עומדת בחצר – אוכל אחת אחת, ופטור. ואם צירף – חייב. גפן נטוע בחצר, כקורנית שבחצר – שהחצר קובעת בדבר שנגמרה מלאכתו, אם צירף. או בלא צירוף, כהנהו שאין רגילין לעשות מהן גורן. והא דתנן פ"ח דשביעית [מ"א] כל שאינו מיוחד, לא לאוכל אדם ולא לאוכל בהמה, חישב עליו לאוכל אדם ולאוכל בהמה – נותנין חומרי אדם וחומרי בהמה, כגון האזוב והקורנית, לא קשה אהא דאמרינן בשמעתין דסתמיה לאדם, דהיינו דוקא בחצר. כדפרישית לעיל.

מין קתני ש"מ. וא"ת: בריש "הגוזל קמא" (ב"ק לד.) קאמר אביי דלר' ישמעאל שינוי אין קונה, דקאמרי רבנן: לא הפריש פאה מן הקמה – יפריש מן העמרים, או מן הכרי, ולא מן העיסה. ולר"ש אף מן העיסה. ודחי רבא: בעלמא שינוי קונה, והכא משום "תעזוב" יתירא. ואביי, "תעזוב" יתירא למפקיר כרמו, אם כן לרבא מפקיר כרמו – פטור מן הפאה לר"ש וא"כ היכי מוכח הכא דמין קתני דילמא מתני' דקתני "כל שחייב בפאה – חייב במעשר" ר"ש היא? וי"ל: דלרבא נמי "תעזוב" יתירא, למפקיר כרמו, ותרתי ש"מ דהא אביי נמי דדריש ליה ב"הגוזל" קמא (שם לד.) למפקיר כרמו לכ"ע דריש לה בפ"ק דתמורה (דף ו.) למילתא אחריתי, דקאמר התם אביי: כל דאמר רחמנא לא תעביד – אי עביד, מהני ליה. מותיב רבא: והרי פאה, דאמר רחמנא "לא תכלה", ואמרינן: דאם לא הפריש מן הקמה – יפריש מן העומרין או מן הכרי לרבנן, או אף מן העיסה לר"ש אלמא דלא מהני! ומשני אביי: התם משום "תעזוב" יתירא. ורבא, "תעזוב" יתירא – למפקיר כרמו. והשתא בין אביי ובין רבא דרשי "תעזוב" למפקיר כרמו. ואביי דסבר דבעלמא אי עביד מהני – דריש נמי מ"תעזוב" דיפריש מן העומרים או מן הכרי, או מעיסה לר"ש דלא נימא: אי עביד – מהני. אבל אי בעלמא שינוי קונה לר"ש כמו בגזל – אין סברא להעמיד "תעזוב" שיפריש מן העיסה, אלא דדוקא מעמרים או מהכרי. ורבא סבר ד"תעזוב" למפקיר כרמו, ולר' שמעון שיפריש מן העיסה, אע"ג דבעלמא שינוי קונה. אבל להפריש מן העומרים או מן הכרי – לא צריך קרא, דבעלמא נמי כל דאמר רחמנא לא תעביד – אי עביד, לא מהני, לרבא. והא

**תוספי הרא"ש**

שם טומאה חמורה בעולם. דאינה צריכה הכשר בשום מקום תימה ליפלוג במחשבה גופה שלא מצינו טומאה חמורה שצריכה מחשבה בשום מקום אבל טומאה קלה צריכה מחשבה בעלמא ונבלת בהמה טמאה ונבלת עוף טהור כדאמרינן לעיל דצריכה מחשבה היינו לצרף פחות מכזית עם פחות מכביצה אוכלין כדפרש"י אבל בכזית ממנה מטמא אדם וכלים בלא מחשבה ומיהו נבלה בעינן שתהא ראויה לגר לבר פדא והיינו כעין מחשבה: אלימא דזרעינו מתחל' לאדם ואם היו נשמרים דקתני היינו דמעיקרא היו נשמרין לאדם: אלא לאו דזרעינהו מתחלה לבהמה. ואם היו נשמרין דקתני היינו שמכאן ולהבא נשמרין לאדם ותימה אמאי קתני שבחצר דבשלמא לפי המסקנא ניחא דמה שהן זרועין בחצר (א)שעלו מאיליהן דאין דרך לזרוע אלא בגנה וגם משום שזרועין בחצר הוו סתמיהו לאדם דנראה כשהן רכין קודם שיתקשו אבל בגינה אין סתמייהו לאדם. לפי שאינן ניכרין מתי יתקשו אבל השתא דמיירי שייחדם לאדם מה לי בחצר מה לי בגינה וי"ל משום דבתרי בבי דרישא תנא נמי גבי חצר תאנה העומדת בחצר אוכל אחת ופטור ואם צירף חייב גפן נטועה בחצר כו'. וכן הקורנית שבחצר כו'. וקמ"ל הני בבי דרישא בחצר (דרישא) קובעת היכא דצירף בדבר שנגמרה מלאכתו וסיאה ואזוב וקורנית אצירוף דלעיל קאי אי נמי בלא צירוף נמי חייבין בחצר שאין רגילין לצרף לעשות מהן גורן וחשיב כמילא גמר מלאכתן והא דתנן פ"ח במס' שביעית כל שאינו מיוחד לא לאוכל אדם ולא לאוכל בהמה חישב עליו לאוכל אדם ואוכל בהמה נותנין עליו חומרי אדם וחומרי בהמה כגון האזוב והקורנית והסיאה לא ק' להך דשמעתין דאמרי דסתמייהו לאדם קיימי דהיינו דוקא בחצר כדפ"ל. ועי"ל דסתמא להאי ולהאי קאי וה"ק אינו מיוחד לא לאוכל אדם גרידא ולא לאוכל בהמה גרידא אם חישב עליו לאוכל אדם לבד או לאוכל בהמה נותנין עליו חומרא של זה וחומרא של זה כלומר הכל לפי מחשבתו אבל אוכל שסתמו לאדם קאי אין יכול לשנותו לבהמה ע"י מחשבתו: אלא לאו ש"מ מין קתני ש"מ. תימה דאמרי' בריש הגוזל קמא דאביי סבר דלר' שמעון שינוי אינו קונה מדקאמר לא הפריש מן הקמה יפריש מן העמרים ר' ישמעאל אומר אף מן העיסה ורבא אמר בעלמא שינוי קונה והכא משום דכתיב תעזוב יתירא. ולאביי תעזוב יתירא למפקיר כרמו. א"כ לרבא מפקיר כרמו פטור מפיאה לר' ישמעאל כיון דדריש תעזוב יתירא לדרשא אחריתי וא"כ היכי מוכח הכא אליבא דרבא דמין קתני דילמא מתניתין דכל שחייב בפיאה חייב במעשר ר' ישמעאל היא וי"ל דאף לרבא תעזוב יתירא אתא נמי למפקיר (עצמו) [כרמו] ותרתי ש"מ דהא אביי גופיה דמוקי תעזוב למפקיר כרמו מוקי לה נמי למפריש מן העיסה בפ"ק דתמורה דלא תימא אי עביד מהני:

**הגהות הב"ח**

(א) תוס' ד"ה אלא וכו' תאנה שהיא עומדת בחצר אוכל אחת אחת ופטור וכו' נותנין עליו חומרי אדם:

**עין משפט נר מצוה**

כה א מיי' פ"ג מהל' אבות הטומאות הל"ח.
כו ב ג ד מיי' פ"ג מהל' טומאת אוכלין הלכה ג.
כז ה ו ז מיי' פ"ב מהל' תרומות הל"ב.
כח ח מיי' פ"ו מהל' בכורים הל"ז.
[נזיר נ. בכורות כג. חולין עח.]
כט ט טוש"ע יו"ד סי' סא סעי' ו.
ל י מיי' פ"ח מהל' מתנות עניים הל' כז.
לא כ מיי' שם פ"ג הל' יח.

**מסורת הש"ס**

שקלים ח. [לעיל נ: וש"נ] ושם איתא שלשה עשר
זבחים קה. חולין קכח. כריתות כא.
מעשרות פ"ג מ"ט
[דף לג.]
[לקמן עמוד ב']
[צ"ל דתניא]
ב"ק לג. חולין קלב: תמורה ו. נדרים מז: [ב"ק כח.]
פאה פ"ג מ"ב
[נזיר נו:]

(א) נראה דצ"ל דמה שכן זרועין בחצר מסתמא עלו מאליהן.

[נ"ל מעשרות פ"ד מ"ה]

לב א מיי' פ"ז מהל' טומאת אוכלין הל' י"ז:
לג ב ג מיי' פ"ז מהל' מעשר שני הל"ט:
לד ד מיי' פ"ז מהל' טומאת אוכלין הל"ו:
לה ה מיי' פ"ט מהל' בכורים הל"ד:
לו ו מיי' פ"ו מהל' שמיטה ויובל הל"ג:
לז ז מיי' שם הל"ד:
לח ח מיי' פ"א מהל' מאכלות אסורות הל' כד סמג עשין סב טוש"ע י"ד סי' פג סעיף ג:
לט ט מיי' פ"ח מהל' ברכות הל"ח:
מ י מיי' שם סמג עשין כז טוש"ע או"ח סי' רכ סעי' א וסימן רז:

וְהָא שֶׁבֶת דְּמִיחַיֵּיב בְּפֵאָה, (א) וּמִיחַיֵּיב בְּמַעֲשֵׂר, דִּתְנַן: כָּל שֶׁחַיָּיב בְּפֵאָה – חַיָּיב בְּמַעֲשֵׂר. וּמִדְּחַיָּיב בְּמַעֲשֵׂר – מְטַמֵּא טוּמְאַת אוֹכָלִין, אַלְמָא: כָּל מִילֵּי דְּעָבֵיד לְטַעֲמָא – מְטַמֵּא טוּמְאַת אוֹכָלִין, דְּהַאי שֶׁבֶת לְטַעֲמָא עֲבִידָא. וּרְמִינְהִי: *הַקּוֹשְׁט, וְהַחִימּוּם, וְרָאשֵׁי בְשָׂמִים, וְהַתִּיאָה, וְהַחִלְתִּית, וְהַפִּלְפְּלִים, וְחַלַּת חָרִיעַ – נִקָּחִין בְּכֶסֶף מַעֲשֵׂר, וְאֵין מְטַמְּאִין טוּמְאַת אוֹכָלִין – דִּבְרֵי רַבִּי עֲקִיבָא. אָמַר לוֹ רַבִּי יוֹחָנָן בֶּן נוּרִי: אִם נִקָּחִין בְּכֶסֶף מַעֲשֵׂר – מִפְּנֵי מָה אֵין מְטַמְּאִין טוּמְאַת אוֹכָלִין? וְאִם [א]אֵינָן מְטַמְּאִין – [ב]אַף הֵם לֹא יִלָּקְחוּ בְּכֶסֶף מַעֲשֵׂר! *וְא"ר יוֹחָנָן בֶּן נוּרִי: נִמְנוּ וְגָמְרוּ שֶׁאֵין נִקָּחִין בְּכֶסֶף מַעֲשֵׂר, וְאֵין מְטַמְּאִין טוּמְאַת אוֹכָלִין. אָמַר רַב חִסְדָּא: כִּי תַּנְיָא הַהִיא – [ג]בְּשֶׁבֶת הָעֲשׂוּיָה לְכָמָךְ. אָמַר רַב אַשִׁי אֲמַרִיתָהּ לִשְׁמַעְתֵּי' קַמֵּיהּ דְּרַב כָּהֲנָא (אֲמַר): לָא תֵּימָא בְּשֶׁבֶת הָעֲשׂוּיָה לְכָמָךְ – הָא סְתָמָא לִקְדֵרָה, אֶלָּא – סְתַם שֶׁבֶת לְכָמָךְ עֲשׂוּיָה, *דִּתְנַן: [ד]הַשֶּׁבֶת מִשֶּׁנָּתְנָה טַעַם בַּקְּדֵרָה – אֵין בָּהּ מִשּׁוּם תְּרוּמָה, וְאֵינָהּ מְטַמְּאָה טוּמְאַת אוֹכָלִין. הָא עַד שֶׁלֹּא נָתְנָה טַעַם בַּקְּדֵרָה – יֵשׁ בָּהּ מִשּׁוּם תְּרוּמָה, וּמְטַמְּאָה טוּמְאַת אוֹכָלִין. וְאִי ס"ד סְתָמָא לִקְדֵרָה – כִּי לָא נָתְנָה נַמִי, סְתָמָא לִקְדֵרָה! אֶלָּא לָאו ש"מ – סְתָמָא לְכָמָךְ עֲשׂוּיָה. ש"מ.§ **מתני'** [ה]כָּל שֶׁחַיָּיב בְּרֵאשִׁית הַגֵּז – חַיָּיב בְּמַתָּנוֹת, וְיֵשׁ שֶׁחַיָּיב בְּמַתָּנוֹת וְאֵינוֹ חַיָּיב בְּרֵאשִׁית הַגֵּז. *כָּל שֶׁיֵּשׁ לוֹ בִּיעוּר – יֵשׁ לוֹ שְׁבִיעִית, וְיֵשׁ שֶׁיֵּשׁ לוֹ שְׁבִיעִית וְאֵין לוֹ בִּיעוּר.§ **גמ'** [ו]כְּגוֹן *עֲלֵה הַלּוּף שׁוֹטֶה, וְהַדַּנְדְּנָה. יֵשׁ שֶׁיֵּשׁ לוֹ שְׁבִיעִית וְאֵין לוֹ בִּיעוּר – *[ז]עִיקַּר הַלּוּף שׁוֹטֶה, וְעִיקַּר הַדַּנְדְּנָה. דִּכְתִיב *°"וְלִבְהֶמְתְּךָ וְלַחַיָּה אֲשֶׁר בְּאַרְצֶךָ תִּהְיֶה כָל תְּבוּאָתָהּ לֶאֱכוֹל", כָּל זְמַן שֶׁחַיָּה אוֹכֶלֶת מִן הַשָּׂדֶה – אַתָּה מַאֲכִיל לִבְהֶמְתְּךָ בַּבַּיִת, כָּלָה לַחַיָּה מִן הַשָּׂדֶה – כַּלֵּה לִבְהֶמְתְּךָ שֶׁבַּבַּיִת, וְהָנֵי לָא כָּלוּ לְהוּ.§ **מתני'** *[ח]כָּל שֶׁיֵּשׁ לוֹ קַשְׂקֶשֶׂת – יֵשׁ לוֹ סְנַפִּיר, וְיֵשׁ שֶׁיֵּשׁ לוֹ סְנַפִּיר וְאֵין לוֹ קַשְׂקֶשֶׂת. כָּל שֶׁיֵּשׁ לוֹ קַרְנַיִם – יֵשׁ לוֹ טְלָפַיִם, וְיֵשׁ שֶׁיֵּשׁ לוֹ טְלָפַיִם וְאֵין לוֹ קַרְנַיִם.§ **גמ'** כָּל שֶׁיֵּשׁ לוֹ קַשְׂקֶשֶׂת – דָּג טָהוֹר, יֵשׁ שֶׁיֵּשׁ לוֹ סְנַפִּיר וְאֵין לוֹ קַשְׂקֶשֶׂת – דָּג טָמֵא. מִכְּדִי, אֲנַן אַקַּשְׂקֶשֶׂת סָמְכִינַן, "סְנַפִּיר" דִּכְתַב רַחֲמָנָא לָמָּה לִי? אִי לָא כָּתַב רַחֲמָנָא סְנַפִּיר, °הֲוָה אָמִינָא: מַאי "קַשְׂקֶשֶׂת" דִּכְתִיב – סְנַפִּיר, וַאֲפִילּוּ דָּג טָמֵא – כָּתַב רַחֲמָנָא "סְנַפִּיר וְקַשְׂקֶשֶׂת". וְהַשְׁתָּא דִּכְתַב רַחֲמָנָא סְנַפִּיר וְקַשְׂקֶשֶׂת, מְנָלַן דְּקַשְׂקֶשֶׂת לְבוּשָׁא הוּא? דִּכְתִיב: °"וְשִׁרְיוֹן קַשְׂקַשִּׂים הוּא לָבוּשׁ". וְלִכְתּוֹב רַחֲמָנָא "קַשְׂקֶשֶׂת" וְלָא בָּעֵי "סְנַפִּיר"! א"ר אַבָּהוּ, וְכֵן תָּנָא דְּבֵי רַבִּי יִשְׁמָעֵאל: °"יַגְדִּיל תּוֹרָה וְיַאְדִּיר".§ **מתני'** *[ט]כָּל הַטָּעוּן בְּרָכָה לְאַחֲרָיו – טָעוּן בְּרָכָה לְפָנָיו, וְיֵשׁ שֶׁטָּעוּן בְּרָכָה לְפָנָיו וְאֵין טָעוּן בְּרָכָה לְאַחֲרָיו.§ **גמ'** *לְאֵתוּיֵי מַאי? לְאֵתוּיֵי יָרָק. וּלְרַבִּי יִצְחָק [י]דִּמְבָרֵךְ אַיָּרָק, לְאֵתוּיֵי מַאי? לְאֵתוּיֵי מַיָּא. וּלְרַב פַּפָּא דִּמְבָרֵךְ אַמַּיָּא, לְאֵתוּיֵי מַאי? לְאֵתוּיֵי מִצְוֹת. וְלִבְנֵי מַעֲרָבָא דִּמְבָרְכִי בָּתַר דְּסַלִּיקוּ תְּפִילַּיְיהוּ "אֲשֶׁר קִדְּשָׁנוּ בְּמִצְוֹתָיו וְצִוָּנוּ לִשְׁמוֹר חוּקָּיו", לְאֵתוּיֵי מַאי? לְאֵתוּיֵי רֵיחָנֵי

רֵיחָנֵי

תורה אור: ויקרא כה; שמואל א יז; ישעיהו מב

וְהָא שֶׁבֶת וכו'. לָאו קוּשְׁיָא הִיא, אֶלָּא מִילְּתֵיהּ דָּיֵיק וְאָזֵיל. לְטַעֲמָא. לְמַתֵּק הַקְּדֵרָה. וְהַחִימּוּם. פיטרטר"א. וְהַתִּיאָה. הַיְינוּ סִיאָה. חַלַּת חָרִיעַ. קרו"ג, וְהוּא כַּרְכּוֹם. אַף הֵם לֹא יִלָּקְחוּ בְּכֶסֶף מַעֲשֵׂר. דְּרַחֲמָנָא אָמַר "וְנָתַתָּ הַכֶּסֶף וגו' וְאָכַלְתָּ לְפָנַי" וגו', וְהָנֵי לְדִידַן לָאו אוֹכֶל נִינְהוּ. נִמְנוּ וְגָמְרוּ כו'. אַלְמָא, כָּל מִידֵי דְּלָא עָבֵיד לְאוֹכְלוֹ אֶלָּא לְהַטְעִים הַקְּדֵירָה – לָא מְטַמֵּא, דְּהָא פִּלְפְּלִין וְכַרְכּוֹם לְטַעֲמָא עֲבִידֵי. לְכָמָךְ. דְּכוֹתְשִׁין אוֹתוֹ וְנוֹתְנִין אוֹתוֹ בְּכוּתָּח, וְעִיקָּרוֹ (ב) שֶׁבְּתוֹכוֹ מַטְבִּילִין כָּל אוֹכֶל, דְּהַאי לָאו לְטַעֲמָא עָבֵיד, דַּהֲוָה עִיקָּר. אֲמַרִיתָהּ לִשְׁמַעְתָּא כו'. הַךְ שְׁמַעְתָּא דְּפָרֵישִׁית לְקַמֵּיהּ: לָא תֵּימָא כו'. הָעֲשׂוּיָה. שֶׁהִצְנִיעָהּ לְכָךְ, הָא סְתָמָא – לִקְדֵרָה וְלָא מְטַמֵּא. אֶלָּא סְתַם שֶׁבֶת לְכָמָךְ. וּמְטַמֵּא. דִּתְנַן הַשֶּׁבֶת. סְתָם שֶׁבֶת מַשְׁמַע. אֵין בָּהּ מִשּׁוּם תְּרוּמָה. שֶׁאִם חָזַר הַקֶּלַח וְנָפַל לְתוֹךְ קְדֵרָה שֶׁל חוּלִּין – אֵינוֹ מְדַמֵּעַ. כִּי לֹא נָתְנָה נַמִי. סְתָמָא לִקְדֵרָה, וְאַמַּאי מְטַמְּאָה? הָא אָמְרִינַן לְעֵיל: דְּמִידֵי דְּעָבֵיד לְטַעֲמָא לָא מְטַמֵּא. **מתני'** כָּל שֶׁיֵּשׁ לוֹ בִּיעוּר. שֶׁהוּא מְלוּוֶּה לְבַעֲרוֹ מִן הַבַּיִת בַּשְּׁבִיעִית כְּשֶׁכָּלָה לַחַיָּה מִן הַשָּׂדֶה. יֵשׁ לוֹ שְׁבִיעִית. לְעִנְיַן שֶׁחַיָּיב לְהַפְקִיר, וְאָסוּר לַעֲשׂוֹתָן סְחוֹרָה וּמְלוּגְמָא וְאַפִּיקְטְוִיזִין. וְיֵשׁ. שֶׁנּוֹהֶגֶת בּוֹ קְדוּשַּׁת שְׁבִיעִית וְאֵין לוֹ בִּיעוּר, כִּדְמְפָרֵשׁ בַּגְּמָרָא: עִיקַּר הַלּוּף וְהַדַּנְדְּנָה, שֶׁאֵין כָּלִים מִן הַשָּׂדֶה בִּימוֹת הַגְּשָׁמִים. **גמ'** לוּף שׁוֹטֶה. שֵׁם לְוַוי הוּא, וַעֲשָׂבִים הֵם. עֲלֵה הַלּוּף שׁוֹטֶה וְהַדַּנְדְּנָה. וְה"ה לְכָל הַכָּלִים בִּימוֹת הַגְּשָׁמִים מֵהַשָּׂדֶה, אֶלָּא הָא דְּנָקַט הָנֵי – מִשּׁוּם דְּסֵיפָא דְּמַתְנִיתִין מִיתּוֹקְמָא בְּעִיקָּרִין, וְאַשְׁמוּעִינַן חִילּוּף בֵּין עִיקָּרָן לַעֲלֵיהֶן. **מתני'** קַשְׂקֶשֶׂת. מַלְבּוּשִׁין שֶׁל דָּג. סְנַפִּיר. אֵלּוּ כְּנָפַיִם שֶׁשָּׁט בָּהֶן עַל פְּנֵי הַמַּיִם. יֵשׁ לוֹ טְלָפַיִם. פַּרְסוֹתָיו סְדוּקוֹת, שֶׁאֵין קַרְנַיִם אֶלָּא לִבְהֵמָה וּלְחַיָּה טְהוֹרָה. וְיֵשׁ שֶׁיֵּשׁ לוֹ טְלָפַיִם. כְּגוֹן חֲזִיר, וְאֵין לוֹ קַרְנַיִם. **גמ'** דָּג טָמֵא. אִיכָּא דְּיֵשׁ לוֹ סְנַפִּיר. אַקַּשְׂקֶשֶׂת סָמְכִינַן. דְּהָאָמַרְתְּ: כָּל שֶׁיֵּשׁ לוֹ קַשְׂקֶשֶׂת. (ג). ה"א מַאי קַשְׂקֶשֶׂת דִּכְתַב רַחֲמָנָא הַיְינוּ סְנַפִּיר. כְּנָפַיִם שֶׁפּוֹרֵחַ בָּהֶן, מִכִּי אִית בֵּיהּ כְּנָפַיִם – שָׁרֵי, וְאָתֵי לְמִישְׁרֵי דָּג טָמֵא. וּלְהָכִי כְּתַב תַּרְוַיְיהוּ, דְּעַל כָּרְחָךְ חַד מִינַּיְיהוּ לְבוּשָׁא הוּא. אייקררי"ן בְּלַעַ"ז. וּפָרְכִינַן: וְהַשְׁתָּא דִּכְתִיבִי תַּרְוַיְיהוּ מְנָלַן דְּקַשְׂקֶשֶׂת לְבוּשָׁא הוּא. דְּקָתָנֵי: "כָּל שֶׁיֵּשׁ לוֹ קַשְׂקֶשֶׂת – יֵשׁ לוֹ סְנַפִּיר", אַלְמָא, פְּשִׁיטָא לַן מַאי קַשְׂקֶשֶׂת, וַדַּאי מֵהַאי קְרָא נָפְקָא "וְשִׁרְיוֹן קַשְׂקַשִּׂים הוּא לָבוּשׁ". אַלְמָא, לְבוּשָׁא מִיקְרֵי. וְכֵיוָן דְּמֵהַאי קְרָא נָפְקָא, לַן הַשְׁתָּא לָא לִכְתּוֹב סְנַפִּיר וְלִכְתּוֹב קַשְׂקֶשֶׂת, דְּהָא לֵיכָּא לְמֵימַר: הֲוָה אָמִינָא, מַאי קַשְׂקֶשֶׂת סְנַפִּיר. דִּמְבָרֵךְ אַיָּרָקָא. לְאַחֲרָיו "בּוֹרֵא נְפָשׁוֹת רַבּוֹת", כִּי הֵיכִי דִּמְבָרְכִינַן אַכָּל מִינֵי מַאֲכָל וְעַל כָּל פְּרִי הָעֵץ, חוּץ מִשִּׁבְעַת הַמִּינִים דְּבָעֵינַן בְּרָכָה אַחַת מֵעֵין ג'. מִצְוֹת. צִיצִית וְלוּלָב וּשְׁאָר מִצְוֹת, שֶׁמְּבָרְכִין עֲלֵיהֶן עוֹבֵר לַעֲשִׂיָּיתָן.

רֵיחָנֵי

**והא** שבת מדחייב בפאה חייב נמי במעשר. הוי מצי לאתויי הא דתנא במס' *(שביעית.) (פ"ד) ומייתי לה בפ"ק דמסכת ע"ז (דף ז:) השבת – מתעשר זרע וירק, ובהדיא תנן ומייתי בסמוך, דשבת משנתנה טעם בקדרה – אינה מטמאה טומאת אוכלין, הא, עד שלא נתנה – מטמאה! אלא דניחא ליה למפרך דרבי עקיבא אדרבי עקיבא.

**התיאה**. פרש"י: דהיינו סיאה. וקשה: דלעיל אמר דסתמיה לאדם, וחייב במעשר, וא"כ מטמא טומאת אוכלין. והכא קאמר: תיאה אין מטמא טומאת אוכלין? וי"ל: דדוקא בשכר, סתמייהו לאדם. אי נמי: ב' מינים הן. **אם** נקח בכסף מעשר מפני מה אין מטמא טומאת אוכלים כו'. וא"ת: והא אמרינן בפרק "בכל מערבין" (עירובין כח:) קור נקח בכסף מעשר, ואין מטמא טומאת אוכלין? וי"ל: דקור נמי, אם שלקו וטגנו – מטמא טומאת אוכלין. ולכך אף קודם שליקה, נקח בכסף מעשר. מידי דהוי אבהמה וחיה, דנקחות בכסף מעשר, לפי שראויין לשחוט, אבל טומאת אוכלים אין להם מחיים. והכא פריך שפיר: אי נקחות בכסף מעשר, לפי שראויה אחר תיקון לאכילה – אם כן, יטמא טומאת אוכלים מיד, שהרי בקל יכול לתקנה, ומעתה יש עליה שם אוכל, ולא דמי לקור שמחוסר שליקה וטגון. ואי אין מטמא טומאת אוכלין, לפי שאחר התקון אינה ראויה בפני עצמה לאכילה – אם כן, גם לא יהו נקחות בכסף מעשר!

**ולכתוב** רחמנא קשקשת כו'. וא"ת: והיכי הוי ידעי מה קשקשת, קודם שנכתב קרא דגלית? ויש לומר: דמקבלה הוה ידעינן. דהכי נמי נגיחה לא ידעינן דהויא בקרן, אלא מקרא ד"ויעש לו צדקיהו בן כנענה קרני ברזל" וגו' (ב"ק דף ב:) וא"ת: ומנלן דבעינן תרוייהו, אימא דטהור בחדא מינייהו, או בהא או בהא, עד שיפרט לך הכתוב יחדו? וי"ל: דומיא דסימני בהמה בעינן מעלת גרה ומפרסת פרסה, מדאסר רחמנא חזיר וגמל.

**כל** הטעון ברכה לאחריו טעון ברכה לפניו. וברכת טבילה, דאמרינן בפ"ק דפסחים (דף ז.) דמברך אחר טבילה, התם נמי דינה להיות לפניה, אלא משום דגברא דלא חזי הוא. **ולבני** מערבא דמברכי כי מסלקין תפילייהו לשמור חוקיו. אומר ר"ת: דעל תפילין לבד הוו מברכי "לשמור חוקיו". דקרא (שמות יג) ד"ושמרת את החוקה הזאת למועדה" ס"ל לבני מערבא דבתפילין כתיב, כדאמר בירושלמי. אבל ציצית, כי קמסלק מעליו – ליכא מאן דמברך. ותפילין נמי, דוקא כשמסלקן סמוך לשקיעת החמה, שמחויב לסלקן, כדאמר ב"הקומץ רבה" (מנחות דף לו:) הניח תפילין לאחר שקיעת החמה – עובר בעשה, דכתיב "ושמרת את החוקה", והשמר דעשה – עשה. אבל ציצית, אע"ג דפטור בלילה, ליכא איסור, ואין חייב לסלקן. ובשמעתין הוי מצי למימר לאתויי ציצית, אלא דניחא למינקט ריחני, משום דפסיקא, דאכל ריחני אין מברך אחריהן. ולדידן לא קי"ל כבני מערבא, ולא מברכין אחר תפילין "לשמור חוקיו". דבפרק "הקומץ רבה" (שם דף לו.) מוכח דלילה זמן תפילין הוא. דהכי סבר רב אשי התם, ומדרבנן הוא דאסור שלא יישן בהן, וקרא ד"ושמרת" מוקמינן לה דבחוקת הפסח הכתוב מדבר. ואף על גב דשבת לאו זמן תפילין הוא, מכל מקום אין מברך עליהם כשמסלקן ע"ש עם חשכה, דאין חייב לסלקן, דנפקא לן (שם) מ"לאות על ידך" – יצאו שבתות ויו"ט שהן גופן אות*).

*) [ועי' תוס' ברכות מז: ותוס' סוכה לט. ד"ה אבל ותוס' מנחות לו: ד"ה ושמרת]

קדושי

## תוספי הרא"ש

**והא** שבת דמיחייב בפאה חייב במעשר. תימה ולמה צריך להך דיוקא והא תני בהדיא במס' שביעית ומייתי לה בפ"ק דע"ז דשבת מתעשר זרע וירק וזירין. ותו אמאי מייתי מדיוקא דמטמא טומאת אוכלין לייתו מתניתין דבסמוך השבת משנתנה טעם בקדירה אינה מטמאה כו' הא עד שלא נתנה טעם בקדירה מטמא וי"ל דניחא ליה למיפרך מדר' עקיבא אדר' עקיב': **והפלפלין** וחלת חריע כו' ואין מטמאין טומאת אוכלין. תימה דבפרק בכל מערבין אמרינן גרגיר מתעשר זרע וירק. ופריך זרע גרגיר למאי חזי ומשני שכן ראשונים לא היה להם פלפלין היו שוחקין אותו ומטבילין בו צלי וכ"ש דפלפלין מתעשר מהאי טעמא וכיון דמתעשר מטמא טומאת אוכלין. וי"ל דה"ק זרע גרגיר שוחקין אותו להטביל בו צלי ולכך מתעשר כי בפני עצמו נמי ראוי לאכילה לאחר שחיקה בלא טיבול אבל אין רגילות לשחוק כדי לאכול בלא טיבול כי אינו ראוי כמו ע"י טיבול אבל פלפלין ע"י שחיקה אינו ראוי כלל בעיניה כ"א ע"י צירוף הלכך אינו מתעשר ואינו מטמ' טומאת אוכלין ואין נראה לחלק בין רטיבתא ליבישתא כדאיתא בפרק בתרא דיומא כם פלפלי ביומא דכיפורי פטור ומוקי לה ביבשתא דהא אפי' ביבישתא ראוי להטביל בו צלי: **אם** ניקחין בכסף מעשר מפני מה אין מטמאין כו'. ותימה והא אמרינן בפ' בכל מערבין דקור ניקח בכסף מעשר ואינו מטמא טומאת אוכלין וי"ל דשאני קור דנעשה אוכל גמור ע"י שליקה דאמרינן דאם שלקו וטגנו מטמא טומאת אוכלין. הילכך ניקח בכסף מעשר אף קודם שליקה מידי דהוה אבהמה וחיה דניקחין בכסף מעשר לפי שראויה לישחט אע"ג דאין מטמאין טומאת אוכלין מחיים. אבל קושט וחימום והנך דחשיבי בהדייהו אינן נעשין אוכל ע"י תיקון אלא לטעמא עבידי או לטיבול ולכך נמנו וגמרו דאין מטמאין טומאת אוכלין הילכך פריך מעיקרא אם ניקחין בכסף מעשר משום דבתיקון כל שהוא חזו למילתייהו או לטעמא או לטיבול מפני מה א)אינן ראויין לאכילה בפני עצמן א"כ לא יהו ניקחין בכסף מעשר: **ולכתוב** קשקשת. ותימה ומנא ידעינן מאי פירושו קודם שנכתב קרא דגלית וי"ל דקבלה היתה בידם ממשה רבינו כמו כי ינח דלא ידענא דהוה בקרן אלא מקרא דויעש לו צדקיהו בן כנענה קרני ברזל. ותימה השתא נמי נימא דבחד טהור או האי או האי עד שיפרט לך הכתוב יחדו וי"ל דומיא דסימני בהמה דמפרסת פרסה ומעלת גרה דבעינן תרוייהו מדאסר רחמנא חזיר וגמל: **ולבני** מערבא דמברכי בתר דמסלקי תפליהו לשמור חוקיו. אר"ת דלאחר שמסלק טליתו מעליו ליכא מאן דמברך דלא שייך ברכה דלשמור חוקיו אלא בתפלין דוקא דכתיב ושמרת את החוקה הזאת למועדה מימים ימימה ודוקא כשמסלקן סמוך לשקיעת החמה דדרשינן ימים ולא לילות ומחוייב לסלקן כדאמרינן בהקומץ רבה המניח תפילין אחר שקיעת החמה עובר בעשה וכן דאיכא מצוה בסילוקן מברך. ובירושלמי דברכות פ' היה קורא נמי אמרינן על מילתא דבני מערבא דמברכי לשמור חוקיו כמ"ד בחוקת תפילין הכתוב מדבר (לא) וא"כ כ"ש דלאחר ציצית לא מברך דלא כתיב ביה חוקה ומיהו הוה מצי למימר לאיתויי ציצית אלא דניחא ליה למימר לאיתויי מהני דפסיקא ליה אבל שאר מצות לא פסיקא ליה כיון דעל תפלין מברכי ולדידן לא מברכינן לשמור חוקיו אפי' לאחר תפלין דבפרק הקומץ רבה מוכח דלילה לאו זמן תפילין הוא ומדרבנן הוא דאסור גזירה שמא ישן בהן וקרא דושמרת את החוקה הזאת בחוקת הפסח הכתוב מדבר ואפי' עם כניסת ע"ש לא מברך אע"ג דמצוה בסילוקן כיון דלא כתוב בהו חוקה דהא דשבת לאו זמן תפלין הוא

א) חסר כאן וצ"ל מפני מה אינן מטמאין טומאת אוכלין ואי אינן מטמאין טומאת אוכלין לפי שאחר התקון אינן ראויין וכו'.

מסורת הש"ס: עוקצין פ"ג מ"ה; [ליתא במשנה]; ג"ז שם מ"ד ברכות לט.; רש"ל מ"ז; [עי' שביעית פ"ז מ"א ומ"ב]; [שביעית פ"ז מ"א]; [שם מ"ב]; [פסחים נב: ע"ש]; חולין סו.; ברכות מד:; [שם ע"ש]

הגהות הב"ח

(א) גמ' בפאה מיחייב במעשר כל"ל ותיבת ו' נמחק: (ב) רש"י ד"ה לכמך וכו' ועיקרו שבתוכו מטבילין כל: (ג) ד"ה אקשקשת וכו' קשקשת יש לו סנפיר הס"ד:

גליון הש"ס

גמ' הוה אמינא מאי קשקשת סנפיר. ע' חולין כב ע"ב תוס' ד"ה ...:

רִיחָנֵי. מְבָרְכִין עֲלֵיהֶן "בּוֹרֵא עֲצֵי בְשָׂמִים", וְאֵין טָעוּן בְּרָכָה לְאַחֲרָיו, דַּהֲנָאָה מוּעֶטֶת הִיא. **מתני'** וְרָאוּי לִהְיוֹת בֵּן סוֹרֵר וּמוֹרֶה. מִשֶּׁיָּבִיא שְׁתֵּי שְׂעָרוֹת עַד שֶׁיַּקִּיף זָקָן, אֲבָל קוֹדֶם ב' שְׂעָרוֹת – לָאו בַּר עוֹנָשִׁין הוּא, וּמִשֶּׁהִקִּיף זָקָן – רָאוּי לְהוֹלִיד, וְרַחֲמָנָא אָמַר "בֵּן" וְלֹא הָרָאוּי לִהְיוֹת אָב. הַתַּחְתּוֹן וְלֹא הָעֶלְיוֹן. תורה אור

**קדושי** טעות. הקשה ריב"ן: וכי לית ליה מתניתין דיבמות (דף ג:) "ואי אתה יכול לומר בחמותו ואם חמותו שמיאנו"? וליכא למימר: דמתני' דהתם – בקדושי קטנות, והכא איירי – בקדושי טעות, כדקתני בהדיא דרבי ישמעאל בקדושי קטנה נמי איירי, שהרי

אריחני.§ **מתני'** בתִּינוֹקֶת שֶׁהֵבִיאָה שְׁתֵּי שְׂעָרוֹת – אוֹ חוֹלֶצֶת אוֹ מִתְיַבֶּמֶת, וְחַיֶּיבֶת בְּכָל מִצְוֹת הָאֲמוּרוֹת בַּתּוֹרָה. וְכֵן תִּינוֹק שֶׁהֵבִיא שְׁתֵּי שְׂעָרוֹת – חַיָּיב בְּכָל מִצְוֹת הָאֲמוּרוֹת בַּתּוֹרָה, גוְרָאוּי לִהְיוֹת בֵּן סוֹרֵר וּמוֹרֶה, *מִשֶּׁיָּבִיא שְׁתֵּי שְׂעָרוֹת עַד שֶׁיַּקִּיף זָקָן. הַתַּחְתּוֹן וְלֹא הָעֶלְיוֹן, אֶלָּא שֶׁדִּבְּרוּ חֲכָמִים בְּלָשׁוֹן נְקִיָּה. דתִּינוֹקֶת שֶׁהֵבִיאָה שְׁתֵּי שְׂעָרוֹת אֵינָהּ יְכוֹלָה לְמָאֵן. *רַבִּי יְהוּדָה אוֹמֵר: עַד שֶׁיִּרְבֶּה הַשָּׁחוֹר.§ **גמ'** וְכֵיוָן דִּתְנַן: "חַיֶּיבֶת בְּכָל מִצְוֹת הָאֲמוּרוֹת בַּתּוֹרָה", "אוֹ חוֹלֶצֶת אוֹ מִתְיַבֶּמֶת" לָמָּה לִי? לְאַפּוּקֵי *מִדְּרַבִּי יוֹסֵי, דְּאָמַר: "אִישׁ" כָּתוּב בַּפָּרָשָׁה, אֲבָל אִשָּׁה – בֵּין גְּדוֹלָה וּבֵין קְטַנָּה, קמ"ל: דְּאִי אַיְיתֵי שְׁתֵּי שְׂעָרוֹת – אִין, אִי לָא – לָא. מַאי טַעְמָא? אִשָּׁה כְּאִישׁ. וְכֵיוָן דְּתָנָא "וְכֵן הַתִּינוֹק שֶׁהֵבִיא ב' שְׂעָרוֹת", "חַיָּיב בְּכָל הַמִּצְוֹת הָאֲמוּרוֹת בַּתּוֹרָה" ל"ל? וְכִי תֵּימָא: מִשּׁוּם דְּקָבָעֵי לְמִתְנֵי "וְרָאוּי לִהְיוֹת בֵּן סוֹרֵר וּמוֹרֶה" תְּנִינָא חֲדָא זִימְנָא: *אֵימָתַי הוּא בֵּן סוֹרֵר וּמוֹרֶה – מִשֶּׁיָּבִיא שְׁתֵּי שְׂעָרוֹת וְעַד שֶׁיַּקִּיף זָקָן, הַתַּחְתּוֹן וְלֹא הָעֶלְיוֹן, אֶלָּא שֶׁדִּבְּרוּ חֲכָמִים בְּלָשׁוֹן נְקִיָּה! אִין ה"נ, אֶלָּא – אַיְּדֵי דְּפָרֵישׁ מִילֵּי דְתִינוֹקֶת – קָמְפָרֵשׁ נַמִּי מִילֵּי דְתִינוֹק.§ "תִּינוֹקֶת שֶׁהֵבִיאָה" כו'.§ א"ר אֲבָהוּ, א"ר אֶלְעָזָר: הֲלָכָה כְּרַבִּי יְהוּדָה. וּמוֹדֶה רַבִּי יְהוּדָה שֶׁאִם נִבְעֲלָה לְאַחַר שֶׁהֵבִיאָה שְׁתֵּי שְׂעָרוֹת – שׁוּב אֵינָהּ יְכוֹלָה לְמָאֵן. חַבְרוּהִי דְּרַב כָּהֲנָא סְבוּר לְמֶעֱבַד עוּבְדָא כְּרַבִּי יְהוּדָה, וְאע"ג דְּנִבְעֲלָה. אֲמַר לְהוּ רַב כָּהֲנָא: לֹא כָּךְ הָיָה מַעֲשֶׂה בְּבִתּוֹ שֶׁל רַבִּי יִשְׁמָעֵאל, שֶׁבָּאת לְבֵית הַמִּדְרָשׁ לְמָאֵן, וּבְנָהּ מוּרְכָּב לָהּ עַל כְּתֵפָהּ. וְאוֹתוֹ הַיּוֹם הוּזְכְּרוּ דְּבָרָיו שֶׁל רַבִּי יִשְׁמָעֵאל בְּבֵית הַמִּדְרָשׁ, *וּבָכְתָה בְּכִיָּיה גְּדוֹלָה בְּבֵית הַמִּדְרָשׁ. אָמְרוּ: דָּבָר שֶׁאָמַר אוֹתוֹ צַדִּיק – יִכָּשֵׁל בּוֹ זַרְעוֹ? *דְּאָמַר רַב יְהוּדָה, אָמַר שְׁמוּאֵל מִשּׁוּם רַבִּי יִשְׁמָעֵאל: °"וְהִיא לֹא נִתְפָּשָׂה" – אֲסוּרָה, ההָא נִתְפְּשָׂה – מוּתֶּרֶת. ווְיֵשׁ לְךָ אַחֶרֶת, שֶׁאע"פ שֶׁלֹּא נִתְפְּשָׂה – מוּתֶּרֶת, וְאֵיזוֹ זוֹ – שֶׁקִּדּוּשֶׁיהָ קִדּוּשֵׁי טָעוּת, שֶׁאע"פ שֶׁבְּנָהּ מוּרְכָּב עַל כְּתֵפָהּ – מְמָאֶנֶת וְהוֹלֶכֶת לָהּ. זוְנִמְנוּ וְגָמְרוּ: עַד מָתַי הַבַּת מְמָאֶנֶת – עַד שֶׁתָּבִיא שְׁתֵּי שְׂעָרוֹת! פָּרוּשׁ וְלָא עֲבוּד עוּבְדָא. רַבִּי יִצְחָק וְתַלְמִידֵי דְּרַבִּי חֲנִינָא עֲבוּד עוּבְדָא כְּרַבִּי יְהוּדָה, וְאע"ג דְּנִבְעֲלָה. אֲזַל רַב שֶׁמֶן בַּר אַבָּא אֲמָרָהּ קַמֵּיהּ דְּר' יוֹחָנָן, אֲזַל רַבִּי יוֹחָנָן אֲמָרָהּ קַמֵּיהּ דְּרַבִּי יְהוּדָה נְשִׂיאָה. שְׁדַר בַּלָּשָׁא, וְאַפְּקוּהָ. אָמַר רַב חִסְדָּא, אָמַר מָר עוּקְבָא: לֹא שֶׁיִּרְבֶּה הַשָּׁחוֹר מַמָּשׁ, אֶלָּא כְּדֵי שֶׁיִּהְיוּ שְׁתֵּי שְׂעָרוֹת שׁוֹכְבוֹת, וְנִרְאוֹת כְּמִי שֶׁיִּרְבֶּה הַשָּׁחוֹר עַל הַלָּבָן. רָבָא אָמַר: שְׁתֵּי שְׂעָרוֹת הַמַּקִּיפוֹת מִשָּׂפָה לְשָׂפָה. א"ר חֶלְבּוֹ, אָמַר רַב הוּנָא: חשְׁתֵּי שְׂעָרוֹת שֶׁאָמְרוּ – צָרִיךְ שֶׁיְּהֵא בְּעִיקָּרָן גּוּמוֹת. *רַב מַלְכִּיו אָמַר רַב אַדָּא בַּר אַהֲבָה: טגּוּמוֹת אע"פ שֶׁאֵין שְׂעָרוֹת. אָמַר רַב חֲנִינָא בְּרֵיהּ דְּרַב אִיקָא: שַׁפּוּד, שְׁפָחוֹת, וְגוּמוֹת – רַב מַלְכִּיו; בְּלוֹרִית, אֵפֶר מִקְלֶה, וּגְבִינָה – רַב מַלְכִּיָּא. רַב פַּפָּא אָמַר: מַתְנִי' וּמַתְנִיתָא – רַב מַלְכִּיָּא, שְׁמַעְתְּתָא – רַב מַלְכִּיו, וְסִימָנָא: מַתְנִיתָא מַלְכְּתָא. מַאי בֵּינַיְיהוּ? אִיכָּא בֵּינַיְיהוּ שְׁפָחוֹת. אָמַר רַב אַשִׁי, אָמַר לִי מָר זוּטְרָא, קָשֶׁה בָּהּ רַבִּי חֲנִינָא מִסּוּרָא: לָא לִישְׁתָּמִיט תַּנָּא וְאַשְׁמוּעִי' גּוּמוֹת! אִי אַשְׁמוּעִינַן גּוּמוֹת – ה"א: עַד שֶׁיְּהוּ שְׁתֵּי שְׂעָרוֹת בִּשְׁתֵּי גּוּמוֹת, קמ"ל – ידַּאֲפִילּוּ שְׁתֵּי שְׂעָרוֹת בְּגוּמָא אַחַת. וּמִי אִיכָּא כְּה"ג? וְהָכְתִיב: °"אֲשֶׁר בִּשְׂעָרָה יְשׁוּפֵנִי וְהִרְבָּה פְצָעַי חִנָּם", *וְאָמַר רָבָא: אִיּוֹב בִּסְעָרָה חֵירֵף, בִּסְעָרָה הֱשִׁיבוּהוּ. בִּסְעָרָה חֵירֵף – אָמַר לְפָנָיו: רבש"ע, שֶׁמָּא רוּחַ סְעָרָה עָבְרָה לְפָנֶיךָ וְנִתְחַלְּפָה לְךָ בֵּין אִיּוֹב לְאוֹיֵב? בִּסְעָרָה הֱשִׁיבוּהוּ: °"וַיַּעַן ה' אֶת אִיּוֹב

בְּאֵיזוֹ הַקָּפַת זָקָן אָמְרוּ? בַּתַּחְתּוֹן שֶׁלְּמַטָּה וְלֹא הָעֶלְיוֹן. ה"ג: רַבִּי יְהוּדָה אוֹמֵר עַד שֶׁיִּרְבֶּה הַשָּׁחוֹר. וְל"ג: "עַל הַלָּבָן", כְּלוֹמַר, שֶׁיַּשְׁחִיר אוֹתוֹ מָקוֹם מִשְּׂעָרוֹת הַרְבֵּה. **גמ'** אִישׁ כְּתִיב בַּפָּרָשָׁה. (דברים כה) "וְאִם לֹא יַחְפּוֹץ הָאִישׁ", הִלְכָּךְ קָטָן לֹא חָלֵין, אֲבָל אִשָּׁה – בֵּין גְּדוֹלָה בֵּין קְטַנָּה. הֲלָכָה כְּרַבִּי יְהוּדָה. שֶׁאִם לֹא בָּא עָלֶיהָ מִשֶּׁהֵבִיאָה שְׁתֵּי שְׂעָרוֹת – שֶׁיְּכוֹלָה לַעֲקוֹר נִשּׂוּאֵי קַטְנוּתֶיהָ, עַד שֶׁיִּרְבֶּה הַשָּׁחוֹר. שׁוּב אֵינָהּ יְכוֹלָה לְמָאֵן. דְּהָךְ בִּיאָה הָווּ לְהוּ קִדּוּשִׁין גְּמוּרִין, דִּגְדוֹלָה הִיא וּבְיָדָהּ לְקַדֵּשׁ עַצְמָהּ. וְכִי פָּלֵיג – כְּשֶׁלֹּא בָּעַל לְאַחַר שֶׁגָּדְלָה פָּלֵיג, וַאפ"ה לְר"מ לֹא מְמָאֶנֶת, דְּכֵיוָן שֶׁהִגְדִּילָה שָׁעָה אַחַת וְלֹא מִיחֲתָה – שׁוּב אֵינָהּ יְכוֹלָה לִמְחוֹת, וְחָלוּ לְהוּ קִדּוּשִׁין קַמָּאֵי. בְּבִתּוֹ שֶׁל רַבִּי יִשְׁמָעֵאל. שֶׁהִשִּׂיאָתָהּ אִמָּהּ כְּשֶׁהָיְתָה קְטַנָּה יְתוֹמָה, וּלְאַחַר שֶׁיָּלְדָה בָּאת לְמָאֵן. וְהִיא. מִיעוּטָא הוּא, וְהָכִי דָּרֵישׁ: "הִיא" – אִשָּׁה סְתָמָא שֶׁקִּדּוּשֶׁיהָ גְּמוּרִין, הִיא דְּכִי לֹא נֶאֶנְסָה – אֲסוּרָה לְבַעְלָהּ, וְיֵשׁ לְךָ אַחֶרֶת, שֶׁאֲפִילּוּ זָנְתָה שֶׁלֹּא בְּאוֹנֶס – מוּתֶּרֶת לַבַּעַל וְלַבּוֹעֵל, וְאֵיזוֹ? זוֹ שֶׁקִּידּוּשֶׁיהָ קִדּוּשֵׁי טָעוּת, כְּגוֹן "ע"מ שֶׁאֲנִי כֹּהֵן", וַהֲרֵי הוּא יִשְׂרָאֵל. וּכְגוֹן קְטַנָּה, דְּאֵין מַעֲשֶׂיהָ כְּלוּם, וְאִמָּהּ נַמִּי אֵין בְּיָדָהּ לְקַדְּשָׁהּ. וַאֲפִילּוּ בְּנָהּ מוּרְכָּב כו'. דְּלָאו נִשּׂוּאִין הָווּ, לְעִנְיַן זְנוּת נַמִּי לֹא מִיתַּסְרָה עֲלֵיהּ, דִּפְנוּיָה בְּעָלְמָא הִיא. וְלָא אָמְרִינַן: בְּעִילוֹת שֶׁבָּעַל מִשֶּׁגָּדְלָה – הָווּ קִדּוּשִׁין, דְּקָסָבַר: כָּל הַבּוֹעֵל – עַל דַּעַת קִדּוּשִׁין הָרִאשׁוֹנִים הוּא בּוֹעֵל, וְלֹא נִתְכַּוֵּין לַחֲזוֹר וּלְקַדְּשָׁהּ. בַּלָּשָׁא. חַיִל. וְאַפְּקוּהָ. מִבַּעְלָהּ הָאַחֲרוֹן שֶׁנְּשָׂאָהּ בְּמֵיאוּן זֶה. שְׁתֵּי שְׂעָרוֹת שׁוֹכְבוֹת. שֶׁיְּהוּ אֲרוּכּוֹת. שְׁפָחוֹת. מַתְנִיתִין הִיא בִּכְתוּבּוֹת, וְאָמַר רַב מַלְכִּיָּא עֲלָהּ: הֲלָכָה כְּר"א. בְּלוֹרִית. מַתְנִיתִין הִיא: גּוֹי הַמִּסְתַּפֵּר מִיִּשְׂרָאֵל, כֵּיוָן שֶׁהִגִּיעַ לִבְלוֹרִית – שׁוֹמֵט אֶת יָדוֹ. וְאָמְרִינַן: וְכַמָּה? וְאָמַר רַב מַלְכִּיָּא עֲלָהּ: ג' אֶצְבָּעוֹת לְכָל רוּחַ. גְּבִינָה. נַמִּי מִשְׁנָה הִיא בְּ"אֵין מַעֲמִידִין": מִפְּנֵי מָה אָסְרוּ גְּבִינוֹת הַגּוֹיִם כו' וְאָמַר רַב מַלְכִּיָּא עֲלָהּ: מִפְּנֵי שֶׁמַּחֲלִיקִין פְּנֵיהֶן בְּשׁוּמַן חֲזִיר. כָּל הָנָךְ תְּלָתָא לֹא אָתָא רַב מַלְכִּיָּא אֶלָּא לְפָרוּשֵׁי טַעֲמָא דְּמַתְנִיתִין, [אוֹ] שִׁיעוּרָא אוֹ לְאוֹקְמֵי הִלְכְתָא. אֲבָל גּוּמוֹת, שַׁפּוּד וְאֵפֶר מִקְלֶה – שְׁמַעְתָּא דְּנַפְשֵׁיהּ הִיא. וְרַב פַּפָּא מַחֲלִיף שְׁפָחוֹת – לְרַב מַלְכִּיָּא, וְאֵפֶר מִקְלֶה – לְרַב מַלְכִּיו. קָשֶׁה בָּהּ רַבִּי חֲנִינָא. אִי סָלְקָא דַּעְתָּךְ: גּוּמוֹת אַף עַל פִּי שֶׁאֵין שְׂעָרוֹת – לָא לִישְׁתַּמֵּיט בְּכוּלֵּיהּ תַּלְמוּד חַד תַּנָּא, וּלְאַשְׁמוּעִי' תִּינוֹקֶת שֶׁהֵבִיאָה שְׁתֵּי גּוּמוֹת. מִן

בתו שבאת למאן הוו קדושי קטנות, דמינה מייתי רב כהנא ראייה דאינה ממאנת אחר הבאת שערות, וקאמר: "דבר שאמר אותו לדיק יכשל בו זרעו" – אלמא ר' ישמעאל בקדושי קטנות נמי איירי. ואע"ג דיש לפרש למה שאמר (א) "אותו לדיק" – היינו, כעין דבר שאמר אותו לדיק, שהוא אומר בקדושי טעות, ובתו באת למאן מחמת קדושי קטנות. מ"מ מדקאמר "נמנו וגמרו עד מתי הבת ממאנת? עד שתביא ב' שערות" משמע דנמנו וגמרו לאפוקי מדר' ישמעאל. דליכא למימר: לאפוקי מדרבי יהודה, דהא רבי יהודה מודה בנבעלה. וזאת, נבעלה, שהרי בנה מורכב על כתפה היה. ושמואל דסבר כרבי ישמעאל, ואמר בפרק "המדיר" (כתובות דף עג:) קדשה על תנאי, וכנסה סתם – אפילו בעל, אינה לריכה הימנו גט, וכי לית ליה לשמואל מתני' דיבמות (דף ג:) ובפ' "המדיר" (כתובות דף עג.) פריך לשמואל ממשניות טובא, ומשני להו, ולא בעי למימר דפליג אסתם משנה! וי"ל: דר' ישמעאל לית ליה מתני' דיבמות. ושמואל לא סבר כר' ישמעאל אלא בקדושי טעות, אבל בקדושי קטנות – לא סבר כוותיה, אלא כמתני' דיבמות (דף ג:) ודמכילתין, דתנן: "עד מתי הבת ממאנת? עד שתביא ב' שערות". ובפרק "מי שמת" (ב"ב דף קנו.) קאמר שמואל בהדיא: בודקין למיאונין, לאפוקי מדרבי יהודה. וכן מוכח נמי בפרק "נושאין" (יבמות דף ק:) דפריך: ממאנת מי קא ילדה? ומשני: בקדושי טעות, וכרבי ישמעאל. משמע, דוקא בקדושי טעות סבר כוותיה, ולא בקדושי קטנות, דאליבא דשמואל איירי התם. והא דאמר שמואל בפ' "ב"ש" (שם דף קט:) ובפ' "המדיר" (כתובות דף עג.) קטנה שלא מיאנה והגדילה ועמדה ונישאת – לריכה גט משני, משמע דאינה מקודשת לראשון, מדלריכה גט משני. היינו, מן התורה, אבל מדרבנן – לריכה גט מראשון, דמשהגדילה אינה יולאה במיאון, כדפרישית. **איכא** בינייהו שפחות. וא"ת: לימא נמי, איכא בינייהו "אפר מקלה", דהוי שמעתתא, ותני לה בדרב מלכיא, א] דרב פפא אמר שמעתתא דרב מלכיו? ויש לומר: דה"ק כולהו מתניתא רב מלכיא, ושמעתתא – יש מהן רב מלכיא ויש מהן רב מלכיו. עד

מא א טוש"ע א"ח סי' רטז סעי' א:
מב ב מיי' פ"ב מהל' אישות הל"א ופ"א מהל' יבום הלי"ז סמג עשין נא טוש"ע אה"ע סי' קסו סעיף ד [וברב אלפס יבמות פי"ג מו]:
מג ג מיי' פי"ז מהל' ממרים הל"ה:
מד ד מיי' פי"א מהל' גירושין הל"ד וע"ש סמג עשין כ טוש"ע אה"ע סי' קנה סעיף יב [וברב אלפס שם]:
מה ה מיי' פי"ח מהל' איסורי ביאה הלי"ז סמג לאוין קכה טוש"ע אה"ע סי' ו סעיף יח:
מו ו מיי' שם פ"ג הל"ב:
מז ז מיי' פי"א מהל' גירושין הלכה ד סמג עשין נ טוש"ע אה"ע סי' קנה סעיף יב:
מח ח ט י מיי' פ"ב מהל' אישות הלי"ז סמג עשין נ טוש"ע שם סעי' טז:

[סנהדרין סח:]
יבמות יב: כתובות לו. ב"ב קנו. חולין כו:
[יבמות קח: ב"ב קנו.]
[סנהדרין סח:]
נ"א ובכתה
יבמות נו: וקף ק: כתובות נח. עג.
במדבר ה
ב"ק כח: כתובות סח: ע"ז כט.
איוב ט
ב"ב טז. [ושם איתא רבא]
שם לח

**הגהות הב"ח**
(א) תוס' ד"ה קדושי כו' ואע"ג דיש לפרש למה שאמר דבר שאמר אותו לדיק:

**הגהות מהר"ב רנשבורג**
א] תוס' ד"ה איכא בינייהו כו' ותני לה בדרב מלכיא. נ"ב עיין פרש"י ובמכות דף כא ע"א בפרש"י ובערוך ערך ספוד וצ"ע:

**תוספי הרא"ש**
הוא נפקא לן מוהיו לך לאות יצאו שבתות וימים טובים שהן עצמן אות: **ואי** זו זו (זו) שקידושיה בטעות. והקשה הריב"ן וכי לית ליה לר' ישמעאל מתני' דפ"ק דיבמות אי אתה יכול לומר בחמותו ואם חמותו שמיאנו. ושמואל נמי דאמר בפ' המדיר קדשה על תנאי וכנסה סתם אפי' בעל אינה צריכה גט. א"כ לדידיה נמי מצינו חמות ממאנת ולא מצינו למימר דאפי' מיאון אינה צריכה דהא קתני הכא ממאנת והולכת וכ"ת מתניתין דהתם לא איירי בקידושי טעות אלא בקידושי קטנות דהא ר' ישמעאל בקידושי קטנות נמי איירי דהא בתו שבאת למאן קידושי קטנה היא דהא מייתי ראיה מינה דאינה ממאנת לאחר הבאת ב' שערות וקאמר דבר שאמר אותו צדיק יכשל בו זרעו אלמא ר' ישמעאל בקידושי קטנות נמי איירי אפי' אם תפרש מעין אותו דבר שאמר אותו צדיק שדיבר בקידושי טעות יכשל בו זרעו לעשות אפי' בקידושי קטנות מ"מ מדאמר נמנו וגמרו עד שתביא שתי שערות אי לאפוקי מדר' יהודה נמנו הא מודה בנבעלה וזאת בנה מורכב על כתיפה היא אלא לאפוקי מדר' ישמעאל וע"י ברייתא זו פרוש חבריא דרב כהנא ולא עבוד עובדא אלמא דר' ישמעאל אף בקידושי קטנות נמי איירי ואין נראה לומר דלית ליה לשמואל מתני' דיבמות וסבר לה כר' ישמעאל דהא בפרק המדיר פריך לשמואל ממשניות טובא ומשני להו וי"ל דשמוא' בקידושי טעות סבר לה כר' ישמעאל אבל בקידושי קטנות פליג עליה והשתא לא פליג שמואל אמתניתין דיבמות ודמכילתין דתנן ממאנת עד שתביא ב' שערות ומתניתין דב"ש דתנן מלמדין את הקטנה שתמאן בו. ר"ג אומר תמתין עד שתגדיל ותצא הלזו משום אחות אשה וכן בס"פ מי שמת אמר שמואל בודקין למיאונין לאפוקי מדר' יהודה וכן משמע בפ' נושאין דקאמר ממאנת מי ילדה ומשני בקידושי טעות וכר' ישמעאל משמע דוקא בקידושי טעות סבר לה כר' ישמעאל דממאנת בגדולות ולא בקידושי קטנות ואליבא דשמואל איירי התם וכן הלכה. והכי פסק בפרק מי שמת הילכתא בכולהו דאמר שמואל וחדא מינייהו הוי בודקין לחליצה ולמיאונין ולגיטין ולקידושין: **עבוד** עובדא כר' יהודה אע"פ שנבעלה. תימה לי מאי קסברי אי טעמא דר' יהודה משום על דעת קידושין הראשונים הוא בועל אפי' רבה השחור נמי ואי קסבר לשם קידושין הוא בועל אפי' הביא שתי שערות נמי וצ"ל דסבירא להו דלר' יהודה על דעת קידושין הראשונים הוא בועל ומי' כשהיא גדולה כל כך שכבר רבה השחור אמור רבנן דלא ממאנת [גזירה] אטו נתקדשה האידנא: **איכא** בינייהו שפחות. פרש"י ושכנגדה דהיינו אפר מקלה דהוי שמעתא ורב מלכיא אמרה. א"נ ה"ק כולהו מתנייתא רב מלכיא ושמעתתא יש מהן רב מלכיו אמרם:

**עד** שתכלכל. לשון גדול שער הוא, כדאמר בריש נזיר (דף ג.) "הריני מכלכל" – הרי זה נזיר, וקאמר בגמרא: *מאי משמע דכלכול לישנא דגדול שער הוא? *דתניא, אמר רבי יהודה: סיד – כדי לסוד כלכול קטן, ואמר: לדעה ובת לדעה. **הלכה** כדברי כולן להחמיר. בפ' "מי שמת" (ב"ב דף קנו.) אמר ר"נ אמר שמואל: בודקין לחלילה ולמיאונין – לאפוקי מדרבי יהודה, דאמר: עד שירבה השחור על הלבן. והתם פסק ככולהו דאמר התם ר"נ אמר שמואל. וה"נ קאמר: הלכה כדברי כולן, להחמיר. הלכך, אינה חולצת עד שתביא שער גדול שבכולן, ועד שיהו ב' שערות במקום אחד, כרב אשי. ואם יש לה דדים גדולים, כשאר נשים – אינה צריכה לבדוק התחתון. ולא תמאן – משהביאה שתי שערות קטנות, ואפי' אחת בגבה ואחת בין קשרי אצבעותיה. ור"ת כתב בספר הישר: דמשהגיעה לכלל שנותיה – לא תמאן בזמן הזה, דאע"ג דהיכא דלא בעל פסקינן בפ' "יוצא דופן" (לעיל דף מו.) דלא חיישינן שמא נשרו, אין אנו בקיאין לבדוק בכל גופה שלא יהו לה שערות, דאפי' אחת בגבה ואחת בכריסה ובקשרי אצבעותיה – מצטרפים, או גומות גרידא.

**שלש** גריסין נמי (ג) בתרי יומי תרתי ופלגא חזיתיה ואידך דם מאכולת הוא. תימה: אמאי לא פריך, דלמא כל ג' גריסין בתרי יומי חזיתיה, כדקאמר בפחות מג' גריסין? ונראה למהר"ם וכן מצאתי, דאי לא דתלינן בדם מאכולת, ונימא: דכל הכתם מגופה חזיתיה – אין לנו להקל ולומר: דבתרי יומי חזיתיה, כיון דיש בו שיעור דאפשר לחלקו לג' ראיות. לכך פריך: דילמא תרי ופלגא בתרי יומי חזיתיה, כיון דראתה מעט פחות מג' גריסין, אע"ג דאית בהו טפי משיעור שתי ראיות – אתה מיקל לתלות המותר באותן ב' ראיות, ולא בראייה ג'. ה"נ בג' גריסין וג' עודות נימא: תרי ופלגא, אע"ג דהוה טפי מב' ראיות נימא: דבתרי יומי חזיתיה, והמותר נתלה בדם מאכולת. וא"ת: מנא ליה לרבא דבג' גריסין במקום א' חיישי רבנן, דילמא דוקא בג' מקומות ומצאתן ביום אחד, ולר' חנינא דוקא בג' חלוקות, או בחלוק א' ומצאתו בג' ימים? וי"ל: דלא מפלגי רבנן. אבל

איוב מן הסערה, ויאמר" *אליו: שוטה שבעולם, הרבה נימין בראתי בראשו של אדם, ולכל נימא ונימא בראתי לו גומא בפני עצמה שלא יהיו שתים יונקות מגומא אחת, שאלמלא שתים יונקות מגומא אחת – מכחיש מאור עיניו של אדם. גומא בגומא לא נתחלף לי, איוב באויב נתחלף לי? לא קשיא, הא – בגופא, הא – ברישא. אמר רב יהודה, אמר שמואל: [א]שתי שערות שאמרו – אפילו אחת על הכף ואחת על הביצים. *תניא נמי הכי: שתי שערות שאמרו – אפילו אחת בגבה ואחת בכריסה, אחת ע"ג קשרי אצבעותיה של יד ואחת ע"ג קשרי אצבעותיה של רגל, דברי ר' שמעון בן יהודה איש כפר עכו שאמר משום רבי שמעון. ורבנן אמר רב (א) חסדא: [ב]עד שיהו ב' שערות במקום אחד. ת"ר: *עד מתי הבת ממאנת? עד שתביא שתי שערות, דברי רבי מאיר. ר' יהודה אומר: עד שירבה השחור. רבי יוסי אומר: עד שתקיף העטרה. בן שלקות אומר: עד שתכלכל. ואמר רבי שמעון, מצאני חנינא בן חכינאי בצידן, ואמר: כשאתה מגיע אצל ר"ע אמור לו "עד מתי הבת ממאנת"? אם יאמר לך "עד שתביא שתי שערות", אמור לו "והלא בן שלקות העיד במעמד כולכם ביבנה עד שתכלכל, ולא אמרתם לו דבר"! כשבאתי אצל רבי עקיבא, אמר לי: כלכול זה – איני יודע מהו, בן שלקות – איני מכיר, עד מתי הבת ממאנת – עד שתביא ב' שערות.§ **מתני'** [ג]שתי שערות האמורות בפרה, ובנגעים, והאמורות בכל מקום – כדי לכוף ראשן לעיקרן – דברי רבי ישמעאל. ר"א אומר: כדי לקרוץ בציפורן, ר' עקיבא אומר: כדי שיהו ניטלות בזוג.§ **גמ'** אמר רב חסדא, אמר מר עוקבא: [ד]הלכה כדברי כולן להחמיר.§ **מתני'** [ה]הרואה כתם – הרי זו מקולקלת וחוששת משום זוב – דברי רבי מאיר, וחכ"א: אין בכתמים משום זוב.§ **גמ'** *מאן חכמים? ר' חנינא בן אנטיגנוס היא, דתניא, ר"ח בן אנטיגנוס אומר: כתמים אין בהן משום זוב. ופעמים שהכתמים מביאין לידי זיבה. [ו]כיצד – לבשה ג' חלוקות הבדוקות לה ומצאה עליהם כתם, או שראתה ב' ימים וחלוק אחד – הן הן הכתמים המביאין לידי זיבה. השתא שלשה חלוקות דלאו מגופה קחזיא – חיישינן, ב' ימים וחלוק אחד מיבעיא? מהו דתימא – כל כי האי גוונא מביאה קרבן ונאכל, קא משמע לן. אמר רבא, בהא זכנהו ר' חנינא בן אנטיגנוס לרבנן: מאי שנא פחות מג' גריסין במקום אחד דלא חיישינן דאמרי': בתרי יומי חזיתיה, שלשה גריסין במקום אחד נמי – נימא: תרתי ופלגא מגופה חזיתיה, ואידך – אגב זוהמא דם מאכולת הוא. ורבנן, כיון דאיכא לפלוגי בגרים ועוד לכל יומא – לא תלינן. ור"ח בן אנטיגנוס ג' גריסין במקום א' הוא דלא חיישינן, הא בג' מקומות – חיישינן? הא אמרת בג' חלוקות – אין, בג' מקומות – לא! לדבריהם דרבנן קאמר להו, לדידי – בג' חלוקות – אין, בג' מקומות – לא: אלא לדידכו, אודו לי מיהת דהיכא דחזאי ג' גריסין במקום אחד, דאמרינן – תרי ופלגא מגופה חזיתיה, ואידך – אגב זוהמא דם מאכולת הוא! ורבנן – כיון דאיכא לפלוגי בגרים ועוד לכל יומא – לא תלינן. ת"ר: [ז]הרואה כתם, אם יש בו כדי לחלק ג' גריסין, שהן כגרים ועוד – חוששת, ואם לאו – אינה חוששת. ר' יהודה בן אגרא אומר משום רבי יוסי: אחת זו ואחת זו – חוששת.

אמר

מן הסערה. כלומר, משער הראש אני משיבך תשובה: הרבה נימין בראתי באדם וכו'. על הכף. גובה שעל האבר, למטה מן הכרס. אפילו אחת על הכף כו'. אע"ג דאינו במקום אחד. אחת בגבה. תחת אותו מקום. בין קשרי אצבעותיה. ואינה מביאה שער עד שתגדיל. שתכלכל. לא שמעתי מהו. ונראה בעיני שחברו במס' שבת (עח.): "כדי *לסוד כלכול", ואמרינן (שם פ.) מאי "כלכול"? לדעה ובת לדעה, ה"נ: עד שיהו שם שערות הרבה, שיהא רצוף ומלובש בשער. ואני מצאתי: "עד שתכלכל" בבי"ת, שער גדול כפוף ומכולכל. ולא ישר בעיני. איני יודע מהו. כלומר, לא סבירא לי. **מתני'** ב' שערות האמורות בפרה. דקיימא לן: ב' שערות שחורות – פוסלות בה, בגמרא ד"אין מעמידין" (ע"ז דף כד.) ובמסכת פרה (פ"ב מ"ה). ובנגעים. שער לבן, דקי"ל בת"כ: מיעוט "שערות" – שתים. והאמורות בכל מקום. בתינוק ובתינוקת. לקרוץ. לאחוז מעט. שיהו ניטלות בזוג. שיעורא רבה (דכולהו). **גמ'** להחמיר. משנקרצות בצפורן – לא ממאנת, שמא גדולה היא. ולענין חליצה – עד דאיכא שיעורא רבה דכולהו. **מתני'** הרי זו מקולקלת. אינה יודעת פתח נדותה לידע מתי יתחילו י"א יום שבין נדה לנדה, דהא לא ידעה אימת חזאי. וחוששת משום זוב. אם עברו עליה ג' ימי זיבה משלבשה חלוק זה, ומצאה עליו כתם גדול שיעור ג' גריסין ועוד – מספקינן להו, דילמא כל חדא וחדא – בחד יומא חזיא, אע"ג דבמקום אחד נמצאו. **גמ'** ג' חלוקות. הבדוקות לה, ולבשתן בשלשת ימי זיבה אחד ליום. או שראתה ב' ימים. ראייה ממש מגופה בתוך י"א יום, ובשלישי לבשה חלוק הבדוק לה, ומצאתה עליו כתם. מהו דתימא כל כי האי גוונא וכו'. להכי נקט ב' ימים וחלוק אחד, לאשמועינן דהשתא נמי חששא בעלמא היא, ומביאה קרבן ואינו נאכל – דשמא לאו מגופה הואי הך כתם שלישי, ומליקת חולין – נבלה. דאי לא אשמועינן, הוה אמינא: הרי רגלים לדבר דודאי זבה היא. זכנהו. תשובה ניצחת השיבן. אגב זוהמא. דנדות אתאי מאכולת, ונתמעכה שם. ורבי חנינא כו'. לרבא פרכינן, דאמר לרבי חנינא שלשה גריסין במקום אחד (ב). תרי ופלגא כו'. אלמא לא פליג רבי חנינא אלא במקום אחד, אבל בשלשה מקומות – מודה, והא קתני רבי חנינא לעיל: לבשה ג' חלוקות כו', אבל בחלוק אחד בג' מקומות – לא. שהן כגרים ועוד. כלומר, שלשה גריסין גסין, דאיכא בכל חד וחד כגרים ועוד. דהכי הוי שיעור כתם לקמן בפרק "הרואה כתם" (דף נט.). אחת זו ואחת זו. אפילו בשתי גריסין – חוששין שמא ראתה אותן בשני בין השמשות, או אחת היום ואחת בין השמשות של מחר, וראיית בין השמשות עולה לשני ימים, שמקצתה מן היום ומקצתה מן הלילה, ויש כאן שלשה רצופין.

א"ר

[שם דף ג.]
[נ"ל דתנן]
[עי' ב"ב טז.]
[תוספתא פ"ו ה"ב]
[נ"ל לסוד]
ב"ק ע: ב"ב נו. סנהדרין ל.
[רש"ל מ"ז וס"ג וזהו שיעורא וע' במ"ל פ"ב מהל' איסות הלט"ז]
[עירובין פג. וש"נ]

מט א ב מיי' פ"ב מהל' איסות הלי"ז סמג עשין כ טוש"ע אה"ע סי' קנה סעי' יז:
נ ג ד מיי' פ"א מהל' פרה אדומה הל"ד ופ"ב מהל' טומאת צרעת הל"א ופ"ב מהל' איסות הלט"ז סמג עשין כ רלל טוש"ע אה"ע סי' קנה סעיף יח:
נא ה מיי' פ"ט מהל' איסורי ביאה הל"ג סמג לאוין קיא:
נב ו ז מיי' שם הלי"ב והלכה יד:

## תוספי הרא"ש

**עד** שתכלכל. לשון גידול שער כדאמרינן בריש נזיר הריני מכלכל הרי זה נזיר. ובשבת פרק המוציא תנן ר' יהודה אומר כדי לסוד כלכול ואמרינן בגמרא צדעא ובת צדעא: **והלכה כדברי** כולם להחמיר. משום דמספקא לן כמאן הילכתא מחמיר לפסוק כשניהם כדלעיל פרק יוצא דופן גבי חצר צורית וגבי סימני בגרות הילכך בשתי שערות קטנות לא תמאן ואינה חולצת עד שיהו גדולות כשיעור הגדול שבכולם וכן נמי אחת בגבה ואחת בקשרי אצבעותיה לא תמאן ואינה חולצת עד שיהו הב' שערות במקום אחד כרב אסי ואם יש לה דדין גדולים אין צריך לבדוק התחתון כדרבנן דריש פירקין דאי אפשר לבוא העליון עד שיבוא התחתון: **דאמרינן** תרי ופלגא מגופיה חזיתיה. ותימה ומנא ליה לרבא דשלשה גריסין במקום אחד חיישי רבנן דלמא בג' מקומות דוקא ואפי' מצאתן ביום אחד ולר' חנינא בן אנטיגנוס דוקא מצאתו בג' חלוקין או בחלוק אחד שמצאתו בג' ימים אבל במקום אחד אפי' רבנן לא חיישי דכיון דבמקום אחד נמצא אמרינן דבפעם אחת יצא מגופה. וי"ל דמשמע ליה דרבנן לא מיפלגי מדתנן הרואה כתם משמשת משום זוב משמע דאפי' בכתם אחד חיישינן:

## הגהות הב"ח

(א) גמ' אמר רב חסדא עד שיהו ב' שערות: (ב) רש"י ד"ה ורבי חנינא וד"ה תרי הד"א: (ג) תוס' ד"ה שלש גריסין נמי נימא בתרי וכו' בתרי יומי חזיתיה דכיון דראתה מעט פחות:

אָמַר רַבִּי: נִרְאִין דִּבְרֵי רַבִּי יְהוּדָה בֶּן אַגְרָא – בְּשֶׁלֹּא בָּדְקָה, וְדִבְרֵי חֲכָמִים – בְּשֶׁבָּדְקָה. מַאי בָּדְקָה וּמַאי לֹא בָּדְקָה? אָמַר רָבָא, אַשְׁכַּחְתִּינְהוּ לְרַבָּנַן דְּבֵי רַב דְּיָתְבִי וְקָאָמְרִי: אהָכָא בְּמַאי עָסְקִינַן – כְּגוֹן שֶׁבָּדְקָה עַצְמָהּ וְלֹא בָּדְקָה חֲלוּקָהּ, וְאַף עַצְמָהּ לֹא בָּדְקָה אֶלָּא בֵּין הַשְּׁמָשׁוֹת *דְּרַבִּי יְהוּדָה, וּבְבֵין הַשְּׁמָשׁוֹת דְּר' יוֹסֵי לֹא בָּדְקָה. דְּרַבָּנַן סָבְרִי בְּבֵין הַשְּׁמָשׁוֹת דְּרַבִּי יוֹסֵי – לֵילְיָא הוּא, וְהָא בָּדְקָה בְּבֵין הַשְּׁמָשׁוֹת דְּרַבִּי יְהוּדָה. וְר' יוֹסֵי לְטַעֲמֵיהּ, דְּאָמַר בֵּין הַשְּׁמָשׁוֹת סְפֵיקָא הֲוֵי. וְאָמִינָא לְהוּ אֲנָא: אִילְמָלֵי יָדֶיהָ בְּעֵינֶיהָ כָּל בֵּין הַשְּׁמָשׁוֹת – יָפֶה אַתֶּם אוֹמְרִים, עַכְשָׁיו – שֶׁמָּא עִם סִלּוּק יָדֶיהָ רָאֲתָה? וְאָמְרוּ לִי: כִּי קָאָמְרִינַן – בכְּשֶׁנְּתוּנָה יָדֶיהָ בְּעֵינֶיהָ כָּל בֵּין הַשְּׁמָשׁוֹת. אָמַר רַבִּי: נִרְאִין דִּבְרֵי רַבִּי יְהוּדָה בֶּן אַגְרָא כְּשֶׁלֹּא בָּדְקָה. מַאי "לֹא בָּדְקָה"? אִילֵימָא דְּבָדְקָה בִּדְרַבִּי יְהוּדָה וְלֹא בָּדְקָה בִּדְרַבִּי יוֹסֵי, מִכְּלָל דְּרַבִּי יְהוּדָה סָבַר אע"ג דְּבָדְקָה בְּתַרְוַיְיהוּ – חָיְישָׁא? הָא בָּדְקָה! אֶלָּא פְּשִׁיטָא דְּלֹא בָּדְקָה לֹא בִּדְרַבִּי יְהוּדָה וְלֹא בִּדְרַבִּי יוֹסֵי, אֲבָל בָּדְקָה בְּדְר' יְהוּדָה וְלֹא בָּדְקָה בִּדְר' יוֹסֵי – לָא חָיְישָׁא. אַלְמָא: בֵּין הַשְּׁמָשׁוֹת דְּר' יוֹסֵי – לְרַבִּי לֵילְיָא הוּא. אֵימָא סֵיפָא: "וְדִבְרֵי חֲכָמִים כְּשֶׁבָּדְקָה". מַאי "בָּדְקָה"? אִילֵימָא דְּבָדְקָה בִּדְרַבִּי יְהוּדָה וְלֹא בָּדְקָה בִּדְרַבִּי יוֹסֵי, מִכְּלָל דְּרַבָּנַן סָבְרִי אע"ג דְּלָא בָּדְקָה בְּתַרְוַיְיהוּ – לָא חָיְישִׁינַן, הָא לֹא בָּדְקָה! אֶלָּא פְּשִׁיטָא – דְּבָדְקָה בֵּין בִּדְר' יְהוּדָה וּבֵין בִּדְרַבִּי יוֹסֵי, אֲבָל בָּדְקָה בִּדְר' יְהוּדָה וְלֹא בָּדְקָה בִּדְר' יוֹסֵי – חָיְישִׁינַן. אַלְמָא: בֵּין הַשְּׁמָשׁוֹת דְּרַבִּי יוֹסֵי – לְרַבִּי סְפֵקָא הֲוֵי. קַשְׁיָא דְּרַבִּי אַדְּרַבִּי! ה"ק: נִרְאִין דִּבְרֵי רַבִּי יְהוּדָה בֶּן אַגְרָא לְרַבָּנַן דְּלֹא בָּדְקָה כְּלָל לֹא בִּדְרַבִּי יְהוּדָה וְלֹא בִּדְרַבִּי יוֹסֵי, שֶׁאַף חֲכָמִים לֹא נֶחְלְקוּ עָלָיו אֶלָּא דְּבָדְקָה בִּדְר' יְהוּדָה, וְלֹא בָּדְקָה בִּדְר' יוֹסֵי. אֲבָל הֵיכָא דְּלֹא בָּדְקָה כְּלָל – מוֹדוּ לֵיהּ. וּרְמִינְהוּ: הָרוֹאָה כֶּתֶם, לִרְאִיָּה מְרוּבָּה – חוֹשֶׁשֶׁת, לִרְאִיָּה מוּעֶטֶת – אֵינָהּ חוֹשֶׁשֶׁת, זוֹ דִּבְרֵי רַבִּי יְהוּדָה בֶּן אַגְרָא שֶׁאָמַר מִשּׁוּם רַבִּי יוֹסֵי. א"ר: אֲנִי שָׁמַעְתִּי מִמֶּנּוּ שֶׁאַחַת זוֹ וְאַחַת זוֹ – חוֹשֶׁשֶׁת, וּמִן הַטַּעַם הַזֶּה אָמַר לִי: וּמָה אִילּוּ נִדָּה שֶׁלֹּא הִפְרִישָׁה בְּטָהֳרָה מִן הַמִּנְחָה וּלְמַעְלָה לֹא תְּהֵא בְּחֶזְקַת טְמֵאָה? וְנִרְאִין דְּבָרָיו כְּשֶׁבָּדְקָה. מַאי בָּדְקָה? אִילֵימָא דְּבָדְקָה בִּדְר' יְהוּדָה וְלֹא בָּדְקָה בִּדְרַבִּי יוֹסֵי, מִכְּלָל דְּרַבִּי יְהוּדָה בֶּן אַגְרָא סָבַר, אע"ג דְּלֹא בָּדְקָה לֹא בִּדְר' יְהוּדָה וְלֹא בִּדְר' יוֹסֵי – לָא חָיְישָׁא? וְהָא לֹא בָּדְקָה! אֶלָּא פְּשִׁיטָא – דְּבָדְקָה בֵּין בִּדְר' יְהוּדָה וּבֵין בִּדְרַבִּי יוֹסֵי, מִכְּלָל דְּרַבִּי יְהוּדָה בֶּן אַגְרָא סָבַר: בָּדְקָה בִּדְר' יְהוּדָה וְלֹא בָּדְקָה בִּדְר' יוֹסֵי – לָא חָיְישָׁא, אַלְמָא: בֵּין הַשְּׁמָשׁוֹת דְּרַבִּי יוֹסֵי לְר' יְהוּדָה בֶּן אַגְרָא – לֵילְיָא הוּא. קַשְׁיָא דְּרַבִּי יְהוּדָה בֶּן אַגְרָא אַדְּר' יְהוּדָה בֶּן אַגְרָא! בִּשְׁלָמָא בְּלָא רַבִּי – לָא קַשְׁיָא, הָתָם – דְּבָדְקָה בִּדְר' יְהוּדָה וְלֹא בָּדְקָה בִּדְר' יוֹסֵי, הָכָא – דְּבָדְקָה נַמִּי בִּדְר' יְהוּדָה וּבִדְר' יוֹסֵי. אֶלָּא בִּדְרַבִּי קַשְׁיָא! תְּרֵי תַּנָּאֵי וְאַלִּיבָּא דְּרַבִּי יְהוּדָה בֶּן אַגְרָא; הַאי תַּנָּא סָבַר: שָׁלֵם בֵּין הַשְּׁמָשׁוֹת דְּר' יְהוּדָה וַהֲדַר

**רש"י**

א"ר נִרְאִין כו'. כּוּלָּהּ מְפָרֵשׁ לָהּ. הָכָא בְּמַאי עָסְקִינַן. פְּלוּגְתָּא דְּרַבָּנַן וְרַבִּי יְהוּדָה בֶּן אַגְרָא. כְּשֶׁבָּדְקָה. עַצְמָהּ כָּל שְׁנֵי בֵּין הַשְּׁמָשׁוֹת. וְלֹא בָּדְקָה חֲלוּקָהּ. בִּשְׁנֵי יָמִים אֶלָּא בַּג', וּמְלֵאָה ב' גְּרִיסִין. וּלְפִי שֶׁלֹּא בָּדְקָה חֲלוּקָהּ עַד הֵנָּה, לֹא יָדְעָה מֵאֵימָתַי הֵן בָּאִין. לְפִיכָךְ יֵשׁ לָחוּשׁ שֶׁמָּא בִּשְׁנֵי בֵּין הַשְּׁמָשׁוֹת רָאֲתָה, אוֹ אַחַת בַּיּוֹם רִאשׁוֹן וְאַחַת בֵּין הַשְּׁמָשׁוֹת שֶׁל מָחָר – דַּהֲווּ לְהוּ ג' רְאִיּוֹת. בֵּין הַשְּׁמָשׁוֹת דְּרַבִּי יְהוּדָה. בְּ"בַמֶּה מַדְלִיקִין": הִכְסִיף הָעֶלְיוֹן וְלֹא הִכְסִיף הַתַּחְתּוֹן, וְשִׁיעוּרוֹ – חֲצִי מִיל, וּלְר' יוֹסֵי – כְּהֶרֶף עַיִן. וּבְסוֹף הַיּוֹם הוּא, זֶה נִכְנָס וְזֶה יוֹצֵא. וְהָא בָּדְקָה בְּבֵין הַשְּׁמָשׁוֹת דְּרַבִּי יְהוּדָה. הִלְכָּךְ לֹא רָאֲתָה אַחַת מֵהֶן בֵּין הַשְּׁמָשׁוֹת, שֶׁתַּעֲלֶה לְחוֹמֶר ב' יָמִים. סְפֵקָא הוּא. דְּחָיְישִׁינַן שֶׁמָּא לְאַחַר סִילּוּק יָדֶיהָ בְּבֵין הַשְּׁמָשׁוֹת דְּרַבִּי יוֹסֵי חָזַאי, וְהוּא עוֹלֶה לִשְׁנֵי יָמִים, וַהֲווּ לְהוּ שְׁלֹשָׁה יָמִים רְצוּפִים. וּלְרַבָּנַן לַיְלָה הוּא, וַאֲפִילּוּ חָזַאי – לָא הֲווּ לְהוּ שְׁלֹשָׁה רְאִיּוֹת. אִילְמָלֵי יָדֶיהָ בְּעֵינֶיהָ. בְּאוֹתוֹ מָקוֹם. כָּל בֵּין הַשְּׁמָשׁוֹת. דְּרַבִּי יְהוּדָה. יָפֶה אַתֶּם אוֹמְרִים. לְרַבָּנַן, דְּלָא חָיְישִׁי, כֵּיוָן דְּכָל בֵּין הַשְּׁמָשׁוֹת דְּר' יְהוּדָה לָא חָזַאי. אֵימוּר עִם סִילּוּק יָדֶיהָ רָאֲתָה. דְּהָא בֵּין הַשְּׁמָשׁוֹת דְּרַבִּי יְהוּדָה אָרוֹךְ הוּא. נִרְאִין דִּבְרֵי רַבִּי יְהוּדָה. דְּחָיֵישׁ. בְּשֶׁלֹּא בָּדְקָה. וּמִדְּקָאָמַר רַבִּי: בְּהָא ס"ל כְּרַבִּי יְהוּדָה, אֲבָל בְּשֶׁבָּדְקָה – לָא ס"ל כְּוָותֵיהּ, מִכְּלָל דְּרַבִּי יְהוּדָה בֶּן אַגְרָא – אֲפִילּוּ בָּדְקָה נַמִּי חָיֵישׁ, וּמַאי "לֹא בָּדְקָה"? אִי נֵימָא: ה"ק רַבִּי: רוֹאֶה אֲנִי אֶת דִּבְרֵי ר' יְהוּדָה בְּשֶׁלֹּא בָּדְקָה בִּדְרַבִּי יוֹסֵי, וְאע"ג דְּבָדְקָה בִּדְר' יְהוּדָה, דְּאִיכָּא לְסַפּוּקֵי בְּבֵין הַשְּׁמָשׁוֹת דְּרַבִּי יוֹסֵי. אֲבָל אֵינִי רוֹאֶה אֶת דְּבָרָיו כְּשֶׁבָּדְקָה בִּשְׁנֵיהֶם. מִכְּלָל דְּרַבִּי יְהוּדָה אֲפִילּוּ בָּדְקָה בְּתַרְוַיְיהוּ. חָיֵישׁ, הָא וַדַּאי בֵּין הַשְּׁמָשׁוֹת לָא חָזַאי, וְאֵין לְךָ לַחֲלוֹק רְאִיָּה אַחַת לִשְׁתַּיִם! אֶלָּא פְּשִׁיטָא דְּלֹא בָּדְקָה. לֹא בְּהָא וְלָא בְּהָא, דְּחוֹשֶׁשֶׁת שֶׁמָּא רָאֲתָה בְּבֵין הַשְּׁמָשׁוֹת דְּר' יְהוּדָה. אֲבָל בָּדְקָה. בִּדְר' יְהוּדָה – אֵין אֲנִי רוֹאֶה אֶת דְּבָרָיו לָחוּשׁ לְזִיבָה. אַלְמָא. קָסָבַר רַבִּי: בֵּין הַשְּׁמָשׁוֹת דְּרַבִּי יוֹסֵי – לַיְלָה הוּא, וְהָרְאִיָּה שֶׁבּוֹ אֵינָהּ עוֹלָה לִשְׁתַּיִם. אִי נֵימָא כְּשֶׁבָּדְקָה בִּדְרַבִּי יְהוּדָה וְלֹא בִּדְרַבִּי יוֹסֵי. וְקָאָמַר רַבִּי: בְּזוֹ אֲנִי רוֹאֶה אֶת דִּבְרֵיהֶם דְּלָא חָיְישִׁינַן, אֲבָל לֹא בָּדְקָה לֹא בְּזוֹ וְלֹא בְּזוֹ – אֵינִי רוֹאֶה אֶת דִּבְרֵיהֶם, דַּאֲנָא סְבִירָא לִי דְּחָיְישָׁא. מִכְּלָל דִּלְרַבָּנַן אע"ג דְּלֹא בָּדְקָה לָא בְּהָא וְלָא בְּהָא לָא חָיְישָׁא וְהָא לֹא בָּדְקָה. וְיֵשׁ לָחוּשׁ לִרְאִיַּית בֵּין הַשְּׁמָשׁוֹת הַמִּתְחַלֶּקֶת לִשְׁתַּיִם. אֶלָּא פְּשִׁיטָא. ד"נִרְאִין דִּבְרֵי חֲכָמִים כְּשֶׁבָּדְקָה" דְּקָאָמַר רַבִּי – שֶׁבָּדְקָה בִּשְׁנֵיהֶם קָאָמַר, אֲבָל בְּאֶחָד מֵהֶן דְּקָאָמְרִי אִינְהוּ: נַמִּי לָא חָיְישָׁא – אֵינִי רוֹאֶה דִּבְרֵיהֶם. דְּכֵיוָן דְּלֹא בָּדְקָה בִּדְר' יוֹסֵי – יֵשׁ לָחוּשׁ לִרְאִיַּית בֵּין הַשְּׁמָשׁוֹת. אַלְמָא, לְרַבִּי סְפֵקָא הוּא כו'. ה"ק. הַאי "נִרְאִין" דְּקָאָמַר רַבִּי, לָאו לְטַעֲמֵיהּ דְּנַפְשֵׁיהּ קָאָמַר, דְּתִידוֹק מִינַּהּ: מִדְּקָאָמַר "בְּזוֹ אֲנִי רוֹאֶה אֶת דִּבְרֵי זֶה, וּבְזוֹ אֵינִי רוֹאֶה" – מִכְּלָל דְּאִינְהוּ בְּתַרְוַיְיהוּ פְּלִיגֵי, וְתִקְשֵׁי לָךְ: אֶלָּא רַבִּי לְפָרוֹשֵׁי פְּלוּגְתַּיְיהוּ אָתָא לְאַשְׁמוֹעִינַן, בְּמַאי פְּלִיגֵי, וה"ק: נִרְאִין דִּבְרֵי ר' יְהוּדָה לַחֲכָמִים, וּמוֹדִים לוֹ דְּחָיְישִׁינַן – כְּשֶׁלֹּא בָּדְקָה לֹא בְּזֶה וְלֹא בְּזֶה. שֶׁדִּבְרֵי חֲכָמִים – כְּשֶׁבָּדְקָה בְּאֶחָד מֵהָנֵי, דְּקָסָבְרֵי: בֵּין הַשְּׁמָשׁוֹת דְּרַבִּי יוֹסֵי – לַיְלָה הוּא. וְרַבִּי יוֹסֵי לְטַעֲמֵיהּ, דְּאָמַר: סְפֵקָא הוּא, הִילְכָּךְ עַד שֶׁתִּבְדּוֹק בִּשְׁנֵיהֶם יֵשׁ לָחוּשׁ בִּרְאִיַּית בֵּין הַשְּׁמָשׁוֹת. לִרְאִיָּה מְרוּבָּה. ג' גְּרִיסִין כְּעוֹוֹלוֹת. לִרְאִיָּה מוּעֶטֶת. שְׁנֵי גְּרִיסִין כְּעוֹוֹלוֹת. מִמֶּנּוּ. מִדְּרַבִּי יוֹסֵי. שֶׁלֹּא הִפְרִישָׁה בְּטָהֳרָה. בַּשְּׁבִיעִי שֶׁלֹּא בָּדְקָה בֵּין הַשְּׁמָשׁוֹת. לֹא תְּהֵא בְּחֶזְקַת טוּמְאָה. וְאֵינָהּ טוֹבֶלֶת לָעֶרֶב, וְאַע"פ שֶׁהִפְרִישָׁה בְּטָהֳרָה שַׁחֲרִית, אַלְמָא מִשֶּׁרָאֲתָה הָוְיָא כָּל הַיּוֹם בְּחֶזְקַת חוֹזֶרֶת וְרוֹאָה עַד גְּמַר הַיּוֹם. אַף זוֹ, הוֹאִיל וְלֹא בָּדְקָה בֵּין הַשְּׁמָשׁוֹת שָׁלֵם, אִיכָּא לְמֵיחַשׁ דִּלְמָא בְּסוֹף בֵּין הַשְּׁמָשׁוֹת רָאֲתָה, וְהִיא עוֹלָה לִשְׁתֵּי רְאִיּוֹת. וְנִרְאִין לִי דְּבָרָיו. וּמוֹדֶה אֲנִי לוֹ. כְּשֶׁבָּדְקָה. בֵּין הַשְּׁמָשׁוֹת שָׁלֵם, תּוּ לָא חָיְישָׁא. וּבְשֶׁלֹּא בָּדְקָה, אֲנִי חוֹלֵק עָלָיו. קַשְׁיָא דְּרַבִּי יְהוּדָה אַדְּר' יְהוּדָה. דִּלְעֵיל ס"ל: בֵּין הַשְּׁמָשׁוֹת דְּרַבִּי יוֹסֵי – סְפֵקָא הוּא. בִּשְׁלָמָא בְּלָא רַבִּי. אִי לָא פֵּירֵשׁ רַבִּי לִפְלוּגְתַּיְיהוּ, בֵּין לְעֵיל בֵּין הָכָא, לָא הֲוָה קַשְׁיָא דְּרַבִּי יְהוּדָה אַדְּר' יְהוּדָה: הָתָם דִּבְדָקָה כו'. אֶלָּא בִּדְרַבִּי. מִכִּי אָתָא רַבִּי לְפָרוֹשֵׁי פְּלוּגְתַּיְיהוּ, וְלָא מוֹקְמָא לַן אֶלָּא כִּדְפֵירְשָׁא, דִּלְרַבִּי יְהוּדָה דִּלְעֵיל סְפֵיקָא הוּא, וְהָכָא מִיתַחֲזֵי דְּלֵילְיָא הוּא – קַשְׁיָא. וְהָדַר.

**תוספות**

**אבל** בדקה בדרבי יהודה כו' וא"ת: דלמא אבל בדקה בדרבי יוסי ולא בדקה בדר' יהודה – לא חיישינן, דבין השמשות דר' יהודה יממא הוא? וי"ל: דהא ר' יהודה בן אגרא מודה דלא חיישינן, כיון דבדקה בדר' יוסי.

**שאף** חכמים לא נחלקו כו' – בכמה דוכתין משני כי הכא, אבל בפרק "הזהב" (ב"מ דף נג.) גבי "חומש ומעשר", ובפרק "כל הבשר" (חולין דף קט.) גבי "אפשר לסוחטו" לא משני הכי, משום שיכול ליישב בענין אחר בהגהה מועטת*. **ומה** אילו נדה שלא הפרישה כו' וא"ת: דבפ"ב (דף סח.) לקמן א"ר יוסי גופיה דהיא בחזקתה וי"ל: דהתם מיירי בשבדקה יום ב' או יום ג' ומצאתה טהורה, (א) שפסקה. והכא – בדלא בדקה. א"נ הכא מיירי שבדקה שחרית של שביעי, ומצאתה טמאה.

*__מכלל__ דרבי יהודה בן אגרא סבר בדקה בדר' יהודה ולא בדקה בדרבי יוסי אינה חוששת. – השתא הוה מצי למיפרך: הא משמיה דרבי יוסי קאמר. וא"ת: ואימא, מכלל דרבי יהודה בן אגרא סבר דבדקה בדר' יוסי גרידא אינה חוששת, ורבי סבר חוששת, כיון דלא בדקה בדרבי יהודה. דבין השמשות דרבי יוסי מישך שייך בדר' יהודה, כדאמר בסוף. והשתא לא הוה צריך למימר: תרי תנאי ואליבא דר' יהודה בן אגרא! וי"ל: דומיא דברייתא דלעיל, דמיירי רבי יהודה בן אגרא כשבדקה בדרבי יהודה ולא בדקה בדרבי יוסי. עצמה

**תוספי הרא"ש**

**אבל** בדקה בדר' יהודה ולא בדקה בדר' יוסי לא חייש וא"ת דילמא בדקה בדר' יוסי ולא בדקה בדר' יהודה לא חייש דבין השמשות דר' יהודה יטמא הוא. וי"ל דבהא ר' יהודה בן (גמדא) [אגרא] מודה דמותרת כיון שבדקה בדר' יוסי: **ומה** אילו נדה שלא הפרישה בטהרה מן המנחה ולמעלה לא תהא בחזקת טמאה. ותימה הא בפרק תינוקת ר' יוסי אומר דהיא בחזקת טהרה וי"ל דהתם מיירי שבדקה ביום ראשון או שני ומצאה טהור (וה"ה) [והכא] בדלא בדקה א"נ הכא מיירי שבדקה שחרית של שביעי ומצאתה (טהורה) [טמא]: **מכלל** דר' יהודה בן אגרא סבר בדקה בדר' ולא [בדקה] בדר' יוסי לא חיישי השתא הוה מצי למיפרך הא משמיה דר' יוסי קאמר. ותימה אימא מכלל דר' יהודה בן אגרא סבר בדקה בדר' יוסי גרידא אינה חוששת ובריית' דלעיל דקאמר ר' יהודה בן אגרא חוששת בבדקה בדר' יהודה ולא בדר' יוסי ורבינו מאיר תירץ דהאי דלא משני הכי משום דמתירוץ זה לא הוה משני מידי דלעולם צ"ל דפליגא תנא דבריית' דלעיל אתנא דברייתא דהכא סבר ר' דבין השמשות דר' יוסי מישך שייך בדר' יהודה הילכך צריכה לבדוק בשניהם ולר' יהודה בן אגרא שלים בין השמשות דר' יהודה והדר מתחיל בין השמשו' דר' יוסי וא"כ מאי קאמר לעיל נראין דברי ר' יהודה בן אגרא לחכמים דהיינו ר' יהודה בשלא בדקה בתרווייהו הא בדקה בדר' יהודה ולא בדר' יוסי אין נראין דבריו לחכמים אבל אליבא דר' יוסי נראין דבריו ולפי תנא דברייתא דהכא אף לר' יוסי אין נראין דבריו אליבא דר' יהודה:

נג א ב מיי' פ"ט מהל' איסורי ביאה הל"ג ועי"ש:

ברכות ב: שבת לד:

[ועי' תוס' ב"מ נב. ד"ה מכלל ותוס' חולין קטו. ד"ה נראין]

עין רש"א ומהר"מ

**הגהות הב"ח**

(א) תוס' ד"ה ומה אילו וכו' ומצאתה טהורה דכיון שפסק פסק והכא בלא בדיקה:

**גליון הש"ס**

**רש"י** ד"ה בין השמשות דר"י וכו' ושיעורו חצי מיל. וכן נקוט רש"י ברכות דף ב ע"ב ד"ה וסוף כאלים. וקשה לי הא בגבלא איתא דלר"י בה"ש תלתא חלקי או ג' רבעי מיל וצ"ע:

דהא כיון דס"ל לר' דבהש"מ דר' יוסי מישך שייך בדר' יהודה ליכא למיחש למידי: [מכאן שייך לגט"ע] **עצמה** וקדשים למפרע. פרש"י עצמה לטהרות. ותימה כיון דתנא מטמאה לטהרות כ"ש לקדשים וי"ל דתנא קדשים לגלויי דעצמה היינו לטהרות חולין שנעשו על טהרת תרומה או על טהרת הקדש. א"נ תנא קדשים לרבותא דרשב"א דאמר אף קדשים אינה מטמאה. ומיהו קשה דלישנא דעצמה לא משמע טהרות ועוד קשה דלרשב"א דאמר בסמוך יומו אבל אם ראתה כתם בשם שלפני ראייה כתם מטמא למפרע ומקולקלת למניינה אלמא כתם חמור מראיה דבראיה ליכא למפרע אבל לענין קלקול למניינה ליכא לעיל בפ"ק אע"ג שאמרו מטמאה מעת לעת אינו מונה אלא משעה שראתה. ומי' מצינו למימר דבסמוך לא איירי אלא לטהרות וקדשים שמטמאה במגע לפני מציאת הכתם מעת לעת. ונראה לפרש דמטמאה עצמה היינו מקולקלת למניינה משעת הכיבוס ור' שמעון אומר אף קדשים שנגעה בהם למפרע אין טמאין משעת הכיבוס אלא מעת לעת וכ"ש שאינה מקולקלת למניינה משעת הכיבוס אבל מעת לעת קודם מציאת הכתם מודו דמקולקלת למניינה כראיה בסמוך. ותימה מ"מ מצינו כתמה חמור מראייתה לר' שמעון דבראיה אינה מקולקלת למניינה כלל וי"ל דלא קאמר שלא יהא כתמה חמור מראייתה בכלל אלא לענין הזמן שלא תטמא בכתם מעת לעת שלא יהא כתמה חמור מראייתה. ומ"מ מעת לעת מתחברא דבראייה אינה מקולקלת כיון דהשתא חזאי מגופה ראיה ודאית נהי דלענין מגע שמטמאין מעת לעת לענין קלקול מניינה לא מחמרינן בה כולי האי. אבל כתם דלא ידעינן מתי נפק אימור מגופה מסתבר דמקולקלת למניינה מעת לעת לדבל טומאת כתם ספק הוא הילכך מעת לעת מחזקינן בה טומאה מספק: אמר רב נחמן אני איפרק. פרש"י נראין דברי מדבריו א"נ שהוא מעוותה ואני מתקנה והמחמיר עדיף: **שהוא מתקן** הלכותיה לידי זוכה. פרש"י שאינה זוכה [מה ר'] [מידו] לר' שמעון כמו לר' שהיא זוכה בה עד יום שמיני לראיתה. ותימה דלר' שמעון נמי מקולקלת למניינה אם ראתה כתם ביום שביעי ואחר נקיה לו כתמה ואדרבה ר' שמעון מחמיר טפי שאפי' מעת לעת לכתמה היא מקולקלת. ועוד תימה גדול לומר דלר' סופרת ז' ימי נדות מיום מציאת הכתם ומובלת דע"ב לא קא' אלא תולה כתמה בראייתה שלא נטמאה מחמת הכתם מפרע אבל לתלות ראייתה בכתמה ולעשות בכתמה

**נד** א מיי' פ"ט מהל' איסורי ביאה הל"ג סמג לאוין קיא:
**נה** ב ג מיי' שם והל"ז סמג שם:
**נו** ד מיי' שם הל"ז יז יח וע"ש בהשגות ובמ"מ ג] סמג שם טוש"ע יו"ד סי' קצ סעי' א:
**נז** ה מיי' פ"ז מהל' איסורי ביאה הלי"ט:
**נח** ו מיי' שם ופ"י הל"כ ופ"ח הל"ז:
**נט** ז מיי' שם פ"ו הלי"ט:

וְהָדַר חָיֵיל בֵּין הַשְּׁמָשׁוֹת דְּר' יוֹסֵי. וְהַאי תַּנָּא סָבַר: בֵּין הַשְּׁמָשׁוֹת דְּר' יוֹסֵי מֵישַׁךְ שַׁיָּיךְ בִּדְר' יְהוּדָה. ת"ר: אהָרוֹאָה כֶּתֶם — מְטַמְּאָה עַצְמָהּ וְקָדָשִׁים לְמַפְרֵעַ — דִּבְרֵי רַבִּי. ר"ש בֶּן אֶלְעָזָר אוֹמֵר: קָדָשִׁים — מְטַמְּאָה, עַצְמָהּ — אֵינָהּ מְטַמְּאָה, שֶׁלֹּא יְהֵא כִּתְמָהּ חָמוּר מֵרְאִיָּיתָהּ. וְהָא מָצִינוּ כִּתְמָהּ חָמוּר מֵרְאִיָּיתָהּ לְעִנְיַן קֳדָשִׁים! אֶלָּא תְּנֵי הָכִי: ר"ש בֶּן אֶלְעָזָר אוֹמֵר אַף קֳדָשִׁים אֵינָהּ מְטַמְּאָה, שֶׁלֹּא יְהֵא כִּתְמָהּ חָמוּר מֵרְאִיָּיתָהּ לְכָל דָּבָר. ת"ר: ברָאֲתָה כֶּתֶם וְאַחַר כָּךְ רָאֲתָה דָּם — תּוֹלָה כִּתְמָהּ בִּרְאִיָּיתָהּ מֵעֵת לְעֵת, דִּבְרֵי רַבִּי. ר"ש בֶּן אֶלְעָזָר אוֹמֵר: יוֹמוֹ. א"ר: נִרְאִין דְּבָרָיו מִדְּבָרַי, שֶׁהוּא — מְתַקְּנָהּ, וַאֲנִי — מְעַוְּותָהּ. מְתַקְּנָהּ? עֲווּתֵי מְעַוֵּית לָהּ! אָמַר רָבִינָא: אֵיפוּךְ. רַב נַחְמָן אָמַר: לְעוֹלָם לָא תֵּיפוּךְ, שֶׁהוּא מְתַקֵּן הִלְכוֹתֶיהָ לִידֵי זִיבָה, וַאֲנִי מְעַוֵּות הִלְכוֹתֶיהָ לִידֵי זִיבָה. בָּעֵי מִינֵּיהּ ר' זֵירָא מֵר' אַסִי: כְּתָמִים צְרִיכִין הֶפְסֵק טָהֳרָה אוֹ לֹא? אִשְׁתִּיק וְלָא א"ל וְלָא מִידֵי. זִימְנִין אַשְׁכְּחֵיהּ דְּיָתֵיב וְקָאָמַר: תּוֹלָה כִּתְמָהּ בִּרְאִיָּיתָהּ מֵעֵת לְעֵת — דִּבְרֵי רַבִּי. אָמַר ר"ל: וְהוּא שֶׁבָּדְקָה, וְרַבִּי יוֹחָנָן אָמַר: גאע"פ שֶׁלֹּא בָּדְקָה. א"ל: מִכְּלָל — דִּכְתָמִים צְרִיכִין הַפְסָקַת טָהֳרָה? א"ל: דאִין. וְהָא זִימְנִין סַגִּיאִין בְּעָא מִינָּךְ וְלָא אָמַרְתְּ וְלָא מִידֵי, [נדה נה:] *דִּלְמָא אַגַּב שִׁיטְפָךְ אָתְיָא לָךְ? א"ל: אִין, אַגַּב שִׁיטְפַאי אָתְיָא לִי.§ **מתני'** ההָרוֹאָה יוֹם י"א בֵּין הַשְּׁמָשׁוֹת — תְּחִלַּת נִדָּה וְסוֹף נִדָּה, תְּחִלַּת זִיבָה וְסוֹף זִיבָה, ויוֹם אַרְבָּעִים לְזָכָר, וְיוֹם שְׁמוֹנִים לִנְקֵבָה, בֵּין הַשְּׁמָשׁוֹת לְכוּלָּן — הֲרֵי אֵלּוּ טוֹעוֹת. א"ר יְהוֹשֻׁעַ: עַד שֶׁאַתֶּם מְתַקְּנִים אֶת הַשּׁוֹטוֹת, בֹּאוּ וְתַקְּנוּ אֶת הַפִּקְחוֹת.§ **גמ'** תְּחִלַּת נִדָּה וְסוֹף נִדָּה? תְּחִלַּת נִדָּה וְסוֹף זִיבָה הִיא! אָמַר רַב חִסְדָּא, זהָכִי קָאָמַר: הָרוֹאָה יוֹם י"א בֵּין הַשְּׁמָשׁוֹת — תְּחִילַּת נִדָּה וְסוֹף זִיבָה, וּבַשְּׁבִיעִי לְנִדָּתָהּ — סוֹף נִדָּה וּתְחִלַּת זִיבָה.§ א"ר יְהוֹשֻׁעַ עַד שֶׁאַתֶּם מְתַקְּנִין אֶת הַשּׁוֹטוֹת" כו'.§ הָנֵי

שוטות

וְהָדַר. מַתְחִיל דְּרַבִּי יוֹסֵי, וּסְפֵקָא הוּא. מֵישַׁךְ שַׁיָּיךְ בִּדְרַבִּי יְהוּדָה. מוּבְלָע הוּא בְּתוֹךְ שֶׁל רַבִּי יְהוּדָה, וְכֵיוָן דִּלְדִידֵיהּ בָּעֵינַן כָּל בֵּין הַשְּׁמָשׁוֹת דְּרַבִּי יְהוּדָה — הֲרֵי בָּדְקָה בִּשְׁנֵיהֶם. מְטַמְּאָה עַצְמָהּ. הָרוֹאָה כֶּתֶם מְטַמְּאָה עַצְמָהּ לְטָהֳרוֹת וְקָדָשִׁים. לְמַפְרֵעַ. עַד שְׁעַת הַכִּבּוּס. חָמוּר מֵרְאִיָּיתָהּ. לְמַפְרֵעַ, דְּלִרְאִיָּיתָהּ — לָא הָוֵי אֶלָּא מֵעֵת לְעֵת, וְכִתְמָהּ — עַד שְׁעַת הַכִּבּוּס. וְהָא מָצִינוּ כו'. דְּהָא מוֹדֶה ר"ש בֶּן אֶלְעָזָר בְּקָדָשִׁים דִּמְטַמְּאָתָן לְמַפְרֵעַ עַד שְׁעַת הַכִּבּוּס. רָאֲתָה כֶּתֶם וְאח"כ רָאֲתָה דָּם. תּוֹךְ מֵעֵת לְעֵת. תּוֹלָה כִּתְמָהּ בִּרְאִיָּיתָהּ. וְאָמְרִינַן: הַאי כֶּתֶם — מִדַּם נִדּוּת זֶה הוּא, וּטְהוֹרָה מִלְּטַמֵּא עַד שְׁעַת הַכִּבּוּס, אֶלָּא מִשֶּׁמְּלָאַתּוּ וּלְהַבָּא. יוֹמוֹ. אִם רָאֲתָה בּוֹ בַּיּוֹם — תּוֹלָה. וְאִם שָׁקְעָה חַמָּה, אַף עַל פִּי שֶׁרָאֲתָה בְּתוֹךְ מֵעֵת לְעֵת — אֵינָהּ תּוֹלָה. שֶׁהוּא מְתַקְּנָהּ. מֵיקֵל עָלֶיהָ, וְכֵיוָן דִּכְתָמִים דְּרַבָּנַן — נִרְאִין דִּבְרֵי הַמֵּיקֵל. וּלְקַמָּן פָּרֵיךְ: עֲווּתֵי מְעַוֵּות לָהּ, דְּהָא ר"ש בֶּן אֶלְעָזָר מַחְמִיר! אֵיפוּךְ. וְאֵימָא: נִרְאִין דְּבָרַי מִדְּבָרָיו. הוּא מְתַקֵּן הִלְכוֹתֶיהָ לִידֵי זִיבָה. לְעִנְיַן זִיבָה הוּא מֵיקֵל. דִּלְדִידֵיהּ, הֵיכָא דְּלָא חָזְיָא בּוֹ בַּיּוֹם — לָא תָּלֵינַן כִּתְמָהּ בִּרְאִיָּיתָהּ, וּמוֹנָה יְמֵי נִדּוּת מִיּוֹם רְאִיָּיתָהּ, וְאֵין יְמֵי זִיבָה מַתְחִילִין עַד יוֹם ח' לִרְאִיָּיתָהּ. לְרַבִּי, מוֹנָה מִיּוֹם מְצִיאַת כִּתְמָהּ. וְאַף לְהָקֵל וְלִטְבּוֹל לֵיל שְׁבִיעִי לְכִתְמָהּ, אִם פָּסְקָה, וּמִיּוֹם ח' לְכִתְמָהּ הָווּ יְמֵי זוֹב. וְנִמְצָא רַבִּי מַחְמִיר לְעִנְיַן זִיבָה, דְּכִי חָזְיָא בַּח' לְכִתְמָהּ — אָמְרִינַן: יוֹם זִיבָה הוּא, וּצְרִיכָה לִשְׁמוֹר תְּשִׁיעִי, יוֹם כְּנֶגֶד יוֹם. וְאִם תִּרְאֶה שְׁנַיִם עִמּוֹ — תְּהֵא זָבָה. וּלְר"ש סוֹף נִדָּה הוּא, וְלֹא מַצְרִיךְ שִׁימּוּר. וְאִם תִּרְאֶה שְׁנַיִם עִמּוֹ — לֹא תִּהְיֶה זָבָה. נִמְצָא הֲנֵי מְבִיאָהּ ע"י כִּתְמָהּ לְזִיבָה, אֲבָל אִיהוּ — לָא. צְרִיכִין הֶפְסֵק טָהֳרָה. בַּשְּׁבִיעִי, לִטְבּוֹל בָּעֶרֶב. צְרִיכָה לִבְדּוֹק בֵּין הַשְּׁמָשׁוֹת לְהַפְסִיק בְּטָהֳרָה אוֹ לֹא. זִימְנִין. פַּעַם אַחֶרֶת. אַשְׁכְּחֵיהּ. רַבִּי זֵירָא לְרַבִּי אַסִי. דְּיָתֵיב וְקָאָמַר. הַךְ מִלְּתָא דְּרַבִּי, וּמְפָרֵשׁ עֲלָהּ, אָמַר ר"ל: וְהוּא שֶׁבָּדְקָה בֵּין הַשְּׁמָשׁוֹת שֶׁל שְׁבִיעִי לְכִתְמָהּ, לְהַפְסִיק בְּטָהֳרָה. אֲבָל לֹא הִפְרִישָׁה בְּטָהֳרָה — גִּלְּיָא דַּעְתָּהּ, דְּמִיּוֹם רְאִיָּיתָהּ נָקְטָה מִנְיָנָא דִּידָהּ, וְהִיא גָּרְמָה לְעַצְמָהּ לְהַבְדִּיל כִּתְמָהּ מֵרְאִיָּיתָהּ, וְכִתְמָהּ מְטַמֵּא לְמַפְרֵעַ מִיּוֹם לְבִישָׁה. וְרַבִּי יוֹחָנָן אָמַר: אַף עַל פִּי שֶׁלֹּא בָּדְקָה. דְּכֵיוָן דִּיכוֹלָה לִתְלוֹת — לָאו בְּגִילּוּי דַּעְתָּהּ תַּלְיָא מִלְּתָא, וְלָא מַפְסְקָא בְּהָכִי. א"ל רַבִּי זֵירָא לְרַבִּי אַסִי. מִדִּפְלִיגִי רַבִּי יוֹחָנָן וְר"ל לְעִנְיַן תָּלְיָא בִּבְדִיקָה וְלֹא בָּדְקָה, מִכְּלָל דְּאוֹרְחָא הוּא לִבְדּוֹק בַּיּוֹם שְׁבִיעִי לְכִתְמָהּ וּלְהַפְסִיק בְּטָהֳרָה. שִׁיטְפָךְ. רִיהֲטָךְ. **מתני'** הָרוֹאָה יוֹם אַחַד עָשָׂר בֵּין הַשְּׁמָשׁוֹת. וְסָפֵק יוֹם הוּא, וְהָוֵי דַּם זִיבָה. אוֹ סָפֵק לַיְלָה, וּתְחִלָּתוֹ נִדָּה. תְּחִלַּת נִדָּה וְסוֹף נִדָּה כו'. וּבַגְּמָרָא פָּרֵיךְ: תְּחִלַּת נִדָּה וְסוֹף זִיבָה הִיא, וְהָוְיָא טוֹעָה, וּבְעַ"כ תֵּשֵׁב שִׁבְעָה. וְאִם רָאֲתָה לְסוֹף שִׁבְעָה יוֹם אֶחָד — נַחְמִיר עָלֶיהָ, לוֹמַר: רְאִיָּה רִאשׁוֹנָה סוֹף זִיבָה הֲוַאי, וְהַשְׁתָּא הָוְיָא תְּחִלַּת נִדָּה, וְתֵשֵׁב שִׁבְעָה. וְאִם שְׁלֹשָׁה תִּרְאֶה — נַחְמִיר עָלֶיהָ, לוֹמַר: רְאִיָּיה רִאשׁוֹנָה תְּחִלַּת נִדָּה הֲוַאי, וְהַשְׁתָּא זָבָה, וּצְרִיכָה שִׁבְעָה נְקִיִּים, וְלֹא תֵּשֵׁב אַרְבָּעָה וָהֵן. וְכֵן לְעוֹלָם הִיא מְקוּלְקֶלֶת, וְתַקָּנָתָהּ כִּדְמְפָרֵשׁ בַּעֲרָכִין (דף ח.). יוֹם אַרְבָּעִים לְזָכָר וְיוֹם שְׁמוֹנִים לְלֵידַת נְקֵבָה בֵּין הַשְּׁמָשׁוֹת לְכוּלָּן. כְּלוֹמַר, בְּאֵיזֶה מֵאֵלּוּ שֶׁתִּרְאֶה בֵּין הַשְּׁמָשׁוֹת — הָוֵי הַאי בֵּין הַשְּׁמָשׁוֹת סָפֵק טָמֵא סָפֵק טָהוֹר. וְאִם תִּרְאֶה לְיוֹם שְׁמִינִי — סָפֵק נִדָּה סָפֵק שׁוֹמֶרֶת יוֹם כְּנֶגֶד יוֹם. וְכֵן לְעוֹלָם, עַד שֶׁתַּפְסוֹק כְּדֵי שִׁיעוּר הַמְפוֹרָשׁ לָהּ בַּעֲרָכִין. אֶת הַשּׁוֹטוֹת. אֶת הַטּוֹעוֹת, כְּגוֹן אֵלּוּ שֶׁרָאוּ בִּשְׁעַת הַסָּפֵק. בֹּאוּ וְתַקְּנוּ אֶת הַפִּקְחוֹת. הָרוֹאוֹת בְּשָׁעָה וַדָּאִית, וּצְרִיכִין אָנוּ לְתַקֵּן פִּתְחֵיהֶן וּלְפָרֵשׁ יְמֵי שִׁימּוּרָן וְתַשְׁמִישָׁן, כִּדְמְפָרֵשׁ בַּבָּרַיְיתָא בַּגְּמָרָא. **גמ'**

שוטות

**עצמה** וקדשים. פירש בקונטרס: עצמה – לטהרות. ותימה: אמאי איצטריך למתני קדשים, דכ"ש הוא? וי"ל: דמשום רשב"א נקטיה, דמסיק: דאפילו קדשים אינה מטמאה. א"נ: תנא קדשים לגלויי דעצמה אף לטהרות. ומיהו לישנא דעצמה לא משמע לטהרות. ועוד קשה: לרשב"א אכתי הוי כתמה חמור מראייתה, דהא איהו גופיה אמר בסמוך דתולה בראיית יומו, אבל כתם שמצאה ביום שלפני הראייה – טמאה למפרע, ומקולקלת למניינה משעת כבוס! ונראה לפרש: דעצמה – היינו, שמקולקלת למניינה משעת כבוס. ורשב"א פליג אתרוייהו: דאינה מקולקלת למניינה, ולא מטמאה קדשים אלא מעת לעת. והא דקאמר רשב"א בסמוך דתולה כתמה בראיית יומו, הא כתם דאתמול לא תליא בראייה – לאו משום שתהא מקולקלת בכתמה דאתמול משעת כבוס, אלא ע"י ראייה דהשתא, וכתם דאתמול היא מקולקלת – דלא ידעה אי מניא מהיום או מכתם. וא"ת: אכתי כתמה חמור מראייתה, דבכתמה – היא מקולקלת למניינה מעל"ע אבל בראייתה, אע"ג דלקדשים ולטהרות מטמאה מעל"ע מ"מ אינה מקולקלת, דמונה מיום שראתה! וי"ל: דלא חייש רשב"א אלא שלא יהיה כתמה חמור מראייתה בזמן לטמאות יותר מעל"ע.

**איפוך**. פ"ה: נראין דברי מדבריו. א"נ איפוך, שהוא מעוותה ואני מתקנה, והמחמיר עדיף.

**שהוא** מתקן הלכותיה לידי זיבה. פ"ה: דלר"ש אם ראתה בח' וט' וי' לכתמה – לא הויא זבה. ולרבי דתולה כתמה בראייתה – הויא זבה. ואין נראה: דלר"ש נמי הויא מקולקלת למניינה, כדפרישית לעיל. ואדרבה, ר"ש מחמיר טפי, שמטמא ממציאת הכתם מעל"ע ומה שפירש נמי דלרבי טובלת בשביעי לכתמה ומשמשת – אין נראה להקל כולי האי, ולא תלינן כתמה בראייתה. ונראה כפר"ח כשמצאה הכתם ביום הראייה. לרבי דתלי כתמה כל מעת לעת בראייה – היא מקולקלת כל מעת לעת, והויא כאילו ראתה שני ימים, יום הראייה ויום שלפניו. ואם ראתה גם למחר – הויא זבה, אם עומדת בימי זובה. ולר"ש דלא תלי אלא יומו א"כ לא חשבינן כאילו ראתה אתמול, ולא תהיה זבה עד שתראה עוד שני ימים. והיינו, ר"ש מתקנה, ורבי מעוותה", דר"ש מיקל טפי. א] ומיהו אם ראתה היום ואתמול ומצאה כתם – רבי שמעון מחמיר, כדפירשנו.

**צריכה** הפסק טהרה. פ"ה צריכה בדיקה להפסיק בשביעי לכתמה, כדי לטבול בערב. ופירש: דלר"ל אם בדקה בשביעי לכתמה, דגליא דעתה דכתמה מראייתה הוא, ב] אבל לא בדקה ומונה מן הראייה – פירש לפי שיטתו, ואין נראה. דאין לה לטבול בליל שמיני לכתמה. דרבי לא אמר שתולין כתמה בראייתה בודאי אלא בספק, כדפי' ותו: היכי מוכח מהכא דבכתם צריכה בדיקה בשביעי, דשאני הכא שראתה ראייה ודאית! ותו: אדרבה, מדקאמר רבי יוחנן אע"פ שלא בדקה בשביעי לכתמה טובלת לערב, א"כ אינה צריכה בדיקה! ונראה לפרש: צריכה הפסקת טהרה בין הכבוס למציאת הכתם – דדלמא הא דתלי רבי כתמה בראייתה ולא מטמא משעת כבוס, היינו כשבדקה בין כבוס למציאת הכתם. וקאמר ריש לקיש: והוא שבדקה – פירוש: סמוך למציאת הכתם, תוך מעת לעת. אבל אם יש מעת לעת (א) מבדיקה למציאת הכתם – מטמאין לה למפרע עד שעת הבדיקה. ורבי יוחנן אמר: אף על פי שלא בדקה – פירוש: סמוך, אלא יש מעת לעת בין בדיקה למציאה, אפילו הכי תלינן הכתם בראייתה, כיון דמשעת כיבוס ליכא, מעת לעת נמי ליכא. אלמא לכולי עלמא צריכה הפסק. דאין נראה לומר דלרבי יוחנן אע"פ ש"לא בדקה כלל" קאמר, דכולי האי לא הוה פליג אריש לקיש.

וארבעה

## תוספי הרא"ש

**כתמים** צריכין הפסק טהרה. אם צריכה בדיקה להפסיק לשביעי בכתמה כדי לטבול לערבית. ופי' דלריש לקיש איגליא בדעתה דכתמה חלוק מראייתה ומונה מן הכתם ואי לא בדקה א"כ לא חלקה ומונה מן הראיה ולא נהירא פירושו. חדא דהא פרישנא דאף לר' אינה יכולה לטבול בשביעי לכתמה ועוד היכי פשיט דבכתם כתם צריך בדיקה בשביעי מהיכא שראתה ראיה ודאית אחר מציאת הכתם. ועוד מה סברא זו שיהא תלוי בדעת האשה אם היא רוצה למנות מכתמה או מראייתה ועוד הא דקאמר ר' יוחנן אע"פ שלא בדקה בז' לכתמה טובלת לערב אלמא אינה צריכה בדיקה ומיירי ע"כ כשהפרישו בטהרה כשאר הימים. ונראה לפרש דאיבעיא ליה אם כתמים צריכין הפסק טהרה בין הכיבוס למציאת הכתם דדילמא הא דתלי ר' כתמה בראייתה ואינו מטמא משעת הכיבוס היינו כי בדקה עצמה לאחר הכיבוס קודם מציאת הכתם הילכך תלינן לקולא כתמה בראייתה דאמרי' ראתה למפרע והיתה מוצאה דם בשעת כתמה או דלמא לא שנא ופשיט מדאמר ריש לקיש והוא שבדקה עצמה פי' לפני מציאת הכתם בסמוך דאין מעת לעת בין בדיקה עד מציאת הכתם אבל יש מעת לעת נהי דמשעת הכיבוס לא מצי לטמויי הכתם מעת לעת מיהא מיטמיא ליה פ"ל ואם לא בדקה כלל תלי' משעת הכיבוס. וה"פ והוא שבדקה כדפרישית אבל לא בדקה כלל לא תלי' כתמה בראייתה וטמאה משעת הכיבוס ר' יוחנן אמר אע"פ שלא בדקה סמוך לכתם אלא יש מעת לעת אפ"ה תולין הכתם בראיה כיון דמשעת הכיבוס ליכא אלמא לכ"ע צריכין הפסק טהרה ורבינו מאיר פי' דאמתניתין קאי הא דתנן לעיל וחכמים אומרים אין בכתמים משום זוב ואוקימנא לעיל דהיינו דוקא בחלוק אחד משום דאיכא למימר בתרתי יומי או בחדא יומא חזיתינהו. והשתא קא מיבעיא לי' הא דמטהרי רבנן משום זוב צריכי הפסק טהרה כגון שהיתה בודקת עצמה בכל יום קודם מציאת הכתם לעיתותי ערב ומיפסקא בטהרה ונהי דלא בדקה חלוקה עד עתה שמצאה הכתם מ"מ כיון דבדקה עצמה בכל יום תלינן דכל הכתם הנמצא בהאי יומא חזיתיה דאם איתא דמאתמול הוה היתה מוצאה דם בשעת בדיקה אבל אם לא בדקה עצמה בכל יום לעיתותי ערב איכא למימר דמודו רבנן דיש בכתמים משום זוב ואמרינן דבב' ימים חזיתינהו ופשיט ליה דהא דא"ר דתולה כתמה בראייתה ואוקימנא לה דר' מיקל לענין זיבה ור' שמעון מחמיר בכתמה כאילו ודאי ראתה משעת הכתם ולטבול בז' לכתמה לא קאמר דאימר הכתם מעלמא אתאי או בימי הזיבה יצא מגופה אלא ודאי להקל לא קאמר ר' לתלות בודאי הראיה מן הכתם. הילכך נראה לפרש שקורא השתא תיקון מה שמחמיר שהיא מקולקלת למניינה והיא ספק זבה לר' שמעון טפי מלר' דאם מצאה הכתם אתמול לר' שמעון מקולקלת למניינה מעת לעת משעת יציאת הכתם ולר' תולה כתמה בראייתה ואינה מקולקל' כלל וכן אם קיימא בימי זיבה וראתה היום ואתמול מצאה כתם דבשביל הכתם חוששין מעת לעת ונחשב לשתי ראיות אם יש בו כשני גריסין ואפי' כגרים א' דאימור בין השמשות ראתה הילכך ספק היא אם ראיה של היום. ולר' דתולה כתמה בראייתה כל מעת לעת אין כאן כ"א שני ימים יום הכתם ויום הראיה ומי' היכא דמצאה הכתם ביום הראיה הוי איפכא דלר' טמאה מעת לעת לפני הראיה והוי כאילו ראתה ב' ימים יום הראיה ויום שלפניו ואם ראתה למחר הוי זיבה דר' לא מפליג בין מצאה הכתם ביום בין מצאתו ביום שלפניו דלעולם חוששת לכתם מעת לעת של ראיה. ולר"ש דתלי דוקא ביומו לא חשבינן לזה כאילו ראתה אתמול ובענין זה פר"ח הוא מתקן הלכותיה לידי זיבה דר' שמעון מיקל לענין שאם ראתה ביום מציאת הכתם לר' שמעון יום אחד הוא ואינה זבה עד שתראה עוד שני ימים ולר' מחזקינן לה בטומאה מאתמול ואם תראה עוד למחרת היא ספק זבה [גדולה] ונמצא שהוא מעוותה וממהר אותה לבא לידי זיבה ואע"ג דברואה למחרת כתמה ר' מיקל טפי דלר' שמעון היא כבר זבה ולר' עד שתראה גם למחרת מ"מ כשרואה ביום כתמה ר' שמעון מיקל טפי. ור"מ היה מיישב פרש"י מה שפי' שטובלת בשביעי לכתמה דהכא מיירי כגון שביום מציאת הכתם הוה ווסתה. ואע"ג דאמרינן בפ"ק דאשה שיש לה וסת כתמה טמא למפרע היכא דראתה בתוך מעת לעת למציאת כתמה יש תולים לבדוק דבשעת ווסתה יצא כתמה כיון דבשעה של טבחים של עברה. והא דאמרינן לעיל תולה לפרק כך היה דאי בשעת והגיע שעת ווסתה ולא בדקה ולבסוף ראתה חוששת לווסתה וחוששת לראייתה. ומסיק לקך לישנא דקשר הכתם ביום ווסתה ומ"מ כיון הכא א"נ י"ל דלעיל איירי כשראתה אחר מעת לעת ומצינו למימר דר' שאני התם דאשה מוצאה דס"ל לעיל פ' כל היד דווסתות דאורייתא גבי הרואה דם מחמת מכתה. ואע"ג דדחי לה תלמודא לעיל דלכ"ע ווסתות דרבנן דיחידאי בעלמא הוא. א"נ אפי' אי ס"ל ווסתות דרבנן היינו דוקא לטמאה למפרע אבל לטמאות ומשתה בשוק של טבחים ועברה וראתה דם בתוך ודאי מגופה אתא:

דאי קיימא בימי זיבה והיום מצאה כתם ולמחר ראתה לר' לא הויא זבה גדולה דלא לשתים לומר דבתרי זימני חזיתיה: **ואמר** ריש לקיש והוא שבדקה לעיתותי ערב. אבל לא בדקה מפלגינן הכתם לשתי ראיות והויא זבה גדולה אפי' לר' ואפי' לר' יוחנן אלא היכא דאיכא יצא כתם בסוף דגלים לדבר שהכתם לשתי ראיות אבל אם לא ראתה אבל הכא עבר אחר ראיה חולה לתרוייהו כתמים בלא ראיה צריכין הפסק טהרה ואם לא הפסיקה בטהרה אפי' נמצא כתם במקום אחר מפלגינן ליה לתלתא ראיות. חלוקה יומי ועוד תרוייהו איירי אליבא דרבנן דמתניתין דאמרי אין בכתמים משום זוב דליכא למימר דאיירי לר' מאיר דמתני' אבל לרבנן בדיק בלא שלא בדקה חדא דמשתמא אליבא דהילכתא (א) היינו דקי"ל כרבנן דמתניתין דתני ר' חנינא בן אנטיגנוס בלשון חכמים ועוד מאי דוחקיה דר"ל לאוקומי כר"מ והוא שבדקה לוקמה כרבנן אע"ג שלא בדקה אלא ש"מ דתרוייהו מוקמי לה אליבא דרבנן כדפרישית:

(א) נראה דצ"ל אליבא דהלכתא דפליגי דוודאי קי"ל כרבנן

## הגהות הב"ח

(א) תוס' ד"ה צריכה כו' מעל"ע מן הבדיקה:

**הגהות מהר"ב רנשבורג** א] תוס' ד"ה שהוא מתקן כו' ומיהו אם ראתה היום ואתמול ומצאה כתם וכו' כצ"ל: ב] ד"ה צריכה הפסק וכו' אבל לא בדקה מונה מן הראייה וכו' כצ"ל: ג] בעין משפט אות ד אחר תיבת ובמ"מ נ"ב נ"ל ועי' פי"א הלכה י"א ובהשגות וכס"מ שם.

שוטות נינהו? טועות נינהו! אֶלָּא תְּנֵי: טועות. דְּתַנְיָא: [א]יום אֶחָד טָמֵא וְיוֹם אֶחָד טָהוֹר — מְשַׁמֶּשֶׁת שְׁמִינִי וְלֵילוֹ עִמּוֹ, וְאַרְבָּעָה לֵילוֹת מִתּוֹךְ שְׁמוֹנָה עָשָׂר יוֹם. וְאִם הָיְתָה רוֹאָה מִבָּעֶרֶב — אֵינָהּ מְשַׁמֶּשֶׁת אֶלָּא שְׁמִינִי בִּלְבַד. [ב]שְׁנֵי יָמִים טְמֵאִין וּשְׁנֵי יָמִים טְהוֹרִין — מְשַׁמֶּשֶׁת שְׁמִינִי, וּשְׁנֵים עָשָׂר, וְשִׁשָּׁה עָשָׂר, וְעֶשְׂרִים. וּתְשַׁמֵּשׁ נַמִי בְּתַשְׁסַר! אָמַר רַב שֵׁשֶׁת: זֹאת אוֹמֶרֶת, *[ג]גַּרְגְּרָן דִּתְנַן — אָסוּר. רַב אַשִׁי אָמַר: נְהִי דְּחַד עָשָׂר לָא בָּעֵי שִׁימּוּר, עֲשִׂירִי מִיהָא בָּעֵי שִׁימּוּר. [ד]שְׁלֹשָׁה יָמִים טְמֵאִין וּשְׁלֹשָׁה יָמִים טְהוֹרִין — מְשַׁמֶּשֶׁת שְׁנֵי יָמִים, וְשׁוּב אֵינָהּ מְשַׁמֶּשֶׁת לְעוֹלָם. [ה]אַרְבָּעָה יָמִים טְמֵאִים וְאַרְבָּעָה יָמִים טְהוֹרִין — מְשַׁמֶּשֶׁת יוֹם אֶחָד, וְשׁוּב אֵינָהּ מְשַׁמֶּשֶׁת לְעוֹלָם. [ו]חֲמִשָּׁה יָמִים טְמֵאִים וַחֲמִשָּׁה יָמִים טְהוֹרִין — מְשַׁמֶּשֶׁת שְׁלֹשָׁה יָמִים, וְשׁוּב אֵינָהּ מְשַׁמֶּשֶׁת לְעוֹלָם. [ז]שִׁשָּׁה יָמִים טְמֵאִין וְשִׁשָּׁה יָמִים טְהוֹרִין — מְשַׁמֶּשֶׁת חֲמִשָּׁה יָמִים, וְשׁוּב אֵינָהּ מְשַׁמֶּשֶׁת לְעוֹלָם. [ח]שִׁבְעָה יָמִים טְמֵאִין וְשִׁבְעָה יָמִים טְהוֹרִין — מְשַׁמֶּשֶׁת רְבִיעַ יָמֶיהָ, מִתּוֹךְ כ"ח יָמִים. [ט]שְׁמוֹנָה יָמִים טְמֵאִין וּשְׁמוֹנָה יָמִים טְהוֹרִין — מְשַׁמֶּשֶׁת חֲמִשָּׁה עָשָׂר יוֹם מִתּוֹךְ אַרְבָּעִים וּשְׁמוֹנָה. הֲרֵי אַרְבֵּיסַר הָווּ! אָמַר רַב אַדָּא בַּר יִצְחָק. [י]זֹאת אוֹמֶרֶת: יְמֵי נִדָּתָהּ שֶׁאֵין רוֹאָה בָּהֶן — עוֹלִין לִסְפִירַת זִיבָתָהּ. דְּאִיבַּעְיָא לְהוּ: יְמֵי

**רש"י**

שׁוֹטוֹת נִינְהוּ. בִּתְמִיָּה. **דְּתַנְיָא.** לְפָרוּשֵׁי "פִּקְחוֹת" דְּמַתְנִיתִין קָאָתֵי. **יוֹם אֶחָד טָמֵא וְיוֹם אֶחָד טָהוֹר.** כׇּל יָמֶיהָ, וְקָמַיְירֵי כְּשֶׁרוֹאָה בַּיּוֹם. **מְשַׁמֶּשֶׁת שְׁמִינִי.** לַיּוֹם שֶׁרָאֲתָה בּוֹ רְאִיָּה רִאשׁוֹנָה, שֶׁהֲרֵי טְהוֹרָה (א) הָוַת. שֶׁהֲרֵי בַּשְּׁבִיעִי לָעֶרֶב טָבְלָה, וְלֹא תִּרְאֶה עַד תְּשִׁיעִי. הִלְכָּךְ, מְשַׁמֶּשֶׁת שְׁמִינִי כּוּלּוֹ לַיְלָה וְיוֹם. **וְלֵילוֹ עִמּוֹ.** לֵיל (ב) אַחֲרָיו, נָגְהֵי תְּשִׁיעִי. **וְאַרְבָּעָה לֵילוֹת מִתּוֹךְ שְׁמוֹנָה עָשָׂר יוֹם.** לִרְאִיָּיה הָרִאשׁוֹנָה. שֶׁהֲרֵי אִשָּׁה זוֹ לֹא תְּהֵא זָבָה לְעוֹלָם, שֶׁאֵינָהּ רוֹאָה ג' רְצוּפִין. וּכְשֶׁהִיא רוֹאָה תְּשִׁיעִי — תְּהֵא שׁוֹמֶרֶת עֲשִׂירִי, וּתְשַׁמֵּשׁ בַּלַּיְלָה, וְתִרְאֶה בְּי"א, וְתִשְׁמוֹר י"ב, וּתְשַׁמֵּשׁ בַּלַּיְלָה — הֲרֵי שְׁתַּיִם. וְתִרְאֶה בִּי"ג, וְתִשְׁמוֹר י"ד, וּתְשַׁמֵּשׁ בַּלַּיְלָה — הֲרֵי שָׁלֹשׁ. וְתִרְאֶה ט"ו, וְתִשְׁמוֹר ט"ז, וּתְשַׁמֵּשׁ לָעֶרֶב — הֲרֵי ד'. וּבְי"ז תִּרְאֶה, וְתִשְׁמוֹר י"ח — הֲרֵי כָּלוּ י"ח וְלֹא שִׁמְּשָׁה אֶלָּא ד' לֵילוֹת לְבַד שְׁמִינִי וְלֵילוֹ, וְתַשְׁמִישׁ אַחֲרוֹן אֵינוֹ בְּתוֹךְ י"ח, וּלְמָחָר בְּי"ט כְּשֶׁתִּרְאֶה — תְּהֵא תְּחִלַּת נִדָּה, שֶׁהֲרֵי שָׁלְמוּ י"א שֶׁבֵּין נִדָּה לְנִדָּה, וְחוֹזֶרֶת לְמִנְיָינָהּ שֶׁאָמַרְנוּ. **וְאִם הָיְתָה רוֹאָה.** בְּכׇל הַיָּמִים הַטְּמֵאִים מִבָּעֶרֶב. **אֵינָהּ מְשַׁמֶּשֶׁת אֶלָּא שְׁמִינִי.** שָׁלֵם, לַיְלָה וָיוֹם. אֲבָל לֹא לֵיל שֶׁל אַחֲרָיו — שֶׁהֲרֵי תִּרְאֶה בּוֹ, וּתְהֵא טְמֵאָה, וּצְרִיכָה לִשְׁמוֹר עֲשִׂירִי. וּבַלַּיְלָה לֹא תִּטְבּוֹל — שֶׁהֲרֵי רוֹאָה. וְכֵן עַד סוֹף י"ח, שֶׁהֵן י"א עִם יְמֵי הַנִּדּוּת. וּבְי"ט תְּהֵא תְּחִלַּת נִדָּה, וְתַחֲזוֹר לְמִנְיָינָהּ וּתְשַׁמֵּשׁ בַּשְּׁמִינִי. וְכֵן לְעוֹלָם. **ב' יָמִים טְמֵאִים כו'.** כְּלָלָא דְּמִילְּתָא: כׇּל יָמִים דִּלְקַמָּן, עַד סוֹף פִּירְקִין — כְּשֶׁרוֹאָה מִבָּעֶרֶב. **מְשַׁמֶּשֶׁת שְׁמִינִי.** שֶׁהוּא מִשְּׁנֵי יָמִים הַטְּהוֹרִים, שֶׁשְּׁבִיעִי וּשְׁמִינִי טְהוֹרִין הֵן. אֶלָּא שֶׁהַשְּׁבִיעִי, מֵהַנִּדּוּת, וְטוֹבֶלֶת לָעֶרֶב, וּמְשַׁמֶּשֶׁת שְׁמִינִי שָׁלֵם. וְלָעֶרֶב תִּרְאֶה, שֶׁהוּא תְּשִׁיעִי, וְכֵן א] עֲשִׂירִי. וְתִשְׁמוֹר י"א יוֹם לְאֵלּוּ שְׁנֵי יָמִים, וְטוֹבֶלֶת לָעֶרֶב וּמְשַׁמֶּשֶׁת י"ב שָׁלֵם. וְתִרְאֶה י"ג וְי"ד, וּתְהֵא שׁוֹמֶרֶת ט"ו, וּתְשַׁמֵּשׁ ט"ז. וְתִרְאֶה י"ז וְי"ח, וְתִשְׁמוֹר י"ט. דְּקָסָבַר: הָרוֹאָה יוֹם י"א — אָסוּר לְשַׁמֵּשׁ לְמָחָר. וּלְקַמָּן פָּרֵיךְ: וּתְשַׁמֵּשׁ בְּתַשְׁסְרֵי, דְּהָא כּוּלּוֹ לְהוּ יָמִים שֶׁצְּרִיכָה שִׁימּוּר! וּמ"מ בְּיוֹם עֶשְׂרִים מְשַׁמֶּשֶׁת, וּכְשֶׁתִּרְאֶה יוֹם כ"א — הֲרֵי הִיא תְּחִלַּת נִדָּה, וְחוֹזֶרֶת לְמִנְיָן זֶה שֶׁאָמַרְנוּ. **וּתְשַׁמֵּשׁ בְּתַשְׁסַר.** דְּקַיְימָא לָן בְּפֶרֶק אַחֲרוֹן (לקמן עב.): יוֹם אַחַד עָשָׂר לִימֵי זִיבָה, לֹא בָּעֵי שִׁימּוּר יוֹם כְּנֶגְדּוֹ. וְזוֹ לָמָּה מְשַׁמֶּרֶת י"ט בִּשְׁבִיל י"ח שֶׁהוּא סוֹף זִיבָה? **גַּרְגְּרָן.** דִּתְנַן בְּפֶרֶק "תִּינוֹקֶת" (שם.): הָרוֹאָה יוֹם י"א וְטָבְלָה לַיּוֹם שֶׁלְּאַחֲרָיו, וְשִׁמְּשָׁה וְרָאֲתָה בּוֹ בַּיּוֹם — בֵּית הִלֵּל אוֹמְרִים: הֲרֵי זֶה גַּרְגְּרָן, שֶׁלֹּא הִמְתִּין יוֹם זֶה. וּמֵהָךְ בָּרַיְיתָא דְּקָתָנֵי "וּמְשַׁמֶּשֶׁת יוֹם עֶשְׂרִים, וְלֹא יוֹם י"ט" שָׁמְעִינַן דְּאָסוּר לִהְיוֹת גַּרְגְּרָן וּלְשַׁמֵּשׁ בְּיוֹם י"ב עִם הָרוֹאָה בְּי"א. **רַב אַשִׁי אָמַר.** לְעוֹלָם אֵינוֹ אָסוּר. וְהָכָא דְּתָנֵי "אָסוּר" מִשּׁוּם שֶׁרָאֲתָה יוֹם עֲשִׂירִי, דְּאִיהוּ בָּעֵי שִׁימּוּר. לְפִיכָךְ תֵּשֵׁב י"ט הַטָּהוֹר, וִיהֵא שִׁימּוּר לְיוֹם י"ז, שֶׁהוּא עֲשִׂירִי לִימֵי זִיבָה. שִׁימּוּר לָא הָוֵי אֶלָּא יוֹם טָהוֹר, דְּהָכִי נָפְקָא לָן: "יִהְיֶה" — מְלַמֵּד שֶׁסּוֹפֶרֶת יוֹם אֶחָד לְאֶחָד, וּסְפִירָה לָא הָוֵי אֶלָּא יוֹם טָהוֹר. **מְשַׁמֶּשֶׁת שְׁנֵי יָמִים.** אַחַד עָשָׂר וְי"ב, שֶׁהַשְּׁמִינִי וּתְשִׁיעִי מִי"א שֶׁבֵּין נִדָּה לְנִדָּה הֵן. וַעֲשִׂירִי, שִׁימּוּר הוּא לָהֶן. וְשׁוּב אֵינָהּ מְשַׁמֶּשֶׁת לְעוֹלָם — שֶׁהֲרֵי תְּהֵא זָבָה בְּי"ג וְי"ד וְט"ו, וּצְרִיכָה לִסְפּוֹר ז' נְקִיִּים, וְהִיא לֹא תִּרְאֶה ז' נְקִיִּים לְעוֹלָם. **יוֹם אֶחָד.** שְׁמִינִי, דְּכוּלָּהּ בָּרַיְיתָא: בְּשֶׁרוֹאָה בָּעֶרֶב. **רְבִיעַ יָמֶיהָ מִתּוֹךְ כ"ח.** שִׁבְעָה יָמִים שֶׁאַחַר שִׁבְעָה הַטְּמֵאִים שֶׁל נִדּוּת — הִיא מְשַׁמֶּשֶׁת, וּבְשִׁבְעָה הַשְּׁלִישִׁיִּים — תְּהֵא זָבָה, וּבְשִׁבְעָה הָאַחֲרוֹנִים — הֵן יְמֵי הַסְּפִירָה. הֲרֵי כ"ח, וּבְיוֹם כ"ט תְּהֵא תְּחִלַּת נִדָּה. וְנִמְצֵאת מְשַׁמֶּשֶׁת רְבִיעַ יָמֶיהָ. וּלְהָכִי נָקַט כ"ח, מִפְּנֵי שֶׁתְּחִלַּת נִדּוּתָהּ שֶׁל זוֹ מִכ"ח לְכ"ח. **ט"ו יוֹם מִתּוֹךְ מ"ח.** כְּגוֹן ח' הָרִאשׁוֹנִים, הַשְּׁמִינִי יְמֵי זִיבָה. וּמִשְּׁמוֹנָה הַשְּׁנִיִּים — תִּשְׁמוֹר יוֹם לַשְּׁמִינִי שֶׁלְּפָנָיו, וּתְשַׁמֵּשׁ שִׁבְעָה. הֲרֵי ט"ז שֶׁעָבְרוּ עָלֶיהָ, וְנִשְׁאֲרוּ ב' לָהּ מִימֵי זִיבָה. וּשְׁמוֹנָה הַשְּׁלִישִׁיִּים — שְׁנַיִם מֵהֶן יְמֵי זוֹב, וְהַשִּׁשָּׁה תְּחִילַּת נִדָּתָהּ. וּשְׁמוֹנָה הָרְבִיעִיִּים, שֶׁהֵן טְהוֹרִים ב] — הָרִאשׁוֹנִים יַשְׁלִים ז' יְמֵי נִדָּה, וְהַשִּׁבְעָה תְּשַׁמֵּשׁ. וְעַכְשָׁיו נוֹתְרוּ ד' יָמִים מִימֵי זִיבָה. שְׁמוֹנָה הַחֲמִישִׁיִּים — הֲרֵי הִיא זָבָה מִשְּׁלֹשָׁה רִאשׁוֹנִים, וְה' שֶׁלְּאַחֲרֵיהֶן, שִׁבְעָה לִסְפִירָה וּשְׁמִינִי לְתַשְׁמִישׁ. הֲרֵי ט"ו יוֹם מִתּוֹךְ מ"ח, וּבְיוֹם מ"ט כְּשֶׁתִּרְאֶה — תְּהֵא תְּחִלַּת נִדָּה, וְתַחֲזוֹר לַמִּנְיָן שֶׁאָמַרְנוּ. **אַרְבֵּיסַר הָווּ.** קָסָבַר: הַאי דְּמוֹתִיב שֶׁהָאִשָּׁה הַזֹּאת לֹא תְּשַׁמֵּשׁ יוֹם מ"ח, לְפִי שֶׁהַשְּׁמוֹנָה הַחֲמִשִּׁיִּים שֶׁנַּעֲשֵׂית בָּהֶן זָבָה, אֵין מֵהֶן אֶלָּא ד' מִימֵי זִיבָה וְד' הָאַחֲרוֹנִים מִימֵי נִדָּה הֵן. וּמִיהוּ תְּחִלַּת נִדָּה לָא הָוֵי, כׇּל זְמַן שֶׁלֹּא סָפְרָה וְלֹא טָהֲרָה מִזּוֹבָהּ. אֲבָל לְהָכִי מְהַנְּיָא הַךְ רְאִיָּיה (ג) ד' הָאַחֲרוֹנִים הָרְאוּיִין לְנִדּוּת — שֶׁכְּשֶׁיָּבֹאוּ שְׁמוֹנָה טְהוֹרִין שֶׁאַחֲרֵיהֶם, לֹא יַעֲלוּ שְׁלֹשָׁה הָרִאשׁוֹנִים לִימֵי הַסְּפִירָה, לְפִי שֶׁהֵן הַשְׁלָמַת יְמֵי נִדָּה. וִימֵי נִדָּתָהּ שֶׁאֵינָהּ רוֹאָה בָּהֶן, אֵין עוֹלִין לִסְפִירַת זִיבָתָהּ. הִלְכָּךְ, אֵין כָּאן אֶלָּא חֲמִשָּׁה לִסְפִירָה, וּכְשֶׁתִּרְאֶה יוֹם מ"ט — סוֹתֶרֶת. וְכֵן כׇּל ח' הַשְּׁבִיעִיִּים, (יום) וְעַד שֶׁיַּגִּיעַ יוֹם ס"ג, לֹא יַשְׁלִימוּ יְמֵי סְפִירָתָהּ. יְמֵי

**תוספות**

**וארבעה** לילות מתוך י"ח. משמע כאן בהדיא דאין נעשה זבה גדולה ולא צריכה ז' נקיים, עד שתראה ג' ימים רצופין בי"א יום. ודלא כאותם שכתבו בשם רבינו סעדיה שצריכה שבעה נקיים, אפילו ראתה בי"א ג' ימים מפוזרים.

**תשמש** בתשסר. וא"ת: כיון דקס"ד דעשירי לא בעי שימור, תקשה ליה רישא אמאי לא משמשת אלא ד' מתוך י"ח דכי ראתה בי"ז — תשמש בי"ח! ותו: דפלוגתא היא בפרק בתרא (לקמן עב:) לרבי יוחנן עשירי בעי שימור, ולר"ל לא בעי שימור! ויש לומר: דהא דקאמר רבי יוחנן עשירי בעי שימור — היינו, בימי זיבה, שאסורה לשמש ביום י"א אפילו פסקה. ולר"ל מותרת, דעשירי כיון דאינה יכולה להיות זבה גדולה — לא בעי שימור. ולהכי ברישא ניחא דאסורה בי"ח דהוו בימי זיבה. דאפילו ר"ל מודה דמדרבנן אסור. אבל בימי נדה סבר המקשה, דאפילו רבי יוחנן מודה דלא בעי שימור. ולכך פריך: תשמש בתשסר! ומשני רב ששת: גרגרן אסור — דאפילו בראיית י"א צריכה שימור מדרבנן ביום י"ב לכ"ע ורב אשי אמר דאינו אסור אלא משום שראתה בעשירי, וצריכה שימור לרבי יוחנן אף בימי נדה מן התורה, כמו בימי זיבה, ולר"ל — מדרבנן. **הני** ארביסר הוו. פ"ה דפריך אמאי משמשת יום מ"ח דשמונה חמישיים שהן טמאין, הן ד' ימי זיבה, וד' ימי נדה. ושמונה טהורין שאחריהם, ג' בימי נדה וחמש בימי זיבה, וג' ימים הראשונים דימי נדה — לא יעלו לה לספירת זיבה, דאין ימי נדה עולין לספירתה. דאע"ג דאינה נדה, שהרי אינה חוזרת לפתח נדתה עד שתספור ז' נקיים, מ"מ כיון דימים הראוים לימי נדה הן — אין עולין לספירת זיבתה. וקשה לפירוש זה: דא"כ תקשה ליה רישא, דקתני "משמשת רביע ימיה מתוך כ"ח הלא ז' שלישיים שהן טמאין, היו ד' בימי זיבה וג' בימי נדה, וא"כ ז' ימים טהורין שאחריהם — לא יעלו לספירת זיבתה, והיאך תחזור חלילה מכ"ח לכ"ח דאסורה לשמש בז' ימים טהורין של כ"ח שניים? ועוד קשה: דמשמע דאי הוה תני "ומשמשת י"ד" הוה ניחא ליה. והא עד ס"ג יום לא יעלו לה ז' לספירתה, כדפירש"י. וא"כ היאך חוזרת חלילה ממ"ח למ"ח? לכן נראה דה"פ: הני י"ד הוו, דבח' רביעיות אינה משמשת רק ו' דהא ח' שלישיים שהיו טמאים, היו ב' בימי זיבה וששה אחריהן ימי נדה, ויום ראשון מרביעיות שהן טהורין — לא תשמש, דהוי מז' ימי נדה. ויום שני — נמי לא תשמש, לרב אשי דאמר לעיל: עשירי בעי שימור, והרי יום שני הוה שימור ליום י"ז שהוא עשירי. ויום ראשון, אע"ג דטהור הוי, סבר המקשה דלא הוי שימור, כיון דהוי מימי נדה, וימים שהיא נדה גמורה — אינן עולין לספירת זיבה קטנה. אבל מיום מ"ח לא פריך, דכיון דאינה נדה גמורה עד שתספור ז' נקיים — עולין לה שפיר לכ"ע, אע"פ שהן ראויין לימי נדה. ולכך ניחא ליה רישא דמשמשת רביע ימיה מתוך כ"ח. ומה שפרש"י דעד ס"ג לא ישלמו ימי זיבה, נראה דלא דק. דאינה טובלת עד ליל פ' שהרי ח' ימים שביעיים הם ששה ימי זיבה ושני ימי נדה, ושמיניים הטהורים הן ה' בימי נדה וג' בימי זיבה, ותשיעיים הטמאות — כל ח' ימי זיבה, והעשיריים ז' לספירת נקיים. (ד) **ולמאי** ג] דמשנה התלמוד ימי לידה וימי נדה, א"כ לר"ת דפסק *) דימי לידתה שאינה רואה בהן, אין עולין לספירת זיבתה (וה"ה) ולפרש"י דימים הראויים לימי נדה אין עולין — אין תקנה לנשים בזמן הזה, דהוי כלהון ספק זבות, וצריכות ז' נקיים. ופעמים דקיימי בימים הראויים לנדה, ולא עלו לה לספירתה. ומיהו לפירוש רש"י אתי שפיר — דהוא פסק דימי לידה עולין לימי ספירתה. ולר"ת נמי: ימי נדה דווקא אין עולין, אבל ימים הראויין — עולין שפיר. אלא

*) [לעיל לז. ד"ה אביי]

נדה אינן עולין לספירת זבה. וקשה לפי' דא"כ תקשי ליה רישא משמעת רביע ימיה מתוך כ"ח יום והלא ז' שלישיים שהם טמאים הם ד' בימי זיבה וג' בימי נדה וא"כ ז' ימים שאחריהן שהיו טהורין לא עלו לספירת זבה והיאך תחזור חלילה מכ"ח לכ"ח הלא לא תוכל לשמש ביום ז' טהורין הראשונים של כ"ח השניים. ותו דמשמע דאי הוה תני משמשת י"ד יום הוה ניחא ליה ואמאי והא עד ס"ג יום לא ישלימו לה ז' לספירת זבה כדפרש"י וא"כ היאך חוזרת חלילה ממ"ח ליום למ"ח יום. אלא נראה לפרש דפריך ארבעיסר הוו משום דח' שלישיים שהיו טמאים הוו שני ימים בימי זיבה וששה בימי נדה ושמונה טהורין שאחריהן הראשון הוא להשלים ז' ימים נדה ועוד צריכה יום אחד לשמור לשני ימים שראתה בימי זיבה ולא נשאר לשימוש אלא ששה ימים אלמא ש"מ ימי נדה גמורה עולין לספירת זבה קטנה ופריך לרב אשי דלעיל דאמר עשירי בעי שימור: אלא

**תוספי הרא"ש**

**שמיני** ולילו וד' לילות מתוך י"ח מכאן משמע דאם ראתה ג' ימים בתוך י"א יום שבין נדה לנדה אם אינם רצופין אינה זבה גדולה לאפוקי מרב סעדיה שכתב שאם ראתה ג' ימים בימי זיבה אפילו היו מפוזרין צריכין ז' נקיים והגיה ר"ת ושיבוש הוא דאחרים כתבוהו ותלו בשמו דאטו רב סעדיה מי חתים עליה: **ותשמש** בתשסר. ותימה כיון דס"ד דעשירי לא בעי שימור א"כ תיקשי ליה דאשה משמשת ד' לילות ולא יותר ואמאי הא כי ראתה יום שבעה עשר תשמש ביום י"ח. עוד דפלוגתא היא דר"י ור"ל בפרק תינוקת ולר' יוחנן בעי שימור [וי"ל דהא דקאמר ר' יוחנן עשירי בעי שימור] היינו דוקא בתוך ימי זיבתה שאסורה לשמש ביום י"ח אפי' פוסקת בו ולר"ל מותרת דדוקא תשיעי שיכול לבא לידי זבה גדולה בעי שימור אבל עשירי שאינו יכול לבא לידי זבה גדולה לא בעי שימור אבל בימי נדה אפי' ר' יוחנן מודה דלא בעי שימור. הלכך פריך ותשמש בתשסר אבל השתא ניחא ליה דאסור לשמש ביום י"ח דהיינו בימי זיבה ואפי' ר"ל מודה דמדרבנן אסור. ורב ששת משני דמדרבנן אסור דאפי' (בראייתה י"א יום) [ברואה ביום י"א גופא] צריכה לשמור מדרבנן ביום י"ב לכ"ע ורב אשי [אמר] גרגרן מותר ואינו אסור אלא מחמת יום עשירי שראת' הלכך צריכה שימור אף בימי נדה לר' יוחנן מן התורה כימי זיבה ולר"ל מדרבנן: **הני** ארביסר הוו. פרש"י דפריך אמאי תשמש יום מ"ח דהא ח' חמשיים שהם טמאים הם ד' בימי זיבה וד' בימי נדה וח' טהורים שאחריהן ג' בימי נדה וה' בימי זיבה ולא יעלו לה לספירת זבה דימי

**עין משפט נר מצוה**

ס א מיי' פ"ז מהלכות איסורי ביאה הלכה יד:
סא ב מיי' שם הלכה טו:
סב ג מיי' שם פ"ו הלכ' יז יח:
סג ד מיי' שם ופ"ז הלכה טז:
סד ה מיי' שם הלכה יז:
סה ו מיי' שם הלכה יח:
סו ז מיי' שם הלכה יט [ז]:
סז ח מיי' שם הלכה כ והלכ' כא:
סח ט י מיי' שם הלכה כב:

[לקמן עב.]

**הגהות הב"ח**

(א) רש"י ד"ה משמשת וכו' טהורה הוא שהרי: (ב) ד"ה ולילו עמו ליל של אחריו: (ג) ד"ה ארביסר וכו' הך דראייה דד' האחרונים: (ד) תוס' ד"ה ולמאי דמשנה התלמוד ימי לידה הס"ד:

**גליון הש"ס**

גמ' משמשת שמיני ולילו עמו. ע' בהרא"ש בפ' בנות כותים סי' ח':

**הגהות מהר"ב רנשבורג**

א] רש"י ד"ה משמשת שמיני שהוא וכו' ועשירי ותשמור יום י"א וכו' כצ"ל: ב] ד"ה ט"ו יום וכו' ושמונה הרביעיים שהן טהורים הראשון ישלים ז' וכו' כצ"ל: ג] תוד"ה ולמאי דמשנה התלמוד וכו':

סט א מיי' פ"ז מהל' איסורי ביאה הלכה כג:
ע ב ג מיי' שם הלכה כד:
א ד מיי' פ"ב מהל' מטמאי משכב ומושב הלכה א סמג עשין רמח:
ב ה מיי' פ"ט מהלכות טומאת מת הלכה ח:
ג ו מיי' פ"ב מהלכות משכב ומושב הלכה ח:
ד ז מיי' פ"ד מהלכות אבות הטומאה הלכה יב:
ה ח מיי' שם פ"ו הלכה ח:
ו ט מיי' שם פ"ה הלכה יד ופ"ב בהלכות מטמאי מו"מ הלכה ח:
ז י מיי' שם:
ח ל מיי' פ"א מהלכות משכב ומושב הלכה ח:
ט מ מיי' פט"ו מהל' טומאת צרעת הלכ' ...
י נ מיי' פ"א מהלכות משכב ומושב הלכה ח:

*ימי לידה שאינה רואה בהן, מהו שיעלו לספירת זיבתה? אמר רב כהנא, ת"ש: ראתה שנים, ולשלישי הפילה, ואינה יודעת מה הפילה – הרי זו ספק זיבה ספק לידה: מביאה קרבן ואינו נאכל, וימי לידתה שאין רואה בהן – עולין לה לספירת זיבתה. אמר רב פפא: שאני התם, כיון דאיכא למימר יולדת זכר היא, וכל הני שבעה יתירי דקיהבינן לה – סלקי לה לספירת זיבתה. אמר ליה רב הונא בריה דרב יהושע לרב פפא: ביולדת זכר – איכא לספוקי, ביולדת נקבה – ליכא לספוקי? אלא לאו שמע מינה: עולין, שמע מינה. אתשעה ימים טמאין ותשעה ימים טהורין – משמשת שמונה ימים מתוך שמונה עשר. בעשרה ימים טמאין ועשרה ימים טהורים – ימי שמושה *כימי זיבתה. גוכן למאה וכן לאלף.§

## הדרן עלך בא סימן

*דם דהנדה הובשר המת – מטמאין לחין ומטמאין יבשין. ואבל הזוב, והניע, והרוק, *זוהשרץ, חוהנבלה, טוהשכבת זרע מטמאין לחין ואין מטמאין יבשין. יואם יכולין להשרות ולחזור לכמות שהן – מטמאין לחין ומטמאין יבשין. *וכמה היא שרייתן? בפושרין כמעת לעת. רבי יוסי אומר: בשר המת יבש, ואינו יכול להשרות ולחזור לכמות שהיה – טהור.§ **גמ'** מנא הני מילי? אמר חזקיה, לדאמר קרא: °"והדוה בנדתה", מדוה כמותה, מה היא מטמאה, אף מדוה מטמאה. אשכחן לח, יבש מנלן? אמר רבי יצחק: אמר קרא °"יהיה" – בהוייתו יהא. ואימא: הני מילי בלח ונעשה יבש, יבש מעיקרו מנלן? ותו, הא דתנן: *המפלת כמין קליפה כמין עפר, כמין שערה, כמין יבחושין אדומים – תטיל למים, אם נמוחו טמא מנלן? "יהיה" רבויא הוא. אי מה היא עושה משכב ומושב לטמא אדם ולטמא בגדים, אף דמה נמי עושה משכב ומושב לטמא אדם ולטמא בגדים? אטו דמה בר משכב ומושב הוא? ולטעמיך, אבן מנוגעת בת משכב ומושב היא, דאיצטריך קרא למעוטי? דתניא: יכול תהא אבן מנוגעת עושה משכב ומושב לטמא אדם לטמא בגדים. ודין הוא, ומה זב שאינו מטמא בביאה עושה משכב ומושב לטמא אדם לטמא בגדים, אבן מנוגעת שמטמאה בביאה אינו דין שמטמאה משכב ומושב לטמא אדם לטמא בגדים – ת"ל: "הזב", הזב – מולא אבן מנוגעת. טעמא דמעטיה קרא, הא לאו הכי מטמאה! ומינה, לאו מי אמרת הזב – ולא אבן מנוגעת, ה"נ אמר קרא: "אשר היא יושבת עליו" נהיא ולא דמה.
אי

ויקרא טו | שם

**תוספות**

**אלא** ש"מ עולין ש"מ. וטעמא דרב הונא בריה דרב יהושע, אע"ג דהוי ספק ספקא, מ"מ אי בעלמא אין עולין – הכא נמי הוה לן למגזר, אטו בעלמא. **וכן** למאה וכן לאלף. ימי שמושה ב] (ב) כימי זיבתה. דמאחר ז' ימי נדה, כל הימים שתראה, אפילו מאה או אלף, מקרו "ימי זיבתה", עד שתספור ז' נקיים.

### הדרן עלך בא סימן

**דם** הנדה, מנא הני מילי. לרבא דאמר בפ' "בנות כותים" (לעיל לה.) "לאחרים גורם טומאה, לעצמו לא כ"ש" ולית ליה ד"שעיר המשתלח יוכיח" – הכא לא צריך קרא. ומיהו לדם נדה של מצורעת אצטריך שפיר קרא, דהדם אינו גורם טומאה. ולקמן דמצריך קרא לטומאת זובו במגע ובמשא, ולא יליף מדם הנדה דהכא – משום דאיכא למפרך: מה לדם הנדה שכן מטמא באונס. ואם תאמר: וכיון דלא ילפינן מהכא, אמאי אצטריך לקמן קרא למעוטי זוב יבש, מהיכא תיתי לטמא? ויש לומר: כיון דהשוה הכתוב דם נדה וזוב לטומאה, ממילא ילפינן מהדדי, דגילוי מילתא בעלמא הוא. **ותו** הא דתנן המפלת כו' – תימה: דהיינו היא קושיא גופיה! וי"ל: דה"ק, וכ"ת: דאין הכי נמי דיבש מעיקרא טהור, והתנן המפלת כו'. אי נמי י"ל: ותו, יבש משונה כמין יבחושין או כמין קליפה, מנלן?

**יכול** תהא אבן מנוגעת כו'. אבן מנוגעת שמטמאה בביאה כו'. וא"ת: מת יוכיח, שמטמא בביאה, ואינו עושה משכב ומושב! ועוד: מצורע גופיה מפרש ר"ת בריש "אלו דברים" (פסחים דף סז:*) דלא עביד משכב ומושב אלא לטמא אוכלין ומשקין! ויש לומר: דמקרא דהכא ממעטינן להו, "הזב" – ולא המצורע, ולא המת.

***אף** מדוה נמי מטמא באבן מסמא. – ואם תאמר: כיון דממעטינן מדוה מ"היא" (ג) לטמא משכב ומושב, ממעטינן נמי מאבן מסמא. דהא מכח משכב ומושב הוי טומאה לאבן מסמא, כדתנן בת"כ: מנין לרבות עשר מצעות זו על גב זו, ועל גביהן אבן מסמא? תלמוד לומר "כל המשכב"! ואור"י: דאבן מסמא נפקא לן משום דרשא, דלא מטמא אלא אוכלין ומשקין. ולהכי אילטריך למעוטי מדוה, אף מאבן מסמא שהיא טומאה קלה.
אבן

עייך לקמן נה.

[ד"ה שכן עושה מו"מ ע"ש]

**רש"י**

ימי לידתה. כגון ילדה בזוב ופסקה מיד. הכי גרסינן: ראתה שנים. ראתה שני ימים בשופי, בתוך י"א שבין נדה לנדה. ספק לידה ספק זיבה. שמא לידה שמא זיבה, שמא לא זו ולא זו. אם ולד הוא ולא ראתה בפתיחת הקבר – הרי היא לידה ולא זיבה. ואם אינו ולד וראתה דם בפתיחת הקבר – הרי היא זיבה, ואין כאן לידה. ואם ולד הוא וראתה דם בלידה – הרי זו יולדת בזוב. ואם נפתח קבר בלא דם, ואינו ולד – אין כאן לא זו ולא זו. הלכך, ספק הוא, ונטיל עליה חומר לידה – לטמא שבועיים, אפילו לא תראה. וחומר זיבה – שכל זמן שלא תפסוק ז' נקיים, לא תטהר. ומביאה קרבן, ואינו נאכל שמא אין כאן לא לידה ולא זיבה. וימי לידתה שאין רואה בהן עולין כו'. ואע"ג דאיכא לספוקי ביולדת בזוב, ויש כאן לידה וזיבה. משום דאיכא למימר כו'. אבל אי הוה פשיטא לן דיולדת נקבה היא, לא סלקי לה. ט' ימים טמאין. תרי מינייהו זיבה, וכי *חזיא טהורין – חד מינייהו הוי שימור, ושמונה לתשמיש, וביום י"ט הויא תחלת נדה. ולעולם לא תהא זבה. ימי שמושה כימי זיבתה. דמעשרה טמאין הוו ז' נדה וג' זיבה, ומעשרה טהורין ז' לספירה וג' לתשמיש. הרי ימי שימוש (א)א] כימי זיבה. וכן למאה. טמאין ז' ימי נדה, וכולהו ימי זיבה, ומאה טהורין ז' לספירה, וכולהו לתשמיש. וכן לאלף.

### הדרן עלך בא סימן

**דם** הנדה. והניע. קר"ק בלע"ז, וממעיינות הזב הן, והוי אב הטומאה. וכמה היא שרייתן. דנימא: אי הדרא בכי האי שיעורא – לחין נינהו? בפושרים מעת לעת. אבל אי בעי טפי מים חמים או יותר ממעת לעת – יבשין הן. **גמ'** מנא הני מילי. דדם נדה מטמא מגעו ומשאו? אשכחן לח. דדוה – לא משמע, כעין שהוא זב. יהיה. "דם יהיה זובה". יבש מעיקרו. כגון הני דתנינן. מין שערה. אדומה. עושה משכב. שיהא משכבו מטמא אדם, ולא יהא ראשון במגעו, אלא אב הטומאה כמשכב נדה עצמה. שאינו מטמא בביאה. אדם הנכנס עם הזב בבית – אינו טמא. אבן המנוגעת. מטמאה בביאה אדם הנכנס עמה לבית, דכתיב: "והבא אל הבית" וגו'. הזב. "אשר ישכב עליו הזב" (ויקרא טו). היא. עושה משכבה אב הטומאה, ולא דמה עושה משכבה אב הטומאה. אבל מטמא הוא את שתחתיו משום משא להיות ראשון, ואף על פי שאין נוגע בו. דהא איתקש לנדה. והכי נמי תנן ב"אבות הטומאה" (כלים פ"א מ"ג) דדם נדה מטמא במשא.
אי

תורה אור

**מסורת הש"ס**

[לעיל לו.]
נ"ל אתיא
עיין מהר"מ
[לעיל כב.]
[ע"ז סח:]
לעיל כב:
לעיל כה. כב.

**הגהות הב"ח**

(א) רש"י ד"ה ימי שמושה וכו' כימי זיבה: (ב) תוס' ד"ה וכן וכו' כימי זיבתה: (ג) ד"ה אף וכו' מהיא מלטמא משכב ומושב ממעטינן ליה נמי וכו' וכל המשכב:

**גליון הש"ס**

מתני' בפושרין מעט לעת. עיין זבחים קט ע"ב תוס' ד"ה אף הכוונה: רש"י ד"ה היא עושה כו' את שתחתיו משום משא. עי' שבת פג ע"ב ברש"י ד"ה כרעו הן:

**הגהות מהר"ב רנשבורג**

א] רש"י ד"ה ימי שמושה וכו' הרי ימי שמוש כימי זיבה כל': ב] תוס' ד"ה וכן למאה וכו' כימי זיבתה וכו' כל"ל:

**תוספי הרא"ש**

**אלא** ש"מ עולין ש"מ. וטעמא דרב הונא בר' דרב יהושע הוי דאע"ג דספק ספיקא הוא מ"מ אם בעלמא אין עולים הכא הוה לן למיגזר אטו בעלמא:

סליק פירקא

**מנה"מ.** ומק"ו לא מטמינן ליה כיון שגורם לאחרים טומאה לעצמו לא כ"ש דאיכא למימר שעיר המשתלח יוכיח ולרבא דלית ליה שעיר המשתלח יוכיח לעיל בפ' בנות כותים איצטריך לדם הנדה של מצורעת שאינו גורם לה טומאה. ותימה לקמן אמאי צריך קרא לטמא זובו במגע ומשא נילף מדם הנדה ואי פרכת שכן מטמא באונס א"כ אמאי איצטריך קרא לקמן למעוטי זוב יבש מהיכא תיתי דהוה טמא וי"ל דעיקר טומאה ודאי לא ילפינן מנדה משום הך פירכא אבל כיון שהשוון הכתוב לטומאה ממילא ילפינן מהדדי לטמאות לח ויבש דגלויי מלתא בעלמא הוא: **ותו** הא דתנן המפלת כמין חתיכה. תימה מאי ותו היינו קמייתא גופה וי"ל דהוי כמו אלמה תנן וכ"ת ה"נ יבש מעיקרו טהור הא תנן המפלת וכו' א"נ ותו יבש משונה כי האי שענשה כמין יבחושין או קליפה מנא לן: **יכול** תהא אבן מנוגעת עושה משכב ומושב לטמויי אדם לטמויי בגדים. ותימה מי חמירא ממצורע גופיה דלא עביד משכב ומושב אלא לטמויי אוכלין ומשקין כדמוכח בפסחים פרק אלו דברים. ולקמן בפרק בתרא אפרשנו בע"ה. וי"ל דעיקר דינא לא בעי' למילף אלא לטמויי אוכלין ומשקין כעין מצורע אלא כיון דמהך ק"ו מצי למילף נמי אדם ובגדים נקט אדם ובגדים הלכך לא חש למימר מצורע יוכיח שמטמא בביאה ואינו עושה משכב ומושב לטמא אדם לטמא בגדים משום דידע דעיקר מילתיה לא יליף אלא לטמויי אוכלין ומשקין כעין מצורע. ועוי"ל דהא המצורע גופיה אינו עושה משכב ומושב אלא לטמא אוכלין ומשקין היינו מהכא הזב ולא המצורע ואבן המנוגעת נמי אפשר דעושה משכב ומושב לטמא אוכלין ומשקין כעין מצורע והא דלא פריך תלמודא אלמא עושה משכב ומושב לטומאה קלה משום דלא היה יודע להוכיח שהוא כך לא ממשנה ולא מברייתא: **אבן** המנוגעת שמטמאה בביאה כו'. ותימה מת יוכיח שמטמא בביאה ואינו עושה משכב ומושב. וי"ל דמת גופיה נמי לא אימעוט אלא מהכא

אי מה היא מטמאה באבן מסמא, אף מדוה נמי מטמאה באבן מסמא? אמר רב אשי, אמר קרא: °"והנושא אותם", "אותם" – מיעוטא הוא.§ "ובשר המת". § מנלן? אמר ר"ל, אמר קרא: °"לכל טומאתו" – לכל טומאות הפורשות ממנו. רבי יוחנן אמר: °"או בעצם אדם או בקבר", אדם דומיא דעצם, מה עצם – יבש, אף כאן – יבש. מאי בינייהו? איכא בינייהו – דאפריך אפרוכי. מיתיבי: [א]בשר המת שהופרך – טהור! התם – [ב]דאקמח והוי עפרא. מיתיבי: *[ג]כל שבמת – מטמא, חוץ מן השינים, והשער, והצפורן. ובשעת חבורן – הכל טמא! אמר רב אדא בר אהבה: דומיא דעצם, מה עצם – שנברא עמו, אף כל – שנברא עמו. והאיכא שער וצפורן, שנבראו עמו – וטהורין! אלא אמר רב אדא בר אהבה: דומיא דעצם, מה עצם – שנברא עמו ואין גזעו מחליף, אף כל שנברא עמו [ד]ואין גזעו מחליף. יצאו השינים – שלא נבראו עמו. יצאו שער וצפורן, שאף על פי שנבראו עמו – גזעו מחליף. והרי עור, דגזעו מחליף, *ותנן: *הגלודה, רבי מאיר מכשיר. וחכמים – [ה]פוסלין. ואפילו רבנן לא קפסלי אלא דאדהכי והכי שליט בה אוירא ומתה, ולעולם גזעו מחליף. *ותנינן: אלו שעורותיהם כבשרן – [ו]עור האדם! הא איתמר עלה, אמר עולא: דבר תורה – עור אדם, טהור. ומאי טעמא אמרו טמא – גזרה שמא יעשה אדם עורות אביו ואמו שטיחין לחמור. ואיכא דאמרי: הרי עור, דאין גזעו מחליף, *ותנן "וחכמים פוסלין". ואפי' רבי מאיר לא קא מכשר – אלא דקריר בשרא וחייא, ולעולם אין גזעו מחליף, ואמר עולא: דבר תורה – עור אדם טהור! כי איתמר דעולא – אסיפא איתמר: א) [ז]וכולן שעבדן או שהילך בהן כדי עבודה – טהורין, [ח]חוץ מעור אדם. ואמר עולא: [ט]דבר תורה – עור אדם כי עבדו, טהור. ומה טעם אמרו טמא – גזרה שמא יעשה אדם עור אביו ואמו שטיחין. והרי בשר, דגזעו מחליף וטמא! אמר מר בר רב אשי: בשר נעשה מקומו צלקת.§ "אבל הזוב". § זוב מנלן? דתניא: *°"זובו טמא" – לימד על הזוב שהוא טמא. והלא דין הוא, לאחרים – גורם טומאה, לעצמו – לא כ"ש? *שעיר המשתלח יוכיח, שגורם טומאה לאחרים – והוא עצמו, טהור. אף אתה אל תתמה על זה, שאע"פ שגורם טומאה לאחרים – הוא עצמו טהור. ת"ל: "זובו טמא" – לימד על הזוב שהוא טמא. ואימא: ה"מ – במגע, אבל במשא – לא, מידי דהוה אשרץ! אמר רב ביבי בר אביי: במגע לא איצטריך קרא – דלא גרע משכבת זרע,

כי

א) פסחים מו. חולין קכב.

**רש"י**

אי מה. משא נדה חמור לטמא אבן מסמא. אבן גדולה המושמה על הכלים, ונדה נשאת עליה – מטמאה בגדים שתחת האבן, כדאמר בתורת כהנים. אף משא דמה חמור, לטמא באבן מסמא. דיש מטמא במשא, ואינו מטמא באבן מסמא, (א) במסכת שבת בפרק "רבי עקיבא" (דף פג.) דאמרינן: במשא – כולי עלמא לא פליגי, דמטמא. כי פליגי – באבן מסמא, דאין משאו אלא בדבר הראוי ליגשא, אבל גדולה – אינה מטלטלת, להיות הטומאה נישאת עליה. וגבי זב הוא דרביה קרא. והנושא אותם. במשכב הזב כתיב. ומשכב הזב הנישא על אבן מסמא – מטמא כלים שתחתיה, כדמפרש בתורת כהנים, וכתיב "אותם" למעוטי דמה. לכל טומאות הפורשות. לא שנא לח ולא שנא יבש. דמפרך אפרוכי. שיבש יותר מדאי, לר' יוחנן טהור, דדומיא דעצם בעינן, ועצם – לא מיפרך. דאקמח. לשון טחינה כקמח. חוץ מן השינים. והא שינים דומיא דעצם הן, וטהורין! וקשיא לתרווייהו. שינים. לא נבראו עמו, שגדלין לאחר זמן. אין גזעו מחליף. אם ניטל, אינו חוזר. הגלודה. בהמה שנקלף עורה מפני טורח מלאכה או מחמת שחין. דתנן ר"מ מכשיר. ואינה טרפה, דהדרא בריא. אלמא, גזעו מחליף. אדהכי והכי. עד שהוא חוזר וגדל. שליט בה אוירא ומתה. הלכך טרפה. שטיחין. מרדעת לחמור. וחכמים פוסלין. דלא הדרא בריא. אלמא, אין גזעו מחליף. קריר עלה בשרא. מתקשה בשרה ונעשה כעור. אסיפא. סיפא ד"ואלו שעורותיהן כבשרן". וכולן. העורות שמנו חכמים להיות מטמאין כבשר, בפ' "העור והרוטב". שעבדן או הילך בהן כדי עבודה. כדרך שרגילין לתת עור לפני דורסן, ושיעור עבודה מפרש *בברכות (דף טו) ובפסחים (דף מו.) כדי *מיל. טהורין. שבטלן מתורת בשר. כי עבדן. נמי טהור, דהא בטילה. נעשה מקומו צלקת. כלומר, רושם נראה בה, חרין או גומא, ואין כולו חוזר. אבל שער וצפורן – אין נטילתן ניכר. לאחרים. לזב. שעיר המשתלח. גורם טומאה למשלחו, דכתיב (ויקרא טז): "והמשלח את השעיר" וגו'. שרץ. מטמא במגע, ולא במשא.

**תוספות**

אבן מסמא. (ב) פ"ה: אבן המונחת על גבי יתדות, וזב יושב עליה, וכלי תחת האבן. וטמא מ"וכל אשר יהיה תחתיו". וקשה: דבת"כ מפיק אבן מסמא מ"וכל המשכב", וקרא ד"וכל אשר יהיה תחתיו" מוקי בפרק "בנות כותים" (לעיל לג.) לעליונו של זב, ובת"כ מוקי לה במרכב! ועוד: דאי מ"וכל אשר יהיה תחתיו" נפקא, אם כן אפילו כלים שאין ראויים למשכב ומושב נמי. ובתורת כהנים מוכח בהדיא דכלים שאינם ראויין למשכב ומושב אין להם אפילו טומאה קלה! ועוד: אמאי נקט "אבן", אפילו דף על גבי יתדות נמי! ועוד: מדקרי ליה "מסמא" – משמע: לשון שימה! ומפרש רבינו תם ורבינו שמואל: ד"אבן מסמא" – היינו, אבן גדולה שהיא כבדה ובגדים תחתיה. וכבדה כל כך, עד שאין ניכר כובד הזב היושב עליה ועל הבגדים. ואין בה אלא טומאה קלה, כדפי' לעיל. והשתא אתי שפיר דמייתי בפ' בתרא (לקמן סט:) "והיתיאת אבן חדא ושומת על פום גובא" – שצריכה שימה ואתוי, לפי שאינה קלה לטלטל. אך קשה: דבת"כ מרבה אבן מסמא מ"וכל המשכב" מטעם משכב ומושב, ובכל התלמוד משמע דהוה מטעם משא. (ג) ובשמעתין ממעט לה מ"והנושא אותם" וכן לקמן בפרק בתרא (דף סט.) תנן: הזב והזבה מטמאין במשא, עד שימוק הבשר. ומפרש בגמרא: מאי "משא"? אבן מסמא. ובשבת פרק "רבי עקיבא" (דף פג.) קאמר: כי פליגי – באבן מסמא, ובמתניתין קתני *"היסט". ובתוספתא דכלים *תניא: אין טומאה לכלי חרס אלא מאוירו ובהסיטו על גבי אבן מסמא, והיסט – היינו משא, כדאמרינן ב"העור והרוטב" (חולין קכד:) אטו נושא לאו מסיט הוא! ועוד: אי היסט מטעם משכב ומושב, הא אמר בפרק "ר"ע" (שבת פד.) דמדרס כלי חרס – טהור! וי"ל: דמה שקרא בכל התלמוד "משא" – היינו, כגון שיד הטהור או רגלו תחת האבן, והזב או דם הנדה על האבן, דנראה דהטהור נשא את הזב או את הדם. אבל כלים תחת האבן, והזב יושב עליה – הוי מטעם משכב ומושב. והא דתנן במסכת זבים (פ"ה מ"ב) כילד אצבעו של זב תחת הנדבך והטהור מלמעלה כו' – נראה דהיינו היסטו על גבי אבן מסמא דתוספתא, וכגון שהנדבך דוחק אצבעו של זב. דאי לאו הכי, הוי כאילו היה אויר בין אצבעו לנדבך, דאין כאן טומאה כלל. מיתיבי בשר המת שהופרך טהור. וא"ת: ולימא, ר' יוסי היא, דאמר במתני' "בשר (ד) שיבש – טהור"? וי"ל: דלא אתיא כרבי יוסי, מדקתני "הופרך", ולא קתני "שיבש". חוץ מן השינים. פ"ה: וקשה לתרוייהו. וקשה: א] דא"כ תקשה ליה קרא ד"או בעצם"! אלא נראה דלר"ל לחוד פריך, ופשיטא דשינים אינם בכלל עצם. אלא אמר רב אדא. אינו חוזר בו ממה שאמר, אלא מפרש והולך מעט מעט. שמא יעשה שטיחין. וא"ת: והלא מת אסור בהנאה, דגמרינן (ע"ז דף כט:) "שם" "שם" מעגלה ערופה! וי"ל: דטומאה חמירא להו טפי, כדאמר בפרק ב' דיומא (דף כג.) ללמדך שקשה עליהם טומאת כלי, יותר משפיכות דמים. ועוד נראה: דעור אינו בכלל בשר, ליאסר בהנאה. א) דהא עגלה ערופה נמי לא נפקאב] אלא מדכתיב בה "כפרה", כקדשים, ב) ועוד קדשים מותרין בהנאה לאחר זריקה, שהוא זמן כפרה. וניחא השתא דאיצטריך בשור הנסקל "לא יאכל" להנאת עורו – דלא אתי מבשרו. בשר נעשה מקומו צלקת ואין גזעו מחליף. הקשה רשב"ם: דאמר בסוף "העור והרוטב" (חולין קכח:) דבשר מן החי אינו מטמא באהל. מה מת, אינו עושה חליפין. אף כל כו'. ובשר עושה חליפין! ותירץ: דאין הכל אחד, ד"גזעו מחליף" משמע: חוזר לגמרי, וזה אינו עושה בבשר. אבל "עושה חליפין" משמע: שגדל קצת ולא לגמרי, וזהו אף בבשר. וא"ת: כיון דמעצם ילפינן, נימא בהאי לישנא: מה עצם, שאינו עושה חליפין. ונמעט אפילו בשר! וי"ל: דשמא גם עצם מתחזק או גדל מעט אחר שחסר. שעיר המשתלח יוכיח. ואם תאמר: ולימא, דם הנדה יוכיח, שגורם משכב ומושב לנדה, ודמה אמעיט לעיל מינייהו! וי"ל: דאין זה יוכיח, כיון שיש לו לדם טומאת משא כמו נדה. וה"נ ליהוי זוב, כמו דם הנדה. אבל שעיר המשתלח, אין לו שום טומאה כלל.

א) עי' תוס' חולין קכב. ד"ה עורות ותוס' זבחים עא: ד"ה ובטריפה] ב) [צ"ל ועור]

**עין משפט נר מצוה**

יא א ב מיי' פ"ג מהל' טומאת מת הלכה י:
יב ג ד מיי' שם הל' יג:
יג ה מיי' פ"ט מהלכות שחיטה הלכה ז סמג עשין סג טוש"ע י"ד סי' נט סעיף א:
יד ו מיי' פ"ג מהלכות טומאת מת הלכה יא:
טו ז מיי' פ"א מהלכות אבות הטומאות הלכה ט:
טז ח ט מיי' פ"ג מהל' טומאת מת הלכה יא:

**הגהות הב"ח**

(א) רש"י ד"ה אי מה וכו' מסמא כדאיתא במסכת שבת: (ב) תום' ד"ה אבן מסמא פ"ה. נ"ב קך דף פ"ה ריש פ' ר' עקיבא: (ג) בא"ד ממעט משא דבשמעתין ממעט: (ד) ד"ה מיתיבי וכו' בשר המת שיבש.

יז א מיי' פ"א מהלכות מטמאי משכב ומושב הלכה יב:
יח ב ג ד מיי' שם הלכה טז:

תורה אור

כִּי אִיצְטְרִיךְ קְרָא – לְמַשָּׂא. וְאֵימָא: בְּמַשָּׂא – מְטַמֵּא אָדָם וּבְגָדִים. בְּמַגַּע אָדָם – מְטַמֵּא, בְּגָדִים – לֹא לְטַמֵּא, מִידֵי דַּהֲוָה אַמַּגַּע נְבֵלָה! לָא ס"ד, דְּתַנְיָא, אֲחֵרִים אוֹמְרִים: °"הַזָּב אֶת [ויקרא טו] זוֹבוֹ לַזָּכָר וְלַנְּקֵבָה" – מַקִּישׁ זוֹבוֹ לוֹ. מַה הוּא – לֹא חִלַּקְתָּ בֵּין מַגָּעוֹ לְמַשָּׂאוֹ לְטַמֵּא אָדָם וּלְטַמֵּא בְּגָדִים, אאַף זוֹבוֹ – כֵּן. וְהַשְׁתָּא דְּנָפְקָא לָן מֵ"הַזָּב אֶת זוֹבוֹ", "זוֹבוֹ טָמֵא" לָמָּה לִי? אָמַר רַב יְהוּדָה מִדִּסְקַרְתָּא: *אִיצְטְרִיךְ, סד"א: שָׂעִיר הַמִּשְׁתַּלֵּחַ יוֹכִיחַ – שֶׁגּוֹרֵם טוּמְאָה לַאֲחֵרִים וְהוּא עַצְמוֹ טָהוֹר, וְאִי מִשּׁוּם "הַזָּב אֶת זוֹבוֹ" – לְמִנְיָינָא הוּא דַּאֲתָא: "זוֹב" – חַד, "זוֹבוֹ" – תַּרְתֵּי, וּבַשְּׁלִישִׁי אַקְשֵׁיהּ רַחֲמָנָא לִנְקֵבָה! כָּתַב רַחֲמָנָא "זוֹבוֹ טָמֵא". וְהַשְׁתָּא דְּאָמַר רַחֲמָנָא "זוֹבוֹ טָמֵא הוּא" – דְּרוֹשׁ בֵּיהּ נַמִי הַאי. § "וְהָרוֹק". § רוֹק מְנָלַן? דְּתַנְיָא: °"וְכִי [שם] יָרוֹק", יָכוֹל אע"פ שֶׁלֹּא נָגַע – ת"ל: "בַּטָּהוֹר" – עַד שֶׁיִּגַּע בַּטָּהוֹר. אֵין לִי אֶלָּא רוּקוֹ, בכִּיחוֹ וְנִיעוֹ וּמֵי הָאַף שֶׁלּוֹ מִנַּיִן? ת"ל: "וְכִי יָרוֹק". אָמַר מָר: יָכוֹל אע"פ שֶׁלֹּא נָגַע, מֵהֵיכָא תֵּיתֵי? סד"א: נֵילַף "רוֹק" "רוֹק" מִיְּבָמָה, מַה הָתָם אע"פ דְּלֹא נָגַע, אַף ה"נ – דְּלֹא נָגַע, קמ"ל. (א) וְאֵימַר: הָנֵי מִילֵּי – בְּמַגָּע, אֲבָל בְּמַשָּׂא – לָא, מִידֵי דַּהֲוָה אַשֶּׁרֶץ! אָמַר רֵישׁ לָקִישׁ, תָּנָא דְּבֵי רַבִּי יִשְׁמָעֵאל: אָמַר קְרָא "בַּטָּהוֹר" – *מַה שֶּׁבְּיַד טָהוֹר טִמֵּאתִי לָךְ. וְאֵימָא: בְּמַשָּׂא – מְטַמֵּא אָדָם וּבְגָדִים, בְּמַגָּע – אָדָם לְטַמֵּא, בְּגָדִים – לָא לְטַמֵּא, מִידֵי דַּהֲוָה אַמַּגַּע נְבֵלָה! אֲמַר רֵישׁ לָקִישׁ, וְכֵן תָּנָא דְּבֵי רַבִּי יִשְׁמָעֵאל: אָמַר קְרָא "בַּטָּהוֹר" – טָהֳרָה שֶׁטִּהַרְתִּי לְךָ בְּמָקוֹם אַחֵר טִמֵּאתִי לְךָ כָּאן, וְאֵיזֶה זֶה – זֶה מַגַּע נְבֵלָה. וְאֵימָא *כְּמַשָּׂא דְּשֶׁרֶץ! א"כ נִכְתּוֹב קְרָא "בָּאָדָם", מַאי "בַּטָּהוֹר" – ש"מ תַּרְתֵּי. § "וּמֵי הָאַף". § מַאי "מֵי הָאַף"? אָמַר רַב: בְּנִגְרָרִין דֶּרֶךְ הַפֶּה, לְפִי שֶׁאִי אֶפְשָׁר לְמֵי הָאַף בְּלֹא צִחְצוּחֵי הָרוֹק. וְר' יוֹחָנָן אָמַר: גאֲפִילּוּ בְּנִגְרָרִין דֶּרֶךְ הַחוֹטֶם, אַלְמָא קָסָבַר: מַעְיָין הוּא, וְרַחֲמָנָא רַבְּיֵיהּ. וְרַב, נַחְשׁוֹב נַמִי דִּמְעַת עֵינוֹ! דְּאָמַר רַב: הַאי מַאן דְּבָעֵי דְּלִסְתַּמְיֵהּ לְעֵינֵיהּ – לִיכְחוֹל מִגּוֹי. וְלֵוִי אָמַר: הַאי מַאן דְּבָעֵי דְּלֵימוּת – לִיכְחוֹל מִגּוֹי. וְאָמַר רַב חִיָּיא בַּר גּוּרְיָא: מ"ט דְּרַב דְּלֹא אָמַר: הַאי מַאן דְּבָעֵי דְּלֵימוּת – הוֹאִיל וְיָכוֹל לְגוֹרְרָן וּלְהוֹצִיאָן דֶּרֶךְ הַפֶּה! וְרַב, נְהִי דְּזִיהֲרָא – נָפֵיק, דִּמְעָתָא גּוּפָא – לָא נָפֵיק. ת"ש, *דתִּשְׁעָה מַשְׁקִין הַזָּב הֵן: הַזֵּיעָה, וְהַלֵּיחָה סְרוּחָה, וְהָרֵיעִי – טְהוֹרִין מִכְּלוּם. דִּמְעַת עֵינוֹ, וְדַם מַגֵּפָתוֹ, וַחֲלֵב הָאִשָּׁה – מְטַמְּאִין טוּמְאַת מַשְׁקִין *בִּרְבִיעִית. אֲבָל זוֹבוֹ, רוּקוֹ, וּמֵימֵי רַגְלָיו – מְטַמְּאִין טוּמְאָה חֲמוּרָה. וְאִילּוּ "מֵי הָאַף" לָא קָתָנֵי. בִּשְׁלָמָא לְרַב לָא קָתָנֵי – דְּלָא פְּסִיקָא לֵיהּ לְמִתְנֵי, זִימְנִין דְּאָתֵי דֶּרֶךְ הַפֶּה וְזִימְנִין דְּאָתֵי דֶּרֶךְ הַחוֹטֶם. אֶלָּא לְר' יוֹחָנָן – לִיתְנֵי! וּלְטַעְמִיךְ – "כִּיחוֹ וְנִיעוֹ" מִי קָתָנֵי? אֶלָּא: תָּנָא רוֹק וְכָל דַּאֲתָא מֵרִבּוּיָא, הָכָא נַמִי – תָּנָא רוּקוֹ, וְכָל דַּאֲתָא מֵרִבּוּיָא. דִּמְעַת עֵינוֹ – דִּכְתִיב: °"וַתַּשְׁקֵמוֹ [תהלים פ] בִּדְמָעוֹת שָׁלִישׁ". וְדַם מַגֵּפָתוֹ – דִּכְתִיב: °"וְדַם חֲלָלִים יִשְׁתֶּה", *מַה לִּי קַטְלֵיהּ כּוּלֵּיהּ, [במדבר כג] מַה לִּי קַטְלֵיהּ פַּלְגֵיהּ. *חֲלֵב הָאִשָּׁה – דִּכְתִיב: °"וַתִּפְתַּח אֶת נֹאד הֶחָלָב וַתַּשְׁקֵהוּ". [שופטים ד] מֵימֵי רַגְלָיו מְנָלַן? דְּתַנְיָא: "זוֹבוֹ טָמֵא וְזֹאת" – לְרַבּוֹת מֵימֵי רַגְלָיו לְטוּמְאָה. וַהֲלֹא דִּין הוּא, וּמָה רוֹק הַבָּא מִמָּקוֹם טָהֳרָה – טָמֵא, מֵימֵי רַגְלָיו הַבָּאִין מִמָּקוֹם

**רש"י**

נְבֵלָה. בְּמַגָּע – מְטַמְּאָה אָדָם וְלֹא בְּגָדִים שֶׁעָלָיו, וּבְמַשָּׂא – מְטַמְּאָה אָדָם וּבְגָדִים שֶׁעָלָיו, כִּדְכְתִיב (ויקרא יא): "וְהַנּוֹגֵעַ בְּנִבְלָתָהּ יִטְמָא עַד הָעָרֶב וְהַנּוֹשֵׂא אֶת נִבְלָתָהּ יְכַבֵּס בְּגָדָיו". אֲבָל בְּמַגָּע – לָא כְּתִיב כִּבּוּס. זָב. אֲפִילּוּ מַגָּעוֹ מְטַמֵּא בְּגָדִים, דִּכְתִיב: "וְהַנּוֹגֵעַ בִּבְשַׂר הַזָּב יְכַבֵּס בְּגָדָיו". וְכֵן מַשָּׂאוֹ, דִּכְתִיב בְּמִשְׁכָּב וּמוֹשָׁב: "וְהַנּוֹשֵׂא אוֹתָם יְכַבֵּס בְּגָדָיו", וְקַל וָחוֹמֶר לְנוֹשֵׂא זָב עַצְמוֹ. וְהַשְׁתָּא דְּנָפְקָא לָן. טוּמְאַת הַזָּב מִ"וְהַזָּב אֶת זוֹבוֹ", דְּאִיתְקַשׁ זוֹבוֹ לוֹ, "זוֹבוֹ טָמֵא" לָמָּה לִי? זָב חֲדָא וְזוֹבוֹ תַּרְתֵּי. וּכְתִיב "לַזָּכָר" דִּבְשְׁתֵּי רְאִיּוֹת רִאשׁוֹנוֹת, דִּין זָכָר עָלָיו, שֶׁאֵינוֹ מְטַמֵּא בְּאוֹנֶס. וּמִכָּאן וְאֵילָךְ, אִיתְקַשׁ לִנְקֵבָה, דַּאֲפִילּוּ רָאָה שְׁלִישִׁי בְּאוֹנֶס – חַיָּיב קָרְבָּן. וְהַשְׁתָּא דִּכְתִיב זוֹבוֹ טָמֵא. דְּנָפְקָא לָן מִינֵּיהּ עִיקַּר טוּמְאַת זוֹב, מֵהַשְׁתָּא דְּרוֹשׁ מִ"וְהַזָּב אֶת זוֹבוֹ" הַךְ דְּרָשָׁה, דְּלֹא תַּחְלוֹק בֵּין מַגָּעוֹ לְמַשָּׂאוֹ, וְאַעַ"פ שֶׁאַתָּה דּוֹרְשׁוֹ לִדְרָשָׁה אַחֲרִינֵי. כִּיחוֹ וְנִיעוֹ. מִין רוֹק הֵן. תַּלְמוּד לוֹמַר וְכִי יָרוֹק. וָי"ו דָּרֵישׁ. בְּמֶה שֶׁבְּיָד טָהוֹר. אִם רַק בְּמֶה שֶׁבְּיַד טָהוֹר, דַּהֲוָה לֵיהּ טָהוֹר נוֹשֵׂא אֶת הָרוֹק. זֶה מַגַּע נְבֵלָה. שֶׁטִּהַרְתִּי לְךָ בְּגָדִים שֶׁעָלָיו, וְטִמֵּאתִים לְךָ כָּאן בְּמַגַּע הָרוֹק. וְאֵימָא מַשָּׂא דְּשֶׁרֶץ. שֶׁטִּהַרְתִּי לְךָ אֶת הַנּוֹשְׂאוֹ, טִמֵּאתִי לְךָ בְּכָאן בְּנוֹשֵׂא הָרוֹק, אֲבָל מַגָּעוֹ – כִּנְבֵלָה. לֵימָא בָּאָדָם. דְּדָרְשִׁינַן: "בְּמֶה שֶׁבְּיַד אָדָם". וְהַיְינוּ, מַשָּׂאוֹ. וּבְלָאו דְּרָשָׁא דְּ"טָהֳרָה שֶׁטִּהַרְתִּי לְךָ" וכו', נָפְקָא לָן מַשָּׂא. מַאי בַּטָּהוֹר. דְּמַשְׁמַע: טָהֳרָה שֶׁטִּהַרְתִּי בְּמָקוֹם אַחֵר, טִמֵּאתִי בְּכָאן. ש"מ תַּרְתֵּי. מַשָּׂא – מֵרִבּוּיָא דְּבֵי"ת שֶׁ"בַּטָּהוֹר", וּמַגָּע לְטַמֵּא בְּגָדִים מִ"טָּהוֹר". בְּנִגְרָרִין דֶּרֶךְ הַפֶּה. שֶׁגּוֹרְרָן וְהוֹצִיאָן דֶּרֶךְ הַפֶּה. וְרַחֲמָנָא רַבְּיֵיהּ. מִ"כִּי יָרוֹק" – כָּל דְּדָמֵי לְרוֹק. וְרַב. כֵּיוָן דְּלָאו מַעְיָן הוּא, אֶלָּא מִפְּנֵי שֶׁגּוֹרְרָן דֶּרֶךְ פִּיו קָתָנֵי לָהּ, וּמִשּׁוּם לִחְלוּחֵי הָרוֹק. לִיחֲשׁוֹב נַמִי בְּמַתְנִיתָא דִּמְעַת עֵינוֹ. וְנוֹקְמָהּ בְּשֶׁגּוֹרְרָהּ דֶּרֶךְ הַפֶּה, דְּהָאָמַר רַב: אֶפְשָׁר לְגוֹרְרָהּ דֶּרֶךְ הַפֶּה? דְּאָמַר רַב הַאי מַאן דְּבָעֵי דְּלִסְתַּמְיֵהּ. שֶׁיִּתְעַוֵּור. לִיכְחוֹל עֵינֵיהּ מִגּוֹי וְלֵוִי אָמַר כו' מַאי טַעְמָא דְּרַב דְּלֹא אָמַר לֵימוּת. דְּסָבַר: אִם נָתַן הַגּוֹי לְתוֹכוֹ סַם הַמָּוֶת – יָכוֹל לְגוֹרְרוֹ וּלְהוֹצִיאוֹ דֶּרֶךְ פִּיו, כְּדֶרֶךְ הָרוֹקְקִין שֶׁמּוֹשְׁכִין מֵי הָאַף בְּפִיהֶם ע"י רוּחַ נְשִׁימָתָם לְגוּפָן. זִיהֲרָא. אֶרֶס שֶׁל סַם הַמָּוֶת. לֵיחָה סְרוּחָה. קויטור"א. מַגֵּפָתוֹ. מַכָּתוֹ. טוּמְאַת מַשְׁקִין. לְטַמֵּא אוֹכָלִין וּמַשְׁקִין, כִּשְׁאָר מַשְׁקִין טְמֵאִים. בִּרְבִיעִית. זֶהוּ שִׁיעוּר מַשְׁקִין לְטוּמְאָה. טוּמְאָה חֲמוּרָה. אָדָם וּבְגָדִים, דְּמַעְיָינוֹת הֵן. בִּשְׁלָמָא לְרַב. דְּאָמַר: הַאי דְּקָתָנֵי לְהוּ תָּנָא דִּלְעֵיל, בְּנִגְרָרִין דֶּרֶךְ הַפֶּה, אִיכָּא לְתָרוּצֵי: דְּהַאי תַּנָּא לְהָכִי לָא תָּנֵי לְהוּ, דְּכֵיוָן דְּטוּמְאָתָן לָאו מֵחֲמַת עַצְמָן הִיא, אֶלָּא מִשּׁוּם לִחְלוּחֵי רוֹק, לָא פְּסִיקָא לֵיהּ. דְּהָא זִימְנִין דְּנָפְקֵי דֶּרֶךְ חוֹטֶם, וּטְהוֹרִין. וּבְמִילְּתָא דְּלָא פְּסִיקָא, לָא קָמַיְירֵי. אֶלָּא לְרַבִּי יוֹחָנָן. דְּאָמַר: לְעוֹלָם טְמֵאִין, לִיתְנֵי. וַתַּשְׁקֵמוֹ בִּדְמָעוֹת שָׁלִישׁ. אַלְמָא, מַשְׁקֶה אִיקְרוּ. דַּם חֲלָלִים יִשְׁתֶּה. אַלְמָא, דַּם חָלָל אִיקְרֵי מַשְׁקֶה. וְדַם מַגֵּפָתוֹ נַמִי, דַּם חֲלָלִים הוּא, דְּהָא קַטְלֵיהּ פַּלְגֵיהּ. זוֹבוֹ טָמֵא וְזֹאת. דִּסְמִיךְ לֵיהּ "וְזֹאת תִּהְיֶה טוּמְאָתוֹ" וגו', וְדָרְשֵׁי הַאי "וְזֹאת" אַקְּרָא דִּלְעֵיל "זוֹבוֹ טָמֵא וְזֹאת" – כְּלוֹמַר, דָּבָר אַחֵר נַמִי כְּזוֹב. מִמָּקוֹם

**תוספות**

**כי** איצטריך קרא למשא. וא"ת: למשא נמי לא איצטריך, מההיא טעמא דלא גרע משכבת זרע. דהא בזב קיימין, ואיכא למ"ד סוף פ"ב דב"ק (דף כה.) שכבת זרע מטמאה במשא, אפילו בלא ליאתוחי זיבה, מק"ו ומה טהור בטהור – פירוש: רוק, טמא בטמא. טמא בטהור, שכבת זרע – אינו דין שיהא טמא בטמא! ויש לומר: דלא קשה מידי, דאין לנו לעשות זאת הזיבה שהיא גורמת טומאה, א] דהיינו ראייה שניה, משאם היתה שכבת זרע וקרי, שאחר ראייה ראשונה טהור, ממשא שאינו זב. וה"ק: דלא גרע מאילו היתה ראייה זו שכבת זרע, דמטמאה במגע ולא במשא. ומק"ו לא אתי – דאין זה טמא בטמא, דאכתי אינו טמא, אלא על ידי ראייה זו הוא נעשה טמא. וא"ת: כיון דמגע נפקא לן בלא קרא, היכי שייך לומר "שעיר המשתלח יוכיח", הא לא דמי. דבזוב איכא טומאת מגע. וכי האי גוונא אמר בפרק "כל הבשר" (חולין קטו:) גבי בשר בחלב, דיליף איסור אכילה מ"ואנשי קדש תהיון", ואיסור הנאה מערלה מק"ו ופריך: ונילף כולה מילתא מערלה? ומשני: משום דאיכא למימר, חוסם פי פרה ודש בה וחורש בשור וחמור יוכיח – שנעבדה בהן עבירה, ומותרין אף באכילה. אבל עכשיו דנפקא לן איסור אכילה מקרא, ליכא למימר תו "יוכיח", דלא דמי דאינהו שרי באכילה? ויש לומר: דשעיר המשתלח נמי, כיון דמטמא אחרים העוסקין בו – אינו טהור גמור, ושייך לטומאת עצמו, והוי כאילו טמא במגע, ודמיא לזוב.

**כיחו** וניעו. כיחו – הוא הבא מכח רב מן החזה, ניעו ע"י נענוע מעט. כך מפרש ר"ת. *ויש לפרש נמי איפכא: ניעו – שמנענע כל גופו, כיחו – בכח מעט. ובמתני' דלא תנא "כיחו" – לא חש להאריך. אבל תימה: דתנן "ניעו" מקמי "רוק" דעיקר, דכתיב בהדיא? וי"ל: דהך דאתיא מדרשא חביבא ליה.

**נילף** רוק רוק מיבמה. תימה: מהכא דהשתא נילף רוק דיבמה דנגע? ויש לומר: דבסיפרי דרשינן ליה מקרא דלא בעינן נגע. "וירקה בפניו" – יכול בפניו ממש? ת"ל: "לעיני הזקנים" – רוק הנראה לזקנים.

דם

[וכ"כ הערוך בערך כח ועי' תוס' ב"ק ג: ד"ה כיחו]

[לעיל לה.]

[שבת יד:]

נ"ל במשא

[כריתות יג.]

[ועי' תוס' כריתות יג: ד"ה וחלב אשה]

[חולין לה:]

[עי' תוס' לעיל יט: ד"ה כתיב]

**הגהות הב"ח**

(א) גמ' ואימא הני מילי במגע:

**הגהות מהר"ב רנשבורג**

א] תוס' ד"ה כי וכו' דהיינו ראייה שניה גרועה משאם היתה וכו' כצ"ל:

**תוספי הרא"ש**

מהני מה שהוא גורם טומאה לאשה שהוא מטמא במגע ובמשא וה"נ ליהוי זוב כדם הנדה. וליכא למימר משכב ומושב יוכיח שהזוב גורם לזב לטמות משכב ומושב והוא עצמו אינו מטמא וה"ה מגע ומשא משום דאי מק"ו יליף ליה הוה מטמא אף משכב ומושב: **כי** איצטריך קרא למשא. תימה היכי שייך למימר שעיר המשתלח יוכיח דאף מגע אינו מטמא ולא שייך למימר יוכיח על זוב שמטמא במגע כדמוכח בפ' כל הבשר דקאמר בשר בחלב אסור באכילה מאנשי קדש תהיון לי. ואיסור הנאה מפיק ליה מערלה שלא נעבדה בו עבירה. ופריך איסור אכילה נמי תיפוק לי מק"ו דערלה ומשני דאיכא למימ' חורש בשור ובחמור יוכיח שנעבדה בו עבירה ומותר. אבל השתא דנפקא לן איסור אכילה מאנשי קדש תהיון לי ליכא למימר דחורש בשור ובחמור יוכיח דמה לחורש בשור ובחמור שמותר אף באכילה. וי"ל דהא דשעיר המשתלח מטמא מעסיקיו הך טומאה דמיא קצת למגע: **איצטריך** סד"א שעיר המשתלח יוכיח. ואי משום הזב למניינא היא דאתאי. ת' למה לי למימר שעיר המשתלח יוכיח לימא סד"א למניינא הוא דאתאי וי"ל דאי לאו דאשכחן כה"ג בשעיר המשתלח לא הוה מוקמינן הזב למניינא. אי נמי י"ל דרב יהודה מדסקרתא לא הוה ידע אלא רישא דברייתא דזובו טמא לימד על הזוב שהוא טמא הלכך קאמר מטעם שגורם טומאה לאחרים לא הוה טמא דשעיר המשתלח יוכיח ואי משום קרא דזובו למניינא הוא דאתא וכן משמע בפ' בנות כותים דלא הוה ידע א)רב יהודה מדסקרתא הך דשעיר המתלח יוכיח: כתב רחמנא זובו טמא דריש ביה נמי האי. כיון דעיקר טומאה ילפינן מזובו דרשינן מוהזב את זובו להקיש זובו לו להשוות מגע למשא אבל ללמוד מזב בהיקשא טומאה דלא כתיבא ביה לא דרשינן הלכך לא פריך אי מה זב עושה משכב ומושב כו' כדפריך לעיל בנדה: **מטמאין** טומאת משקין ברביעית וטומאתן דרבנן בעלמא וקראי אסמכתא בעלמא נינהו הלכך בעינן רביעית דאי הוו משקין מדאורייתא הוו מטמאין בכל שהן כדמוכח בפ"ק דפסחים דקאמר כגון שהיה המשקה טופח עליו דבשר ואמרינן נמי התם משקה בית מטבחייא דכן לא אמרן אלא דהוו רביעית דחזו להטביל בהן מחטין וצינוריות אבל פחות מרביעית טמאין:

דם

א) נ"ל דלא הוה ידע רבא הך וכו' ועי' שם בתוס' (דף לב ע"ב) ד"ה אילימא.

ממקום טמא — אינו דין שיהו טמאין? דם היוצא מפי האמה יוכיח, שבא ממקום טמא — וטהור, אף אתה אל תתמה על זה, שאע"פ שבא ממקום טומאה — יהיה טהור, ת"ל: "זובו טמא וזאת" — לרבות מימי רגליו לטומאה. דם היוצא מפי האמה מנלן דטהור? *דתניא: יכול יהא דם היוצא מפיו ומפי האמה טמאין — ת"ל: (ויקרא טו) °"זובו טמא הוא" — הוא, טמא. אואין דם היוצא מפיו ומפי האמה טמא, אלא טהור. ואיפוך אנא! אמר רבי יוחנן משום רבי שמעון בן יוחי: *דומיא דרוק, מה רוק — שמתעגל ויוצא, אף כל — שמתעגל ויוצא, יצא דם — שאין מתעגל ויוצא. והרי חלב שבאשה, שמתעגל ויוצא, ואמר מר: חלב שבאשה — מטמא טומאת משקין. טומאת משקין — אין, אבל לא טומאה חמורה! אלא אמר ר' יוחנן משום רבי שמעון בן יוחי: דומיא דרוק, מה רוק — מתעגל ויוצא וחוזר ונבלע, אף כל — מתעגל ויוצא וחוזר ונבלע, יצא דם — שאינו מתעגל ויוצא, יצא חלב שבאשה שאע"פ שמתעגל ויוצא, אינו חוזר ונבלע. וניליף מזובו: מה זובו שאין מתעגל ויוצא — מטמא, אף כל! אמר רבא: מזובו ליכא למילף — שכן גורם טומאה לאחרים.§ "והשרץ".§ אמר ריש לקיש: בשרץ שיבש ושלדו קיימת — טמא. והאנן תנן: מטמאין לחין ואין מטמאין יבשין! אמר רבי זירא: לא קשיא, גהא — בכולן, הא — במקצתן. *דתניא, א"ר יצחק ברבי ביסנא, אמר רבי שמעון בן יוחי: (שם יא) °"בהם", יכול בכולן? ת"ל: "מהם". אי "מהם" — יכול במקצתן? תלמוד לומר: "בהם". הא כיצד? כאן — בלח, כאן — ביבש. אמר רבא: הני זבוגי דמחוזא, כי שלדן קיימת — טמאין. ואמר ריש לקיש: דשרץ שנשרף ושלדו קיימת — טמא. מיתיבי: *הנמצא שרץ שרוף על גבי הזיתים, וכן מטלית המהוהא — טהורין, שכל הטמאות כשעת מציאתן! א"ר זירא: לא קשיא, הא — בכולן, הא — במקצתן. דתניא, אמר רבי יצחק בר' ביסנא משום ר"ש בן יוחי: "בהם", יכול בכולן? ת"ל: "מהם". אי "מהם" — יכול במקצתן? ת"ל: "בהם". הא כיצד? כאן — בשרוף, כאן — בשאינו שרוף.§ (שם טו) "מטמאין לחין".§ זב — דכתיב: °"רר בשרו". כיחו וניעו ורוקו — דכתיב: (שם) °"כי ירוק הזב", כעין רוק. (שם יא) שרץ — *°"במותם" אמר רחמנא, כעין מיתה. (שם) שכבת זרע — *הראויה להזריע. נבלה — דכתיב: °"כי ימות" — כעין מיתה.§ "אם יכולין להשרות".§ בעי רבי ירמיה: תחילתו וסופו בפושרין, או דלמא תחילתו אף על פי שאין סופו? ת"ש, דתניא: כמה היא שרייתן בפושרין? יהודה בן נקוסא אומר: ומעת לעת, תחילתו אף על פי שאין סופו. רשב"ג אומר: צריכין שיהו פושרין מעת לעת.§ "רבי יוסי אומר בשר המת" כו'.§ אמר שמואל: טהור מלטמא בכזית, אבל מטמא טומאת רקב. תניא נמי הכי, רבי יוסי אומר: בשר המת שיבש ואין יכול לשרות ולחזור כמות שהיה — טהור מלטמא בכזית, אבל טמא טומאת רקב.§

**מתני'** *זהשרץ שנמצא במבוי — מטמא למפרע, עד שיאמר "בדקתי את המבוי הזה, ולא היה בו שרץ", או עד שעת כבוד. וכן חכתם שנמצא בחלוק — מטמא למפרע, עד שיאמר "בדקתי את החלוק הזה, ולא היה בו כתם", או עד שעת הכבוס. ומטמא בין לח בין יבש. ר"ש אומר: טהיבש — מטמא למפרע, והלח — אינו מטמא אלא עד שעת *שיהא יכול לחזור ולהיות לח.§

**גמ'** איבעיא להו: עד שעת כבוד חזקתו בדוק, או דלמא חזקתו מתכבד? ומאי נפקא מינה — דאמר "כביד ולא בדיק". אי אמרת חזקתו בדוק — הא לא בדק, אי אמרת חזקתו מתכבד — הא מתכבד.

אי

---

**רש"י**

ממקום טומאה. ממקום שזובו יוצא, שהוא טמא בשבילו. דם היוצא מפי אמתו. של זב גמור, יליף ליה לקמן דטהור. יכול דם היוצא מפיו. של זב יהא נדון כרוק, ודם היוצא מפי אמתו יהא נדון כזוב? ואיפוך אנא. "וזאת" – לרבות דם, ו"הוא" – להוציא מי רגלים. שמתעגל. מתאסף הרבה כאחד, ואח"כ יוצא, כגון רוק ומי רגלים ושכבת זרע. דם. אין מתעגל ויוצא, דכי אתא – קמא קמא נפיק. וחוזר ונבלע. כשאינו מוציאו. אף כל כו'. כגון סילון של מי רגלים – חוזר ונבלע. יצא דם – שאינו מתעגל ויוצא. חלב – אע"ג שמתעגל, אינו חוזר ונבלע. ושלדו. דפוס צורתו. קיימת. שלא נשבר ונתפזר. בכולן. כשכולו שלם טמא, אפילו יבש. בהם. בשרצים כתיב (ויקרא יא): "כל הנוגע בהם". מהם. "וכל אשר יפול עליו מהם במותם יטמא" (שם). זבוגי. פרוי"ט הנמלאים יבשים במחוזא, והוא צב. ויש שקורין אותו בלע"ז בו"ט. המהוהא. בלויה ונרקבת. רר. כעין ריר שהוא לח, כמו (שמואל א כא): "ויורד רירו על זקנו". תחילתו אע"פ שאין סופו. אין צריך שיהו המים פושרין בסוף, כשיכלה מעת לעת. יהודה בן נקוסא אומר. אין צריך שיהו המים פושרין בסוף, אלא יהו על הארץ כמעת לעת, אע"פ שאין סופן. וקולא היא, דאי לא הדר בהכי – טהור. ואע"ג דאי הוו פושרין כל מעת לעת, הוה הדר. טומאת רקב. מלא תרווד ממנו °מטמא במגע ובמשא ובאהל. **מתני'** ומטמא בין לח ובין יבש. הכתם או השרץ, בין שנמצאו לחין בין שנמצאו יבשין – מטמא כל טהרות שנעשו במבוי מיום כיבודו, ושעשתה האשה מיום כבוס. היבש מטמא למפרע. עד שעת כיבוד או כיבוס. דאיכא למימר: לאחר כיבוס, מיד נפל. אבל הלח אינו מטמא למפרע, אלא עד שעה שיוכל לומר: אם נפל באותו יום, עדיין הוא יכול להיות עכשיו לח. אבל עד שעת הכיבוד לזמן מרובה – לא, דהא לח הוא. ואי מההיא שעתא נפל, הוה מתעביד יבש. **גמ'** חזקתו בדוק. מי מחזקינן דבדיק ליה בשעת הכיבוד, ומשום הכי טהרות דקודם כיבוד – טהורות. או משום דחזקתו מתכבד. דאי הוה התם בשעת כיבוד, הוי נפיק האי שרץ מחמת כיבוד. דאמר כביד ולא בדיק. "כבדתיו, ולא בדקתיו". אי אמרת דהא דמטהרין הנך דמקמי כיבוד, משום דחזקתו שבדקו בשעת כיבוד – הא לא בדיק, וטהרות דמקמי כיבוד נמי טמאו' ואי אמרת כו'.

אי

---

**תוספות**

**דם** היוצא מפיו טהור. בפרק "מצות חליצה" (יבמות דף קה.) מוקי בשותת. דאי לאו הכי, טמא משום לחלוחי הרוק.

**דם** היוצא מפי האמה. ואם תאמר: הא כבר ממעטינן בריש "בנות כותים" (לעיל דף לג:) איש מאודם? ויש לומר: דהיינו דאין נעשה זב ע"י ראיית אודם. אבל אם כבר נעשה זב – ליהוי דם היוצא מפי האמה טמא, כמו רוקו. ולכך צריך קרא הכא למעוטי.

**וזאת** לרבות מימי רגליו לטומאה. מוי"ו ד"וזאת" קדריש. כי היכי דדרשינן לעיל כיחו וניעו מוי"ו ד"וכי ירוק". אבל "זאת" בכל דוכתי אתא למעוטי. והאי "זאת" נמי אתא למעוטי, דבת"כ מצריך תרי מיעוטי, "זאת" ו"טמא הוא" – חד, למעוטי זיעה וליחה סרוחה. וחד, למעוטי דם היוצא מפיו ומפי האמה.

**מה** רוק שמתעגל ויוצא כו'. מכח ריבויא ד"וכי ירוק הזב בטהור" ד"וזאת" דריש הכי. אבל אי לאו הני קראי, הוה ממעטינן כולהו כיחו וניעו ומי רגלים מטמא הוא כמו דם היוצא מפי האמה. וא"ת: ולמה לי תרי קראי "וכי ירוק" – לכיחו וניעו, "וזאת" – למי רגלים וי"ל: דמ"וכי ירוק" לא הוה דרשינן אלא כיחו וניעו שיוצא דרך הפה, או מי האף נמי לרבי יוחנן דדמי כמו רוק. ומ"וזאת" לא הוה מרבינן אלא מי רגלים שיוצאין מפי האמה כמו זוב. דקרא ד"וזאת" – גבי זוב כתיב. או משום דבאין ממקום טמא. מיהו קשה: דמשמע דהוה מרבינן חלב האשה מ"וזאת" אם היה חוזר ונבלע, ואמאי? והא אפילו כיחו וניעו לא הוה מתרבי מ"וזאת" אי לאו ריבויא ד"וכי ירוק"! וצריך לומר: דאי לאו ריבויא ד"וכי ירוק", הוה מוקמינן "וזאת" לכיחו וניעו דוקא, דהוי כעין רוק. אבל השתא דכתיב "וכי ירוק", אייתר "וזאת" לכל דבר המתעגל ויוצא וחוזר ונבלע.

**וניליף** מזובו. אי זיבה לאו מעין הוה, דבעיא היא בפרק "בנות כותים" (לעיל לד:).

**אי** בהם אי מהם כו' ואע"ג דמהאי "בהם" ו"מהם" דרשינן בפ"ק דחגיגה (דף יא.) ששיעורו בכעדשה – התם אסמכתא הוא, דשיעורים הלכה למשה מסיני*.

**שרץ** שנשרף. ק"ק דלא עריב יבש ושרוף בהדי הדדי, דמחד קרא קדריש להו.

**שכבת** זרע בראויה להזריע. ואם תאמר: והלא *שכבת זרע שאינו יורה כחץ אינו ראוי להזריע, ומטמא! ויש לומר: דמין ראוי להזריע בעינן, ואפי' שאינו יורה כחץ, כיון שהוא לח – חשיב מין שכבת זרע הראוי להזריע.

בגומא

מיעוטין. וכה"ג פריך פ"ק דזבחים בכל אתר מן להוציא וכאן לרבות. וי"ל דואת נמי הוי מיעוטא ומוא"ו דוזאת קא דריש כדדרשינן לעיל כיחו וניעו ומוא"ו דוכי ירוק. ובת"כ דרשינן האי זאת למעוטי זיעה וליחה סרוחה והרעי: **מה** רוק מתעגל ויוצא וחוזר ונבלע. ותימה למה לי קרא לרבות כיחו וניעו ומימי רגליו הא הוי דומיא דרוק שמתעגלין ויוצאין וחוזרין ונבלעין וי"ל דאפ"ה לא מרבינן אי לאו דכתיב בהדיא דהוה ממעיטנא להו מהוא אמה. כי היכי דממעיטנא מיניה דם היוצא מפיו ומפי האמה. ותימה לי תרי קראי וכי ירוק לכיחו וניעו וזאת למי רגלים וי"ל דאי לאו רבויא דוכי הוה מוקמינן וזאת לכיחו וניעו דוקא היוצאים מן הפה כמין רוק. אבל השתא דכתיב וכי אייתר וזאת לרבות כל דבר שמתעגל ויוצא וחוזר ונבלע: נילף מזובו. בפ' בנות כותיים מיבעיא ליה אי מקום זיבה מעיין הוא או לא והכא פריך אי לאו מעיין הוא:

**אמר** ריש לקיש שרץ שנשרף ושלדו קיימת טמא. אע"ג דאמר ריש לקיש שרץ שיבש הו"א נשרף גרע טפי. ומיהו לענין לרבויינהו מקרא שקולין הן:

---

**תוספי הרא"ש**

**דם** היוצא מפיו טהור. בפרק מצות חליצה מוקי לה בשותת דאי לאו הכי טמא משום צחצוחי הרוק: **דם** היוצא מפי האמה. אע"ג דממעטינן ליה בפ' בנות כותים היינו לענין שאינו נעשה זב ע"י אותו דם והכא איצטריך קרא אם כבר הוא זב שאינו טמא כמו רוקו: **וזאת** לרבות מימי רגליו. ותימה בכל דוכתא אמרינן וזאת למעט כדלעיל בפרק יוצא דופן זאת היא העולה הרי אלו ג'

בגומא

---

**עין משפט נר מצוה**

יט א מיי' פ"א מהל' משכב ומושב הלכה טז:

כ ב ג ד מיי' פ"ד מהל' אבות הטומאה הלכה יב:

כא ה מיי' שם פט"ו הלכה י:

כב ו מיי' פ"ב מהלכות משכב ומושב הלכה א:

כג ז מיי' פ"ח מהלכות אבות הטומאה הלכה ד:

כד ח מיי' פ"ג מהלכות משכב ומושב הלכה ז:

כה ט מיי' פי"ח מהל' אבות הטומאה הלכה ד:

[ובחגיגה יא. ד"ה הא תירצו דתרתי שמעינן מיניה עוד תירצו דתרי קראי כתיב]

[לעיל מג.]

---

**מסורת הש"ס**

יבמות קה.

[לעיל יט:]

חגיגה יא. [ועי' תוס' נזיר נב. ד"ה ת"ש]

טהרות פ"ט מ"ט לעיל ד.

[ע"ז סח: חולין עד.]

[ע"ז סה:]

לעיל ג.

גי' רש"א שיהא יכול להיות לח

**גליון הש"ס**

**רש"י** ד"ה טומאת רקב כו' מטמא במגע. עי' פ"ב מ"ב דאהלות ובהרע"ב שם. ועי' בהרע"ב פ"ד מ"ה דטהרות ול"ע:

עין משפט נר מצוה

כו א טוש"ע י"ד סימן קצ סעיף מו מז: כז ב מיי' פי"ח מהלכות אבות הטומאות הל' ז ופ"ג מהלכות משכב ומושב הלכה ז:

כח ג מיי' פ"ג מהלכות משכב ומושב הלכה ז: כט ד ה ו מיי' שם פ"ד הלכה ו:

מסורת הש"ס

אִי נַמִּי — דְּאִשְׁתַּכַּח בְּגוּמָא. אִי אָמְרַתְּ חֶזְקָתוֹ בָּדוּק, מַאן דְּבָדַק — בְּגוּמָא נַמִּי בָּדֵיק, אִי אָמְרַתְּ חֶזְקָתוֹ מִתְכַּבֵּד — גּוּמָא לָא מִתְכַּבְּדָא.§ "וְכֵן הַכֶּתֶם" וכו'.§ אִיבַּעְיָא לְהוּ: עַד שְׁעַת כִּבּוּס חֶזְקָתוֹ בָּדוּק, אוֹ דִּלְמָא חֶזְקָתוֹ מִתְכַּבֵּס? לְמַאי נָפְקָא מִינַּהּ — דְּאָמַר כִּיבֵּס וְלָא בְּדַק. אִי אָמְרַתְּ חֶזְקָתוֹ בָּדוּק — הָא לָא בְּדַק, אִי אָמְרַתְּ חֶזְקָתוֹ מִתְכַּבֵּס — הָא מִתְכַּבֵּס. אִי נַמִּי, דְּאִשְׁתַּכְּחָה בְּסִטְרָא. אִי אָמְרַתְּ חֶזְקָתוֹ בָּדוּק — מַאן דִּבְדַק, בְּסִטְרָא נַמִּי בָּדֵיק. אִי אָמְרַתְּ חֶזְקָתוֹ מִתְכַּבֵּס — בְּסִטְרָא לָא מִתְכַּבֵּס. מַאי? תָּא שְׁמַע, דְּתַנְיָא, א"ר מֵאִיר: מִפְּנֵי מָה אָמְרוּ הַשֶּׁרֶץ שֶׁנִּמְצָא בְּמָבוֹי — מְטַמֵּא לְמַפְרֵעַ, עַד שֶׁיֹּאמַר "בָּדַקְתִּי אֶת הַמָּבוֹי הַזֶּה, וְלֹא הָיָה בּוֹ שֶׁרֶץ", אוֹ עַד שְׁעַת כִּיבּוּד? — מִפְּנֵי שֶׁחֶזְקַת בְּנֵי יִשְׂרָאֵל בּוֹדְקִין מְבוֹאוֹתֵיהֶן בִּשְׁעַת כִּבּוּדֵיהֶם, וְאִם לֹא בָּדְקוּ — הִפְסִידוּהוּ לְמַפְרֵעַ. וּמִפְּנֵי מָה אָמְרוּ כֶּתֶם שֶׁנִּמְצָא בְּחָלוּק מְטַמֵּא לְמַפְרֵעַ, עַד שֶׁיֹּאמַר "בָּדַקְתִּי אֶת הֶחָלוּק וְלֹא הָיָה בּוֹ כֶּתֶם", אוֹ עַד שְׁעַת הַכִּבּוּס? — מִפְּנֵי שֶׁחֶזְקַת בְּנוֹת יִשְׂרָאֵל בּוֹדְקוֹת חֲלוּקֵיהֶן בִּשְׁעַת כִּבּוּסֵיהֶן, וְאִם לֹא בָּדְקוּ — הִפְסִידוּ לְמַפְרֵעַ. ר' אַחָא אָמַר: תַּחֲזוֹר וּתְכַבְּסֶנּוּ, אִם נִדְחָה מַרְאִיתוֹ — בְּיָדוּעַ שֶׁלְּאַחַר כִּבּוּס, (א) וְאִם לָאו — *בְּיָדוּעַ שֶׁלִּפְנֵי הַכִּבּוּס. רַבִּי אוֹמֵר: [א]אֵינוֹ דּוֹמֶה כֶּתֶם שֶׁלְּאַחַר הַכִּבּוּס לְכֶתֶם שֶׁלִּפְנֵי הַכִּבּוּס, שֶׁזֶּה מַקְדִּיר וְזֶה מַגְלִיד. [ב]ש"מ חֶזְקָתוֹ בָּדוּק, ש"מ.§ "וּמְטַמֵּא בֵּין לַח" וכו'.§ א"ר אֶלְעָזָר: [ג]לֹא שָׁנוּ — אֶלָּא שֶׁרֶץ, אֲבָל כֶּתֶם לַח — נַמִּי מְטַמֵּא לְמַפְרֵעַ, אֵימַר יָבֵשׁ הָיָה וּמַיָּא נָפֵיל עֲלֵיהּ. שֶׁרֶץ נַמִּי, אֵימַר: יָבֵשׁ הָיָה — וּמַיָּא נָפֵיל עֲלֵיהּ! אִם אִיתָא דְּהָכִי הוּא — אִמַּרְטוּטֵי אִימַּרְטֵט.§

**מתני'** *כָּל הַכְּתָמִין הַבָּאִין מֵרֶקֶם — טְהוֹרִין. רַבִּי יְהוּדָה מְטַמֵּא, מִפְּנֵי שֶׁהֵם גֵּרִים וְטוֹעִין. [ד]הַבָּאִין מִבֵּין הַגּוֹיִם — טְהוֹרִין. מִבֵּין יִשְׂרָאֵל וּמִבֵּין הַכּוּתִים — רַבִּי מֵאִיר מְטַמֵּא, וַחֲכָמִים מְטַהֲרִים, מִפְּנֵי שֶׁלֹּא נֶחְשְׁדוּ עַל כִּתְמֵיהֶן.§

**גמ'** *קָפָסֵיק וְתָנֵי, אֲפִילּוּ מִתַּרְמוֹד! א"ר יוֹחָנָן, זֹאת אוֹמֶרֶת: מְקַבְּלִין גֵּרִים מִתַּרְמוֹד. אִינִי, וְהָא רַבִּי יוֹחָנָן וְסָבַיָּא דְּאָמְרִי תַּרְוַיְיהוּ: אֵין מְקַבְּלִין גֵּרִים מִתַּרְמוֹד! וְכִי תֵּימָא: "זֹאת", וְלָא סְבִירָא לֵיהּ, *וְהָאָמַר רַבִּי יוֹחָנָן: הֲלָכָה כִּסְתָם מִשְׁנָה! *אֲמוֹרָאֵי נִינְהוּ, וְאַלִּיבָּא דְּרַבִּי יוֹחָנָן.§ "מִבֵּין יִשְׂרָאֵל" וכו'.§ וְרַבָּנַן, אִי דְּיִשְׂרָאֵל מְטַהֲרֵי, דְּמַאן מְטַמּוּ? חַסּוּרֵי מִחַסְּרָא, וְהָכִי קָתָנֵי: מִבֵּין יִשְׂרָאֵל — טָמֵא. מִבֵּין הַכּוּתִים — רַבִּי מֵאִיר מְטַמֵּא, *דְּכוּתִים גֵּרֵי אֲרָיוֹת הֵן. וַחֲכָמִים מְטַהֲרִין, דְּכוּתִים גֵּרֵי אֱמֶת הֵן. אִי הָכִי, "שֶׁלֹּא נֶחְשְׁדוּ עַל כִּתְמֵיהֶן" "גֵּרֵי אֲרָיוֹת" מִבָּעֵי לֵיהּ! אֶלָּא הָכִי קָאָמַר: מִבֵּין יִשְׂרָאֵל וּמִבֵּין הַכּוּתִים — טְמֵאִין, דְּכוּתִים גֵּרֵי אֱמֶת הֵן. [ה]הַנִּמְצָאִין בְּעָרֵי יִשְׂרָאֵל טְהוֹרִין, שֶׁלֹּא נֶחְשְׁדוּ עַל כִּתְמֵיהֶם, וְאַצְנוֹעֵי מַצְנְעֵי לְהוּ. הַנִּמְצָאִין בְּעָרֵי כוּתִים — רַבִּי מֵאִיר מְטַמֵּא, דְּנֶחְשְׁדוּ עַל כִּתְמֵיהֶם. וַחֲכָמִים מְטַהֲרִין, שֶׁלֹּא נֶחְשְׁדוּ עַל כִּתְמֵיהֶן.§

**מתני'** [י]כָּל הַכְּתָמִים הַנִּמְצָאִים בְּכָל מָקוֹם — טְהוֹרִין, חוּץ מִן הַנִּמְצָאִים בַּחֲדָרִים וּבִסְבִיבוֹת בֵּית הַטְּמֵאוֹת. בֵּית הַטְּמֵאוֹת שֶׁל כּוּתִים מְטַמְּאִין בְּאֹהֶל, מִפְּנֵי שֶׁהֵם קוֹבְרִין שָׁם אֶת הַנְּפָלִים. ר' יְהוּדָה אוֹמֵר: לֹא הָיוּ קוֹבְרִין, אֶלָּא מַשְׁלִיכִין, וְחַיָּה גּוֹרַרְתּוֹ. נֶאֱמָנִים לוֹמַר "קָבַרְנוּ שָׁם אֶת הַנְּפָלִים", אוֹ "לֹא קָבַרְנוּ". נֶאֱמָנִים לוֹמַר עַל הַבְּהֵמָה אִם בִּכְּרָה אִם לֹא בִּכְּרָה. נֶאֱמָנִים עַל צִיּוּן קְבָרוֹת. וְאֵין נֶאֱמָנִין לֹא עַל הַסְּכָכוֹת, וְלֹא עַל הַפְּרָעוֹת, וְלֹא עַל בֵּית הַפְּרָס. זֶה הַכְּלָל דָּבָר שֶׁחֲשׁוּדִים בּוֹ — אֵין נֶאֱמָנִין עָלָיו.§ **גמ'**

מַאי

---

אִי נַמִּי. בִּסְתָמָא, דְּלָא אָמַר "לָא בָּדַקְתִּי", וְאִשְׁתַּכַּח שֶׁרֶץ בְּגוּמָא. בְּסִטְרָא. בְּצִדֵּי הַבֶּגֶד, שֶׁיֵּשׁ שָׁם קְמָטִים וּתְפִירוֹת שֶׁקּוֹרִין וירונ"ש. מִפְּנֵי מָה אָמְרוּ כו'. כְּלוֹמַר, מִפְּנֵי מָה תָּלוּ בְּכִיבּוּד וְטִיהֲרוּ טְהָרוֹת דְּקוֹדֶם כִּיבּוּד? לְמַפְרֵעַ. אֲפִילּוּ דְּקוֹדֶם כִּיבּוּד — טְמֵאוֹת. וּמִפְּנֵי מָה אָמְרוּ. וּמִפְּנֵי מָה תָּלוּ טָהֳרָה בְּכִבּוּס? תַּחֲזוֹר וּתְכַבְּסֶנּוּ. אִם לֹא בְּדָקְתּוֹ בִּשְׁעַת כִּבּוּסוֹ, וּלְאַחַר זְמַן נִמְצָא בּוֹ כֶּתֶם, וְאֵין יָדוּעַ אִם קוֹדֶם כִּבּוּס הָיָה בּוֹ לְטַמֵּא טְהָרוֹת שֶׁל קוֹדֶם לָכֵן. אִם נִדְחוּ. מַרְאָיו מֵחֲמַת כִּבּוּס זֶה. בְּיָדוּעַ שֶׁלְּאַחַר כִּבּוּם. רִאשׁוֹן נָפַל בּוֹ, וּטְהָרוֹת שֶׁל קוֹדֶם כִּבּוּס רִאשׁוֹן — טְהוֹרוֹת. דְּאִי קוֹדֶם כִּבּוּס קַמָּא הֲוָה בֵּיהּ, כְּבָר נִדְחוּ מַרְאָיו מֵחֲמַת כִּבּוּס רִאשׁוֹן. מַקְדִּיר. נִכְנָס בַּבֶּגֶד. טרשטריי"ש. כֶּתֶם שֶׁלִּפְנֵי כִּבּוּס — מַגְלִיד, וְגִלְדּוֹ עָבֶה. לֹא שָׁנוּ. אַדְּר' שִׁמְעוֹן קָאֵי. לְמַפְרֵעַ. עַד שְׁעַת הַכִּבּוּס. **מתני'** בָּאִין מֵרֶקֶם טְהוֹרִים. שֶׁהֵן גּוֹיִם, וְדָמָן טָהוֹר. שֶׁהֵן גֵּרִים. וְדָמָן טָמֵא. וְטוֹעִין. שֶׁאֵין מַצְנִיעִין אֶת כִּתְמֵיהֶם. וַחֲכָמִים מְטַהֲרִין. בַּגְּמָרָא פָּרֵיךְ: וְאִי דְּיִשְׂרָאֵל טָהוֹר, דְּמַאן טָמֵא? שֶׁלֹּא נֶחְשְׁדוּ. וּמְכַבְּסִין אוֹתָם. **גמ'** קָא פָּסֵיק וְתָנֵי. הַבָּאִין מִבֵּין הַגּוֹיִם טְהוֹרִין, וַאֲפִילּוּ מִתַּרְמוֹד. אַלְמָא, בְּנֵי תַּרְמוֹד גּוֹיִם גְּמוּרִים הֵן. זֹאת אוֹמֶרֶת מְקַבְּלִין גֵּרִים מִן הַתַּרְמוֹד. וּכְשֵׁרִין לָבֹא בַּקָּהָל, וְלָא אָמְרִינַן מַמְזֵרִים הֵן, שֶׁנִּתְעָרְבוּ בִּבְנוֹת עֲשֶׂרֶת הַשְּׁבָטִים, וְגוֹי וְעֶבֶד הַבָּא עַל בַּת יִשְׂרָאֵל — הַוָּלָד מַמְזֵר. גֵּרֵי אֲרָיוֹת הֵן. מְפוֹרָשׁ בְּסֵפֶר מְלָכִים (ב, יז): "וַיְשַׁלַּח ה' בָּהֶם אֶת הָאֲרָיוֹת" וגו'. גֵּרֵי אֱמֶת הֵן. וְדָמָן טָמֵא. בְּעָרֵי יִשְׂרָאֵל. בְּמָקוֹם גָּלוּי. נֶחְשְׁדוּ עַל כִּתְמֵיהֶן. דְּלָא מַצְנְעֵי לְהוּ. **מתני'** בְּכָל מָקוֹם. בִּמְקוֹם יִשְׂרָאֵל. בַּחֲדָרִים. מִסְּתָמָא מִדְּאַצְנְעֵי, דַּם נִדָּה הוּא. בֵּית הַטְּמֵאוֹת. חֶדֶר שֶׁהַנָּשִׁים מִשְׁתַּמְּשׁוֹת בּוֹ בִּימֵי נִדּוּתָן. סְכָכוֹת וּפְרָעוֹת. בַּגְּמָ' מְפָרֵשׁ לְהוּ, וְסָפֵק נִינְהוּ וּמִדְּרַבָּנַן, וְכוּתִיִּים לֵית לְהוּ. **גמ'** מַאי

---

**בגומא** נמי בדיק. והא דאמר בפ"ק דפסחים (דף ז.) דגומא אינה נבדקת, גבי תיבה שנשתמשו בה מעות מעשר (ג)שני — התם בחריץ המכוסה בקרשי התיבה, דהויא גומא אינה נבדקת. **וכן** הכתם עד שעת כבוס חזקתו בדוק כו' ל"ג "איבעיא להו", דקאי א"איבעיא להו" דלעיל גבי שרץ. *__בודקות__ חלוקיהן בשעת כבוסיהן. לאחר הכבוס בודקות, ואם לא מצאה הכתם — טהור החלוק, אע"פ שהיה בו בודאי כתם קודם כבוס, וכגון שהטבילתו. והא דאמר לקמן בפרק "האשה" (דף סא.) "בגד שאבד בו כתם, מעבירים עליו ז' סממנים לבטלו" ה"ה דאזיל ליה לכתם ע"י כבוס סתם. והא דמסיק דאין חזקתו מתכבס — היינו, כשהכתם בסיטרא או בזוית. אי נמי: ע"י כבוס סתם לא אזיל, ו"בודקות חלוקיהן" — היינו, לפני כבוס. ואי מצאה הכתם — מעבירה עליו ז' סממנים, או תעשה כבוס גמור וטוב. דהא חזינן דע"י כבוס טוב, הולך הכתם בלא סממנים. **שמע** מינה חזקתו בדוק. והא דאמר בפ"ק דפסחים (דף ז.) ובאלו מציאות" (ב"מ דף כו.) "מעות שנמצאו בירושלים בשאר ימות השנה, חולין. לפי ששוקי ירושלים עשויין להתכבד בכל יום" — לא שחזקתן מתכבדים, אלא בשעת כבוד רגילים לעיין ולחפש אם יש שם מעות. אי נמי: כשבודקין השוקים שלא יהא שם עפר כשעורה או כעדשה מן השרץ, אם היו שם מעות, היו נמצאות. **הבאים** מרקם. ר"ת גריס *"רקם". דאילו ברקם, היו ישראל, כדאמר בריש מסכת גיטין (דף ב.) אף המביא מן הרקם ומן החגר. ולא קשה מידי, דטובי "רקם" הוו, כדפרישית שם. ועוד: אע"ג דברקם ישראל הוו, קאמר הכא דכתמן טהורין — דישראל מצניעים כתמיהן, אלא של גוים הן, וטהורין. ורבי יהודה מטמא — משום שיש שם גרים, וטועים (ג) להשתמש. אי נמי: הכא איירי בידוע שהן של גוים הדרים שם. **מבין** הגוים טהורים. אע"ג דבפרק "בנות כותים" (לעיל לד.) אמר דדם גויה מטמא כרוקה וכמימי רגליה — בכתמים דרבנן לא גזרו עליהם. **אמוראי** נינהו כו' — ואם תאמר: א"כ מ"מ תקשה לרבי יוחנן דאמר: אין מקבלין גרים מן התרמוד. אע"ג דסתם מתניתין ד"עשרה יוחסין" (קדושין דף עה:) ודפרק "אלמנה" (יבמות סח:) וכמה תנאי סברי דגוי ועבד הבא על בת ישראל הולד ממזר, מ"מ תקשה ליה ממתניתין דסברה דלא באו גוים על בנות ישראל. דאי באו — הוי כתמן טמא. דבין אם הולד ממזר או כשר — ישראל הוי! ויש לומר: דרבי יוחנן וסביא סברי כדתני רמי בר יחזקאל בפ"ק דיבמות (דף טז.) דאין מקבלין גרים מן הקרמיין ומן התרמודין. דפליג אמתניתין דהכא דמטהר כתמי כל הגוים. ולא בעי לשנויי "לא, לבר מתרמוד", כדמשני בפ"ק דגיטין (דף ו.) "לא, לבר מבבל" — מדמחלק ברקם ולא בשאר גוים, משמע דכולהו טהורים.* **קוברין** שם הנפלים. ואם תאמר: והיאך משתמשים שם בימי טומאתן, והלא נזהרים הם מטומאת מת ונפלים, כדתניא: נאמנים לומר "לא קברנו שם הנפלים". ומוקי לה בגמרא בכותי כהן עומד שם.א] ובפרק "בנות כותים" (לעיל דף לג.) אמר דנשוי מטמא משום בועל נדה, אבל פנוי — לא! וי"ל: דלפי שעה קוברין שם נפלין, ולאחר זמן מסלקין אותם לקוברן בבית הקברות, ואין אנו יודעין מתי מסירין אותן. **לא** נחשדו על כתמיהם. ואע"ג דכתמים דרבנן, הך טומאה אית להו. דסברה: דמגופה אתא. ולמאי

---



תוספי הרא"ש

**בגומא** נמי בדיק. והא דאמרינן בפ"ק דפסחים גבי תיבה שנשתמשו בה מעות מעשר דגומא אינה נבדקת התם בגומא מכוסה בדפי התיבה ואינה נראית: ה"ג וכן הכתם כו' עד שעת כיבוס חזקתו בדוק ול"ג איבעיא להו דקאי אאיבעיא דבעי לעיל: **ש"מ** חזקתו בדוק. אבל ע"י כיבוד אינו נמצא. והא דאמרינן בפ"ק דפסחים ובפ' אלו מציאות מעות שנמצאו שם חולין לפי ששוקי ירושלים עשוין להתכבד בכל יום. שאני מעות דבשעת הכיבוד רגילין לעיין עליהם ולבקש מעות שנפלו שם: **אימרטוטי** אימרטוט. אילו נפלו מים עליהם כל כך עד שחזר להיות לח היה נמרט ונפרך: **הבאין** מרקם. תימה דהכא משמע שלא היו דרין בו אלא גוים וגרים ובגיטין אמרינן אף המביא מרקם ומן החגר אלמא ישראלים היו דרין בו. ר"ת היה גורס הבא ריקם ושמא ריקם המלך בנאה וקרא על שמו. ומיהו לא קשה מידי דבלאו הכי צריך לומר התם דטובי ריקם היו. ועוד אפי' אם ישראלים וגוים דרים בריקם הני כתמים דמשתכחי בחוץ לאו דישראל הם דהא מצניעי כתמיהו ור' יהודה קאמר אף הגוים ישראלים הם אלא שטעו להשתמר א"נ הכא מיירי בכתמים שידועין בודאי דשל גוים: **מבין** הגוים טהורין אע"ג דדם גויה טמא כרוקה כדאמרינן לעיל בפרק בנות כותיים לא גזרו חכמים בכתמיהם כיון דדמן לאו דאורייתא הוא: **אמוראי** ניניהו ואליבא דר' יוחנן. ותימה מ"מ ר' יוחנן לאו תנא הוא ותיקשי ליה מתניתין דהשתא קסבר ר' יוחנן כמ"ד גוי ועבד הבא על בת ישראל הולד ממזר ובסתם מתניתין בפרק האומר ובפרק אלמנה מ"מ מתניתין סברה דלא באו גוים על בנות ישראל כלל דאי באו גוים הולד ודמן טמא ולא אשכחן תנא דפליג על מתניתין בהא וי"ל דר' יוחנן וסביא ס"ל כדתני דמי בר יחזקאל בפ"ק דיבמות אין מקבלין גרים מן הקרתויים וההיא פליגא אמתניתין דמטהרת כתמי כל גוים הן. ותימה ונשיהן נדות היאך משמשין שם וגם האנשים בימי טומאתן ואי אין נזהרין בטומאת מת של נפלים א"כ בפ' בנות כותיים דאמרינן בכותי שטבל ועלה ודרס על בגדי חבר שטהור גמור אי בקרוב. וגם דהא דתנן התם הכותיים מטמאין משכב תחתון כעליון מוקמינן לה בנשוי אבל בפנוי לא ואמאי והלא טמאין טומאת מת וי"ל דלפי שעה קוברין שם נפליהן ואז נזהרין מטומאה ולאחר זמן מסירין אותו לקוברו בבית הקברות ולדידן לעולם הן בספק טומאה: **לא** נחשדו על כתמיהן. אף על גב דכתמים דרבנן מיסתבר להו דמגופה אתא:

הגהות הב"ח

(א) גמ' ואם לאו בידוע. נ"ב ע"ל בדף סד ע"ב בתוספות בד"ה על גבי כולם: (ב) תוס' ד"ה בגומא וכו' שאני התם: (ג) ד"ה הבאים וכו' וטועים להשתמר אי נמי:

הגהות מהר"ב רנשבורג

א] תוס' ד"ה קוברין וכו' ובפ' בנות כותים אמר. נ"ב עיין ספר עמודי שלמה:

יבמות טז. ב"ק לח: | יבמות שם | [שבת מו. וש"נ] [יבמות טז: גיטין כג. מנחות נב: חולין מג.] | יבמות נז: קדושין עה: סנהדרין פה: [ב"ק לח: חולין ג.] | [ועי' תוס' לקמן סד: ד"ה על גבי כולם] | [ועי' היטב תוספות יבמות טז: ד"ה אמוראי]

מאי דרוש? "לא תסיג גבול רעך אשר גבלו ראשונים בנחלתך", כל שיש לו נחלה – יש לו גבול, כל שאין לו נחלה – אין לו גבול. "נאמנים לומר קברנו". והא לית להו "ולפני עור לא תתן מכשול"! א"ר אבהו: בכהן עומד שם. ודלמא כהן טמא הוא? דנקיט תרומה בידיה. ודלמא תרומה טמאה היא? דקאכיל מינה. אי הכי, מאי למימרא? מהו דתימא: לא בקיאי ביצירה, קמ"ל. § "נאמנין על הבהמה" וכו'. § והא לית להו "ולפני עור לא תתן מכשול"! א"ר חייא בר אבא, א"ר יוחנן: בגוזז ועובד. אי הכי, מאי למימרא? מהו דתימא: לא בקיאי בטינוף, קמ"ל. § "נאמנין על ציון" וכו'. § ואע"ג דמדרבנן הוא, כיון דכתיבא – מזהר זהירי ביה, דכתיב: "וראה עצם אדם ובנה אצלו ציון". § "אבל אין נאמנין לא על הסככות" וכו'. § סככות – *דתנן: *אלו הן סככות – אילן המיסך על הארץ. פרעות – דתנן: [א] *אבנים פרעות היוצאות מן הגדר. "בית הפרס" – *א"ר יהודה, א"ר שמואל: מנפח אדם בית הפרס והולך. *רב יהודה בר אמי משמיה דרב יהודה אמר: בית הפרס שנידש – טהור. ותנא: החורש בית הקברות – הרי זה עושה בית הפרס. ועד כמה הוא עושה? מלא מענה מאה אמה, בית ארבעת סאין. רבי יוסי אומר: חמש. ולא מהימני? והתניא: שדה שאבד בה קבר – נאמן כותי לומר "אין שם קבר", לפי שאינו מעיד אלא על גופו של קבר. אילן שהוא מיסך על הארץ – נאמן לומר "אין תחתיו קבר", לפי שאינו מעיד אלא על גופו של קבר! א"ר יוחנן: במהלך ובא על פני כולה. אי הכי, מאי למימרא? מהו דתימא: *רצועה נפקא, קמ"ל. § "זה הכלל" כו'. § "זה הכלל" לאתויי מאי? לאתויי תחומין ויין נסך. §

## הדרן עלך דם הנדה

**רש"י**

מאי דרוש. כותיים, שאין קוברים את הנפלים, ומוקמינן לה בספרי: במוכר קברי אבותיו. נאמנין לומר קברנו. דמידי דאורייתא הוא טומאת המת. והא לית להו ולפני עור לא תתן מכשול. לא דרשי ליה: במחטיא את חבירו, ולא איכפת להם אם אנו חוטאים על פיהם. בכהן. כותי עומד שם. דקאכיל מינה. ותרומה טמאה, באזהרה לטהור, וכ"ש לטמא. לא בקיאי ביצירה. וכי קברי נפל, לא ידעי דהוא בן מ' יום, וסברי: מיא בעלמא הוא, ואינו מטמא. בטינוף. בבהמה דקה, ופוטר את הבהמה מן הבכורה. ובבכורות (דף כא:) מפרש: מאי "טינוף" – שמגלגלת ומוציאה דם דרך רחם, וזהו הולד שנימוח ויוצא. הלכך, הבא אחריו – אינו בכור. והני כותיים לא בקיאי בטינוף, וזימנין דלא טניף, ואמרו: טינוף הוא, ופוטרין את הבא אחריו. קמ"ל. על ציון. לציין, וסומכין עליהן, ועבדינן טהרות היכא דלא ליינו. אילן המיסך על הארץ. והוא סמוך לדרך בית הקברות. וזימנין דמיתרמי בין השמשות, וקברי התם. ואם הענפים מובדלים, שאין האהל שלם, וידוע ודאי שיש קבר תחת (א) האהלות, ואין ידוע איזה הוא. והכותי מעיד על אחד "זה טהור" – אינו נאמן, לפי שאינו חש על הספק, ותולה הטומאה באהל שני מספק. פרעות. (ב) גדולות ובולטות מן הגדר. וקברו תחת אחת מהן, ואין אנו יודעין תחת איזהו מהן. ובא כותי והעיד על מקצתן שהן טהורות – אינו נאמן, משום דלספקא לא חייש, ותולה הספק באחרות. בית הפרס. שדה שנחרש בה קבר. ואוקמי רבנן (ג) על סביבות הקבר מאה אמה בספק טומאה, שדיקדקה המחרישה את העצמות ומגלגלתן. מנפח. דבשר – ליכא, ועצם כשעורה – לא מטמא אלא במגע ובמשא. הלכך, מנפח כדי שלא יגעו רגליו בו, והולך. שנידש. ברגלי אדם. שהרגלים נושאים את העצמות, ושחקום. פרס. לשון דבר שבור ופרוס, על שם שנפרסו העצמות. בית ארבעת סאין. היינו ק' על ק', שהרי חצר המשכן מאה על חמשים, והוא "בית סאתים". שדה שאבד בה קבר. מיקרי נמי "בית הפרס", ורבנן גזרו בכולה. דתניא במועד קטן (דף ה:): ג' בית הפרס הן, שדה שאבד בה קבר, ושנחרש בה קבר, ושדה בוכין. שאין מעיד אלא על גופו של קבר. דכיון דאמרי "אין שם קבר ברוח זה" – על גופו של קבר הוא מעיד. וגופו של קבר – דאורייתא, ובדאורייתא מהימני. אלמא נאמנין על בית הפרס ועל (בית) הסככות (ד). מהלך על פני כל השדה. דכיון דעל פני כולה מהלך, ודאי פשיטא ליה דניטלה הטומאה משם. ומתני' דקתני דאין נאמן – כגון שאינו מהלך על פני כולה, שמשייר רוח אחת. הלכך, אפילו במקום שעבר אינו נאמן, משום דאיהו לספקא לא חייש. מאי למימרא. נהי דלספק לא חייש, לודאי – חייש. וכיון דפשיטא לן דקבר הוה בה, והוא מהלך על פני כולה – הרי עובר על מקום הקבר. ואי לאו דקים ליה שניטלה הטומאה, לא עבר. רצועה נפקא. מן השדה, ונקראת על שם שדה זו. ושם הוא תולה את מקום הטומאה, והכא עבר מספקא, דלספקא לא חייש. קמ"ל. כיון דעל כל ד' רוחותיה עובר (ה) בתוכה. לרצועה לא חיישינן. לאתויי תחומין. אין נאמנין לומר "עד כאן תחום שבת" – דתחומין דרבנן, וכותיים לא סבירא להו. ויין נסך. דאין כותי מקפיד על מגע גוי.

**תוספות**

ודלמא כהן טמא הוא. ואע"ג דטמא נמי אסור לשהות בבית הקברות, דבנזיר בפרק "מי שאמר" (דף יז.) בעי: נזיר והוא בבית הקברות, מי בעי שהייה למלקות או לא? ובפרק "ג' מינין" (שם דף מג:) אמר רב הונא: נזיר שעומד בבית הקברות והשיטו לו מתו או מת אחר – חייב. וטעמא: לפי שמוסיף טומאה עליו, דבחבורים עושין את האחר אב הטומאה, כדאמר התם – כותיים לית להו הנך (ו) מימרות. ובנה אצלו ציון. במועד קטן (דף ה.) מפיק מהכא ציון של בית הקברות. וא"ת: ולר"ש דאמר* אין קברי גוים מטמאין באהל, היכי מפיק מהכא? הא אמר במו"ק דאין מציינין אלא על טומאת אהל! וי"ל: מדמציינין לפי שעה ציון, משום טומאת מגע ומשא, אם כן לכל הפחות יש לציין בטומאת אהל. ולמאי דבעי למימר ב"הבא על יבמתו" (יבמות דף סא.) דלר"ש אתי גוים לא מטמאי אפילו במגע ובמשא, נפיק ליה לר"ש ציון מדרשא אחריתי דהתם, וציון דגבי גוג – לאו משום טומאה, אלא לנקות הארץ מן המתים. וא"ת: ולר"ש דדריש (שם) דאין גוים קרויין "אדם", הא כתיב "וראה עצם אדם"? וי"ל: דנקט "אדם" – לאפוקי דס"ד דקברו שם עצמות בהמה. אילן המיסך. מיירי בידוע שיש מת קבור שם, אך שאין ידוע תחת איזו ענף. ואין כותי נאמן לומר שאינו קבור תחת ענף זה, אפילו הולך תחתיו – דאין מקפיד על ספק טומאה. ודוקא במאהיל על פני כולה אמר בסמוך דנאמן. ומה שפ"ה: אילן בסמוך לבית הקברות, ופעמים קוברין שם – בחנם פירש כן. כיון שצריך לפרש בידוע שמת קבור שם, דבספק – לא היה נאמן, אפילו היה מהלך על פני כולה. ואע"ג דספק טומאה ברה"ר טהור – הכא, גזור רבנן. והא דקאמר לקמן בפ"ב (דף סח:) דסככות ופרעות לאו אהל הוא, ורבנן גזרו עלייהו – לאו דוקא קאמר דלאו אהל הוא, דבודאי קבור שם איירי, כדפי' אלא כלומר, הך טומאת אהל אינה אלא מדרבנן, דברה"ר ספקו טהור. א"נ: הענפים המובדלין זה מזה, רואים אותם כאילו הן סמוכות, ליחשב אהל. *כדאמר באהלות (דף סט) המיסך על הארץ – רבי יהודה אומר: רואין התחתונות כאילו עולות למעלה, והעליונות כאילו יורדות למטה. ואם היו נוגעות זו בזו כפותח טפח – מביאות וחוללות כו'. בית הפרס. על שם פריסה. שהעצמות נפרסים במדרס רגלים, או ע"י מחרישה. ובשדה שאבד בה קבר, לא שייך האי טעמא, וקרי ליה בפ"ק דמועד קטן (דף ה:) "בית הפרס"! ושמא אגב דקרי "בית הפרס" לשדה שנחרש בה קבר, קרי גם לאבד "בית הפרס". א"נ: לשון "בית הפרס" – על שם שפרסות רגלי אדם נמנעות מלילך שם, מפני הטומאה. ובפ"ק דמו"ק (דף ה:) תניא גבי בית הפרס: הוא שדה שנחרש בה קבר, ושאבד בה קבר, ושדה בוכים. ומפרש טעמא דשדה בוכים – משום יאוש בעלים. ומפרש בערוך: *שדה מיוחד, שקרובי המת מביאין אותו על אותו שדה. ואנשי בית הקברות באין לקראתו, ובוכים יחד (ז) וכו'. והראשונים חוזרים לביתם, ואלו נוטלין אותו ומוליכין אותו לקוברו. ואותו שדה – טמא, דשמא נתדלדל ונתנענע מעט מעט ממנו, ונפל, ושכחוהו. ורבינו שמואל פי': פעמים שבני העיר מניחין אותו שם, לפי שסוברין שאנשי בית הקברות יבואו ויטלו אותו. ובני בית הקברות יסברו, שאנשי העיר יוליכוהו לבית הקברות. ונשאר שם. ועוד פי' שם: "שדה בוכין" שדה שיש בה בוכין, ומניחין המת שם לפי שעה, עד שיהו פנוים להוליכו לבית הקברות לקוברו. ופעמים שנשכח שם, ולא הוסר, וזהו יאוש בעלים. בית הפרס שנידש טהור. אשדה שנחרש בה קבר קאי, דמספקינן לעלם כשעורה ק' אמה סביבות הקבר. דכיון שנידש ונרמס ברגלים, י"ל: שהוליכו כשעורה משם. אבל אשדה שאבד בה קבר, לא שייכא הך קולא. מלא מענה ק' אמה. בתוספתא דאהלות [רפי"ז] מפרש דהנך ק' אמה – היינו, לכל רוח. אמר ר' יוחנן במהלך ובא על פני כולה. אבל בשדה שנחרש בה קבר – אפילו מהלך ובא על פני כולה, לא מהימן. דאין כאן אלא ספקא דרבנן, שמא הסיט עצם כשעורה, ואין הכותי חושש עליה. וא"ת: כי היכי דליון קברות דמהימן אדאורייתא, דאוקימנא בכהן עומד שם, ה"נ ליתני במתני' דמהימן אסככות ופרעות ובמהלך על פני כולה! וי"ל: דלא חשיבא ליה למתני' רבותא לאשמועינן דלא חיישינן לרצועה נפקא. ועוד: אבית הפרס דנחרש בה קבר – לא מהני מהלך ובא על פני כולה, כדפרישית, אלא דוקא באבד בה קבר וא"ת: ובאבד נמי היכי מהני, דלמא (ח) טמאה היא? וי"ל: דמיירי דנקיט תרומה ואכיל מינה, כדקאמר לעיל. וה"ה דנקט ולא אכיל, וכגון שידוע לנו שהיא טהורה, דלא הוה כותי מטמא לה.

## הדרן עלך דם הנדה

**תוספי הרא"ש**

בכהן טמא. ותימה ומה בכך אפי' הוא טמא אסור ליכנס בבית הקברות דבנזיר מבעיא ליה בנזיר וכהן [בבית הקברות] אי בעו שהייה למלקות. ואמרינן נמי בפ"ג מינין אמר רב הונא נזיר שהוא עומד בבית הקברות והושיטו לו מתו ומת אחר חייב. וי"ל דכותאי לית להו הא דרב הונא אלא סברי כשהוא טמא אינו מוזהר עוד מלהוסיף טומאה: אילן המיסך על הארץ. מיירי שידוע לנו בודאי שמת קבור תחתיו ואינו ידוע לנו תחת איזה מן הענפים ואין הכותי נאמן לומר תחת ענף אחד הוא קבור אפי' הוא הולך תחת שאר הענפים שאינו מקפיד על ספק טומאה כדמוכח בסמוך דאינו נאמן אלא בהולך על פני כולה. ומה שפרש"י אילן הסמוך לבית הקברות ופעמים קוברין שם אורחא דמילתא נקט אבל לעולם צריך שיהא ודאי (שיש מת קבור תחתיו שאם היה ספק לא היה הכותי נאמן אפי' הולך) על פני כולה ואע"ג בספק טומאה ברה"ר ספיקו טהור הכא גזור רבנן: בית הפרס. פרש"י על שם שהעצמות נפרסין ונפרכין כמדרס רגלי אדם או ע"י המחרישה ואע"ג דבשדה שאבד בו קבר לא שייך האי טעמא וא"ה קרי ליה בית הפרס בפ"ק דמועד קטן. וי"ל דאגב שקרי לשדה (שנאבד) [שנחרש] בו קבר בית הפרס קרי ליה נמי להאי הכי א"נ לשון בית הפרס הוי על שם שפרסות רגלים נמנעין לילך שם מפני הטומאה. בפ"ק דמועד קטן (וי"ל דאגב) תניא ג' בית הפרס הן שדה שאבד בו קבר ושדה שנחרש בו קבר ושדה בוכין ומפרש שדה בוכים משום יאוש בעלים ומפרש בערוך דשדה מיוחד יש שקרובי המת מביאין אותו עד אותו מקום ואנשי בית הקברות באין לקראתם ובוכין ומספידין שם ביחד והראשונים חוזרים לביתם ואלו נוטלים אותו ומוליכים אותו לבית הקברות ואותו השדה טמא שמא נדלדל ונתנענע ממנו מעט ונפל שם ושכחוהו. ורשב"ם פי' פעמים שבני העיר מביאין אותו שם וסבורין שאנשי בית הקברות יטלוהו משם ובני הקברות סבורין שאנשי העיר יוליכוהו לבית הקברות ונשאר שם וזהו יאוש בעלים: במהלך ובא על פני כולה. ובכהן אוכל תרומה כדלעיל. אבל בשדה שנחרש בה קבר אפי' אם מהלך על פני כולה אינו נאמן דספק הוא אם יש טומאה כלל דשמא לא נשאר עצם כשעורה שלא נחרש במחרישה וכותי לא חייש לספק טומאה: רצועה נפקא. ובאילן שמא היה ענף יוצא מן האילן ונקצץ ותולה בו הטומאה. ותימה כיון שאומר מתניתין דאינו נאמן על (הסככות) [הסככות ופרעות] ולוקמא במהלך על פני כולה וי"ל דלא חשיב ליה חדוש הך דאימור רצועה נפקא כמו אימור לא בקיאי ביצירה ובטינוף וציון שהוא מדרבנן: סליק פירקא.

**עין משפט נר מצוה**

ל א ב מיי' פי"א מהל' טומאת מת הלכה ב:
לא ג מיי' פ"ו מהל' קרבן פסח הלכה ח:
לב ד ה מיי' פ"י מהלכ' טומאת מת הלכה ה:

**מסורת הש"ס**

[יבמות סא.]
ברכות יט: עירובין ל: מו"ק ה: חגיגה כה: פסחים לב: כתובות כח: בכורות כט.
[תוספתא פ"ט דאהלות נזיר נד:] אהלות פ"ח מ"ב
תוספתא שם
[עמ"ש ברכות יט: על הגליון]
גיטין ז: קדושין עב.
דברים יט | ויקרא יט | יחזקאל לט

**הגהות הגר"א**

[א] גמ' אבנים פרעות. תיבת אבנים נמחק:

נ"ל כדאמר בתוספתא דאהלות (פ"ט) ואלו הן סככות אילן המיסך על הארץ ר' יהודה אומר כו' וחוללים כו' ועי' ברבינו שמשון פ"ח דאהלות (מ"ב)

**הגהות הב"ח**

(א) רש"י ד"ה אילן וכו' קבר תחת אחד האהלות: (ב) ד"ה פרעות אבנים גדולות: (ג) ד"ה בית הפרס וכו' רבנן כל סביבות: (ד) ד"ה שאין וכו' והסככות הס"ד ואח"כ מ"ה במהלך וכו' שהכותי מהלך על פני: (ה) ד"ה קמ"ל וכו' עובר לרצועה כנ"ל ותיבת בתוכה נמחק: (ו) תוס' ד"ה ודלמא וכו' הנך חומרות הס"ד: (ז) ד"ה בית הפרס וכו' ובוכים יחד כולם והראשונים: (ח) ד"ה אמר וכו' דלמא טמא הוא וכו':

**גליון הש"ס**

רש"י ד"ה דקאכיל מינה ותרומה טמאה באזהרה וכו'. תמיהני הא אכילת תרומה טמאה אסור רק בעשה עי' יבמות עד ע"ב וצ"ע:

**הגהות מהר"ב רנשבורג**

[א] גמ' מאי דרוש לא תסיג. נ"ב עיין מג"א סי' תקכו ס"ק כ ובפירוש משניות לרמב"ם במשנתינו ודו"ק:

א מיי' פ"ט מהלכות איסורי ביאה הלכה ח סמג לאוין קיא טוש"ע י"ד סי' קצ סעיף יא:
ב ב מיי' שם הלכה י טוש"ע שם סעיף יב:
ג ג מיי' שם טוש"ע שם סעיף יג:
ד ד מיי' שם הלכה יא טוש"ע שם סעיף יד:
ה ה מיי' שם הלכה ז סמג שם טור ש"ע שם סעיף י ועיין בטור:
ו ו מיי' פ"ה שם הלכה יז סמג שם טוש"ע י"ד סימן קנא:
ז ז מיי' שם פ"ד הלכה יח סמג שם טוש"ע י"ד סימן קצ סעיף לז:
ח ח ט י מיי' שם פ"ט הלכה יט והלכה כ והלכה כא ועיין בהשגות ובמ"מ סמג שם טור ש"ע י"ד סי' קצ סעיף יא וסעיף יב וע"ש:

תורה אור

**הרואה** [א]כתם על בשרה, כנגד בית התורפה – מטמאה, ושלא כנגד בית התורפה – טהורה. על עקבה ועל ראש גודלה – טמאה. על שוקה ועל פרסותיה, מבפנים – טמאה, מבחוץ – טהורה, ועל הצדדין מכאן ומכאן – טהורה. [ב]ראתה על חלוקה, מן החגור ולמטה – טמאה, מן החגור ולמעלה – טהורה. [ג]ראתה על בית יד של חלוק, אם מגיע כנגד בית התורפה – טמאה, ואם לאו – טהורה. [ד]היתה פושטתו ומתכסה בו בלילה, כל מקום שנמצא בו כתם – טמאה, מפני שהוא חוזר. וכן בפוליום.§ **גמ'** אמר שמואל: [ה]בדקה קרקע עולם וישבה עליה, ומצאה דם עליה – טהורה, שנאמר °"בבשרה" – עד שתרגיש בבשרה. (ויקרא טו) האי "בבשרה" – מיבעי ליה *שמטמאה בפנים כבחוץ! *א"כ לימא קרא "בבשר", מאי "בבשרה" – שמע מינה: עד שתרגיש בבשרה. ואכתי מיבעי ליה: *"בבשרה" ולא בשפיר, ולא בחתיכה! תרתי שמע מינה. תא שמע, *האשה שהיא עושה צרכיה וראתה דם, רבי מאיר אומר: אם עומדת – טמאה, ואם יושבת – טהורה. היכי דמי? אי דארגשה – יושבת אמאי טהורה? אלא לאו – דלא ארגשה, וקתני: עומדת – טמאה! [ו]לעולם – דארגשה, ואימור: הרגשת מי רגלים הואי. עומדת – הדור מי רגלים למקור, ואייתי דם, ויושבת טהורה. ת"ש: [ז]עד שהיה נתון תחת הכר ונמצא עליו דם, אם עגול – טהור, ואם משוך – טמא. היכי דמי? אי דארגישה – עגול אמאי טהור? אלא לאו – דלא ארגישה, וקתני: משוך – טמא! לא, לעולם – דארגישה, ואימור: הרגשת עד הואי, משוך – ודאי מגופה אתא, עגול – טהור. תא שמע: *נמצא על שלו – טמאין וחייבין בקרבן, נמצא על שלה אתיום – טמאין, וחייבין בקרבן. נמצא על שלה לאחר זמן – טמאים מספק, ופטורין מן הקרבן. היכי דמי? אי דארגישה – לאחר זמן אמאי פטורין מן הקרבן? אלא לאו – דלא ארגישה, וקתני: נמצא על שלה אתיום – טמאין, וחייבין בקרבן! לא, לעולם – דארגישה, ואימא: הרגשת שמש הוה. תא שמע: נמצאת אתה אומר, ג' ספקות באשה: [ח]על בשרה, ספק טמא ספק טהור – טמא; על חלוקה, ספק טמא ספק טהור – טהור; ובמגעות ובהיסטות – הלך אחר הרוב. מאי "הלך אחר הרוב"? לאו אם רוב ימיה טמאין – טמאה, ואע"ג דלא ארגשה! לא, אם רוב ימיה בהרגשה חזיא – טמאה, דאימור: ארגשה ולאו אדעתה. אמר מר: על בשרה, ספק טמא ספק טהור – טמא; על חלוקה, ספק טמא ספק טהור – טהור. ה"ד? אי מחגור ולמטה – על חלוקה אמאי טהור? והא תנן: מן החגור ולמטה – טמא! ואי מחגור ולמעלה – על בשרה אמאי טמא? והתנן: ראתה דם על בשרה שלא כנגד בית התורפה – טהורה! אב"א מחגור ולמטה, ואב"א מחגור ולמעלה. אי בעית אימא: מחגור ולמטה – [ט]כגון שעברה בשוק של טבחים, על בשרה – מגופה אתאי, דאי מעלמא אתאי – על חלוקה מיבעי ליה אשתכוחי. על חלוקה – מעלמא אתא, דאי מגופה אתא – על בשרה מיבעי ליה אשתכוחי. ואיבעית אימא: מחגור ולמעלה – [י]כגון דאזדקרה. על בשרה – ודאי מגופה אתאי, דאי מעלמא אתאי – על חלוקה איבעי ליה אשתכוחי, על חלוקה – מעלמא אתאי, דאי מגופה אתאי – על בשרה איבעי ליה אשתכוחי. קתני מיהת "על בשרה ספק טמא ספק טהור – טמא", ואע"ג דלא הרגישה! ועוד, תנן: הרואה כתם על בשרה כנגד בית התורפה – טמאה, ואע"ג דלא הרגישה! אמר רב ירמיה מדפתי: מודה שמואל שהיא טמאה מדרבנן

**הרואה** כתם. ת"ש האשה שעושה צרכיה. תימה: מאי מהדר אפירכות, הא כמה משניות פ' "בא סימן" ו"דם הנדה" בדיני כתמים, וליפרוך מינייהו. ולא שייך לשנויי עלייהו, לא הרגשת עד ולא הרגשת שמש! ואומר הר"י: דמדיני כתמים ליכא למפרך – דהיינו יכולין להעמיד שיש זמן מרובה משעת הכבוס, ואימור: הרגישה, ולאו אדעתה. אבל בשמעתין פריך מכתמים דבבשרה – דאין רגילות שיהות כתם בבשר בלא דעתה שלא ייבש ויפול. מיהו ברייתא דג' ספקות דמייתי לקמן פריך מחלוקה, כמו שנפרש בההיא. וי"ל: דמשמע דזמן מועט היה שם, דומיא דבשר. ומשני: דמזמן רחוק הוה, ואימור: ארגשה ולא אדעתה. אי נמי: כיון דרוב ימיה טמאים, יש לחוש. **אימור** הרגשת שמש הואי. וא"ת: אמאי לא נקט הרגשת מי רגלים, כמו לעיל. ואע"פ שלא הטילה, כדאמר בריש מכילתין, והל"ל: כסבור' הרגשת מי רגלים הוא! וי"ל: דהכא זמן מועט בין תשמיש למציאת הדם – והיתה יודעת אם תרגיש במי רגלים. אבל לעיל בין פקידה לפקידה – יש זמן ארוך, והרבה פעמים יש הרגשת מי רגלים בינתיים. **ובמגעות** ובהיסטות הלך אחר הרוב. פ"ה: אשה שאין לה וסת, ורגילה לראות תדיר ובודקת עצמה תמיד, וכל זמן שלא בדקה עצמה – מחזקת עצמה בטומאה. הלכך, אם רוב ימיה היא טמאין – טמאה. וזהו תימה: שזו החומרא לא מצינו בשום מקום. דהא אשה שיש לה וסת – דיה שעתה, וטומאה דמעת לעת – אינה אלא באין לה וסת, ולא מפקידה לפקידה. ואפי' ברואה, וכ"ש הכא, דאין כאן אלא כתם. ואין לחלק בין ברואה תדיר בין שאינה רואה תדיר. ונראה: דקאי א"נמצא על חלוקה" (ספק טמא ספק טהור) וקאמר: דאם *) אחרי מציאת הכתם, רוב ימיה טמאין – טמאה, ואף על גב דעברה בשוק של טבחים. ולא אמרינן: אי מגופה אתא – על בשרה איבעי ליה לאשתכוחי. **אמר** מר על בשרה כו' – ולבסוף פריך מינה לשמואל. והא דלא פריך מינה ברישא אלא פריך ממגעות והיסטות דסיפא ברישא – משום דפשוט הוא יותר. אבל רישא מיבעי ליה לתרולי ברישא, והדר פריך מינה. **על** בשרה ודאי מגופה אתאי. וא"ת: מאי שנא דלקמן בשמעתין גבי "לבשה שלשה חלוקות ועברה בשוק של טבחים – תולה אפילו בתחתון", ולא אמרינן: אי איתא דמעלמא אתאי, אעליון ה"ל לאשתכוחי? ויש לומר: דהתם, לפעמים שהיא מגלה חלוקה העליון ואתי על התחתון. אבל אין דרך לגלות בשרה. **קתני** מיהא על בשרה כו' וא"ת: ומאי קושיא, ה"נ אימור: ארגשה ולאו אדעתה, כדאמר לעיל? וי"ל: דהתם, דרוב ימיה טמאין – יש רגלים לדבר, שיש לתלות בהרגשה ולאו אדעתה. אבל הכא – אין שום הוכחה שנתלה בהרגשה ולאו אדעתה, שאין רק שעה מועטת שהוא על בשרה.

*) גי' ר"מ קודס

**הרואה**. כנגד בית התורפה. אותו מקום, דאיכא למימר: דם מאותו מקום נפל להתם, וטמאה. על עקבה ועל ראש גודלה טמאה. ראש גודלה של רגל. ובגמרא מפרש טעמא. מבפנים. בין שני שוקים, כל גובהן מן הארץ. מבחוץ. מכאן ומכאן. צדדים. אחורי השוק – כל גובהן כנגד העקב, ולפניו – כל גובהן כנגד הרגל. מן החגור ולמטה. כנגד בית התורפה הוא. אם מגיע כנגד בית התורפה. כגון שנמלא בראש בית ידה סמוך ליד, שפעמים שפושטתן מזרועה ונופל כנגד מטה. שלא כנגד בית התורפה. כגון שנמלא סמוך לכתפה. שהוא חוזר. פעמים שראש החלוק נהפך כלפי פניה שלמטה. וכן בפוליום. מעפורת שמתכסה בו. אירי"ל בלע"ז. **גמ'** צרכיה. מטלת מים. עומדת טמאה. דאיידי דדחיק לה עלמא דמעומד השתינה, ולא יכלה לעכור – הדור מי רגלים למקור, ואייתו דם. יושבת טהורה. דמכה יש לה במקום מי רגלים, שאין דרך דם נדה לצאת עם מי רגלים. עד. סדין שבודקת בו. עגול. אין זה דם בדיקה, דדרך קינוח להיות משוך. דארגישה. בשעת בדיקה. ועגול להכי טהור לעולם – דאימור הרגשת עד הואי, שליערתה בדיקת העד. על בשרה ספק טמא ספק טהור טמא. כולו מפרש לקמן. ובמגעות ובהיסטות הלך אחר הרוב. אשה שלא מצאה כתם, והרי היא מחזקת עצמה בספק נדה. כגון שאין לה וסת ורגילה לראות תדיר, ונגעה או הסיטה – הלך אחר רוב ימיה. אם רוב ימיה רגילה לראות – מגעה והסיטה טמא, ואע"ג דהשתא לא ארגישה. דאזדקרה. זקפה עצמה לאחוריה, ואע"ג דעברה בשוק של טבחים – טמאה. דאי מעלמא אתאי – על חלוקה אבעי ליה לאשתכוחי. מדרבנן.

[לעיל כה: מ. מח:]
[לעיל כה:]
לעיל כח:
לקמן נט: [לעיל יד:]
לעיל יד. וש"נ

### תוספי הרא"ש

**הרואה** כתם. עד שתרגיש בבשרה. קס"ד דשמואל מטהר לגמרי משום דלא ארגש' ותימה אמאי לא פריך לשמואל מכמה מתני' דאיירו בכתמים טמאים אע"ג דלא ארגשה הא דתנן בפ' בא סי' הרואה כתם הרי זו מקולקלת. ובפ' דם הנדה הכתם שנמצא בחלוק. ובפרקין דתנן מחגור ולמטה טמאה וליכא לשנויי בה לא הרגשת עד ולא הרגשת שמש. וע"ק כיון דשני ממגעות והיסטות אימור הרגישה ולא אדעתה מאי פריך ליה תו מעל בשרה ספק טהור ספק טמא ומתניתין דכנגד התורפה דבהנהו נמי איכא למימר אימור ארגישה ולאו אדעתה אע"ג דקאמר אם רוב ימיה בהרגשה חזאי רוב נשים אינן רואות אלא בהרגשה וי"ל דמכולהו הנהו מתניתין דכתמים לא הוה מצי לאקשויי משום דאיסור מזמן מרובה יצא הכתם מגופה ואימר ארגשה ושכחה לפיכך פריך ליה מכל הנך מתניתין שיצא ממנה הדם מזמן קרוב ואי ארגישה היתה יודעת וכן מכתם שנמצא על בשרה מזמן קרוב בא ואי מזמן רחוק אתא אין דרך כתם להתקיים על בשרה כי הזיעה מעבירתו. אף על גב דבמגעות והיסטות דפריך מינה היינו שנמצא הכתם על חלוקה משום דכיון דרוב ימיה טהורים מסתמא מזמן קרוב בא הכתם א"ה משני ליה שמא מזמן רחוק בא וארגשה ולאו אדעתה: **וקתני** עומדת טמאה. הק' ר"מ אדמקשי ליה מדר' מאיר ליסייעה מר' יוסי דפליג עליה ואמר בין כך ובין כך טהורה ושמואל גופיה פסיק לקמן כותיה ותירץ דפריך הכא אפי' מר' יוסי דע"כ לא פליג ר' יוסי אלא משום דאין דרך דם המקור לצאת עם מי רגלים. אבל עומדת ויושבת בלא מי רגלים טמאה אע"ג דלא ארגישה דאי בלא מי רגלים מטהר ר' יוסי והאי דנקט מי רגלים להודיעך כחו דר"מ אדרבה לשמעינן בלא מי רגלים להודיעך כחו דרבי יוסי דהוא כח דהיתירא והלכתא כותיה: **משוך** טמא. אפי' בכל שהוא דאי מבאכולת אהא לא הוה משוך: עגול טהור כי ליכא כגרים. ועוד הני מפרש לה בשילהי פירקין: **רוב** ימיה טמאין. פרש"י אין לה ווסת ורגילה תדיר לראות וקשה לפירושו אמאי היא בחזקת טמאה והלא אפי' בודאי ראתה לא מטמינן אלא מעת לעת אשה שאין לה ווסת והיכא שלא ראתה פשיטא דלא מוקמינן לה ברואה. ונראה לפרש דקאי על חלוקה ספק טמא ספק טהור ומפרש לה בסמוך שעברה בשוק של טבחים וטהור דקאמר מיירי לבעלה אבל לטהרות אי רוב ימיה טמאה אמרינן דמגופה אתא דאם איתא דמעלמא אתאי על חלוקה איבעי לאישתכוחי אע"ג דלקמן אמרינן לבשה ג' חלוקין ועברה בשוק של טבחים תולה אפי' בתחתון ולא אמרינן אעליון איבעי ליה לאישתכוחי משום דזימנין דמגבהת שני חלוקין העליונים אבל כולם אינה רגילה להגביה משום שלא יראה בשרה: **קתני** מיהא על בשרה. מהך רישא הו"ל למיפרך תחילה אלא משום דפריך מסיפא דפשיטא

פריך

כרדי

מְדְּרַבָּנַן. רַב אַשִׁי אָמַר: שְׁמוּאֵל הוּא דְּאָמַר כְּר' נְחֶמְיָה. דִּתְנַן, *ר' נְחֶמְיָה אוֹמֵר: [א]כָּל דָּבָר שֶׁאֵינוֹ מְקַבֵּל טוּמְאָה — אֵינוֹ מְקַבֵּל כְּתָמִים. בִּשְׁלָמָא לְרַב אַשִׁי — הַיְינוּ דְּקָאָמַר קַרְקַע, אֶלָּא לְרַב יִרְמְיָה — מַאי אִירְיָא קַרְקַע? אֲפִילּוּ גְּלִימָא נַמִּי! לָא מִיבָּעֲיָא קָאָמַר, לָא מִיבָּעֲיָא גְּלִימָא — דְּלָא מְבַדֵּק שַׁפִּיר, וְאִיכָּא לְמֵימַר מֵעָלְמָא אֲתָא, אֶלָּא אֲפִילּוּ קַרְקַע דִּמְבַדֵּק שַׁפִּיר, דְּאִיכָּא לְמֵימַר מִגּוּפָהּ אָתְיָא — טָהוֹר. § "עַל עֲקֵבָהּ וְעַל רֹאשׁ גּוּדָלָהּ טְמֵאָה" וכו'. § בִּשְׁלָמָא עֲקֵבָהּ — עָבֵיד דְּנָגַע בְּאוֹתוֹ מָקוֹם, אֶלָּא רֹאשׁ גּוּדָלָהּ, מַאי טַעְמָא? וְכִי תֵּימָא: זִימְנִין דְּנָגַע בַּעֲקֵבָהּ, וּמִי מַחְזְקִינַן טוּמְאָה מִמָּקוֹם לְמָקוֹם? וְהַתַּנְיָא: [ב]הָיְתָה לָהּ מַכָּה בְּצַוָּארָהּ (א) שֶׁתּוּכַל לִתְלוֹת — תּוֹלָה, עַל כְּתֵפָהּ, שֶׁאֵינָהּ יְכוֹלָה לִתְלוֹת — אֵינָהּ תּוֹלָה, וְאֵין אוֹמְרִים שֶׁמָּא בְּיָדָהּ נְטָלַתּוּ וְהֱבִיאַתּוּ לְשָׁם! אֶלָּא: [ג]שָׁאנֵי רֹאשׁ גּוּדָלָהּ, דְּבַהֲדֵי דְּפָסְעָה, עָבֵיד דְּמִתְרַמֵּי. וְלָא מַחְזְקִינַן טוּמְאָה מִמָּקוֹם לְמָקוֹם? וְהַתַּנְיָא: נִמְצֵאת עַל קִשְׁרֵי אֶצְבְּעוֹתֶיהָ — טְמֵאָה, מִפְּנֵי שֶׁיָּדַיִם עַסְקָנִיּוֹת הֵן. מַאי טַעְמָא — לָאו מִשּׁוּם דְּאָמְרִינַן: בָּדְקָה בְּחַד יְדָא וְנָגְעָה בְּאִידָךְ יְדָא? לָא, [ד]שָׁאנֵי יָדָהּ — דְּכוּלָּהּ עֲבִידָא דְּנָגְעָה. § "עַל שׁוֹקָהּ וְעַל פַּרְסוֹתֶיהָ מִבִּפְנִים" וכו'. § מִבִּפְנִים עַד הֵיכָא? אָמְרִי דְּבֵי רַבִּי יַנַּאי: עַד מְקוֹם חֲבָק. אִיבַּעְיָא לְהוּ: מְקוֹם חֲבָק כְּלִפְנִים אוֹ כְּלַחוּץ? ת"ש, דְּתָנֵי רַב קְטִינָא: [ה]עַד מְקוֹם חֲבָק, וַחֲבָק עַצְמוֹ — כְּלִפְנִים. רַב חִיָּיא בְּרֵיהּ דְּרַב אָוְיָא מַתְנֵי לָהּ בְּהֶדְיָא, אָמְרִי דְּבֵי רַבִּי יַנַּאי: עַד מְקוֹם חֲבָק, וַחֲבָק עַצְמוֹ — כְּלִפְנִים. בָּעֵי רַבִּי יִרְמְיָה: כְּשִׁיר מַהוּ, כְּשׁוּרָה מַהוּ, טִיפִּין טִיפִּין מַהוּ, לְרוֹחַב יְרֵכָהּ מַהוּ? [ו]ת"ש: עַל בְּשָׂרָהּ, סָפֵק טָמֵא סָפֵק טָהוֹר — טָמֵא. עַל בְּשָׂרָהּ — מַאי לָאו כִּי הַאי גַּוְונָא? לָא, דִּלְמָא דְּעָבֵיד כִּרְצוּעָה. הַהִיא אִיתְּתָא דְּאִשְׁתַּכַּח לָהּ דָּמָא בְּמַשְׁתִּיתָא, אֲתַאי לְקַמֵּיהּ דְּרַבִּי יַנַּאי, אֲמַר לָהּ: [ז]תֵּיזִיל וְתֵיתֵי. וְהַתַּנְיָא: *אֵין שׁוֹנִין בְּטָהֳרוֹת! כִּי אָמְרִינַן "אֵין שׁוֹנִין" לְקוּלָּא, אֲבָל לְחוּמְרָא — שׁוֹנִין. § "הָיְתָה פּוֹשַׁטְתּוֹ" וכו'. § תַּנְיָא, אר"א בְּר' יוֹסֵי: דָּבָר זֶה הוֹרֵיתִי בְּעִיר רוֹמִי לְאִיסּוּר. וּכְשֶׁבָּאתִי אֵצֶל חֲכָמִים שֶׁבַּדָּרוֹם אָמְרוּ לִי יָפֶה הוֹרֵיתָ. ת"ר: [ח]אֲרוּכָּה שֶׁלָּבְשָׁה חֲלוּקָהּ שֶׁל קְצָרָה, וּקְצָרָה שֶׁלָּבְשָׁה חֲלוּקָהּ שֶׁל אֲרוּכָּה, אִם מַגִּיעַ כְּנֶגֶד בֵּית הַתּוֹרְפָה שֶׁל אֲרוּכָּה — שְׁתֵּיהֶן טְמֵאוֹת. וְאִם לָאו, אֲרוּכָּה — טְהוֹרָה, וּקְצָרָה — טְמֵאָה. תַּנְיָא אִידָךְ: בָּדְקָה חֲלוּקָהּ (ב) וְהִשְׁאִילַתּוּ לַחֲבֵירְתָּהּ, הִיא — טְהוֹרָה, וַחֲבֵירְתָּהּ — תּוֹלָה בָּהּ. אָמַר רַב שֵׁשֶׁת: וּלְעִנְיַן דִּינָא תְּנַן, [ט]אֲבָל לְעִנְיַן טוּמְאָה — הִיא טְהוֹרָה, וַחֲבֵירְתָּהּ טְמֵאָה.

מַאי

מְדְּרַבָּנַן. דִּלְמָא אַרְגְּשָׁה, וְלָאו אַדַּעְתָּהּ. רַב אַשִׁי אָמַר. טַעְמָא דִּשְׁמוּאֵל דְּאָמַר לְעֵיל: בָּדְקָה קַרְקַע עוֹלָם כו' – לָאו מִשּׁוּם הַרְגָּשָׁה, אֶלָּא כְּרַבִּי נְחֶמְיָה ס"ל, דְּאָמַר: לֹא הִזְכִּירוּ חֲכָמִים גְּזֵרַת כֶּתֶם, אֶלָּא עַל דָּבָר הַמְקַבֵּל טוּמְאָה. הִלְכָּךְ, כָּל הָנָךְ תְּיוּבְתָּא – לָאו קוּשְׁיָא נִינְהוּ, דִּשְׁמוּאֵל לָא אַיְירֵי בְּהַרְגָּשָׁה כְּלָל. אֶלָּא רַב יִרְמְיָה מְדַפְּתִי. דְּקִבְּלָהּ לִתְיוּבְתָּא דִּלְעֵיל, וְשַׁנֵּי: מוֹדֶה שְׁמוּאֵל כו', וּמִדְּקִבְּלָהּ לִתְיוּבְתָּא – מִכְּלָל דְּטַעֲמָא דִּשְׁמוּאֵל מִשּׁוּם הַרְגָּשָׁה. וְאִי מִשּׁוּם הַרְגָּשָׁה – מַאי אִירְיָא "קַרְקַע", אֲפִילּוּ גְּלִימָא נַמִּי! בָּדְקָה בְּטַלִּית, וְיָשְׁבָה עָלֶיהָ, וְאַחַר כָּךְ מָצְאָה דָּם – טְהוֹרָה, שֶׁלֹּא הִרְגִּישָׁה! בְּצַוָּארָהּ. אִם נִמְצָא דָּם כְּנֶגֶד תּוֹרְפָהּ – יְכוֹלָה לִתְלוֹת בְּמַכָּה שֶׁל צַוָּארָהּ. שֶׁפְּעָמִים שֶׁמַּטָּה אֶת צַוָּארָהּ לְפָנֶיהָ, וְנוֹפֵל דַּם הַמַּכָּה עַל תַּחְתִּית חֲלוּקָהּ. עַל כְּתֵפָהּ. שֶׁאֵינָהּ יְכוֹלָה לִתְלוֹת, שֶׁאֵין דָּם בָּא מִכְּתֵפָהּ וְנוֹפֵל לְפָנֶיהָ – אֵין תּוֹלָה. וְאֵין אוֹמְרִים בְּיָדָהּ נְטָלַתּוּ. מִמַּכָּה שֶׁבִּכְתֵפָהּ, וֶהֱבִיאַתּוּ לְפָנֶיהָ. עָבֵיד דְּמִתְרַמֵּי. תַּחַת אוֹתוֹ מָקוֹם, וְדָם נוֹטֵף עָלָיו. עַל קִשְׁרֵי אֶצְבְּעוֹתֶיהָ. הַיְינוּ, "גַּב הַיָּד". וְהָא גַּב הַיָּד, אֲפִילּוּ בִּשְׁעַת בְּדִיקָה, לֹא נָגְעָה – מ"ט טְמֵאָה? לָאו מִשּׁוּם דְּאָמְרִינַן. בָּדְקָה בְּאִידָךְ יָדָא, וְנָגְעָה יָד שֶׁבָּדְקָה עַל גַּב חֲבֵירְתָּהּ. עַד הֵיכָא. קָרוּי "פְּנִים מֵעוֹבִי הַשּׁוֹק", וְלָא אָמְרִינַן לְדָדִין נִינְהוּ? עַד מְקוֹם חֲבָק. סָפֵק. וְכִמְדוּמֶּה לִי שֶׁהוּא קֶפֶן הַיָּרֵךְ וְהַשּׁוֹק, שֶׁקּוֹרִין ייר"ט. וְקָאָמַר: עַד מָקוֹם שֶׁהוּא מַתְחִיל – קָרוּי "פְּנִים". וַחֲבָק הִיא מְתִיחַת הַגִּידִין שֶׁחוֹבְקִין הַיָּרֵךְ וְהַשּׁוֹק יַחַד, סָמוּךְ לְאוֹתוֹ קֶפֶן, כְּמוֹ (שבת דף סד.) "אֶת הַקִּילְקִי וְאֶת הַחֲבָק". כְּשִׁיר. רְלוּעָה בְּעִיגּוּל, כְּצָמִיד. מַהוּ. מִי מְסַפְּקִינַן בְּדַם הַנִּדָּה אוֹ לָאו? כִּרְצוּעָה. לְאוֹרֶךְ הַיָּרֵךְ דְּהַיְינוּ אוֹרְחֵיהּ כְּשֶׁנּוֹפֵל וְשׁוֹתֵת נַעֲשֶׂה כִּרְלוּעָה. בְּמַשְׁתִּיתָא. "עִם הַמַּסֶּכֶת" דְּשִׁמְשׁוֹן (שופטים טז) מְתַרְגְּמִינַן: עִם מַשְׁתִּיתָא. שֶׁהָיְתָה מַסֶּכֶת טָווּי לֶאֱרִיג, וְנִמְצָא דָּם עַל הַשְּׁתִי. תֵּיזִיל וְתֵיתֵי. כְּדֶרֶךְ שֶׁעָשְׂתָה עַד עַכְשָׁיו, שֶׁהָלְכָה וְשָׁבָה. אִי מִתְרַמֵּי שֶׁהַטָּווּי הַמּוּסָּךְ, שֶׁקּוֹרִין אורדי"ר, בָּא בֵּין רַגְלֶיהָ כְּנֶגֶד אוֹתוֹ מָקוֹם – טְמֵאָה. וְהָתַנְיָא אֵין שׁוֹנִין בְּטָהֳרוֹת. גַּבֵּי "מִתְעַטֵּף בְּטַלִּיתוֹ וְטָהֳרוֹת וּטְמֵאוֹת בְּלִבּוֹ", בְּפ"ק (לעיל דף ה:) סָפֵק נָגַע סָפֵק לֹא נָגַע – טָהוֹר. וְאִם אִי אֶפְשָׁר אא"כ נָגַע – טָמֵא. רַבָּן שִׁמְעוֹן בֶּן גַּמְלִיאֵל אוֹמֵר: אע"פ דְּלֹא אֶפְשָׁר – לָא מְטַמֵּינַן לֵיהּ, אֶלָּא אוֹמְרִים לוֹ "שְׁנֵה", וְאִי לָא נָגַע – מְטַהֲרִינַן לֵיהּ. אָמְרוּ לוֹ: אֵין שׁוֹנִין בְּטָהֳרוֹת. דְּאַף עַל גַּב דְּהַשְׁתָּא לָא מִיתְרַמֵּי, דִּלְמָא מֵעִיקָּרָא לָא הֲוָה הָכִי! כִּי אָמְרִינַן אֵין שׁוֹנִין לְקוּלָּא. כְּגוֹן בְּהַהִיא דְּלָא לוֹ אא"כ נָגַע, וְטָמֵא, וַאֲנַן נֵיקוּ וְנֵימָא לֵיהּ "שְׁנֵה", לְהָקֵל. אֲבָל הָכָא חוּמְרָא הוּא: דְּמִסְּתָמָא טְהוֹרָה, דְּהָא לֹא עַל בְּשָׂרָהּ וְלֹא עַל חֲלוּקָהּ אִשְׁתַּכַּח. וְהַאי דְּאָמַר "תֵּיזִיל וְתֵיתֵי, וְאִי מִתְרַמֵּי, מְטַמֵּינַן לָהּ" – חוּמְרָא הִיא. דָּבָר זֶה. הָיְתָה פוֹשַׁטְתּוֹ וּמִתְכַּסָּה בּוֹ בַּלַּיְלָה כו'. חֲלוּקָהּ שֶׁל קְצָרָה. וְלֹא בְּדָקַתּוּ קוֹדֶם לְבִישָׁה, וְאַחַר כָּךְ נִמְצָא עָלָיו דָּם. אִם מַגִּיעַ. כֶּתֶם. כְּנֶגֶד בֵּית הַתּוֹרְפָה. שֶׁל אֲרוּכָּה – טְמֵאָה אַף אֲרוּכָּה, וְכ"ש קְצָרָה. וְאִם לָאו טְהוֹרָה. הָאֲרוּכָּה, אֲבָל קְצָרָה – טְמֵאָה, שֶׁהֲרֵי כְּנֶגֶד בֵּית הַתּוֹרְפָה שֶׁלָּהּ הוּא מַגִּיעַ. הִיא טְהוֹרָה. הָרִאשׁוֹנָה. וּלְעִנְיַן דִּינָא. דִּכְבוּס הַכֶּתֶם מִן הֶחָלוּק תְּנַן דַּחֲבֵירְתָּהּ תּוֹלָה בָּהּ, דְּאָמְרָה אַחֲרוֹנָה: "לָא מְהֵימַנְתְּ לִי, דְּאַתְּ בְּדַקְתֵּיהּ". שְׁתֵּיהֶן

**כרבי** נחמיה דאמר כל דבר שאינו מקבל טומאה כו' – טעמא דרבי נחמיה: כיון דדבר שהכתם בו – טהור, גם על האשה לא גזרו טומאה. והיא (ג) משתיתא דבסמוך, נהי דלא מקבלה טומאה, מ"מ מקבל טומאה בנגעים. ***מודה** שמואל שהיא טמאה מדרבנן. פי' הקונטרס: דתלינן דלמא ארגשה, ולאו אדעתה. ואין נראה: דאפילו מוחזק לה שלא הרגישה – טמאה, הואיל וראתה דם נדות. ורב אשי נמי מודה א] דלשמואל, היכא דלא הרגישה – טהורה מן התורה, וטמאה מדרבנן. אלא אתי לפרושי דכי נמצא אקרקע דטהורה – אפילו מדרבנן. **ומי** מחזקינן טומאה ממקום למקום. – וקשה: דמאי פריך, דודאי להקל – לא מחזקינן, אבל להחמיר, כי הכא – מחמרינן. דהכי אמר לקמן: אין שונין בטהרות להקל, אבל לחומרא שונין! ויש לומר: כיון דכתמים דרבנן, אי איתא דתלינן להחמיר – להקל נמי היה לנו לתלות, בדבר הרגיל קצת. אבל לענין ממקום למקום, שאין רגילות כל כך – אמרינן לקמן בסמוך, דאפילו בכתמים שונין לחומרא, ולא להקל. תימה: דליפרוך ממתניתין "שלא כנגד התורפה – טהורה", ולא אמר: בדקה בהאי ידא ונגעה בבשרה למעלה מן התורפה! וי"ל: דאם איתא דבדקה ומצאה טמאה – היתה זכורה, והויא רמיא אדעתה שהיא טמאה. אבל כי נגעה בדם שעל כתפה – לא רמיא אנפשה, כיון דאין זה דם טמא. ובסמוך גבי דם טמא, דפריך: ואימא דבדקה בהאי ידא ונגעה באידך – פריך מכ"ש וממתניתין נמי הוה מצי למפרך. (ד) *ויש לחלק בין "ממקום למקום" דהכא, להההוא דפ"ק (לעיל דף ד.) דהתם – טומאה עצמה באה ממקום למקום, והכא – טומאה עצמה במקום אחד עומדת. **מקום** חבק. פרש"י: שהוא קפן הירך והשוק. ו"חבק" הוא מקום מתיחת הגידים, שחובקים הירך והשוק. ובערוך פירש: שנועלין אנפליאות שיש בה לולאות, ומקום חבור הלולאות קרי "חבק". ועוד פירש פירוש אחר: שכופף השוק על הירך, מה שמתכסה הבשר ע"י כפיפת השוק על ירך שחובקין זה את זה קרי "מקום חבק". **כשורה** מהו. אומר ר"י: דהיינו, טיפין טיפין. דאי מחוברת השורה יחד – היינו "רלועה", דבסמוך. וטיפין טיפין – היינו מעורבין, שאינו לא כשיר ולא כשורה. והא דאמר לקמן: טיפין טיפין, אין מצטרפין – היינו, על הבגד. והכא איירי על בשרה. דיש יותר לתלות בדם מאכולת על הבגד מעל בשרה. **ולענין** דינא תנן. וא"ת: מדינא נמי תתחייב השניה לכנסו, כדאמר ב"המדיר" (כתובות עו:) כל שנולד ספק ברשותו – עליו להביא ראיה! וי"ל: כיון דאינה לשניה אלא בתורת שאלה – אינה ממש ברשותו. ועוד יש לומר: דהתם קאמר שאם ירצה להוציא – יוציא ראיה. אבל הכא – לא תתחייב האחרונה לכנסו *).

*) (ועי' היטיב סוגיא בהמדיר דף עו: וע"ע תוס' חולין נא. ד"ה המוליך)

[לקמן נט:]

[לעיל ה:]

שייך לעיל

ט א מיי' פ"ט מהל' איסורי ביאה הל"ז [סמג לאוין קיא] טוש"ע יו"ד סי' קצ סעי' י:
י ב מיי' פ"ט מהל' איסורי ביאה הל' כה סמג לאוין קיא טוש"ע יו"ד סי' קצ סעי' יא וסעיף יח:
יא ג ד ה מיי' שם הל"ח טוש"ע שם סעיף יא:
יב ו מיי' שם הל"ט טוש"ע שם סעי' ט:
יג ז טוש"ע שם סעי' לב:
יד ח מיי' שם הל' לא טוש"ע שם סעי' מח:
טו ט מיי' שם הל' ל וע"ש טוש"ע שם סעיף מ:

גי' מהר"מ ויש לחלק בין כו' והוא ענין בפני עצמו

### הגהות הב"ח

(א) גמ' מכה בצוארה מקום שתוכל: (ב) שם תניא אידך בדקה חלוקה. נ"ב ס"א עצמה וחלוקה: (ג) תוס' ד"ה כר' נחמיה וכו' והיא משתיתא. נ"ב עי' באשר"י בפי' האשה: (ד) ד"ה ומי וכו' הוה מצי למפרך והא דאמר בפ"ק דלא מחזקינן טומאה ממקום למקום כו' יש לחלק בין:

### הגהות מהר"ב רנשבורג

א] תוד"ה מודה וכו' ורב אשי נמי מודה. נ"ב עי' שו"ת רמ"א סי' לז בריש דבריו דלא משמע הכי ועי' סד"ט סי' קצ דף מה ע"א ד"ה וטרם אכלה בדיני כתמים ויעו"ש עוד סי' קפג ס"ק ב':

### תוספי הרא"ש

פריך מינה תחילה: **על** כתיפה אינה תולה. וא"ת דילמא לקולא דוקא אבל לחומרא כמו על גודלה מחזקינן טומאה ממקום למקום. וי"ל כיון דכל עיקר כתמים הם מדרבנן ומקילינן בהו כדתנן בפירקין אי מחזקינן דם ממקום למקום לחומרא ה"ה לקולא. ותימה ליפרוך ממתניתין שלא כנגד בית התורפה טהורה ולא אמרינן שמא בדקה בחד ידא ונגעה בבשרה שלא כנגד בית התורפה. וי"ל דאם איתא דבדקה בידה ומצאה טמא היתה זכורה שאין דרך אשה לשכוח כשהיא בודקת ומוצאה עצמה טמאה. והא דפריך בסמוך גבי דם טמא דאימר בדקה בחד ידא ונגעה באידך ידא מכ"ש פריך דבעלמ' אית לן למימר הכי ועל מתנינין הוה מצי למיפרך: **עד** מקום חבק. פרש"י חבק מקום מתיחת הגידים שחובקים הירך והשוק וכנגד אותו חבק למטה עד פרסת רגלי' ולמעלה עד אותו מקום גרוי בפנים ומקום חבק דהיינו רוחב הגידים מיבעיא ליה אי כלפנים אי כלחוץ. ובערוך פ' כשמעלין את השוק באנפלאות שיש להם לולאות ומקום חיבוק הלולאות קרי ליה חבק. עוד פי' כשכופפת שוקה על ירכה מה שמכוסה מן הבשר על ידי כפיפת השוק על הירך הוי מקום חבק על שם שמחבקין זה את זה: **כשורה** היינו טיפין עשויין כשורה דאי בלא טיפין היינו כרצועה דקאמר בסמוך. וטיפין טיפין היינו עשויין בשינוי דאי לאו הכי למה יש להסתפק בטיפין ורבינו שמואל פירש כשורה היינו הרבה שורות. וטיפין טיפין מצינן לפרושי עשויין כשורה או כשיר והא דאמרינן בשילהי פירקין טיפין טיפין אין מצטרפין היינו כי נמצאו על הבגד שיש לספק כל טיפה בדם מאכולת: **לאו** לאיתויי כה"ג. תימה מנא ליה דאתא לאיתויי דילמא בכתם כי אורחיה מיירי. וי"ל מדקאמר האי לישנא ספק טהור ספק טמא ולא קאמר על בשרה ספק טמא משמע דאתא לאשמועינן שום חידוש בכתם משונה: **לענין** דינא תנן. הקשה הריב"י לענין דינא נמי נימא כאן נמצאו כאן היו כדאמרינן בשילהי המדיר גבי מומין וגבי טריפות. י"ל דהתם נשתנית האשה מרשות האב עצמה לרשות הבעל והפרה מרשות המוכר לרשות לוקח אבל הכא לא יצא החלוק מרשות בעלת החלוק דאינו ביד השניה בתורת מתנה ומכר אלא בתורת שאלה. ועי"ל דלא אמרינן כאן נמצאו וכאן היו אלא שאם השני בא להוציא מיד הראשון כי התם שהוא בא להוציא האשה מביתו ולפוטרה בלא כתובה ולהוציאה מחזקתה הילכך אומרת לו ברשותך נולדו המומין

טז א מיי' פ"ט מהל' איסורי ביאה הלכ"ו סמג לאוין קיח טוש"ע יו"ד סי' קצ סעי' כה:
יז ב ג מיי' שם הל' כז טוש"ע שם סעי' יח:
יח ד מיי' שם הל' כג טוש"ע שם סעיף ה:
יט ה מיי' שם הל' כד טוש"ע שם סעי' יט:
כ ו ז מיי' שם הל' כב טוש"ע שם סעי' יח:
כא ח מיי' שם פ"ד הל' יח סמג שם טוש"ע שם סעיף לד:
כב ט מיי' שם פ"ט הל' כז סמג שם טוש"ע שם סעי' יח:
כג י מיי' הל' שם טוש"ע שם סעי' כב:
כד כ טוש"ע שם סעי' ז:
כה ל מיי' פ"י מהל' תרומות הלי"ג:
כו מ מיי' פ"ט מהל' איסורי ביאה הל' כח סמג לאוין קיא טוש"ע יו"ד סי' קצ סעי' כב:
כז נ מיי' שם הל' כג טוש"ע שם סעיף ה:

מאי שְׁנָא מֵהָא דְּתַנְיָא: *אשְׁתֵּי נָשִׁים שֶׁנִּתְעַסְּקוּ בְּצִפּוֹר אֶחָד, וְאֵין בּוֹ אֶלָּא כְּסֶלַע דָּם, וְנִמְצָא כְּסֶלַע עַל זוֹ וּכְסֶלַע עַל זוֹ — שְׁתֵּיהֶן טְמֵאוֹת? שָׁאנֵי הָתָם — דְּאִיכָּא סֶלַע יְתֵירָה. ת"ר: בלָבְשָׁה שְׁלֹשָׁה חֲלוּקוֹת הַבְּדוּקִין לָהּ, אִם יְכוֹלָה לִתְלוֹת — תּוֹלָה, וַאֲפִילּוּ בַּתַּחְתּוֹן. *אֵין יְכוֹלָה לִתְלוֹת — אֵינָהּ תּוֹלָה, וַאֲפִי' בָּעֶלְיוֹן. כֵּיצַד, עָבְרָה בְּשׁוּק שֶׁל טַבָּחִים — תּוֹלָה, אֲפִילּוּ בַּתַּחְתּוֹן. לֹא עָבְרָה בְּשׁוּק שֶׁל טַבָּחִים — אַף בָּעֶלְיוֹן אֵינָהּ תּוֹלָה.§ **מתני'** גוְתוֹלָה בְּכָל דָּבָר שֶׁהִיא יְכוֹלָה לִתְלוֹת: שָׁחֲטָה בְּהֵמָה חַיָּה וְעוֹף, נִתְעַסְּקָה בִּכְתָמִים, אוֹ שֶׁיָּשְׁבָה בְּצַד הָעֲסוּקִין בָּהֶן, *הָרְגָה מַאֲכוֹלֶת — הֲרֵי זוֹ תּוֹלָה בָּהּ. עַד כַּמָּה תּוֹלָה? רַבִּי חֲנִינָא בֶּן אַנְטִיגְנוֹס אוֹמֵר: דעַד כִּגְרִיס שֶׁל פּוֹל, וְאַף עַל פִּי שֶׁלֹּא הָרְגָה. *הוְתוֹלָה בִּבְנָהּ אוֹ בְּבַעְלָהּ. ואִם יֵשׁ בָּהּ מַכָּה, וְהִיא יְכוֹלָה לְהִגָּלַע וּלְהוֹצִיא דָּם — הֲרֵי זוֹ תּוֹלָה. מַעֲשֶׂה בְּאִשָּׁה אַחַת שֶׁבָּאת לִפְנֵי ר"ע, אָמְרָה לוֹ: רָאִיתִי כֶּתֶם. אָמַר לָהּ: שֶׁמָּא מַכָּה הָיְתָה בִּיךְ? אָמְרָה לוֹ: הֵן, וְחָיְתָה. אָמַר לָהּ: שֶׁמָּא יְכוֹלָה לְהִגָּלַע וּלְהוֹצִיא דָּם? אָמְרָה לוֹ: הֵן. זוְטִהֲרָהּ ר"ע. *רָאָה תַּלְמִידָיו מִסְתַּכְּלִין זֶה בָּזֶה, אָמַר לָהֶם: מַה הַדָּבָר קָשֶׁה בְּעֵינֵיכֶם? *שֶׁלֹּא אָמְרוּ חֲכָמִים הַדָּבָר לְהַחְמִיר — אֶלָּא לְהָקֵל, שֶׁנֶּאֱמַר: °"וְאִשָּׁה כִּי תִהְיֶה זָבָה דָּם יִהְיֶה זוֹבָהּ בִּבְשָׂרָהּ", "דָּם" — וְלֹא כֶּתֶם. [ויקרא טו] חעַד שֶׁהוּא נָתוּן תַּחַת הַכַּר וְנִמְצָא עָלָיו דָּם, עָגוֹל — טָהוֹר, מָשׁוּךְ — טָמֵא, דִּבְרֵי ר"א בְּרַבִּי צָדוֹק.§ **גמ'** תָּנֵינָא לְהָא דְּת"ר: *מַעֲשֶׂה וְתָלָה ר"מ בְּקִילוֹר, וְרַבִּי תָּלָה בְּשְׂרַף שִׁקְמָה.§ "אוֹ שֶׁיָּשְׁבָה".§ יָשְׁבָה — אִין, לֹא יָשְׁבָה — לָא. תָּנֵינָא לְהָא דְּת"ר: טעָבְרָה בְּשׁוּק שֶׁל טַבָּחִים, סָפֵק נִיתַּז עָלֶיהָ סָפֵק לֹא נִיתַּז עָלֶיהָ — תּוֹלָה, יסָפֵק עָבְרָה סָפֵק לֹא עָבְרָה — טְמֵאָה.§ "הָרְגָה מַאֲכוֹלֶת".§ הָרְגָה — אִין, לֹא הָרְגָה — לָא. מַתְנִי' מַנִּי? רשב"ג הִיא, דְּתַנְיָא: הָרְגָה — תּוֹלָה, לֹא הָרְגָה — אֵינָהּ תּוֹלָה, דִּבְרֵי רשב"ג. וַחכ"א: בֵּין כָּךְ וּבֵין כָּךְ — תּוֹלָה. אָמַר רשב"ג: לְדִבְרֵי אֵין קֵץ, וּלְדִבְרֵי חֲבֵרַי אֵין סוֹף. לְדִבְרַי אֵין קֵץ — שֶׁאֵין לְךָ אִשָּׁה שֶׁטְּהוֹרָה לְבַעְלָהּ, שֶׁאֵין לְךָ כָּל מִטָּה וּמִטָּה שֶׁאֵין בָּהּ כַּמָּה טִיפֵּי דַּם מַאֲכוֹלֶת. לְדִבְרֵי חֲבֵרַי אֵין סוֹף — שֶׁאֵין לְךָ אִשָּׁה שֶׁאֵינָהּ טְהוֹרָה לְבַעְלָהּ, שֶׁאֵין לְךָ כָּל סָדִין וְסָדִין שֶׁאֵין בּוֹ כַּמָּה טִיפֵּי דָּם. אֲבָל נִרְאִין דִּבְרֵי ר' חֲנִינָא בֶּן אַנְטִיגְנוֹס מִדְּבָרַי וּמִדִּבְרֵיהֶם, שֶׁהָיָה אוֹמֵר: עַד כַּמָּה הִיא תּוֹלָה — עַד כִּגְרִיס שֶׁל פּוֹל, א]וְלִדְבָרָיו אָנוּ מוֹדִים. וּלְרַבָּנַן דְּאָמְרִי תּוֹלָה, עַד כַּמָּה? אָמַר ר"נ בַּר יִצְחָק: כתּוֹלָה בְּפִשְׁפֵּשׁ — וְעַד *כְּתוּרְמוּס. ת"ר: פִּשְׁפֵּשׁ זֶה, אָרְכּוֹ כְּרָחְבּוֹ, וְטַעְמוֹ כְּרֵיחוֹ, בְּרִית כְּרוּתָה לוֹ — שֶׁכָּל הַמּוֹלְלוֹ מֵרִיחַ בּוֹ. אָרְכּוֹ כְּרָחְבּוֹ — לְעִנְיַן כְּתָמִים, טַעְמוֹ כְּרֵיחוֹ — לְעִנְיַן תְּרוּמָה. *דִּתְנַן: לאוֹ שֶׁטָּעַם טַעַם פִּשְׁפֵּשׁ בְּפִיו — ה"ז יִפְלוֹט. מְנָא יָדַע? טַעְמוֹ כְּרֵיחוֹ. וְאַכַּתִּי מְנָא יָדַע? בְּרִית כְּרוּתָה לוֹ, שֶׁכָּל הַמּוֹלְלוֹ מֵרִיחַ בּוֹ. אָמַר רַב אַשִׁי: מעִיר שֶׁיֵּשׁ בָּהּ חֲזִירִים — אֵין חוֹשְׁשִׁין לִכְתָמִים. אָמַר ר"נ בַּר יִצְחָק: *וְהָא דְּדוּקֶרֶת — כְּעִיר שֶׁיֵּשׁ בָּהּ חֲזִירִים דָּמְיָא.§ "עַד כַּמָּה הִיא תּוֹלָה" וכו'.§ אָמַר רַב הוּנָא: כִּגְרִיס — אֵינָהּ תּוֹלָה, פָּחוֹת מִכִּגְרִיס — תּוֹלָה. וְרַב חִסְדָּא אָמַר: נכִּגְרִיס — תּוֹלָה, יָתֵר מִכִּגְרִיס — אֵינָהּ תּוֹלָה. לֵימָא בְּעַד וְעַד בִּכְלָל קָא מִיפַּלְגִי, דְּרַב הוּנָא סָבַר: *עַד — וְלֹא עַד בִּכְלָל, וְרַב חִסְדָּא סָבַר: עַד — וְעַד בִּכְלָל. אָמַר לְךָ רַב הוּנָא: אִיכָּא עַד וְעַד בִּכְלָל, וְאִיכָּא עַד וְלֹא עַד בִּכְלָל, וְהָכָא לְחוּמְרָא וְהָכָא לְחוּמְרָא. וְרַב חִסְדָּא אָמַר לְךָ: בְּעָלְמָא אֵימָא לְךָ — לְחוּמְרָא אָמְרִינַן, לְקוּלָּא לָא אָמְרִינַן. וְהָכָא — כִּדְרַבִּי אַבָּהוּ, *דְּא"ר אַבָּהוּ: כָּל שִׁיעוּרֵי חֲכָמִים — לְהַחְמִיר, חוּץ מִכִּגְרִיס שֶׁל כְּתָמִים — לְהָקֵל. אִיכָּא דְּאָמְרִי לָהּ לְהָא שְׁמַעְתָּא בְּאַפֵּי נַפְשָׁהּ. רַב הוּנָא אָמַר: כִּגְרִיס — כְּיָתֵר מִכִּגְרִיס, וְרַב חִסְדָּא אָמַר: כִּגְרִיס — כְּפָחוֹת מִכִּגְרִיס, וְקָמִיפַּלְגִי בְּ"עַד וְעַד" דְּהָכָא, כִּדְאָמְרִינַן. מֵיתִיבֵי:

הָיוּ

**רש"י**

שְׁתֵּיהֶן טְמֵאוֹת. וְלָא תָּלִינַן אֶחָד מִן הַכְּתָמִים בַּצִּפּוֹר, וְאַע"ג דְּאִיכָּא לְמִתְלֵי. וְה"נ, אַע"ג דְּבָדְקָה, לֵימָא: שְׁתֵּיהֶן טְמֵאוֹת. דְּאֵימוֹר: לָאו יָפֶה בָּדְקָה. סֶלַע יְתֵירָה. וּמַאי חֲזֵית דְּתָלֵית לֵיהּ לְסֶלַע יְתֵירָה דִּטְמֵאָה בְּהַךְ? תָּלְיֵיהּ בְּהַךְ! הִלְכָּךְ, שְׁתֵּיהֶן טְמֵאוֹת. אֲבָל הָכָא – טוּמְאָה תְּלוּיָה בְּהַךְ דְּלָא בָּדְקָה. שְׁלֹשָׁה חֲלוּקוֹת. זֶה עַל גַּב זֶה. יְכוֹלָה לִתְלוֹת. כִּדְמְפָרֵשׁ: עָבְרָה בְּשׁוּק שֶׁל טַבָּחִים. [תוספתא דמקואות פ"ב] **מתני'** עַד כַּמָּה הִיא תּוֹלָה. בְּדַם מַאֲכוֹלֶת? כִּגְרִיס. אֲבָל טְפֵי מֵהָכִי – אֵין דַּם מַאֲכוֹלֶת כָּל כָּךְ גָּדוֹל, וּבְהָכִי מִיהָא תָּלְיֵיהּ. וְאַע"פ שֶׁלֹּא הָרְגָה. וְרַבִּי חֲנִינָא פָּלֵיג אַדְּרַבָּנַן, דְּקָאָמְרִי: הָרְגָה – אִין, לֹא הָרְגָה – לָא. [נ"ל אינה] וְתוֹלָה בִּבְנָהּ וּבְבַעְלָהּ. אִם יֵשׁ בָּהֶם מַכָּה. וְאִם יֵשׁ בָּהּ מַכָּה. יְבֵשָׁה וּרְאוּיָה לְהִגָּלַע, כְּלוֹמַר, לְהִתְקַלְקֵל וּלְהוֹצִיא דָּם – תּוֹלָה. **גמ'** קִילוֹר. אִפְלַשְׁטוּר"א, חָדוּשׁ. לֹא יָשְׁבָה לָא. וְלָא אָמְרִינַן: דִּלְמָא יָשְׁבָה וְלָאו אַדַּעְתָּהּ. לְדִבְרַי אֵין קֵץ. שֶׁאֲנִי נוֹתֵן שִׁיעוּר, וְאִם לֹא הָרְגָה – אֲפִילּוּ כְּחַרְדָּל, טְמֵאָה. [לעיל יט:] "וּלְדִבְרֵי חֲבֵרַי אֵין סוֹף" – שֶׁהֵם מְקִילִּים יוֹתֵר מִדַּאי, דַּאֲפִילּוּ לֹא הָרְגָה – תּוֹלָה. וְאֵין נוֹתְנִין שִׁיעוּר, אֶלָּא אֲפִילּוּ כְּסֶלַע – תּוֹלָה, אוֹ יוֹתֵר. [שם] עַד כִּגְרִים. וַאֲפִילּוּ לֹא הָרְגָה. וְיָתֵר מִכִּגְרִים – לֹא, וַאֲפִילּוּ הָרְגָה. וְלִדְבָרָיו יֵשׁ לְטַמֵּא כִּגְרִים וְעוֹד, וּלְטַהֵר פָּחוֹת מִכִּגְרִים. עַד כַּמָּה. כְּלוֹמַר, וְכִי אֶפְשָׁר לִתְלוֹת כֶּתֶם גָּדוֹל בְּמַאֲכוֹלֶת? אָמַר ר"נ תּוֹלָה בְּפִשְׁפֵּשׁ עַד כְּתוּרְמוּס. [לעיל מה.] כֶּתֶם רָחָב כְּתוּרְמוּס – יְכוֹלָה לִתְלוֹת, וְלֹא בְּמַאֲכוֹלֶת אֶלָּא בְּפִשְׁפֵּשׁ. שֶׁמָּא פִּשְׁפֵּשׁ הָרְגָה, שֶׁכִּתְמוֹ גָּדוֹל. [חולין נה. ע"ש] פִּשְׁפֵּשׁ – פּוּנֵייש"א בְּלַעַ"ז. בְּרִית כְּרוּתָה לוֹ. כְּלוֹמַר, רֵיחוֹ נוֹדֵף וּמַבְאִישׁ. וְכָל הַמּוֹלְלוֹ, עַל כָּרְחוֹ מֵרִיחַ רֵיחוֹ. [לעיל יט:] לְעִנְיַן כְּתָמִים. דְּאִי הָוֵה כֶּתֶם אָרְכּוֹ כְּרָחְבּוֹ, אֲפִילּוּ יוֹתֵר מִכִּגְרִים – תָּלִינַן בְּפִשְׁפֵּשׁ. אוֹ שֶׁטָּעַם טַעַם פִּשְׁפֵּשׁ. בְּאוֹכֵל תְּרוּמָה מַיְירֵי, *וְכ"ש חוּלִּין – דְּהָא שֶׁרֶץ הוּא. [נ"ל וה"ה] אֶלָּא הַאי דְּנָקַט "תְּרוּמָה" – מִשּׁוּם דִּפְלִיגֵי לְעֵיל מִינֵּיהּ: אָמְרוּ לוֹ "נִטְמֵאתָ, וְנִטְמֵאת הַתְּרוּמָה" – ר"א אוֹמֵר: יִבְלַע. ר' יְהוֹשֻׁעַ אוֹמֵר: יִפְלוֹט. אֲבָל (א) אוֹמֵר לוֹ "טָמֵא הָיִיתָ, וּטְמֵאָה הָיְתָה הַתְּרוּמָה", אוֹ שֶׁנּוֹדַע שֶׁהוּא טֶבֶל, אוֹ שֶׁטָּעַם טַעַם פִּשְׁפֵּשׁ לְתוֹךְ פִּיו – ה"ז יִפְלוֹט. הוֹאִיל וְעַד שֶׁלֹּא נְתָנָהּ לְתוֹךְ פִּיו, אֵירַע בָּהּ פְּסוּל זֶה – לָא חָיְישִׁינַן לְהֶפְסֵד תְּרוּמָה. [פירש"י בפ' אין לדין (דף כה:) שהוא מין קיטנית עגול כמין עדשה ורחב כמעה קטנה כו'] [תרומות פ"ח מ"ב] מְנָא יָדַע. טַעַם פִּשְׁפֵּשׁ? וְאַכַּתִּי מְנָא יָדַע. וַהֲלֹא לָא הֵרִיחַ בּוֹ? חֲזִירִים. אוֹכְלִים שְׁקָלִים וּרְמָשִׂים, וּמַתִּיזִים דָּם. דְּדוּקֶרֶת. טַבָּחִים הַרְבֵּה וְאַשְׁפּוֹת וּשְׁקָלִים מְצוּיִין בָּהּ. [נ"ל והאי] וְהָכָא לְחוּמְרָא. הִלְכָּךְ, עַד וְלֹא עַד בִּכְלָל. דְּאִי עַד וְעַד בִּכְלָל – הָוֵה לֵיהּ קוּלָּא, דְּקָתָנֵי "עַד כִּגְרִיס תּוֹלָה". וְקַיְימָא לָן בְּ"אֵלּוּ טְרֵיפוֹת" (חולין נה.) דְּבָכָל עַד אָזְלִינַן לְחוּמְרָא: אִי עַד וְעַד חוּמְרָא הוּא – אָזְלִינַן בָּתְרֵיהּ, וְאִי עַד וְלֹא עַד חוּמְרָא הוּא – אָזְלִינַן בָּתְרֵיהּ. [ברכות כו: וש"נ] אָמְרִי לָהּ בְּאַנְפֵּי נַפְשָׁהּ. וְלָאו אַמַּתְנִי'. ה"ג: וְקָמִיפַּלְגִי בְּעַד וְעַד דְּהָכָא. כִּדְאָמַר רַב הוּנָא: לְחוּמְרָא, כִּדְאָמְרִינַן בְּכָל דּוּכְתֵּי. הִלְכָּךְ, עַד וְלֹא עַד בִּכְלָל. וּלְרַב חִסְדָּא כְּרַבִּי אַבָּהוּ. [חולין נה. ע"ש]

טִיפֵּי

**תוספות**

**מאי** שנא מהא דתניא ב' נשים כו'. תימה: מה דומה להך דלעיל? דהכא – אין לתלות בזו יותר מבזו, אבל לעיל – אין לתלות בראשונה, הואיל ובדקה! ואומר ר"ת: דברייתא איירי שנתעסקה בצפור זו אחר זו. ואם היתה נשאלת הראשונה – היינו מטהרין אותה, הואיל ונתעסקה. ובשביל חברתה – אנו מטמאין הראשונה שהיא טהורה גמורה. גם למעלה, אע"פ שהראשונה בדוקה – נטמאנה, הואיל ושניה תולה בה לענין דינא.

**אין** לך כל מטה ומטה. הכא לא נקט "סדין וסדין", כדבסמוך – משום דהכא בעי למימר: מטה, אפילו של איש, שאין בה כמה טיפין של דם מאכולת – אם כן ה"נ של אשה יש לנו לתלות במאכולת. אבל בסמוך לא איירי אלא בשל אשה, להכי נקט סדין. (ב) **וכדבריו** אנו מודים. ומיהו היכא דהרגה הרבה מאכולת או פשפש – תולה, כפי מה שהרגה, מידי דהוה אשוק של טבחים. **עיר** שיש בה חזירים אין חוששין בכתמים. אומר רשב"ם: דאפי' יותר מכגרים, ואפי' מן החגור ולמטה, ואפילו לא נתעסקה, ואין לה מכה שיש לה להגלע ולהוציא דם. מיהו אור"י: דאין לסמוך על זה עכשיו להקל, כשמוצאה כתמים במקום שאין רגילות ליגע בהן חזירים. וכן מנהג דלא תלינן. ומיהו במקום שיש רגילים לדבר שיש לתלות בחזירים וכיוצא בהן – תלינן, כדקאמר התלמוד.

היו

**הגהות הגר"א**

א] גמ' ולדבריו אנו מודים נמחק ונ"ב וכדבריו אנו מודים:

**הגהות הב"ח**

(א) רש"י ד"ה או שטעם וכו' אבל אמרו לו טמא היית וטמאה היתה התרומה: (ב) תום' ד"ה ולדבריו נו:

**תוספי הרא"ש**

המומין. וכן לענין טריפות בא הלוקח להוציא מיד המוכר אבל לחייב השני לא: **ואין** בו אלא סלע כו'. תימה מאי פירכא היא זו שאני הכא דהי מינייהו מפקת אבל לעיל שבדקה הראשונה למה נטמאה. ותירץ ר"ת דהכא מיירי שנתעסקה האחת תחלה ואח"כ חברתה ואפי' נתעסקו ביחד אי אפשר לצמצם שלא התחילה האחת תחלה וא"כ היה לנו לתלות דם צפור בראשונה ולטהרה כהך דלעיל שהיתה בדוקה ומשני כיון דאיכא סלע יתירה איכא לתלות בזו כמו בזו אע"ג דהתחילה קודם חברתה אימור לא בא מיד דם הצפור עליה אבל לעיל הבדוקה בחזקת טהרה היא: **לא** ישבה לא. פי' לא ידעה אם ישבה אם לאו: **אין** לך כל מטה ומטה ובסמוך נקט כל סדין וסדין משום דעכשיו קאמר אין לך כל מטה ומטה של איש ואשה שאין בו כמה טיפי דמים של מאכולת. וא"כ של אשה נמי יש לתלות במאכולת כמו מטה של איש והדר קאמר אין לך כל סדין וסדין של אשה שאין בה כמה טיפי דמים ואין לתלות כולם בדם מאכולת: **וכדבריו** אנו מודים. פי' ר"מ דבכלל דבריו דבריהם דרבנן מודים לדבריו דכגרים תולה ובכלל דבריו דברינו דגם אני מודה לדבריו דהיכא (דהיכינה) [דהרגה] הוי שיעורא כגרים דתולה וכיון שבכלל דבריו א)נראין דברינו ונראין דבריו ודמיא לההיא דתנן בבמסכת אבות רואה אני את דברי ר' אלעזר בן ערך מדבריכם שבכלל דבריו דבריכם: **עיר** שיש בה חזירין אין חוששין לכתמים. פירש"י אפי' לא עברה בשוק של טבחים ואפי' אין מכה עליה ואפי' מחגור ולמטה כיון דשכיחי בה חזירין שהן מנקרין באשפה ומתזין דם נבילות וטריפות הוי בכל פעם כאילו עברה בשוק של טבחים. ונראה דהאידנא אין לתלות בחזירים אם מצאה כתם שאינו מצוי שיהו חזירים מתיזין דם אבל אין לומר דלטהרות דוקא קאמר כשיש לתלות בחזירים. ודדוקרת דקאמר לאותם שעושים בה טהרות בימי רב נחמן ב)(אלא כמו זבוני דמחתא דאמר רב לעיל בשלדו קיים הן טמאין דלאו היינו לבני בבל אלא לשאר מקומות שעושין בו טהרות) דהא לטהרות מחמרינן טפי מלבעלה וכיון דתלינן לטהרות לחזירים כ"ש לבעלה:

א) נראה דצ"ל וכיון שבכלל דבריו דברינו ובדבריהם משו"ה נראין דבריו להסיא וכו'. ב) צ"ל כמו אבוגי דמחוזא דאמר רבא לעיל [דף ט ע"א] דאם שלכן קיימת טמאין וע"כ דכ"מ לענין טהרות קאמר ולאו היינו וכו'.

אָהָיוּ עָלֶיהָ טִיפֵּי דָמִים לְמַטָּה, וְטִיפֵּי דָמִים לְמַעְלָה — תּוֹלָה *בָּעֶלְיוֹן עַד כִּגְרִים. מַאי לָאו — כִּגְרִים מִלְּמַטָּה? לָא, כִּגְרִים מִלְּמַעְלָה. אִיתְּמַר, נִמְצָא עָלֶיהָ כִּגְרִים וָעוֹד, וְאוֹתוֹ עוֹד — רְצוּפָה בּוֹ מַאֲכוֹלֶת, ר' חֲנִינָא אוֹמֵר: טְמֵאָה. ר' יַנַּאי אוֹמֵר: בטְהוֹרָה. רַבִּי חֲנִינָא אוֹמֵר: טְמֵאָה, כִּי תָּלְיָא — בִּכְגְרִים, בִּכְגְרִים וְעוֹד — לָא תָּלְיָא. רַבִּי יַנַּאי אוֹמֵר: טְהוֹרָה, הָנֵי מִילֵּי — הֵיכָא דְּלָא רְצוּפָה בּוֹ מַאֲכוֹלֶת, אֲבָל הֵיכָא דִּרְצוּפָה בּוֹ מַאֲכוֹלֶת — מוֹכְחָא מִילְּתָא דְּהַאי וְעוֹד דַּם מַאֲכוֹלֶת הוּא. פָּשׁ לֵיהּ — כִּגְרִים, כֵּיוָן דִּבְעָלְמָא תָּלְיָא, הָכָא נַמִי תָּלְיָא. בָּעֵי רַבִּי יִרְמְיָה: נִתְעַסְּקָה בִּכְגְרִים, וְנִמְצָא עָלֶיהָ בִּכְגְרִים וְעוֹד, מַהוּ? תִּבָּעֵי לְר' חֲנִינָא, תִּבָּעֵי לְר' יַנַּאי. תִּבָּעֵי לְר' חֲנִינָא — עַד כָּאן לָא קָאָמַר ר' חֲנִינָא הָתָם טְמֵאָה — אֶלָּא דְּלָא נִתְעַסְּקָה, אֲבָל הָכָא דְּנִתְעַסְּקָה — גתָּלְיָא? אוֹ דִּלְמָא: אֲפִילּוּ לְרַבִּי יַנַּאי דְּאָמַר טְהוֹרָה, הָנֵי מִילֵּי — הֵיכָא דִּרְצוּפָה בּוֹ מַאֲכוֹלֶת, אֲבָל הֵיכָא דְּאֵין רְצוּפָה בּוֹ מַאֲכוֹלֶת — לָא תָּלְיָא? תָּא שְׁמַע: דנִתְעַסְּקָה בְּאָדוֹם — אֵין תּוֹלָה בָּהּ שָׁחוֹר, בְּמוּעָט — אֵין תּוֹלָה בּוֹ מְרוּבֶּה. הֵיכִי דָּמֵי? לָאו כִּי הַאי גַּוְונָא? לָא, הכְּגוֹן דְּנִתְעַסְּקָה בִּכְגְרִים, וְנִמְצָא עָלֶיהָ שְׁנֵי גְרִיסִין וְעוֹד. אִי הָכִי, מַאי לְמֵימְרָא? מַהוּ דְּתֵימָא: שְׁקוֹל כִּגְרִים צִפּוֹר — שְׁדֵי בֵּי מִצְעֵי, זִיל הָכָא, לֵיכָּא שִׁיעוּרָא, זִיל הָכָא — לֵיכָּא שִׁיעוּרָא, קמ"ל. אָמַר רָבָא: נִמְצָא עָלֶיהָ מִין אֶחָד — תּוֹלָה בּוֹ כַּמָּה מִינִין. מֵיתִיבֵי: נִתְעַסְּקָה בְּאָדוֹם — אֵין תּוֹלָה בּוֹ שָׁחוֹר! נִתְעַסְּקָה שָׁאנֵי. אִיכָּא דְּאָמְרִי, אָמַר רָבָא: נִתְעַסְּקָה בְּמִין אֶחָד — תּוֹלָה בּוֹ כַּמָּה מִינִין. מֵיתִיבֵי: נִתְעַסְּקָה בְּאָדוֹם — אֵין תּוֹלָה בּוֹ שָׁחוֹר! כִּי קָאָמַר רָבָא — ודְּאִתְעַסְּקָה בְּתַרְנְגוֹלֶת, דְּאִית בָּהּ כַּמָּה מִינֵי דְּמָא.§ "מַעֲשֶׂה בְּאִשָּׁה" [וכו'].§ וְהַתַנְיָא: לֹא אָמְרוּ חֲכָמִים אֶת הַדָּבָר לְהָקֵל, אֶלָּא לְהַחְמִיר! אָמַר רָבִינָא: לֹא לְהָקֵל עַל דִּבְרֵי תוֹרָה — אֶלָּא לְהַחְמִיר עַל דִּבְרֵי תוֹרָה, זוּכְתָמִים עַצְמָן דְּרַבָּנַן.§ "עַד שֶׁהוּא נָתוּן".§ אִיבַּעְיָא לְהוּ: מִי פְּלִיגִי רַבָּנַן עֲלֵיהּ דר"א בְּרַבִּי צָדוֹק, אוֹ לָא? תָּא שְׁמַע: חכֶּתֶם אָרוֹךְ — מִצְטָרֵף, טטִפִּין טִפִּין — אֵין מִצְטָרְפִין. מַנִּי? אִי רַבִּי אֱלִיעֶזֶר בְּר' צָדוֹק — לָמָּה לִי צֵירוּף? הָאָמַר: מָשׁוּךְ כָּל שֶׁהוּא — טָמֵא! אֶלָּא לָאו — רַבָּנַן, שְׁמַע מִינַּהּ: פְּלִיגִי. לָא, לְעוֹלָם ר' אֱלִיעֶזֶר בְּרַבִּי צָדוֹק, וְכִי אָמַר רַבִּי אֱלִיעֶזֶר בְּרַבִּי צָדוֹק — בְּעֵד, אֲבָל בְּכֶתֶם — לָא. ת"ש: דְּאָמַר רַב יְהוּדָה, אָמַר שְׁמוּאֵל: הֲלָכָה כְּרַבִּי אֱלִיעֶזֶר בְּרַבִּי צָדוֹק. *הֲלָכָה מִכְּלָל דִּפְלִיגִי, שְׁמַע מִינַּהּ.§

## הדרן עלך הרואה כתם

ס"א עליון

[שבת קו: וש"נ]

---

**רש"י**

טִיפֵּי דָמִים לְמַטָּה. כְּלוֹמַר, קְטַנִּים. לְמַעְלָה. גְּדוֹלִים. כִּגְרִים מִלְּמַטָּה. (א) בִּפְחוּת מִכִּגְרִים, וְתָלֵינַן. נִמְצָא עָלֶיהָ כִּגְרִים וְעוֹד. דְּהִלְכְתָא כְּרַב חִסְדָּא, דְּמֵיקֵל. כֵּיוָן דִּבְעָלְמָא. הֵיכָא דְּלֵיכָּא וְעוֹד – תָּלְיָא כִּגְרִים בְּמַאֲכוֹלֶת, הָשְׁתָּא נַמִי תָּלְיָא הַאי גְּרִים בְּמַאֲכוֹלֶת אַחֲרִינָא. נִתְעַסְּקָה בִּכְגְרִים. דַּם צִפּוֹר אוֹ קִילוֹר. אֲבָל הָכָא דְּנִתְעַסְּקָה תָּלְיָא. כִּגְרִים בְּדַם צִפּוֹר, וְעוֹד – דַּם מַאֲכוֹלֶת הֲוֵה. מַאי לְמֵימְרָא. הָא אֲפִילּוּ תַּלְיָא כִּגְרִים בְּצִפּוֹר, אַכַּתִּי פָּשׁ לֵיהּ גְּרִיס וְעוֹד! מַהוּ דְּתֵימָא שָׁקוֹל כִּגְרִים. דַּם צִפּוֹר וְשָׁדֵי בֵּי מִצְעֵי. נִמְצָא עָלֶיהָ מִין אֶחָד. מִדָּבָר הַדּוֹמֶה לְכֶתֶם, כְּגוֹן קִילוֹר אוֹ שָׂרָף, וְאַחַר כָּךְ מָצְאָה עַל חֲלוּקָהּ כֶּתֶם אַף עַל פִּי אֵין מַרְאִיתוֹ דּוֹמֶה לְאוֹתוֹ הַמִּין, תּוֹלָה בּוֹ. נִתְעַסְּקָה שָׁאנֵי. דְּכֵיוָן דְּנִתְעַסְּקָה בְּמִין אָדוֹם – הֵיכִי תָּלֵינַן בֵּיהּ כֶּתֶם שָׁחוֹר? אֲבָל נִמְצָא עָלֶיהָ מִין אָדוֹם – תּוֹלָה בָּהּ כֶּתֶם שָׁחוֹר, דְּאָמְרִינַן: כִּי הֵיכִי דְּנִיתַּן עָלֶיהָ הַאי מִין, בְּדְלָא יָדְעָה – הָכִי נַמִי הֲוָה עֲלָהּ מִינָא אַחֲרִינָא, וְלָא יָדְעָה. לֹא לְהָקֵל עַל דִּבְרֵי תוֹרָה. הַאי דִּגְזוּר רַבָּנַן בִּכְתָמִים – לְהַחְמִיר עַל ד"ת, שֶׁלֹּא לְהָקֵל בְּנִדָּה גְּמוּרָה. וּמִיהוּ כְּתָמִים עַצְמָן – דְּרַבָּנַן, וְאָזְלִינַן בָּהֶן לְקוּלָּא, וְתָלִינַן בְּכָל מִידֵּי. כֶּתֶם אָרוֹךְ מִצְטָרֵף. לִכְגְרִים וְעוֹד. מָשׁוּךְ כָּל דְּהוּ טָמֵא. דְּכֵיוָן דְּאָמַר: מָשׁוּךְ מִגּוּפָהּ אָתֵי, וּבִמְשִׁיכָה תַּלְיָא טַעֲמָא – אֲפִילּוּ בְּכַחַרְדָּל טָמֵא. לְעוֹלָם. אַף עַל פִּי לְרַבִּי אֱלִיעֶזֶר בָּעֵי צֵירוּף. וְכִי אָמַר רַבִּי אֱלִיעֶזֶר. מָשׁוּךְ וַדַּאי מִגּוּפָהּ אַתָּא. בְּעֵד. שֶׁבּוֹדֶקֶת בּוֹ. אֲבָל בְּכֶתֶם. שֶׁעַל חֲלוּקָהּ – כִּגְרִים וְעוֹד בָּעֵינַן.

## הדרן עלך הרואה כתם

---

**תוספות**

**היו** בה טיפי דמים למטה וטיפי דמים למעלה תלינן בעליון עד כגרים. פ"ה: "למטה" – קטנים, "למעלה" – גדולים, "תלינן בעליון" – הגדול בדם מאכולת, "עד כגרים, מאי לאו עד כגרים כלמטה" – (ב) בפחות מכגרים. "לא, כלמעלה" – ביותר מכגרים. וזהו תימה: אמאי נקט "למעלה" ו"למטה" הוה ליה למנקט "גדולים" ו"קטנים" ועוד: היכי משמע ליה כלמטה, מאי אולמיה ממתניתין? ועוד: דלא הוה ליה למנקט "כלמעלה" ו"כלמטה" דהוה ליה למימר "כפחות מכגרים" ו"יותר מכגרים", לישנא דנקט עד הכא! ונראה לי דה"פ: "למטה" – למטה מן החגור, "למעלה" – למעלה מן החגור. "תולה בעליון" – אותו שלמטה נתלה בעליון, *דשמא כמו שעליון מעלמא אתי, תחתון נמי מעלמא אתי. (ג) ועוד כגרים נתלה בו וקאמר: "מאי לאו כגרים למטה" ד"עד כגרים" דקתני, איירי שהתחתון עד כגרים – תולה בעליון, שממקום שבא העליון בא התחתון. מכלל דאי לאו עליון – מטמינן ליה, ולא תלינן בדם מאכולת. אלמא, כגרים כיותר מכגרים! ומשני: "לא, כגרים ולמעלה" – כלומר, תולה תחתון בעליון כשהעליון עד כגרים, ולמלעלה למטה קאשיב, כשהעליון ג' גריסין או שני גריסין, עד כגרים – שאז אין אנו תולין עליון בדם מאכולת אלא מעלמא אתי, אז נתלה בו התחתון. ומיירי כשתחתון יותר מכגרים. אבל אם היה העליון כגרים, אז לא יהיה התחתון טהור, שאין רגלים לדבר דאתא דם זה מעלמא, שהרי העליון יש לתלותו בדם מאכולת. **נתעסקה** בכגרים ומצאה עליה כגרים ועוד. אור"י: הוא הדין נתעסקה בפחות מכגרים ונמצא עליה כגרים ועוד, דבכלל בעיא זו. דאין לומר דהא פשיטא ליה דאינה תולה אפי' לרבי ינאי דא"כ, כי פשיט לקמן מאי לאו בכה"ג לוקמה בשנתעסקה בפחות מכגרים דפשיטא ליה דאינה תולה! אלא ודאי בכל ענין בעי. **נמצא** עליה מין אחד. פ"ה: מדבר הדומה לכתם, כגון שרף או קילור. דהא, ודאי מעלמא אתא – תולה בו כמה מיני כתמים, ואינה מכרת אם דם היא. ור"י מפרש: "נמצא" – שמצאה, "מין אחד" – למעלה מן החגור, "תולה בו כמה מינים" – שלמטה מן החגור. משום שכמו שהעליון ודאי מעלמא אתא, כך נאמר בתחתון דמעלמא אתא.

## הדרן עלך הרואה כתם

---

**עין משפט נר מצוה**

כח א (מיי' פ"ט מהל' איסורי ביאה) סמג לאוין קיא טוש"ע יו"ד סי' קצ סעי' יז:

כט ב מיי' שם הל' כג סמג שם טוש"ע שם סעי' כח:

ל ג מיי' שם הל' כו טוש"ע שם סעי' כו:

לא ד מיי' שם הל' כז טוש"ע שם סעי' כג:

לב ה מיי' שם הל' כו טוש"ע שם סעי' כו:

גי' מהר"מ דאמרי' כמו וכו'

לג ו מיי' שם הל' כז טוש"ע שם סעי' כד:

לד ז מיי' שם הל"ב טוש"ע שם סעי' א:

לה ח מיי' שם הל"ו טוש"ע שם סעי' ה:

לו ט מיי' שם הל"ז טוש"ע שם סעי' ח:

---

**תוספי הרא"ש**

**טיפי** דמים למטה. פרש"י טיפין קטנים ולמעלה היינו טיפין גדולים ופריך מאי לאו כגרים כלמטה אלמא עד ולא עד בכלל. ולא נהירא פי' שפי' טיפי למעלה גדולים (טיפה) ולמטה קטנים. ותו מאי אולמא הך ברייתא ממתני' דקתני עד כמה היא תולה עד כגרים ופליגי באי עד ועד בכלל או לא ומפרש ר"ת טיפי דמים למטה מן החגור וטיפי דמים למעלה מן החגור תולה התחתון בעליון עד כגרים כלומר כמו שבא העליון ממקום אחר ולא מגופה כך אנו תולין שבא התחתון ממקום אחר: מאי לאו כגרים דלמטה. ה"ג בספרים ישנים וה"פ מאי לאו שיתלו הגרים שהוא למטה בכתם העליון לומר שבא מעלמא א"כ אי לאו עליון ה"א כגרים שהוא למטה מגופה אתאי אלמא עד ולא עד בכלל ומשני כגרים דלמעלה. כלומר הכתם התחתון יתלו בעליון לומר מעלמא אתאי עד כגרים אם העליון הוא גדול כג' גריסין או ב' גריסין עד כגרים אבל אם כתם העליון אינו אלא כגרים אימור דם מאכולת הוא ולא תלינן כתם התחתון שהוא גדול יותר מכגרים העליון. והכי מוכח בתוספתא דקתני היו עליה שני כתמים אחד למעלה ואחד למטה אע"פ שהתחתון גדול והעליון קטן תולין התחתון עד כגרים שאני אומר ממקום שבא העליון בא התחתון: **היו** עליה כגרים ועוד. ובאותו ועוד רצופה בו מאכולת. נראה לי דהה"נ אם היו עליה כשני גריסין לר' ינאי טהורה כיון דכי מדלת כגרים של מאכולת לא נשאר בו גרים ועוד והא דנקט כגרים ועוד לרבותא דר' חנינא נקטי' דאפי' בהכי מטמאה: **נתעסקה** בכגרים ונמצא עליה בכגרים ועוד. נ"ל דהה"נ אם נמצא עליה כשני גריסין מיבעיא ליה אי מטמיא לה והא דנקט כגרים ועוד משום דאפי' בכה"ג מספקא ליה דילמא טמאה וה"ה דהוה מצי למיבעי נתעסקה בפחות מכגרים ונמצא עליו כגרים ועוד דאי בהא פשיטא ליה שאינה תולה א"כ לקמן לוקי כה"ג נתעסקה במועט אין תולה בו מרובה. נמצא עליה מין אחד תולה בו מינין הרבה. וכגון שאותו המין אין לספק בכתם כגון שהוא למעלה מן החגור: ת"ש כתם ארוך מצטרף. לפי מה שרוצה לפשוט מכאן דפליגי לא משמע ליה שיהא שום חילוק בין כתם לעד. ולר' אליעזר בן צדוק משוך כל שהוא טמא אפי' על חלוקה או על גבי הסדין. ולכאורה דשמעתין משמע דכי מסיק דפליגי רבנן עליה מהיא דשמואל היינו כדבעינן למימר השתא וזו הוא חומרא גדולה אם נטמא כתם משוך בכל שהוא דהא פסקינן הילכתא כר' אליעזר ונראה לפרש דהך שינויא דשני כי קאמר ר' אליעזר בר צדוק בעד אבל בכתם לא קיימא אף לפי המסקנא וכן משמע לשון התוספתא דקתני משוך טמא מפני דם הקינוח: סליק פרק הרואה כתם בס"ד

---

**הגהות הב"ח**

(א) רש"י ד"ה כגרים מלמטה כפחות: (ב) תום' ד"ה היו וכו' כלמטה בפחות מכגרי' לא כלמעלה כיותר מכגרים: (ג) בא"ד מעלמא אתי ועד כגרים כו' כגרים מלמטה דעד כו' כיותר מכגרים ומשני לא כגרים מלמעלה:

**עין משפט נר מצוה**

**א** א מיי' פ"ה מהל' איסורי ביאה הלי"ז סמג לאוין קיא טוש"ע יו"ד סי' קנא סעי' ב ועי"ש בהגה"ה:
**ב** ב ג שם בהג"ה:
**ג** ד מיי' פ"ט שם הל' כט ועי"ש סמג שם טוש"ע יו"ד סי' קל סעיף מא:
**ד** ה מיי' שם הל' לב ועי"ש טוש"ע שם סעיף מט:
**ה** ו ז מיי' שם הל"ז ועי"ש טוש"ע שם סעיף י:

**מתני'** *הָאִשָּׁה שֶׁהִיא עוֹשָׂה צְרָכֶיהָ, וְרָאֲתָה דָּם. רַבִּי מֵאִיר אוֹמֵר: אִם עוֹמֶדֶת — טְמֵאָה, וְאִם יוֹשֶׁבֶת — טְהוֹרָה. ר' יוֹסֵי אוֹמֵר: אבֵּין כָּךְ וּבֵין כָּךְ — טְהוֹרָה. אִישׁ וְאִשָּׁה שֶׁעָשׂוּ צָרְכֵיהֶן לְתוֹךְ הַסֵּפֶל, וְנִמְצָא דָּם עַל הַמַּיִם, רַבִּי יוֹסֵי — במְטַהֵר, וְרַבִּי שִׁמְעוֹן — מְטַמֵּא, שֶׁאֵין דֶּרֶךְ הָאִישׁ לְהוֹצִיא דָּם, אֶלָּא שֶׁחֶזְקַת דָּמִים מִן הָאִשָּׁה.§ **גמ'** מַאי שְׁנָא עוֹמֶדֶת — דְּאָמְרִינַן מֵי רַגְלַיִם הֲדוּר לַמָּקוֹר וְאַיְיתֵי דָּם, יוֹשֶׁבֶת נַמִי נֵימָא מֵי רַגְלַיִם הֲדוּר לַמָּקוֹר וְאַיְיתֵי דָּם! אָמַר שְׁמוּאֵל: גבִּמְזַנֶּקֶת. מְזַנֶּקֶת נַמִי, דִּלְמָא בָּתַר דִּתְמוּ מַיָּא אֲתָא דָּם? אָמַר ר' אַבָּא: בְּיוֹשֶׁבֶת עַל שְׂפַת הַסֵּפֶל, וּמְזַנֶּקֶת בְּתוֹךְ הַסֵּפֶל, וְנִמְצָא דָּם בְּתוֹךְ הַסֵּפֶל. דְּאִם אִיתָא דְּבָתַר דִּתְמוּ מַיָּא אֲתָא — עַל שְׂפַת הַסֵּפֶל אִיבָּעֵי לֵיהּ לְאִשְׁתַּכּוּחֵי. אָמַר שְׁמוּאֵל, וְאָמְרִי לָהּ אָמַר רַב יְהוּדָה, אָמַר שְׁמוּאֵל: הֲלָכָה כְּר' יוֹסֵי. וְכֵן אוֹרֵי לֵיהּ רַבִּי אַבָּא לְקָלָא: הֲלָכָה כְּרַבִּי יוֹסֵי.§ "אִישׁ וְאִשָּׁה" [וכו'].§ אִיבַּעְיָא לְהוּ: אִישׁ וְאִשָּׁה עוֹמְדִין. מַה לִּי א"ר מֵאִיר? כִּי אָמַר רַבִּי מֵאִיר — בְּחַד סְפֵקָא, אֲבָל בִּסְפֵק סְפֵקָא — לָא מְטַמֵּא, אוֹ דִּלְמָא לֹא שְׁנָא? אָמַר רֵישׁ לָקִישׁ: הִיא הִיא, מִמַּאי — מִדְּלָא קָתָנֵי "ר' מֵאִיר וְרַבִּי יוֹסֵי מְטַהֲרִין". א"ה הַשְׁתָּא רַבִּי מֵאִיר בִּסְפֵק סְפֵקָא מְטַמֵּא, בְּחַד סְפֵקָא מִיבַּעְיָא? לְהוֹדִיעֲךָ כֹּחוֹ דְּרַבִּי יוֹסֵי — דַּאֲפִילּוּ בְּחַד סְפֵקָא מְטַהֵר. וְאַדְּמִיפַּלְגִי בְּחַד סָפֵק — לְהוֹדִיעֲךָ כֹּחוֹ דר' יוֹסֵי, לִיפַּלְגוּ בִּסְפֵק סְפֵקָא — לְהוֹדִיעֲךָ כֹּחוֹ דר' מֵאִיר! *כֹּחַ דְּהֶיתֵּרָא עָדִיף לֵיהּ. ור' יוֹחָנָן אָמַר: כִּי קָאָמַר רַבִּי מֵאִיר — בְּחַד סְפֵקָא. אֲבָל בִּסְפֵק סְפֵקָא — לָא אָמַר. אִם כֵּן, לִיתְנֵי ר"מ ור' יוֹסֵי מְטַהֲרִין"! אִין הָכִי נַמִי, וְאַיְּידֵי דִּסְלֵיק מֵרַבִּי יוֹסֵי — פְּתַח בְּדְרַבִּי יוֹסֵי. וְרַבִּי יוֹסֵי, בְּחַד סְפֵקָא — מְטַהֵר, בִּסְפֵק סְפֵקָא מִיבַּעְיָא? מַהוּ דְּתֵימָא: הָנֵי מִילֵּי — דִּיעֲבַד, אֲבָל לְכַתְחִלָּה — לָא, קָא מַשְׁמַע לָן. תַּנְיָא כְּוָותֵיהּ דְּרַבִּי יוֹחָנָן: אִישׁ וְאִשָּׁה שֶׁעָשׂוּ צָרְכֵיהֶן לְתוֹךְ הַסֵּפֶל, וְנִמְצָא דָּם עַל הַמַּיִם — רַבִּי מֵאִיר וְרַבִּי יוֹסֵי מְטַהֲרִין, ור' שִׁמְעוֹן מְטַמֵּא. אִיבַּעְיָא לְהוּ: אִשָּׁה יוֹשֶׁבֶת, מַה לִּי אָמַר רַבִּי שִׁמְעוֹן? כִּי אָמַר רַבִּי שִׁמְעוֹן — בְּעוֹמֶדֶת, דְּדָחֵיק לָהּ עָלְמָא אֲבָל יוֹשֶׁבֶת — לָא. אוֹ דִּלְמָא לָא שְׁנָא? ת"ש דְּתַנְיָא, יוֹשֶׁבֶת — תּוֹלָה, עוֹמֶדֶת — אֵינָהּ תּוֹלָה, דִּבְרֵי ר"מ רַבִּי יוֹסֵי אוֹמֵר: בֵּין כָּךְ וּבֵין כָּךְ — תּוֹלָה. ר"ש אוֹמֵר: בֵּין כָּךְ וּבֵין כָּךְ — אֵינָהּ תּוֹלָה. אִיבַּעְיָא לְהוּ: אִישׁ וְאִשָּׁה יוֹשְׁבִין. מַה לִּי א"ר שִׁמְעוֹן? כִּי אָמַר רַבִּי שִׁמְעוֹן עוֹמֶדֶת — דְּדָחֵיק לָהּ עָלְמָא, וְיוֹשֶׁבֶת — דְּחַד סָפֵק, אֲבָל בִּסְפֵק סְפֵקָא — לָא אָמַר. אוֹ דִּלְמָא ל"ש ת"ש כֵּיוָן דא"ר שִׁמְעוֹן "חֶזְקַת דָּמִים מִן הָאִשָּׁה" ל"ש עוֹמְדִין, וְלָא שְׁנָא יוֹשְׁבִין.§ **מתני'** דהַשְׁאִילָה חֲלוּקָהּ לְנָכְרִית אוֹ לְנִדָּה — הֲרֵי זוֹ תּוֹלָה בָּהּ. הג' נָשִׁים שֶׁלָּבְשׁוּ חָלוּק אֶחָד, אוֹ שֶׁיָּשְׁבוּ עַל סַפְסָל אֶחָד וְנִמְצָא עָלָיו דָּם — כּוּלָּן טְמֵאוֹת. ויָשְׁבוּ עַל סַפְסָל שֶׁל אֶבֶן, אוֹ עַל הָאִיצְטְבָא שֶׁל מֶרְחָץ — רַבִּי נְחֶמְיָה מְטַהֵר. שֶׁהָיָה *רַבִּי נְחֶמְיָה אוֹמֵר: זכָּל דָּבָר שֶׁאֵינוֹ מְקַבֵּל טוּמְאָה — אֵינוֹ מְקַבֵּל כְּתָמִים.§ **גמ'** אָמַר רַב: בְּגוֹיָה

הרואה

**רש"י**

**הָאִשָּׁה.** אִם עוֹמֶדֶת. מְפָרֵשׁ בַּגְּמָרָא. צָרְכֵיהֶן. מֵי רַגְלַיִם. ר' יוֹסֵי מְטַהֵר. דְּהָא אֲפִי' בְּאִשָּׁה גְּרֵידְתָּא מְטַהֵר, דְּלֵיכָּא אֶלָּא חַד סָפֵק: סָפֵק בָּא מִן הַמָּקוֹר, סָפֵק בָּא מִמְּקוֹם מֵי רַגְלַיִם. וְכ"שׁ הָכָא, דְּדִלְמָא מֵאִישׁ אָתוּ. וּבַגְּמָרָא פָּרְכִינַן: הַשְׁתָּא בְּחַד סָפֵק מְטַהֵר, בִּתְרֵי סְפֵקֵי מִיבַּעְיָא? **גמ'** בִּמְזַנֶּקֶת. מְקַלַּחַת. דְּכֵיוָן דְּנָפֵק בְּקִילּוּחַ כִּי אוֹרְחָא, לָא דְּחִיקָא, וְלָא הָדוּר מֵי רַגְלַיִם לַמָּקוֹר, וְאֵין דֶּרֶךְ דַּם מָקוֹר לָצֵאת עִם מֵי רַגְלַיִם. אֲבָל שׁוֹתֶתֶת, אַיְּידֵי דְּאוֹקְמָהּ אַנַּפְשָׁהּ הוּא, וְאִיכָּא לְמֵימַר: הָדוּר, כְּאִילּוּ עוֹמֶדֶת. אֲבָל עוֹמֶדֶת, אִי אֶפְשָׁר לָהּ לְזַנֵּק. מְזַנֶּקֶת. (א) נְהִי נַמִי דְּלָא הָדוּר לַמָּקוֹר, מִיהוּ מַאן לֵימָא לָן דִּבַהֲדֵי מֵי רַגְלַיִם אֲתָא, דְּנֵימָא: וַדַּאי לָאו מִמָּקוֹר הוּא, מִדַּאֲתָא בַּהֲדֵי מֵי רַגְלַיִם, אֶלָּא מִמְּקוֹם מֵי רַגְלַיִם (ב) וּמַכָּה יֵשׁ בָּהּ? דִּלְמָא בָּתַר דִּתְמוּ מַיָּא. אֲתָא דָּם מִמָּקוֹר, וְלָא מֵחֲמַת מֵי רַגְלַיִם. וְכֵן אוֹרֵי לֵיהּ לְקָלָא. שֵׁם אָדָם שֶׁהוּצְרַךְ לַדָּבָר. אִישׁ וְאִשָּׁה עוֹמְדִין מַאי אָמַר בָּהּ ר' מֵאִיר. דִּמְטַמֵּא בְּאִשָּׁה עוֹמֶדֶת, הָכָא אִיכָּא סְפֵק סְפֵקָא לְהָקֵל: דִּלְמָא מֵאִישׁ אָתֵי, וַאֲפִילּוּ אִם תִּמְצֵי לוֹמַר דְּמִינָּהּ אֲתָא — דִּלְמָא לָא הָדוּר מֵי רַגְלַיִם לַמָּקוֹר, וּמִמְּקוֹם מַכָּה בָּא. הִיא הִיא. כִּי הֵיכִי דִּמְטַמֵּא ר' מֵאִיר בְּאִשָּׁה לְחוּדָהּ, הָכִי נַמִי מְטַמֵּא בְּאִישׁ וְאִשָּׁה עוֹמְדִין. בְּחַד סְפֵקָא מִיבַּעְיָא. וְלָמָּה לֵיהּ לְפַלּוּגֵי ר"מ בְּרֵישָׁא, לְאַשְׁמוּעִינַן בְּסֵיפָא "ר"מ מְטַמֵּא", דְּלִישְׁתַּמְעוּ תַּרְוַיְיהוּ. דִּיעֲבַד. כְּגוֹן שֶׁנִּתְעַסְּקָה בְּטָהֳרוֹת, אֲבָל לְכַתְחִלָּה — אוֹמְרִין לָהּ "אַל תִּתְעַסֵּק". קמ"ל. מִמִּשְׁנָה יְתֵירָתָא דְּלָא אִצְטְרִיךְ, דַּאֲפִי' לְכַתְחִלָּה קָאָמַר. אִשָּׁה. לְחוּדָהּ יוֹשֶׁבֶת וְעוֹשָׂה צְרָכֶיהָ, וְנִמְצָא דָּם בַּסֵּפֶל. מַה לִּי א"ר שִׁמְעוֹן. מִי אָמְרִי': כִּי א"ר שִׁמְעוֹן — בְּעוֹמֶדֶת. דְּכֵיוָן דְּעוֹמֶדֶת, אֲפִי' אִיכָּא אִישׁ בַּהֲדָהּ — מְטַמֵּא, דְּכֵיוָן דְּאָמַר ר"ש: חֶזְקַת דָּמִים מִן הָאִשָּׁה — אֵין כָּאן סְפֵק סְפֵקָא. אֲבָל יוֹשֶׁבֶת — וַדַּאי מִמְּקוֹם מֵי רַגְלַיִם אָתָא, וְתוֹלָה בְּמַכָּה. אִישׁ וְאִשָּׁה יוֹשְׁבִין מַה לִּי אָמַר ר"ש. מִי אָמְרִי': כִּי אָמַר מַתְנִי' — בְּעוֹמְדִין, וְאַלִּימָא לֵיהּ עוֹמֶדֶת, דַּאֲפִי' בִּתְרֵי סְפֵקֵי מְטַמֵּא. וּבָרַיְיתָא נַמִי דִּמְטַמֵּא ר"ש — בְּיוֹשֶׁבֶת, מִשּׁוּם דְּלֵיכָּא אִישׁ בַּהֲדָהּ. אֲבָל הָכָא, דְּתַרְתֵּי לְקוּלָּא, יוֹשֶׁבֶת וְאִישׁ בַּהֲדָהּ — לָא. ת"שׁ. מִדְּקָתָנֵי "חֶזְקָה", אַלְמָא לָא מְסַפְּקָא דַּם בְּאִישׁ כְּלָל. **מתני'** הִשְׁאִילָה חֲלוּקָהּ לְנָכְרִית אוֹ לְנִדָּה. וְאַחַר כָּךְ לְבָשַׁתּוּ הִיא, וּמָצְאָה עָלֶיהָ כֶּתֶם. הֲרֵי זוֹ תּוֹלָה בָּהּ. וּטְהוֹרָה. דְּכֵיוָן דְּנִדָּה הִיא, לָא מְקַלְקְלָה לַהּ מִידֵּי. וְנָכְרִית נַמִי טְמֵאָה, וְתָלְיָא בָּהּ. אֲבָל יִשְׂרְאֵלִית טְהוֹרָה שֶׁשָּׁאֲלָה חָלוּק מֵחֲבֶירְתָּהּ טְהוֹרָה, וְאַחַר כָּךְ לְבָשַׁתּוּ חֲבֶירְתָּהּ — שְׁתֵּיהֶן טְמֵאוֹת, כִּדְקָתָנֵי "שָׁלֹשׁ נָשִׁים" כו'. דְּכֵיוָן דְּאִי תָּלְיָא בָּהּ — מְקַלְקְלָה לָהּ, מַאי חָזֵית דִּמְקַלְקְלָה לָהּ לְהַךְ טְפֵי מֵהַךְ? שֶׁל אֶבֶן. שֶׁאֵינוֹ מְקַבֵּל טוּמְאָה, וְסַפְסָל דְּרֵישָׁא — בְּשֶׁל עֵץ, דְּרָאוּי לִיטָּמֵא בְּמוֹשַׁב הַזָּב וְהַנִּדָּה. אֵין מְקַבֵּל כְּתָמִים. כְּלוֹמַר, לֹא גָּזְרוּ עַל כְּתָמִים. טַעֲמָא דְּרַבִּי נְחֶמְיָה מְפָרֵשׁ בַּגְּמָרָא.

[לעיל יד. נז:]
[ברכות ס. וש"נ]
[לעיל נח.]

**תוספות**

**האשה** . מאי שנא עומדת דאמר הדור מי רגלים למקור ואייתי דם. פרש"י בריש פירקין דלעיל: דאיידי דדחיק לה עלמא, דמעומד השתינה, ולא יכלה לעצור – הדור מי רגלים למקור, ואייתי דם. יושבת נמי, לימא: הדור מי רגלים למקור. דס"ד השתא בשותתת, דהשתא נמי דחיק לה עלמא. ומשני: במזנקת – מקלחת, כיון דנפיק כי אורחיה – לא דחיק לה, ולא הדור מי רגלים למקור, (ג) דאין דרך לדם מקור לצאת עם מי רגלים. אבל שותתת, איידי דמוקמה אנפשה – איכא למימר: הדור, כאילו עומדת. אבל עומדת, אי אפשר לה לזנק. ופריך: מזנקת נמי, נהי דלא הדור למקור, מיהו מאן לימא לן דבהדי מי רגלים אתא, דנימא: ודאי לאו ממקור הוא דאתא, כיון דאתו בהדי מי רגלים, אלא ממקום מי רגלים באו ומכה יש בה. דלמא בתר דתמו מיא אתא דם ממקור, ולא ממי רגלים? ע"כ לשון רש"י. וקשה על מה שפי' דעומדת אי אפשר לה לזנק א"כ אמאי נקט כלל עומדת? לא ליתני אלא יושבת, וליפלוג בין מזנקת לשותתת! ויש ליישב פ"ה דנקט עומדת, משום דפסיקא ליה דלעולם שותתת היא. אי נמי: משום ר' יוסי נקט לה, דאפי' בעומדת, שאין רחמה נפתח – מטהר. ועוד יש לומר: דעומדת שפיר אפשר לה לזנק. והמקשה היה סבור דמתניתין איירי בכל ענין, בין בשתיתה בין בזנוק, ולהכי פריך: מאי שנא עומדת דטמאה, משום חדא ריעותא דאין רחמה נפתח, אע"ג דמזנקת – יושבת נמי תהא טמאה, היכא דשותתת! ומשני: דכולה איירי דווקא במזנקת. והא דלא מפליג ביושבת גופה, וליתני דטמאה בשותתת – משום דבעי לאשמועינן דעומדת טמאה היא, אפי' מזנקת. ועוד י"ל: דהמקשה סבר דאיירי מתני' בשותתת. דבמזנקת, אפי' עומדת טהורה, דליכא למימר הדור, הואיל ומזנקת. ולהכי פריך: יושבת, כיון דשותתת, ואיכא חדא לריעותא. ומשני: דאיירי במזנקת, ואפילו הכי עומדת טמאה, דאיכא למימר הדור כו', ובעינן תרתי לטיבותא.

**דלמא** בתר דתמו מיא. פירוש: אפילו במזנקת, דלמא בתר שהניחה מלזנק ושותתת, הדור למקור ואתי דם. אבל על פי' הקונטרס דפי' דלאחר שכלו מי רגלים אתא דם כי אורחא, קשה: דאם כן, בשעה שמזנקת, נמי לפרוך: דילמא בא דם כדרכו, כשאר אשה שהיא רואה? אלא ודאי פשיטא ליה, מדלא חזאי קודם עשיית צרכיה או אחר כך, אם כן הדם לאו ממילא אתא, אלא על ידי מי רגלים שחזרו למקור ואתא דם. ושמא בשעת זינוק, אי אפשר לדם לבא כדרכו, שמחמת הזינוק נסתם המעיין של דם.

**וכן** אורי ליה רבי אבא לקלא. נראה דקלא שם חכם. אבל ל"ג "לקולא", דמה לו להזכירו.

**מדלא** קאמר ר' מאיר ור' יוסי מטהרין. וא"ת: אדרבה, מדלא קאמר "רבי מאיר ורבי שמעון מטמאין" שמע מינה שרבי מאיר מטהר! וי"ל: דלא הוה מצי למיתני הכי, דהא מסיק דחזקת דמים מן האשה, ומהא מסיק לקמן דר' שמעון מטמא אפילו באיש ואשה יושבים, ורבי מאיר מטהר אפילו באשה יושבת.

תולה

**תוספי הרא"ש**

**האשה.** במזנקת. פרש"י אבל עומדת אי אפשר לה לזנק וקשה לפירושו דא"כ ליפלוג ביושבת בין מזנקת לשותתת דהוי רבותא טפי לאשמועינן דאפי' יושבת טמאה בשותתת. וי"ל דעומדת פסיק ליה דאין צריך לפרש בשותתת משום דכל עומדת שותתת א"נ לרבותא דר' יוסי נקטיה דאפי' בעומדת ושותתת מטהר. מיהו נראה לפרש דעומדת אפשר לה לזנק וה"פ דסוגיא דשמעתין יושבת נמי נימא מי רגלים הדור למקור ואייתו דם. דס"ד דמתניתין איירי בכל ענין בין במזנקת בין בשותתת הילכך פריך כי היכי דעומדת טמאה בחדא לריעותא במה שאין נפתח שיוכלו ממימי רגליה לצאת בהדיא אלא נעצרין שם ואיכא למימר דהדור למקור ואייתי דם. אע"ג דאיכא חדא לטיבותא דמזנקת יושבת נמי תהא טמאה היכא דשותתת כיון דאיכא חדא לריעותא ומשני כולה מתניתין מיירי במזנקת ותרתי לטיבותא בעינן הילכך עומדת אע"ג דמזנקת טמאה דאין רחמה נפתח ויושבת נמי אי שותתת טמאה והא דלא מפליג ביושבת לטמא היכא דלא זינקה דניחא ליה טפי לאשמועינן דעומדת טמאה אע"ג דזינקה: **דילמא** בתר דתמו מיא אתו דם. אין לפרש שאחר שכלו מימי רגליה אתא דמה כי אורחיה מן המקור דא"כ בשעה שמזנקת נמי לפרוך דילמא אתא דם מן המקור כי אורחיה כשאר אשה שהיא רואה אלא ודאי פשיטא ליה מדלא חזיא קודם שהתחילה לעשות צרכיה אלא אחרי כן האי דם לאו ממילא אתא כ"א ע"י מי רגלים שחזרו למקור והביאו הדם עמהם והכי פריך אפי' מזנקת דילמא בתר דפסקה מלזנק בעידנא דסיימי מיא שאינן באין עוד בגבורה אלא שותתין הדור למקור ואייתו דם: **וכן** אורי ליה ר' אבא לקולא הלכה כר' יוסי. וי"מ לקלא שם גברא הוא משום דקשיא להו אמאי איצטריך ליה למימר לקולא ממילא ידעינן דר' יוסי הוא דמיקל. ונ"ל לפרש לקולא בכל מקום שהוא מיקל דלא תימא דוקא בספק דאיכא ספק ספיקא אלא אפי' ברישא דחדא ספיקא אורי כותיה: **מדלא** קתני ר"מ ור' יוסי מטהרין. ותימה אי מטמא א"כ ליתני בסיפא ר"מ ור"ש מטמאין. וי"ל משום דר"ש מטמא אפי' באשה יושבת כדאמרינן בסמוך. **תניא** כוותיה דרד' יוחנן איש ואשה וכו'. הקשה ר' מאיר דילמא הכא ביושבין איירי ובהא מודי ר"ל דר"מ מטהר וכ"ת אי ביושבים מאי איריא איש ואשה דהוי ספק ספיקא אפי' אשה לחודה יושבת מטהר ר"מ דילמא להודיעך כחו דר"ש איצטריך א)דכבר שמעינן ליה ממתניתין דאפי' באיש ואשה מטמא כדדייק לקמן ממתניתין. ועוי"ל דמסתמא כח דר"מ ור' יוסי דאתא לאשמועינן דהוי כח דהיתירא וכה דהילכתא: **אשה** יושבת מה לי א"ר שמעון וא"ת דנפשוט דאפי' ביושבת מטמא מדלא תנא ר"ש מטמא בהדי ר"מ וי"ל דאיבעיא ליה אליבא דר' יוחנן דאמר דר"מ מטהר בסיפא אפי' בעומדת. ותימה לר' יוחנן נמי תפשוט אי ר"ש מטהר א"כ ליתני נמי ר"ש ב)בהדי ר"מ וי"ל דעדיפא איתי ליה מברייתא:

א) נ"ל וי"ל דלר"ש לא אילטריך דכבר שמעינן וכו'. ב) נראה דר"ל דמ"מ ליתני ברישא בהדי ר"מ.

**הגהות הב"ח**

(א) רש"י ד"ה מזנקת נמי נהי דלא כו' ל"ל: (ב) באד"ה מי רגלים באו ומכה. (ג) תוס' ד"ה האשה וכו' למקור ואין דרך:

הרואה. שגדולה היא, וידעינן בה דכבר ראתה. ראויה לראות. שהגיעו ימי הנעורים. ותסברא רבי מאיר לחומרא הוא. דתימא: דלתנא קמא, אפילו אינה ראויה, ותשמע מינה דלתרוייהו לא בעינן שראתה כבר – והא תניא דרבי מאיר לקולא, מכלל דלת"ק לא סגי בראויה לראות, עד שתהא רואה ממש. ופרכינן: אלא קשיא הך. קמייתא דמשמע דר' מאיר לחומרא. [יבמות כב: וש"נ] תריץ הכי כו'. וברייתא דקתני: "אינה תולה בנכרית" לת"ק הכי קאמר: אינה תולה בנכרית הראויה לראות, אלא אם כן רואה. ר' מאיר אומר: תולה. ותרוייהו מתניתא חדא מילתא אמרי, ורב דאמר – כתנא קמא דתרוייהו. בשני שלה. אם השאילתה לשומרת יום בשני שלה – תולה בה, ואף על גב דלא הוחזקה רואה היום. כיון דמעיינה פתוח – תולה בה. ואע"ג דמקלקלה לה פורתא, דצריכה לשמור יום המחרת – כיון דטמאה השתא. ובסופרת ז'. נקיים אחר זיבה, ואף ע"פ שמקלקלה הרבה, שסותרה כל ימי ספירתה וצריכה לספור ז' נקיים – הואיל ועכשיו טמאה, תולה בה. וחברתה מקולקלת. שומרת יום צריכה עוד לשמור שלישי, בשביל כתם זה. ואם סופרת – היא סותרת כל שלפניה. רבי אומר אינה תולה. הואיל ומקלקלה לה. מאי חזית דמקלקלת להך טפי מהך? ושוין שתולה בשומרת יום כנגד יום בראשון שלה. דלא מקלקלה מידי. וביושבת על דם טוהר ובבתולה שדמיה טהורין. דלא מקלקלה לה מידי, שאין לה כתם, כדאמרי' בפ' קמא (דף י:): זו שירפה מלוי, ותלינן כתמה בדם בתולים. לפיכך דרבן שמעון למה לי. כיון דתנא: תולה בה – פשיטא דהיא מתוקנת, וזו מקולקלת! שהלכו בשני שבילין. ולא ידענא הי להאי על, והי להאי על. באנו למחלוקת. לרבן שמעון, (א) דאמר: תולין כתם בשומרת יום – הכא נמי תולין שביל טמא באדם טמא וטהור בטהור. ולרבי – שניהם טמאים. עד כאן לא אמר רבי. *דשניה טמאה. אלא משום דכי הדדי נינהו. שתיהן היו בחזקת טהרה, (ב) השומרת יום בשני שלה – ראויה לטבול כל שעה שתרצה, כיון שספרה שעה אחת. הילכך, אין כאן טומאה שתוכל לתלות בה יותר מזאת, לפיכך שתיהן טמאות. אבל הכא דטמא הוא – מאי נפקא ליה מינה אי תלית ביה? הילכך, אפילו לרבי תלינן. ורב חסדא אמר סוף סוף. הך שומרת יום טבילה היא בעיא. הילכך, טמאה הואי. ואפילו הכי קאמר רבי: לא תלינן בה. איתמר נמי. כרב אדא דאמר: אפילו לרבי תלינן שביל טמא בטמא. וכמדומה לי דלא גרס "נמי". טמא וטהור. או אפילו טהור ותלוי שהלכו כו' – תולה טהור את שביל טמא בתלוי. לדברי הכל. ואפילו לרבי, וכדאמרינן: דהתם הוא דכי הדדי נינהו, אבל הכא דתלוי טמא מספק וטהור טהור גמור – תולין טומאה בתלוי. כתם בכתם. השאילה חלוקה לבעלת הכתם, ואח"כ לבשתה היא – מהו שתתלה בראשונה, להיות היא טהורה? שומרת יום. חזאי אתמול מגופה. לא תליא. ושתיהן טמאות. לפי שאין תולין. דמעלמא אתי לה טומאת כתם קמא, ולא בחזקת רואה היא. בשני שלה. אינה תולה, דמקלקלה לה, שמאחרת ימי טומאת כתמה יום אחד. אבל ביום ראשון, שלבשה חלוק זה ביום ראשון (לכתמה הראשון) – תולה, דלא מקלקלה לה מידי.

א) עיין במשנה למלך פ"ט מהלכות א"ב הלכה כ"ט שכתב דהך שתי תיבות בין לרבי הם ט"ס ומפרש כוונת התוס' ע"ש.

אהרואה. ממאי? – דומיא דנדה, מה נדה – דקחזיא, אף גויה – דקא חזיא. *אמר רב ששת: כי נייס ושכיב רב אמרה להא שמעתא. דתניא: תולה בנכרית. רבי מאיר אומר: בנכרית הראויה לראות. ואפילו ר"מ לא קאמר – אלא בראויה לראות, אבל רואה – לא איצטריך. אמר רבא: ותסברא ר"מ לחומרא? רבי מאיר לקולא. דתניא: אינה תולה בנכרית. רבי מאיר אומר: תולה. ואלא קשיא הך! תריץ הכי: והיא שרואה. ר' מאיר אומר – בראויה לראות, ואף ע"פ שאינה רואה. ת"ר: תולה בשומרת יום כנגד יום בשני שלה, ובסופרת שבעה שלא טבלה. לפיכך היא – מתוקנת. וחברתה – מקולקלת, דברי רשב"ג. רבי אומר: באינה תולה, לפיכך שתיהן מקולקלות. גושוין שתולה בשומרת יום כנגד יום בראשון שלה, וביושבת על דם טוהר, ובבתולה שדמיה טהורין. *"לפיכך" דרשב"ג למה לי? משום דרבי. "לפיכך" דרבי למה לי? מהו דתימא: ההיא דאשתכח כתם גבה – תתקלקל, אידך – לא תתקלקל, קמשמע לן. אמר רב חסדא: טמא וטהור שהלכו בשני שבילין, אחד טהור ואחד טמא – *באנו למחלוקת רבי ורשב"ג. מתקיף לה רב אדא: עד כאן לא קאמר רבי התם אלא דתרוייהו כי הדדי נינהו, הכא – מאי נפקא לן מינה? ורב חסדא – סוף סוף איהי טבילה בעיא. איתמר, א"ר יוסי בר' חנינא: דטמא וטהור, ואפילו טהור ותלוי, שהלכו בשני שבילין, אחד טמא ואחד טהור – תולה טמא בתלוי, וטהור בטהור – לדברי הכל. בעא מיניה ר' יוחנן מרבי יהודה בר ליואי: מהו לתלות כתם בכתם? אליבא דרבי – לא תבעי לך, השתא, ומה התם דקא חזיא מגופה – אמרת אינה תולה, הכא דמעלמא קא אתי – לא כל שכן? כי תבעי לך – אליבא דרשב"ג, התם הוא דקא חזיא מגופה – תליא, הכא דמעלמא קאתי – לא תליא, או דלמא לא שנא? הא"ל אין תולין. מה טעם? *לפי שאין תולין. איתיביה: אין תולין כתם בכתם. השאילה חלוקה לנכרית או ליושבת על הכתם – הרי זו תולה בה. הא גופה קשיא! רישא אמרת אין תולין, סיפא אמרת תולין הא לא קשיא, הא – רבי, והא – רשב"ג. איכא דאמרי: הא והא – רבי, הא – בראשון שלה, הא – בשני שלה. רב אשי אמר: הא והא רשב"ג ולא קשיא, כאן

*תולה בשומרת יום כנגד יום. מספקא ליה להר"י אם טמא קל, כגון סופרת מקצת או הכל ולא טבלה, תולה בלא ספרה כלל, בין בנדה בין בטמא מת, ושבילי דשמעתין לא איירי אלא בטהור וטמא. (לעיל) יושבת מה לי אמר ר"ש. מדלא קאמר ר"מ ור' שמעון מטמאים" ליכא למפשט דלרבי יוחנן מטהר ר"מ בספק ספקא. ומיהו מרישא ה"מ למפשט: מדלא קאמר ר' מאיר ור"ש אומרים: "עומדת – טמאה, יושבת – טהורה", אלא דעדיפא מייתי מברייתא. טמא וטהור שהלכו בשני שבילין. הך "טמא" לא מיירי בטמא שספר והזה, אלא שלא טבל. מדקאמר רב אדא "התם כי הדדי נינהו, הכא מאי נפקא ליה מינה", משמע דלאו דומיא דפלוגתא לעיל הוא. ובטמא שלא ספר כלל, נמי לא איירי – דאפילו רבי מודה דתולה, כדאמר "ושוין" כו', ואמאי קאמר רב חסדא "באנו למחלוקת"? אלא מיירי בטמא שספר קצת. וס"ל לרב חסדא, דלרבי אפי' בספרה קצת *אינה תולה. ורב אדא דקאמר "מאי נפקא ליה מינה" – לא קרי הפסד, כיון דלא סתר הכל. והא דנקט "סופרת ז' שלא טבלה" – לרבותא דרשב"ג נקטיה, דאפ"ה תולה. באנו למחלוקת דרבי ורשב"ג. וא"ת: ורב חסדא אמאי לא נקט מילתיה בזבה גופה, ולימא: זבה שספרה מקצתה, באנו למחלוקת כו'? וי"ל: דניחא ליה לאשמועינן דאפי' בב' שבילין מטמא, דאע"ג דהוי ספק טומאה ברה"ר. וא"ת: אם כן, מה ענין כתמים לשבילין? דאע"ג דבתרוייהו אתרע חזקת טהרה דידהו קצת, מ"מ יש לטהר יותר בשבילין – משום ספק טומאה ברה"ר! וי"ל: דגבי כתם נמי איכא למימר דלא אתרע חזקתה כלל, דאיכא למתלי בחברתה, כמו בשוק של טבחים. ואפ"ה, לרבי אינה תולה משום דמ"ש זו מזו, כיון ששניהם טהורין, שספרה כבר ז' ימים – הכי נמי, מאי חזית דתלינן בטמא שספר מקצת טפי מבטהור גמור, ואע"ג דאית ליה חזקה דטהרה, מיחזי כי חוכא ואטלולא. דמהאי טעמא מטמינן ב' טהורין שהלכו בשני שבילין ובאו לשאול בבת אחת – דטהורין מדינא, ומטמינא להו כי היכי דלא ליהוי כי חוכא. ואע"ג דלא דמי: דהתם אי מטהרין לתרוייהו – הוי חוכא, דאי אפשר להיות ששניהם טהורין. אבל הכא – אפשר דטהור הלך בטהור. מ"מ הוי חוכא: דאמאי תלינן טפי בטמא מבטהור? כדאמר לעיל גבי נשים. וא"ת: מ"ש משני קופות, דאמרינן "חולין לתוך חולין נפלו"? וי"ל: דהתם אינו מפסיד לחברתה בתלייתו כלום, והכא נמי אפילו רבי מודה שתולה בנדה גמורה שלא טבלה כלל. מהו לתלות כתם בכתם. אומר הר"י: דליכא למימר דבעי לתלות בסופרת שבעה שלא טבלה, אבל בראשון פשיטא ליה דתולה – דאם כן, מאי קאמר לקמן מ"מ קשיא, הא איכא לשנויא) בין לרבי בין לרשב"ג בראשון שלה איירי ברייתא. ועוד: דאליבא דרבי נמי ה"ל למבעי בראשון שלה, כיון דלא חזיא מגופה. אלא אפי' בראשון שלה מבעי ליה. ופשיט ליה דאין תולין אפי' לרשב"ג, אלא לחזיא מגופה. והשתא לכולהו שינויי קשה לר' יהודה בר ליואי. והא דקמשני "הא והא רבי, הא – בראשון שלה, והא – בשני שלה", התלמוד הוא דקמהדר לשנויי בכל ענין שיכול לתרץ. ולא בשיטתיה דר"י דהא קאמר "אליבא דרבי לא תבעי לך", ואוקימנא בעיא שלו אפילו בראשון שלה, וקאמר "כיון דהיכא דמגופה חזיא לא תלינן בשני שלה", לרבי בכתם לא תלינן, אפילו בראשון שלה.

כאן

### תוספי הרא"ש

דתניא תולה בנכרית ר"מ אומר בראויה לראות. לפי מאי דס"ד השתא דר"מ לחומרא ולרבנן [לא] בעו (שלא) שתהא ראויה לראות. כתב רבינו מאיר דהוה מצי למימר ולטעמיך מאי אידיא נכרית אפי' ישראלית נמי דכיון דלא הגיע זמנה לראות ולא ראתה כתמה טהור כדאמרינן לעיל דאפי' סדיניה מלוכלכין בדם אין חוששין לה וכיון דלא מקלקלא ליה תולה: בנכרית הרואה. פי' שראתה כבר אבל אין צ"ל שראתה עכשיו א"כ אפי' ישראלית נמי והא דקאמר דומיא דנדה מה נדה דקא חזיא לאו דומיא דנדה ממש אלא כמו נדה שראתה אף נכרית שכבר ראתה: טמא וטהור שהלכו בשני שבילין. האי טמא לאו שכבר ספר שבעה דא"כ היכי קאמר הכא רב אדא (בר אהבה) מאי נפקא ליה מינה נפקא ונפקא שהרי סותר כל מה שספר ולא איירי נמי בלא ספר כלל דא"כ היכי קאמר רב חסדא באנו למחלוקת ר' ורשב"ג הא תניא לעיל ושוין שתולה בשומרת יום בראשון שלה משום דלא מפסדא מידי אלא מיירי כשספר ג' או ד' ובהא פליגי דרב אדא ורב חסדא רב אדא סבר כיון שאינו סותר הכל לא קרי ליה הפסד ורב חסדא סבר אפי' סותר במקצת קרי ליה הפסד ותימה ומנא ליה לרב אדא דרב חסדא איירי בספר מקצת ולכך פריך ליה מאי נפקא ליה מינה דילמא דרב חסדא בשספר כל שבעה איירי וי"ל דא"כ מאי חידושא דרב חסדא היינו פלוגתייהו דלעיל. ותימה אמאי קאמר לעיל ספרה שבעה לרב חסדא וי"ל דלרבותא דרשב"ג נקטיה דא"ה תולה בה. ותימה ורב חסדא לימא מילתיה בזבה גופה שספרה מקצתה באנו למחלוקת רשב"ג ור' וי"ל דניחא ליה למימר בשני שבילין לרבותא דר' דמטמא אע"ג דהוי ספק טומאה ברה"ר מטמיא להו כיון דבאו לישאל בבת אחת ולא תלינן טהור בטהור וטמא בטמא. מיהו קשיא לרב אדא אמאי נקט לעיל דשוין שתולה בראשון ליתני חמישי וששי דהוי רבותא טפי [ובלא"ה] פי' זה נראה דוחק לר"מ דלכאורה משמע דאיירי דומיא דפלוגתייהו דלעיל דאי מיירי בע"א היה לו לפרש ופי' הוא דאיירי טמא במת בשביעי שלו קודם שטבל והוה דומיא דפלוגתייהו דלעיל וא"ה קאמר רב אדא בר אהבה דלא דמי לדלעיל [דהתם] תרוייהו כי הדדי נינהו דסופרת בשביעי שלה חשובה כטהורה כיון שטהרתה תלוי בידה אימתי שתרצה תטבול ותטהר אבל הכא מאי נפקא ליה מינה כיון שאין טהרתו תלויה בידו שצריך אדם טהור להזות עליו חשוב הוא כטמא גמור דמי יימר דמזדקק. ועוד דקדק מדלא קאמר הכא לאו כי הדדי נינהו אלא קאמר הכא מאי נפקא ליה מינה משמע שבא להוסיף ולומר אפי' אי הוו כי הדדי מאי נפקא ליה מינה לטמא שטהור תולה בו הרי ספק טומאה בר"ה הוא וטהור ולא מקלקלין ליה אלא אם באו שנים לישאל בבת אחת ואהא קאמר דתולה הטהור בטמא ולא נפקא ליה מינה כולי האי שהרי בקל יכול ליזהר שלא יבא לישאל בבת אחת הילכך אי מיתרמי ליה מילתא דבאו לישאל בבת אחת תלינן ביה: מהו לתלות כתם בכתם. לכאורה משמע דבעי כגון שספרה ג' או ד' דומיא דלעיל אבל בראשון לכ"ע תולה כיון דלא מפסדא מידי ואי אפשר לומר כן דא"כ לבעי בראשון שלה לרבי שמא אינה תולה משום דלא הוי מגופה. ותו אי פשיטא ליה דבראשון שלה תולה אמאי איתותב רב ליואי מברייתא דלקמן לישני הא בראשון הא בז'. הילכך נראה דאף בראשון מבעיא ליה והק אליבא דר' פשיטא כיון דלא חזיא מגופה דאינה תולה אף בראשון כיון דכי חזיא מגופה קאמר דאינה תולה בז'. ומיבעיא ליה אליבא דרשב"ג דקאמר דכי חזיא מגופה תליא אפי' בשביעי הכי נמי א)דמעלמא קאתי דילמא אף בראשון לא תליא:

א) נראה דצ"ל הכי נמי הכא בכתם דמעלמא קאתי נמי תלינן או דלמא וכו'.

עי' במל"מ בפ"ט הלכ"ט מהלכות איסורי ביאה

ו א מיי' פ"ט מהל' איסורי ביאה הל' כט ועי' במ"מ וכ"מ סמג לאוין קיא טוש"ע יו"ד סי' קצ סעי' מה:

ז ב מיי' שם הל' כט סמג שם טוש"ע יו"ד שם:

ח ג מיי' שם הל' כט ועי' במ"מ וכ"מ סמג שם טוש"ע יו"ד שם סעי' מב וע"ש:

ט ד מיי' פי"ט מהל' שאר אבות הטומאות הלכה ז:

י ה מיי' פ"ט מהל' איסורי ביאה הל' כט סמג לאוין קיא טוש"ע יו"ד סי' קצ סעי' מב:

גי' מהר"מ אינה תולה והא דנקט כו' דאפ"ה תולה ורב אדא כו' סתר הכל כל"ל

#### הגהות הב"ח

(א) ד"ה באנו למחלוקת כו' לרשב"ג דאמר: (ב) ד"ה אלא משום וכו' טהרה השומרת:

נ"א דשתיהן טמאות

[פי' קבלה היא כך לבני אדם. ערוך ערך לפי א']

#### גליון הש"ס

גמ' לפיכך דרשב"ג. כעין זה לעיל ט ע"א ובכ"מ כט ע"א: שם אין תולין מה טעם לפי שאין תולין. כעין זה שבת כא ע"א גיטין כח ע"א:

יא א ב מיי' פ"ט מהל' איסורי ביאה הל"ז:
יב ג טוש"ע יו"ד סי' קל סעי' נב:
יג ד מיי' שם הל' לב ועי' במ"מ סמג שם טוש"ע שם סעי' ג וע"ש:
יד ה ו מיי' הל' שם ועי' בכ"מ טוש"ע שם סעי' לא:
טו ז מיי' שם הל' לג טוש"ע שם סעיף נב:

כָּאן לְמַפְרֵעַ כָּאן — לְהַבָּא. מִכׇּל מָקוֹם קַשְׁיָא! אֲמַר רָבִינָא: לָא קַשְׁיָא, הָכִי קָאָמַר: הִשְׁאִילָה חֲלוּקָהּ לְנׇכְרִית — בַּעֲלַת כֶּתֶם הֲרֵי זוֹ תּוֹלָה בָּהּ, וְהָא "אוֹ לְיוֹשֶׁבֶת עַל הַכֶּתֶם" קָתָנֵי! הָכִי קָאָמַר: אוֹ לְיוֹשֶׁבֶת עַל דַּם טוֹהַר — בַּעֲלַת כֶּתֶם תּוֹלָה בָּהּ.§ "שָׁלֹשׁ שֶׁלָּבְשׁוּ כו' שֶׁהָיָה ר' נְחֶמְיָה" כו'.§ אֲמַר רַב מַתָּנָה: מ"ט דר' נְחֶמְיָה — דִּכְתִיב °"וְנִקָּתָה לָאָרֶץ תֵּשֵׁב", כֵּיוָן שֶׁיָּשְׁבָה לָאָרֶץ — נִקְּתָה. (ישעיהו ג) אָמַר רַב הוּנָא, אָמַר רַבִּי חֲנִינָא: אמְטַהֵר הָיָה רַבִּי נְחֶמְיָה אֲפִילּוּ בַּאֲחוֹרֵי כְּלִי חֶרֶס. פְּשִׁיטָא! מַהוּ דְּתֵימָא: לִיגְזוֹר גַּבּוֹ אַטּוּ תּוֹכוֹ, קמ"ל. אֲמַר אַבַּיֵי: מְטַהֵר הָיָה ר' נְחֶמְיָה בבְּמַטְלָנִיּוֹת שֶׁאֵין בָּהֶן שָׁלֹשׁ עַל שָׁלֹשׁ, דְּלָא חַזְיָין לָא לַעֲנִיִּים וְלָא לַעֲשִׁירִים. דָּרַשׁ רַב חִיָּיא בַּר רַב מַתָּנָה מִשְּׁמֵיהּ דְּרַב: הֲלָכָה כר' נְחֶמְיָה. אֲמַר לֵיהּ רַב נַחְמָן: אַבָּא תָּנֵי מַעֲשֶׂה בָּא לִפְנֵי חֲכָמִים וְטִמְּאוּם, וְאַתְּ אָמְרַתְּ הֲלָכָה כְּרַבִּי נְחֶמְיָה?! מַאי הִיא? דְּתַנְיָא: גשְׁתֵּי נָשִׁים שֶׁהָיוּ טוֹחֲנוֹת בְּרֵחַיִם שֶׁל יָד, וְנִמְצָא דָּם תַּחַת הַפְּנִימִית — שְׁתֵּיהֶן טְמֵאוֹת, תַּחַת הַחִיצוֹנָה — הַחִיצוֹנָה טְמֵאָה, וְהַפְּנִימִית טְהוֹרָה, בֵּינְתַיִם — שְׁתֵּיהֶן טְמֵאוֹת. [א] הָיָה מַעֲשֶׂה וְנִמְצָא דָּם עַל שְׂפָתָהּ שֶׁל אַמְבָּטִי, וְעַל עָלֶה שֶׁל זַיִת בְּשָׁעָה שֶׁמַּסִּיקוֹת אֶת הַתַּנּוּר, וּבָא מַעֲשֶׂה לִפְנֵי חֲכָמִים — וְטִמְּאוּם. תַּנָּאֵי הִיא, דְּתַנְיָא: ר' יַעֲקֹב מְטַמֵּא, וְרַבִּי נְחֶמְיָה מְטַהֵר, וְהוֹרוּ חֲכָמִים כְּרַבִּי נְחֶמְיָה.§

**מתני'** *דשָׁלֹשׁ נָשִׁים שֶׁהָיוּ יְשֵׁנוֹת בְּמִטָּה אַחַת, וְנִמְצָא דָּם תַּחַת אַחַת מֵהֶן — כּוּלָּן טְמֵאוֹת. הבָּדְקָה אַחַת מֵהֶן וְנִמְצֵאת טְמֵאָה — הִיא טְמֵאָה וּשְׁתֵּיהֶן טְהוֹרוֹת. וְתוֹלוֹת זוֹ בָּזוֹ, וְאִם לֹא הָיוּ רְאוּיִן לִרְאוֹת — רוֹאִין אוֹתָן כְּאִילּוּ הֵן רְאוּיוֹת.§

**גמ'** אָמַר רַב יְהוּדָה, אָמַר רַב: ווְהוּא שֶׁבָּדְקָה עַצְמָהּ בְּשִׁיעוּר וֶסֶת. סְבַר לָהּ כְּבַר פַּדָּא, דְּאָמַר: כׇּל שֶׁבַּעְלָהּ בְּחַטָּאת — טָהֳרוֹתֶיהָ טְמֵאוֹת, בַּעְלָהּ בְּאָשָׁם תָּלוּי — טָהֳרוֹתֶיהָ תְּלוּיוֹת, בַּעְלָהּ פָּטוּר — טָהֳרוֹתֶיהָ טְהוֹרוֹת. וְרַבִּי אוֹשַׁעְיָא אָמַר: אֲפִילּוּ בַּעְלָהּ בְּחַטָּאת — טָהֳרוֹתֶיהָ תְּלוּיוֹת. בִּשְׁלָמָא הָתָם — אֵימַר שַׁמָּשׁ עַכְּבֵיהּ לַדָּם [אֲבָל] הָכָא — אִם אִיתָא דַּהֲוֵי דָּם מַאן עַכְּבֵיהּ? א"ר יִרְמְיָה: מָשָׁל דר' אוֹשַׁעְיָא לְמָה הַדָּבָר דּוֹמֶה — לְיֶלֶד וְזָקֵן שֶׁהָיוּ מְהַלְּכִין בַּדֶּרֶךְ, כׇּל זְמַן שֶׁהָיוּ בַּדֶּרֶךְ — יֶלֶד שׁוֹהֵא לָבֹא, נִכְנְסוּ לָעִיר — יֶלֶד מְמַהֵר לָבֹא. וְאָמַר אַבַּיֵי: מָשָׁל דר' אוֹשַׁעְיָא לְמָה הַדָּבָר דּוֹמֶה — לְאָדָם שֶׁנּוֹתֵן אֶצְבַּע בָּעַיִן, כׇּל זְמַן שֶׁאֶצְבַּע בָּעַיִן — דִּמְעָה שׁוֹהָא לָבֹא, נָטַל הָאֶצְבַּע — דִּמְעָה מְמַהֶרֶת לָבֹא.§ "וְתוֹלוֹת זוֹ בָּזוֹ".§ ת"ר: זכֵּיצַד תּוֹלוֹת זוֹ בָּזוֹ. עוּבָּרָה וְשֶׁאֵינָהּ עוּבָּרָה — תּוֹלָה עוּבָּרָה בְּשֶׁאֵינָהּ עוּבָּרָה, מֵנִיקָה וְשֶׁאֵינָהּ מֵנִיקָה — תּוֹלָה מֵנִיקָה בְּשֶׁאֵינָהּ מֵנִיקָה, זְקֵנָה וְשֶׁאֵינָהּ זְקֵנָה — תּוֹלָה זְקֵנָה בְּשֶׁאֵינָהּ זְקֵנָה, בְּתוּלָה וְשֶׁאֵינָהּ בְּתוּלָה — תּוֹלָה בְּתוּלָה בְּשֶׁאֵינָהּ בְּתוּלָה. הָיוּ שְׁתֵּיהֶן עוּבָּרוֹת, שְׁתֵּיהֶן מֵנִיקוֹת, שְׁתֵּיהֶן זְקֵנוֹת, שְׁתֵּיהֶן בְּתוּלוֹת — זוֹ הִיא שֶׁשָּׁנִינוּ, לֹא הָיוּ רְאוּיוֹת לִרְאוֹת — רוֹאִין כְּאִילּוּ

---

**רש"י**

כָּאן לְמַפְרֵעַ. לְעִנְיַן טוּמְאַת מַפְרֵעַ — תּוֹלִין, דְּלָא מְקַלְקְלָה לָהּ בְּהָכִי, וְלָא תִּטַמֵּא לְמַפְרֵעַ. אֲבָל מִכָּאן וּלְהַבָּא — אֵין תּוֹלָה, דִּמְקַלְקְלָה לָהּ. וּמַאי חֲזֵית דִּמְקַלְקְלָה לָהּ טְפֵי מִינָּהּ? מִכׇּל מָקוֹם קַשְׁיָא. דִּלְרַבָּן שִׁמְעוֹן תּוֹלִין, וְקַשְׁיָא לְבַר לֵיוָאי. אָמַר רָבִינָא. תָּרֵיץ רֵישָׁא וְסֵיפָא הָכִי, וְלָא תִּקְשֵׁי לְבַר לֵיוָאי. לְנׇכְרִית. בַּעֲלַת הַכֶּתֶם — הֲרֵי זוֹ תּוֹלָה בָּהּ. כְּלוֹמַר, לְנׇכְרִית הָרוֹאָה — הֲרֵי בַּעֲלַת הַכֶּתֶם זוֹ תּוֹלָה בַּנׇּכְרִית. וְהָא אוֹ לְיוֹשֶׁבֶת קָתָנֵי. וְהַךְ לָאו "יוֹשֶׁבֶת" הִיא, דְּהָא הַשְׁתָּא הִיא דְּאִישְׁתַּכַּח עֲלָהּ, וְ"יוֹשֶׁבֶת" מַשְׁמַע שֶׁהִתְחִילָה לִמְנוֹת שִׁבְעַת יָמִים. הָכִי קָאָמַר. הִשְׁאִילָה חֲלוּקָהּ לְנׇכְרִית, אוֹ לְיִשְׂרְאֵלִית יוֹשֶׁבֶת עַל דַּם טוֹהַר דְּדָמֶיהָ טְהוֹרִין, וְאֵין כָּאן קִלְקוּל — הֲרֵי בַּעֲלַת כֶּתֶם תּוֹלָה בָּהּ. אַטּוּ תּוֹכוֹ. דְּדָבָר הַמְקַבֵּל טוּמְאָה הוּא, וּמְקַבֵּל גְּזֵרַת כְּתָמִים לְטַמֵּא אִשָּׁה מִדְּרַבָּנַן. פְּנִימִית. שֶׁאֵצֶל הָרֵחַיִם. שְׁתֵּיהֶן טְמֵאוֹת. שֶׁחִיצוֹנָה דּוֹחֶקֶת עַצְמָהּ לְהִתְקָרֵב אֶל הָרֵחַיִם, וְעוֹבֶרֶת וְנִכְנֶסֶת (א) לְמַעֲמָדָהּ הַפְּנִימִית. הִילְכָּךְ, שְׁתֵּיהֶן עָבְרוּ שָׁם, וְלָא יָדְעִינַן מֵהֵי נְפַל. הַפְּנִימִית טְהוֹרָה. שֶׁהַפְּנִימִית אֵינָהּ מִתְרַחֶקֶת מִן הָרֵחַיִם לִיכָּנֵס בְּמַעֲמַד הַחִיצוֹן. אַמְבָּטִי. מֶרְחָץ, שֶׁהָיוּ בָּאוֹת לִרְחוֹץ. וְטִמְּאוּם. וְהָא עָלֶה שֶׁל זַיִת, דְּלָא מְקַבֵּל טוּמְאָה, וּמְקַבֵּל כְּתָמִים. וּמִדְּקָתָנֵי: "וֶהֱבִיאוּם לִפְנֵי חֲכָמִים", מִכְּלָל דְּרַבִּים פְּלִיגֵי עֲלֵיהּ! תַּנָּאֵי הִיא. דְּאִיכָּא תַּנָּא דְּתַנָּא דִּיחִידָאָה פָּלֵיג עֲלֵיהּ, וְרַבָּנַן מוֹדוּ לֵיהּ. מתני' וְתוֹלוֹת זוֹ בְּזוֹ. בַּגְּמָרָא מְפָרֵשׁ לָהּ: שֶׁאִם הָיְתָה הָאַחַת מְעוּבֶּרֶת — תּוֹלָה הַדָּם בְּשֶׁאֵינָהּ מְעוּבֶּרֶת, וְהִיא טְהוֹרָה. וְאִם לֹא הָיוּ רְאוּיוֹת וכו'. בַּגְּמָ' מְפָרֵשׁ: שֶׁאִם הָיוּ כּוּלָּן מְעוּבָּרוֹת אוֹ כּוּלָּן מֵנִיקוֹת — כּוּלָּן טְמֵאוֹת, כְּאִילּוּ רְאוּיוֹת לִרְאוֹת. דַּאֲמָרַן: דָּם מִבֵּינַיְיהוּ נְפַק. גמ' וְהוּא שֶׁבָּדְקָה עַצְמָהּ כְּשִׁיעוּר וֶסֶת. שֶׁל מְלַאכְתָּהּ. הִילְכָּךְ, מַחְזְקִינַן הַאי דָּם בְּדִידָהּ, וְאִינָךְ — טְהוֹרוֹת. כְּבַר פַּדָּא דְּאָמַר כׇּל שֶׁבַּעְלָהּ בְּחַטָּאת כו'. אִשָּׁה שֶׁנִּתְעַסְּקָה בְּטָהֳרוֹת, וּפָרְשָׁה וְרָאֲתָה דָּם כְּשִׁיעוּר וֶסֶת. דִּלְגַבֵּי בַּעְלָהּ בְּכִי הַאי שִׁיעוּרָא — הָוֵי בַּעְלָהּ בְּחַטָּאת, דְּמַחְזְקִינַן הַאי דָּם בִּשְׁעַת בְּעִילָה וַדַּאי. הָכָא נַמִי מַחְזְקִינַן לֵיהּ בְּוַדַּאי בִּשְׁעַת עֲסִיקָתָהּ בְּהָנָךְ טָהֳרוֹת, וְטָהֳרוֹת טְמֵאוֹת וַדַּאי, וְשׂוֹרְפִין, (ב) וְאֵינוֹ כִּשְׁאָר מֵעֵת לְעֵת לִתְלוֹת. בַּעְלָהּ בְּאָשָׁם תָּלוּי. אִם לְאַחַר שֶׁפֵּירְשָׁה מִן הַטָּהֳרוֹת, שָׁהֲתָה כְּדֵי שֶׁתֵּרֵד מִן הַמִּטָּה וְתָדִיחַ פָּנֶיהָ. דְּאִי לְגַבֵּי בַּעְלָהּ בְּכִי הַאי שִׁיעוּרָא — הָוֵי בַּעְלָהּ בְּאָשָׁם תָּלוּי, דְּסָפֵק דָּם הָוָה בִּשְׁעַת בִּיאָה סָפֵק בָּתַר הָכִי. ה"נ סָפֵק הוּא, אִי הָוָה דָּם בִּשְׁעַת טָהֳרוֹת אוֹ לָאו — טָהֳרוֹתֶיהָ תְּלוּיוֹת. בַּעְלָהּ פָּטוּר. כְּגוֹן שֶׁשָּׁהֲתָה יוֹתֵר מִכֵּן. דִּלְגַבֵּי בַּעְלָהּ — פָּטוּר, דַּאֲפִי' אָשָׁם תָּלוּי לֵיכָּא, דְּמַחְזְקִי' לְהַאי דָּם לְאַחַר בִּיאָה. הָכָא נַמִי טָהֳרוֹתֶיהָ טְהוֹרוֹת. וְלֵית לֵיהּ לְבַר פַּדָּא טוּמְאָה מֵעֵת לְעֵת כְּשַׁמַּאי, דְּאָמַר: דַּיָּין שְׁעָתָן. אוֹ בְּאַרְבַּע נָשִׁים שֶׁאָמְרוּ: דַּיָּין שְׁעָתָן. וּמַתְנִי' נַמִי דְּקָתָנֵי: "הִיא טְמֵאָה וְכוּלָּן טְהוֹרוֹת" — אַלְמָא וַדַּאי בְּדִידָהּ מַחְזְקִינַן, דִּמְטַהֲרִינַן לְהָנָךְ, אַלְמָא כְּבַר פַּדָּא הוּא דְּמַשְׁוֵי לְטָהֳרוֹת טוּמְאָה וַדָּאִית הֵיכָא דִּבְדָקָה שִׁיעוּר וֶסֶת. וְלָא כר' אוֹשַׁעְיָא דְּאָמַר: אֲפִי' בַּעְלָהּ בְּחַטָּאת — טָהֳרוֹתֶיהָ תְּלוּיוֹת, וַאֲפִי' כְּשִׁיעוּר וֶסֶת לֵית לֵיהּ טוּמְאָה וַדָּאִית. בִּשְׁלָמָא הָתָם. גַּבֵּי בְּעִילָה, כִּי רָאֲתָה כְּשִׁיעוּר וֶסֶת, אָמְרִינַן: בִּשְׁעַת בִּיאָה הֲוָה דָּם, וְהַאי דְּלָא אֲתָא עַד הַשְׁתָּא — שַׁמָּשׁ עַכְּבֵיהּ. אֲבָל גַּבֵּי טָהֳרוֹת, אִם אִיתָא דַּהֲוָה דָּם בִּשְׁעַת טָהֳרוֹת — מַאן עַכְּבֵיהּ? הִלְכָּךְ, וַדַּאי טוּמְאָה לֵיכָּא, אֶלָּא גְּזֵרַת מֵעֵת לְעֵת מִדְּרַבָּנַן. מָשָׁל דר' אוֹשַׁעְיָא. דְּאָמַר: שַׁמָּשׁ מְעַכֵּב אֶת הַדָּם. יֶלֶד שׁוֹהֶא לָבֹא. הוֹלֵךְ בְּנַחַת, וּמַמְתִּין לַזָּקֵן. נִכְנְסוּ לָעִיר. וְנִפְרְדוּ זֶה לָלֶכֶת בֵּיתוֹ וְזֶה לָלֶכֶת בֵּיתוֹ, אָז הַיֶּלֶד מְמַהֵר לָבֹא. עוּבָּרָה. דָּמֶיהָ מְסוּלָּקִין, וְכֵן מֵנִיקָה, וּזְקֵנָה, בְּתוּלָה. הַאי "בְּתוּלָה" — בְּתוּלַת דָּמִים, שֶׁלֹּא רָאֲתָה מִימֶיהָ, וַאֲפִילּוּ הִיא נְשׂוּאָה קָרֵי לָהּ בְּתוּלָה לְהָכִי, כִּדְאָמְרִינַן בְּפֶרֶק קַמָּא (לעיל דף ח.). כְּאִילּוּ

---

**תוספות**

**כאן** למפרע כאן להבא. פרש"י: למפרע – תולה, דלא מקלקלה לה בהכי, ולא תטמא למפרע. להבא – אינה תולה בבעלת כתם בשני שלה, דמקלקלה לה, ומאי חזית דמקלקלה לה להך טפי מינה? וזהו תימה: שנתלה זה הכתם בחברתה לחלאין! ומפרש הר"י: "למפרע" – אם בעלת הכתם הכירה בכתמה, ואח"כ לבשה היא וחברתה חלוק, ונמלא בה כתם – תולה בה, כיון שכבר הכירה בטומאה קודם שבא הספק בשתיהן. "כאן להבא" – שלבשו שתיהן חלוק ונמלא בו כתם, ולא נודע ממי הוא, ואח"כ לבשה חלוק, ונמלא בו כתם. אע"ג שזאת ודאי טמאה ע"י כתם שלה, הואיל ולא נודע בה עד אחר שאירע בה ובחברתה הספק – אינה תולה. ויש לפרש לשון הש"ס איפכא: למפרע – אין תולין, ולהבא – תולין. וקאי "למפרע" ולהבא אשאלת החלוק: אם שאלת החלוק היה למפרע – קודם שבעלת החלוק הכירה כתמה. ולהבא – ששאלת החלוק שממנו אירע הספק בשתיהן היתה אחר מציאת הכתם של בעלת הכתם – תולין. והיא היא.

**במטלניות** שאין בהן שלש על שלש. והכא לא פריך "פשיטא?", כמו לעיל – דזובחים פרק "דם חטאת" (דף לד.) °משמע דאי חשיב עלייהו ויחדם, מקבלים טומאה. **והוא** שבדקה עצמה כשיעור וסת. לאו דוקא בדקה אלא קנחה, כדאמר בפ"ק (לעיל דף יב.) דלא משכחת בדיקה כשיעור וסת. **בעלה** פטור טהרותיה טהורות. פ"ה: ולית ליה טומאה מעת לעת כשמאי. אי נמי: בד' נשים שדיין שעתן. ועוד י"ל: באשה שיש לה וסת. אי נמי: בחולין שאין בהן טומאה מעת לעת. **אימא** שמש עכביה לדם אבל הכא כו' וא"ת: כיון דיכול להיות דאע"ג דנמצא כשיעור וסת, שלא היה דם בשעת ביאה. אם כן, אמאי בעלה בחטאת? הא ספק הוא! וי"ל: כיון דרוב פעמים בא מקודם ובתשמיש, דאיכא למתלי בעיכוב שמש – טמא מן התורה.

**עוברה** ושאינה עוברה כו' אור"י: דדוקא בהך עניגא דקאמר הש"ס תולין, אבל יש לה וסת דמסולקת בדמים, דהא אמרינן בה דיה שעתה – אינה תולה באין לה וסת. וכן יש לה וסת, ולא הגיע שעת וסתה – אין תולה בהגיע שעת וסתה. אמר

---

**תוספי הרא"ש**

**כאן** למפרע כאן להבא. פרש"י דלמפרע תולה דלא מקלקלא בהכי אבל מכאן ולהבא (לא) [קא] מקלקלא לה. ולא נהירא לתלות בחברתה לחצאין. ונראה כפי' הר"י דפי' כאן למפרע כגון שבשעה שלבשה השניה החלוק עדיין לא היתה הראשונה טמאה משום כתם ולאחר כך מצאה כתם בחלוק אחר אינה תולה בה כיון דבשעה מציאת הכתם לא היתה הראשונה טמאה משום כתם אע"ג דאיגלאי מילתא השתא שהיתה טמאה באותה שעה א)אינה תולה: **כאן** למפרע כאן להבא. כגון שלבשה השניה החלוק היתה הראשונה טמאה משום כתם שמצאה בחלוק אחר הרי זו תולה בה כיון דמיד יכולה לתלות מכאן ולהבא: **באחורי** כלים. מכאן ראיה שאין לפרש הא דאמרי' בפ' על אלו מומין נטמא גבו לא נטמא תוכו הא גבי טמא דא"כ אמאי מטהר ר' נחמיה ומאי פריך פשיטא אלא אף גבו לא נטמא: **מטהר** היה ר' נחמיה אף מטלניות שאין בהן ג' על ג'. ואע"ג דאתו מכח דבר המקבל טומאה דמהאי טעמא פסולין לסכך הסוכה: **זה** היה מעשה. כלומר כיוצא בזה היה מעשה שנמצא דם על שפתה של אמבטי ושל עלה של זית במקום שהיו שתיהן ראויין לעבור: **כל** שבעלה פטור טהרות טהורות. פרש"י כב"ש דאמר דיין שעתן או בד' נשים אי נמי בשיש לה ווסת אי נמי לחולין. ור' אושעיא אמר (אף) אפי' בעלה בחטאת טהרותיה תלויות ולית ליה לר' אושעיא הא דאמר רב הונא והוא שבדקה כשיעור ווסת דאין חילוק [בין כשיעור] ווסת בין לאחר שיעור ווסת דלענין טהרות אפי' כשיעור ווסת טהרותיה תלויות דאם איתא לדם מעיקרא מאן עכביה ולענין כתמים תלינן לקולא דאפי' לאחר שיעור ווסת מטהרי' חברותיה. ותימה כיון שיכול להיות שלא בא הדם מקודם אמאי בעלה בחטאת ושמא יביא חולין לעזרה. י"ל דכיון שרוב פעמים בא מקודם ובתשמיש איכא למיתלי בעיכוב שמש איכא ודאי טומאה מן התורה:

א) נראה דל"ל אינה תולה. כאן להבא כגון שבשעה שלבשה החלוק כבר היתה וכו'.

---

קדושין עג: [ע' תוס' סוטה כח. ד"ה בר"ה]

**הגהות הב"ח**
(א) רש"י ד"ה שתיהן וכו' למעמד הפנימית: (ב) ד"ה כבר פדא וכו' ושורפין ואינו כשאר:

רש"ל

**הגהות הגר"א**
[א] גמ' היה מעשה. נמחק תיבת היה:

**גליון הש"ס**
תום' ד"ה במטלניות וכו' משמע דאי חשיב כו'. ע' סוכה טז ע"א תד"ה דלא חזי:

תורה אור

כאילו הן ראויות.§ **מתני'** [א]שלש נשים שהיו ישנות במטה אחת, ונמצא דם תחת האמצעית — כולן טמאות. תחת הפנימית — שתים הפנימיות טמאות, והחיצונה טהורה. תחת החיצונה — שתים החיצונות טמאות, והפנימית טהורה. *[ב]אימתי — בזמן שעברו דרך מרגלות המטה, אבל אם עברו דרך עליה — כולן טמאות. בדקה אחת מהן, ונמצאת טהורה — היא טהורה, ושתים טמאות. בדקו שתים, ומצאו טהורות — הן טהורות, ושלישית טמאה. שלשתן, ומצאו טהורות — כולן טמאות. למה הדבר דומה — [ג]לגל טמא שנתערב בין שני גלים טהורים, *ובדקו אחת מהן ומצאו טהור — הוא טהור, ושנים טמאים. שנים, ומצאו טהורין — הם טהורין, ושלישי טמא. שלשתן, ומצאו טהורין — כולן טמאים, דברי ר"מ. שר"מ *אומר: כל דבר שהוא בחזקת טומאה — לעולם הוא בטומאתו, עד שיודע לך טומאה היכן היא. וחכמים אומרים: [ד]בודק עד שמגיע לסלע או לבתולה.§ **גמ'** מאי שנא רישא — דלא מפליג, ומאי שנא סיפא דקמפליג? אמר רבי אמי: [ה]במשולבות.§ "בדקה אחת" [וכו'].§ למה ליה למתני "למה זה דומה"? הכי קאמר להו ר' מאיר לרבנן: מ"ש בדם דלא פליגיתו, ומ"ש בגל דפליגיתו? ורבנן, בשלמא התם — אימא עורב נטלה, אלא הכא — האי דם מהיכא אתא?! תניא, אמר ר"מ מעשה בשקמה של כפר סבא שהיו מחזיקין בה טומאה, ובדקו ולא מצאו, לימים נשבה בו הרוח ועקרתו, ונמצא גולגולת של מת תחובה לו בעיקרו. אמרו לו: משם ראיה? אימר לא בדקו כל צרכו. תניא, א"ר יוסי: מעשה במערה של שיחין שהיו מחזיקין בה טומאה, ובדקו עד שהגיעו לקרקע שהיתה חלקה כצפורן, ולא מצאו. לימים נכנסו בה פועלים מפני הגשמים. ונתיזו בקרדומותיהן, ומצאו מכתשת מלאה עצמות. *אמרו לו: משם ראיה? אימר לא בדקו כל צרכו. תניא, אבא שאול אומר: מעשה בסלע בית חורון שהיו מחזיקין בה טומאה, ולא יכלו חכמים לבדוק, מפני שהיתה מרובה. והיה שם זקן אחד, ורבי יהושע בן חנניא שמו, אמר להן: הביאו לי סדינים! הביאו לו סדינים, ושראן במים, ופרסן עליהם. מקום טהרה — יבש, מקום טומאה — לח. ובדקו ומצאו בור גדול מלא עצמות. תנא: הוא הבור שמילא ישמעאל בן נתניה חללים, דכתיב: °"והבור אשר השליך שם ישמעאל את כל פגרי אנשים אשר הכה ביד גדליה". וכי גדליה הרגן? והלא ישמעאל הרגן! אלא מתוך שהיה לו לחוש לעצת יוחנן בן קרח ולא חש — מעלה עליו הכתוב כאילו הרגן. אמר רבא: האי לישנא בישא, אע"פ דלקבולי לא מבעי — *מיחש ליה מבעי. הנהו בני גלילא דנפק עלייהו קלא דקטול נפשא, אתו לקמיה דרבי טרפון, אמרו ליה: לטמרינן מר! אמר להו: היכי נעביד? אי לא אטמרינכו — חזו יתייכו, אטמרינכו — הא אמור רבנן האי לישנא בישא, אע"ג דלקבולי לא מבעי — מיחש ליה מבעי, זילו אתון טמרו נפשייכו. °"ויאמר ה' אל משה אל תירא" — מכדי, סיחון ועוג אחי הוו, דאמר מר: סיחון ועוג בני אחיה בר שמחזאי הוו. מאי שנא מעוג — דקמסתפי, ומאי שנא מסיחון דלא קמסתפי? א"ר יוחנן, אר"ש בן יוחי: מתשובתו של אותו צדיק אתה יודע מה היה בלבו, אמר: שמא תעמוד לו זכות של אברהם אבינו, שנאמר °"ויבא הפליט ויגד לאברם העברי", ואמר רבי יוחנן: זה עוג שפלט מדור המבול. תנו רבנן: [ו]בגד שאבד בו כתם — מעביר עליו שבעה סממנין ומבטלו, רבי שמעון בן אלעזר אומר: בודקו

ירמיהו מא | [פסחים קי:] | במדבר כא | בראשית יד

**רש"י**

כאילו הן ראויות. לראות, ושתיהן טמאות — דמכל מקום דם מביניהו נפיק. **מתני'** חיצונה. קרי להך דלצד דרך עליית המטה. "פנימית" — אותה שלצד הקיר. ובגמרא מפרש מאי שנא הכא דמפליג בין נמצא תחת הפנימית לנמצא תחת אמצעית, וברישא קתני "תחת אחת מהן — כולן טמאות", אפילו נמצא תחת פנימית או חיצונה. **אימתי.** אמרו "נמצא תחת חיצונה, פנימית טהורה" — בזמן שעלו דרך מרגלות המטה, דלא עברה פנימית על מקום מציאת הדם. **אבל עברו.** שלשתן דרך (א) עלייה, שהן דורסות ועוברות על החיצונה — כולן טמאות, ואפי' פנימית, דשמא כשעברה פנימית דרך שם נפל ממנה. **גל טמא.** שהיה שם כזית מן המת. **לבתולה.** קרקע בתולה, ואם לא מצא — הגל טהור. **גמ' מאי שנא רישא.** דקתני לעיל "נמצא דם תחת אחת מהן — כולן טמאות", ולא מפליג בין נמצא תחת אמצעית לנמצא תחת פנימית או חיצונה? **א"ר אמי רישא במשולבות.** תכופות ודבוקות יחד. הלכך, אפילו נמצא תחת הפנימית — איכא לספוקי נמי בחיצונה. **מאי שנא בדם דלא פליגיתו.** דמודים אתם לי דהיכא דנמצא שלשתן טהורות כולן טמאות. **ובגל.** אתם חלוקים עלי, דאם בדק ולא מצא — טהור, ואע"ג דמוחזק לן דהואי טומאה בחד מינייהו? **לקרקע חלקה כצפורן.** לקרקע חלקה שלא נזרעה מעולם. **מקום הטומאה לח.** שנבלעו שם מים של סדין, מתוך שהיה העפר רך. **יוחנן בן קרח.** אמר לו לגדליה: שמעתי שבא ישמעאל בן נתניה להרגך (ירמיה מ). **ביד גדליה.** משמע, שע"י גדליה נהרגו. **מיחש ליה מיבעי.** ושמא הרגתם, ואסור להציל אתכם. **בני אחיה.** שבא משמחזאי ועזאל, שני מלאכים שירדו בדור אנוש. **מתשובתו של אותו צדיק.** (ב) הוצרך הקב"ה להשיב שלא יירא ממנו. **עוג פלט מן המבול.** שברח לא"י, כדאמרינן ב"חלק"*. **שאבד בו כתם.** כגון שנכנס במים או נגלל בדם בהמה, ואין נודע מקום הנדות, וקי"ל במתני': אין דם הנדות טהור בלא שבעה סממנין. **מעביר [עליו] ז' סממנין.** על הבגד. **ומבטלו.** לדם. והאי דנקט הך ברייתא הכא — משום דאיירי לעיל בגלים שאבדה בהם טומאה ואין ידוע מקומה. בודקו

[בסדר המשנה גרים א"ר יהודה] | [בסדר המשנה גרים ובדק אחר] | פסחים י. בכורות כה: | לא נמצא שם [אבל נמצא בזבחים קיג: ועיין ח"א בסוגיא דהכא וכן עוד בח"א זבחים שם]

**תוספות**

**אמר רבי אמי [רישא] במשולבות.** פ"ה "רישא" — דלא מפליג, איירי "במשולבות" — ותכופות זו לזו, ולהכי איכא לספוקי בכולהו. ובהרבה ספרים לא גרסינן "רישא". ואומר הר"י דיש לפרש: דסיפא איירי במשולבות — כלומר, מכוונות כל אחת במקומה, ולא היו תכופות ומעורבות זו בזו. ובפירוש ר"ח כתוב "דמשלחפי שלחופי" — שמתפרדות זו מזו. **מקום טהרה לח.** אסדינים קאי, דמתוך שהיה הקרקע קשה — לא בלע מים שבהסדינין, ומקום הטומאה יבש. ואית ספרים דגרסינן איפכא "מקום טומאה לח", ואקרקע קאי, שהיה לח מחמת הסדינין, שבלע לפי שהיה רך ותיחוח. וכה"ג בדק רבי יוחנן בן זכאי כשקלן תורמוסי תרומה, בעובדא דרבי שמעון בן יוחי במסכת שבת (דף לג:). **אטמרינכו הא אמור רבנן האי לישנא בישא** כו'. פי' בקונטרס: ושמא הרגתם, ואסור להצילכם. ובשאלתות דרב אחאי* מפרש: שמא הרגתם, ואם אטמין אתכם — חייבתם ראשי למלך. והיינו "מיחש מיבעי ליה למיחש" — שיש לחוש ללשון הרע להאמינו, לגבי זה שיזהר שלא יבא לו הפסד ולא לאחרים. **זה עוג שפלט מדור המבול.** הכי נמי נפלט סיחון מדור המבול, כיון דאחי הוו. אלא דהך "הפליט" קים ליה דהוא עוג ולא סיחון, מהאי טעמא גופיה כיון דדחיל ליה משה. ועוד אמר (*בפרק "רבי אליעזר") (דף לד) שעוג מצאו לאברהם אבינו שהיה עומד בגרנות לתקן עוגות לפסח. ועל שם זה נקרא "עוג". ומייתי ליה — משום דמחזי כלישנא בישא. דאמר במדרש: *עוג אמר בלבו, אלך ואומר לאברהם וילחם וימות, ואשא שרה אשתו. אפילו הכי היה ירא משה, שמא תעמוד לו זכות אברהם. **מעביר עליו שבעה סממנין.** וא"ת: ומה צריך להעביר עליו? הלא כיון שאבד ואינו ניכר — אינו מקפיד עליו, ובטל ממילא. כדקתני ר' חייא לקמן (דף סב:) דם הנדה ודאי — מעביר עליו ז' סממנין, ומבטלו. שכיון שהעביר עליו — אזל ליה חזותא, ואינו מקפיד עליו יותר, א] אע"פ שניכר. *אלא בקפידא תליא מילתא! ויש לומר: דהכא קרי שפיר מקפיד עליו דאם אינו מולאו עכשיו, שמא ימצאנו פעם אחרת. בודקו

[סוף פ' שלח סי' קכט] | [נ"ל בפרקי דר"א ובפרקי דר"א שלפני לא מצאתי אלא רק בב"ר פ' לך לך פ' מ"ב] | [בראשית רבה פ' מ"ב]

**עין משפט נר מצוה**

רס"א

טז א ב מיי' פ"ט מהל' איסורי ביאה הל' לב (וגורס תחת א' מהן ועי' במ"מ ובכ"מ) סמג לאוין קיא טוש"ע יו"ד סי' קצ סעי' נ:

יז ג ד מיי' פ"ט מהל' טומאת מת הל"י:

יח ה מיי' פ"ט מהל' איסורי ביאה הל' לב לד וע' מ"מ סמג שם טוש"ע יו"ד סי' קצ סעיף נ:

יט ו מיי' פ"ד מהל' משכב ומושב הלי"ב סמג לאוין קיא:

**הגהות הב"ח**

(א) רש"י ד"ה אבל כו' דרך עליה שהן: (ב) ד"ה מתשובתו וכו' שהוצרך:

**הגהות מהר"י לנדא**

א] תוס' ד"ה מעביר וכו' אע"פ שניכר אלמא בקפידא תלי' מילתא. עי' בבכורות דף כה ע"ב:

**תוספי הרא"ש**

**רישא** במשולבות. י"ס שאין כתוב רישא אלא במשולבות גרידא. ויש לפרש סיפא במשולבו' ומכוונו' כל אחת (במקוה) במקומה ולא דחקו זה את זה. ור"ח פי' סיפא דמשלחפי שלחופי פי' שמופרדות זו מזו: **מקום** טומאה נגוב מקום טהרה לח. פירוש במקום הטומאה היתה הקרקע חפור ונכנס בו לחלוחית המים ונתנגב הסדין ובמקום טהרה שלא חפרו שם הקרקע היה קשה ולא נבלע המים ונשאר הסדין לח. וי"ס דגרסי מקום טומאה לח מקום טהרה נגוב וקאי לח ונגוב אקרקע ולא אסדין: **איטמרינכו** הא אמור רבנן האי לישנא בישא איבעי ליה למיחש. פרש"י ושמא הרגתם ואסור להציל אתכם. ותימה הוא לומר כן שאם יצא קול על האדם שחטא שבשביל זה אסור להציל נפשו. ונראה דברי רב אחאי שפי' בשאלתות אם הרגתם חייבתם ראשי למלך שהתורה מלקבל רוצחים. ובענין זה דוקא יש לחוש ללישנא בישא היכא שיכול לבא לידי היזק לו או לאחרים אם לא יחוש לו וכגון ההוא דגדליה בן אחיקם אבל בענין אחר אסור אפי' לחוש ללשון הרע ולהאמינו כלל וכלל: **זה** עוג שפלט מדור המבול. ה"ה סיחון פלט מדור המבול כיון דאחי הוו אלא דקים להו דקרא דויבא הפליט בעוג מיירי ובמדרש יש דבאותה שעה מצא אברהם שהיה עושה עוגות לפסח ועל שם כך נקרא עוג. ותימה מאי שייך לאיתויי הכא וי"ל משום דאיירי בלישנא בישא שיש לחוש וכן עוג כוון לרעה מה שהגיד לאברהם שנשבה לוט כי אמר בלבו אלך ואגיד לאברהם וילחם עם המלכים ויהרגוהו ואשא שרה אשתו וא"ה ירא משה שמא תעמוד לו זכות של אברהם: **בגד** שאבד בו כתם מעביר עליו ז' סמנין ומבטלו. וא"ת אמאי צריך לבטלו הא קתני ר' חייא לקמן דם נדה מעביר עליו ז' סממנין ומבטלו אע"ג דאכתי ניכר הדם קצת טהור כיון שאינו מקפי' עליו דבקפידא תליא מילתא דאמרינן לקמן כ"ש הכא שאינו רואהו ואינו מקפיד עליו וי"ל דנהי דעכשיו אינו מקפיד עליו לאחר זמן ימצאנו ויקפיד עליו הילכך צריך לבטלו בז' סממנין: [מכאן שייך לע"ב] **בודקו שכונות** שכונות. ויעיין יפה יפה אם יוכל להכירו ולמוצאו ולא בדקו ולא מצאו אמרינן דמסתמא נפל הכתם מן הבגד. ותימה לר' מאיר דאמר לעיל כל דבר שהוא בחזקת טומאה לעולם הוא בחזקת טומאה עד שתוודע הטומאה א"כ מה תועיל בדיקה זו וי"ל דהתם שאני דאי דם מהיכא אתי אי לא מהני נשי אבל הכתם אימור נתכבס ולאו אדעתיה אע"ג דר' מאיר לית ליה האי טעמא גבי טומאת מת הכא מודה דבבדיקה סגי דאפשר להיות שנפל הכתם או שנתכבס ואינה זכורה: **בודקו** בחמה. ודוקא קרי דסמיך ועב אבל דם דקליש אינו ניכר בחמה: **בגד** שאבד בו כלאים. ותימה למה לא יבטל דבר מועט שנתערב בו ואין מקומו ניכר בכל הבגד דהא אמרינן בשלהי תמורה דצמר בכור ושער נזיר שארגו בשק שבטל אי לאו דעבד מיניה כעין ציפרתא שארג צורת צפור מן השער דחשיב ולא בטיל וי"ל דלא שייך ביטול ברוב אלא איסור שנתערב בהיתר אבל היתר שנתערב בהיתר וע"י תערובת זה נאסר לא שייך ביטול ברוב (אלא איסור שנתערב) דאין כאן אלא חתיכה של איסור דאפי' אם אורך הבגד אלף אמה ויש בו חוט של כלאים מצד אחד כולו אסור שכל הבגד נקרא שעטנז. והא דבעינן נתינת טעם בבשר בחלב כמו בשאר איסורין אע"ג דהוי היתר בהיתר ולא שייך בו ביטול כיון שע"י תערובת זה נאסר שאני התם דהדרך בישול אסרה תורה ולא מיקרי בשר בחלב בלא נתינת טעם: **ולא** יעשנו מרדעת לחמור. ודוקא שאבד בו כלאים דחיישינן שמא יקח חתיכה ממנה ויתפרנה בבגדו או שמא יעלה עליו המרדעת עצמה אבל ודאי כלאים מותר לעשות מרדעת כדתנן בפ' בתרא דכלאים מרדעת החמור ותכריכי המת אין בה משום כלאים ודוקא לישב עליו אבל בהעלייה אסור כדתנן ולא יעלנה על כתפו אפי' להניח עליה את הזבל וטעמא משום דלהציעו אינו אסור אלא מדרבנן כדאמרינן בספ"ק דביצה לא יעלה עליך אבל אתה מותר להציע תחתיך אבל א"ח אסור לעשות כן שמא תיכרך עליו נימא ובמרדעת שהוא קשה וליכא למיחש שמא תיכרך עליו נימא לא גזור והיינו טעמא נמי דתנן התם הכרים והכסתות אין בהן משום כלאים וכן נמי במרדעת בעינן שלא יהא בשרו נוגע בהן. וצ"ל מדקתני בכרים ולכבד שלא יהא בשרו נוגע בהם ובמרדעת לא קתני הכי מכלל דבמרדעת א)רכין הן כדמוכח בזבחים פרק דם חטאת דאמרינן התם הא כרים וכסתות דרכין נינהו ותנן היתה של עור כו' הילכך בעינן שלא יהא נוגע בשרו בהם שלא תיכרך עליו נימא: **אבל** עושין ממנו תכריכין למת. וה"ה בלא אבד אלא רבותא נקט דאבד שרי ולא גזרינן שמא ילבשם לפי שהם אסורים בהנאה וכ"ש בכלאים ידועים דשרי כדתנן במס' כלאים. ותימה ואמאי לא מיחזי משום לועג לרש דאפי' ציצית כמו כן רמינן להו בההיא שעתא כדאמרינן בפ' התכלת אמר שמואל כלי קופסא חייבין בציצית ומודה שמואל בזקן שעשאה לכבודו שפטורה מן הציצית וההיא שעתא ודאי רמינן ליה משום לועג לרש חרף עושהו. ותירץ רשב"ם דאין כאן לועג לרש דאפי' בחי כה"ג אי לביש כלאים שלא להנאתו שרי כדאמרינן מוכרי כסות מוכרין כסותם כדרכן ול"נ דא"כ בחי נמי כה"ג מיפטר בציצית כיון שאינו נהנה דלא קרינן ביה כסותך אשר תכסה בה ומוכרי כסות אינן חייבין לעשות בהן ציצית. ור"ת תירץ דשאני ציצית שהיא מצוה חשובה ושקולה כנגד כל המצות כדדרשינן במנחות וזכרתם את כל מצותי וגם ציצית וח' חוטין וה' קשרים עולין למנין תרי"ג מצות להכי איכא לועג לרש. וי"מ דההיא שעתא ודאי רמינן ליה פי' בההיא שעתא כשנותנין אותו במיטה דאיכא לועג לרש משום דנושאי המטה יש להם ציצית בבגדיהם ולדידיה לית ליה אבל בקבר אין צריך לשום ציצית בבגדו ותכריכי המת של כלאים נמי מלבישין אותו כשמשימין אותו בקבר וליכא השתא לועג לרש. ומה שנהגו להסיר הציצית מטליתות של מתים אין להביא ראיה מההיא דברכות דא"ל ר'

א) חסר כאן וצ"ל מכלל דבמרדעת אפי' בשרו נוגע בהן מותר והטעם משום דמרדעת קשה ביותר אבל כרים וכסתות רכין הם וכו'. וכ"ה בדברי רבינו בפי' למס' כלאים פ"ט מ"ה ע"ש.

כ א מיי' פ"ד מהל' משכב ומושב הל"ב סמג לאוין קיא:
כא ב מיי' פ"י מהל' כלאים הל' כו (וע' בהשגות ובכ"מ) סמג לאוין רפג טוש"ע יו"ד סי' שא סעי' ח [וברב אלפס בילה פ"ק קפח:]
כב ג ד מיי' שם הל' כה טוש"ע שם סעי' ז:
כג ה מיי' שם הל' כז:
כד ו מיי' פ"ט מהל' איסורי ביאה הל"ז (ועי' במ"מ וכב"מ) סמג לאוין קיא טוש"ע יו"ד סי' קצ סעי' י:
כה ז מיי' פ"ה מהל' תעניות הלכ"ו סמג עשין מד"ס ג טוש"ע או"ח סי' תקס סעיף ד:
כו ח מיי' פ"ט מהל' איסורי ביאה הל' לו וה"ה מהל' משכב ומושב הל"ג טוש"ע יו"ד סי' קצ סעי' לג:

בודקו שכונות שכונות. כל שלש ושלש אצבעות לבד. במחט. מקום הזרע קשה, והמחט מתעכב ליכנס בו. חדש. אין נבדק בחמה, לפי שהוא עב ומהודק. אבל שחוק נבדק בחמה: שוטחו כנגד עיניו, מקום הזרע הוי סתום, ואין החמה נראית בבגדו כל כך. שאבד בו כלאים. שאם היה מכיר חוט הצמר בבגד הפשתן – נותקו, וכשר. לא ימכרנו לגוי. דאתא הגוי ומזבן ליה לישראל. צובעו ומותר. שעל ידי הצבע הוא ניכר, כדמפרש: עמרא וכיתנא לא שליט בהו צבעא כי הדדי, שהפשתן קשה לקבל הצבע יותר מן הצמר. ואי לא מינכר בצביעה – ודאי נפל. מנליה לסבא הא. דסמכינן אהכי? שוע. לשון חלק. תרגום של "חלק": שעיע. כלומר, שיהו חלוקין יחד במסרק. וטווי. יחד. ונוז. ארוג. ורבנן הוא דגזור בארוג, בלא שוע וטווי. להקל על כתמיהן. שאין הכתם ניכר בו כמראה דם גמור. בפולמוס. חיל. אירוס. מפרש בגמרא בסוטה (דף מט.) טבלא דחד פומא. והיינו, זוג המקשקש. **מתני'** מעבירין על הכתם. שאין הדם בטל, עד שיעבירו כולן עליו. רוק תפל. לקמן מפרש: שלא טעם כלום כל אותו היום קודם לכן. והיינו "תפל" – בלא טעם. מי גריסין. מפרש לקמן.

**בודקו** שכונות. תימה: דמשמע דאם לא נמצא – טהור, ותימה: דאמר לעיל לר"מ, כל דבר שבחזקת טומאה – לעולם הוא בטומאתו, עד שיודע לך טומאה היכן היא. ואפילו רבנן לא פליגי לגבי דם, כדאמרן לעיל "האי דם, מהיכא אתי"? וי"ל: דהכא נמי דמי לגל. דשמא מעצמו הלך או נתכבס על ידי שום דבר, ולאו אדעתיה. ואפשר דאפילו ר"מ מודה הכא, דשכיח טפי מלמימר "עורב בא ונטלה". **בגד** שאבד בו כלאים לא ימכרנו לגוי. וא"ת: וליבטיל ברובא, כדפרכינן בסוף תמורה (דף לד.) גבי שער נזיר שנארג בבגד: ידלק, וליבטיל ברובא! ומשני: בצפרתא, שארג בו צורת צפור, דחשיב, ולא בטיל. וי"ל: דלא שייך בטול ברוב א] אלא כשהאיסור מעורב בהיתר. אבל כלאים, ששניהם היתר, ונאסרין על ידי תערובות – כך אסור המרובה כמו המועט. **לא** ימכרנו לגוי. – פרש"י: דנקט "אבד", שאם היה מכירו – נותקו מן הבגד, ומותר. וכן י"ל: שהיה מותר למוכרו לגוי אם היה ניכר, אף בלא נתיקה, וכן לעשות מרדעת לחמור, וכל שכן תכריכים למת – כיון שהכלאים ניכרין, לא קני ליה ישראל מגוי. וכן המרדעת לא חיישינן דלמא מימליך לעשות בגד, כדתנן במסכת כלאים (פ"ט מ"ד) מרדעת החמור ותכריכי המת – אין בהם משום כלאים. אי נמי: לא חיישינן בעודה מרדעת שיעלנה על כתפו, דתנן בהך סיפא: לא יעלה את המרדעת על כתפו, ואפי' להוציא בה את הזבל. אבל בהצעה לא גזרינן – הואיל ואין דרכה בהעלאה. דמן התורה לא אסור אלא העלאה, אבל להציעו תחתיו – שרי. ורבנן גזרו אפילו עשר מצעות זו ע"ג זו בשאר כלאים, אטו העלאה. ובאין דרכו בהעלאה – שרי להציעו תחתיו, ואפילו מדרבנן, ובלבד שלא יהא בשרו נוגע בהן. אבל אבד בו כלאים – אסור למרדעת, אע"ג דאין דרכו בהעלאה. והיינו טעמא, דתנן במסכת כלאים (שם מ"ג) הכרים והכסתות – אין בהם משום כלאים, ובלבד שלא יהא בשרו נוגע בהן. לפי שאין דרכן בהעלאה, לא גזרו חכמים בהצעתן. ובמרדעת נמי בעינן שלא יהא בשרו נוגע בהם, דתו ליכא למיחש לכריכת נימא. וכל שכן אם לא אבד. ו"אבד" דנקט – לרבותא, דאע"ג דאסירא. **אבל** עושה אותם תכריכין למת. כדפרישית דתכריכי המת שרו, כדאמר במסכת כלאים (פ"ט מ"ד) תכריכי המת אין בהן משום כלאים. דכיון דאסירי בהנאה – לא משתמשי בהו, ולא אתי לזבוני לגוי. וא"ת: והאיכא "לועג לרש", שמלבישו בדבר האסור, ומראה לו שאין לו עוד חלק במצות. כדאמר ב"התכלת" (מנחות דף מא.) גבי ציצית: והאידנא שעתא דאי רמינן ליה, משום "לועג לרש". ופרשב"ם: דאין בו איסור, ואפילו לחי, כי האי גוונא שאין המת נהנה בו. וקשה: דהא ציצית נמי אין החי חייב בו אם אין בו הנאת לבישה. ומוכרי כסות דפטירי מכלאים, פטורים נמי מציצית! ומפרש רבינו תם: דדוקא שייך "לועג לרש" בציצית, משום דשקולה כנגד כל המצות, כדנפקא לן במנחות (דף מג:) מ"וזכרתם את כל מצות ה'". והא דאמר בפרק "מי שמתו" (ברכות דף יח.) אמר ליה א) (רבי לרבי חייא) דליה לכנפך, דלא לימרו "למחר באין אצלנו, ועכשיו מלעיגים אותנו!" אע"ג דיש למתים ציצית, מכל מקום מה שאנו מראים עצמנו בפניהם מקיימי מצות, והם אינם מצווין – קרי "לועג לרש". ואם תאמר: ועכשיו שאנו רגילין להסיר ציצית מטליתות המתים, היאך הוא זה? והא אמרינן במנחות (דף מא.) שלכתחילה צריך ליתן ציצית בבגדי המתים, משום "לועג לרש"! ובמתי מדבר מצינו ב"המוכר הספינה" (ב"ב דף עד.) שהיה להם ציצית. מיהו מהא לא קשה – שבכל ט' באב היו נכנסים בקבריהם חיים, ולמחר הכרוז יצא "הבדלו חיים מתוך המתים", כדאיתא באיכה רבתי. אבל על מנהגנו יש לתמוה מכח ההיא ד"התכלת" (מנחות דף מא.) ואור"י: דבימי חכמים שכולן היו לובשים ציצית, אם לא היה להם גם במותם – לעג גדול היה, שדומה כמו שהיו אומרים: הואיל ומת, אין צריך עוד ציצית. אבל עכשיו שאין הכל לובשים ציצית בחייהם – אם ישימו ציצית לכולן, הוא יותר "לועג לרש". שבחייו – לא קיים, ובמותו – יקיים! ואם ישים למי שהיה לו בחייו, ולא למי שלא היה לו – יתביישו החיים. כדתניא בפ' בתרא (לקמן דף עא.) בראשונה היו מטבילין על גב נדות מתות, והיו החיות מתביישות, התקינו שיהיו מטבילין על הכל. ועוד יש קצת סמך למנהגנו שמסירין הציצית ממסכת שמחות (פי"ב) שאבא שאול צוה את בניו: קברוהו תחת מרגלותיו של אביו, והתירו תכלת מאפליונו. מיהו טעמא של אבא שאול לא נתברר ב). **אמר** רב יוסף זאת אומרת מצות בטילות לעתיד לבא. תימה: אמאי לא קאמר רב יוסף מילתיה אמתניתין דכלאים, דתנן בהדיא: תכריכין למת, אין בהם משום כלאים? ויש לומר: דמהך מתניתין לא משמע אלא שכל זמן שהוא מת – אין עליו משום איסור כלאים. אבל הך דקתני דלכתחילה עושה לו תכריכין מכלאים, אע"פ שכשיעמוד לעתיד יעמוד במלבושיו שנקבר בהן, שמע מינה שמצות בטילות לעתיד לבא.

**שוע** טווי ונוז. פירש"י: תרגום של "חלק" שעיע, שחולקין אותו יחד במסרק, וטווי יחד, ונוז – ארוג. ורבנן גזור בארוג בלא שוע וטווי. וקשה: דא"כ כלאים בציצית היכי משכחת לה דאיצטריך קרא למשרי, והלא חוטי תכלת חלוקין במסרק וטווי לבדם? וע"ק: דאי נוז ארוג הוא, מאי פריך "ואימא או שוע או טווי או נוז?", היאך יהיה שוע או טווי כלאים בלא נוז? שהאריגה היא החיבור! ועוד: דלמה לי קרא דנוז לאריגה, מ"יחדו" נפקא, דדרשינן מינה: ג) שתי תכיפות, וכל שכן ארוג! ומפרש רבינו תם: דמדאורייתא "שעטנז" כתיב עד שיהיה שוע טווי ונוז שוע – כל אחד לבדו. וכן נמי טווי, וכן נוז לבדו, ואחר כך "יחדיו" – לחברם. ופירוש "נוז" – היינו, שזור. כדאיתא במשניות (כלאים פ"ט מ"ח) נוז – נלוז ומליז הוא לאביו שבשמים. אלטוו"ש הוא בלע"ז לשון "עקש ופתלתול" (דברים לב) ומשום הכי איצטריך קרא למשרי כלאים בציצית – שחוטי הציצית שזורין, כדאיתא בספרי: "פתיל תכלת" – טווי ושזור. אין לי אלא תכלת, לבן מנין? אמרה תורה: תן תכלת ותן לבן, מה תכלת – שזור, אף לבן – שזור. וארוג – נפקא לן מ"יחדו" כדפרישית. וחוטי דכיתנא – מיירי בשלא נשזר. ופריך: ואימא או שוע – כל אחד לבדו, ואחר כך חברם. או טווי – כל אחד לבדו, וחברם. או נוז – כל אחד לבדו, וחברם אחר כך! ומשני: דהלכה כמר זוטרא, מדאפקינהו קרא בחד לישנא. [וע"ע תוס' יבמות ה, ד"ה "עד שיהא"].

בודקו שכונות שכונות. א אבדה בו שכבת זרע, חדש – בודקו במחט, שחוק – בודקו בחמה. תנא: אין שכונה פחותה משלש אצבעות. *ת"ר: ב בגד שאבד בו כלאים – הרי זה *לא ימכרנו לגוי, ולא יעשנו מרדעת לחמור. ג אבל עושה ממנו תכריכין למת. אמר רב יוסף: זאת אומרת – מצות בטלות לעתיד לבא. א"ל אביי ואי תימא רב דימי: והא א"ר מני, א"ר ינאי, לא שנו – אלא לספדו, אבל לקוברו – אסור! א"ל: לאו איתמר עלה, א"ר יוחנן ד אפילו לקוברו? ור' יוחנן לטעמיה, *דא"ר יוחנן: מאי דכתיב "במתים חפשי" (תהלים פח) כיון שמת אדם, נעשה חפשי מן המצות. אמר רפרם בר פפא, אמר רב חסדא: ה בגד שאבד בו כלאים – צובעו, ומותר. א"ל רבא לרפרם בר פפא: מנא ליה לסבא הא? א"ל מתני' היא, דתנן, בודק, עד שמגיע לסלע, ואי ליכא – אימר עורב נטלה! הכי נמי: עמרא וכיתנא בהדדי – לא סליק להו צבעא, וכיון דלא ידיע – אימר מנתר נתר. אמר רב אחא בריה דרב ייבא משמיה דמר זוטרא: האי מאן דרמי חוטא דכיתנא בגלימיה דעמרא ונתקיה, ולא ידע אי נתיק אי לא נתיק – שפיר דמי. מ"ט? מדאורייתא "שעטנז" כתיב – *עד שיהיה שוע טווי ונוז, ורבנן הוא דגזרו ביה. וכיון דלא ידע אי נתקיה – שרי. מתקיף לה רב אשי: אימר – או שוע או טווי או נוז! והלכתא כמר זוטרא, מדאפקינהו רחמנא בחדא לישנא. ת"ר: בגד צבוע – מטמא משום כתם, רבי נתן בר יוסף אומר: ו אינו מטמא משום כתם, שלא תקנו בגדי צבעונין לאשה אלא להקל על כתמיהן. תקנו? מאי תקנינהו? אלא שלא הותרו בגדי צבעונין לאשה אלא להקל על כתמיהן. הותרו – מכלל דאסירי? אין, א) ז דתנן: בפולמוס של אספסינוס גזרו על עטרות חתנים ועל האירוס. בקשו לגזור על בגדי צבעונין, אמרי: הא עדיפא – כדי להקל על כתמיהן.§ **מתני'** ב) ח שבעה סמנין מעבירין על הכתם: רוק תפל, ומי גריסין, ומי רגלים, ונתר, ובורית, קמוניא

א) סוטה מט. גיטין ז. ב) סנהדרין מט: ע"ש זבחים לה.

א) [צ"ל ר' חייא לר' יוחנן] ב) [וע"ע תוס' ברכות יח. ד"ה למחר ותוס' ב"ב עד. ד"ה פסקי ותוס' ע"ז סה: ד"ה אבל ותוס' פסחים מ: ד"ה אבל] ג) [יבמות ה:]

פסחים מ: ע"ז סה:
[עי' תוס' חולין נח. סד"ה וכנמלא]
[שבת ל. קנח:]
כלאים פ"ט מ"ח

### הגהות מהר"ב רנשבורג

א] תוס' ד"ה בגד וכו' וי"ל דלא שייך ביטול ברוב. נ"ב עי' חולין נח ע"א תוס' ד"ה וכנמלא וכו' לדרך אחרת לגמרי בזה.

### תוספי הרא"ש

חנינא לר' יונתן דלייה שלא יאמרו למחר באין אצלנו ועכשיו מלעיגין עלינו דאפי' אם היו משימין ציצית בתכריכי המת איכא לועג שמראין עצמן כמקיימי מצות והמתים אינם יכולין לקיים וממתי מדבר אין קשה למנהג שלנו דאמרינן בב"ב פרק הספינה גבי רבה בר בר חנה שנטל ציצית בבגדיהם אלמא שמטילין ציצית למתים. שאני התם שהיו מכניסין חיים בקבריהם ובבקר היה הכרוז יוצא הבדלו החיים מן המתים. אומר ר"ת ששמע מזקני (לוטיה) [לותיר] משום שציצית מצוה גדולה היא והוי כמו עדות שקיים את התורה כדאיתא במדרש לדורתם חסר וא"ו לדורתם ואין הדור הזה ראוי לאותו עדות. ועי"ל כי בימיהן היו לכולם טליתות בן ד' כנפים וכיון שהיה להם בחייהם היו עושים גם במותם אבל עכשיו שאין לכולם בחייהן לא יתכן שיעשו לו במותו מה שלא עשה בחייו. ואי תימא עשו לאותו שהיו לו בחייו נמצא אחרים מתביישים. וכה"ג אמרינן לקמן בפרק בתרא בתחלה היו מטבילין כלים על גבי נדות מתות והיו נדות חיות מתביישות התקינו שיהו מטבילין על הכל. וכ"ת דלא דמי להך דהכא דנכספו שם עבירה שלא היתה בחייהן הא ליתא דאין כל כך עבירה דלא חייבה תורה לעשות ציצית אלא מי שיש לו טלית בת ד' כנפות דאמרינן בפ' התכלת א"ל מלאכא לרב קטינא סרבלא בסיתוא וסדינא בקייטא מצדקי למיפטר נפשי' מציצית ומסיק התם דבעידן ריתחא ענשי עלה היינו דוקא בימיהן שכל עיטופן היה בטלית בת ד' כנפות הילכך העושה טלית פטורה מיענש אבל האידנא שכל מלבושינו אין לו ד' כנפות אפי' בעדן ריתחא לא מיענשי. ומ"מ נכון לכל ירא שמים לקנות טלית בת ד' כנפות לחייב עצמו בציצית שהיא מצוה גדולה וחשובה כדאמרינן בב"ר וכי משה רבינו היה דחוק ליכנס לארץ לאכול מפריה ולשבוע מטובה אלא כך אמר משה מצות שיוכלו להתקיים על ידם יתקיימו על ידי. עוי"ל כי סמך לדבר במסכת שמחות דקאמר התם אבא שאול צוה את בניו קברוני תחת מרגלותיו של אבא והתירו תכלת מאפליוני. א) ועל פי ספרים החיצונים אנו עושים כמה דברים כמו ויחל משה בתענית ובמגלה קאמר בברכות וקללות וכן איתא במגילה ר"ח אב שחל להיות בשבת מפטירין חזון ישעיהו ואנו נוהגין על פי מדרש פסיקתא לומר חזון ישעיהו בשבת שלפני ט' באב: **זאת** אומרת מצות בטילות לעתיד לבא. תימה שלא אמר דבריו על המשנה וי"ל משום דבברייתא קתני עושין אותו תכריכין למת לכתחלה: **לא שנו** אלא לסופדו דבעולם הזה לאו בר מצוה הוא אבל לקוברו אסור דלעתיד לבא כשיחיו ויעמדו בלבושיהם יתחייבו במצות: שוע טווי ונוז. פרש"י שיהיה הצמר והפשתן מתוקנים יחד במסרק וטווין יחד ונוז היינו ארוג. וקשה דא"כ אמאי הצריך להתיר כלאים בציצית והלא התכלת צריך להיות סרוק לבדו וטווי לבדו. וי"מ שוע לבד וטווי לבד ונוז יחד דהיינו ארוג. וקשה דא"כ אמאי הוי האי חוטא דכיתנא בגלימא דעמרא ספקא דרבנן והלא כל אחד היה שוע או טווי לבד וארוג יחד ודוחק הוא לומר דבאותו חוט לא היה שוע או לא היה טווי ועוד מאי פריך ואימא או שוע או טווי או נוז דשוע ולא נוז לאו בגד הוא כיון שאינו ארוג. ואין לפרש ואימא שוע בהדי טווי או טווי בהדי נוז או נוז לחודיה דא"כ שוע וטווי דכתב רחמנא למה לי כיון דבנוז לחודיה חייב. ועוד מאי שנא שוע וטווי דקאי על כל חד וחד ונוז קאי אצמר ופשתים בהדי הדדי. ועוד הכי משכחת לה נוז לחודיה בלא שוע ובלא טווי. ועוד אמאי צריך קרא לארוג הא מיחדו נפקא לן דשתי תפירות חיבור כ"ש ארוג. הילכך נראה לר"ת לפרש שעטנז יחדו שיהא כל אחד שוע לבד טווי לבד ונוז לבד ואח"כ מחובר יחדיו. ונוז היינו שזור כדתנן במס' כלאים נלוז ומליז הוא לאביו שבשמים לשון עקש ופתלתול לפי שחוט משזר מעוקם ונפתל והך חוטא הוי ספיקא דרבנן לפי שלא היה שזור ופריך מנלן דבעינן כל שלשתן בהדי יחדיו אימא או שוע וחברו כעין לבדים או טווי בלא שוע נוז וחברו כעין בגדים גרועים דלא שזירי ולא שעי או נוז ששזור פתילה של צמר ושל פשתים וחברם. והא דאיצטריך למישרי כלאים בציצית משום דבעינן שיהא חוט של תכלת שזור כדאשכחן בעירובין פרק המוצא תפילין. המוצא תכלת בשוק לשונות פסולה חוטין כשרה. ומוקי לה בשזורין דכיון ששזרו ודאי לשם ציצית טוואן. ובסיפרי מפיק לה מקרא דשזורים בעינן דקאמר התם פתיל תכלת טווי ושזור אין לי אלא תכלת לבן מנין אמרה תורה תן תכלת בציצית ותן לבן מה תכלת טווי ושזור אף לבן טווי ושזור וסתם בגדים נמי יש להן חוטין שזורין בסוף הבגד כדי שלא יפסיד הבגד כדאמרינן בעירובין פרק המוצא תפילין. ודילמא אדעתא דשיפתא דגלימא טיבינהו הילכך הוי תכלת בסדין כלאים דאורייתא. והא דתנן בפרק בתרא דמסכת כלאים אין חייבין משום כלאים אלא על טווי וארוג שנאמר שעטנז שוע טווי ונוז לאו משום דנוז היינו ארוג דא"כ היה לו לומר שאינו חייב אלא על שוע טווי וארוג אלא לאו למידרש כולי שעטנז הוא דאתא אלא משום טווי לחודיה נקטיה אבל ארוג נפקא לן מיחדו:

א) ועי' בדברי הרמב"ן ז"ל בס' תורת האדם בשער ההוצאה ובמלחמות ה' בסוף מו"ק שכתב דבברייתא דמס' צילית איתא דחכמים פליגי על אבא שאול והלכה כחכמים ע"ש היטב. וטעמו של אבא שאול מבואר שם משום דס"ל דצילית יש בו משום קדושה.

קמוניא, ואשלג, אהטבילו ועשה על גביו טהרות, העביר עליו שבעה סמנין ולא עבר – הרי זה צבע, הטהרות טהורות ואינו צריך להטביל. עבר או שדיהה – הרי זה כתם, והטהרות טמאות, וצריך להטביל. באיזהו רוק תפל – כל שלא טעם כלום. מי גריסין – לעיסת גריסין של פול *חלוקת נפש. מי רגלים – *שהחמיצו. וצריך לכסכס שלש פעמים לכל אחד ואחד. *געבירן שלא כסדרן, או שהעביר שבעה סמנין כאחת – לא עשה ולא כלום.§ **גמ'** תנא: *נתר אלכסנדרית ולא נתר אנטפטרית.§ "בורית".§ אמר רב יהודה: זה אהלא. והתניא: הבורית והאהל! אלא, מאי בורית – כבריתא. ורמינהי: *הוסיפו עליהן הלביצין, והלעונין, הבורית, והאהל. ואי בורית כבריתא, מי אית ליה שביעית? *והתנן, *זה הכלל: כל שיש לו עיקר – יש לו שביעית, וכל שאין לו עיקר – אין לו שביעית! אלא מאי בורית – אהלא. והתניא: הבורית והאהל? – תרי גווני אהלא.§ "קמוניא".§ אמר רב יהודה: שלוף דוץ.§ "ואשלג".§ *אמר שמואל: שאלתינהו לנחותי ימא, ואמרו: אשלגא שמיה, ומשתכח ביני נקבי מרגניתא, ומפקי לה ברמצא דפרזלא.§ "הטבילו ועשה" [כו'].§ תנו רבנן: העביר עליו שבעה סמנין, ולא עבר. צפון, ועבר – טהרותיו טמאות. צפון, צבע נמי מעבר! אלא: דהעביר עליו ששה סמנין ולא עבר, העביר עליו צפון ועבר – טהרותיו טמאות, שאם העביר שביעי מתחילה – שמא עבר. תניא אידך: ההעביר עליו שבעה סמנין ולא עבר, שנאן ועבר – טהרותיו טהורות. א"ר זירא: ולא שנו – אלא הטהרות שנעשו בין תכבוסת ראשונה לשניה, אבל טהרות שנעשו אחר תכבוסת שניה – טהרותיו טמאות, שהרי הקפיד עליו ועבר.
אמר

**רש"י**

קמוניא ואשלג. מפרש בגמ'. הטבילו. קודם שהעבירן עליו. הרי זה צבע. דאי הוה דם, הוה עבר. שדיהה. נשתנה מאדמימותו. לעיסת גריסין של פול חלוקת נפש. שנחלק האוכל מן הקליפה, לועסה לגריסת הפול, ומעבירו על הכתם. לכסכס. לשפשף. שלש פעמים. בין שתי ידיו, כדרך כיבוס בגדים. שכופל לדו עם לדו, ומשפשף ומוליך ומביא. כסדרן. כדרך ששנויין כאן. לא עשה ולא כלום. לא לבדוק ולא לבטל. **גמ'** כבריתא. גפרית. הוסיפו עליהן. לענין שביעית הלבלין. עיקר. שורש שממנו חי, וגפרית – קרקע בעלמא הוא. רמצא דפרזלא*. צפון. שבו"ן בלע"ז. שנאן ועבר טהרותיו טהורות. דאם איתא דדם הוא – בהעברה קמייתא הוה עבר. תכבוסת. העברת סממנין. שהרי הקפיד עליו. כשחזר והעבירן גילה דעתו שמקפיד עליו בספק דם. ועבר. על ידי העברה זו ונעשה בו מעשה דם, שכן דרך דם לעבור על ידי שבעה הסממנים.
מידי

**תוספות**

**אמר** רב יהודה זה אהל. בשבת פרק "רבי עקיבא" (דף צ.) איכא ספרים דגרסי "זה החול", ופריך: והתניא "הבורית והחול"? ותימה: דהתנן "חול" בפרק "המוציא" (שם פ:) וי"ל: דתרי גווני "חול", חד – לבנין, וחד – לחפיפה וכבוס. ואתי שפיר להאי גירסא במסקנא דקאמר: אלא מאי "בורית"? אהל. ולא קאמר "אלא לעולם" כו'. **והתניא** הבורית והאהל. פי' לענין שביעית נשנית. אבל לפי גירסת הספרים דשבת דגרס "הבורית והחול", תימה היא: לענין מה נשנית? ואי לענין הוצאת שבת – הא קאמר רבי יהודה שיעור בנתר ובורית כדי להעביר בו את הכתם, והך שיעורא לא שייך רק מהני ז' מיני סמנים! ומיהו אפשר דרבנן אית להו דבורית וחול הראויין לחפיפה וכבוס, אית להו חד שיעורא לענין שבת. ורבי יהודה פליג אבורית לחוד, וקאמר: כדי להעביר בו את הכתם. **כבריתא.** פירש"י: גפרית. וכן בערוך:* "אש וגפרית" – תרגום: אשתא וכבריתא (תהלים יא) והקשה הר"ר יעקב מאורליינ"ש: בשבת, כי פריך "כבריתא מי אית ליה שביעית?" לפרוך ממתני' דשבת, דתנן בפ' "המוציא" (דף עח:) שיעור אחרינא בגפרית וזפת "כדי לסתום נקב"? ומיהו לא קשה: דבכמה מקומות מצי למפרך ממשנה, וכשהפירכא יותר פשוטה מן הברייתא – פריך מינה. ועוד: כיון שסידר התלמוד הכא, הובאה שם והוקבעה. **כל** שאין לו עיקר. פירש בקונטרס במסכת עבודה זרה (דף יד.) עיקר המתקיים בארץ בימות החמה ובימות הגשמים. וזה קשה: דא"כ תבואה לא יהא נוהג בה שביעית – שאינה מתקיימת בימות הגשמים! ונראה כמו שפירש הכא: שאין לו שורש בארץ, כמו גפרית. וגם מה שפירש שם: תורניתא – מין ארז, כדאיתא בראש השנה (דף כג.) שיטה תורניתא. זה אינו נראה, דבמסכת ע"ז (דף יד.) פריך כי הכא: "ומי אית ליה שביעית, והתניא" כו', והרי ודאי לארז יש לו שורש! על כן נראה כמו שפי' רש"י בשבת (דף צ.) שהוא כעין מחפורת, צריך שקורין אלו"ם, ומין קרקע הוא, וכמו גפרית הוא, שאינו נשרש בארץ. **תרי** גווני אהלא. תימה: לספרים דגרסי בשבת (שם) "והתניא הבורית והחול", אמאי לא משני מעיקרא "תרי גווני חול", כדמשני במסקנא גבי אהל? וי"ל: דקים ליה להתלמוד דלא הוו תרי גווני חול לכבוס. ***הטבילו** ועשה על גביו טהרות כו' הרי זה צבע. אין לפרש: הרי זה ודאי צבע, כדפירש בקונטרס בפרק "ארבע מיתות" (סנהדרין דף מט.) דאם כן, לקמן אמאי קאמר "אבל טהרות שאחר תכבוסת שניה, טמאות" – הלא כיון שלא עבר מתחלה בז' סממנים, ודאי צבע הוא! ועוד: כי פריך לקמן לר"ל דאמר בלוע שיכול לצאת ע"י הדחק לא שמיה בלוע ממתניתין ד"הרי זה צבע" – מאי פירכא היא? הרי היא ודאי צבע, ואין כאן טומאה בלועה כלל! ואמאי נקט נמי "והטבילו", אפי' לא הטבילו, נמי! על כן צריך לפרש: הרי זה ספק צבע. כלומר, יש לנו לתלות בצבע. ואע"פ דפעמים דדם נדה [אינו] עובר ע"י ז' סמנין, הכא איכא ספק ספקא, מלבד טעמא דבטול: דשמא צבע הוא, כיון דלא עבר. ואם תמצי לומר דדם הוא, אימא מעלמא אתא. הילכך, מטהרינן אפילו למפרע. אבל טעמא דבטול לחוד לא מהני, דגבי דם נדה דקאמר "מעביר עליו ז' סמנין ומבטלו" – אינו אלא לטהר מכאן ולהבא, אבל למפרע – טמא מדרבנן, הואיל והקפיד, שסבור שיכול לצאת ע"י ז' סממנין, ואכתי לא בטלו. ואע"ג דמן התורה טהור, דהואיל ואין סופו לצאת ע"י ז' סממנין נתבטל. אבל כאן, כיון דאיכא ספק ספקא ובטול – טהור אף מדרבנן למפרע. ומיהו מטעם ספק ספקא לחוד לא הוה מטהרינן ליה, אי לאו טעמא דבטול – משום דרגילות לבא דם מגופה. כדאמרינן בפרק קמא (לעיל דף ג.) בצפור לא נתעסקה, בשוק של טבחים לא עברה – האי דם מהיכא אתא? דעל כרחך בלא טעמא דבטול לא מטהרינן ליה מטעם ספק ספקא, מדנקט "הטבילו". אע"ג דמקילינן בשאר ספק ספקא. ומשום הכי פריך מינה לר"ל דבטל, אע"ג דיכול לצאת ע"י הדחק בצפון. ואם תאמר: אכתי למה לי הטבילו, כיון דטהור מטעם בטול וספק ספקא? וי"ל: דנהי דכשנתייבש הבגד – נתבטל, מיהו בעודו לח – לא נתבטל, ובעודו לח נגע בו הבגד, ומשום הכי צריך להטביל. ועוד יש לומר: "הרי זה צבע" – צביעות דם בעלמא, ונתבטל, ולא נצטרך לטעם דספק ספקא. והשתא נתפרש טעם בטול במשנה דמינה פריך לריש לקיש. ומיהו פירוש ראשון נראה עיקר, דלשון "צבע" לא משמע צביעות דם, אלא צבע ממש.
**צפון** צבע נמי מעבר. וא"ת: ומה בכך, והא הקפיד עליו, כיון שהעביר צפון אחר שבעה סמנין, ונימא ד"טהרותיו טמאות" דקאמר – קאי אתכבוסת שניה. ומהאי טעמא נמי קאמרינן לקמן: שנאן ועבר, דטהרות שנעשו אחר תכבוסת שניה – טמאות. והכא נמי, ליטמא! וליכא למימר: דקפידא לא מהני אלא כשעובר בז' סממנין שמעבירין בקל, אבל צפון שמעביר על ידי הדחק – אפילו הקפיד, טהורות. דלקמן מסיק רב פפא: יכול לצאת, והקפיד עליו – דברי הכל טמא, אע"פ שאין יכול לצאת אלא ע"י הדחק. והיינו, שיכול לצאת על ידי צפון. דהא ממתני' פריך רבי יוחנן לריש לקיש אמאי טהורה, כי לא עבר ע"י ז' סמנין, הא יכול לצאת ע"י צפון! וי"ל: דברייתא לא מיירי בטהרות דאחר תכבוסת שניה, דיותר היה ראוי לאשמועינן "טהרותיו טהורות" אטהרות דאחר תכבוסת ראשונה, כדקאמר בברייתא דלקמן, אלא אתכבוסת ראשונה נמי קאי. והוה מצי למפרך מברייתא דבסמוך, דקתני "שנאן ועבר – טהרותיו טהורות", אלא דניחא ליה למיפרך מגופה.
**העביר** עליו ששה סמנין ולא עבר העביר עליו צפון ועבר כו' – תימה: פשיטא, והלא אינו מזכיר במשנתינו צפון במנין ז' סממנין, ומאי קא משמע לן? והא פשיטא דבששה לא סגי! ויש לומר: דאשמועינן, דאע"ג דלא עבר כלל, ולא נשתנה ע"י ו' סמנין, איכא למימר משום השביעי לא יעבור – קא משמע לן דיש להחמיר, דשמא בשביעי אם העביר קודם הצפון, היה עוכר. **שנאן** ועבר. נראה לר"י: דע"י שנאן צבע נמי עוכר. דאי לאו הכי, אמאי טהורות אפילו למפרע? הא ליכא הכא ספק ספקא ויהיו טמאות למפרע, כיון דליכא אלא חדא ספקא, כדפרישית במתניתין. **שהרי** הקפיד עליו. וא"ת: (א) אמתני' דקתני "הרי זה צבע", מ"מ כשיכבסנו הרי מקפיד עליו, וליטמא טהרות דאחר תכבוסת? וי"ל: דכבוס אינו קפידא, דאינו אלא ללבנו. וא"ת: מ"מ כשיכבסנו יטמא הבגד, שילא הדם, ואינו בלוע? וי"ל: דדיליאתו יבטל נמי בתכבוסת. **שהרי** הקפיד עליו ועבר. וא"ת: מה צריך לומר "ועבר"? וכי תימא: משום דנפלט וטמא הבגד א"כ אמאי נקט "והקפיד"? וי"ל: דנקט "ועבר", דאז קפידתו קפידא, הואיל והועילה מחשבתו שעבר. ומשום הכי נמי קתני במתניתין דכי לא עבר – טהור, ואף על גב דהקפיד.
אמר

**תוספי הרא"ש**

**אלא** מאי בורית אהל. ק"ק דה"ל למימר אלא לעולם מאי בורית אהל הילכך נראה כגירסא דשבת פרק אמר רבי עקיבא דגרים מעיקרא בורית אמר רב יהודה זה החול והתניא והבורית והחול כו': **והטבילו** ועשה על גביו טהרות העביר עליו ז' סמנין ולא עבר הרי זה צבע. אין לפרש דהוי ודאי צבע מדלא עבר דא"כ אמאי [נקט] הטבילו אפי' לא הטבילו נמי טהרותיו טהורות ועוד מאי מותיב מינה ר' יוחנן לר"ל בגמ' דאמר טומאה בלועה מטמאה כיון דצבע הוא אין כאן טומאה בלועה כלל. ועוד תניא בגמ' שנאן ועבר טהורתיו טהורות ומפרש דהיינו טהרות שבין תכבוסת ראשונה לשניה אבל טהרות שאחר תכבוסת שניה טמאות עד שיטביל כיון שהקפיד עליו ואי ודאי צבע הוא כשלא עבר בראשון מה תלוי בקפידא כיון דודאי אין כאן דם. אלא ה"פ הרי זה ספק צבע והוי כעין ספק ספיקא ספק צבע ספק דם ואפי' את"ל דם אימור מעלמא אתא ולא ספק ספיקא ממש. דא"כ בלא העברת סמנין יהא טהור אלא אינו כשאר ספק ספיקא דעלמא משום דרוב פעמים מגופה אלא ע"י שלא עבר ע"י ז' סמנין ה"ל ספק ספיק' ומטהרינן ליה אבל דם נדה ודאי אע"ג דאמרינן בגמ' דמעביר עליו ז' סממנין ומבטלו ה"מ לטהרות דלאחר תכבוסת דכיון שביטלו גלי אדעתיה שאינו מקפיד עליו עוד. אבל טהרות דקודם לכן טמאות שהרי לא ביטלו עדיין. ודוקא מדרבנן אבל מדאורייתא טהורות כיון שהוא בלוע כל כך שאינו סופו לעבור ע"י סממנין הילכך דוקא הטבילו הוא דמטהרינן משום דאיכא לספוקי בצבעים דאפי' היה דם נדה ודאי לא היו טמאות מדאורייתא אלא מדרבנן אבל אם לא הטבילו דאם היה דם נדה ודאי היו טמאות מדאורייתא שהרי נטמא הבגד מתחלה כשנפל עליו הדם הלח אין לטהר מטעם דאיכא לספוקי בצבע. זו היא שיטת רבינו שמשון. ונדחק לפרש ולחלק לר' יוחנן בין כתם לדם נדה ממש דבכתם טהרות הראשונות טהורות ובדם נדה טמאות. וק"ל מאי שנא דם נדה שהוא כל כך שאינו יכול לצאת כ"א ע"י צפון מחרסין הבלוען משקין טמאין ואינן יכולין [לצאת] כ"א ע"י הסק תנור דמטהר ר' יוחנן הילכך נראה לפרש הרי זה צבע כיון שהעביר עליו ז' סמנין ולא עבר הוברר הדבר שהיה בלוע מעיקרו כל כך שאינו יכול [לצאת] כ"א ע"י צפון ונתבטל מתורת דם ואין כאן צביעת דם בעלמא. וה"ה דם נדה ודאי אם הטבילו ועשה על גביו טהרות והעביר עליו ז' סמנין ולא עבר טהרותיו טהורות והאי דנקט כתם משום דמתניתין איירי בכתמים וה"ה דם נדה ודאי והיינו דקתני ר' חייא דם הנדה ודאי מעביר עליו ז' סמנין ומבטלו דאם עבר נטהר הכתם ואם לא עבר הוברר שהיה בלוע כל כך שלא היה יכול לעבור כ"א ע"י צפון ואפי' טהרות הראשונות טהורות: **צפון** ציבעא נמי מעבר. פי' כיון שע"י ז' סמנין לא עבר בלוע הוי וטהור כדתנן במתניתין ומה שעבר ע"י צפון לא יצא ע"י כך מתורת בלוע דאפי' ציבעא נמי מעבר. ותימה מאי קשיא ליה דילמא טהרותיו טמאות דקאמר היינו לאחר העברת צפון שהרי הקפיד עליו ועבר כדאמרינן בסמוך דטהרות דלאחר תכבוסת שניה טמאות וכ"ת דוקא כי עבר ע"י ז' סמנין אהני קפידתו לטמא אח"כ אבל כי לא עברי אלא ע"י צפון אין קפידתו קפידא לפי שהוא בלוע יותר מדאי דהא אמרינן בסוף שמעתין אמר רב פפא יכול לצאת ע"י הדחק והקפיד עליו והיינו בליעת חרסים ע"י היסק תנור דפליגי ביה ויכול לצאת ע"י צפון כיוצא בו דהא פריך ר' יוחנן לר"ל ממתניתין אמאי טהורות כי לא עבר הא יכול לצאת ע"י צפון והוי כמו יכול לצאת ע"י היסק דמטמא ר"ל אע"פ שלא יצא. וי"ל דא"כ ה"ל למימר טהרותיו טהורות. ונימא דקאי אתכבוסת ראשונה כדאמר בסמוך דמסתמא תחלת דבריו יש לו לפ' אלא ודאי טמאות אתכבוסת ראשונה נמי קאי ואפי' לא היה צפון מעביר הצבע היה יכול להקשות מברייתא דבסמוך שנאן ועבר טהרותיו טהורות אלא דניחא ליה למיפרך מגופה: שאם העביר עליו סם שביעי שמא עבר. ותימה פשיטא דבששה סמנין לא סגי ואם לא העביר כל השבעה טמא. וי"ל דמיירי כגון שלא דיהה מראה אדמימותו כלל בהעברת ששה סממנין סד"א בשביל השביעי מסתמא לא יעבור וצבע הוא: **לא** שאנו אלא טהרות שנעשו אחר תכבוסת ראשונה מטבילה עד תכבוסת שניה. אבל טהרות דמתכבוסת שניה עד שיטבול טמאות דכיון שהקפיד עליו ונהג בו מנהג דם אלמא לא מחשיב ליה בלוע ע"י מה שלא עבר בז' סמנין הראשונים. ותימה אמאי קתני מתניתין דהרי זה צבע ואין צריך להטביל הא כיון שהקפיד עליו להעבירו בז' סמנין נהג בו מנהג דם ויהא טמא עד שיטבול וי"ל דהעברת ז' סמנין דמתניתין אינן כדי להעביר הכתם דאדרבה ניחא ליה טפי שלא יעבור דאז יהיו טהרותיו טהורות. ועוד י"ל דדוקא הכא דאהנו מעשיו דשנאן ועבר אבל לא עבר לא הוי קפידיה קפידא:

**עין משפט נר מצוה**

כז א מיי' פ"ד מהל' מטמאי משכב ומושב הלכה יג:

כח ב מיי' פ"ט מהל' איסורי ביאה הל' לח סמג לאוין קיא וסמג עשין רמג:

כט ג מיי' שם הל' לז: ד ה ו מיי' פ"ד מהל' מטמאי משכב ומושב הלכה יד:

**מסורת הש"ס**

[בערוך ערך חלק ג' הגירס' כפי' זה ע"ש וע"ע בערך לעס א]

זבחים לה: סנהדרין מט:

שבת צ. ע"ש

שם ע"ש. חסר כאן כמסמר ארוך של ברזל כמו שפי' שבת קכג. ועי' כאן בגמ' ה"ל [ג"ל והתניא]

שבת צ.

[ע' כבר ב']

[בפיסקא לקמן סג. פרש"י ד"ה שמתמאי שמשמעמו]

שייך למתני'

**הגהות הב"ח**

(א) תד"ה שהרי הקפיד וכו' במתניתין דקתני:

לא א מיי' פ"ד מהל' מטמאי משכב ומושב הלכה יא:

רש"א מ"ז

לב ב ג מיי' פי"ד מהל' כלים הל"ו:
לג ד ה מיי' פ"ד מהל' טומאת מת הל"ח:
לד ו ז מיי' שם הל"ג:
לה ח מיי' פ"ד מהל' כלים הל"ו:

אֲמַר לֵיהּ רַבִּי אַבָּא לְרַב אַשִׁי: מִידֵי בִּקְפֵידָא תַּלְיָא מִילְּתָא? א"ל: אִין. דְּתַנְיָא, רַבִּי חִיָּיא אוֹמֵר: [א]דַּם הַנִּדָּה וַדַּאי – מַעֲבִיר עָלָיו ז' סַמָּנִין וּמְבַטְּלוֹ, וְאַמַּאי? הָא דַּם נִדָּה הוּא! אַלְמָא – בִּקְפֵידָא תַּלְיָא מִילְּתָא, ה"נ – בִּקְפֵידָא תַּלְיָא מִילְּתָא. *תְּנַן הָתָם: [ב]חֲרָסִין שֶׁנִּשְׁתַּמֵּשׁ בָּהֶן זָב, שֶׁבָּלְעוּ מַשְׁקִין, וְנָפְלוּ לַאֲוִיר הַתַּנּוּר, וְהוּסַּק הַתַּנּוּר – הַתַּנּוּר טָמֵא, שֶׁסּוֹף מַשְׁקֶה לָצֵאת. אָמַר ר"ל: לֹא שָׁנוּ – אֶלָּא מַשְׁקִין קַלִּים, אֲבָל מַשְׁקִין חֲמוּרִין – טָמֵא, אע"פ שֶׁלֹּא הוּסַּק הַתַּנּוּר. רַבִּי יוֹחָנָן אָמַר: [ג]אֶחָד מַשְׁקִין קַלִּין וְאֶחָד מַשְׁקִין חֲמוּרִין, אִם הוּסַּק הַתַּנּוּר – אִין, אִי לָא – לָא. אֵיתִיבֵיהּ רַבִּי יוֹחָנָן לְרֵישׁ לָקִישׁ: הִטְבִּילוֹ וְעָשָׂה עַל גַּבָּיו טְהָרוֹת, וְהֶעֱבִיר עָלָיו ז' סַמָּנִין וְלֹא עָבַר – הֲרֵי זֶה צֶבַע, וְטָהֳרוֹתָיו טְהוֹרוֹת, וְאֵין צָרִיךְ לְהַטְבִּיל! אֲמַר לֵיהּ: הַנַּח לִכְתָמִים – דְּרַבָּנַן. וְהָתָנֵי רַבִּי חִיָּיא: דַּם הַנִּדָּה וַדַּאי – מַעֲבִיר עָלָיו ז' סַמָּנִין, וּמְבַטְּלוֹ! אֲמַר לֵיהּ: רַבִּי לֹא שָׁנָה, רַבִּי חִיָּיא מְנָא לֵיהּ? אֵיתִיבֵיהּ רַבִּי יוֹחָנָן לְרֵישׁ לָקִישׁ: *[ד]רְבִיעִית דָּם שֶׁנִּבְלַע בַּבַּיִת – הַבַּיִת טָמֵא. וְאָמְרִי לָהּ: הַבַּיִת טָהוֹר, [ה]וְלָא פְּלִיגִי, הָא – בְּכֵלִים דְּמֵעִיקָּרָא, הָא – בְּכֵלִים דְּבַסּוֹף. *[ו]נִבְלְעָה בִּכְסוּת, אִם מִתְכַּבֶּסֶת וְיוֹצֵא מִמֶּנָּה רְבִיעִית דָּם – טְמֵאָה, וְאִם לָאו – טְהוֹרָה! אֲמַר רַב כָּהֲנָא: מִקּוּלֵּי רְבִיעִיּוֹת שָׁנוּ כָּאן, שֶׁאֲנִי דַּם תְּבוּסָה – דְּרַבָּנַן. אֵיתִיבֵיהּ ר"ל לְרַבִּי יוֹחָנָן: *[ז]כָּל הַבָּלוּעַ שֶׁאֵינוֹ יָכוֹל לָצֵאת – טָהוֹר, הָא יָכוֹל לָצֵאת – טָמֵא, וְאַף ע"ג דְּלָא נָפֵיק! *א"ר פַּפָּא: [ח]כָּל הֵיכָא דְּאֵין יָכוֹל לָצֵאת, וְלֹא הִקְפִּיד עָלָיו – דִּבְרֵי הַכֹּל טָהוֹר, יָכוֹל לָצֵאת וְהִקְפִּיד עָלָיו – דִּבְרֵי הַכֹּל טָמֵא, כִּי פְּלִיגִי – דְּיָכוֹל לָצֵאת וְלֹא הִקְפִּיד עָלָיו. מָר סָבַר: כֵּיוָן דְּיָכוֹל לָצֵאת – אַף עַל גַּב דְּלָא הִקְפִּיד עָלָיו. וּמָר סָבַר: אע"ג דְּיָכוֹל לָצֵאת,
אִם

**מִידֵי בִּקְפֵידָא תַּלְיָא מִילְּתָא.** בִּתְמִיָּה. כֵּיוָן דְּטָהֳרוֹת שֶׁבֵּינְתַיִים טְהוֹרוֹת – אַלְמָא, לָאו דָּם הוּא. אַחֲרוֹנוֹת, מִשּׁוּם קְפֵידָא אַמַּאי טְמֵאוֹת? **דַּם הַנִּדָּה וַדַּאי.** כְּגוֹן נִדָּה שֶׁקִּינְּחָה בְּסָדִין דָּם, אַף עַל גַּב דְּוַדַּאי דָּם הוּא. **מַעֲבִיר עָלָיו ז' סַמָּנִין וּמְבַטְּלוֹ.** וַאֲפִילּוּ לֹא עָבַר – הֲרֵי הוּא בָּטֵל, וְטָהוֹר הוּא. הוֹאִיל וְאֵין אָדָם מַקְפִּיד עָלָיו אַחַר הַעֲבָרַת הַסַּמָּנִין, מִדְּאַזֵּל לָהּ חֲזוּתָא. **חֲרָסִין.** כְּגוֹן עָבִיט שֶׁל מֵי רַגְלַיִם שֶׁל זָב וְשֶׁל זָבָה. **שֶׁסּוֹף מַשְׁקֶה לָצֵאת.** כְּלוֹמַר, דֶּרֶךְ מַשְׁקֶה לָצֵאת ע"י לִיבּוּן הַחֶרֶס. וְכֵיוָן שֶׁהָיוּ חֲרָסִין אֵלּוּ בַּתַּנּוּר בִּשְׁעַת הֶיסֵּקוֹ, יָצְאוּ הַמַּשְׁקִין, וְנִטְמָא תַּנּוּר מֵאֲוִירוֹ. **לֹא שָׁנוּ.** הָא דְּקָתָנֵי "הוּסַּק" – אִין, לֹא הוּסַּק – לָא. דְּכָל זְמַן שֶׁהֵן נִבְלָעִין בַּחֲרָסִין – אֵין מְטַמְּאִין אֶת אֲוִיר הַתַּנּוּר אֶלָּא מַשְׁקִין קַלִּין שֶׁאֵינָן אַב הַטּוּמְאָה, כְּגוֹן דִּמְעַת עֵינוֹ וְדַם מַגֵּפָתוֹ אוֹ מֵי רַגְלַיִם דִּטְמֵא מֵת אוֹ טְמֵא שֶׁרֶץ. דַּאֲפִילּוּ כְּשֶׁהוּסַּק וְיָצְאוּ, וְהָיוּ הֵן מַמָּשׁ בַּאֲוִיר הַתַּנּוּר – לֹא טִמְּאוּהוּ אֶלָּא מִדְּרַבָּנַן. דְּאֵין מַשְׁקֶה מְטַמֵּא כְּלִי, חוּץ מִמַּשְׁקֶה אַב הַטּוּמְאָה. **אֲבָל מַשְׁקִין חֲמוּרִין.** כְּגוֹן מֵי רַגְלַיִם שֶׁל זָב וְשֶׁל זָבָה, שֶׁרִיבָּה בָּהֶן הַכָּתוּב מַעְיָינוֹת לְטַמֵּא אָדָם וְכֵלִים. **טָמֵא.** הַתַּנּוּר, אֲפִילּוּ לֹא הוּסַּק, כֵּיוָן דְּיְכוֹלִין לָצֵאת ע"י הֶיסֵּק – לָאו טוּמְאָה בְּלוּעָה הִיא, וּמְטַמְּאָה. **אִי לָא לָא.** דַּהֲוָה לֵיהּ טוּמְאָה בְּלוּעָה בַּחֲרָסִין, וְטוּמְאָה בְּלוּעָה – לָא מְטַמְּיָא, כִּדְאָמַר בְּ"בְּהֵמָה הַמַּקְשָׁה" (חולין עא.). **טָהֳרוֹתָיו טְהוֹרוֹת.** אִי אָמְרַתְּ בִּשְׁלָמָא בָּלוּעַ שֶׁאֵינוֹ יָכוֹל לָצֵאת אֶלָּא ע"י הַדְּחָק, טָהוֹר – מִשּׁוּם הָכִי תָּלֵינַן לְקוּלָּא, וְאָמְרִינַן: לֶבַע הוּא, וְטָהוֹר. מִשּׁוּם דְּאִי נַמִי דָּם הוּא, כֵּיוָן דְּנִבְלַע כָּל כָּךְ, דְּאֵין הַסַּמְמָנִין יְכוֹלִין לְהַעֲבִירוֹ, וְאַף עַל פִּי שֶׁיָּכוֹל לָצֵאת עַל יְדֵי צָפוֹן – טָהוֹר. אֶלָּא לְדִידָךְ, דְּאָמְרַתְּ: הוֹאִיל וִיכוֹלִין לָצֵאת עַל יְדֵי הֶיסֵּק, כִּי לֹא יָצְאוּ נַמִי טְמֵאִין – הָכָא הֵיכִי תָּלֵינַן לְקוּלָּא לֶאֱכוֹל תְּרוּמָה תְּלוּיָה, דִּלְמָא דָּם הוּא? **אֲמַר לֵיהּ הַנַּח לִכְתָמִים.** דְּעִיקַּר תְּחִילַּת גְּזֵרָתָן אֵינָהּ אֶלָּא מִדְּרַבָּנַן. הִילְכָּךְ, מְקִילִּינַן. דְּמִדְּאוֹרַיְיתָא, עַד שֶׁתַּרְגִּישׁ בִּבְשָׂרָהּ. **מַעֲבִיר עָלָיו** כו'. וְהָא הָכָא דְּוַדַּאי דָּם הוּא – מְטַהֲרִינַן לֵיהּ, מִשּׁוּם דְּנִבְלַע כָּל כָּךְ, וְאע"פ שֶׁיָּכוֹל לָצֵאת ע"י צָפוֹן. **אָמַר לוֹ זוֹ אֵינָהּ מִשְׁנָה.** וּמְשׁוּבֶּשֶׁת הִיא, הוֹאִיל וְרַבִּי לֹא שְׁנָאָהּ בְּמִשְׁנָתֵינוּ שֶׁסִּידֵּר אֶת הַמִּשְׁנָה. **ר' חִיָּיא.** תַּלְמִידוֹ, מִנַּיִן לוֹ? **רְבִיעִית דָּם.** שֶׁל מֵת מְטַמֵּא בְּאֹהֶל. **הַבַּיִת טָמֵא.** כְּלֵי הַבַּיִת טְמֵאִין בְּאֹהֶל. **בְּכֵלִים דְּמֵעִיקָּרָא.** שֶׁהָיוּ שָׁם קוֹדֶם שֶׁנִּבְלְעָה – טְמֵאִים, שֶׁנִּטְמְאוּ בְּאֹהֶל. **וְהָא בְּכֵלִים דִּלְבַסּוֹף.** שֶׁבָּאוּ לַבַּיִת לְאַחַר שֶׁנִּבְלַע הַדָּם בַּקַּרְקַע – טְהוֹרִים, דְּתוּ לָא מְטַמְּיָא. **וְאִם לָאו טְהוֹרָה.** וְאע"ג דִּרְבִיעִית שְׁלֵמָה נִבְלַעַת בּוֹ. אַלְמָא, בָּלוּעַ שֶׁאֵינוֹ יָכוֹל לָצֵאת לְהֶדְיָא אֶלָּא ע"י הַדְּחָק, כִּי הָכָא דְּע"י צָפוֹן נָפְקָא כּוּלָּהּ, וְקָתָנֵי: טְהוֹרָה. **דַּם תְּבוּסָה.** הַאי רְבִיעִית דִּמְקִילִּין בָּהּ – לֹא בְּבָאָה מַמָּשׁ מִן הַמֵּת, אֶלָּא בִּרְבִיעִית דַּם תְּבוּסָה, שֶׁהוּא סָפֵק. וַאֲפִי' לֹא נִבְלְעָה – אֵין לָהּ טוּמְאָה וַדָּאִית, כִּדְתַנְיָא בְּפֶ' בַּתְרָא (לקמן דף עא.): אֵיזֶהוּ דַּם תְּבוּסָה? הָרוּג שֶׁיָּצָא מִמֶּנּוּ רְבִיעִית דָּם בְּחַיָּיו וּבְמוֹתוֹ, סָפֵק יָצָא רוּבּוֹ מֵחַיִּים, סָפֵק יָצָא רוּבּוֹ לְאַחַר מִיתָה, וְטָמֵא. **כֵּיוָן דְּיָכוֹל לָצֵאת** כו'. וְהָנָךְ חֲרָסִין, אע"ג דְּלָא קָפֵיד בְּהוּ לְהוֹצִיא כָּל מַה שֶּׁבְּתוֹכָן – טְמֵאִין, כָּל זְמַן שֶׁלֹּא יָצָא, הוֹאִיל וְיָכוֹל לָצֵאת עַל יְדֵי הֶיסֵּק.
אִם

**אמר** רבי אבא מידי בקפידא תליא מילתא. דכיון דלא עבר בראשונה – נתבטל בבגד, וכי עבר נמי בשניה – לא טמא הבגד ביציאתו לחוץ, לפי שנתבטל כמי תכבוסת. וא"ת: ולר' אבא תקשה, אמאי נקט במתניתין "הרי זה לבע", אפילו דם (נדה) ודאי טהור אף למפרע. דכיון דלא עבר – איגלאי מילתא למפרע שנתבטל בבגד, אלא ודאי בקפידא תליא מילתא! וי"ל: דלא איגלאי מילתא למפרע שלא היה ראוי לעבור מתחלה ע"י שלא עבר עתה, שהרי כל שעה הוא מתייבש יותר ויותר, ומעיקרא שמא היה ראוי לעבור. אי נמי: היה סבור כריש לקיש דמטמא טומאה בלועה, לכך אלטריך לומר "ה"ז לבע". **אלמא** בקפידא תליא מילתא. וא"ת: אם כן, מה לורך בהעברת סמנים, כיון דמבטל בלבו – סגי! וי"ל: דבטלה דעתו אלל כל אדם, אם יבטלנו בלא שבעה סממנים. **הנח** לכתמים דרבנן. מיהו כיון דרגילות לבא כתם מגופה – לא מקילינן, אי לאו משום דאיכא למתלי בלבע, (א) כדפירש במתניתין. ולא דמי לדם תבוסה דלקמן, דמקילינן משום דהוי מדרבנן. אי נמי: כדי לטהר אפילו למפרע, נקט "הרי זה לבע". או שמא מתחלה שלא נתייבש כל כך, היה יכול ללאת. **רבי** חייא מנא ליה. וא"ת: אם כן, לעולם לא ניתיב תיובתא מברייתא דמתני בי ר' חייא ובי רבי אושעיא! וי"ל: דבכולהו איכא למימר, כדאמר אילפא בתענית (דף כא.) ובכתובות (דף סט:) כל דאמר מילתא דבי ר' חייא ור' אושעיא ולא פשיטנא ליה ממתני' כו'. והך הוה פשיטא ליה לר"ל: דלא רמיזא במתניתין. ועוד: דסברא הוא, מדנקט מתניתין כתם ולא דם נדה – שמע מינה דדם נדה ודאי לא מלי לבטל, ולית ליה חילוק בין להבא בין למפרע. **אם** מתכבסת ויוצא ממנה רביעית דם. פרש"י ב"הגוזל" (ב"ק קא:) שיתנו מים במדה, ואם כשיסחטנו לחוץ ימלאו רביעית יותר א"כ ודאי היה בו רביעית דם. וקשה: דאפילו לא ימלאו רביעית יותר, מ"מ יכול להיות שהיה בו רביעית. שהרי הכסות בלועה גם מן המים וגם מן הדם, שאין הכל יכול ללאת! ונראה: כדתניא בתוספתא דאהלות (פ"ד) רביעית דם שבלוע בכסות, כילד משערין אותו? מביא מים במדה, ומכבס. ומביא מים אחרים, ונותן בתוכו רביעית דם. ואם היה שוה מראיהן – טמאה. שאם כן, גם מן הבגד ילא רביעית דם. שהרי גם מן המים ומן הדם נשארו בבגד, ולא יהיה מראהו שוה, אם לא היה בו רביעית דם מתחלה. ואם תאמר: ומה לריך מדה למים הראשונים? לא היה לריך אלא שיתן מים במדה שילא מן הבגד פחות רביעית, ויתן רביעית דם לתוכו. ואם ישוה מראיהן – טמא! וכ"ת: שלא הזכיר מדה ראשונה אלא לתת מן השניה כמדתה – הלא על כרחך אינו לריך מן השניים כשיעור שבלעה כסות מן הראשונים! ויש לומר: דמשום הכי נקט מדה בראשונה, שאם ימלא רביעית יותר א"ל לחזור ולטרוח ולהביא מים שניים, כדפרש"י. **ואם** לאו טהורה. אע"ג דכל הרביעית נבלע בבגד. וא"ת: משעה שנפל עליה יחד, נטמא הכסות! וי"ל: דמיירי דקודם שנפל רביעית נבלע בכסות מה שאינו יכול ללאת ע"י סתם כבוס, ונתבטל בבגד, ולא היה (ב) רביעית שלם מעולם. **מקולי** רביעיות שנו כאן. תימה: דב"הגוזל קמא" (ב"ק דף קא.) פריך: תנא "בגד שלבעו בקליפי ערלה – ידלק", אלמא: חזותא מילתא היא. ורמינהי: "רביעית דם שנבלע בבגד" כו'! ומשני: מקולי רביעיות שנו כאן. והא הך שינויא לא הוי אלא לר"ל א"כ תקשה לר' יוחנן! וי"ל: דלר' יוחנן לא קשה מידי טומאה לערלה, דגבי טומאה – משום קפידא. וכיון דאינו יכול ללאת אלא ע"י הדחק – בטל, דטומאה בלועה לא מטמיא. אבל גבי ערלה – ניחא ליה בחזותא, ולא מבטל ליה. והתם משני שינויא דמהני לר"ל וה"ק: אפילו לפי דבריך שאתה מדמה טומאה לאיסור – לא קשה, דדם תבוסה דרבנן. **הא** יכול ללאת טמא. ואם תאמר: ומאי קושיא, דלמא הכי פירושו: כל הבלוע שאינו יכול ללאת על ידי סתם תכבוסת – טהור, אע"ג דיכול ללאת על ידי הדחק בלפון, הא יכול ללאת ע"י סתם תכבוסת – טמא. דהא הך ד"כל הבלוע" סיפא דהך דלעיל "שנבלע בכסות", והאי – בסתם תכבוסת אוקמינן. ופרישנא "ואם לאו, טהורה" אע"ג דיכול ללאת ע"י הדחק בלפון. ואדרבה, קשיא לריש לקיש! ויש לומר: דהך ד"כל הבלוע" משמע: שאינו יכול ללאת כלל, דסתמא קתני, ואפילו הכי קיימא שפיר ארישא.
דה"פ

כלים פ"ט מ"ה וסם איתא וז"ל חרסין שנשתמש בהן זב מסקין טמאין ונפלו לאויר התנור וכו'. ועי' תוס' כריתות טו: ד"ה מגד]

ב"ב קה: אהלות פ"ג מ"ב ע"ש

שם מ"ב

[שם מ"ב]

גי' רש"א א"ר פפא כל היכא דאין יכול לצאת וכו' ד"ה טהור יכול וכו' וכן הוא בגמרות ישנות

הגהות הב"ח

(א) תד"ה הנח וכו' בלבע כדפירשנו: (ב) ד"ה ואם לאו וכו' ולא היה בו רביעית:

## תוספי הרא"ש

ר' לא שנאה ר' חייא מנין לו. תימה וכי מילתא דתמיה היא אי ר' חייא הוסיף לפרש מה שלא פי' ר'. וי"ל דמשמע ליה לר"ל דר' חייא פליג אדר' משום דקתני מתניתין כתם דמשמע דוקא בכתמים משום דכתמים מדרבנן אבל דם נדה לא מהני ליה ביטול. ועוד אפי' לא פליג כל ברייתא דלית לה רמז מהמשנה לא מותבינן מינה תיובתא כדאמרינן בסוף מציאת האשה גבי אילפא תלא נפשיה באיסקרתא ואמר כל דבעי ליה מתניתא דתני בי ר' חייא ור' אושעיא ולא פשיטנא ליה ממתניתין טבענא בימא: **אם** מתכבסת ויוצאה ממנה רביעית דם טמאה. בפרק הגוזל קמא פרש"י דמשערינן אם יש במים שנתכבסו בו רביעית יותר לאחר תכבוסת מקודם תכבוסת ואי אפשר לצמצם שיעור זה יפה בענין זה שהרי נשתייר בבגד מן המים ובפ' ד' דתוספתא דאהלות קתני רביעית דם שנבלעה בכסות כיצד מטהרינן אותה מביא מים במדה ומכבסה בהם ומביא מים אחרים ונותן לתוכן רביעית דם אם מראיהן שוין הרי זו טמאה ואם לאו טהורה. ועתה אין לחוש אם נשאר המים בבגד שהרי הדם נתן מראה אדמומית אף במה שנבלע בבגד. וה"ה שלא היה צריך למדוד המים מתחלה אלא לאחר הכיבוס מודד מי התכבוסת ויקח מים אחרים באותה מדה פחות רביעית. ויתן רביעית דם באותם מים לידע אם מראיהן שוין אלא לכך מודד קודם הכיבוס שאם מוצא בהם רביעית יותר שוב אין צריך להביא אחרים: **ואם** לאו טהור. פי' טהור הבית שהכסות בתוכו. ואי גרס טהורה קאי אכסות אחר שהטבילה. ותימה מאי קשה לר"ל הא דמטמא ר"ל היינו משום שיכול לצאת בהיסק אבל אם אינו יכול לצאת מודה דטהור. וי"ל דה"פ דמתניתין אם יוצא בכיבוס קל טמאה ואם לאו שאינה יוכלה לצאת בקל אלא ע"י הדחק טהורה. **הא** יכול לצאת טמא. ותימה מאי קשה ליה דילמא ה"ק הא יכול לצאת בדבר קל טמא. ור' יוחנן נמי דמטהר היינו במשקין שאין יכולין לצאת אלא ע"י הדחק כגון בהיסק תנור ובצפון דאם יכולין לצאת בז' סממנין מודה דטמא. ואדרבה קשה לר"ל דקתני אין יכולין לצאת טהור דמשמע אין יכול לצאת בקל אע"ג דיכול לצאת ע"י הדחק טהור. וי"ל דמשמע לישנא אין יכול לצאת כלל אפי' ע"י הדחק טהור ובהא מודה ר"ל הא יכול לצאת ע"י הדחק טמא הילכך פריך שפיר לר' יוחנן. ותימה והא סיפא דההיא דכסות דלעיל היא במס' אהלות ופרישית לה אם מתכבסת ויוצא ממנו רביעית דם בדבר קל טמאה ואם לאו שאינו יכול לצאת בקל טהור ועליה קאי הך סיפא ה"ק כל הבלוע שאינו יכול לצאת בקל (טמא) [טהור]. וי"ל דע"כ כל הבלוע שאינו יכול לצאת משמע דאינו יכול לצאת כלל אף על ידי הדחק. וה"פ לר"ל ואם לאו שאין הרביעית של דם תבוסה יכול לצאת בכיבוס קל טהורה שהרי כל הבלוע שאינו יכול לצאת כלל בשום ענין טהור אף בטומאה דאורייתא. הילכך בדם תבוסה דרבנן יש לטהר כשאין יכול לצאת בקל אע"פ שיכול לצאת ע"י הדחק ואליבא דר' יוחנן מפרש רב פפא הכי ואם לאו טהורה כיון שאינו יכול לצאת בקל דמסתמא אינו מקפיד עליו אע"פ שהיה יכול יצאת ע"י הדחק שהרי כל הבלוע שאינו יכול לצאת כלל טהור אע"פ שמקפיד עליו בפי' הילכך היכא דאינו מפרש דמקפיד דין הוא אפי' יכול לצאת ע"י הדחק כיון דאינו יכול לצאת בקל (טמא) [טהור] אף בטומאה דאורייתא הילכך פריך מינה שפיר ר' יוחנן לר"ל:

אִם הִקְפִּיד עָלָיו — אִין, אִי לָא — לָא.§ "אֵיזֶהוּ רוֹק תָּפֵל".§ תָּנָא: אכָּל שֶׁלֹּא טָעַם כְּלוּם מִבָּעֶרֶב. סְבַר רַב פָּפָּא קַמֵּיהּ דְּרָבָא לְמֵימַר: כְּמַאן דַּאֲמַר לָא טְעֵם מִידֵּי בְּאוֹרְתָא. אֲמַר לֵיהּ רָבָא: מִי קָתָנֵי "בָּעֶרֶב" ב"מִבָּעֶרֶב" קָתָנֵי, לְאַפּוּקֵי הֵיכָא דְּקָדֵים וְאָכֵיל. אֲמַר רַבָּה בַּר בַּר חָנָה, אָמַר רַבִּי יוֹחָנָן: גאֵיזֶהוּ רוֹק תָּפֵל — כָּל שֶׁעָבַר עָלָיו חֲצוֹת לַיְלָה, וּבְשֵׁינָה. לְמֵימְרָא דְּבְשֵׁינָה תַּלְיָא מִילְּתָא? *וְהָתְנַן: יָשֵׁן כָּל הַיּוֹם — אֵין זֶה רוֹק תָּפֵל, נֵיעוֹר כָּל הַלַּיְלָה — הֲרֵי זֶה רוֹק תָּפֵל הָתָם — בְּמִתְנַמְנֵם. *הֵיכִי דָּמֵי מִתְנַמְנֵם? אָמַר רַב אָשֵׁי: נִים וְלָא נִים, תִּיר וְלָא תִּיר, דְּקָרוּ לֵיהּ — וְעָנֵי, וְלָא יָדַע לְאַהֲדוּרֵי סְבָרָא, וְכִי מַדְכְּרוּ לֵיהּ — מִדְכַּר. תָּנָא: דהִשְׁכִּים וְשָׁנָה פִּרְקוֹ — אֵין זֶה רוֹק תָּפֵל. וְעַד כַּמָּה? אָמַר רַב יְהוּדָה בַּר שֵׁילָא, אָמַר רַב אַשִׁי, אָמַר רַבִּי אֶלְעָזָר: הכָּל שֶׁיָּצָא רוֹב דִּבּוּרוֹ שֶׁל שָׁלֹשׁ שָׁעוֹת.§ "מֵי גְרִיסִין לְעִיסַּת גְּרִיסִין שֶׁל פּוֹל" וכו'.§ לֵימָא מְסַיֵּיע לֵיהּ לְרֵישׁ לָקִישׁ, דַּאֲמַר ר"ל: רוֹק תָּפֵל צָרִיךְ שֶׁיְּהֵא עִם כָּל אֶחָד וְאֶחָד? דִּלְמָא והַבְלָא דְּפוּמָא מַעֲלֵי. מַתְנִיתִין דְּלָא כְּרַבִּי יְהוּדָה, דְּתַנְיָא, ר' יְהוּדָה אוֹמֵר: מֵי גְרִיסִין רוֹתֵחַ, וְעוֹבֵר שֶׁיִּתֵּן לְתוֹכוֹ מֶלַח. *מַאי מַשְׁמַע דְּהַאי "עוֹבֵר" לִישָּׁנָא דְּאַקְדּוּמֵי הוּא? אָמַר ר"נ בַּר יִצְחָק: דַּאֲמַר קְרָא (שמואל ב יח) "וַיָּרָץ אֲחִימַעַץ דֶּרֶךְ הַכִּכָּר וַיַּעֲבוֹר אֶת הַכּוּשִׁי". אַבַּיֵי אָמַר מֵהָכָא: (בראשית לג) "וְהוּא עָבַר לִפְנֵיהֶם". וְאִיבָּעֵית אֵימָא מֵהָכָא: (מיכה ב) "וַיַּעֲבוֹר מַלְכָּם לִפְנֵיהֶם וַה' בְּרֹאשָׁם".§ "מֵי רַגְלַיִם שֶׁהֶחְמִיצוּ".§ תָּנָא: זכַּמָּה חִימּוּצָן? שְׁלֹשָׁה יָמִים. א"ר יוֹחָנָן: כָּל שִׁיעוּרֵי חֲכָמִים בִּכְתָמִים, צָרִיךְ שִׁיעוּר לְשִׁיעוּרָן. דְּיֶלֶד אוֹ דְּזָקֵן? דְּאִישׁ אוֹ דְּאִשָּׁה? מְכוּסִּים אוֹ מְגוּלִּים? בִּימוֹת הַחַמָּה אוֹ בִּימוֹת הַגְּשָׁמִים?§ ח"וְצָרִיךְ לְכַסְכֵּס שָׁלֹשׁ פְּעָמִים".§ *בָּעֵי רַבִּי יִרְמְיָה: אַמְטוּיֵי וְאַתּוּיֵי — חַד, אוֹ דִּלְמָא אַמְטוּיֵי וְאַתּוּיֵי — תַּרְתֵּי, מַאי? טתֵּיקוּ.§ "הֶעֱבִירָן שֶׁלֹּא כְּסִדְרָן".§ ת"ר: הִקְדִּים שְׁנַיִים לָרִאשׁוֹנִים, תָּנֵי חֲדָא: שְׁנַיִים — עָלוּ לוֹ, רִאשׁוֹנִים — לֹא עָלוּ לוֹ. וְתַנְיָא אִידָךְ: רִאשׁוֹנִים — עָלוּ לוֹ, שְׁנַיִים — לֹא עָלוּ לוֹ. אָמַר אַבַּיֵי: יאִידֵי וְאִידֵי — שְׁנַיִים עָלוּ לוֹ, וְלֹא רִאשׁוֹנִים. וּמַאי "רִאשׁוֹנִים" — רִאשׁוֹנִים לְכְסִדְרָן, וּשְׁנַיִים לְהַעֲבָרָתָן.§

**מתני'** כּכָּל אִשָּׁה שֶׁיֵּשׁ לָהּ וֶסֶת — דַּיָּהּ שְׁעָתָהּ. לוְאֵלּוּ הֵן הַוְּסָתוֹת: מְפַהֶקֶת, וּמְעַטֶּשֶׁת, וְחוֹשֶׁשֶׁת בְּפִי כְרֵיסָהּ וּבְשִׁפּוּלֵי מֵעֶיהָ, וְשׁוֹפַעַת, וּכְמִין צְמַרְמוֹרוֹת אוֹחֲזִין אוֹתָהּ, וְכֵן כַּיּוֹצֵא בָּהֶן. מוְכָל שֶׁקָּבְעָה לָהּ שְׁלֹשָׁה פְּעָמִים — הֲרֵי זֶה וֶסֶת.§

**גמ'** תְּנֵינָא חֲדָא זִימְנָא: *כָּל אִשָּׁה שֶׁיֵּשׁ לָהּ וֶסֶת — דַּיָּהּ שְׁעָתָהּ! הָתָם — בְּוֶסֶתוֹת דְּיוֹמֵי, הָכָא — בְּוֶסֶתוֹת דְּגוּפָא. כִּדְקָתָנֵי: אֵלּוּ הֵן וְסָתוֹת — הָיְתָה מְפַהֶקֶת, מְעַטֶּשֶׁת, וְחוֹשֶׁשֶׁת בְּפִי כְרֵיסָהּ, וּבְשִׁפּוּלֵי מֵעֶיהָ, וְשׁוֹפַעַת. שׁוֹפַעַת? הָא שָׁפְעָה וְאָזְלָא! אָמַר עוּלָּא בְּרֵיהּ דְּרַב עִלַּאי: בְּשׁוֹפַעַת

---

**רש"י**

אם הקפיד עליו אין. והא דקתני "אם יכול לצאת, טמא" — כשהקפיד. באורתא. שאפילו אמש לא טעם כלום. מבערב קתני. אבל אמש אכל כשאר ב"א. לאפוקי דקדים. קודם היום לאחר שניעור משנתו ואכיל, דלא הוי רוק תפל. לפי שהשינה — ממררת את הרוק ומחזקתו, והאוכל — ממתקו ומעביר את כחו. התם. דקתני "ניעור כל הלילה, הרי זה רוק תפל" — לא דניעור ממש, אלא מתנמנם, דודאי שינה של לילה בעינן. ושינת היום, אע"ג דישן — לאו תפל הוא, הואיל וטעם כלום. שהטועם שחרית — נהנה כל היום כולו. השכים ושנה פרקו. הדבור מעביר כח הרוק. של שלש שעות. שהוא עשוי לדבר בשלש שעות. לימא מתני'. דבעי לעיסה כדי שיהא רוק מעורב בגריסין, מסייע ליה לריש לקיש. עובר. קודם, שהמלח מעביר כח הגריסין. ויעבור את הכושי. קדם לפניו. שהחמיצו. שהסריחו. הני מי רגלים דילד או דזקן. של זקן מעלו טפי. מכוסין. מעלו טפי. בימות החמה. מעלו טפי. בעי רבי ירמיה האי שלש פעמים דקתני אמטויי ואתויי חד. הולכה והובאה חשיב חד, או דלמא: אמטויי חשיב חד, ואתויי — חד, דהוו להו תרי. שניים לראשונים. נתר ובורית וקמוניא ואשלג, לרוק תפל ומי גריסין ומי רגלים. תני חדא שניים עלו לו. אותם שהעביר בשנייה — עלו לו. ראשונים לא עלו לו. וכי הדר מעביר נתר ובורית וקמוניא ואשלג זימנא אחריתי, בתר רוק וגריסין ומי רגלים — נמצא עוברין עליו כסדרן. ותניא אידך כו'. וקשיין אהדדי. אמר אביי הא והא סבירא להו שניים שהעביר. (א) שניים שהיה לו להעביר ראשון — עלו לו, וראשונים שהעביר ראשון — לא עלו לו. דהכי שפיר, דכי הדר מצרכינן לעבורינהו בתר שניים — הוי ליה כסדרן. ומאי ראשונים. דקתני באידך ברייתא: "עלו לו"? ראשונים לכסדרן. שהיה לו להעביר תחלה, שהוא העביר לבסוף, דהוו להו הנך ראשונים — לכסדרן, שניים — להעברתן. **מתני'** מפהקת. *אישטרליי"ר בלע"ז. פי כרסה. נגד טבורה. שפולי מעיה. בית הרחם. ושופעת. בגמרא פריך: מאי קאמר? צמרמורות. פרילונ"ש. אוחזין אותה. בכך למודה להיות בכל עת שהיא רואה. דיה שעתה. בכל ראיות שתראה ע"י וסתות אלו. כיוצא בהן. מפרש בגמרא. **גמ'** בוסתות דיומי. כגון מט"ו לט"ו. הא קא שפעה ואזלא. והיכן הוא הוסת, הואיל וכל ימיה רואה?

---

**תוספות**

דה"פ לריש לקיש: שכל הבלוע שאינו יכול לצאת אפילו על ידי הדחק בגפון — טהורה. א] ואם לאו, דיכול לצאת ע"י הדחק — טמאה אפילו בטומאה דאורייתא. ואם כן, בדם תבוסה דרבנן, אפילו יוצא על ידי הדחק — טהור. והשתא מפרש בסיפא ויהיב טעמא לרישא (ב) בטומאה דאורייתא, דכי אינו יכול לצאת — טהורה, אבל יכול לצאת על ידי הדחק — טמאה. ולר' יוחנן דמפרש כדמשני רב פפא — פירוש: דרישא אם מתכבסת ויוצא ממנו בתכבוסת סתם — טמא, שכן דרך להקפיד עליו הואיל ויוצא בקל. ואם לאו — טהורה, ואפילו יוצא ע"י צפון, דאין דרך להקפיד עליו כיון שאינו יוצא בתכבוסת סתם. ומייתי כל הבלוע, ליתן טעם לרישא, דכיון (ג) דאינו יכול לצאת כלל, אפילו הקפיד בפירוש — אין קפידתו קפידא, דבטלה דעתו אצל כל אדם שאין דרכן להקפיד. ברישא נמי יכול לצאת על ידי הדחק, ועל ידי כבוס סתם אינו יכול לצאת — טהור, הואיל ואין דרך להקפיד בסתם. והיינו כדמשני רב פפא כל היכא דאינו יכול לצאת כו'. והשתא רב פפא אינו סותר מה שאמר למעלה, אלא בא לתרץ דה"פ: הא יכול לצאת על ידי הדחק, והקפיד עליו להוציאו — טמא. וכי קאמר לעיל טהור — בשלא הקפיד עליו להוציאו. ולא היה צריך רב פפא לומר אלא "התם בדקפיד", אלא בא להשמיענו פלוגתא דרבי יוחנן ור"ל: דפליגי בדלא קפיד ויכול לצאת על ידי הדחק, דר"ל מטמא ור"י מטהר.

**נים** ולא נים תיר ולא תיר. פי': נים ולא נים — בתחלת שינה, תיר ולא תיר — בסוף שינה, כשהוא ניעור משנתו. וב"ערבי פסחים" (פסחים קכ:) נמי גבי "נתנמנמו יאכלו", ונקט כי האי לישנא "נים ולא נים, תיר ולא תיר". איכא לפרושי בכי האי גוונא: נים ולא נים — שעתה בחצות הלילה מתחיל להתנמנם, תיר ולא תיר — שישן בחצי הראשון ועתה כשמגיע בחצות הלילה היה מתחיל ליעור, והוא תיר ולא תיר*.

**תנא** כמה חימוצן שלשה ימים. קשה: דבפרק "רבי עקיבא" (שבת דף צ.) קאמר גבי "מי רגלים שהחמילו", בני מ' יום — משמע: ולא קודם לכן! ואיכא ספרים דגרסי "עד ארבעים יום". ולפי זה ניחא, דאיכא למימר: משלשה ועד ארבעים מעלו. ואיכא ספרים דגרסי "בן ארבעים", וקאי אתינוק שהוא בן מ' יום. וקשה: דהא לקמן איבעיא להו דילד או דזקן? וי"ל דה"פ: דילד דווקא, או אפילו דזקן נמי, ולא כפ"ה דפירש דזקן מעלו טפי. וכן משמע מדקאמר "דאיש או דאשה" — וליכא למימר או דאשה דוקא, דהא "דילד או דזקן" נקט לשון זכר. וכן בשבת "בן מ' — לשון איש. מיהו תימה: אמאי לא מייתי הכא הך ברייתא דשבת ד"בן מ' יום" *ועוד מילי טובא שמאריך באותה ברייתא יותר מהכא, והכא מאריך בדין מי רגלים יותר מהתם? ונראה לומר: דברייתא דהתם קאי אמילתא דת"ק דאמר "כדי לכבס בו בגד קטן", והתם לא מעלו אלא בני מ' יום. והכא, לגבי כתם איירי, ומעלו בני שלשה ימים, ולא שייכי כולהו מילי דהתם הכא, ומשום הכי לא מייתי ההיא ברייתא הכא*.

**מפהקת**. פי' בקונטרס: אשטריליי"ר בלע"ז. ואין נראה, אלא כמו שפירש בשבת (דף קלו.) גבי "פיהק ומת": באליי"ר, כדאמר בברכות (דף כד:) גבי רבי שהיה מפהק, ומניח ידו תחת סנטרו. **מעטשת**. אישטרנויי"ר. וגוסה פירש רש"י בגמרא: באליי"ר. ואין נראה, אלא פירוש: רוטי"ר. וכן *"גיהק בתפלה" — רוטי"ר. ובערוך פירש: קול היוצא מן הגרון מתוך מאכל כבד, וזה רוטי"ר. ואין נראה לפרש סנגלוטי"ר. וכולהו הני וסתות איירי שמפהקת או מעטשת שעה או שתים בעת שרגילה לראות, אבל משום פיהוק או עיטוש חדא זימנא — לא קבעה. מדמפליג *בין תחלת וסת לסוף וסת, ובחד פיהוק וחד עיטוש לא שייך תחלה וסוף.

לימים

---

**תוספי הרא"ש**

**וכמה** חימוצה ג' ימים. בשבת פרק ר' עקיבא מפרש בגמרא מ' יום ובמי רגלים דהכא איירי דקתני התם ר' יהודה אומר כדי להעביר את הכתם [וי"ל] דכאן פי' דפחות מג' ימים לא מהני והתם [אמר] דטפי ממ' יום לא מהני. וי"מ הא דקאמר התם בן מ' יום היינו של תינוק בן מ' יום והא דמיבעיא ליה הכא דילד או זקן י"ל דה"ק דילד או אפי' דזקן. וקצת תימה דלא מייתי בשמעתין ההיא דשבת: **דילד** או דזקן. כולה שמעתין מוכחא דמי רגלים דמתניתין מי רגלים ממש ולא עשב שכך שמו ומי רגלים דפיטום הקטרת ומי רגלים דהכא שוין כדמוכח בפ' דם חטאת דפריך והא בעינן לאעבורי סממנין על הכתם ותנן אין מכניסין מי רגלים למקדש ודלא כדברי המפרשים שהוא עשב ששמו מי רגלים ובשביל ששמו מכוער אין מכניסין אותו למקדש: **ותניא** אידך ראשונים עלו לו שניים לא עלו לו. וקשה ליה מברייתא אברייתא וגם פי' דברייתא תנינא לא ידע: **מפהק**. פרש"י אשטורלייה. אדם שפושט אבריו. ובפ' אם לא הביא גבי פיהק ומת פי' פלייר אדם הפותח פיו. וכן נראה מהא דאמרינן בברכות גבי ר' כשהיה מפהק היה מניח ידו על סנטרו. ובערוך פי' קול היוצא מן הגרון מתוך שאכל מאכל כבד. ונראה דלא איירי בקביעות וסת דגיהוק ופיהוק דחדא זימנא אלא כמה פעמים היא עושה כן בשעת וסתה דבחד פיהוק ובחד עיטוש לא שייך תחלה וסוף וכל אלו וסתות דגופה אין להם זמן קבוע:

---

**עין משפט נר מצוה**

לו א ב ג ד ה ו ז מיי' פ"ט מהל' איסורי ביאה הל' לח:

לז ח ט י מיי' שם הלכה לז ולחומרא:

לח כ מיי' שם הל"ד ופי"ד מהל' משכב ומושב הל"ז:

לט ל מ מיי' שם פ"ח הל"ב ופ"ג מהל' משכב ומושב הל"ו סמג לאוין קיא טוש"ע יו"ד סי' קפט סעי' יט:

**הגהות מהר"ב רנשבורג**

א] תוד"ה (בדף סב ע"ב) הא יכול וכו' ואם לאו דיכול לצאת אפי' ע"י הדחק טמאה טומאה דאורייתא וכו' כצ"ל לענ"ד ועי' מהרש"א והיא היא:

[ועי"ע תוס' תענית יב: ד"ה נים]

אבל בגמרות שלפנינו ליתא התם אלא הך מילתא דבן מ' יום ע"ש רש"א

**מסורת הש"ס**

גי' יעב"ץ והתניא

פסחים קכ: תענית יב. מגילה יח: יבמות נד.

סוכה לט. פסחים ז: קיט. מגילה כא: [מנחות לה]

[מנחות עו. ב"ק קיט:]

[והא אדם שפושט אבריו כ"כ הרא"ש]

לעיל ג.

[ועי' מנחות מג. וכתוס' שם ד"ה בן ארבעים]

[ברכות כד.]

[במתניתין לקמן ע"ב]

**הגהות הב"ח**

(א) רש"י ד"ה אמר אביי וכו' שניים שהעביר שניה שהיה: (ב) תוס' ד"ה (בדף סב ע"ב) הא יכול וכו' לריכה טומאה דאורייתא וכו': (ג) בא"ד דכיון דבלאו הכי יכול לצאת וכו' נמי יכול לצאת ע"י הדחק:

בשופעת דם טמא מתוך דם טהור.§ "וכמין צמרמורות" וכו'.§ "וכן כיוצא בהן" לאתויי מאי? אמר רבה בר עולא: לאתויי אשה שראשה כבד עליה, ואבריה כבדים עליה, ורותתת, וגוסה. אמר רב הונא בר חייא, אמר שמואל: הרי אמרו לימים – שנים, לוסתות – אחת, למה שלא מנו חכמים – שלשה. "למה שלא מנו חכמים" – לאתויי מאי? אמר רב יוסף: לאתויי ראשה כבד עליה, ואבריה כבדין עליה, ורותתת, וגוסה. א"ל אביי: מאי קא משמע לן? מתני' היא, דהא פרשה רבה בר עולא! אלא אמר אביי: לאתויי – אכלה שום וראתה, ואכלה בצלים וראתה, כססה פלפלים וראתה. *אמר רב יוסף: לא שמיע לי הא שמעתא. *אמר ליה אביי: את אמריתה ניהלן, ואהא אמריתה ניהלן: היתה למודה להיות רואה יום חמשה עשר ושינתה ליום עשרים – זה וזה אסורין. שלש פעמים ליום עשרים – הותר יום חמשה עשר, וקבעה לה יום עשרים, שאין אשה קובעת לה וסת – עד שתקבענה שלש פעמים. ואמרת לן עלה אמר רב יהודה, אמר שמואל: זו דברי ר"ג בר רבי שאמר משום רשב"ג, אבל חכמים אומרים: ראתה – אינה צריכה לא לשנות ולא לשלש. ואמרינן לך: לשנות אמרת לן, לשלש מיבעיא? ואמרת לן לשנות – בוסתות, לשלש – בימים. ונימא זו דברי רשב"ג! הא קמ"ל שמואל: דר"ג ברבי כרשב"ג סבירא ליה.§ מתני' היתה למודה להיות רואה בתחלת הוסתות, כל הטהרות שעשתה בתוך הוסתות – טמאות. בסוף הוסתות – כל הטהרות שעשתה בתוך הוסתות טהורות. רבי יוסי אומר: אף ימים ושעות וסתות. היתה למודה להיות רואה עם הנץ החמה – אינה אסורה אלא עם הנץ החמה. רבי יהודה אומר: כל היום שלה. גמ' תנא, כיצד א"ר יוסי: ימים ושעות וסתות – היתה למודה להיות רואה מיום עשרים ליום עשרים, ומשש שעות לשש שעות, הגיע יום עשרים ולא ראתה – אסורה לשמש כל שש שעות ראשונות – דברי רבי יהודה, ורבי יוסי מתיר עד שש שעות, וחוששת בשש שעות. עברו שש שעות ולא ראתה – אסורה לשמש כל היום כולו – דברי ר' יהודה, ורבי יוסי מתיר מן המנחה ולמעלה.§ "היתה למודה".§ והתניא, רבי יהודה אומר: כל הלילה שלה! לא קשיא, הא – דרגילה לראות בתחלת יממא, והא – דרגילה לראות בסוף ליליא. תני חדא: רבי יהודה אוסרה לפני וסתה, ומתירה לאחר וסתה. ותניא אידך: אוסרה לאחר וסתה, ומתירה לפני וסתה. ולא קשיא, הא – דרגילה למחזי בסוף ליליא, הא – דרגילה למחזי בתחלת יממא. אמר רבא: הלכה כרבי יהודה. ומי אמר רבא הכי? *והתניא: "והזרתם את בני ישראל מטומאתם", מכאן א"ר *ירמיה: אזהרה לבני ישראל שיפרשו מנשותיהן *סמוך לוסתן. וכמה? אמר *)רבא: עונה. מאי לאו – עונה אחריתי? לא, אותה עונה. ותרתי למה לי? צריכא, דאי אשמועינן הא הוה אמינא: ה"מ – לטהרות, אבל לבעלה – לא, קמ"ל. ואי מההיא – הוה אמינא: סמוך לוסתה עונה אחריתי, קמ"ל אותה עונה.§ מתני' *היתה למודה להיות רואה יום ט"ו ושינתה להיות רואה ליום כ' זה וזה אסורין. שינתה פעמים ליום כ' – זה וזה אסורין. שינתה ג' פעמים ליום כ' – הותר ט"ו וקבעה לה יום כ' שאין אשה קובעת לה וסת עד שתקבענה ג' פעמים, ואינה מטהרת מן הוסת – עד שתעקר ממנה ג' פעמים.§ גמ'

*) נ"ל רבה

ויקרא טו

---

**רש"י**

בשופעת דם טמא מתוך דם טהור. רגילה לראות דם טהור תחלה ואח"כ דם טמא – הוי וסת, וכל שעה שתראה דם טמא אחר דם טהור – אמרינן דדיה שעתה. גוסה. בלאיי"ר. הרי אמרו. לקמן בשמעתין "אינה צריכה לא לשנות ולא לשלש", ומפרש לה: לשנות בוסתות כו'. לימים שנים. וסתות דיומי, משתקבעתן שתי פעמים – הוי וסת. לוסתות. דגופה, כגון הני דמתניתין, משתקבעתן פעם אחת – הוי וסת. למה שלא מנו חכמים. וסת שלש. וקמיבעיא ליה לשמואל: "למה שלא מנו חכמים", מאי היא? והכי קאמר שמואל: אני שמעתי כן, "למה שלא מנו חכמים שלש", אבל איני יודע מהו. מתניתין היא. דקתני: "וכן כיוצא בהן", ופירשה רבה בר עולא: לאתויי הני. הא שמעתתא. דשמואל, דאמר: לימים שנים, לוסתות אחד. זה וזה. כשיגיע עוד חמשה עשר – אסורה לשמש, שמא תחזור לוסתה. וכשיגיע יום עשרים – נמי תאסר, שמא מעכשיו תקבע וסת ליום עשרים. שאמר משום רבן שמעון בן גמליאל. דלא הוי חזקה בציר מתלת זימני, כדשמעינן ליה לרבן שמעון בן גמליאל בכל דוכתי: לשלישי תנשא, לרביעי לא תנשא (יבמות דף סד:). ונימא זו דברי רשב"ג. דהא קיימא לן בכל דוכתי, דבעי שלשה זימני לחזקה. מתני' בתוך וסתות. בוסתות דגופה קאמר. אף ימים ושעות. בגמ' מפרש. אינה אסורה אלא עם הנץ החמה. וכל הלילה משמשת, ואם עבר הנץ החמה ולא ראתה – משמשת כל היום. ורבי יוסי קתני לה, דדייק שעת הוסתות, ותו לא. רבי יהודה אומר כל היום שלה. מותרת לשמש משעבר הנץ החמה ולא ראתה, אבל כל הלילה שלפני הנץ החמה של וסתה – אסורה לשמש. ומפרש בגמרא דהאי "למודה עם הנץ החמה" דקתני – דרגילה למחזי בסוף ליליא מקמי דלימטי תחלת יממא. ואנן אסרינן לה כל עונת וסתה – נמצאת אסורה כל הלילה, שהיא עונת וסתה. ורבי יהודה מחמיר. גמ' אסורה לשמש כל היום כולו דברי רבי יהודה. ורבי יהודה לטעמיה, דאמר: כל עונת וסתה אסורה, ועונה הוי או יום או לילה. ומי שוסתה בלילה, ואפילו בסופה – אסורה כל הלילה. ואם וסתה ביום, ואפי' בסופו – כל היום אסורה. עד שש שעות. דשעות דייקינן, הואיל ווסתה בשעה ששית – אינה אסורה לא לפניה ולא לאחריה. וחוששת לשש שעות. שעה ששית היא אסורה, שהוא וסתה. מן המנחה. היינו משש שעות ולמעלה, מכי יטו צללי ערב. וכשבע, כבר נטו הצללים, שהחמה במערב. עם הנץ. דמתניתין, בסוף לילה. לפיכך, כל היום שלה, (א) והלילה אסורה. "עם הנץ" דברייתא – בתחלת יממא, ולפיכך לילה מותרת ויום אסורה. והזרתם את בני ישראל. וסמיך ליה "והדוה בנדתה". עונה אחריתי. דאם וסתה ביום – אסורה כל היום וכל הלילה שלפניו. ורבי יהודה לא אסר אלא עונת וסתה. ותרתי למה ליה. לרבא לאשמועינן? מתני' ואינה מטהרת מן הוסת. דאסורה כל ימי וסתה, שמא תראה. גמ' קבעה

---

**תוספות**

לימים שנים. היינו כרבי, דאמר: *בתרי זימני הויא חזקה. ושלא מנו חכמים – ג' הואיל ואינו וסת גמור, מודה רבי דבעי ג' זימני, והכי קים ליה. אכלה שום וראתה. הואיל ועל ידי מעשה הם – אינו וסת גמור, ולא הוה בכלל דמתני' וא"ת: ואמאי לא קאמר נמי "קפצה וראתה", דהוו נמי על ידי מעשה? ויש לומר: דאינה קובעת וסת לקפיצות לחודיהו, כדאמר בפרק קמא (לעיל יא.) דכל שתקבענה מחמת אונס, אפי' כמה פעמים – לא קבעה. אבל אכלה שום לא חשיב אונס כמו טורח של קפיצה, שאין הראייה באה על ידי טורח אלא ממילא. זו דברי רשב"ג אבל חכמים אומרים כו' – לכאורה משמע: "זו", ולא סבירא ליה. מדלא קאמר "אבל רבי אומר". ואפילו את"ל הכי, לא תקשי לקמן גבי דילוג דמוקמינן שמואל כרשב"ג דאליבא דמתניתין פליגי רב ושמואל. ולמאי דאמר מעיקרא התלמוד דפליגי בפלוגתא דרבי ורשב"ג צריך לומר: "זו" וסבירא ליה, כדמשני בפרק "שור שנגח" (ב"ק דף לז:). אסורה לשמש כל שש שעות דברי רבי יהודה. לר' יהודה הוה שייך למתני "כל היום כולו", כדמוכח בסיפא שהוא אוסר כל היום, אלא משום רבי יוסי תני לה בתרתי בבי. וחוששת בששה שעות. היינו, כל שעה ששית. מן המנחה ולמעלה. פירש"י: סוף שש, שמאז נוטי' צללי ערב. ופי' רשב"ם: דאף על גב דאמר ב"תמיד נשחט" (פסחים נח.) דזמן המנחה לכל המוקדם הוי משש שעות ומחצה ואילך – היינו, משום דלא קים לן שפיר בשיעור שעות היום. אבל מן הדין הוא מתחילת ז' ומיהו לגבי וסת נמי אסורה עד חצי שעה שביעית, דהיינו "מן המנחה ולמעלה". איתמר

---

**עין משפט נר מצוה**

[עירובין נז.]

מ א מיי' פ"א מהל' איסורי ביאה הל"ב וע"ש ומיי' פ"ב מהל' משכב ומושב הל"ו סמג לאוין קיא טוש"ע יו"ד סי' קפט סעי' יט:

מא ב שם סעי' כג בהגה"ה:

מב ג מיי' פ"ג מהל' משכב ומושב הל"ו סמג שם טוש"ע שם סעיף כל:

מג ד ה מיי' פ"ח מהל' איסורי ביאה הל' ג וע"ש סמג שם טוש"ע שם סי' קפד סעיף ב:

מד ו מיי' שם הל"ד סמג שם טוש"ע שם סימן קפט סעיף יד:

מה ז מיי' שם טוש"ע שם סעי' ב:

**תוספי הרא"ש**

לימים שנים. כר' דאמר בתרי זימני הויא חזקה אבל ווסתות דגופה קים ליה לשמואל דלר' סגיא ליה בחדא זימנא. ולמה שלא מנו חכמים כגון ע"י מעשה באים מודה ר' דאינן ראויין לקבוע בפחות מג': לאיתויי אכלה שום ובצל וכססה פלפלין. ולא הוו ככל הנהו דפי' רבה בר עולא דהנהו אתו ממילא והנך ע"י מעשה לכך צריך ג' זימני ולא בעי למימר לאיתויי קפצה וראתה דהא תניא בפ"ק כל שתקבענה מחמת אונס לא הוי וסת אבל אכלה שום ובצל לא חשיב אונס דאין הראיה באה ע"י טורח אלא ממילא: אמר שמואל זו דברי רשב"ג. אם נפרש זו ולא ס"ל אלא סבר כר' דאמר בתרי זימני הוי חזקה כדמשמע בכל דוכתא זו ולא ס"ל לא תיקשי לך הא דפליגי רב ושמואל בסמוך ואמר שמואל עד שתשלש בדילוג דהתם אליבא דרשב"ג פליגי אבל מ"מ שמואל כר' ס"ל אבל מעיקרא דבעי למימר תלמודא דפליגי מפלוגתא דר' ורשב"ג ע"כ זו וס"ל קאמר וה"נ אשכחן בריש שור שנגח ד' וה': מן המנחה ולמעלה. פרש"י מתחלת ז' נוטין צללי ערב ואינה אסורה אלא עד סוף שעה ששית. אע"ג דלכל המוקד' בחצי שביעית הוי זמן התמיד היינו לפי שאין אנו בקיאין בשעות היום כדאמרינן בפ' אמר להם הממונה אבל מן הדין הוי מתחלת שעה שביעית. א"נ חצי שביעית וחצי ששית חמה עומדת בראש כל אדם ולכך הוי בכלל חצות עד שש שעות ומחצה: ומי אמר רבא הכי והתניא והזרתם כו' כ"ש אי הוה סבר כר' יוסי דקשיא ליה טפי אלא לא נחת אלא לפרושי תרתי מילי דרבא דצריכי תרווייהו: שינתה ליום עשרים זה וזה אסורין וחוששת ליום ט"ו שאחר ראיית עשרים ואם [לא] תראה ביום ט"ו חוששת ליום עשרים שאחר ראיית יום כ' זה:

---

**מסורת הש"ס**

תורה אור

[עירובין י. וש"נ]

[שם וש"נ]

יבמות סב: שבועות יח:

[בשבועו' איתא ר' יאשיה]

[יבמות סב: שבועות יח.]

[לעיל לט.]

יבמות סד: ודף סב.

**הגהות הב"ח**

(א) רש"י ד"ה עם הנץ וכו' כל היום שלה מותרת והלילה אסורה:

**גמ'** אִיתְּמַר, *רָאֲתָה יוֹם חֲמִשָּׁה עָשָׂר לְחֹדֶשׁ זֶה, וְיוֹם ט"ז לְחֹדֶשׁ זֶה, וְיוֹם שִׁבְעָה עָשָׂר לְחֹדֶשׁ זֶה. רַב אָמַר: קָבְעָה לָהּ וֶסֶת לְדִילּוּג. וּשְׁמוּאֵל אָמַר: [א]עַד שֶׁתְּשַׁלֵּשׁ בְּדִילּוּג. נֵימָא רַב וּשְׁמוּאֵל בִּפְלוּגְתָּא דְּרַבִּי ורשב"ג קָמִיפַּלְגִי; דְּתַנְיָא, *[ב]נִיסֵּת לָרִאשׁוֹן – וּמֵת, לַשֵּׁנִי – וּמֵת, לַשְּׁלִישִׁי – לֹא תִּנָּשֵׂא, דִּבְרֵי רַבִּי. רשב"ג אוֹמֵר: לג' תִּנָּשֵׂא, לד' – לֹא תִּנָּשֵׂא. לָא, דכ"ע כרשב"ג וְהָכָא בְּהָא קָמִיפַּלְגִי; רַב סָבַר – חֲמִשָּׁה עָשָׂר מִמִּנְיָנָא, וּשְׁמוּאֵל סָבַר – כֵּיוָן דְּלָאו בְּדִילּוּג חֲזִיתֵיהּ, לָאו מִמִּנְיָנָא הוּא. אֵיתִיבֵיהּ: [ג]הָיְתָה לְמוּדָה לִהְיוֹת רוֹאָה יוֹם ט"ו וְשִׁינְּתָה לְיוֹם שִׁשָּׁה עָשָׂר – זֶה וָזֶה אֲסוּרִין. שִׁינְּתָה לְיוֹם שִׁבְעָה עָשָׂר – הוּתַּר שִׁשָּׁה עָשָׂר וְנֶאֱסַר חֲמִשָּׁה עָשָׂר וְשִׁבְעָה עָשָׂר. שִׁינְּתָה לְיוֹם שְׁמוֹנָה עָשָׂר – הוּתְּרוּ כּוּלָּן, וְאֵין אָסוּר אֶלָּא מִשְּׁמוֹנָה עָשָׂר וְאֵילָךְ. קַשְׁיָא לְרַב! אָמַר לָךְ רַב: לְמוּדָה שָׁאנֵי. [ו]וְדְקָאָרֵי לָהּ, מַאי קָאָרֵי לָהּ לְמוּדָה אִצְטְרִיכָא לֵיהּ. מַהוּ דְּתֵימָא: כֵּיוָן דִּלְמוּדָה, וַעֲקַרְתֵּיהּ – בִּתְרֵי זִימְנֵי עָקְרָה לֵיהּ, קמ"ל. מֵיתִיבֵי: רָאֲתָה יוֹם עֶשְׂרִים וְאֶחָד בְּחֹדֶשׁ זֶה, יוֹם עֶשְׂרִים וּשְׁנַיִם בְּחֹדֶשׁ זֶה, יוֹם עֶשְׂרִים וּשְׁלֹשָׁה בְּחֹדֶשׁ זֶה – קָבְעָה לָהּ וֶסֶת. סֵירְגָה לְיוֹם עֶשְׂרִים וְאַרְבָּעָה – לֹא קָבְעָה לָהּ וֶסֶת. תְּיוּבְתָּא דִּשְׁמוּאֵל! אָמַר לָךְ שְׁמוּאֵל: הָכָא בְּמַאי עָסְקִינַן – כְּגוֹן דִּרְגִילָה לְמֶחֱזֵי בְּיוֹם עֶשְׂרִים, וְשִׁינְּתָה לְיוֹם עֶשְׂרִים וְאֶחָד. דַּיְקָא נַמִי, דְּשָׁבְקִינַן לְיוֹם עֶשְׂרִים, וְנָקַט לְיוֹם עֶשְׂרִים וְאֶחָד ש"מ. § "שֶׁאֵין הָאִשָּׁה קוֹבַעַת לָהּ וֶסֶת עַד שֶׁתִּקְבָּעֶנָּה" וכו'. § א"ר פַּפָּא: [ד]לָא אֲמָרַן – אֶלָּא לְמִקְבְּעָה, אֲבָל לְמֵיחַשׁ לָהּ – בַּחֲדָא זִימְנָא חָיְישָׁא. מַאי קמ"ל? תָּנֵינָא: הָיְתָה לְמוּדָה לִהְיוֹת רוֹאָה יוֹם חֲמִשָּׁה עָשָׂר, וְשִׁינְּתָה לְיוֹם עֶשְׂרִים – זֶה וָזֶה אֲסוּרִין! אִי מֵהָתָם – ה"א: ה"מ – הֵיכָא דְּקַיְימָא בְּתוֹךְ יְמֵי נִדָּתָהּ, אֲבָל הֵיכָא דְּלָא קַיְימָא בְּתוֹךְ יְמֵי נִדָּתָהּ – אֵימָא לָא, קמ"ל. § "וְאֵינָהּ מְטַהֶרֶת מִן הַוֶּסֶת" וכו'. § א"ר פַּפָּא: [ה]לָא אֲמָרַן, אֶלָּא דִּקְבַעְתֵּיהּ תְּלָתָא זִימְנֵי – דִּצְרִיכִי תְּלָתָא זִימְנֵי לְמֶעְקְרֵיהּ, אֲבָל תְּרֵי זִימְנֵי – בַּחֲדָא זִימְנָא מִיעֲקַר. מַאי קמ"ל? תָּנֵינָא: אֵין הָאִשָּׁה קוֹבַעַת לָהּ וֶסֶת עַד שֶׁתִּקְבָּעֶנָּה שָׁלֹשׁ פְּעָמִים! מַהוּ דְּתֵימָא: חֲדָא – לְחַד, תְּרֵי – לְתַרְתֵּי, וּתְלָתָא – לִתְלָתָא, קָא מַשְׁמַע לָן. תַּנְיָא כְּוָתֵיהּ דְּרַב פַּפָּא: [ו]הָיְתָה לְמוּדָה לִהְיוֹת רוֹאָה יוֹם עֶשְׂרִים, וְשִׁינְּתָה לְיוֹם שְׁלֹשִׁים – זֶה וָזֶה אֲסוּרִין, הִגִּיעַ יוֹם עֶשְׂרִים וְלֹא רָאֲתָה – מוּתֶּרֶת לְשַׁמֵּשׁ עַד יוֹם שְׁלֹשִׁים, וְחוֹשֶׁשֶׁת לְיוֹם שְׁלֹשִׁים. הִגִּיעַ יוֹם שְׁלֹשִׁים וְרָאֲתָה, הִגִּיעַ יוֹם עֶשְׂרִים וְלֹא רָאֲתָה, וְהִגִּיעַ יוֹם שְׁלֹשִׁים וְלֹא רָאֲתָה, וְהִגִּיעַ יוֹם עֶשְׂרִים וְרָאֲתָה – הוּתַּר יוֹם שְׁלֹשִׁים וְנֶאֱסַר

---

**רש"י**

קָבְעָה לָהּ וֶסֶת לְדִילּוּג. וַאֲסוּרָה לְיוֹם י"ח לְחֹדֶשׁ רְבִיעִי, וּלְיוֹם י"ט בְּחֹדֶשׁ חֲמִישִׁי, וְכֵן לְעוֹלָם. עַד שֶׁתְּשַׁלֵּשׁ בְּדִילּוּג. וְיוֹם ט"ו אֵינוֹ מִן הַמִּנְיָן – שֶׁהוּא תְּחִלַּת רְאִיָּיתָהּ, וְאֵין שָׁם דִּילּוּג. הָיְתָה לְמוּדָה. וֶסֶת קָבוּעַ לְט"ו, וְשִׁינְּתָה לְי"ו – זֶה וָזֶה אֲסוּרִין. כְּלוֹמַר, כְּשֶׁיַּגִּיעַ ט"ו וְי"ו עוֹד – תֵּאָסֵר. חָזְרָה וְשִׁינְּתָה בַּשְּׁנִיָּה [לְשִׁבְעָה עָשָׂר] – הוּתַּר ט"ז מִכָּאן וְאֵילָךְ, שֶׁלֹּא קְבָעַתּוֹ אֶלָּא פַּעַם אַחַת. הִלְכָּךְ, בְּפַעַם אַחַת הוּא נֶעֱקָר. הוּתְּרוּ כּוּלָּן. ט"ו – שֶׁהֲרֵי עֲקַרְתּוֹ שְׁלֹשָׁה פְּעָמִים, וְט"ז וְי"ז – בַּחֲדָא זִימְנָא מִיעֲקַר, וַאֲפִילּוּ י"ח הַבָּא לֹא יֵאָסֵר, אֶלָּא י"ט. כִּדְקָתָנֵי: "מִשְּׁמוֹנָה עָשָׂר וְאֵילָךְ", שֶׁהֲרֵי שִׁילְּשָׁה בְּדִילּוּג וְקָבְעָה לָהּ וֶסֶת לְדִילּוּג. תְּיוּבְתָּא דְּרַב. דְּהָא קָתָנֵי: שִׁינְּתָה לְשִׁבְעָה עָשָׂר – נֶאֱסַר ט"ו וְי"ו, וְלָא קָתָנֵי מִי"ז וְאֵילָךְ, וְאַע"ג דְּדִילְּגָה ב' זִימְנֵי. אַלְמָא, רְאִיָּיה קַמַּיְיתָא – לָאו מִמִּנְיָנָא. לְמוּדָה שָׁאנֵי. כֵּיוָן דְּוִסְתָּהּ קָבוּעַ לְט"ו – שָׁדֵינַן רְאִיָּיה שֶׁל ט"ו עִם רְאִיּוֹת שֶׁעָבְרוּ עָלֶיהָ, שֶׁהֲרֵי בִּזְמַנָּהּ רָאֲתָה, וְהֵיכִי הֲוָה מָלֵינַן לְמִימְנְיֵיהּ עִם הָנֵי דְּדִילּוּג?! וְכִי אָמֵינָא אֲנָא – הֵיכָא דִּרְאִיַּית ט"ו שֶׁהָיְתָה תְּחִלַּת רְאִיָּיתָהּ, אוֹ שֶׁלֹּא הָיָה לָהּ וֶסֶת קוֹדֶם לָכֵן, אוֹ שֶׁהָיָה לָהּ וֶסֶת לְיוֹם עֶשְׂרִים. וּדְקָאָרֵי לָהּ מַאי קָאָרֵי לָהּ. הָא וַדַּאי הֵיכִי מָצֵי לְאַקְשׁוּיֵי מִלְּמוּדָה? קס"ד. ה"ה לְשֶׁאֵינָהּ לְמוּדָה בָּעֵינַן תְּלָתָא זִימְנֵי דִּילּוּג, וְהַאי דְּנָקַט "לְמוּדָה" – לָאו מִשּׁוּם *עֲקִירַת וֶסֶת דִּילּוּג, לְמֵידַק דִּלְמוּדָה הוּא דְּבָעֵי שֶׁתְּשַׁלֵּשׁ בְּדִילּוּג. אֶלָּא מִשּׁוּם עֲקִירַת וֶסֶת רִאשׁוֹן, דְּקָתָנֵי "חָזְרָה וְשִׁינְּתָה לְי"ז – הוּתַּר ט"ז וְנֶאֱסַר ט"ו וְי"ז", וְאַע"ג דַּעֲקַרְתֵּיהּ לְט"ו תְּרֵי זִימְנֵי. דְּסד"א: כֵּיוָן דִּלְמוּדָה הֲוַאי בְּט"ו, וַעֲקַרְתֵּיהּ ב' זִימְנֵי – תּוּ לָא הָדְרָה, וְתִשְׁתְּרֵי לְט"ו הַבָּא. קמ"ל. דְּאֵין וֶסֶת קָבוּעַ נֶעֱקָר בְּפָחוֹת מִשָּׁלֹשׁ פְּעָמִים. סֵירְגָה. מִיּוֹם כ"ב לְיוֹם כ"ד. לֹא קָבְעָה לָהּ וֶסֶת. שֶׁאֵין דִּילּוּג זֶה דּוֹמֶה לָרִאשׁוֹן. דְּרִאשׁוֹן – יוֹם אֶחָד, וְזֶה – שְׁנֵי יָמִים כְּאֶחָד. קָתָנֵי מִיהָא: קָבְעָה לָהּ וֶסֶת בְּג' רְאִיּוֹת, וְרִאשׁוֹנָה בִּכְלָל. וְשִׁינְּתָה לְיוֹם כ"א. דְּאִיכָּא דִּילּוּג תְּלָת זִימְנֵי. דַּיְקָא נַמִי. מִדְּשָׁבְקִינַן לְיוֹם עֶשְׂרִים, דַּהֲוָה לֵיהּ לְמִיתְנֵי "רָאֲתָה בְּיוֹם עֶשְׂרִים בְּחֹדֶשׁ זֶה, וְיוֹם עֶשְׂרִים וְאֶחָד בְּחֹדֶשׁ זֶה, וְיוֹם עֶשְׂרִים וּשְׁנַיִם בְּחֹדֶשׁ זֶה", שֶׁכֵּן דֶּרֶךְ לְשׁוֹן תַּנָּאִים לִשְׁנוֹת כְּלָל וּלְשׁוֹן קְצָרָה. לָא אֲמָרַן. דְּאֵין קוֹבַעַת עַד שֶׁתִּקְבָּעֶנּוּ שָׁלֹשׁ פְּעָמִים, אֶלָּא לְמִקְבְּעֵיהּ דְּתֶהֱוֵי דַּיָּהּ שַׁעְתָּהּ וְלֹא יֵעָקֵר בְּפָחוֹת מִג'. אֲבָל לְמֵיחַשׁ. בַּחֲדָא זִימְנָא חָיְישָׁא לֵיהּ. שֶׁאִם רָאֲתָה בְּיוֹם ט"ו פַּעַם אַחַת – חוֹשֶׁשֶׁת לְט"ו הַבָּא, וְלֹא תְּשַׁמֵּשׁ. הָנֵי מִילֵּי. הֵיכָא דְּקָאֵים לֵיהּ אוֹתוֹ יוֹם שֶׁשִּׁינְּתָה בּוֹ בְּתוֹךְ יָמִים שֶׁרְאוּיָה לִהְיוֹת בָּהֶן נִדָּה. כִּי מַתְנִי' שֶׁהִיא לְמוּדָה לִהְיוֹת רוֹאָה בְּיוֹם ט"ו לִטְבִילָתָהּ, שֶׁהוּא כ"ב לִרְאִיָּיתָהּ, וְכִדְאוֹקִימְנָא בִּ"בְנוֹת כּוּתִים" (לעיל לט.). וְשִׁינְּתָה לְיוֹם עֶשְׂרִים לִטְבִילָה, שֶׁהֵן עֶשְׂרִים וָשֶׁבַע לִרְאִיָּיה. דְּכִי הָדַר מָטֵי יוֹם ט"ו לִטְבִילָתָהּ, קַיְימָא לָהּ בַּיָּמִים הָרְאוּיִים לְנִדָּה. שֶׁהֲרֵי שָׁלְמוּ לְאַחַר טְבִילָה י"א שֶׁבֵּין נִדָּה לְנִדָּה, וְנִכְנְסָה אַרְבָּעָה יָמִים בַּיָּמִים הָרְאוּיִים לְנִדּוּת. אֲבָל הֵיכָא דְּקָאֵי בְּתוֹךְ יְמֵי זִיבָתָהּ, כְּגוֹן שֶׁהָיְתָה לְמוּדָה לִרְאוֹת לְיוֹם חֲמִשָּׁה עָשָׂר לִטְבִילָתָהּ, וְהִקְדִּימָה וְרָאֲתָה בְּתוֹךְ יְמֵי הַזּוֹב, כְּגוֹן לְיוֹם עֲשִׂירִי לִטְבִילָה. אֵימָא לֹא תֵּיחוּשׁ לָהּ. דְּכִי מָטְיָא טְבִילָתָהּ אַחֲרִיתִי, וְתִטְבּוֹל, וְיַגִּיעַ יוֹם *עֶשְׂרִים – לֹא תֵּאָסֵר לְשַׁמֵּשׁ, דְּהָא קַיְימָא לָן בְּפֶרֶק דִּלְעֵיל (דף לט.): כָּל אַחַד עָשָׂר – בְּחֶזְקַת טְהֹרָה, שֶׁאֵינָהּ מוּחְזֶקֶת רוֹאָה. הִלְכָּךְ, מִשּׁוּם חֲדָא זִימְנָא לֹא תֵּיחוּשׁ לָהּ, דְּאַקְרַאי בְּעָלְמָא הֲוָה, קמ"ל. **תְּנֵינָא** אֵין הָאִשָּׁה קוֹבַעַת. וְאֵינָהּ מְטַהֶרֶת. וּמִדְּתָנָא לְהוּ גַּבֵּי הֲדָדֵי – מַשְׁמַע דְּלָא בָּעֵי עֲקִירָה שָׁלֹשׁ פְּעָמִים אֶלָּא לְמִי שֶׁנִּקְבַּע שָׁלֹשׁ פְּעָמִים. חַד לְחַד. חֲדָא עֲקִירָה לְחַד קְבִיעוּת, וְקָא מַשְׁמַע לָן: דַּאֲפִילּוּ קְבַעְתֵּיהּ תְּרֵי זִימְנֵי – מִיעַקְרָא בְּחַד זִימְנָא. כְּוָתֵיהּ. דַּאֲפִילּוּ קְבַעְתֵּיהּ תְּרֵי זִימְנֵי – מִיעֲקַר בְּחַד זִימְנָא. ה"ג: מוּתֶּרֶת לְשַׁמֵּשׁ עַד יוֹם שְׁלֹשִׁים. כָּל יָמִים שֶׁבֵּינְתַיִים מוּתָּרִים. הִגִּיעַ יוֹם שְׁלֹשִׁים וְלֹא רָאֲתָה הִגִּיעַ יוֹם עֶשְׂרִים וְרָאֲתָה הוּתַּר שְׁלֹשִׁים. הֶעָתִיד לָבֹא, דְּהָא אִיעֲקַר מִינָּהּ. וְאַף עַל גַּב דִּקְבַעְתֵּיהּ תְּרֵי זִימְנֵי – מִיעֲקַר בְּחַד זִימְנָא. וְנֶאֱסַר

---

**תוספות**

**איתמר** ראתה ט"ו בחדש זה וט"ז בחדש זה. פי': דווקא בכי האי גוונא, אבל ראתה בג' חדשים או בב' לחדש או באחד לכ"ע אין צריך יותר, כדאמר לעיל בסוף "בנות כותים" (דף לט:) דאזלי ריש ירחא וריש ירחא כו'. ואפילו שאחד מלא ואחד חסר, ואין הימים שבין ראייה לראייה שוין מ"מ קביעות החדש גורם. והיכא דבראשונה אין לה שיעור בחדש, שתהא השניה נראת דילוג מן הראשונה דכ"ע דאין הראשונה מן המנין, ובעינן שתשלש בדילוג. כגון ראתה עכשיו, ושניה בעשרים לה, ושלישית בכ"א לשניה. ומשום הכי נקט "ט"ו בחדש זה". ולפירוש זה קשה: דבפרק "שור שנגח ד' וה'" (ב"ק לז:) מדמה נגח יום חמשה עשר בחדש זה וששה עשר בחדש זה ושבעה עשר בחדש זה, לפלוגתא דהכא. ואם כן, היכי קאמר התם לעיל גבי "ראה שור ונגח, שור ולא נגח" דהויא ראשונה מן המנין? הא בכי האי גוונא אפי' רב מודה דלא הוי ראשונה מן המנין, שהרי לא היתה לשום זמן לא לחדש ולא לשבת! ויש לחלק בין סירוגין דימים לסירוגין דשוורים. ור"ח פי' "קבעה לה וסת לדילוג" – כשעשתה שלש פעמים כסדר הזה, כגון שראתה ט"ו בניסן וי"ו באייר וי"ז בסיון, וכן ראתה ט"ו בתמוז וי"ו באב וי"ז באלול, ועוד ראתה ט"ו בתשרי וי"ו במרחשון וי"ז בכסליו – חוששת מכאן ואילך ט"ו לחדש זה וי"ו לשני וי"ז לשלישי. ולשמואל צריכה "שתשלש בדילוג" – שתראה בחדש רביעי יום י"ח ובג' חדשים שאחריהם יום י"ו וי"ז וי"ח, וכן בשלישי עוד שאחרי כן. דראייה של ט"ו יום בחדש הראשון, לא היה ממנינא. ותימה: למה פי' כן, דא"כ כשאל התלמוד "לימא כדרבי ורשב"ג קמיפלגי" – לא פליגי בראייה ראשונה לחוד אלא בשלש ראיות של דילוג ראשון, ובמסקנא יהיה הפירוש בע"א ואמאי לא סגי בג' חדשים כדפי' בקונטרס? **ואינה** אסורה אלא מי"ח ואילך. וא"ת ויאסר נמי יום י"ח כי שינתה לי"ז שהרי דילגה. ויהיה בכלל וסת דילוג, כמו ט"ו וי"ו דחיישינן בחדא זימנא? ואומר הר"י: דאין לחוש בדילוג משום חדא זימנא. **מיחש** בחדא זימנא חיישינן. פירש"י: דחיישינן לתשמיש. וכן צריך לפרש, מדלא פרי' התלמוד בהדיא לטהרות. ואין להזכיר בשום קביעות וסת ג' פעמים לגבי תשמיש – דהא בחדא זימנא חיישינן, אלא לגבי שאם נקבעו שלש פעמים – חוששין לו, עד שיעקר שלש פעמים.

הדרן עלך האשה

---

**תוספי הרא"ש**

**רב** אמר קבעה לה וסת לדילוג. ודוקא שראייה ראשונה היתה בט"ו לחדש והשניה בט"ז בחדש והשלישי בי"ז בחדש דבכהא"ג דוקא ס"ל לרב דראשונה ממנין הדילוג כיון דזמן ראיותיה למנין ימות החדש אבל אם ראייה ראשונה היה בר"ח ושניה בט"ו לראייה זו ושלישית בי"ו לאותה ראייה מודה רב דלא קבעה לה וסת דראייה ראשונה אינה מן המנין. וכן מוכח בפ' שור שנגח ד' וה' דמדמי נגח ט"ו בחדש זה וט"ז בחדש זה וי"ז בחדש זה לפלוגתא דהכא אע"ג דהתם קאמר ראה שור ונגח [שור ולא נגח] שור נגח שור ולא נגח שור נגח נעשה מועד לסירוגין. אע"ג דהתם ליכא לא חדש ולא שבת. י"ל דהתם תלוי בווסת בראיית השוורים. ור"ח פירש דפלוגתא דהכא מיירי כגון שראתה בדילוג ג' חדשים שניים ושלישיים כענין דילוג שראתה בג' חדשים ראשונים וקבעה לה וסת אליבא דרב מחדש תשיעי ואילך יום ט"ו לחדש עשירי ויום ט"ז לחדש י"א ויום י"ז לחדש י"ב וכן לעולם בכל ג' וג' חדשים. ולשמואל צריכה שתשלש בדילוג שתראה בחדש רביעי יום י"ח כי חדש הראשון אינו מן המנין א)והג' חדשים שאחרי כן יום ט"ז ויום י"ז ויום י"ח וכן עוד בשלשה שאחרי כן. ותימה לפירושו דלמה לא סגי בג' חדשים לבד כדפרישית: **זה** וזה אסורין דבחדא זימנא חייש לה. ותימה כי שינתה ליום י"ז למה לא תהא אסורה יום י"ח בחדש שאחריו דהא דילגה חדא זימנא וי"ל דלא חיישינן גבי דילוג בחדא זימנא: **תיובתא** דרב. נ"ל דהוה מצי לשנויי דהכא לא איירי בקביעות ימי החדש אלא מט"ו לט"ו אלא דבלאו הכי משני ליה שפיר למודה שאני: **מהו** דתימא כיון דלמודה היא ועקרתיה תרי זימני כו'. לישנא דכיון קשה לי דה"ל למימר אע"ג דלמודה היא. ונ"ל לפרש מהו דתימא כיון דלמודה היא לראות מט"ו לחדש ועקרתיה בתרי זימני לראות בדילוג עקרה ליה דנהי דלא הויא ט"ו בכלל לקבוע וסת לדילוג להוי בכלל לעקור וסת הראשון שהיה בלא דילוג: **תיובתא** דשמואל. אומר ר"מ דהוה מצי למימר הא מני רבי היא אלא דבלאו הכי משני ליה שפיר בחדא זימנא חיישא אפילו לבעלה ואין נראה לומר דלטהרות דוקא קאמר מדלא פי' התלמוד: ה"ג רש"י הגיע יום עשרים ולא ראתה יום שלשים ולא ראתה הותר יום שלשים ונאסר יום עשרים ואע"ג דלא ראתה ג' פעמים ביום כ' לא נעקר יום כ' כיון דלא ראתה יום ל' כמו שהתחילה כבר שני פעמים דאם אשה מדלגת וסת אחד או שנים או אפי' ג' ואינה רואה בנתים לזמן אחר וחוזרת לראות בזמן ווסתה לא נעקר הווסת בכך: **סליק פרק האשה**

---

**עין משפט נר מצוה**

מו א מיי' פ"ח מהל' איסורי ביאה הל"ו ועיין בכ"מ סמג לאוין קיא טוש"ע יו"ד סי' קפט סעיף ה וסעי' ז:

מז ב מיי' שם הל' לא סמג לאוין קיא טוש"ע יו"ד סי' קפט סעיף ח:

מח ג מיי' שם פ"ח הל' ז סמג שם:

מט ד ה מיי' שם הל"ו והל"ח טוש"ע יו"ד סי' קפט סעיף ב:

נ ו טוש"ע שם סעיף יד:

---

**מסורת הש"ס**

[ב"ק לז:]

[יבמות סד: תוספתא שבת פט"ו]

ג"א קביעות

ר"מ עשירי ועיין רש"א שמאריך

**גליון הש"ס**

גמ' ודקארי לה מאי קארי לה. ע' ב"ב ב ע"ב תד"ה וקארי.

---

א) נראה דצ"ל רק המנין מתחיל מג' חדשים שאחרי כן שראתה בהם יום ט"ז וכו'.

**עין משפט נר מצוה**

א א מיי' פ"ה מהל' איסורי ביאה הל"ח ופ"א שם הל"ח סמג לאוין קיא טוש"ע יו"ד סי' קנג וטוש"ע אה"ע סי' סב סעי' א:
ב ב מיי' פ"ה שם הל"ט ועי' בפ"א וכטוש"ע שם:
ג ג מיי' שם פ"ה וע' בהשגות וכמ"מ:
ד ד מיי' שם הל"ח:
ה ה מיי' שם הל"ט: כג:
ו ו מיי' שם הל"ט:
ז ז טוש"ע אה"ע סי' סב סעי' ח:
ח ח מיי' שם הל' כה [וברב אלפס שבועות פ"ב דף לב.]:
ט ט מיי' שם הל' יט:
י י מיי' שם הל' כ:

**תוספות**

**תינוקת** ד' לילות. ב"ה לא בעו רצופין, כדאמר בגמרא: מעשה ונתן לה רבי ד' לילות מתוך שנים עשר חדש. וכן נראה דד' לילות לב"ש א] אפילו מפוזרות, כמו לב"ה. **כל** זמן שהרוק מצוי בתוך הפה. שרואה מחמת תשמיש, תלינן כל היום המחרת וכל הלילה שאחריו, אפילו לא שמשה בהם בדם בתולים, ואפי' אינה נוחרת. אבל תו – לא תלינן, הואיל ולא שמשה, כדאמר לעיל בספ"ק (דף יא:) עבר עליה לילה אחת בלא תשמיש – טמאה. ורב מחמיר טפי, דדוקא כשנוחרת ביום שלאחר תשמיש תלינן בו ובלילה שלאחריו, אבל בלא נחירה – לא. **על** גבי כולם ורואה על גבי כולם ואינה רואה בידוע שחיתה המכה. לספרים (ג) דגרסינן הכי "על גבי *כלים ורואה" ליכא לפרושי "בידוע" דאיכא הוכחה, דהא לא מוכח ולא מידי, הואיל ורואה. אלא ה"פ: בידוע שיש לתלות שחיתה המכה. וכן צריך לומר בפ' "דם הנדה" לעיל (דף נו:) "בידוע שלפני הכנוס" – כלומר, שיש לתלותו לפני הכנוס. **רב** אמר לא הפסידה לילות עד מוצאי שבת תנן. וא"ת: בפ"ק דכתובות (דף ו:) דפריך למאן דאסר לבעול בשבת מדקאמר הכא "עד מוצאי שבת", וקאמר: מאי לאו, דאי לא בעיל – מאי בעיל! ומשני: לא, כשבעל. ופריך: אי כשבעל, מאי למימרא? ומשני: הא קמ"ל כדשמואל, דאמר: פרצה דחוקה כו'. והשתא, מאי פריך "מאי למימרא", הא אשמעינן טובא, דלא הפסידה לילות, כדקאמר הכא! וי"ל: דהתם איכא לישנא דשמואל אוסר למבעל לכתחלה, וכן לרב, ואיצטריך ליה לשנויי הכי לשמואל, דאפילו אי (ג) כלוי סבירא ליה, דהפסידה לילות. **דשרי** למבעל לכתחלה כדשמואל כו' – אף על גב דבפ"ק דכתובות (דף ו:) מייתי הך דשמואל אבעילה שניה, מ"מ לפי האמת דשרי למבעל בתחלה נקט הכא, דהוי רבותא טפי. **רבי** אסי אמר טהורה. ואף על גב דלית ליה הך סברא דאם איתא דהוה דם מעיקרא הוה אתי, מיהו ס"ל שפיר הא דרב גידל דלעיל, ספ"ק (דף יא:) דאם פסקה מחמת תשמיש וראתה אפילו מחמת תשמיש – טמאה. דאם איתא דדם בתולין הוא – מעיקרא כששמשה הוה אתי, ולא הוה לה למפסק מחמת תשמיש. כיון דבתחלה בעל ומצא דם, אם איתא שנשאר עוד דם בתולין – לא היה לה לפסוק כששמשה. אבל הכא איירי דבעל ולא מצא דם, ולהכי איכא למימר דבעל כדשמואל.

**שאני** שמואל דרב גובריה. משמע הכא דשמואל לא שכיחא, וכן בפרק *קמא דחגיגה (דף יד:) גבי בתולה שעיברה, פירוש: שהושיבוה על פי החבית, ואין ריחה נודף – ובזה נודע שהיא בתולה, *ומפיק דכשרה לכהן גדול, דאיכא למימר: באמבטי עיברה, דשכיח טפי מדשמואל. וקשה: דבפרק קמא דכתובות (דף ו:) קאמר: רוב בקיאין בהטיה! ויש לומר: דהטיה דכתובות אינה בעילה גמורה שתתעבר בה, כבשאר ביאות.

**גמרא**

וְנֶאֱסָר יוֹם עֶשְׂרִים, מִפְּנֵי *שֶׁאוֹרַח בִּזְמַנּוֹ בָּא.§ **מתני'** נָשִׁים בִּבְתוּלֵיהֶם כִּגְפָנִים: יֵשׁ גֶּפֶן שֶׁיֵּינָהּ אָדוֹם, וְיֵשׁ גֶּפֶן שֶׁיֵּינָהּ שָׁחוֹר, וְיֵשׁ גֶּפֶן שֶׁיֵּינָהּ מְרוּבֶּה, וְיֵשׁ גֶּפֶן שֶׁיֵּינָהּ מוּעָט. ר' יְהוּדָה אוֹמֵר: כָּל גֶּפֶן יֵשׁ בָּהּ יַיִן, וְשֶׁאֵין בָּהּ יַיִן ה"ז דּוּרְקְטִי.§ **גמ'** תָּנָא: דּוֹר קָטוּעַ. *תָּנֵי רַבִּי חִיָּיא: כְּשֵׁם שֶׁהַשְּׂאוֹר יָפֶה לָעִיסָּה – כָּךְ דָּמִים יָפִין לָאִשָּׁה. תָּנָא מִשּׁוּם ר"מ כָּל אִשָּׁה שֶׁדָּמֶיהָ מְרוּבִּין – בָּנֶיהָ מְרוּבִּין.§

## הדרן עלך האשה

**תִּינוֹקֶת** *שֶׁלֹּא הִגִּיעַ זְמַנָּהּ לִרְאוֹת, וְנִיסֵּת, ב"ש אוֹמְרִים: נוֹתְנִין לָהּ אַרְבַּע לֵילוֹת, וב"ה אוֹמְרִים: [א]עַד שֶׁתִּחְיֶה הַמַּכָּה. הִגִּיעַ זְמַנָּהּ לִרְאוֹת וְנִיסֵּת, ב"ש אוֹמְרִים: נוֹתְנִין לָהּ לַיְלָה הָרִאשׁוֹן, וב"ה אוֹמְרִים: [ב]עַד מוֹצָאֵי שַׁבָּת, אַרְבַּע לֵילוֹת. רָאֲתָה וְעוֹדָהּ בְּבֵית אָבִיהָ, ב"ש אוֹמְרִים: [ג]נוֹתְנִין לָהּ בְּעִילַת *מִצְוָה, וב"ה אוֹמְרִים: כָּל הַלַּיְלָה כּוּלָּהּ.§ **גמ'** אָמַר רַב נַחְמָן בַּר יִצְחָק: וַאֲפִילּוּ רָאֲתָה. מִמַּאי – מִדְּקָא מַפְלִיג בְּסֵיפָא בֵּין רָאֲתָה בֵּין בְּשֶׁלֹּא רָאֲתָה, מִכְּלָל דְּרֵישָׁא – לָא שְׁנָא הָכִי וְלָא שְׁנָא הָכִי. תַּנְיָא נַמִי הָכִי, ב"ה אוֹמְרִים: עַד שֶׁתִּחְיֶה הַמַּכָּה, [ד]בֵּין רָאֲתָה בֵּין לֹא רָאֲתָה.§ "עַד שֶׁתִּחְיֶה הַמַּכָּה".§ עַד כַּמָּה? אָמַר רַב יְהוּדָה אָמַר רַב: כָּל זְמַן שֶׁנּוֹחֶרֶת. כִּי אֲמַרִיתָהּ קַמֵּיהּ דִּשְׁמוּאֵל, אֲמַר לִי: נְחִירָה זוֹ – אֵינִי יוֹדֵעַ מַה הִיא, אֶלָּא – כָּל זְמַן שֶׁהָרוֹק מָצוּי בְּתוֹךְ הַפֶּה מֵחֲמַת תַּשְׁמִישׁ. נְחִירָה דְּקָאָמַר רַב הֵיכִי דָּמֵי? אֲמַר רַב שְׁמוּאֵל בַּר רַב יִצְחָק לְדִידִי מְפָרְשָׁא לִי מִינֵּיהּ דְּרַב: [ה]עוֹמֶדֶת וְרוֹאָה, יוֹשֶׁבֶת וְאֵינָהּ רוֹאָה – בְּיָדוּעַ שֶׁלֹּא חָיְתָה הַמַּכָּה. עַל גַּבֵּי קַרְקַע וְרוֹאָה, עַל גַּבֵּי כָּרִים וּכְסָתוֹת וְאֵינָהּ רוֹאָה – בְּיָדוּעַ שֶׁלֹּא חָיְתָה הַמַּכָּה. עַל גַּבֵּי כּוּלָּם וְרוֹאָה, ע"ג כּוּלָּם וְאֵינָהּ רוֹאָה – בְּיָדוּעַ שֶׁחָיְתָה הַמַּכָּה.§ "הִגִּיעַ זְמַנָּהּ" וכו'.§ אִיתְּמַר: שִׁימְּשָׁה בַּיָּמִים, רַב אָמַר: לֹא הִפְסִידָה לֵילוֹת, וְלֵוִי אָמַר: הִפְסִידָה לֵילוֹת. רַב אָמַר: [ו]לֹא הִפְסִידָה לֵילוֹת, "עַד מוֹצָאֵי שַׁבָּת" תְּנַן. וְלֵוִי אָמַר: הִפְסִידָה לֵילוֹת, מַאי "אַרְבַּע לֵילוֹת" דְּקָתָנֵי? – אַרְבָּעָה עוֹנוֹת. וּלְרַב, לָמָּה לִי לְמִיתְנָא "אַרְבַּע לֵילוֹת"? אוֹרַח אַרְעָא קמ"ל דְּדַרְכָּהּ דְּבִיאָה בַּלֵּילוֹת. וּלְלֵוִי, לִיתְנֵי "אַרְבַּע לֵילוֹת", "עַד מוֹצָאֵי שַׁבָּת" לָמָּה לִי? הָא קמ"ל [ז]דְּשָׁרֵי לְמִבְעַל לְכַתְּחִלָּה בְּשַׁבָּת. כִּדְשְׁמוּאֵל, *דַּאֲמַר שְׁמוּאֵל: פִּרְצָה דְּחוּקָה – מוּתָּר לִיכָּנֵס בָּהּ בְּשַׁבָּת, ואע"פ שֶׁמֵּשִׁיר צְרוֹרוֹת. אִיתְּמַר: בָּעַל וְלֹא מָצָא דָּם, וְחָזַר וּבָעַל וּמָצָא דָּם – רַבִּי חֲנִינָא אָמַר: טְמֵאָה, וְרַבִּי אַסִּי אָמַר: טְהוֹרָה. ר' חֲנִינָא אָמַר: [ח]טְמֵאָה, דְּאִם אִיתָא דַּהֲוָה דַּם בְּתוּלִים – מֵעִיקָּרָא הֲוֵי אָתֵי. וְרַבִּי אַסִּי אָמַר: טְהוֹרָה, דִּילְמָא אִתְרְמֵי לֵיהּ כִּדְשְׁמוּאֵל. *דַּאֲמַר שְׁמוּאֵל: יָכוֹלְנִי לִבְעוֹל כַּמָּה בְּעִילוֹת בְּלֹא דָּם. וְאִידָךְ *שָׁאנֵי שְׁמוּאֵל דְּרַב גּוּבְרֵיהּ. *אָמַר רַב: [ט]בּוֹגֶרֶת נוֹתְנִין לָהּ לַיְלָה הָרִאשׁוֹן. וה"מ – שֶׁלֹּא רָאֲתָה, אֲבָל רָאֲתָה – אֵין לָהּ אֶלָּא בְּעִילַת מִצְוָה, וְתוּ לָא. מֵיתִיבִי: [י]מַעֲשֶׂה וְנָתַן לָהּ רַבִּי אַרְבַּע לֵילוֹת מִתּוֹךְ י"ב חֹדֶשׁ. ה"ד? אִילֵימָא דִּיהֵיב לָהּ כּוּלְּהוּ בִּימֵי קַטְנוּת

עַד

**רש"י**

וְנֶאֱסָר יוֹם עֶשְׂרִים. הַבָּא. שֶׁהֲרֵי לְמוּדָה בְּעֶשְׂרִים וְלָא עֲקַרְתּוֹ אֶלָּא שְׁנֵי פְּעָמִים. שֶׁהֲרֵי עֲקִירָה הָאַחֲרוֹנָה שֶׁל עֶשְׂרִים הָאַחֲרוֹנָה שֶׁלֹּא רָאֲתָה, שֶׁאַחַר הַשְּׁלֹשִׁים שְׁנִיִּים – לָאו עֲקִירָה הִיא, שֶׁהֲרֵי לֹא שִׁינְּתָה לְיוֹם שְׁלֹשִׁים הַשְּׁלִישִׁיִּים וְלֹא רָאֲתָה עַד יוֹם עֶשְׂרִים לַחֹדֶשׁ כְּווֹסְתָּהּ. מִפְּנֵי שֶׁאוֹרַח. זֶה שֶׁחָזַר לָשׁוּב יוֹם עֶשְׂרִים בִּזְמַנּוֹ הָרִאשׁוֹן בָּא. **מתני'** כָּל גֶּפֶן יֵשׁ בָּהּ יַיִן. כָּל אִשָּׁה יֵשׁ לָהּ בְּתוּלִים וְדָמִים. וְשֶׁאֵין לָהּ הֲרֵי זֶה דּוֹר קָטוּעַ. (א) וְכֵיוָן שֶׁאֵין לָהֶן דָּמִים מְרוּבִּים אֵין בְּנֵיהֶן מְרוּבִּין.

## הדרן עלך האשה

**תִּינוֹקֶת**. נוֹתְנִין לָהּ אַרְבַּע לֵילוֹת. לְשַׁמֵּשׁ, וַאֲפִי' רוֹאָה – אָמְרִינַן: דַּם בְּתוּלִים הוּא. עַד שֶׁתִּחְיֶה הַמַּכָּה. מְפָרֵשׁ בַּגְּמָרָא. הִגִּיעַ זְמַנָּהּ לִרְאוֹת. וְלֹא רָאֲתָה. עַד מוֹצָאֵי שַׁבָּת. וְהִיא נִיסֵּת בָּרְבִיעִי. **גמ'** אֲפִילּוּ רָאֲתָה. בְּבֵית אָבִיהָ, אָמְרוּ ב"ה: הוֹאִיל וְלֹא הִגִּיעַ זְמַנָּהּ לִרְאוֹת – נוֹתְנִין לָהּ עַד שֶׁתִּחְיֶה הַמַּכָּה. מִדְּפָלֵיג בְּסֵיפָא. בְּהִגִּיעַ זְמַנָּהּ, קָתָנֵי חִילּוּק בֵּין רָאֲתָה לְלֹא רָאֲתָה. שֶׁנּוֹחֶרֶת. לְקַמָּן מְפָרֵשׁ. שֶׁהָרוֹק מָצוּי. שֶׁרוֹאָה מֵחֲמַת תַּשְׁמִישׁ. עַד מוֹצָאֵי שַׁבָּת תְּנַן. בַּיּוֹם וּבַלַּיְלָה. דְּשָׁרֵי לְמִבְעַל בְּשַׁבָּת. אַף ע"פ שֶׁלֹּא בָּעַל עֲדַיִין כִּי אִם שְׁתֵּי בְּעִילוֹת, וּפֶתַח דָּחוּק. וְחָזַר וּבָעַל. בְּתוֹךְ אַרְבַּע לֵילוֹת. טְמֵאָה. דְּדַם נִדָּה הוּא. בּוֹגֶרֶת נוֹתְנִין לָהּ לַיְלָה הָרִאשׁוֹן. וַאֲפִי' לב"ה דְּאָמְרֵי דְּהִגִּיעַ זְמַנָּהּ לִרְאוֹת אַרְבָּעָה – הָנֵי מִילֵּי נַעֲרָה, דְּמִשֶּׁהִגִּיעוּ יְמֵי הַנְּעוּרִים, הָוֵי זְמַנָּהּ. אֲבָל בּוֹגֶרֶת – לַיְלָה הָרִאשׁוֹן, וְתוּ לָא. מִתּוֹךְ שְׁנֵים עָשָׂר חֹדֶשׁ. שֶׁבָּעַל לַיְלָה הָרִאשׁוֹן וְהָלַךְ בַּדֶּרֶךְ מִיָּד. וְשָׁהָה שְׁלֹשָׁה חֳדָשִׁים, וְחָזַר וּבָעַל וּמָצָא דָּם, וְכֵן פַּעַם שְׁנִיָּה וּשְׁלִישִׁית, וּבָא לִפְנֵי רַבִּי. וְאָמַר: דַּם בְּתוּלִים הוּא.

**תוספי הרא"ש**

**עד** שתחיה המכה. פרשתי לעיל בפ"ק: מכלל דרישא לא שנא. ואין נראה לומר דראתה ועודה בבית אביה ארישא קאי דא"כ אמאי הפסיק בההיא דהגיע זמנה לראות ואין לומר דאתרווייהו קאי דלא מיסתבר להשוותם בראתה כיון דבלא ראתה מקילינן טפי בלא הגיע: **כל** זמן שהרוק מצוי בתוך הפה מחמת תשמיש. שלא פסקה לראות מחמת תשמיש הילכך כל ראיות דמחר ודליליא דאחרי כן אפי' לא שמשה תלינן בדם בתולים אבל אם ראתה ביום שני הוי דם נדה כדאמרינן בפ"ק עבר עליה לילה אחת בלא תשמיש וראתה טמאה ואם אח"כ שימשה וראתה דם מחמת תשמיש טהורה כל יום של מחרת ולילה שאחר כן אפי' לא שימשה כדאמרינן מעשה ונתן לה ר' ד' לילות מתוך י"ב חדש וכן לרב דאמר כל זמן שנוחרת כל הראייה של אותה הלילה ויום של אחריו אף בלא נחירה טהורה וביום שלאחריו אם ראתה בלא נחירה טמאה: **מאי** ד' לילות דקתני ד' עונות. י"ס דגר' בתר הכי וליתני ד' עונות אורח ארעא קמ"ל דדרכה דעונה בליליא. וליתני ד' לילות עד מוצאי שבת למה לי הא קמ"ל כו'. והוה מצי למיפרך נמי לרב ד' לילות למה

[ולמשני נמי] קמ"ל דרכה דעונה בליליא אלא משום דסליק ממילתיה לוי פריך אליביה. וי"ס דגרסי לרב למה לי למיתני ד' לילות. אורח ארעא קמ"ל דאורחא דביאה בליליא. וללוי ליתני ד' עונות. ואע"ג דכבר [הקשה לרב הדר] תו פריך ללוי דלתני ד' עונות לאשמועינן בפי' דהפסידה לילות ומשני קמ"ל דבליליא כלומר תרתי קמ"ל דאותם ד' עונות דוקא בלילה. וגם דאורחא דעונה בליליא: **הא קמ"ל** דשרי למיבעל בשבתא [כדשמואל. י"ס] דגרסי דשרי למיבעל בתחילה. ואע"ג דבפ"ק דכתובות מייתי דשמואל על ביאה שניה היינו משום דהתם איירי למ"ד אסור לבעול בתחלה בשבת והכא נקט אליבא דהילכתא דשרי ובלאו הכי הוה מצי [למימר דמותר] לבעול בתחלה בשבת אלא אגב ריהטא דתלמודא דמייתי דשמואל התם נקטיה נמי הכא: **ור'** אסי (נמי) אמר טהורה. ואע"ג דלית ליה אם איתא דהוה דם מעיקרא הוה אתי מ"מ מצי סבר האי דאמר רב גידל [בפ"ק דאם פסקה] מחמת תשמיש וראתה טמאה אפי' ראתה מחמת תשמיש דאם איתא דאישתייר מדם בתולים לא היתה פוסקת הואיל וכבר התחילו לצאת אבל הכא דלא התחילו לצאת איכא למימר דילמא אתרמי ליה: **שאני** שמואל דרב גובריה. וכן בפ"ק דחגיגה אמרינן דשמואל לא שכיחי. ותימה דבפ"ק דכתובות אמרינן דרוב בקיאין בהטייה. וי"ל דשמואל איירי בבעילה גמורה שראויה להתעבר בה דהכי מייתי לה בפ"ק חגיגה. וכן הכא מיירי שבעל בעילה גמורה ואין הכל בקיאין לבעול בעילה גמורה בהטייה רק שמואל דרב גובריה:

**מסורת הש"ס**

[לעיל טז.]
[לעיל ח: כתובות י:]
כתובות ו. לעיל יא:
[ע' תוס' כתובות ז. ד"ה בעילת]
כתובות ו:
חגיגה טו. [לעיל כה:]
[כתובות לו.]
נ"ל שני
[נ"ל ומסיק]

**הגהות הב"ח**

(א) רש"י ד"ה תינוקת וכו' וכיון שאין: (ג) תוס' ד"ה על גבי וכו' לספרים דגרסי הכי על גבי כולם ורואה: (ג) ד"ה רב וכו' דאפילו אי שמואל כלוי סבירא ליה:

**הגהות מהר"ב רנשבורג**

א] תוד"ה תינוקת וכו' לב"ש אפי' מפוזרות. נ"ב וכ"ה להדיא בתוספתא:

"עַד שֶׁתְּהֵא הַמַּכָּה" תְּנַן. אֶלָּא דְּיָהֵיב לָהּ כּוּלְּהוּ בִּימֵי נַעֲרוּת — נַעֲרוּת י"ב חֹדֶשׁ מִי אִיכָּא? וְהָא *אָמַר שְׁמוּאֵל: אאֵין בֵּין נַעֲרוּת לְבַגְרוּת אֶלָּא ו' חֳדָשִׁים בִּלְבַד! וְכִי תֵּימָא: בָּצִיר מֵהָכִי — הוּא דְּלֵיכָּא, הָא טְפֵי — אִיכָּא, הָא "בִּלְבַד" קָאָמַר! אֶלָּא דְּיָהֵיב לָהּ שְׁתַּיִם בִּימֵי קַטְנוּת וּשְׁתַּיִם בִּימֵי נַעֲרוּת — הָא בְּעָא מִינֵּיהּ רַב חִינָּנָא בַּר שֶׁלֶמְיָא מֵרַב: הִגִּיעַ זְמַנָּהּ לִרְאוֹת תַּחַת בַּעְלָהּ מַהוּ? אֲמַר לֵיהּ: בכׇּל בְּעִילוֹת שֶׁאַתָּה בּוֹעֵל — אֵינָן אֶלָּא אַחַת, וְהַשְּׁאָר מַשְׁלִימִין לְד' לֵילוֹת. אֶלָּא: דְּיָהֵיב לָהּ אַחַת בִּימֵי קַטְנוּת, וּשְׁתַּיִם בִּימֵי נַעֲרוּת, וְאַחַת בִּימֵי בַּגְרוּת — אִי אָמְרַתְּ בִּשְׁלָמָא בּוֹגֶרֶת בְּעָלְמָא יָהֲבִינַן לָהּ טְפֵי, כִּי הֵיכִי דְּאָהֲנֵי קַטְנוּת בִּימֵי נַעֲרוּת לְמִבְצַר לָהּ חֲדָא, אָהֲנֵי נָמֵי נַעֲרוּת לְבַגְרוּת לְמִבְצַר לָהּ חֲדָא. אֶלָּא אִי אָמְרַתְּ בּוֹגֶרֶת דְּעָלְמָא לָא יָהֲבִינַן לָהּ טְפֵי, לָא לֵיתַב לָהּ אֶלָּא בְּעִילַת מִצְוָה וְתוּ לָא! לְעוֹלָם דְּיָהֵיב לָהּ אַחַת בִּימֵי קַטְנוּת וְג' בִּימֵי נַעֲרוּת, מִי סָבְרַתְּ כׇּל תְּלָתָא יַרְחֵי — חֲדָא עוֹנָה? כׇּל תְּרֵי יַרְחֵי — חֲדָא עוֹנָה. מְנִימִין סַקְסְנָאָה הֲוָה שָׁקֵיל וְאָזֵיל לְאַתְרֵיהּ דִּשְׁמוּאֵל סְבַר לְמֶעֱבַד עוּבְדָא כְּוָותֵיהּ דְּרַב אֲפִילּוּ רָאֲתָה. אֲמַר: לָא פְּלִיג רַב בֵּין רָאֲתָה בֵּין לֹא רָאֲתָה. קָדֵים שָׁכֵיב בְּאוֹרְחָא. *קָרֵי שְׁמוּאֵל עֲלֵיהּ דְּרַב: °"לֹא יְאוּנֶּה (משלי יב) לַצַּדִּיק כׇּל אָוֶן". אֲמַר רַב חִינָּנָא בַּר שֶׁלֶמְיָא מִשְּׁמֵיהּ דְּרַב: כֵּיוָן שֶׁנִּתְּקוּ שִׁנָּיו שֶׁל אָדָם — נִתְמַעֲטוּ מְזוֹנוֹתָיו, שֶׁנֶּאֱמַר: °"גַּם *(אָנֹכִי נָתַתִּי לָךְ) נִקְיוֹן שִׁנַּיִם (עמוס ד) בְּכׇל עָרֵיכֶם וְחוֹסֶר לֶחֶם בְּכׇל מְקוֹמוֹתֵיכֶם". § "רָאֲתָה וְעוֹדָהּ". § תָּנוּ רַבָּנַן, רָאֲתָה וְעוֹדָהּ בְּבֵית אָבִיהָ, בֵּית הִלֵּל אוֹמְרִים: כׇּל הַלַּיְלָה שֶׁלָּהּ, וְנוֹתְנִין לָהּ עוֹנָה שְׁלֵמָה. וְכַמָּה עוֹנָה שְׁלֵמָה? פֵּירַשׁ רַבָּן שִׁמְעוֹן בֶּן גַּמְלִיאֵל: לַיְלָה וַחֲצִי יוֹם. וּמִי בָּעֵינַן כּוּלֵּי הַאי? וּרְמִינְהִי: *"הֲרֵי שֶׁהָיוּ גִּתָּיו וּבֵית בַּדָּיו טְמֵאוֹת, וּבִקֵּשׁ לַעֲשׂוֹתָן בְּטׇהֳרָה, גכֵּיצַד הוּא עוֹשֶׂה, הַדַּפִּין וְהַלּוּלָבִין וְהָעֲדָשִׁין — מַדִּיחָן, הָעֲקָלִים

**רש"י**

עַד שֶׁתְּהֵא הַמַּכָּה תְּנַן. וְ"ד' לֵילוֹת לִקְטַנָּה", מַאי עֲבִידְתַּיְיהוּ? אֵינָן אֶלָּא אַחַת. וְשָׁלֹשׁ בָּעֵי לְמֵיתַב לָהּ, לְבַד ד' דִּקְטַנּוּת. אִי אָמְרַתְּ בִּשְׁלָמָא בּוֹגֶרֶת בְּעָלְמָא. שֶׁנִּיסֵּת לְאַחַר שֶׁבָּגְרָה. אִית לָהּ טְפֵי. מִלַּיְלָה אַחַת, דְּאִית לָהּ ד' לֵילוֹת. מִשּׁוּם הָכִי יָהֵיב לְהַךְ מִשֶּׁבָּגְרָה לַיְלָה אַחַת שְׁלֵמָה, וְאַף עַל גַּב דְּנִבְעֲלָה קוֹדֶם לָכֵן. דְּכִי הֵיכִי דְּאַהֲנֵי בְּעִילוֹת קַטְנוּת לְמִבְצַר חֲדָא מִד' לֵילוֹת הַנִּיתָּנוֹת לְנַעֲרָה, דְּהָא אָמְרִינַן: כׇּל בְּעִילוֹת שֶׁבָּעַל אֵינָן אֶלָּא אַחַת, הָא לַיְלָה אַחַת מִיהָא מִבַּצְרִי, דְּתוּ לָא יָהֲבִינַן לָהּ ד' אֶלָּא ג'. אַהֲנֵי נָמֵי בְּעִילַת נַעֲרוּת לְמִבְצַר חֲדָא. מִלֵּילוֹת דְּבַגְרוּת, וְתוּ לָא. הִלְכָּךְ, לְהַךְ בּוֹגֶרֶת שֶׁנִּבְעֲלָה קוֹדֶם לָכֵן יָהֲבִינַן מִיהָא לַיְלָה אַחַת מֵהַשְּׁתַּיִם. אֶלָּא אִי אָמְרַתְּ בּוֹגֶרֶת. לַיְלָה הָרִאשׁוֹן וְתוּ לָא, אַמַּאי יָהֵיב לָהּ (א) לְהַךְ אַחַת בִּימֵי בַּגְרוּת? אִם כֵּן בְּעִילוֹת דְּקוֹדֶם לָכֵן מַאי אַהֲנוּ, הָא בְּעִילָה הוּא דְּבָעֵי לְמֵיתַב לָהּ בִּימֵי בַּגְרוּת, וְלֹא כׇּל הַלַּיְלָה! וְג' בִּימֵי נַעֲרוּת. וְלֵיכָּא הָכָא בַּגְרוּת כְּלָל. וּדְקַשְׁיָא לָךְ: הָא לָא מַשְׁכַּחַתְּ ג' עוֹנוֹת שֶׁל ג' חֳדָשִׁים בִּימֵי נַעֲרוּת? מִי סָבְרַתְּ כו'. כְּוָותֵיהּ דְּרַב. בּוֹגֶרֶת, כׇּל לַיְלָה הָרִאשׁוֹן. לֹא יְאוּנֶּה כו'. שֶׁלֹּא נִכְשַׁל זֶה בִּדְבָרָיו. מִשֶּׁנִּתְּקוּ שִׁנָּיו. זָקֵן. נִתְמַעֲטוּ מְזוֹנוֹתָיו. קָשֶׁין לָאו. גִּתָּיו. לְיַיִן. וּבֵית בַּדָּיו. לְשֶׁמֶן. הַדַּפִּין. זֶהוּ הַדֶּלֶת שֶׁנּוֹתְנִין עַל הָעֲנָבִים. הַלּוּלָבִים. הַיְינוּ סוּפְיָא, אִיסְקוּבָ"א שֶׁמְּנַקִּים בָּהּ אֶת הַגַּת. וְהָעֲדָשִׁין. זוֹ הִיא הַגַּת עַצְמָהּ, שֶׁהָעֲנָבִים נְתוּנִים שָׁם. הָעֲקָלִים.

**תוספות**

**וכי** תימא בציר הוא דליכא הא טפי איכא. במסכת קדושין (דף עט.) פרש"י דלא גרסי' ליה (בלבד) דבלאו "בלבד" נמי משמע לא פחות ולא יותר. *מיהו נראה דאי לאו "בלבד", מצינו לפרושי הכי: אין שיעור הקטן שבין נערות לבגרות אלא ו' חדשים, והוה משמע שפיר דאיכא טפי. **אלא** דיהיב לה אחת בימי קטנות ושתים בימי נערות כו'. מדמסיק לקמן "מי סברת דכל תלתא ירחי חדא עונה", מכלל דכך היה סבור מתחלה. וע"כ או הראשונה שבקטנות רחוקה מן השניה ו' חדשים והשאר ג' ג' או הרביעית רחוקה ו' חדשים מהשלישית והשאר ג' ג'. שאם לא כן, לא היו מתוך י"ב חדש. וא"כ כי מסיק "תלתא בימי נערות, וכל תרי ירחי חדא עונה", לא היה צריך לשנות סדר העונות, אלא כל תלתא ירחי חדא עונה: הראשונה – לפני הנערות, והשניה – בתחלת נערות, והשלישית – באמצע נערות ג' ירחים אחרים, והרביעית – בסוף נערות! ויש לומר: דניחא ליה להתלמוד להשוות הפסקות הביאות זו מזו כמו שהוא יכול. ואע"ג דביאת קטנות צריך שתהא ו' חדשים לפני נערות, דאם לא כן – לא היו י"ב חדש, מ"מ נראה דלאו דוקא בשלא בעל אלא ו' חדשים לפני נערות. דהא אפילו בעל כל ימי משך קטנות, קאמר דאינו אלא בעילה אחת. הילכך, אי כל חדא תלתא ירחי – תהיה השניה שבתחלת נערות סמוך לביאה אחרונה של קטנות. מש"ה קאמר "כל תרי ירחי חדא עונה", השניה תהיה בסוף ב' חדשים של נערות רחוק מסוף קטנות, והשלישית – לסוף ד' חדשים, והרביעית – לסוף ו' חדשים, וריחוקם שוה – תרי תרי ירחי. וכן כדקס"ד מעיקרא בכל תלתא ירחי חדא עונה היא, שוה בזה הענין ג' חדשים לפני קטנות, ונמשכות הביאות עד סוף קטנות, דאינה אלא ביאה אחת. ומשם – לג' חדשים באמצע נערות, ומשם לג' חדשים בסוף נערות, ורביעית – ג' חדשים בבגרות. *או ראשונה – בסוף קטנות, ושניה – באמצע נערות, ושלישית – בסוף נערות, ורביעית ג' חדשים בבגרות. **סבר** למעבד עובדא כוותיה דרב ואפילו ראתה. וא"ת: והא אפילו אי לא הוה מפליג בין ראתה ללא ראתה, מ"מ לא ה"ל למעבד כרב, דהא מסקינן לקמן "רב ושמואל דאמרי תרוייהו: הלכה, בועל בעילת מצוה ופורש"! וי"ל: דאי לא עביד כהך דלקמן – לא הוה מקפיד שמואל, דמ"מ הוה עביד כמתני' אבל בהך שהיה רוצה לעשות מה שלא אמר רב מעולם – בזה היה מקפיד שמואל.

**הדפין** והלולבים והעדשין. העדשין, פ"ה: זו היא הגת עצמה, שהענבים נתונים בה. ובס"פ בתרא דמסכת ע"ז (דף עה.) קאמר: בעו מיניה מר' אבהו, הני גורגי דגוים מהו? פרש"י, וכן בערוך: "גורגי" – עקלים. ופשיט ליה מהא מתני' ד"הדפין והלולבין" וכו' דעקלים – מנגבן. ופרש"י התם: דמדפשיט מהך מתני' ש"מ דעיקר היא. הילכך, סמכינן עלה למשרי גת בהדחה. ולא סמכינן אברייתא דלעיל "הגת והמחץ", דקתני: של עץ ושל אבן – מנגבן, והן טהורין. וזהו תימה אי מייתי ההיא ברייתא ד"הדפין" לגבי עקלין, דליכא דפליג (ב) גבי שאר דברים דפליג אידך ברייתא עלה, וליכא טעמא למסמך עליה! ומיהו, מטעם ד"בשל סופרים הלך אחר המיקל" הוה מצי פסיק כוותיה. ועוד: דבתוספתא דטהרות גרסינן "הדפין והלולבין והעדשין – מנגבן, והן טהורין". ומיהו אומר ר"י: דאפי' אי גרסינן "מדיחן" כגירסת הספרים, ל"ק לברייתא דלעיל. דעדשין – לאו גת עצמה הוא, אלא עיגול של טיט שמכביד על ענבים שבגת לדורכן, וכן פי' בערוך בערך "טלפח". והוא "יס" דאמר בפ' "המוכר הבית" (ב"ב דף סז:) מאי "יס"? טלפחא. ולפי שהוא עגול קרוי "עדשים" ו"טלפחא" ונקרא "יס" – על שם שהענבים נעצרים על ידו, ומתמלאת יין כמים יכסו על ים. ומה שלא שנה הכא דין גת – היינו משום שהיא כבדה, ואינה מטלטלת כל כך, ומשתמרת יותר מטומאה מכל כלי הגת, שיד הכל ממשמשין בהן. וכן ב"המוכר הבית" לא הוצרך לשנות *גת – כי פשיטא שמכר את *)הגת עצמו. ו"מכר את היקבים" דקתני בגמרא – לאו היינו גת כפרשב"ם, אלא כמו שפירש הערוך: סלים שמביאין בהן זיתים לבית הבד. ור"ת מפרש דהך מתני', בכלי בית הבד איירי. כדאמר ב"איזהו נשך" (ב"מ דף עד.) גבי "מעטן של זיתים": והא מחסר מכמר ועיולי לבי דפיה? וגבי "עביט של ענבים" נקט: ועיולי לבי מעצרתא. וכן עדשין דפרק "המוכר את הבית" (ב"ב דף סז:) קאמר להו גבי בית הבד, דקאמר: המוכר את בית הבד – מכר את הים. ומפרש: מאי "יס"? טלפחא, והיינו עדשין דהכא. וכן עקלים מצינו בבד, בפרק "זה בורר" (סנהדרין כו.) לעקל בית הבד אני צריך, וב"הגוזל בתרא" (ב"ק קטו:) כשעקל בית הבד כרוך עליה. ואע"ג דפתח בתרתי: "גתיו ובית בדיו טמאים" – גת, שייריה. כדקאמר ב"החולץ" (יבמות דף לח:) כתובה לב"ש שייריה. ומיהו קשה: דלא דמי, אי התם שייר לב"ש מ"מ תני לב"ה אבל הכא, אמאי תנא "גת" כלל, אי לאו לאשמועינן בהו מידי? אלא ע"כ משמיענו בבד, ומינה שמעינן דגת כיוצא בו! וע"ק: אי לא מיירי אלא בבד, היכי פשיט דגורגי דגוים, דהיינו עקלין דגבי גת דלענין יין נסך, מעקלין דברייתא דאיירי בכלי בד? אלא ע"כ צ"ל דתנא "בד", ומיניה נשמע גת וכיוצא בו. ורשב"ג נמי קאמר "מגת לגת ומבד לבד", דדינם שוה. ועוד אומר ר"י: דאפילו לפירש"י דפי' דעדשין היינו גת, ולגירסת הספרים דגרסי' "מדיחן" – לא פליג אברייתא דגת ומחץ, דקתני "מנגבן והן טהורין". דהתם – בשל גוים מיירי, לפיכך מחמרינן לנגב, אע"ג דאין מזופפין, כדקתני: אם היו מזופפין – אסורין. והך דהכא – איירי בשל ישראל, ונגע בהן גוי. כדקתני: מי שהיו גתיו ובית בדיו טמאין. ומש"ה סגי בהדחה. וכן צ"ל לרבא, דאמר התם: "ל"ש" – פירוש: דבעי ניגוב, "אלא שזפתה, אבל דרך בה בלא זפיתה – לא". ובהך ברייתא קתני "של עץ ושל אבן – מנגבן, והם טהורין. ואם היו מזופפין – אסורין". אלמא, בלא זפיתה נמי בעי ניגוב. אלא מתניתא איירי בשל גוי. ומיהו קשה: דהיכי פשיט גורגי דגוים מעקלין דברייתא דשמעתין? דלמא דגוים חמירי! וי"ל: דאע"ג דבגת מפלגינן בין ישראל לשל גוים, יש דברים דלא שייך לאפלוגי בהו כמו גבי נודות, וגבי דבר שמכניסו לקיום, דאפי' לפי שעה עוזרו בהו רבנן, ל"ש דישראל, ל"ש דגוים. ומש"ה מייתי ראייה שפיר מעקלים, *אי (ג) בגורגי של שיפא ושל גמי איירי, ומייתי ראיה דאפי' בשל ישראל מיישנה שנים עשר חדש. היינו

*) גי' רש"א הבד וע"ש בתוס'

**תוספי הרא"ש**

**לעולם** דיהב לה אחת בימי קטנות וג' בימי נערות. וכדמסיק דתרתי ירחי. הוה חד עונה וכגון שבעל ששה חדשים לפני נערות בעילה ראשונה ואחת בסוף שני חדשים לנערות ואחת לסוף ד' חדשים לנערות ואחת לסוף נערות. ותימה ואמאי חזר בו טמאי דהוה ס"ד דתלתא ירחי הוו חד עונה השתא נמי נימא הכי וכגון שבעל שניה בתחלת נערות וג' באמצע נערות וד' בסוף נערות. ור"מ תירץ מדקאמר ד' לילות מתוך י"ב חדש משמע דכל הביאות היו מופלגות זו מזו. ואי ביאה שניה הויא בתחלת נערות א"כ לא היו ראשונה ושניה מופלגות זו מזו. דכל מה שבעל בתוך ו' חדשים חשיב כלילה אחת ואפי' היה המעשה כך שלא בעל אלא בעילה ראשונה בקטנות כשנשאה מ"מ כיון דאפי' אי בעל כל ששה חדשים דקטנות הוו כמו לילה אחת בעי לאוקומי דאיכא הפלגה בין ביאת קטנות לביאה ראשונה דנערות: **סבר** למיעבד עובדא כוותיה דרב. ואע"ג דרב עצמו פסק לקמן בועל בעילה מצוה ופורש (או) דילמא לא שמיע ליה. א"נ מנימין סבר לה כמתני' ובזה לא היה מקפיד שמואל. אבל במה שהיה רוצה לסמוך על מילתיה דרב מה שלא אמר מעולם על זה שייך למימר לא יאונה לצדיק כל און שלא יכשלו בדבריו: **העדשים** פרש"י גת עצמה. ולא נהירא לר"ת דא"כ הו"ל למיתני ברישא דכולהו. אלא היינו עיגול של טיט שמניחין על הדפין שעל התפוח להכביד על הענבים ולסוחטן. וכן פי' בערוך בערך טלופחא. והוא ים דתנן בפ' המוכר את הבית המוכר את בית הבד מכר את הים. ומפרש התם מאי ים טלופחא ולפי שהוא עגול כעדשה נקרא טלופחא דעדשים מתרגמינן טלופחי'. ומה שנקרא ים. לפי שעל ידו נעצרים הענבים בגת ושופעין כים. ותדע לך דקתני התם המוכר את בית הבד מכר את הים ואי ים היינו גת עצמה או בד עצמה מאי איצטריך למיתנייה פשיטא שמכרו:

**עין משפט נר מצוה**

[וע' תוס' כתובות לט: ד"ה וכ"ת]

יא א מיי' פ"ב מהל' אישות הל"ב סמג עשין מח טוש"ע יו"ד סי' רלד סעי' א בהג"ה:

יב ב מיי' פ"ה מהל' איסורי ביאה הל' כב:

יג ג מיי' פי"א מהל' מאכלות אסורות הל' כב ופי"א מהל' טומאת אוכלים הלי"ז:

**מסורת הש"ס**

כתובות לט. קדושין עט.

[יבמות קכא. חולין נט.]

[נ"ל אני נתתי לכם]

ע"ז עה. [תוספתא פי"א דטהרות ע"ש וע' בר"ש מ"ח פ"י דטהרות]

ועיין רש"א שכתב דלפי גי' שלפנינו ורביעית ג' חדשים והיא גי' רש"ל צריך להגיה הכא אז במקום או

גי' רש"א בד

[נ"ל או]

**הגהות הב"ח**

(א) רש"י ד"ה אלא וכו' אמאי יהיב לה רבי להך אחת: (ב) תוס' ד"ה הדפין וכו' דליכא דפליג על זה גבי שאר: (ג) בסה"ד מעקלים אי נמי בגורגי של שיפא:

הָעֲקָלִים שֶׁל נְצָרִים וְשֶׁל *בִּצְבּוּץ – מְנַגְּבָן, שֶׁל שִׁיפָא וְשֶׁל גֶּמִי – מְיַישְּׁנָן. וְכַמָּה מְיַישְּׁנָן? י"ב חֹדֶשׁ. רשב"ג אוֹמֵר: מַנִּיחָן מִגַּת לַגַּת וּמִבַּד לַבַּד. הַיְינוּ ת"ק: אִיכָּא בֵּינַיְיהוּ חָרְפֵי וְאָפְלֵי. רַבִּי יוֹסֵי אוֹמֵר: הָרוֹצֶה לְטַהֵר מִיָּד – מַגְעִילָן בְּרוֹתְחִין, אוֹ חוֹלְטָן בְּמֵי זֵיתִים. רשב"ג אוֹמֵר מִשּׁוּם ר' יוֹסֵי: מַנִּיחָן תַּחַת הַצִּינוֹר שֶׁמֵּימָיו מְקַלְּחִין, אוֹ בְּמַעְיָן שֶׁמֵּימָיו רוֹדְפִין. וְכַמָּה? – עוֹנָה. כְּדֶרֶךְ שֶׁאָמְרוּ בְּיֵין נֶסֶךְ, כָּךְ אָמְרוּ בְּטָהֳרוֹת. כְּלַפֵּי לַיָּיא בְּטָהֳרוֹת קָיְימִינַן! אֶלָּא: כְּדֶרֶךְ שֶׁאָמְרוּ בְּטָהֳרוֹת [א]כָּךְ אָמְרוּ בְּיֵין נֶסֶךְ. וְכַמָּה עוֹנָה? א"ר חִיָּיא בַּר אַבָּא, א"ר יוֹחָנָן: [ב]אוֹ יוֹם אוֹ לַיְלָה. ר' חָנָה שְׁאוֹנָא, וְאָמְרִי לָהּ רַבִּי חָנָה בַּר שְׁאוֹנָא אָמַר רַבָּה בַּר בַּר חָנָה א"ר יוֹחָנָן: חֲצִי יוֹם וַחֲצִי לַיְלָה. וַאֲמַר רַב שְׁמוּאֵל בַּר רַב יִצְחָק: וְלָא פְּלִיגִי, הָא בִּתְקוּפַ' נִיסָן וְתִשְׁרֵי, הָא – בִּתְקוּפַת תַּמּוּז וְטֵבֵת. הָכָא נַמִי, אֵימָא גַּבֵּי נִדָּה: חֲצִי יוֹם וַחֲצִי לַיְלָה! וְהָא לַיְלָה וַחֲצִי יוֹם קָאָמַר! אֶלָּא: אִי לַיְלָה דְּנִיסָן וְתִשְׁרֵי, אִי חֲצִי יוֹם וַחֲצִי לַיְלָה דְּטֵבֵת וְתַמּוּז. ואב"א: שָׁאנֵי כְּתוּבָּה.* (א) דְּמַגְבֵּי בָּהּ טְפֵי עַד דְּחָתְמֵי. רַב וּשְׁמוּאֵל דְּאָמְרִי תַּרְוַיְיהוּ: הֲלָכָה *בּוֹעֵל בְּעִילַת מִצְוָה, וּפוֹרֵשׁ. מְתִיב רַב חִסְדָּא: מַעֲשֶׂה וְנָתַן לָהּ רַבִּי ד' לֵילוֹת מִתּוֹךְ י"ב חֹדֶשׁ! א"ל *רָבָא: *הֲדוּרֵי אַפִּירְכָא לָמָּה *לִי? אוֹתֵיב מִמַּתְנִי' הוּא סָבַר – *מַעֲשֶׂה רַב. מ"מ לְרַב וּשְׁמוּאֵל קַשְׁיָא! *אִינְהוּ דְּעָבְדוּ כְּרַבּוֹתֵינוּ. דְּתַנְיָא, רַבּוֹתֵינוּ [ג]חָזְרוּ וְנִמְנוּ: (ב) בּוֹעֵל בְּעִילַת מִצְוָה, וּפוֹרֵשׁ. אֲמַר עוּלָּא: כִּי הֲווּ בָּהּ ר' יוֹחָנָן ור"ל בְּתִינוֹקֶת, *לָא הֲווּ מַסְּקֵי מִינָּהּ אֶלָּא כִּדְמָסֵיק תַּעֲלָא מִבֵּי כְּרָבָא, וּמְסַיְּימִי בָּהּ הָכִי: בּוֹעֵל בְּעִילַת מִצְוָה, וּפוֹרֵשׁ. א"ל ר' אַבָּא לְרַב אַשִׁי: אֶלָּא מֵעַתָּה בַּעַל נֶפֶשׁ לֹא יִגְמוֹר בִּיאָתוֹ! א"ל: *[ד]א"כ לִבּוֹ נוֹקְפוֹ וּפוֹרֵשׁ. ת"ר: וְכוּלָּן שֶׁהָיוּ שׁוֹפְעוֹת דָּם וּבָאוֹת מִתּוֹךְ ד' לֵילוֹת לְאַחַר ד' לֵילוֹת, מִתּוֹךְ הַלַּיְלָה לְאַחַר הַלַּיְלָה – כּוּלָּן צְרִיכוֹת לִבְדּוֹק אֶת עַצְמָן. וּבְכוּלָּן ר"מ מַחְמִיר כְּדִבְרֵי ב"ש [א] וּשְׁאָר רְאִיּוֹת שֶׁבֵּין ב"ש וב"ה – הַלֵּךְ אַחַר מַרְאֵה דָּמִים. שֶׁהָיָה ר"מ אוֹמֵר: מַרְאֵה דָּמִים מְשׁוּנִּים הֵן זֶה מִזֶּה. כֵּיצַד: דַּם נִדָּה – אָדוֹם, דַּם בְּתוּלִים – אֵינוֹ אָדוֹם. דַּם נִדָּה – זִיהוּם, דַּם בְּתוּלִים – אֵינוֹ זִיהוּם. דַּם נִדָּה – בָּא מִן הַמָּקוֹר, [ה]דַּם בְּתוּלִים – בָּא מִן הַצְּדָדִין. אָמַר רַבִּי יִצְחָק בַּר רַבִּי יוֹסֵי, אָמַר רַבִּי יוֹחָנָן: זוֹ דִּבְרֵי ר' מֵאִיר, אֲבָל חֲכָמִים אוֹמְרִים כָּל מַרְאֵה דָּמִים – אַחַת הֵן. תָּנוּ רַבָּנַן: [א] [ו]הָרוֹאָה דָּם מֵחֲמַת תַּשְׁמִישׁ – מְשַׁמֶּשֶׁת פַּעַם רִאשׁוֹנָה וּשְׁנִיָּה וּשְׁלִישִׁית. מִכָּאן וְאֵילָךְ – לֹא תְּשַׁמֵּשׁ, עַד שֶׁתִּתְגָּרֵשׁ, וְתִנָּשֵׂא

[חולין פט:]

**רש"י**

הָעֲקָלִים. רדוט"ש. יֵשׁ מְקוֹמוֹת שֶׁקּוֹשְׁרִין אֶת הַתַּפּוּחַ שֶׁל חַרְצַנִּים בַּעֲקָלִים סָבִיב. בִּצְבּוּץ. קַנְבּוּס. מְנַגְּבָן. שֶׁאֵינָם בּוֹלְעִין כָּל כָּךְ. שִׁיפָא. גּוֹמֶא גליי"ד בְּלַעַ"ז. חָרְפֵי וְאָפְלֵי. לְר"ש, פְּעָמִים שֶׁהֵן יוֹתֵר מִי"ב חֹדֶשׁ, פְּעָמִים שֶׁהֵן פָּחוֹת. לָא פְּלִיגִי. רַבִּי חִיָּיא וְרַבָּה בַּר בַּר חָנָה. בִּתְקוּפַת נִיסָן וְתִשְׁרֵי. שֶׁהַיּוֹם וְהַלַּיְלָה שָׁוִים, אוֹ יוֹם אוֹ לַיְלָה. בִּתְקוּפַת תַּמּוּז וְטֵבֵת. שֶׁאֵינָם שָׁוִין, חֲצִי יוֹם וַחֲצִי לַיְלָה – דְּהָוֵי עוֹנָה שְׁלֵימָה שֶׁל י"ב שָׁעוֹת. שָׁאנֵי כְּתוּבָּה (ג) דְּמַגְּבֵי בָּהּ טְפֵי. יֵשׁ עִיכּוּב בַּדָּבָר לְדַקְדֵּק בַּכֹּל וּלְחוֹתְמָהּ, הִילְכָּךְ בָּעֵינַן לַיְלָה שְׁלֵימָה וַחֲצִי יוֹם. הֲלָכָה בּוֹעֵל בְּעִילַת מִצְוָה. בֵּין הִגִּיעַ זְמַנָּהּ, בֵּין לֹא הִגִּיעַ. כִּי הֲווּ מְעַיְּינֵי בְּתִינוֹקֶת. בְּהַאי פִּרְקָא שֶׁשְּׁמָהּ "תִּינוֹקֶת". תַּעֲלָא. שׁוּעָל. מִבֵּי כְּרָבָא. מִן הַמַּחֲרֵישָׁה, שֶׁאֵינוֹ מוֹצִיא מִשָּׁם אֶלָּא אָבָק בְּרַגְלָיו. הָכִי נַמִי לָא יָלְפִינַן מִפִּרְקָא דְּמַתְנִי' מִידֵי, אֶלָּא מִבָּרַיְיתָא. וּכְרַבּוֹתֵינוּ, דְּאָמְרֵי: בּוֹעֵל בְּעִילַת מִצְוָה, וּפוֹרֵשׁ. מִתּוֹךְ ד' לֵילוֹת. לְלֹא רָאֲתָה בְּבֵית אָבִיהָ. אוֹ מִתּוֹךְ הַלַּיְלָה, לְרָאֲתָה בְּבֵית אָבִיהָ – צְרִיכוֹת לִבְדּוֹק, שֶׁאֵין סוֹמְכוֹת לוֹמַר: הוֹאִיל וְשׁוֹפְעוֹת דָּם – מִדַּם בְּתוּלִים הוּא, וַאֲפִילּוּ אַחַר ד' לֵילוֹת. אֶלָּא בּוֹדְקוֹת אִם נִשְׁתַּנּוּ מַרְאֶה דָּמִים, כִּדְמְפָרֵשׁ. וּבְכוּלָּן ר"מ מַחְמִיר כְּדִבְרֵי ב"ש. לִקְטַנָּה, ד' לֵילוֹת. לְהַצְרִיכָהּ בְּדִיקָה, אִם שׁוֹפַעַת מִתּוֹךְ ד' לְאַחַר ד'. וּלְנַעֲרָה, לַיְלָה אֶחָד. וּשְׁאָר רְאִיּוֹת. הֵיכָא דְּאֵינָהּ שׁוֹפַעַת, שֶׁבֵּין ב"ש וב"ה. דְּלְב"ה – טְהוֹרִין, וַאֲפִי' נִשְׁתַּנּוּ. (ד) וְאָמַר ר"מ: הַלֵּךְ אַחַר מַרְאֵה דָּמִים. וּבְהָא לָא ס"ל כְּב"ש לְגַמְרֵי. דְּלְב"ש, אֲפִילּוּ לֹא נִשְׁתַּנּוּ – טְמֵאִין, כֵּיוָן דְּאֵינָהּ שׁוֹפַעַת מִתּוֹךְ ד' לְאַחַר ד' לִקְטַנָּה, וּמִתּוֹךְ לַיְלָה לְאַחַר לַיְלָה לְהַגִּיעַ זְמַנָּהּ וְלֹא רָאֲתָה. הָרוֹאָה דָּם. לָאו בִּבְתוּלָה קָא מַיְירֵי, אֶלָּא בְּדַם נִדּוּת. וְתִנָּשֵׂא

[פי' פשתן מלוכן כמו עריך ערך כן ד'] [ס"א דמגהי [ובערוך או' דמגחי בה טפי פי' טשאין ונותנין בה טובא ומאחרין עד חצי הלילה. ערוך ערך גח א'] [נ"ל לא] [שבת כח. וש"נ] [יומא מג:] [לעיל ג: וש"נ]

**תוספות**

**היינו** ת"ק. וא"ת: טובא איכא בינייהו, דהא ת"ק מצריך י"ב חדש, ורשב"ג קאמר דכשנטמא בזה הגת – ישתמש בהן בגת הבאה. א"כ הוא מסוף גת לתחלת גת, וחסר משנה כל ימי משך הגת! וי"ל: דס"ל דת"ק לא מחמיר טפי מי"ב חדשי לבנה, ובישול פירות הולך אחר החמה, אם כן מסוף גת לתחלת גת איכא י"ב חדשי לבנה. ומשני: "איכא בינייהו חרפי ואפלי" – כלומר, אשתקד הוו אפלי, ועכשיו חרפי, ואיכא פחות מי"ב חדשי לבנה מגת לגת. א"נ: פשיטא ליה דת"ק לא קאמר י"ב חדש משנתרוקנה הגת דא"כ כלו ימי בציר, ולא יכול להשתמש עד כ"ד חודש, והיא גת אחרת. אלא "י"ב חדש" דקאמר ת"ק – עם זמן שהיין בו. והיינו כרשב"ג דאמר "לגת הבאה"! ומשני: "איכא בינייהו חרפי ואפלי", כדפירש רש"י: "חרפי" – שממהר הבציר של שנה זו משל אשתקד. רשב"ג מיקל, דליכא י"ב חדש, "ואפלי" – שמאחר הבציר של שנה זו משל אשתקד. רשב"ג מחמיר. אבל ת"ק מודה נמי, דכל זמן שיש בו י"ב חדש עם זמן שהיין בגת – די בכך, וזו היא קולא.

**וכולן** ששופעות ובאות מתוך ד' לילות לאחר ד' לילות כולן צריכות לבדוק **את עצמן**. אור"י: דלאו דוקא כשםלמו כל ד' לילות, דה"ה מכל לילה מתוך ד' לילות ליום של אחרי כן. דהא אם ראתה ביום – טמאה ללוי, דאמר: ד' עונות. ואפילו לרב, דאמר: לא הפסידה לילות, מ"מ מודה דאם נשתנו, תהא ראייה טמאה. הילכך, צריכה לבדוק אולי נשתנה. אע"ג דבלילה נמי אם נשתנה טמאה מ"מ לא בעיא בדיקה. אבל ביום בעי' בדיקה, ולא סמכינן למימר: הואיל ושופעת דם בתולים. (ה) והך הוא בדיקה, אפילו לרבנן דפליגי לקמן עליה דר"מ דאמר: כל מראה דמים אחת הן. דודאי אית להו הא דספ"ק (לעיל יט.) אם נשתנו מראה דמים שלה – טמאה. ולקמן לא פליגי בנשתנה הדם מבתחלה, אלא אם בין זה ובין הראשון דומה לדם נדה. וה"פ: "ובכולן ר"מ מחמיר כב"ש" – בכל מחלוקת שבין ב"ש וב"ה (וב"ה) דמתניתין *מחמירין. ודוקא באותן ד' לילות לתינוקת שלא הגיע זמנה לראות, ובלילה לתינוקת שהגיע זמנה, מטהר ר"מ אפילו דומה לדם נדה – תלינן ליה בדם בתולים. "ושאר ראיות שבין ב"ש וב"ה" – כגון מד' לילות ועד שתחיה המכה לתינוקת שלא הגיע זמנה, וכגון מלילה הראשונה לד' לילות בהגיע זמנה. דלב"ש לא תלינן כלל בדם בתולים, ולב"ה תלינן בבתולים אפי' דומה לדם נדה. התם מחלק ר"מ שאם דומה לדם נדה – טמאה, אע"פ שבתוך הלילות או הלילה היינו תולין בדם בתולים, עכשיו לא נתלה. ואם דומה כל הדם שאחרי הד' לילות או הלילה לדם בתולים – טהור. וחכ"א: כל מראה דמים אחת הן, וסבירא להו לגמרי כב"ה ולעולם תלינן בדם בתולים, עד שתחיה המכה או עד ד' לילות, רק שלא ישתנה הדם מכמות שהיה. ושפיר סבירא להו לרבנן הך דספ"ק דאם נשתנו מכמות שהיו מראה דמים שלה – טמאה. ולא כפירש"י שפירש: דאפי' נשתנו מכמות שהיו מראה דמים – טהורה לרבנן. וא"ת: מאי קמ"ל בהך בדיקה, והא אפי' בתוך זמן תליית דם בתולים, כמו בלא הגיע זמנה לראות לב"ה דתלינן בדם בתולים עד שתחיה המכה, אמר בפ"ק (לעיל יא:) דבתולה בודקת שחרית וערבית, שמא נשתנו מראה דמיה. כ"ש לאחר שעבר זמן תלייתה בבתולים, שצריכה לבדוק, דהך בדיקה שחרית היא! וכי תימא: משום שופעת נקט. דכיון דשופעת, איכא למתלי בבתולים חוץ לזמנה כמו תוך הזמן – אדרבה, כיון דאפילו בשאינה מרגשת בשום ראייה צריכה לבדוק, כ"ש כשמרגשת בראייה! וי"ל: דבדיקה דלעיל שחרית וערבית אוקמינן לטהרות, אבל לבעלה – לא בעיא בדיקה. והכא איירי לבעלה – דבעיא בדיקה. ב] א"נ: הך בדיקה הויא בשפופרת, אם בא ממקור או מן הצדדים, וכן משמע בתוספתא. וניחא, דמשום הכי קתני בסיפא "דם נדה בא מן המקור". ונאמנת

**עין משפט נר מצוה**

יד א מיי' פי"א מהל' מאכלות אסורות הל' כא סמג לאוין קמא טוש"ע יו"ד סי' קלח סעי' ו:

טו ב מיי' שם ופי"א מהל' טומאת אוכלין הלי"ז סמג שם טוש"ע שם:

טז ג ד מיי' פי"א מהל' איסורי ביאה הל"ח ופ"ה שם הל' יט סמג לאוין קיא טוש"ע יו"ד סימן קצג וטוש"ע אה"ע סי' סג סעי' א [וברב אלפס שבועות פ"ב דף רל.]:

יז ה מיי' שם פ"ה הלי"ח:

יח ו מיי' שם פ"ד הל"כ. סמג שם טוש"ע יו"ד סי' קפז סעי' א [וברב אלפס שבועות פ"ב דף רפח.]:

**גליון הש"ס**

**גמ'** אינהו דעבדו כרבותינו. כעין זה כתובות עח ע"ב:

כתובות ז.

נ"ל רבה

רש"ל מ"ז

מחמיר רש"ל

**הגהות הב"ח**

(א) גמ' שאני כתובה דמהני בה טפי: (ב) שם חזרו ונמנו שיהא בועל: (ג) רש"י ד"ה שאני כתובה דמהני בה: (ד) ד"ה ושאר וכו' נשתנו אמר ר"מ: (ה) תום' ד"ה וכולן וכו' דם בתולים הוא והך:

**הגהות הגר"א**

[א] גמ' ושאר ראיות. נ"ב נ"ל וכן שאר ראיות:

**הגהות מהר"ב רנשבורג**

א] גמ' ת"ר הרואה דם מחמת תשמיש וכו'. נ"ב עי' שו"ת הב"ח סי' פ"ג פ"ד פ"ה: ב] תוד"ה וכולן וכו' א"נ הך בדיקה הויא בשפופרת. נ"ב עי' ת"י סס"י קפז ס"ק יד ובסד"ט שם ס"ק כט:

**תוספי הרא"ש**

**רשב"ג** היינו ת"ק. תימה מאי קשה ליה הא רשב"ג שרי מגת לגת אע"ג דזמן בציר נמשך חדש או חדשים ונשתהה האיסור בכלי כל זמן הבציר וליכא י"ב חדש שנתרוקן הכלי מן האיסור וי"ל דפשיטא ליה דמגת לגת דקאמר רשב"ג היינו מתחלת גת לתחלת גת או מסוף גת לסוף גת דאי מסוף גת לתחלת גת אין זה דבר מסויים ושיעור שוה דבשנה אחת יש ענבים הרבה ונמשך הבציר זמן גדול ופעמים שאין ענבים הלכך פריך היינו ת"ק ומשני איכא בינייהו חרפי ואפלי דלת"ק לעולם י"ב חדש ורשב"ג מגת לגת הן פחות מי"ב חדש הן יותר וחשיב שפיר דבר מסויים דרוב שנים הפירות מתבשלים אחר חדשי חמה: **רב** ושמואל דאמרי תרווייהו הילכתא בועל בעילת מצוה ופורש. והא דאמר רב לעיל בוגרת נותנין לה לילה ראשון אליבא דמתניתין קאמר. ומי' פסיק הלכתא כרבותינו: **וכולם** שהיו שופעות דם צריכות לבדוק עצמן. פרש"י אם נשתנה הדם. וה"נ בתוך ד' לילות אם ראתה מחמת תשמיש לילה הראשונה דם שאינו אדום כדם נדה ולמחר ראתה דם בלא תשמיש דם אדום כדם נדה טמאה כדאמרינן בפ"ק נשתנו מראה דמים שלה טמאה. הילכך אם היתה שופעת מלילה הראשונה ששמשה עד למחרת דסד"א דדם בתולים הוא. א"ה אם נשתנה להיות אדום כדם הנדה טמאה. ומיהו אם בשעת תשמיש ראתה דם אדום ומזוהם כדם נדה דתלינן ליה בדם בתולים כיון דמחמת תשמיש ראתה ולמחרת בלא תשמיש ראתה דם משונה שאינו אדום כדם נדה או ראתה דם אדום ומזוהם כדם נדה טהורה כיון דלא נשתנה אלא ראתה מראית דם זה בשעת תשמיש. והך דרישא אתיא אפי' כרבנן דבסמוך דלא חיישי לשינוי מראה דמים דבסיפא דוקא פליגי בימים שב"ה מוסיפין על ב"ש: **ובכולם** ר' מאיר מחמיר כדברי ב"ש. והולך ומפרש היאך מחמיר דשאר ראיות שבין ב"ש לב"ה כגון תינוקת שלא הגיע זמנה לראות מד' לילות עד שתחיה המכה והגיע זמנה לראות ולא ראתה מלילה הראשונה עד ד' לילות ובראתה מביאת מצוה עד סוף הלילה דב"ש מטמאין אפי' ראתה בשעת תשמיש דם שאינו אדום כדם הנדה אלא דיהה קצת ואינו מזוהם ומראהו כדם בתולים. וב"ה מטהרים אפי' ראתה מחמת תשמיש דם אדום ומזוהם כדם נדה. ואפילו שלא מחמת תשמיש אם לא נשתנה. ור' מאיר מחמיר דאם ראתה בהם דם אדום ומזוהם כדם נדה שלא בשעת תשמיש. אע"פ שראתה מראה דם זה בלילה ראשונה בשעת תשמיש או אפי' בשעת תשמיש נמי ראתה דם אדום ומזוהם לאחר ד' לילות הויא טמאה אבל אם ראתה דם שאינו אדום ומזוהם בין בשעת תשמיש בין שלא בשעת תשמיש [טהורה] כב"ה: **וחכ"א** כל מראה דם אחת הם עד שתחיה המכה. או כל ד' לילות בהגיע ולא ראתה אף אם ראתה דם אדום ומזוהם בשעת תשמיש או שלא בשעת תשמיש רק שלא נשתנה טהור כב"ה. ותימה מאי קמ"ל דבודקת בשופעת לאחר ד' לילות דמשמע דמשום דהתחילו ימי טומאה הלא אף בתוך ד' לילות בודקת שחרית וערבית אם נשתנו מראה דמים כדאמרינן פ"ר בתולה שדמיה טהורין בודקת שחרית וערבית רק שאחר תשמיש אינה צריכה לבדוק משום דאימר שמש עכרו. ואף בלא הגיע זמנה לראות דאמרינן בפ"ק דהיא בחזקת טהרה היינו כשלא ראתה מעולם. אבל בפעם ראשונה ושניה הרי היא ככל הנשים ומטמאה מעת לעת ומפקידה לפקידה כדאיתא בפ"ק ומתניתין עד שתחיה המכה איירי דאפי' ראתה כמה פעמים בבית אביה כדאמרינן בריש פירקין. וא"כ צריכה בדיקה שחרית וערבית לידע אם נשתנו דמיה. וי"ל דה"מ לטהרות אבל לאחר ד' לילות שנכנסו ימי טומאה אם היתה שופעת בודקת אף לבעלה דאם נשתנו דמים טמאה ואם לא נשתנו טהורה כיון דשופעת מימי טהרה. א"נ כגון שהתחילה לשמש בחצי הלילה וכלתה עונתה בחצי היום כדאמרינן לעיל. ושופעת מחצי היום ואילך בודקת אע"פ שאינו שחרית וערבית. א"נ הך בדיקה בשפופרת לידע אם בא מן המקור או מן הצדדין אבל קודם ד' לילות אף אם שופעת לא בדקתה בשפופרת. והכי משמע בתוספתא דתאני התם וכולם שהיו שופעות דם בודקות עצמן בשפופרת חוץ מן הבתולה שדמיה טהורין מפני שדם בתולים טהור ובכולן היה ר"מ מחמיר כדברי ב"ש כו. ועי"ל דרישא דהך ברייתא לא איירי כלל בשינוי מראה דמים אלא ה"פ אם שופעת מתוך ימי טהרה לימי טומאה בודקת עצמה דאם ראתה דם אדום ומזוהם כדם נדה טמאה אע"פ ששופעת מתוך לילה ראשונה ששימשה וראתה דם ממראה זה. אבל בתוך ד' לילות אף שפעה מלילה שראתה בשעת תשמיש דם אדום ומזוהם ולמחרת נמי ראתה מראית זה אף בלא תשמיש טהורה:

וְתִנָּשֵׂא לְאַחֵר. נִיסֵּת לְאַחֵר וְרָאֲתָה דָּם מֵחֲמַת תַּשְׁמִישׁ — מְשַׁמֶּשֶׁת פַּעַם רִאשׁוֹנָה וּשְׁנִיָּה וּשְׁלִישִׁית, מִכָּאן וְאֵילָךְ — לֹא תְּשַׁמֵּשׁ, עַד שֶׁתִּתְגָּרֵשׁ וְתִנָּשֵׂא לְאַחֵר. נִיסֵּת לְאַחֵר וְרָאֲתָה דָּם מֵחֲמַת תַּשְׁמִישׁ — מְשַׁמֶּשֶׁת פַּעַם רִאשׁוֹנָה וּשְׁנִיָּה וּשְׁלִישִׁית, מִכָּאן וְאֵילָךְ לֹא תְּשַׁמֵּשׁ עַד שֶׁתִּבְדּוֹק עַצְמָהּ. [א]כֵּיצַד בּוֹדֶקֶת אֶת עַצְמָהּ — מְבִיאָה שְׁפוֹפֶרֶת וּבְתוֹכָהּ מִכְחוֹל, וּמוֹךְ מוּנָּח עַל רֹאשׁוֹ, אִם נִמְצָא דָּם עַל רֹאשׁ הַמּוֹךְ — בְּיָדוּעַ שֶׁמִּן הַמָּקוֹר הוּא בָּא, לֹא נִמְצָא דָּם עַל רֹאשׁוֹ — בְּיָדוּעַ שֶׁמִּן הַצְּדָדִין הוּא בָּא. [ב]וְאִם יֵשׁ לָהּ מַכָּה בְּאוֹתוֹ מָקוֹם תּוֹלָה בְּמַכָּתָהּ, [ג]וְאִם יֵשׁ לָהּ וֶסֶת — תּוֹלָה בְּוִסְתָּהּ. [ד]וְאִם הָיָה דַּם מַכָּתָהּ מְשׁוּנֶּה מִדַּם רְאִיָּיתָהּ — אֵינָהּ תּוֹלָה. [ה]וְנֶאֱמֶנֶת אִשָּׁה לוֹמַר "מַכָּה יֵשׁ לִי בַּמָּקוֹר שֶׁמִּמֶּנָּה דָּם יוֹצֵא", דִּבְרֵי רַבִּי. רשב"ג אוֹמֵר: דַּם מַכָּה הַבָּא מִן הַמָּקוֹר — טָמֵא. וְרַבּוֹתֵינוּ הֵעִידוּ עַל דַּם הַמַּכָּה הַבָּא מִן הַמָּקוֹר שֶׁהוּא טָהוֹר. מַאי בֵּינַיְיהוּ? אָמַר עוּלָּא *מָקוֹר מְקוֹמוֹ טָמֵא אִיכָּא בֵּינַיְיהוּ. שְׁפוֹפֶרֶת, אַפְּגוּרֵי מִפְגְּרָא לָהּ! אָמַר שְׁמוּאֵל: [ו]בִּשְׁפוֹפֶרֶת שֶׁל אֵבֶר, וּפִיהָ רָצוּף לְתוֹכָהּ. אָמַר לֵיהּ רֵישׁ לָקִישׁ לְרַבִּי יוֹחָנָן: [ז]וְתִבְדּוֹק עַצְמָהּ בְּבִיאָה שְׁלִישִׁית שֶׁל בַּעַל הָרִאשׁוֹן? אָמַר לֵיהּ: לְפִי *שֶׁאֵין כָּל הָאֶצְבָּעוֹת שָׁוֹת. אָמַר לֵיהּ: וְתִבְדּוֹק עַצְמָהּ בְּבִיאָה רִאשׁוֹנָה שֶׁל בַּעַל שְׁלִישִׁי? לְפִי שֶׁאֵין כָּל הַכֹּחוֹת שָׁווֹת. הַהִיא דַּאֲתַאי לְקַמֵּיהּ דְּרַבִּי, אָמַר לֵיהּ לְאַבְדָּן: זִיל בְּעַתָהּ. אֲזַל בְּעָתָהּ, וְנָפַל מִמֶּנָּה חֲרָרַת דָּם. אָמַר רַבִּי: [ח]נִתְרַפְּאָה זֹאת. הַהִיא אִתְּתָא דַּאֲתַאי לְקַמֵּיהּ דְּמָר שְׁמוּאֵל, אָמַר לֵיהּ לְרַב דִּימִי בַּר יוֹסֵף: זִיל בְּעַתָהּ! אֲזַל בְּעָתָהּ, וְלָא נְפַל מִמֶּנָּה וְלָא מִידֵּי. אָמַר שְׁמוּאֵל: זוֹ — מְמַלְאָה וְנוֹפֶצֶת הִיא, וְכָל הַמְמַלְאָה וְנוֹפֶצֶת — אֵין לָהּ תַּקָּנָה. הַהִיא דַּאֲתַאי לְקַמֵּיהּ דְּרַבִּי יוֹחָנָן, דְּכָל אֵימַת (א) דַּהֲוַת סָלְקָא מִטְּבִילַת מִצְוָה הֲוַת קָחָזְיָא דָּמָא. א"ל שֶׁמָּא דִּימַת עִירֵיךְ עָלְתָה בֵּיךְ, לְכִי וְהִבָּעֲלִי לוֹ ע"ג הַנָּהָר. אִיכָּא דְּאָמַר, אָמַר לָהּ: תְּגַלִּי לְחַבְרוֹתַיִךְ. כִּי הֵיכִי דְּתֶהֱווּ עֲלַיִךְ לְהַךְ גִּיסָא — נִתְהֲווּ עֲלָךְ לְהַךְ גִּיסָא. וְאִיכָּא דְּאָמַר, אָמַר לָהּ: גַּלִּי לְחַבְרוֹתַיִךְ, כִּי הֵיכִי דְּלִבְעוּ עֲלַיִךְ רַחֲמִים. דְּתַנְיָא: °"וְטָמֵא טָמֵא יִקְרָא" — *צָרִיךְ לְהוֹדִיעַ צַעֲרוֹ לָרַבִּים, וְרַבִּים מְבַקְּשִׁים עָלָיו רַחֲמִים. ויקרא יג אָמַר רַב יוֹסֵף: הֲוָה עוּבְדָּא בְּפוּמְבְּדִיתָא — וְאִתַּסֵּי. אָמַר רַב יוֹסֵף, אָמַר רַב יְהוּדָה, אָמַר רַב, הִתְקִין רַבִּי *בַּשָּׂדוֹת: רָאֲתָה יוֹם אֶחָד — תֵּשֵׁב שִׁשָּׁה וְהוּא, שְׁנַיִם — תֵּשֵׁב שִׁשָּׁה וְהֵן, שְׁלֹשָׁה — תֵּשֵׁב שִׁבְעָה נְקִיִּים. אָמַר ר' זֵירָא: [ט]בְּנוֹת יִשְׂרָאֵל א) הֶחְמִירוּ עַל עַצְמָן, שֶׁאֲפִילּוּ רוֹאוֹת טִפַּת דָּם כְּחַרְדָּל — יוֹשְׁבוֹת עָלֶיהָ שִׁבְעָה נְקִיִּים. אַדְבְּרֵיהּ רָבָא לְרַב שְׁמוּאֵל וְדָרַשׁ: קָשְׁתָה שְׁנֵי יָמִים וְלַשְּׁלִישִׁי הִפִּילָה — תֵּשֵׁב שִׁבְעָה נְקִיִּים. קָסָבַר: אֵין קִשּׁוּי לִנְפָלִים, *וְאִי אֶפְשָׁר לִפְתִיחַת הַקֶּבֶר בְּלֹא דָּם. א"ל רַב פַּפָּא לְרָבָא: מַאי אִרְיָא, קָשְׁתָה שְׁנֵי יָמִים — אֲפִילּוּ מַשֶּׁהוּ בְּעָלְמָא! *דְּהָא א"ר זֵירָא: בְּנוֹת יִשְׂרָאֵל הֶחְמִירוּ עַל עַצְמָן, שֶׁאֲפִילּוּ רוֹאוֹת טִפַּת דָּם כְּחַרְדָּל — יוֹשְׁבוֹת עָלֶיהָ שִׁבְעָה נְקִיִּים! א"ל: *אָמֵינָא לָךְ (ב) אִיסּוּרָא, וְאַתְּ אָמְרַתְּ מִנְהָגָא? הֵיכָא דְּאַחְמוּר — אַחְמוּר, הֵיכָא דְּלָא אַחְמוּר — לָא אַחְמוּר. (תִּבְעוּהָ, נֶתֶר, בְּחַמִּין, לִטְבּוֹל, קְמָטִים, ע"ג גָּמָל, סי') *אָמַר רָבָא: [י]תְּבָעוּהָ לִינָּשֵׂא וְנִתְפַּיְּיסָה — צְרִיכָה שֶׁתֵּשֵׁב שִׁבְעָה נְקִיִּים. רָבִינָא אִיעֲסַק לֵיהּ לִבְרֵיהּ בֵּי רַב (ג) חֲנִינָא, ב) א"ל: סָבַר לֵיהּ מָר לְמִכְתַּב כְּתוּבָּה *לְאַרְבָּעָה יוֹם? א"ל: אִין. כִּי מְטָא לְאַרְבָּעָה — נְטַר עַד אַרְבָּעָה אַחֲרִינָא, אִיעַכַּב שִׁבְעָה יוֹמֵי בָּתַר הַהוּא יוֹמָא. א"ל מַאי הַאי? א"ל: לָא סְבַר לַהּ מָר לְהָא דְּרָבָא, דְּאָמַר רָבָא: תְּבָעוּהָ לִינָּשֵׂא וְנִתְפַּיְּיסָה — צְרִיכָה לֵישֵׁב שִׁבְעָה נְקִיִּים. א"ל: אֵימַר דְּאָמַר רָבָא — בִּגְדוֹלָה דְּקָחָזְיָא דָּמָא, אֲבָל בִּקְטַנָּה דְּלָא חָזְיָא דָּמָא — מִי אָמַר? א"ל: בְּפֵירוּשׁ אָמַר רָבָא: [כ]ל"ש גְּדוֹלָה לָא שְׁנָא קְטַנָּה. גְּדוֹלָה טַעְמָא מַאי? — מִשּׁוּם דְּמַחְמְדָא, קְטַנָּה נַמִּי מַחְמְדָא. אָמַר רָבָא: אִשָּׁה

לא

א) [פרש"י ותוס' ע"ז תמלא באריכות במגילה כח: ובתר"י ברכות פ' אין עומדין ברי"ף דף כה. באריכות] ב) גי' הרב המגיד א"ל ליום פלן נכתוב כתובה איעכב ז' יומי בר מההוא יומא אתא א"ל מ"ט עבד מר הכי כו'

---

**רש"י**

וְתִנָּשֵׂא לְאַחֵר. כִּדְמְפָרֵשׁ לְקַמֵּיהּ, שֶׁאֵין כָּל הָאֶצְבָּעוֹת שָׁווֹת. וְתִנָּשֵׂא לְאַחֵר. דִּתְלָתָא זִימְנֵי בָּעֵינַן לַחֲזָקָה, כְּרשב"ג. בְּכוּלֵּהּ גָּרְסִינַן "וּשְׁלִישִׁית". מִכְחוֹל. קֵיסָם אָרוֹךְ, וּמוֹךְ עַל רֹאשׁוֹ שֶׁל מִכְחוֹל. מִן הַצְּדָדִין. וְטָהוֹר. וְאִם יֵשׁ לָהּ וֶסֶת. לְקִלְקוּל הַזֶּה, שֶׁאֵינָהּ רוֹאָה כָּל שָׁעָה מֵחֲמַת תַּשְׁמִישׁ אֶלָּא לִפְרָקִים — תּוֹלָה בְּוִסְתָּהּ, וּמְשַׁמֶּשֶׁת בְּלֹא בְּדִיקָה בֵּין וֶסֶת לְוֶסֶת. דִּבְרֵי רַבִּי. הַךְ מִילְּתָא לְחוּדָהּ דְּ"נֶאֱמֶנֶת אִשָּׁה" קָאָמַר רַבִּי, אֲבָל רֵישָׁא — כּוּלָּהּ רַבָּן שִׁמְעוֹן הִיא. אַפְּגוּרֵי מִפְגְּרָא. שֶׁהָעֵץ אֵינוֹ חָלָק, וּמְסָרֵט וּמוֹצִיא דָּם. רָצוּף. כָּפוּל. וְתִבְדּוֹק בְּבִיאָה שְׁלִישִׁית שֶׁל בַּעַל רִאשׁוֹן. כְּלוֹמַר, מִבִּיאָה שְׁלִישִׁית שֶׁל רִאשׁוֹן וְאֵילָךְ, תְּשַׁמֵּשׁ ע"י בְּדִיקָה, וְלָמָּה תִּתְגָּרֵשׁ? לְפִי שֶׁאֵין כָּל הָאֶצְבָּעוֹת שָׁווֹת. וְשֶׁמָּא בְּבַעַל אַחֵר לֹא תִּצְטָרֵךְ בְּדִיקָה. וּמוּטָב שֶׁתִּתְגָּרֵשׁ וְתִתַּקֵּן, וְלֹא תָּבֹא לִידֵי (ד) כָּרֵת. הִלְכָּךְ, מִתְגָּרֶשֶׁת עַד שֶׁתִּתְחַזֵּק בְּשָׁלֹשׁ אֶצְבָּעוֹת. וְתִבְדּוֹק בְּבִיאָה רִאשׁוֹנָה שֶׁל בַּעַל שְׁלִישִׁי. מֵאַחַר שֶׁעָלֶיהָ פַּעַם אַחַת — לֹא תְּשַׁמֵּשׁ שְׁנִיָּה בְּלֹא בְּדִיקָה, שֶׁהֲרֵי הוּחְזְקָה בְּג' אֶצְבָּעוֹת. וּמְשַׁנֵּינַן: אֵין חֶזְקַת בִּיאָה אַחַת — חֲזָקָה, דְּאֵין כָּל הַכֹּחוֹת שָׁוִין, וְשֶׁמָּא בְּעִילָה זוֹ הָיְתָה בְּכֹחַ מְרוּבֶּה. הִלְכָּךְ, עַד שֶׁתִּתְחַזֵּק בְּג' בִּיאוֹת לְכָל אֶחָד וְאֶחָד, וַהֲדַר תִּבָּעֵי בְּדִיקָה לְבִיאָה רְבִיעִית שֶׁל בַּעַל שְׁלִישִׁי. הַהִיא דַּאֲתַאי. שֶׁהָיְתָה רוֹאָה דָּם מֵחֲמַת תַּשְׁמִישׁ. בְּעָתָהּ. הַבְהִילָהּ פִּתְאוֹם. מְמַלְאָה וְנוֹפֶצֶת. מִתְמַלְּאָה דָּם וּמְנַפַּלְתּוֹ בִּשְׁעַת תַּשְׁמִישׁ. דִּימַת עִירֵיךְ. בְּנוֹת עִירֵךְ, שֶׁהָיוּ מִתְקַנְּאוֹת בָּךְ בְּחִיבָּה שֶׁבֵּינֵיךְ לְבַעֲלֵיךְ. "דִּימַת" לְשׁוֹן לִיעוּז פרליר"ן, כְּמוֹ (יבמות דף נג.): "מֵידַס דַּיְימָא", וּכְמוֹ (סוטה דף כז.): "לֹא יִשָּׂא אָדָם דּוּמָה". כִּי הֵיכִי דְּתֶהֱווּ עֲלַיִךְ. עַד הַשְׁתָּא לְהַאי גִּיסָא, עַל חִיבָּה יְתֵירָה שֶׁבֵּינֵיכֶם. נִתְהֲווּ עֲלַיִךְ לְאִידָךְ גִּיסָא. וְיֹאמְרוּ "כַּמָּה שְׂנוּאָה זוֹ", וְתָשׁוּב קִנְאָה מִמֵּךְ. הֲוָה עוּבְדָּא. וְגִילְּתָה לְצָרָהּ לָרַבִּים, וּבִקְשׁוּ עָלֶיהָ רַחֲמִים, וְנִתְרַפְּאָה. בַּשָּׂדוֹת. מָקוֹם שֶׁאֵין בְּנֵי תּוֹרָה, וְאֵינָן יוֹדְעוֹת לִמְנוֹת פֶּתַח נִדּוּת, מָתַי הֵן יְמֵי נִדָּה, מָתַי הֵן יְמֵי זוֹב. שִׁשָּׁה וְהוּא. כְּדִין תּוֹרָה, וְשֶׁמָּא בִּימֵי נִדָּה הוּא. שְׁנַיִם תֵּשֵׁב שִׁשָּׁה וְהֵן. לְחוּמְרָא, שֶׁמָּא רִאשׁוֹן — סוֹף זוֹב, וְשֵׁנִי — תְּחִלַּת נִדָּה, וּצְרִיכָה עוֹד שִׁשָּׁה. אֲבָל שְׁלֹשָׁה, דְּאִילּוּ הֲוֵי יְמֵי זִיבָה — צְרִיכָה ז' נְקִיִּים, הַשְׁתָּא נַמִּי תֵּשֵׁב שִׁבְעָה נְקִיִּים, שֶׁמָּא בִּימֵי זִיבָה עוֹמֶדֶת. קָשְׁתָה שְׁנַיִם. וְרָאֲתָה בִּימֵי זוֹב. אִיסּוּרָא. דַּאֲפִי' הֵיכָא דְּלָא אַחְמוּר — תֵּשֵׁב עַל כָּרְחָהּ מִן הַתּוֹרָה. צְרִיכָה לֵישֵׁב שִׁבְעָה נְקִיִּים. שֶׁמָּא מֵחֲמַת תַּאֲוַת חִימּוּד רָאֲתָה דָּם. אִיעַכַּב ז' יוֹמֵי. בָּתַר יוֹמָא שֶׁנִּתְפַּיְּיסָה לִינָּשֵׂא.

לא

---

**תוספות**

וְנֶאֱמֶנֶת אשה לומר וכו' דברי רבי. פרש"י: דדוקא הך סיפא ד"נאמנת" כרבי, אבל כולה רישא כרשב"ג דסבירא ליה* בג' זימני הוי חזקה. ור"י מפרש: דאפילו רבי מודה ברואה מחמת תשמיש, דבעי ג' זימנין לאחזוקה. דומיא דהך דלעיל,* דאמר: "לימים ב' ולמה שלא מנו חכמים — ג' כגון אכלה שום או פלפלין". דאפילו לרבי בעי תלת זימני.

ותבדוק עצמה בביאה שלישית כו'. פירש בקונטרס: מביאה שלישית ואילך, תשמש על ידי בדיקה, ולמה תתגרש? מתוך לשונו משמע דאסורה לראשון, אפי' בבדיקה. וה"ה דהוה מצי למיפרך לפי פירושו: דגם לשני לא תשתרי אלא ע"י בדיקה, כיון דלא ידע שינויא ד"לאו כל האצבעות שוות". ור"ת מתיר לראשון בבדיקה. ויש להעמיד הברייתא כשאינה רוצה לטרוח בבדיקה, או שאינה יודעת לבדוק. וכן משמע בירושלמי בפ' "דם הנדה", דפריך: ותבדוק עצמה בבעל שני? ומשני: לפי שאין כל האצבעות שוות. כן י"ל דהתלמוד דידן נמי פריך אשני. ובתוספתא (פ"ח) נמי תניא: עד כמה מותרת לינשא? עד שלשה כו' — פירוש: עד כמה מותרת בלא בדיקה. ומדלא מהדר אאיסורא לפרש "עד כמה היא אסורה, אפילו בבדיקה", משמע דבבדיקה שריא, אפילו לראשון. ואתי שפיר לפירוש ר"ת, דפירכא קמייתא הוי כמו פירכא שניה.

ותבדוק עצמה בביאה ראשונה של בעל שלישי. תימה: למאי דלא ידע שינויא ד"אין כל הכחות שוות", ליפרוך: דתבדוק עצמה בביאה שניה של בעל שני. דלענין אצבע שלו, אין לומר "לא כל האצבעות שוות", שהרי כבר ראתה פעם ראשונה על ידי בעילתו. ומשום חזקת כחות אין להתירה, שהרי הוחזקה בג' כחות של בעל ראשון. ואין להתירה אלא מטעם זה ד"אין כל הכחות שוין", ואין חזקת כחו של ראשון מועלת לשני, ואכתי לא ידעינן הך טעמא.

כי היכי דתהוו עליך להך גיסא. פירש"י: תחת אשר קנאו באהבת אישך, יאמרו "כמה שנאה גדולה", ותשוב קנאתם ממך. ובערוך* פי' ששלטו בך עינים להתרחק מבעליך, תודיעם עכשיו שאת בת דמים מרובים, שבניך מרובין ביותר. ויתנו עיניהם בך, ויאמרו "אשריה שדמיה מרובים, שמתוך כך בניה מרובים", ומתוך העין שיתנו בך יפסקו הדמים ותתרפא.

שנים תשב ששה. א] שמא ראתה יום ראשון דם ירוק, ואינו מן המנין.

כל

---

**תוספי הרא"ש**

דברי ר'. פרש"י אבל רישא לאו רבי היא דלר' בתרי זימני הויא חזקה. ומיהו י"ל דאף לר' בעינן ג' זימני כדאמרינן לעיל לימים שנים והיינו כר' וקאמר למה שלא מנו חכמים ג' כמו אכלה שום וראתה כו' אלמא גם לר' יש דבר שצריך שתתחזק ג' פעמים: **לפי** שאין כל האצבעות שוות. פירש"י ושמא בבעל אחר לא תצטרך בדיקה ומוטב שתתגרש ותתקן ולא תבא לידי חשש כרת הלכך מתגרשת עד שתתחזק בג' אצבעות. ומשמע לפי' שאסורה לראשון מתשמיש שלישי ואילך אפילו בבדיקה שלא תהא בחשש כרת. ול"נ פי' דאם יש חשש בבדיקה זו ואסרינן לה לראשון ע"י בדיקה א"כ למה לא נתיר אותה לבעל שלישי ע"י בדיקה בפעם רביעית וכי מחמת תקנת נשואי אשה נתיר חשש איסור ואם אין חשש איסור בבדיקה א"כ גם לראשון תהא מותרת. הלכך נ"ל דה"פ ותבדוק עצמה מביאה שלישית של בעל ראשון כלומר ואמאי מותרת לשני בלא בדיקה כיון שכבר הוחזקה לראות ג' פעמים בשעת תשמיש דומיא דפירכא שניה דפריך ותבדוק עצמה בביאה ראשונה של בעל שלישי כדפי' התם שתהא אסורה לשמש בלא בדיקה הכי נמי פריך הכא שתהא אסורה לשמש מכאן ואילך אפילו לבעל אחר ומשני לפי שאין כל האצבעות שוות וחזקת בעל ראשון אינה אוסרתה על בעל שני. וה"נ אי בעיא לבדוק בביאה רביעית של בעל ראשון דשריא ליה אלא עצה טובה קמ"ל דמוטב שתתגרש ותינשא לשוק ולא תצטרך בדיקה: **ותבדוק** עצמה מביאה ראשונה של בעל שלישי. ותי' כיון דאכתי לא ידע טעמא דכל הכחות שוין ליפרוך נמי ותבדוק עצמה מביאה ראשונה של בעל שני שהרי אצבע שלו שוה לאצבע של ראשון. וי"ל דידע שפיר המקשה דאית לן למימר אין כל הכחות שוין כל זמן שלא הוחזקה באצבעות: **נתהוו** לאידך גיסא. פי' בערוך שתאמרי להם שאת בת דמים מרובין ויתנו בך עין לומר בניך מרובין ויפסקו ממך הדמים: **יום** אחד תשב ששה והוא. וצריך שיהו נקיים שבכל יום שתראה מספקי' דלמא השתא הוי תחלת נדה. והא דלא קאמר נקיים משום דלא שייך לומר נקיים אלא כשהם ימי ספירה **שנים** תשב ששה והן. ותי' אמאי סגי לה בששה דלמא ראשון הוה בימי זבה וימי נדה שאיהה רואה בהן אין עולין לספירת זיבתה כדפסק ר"ת בימי לידה. ובשילהי בא סימן משוה יחד ימי נדה לימי לידה ונמצא שהיא צריכה עדיין לשמור יום אחד כנגד אותו יום שראתה בימי זבה. וי"ל אי מספקי' לשני בתחלת נדה א"כ הוי הראשון י"א יום של זיבה ולא בעי שימור מדאורייתא ואפילו אי בעי שימור מדרבנן לא היה ר' מחמיר על עם שבשדות כל כך: **טפת** דם כחרדל. ותי' כיון דרואה ודאה מאי רבותא בטפת דם כחרדל. פשיטא דמטמא בכל שהוא תנן. וי"ל דטעמא דיושבת ז' נקיים היינו משום דאימור תמול ושלשום ראתה ולאו אדעתה וסד"א אלו ראתה לפני שני ימים היתה רואה עתה ראיה מרובה שכבר מעיינה פתוח ומדלא אשכה אלא כחרדל ש"מ מעיינה סתום קמ"ל: **אדבריה** רבא כו'. ואי אפשר לפתיחת הקבר בלא דם. והא דאמרינן בפ"ב דכריתות ולרבא דאמר מחוסר כפורים דזב כזב דמי הא מתניתא היכי מתרץ לה אמר רב אשי מתרץ לה ביום מ' ליצירת זכר וביום פ' ליצירת נקבה ור' ישמעאל היא ואפשר לפתיחת הקבר בלא דם אליבא דהאי ברייתא קאמר הכי אבל איהו סבר אי אפשר לפתיחת קבר בלא דם כדקאמר הכא. אבל בשאילתות דרב אחאי כתב דהא דקאמר התם אפשר לפתיחת הקבר בלא דם היינו ביום ארבעים שעדיין לא נגמר צורת הוולד. ואפשר הקבר ליפתח בלא דם וליתא דהא לעיל בפ' המפלת אמרי' גבי המפלת חתיכה דפליגי ר' יהודה ורבנן בפלוגתא דהני תנאי אם אפשר לפתיחת הקבר בלא דם. אלמא מאן דאית ליה א"א לפתיחת הקבר אפי' בחתיכה קטנה

---

**עין משפט נר מצוה**

[יבמות סד:]

[סג ע"ב]

יט א מיי' פ"ד מהל' איסורי ביאה הל' כב סמג לאוין קיא טוש"ע י"ד סי' קפז סעיף ב [וברב אלפס שבועות פ"ב דף רפח:]:

כ ב מיי' שם הל' כ טוש"ע שם סעיף ה [וברב אלפס שם]:

כא ג מיי' שם טוש"ע שם סעיף ד:

כב ד מיי' שם טוש"ע שם ס"ה:

כג ה מיי' שם טוש"ע שם סעיף ו [וברב אלפס שם]:

כד ו מיי' שם הל' כב טוש"ע שם סעיף ב:

כה ז מיי' שם הלכה כ טוש"ע שם סעיף ג וע"ש [וברב אלפס שם]:

כו ח טוש"ע שם סעיף ט ע"ש:

כז ט מיי' שם פי"א הלכה ד סמג שם טור ש"ע שם סי' קפג [וברב אלפס שם]:

כח י כ מיי' שם פי"א הלכה ט וע' בהשגות ובמ"מ ובכ"מ שם סמג שם טוש"ע שם סי' קצב סעיף א [וברב אלפס שבועות פ"ב דף רלו:]:

---

**מסורת הש"ס**

תורה אור

[לעיל טז. וש"נ]

[פסחים קיב:]

שבת סז. מו"ק ה. חולין עח. סוטה לב:

[כרי"ף וכר"ן פ"ב דשבועות או' בסוודית]

[לעיל טז. וש"נ]

ברכות לא. מגילה כח:

[יבמות יג:]

יבמות לז: יומא יח:

ס"א ליום ארבעה ועי' רש"א

**הגהות הב"ח**

(א) גמ' דהות סלקא מטבילת נ"ב פי' הראב"ד דכשהיתה נכנסת לעיר היתה רואה דם א"ל מפני שהכותיות רואות ביך שבאה נכנסת ומתקנאות ביך לפיכך אמר לה לכי והבעלי על גב הנהר קודם שיראו אותך: (ב) שם אמינא לך אנא איסורא כצ"ל: (ג) שם איעסק ליה לבריה בי רב חנינא כצ"ל: (ד) רש"י ד"ה לפי שאין וכו' ולא תבא לידי ספק כרת.

**גליון הש"ס**

גמ' א"ל אמינא לך איסורא. עיין ברמב"ן סי' קכ"ב שהיה לו גי' אחרת כאן: שם לבריה בי רב חנינא. בריי"ף והרשב"א ורא"ש איתא בי רב חביבא:

**הגהות מהר"ב רנשבורג**

א] תוד"ה שנים וכו' שמא ראתה יום ראשון. נ"ב פי' ידי אלינו פי"א מהל' איסורי ביאה דין ג' תיקון פ"ה בסוף דבריו בזה:

אלא תחוף לא בנתר ולא *בחול. בנתר — משום דמקטף, ובחול — משום דמסריך. ואמר אמימר משמיה דרבא: *באשה לא תחוף אלא בחמין, (א) אבל לא בצונן, ואפילו בחמי חמה. צונן מאי טעמא לא — משום דקרירי, (ב) ומשרו מזייא ואמר רבא: גלעולם ילמד אדם בתוך ביתו שתהא אשה מדיחה בית קמטיה במים. א] מיתיבי דבית הקמטים ובית הסתרים אינן צריכין לביאת מים! הנהי דביאת מים — לא בעינן, מקום הראוי לביאת מים — בעינן, כדר' זירא. *דא"ר זירא: וכל הראוי לבילה — אין בילה מעכבת בו, ושאין ראוי לבילה בילה מעכבת בו. *אמר רבין בר רב אדא, אמר רבי יצחק: מעשה בשפחתו של רבי שטבלה ועלתה, ונמצא לה עצם חוצץ בין שיניה, זוהצריכה רבי טבילה אחרת. ואמר רבא: חטבלה ועלתה ונמצא עליה דבר חוצץ, אם סמוך לחפיפה טבלה — אינה צריכה לחוף ולטבול, ואם לאו — צריכה לחוף ולטבול. איכא דאמרי: טאם באותו יום שחפפה טבלה — אינה צריכה לחוף ולטבול ואם לאו — צריכה לחוף ולטבול. מאי בינייהו? איכא בינייהו: ילמסמך לחפיפה טבילה, למיחף בימָמא ולמטבל בליליא. אמר רבא: כאשה לא תעמוד על גבי כלי חרס ותטבול. סבר רב כהנא למימר: טעמא מאי — משום גזירת מרחצאות, הא על גבי סילתא — שפיר דמי. א"ל רב חנן מנהרדעא: התם טעמא מאי — למשום דבעית, סילתא נמי מבעיתא. אמר רב שמואל בר רב יצחק: נאשה לא תטבול בנמל,

**רש"י**

לא תחוף. שערה. מקטף. נותק שער, ומתבלבל, וחוצץ. סריך. מדביק השער, וחוצץ. ואפילו בחמי חמה. די לה בחמין שהוחמו בשמש. (ג) דמשרו מזיא. מקשין את השערות, ואין לכלוכן עובר. קמטיה. בית השחי ובית הסתרים שלה. כל הראוי לבילה. במסכת מנחות: ששים עשרונים הבאים בכלי אחד — ראוין לבלול, ואין בילה מעכבת בו, שאם לא בלל — כשר. ושאין ראוי לבילה, כגון ששים ואחד עשרונים בכלי אחד — בילה מעכבת בו, ופסולה. הואיל ואי בעי לבלול, לא מצי למבלל. אינה צריכה לחוף ולטבול. דודאי לאחר שטבלה בא עליה. איכא בינייהו כו'. ללישנא קמא בעינן סמוך לחפיפה טבילה. גזירת מרחצאות. שדרך מרחצאות לישב ע"ג אצטבאות של אדמה, דדמי לכלי חרס, ואתי למימר: טבילה עולה בהן. סילתא. בקעת עצה, כמו "בחברתה ולא בסילתא", (ד) *[ביבמות] (דף סג:). דבעיתא. שלא תפול, ולא טבלה שפיר.

בנמל

**תוספות**

כל הראוי לבילה אין בילה מעכבת בו. וא"ת: הא בכמה מקומות כתיב "בלולה", ונימא: שנה עליו הכתוב לעכבו! וי"ל: דכולהו צריכי לגופייהו. וקשה: דנימא, מדתנא בהו קרא בפרשת נשיאים תריסר זימני "בלולה בשמן", דמעכבא. דהכי אמרינן ב"הקומץ רבה" (מנחות יט.) דפריך לשמואל גבי מנחה דלא יליף דורות משעה, דכתיב "וימלא כפו ממנה" – לומר דשנה עליו הכתוב לעכב על מלא קומצו. ופריך: והא אמר שמואל, מזרקות מקדשים את היבש, דכתיב "שניהם מלאים סולת"! ומשני: שאני התם, דתנא בהו קרא תריסר זימני לעכב! ויש לומר: דשמא יש שום דרשא בשום מקום דבילה לא מעכבא. וא"ת: כיון דלא מעכבא, היכא דאין ראוי לבילה נמי ליתכשר! ויש לומר: דסברא הוא, דכיון דקפיד קרא לכתחלה לעשות המצוה, בעינן שיהא ראוי לכך, אע"פ שאינו מעכב. דאם לא כן, נתבטלה המצוה לגמרי, שלא היה יכול לעשותה. וכן בכמה מקומות, כגון ביאת מים, דכתיב "כל בשרו", וממעטים בית הסתרים. ומ"מ בעינן ראוי לביאת מים בכל בשרה. וכן בכמה דוכתי. וגבי ערל וטמא, דמשלחין קרבן אף על פי שאינן ראויים לסמיכה. *ולא מעכבין, דהא רבינהו קרא דמזובו ולא מנגעו, וקרא בהבאת קרבן מיירי. ואמאי? הא לא מצי סמיך! ובפרק "כל *פסולי המוקדשין" (זבחים לג.) דתכף לסמיכה שחיטה דאורייתא, ואע"ג דלא טהר מנגעו, משלח קרבן זיבה. וא"ת: אמאי לא בעינן ביאת מים לכתחילה בבית הסתרים, כמו בילה וקריאה בחליצה ובביכורים? וי"ל: דאין סברא גבי טבילה, שלא הקפידה תורה אלא שיטהר האדם. ואין לומר: דלכתחילה לבעי – דכיון דבדיעבד טהור, לכתחלה נמי לא בעי, ותעלה לו טבילה. אבל בילה ומקרא בכורים וחליצה – מצות נינהו, הלכך לכתחלה ליעבד. וא"ת: כיון דלכתחלה בעי' בילה במנחות (ד' יח:) גבי עיקר מילתיה דרבי זירא, דקאמר: מתנדב אדם מנחה של ס' עשרון, ומביאה בכלי אחד. מנחה של ס"א – מביא ס' בכלי אחד, ואחד בכלי אחד. דקים להו דס' נבללין, וס"א אין נבללין. ופריך: וכי אין נבללין, מאי הוי? והא תנן "אם לא בלל – כשר"! ומשני, א"ר זירא: כל הראוי וכו'. ומאי פירכא, כיון דלכתחילה מצוה לבלול, משום הכי מצוה להביא בב' כלים, לקיים בה מצות בלילה? ואומר ר"י: כיון שנדר מנחה של ס"א – אינו יוצא ידי נדרו אם לא יביא מנחה גדולה. הלכך, כיון דדיעבד כשר בלא בילה, יש לו להביא בכלי אחד, לקיים נדרו. ואע"ג דגבי ב' עשרונים קאמר "אם רוצה מביא בב' כלים", מ"מ גבי ס"א מוכח מילתא דנתכוין לקרבן גדול. אי נמי: "מתנדב אדם מנחה" קאי אמנחה אחת דאמרינן התם לעיל. ומשום הכי לא בעי לפלוגינהו בשני כלים משום בילה, כיון דאינה מעכבת. מיהו קשה: דהך סוגיא דהתם לר"ש דאית ליה דס"א אין נבללים, ור"ש פליג אדרבנן דקאמרי: "הרי עלי מנחה להביא בכלי אחד", והביא בב' כלים, דאף ידי נדרו יצא. וכיון דבדיעבד יצא בשני כלים, שפיר אית ליה לפלוגינהו, כדי לקיים מצות בלילה. ואכתי קשה: מאי פירכא? וי"ל: דמנחה של ס"א משמע יותר מנחה אחת ממנחה קבועה סתם, אע"ג דפריש בהדיא "בכלי אחד". אי נמי: הך פירכא ד"וכי אין נבללין, מאי הוי?" לרבנן פריך, ונאמר: דאית ליה להאי תנא טעמא דר"ש דס"א אין נבללים יפה. **אם** סמוך לחפיפה טבלה אינה צריכה לחוף ולטבול. והא דאמר בפ"ק דחולין (דף י.) טבל ועלה ונמצא עליו דבר חוצץ, אפילו נתעסק באותו המין כל היום כולו, לא עלתה לו טבילה, עד שיאמר "ברי לי שלא היה עלי קודם לכן" – התם בשלא טבל סמוך לחפיפה, אע"ג דהתם לא מפליג. ועוד אומר ר"ת: דההיא דחולין – לטהרות, ומחמרינן טפי, דאפילו טבל סמוך לחפיפה – לא מועלת לו טבילה. והכא איירי לבעלה. והא דאמרינן בסוף שמעתין: ולית הילכתא ככל הני שמעתתא, כי איתמר הני, לטהרות – לא קאי אהך מימרא, אלא קאי אכולהו מימרות דמכלי חרס ואילך. ועוד אומר ר"י: דאי הך דחולין מיירי לטהרות – איכא לאוקמיה בשלא חפפה כלל, כדאיתא בירושלמי דמסכת פסחים סוף פרק "כל שעה": נדה – חופפת וסורקת וטובלת, כהנת – אינה חופפת וסורקת. נדה כהנת – חופפת וסורקת, שלא תחלוק בין נדה לנדה. וטעמא מפרש התם: לפי שכהנת תדירה בטבילה – לא החמירו עליה, ובעיוני סגי לה. ושוב פירש ר"ת: דחפיפה לא שייכא אלא בראש, והך דחולין איירי בשאר הגוף דליכא חפיפה. וכן משמע לעיל, דקאמר "אשה לא תחוף אלא בחמין" כו', וקאמר: טעמא, דמשרו מזיא. ומדלא קאמר "לא תחוף ראשה" ש"מ דכ"מ חפיפה שייך טעמא דמשרו מזיא, דבמקום שער הוא. ועוד מביא ר"י ראיה: דאמרינן בפרק "מרובה" (ב"ק דף פב.) גבי עשר תקנות דעזרא "שתהא אשה חופפת וטובלת". ופריך: מדאורייתא הוא וכו', מאי נינהו שערות? ומשני: לעיוני – מדאורייתא, דילמא מיקטר. ואתא איהו ותקן חפיפה. ומדקאמר "דילמא מיקטר", שמע מינה: דליכא חפיפה בראש. ובכמה מקומות הוזכרה חפיפה אצל הראש. אבל במחזור ה"ר שמריה מפרש בשם רש"י דבכל הגוף שייך חפיפה, כדאמרינן בפ' "כל כתבי" (שבת דף קכ:) הרי שהיה שם כתוב על בשרו ה"ז לא יחוף. ומיהו בכל הספרים ליכא אלא "לא ירחץ ולא יסוך". ועוד מייתי ראיה: מדמייתי לקמן (דף סז:) אההיא ד"אשה חופפת בלילה וטובלת בלילה" מעובדא דהוה בי ריש גלותא, ואמר לה: "עבדי חסרת, דודי חסרת, טשטקי חסרת?" פי' "עבדי חסרת": להביא מים להחם לרחוץ כל הגוף. דאילו חפיפת הראש – לא בעי כולי האי. ומיהו לפירוש ר"ת – אין ראיה, שפירש "עבדי חסרת": להחם מים להטיל לתוך מי הטבילה הצוננין להחם, וטשטקי – הוא טשטקי דפיזא, והוא כסא לישב עליו בבית המרחץ. ורבינו סעדיה פירש "טשטקי" – מסרקות, היינו לחוף הראש. הילכך אין לנו ראייה שיצטרך חפיפה בגוף, אלא לעיוני בעלמא, כמו בראש מדאורייתא. ואע"פ שאנו מדמין – אין לעשות מעשה, אלא צריך לחפוף כל הגוף. וכן מנהג כל הנשים לרחוץ כל הגוף עכשיו. [ועי' תוס' ב"ק פ"ב. ד"ה "ושתהא"]. **איכא** בינייהו סמוך לחפיפה טבילה. לא מיירי (ה) הכא מידי בהצרכת סמוך לחפיפה טבילה, אלא לענין לתלות אחר הטבילה אם נמצא עליה דבר חוצץ קאמר דפליגי, אם צריך לענין זה סמוך לחפיפה טבילה. **על** גבי כלי חרס. גרסי' דשייך ביה גזירות מרחצאות, שרגיל להיות ומצוי שם כלי חרס לצורך חמין. **אשה** לא תטבול בנמל. כתוב בספרים: אע"ג דהשתא ליכא "אימור ברדיוני נפל" ופירש"י: "בנמל" – מפני שהספינות רגילות להיות שם, כל שעה מצוי שם טיט. ואע"ג דהשתא ליכא עליה טיט, "אימור ברדיוני" – בצאתה מן המים שכשכה רגליה במים, ונפל. ופי' נמי: "מפלי ביומי תשרי" דבסמוך – מחצלות תחתיהן מפני הטיט. ולרבינו תם נראה כפירוש ר"ח "לא תטבול בנמל" כי בני אדם מצויין שם, ובעיתא וממהרת מפני שבושה מבני אדם המצויין שם. והוי דומיא דסילתא, דהוי טעמא משום דבעיתא. ופירש "מפלי" – מחצלות כמין גדר בנהר, לצניעות שלא יראוה עוברין ושבין. ול"ג הכא "אע"ג דהשתא ליכא" כו', עד בסמוך גבי "נתנה תבשיל לבנה וטבלה – לא עלתה לה טבילה. אע"ג דהשתא ליכא – אימור ברדיוני נפל". ומפרש ר"ת: בשני דלתי"ן, לשון נדידה. ור"ח פי': לשון הוחלקה, ונפל בירידה. ובערוך א) פירש: מפלי – משום צניעות. ור"ח פי': מקוואות ביומי ניסן – משום דחייש לשאובין, וכן פי' בערוך. ותימה הוא: מה שאיבה שייך? וי"ל: כי כמה צינורות מושכין לתוך הנהרות, שהם בכלים שחקקן ולבסוף קבען. אבל פירש"י עיקר: דנוטפין כמקוה, ואינם מטהרין אלא באשבורן, ולא דרך זחילה. ומשום מים חיים ליכא לפרושי, כדפירש"י: דתניא בתוספתא, ב) חומר בזב מבזבה – שהזב טעון מים חיים [כו'].

נתנה

א) [ערך כף ב'] ב) [פ"ג דזבים ופ"א דמגילה]

**עין משפט נר מצוה**

כט א ב מיי' פ"ב מה' מקוואות הל' יח סמג עשין רמח טוש"ע י"ד סי' קצח סעיף ב [וברב אלפס שבועות רלב.]:

ל ג ד ה מיי' שם פ"א הל' י סמג שם טוש"ע שם סעיף א וסי' קצח סעיף כה וסעיף מג ובהג"ה [וברב אלפס שם]:

[בהרא"ש אי' אשה לא תחוף אלא בחמין ואפי' בחמי חמה אבל לא בצונן וכו' וכזה מובן פירש"י ד"ה ואפילו]

לא ו מיי' פי"ז מהל' מעשה הקרבנות הלכה ו:

לב ז מיי' פ"ב מהלכות מקוואות הל' יג סמג עשין רמח טוש"ע י"ד סי' קצח סעיף כד:

לג ח ט מיי' שם הלכה יז ועיין בהשגות ובכ"מ סמג שם טוש"ע י"ד סי' קצח סעיף י:

לד י מיי' שם הל' טז טוש"ע שם סעיף ג וסעיף ח:

לה כ ל מ מיי' שם פ"א הל' יא סמג שם טוש"ע י"ד סי' קצח סעיף לא:

לו נ מיי' שם טוש"ע שם סעיף לג וסעיף לד:

נ"ל ולא מעכבין ואמאי הא לא מצי סמיך ובפ' כל פסולי המוקדשין כו' שחיטה דאורייתא והא רבינהו קרא דמזובו ולא מנגעו וקרא דמזובו ולא מנגעו וקרא בהבאת קרבן מיירי ואע"ג דלא טהר כו'. רש"א ועיין בתוס' ר"פ כסוי דם ופ' מצות חליצה

**מסורת הש"ס**

[נ"ל באהל גי' הערוך בערך עפר א' וכ"ה ברי"ף [וברא"ש] פ"ב דשבועות וכן בטוש"ע וכ"כ הב"י דגרסי כל הפוסקים באהל]

(ר"ה יג פסחים עא: קדושין כה. יבמות קד: חולין פג: מנחות יח: קג: מכות יח: נדרים עג. ב"ב פא:)

**הגהות הב"ח**

(א) גמ' לא תחוף אלא בחמין ואפילו בחמי חמה אבל לא בצונן כצ"ל: (ב) שם דקרירי משרו מזייא: (ג) רש"י ד"ה משרו מזייא: (ד) ד"ה סילתא וכו' ולא בסילתא במגילה נ"ב לא נמצא כן במגילה אלא בפ' הבע"י בדף סג ואולי רש"י היה גורס כך גם בפ"ק דמגילה אלא אין אסתר מגדת ע"ש דיהיב מרדכי עצה אין אשה מתקנאת אלא בירך חברתה: (ה) תוס' ד"ה איכא וכו' לא מיירי נ"ב דאל"כ קשיא דרבא דהכא לרבא דסוף שמעתתא דדרש רבא אשה חופפת כו':

**הגהות מהר"ב רנשבורג**

א] גמ' מיתיבי בית הקמטים. נ"ב מקוואות פ"ח:

**תוספי הרא"ש**

קטנה ס"ל דא"א כ"ש יום מ' לזכר: **אשה** לא תחוף אלא בחמין ואפי' בחמי חמין אבל בקרירי לא. ובפר"ח גרס אשה לא תחוף בקרירי ואפי' בחמי חמה. פי' אסור לחוף. ובפרק כל שעה אמרינן לא תלוש בחמין ולא בחמי חמה אלמא מדמי חמי חמה לחמין. ומיהו לא קשה לפר"ח דגבי חימוץ בחמין כל דהו מתחמץ: **דאמר** ר' זירא כל הראוי לבילה אין בילה מעכבת בו. האי מילתא דר' זירא בפ' המנחות והנסכים גבי הא דתנן הרי עלי למנחה של ס"א עשרונים מביא ששים בכלי אחד ועשרון אחד בכלי אחר. ומפרש טעמא משום דששים נבללין ששים ואחד אין נבללין. ופריך כי אין נבללין מאי הוי והתנן אם לא בלל כשר א"ר זירא כל הראוי לבילה כו'. תימה מאי פריך נהי דבדיעבר אמרינן אם לא בלל כשר מ"מ לכתחילה צריך לבלול הלכך צריך להביא בשני כלים. וי"ל משום דההוא גברא לקרבן גדול איכוון. ותנן הרי עלי להביא בכלי אחד והביא בשני כלים לא יצא. הלכך ס"ד דשפיר טפי להביא בכלי אחד אפי' בלא בלילה. ומשני דאפ"ה ראוי לבלילה בעינן: **אין** בילה מעכבת. והיינו טעמא משום דלא שנה הכתוב עליו לעכב אע"ג דגבי נשיאים כתיב תריסר זימני בלולה בשמן התם מעשה קא חשיב האיך עשו ולא לעיכובא איצטריך. ואע"ג דבהקומץ יליף דכלי מקדש אף מה שבתוכו מדכתיב שניהם מלאים סולת עיכובא לא יליף. ואע"ג דלא שנה קרא לעכב. מ"מ מיסתבר דראוי לבילה בעינן דכיון דהצריך הכתוב בלילה מסתמא צריך שיהא הקרבן ראוי למה שצוה הכתוב לעשות כן. וכן גבי קריאת חליצה אע"ג דלא מעכבא ראוי לקריאה בעינן כדאמרינן אלם ואלמת פסולין לפי שאינן באמר ואמר. וכן גבי קריאת בכורים בעינן ראוי לקריאה בפ' המוכר את הספינה. ותי' אמאי לא בעינן הכא (ראוי) ביאת מים לכתחלה בבית הסתרים. וי"ל דשאני הכא דלא הזכיר ביאת מים בבית הסתרים כמו שהזכיר קריאה בחליצה ובכורים דורחץ את בשרו משמע מאבראי. ומי' ראוי לביאת מים בעינן כיון דלפעמים נכנס בו המים: **אינה** צריכה לחוף ולטבול. והא דאמרינן בפ"ק דחולין טבל ועלה ונמצא עליו דבר חוצץ לא עלתה לו טבילה עד שיאמר ברי לי שלא היה עלי מקודם לכן. התם בשלא חפף סמוך לטבילה. או א"נ התם לטהרות והכא לבעלה. אע"ג דלמקן גר"ת ה"מ לטהרות היינו מכלי חרס ואילך. א"נ התם מיירי לטהרות ומשום דלא בעי חפיפה כלל הלכך צ"ל ברי לי. והכי אמרי' בירושלמי פ' כל שעה נדה חופפת וסורקת כהנת אינה חופפת וסורקת נדה כהנת חופפת וסורקת שלא תחלוק בין נדה לנדה. ומפ' התם לפי שרגילה בטבילה לא החמירו להצריכה חפיפה רק לעיוני בעלמא. ר"ת מפרש דבחולין מיירי שנמצא דבר חוצץ על גופו דלא בעי חפיפה והכא בנמצא בראשו דחפיפה לא שייך אלא בראש ובמקום השער וכן לא מצינו חפיפה בכל מקום בתלמוד אלא במקום שער בשמעתין לעיל אבל בקרירי לא משום דמשרו מזיא: לא תחוף בנתר דמיקטף. ובפ"ק דשבת גבי הלל שהיה חופף ראשו ובפ' חלק דהוה חפיף רישיה וכן נזיר חופף ומפספס אבל לא סורק וכן גבי עיקר תקנת חפיפה דתקין עזרא בפ' מרובה פריך מדאורייתא היא דכתיב את כל בשרו שלא יהיה דבר חוצץ כו'. ומשני דאורייתא לעיוני דלמא מקטר. ועזרא תיקן חפיפה ולישנא דמיקטר לא שייך אלא גבי שער אבל שאר הגוף לא בעי הדחה כלל: מדקאמר שתהא אשה מדחה קמטיה מכלל דלשאר הגוף לא בעי הדחה דאי קמטיה לרבותא קאמר דאע"ג שאין צריך ביאת מים צריך הדחה וה"ה שאר הגוף. א"כ הו"ל למימר אפילו בית קמטיה. ורבינו שמעיה כתב בשם רש"י דחפיפה הוא בכל הגוף כדאמרינן בפרק כל כתבי מי שהיה לו שם כתוב על בשרו לא יחוף וליתא התם אלא [לא] ירחוץ ולא יסוך. ועוד הביא ראיה מההיא דפ"ב כתובות מישהא דחפיפותא קאמר מר. ואינה ראיה דמיירי בשמן שסכין לאדם שיש לו חטטין בראשו. ועוד הביא מדאמרינן לקמן בפירקין עבדי חסרת טשטקי חסרת דודי חסרת. ואי לחפיפת הראש גרידא מה צריך כולי האי וגם זו אינה ראיה לפר"ת דמפרש דודי להחם חמין ולהטילן במי הטבילה אם יראה מן הצינה. וטשטקי. פי' רב סעדיה מסרקות גדולות. ומיהו בערוך פי' והלא יש לך עבדים הרבה. ויורות להחם חמין בלילה ולחוף וכן נהגו לחוף כל הגוף ומנהג כשר הוא: **איכא** בינייהו סמוך לחפיפה טבילה. פי' היכא דלא חפפה סמוך לטבילה אבל לכ"ע בעינן חפיפה סמוך לטבילה לכתחלה: **סבר** רב הונא למימר משום גזירת מרחצאות. דלמא אתי למיטבל במים שאובין במרחצאות

בנמל, אע"ג דהשתא ליכא — אימר ברדיוני נפל. *אבוה דשמואל [א]עבד לבנתיה מקוואות ביומי ניסן, ומפצי ביומי תשרי. אמר רב גידל, אמר רב: [ב]נתנה תבשיל לבנה וטבלה ועלתה — לא עלתה לה טבילה, אף על גב דהשתא ליכא — אימר ברדיוני נפל. אמר רמי בר *אבא: [ג]הני רבדי דכוסילתא, עד תלתא יומי — לא חייצי, מכאן ואילך — חייצי. אמר מר עוקבא: *[ד]לפלוף שבעין, לח אינו חוצץ, יבש — חוצץ. אימתי נקרא יבש — משעה שמתחיל לירק. אמר שמואל: [ה]כחול שבתוך העין — אינו חוצץ. ושעל גבי העין — חוצץ. אם היו עיניה פורחות אפי' על גבי העין אינו חוצץ. א"ר יוחנן: [ו]פתחה עיניה ביותר, או עצמה עיניה ביותר — לא עלתה לה טבילה. אמר ריש לקיש: [ז]האשה לא תטבול אלא דרך גדילתה. *כדתנן: [ח]האיש נראה כעודר (א) ומוסק זיתים, אשה נראית כאורגת וכמניקה את בנה. *אמר רבה בר רב הונא: [ט]נימא אחת קשורה — חוצצת, שלש

**רש"י**

בנמל. פורט"ו, מקום שהספינות נקבעות, שמעלות טיט, וחולץ. ברדיוני נפל. הטיט מעליה. "ברדיוני" — איני יודע לשונו, ונראה שהוא לשון שיכשוך, שכששכשכה רגליה במים בהלכתה נפל. מקוואות בימי ניסן. מקוה מים מכונסין. ואין טובלות בנהר — לפי שרבו המים בימות הגשמים מגשמים שנפלו, וחייש שמא ירבו נוטפין על הזוחלין. ותניא בתורת כהנים: (ב) מה מעין מטהר בזוחלין, אף מקוה מטהר בזוחלין. כלומר, שמטבילין במכונסין דרך זחילתן קודם שנקוו ונחו במקוה — ת"ל: "אך מעין": מעין מטהר בזוחלין, והמקוה מטהר באשבורן. ומהו "אשבורן"? דקוו וקיימי. דאין מטבילין במכונסים אלא משנקוו למקוויהם ונחו מזחילתן. ותנן במסכת מקוואות (פ"ה מ"ה): "הזוחלין — כמעין". כלומר, זוחלין שבנהרות — כמעין. "והנוטפין — כמקוה". ומים הנוטפין מטהרים, הרי הן כמקוה, ואין מטהרים בזחילה. הילכך, בימי ניסן שנתרבה הנהר על ידי גשמים — חייש שמא רבו נוטפין שבו על חיים שבו, ובטלו זוחלין, ואין מטהרין את הטמא הטובל בהן דרך זחילה. וכל הנהרות לעולם הן הולכים וזוחלין — לפיכך עביד להו מקוה באשבורן לטבול בתוכו. יש מפרשים: דבעינן מים חיים לזבה — ולאו מילתא היא, דתניא בתוספתא:* חומר בזב מבזבה, שהזב טעון מים חיים כו'. ומפצי ביומי תשרי. שטובלין בנהר, שהזוחלין מרובין. אבל מפני חלילת הטיט, נותן מחצלות בנהר שעוברות עליהן. רבדי. פוינטור"ט. כוסילתא. פלומ"א, ודרכן של מכות של הקזת דם להעלות גלד. תלתא יומי. גלדן רך ומחובר, והוי כגוף הבשר, ולא חייצי. לפלוף. קליד"א. פורחות. פותחת ועוצמת תדיר בין כך ובין כך. אינו חוצץ — לפי שפריחתה מעבירתו, ואינו עב על גב העין, ואין בו ממש. ל"א: דומעות. שהדמעה מלחלחת את הכחול, ואינו חוצץ. פתחה עיניה ביותר. הויא חלילה למעלה. עצמה עיניה ביותר. הויא חלילה למטה. לא תטבול אלא כדרך גדילתה. כלומר, לא תדחק זרועותיה על בשרה, ולא רגליה ושוקיה זה בזה, אלא כדרך הליכתה ותשמישה תמיד. ומה שנכסה וקמוט, ואין מים באין בו — לא איכפת לן. ואינה צריכה לפשט בית קמטיה וסתריה, אלא כדרכן תמיד. כדתנן. גבי ראיית נגעים, שטיהר כהן הכתוב בית הסתרים, דכתיב (ויקרא יג): "לכל מראה עיני הכהן", ותנן: האיש מראה נגעו לכהן כעודר וכמוסק זיתים. כעודר. בבית השחי, וכמוסק זיתים — בבית הערוה. דאם יש לו נגע בבית השחי — אין צריך להגביה זרועותיו יותר מדאי להראותו, אלא כעודר שמגביה ואינו מאמץ עצמו. ומה שיוכל כהן לראות — יראה, ואם לא יוכל לראות — טהור. ובבית הערוה א"צ לכוף ולשוח יותר מדאי, אלא כמוסק זיתים אחר שנשרו מן האילן ומלקטן (ג) על הארץ. והאשה נראית. לכהן בנגעה. כאורגת. בבית השחי, ואם בבית הערוה — היא יושבת עצמה כמניקה את בנה. נימא אחת. מיהדקא שפיר, וחוצצת. שלש.

**תוספות**

נתנה תבשיל לבנה. בפירוש ר"ח כתוב עוד מימרא אחרת, שאינה כתובה בספרים שלנו, וזו היא: "מפשלת את בנה וטובלת — לא עלתה לה טבילה". ויש לפרש: "מפשלת את בנה" — לאחוריה, והיא ערומה ולא היו בגדיה עליה, וטבלה. לא עלתה לה טבילה — דחיישינן שמא הוה עליה דינוקא טיט וכיולא בו, ונדבק באמו, וחוצץ בטבילתה, ולא ידעה לה. אף על גב דחזינן לה השתא דליכא מידי עליה — חיישינן דלמא בעלייתה מן הטבילה "נפל ברדיוני" — הוחלק ונפל דרך ירידה, כפי' ר"ח. ונ"ל: שהיתה מפשלת בנה אפי' לפני טבילתה בסמוך, ולאו דוקא בטבילתה.

לפלוף שבעין לח אינו חוצץ יבש חוצץ. דדוקא שבתוך העין, מפני שהדמעה שבעין מלחלחתו ואינו מניחתו להיות יבש. אבל לפלוף חוץ לעין, אפי' לח — חוצץ. והכי משמע במסכת מקוואות פ"ט (מ"ב) דגבי "אלו חוצצין" קתני "לפלוף שחוץ לעין", וגבי "שאין חוצצין" קתני "לפלוף שבעין", ולא מפליג בין לח ליבש אלא בין חוץ לעין לתוך העין. והיינו, בלח דיבש — בעין נמי חוצץ. וצואה שתחת הצפורן יבשה — חוצץ. והא דתנן התם במס' מקוואות גבי "ואלו שאין חוצצין בטבילה: לכלוכי צואה שעל הבשר וצואה שתחת הצפורן" א) (וצפורן המדולדלת) — מיירי בלח, דומיא דלכלוכי צואה שעל הבשר. דאי ביבש, אמאי לא חייצי? ועוד: דלעיל גבי "ואלו חוצצין" קתני "גלדי צואה שעל בשרה ובצק שתחת הצפורן".

פתחה עיניה ביותר או עצמה עיניה ביותר. לכך יש ללמוד לכל אשה הטובלת, שלא תטבול ותפתח עיניה, ולא תעצים עיניה ביותר, לפירש"י דלא גרסינן בסמוך דהני שמעתתא "לטהרות". ולכל הפירושים, צריך ללמדה לפתוח פיה, שיהא ראוי לביאת מים. כדאמרינן לעיל דכל בית הסתרים בעינן שיהא ראוי לביאת מים. ומייתי נמי משפחתו של רבי, שטבלה ונמצא עצם בין שיניה, והצריכה רבי טבילה אחרת.

מו א מיי' פ"ב מהל' מקוואות הל' טו סמג עשין רמח טוש"ע י"ד סי' קצח סעיף ה [רב אלפס שבועות רלג.]:

נ"ל רבה

מז ב ג ד מיי' שם פ"א הלכה יב סמג שם טוש"ע י"ד שם סעיף א:

נ"ל ורבה ואביי רש"א

מח ה מיי' פ"ד מהל' איסורי ביאה הל' ז סמג עשין רמח טוש"ע י"ד סי' קצז סעיף ג:

מט ו ז ח ט מיי' שם הל' ח טוש"ע שם סעיף ז [וברב אלפס שם רלב.]

נ י מיי' פ"ב מהלכות מקוואות הל' טז סמג שם טוש"ע י"ד סי' קצט סעיף ו:

[נ"ל לאביי ורבא כן נכון להיות וכן העתיקו תד"ה משום וכרי"ף פ"ב דשבועות אי' אמר ליה ר"פ לרבא מכדי וכו' ולפי הגי' שלפנינו דאמר לתרווייהו נ"ל אמר להו ר"פ וכו']

שָׁלֹשׁ – אֵינָן חוֹצְצוֹת, שְׁתַּיִם – אֵינִי יוֹדֵעַ. ור' יוֹחָנָן אָמַר: אָנוּ אֵין לָנוּ אֶלָּא אַחַת. *אָמַר ר' יִצְחָק, דְּבַר תּוֹרָה: רוּבּוֹ הַמַּקְפִּיד עָלָיו – חוֹצֵץ, רוּבּוֹ וְאֵינוֹ מַקְפִּיד עָלָיו – אֵינוֹ חוֹצֵץ. וְגָזְרוּ עַל רוּבּוֹ שֶׁאֵינוֹ מַקְפִּיד – מִשּׁוּם רוּבּוֹ הַמַּקְפִּיד, וְגָזְרוּ עַל מִיעוּטוֹ הַמַּקְפִּיד – מִשּׁוּם רוּבּוֹ הַמַּקְפִּיד. וְלִגְזוֹר נַמִּי עַל מִיעוּטוֹ שֶׁאֵינוֹ מַקְפִּיד, מִשּׁוּם מִיעוּטוֹ הַמַּקְפִּיד! *הִיא גּוּפָהּ גְּזֵרָה, וַאֲנַן נֵיקוּם וְנִגְזוֹר גְּזֵרָה לִגְזֵרָה?! אָמַר רַב: נִדָּה בִּזְמַנָּהּ – אֵינָהּ טוֹבֶלֶת אֶלָּא בַּלַּיְלָה, וְשֶׁלֹּא בִּזְמַנָּהּ – טוֹבֶלֶת בֵּין בַּיּוֹם בֵּין בַּלַּיְלָה. רַבִּי יוֹחָנָן אָמַר: בֵּין בִּזְמַנָּהּ בֵּין שֶׁלֹּא בִּזְמַנָּהּ – אֵינָהּ טוֹבֶלֶת אֶלָּא בַּלַּיְלָה, מִשּׁוּם סְרַךְ בִּתָּהּ. וְאַף רַב הֲדַר בֵּיהּ, דְּאָמַר רַבִּי חִיָּיא בַּר אַשִׁי, אָמַר רַב: נִדָּה, בֵּין בִּזְמַנָּהּ בֵּין שֶׁלֹּא בִּזְמַנָּהּ – אֵינָהּ טוֹבֶלֶת אֶלָּא בַּלַּיְלָה, מִשּׁוּם סְרַךְ בִּתָּהּ. אַתְקֵין רַב אִידִי בְּנַרֶשׁ לְמִטְבַּל בְּיוֹמָא דִּתְמַנְיָא, מִשּׁוּם אַרְיָוָתָא, רַב אַחָא בַּר יַעֲקֹב בְּפַפּוּנְיָא – מִשּׁוּם גַּנָּבֵי, רַב יְהוּדָה בְּפוּמְבְּדִיתָא – מִשּׁוּם צִנָּה, *רָבָא בְּמְחוֹזָא – מִשּׁוּם אַבּוּלָאֵי. אֲמַר לֵיהּ רַב פַּפָּא *לְרָבָא וּלְאַבַּיֵי: מִכְּדֵי הָאִידָּנָא כּוּלְּהוּ סְפֵק זָבוֹת שָׁוִינְהוּ רַבָּנַן, לִיטְבְּלִינְהוּ בְּיָמָמָא דִּשְׁבִיעָאָה? מִשּׁוּם דְּרַבִּי שִׁמְעוֹן, *דְּתַנְיָא: "אַחַר תִּטְהָר" (ויקרא טו) – אַחַר אַחַר לְכוּלָּן, שֶׁלֹּא תְּהֵא טוּמְאָה מַפְסֶקֶת בֵּינֵיהֶן. *ר' שִׁמְעוֹן אוֹמֵר: "אַחַר תִּטְהָר" – אַחַר מַעֲשֶׂה תִּטְהַר. *אֲבָל אָמְרוּ חֲכָמִים: אָסוּר לַעֲשׂוֹת כֵּן, שֶׁמָּא תָּבֹא לִידֵי סָפֵק. אָמַר רַב הוּנָא: אִשָּׁה חוֹפֶפֶת בְּאֶחָד בַּשַּׁבָּת וְטוֹבֶלֶת בַּשְּׁלִישִׁי בַּשַּׁבָּת – שֶׁכֵּן אִשָּׁה חוֹפֶפֶת בְּעֶרֶב שַׁבָּת וְטוֹבֶלֶת בְּמוֹצָאֵי שַׁבָּת. אִשָּׁה חוֹפֶפֶת בְּאֶחָד בַּשַּׁבָּת וְטוֹבֶלֶת בָּרְבִיעִי בַּשַּׁבָּת – שֶׁכֵּן אִשָּׁה חוֹפֶפֶת בְּעֶרֶב שַׁבָּת וְטוֹבֶלֶת בְּמוֹצָאֵי יו"ט שֶׁחָל לִהְיוֹת אַחַר הַשַּׁבָּת. אִשָּׁה חוֹפֶפֶת בְּאֶחָד בַּשַּׁבָּת וְטוֹבֶלֶת בַּחֲמִישִׁי בַּשַּׁבָּת – שֶׁכֵּן אִשָּׁה חוֹפֶפֶת בְּעֶרֶב שַׁבָּת וְטוֹבֶלֶת בְּמוֹצָאֵי שְׁנֵי יָמִים טוֹבִים שֶׁל רֹאשׁ הַשָּׁנָה שֶׁחָל לִהְיוֹת אַחַר הַשַּׁבָּת. וְרַב חִסְדָּא אָמַר: כּוּלְּהוּ – אָמְרִינַן, "שֶׁכֵּן" – לָא אָמְרִינַן, הֵיכָא דְּאֶפְשָׁר – אֶפְשָׁר, הֵיכָא דְּלָא אֶפְשָׁר – לָא אֶפְשָׁר. וְרַב יֵימָר אָמַר: אֲפִילּוּ "שֶׁכֵּן" – נַמִּי אָמְרִינַן, לְבַר מֵאִשָּׁה חוֹפֶפֶת בְּאֶחָד בַּשַּׁבָּת וְטוֹבֶלֶת בַּחֲמִישִׁי בַּשַּׁבָּת, דִּלְמוֹצָאֵי שְׁנֵי יָמִים טוֹבִים שֶׁל רֹאשׁ הַשָּׁנָה שֶׁלְּאַחַר הַשַּׁבָּת לֵיתָא, דְּאֶפְשָׁר דְּחוֹפֶפֶת בַּלַּיְלָה וְטוֹבֶלֶת בַּלַּיְלָה. דָּרַשׁ מָרֵימָר: הִלְכְתָא כְּרַב חִסְדָּא, וּכְדִמְתָרֵץ רַב יֵימָר. אִיבַּעְיָא לְהוּ: אִשָּׁה מַהוּ שֶׁתָּחוֹף בַּלַּיְלָה וְתִטְבּוֹל בַּלַּיְלָה? מָר זוּטְרָא אוֹסֵר, וְרַב חִינָּנָא מִסּוּרָא שָׁרֵי. א"ל רַב אַדָּא (א) [לְרַב חִינָּנָא מִסּוּרָא:] לָאו הָכִי הֲוָה עוּבְדָּא בִּדְבֵיתְהוּ דְּאַבָּא מָרִי רֵישׁ גָּלוּתָא דְּאִיקּוּט, אֲזַל ר"נ בַּר יִצְחָק לְפַיּוֹסָהּ. וְאָמְרָה לֵיהּ: מַאי אִיתֵיהּ הָשְׁתָּא? תִּסְגֵּי

שָׁלֹשׁ. לָא מִיהַדְּקֵי. דְּבַר תּוֹרָה. הֲלָכָה לְמֹשֶׁה מִסִּינַי, דְּאָמַר מָר (סוכה דף ה:): שִׁיעוּרִין חֲלִיצִין וּמְחִיצִין – הֲלָכָה לְמֹשֶׁה מִסִּינַי. רוּבּוֹ. רוֹב שְׂעָרוֹ קָשׁוּר אַחַת אַחַת. בִּזְמַנָּהּ. בַּשְּׁבִיעִי, וּבְנִדָּה דְּאוֹרַיְיתָא קָמַיְירֵי, שֶׁלֹּא סָפְרָה ז' נְקִיִּים. בַּלַּיְלָה. דִּכְתִיב בָּהּ (ויקרא טו): "תִּהְיֶה" – בְּנִדָּתָהּ תְּהֵא בְּנִדָּתָהּ כָּל ז'. שֶׁלֹּא בִּזְמַנָּהּ. בַּשְּׁמִינִי. מִשּׁוּם סְרַךְ בִּתָּהּ. שֶׁנּוֹהֶגֶת אַחֲרֶיהָ לִטְבּוֹל בַּיּוֹם, וַאֲפִילּוּ בִּזְמַנָּהּ, וְאָתְיָא לִידֵי כָּרֵת. וְלָא יָדְעָה דְּאִמָּהּ בַּשְּׁמִינִי הוּא דְּטָבְלָה בַּיּוֹם. אַבּוּלָאֵי. שׁוֹעֲרֵי הָעִיר, וְגוֹיִם הֵן. ל"א: בִּנְיָנִים שֶׁל מְעָרוֹת הָיוּ בְּדֶרֶךְ בֵּית הַטְּבִילָה, וְאִם תִּפּוֹל שָׁם – תִּסְתַּכֵּן. סְפֵק זָבוֹת שָׁוִינְהוּ. שֶׁאֲפִילּוּ נִדָּה סוֹפֶרֶת ז' נְקִיִּים, דְּהֶחְמִירוּ עַל עַצְמָן כְּדְר' זֵירָא. לִיטְבְּלָה בִּימָמָא. דְּשִׁבְעָה, מִמָּה נַפְשָׁךְ: אִם נִדָּה הִיא – הֲרֵי יוֹם טְבִילָתָהּ יוֹתֵר מִז' לִרְאִיָּיתָהּ, וְאִם זָבָה הִיא – טוֹבֶלֶת זָבָה בַּיּוֹם. אַחַר מַעֲשֶׂה. כֵּיוָן שֶׁסָּפְרָה מִקְצָת הַיּוֹם שֶׁל ז', תִּטְהַר ע"י טְבִילָה. לִידֵי סָפֵק. שֶׁמָּא תְּשַׁמֵּשׁ בּוֹ בַּיּוֹם וְתִרְאֶה מִיַּד לְאַחַר תַּשְׁמִישׁ – וְנִמְצָא סוֹתֶרֶת כָּל שֶׁלְּפָנֶיהָ, וּטְבִילָתָהּ פְּסוּלָה. שֶׁכֵּן אִשָּׁה חוֹפֶפֶת בְּעֶ"שׁ וְטוֹבֶלֶת לְמוֹצָ"שׁ. דְּהָא אֵינָהּ יְכוֹלָה לָחוֹף בְּשַׁבָּת, וְדָנִין אֶפְשָׁר מִשֶּׁאִי אֶפְשָׁר. כּוּלְּהוּ אָמְרִי'. הֵיכָא דְּהִגִּיעַ טְבִילָתָהּ בְּמוֹצָ"שׁ – חוֹפֶפֶת בְּעֶ"שׁ. וְאִם הִגִּיעַ טְבִילָתָהּ בְּמוֹצָאֵי י"ט אַחַר הַשַּׁבָּת, אוֹ לְמוֹצָאֵי ב' יָמִים טוֹבִים שֶׁל ר"ה אַחַר הַשַּׁבָּת – חוֹפֶפֶת נַמִּי מִבְּעֶ"שׁ, דְּהָא לֹא אֶפְשָׁר לָחוֹף בְּיו"ט. שֶׁכֵּן לָא אָמְרִי'. הֵיכָא דְּטוֹבֶלֶת בְּלֵיל יוֹם חוֹל, שֶׁיְּכוֹלָה לָחוֹף הַיּוֹם – אֲסוּרָה לָחוֹף מֵאֶתְמוֹל, (ב) כִּדְקָאָמְרָן מִשּׁוּם טַעֲמָא דְּ"שֶׁכֵּן אִשָּׁה חוֹפֶפֶת בְּעֶ"שׁ וְטוֹבֶלֶת לְמוֹצָאֵי שַׁבָּת". דְּהָתָם – לֹא אֶפְשָׁר, אֲבָל מוֹצָאֵי יוֹם חוֹל – אֶפְשָׁר לָחוֹף הַיּוֹם. אֲפִילּוּ שֶׁכֵּן אָמְרִינַן. דַּאֲפִילּוּ טָבְלָה מוֹצָאֵי יוֹם חוֹל – יְכוֹלָה לָחוֹף מֵאֶתְמוֹל. לְבַד מֵאִשָּׁה חוֹפֶפֶת בְּאֶחָד בַּשַּׁבָּת וְטוֹבֶלֶת בַּחֲמִישִׁי בַּשַּׁבָּת. דְּרָחוֹק יוֹתֵר מִדַּאי, וַאֲפִילּוּ טַעֲמָא דְּ"שֶׁכֵּן" לֵיכָּא לְמֵימַר – דַּאֲפִילּוּ בְּמוֹצָאֵי שְׁנֵי יָמִים טוֹבִים שֶׁל ר"ה שֶׁאַחַר הַשַּׁבָּת אֲסוּרָה לָחוֹף בְּעֶ"שׁ, וּמוּטָב שֶׁתָּחוֹף בְּלֵיל טְבִילָתָהּ. וְהִלְכְתָא כְּרַב חִסְדָּא. לְחוּמְרָא, דְּאָמַר: "שֶׁכֵּן" לָא אָמְרִינַן. דְּהֵיכָא דְּטָבְלָה מוֹצָאֵי יוֹם חוֹל – לָא תָּחוֹף מֵאֶתְמוֹל. וּכְמַאי דְּאָמַר רַב חִסְדָּא: כּוּלְּהוּ אָמְרִינַן, דְּהֵיכָא דְּטָבְלָה בְּמוֹצָאֵי ב' יָמִים טוֹבִים [שֶׁל רֹאשׁ הַשָּׁנָה] אַחַר הַשַּׁבָּת, חוֹפֶפֶת בְּעֶ"שׁ – לֵית הִלְכְתָא כְּוָותֵיהּ, אֶלָּא כִּדְמְתָרֵץ רַב יֵימָר: חָיְיפָא בְּלֵילְיָא, וְטָבְלָה בְּלֵילְיָא. מָרֵימָר חוּמְרֵי נָקַט, מִדְּרַב חִסְדָּא וּמִדְּרַב יֵימָר. מַהוּ שֶׁתָּחוֹף בַּלַּיְלָה. בְּלֵיל טְבִילָתָהּ: מִי אָמְרִינַן, מִתּוֹךְ שֶׁמְּמַהֶרֶת לִטְבִילָתָהּ – לָא חָיְיפָא שַׁפִּיר? דְּאִיקּוּט. לְשׁוֹן קְטָטָה, וְלֹא רָצְתָה לִטְבּוֹל. מַאי אִיתֵיהּ הָשְׁתָּא. מַה לָּךְ לְמַהֵר הַלַּיְלָה?

תִּסְגֵּי

משום סרך בתה. ליכא לפרושי דדוקא בנדה אסור משום סרך בתה, שתהא סבורה שהוא שביעי, ותטבול בשביעי ותשמש ואיכא כרת. אבל זבה, אפילו אם בתה סבורה שהוא שביעי, ליכא איסורא דאורייתא אלא חששא בעלמא, שמא תראה אחר שתטבול ביום שביעי, כדר"ש – הא ליכא למימר, דהא אתקין *רבא למטבל ביממא דתמיניא במחוזא משום אבולאי, משמע: הא לאו אבולאי – אסור, אע"ג דחומרא דרבי זירא היתה נוהגת בימיו וטובלת בשמיני, כדא"ל רב פפא לאביי ולרבא: מכדי האידנא כולהו ספק זבות שוינהו רבנן, *ואביי ורבא בדור אחד היו. הילכך, אפי' בזמן הזה אסור לטבול, בין בח' בין בט' ביום. ומיהו אומר ר"ת: שאין קפידא רק כשתשוב לביתה שיהיה לילה, וא"כ שתצא בלילה מביתה – דשוב לא יבוא לידי ספק, ליכא למיחש אם תטבול היא ביום סמוך לחשיכה תטבול בתה בעוד היום גדול. דמרגשת הבת בכך שתטבול סמוך לחשיכה כאמה. אבל במקום שיש לירא מפריצי העיר או מגנבים – שרי, כדאיתא בשמעתין. ורבינו משולם התיר לאשה בעיר שהיה לחוש לגנבים, לחוף בע"ש בז' שלה, ולטבול ביום שבת שהוא שמיני מבעוד יום, משום גנבים. ור"ת אוסר – דתרי קולי לא אשכחן דשרי התלמוד, הרחקת חפיפה מטבילה וסרך בתה. **אבל** אמרו חכמים אסור לעשות כן שלא תבוא לידי ספק. נ"ל: אסור לעשות כן לטבול, דאי אתשמיש – מהו "שלא תבוא לידי ספק"? הא כבר באה בשעת תשמיש שמא תראה, והוה ליה למימר "שלא תבא לידי ודאי"! ועוד: היכי שרו (ג) רבנן לשמש? הא ודאי אמרי' לקמן במתני' (דף עב.) "הרי זה תרבות רעה" גבי שומרת יום כנגד יום שטבלה בשני לראייתה, וקאמר: מגעה ובעילתה תלויה. וכן משמע בשמעתין, מדפריך: ונטבלינהו ביממא דז' ומשני: משום דר"ש, אלמא אטבילה קאמר ר"ש דאסור. ומיהו זה יש לדחות: דלעולם קאי אתשמיש, אבל טבילה שריא לר"ש אלא אח"כ החמירו לאסור בה הטבילה, גזרה שמא תשמש. אבל קשה: דלעיל פ' "המפלת" (דף כט:) בשמעתין דטועה פריך: בכ"א תשמש? ומשני: ר"ש היא, דאמר: אבל אסור לעשות כן. אם כן, אתשמיש קאי, דהא ודאי ביממא מטבלינן לה משום "טבילה בזמנה מצוה"! וי"ל: דה"פ: ר"ש היא, דאמר גבי ודאי זבה דאסור לעשות כן לטבול ביום שמא תבא לידי ספק לשמש, שבעילתה תהא תלויה, הילכך בהך טועה. אע"ג דאיכא בה כמה ספקות: דשמא לא היתה זבה כלל, ואם היתה זבה – אימר: הרחיקה לידתה, ושמא לא תראה אסורה לשמש לר' שמעון, אבל טבילה תהא מותרת אפילו לר"ש דשרי לה לטבול משום "טבילה בזמנה מצוה".

כך

## תוספי הרא"ש

השחי. וכמוסק זיתים לבית הערוה. ובת"כ מיתניא איפכא לכל מראה עיני הכהן פרט לבית הסתרים מכאן אמרו האיש כעודר לבית הסתרים פי' בית הערוה זיתים לבית השחי והאשה כאורגת לבית הסתרים וכמניקה תחת הדד: **רובו** ומקפיד עליו חוצץ. פרש"י דהיינו בשערו אבל בגופו אפילו מיעוט ואינו מקפיד חוצץ. וקשה לפירושו מהא דאמר בהערל מעוברת שנתגיירה בנה אין צריך טבילה. ופריך אי מדר' יצחק אימר דא"ר יצחק רובו כולו מי אמר ולא קאמר אימר דאמר ר' יצחק שערו בשרו מי אמר. אלמא ר' יצחק אכל הגוף קאי. ועוד גבי כגרים תנן שיעור בחציצתן במס' מקואות ומייתי לה בפרק אלו קשרים על המרדעת חוצץ רשב"ג אומר עד כאיסר האיטלקי ובזבחים בשילהי דם חטאת אמרינן רבב על בגדו חוצץ ואם מוכר רבב אינו חוצץ אלמא בגוף הכלי תלוי בשיעורא ובקפידא וה"ה נ באדם. וע"ק דקתני אי איצטריך את בשרו את הטפל לבשרו ומאי ניהו שערו תיפוק לי מהלכה כיון דלא נשתנית אלא בשער. אלא ודאי ר' יצחק בחציצת הגוף איירי הלכך איצטריך את בשרו לרבות שערו: **ליטבל** ביממא דז'. צ"ל משום סרך בתה שהיא סוברת שאמה טובלת ביום ז' ותעשה גם היא כן ותבא לידי ספק. ואין לומר דלא שייך סרך בתה אלא לדידהו שהיו נוהגין כדין נדה דאורייתא ואיכא למיחש שמא תטבול בתה בשביעי לנדתה ביום וטבילתה זו כמאן דליתא אבל משום סרך בתה שתטבול בשביעי האידנא מדרבנן בעלמא הוא ולא חיישינן. הא ליתא דהא רבא במחוזא תיקן משום אבולאי למיטבל ביממא דתמניא הא לאו משום אבולאה הוה אסור משום סרך בתה. ובימיו כבר היה תקנת ר' זירא כדא"ל רב פפא לרבא מכדי האידנא כולהו נשי ספק זבות נינהו כו'. ורשב"ם היה מחמיר שלא תטבול עד שתחשך. מיהו ר"ת אומר שאין להחמיר כל כך רק שתטבול סמוך לחשיכה ותשוב לביתה משחשיכה

## תוספי הרא"ש

משחשיכה אז ליכא למיחש לסרך בתה: **אסור** לעשות כן שמא תבא לידי ספק. פי' אסורה לטבול שמא תשמש ותהיה בספק אבל אין לפרש דקאי אתשמיש אבל הטבילה שריא לר' שמעון אלא דאמוראי בתראי אסרו גם טבילה גזירה שמא תשמש שאסור לר' שמעון והכי משמע בפרק המפלת גבי טועה דפריך ביום כ"א תשמש ומשני משום דר' שמעון משמע דאתשמיש קאי דהא התם טובלת ביום כ"א משום טבילה בזמנה מצוה. וכן משמע נמי קצת בת"כ דקתני ר' שמעון אומר אחר מעשה תטהר כיון שטבלה טהורה להתעסק בטהרות. אבל אמרו חכמים אסור לעשות כן משמע דאלהתעסק בטהרות קאי. ואי אפשר לומר כן דע"כ גם הטבילה אוסר ר' שמעון דלא מיסתבר דפליגי רבנן עליה להתיר תשמיש כיון שאם תראה נמצא בועל זבה למפרע. ועוד דתנן במתני' טבלה ביום שלאחריו ושמשה הרי זו תרבות רעה ומגען ובעילתן תלוין. ומסתמא תרבות רעה דקאמר אסור. ובגמרא נמי א"ר יהודה וכי לית אתם קורין תרבות רעה והלא לא נתכוון זה אלא לבעול שומרת יום כנגד יום משמע דלכ"ע אסור ולא מיסתבר לחלק בין יום שביעי לפי שכבר נסתלקו דמיה. ועוד דאחר מעשה תטהר דקאמר היינו הטבילה ועל המעשה שהזכיר אמר דאסור לעשות כן. ועוד אי אתשמיש קאי מאי קאמר שמא תבא לידי ספק כיון דשמשה כבר באה לידי ספק שמא תראה וה"ל למימר שמא תבא לידי ודאי. ובטועה דהמפלת פריך יום כ"א תשמש דכיון דאיכא ספיקות טובא תהא מותרת אף לשמש. ומשני משום

## הגהות הב"ח

(א) גמ' א"ל רב אדא מסורא למר זוטרא לאו הכי הוה עובדא בדביתהו: (ב) רש"י ד"ה שכן לא וכו' מאתמול כדקאמרת משום: (ג) תום' ד"ה אבל וכו' היכי שרו רבנן. נ"ב פי' רבנן דפליגי אר' שמעון וע"ל פרק המפלת דף כט ע"כ בתוס' בד"ה ר"ש:



תורה אור: ויקרא טו

עירובין ד: סוכה ו: יבמות עח.

עירובין ד: [שבת יא: ביצה ג. וש"נ]

נ"ל רבה רש"א בשם ס"י

לעיל לג: [לז. לקמן סח:]

[לעיל כט: ל.]

[שם]

תסגי (א) אייתי למחר. וידע מאי קאמרה ליה. אמר: *דודי חסרת, *טשטקי חסרת, עבדי חסרת? דרש רבא: אשה חופפת בערב שבת וטובלת במוצאי שבת. אמר ליה רב פפא לרבא: והא שלח רבין באגרתיה, אשה לא תחוף בערב שבת ותטבול במוצאי שבת. ותמה על עצמך היאך חופפת ביום וטובלת בלילה – הא בעינן "תכף לחפיפה טבילה", וליכא! *הדר אוקי רבא אמורא עליה ודרש: דברים שאמרתי לפניכם טעות הן בידי, ברם כך אמרו משמיה דרבי יוחנן אשה לא תחוף בערב שבת ותטבול במוצאי שבת, ותמה על עצמך היאך חופפת ביום וטובלת בלילה – הא בעינן "סמוך לחפיפה טבילה" וליכא! [א]והלכתא: אשה חופפת ביום וטובלת בלילה. והלכתא: אשה לא תחוף אלא בלילה. (אלא) קשיא הלכתא אהלכתא! לא קשיא, [ב]הא – דאפשר, הא – דלא אפשר.§ **מתני'** נדה שבדקה עצמה יום שביעי שחרית ומצאה טהורה, ובין השמשות לא הפרישה, ולאחר ימים בדקה ומצאה טמאה – הרי היא בחזקת טהורה. בדקה עצמה ביום שביעי שחרית ומצאה טמאה, ובין השמשות לא הפרישה, ולאחר זמן בדקה ומצאה טהורה – הרי זו בחזקת טמאה, ומטמאה מעת לעת ומפקידה לפקידה. ואם יש לה וסת – דיה שעתה. *ור' יהודה אומר: כל שלא הפרישה בטהרה מן המנחה ולמעלה – הרי זו בחזקת טמאה. וחכמים אומרים: [ג]אפילו בשנים לנדתה בדקה ומצאה טהורה, ובין השמשות לא הפרישה, ולאחר זמן בדקה ומצאה טמאה – הרי זו בחזקת טהורה.§ **גמ'** איתמר, רב אמר: זבה ודאי, ולוי אמר: זבה ספק. אהייא? אילימא ארישא "הרי זו בחזקת טהורה" קתני. אלא אסיפא. בשלמא ספק זבה – אמרינן, אלא זבה ודאי נמי? הרי בדקה ומצאה טהורה! אלא כי איתמר דרב ולוי – שמעתא באפי נפשה איתמר: נדה שבדקה עצמה ביום השביעי שחרית ומצאה טמאה, ובין השמשות לא הפרישה, ולאחר ימים בדקה ומצאה טמאה, רב אמר – [ד]זבה ודאי, ולוי אמר – זבה ספק. רב אמר: זבה ודאי, כיון דמעיקרא נמצאת טמאה, ועכשיו נמצאת טמאה – טמאה ודאי. ולוי אמר: ספק זבה, אימר, פסקה ביני וביני.
וכן

**רש"י**

תסגי ואייתי למחר. די לך אם אטבול למחר. וידע. רב נחמן. מאי קאמרה ליה. שלא חפפה. עבדי חסרת. להביא מים ולחמם. דודי. קדרות לחמם בהם חמין. טשטקי. פלדוסטו"ל לישב עליהן. ותמה על עצמך היאך אשה כו'. שהרי בקושי התירו להרחיק חפיפתה מטבילתה כל כך, אלא משום דאי חפפה בליל טבילתה – איסור: לא חייפא שפיר, משום דממהרת לטבילתה, מתוך שמהומה לביתה. הא דאפשר. לחוף ביום – חופפת ביום. הא דלא אפשר. לחוף, כגון מוצאי (ב) *יום טוב – לא תחוף אלא בלילה.

**מתני'** לא הפרישה. לא בדקה עצמה להפריש בטהרה. הרי זו בחזקת טהורה. בימים שבינתיים, וטהרותיה שנגעה בהן לאחר שטבלה בליל שמיני – טהורות, דהשתא הוא דחזאי. ומטמאה מעת לעת. ארישא קאי, דקתני: "אחר ימים בדקה ומצאה טמאה" – מטמאה מעת לעת של ראייה זו. אפילו בשנים לנדתה בדקה. שחרית ומצאה טהורה, ובין השמשות לא הפרישה, ולסוף ז' טבלה, ואחר ימים בדקה ומצאה טמאה – הרי זו עד עכשיו בחזקת טהורה. ושלש מחלוקות בדבר: לתנא קמא: שביעי הוא דמטהרתה בדיקת שחרית, אבל שני – לא. ולר' יהודה: אפילו בדיקת שביעי שחרית – לא מטהרה, עד שתפריש בין השמשות. ולרבנן בתראי: אפילו בשני. **גמ'** זבה ודאי. מפרש ואזיל. אהייא. קאי? אסיפא. "בדקה שביעי שחרית ומצאה טמאה, ובין השמשות לא הפרישה". בשלמא ספק זבה לחיי. דכיון דלא הפרישה בטהרה, לא שחרית ולא ערבית – איכא לספוקי ברואה ח' וט' וי'. אלא זבה ודאי נמי. בתמיה, והרי בדקה לאחר הימים ומצאה טהורה, ואיכא למימר: כיון דמצאה טהורה, עד השתא נמי לא חזאי! באפי נפשה. ולאו אמתניתין.

**תוספות**

**כך** אמרו משמיה דרבי יוחנן אשה לא תחוף בערב שבת ותטבול למוצאי שבת ותמה על עצמך היאך אשה חופפת ביום וטובלת בלילה. שהרי בקושי התירו לה להרחיק חפיפתה כל כך, אלא משום דאי חופפת בליל טבילתה – איכא: לא חייפא שפיר, מתוך שמהומה לביתה ממהרת לטבילתה. ופירש רש"י: "הא דאפשר" – לחוף ביום, כגון בימי החול, חופפת ביום וטובלת בלילה. "הא דלא אפשר" – לחוף ביום, כגון שאירעה טבילתה במוצאי שבת, ואם תחוף בע"ש תרחיק יותר מדאי מטבילתה, חופפת בליל טבילתה במוצאי שבת. וא"ת: הא דפסקינן לעיל הלכתא כרב חסדא וכדמתרץ רב יימר, לא קאי. דהכא אמרינן דאינה חופפת ע"ש וטובלת למוצאי שבת! וי"ל: דאיכא לאוקמי פסק דלעיל, שליל טבילתה במוצ"ש והוא יו"ט – אז ודאי תחוף מע"ש ולא תפסיד עונתה. הואיל ואינה יכולה לחוף בליל טבילתה, ולא ביום שלפני טבילה. מ"מ לפירוש רש"י נראה דמותר לחוף בליל טבילה, אלא שטוב לה יותר לחוף ביום, מפני שמהומה לביתה. וכן משמע מדקאמר "אשה חופפת ביום", ולא קאמר "אשה לא תחוף אלא ביום" כדקאמר "אשה לא תחוף אלא בלילה". וכן משמע לעיל בעובדא דבי ריש גלותא, דמותר לחוף בליל טבילה. ולא מסתבר לפלוגי משום דאיקוט – מדמייתי מההוא עובדא דנדה חופפת בלילה, משמע: אף בלא אונס. ובשאלתות דרב אחאי פרשת אחרי מות [סי' נו] פירשה: "הא דאפשר" – לחוף בליל טבילה שהוא חול, לא תרחיק חפיפה מטבילה כלל. ואפילו אם היום כמו כן חול – לא תחוף אלא בלילה. ו"הא דלא אפשר" – כגון שליל טבילה יום טוב או שבת, אז תחוף ביום שלפני הטבילה. ואפילו אם יום שלפני הטבילה כמו כן יו"ט או שבת, אז תחוף מערב שבת או מערב יו"ט כפסק שלמעלה דדריש מרימר דהילכתא כרב חסדא וכדמתרץ רב יימר. ולדברי השאלתות, כל זמן שתוכל – אין לחוף אלא בליל טבילה. מיהא לפי מנהג הנשים של עכשיו ששוהות במרחץ עד הלילה – מותר לחוף ביום, אף לפי השאלתות. ואינו אסור אלא לחוף מבעוד יום, ולצאת מן המרחץ קודם הלילה. אבל כששהתה שם עד הלילה – חפיפה אריכתא היא, שכל שעה עוסקת בחפיפת גופה ושערה, ותבא עליה ברכה. ועוד יש שמחמירות: אע"פ שחופפת, נושאות עמהן מסרק, וסורקות עצמן בבית הטבילה. ור"ת פירש: "ותמה על עצמך" – זהו כפל מלה. כלומר, היאך אתה אומר דבר זה שאשה חופפת ביום וטובלת בליל מוצאי שבת, והא בעינן "סמוך לחפיפה טבילה"?! ואומר ר"י: דכי האי גוונא איכא בפסחים "פרק כל שעה" (דף כג.) ותמה על עצמך היאך חמץ אסור בהנאה כל שבעה. (ג).

**והלכתא** אשה חופפת ביום וטובלת בלילה. פי' בערב שבת, וטובלת במוצאי שבת. "והלכתא: אשה לא תחוף אלא בלילה" – פירוש: במוצאי שבת, ולא תמהר לחוף בערב שבת. **הא** דאפשר. לחוף במוצאי שבת שהוא חול – תחוף בו, ולא תמהר לחוף מערב שבת. ו"הא דלא אפשר" לחוף במוצאי שבת ליל טבילתה, כגון שהוא יום טוב – חופפת מערב שבת, אף על פי שטבילתה למוצאי שבת, או ליל שני בשבת והם שני ימים טובים אחר השבת. ולא איירי כלל התלמוד באיסור חפיפה שחרית וטבילה ערבית בלא הפסקת יום, וכן לא איירי באיסור חפיפת לילה. ואומר ר"י: דאם אירע טבילתה ליל תשעה באב – אסורה לטבול, דלית הלכתא כהך ברייתא (א) ד"כל כתבי הקדש" (שבת קיא.) דכל חייבי טבילות טובלין כדרכן, בין בט' באב בין ביה"כ. אלא קי"ל כרבי חנינא סגן הכהנים דאמר סוף פרק קמא דתענית (דף יג.) כדי הוא בית אלהינו לאבד עליו טבילה אחת בשנה. ואומר עלה בירושלמי בפ"ב דביצה: אורי רבי לוי כהדא דרבי חנינא סגן הכהנים. ועוד יש לפרש: דההיא (ב) ד"כל כתבי" – בימי התנאים, שהיו עסוקים בטהרות, והיו צריכים ביום תשעה באב להתעסק בטהרות, לפיכך טובלת מבערב. אבל בזמן הזה, לבעלה דוקא – אפשר לה לחוף ולטבול במוצאי תשעה באב. ואם אין לה פנאי לרחוץ ולחוף בלילה – תרחוץ ותחוף ערב תשעה באב, כדי שיהיה בקל לה עדיין לחוף קצת מוצאי תשעה באב ולטבול.

א) נ"ל דה' שרלים ב) נ"ל דה' שרלים

**תוספי הרא"ש**

בע"ש ותטבול בלילה למוצאי שבת והא בעינן סמוך לחפיפה טבילה דלמא לא תחוף אלא בליל מוצאי שבת. ודוגמתו איכא בפ' כל שעה ר' יוסי הגלילי אומר ותמה על עצמך היאך חמץ אסור בהנאה כל ז' כלומר היאך תוכל לאוסרו אלא מותר הוא בהנאה ובתר הכי קאמר והלכתא אשה חופפת ביום פי' בע"ש וטובלת בלילה פי' למוצאי שבת לא קשה הא דאפשר לחוף בליל מוצאי שבת תחוף בלילה ולא תאריך חפיפתה מע"ש. הא דלא אפשר לחוף במוצאי שבת כגון יו"ט שחל להיות במוצאי שבת אז חופפת ביום בע"ש. וכן נוהגות הנשים האידנא ונזהרות בשבת מליתן תבשיל לבנה ומלהתעסק בדבר שיכול לבא לידי חציצה ומחממין קיתון של מים להדיח בית הסתרים ובית הקמטים כב"ה דמתירין להחם חמין לרגליו בי"ט אבל לא כל גופו וגם קושרות שערותיהן יפה שלא יתבלבל. וה"ר משולם התיר בעירו לחוף בע"ש שהיה שביעי שלה ולטבול ביום השבת כי היו יראות מלטבול בלילה. ור"ת כתב דתרי קולי בהדי הדדי לא אשכחן קולא דסרך בתה וקולא דהרחקת חפיפה מטבילה: **נדה** שבדקה ביום ז' ומצאה טהורה. משמע טעמא דבדקה בז' ומצאה טהורה הא לא בדקה הויא בחזקת טומאה ובסיפא קתני בדקה בז' שחרי' ומצאה טמא טעמ' דבדקה ומצאה טמא הא לא בדקה הויא בחזקת טהרה ואיכא למימר דרישא כי לא בדקה בשביעי הויא בחזקת טומאה משום דלאחר ימים מצאה טמא וסיפא כי לא בדקה הויא בחזקת טהרה משום דלאחר ימים בדקה ומצאה טהורה. אבל אי אפשר לומר כן דאם לא בדקה בשביעי דמוקמינן לה בחזקת טהרה

אמרו

לחוף ביום כגון בימי חול חופפת היכא דלא אפשר לחוף אלא בלילה כגון שחל טבילתה במוצאי שבת שאם תחוף בערב שבת לא תהיה חפיפתה סמוך לטבילתה הילכך חופפת בליל טבילתה במוצאי שבת. ולפיכך פי' אם אפ' אם חל במוצאי שבת נראה שלא להתיר לחוף (אלא בלילה כגון שחל טבילתה במוצאי שבת) בע"ש ולטבול במוצאי שבת שהרי פ' דבקושי התירו לחוף ביום ולטבול בלילה אלא דעדיף טפי משום שמצוה להרחיק כולי האי מע"ש למו"ש אסור אף אם חל יו"ט במוצאי שבת ומוטב שתדחה בשאלתות דרב אחאי בפרשה אחרי מות פירש הא דאפשר לחוף בלילה כגון בימות החול לא תחוף אלא בלילה היכא דלא אפשר לה לחוף בלילה כגון שחל ליל טבילתה בשבת או ביו"ט אז חופפת ביום ואפילו אם היה יו"ט חמישי וששי וחל ליל טבילתה בשבת חופפת ביום רביעי ולא תתבטל בעונתה. וסוגיא דתלמודא לא משמע כפי' דקא מיבעיא ליה נדה מהו שתחוף בלילה ותטבול בלילה אלמא משמע דיותר טוב הוא לחוף ביום דחיישינן דלא תחוף בטוב בלילה מתוך שמהומה לביתה (ותטבול בלילה אלמא משמע). ומיהו גם לפירוש השאלתות מנהג יפה הוא לנשים שלנו שמתחילות לחוף מבעוד יום ועוסקות בחפיפה עד שחושך ואז טובלות. ועוד מחמירות על עצמן אע"פ שחפפו נושאות עמהן מסרק וסורקות עצמן בבית הטבילה. ור"ת פי' דאפשר ולא אפשר לא בא להורות כלל על דין חפיפה אם הוא ביום או בלילה אלא קאי אהא דקאמר אשה לא תחוף בע"ש ותמה על עצמך כו'. היאך תוכל לומר חופפת ביום בע"ש

(כלאחר ימים בדקה ומצאה טהור אבל אי אפשר לומר כן דאם לא בדקה בשביעי) אע"פ שראתה ודאי בששי דמאי שנא כשבדקה בששי ומצאה טמא משום שאנו חוששין לומר שמא ראתה בשמיני ובתשיעי ועשירי נמי כשבדקה בששי ומצאה טמא יש לנו לחוש שמא ראתה בשביעי שהוא עדיין בימי טומאה וראתה גם בתשיעי ובעשירי דמה לי חשש ג' ימים מחמת ראיה של שביעי ומה לי חשש ד' ימים. מחמת יום ששי. הלכך נראה דה"ה לא בדקה בשביעי ומצאה טמא אלא בששי או בשאר הימים אף בראשון רק שלא הפרישה בטהרה באחד מן הימים וגם בין השמשות לא הפרישה ולאחר ימים בדקה ומצאה טהור הרי זו בחזקת טומאה והאי דנקט בדקה עצמה ביום השביעי ומצאה טמא לאו דוקא אלא ה"ה באחד משאר הימים אלא משום דבעי למיתני ובין השמשות לא הפרישה נקט נמי בשביעי שחרית: **וחכ"א** אף בשני לנדתה בדקה ומצאה טהור. וכדפרש"י הג' מחלוקות בדבר ת"ק סבר דוקא בשביעי ור' יהודה דוקא בין השמשות וחכמים אומרים אף בשני ולפירושו איכא עדיין תנא רביעי דבגמרא קאמר אפילו בראשון הלכך נראה דליכא אלא תרי תנאי וחכמים מפרשי מילי דת"ק משום דר' יהודה בעי הפרשה מן המנחה ולמעלה ולא סגי בהפרשה דשביעי שחרית ואתו רבנן לפרושי דאפילו בשפרשה בשני סגיא וה"ה בהפרשה בראשון אלא שאין דרך אשה לבדוק ביום ראשון אחרי שכבר בדקה פעם אחת ומצאה. טמאה א"כ נשנית לפי הטעות שטעה ר' שלא שאל בראשון: **רב** אמר זבה ודאי.
תמיה'

**עין משפט נר מצוה**

נא א מיי' פ"ב מה' מקוואות הלכה טז סמג עשין רמח טוש"ע י"ד סימן קצט סעיף ג וסעיף ז [וברב אלפס שבועות פ"ב דף רלג.]:

נב ב ד מיי' פ"ו מהל' איסורי ביאה הל' כ:

[פי' קדירות רק אר' בערוך ערך טשטק ועי' לעיל סו: בתוס' ד"ה אם סמוך]

**מסורת הש"ס**

[פי' יורות]

ס"א שבת

[שבת סג: וש"נ]

[נ"ל רבי]

**הגהות הב"ח**

(א) גמ' תסגי ואייתי למחר: (ב) רש"י ד"ה הא דלא אפשר לחוף ביום כגון מוצאי שבת ויום טוב: (ג) תוס' ד"ה כך וד"ה והלכתא וד"ה הא דאפשר הס"א:

וכן תנא לוי במתניתא: אחר הימים, בין בדקה ומצאה טהורה, בין בדקה ומצאה טמאה — הרי זו ספק זבה.§ "ומטמאה מעת לעת".§ לימא תהוי תיובתא דרבא! דאמר רבא: *לומר שאין האשה מטמאה מעת לעת בתוך ימי זיבתה! ולאו אותביניה לרבא חדא זימנא! הכי קאמרינן: לימא תהוי תיובתא דרבא נמי מהא! אמר לך רבא: כי קתני "מטמאה מעת לעת" — אריש פרקין קאי, א"ראתה ועודה בבית אביה". סד"א — כיון דמפסקי להו ימים טהורין — כתחלת נדתה דמיא, ולא תטמא מעת לעת, קמ"ל.§ "אם יש לה וסת".§ נימא תהוי תיובתא דרב הונא בר חייא אמר שמואל, *דאמר רב הונא בר חייא אמר שמואל: לומר שאין האשה קובעת לה וסת בימי זיבתה. אמר לך רב הונא בר חייא: כי אמרינן אין אשה קובעת לה וסת בימי זיבתה — אדלא בעיא תלתא זימני למיעקר. דאמרינן דמיה מסולקין, וכיון דדמיה מסולקין — דיה שעתה.§ "רבי יהודה אומר".§ תניא, אמרו לו לר' יהודה: אלמלי ידיה מונחות בעיניה כל בין השמשות — יפה אתה אומר, עכשיו — אימר עם סלוק ידיה ראתה, מה לי הפרישה בטהרה בז' מן המנחה ולמעלה — מה לי הפרישה בטהרה בראשון. בראשון — במי איכא למאן דאמר? אין, והתניא, אמר רבי: שאלתי את רבי יוסי ור' שמעון כשהיו מהלכים בדרך, נדה שבדקה עצמה יום ז' שחרית ומצאה טהורה, ובין השמשות לא הפרישה, ולאחר הימים בדקה ומצאה טמאה, מהו? *אמרו לו: הרי זו בחזקת טהרה. ששי, חמישי, רביעי, שלישי, שני, מאי? א"ל: לא שנא. בראשון לא שאלתי, וטעיתי שלא שאלתי. *אטו כולהו לאו בחזקת טומאה קיימי? וכיון דפסק — פסק, ראשון נמי, כיון דפסק — פסק. ומעיקרא מאי סבר? גהואיל והוחזק מעין פתוח.§

**מתני'** *דהזב והזבה שבדקו עצמן ביום ראשון ומצאו טהור, וביום השביעי ומצאו טהור, ושאר ימים שבינתיים לא בדקו, רבי אליעזר אומר: הרי הן בחזקת טהרה. ר' יהושע אומר: אין להם אלא יום ראשון ויום שביעי בלבד. ר' עקיבא אומר: אין להם אלא יום ז' בלבד.§

**גמ'** תניא, אמר לו רבי אליעזר לר' יהושע: לדבריך אתה מונה בסירוגין, והתורה אמרה °"אחר תטהר" — *"אחר אחר לכולן, שלא תהא טומאה מפסקת ביניהן! אמר לו רבי יהושע: ואתה, אי אתה מודה בזב שראה קרי, ובנזיר שהילך סככות ופרעות, שמונה בסירוגין? והתורה אמרה °"והימים הראשונים יפלו". ורבי אליעזר; בשלמא התם °"לטמאה בה" אמר רחמנא — שאינה סותרת אלא יומה, ואי משום איחלופי — זב בבעל קרי לא מיחלף. נזיר שהילך על גבי סככות ופרעות נמי °מדאורייתא אהל מעליא בעינן, ורבנן הוא דגזור — ורבנן בדאורייתא לא מיחלף. אבל הכא, אי חיישינן דלמא חזאי בספק, אתי לאיחלופי בודאי. תני, *ר' יוסי ור' שמעון אמרי: נראין דברי רבי אליעזר מדברי רבי יהושע, ודברי רבי עקיבא מדברי כולן, אבל הלכה כרבי אליעזר. איבעיא להו: הזב והזבה שבדקו עצמן יום ראשון ויום שמיני ומצאו טהור, ושאר הימים לא בדקו, לרבי

[ויקרא טו] [במדבר ו] [ויקרא טו]

וכן תנא לוי במתניתא. אסיפא דמתני' תני הכי: בדקה ז' שחרית ומצאה טמאה, ובין השמשות לא הפרישה. ואחר הימים, בין בדקה ומצאה טהורה, בין בדקה ומצאה טמאה — הרי זו ספק זבה. לומר שאינה מטמאה מעת לעת. בפ' "בנות כותים" (לעיל לט.) קתני: כל אחד עשר — בחזקת טהרה. ואמרינן: למאי הלכתא? ואמר רבא: לומר, שאם תראה בתוך י"א — אינה מטמאה מעת לעת. ומתניתין קתני: "מטמאה מעת לעת" — ארישא, דקתני: "אחר הימים, בדקה ומצאה טמאה". ומתמה התלמוד: ולאו אותביניה בפ' "בנות כותים" (שם) ולא איפרוק? כי קתני. "ומטמאה מעת לעת". אריש פירקין קאי. "ראתה ועודה בבית אביה ב"ה אומרים: כל הלילה שלה", וקאמר: ראם ראתה לאחר מכאן — מטמאה מעת לעת. כתחלת נדה. כבתולת דמים, דקי"ל (לעיל דף ז.) דיה שעתה בראייה ראשונה. ואם יש לה וסת. קא סלקא דעתך: אסיפא דמתני' קאי, דקתני: "אחר הימים בדקה ומצאה טמאה — מטמאה מעת לעת". ואם יש לה וסת קבוע לאחר הימים, דהיינו ימי זיבה וראתה בו — דיה שעתה. לומר שאינה קובעת. בפ' "בנות כותים" גבי "כל י"א בחזקת טהרה". אמר לך שמואל. כי אמרי אנא: לקולא, דלא בעינן תלת זימני למיעקריה. דהא קתני "כל י"א בחזקת טהרה" דהיינו, קולא, דדמיה מסולקין. אבל לענין "דיה שעתה" — כל שכן דהוי וסת, דהא דמיה מסולקין. עם סילוק ידיה ראתה. ואפילו הכי אמרת טהורה. הלכך, מה לי הפסיקה בטהרה בראשון כו'. מי איכא למאן דאמר כו'. והא אפילו רבנן בתראי — בשני שלה הוא דקאמרי, אבל בראשון דהוי פתיחת מעיינה ליכא למאן דאמר דאם בדקה בצהרים ומצאה טהור, דתהוי הפרשה. וטעיתי שלא שאלתי. שאילו שאלתי, היו מטהרין. מעיקרא מאי סבר. שלא רצה לשאול? **מתני'** הזב והזבה. שפסקו, והתחילו לספור ז' ובדקו יום ראשון ושביעי כו'. רבי עקיבא אומר אין להם אלא שביעי. שמא ראו בינתיים, וסתרו ספירתן הראשונה. **גמ'** אי אתה מודה בזב שראה קרי. בימי ספירו, שאינו מונה אותו יום, דקיימא לן דסותר יום א' ומונה לסירוגין. ונזיר שהילך סככות ופרעות. שהן ספק אהל — אין אותו יום עולה למנין נזירותו, ונמצא שמונה ל' יום של סתם נזירות בסירוגין. התם. זב שראה קרי. לטמאה בה כתיב. "זאת תורת הזב ואשר תצא ממנו שכבת זרע" וגו' (ויקרא טו) — מה זיבה *סותרת, אף קרי סותר. אי מה זיבה סותרת הכל, אף קרי סותר הכל? ת"ל: "לטמאה בה" — אין לך סתירה אלא בטומאתה האמור בה, מה טומאת קרי יום אחד, אף סתירתה יום אחד. ואי משום איחלופי. דלא ליתי למנות לסירוגין בזיבה גמורה? אהל מעליא בעינן. אין נזיר מטמא אלא באהל מת ודאי, כדכתיב (במדבר ו): "וכי ימות מת עליו" — במחוורת עליו, כדאמר ב"כילד צולין" (פסחים פא:). ורבנן גזור ביה. לסתור אותו יום. וא"ת: אתי לאיחלופי באהל מת גמור, ולא יסתור אלא יום א'? דרבנן בדאורייתא. אהל ספק דרבנן באהל דאורייתא — לא מיחלף. אבל הכא. אי חיישינן ולא תמנה יום שבינתיים, משום דלמא חזאי בספק — אתי למיחלף בודאי, דאמרינן: מדלא מנינן הני ימים, ודאי חזאי בינתיים, וקא מניא לראשון, ואתיא למנות ודאי רואה בסירוגין. נראין דברי ר"א מדברי רבי יהושע. דכיון דחייש רבי יהושע לשמא ראה בינתיים, היה לו לסתור אף הראשון. ודברי ר"ע מדברי כולן. דבעי ספורין ודוקין. יום שמיני. כבר עברו ימי הספירה, ולא היה סופן בטהרה, דלא בדקה יום ז'.

לרבי

**אמרו** ליה הרי זו בחזקת טהרה. וא"ת: תקשה דרבי יוסי דהכא דקאמר דסגי לה בהפרשה שחרית, אדרבי יוסי דפרק "בא סימן" (לעיל דף נג.) דקאמר: ומה אילו נדה שלא הפרישה בטהרה מן המנחה ולמעלה לא תהא בחזקת טומאה — אלמא, בעי הפרשה מן המנחה ולמעלה! ויש לומר: דהתם מיירי כשהפרישה ביום שראתה בו שחרית, (א) והכא מיירי בבדקה שחרית ומצאה טהורה. וקשה: דאם כן, כי פרכינן לרבי יהודה "אילו ידיה בעיניה כל בין השמשות" וכו', לימא ר' יוסי לנפשיה, דהא איהו נמי מצריך הפרשה מן המנחה ולמעלה כשהפרישה ביום שראתה, ומה מועיל עיכוב זה? שמא עם סילוק ידיה ראתה! וי"ל: דלנפשיה לא קשה, דכיון דהוחזקה רואה שחרית — דין הוא להצריכה הפרשה מן המנחה ולמעלה בלא חומרא אלא מן הדין. ואין לנו להחמיר ולספק שמא עם סילוק ידיה ראתה, להצריכה בדיקה בסוף היום. אבל רבי יהודה, שבא להחמיר ולספק דאפילו בשלא ראתה שחרית אלא בבדקה עצמה ומצאה טהורה הוא מצריך הפרשה — גם בסוף היום היה לו להחמיר ולבדוק מספק שמא עם סילוק ידיה ראתה.

**אבל** הלכה כרבי אליעזר. אע"ג דאין למדין הלכה מפי התלמוד, הא פסקינן בפ"ק לעיל (דף ז:) כרבי אליעזר בארבע, והא חד מינייהו. והכא

עין משפט נר מצוה

נג א מיי' פ"ח מהל' איסורי ביאה הל' ט טור י"ד סי' קפט:
נד ב ג מיי' שם פ"ו הלכה כ:
נה ד מיי' פ"ו מהל' איסורי ביאה הלכה כא ופ"ג מהל' מחוסרי כפרה הל' ג טוש"ע י"ד סימן קצו סעיף ד:

גליון הש"ס

**גמ'** מדאורייתא אהל מעליא בעינן. לעיל נז ע"א תוס' ד"ה אילן:

[גי' הרשב"א בתה"א התם טעמא מאי כולהו כו']

לעיל ז:

[לעיל לג: וש"נ]

מסורת הש"ס

[לעיל לט.]

שם

[נ"ל אמרו לי יעב"ץ]

[לעיל ז:]

[לעיל כב.]

הגהות הב"ח

(א) תוס' ד"ה אמרו ליה הרי וכו' שחרית אבל הכא מיירי:

תוספי הרא"ש

תמיה' לי איך תביא קרבן מספק כיון דקי"ל דכל י"א בחזקת טהרה:
**לימא** תיהוי תיובתיה דרבא דאמר רבא לומר שאינה מטמאה מעת לעת בתוך ימי זיבתה. ולא משמע ליה לפרושי דלאחר מכאן בדקה ומצאה טמאה היינו לאחר י"א יום משום דלאחר מכאן משמע אפילו בסמוך: **תיהוי** כתחלת נדה. פרש"י כתחלת דמים דקי"ל דיה שעתה בראייה ראשונה. ול"נ דלמה תיסוק אדעתין דחזרה לקדמותה בשביל הפסק ימים טהורים. ונראה לפרש (כד"א) לימא תיהוי כתחלת נדה כלומר כימי רואה אחר דם טוהר דאמרינן בפ' בנות כותים דדיה בעתה אפי' לרב דאמר מעיין אחד הוא היכא דליכא שהות קמ"ל הכא דמטמאה מעת לעת ומפקידה לפקידה ולאו דוקא מעת לעת ממש אלא שעה שראוי לתלות בדם בתולים והא דלא אמרינן הכי ברואה אחר דם טוהר משום דהתם ליכא שהות כלל לטמויי

קאמר ר' גופיה משום ר' יוסי ומזה הטעם אמר לי ומה נדה שלא הפרישה בטהרה מן המנחה ולמעלה לא תהא בחזקת טומאה. וי"ל דהתם מיירי כשלא הפרישה בערב כשמצאה בבקר טמא הכא בבדקה בשחרית ומצאתה טהורה והא דא"ל לר' יהודה אלמלי ידיה בין עיניה וכו' ולא קא"ל ר' יוסי לנפשיה דגם הוא מצריך הפרשה מן המנחה ולמעלה כשראתה בו ביום. וי"ל דדוקא לר' יהודה שייך להקשות משום שמחמיר כל כך מן המנחה ולמעלה יש לו להחמיר ולחוש שמא עם סילוק ידיה ראתה כמו שרושש באותה

תוספי הרא"ש

לטמויי מעת לעת דאי אפשר לה לראות שום דם שתהיה טמאה בו מאתמול אבל הכא אפשר לראות מאתמול דם טמא כגון אם נשתנה הדם: **הרי** זו בחזקת טהרה. תימה דלעיל בס"פ בא סימן

לרבי אליעזר מהו? תחלתן וסופן בעינן, והכא – תחלתן איכא, סופן ליכא. או דילמא – תחלתן אף על גב שאין סופן? אמר רב: [א]היא היא, תחלתן אע"פ שאין סופן. ורבי חנינא אמר: תחלתן וסופן בעינן, הכא – תחלתן איכא, סופן ליכא. מיתיבי: ושוין בזב ובזבה שבדקו עצמן יום ראשון ויום שמיני ומצאו טהור – שאין להם אלא שמיני בלבד. מאן "שוין"? לאו רבי אליעזר ורבי יהושע? לא, ר' יהושע ור' עקיבא. אמר רב ששת, אמר רב ירמיה בר אבא, אמר רב: נדה שהפרישה בטהרה בשלישי שלה – סופרתו למנין שבעה נקיים. נדה, ספירה למה לה? אלא אימא: זבה שהפרישה בטהרה בשלישי שלה – [ב]סופרתו למנין ז' נקיים. אמר ליה רב ששת לרב ירמיה בר אבא: רב כבותאי אמרה לשמעתיה, דאמרי יום שפוסקת בו סופרתו למנין ז' כי קאמר רב, [ג]לבר משלישי. בר משלישי, פשיטא! לא צריכא, [ד]כגון דלא בדקה עד שביעי, ואשמועינן התם – תחלתן אע"פ שאין סופן, והכא קמ"ל – סופן אע"פ שאין תחלתן. דמהו דתימא: תחלתן אף על פי שאין סופן הוא דאמרינן, דאוקמינהו אחזקייהו, אבל סופן אע"פ שאין תחלתן – לא, קמ"ל. איני, והא *כי אתא רבין אמר: מתיב ר' יוסי ברבי חנינא "טועה", ולא ידענא מאי תיובתיה. (א) דקי"ל שבוע קמא דאתיא לקמן – בלילותא מטבלינן לה, בימָמא לא מטבלינן לה. ואי ס"ד לא בעינן ספורין לפנינו – בימָמא נמי נטבלינה, דילמא יולדת זכר בזוב היא, ועבדה לה ספורין! אלא לאו שמע מינה – בעינן ספורין בפנינו! ולאו מי אוקימנא *כר"ע דאמר בעינן ספורין לפנינו ומנא תימרא דלרבנן לא בעינן ספורין לפנינו – *דתנן: טועה שאמרה "יום אחד טמא ראיתי" מטבילין אותה ט' טבילות, ז' לנדה ותרי לזיבה. "בין השמשות טמא ראיתי" – מטבילין אותה י"א טבילות. י"א מאי עבידתייהו? אמר רב ירמיה מדפתי: כגון שבאת לפנינו בין השמשות, והויין תמני לנדה ותלת לזיבה. "לא ראיתי כל עיקר" – מטבילין אותה ט"ו טבילות. אמר רבא: האי דינא דלא דינא, דייני בגלחי, *דאית ליה תורא – לירעי חד יומא, דלית ליה תורא – לירעי תרי יומי. אתרמי להו יתמא בר ארמלתא, יהבי ליה תורי, אזל נכסינהו. אמר להו: *דאית ליה תורא – לשקול חד משכא, דלית ליה תורא – לשקול תרי משכי. אמרי ליה: מאי האי דקאמרת? אמר להו: סוף דינא כתחלת דינא. תחלת דינא לאו מאן דלית ליה עדיף? סוף דינא נמי – מאן דלית ליה עדיף! הכא נמי, ומה היכא דאמרה "ראיתי" – סגי לה אי בתשע טבילות אי בי"א טבילות, היכא דקאמרה איהי "לא ראיתי" בעיא חמש עשרה טבילות?! אלא אימא הכי: "ראיתי ואיני יודע כמה ראיתי, אי בימי נדה ראיתי או בימי זיבה ראיתי" – מטבילין אותה ט"ו טבילות. אתאי קמן בימָמא – יהבינן לה שב לנדה ותמני

---

**רש"י**

לרבי אליעזר. דמכשר בבדיקת שביעי עם הראשון. מהו. דלרבי יהושע, ודאי אין להם אלא שמיני בלבד. דאף ע"ג דתליא מילתיה בבדיקה, ומונה ימים הבדוקין אפילו בסירוגין – הני מילי בראשון ושביעי, דחזו לאיצטרופי לחד מנינא. אבל שמיני – לאו מסדר ספירת הראשון הוא, ולא מצטרף. ולר' עקיבא נמי, אין לו אלא שמיני בלבד, שמא ראה בינתים, ומכאן ואילך צריך לספור ששה. אלא לרבי אליעזר, מי מחזקינן כל ז' בטהרה משום בדיקת ראשון, דהוו תחלתן בטהרה, או לא? היא היא. טהורין. לאו רבי אליעזר ורבי יהושע. דאע"ג דפליגי עליה דרבי עקיבא בראשון ושביעי, הכא – מודו. לא רבי יהושע ורבי עקיבא. כדפרישית. אבל לרבי אליעזר, הואיל ותחלתן בטהרה, מחזקינן לכולהו בטהרה. כבותאי אמרה לשמעתיה. בפרק "בנות כותים" (לעיל דף לג.). דלא בדקה עד שביעי. דלא הוי תחילת ימי ספירה בטהרה, דלא בדקה בראשון משהפרישה בבין השמשות של שלישי לזיבה שראתה בו ביום, עד ז' לספירה. ותרי קולי אשמועי' רב בספירה. התם. דאמר רב לעיל דמטהר רבי אליעזר בבודק ראשון ושמיני – אשמועינן תחלתן אע"פ שאין סופן. והכא אשמועינן סופן אע"פ שאין תחלתן. דמשום בדיקת ז' מחזקינן כל ששה לפניו בטהרה, הואיל ופסקה בשלישי. ומיהו הפרשה בטהרה בעינן, דמשהוחזק מעין פתוח ליכא לאחזוקי בטהרה עד שתבדוק ותמצא שפסק, כדאמרינן במתני' דהפרשה בטהרה בעינן. איני. לרב פריך, דלא בעי ספורין (ב) ובודקין ודאי וקיימא לן ב"המפלת" (לעיל דף כט:) ד"שבוע קמא בלילותא מטבלינן לה" – כל ליליא, דילמא השתא שלמו שבעה של טומאת זכר. "בימָמא לא מטבילין לה" – לספוקה ביולדת בזוב, ולמימר בכל יומא: היום כלין ז' נקיים שאחר טומאת לידה. ומשום הכי לא מטבילין לה: דאי נמי מתרמי האידנא ז' של נקיים – משום דטבילה בזמנה מצוה, ונדה ויולדת טבילתן בלילה, וזבה טבילתה ביום, לא הויא ספירה, הואיל ולא ספרה בפנינו, עד שתשב בפנינו שבוע טהור. יום אחד טמא ראיתי. "ואיני יודע אימתי", ואפילו היום י"ל זהו. ואינה יודעת אם יום ראייתה בימי נדה אם בימי זבה – מטבילין אותה, משום טבילה בזמנה מצוה. תשע טבילות ז' לנדה ותרתי לזיבה. וכגון דאתאי לקמן בימָמא. ומטבילין אותה הלילה – שמא נדה היא, והלילה כלו ז' ימי נדה, וכן לליל יום ז', וכן כל ליל שבוע זה, וטפי לא איכא לספוקי. ותרתי לזיבה בימָמא – ביומא דאתאי לקמן מטבילין לה, דלמא אתמול חזאי, וימי זיבה הוו, והאי שומרת יום כנגד יום. ולמחר נמי טבלה, דילמא ביומא דאתאי לקמן הוא דחזאי, וטפי ליכא לספוקי. אבל אתיא לקמן בליליא – איכא י' טבילות, ח' לנדה וב' לזיבה. דההוא ליליא גופיה איכא לספוקי: השתא זמן טבילתה, וכן כל לילות שבוע זה. ולמוצאי שביעי נמי טבלה – משום דילמא בליליא דאתאי קמן חזאי, והשתא הואי זמן טבילה. והאי דלא קא תני י' טבילות – משום מילתא דלא פסיקא היא, דהא כי אתיא בימָמא ליכא אלא ט'. אבל ט' פסיקא ליה, דבליר מהכי ליכא, והכי מוקי לקמן. מאי עבידתייהו. אם באתה ביום או בלילה ואומרת "בין השמשות טמא ראיתי" – אין כאן טבילה יתירתא, דהא כי אמרה נמי "יום טמא ראיתי, ואיני יודע מתי אם בימי נדה ואם בימי זיבה", מספקי ליה: דילמא האידנא ביום שבאת לפנינו חזאי? תמני לנדה. כגון באת לפנינו בין השמשות של ערב שבת – טובלת מיד בלילי שבת, שמא השתא זמן טבילתה, וכן כל שבוע זה. ולילי שבת הבאה – שמא בין השמשות שבאת לפנינו ראתה, ולילה היא, ומשכה ז' ימי נדה עד עכשיו. ולפי שיום שבת הבא היה תחלת נדתה – הרי ח' טבילות לנדה. ותלת לזיבה – דמטבילין לה בין השמשות דאתאי לקמן, דילמא בין השמשות דאתמול חזאי, ומיום ה' בשבת היא, ושמרה ערב שבת כנגד יום ה', וטובלת בין השמשות עד שלא תחשך – דשמא עדיין יום הוא, ולאו לטבילת זוב. ולמחר בשבת נמי טבלה – שמא בין השמשות דאתמול כשבאת לפנינו ראתה, ומיום ששי היה, והיום טובלת ליום כנגד יום. ולאחד בשבת נמי טבלה – משום ספק ההוא בין השמשות גופיה, שמא לילה הוא כשבאת לפנינו, ובכל יום השבת הוי ראשון, ואחד בשבת הוי שימור, וטבלה. האי דינא דלא דינא דייני בגלחי. דין זה שאינו דין היו דנין באותו מקום. לירעי חד יומא. כל הבהמות לרעיה. אזל יתמא. שלא היה לו שור וכשהוצרכו לרעות בהמותיהן ב' ימים. נכסינהו. שחטן. כמה ראיתי. אם א' אם ג'. שב לנדה. כשבאת בשבת – טובלת למוצאי שבת, שמא באחד בשבת שעברה ראתה תחלה, וכן עד לילי שבת הבאה. ולילי שבת בכלל – שמא בשבת שבאת לפנינו ראתה, ואותו היום לבד ראתה. ותמני

---

**תוספות**

**והכא** קמ"ל סופן אע"פ שאין תחלתן. ואם תאמר: (א"כ) לרב, כל זבה צריכה הפרשה ביום שפוסקת בו, כמו נדה. ואמאי קתני במתני' "שבדקה עצמה יום ראשון", הא כבר בדקה עצמה מאתמול, והפרישה בטהרה? ואי הוה אומר דלא בעינן הפרשה ביום ג' הוה ניחא. וי"ל: דליכא למידק הכי, דאפי' אי סגי בהפרשת שלישי, לרבי אליעזר לא סגי. דלא תני "שבדקה ביום ראשון" משום פלוגתא דרבי יהושע ורבי עקיבא. כמו "ראשון ושמיני" דקאמר רב לרבי אליעזר "היא היא", ולא תני במתני', אע"ג דלר' אליעזר הוי רבותא טפי – משום דלא מיתני ליה תו פלוגתא דר' יהושע ור' עקיבא. **שבעה** לנדה ושנים לזיבה. מכאן אין יכול לדקדק דלא בעינן ספורים בפנינו, מדטובלת אע"פ שלא הפסיקה בטהרה, ולא בדקה נמי בתחלת ספורים. דאע"ג דלא בעינן ספורים בפנינו בזבה קטנה, בזבה גדולה בעינן. ועוד: דסוף סוף סגי לה במה שבדקה ביום הספירה ומצאה טהורה. דאי אין בדיקת סוף היום עולה לספירה – לא היה תקנה לבנות ישראל אלא אם כן יבדקו בעליית עמוד השחר, דספירת לילה אינה ספירה. מה

---

**מסורת הש"ס**

[לעיל כט. יח:]

[לעיל ל.]

[נ"ל דתניא]

[סנהדרין קט.]

שם

**הגהות הב"ח**

(א) גמ' וקיימא לן שבוע קמא: (ב) רש"י ד"ה איני וכו' ובודקין ודאי הס"ד ואח"כ מ"ה וקיימא לן וכו' זכר הס"ד ואח"כ מ"ה בימָמי לא וכו' של נקיים והוה בעיא טבילה כו' משום דטבילה בזמנה מצוה דנדה ויולדת וכו' ולא ספרתן בפנינו:

**עין משפט נר מצוה**

רש"א מ"ז

נו א ב ג ד מיי' פ"ו מהל' איסורי ביאה הל' כב טוש"ע י"ד סי' קצו סעיף ז:

**תוספי הרא"ש**

באותה בדיקה דקודם המנחה: **רב** אמר היא היא תחלתן אע"פ שאין סופן. והאי דקתני במתניתין ביום השביעי משום ר' יהושע נקטיה: הכא קמ"ל סופן אע"פ שאין תחלתן. והאי דנקט מתניתין יום ראשון משום ר' יהושע ור' עקיבא נקטיה: **איני** והא כי אתא רבין כו'. אע"ג דאליביה דר' אליעזר קאמר מ"מ פריך ליה דלא אשכחן תנא דס"ל סופן אע"פ שאין תחלתן הלכך לא מיבעיא ליה לפרושי דברי ר' אליעזר הכי: **ואי** ס"ד לא בעינן ספורי' לפנינו בימָמי ליטבלה. ואי משום דבעינן הפסקה בשלישי כדקאמר רבא לעיל נדה שהפרישה בטהרה בשלישי שלה אלמא בלא הפרשה אינה יכולה לספור. חומרא בעלמא היא ומדרבנן ואינה נמנעת בשביל זה מלטבול כיון שטבילה בזמנה מצוה ואפילו בעיא הפסקה מן התורה טובלת דשמא הפסיקה ולאו אדעתה כיון דבאיזה יום שהפסיקה מועלת הפסקתה אבל אין לחוש ולומר שמא בדקה ביום ראשון של ספירה ואיכא תחלתן וסופן שבאתה שעתה שבדקה לפנינו יום שביעי של יום זה: **לאו** מי אוקימנא כר' עקיבא. משמע דר' חנינא לא מיבעי ליה לאוקומי כר' עקיבא דאתיא שפיר כר' אליעזר. מתוך כך נראה דהלכה כרב דסופן אע"פ שאין תחלתן. דסוגיין דסוף המפלת כוותיה וכ"ש בתחלתן ואע"פ שאין סופן. מיהו יש לדחות דר' חנינא נמי לא מיתוקמא כר' אליעזר דכיון דלא בעינן ספורי' לפנינו בכל הימים א"כ חומרא בעלמא היא דבעי סופן ותחלתן ולאו מדאורייתא הלכך מטבלינן לה משום טבילה בזמנה מצוה. וכי פריך הכא לרב הוה מצי לאקשויי. ולטעמיך היכי מצי מוקמת לה בשום ענין כר' אליעזר ולישנא משמע כן דקאמר לאו מי אוקימנא כר' עקיבא משמע אפי' ליתא לדרב: ז' לנדה ותרי לזבה. מכאן אינו יכול לדקדק דלא בעינן ספורים לפנינו דחשבינן להך יום ספירה אע"פ שלא הפסיקה בטהרה אתמול בתחלתן יום הספירה משום שאין לחוש מה שלא הפסיקה בטהרה כיון שיום הספירה בדקה ומצאה טמא טהור. א"נ אפי' לא בעינן ספורים לפנינו לגמרי גבי שומרת יום לענין זבה גדולה אפשר דבעינן ספורים לפנינו כגון שבאת לפנינו בין השמשות. והא דקתני בין השמשות אמרה ראיתי ה"פ באתה לפנינו בין השמשות ואמרה טמא ראיתי אבל לא אמרה שהראיה היתה בין השמשות: הזוב

נז א ב ג ד ה מיי' פ"ו מהל' מטמאי משכב ומושב הלכה ז:

ותמני לזיבה, אתאי קמן בלילותא — יהבינן לה תמני לנדה ושב לזיבה. זיבה — תמני בעיא! אלא, אידי ואידי שב לנדה ותמני לזיבה. בלילותא, תמני לנדה בעי! זיבה דפסיקא ליה, דלא שנא כי אתיא קמן בימא, לא שנא כי אתיא קמן בליליא — חשיב לה. נדה דלא פסיקא ליה, דכי אתיא קמן בלילותא — בעי תמני, בימא — לא קבעי תמני, לא קחשיב לה. ואי ס"ד ספורין לפנינו בעינן — כל הני טבילות למה לי? תספור ז' והדר תטבול! אלא לאו שמע מינה — רבנן היא, דאמרי לא בעינן ספורין לפנינו. אמר ליה רב אחא בריה דרב יוסף לרב אשי: לאו תרוצי קמתרצינן לה?! תריץ ואימא הכי "ספרתי ואיני יודעת כמה ספרתי, אם בימי נדה ספרתי ואם בימי זיבה ספרתי" — מטבילין אותה ט"ו טבילות. "ספרתי ואיני יודעת כמה ספרתי" — חד יומא מיהא אי אפשר דלא ספרה, חסרה לה טבילה! אלא אימא: "איני יודעת אם ספרתי אם לא ספרתי".§

**מתני'** [א]הזב, והזבה, והנדה, והיולדת, והמצורע שמתו — מטמאין במשא, עד שימוק הבשר. [ב]גוי שמת — טהור מלטמא. בית שמאי אומרים: כל הנשים מתות נדות. וב"ה אומרים: אין נדה אלא שמתה נדה.§

**גמ'** מאי "במשא"? אילימא במשא ממש — אטו כל מת מי לא מטמא במשא! אלא: מאי "במשא"? — [ג]באבן מסמא, דכתיב: (דניאל ו) "והיתית אבן חדא ושומת על פום גובא". מאי טעמא? אמר רב: [ד]גזרה שמא יתעלפה. תנא, משום ר' אליעזר אמרו: עד שיבקע כריסו.§ "גוי שמת" [כו'].§ תניא, אמר רבי: מפני מה אמרו גוי שמת טהור מלטמא במשא — [ה]לפי שאין טומאתו מחיים מדברי תורה, אלא מדברי סופרים. ת"ר: שנים עשר דברים שאלו אנשי אלכסנדריא את רבי יהושע בן *חיננא: ג' דברי חכמה, ג' דברי הגדה, ג' דברי בורות, ג' דברי דרך ארץ. ג' דברי חכמה: הזב והזבה והנדה והיולדת והמצורע שמתו, עד מתי מטמאין במשא? אמר להן: עד שימוק הבשר. בת משולחת, מה היא לכהן? מי אמרינן קל וחומר: *ומה אלמנה לכ"ג שאין איסורה שוה בכל — בנה פגום, זו שאיסורה שוה בכל — אינו דין שבנה פגום? או דילמא: מה לאלמנה לכהן גדול — שהיא עצמה מתחללת? אמר להן:

היא

---

**ותמני לזיבה.** בשבת גופה אתאי — מטבילין לה, שמא שלשה ימים ראתה בימות זוב, והיום כלין ספורין. וכן למחר, וכן ביום שבת הבאה יש לומר: ביום שבאתה לפנינו ראתה, והוא שלישי לזיבה, והיום כלו ספורין שלה. **בלילותא.** אם באת לפנינו בלילה — תמני לנדה. באת בלילי שבת — טובלת מיד, שמא הלילה כלו ימי נדה. וכן כל לילות שבוע זה ולילי יום שבת הבא, משום דשמא בליל שבאת לפנינו ראתה — הרי ח'. **ושב לזיבה.** לאו מילתא היא, דהא פרכינן: זבה תמני הויין, דהא למחר בשבת טבלה, ויום שבת הבא נמי טבלה, שמא בלילי שבת כשבאת לפנינו ראתה והוא שלישי לזיבתה, והיום כלין ימי הספירה. **אידי ואידי.** בין באת לפנינו ביום בין באת לפנינו בלילה. וקא פריך: נדה בלילותא כו' — כלומר, כשבאת לפנינו בלילה, איכא טבילה יתירתא, שטובלת מיד משום נדה! ומהדר: (א) ומשום זיבה דפסיקא ליה טבילה, ספק זיבה דפסיקא ליה דתמני נינהו, לעולם חשיב להו כתמני. **למה לי.** כל הני טבילות? הטבילות דימי דזיבה קא פריך, לספור שבעה קמן, ולטבלה בשביעית! ומקמי הכי — לא, דאפילו שלמי נקיים דילה, לאו בת טבילה היא, הואיל ולא בדקה. **אלא לאו ש"מ רבנן היא.** דפליגי עליה דרבי עקיבא, א] ורבי דאמר "לא בעינן ספורין לפנינו" — כרבנן סבירא ליה. **ספרתי.** "בדקתי קצת נקיים או כולן, ואיני יודעת כמה. או שמא נקיים שראיתי — לאו אחר ימי הזוב היו, אלא לאחר ימי נדות" — מטבילין אותה ט"ו טבילות, שמא עכשיו כלין, וכדפרישית. **חד יומא מיהא אי אפשר דלא ספרה.** וליכא לספוקה ברואה יום שבאת לפנינו, ובעיי להו טבילות דשביעי. **אימא איני יודעת אם ספרתי אם לא ספרתי.** הלכך אפילו יומא קמא טבלה, דלמא כל ז' (*שלפנינו) ספרה ובדקה, דהא קאמרה "שמא ספרתי", ויום ז' נמי טבלה — שמא לא ספרה קודם לכן.

**מתני' מטמאין במשא.** בגמרא פריך: כל מת נמי מטמא במשא? ומשנינן: באבן מסמא, דשאר מתים — לא מטמו, הכא — מטמו מדרבנן. הואיל ומחיים מטמו באבן מסמא מדאורייתא, שהרי מטמאין מושב כל שתחתיהם, גזור בהו רבנן לאחר מיתה, כדמפרש טעמא בגמרא: גזרה שמא יתעלפה. **עד שימוק הבשר.** דמהשתא הוי מת ודאי. **גוי שמת.** אע"ג דמחיים הרי הוא כזב לכל דבריו, *ולטמא באבן מסמא — משמת, טהור מלטמא באבן מסמא, כדמפרש בגמרא: הואיל וטומאת זיבה שעליו מחיים אינה אלא מדברי סופרים. **כל הנשים** מחזקינן להו בנדות. ומטבילין כלים שהיו עליהן סמוך ליציאת נשמה, וטעמא מפרש בגמרא. **גמ'** כדכתיב **והיתית אבן חדא ושומת על פום גובא.** לשון "מסמא" קא מפרש, דהיינו אבן כבדה העשויה להיונח ואינה מטלטלת. הלכך, כשהיא על גבי כלים ומת נתון עליה — אין זה משא, הואיל ואינה ראויה להטלטל עמו. **מאי טעמא.** גזור רבנן בזב וזבה לטמא אף לאחר מיתה באבן מסמא? **גזרה שמא יתעלפה.** פאשמיי"ר, ודומה למת. ואי אמרת: זב מת לא מטמא, בזב חי אתי נמי לטהורי כי האי. **דברי חכמה.** הלכה. **דברי בורות.** שטות. **בת משולחת.** ישראל שהחזיר גרושתו משנישאת לאחר, והוליד בת. **אלמנה אינה אסורה. אלא לכ"ג. בנה פגום.** חלל, דכתיב (ויקרא כא): "לא יחלל זרעו". **זו שאיסורה שוה בכל.** בישראל ובכהנים אסור להחזיר גרושתו משנישאת. **היא עצמה.** משנישאת לכהן גדול — מתחללת, שאם מת — אסורה להנשא להדיוט, ואם היתה כהנת — נפסלת מן התרומה בביאתו, דכתיב: "לא יחלל זרעו בעמיו", ו"עמיו" — זו אשתו.

היא

---

**מה** לאלמנה לכהן גדול שכן היא עצמה מתחללת תאמר במחזיר גרושתו שאינה מתחללת. פי' מן התרומה, לפירוש רש"י. ד"כי תהיה לאיש זר", דמיניה ילפינן (יבמות דף סח.) כיון שנבעלה לפסול לה — פסלה מן הכהונה, איירי באלמנה לכ"ג דלא איירי במחזיר גרושתו, דלאו זר מעיקרא הוא אצלה. מיהו קשה: דנהי דלא מצינן למילף מהאי קרא, מ"מ תתחלל מהאי קל וחומר גופיה! וכן בפ' "החולץ" (שם דף מד.) דיליף לר' יהושע דחייבי כריתות בנה פגום מהאי קל וחומר דאלמנה לכ"ג ופריך כי הכא: לימא היא עצמה מתחללת מק"ו ותאסר אף מתרומה! וי"ל: כיון דאין חלל אלא מאיסור כהונה, ליכא למילף בעלמא לפסול האשה עצמה מאיסור כהונה. דלהכי אייתר התם "חללה" — למימר דאין חללה אלא מאיסור כהונה, דהיינו פסול האשה שהיתה כשרה ונתחללה. ואף ע"ג דגר עמוני ומואבי פוסלין, אע"ג דלא הוו איסור כהונה — התם מקרא דרשינן ליה, אבל מק"ו ליכא למילף. ומיהו קשה: נילף מאלמנה לכה"ג ומגוי ועבד, אי נמי מחלל וגוי ועבד, או גר עמוני ומצרי ואדומי, במה הצד דהיא עצמה מתחללת! דכי פרכינן: מה לאלמנה לכ"ג או לחלל, שכן איסור כהונה — איכא למימר: גוי ועבד יוכיחו, דלאו איסור כהונה, ופוסלין בביאתם. מה לגוי ועבד, שכן אסורין לבא בקהל, או דלא תפסי בהו קדושין — אלמנה לכ"ג או חלל יוכיחו. הצד השוה שבהן: שאינם ברוב הקהל, ופוסלין בביאתן — אף מחזיר גרושתו יפסלנה בביאתו. והכי מייתי ר' יהודה דגר פוסל בביאתו בפ' בתרא דקדושין (דף עח.) במה הצד דאיסור כהונה ומילתא אחריתי בהדה, דהיינו מחלל ומצרי ראשון. וכן נמי תקשה: אמאי מצריך בפ' "אלמנה לכה"ג" (יבמות דף סח.) קרא ד"וכי תהיה לאיש זר" לגר עמוני ומואבי דפוסלין בביאתם? נילף במה הצד מחלל וגוי ועבד, כדפירשתי! ויש לומר: כיון דבגוי ועבד הולד ממזר — ליכא למילף תו מינייהו פסול ביאה, כיון דחמירי כולי האי דוולדן ממזר. דדוקא רבי יהודה יליף בקדושין (שם) דגר פוסל בביאתו ממצרי ראשון, אף על גב דבתו פסולה לבא בקהל. אבל רבנן פליגי עליה, דלית להו הך סברא. ומתוך האי שינויא מתרצא נמי קושיא אחריתי בפרק "הערל" (יבמות דף עז.) *)דקאמר: עמוני שנשא בת ישראל — בתו כשרה לכהונה. ופריך: ונימא דפסול במה הצד דאלמנה לכה"ג וחלל? ומשני: דאיכא למפרך, מה להצד השוה שבהן שכן יש בהן צד עבירה. ואמאי לא קאמר: מצרי ראשון יוכיח, דהכי יליף בקדושין (דף עח.) לר' יהודה? אלא כיון דבתו פסולה (ב) — לא ילפינן מיניה פסול ביאה, אלא דוקא לר' יהודה. וא"ת: למאן דאמר (יבמות דף מה.) גוי ועבד הבא על בת ישראל — הולד כשר, אם כן נילף דהיא עצמה מתחללת, כדפי'. ויש לומר: דלא ילפינן מאיסור כהונה ומילתא אחריתי בהדה, אלא לר' יהודה דוקא, כדאשכחן בקדושין. אבל לרבנן, לית להו הך סברא.

היא

---

## תוספי הרא"ש

**הזב** והזב והיולדת והמצורע. והא דלא תני והמצורעת בב"מ כדקתני זב וזבה. מפרש בברייתא פרק ד' מחוסרי כפרה משום דזב וזבה חלוקין בטומאתן דזב מטמא בראיות וזבה בימים זב טהור באונס וזבה טמאה באונס אבל מצורע ומצורעת אין חלוקין בעיקר טומאתן. ומה שמדקדק התלמוד שם יותר מבשאר מקומות משום דקתני התם מטמא ד' מחוסרי כפרה. ומדקדק אמאי חשיב זב וזבה בתרי ומצורע ומצורעת לא חשיב בתרי: **ומטמא** באבן מוסמא. תימה דמשמע הכא דמצורע מטמא משכב ומושב דאבן מוסמא מדין משכב ומושב מטמא דתניא בת"כ מנין לרבות י' מצעות זו על גב זו ואפי' באבן מסמא ת"ל בכל המשכב. ואמרינן נמי בריש בכל מערבין כל שהזב נישא עליו טהור חוץ מן הראוי למשכב ומושב והאדם אלמא דאבן מסמא נמי בעיא דחזיא למשכב ומושב. ובת"כ בתחלת פרשה זאת תהיה דריש התם דמצורע [עושה] משכב ומושב. וקשה דבפסחים בריש אלו דברים קאמר דמצורע אינו עושה משכב ומושב ואינו מטמא כלי חרס בהיסט ואומר ר"ת דמצורע [עושה] משכב ומושב לטמא אוכלין ומשקין אבל [לא] לטמא אדם וכלים. וכן פרש"י במסכת פסחים ונראה דממעטי ליה מהזב ולא מצורע כי היכי דמתמעטי בבית המנוגעת לעיל בפרק דם הנדה. ודוקא מטומאה חמורה אבל אוכלין ומשקין מטמא. ולעיל בפרק דם הנדה פרש"י דאבן מסמא דהכא לאו מדין משכב ומושב מטמא מדקרי ליה משא: **מה** לאלמנה שכן היא עצמה מתחללת. ותימה היא גופה ניליף שתתחלל מק"ו מאלמנה. ור"ש פי' בפ"ק דיבמות תאמר במחזיר גרושתו דאינה מתחללת דאי להנשא לכהן כבר נפסלה משעת גירושין ואי לתרומה דנטמא לא מיפסלא כדאמרי' בפרק אלמנה דאינה מתחללת בביאת חייבי לאוין אלא בזר אצלה מעיקרא לאפוקי מחזיר גרושתו ויבמה לשוק דלאו זר אצלה מעיקרא הוא. וקשה לפירושו דנהי דלא ילפינן מכי תהיה לאיש זר אלא דהוי זר אצלה מעיקרו מ"מ תתחלל מק"ו. ונראה מפרש דמק"ו לא מצי למילף שתתחלל דאין חללה אלא מאיסורי כהונה כדאמרינן בפ' י' יוחסין ישראל הבא על אחותו זונה משוי לה ולא חללה משוי לה. משום דאין חללה אלא מאיסור כהונה אע"ג דאשכחן שמתחללת בלא איסור כהונה כדאמרינן בפ' אלמנה גר עמוני ומואבי ומצרי ואדומי כותי נתין חלל וממזר שבאו על הכהנת על הלויה ועל הישראלית שפסלוה התם מקרא דריש לה אבל מק"ו לא שייך למילף מחללות אלא מאיסור כהונה דלהכי אייתר לן חללה לומר דלא ילפינן מק"ו אע"ג דילפינן מק"ו דבנה פגום היינו דוקא פסול הזרע אבל פסול האשה דהיינו לשון חללות שהיתה כשרה ונתחללה לא יליפנן:

א"ל

---

### הגהות מהר"ב רנשבורג

א] רש"י ד"ה אלא לאו ש"מ וכו' דפליגי עליה דר"ע ורבי וכו' כצ"ל.

נ"ל שלא לפנינו רש"א

[נ"ל דתניא]

[יבמות טו: מד: מה.]

*) נ"ל דקאמר גר עמוני בתו כשירה לכהונה ופריך כו' אלא כיון דבתו פסולה לקהל לא ילפינן מיניה הרי פסול כהונה אלא דוקא לר"י וא"ת כו' רש"א וכן מנא מוגה. וגו' מהר"ש דקאמר עמוני שנשא עמונית וע"ש בסוגיא דיבמות

### הגהות הב"ח

(א) רש"י ד"ה אידי ואידי וכו' ומהדר זיבה כצ"ל ותיבת ומשום נמחק:

(ב) תוס' ד"ה מה לאלמנה וכו' כיון דבתו פסולה לבא בקהל לא ילפינן מיניה:

*אהיא תועבה, ואין בניה תועבין. *שני מצורעין שנתערבו קרבנותיהן זה בזה, וקרב קרבנו של אחד מהן, ומת אחד מהן, השני מה תהא עליו? אמר להן: בכותב נכסיו לאחרים — והוי עני, ומביא חטאת העוף הבא על הספק. והאיכא אשם! אמר שמואל: כשקרב אשמו. אמר רב ששת: גברא רבה כשמואל לימא כי האי מילתא. כמאן, אי כר' יהודה *דאמר אשם קבעה — וכיון דקבעה לה אשם בעשירות, לא מצי מייתי חטאת בדלות. דתנן: *מצורע שהביא קרבן עני והעשיר, או עשיר והעני — הכל הולך אחר חטאת, דברי ר' שמעון. *ורבי יהודה אומר: גהכל הולך אחר אשם. רבי אליעזר בן יעקב אומר: הכל הולך אחר צפורים. ואי כרבי שמעון דאמר חטאת קבעה אע"ג דלא קרב אשם, ניתי אחר. דהא שמעינן ליה לרבי שמעון דאמר לייתי ולתני. *דתניא, אמר ר"ש: למחרת מביא אשמו ולוגו עמו, ומעמידו בשער נקנור, ומתנה עליו ואומר "אם מצורע הוא — הרי אשמו ולוגו עמו. ואם לאו — אשם זה יהא שלמי נדבה". ואותו אשם טעון שחיטתו

**רש"י**

היא תועבה. במחזיר גרושתו כתיב (דברים כד): "כי תועבה היא". השני מה תהא עליו. היאך יטהר לקדשים? שאילו היה מצורע חבירו חי, אע"פ שנתערבו קרבנותיהם — זה יקרב לשם מי שהוא, וזה יקרב לשם מי שהוא. או אם מת האחד, והיו שני הקרבנות בפנינו — היו הקרבנות מתים, וזה מקריב קרבן אחר. אבל עכשיו אינו יכול להקריב את זה — שמא של מת הוא, והוי חטאת שמתו בעליה. וקרבן אחר נמי אינו יכול להביא — שמא אותו שקרב היה שלו, ונפטר, ונמצא מביא חולין לעזרה. ואינו יכול להתנות בנדבה — שאין חטאת באה נדבה. ואפי' לרבי שמעון דאמר לקמן: אשם קרב מספק על תנאי: "אם הוא חייב אשם, הרי זה לאשם. ואם לאו, הרי זה שלמי נדבה" — הני מילי אשם, שמתן דמו דומה לשלמים. אבל חטאת, שאין מתן דמה דומה לשלמים, אינו יכול להתנות ולומר: "אם קרבה חטאתי, הרי חטאת זו שלמי נדבה", דמתן דמה היכי ליעביד? ליעביד ארבעה מתנות ולמעלה מחוט הסיקרא — שמא שלמי נדבה נינהו, ואם שתי מתנות ולמטה מחוט הסיקרא — שמא חטאת הוא. והוי ליה עני. וראוי להביא בדלות. וחטאת העוף באה בספק, ואין שם משום מביא חולין בעזרה. והא איכא אשם. ששוה בעשיר ובעני, והיאך הוא מביא אשם מספק דלמא מייתי חולין בעזרה? אמר שמואל. הך תקנתא דרבי יהושע, כשהביא את אשמו קודם מיתת חבירו. אבל אם לא קרב — אין לו תקנה. אי כרבי יהודה. דאמר: אין אשם בא על תנאי, ומשום הכי ליכא תקנתא באשם. הא אמר אשם קבע. ואם קרב את אשמו, לית ליה תקנתא בחטאת. דאשם שהביא בעשירות קבע את שאר קרבנותיו בעשירות, ואין יכול להביא את חטאתו עני. מצורע שהביא. אחד מקרבנותיו. והעשיר. עד שלא הספיק להביא את כולו, או עשיר והעני. הכל הולך אחר חטאת. אם הביא חטאת בדלות — מקריב נמי עולתו בדלות, ואם בעשירות — מקריב נמי עולה בעשירות. אחר אשם. אם כשהקריב אשמו היה עשיר — יקריב את האחרים בעשירות. אחר צפורים. שתי צפרים חיות טהורות, שהיה כהן מטהר בהם את המצורע שבעה ימים קודם תגלחתו, ולאו קרבן הן, ושוות בעשיר ובעני. ואם באותה שעה היה עשיר — מביא כל קרבנותיו בעשירות. וטעמא דכולהו מפרש בכריתות: "אשר לא תשיג ידו בטהרתו" — רבי שמעון סבר: "טהרתו" — דבר המכפרו. ורבי יהודה סבר: דבר המכשירו, והיינו אשם שממנו נותן על הבהונות. ורבי אליעזר סבר: דבר הגורם לו טהרה, ומאי נינהו? צפורין. ואי כרבי שמעון. דאמר: אשם לא קבע, והלכך אפילו הקריב את אשמו כשהוא עשיר, יכול להביא חטאת עני — למה ליה לשמואל לאוקמי כשקרב אשמו כשהוא עשיר, יכול להביא חטאת עני. אפילו לא קרב נמי איכא תקנתא באשם, לאתויי אשם מביתו ולומר: אם קרבן שקרב של חבירי — הרי זה שלי, ואם שלי היה — הרי זה לשלמים. למחרת. בספק מצורע קאי, וקאמר: למחר של טבילתו, שהוא יום הבאת קרבנותיו, מביא את אשמו כו'.

**תוספות**

היא תועבה ואין בניה תועבין. וא"ת: מה צריך, והא פרכינן אקל וחומר דאלמנה לכהן גדול "מה לאלמנה לכהן גדול, שכן היא עצמה מתחללת"? וליכא למימר, דלאו פירכא גמורה היא — דהא על ידי הך פירכא הדר ביה בפ' "החולץ" (יבמות דף מד.) מהא דקאמר "הכל מודים במחזיר גרושתו שהולד פגום, מקל וחומר דאלמנה לכהן גדול", ואומר "אלא אי איתמר הכי איתמר"! ועוד קשה: דבפ"ק דיבמות (דף יד:) קאמר רבי יוחנן בן נורי: כילד נעשה כדברי ב"ה שמתירין את הצרות לשוק בלא חליצה ויבום, הולד פגום לדברי ב"ש ומנלן דהוי פגום? אי מקל וחומר דאלמנה לכהן גדול — איכא למיפרך כי הכא! וי"ל: אהך קושיא בתרייתא: דנפקא לן הולד פגום בצרות לשוק מ"היא תועבה ואין בניה תועבין" מכלל דבעלמא, אפילו בניה תועבין. מיהו בשמעתא ליכא למימר דמשום הכי נקט האי קרא אע"ג דלא צריך, משום דאשמועינן דאיצטריך ליה ר' יהושע למדרש בעלמא, כגון ביבמה לשוק דבניה תועבין. דבשמעתין דיבמות אית ליה לר' יהושע דהולד של צרות כשר לשוק, דקאמר: בני צרות אני מעיד לכם וי"ל: אי לאו מיעוט דהיא הוה מפקינן דולד פגום משום דטומאה כתיב בה כעריות. ואפי' למ"ד דלא קאי טומאה אלא אסוטה, דכיון דאיעקר איעקר מ"מ לשון "תועבה" הוה אמינא דקאי נמי אבנים, אי לאו "היא". א"נ: הא דמייתי הכא קרא ד"היא תועבה" — היינו משום דלא נילף מאלמנה לכהן גדול ומעבד ונכרי דתתחלל כר' יהודה דבפ' בתרא דקדושין (דף עח.). **ומת** אחד מהן. תימה: למאי דס"ד דלא קרב אשמו, וכדבעי רב ששת לאוקומי, בלא מת נמי היינו יכולין לשאול היאך יקרב השני, הלא אינם יודעין מי נפטר כבר מקרבן ולמי יעשו מתן בהונות מדם האשם שלא קרב? וי"ל: יכולין לעשות לשניהם, ואי משום סמיכה — יקריבו בלא סמיכה, משום תקוני גברא. **ומביא** חטאת העוף הבא על הספק. וקשה: דבגיטין פרק "כל הגט" (דף כח:) גבי "השולח חטאתו ממדינת הים", ואוקמיה רב פפא בחטאת העוף, היכי קאמר בתר הכי "ולריכי כו' אבל חטאת העוף, מספקא לא לייתי חולין לעזרה", והא אמרינן בשמעתין דבא על הספק! וי"ל: דהכא כשהמצורע לפנינו — משום תקוני גברא מקריבין אותו אספקא, הואיל ואינו יכול לתקן בענין אחר. אבל התם שהבעלים במדינת הים, אם היה מת — אין לו דין חטאת להיות קרב, ואז לא יקריבוהו מספק. **דתנן** מצורע שהביא קרבן עני וכו'. "דתנן" גרסי' ואע"ג דלדברי ר' אליעזר אינן שנויין במשנה — לא חש להאריך ולומר "תניא" על דבריו, הואיל ולא היה צריך לדבריו כ"כ, אלא לדברי ר"ש ור"י אבל בערכין פרק "השג יד" (דף יז:) קאמר: תניא ר' אליעזר בן יעקב אומר כו', ושלשתן מקרא אחד דרשו. **למחרת** מביא אשמו ולוגו עמו. פירש"י: בספק מצורע איירי. (א) למחרת טבילתו, שהוא יום הבאת קרבנותיו. והך ברייתא מייתי לה בזבחים פ' "התערובת" (דף עו.) ושם פי' רש"י "למחרת" — ביום שמיני לצרעתו, וה"נ מייתי לה במנחות פרק בתרא (דף קה.) ופי' רש"י שם: "למחרת" — ביום ס"א והכל אחד הוא, שיום ס"א במקום שמיני לצרעתו, אלא שהוצרך להתאחר ס' יום משום דשמא נזיר טמא הוא, ואז תגלחת שניה שלו. והכי מתניא בתוספתא דנזיר: "ספק נזיר טמא ספק נזיר טהור, אבל ודאי נזיר היה. ספק מצורע טמא ספק מצורע טהור, אבל ודאי מצורע היה" — פירוש: הוא יודע שהיה נזיר, אבל אינו יודע אם נטמא למת או לאו. וכן יודע הוא שמצורע היה, אבל אינו יודע אם (ב) נטמא בצרעתו אי לאו. "אוכל בקדשים לאחר ס"א יום, ושותה יין ומטמא למתים לאחר מאה וכ' יום. כילד? אומרים לו: נזיר טמא אתה, וצריך אתה לעשות כל דין נזיר טמא, ואחר תתחיל נזירות טהרה. הזה ושנה וגלח, והביא קרבן. מנה ז' והזה ושנה ומבקש לגלח, אומר לו: טהור אתה, ואין טהור מגלח פחות מל' יום" — פירוש: שמא נזיר טהור אתה. "לא ומנה כ"ג" — פירוש: כדי "להשלים ל'": "מנה ל' ובקש לגלח, אומרים לו: נזיר טהור אתה, ואי אתה מגלח אלא על הדמים" — פירוש: עד שיזרק הדם עליו מאחד מקרבנותיו, שהוא מביא ג' בהמות, חטאת עולה ושלמים, ואין מעכב אותו מלגלח אלא אחד מהן. "כילד הוא עושה? מביא עולת בהמה ומתנה: אם טהור הוא — זו חובה, ואם לאו — נדבה. וכשיזורק דמה יכול לגלח" — פירוש: לכך יתנה מן העולה ולא מן החטאת — שאין חטאת בהמה באה על הספק. וכן לא על השלמים — ששלמי נזיר טעונים תנופה, וזהו ספק מצורע, ואינו יכול להניף. ועוד: שהן טעונין לחם וזרוע בשלה, ואין שלמים כאלו באין נדבה. הילכך, אין יכול להתנות שיהיה מוכשר לגלח אלא בזריקת דמי העולה. "כילד יעשה להחמיר עליו? מביא פיילי חרס חדשה, ונותן לתוכה רביעית מים חיים, ומביא צפור דרור" — פירוש: כדרך כל המצורעים בתגלחת הראשונה, וחטאת העוף כדין טמא — פירוש: דשמא נזיר טמא הוא, ותגלחת זו של טומאה היא. ואין מתחיל נזירות טהרה עד שיביא חטאת טומאה — שחטאתו מעכבתו, אבל אשמו אינו מעכבו. וישחט אותו

עד

**מסורת הש"ס**

[קדושין עז.] יבמות יח: מד:

נ"א האמר

נגעים פי"ד מי"א ערכין יז: כריתות ט:

[נ"ל רבי]

נזיר ס. זבחים עו. מנחות קה.

**עין משפט נר מצוה**

נח א מיי' פט"ו מהל' איסורי ביאה הל"ב:
נט ב מיי' פ"ה מהל' מחוסרי כפרה הל"י:
ס ג מיי' שם הל"ט ועי' בכ"מ:

נגעים פי"ד מי"ג

**הגהות הב"ח**

(א) תוס' ד"ה למחרת וכו' בספק מצורע איירי וקאמר למחרת טבילתו שהוא יום הבאת קרבנותיו מביא את אשמו כו' והך ברייתא: (ב) בא"ד אינו יודע אם נטהר מצרעתו אי לאו:

**תוספי הרא"ש**

א"ל היא תועבה ואין בניה תועבין. תימה למה לי קרא כיון דק"ו דאלמנה פריכא הוא ופירכא גמורה היא דבפ' החולץ חזר בו רב יוסף מדבריו מתוך פירכא זו גבי הכל מודים במחזיר גרושתו דהולד פגום ור' יהושע גופיה חשיב ליה פירכא דמכשר בני צרות דב"ה לב"ש דקאמר התם מעידני בכם. וי"ל דאיצטריך למימר היא תועבה ואין בניה תועבין דלא תימא בניה תועבין משום דכתיב ביה טומאה כעריות כדאמרינן בפ"ק דיבמות ואפי' רבנן דר' יוסי בן כפר דדרשינן לרבות סוטה הנסתרה הא אמרינן אין מקרא יוצא מידי פשוטו ואפי' למ"ד כיון דאיעקר איעקר מ"מ שפיר איצטריך היא תועבה דלא תימא דאמחזיר גרושתו נמי קאי: **השני** מה תהא עליו. שאילו היה חי מצורע חבירו זה יקרב לשם מי שהוא וזה יקרב לשם מי שהוא: ואפי' לא קרב אשמו כדבעי רב ששת לאוקומי ויכול לעשות מכל אחד ואחד מתן בהונות לשניהם ואי משום סמיכה יקריבוהו בלא סמיכה משום תקוני גברא: **דתנן** מצורע שהביא קרבן עני והעשי' כו'. ומשנה היא בפרק בתרא דמסכת נגעים אבל מילתא דר' אליעזר ב"י לא מיתניא התם ובריי‍תא היא מילתיה דר' אליעזר ב"י ובמס' ערכין פרק השג יד בתר דמייתי מתניתין דפליגי בה ר' שמעון ור' יהודה קאמר ותניא ר' אליעזר ב"י אומר הכל הולך אחר הצפורים ופי' התם דשלשתם מקרא אחד דרשו ואע"פ שלא היה צריך כן אלא מילתיה דר' יהודה ור' שמעון ניחא ליה להביא כולה פלוגתא דהדך מילתא: **ואם** לאו אשם זה יהא שלמי נדבה. ותימה והיכי מצי מתנה בשלמים והלא צריך לקבל דמו של זה האשם כדאמרינן בריש איזהו מקומן דשני כהנים מקבלין את דמו אחד ביד ואחד בכלי ואם שלמי' קא עבר מדאוריי' כדאמרינן בפ"ב דזבחים שצריך לקבל כל דמו של זבח. וי"ל דתקוני גברא שאני כדאיתא בפ' התערובות:

עד תגלחת שניה שיעשה, כשיטהר בודאי מן הצרעת. או שמא לא יביא אשמו כלל, כיון שאינו אלא ספק טמא, וא"צ לו להביא להכשירו שום דבר, ומה שמביא חטאתו ביום תגלחתו – היינו כר"ע, דאמר במסכת נזיר שאם גלח בשמיני – מביא קרבנותיו בו ביום. והכא זהו כמו גילוח בשמיני, שהא אותו מפני נזירות טהרה. "ומתנה על חטאתו: אם טמא אני – חטאתי זו חובתי לנזירות טומאה, ועולה נדבה" – פירוש: עולת בהמה שהיא ספק משום נזירות טומאה. "ואם טהור אני – עולה זו חובתי, וחטאת מספק. ומגלח ראשו וזקנו וגבות עיניו, כדרך שהמצורעים מגלחים". ואחר גילוח זה כתוב בתוספתא (פ"ו) מביא עולת בהמה כו'. ונראה שחסר כאן "וסופר שלשים יום" – פירוש: לימי נזירות טהרה, וספק נזירות טהרה הוא מונה. ואינו יכול לגלח לצרעתו תגלחת שניה, הראויה להיות לסוף ח' ימים של ראשונה, עד שיזרוק עליו מן הדמים, ושמא נזיר טהור הוא, וטוב לו להביא עולה מספק מחטאת ושלמים, כדפירשתי לעיל. לפיכך ישהא החטאת והשלמים עד סוף נזירות טהרה, שיהא אחר טהרת צרעתו בודאי. "ומתנה על העולה שהוא מביא עכשיו, ואומר: אם טמא אני" – פירוש: אם טמא הייתי בתגלחת ראשונה, "העולה ראשונה היא נדבה, וחטאת העוף חובה, וזו תהא חובה. ואם טהור אני – עולה ראשונה היא חובה, וזו נדבה" – כי תגלחת זו של עכשיו אינה כלום, שאינה צריכה לא לנזירות ולא לצרעת. כי אם הראשונה היתה של נזירות טהרה, א"כ לא היה מצורע, שימי צרעתו אינן עולין לימי נזירות, כדאמרינן בפרק "מי שאמר הריני נזיר מגלח" (נזיר יז.) וכן בפ' "ב' נזירים" (שם דף ס:) "וחטאת העוף שהבאתי אז, ספק. ומגלח ראשו וזקנו וגבות עיניו, כדרך שהמצורעים מגלחים" – וזו היא תגלחת שניה של מצורע, הראויה להיות בסוף ז' ימי ספירות מתגלחת ראשונה, אלא שאינו יכול לעשות עד עכשיו מפני ספק נזירות שעליו, שגילוח ספק מצורע אינו דוחה איסור גילוח נזיר, כדפירשנו. "רבי שמעון אומר: למחר מביא אשמו" כו', כדין מצורע בשמיני שלו, והוא יום ס"א "ומתנה עליו כו', ואוכל בקדשים מיד" – היינו, אוכל בקדשים אחר ששים יום דקתני לעיל, ומוכח בהדיא שיום הס"א בשמיני שלו, ומוכח נמי דלמחרת זהו למחרת של ס"א והוא במקום יום שמיני לתגלחתו, כדפרישית.

תורה אור

שְׁחִיטָתוֹ בַּצָּפוֹן, וְטָעוּן מַתְּנַת בְּהוֹנוֹת, וּסְמִיכָה, וּנְסָכִים, וּתְנוּפָה, וְחָזֶה וְשׁוֹק, וְנֶאֱכָל לְזִכְרֵי כְהוּנָּה לְיוֹם וְלַיְלָה. וְלֹא הוֹדוּ לוֹ חֲכָמִים לר' שִׁמְעוֹן, מִפְּנֵי *שֶׁמֵּבִיא קָדָשִׁים לְבֵית הַפְּסוּל! שְׁמוּאֵל סָבַר לָהּ כְּרַבִּי שִׁמְעוֹן בַּחֲדָא, וּפָלֵיג עֲלֵיהּ בַּחֲדָא.§ שְׁלֹשָׁה דִּבְרֵי אַגָּדָה: כָּתוּב אֶחָד אוֹמֵר (א) °"כִּי לֹא אֶחְפּוֹץ בְּמוֹת הַמֵּת", וְכָתוּב אֶחָד אוֹמֵר °"כִּי חָפֵץ ה' לַהֲמִיתָם" כָּאן – בְּעוֹשִׂין תְּשׁוּבָה, כָּאן – בְּשֶׁאֵין עוֹשִׂין תְּשׁוּבָה. כָּתוּב אֶחָד אוֹמֵר °*"כִּי... *לֹא יִשָּׂא פָנִים וְלֹא יִקַּח שֹׁחַד", וְכָתוּב אֶחָד אוֹמֵר °"יִשָּׂא ה' פָּנָיו אֵלֶיךָ"! כָּאן – קוֹדֶם גְּזַר דִּין, כָּאן – לְאַחַר גְּזַר דִּין. כָּתוּב אֶחָד אוֹמֵר °"כִּי בָחַר ה' בְּצִיּוֹן", וְכָתוּב אֶחָד אוֹמֵר °"כִּי עַל אַפִּי וְעַל חֲמָתִי *הָיְתָה הָעִיר הַזֹּאת לְמִן הַיּוֹם אֲשֶׁר בָּנוּ אוֹתָהּ עַד הַיּוֹם הַזֶּה"! כָּאן – קוֹדֶם שֶׁנָּשָׂא שְׁלֹמֹה אֶת בַּת פַּרְעֹה, כָּאן – לְאַחַר שֶׁנָּשָׂא שְׁלֹמֹה אֶת בַּת פַּרְעֹה.§ שְׁלֹשָׁה דִּבְרֵי בּוּרוּת: אִשְׁתּוֹ שֶׁל לוֹט מַהוּ שֶׁתְּטַמֵּא? אָמַר לָהֶם: מֵת מְטַמֵּא, וְאֵין נְצִיב מֶלַח מְטַמֵּא. בֶּן שׁוּנַמִּית מַהוּ שֶׁיְּטַמֵּא? אָמַר לָהֶן: מֵת מְטַמֵּא, וְאֵין חַי מְטַמֵּא. מֵתִים לֶעָתִיד לָבֹא, צְרִיכִין הַזָּאָה שְׁלִישִׁי וּשְׁבִיעִי, אוֹ אֵין צְרִיכִין? אָמַר לָהֶן: לִכְשֶׁיָּחְיוּ, נְחַכֵּם לָהֶן. אִיכָּא דְּאָמְרִי: לִכְשֶׁיָּבֹא מֹשֶׁה רַבֵּינוּ עִמָּהֶם.§ שְׁלֹשָׁה דִּבְרֵי דֶּרֶךְ אֶרֶץ: מַה יַּעֲשֶׂה אָדָם וְיֶחְכַּם? אָמַר לָהֶן: יַרְבֶּה בִּישִׁיבָה, וִימַעֵט בִּסְחוֹרָה. אָמְרוּ: הַרְבֵּה עָשׂוּ כֵן, וְלֹא הוֹעִיל לָהֶם! אֶלָּא: יְבַקְשׁוּ רַחֲמִים מִמִּי שֶׁהַחָכְמָה שֶׁלּוֹ, שֶׁנֶּאֱמַר °"כִּי ה' יִתֵּן חָכְמָה מִפִּיו דַּעַת וּתְבוּנָה". תָּנֵי ר' חִיָּיא: מָשָׁל לְמֶלֶךְ בָּשָׂר וָדָם שֶׁעָשָׂה סְעוּדָה לַעֲבָדָיו, וּמְשַׁגֵּר לְאוֹהֲבָיו מִמַּה שֶּׁלְּפָנָיו. מַאי קמ"ל? דְּהָא בְּלָא הָא, לָא סַגְיָא. מַה יַּעֲשֶׂה אָדָם וְיִתְעַשֵּׁר? אָמַר לָהֶן: [א] יַרְבֶּה בִּסְחוֹרָה, וְיִשָּׂא וְיִתֵּן בֶּאֱמוּנָה. אָמְרוּ לוֹ: הַרְבֵּה עָשׂוּ כֵן וְלֹא הוֹעִילוּ! אֶלָּא: יְבַקֵּשׁ רַחֲמִים מִמִּי שֶׁהָעוֹשֶׁר שֶׁלּוֹ. שֶׁנֶּאֱמַר °"לִי הַכֶּסֶף וְלִי הַזָּהָב". מַאי קמ"ל? דְּהָא בְּלָא הָא לָא סַגִּי, מַה יַּעֲשֶׂה אָדָם וְיִהְיוּ לוֹ בָּנִים זְכָרִים? אָמַר לָהֶם: יִשָּׂא אִשָּׁה הַהוֹגֶנֶת לוֹ, וְיִקַדֵּשׁ

שְׁחִיטָתוֹ בַּצָּפוֹן וּמַתַּן בְּהוֹנוֹת וּלְיוֹם וְלַיְלָה. כְּחוֹמֶר אָשָׁם, וּתְנוּפָה וּסְמִיכָה וְחָזֶה וְשׁוֹק – כְּחוֹמֶר שְׁלָמִים, דִּבְאָשָׁם לֵיכָּא סְמִיכָה, כִּדְאָמְרִינַן בִּמְנָחוֹת בְּפֶ' "שְׁתֵּי מִדּוֹת". לְבֵית הַפְּסוּל. דִּלְמָא לָא מְצוֹרָע הוּא, וַהֲוֵי שְׁלָמִים, וּמְמַעֵט זְמַן אֲכִילָתָן – שֶׁשּׂוֹרֵף אֶת הַנּוֹתָר לְיוֹם וְלַיְלָה, וְהָיָה לוֹ לְאוֹכְלוֹ בִּשְׁנֵי יָמִים. כְּוָותֵיהּ בַּחֲדָא. דְּאָשָׁם לָא קָבַע. וּפָלֵיג עֲלֵיהּ בַּחֲדָא. שֶׁאֵין אָשָׁם בָּא עַל תְּנַאי. בֶּן הַשּׁוּנַמִּית. שֶׁהֶחֱיָה אֱלִישָׁע, מַהוּ שֶׁיְּטַמֵּא לְאַחַר שֶׁהֶחֱיָהוּ, מִי חָשׁוּב כַּמֵּת? נְחַכֵּם לָהֶן. נִתְיַישֵּׁב בַּדָּבָר. לְאוֹהֲבָיו מְשַׁגֵּר מִמַּה שֶּׁלְּפָנָיו. כָּךְ חָכְמָה, שֶׁהִיא לְאוֹהֲבָיו שֶׁל מָקוֹם, נְתָנָהּ לָהֶם מִפִּיו, וְלֹא מֵאוֹצָר אַחֵר. מַאי קמ"ל. לָמָּה לֵיהּ לְמֵימַר לְהוּ "יַרְבֶּה בִּישִׁיבָה", הוֹאִיל וּבְרַחֲמִים הַדָּבָר תָּלוּי?

פי' בקונטרס: דבאשם ליכא סמיכה, כדאמרינן במנחות פרק "שתי מדות" (דף צג.) ולא עיין בה, דתנן: *כל קרבנות היחיד טעונין סמיכה, חוץ מבכור ומעשר ופסח. *ואילו אשם, לא מפיק. ובפרק "כל הפסולין" (זבחים דף לג.) פליגי אי סמיכת אשם מצורע דאורייתא או לא, ומיהו לכ"ע סמיכה בעי. ובפ"ב דנגעים (מ"ח) תנן: בא לו [אצל] אשם, סומך ב' ידיו עליו. והא דקאמר הכא "ואותו אשם טעון סמיכה" – היינו, באקופי ידא, למ"ד סמיכת אשם מצורע לאו דאורייתא. ומשום דסמיכתו חלוקה משאר אשמות, קאמר הכי. וכן נסכים נמי לא קתני משום ספקא דשלמים, דהא תנן (מנחות דף צ.) דכל חטאת ואשם אין טעונין נסכים, אלא שחטאתו ואשמו של מצורע טעונים נסכים, אלא משום דחלוקה משאר אשמות קא חשיב לכל הנהו מילי דחלוק מינייהו. **כתוב** אחד אומר ישא ה' פניו אליך. א] – לפי הפשט לא משמע שהקב"ה נושא את פניהם, דלא כתיב "ישא ה' פניך", ומשמע שיפנה אליך *להשים לך שלום. ובספרי נמי דריש: שיסיר הקב"ה פנים של זעם. מיהו התלמוד חשיב ליה כאילו כתיב "פניך". וטפי ה"ל להתלמוד לאקשויי מ"הנה נשאתי פניך גם לדבר הזה" דלוט (בראשית יט) ומן "וישא ה' פני איוב" (איוב מב)*. **כאן** קודם גזר דין וכו' – תימה: דבפרק "מי שמתו" (ברכות דף כ.) קאמר: אמרו מלאכי השרת לפני הקב"ה, רבש"ע, כתוב בתורתך "אשר לא ישא פנים", מפני מה אתה נושא פנים לישראל? אמר להם: לא אשא פנים לישראל?! אני אמרתי "ואכלת ושבעת", והם מדקדקים עד כזית ועד כביצה. משמע שמחלק בין גוים לישראל, ואמאי לא משני כי הכא, או הכא כהתם? ויש לומר: דלעולם שינויא דהכא עיקר, וקרא *דאמר "לא ישא פנים" מיירי בין בישראל בין בגוים. בגוים – אפילו קודם גזר דין, שזהו קו המשפט, ולישראל – לאחר גזר דין. אבל הוא נכנס להם לישראל לפנים משורת הדין, ונושא להם פנים קודם גזר דין כדמשמע הכא מקרא ד"ישא ה' פניו אליך". ומלאכי השרת אמרו לפני הקדוש ברוך הוא: למה נכנסת לישראל לפנים משורת הדין יותר מלגוים, לישא להם פנים קודם גזר דין? והשיב: לא אשא להם פנים?! וכו'. ***כאן** בעושה תשובה וכו'. בספרי משני אהך קושיא: כאן קודם גזר דין, כו'. ותימה: דבר"ה פ"ק (דף יז:) אמר: גדולה תשובה שמקרעת גזר דינו של אדם, שנאמר "ושב ורפא לו". מיתיבי: השב בינתיים – מוחלין לו, לא שב בינתיים" פירוש: קודם גזר דין, "אפילו הביא כל אילי נביות – אין מוחלין לו"! ומשני: "לא קשיא, הא – ביחיד, הא – בצבור". אלמא, ביחיד אין תשובה מקרעת גזר דין של אדם, ובשמעתין משמע דמועלת תשובה אפי' ביחיד, דומיא דבני עלי, ואפי' לאחר גזר דין. דאילו קודם גזר דין, פשיטא דהקב"ה מקבל תשובה. ועוד: דלהמיתם משמע לאחר גזר דין! וי"ל: דסוגיא דשמעתין, כרבי יצחק, דאמר: *יפה צעקה, (ג) בין קודם גזר דין בין לאחר גזר דין. **ואין** נציב מלח מטמא. משמע: אבל אי לא הוה נציב מלח – מטמא, אפילו לרבי שמעון נמי איכא למימר דמטמא אפילו באהל. וכן נמי ליון מערתא דרבי בנאה, בפרק "חזקת הבתים" (ב"ב דף נח.) אתי נמי כר"ש, דאחר מתן תורה דאיקרו ישראל "אדם", איכא לפלוגי. אבל קודם מתן תורה, אין חילוק. והרב רבי משה מפונטויז"א פירש: דבנזיר פרק "כהן גדול" (דף נד.) מרבי מ"או בקבר" קברי מתים שלפני הדבור. אלמא, קודם מתן תורה מטמא, אע"ג דלא איקרו "אדם"! ואי אפשר לומר כך, דהך סוגיא ד"כהן גדול" לא אתיא אלא כרבי שמעון, דממעט להו מ"אדם" ועוד: "או בקבר" גבי מגע כתיב, ואחר מתן תורה מטמאין קברי גוים במגע, ולא אימעוט לרבי שמעון אלא מאהל. והכי מסיק בפרק "הבא על יבמתו" (יבמות דף סא.) ונראה לפרש: ד"לפני הדבור" – היינו, קודם שנאמר פרשת אהל. דהיינו, קודם שהוקם המשכן. כדאיתא בגיטין פ' "הניזקין" (דף ס.) שמונה פרשיות נאמרו ביום הקמת המשכן, וחשיב פרשת פרה ופרשת טמאין. דס"ד "כי ימות באהל" מכאן ולהבא כתיב, ולהכי איצטריך "או בקבר", וקאי ריבויא א"כי ימות", ולא א"אדם" וכי האי גוונא איכא בפ' בתרא דהוריות (דף י.) "כי יהיה" – פרט שלפני הדבור, דגבי זיבה*). **מתים** לעתיד לבא צריכים הזאה. ואם תאמר: אמאי לא בעי הך בעיא על בן השונמית, דאיירי ביה? וי"ל: שמא משום דכתיב קרא לעתיד לבא (יחזקאל לו) "וזרקתי עליכם מים טהורים", ומספקא ליה אי הך זריקה הויא שלישי ושביעי, אי לא. אבל בן השונמית, פשיטא ליה דלא בעי הזאה. והאנן

**סמיכה** ונסכים. פרש"י סמיכה משום שלמים דבאשם ליכא סמיכה כדאמרינן בפ' שתי מדות. וליתא דאדרבה מוכח התם דטעון סמיכה דתנן התם כל קרבנות היחיד טעונין סמיכה חוץ מבכור מעשר ופסח ואלו אשם לא קא חשיב ועוד בפרק כל הפסולין איכא למ"ד סמיכות אשם מצורע לאו דאורייתא משום דבעינן תכף לסמיכה שחיטה מדאורייתא ומצורע אינו יכול ליכנס לעזרה ואיכא מ"ד סמיכות אשם דאורייתא ותכף לסמיכה שחיטה לאו דאורייתא אלמא דכ"ע מיהא בעי סמיכה ובהדיא תנן הכי במסכת נגעים בא לו אצל אשם וסמך שתי ידיו עליו. אלא י"ל דתנא סמיכה משום דסמיכה זו חלוקה משאר סמיכות שהרי באקפויי ידא. למ"ד סמיכה אשם מצורע לאו דאורייתא דלא תהוי עבודה בקדשים וה"ק ואותו אשם טעון סמיכת אשם דהיינו באקפויי ידא. ונסכים דקתני לאו משום דספיקא דשלמים דהא תנן בפ' ב' מדות דכל חטאת ואשם אין טעון נסכים. אלא שחטאתו ואשמו של מצורע טעונין נסכים. אלא מפני שאשם זה חלוק משאר אשמות דעלמא שטעון תנופת חזה ושוק כשלמים מזכיר כן כל הדברים שהוא חלוק מדין שאר אשמות אע"פ שבנסכים אינו חלוק משאר אשם מצורע. ומיהו למ"ד סמיכת אשם [מצורע] דאורייתא דהשתא הויא סמיכה גמורה כדי נסבה אלא אגב רידטא דכולי תלמודא פריך מה לשלמים שכן טעונין סמיכה נסכים ותנופה חזה ושוק נקטיה נמי הכא ולמ"ד סמיכת אשם [מצורע] לאו דאורייתא הא דתקינו ביה רבנן סמיכה באקפויי ידא יותר מבשאר קדשים כגון מעשר בכור ופסח יש ליתן טעם משום דשאר אשמות סמיכתן דאורייתא. והא דאין נמנעין כאן מלהביא קרבן זה משום דאם שלמים הוא טעון סמיכה גמורה והך סמיכה באקפויי ידא למ"ד לאו דאורייתא אין יוצא בה ידי סמיכה גם היא שלמים. וכה"ג אשכחן בפרק האשה גבי חמשה שנתערבו עורות פסחיהם ונמצא יבלת באחד מהם שפטורין מלעשות פסח שני ולא מתנה בשלמים משום דשלמים טעונין סמיכה ופסח אין טעון סמיכה. יש ליתן טעם משום דתקיני גברא כדפ"ל: **ונאכל** ליום ולילה. ותימה ולתנייה בתודה דאם אינו אשם מצורע שהיא תודת נדבה. והכי שפיר טפי דלא ממעט כל כך באכילת קדשים דנאכלין ליום ולילה. י"ל דתודה לא מצי מתני משום לחם דלא משכח ליה תקנה לבוא על תנאי וכדאמרי' בפ' התודה: **כתוב** אחד אומר ישא ה' פניו אליך. כ"ש היה תמיהא על קשיא זו דלא כתיב ישא פניך אלא ישא פניו דמשמע יפנה אליך וישם לך שלום. א"נ כדדריש בספרי ישא פניו אליך ויסיר כעסו ממך כלומר פנים של זעם יסיר ממך. ויותר היה ראוי להקשות מוישא ה' את פני איוב או מהנה לדבר הזה נשאתי פניך דלוט. ובספרי מייתי ליה לקרא דלוט ובפ' מי שמתו אמרינן שאמרו מלאכי השרת לפני הקב"ה כתוב בתורה לא ישא פנים ולא יקח שוחד ואתה נושא פנים לישראל שנאמר ישא ה' פניו א"ל ולא אשא פנים לישראל שאני אמרתי ואכלת ושבעת וברכת והם החמירו על עצמן עד כזית עד כביצה. והך נשיאות כפים דהתם הוי קודם גמר דין וא"ה אמרו מלאכי השרת שלא היה לו לישא פנים לישראל אפי' קודם גמר דין כמו שאינו נושא [פנים] לאומות: **כאן** קודם תשובה כו'. בספרי מתרץ הך קושיא כההיא דלעיל כאן קודם גזר דין כו' ותימה מדמוקי הכא כי לא אחפוץ במות המת אחר תשובה ש"מ דמועלת תשובה אפי' ליחיד דומיא דבני עלי. וקשה דבפ"ק דר"ה מוקמינן הא דא"ר יוחנן גדולה תשובה שקורעת גזר דינו של אדם שנאמר ושב ורפא לו בצבור אבל לא ביחיד כו'. וי"ל דשמעתין דהכא כר' יצחק דאמר התם יפה צעקה לאדם בין קודם גזר דין בין לאחר גזר דין ואפי' ביחיד מיירי: **ואין** נציב מלח מטמא. ואפי' לר' שמעון דאמר קברי עובדי כוכבים אין מטמאין ואיכא למ"ד בפ' הבא על יבמתו דאפי' במגע לא מטמא היינו דוקא בעובדי כוכבים שלאחר מתן תורה אבל קודם לכן אין חילוק בין ישראלים לעובדי כוכבים: **מתים** לעתיד לבא צריכין הזאה. מה שלא שאלו אם מטמאין. משום דכבר השיב להם דאין החי מטמא ומה שלא שאלו בבן השונמית אם צריך הזאה י"ל דדוקא במתים לעתיד שאלו משום דכתיב בקרא וזרקתי עליכם מים טהורים:

[פסחים יג: ביצה יט: זבחים עה: בכורות ס:]

[ג"ל אשר]

יחזקאל יח | שמואל א ב | דברים י | במדבר ו | תהלים קלב | ירמיהו לב | משלי ב | חגי ב

## הגהות הגר"א

[א] גמ' ירבה בסחורה נמחק:

[ברכות כ: ר"ה יז: וע"ש]

[נ"ל היתה לי העיר]

## הגהות מהר"ב רנשבורג

א] תוס' ד"ה כתוב א' אומר ישא ה' פניו אליך. נ"ב עי' מהרא"ח בדרושיו פ' ויקהל דף מח ע"ד וכס' רצוף אהבה בחידושי נדה:

[מנחות צג.]

[ע' תוס' קדושין נה: ד"ה ולדמאי אשם הוא וכו' ואשם אין טעון סמיכה כו' ע"ש]

להשים רש"ל

ע' תוס' ר"ה יז. סוף ד"ה אשר וכו' כתבו ישוב על זה]

נ"ל דאמר

[דיבור זה שייך לעיל קודם ד"ה כתוב]

[ר"ה טז: יח.]

*) [וע' תוס' נזיר נד. ד"ה או תוס' יבמות סא. ד"ה ואין ותוס' ע"ז ג. ד"ה כהנים ותוס' סנהדרין ... ד"ה אלא ותוס' ב"ק לח. ד"ה אלא ותוס' ב"מ ... ד"ה מגיין]

**הגהות הב"ח** (א) גמ' שלשה דברי אגדה כתוב אחד אומר כי לא ישא פנים וכו' לאחר גזר דין כתוב אחד אומר כי לא אחפוץ וכו' תשובה כתוב אחד אומר כי בחר כצ"ל: (ג) תוס' ד"ה כאן בעושה וכו' יפה צעקה לאדם בין:

וִיקַדֵּשׁ עַצְמוֹ בִּשְׁעַת תַּשְׁמִישׁ. אָמְרוּ: הַרְבֵּה עָשׂוּ כֵּן, וְלֹא הוֹעִילוּ. אֶלָּא: יְבַקֵּשׁ רַחֲמִים מִמִּי שֶׁהַבָּנִים שֶׁלּוֹ, שֶׁנֶּאֱמַר: °"הִנֵּה נַחֲלַת ה' בָּנִים שָׂכָר פְּרִי הַבָּטֶן". מַאי קָא מַשְׁמַע לָן – דְּהָא בְּלָא הָא לָא סַגִּי. מַאי "שָׂכָר פְּרִי הַבָּטֶן"? א"ר חָמָא בְּרַבִּי חֲנִינָא: בִּשְׂכַר *שֶׁמַּשְׁהִין עַצְמָן בַּבֶּטֶן כְּדֵי שֶׁתַּזְרִיעַ אִשְׁתּוֹ תְּחִילָּה – נוֹתֵן לוֹ הקב"ה שְׂכַר פְּרִי הַבָּטֶן.§ "בֵּית שַׁמַּאי אוֹמְרִים" [וכו'].§ מַאי טַעֲמַיְיהוּ דְּבֵית שַׁמַּאי? אִי נֵימָא מִשּׁוּם דִּכְתִיב °"וַתִּתְחַלְחַל הַמַּלְכָּה" *וְאָמַר רַב: מְלַמֵּד שֶׁפֵּירְסָה נִדָּה, הָכָא נַמִי – אַגַּב בִּיעֲתוּתָא דְּמַלְאֲכָא דְּמוֹתָא חַזְיָא. וְהָאֲנַן תְּנַן: *שֶׁחֲרָדָה מְסַלֶּקֶת אֶת הַדָּמִים! הָא לָא קַשְׁיָא, פַּחְדָּא – צָמֵית, בִּיעֲתוּתָא – מְרַפְיָא. אֶלָּא, הָא *דִּתְנַן, ב"ש אוֹמְרִים: כָּל הָאֲנָשִׁים מֵתִים זָבִין, וּבֵ"ה אוֹמְרִים: אֵין זָב אֶלָּא מִי שֶׁמֵּת זָב. *אִקְרִי כָּאן "מִבְּשָׂרוֹ" – וְלֹא מֵחֲמַת אוֹנְסוֹ! אֶלָּא, טַעֲמָא דב"ש כִּדְתַנְיָא: *בָּרִאשׁוֹנָה הָיוּ מַטְבִּילִין כֵּלִים עַל גַּבֵּי נִדּוֹת מֵתוֹת, וְהָיוּ נִדּוֹת חַיּוֹת מִתְבַּיְּישׁוֹת. הִתְקִינוּ שֶׁיְּהוּ מַטְבִּילִין עַל גַּבֵּי כָּל הַנָּשִׁים, מִפְּנֵי כְּבוֹדָן שֶׁל נִדּוֹת חַיּוֹת. בָּרִאשׁוֹנָה הָיוּ מַטְבִּילִין עַל גַּבֵּי זָבִין מֵתִין, וְהָיוּ זָבִין חַיִּין מִתְבַּיְּישִׁין. הִתְקִינוּ שֶׁיְּהוּ מַטְבִּילִין עַל גַּבֵּי כָּל הָאֲנָשִׁים, מִפְּנֵי כְּבוֹדָן שֶׁל זָבִין חַיִּים.§

**מתני'** [א]הָאִשָּׁה שֶׁמֵּתָה וְיָצְאָה מִמֶּנָּה רְבִיעִית דָּם – מְטַמְּאָה מִשּׁוּם כֶּתֶם, *וּמְטַמְּאָה בְּאֹהֶל. רַבִּי יְהוּדָה אוֹמֵר: אֵינָהּ מְטַמְּאָה מִשּׁוּם כֶּתֶם, מִפְּנֵי שֶׁנֶּעֱקַר מִשֶּׁמֵּתָה. וּמוֹדֶה רַבִּי יְהוּדָה בְּיוֹשֶׁבֶת עַל מַשְׁבֵּר וּמֵתָה, וְיָצְאָה מִמֶּנָּה רְבִיעִית דָּם שֶׁהִיא מְטַמְּאָה מִשּׁוּם כֶּתֶם. אָמַר רַבִּי יוֹסֵי: לְפִיכָךְ אֵינָהּ מְטַמְּאָה בְּאֹהֶל.§

**גמ'** מִכְּלָל דְּתַנָּא קַמָּא סָבַר: אַף עַל גַּב דְּנֶעֱקַר דָּם מִשֶּׁמֵּתָה – מְטַמְּאָה מִשּׁוּם כֶּתֶם? אָמַר (רַבִּי) זְעִירִי: *[ב]מָקוֹר מְקוֹמוֹ טָמֵא אִיכָּא בֵּינַיְיהוּ.§ "וּמוֹדֶה רַבִּי יְהוּדָה".§ מִכְּלָל *דְּתַנָּא קַמָּא סָבַר בְּאֹהֶל נַמִי מְטַמֵּא? אָמַר רַב יְהוּדָה: דַּם תְּבוּסָה אִיכָּא בֵּינַיְיהוּ. דְּתַנְיָא, *אֵיזֶהוּ דַּם תְּבוּסָה? פֵּירַשׁ ר"א בְּרַבִּי יְהוּדָה: הָרוּג שֶׁיָּצָא מִמֶּנּוּ דָּם בֵּין בְּחַיָּיו בֵּין בְּמוֹתוֹ, סָפֵק בְּחַיָּיו יָצָא סָפֵק בְּמוֹתוֹ יָצָא, סָפֵק בְּחַיָּיו וּבְמוֹתוֹ – זֶהוּ דַּם תְּבוּסָה. וַחֲכָמִים אוֹמְרִים: [ג]ברה"י – סְפֵקוֹ טָמֵא, ברה"ר סְפֵקוֹ טָהוֹר. אֶלָּא אֵיזֶהוּ דַּם תְּבוּסָה – [ד]הָרוּג שֶׁיָּצָא הֵימֶנּוּ רְבִיעִית דָּם בְּחַיָּיו וּבְמוֹתוֹ, וַעֲדַיִין לֹא פָּסַק, סָפֵק רוּבּוֹ בְּחַיָּיו וּמִיעוּטוֹ בְּמוֹתוֹ, סָפֵק מִיעוּטוֹ בְּחַיָּיו וְרוּבּוֹ בְּמוֹתוֹ – זֶהוּ דַּם תְּבוּסָה. רַבִּי יְהוּדָה אוֹמֵר: הָרוּג שֶׁיָּצָא מִמֶּנּוּ רְבִיעִית דָּם, וְהָיָה מוּטָּל בְּמִטָּה וְדָמוֹ מְטַפְטֵף לְגוּמָּא – טָמֵא, מִפְּנֵי שֶׁהַטִּפָּה שֶׁל מִיתָה מְעוֹרֶבֶת בּוֹ. וַחֲכָמִים [ה]מְטַהֲרִין, מִפְּנֵי שֶׁרִאשׁוֹן

---

**רש"י**

וִיקַדֵּשׁ עַצְמוֹ. לְשַׁמֵּשׁ בִּצְנִיעוּת. שֶׁמַּשְׁהִין. לְהוֹצִיא אֶת הַזֶּרַע. פַּחֲדָא צָמֵית. דַּאֲגַת יִרְאָה כִּי הָכָא, מִפְּנֵי פַּחַד כַּרְכּוֹם, וְהִגִּיעַ שְׁעַת וִסְתָּהּ וְלֹא בָּדְקָה – טְהוֹרָה, שֶׁהַחֲרָדָה מְסַלֶּקֶת הַדָּמִים. בִּיעֲתוּתָא. הַבֶּהָלוֹת פִּתְאוֹם, שֶׁאָדָם רוֹאֶה אוֹ שׁוֹמֵעַ – נִבְהָל, מְרַפְיָא. אֶלָּא הָא דִּתְנַן כָּל הָאֲנָשִׁים. הַמֵּתִים מַחְזְקִינַן לְהוּ כְּזָבִין סָמוּךְ לְמִיתָתָן, וְאִי טַעֲמַיְיהוּ דְּב"ש מִשּׁוּם בִּיעֲתוּתָא דְּמַלְאַךְ הַמָּוֶת – זְכָרִים הֵיכִי מְטַמְּאוּ? הָא זָכָר אֵינוֹ מְטַמֵּא בְּאוֹנֶס, דְּקָרֵינַן בֵּיהּ "מִבְּשָׂרוֹ" – וְלֹא מֵחֲמַת אוֹנְסוֹ. אֶלָּא טַעֲמַיְיהוּ דְּב"ש. מִדְּרַבָּנַן, מִשּׁוּם כְּבוֹד זָבִין הִתְקִינוּ שֶׁיְּהוּ מַטְבִּילִין כֵּלִים שֶׁל סָמוּךְ לְמִיתָה, אַף עַל פִּי שֶׁלֹּא נָגְעוּ בָּהֶם לְאַחַר מִיתָה. [כֵּלִים]. אַף הַכֵּלִים שֶׁל קוֹדֶם לְמִיתָה. מִתְבַּיְּישִׁין. שֶׁאֲפִילּוּ בְּמִיתָתָן הֵם מְשׁוּנִּין מִכָּל אָדָם. **מתני'** מְטַמֵּא מִשּׁוּם כֶּתֶם. דְּדַם נִדָּה בְּמַשֶּׁהוּ, דְּאִי מִשּׁוּם טוּמְאַת מֵת – לֹא מְטַמֵּא אֶלָּא בִּרְבִיעִית. וּמְטַמֵּא בְּאֹהֶל. אִם כָּל הָרְבִיעִית יַחַד. שֶׁמְּטַמְּאָה מִשּׁוּם כֶּתֶם. שֶׁנֶּעֱקַר מֵחַיִּים. **גמ'** לְת"ק מָקוֹר מְקוֹמוֹ טָמֵא. הִילְכָּךְ, אַף עַל גַּב שֶׁנֶּעֱקַר לְאַחַר מִיתָה – מְטַמֵּא בְּנִדּוּת, מִפְּנֵי שֶׁהָיָה בַּמָּקוֹר מֵחַיִּים, וְאע"ג דִּלְאַחַר מִיתָה לָאו רוֹאָה הִיא. בְּאֹהֶל נַמִי מְטַמֵּא. בִּתְמִיָּה. הֲרֵי יוֹצֵא מֵחַיִּים? דַּם תְּבוּסָה אִיכָּא בֵּינַיְיהוּ. לְר' יְהוּדָה, הוֹאִיל וְסָפֵק הוּא: סָפֵק אִם נֶעֱקַר כּוּלּוֹ מֵחַיִּים, סָפֵק אִם נֶעֱקַר מִקְצָתוֹ לְאַחַר מִיתָה – הֲוָה דַּם תְּבוּסָה, וּמִדְּרַבָּנַן מְטַמֵּא בְּאֹהֶל. דְּמִדְּאוֹרַיְיתָא – עַד שֶׁתְּהֵא רְבִיעִית לְאַחַר מִיתָה. וְר' יוֹסֵי סָבַר: הַאי לָאו דַּם תְּבוּסָה הוּא, דְּכֵיוָן דְּכוֹרַעַת לֵילֵד הוּא – כּוּלּוֹ נֶעֱקַר מֵחַיִּים. אֵיזֶהוּ דַּם תְּבוּסָה. דְּאָמְרִינַן בְּפִירְקִין דִּלְעֵיל (דף סב:) דְּטוּמְאָתוֹ דְּרַבָּנַן. בְּחַיָּיו וּבְמוֹתוֹ. שֶׁהִתְחִילָה הָרְבִיעִית לָצֵאת מֵחַיִּים: סָפֵק כּוּלּוֹ מֵחַיִּים, סָפֵק כּוּלּוֹ בְּמוֹתוֹ – זֶהוּ דַּם תְּבוּסָה, וְטָמֵא מִדְּרַבָּנַן בְּאֹהֶל, כִּדְאָמְרִי' בְּפִירְקִין דִּלְעֵיל: דַּם תְּבוּסָה – דְּרַבָּנַן. וַחכ"א. זֶה אֵינוֹ, הוֹאִיל וְאִיכָּא לְסַפּוּקֵי: שֶׁמָּא כּוּלּוֹ בְּמוֹתוֹ – הֲוָה לֵיהּ סָפֵק טוּמְאָה דְּאוֹרַיְיתָא בִּרה"י, וּסְפֵקוֹ טָמֵא. אֶלָּא אֵיזֶהוּ דַּם תְּבוּסָה. דְּטוּמְאָתוֹ מִדִּבְרֵי סוֹפְרִים. הָרוּג שֶׁיָּצָא כו'. דִּפְשִׁיטָא לָן דְּלָא נָפֵיק מִינֵּיהּ רְבִיעִית שְׁלֵמָה לְאַחַר מִיתָה, וְסָפֵק רוּבּוֹ מֵחַיִּים כו' רְבוּתָא אַשְׁמוּעִינַן: דְּאע"ג דְּמְסַפְּקָא לָן אִי רוּבּוֹ מֵחַיִּים, גְּזַר עֲלֵיהּ טוּמְאָה. וּמִיהוּ אִי הֲוָה נַמִי רוּבָּא לְאַחַר מִיתָה – אֵין טוּמְאָתוֹ מִן הַתּוֹרָה, דִּרְבִיעִית שְׁלֵמָה דְּמֵת בָּעֵינַן. וּמִיהוּ אִי הֲוָה פְּשִׁיטָא לָן דְּרוּבָּא מֵחַיִּים – לָא גָּזְרוּ עֲלֵיהּ.

---

**תוספות**

**והאנן** תנן שחרדה מסלקת הדמים. בלאו מתניתין דהכא, הוה מצי למפרך אדרב, אלא אגב דקאי לפרושי מתני' פריך אמתניתין. **אלא** טעמא דבית שמאי *כדתנן בראשונה. משמע דהך לא אתי כב"ה, ותימה: דבסוף מועד קטן (דף כז:) תני לה גבי שאר "בראשונה" דקתני התם, דהוי הילכתא פסיקתא. משמע, דכולהו הלכתא כמו שהתקינו לבסוף, ובתוספת' דמכילתין (פ"ט) קתני לכולהו! ואומר ר"ת: דברייתא דהכא איירי בכלים שהיו עליה סמוך למיתה, ומודו ב"ה בכלים שיש עליהם טומאת זבה. אבל פלוגתא דמתניתין ארישא, דזב וזבה מטמאין באבן מסמא עד שימוק הבשר כו' שמא יתעלפה. והך חומרא מוקי בית שמאי בכל הנשים שמטמאין באבן מסמא עד שימוק הבשר, ואהא דוקא פליגי ב"ה. ועוי"ל: ד"בראשונה" דהכא, היינו דמתחילה היו נוהגין כב"ה, ולבסוף התקינו לכ"ע שיהיו נוהגין כבית שמאי. **מטמא** משום כתם. פי': כדם נדה במשהו, דאי משום מת – בעי רביעית. **מקור** מקומו טמא איכא בינייהו. לת"ק מקומו טמא. ולא לענין שיהא הדם הנוגע בו טמא טומאת מגע, דאפילו בלא מקור ליטמא אפי' *פחות מרביעית, משום דנגע במת. אלא כתם ראייה גמורה קאמר, שיטמא הדם במגע ובמשא אע"ג דלאו רואה היא לאחר מיתה, הואיל והיה במקור מחיים. ומשעת כבוס ליכא לטמויי כמו כתם – דהא ודאי השתא הוא דאתא דם, ולא מהני טומאת כתם אלא להיות טומאה בפחות מרביעית [במשהו]. **בין** בחייו בין במותו. מפרש ואזיל: ספק בחייו כולו, ספק במותו כולו. ספק בחייו ובמותו, קצת בחייו קצת במותו. **ה"ג** בפי' ר"ח ובתוספתא דאהלות (פ"ד): הרוג שיצא ממנו רביעית דם בחייו ובמותו, ועדיין לא פסק, ספק רובו מחיים כו' – ורבינו שמואל כתב דלא איתפרש. ומפרש ר"י "ועדיין לא פסק" – הדם משמת, ושמא הולך ורבה עד שיהא רביעית שלמה. ואף ע"ג דהשתא ליכא אלא רובו לאחר מיתה – דגזרו אטו כולו מדין דם תבוסה. אבל כשראינו כשפסק משמת – לא גזרו עליו דין דם תבוסה, כי בודאי לא יצא רביעית לאחר מיתה במה שיצא אחרי כן. "ודמו מטפטף לגומא" (שמא) מספקא ליה לר"י אי בעי רבי יהודה ועדיין לא פסק כרבנן, ו"טיפה של מיתה" – לאו דוקא. אלא הכי קאמר: ומה שיטפטף לאחר מיתה – אינו מתבטל ראשון ראשון, אלא מצטרפין כולן עד שיהא בו שיעור לטמא. ורבנן מטהרים – *דראשון ראשון בטל. או דילמא: לא בעי "עדיין לא פסק" ו"טיפה" דנקט דוקא, מדקאמר לקמן "שאני אומר טיפה של מיתה עומדת לה על העץ", הא אם ירדה למטה – הוה מטמא רבי יהודה, אע"ג דאין דרך לעמוד על העץ אלא מעט. ורבנן דקאמרי "ראשון ראשון נפסק" – רבותא קאמר: אפילו לא פסק, כיון דאינו אלא מטפטף, ראשון ראשון בטל. והרב ר' יהודה בן ה"ר י"ט מפרש: "ועדיין לא פסק" – פירוש: מלהיות שותת, אילו היה מטפטף – היה טהור, דראשון ראשון בטל. וחכמים דבתר הכי היינו תנא קמא, דמפרשי טעמייהו אמאי פליגי אדרבי יהודה: מפני שראשון ראשון נפסק. וכן נמי ר' יהודה בתר הכי מפרש טעמא אמאי פליג אדר"ש "שאני אומר טיפה של מיתה עמדה על העץ". ור"ת מפרש: "ועדיין לא פסק" – שאחר שנודע לנו שמת, ראינו שלא פסק. ובודאי איכא מיעוט לאחר מיתה, כדמפרש ואזיל "ספק רובא מחיים, ספק מיעוט" כו'. ואתא לאפוקי מתנא קמא דאמר אפי' היכא דאיכא לספוקי שמא יצא כולו מחיים, טמא. **ודמו** מטפטף לגומא. רבי יהודה נקט "גומא" – משום שהזכיר טפטוף שיהא יחד ומצטרף. דבלאו גומא אינו מתערב יפה, אלא נוטף כאן וכאן. אבל רבי שמעון דנקט "שותת" – אפילו בארץ מתערב יפה.

רבי

---

**תוספי הרא"ש**

**אלא** טעמא דב"ש כדתניא בראשונה כו'. תימה דמשמע דהך בריית' דב"ש היא ובמוע' קטן מייתי לה בהדי שאר בראשונה דקאמר בראשונה היו מוליכין לבית האבל כו'. בראשונ'

---

היתה הוצאת המת קשה לקרוביו כו'. ובתוספתא קתני להו לכולהו בהדי הדדי ומשמע דקי"ל הכי כמו שהתקינו לבסוף. ואומר ר"ת דברייתא דהכא איירי בכלים שהיו עליה סמוך למיתה דמודו ב"ה דאותו יש להם טומאת זיבה. ופלוגתא דמתניתין קיימא ארישא דקתני דנדה מטמאה באבן מסמא עד שימוק הבשר והך חומרא מוקמי ב"ש בכל הנשים. וב"ה פליגי עלייהו בהא. והכי מייתי מהך ברייתא דכי היכי דתקינו חכמים על כל בגדים סמוך למיתה משום כבוד זבין חיים ה"נ תקינו לב"ש דכל הנשים (מחמירות) [מטמאות] באבן מסמא. או א"נ הכי קתני בראשונה היו נוהגין כב"ה ולבסוף התקינו כב"ש: **מקור** מקומו טמא. ותימה תיפוק לי בלא טעם דמקור שהרי נגע במת. וצ"ל שמחמת טומאת מקור חשיב כדם נדה אע"פ שנעקר ממנה משמתה ומטמאה במשא כדין דם הנדה וכעין החרדל: **מכלל** דר' יהודה סבר באהל נמי מטמא. הא כיון דא"ר יוסי אינו מטמא באהל א"כ מיירי בשנעקר הדם מחיים: **דרה"ר** ספיקו טהור. ולא החמירו בו חכמים לעשות אותו דם תבוסה כיון דשמא יצא כולו מחיים. ורש"י פירש דחכמים באין להחמיר ולומר דטמא מדאורייתא ברשות היחיד וברשות הרבים ספיקו טהור מן התורה אבל מטמא משום דם תבוסה דרבנן. אלא איזהו דם תבוסה דאינו אלא מדרבנן אפי' ברה"י כגון היכא דפשיטא לן דלא נפיק רביעית שלם לאחר מיתה: **הרוג** שיצא ממנו רביעית דם בחייו ובמותו ועדיין לא פסק. כך כתוב הגירסא (בס"פ) [בתוספתא] וה"פ ועדיין לא פסק ויכול להיות רבה עד שיהא בו רביעית מדם שלאחר מיתה או גזרו בו טומאה אע"פ שאין בו רביעית אבל אם פסק כבר דידעינן דתו לא יהיה רביעית לאחר מיתה לא גזרו בו. י"מ ולא פסק כלומר שותת (ששתת) דאי מטפטף ונפסק ראשון ראשון בטל והיינו כרבנן [דסיפא] דמטהרי בהכי. י"ם דגרסי ועדיין לח וה"פ דאי נקרש מקצתו אותו שנקרש בא מחיים וכאילו הוא בפני עצמו ואין כאן רביעית:

---

סא א ב מיי' פ"ד מהל' מטמאי משכב ומושב הלכ' ו' סמג עשין רמח: סב ג מיי' פ"ב מהל' טומאת מת הל' ד' סמג שם: סג ד מיי' שם הל' ד': סד ה מיי' שם הל' ד':

תהלים קכז | אסתר ד | [לעיל לא.] | סוטה כ: מגילה טו. | לעיל לט. סוטה כ: | [נ"ל דתניא] | [לעיל לה. וש"נ] | [תוספתא פ"ט] מ"ק כז: | חולין פז: | [לעיל נז. וש"נ] | [תוספתא דאהלות פ"ד]

**עין משפט נר מצוה**

**סה** א מיי' פ"ה מהל' מטמאי משכב ומושב הלכה ד:
**סו** ב מיי' פי"א מהל' אבות הטומאה הל"ט:
**סז** ג ד מיי' פ"ה מהל' מטמאי משכב ומושב הלכה ד:
[תוספתא דאהלות פ"ד ע"ש]
**סח** ה מיי' פ"ג מהל' מעשר שני הל"ד:
**סט** ו מיי' פי"ב מהל' תרומות הל"א:
**ע** ז מיי' פ"ג מהל' תרומות הלי"ז:
**עא** ח מיי' פ"י מהל' אבות הטומאה הל"ד:
**עב** ט מיי' פ"ה מהל' משכב ומושב הל"ז ופ"ו מהל' איסורי ביאה הלי"ז:

שֶׁרִאשׁוֹן רִאשׁוֹן נִפְסָק. שַׁפִּיר קָאָמְרִי לֵיהּ רַבָּנַן לר' יְהוּדָה! ר' יְהוּדָה לְטַעְמֵיהּ, *דְּאָמַר אֵין דָּם מְבַטֵּל דָּם. *ר"ש אוֹמֵר: צָלוּב עַל הָעֵץ, שֶׁדָּמוֹ שׁוֹתֵת לָאָרֶץ, וְנִמְצָא תַּחְתָּיו רְבִיעִית דָּם — טָמֵא. רַבִּי יְהוּדָה מְטַהֵר, שֶׁאֲנִי אוֹמֵר טִפָּה שֶׁל מִיתָה עוֹמֶדֶת לוֹ עַל גַּב הָעֵץ. וְרַבִּי יְהוּדָה נֵימָא אִיהוּ לְנַפְשֵׁיהּ: שֶׁאֲנִי אוֹמֵר טִפָּה שֶׁל מִיתָה עוֹמֶדֶת עַל גַּב הַמִּטָּה! שָׁאנֵי בַּמִּטָּה דִּמְחַלְחֲלָה.§ **מתני'** בָּרִאשׁוֹנָה הָיוּ אוֹמְרִים: הַיּוֹשֶׁבֶת עַל דַּם טָהוֹר — הָיְתָה מְעָרָה מַיִם לַפֶּסַח. אחָזְרוּ לוֹמַר: הֲרֵי הִיא כְּמַגַּע טְמֵא מֵת לְקָדָשִׁים — כְּדִבְרֵי ב"ה ב"ש אוֹמְרִים: אַף כִּטְמֵא מֵת.§ **גמ'** [א] מְעָרָה — אִין, נוֹגַעַת — לָא, אַלְמָא *חוּלִּין שֶׁנַּעֲשׂוּ עַל טָהֳרַת הַקֹּדֶשׁ — כְּקֹדֶשׁ דָּמוּ. אֵימָא סֵיפָא: חָזְרוּ לוֹמַר הֲרֵי הִיא כְּמַגַּע טְמֵא מֵת לְקָדָשִׁים, לְקָדָשִׁים — אִין, לְחוּלִּין — לָא, אַלְמָא: *חוּלִּין שֶׁנַּעֲשׂוּ עַל טָהֳרַת הַקֹּדֶשׁ בלָאו כְּקֹדֶשׁ דָּמוּ! [ב] מתני' מַנִּי אַבָּא שָׁאוּל הִיא, דְּתַנְיָא, *אַבָּא שָׁאוּל אוֹמֵר: טְבוּל יוֹם תְּחִילָּה לַקֹּדֶשׁ, לְטַמֵּא שְׁנַיִם, וְלִפְסוֹל אֶחָד.§ **מתני'** גוּמוֹדִים שֶׁהִיא אוֹכֶלֶת בְּמַעֲשֵׂר, וְקוֹצָה לָהּ חַלָּה, וּמַקֶּפֶת וְקוֹרָא לָהּ שֵׁם, וְאִם נָפַל מֵרוֹקָהּ וּמִדַּם טָהֳרָה עַל כִּכָּר שֶׁל תְּרוּמָה — שֶׁהוּא טָהוֹר. *ב"ש אוֹמְרִים: צְרִיכָה טְבִילָה בָּאַחֲרוֹנָה, וּבֵית הִלֵּל אוֹמְרִים: דאֵינָהּ צְרִיכָה טְבִילָה בָּאַחֲרוֹנָה.§ **גמ'** *דְּאָמַר מָר: הטָבַל וְעָלָה — אוֹכֵל בְּמַעֲשֵׂר.§ ו"וְקוֹצָה לָהּ חַלָּה".§ *חוּלִּין הַטְּבוּלִין לְחַלָּה — לָאו כְּחַלָּה דָּמוּ.§ "וּמַקֶּפֶת".§ דְּאָמַר מָר: *זמִצְוָה לִתְרוֹם מִן הַמּוּקָּף.§ "וְקוֹרָא לָהּ שֵׁם".§ סד"א נִגְזוֹר דִּלְמָא אָתֵי לְמִנְגַּע בָּהּ מֵאַבְרָאֵי קמ"ל.§ "וְאִם נָפַל מֵרוֹקָהּ".§ *דִּתְנַן: חמַשְׁקֵה טְבוּל יוֹם *(מַשְׁקִין הַיּוֹצְאִין מִמֶּנּוּ) כְּמַשְׁקִין הַנּוֹגֵעַ בָּהֶם, וְאֵלּוּ וָאֵלּוּ אֵינָן מְטַמְּאִין, [א] חוּץ מִמַּשְׁקֵה הַזָּב — שֶׁהוּא אַב הַטּוּמְאָה.§ "בֵּית שַׁמַּאי".§ מַאי בֵּינַיְיהוּ? אָמַר רַב קְטִינָא: טְבוּל יוֹם אָרוּךְ אִיכָּא בֵּינַיְיהוּ.§ **מתני'** הָרוֹאָה יוֹם אַחַד עָשָׂר, וְטָבְלָה לָעֶרֶב וּמְשַׁמְּשָׁה ב"ש אוֹמֵר: טמְטַמְּאִין מִשְׁכָּב וּמוֹשָׁב, וְחַיָּיבִין בְּקָרְבָּן. וב"ה

[פירושין ל: וש"נ]

**רש"י**

שֶׁאֵין זָב בְּקִילּוּחַ, אֶלָּא נוֹטֵף. וְהִלְכָּךְ, אֲפִי' הָיָה רוֹב לְאַחַר מִיתָה – טָהוֹר, שֶׁהֲרֵי מִתְּחִילָּה דָּם נָפַל מֵחַיִּים בְּתוֹךְ הַגּוּמָא, וְאַחַ"כ נָפַל דַּם מִיתָה עָלָיו טִיפִּין טִיפִּין. כָּל טִיפָּה וְטִיפָּה שֶׁנָּפְלָה, בָּטְלָה בְּדָם הָרִאשׁוֹן שֶׁהָיָה בַּגּוּמָא מֵחַיִּים. וְהֵיכָא אָמְרִי' דַּם תְּבוּסָה? בְּשׁוֹכֵב עַל הָאָרֶץ וְדָמוֹ זָב וְאֵינוֹ נִפְסָק, הַהוּא כִּי הָוֵי לְאַחַר מִיתָה רוּבָּא, אָזְלִינַן בָּתְרֵיהּ מִדְּרַבָּנַן. וְאִי נַמִּי מְסַפְּקָא לָן, גְּזוֹר בָּהּ טוּמְאָה. דְּאֵין דָּם מְבַטֵּל דָּם. בְּפֶרֶק "כִּסּוּי הַדָּם". שׁוֹתֵת לָאָרֶץ. שֶׁאֵינוֹ נוֹטֵף, אֶלָּא שׁוֹתֵת וְאֵינוֹ נִפְסָק. הִילְכָּךְ, לֹא מְבַטֵּל הַהוּא דִּלְאַחַר מִיתָה שֶׁהוּא הַרְבֵּה. אֲבָל נוֹטֵף רִאשׁוֹן בָּטֵל, וַאֲפִילּוּ טִפָּה שֶׁלְּאַחַר מִיתָה מְרוּבָּה – בָּטְלָה, שֶׁלֹּא נָפַל בְּיַחַד. **מתני'** מְעָרָה מַיִם לַפֶּסַח. מִכְּלִי אֶל כְּלִי לִרְחוֹץ בּוֹ אֶת בְּשַׂר הַפֶּסַח. אֲבָל בַּמַּיִם אֵינָהּ נוֹגַעַת, שֶׁהִיא טְבוּלַת יוֹם שֶׁטָּבְלָה לְסוֹף שְׁבוּעַיִים. וְאֵין לָהּ הֶעֱרֵב שֶׁמֶשׁ עַד יוֹם שְׁמוֹנִים, שֶׁהוּא תֵּכֶף לַהֲבָאַת כַּפָּרָתָהּ. וְהַכָּתוּב עֲשָׂאָהּ טְבוּלַת יוֹם, דִּכְתִיב (ויקרא יב): "בְּכָל קֹדֶשׁ לֹא תִגָּע", וְקי"ל: *"בְּכָל קֹדֶשׁ" – לְרַבּוֹת אֶת הַתְּרוּמָה. וּטְבוּל יוֹם, שֵׁנִי הוּא. וּכְשֶׁהִיא מְעָרָה, אֵינָהּ נוֹגַעַת בַּמַּיִם אֶלָּא בַּכֵּלִים, וְשֵׁנִי אֵינוֹ מְטַמֵּא כְּלִי. חָזְרוּ לוֹמַר הֲרֵי הִיא כְּמַגַּע טְמֵא מֵת. שֶׁהוּא רִאשׁוֹן לְקָדָשִׁים, אֲבָל לְחוּלִּין – לֹא. הִילְכָּךְ, אֲפִילּוּ נוֹגַעַת בַּמַּיִם אִם תִּרְצֶה, שֶׁהַמַּיִם חוּלִּין הֵם וּטְבוּל יוֹם שֵׁנִי הוּא וְאֵין שֵׁנִי עוֹשֶׂה שְׁלִישִׁי בְּחוּלִּין. וְאַף ע"פ שֶׁהַמַּיִם הַלָּלוּ נַעֲשִׂים עַל טָהֳרַת הַקֹּדֶשׁ שֶׁהֲרֵי לִרְחִיצַת פֶּסַח עֲשׂוּיוֹת – לָא מְהַנֵּי בְּהוּ שֵׁנִי, דְּחוּלִּין הַנַּעֲשֶׂה עַל טָהֳרַת הַקֹּדֶשׁ לָאו כְּקֹדֶשׁ דָּמוּ. **גמ'** נוֹגַעַת. בַּמַּיִם – לָא. כְּקֹדֶשׁ דָּמוּ. וּמְהַנֵּי בְּהוּ שֵׁנִי. **מתני'** וּמוֹדִים שֶׁאוֹכֶלֶת בְּמַעֲשֵׂר. כְּדִין טְבוּל יוֹם. וְקוֹצָה לָהּ חַלָּה. עַד שֶׁלֹּא תִּקְרָא עָלֶיהָ שֵׁם, וּמַנְחָתָהּ בִּכְלִי. וּמַקֶּפֶת. וּמְקָרֶבֶת הַכְּלִי אֵצֶל הָעִיסָּה, כְּמוֹ "אַקְפִינְהוּ, וְלָא אִדְמוּ", בִּ"שְׁחִיטַת חוּלִּין" (דף ג.). וּכְמוֹ "אֵין מַקִּיפִין שְׁתֵּי חָבִיּוֹת", בְּמַסֶּ' בֵּיצָה (דף לג:). וּבַגְּמָרָא מְפָרֵשׁ: דְּמִצְוָה לִתְרוֹם מִן הַמּוּקָּף – מִן הַקָּרוֹב לַדָּבָר שֶׁהוּא תּוֹרֵם עָלָיו. **וְאִם נָפַל מֵרוֹקָהּ**. דַּהֲווּ לְהוּ מַשְׁקִים הַיּוֹצְאִין מִן הַטְּבוּל יוֹם, וּטְהוֹרִים, כִּדְתַנְיָא בַּגְּמָרָא. **צְרִיכָה טְבִילָה**. לֵיל שְׁמוֹנִים לִתְרוּמָה, מִפְּנֵי שֶׁטְּבוּלַת יוֹם אָרוֹךְ הִיא, וְהִסִּיחָה דַּעְתָּהּ מִן הַתְּרוּמָה. וְאִם יִשְׂרְאֵלִית הִיא – טוֹבֶלֶת לְבִיאַת מִקְדָּשׁ. **אֵינָהּ צְרִיכָה**. אֲבָל לְקָדָשִׁים – מוֹדוּ ב"ה דְּקַיְימָא לָן (חגיגה דף כא.): הָאוֹנֵן וּמְחוּסַּר כִּפּוּרִים צְרִיכִין טְבִילָה לַקֹּדֶשׁ. הִילְכָּךְ, לְאַחַר שֶׁהֵבִיאָה כַּפָּרָתָהּ טוֹבֶלֶת לְקָדָשִׁים. **גמ'** לָאו כְּחַלָּה דָּמוּ. וְלָא מְהַנֵּי בְּהוּ שֵׁנִי. **מתני'** הָרוֹאָה יוֹם י"א. שֶׁהִיא סוֹף יְמֵי זוֹב, וְאֵין יוֹם שֶׁלְּאַחֲרָיו מִצְטָרֵף עִמּוֹ לְזִיבָה. מִשְׁכָּב וּמוֹשָׁב. אֲפִילּוּ בַּעְלָהּ מְטַמֵּא מִשְׁכָּב וּמוֹשָׁב לְטַמֵּא אוֹכָלִין וּמַשְׁקִין, שֶׁהוּא כְּבוֹעֵל שׁוֹמֶרֶת יוֹם כְּנֶגֶד יוֹם, דְּקָסָבַר: יוֹם י"א בָּעֵי שִׁימּוּר. וב"ה

**תוספות**

**רבי** יהודה לטעמיה דאמר אין דם מבטל דם. וא"ת: לרבא דמשני אליבא דרבי יהודה בזבחים בפרק "התערובת" (דף עט.) דבכ"מ אית ליה לר' יהודה מין במינו לא בטיל, וכן נמי בפ' "הערל" (יבמות דף פא:) גבי "חתיכה של חטאת" וגבי "פרוסה של לחם הפנים", דקאמר התם ר' יהודה: לא תעלה, ומוקי לה התם רבה בר רב הונא: כשנמוחה. ופריך: אי הכי, מ"ט דר' יהודה? ומשני: ר' יהודה לטעמיה, דאמר מין במינו לא בטיל. והשתא דקאמר התם בטיל – היינו בטומאה דרבנן, דמדאורייתא – בכל שהוא סגי. א"כ, ה"נ דם תבוסה דרבנן, וליבטל ברובא! ויש לומר: כיון דשייך ביה טומאה רביעית דם דמטמא באהל – ראוי להחמיר בו יותר, ולא בטל ברובו במינו. וא"ת: ולפרוך מהכא לרב חסדא, דאמר בפ' "הקומץ רבה" (מנחות דף כג.) נבלה בטלה בשחוטה, דבתר מבטל אזלינן, ואי אפשר לשחוטה שתעשה נבלה, והוי ליה מין בשאינו מינו. והכא נמי, אי אפשר לדם המבטל להיות טמא וליבטל ביה דם של אחר מיתה! ויש לומר: דהתם אליבא דתנא דבי ר' חייא פליגי רב חסדא ורבי חנינא, דסבר התם כרבי יהודה. אבל לרבי יהודה גופיה אין חילוק, ולעולם לא בטיל.*. **מערה** אין נוגעת לא. וא"ת: וליתני "אינה נוגעת", דלגופיה לא איצטריך, דפשיטא דמערה, דהא אינה מטמאה *בהיסט! ויש לומר: דאיצטריך לאשמועינן דלא חיישינן שמא נגעה. והכי נמי איכא לפרושי הא °דתניא במסכת ידים "כל שאינו מטמא את המים במשא כשר לנטילת ידים ויש שרוצים לדקדק הא מטמא במשא אינו – כשר לנטילת ידים". ומתוך כך אוסרין לקבל מים מן גוי. ושיבוש הוא: דהא נדה ויולדת נוטלות ידיהן, אף על פי שמטמאות במשא. וכ"ש עכשיו, שאנו נוטלין כולנו ממי טמאים. ונראה דהתם איירי לתרומה או לחולין שנעשו על טהרת תרומה, ולא אתא לדיוקא אלא לגופיה דכשר לערות לידים. ואף ע"ג דמטמא במגע – לא חיישינן שמא יגע. ולעיל מיניה תניא: הכל כשרין ליטול ידים, ואפילו טמא מת, ואפילו בועל נדה שאינו מטמא (בהיסט) ושמא כי היכי דקיל מנדה, שאינו מטמא משכב תחתון [אלא] כעליון, ושטבילתו ביום, ה"נ °יקיל מנדה שאינו מטמא בהיסט. ומיהו קשיא: הא דתנן במסכת כלים (פ"א מ"ג) למעלה מהן נבלה, דמטמא במשא. למעלה מהן בועל נדה, שמטמא משכב תחתון כעליון. אלמא, מטמא נמי במשא! מיהו מצינן למימר: דאע"ג דאינו מטמא במשא, קאמר שפיר "למעלה מנבלה" – כיון דאיכא חומרא חדא, דלית בנבלה. דה"נ תנן לעיל "ומטמא באבן מסמא", ותנן בתר הכי "למעלה מהן מת שמטמא באהל", אע"ג דאינו מטמא באבן מסמא. ואומר ר"י: דלא קשה מידי, אפילו אי מטמא במשא כנבלה – היינו, דמטמא את הטהור הנושא. אבל כשהוא נושא את הטהור, כגון הכא שהוא נושא את המים – לא מטמא. כדאמר בפ' "ר"ע" בשבת (דף פג.) זה הסיטו של זב, שלא מצינו לו חבר בכל התורה כולה, שאם תכריע טומאה את הטהרה בכף מאזנים, שיהא טמא. **חולין** הטבולין לחלה לאו כחלה דמו. דוקא לענין טבול יום, כדאמרינן לעיל בפרק קמא (דף ז.) כל שודאי מטמא חולין כו'. **ואם** נפל מרוקה ומדם טהרה על ככר של תרומה שהוא טהור. והכי תנן בריש פ"ב דטבול יום "משקין היוצאין ממנו" – מפ' ר"ת: במשקה תרומה הנוגע בהן, אלו ואלו אין מטמאין את הקדשים, אבל מפסל פסלי ליה. אבל תרומה – אפילו אינה פוסלת, כדתני הכא "שאם נפל רוקה ודם טהרה על ככר של תרומה, שטהורה". ואין לפרש במשקה חולין הנוגע בהן, דהא טבול יום אינו מטמא משקה חולין – ומאי קאמר "אלו ואלו אין מטמאין" (קדשים) אפילו מפסל נמי לא פסלי! ואין לפרש במשקה חולין שנעשו על טהרת הקדש – דהא חזרו לומר בשמעתין דלאו כקדש דמו.

**הרואה** יום אחד עשר וטבלה לערב כו' – דספירת ערב, לאו ספירה היא, כדקאמר בגמרא: ושוין בטבילת לילה שאינה טבילה. מכאן קשה לפירוש רש"י שפירש בפ' ב' דזבחים (דף כג.) ובפסחים פרק "כילד צולין" (דף פא.) דקאמר לר' יוסי דקאמר: מקצת היום ככולו, וזבה שראתה בשביעי שלה – אינה סותרת לאחר טבילה. ופריך התם: אלא זבה גמורה, היכי משכחת לה? ומשני: בשופעת. אי נמי: ברואה בשני בין השמשות. ופי' רש"י: הא דלא משני "ברואה בלילות" – משום דלמ"ד מקצת היום ככולו, לילה חשיבא ספירה, ולא צריך עמוד השחר לטבול. והשתא קשה: דא"כ מתני' דלא כר' יוסי! וכן מתני' דמגילה פ' "הקורא" (דף כ.) דתנן: כולן שעשו משעלה עמוד השחר – כשר. משמע דבלילה לא הוי ספירה! ומפ'

**תוספי הרא"ש**

**מערה** מים לפסח. אבל לא תגע בהן דחולין שנעשו על טהרת הקדש כקדש דמו. והאי דנקט מערה ולא נקט אינה נוגעת לאשמועינן דאע"ג דאינה נוגעת לא אסרו לערות שמא תגע: **בקודש** דמו. הכי נמי הוה מצי למימר כתרומה דמו דאשכחן מאן דסבר הכי בפ' אין דורשין: אלו ואלו אין מטמאין. אומר ר"ת דהכי פירושו במשקין של תרומה הנוגע בהם דאילו כמשק' חולין טהורין גמורים הן דאין טבול יום מטמא משקה חולין. אלו ואלו אין מטמאין היינו אין מטמאין קדש אלא פוסלין. אבל תרומה אפי' מיפסל נמי לא פסלי כדקתני מתניתין ואם נפל מרוקה או מדם טהרה שלה על ככר של תרומה טהור. ואין לפרש דמשקה חולין קאמר ובחולין שנעשו על טהרת הקדש דהא סבירא לן השתא דלאו בקדש דמו כמו שחזרו לומר הרי הן כמגע [טמא] מת לקדשים ומותרת אף ליגע בידים ואינן פוסלין את הפסח ואלו משקין היוצאין ממנו פוסלין את הקדש מדקתני על ככר של תרומה טהור מכלל דשל קדש טמא:

**הרואה** י"א. ה"ה עשירי למ"ד בגמרא לא בעי שימור:

**מסורת הש"ס**

חולין פז: [זבחים עח. לה: לו. מנחות כב. פסחים סה:]
[חגיגה יט: חולין ב:]
[יבמות עה.]
[חולין ג:]
[סוטה כט: מעילה ח. ע"ש תוספתא דטהרות פ"א]
[לעיל כט:]
פסחים לה: יבמות פד: [נגעים פי"ד מ"ג וע' בר"ש בחג"ה]
[במשנה ליתא]
[תוספתא דאהלות פ"ד ע"ש]
[וע"ע תוס' מנחות כב: ד"ה ור' יהודה סבר]
ס"א במשא
לעיל ז.
טבול יום פ"ב [מ"א ע"ש חולין פז:]
רש"ל במשא
רש"א

**הגהות הגר"א**

[א] גמ' חוץ ממשקה הזב. שהוא אב הטומאה נמחק:

**גליון הש"ס**

**תום'** ד"ה מערה וכו' דתניא במס' ידים וכו'. בתוספתא הובא בר"ש ספ"א דידים: **בא"ד** קיל מנדה שאינה מטמא בהיסט כו'. ע' יומא ו ע"ב תד"ה שמטמא:

**הגהות מהר"ב רנשבורג**

א] גמ' מערה אין נוגעת לא אלמא חולין וכו' אימא סיפא חזרו לומר כו' אלמא חולין. ד' מלות אלו אלמא. אימא סיפא. אלמא. נמחקו. וכ"ב כ"ז נמחק לדעת מהרש"א וכ"ה בר"ש משנה א' פ"ב דטבו"י יעו"ש: ב] שם מתני' מני אבא שאול היא. כ"ב עי' פאר הלכה דף ה ע"ג באורך ועוד שם דף ו' ע"ב ד"ה בזה:

**וב"ה פוטרין מן הקרבן.** דלא בעי שימור. אבל לענין טומאה – מודו מדרבנן להחמיר, גזרה יום י"א אטו תוך י"א יום, דמטמאה בועלה מדאורייתא עד שתספור קצת יום המחרת, כדיליף לקמן מ"יהיה לה". **טבלה יום שלאחריו.** דעבדה שימור קצת. ושימור מעליא הוא, אלא שמתוך י"א יום – אסור לעשות כן, שלא תבא לידי ספק שמא תראה לאחר תשמיש, ומצטרפין הימים לזיבה, ואין טבילתה טבילה. **מטמאין משכב ומושב.** ואפילו בועלה, מדרבנן גזרו אטו תוך י"א יום. **ופטורין מן הקרבן.** דהא עבדי שימור, ואע"פ שחזרה וראתה – אין מצטרפין לזיבה, שהרי תחילת נדה היא. **גרגרן.** ממהר לחטוא, שמא ירגיל בכך תוך י"א. אבל לענין טומאה – טהור. **וחייבין בקרבן.** ואפילו לא תראה למחר, דהא בעי שימור, והרי בעל זבה קטנה. **טבלה יום שלאחריו.** דעבדה קצת שימור, ושמשה. **ה"ז תרבות רעה.** שמא תראה אחר כן, ותצטרף לשלפניו, ואין טבילתה טבילה. **ומגען.** לענין טומאה וטהרה. **ובעילתן.** לענין קרבן. **תלויין.** שאם תראה – מגען מגע זבה, וחייבין בקרבן. ואם לא תראה – מגען טהור ובעילתן פטורה. **גמ' ת"ר ושוין בטובלת לילה לזבה.** ואע"פ שחלוקין ב"ה ברואה יום י"א וטבלה לערב שפטורין מן הקרבן – התם, משום דיום י"א לא בעי שימור. הילכך, לאו זבה הואי. אבל זבה קטנה של תוך י"א יום בעיא שימור, דאין טבילת לילה עולה עד שתשמור יום המחרת קצת ותטבול. **ושוין ברואה תוך י"א יום וטבלה לערב ושמשה שחייבין בקרבן.** ואפילו בועלה ביום, והך סיפא פירושא דרישא הוא. **אם שוה לו לטומאה.** שאתם מודים שמטמאה בועלה משכב ומושב ליל מוצאי י"א. **בתוך י"א מצטרף עמו לזיבה.** הילכך, צריכה לשמור יום המחרת כנגד יום הראייה. **להחמיר.** מדרבנן. **להקל.** להביא חולין לעזרה. **נושכים.** מוקשין. **אמר רב הונא משכבות ומושבות שבשני.** לראייתה. הרואה תוך י"א וטבלה יום שלאחריו, לב"ש דמחמירי ומטמאין משכב ומושב מדרבנן לאחר טבילה, ואפילו לא ראתה, מאי טעמא? דכיון דכי חזיא – מטמאה למפרע מדאורייתא, שהרי מצטרף לזיבה. כי לא חזיא נמי – גזרינן מדרבנן אטו ראתה. **תנינא טבלה יום שלאחריו.** יום י"ב שאינו מצטרף, ואחר כן ראתה. וקס"ד: האי ראתה דלאחריו – כאילו לא ראתה תוך י"א דמיא, דהא עכשיו היא מטמאה מתחילת נדה, ואינה פוסלת טבילה שחרית. והך טומאה, מדרבנן היא, דגזרינן י"ב אטו י"א, ה"נ גזרינן לא ראתה אטו ראתה. **ראיית נדה היא.** ואינה מצטרפת, אלא מעכשיו מטמאה. וטומאת מעת לעת הוא דאיכא עליה, וטומאת מעת לעת אינה מטמאה את בועלה אלא משום דגזרינן יום שלאחר י"א אטו תוך י"א דאורייתא. ה"נ, תוך י"א לא ראתה בשני אחר טבילתה, גזרינן אטו ראתה. **א"ל אביי לרב יוסף רב כהנא.** דאמר, ראתה שאני – הכי קא קשיא ליה: אע"ג דהך טומאה מדרבנן, ליכא למימר דכי היכי דגזרי ב"ש ראייה שניה דלאחר י"א אטו ראייה שניה תוך י"א, ה"נ נגזור לא ראתה אטו ראתה – דראייה בראייה מיחלפא, ראתה בלא ראתה לא מיחלפא. **ועוד תנן.** דלא כרב הונא. **הרואה ראייה אחת של זוב.** באיש מיירי. **כשומרת יום כנגד יום.** בשני שלה, שמגעה תלוי אחר טבילה, אף זה מגעו תלוי. אם טבל לאחר ראייה ונגע במעשר – מגעו תלוי, שמא יראה ראייה שניה, ומצטרף לזיבה. **כבעל קרי.** וטהור למעשר, לאחר טבילה מיד. קתני מיהא לב"ש שומרת יום וזב בראייה ראשונה שוין. ותניא.

[לעיל נד.]

וב"ה אומרים: [א]פטורים מן הקרבן. טבלה ביום של אחריו ושמשה את ביתה, ואח"כ ראתה [א]ב"ש אומרים: מטמאין משכב ומושב, ופטורין מן הקרבן. וב"ה אומרים: [ב]ה"ז *גרגרן. [ג]ומודים ברואה בתוך י"א יום, וטבלה לערב ושמשה – שמטמאין משכב ומושב. וחייבין בקרבן. [ד]טבלה ביום של אחריו ושמשה ה"ז תרבות רעה, ומגען ובעילתן תלויין.§ **גמ'** ת"ר [ה]ושוין בטובלת לילה לזבה – שאינה טבילה. ושוין ברואה בתוך י"א יום, וטבלה לערב ושמשה – שמטמאה משכב ומושב, וחייבין בקרבן. לא נחלקו אלא ביום י"א יום, שב"ש אומרים: מטמאין משכב ומושב, וחייבין בקרבן. ובית הלל – פוטרין מקרבן. אמרו להן ב"ש לב"ה מ"ש יום י"א מיום תוך י"א אם שוה לו לטומאה, לא ישוה לו לקרבן? אמרו להן ב"ה לב"ש לא אם אמרת בתוך י"א יום – שכן יום שלאחריו מצטרף עמו לזיבה, תאמרו ביום י"א – שאין יום שלאחריו שנצטרף עמו לזיבה! אמרו להם בית שמאי: השוו מדותיכם, אם שוה לו לטומאה – ישוה לו לקרבן, ואם לא שוה לו לקרבן – לא ישוה לו לטומאה. אמרו להם ב"ה אם הביאנוהו לידי טומאה – להחמיר, לא נביאהו לידי קרבן – להקל. ועוד, מדבריכם אתם נושכין, שאתם אומרין, טבלה יום שלאחריו ושמשה, ואח"כ ראתה – מטמא משכב ומושב, ופטורה מן הקרבן אף אתם השוו מדותיכם – אם שוה לו לטומאה – ישוה לו לקרבן, ואם לא שוה לו לקרבן – לא ישוה לו לטומאה! אלא – להחמיר ולא להקל הכא נמי – להחמיר ולא להקל. אמר רב הונא: משכבה ומושבה שבשני ב"ש מטמאין, אע"פ שטבלה, אע"פ שלא ראתה. מאי טעמא? – כיון דאילו חזיא – מטמאה, השתא נמי מטמיא. אמר רב יוסף: מאי קמ"ל תנינא: טבלה יום שלאחריו ושמשה את ביתה, ואח"כ ראתה. ב"ש אומרים: מטמאה משכבות ומושבות ופטורה מן הקרבן! אמר רב כהנא: ראתה שאני. אמר רב יוסף: וכי ראתה מאי הוי? ראייה דנדה היא! א"ל אביי לרב יוסף: רב כהנא הכי קא קשיא ליה, בשלמא היכא דראתה – גזרינן ראייה דנדה אטו ראייה דזבה, אלא היכא דלא ראתה – מאי נגזר בה? ועוד: תנן, *הרואה ראייה אחת של זוב ב"ש אומרים: כשומרת יום כנגד יום, וב"ה א' [ו]כבעל קרי. ותניא

זבים פ"א מ"א

ומפ' ר"ת: דהכי פריך, זבה בימימא היכי משכחת לה, מדכתיב "כל ימי זוב טומאתה" אמרי' לקמן: אימר בימימא תהוי זבה. משמע דבראיית ימים היא נעשית זבה. מיהא תימה: מאי קא משני "ברואה בשני בין השמשות", מ"מ ליכא אלא ב' ראיות ביום! וי"ל: דלא חש להזכיר השלישית, כיון שהזכיר השניה, ממילא ידעי' השלישית. וכן צ"ל: לפירש"י דבסוף פרק ב' דנזיר (דף טז.) דאיכא נמי הך סוגיא ד"כילד צולין" (פסחים דף פא.) ומשני: דחזאי תלתא יומי סמוך לשקיעת החמה, דלא הוי שהות דסליק ליה למניינא. ב] ו"תלתא יומי" – לאו דוקא, דבחדא סגי כשראתה בשני עד הלילה. ור"י מפרש: "זבה גמורה לר' יוסי, היכי משכחת לה?" – כיון דאית ליה לרבי יוסי מקצת היום ככולו בתחילת היום, דקאמר: זב הרואה בשביעי שלו – אינו סותר התחלת היום, וישלים ז'. ה"ה נמי דסוף היום ככולו, ואפי' ראתה בלילה – מה בכך? מ"מ מקצת היום ככולו, וסוף היום להוי שימור! וכן משמע בנזיר (דף טז.) דקאמר: "ולרבי יוסי כו' כיון דחזאי פלגא דיומא, אידך פלגא סליק לה שימור" – משמע שסוף היום, מחצות ואילך, הוי שימור דאידך פלגא! ומשני: "דחזאי תלתא יומי סמוך לשקיעת חמה, דלא הוי שהות" פי' סוף היום סליק לה למנינא דראייתה. וא"ת: ולרבי יוסי נימא "וכי כותאי אמרה לשמעתיה, דאית ליה מקצת היום ככולו", ושמעתיה דרב אוקמינן לעיל (דף סט.) דלא ככותאי, ובנזיר אוקמינן רב כרבי יוסי! וי"ל: דכי אית ליה מקצת היום ככולו – היינו, בשביעי לזבה, שהוא יום אחרון של חשבונה. וכן בשומרת יום כנגד יום, מקצת יום ספירה עולה, ואינה סותרת. שאין לה למנות יותר, והוא סוף חשבונה. אבל בתחילת הספירה – לא אמרינן שסוף היום שהיא פוסקת בו, שיהא ככולו. מיהו קשה: דאמרי' בפ"ק דר"ה (דף י.): אמר רבא, ק"ו: ומה נדה, שאין תחילת היום עולה לה בסופה – סוף היום עולה לה בתחילתה. שנה, שתחילת היום עולה לה בסופה – אינו דין שסוף היום עולה לה בתחילתה. ומאי קושיא? זבה תוכיח לרבי יוסי, שתחילת היום עולה לה בסופה, ואין סוף היום עולה לה בתחילתה! ואור"י: דאליבא דרבנן קאמר רבא, ולא אליבא דר' יוסי. ועוד נ"ל: דאפילו לרבי יוסי אין שייך לומר "יוכיח" מזבה לנדה, דגבי נדה – דין הוא שיהיה יום ראשון מן החשבון, כי למה לא יהיה ככל הטומאות שאין צריכין נקיים? אבל זבה, דצריכה נקיים – נהי דבסוף החשבון יעלה, שמיד שנכנס השביעי, נכנס בטהרה. מ"מ יום שפוסקת בו, שאינו טהור – אינו דין שיעלה לה לחשבון הנקיים.*. **אף** אתם השוו מדותיכם. וא"ת: ומאי ס"ד דב"ש הא ודאי לדידהו נמי איכא לאקשויי הכי! וי"ל: דקסברי ב"ש דיום י"א שהוא מדאורייתא, אי מחמירינן ביה לטמא משכב ומושב – אתי למימר ביה חיוב קרבן. אבל ביום שלאחריו, שהכל יודעין שהוא מדרבנן – לא אתי לחיובי קרבן אי מחמירין ביה לטמויי משכב ומושב. **אמר** רב כהנא ראתה שאני. ואדרבה, מגליה לרב הונא בתוך י"א יום בלא ראתה. והיינו דקאמר "רב כהנא הכי קא קשיא ליה" פי' אדרב הונא. ועוד: תניא דלא כרב הונא. אלא

[וע' תוס' לעיל נג: ד"ה סופרתו ותוס' פסחים פא. ד"ה א"ן]

עג א מיי' פ"ו מהל' איסורי ביאה הלי"ז:
עד ב מיי' שם הלי"ח ופ"ה מהל' משכב ומושב הלכה ח:
עה ג מיי' פ"ו מהל' איסורי ביאה הלי"ב ופ"ה מהל' משכב ומושב הל"ו:
עו ד מיי' פ"ו מהל' איסורי ביאה הלי"ג ופ"ה מהל' משכב ומושב שם:
עז ה מיי' פ"ה מהל' משכב ומושב שם ופ"ו מהל' איסורי ביאה הלי"ב:
עח ו מיי' פ"ב מהל' מחוסרי כפרה הל' ו:

## תוספי הרא"ש

ושוין בטבילת לילה לזבה שאינה טבילה. פרש"י דשוין דסיפא [הוא פירושא] לשוין דרישא. ורבינו מאיר פירש דקאי אהא דתנן במתניתין גבי זבה קטנה היכא דחל יום י"ב יום טבילתה וקדמה וטבלה בלילה דלב"ש מטמא משכב ומושב וחייבין בקרבן ולב"ה פטורין מן הקרבן שוין הן ומודו להו ב"ה לב"ש היכא דחל שביעי לספירתה יום י"ב וקדמה וטבלה בלילה שחייבין בקרבן: **אף** אתם השוו מדותיכם כו'. (וב"ש) [וב"ה] סברי דביום י"א כשטבלה לערב אין לגזור טומאה דלמא אתי למימר טומאה דאורייתא היא לפי שהוא מי"א ימי זיבה ויבא לחייבה קרבן ותביא חולין לעזרה. אבל ביום שלאחריו מידע ידעי כ"ע דתחלת נדה [הוא] וחומרא דרבנן בעלמא הוא ולא יבא לטעות לענין קרבן:

## הגהות מהר"ב רנשבורג

א] גמ' בש"א מטמאין משכבות ומושבות ופטורים מן הקרבן כצ"ל: ב] תוס' ד"ה (בדף עא ע"ב) הרואה וכו' ותלתא יומי ל"ד דבחדא. מלת דבחדא נמחק. ונ"ב דבתרתי כצ"ל וכמ"ש רש"א:

וְתַנְיָא הַמֵּסִיט אֶת הָרְאִיָּה ב"ש אוֹמְרִים: תּוֹלִין, וב"ה א מְטַהֲרִין. מִשְׁכָּבוֹת וּמוֹשָׁבוֹת שֶׁבֵּין רְאִיָּה רִאשׁוֹנָה לִרְאִיָּה שְׁנִיָּה ב"ש תּוֹלִין וב"ה ב מְטַהֲרִין. וְקָתָנֵי רֵישָׁא: הָרוֹאָה רְאִיָּה אַחַת שֶׁל זוֹב ב"ש אוֹמְרִים: כְּשׁוֹמֶרֶת יוֹם כְּנֶגֶד יוֹם. אַלְמָא: שׁוֹמֶרֶת יוֹם כְּנֶגֶד יוֹם, לב"ש תּוֹלִין! לָא תֵּימָא "שׁוֹמֶרֶת יוֹם כְּנֶגֶד יוֹם", אֶלָּא אֵימָא "כְּבוֹעֵל שׁוֹמֶרֶת יוֹם כְּנֶגֶד יוֹם". מַאי שְׁנָא אִיהוּ דְּלָא מְטַמֵּא מִשְׁכָּב וּמוֹשָׁב, וּמַאי שְׁנָא אִיהִי דִּמְטַמְּיָא לֵיהּ? אִיהוּ דְּלָא שְׁכִיחִי בֵּיהּ דָּמִים — לָא גְּזוּר בֵּיהּ רַבָּנַן, אִיהִי דִּשְׁכִיחִי בָּהּ דָּמִים — גְּזוּר בָּהּ רַבָּנַן. וּמַאי שְׁנָא מִשְׁכָּב וּמוֹשָׁב דִּמְטַמְּיָא לֵיהּ, וּמַאי שְׁנָא בּוֹעֵל דְּלָא מְטַמְּיָא לֵיהּ? מִשְׁכָּב וּמוֹשָׁב דִּשְׁכִיחַ — מְטַמְּיָא לֵיהּ, בּוֹעֵל דְּלָא שְׁכִיחַ — לָא מְטַמְּיָא. תְּנַן: טָבְלָה יוֹם שֶׁלְּאַחֲרָיו וְשִׁמְּשָׁה — הֲרֵי זוֹ תַּרְבּוּת רָעָה, מַגָּעָן וּבְעִילָתָן תְּלוּיִין. מַאי לָאו, דִּבְרֵי הַכֹּל הִיא? לָא ב"ה הִיא. דְּתַנְיָא, [א]אָמַר לָהֶם רַבִּי יְהוּדָה לב"ה וְכִי לָזוֹ אַתֶּם קוֹרִין "תַּרְבּוּת רָעָה"? וַהֲלֹא לֹא נִתְכַּוֵּון זֶה אֶלָּא לִבְעוֹל אֶת הַנִּדָּה! נִדָּה ס"ד אֶלָּא אֵימָא "לִבְעוֹל אֶת הַזָּבָה". זָבָה ס"ד אֶלָּא אֵימָא "לִבְעוֹל שׁוֹמֶרֶת יוֹם כְּנֶגֶד יוֹם". אִיתְּמַר: *עֲשִׂירִי — רַבִּי יוֹחָנָן אָמַר: ג עֲשִׂירִי כִּתְשִׁיעִי, מַה תְּשִׁיעִי — בָּעֵי שִׁימּוּר, אַף עֲשִׂירִי — בָּעֵי שִׁימּוּר. ר"ל אָמַר: עֲשִׂירִי כְּאַחַד עָשָׂר, מָה אַחַד עָשָׂר — לָא בָּעֵי שִׁימּוּר, אַף עֲשִׂירִי — לָא בָּעֵי שִׁימּוּר. אִיכָּא דְּמַתְנֵי לַהּ אַהָא, *אָמַר לוֹ רַבִּי אֶלְעָזָר בֶּן עֲזַרְיָה לר"ע *אֲפִי' אַתָּה מַרְבֶּה "בְּשֶׁמֶן" (א) ["בְּשֶׁמֶן"] כָּל הַיּוֹם כּוּלּוֹ — אֵינִי שׁוֹמֵעַ לְךָ! אֶלָּא, ד חֲצִי לוֹג שֶׁמֶן לְתוֹדָה, ה וּרְבִיעִית א] יַיִן לְנָזִיר ו וְאַחַד עָשָׂר יוֹם שֶׁבֵּין נִדָּה לְנִדָּה — הֲלָכָה לְמֹשֶׁה מִסִּינַי. מַאי "הֲלָכָה"? ר' יוֹחָנָן אָמַר: הֲלָכָה י"א ר"ל אוֹמֵר: הִלְכוֹת אַחַד עָשָׂר. ר' יוֹחָנָן אָמַר: הֲלָכָה אַחַד עָשָׂר, אַחַד עָשָׂר הוּא דְּלָא בָּעֵי שִׁימּוּר — הָא לַאֲחֲרִינֵי עָבֵיד שִׁימּוּר. ור"ל אָמַר: הִלְכוֹת אַחַד עָשָׂר, לָא אַחַד עָשָׂר בָּעֵי שִׁימּוּר, וְלָא שִׁימּוּר לַעֲשִׂירִי הָוֵי. הָנֵי הֲלָכוֹת נִינְהוּ? הָנֵי קְרָאֵי נִינְהוּ! דְּתַנְיָא: יָכוֹל הָרוֹאָה ג' יָמִים בִּתְחִילַּת נִדָּה רְצוּפִים. תְּהֵא זָבָה. וּמָה אֲנִי מְקַיֵּים °"אִשָּׁה כִּי תִהְיֶה זָבָה דָּם יִהְיֶה זוֹבָהּ" — בְּרוֹאָה יוֹם אֶחָד (אֲבָל הָרוֹאָה ג' יָמִים בַּתְּחִילָּה תִּהְיֶה זָבָה) תַּלְמוּד לוֹמַר: בְּלֹא

ויקרא טו

תורה אור

וְתַנְיָא. בְּזָב בִּרְאִיָּיה רִאשׁוֹנָה. הַמֵּסִיט אֶת הָרְאִיָּה. טָהוֹר שֶׁהֵסִיט אֶת הַטִּפָּה רִאשׁוֹנָה. ב"ש אוֹמְרִים תּוֹלִין. אִם יַחֲזוֹר הַזָּב וְיִרְאֶה הַיּוֹם שֵׁנִים — נִמְצָא זָב גָּמוּר לְמַפְרֵעַ, וְזוֹב מְטַמֵּא בְּמַשָּׂא. וּב"ה מְטַהֲרִין. כְּמֵסִיט אֶת הַקֶּרִי, דְּלָא מְטַמֵּא בְּמַשָּׂא. מִשְׁכָּבוֹת וּמוֹשָׁבוֹת כו'. אַלְמָא מִדְּמַקְּשֵׁי ב"ש רְאִיָּיה רִאשׁוֹנָה לְשׁוֹמֶרֶת יוֹם, וְקָתָנֵי: מִשְׁכָּב וּמוֹשָׁב שֶׁל בֵּין רְאִיָּיה רִאשׁוֹנָה לִשְׁנִיָּה תּוֹלִין, אַלְמָא מִשְׁכָּב וּמוֹשָׁב דְּשׁוֹמֶרֶת יוֹם בְּשֵׁנִי שֶׁלָּהּ תּוֹלִין, וְאִם לֹא תִּרְאֶה — טְהוֹרָה. וְדַוְקָא בְּשֵׁנִי, אֲבָל בָּרִאשׁוֹן — לָא סָלְקָא לָהּ טְבִילָה, עַד שֶׁתִּשְׁמוֹר קְצָת שֵׁנִי, וְכָל זְמַן שֶׁלֹּא טָבְלָה — זָבָה הִיא. אֶלָּא אֵימָא כְּבוֹעֵל שׁוֹמֶרֶת יוֹם. דְּמוֹדֶה רַב הוּנָא בִּבְעִילָה בְּשֵׁנִי לְאַחַר טְבִילָתָהּ, שֶׁהִיא תּוֹלָה כָּל זְמַן שֶׁלֹּא רָאֲתָה, וְאֵין טוּמְאָתָהּ עָלָיו אֲפִילּוּ מִדְּרַבָּנַן. מַאי שְׁנָא אִיהוּ. בּוֹעֵל. דְּלָא מְטַמֵּא מִשְׁכָּב וּמוֹשָׁב. דִּילֵיהּ, וּמַאי שְׁנָא אִיהִי דִּמְטַמְּאָה? אִיהוּ דְּלָא שְׁכִיחַ בֵּיהּ דָּמִים לָא גְּזַרוּ בֵּיהּ רַבָּנַן. לְטַמֵּא מִשְׁכָּב וּמוֹשָׁב, כָּל זְמַן שֶׁלֹּא רָאֲתָה לְאַחַר תַּשְׁמִישׁ. וּמַאי שְׁנָא מִשְׁכָּב וּמוֹשָׁב. כֵּיוָן דְּאָמַרְתְּ: "אִיהִי דִּשְׁכִיחִי בָּהּ דָּמִים, גְּזַרוּ בָּהּ רַבָּנַן" — מַאי שְׁנָא בּוֹעֵל, דְּלָא גְּזַרוּ בֵּיהּ רַבָּנַן שֶׁתְּטַמְּאֶנּוּ? דִּבְרֵי הַכֹּל. וַאֲפִילּוּ ב"ש, וְקָתָנֵי בְּשֵׁנִי שֶׁבְּתוֹךְ י"א מַגָּעָהּ תָּלוּי, וְקַשְׁיָא לְרַב הוּנָא! עֲשִׂירִי. אֵין לוֹ צֵרוּף לְזִיבָה, שֶׁאֵין מִצְטָרֵף עִמּוֹ אֶלָּא י"א דְּהָוֵי לְהוּ תְּרֵי. כִּתְשִׁיעִי. דִּפְשִׁיטָא לָן בֵּיהּ דְּבָעֵי שִׁימּוּר אִם רָאֲתָה בּוֹ, דְּהָא רָאוּי לַהֲבִיאָהּ לִידֵי זָבָה גְּמוּרָה. אַף עֲשִׂירִי. אִם הִתְחִילָה לִרְאוֹת בּוֹ. בָּעֵי שִׁימּוּר. י"א כְּנֶגְדּוֹ, אע"ג דְּאֵינָהּ רְאוּיָה לָבֹא לִידֵי זָבָה גְּמוּרָה. כִּי"א. לְב"ה דְּאָמְרֵי: לָא בָּעֵי שִׁימּוּר. בְּשֶׁמֶן בְּשֶׁמֶן. גַּבֵּי רְבוּכָה שֶׁל תּוֹדָה בִּמְנָחוֹת בְּפֶ' "ב' מִדּוֹת" (דף פט.) דִּכְתִיב: "וְהִקְרִיב עַל זֶבַח הַתּוֹדָה", וּכְתִיב תְּלָתָא "בַּשֶּׁמֶן". וְתַנְיָא: אִילּוּ נֶאֱמַר "בַּשֶּׁמֶן" — הָיִיתִי אוֹמֵר כָּל הַמְּנָחוֹת לְלוֹג. ת"ל: "בַּשֶּׁמֶן" "בַּשֶּׁמֶן" דְּחַלּוֹת וּרְקִיקִין — הָוֵי רִיבּוּי אַחַר רִיבּוּי, לְמַעֵט לַחֲצִי לוֹג. אֵינִי שׁוֹמֵעַ לְךָ. לְלַמֵּד דָּבָר זֶה מִן הַמִּקְרָא, שֶׁהֲלָכָה לְמֹשֶׁה מִסִּינַי עַל פֶּה הוּא. שֶׁבֵּין נִדָּה לְנִדָּה. בֵּין סוֹף נִדָּה לִתְחִילַּת נִדָּה, מִשֶּׁכָּלוּ יְמֵי נִדָּה אֵינָהּ חוֹזֶרֶת לִהְיוֹת נִדָּה לֵישֵׁב לִרְאִיָּיה אַחַת שִׁבְעָה וְהוּא, עַד שֶׁיִּכְלוּ י"א יוֹם. מַאי הֲלָכָה. דְּמַשְׁמַע אַיּוֹם י"א קָאָמַר רַבִּי אֶלְעָזָר בֶּן עֲזַרְיָה דַּהֲוֵי הֲלָכָה לְמֹשֶׁה מִסִּינַי, וּבָעֵי הַתַּלְמוּד מַאי הִלְכוֹתָיו מִשְּׁאָר הַיָּמִים שֶׁלְּפָנָיו? הֲלָכָה י"א. כְּדָבָר אֶחָד הוּא חָלוּק מִשֶּׁלְּפָנָיו. הִלְכוֹת י"א. בִּשְׁנֵי דְבָרִים הוּא חָלוּק. שִׁימּוּר לַאֲחֲרִינֵי. לַעֲשִׂירִי. לָא אִיהוּ בָּעֵי שִׁימּוּר. מִדְּאוֹרַיְיתָא לִשְׁמוֹר *י"א כְּנֶגְדּוֹ, וְלָא לַאֲחֲרִינֵי הָוֵי שִׁימּוּר. דַּעֲשִׂירִי לָא בָּעֵי שִׁימּוּר מִדְּאוֹרַיְיתָא, הוֹאִיל וְלֹא תָּבֹא בָּהֶן לִידֵי זִיבָה. וּמִדְּרַבָּנַן מִיהָא אֲפִילּוּ רוֹאָה יוֹם י"א — אֲסוּרָה לְשַׁמֵּשׁ בַּיּוֹם שֶׁלְּאַחֲרָיו, כִּדְקָתָנֵי מַתְנִי': "ה"ז גַּרְגְּרָן", וְאָמְרִינַן בְּפֶרֶק "בָּא סִימָן" (לעיל דף נד.): "גַּרְגְּרָן" דִּתְנַן — אָסוּר. יָכוֹל הָרוֹאָה ג' יָמִים בִּתְחִלַּת נִדָּה רְצוּפִים תְּהֵא זָבָה. לִסְפִירַת ז' נְקִיִּים וּלְקָרְבָּן, דִּכְתִיב (ויקרא טו): "יָמִים רַבִּים", וְקָמְצָרִיךְ לָהּ סְפִירָה וְקָרְבָּן? מָה אֲנִי מְקַיֵּים וְאִשָּׁה כִּי תִהְיֶה זָבָה. הָאָמוּר בְּפָרָשָׁה רִאשׁוֹנָה, שֶׁלֹּא הִצְרִיכָהּ סְפִירַת נְקִיִּים וְקָרְבָּן. בְּרוֹאָה יוֹם אֶחָד. אֲבָל רָאֲתָה ג' — תְּהֵא זָבָה. תַּלְמוּד לוֹמַר. בְּפָרָשָׁה שְׁנִיָּה. בְּלֹא

אין

*אלא אימא כבועל שומרת יום כנגד יום. וקשה: דא"כ מסקינן דשומרת יום כנגד יום בשני שלה אין בועלה מטמא משכב ומושב, והא תניא: "טבלה ביום שלאחריו, ושמשה את ביתה, ואח"כ ראתה — מטמאין משכב ומושב", ו"מטמאין" משמע לשון רבים, דקאי אתרווייהו, היא ובועלה! וליכא למימר: "ראתה שאני", דהא מתרצא מילתא דרב יוסף, ואידחי רב כהנא. וי"ל: דהך מסקנא דהכא, ליישובי מילתא דרב הונא אתא, דלא תקשי ליה מברייתא, ומיהו מילתא דרב יוסף אדחי. וניחא נמי טפי לרב הונא דלא תקשי "מאי קמ"ל דודאי ראתה שאני", כדמתרץ אביי מילתיה דרב כהנא. וסבר רב הונא דלענין בועלה, דלא שכיח, אית לן למימר "ראתה שאני". אבל איהי, דשכיחי בה דמים, אפי' לא ראתה — גזרינן אטו ראתה. כי היכי דגזרינן ראתה ביום י"ב, אטו ראתה תוך י"א, ואע"ג דראיית י"ב אינה סותרת. ועוד אור"י: דאפילו קיימא מילתא דרב יוסף, ניחא דלא קשה ממתני' דודאי ביום שלאחריו, דהיינו ביום י"ב דשכיח בועל גבה, דליכא איסור דאורייתא — מטמא בועל משכב ומושב, אע"ג דלא ראתה. אבל תוך י"א יום בשני שלה, אע"ג דגבי דידה לא מפלגינן בין ראתה ללא ראתה מ"מ בועל אינו מטמא משכב ומושב, אלא בראתה. **מאי** שנא איהו. פי' בקונטרס: מאי שנא בועל, דלא מטמא משכב ומושב. *ותימה: דהיינו האי דפריך בתר הכי "מאי שנא בועל דלא מטמא משכב ומושב"? וי"ל: דמעיקרא פריך משום לתאי דידיה. וכי משני דלא שכיח ביה דמים, פריך: ולטמא משום לתאי דידה. ור"י מפרש: מ"ש דאיהו רואה ראייה אחת של זוב, דתולין משכבות ומושבות שבין ראשונה לשניה, ואין מטמא אלא ע"י תלייה אם יראה, ואם לא יראה — טהורין. "ומאי שנא איהי", דכי רואה תוך י"א יום דמטמאה משכב ומושב, ואע"ג דלא ראתה לרב הונא. מיהו לא דמי: דהתם — משום דכי ראתה, סתרה. ולכך החמירו בלא ראתה. אבל זב — אפילו יראה, לא יסתור. לכך נראה: "מאי שנא איהי", דכי טבלה יום שלאחר י"א יום ושמשה וראתה — דמטמאה משכב ומושב בלא תלייה, אע"ג דהתם נמי אין סתירה. ולהאי פירוש דפרשינן דראתה לאו דוקא, פריך. אבל לאידך פירושא דאמרינן ראתה שאני, אבל לא ראתה תולין — שוין איהו ואיהי. **אלא** חצי לוג שמן לתודה] ורביעית יין לנזיר. — נראה דהכי שמע מרביה, וגרסינהו. א"נ: ר"ע חלק עליו מכל שלשה אלה, כדאמר לקמן גבי אחד עשר יום, הלכתא לר' אלעזר בן עזריה, קראי לרבי עקיבא. והוא הדין נמי דבשלישי פליג, אע"ג דלא אשכחן. **רבי** יוחנן אמר הלכה אחד עשר. תימה: במאי פליגי ר' יוחנן ור"ל? הא רבי אלעזר בן עזריה לא איירי אלא בחשבון הימים שבתוך אחד עשר, דשייכא בהו זיבה. אבל בשימור אחד עשר — לא איירי כלל. וכן משמע, מדפריך לקמן "הני קראי נינהו", ואי איהו איירי בהלכתא אחד עשר — לישני: קרא, למנין הימים שהיא זבה. והלכתא, לשימור אחד עשר! ויש לומר: דודאי "הלכה" דקאמר רבי אלעזר בן עזריה, לא איירי אלא במנין הימים דשייכי בהו זיבה. ורבי יוחנן ור"ל בסברא בעלמא פליגי, דרבי יוחנן קאמר: כיון דיום שאחר י"א הוא נדות — אין י"א צריך ספירה. (ב) ור"ל סבר: דאפילו שימור אינו נעשה לעשירי, כיון דאינו ראוי להצטרף לזיבה גדולה, דליכא אלא ב' ימים. והשתא ניחא דהש"ס פריך שפיר "קראי נינהו".

ע' רש"א

עט א ב מיי' פ"א מהל' משכב ומושב הלכה יב:

פ ג מיי' פ"ה הל"ח:

פא ד מיי' פ"ו מהל' מעשה הקרבנות הל"כ:

פב ה גן מיי' פ"ה מהל' נזירות הל"ב:

פג ו מיי' פ"ו מהל' איסורי ביאה הל"ב:

הגהות מהר"ב רנשבורג

א] גמ' חצי לוג שמן לתודה ורביעית שמן לנזיר כו'. ב] תוס' ד"ה אלא חצי כו' ורביעית שמן לנזיר כו'. ג] בעין משפט אות ה' נ"ל מיי' פ"ח מה' נזירות ה"ח:

נ"ל כבספרים של תוס' היה הגירסא בקושיא דפריך בתר הכי בגמ' כמו בספרים שלנו דגרסי' מ"ש משכב ומושב דמטמאין ליה לפני גי' זו לא מקשי תוס' מידי. מהר"מ

[סנהדרין פז.]

[מנחות פט.]

[זבחים פב.]

רש"ל

הגהות הב"ח

(א) גמ' אתה מרבה בשמן כל היום: (ב) תוס' ד"ה ר' יוחנן וכו' אין י"א צריך ספירה אבל מ"מ נעשה שמור לעשירי ור"ל סבר:

רש"ל מ"ז

נ"ל י"ב

הגהות הגר"א

[א] גמ' א"ל (ר' יהודה) נמחק וצ"ל בית שמאי:

תוספי הרא"ש

וקתני רישא הרואה ראיה של זוב בש"א כשומרת יום כנגד יום. אלמא לב"ש שומרת יום כנגד יום תולין. תמיה לי מאי קא פריך דב"ש וב"ה פליגי ברואה ראיה אחת דטומאה דאורייתא דב"ה משוי ליה לבעל קרי וב"ש משוי ליה כשומרת יום כנגד יום דאורייתא. א"נ דאם איתא דלב"ש דטמאה משכב ומושב בשני אפילו לא ראתה להו למימר בשומרת יום כנגד יום דלא ליהוי למיטעי למהר אותה בשלא ראתה קודם כמו רואה ראיה אחת של זוב: **לא** תימא כשומרת יום כנגד יום אלא אימא כבועל שומרת יום כנגד יום. תימה דרב הונא מדמי תוך י"א בלא ראתה כמו י"ב בשראתה כדקאמר רב הונא לעיל אף אנן נמי תנינא וא"כ היכי קאמר דבתוך י"ב בשלא ראתה דבועלה טהור הא תנן במתניתין טבלה ביום שלאחריו ושמשה את ביתה ואח"כ ראתה בש"א מטמאה משכב אלמא בועלה טמא ביום י"ב כשראתה וא"כ ה"ה יום י"א אע"פ שלא ראתה. וי"ל דס"ל לרב הונא דאע"ג דגזרו תוך י"א בשני שלה היכא שלא ראתה אטו ראתה לענין משכב ומושב כי היכי דגזרו חכמים ביום י"ב שראתה אע"ג דאינה סותרת אטו ראייה דתוך י"א יום. לענין בועלה דלא שכיח לא רצו להחמיר בלא ראתה בשני שלה אטו ראתה אע"פ שגזרו חכמים בבועל בשראתה ביום י"ב אטו ראתה תוך י"א: **מאי** שנא איהו ומאי שנא איהי. פרש"י מאי שנא בועל דלא מטמא משכב ומושב כל זמן שלא ראתה אחר תשמיש דיליה ומאי שנא איהי דמטמא. ותימה דהיינו איך קושיא דפריך בתר הכי מאי שנא משכבות ומושבות דמטמיא ומאי שנא בועל דלא מטמיא ונראה דה"פ מאי שנא איהו רואה ראיה אחת של זוב דמשכבות ומושבות שבין ראשונה לשניה לב"ש תולין ואם לא ראתה ראייה שניה טהורין ומאי שנא איהי רואה תוך י"א יום דמטמאה משכב ומושב אפי' לא ראתה כדקאמר רב הונא. ומיהו המדקדק פרש"י לא קשה מידי דה"פ מאי שנא איהו בועל דלא מטמא משכב ומושב אחר תשמיש ומאי שנא איהי דמטמאה והדר תו פריך מאי שנא משכבות ומושבות דגזור ביה משום דשכיחי ביה דמים ומאי שנא דלא גזור בה שתטמאנו במגע אלא טהור גמור הוי: ר' יוחנן אמר הילכתא י"א. תימה במאי קא מיפלגי ר' יוחנן ור"ל בדברי ר' אלעזר בן עזריה הא איהו לא איירי כלל ביום י"א אי הוי שימור אי לא אלא קאמר שיש י"א בין נדה לנדה דשייכא בהו זיבות ולא נדות. ועוד לפי דברי ר' יוחנן ור"ל מאי קא פריך קראי נינהו הא לא איירי קרא בדין יום אי בעי שימור או לא. או אי הוי שימור לאחריני ומתוך לשון רש"י משמע דהגרס במילתיה דר' אלעזר בן עזריה ויום י"א יום שבין נדה לנדה ול"ג י"א יום כו' דפרש"י מאי הילכתא דמשמע איום י"א קאמר ר' אלעזר דהוי הלכה למשה מסיני ובעי תלמודא מה הן הלכותיו משאר הימים שהיו לפניו. והא דפריך קראי נינהו ולא קפריך הילכתא למה לי אלא קשה ליה קרא למה לי דכיון דהילכתא היא די"א לא בעי שימור ממילא שמעינן שיש י"א בין נדה לנדה. ומיהו קשה הא דמשני קראי לר' עקיבא הילכתא לר' אלעזר ב"ע הא מקראי דר' עקיבא לא שמעינן אי בעי שימור או הוי שימור לאחריני. וי"ל דלר' עקיבא שמעינן להו מסברא:

ויקרא טו °"בְּלֹא עֵת נִדָּתָהּ" (*עַל נִדָּתָהּ) אסָמוּךְ לְנִדָּתָהּ. וְאֵין לִי אֶלָּא סָמוּךְ לְנִדָּתָהּ, מוּפְלָג לְנִדָּתָהּ יוֹם אֶחָד מִנַּיִן? ת"ל °"אוֹ כִּי תָזוּב". אֵין לִי אֶלָּא יוֹם אֶחָד, מִנַּיִן לְרַבּוֹת מוּפְלָג שְׁנַיִם, שְׁלֹשָׁה, אַרְבָּעָה, חֲמִשָּׁה, שִׁשָּׁה, וְשִׁבְעָה, שְׁמוֹנָה, תִּשְׁעָה, עֲשָׂרָה, מִנַּיִן? אָמַרְתָּ: מַה מָּצִינוּ בָּרְבִיעִי — שֶׁרָאוּי לספירה וְרָאוּי לְזִיבָה, אַף אֲנִי אָבִיא הָעֲשִׂירִי — שֶׁרָאוּי לִסְפִירָה וְרָאוּי לְזִיבָה. וּמִנַּיִן לְרַבּוֹת אַחַד עָשָׂר? ת"ל "בְּלֹא עֵת נִדָּתָהּ". יָכוֹל שֶׁאֲנִי מַרְבֶּה אַף שְׁנֵים עָשָׂר? אָמַרְתָּ: לָאו. וּמָה רָאִיתָ לְרַבּוֹת אַחַד עָשָׂר וּלְהוֹצִיא שְׁנֵים עָשָׂר? מְרַבֶּה אֲנִי אַחַד עָשָׂר — שֶׁרָאוּי לִסְפִירַת "אוֹ כִּי תָזוּב". וּמוֹצִיא אֲנִי י"ב — שֶׁאֵין רָאוּי לִסְפִירַת "אוֹ כִּי תָזוּב". וְאֵין לִי אֶלָּא שְׁלֹשָׁה יָמִים, שְׁנֵי יָמִים מִנַּיִן? ת"ל "יְמֵי". יוֹם אֶחָד מִנַּיִן? ת"ל "כָּל יְמֵי טֻמְאָה" — מְלַמֵּד בשֶׁמְּטַמְּאָה אֶת בּוֹעֲלָהּ כְּנִדָּה. "הִיא" — הִיא מְטַמְּאָה אֶת בּוֹעֲלָהּ, גוְאֵין הַזָּב מְטַמֵּא מַה שֶּׁהוּא בּוֹעֵל. וַהֲלֹא דִּין הוּא: וּמַה הִיא שֶׁאֵינָהּ מְטַמְּאָה בִּרְאִיּוֹת כְּבְיָמִים — מְטַמְּאָה אֶת בּוֹעֲלָהּ, הוּא שֶׁמְּטַמֵּא בִּרְאִיּוֹת כְּבְיָמִים — אֵינוֹ דִּין שֶׁמְּטַמֵּא מַה שֶּׁהוּא בּוֹעֵל? ת"ל "הִיא" — הִיא מְטַמְּאָה אֶת בּוֹעֲלָהּ, וְאֵין הַזָּב מְטַמֵּא מַה שֶּׁהוּא בּוֹעֵל. א] וּמִנַּיִן שֶׁהוּא עוֹשֶׂה מִשְׁכָּב וּמוֹשָׁב? ת"ל °"כְּמִשְׁכַּב נִדָּתָהּ". וְאֵין לִי אֶלָּא שְׁלֹשָׁה יָמִים, שְׁנֵי יָמִים מִנַּיִן? ת"ל "יְמֵי". יוֹם אֶחָד מִנַּיִן? דת"ל "כָּל יְמֵי". וּמִנַּיִן *שֶׁסּוֹפֶרֶת אֶחָד לְאֶחָד? ת"ל "יִהְיֶה לָּהּ". ב] יָכוֹל תִּסְפּוֹר שִׁבְעָה לִשְׁנַיִם, וְדִין הוּא: וּמַה הוּא שֶׁאֵין סוֹפֵר אֶחָד לְאֶחָד — סוֹפֵר שִׁבְעָה לִשְׁנַיִם, הִיא שֶׁסּוֹפֶרֶת אֶחָד לְאֶחָד — אֵינוֹ דִּין שֶׁתִּסְפּוֹר שִׁבְעָה לִשְׁנַיִם? ת"ל "יִהְיֶה לָּהּ" — האֵינָהּ סוֹפֶרֶת אֶלָּא יוֹמָהּ. אַלְמָא קְרָאֵי נִינְהוּ! לר"ע — קְרָאֵי, לר' אֶלְעָזָר בֶּן עֲזַרְיָה — הִלְכְתָא. א"ל *רַב שְׁמַעְיָה לר' אַבָּא: אֵימָא, בִּימָמָא — תֶּהֱוֵי זָבָה, בְּלֵילְיָא — תֶּהֱוֵי נִדָּה! א"ל עֲלָךְ אֲמַר קְרָא °"עַל נִדָּתָהּ" — סָמוּךְ לְנִדָּתָהּ, סָמוּךְ לְנִדָּתָהּ אֵימַת הָוֵי? — בְּלֵילְיָא, וְקָא קָרֵי לָהּ "זָבָה". תָּנָא *דְּבֵי אֵלִיָּהוּ: כָּל הַשּׁוֹנֶה הֲלָכוֹת בְּכָל יוֹם — מוּבְטָח לוֹ שֶׁהוּא בֶּן הָעוֹלָם הַבָּא, שֶׁנֶּאֱמַר °"הֲלִיכוֹת עוֹלָם לוֹ" — אַל תִּקְרֵי "הֲלִיכוֹת" אֶלָּא "הֲלָכוֹת".§

[ויקרא טו | שם | שם | שם | מגילה כח: | חבקוק ג]

## הדרן עלך תינוקת וסליקא לה מסכת נדה

**רש"י**

**בלא** עֵת נִדָּתָהּ. אֵינוֹ אוֹמֵר לָךְ אֶלָּא בָּרוֹאָה שְׁלֹשָׁה אַחַר יְמֵי נִדָּתָהּ, סָמוּךְ לְנִדָּתָהּ: שֶׁרָאֲתָה יוֹם רִאשׁוֹן אַחַר ז' יְמֵי נִדָּתָהּ, וְרָאֲתָה שְׁמִינִי, וּתְשִׁיעִי, וַעֲשִׂירִי. **או** כִּי תָזוּב. לְרַבּוֹת רוֹאָה ט' וי' וְאַחַד עָשָׂר. מִנַּיִן לְרַבּוֹת שְׁנַיִם שְׁלֹשָׁה כו'. שֶׁכּוּלָּן יֵשׁ לָהֶן דִּין אֶחָד? אָמַרְתָּ מַה מָּצִינוּ בָּרְבִיעִי. לַיָּמִים שֶׁאַחַר הַנִּדָּה. **שהוא** רָאוּי. לִסְפִירַת נְקִיִּים אִם רָאֲתָה אב"ג וּפָסְקָה. **וראוי** לְזִיבָה. (א) לְצָרֵף עִם בג"ד, אִם לֹא רָאֲתָה בְּא'. דְּהָא אִתְרַבֵּי מוּפְלָג יוֹם אֶחָד מִקְּרָא ד"אוֹ כִּי תָזוּב", ג) דְּהַיְינוּ בג"ד. אַף אֲנִי מְרַבֶּה כָּל אֵלּוּ עַד י', וְיוֹ"ד בִּכְלָל שֶׁהֵן רְאוּיִין לִסְפִירָה, אִם רָאֲתָה שְׁלֹשָׁה רִאשׁוֹנִים — מָשְׁכֵי ז' נְקִיִּים עַד שֶׁיְּהוּ נַמִּי נִרְאִין לְזִיבָה בְּאֵיזֶה מֵהֶם שֶׁתִּרְאֶה שְׁלֹשָׁה רְצוּפִין. **מנין** לְרַבּוֹת י"א. שֶׁיִּצְטָרֵף עִם הָרִאשׁוֹנִים לְזִיבָה לְג' רְצוּפִין, וְאַע"ג שֶׁאֵינוֹ רָאוּי לִסְפִירַת נְקִיִּים שֶׁל זִיבַת ג' רִאשׁוֹנִים? ת"ל בְּלֹא עֵת נִדָּתָהּ. וַאֲפִילּוּ מוּפְלָג לְיָמִים הַרְבֵּה. יָכוֹל. כֵּיוָן דִּכְתִיב "בְּלֹא עֵת נִדָּתָהּ", שֶׁאֲנִי מְרַבֶּה אַף י"ב. שֶׁאִם רָאֲתָה י' י"א י"ב — תְּהֵא זָבָה גְּמוּרָה, וְלֹא תְּהֵא תְּחִלַּת נִדָּה בִּרְאִיַּית י"ב אֶלָּא מִצְטָרֵף לְזִיבָה? יוֹם י"א. שֶׁהוּא רָאוּי לִסְפִירַת זִיבָה, "אוֹ כִי תָזוּב" — דְּזִיבָה רְבִיעִי מִתְרַבֵּי מֵ"אוֹ כִי תָזוּב", וּלְאוֹתָהּ זִיבָה מָשְׁכֵי יְמֵי סְפִירָה עַד י"א. **ואין** לִי. שֶׁתִּקָּרֵא זָבָה לְטוּמְאָה אֶלָּא רוֹאָה שְׁלֹשָׁה רְצוּפִין. ת"ל יְמֵי. "כָּל יְמֵי זוֹב טוּמְאָתָהּ כִּימֵי נִדָּתָהּ תִּהְיֶה". **טמאה**. מְלַמֵּד שֶׁמְּטַמְּאָה אֶת בּוֹעֲלָהּ כְּנִדָּה, שֶׁמְּפוֹרָשׁ בָּהּ "אֲשֶׁר יִשְׁכַּב אִישׁ" וגו'. **היא** שֶׁאֵינָהּ מְטַמְּאָה. בִּשָׁלֹשׁ רְאִיּוֹת בְּיוֹם אֶחָד טוּמְאַת זוֹב גָּמוּר לְקָרְבָּן, כְּאִילּוּ רָאֲתָה שְׁלֹשָׁה יָמִים. אֲבָל זָב — מְטַמֵּא בֵּין בְּג' רְאִיּוֹת בְּיוֹם אֶחָד, בֵּין בְּג' יָמִים רְצוּפִין, בְּב"ק בְּפֶ' "כֵּיצַד הָרֶגֶל" (דף כד.). **ואין** לִי. עוֹשָׂה מִשְׁכָּב וּמוֹשָׁב בַּיָּמִים שֶׁאַחַר הַנִּדָּה, אֶלָּא הָרוֹאָה שְׁלֹשָׁה יָמִים, שְׁנֵי יָמִים מִנַּיִן? ת"ל. "כָּל הַמִּשְׁכָּב אֲשֶׁר (ב) יִשְׁכַּב עָלָיו כָּל יְמֵי זוֹבָהּ כְּמִשְׁכַּב נִדָּתָהּ". יִהְיֶה לָהּ. הוֹסִיף לָהּ הֲוָיָה שֶׁל שִׁמּוּר. **הוא** שֶׁאֵינוֹ סוֹפֵר אֶחָד לְאֶחָד. זָב בַּעַל רְאִיָּיה אַחַת — כְּבַעַל קֶרִי, וְטוֹבֵל בּוֹ בַּיּוֹם, סוֹפֵר שִׁבְעָה — לִשְׁנַיִם. **אלמא** קְרָאֵי נִינְהוּ. כָּל דִּין י"א שֶׁבֵּין נִדָּה לְנִדָּה, מִכָּאן לָמַדְנוּ שֶׁהֵן י"א יוֹם, וְהָרוֹאָה בָּהֶם ג' — הֲרֵי זוֹ זָבָה. וְהָרוֹאָה בְּא' בְּב' — סוֹפֶרֶת יוֹם כְּנֶגֶד יוֹם. וּלְסוֹף י"א מַתְחִילִין יְמֵי נִדָּה, אִם תִּרְאֶה אֶחָד — תֵּשֵׁב שִׁשָּׁה וְהוּא, שֶׁהֲרֵי לֹא רִבִּינַן לְדִין יוֹם זוֹבָהּ אֶלָּא י"א, וּמִכָּאן וְאֵילָךְ הֲרֵי הִיא בְּדִין פָּרָשָׁה רִאשׁוֹנָה דִּכְתִיב בָּהּ: "שִׁבְעַת יָמִים תִּהְיֶה בְנִדָּתָהּ". **לְרַבִּי עֲקִיבָא** קְרָאֵי. דְּלֹא גָּמַר הַךְ הִלְכְתָא הֲלָכָה לְמֹשֶׁה מִסִּינַי דְּקָאָמַר ר' אֶלְעָזָר בֶּן עֲזַרְיָה. וְכִי הֵיכִי דְּיָלֵיף חֲצִי לוֹג שֶׁמֶן לְתוֹדָה מִקְּרָאֵי, הָכִי נַמִּי יָלֵיף אַחַד עָשָׂר יוֹם שֶׁבֵּין נִדָּה לְנִדָּה מִקְּרָאֵי. **בימָמֵי**. רָאֲתָה בַּיּוֹם — תִּהְיֶה זָבָה, כִּדְכְתִיב (ויקרא טו): "יָמִים רַבִּים". אֲבָל רָאֲתָה בַּלֵּילוֹת — לֹא תְּהֵא זָבָה. **סמוך לנדתה**. לֵיל שְׁמִינִי. שֶׁהֲרֵי יְמֵי נִדּוּת, כָּל שִׁבְעָה עַד הַלַּיְלָה, כִּדְכְתִיב: "שִׁבְעַת יָמִים תִּהְיֶה #בְנִדָּתָהּ". **הֲלָכוֹת**. מִשְׁנָה וּבָרַיְיתָא, הֲלָכָה לְמֹשֶׁה מִסִּינַי.

## הדרן עלך תינוקת וסליקא לה מסכת נדה

**תוספות**

**אין** לי אלא יום אחד מנין לרבות מופלג שנים ושלשה. אגב ריהטא נקט "שנים", ד"שנים" היינו יום שני לימי זיבה, דהיינו מופלג יום אחד שריבה כבר, דהא מני ואזיל עד י' וי"א. וא"כ, "שנים" היינו שני. **הוא** שמטמא בראיות כבימים אינו דין כו'. תימה: דאיכא למפרך, מה להיא – שכן מטמאה באונס! והכי אמרינן בריש פרק "בנות כותים" (לעיל לב:) דלא ילפינן מהדדי. וכן לקמן, דקאמר: מה הוא שאינו סופר אחד לאחד כו' – איכא למפרך: מה להוא – שכן מטמא בראיות כבימים! מיהו בזה מצינן שפיר למילף, דלגבי ספירה אחמיר רחמנא באשה מבאיש. ולענין ספירה עביד שפיר ק"ו הואיל ולענין ספירה מצינו שהחמיר באשה מבאיש. וי"ל: שאינו קל וחומר גמור, אלא כמו גילוי מילתא בעלמא, לגלות זה על זה. וי"ע: דאיכא מקומות דאיכא תרי קראי לדם נדות ולזיבות, ויש מקומות דנפקא מחד קרא.

**ת"ל** כל ימי (ג) נדתה. תימה: דהך מוקמינן כר"ע אלמא, ר"ע קא דריש "כל". וכן בשלהי פ' "התערובת" (זבחים פב.) דריש ר"ע "כל". וא"כ, כי קאמר בפסחים פרק "אלו עוברין" (דף מג:) מאן שמעת ליה דדריש "כל"? ר' אליעזר הוא – דלמא ר"ע הוא, דדריש נמי "כל"? ויש לומר: דאין לדמות דרשות ד"כל" להדדי, דיש "כל" דשייך למדרש לכ"ע והאי דשמעתין, דלמניגא – מדרש שפיר, דמד"ימי" למניגא, "כל" נמי למניגא.*.

**תנא** דבי אליהו כל השונה הלכות. אית ספרים דלא גרסינן ליה, מיהו בפירוש רש"י איתא, ור"ת הגיהו בספרו. וכן נראה דאיידי דאיירי לעיל בהלכתא, מייתי לה לסיים בדבר טוב. ואיתא נמי כן במגילה פרק בתרא (דף כח:) והכי נמי אמרינן ב"אין עומדין" (ברכות לא.) שכן מצינו בנביאים הראשונים, שסיימו דבריהן בדברי שבח ותנחומין.

[וע"ע תוס' מנחות נו: ד"ה אמר ותוס' זבחים פב. ד"ה ת"ל ותוס' פסחים מג: ד"ה מאן ותוס' מנחות יח: ד"ה קומץ]

## הדרן עלך תינוקת וסליקא לה מסכת נדה

### תוספי הרא"ש

**מנין** לרבות שני ושלישי כו'. מדקא חשיב עד עשירי ואחד עשר אלמא האי שני הוא יום שני לימי זיבה וכדי נסבה דהיינו מופלג יום א' מנדתה וכבר ריבה אותו מאו כי תזוב אלא אגב ריהטא חוזר וכופלו בהדי אחריני: **מנין** לרבות יום י"א (יום). דס"ד לא מרבינן ראוי לספירה אלא לעיקר זיבות הכתובה בפסוק אבל לא לספירה דמרבינן מאו כי תזוב **ומה** היא שאינה מטמאה בראיות כבימים. ותימה מה להיא שכן מטמאה באונס כו' ובסמוך דקאמר ומה הוא שאין סופר אחד לאחד וכו' איכא למיפרך מה להוא שכן מטמא בראיות כבימים כדאמרינן בריש בנות כותים דלא ילפי מהדדי מכח הנך פירכי. וי"ל דאינו סומך עיקר על הק"ו אלא כמו ילמד סתום מן המפורש. ויש דברים דילפי מהדדי כדמפרש בריש בנות כותים: **תאנא** דבי אליהו כל השונה הלכות. איידי דאיירי לעיל בהלכות י"א שהיא הל"מ קא מייתי לה הכא כדפרש"י. הלכות משנה ובריי תא והלכה למשה מסיני. ומיהו לא שייכא כל כך הכא טפי מבשאר דוכתי דלא מייתי לה אגב גררא זו אלא משום דניחא ליה לסיים בדבר טוב כדאמרינן באין מעמידין שכן מצינו בנביאים הראשונים שסיימו בדברי שבח ותנחומין:

סליק פרק תינוקת בס"ד ובסליקותיה מסכת נדה ברחמי שמיא

**הכותב נסים ק' כה"ר אברהם מוליכה נ"ע**

**עין משפט נר מצוה**

**פד** א מיי' פ"ו מהל' איסורי ביאה הל"ב:
**פה** ב מיי' פ"ג מהל' מטמאי משכב ומושב הל"א ופ"ד מהל' איסורי ביאה הל"ב:
**פו** ג מיי' פ"ג מהל' מטמאי משכב ומושב הלכה ג:
**פז** ד מיי' פ"ו מהל' איסורי ביאה הל"ז ופ"א מהל' מטמאי משכב ומושב הל"ב:
**פח** ה מיי' פ"ו מהל' איסורי ביאה הל"ח והלכה ט:

**מסורת הש"ס**

לפי' גי' רש"י צריך למחוק תיבות אלו וכצ"ל לקמן מנין לרבות י"א ת"ל על נדתה ולקמן א"ל עלך אמר קרא בלא עת נדתה סמוך לנדתה כו' וע' רש"א

הוריות ד.

[ילקוט איתא ר' ישעיה]

### הגהות הב"ח

(א) רש"י ד"ה וראוי לזיבה להצטרף עם ב"ג אם לא ראתה וכו' ז' נקיים עד עשירי שיהו נמי: (ב) ד"ה ת"ל כל המשכב אשר תשכב: (ג) תוס' ד"ה ת"ל כל ימי זובה כמשכב נדתה תימה:

### הגהות מהר"ב רנשבורג

א] גמ' ומנין שהוא עושה משכב ומושב. מלת שהוא נמחק. ונ"ב שהיא כצ"ל וכ"ה בת"כ: ב] שם יכול תספור שבעה לשנים. נ"ב עי' ת"כ וקרבן אהרן דף קע ע"א וע"ב: ג] רש"י ד"ה וראוי לזיבה וכו' דהיינו בג"ד כאן הס"ד ואח"כ מה"ד אף אני וכו' משכי ז' נקיים עד העשירי שיהו וכו' כצ"ל:

*The following paragraph is recited three times:*

הַדְרָן עֲלָךְ מַסֶּכֶת נִדָּה וְהַדְרָךְ עֲלָן, דַּעְתָּן עֲלָךְ מַסֶּכֶת נִדָּה וְדַעְתָּךְ עֲלָן, לָא נִתְנְשֵׁי מִנָּךְ מַסֶּכֶת נִדָּה וְלָא תִתְנְשֵׁי מִנָּן, לָא בְּעָלְמָא הָדֵין וְלָא בְּעָלְמָא דְאָתֵי.

יְהִי רָצוֹן מִלְּפָנֶיךָ יהוה אֱלֹהֵינוּ וֵאלֹהֵי אֲבוֹתֵינוּ, שֶׁתְּהֵא תוֹרָתְךָ אֻמָּנוּתֵנוּ בָּעוֹלָם הַזֶּה, וּתְהֵא עִמָּנוּ לָעוֹלָם הַבָּא. חֲנִינָא בַּר פַּפָּא, רָמֵי בַּר פַּפָּא, נַחְמָן בַּר פַּפָּא, אֲחַאי בַּר פַּפָּא, אַבָּא מָרִי בַּר פַּפָּא, רַפְרָם בַּר פַּפָּא, רָכִישׁ בַּר פַּפָּא, סוּרְחַב בַּר פַּפָּא, אַדָּא בַּר פַּפָּא, דָּרוּ בַּר פַּפָּא.

הַעֲרֶב נָא יהוה אֱלֹהֵינוּ אֶת דִּבְרֵי תוֹרָתְךָ בְּפִינוּ וּבְפִי עַמְּךָ בֵּית יִשְׂרָאֵל, וְנִהְיֶה אֲנַחְנוּ וְצֶאֱצָאֵינוּ (וְצֶאֱצָאֵי צֶאֱצָאֵינוּ) וְצֶאֱצָאֵי עַמְּךָ בֵּית יִשְׂרָאֵל, כֻּלָּנוּ יוֹדְעֵי
תהלים קיט שְׁמֶךָ וְלוֹמְדֵי תוֹרָתְךָ לִשְׁמָהּ. מֵאֹיְבַי תְּחַכְּמֵנִי מִצְוֺתֶךָ כִּי לְעוֹלָם הִיא־לִי: יְהִי־לִבִּי תָמִים בְּחֻקֶּיךָ לְמַעַן לֹא אֵבוֹשׁ: לְעוֹלָם לֹא־אֶשְׁכַּח פִּקּוּדֶיךָ כִּי־בָם חִיִּיתָנִי: בָּרוּךְ אַתָּה יהוה לַמְּדֵנִי חֻקֶּיךָ: אָמֵן אָמֵן אָמֵן סֶלָה וָעֶד.

מוֹדִים אֲנַחְנוּ לְפָנֶיךָ יהוה אֱלֹהֵינוּ וֵאלֹהֵי אֲבוֹתֵינוּ שֶׁשַּׂמְתָּ חֶלְקֵנוּ מִיּוֹשְׁבֵי בֵּית הַמִּדְרָשׁ, וְלֹא שַׂמְתָּ חֶלְקֵנוּ מִיּוֹשְׁבֵי קְרָנוֹת. שֶׁאָנוּ מַשְׁכִּימִים וְהֵם מַשְׁכִּימִים, אָנוּ מַשְׁכִּימִים לְדִבְרֵי תוֹרָה, וְהֵם מַשְׁכִּימִים לִדְבָרִים בְּטֵלִים. אָנוּ עֲמֵלִים וְהֵם עֲמֵלִים, אָנוּ עֲמֵלִים וּמְקַבְּלִים שָׂכָר, וְהֵם עֲמֵלִים וְאֵינָם מְקַבְּלִים שָׂכָר. אָנוּ רָצִים וְהֵם רָצִים, אָנוּ רָצִים לְחַיֵּי הָעוֹלָם הַבָּא, וְהֵם רָצִים לִבְאֵר
תהלים נה שַׁחַת, שֶׁנֶּאֱמַר: וְאַתָּה אֱלֹהִים תּוֹרִדֵם לִבְאֵר שַׁחַת אַנְשֵׁי דָמִים וּמִרְמָה לֹא־יֶחֱצוּ יְמֵיהֶם וַאֲנִי אֶבְטַח־בָּךְ:

יְהִי רָצוֹן מִלְּפָנֶיךָ יהוה אֱלֹהַי, כְּשֵׁם שֶׁעֲזַרְתַּנִי לְסַיֵּם מַסֶּכֶת נִדָּה כֵּן תְּעַזְרֵנִי לְהַתְחִיל מַסֶּכְתּוֹת וּסְפָרִים אֲחֵרִים וּלְסַיְּמָם, לִלְמֹד וּלְלַמֵּד לִשְׁמֹר וְלַעֲשׂוֹת וּלְקַיֵּם אֶת כָּל דִּבְרֵי תַלְמוּד תּוֹרָתְךָ בְּאַהֲבָה, וּזְכוּת כָּל הַתַּנָּאִים וְאָמוֹרָאִים וְתַלְמִידֵי חֲכָמִים יַעֲמֹד לִי וּלְזַרְעִי שֶׁלֹּא תָמוּשׁ הַתּוֹרָה מִפִּי וּמִפִּי זַרְעִי וְזֶרַע זַרְעִי
משלי ו עַד עוֹלָם, וְיִתְקַיֵּם בִּי: בְּהִתְהַלֶּכְךָ תַּנְחֶה אֹתָךְ בְּשָׁכְבְּךָ
משלי ט תִּשְׁמֹר עָלֶיךָ וַהֲקִיצוֹתָ הִיא תְשִׂיחֶךָ: כִּי־בִי יִרְבּוּ יָמֶיךָ
משלי ג וְיוֹסִיפוּ לְּךָ שְׁנוֹת חַיִּים: אֹרֶךְ יָמִים בִּימִינָהּ בִּשְׂמֹאולָהּ
תהלים כט עֹשֶׁר וְכָבוֹד: יהוה עֹז לְעַמּוֹ יִתֵּן יהוה יְבָרֵךְ אֶת־עַמּוֹ בַשָּׁלוֹם:

*The following paragraph is recited three times:*

הַדְרָן We shall return to you, tractate *Nidda,* and your glory is upon us. Our thoughts are upon you, tractate *Nidda,* and your thoughts are upon us. We will not be forgotten from you, tractate *Nidda,* and you will not be forgotten from us; neither in this world nor in the World-to-Come.

יְהִי רָצוֹן May it be Your will, Lord our God and God of our ancestors, that Your Torah will be our avocation in this world and will accompany us to the World-to-Come. Ḥanina bar Pappa, Ramei bar Pappa, Naḥman bar Pappa, Aḥai bar Pappa, Abba Mari bar Pappa, Rafram bar Pappa, Rakhish bar Pappa, Surḥav bar Pappa, Adda bar Pappa, Daru bar Pappa.

הַעֲרֶב נָא Please, Lord our God, make the words of Your Torah sweet in our mouths and in the mouths of Your people, the house of Israel, so that we, our descendants (and their descendants), and the descendants of Your people, the house of Israel, may all know Your name and
study Your Torah for its own sake. Your commandments *Psalms 119*
make me wiser than my enemies, for they are ever with me. Let my heart be undivided in Your statutes, in order that I may not be put to shame. I will never forget Your precepts, for with them You have quickened me. Blessed are You, O Lord; teach me Your statutes. Amen, Amen, Amen, Selah, Forever.

מוֹדִים We give thanks before You, Lord Our God and God of our ancestors, that You have placed our lot among those who sit in the study hall and that you have not given us our portion among those who sit idly on street corners. We rise early and they rise early. We rise early to pursue matters of Torah and they rise early to pursue frivolous matters. We toil and they toil. We toil and receive a reward and they toil and do not receive a reward. We run and they run. We run to the life of the World-to-Come and they run to the pit of destruction,
as it is stated: But You, God, will bring them down into *Psalms 55*
the pit of destruction; men of blood and deceit shall not live out half their days; but as for me, I will trust in You.

יְהִי רָצוֹן May it be Your will, Lord my God, just as you have assisted me in completing tractate *Nidda* so assist me to begin other tractates and books and conclude them to learn and to teach, to observe and to perform, and to fulfill all the teachings of Your Torah with love. And may the merit of all the *tanna'im* and *amora'im* and Torah scholars stand for me and my descendants so that the Torah will not move from my mouth and from the mouths of my descendants and the descendants of my
descendants forever. And may the verse: When you *Proverbs 6*
walk, it shall lead you, when you lie down, it shall watch over you; and when you awaken, it shall talk with you
be fulfilled in me. For in the Torah your days shall be *Proverbs 9*
multiplied, and the years of your life shall be increased.
Length of days is in her right hand; in her left hand are *Proverbs 3*
riches and honor. May the Lord give strength to His *Psalms 29*
people; the Lord will bless His people with peace.

*The following* קדיש *requires the presence of a* מנין.

יִתְגַּדַּל וְיִתְקַדַּשׁ שְׁמֵהּ רַבָּא
בְּעָלְמָא דְּהוּא עָתִיד לְאִתְחַדָּתָא
וּלְאַחֲיָאָה מֵתַיָּא, וּלְאַסָּקָא יָתְהוֹן לְחַיֵּי עָלְמָא
וּלְמִבְנֵא קַרְתָּא דִירוּשְׁלֵם, וּלְשַׁכְלְלָא הֵיכְלֵהּ בְּגַוַּהּ
וּלְמֶעְקַר פָּלְחָנָא נֻכְרָאָה מֵאַרְעָא
וְלַאֲתָבָא פָּלְחָנָא דִשְׁמַיָּא לְאַתְרֵהּ
וְיַמְלִיךְ קֻדְשָׁא בְּרִיךְ הוּא בְּמַלְכוּתֵהּ וִיקָרֵהּ
(נוסח ספרד: וְיַצְמַח פֻּרְקָנֵהּ וִיקָרֵב מְשִׁיחֵהּ)
בְּחַיֵּיכוֹן וּבְיוֹמֵיכוֹן וּבְחַיֵּי דְכָל בֵּית יִשְׂרָאֵל
בַּעֲגָלָא וּבִזְמַן קָרִיב, וְאִמְרוּ אָמֵן.

יְהֵא שְׁמֵהּ רַבָּא מְבָרַךְ לְעָלַם וּלְעָלְמֵי עָלְמַיָּא.

יִתְבָּרַךְ וְיִשְׁתַּבַּח וְיִתְפָּאַר וְיִתְרוֹמַם וְיִתְנַשֵּׂא
וְיִתְהַדָּר וְיִתְעַלֶּה וְיִתְהַלָּל
שְׁמֵהּ דְּקֻדְשָׁא בְּרִיךְ הוּא
לְעֵלָּא מִן כָּל בִּרְכָתָא
/בעשרת ימי תשובה: לְעֵלָּא לְעֵלָּא מִכָּל בִּרְכָתָא/
וְשִׁירָתָא, תֻּשְׁבְּחָתָא וְנֶחֱמָתָא, דַּאֲמִירָן בְּעָלְמָא
וְאִמְרוּ אָמֵן. (קהל: אָמֵן)

עַל יִשְׂרָאֵל וְעַל רַבָּנָן
וְעַל תַּלְמִידֵיהוֹן וְעַל כָּל תַּלְמִידֵי תַלְמִידֵיהוֹן
וְעַל כָּל מָאן דְּעָסְקִין בְּאוֹרַיְתָא
דִּי בְּאַתְרָא (בארץ ישראל: קַדִּישָׁא) הָדֵין, וְדִי בְּכָל אֲתַר וַאֲתַר
יְהֵא לְהוֹן וּלְכוֹן שְׁלָמָא רַבָּא
חִנָּא וְחִסְדָּא, וְרַחֲמֵי, וְחַיֵּי אֲרִיכֵי, וּמְזוֹנֵי רְוִיחֵי
וּפֻרְקָנָא מִן קֳדָם אֲבוּהוֹן דִּי בִשְׁמַיָּא
וְאִמְרוּ אָמֵן.

יְהֵא שְׁלָמָא רַבָּא מִן שְׁמַיָּא
וְחַיִּים (טוֹבִים) עָלֵינוּ וְעַל כָּל יִשְׂרָאֵל
וְאִמְרוּ אָמֵן.

*Bow, take three steps back, as if taking leave of the Divine Presence, then bow, first left, then right, then center, while saying:*

עֹשֶׂה שָׁלוֹם/ בעשרת ימי תשובה: הַשָּׁלוֹם/ בִּמְרוֹמָיו
הוּא יַעֲשֶׂה בְרַחֲמָיו שָׁלוֹם, עָלֵינוּ וְעַל כָּל יִשְׂרָאֵל
וְאִמְרוּ אָמֵן.

*The following Kaddish requires the presence of a minyan.*

Magnified and sanctified may His great name be,
in the world that will in future be renewed,
reviving the dead and raising them up to eternal life.
He will rebuild the city of Jerusalem
and in it re-establish His Temple.
He will remove alien worship from the earth
and restore to its place the worship of Heaven.
Then the Holy One, blessed be He,
will reign in His sovereignty and splendor.
May it be in your lifetime and in your days,
(*Nusaḥ Sepharad:* make His salvation flourish,
and hasten His messiah,)
and in the lifetime of all the House of Israel,
swiftly and soon – and say: Amen.

May His great name be blessed for ever and all time.

Blessed and praised,
glorified and exalted,
raised and honored,
uplifted and lauded
be the name of the Holy One,
blessed be He,
beyond any blessing,
song, praise and consolation uttered in the world –
and say: Amen.

To Israel, to the teachers,
their disciples and their disciples' disciples,
and to all who engage in the study of Torah,
in this (*in Israel add:* holy) place or elsewhere,
may there come to them and you great peace,
grace, kindness and compassion,
long life, ample sustenance and deliverance,
from their Father in Heaven –
and say: Amen.

May there be great peace from heaven,
and (good) life for us and all Israel –
and say: Amen.

*Bow, take three steps back, as if taking leave of the Divine Presence, then bow, first left, then right, then center, while saying:*

May He who makes peace in His high places,
in His compassion make peace for us and all Israel –
and say: Amen.